THE
American Tradition in Literature

FOURTH EDITION

Edited by

Sculley Bradley

PROFESSOR EMERITUS OF ENGLISH
UNIVERSITY OF PENNSYLVANIA

Richmond Croom Beatty

LATE OF VANDERBILT UNIVERSITY

E. Hudson Long

PROFESSOR OF AMERICAN LITERATURE AND
CHAIRMAN OF THE ENGLISH DEPARTMENT
BAYLOR UNIVERSITY

George Perkins

PROFESSOR OF ENGLISH
EASTERN MICHIGAN UNIVERSITY

SHORTER EDITION
IN ONE VOLUME

GROSSET & DUNLAP

DISTRIBUTED BY W. W. NORTON & COMPANY, INC.

Book design by John Woodlock

Contents

The New Nation and the House Divided   201

ROMANTIC REDISCOVERY: NATURE, MAN, SOCIETY

TRANSCENDENTAL IDEALISM

The Emergence of Modern American Literature 873

PIONEERS OF A NEW POETRY

THE ATTACK ON CONVENTION

FICTION: THE FIFTIES

THE PROSE WRITER AS SUBJECT

RECENT FICTION

Preface

This shorter edition of *The American Tradition in Literature* includes in one volume considerably more than half the literature contained in the two volumes of the complete edition. The contents have been thoroughly examined in order to bring them in line with the changes incorporated in the longer version, an anthology that has met with widespread favor in its first three editions and has now been revised because of the passage of time that has seen new writers emerge, prevailing critical attitudes change, and new scholarship appear. It should be emphasized that in the years since Sculley Bradley, Richmond Croom Beatty, and E. Hudson Long first edited this work, the aims have remained substantially the same. The following paragraphs, taken from the first edition, remain essentially as appropriate now as they were when they were first printed:

"In compiling this work we have intended to provide a freshly considered collection of great American writings representing the range and power of our literature as a whole. Our effort has been to represent major authors in the fullness of their stature and variety. Besides the titans, we have included writers of lesser stature whose works endure; but no author was introduced primarily for the purpose of illustrating literary or social history. * * *

"While we have made literary merit our final criterion for selection, we have attempted in our critical apparatus to emphasize the relations between the literary work and the general movements in American civilization and intellectual history. In the textual annotations, as in the introductory essays and biographical sketches, we have attempted to secure as much objectivity as possible, to suppress individualistic critical tendencies of our own in favor of the consensus of our professional peers, and to leave the reader free to pursue his own ideas and values without having to contend with ours. Yet we have annotated liberally, believing it our function as editors to elucidate any substantial obscurity that would handicap a reader lacking immediate access to the appropriate reference books. * * *

"The study of American literature can be acceptably organized in several ways; we have therefore attempted to provide a certain flexibility in our sequence of authors and texts. In general we have followed a chronological order, but by a few slight departures we were also able to bring authors together under topical headings which represent the pronounced response of our literature, at one time or another, to regional influence, social forces, dominant ideas, historical events, or aesthetic values."

In this revision, a major effort has been directed toward making the selections from the twentieth century more broadly representative, but there are some new inclusions from earlier times as well. The Indian heritage is newly represented by a gathering of tales, speeches, and poems. The Ralph Waldo Emerson representation has been changed by adopting the Center for Editions of American Authors texts of *Nature*, "The American Scholar," and "The Divinity School Address," all of which are here liberally annotated. Emerson's important essay "Fate" is newly included. Also new to this edition are the excerpts from *Narrative of the Life of Frederick Douglass*. Walt Whitman's "The Wound-Dresser" has been added to the Whitman selections previously included. Emily Dickinson's poems now appear in the Thomas H. Johnson texts, and "Of Bronze—and Blaze" (J. 290) and "We play at Paste" (J. 320) have been added to the previous representation.

The selections from twentieth-century poets previously represented have been strengthened by the inclusion of Robert Frost's "Directive"; Edna St. Vincent Millay's "I Shall Go Back Again to the Bleak Shore" and "Those Hours When Happy Hours Were My Estate"; Wallace Stevens's "The Idea of Order at Key West"; and Robert Lowell's "Skunk Hour." Poets new to this edition are Langston Hughes, Randall Jarrell, John Berryman, William Stafford, James Dickey, Robert Bly, Allen Ginsberg, W. D. Snodgrass, Gary Snyder, and Sylvia Plath.

Among twentieth-century writers of fiction, F. Scott Fitzgerald, omitted earlier, is now represented by "Babylon Revisited." Other writers of fiction included for the first time are Richard Wright, Vladimir Nabokov, Ralph Ellison, Saul Bellow, William Gass, John Barth, and Joyce Carol Oates. Twentieth-century drama is now represented by Tennessee Williams's *The Glass Menagerie*. To the earlier examples of nonfiction prose there have now been added James Baldwin's long essay "Notes of a Native Son" and a substantial selection from Henry Miller's *The Time of the Assassins*.

Besides the new material in the headnotes and bibliographies accompanying the writers who are new to this edition, the revisions include changes in the general introductions, individual headnotes, footnotes, and bibliographies accompanying material carried over from the previous edition. The aim has been to bring the work as a whole completely up to date.

This edition continues the textual tradition established by Sculley Bradley, Richmond Croom Beatty, and E. Hudson Long in the first edition of the complete version and carried faithfully through each revision. Considerable pains have been taken to provide in each instance a faithful copy of the text that in the judgment of the editor is the best edition of the work. The following guidelines, as stated in the preface to the third edition, remain in effect:

"The textual source of any text, unless it is obvious, will be stated in the bibliographical note or a footnote. In editing the difficult texts of Colonial writers we have been guided by the condition of the particular texts. Those, like Bradford's *Of Plymouth Plantation,* in which archaic spelling, punctuation, and abbreviations are a mechanical handicap for many readers, have been normalized in accordance with present practice. But the language has not been altered or 'modernized'; the texts of Colonial poets are untouched and, like most of the prose, clarified only by annotation. Significant dates appear at the end of a selection; that of first publication in a volume by the author at the right margin, preceded by the date of first serial publication; an established date of composition, if of significance, in the left margin. In all instances the omission of text has been indicated by three asterisks, and titles are those of the original except where printed between square brackets."

The guiding spirit of this revision has been Phillip Leininger, the publisher's editor who initiated the complex negotiations that made a fourth edition possible. From beginning to end his judgment has been a constant and welcome check on my own and I wish to give here grateful acknowledgment of his help. I have also been sustained by the approval given by Professors Bradley and Long and by Mrs. Flora Beatty to the general plans for revisions, although the responsibility for the detailed implementation of the plans and for seeing the work through the press remains my own. Other debts are many. The editorial work of Nancy B. Brooks, of Grosset & Dunlap, has been consistently excellent. Neda M. Westlake, Librarian of the Rare Book Collection of the Library of the University of Pennsylvania, kindly sent on the file of bibliographical clippings that she had compiled for use in a fourth edition. The library staffs of Eastern Michigan University and the University of Michigan were most helpful in providing trustworthy texts. The Eastern Michigan University Department of English supplied the assistance of five graduate students: Jan Bender, Kenneth Buckshi, Mary Alice Ervin, Charles Myers, and Satya Tandon.

Leita Hamill served as an able permissions secretary. Among friends and colleagues at Eastern Michigan University, Naomi Madgett, Walter Brylowski, Jeffrey Duncan, Milton Foster, and Glenn Ruihley made particularly helpful suggestions for additions or alterations in the texts. Among the many suggestions from scholars elsewhere, those by William M. Gibson, Charles Neider, Frank K. Robinson, Per Seyersted, Henry Nash Smith, and Linda Welshimer Wagner were perhaps most helpful in giving final shape to the work. The aid of my wife, Barbara Miller Perkins, was, as always, invaluable.

GEORGE PERKINS

THE
American Tradition in Literature
FOURTH EDITION

SHORTER EDITION

The Literature of the Colonies and the Revolution

There was an enormous amount of writing in America during the first century of settlement. The adventurers and settlers wrote descriptions of the country, like those by Captain John Smith of Virginia, the most famous of the scores of chroniclers; they wrote picturesquely of explorations and discoveries, of Indian wars and captivities; they made personal journals of their experiences. They created their instruments of government and law; they recorded the history of their colonies, often for political or economic purposes, but also, in New England especially, to "justify the ways of God to men" in the New Jerusalem. A large number of these works were printed, in England or on the Continent. Most of them were merely timely, although useful for future historians; but with a frequency quite amazing, in view of the physical conditions of life in the New World, there appeared the writer who

was also a great person, who communicated the richness of his spirit or character in writings that time has not tarnished. Our colonial literature became a great reservoir of material and inspiration for that of the nineteenth century; for readers today it still provides an understanding of those bedrock American experiences which developed the national character and our peculiarly American institutions.

Although the people of the colonies derived their language and political institutions from Great Britain, they were to become increasingly indebted, as the British themselves had, to a variety of European cultures. The French, Germans, Swedes, and Dutch—and the Jews from Germany and Portugal, who appeared in the Middle Colonies especially during the eighteenth century—were merely following in the wake of European continentals as far back as Eric the Red and Leif Ericsson. Also before the British, the Spaniards, in the half century following the voyage of Columbus, had rimmed the Gulf of Mexico and pushed westward to the Pacific. For all their hardihood, the early settlers could only vaguely comprehend the natural immensity that confronted their efforts—an unimaginable empire, between the Isthmus of Panama and the Arctic, of nearly eight million square miles, more than half of it covered by ancient forests of fabulous density. The land stretched before them in majesty and mystery, while the Indians told of wonders yet unseen—vast peaks and mighty rivers, shifting sands and ancient golden cities overrun by ruin.

It is no wonder if the American imagination bears, to this day, the indelible mark of this immeasurable richness, and of those dark people who possessed the land before them. America was El Dorado, the golden western limit of Renaissance energies; and this great tide was still at flood when the Reformation flung out another restless host for whom America became the Promised Land of the human spirit. At the same time that the New World invited the colonial ambitions of rival empires, or lured the adventurer for pelts and pelf, it was also holding out the promise of new freedom and new hope for men of some sober purpose or lofty idealism forbidden in the Old World. The majority of them, and predominantly those who came to rest in New England and the Middle Colonies, were products, in some sort, of the Protestant Reformation, a fact which continues to influence the life and thought of the United States.

VIRGINIA AND THE SOUTH

However, the first permanent English settlement was the result not of religious but of mercantile motives. The Virginia Company promoted the Jamestown colony (1607), expecting that its plantations would provide goods for the British trade and would attract the Englishmen who needed homes and land. Their conception of the New World was so unrealistic that they brought with them to Virginia a perfumer and several tailors. Epidemic fevers and Indian raids during the first few years reduced the colony as fast as new recruits could be brought in on the infrequent supply ships. The Indians, who had been counted on for cheap labor, refused to be enslaved or even to work. Innocent of the European concept of property, they resented the settlers who fenced and cultivated their hunting grounds, and they retaliated with blood and fire. Still, somehow the colony increased, first at Jamestown, then at Williamsburg, the handsome colonial capital where, in 1693, William and Mary was founded as the second college in North America.

During the seventeenth century the South was not a land of large plantations. However, the eventual shift from a yeoman to a slave-holding plantation economy was an inevitable result of British mercantilism, an abusive colonial system to be sure, but one which, for a time, perhaps actually benefited the agricultural colonies of the South. The Navigation Acts of the late seventeenth century were intended to compel the colonists to sell to the mother country all their raw materials and agricultural exports, for which they were to receive in exchange British manufactured products. Since British shipping was given a monopoly of the carriage, at rates fixed in England, the mother country was assured of a credit balance. In the northern colonies, where natural conditions favored manufactures and commerce, this exploitation in time became intolerable, and provided one of the deep-rooted reasons for the Revolution. Although the southern plantation colonies were restless at being confined to the British market, their crops were generally salable there. The southern plantation wealth grew steadily, supporting, in the eighteenth century, a tidewater aristocracy that produced some families of great culture, whose sons enjoyed the advantages of British and continental universities and built up fine private libraries. They ultimately produced such leaders and statesmen as the Byrds, Jefferson, and Madison. Yet, before the period of the Revolution, they added but little to the creative literature of the colonies. This does not seem surprising. The urban centers were small and widely separated; and the population, much dispersed, was composed of a few privileged aristocrats, thousands of slaves, and a white middle class of generally unlettered frontiersmen and small yeoman farmers.

NEW ENGLAND

In the New England colonies, as has been implied, the situation was quite different. At Plymouth (1620), Salem (1628), Massachusetts Bay (1630), and other nearby spots soon settled, more than twenty thousand Englishmen found new homes. A considerable number were learned, especially the Puritan clergymen and governors; and some of them were great men. Even in the seventeenth century they produced a considerable body of writing. Yet they were not literary people in the professional sense, and they were intent upon subduing a wilderness, making homes, and building a new civil society, on which they had staked their lives, and in some instances, their fortunes.

It was not long until the colony at Massachusetts Bay assumed the natural hegemony of New England. Here was the physical situation—a harbor and river—for expansion into a cluster of small towns in close association with each other. The governor of the Massachusetts Bay Company, John Winthrop, a strong Puritan, moved the seat of his company from London to Boston Bay, thus making the chartered company into an overseas colony with limited, but then quite unprecedented, powers of self-government. The Puritans who followed Winthrop were thrifty, and they thrived. They initiated a town-meeting government, popular elections, a bicameral council, and other novelties that were to become parts of the machinery of democracy. They can justly be charged with intolerance, of course, for they soon achieved a consensus on matters of dogma, and they had no such problems of diversity as made toleration inevitable in the Middle Colonies. But in New England such outcasts as Roger Williams and Anne Hutchinson soon founded colonies of their own, thus accelerating the outward flow of forces from Boston into New Hampshire, Connecticut, and Rhode Island. By 1643 there was the beginning of the New England Federation for mutual security and co-operative economic enterprise.

PURITANISM

The earliest English Puritans were devout members of the Church of England and had no desire to produce a schism. By the time of Elizabeth's reign the Church of England was clearly Protestant in respect to its separation from Rome. The Puritans wished the reform to be carried much further, in order to simplify or "purify" the creeds and rituals and to diminish the authority of the bishops, but still no official break was intended. In 1633, however, the elevation of Archbishop Laud put the Church of England in the control of a tyrant who was determined to root out "Calvinist" dissenters, Presbyterian or Puritan, by legal persecution. The consequent soul-searching among Puritans, who were never a "sect" in the sense that the Presbyterians were, carried them closer to certain fundamental tenets of John Calvin (1509–1564); and the most powerful and radical of them, unwilling to submit to the abu-

sive and cruel laws against them, soon formed the core of the New England clergy. It should be emphasized, however, that the Puritans did not regard the word of Calvin as the word of authority. They agreed with him when they thought him reasonable, but there were many aspects of his theology that they found unreasonable and so disregarded.

The ideas of Martin Luther (1483–1546), the earlier leader of the great Reformation, likewise became a permanent influence on both religious and civil institutions of American democracy. Concepts of authority, both civil and ecclesiastical, had been everywhere slowly weakening; they were shattered, wherever Luther's words were received, by his doctrine of the "priesthood of believers." "Neither Pope or Bishop nor any other man," he said, "has a right to impose a single syllable of law upon a Christian man without his consent."

Calvin's *Institutes*, on the other hand, authorized a theological system in certain respects as rigid as that of the Church of Rome, but its ultimate official authority was the consensus of its constituents, and not a hierarchy. In this system the New England "congregational meeting" was inherent from the beginning. In earlier stages of the Reformation it was held that the religion of the ruler should be the religion of the country he dominated, but Calvin, like Catholic thinkers, insisted that the church should be independent. The state should, in fact, be its servant. The result, in early New England during the Puritan period, was that the leading clergymen, powerful and well-trained, were for a time the dominating temporal as well as spiritual authority; but by 1700 their civil powers began to crumble under the weight of new secular influence.

In common with all advocates of strict Christian orthodoxy, American Puritans subscribed to Calvin's insistence that the omnipotent God had created the first man, Adam, in his own perfect image, that Adam in his willfulness had broken God's covenant, and that, as *The New England Primer* put it, "In Adam's fall we sinned all." It was Calvin's dogmas of predestination and grace that set him sharply apart from Luther on the one hand and the Roman Catholic Church on the other. The redemption of the individual came only by regeneration, the work of the spirit of God "in the souls of the elect and of them alone." Calvin and the Puritans put a special emphasis on the doctrine of original depravity. Adam's children were not mere automatons of evil impulse, since they possessed, as Adam had, a limited freedom of the will to make the good or evil choice. Still, nothing in man's personal power could mitigate the original sinfulness of his nature. Hence, redemption must be a free gift of God's saving grace, made to those predestined to receive it. No person could earn grace by good works, since good works, in themselves, could only be the result and fruition of grace. These doctrines were characteristically reflected in the interpretation of Christ the Redeemer as representing God's New Covenant with mankind, as Adam represented the Old Covenant.

These doctrines, to which Jonathan Edwards gave the classic recapitulation when Puritanism was already waning, have been interpreted by many modern critics as excessively grim and gloomy. A stereotype of the Puritan has been created, depicting him as a dour, thinly ascetic fellow employing censorship and blue laws to impose his prudish standards on others. Most of the Puritans would have voted to put him in the stocks. It is true that extreme zealots among them, overinterpreting their dogmas, despised this mortal life in contrast to the next. The same zealots, during an outbreak of hysterical superstition, persecuted the "witches." Yet the Puritans in general were lovers of life; their clergy were well-educated scholars in whom the Renaissance lamp of humanism still burned. They did not forbid gaily colored clothes if they could get them; they developed a pleasing domestic architecture and good arts and crafts on American soil; they liked the drink even if they despised the drunkard; they feared both ignorance and emotional evangelism, and made of their religious thought a rigorous intellectual discipline. They were the earliest colonists to insist on common schools; they had the first college (Harvard, 1636) and the first printing press in the colonies (Cambridge, 1638); and they were responsible for the most abundant and memorable literature created in the colonies before 1740. In their influence on American life, there is much more to bless them for than to condemn.

THE MIDDLE COLONIES

Lying between New England to the northeast and the sprawling farmlands of the southern colonies stretched the provinces of New York, New Jersey, Delaware, and Pennsylvania. The seed of American toleration was sown in this area, with its diversity of national strains, for here the melting pot that produced Crèvecœur's conception of an American boiled with a briskness unknown elsewhere along the Atlantic seaboard. Dutch and Swedish colonies were established in New York and Pennsylvania before the British came; the tolerance of Pennsylvania attracted large numbers of German and French-Huguenot refugees; and Jewish merchants early appeared in New York and Philadelphia.

Of all the colonies, the Middle Colonies enjoyed the best geographical location, the easiest access to the great inland waterways and stored natural resources of the continent, the largest economic promise, resulting from a fine balance of agricultural, manufacturing, and commercial potentials. By 1750, the Quaker city of Philadelphia had become the unofficial colonial capital by virtue of its location, the size of its population, and the volume of its commercial activity, in which respects it surpassed any city, except London, in the British Empire. The cultural institutions of the Middle Colonies, somewhat different from those of New England, were to prove quite as important in providing those basic conditions and ideas which, during the revolutionary crises of the eighteenth century, were formally welded into a national character and a frame of democratic government then unique among the nations of the world.

Of the many groups present in the Pennsylvania colony, the Quakers were the most homogeneous. Although these Friends, in the beginning, were drawn primarily from the humbler ranks of the English middle classes—they were artisans, tradesmen, and yeoman farmers for the most part—their American leader, William Penn, was one of the best-trained men in the colonies, and one of the greatest. He was a follower of George Fox, the English shepherd and cobbler whose powerful evangelism welded his disciples into the Religious Society of Friends. The early Quaker theology was fundamentally closer to Luther's than to Calvin's. It was less concerned with the original depravity of man than with the abounding grace of God. But Fox and his followers went far beyond Luther's rebellion against the delegated authority of pope or bishop; Fox taught that the ultimate authority for any person was the "inner light," the divine immanence, revealed to his own soul. Thus the Quaker worshiped in quiet, waiting upon the inward revelation of unity with the Eternal.

Penn had inherited from his

father a large financial claim upon the government of Charles II, and in 1681 he secured in settlement the vast colonial estate which the King named Pennsylvania. As Proprietor, Penn exercised great powers, but in writing his famous "Frame of Government" he ordained a free commonwealth, bestowing wide privileges of self-government upon the people. Convinced that "the nations want a precedent," he declared that "any government is free to the people where the laws rule * * * and the people are party to the laws. * * * Liberty without obedience is confusion, and obedience without liberty is slavery." These words, and the precedent which he established by his "Holy Experiment," remained alive in the American colonies, much later to be embodied in the Declaration of Independence of the nation and in its constitutional instrument of government, both written in Penn's city.

Under these favorable conditions the colony thrived. Like the Puritans, the Quakers quickly made provision for education. Four years after Penn's arrival, they had their first press (1686) and a public school chartered by the Proprietor. In 1740 Philadelphians chartered the Charity School, soon called the Academy, and later the University of Pennsylvania, the fourth colonial college (following Harvard, William and Mary, and Yale). During the same period the Middle Colonies founded three other colleges: Princeton (the College of New Jersey, 1746), Co-

lumbia (King's College, 1754), and Rutgers (Queen's College, 1766).

The energies of the inhabitants of these colonies of mixed cultures, centering upon Pennsylvania, fostered the development of science and medicine, technical enterprise and commerce, journalism and government—Penn, for example, made the first proposal for a union of the colonies—but in spite of the remarkable currency of the printed word among them, they produced less than New England of lasting literary value until after the first quarter of the eighteenth century. William Penn, however, proved to be a genuine writer, if on a limited scale. Besides his famous "Frame of Government," two of his works have continued to live: *No Cross No Crown* (1669), a defense of his creed, and *Some Fruits of Solitude* (1693), a collection of essays on the conduct of life and his Christian faith. Many of the early American Friends published journals, but only one, that of John Woolman, survives as great literature. Of the many early colonial travelers and observers, some from the Middle Colonies produced literary records comparable with those of Byrd of Virginia and Madam Knight of Boston. Crèvecœur, perhaps the most gifted of the colonial travelers, settled in Pennsylvania and later in upstate New York. John Bartram and his more famous son, William, established a long tradition of natural history in Philadelphia. Each left an important record of his travels and observations of American natural history, scientifically valuable, and, in William's case, a work of genuine literature. On settling in this country in 1804, the greater naturalist and painter John James Audubon made Philadelphia his home.

THE ENLIGHTENMENT

These Middle Colonies, as a result of their mixed culture and central location, became the natural center for activities of mutual interest, such as the intercolonial convention or congress. A growing sense of unity and independence characterized the second great period of American cultural history, beginning about 1725. Politically, this spirit encouraged the growth of a loose confederation, disturbed by the British colonial wars on the frontier and by "intolerable" British trade and taxation policies. In succession it produced the Revolution, the federal and constitutional union of the states, and the international recognition of the hegemony of the United States on the North American continent by about 1810, roughly the time of Jefferson's retirement as president, when a new national period began in literature and political life. During these years, the frontier moved beyond the Alleghenies, leaving behind it an established seaboard culture, and, in such cities as Philadelphia, Boston, and New York, a growing spirit of metropolitan sophistication.

The Enlightenment and its rationalistic spirit infused the minds and the acts of American leaders. Earlier religious mysticisms, local in character, were now overlaid by larger concerns for general toleration, civil rights, and a more comprehensive democracy in government. The conflict of ideas at the beginning of this period is well represented in a comparison of the contemporaries Jonathan Edwards and Benjamin Franklin, both among the greatest early Americans. Edwards represented the fullest intellectual development of the Calvinistic Puritan; his hard intellect and authoritarian convictions were tempered by human tenderness and spiritual sensitivity. Yet the last member of the Puritan hierarchy, Cotton Mather, had met fundamental and final opposition about the time Edwards was born. The secular spirit, the immigration of a new population, and the development of the urban spirit of enterprise and commerce would have doomed the Puritan commonwealth even if the Puritans themselves had not outgrown it.

The Age of Reason manifested a rationalistic conception of man in his relations with nature and God, suggested the extension of principles of equality and social justice, and encouraged the belief that man might assume greater control of nature without offending the majesty of God. If the universe, as Newton suggested, somewhat resembled a clock of unimaginable size, why might not man, by studying its laws, learn to utilize them for his benefit? The writings of John Locke (1632–1704) had enormous influence, and American readers also knew the writings of Locke's early student, Shaftesbury, and of various other British and French rationalists. Among the French writers, Rousseau and Quesnay, the best known in America, were both influential in their sociological ideas. Rousseau, in emphasizing the social contract as the "natural" basis for government, suggested a consistency between the laws of nature and those of society. Quesnay and his physiocratic followers strengthened this doctrine by asserting that society was based on the resources of nature, on land itself, thus stimulating the agrarian thought that was so attractive to Jefferson. Rationalism applied to theology produced Deism, but the degrees of Deism ranged widely, from the casual to the dialectical severity of Tom Paine. For the confirmed Deist, God was the first cause, but the hand of God was more evident in the mechanism of nature than in scriptural revelation; the Puritan belief in miraculous intervention and supernatural manifestations was regarded as blasphemy against the divine Creator of the immutable harmony and perfection of all things. But most enlightened rationalists confined their logic to practical affairs, or, like Franklin and Jefferson, entertained a mild Deism that diminished as they grew older.

THE BROADENING OF EIGHTEENTH-CENTURY LITERATURE

During this revolutionary end of the eighteenth century, Rationalism, reflected in the neoclassical spirit in literature, began to wane; at the same time a nascent romanticism appeared in life and literature. In England the influence of Pope was quickly superseded by the romanticism of Gray, Chatterton, Goldsmith, and the periodical essayists. Before Tom Paine wrote *The Age of Reason*, the age of revolution was well advanced; and the American and French revolutions advocated rationalistic instruments of government in support of romantic ideals of freedom and individualism. American writers, like the British, responded to these commingled influences, as for example, in the case of Jefferson or Freneau. The latter, an avowed Deist and a neoclassicist in his earliest poems, became in his later nature lyrics a forerunner of the romantic Bryant. This was the pattern of his age, in which the romantic movement, which was to dominate our literature after 1810, was already present in embryo. It was an age of magnificent literary energies, of vast upheaval, spiritual and social; and the rapid growth of publishing provided a forum for contestants of all ranks. The first newspaper to succeed in the colonies, the Boston *News-Letter*, had appeared in 1704; by the time of the Revolution there were nearly fifty. No magazine appeared until 1741, but after that date magazines flourished, and by the time of Washington's inauguration (1789) there had been nearly forty. Periodical publication gave a hearing to scores of essayists, propagandists, and political writers; to such leading authors as Paine and Freneau; and to lesser writers still remembered, such as Francis Hopkinson, whose verse satires plagued the British, and John Dickinson, a lawyer whose *Letters from a Farmer in Pennsylvania* (1767–1768) skillfully presented the colonial position in various newspapers in the hope of securing British moderation before it was too late. William Smith, Provost of the College of Philadelphia, made his *American Magazine* (1757–1758) a vehicle for a talented coterie of his protégés and students—the short-lived Nathaniel Evans, Francis Hopkinson, and Thomas Godfrey, the first American playwright. Such verse as theirs, both satirical and sentimental, abounded in the periodicals, but although there had been scores of American poets by the time of the Revolution, only Freneau and Taylor have been greatly admired for their literary values. Among still earlier poets, Anne Bradstreet, who died in 1672, is remembered for her small but genuine lyric gift, appearing amid inhospitable conditions in Puritan Massachusetts, and Michael Wigglesworth is remembered for *The Day of Doom* (1662), the most popular Puritan poem, whose lengthy description of the Last Judgment conferred the benison of penance along with the fascinations of melodrama.

Theatrical activity had appeared sporadically ever since the beginning of the century. By 1749 a stock company was established in Philadelphia, and its seasonal migrations encouraged the building of theaters and the growth of other companies of players, in New York, Boston, Williamsburg, and Charleston. The native players, and visiting actors from England, devoted themselves principally to Elizabethan revivals and classics of the French theater, but it was an age of great talent on the stage, and the support of the theater, in spite of continuous opposition from religious objectors, illustrates the steady increase of urban sophistication. Thomas Godfrey's *Prince of Parthia*, the first native tragedy to be performed, reached the stage in 1767. During the Revolution, drama survived only as effective political satire. Native authorship revived in 1787, with the appearance of Royall Tyler's *The Contrast*, which still retains an archaic vitality; in its day it established the stereotype of "Brother Jonathan" for the homespun American character. Early native playwrights included two prominent writers of fiction, Susannah Rowson and H. H. Brackenridge. William Dunlap, a portrait painter, among whose many plays *André* (1798) remains a genuine, if now outdated work, lived far into the Knickerbocker period and was the first large-scale producer-playwright of our literature, although he went bankrupt in this enterprise.

Meanwhile, a native fiction had taken root. The great age of British fiction had begun about 1719, and such English novelists as Defoe, Fielding, Richardson, and even Smollett and Sterne were widely read in the colonies. Soon after the Revolution, however, fiction of native authorship appeared, first represented in two domestic novels, *The Power of Sympathy* (1789), by William Hill Brown, and *Char-*

lotte Temple (1794), by the English-born Susannah H. Rowson, which has been reprinted even in the twentieth century. A really fine picaresque novel, *Modern Chivalry*, by the Pennsylvania jurist H. H. Brackenridge, appeared in five parts between 1792 and 1815. Its author's learning in the classics and his familiarity with the great picaresque tradition of Cervantes were here combined with an acid and clever satire of early American failures in democratic politics. A third European fictional tradition, the Gothic romance of terror, found its American exemplar in Charles Brockden Brown, another Philadelphian, four of whose romances made literary history, if not great literature, between 1798 and 1800.

Freneau is the most important bridge between the classicism of the eighteenth century and the full-fledged romanticism of the nineteenth. Late in the eighteenth century, however, the seven so-called Connecticut Wits, most of them associated with Yale, attracted great attention by devoting themselves to a new national poetic literature. Three of them achieved a considerable distinction in life, but none of them affected the literature of America except in the historical sense. John Trumbull (1750–1831) is best remembered for his satires: *The Progress of Dullness* (1772), an amusing attack on "educators" which makes excellent sense if

only passable poetry, and *M'-Fingal* (1775–1782), a burlesque epic blasting American Toryism. Timothy Dwight reached distinction as president of Yale, but of his poems only *Greenfield Hill* (1794) rises occasionally above his didactic solemnity. Joel Barlow (1754–1812) was a large-minded liberal and an American patriot, but no one who has been condemned to read his pioneer American epic, *The Vision of Columbus* (1787), or its even longer later version, *The Columbiad* (1807), can quite forgive him. His shorter mock-epic, *The Hasty-Pudding* (1796), however, is the very entertaining work of a generous mind.

The literature of America up to the end of the eighteenth century needs no apology. The minor literature was abundant; it was serviceable to its time, and in retrospect it seems no more odd or feeble than the common stock of popular expression of the earlier periods of any nation. What is profoundly important is the wealth of true literature, the inspired expression of great men writing often under conditions unfavorable to literary expression, which appeared from the first, and increasingly through the years, in an abundance entirely out of proportion to the size of the population and the expectations that might be entertained for a country so new and so wild and sparsely settled.

The Puritan Culture

WILLIAM BRADFORD

(1590–1657)

William Bradford was one of the greatest of colonial Americans, a man large in spirit and wisdom, wholly consecrated to a mission in which he regarded himself as an instrument of God. The early history of Plymouth Colony was the history of his leadership, and tiny Plymouth occupies a position in history wholly incommensurate with its size.

Like the patriarchs of the Old Testament, William Bradford in his annals recorded God's "choosing" of His people, their exile, and their wanderings. Even after twelve years in Holland, as Bradford wrote in the language of *Hebrews*, "they knew they were pilgrims," and must follow the cloud and fire to a land promised, if at first unpromising, their new Zion. In 1630 Bradford wrote his first ten chapters, dealing with the persecutions of the Separatists in Scrooby, England, their flight to Holland in 1608, and their history until they landed at Plymouth in 1620. His "Second Book," dealing with their history in Plymouth from 1620 until 1647, was

written "in pieces," most of it before 1646.

Bradford was born of a yeoman farmer and a tradesman's daughter in Yorkshire. Orphaned in his first year by his father's death and trained for farming by relatives, almost without formal education, he was a well-read man who brought a considerable library with him to Plymouth at the age of thirty. When he was twelve he had begun the earnest study of the Bible; at sixteen he joined the Separatist group then forming at nearby Scrooby, an act which taxed both courage and conviction; at eighteen he accompanied the group to Holland to escape persecution, perhaps death. In Holland he lost a small patrimony in business, became a weaver, and achieved relative prosperity. He also read widely in English and Dutch, and somewhat in French, Greek, and Hebrew. At twenty-seven he was a leader of his people in Leyden, a member of the committee which arranged their pilgrimage. On November 11, 1620, just after the *Mayflower* made land-

14

fall at Cape Cod, he signed the Mayflower Compact; he was one of the group that explored the unknown shore; he was one of those who, on December 11, entered Plymouth Bay in the teeth of a snowstorm, and stepped ashore—according to legend—on Plymouth Rock. His first wife was lost overboard in his absence, one of the fifty who, out of the 102 Pilgrims who reached Plymouth, were to die within the year. Among these was the first elected governor, John Carver.

Bradford, elected to succeed Governor Carver, probably had already begun to write a sort of history of the colony. The evidence is inconclusive, but it is believed that Bradford and Edward Winslow consolidated their journals and sent them for anonymous publication to George Morton, English agent for the Pilgrims. Morton, as compiler, signed himself "G. Mourt," possibly for political reasons, and *A Relation or Journall of the Beginning and Proceedings of the Plantation Setled at Plimoth*, generally known as *Mourt's Relation*, appeared in London in 1622.

From 1621 until his death, Bradford probably possessed more power than any other colonial governor; yet he refused the opportunity to become sole proprietor, and maintained the democratic principles suggested in the Mayflower Compact. He was re-elected thirty times, for a total term of thirty-three years —in two years no elections were held, and in five terms, "by importunity," he succeeded in passing his authority to another. He persuaded the surviving Pilgrim Fathers to share their original rights with the entire body of Freemen; at the same time he led the small group of "Old Comers" who controlled the fishing and trading monopolies, not for private gain, but to liquidate the debt to the British investors who had financed their undertaking. He seldom left Plymouth, where he died. His worldly estate was a small house and some orchards and little else, but he was one of his country's first great men.

The first edition of the *History of Plymouth Plantation*, edited by Charles Deane, appeared in Boston, 1856, but it has been superseded. The standard edition is *History of Plymouth Plantation, 1620–1647*, 2 vols., edited, with notes, by W. C. Ford, Boston, Massachusetts Historical Society, 1912; but even this edition is unreliable, there being some twenty-five minor errors in the transcription of the Mayflower Compact alone. For the general reader the best edition is *Of Plymouth Plantation, 1620–1647*, edited by Samuel Eliot Morison, New York, 1952. The selections in this text have been reproduced from this edition, in which spelling and punctuation follow modern practice.

Mourt's Relation, first published as *A Relation or Journall of the Beginning and Proceedings of the Plantation Setled at Plimoth*, London, 1622, is available in new editions, edited by Theodore Besterman, London, 1939, and Dwight B. Heath, 1963.

Good biographical studies are Bradford Smith, *Bradford of Plymouth*, 1951; Samuel Eliot Morison, "Introduction," *Of Plymouth Plantation, 1620–1647*, 1952; and Samuel Eliot Morison, "William Bradford," *Dictionary of American Biography*, 1933.

From Of Plymouth Plantation

Chapter IX: Of their Voyage, and how they Passed the Sea;
and of their Safe Arrival at Cape Cod

* * *

Being thus arrived in a good harbor, and brought safe to land, they fell upon their knees and blessed the God of Heaven who had brought them over the vast and furious ocean, and delivered them from all the perils and miseries thereof, again to set their feet on the firm and stable earth, their proper element. And no marvel if they were thus joyful, seeing wise Seneca was so affected with sailing a few miles on the coast of his own Italy, as he affirmed, that he had rather remain twenty years on his way by land than pass by sea to any place in a short time, so tedious and dreadful was the same unto him.[1]

But here I cannot but stay and make a pause, and stand half amazed at this poor people's present condition; and so I think will the reader, too, when he well considers the same. Being thus passed the vast ocean, and a sea of troubles before in their preparation (as may be remembered by that which went before), they had now no friends to welcome them nor inns to entertain or refresh their weatherbeaten bodies; no houses or much less towns to repair to, to seek for succour. It is recorded in Scripture [2] as a mercy to the Apostle and his shipwrecked company, that the barbarians showed them no small kindness in refreshing them, but these savage barbarians, when they met with them (as after will appear) were readier to fill their sides full of arrows than otherwise. And for the season it was winter, and they that know the winters of that country know them to be sharp and violent, and subject to cruel and fierce storms, dangerous to travel to known places, much more to search an unknown coast. Besides, what could they see but a hideous and desolate wilderness, full of wild beasts and wild men—and what multitudes there might be of them they knew not. Neither could they, as it were, go up to the top of Pisgah [3] to view from this wilderness a more goodly country to feed their hopes; for which way soever they turned their eyes (save upward to the heavens) they could have little solace or content in respect of any outward objects. For summer being done, all things stand upon them with a weatherbeaten face, and the whole country, full of woods and

1. Bradford cites Epistle LIII. His words, "he had rather remain * * * in a short time," are translated from Seneca. *Epistulae Morales ad Lucilium,* LIII, Section 5.
2. Bradford cites Acts xxviii. Verse 2 refers to the Melitans' kindness to the shipwrecked Paul.
3. From Mount Pisgah in Palestine (also called Mount Nebo; in Arabic, Ras Siyagha; now in Jordan), Moses saw the Promised Land (Deuteronomy xxxiv: 1–4).

thickets, represented a wild and savage hue. If they looked behind them, there was the mighty ocean which they had passed and was now as a main bar and gulf to separate them from all the civil parts of the world. If it be said they had a ship to succour them, it is true; but what heard they daily from the master and company? But that with speed they should look out a place (with their shallop) where they would be, at some near distance; for the season was such as he would not stir from thence till a safe harbor was discovered by them, where they would be, and he might go without danger; and that victuals consumed apace but he must and would keep sufficient for themselves and their return. Yea, it was muttered by some that if they got not a place in time, they would turn them and their goods ashore and leave them. Let it also be considered what weak hopes of supply and succour they left behind them, that might bear up their minds in this sad condition and trials they were under; and they could not but be very small. It is true, indeed, the affections and love of their brethren at Leyden [4] was cordial and entire towards them, but they had little power to help them or themselves; and how the case stood between them and the merchants at their coming away hath already been declared.

What could now sustain them but the Spirit of God and His grace? May not and ought not the children of these fathers rightly say: "Our fathers were Englishmen which came over this great ocean, and were ready to perish in this wilderness; but they cried unto the Lord, and He heard their voice and looked on their adversity," [5] etc. "Let them therefore praise the Lord, because He is good: and His mercies endure forever. Yea, let them which have been redeemed of the Lord, shew how He hath delivered them from the hand of the oppressor. When they wandered in the desert wilderness out of the way, and found no city to dwell in, both hungry and thirsty, their soul was overwhelmed in them." "Let them confess before the Lord His lovingkindness and His wonderful works before the sons of men." [6]

Chapter X: *Showing How they Sought out a place of Habitation; and What Befell them Thereabout*

* * *

After this,[7] the shallop being got ready, they set out again for the better discovery of this place, and the master of the ship desired to go himself. So there went some thirty men but found it to be no

4. Leyden in Holland, where nearly half the exiled Separatists remained when these Pilgrims set out for America by way of England.
5. Bradford cites Deuteronomy xxvi: 5–7, referring to God's deliverance of Israel from bondage in Egypt.
6. Bradford cites "107 Psa: v. 1, 2, 4, 5, 8," of which these closing lines, beginning with "Let them therefore praise the Lord . . .", are a paraphrase.
7. The Pilgrims have already explored the shore, finding a pond and a creek and, close by, some caches of Indian corn.

harbor for ships but only for boats. There was also found two of their houses covered with mats, and sundry of their implements in them, but the people were run away and could not be seen. Also there was found more of their corn and of their beans of various colours; the corn and beans they brought away, purposing to give them full satisfaction when they should meet with any of them as, about some six months afterward they did, to their good content.[8]

And here is to be noted a special providence of God, and a great mercy to this poor people, that here they got seed to plant them corn the next year, or else they might have starved, for they had none nor any likelihood to get any till the season had been past, as the sequel did manifest. Neither is it likely they had had this, if the first voyage had not been made, for the ground was now all covered with snow and hard frozen; but the Lord is never wanting unto His in their greatest needs; let His holy name have all the praise. * * *

From hence they departed and coasted all along [9] but discerned no place likely for harbor; and therefore hasted to a place that their pilot (one Mr. Coppin who had been in the country before) did assure them was a good harbor, which he had been in, and they might fetch it before night; of which they were glad for it began to be foul weather.

After some hours' sailing it began to snow and rain, and about the middle of the afternoon the wind increased and the sea became very rough, and they broke their rudder, and it was as much as two men could do to steer her with a couple of oars. But their pilot bade them be of good cheer for he saw the harbor; but the storm increasing, and night drawing on, they bore what sail they could to get in, while they could see. But herewith they broke their mast in three pieces and their sail fell overboard in a very grown sea, so as they had like to have been cast away. Yet by God's mercy they recovered themselves, and having the flood [1] with them, struck into the harbor. But when it came to, the pilot was deceived in the place, and said the Lord be merciful unto them for his eyes never saw that place before; and he and the master's mate would have

8. Morison notes that this second expedition explored the Pamet and Little Pamet rivers from November 28 to November 30, and that descendants of these Nauset Indians still survive at Mashpee, Cape Cod.
9. This is the third exploring expedition, begun on December 6/16, 1620, after several weeks of confinement on the *Mayflower* by "foul weather." Ten men, including Bradford, in their shallop, are to explore as far as Plymouth, seeking a better ship's harbor than the Pamet or Ipswich, previously examined. They have successfully with-

stood the first severe Indian attack, and are now proceeding to Plymouth. The dates in Bradford's manuscript are Old Style (following the Julian calendar), ten days earlier than the same dates according to the present (Gregorian) calendar. In these notes, important verifiable dates are given in both forms, as above.
1. "The mean rise and fall of tide there is about 9 ft. Plymouth Bay * * * is a bad place to enter in thick weather with a sea running and night coming on" [Morison's note].

run her ashore in a cove full of breakers before the wind. But a lusty seaman which steered bade those which rowed, if they were men, about with her or else they were all cast away; the which they did with speed. So he bid them to be of good cheer and row lustily, for there was a fair sound before them, and he doubted not but they should find one place or other where they might ride in safety. And though it was very dark and rained sore, yet in the end they got under the lee of a small island and remained there all that night in safety.[2] But they knew not this to be an island till morning, but were divided in their minds; some would keep the boat for fear they might be amongst the Indians, others were so wet and cold they could not endure but got ashore, and with much ado got fire (all things being so wet); and the rest were glad to come to them, for after midnight the wind shifted to the northwest and it froze hard.

But though this had been a day and night of much trouble and danger unto them, yet God gave them a morning of comfort and refreshing (as usually He doth to His children) for the next day was a fair, sunshining day, and they found themselves to be on an island secure from the Indians, where they might dry their stuff, fix their pieces and rest themselves; and gave God thanks for His mercies in their manifold deliverances. And this being the last day of the week, they prepared there to keep the Sabbath.

On Monday they sounded the harbor and found it fit for shipping, and marched into the land and found divers cornfields and little running brooks, a place (as they supposed) fit for the situation.[3] At least it was the best they could find, and the season and their present necessity made them glad to accept of it. So they returned to their ship again with this news to the rest of the people, which did much comfort their hearts.

On the 15th of December they weighed anchor to go to the place they had discovered, and came within two leagues of it, but were fain to bear up again; but the 16th day, the wind came fair, and they arrived safe in this harbor. And afterwards took better view of the place, and resolved where to pitch their dwelling; and the 25th day began to erect the first house for common use to receive them and their goods.[4]

---

2. Morison identifies the anchorage as the lee of Saquish Head, and the island there as Clarks Island, where they spent Saturday and Sunday, December 9/19–10/20.
3. "Here is the only contemporary authority for the 'Landing of the Pilgrims on Plymouth Rock' on Monday, 11/21 Dec. 1620. * * * The landing took place from the shallop, not the *Mayflower* * * * Nor is it clear that they landed on * * * Plymouth Rock, [although] it would have been very convenient for that purpose at half tide" [Morison's note].
4. *I.e.,* the *Mayflower* reached Plymouth Harbor on December 16/26, but the Pilgrims did not actually begin to build ashore for nine more days. *Mourt's Relation* shows that the interval was used in exploring for the best possible site.

From Of Plymouth Plantation, Book II

[*The Mayflower Compact* (1620)]

I shall a little return back, and begin with a combination made by them before they came ashore; being the first foundation of their government [5] in this place. Occasioned partly by the discontented and mutinous speeches that some of the strangers amongst them had let fall from them in the ship: That when they came ashore they would use their own liberty, for none had power to command them, the patent they had being for Virginia and not for New England, which belonged to another government, with which the Virginia Company had nothing to do.[6] And partly that such an act by them done, this their condition considered, might be as firm as any patent, and in some respects more sure.

The form was as followeth: [7]

In the Name of God, Amen.

We whose names are underwritten, the loyal subjects of our dread Sovereign Lord King James, by the Grace of God of Great Britain, France, and Ireland King, Defender of the Faith, etc.

Having undertaken, for the Glory of God and advancement of the Christian Faith and Honour of our King and Country, a Voyage to plant the First Colony in the Northern Parts of Virginia, do by these presents solemnly and mutually in the presence of God and one of another, Covenant and Combine ourselves together into a Civil Body Politic, for our better ordering and preservation and furtherance of the ends aforesaid; and by virtue hereof to enact, constitute and frame such just and equal Laws, Ordinances, Acts, Constitutions and Offices, from time to time, as shall be thought most meet and convenient for the general good of the Colony, unto which we promise all due submission and obedience. In witness whereof we have hereunder subscribed our names at Cape Cod, the 11th of November, in the year of the reign of our Sovereign Lord King James, of England, France and Ireland the eighteenth, and of Scotland the fifty-fourth. Anno Domini 1620.

5. The Mayflower Compact is important as an early American covenant instituting civil government by common consent with reference to the common good. Although it was enacted in an emergency, it followed the precedent of the church covenants already familiar to Puritans, and, as Bradford's words suggest, it was the "first foundation" of direct popular government in America, while feudal forms persisted in Europe. 6. The Pilgrims and the "Adventurers" who sailed with them were alike authorized by patent from the Virginia Company, whose territory extended northward only to Manhattan Island. 7. A text differing from this one only in a few insignificant words was published in *Mourt's Relation* in 1622.

After this they chose, or rather confirmed, Mr. John Carver (a man godly and well approved amongst them) their Governor ᵔ that year. And after they had provided a place for their goods, or common store (which were long in unlading for want of boats, foulness of the winter weather and sickness of divers [8]) and begun some small cottages for their habitation; as time would admit, they met and consulted of laws and orders, both for their civil and military government as the necessity of their condition did require, still adding thereunto as urgent occasion in several times, and as cases did require.

In these hard and difficult beginnings they found some discontents and murmurings arise amongst some, and mutinous speeches and carriages in other; but they were soon quelled and overcome by the wisdom, patience, and just and equal carriage of things, by the Governor and better part, which clave faithfully together in the main.

ANNE BRADSTREET

(1612?–1672)

In 1650 a woman poet was a rarity, but Anne Bradstreet's place in literary history is the result not only of her uniqueness but of a genuine if limited inspiration and a force of character which have survived for three hundred years in a few of her poems. This first noteworthy American poet was born in Northampton, England, probably in 1612. Her father, Thomas Dudley, by conviction a sturdy Puritan, had turned from a military career to business; when Anne was born he was steward of the estates of the Earl of Lincoln, a learned and aristocratic Puritan. Thomas Dudley was himself a man of studious character, and his daughter had the advantages of good tutoring, with access to the Earl's considerable library at Sempringham Castle. She was widely read but not learned, drawn chiefly toward the serious and religious writings of the Puritan world, and very little toward those of that other world, just waning, in which there still lived at her birth Shakespeare and Cervantes, Ben Jonson and Bacon.

In 1628, at the age of sixteen, she married Simon Bradstreet, a grave and brilliant young Puritan who had been trained at Cambridge and afterward by her father. Two years later, Bradstreet gave up his position as steward of the Countess of Warwick, and with his young wife embarked upon the *Arabella* for America. Dudley and his family also sailed on that ship, which brought the first settlers to the colony at Massachusetts Bay. One of the most active men in the colony, Dudley served four terms as governor. Simon Brad-

8. Several; various persons.

street was governor of the colony for ten years; he served also as judge, and represented Massachusetts at the court of Charles II when curtailment of the charter was threatened in 1661.

In spite of the hardships of early colonial life and the duties of her household, Anne Bradstreet seems to have turned resolutely to authorship whenever she had the opportunity. Manuscripts of the poems in her first volume bear dates from 1632 to 1643. Whether she intended publication or not, she wrote a dedicatory poem to her father in 1642. In 1647 her sister's husband, John Woodbridge, pastor of the church of Andover, sailed to England and took her manuscript volume with him. Without her consent he had it published in London, in 1650, with the title, *The Tenth Muse Lately Sprung Up in America, * * * By a Gentlewoman of Those Parts.* About 1666 she revised all her poems for an authorized edition, which was not published until after her death.

The first edition of Anne Bradstreet's writings was *The Tenth Muse Lately Sprung Up in America * * *, London, 1650, unsigned. The second edition, revised and enlarged by the author, for the first time including the "Contemplations," was posthumously published as *Several Poems Compiled with Great Variety of Wit and Learning,* Boston, 1678. This was reprinted in 1758. The best edition, with biographical and critical comment, is *The Works of Anne Bradstreet in Prose and Verse,* edited by J. H. Ellis, 1867; reprinted 1932. In this edition the prose "Meditations" first appeared. A collection, *The Tenth Muse* (1650), *Meditations * * * and Other Works,* ed. by Josephine K. Piercy, appeared in 1966. The texts below are from Ellis' edition, which reproduces those of the 1678 edition. The capitalization, spelling, and punctuation have been normalized.

Biographies are Helen S. Campbell, *Anne Bradstreet and Her Time,* 1891, L. Caldwell, *An Account of Anne Bradstreet,* 1898, and Elizabeth Wade White, *Anne Bradstreet: "The Tenth Muse,"* 1971. Excellent sketches are by Moses C. Tyler, in *A History of American Literature During the Colonial Period,* 1878, revised 1897, 1949; and by Lyon N. Richardson, in the *Dictionary of American Biography,* 1929. Josephine K. Piercy, *Anne Bradstreet,* 1965, is a critical study.

The Prologue[1]

1

To sing of wars, of captains, and of kings,
Of cities founded, commonwealths begun,
For my mean pen are too superior things;
Or how they all, or each, their dates have run;
Let poets and historians set these forth;
My obscure lines shall not so dim their worth.   5

2

But when my wond'ring eyes and envious heart
Great Bartas'[2] sugared lines do but read o'er,
Fool, I do grudge the muses did not part

---

1. Anne Bradstreet apparently intended this poem as a prologue for her lengthy "Quaternions" on the history of mankind and the "four monarchies." In the 1650 edition it stood at the beginning of that work, preceded only by her poem dedicating her poems to her father.
2. Guillaume de Salluste du Bartas (1544–1590), French writer of religious epics, by whom she was inspired.

'Twixt him and me that overfluent store. 10
A Bartas can do what a Bartas will;
But simple I according to my skill.

3

From schoolboy's tongue no rhet'ric we expect,
Nor yet a sweet consort from broken strings,
Nor perfect beauty where's a main defect. 15
My foolish, broken, blemished Muse so sings;
All this to mend, alas, no art is able,
'Cause nature made it so irreparable.

4

Nor can I, like that fluent, sweet-tongued Greek
Who lisped at first, in future times speak plain. 20
By art he gladly found what he did seek;
A full requital of his striving pain.
Art can do much, but this maxim's most sure:
A weak or wounded brain admits no cure.

5

I am obnoxious to each carping tongue 25
Who says my hand a needle better fits;
A poet's pen all scorn I should thus wrong,
For such despite they cast on female wits.
If what I do prove well, it won't advance;
They'll say it's stol'n, or else it was by chance. 30

6

But sure the antique Greeks were far more mild;
Else of our sex why feignèd they those nine,[3]
And Poesy made Calliope's own child?
So 'mongst the rest they placed the arts divine,
But this weak knot they will full soon untie: 35
The Greeks did nought but play the fools and lie.

7

Let Greeks be Greeks, and women what they are;
Men have precedency and still excel.
It is but vain unjustly to wage war;
Men can do best, and women know it well. 40
Pre-eminence in all and each is yours;
Yet grant some small acknowledgement of ours.

8

And O ye high-flown quills [4] that soar the skies,
And ever with your prey still catch your praise,
If e'er you deign these lowly lines your eyes, 45

---

3. All nine of the Greek Muses were female deities, each patronizing a different art. That of Calliope, mentioned in the following line, was the epic, which Mrs. Bradstreet was attempting in her "Quaternions."

4. The quill pen, then in general use.

Give thyme or parsley wreath; I ask no bays.
This mean and unrefinèd ore of mine
Will make your glistering gold but more to shine.

1643?   1650

To My Dear and Loving Husband [5]

If ever two were one, then surely we.
If ever man were loved by wife, then thee;
If ever wife was happy in a man,
Compare with me ye women if you can.
I prize thy love more than whole mines of gold,   5
Or all the riches that the East doth hold.
My love is such that rivers cannot quench,
Nor ought but love from thee give recompense.
Thy love is such I can no way repay;
The heavens reward thee manifold, I pray.   10
Then while we live, in love let's so persever,
That when we live no more we may live ever.

                                                                        1678

A Letter to Her Husband [6]

Phoebus,[7] make haste, the day's too long, be gone;
The silent night's the fittest time for moan.
But stay this once, unto my suit give ear,
And tell my griefs in either hemisphere;
And if the whirlings of thy wheels don't drown'd   5
The woful accents of my doleful sound,
If in thy swift carrier [8] thou canst make stay,
I crave this boon, this errand by the way:
Commend me to the man more loved than life,
Shew him the sorrows of his widowed wife,   10
My dumpish thoughts, my groans, my brakish tears,
My sobs, my longing hopes, my doubting fears,
And if he love, how can he there abide?
My interest's more than all the world beside.
He that can tell the stars or ocean sand,   15

5. In the 1678 edition, posthumously published, the anonymous editor included this among "several other poems made by the author upon diverse occasions, * * * found among her papers after her death, which she never meant should come to publick view." 6. First published in the 1678 edition. There it is simply entitled "Another,"
following a short poem called "A Letter to Her Husband, Absent upon Publick Employment." These were among the manuscript poems of an intimate nature which Mrs. Bradstreet had apparently not intended to publish. 7. The sun. 8. *I.e.*, "career," or "course."

Or all the grass that in the meads do stand,
The leaves in the woods, the hail or drops of rain,
Or in a cornfield number every grain,
Or every mote that in the sunshine hops,
May count my sighs and number all my drops.   20
Tell him the countless steps that thou dost trace,
That once a day thy spouse thou mayst embrace;
And when thou canst not treat by loving mouth,
Thy rays afar salute her from the south.
But for one month I see no day, poor soul,   25
Like those far situate under the pole,
Which day by day long wait for thy arise:
O how they joy when thou dost light the skys.
O Phoebus, hadst thou but thus long from thine
Restrained the beams of thy beloved shine,   30
At thy return, if so thou could'st or durst,
Behold a Chaos blacker than the first.
Tell him here's worse than a confused matter—
His little world's a fathom under water;
Nought but the fervor of his ardent beams   35
Hath power to dry the torrent of these streams.
Tell him I would say more, but cannot well:
Oppressed minds abruptest tales do tell.
Now post with double speed, mark what I say;
By all our loves conjure him not to stay.   40

1678

The Author to Her Book [9]

Thou ill-formed offspring of my feeble brain,
Who after birth did'st by my side remain,
Till snatched from thence by friends, less wise than true,
Who thee abroad exposed to public view;
Made thee in rags, halting, to the press to trudge,   5
Where errors were not lessened, all may judge.
At thy return my blushing was not small,
My rambling brat (in print) should mother call;
I cast thee by as one unfit for light,
Thy visage was so irksome in my sight;   10

9. This casual poem is one of Anne Bradstreet's most delightful and genuine. It recounts with humor her feelings at seeing her poems in print in 1650 without her authorization or correction, and her subsequent efforts to improve them. It appears that she intended this to stand last among her poems when she revised them about 1666 for a proposed second edition. Whoever sent the volume to the printer after her death added a subsequent section of thirteen "Posthumous Poems."

Yet being mine own, at length affection would
Thy blemishes amend, if so I could:
I washed thy face, but more defects I saw,
And rubbing off a spot, still made a flaw.
I stretched thy joints to make thee even feet,   15
Yet still thou run'st more hobbling than is meet;
In better dress to trim thee was my mind,
But nought save homespun cloth, in the house I find.
In this array, 'mongst vulgars may'st thou roam;
In criticks hands beware thou dost not come;   20
And take thy way where yet thou are not known.
If for thy Father asked, say thou had'st none;
And for thy Mother, she alas is poor,
Which caused her thus to send thee out of door.

1666?   1678

SAMUEL SEWALL

(1652–1730)

The New England Puritans were closely united by their common faith, but they produced the varied individualism of Bradford, John Eliot, the Mathers, and Jonathan Edwards, among others. Samuel Sewall represents a distinct type of the second and third generations, in which a more secular spirit gradually defeated the waning theocracy. Devoutly religious in private and public life, Sewall resisted an early religious vocation in favor of wealth, public office, and the pursuit of his hobbies. Shortly after his graduation from Harvard in 1671, he married Hannah, daughter of John Hull, Master of the Mint and reputed to be the wealthiest person in Massachusetts. His position was soon further strengthened by a small inheritance from his father. Sewall became an early example of the American aristocrat who regards public service

as his natural expression. His father, avoiding the consequences of the Restoration of 1660, had brought him at the age of nine to Boston, and he seldom left it afterward. His *Diary*, for which he is best known, is a social history of that city during more than a half century.

Sewall began his public service in his late twenties. He managed the colony's printing press for several years, acting concurrently as deputy of the general court (1683) and later as member of the Council (1684–1686). In England on business in 1688, he assisted Increase Mather, the appointed envoy of the Massachusetts churches, in his unsuccessful efforts to secure the restoration of the charter of the colony. Under the new charter of 1692, Sewall again became a member of the Council, and served for thirty-three years. In the same year, 1692, he achieved his professional objective, being appointed as justice of the Superior Court; and he rose in the judiciary until, from 1718 to 1728, he was chief justice of Massachusetts.

One judicial act above all others is memorable in his life; he was a member of the special court of three which condemned the witches of Salem in 1692. That the blood of these innocents rested heavily on his soul is shown by his public confession of error five years later, and by other acts of contrition recorded in the text of his diary.

Sewall becomes the more interesting, since he represents not only himself but also an epoch. With the rapid influx of new people, the fervid dedication of the Puritan Fathers was doomed. Sewall's *Diary* depicts the resultant secularization, and the daily life of the generation that, within his time, first fully expressed those practical traits that came to be called "Yankee." He was shrewdly aware of the value of money, but wished to earn it honestly; he was ambitious for honors, position, and esteem, but affectionate and neighborly; he was of moderate

intelligence, often quaintly obtuse, but he had a quick sense of responsibility, the courage to confess his sins and acknowledge God publicly, and the humanitarian inspiration to become the author of perhaps the first tract published against Negro slavery in this country, *The Selling of Joseph* (1700).

The now famous *Diary* was not published until 1878. His first entries were made in 1673, and the record was copiously continued for most of the years through 1729, a total span of fifty-seven years. In spite of occasional lapses, the style bears the interesting stamp of the man himself, at his best when he portrays with a few suggestive strokes the dramatic essentials of a scene, a conversation, or even a gathering of people.

The Diary of Samuel Sewall was published in the *Collections of the Massachusetts Historical Society*, Fifth Series, Vols. V–VII, 1878–1882, the source of the present text. A recent definitive edition including new material on Sewall and his times is M. Halsey Thomas, *The Diary of Samuel Sewall*, 1973. Biographical studies are N. H. Chamberlain, *Samuel Sewall * * * *, 1897, Ola E. Winslow, *Samuel Sewall of Boston*, 1964, and T. B. Strandness, *Samuel Sewall: A Puritan Portrait*, 1967.

From The Diary of Samuel Sewall

[*Customs, Courts, and Courtships*]

April 29, 1695. The morning is very warm and Sunshiny; in the Afternoon there is Thunder and Lightening, and about 2 P.M. a very extraordinary Storm of Hail, so that the ground was made white with it, as with the blossoms when fallen; 'twas as bigg as pistoll and Musquet Bullets; It broke of the Glass of the new House about 480 Quarrels [1] of the Front; of Mr. Sergeant's about as much; Col. Shrimpton, Major General, Govr. Bradstreet, New

---

1. Squares; panes set diagonally in a window.

Meetinghouse, Mr. Willard, &c. Mr. Cotton Mather dined with us, and was with me in the new Kitchen when this was; He had just been mentioning that more Ministers Houses than others proportionably had been smitten with Lightening; enquiring what the meaning of God should be in it. Many Hail-Stones broke throw the Glass and flew to the middle of the Room, or farther: People afterward Gazed upon the House to see its Ruins. I got Mr. Mather to pray with us after this awful Providence; He told God He had broken the brittle part of our house, and prayd that we might be ready for the time when our Clay-Tabernacles should be broken. Twas a sorrowfull thing to me to see the house so far undon again before twas finish'd. * * *

Jan. 14, 1697. Copy of the Bill I put up on the Fast day; [2] giving it to Mr. Willard as he pass'd by, and standing up at the reading of it, and bowing when finished; in the Afternoon.

Samuel Sewall, sensible of the reiterated strokes of God upon himself and family; and being sensible, that as to the Guilt contracted upon the opening of the late commission of Oyer and Terminer at Salem (to which the order for this Day relates) he is, upon many accounts, more concerned than any that he knows of, Desires to take the Blame and shame of it, Asking pardon of men, And especially desiring prayers that God, who has an Unlimited Authority, would pardon that sin and all other his sins; personal and Relative: And according to his infinite Benignity, and Sovereignty, Not Visit the sin of him, or of any other, upon himself or any of his, nor upon the Land: But that He would powerfully defend him against all Temptations to Sin, for the future; and vouchsafe him the efficacious, saving Conduct of his Word and Spirit. * * *

Saturday, Feb. 6, 1714. * * * My neighbour Colson knocks at our door about 9. or past to tell of the Disorders at the Tavern [3] at the Southend in Mr. Addington's house, kept by John Wallis. He desired me that I would accompany Mr. Bromfield and Constable Howell thither. It was 35. Minutes past Nine at Night before Mr. Bromfield came; then we went. I took Æneas Salter with me. Found much Company. They refus'd to go away. Said were there to drink the Queen's Health, and they had many other Healths to drink. Call'd for more Drink: drank to me, I took notice of the Affront to them. Said must and would stay upon that Solemn occasion. Mr. John Netmaker drank the Queen's Health to me. I told him I drank none; upon that he ceas'd. Mr. Brinley put on

---

2. Devout persons often made public confession of sin by posting acknowledgments in the church. Sewall refers to his activity as a judge in 1692 in the Salem witchcraft trials, which condemned nineteen to be hanged and one to be pressed to death, while scores were tortured and publicly disgraced.

3. This event occurred on Queen Anne's birthday, which the worldly would celebrate in a spirited fashion.

his Hat to affront me. I made him take it off. I threaten'd to send
some of them to prison; that did not move them. They said they
could but pay their Fine, and doing that they might stay. I told
them if they had not a care, they would be guilty of a Riot. Mr.
Bromfield spake of raising a number of Men to Quell them, and
was in some heat, ready to run into Street. But I did not like
that. Not having Pen and Ink, I went to take their Names with my
Pensil, and not knowing how to Spell their Names, they themselves
of their own accord writ them. Mr. Netmaker, reproaching the
Province, said they had not made one good Law.

At last I address'd myself to Mr. Banister. I told him he had
been longest an Inhabitant and Freeholder, I expected he should
set a good Example in departing thence. Upon this he invited
them to his own House, and away they went; and we, after them,
went away. The Clock in the room struck a pretty while before
they departed. I went directly home, and found it 25. Minutes
past Ten at Night when I entred my own House. * * *

May 26, [1720]. About midnight my dear wife [4] expired to our
great astonishment, especially mine. May the Sovereign Lord pardon
my Sin, and Sanctify to me this very Extraordinary, awful Dispensation.

May 29, [1720]. God having in his holy Sovereignty put my Wife
out of the Fore-Seat, I aprehended I had Cause to be asham'd of my
Sin, and to loath my self for it; and retired to my Pue. * * * I
put a Note to this purpose: Samuel Sewall, depriv'd of his Wife by
a very sudden and awfull Stroke, desires Prayers that God would
sanctify the same to himself, and Children, and family. Writ and
sent three; to the South, Old, and Mr. Colman's church.

Sept. 5, 1720. Going to Son Sewall's I there meet with Madam
Winthrop, told her I was glad to meet her there, had not seen her
a great while; gave her Mr. Homes's Sermon.

Sept. 30, 1720. Mr. Colman's Lecture: Daughter Sewall acquaints Madam Winthrop that if she pleas'd to be within at 3.
p.m. I would wait on her. She answer'd she would be at home.

Oct. 1, 1720. Satterday, I dine at Mr. Stoddard's: from thence
I went to Madam Winthrop's just at 3. Spake to her, saying, my
loving wife died so soon and suddenly, 'twas hardly convenient for
me to think of Marrying again; however I came to this Resolution,
that I would not make my Court to any person without first Consulting with her. Had a pleasant discourse about 7 Single persons
sitting in the Fore-seat [5] September 29th viz. Madm Rebekah Dud-

4. In August, 1719, Sewall, then a widower, began to court the widow Abigail
Tilly. Two months later, in October,
1719, they were married. However,
after seven months, Abigail suddenly
died in the night, as the diarist
records below.
5. It was customary for widows to sit
in a pew reserved for them at the front
of the church.

ley, Catharine Winthrop, Bridget Usher, Deliverance Legg, Rebekah Loyd, Lydia Colman, Elizabeth Bellingham. She propounded one and another for me; but none would do, said Mrs. Loyd was about her Age.

Oct. 3, 1720. Waited on Madam Winthrop again; 'twas a little while before she came in. Her daughter Noyes being there alone with me, I said, I hoped my Waiting on her Mother would not be disagreeable to her. She answer'd she should not be against that that might be for her Comfort. I Saluted her, and told her I perceiv'd I must shortly wish her a good Time; (her mother had told me, she was with Child, and within a Moneth or two of her Time). By and by in came Mr. Airs, Chaplain of the Castle,[6] and hang'd up his Hat, which I was a little startled at, it seeming as if he was to lodge there. At last Madam Winthrop came too. After a considerable time, I went up to her and said, if it might not be inconvenient I desired to speak with her. She assented, and spake of going into another Room; but Mr. Airs and Mrs. Noyes presently rose up, and went out, leaving us there alone. Then I usher'd in Discourse from the names in the Fore-seat; at last I pray'd that Katharine[7] might be the person assign'd for me. She instantly took it up in the way of Denyal, as if she had catch'd at an Opportunity to do it, saying she could not do it before she was asked. Said that was her mind unless she should Change it, which she believed she should not; could not leave her Children. I express'd my Sorrow that she should do it so Speedily, pray'd her Consideration, and ask'd her when I should wait on her agen. She setting no time, I mention'd that day Sennight.[8] Gave her Mr. Willard's Fountain open'd[9] with the little print and verses; saying, I hop'd if we did well read that book, we should meet together hereafter, if we did not now. She took the Book, and put it in her Pocket. Took Leave. * * *

Oct. 11, 1720. I writ a few Lines to Madam Winthrop to this purpose: "Madam, These wait on you with Mr. Mayhew's[1] Sermon, and Account of the state of the Indians on Martha's Vinyard. I thank you for your Unmerited Favours of yesterday; and hope to have the Happiness of Waiting on you to-morrow before Eight a-clock after Noon. I pray God to keep you, and give you a joyfull entrance upon the Two Hundred and twenty ninth year of Christopher Columbus his Discovery; and take Leave, who am, Madam, your humble Servt. S.S.

Oct. 12, 1720. Mrs. Anne Cotton came to door (twas before 8.)

---

6. Castle Island, in Boston Harbor, a small fortress with a garrison.
7. Mrs. Winthrop.
8. Seven nights; a week.
9. *The Fountain Opened, or the Great Gospel Privilege of Having Christ Ex-*
hibited to Sinful Men * * * , by Samuel Willard (Boston, 1700).
1. Experience Mayhew was a well-known Puritan evangelist and Indian missionary of Martha's Vineyard.

said Madam Winthrop was within, directed me into the little Room, where she was full of work behind a Stand; Mrs. Cotton came in and stood. Madam Winthrop pointed to her to set me a Chair. Madam Winthrop's Countenance was much changed from what 'twas on Monday, look'd dark and lowering. At last, the work, (black stuff or Silk) was taken away, I got my Chair in place, had some Converse, but very Cold and indifferent to what 'twas before. Ask'd her to acquit me of Rudeness if I drew off her Glove. Enquiring the reason, I told her twas great odds between handling a dead Goat, and a living Lady. Got it off. I told her I had one Petition to ask of her, that was, that she would take off the Negative she laid on me the third of October; She readily answer'd she could not, and enlarg'd upon it; She told me of it so soon as she could; could not leave her house, children, neighbours, business. I told her she might do som Good to help and support me. Mentioning Mrs. Gookin, Nath, the widow Weld was spoken of; said I had visited Mrs. Denison. I told her Yes! Afterward I said, If after a first and second Vagary she would Accept of me returning, Her Victorious Kindness and Good Will would be very Obliging. She thank'd me for my Book, (Mr. Mayhew's Sermon), But said not a word of the Letter. When she insisted on the Negative, I pray'd there might be no more Thunder and Lightening, I should not sleep all night. I gave her Dr. Preston,[2] The Church's Marriage and the Church's Carriage, which cost me 6s at the Sale. The door standing open, Mr. Airs came in, hung up his Hat, and sat down. After awhile, Madam Winthrop moving, he went out. Jno Eyre look'd in, I said How do ye, or, your servant Mr. Eyre: but heard no word from him. Sarah fill'd a Glass of Wine, she drank to me, I to her, She sent Juno home with me with a good Lantern, I gave her 6d and bid her thank her Mistress. In some of our Discourse, I told her I had rather go to the Stone-House [3] adjoining to her, than to come to her against her mind. Told her the reason why I came every other night was lest I should drink too deep draughts of Pleasure. She had talk'd of Canary, her Kisses were to me better than the best Canary. Explain'd the expression Concerning Columbus. * * *

Oct. 19, 1720. Midweek, Visited Madam Winthrop; Sarah told me she was at Mr. Walley's, would not come home till late. I gave her Hannah 3 oranges with her Duty, not knowing whether I should find her or no. Was ready to go home: but said if I knew she was there, I would go thither. Sarah seem'd to speak with pretty good Courage, She would be there. I went and found her there, with Mr. Walley and his wife in the little Room below. At 7 a-clock I

---

2. John Preston (1587–1628), English Puritan of Cambridge University, teacher of many early American Puritans.
3. *I.e.*, the prison.

mentioned going home; at 8. I put on my Coat, and quickly waited on her home. She found occasion to speak loud to the servant, as if she had a mind to be known. Was Courteous to me; but took occasion to speak pretty earnestly about my keeping a Coach: I said 'twould cost £100. per annum: she said twould cost but £40. * * * Exit. Came away somewhat late.

Oct. 20, 1720. * * * Madam Winthrop not being at Lecture, I went thither first; found her very Serene with her dâter [4] Noyes, Mrs. Dering, and the widow Shipreev sitting at a little Table, she in her arm'd Chair. She drank to me, and I to Mrs. Noyes. After awhile pray'd the favour to speak with her. She took one of the Candles, and went into the best Room, clos'd the shutters, sat down upon the Couch. She told me Madam Usher had been there, and said the Coach must be set on Wheels, and not by Rusting. She spake somthing of my needing a Wigg. Ask'd me what her Sister said to me. I told her, She said, If her Sister were for it, She would not hinder it. But I told her, she did not say she would be glad to have me for her Brother. Said, I shall keep you in the Cold, and asked her if she would be within to morrow night, for we had had but a running Feat. She said she could not tell whether she should, or no. I took Leave. As were drinking at the Governour's, he said: In England the Ladies minded little more than that they might have Money, and Coaches to ride in. I said, And New-England brooks its Name. At which Mr. Dudley smiled. Govr said they were not quite so bad here.

Oct. 21, 1720. Friday, My Son, the Minister, came to me p.m. by appointment and we pray one for another in the Old Chamber; more especially respecting my Courtship. About 6. a-clock I go to Madam Winthrop's; Sarah told me her Mistress was gon out, but did not tell me whither she went. She presently order'd me a Fire; so I went in, having Dr. Sibb's Bowels [5] with me to read. I read the two first Sermons, still no body came in: at last about 9. a-clock Mr. Jno Eyre came in; I took the opportunity to say to him as I had done to Mrs. Noyes before, that I hoped my Visiting his Mother would not be disagreeable to him; He answered me with much Respect. When twas after 9. a-clock He of himself said he would go and call her, she was but at one of his Brothers: A while after I heard Madam Winthrop's voice, enquiring something about John. After a good while and Clapping the Garden door twice or thrice, she came in. I mentioned something of the lateness; she banter'd me, and said I was later. She receiv'd me Courteously. I ask'd when our proceedings should be made publick: She said They were like

---

4. Daughter.
5. Dr. Richard Sibbes, prominent English Puritan, published in 1639 his *Bowels Opened; or a discovery of the* *Neere and deere Love, Union and communion between Christ and the Church.* Here again "bowels" denotes a supposed inner organ of compassion.

to be no more publick than they were already. Offer'd me no Wine that I remember. I rose up at 11 a-clock to come away, saying I would put on my Coat, She offer'd not to help me. I pray'd her that Juno might light me home, she open'd the Shutter, and said twas pretty light abroad; Juno was weary and gon to bed. So I came hôm by Star-light as well as I could. At my first coming in, I gave Sarah five Shillings. I writ Mr. Eyre his Name in his book with the date Octobr 21, 1720. It cost me 8s. Jehovah jireh! [6] Madam told me she had visited M. Mico, Wendell, and Wm Clark of the South [Church].

Oct. 22, 1720. Dâter Cooper visited me before my going out of Town, staid till about Sun set. I brought her going near as far as the Orange Tree.[7] Coming back, near Leg's Corner, Little David Jeffries saw me, and looking upon me very lovingly, ask'd me if I was going to see his Grandmother? [8] I said, Not to-night. Gave him a peny, and bid him present my Service to his Grandmother.

Oct. 24, 1720. I went in the Hackny Coach through the Common, stop'd at Madam Winthrop's (had told her I would take my departure from thence). Sarah came to the door with Katee in her Arms: but I did not think to take notice of the Child. Call'd her Mistress. I told her, being encourag'd by David Jeffries loving eyes, and sweet Words, I was come to enquire whether she could find in her heart to leave that House and Neighbourhood, and go and dwell with me at the Southend; I think she said softly, Not yet. I told her It did not ly in my Lands [9] to keep a Coach. If I should, I should be in danger to be brought to keep company with her Neighbour Brooker, (he was a little before sent to prison for Debt). Told her I had an Antipathy against those who would pretend to give themselves; but nothing of their Estate. I would a proportion of my Estate with my self. And I suppos'd she would do so. As to a Perriwig, My best and greatest Friend, I could not possibly have a greater, began to find me with Hair before I was born, and had continued to do so ever since; and I could not find in my heart to go to another. She commended the book I gave her, Dr. Preston, the Church Marriage; quoted him saying 'twas inconvenient keeping out of a Fashion commonly used. I said the Time and Tide did circumscribe my Visit. She gave me a Dram of Black-Cherry Brandy, and gave me a lump of the Sugar that was in it. She wish'd me a good Journy. I pray'd God to keep her, and came away. Had a very pleasant Journy to Salem. * * *

Nov. 2, 1720. Midweek, went again, and found Mrs. Alden

---

6. God will provide. See Genesis xxii: 14. These were Abraham's words when God provided him with a ram to use for the sacrifice instead of his son, Isaac.
7. That is, "I accompanied her nearly to the Orange Tree" (an inn on the road).
8. Madam Winthrop.
9. *I.e.*, "It did not accord with my income."

there, who quickly went out. Gave her about ½ pound of Sugar Almonds, cost 3s per £. Carried them on Monday. She seem'd pleas'd with them, ask'd what they cost. Spake of giving her a Hundred pounds per anum if I dy'd before her. Ask'd her what sum she would give me, if she should dy first? Said I would give her time to Consider of it. She said she heard as if I had given all to my Children by Deeds of Gift. I told her 'twas a mistake, Point-Judith was mine &c. That in England, I own'd, my Father's desire was that it should go to my eldest Son; 'twas 20£ per anum; she thought 'twas forty. I think when I seem'd to excuse pressing this, she seem'd to think twas best to speak of it; a long winter was coming on. Gave me a Glass or two of Canary.

Nov. 4, 1720. Friday, Went again about 7. a-clock; found there Mr. John Walley and his wife: sat discoursing pleasantly. I shew'd them Isaac Moses's [an Indian] Writing. Madam W. serv'd Comfeits to us. After awhile a Table was spread, and Supper was set. I urg'd Mr. Walley to Crave a Blessing; but he put it upon me. About 9. they went away. I ask'd Madam what fashioned Neck-lace I should present her with, She said, None at all. I ask'd her Whereabout we left off last time; mention'd what I had offer'd to give her; Ask'd her what she would give me; She said she could not Change her Condition: She had said so from the beginning; could not be so far from her Children, the Lecture. Quoted the Apostle Paul affirming that a single Life was better than a Married. I answer'd That was for the present Distress. Said she had not pleasure in things of that nature as formerly: I said, you are the fitter to make me a Wife. If she hald in that mind, I must go home and bewail my Rashness in making more haste than good Speed. However, considering the Supper, I desired her to be within next Monday night, if we liv'd so long. Assented. * * *

Nov. 7, 1720. My Son pray'd in the Old Chamber. Our time had been taken up by Son and Daughter Cooper's Visit; so that I only read the 130th and 143 Psalm. Twas on the Account of my Courtship. I went to Mad. Winthrop; found her rocking her little Katee in the Cradle. I excus'd my Coming so late (near Eight). She set me an arm'd Chair and Cusheon; and so the Cradle was between her arm'd Chair and mine. Gave her the remnant of my Almonds; She did not eat of them as before; but laid them away; I said I came to enquire whether she had alter'd her mind since Friday, or remained of the same mind still. She said, Thereabouts. I told her I loved her, and was so fond as to think that she loved me: She said had a great respect for me. I told her, I had made her an offer, without asking any advice; she had so many to advise with, that twas a hindrance. The Fire was come to one short Brand besides the Block, which Brand was set up in end; at last it fell to pieces, and no Recruit was made: She gave me a Glass of Wine. I think I repeated again that I would go home and bewail my Rashness in making more haste than good Speed. I would endeavour to contain myself, and not go on to sollicit her to do that which she could not Consent to. Took leave of her. As came down the steps she bid me have a Care. Treated me Courteously. Told her she had enter'd the 4th year of her Widowhood. I had given her the News-Letter before; I did not bid her draw off her Glove as sometime I had done. Her Dress was not so clean as sometime it had been. Jehovah jireh! [1]

1673–1729   1878

EDWARD TAYLOR
(1645?–1729)

During the lifetime of Edward Taylor only a few friends read his poems, which remained in manuscript. The quiet country pastor tended his flock at Westfield, then a frontier village, in the Connecticut valley, and regarded his poems as sacramental acts of private devotion and worship. Ezra Stiles, the poet's grandson, inherited the manuscript, along with Taylor's command "that his heirs should never publish" it; he therefore deposited it in the library at Yale College, of which he was the president. More than two centuries passed before it was discovered, and by that time little could be learned of the man besides what appears in the poetry.

The poetry alone is sufficient to establish him as a writer of a genuine power unequaled by any American poet until Bryant appeared, 150 years later. "A man of small stature but firm: of quick Passions—yet serious and

grave," wrote his grandson Ezra Stiles; and Samuel Sewall remembered a sermon he had preached at the Old South Church in Boston, which "might have been preached at Paul's Cross." This poet was clearly a man of great spiritual passion, of large and liberal learning, enraptured by the Puritan dream to such a degree that he could express it in living song. His success was by no means invariable, but his best poems, a considerable number, justify the position that he at once attained in our literature when in 1939 Thomas H. Johnson published from manuscript a generous selection.

Taylor was born in Coventry, England, or nearby, probably in 1645, and most likely in a family of dissenters. Johnson points out that an ardent young Congregationalist was not then welcome at the British universities, and concludes that the persecutions of 1662 confirmed Taylor's

1. Again, "God will provide"; and although Sewall acknowledged defeat with Mrs. Winthrop, he achieved a

third marriage sixteen months later, in his seventy-first year.

resolution to emigrate. He taught school for a few years, but finally, in July, 1668, he arrived in Boston, seeking liberty and education. He carried letters to Increase Mather, already a prominent clergyman, and to John Hull, the Master of the Mint, the leading capitalist of the colony, and father of Sewall's first wife. The earnest young seeker captured the affections of his hosts—the Mathers became his intimates for life—and in a few days it was arranged for him to be off for Harvard, where he and Samuel Mather, a nephew of Increase, were classmates. He and Sewall were still closer—"Chamberfellows and Bed-fellows," as the latter records, adding that "he * * * drew me thither." Quite certainly young Taylor captivated everyone, although his college life was otherwise uneventful, save for some academic distinctions.

Upon graduation in 1671 he accepted a call from the congregation of Westfield, and spent the remaining fifty-eight years of his life in quiet usefulness as pastor to his Congregational flock. He married twice and became the father of thirteen children, most of whom he outlived. In 1720 Harvard conferred on him the degree of Master of Arts. Taylor died in 1729, "entirely enfeebled * * * longing and waiting for his Dismission." Taylor's manuscript book is in several sections: "God's Deter-

minations," which includes "The Preface" and "The Glory of and Grace in the Church Set Out"; "Miscellaneous Poems," the source of "Huswifery" and "Upon a Spider * * * "; and the "Preparatory Meditations," in two series, from which are drawn the remaining poems included in this volume. Never a servile imitator, Taylor was quite evidently acquainted with the serious British poetry of his times, especially the metaphysical poets—such as Donne, Crashaw, and Herbert—and the contemporaries of Milton, who published *Paradise Lost* the year before young Taylor set out for America.

Taylor's work was uneven; yet at his best he produced lines and passages of startling vitality, fusing lofty concept and homely detail in the memorable fashion of great poetry. He was a true mystic whose experience still convinces us, and one of the four or five American Puritans whose writings retain the liveliness of genuine literature.

A judicious selection of Edward Taylor's poems, along with an authoritative biographical sketch, a critical introduction, and notes, may be found in Thomas H. Johnson's edition of *The Poetical Works of Edward Taylor*, 1939, supplemented in "Some Edward Taylor Gleanings," *New England Quarterly*, XVI (June, 1943), 280–296, and in "The Topical Verses of Edward Taylor," *Publications of the Colonial Society of Massachusetts*, XXXIV (1943), 513–554. *The Poems of Edward Taylor*, edited by Donald E. Stanford, 1960, is the complete, annotated edition. Recent studies by Norman S. Grabo are *Edward Taylor*, 1962, and *Edward Taylor's "Christographia,"* 1962.

The Preface

in iambic pentameter couplets

Infinity, when all things it beheld
In Nothing, and of Nothing all did build,

Upon what Base was fixt the Lath,[1] wherein
He turn'd this Globe, and riggalld [2] it so trim?
Who blew the Bellows of his Furnace Vast?   5
Or held the Mould wherein the world was Cast?
Who laid its Corner Stone? Or whose Command?
Where stand the Pillars upon which it stands?
Who Lac'de and Filletted [3] the earth so fine,
With Rivers like green Ribbons Smaragdine? [4]   10
Who made the Sea's its Selvedge,[5] and it locks
Like a Quilt Ball [6] within a Silver Box?
Who Spread its Canopy? Or Curtains Spun?
Who in this Bowling Alley bowld the Sun?
Who made it always when it rises set   15
To go at once both down, and up to get?
Who th'Curtain rods made for this Tapistry?
Who hung the twinckling Lanthorns in the Sky?
Who? who did this? or who is he? Why, know
Its Onely Might Almighty this did doe.   20
His hand hath made this noble worke which Stands
His Glorious Handywork not made by hands.
Who spake all things from nothing; and with ease
Can speake all things to nothing, if he please.
Whose Little finger at his pleasure Can   25
Out mete [7] ten thousand worlds with halfe a Span:
Whose Might Almighty can by half a looks [8]
Root up the rocks and rock the hills by th'roots.
Can take this mighty World up in his hande,
And shake it like a Squitchen [9] or a Wand.   30
Whose single Frown will make the Heavens shake
Like as an aspen leafe the Winde makes quake.
Oh! what a might is this Whose single frown
Doth shake the world as it would shake it down?
Which All from Nothing fet,[1] from Nothing, All: 35
Hath All on Nothing set, lets Nothing fall.
Gave all to nothing Man indeed, whereby
Through nothing man all might him Glorify.
In Nothing then imbosst the brightest Gem

---

1. Lathe.
2. To make a groove for. *Cf.* archaic "regal" or "riggal," a groove or slot for a moving mechanical member.
3. A filet was a lace mesh often used in binding women's hair.
4. Emerald green, from the Latin *smaragdus,* "emerald."
5. The woven or finished edge of a fabric.
6. A ball with a cover quilted of small patches of contrasting colors, used as a toy or trinket.
7. Measure out.
8. *half a looks:* So reads the original manuscript in the Yale University Library.
9. "Possibly * * * the obsolete substantive *switching,* a switch or stick" [Johnson's note].
1. Fetched.

More pretious than all pretiousness in them.   40
But Nothing man did throw down all by Sin:
And darkened [2] that lightsom Gem in him.
    That now his Brightest Diamond is grown
    Darker by far than any Coalpit Stone.

1682   1939

Meditation One

What Love is this of thine, that Cannot bee
    In thine Infinity, O Lord, Confinde,
Unless it in thy very Person see,
    Infinity, and Finity Conjoyn'd?
    What hath thy Godhead, as not satisfide   5
    Marri'de our Manhood, making it its Bride?

Oh, Matchless Love! Filling Heaven to the brim!
    O're running it: all running o're beside
This World! Nay Overflowing Hell; wherein
    For thine Elect, there rose a mighty Tide!   10
    That there our Veans might through thy Person bleed,
    To quench those flames, that else would on us feed.

Oh! that thy Love might overflow my Heart!
    To fire the same with Love: for Love I would.
But oh! my streight'ned [3] Breast! my Lifeless Sparke!   15
    My Fireless Flame! What Chilly Love, and Cold?
    In measure small! In Manner Chilly! See.
    Lord, blow the Coal: Thy Love Enflame in mee.

1682   1939

Huswifery

Make me, O Lord, thy Spin[n]ing Wheele compleate.
    Thy Holy Worde my Distaff make for mee.
Make mine Affections thy Swift Flyers neate
    And make my Soule thy holy Spoole to bee.
    My Conversation make to be thy Reele [4]   5
    And reele the yarn thereon spun of thy Wheele.

Make me thy Loome then, knit therein this Twine:
    And make they Holy Spirit, Lord, winde quills: [5]

2. Read "darkenèd."
3. *I.e.*, straightened, here meaning "constricted."
4. Among the parts of a spinning wheel,
the *distaff* holds the raw wool or flax,
the *flyers* regulate the spinning, the
spool twists the yarn, and the *reel* receives the finished thread.
5. The spools of a loom.

Then weave the Web thyselfe. The yarn is fine.
Thine Ordinances make my Fulling Mills.[6]   10
Then dy the same in Heavenly Colours Choice,
All pinkt [7] with varnisht [8] Flowers of Paradise.

Then cloath therewith mine Understanding, Will,
Affections, Judgment, Conscience, Memory
My Words, and Actions, that their shine may fill   15
My wayes with glory and thee glorify.
Then mine apparell shall display before yee
That I am Cloathd in Holy robes for glory.

1685?   1939

Meditation Eight

John VI: 51. I am the living bread.[9]

I ken[n]ing [1] through Astronomy Divine
The Worlds bright Battlement, wherein I spy
A Golden Path my Pensill cannot line,
From that bright Throne unto my Threshold ly.
And while my puzzled thoughts about it pore,   5
I finde the Bread of Life in't at my doore.

When that this Bird of Paradise put in   *soul*
The Wicker Cage (my Corps) to tweedle [2] praise *body*
Had peckt the Fruite forbad: and so did fling *sin*
Away its Food; and lost its golden dayes; *The fall*   10
It fell into Celestiall Famine sore:
And never could attain a morsell more.

Alas! alas! Poore Bird, what wilt thou doe?
The Creatures field no food for Souls e're gave.
And if thou knock at Angells dores they show   15
An Empty Barrell: they no soul bread have.
Alas! Poore Bird, the Worlds White Loafe is done.
And cannot yield thee here the smallest Crumb.

In this sad state, Gods Tender Bowells [3] run *metaphysical*
Out streams of Grace: and he to end all strife *conceit*   20
The Purest Wheate in Heaven, his deare-dear Son
Grinds, and kneads up into this Bread of Life.

6. Mills in which the cloth is cleansed
with fuller's earth or soap.
7. *I.e.*, pinked, meaning "ornamented."
8. Here meaning "lustrous, glossy."
9. In ll. 21–36 the poet elaborates the
passage: "I am the living bread which
came down out of heaven; if any man
eat of this bread he shall live forever,"
in support of the doctrine of grace, the
New Covenant between God and Adam's
fallen children.
1. Recognizing, knowing.
2. *I.e.*, twiddle, here signifying "warble," in reference to the bird of paradise, his soul.
3. Here referring to a supposed inward
center of compassion.

Which Bread of Life from Heaven down came and stands
Disht on thy Table up by Angells Hands.

Did God mould up this Bread in Heaven, and bake,   25
Which from his Table came, and to thine goeth?
Doth he bespeake thee thus, This Soule Bread take.
Come Eate thy fill of this thy Gods White Loafe?
Its Food too fine for Angells, yet come, take
And Eate thy fill. Its Heavens Sugar Cake.   30

What Grace is this knead in this Loafe? This thing
Souls are but petty things it to admire.
Yee Angells, help: This fill would to the brim
Heav'ns whelm'd-down Chrystall meele Bowle, yea and higher.
This Bread of Life dropt in thy mouth, doth Cry.   35
Eate, Eate me, Soul, and thou shalt never dy.

1682   1939

The Glory of and Grace in
the Church set out

Come now behold
With this Knot ⁴ What Flowers do grow:
Spanglde like gold:
Whence Wreaths of all Perfumes do flow.
Most Curious ⁵ Colours of all sorts you shall   5
With all Sweet Spirits ⁶ s[c]ent. Yet thats not all.

Oh! Look, and finde
These Choicest Flowers most richly sweet
Are Disciplinde
With Artificiall Angells meet.⁷   10
An heap of Pearls is precious: but they shall
When set by Art Excell: Yet that's not all.

Christ's Spirit showers
Down in his Word, and Sacraments
Upon these Flowers
The Clouds of Grace Divine Contents.   15
Such things of Wealthy Blessings on them fall
As make them sweetly thrive: Yet that's not all.

Yet Still behold!
All flourish not at once. We see   20

---

4. Clump.
5. Amazing.
6. Essences, perfumes.

7. *Disciplinde * * * meet:* Taught
suitably by angel artificers.

While some Unfold
Their blushing Leaves, some buds there bee.
Here's Faith, Hope, Charity in flower, which call
On yonders in the Bud. Yet that's not all.

But as they stand   25
Like Beauties reeching [8] in perfume
    A Divine Hand
Doth hand them up to Glories room:
Where Each in sweet'ned Songs all Praises shall
Sing all ore Heaven for aye. And that's but all.   30

1682   1939

Upon a Spider Catching a Fly

Thou sorrow, venom Elfe:
    Is this thy play,
To spin a web out of thyselfe
    To Catch a Fly?
        For why?   5

I saw a pettish [9] wasp
    Fall foule therein.
Whom yet thy whorle [1] pins did not clasp
    Lest he should fling
        His sting.   10

But as affraid, remote
    Didst stand hereat
And with thy little fingers stroke
    And gently tap
        His back.   15

Thus gently him didst treate
    Lest he should pet,
And in a froppish,[2] waspish heate
    Should greatly fret
        Thy net.   20

Whereas the silly Fly,
    Caught by its leg
Thou by the throate tookst hastily,
    And 'hinde the head
        Bite Dead.   25

8. *Cf.* "reeking"; an obsolete meaning was "to emit sweet odors."
9. Peevish, ill-humored. *Cf.* "pet," l. 17.
1. The whorl, or small flywheel of the spindle, whose "pins" secure the spinning thread, as the whirling legs of the spider enmesh his victim.
2. Fretful.

This goes to pot, that not
   Nature doth call.[3]
Strive not above what strength hath got
   Lest in the brawle
     Thou fall.   30

This Frey [4] seems thus to us.
   Hells Spider gets
His intrails spun to whip Cords [5] thus
   And wove to nets
     And sets.   35

To tangle Adams race
   In's stratigems
To their Destructions, spoil'd, made base
   By venom things
     Damn'd Sins.   40

But mighty, Gracious Lord
   Communicate
Thy Grace to breake the Cord, afford
   Us Glorys Gate
     And State.   45

We'l Nightingaile sing like
   When pearcht on high
In Glories Cage, thy glory, bright,
   [Yea,] thankfully,
     For joy.   50

1685?   1939

[Two Meditations on "The Song of Solomon," Canticle VI] [6]

Meditation 142, Second Series

Canticles VI: 9. My Dove is One the onely One of her mother the Choice One of her that bare her etc.

What shall I say, my Deare Deare Lord? most Deare
Of thee! My choisest words when spoke are then

---

3. *that not / Nature doth call:* I.e., he "goes to pot" who does not call upon "Natural Reason," which, in the Puritan Covenant theology, was man's inherent endowment of capacity to know God's Truth.
4. *I.e.*, fray, or affray, here meaning "attack."

5. Tough cord, now of hemp, formerly of animal entrails, like catgut.
6. Among the biblical texts which inspired Taylor's *"Preparatory Meditations"* the Canticles, with their luxuriant tonality and imagery, moved him most deeply. Solomon's eight Canticles, independently striking, are at the same time an integrated totality of the erotic

Articulated Breath, soon disappeare.
   If wrote are but the Drivle of my pen
   Beblackt with my inke, soon torn worn out unless   5
   Thy Holy Spirit be their inward Dress.

What, what a Say is this. Thy Spouse doth rise.
   Thy Dove all Undefiled doth excell
All though but one the onely in thine Eyes
   All Queen and Concubines that bear the bell.   10
   Her excellence all excellency far
   Transcends as doth the Sun a pinking Star.

She is the Onely one her mother bore
   Jerusalem ever above esteems
Her for her Darling her choice one therefore   15
   Thou holdst her for the best that ere was seen.
   The Sweetest Flower in all thy Paradise
   And she that bore her Made her hers most Choice.

That power of thine that made the Heavens bow,
   And blush with shining glory ever cleare   20
Hath taken her within his glorious brow
   And made her Madam of his Love most Deare
   Hath Circled her within his glorious arms
   Of Love most rich, her shielding from all harms.

She is thy Dove, thy Undefiled, she shines   25
   In thy rich Righteousness all Lovely, White
The onely Choice one of her Mother, thine
   Most beautifull beloved, thy Delight.
   The Daughters saw and blessed her, the Queens
   And Concubines her praisd and her esteem.   30

---

experience as sublime and indispensable to the human condition. Early Christian theology retained this work in the canon by a mystical sublimation of the erotic to the level at which the love of God, of Christ and His Church, and mankind coexist. Solomon's sixth Canticle reconstructs his young love for the Shulamite girl, early lost but passionately remembered. For this Canticle alone Taylor wrote twenty poems in the Second Series, of which we represent the dominant theme in "Meditation 142" and "Meditation 146."

The story of the Shulamite appears in I Kings i: 1–6 and I Kings ii: 17. When King David, Solomon's father, lay stricken with the chill of age, his courtiers, as was customary, "sought a young virgin * * * throughout all Israel, and found Abishag, a Shunamite" [Shulamite]. Young Solomon saw that she "was very fair and cherished the King, and ministered to him, but he knew her not." After David named Solomon to succeed him and was dead, Solomon ordered the death of his half-brother who, having failed in an attempt to seize the throne, plotted to secure David's handmaiden. The Shulamite appears no more in the record, but she was still in Solomon's memory when he wrote the Canticles.

"Meditation 142" is based on stanza ix of Canticle VI. Here Solomon, at the height of power and splendor, and in spite of the luxury of his household (*cf.* lines 10 and 29–30), holds in memory a discourse with the "onely one," which Taylor expresses in terms of Christ and the mortal.

"Meditation 146" is based on stanza xiii, in which the lover, or Solomon, recognizes the anguish of long and hopeless separation from this "one." Taylor, again in religious terms, expresses the anguish of mankind's search for God.

Thy Love that fills the Heavens brimfull throughout
    Coms tumbling on her with transcendent bliss
Even as it were in golden pipes that spout
    In Streams from heaven, Oh! what love like this?
    This comes upon her, hugs her in its Arms   35
    And warms her Spirits. Oh! Celestiall Charms.

Make me a member of this Spouse of thine
    I humbly beg deck thus, as Tenis Ball
I shall struck hard on th'ground back bounce with Shine
    Of Praise up to the Chamber floor thy Hall,   40
    Possesses. And at that bright Doore I'l sing
    Thy sweetest praise untill thou'st take me in.

1718   1960

Meditation 146, Second Series

Canticles VI: 13. Return, oh Shulamite, return return.

My Deare Deare Lord, I know not what to say:
    Speech is too Course a web for me to cloath
My Love to thee in or it to array,
    Or make a mantle. Wouldst thou not such loath?
    Thy Love to mee's too great, for mee to shape   5
    A Vesture for the Same at any rate.

When as thy Love doth Touch my Heart down tost
    It tremblingly runs, seeking thee its all,
And as a Child when it his nurse hath lost
    Runs seeking her, and after her doth Call.   10
    So when thou hidst from me, I seek and sigh.
    Thou saist return return Oh Shulamite.

Rent out on Use thy Love thy Love I pray.
    My Love to thee shall be thy Rent and I
Thee Use on Use, Intrest on intrest pay.   15
    There's none Extortion in such Usury.

I'le pay thee Use on Use for't and therefore
    Thou shalt become the greatest Usurer.
But yet the principall I'le neer restore.
    The Same is thine and mine. We shall not Jar.   20
    And so this blessed Usury shall be
    Most profitable both to thee and mee.

And shouldst thou hide thy shining face most fair
    Away from me. And in a sinking wise

My trembling beating heart brought nigh t'dispare   25
Should cry to thee and in a trembling guise
Lord quicken it. Drop in its Eares delight
Saying Return, Return my Shulamite.

1718   1960

JONATHAN EDWARDS
(1703–1758)

Jonathan Edwards, the last and most gifted defender of New England Calvinism, was in several respects the most remarkable American Puritan. Later even than Cotton Mather he attempted to revive the Puritan idealism in a new age of science, secularism, and mercantile activity. Where Mather militantly supported an institutional heirarchy, Edwards relied on spiritual insight; where Mather was aggressive and pedantic, Edwards possessed a profound learning supported by genuine mystical experience and the persuasive gifts of the logician. Unlike Mather, Edwards saw the fruits of his evangelism in the temporary revival of Puritan orthodoxy, but within sixteen years his own congregation had repudiated him. He was in all things too late born. If as a result he was at once identified with the past, he has at least held his position in history.

Edwards was born in 1703, in East Windsor, Connecticut. In childhood he wrote serious works, including a logical refutation of materialism and a pioneer study of the behavior of spiders. At thirteen he was enrolled at Yale. About 1717, before any other American thinker, he discovered, in Locke's *Essay Concerning Human Understanding*, a new empiricism, a theory of knowledge, and a psychology which he later used in support of such Calvinistic doctrines as predestination and the sovereignty of God, doctrines which, as *Personal Narrative* reveals, he had accepted for himself only after much soul-searching.

They became his foundation stone of faith during his ministry at Northampton, Massachusetts, where he was pastor from 1726 to 1750; they are equally fundamental to the fifteen books that he published, principally from Northampton. The "Great Awakening" of religious faith began there with his preaching, and spread in a wave of evangelism through the middle colonies, ironically producing, in a few years, organized schisms from Congregational and Presbyterian orthodoxy. This schismatic tendency was reflected in his own congregation after 1744. While his influence was being carried abroad by his writings, Edwards was confronted at home with a growing resistance to his severe orthodoxy, and finally, in 1750, with the decree of exclusion memorialized by his famous *Farewell Sermon* to his congregation.

At Stockbridge, Massachusetts, then a frontier village, he was appointed as pastor and Indian missionary, and there he completed his greatest writings, including *Freedom of the Will* (1754). Elected president of Nassau Hall (Princeton) in 1757, he assumed office in January, 1758, but died within three months as the result of an inoculation against smallpox.

He had gained a position as our country's first systematic philosopher, and earned a permanent place among those who have advanced the thought of the western world. For his use of the empiricism and psychology of Locke was truly an advance, although he employed it to defend a primitive Calvinistic orthodoxy that could not long sustain itself against the rationalistic "enlightenment" of the age of science which had already dawned. Yet no other writer has been so successful in suffusing this grim, Puritan determinism with "a divine and supernatural light" (as he said), in showing human predestination as the necessary corollary to the beauty of God's majestic sovereignty, in combining cold logic with the warmth of mystical insight.

His best and most representative sermon, "Sinners in the Hands of an Angry God," holds the "rebellious and disorderly" congregation of Enfield over the flaming pit of hell. Even in that sermon, as the notes will show, he was less concerned with God's wrath than with His Grace, which was freely extended to sinners who repented. This is also his theme in his masterpiece, *Freedom of the Will*, in *Personal Narrative*, and in such essays as "The Nature of True Virtue."

Except in the expression of mystical experience, and of the joy of nature and thought, Edwards's style tends to be reserved and somewhat tiresomely scrupulous; Perry Miller remarks (in *Jonathan Edwards*), even in controversy "he demolishes at tedious length all possible positions of his opponents, including some that they do not hold * * * , and all the time hardly declares his own." But the beauty of this method is that there is nothing left but his own position, and whatever may be thought of his style, it enabled him, very often, to perform that miracle of metaphysics which he called "seeing the perfect idea of a thing."

Collected editions entitled *The Works of President Edwards* were edited by Edward Williams and Edward Parsons, 8 vols., Leeds, 1806–1811, and (source of this text) the American edition, 8 vols., edited by Samuel Austin, 1808–1809; reprinted, 4 vols., New York, 1843. An adequate selection is *Jonathan Edwards: Representative Selections*, edited by Clarence H. Faust and Thomas H. Johnson, 1935. For biography, see Ola E. Winslow's *Jonathan Edwards*, 1940, and Perry Miller's *Jonathan Edwards*, 1949, and see A. O. Aldridge, *Jonathan Edwards*, 1964, and Edward Davidson, *Jonathan Edwards* * * * , 1966. A Yale University definitive edition is in progress, general editor, Perry Miller.

Sarah Pierrepont

They say there is a young lady in——¹ who is beloved of that Great Being, who made and rules the world, and that there are certain seasons in which this Great Being, in some way or other invisible, comes to her and fills her mind with exceeding sweet delight, and that she hardly cares for anything, except to meditate on him—that she expects after a while to be received up where he is, to be raised up out of the world and caught up into heaven; being assured that he loves her too well to let her remain at a distance from him always. There she is to dwell with him, and to be ravished with his love and delight forever. Therefore, if you present all the world before her, with the richest of its treasures, she disregards it and cares not for it, and is unmindful of any pain or affliction. She has a strange sweetness in her mind, and singular purity in her affections; is most just and conscientious in all her conduct; and you could not persuade her to do any thing wrong or sinful, if you would give her all the world, lest she should offend this Great Being. She is of a wonderful sweetness, calmness and universal benevolence of mind; especially after this Great God has manifested himself to her mind. She will sometimes go about from place to place, singing sweetly; and seems to be always full of joy and pleasure; and no one knows for what. She loves to be alone, walking in the fields and groves, and seems to have some one invisible always conversing with her.

1723?   1830

From A Divine and Supernatural Light ²

A Divine and Supernatural Light, immediately imparted to the Soul by the Spirit of God, shown to be both a Scriptural and Rational Doctrine.

MATTHEW XVI. 17. *And Jesus answered and said unto him, Blessed art thou, Simon Barjona: for flesh and blood hath not revealed it unto thee, but my Father which is in heaven.*

* * *

DOCTRINE

That there is such a thing as a Spiritual and Divine Light, immediately imparted to the soul by God, of a different nature from any that is obtained by natural means.

1. New Haven, Connecticut. Sarah was only thirteen when Edwards wrote this, about 1723. In 1727 he married Sarah, and she became a principal inspiration in his life and writing.

2. The present sermon contrasts with the later "Sinners in the Hands of an Angry God" (see below), although both deal with an aspect of regeneration. The later sermon grimly warned the

In what I say on this subject, at this time, I would,

I. Show what divine light is.

II. How it is given immediately by God, and not obtained by natural means.

III. Show the truth of the doctrine.

And then conclude with a brief improvement.

I. I would show what this spiritual and divine light is. And in order to it, would shew,

First, In a few things what it is not. And here,

1. Those convictions that natural men may have of their sin and misery, is not this spiritual and divine light. Men in a natural condition may have convictions of the guilt that lies upon them, and of the anger of God, and their danger of divine vengeance. Some convictions are from light or sensibleness of truth. That some sinners have a greater conviction of their guilt and misery than others, is because some have more light, or more of an apprehension of truth than others. And this light and conviction may be from the Spirit of God; the Spirit convinces men of sin. But yet nature is much more concerned in it than in the communication of that spiritual and divine light that is spoken of in the doctrine; it is from the Spirit of God only as assisting natural principles, and not as infusing any new principles. Common grace differs from special, in that it influences only by assisting of nature; and not by imparting grace, or bestowing any thing above nature. The light that is obtained is wholly natural, or of no superior kind to what mere nature attains to, though more of that kind be obtained than would be obtained if men were left wholly to themselves: Or, in other words, common grace only assists the faculties of the soul to do that more fully which they do by nature, as natural conscience or reason will, by mere nature make a man sensible of guilt, and will accuse and condemn him when he has

---

unregenerate that the saving grace is not to be won simply by church membership. "A Divine and Supernatural Light," by contrast, is a serene attempt to explain the spiritual experience of regeneration itself. Making use of a new psychology inspired by Locke and later writers, Edwards argues that the indwelling light of regeneration—of redeeming grace—is the very presence of God. This, if supernatural, is still certainly a reality, but a reality apprehended directly by consciousness without the necessary and "natural" intervention of the senses or the rational faculty.

The second of the works of Edwards to be printed, this bore a footnote, "Preached at Northampton and published at the desire of some of the hearers, in the year 1734." The sermon was delivered in August, 1733. The text below is that of the first American collection of Edwards's *Works*, 1808–9, which reproduced the first edition text of this sermon except for typography.

In the present text we have retained the Doctrine and the Defense of Doctrine, omitting the demonstration, or exegesis, of biblical text supporting the Doctrine, then a conventional but not universal requirement of homiletics.

done amiss. Conscience is a principle natural to men; and the work that it doth naturally, or of itself, is to give up an apprehension of right and wrong, and to suggest to the mind the relation that there is between right and wrong, and a retribution. The Spirit of God, in those convictions which unregenerate men sometimes have, assists conscience to do this work in a further degree than it would do if they were left to themselves: He helps it against those things that tend to stupify it, and obstruct its exercise. But in the renewing and sanctifying work of the Holy Ghost, those things are wrought in the soul that are above nature, and of which there is nothing of the like kind in the soul by nature; and they are caused to exist in the soul habitually, and according to such a stated constitution or law that lays such a foundation for exercises in a continued course, as is called a principle of nature. Not only are remaining principles assisted to do their work more freely and fully, but those principles are restored that were utterly destroyed by the fall; and the mind thenceforward habitually exerts those acts that the dominion of sin had made it as wholly destitute of, as a dead body is of vital acts.

The Spirit of God acts in a very different manner in the one case, from what he doth in the other. He may indeed act upon the mind of a natural man, but he acts in the mind of a saint as an indwelling vital principle. He acts upon the mind of an unregenerate person as an extrinsic, occasional agent; for in acting upon them, he doth not unite himself to them; for notwithstanding all his influences that they may be the subjects of, they are still sensual, having not the Spirit. Jude 19. But he unites himself with the mind of a saint, takes him for his temple, actuates and influences him as a new supernatural principle of life and action. There is this difference, that the Spirit of God, in acting in the soul of a godly man, exerts and communicates himself there in his own proper nature. Holiness is the proper nature of the Spirit of God. The Holy Spirit operates in the minds of the godly, by uniting himself to them, and living in them, and exerting his own nature in the exercise of their faculties. The Spirit of God may act upon a creature, and yet not in acting communicate himself. The Spirit of God may act upon inanimate creatures; as, the *Spirit moved upon the face of the waters,* in the beginning of the creation; so the Spirit of God may act upon the minds of men many ways, and communicate himself no more than when he acts upon an inanimate creature. For instance, he may excite thoughts in them, may assist their natural reason and understanding, or may assist other natural principles, and this without any union with the soul, but may act, as it were, as upon an external object. But as he acts in his holy influences and spiritual operations, he acts in a way of peculiar communication of himself; so that the subject is thence denominated spiritual.

2. This spiritual and divine light does not consist in any impression made upon the imagination. It is no impression upon the mind, as though one saw any thing with the bodily eyes: It is no imagination or idea of an outward light or glory, or any beauty of form or countenance, or a visible lustre or brightness of any object. The imagination may be strongly impressed with such things; but this is not spiritual light. Indeed when the mind has a lively discovery of spiritual things, and is greatly affected by the power of divine light, it may, and probably very commonly doth, much affect the imagination; so that impressions of an outward beauty or brightness may accompany those spiritual discoveries. But spiritual light is not that impression upon the imagination, but an exceeding different thing from it. Natural men may have lively impressions on their imaginations; and we cannot determine but that the devil, who transforms himself into an angel of light, may cause imaginations of an outward beauty, or visible glory, and of sounds and speeches, and other such things; but these are things of a vastly inferior nature to spiritual light.

3. This spiritual light is not the suggesting of any new truths or propositions not contained in the word of God. This suggesting of new truths or doctrines to the mind, independent of any antecedent revelation of those propositions, either in word or writing, is inspiration; such as the prophets and apostles had, and such as some enthusiasts pretend to. But this spiritual light that I am speaking of, is quite a different thing from inspiration: It reveals no new doctrine, it suggests no new proposition to the mind, it teaches no new thing of God, or Christ, or another world, not taught in the Bible, but only gives a due apprehension of those things that are taught in the word of God.

4. It is not every affecting view that men have of the things of religion that is this spiritual and divine light. Men by mere principles of nature are capable of being affected with things that have a special relation to religion as well as other things. A person by mere nature, for instance, may be liable to be affected with the story of Jesus Christ, and the sufferings he underwent, as well as by any other tragical story: He may be the more affected with it from the interest he conceives mankind to have in it: Yea, he may be affected with it without believing it; as well as a man may be affected with what he reads in a romance, or sees acted in a stage play. He may be affected with a lively and eloquent description of many pleasant things that attend the state of the blessed in heaven, as well as his imagination be entertained by a romantic description of the pleasantness of fairy land, or the like. And that common

belief of the truth of the things of religion, that persons may have from education or otherwise, may help forward their affection. We read in Scripture of many that were greatly affected with things of a religious nature, who yet are there represented as wholly graceless, and many of them very ill men. A person therefore may have affecting views of the things of religion, and yet be very destitute of spiritual light. Flesh and blood may be the author of this: One man may give another an affecting view of divine things with but common assistance; but God alone can give a spiritual discovery of them.

But I proceed to show,

Secondly, Positively what this spiritual and divine light is.

And it may be thus described: A true sense of the divine excellency of the things revealed in the word of God, and a conviction of the truth and reality of them thence arising.

This spiritual light primarily consists in the former of these, viz. A real sense and apprehension of the divine excellency of things revealed in the word of God. A spiritual and saving conviction of the truth and reality of these things, arises from such a sight of their divine excellency and glory; so that this conviction of their truth is an effect and natural consequence of this sight of their divine glory. There is therefore in this spiritual light,

1. A true sense of the divine and superlative excellency of the things of religion; a real sense of the excellency of God and Jesus Christ, and of the work of redemption, and the ways and works of God revealed in the gospel. There is a divine and superlative glory in these things; an excellency that is of a vastly higher kind, and more sublime nature than in other things; a glory greatly distinguishing them from all that is earthly and temporal. He that is spiritually enlightened truly apprehends and sees it, or has a sense of it. He does not merely rationally believe that God is glorious, but he has a sense of the gloriousness of God in his heart. There is not only a rational belief that God is holy, and that holiness is a good thing, but there is a sense of the loveliness of God's holiness. There is not only a speculatively judging that God is gracious, but a sense how amiable God is upon that account, or a sense of the beauty of this divine attribute.

There is a twofold understanding or knowledge of good that God has made the mind of man capable of. The first, that which is merely speculative and notional; as when a person only speculatively judges that any thing is, which, by the agreement of mankind, is called good or excellent, viz. that which is most to general advantage, and between which and a reward there is a suitableness, and the like. And the other is, that which consists in the sense of the heart: As when there is a sense of the beauty, amiable-

ness, or sweetness of a thing; so that the heart is sensible of pleasure and delight in the presence of the idea of it. In the former is
exercised merely the speculative faculty, or the understanding,
strictly so called, or as spoken of in distinction from the will or
disposition of the soul. In the latter, the will, or inclination, or
heart, is mainly concerned.

Thus there is a difference between having an opinion, that God
is holy and gracious, and having a sense of the loveliness and
beauty of that holiness and grace. There is a difference between
having a rational judgment that honey is sweet, and having a sense
of its sweetness. A man may have the former, that knows not how
honey tastes; but a man cannot have the latter unless he has an
idea of the taste of honey in his mind. So there is a difference
between believing that a person is beautiful, and having a sense
of his beauty. The former may be obtained by hearsay, but the
latter only by seeing the countenance. There is a wide difference
between mere speculative rational judging any thing to be excellent, and having a sense of its sweetness and beauty. The former
rests only in the head, speculation only is concerned in it; but the
heart is concerned in the latter. When the heart is sensible of
the beauty and amiableness of a thing, it necessarily feels pleasure
in the apprehension. It is implied in a person's being heartily
sensible of the loveliness of a thing, that the idea of it is sweet
and pleasant to his soul; which is a far different thing from
having a rational opinion that it is excellent.

2. There arises from this sense of divine excellency of things
contained in the word of God, a conviction of the truth and
reality of them: And that either directly or indirectly.

First, Indirectly, and that two ways.

1. As the prejudices that are in the heart, against the truth of
divine things, are hereby removed; so that the mind becomes
susceptive of the due force of rational judgments for their truth.
The mind of man is naturally full of prejudices against the truth
of divine things: It is full of enmity against the doctrines of the
gospel; which is a disadvantage to those arguments that prove
their truth, and causes them to lose their force upon the mind.
But when a person has discovered to him the divine excellency of
Christian doctrines, this destroys the enmity, removes those prejudices, and sanctifies the reason, and causes it to lie open to the
force of arguments for their truth.

Hence was the different effect that Christ's miracles had to
convince the disciples, from what they had to convince the Scribes
and Pharisees. Not that they had a stronger reason, or had their
reason more improved; but their reason was sanctified, and those
blinding prejudices, that the Scribes and Pharisees were under,

were removed by the sense they had of the excellency of Christ and his doctrine.

2. It not only removes the hindrances of reason, but positively helps reason. It makes even the speculative notions the more lively. It engages the attention of the mind, with the more fixedness and intenseness to that kind of objects; which causes it to have a clearer view of them, and enables it more clearly to see their mutual relations, and occasions it to take more notice of them. The ideas themselves that otherwise are dim and obscure, are by this means impressed with the greater strength, and have a light cast upon them; so that the mind can better judge of them. As he that beholds the objects on the fact of the earth, when the light of the sun is cast upon them, is under greater advantage to discern them in their true forms and mutual relations, than he that sees them in a dim star light or twilight.

The mind having a sensibleness of the excellency of divine objects, dwells upon them with delight; and the powers of the soul are more awakened and enlivened to employ themselves in the contemplation of them, and exert themselves more fully and much more to the purpose. The beauty and sweetness of the objects draws on the faculties, and draws forth their exercises: So that reason itself is under far greater advantages for its proper and free exercises, and to attain its proper end, free of darkness and delusion. But,

Secondly. A true sense of the divine excellency of the things of God's word doth more directly and immediately convince of the truth of them; and that because the excellency of these things is so superlative. There is a beauty in them that is so divine and godlike, that is greatly and evidently distinguishing of them from things merely human, or that men are the inventors and authors of; a glory that is so high and great, that when clearly seen, commands assent to their divinity and reality. When there is an actual and lively discovery of this beauty and excellency, it will not allow of any such thought as that it is an human work, or the fruit of men's invention. This evidence that they that are spiritually enlightened have of the truth of the things of religion, is a kind of intuitive and immediate evidence. They believe the doctrines of God's word to be divine, because they see divinity in them. i.e. They see a divine, and transcendent, and most evidently distinguishing glory in them; such a glory as, if clearly seen, does not leave room to doubt of their being of God, and not of men.

Such a conviction of the truth of religion as this, arising, these ways, from a sense of the divine excellency of them, is that true spiritual conviction that there is in saving faith. And this original of it, is that by which it is most essentially distinguished from that common assent, which unregenerate men are capable of.

II. I proceed now to the second thing proposed, viz. To show how this light is immediately given by God, and not obtained by natural means. And here,

1. It is not intended that the natural faculties are not made use of in it. The natural faculties are the subject of this light: And they are the subject in such a manner, that they are not merely passive, but active in it; the acts and exercises of man's understanding are concerned and made use of in it. God, in letting in this light into the soul, deals with man according to his nature, or as a rational creature; and makes use of his human faculties. But yet this light is not the less immediately from God for that; though the faculties are made use of, it is as the subject and not as the cause; and that acting of the faculties in it, is not the cause, but is either implied in the thing itself (in the light that is imparted) or is the consequence of it. As the use that we make of our eyes in beholding various objects, when the sun arises, is not the cause of the light that discovers those objects to us.

2. It is not intended that outward means have no concern in this affair. As I have observed already, it is not in this affair, as it is in inspiration, where new truths are suggested: For here is by this light only given a due apprehension of the same truths that are revealed in the word of God; and therefore it is not given without the word. The gospel is made use of in this affair: This light is the "light of the glorious gospel of Christ." 2. Cor. iv. 4. The gospel is as a glass, by which this light is conveyed to us. 1 Cor. xiii. 12. "Now we see through a glass." . . . But,

3. When it is said that this light is given immediately by God, and not obtained by natural means, hereby is intended, that it is given by God without making use of any means that operate by their own power, or a natural force. God makes use of means; but it is not as mediate causes to produce this effect. There are not truly any second causes of it; but it is produced by God immediately. The word of God is no proper cause of this effect: It does not operate by any natural force in it. The word of God is only made use of to convey to the mind the subject matter of this saving instruction: And this indeed it doth convey to us by natural force or influence. It conveys to our minds these and those doctrines; it is the cause of the notion of them in our heads, but not of the sense of the divine excellency of them in our hearts. Indeed a person cannot have spiritual light without the word. But that does not argue, that the word properly causes that light. The mind cannot see the excellency of any doctrine, unless

that doctrine be first in the mind; but the seeing of the excellency of the doctrine may be immediately from the Spirit of God; though the conveying of the doctrine or proposition itself may be by the word. So that the notions that are subject matter of this light, are conveyed to the mind by the word of God; but that due sense of the heart, wherein this light formally consists, is immediately by the Spirit of God. As for instance, that notion that there is a Christ, and that Christ is holy and gracious, is conveyed to the mind by the word of God: But the sense of the excellency of Christ by reason of that holiness and grace, is nevertheless immediately the work of the Holy Spirit.[3]

* * *

1733   1808–9

Sinners in the Hands of an Angry God [4]

DEUT. XXXII. 35. *Their foot shall slide in due time.*

In this verse is threatened the vengeance of God on the wicked unbelieving Israelites, that were God's visible people, and lived under means of grace [5] and that, notwithstanding all God's won-

3. Here concludes Edwards's analysis of his Doctrine and its application to religious experience. As indicated in his initial outline (see above) Part III, here excluded, is the conventional defense of the Doctrine: one, by reference to sixteen quoted Biblical texts from the Gospels, the Epistles, and the Psalms; and, two, by asserting the "rational" probability of there being such "transcendent excellence" in "divine things" that it could be communicated to man only by revelation that transcends reason, as the quoted scriptures had suggested. The usual brief recapitulation of the entire argument ends the sermon.

4. Edwards delivered this sermon on July 8, 1741, at Enfield, Connecticut, at the height of the Great Awakening, a revival of some ten years' duration for which he was largely responsible. The preacher was attempting to bring the members of the congregation to share his understanding of the truth, not merely to terrify them with as vivid a glimpse into Hell as the imagination of man has been able to conceive. That he succeed in this last effect there can be no doubt; in fact, to the modern reader, the sermon may seem an unnecessarily vehement attack on the sober congregation at Enfield. Many of Edwards's listeners were, however, members of the church only by reason of the Half-Way Covenant, a New England revision of Congregationalist doctrine then almost a century old. Church membership had originally been granted to the children of parents who had confessed to a personal experience of conversion; the Half-Way Covenant extended this provision to the third generation, even though neither they nor their parents had made a confession.

Edwards's real purpose, therefore, was to destroy his listeners' lethargic assumption that once they were members of the visible church they were also quite surely regenerated children of God. For their own salvation, they must recognize their total and inherited depravity and that the "mere good pleasure" of God must determine whether or not they should be saved.

The sermon follows the traditional three-part pattern: an elucidation of a Biblical text, the Calvinistic doctrine depending upon it, and the application of the text to the contemporary situation. The text is that of the first edition of 1741, except that we have reduced capital initials to lower case whenever they represent the arbitrary adornment of the period but distract the modern reader's attention.

5. In Calvinistic doctrine as formulated in the Westminster Confession, the "means of grace" are supplied by the ordinances, which "are the preaching of the word and the administration of the sacraments of baptism and the Lord's Supper." Edwards is here drawing a parallel between his own people and the Israelites, both "God's visible people": the Israelites' "means of grace" were embodied in the Ten Commandments.

derful works that he had wrought towards that people, yet remained, as is expressed, ver. 28, void of counsel, having no understanding in them; and that, under all the cultivations of Heaven, brought forth bitter and poisonous fruit; as in the two verses next preceding the text.[6]

The expression that I have chosen for my text, *Their foot shall slide in due time*, seems to imply the following things, relating to the punishment and destruction that these wicked Israelites were exposed to.

1. That they were *always* exposed to destruction, as one that stands or walks in slippery places is always exposed to fall. This is implied in the manner of their destruction's coming upon them, being represented by their foot's sliding. The same is expressed, Psal. lxxiii.18. *Surely thou didst set them in slippery places; thou castedst them down into destruction.*

2. It implies that they were always exposed to *sudden* unexpected destruction. As he that walks in slippery places is every moment liable to fall; he can't foresee one moment whether he shall stand or fall the next; and when he does fall, he falls at once, without warning. Which is also expressed in that, Psal. lxxiii. 18, 19. *Surely thou didst set them in slippery places; thou castedst them down into destruction. How are they brought into desolation as in a moment?*

3. Another thing implied is that they are liable to fall of *themselves*, without being thrown down by the hand of another. As he that stands or walks on slippery ground, needs nothing but his own weight to throw him down.

4. That the reason why they are not fallen already, and don't fall now, is only that God's appointed time is not come. For it is said, that when that due time, or appointed time comes, *their foot shall slide*. Then they shall be left to fall as they are inclined by their own weight. God won't hold them up in these slippery places any longer, but will let them go; and then, at that very instant, they shall fall into destruction; as he that stands in such slippery declining ground on the edge of a pit that he can't stand alone, when he is let go he immediately falls and is lost.

The observation from the words that I would now insist upon is this,

There is nothing that keeps wicked men, at any one moment, out of Hell, but the mere pleasure of God.

---

6. Much of this chapter of Deuteronomy is a song sung by Moses to the Israelites, exhorting them to repent and prepare for the promised land after they had fallen into the ways of transgression that culminated in the worship of the golden calf.

By the mere pleasure of God, I mean his sovereign pleasure, his arbitrary will, restrained by no obligation, hindered by no manner of difficulty, any more than if nothing else but God's mere will had in the last degree, or in any respect whatsoever, any hand in the preservation of wicked men one moment.[7]

The truth of this observation may appear by the following considerations.

1. There is no want of *power* in God to cast wicked men into Hell at any moment. Men's hands can't be strong when God rises up: the strongest have no power to resist him, nor can any deliver out of his hands.

He is not only able to cast wicked men into Hell, but he can most *easily* do it. Sometimes an earthly prince meets with a great deal of difficulty to subdue a rebel, that has found means to fortify himself and has made himself strong by the numbers of his followers. But it is not so with God. There is no fortress that is any defence from the power of God. Tho' hand join in hand, and vast multitudes of God's enemies combine and associate themselves, they are easily broken in pieces: they are as great heaps of light chaff before the whirlwind; or large quantities of dry stubble before devouring flames. We find it easy to tread on and crush a worm that we see crawling on the earth; so 'tis easy for us to cut or singe a slender thread that any thing hangs by; thus easy is it for God when he pleases to cast his enemies down to Hell. What are we, that we should think to stand before him, at whose rebuke the earth trembles, and before whom the rocks are thrown down?

2. They *deserve* to be cast into Hell; so that divine Justice never stands in the way, it makes no objection against God's using his power at any moment to destroy them. Yea, on the contrary, justice calls aloud for an infinite punishment of their sins. Divine Justice says of the tree that brings forth such grapes of Sodom, *Cut it down, why cumbreth it the ground,* Luke xiii. 7. The sword of divine Justice is every moment brandished over their heads, and 'tis nothing but the hand of arbitrary mercy, and God's mere will, that holds it back.

3. They are *already* under a sentence of condemnation to Hell. They don't only justly deserve to be cast down thither; but the sentence of the law of God, that eternal and immutable rule of righteousness that God has fixed between him and mankind, is gone out against them, and stands against them; so that they are bound over already to Hell. John iii. 18. *He that believeth not is*

7. It is implicit in the doctrine of unconditional election that God is sovereign and under no obligation to rescue unregenerate man who has disobeyed God's commands.

condemned already. So that every unconverted man properly belongs to Hell; that is his place; from thence he is. John viii. 23. *Ye are from beneath.* And thither he is bound; 'tis the place that justice, and God's word, and the sentence of his unchangeable law assigns to him.

4. They are now the objects of that very *same* anger and wrath of God that is expressed in the torments of Hell: and the reason why they don't go down to Hell at each moment, is not because God, in whose power they are, is not then very angry with them; as angry as he is with many of those miserable creatures that he is now tormenting in Hell, and do there feel and bear the fierceness of his wrath. Yea God is a great deal more angry with great numbers that are now on earth, yea doubtless with many that are now in this congregation, that it may be are at ease and quiet, than he is with many of those that are now in the flames of Hell.

So that it is not because God is unmindful of their wickedness, and don't resent it, that he don't let loose his hand and cut them off. God is not altogether such an one as themselves, tho' they may imagine him to be so. The wrath of God burns against them, their damnation don't slumber, the pit is prepared, the fire is made ready, the furnace is now hot, ready to receive them, the flames do now rage and glow. The glittering sword is whet, and held over them, and the pit hath opened her mouth under them.

5. The *Devil* stands ready to fall upon them and seize them as his own, at what moment God shall permit him. They belong to him; he has their souls in his possession, and under his dominion. The Scripture represents them as his *goods*, Luke xi. 21. The devils watch them; they are ever by them, at their right hand; they stand waiting for them, like greedy hungry lions that see their prey, and expect to have it, but are for the present kept back; if God should withdraw his hand, by which they are restrained, they would in one moment fly upon their poor souls. The old Serpent is gaping for them; Hell opens its mouth wide to receive them; and if God should permit it, they would be hastily swallowed up and lost.

6. There are in the souls of wicked men those hellish *principles* reigning, that would presently kindle and flame out into hell fire, if it were not for God's restraints. There is laid in the very nature of carnal men a foundation for the torments of Hell: there are those corrupt principles, in reigning power in them, and in full possession of them, that are seeds of hell fire. These principles are active and powerful, and exceeding violent in their nature, and if it were not for the restraining hand of God upon them, they would soon break out, they would flame out after the same manner as the same corruptions, the same enmity does in the

hearts of damned souls, and would beget the same torments in 'em as they do in them. The souls of the wicked are in Scripture compared to the troubled sea, Isai. lvii. 20. For the present God restrains their wickedness by his mighty power, as he does the raging waves of the troubled sea, saying, *hitherto shalt thou come, and no further*; but if God should withdraw that restraining power, it would soon carry all afore it. Sin is the ruin and misery of the soul; it is destructive in its nature; and if God should leave it without restraint, there would need nothing else to make the soul perfectly miserable. The corruption of the heart of man is a thing that is immoderate and boundless in its fury; and while wicked men live here, it is like fire pent up by God's restraints, whenas if it were let loose it would set on fire the course of nature; and as the heart is now a sink of sin, so, if sin was not restrained, it would immediately turn the soul into a fiery oven, or a furnace of fire and brimstone.

7. It is no security to wicked men for one moment, but there are no *visible means of death* at hand. 'Tis no security to a natural man, that he is now in health, and that he don't see which way he should now immediately go out of the world by any accident, and that there is no visible danger in any respect in his circumstances. The manifold and continual experience of the world in all ages, shews that this is no evidence that a man is not on the very brink of eternity, and that the next step won't be into another world. The unseen, unthought of ways and means of persons going suddenly out of the world are innumerable and inconceivable. Unconverted men walk over the pit of Hell on a rotten covering, and there are innumerable places in this covering so weak that they won't bear their weight, and these places are not seen. The arrows of death fly unseen at noon-day; the sharpest sight can't discern them. God has so many different unsearchable ways of taking wicked men out of the world and sending 'em to Hell, that there is nothing to make it appear that God had need to be at the expence of a miracle, or go out of the ordinary course of his Providence, to destroy any wicked man, at any moment. All the means that there are of sinners going out of the world, are so in God's hands, and so universally absolutely subject to his power and determination, that it don't depend at all less on the mere will of God, whether sinners shall at any moment go to Hell, than if means were never made use of, or at all concerned in the case.

8. Natural men's *prudence* and *care* to preserve their own *lives*, or the care of others to preserve them, don't secure 'em a moment. This divine Providence and universal experience does also bear testimony to. There is this clear evidence that men's own wisdom

is no security to them from death; that if it were otherwise we should see some difference between the wise and politick men of the world, and others, with regard to the liableness to early and unexpected death; but how is it in fact? Eccles. ii. 16. *How dieth the wise man? as the fool.*

9. All wicked men's *pains* and *contrivance* they use to escape *Hell*, while they continue to reject Christ, and so remain wicked men, don't secure 'em from Hell one moment. Almost every natural man that hears of Hell, flatters himself that he shall escape it; he depends upon himself for his own security; he flatters himself in what he has done, in what he is now doing, or what he intends to do; every one lays out matters in his own mind how he shall avoid damnation, and flatters himself that he contrives well for himself, and that his schemes won't fail. They hear indeed that there are but few saved, and that the bigger part of men that have died heretofore are gone to Hell; but each one imagines that he lays out matters better for his own escape than others have done: he don't intend to come to that place of torment; he says within himself, that he intends to take care that shall be effectual, and to order matters so for himself as not to fail.

But the foolish children of men do miserably delude themselves in their own schemes, and in their confidence in their own strength and wisdom; they trust to nothing but a shadow. The bigger part of those that heretofore have lived under the same means of grace, and are now dead, are undoubtedly gone to Hell; and it was not because they were not as wise as those that are now alive; It was not because they did not lay out matters as well for themselves to secure their own escape. If it were so, that we could come to speak with them, and could inquire of them, one by one, whether they expected when alive, and when they used to hear about Hell, ever to be the subjects of that misery, we doubtless should hear one and another reply, "No, I never intended to come here; I had laid out matters otherwise in my mind; I thought I should contrive well for myself; I thought my scheme good; I intended to take effectual care; but it came upon me unexpected; I did not look for it at that time, and in that manner; it came as a thief; death outwitted me; God's wrath was too quick for me; O my cursed foolishness! I was flattering myself, and pleasing myself with vain dreams of what I would do hereafter, and when I was saying peace and safety, then sudden destruction came upon me."

10. God has laid himself under *no obligation* by any promise to keep any natural man out of Hell one moment. God certainly has made no promises either of eternal life, or of any deliverance or preservation from eternal death, but what are contained in the

Covenant of Grace, the promises that are given in Christ, in whom all the promises are yea and amen. But surely they have no interest in the promises of the Covenant of Grace [8] that are not the children of the Covenant, and that don't believe in any of the promises of the Covenant, and have no interest in the *Mediator* of the Covenant.

So that whatever some have imagined and pretended about promises made to natural men's earnest seeking and knocking, 'tis plain and manifest that whatever pains a natural man takes in religion, whatever prayers he makes, till he believes in Christ, God is under no manner of obligation to keep him a *moment* from eternal destruction.

So that thus it is, that natural men are held in the hand of God over the pit of Hell; they have deserved the fiery pit, and are already sentenced to it; and God is dreadfully provoked, his anger is as great towards them as to those that are actually suffering the executions of the fierceness of his wrath in Hell, and they have done nothing in the least to appease or abate that anger, neither is God in the least bound by any promise to hold 'em up one moment; the Devil is waiting for them, Hell is gaping for them, the flames gather and flash about them, and would fain lay hold on them, and swallow them up; the fire pent up in their own hearts is struggling to break out; and they have no interest in any mediator, there are no means within reach that can be any security to them. In short, they have no refuge, nothing to take hold of, all that preserves them every moment is the mere arbitrary will, and uncovenanted unobliged forbearance of an incensed God.

APPLICATION

The use may be of *awakening* to unconverted persons in this congregation.[9] This that you have heard is the case of every one of you that are out of Christ. That world of misery, that lake of burning brimstone is extended abroad under you. *There* is the dreadful pit of the glowing flames of the wrath of God; there is Hell's wide gaping mouth open; and you have nothing to stand upon, nor any thing to take hold of: there is nothing between you and Hell but the air; 'tis only the power and mere pleasure of God that holds you up.

You probably are not sensible of this; you find you are kept out of Hell, but don't see the hand of God in it, but look at other things, as the good state of your bodily constitution, your

---

8. The new covenant, made by God after the fall of Adam, whereby he offered salvation and eternal life after physical death to those who accepted the atonement of Christ.

9. *Cf.* note 1, with reference to the Half-Way Covenant.

care of your own life, and the means you use for your own preservation. But indeed these things are nothing; if God should withdraw his hand, they would avail no more to keep you from falling, than the thin air to hold up a person that is suspended in it.

Your wickedness makes you as it were heavy as lead, and to tend downwards with great weight and pressure towards Hell; and if God should let you go, you would immediately sink and swiftly descend and plunge into the bottomless gulf, and your healthy constitution, and your own care and prudence, and best contrivance, and all your righteousness, would have no more influence to uphold you and keep you out of Hell, than a spider's web would have to stop a falling rock. Were it not that so is the sovereign pleasure of God, the earth would not bear you one moment; for you are a burden to it; the creation groans with you; the creature is made subject to the bondage of your corruption, not willingly; the sun don't willingly shine upon you to give you light to serve sin and Satan; the earth don't willingly yield her increase to satisfy your lusts; nor is it willingly a stage for your wickedness to be acted upon; the air don't willingly serve you for breath to maintain the flame of life in your vitals, while you spend your life in the service of God's enemies. God's creatures are good, and were made for men to serve God with, and don't willingly subserve to any other purpose, and groan when they are abused to purposes so directly contrary to their nature and end. And the world would spue you out, were it not for the sovereign hand of him who hath subjected it in hope. There are the black clouds of God's wrath now hanging directly over your heads, full of the dreadful storm, and big with thunder; and were it not for the restraining hand of God it would immediately burst forth upon you. The sovereign pleasure of God for the present stays his rough wind; otherwise it would come with fury, and your destruction would come like a whirlwind, and you would be like the chaff of the summer threshing floor.

The wrath of God is like great waters that are dammed for the present; they increase more and more, and rise higher and higher, till an outlet is given, and the longer the stream is stopped, the more rapid and mighty is its course, when once it is let loose. 'Tis true, that judgment against your evil works has not been executed hitherto; the floods of God's vengeance have been withheld; but your guilt in the meantime is constantly increasing, and you are every day treasuring up more wrath; the waters are continually rising and waxing more and more mighty; and there is nothing but the mere pleasure of God that holds the waters back that are unwilling to be stopped, and press hard to go forward; if God should only withdraw his hand from the flood-gate, it would immediately fly open, and the fiery floods of the fierceness and wrath of God would rush forth with inconceivable fury, and would come upon you with omnipotent power; and if your strength were ten thousand times greater than it is, yea ten thousand times greater than the strength of the stoutest, sturdiest devil in Hell, it would be nothing to withstand or endure it.

The bow of God's wrath is bent, and the arrow made ready on the string, and justice bends the arrow at your heart, and strains the bow, and it is nothing but the mere pleasure of God, and that of an angry God, without any promise or obligation at all, that keeps the arrow one moment from being made drunk with your blood.

Thus are all you that never passed under a great change of heart, by the mighty power of the spirit of God upon your souls; all that were never born again, and made new creatures, and raised from being dead in sin, to a state of new, and before altogether unexperienced light and life, (however you may have reformed your life in many things, and may have had religious affections, and may keep up a form of religion in your families and closets, and in the house of God, and may be strict in it,) you are thus in the hands of an angry God; 'tis nothing but his mere pleasure that keeps you from being this moment swallowed up in everlasting destruction.

However unconvinced you may now be of the truth of what you hear, by and by you will be fully convinced of it. Those that are gone from being in the like circumstances with you, see that it was so with them; for destruction came suddenly upon most of them, when they expected nothing of it, and while they were saying, *peace and safety:* Now they see, that those things that they depended on for peace and safety, were nothing but thin air and empty shadows.

The God that holds you over the pit of Hell, much as one holds a spider, or some loathsome insect, over the fire, abhors you, and is dreadfully provoked; his wrath towards you burns like fire; he looks upon you as worthy of nothing else, but to be cast into the fire; he is of purer eyes than to bear to have you in his sight; you are ten thousand times so abominable in his eyes as the most hateful venomous serpent is in ours. You have offended him infinitely more than ever a stubborn rebel did his prince: and yet 'tis nothing but his hand that holds you from falling into the fire every moment: 'tis to be ascribed to nothing else, that you did not go to Hell the last night; that you was suffered to awake again in this world, after you closed your eyes to sleep: and there is no other reason to be given why you have not dropped into Hell since you arose in the morning, but that God's hand has held you up: there is no other reason to be given why you have not gone to Hell since you have sat here in the house of God, provoking his pure eyes by your sinful wicked manner of attending his solemn worship: yea, there is nothing else that is to be given as a reason why you don't this very moment drop down into Hell.

O sinner! Consider the fearful danger you are in: 'tis a great furnace of wrath, a wide and bottomless pit, full of the fire of wrath, that you are held over in the hand of that God, whose wrath is provoked and incensed as much against you as against many of the damned in Hell: you hang by a slender thread, with the flames of divine wrath flashing about it, and ready every moment to singe it, and burn it asunder; and you have no interest in any mediator, and nothing to lay hold of to save yourself, nothing to keep off the flames of wrath, nothing of your own, nothing that you ever have done, nothing that you can do, to induce God to spare you one moment.

And consider here more particularly several things concerning that wrath that you are in such danger of.

1. *Whose* wrath it is; it is the wrath of the infinite God. If it were only the wrath of man, tho' it were of the most potent prince, it would be comparatively little to be regarded. The wrath of kings is very much dreaded, especially of absolute monarchs, that have the possessions and lives of their subjects wholly in their power, to be disposed of at their mere will. Prov. xx. 2. *The fear of a king is as the roaring of a lion: whoso provoketh him to anger, sinneth against his own soul.* The subject that very much enrages an arbitrary prince, is liable to suffer the most extreme torments, that human art can invent or human power can inflict. But the greatest earthly potentates, in their greatest majesty and strength, and when clothed in their greatest terrors, are but feeble despicable worms of the dust, in comparison of the great and almighty Creator and King of heaven and earth: it is but little that they can do, when most enraged, and when they have exerted the utmost of their fury. All the kings of the earth before God are as grasshoppers, they are nothing and less than nothing: both their love and their hatred is to be despised. The wrath of the great King of Kings is as much more terrible than theirs, as his majesty is greater. Luke xii. 4, 5. *And I say unto you my friends, be not afraid of them that kill the body, and after that have no more that they can do: but I will forewarn you whom ye shall fear; fear him, which after he hath killed, hath power to cast into Hell; yea I say unto you, fear him.*

2. 'Tis the *fierceness* of his wrath that you are exposed to. We often read of the *fury* of God; as in Isai. lix. 18. *According to their deeds, accordingly he will repay fury to his adversaries.*

So Isai. lxvi. 15. *For behold, the Lord will come with fire, and with chariots like a whirlwind, to render his anger with fury, and his rebukes with flames of fire.* And so in many other places. So we read of God's fierceness. Rev. xix. 15. There we read of *the winepress of the fierceness and wrath of Almighty God.* The words are exceeding terrible; if it had only been said, *the wrath of God,* the words would have implied that which is infinitely dreadful: but 'tis not only said so, but the *fierceness and wrath of God:* the fury of God! the fierceness of Jehovah! Oh how dreadful must that be! Who can utter or conceive what such expressions carry in them! But it is not only said so, but *the fierceness and wrath of Almighty God.* As tho' there would be a very great manifestation of his almighty power, in what the fierceness of his wrath should inflict, as tho' omnipotence should be as it were enraged, and exerted, as men are wont to exert their strength in the fierceness of their wrath. Oh! then what will be the consequence! What will become of the poor worm that shall suffer it! Whose hands can be strong? and whose heart endure? To what a dreadful, inexpressible, inconceivable depth of misery must the poor creature be sunk, who shall be the subject of this!

Consider this, you that are here present, that yet remain in an unregenerate state. That God will execute the fierceness of his anger, implies that he will inflict wrath without any pity: when God beholds the ineffable extremity of your case, and sees your torment to be so vastly disproportioned to your strength, and sees how your poor soul is crushed and sinks down, as it were into an infinite gloom, he will have no compassion upon you, he will not forbear the executions of his wrath, or in the least lighten his hand; there shall be no moderation or mercy, nor will God then at all stay his rough wind; he will have no regard to your welfare, nor be at all careful lest you should suffer too much, in any other sense than only that you shall not suffer beyond what strict justice requires: nothing shall be withheld, because it's so hard for you to bear. Ezek. viii. 18. *Therefore will I also deal in fury; mine eye shall not spare, neither will I have pity; and tho' they cry in mine ears with a loud voice, yet I will not hear them.* Now God stands ready to pity you; this is a day of mercy; you may cry now with some encouragement of obtaining mercy: but when once the day of mercy is past, your most lamentable and dolorous cries and shrieks will be in vain; you will be wholly lost and thrown away of God as to any regard to your welfare; God will have no other use to put you to but only to suffer misery; you shall be continued in being to no other end; for you will be a vessel of wrath fitted to destruction; and there will be no other use of this vessel but only to be filled full of wrath: God will be so

mighty power that is to be seen in it. Isai. xxxiii. 12, 13, 14. *And the people shall be as the burning of lime, as thorns cut up shall they be burnt in the fire. Hear ye that are far off what I have done; and ye that are near acknowledge my might. The sinners in Zion are afraid, fearfulness hath surprized the hypocrites, etc.*

Thus it will be with you that are in an unconverted state, if you continue in it; the infinite might, and majesty and terribleness of the omnipotent God shall be magnified upon you, in the ineffable strength of your torments: you shall be tormented in the presence of the holy angels, and in the presence of the Lamb;[2] and when you shall be in this state of suffering, the glorious inhabitants of Heaven shall go forth and look on the awful spectacle, that they may see what the wrath and fierceness of the Almighty is, and when they have seen it, they will fall down and adore that great power and majesty. Isai. lxvi. 23, 24. *And it shall come to pass, that from one new moon to another, and from one sabbath to another, shall all flesh come to worship before me, saith the Lord; and they shall go forth and look upon the carcasses of the men that have transgressed against me; for their worm shall not die, neither shall their fire be quenched, and they shall be an abhorring unto all flesh.*

4. 'Tis *everlasting* wrath. It would be dreadful to suffer this fierceness and wrath of Almighty God one moment; but you must suffer it to all eternity: there will be no end to this exquisite horrible misery: when you look forward, you shall see a long forever, a boundless duration before you, which will swallow up your thoughts, and amaze your soul; and you will absolutely despair of ever having any deliverance, any end, any mitigation, any rest at all; you will know certainly that you must wear out long ages, millions of millions of ages, in wrestling and conflicting with this almighty merciless vengeance; and then when you have so done, when so many ages have actually been spent by you in this manner, you will know that all is but a point to what remains. So that your punishment will indeed be infinite. Oh who can express what the state of a soul in such circumstances is! All that we can possibly say about it, gives but a very feeble faint representation of it; 'tis inexpressible and inconceivable: for *who knows the power of God's anger?*

How dreadful is the state of those that are daily and hourly in danger of this great wrath, and infinite misery! But this is the dismal case of every soul in this congregation, that has not been born again, however moral and strict, sober and religious they may otherwise be. Oh that you would consider it, whether you be young

2. Christ in his priestly office, having sacrificed himself for sinners (*cf.* John i: 29).

as precious as the souls of the people at Suffield,[3] where they are flocking from day to day to Christ?

Are there not many here that have lived *long* in the world, that are not to this day born again, and so are aliens from the commonwealth of Israel, and have done nothing ever since they have lived, but treasure up wrath against the day of wrath? Oh sirs, your case in an especial manner is extremely dangerous; your guilt and hardness of heart is extremely great. Don't you see how generally persons of your years are passed over and left, in the present remarkable and wonderful dispensation of God's mercy? You had need to consider yourselves, and wake thoroughly out of sleep; you cannot bear the fierceness and wrath of the infinite God.

And you that are *young men*, and *young women*, will you neglect this precious season that you now enjoy, when so many others of your age are renouncing all youthful vanities, and flocking to Christ? You especially have now an extraordinary opportunity; but if you neglect it, it will soon be with you as it is with those persons that spent away all the precious days of youth in sin, and are now come to such a dreadful pass in blindness and hardness.

And you *children* that are unconverted, don't you know that you are going down to Hell, to bear the dreadful wrath of that God that is now angry with you every day, and every night? Will you be content to be the children of the Devil, when so many other children in the land are converted, and are become the holy and happy children of the King of kings?

And let every one that is yet out of Christ, and hanging over the pit of Hell, whether they be old men and women, or middle aged, or young people, or little children, now hearken to the loud calls of God's word and providence. This acceptable year of the Lord, that is a day of such great favour to some, will doubtless be a day of as remarkable vengeance to others. Men's hearts harden, and their guilt increases apace at such a day as this, if they neglect their souls: and never was there so great danger of such persons being given up to hardness of heart, and blindness of mind. God seems now to be hastily gathering in his elect in all parts of the land; and probably the bigger part of adult persons that ever shall be saved, will be brought in now in a little time, and that it will be as it was on that great out-pouring of the Spirit upon the Jews in the Apostles' days,[4] the election will obtain, and the rest will be blinded. If this should be the case with you, you will eternally curse this day, and will curse the day that ever you was

3. "The next neighbour town" [Edwards's note].
4. Pentecost, when after Christ's ascension, the Holy Spirit, as the third person of the Trinity, was given to the apostles (Acts ii).

born, to see such a season of the pouring out of God's Spirit; and will wish that you had died and gone to Hell before you had seen it. Now undoubtedly it is, as it was in the days of John the Baptist, the ax is in an extraordinary manner laid at the root of the trees, that every tree that brings not forth good fruit, may be hewn down, and cast into the fire.

Therefore let every one that is out of Christ, now awake and fly from the wrath to come. The wrath of Almighty God is now undoubtedly hanging over great part of this congregation: let every one fly out of Sodom. *Haste and escape for your lives, look not behind you, escape to the mountain, lest you be consumed.*

1741   1741

Personal Narrative [5]

I had a variety of concerns and exercises about my soul from my childhood; but had two more remarkable seasons of awakening, before I met with that change by which I was brought to those new dispositions, and that new sense of things, that I have since had. The first time was when I was a boy, some years before I went to college, at a time of remarkable awakening in my father's congregation. I was then very much affected for many months, and concerned about the things of religion, and my soul's salvation; and was abundant in duties. I used to pray five times a day in secret, and to spend much time in religious talk with other boys, and used to meet with them to pray together. I experienced I know not what kind of delight in religion. My mind was much engaged in it, and had much self-righteous pleasure; and it was my delight to abound in religious duties. I with some of my schoolmates joined together, and built a booth in a swamp, in a very retired spot, for a place of prayer. And besides, I had particular secret places of my own in the woods, where I used to retire by myself; and was from time to time much affected. My affections seemed to be lively and easily moved, and I seemed to be in my element when engaged in religious duties. And I am ready to think, many are deceived with such affections, and such a kind of delight as I then had in religion, and mistake it for grace.

But in process of time, my convictions and affections wore off; and I entirely lost all those affections and delights and left off secret prayer, at least as to any constant performance of it; and

5. Celebrated for "mysticism" and "charm," this classic of religious experience was actually "the apparatus of psychological investigation * * * devoted, not to the defense of emotion against reason, but to a winnowing out of the one pure spiritual emotion from the horde of imitations" (Miller, *Jonathan Edwards*, p. 106). Written about 1740–1742, this essay was first published in a *Life* of Edwards by Samuel Hopkins (1765).

returned like a dog to his vomit,[6] and went on in the ways of sin. Indeed I was at times very uneasy, especially towards the latter part of my time at college; when it pleased God, to seize me with the pleurisy; in which he brought me nigh to the grave, and shook me over the pit of hell. And yet, it was not long after my recovery, before I fell again into my old ways of sin. But God would not suffer me to go on with my quietness; I had great and violent inward struggles, till, after many conflicts, with wicked inclinations, repeated resolutions, and bonds that I laid myself under by a kind of vows to God, I was brought wholly to break off all former wicked ways, and all ways of known outward sin; and to apply myself to seek salvation, and practice many religious duties; but without that kind of affection and delight which I had formerly experienced. My concern now wrought more by inward struggles and conflicts, and self-reflections. I made seeking my salvation the main business of my life. But yet, it seems to me, I sought after a miserable manner; which has made me sometimes since to question, whether ever it issued in that which was saving; being ready to doubt, whether such miserable seeking ever succeeded. I was indeed brought to seek salvation in a manner that I never was before; I felt a spirit to part with all things in the world, for an interest in Christ.——My concern continued and prevailed, with many exercising thoughts and inward struggles; but yet it never seemed to be proper to express that concern by the name of terror.

From my childhood up, my mind had been full of objections against the doctrine of God's sovereignty, in choosing whom he would to eternal life, and rejecting whom he pleased; leaving them eternally to perish, and be everlastingly tormented in hell. It used to appear like a horrible doctrine to me.[7] But I remember the time very well, when I seemed to be convinced, and fully satisfied, as to this sovereignty of God, and his justice in thus eternally disposing of men, according to his sovereign pleasure. But never could give an account, how, or by what means, I was thus convinced, not in the least imagining at the time, nor a long time after, that there was any extraordinary influence of God's Spirit in it; but only that now I saw further, and my reason apprehended the justice and reasonableness of it. However, my mind rested in it; and it put an end to all those cavils and objections. And there has been a wonderful alteration in my mind, with respect to the doctrine of God's sovereignty, from that day to this; so that I scarce ever have found so much as the rising of an objection

6. "—so a fool to his folly" (Proverbs xxvi: 11).
7. Referring to the Covenant theology of the Puritans. God's first covenant with Adam was eternal life in return for obedience—a covenant of justice. In Adam's fall, mankind forfeited this covenant. The New Covenant revealed through Jesus Christ was one of mercy; no one could earn or deserve God's grace.

against it, in the most absolute sense, in God's shewing mercy to whom he will shew mercy, and hardening whom he will.[8] God's absolute sovereignty and justice, with respect to salvation and damnation, is what my mind seems to rest assured of, as much as of any thing that I see with my eyes; at least it is so at times. But I have often, since that first conviction, had quite another kind of sense of God's sovereignty than I had then. I have often since had not only a conviction, but a delightful conviction. The doctrine has appeared exceeding pleasant, bright, and sweet.

Absolute sovereignty is what I love to ascribe to God. But my first conviction was not so.

The first instance that I remember of that sort of inward, sweet delight in God and divine things that I have lived much in since, was on reading those words, 1 Tim. i: 17. *Now unto the King eternal, immortal, invisible, the only wise God, be honor and glory forever and ever, Amen.* As I read the words, there came into my soul, and was as it were diffused through it, a sense of the glory of the Divine Being; a new sense, quite different from any thing I ever experienced before. Never any words of scripture seemed to me as these words did. I thought within myself, how excellent a being that was, and how happy I should be, if I might enjoy that God, and be wrapt up in heaven, and be as it were swallowed up in him forever! I kept saying, and as it were singing over these words of scripture to myself; and went to pray to God that I might enjoy him, and prayed in a manner quite different from what I used to do; with a new sort of affection. But it never came into my thought, that there was any thing spiritual, or of a saving nature in this.

From about that time, I began to have a new kind of apprehensions and ideas of Christ, and the work of redemption, and the glorious way of salvation by him. An inward, sweet sense of these things, at times, came into my heart; and my soul was led away in pleasant views and contemplations of them. And my mind was greatly engaged to spend my time in reading and meditating on Christ, on the beauty and excellency of his person, and the lovely way of salvation by free grace in him. I found no books so delightful to me, as those that treated of these subjects. Those words, Cant.[9] ii: 1, used to be abundantly with me. *I am the Rose of Sharon, and the Lily of the valleys.* The words seemed to me, sweetly to represent the loveliness and beauty of Jesus Christ. The whole book of Canticles used to be pleasant to me, and I used to be much in reading it, about that time; and found, from time to

---

8. Romans ix: 18. Paul's words were often quoted in support of the doctrine of grace.

9. Canticles, or the Song of Solomon, a love poem interpreted by theologians as applying to Christ and mankind.

time, an inward sweetness, that would carry me away, in my contemplations. This I know not how to express otherwise, than by a
calm, sweet abstraction of soul from all the concerns of this world;
and sometimes a kind of vision, or fixed ideas and imaginations, of
being alone in the mountains, or some solitary wilderness, far
from all mankind, sweetly conversing with Christ, and wrapt and
swallowed up in God. The sense I had of divine things, would
often of a sudden kindle up, as it were, a sweet burning in my
heart; an ardor of soul, that I know not how to express.

Not long after I began to experience these things, I gave an
account to my father of some things that had passed in my mind.
I was pretty much affected by the discourse we had together; and
when the discourse was ended, I walked abroad alone, in a solitary
place in my father's pasture for contemplation. And as I was
walking there and looking up on the sky and clouds, there came
into my mind so sweet a sense of the glorious *majesty* and *grace*
of God, that I know not how to express. I seemed to see them
both in a sweet conjunction; majesty and meekness joined together;
it was a gentle, and holy majesty; and also a majestic meekness; a
high, great, and holy gentleness.

After this my sense of divine things gradually increased, and became more and more lively, and had more of that inward sweetness.
The appearance of every thing was altered; there seemed to be,
as it were, a calm, sweet cast, or appearance of divine glory, in
almost every thing. God's excellency, his wisdom, his purity and
love, seemed to appear in every thing; in the sun, moon, and stars;
in the clouds, and blue sky; in the grass, flowers, trees; in the water,
and all nature; which used greatly to fix my mind. I often used to
sit and view the moon for continuance; and in the day, spent
much time in viewing the clouds and sky, to behold the sweet
glory of God in these things; in the mean time, singing forth, with
a low voice, my contemplations of the Creator and Redeemer. And
scarce any thing, among all the works of nature, was so delightful
to me as thunder and lightning; formerly, nothing had been so
terrible to me. Before, I used to be uncommonly terrified with
thunder, and to be struck with terror when I saw a thunder storm
rising; but now, on the contrary, it rejoiced me. I felt God, so to
speak, at the first appearance of a thunder storm; and used to
take the opportunity, at such times, to fix myself in order to view
the clouds, and see the lightnings play, and hear the majestic and
awful voice of God's thunder, which oftentimes was exceedingly
entertaining, leading me to sweet contemplations of my great and
glorious God. While thus engaged, it always seemed natural to me
to sing, or chant for my meditations; or, to speak my thoughts in
soliloquies with a singing voice.

I felt then great satisfaction, as to my good state; but that did not content me. I had vehement longings of soul after God and Christ, and after more holiness, wherewith my heart seemed to be full, and ready to break; which often brought to my mind the words of the Psalmist, Psal. cxix. 28: *My soul breaketh for the longing it hath.* I often felt a mourning and lamenting in my heart, that I had not turned to God sooner, that I might have had more time to grow in grace. My mind was greatly fixed on divine things; almost perpetually in the contemplation of them. I spent most of my time in thinking of divine things, year after year; often walking alone in the woods, and solitary places, for meditation, soliloquy, and prayer, and converse with God; and it was always my manner, at such times, to sing forth my contemplations. I was almost constantly in ejaculatory prayer, wherever I was. Prayer seemed to be natural to me, as the breath by which the inward burnings of my heart had vent. The delights which I now felt in the things of religion, were of an exceedingly different kind from those before mentioned, that I had when a boy; and what I then had no more notion of, than one born blind has of pleasant and beautiful colors. They were of a more inward, pure, soul-animating and refreshing nature. Those former delights never reached the heart; and did not arise from any sight of the divine excellency of the things of God; or any taste of the soul-satisfying and life-giving good there is in them.

My sense of divine things seemed gradually to increase, until I went to preach at New York,[1] which was about a year and a half after they began; and while I was there, I felt them, very sensibly, in a higher degree than I had done before. My longings after God and holiness, were much increased. Pure and humble, holy and heavenly Christianity, appeared exceedingly amiable to me. I felt a burning desire to be in every thing a complete Christian; and conform to the blessed image of Christ; and that I might live, in all things, according to the pure and blessed rules of the gospel. I had an eager thirsting after progress in these things; which put me upon pursuing and pressing after them. It was my continual strife day and night, and constant inquiry, how I should *be* more holy, and *live* more holily, and more becoming a child of God, and a disciple of Christ. I now sought an increase of grace and holiness, and a holy life, with much more earnestness, than ever I sought grace before I had it. I used to be continually examining myself, and studying and contriving for likely ways and means, how I should live holily, with far greater diligence and earnestness, than ever I pursued any thing in my life; but yet with too great a de-

1. August, 1722–May, 1723.

pendance on my own strength; which afterwards proved a great damage to me. My experience had not then taught me, as it has done since my extreme feebleness and impotence, every manner of way; and the bottomless depths of secret corruption and deceit there was in my heart. However, I went on with my eager pursuit after more holiness, and conformity to Christ.

The heaven I desired was a heaven of holiness; to be with God, and to spend my eternity in divine love, and holy communication with Christ. My mind was very much taken up with contemplations on heaven, and the enjoyments there; and living there in perfect holiness, humility and love. And it used at that time to appear a great part of the happiness of heaven, that there the saints could express their love to Christ. It appeared to me a great clog and burden, that what I felt within, I could not express as I desired. The inward ardor of my soul, seemed to be hindered and pent up, and could not freely flame out as it would. I used often to think, how in heaven this principle should freely and fully vent and express itself. Heaven appeared exceedingly delightful, as a world of love; and that all happiness consisted in living in pure, humble, heavenly, divine love.

I remember the thoughts I used then to have of holiness; and said sometimes to myself, "I do certainly know that I love holiness, such as the gospel prescribes." It appeared to me, that there was nothing in it but what was ravishingly lovely; the highest beauty and amiableness—a *divine* beauty; far purer than any thing here upon earth; and that every thing else was like mire and defilement, in comparison of it.

Holiness, as I then wrote down some of my contemplations on it, appeared to me to be of a sweet, pleasant, charming, serene, calm nature; which brought an inexpressible purity, brightness, peacefulness and ravishment to the soul. In other words, that it made the soul like a field or garden of God, with all manner of pleasant flowers; all pleasant, delightful, and undisturbed; enjoying a sweet calm, and the gently vivifying beams of the sun. The soul of a true Christian, as I then wrote my meditations, appeared like such a little white flower as we see in the spring of the year; low and humble on the ground, opening its bosom to receive the pleasant beams of the sun's glory; rejoicing as it were in a calm rapture; diffusing around a sweet fragrancy; standing peacefully and lovingly, in the midst of other flowers round about; all in like manner opening their bosoms, to drink in the light of the sun. There was no part of creature holiness, that I had so great a sense of its loveliness, as humility, brokenness of heart and poverty of spirit; and there was nothing that I so earnestly longed for. My heart panted after this, to lie low before God, as in the dust; that I might be nothing, and that God might be ALL, that I might become as a little child.[2]

While at New York, I was sometimes much affected with reflections on my past life, considering how late it was before I began to be truly religious; and how wickedly I had lived till then; and once so as to weep abundantly, and for a considerable time together.

On *January* 12, 1723, I made a solemn dedication of myself to God, and wrote it down; giving up myself, and all that I had to God; to be for the future in no respect my own; to act as one that had no right to himself, in any respect. And solemnly vowed to take God for my whole portion and felicity; looking on nothing else as any part of my happiness, nor acting as if it were; and his law for the constant rule of my obedience; engaging to fight with all my might, against the world, the flesh and the devil, to the end of my life. But I have reason to be infinitely humbled, when I consider how much I have failed of answering my obligation.

I had then abundance of sweet religious conversation in the family where I lived, with Mr. John Smith and his pious mother. My heart was knit in affection to those in whom were appearances of true piety; and I could bear the thoughts of no other companions, but such as were holy, and the disciples of the blessed Jesus. I had great longings for the advancement of Christ's kingdom in the world; and my secret prayer used to be, in great part, taken up in praying for it. If I heard the least hint of any thing that happened, in any part of the world, that appeared, in some respect or other, to have a favorable aspect on the interest of Christ's kingdom, my soul eagerly catched at it; and it would much animate and refresh me. I used to be eager to read public news letters, mainly for that end; to see if I could not find some news favorable to the interest of religion in the world.

I very frequently used to retire into a solitary place, on the banks of Hudson's river, at some distance from the city, for contemplation on divine things, and secret converse with God; and had many sweet hours there. Sometimes Mr. Smith and I walked there together, to converse on the things of God; and our conversation used to turn much on the advancement of Christ's kingdom in the world, and the glorious things that God would accomplish for his church in the latter days. I had then, and at other times the greatest delight in the holy scriptures, of any book whatsoever. Oftentimes in reading it, every word seemed to touch my heart. I felt a harmony between something in my heart, and those sweet

2. This is the first climax of *Personal Narrative*, a theological case history of divine grace. In the Calvinistic theology, grace functioned through the stages of "regeneration"—after conviction of sin, repentence, and humiliation, man arrives at the stage of "justification"; he is relieved, not of original sin, but of its consequences. In the passages above, Edwards has been testing the psychological reality of his experience of "justification." *Cf.* Mark x: 15.

and powerful words. I seemed often to see so much light exhibited by every sentence, and such a refreshing food communicated, that I could not get along in reading; often dwelling long on one sentence, to see the wonders contained in it; and yet almost every sentence seemed to be full of wonders.

I came away from New York in the month of April, 1723, and had a most bitter parting with Madam Smith and her son. My heart seemed to sink within me at leaving the family and city, where I had enjoyed so many sweet and pleasant days. I went from New York to Weathersfield, by water, and as I sailed away, I kept sight of the city as long as I could. However, that night, after this sorrowful parting, I was greatly comforted in God at Westchester, where we went ashore to lodge; and had a pleasant time of it all the voyage to Saybrook. It was sweet to me to think of meeting dear Christians in heaven, where we should never part more. At Saybrook we went ashore to lodge, on Saturday, and there kept the Sabbath; where I had a sweet and refreshing season, walking alone in the fields.

After I came home to Windsor, I remained much in a like frame of mind, as when at New York; only sometimes I felt my heart ready to sink with the thoughts of my friends at New York. My support was in contemplations on the heavenly state; as I find in my Diary of May 1, 1723. It was a comfort to think of that state, where there is fulness of joy; where reigns heavenly, calm, and delightful love, without alloy; where there are continually the dearest expressions of this love; where is the enjoyment of the persons loved, without ever parting; where those persons who appear so lovely in this world, will really be inexpressibly more lovely and full of love to us. And how sweetly will the mutual lovers join together to sing the praises of God and the Lamb! [3] How will it fill us with joy to think, that this enjoyment, these sweet exercises will never cease, but will last to all eternity! I continued much in the same frame, in the general, as when at New York, till I went to New Haven as tutor to the college; particularly once at Bolton, on a journey from Boston, while walking out alone in the fields. After I went to New Haven I sunk in religion; my mind being diverted from my eager pursuits after holiness, by some affairs that greatly perplexed and distracted my thoughts.

In September, 1725, I was taken ill at New Haven, and while endeavoring to go home to Windsor, was so ill at the North Village, that I could go no further; where I lay sick for about a

---

3. John repeatedly referred to Christ as the Lamb of God; he envisioned the heavenly host singing praises to God and the Lamb in Revelation xiv: 2–3 and xix: 5–7.

quarter of a year. In this sickness God was pleased to visit me again with the sweet influences of his Spirit. My mind was greatly engaged there in divine, pleasant contemplations, and longings of soul. I observed that those who watched with me, would often be looking out wishfully for the morning; which brought to my mind those words of the Psalmist, and which my soul with delight made its own language, *My soul waiteth for the Lord, more than they that watch for the morning, I say, more than they that watch for the morning;* [4] and when the light of day came in at the windows, it refreshed my soul from one morning to another. It seemed to be some image of the light of God's glory.

I remember, about that time, I used greatly to long for the conversion of some that I was concerned with; I could gladly honor them, and with delight be a servant to them, and lie at their feet, if they were but truly holy. But some time after this, I was again greatly diverted in my mind with some temporal concerns that exceedingly took up my thoughts, greatly to the wounding of my soul; and went on through various exercises, that it would be tedious to relate, which gave me much more experience of my own heart, than ever I had before.

Since I came to this town, [5] I have often had sweet complacency in God, in views of his glorious perfections and the excellency of Jesus Christ. God has appeared to me a glorious and lovely being, chiefly on the account of his holiness. The holiness of God has always appeared to me the most lovely of all his attributes. The doctrines of God's absolute sovereignty, and free grace, in shewing mercy to whom he would shew mercy; and man's absolute dependance on the operations of God's Holy Spirit, have very often appeared to me as sweet and glorious doctrines. These doctrines have been much my delight. God's sovereignty has ever appeared to me, a great part of his glory. It has often been my delight to approach God, and adore him as a sovereign God, and ask sovereign mercy of him.

I have loved the doctrines of the gospel; they have been to my soul like green pastures. The gospel has seemed to me the richest treasure; the treasure that I have most desired, and longed that it might dwell richly in me. The way of salvation by Christ has appeared, in a general way, glorious and excellent, most pleasant and most beautiful. It has often seemed to me, that it would in a great measure spoil heaven, to receive it in any other way. That text has often been affecting and delightful to me. Isa. xxxii: 2. *A man shall be an hiding place from the wind, and a covert from the tempest,* &c.

It has often appeared to me delightful, to be united to Christ; to have him for my head, and to be a member of his body; also to have Christ for my teacher and prophet. I very often think with sweetness, and longings, and pantings of soul, of being a little child, taking hold of Christ, to be led by him through the wilderness of this world. That text, Matth. xviii: 3, has often been sweet to me, *except ye be converted and become as little children,* &c. I love to think of coming to Christ, to receive salvation of him, poor in spirit, and quite empty of self, humbly exalting him alone; cut off entirely from my own root, in order to grow into, and out of Christ; to have God in Christ to be all in all; and to live by faith on the Son of God, a life of humble unfeigned confidence in him. That scripture has often been sweet to me, Psal. cxv: 1. *Not unto us, O Lord, not unto us, but to thy name give glory, for thy mercy and for thy truth's sake.* And those words of Christ, Luke x: 21. *In that hour Jesus rejoiced in spirit, and said, I thank thee, O Father, Lord of heaven and earth, that thou hast hid these things from the wise and prudent, and hast revealed them unto babes; even so, Father, for so it seemed good in thy sight.* That sovereignty of God which Christ rejoiced in, seemed to me worthy of such joy; and that rejoicing seemed to show the excellency of Christ, and of what spirit he was.

Sometimes, only mentioning a single word caused my heart to burn within me; or only seeing the name of Christ, or the name of some attribute of God. And God has appeared glorious to me, on account of the Trinity. It has made me have exalting thoughts of God, that he subsists in three persons; Father, Son and Holy Ghost. The sweetest joys and delights I have experienced, have not been those that have arisen from a hope of my own good estate; but in a direct view of the glorious things of the gospel. When I enjoy this sweetness, it seems to carry me above the thoughts of my own estate; it seems at such times a loss that I cannot bear, to take off my eye from the glorious pleasant object I behold without me, to turn my eye in upon myself, and my own good estate.

My heart has been much on the advancement of Christ's kingdom in the world. The histories of the past advancement of Christ's kingdom have been sweet to me. When I have read histories of past ages, the pleasantest thing in all my reading has been, to read of the kingdom of Christ being promoted. And when I have expected, in my reading, to come to any such thing, I have rejoiced in the prospect, all the way as I read. And my mind has been much entertained and delighted with the scripture promises and prophecies, which relate to the future glorious advancement of Christ's kingdom upon earth.

I have sometimes had a sense of the excellent fulness of Christ, and his meetness and suitableness as a Saviour, whereby he has appeared to me, far above all, the chief of ten thousands. His blood and atonement have appeared sweet, and his righteousness sweet: which was always accompanied with ardency of spirit; and inward strugglings and breathings, and groanings that cannot be uttered, to be emptied of myself, and swallowed up in Christ.

Once as I rode out into the woods for my health, in 1737, having alighted from my horse in a retired place, as my manner commonly has been, to walk for divine contemplation and prayer, I had a view that for me was extraordinary, of the glory of the Son of God, as Mediator between God and man, and his wonderful, great, full, pure and sweet grace and love, and meek and gentle condescension. This grace that appeared so calm and sweet, appeared also great above the heavens. The person of Christ appeared ineffably excellent with an excellency great enough to swallow up all thought and conception—which continued as near as I can judge, about an hour; which kept me the greater part of the time in a flood of tears, and weeping aloud. I felt an ardency of soul to be, what I know not otherwise how to express, emptied and annihilated; to lie in the dust, and to be full of Christ alone; to love him with a holy and pure love; to trust in him; to live upon him; to serve and follow him; and to be perfectly sanctified and made pure, with a divine and heavenly purity. I have, several other times, had views very much of the same nature, and which have had the same effects.

I have many times had a sense of the glory of the third person in the Trinity, in his office of Sanctifier; in his holy operations, communicating divine light and life to the soul. God, in the communications of his Holy Spirit, has appeared as an infinite fountain of divine glory and sweetness; being full, and sufficient to fill and satisfy the soul; pouring forth itself in sweet communications; like the sun in its glory, sweetly and pleasantly diffusing light and life. And I have sometimes had an affecting sense of the excellency of the word of God, as a word of life; as the light of life; a sweet, excellent, life-giving word; accompanied with a thirsting after that word, that it might dwell richly in my heart.

Often, since I lived in this town, I have had very affecting views of my own sinfulness and vileness; very frequently to such a degree as to hold me in a kind of loud weeping, sometimes for a considerable time together; so that I have often been forced to shut myself up. I have had a vastly greater sense of my own wickedness, and the badness of my own heart, than ever I had before my conversion. It has often appeared to me, that if God should mark iniquity against me, I should appear the very worst of all mankind; of all that have been, since the beginning of the world to this time; and that I should have by far the lowest place in hell. When others, that have come to talk with me about their soul concerns, have expressed the sense they have had of their own wickedness, by saying that it seemed to them, that they were as bad as the devil himself; I thought their expression seemed exceedingly faint and feeble, to represent my wickedness.

My wickedness, as I am in myself, has long appeared to me perfectly ineffable, and swallowing up all thought and imagination; like an infinite deluge, or mountains over my head. I know not how to express better what my sins appear to me to be, than by heaping infinite upon infinite, and multiplying infinite by infinite. Very often, for these many years, these expressions are in my mind, and in my mouth, "Infinite upon infinite—Infinite upon infinite!" When I look into my heart, and take a view of my wickedness, it looks like an abyss infinitely deeper than hell. And it appears to me, that were it not for free grace, exalted and raised up to the infinite height of all the fulness and glory of the great Jehovah, and the arm of his power and grace stretched forth in all the majesty of his power, and in all the glory of his sovereignty, I should appear sunk down in my sins below hell itself; far beyond the sight of every thing, but the eye of sovereign grace, that can pierce even down to such a depth. And yet, it seems to me, that my conviction of sin is exceedingly small, and faint; it is enough to amaze me, that I have no more sense of my sin. I know certainly, that I have very little sense of my sinfulness. When I have had turns of weeping and crying for my sins, I thought I knew at the time, that my repentance was nothing to my sin.

I have greatly longed of late, for a broken heart, and to lie low before God; and, when I ask for humility, I cannot bear the thoughts of being no more humble than other Christians. It seems to me, that though their degrees of humility may be suitable for them, yet it would be a vile self-exaltation to me, not to be the lowest in humility of all mankind. Others speak of their longing to be "humbled to the dust"; that may be a proper expression for them, but I always think of myself, that I ought, and it is an expression that has long been natural for me to use in prayer, "to lie infinitely low before God." And it is affecting to think, how ignorant I was, when a young Christian, of the bottomless, infinite depths of wickedness, pride, hypocrisy and deceit, left in my heart.

I have a much greater sense of my universal, exceeding dependance on God's grace and strength, and mere good pleasure, of late, than I used formerly to have; and have experienced more of an abhorrence of my own righteousness. The very thought of any joy arising in me, on any consideration of my own amiableness, performances, or experiences, or any goodness of heart or life, is nauseous and detestable to me. And yet I am greatly afflicted with a proud and self-righteous spirit, much more sensibly than I used to be formerly. I see that serpent rising and putting forth its head continually, every where, all around me.

Though it seems to me, that, in some respects, I was a far better Christian, for two or three years after my first conversion, than I am now; and lived in a more constant delight and pleasure; yet, of late years, I have had a more full and constant sense of the absolute sovereignty of God, and a delight in that sovereignty; and have had more of a sense of the glory of Christ, as a Mediator revealed in the gospel. On one Saturday night, in particular, I had such a discovery of the excellency of the gospel above all other doctrines, that I could not but say to myself, "This is my chosen light, my chosen doctrine;" and of Christ, "This is my chosen Prophet." It appeared sweet, beyond all expression, to follow Christ, and to be taught, and enlightened, and instructed by him; to learn of him, and live to him. Another Saturday night, (*January*, 1739) I had such a sense, how sweet and blessed a thing it was to walk in the way of duty; to do that which was right and meet to be done, and agreeable to the holy mind of God; that it caused me to break forth into a kind of loud weeping, which held me some time, so that I was forced to shut myself up, and fasten the doors. I could not but, as it were, cry out, "How happy are they which do that which is right in the sight of God! They are blessed indeed, they are the happy ones!" I had, at the same time, a very affecting sense, how meet and suitable it was that God should govern the world, and order all things according to his own pleasure; and I rejoiced in it, that God reigned, and that his will was done.

1740?–1742   1765

From Dissertation: Concerning the End for Which God Created the World [6]

Chapter I: What Reason Teaches Concerning Creation

SECTION II. *Some farther observations concerning those things which reason leads us to suppose God aimed at in the creation of the world, shewing particularly what things that are absolutely good, are actually the consequence of the creation of the world.*

6. Like "The Nature of True Virtue," this work of his Stockbridge period represents the fullness of Edwards's faith and power. Indeed, this disserta- tion as a whole takes him back to the mysticism of his youth, but now balanced with accumulated knowledge and experience. His vision of God as the

From what was last observed it seems to be the most proper and just way of proceeding, as we would see what light reason will give us respecting the particular end or ends God had ultimately in view in the creation of the world; to consider what thing or things, are actually the effect or consequence of the creation of the world, that are simply and originally valuable in themselves. And this is what I would directly proceed to, without entering on any tedious metaphysical inquiries wherein fitness, amiableness, or valuableness consists; or what that is in the nature of some things, which is properly the foundation of a worthiness of being loved and esteemed on their own account. In this I must at present refer what I say to the sense and dictates of the reader's mind, on sedate and calm reflection.

I proceed to observe,

1. It seems a thing in itself fit, proper and desirable, that the glorious attributes of God, which consist in a sufficiency to certain acts and effects, should be exerted in the production of such effects, as might manifest the infinite power, wisdom, righteousness, goodness, &c. which are in God. If the world had not been created, these attributes never would have had any exercise. The power of God, which is a sufficiency in him to produce great effects, must for ever have been dormant and useless as to any effect. The divine wisdom and prudence would have had no exercise in any wise contrivance, any prudent proceeding or disposal of things; for there would have been no objects of contrivance or disposal. The same might be observed of God's justice, goodness and truth. Indeed God might have known as perfectly that he possessed these attributes, if they had never been exerted or expressed in any effect. But then if the attributes which consist in a sufficiency for correspondent effects, are in themselves excellent, the exercises of them must likewise be excellent. If it be an excellent thing that there should be a sufficiency for a certain kind of action or operation, the excellency of such a sufficiency must consist in its relation to this kind of operation or effect; but that could not be, unless the operation itself were excellent. A sufficiency for any act or work is no farther valuable, than the work or

---

infinite love and fullness, from which all creation emanates cosmically infused by God, is not the patriarchal and personalized God of the Old Testament; even as the God of Love there is a dimension obtained perhaps from the Newtonian universe, and this quality has caused some commentators to find a foreshadowing of the later transcendentalism in this latest aspect of his writings.

This Dissertation is composed of two short chapters, of which the first, "What Reason Teaches Concerning Creation," is much more interesting, ideologically, than the second, "What the Scriptures Teach." Section II of Chapter I, as an entity one of the best of Edwards's essays, is also a remarkable statement of infinite divine love and its creativity.

This work appeared with "The Nature of True Virtue" in the posthumous volume *Two Dissertations*, 1765.

effect is valuable.[7] As God therefore esteems these attributes themselves valuable, and delights in them; so it is natural to suppose that he delights in their proper exercise and expression. For the same reason that he esteems his own sufficiency wisely to contrive and dispose effects, he also will esteem the wise contrivance and disposition itself. And for the same reason as he delights in his own disposition, to do justly, and to dispose of things according to truth and just proportion; so he must delight in such a righteous disposal itself.

2. It seems to be a thing in itself fit and desirable, that the glorious perfections of God should be known, and the operations and expressions of them seen by other beings besides himself. If it be fit, that God's power and wisdom, &c. should be exercised and expressed in some effects, and not lie eternally dormant, then it seems proper that these exercises should appear, and not be totally hidden and unknown. For if they are, it will be just the same as to the above purpose, as if they were not. God as perfectly knew himself and his perfections, had as perfect an idea of the exercises and effects they were sufficient for, antecedently to any such actual operations of them, as since. If therefore it be nevertheless a thing in itself valuable, and worthy to be desired, that these glorious perfections be actually expressed and exhibited in their correspondent effects; then it seems also, that the knowledge of these perfections, and the expressions and discoveries that are made of them, is a thing valuable in itself absolutely considered; and that it is desirable that this knowledge should exist. As God's perfections are things in themselves excellent, so the expression of them in their proper acts and fruits is excellent; and the knowledge of these excellent perfections, and of these glorious expressions of them, is an excellent thing, the existence of which is in itself valuable and desirable. It is a thing infinitely good in itself that God's glory should be known by a glorious society of created beings. And that there should be in them an increasing knowledge of God to all eternity, is an existence, a reality infinitely worthy to be, and worthy to be valued and regarded by him, to whom it belongs to order that to be, which, of all things possible, is fittest and best. If existence is more worthy than defect and nonentity, and if any created existence is in itself worthy to be, then knowledge or understanding is a thing worthy to be; and if any knowl-

---

7. "As we must conceive of things, the end and perfection of these attributes does as it were consist in their exercise: 'The end of wisdom (says Mr. G. Tennent, in his Sermon at the opening of the Presbyterian church of Philadelphia) is design; the end of power is action; the end of goodness is doing good. To suppose these perfections not to be exerted, would be to represent them as insignificant. Of what use would God's wisdom be, if it had nothing to design or direct? To what purpose his almightiness, if it never brought any thing to pass? And of what avail his goodness, if it never did any good?'" [Edwards's note].

edge, then the most excellent sort of knowledge, viz. that of God and his glory. The existence of the created universe consists as much in it as in any thing: Yea this knowledge, is one of the highest, most real and substantial parts, of all created existence, most remote from nonentity and defect.

3. As it is a thing valuable and desirable in itself that God's glory should be seen and known, so when known, it seems equally reasonable and fit, it should be valued and esteemed, loved and delighted in, answerably to its dignity. There is no more reason to esteem it a fit and suitable thing that God's glory should be known, or that there should be an idea in the understanding corresponding unto the glorious object, than that there should be a corresponding disposition or affection in the will. If the perfection itself be excellent, the knowledge of it is excellent, and so is the esteem and love of it excellent. And as it is fit that God should love and esteem his own excellence, it is also fit that he should value and esteem the love of his excellency. For if it becomes any being greatly to value another, then it becomes him to love to have him valued and esteemed: And if it becomes a being highly to value himself, it is fit that he should love to have himself valued and esteemed. If the idea of God's perfection in the understanding, be valuable, then the love of the heart seems to be more especially valuable, as moral beauty especially consists in the disposition and affection of the heart.

4. As there is an infinite fulness of all possible good in God, a fulness of every perfection, of all excellency and beauty, and of infinite happiness; and as this fulness is capable of communication or emanation *ad extra*; so it seems a thing amiable and valuable in itself that it should be communicated or flow forth, that this infinite fountain of good should send forth abundant streams, that this infinite fountain of light should, diffusing its excellent fulness, pour forth light all around. . . . And as this is in itself excellent, so a disposition to this, in the divine being, must be looked upon as a perfection or an excellent disposition, such an emanation of good is, in some sense, a multiplication of it; so far as the communication or external stream may be looked upon as any thing besides the fountain, so far it may be looked on as an increase of good. And if the fulness of good that is in the fountain, is in itself excellent and worthy to exist, then the emanation, or that which is as it were an increase, repetition or multiplication of it, is excellent and worthy to exist. Thus it is fit, since there is an infinite fountain of light and knowledge, that this light should shine forth in beams of communicated knowledge and understanding: And as there is an infinite fountain of holiness, moral excellence and beauty, so it should flow out in communicated holi-

ness. And that as there is an infinite fulness of joy and happiness, so these should have an emanation, and become a fountain flowing out in abundant streams, as beams from the sun.

From this view it appears another way to be a thing in itself valuable, that there should be such things as the knowledge of God's glory in other beings, and an high esteem of it, love to it, and delight and complacence in it: This appears I say in another way, viz. as these things are but the emanations of God's own knowledge, holiness and joy.

Thus it appears reasonable to suppose, that it was what God had respect to as an ultimate end of his creating the world, to communicate of his own infinite fulness of good; or rather it was his last end, that there might be a glorious and abundant emanation of his infinite fulness of good *ad extra*, or without himself, and the disposition to communicate himself, or diffuse his own FULNESS,[8] which we must conceive of as being originally in God as a perfection of his nature, was what moved him to create the world. But here as much as possible to avoid confusion, I observe, that there is some impropriety in saying that a disposition in God to communicate himself *to the creature*, moved him to create the world. For though the diffusive disposition in the nature of God, that moved him to create the world, doubtless inclines him to communicate himself to the creature, when the creature exists; yet this cannot be all: Because an inclination in God to communicate himself to an object, seems to presuppose the existence of the object, at least in idea. But the diffusive disposition that excited God to give creatures existence, was rather a communicative disposition in general, or a disposition in the fulness of the divinity to flow out and diffuse itself. Thus the disposition there is in the root and stock of a tree to diffuse and send forth its sap and life, is doubtless the reason of the communication of its sap and life to its buds, leaves and fruits, after these exist. But a disposition to communicate of its life and sap to its fruits, is not so properly the cause of its producing those fruits, as its disposition to communicate itself, or diffuse its sap and life in general. Therefore to speak more strictly according to truth, we may suppose, *that a disposition in God, as an original property of his nature, to an emanation of his own infinite fulness, was what excited him to create the world; and so that the emanation itself was aimed at by him as a last end of the creation.*

1756–1758   1765

---

8. " I shall often use the phrase *God's fulness*, as signifying and comprehending all the good which is in God natural and moral, either excellence or happiness; partly because I know of no better phrase to be used in this general meaning; and partly because I am led hereto by some of the inspired writers, particularly the Apostle Paul, who often useth the phrase in this sense " [Edwards's note].

WILLIAM BYRD

(1674–1744)

William Byrd was born March 28, 1674, at the fall of the James River, in what is now Richmond, Virginia, a city he founded and named. At the age of seven he was sent to England for his education, under the direction of a grandfather. After a brief interval in Holland, where he learned something about the Dutch commercial system, he took up quarters in the Middle Temple, in London, for the study of law. He had already been elected a member of the Royal Society when, at the age of twenty-two, he returned to Virginia. In the tradition of his family, he was elected a member of the House of Burgesses, and he represented the colony on several occasions in England. In 1705, upon his father's death, he returned to Virginia, where he remained for the next ten years. Byrd inherited the family property—some 26,-000 acres—and succeeded his father as Receiver-General of Revenues. He progressed from this office to membership in the Supreme Council, which functioned as a sort of Senate for the colony, retaining membership until his death, although exactly half of his seventy years were spent abroad.

His secret diaries—kept in an obsolete shorthand—form a unique and valuable account of life, day by day, on a colonial southern plantation. They defeat the myth that southern plantation life was characterized chiefly by silken ease, horse racing, and mint juleps. They further establish Byrd as a systematic student of literature: he read Greek, Hebrew, Latin, and French with facility. His library of 3,600 volumes was one of the largest private collections to be assembled in America before the Revolution. At the time of his death he had completed the building of Westover, one of the finest colonial Virginia mansions. His holdings in land amounted to approximately 186,000 acres in Virginia and North Carolina.

Byrd's writings hold their place for the literary pleasure that they still provide, for the vitality and usefulness of their observation of American life, and for their foreshadowing, in the character of their author, of the liberal, patrician leadership which produced Washington and Jefferson in the next generation. If Byrd was the cavalier, he was an Americanized cavalier, who opposed the authoritarian pretensions of Governor Spotswood, and defended the American planter gentry in their effort to preserve local determination of their own government and taxation. He was at home with the society, literature, and learning of London in that brilliant first quarter of the eighteenth century—with Wycherley and Congreve, or with the Earl of Orrery; but he also loved Williamsburg, by contrast a rustic capital. His literary style reflected the enlightened humanism and worldly security of his British literary contemporaries, but he employed it, without deterioration, in the description of a rugged frontier. Trained in science and the practical arts as well as in literature, he brought a practical observation to bear on the products of the land and the customs and characters of its inhabitants, both the Indians and the white frontiersmen. A Virginia gentleman, he was aware of the great social contrasts present in Virginia life, but he saw the potentialities both in the land and in its people.

The first publication of *The Westover Manuscripts* (containing the *History*, the *Progress*, and the *Journey*) was in 1841. A recent edition of these works is that edited by Mark Van Doren under the title *A Journey to the Land of Eden*, 1928. The Dietz Press, Richmond, published *The Secret Diary of William*

Byrd of Westover, 1709–1712, edited by Louis B. Wright and Marion Tinling, 1941 (abridged by the same editors as *The Great American Gentleman: William Byrd of Westover*, 1963); *Another Secret Diary of William Byrd of Westover, 1739–1741*, edited by Maude H. Woodfin and Marion Tinling, 1942; and also *William Byrd's Natural History of Virginia*, edited by R. C. Beatty and William Mulloy, 1940. A third portion of the diaries is *William Byrd of Virginia: The London Diary (1717–1721) and Other Writings*, edited by Louis B. Wright and Marion Tinling, 1958.

The most reliable edition of the *History* and related materials is *William Byrd's Histories of the Dividing Line Betwixt Virginia and North Carolina*, edited by W. K. Boyd, 1929. This volume includes the previously unpublished *Secret History*. The present text is based on this edition, with the reduction of irregular capitals and the regularizing of abbreviated words.

R. C. Beatty's *William Byrd of Westover*, 1932, is a full-length biography; and Byrd is included in Louis B. Wright's *The First Gentlemen of Virginia*, 1940.

From The History of the Dividing Line [1]

[*Indian Neighbors*]

* * * I am sorry I cannot give a better account of the state of the poor Indians with respect to Christianity, although a great deal of pains has been and still continues to be taken with them. For my part, I must be of opinion, as I hinted before, that there is but one way of converting these poor infidels, and reclaiming them from barbarity, and that is, charitably to intermarry with them, according to the modern policy of the most Christian king in Canada and Louisiana.[2] Had the English done this at the first settlement of the colony, the infidelity of the Indians had been worn out at this day, with their dark complexions, and the country had swarmed with people more than it does with insects. It was certainly an unreasonable nicety, that prevented their entering into so good-natured an alliance. All nations of men have the same natural dignity, and we all know that very bright talents may be lodged under a very dark skin. The principal difference between one people and another proceeds only from the different opportunities of improvement. The Indians by no means want under-

1. The official party, including commissioners and surveyors from both states, met on March 5, 1728, to begin the survey intended to establish the long-disputed boundary line between Virginia and North Carolina.
2. Louis XV of France, reigned 1715–1774.

standing, and are in their figure tall and well-proportioned. Even their copper-colored complexion would admit of blanching, if not in the first, at the farthest in the second generation. I may safely venture to say, the Indian women would have made altogether as honest wives for the first planters, as the damsels they used to purchase from aboard the ships. It is strange, therefore, that any good Christian should have refused a wholesome, straight bed-fellow, when he might have had so fair a portion with her, as the merit of saving her soul.

[March 13, 1728.] This being Sunday, we rested from our fatigue, and had leisure to reflect on the signal mercies of Providence.

The great plenty of meat wherewith Bearskin [3] furnished us in these lonely woods made us once more shorten the men's allowance of bread, from five to four pounds of biscuit a week. This was the more necessary, because we knew not yet how long our business might require us to be out.

In the afternoon our hunters went forth, and returned triumphantly with three brace of wild turkeys. They told us they could see the mountains distinctly from every eminence, though the atmosphere was so thick with smoke that they appeared at a greater distance than they really were.

In the evening we examined our friend Bearskin, concerning the religion of his country, and he explained it to us, without any of that reserve to which his nation is subject. He told us he believed there was one supreme God, who had several subaltern deities under him. And that this master God made the world a long time ago. That he told the sun, the moon, and stars, their business in the beginning, which they, with good looking after, have faithfully performed ever since. That the same Power that made all things at first has taken care to keep them in the same method and motion ever since. He believed that God had formed many worlds before he formed this, but that those worlds either grew old and ruinous, or were destroyed for the dishonesty of the inhabitants. That God is very just and very good—ever well pleased with those men who possess those god-like qualities. That he takes good people into his safe protection, makes them very rich, fills their bellies plentifully, preserves them from sickness, and from being surprised or overcome by their enemies. But all such as tell lies, and cheat those they have dealings with, he never fails to punish with sickness, poverty and hunger, and, after all that, suffers them to be knocked on the head and scalped by those that fight against them. He believed that after death both good

3. Their Indian guide and hunter.

and bad people are conducted by a strong guard into a great road, in which departed souls travel together for some time, till at a certain distance this road forks into two paths, the one extremely level, and the other stony and mountainous. Here the good are parted from the bad by a flash of lightning, the first being hurried away to the right, the other to the left. The right hand road leads to a charming warm country, where the spring is everlasting, and every month is May; and as the year is always in its youth, so are the people, and particularly the women are bright as stars, and never scold. That in this happy climate there are deer, turkeys, elks, and buffaloes innumerable, perpetually fat and gentle, while the trees are loaded with delicious fruit quite throughout the four seasons. That the soil brings forth corn spontaneously, without the curse of labor, and so very wholesome, that none who have the happiness to eat of it are ever sick, grow old, or die. Near the entrance into this blessed land sits a venerable old man on a mat richly woven, who examines strictly all that are brought before him, and if they have behaved well, the guards are ordered to open the crystal gate, and let them enter into the land of delight. The left hand path is very rugged and uneven, leading to a dark and barren country, where it is always winter. The ground is the whole year round covered with snow, and nothing is to be seen upon the trees but icicles. All the people are hungry, yet have not a morsel of anything to eat, except a bitter kind of potato, that gives them the dry gripes, and fills their whole body with loathsome ulcers, that stink, and are insupportably painful. Here all the women are old and ugly, having claws like a panther, with which they fly upon the men that slight their passion. For it seems these haggard old furies are intolerably fond, and expect a vast deal of cherishing. They talk much, and exceedingly shrill, giving exquisite pain to the drum of the ear, which in that place of torment is so tender, that every sharp note wounds it to the quick. At the end of this path sits a dreadful old woman on a monstrous toad-stool, whose head is covered with rattle-snakes instead of tresses, with glaring white eyes, that strike a terror unspeakable into all that behold her. This hag pronounces sentence of woe upon all the miserable wretches that hold up their hands at her tribunal. After this they are delivered over to huge turkey-buzzards, like harpies, that fly away with them to the place above mentioned. Here, after they have been tormented a certain number of years, according to their several degrees of guilt, they are again driven back into this world, to try if they will mend their manners, and merit a place the next time in the regions of bliss. This was the substance of Bearskin's religion, and was as much to the purpose as could be expected from a mere state of nature,

without one glimpse of revelation or philosophy. It contained, however, the three great articles of natural religion: the belief of a
God; the moral distinction betwixt good and evil; and the expectation of rewards and punishments in another world. Indeed, the
Indian notion of a future happiness is a little gross and sensual,
like Mahomet's paradise. But how can it be otherwise, in a people
that are contented with Nature as they find her, and have no other
lights but what they receive from purblind tradition?

1728   1841

From A Progress to the Mines [4]
[*Reading a Play in the Backwoods*]

[Sept. 20, 1732.] I continued the bark,[5] and then tossed down
my poached eggs, with as much ease as some good breeders slip
children into the world. About nine I left the prudentest orders I
could think of with my vizier, and then crossed the river to Shac-
co's. I made a running visit to three of my quarters,[6] where, besides finding all the people well, I had the pleasure to see better
crops than usual both of corn and tobacco. I parted there with
my intendant, and pursued my journey to Mr. Randolph's, at
Tuckahoe, without meeting with any adventure by the way. Here
I found Mrs. Fleming, who was packing up her baggage with
design to follow her husband the next day, who was gone to a
new settlement in Goochland. Both he and she have been about
seven years persuading themselves to remove to that retired part
of the country, though they had the two strong arguments of
health and interest for so doing. The widow smiled graciously
upon me, and entertained me very handsomely. Here I learned all
the tragical story of her daughter's humble marriage with her
uncle's overseer. Besides the meanness of this mortal's aspect, the
man has not one visible qualification, except impudence, to recom-
mend him to a female's inclinations. But there is sometimes such a
charm in that Hibernian endowment, that frail woman cannot
withstand it, though it stand alone without any other recommendation. Had she run away with a gentleman or a pretty fellow,
there might have been some excuse for her, though he were of inferior fortune: but to stoop to a dirty plebeian, without any kind
of merit, is the lowest prostitution. I found the family justly enraged at it; and though I had more good nature than to join in her

4. An account of a journey to the home
and iron mines of former Governor
Alexander Spotswood in the highlands
of western Virginia. Byrd hoped to develop the iron on his own land. Goochland, named below as a stage, was about
half the distance.
5. Suffering from a fever, he has been
taking doses of "bark" (quinine) and
brandy.
6. *I.e.*, the living "quarters" for the
slaves.

condemnation, yet I could devise no excuse for so senseless a
prank as this young gentlewoman had played. Here good drink
was more scarce than good victuals, the family being reduced to
the last bottle of wine, which was therefore husbanded very
carefully. But the water was excellent. The heir of the family
did not come home till late in the evening. He is a pretty young
man, but had the misfortune to become his own master too soon.
This puts young fellows upon wrong pursuits, before they have
sense to judge rightly for themselves. Though at the same time
they have a strange conceit of their own sufficiency, when they
grow near twenty years old, especially if they happen to have a
small smattering of learning. It is then they fancy themselves
wiser than all their tutors and governors, which makes them headstrong to all advice, and above all reproof and admonition.

[Sept. 21, 1732.] I was sorry in the morning to find myself
stopped in my career by bad weather brought upon us by a northeast wind. This drives a world of raw unkindly vapors upon us
from Newfoundland, laden with blight, coughs, and pleurisies.
However, I complained not, lest I might be suspected to be tired of
the good company. Though Mrs. Fleming was not so much
upon her guard, but mutinied strongly at the rain, that hindered
her from pursuing her dear husband. I said what I could to comfort a gentlewoman under so sad a disappointment. I told her a
husband, that stayed so much at home as her's did, could be no
such violent rarity, as for a woman to venture her precious health,
to go daggling through the rain after him, or to be miserable if
she happened to be prevented. That it was prudent for married
people to fast sometimes from one another, that they might come
together again with the better stomach. That the best things in
this world, if constantly used, are apt to be cloying, which a little
absence and abstinence would prevent. This was strange doctrine
to a fond female, who fancies people should love with as little
reason after marriage as before. In the afternoon monsieur Marij,
the minister of the parish, came to make me a visit. He had been a
Romish priest, but found reasons, either spiritual or temporal, to
quit that gay religion. The fault of this new convert is, that he
looks for as much respect from his protestant flock, as is paid to
the popish clergy, which our ill-bred Hugonots do not understand.
Madam Marij had so much curiosity as to want to come too; but
another horse was wanting, and she believed it would have too
vulgar an air to ride behind her husband. This woman was of the
true exchange breed, full of discourse, but void of discretion,
and married a parson, with the idle hopes he might some time or
other come to be his grace of Canterbury. The gray mare is the
better horse in that family, and the poor man submits to her wild

vagaries for peace' sake. She has just enough of the fine lady to run in debt, and be of no signification in her household. And the only thing that can prevent her from undoing her loving husband will be, that nobody will trust them beyond the sixteen thousand,[7] which is soon run out in a Goochland store. The way of dealing there is for some small merchant or peddler to buy a Scots penny-worth of goods, and clap one hundred and fifty per cent. upon that. At this rate the parson cannot be paid much more for his preaching than it is worth. No sooner was our visitor retired, but the facetious widow was so kind as to let me into all this secret history, but was at the same time exceedingly sorry that the woman should be so indiscreet, and the man so tame as to be governed by an unprofitable and fantastical wife.

[Sept. 22, 1732.] We had another wet day, to try both Mrs. Fleming's patience and my good breeding. The northeast wind commonly sticks by us three or four days, filling the atmosphere with damps, injurious both to man and beast. The worst of it was, we had no good liquor to warm our blood, and fortify our spirits against so strong a malignity. However, I was cheerful under all these misfortunes, and expressed no concern but a decent fear lest my long visit might be troublesome. Since I was like to have thus much leisure, I endeavored to find out what subject a dull married man could introduce that might best bring the widow to the use of her tongue. At length I discovered she was a notable quack, and therefore paid that regard to her knowledge, as to put some questions to her about the bad distemper that raged then in the country. I mean the bloody flux, that was brought us in the negro-ship consigned to Col. Braxton. She told me she made use of very simple remedies in that case, with very good success. She did the business either with hartshorn drink, that had plan-tain leaves boiled in it, or else with a strong decoction of St. Andrew's cross, in new milk instead of water. I agreed with her that those remedies might be very good, but would be more effectual after a dose or two of Indian physic. But for fear this conversation might be too grave for a widow, I turned the dis-course, and began to talk of plays, and finding her taste lay most towards comedy, I offered my service to read one to her, which she kindly accepted. She produced the second part of the Beggar's Opera,[8] which had diverted the town for forty nights successively, and gained four thousand pounds to the author. This was not owing altogether to the wit or humor that sparkled in it, but to some political reflections, that seemed to hit the ministry. But

---

7. *I.e.,* "sixteen thousand" pounds of tobacco, as this country clergyman's salary was reckoned.
8. *The Beggar's Opera,* by John Gay (1685–1732), on the London stage in 1728, had proved one of the most suc-cessful of British plays.

the great advantage of the author was, that his interest was solicited by the dutchess of Queensbury, which no man could refuse who had but half an eye in his head,[9] or half a guinea in his pocket. Her grace, like death, spared nobody, but even took my lord Selkirk [1] in for two guineas, to repair which extravagance he lived upon Scots herrings two months afterwards. But the best story was, she made a very smart officer in his majesty's guards give her a guinea, who swearing at the same time it was all he had in the world, she sent him fifty for it the next day, to reward his obedience. After having acquainted my company with the history of the play, I read three acts of it, and left Mrs. Fleming and Mr. Randolph to finish it, who read as well as most actors do at a rehearsal. Thus we killed time, and triumphed over the bad weather.

1732   1841

JOHN WOOLMAN
(1720–1772)

John Woolman's *Journal* (1774) is a "Quaker classic of the inner Light," and countless non-Quaker readers have been touched by its "exquisite purity and grace." Among the enduring autobiographies of the world, it shines apart, one of the few in which the record of the temporal life radiates a wholly spiritual and eternal light. The sentence with which, at thirty-six, Woolman began his *Journal*, contains the clue to its perfect candor and purity: "I have often felt a motion of love to leave some hints in writing of my experience of the goodness of God."

Such a vision of the interpenetration of the divine with the human had enkindled the evangelism of George Fox in England, about 1650. His followers called themselves Friends but found an unfriendly world, for they were double-dyed dissenters, differing both from the established church and from the Puritan sects. The American Puritans, themselves fugitives from persecution, had grievously persecuted the Quakers, whose "heresies" certainly threatened a hierarchy founded on belief in original depravity, predestination, and limited election for salvation by grace. Quakers believed that Christ was the atonement for all mankind's sins, that the "inward light" of God's immanence was available to all who sought "in the spirit and in truth."

Woolman's *Journal* is clearer to the reader who understands

---

9. In the tradition of that age of literary patronage, the Duchess became his patroness, and Gay passed several years, before his death at forty-seven, in the household of the Duke of Queens-berry.

1. The first earl of Selkirk, William Douglas, of the ancient Scottish line; the jest concerning the frugality of the Scots is perennial.

these principles of the Quakers, and their other fundamental testimony, that of quietness. The hysterical outbreaks of revivalism which marked the Puritan history are rare in the Quaker records; the Quaker trusted his "light" only in the controlled retrospect of his judgment. This is nowhere better illustrated than in Woolman's strict discipline of impulsive "concerns" by means of "religious exercise" and the "draught" or "leading" of his mind. That this discipline of responsibility inevitably compelled Friends toward the service of the human community is illustrated by Woolman's unflagging interest in the whole life about him. For the Quaker mystic, salvation did not await a millennium; mortal and immortal life were wonderfully and strangely one.

John Woolman was born in 1720, on a farm on the Rancocas in New Jersey, twenty miles from the Quaker city of the Penns. The young farmer experienced a growing companionship with nature, and a quietness favorable to the natural unfolding of a spirit essentially mystical. For his education there was the dame school, the Bible, the journals of Friends, some of them truly inspired, and always the close-knit community of the Quaker family and its meeting. At twenty he became a shopkeeper in nearby Mount Holly, and also learned the trade of the tailor. He prospered in his business and in his marriage, while his vocation soon led to his being "recorded" as a minister— the Friends' way of acknowl-

edging by consensus the acceptability of the voluntary ministry that then provided their only leadership.

As his religious vocation grew, Woolman was led, at the age of thirty-six, to give up his shop altogether and live upon the income from intermittent tailoring, which provided sufficient means for his frugal life. Thus he was enabled to respond to his evangelical "concern"; he made extensive visitations among Friends throughout the colonies, sometimes for months at a time, preaching the way of "Divine Love." In his ministry and in the tracts which he published from time to time, he became a force in the growing movement for toleration; he attacked the economic exploitation which was already producing poverty and wretchedness among the masses; he preached unceasingly against slavery, and published one of the earliest works in the American literature of abolition. He led the movement which secured the freedom of slaves held by American Quakers—the first general emancipation of slaves in America. The abolition of slavery was one of the concerns which he carried abroad in 1772, on a visit to the Friends' Meetings in England. In protest against the poverty of the British workers and the cruel conditions imposed upon the coachmen, he traveled through England on foot, preaching at various Meetings.

The standard collection is *The Journal and Essays of John Woolman*, edited by Amelia M. Gummere, 1922. This contains a biography. Other biographies are Janet Whitney, *John Woolman, American Quaker*, 1942, and C. O.

Peare, *John Woolman, Child of Light,* 1954. For material on the Society of Friends, see Rufus M. Jones, *The Quakers in the American Colonies,* 1921; and Elbert Russell, *The History of Quakerism,* 1942. Since Woolman left two revisions of the manuscript of the *Journal,* and since the first edition of the *Works,* 1774, was not accurate, it is natural that many variant readings appear in the more than forty editions that have been published in America and England. The Boston edition of 1871, with an introduction by J. G. Whittier, is followed here. The most recent one has been edited by Janet Whitney, 1950. Critical works are Edwin H. Cady, *John Woolman,* 1965, and P. Rosenblatt, *John Woolman,* 1969.

From The Journal of John Woolman

[*Quaker Faith and Practice*]

I was born in Northampton, in Burlington county, West-Jersey,[1] in the year 1720; and before I was seven years old I began to be acquainted with the operations of divine love. Through the care of my parents, I was taught to read nearly as soon as I was capable of it; and, as I went from school one seventh day,[2] I remember, while my companions went to play by the way, I went forward out of sight, and, sitting down, I read the 22d chapter of the Revelations. "He shewed me a pure river of water of life, clear as chrystal, proceeding out of the throne of God and of the lamb, &c." and, in reading it, my mind was drawn to seek after that pure habitation, which, I then believed, God had prepared for his servants. The place where I sat, and the sweetness that attended my mind, remain fresh in my memory.

This, and the like gracious visitations, had that effect upon me, that when boys used ill language it troubled me; and, through the continued mercies of God, I was preserved from it.

The pious instructions of my parents were often fresh in my mind when I happened to be among wicked children, and were of use to me. My parents, having a large family of children, used frequently, on first days after meeting,[3] to put us to read in the holy scriptures, or some religious books, one after another, the rest sitting by without much conversation; which, I have since often thought, was a good practice. From what I had read and heard, I believed there had been, in past ages, people who walked in uprightness before God, in a degree exceeding any that I knew, or heard of, now living; and the apprehension of there being less steadiness and firmness, amongst people in this age than in past ages, often troubled me while I was a child. * * *

1. The colonial "Jerseys" included East Jersey and West Jersey. The Woolman plantation (farm) was near Mount Holly, site of an early Quaker community affiliated with the Philadelphia Friends, twenty miles distant.
2. *I.e.,* Saturday. Quakers substituted numbers for the usual names of the days of the week, both to gain simplicity and to avoid celebration of pagan gods.
3. Quakers, like the early Puritans, replaced the formal "church" by a simple "meetinghouse."

Advancing in age, the number of my acquaintances increased, and thereby my way grew more difficult; though I had found comfort in reading the holy scriptures, and thinking on heavenly things, I was now estranged therefrom: I knew I was going from the flock of Christ, and had no resolution to return; hence serious reflections were uneasy to me, and youthful vanities and diversions my greatest pleasure. Running in this road I found many like myself; and we associated in that which is the reverse to true friendship.[4]

But in this swift race it pleased God to visit me with sickness, so that I doubted of recovering; and then did darkness, horror, and amazement, with full force, seize me, even when my pain and distress of body was very great. I thought it would have been better for me never to have had a being, than to see the day which I now saw. I was filled with confusion; and in great affliction, both of mind and body, I lay and bewailed myself. I had not confidence to lift up my cries to God, whom I had thus offended; but, in a deep sense of my great folly, I was humbled before him; and, at length, that word which is as a fire and a hammer, broke and dissolved my rebellious heart,[5] and then my cries were put up in contrition; and in the multitude of his mercies I found inward relief, and felt a close engagement, that, if he was pleased to restore my health, I might walk humbly before him.

After my recovery, this exercise [6] remained with me a considerable time; but, by degrees, giving way to youthful vanities, they gained strength, and, getting with wanton [7] young people, I lost ground. The Lord had been very gracious, and spoke peace to me in the time of my distress; and I now most ungratefully turned again to folly; on which account, at times, I felt sharp reproof. I was not so hardy as to commit things scandalous; but to exceed in vanity, and promote mirth, was my chief study. Still I retained a love for pious people, and their company brought an awe upon me. My dear parents, several times, admonished me in the fear of the Lord, and their admonition entered into my heart, and had a good effect for a season; but, not getting deep enough to pray rightly, the tempter, when he came, found entrance. I remember once, having spent a part of the day in wantonness, as I went to bed at night, there lay in a window, near my bed, a Bible, which I opened, and first cast my eye on this text, "We lie down in our shame, and our confusion covers us":[8] this I

---

4. The people known as Quakers called themselves Friends, or officially, the Religious Society of Friends.
5. *Cf.* Jeremiah xxiii: 29: "Is not my word like as a fire? saith the Lord; and like a hammer that breaketh the rock in pieces?"
6. In the language of Friends, an experience or act conducive to religious faith.
7. Here meaning "worldly."
8. Jeremiah iii: 25.

knew to be my case: and, meeting with so unexpected a reproof, I was somewhat affected with it, and went to bed under remorse of conscience; which I soon cast off again. * * *

There is a harmony in the sound of that voice to which divine love gives utterance, and some appearance of right order in their temper and conduct, whose passions are regulated; yet all these do not fully shew forth that inward life to such as have not felt it: But this white stone [9] and new name is known rightly to such only as have it.

Though I have been thus strengthened to bear the cross, I still found myself in great danger, having many weaknesses attending me, and strong temptations to wrestle with; in the feeling whereof I frequently withdrew into private places, and often with tears besought the Lord to help me, whose gracious ear was open to my cry.

All this time I lived with my parents, and wrought on the plantation; and, having had schooling pretty well for a planter, I used to improve it in winter-evenings, and other leisure times; and, being now in the twenty-first year of my age, a man, in much business at shopkeeping and baking, asked me, if I would hire with him to tend shop and keep books. I acquainted my father with the proposal; and, after some deliberation, it was agreed for me to go.

At home I had lived retired; and now, having a prospect of being much in the way of company, I felt frequent and fervent cries in my heart to God, the father of mercies, that he would preserve me from all corruption; that in this more publick employment, I might serve him, my gracious Redeemer, in that humility and self-denial, with which I had been, in a small degree, exercised in a more private life. The man, who employed me, furnished a shop in Mount-Holly, about five miles from my father's house, and six from his own; and there I lived alone, and tended his shop.

* * * Every trial was a fresh incitement to give myself up wholly to the service of God, for I found no helper like him in times of trouble. After a while, my former acquaintance gave over expecting me as one of their company; and I began to be known to some whose conversation was helpful to me: and now, as I had experienced the love of God, through Jesus Christ, to redeem me from many pollutions, and to be a succour to me through a sea of conflicts, with which no person was fully acquainted; and as my heart was often enlarged in this heavenly principle, I felt a tender compassion for the youth, who remained entangled in snares, like those which had entangled me from one time to another: this love and tenderness increased; and my mind was more

9. Revelation ii: 17: "To him that overcometh will I give * * * a white stone, and in the stone a new name written * * * "

strongly engaged for the good of my fellow-creatures. I went to meetings in an awful frame of mind, and endeavoured to be inwardly acquainted with the language of the true Shepherd; and, one day, being under a strong exercise of spirit, I stood up, and said some words in a meeting; but, not keeping close to the divine opening, I said more than was required of me; and being soon sensible of my error, I was afflicted in mind some weeks, without any light or comfort, even to that degree that I could not take satisfaction in any thing: I remembered God, and was troubled, and, in the depth of my distress, he had pity upon me, and sent the Comforter. I then felt forgiveness for my offence, and my mind became calm and quiet, being truly thankful to my gracious Redeemer for his mercies; and, after this, feeling the spring of divine love opened, and a concern [1] to speak, I said a few words in a meeting, in which I found peace; this, I believe, was about six weeks from the first time: and, as I was thus humbled and disciplined under the cross, my understanding became more strengthened to distinguish the pure spirit which inwardly moves upon the heart,[2] and taught me to wait in silence sometimes many weeks together, until I felt that rise which prepares the creature.

[Cases of Conscience]

* * *

My employer having a negro woman, sold her, and desired me to write a bill of sale, the man being waiting who bought her: the thing was sudden; and, though the thoughts of writing an instrument of slavery for one of my fellow-creatures felt uneasy, yet I remembered I was hired by the year, that it was my master who directed me to do it, and that it was an elderly man, a member of our society,[3] who bought her; so, through weakness, I gave way, and wrote; but, at the executing it, I was so afflicted in my mind, that I said, before my master and the friend, that I believed slave-keeping to be a practice inconsistent with the Christian religion. This in some degree abated my uneasiness; yet, as often as I reflected seriously upon it, I thought I should have been clearer, if I had desired to have been excused from it, as a thing against my conscience; for such it was. And, some time after this, a young man, of our society, spoke to me to write a conveyance of a slave to him, he having lately taken a negro into his house: I told him I was not easy to write it; for, though many of our meeting and

1. In the Friends' terminology, a compelling inward motivation for an action or message approved by the judgment.
2. Friends hold themselves responsible to an "inward light" which, however, is genuine only when "disciplined understanding" distinguishes between selfish desire and the immanent radiance of God.
3. The Society of Friends. Woolman later led the successful movement to liberate the slaves held by Quakers—the first American emancipation.

in other places kept slaves, I still believed the practice was not right, and desired to be excused from the writing. I spoke to him in good will; and he told me that keeping slaves was not altogether agreeable to his mind; but that the slave being a gift to his wife, he had accepted of her.

Until the year 1756, I continued to retail goods, besides following my trade as a tailor; about which time I grew uneasy on account of my business growing too cumbersome. I began with selling trimmings for garments, and from thence proceeded to sell cloths and linens; and at length, having got a considerable shop of goods, my trade increased every year, and the road to large business appeared open: but I felt a stop in my mind.

Through the mercies of the Almighty, I had, in a good degree, learned to be content with a plain way of living.[4] I had but a small family; and on serious reflection, I believed Truth did not require me to engage in many cumbering affairs. It had generally been my practice to buy and sell things really useful. Things that served chiefly to please the vain mind in people, I was not easy to trade in; seldom did it, and whenever I did, I found it to weaken me as a Christian.

The increase of business became my burthen; for though my natural inclination was toward merchandise, yet I believed Truth required me to live more free from outward cumbers. There was now a strife in my mind betwixt the two, and in this exercise my prayers were put up to the Lord, who graciously heard me, and gave me a heart resigned to his holy will; I then lessened my outward business; and as I had opportunity, told my customers of my intention, that they might consider what shop to turn to; and so in a while, wholly laid down merchandise, following my trade as a tailor, myself only, having no prentice. I also had a nursery of apple trees, in which I spent a good deal of time hoeing, grafting, trimming, and inoculating.

In merchandise it is the custom, where I lived, to sell chiefly on credit, and poor people often get in debt; and when payment is expected, having not wherewith to pay, and so their creditors often sue for it at law. Having often observed occurrences of this kind, I found it good for me to advise poor people to take such goods as were most useful and not costly.

In the time of trading, I had an opportunity of seeing that a too liberal use of spirituous liquors, and the custom of wearing too costly apparel, led some people into great inconveniences; and these two things appear to be often connected one with the other; for by not attending to that use of things which is consistent with

4. Friends adopted "plainness," not to achieve asceticism, but to retain "the simplicity that is in Christ" described by Paul (II Corinthians xi: 3, and i: 12).

universal righteousness, there is an increase of labor which extends beyond what our heavenly Father intends for us; and by great labor, and often by much sweating in the heat, there is, even among such who are not drunkards, a craving of some liquor to revive the spirits; that, partly by the luxurious drinking of some, and partly by the drinking of others, led to it through immoderate labor, very great quantities of rum are annually expended in our colonies; of which we should have no need, did we steadily attend to pure wisdom. * * *

As every degree of luxury hath some connection with evil; for those who profess to be disciples of Christ, and are looked upon as leaders of the people, to have that mind in them, which was also in Christ, and so stand separate from every wrong way, is a means of help to the weaker. * * * I have felt an increasing care to attend to that holy Spirit which sets right bounds to our desires, and leads those who faithfully follow it, to apply all the gifts of Divine Providence to the purposes for which they were intended.

1756   1774

ST. JEAN DE CRÈVECŒUR
(1735–1813)

St. Jean de Crèvecœur (christened Michel-Guillaume Jean de Crèvecœur), born of a distinguished and ancient family near Caen, was educated strictly but well in a Jesuit school, and then visited England. At the age of nineteen he was in Canada, a lieutenant in the French army under Montcalm. In this service he surveyed and mapped large areas around the Great Lakes and in the Ohio country. He was in New York by 1759; he later roamed, an observant pilgrim, through the frontiers of New York, Pennsylvania, and the southern colonies. He became a citizen of New York in 1765, soon acquired a plantation in Orange County some sixty miles from the city, and married in 1769. There he remained, a successful planter, until the Revolution, writing down his impressions of rural America, "a land of happy farmers" and a haven of equality and freedom for the oppressed and dispossessed of Europe.

In spite of these liberal enthusiasms, his training was aristocratic, and he had sworn allegiance to Britain; his mildly Tory inclinations appear repeatedly in the *Letters*, particularly in those that he suppressed in his lifetime. In this equivocal mood he found himself suspected by both sides, and returned to France in 1780. *Letters from an American Farmer* appeared in London two years later; an enlarged but sentimentalized version in French was published in Paris in 1783.

The influence of Franklin and French friends secured his appointment as French consul to New York, New Jersey, and Connecticut. He returned to America in 1783, to find his wife dead, his children safe with a Boston family, and his plantation home wrecked by an Indian raid. Until 1790 he remained in New York, devoting himself to the cause of good relations between his mother country and his adopted land. The last twenty-three years of his life were spent in his ancestral Normandy. His only later publication was the *Voyage dans la Haute Pensylvanie et dans l'État de New-York* (1801). His suppressed letters from the earlier series remained unpublished and forgotten until their rediscovery by American scholars resulted in the *Sketches of Eighteenth Century America* (1925).

Crèvecœur exemplifies a number of ideals prevalent both in America and in Europe during the late eighteenth century. He subscribed in some degree to

Rousseau's idealization of natural man as inherently good when free, and subject to corruption only by artificial urban society. He was an anticlerical like Thomas Paine, with a strong distrust for organized religion. Along with Jefferson and Franklin he held the physiocratic faith that agriculture was the basis of our economy; and he believed in humanitarian action to correct such abuses as slavery, civil disturbance, war, and the poverty of the masses.

A good and available edition of Crèvecœur is the *Letters from an American Farmer*, edited by W. P. Trent and Ludwig Lewisohn, 1904; see also *Sketches of Eighteenth Century America*, edited by H. L. Bourdin, R. H. Gabriel, and S. T. Williams, 1925, and Percy G. Adams, ed., *Crèvecoeur's 18th-Century Travels in Pennsylvania and New York*, 1962. For biography and criticism, see Julia P. Mitchell, *St. Jean de Crèvecœur*, 1916; H. C. Rice, *Le Cultivateur American: * * * *, 1933; Thomas Philbrick, *St. John de Crèvecœur*, 1970; and the essay by Stanley T. Williams in the *Dictionary of American Biography*, 1930.

From Sketches of Eighteenth Century America

Manners of the Americans [1]

Let us view now the new colonist as possessed of property. This has a great weight and a mighty influence. From earliest infancy we are accustomed to a greater exchange of things, a greater transfer of property than the people of the same class in Europe. Whether it is occasioned by that perpetual and necessary emigrating genius which constantly sends the exuberancy of full societies

1. This portion from the essay "Manners of the Americans" is a distillation of the American experience. The author defines the progression of the colonist from his first position of strength on the frontier to his ultimate place of shrewdly-won, conservative security. Crèvecœur follows the process of the developing American character as it diverges from the European pattern of patronage and of religious and political rigidity to become a new identity, in many ways admirable and desirable. However,

Americans are not sanctified residents of Utopia: if they are no longer subservient to "a supercilious prince or a proud lord," they have achieved survival by the adaptation of European cunning.

This selection is from *Sketches of Eighteenth Century America*, pp. 66–78. Henri L. Bourdin, Ralph H. Gabriel, and Stanley T. Williams, eds., New Haven, 1925, from manuscripts then recently discovered in the Crèvecœur estate in France.

to replenish new tracts; whether it proceeds from our being richer; whether it is that we are fonder of trade which is but an exchange, —I cannot ascertain. This man, thus bred, from a variety of reasons is determined to improve his fortune by removing to a new district, and resolves to purchase as much land as will afford substantial farms to every one of his children,—a pious thought which causes so many even wealthy people to sell their patrimonial estates to enlarge their sphere of action and leave a sufficient inheritance to their progeny.

No sooner he is resolved than he takes all the information he can with regard to the country he proposes to go to inhabit. He finds out all travellers who have been on the spot; he views maps; attentively weighs the benefits and disadvantages of climate, seasons, situation, etc.; he compares it with his own. A world of the most ponderous reflections must needs fill his mind. He at last goes to the capital and applies to some great land-holders. He wants to make a purchase. Each party sets forth the peculiar goodness of its tracts in all the various possible circumstances of health, soil, proximity of lakes, rivers, roads, etc. Maps are presented to him; various lots are spread before him as pieces of linen in the shop of a draper. What a sagacity must this common farmer have, first, to enable him to choose the province, the country, the peculiar tract most agreeable to his fortune; then to resist, to withstand the sophistry of these learned men armed with all the pomp of their city arguments! Yet he is a match for them all. These mathematical lines and sheets of paper would represent nothing to a man of his class in Europe, yet he understands their meaning, even the various courses by which the rivers and mountains are known. He remembers them while in the woods, and is not at a loss to trace them through the impervious forest, and to reason accurately upon the errors and mistakes which may have been made by the surveyor's neglect or ignorance in the representation of them. He receives proper directions and departs for the intended place, for he wants to view and examine ere he purchases.

When near the spot, he hires a man, perhaps a hunter, of which all the frontiers are full, and instead of being lost and amazed in the middle of these gloomy retreats, he finds the place of beginning on which the whole survey is founded. This is all the difficulty he was afraid of; he follows the ancient blazed trees with a sagacity and quickness of sight which have many times astonished me, though bred in the woods. Next he judges of the soil by the size and the appearance of the trees; next he judges of the goodness of the timber by that of the soil. The humble bush which delights in the shade, the wild ginseng, the spignet,[2] the weeds on which he

2. A corruption of "spikenard."

treads teach him all he wants to know. He observes the springs, the moisture of the earth, the range of the mountains, the course of the brooks. He returns at last; he has formed his judgment as to his future buildings; their situation, future roads, cultivation, etc. He has properly combined the future mixture of conveniences and inconveniences which he expects to meet with. In short the complicated arrangement of a great machine would not do greater honour to the most skilful artist than the reduction and digesting of so many thoughts and calculations by this hitherto obscure man.

He meets once more the land-proprietors; a new scene ensues. He is startled at the price. He altercates with them, for now he has something to say, having well explored the country. Now he makes them an offer; now he seems to recede; now wholly indifferent about the bargain; now willing to fulfil it if the terms are reasonable. If not, he can't but stay where he is, or perhaps accept of better offers which have been made to him by another person. He relinquishes, he pursues his object—that is his advantage—through a more complex labyrinth than a European could well imagine. He is diffident; he is mistrustful as to the title, ancientness of patent, priority of claim, etc. The idea that would occur to an Englishman of his class would be that such great and good men would not deceive such a poor farmer as he is; he would feel an inward shame to doubt their assertions. You are wrong, my friends; these are not your country parish-squires who would by so gross a deceit defame their characters and lose your vote. Besides, the price of things is better ascertained there in all possible bargains than here. This is a land-merchant who, like all other merchants, has no other rule than to get what he can. This is the general standard except where there is some competition. The native sagacity of this American colonist carries him at last through the whole bargain. He purchases fifteen hundred acres at three dollars [3] per acre to be paid in three equal yearly payments. He gives his bond for the same, and the whole tract is mortgaged as a security. On the other hand, he obtains bonds of indemnity to secure him against the miscarriages of the patent and other claims.

He departs with all his family, and great and many are the expenses and fatigues of this removal with cows and cattle. He at last arrives on the spot. He finds himself suddenly deprived of the assistance of friends, neighbours, tradesmen, and of all those inferior links which make a well-established society so beautiful and pleasing. He and his family are now alone. On their courage, perseverance, and skill their success depends. There is now no retreating; shame and ruin would infallibly overtake them. What

---

3. The original editor noted that the text had read forty shillings, but the author corrected the amount to three dollars.

is he to do in all possible cases of accidents, sickness, and other casualties which may befall his family, his cattle and horses, breaking of the implements of husbandry, etc.? A complicated scene presents itself of the contemplative mind, which does the Americans a superlative honour. Whence proceed that vigour and energy, those resources which they never fail to show on these trying occasions? From the singularity of their situation, from that locality of existence which is peculiar to themselves as a new people improving a new country?

I have purposely visited many who have spent the earliest part of their lives in this manner; now ploughmen, now mechanics, sometimes even physicians. They are and must be everything. Nay, who would believe it? This new man will commence as a hunter and learn in these woods how to pursue and overtake the game with which it abounds. He will in a short time become master of that necessary dexterity which this solitary life inspires. Husband, father, priest, principal governor,—he fills up all these stations, though in the humble vale of life. Are there any of his family taken sick, either he or his wife must recollect ancient directions received from aged people, from doctors, from a skilful grandmother, perhaps, who formerly learned of the Indians of her neighbourhood how to cure simple diseases by means of simple medicines. The swamps and woods are ransacked to find the plants, the bark, the roots prescribed. An ancient almanac, constituting perhaps all his library, with his Bible, may chance to direct him to some more learned ways.

Has he a cow or an ox sick, his anxiety is not less, for they constitute part of his riches. He applies what recipes he possesses; he bleeds, he foments; he has no farrier at hand to assist him. Does either his plough or his cart break, he runs to his tools; he repairs them as well as he can. Do they finally break down, with reluctance he undertakes to rebuild them, though he doubts of his success. This was an occupation committed before to the mechanic of his neighbourhood, but necessity gives him invention, teaches him to imitate, to recollect what he has seen. Somehow or another 'tis done, and happily there is no traveller, no inquisitive eye to grin and criticize his work. It answers the purposes for the present. Next time he arrives nearer perfection. Behold him henceforth a sort of intuitive carpenter! Happy man, thou hast nothing to demand of propitious heaven but a long life to enable thee to finish the most material part of thy labours, in order to leave each of thy children an improved inheritance. Thank God and thy fate, thy wife can weave. This happy talent constitutes the most useful part of her portion. Then all is with thee as well as it can be. The yarn which thy daughters have spun will now be converted into coarse but substantial cloth. Thus his flax and the wool clothes all the family; most women are something of tailors. Thus if they are healthy, these settlers find within themselves a resource against all probable accidents.

His ingenuity in the fields is not less remarkable in executing his rural work in the most expeditious manner. He naturally understands the use of levers, handspikes, etc. He studies how to catch the most favourable seasons for each task. This great field of action deters him not. But what [shall] he do for shoes? Never before did he find himself so near going barefooted. Long wintry nights come on. It ought to be a time of inactivity and repose, considering the amazing fatigues of the summer. The great fire warms the whole house; cheers all the family; it makes them think less of the severity of the season. He hugs himself with an involuntary feeling; he is conscious of present ease and security. He hears the great snowstorm driving by his door; he hears the impotent wind roaring in his chimney. If he regrets his ancient connections, the mug of cider and other conveniences he enjoyed before, he finds himself amply remunerated by the plenty of fuel he now possesses, etc. The rosy children sitting round the hearth, sweat and sleep with their basins of samp [4] on their laps; the industrious mother is rattling at her loom, avariciously improving every minute of her time. Shall the master, the example of so happy a family, smoke and sleep and be idle? No, he has heard the children complain of sores and chilblains for want of shoes; he has leather, but no shoemaker at hand. A secret wish arises, natural enough to a father's heart: he wants to see them all happy. So noble a motive can't but have a successful end. He has, perhaps, a few lasts and some old tools; he tries to mend an old pair. Heaven be praised! The child can walk with them, and boast to the others of his new acquisition. A second pair is attempted; he succeeds as well. He ventures at last to make a new one. They are coarse, heavy, ponderous, and clumsy, but they are tight and strong, and answer all the intended purposes. What more can he want? If his gears break, he can easily repair them. Every man here understands how to spin his own yarn and to [make] his own ropes. He is a universal fabricator like Crusoe. With bark and splinters the oldest of the children amuse themselves by making little baskets. The hint being praised by the father is further improved, and in a little time they are supplied with what baskets they want.

Casks require too much labour and particular ingenuity. He in vain attempts it; he cannot succeed, but indulgent Nature offers him a sufficient compensation. In the woods which surround him hollow trees present themselves to him; he can easily distinguish

4. Porridge made of coarsely ground Indian corn.

them by the sound they yield when struck with the ax. They have long served as winter habitations to squirrels and other animals. Now they are cut into proper lengths, smoothed on the inside. They are placed on the floor and [are] ready to contain anything but liquids. Tight vessels are not wanted as yet, for he has no fermented liquor to preserve (save spruce beer), until his young orchard begins to bear, and by that time the natural improvement of the country will bring the necessary tradesmen into his neighbourhood.

Happy man, did'st thou but know the extent of thy good fortune! Permit me to hold for a minute the sketch of thy political felicity, that thou mayest never forget that share of gratitude which thou owest to the mild government under which thou livest. Thou hast no church-dues to pay derived from the most unaccountable donations, the pious offerings of rough ignorance or mistaken zeal; those ancient calamities are unknown to thy land. Thou mayest go to toil and exert the whole energy and circle of thy industry, and try the activity of human nature in all situations. Fear not that a clergyman whom thou never hearest, or any other, shall demand the tenth part of thy labour. Thy land, descended from its great Creator, holds not its precarious tenure either from a supercilious prince or a proud lord. Thou need'st not dread any contradictions in thy government and laws of thy country; they are simple and natural, and if they are sometimes burdensome in the execution, 'tis the fault of men. Thou need'st not fear those absurd ordinances alternately puzzling the understanding and the reason of subjects, and crushing all national industry. Thou need'st not tremble lest the most incomprehensible prohibitions shall rob thee of that sacred immunity with which the produce of thy farm may circulate from hand to hand until it reaches those of the final exporter. 'Tis all as free as the air which thou breathest. Thy land, thy canton is not claimed by any neighbouring monarch who, anxious for the new dominion, ravages, devastates, and despoils its peaceable inhabitants. Rest secure: no cruel militia-laws shall be enacted to ravish from thee thy son, and to make him serve an unknown master in his wars; to enrich a foreign land with his carcass, unrelieved in his pains and agonies, unpitied in his death. The produce of thy loins shall not feed foreign wolves and vultures.

No, undisturbed, this offspring of thine shall remain with thee to coöperate in that family partnership of which thou art the first director and manager. At a proper season thou shalt see him marry, perhaps thy neighbour's daughter. Thou then shalt have the pleasure of settling him on that land which he has helped thee to earn and to clear; henceforth he shall become also a new neighbour to thee, still remaining thy son and friend. Thy heart shall swell with inward exultation when thou shalt see him prosper and flourish, for his future prosperity will be a part of thine in the same proportion as thy family happiness is a part of that diffusive one which overspreads thy country's. In the future extensive harvests thou shalt raise; and other laborious undertakings which the seasons and the elements bid thee execute quickly. The reunited aid of the combined family by a reciprocal assistance will often throughout the year combine together to accomplish the most painful tasks.

Humanity is not obliged here, as in the old world, to pass through the slow windings of the alembic.[5] Here 'tis an abundant spring, running and dividing itself everywhere agreeable to the nature and declivity of the ground. Neither dams nor mounds nor any other obstructions restrain it; 'tis never artificially gathered as a turbid flood to exhale in the sun, nor sunken under ground for some sinister purposes. 'Tis a regular fecundating stream left to the laws of declivity and invariably pursuing its course.

Thus this man devoid of society learns more than ever to center every idea within that of his own welfare. To him all that appears good, just, equitable, has a necessary relation to himself and family. He has been so long alone that he has almost forgot the rest of mankind except it is when he carries his crops on the snow to some distant market.

The country, however, fills with new inhabitants. His granary is resorted to from all parts by other beginners who did not come so well prepared. How will he sell his grain to these people who are strangers to him? Shall he deduct the expense of carrying it to a distant mill? This would appear just, but where is the necessity of this justice? His neighbours absolutely want his supply; they can't go to other places. He, therefore, concludes upon having the full price. He remembers his former difficulties; no one assisted him then. Why should he assist others? They are all able to work for themselves. He has a large family, and it would be giving its lawful substance away; he cannot do it. How should he be charitable? He has scarcely seen a poor man in his life. How should he be merciful, except from native instinct? He has never heard that it was a necessary qualification, and he has never seen objects that required the benefits of his sympathy. He has had to struggle alone through numbers of difficult situations and inconveniences; he, therefore, deals hardly with his new neighbours. If they are not punctual in their payment, he prosecutes them at law, for by this time its benefits have reached him. 'Tis laid out into a new

5. A convoluted chemical device for extracting and purifying.

county, and divided into townships. Perhaps he takes a mortgage
on his neighbour's land. But it may happen that it is already encumbered by anterior and more ponderous debts. He knows instinctively the coercive power of the laws: he impeaches the cattle;
he has proper writings drawn; he gets bonds in judgment. He secures himself; and all this is done from native knowledge; he has
neither counsellor nor adviser. Who can be wiser than himself in
this half-cultivated country? The sagacity peculiar to the American
never forsakes him; it may slumber sometimes, but upon the appearance of danger it arises again as vigorous as ever.

But behold him happily passed through the course of many
laborious years; his wealth and, therefore, his consequence increase
with the progress of the settlement. If he is litigious, overbearing,
purse-proud, which will very probably be the bent of his mind, he
has a large field. Among so many beginners there need be many
needy, inconsiderate, drunken, and lazy. He may bring the necessary severity of the law to flourish even in these wilds. Well may
we be subjects to its lash, or else we would be too happy, for
this is almost all the tribute we pay.

Now advanced in life and grown rich, he builds a good substantial
stone or frame house, and the humble log one, under which he
has so much prospered, becomes the kitchen. Several roads inter-
sect and meet near this spot, which he has contrived on purpose.
He becomes an innholder and a country-merchant. This introduces
him into all the little mysteries of self-interest, clothed under
the general name of profits and emoluments. He sells for good
that which perhaps he knows to be indifferent, because he also
knows that the ashes he has collected, the wheat he has taken in
may not be so good or so clean as it was asserted. Fearful of fraud
in all his dealings and transactions, he arms himself, therefore,
with it. Strict integrity is not much wanted, as each is on his guard
in his daily intercourse, and this mode of thinking and acting becomes habitual. If any one is detected in anything too glaring
but without the reach of the law, where is the recollection of
ancient principles, either civil or religious, that can raise the blush
of conscious shame? No minister is at hand by his daily admoni-
tions to put him in remembrance of a vindictive God punishing
all frauds and bad intentions, rewarding rectitude and justice.
Whatever ideas of this kind they might have imbibed when
young; whatever conscience may say; these voices have been so long
silent, that they are no longer heard. The law, therefore, and its
plain meaning are the only forcible standards which strike and
guide their senses and become their rule of action. 'Tis to them an
armour serving as well for attack as for defence; 'tis all that

seems useful and pervading. Its penalties and benefits are the only thing feared and remembered, and this fearful remembrance is what we might call in the closet a reverence for the law.

With such principles of conduct as these, follow him in all these situations which link men in society, in that vast variety of bargains, exchanges, barters, sales, etc.; and adduce the effects which must follow. If it is not "bellum omnium contra omnes," [6] 'tis a general mass of keenness and sagacious acting against another mass of equal sagacity; 'tis caution against caution. Happy, when it does not degenerate into fraud against fraud! The law, which cannot pervade and direct every action, here leaves her children to themselves, and abandons those peccadilloes (which convulse not though they may [dim] some of the most beautiful colours of society) to the more invisible efficacy of religion.

But here this great resource fails in some measure, at least with a great many of them, from the weakness of their religious education, from a long inattention, from the paucity of instructions received. Is it a wonder that new rules of action should arise? It must constitute a new set of opinions, the parent of manners. You have already observed this colonist is necessarily different from what he was in the more ancient settlements he originally came from; become such by his new local situation, his new industry, that share of cunning which was absolutely necessary in consequence of his intercourse with his new neighbours.

1925

6. "War of all against all"; in the context, "each man for himself."

Reason and Revolution

BENJAMIN FRANKLIN
(1706–1790)

Franklin was the epitome of the Enlightenment, the versatile, practical embodiment of rational man in the eighteenth century. His mind approved and his behavior demonstrated the fundamental concepts of the Age of Reason—faith in the reality of the world as revealed to the senses, distrust of the mystical or mysterious, confidence in the attainment of progress by education and humanitarianism, and the assurance that an appeal to Reason would provide solutions for all human problems, including those of the society and the state. Many of his contemporaries ordered their personal lives by such beliefs, but it was Franklin's particular genius to make the rational life comprehensible and practicable to his countrymen.

In the years between his birth in Boston, in 1706, and his death in Philadelphia, in 1790, incredible political and economic changes occurred; after a successful struggle with France for domination of the North American continent, England recognized the independence of thirteen of her colonies in a treaty signed in Paris; the philosophy of rational individualism undermined the position of established church and aristocracy; and the new empirical science, responding to Newton's discoveries, again awakened man's dream of mastering his physical world. Other men were pioneers in some of these events, but in all of them Benjamin Franklin actively participated—and left a written record unsurpassed for its penetration, objectivity, and wit.

His early years in Boston, spent reluctantly in his father's tallow shop and sporadically at school, were typical of the experience of a child in a colonial town; then, at the age of twelve, the boy was apprenticed to his brother James, a printer. There followed the long hours of work and the regimen of self-education so graphically recalled in Franklin's *Autobiography*, written many years later for his son, William. In 1722, when his brother was jailed for offending the authorities in his *New England Courant*, sixteen-year-old Benjamin took over the editorship of the paper, and under the pseudonym of Silence Dogood, continued his editorials on subjects ranging from the merits of higher education to freedom of the press. The next year, after disagreements with his brother, he took ship for Philadelphia, arriving in October, 1723, and created a favorite American anecdote by walking up from the Market Street wharf in the morning, munching on one of the "three great puffy rolls" he had purchased with his last pennies. He quickly found employment with Keimer, a printer, and after various activities, including a two-year stay in London, became sole owner of a printing firm which by his industry, frugality, and wise investments enabled him to retire from active business in 1748, when he was only forty-two years old. The years that lay ahead were to give him the varied experiences of a politician, statesman, and public citizen, but the discipline and adaptability which he urged upon his fellow citizens were characteristics of a proficient artisan devoted to his craft. Years later, although academic and international honors had been pressed upon him, he wrote as the opening words of his will, "I, Benjamin Franklin, of Philadelphia, printer. * * *"

It was characteristic of Franklin that he not only printed legal forms, copies of Indian treaties, *The Pennsylvania Gazette*, 1729–1766, and acts of the Pennsylvania Assembly, but also made the yearly almanac a characteristically American thing. *Poor Richard's Almanack* gave the usual information on weather and currency, but

the aphorisms, their sources ranging from Greek to English writers, became, by the turn of a phrase, American in vocabulary and implication.

His profession may have provided opportunity for acquaintance with the colonial leaders of Pennsylvania, but it was his unceasing energy and interest in humanity that directed his talents into a variety of civic projects. Franklin brought them about by perseverant ingenuity —such far-reaching institutions as the first circulating library, and more immediate measures, such as the lottery for the erection of steeple and chimes for Christ Church. Among the surviving monuments to his genius for the practical utilization of humane ideas are our first learned society—the American Philosophical Society; our first colonial hospital—the Pennsylvania Hospital; and the University of Pennsylvania, the first such institution to be founded upon the ideal of secular education which he formulated in a number of his writings.

His inquiring mind, energized by his confidence in the progress of rational man, turned as naturally to speculative thought as to ingenious inventions and to the improvement of the institutions of daily life. Nothing was more engrossing to Franklin than the manifestations of nature, so long in the realm of the theoretical or mystical, but now, with the stirring advance of eighteenth-century science, convincingly demonstrated to men's minds by scrupulous techniques of experimental observation. Franklin's curiosity ranged from the causes of earthquakes and the benefits of the Gulf Stream to navigation, to the possible association of lightning and electricity. As early as 1746 he became acquainted through correspondence with English scientists, and his enthusiastic assimilation of their information led to experiments with the Leyden jar and culminated in the famous kite-and-key experiment in 1752. His *Experiments and Observations on Electricity* (1751–1753) brought him international fame.

With the interest in science, the eighteenth century saw a corresponding growth of rationalism and skepticism in religion. Largely derivative from Shaftesbury and Locke, Deism, which stood a pole apart from the orthodoxy of the time, offered minds such as Franklin's an opportunity for reliance on a creative deity and freedom from the strictures of traditional theology. Franklin's earlier doubts became tempered in his later life to that benevolent eclecticism of moderation in action and a reasoned faith in God.

His leadership in civic enterprises and business might in itself have involved Franklin in the struggle for independence from England, but long before 1776 he had demonstrated qualities of statesmanship. He had learned the intricacies and intrigues of a proprietary colonial government in the fifteen years before 1751 during which he served as clerk of the Pennsylvania Assembly. And his consummate skill as diplomat in England, and in France in 1783, was the result of long experience,

which had begun with his mission, many years earlier, to obtain a treaty with the Ohio Indians.

In two lengthy trips to England between 1757 and 1775, he had served as colonial agent for Pennsylvania, Georgia, Massachusetts, and New Jersey, hoping for conciliation between England and the American colonies, but making a masterful defense against the Stamp Act. He returned to Philadelphia in time to serve in the Second Continental Congress and to be chosen, with Jefferson, as a member of the committee to draft the Declaration of Independence. After two years in France as the agent of Congress, Franklin successfully negotiated a treaty of alliance in 1778; and with John Jay and John Adams, he arranged the terms and signed the Treaty of Paris that ended the Revolution. The nine years he spent at Passy, near Paris, brought him the affectionate adulation of the French, and from his private press came beautifully printed and whimsical "Bagatelles," such as "The Whistle," "The Ephemera," and "To Madame Helvetius."

Franklin returned to Philadelphia in 1785, became president of the executive council of Pennsylvania for three years, and closed his brilliant career by serving as a member of the Constitutional Convention. His death in 1790 was the occasion for international mourning for a man who had become a symbol of democratic action in America and Europe. Six years earlier, when Jefferson was congratulated on replacing Franklin as minister at Paris, he responded, "No one can replace him, Sir; I am only his successor." There has been, in fact, no one since to replace him; he stands alone.

The definitive edition (in progress) is *The Papers of Benjamin Franklin*, Yale University Press, 1959—16 vols. to 1972. Significant verbal variants will be shown in our footnotes as "Yale reads:" Our other texts are from the 10-vol. edition by A. H. Smyth (1905). The Bigelow edition (1887–1889) supplements Smyth. A well balanced selection is *Franklin: Representative Selections*, edited by F. L. Mott and C. L. Jorgensen, American Writers Series, 1936. Modern critical biographies are Carl Van Doren, *Benjamin Franklin*, 1938; Bruce I. Granger, *Benjamin Franklin, An American Man of Letters*, 1964; Alfred O. Aldridge, *Benjamin Franklin, Philosopher and Man*, 1965; Ralph Ketcham, *Benjamin Franklin*, 1965; and Richard Amacher, *Benjamin Franklin*, 1962.

For Franklin's years in London and Paris see Roger Burlingame, *Benjamin Franklin: Envoy Extraordinary*, 1967. For special study, several other works are useful, especially James Parton, *Life and Times of Benjamin Franklin*, 2 vols., 1864; *The Life of Benjamin Franklin * * **, 3 vols., edited by John Bigelow, 1874 (1916); J. B. McMaster, *Benjamin Franklin as Man of Letters*, 1887; P. L. Ford, *The Many-Sided Franklin*, 1899; Bernard Fay, *Franklin, the Apostle of Modern Times*, 1929; and Paul W. Conner, *Poor Richard's Politics: Benjamin Franklin and His New America*, 1965.

For special topics, and for the various recent collections of Franklin letters, see Bibliography, *Literary History of the United States*, edited by Robert E. Spiller, Willard Thorp, Thomas H. Johnson, and Henry Seidel Canby, Vol. III and supplements. On the text of the *Autobiography*, see Max Farrand, *The Autobiography of Benjamin Franklin: A Restoration of a "Fair Copy,"* 1949; and *Benjamin Franklin's Memoirs, Parallel Text Edition*, edited by Max Farrand, 1949. Except for the selections from *Poor Richard's Almanack*, all texts conform to modern practice in respect to spelling and punctuation.

From The Autobiography [1]

TWYFORD,[2] at the Bishop of St. Asaph's, 1771.

DEAR SON:

I have ever had a pleasure in obtaining any little anecdotes of my ancestors. You may remember the inquiries I made among the remains of my relations when you were with me in England,[3] and the journey I undertook for that purpose. Now imagining it may be equally agreeable to you to know the circumstances of *my* life, many of which you are yet unacquainted with, and expecting a week's uninterrupted leisure in my present country retirement, I sit down to write them for you. To which I have besides some other inducements. Having emerged from the poverty and ob-

1. At sixty-five, Franklin wrote an account of his first twenty-four years, intended for his son, William, then colonial governor of New Jersey. Years later he was persuaded by friends to continue it. Additions in 1783, 1784, and 1788 more than doubled the size of the original manuscript, but brought the account only to the years 1757–1759, before the great period of Franklin's public service and international influence. He did not publish this work. The selections below are based on the collation of Bigelow with Farrand's original manuscript readings in *Ben-*

jamin Franklin's Memoirs. Verbal variants in *The Papers* (Vol. X) are shown in footnotes. The language of the present text is not "modernized," but mechanical conventions have been regularized.

2. In England, near Winchester. Franklin had become intimate with Jonathan Shipley, Bishop of St. Asaph's, who approved a more liberal policy for the colonies.

3. His son, William Franklin, went to England as his father's secretary in 1757, studied law there, and later served as royal governor of New Jersey.

scurity in which I was born and bred to a state of affluence and some degree of reputation in the world, and having gone so far through life with a considerable share of felicity, the conducing means I made use of, which with the blessing of God so well succeeded, my posterity may like to know, as they may find some of them suitable to their own situations, and therefore fit to be imitated. That felicity, when I reflected on it, has induced me sometimes to say that were it offered to my choice I should have no objection to a repetition of the same life from its beginning, only asking the advantages authors have in a second edition to correct some faults of the first. So would I, if I might, besides correcting the faults, change some sinister accidents and events of it for others more favorable, but though this was denied, I should still accept the offer. However, since such a repetition is not to be expected, the next thing most like having one's life over again seems to be a *recollection* of that life, and to make that recollection as durable as possible the putting it down in writing. * * *

The notes one of my uncles (who had the same kind of curiosity in collecting family anecdotes) once put into my hands furnished me with several particulars relating to our ancestors. From these notes I learned that the family had lived in the same village, Ecton, in Northamptonshire, for three hundred years, and how much longer he knew not (perhaps from the time when the name Franklin, that before was the name of an order of people, was assumed by them for a surname when others took surnames all over the kingdom),[4] on a freehold of about thirty acres, aided by the smith's business, which had continued in the family till his time, the eldest son being always bred to that business—a custom which he and my father both followed as to their eldest sons. * * *

Josiah, my father, married young, and carried his wife with three children into New England about 1682. The conventicle[5] having been forbidden by law and frequently disturbed induced some considerable men of his acquaintance to remove to that country, and he was prevailed with to accompany them thither, where they expected to enjoy their mode of religion with freedom. By the same wife he had four children more born there, and by a second wife ten more, in all seventeen; of which I remember thirteen sit-

4. Yale notes a memorandum, written perhaps by Benjamin Franklin, in Temple Franklin's edition, quoting on this subject a fifteenth-century English legal authority. Benjamin's father wrote him, May 26, 1739, discussing the origin of the name and giving some account of the English Franklins. *Papers*, II, 229–

32. Franklin properly associated the name with "an order of people"; the "freehold" tenant had tax privileges. *Cf.* Chaucer's tale of the Franklin.
5. Religious assemblies of dissenters, made illegal by the Act of Uniformity, 1662.

ting at one time at his table, who all grew up to be men and women, and married; I was the youngest son, and the youngest child but two, and was born in Boston, New England. My mother, the second wife, was Abiah Folger, a daughter of Peter Folger,[6] one of the first settlers of New England, of whom honorable mention is made by Cotton Mather, in his church history of that country, entitled *Magnalia Christi Americana*, as "a godly, learned Englishman," if I remember the words rightly. I have heard that he wrote sundry small occasional pieces, but only one of them was printed, which I saw now many years since. * * *

My elder brothers were all put apprentices to different trades. I was put to the grammar school at eight years of age, my father intending to devote me, as the tithe of his sons, to the service of the church. My early readiness in learning to read (which must have been early, as I do not remember when I could not read) and the opinion of all his friends that I should certainly make a good scholar encouraged him in this purpose of his. My uncle Benjamin, too, approved of it, and proposed to give me all his shorthand volumes of sermons, I suppose as a stock to set up with, if I would learn his character.[7] I continued, however, at the grammar school not quite one year, though in that time I had risen gradually from the middle of the class of that year to be the head of it, and farther was removed into the next class above it, in order to go with that into the third at the end of the year. But my father, in the meantime, from a view of the expense of a college education, which having so large a family he could not well afford, and the mean living many so educated were afterwards able to obtain—reasons that he gave to his friends in my hearing—altered his first intention, took me from the grammar school, and sent me to a school for writing and arithmetic, kept by a then famous man, Mr. George Brownell, very successful in his profession generally, and that by mild, encouraging methods. Under him I acquired fair writing pretty soon, but I failed in the arithmetic, and made no progress in it. At ten years old I was taken home to assist my father in his business, which was that of a tallow-chandler and soap-boiler; a business he was not bred to, but had assumed on his arrival in New England, and on finding his dying trade would not maintain his family, being in little request. Accordingly, I was employed in cutting wick for the candles, filling the dipping mold and the molds for cast candles, attending the shop, going of errands, etc. * * *

From a child I was fond of reading, and all the little money

6. Peter Folger (1617–1690), pioneer of Nantucket, a schoolmaster, published a volume of ballads condemning the Puritans for lack of religious toleration.
7. His shorthand.

that came into my hands was ever laid out in books. Pleased with the *Pilgrim's Progress,* my first collection was of John Bunyan's works in separate little volumes. I afterwards sold them to enable me to buy R. Burton's *Historical Collections;* they were small chapman's books, and cheap, forty or fifty in all. My father's little library consisted chiefly of books in polemic divinity, most of which I read and have since often regretted that at a time when I had such a thirst for knowledge, more proper books had not fallen in my way, since it was now resolved I should not be a clergyman. *Plutarch's Lives* there was, in which I read abundantly, and I still think that time spent to great advantage. There was also a book of Defoe's,[8] called an *Essay on Projects,* and another of Dr. Mather's,[9] called *Essays to do Good,* which perhaps gave me a turn of thinking that had an influence on some of the principal future events in my life.

This bookish inclination at length determined my father to make me a printer, though he had already one son (James) of that profession. In 1717 my brother James returned from England with a press and letters to set up his business in Boston. I liked it much better than that of my father, but still had a hankering for the sea. To prevent the apprehended effect of such an inclination, my father was impatient to have me bound to my brother. I stood out some time, but at last was persuaded, and signed the indentures when I was yet but twelve years old. * * *

And after some time an ingenious tradesman, Mr. Matthew Adams, who had a pretty collection of books, and who frequented our printing-house, took notice of me, invited me to his library, and very kindly lent me such books as I chose to read. I now took a fancy to poetry, and made some little pieces; my brother, thinking it might turn to account, encouraged me, and put me on composing two occasional ballads. One was called *The Lighthouse Tragedy,* and contained an account of the drowning of Captain Worthilake with his two daughters; the other was a sailor's song, on the taking of Teach (or Blackbeard), the pirate.[1] They were wretched stuff, in the Grub-street-ballad style; and when they were printed he sent me about the town to sell them. The first sold wonderfully, the event being recent, having made a great noise. This flattered my vanity; but my father discouraged me by ridiculing my performances and telling me verse-makers were

8. Daniel Defoe's *Essay upon Projects* (1697) advanced such liberal social proposals as insurance and popular education.
9. Cotton Mather's essays, originally entitled *Bonifacius* (1710), emphasized practical virtues, and influenced Franklin's early *Dogood Papers* (1722).

1. During 1717–1718, George Worthilake, keeper of the Boston Light, was drowned with his family while rowing to Boston; and "Blackbeard," or Edward Teach, famed pirate of the southern coast, was killed by a British naval expedition.

generally beggars. So I escaped being a poet, most probably a very bad one; but as prose writing has been of great use to me in the course of my life, and was a principal means of my advancement, I shall tell you how, in such a situation, I acquired what little ability I have in that way. * * *

About this time I met with an odd volume of the *Spectator*.[2] It was the third. I had never before seen any of them. I bought it, read it over and over, and was much delighted with it. I thought the writing excellent, and wished, if possible, to imitate it. With that view I took some of the papers, and making short hints of the sentiment in each sentence, laid them by a few days, and then, without looking at the book, tried to complete the papers again by expressing each hinted sentiment at length, and as fully as it had been expressed before, in any suitable words that should come to hand. Then I compared my *Spectator* with the original, discovered some of my faults, and corrected them. But I found I wanted a stock of words, or a readiness in recollecting and using them, which I thought I should have acquired before that time if I had gone on making verses; since the continual occasion for words of the same import, but of different length to suit the measure, or of different sound for the rhyme, would have laid me under a constant necessity of searching for variety and also have tended to fix that variety in my mind and make me master of it. Therefore, I took some of the tales and turned them into verse, and, after a time, when I had pretty well forgotten the prose, turned them back again. I also sometimes jumbled my collections of hints into confusion, and after some weeks endeavored to reduce them into the best order, before I began to form the full sentences and complete the paper. This was to teach me method in the arrangement of thoughts. By comparing my work afterwards with the original, I discovered many faults and amended them. * * *

While I was intent on improving my language, I met with an English grammar (I think it was Greenwood's), at the end of which there were two little sketches of the arts of rhetoric and logic, the latter finishing with a specimen of a dispute in the Socratic method; and soon after I procured Xenophon's *Memorable Things of Socrates*,[3] wherein there are many instances of the same method. I was charmed with it, adopted it, dropped my abrupt contradiction and positive argumentation and put on the humble inquirer and doubter. And being then, from reading Shaftesbury and Collins,[4] become a real doubter in many points of our re-

2. Famous British periodical (1711–1712) largely the work of Joseph Addison and Sir Richard Steele.
3. Title of Edward Bysshe's translation (1712) of Xenophon's *Memorabilia*. Note that Franklin was already familiar

with the "Socratic method" of argument from reading James Greenwood's *Grammar* (1711), which emphasized, in the fashion of the day, the logical bases of grammar and rhetoric.
4. The Earl of Shaftesbury's collected

ligious doctrine, I found this method safest for myself and very embarrassing to those against whom I used it; therefore I took a delight in it, practiced it continually, and grew very artful and expert in drawing people, even of superior knowledge, into concessions, the consequences of which they did not foresee, entangling them in difficulties out of which they could not extricate themselves, and so obtaining victories that neither myself nor my cause always deserved. I continued this method some few years, but gradually left it, retaining only the habit of expressing myself in terms of modest diffidence, never using, when I advanced anything that may possibly be disputed, the words *certainly, undoubtedly*, or any others that give the air of positiveness to an opinion; but rather say, I conceive or apprehend a thing to be so or so; it appears to me, or I should think it so or so, for such and such reasons; or I imagine it to be so; or it is so, if I am not mistaken. This habit, I believe, has been of great advantage to me when I have had occasion to inculcate my opinions and persuade men into measures that I have been from time to time engaged in promoting; and, as the chief ends of conversation are to *inform* or to be *informed*, to *please* or to *persuade*, I wish well-meaning, sensible men would not lessen their power of doing good by a positive, assuming manner that seldom fails to disgust, tends to create opposition and to defeat every one of those purposes for which speech was given to us, to wit, giving or receiving information or pleasure. * * *

My brother had, in 1720 or 21, begun to print a newspaper. It was the second that appeared in America, and was called the *New England Courant*.⁵ The only one before it was the *Boston News-Letter*. * * *

He had some ingenious men among his friends, who amused themselves by writing little pieces for this paper, which gained it credit and made it more in demand, and these gentlemen often visited us. Hearing their conversations, and their accounts of the approbation their papers were received with, I was excited to try my hand among them; but, being still a boy, and suspecting that my brother would object to printing anything of mine in his paper if he knew it to be mine, I contrived to disguise my hand and, writing an anonymous paper, I put it in at night under the door of the printing-house. It was found in the morning and communicated to his writing friends when they called in as usual. They

essays, *Characteristics* * * * (1711, 1713), are here associated with Anthony Collins' *Discourse* * * * (1713), because both are "free thinking" in theology; Shaftesbury also influenced Franklin's rational view of morality.
5. Actually, James Franklin's *New* *England Courant* (1721–1726), was the fifth American newspaper. *Publick Occurrences* appeared in Boston, for one issue only, in 1690; it was followed by the Boston *News-Letter*, 1704, the Boston *Gazette*, 1719, and, in Philadelphia, the *American Weekly Mercury*, 1719.

read it, commented on it in my hearing, and I had the exquisite pleasure of finding it met with their approbation, and that, in their different guesses at the author, none were named but men of some character among us for learning and ingenuity. I suppose now that I was rather lucky in my judges, and that perhaps they were not really so very good ones as I then esteemed them.

Encouraged, however, by this, I wrote and conveyed in the same way to the press several more papers which were equally approved; [6] and I kept my secret till my small fund of sense for such performances was pretty well exhausted, and then I discovered it, when I began to be considered a little more by my brother's acquaintance, and in a manner that did not quite please him, as he thought, probably with reason, that it tended to make me too vain. And perhaps this might be one occasion of the differences that we began to have about this time. Though a brother, he considered himself as my master, and me as his apprentice, and accordingly expected the same services from me as he would from another, while I thought he demeaned me too much in some he required of me, who from a brother expected more indulgence. * * * [7]

One of the pieces in our newspaper on some political point, which I have now forgotten, gave offense to the Assembly. He was taken up, censured, and imprisoned for a month, by the speaker's warrant, I suppose because he would not discover his author. * * *

During my brother's confinement, which I resented a good deal, notwithstanding our private differences, I had the management of the paper; and I made bold to give our rulers some rubs in it, which my brother took very kindly, while others began to consider me in an unfavorable light, as a young genius that had a turn for libeling and satire. My brother's discharge was accompanied with an order of the House (a very odd one), that "James Franklin should no longer print the paper called the *New England Courant*."

There was a consultation held in our printing-house among his friends what he should do in this case. Some proposed to evade the order by changing the name of the paper; but my brother seeing inconveniences in that, it was finally concluded on as a better way to let it be printed for the future under the name of *Benjamin Franklin*,[8] and to avoid the censure of the Assembly, that might fall on him as still printing it by his apprentice, the contrivance was that my old indenture should be returned to me, with a full

6. *The Dogood Papers* (1722), his first published prose.
7. "I fancy his harsh and tyrannical treatment of me might be a means of impressing me with that aversion to arbitrary power that has stuck to me through my whole life" [Franklin's note].

8. In fact, James Franklin was arrested twice, on different charges; consequently, Benjamin edited the *Courant* for three weeks in June and July, 1722, and again for a week in February, 1723, before his name appeared as ostensible editor on February 11, 1723.

discharge on the back of it, to be shown on occasion; but to secure to him the benefit of my service, I was to sign new indentures for the remainder of the term, which were to be kept private. A very flimsy scheme it was; however, it was immediately executed, and the paper went on accordingly under my name for several months.

At length, a fresh difference arising between my brother and me, I took upon me to assert my freedom, presuming that he would not venture to produce the new indentures. It was not fair in me to take this advantage, and this I therefore reckon one of the first errata of my life; but the unfairness of it weighed little with me when under the impression of resentment for the blows his passion too often urged him to bestow upon me, though he was otherwise not an ill-natured man; perhaps I was too saucy and provoking.

When he found I would leave him, he took care to prevent my getting employment in any other printing-house of the town, by going round and speaking to every master, who accordingly refused to give me work. I then thought of going to New York, as the nearest place where there was a printer; and I was rather inclined to leave Boston when I reflected that I had already made myself a little obnoxious to the governing party, and, from the arbitrary proceedings of the Assembly in my brother's case, it was likely I might, if I stayed, soon bring myself into scrapes; and farther, that my indiscreet disputations about religion began to make me pointed at with horror by good people as an infidel or atheist. I determined on the point, but my father now siding with my brother, I was sensible that, if I attempted to go openly, means would be used to prevent me. My friend Collins, therefore, undertook to manage a little for me. He agreed with the captain of a New York sloop for my passage, under the notion of my being a young acquaintance of his, that had got a naughty girl with child, whose friends would compel me to marry her, and therefore I could not appear or come away publicly. So I sold some of my books to raise a little money, was taken on board privately, and as we had a fair wind, in three days I found myself in New York, near three hundred miles from home, a boy of but seventeen, without the least recommendation to, or knowledge of, any person in the place, and with very little money in my pocket.

My inclinations for the sea were by this time worn out, or I might now have gratified them. But, having a trade, and supposing myself a pretty good workman, I offered my service to the printer in the place, old Mr. William Bradford,[9] who had been the first

9. William Bradford, the first Philadelphia printer (1685). In 1692 he supported George Keith in a schismatic attack on Penn's doctrines. In 1693 in New York he became the royal printer, and he founded that colony's first newspaper, the New York *Gazette* (1725).

printer in Pennsylvania, but removed from thence upon the quarrel of George Keith. He could give me no employment, having little to do and help enough already; but, says he, "My son [1] at Philadelphia has lately lost his principal hand, Aquila Rose,[2] by death; if you go thither, I believe he may employ you." Philadelphia was one hundred miles further; I set out, however, in a boat for Amboy,[3] leaving my chest and things to follow me round by sea. * * *

When we drew near the island, we found it was at a place where there could be no landing, there being a great surf on the stony beach. So we dropped anchor, and swung round towards the shore. Some people came down to the water edge and hallowed to us, as we did to them; but the wind was so high, and the surf so loud, that we could not hear so as to understand each other. There were canoes on the shore, and we made signs, and hallowed that they should fetch us; but they either did not understand us, or thought it impracticable, so they went away, and night coming on, we had no remedy but to wait till the wind should abate; and in the mean time the boatman and I concluded to sleep if we could; and so crowded into the scuttle, with the Dutchman, who was still wet, and the spray, beating over the head of our boat, leaked through to us, so that we were soon almost as wet as he. In this manner we lay all night, with very little rest; but, the wind abating the next day, we made a shift to reach Amboy before night, having been thirty hours on the water, without victuals or any drink but a bottle of filthy rum, the water we sailed on being salt. * * * In the morning, crossing the ferry, I proceeded on my journey on foot, having fifty miles to Burlington, where I was told I should find boats that would carry me the rest of the way to Philadelphia. * * *

I have been the more particular in this description of my journey, and shall be so of my first entry into that city, that you may in your mind compare such unlikely beginning with the figure I have since made there. I was in my working dress, my best clothes being to come round by sea. I was dirty from my journey; my pockets were stuffed out with shirts and stockings; I knew no soul nor where to look for lodging. I was fatigued with traveling, rowing, and want of rest; I was very hungry; and my whole stock of cash consisted of a Dutch dollar and about a shilling in copper. The latter I gave the people of the boat for my passage, who at first re-

1. Andrew Bradford (1686–1742), later Franklin's principal rival as a printer.
2. Aquila Rose (1695?–1723). His posthumous *Poems* * * * (1740) survives because Franklin assisted the poet's son in publishing them.
3. Perth Amboy, then the coastal capital of New Jersey. From there the shortest route across New Jersey was to Burlington, then capital of West Jersey, where the Delaware River would provide an easy passage of twenty miles to Philadelphia.

fused it, on account of my rowing; but I insisted on their taking it, a man being sometimes more generous when he has but a little money than when he had plenty, perhaps through fear of being thought to have but little.

Then I walked up the street, gazing about, till near the market-house I met a boy with bread. I had made many a meal on bread, and, inquiring where he got it, I went immediately to the baker's he directed me to, in Second Street, and asked for biscuit, intending such as we had in Boston; but they, it seems, were not made in Philadelphia. Then I asked for a three-penny loaf, and was told they had none such. So, not considering or knowing the difference of money, and the greater cheapness nor the names of his bread, I bade him give me three-penny-worth of any sort. He gave me, accordingly, three great puffy rolls. I was surprised at the quantity, but took it, and, having no room in my pockets, walked off with a roll under each arm, and eating the other. Thus I went up Market Street as far as Fourth Street, passing by the door of Mr. Read, my future wife's father; when she, standing at the door, saw me, and thought I made, as I certainly did, a most awkward, ridiculous appearance. Then I turned and went down Chestnut Street and part of Walnut Street, eating my roll all the way, and, coming round, found myself again at Market Street wharf, near the boat I came in, to which I went for a draught of the river water; and, being filled with one of my rolls, gave the other two to a woman and her child that came down the river in the boat with us, and were waiting to go farther.

Thus refreshed, I walked again up the street, which by this time had many clean-dressed people in it, who were all walking the same way. I joined them, and thereby was led into the great meeting-house of the Quakers near the market. I sat down among them, and, after looking round awhile and hearing nothing said, being very drowsy through labor and want of rest the preceding night, I fell fast asleep, and continued so till the meeting broke up, when one was kind enough to rouse me. This was, therefore, the first house I was in, or slept in, in Philadelphia. * * *

Keimer's printing-house,[4] I found, consisted of an old shattered press, and one small, worn-out font of English,[5] which he was then using himself, composing an elegy on Aquila Rose, before mentioned, an ingenious young man, of excellent character, much respected in the town, clerk of the Assembly, and a pretty poet. Keimer made verses too, but very indifferently. He could not be said to write them, for his manner was to compose them in the

---

4. Andrew Bradford could not employ him; he accordingly sought work with Bradford's competitor, Samuel Keimer.

5. The English, or 14-point, type would be oversized for most book and newspaper work.

types directly out of his head. So there being no copy, but one pair of cases,[6] and the elegy likely to require all the letter, no one could help him. I endeavored to put his press (which he had not yet used, and of which he understood nothing) into order fit to be worked with; and, promising to come and print off his elegy as soon as he should have got it ready, I returned to Bradford's, who gave me a little job to do for the present, and there I lodged and dieted. A few days after, Keimer sent for me to print off the elegy. And now he had got another pair of cases, and a pamphlet to reprint, on which he set me to work. * * *

Sir William Keith,[7] governor of the province, was then at Newcastle, and Captain Holmes, happening to be in company with him when my letter came to hand, spoke to him of me, and showed him the letter. The Governor read it, and seemed surprised when he was told my age. He said I appeared a young man of promising parts, and therefore should be encouraged; the printers at Philadelphia were wretched ones; and if I would set up there he made no doubt I should succeed; for his part, he would procure me the public business, and do me every other service in his power. This my brother-in-law afterwards told me in Boston, but I knew as yet nothing of it; when, one day, Keimer and I being at work together near the window, we saw the Governor and another gentleman (which proved to be Colonel French of Newcastle), finely dressed, come directly across the street to our house, and heard them at the door.

Keimer ran down immediately, thinking it a visit to him; but the Governor inquired for me, came up, and with a condescension and politeness I had been quite unused to, made me many compliments, desired to be acquainted with me, blamed me kindly for not having made myself known to him when I first came to the place, and would have me away with him to the tavern, where he was going with Colonel French to taste, as he said, some excellent Madeira. I was not a little surprised, and Keimer stared like a pig poisoned. I went, however, with the Governor and Colonel French to a tavern at the corner of Third Street, and over the Madeira he proposed my setting up my business, laid before me the probabilities of success, and both he and Colonel French assured me I should have their interest and influence in procuring the public business of both governments. On my doubting whether my father would assist me in it, Sir William said he would give me a letter to him, in which he would state the advantages, and he

6. The hand typesetter picked his capitals from boxes in the "upper case," his small letters from those in the "lower case."
7. Sir William Keith (1680–1749),

governor of Pennsylvania (1717–1726), sided with the Assembly and the people; he opposed the Proprietors, who caused his dismissal.

did not doubt of prevailing with him. So it was concluded I should return to Boston in the first vessel, with the Governor's letter recommending me to my father. In the mean time the intention was to be kept secret, and I went on working with Keimer as usual, the Governor sending for me now and then to dine with him—a very great honor I thought it—and conversing with me in the most affable, familiar, and friendly manner imaginable.[8] * * *

We proceeded to Philadelphia. I received on the way Vernon's money, without which we could hardly have finished our journey. Collins wished to be employed in some counting-house; but, whether they discovered his dramming by his breath, or by his behavior, though he had some recommendations, he met with no success in any application, and continued lodging and boarding at the same house with me, and at my expense. Knowing I had that money of Vernon's, he was continually borrowing of me, still promising repayment as soon as he should be in business. At length he had got so much of it that I was distressed to think what I should do in case of being called on to remit it. * * *

The breaking into this money of Vernon's was one of the first great errata of my life; and this affair showed that my father was not much out in his judgment when he supposed me too young to manage business of importance. But Sir William, on reading his letter, said he was too prudent. There was great difference in persons; and discretion did not always accompany years, nor was youth always without it. "And since he will not set you up," says he, "I will do it myself. Give me an inventory of the things necessary to be had from England, and I will send for them. You shall repay me when you are able; I am resolved to have a good printer here, and I am sure you must succeed." This was spoken with such an appearance of cordiality, that I had not the least doubt of his meaning what he said. * * *

I presented him an inventory of a little printing-house, amounting by my computation to about one hundred pounds sterling. He liked it, but asked me if my being on the spot in England to choose the types and see that everything was good of the kind might not be of some advantage. "Then," says he, "when there, you may make acquaintances, and establish correspondences in the bookselling and stationery way." I agreed that this might be advantageous. "Then," says he, "get yourself ready to go with *Annis*," which was the annual ship[9] and the only one at that time usually

---

8. In April, 1724, Franklin returned to Boston, but could not win financial backing from his father, who thought him to be too young for the responsibility. His Boston friend John Collins, however, was impressed by his account and decided to move to Philadelphia.
9. Yale footnote: Capt. Thomas Annis, master of the "Annual Ship."

passing between London and Philadelphia. But it would be some months before *Annis* sailed, so I continued working with Keimer, fretting about the money Collins had got from me, and in daily apprehensions of being called upon by Vernon, which, however, did not happen for some years after. * * *

My chief acquaintances at this time were Charles Osborne, Joseph Watson, and James Ralph,[1] all lovers of reading. The first two were clerks to an eminent scrivener or conveyancer in the town, Charles Brogden;[2] the other was clerk to a merchant. Watson was a pious, sensible young man, of great integrity; the others rather more lax in their principles of religion, particularly Ralph, who, as well as Collins, had been unsettled by me, for which they both made me suffer. * * *

Ralph, though married, and having one child, had determined to accompany me in this voyage. It was thought he intended to establish a correspondence and obtain goods to sell on commission; but I found afterwards, that through some discontent with his wife's relations he purposed to leave her on their hands and never return again. Having taken leave of my friends, and interchanged some promises with Miss Read, I left Philadelphia in the ship, which anchored at Newcastle.[3] The Governor was there; but when I went to his lodging, the secretary came to me from him with the civillest message in the world, that he could not then see me, being engaged in business of the utmost importance, but should send the letters to me on board, wished me heartily a good voyage and a speedy return, etc. I returned on board a little puzzled, but still not doubting.

Mr. Andrew Hamilton,[4] a famous lawyer in Philadelphia, had taken passage in the same ship for himself and son, and with Mr. Denham, a Quaker merchant, and Messrs. Onion and Russel, masters of an iron work in Maryland, had engaged the great cabin; so that Ralph and I were forced to take up with a berth in the steerage and, none on board knowing us, were considered as ordinary persons. But Mr. Hamilton and his son (it was James, since Governor), returned from Newcastle to Philadelphia, the father being recalled by a great fee to plead for a seized ship; and, just

---

1. Ralph (died 1762) accompanied Franklin to England. He became known as a Neoclassical poet and as collaborator with Henry Fielding on the *Champion*, a periodical, and was author of an authoritative *History of England*.
2. Yale prints "Charles Brogden" but footnotes it as "Charles Brockden."
3. Now New Castle, Delaware; originally a Swedish settlement, and an active port of entry. Delaware and Pennsylvania, both part of the grant to William Penn, remained long under the same governor.
4. Andrew Hamilton (died 1741), whose defense of John Peter Zenger, publisher of the New York *Weekly Journal*, established the principle of political freedom for the colonial press. His son James, four times governor of Pennsylvania before 1773, was a strongly conservative Tory.

before we sailed, Colonel French coming on board and showing me great respect, I was more taken notice of, and with my friend Ralph invited by the other gentlemen to come into the cabin, there being now room. Accordingly, we removed thither. * * *

When we came into the Channel, the captain kept his word with me, and gave me an opportunity of examining the bag for the Governor's letters. I found none upon which my name was put as under my care * * * and after recollecting and comparing circumstances, I began to doubt his sincerity. I found my friend Denham, and opened the whole affair to him. He let me into Keith's character; told me there was not the least probability that he had written any letters for me; that no one who knew him had the smallest dependence on him; and he laughed at the notion of the Governor's giving me a letter of credit, having, as he said, no credit to give. On my expressing some concern about what I should do, he advised me to endeavor getting some employment in the way of my business. "Among the printers here," says he, "you will improve yourself, and when you return to America, you will set up to greater advantage." * * *

Ralph and I were inseparable companions. We took lodgings together in Little Britain [5] at three shillings and sixpence a week —as much as we could then afford. He found some relations, but they were poor and unable to assist him. He now let me know his intentions of remaining in London, and that he never meant to return to Philadelphia. He had brought no money with him, the whole he could muster having been expended in paying his passage. I had fifteen pistoles; [6] so he borrowed occasionally of me to subsist while he was looking out for business. * * *

I immediately got into work at Palmer's,[7] then a famous printing-house in Bartholomew Close, and here I continued near a year. I was pretty diligent, but spent with Ralph a good deal of my earnings in going to plays and other places of amusement. We had together consumed all my pistoles, and now just rubbed on from hand to mouth. He seemed quite to forget his wife and child, and I, by degrees, my engagements with Miss Read, to whom I never wrote more than one letter, and that was to let her know I was not likely soon to return. This was another of the great errata of my life, which I should wish to correct if I were to live it over again. In fact, by our expenses, I was constantly kept unable to pay my passage.

5. In the heart of London, near St. Paul's.
6. The pistole, or quarter doubloon, a Spanish coin, was then worth eighteen shillings in English currency.
7. Samuel Palmer (died 1732) was a prominent printer. Bartholomew Close was associated with the shops and lodgings of publishers, just as the Temple housed the legal profession. Both were in the center of London.

At Palmer's I was employed in composing for the second edition of Wollaston's *Religion of Nature*.[8] Some of his reasonings not appearing to me well founded, I wrote a little metaphysical piece in which I made remarks on them. It was entitled A *Dissertation on Liberty and Necessity, Pleasure and Pain*. I inscribed it to my friend Ralph; I printed a small number. It occasioned my being more considered by Mr. Palmer as a young man of some ingenuity, though he seriously expostulated with me upon the principles of my pamphlet, which to him appeared abominable. My printing this pamphlet was another erratum. While I lodged in Little Britain, I made an acquaintance with one Wilcox, a bookseller, whose shop was at the next door. He had an immense collection of second-hand books. Circulating libraries were not then in use; but we agreed that, on certain reasonable terms, which I have now forgotten, I might take, read, and return any of his books. This I esteemed a great advantage, and I made as much use of it as I could.

My pamphlet by some means falling into the hands of one Lyons,[9] a surgeon, author of a book entitled *The Infallibility of Human Judgment*, it occasioned an acquaintance between us. He took great notice of me, called on me often to converse on those subjects, carried me to the Horns, a pale alehouse in —— Lane, Cheapside, and introduced me to Dr. Mandeville,[1] author of the *Fable of the Bees*, who had a club there, of which he was the soul, being a most facetious, entertaining companion. Lyons, too, introduced me to Dr. Pemberton,[2] at Batson's Coffeehouse, who promised to give me an opportunity, some time or other, of seeing Sir Isaac Newton, of which I was extremely desirous; but this never happened.

I had brought over a few curiosities, among which the principal was a purse made of the asbestos, which purifies by fire. Sir Hans Sloane[3] heard of it, came to see me, and invited me to his house in

8. *The Religion of Nature Delineated* (1772), by William Wollaston (1660–1724). According to Van Doren (*Benjamin Franklin*, pp. 51, 80), the book influenced his Deism. Wollaston argued that judgments of good and bad refer not only to religious revelation, but to a principle in Nature itself. Franklin's *Dissertation* * * * (1725), mentioned here, was a rebuttal, arguing that there are no natural vices or virtues—men simply respond to "necessity" on the basis of pain or pleasure. He soon abandoned this extreme materialism in favor of an eclectic Deism similar to Wollaston's represented in his *Articles of Belief and Acts of Religion*, written in 1728 as his private creed.
9. According to Van Doren, William Lyons; his book is insignificant.
1. Bernard Mandeville (1670?–1733), Dutch-born physician. His political satire, *The Fable of the Bees: or, Private Vices, Public Benefits* (1714, revision of an earlier title, 1705) created sensational controversy by arguing that all acts of "virtue" spring from some selfishness.
2. Henry Pemberton was an editor and explicator of Newton; the latter, then eighty-four, was the scientific fountain-head of the Enlightenment.
3. Sir Hans Sloane (1660–1753), eminent botanist and physician, who left many thousands of bound volumes and manuscripts as the beginning of the British Museum collection.

Bloomsbury Square, where he showed me all his curiosities, and persuaded me to let him add that to the number, for which he paid me handsomely. * * *

Thus I spent about eighteen months in London; most part of the time I worked hard at my business, and spent but little upon myself except in seeing plays and in books. My friend Ralph had kept me poor; he owed me about twenty-seven pounds, which I was now never likely to receive; a great sum out of my small earnings! I loved him, notwithstanding, for he had many amiable qualities, though I had by no means improved my fortune; but I had picked up some very ingenious acquaintance, whose conversation was of great advantage to me; and I had read considerably. * * *

My brother-in-law, Holmes, being now at Philadelphia, advised my return to my business; and Keimer tempted me, with an offer of large wages by the year, to come and take the management of his printing-house, that he might better attend his stationer's shop. I had heard a bad character of him in London from his wife and her friends, and was not fond of having any more to do with him. I tried for farther employment as a merchant's clerk; but not readily meeting with any I closed again with Keimer. * * *

I soon perceived that the intention of engaging me at wages so much higher than he had been used to give was to have these raw, cheap hands formed through me; and, as soon as I had instructed them, then they being all articled to him, he should be able to do without me. I went on, however, very cheerfully, putting his printing-house in order, which had been in great confusion, and brought his hands by degrees to mind their business and to do it better. * * *

But, however serviceable I might be, I found that my services became every day of less importance, as the other hands improved in the business; and when Keimer paid my second quarter's wages, he let me know that he felt them too heavy, and thought I should make an abatement. He grew by degrees less civil, put on more of the master, frequently found fault, was captious, and seemed ready for an outbreaking. I went on, nevertheless, with a good deal of patience, thinking that his encumbered circumstances were partly the cause. At length a trifle snapped our connection; for a great noise happening near the courthouse, I put my head out of the window to see what was the matter. Keimer, being in the street, looked up and saw me, called out to me in a loud voice and angry tone to mind my business, adding some reproachful words, that nettled me the more for their publicity, all the neighbors who were looking out on the same occasion being witnesses how I was treated. He came up immediately into the printing-house, continued the quarrel, high words passed on both sides, he gave me the quarter's warning we had stipulated, expressing a wish that he had not been obliged to so long a warning. I told him his wish was unnecessary, for I would leave him that instant; and so, taking my hat, walked out of doors, desiring Meredith, whom I saw below, to take care of some things I left, and bring them to my lodging.

Meredith came accordingly in the evening, when we talked my affair over. He had conceived a great regard for me, and was very unwilling that I should leave the house while he remained in it. He dissuaded me from returning to my native country, which I began to hint of; he reminded me that Keimer was in debt for all he possessed; that his creditors began to be uneasy; that he kept his shop miserably, sold often without profit for ready money, and often trusted without keeping accounts; that he must therefore fail, which would make a vacancy I might profit of. I objected my want of money. He then let me know that his father had a high opinion of me, and, from some discourse that had passed between them, he was sure would advance money to set us up, if I would enter into partnership with him. "My time," says he, "will be out with Keimer in the spring; by that time we may have our press and types in from London. I am sensible I am no workman; if you like it, your skill in the business shall be set against the stock I furnish, and we will share the profits equally."

The proposal was agreeable, and I consented; his father was in town and approved of it; the more as he saw I had great influence with his son, had prevailed on him to abstain long from dram-drinking, and he hoped might break him off that wretched habit entirely, when we came to be so closely connected. * * *

Before I enter upon my public appearance in business, it may be well to let you know the then state of my mind with regard to my principles and morals, that you may see how far those influenced the future events of my life. My parents had early given me religious impressions, and brought me through my childhood piously in the dissenting way. But I was scarce fifteen, when, after doubting by turns of several points, as I found them disputed in the different books I read, I began to doubt of Revelation itself. Some books against deism fell into my hands; they were said to be the substance of sermons preached at Boyle's lectures.[4] It happened that they wrought an effect on me quite contrary to what was intended by them; for the arguments of the deists, which were quoted to be refuted, appeared to me much stronger than the refutations; in short, I soon became a thorough deist. My arguments perverted

4. Robert Boyle (1627–1691), famous British pioneer physicist, discoverer of Boyle's law; endowed the Boyle Lectures for defense of Christianity.

some others, particularly Collins and Ralph; but each of them having afterwards wronged me greatly without the least compunction, and recollecting Keith's conduct towards me (who was another free thinker), and my own towards Vernon and Miss Read, which at times gave me great trouble, I began to suspect that this doctrine, though it might be true, was not very useful. My London pamphlet,[5] which had for its motto these lines of Dryden—

> "Whatever is, is right. Tho' purblind Man
> Sees but a Part of the Chain, the nearest Link,
> His Eyes not carrying to the equal Beam,
> That poises all, above." [6]

—and from the attributes of God, his infinite wisdom, goodness, and power, concluded that nothing could possibly be wrong in the world, and that vice and virtue were empty distinctions, no such things existing, appeared now not so clever a performance as I once thought it; and I doubted whether some error had not insinuated itself unperceived into my argument, so as to infect all that followed, as is common in metaphysical reasonings.

I grew convinced that *truth, sincerity* and *integrity* in dealings between man and man were of the utmost importance to the felicity of life; and I formed written resolutions (which still remain in my journal book), to practice them ever while I lived. Revelation had indeed no weight with me as such; but I entertained an opinion that, though certain actions might not be bad *because* they were forbidden by it, or good *because* it commanded them, yet probably these actions might be forbidden *because* they were bad for us, or commanded *because* they were beneficial to us in their own natures, all the circumstances of things considered. And this persuasion, with the kind hand of Providence or some guardian angel, or accidental favorable circumstances and situations, or all together, preserved me through this dangerous time of youth, and the hazardous situations I was sometimes in among strangers, remote from the eye and advice of my father, without any *wilful* gross immorality or injustice, that might have been expected from my want of religion. I say *wilful*, because the instances I have mentioned had something of *necessity* in them, from my youth, inexperience, and the knavery of others. I had therefore a tolerable character to begin the world with; I valued it properly, and determined to preserve it.

We had not been long returned to Philadelphia before the new types arrived from London. We settled with Keimer, and left him

---

5. "Of Liberty and Necessity, Pleasure and Pain" (see above).
6. He apparently quotes from memory, with some slight variations. *Cf.* Dryden's *Oedipus* (London, 1679), Act III, Scene 2.

by his consent before he heard of it. We found a house to hire near the market, and took it. To lessen the rent, which was then but twenty-four pounds a year, though I have since known it to let for seventy, we took in Thomas Godfrey,[7] a glazier, and his family, who were to pay a considerable part of it to us, and we to board with them. We had scarce opened our letters and put our press in order, before George House, an acquaintance of mine, brought a countryman to us, whom he had met in the street inquiring for a printer. All our cash was now expended in the variety of particulars we had been obliged to procure, and this countryman's five shillings, being our first-fruits, and coming so seasonably, gave me more pleasure than any crown [8] I have since earned; and from the gratitude I felt towards House, has made me often more ready than perhaps I should otherwise have been to assist young beginners. * * *

I should have mentioned before that in the autumn of the preceding year, I had formed most of my ingenious acquaintance into a club of mutual improvement, which we called the Junto.[9] We met on Friday evenings. The rules that I drew up required that every member, in his turn, should produce one or more queries on any point of morals, politics, or natural philosophy, to be discussed by the company; and once in three months produce and read an essay of his own writing, on any subject he pleased. Our debates were to be under the direction of a president, and to be conducted in the sincere spirit of inquiry after truth, without fondness for dispute, or desire of victory; and, to prevent warmth, all expressions of positiveness in opinions, or direct contradiction, were after some time made contraband, and prohibited under small pecuniary penalties.

The first members were Joseph Breintnal,[1] a copier of deeds for the scriveners, a good-natured, friendly, middle-aged man, a great lover of poetry, reading all he could meet with, and writing some that was tolerable; very ingenious in many little nicknackeries, and of sensible conversation. Thomas Godfrey, a self-taught mathematician, great in his way, and afterwards inventor of what is now called Hadley's quadrant. But he knew little out of his way, and was not a pleasing companion; as, like most great mathematicians I have met with, he expected universal precision [2] in everything said, or was forever denying or distinguishing upon trifles,

7. Thomas Godfrey, later a member of the Junto mentioned in the following paragraph, a mathematician and the inventor of a quadrant long standard for navigation, was the father of Thomas Godfrey (1736–1763), who wrote the first American tragedy, *The Prince of Parthia*, produced in 1767.
8. Five shillings.

9. A faction or cabal, often secret (from the Spanish *junta*). This is the first American literary society of any duration; as Franklin shows, a number of its members achieved high distinction.
1. Yale reads: Joseph Brientnal.
2. Yale reads; expected unusual Precision.

to the disturbance of all conversation. He soon left us. Nicholas Scull, a surveyor, afterwards surveyor-general, who loved books, and sometimes made a few verses. William Parsons, bred a shoemaker, but loving reading, had acquired a considerable share of mathematics, which he first studied with a view to astrology, that he afterwards laughed at. He also became surveyor-general. William Maugridge, a joiner,[3] a most exquisite mechanic, and a solid, sensible man. Hugh Meredith, Stephen Potts, and George Webb I have characterized before. Robert Grace, a young gentleman of some fortune, generous, lively, and witty; a lover of punning and of his friends. And William Coleman, then a merchant's clerk, about my age, who had the coolest, clearest head, the best heart, and the exactest morals of almost any man I ever met with. He became afterwards a merchant of great note, and one of our provincial judges. Our friendship continued without interruption to his death, upwards of forty years. And the club continued almost as long, and was the best school of philosophy and politics[4] that then existed in the province; for our queries, which were read the week preceding their discussion, put us on reading with attention upon the several subjects, that we might speak more to the purpose, and here, too, we acquired better habits of conversation, everything being studied in our rules which might prevent our disgusting each other. From hence the long continuance of the club, which I shall have frequent occasion to speak farther of hereafter. * * *

George Webb, who had found a female friend that lent him wherewith to purchase his time of Keimer, now came to offer himself as a journeyman to us. We could not then employ him; but I foolishly let him know, as a secret, that I soon intended to begin a newspaper, and might then have work for him. My hopes of success, as I told him, were founded on this, that the then only newspaper,[5] printed by Bradford, was a paltry thing, wretchedly managed, no way entertaining, and yet was profitable to him; I therefore thought a good paper could scarcely fail of good encouragement. I requested Webb not to mention it; but he told it to Keimer, who immediately, to be beforehand with me, published proposals for printing one himself,[6] on which Webb was to be employed. I resented this; and to counteract them, as I could not yet begin our

3. Cabinetmaker.
4. Yale reads: school of Philosophy, Morals and Politics.
5. *American Weekly Mercury* (1719–1746). As Franklin explains, six of his "Busy Body Papers" in the *Mercury* (1729) "burlesqued and ridiculed" Keimer's new *Gazette* until Franklin was able to buy it himself.
6. Samuel Keimer published the first number of *The Universal Instructor in All Arts and Sciences and Pennsylvania Gazette* on December 24, 1728. Franklin bought him out "for a trifle," and assumed its publication as *The Pennsylvania Gazette*, dated September 25–October 2, 1729. It made him a fortune. In 1766 he relinquished it to David Hall, his partner; it continued publication until 1815.

paper, I wrote several pieces of entertainment for Bradford's paper, under the title of the Busy Body, which Breintnal [7] continued some months. By this means the attention of the public was fixed on that paper, and Keimer's proposals, which we burlesqued and ridiculed, were disregarded. He began his paper, however, and after carrying it on three quarters of a year, with at most only ninety subscribers, he offered it me for a trifle; and I, having been ready some time to go on with it, took it in hand directly; and it proved in a few years extremely profitable to me. * * *

About this time [8] there was a cry among the people for more paper money, only fifteen thousand pounds being extant in the province, and that soon to be sunk. The wealthy inhabitants opposed any addition, being against all paper currency, from an apprehension that it would depreciate, as it had done in New England, to the prejudice of all creditors. We had discussed this point in our Junto, where I was on the side of an addition, being persuaded that the first small sum struck in 1723 had done much good by increasing the trade, employment, and number of inhabitants in the province, since I now saw all the old houses inhabited, and many new ones building: whereas I remembered well, that when I first walked about the streets of Philadelphia, eating my roll, I saw most of the houses in Walnut Street, between Second and Front streets, with bills on their doors to be let; and many likewise in Chestnut Street and other streets, which made me then think the inhabitants of the city were deserting it one after another.

Our debates possessed me so fully of the subject, that I wrote and printed an anonymous pamphlet [9] on it, entitled *The Nature and Necessity of a Paper Currency*. It was well received by the common people in general; but the rich men disliked it, for it increased and strengthened the clamor for more money; and they happening to have no writers among them that were able to answer it, their opposition slackened, and the point was carried by a majority in the House. My friends there, who conceived I had been of some service, thought fit to reward me by employing me in printing the money, a very profitable job and a great help to me.[1] This was another advantage gained by my being able to write.

The utility of this currency became by time and experience so evident as never afterwards to be much disputed; so that it grew soon to fifty-five thousand pounds, and in 1739 to eighty thousand pounds, since which it arose during war to upwards of three hundred and fifty thousand pounds—trade, building, and inhabitants all the while increasing—though I now think there are limits beyond which the quantity may be hurtful.

7. Yale reads: Brientnal.
8. The winter of 1728–1729.
9. Dated April 3, 1729.

1. Franklin had bought out his partner, Hugh Meredith, in July, 1730, having borrowed money for the transaction.

I soon after obtained through my friend Hamilton the printing of the Newcastle [2] paper money, another profitable job as I then thought it, small things appearing great to those in small circumstances; and these, to me, were really great advantages, as they were great encouragements. He procured for me, also, the printing of the laws and votes of that government, which continued in my hands as long as I followed the business. * * *

I began now gradually to pay off the debt I was under for the printing-house. In order to secure my credit and character as a tradesman, I took care not only to be in *reality* industrious and frugal, but to avoid all *appearances* of the contrary. I dressed plainly; I was seen at no places of idle diversion. I never went out afishing or shooting; a book, indeed, sometimes debauched me from my work, but that was seldom, snug, and gave no scandal; and, to show that I was not above my business, I sometimes brought home the paper I purchased at the stores through the streets on a wheelbarrow. Thus being esteemed an industrious, thriving young man, and paying duly for what I bought, the merchants who imported stationery solicited my custom; others proposed supplying me with books; I went on swimmingly. In the meantime, Keimer's credit and business declining daily, he was at last forced to sell his printing-house to satisfy his creditors.[3] He went to Barbados, and there lived some years in very poor circumstances. * * *

There remained now no competitor with me at Philadelphia but the old one, Bradford, who was rich and easy, did a little printing now and then by straggling hands, but was not very anxious about it. However, as he kept the post-office, it was imagined he had better opportunities of obtaining news; his paper was thought a better distributer of advertisements than mine, and therefore had many more, which was a profitable thing to him, and a disadvantage to me; for, though I did indeed receive and send papers by the post, yet the public opinion was otherwise, for what I did send was by bribing the riders, who took them privately, Bradford being unkind enough to forbid it, which occasioned some resentment on my part; and I thought so meanly of him for it, that when I afterward came into his situation [4] I took care never to imitate it. * * *

And now I set on foot my first project of a public nature, that for a subscription library. I drew up the proposals, got them put into form by our great scrivener, Brockden, and, by the help of my friends in the Junto, procured fifty subscribers of forty shillings

---

2. *I.e.*, for Delaware.
3. In 1729, according to Van Doren, Keimer's apprentice, David Harry, took over his print shop, but he, too, failed in a few months.

4. Franklin became Deputy Postmaster-General for all the colonies in 1753. He required a fee for the carriage of newspapers, and made the service available to all publishers.

each to begin with, and ten shillings a year for fifty years, the term our company was to continue.[5] We afterwards obtained a charter, the company being increased to one hundred. This was the mother of all the North American subscription libraries, now so numerous. It is become a great thing itself, and continually increasing. These libraries have improved the general conversation of the Americans, made the common tradesmen and farmers as intelligent as most gentlemen from other countries, and perhaps have contributed in some degree to the stand so generally made throughout the colonies in defence of their privileges.[6] * * *

This library afforded me the means of improvement by constant study, for which I set apart an hour or two each day, and thus repaired in some degree the loss of the learned education my father once intended for me. Reading was the only amusement I allowed myself. I spent no time in taverns, games, or frolics of any kind; and my industry in my business continued as indefatigable as it was necessary. I was indebted for my printing-house; I had a young family coming on to be educated, and I had to contend with, for business, two printers who were established in the place before me. My circumstances, however, grew daily easier. My original habits of frugality continuing, and my father having, among his instructions to me when a boy, frequently repeated a proverb of Solomon,[7] "Seest thou a man diligent in his calling, he shall stand before kings, he shall not stand before mean men," I from thence considered industry as a means of obtaining wealth and distinction, which encouraged me, though I did not think that I should ever literally *stand before kings*, which, however, has since happened; for I have stood before *five*, and even had the honor of sitting down with one—the King of Denmark—to dinner. * * *

It was about this time I conceived the bold and arduous project of arriving at moral perfection. I wished to live without committing any fault any time; I would conquer all that either natural inclination, custom, or company might lead me into. As I knew, or thought I knew, what was right and wrong, I did not see why I might not always do the one and avoid the other. But I soon found I had undertaken a task of more difficulty than I had imagined. While my care was employed in guarding against one fault, I was often surprised by another; habit took the advantage of inattention; inclination was sometimes too strong for reason. I

5. Founded in 1731, the Library Company of Philadelphia is an important collection of rare books, especially Americana.
6. The first manuscript, dated 1771, ends here. It is followed by a brief correspondence, dated 1783, in which friends urge him to complete his autobiography. The third section, which is given in part below, is headed "Continuation of the Account of my Life, begun at Passy, near Paris, 1784."
7. Proverbs xxii: 29.

concluded at length, that the mere speculative conviction that it was our interest to be completely virtuous was not sufficient to prevent our slipping; and that the contrary habits must be broken, and good ones acquired and established, before we can have any dependence on a steady, uniform rectitude of conduct. For this purpose I therefore contrived the following method.

In the various enumerations of the moral virtues I had met with in my reading, I found the catalogue more or less numerous, as different writers included more or fewer ideas under the same name. Temperance, for example, was by some confined to eating and drinking, while by others it was extended to mean the moderating every other pleasure, appetite, inclination, or passion, bodily or mental, even to our avarice and ambition. I proposed to myself, for the sake of clearness, to use rather more names, with fewer ideas annexed to each, than a few names with more ideas; and I included under thirteen names of virtues all that at that time occurred to me as necessary or desirable, and annexed to each a short precept, which fully expressed the extent I gave to its meaning.

These names of virtues, with their precepts, were:

1. TEMPERANCE. Eat not to dullness; drink not to elevation.

2. SILENCE. Speak not but what may benefit others or yourself; avoid trifling conversation.

3. ORDER. Let all your things have their places; let each part of your business have its time.

4. RESOLUTION. Resolve to perform what you ought; perform without fail what you resolve.

5. FRUGALITY. Make no expense but to do good to others or yourself; *i.e.*, waste nothing.

6. INDUSTRY. Lose no time; be always employed in something useful; cut off all unnecessary actions.

7. SINCERITY. Use no hurtful deceit; think innocently and justly, and, if you speak, speak accordingly.

8. JUSTICE. Wrong none by doing injuries, or omitting the benefits that are your duty.

9. MODERATION. Avoid extremes; forbear resenting injuries so much as you think they deserve.

10. CLEANLINESS. Tolerate no uncleanliness in body, clothes, or habitation.

11. TRANQUILITY. Be not disturbed at trifles, or at accidents common or unavoidable.

12. CHASTITY. Rarely use venery but for health or offspring, never to dullness, weakness, or the injury of your own or another's peace or reputation.

13. HUMILITY. Imitate Jesus and Socrates.

My intention being to acquire the *habitude* of all these virtues, I judged it would be well not to distract my attention by attempting the whole at once, but to fix it on one of them at a time; and, when I should be master of that, then to proceed to another, and so on, till I should have gone through the thirteen; and, as the previous acquisition of some might facilitate the acquisition of certain others, I arranged them with that view, as they stand above. *Temperance* first, as it tends to procure that coolness and clearness of head, which is so necessary where constant vigilance was to be kept up, and guard maintained against the unremitting attraction of ancient habits, and the force of perpetual temptations. This being acquired and established, *Silence* would be more easy; and my desire being to gain knowledge at the same time that I improved in virtue, and considering that in conversation it was obtained rather by the use of the ears than of the tongue, and therefore wishing to break a habit I was getting into of prattling, punning, and joking, which only made me acceptable to trifling company, I gave *Silence* the second place. This and the next, *Order*, I expected would allow me more time for attending to my project and my studies. *Resolution*, once become habitual, would keep me firm in my endeavors to obtain all the subsequent virtues; *Frugality* and *Industry* freeing me from my remaining debt, and producing affluence and independence, would make more easy the practice of *Sincerity and Justice*, etc., etc. Conceiving then, that, agreeably to the advice of Pythagoras [8] in his Golden Verses, daily examination would be necessary, I contrived the following method for conducting that examination. * * *

The precept of *Order* requiring that *every part of my business should have its allotted time*, one page in my little book contained the following scheme of employment for the twenty-four hours of a natural day.

THE MORNING *Question.* What good shall I do this day?	5 6 7	Rise, wash and address *Powerful Goodness!* [9] Contrive day's business, and take the resolution of the day; prosecute the present study, and breakfast.

8. Influential Greek philosopher-mathematician (*fl.* 530 B.C.), whose teachings survive only in the traditions of his disciples. Franklin refers to the Pythagorean discipline of "passionate intellectual contemplation."
9. Franklin's daily prayer, prefixed to his "tables of examinations," was as follows: "O powerful Goodness! bountiful Father! merciful Guide! Increase in me that wisdom which discovers my truest interest. Strengthen my resolutions to perform what that wisdom dictates. Accept my kind offices to Thy other children as the only return in my power for Thy continual favours to me."

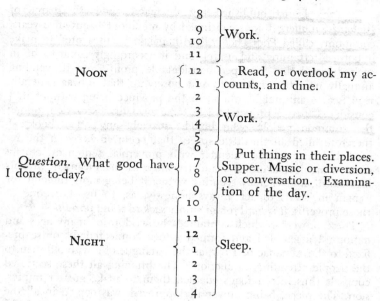

My list of virtues contained at first but twelve; but a Quaker friend having kindly informed me that I was generally thought proud; that my pride showed itself frequently in conversation; that I was not content with being in the right when discussing any point, but was overbearing, and rather insolent, of which he convinced me by mentioning several instances; I determined endeavoring to cure myself, if I could, of this vice or folly among the rest, and I added *Humility* to my list, giving an extensive meaning to the word.

I cannot boast of much success in acquiring the *reality* of this virtue, but I had a good deal with regard to the *appearance* of it. * * *

In reality, there is, perhaps, no one of our natural passions so hard to subdue as *pride*. Disguise it, struggle with it, beat it down, stifle it, mortify it as much as one pleases, it is still alive, and will every now and then peep out and show itself; you will see it, perhaps, often in the history; for, even if I could conceive that I had completely overcome it, I should probably be proud of my humility.[1] * * *

1. "Thus far written at Passy, 1784" [Franklin's note]. Then, beginning a new manuscript, Franklin wrote: "I am now about to write at home [Philadelphia], August, 1788, but cannot have the help expected from my papers, many of them being lost in the war. * * *" The selections following describe some of the practical projects, from 1731 to 1753, which increased his reputation prior to his call to highest national service in the period of the Revolution.

In 1732 I first published my almanac,[2] under the name of *Richard Saunders;* it was continued by me about twenty-five years, commonly called *Poor Richard's Almanack.* I endeavored to make it both entertaining and useful, and it accordingly came to be in such demand that I reaped considerable profit from it, vending annually near ten thousand. And observing that it was generally read, scarce any neighborhood in the province being without it, I considered it as a proper vehicle for conveying instruction among the common people, who bought scarcely any other books; I therefore filled all the little spaces that occurred between the remarkable days in the calendar with proverbial sentences, chiefly such as inculcated industry and frugality, as the means of procuring wealth, and thereby securing virtue; it being more difficult for a man in want, to act always honestly, as, to use here one of those proverbs, *it is hard for an empty sack to stand upright.*

These proverbs, which contained the wisdom of many ages and nations, I assembled and formed into a connected discourse prefixed to the Almanac of 1757, as the harangue of a wise old man to the people attending an auction.[3] The bringing all these scattered counsels thus into a focus enabled them to make greater impression. The piece, being universally approved, was copied in all the newspapers of the continent; reprinted in Britain on a broadside, to be stuck up in houses; two translations were made of it in French, and great numbers bought by the clergy and gentry, to distribute gratis among their poor parishioners and tenants. In Pennsylvania, as it discouraged useless expense in foreign superfluities, some thought it had its share of influence in producing that growing plenty of money which was observable for several years after its publication.

I considered my newspaper, also, as another means of communicating instruction, and in that view frequently reprinted in it extracts from the *Spectator,* and other moral writers; and sometimes published little pieces of my own, which had been first composed for reading in our Junto. Of these are a Socratic dialogue, tending to prove that, whatever might be his parts and abilities, a vicious man could not properly be called a man of sense; and a discourse on self-denial showing that virtue was not secure till its practice became a habitude, and was free from the opposition of contrary inclinations. These may be found in the papers about the beginning of 1735. * * *

In 1739 arrived among us from Ireland the Reverend Mr. White-

2. *Poor Richard's Almanack.* He published it from 1733 to 1758, then sold it. See the selections in this volume, immediately following the *Autobiography.*

3. "The Way to Wealth"; included in this volume.

field,[4] who had made himself remarkable there as an itinerant preacher. He was at first permitted to preach in some of our churches; but the clergy taking a dislike to him soon refused him their pulpits, and he was obliged to preach in the fields. The multitudes of all sects and denominations that attended his sermons were enormous, and it was matter of speculation to me, who was one of the number, to observe the extraordinary influence of his oratory on his hearers, and how much they admired and respected him, notwithstanding his common abuse of them, by assuring them they were naturally *half beasts and half devils.* It was wonderful to see the change soon made in the manners of our inhabitants. From being thoughtless or indifferent about religion, it seemed as if all the world were growing religious, so that one could not walk through the town in an evening without hearing psalms sung in different families of every street.

And it being found inconvenient to assemble in the open air, subject to its inclemencies, the building of a house to meet in was no sooner proposed, and persons appointed to receive contributions, but sufficient sums were soon received to procure the ground and erect the building, which was one hundred feet long and seventy broad, about the size of Westminster Hall; and the work was carried on with such spirit as to be finished in a much shorter time than could have been expected.[5] Both house and ground were vested in trustees, expressly for the use of any preacher of any religious persuasion who might desire to say something to the people at Philadelphia; the design in building not being to accommodate any particular sect, but the inhabitants in general; so that even if the Mufti of Constantinople were to send a missionary to preach Mohammedanism to us, he would find a pulpit at his service. * * *

I had, on the whole, abundant reason to be satisfied with my being established in Pennsylvania. There were, however, two things that I regretted, there being no provision for defense, nor for a complete education of youth; no militia, nor any college. I therefore, in 1743, drew up a proposal for establishing an academy; and at that time, thinking the Reverend Mr. Peters,[6] who was out of employ, a fit person to superintend such an institution, I

---

4. George Whitefield (1714–1770), a British evangelist, was associated with the founding of the Methodist denomination, but split from the Wesleys on theological grounds, to become the leader of the Calvinistic Methodists. In his early American pilgrimages (1738–41) he became an evangelist of the "Great Awakening" (*cf.* the headnote to Jonathan Edwards).

5. Then called the New Building, it was used before completion (1739) for Whitefield's audiences, and later housed the Charity School, Academy, and College of Philadelphia (the University of Pennsylvania).

6. Richard Peters had been Rector of Christ's Church, Philadelphia, and was expecting appointment as Secretary of the colony.

communicated the project to him; but he, having more profitable views in the service of the proprietaries, which succeeded, declined the undertaking; and, not knowing another at that time suitable for such a trust, I let the scheme lie a while dormant. I succeeded better the next year, 1744, in proposing and establishing a Philosophical Society.[7] The paper I wrote for that purpose will be found among my writings, when collected. * * *

Peace being concluded, and the association business therefore at an end, I turned my thoughts again to the affair of establishing an academy. The first step I took was to associate in the design a number of active friends, of whom the Junto furnished a good part; the next was to write and publish a pamphlet, entitled *Proposals Relating to the Education of Youth in Pennsylvania.*[8] This I distributed among the principal inhabitants gratis; and as soon as I could suppose their minds a little prepared by the perusal of it, I set on foot a subscription for opening and supporting an academy; it was to be paid in quotas yearly for five years; by so dividing it, I judged the subscription might be larger, and I believe it was so, amounting to no less, if I remember right, than five thousand pounds.

In the introduction to these proposals, I stated their publication, not as an act of mine, but of some *public-spirited gentleman,* avoiding as much as I could, according to my usual rule, the presenting myself to the public as the author of any scheme for their benefit.

The subscribers, to carry the project into immediate execution, chose out of their number twenty-four trustees, and appointed Mr. Francis, then attorney-general, and myself to draw up constitutions for the government of the academy; which being done and signed, a house was hired, masters engaged, and the schools opened, I think, in the same year, 1749.

The scholars increasing fast, the house was soon found too small, and we were looking out for a piece of ground, properly situated, with intention to build, when Providence threw into our way a large house ready built, which, with a few alterations, might well serve our purpose. This was the building before mentioned, erected by the hearers of Mr. Whitefield, and was obtained for us in the following manner.

It is to be noted that the contributions to this building being

---

7. The American Philosophical Society (1743–), first learned scientific society in North America. Its first three presidents were Franklin, David Rittenhouse, and Thomas Jefferson.
8. This pamphlet, which appeared in 1749, made the proposal, then radical, for college education on a secular basis, free from ecclesiastical concerns and denominational bias. It carried over the spirit of the "Proposal for Promoting Useful Knowledge" (1743) which he mentions in the preceding paragraph.

made by people of different sects, care was taken in the nomination of trustees, in whom the building and ground was to be vested, that a predominancy should not be given to any sect, lest in time that predominancy might be a means of appropriating the whole to the use of such sect, contrary to the original intention. It was therefore that one of each sect was appointed, viz., one Church-of-England man, one Presbyterian, one Baptist, one Moravian, etc.; those, in case of vacancy by death were to fill it by election from among the contributors. The Moravian happened not to please his colleagues, and on his death they resolved to have no other of that sect. The difficulty then was, how to avoid having two of some other sect, by means of the new choice.

Several persons were named, and for that reason not agreed to. At length one mentioned me, with the observation that I was merely an honest man, and of no sect at all, which prevailed with them to choose me. The enthusiasm which existed when the house was built had long since abated, and its trustees had not been able to procure fresh contributions for paying the ground-rent and discharging some other debts the building had occasioned, which embarrassed them greatly. Being now a member of both sets of trustees, that for the building and that for the academy, I had a good opportunity of negotiating with both, and brought them finally to an agreement, by which the trustees for the building were to cede it to those of the academy, the latter undertaking to discharge the debt, to keep forever open in the building a large hall for occasional preachers, according to the original intention, and maintain a free school for the instruction of poor children. Writings were accordingly drawn, and on paying the debts the trustees of the academy were put in possession of the premises; and by dividing the great and lofty hall into stories, and different rooms above and below for the several schools, and purchasing some additional ground, the whole was soon made fit for our purpose, and the scholars removed into the building. The care and trouble of agreeing with the workmen, purchasing materials, and superintending the work, fell upon me; and I went through it the more cheerfully, as it did not then interfere with my private business, having the year before taken a very able, industrious, and honest partner, Mr. David Hall, with whose character I was well acquainted, as he had worked for me four years. He took off my hands all care of the printing-office, paying me punctually my share of the profits. This partnership continued eighteen years, successfully for us both.

The trustees of the academy, after a while, were incorporated by a charter from the governor; their funds were increased by contributions in Britain and grants of land from the proprietaries, to which the Assembly has since made considerable addition; and thus was established the present University of Philadelphia.[9] I have been continued one of its trustees from the beginning, now near forty years, and have had the very great pleasure of seeing a number of the youth who have received their education in it distinguished by their improved abilities, serviceable in public stations, and ornaments to their country. * * *

Before I proceed in relating the part I had in public affairs * * * , it may not be amiss here to give some account of the rise and progress of my philosophical reputation.

In 1746, being at Boston, I met there with a Dr. Spence, who was lately arrived from Scotland and showed me some electric experiments. They were imperfectly performed, as he was not very expert; but, being on a subject quite new to me, they equally surprised and pleased me. Soon after my return to Philadelphia, our library company received from Mr. P. Collinson,[1] Fellow of the Royal Society of London, a present of a glass tube, with some account of the use of it in making such experiments. I eagerly seized the opportunity of repeating what I had seen at Boston; and by much practice, acquired great readiness in performing those, also, which we had an account of from England, adding a number of new ones. I say much practice, for my house was continually full for some time with people who came to see these new wonders. * * *

Obliged as we were to Mr. Collinson for his present of the tube, etc., I thought it right he should be informed of our success in using it, and wrote him several letters containing accounts of our experiments. He got them read in the Royal Society, where they were not at first thought worth so much notice as to be printed in their *Transactions*. One paper, which I wrote for Mr. Kinnersley on the sameness of lightning with electricity, I sent to Dr. Mitchel,[2] an acquaintance of mine, and one of the members also of that society, who wrote me word that it had been read, but was laughed at by the connoisseurs. The papers, however, being shown to Dr. Fothergill,[3] he thought them of too much value to be stifled, and

9. Now the University of Pennsylvania. The University dates from 1765, when the medical school was added to the College of Philadelphia. The latter, chartered 1755, absorbed the Academy, chartered 1749, and the Charity School, whose charter, granted to the trustees of the New Building, is dated 1740. Instruction was continued in the Charity School and the Academy for more than a century under these trusts, which sprang chiefly from Franklin's efforts.
1. Peter Collinson (1694–1768), Quaker merchant, transmitted in London the reports of Franklin's electrical experiments. One of Franklin's letters to Collinson is reprinted in this volume.
2. Dr. John Mitchell of Virginia and London, one of Franklin's earliest scientific correspondents. Years later, in negotiating the peace treaty with England (1783), Franklin used a map of the southern colonies made by Mitchell.
3. John Fothergill (1712–1780), London Quaker and physician, developed internationally famous botanical gardens. A longtime friend and correspondent, he aided Franklin in drafting the scheme of reconciliation rejected by Parliament (1774).

advised the printing of them. Mr. Collinson then gave them to Cave for publication in his *Gentleman's Magazine*,[4] but he chose to print them separately in a pamphlet, and Dr. Fothergill wrote the preface. Cave, it seems, judged rightly for his profit, for by the additions that arrived afterward they swelled to a quarto volume, which has had five editions, and cost him nothing for copy-money.

* * *

1771, 1783, 1784, 1788

From Poor Richard's Almanack [5]

Preface to Poor Richard, 1733

Courteous Reader,

I might in this place attempt to gain thy Favour, by declaring that I write Almanacks with no other View than that of the publick Good; but in this I should not be sincere; and Men are nowadays too wise to be deceiv'd by Pretences how specious soever. The plain Truth of the Matter is, I am excessive poor, and my Wife, good Woman, is, I tell her, excessive proud; she cannot bear, she says, to sit spinning in her Shift of Tow, while I do nothing but gaze at the Stars; and has threatned more than once to burn all my Books and Rattling-Traps (as she calls my Instruments) if I do not make some profitable Use of them for the Good of my Family. The Printer has offer'd me some considerable share of the Profits, and I have thus begun to comply with my Dame's Desire.

Indeed this Motive would have had Force enough to have made me publish an Almanack many Years since, had it not been overpowered by my Regard for my good Friend and Fellow Student Mr. *Titan Leeds*,[6] whose Interest I was extremely unwilling to hurt: But this Obstacle (I am far from speaking it with Pleasure) is

4. A famous periodical (1731–1754) published in London by Edward Cave, prominent printer and journalist.
5. Franklin published his almanac annually from 1733 to 1758, then sold it, but it continued publication until 1796. Besides the usual astronomical and agricultural data of an almanac, Franklin inserted useful information, literary selections, and especially the editorial wisdom of the fictional Richard Saunders, who, with his wife, Bridget, became favorite literary characters. Poor Richard's proverbs, often old, but always newly minted for Americans, are still current homely wisdom. *The Way to Wealth* was a collection of the most utilitarian, hence the best remembered, of these maxims, prepared for Poor Richard's preface of 1758. This is preceded in the present selections by Poor Richard's first preface, that of 1733. See also Franklin's account in the *Autobiography*. The selections from the *Almanack* follow Franklin's original text without typographical alterations.
6. Titan Leeds (1699–1738), Franklin's rival in Philadelphia, publisher of *The American Almanack*. Inspired by Swift's famous Bickerstaff hoax, Franklin immortalized Leeds by the mock prediction, from astronomical "evidence," of his imminent death. Leeds' denial only served to publicize the controversy, in which Poor Richard was still persisting when his victim died, five years later.

soon to be removed, since inexorable Death, who was never known to respect Merit, has already prepared the mortal Dart, the fatal Sister has already extended her destroying Shears, and that ingenious Man must soon be taken from us. He dies, by my Calculation made at his Request on Oct. 17, 1733. 3 h. 29 m. P.M. at the very instant of the ♂ of ☉ and ☿ : By his own Calculation he will survive till the 26th of the same Month. This small Difference between us we have disputed whenever we have met these 9 Years past; but at length he is inclinable to agree with my Judgment: Which of us is most exact, a little Time will now determine. As therefore these Provinces may not longer expect to see any of his Performances after this Year, I think myself free to take up the Task, and request a share of the publick Encouragement; which I am the more apt to hope for on this Account, that the Buyer of my Almanack may consider himself, not only as purchasing an useful Utensil, but as performing an Act of Charity, to his poor *Friend and Servant*

R. Saunders.

The Way to Wealth: Preface to Poor Richard, 1758 [7]

Courteous Reader,

I have heard that nothing gives an Author so great Pleasure, as to find his Works respectfully quoted by other learned Authors. This Pleasure I have seldom enjoyed; for tho' I have been, if I may say it without Vanity, an *eminent Author* of Almanacks annually now a full Quarter of a Century, my Brother Authors in the same Way, for what Reason I know not, have ever been very sparing in their Applauses; and no other Author has taken the least Notice of me, so that did not my Writings produce me some *solid Pudding*, the great Deficiency of *Praise* would have quite discouraged me.

I concluded at length, that the People were the best Judges of my Merit; for they buy my Works; and besides, in my Rambles, where I am not personally known, I have frequently heard one or other of my Adages repeated, with, *as poor Richard says*, at the End on't; this gave me some Satisfaction, as it showed not only that my Instructions were regarded, but discovered likewise some Respect for my Authority; and I own, that to encourage the Prac-

---

7. In 1757, on a voyage to England to represent the grievances of Pennsylvania against the Crown and the Proprietors, Franklin wrote the preface for his almanac of 1758. He imagined an old man, Father Abraham, addressing an auction, in a speech drawn almost entirely from Poor Richard's maxims on virtue and economy over the past twenty-five years. The result was an American classic of prudential virtue. In 1759 it was separately published as *Father Abraham's Speech*. It has been republished many times. It omits Poor Richard's many worldly and even sophisticated epigrams, but it remains a compendium of the homely practicality of the common American folk. It has been here printed in its original spelling and punctuation.

tice of remembering and repeating those wise Sentences, I have sometimes *quoted* myself with great Gravity.

Judge then how much I must have been gratified by an Incident I am going to relate to you. I stopt my Horse lately where a great Number of People were collected at a Vendue of Merchant Goods. The Hour of Sale not being come, they were conversing on the Badness of the Times, and one of the Company call'd to a plain clean old Man, with white Locks, *Pray, Father* Abraham, *what think you of the Times? Won't these heavy Taxes quite ruin the Country? How shall we ever be able to pay them? What would you advise us to?*—Father *Abraham* stood up, and reply'd, If you'd have my Advice, I'll give it you in short, for a *Word to the Wise is enough*, and *many Words won't fill a Bushel*, as *Poor Richard* says. They join'd in desiring him to speak his Mind, and gathering round him, he proceeded as follows;

"Friends, says he, and Neighbours, the Taxes are indeed very heavy, and if those laid on by the Government were the only Ones we had to pay, we might more easily discharge them; but we have many others, and much more grievous to some of us. We are taxed twice as much by our *Idleness*, three times as much by our *Pride*, and four times as much by our *Folly*, and from these Taxes the Commissioners cannot ease or deliver us by allowing an Abatement. However let us hearken to good Advice, and something may be done for us; *God helps them that help themselves*, as *Poor Richard* says, in his Almanack of 1733.

It would be thought a hard Government that should tax its People one tenth Part of their *Time*, to be employed in its Service. But *Idleness* taxes many of us much more, if we reckon all that is spent in absolute *Sloth*, or doing of nothing, with that which is spent in idle Employments or Amusements, that amount to nothing. *Sloth*, by bringing on Diseases, absolutely shortens Life. *Sloth, like Rust, consumes faster than Labour wears, while the used Key is always bright*, as *Poor Richard* says. But *dost thou love Life, then do not squander Time, for that's the Stuff Life is made of*, as *Poor Richard* says.—How much more than is necessary do we spend in Sleep! forgetting that *The sleeping Fox catches no Poultry*, and that *there will be sleeping enough in the Grave*, as *Poor Richard* says. If Time be of all Things the most precious, *wasting Time* must be, as *Poor Richard* says, *the greatest Prodigality*, since, as he elsewhere tells us, *Lost Time is never found again*; and what we call *Time-enough, always proves little enough*: Let us then up and be doing, and doing to the Purpose; so by Diligence shall we do more with less Perplexity. *Sloth makes all Things difficult, but Industry all easy*, as *Poor Richard* says; and *He that riseth late, must trot all Day, and shall scarce overtake his Business at Night*. While

Laziness travels so slowly, that Poverty soon overtakes him, as we read in *Poor Richard,* who adds, *Drive thy Business, let not that drive thee;* and *Early to Bed, and early to rise, makes a Man healthy, wealthy and wise.*

So what signifies *wishing* and *hoping* for better Times. We may make these Times better if we bestir ourselves. *Industry need not wish,* as *Poor Richard* says, and *He that lives upon Hope will die fasting. There are no Gains, without Pains;* then *Help Hands, for I have no Lands,* or if I have, they are smartly taxed. And, as *Poor Richard* likewise observes, *He that hath a Trade hath an Estate,* and *He that hath a Calling, hath an Office of Profit and Honour;* but then the *Trade* must be worked at, and the *Calling* well followed, or neither the *Estate,* nor the *Office,* will enable us to pay our Taxes.—If we are industrious we shall never starve; for, as *Poor Richard* says, *At the working Man's House* Hunger *looks in, but dares not enter.* Nor will the Bailiff or the Constable enter, for *Industry pays Debts, while Despair encreaseth them,* says *Poor Richard.*—What though you have found no Treasure, nor has any rich Relation left you a Legacy, *Diligence is the Mother of Good luck,* as *Poor Richard* says, *and God gives all Things to Industry.* Then *plough deep, while Sluggards sleep, and you shall have Corn to sell and to keep,* says *Poor Dick.* Work while it is called To-day, for you know not how much you may be hindered To-morrow, which makes *Poor Richard* say, *One To-day is worth two To-morrows;* and farther, *Have you somewhat to do To-morrow, do it To-day.* If you were a Servant, would you not be ashamed that a good Master should catch you idle? Are you then your own Master, *be ashamed to catch yourself idle,* as *Poor Dick* says. When there is so much to be done for yourself, your Family, your Country, and your gracious King, be up by Peep of Day; *Let not the Sun look down and say, Inglorious here he lies.* Handle your Tools without Mittens; remember that *the Cat in Gloves catches no Mice,* as *Poor Richard* says. 'Tis true there is much to be done, and perhaps you are weak handed, but stick to it steadily, and you will see great Effects, for *constant Dropping wears away Stones,* and by *Diligence and Patience the Mouse ate in two the Cable;* and *little Strokes fell great Oaks,* as *Poor Richard* says in his Almanack, the Year I cannot just now remember.

Methinks I hear some of you say, *Must a Man afford himself no Leisure?*—I will tell thee, my Friend, what *Poor Richard* says *Employ thy Time well if thou meanest to gain Leisure;* and *since thou art not sure of a Minute, throw not away an Hour.* Leisure, is Time for doing something useful; this Leisure the diligent Man will obtain, but the lazy Man never; so that, as *Poor Richard* says, a *Life of Leisure and a Life of Laziness are two Things*. Do you imagine that Sloth will afford you more Comfort than Labour? No, for as *Poor Richard* says, *Trouble springs from Idleness, and grievous Toil from needless Ease*. *Many without Labour, would live by their* WITS *only, but they break for want of Stock*. Whereas Industry gives Comfort, and Plenty, and Respect: *Fly Pleasures, and they'll follow you*. *The diligent Spinner has a large Shift*; and *now I have a Sheep and a Cow, every Body bids me Good morrow*; all which is well said by *Poor Richard*.

But with our Industry, we must likewise be *steady, settled* and *careful*, and oversee our own Affairs *with our own Eyes*, and not trust too much to others; for, as *Poor Richard* says,

> I never saw an oft removed Tree,
> Nor yet an oft removed Family,
> That throve so well as those that settled be.

And again, *Three Removes is as bad as a Fire*; and again, *Keep thy Shop, and thy Shop will keep thee*; and again, *If you would have your Business done, go; If not, send*. And again,

> He that by the Plough would thrive,
> Himself must either hold or drive.

And again, *The Eye of a Master will do more Work than both His Hands*; and again, *Want of Care does us more Damage than Want of Knowledge*; and again, *Not to oversee Workmen, is to leave them your Purse open*. Trusting too much to others Care is the Ruin of many; for, as the *Almanack* says, *In the Affairs of this World, Men are saved, not by Faith, but by the Want of it*; but a Man's own Care is profitable; for, saith *Poor Dick*, *Learning is to the Studious, and Riches to the Careful*, as well as *Power to the Bold, and Heaven to the Virtuous*. And farther, *If you would have a faithful Servant, and one that you like, serve yourself*. And again, he adviseth to Circumspection and Care, even in the smallest Matters, because sometimes *a little Neglect may breed great Mischief*; adding, *For want of a Nail the Shoe was lost; for want of a Shoe the Horse was lost; and for want of a Horse the Rider was lost*, being overtaken and slain by the Enemy, all for want of Care about a Horse shoe Nail.

So much for Industry, my Friends, and Attention to one's own Business; but to these we must add *Frugality*, if we would make our *Industry* more certainly successful. A Man may, if he knows not how to save as he gets, *keep his Nose all his Life to the Grindstone*, and die not worth a *Groat* at last. *A fat Kitchen makes a lean Will*, as *Poor Richard* says; and,

> *Many Estates are spent in the Getting,*
> *Since Women for Tea forsook Spinning and Knitting,*
> *And Men for Punch forsook Hewing and Splitting.*

If you would be wealthy, says he, in another Almanack, *think of Saving as well as of Getting: The* Indies *have not made* Spain *rich, because her* Outgoes *are greater than her* Incomes. Away then with your expensive Follies, and you will not have so much Cause to complain of hard Times, heavy Taxes, and chargeable Families; for, as *Poor Dick* says,

> *Women and Wine, Game and Deceit,*
> *Make the Wealth small, and the Wants great.*

And farther, *What maintains one Vice, would bring up two Children.* You may think perhaps, That a *little Tea,* or a *little* Punch now and then, Diet a *little* more costly, Clothes a *little* finer, and a *little* Entertainment now and then, can be no *great* Matter; but remember what *Poor Richard* says, Many a Little *makes a Mickle;* and farther, *Beware of* little *Expences; a small Leak will sink a great Ship;* and again, *Who Dainties love, shall Beggars prove;* and moreover, *Fools make Feasts, and wise Men eat them.*

Here you are all got together at this Vendue of *Fineries* and *Knicknacks.* You call them *Goods,* but if you do not take Care, they will prove *Evils* to some of you. You expect they will be sold *cheap,* and perhaps they may for less than they cost; but if you have no Occasion for them, they must be *dear* to you. Remember what *Poor Richard* says, Buy what thou hast no Need of, and ere *long thou shalt sell thy Necessaries.* And again, *At a great Pennyworth pause a while:* He means, that perhaps the Cheapness is *apparent* only, and not *real;* or the Bargain, by straitning thee in thy Business, may do thee more Harm than Good. For in another place he says, *Many have been ruined by buying good Pennyworths.* Again, *Poor Richard* says, *'Tis foolish to lay out Money in a Purchase of Repentance;* and yet this Folly is practised every Day at Vendues, for want of minding the Almanack. *Wise Men,* as *Poor Dick* says, *learn by others Harms, Fools scarcely by their own;* but *Felix quem faciunt aliena Pericula cautum.*[8] Many a one, for the Sake of Finery on the Back, have gone with a hungry Belly, and half starved their Families; *Silks and Sattins, Scarlet and Velvets,* as *Poor Richard* says, *put out the Kitchen Fire.* These are not the *Necessaries* of Life; they can scarcely be called the *Conveniences,* and yet only because they look pretty, how many *want* to *have* them. The *artificial* Wants of Mankind thus become more numerous than the *natural;* and, as *Poor Dick* says, For one poor *Person, there are an*

8. He is fortunate who is made cautious by the misfortunes of another.

hundred indigent. By these, and other Extravagancies, the Genteel are reduced to Poverty, and forced to borrow of those whom they formerly despised, but who through *Industry* and *Frugality* have maintained their Standing; in which Case it appears plainly, that a *Ploughman on his Legs is higher than a Gentleman on his Knees*, as *Poor Richard* says. Perhaps they have had a small Estate left them which they knew not the Getting of; they think *'tis Day, and will never be Night*; that a little to be spent out of *so much*, is not worth minding; (*a Child and a Fool*, as *Poor Richard* says, *imagine* Twenty Shillings *and Twenty Years can never be spent*) but, *always taking out of, the Mealtub, and never putting in, soon comes to the Bottom*; then, as *Poor Dick* says, *When the Well's dry, they know the Worth of Water*. But this they might have known before, if they had taken his Advice; *If you would know the Value of Money, go and try to borrow some*; for, *he that goes a borrowing goes a sorrowing*; and indeed so does he that lends to such People, when he goes *to get it in again*.—*Poor Dick* farther advises, and says,

> *Fond* Pride of Dress *is sure a very Curse;*
> *E'er* Fancy *you consult, consult your Purse.*

And again, *Pride is as loud a Beggar as Want, and a great deal more saucy*. When you have bought one fine Thing you must buy ten more, that your Appearance may be all of a Piece; but *Poor Dick* says, *'Tis easier to suppress the first Desire, than to* satisfy *all that follow it*. And 'tis as truly Folly for the Poor to ape the Rich, as for the Frog to swell, in order to equal the Ox.

> *Great Estates may venture more,*
> *But little Boats should keep near Shore.*

'Tis however a Folly soon punished; for *Pride that dines on Vanity sups on Contempt*, as *Poor Richard* says. And in another Place, *Pride breakfasted with Plenty, dined with Poverty, and supped with Infamy*. And after all, of what Use is this *Pride of Appearance*, for which so much is risked, so much is suffered? It cannot promote Health, or ease Pain; it makes no Increase of Merit in the Person, it creates Envy, it hastens Misfortune.

> *What is a Butterfly? At best*
> *He's but a Caterpillar drest.*
> *The gaudy Fop's his Picture just,*

as *Poor Richard* says.

But what Madness must it to be to *run in Debt* for these Superfluities! We are offered, by the Terms of this Vendue, *Six Months Credit*; and that perhaps has induced some of us to attend it, because we cannot spare the ready Money, and hope now to be fine without it. But, ah, think what you do when you run in Debt; *You give to another, Power over your Liberty*. If you cannot pay at the Time, you will be ashamed to see your Creditor; you will be in Fear when you speak to him; you will make poor pitiful sneaking Excuses, and by Degrees come to lose your Veracity, and sink into base downright lying; for, as *Poor Richard* says, *The second Vice is Lying, the first is running in Debt*. And again, to the same Purpose, *Lying rides upon Debt's Back*. Whereas a freeborn *Englishman* ought not to be ashamed or afraid to see or speak to any Man living. But Poverty often deprives a Man of all Spirit and Virtue: *'Tis hard for an empty Bag to stand upright*, as *Poor Richard* truly says. What would you think of that Prince, or that Government, who should issue an Edict forbiding you to dress like a Gentleman or a Gentlewoman, on Pain of Imprisonment or Servitude? Would you not say, that you are free, have a Right to dress as you please, and that such an Edict would be a Breach of your Privileges, and such a Government tyrannical? And yet you are about to put yourself under that Tyranny when you run in Debt for such Dress! Your Creditor has Authority at his Pleasure to deprive you of your Liberty, by confining you in Goal [*sic*] for Life, or to sell you for a Servant, if you should not be able to pay him! When you have got your Bargain, you may, perhaps, think little of Payment; but *Creditors, Poor Richard* tells us, *have better Memories than Debtors*; and in another Place says, *Creditors are a superstitious Sect, great Observers of set Days and Times*. The Day comes round before you are aware, and the Demand is made before you are prepared to satisfy it. Or if you bear your Debt in Mind, the Term which at first seemed so long, will, as it lessens, appear extreamly short. *Time* will seem to have added Wings to Heels as well as Shoulders. *Those have a short Lent*, saith *Poor Richard, who owe Money to be paid at Easter*. Then since, as he says, *The Borrower is a Slave to the Lender, and the Debtor to the Creditor*, disdain the Chain, preserve your Freedom; and maintain your Independence: Be *industrious* and *free*; be *frugal* and *free*. At present, perhaps, you may think yourself in thriving Circumstances, and that you can bear a little Extravagance without Injury;

> *For Age and Want, save while you may;*
> *No Morning Sun lasts a whole Day,*

as *Poor Richard* says—Gain may be temporary and uncertain, but ever while you live, Expence is constant and certain; and *'tis easier to build two Chimnies than to keep one in Fuel*, as *Poor Richard* says. So *rather go to Bed supperless than rise in Debt*.

> *Get what you can, and what you get hold;*
> *'Tis the Stone that will turn all your Lead into Gold,*

as *Poor Richard* says. And when you have got the Philosopher's Stone, sure you will no longer complain of bad Times, or the Difficulty of paying Taxes.

This Doctrine, my Friends, is *Reason* and *Wisdom*; but after all, do not depend too much upon your own *Industry*, and *Frugality*, and *Prudence*, though excellent Things, for they may all be blasted without the Blessing of Heaven; and therefore ask that Blessing humbly, and be not uncharitable to those that at present seem to want it, but comfort and help them. Remember *Job* suffered, and was afterwards prosperous.

And now to conclude, *Experience keeps a dear School, but Fools will learn in no other, and scarce in that*; for it is true, *we may give Advice, but we cannot give Conduct*, as *Poor Richard* says: However, remember this, *They that won't be counselled, can't be helped*, as *Poor Richard* says: And farther, *That if you will not hear Reason, she'll surely rap your Knuckles.*"

Thus the old Gentleman ended his Harangue. The People heard it, and approved the Doctrine and immediately practised the contrary, just as if it had been a common Sermon; for the Vendue opened, and they began to buy extravagantly, notwithstanding all his Cautions, and their own Fear of Taxes.—I found the good Man had thoroughly studied my Almanacks, and digested all I had dropt on those Topicks during the Course of Five-and-twenty Years. The frequent Mention he made of me must have tired any one else, but my Vanity was wonderfully delighted with it, though I was conscious that not a tenth Part of the Wisdom was my own which he ascribed to me, but rather the *Gleanings* I had made of the Sense of all Ages and Nations. However, I resolved to be the better for the Echo of it; and though I had at first determined to buy Stuff for a new Coat, I went away resolved to wear my old One a little longer. *Reader*, if thou wilt do the same, thy Profit will be as great as mine.

I am, as ever,
Thine to serve thee,

July 7, 1757.   RICHARD SAUNDERS.

The Speech of Polly Baker [9]

The Speech of Miss Polly Baker before a Court of Judicature, at Connecticut near Boston in New England; where she was prosecuted the fifth time, for having a Bastard Child: Which influenced

9. "The Speech of Polly Baker" is one of the most famous of Franklin's comic satires. It was probably first printed in Philadelphia, but that printing remains

the Court to dispense with her Punishment, and which induced one of her Judges to marry her the next Day—by whom she had fifteen Children.

"May it please the honourable bench to indulge me in a few words: I am a poor, unhappy woman, who have no money to fee lawyers to plead for me, being hard put to it to get a living. I shall not trouble your honours with long speeches; for I have not the presumption to expect that you may, by any means, be prevailed on to deviate in your Sentence from the law, in my favour. All I humbly hope is, that your honours would charitably move the governor's goodness on my behalf, that my fine may be remitted. This is the fifth time, gentlemen, that I have been dragg'd before your court on the same account; twice I have paid heavy fines, and twice have been brought to publick punishment, for want of money to pay those fines. This may have been agreeable to the laws, and I don't dispute it; but since laws are sometimes unreasonable in themselves, and therefore repealed; and others bear too hard on the subject in particular circumstances, and therefore there is left a power somewhere to dispense with the execution of them; I take the liberty to say, that I think this law, by which I am punished, both unreasonable in itself, and particularly severe with regard to me, who have always lived an inoffensive life in the neighbourhood where I was born, and defy my enemies (if I have any) to say I ever wrong'd any man, woman, or child. Abstracted from the law, I cannot conceive (may it please your honours) what the nature of my offense is. I have brought five fine children into the world, at the risque of my life; I have maintain'd them well by my own industry, without burthening the township, and would have done it better, if it had not been for the heavy charges and fines I have paid. Can it be a crime (in the nature of things, I mean) to add to the king's subjects, in a new country, that really wants people? I own it, I should think it rather a praiseworthy than a punishable action. I have debauched no other woman's husband, nor enticed any other youth; these things I never was charg'd with; nor has any one the least cause of complaint against me, unless, perhaps, the ministers of justice, because I have had children without being married, by which they have missed a wedding fee. But can this be a fault of mine? I appeal to your honours. You are pleased to allow I don't want sense; but I must be stupefied

---

undiscovered. When he was an old man at Passy, he told Thomas Jefferson and others, in conversation, that "Polly Baker is a story of my own making," an ephemeral piece used in some periodical that he published. (*Writings of Thomas Jefferson*, 1892–1899, Vol. X, p. 121, note.) The first confirmed publication of the piece is extant in *The*

to the last degree, not to prefer the honourable state of wedlock to the condition I have lived in. I always was, and still am willing to enter into it; and doubt not my behaving well in it, having all the industry, frugality, fertility, and skill in economy appertaining to a good wife's character. I defy any one to say I ever refused an offer of that sort: on the contrary, I readily consented to the only proposal of marriage that ever was made me, which was when I was a virgin, but too easily confiding in the person's sincerity that made it, I unhappily lost my honour by trusting to his; for he got me with child, and then forsook me.

"That very person, you all know, he is now become a magistrate of this country; and I had hopes he would have appeared this day on the bench, and have endeavoured to moderate the Court in my favour; then I should have scorn'd to have mentioned it; but I must now complain of it, as unjust and unequal, that my betrayer and undoer, the first cause of all my faults and miscarriages (if they must be deemed such), should be advanced to honour and power in this government that punishes my misfortunes with stripes and infamy. I should be told, 'tis like, that were there no act of Assembly in the case, the precepts of religion are violated by my transgressions. If mine is a religious offense, leave it to religious punishments. You have already excluded me from the comforts of your church communion. Is not that sufficient? You believe I have offended heaven, and must suffer eternal fire: Will not that be sufficient? What need is there then of your additional fines and whipping? I own I do not think as you do, for, if I thought what you call a sin was really such, I could not presumptuously commit it. But, how can it be believed that heaven is angry at my having children, when to the little done by me towards it, God has been pleased to add his divine skill and admirable workmanship in the formation of their bodies, and crowned the whole by furnishing them with rational and immortal souls?

"Forgive me, gentlemen, if I talk a little extravagantly on these matters; I am no divine, but if you, gentlemen, must be making laws, do not turn natural and useful actions into crimes by your prohibitions. But take into your wise consideration the great and growing number of batchelors in the country, many of whom, from the mean fear of the expences of a family, have never sincerely and honourably courted a woman in their lives; and by their manner of living leave unproduced (which is little better than murder) hundreds of their posterity to the thousandth generation. Is not this a greater offense against the publick good than mine? Compel them, then, by law, either to marriage, or to pay double the fine of fornication every year. What must poor young women do, whom customs and nature forbid to solicit the men, and who cannot force themselves upon husbands, when the laws take no care to provide them any, and yet severely punish them if they do their duty without them; the duty of the first and great command of nature and nature's God, *encrease and multiply*; a duty, from the steady performance of which nothing has been able to deter me, but for its sake I have hazarded the loss of the publick esteem, and have frequently endured publick disgrace and punishment; and therefore ought, in my humble opinion, instead of a whipping, to have a statue erected to my memory."

1747

The Sale of the Hessians [1]

From the Count de Schaumbergh to the Baron Hohendorf, Commanding the Hessian Troops in America

ROME, February 18, 1777.

MONSIEUR LE BARON:—

On my return from Naples, I received at Rome your letter of the 27th December of last year. I have learned with unspeakable pleasure the courage our troops exhibited at Trenton,[2] and you cannot imagine my joy on being told that of the 1,950 Hessians engaged in the fight, but 345 escaped. There were just 1,605 men killed, and I cannot sufficiently commend your prudence in sending an exact list of the dead to my minister in London. This precaution was the more necessary, as the report sent to the English ministry does not give but 1,455 dead. This would make 483,450 florins instead of 643,500 which I am entitled to demand under our convention. You will comprehend the prejudice which such an error would work in my finances, and I do not doubt you will take the necessary pains to prove that Lord North's [3] list is false and yours correct.

The court of London objects that there were a hundred wounded who ought not to be included in the list, nor paid for as dead; but I trust you will not overlook my instructions to you on quitting

---

1. The exact date and place of the first publication of this satire are unknown. It is reported first in French; the English version was in circulation in 1778, and it has reappeared many times. The English purchase of thousands of mercenaries from Hesse evoked profound anger in America, and Franklin distorted the facts for satiric effect. It has not been proved (but was generally suspected) that Frederick II, Landgrave of Hesse-Cassel, pocketed a profit on the death indemnities. He was re-portedly paid £30 per head for at least 15,700 Hessians killed on American soil (J. F. Watson, *Annals of Philadelphia*, Vol II, p. 66).

2. At the Battle of Trenton (Christmas night, 1776) Washington routed the Hessian defenders and took 950 prisoners, leaving twenty or thirty dead, including their commander. Franklin's exaggeration is a satiric license.

3. Frederick North, Earl of Guilford, British prime minister (1770–1782).

Cassel, and that you will not have tried by human succor to recall the life of the unfortunates whose days could not be lengthened but by the loss of a leg or an arm. That would be making them a pernicious present, and I am sure they would rather die than live in a condition no longer fit for my service. I do not mean by this that you should assassinate them; we should be humane, my dear Baron, but you may insinuate to the surgeons with entire propriety that a crippled man is a reproach to their profession, and that there is no wiser course than to let every one of them die when he ceases to be fit to fight.

I am about to send to you some new recruits. Don't economize them. Remember glory before all things. Glory is true wealth. There is nothing degrades the soldier like the love of money. He must care only for honour and reputation, but this reputation must be acquired in the midst of dangers. A battle gained without costing the conqueror any blood is an inglorious success, while the conquered cover themselves with glory by perishing with their arms in their hands. Do you remember that of the 300 Lacedæmonians who defended the defile of Thermopylæ, not one returned? How happy should I be could I say the same of my brave Hessians!

It is true that their king, Leonidas, perished with them: but things have changed, and it is no longer the custom for princes of the empire to go and fight in America for a cause with which they have no concern. And besides, to whom should they pay the thirty guineas [4] per man if I did not stay in Europe to receive them? Then, it is necessary also that I be ready to send recruits to replace the men you lose. For this purpose I must return to Hesse. It is true, grown men are becoming scarce there, but I will send you boys. Besides, the scarcer the commodity the higher the price. I am assured that the women and little girls have begun to till our lands, and they get on not badly. You did right to send back to Europe that Dr. Crumeras who was so successful in curing dysentery. Don't bother with a man who is subject to looseness of the bowels. That disease makes bad soldiers. One coward will do more mischief in an engagement than ten brave men will do good. Better that they burst in their barracks than fly in a battle, and tarnish the glory of our arms. Besides, you know that they pay me as killed for all who die from disease, and I don't get a farthing for runaways. My trip to Italy, which has cost me enormously, makes it desirable that there should be a great mortality among them. You will therefore promise promotion to all who expose themselves; you will exhort them to seek glory in the midst

4. The exact death bounty is not known, but Franklin's figure here verifies that quoted by Watson from an independent source.

of dangers; you will say to Major Maundorff that I am not at all content with his saving the 345 men who escaped the massacre of Trenton. Through the whole campaign he has not had ten men killed in consequence of his orders. Finally, let it be your principal object to prolong the war and avoid a decisive engagement on either side, for I have made arrangements for a grand Italian opera, and I do not wish to be obliged to give it up. Meantime I pray God, my dear Baron de Hohendorf, to have you in his holy and gracious keeping.

Letter to Peter Collinson [5]

[*Kite and Key*]

[PHILADELPHIA] Oct. 19, 1752.

SIR,

As frequent mention is made in public papers from *Europe* of the success of the *Philadelphia* experiment for drawing the electric fire from clouds by means of pointed rods of iron erected on high buildings, &c., it may be agreeable to the curious to be informed, that the same experiment has succeeded in *Philadelphia*, though made in a different and more easy manner, which is as follows:

Make a small cross of two light strips of cedar, the arms so long as to reach to the four corners of a large thin silk handkerchief when extended; tie the corners of the handkerchief to the extremities of the cross, so you have the body of a kite; which being properly accommodated with a tail, loop, and string, will rise in the air, like those made of paper; but this being of silk, is fitter to bear the wet and wind of a thunder-gust without tearing. To the top of the upright stick of the cross is to be fixed a very sharp-pointed wire, rising a foot or more above the wood. To the end of the twine, next the hand, is to be tied a silk ribbon, and where the silk and twine join, a key may be fastened. This kite is to be raised when a thunder-gust appears to be coming on, and the person who holds the string must stand within a door or window, or under some cover, so that the silk ribbon may not be wet; and care must be taken that the twine does not touch the frame of the door or window. As soon as any of the thunder-clouds come over

5. Franklin gives an account of these experiments in the *Autobiography*, above. This letter was among the documents read to the Royal Society in London on December 21, 1752, concerning Franklin's identification of lightning wtih electricity, for which he received the Copley Medal in 1753 and was elected a Fellow of the Society in 1756. The letter was printed in the *Gentleman's Magazine*, December, 1752. (Franklin had experimented with lightning rods without proving his theory of electricity two years earlier.)

the kite, the pointed wire will draw the electric fire from them, and the kite, with all the twine, will be electrified, and the loose filaments of the twine will stand out every way, and be attracted by an approaching finger. And when the rain has wet the kite and twine, so that it can conduct the electric fire freely, you will find it stream out plentifully from the key on the approach of your knuckle. At this key the phial [6] may be charged; and from electric fire thus obtained, spirits may be kindled, and all the other electric experiments be performed, which are usually done by the help of a rubbed glass globe or tube, and thereby the sameness of the electric matter with that of lightning completely demonstrated.

B. Franklin.

The Ephemera [7]

You may remember, my dear friend, that when we lately spent that happy day in the delightful garden and sweet society of the Moulin Joly,[8] I stopt a little in one of our walks, and staid some time behind the company. We had been shown numberless skeletons of a kind of little fly, called an ephemera, whose successive generations, we were told, were bred and expired within the day. I happened to see a living company of them on a leaf, who appeared to be engaged in conversation. You know I understand all the inferior animal tongues; my too great application of the study of them is the best excuse I can give for the little progress I have made in your charming language.[9] I listened through curiosity to the discourse of these little creatures; but as they, in their national vivacity, spoke three or four together, I could make but little of their conversation. I found, however, by some broken expressions that I heard now and then, they were disputing warmly on the merits of two foreign musicians, one a *cousin*, the other a *moscheto*;[1] in which dispute they spent their time, seemingly as re-

6. The Leyden jar, an early experimental electrical condenser.
7. In France as American representative (1776–85) Franklin had a small press for propaganda releases, on which he also printed his "Bagatelles," charming trifles to amuse his friends. "The Ephemera," unlike most of these essays, shows his characteristic speculative curiosity as well as the wit that captivated the French. Madame Brillon, for whom he wrote this, was a young Passy matron at least thirty-five years his junior, with whom he played simultaneously the father and gallant. Franklin wrote this, the first Bagatelle, in 1778; it was printed both in French and English, but the dates are not established.
8. Name of an island in the Seine, location of the home of a friend, where they had spent a day together.
9. He had asked her to correct his French; she thought correction impaired his style and distracted him with the statement that it was "always good French to say: *'Je vous aime'*" (Van Doren).
1. The *cousin* is a gnat, the *moscheto* a mosquito; Franklin here makes a playful reference to the continuous rivalries, in Paris, between opposing musical schools.

gardless of the shortness of life as if they had been sure of living a month. Happy people! thought I, you live certainly under a wise, just, and mild government, since you have no public grievances to complain of, nor any subject of contention but the perfections and imperfections of foreign music. I turned my head from them to an old grey-headed one, who was single on another leaf, and talking to himself. Being amused with his soliloquy, I put it down in writing, in hopes it will likewise amuse her to whom I am so much indebted for the most pleasing of all amusements, her delicious company and heavenly harmony.[2]

"It was," said he, "the opinion of learned philosophers of our race, who lived and flourished long before my time, that this vast world, the Moulin Joly, could not itself subsist more than eighteen hours; and I think there was some foundation for that opinion, since, by the apparent motion of the great luminary that gives life to all nature, and which in my time has evidently declined considerably towards the ocean at the end of our earth, it must then finish its course, be extinguished in the waters that surround us, and leave the world in cold and darkness, necessarily producing universal death and destruction. I have lived seven of those hours, a great age, being no less than four hundred and twenty minutes of time. How very few of us continue so long! I have seen generations born, flourish, and expire. My present friends are the children and grandchildren of the friends of my youth, who are now, alas, no more! And I must soon follow them; for, by the course of nature, though still in health, I cannot expect to live above seven or eight minutes longer. What now avails all my toil and labor, in amassing honey-dew on this leaf, which I cannot live to enjoy! What the political struggles I have been engaged in, for the good of my compatriot inhabitants of this bush, or my philosophical studies for the benefit of our race in general! for, in politics, what can laws do without morals? Our present race of ephemeræ will in a course of minutes become corrupt, like those of other and older bushes, and consequently as wretched. And in philosophy how small our progress! Alas! art is long, and life is short! My friends would comfort me with the idea of a name, they say, I shall leave behind me, and they tell me I have lived long enough to nature and to glory. But what will fame be to an ephemera who no longer exists? And what will become of all history in the eighteenth hour, when the world itself, even the whole Moulin Joly, shall come to its end, and be buried in universal ruin?"

To me, after all my eager pursuits, no solid pleasures now remain, but the reflection of a long life spent in meaning well, the

2. Madame Brillon, an accomplished musician, played and sang, and set verses to music for Franklin.

sensible conversation of a few good lady ephemeræ, and now and then a kind smile and a tune from the ever amiable *Brillante*.[3]

B. FRANKLIN.

1778

To Madame Helvetius[4]

Mortified at the barbarous resolution pronounced by you so positively yesterday evening, that you would remain single the rest of your life as a compliment due to the memory of your husband, I retired to my chamber. Throwing myself upon my bed, I dreamt that I was dead, and was transported to the Elysian Fields.

I was asked whether I wished to see any persons in particular; to which I replied that I wished to see the philosophers. "There are two who live here at hand in this garden; they are good neighbors, and very friendly towards one another."—"Who are they?"—"Socrates and Helvetius."—"I esteem them both highly; but let me see Helvetius first, because I understand a little French, but not a word of Greek." I was conducted to him, he received me with much courtesy, having known me, he said, by character, some time past. He asked me a thousand questions relative to the war, the present state of religion, of liberty, of the government in France. "You do not inquire, then," said I, "after your dear friend, Madame Helvetius; yet she loves you exceedingly. I was in her company not more than an hour ago." "Ah," said he, "you make me recur to my past happiness, which ought to be forgotten in order to be happy here. For many years I could think of nothing but her, though at length I am consoled. I have taken another wife, the most like her that I could find; she is not indeed altogether so handsome, but she has a great fund of wit and good-sense, and her whole study is to please me. She is at this moment gone to fetch the best nectar and ambrosia to regale me; stay here awhile and you will see her." "I perceive," said I, "that your former friend is more faithful to you than you are to her; she has had several good offers, but has refused them all. I will confess to you that I loved her extremely; but she was cruel to me, and rejected me peremptorily for your sake." "I pity you sincerely," said he, "for she is an excellent woman, handsome and amiable.

3. This pun on her name, Brillon, appears also in Franklin's letters.
4. Another Bagatelle. Madame Helvetius, widow of the philosopher Claude Adrien Helvetius, who had died in 1771, was Franklin's neighbor at Auteuil; a famous beauty in her youth, she was now the gay and sympathetic hostess of two generations of intellectuals. Franklin became her intimate companion and proposed marriage, which she wisely declined; he immortalized the offer in such pleasantries as this famous essay, which he gave her, in French, in December, 1779. The first printings, in French and English, are not dated; however, it has been many times reprinted.

But do not the Abbé de la R * * * * and the Abbé M * * * *
visit her?" [5]—"Certainly they do; not one of your friends has
dropped her acquaintance."—"If you had gained the Abbé M
* * * * with a bribe of good coffee and cream, perhaps you
would have succeeded; for he is as deep a reasoner as Duns Scotus
or St. Thomas; [6] he arranges and methodizes his arguments in
such a manner that they are almost irresistible. Or if by a fine
edition of some old classic you had gained the Abbé de la R
* * * * to speak *against* you, that would have been still better,
as I always observed that when he recommended any thing to her,
she had a great inclination to do directly the contrary." As he
finished these words the new Madame Helvetius entered with the
nectar, and I recognized her immediately as my former American
friend, Mrs. Franklin! [7] I reclaimed her, but she answered me
coldly: "I was a good wife to you for forty-nine years and four
months, nearly half a century; let that content you. I have formed a
new connection here, which will last to eternity."

Indignant at this refusal of my Eurydice,[8] I immediately resolved to quit those ungrateful shades, and return to this good
world again, to behold the sun and you! Here I am; let us *avenge
ourselves!*

1779

Letter to Joseph Priestley [9]

[*Science and Humanity*]

PASSY, Feb. 8, 1780.

DEAR SIR,

Your kind letter of September 27 came to hand but very lately,
the bearer having stayed long in Holland. I always rejoice to hear
of your being still employed in experimental researches into nature, and of the Success you meet with. The rapid Progress *true*
Science now makes, occasions my regretting sometimes that I was

5. Van Doren writes (*Benjamin Franklin*, p. 648): "The witty Abbé Morellet,
who had met Franklin in England, lived
near Madame Helvetius if not in her
house. The book-loving Abbé de la
Roche was comfortably domesticated
with her. * * *"
6. Duns Scotus (1265?–1308), Scottish
scholastic theologian, and St. Thomas
Aquinas (1225?–1274), Italian scholastic and founder of Thomist philosophy—both proverbial for skill in dialectics.
7. Franklin's wife, Deborah, had died

in 1774.
8. In the Greek myth, Eurydice, having
died, was sought by her husband, Orpheus, in Pluto's realm of death.
9. Joseph Priestley (1733–1804), British chemist and liberal, supported the
American and French revolutions. Subjected to hostility and violence, he emigrated to Philadelphia (1791). His research and writing advanced science and
religious liberalism, especially Unitarianism. His correspondence with
Franklin was considerable.

born so soon. It is impossible to imagine the height to which may be carried, in a thousand years, the power of man over matter. We may perhaps learn to deprive large masses of their gravity, and give them absolute levity,[1] for the sake of easy transport. Agriculture may diminish its labour and double its produce; all diseases may by sure means be prevented or cured, not excepting even that of old age, and our lives lengthened at pleasure even beyond the antediluvian standard. O that moral science were in as fair a way of improvement, that men would cease to be wolves to one another, and that human beings would at length learn what they now improperly call humanity! [2]

I am glad my little paper on the *Aurora Borealis* pleased. If it should occasion further enquiry, and so produce a better hypothesis, it will not be wholly useless. I am ever, with the greatest and most sincere esteem, dear sir, yours very affectionately

B. FRANKLIN.

THOMAS PAINE
(1737–1809)

Thomas Paine, with his natural gift for pamphleteering and rebellion, was appropriately born into an age of revolution. "My country is the world, and my religion is to do good," he once declared; and he served the rebels of three countries.

This "Great Commoner of Mankind," son of a nominal Quaker of Thetford, England, was early apprenticed to his father, a staymaker. At nineteen, he went to sea for perhaps two years, then followed his father's trade again as master staymaker in several English communities. For nearly twelve years, beginning in 1762, he was employed as an excise officer. His leisure was devoted to the eager pursuit of books and ideas, particularly the study of social philoso-

phy and the new science. After three years in the excise service, he was dismissed for a neglect of duty, but he was reinstated following a year spent as a teacher near London.

The young excise collector learned social science at first hand, seeing the hardships of the tax-burdened masses and the hopelessness of humble workers of his own class. His first wife having died, he acquired, in his second marriage, a small tobacconist's shop in Lewes, where he was stationed; but he still lived constantly on the edge of privation. In 1772 he wrote his first pamphlet, *The Case of the Officers of the Excise,* and he spent the next winter in London, representing his fellow workers in a petition to Parlia-

1. *Cf.* Latin: "weight," "lightness."
2. The belief in moral progress, common to the thought of the Enlighten-

ment, persists in Franklin's writing and correspondence. Often he expressed its goal as the abolition of war.

ment for a living wage. Suddenly he was dismissed, possibly for his agency in this civil revolt, although the official charge was that he had neglected his duties at Lewes. Within two months of losing his position, he lost his shop through bankruptcy and his wife by separation. This was his unhappy situation at thirty-seven, when Franklin met him in London and recognized his peculiar talents in their American perspective. In 1774 Paine made his way to Philadelphia, bearing a cautious letter from Franklin recommending him as "an ingenious worthy young man."

In Philadelphia, Paine edited the *Pennsylvania Magazine*, and contributed to the *Pennsylvania Journal*. Readers of the two Philadelphia papers recognized a political satirist of genius. On January 10, 1776, his famous pamphlet *Common Sense* appeared. It boldly advocated a "Declaration for Independence," a courageous act of high treason against England; Paine knew quite well that publication of the pamphlet could cost him his life. In three months it sold probably a hundred thousand copies; they circulated from hand to hand. Paine became forthwith the most articulate spokesman of the American Revolution. Appointed aide-de-camp to General Greene, he served through the engagements of 1776 in New York, New Jersey, and Pennsylvania; but his chief contribution was a series of sixteen pamphlets (1776–1783) entitled *The American Crisis* and signed "Common

Sense." The first of these, with its blast at the "summer soldier and the sunshine patriot," appeared in the black month of December, 1776, just after Washington's retreat across New Jersey. It was read at once to all regiments, and like the twelve later *Crisis* pamphlets that dealt directly with the military engagements, it restored the morale and inspired the success of that citizens' army. Paine had served on various committees of the Continental Congress; he was clerk of the Pennsylvania Assembly; he received an honorary degree from the College of Philadelphia (the University of Pennsylvania); and went to France to help negotiate a loan for the colonies.

In 1787 he went to Paris and London. In both countries he was received as an important international figure. In England, the patronage of the great terminated suddenly. Paine's *Rights of Man* (Part I, 1791; Part II, 1792), answering Burke's recent *Reflections on the French Revolution*, suggested the overthrow of the British monarchy. Indicted for treason, he was forced to seek refuge in France.

The French revolutionaries received him enthusiastically; but when he opposed the execution of Louis XVI and the Reign of Terror, he was imprisoned. He had already sent to press in Paris the first part of *The Age of Reason*, a deistic treatise advocating a rationalistic view of religion. Set free as a result of the friendly intercession of James Monroe, then

American ambassador to France, he completed *The Age of Reason* (1794–1795), and wrote his last important treatise, *Agrarian Justice* (1797). In 1802 he returned to America, only to find that his patriotic services had been forgotten in the wave of resentment against his "atheistical" beliefs and the reaction of conservatives against the French Revolution. Neglected by all but his vilifiers, he remained in obscurity, for the most part on his farm in New Rochelle.

His excellence lies in the fiery ardor and determination of his words, the conviction of his courageous and indomitable spirit, and the sincerity and passion of his belief in the rights of the humblest man.

The comprehensive edition of Paine's works is that of Moncure D. Conway, *The Writings of Thomas Paine*, 4 vols., 1894–1896; and the most nearly definitive biography is Conway's *The Life of Thomas Paine*, 2 vols., 1892. Shorter lives have been written by F. J. Gould, 1925; by Crane Brinton in the *Dictionary of American Biography*, 1934; and by Hesketh Pearson, 1937. Longer, and authoritative, is Alfred O. Aldridge, *Man of Reason: The Life of Thomas Paine*, 1959. A careful text is the one-volume edition of A. W. Peach, *Selections from the Works of Thomas Paine*, 1928; an excellent one-volume scholarly edition with introduction is *Thomas Paine: Representative Selections*, edited by H. H. Clark, American Writers Series, 1944. In this volume the Conway edition is followed.

From Common Sense

Thoughts on the Present State of American Affairs [1]

In the following pages I offer nothing more than simple facts, plain arguments, and common sense; and have no other preliminaries to settle with the reader, than that he will divest himself of prejudice and prepossession, and suffer his reason and his feelings to determine for themselves; that he will put on, or rather that he will not put off, the true character of a man, and generously enlarge his views beyond the present day.

Volumes have been written on the subject of the struggle between England and America. Men of all ranks have embarked in the controversy, from different motives, and with various designs; but all have been ineffectual, and the period of debate is closed. Arms as the last resource decide the contest; the appeal was the choice of the king, and the continent has accepted the challenge.

It hath been reported of the late Mr. Pelham [2] (who though an able minister was not without his faults) that on his being attacked in the House of Commons on the score that his measures were only of a temporary kind, replied, *"They will last my time."* Should a thought so fatal and unmanly possess the colonies in the present

1. "Thoughts on the Present State of American Affairs" was Part III of *Common Sense.* Part I discussed the British constitution in relation to "the origin and design of government"; Part II analyzed the weaknesses of "monarchy and hereditary succession." The American Declaration of Independence was promulgated six months later, on July 4.
2. Henry Pelham, British prime minister (1743–1754).

contest, the name of Ancestors will be remembered by future generations with detestation.

The sun never shined on a cause of greater worth. 'Tis not the affair of a city, a county, a province, or a kingdom; but of a continent —of at least one-eighth part of the habitable globe. 'Tis not the concern of a day, a year, or an age; posterity are virtually involved in the contest, and will be more or less affected even to the end of time by the proceedings now. Now is the seedtime of continental union, faith, and honor. The least fracture now will be like a name engraved with the point of a pin on the tender rind of a young oak; the wound would enlarge with the tree, and posterity read it in full grown characters.

By referring the matter from argument to arms, a new era for politics is struck—a new method of thinking has arisen. All plans, proposals, &c. prior to the nineteenth of April,[3] i.e. to the commencement of hostilities, are like the almanacks of the last year; which though proper then, are superseded and useless now. Whatever was advanced by the advocates on either side of the question then, terminated in one and the same point, viz. a union with Great Britain; the only difference between the parties was the method of effecting it; the one proposing force, the other friendship; but it has so far happened that the first has failed, and the second has withdrawn her influence.

As much has been said of the advantages of reconciliation, which, like an agreeable dream, has passed away and left us as we were, it is but right that we should examine the contrary side of the argument, and inquire into some of the many material injuries which these colonies sustain, and always will sustain, by being connected with and dependent on Great Britain. To examine that connection and dependence on the principles of nature and common sense; to see what we have to trust to, if separated, and what we are to expect, if dependent.

I have heard it asserted by some, that as America has flourished under her former connection with Great Britain, the same connection is necessary towards her future happiness, and will always have the same effect. Nothing can be more fallacious than this kind of argument. We may as well assert that because a child has thrived upon milk, that it is never to have meat, or that the first twenty years of our lives is to become a precedent for the next twenty. But even this is admitting more than is true; for I answer roundly that America would have flourished as much, and probably much more, had no European power taken any notice of her. The commerce by which she hath enriched herself are the necessaries of life, and will

3. April 19, 1775, the date of the battles of Lexington and Concord, where American minutemen defended their ammunition stores against British troops—the first armed engagements of the Revolution.

always have a market while eating is the custom of Europe.

But she has protected us, say some. That she hath engrossed us is true, and defended the continent at our expense as well as her own is admitted; and she would have defended Turkey from the same motive, viz. for the sake of trade and dominion.

Alas! we have been long led away by ancient prejudices and made large sacrifices to superstition. We have boasted the protection of Great Britain without considering that her motive was *interest*, not *attachment*; and that she did not protect us from *our enemies* on *our account*, but from her enemies on her own account, from those who had no quarrel with us on any *other account*, and who will always be our enemies on the *same account*. Let Britain waive her pretensions to the continent, or the continent throw off the dependence, and we should be at peace with France and Spain were they at war with Britain. The miseries of Hanover's[4] last war ought to warn us against connections. * * *

I challenge the warmest advocate for reconciliation to show a single advantage that this continent can reap, by being connected with Great Britain. I repeat the challenge, not a single advantage is derived. Our corn will fetch its price in any market in Europe, and our imported goods must be paid for, buy them where we will.

But the injuries and disadvantages which we sustain by that connection are without number; and our duty to mankind at large, as well as to ourselves, instructs us to renounce the alliance: because any submission to, or dependence on, Great Britain, tends directly to involve this continent in European wars and quarrels, and set us at variance with nations who would otherwise seek our friendship, and against whom we have neither anger nor complaint. As Europe is our market for trade, we ought to form no partial connection with any part of it. 'Tis the true interest of America to steer clear of European contentions, which she never can do while by her dependence on Britain she is made the makeweight in the scale of British politics.

Europe is too thickly planted with kingdoms to be long at peace, and whenever a war breaks out between England and any foreign power, the trade of America goes to ruin, *because of her connection with Britain*. The next war may not turn out like the last,[5] and should it not, the advocates for reconciliation now will be wishing for separation then, because neutrality in that case would be a safer convoy than a man of war. Everything that is right or reasonable pleads for separation. The blood of the slain, the weep-

---

4. The Prussian house of Hanover occupied the British throne from 1714 to 1901. Paine thus connects the repeated French invasions of Hanover, during the Seven Years' War (1756–1763), with the Franco-British rivalries.

5. The British were victorious in the French and Indian War, the American phase of the Seven Years' War.

ing voice of nature cries, 'TIS TIME TO PART. Even the distance at which the Almighty hath placed England and America is a strong and natural proof that the authority of the one over the other, was never the design of heaven. The time likewise at which the continent was discovered, adds weight to the argument, and the manner in which it was peopled, increases the force of it. The Reformation was preceded by the discovery of America, as if the Almighty graciously meant to open a sanctuary to the persecuted in future years, when home should afford neither friendship nor safety.
* * *

Men of passive tempers look somewhat lightly over the offenses of Great Britain, and, still hoping for the best, are apt to call out, *Come, come, we shall be friends again for all this.* But examine the passions and feelings of mankind; bring the doctrine of reconciliation to the touchstone of nature, and then tell me whether you can hereafter love, honor, and faithfully serve the power that hath carried fire and sword into your land? If you cannot do all these, then are you only deceiving yourselves, and by your delay bringing ruin upon posterity. Your future connection with Britain, whom you can neither love nor honor, will be forced and unnatural, and being formed only on the plan of present convenience, will in a little time fall into a relapse more wretched than the first. But if you say you can still pass the violations over, then I ask, Hath your house been burnt? Hath your property been destroyed before your face? Are your wife and children destitute of a bed to lie on, or bread to live on? Have you lost a parent or child by their hands, and yourself the ruined and wretched survivor? If you have not, then are you not a judge of those who have. But if you have, and can still shake hands with the murderers, then you are unworthy the name of husband, father, friend, or lover; and whatever may be your rank or title in life, you have the heart of a coward, and the spirit of a sycophant.

This is not inflaming or exaggerating matters, but trying them by those feelings and affections which nature justifies, and without which we should be incapable of discharging the social duties of life, or enjoying the felicities of it. I mean not to exhibit horror for the purpose of provoking revenge, but to awaken us from fatal and unmanly slumbers, that we may pursue determinately some fixed object. 'Tis not in the power of Britain or of Europe to conquer America, if she doth not conquer herself by *delay* and *timidity*. The present winter is worth an age if rightly employed, but if lost or neglected the whole continent will partake of the misfortune; and there is no punishment which that man doth not deserve, be he who, or what, or where he will, that may be the means of sacrificing a season so precious and useful.

It is repugnant to reason, to the universal order of things, to all examples from former ages, to suppose that this continent can long remain subject to any external power. The most sanguine in Britain doth not think so. The utmost stretch of human wisdom cannot, at this time, compass a plan, short of separation, which can promise the continent even a year's security. Reconciliation is *now* a fallacious dream. Nature has deserted the connection, and art cannot supply her place. For, as Milton wisely expresses, "Never can true reconcilement grow where wounds of deadly hate have pierced so deep." [6] * * *

But the most powerful of all arguments is, that nothing but independence, i.e. a continental form of government, can keep the peace of the continent and preserve it inviolate from civil wars. I dread the event of a reconciliation with Britain *now*, as it is more than probable that it will be followed by a revolt somewhere or other, the consequences of which may be far more fatal than all the malice of Britain.

Thousands are already ruined by British barbarity; (thousands more will probably suffer the same fate). Those men have other feelings than us who have nothing suffered. All they *now* possess is liberty; what they before enjoyed is sacrificed to its service, and having nothing more to lose they disdain submission. Besides, the general temper of the colonies towards a British government will be like that of a youth who is nearly out of his time; they will care very little about her. And a government which cannot preserve the peace is no government at all, and in that case we pay our money for nothing; and pray what is it that Britain can do, whose power will be wholly on paper, should a civil tumult break out the very day after reconciliation? I have heard some men say, many of whom I believe spoke without thinking, that they dreaded an independence, fearing that it would produce civil wars. It is but seldom that our first thoughts are truly correct, and that is the case here; for there is ten times more to dread from a patched up connection than from independence. I make the sufferer's case my own, and I protest, that were I driven from house and home, my property destroyed, and my circumstances ruined, that as a man, sensible of injuries, I could never relish the doctrine of reconciliation, or consider myself bound thereby.

The colonies have manifested such a spirit of good order and obedience to continental government as is sufficient to make every reasonable person easy and happy on that head. No man can assign the least pretense for his fears on any other grounds than such as are truly childish and ridiculous, viz., that one colony will be striving for superiority over another. * * *

6. *Paradise Lost,* Book IV, ll. 98–99.

But where, say some, is the king of America? I'll tell you, friend, he reigns above, and doth not make havoc of mankind like the Royal Brute of Great Britain. Yet that we may appear to be defective even in earthly honors, let a day be solemnly set apart for proclaiming the charter; let it be brought forth placed on the divine law, the Word of God; let a crown be placed thereon, by which the world may know, that so far as we approve of monarchy, that in America THE LAW IS KING. For as in absolute governments the king is law, so in free countries the law *ought* to BE king, and there ought to be no other. But lest any ill use should afterwards arise, let the crown at the conclusion of the ceremony be demolished, and scattered among the people whose right it is.[7] * * *

O ye that love mankind! Ye that dare oppose not only the tyranny but the tyrant, stand forth! Every spot of the old world is overrun with oppression. Freedom hath been hunted round the globe. Asia and Africa have long expelled her. Europe regards her like a stranger, and England hath given her warning to depart. O receive the fugitive, and prepare in time an asylum for mankind.

1776

The American Crisis [8]

These are the times that try men's souls: The summer soldier and the sunshine patriot will in this crisis, shrink from the service of his country; but he that stands it Now, deserves the love and thanks of man and woman. Tyranny, like hell, is not easily conquered; yet we have this consolation with us, that the harder the conflict, the more glorious the triumph. What we obtain too cheap, we esteem to[o] lightly:——'Tis dearness only that gives everything its value. Heaven knows how to put a proper price upon its goods; and it would be strange indeed, if so celestial an article as FREEDOM should not be highly rated. Britain, with an army to enforce her tyranny, has declared that she has a right (not only to) TAX but "to BIND *us in* ALL CASES WHATSOEVER", and if being *bound in that manner*, is not slavery, then is there not such a thing as slavery upon earth. Even the expression is impious for so unlimited a power can belong only to God.

Whether the Independence of the Continent was declared too

---

7. Popular sovereignty and a government by social contract are recurrent themes in Paine's later writings; *cf.* also the Declaration of Independence.
8. The first of the sixteen pamphlets now known as *The Crisis*, this originally appeared undated in the *Pennsylvania Journal*, December 19, 1776.

There were three pamphlet editions within the week, one undated, one dated December 19, and one dated December 23. Since Paine later referred to the last as authoritative, it is reproduced here. The last number of *The Crisis*, the sixteenth, appeared on December 9, 1783.

soon, or delayed too long, I will not now enter into as an argument; my own simple opinion is, that had it been eight months earlier, it would have been much better. We did not make a proper use of last winter, neither could we, while we were in a dependent state. However, the fault, if it were one, was all our own; we have none to blame but ourselves. But no great deal is lost yet; all that Howe [9] has been doing for this month past, is rather a ravage than a conquest, which the spirit of the Jersies [1] a year ago would have quickly repulsed, and which time and a little resolution will soon recover.

I have as little superstition in me as any man living, but my secret opinion has ever been, and still is, that God Almighty will not give up a people to military destruction, or leave them unsupportedly to perish, who have so earnestly and so repeatedly sought to avoid the calamities of war, by every decent method which wisdom could invent. Neither have I so much of the infidel in me, as to suppose that he has relinquished the government of the world, and given us up to the care of devils; and as I do not, I cannot see on what grounds the king of Britain can look up to heaven for help against us: a common murderer, a highwayman, or a housebreaker, has as good a pretence as he.

'Tis surprising to see how rapidly a panic will sometimes run through a country. All nations and ages have been subject to them: Britain has trembled like an ague at the report of a French fleet of flat-bottomed boats; and in the fourteenth century the whole English army, after ravaging the kingdom of France, was driven back like men petrified with fear; and this brave exploit was performed by a few broken forces collected and headed by a woman, Joan of Arc. Would that heaven might inspire some Jersey maid to spirit up her countrymen, and save her fair fellow sufferers from ravage and ravishment! Yet panics, in some cases, have their uses; they produce as much good as hurt. Their duration is always short; the mind soon grows through them, and acquires a firmer habit than before. But their peculiar advantage is, that they are the touchstones of sincerity and hypocrisy, and bring things and men to light, which might otherwise have lain forever undiscovered. In fact, they have the same effect on secret traitors which an imaginary apparition would have upon a private murderer. They sift out the hidden thoughts of man, and hold them up in public to the world. Many a disguised tory has lately shown his head, that shall penitentially solemnize with curses the day on which Howe arrived upon the Delaware.

---

9. Lord William Howe had taken command of the British troops in America in 1775.

1. The colony was divided into East and West Jersey.

As I was with the troops at Fort-Lee, and marched with them to the edge of Pennsylvania, I am well acquainted with many circumstances, which those who live at a distance, know but little or nothing of.[2] Our situation there was exceedingly cramped, the place being a narrow neck of land between the North-River[3] and the Hackensack. Our force was inconsiderable, being not one-fourth so great as Howe could bring against us. We had no army at hand to have relieved the garrison, had we shut ourselves up and stood on our defence. Our ammunition, light artillery, and the best part of our stores, had been removed, on the apprehension that Howe would endeavor to penetrate the Jerseys,[4] in which case Fort-Lee could be of no use to us; for it must occur to every thinking man, whether in the army or not, that these kind of field forts are only for temporary purposes, and last in use no longer than the enemy directs his force against the particular object, which such forts are raised to defend.[5] Such was our situation and condition at Fort-Lee on the morning of the 20th of November, when an officer arrived with information that the enemy with 200 boats had landed about seven miles above: Major General Green,[6] who commanded the garrison, immediately ordered them under arms, and sent express to General Washington at the town of Hackensack, distant by the way of the ferry, six miles. Our first object was to secure the bridge over the Hackensack, which laid up the river between the enemy and us, about six miles from us, and three from them. General Washington arrived in about three-quarters of an hour, and marched at the head of the troops towards the bridge, which place I expected we should have a brush for; however, they did not choose to dispute it with us, and the greatest part of our troops went over the bridge, the rest over the ferry, except some which passed at a mill on a small creek, between the bridge and the ferry, and made their way through some marshy grounds up to the town of Hackensack, and there passed the river. We brought off as much baggage as the wagons could contain, the rest was lost. The simple object was to bring off the garrison, and march them on till they could be strengthened by the Jersey or Pennsylvania militia, so as to be enabled to make a stand. We staid four days at

2. On November 20, General Greene made the hasty retreat southward from the Hudson forts to Newark, New Jersey. There, according to tradition, Paine wrote this *Crisis* paper on a drumhead. In less than a month it was printed, and Washington had it read to each regiment of the army, now encamped in Pennsylvania. A few days later, on Christmas night, they struck successfully across the Delaware at Trenton, and nine days later they attacked at Princeton. Paine participated in both battles.

3. The Hudson.
4. Cf. "Jersies" above. The *Crisis* papers, printed, sometimes reprinted, under pressure, were never definitively edited by Paine.
5. Propagandist Paine naturally belittles the British success—actually the capture of Fort Lee and Fort Washington, the strategic defenses of the Hudson, together with enough men and materiel to make a field regiment.
6. *I. e.*, Greene. Nathaniel Greene commanded one of the divisions against Trenton, a month later.

Newark, collected our out-posts with some of the Jersey militia, and marched out twice to meet the enemy, on being informed that they were advancing, though our numbers were greatly inferior to theirs. Howe, in my little opinion, committed a great error in generalship in not throwing a body of forces off from Staten-Island through Amboy, by which means he might have seized all our stores at Brunswick,[7] and intercepted our march into Pennsylvania; but if we believe the power of hell to be limited, we must likewise believe that their agents are under some providential control.

I shall not now attempt to give all the particulars of our retreat to the Delaware; suffice it for the present to say, that both officers and men, though greatly harassed and fatigued, frequently without rest, covering, or provision, the inevitable consequences of a long retreat, bore it with a manly and martial spirit. All their wishes centered in one, which was, that the country would turn out and help them to drive the enemy back. *Voltaire* [8] has remarked that King William never appeared to full advantage but in difficulties and in action; the same remark may be made on General Washington, for the character fits him. There is a natural firmness in some minds which cannot be unlocked by trifles, but which, when unlocked, discovers a cabinet of fortitude; and I reckon it among those kind of public blessings, which we do not immediately see, that God hath blessed him with uninterrupted health, and given him a mind that can even flourish upon care. * * *

Quitting this class of men, I turn with the warm ardor of a friend to those who have nobly stood, and are yet determined to stand the matter out: I call not upon a few, but upon all: not on THIS state or THAT state, but on EVERY STATE: up and help us; lay your shoulders to the wheel; better have too much force than too little, when so great an object is at stake. Let it be told to the future world, that in the depth of winter, when nothing but hope and virtue could survive, that the city and the country, alarmed at one common danger, came forth to meet and to repulse it. Say not that thousands are gone, turn out your tens of thousands; [9] throw not the burden of the day upon Providence, but *"show your faith by your works,"* [1] that God may bless you. It matters not where you live, or what rank of life you hold, the evil or the blessing will reach you all. The far and the near, the home counties and the back,[2] the rich and the poor, will suffer or rejoice alike.

---

7. Now Perth Amboy and New Brunswick. By holding this line Howe could have blocked Greene's only strategic retreat to Pennsylvania.
8. The French man of letters Voltaire (1694–1778), then very popular in America, made this remark concerning William III of England (died 1702) in his principal historical treatise, *Le Siècle de Louis XIV* (1751), Chapter 17.
9. *Cf.* I Samuel xviii: 7: "Saul hath slain his thousands, and David his ten thousands."
1. *Cf.* James ii: 18.
2. *I.e.*, both well-settled "counties," and backwoods.

The heart that feels not now is dead; the blood of his children will curse his cowardice, who shrinks back at a time when a little might have saved the whole, and made *them* happy. I love the man that can smile in trouble, that can gather strength from distress, and grow brave by reflection. 'Tis the business of little minds to shrink; but he whose heart is firm, and whose conscience approves his conduct, will pursue his principles unto death. My own line of reasoning is to myself as straight and clear as a ray of light. Not all the treasures of the world, so far as I believe, could have induced me to support an offensive war, for I think it murder; but if a thief breaks into my house, burns and destroys my property, and kills or threatens to kill me, or those that are in it, and to *"bind me in all cases whatsoever"* to his absolute will, am I to suffer it? What signifies it to me, whether he who does it is a king or a common man; my countryman or not my countryman; whether it be done by an individual villain, or an army of them? If we reason to the root of things we shall find no difference; neither can any just cause be assigned why we should punish in the one case and pardon in the other. Let them call me rebel, and welcome, I feel no concern from it; but I should suffer the misery of devils, were I to make a whore of my soul by swearing allegiance to one whose character is that of a sottish, stupid, stubborn, worthless, brutish man. I conceive likewise a horrid idea in receiving mercy from a being, who at the last day shall be shrieking to the rocks and mountains to cover him, and fleeing with terror from the orphan, the widow, and the slain of America. * * *

I thank God that I fear not. I see no real cause for fear. I know our situation well, and can see the way out of it. While our army was collected, Howe dared not risk a battle; and it is no credit to him that he decamped from the White Plains,[3] and waited a mean opportunity to ravage the defenceless Jerseys; but it is great credit to us, that, with a handful of men, we sustained an orderly retreat for near an hundred miles, brought off our ammunition, all our fieldpieces, the greatest part of our stores, and had four rivers to pass. None can say that our retreat was precipitate, for we were near three weeks in performing it, that the country [4] might have time to come in. Twice we marched back to meet the enemy, and remained out till dark. The sign of fear was not seen in our camp, and had not some of the cowardly and disaffected inhabitants spread false alarms through the country, the Jersies had never been ravaged. Once more we are again collected and collecting, our new army at both ends of the continent is recruiting fast, and we shall

3. At White Plains, New York, Howe had successfully attacked Washington's position in October, but failed to follow up his advantage.
4. The militia, or local volunteers.

be able to open the next campaign with sixty thousand men, well-armed and clothed. This is our situation, and who will may know it. By perserverance and fortitude we have the prospect of a glorious issue; by cowardice and submission, the sad choice of a variety of evils—a ravaged country—a depopulated city—habitations without safety, and slavery without hope—our homes turned into barracks and bawdy-houses for Hessians, and a future race to provide for, whose fathers we shall doubt of. Look on this picture and weep over it! and if there yet remains one thoughtless wretch who believes it not, let him suffer it unlamented.

COMMON SENSE.

December 23, 1776

THOMAS JEFFERSON

(1743–1826)

It may be that Thomas Jefferson's thought and personality have influenced his countrymen more deeply, and remained more effectively alive, than those of any other American. Yet, of the eight titles published by him, only one represents what can be called a book in the usual sense. It is estimated that fifty volumes will be required for the definitive edition of his writings, composed chiefly of state papers, a few treatises, and the incredible twenty-five thousand letters, many of great length, by which he was always "sowing useful truths," as he called it. His words could not be contained by a letter or confined at their first destination; they were reborn in the public ideals and acts of the American people, and indeed in their daily speech. This is partly because he embodied their best meanings in such public utterances as the Virginia Statute for Religious Freedom, in the Declaration of Independence, of which he was the principal au-

thor, in the *Notes on the State of Virginia,* a veritable storehouse of humane ideas and liberal democracy, which he published in 1784–1785, in his addresses as president, and in his autobiography, published three years after his death.

This Virginian planter-aristocrat had as vigorous humanitarian sympathies as Franklin, and though thirty-seven years his junior, he was just as much a product of the Enlightenment. His mind, like Franklin's, ranged curiously over many fields of knowledge—law, philosophy, government, architecture, education, religion, science, agriculture, mechanics—and whatever he touched, he enriched in some measure. He knew that he was not profound, but he read widely, impelled by the same practical reason as Franklin—to gain understanding. The development of rational science from Bacon to Newton; the history of English law from King Alfred to Blackstone; the tradition of

English liberty in Harrington, Milton, Hobbes, Locke, and Algernon Sydney; the challenging ideas of contemporary French liberalism in Montesquieu, Helvetius, Voltaire, and the physiocrats—from acquaintance with these, indeed, he did gain understanding. This understanding he applied, with simple American directness, to a conception of democracy for a new land of plenty, where the people might have a fresh start toward liberty, selfhood, and that excellence which he sought in all things. This patrician humanist looked to merit and ability alone, not to privilege; the natural rights of man must be secured by law inalienably for all, irrespective of station. For him, government, a necessary evil, found sanction only in the common consent of a social contract; its purpose was the benefit of the individual, not his exploitation; it must provide freedom of speech, thought, association, press, worship, education, and enterprise. In a letter to Benjamin Rush in 1800, he stated his conviction, unaltered throughout his life: "I have sworn upon the altar of God, eternal hostility against every form of tyranny over the mind of man."

These ideas found practical expression in Jefferson's forty years of a public life so active that only its highest moments can be mentioned here. He was born in Albemarle County, Virginia, April 13, 1743. Years of private study were supplemented by two years at William and Mary College. He then prepared for the practice of law, but his election to the Virginia House

of Burgesses in 1769 drew him into public life. He represented Virginia in the Second Continental Congress in 1775; the following year—with John Adams, Benjamin Franklin, Roger Sherman, and Robert R. Livingston—he drafted the Declaration of Independence. Again in the Virginia legislature, he devoted himself to codifying and liberalizing the laws and to the cause of toleration represented in his bill for the establishment of religious freedom, finally adopted later, in 1786. He was governor of Virginia (1779–1781), and delegate to the Congress of the Confederation, before going to Paris to assist Franklin and Adams in treaty negotiations (1784). He remained in Paris to succeed Franklin as American minister (1785–1789). As the first American secretary of state (1790–1793) in Washington's cabinet, his opposition to the extreme Federalism and the aristocratic tendencies of Alexander Hamilton, secretary of the treasury, drew the support of those who favored equalitarian measures and greater local independence, thus defining the constitutional questions that have since continued to provide the issues for the two American parties. On these issues he was narrowly defeated by John Adams in 1796, and accepted the vice-presidency, then awarded the unsuccessful candidate. On the same issues he won the election of 1800, and served for two terms as president. Among the many acts of his administration may be noted his measures to prevent unwarranted encroachment of the federal powers upon the domain of the states, and his concern for the expansion of the country, reflected in the Louisiana Purchase (1803) and in his sponsorship of the expedition of Lewis and Clark (1803–1806).

In 1809 he "retired" to a very active life at Monticello, a monument to his architectural genius, whose gradual perfection had been his hobby since 1767. The sale of his library of ten thousand volumes to the national government partially relieved his financial obligations and provided the foundation of the national library of his dreams (now the Library of Congress). His democratic theories of education, formulated through the years, soon took concrete form in the University of Virginia (1819), whose notable buildings he designed, and whose first Rector he became. His correspondence, in which he now expressed the seasoned experience and the accumulated wisdom of a lifetime, grew to enormous proportions, which, as he said, often denied him "the leisure of reading a single page in a week." The only American of his time to be elected to the Institute of France, Jefferson experimented in agriculture, paleontology, geography, and botany, and was president of the American Philosophical Society for eighteen years. It was fitting that his death in 1826 should occur on the fiftieth anniversary of the signing of the Declaration of Independence.

The earliest reliable edition of Jefferson's works is *The Writings of Thomas Jefferson*, 10 vols., edited by P. L. Ford, 1892–1899. The Memorial Edition, edited by A. A. Lipscomb and A. E. Bergh, 20 vols., 1903–1907, contains additional texts not in the Ford edition. A definitive edition, in preparation under the direction of Julian P. Boyd, is expected to comprise at least fifty volumes, of which 18 have appeared at this date (1973), entitled *Papers of Thomas Jefferson* (Princeton University Press). For correspondence, see: *Thomas Jefferson Correspondence* * * * , edited by W. C. Ford, 1916; *Correspondence Between John Adams and Thomas Jefferson*, edited by Paul Wilstach, 1925; and *The Adams-Jefferson Letters*, edited by L. J. Cappon, 1959. Single-volume collections are *The Complete Jefferson* * * * *except his Letters*, edited by Saul K. Padover, 1943; *Life and Selected Writings of Thomas Jefferson*, edited by A. Koch and W. Peden, 1944; *Alexander Hamilton and Thomas Jefferson: Representative Selections*, edited by F. C. Prescott, 1934. W. Peden edited *Notes on the State of Virginia*, 1955.

Biographies and special studies are numerous: see A. J. Nock, *Jefferson*, 1926; and Gilbert Chinard, *Thomas Jefferson: The Apostle of Americanism*, 1929. Dumas Malone has in progress a five-volume biography, of which four have appeared: *Jefferson, The Virginian*, 1948; *Jefferson and the Rights of Man*, 1951; *Jefferson and the Ordeal of Liberty*, 1962; and *Jefferson the President: First Term*, 1970. Other important studies are Adrienne Koch, *The Philosophy of Thomas Jefferson*, 1943, 1957; C. G. Bowers, *Jefferson and Hamilton*, 1925, and *Jefferson in Power*, 1936; J. B. Conant, *Jefferson and the Development of American Public Education*, 1965; and Merrill D. Peterson, *Thomas Jefferson and the New Nation: A Biography*, 1970.

The Declaration of Independence

In CONGRESS, July 4, 1776.

THE UNANIMOUS DECLARATION of the thirteen united STATES OF AMERICA.[1]

When in the Course of human events, it becomes necessary for one people to dissolve the political bands which have connected them with another, and to assume among the powers of the earth, the separate and equal station to which the Laws of Nature and of Nature's God entitle them, a decent respect to the opinions of mankind requires that they should declare the causes which impel them to the separation.————We hold these truths to be self-evident, that all men are created equal, that they are endowed by their Creator with certain unalienable Rights, that among these are Life, Liberty and the pursuit of Happiness.[2]——That to secure these rights, Governments are instituted among Men, deriving their just powers from the consent of the governed,—That whenever any Form of Government becomes destructive of these ends, it is the Right of the People to alter or to abolish it, and to institute new Government, laying its foundation on such principles and organizing its powers in such form, as to them shall seem most likely to effect their Safety and Happiness. Prudence, indeed, will dictate that Governments long established should not be changed for light and transient causes; and accordingly all experience hath shewn, that mankind are more disposed to suffer, while evils are sufferable, than to right themselves by abolishing the forms to which they are accustomed. But when a long train of abuses and usurpations, pursuing invariably the same Object evinces a design to reduce them under absolute Despotism, it is their right, it is their duty, to throw off such Government, and to provide new Guards

1. Richard Henry Lee of Virginia, on June 7, 1776, proposed a resolution in Congress that "these united Colonies are, and of right ought to be, free and independent States." Final action was postponed, but on June 11 a committee of five was appointed, which on June 28 presented the draft of a Declaration of Independence. It was substantially the work of Jefferson, although Franklin made fundamental contributions, and the influence of John Adams is evident. On July 2, Lee's original resolution was passed. On July 4, the Declaration was passed after some changes during debate; the Liberty Bell rang from the State House steeple in Philadelphia, and that night printed broadside copies were hastily run off for public distribution. On August 2, an engrossed parchment copy was signed by all the delegates but three, who also signed shortly thereafter. Printed copies, with all the signatures, appeared in January, 1777. The philosophical and political ideals expressed in the Declaration can be traced far back in history, and their immediate roots are found in eighteenth-century thought, while the final draft represented a consensus among the delegates; however, the document still reflects the authorship of Jefferson, his precise clarity and powerful grace of thought. The text printed here is that authorized by the State Department: *The Declaration of Independence, 1776* (1911).

2. *Cf.* John Locke, *Second Treatise of Government*, where he identified natural rights as those to "life, liberty, and estate [property]."

for their future security.—Such has been the patient sufferance of these Colonies; and such is now the necessity which constrains them to alter their former Systems of Government. The history of the present King of Great Britain [3] is a history of repeated injuries and usurpations, all having in direct object the establishment of an absolute Tyranny over these States. To prove this, let Facts be submitted to a candid world.———He has refused his Assent to Laws, the most wholesome and necessary for the public good.——— He has forbidden his Governors to pass Laws of immediate and pressing importance, unless suspended in their operation till his Assent should be obtained; and when so suspended, he has utterly neglected to attend to them.———He has refused to pass other Laws for the accommodation of large districts of people, unless those people would relinquish the right of Representation in the Legislature, a right inestimable to them and formidable to tyrants only.———He has called together legislative bodies at places unusual, uncomfortable, and distant from the depository of their public Records, for the sole purpose of fatiguing them into compliance with his measures.———He has dissolved Representative Houses repeatedly, for opposing with manly firmness his invasions on the rights of the people.———He has refused for a long time, after such dissolutions, to cause others to be elected; whereby the Legislative powers, incapable of Annihilation, have returned to the People at large for their exercise; the State remaining in the mean time exposed to all the dangers of invasion from without, and convulsions within.———He has endeavoured to prevent the population of these States; for that purpose obstructing the Laws for Naturalization of Foreigners; refusing to pass others to encourage their migrations hither, and raising the conditions of new Appropriations of Lands.———He has obstructed the Administration of Justice, by refusing his Assent to Laws for establishing Judiciary powers.——— He has made Judges dependent on his Will alone, for the tenure of their officers, and the amount and payment of their salaries. ———He has erected a multitude of New Offices, and sent hither swarms of Officers to harass our people, and eat out their substance.———He has kept among us, in times of peace, Standing Armies without the Consent of our legislatures.———He has affected to render the Military independent of and superior to the Civil power.———He has combined with others [4] to subject us to a jurisdiction foreign to our constitution, and unacknowledged by our laws; giving his Assent to their Acts of pretended Legislation: —For Quartering large bodies of armed troops among us:—For

---

3. George III, king from 1760 to 1820, was the responsible engineer of those policies of his government which evoked rebellion.

4. The British Parliament.

protecting them, by a mock Trial, from punishment for any Murders which they should commit on the Inhabitants of these States:—For cutting off our Trade with all parts of the world:—For imposing Taxes on us without our Consent:—For depriving us in many cases, of the benefits of Trial by Jury:—For transporting us beyond Seas to be tried for pretended offences:—For abolishing the free System of English Laws in a neighbouring Province,[5] establishing therein an Arbitrary government, and enlarging its Boundaries so as to render it at once an example and fit instrument for introducing the same absolute rule into these Colonies:—For taking away our Charters, abolishing our most valuable Laws, and altering fundamentally the Forms of our Governments:—For suspending our own Legislatures, and declaring themselves invested with power to legislate for us in all cases whatsoever.—He has abdicated Government here, by declaring us out of his Protection and waging War against us:—He has plundered our seas, ravaged our Coasts, burnt our towns, and destroyed the lives of our people.—He is at this time transporting large Armies of foreign Mercenaries[6] to compleat the works of death, desolation and tyranny, already begun with circumstances of Cruelty & perfidy scarcely paralleled in the most barbarous ages, and totally unworthy the Head of a civilized nation.—He has constrained our fellow Citizens taken Captive on the high Seas to bear Arms against their Country, to become the executioners of their friends and Brethren, or to fall themselves by their Hands.—He has excited domestic insurrections amongst us, and has endeavoured to bring on the inhabitants of our frontiers, the merciless Indian Savages, whose known rule of warfare, is an undistinguished destruction of all ages, sexes and conditions. In every stage of these Opressions We have Petitioned for Redress in the most humble terms: Our repeated Petitions have been answered only by repeated injury. A Prince, whose character is thus marked by every act which may define a Tyrant, is unfit to be the ruler of a free people. Nor have We been wanting in attentions to our British brethren. We have warned them from time to time of attempts by their legislature to extend an unwarrantable jurisdiction over us. We have reminded them of the circumstances of our emigration and settlement here. We have appealed to their native justice and magnanimity, and we have conjured them by the ties of our common kindred to disavow these usurpations, which, would inevitably interrupt our connections and correspondence. They too have been deaf to the

---

5. The Quebec Act (1774) promised concessions to the French Catholics, and restored the French civil law, thus alienating the Province of Quebec from the seaboard colonies in the growing controversy.

6. German soldiers, principally Hessians, hired by the British for colonial service.

voice of justice and of consanguinity. We must, therefore, acquiesce in the necessity, which denounces [7] our Separation, and hold them, as we hold the rest of mankind, Enemies in War, in Peace Friends.

WE, THEREFORE, the Representatives of the UNITED STATES OF AMERICA, in General Congress Assembled, appealing to the Supreme Judge of the world for the rectitude of our intentions, do, in the Name and by Authority of the good People of these Colonies, solemnly publish and declare, That these United Colonies are, and of Right ought to be FREE AND INDEPENDENT STATES; that they are Absolved from all Allegiance to the British Crown, and that all political connection between them and the State of Great Britain, is and ought to be totally dissolved; and that as Free and Independent States, they have full Power to levy War, conclude Peace, contract Alliances, establish Commerce, and to do all other Acts and Things which Independent States may of right do.——And for the support of this Declaration, with a firm reliance on the protection of divine Providence, we mutually pledge to each other our Lives, our Fortunes and our sacred Honor.

1776

First Inaugural Address [8]

Friends and Fellow-Citizens:

Called upon to undertake the duties of the first executive office of our country, I avail myself of the presence of that portion of my fellow-citizens which is here assembled, to express my grateful thanks for the favor with which they have been pleased to look towards me, to declare a sincere consciousness that the task is above my talents, and that I approach it with those anxious and awful presentiments which the greatness of the charge and the weakness of my powers so justly inspire. A rising nation spread over a wide and fruitful land, traversing all the seas with the rich productions of their industry, engaged in commerce with nations who feel power and forget right, advancing rapidly to destinies beyond the reach of mortal eye; when I contemplate these transcendent objects, and see the honor, the happiness, and the hopes of this beloved

7. Proclaims.
8. In accordance with Article II of the Constitution, subsequently changed by the Twelfth Amendment, Jefferson had become vice-president in 1796, as the candidate defeated by the Federalist, John Adams. In 1800 he ran against Aaron Burr, both of them Democratic Republicans (Democrats). The electoral vote was a tie, a result that prompted the adoption of the Twelfth Amendment. The election was settled by a vote in the House of Representatives, where Jefferson, supported by Hamilton, defeated Burr, whose resentment ultimately led to the Burr-Hamilton duel and Hamilton's death. The inauguration occurred on March 4, 1801, before the Congress, in the Senate Chamber of the still-unfinished Capitol.

country committed to the issue and the auspices of this day, I shrink from the contemplation, and humble myself before the magnitude of the undertaking.

Utterly, indeed, should I despair, did not the presence of many whom I here see remind me that in the other high authorities provided by our constitution I shall find resources of wisdom, of virtue, and of zeal on which to rely under all difficulties. To you then, gentlemen, who are charged with the sovereign functions of legislation, and to those associated with you, I look with encouragement for that guidance and support which may enable us to steer with safety the vessel in which we are all embarked, amidst the conflicting elements of a troubled sea.

During the contest of opinion [9] through which we have passed, the animation of discussions and of exertions has sometimes worn an aspect which might impose on strangers unused to think freely and to speak and to write what they think. But this being now decided by the voice of the nation, announced according to the rules of the Constitution, all will, of course, arrange themselves under the will of the law, and unite in common efforts for the common good. All too will bear in mind this sacred principle, that though the will of the majority is in all cases to prevail, that will, to be rightful, must be reasonable; that the minority possess their equal rights, which equal laws must protect, and to violate would be oppression. Let us then, fellow-citizens, unite with one heart and one mind; let us restore to social intercourse that harmony and affection without which liberty, and even life itself, are but dreary things. And let us reflect that having banished from our land that religious intolerance under which mankind so long bled and suffered, we have yet gained little if we countenance a political intolerance as despotic, as wicked, and capable of as bitter and bloody persecutions. During the throes and convulsions of the ancient world, during the agonizing spasms of infuriated man, seeking through blood and slaughter his long-lost liberty, it was not wonderful that the agitation of the billows should reach even this distant and peaceful shore; [1] that this should be more felt and feared by some and less by others; and should divide opinions as to measures of safety. But every difference of opinion is not a difference of principle. We have called by different names brethren of the same principle. We are all republicans; we are all federalists.[2] If there be any among us who would wish to dissolve this Union, or to change its republican form, let them stand undisturbed as monuments of

9. *I.e.*, the bitterly contested election.
1. The **Reign of Terror** (1794) in the French Revolution alarmed American conservatives and intensified the strife between the parties.

2. The two contesting political parties. The "Democratic Republicans" (the official name) were the ancestors of the Democratic party; Jefferson is referring not to politics but to common principles.

the safety with which error of opinion may be tolerated, where reason is left free to combat it.[3] I know, indeed, that some honest men have feared that a republican government cannot be strong; that this Government is not strong enough. But would the honest patriot, in the full tide of successful experiment, abandon a government which has so far kept us free and firm, on the theoretic and visionary fear that this Government, the world's best hope, may by possibility want energy to preserve itself? I trust not. I believe this, on the contrary, the strongest government on earth. I believe it the only one where every man, at the call of the law would fly to the standard of the law; would meet invasions of the public order as his own personal concern. Sometimes it is said that man cannot be trusted with the government of himself. Can he then, be trusted with the government of others? Or have we found angels in the form of kings to govern him? Let history answer this question.

Let us then, pursue with courage and confidence our own federal and republican principles, our attachment to union and representative government. Kindly separated by nature and a wide ocean from the exterminating havoc of one quarter of the globe; too high-minded to endure the degradations of the others; possessing a chosen country, with room enough for our descendants to the hundredth and thousandth generation;[4] entertaining a due sense of our equal right to the use of our own faculties, to the acquisitions of our own industry, to honor and confidence from our fellow-citizens, resulting not from birth, but from our actions and their sense of them; enlightened by a benign religion, professed indeed and practiced in various forms yet all of them inculcating honesty, truth, temperance, gratitude, and the love of man, acknowledging and adoring an overruling Providence, which by all its dispensations proves that it delights in the happiness of man here and his greater happiness hereafter: with all these blessings, what more is necessary to make us a happy and a prosperous people? Still one thing more, fellow-citizens—a wise and frugal government, which shall restrain men from injuring one another, shall leave them otherwise free to regulate their own pursuits of industry and improvement, and shall not take from the mouth of labor the bread it has earned. This is the sum of good government; and this is necessary to close the circle of our felicities.

About to enter, fellow-citizens, on the exercise of duties which comprehend everything dear and valuable to you, it is proper you should understand what I deem the essential principle of this

3. This is probably the first important official recognition of the guarantee of freedom of thought and opinion.
4. The pessimistic "law" of Malthus on the imbalance of population and subsistence had just been propounded in *An Essay on the Principle of Population* (1798).

government, and consequently those which ought to shape its administration. I will compress them in the narrowest compass they will bear, stating the general principle but not all its limitations. Equal and exact justice to all men of whatever state or persuasion, religious or political; peace, commerce and honest friendship with all nations, entangling alliances with none; [5] the support of the state governments in all their rights, as the most competent administrations for our domestic concerns, and the surest bulwarks against anti-republican tendencies; the preservation of the general government in its whole constitutional vigor, as the sheet-anchor of our peace at home and safety abroad; a jealous care of the right of election by the people; a mild and safe corrective of abuses which are lopped by the sword of revolution, where peaceable remedies are unprovided; absolute acquiescence in the decisions of the majority, the vital principle of republics, from which is no appeal but to force, the vital principle and immediate parent of despotism; a well-disciplined militia, our best reliance in peace and for the first moments of war, till regulars may relieve them; the supremacy of the civil over the military authority—economy in the public expense, that labor may be lightly burdened; the honest payment of our debts, and sacred preservation of the public faith; encouragement of agriculture, and of commerce as its handmaid; the diffusion of information and arraignment of all abuses at the bar of the public reason; freedom of religion, freedom of the press, and freedom of person, under the protection of the habeas corpus; [6] and trial by juries impartially selected. These principles form the bright constellation which has gone before us, and guided our steps through an age of revolution and reformation. The wisdom of our sages and blood of our heroes have been devoted to their attainment; they should be the creed of our political faith; the text of civic instruction; the touchstone by which to try the services of those we trust; and should we wander from them in moments of error or alarm, let us hasten to retrace our steps and to regain the road which alone leads to peace, liberty, and safety.

I repair then, fellow-citizens, to the post which you have assigned me. With experience enough in subordinate stations to know the difficulties of this, the greatest of all, I have learned to expect that it will rarely fall to the lot of imperfect man to retire from this station with the reputation and the favor which bring him into it. Without pretentions to that high confidence you reposed in our first and greatest revolutionary character, [7] whose preëminent services had entitled him to the first place in his country's love, and

---

5. Reaffirming Washington's injunction, in the "Farewell Address," that we must not "entangle our peace and prosperity" in foreign alliances.

6. The guarantee that the individual will not be held under unlawful arrest.
7. George Washington.

had destined for him the fairest page in the volume of faithful history, I ask so much confidence only as may give firmness and effect to the legal administration of your affairs. I shall often go wrong through defect of judgment. When right, I shall often be thought wrong by those whose positions will not command a view of the whole ground. I ask your indulgence for my own errors, which will never be intentional; and your support against the errors of others who may condemn what they would not, if seen in all its parts. The approbation implied by your suffrage is a great consolation to me for the past; and my future solicitude will be to retain the good opinion of those who have bestowed it in advance, to conciliate that of others by doing them all the good in my power, and to be instrumental to the happiness and freedom of all.

Relying then on the patronage of your good-will, I advance with obedience to the work, ready to retire from it whenever you become sensible how much better choice it is in your power to make. And may that Infinite Power which rules the destinies of the universe lead our councils to what is best, and give them a favorable issue for your peace and prosperity.

1801

From Notes on the State of Virginia [8]

[*A Southerner on Slavery*] [9]

There must doubtless be an unhappy influence on the manners of our people produced by the existence of slavery among us. The whole commerce between master and slave is a perpetual exercise of the most boisterous passions, the most unremitting despotism on the one part, and degrading submissions on the other. Our children see this and learn to imitate it, for man is an imitative animal. This quality is the germ of all education in him. From his cradle to his grave he is learning to do what he sees others do. If a parent could find no motive either in his philanthropy or his self-love for restraining the intemperance of passion toward his slave, it should always be a sufficient one that his child is present. But generally it

8. *Notes on the State of Virginia* resulted from an official inquiry received by Jefferson in 1781, the year of his retirement as governor of his state. The Marquis de Barbé-Marbois, secretary of the French legation at Philadelphia, formulated a series of questions of interest to him in official negotiations. Jefferson's extended reply, in twenty-three sections, dealt with natural resources, geography, landscape, inhabitants (including the Indians), slavery, government, laws and civil rights, education, religious freedom, social customs, and a number of other topics. Two hundred copies, dated 1782, were printed for private distribution in 1784–1785. The appearance of a French translation caused Jefferson to issue an authorized London edition in 1787, reprinted in Philadelphia in 1788. Additional material and notes appeared in the editions of 1800 and 1853.
9. From Query 18.

is not sufficient. The parent storms, the child looks on, catches the lineaments of wrath, puts on the same airs in the circle of smaller slaves, gives a loose to the worst of passions, and thus nursed, educated, and daily exercised in tyranny, cannot but be stamped by it with odious peculiarities. The man must be a prodigy who can retain his manners and morals undepraved by such circumstances. And with what execration should the statesman be loaded who, permitting one-half of the citizens thus to trample on the rights of the others, transforms those into despots, and these into enemies, destroys the morals of the one part, and the *amor patriae* [1] of the other. For if a slave can have a country in this world, it must be any other in preference to that in which he is born to live and labor for another; in which he must lock up the faculties of his nature, contribute as far as depends on his individual endeavors to the evanishment of the human race, or entail [2] his own miserable condition on the endless generations proceeding from him. With the morals of the people, their industry also is destroyed. For in a warm climate, no man will labor for himself who can make another labor for him. This is so true that, of the proprietors of slaves, a very small proportion indeed are ever seen to labor. And can the liberties of a nation be thought secure when we have removed their only firm basis, a conviction in the minds of the people that these liberties are of the gift of God? That they are not to be violated but with His wrath? Indeed, I tremble for my country when I reflect that God is just; that His justice cannot sleep forever; that considering numbers, nature, and natural means only, a revolution of the wheel of fortune, an exchange of situation, is among possible events; that it may become probable by supernatural interference! The Almighty has no attribute which can take side with us in such a contest. But it is impossible to be temperate and to pursue this subject through the various considerations of policy, of morals, of history natural and civil. We must be contented to hope they will force their way into everyone's mind. I think a change already perceptible, since the origin of the present revolution. [3] The spirit of the master is abating, that of the slave rising from the dust, his condition mollifying, the way, I hope, preparing, under the auspices of heaven, for a total emancipation, and that this is disposed, in the order of events, to be with the consent of the masters, rather than by their extirpation.

1. Love of country.
2. A legal term meaning "to settle on an heir" (as by bequest or inheritance).
3. *I.e.*, the American Revolution.

Letter to John Adams [4]

[*The True Aristocracy*]

MONTICELLO, OCTOBER 28, 1813.

* * * I agree with you that there is a natural aristocracy among men. The grounds of this are virtue and talents. Formerly, bodily powers gave place among the aristoi.[5] But since the invention of gunpowder has armed the weak as well as the strong with missile death, bodily strength, like beauty, good humor, politeness and other accomplishments, has become but an auxiliary ground for distinction. There is also an artificial aristocracy, founded on wealth and birth, without either virtue or talents; for with these it would belong to the first class. The natural aristocracy I consider as the most precious gift of nature, for the instruction, the trusts, and government of society. And indeed, it would have been inconsistent in creation to have formed man for the social state, and not to have provided virtue and wisdom enough to manage the concerns of the society. May we not even say, that that form of government is the best, which provides the most effectually for a pure selection of these natural aristoi into the offices of government? The artificial aristocracy is a mischievous ingredient in government, and provision should be made to prevent its ascendency. On the question, what is the best provision, you and I differ; but we differ as rational friends, using the free exercise of our own reason, and mutually indulging its errors. You think it best to put the pseudo-aristoi [6] into a separate chamber of legislation, where they may be hindered from doing mischief by their coordinate branches, and where, also, they may be a protection to wealth against the Agrarian and plundering enterprises of the majority of the people. I think that to give them power in order to prevent them from doing mischief, is arming them for it, and increasing instead of remedying the evil. For if the co-ordinate branches can arrest their action, so may they that of the co-ordinates. Mischief may be done negatively as well as positively. Of this, a cabal in the Senate of the United States has furnished many proofs. Nor do I believe them necessary

4. The Jefferson–Adams correspondence, comprising more than 150 letters, is one of the greatest in the annals of history. The two patriots had become estranged in politics; the Federalist Adams won the presidency in 1796, despite the opposition of Jefferson, who then succeeded him in 1801, when his Democratic Republican party bitterly attacked the conservatism of the Massachusetts incumbent. Reconciled in 1812, they exchanged their experienced wisdom on the issues of their world until they died, both on the anniversary of national independence, in 1826.

5. In Greek, literally, "the best." In two letters Adams has learnedly argued from ancient and recent examples that, without attention to aristocracy, "no society can pretend to establish a free government. * * * The five pillars of aristocracy are beauty, wealth, birth, genius, and virtue"; but "any one of the first three" outweighs either or both of the others. Jefferson emphasizes genius and virtue.

6. See above, "artificial aristocracy, founded on wealth and birth."

to protect the wealthy; because enough of these will find their way into every branch of the legislation, to protect themselves. From fifteen to twenty legislatures of our own, in action for thirty years past, have proved that no fears of an equalization of property are to be apprehended from them. I think the best remedy is exactly that provided by all our constitutions, to leave to the citizens the free election and separation of the aristoi from the pseudo-aristoi, of the wheat from the chaff. In general they will elect the really good and wise. In some instances, wealth may corrupt, and birth blind them; but not in sufficient degree to endanger the society.

It is probable that our difference of opinion may, in some measure, be produced by a difference of character in those among whom we lived. From what I have seen of Massachusetts and Connecticut myself, and still more from what I have heard, and the character given of the former by yourself (volume I, page 111),[7] who know them so much better, there seems to be in those two States a traditional reverence for certain families, which has rendered the offices of the government nearly hereditary in those families. I presume that from an early period of your history, members of those families happening to possess virtue and talents, have honestly exercised them for the good of the people, and by their services have endeared their names to them. In coupling Connecticut with you, I mean it politically only, not morally. For having made the Bible the common law of their land, they seemed to have modeled their morality on the story of Jacob and Laban.[8] But although this hereditary succession to office with you, may, in some degree, be founded in real family merit, yet in a much higher degree, it has proceeded from your strict alliance of Church and State. These families are canonised in the eyes of the people on common principles, "you tickle me, and I will tickle you." In Virginia we have nothing of this. Our clergy, before the revolution, having been secured against rivalship by fixed salaries, did not give themselves the trouble of acquiring influence over the people. Of wealth, there were great accumulations in particular families, handed down from generation to generation, under the English law of entails.[9] But the only object of ambition for the wealthy was a seat in the King's Council. All their court then was paid to the crown and its creatures; and they Philipised[1] in all collisions between the King and the people. Hence they were unpopular; and

7. Referring to Adams's *Defense of the Constitutions of Government of the United States of America* (3 vols., Philadelphia, 1797; earlier editions, London, 1787 and 1794).
8. Genesis xxvii–xxxi. A dynastic family was founded on the relations in marriage between Jacob and Laban's daughters.
9. An entailed estate could not be sold or given away and was passed on as a whole from generation to generation.
1. In reference to the leaders whom Philip II of Macedon bribed to support his policies intended to destroy the independence of the Greek cities.

that unpopularity continues attached to their names. A Randolph, a Carter, or a Burwell must have great personal superiority over a common competitor to be elected by the people even at this day. At the first session of our legislature after the Declaration of Independence, we passed a law abolishing entails. And this was followed by one abolishing the privilege of primogeniture, and dividing the lands of intestates equally among all their children, or other representatives.[2] These laws, drawn by myself, laid the ax to the foot of pseudo-aristocracy. And had another which I prepared been adopted by the legislature, our work would have been complete. It was a bill for the more general diffusion of learning. This proposed to divide every county into wards of five or six miles square, like your townships; to establish in each ward a free school for reading, writing and common arithmetic; to provide for the annual selection of the best subjects from these schools, who might receive, at the public expense, a higher degree of education at a district school; and from these district schools to select a certain number of the most promising subjects, to be completed at an University, where all the useful sciences should be taught. Worth and genius would thus have been sought out from every condition of life, and completely prepared by education for defeating the competition of wealth and birth for public trusts. My proposition had, for a further object, to impart to these wards those portions of self-government for which they are best qualified, by confiding to them the care of their poor, their roads, police, elections, the nomination of jurors, administration of justice in small cases, elementary exercises of militia; in short, to have made them little republics, with a warden at the head of each, for all those concerns which, being under their eye, they would better manage than the larger republics of the county or State. A general call of ward meetings by their wardens on the same day through the State, would at any time produce the genuine sense of the people on any required point, and would enable the State to act in mass, as your people have so often done, and with so much effect by their town meetings. The law for religious freedom, which made a part of this system, having put down the aristocracy of the clergy, and restored to the citizen the freedom of the mind, and those of entails and descents nurturing an equality of condition among them, this on education would have raised the mass of the people to the high ground of moral respectability necessary to their own safety, and to orderly government; and would have completed the great object of qualifying them to select the veritable aristoi, for the trusts of government, to the exclusion of the pseudalists; and the

2. Jefferson had fostered this legislation against hereditary wealth in Virginia. Primogeniture secured the estate to the oldest son. Intestates are those who leave no will and testament at death.

same Theognis who has furnished the epigraphs of your two letters, assures us that Οὐδεμίαν πω Κύρν᾽, ἀγαθοὶ πόλιν ὤλεσαν ἄνδρες.[3]

Although this law has not yet been acted on but in a small and inefficient degree, it is still considered as before the legislature, with other bills of the revised code, not yet taken up, and I have great hope that some patriotic spirit will, at a favorable moment, call it up, and make it the keystone of the arch of our government.

With respect to aristocracy, we should further consider, that before the establishment of the American States, nothing was known to history but the man of the old world, crowded within limits either small or overcharged, and steeped in the vices which that situation generates. A government adapted to such men would be one thing; but a very different one, that for the man of these States. Here every one may have land to labor for himself, if he chooses; or, preferring the exercise of any other industry, may exact for it such compensation as not only to afford a comfortable subsistence, but wherewith to provide for a cessation from labor in old age. Every one, by his property, or by his satisfactory situation, is interested in the support of law and order. And such men may safely and advantageously reserve to themselves a wholesome control over their public affairs, and a degree of freedom, which, in the hands of the *canaille* [4] of the cities of Europe, would be instantly perverted to the demolition and destruction of everything public and private. The history of the last twenty-five years of France,[5] and of the last forty years in America, nay of its last two hundred years, proves the truth of both parts of this observation.

But even in Europe a change has sensibly taken place in the mind of man. Science had liberated the ideas of those who read and reflect, and the American example had kindled feelings of right in the people. An insurrection has consequently begun, of science, talents, and courage, against rank and birth, which have fallen into contempt. It has failed in its first effort, because the mobs of the cities, the instrument used for its accomplishment, debased by ignorance, poverty and vice, could not be restrained to rational action. But the world will recover from the panic of this first catastrophe. Science is progressive, and talents and enterprise on the alert. Resort may be had to the people of the country, a more governable power from their principles and subordination; and rank, and birth, and tinsel-aristocracy will finally shrink into insignificance, even there. This, however, we have no right to meddle with. It suffices for us, if the moral and physical condition of our own citizens qualifies them to select the able and good for

3. Good men, Curnus, have not yet destroyed any state (Theognis, I, 43).
4. Rabble.

5. *I.e.*, since the beginning of the French Revolution.

the direction of their government, with a recurrence of elections at such short periods as will enable them to displace an unfaithful servant, before the mischief he meditates may be irremediable.

I have thus stated my opinion on a point on which we differ, not with a view to controversy, for we are both too old to change opinions which are the result of a long life of inquiry and reflection; but on the suggestions of a former letter of yours, that we ought not to die before we have explained ourselves to each other. We acted in perfect harmony, through a long and perilous contest for our liberty and independence. A constitution has been acquired, which, though neither of us thinks perfect, yet both consider as competent to render our fellow citizens the happiest and the securest on whom the sun has ever shone. If we do not think exactly alike as to its imperfections, it matters little to our country, which, after devoting to it long lives of disinterested labor, we have delivered over to our successors in life, who will be able to take care of it and of themselves.

Of the pamphlet on aristocracy which has been sent to you, or who may be its author, I have heard nothing but through your letter. If the person you suspect, it may be known from the quaint, mystical, and hyperbolical ideas, involved in affected, new-fangled and pedantic terms which stamp his writings. Whatever it be, I hope your quiet is not to be affected at this day by the rudeness or intemperence of scribblers; but that you may continue in tranquillity to live and to rejoice in the prosperity of our country, until it shall be your own wish to take your seat among the aristoi who have gone before you. Ever and affectionately yours.

PHILIP FRENEAU

(1752–1832)

Judged in his own time by his political opponents as "a writer of wretched and insolent doggerel, an incendiary journalist," Philip Freneau was nevertheless our third important poet. His double rôle as poet and political journalist in the transitional age of the Revolution is consistent with the contradictions of his poetry. Freneau was neoclassical by training and taste yet romantic in essential spirit. He was also at once a satirist and a sentimentalist, a humanitarian but

also a bitter polemicist, a poet of Reason yet the celebrant of "lovely Fancy," and a deistic optimist most inspired by themes of death and transience.

Feneau was born on January 2, 1752, in New York, of French Huguenot and Scottish stock. He was tutored for Princeton ("that hotbed of Whiggery") where he established close friendships with a future president, James Madison, and a future novelist, Hugh Henry Brackenridge. In collaboration with the latter he produced his earliest work; slightly later, in "The Power of Fancy" (1770), a genuine independence appears. After graduation and an unsatisfactory teaching experience, he gained his first popular success in New York in 1775 as a satirist of the British. In 1776 Freneau made his first voyage to the West Indies, where he wrote "The House of Night," foreshadowing the Gothic mood of Poe and Coleridge—F. L. Pattee calls it "the first distinctly romantic note heard in America" —and "The Beauties of Santa Cruz," blending the praise of nature with social protest in his characteristic later manner. This poetry foretold achievement of a distinguished order, but he was soon diverted from literature into the tide of revolution. As passenger on an American ship attacked by the British in 1780, he was taken prisoner. "The British Prison Ship" (1781), a good piece of invective, reveals the rigors and brutality of his captivity. In truth he now could say: "An age employed in edging steel / Can no poetic rapture feel." In the closing year of the war he became the prolific propagandist, celebrating American victories and leaders, while continuing to hurl his vitriol at the British in many poems. "The poet of the Revolution" they called him, a compliment not wholly to his advantage, since its persistence long obscured the fact that his later poems were his best, and these were quite different. The earlier poems were collected (1786) in *The Poems of Philip Freneau Written Chiefly During the Late War.*

For a few years, writing with sporadic fluency, Freneau earned his living variously as farmer, journalist, and sea captain. His *Miscellaneous Works,* essays and new poems, appeared in 1788. In 1790 he married, and almost literally flung himself, as political journalist, into the raging controversies between the Jeffersonian Democrats, whom he supported, and Hamilton's Federalists. In New York he edited the *Daily Advertiser.* In 1791, probably with Jefferson's support, he established in Philadelphia the *National Gazette,* and campaigned against the opinions of the powerful *Gazette of the United States,* edited by John Fenno, and supported by Hamilton. Simultaneously he served as translating clerk in Jefferson's Department of State. He was soon a power in journalism and politics. When Jefferson withdrew from politics temporarily in 1793, Freneau resigned and his paper failed, in the midst of a Federalist tide which ended only with Jefferson's election to the presidency in 1801. Freneau's social and religious liberalism, in which he resembled Paine, gave the Federalists a deadly weapon against him; indeed his political enemies so besmirched his reputation that he has only recently been recognized as a courageous champion of American popular government.

Reduced in fortune and political ambition, he settled in 1794 at his plantation homestead, Mount Pleasant, near Freehold, New Jersey, where for a time he edited a New Jersey paper. On his own hand press he published new essays and poems, and revisions of earlier pieces. Collections appeared in 1795 and 1799. His poverty drove him at fifty to resume plowing the sea instead of his "sandy patrimony"; he was captain of coastwise trading vessels from 1803 to 1807. Again he turned to his farm for subsistence, but in 1818 his home burned down, and he gathered together the remnants of his family and possessions in a little farmhouse nearer town. In 1815 he collected in two volumes the poems of his later period, including the interesting work inspired by the War of 1812, in *A Collection of Poems * * * Written Between the Year 1797 and the Present Time.* After he was seventy, he worked on the public roads; "he went," says Leary, "from house to house as tinker, mending clocks, and doing other

small jobs of repairing." He continued almost until his death to send poems to the newspapers. Poor and nearly forgotten, he died of exposure in 1832 at the age of eighty, after losing his way in a blizzard, as he returned, it is said, from a tavern.

The standard edition of the poetry is *The Poems of Philip Freneau,* 3 vols., edited by F. L. Pattee, 1902–1907. Selections are *Poems of Freneau,* edited by H. H. Clark, 1929, and Philip M. Marsh, ed., *A Freneau Sampler,* 1963. Additional poems are found in *The Last Poems of Philip Freneau,* edited by Lewis Leary, 1946. Philip M. Marsh edited *The Prose of Philip Freneau,* 1955. H. H. Clark has published a facsimile of the 1799 edition of *Letters on Various Interesting and Important Subjects,* 1943. An authoritative critical biography is *That Rascal Freneau: A Study in Literary Failure,* by Lewis Leary, 1941. More recent is Jacob Axelrad, *Philip Freneau: Champion of Democracy,* 1967. Another biography is that of Pattee, in Volume I of his edition of the *Poems;* while H. H. Clark's edition contains a penetrating critical introduction.

To the Memory of the Brave Americans [1]

UNDER GENERAL GREENE, IN SOUTH CAROLINA, WHO FELL
IN THE ACTION OF SEPTEMBER 8, 1781.

At Eutaw Springs the valiant died;
  Their limbs with dust are covered o'er—
Weep on, ye springs, your tearful tide;
  How many heroes are no more!

If in this wreck of ruin, they
  Can yet be thought to claim a tear,   5
O smite your gentle breast, and say
  The friends of freedom slumber here!

Thou, who shalt trace this bloody plain,
  If goodness rules thy generous breast,   10

1. General Nathaniel Greene's fine generalship in the South in 1781 was crucial. Although he lost several hundred men at Eutaw Springs, he prevented the relief of Cornwallis, who surrendered at Yorktown October 19. The poem appeared in the *Freeman's Journal,* November 21, 1781.

Sigh for the wasted rural reign;
Sigh for the shepherds, sunk to rest!

Stranger, their humble graves adorn;
You too may fall, and ask a tear;
'Tis not the beauty of the morn   15
That proves the evening shall be clear.—

They saw their injured country's woe;
The flaming town, the wasted field;
Then rushed to meet the insulting foe;
They took the spear—but left the shield.   20

Led by thy conquering genius, Greene,
The Britons they compelled to fly;
None distant viewed the fatal plain,
None grieved, in such a cause to die—

But, like the Parthian,[2] famed of old,   25
Who, flying, still their arrows threw,
These routed Britons, full as bold,
Retreated, and retreating slew.

Now rest in peace, our patriot band;
Though far from nature's limits thrown,   30
We trust they find a happier land,
A brighter sunshine of their own.

1781   1781, 1786

The Wild Honey Suckle[3]

[handwritten: Seasons in the year]
[handwritten: also possibly the seasons in a man's life]

Fair flower, that dost so comely grow,
Hid in this silent, dull retreat,   *[handwritten: the body]*
Untouched thy honied blossoms blow,
Unseen thy little branches greet:
No roving foot shall crush thee here,   5
No busy hand provoke a tear.

By Nature's self in white arrayed,   *[handwritten: innocence]*
She bade thee shun the vulgar eye,
And planted here the guardian shade,
And sent soft waters murmuring by;   10

---

2. The Parthians, famous cavalrymen of ancient Persia, destroyed their enemies by feigning flight, then suddenly wheeling to discharge their arrows.

3. Then the popular name for a familiar shrub, *azalea viscosa*, sometimes "swamp honeysuckle." *Cf.* Emerson, "The Rhodora."

Thus quietly thy summer goes,
Thy days declining to repose.

Smit with those charms, that must decay,   *aging*
I grieve to see your future doom;
They died—nor were those flowers more gay,
The flowers that did in Eden bloom;   *common in flower.*
   Unpitying frosts, and Autumn's power   *lit : a new land*
   Shall leave no vestige of this flower.

From morning suns and evening dews
At first thy little being came:
If nothing once, you nothing lose,   *Of dust ..*   20
For when you die you are the same;   *. . return to dus*
   The space between, is but an hour,
   The frail duration of a flower.

1786   1786, 1788

The Indian Burying Ground

In spite of all the learned have said,
   I still my old opinion keep;
The posture, that we give the dead,
   Points out the soul's eternal sleep.

Not so the ancients of these lands—   *generalized*
   The Indian, when from life released,   *images : nature*
Again is seated with his friends,   *dressed, poeticized*
   And shares again the joyous feast.[4]

His imaged birds, and painted bowl,
   And venison, for a journey dressed,
archaic → Bespeak the nature of the soul,   10
   Activity, that knows no rest.

His bow, for action ready bent,   *not natural lang*
   And arrows, with a head of stone,   *poeticized*
Can only mean that life is spent,   15
   And not the old ideas gone.

Thou, stranger, that shalt come this way,
   No fraud upon the dead commit—

4. "The North American Indians bury their dead in a sitting posture; decorating the corpse with wampum, the images of birds, quadrupeds, &c: And (if that of a warrior) with bows, arrows, tomhawks [sic], and other military weapons" [Freneau's note].

Observe the swelling turf, and say
    They do not lie, but here they sit.   20

Here still a lofty rock remains,
    On which the curious eye may trace
(Now wasted, half, by wearing rains)
    The fancies of a ruder race.

Here still an aged elm aspires,   25
    Beneath whose far-projecting shade
(And which the shepherd still admires)
    The children of the forest played!

There oft a restless Indian queen
    (Pale Shebah,[5] with her braided hair)   30
And many a barbarous form is seen
    To chide the man that lingers there.

By midnight moons, o'er moistening dews;
    In habit for the chase arrayed,
The hunter still the deer pursues,   35
    The hunter and the deer, a shade!

And long shall timorous fancy see
    The painted chief, and pointed spear,
And Reason's self shall bow the knee
    To shadows and delusions here.   40

1787   1788

On a Honey Bee

DRINKING FROM A GLASS OF WINE AND DROWNED THEREIN [6]

Thou, born to sip the lake or spring,
    Or quaff the waters of the stream,
Why hither come, on vagrant wing?—
    Does Bacchus tempting seem—
        Did he for you this glass prepare?—   5
        Will I admit you to a share?

Did storms harass or foes perplex,
    Did wasps or king-birds bring dismay—

---

5. The Queen of Sheba, a powerful Arabian country, paid a visit in homage to Solomon (I Kings x; II Chronicles ix) and became legendary in literature for her beauty and wisdom.

6. Originally, "On a Bee Drinking from a Glass of Water" (*Time-Piece*, Sept. 6, 1797), this was twice revised, and reprinted with the present title in *Poems* (1809).

Did wars distress, or labors vex,
 Or did you miss your way?—
  A better seat you could not take
  Than on the margin of this lake.   10

Welcome!—I hail you to my glass:
 All welcome, here, you find;
Here, let the cloud of trouble pass,   15
 Here, be all care resigned.—
  This fluid never fails to please,
  And drown the griefs of men or bees.

What forced you here we cannot know,
 And you will scarcely tell—   20
But cheery we would have you go
 And bid a glad farewell:
  On lighter wings we bid you fly,
  Your dart will now all foes defy.

Yet take not, oh! too deep a drink,   25
 And in this ocean die;
Here bigger bees than you might sink,
 Even bees full six feet high.
  Like Pharaoh, then, you would be said
  To perish in a sea of red.[7]   30

Do as you please, your will is mine;
 Enjoy it without fear—
And your grave will be this glass of wine,
 Your epitaph—a tear;
  Go, take your seat on Charon's [8] boat,   35
  We'll tell the hive, you died afloat.

1797, 1809

To a Caty-Did [9]

In a branch of willow hid
Sings the evening Caty-did:
From the lofty locust bough
Feeding on a drop of dew,
In her suit of green array'd   5

7. Pharaoh, king of Egypt, attempting to pursue the Israelites across the Red Sea, lost his army by drowning (Exodus xiv: 1–27).
8. The ferryman of the dead.
9. "A well-known insect, when full grown, about two inches in length, and of the exact color of a green leaf. It is of the genus cicada, or grasshopper kind, inhabiting the green foliage of trees and singing such a song as Caty-did in the evening, towards autumn" [Freneau's note].

Hear her singing in the shade
Caty-did, Caty-did, Caty-did!

While upon a leaf you tread,
Or repose your little head,
On your sheet of shadows laid,   10
All the day you nothing said:
Half the night your cheery tongue
Revell'd out its little song,
Nothing else but Caty-did.

From your lodgings on the leaf   15
Did you utter joy or grief?—
Did you only mean to say,
I have had my summer's day,
And am passing, soon, away
To the grave of Caty-did:—   20
Poor, unhappy Caty-did!

But you would have utter'd more
Had you known of nature's power—
From the world when you retreat,
And a leaf's your winding sheet,   25
Long before your spirit fled,
Who can tell but nature said,
Live again, my Caty-did!
Live and chatter, Caty-did.

Tell me, what did Caty do?   30
Did she mean to trouble you?—
Why was Caty not forbid
To trouble little Caty-did?—
Wrong, indeed at you to fling,
Hurting no one while you sing   35
Caty-did! Caty-did! Caty-did!

Why continue to complain?
Caty tells me, she again
Will not give you plague or pain:—
Caty says you may be hid,   40
Caty will not go to bed
While you sing us Caty-did.
Caty-did! Caty-did! Caty-did!

But, while singing, you forgot
To tell us what did Caty not: 45
Caty-did not think of cold,
Flocks retiring to the fold,

Winter, with his wrinkles old,
Winter, that yourself foretold
　　When you gave us Caty-did. 　　　　50

　Stay securely in your nest;
Caty now, will do her best,
All she can, to make you blest;
But, you want no human aid—
Nature, when she form'd you, said, 　　　55
"Independent you are made,
My dear little Caty-did:
Soon yourself must disappear
With the verdure of the year,"—
And to go, we know not where, 　　　　60
　　With your song of Caty-did.

　　　　　　　　　　　　　1815

On the Universality and Other Attributes of the God of Nature[1]

All that we see, about, abroad,
What is it all, but nature's God?
In meaner works discovered here
No less than in the starry sphere.

In seas, on earth, this God is seen; 　　5
All that exist, upon him lean;
He lives in all, and never strayed
A moment from the works he made:

His system fixed on general laws
Bespeaks a wise creating cause; 　　　10
Impartially he rules mankind
And all that on this globe we find.

Unchanged in all that seems to change,
Unbounded space is his great range;
To one vast purpose always true, 　　15
No time, with him, is old or new.

In all the attributes divine
Unlimited perfectings shine;
In these enwrapt, in these complete,
All virtues in that centre meet. 　　　20

1. Characteristic phrase of Deism, the rationalistic creed of Freneau now at sixty-three as in his youth. For Deism, see Franklin, Paine, and Jefferson, above.

This power doth all powers transcend,
To all intelligence a friend
Exists, the greatest and the best [2]
Throughout all the worlds, to make them blest.

All that he did he first approved,   25
He all things into being loved;
O'er all he made he still presides,
For them in life, or death provides.

1815

2. "*Jupiter, optimus, maximus.—Cicero*" [Freneau's note]. The comparison of pagan and Christian concepts of God was characteristic of Deism; *Cf.* Paine, *The Age of Reason*.

The New Nation and the House Divided

The history of the United States from the beginning of the nineteenth century to the Civil War had almost an epical character. During the early years the new nation successfully defended itself against the sniping of three foreign enemies, while such American statesmen as Washington and Jefferson, Madison and Monroe slowly won for their country the respect if not the affection of European powers. Within a half century, American pioneers had pushed across the forest and mountain barriers, the great rivers and deserts, to the shores of the Pacific, and northwest into Alaska. The power, imagination, and opportunity quickened by political freedom and nationalism were expressed in the development, more rapid than ever before seen, of government, trade, shipping, manufactures, agricultural wealth, and an expanding system of roads and waterways. While the material genius of the country expressed itself luxuriantly, cultural institutions, already strong in the colonies, expanded rapidly; and such authors as Irving, Cooper, Hawthorne,

Poe, Emerson, Longfellow, Melville, and Whitman forged a new literature, rich in native character and tradition, and recognized as American by the world at large. If American literature, like the European literature of the time, was romantic in character, it was not so by imitation, but by virtue of the abounding strangeness of this new continent, and the experience of a way of life in which, for a time, it seemed that the theoretical possibility of uninterrupted human progress might be concretely realized. And then, slowly revealed, the tragic flaw in the American state came into view, the widening, unhealing breach between the sections—and the appalling catastrophe of the Civil War rang down the curtain on an epoch.

REGIONAL INFLUENCES

The city of New York, which by 1800, with a population of sixty thousand, had become the largest city in the United States, was destined to be for several decades the literary capital, the city of the so-called Knickerbocker authors, who derived this label from Washington Irving's

Knickerbocker's History of New York (1809). Prominent among the Knickerbockers were many writers now of only minor interest: such poets as Drake and Halleck, and such men of letters as Charles Fenno Hoffman, Paulding, Verplanck, and Willis. Irving was the only author of this immediate group to achieve high literary distinction, but two other great New York writers, Bryant and Cooper, shared to some degree the Knickerbocker spirit. This spirit was a large-minded, romantic acceptance of life, ranging from Bryant's serious religion of nature to Irving's fantasy and burlesque, and encouraging, especially among its essayists, a worldly sophistication and witty gaiety. The New York theater flourished, and in the development of newspaper journalism the city soon led the nation.

Philadelphia, which had been called "the Athens of America" during the late colonial period, continued to produce literary works, but few of its writers rose to prominence, and many of the more talented found their way to New York, as they have been doing ever since. Philadelphia continued as the center of a new popular periodical literature, represented by *Godey's* and *Graham's*; it long remained an incubating ground for liberal ideas and humanitarian reform; and it maintained leadership in the development of science and technology. Meanwhile, the South built a flourishing agrarian civilization and a distinguished planter-aristocracy on the shaky foundations of slavery, while expending a great deal of its energy, and much of its traditional genius for statesmanship, in defending that doomed institution. At Richmond, and more importantly at Charleston, there developed small coteries of writers, but none were of national prominence except Poe and the Charlestonian William Gilmore Simms. The latter was greatly praised and widely popular, but today few besides the literary specialist are acquainted with his faintly Byronic poetry, or with his many novels of frontier adventure. Cooper has outlived this later rival because of his true sense of history and his creation of a few living characters.

In this first period of our national literature, however, the most spectacular development was the movement generally known as the "renaissance" of New England. It began in a new intellectualism, Unitarian and transcendental, which was crowned by the appearance of the works of Emerson in the late thirties, and by the later masterpieces of Thoreau. New England contributed vitally to the reform movements, especially abolition; it produced, in such figures as Hawthorne, Longfellow, Holmes, and Lowell, creators of a literature which combined a high democratic idealism with a patrician intellectual leadership.

ROMANTICISM

The remarkable and opulent literature which developed in various regions is best explained by reference to certain stirring events of our national history, infused by the surging romanticism which had its sources both at home and abroad. Romanticism is not an organized system, but rather a particular attitude toward the realities of man, nature, and society. From the middle of the eighteenth century, the romantic spirit gradually strengthened, especially in Germany, France, and England; in English literature it flourished earlier than in America, particularly among such writers as Burns, Wordsworth, Coleridge, Shelley, Keats, and Byron. In reaction against the neoclassical spirit, the romantic preferred freedom to formalism and emphasized individualism instead of authority. He exalted the imagination above either rationalism or strict fidelity to factual delineation. He rejected the validity of material reality in favor of innate or intuitive perception by the heart of man: *"intimations* of immortality" were taken to *prove* immortality. In consequence, the romantic gave faith and credence to ideality and elevation—to a reality that was considered more lofty, and truer, than the evidence of substantial things. Romantic reliance upon the importance of the subconscious, inner life was illustrated in Emerson's intuitionalism, and also produced a profound interest in abnormal psychology, shown, for instance, by Poe and Hawthorne.

Yet in its view of nature, the romantic movement was essentially simple, as compared with that of rationalism: its universe was beautiful, and man was the chosen and favored creature in it, as in the nature poems of Wordsworth, Bryant, or Longfellow. In another manifestation, romanticism reveled in strangeness and mystery, producing in one direction the medievalism of Keats and Lowell, and in another the fantastic visions of Coleridge or Poe.

One impulse of romanticism was humanitarian; it romanticized the "common man"; it produced an age of reform movements; it developed a lavish enthusiasm for the primitive—for ancient ballads, epics, and folk literature, and for the "noble savage," usually in the idealization of the American Indian. In some manifestations, especially in America, it reveled in broad forms of humor and burlesque. In every country, romanticism produced a luxuriant new literature, with wide variations among authors, but everywhere certain characteristics persisted: opulence and freedom, devotion to individualism, a reliance upon the good of nature and "natural" man, and an abiding faith in the boundless resources of the human spirit and imagination.

Basically, the romantic spirit is rebellious; it thrives in turbulent times, in revolution and conflict; it encourages an optimistic expectation of improvement. These conditions of romanticism had been present in the American and French revolutions. The later period, which produced such American romantics as Bryant, Irving, and Cooper, was also a time of hopeful challenge. During the youth of this generation, the young republic asserted its independence over and over again: in two diplomatic victories over the French, in leading the world against the Barbary pirates, in resisting British pretensions by war in 1812; and finally, in announcing its western hegemony by the Monroe Doctrine of 1823. Internally an even more astonishing accomplishment extended the American dominion from the Northwest Territory to Oregon, from Louisiana to the Rockies, and (by means of the Mexican War in 1848) through the southwest from Texas to California. For such romantics as Bryant, Irving, Cooper, and their lesser emulators this expansion was a contagious influence, and these frontiers were an invitation to adventure, strongly reflected in their writings.

However, a number of our most powerful romantic authors had been brooding upon problems for which optimism and expansion provided no answers. In Poe and Hawthorne the spiritual questioning of romanticism found its first great American representatives. In their chief works they sought the reality of man in the hidden recesses of the mind and the spirit, and probed these obscure sources of behavior and moral judgment. Poe, like Keats and Coleridge, embodied his revelations in aesthetic symbolism, except in his tales of detection and science— a form of narrative that he invented. By contrast, Hawthorne, equipped with a penetrating sense of history, found his symbolism in man's conflict with the vestiges of the past, indelibly fixed in his moral nature and his social environment. Before Poe and Hawthorne, symbolic literature had appeared in America only in the expression of the rapt visions of early religious mystics, such as Edwards and Woolman; now Poe especially carried symbolic idealism to a level so advanced that he became the inspiration for certain of the French symbolists, and hence a strong influence on the literary expression of the twentieth century. Melville, another great original, stands closer to the tradition of Hawthorne than to any other. Like Hawthorne, he was obsessed by the enigma of evil, but while the New Englander prevailingly took the Puritan morality as a point of departure, Melville drew symbols from land and sea for his explorations into the shadowed heart of the universe.

THE SPIRIT OF REFORM

Early in the nineteenth century the new republic began to experience the social disorders inevitably attendant upon its unprecedented expansion in territory, population, and industrial activity. American writers responded with a swelling tide of literature devoted to humanitarian reform movements. During the thirty years before the Civil War the population of the United States increased from thirteen to thirty million white Americans. Although nearly half of the nation's population had pushed beyond the Alleghenies by 1830, there were already at that time increasing concentrations in eastern urban and industrial centers, where recent immigrants accounted for about 12 per cent of the nation. The remarkable development of industry and financial institutions was accompanied by economic crises and a kind of poverty that the younger agrarian nation had not known. Even the frontier, for all its glamor, adventure, and homestead land, was the scene of back-breaking labor, and of stringently limited educational and cultural opportunity. The election in 1800 of Jefferson, a patrician who trusted the people, has been regarded as breaking the ruling authority of "the rich, the well-born, and the able," and in 1828 the frontier elected its own popular hero, Andrew Jackson, with a direct mandate from the common people. The increasing determination of these masses to be heard in the national government remained a powerful influence against the entrenchment of monopoly and privilege. For these masses Negro slavery was an intolerable threat against the enterprise of free men; and the spirit of the frontier, no less than the moral abhorrence which impelled the North, was influential in precipitating the Civil War.

Respect for the common man and a belief in his capacities was a romantic assumption honored by writers on every hand. Bryant, as a great metropolitan editor, espoused human and civil rights, supported the nascent labor movement and many other reforms, and steadily opposed the extension of slavery. Hawthorne and Melville continued to regard the improvement of society as indispensable for the spirit of mankind. The transcendentalists in general resembled Thoreau rather than Emerson in their active and often rebellious participation in support of various reforms, and especially abolition. Fundamen-

tally, if in varying measure, the reform spirit infused the writing of such New England Brahmins as Longfellow, Lowell, and even Holmes, while Whittier, a man of the people, spent himself, and perhaps mortgaged his artistic potential, in humanitarian causes. New reform movements and organizations flourished, and reform became a profession attracting talented and powerful leadership. Well-directed groups joined forces with British reformers to improve the standards of criminology, to abolish inhuman punishments and imprisonment for debt, to clean up the loathsome jails and provide rehabilitation instead of punishment. Societies for aid to the physically handicapped bore fruit in schools for the deaf and the blind, and asylums for the insane—Dorothea Dix added this interest to her earlier crusade for prison reform.

The American Temperance Society was founded in 1826, and many lecturers, some as prominent as Channing, Beecher, and Garrison, drew large audiences, while local church communities organized auxiliaries of pledge-signers. The women's rights movement drew such leaders as Margaret Fuller, journalist of transcendentalism, Elizabeth Cady Stanton, and Lucretia Mott. In 1848, the movement rose to the national scale with the meeting of the first women's congress at Seneca Falls, New York. Women crusaded for equality with men in educational opportunities and employment, in marriage and property ownership; and they were a vigorous auxiliary to the temperance movement and to the campaigns for factory reforms affecting women and child workers, especially in the New England cotton mills.

TRANSCENDENTALISM

The many important modifications in religious doctrine and in sectarian organizations, especially among Protestant denominations, were of importance for literature principally in New England, where a strong intellectualist mysticism among Unitarian thinkers stimulated the transcendental movement. Even so, Unitarianism and transcendentalism became a concern of our major literature only because of the great stature of Emerson and Thoreau. All other transcendental writers, for example, Bronson Alcott, Margaret Fuller, the Channings, and Orestes Brownson, were at most of secondary importance.

Yet for the history of ideas in the United States, transcendentalism wrote an important chapter. It was the expression for one age of an intuitional idealism which has taken various forms in American thought as a counter-current to rationalistic and authoritarian orthodoxies from early times; whether among dissenters from Puritanism, or Puritan and Quaker mystics, or, as late as 1897, in William James's hypothesis of a "Will to Believe."

Transcendentalism was a philosophical dissent from Unitarianism, which represented the compromise of rational Deism with Calvinism, retaining the rationalists' acceptance of liberal scientific thought, and rejecting extreme concepts concerning the original depravity and the inherited guilt of man. In Unitarianism the Godhead was conceived as Unity, not Trinity; it was the human potential in the acts and words of Jesus that gave them sublime importance; and the Holy Ghost was the divine spark in every man. The rising young transcendentalists asserted that the Unitarian creed had become conventional and complacent in its orthodox fidelity to Christian dogmas of supernaturalism. Transcendentalists rejected Locke's materialistic psychology in favor of the idealism of the German thinker Immanuel Kant (*The Critique of Pure Reason,* 1781), who declared that the "transcendental" knowledge in the mind of man was innate, or *a priori;* the transcendentalists interpreted this view as supporting the belief that intuition surpassed reason as a guide to the truth. Thus they evolved a theological monism, in which the divine immanence of God coexisted with the universe and the individual; they asserted the doctrine of correspondence between the microcosm of the individual mind and the macrocosmic Oversoul of the universe; and hence they derived an enlarged conception of the sanctity of the individual and his freedom to follow his intuitional knowledge.

American transcendentalists were influenced by such British writers as Wordsworth, Coleridge, and Carlyle; they drew on such German idealistic philosophers as Kant, Hegel, Fichte, and Schelling, and on the writings of Goethe, Richter, Herder, and others; they sought confirmation among the ancients: the Greek philosophers, especially Plato, the Neoplatonists, and the Hindu wisdom of the age-old Vedas. They read the Christian mystics from the Middle Ages to Swedenborg.

The Transcendental Club, an informal group, met oftenest at Emerson's Concord home, and its members were chiefly responsible for *The Dial* (1840–1844), the famous little magazine that Emerson edited for two of its four years. One group of transcendentalists concerned themselves with reform movements and social revolt; Thoreau is the most noteworthy of these in respect to literary values. Brook Farm (1841) and Fruitlands (1842) were agrarian experiments in communal living supported briefly by transcendentalists concerned with the social order.

INEVITABLE CONFLICT

From colonial days, antislavery leaders had preached gradual emancipation; but in 1831, a group led by William Lloyd Garrison, editor of the newly founded abolition magazine, *The Liberator*, had formed the militant New England Anti-Slavery Society. Two years later, all such organizations met together in Philadelphia to found the American Anti-Slavery Society. Among the many who attended was Whittier, who thereafter gave the bulk of his limited strength to the cause. The crusade for abolition was carried on in press and pulpit, and on the lecture platform. The succeeding events are too well-known to require formal discussion.

When the Mexican War threatened, Lowell abandoned the dream world of *Sir Launfal* and lighted the caustic flame of the *Biglow Papers*. Longfellow's "Building of the Ship," like Whittier's "Ichabod," reveals the varied emotional reactions of the period. Thoreau's resistance to the Mexican War involved an act of civil disobedience, and he then published the famous essay of that title, initiating a philosophy of pacific resistance. Upon the enactment of the strengthened Fugitive Slave Law of 1850, even the pacifistic Emerson wrote firmly in his *Journal*, "I will not obey it, by God." Act by act, as the following texts reveal, our literature reflects the later events of the drama: the Kansas-Nebraska Bill, the Kansas insurrections, John Brown's life and death, the Lincoln-Douglas debates, the disruption of the Democrats, the new Republican party, the election of Lincoln, and the war itself.

Romantic Rediscovery: Nature, Man, Society

WASHINGTON IRVING
(1783–1859)

As a writer, Washington Irving was so naturally endowed that he seemed to drift into his career at the whim of circumstances and his own inclinations. Humorists are always likely to be taken for granted, and there has been no searching revaluation of Irving such as should have been provoked by the perceptive biography by Stanley T. Williams (1935). With Cooper, Poe, and Hawthorne, Irving has survived all other American writers of fiction before Melville, and he still finds new readers with every passing generation. He was the first great prose stylist of American romanticism, and his familiar style was destined to outlive the formal prose of such contemporaries as Scott and Cooper, and to provide a model for the prevailing prose narrative of the future.

The apparent ease of his writing is not simply that of the gifted amateur; it results from his purposeful identification of his whole personality with what he wrote. He was urbane and worldly, yet humorous and gentle; a robust connoisseur, yet innately reserved; a patrician, yet sympathetic toward the people. His vast reading, following only the impulse of his own enthusiasms, resulted in a rich if random literary inheritance, revealed in all that he wrote. His response to the period of Addison, Swift, and Johnson, with its great and graceful style, and his enthusiasm for the current European romanticism, enabled him to combine these with his independent literary personality and American roots.

It is instructive to consider the number of his literary innovations. He was our first great belletrist, writing always for pleasure, and to produce pleasure; yet readers of all classes responded to him in a country in which the didactic and utilitarian had formerly prevailed. He gave an impetus both to the extravagant American humor of which Mark Twain became the classic, and to the urbane wit that has survived in writers ranging from Holmes and Lowell to the *New Yorker* wits of the present century. In his *Sketch Book* appeared the first modern short stories and the first great American juvenile literature. He was among the first of the moderns to write good history and biography as literary entertainment. He introduced the familiar essay to America. On his own whimsical terms, Irving restored the waning Gothic romances which Poe soon infused with psychological subtleties. The scope of his life and his writing was international, and produced a certain breadth of view in his readers; yet his best-known stories awakened an interest in the life of American regions from the Hudson valley to the prairies of the West. His influence abroad, as writer, as visitor, and as diplomat, was that of a gifted cultural ambassador, at home on both continents, at a time when his young country badly needed such representation. He was the only American writer of his generation who could chide the British in an atmosphere of good humor.

The events of Irving's life are characterized by the same casual approach and distinguished results. Gently born and well educated, the youngest of eleven children of a prosperous New York merchant, he began a genteel reading for the law at sixteen, but preferred a literary Bohemianism. At nineteen he published, in his brother's newspaper, his "Jonathan Oldstyle" satires of New York life. By the age of twenty-three, when he was admitted to the New York bar, he had roamed the Hudson

valley and been a literary vagabond in England, Holland, France, and Italy, reading and studying what pleased him, which was a great deal, and reveling in the gay world of the theater. Back in New York, he joined with his brother, William, and James Kirke Paulding, in 1807, in producing the *Salmagundi* papers, Addisonian commentaries on New York society and frivolities. *A History of New York, by Diedrich Knickerbocker* (1809), a rollicking burlesque of a current serious history of the early Dutch settlers, has become a classic of humor, and might have launched an immediate career for its author.

A personal tragedy, however, changed his course for a time; the death of his fiancée, Matilda Hoffman, coincided with the demands of the family cutlery firm, and in 1810 he went to Washington as representative of the business. In 1815 he again turned restlessly to his European roving, with headquarters in England during the next seventeen years, but his literary career was soon to catch up with him again. In 1818 the failure of the Irving firm, which had bountifully supported his leisure, threw family responsibilities upon him, and he loyally plunged into the authorship for which he had almost unconsciously prepared himself. The *Sketch Book* appeared serially in 1819–1820, and in volume form shortly thereafter it at once had an international success. *Bracebridge Hall* followed in 1822; then he first went to Germany in pursuit of an interest in German romanticism, which flavored the *Tales of a Traveller* (1824) and other later writings. Meanwhile in Paris he had met John Howard Payne, the American dramatist and actor; his collaboration with him resulted brilliantly in *Charles the Second, or The Merry Monarch*, one of the most successful social comedies of its time.

From 1826 to 1829 he was in Spain on diplomatic business, residing for a time in the Alhambra. His reading at that period, including the study of Spanish historical sources, resulted in a number of important works: *A History of the Life and Voyages of Christopher Columbus* (1828), *A Chronicle of the Conquest of Granada* (1829), *Voyages and Discoveries of the Companions of Columbus* (1831), a famous volume of stories and sketches—The *Alhambra* (1832), and "Legends of the Conquest of Spain" (in *The Crayon Miscellany*, 1835).

Before *The Alhambra* appeared, he was on his way back to the United States after two years as secretary of the American legation in London (1829–1831). American reviewers had commented, often with irritation, on his seeming preference for Europe, but the charges were exaggerated. After seventeen years abroad he returned with the desire to portray his own country again, and although such western adventures as *A Tour on the Prairies* (1835), *Astoria* (history of Astor's fur trade, 1836), and *The Adventures of Captain Bonneville* (explorations in the Rocky Mountains, 1837), are not among his best work, they broke new trails in our literature. In 1836 he

made his home at Sunnyside, near Tarrytown, so lovingly described years before as "Sleepy Hollow." He had already declined a nomination to Congress; now he declined to run for mayor of New York, or to become Van Buren's secretary of the navy. Instead he wrote a good *Life of Oliver Goldsmith* (1840), and began the *Life of George Washington* (published 1855–1859), long a standard work. From 1842 to 1845 he served as minister to Spain, then settled at Sunnyside, which he remodeled and enlarged, while preparing the revised edition of his works, and completing his *Washington*. The fifth and last volume of the latter appeared just before his death in 1859.

The standard edition of Irving's work is *The Works of Washington Irving*, Author's Uniform Revised Edition, 21 vols., 1860–1861, reissued in 12 vols., 1881, the source of the texts here reprinted. *The Complete Works of Washington Irving* in 28 vols., with Henry A. Pochmann as general editor, is now being published by the University of Wisconsin Press under the auspices of the CEAA. *The Journals of Washington Irving*, 3 vols., 1919, were edited by W. P. Trent and G. S. Hellman, and a number of volumes of the letters have been published. Several later editions, individual volumes, are easily available; note especially *Knickerbocker's History of New York*, edited by Stanley T. Williams and Tremaine McDowell, 1927, and Edwin T. Bowden, ed., *A History of New York*, 1964. *Washington Irving: Representative Selections*, edited by Henry A. Pochmann, American Writers Series, 1934, has a useful introduction and bibliography.

Pierre M. Irving published the first standard *Life and Letters * * ** , 4 vols., 1862–1864; other good lives are those by Charles Dudley Warner, 1890, and G. S. Hellman, 1925. However, the definitive biographical and critical study is that by Stanley T. Williams: *The Life of Washington Irving*, 2 vols., 1935. See also Edward Wagenknecht, *Washington Irving: Moderation Displayed*, 1962, and William L. Hedges, *Washington Irving, An American Study*, 1965.

From A History of New York, by Diedrich Knickerbocker [1]

Book III: In Which Is Recorded the Golden Reign of Wouter Van Twiller

CHAPTER I: OF THE RENOWNED WOUTER VAN TWILLER,[2] HIS UNPARAL-
LELED VIRTUES—AS LIKEWISE HIS UNUTTERABLE WISDOM IN THE LAW
CASE OF WANDLE SCHOONHOVEN AND BARENT BLEECKER—AND THE
GREAT ADMIRATION OF THE PUBLIC THEREAT

* * *

It was in the year of our Lord 1629 [3] that Mynheer Wouter Van
Twiller was apointed governor of the province of Nieuw Neder-
landts, under the commission and control of their High Mighti-
nesses the Lords States General of the United Netherlands, and
the privileged West India Company.

This renowned old gentleman arrived at New Amsterdam in the
merry month of June, the sweetest month in all the year; when
Dan Apollo seems to dance up the transparent firmament—when
the robin, the thrush, and a thousand other wanton songsters
make the woods to resound with amorous ditties, and the luxurious little boblincon revels among the clover blossoms of the
meadows—all which happy coincidence persuaded the old dames
of New Amsterdam, who were skilled in the art of foretelling
events, that this was to be a happy and prosperous administration.

The renowned Wouter (or Walter) Van Twiller, was descended
from a long line of Dutch burgomasters, who had successively
dozed away their lives, and grown fat upon the bench of magis-
tracy in Rotterdam; and who had comported themselves with such
singular wisdom and propriety, that they were never either heard
or talked of—which, next to being universally applauded, should
be the object of ambition of all magistrates and rulers. There are
two opposite ways by which some men make a figure in the world;

1. Published on December 6, 1809,
simultaneously in Philadelphia, New
York, Boston, Baltimore, and Charleston, this work was conceived as a
parody of a serious history—Samuel
Mitchell's *Picture of New York* (1807).
But the element of parody was almost
lost in the gusty independence of Irving's burlesque, a classic of humorous
literature. In the comic treatment of
the early Dutch governors there are
satirical resemblances to the persons
and policies of American leaders—
especially John Adams, Jefferson, and
Madison. (See the verbatim reprint of
1809 text, with notes by Stanley
T. Williams and Tremaine McDowell,
1927; and the Notes, pp. 379–383, in
Pochmann's *Washington Irving: Repre-*
sentative Selections, 1934.) In several
revisions Irving refined the broadest extravagances of the first text. His last
edition (1848) is followed here. The
work is in eight books. The first two,
ridiculing pedantry and solemnity in historical writing, are a burlesque history
of the world from the Creation to the
establishment of New Amsterdam. The
subsequent books deal with governors
Wouter Van Twiller (in the section here
given in part), William the Testy, and
Peter Stuyvesant "the Headstrong."
2. Wouter Van Twiller (1580?–1656),
Dutch governor of New Netherland,
1633–1637.
3. Actually 1633. Van Twiller was not,
as Irving suggests, the first governor.

one by talking faster than they think; and the other by holding their tongues and not thinking at all. By the first, many a smatterer acquires the reputation of a man of quick parts; by the other, many a dunderpate, like the owl, the stupidest of birds, comes to be considered the very type of wisdom. This, by the way, is a casual remark, which I would not, for the universe, have it thought I apply to Governor Van Twiller. It is true he was a man shut up within himself, like an oyster, and rarely spoke except in mono-syllables; but then it was allowed he seldom said a foolish thing. So invincible was his gravity that he was never known to laugh or even to smile through the whole course of a long and prosperous life. Nay if a joke were uttered in his presence, that set light minded hearers in a roar, it was observed to throw him into a state of perplexity. Sometimes he would deign to inquire into the mat-ter, and when, after much explanation, the joke was made as plain as a pike-staff, he would continue to smoke his pipe in silence, and at length, knocking out the ashes would exclaim, "Well! I see nothing in all that to laugh about."

With all his reflective habits, he never made up his mind on a subject. His adherents accounted for this by the astonishing mag-nitude of his ideas. He conceived every subject on so grand a scale that he had not room in his head to turn it over and examine both sides of it. Certain it is that if any matter were propounded to him on which ordinary mortals would rashly determine at first glance, he would put on a vague, mysterious look; shake his capacious head; smoke some time in profound silence, and at length observe that "he had his doubts about the matter"; which gained him the reputation of a man slow of belief and not easily imposed upon. What is more, it gained him a lasting name: for to this habit of the mind has been attributed his surname of Twiller; which is said to be a corruption of the original Twijfler, or, in plain English, *Doubter*.

The person of this illustrious old gentleman was formed and proportioned, as though it had been moulded by the hands of some cunning Dutch statuary,[4] as a model of majesty and lordly grandeur. He was exactly five feet six inches in height, and six feet five inches in circumference. His head was a perfect sphere, and of such stupendous dimensions, that dame Nature, with all her sex's ingenuity, would have been puzzled to construct a neck capable of supporting it; wherefore she wisely declined the at-tempt, and settled it firmly on the top of his back bone, just between the shoulders. His body was oblong and particularly capacious at bottom; which was wisely ordered by Providence, seeing that he was a man of sedentary habits, and very averse to

4. Then meaning "sculptor."

the idle labor of walking. His legs were short, but sturdy in proportion to the weight they had to sustain; so that when erect he had not a little the appearance of a beer barrel on skids. His face, that infallible index of the mind, presented a vast expanse, unfurrowed by any of those lines and angles which disfigure the human countenance with what is termed expression. Two small grey eyes twinkled feebly in the midst, like two stars of lesser magnitude in a hazy firmament; and his full-fed cheeks, which seemed to have taken toll of every thing that went into his mouth, were curiously mottled and streaked with dusky red, like a spitzenberg apple.

His habits were as regular as his person. He daily took his four stated meals, appropriating exactly an hour to each; he smoked and doubted eight hours, and he slept the remaining twelve of the four and twenty. Such was the renowned Wouter Van Twiller—a true philosopher, for his mind was either elevated above, or tranquilly settled below, the cares and perplexities of this world. He had lived in it for years, without feeling the least curiosity to know whether the sun revolved round it, or it round the sun; and he had watched, for at least half a century, the smoke curling from his pipe to the ceiling, without once troubling his head with any of those numerous theories, by which a philosopher would have perplexed his brain, in accounting for its rising above the surrounding atmosphere.

In his council he presided with great state and solemnity. He sat in a huge chair of solid oak, hewn in the celebrated forest of the Hague, fabricated by an experienced timmerman [5] of Amsterdam, and curiously carved about the arms and feet, into exact imitations of gigantic eagle's claws. Instead of a sceptre he swayed a long Turkish pipe, wrought with jasmin and amber, which had been presented to a stadtholder [6] of Holland, at the conclusion of a treaty with one of the petty Barbary powers. [7] In this stately chair would he sit, and this magnificent pipe would he smoke, shaking his right knee with a constant motion, and fixing his eye for hours together upon a little print of Amsterdam, which hung in a black frame against the opposite wall of the council chamber. Nay, it has even been said, that when any deliberation of extraordinary length and intricacy was on the carpet, the renowned Wouter would shut his eyes for full two hours at a time, that he might not be disturbed by external objects—and at such times the internal commotion of his mind was evinced by certain regular guttural sounds, which his admirers declared were merely the

5. Dutch, "cabinetmaker."
6. Dutch, "governor."
7. The Barbary States of North Africa, whose centuries of piracy on Christian shipping Jefferson had just quelled in expeditions, 1801–1805.

noise of conflict, made by his contending doubts and opinions.

It is with infinite difficulty I have been enabled to collect these biographical anecdotes of the great man under consideration. The facts respecting him were so scattered and vague, and divers of them so questionable in point of authenticity, that I have had to give up the search after many, and decline the admission of still more, which would have tended to heighten the coloring of his portrait.

I have been the more anxious to delineate fully the person and habits of Wouter Van Twiller, from the consideration that he was not only the first, but also the best governor that ever presided over this ancient and respectable province; and so tranquil and benevolent was his reign, that I do not find throughout the whole of it, a single instance of any offender being brought to punishment—a most indubitable sign of a merciful governor, and a case unparalleled, excepting in the reign of the illustrious King of Log,[8] from whom, it is hinted, the renowned Van Twiller was a lineal descendant. * * *

CHAPTER IV: CONTAINING FURTHER PARTICULARS OF THE GOLDEN
AGE, AND WHAT CONSTITUTED A FINE LADY AND GENTLEMAN
IN THE DAYS OF WALTER THE DOUBTER

In this dulcet period of my history, when the beauteous island of Manna-hata presented a scene, the very counterpart of those glowing pictures drawn of the golden reign of Saturn,[9] there was, as I have before observed, a happy ignorance, an honest simplicity prevalent among its inhabitants, which, were I even able to depict, would be but little understood by the degenerate age for which I am doomed to write. Even the female sex, those arch innovators upon the tranquillity, the honesty, and gray-beard customs of society, seemed for a while to conduct themselves with incredible sobriety and comeliness.

Their hair, untortured by the abominations of art, was scrupulously pomatumed back from their foreheads with a candle, and covered with a little cap of quilted calico, which fitted exactly to their heads. Their petticoats of linsey-woolsey were striped with a variety of gorgeous dyes—though I must confess these gallant garments were rather short, scarce reaching below the knee; but then they made up in the number, which generally equalled that of the gentleman's small clothes; and what is still more praiseworthy, they were all of their own manufacture—of which circumstance, as may well be supposed, they were not a little vain.

8. See "The Frogs Desiring a King," in *Aesop's Fables*. The gods appointed a log, which served them silently; they grew dissatisfied, and were sent a stork, which ate them.
9. Roman god of a fabled Golden Age.

These were the honest days in which every woman staid at home, read the Bible, and wore pockets—ay, and that too of a goodly size, fashioned with patchwork into many curious devices, and ostentatiously worn on the outside. These, in fact, were convenient receptacles, where all good housewives carefully stored away such things as they wished to have at hand; by which means they often came to be incredibly crammed—and I remember there was a story current when I was a boy that the Lady of Wouter Van Twiller once had occasion to empty her right pocket in search of a wooden ladle, when the contents filled a couple of corn baskets, and the utensil was discovered lying among some rubbish in one corner—but we must not give too much faith to all these stories; the anecdotes of those remote periods being very subject to exaggeration. * * *

From the sketch here given, it will be seen that our good grandmothers differed considerably in their ideas of a fine figure from their scantily dressed descendants of the present day. A fine lady, in those times, waddled under more clothes, even on a fair summer's day, than would have clad the whole bevy of a modern ballroom. Nor were they the less admired by the gentlemen in consequence thereof. On the contrary, the greatness of a lover's passion seemed to increase in proportion to the magnitude of its object—and a voluminous damsel arrayed in a dozen of petticoats, was declared by a Low Dutch [1] sonneteer of the province to be radiant as a sunflower, and luxuriant as a full-blown cabbage. Certain it is, that in those days the heart of a lover could not contain more than one lady at a time; whereas the heart of a modern gallant has often room enough to accommodate half a dozen. The reason of which I conclude to be, that either the hearts of the gentlemen have grown larger, or the persons of the ladies smaller—this, however, is a question for physiologists to determine.

But there was a secret charm in these petticoats, which, no doubt, entered into the consideration of the prudent gallants. The wardrobe of a lady was in those days her only fortune; and she who had a good stock of petticoats and stockings, was as absolutely an heiress as is a Kamschatka [2] damsel with a store of bearskins, or a Lapland belle with a plenty of reindeer. The ladies, therefore, were very anxious to display these powerful attractions to the greatest advantage; and the best rooms in the house, instead of being adorned with caricatures of dame Nature, in water colors and needle work, were always hung round with abundance of homespun garments, the manufacture and the property of the

---

1. That is, of Holland; *cf.* the "Low Countries" (Holland, Belgium, and Luxembourg).

2. A Russian peninsula on the Bering Sea.

females—a piece of laudable ostentation that still prevails among the heiresses of our Dutch villages. * * *

Such was the happy reign of Wouter Van Twiller, celebrated in many a long forgotten song as the real golden age, the rest being nothing but counterfeit copper-washed coin. In that delightful period, a sweet and holy calm reigned over the whole province. The burgomaster smoked his pipe in peace—the substantial solace of his domestic cares, after her daily toils were done, sat soberly at the door, with her arms crossed over her apron of snowy white, without being insulted with ribald street walkers or vagabond boys —those unlucky urchins who do so infest our streets, displaying, under the roses of youth, the thorns and briers of iniquity. Then it was that the lover with ten breeches, and the damsel with petticoats of half a score, indulged in all the innocent endearments of virtuous love without fear and without reproach; for what had that virtue to fear, which was defended by a shield of good linsey-woolseys, equal at least to the seven bull hides of the invincible Ajax? [3]

Ah blissful, and never to be forgotten age! when every thing was better than it has ever been since, or ever will be again—when Buttermilk Channel [4] was quite dry at low water—when the shad in the Hudson were all salmon, and when the moon shone with a pure and resplendent whiteness, instead of that melancholy yellow light which is the consequence of her sickening at the abominations she every night witnesses in this degenerate city! * * *

1809, 1860–1861

From THE SKETCH BOOK

Rip Van Winkle [5]

A POSTHUMOUS WRITING OF DIEDRICH KNICKERBOCKER

By Woden, [6] *God of Saxons,*
From whence comes Wensday, that is Wodensday.
Truth is a thing that ever I will keep

3. Referring to the legendary shield of Ajax, one of the greatest warriors of the Greeks in the siege of Troy: *cf.* Homer's *Iliad.*
4. In New York harbor, between Governor's Island and Long Island (Brooklyn).
5. This famous tale (ending the first installment of *The Sketch Book*) has been regarded as the first American

short story. Within ten years (1829) it began in Philadelphia its long stage career. This involved adaptations and inheritance by many authors and actors, until it was stabilized in the version acted by the third Joseph Jefferson (1829–1905).
6. Sometimes Wodan or Odin; in Norse and Teutonic mythology, the god of war and wisdom—also "the Thunderer."

> Unto thylke day in which I creep into
> My sepulchre—
>
> —CARTWRIGHT [7]

[The following Tale was found among the papers of the late Diedrich Knickerbocker, an old gentleman of New York, who was
very curious in the Dutch history of the province, and the manners of the descendants from its primitive settlers. His historical
researches, however, did not lie so much among books as among
men; for the former are lamentably scanty on his favorite topics;
whereas he found the old burghers, and still more their wives,
rich in that legendary lore, so invaluable to true history. Whenever, therefore, he happened upon a genuine Dutch family, snugly
shut up in its low-roofed farmhouse, under a spreading sycamore, he looked upon it as a little clasped volume of black-letter,
and studied it with the zeal of a bookworm.[8]

The result of all these researches was a history of the province
during the reign of the Dutch govenors, which he published some
years since. There have been various opinions as to the literary
character of his work, and, to tell the truth, it is not a whit better
than it should be. Its chief merit is its scrupulous accuracy, which
indeed was a little questioned on its first appearance, but has
since been completely established; and it is now admitted into all
historical collections, as a book of unquestionable authority.

The old gentleman died shortly after the publication of his work,
and now that he is dead and gone, it cannot do much harm to his
memory to say that his time might have been much better employed in weightier labors. He, however, was apt to ride his
hobby his own way; and though it did now and then kick up the
dust a little in the eyes of his neighbors, and grieve the spirit of
some friends, for whom he felt the truest deference and affection;
yet his errors and follies are remembered "more in sorrow than in
anger," [9] and it begins to be suspected, that he never intended to
injure or offend. But however his memory may be appreciated by
critics, it is still held dear by many folk, whose good opinion is
well worth having; particularly by certain biscuit-bakers, who have

---

7. William Cartwright (1611–1643),
short-lived prodigy of the "Tribe of
Ben," of whom Jonson said, "My son
Cartwright writes all like a man."
8. Thus, in *The Sketch Book*, Irving
continued to use the fictitious Dutch
historian, Knickerbocker, from his
earlier *History of New York*. But in a
footnote at the end of "Rip Van
Winkle" he gave a clue to the German
source of the folk tale by denying that
Knickerbocker had based it on a

"superstition about the Emperor Frederick *der Rothbart*." This led to the
identification of a probable source,
"Peter Klaus the Goatherd," in a
collection of German legends that Irving had read (see H. A. Pochmann,
"Irving's German Sources in *The Sketch
Book*," *Studies in Philology*, XXVII,
July, 1930, 477–507).
9. Shakespeare's *Hamlet*, Act I, Scene
2, ll. 231–232.

gone so far as to imprint his likeness on their new-year cakes; and have thus given him a chance for immortality, almost equal to the being stamped on a Waterloo Medal,[1] or a Queen Anne's Farthing.[2]]

Whoever has made a voyage up the Hudson must remember the Kaatskill mountains. They are a dismembered branch of the great Appalachian family, and are seen away to the west of the river, swelling up to a noble height, and lording it over the surrounding country. Every change of season, every change of weather, indeed, every hour of the day, produces some change in the magical hues and shapes of these mountains, and they are regarded by all the good wives, far and near, as perfect barometers. When the weather is fair and settled, they are clothed in blue and purple, and print their bold outlines on the clear evening sky; but, sometimes, when the rest of the landscape is cloudless, they will gather a hood of gray vapors about their summits, which, in the last rays of the setting sun, will glow and light up like a crown of glory.

At the foot of these fairy mountains, the voyager may have descried the light smoke curling up from a village, whose shingle-roofs gleam among the trees, just where the blue tints of the upland melt away into the fresh green of the nearer landscape. It is a little village, of great antiquity, having been founded by some of the Dutch colonists, in the early times of the province, just about the beginning of the government of the good Peter Stuyvesant, (may he rest in peace!) and there were some of the houses of the original settlers standing within a few years, built of small yellow bricks brought from Holland, having latticed windows and gable fronts, surmounted with weathercocks.

In that same village, and in one of these very houses (which, to tell the precise truth, was sadly time-worn and weather-beaten), there lived many years since, while the country was yet a province of Great Britain, a simple good-natured fellow, of the name of Rip Van Winkle. He was a descendant of the Van Winkles who figured so gallantly in the chivalrous days of Peter Stuyvesant, and accompanied him to the siege of Fort Christina.[3] He inherited, however, but little of the martial character of his ancestors. I have observed that he was a simple good-natured man; he was, moreover, a kind neighbor, and an obedient hen-pecked husband. Indeed, to the latter circumstance might be owing that meekness of

---

1. A silver medal presented by the British crown to all participants in the Battle of Waterloo (June 18, 1815) or in the engagements of the two previous days.
2. In the reign of Queen Anne (1702–1714) farthings (bronze coins worth a quarter of a penny) bearing her image were minted.
3. Referring to events treated in his *History of New York.* Stuyvesant was the autocratic governor of New Amsterdam (1647–1664); he seized Fort Christina on the Delaware from the Swedes in 1655.

spirit which gained him such universal popularity; for those men are most apt to be obsequious and conciliating abroad, who are under the discipline of shrews at home. Their tempers, doubtless, are rendered pliant and malleable in the fiery furnace of domestic tribulation; and a curtain lecture is worth all the sermons in the world for teaching the virtues of patience and longsuffering. A termagant wife may, therefore, in some respects, be considered a tolerable blessing; and if so, Rip Van Winkle was thrice blessed.

Certain it is, that he was a great favorite among all the good wives of the village, who, as usual, with the amiable sex, took his part in all family squabbles; and never failed, whenever they talked those matters over in their evening gossipings, to lay all the blame on Dame Van Winkle. The children of the village, too, would shout with joy whenever he approached. He assisted at their sports, made their playthings, taught them to fly kites and shoot marbles, and told them long stories of ghosts, witches, and Indians. Whenever he went dodging about the village, he was surrounded by a troop of them, hanging on his skirts, clambering on his back, and playing a thousand tricks on him with impunity; and not a dog would bark at him throughout the neighborhood.

The great error in Rip's composition was an insuperable aversion to all kinds of profitable labor. It could not be from the want of assiduity or perseverance; for he would sit on a wet rock, with a rod as long and heavy as a Tartar's lance, and fish all day without a murmur, even though he should not be encouraged by a single nibble. He would carry a fowling-piece on his shoulder for hours together, trudging through woods and swamps, and up hill and down dale, to shoot a few squirrels or wild pigeons. He would never refuse to assist a neighbor even in the roughest toil, and was a foremost man at all country frolics for husking Indian corn, or building stone-fences; the women of the village, too, used to employ him to run their errands, and to do such little old jobs as their less obliging husbands would not do for them. In a word Rip was ready to attend to anybody's business but his own; but as to doing family duty, and keeping his farm in order, he found it impossible.

In fact, he declared it was of no use to work on his farm; it was the most pestilent little piece of ground in the whole country; every thing about it went wrong, and would go wrong, in spite of him. His fences were continually falling to pieces; his cow would either go astray, or get among the cabbages; weeds were sure to grow quicker in his fields than anywhere else; the rain always made a point of setting in just as he had some outdoor work to do; so that though his patrimonial estate had dwindled away under his management, acre by acre, until there was little more left than a mere patch of Indian corn and potatoes, yet it was the worst conditioned farm in the neighborhood.

His children, too, were as ragged and wild as if they belonged to nobody. His son Rip, an urchin begotten in his own likeness, promised to inherit the habits, with the old clothes of his father. He was generally seen trooping like a colt at his mother's heels, equipped in a pair of his father's cast-off galligaskins,[4] which he had much ado to hold up with one hand, as a fine lady does her train in bad weather.

Rip Van Winkle, however, was one of those happy mortals, of foolish, well-oiled dispositions, who take the world easy, eat white bread or brown, whichever can be got with least thought or trouble, and would rather starve on a penny than work for a pound. If left to himself, he would have whistled life away in perfect contentment; but his wife kept continually dinning in his ears about his idleness, his carelessness, and the ruin he was bringing on his family. Morning, noon, and night, her tongue was incessantly going, and every thing he said or did was sure to produce a torrent of household eloquence. Rip had but one way of replying to all lectures of the kind, and that, by frequent use, had grown into a habit. He shrugged his shoulders, shook his head, cast up his eyes, but said nothing. This, however, always provoked a fresh volley from his wife; so that he was fain to draw off his forces, and take to the outside of the house—the only side which, in truth, belongs to a hen-pecked husband.

Rip's sole domestic adherent was his dog Wolf, who was as much hen-pecked as his master; for Dame Van Winkle regarded them as companions in idleness, and even looked upon Wolf with an evil eye, as the cause of his master's going so often astray. True it is, in all points of spirit befitting an honorable dog, he was as courageous an animal as ever scoured the woods—but what courage can withstand the ever-during and all-besetting terrors of a woman's tongue? The moment Wolf entered the house his crest fell, his tail drooped to the ground, or curled between his legs, he sneaked about with a gallows air, casting many a sidelong glance at Dame Van Winkle, and at the least flourish of a broomstick or ladle, he would fly to the door with yelping precipitation.

Times grew worse and worse with Rip Van Winkle as years of matrimony rolled on; a tart temper never mellows with age, and a sharp tongue is the only edged tool that grows keener with constant use. For a long while he used to console himself, when driven from home, by frequenting a kind of perpetual club of the

4. Knee breeches.

sages, philosophers, and other idle personages of the village; which held its sessions on a bench before a small inn, designated by a rubicund portrait of His Majesty George the Third. Here they used to sit in the shade through a long lazy summer's day, talking listlessly over village gossip, or telling endless sleepy stories about nothing. But it would have been worth any statesman's money to have heard the profound discussions that sometimes took place, when by chance an old newspaper fell into their hands from some passing traveller. How solemnly they would listen to the contents, as drawled out by Derrick Van Bummel, the schoolmaster, a dapper learned little man, who was not to be daunted by the most gigantic word in the dictionary; and how sagely they would deliberate upon public events some months after they had taken place.

The opinions of this junto were completely controlled by Nicholas Vedder, a patriarch of the village, and landlord of the inn, at the door of which he took his seat from morning till night, just moving sufficiently to avoid the sun and keep in the shade of a large tree; so that the neighbors could tell the hour by his movements as accurately as by a sun-dial. It is true he was rarely heard to speak, but smoked his pipe incessantly. His adherents, however (for every great man has his adherents), perfectly understood him, and knew how to gather his opinions. When any thing that was read or related displeased him, he was observed to smoke his pipe vehemently, and to send forth short, frequent and angry puffs; but when pleased, he would inhale the smoke slowly and tranquilly, and emit it in light and placid clouds; and sometimes, taking the pipe from his mouth, and letting the fragrant vapor curl about his nose, would gravely nod his head in token of perfect approbation.

From even this stronghold the unlucky Rip was at length routed by his termagant wife, who would suddenly break in upon the tranquillity of the assemblage and call the members all to naught; nor was that august personage, Nicholas Vedder himself, sacred from the daring tongue of this terrible virago, who charged him outright with encouraging her husband in habits of idleness.

Poor Rip was at last reduced almost to despair; and his only alternative, to escape from the labor of the farm and clamor of his wife, was to take gun in hand and stroll away into the woods. Here he would sometimes seat himself at the foot of a tree, and share the contents of his wallet with Wolf, with whom he sympathized as a fellow-sufferer in persecution. "Poor Wolf," he would say, "thy mistress leads thee a dog's life of it; but never mind, my lad, whilst I live thou shalt never want a friend to stand by thee!" Wolf would wag his tail, look wistfully in his

master's face, and if dogs can feel pity I verily believe he recipro-
cated the sentiment with all his heart.

In a long ramble of the kind on a fine autumnal day, Rip had
unconsciously scrambled to one of the highest parts of the Kaatskill mountains. He was after his favorite sport of squirrel shooting, and the still solitudes had echoed and re-echoed with the
reports of his gun. Panting and fatigued, he threw himself, late
in the afternoon, on a green knoll, covered with mountain herbage,
that crowned the brow of a precipice. From an opening between
the trees he could overlook all the lower country for many a mile
of rich woodland. He saw at a distance the lordly Hudson, far, far
below him, moving on its silent but majestic course, with the
reflection of a purple cloud, or the sail of a lagging bark, here and
there sleeping on its glassy bosom, and at last losing itself in the
blue highlands.

On the other side he looked down into a deep mountain glen,
wild, lonely, and shagged, the bottom filled with fragments from
the impending cliffs, and scarcely lighted by the reflected rays of
the setting sun. For some time Rip lay musing on this scene;
evening was gradually advancing; the mountains began to throw
their long blue shadows over the valleys; he saw that it would be
dark long before he could reach the village, and he heaved a heavy
sigh when he thought of encountering the terrors of Dame Van
Winkle.

As he was about to descend, he heard a voice from a distance,
hallooing, "Rip Van Winkle! Rip Van Winkle!" He looked
round, but could see nothing but a crow winging its solitary flight
across the mountain. He thought his fancy must have deceived
him, and turned again to descend, when he heard the same cry
through the still evening air; "Rip Van Winkle! Rip Van Winkle!"
—at the same time Wolf bristled up his back, and giving a low
growl, skulked to his master's side, looking fearfully down into
the glen. Rip now felt a vague apprehension stealing over him; he
looked anxiously in the same direction, and perceived a strange
figure slowly toiling up the rocks, and bending under the weight of
something he carried on his back. He was surprised to see any
human being in this lonely and unfrequented place, but supposing it to be some one of the neighborhood in need of his assistance, he hastened down to yield it.

On nearer approach he was still more surprised at the singularity of the stranger's appearance. He was a short square-built
old fellow, with thick bushy hair, and a grizzled beard. His dress
was of the antique Dutch fashion—a cloth jerkin strapped round
the waist—several pair of breeches, the outer one of ample volume,
decorated with rows of buttons down the sides, and bunches at

the knees. He bore on his shoulder a stout keg, that seemed full of liquor, and made signs for Rip to approach and assist him with the load. Though rather shy and distrustful of this new acquaintance, Rip complied with his usual alacrity; and mutually relieving one another, they clambered up a narrow gully, apparently the dry bed of a mountain torrent. As they ascended, Rip every now and then heard long rolling peals, like distant thunder, that seemed to issue out of a deep ravine, or rather cleft, between lofty rocks, toward which their rugged path conducted. He paused for an instant, but supposing it to be the muttering of one of those transient thunder-showers which often take place in mountain heights, he proceeded. Passing through the ravine, they came to a hollow, like a small amphitheatre, surrounded by perpendicular precipices, over the brinks of which impending trees shot their branches, so that you only caught glimpses of the azure sky and the bright evening cloud. During the whole time Rip and his companion had labored on in silence; for though the former marvelled greatly what could be the object of carrying a keg of liquor up this wild mountain, yet there was something strange and incomprehensible about the unknown, that inspired awe and checked familiarity.

On entering the amphitheatre, new objects of wonder presented themselves. On a level spot in the centre was a company of odd-looking personages playing at nine-pins. They were dressed in a quaint outlandish fashion; some wore short doublets, others jerkins, with long knives in their belts, and most of them had enormous breeches, of similar style with that of the guide's. Their visages, too, were peculiar: one had a large head, broad face, and small piggish eyes: the face of another seemed to consist entirely of nose, and was surmounted by a white sugar-loaf hat, set off with a little red cock's tail. They all had beards, of various shapes and colors. There was one who seemed to be the commander. He was a stout old gentleman, with a weather-beaten countenance; he wore a laced doublet, broad belt and hanger,[5] high crowned hat and feather, red stockings, and high-heeled shoes, with roses [6] in them. The whole group reminded Rip of the figures in an old Flemish painting, in the parlor of Dominie Van Shaick, the village parson, and which had been brought over from Holland at the time of the settlement.

What seemed particularly odd to Rip was, that though these folks were evidently amusing themselves, yet they maintained the gravest faces, the most mysterious silence, and were, withal, the most melancholy party of pleasure he had ever witnessed.

5. A short, curved sword worn at the side.   6. Rosettes.

Nothing interrupted the stillness of the scene but the noise of the balls, which, whenever they were rolled, echoed along the mountains like rumbling peals of thunder.

As Rip and his companion approached them, they suddenly desisted from their play, and stared at him with such fixed statue-like gaze, and such strange, uncouth, lack-lustre countenances, that his heart turned within him, and his knees smote together. His companion now emptied the contents of the keg into large flagons, and made signs to him to wait upon the company. He obeyed with fear and trembling; they quaffed the liquor in profound silence, and then returned to their game.

By degrees Rip's awe and apprehension subsided. He even ventured, when no eye was fixed upon him, to taste the beverage, which he found had much of the flavor of excellent Hollands.[7] He was naturally a thirsty soul, and was soon tempted to repeat the draught. One taste provoked another; and he reiterated his visits to the flagon so often that at length his senses were overpowered, his eyes swam in his head, his head gradually declined, and he fell into a deep sleep.

On waking, he found himself on the green knoll whence he had first seen the old man of the glen. He rubbed his eyes—it was a bright sunny morning. The birds were hopping and twittering among the bushes, and the eagle was wheeling aloft, and breasting the pure mountain breeze. "Surely," thought Rip, "I have not slept here all night." He recalled the occurrences before he fell asleep. The strange man with a keg of liquor—the mountain ravine—the wild retreat among the rocks—the wobegone party at nine-pins—the flagon—"Oh! that flagon! that wicked flagon!" thought Rip—"what excuse shall I make to Dame Van Winkle!"

He looked round for his gun, but in place of the clean well-oiled fowling-piece, he found an old firelock lying by him, the barrel incrusted with rust, the lock falling off, and the stock worm-eaten. He now suspected that the grave roysters of the mountain had put a trick upon him, and, having dosed him with liquor, had robbed him of his gun. Wolf, too, had disappeared, but he might have strayed away after a squirrel or partridge. He whistled after him and shouted his name, but all in vain; the echoes repeated his whistle and shout, but no dog was to be seen.

He determined to revisit the scene of the last evening's gambol, and if he met with any of the party, to demand his dog and gun. As he rose to walk, he found himself stiff in the joints, and wanting in his usual activity. "These mountain beds do not agree with me," thought Rip, "and if this frolic should lay me up with

7. A Dutch gin long famous for excellence.

a fit of the rheumatism, I shall have a blessed time with Dame Van Winkle." With some difficulty he got down into the glen: he found the gully up which he and his companion had ascended the preceding evening; but to his astonishment a mountain stream was now foaming down it, leaping from rock to rock, and filling the glen with babbling murmurs. He, however, made shift to scramble up its sides, working his toilsome way through thickets of birch, sassafras, and witch-hazel, and sometimes tripped up or entangled by the wild grapevines that twisted their coils or tendrils from tree to tree, and spread a kind of network in his path.

At length he reached to where the ravine had opened through the cliffs to the amphitheatre; but no traces of such opening remained. The rocks presented a high impenetrable wall over which the torrent came tumbling in a sheet of feathery foam, and fell into a broad deep basin, black from the shadows of the surrounding forest. Here, then, poor Rip was brought to a stand. He again called and whistled after his dog; he was only answered by the cawing of a flock of idle crows, sporting high in air about a dry tree that overhung a sunny precipice; and who, secure in their elevation, seemed to look down and scoff at the poor man's perplexities. What was to be done? the morning was passing away, and Rip felt famished for want of his breakfast. He grieved to give up his dog and gun; he dreaded to meet his wife; but it would not do to starve among the mountains. He shook his head, shouldered the rusty firelock, and, with a heart full of trouble and anxiety, turned his steps homeward.

As he approached the village he met a number of people, but none whom he knew, which somewhat surprised him, for he had thought himself acquainted with every one in the country round. Their dress, too, was of a different fashion from that to which he was accustomed. They all stared at him with equal marks of surprise, and whenever they cast their eyes upon him, invariably stroked their chins. The constant recurrence of this gesture induced Rip, involuntarily, to do the same, when, to his astonishment, he found his beard had grown a foot long!

He had now entered the skirts of the village. A troop of strange children ran at his heels, hooting after him, and pointing at his gray beard. The dogs, too, not one of which he recognized for an old acquaintance, barked at him as he passed. The very village was altered; it was larger and more populous. There were rows of houses which he had never seen before, and those which had been his familiar haunts had disappeared. Strange names were over the doors—strange faces at the windows—every thing was strange. His mind now misgave him; he began to doubt whether both he and the world around him were not bewitched. Surely this was his native village, which he had left but the day before. There stood the Kaatskill mountains—there ran the silver Hudson at a distance —there was every hill and dale precisely as it had always been— Rip was sorely perplexed—"That flagon last night," thought he, "has addled my poor head sadly!"

It was with some difficulty that he found the way to his own house, which he approached with silent awe, expecting every moment to hear the shrill voice of Dame Van Winkle. He found the house gone to decay—the roof fallen in, the windows shattered, and the doors off the hinges. A half-starved dog that looked like Wolf was skulking about it. Rip called him by name, but the cur snarled, showed his teeth, and passed on. This was an unkind cut indeed—"My very dog," sighed poor Rip, "has forgotten me!"

He entered the house, which, to tell the truth, Dame Van Winkle had always kept in neat order. It was empty, forlorn, and apparently abandoned. This desolateness overcame all his connubial fears—he called loudly for his wife and children—the lonely chambers rang for a moment with his voice, and then all again was silence.

He now hurried forth, and hastened to his old resort, the village inn—but it too was gone. A large rickety wooden building stood in its place, with great gaping windows, some of them broken and mended with old hats and petticoats, and over the door was painted, "the Union Hotel, by Jonathan Doolittle." Instead of the great tree that used to shelter the quiet little Dutch inn of yore, there now was reared a tall naked pole, with something on the top that looked like a red night-cap,[8] and from it was fluttering a flag, on which was a singular assemblage of stars and stripes— all this was strange and incomprehensible. He recognized on the sign, however, the ruby face of King George, under which he had smoked so many a peaceful pipe; but even this was singularly metamorphosed. The red coat was changed for one of blue and buff, a sword was held in the hand instead of a sceptre, the head was decorated with a cocked hat, and underneath was painted in large characters, GENERAL WASHINGTON.

There was, as usual, a crowd of folk about the door, but none that Rip recollected. The very character of the people seemed changed. There was a busy, bustling, disputatious tone about it, instead of the accustomed phlegm and drowsy tranquillity. He looked in vain for the sage Nicholas Vedder, with his broad face, double chin, and fair long pipe, uttering clouds of tobacco-smoke instead of idle speeches; or Van Bummel, the schoolmaster, doling forth the

8. The "liberty cap," familiar symbol of the French Revolution, was often displayed in the United States.

contents of an ancient newspaper. In place of these, a lean, bilious-looking fellow, with his pockets full of handbills, was haranguing vehemently about rights of citizens—elections—members of congress—liberty—Bunker's Hill—heroes of seventy-six—and other words, which were a perfect Babylonish jargon [9] to the bewildered Van Winkle.

The appearance of Rip, with his long grizzled beard, his rusty fowling-piece, his uncouth dress, and an army of women and children at his heels, soon attracted the attention of the tavern politicians. They crowded round him, eyeing him from head to foot with great curiosity. The orator bustled up to him, and, drawing him partly aside, inquired "on which side he voted?" Rip stared in vacant stupidity. Another short but busy little fellow pulled him by the arm, and, rising on tiptoe, inquired in his ear, "Whether he was Federal or Democrat?" [1] Rip was equally at a loss to comprehend the question; when a knowing, self-important old gentleman, in a sharp cocked hat, made his way through the crowd, putting them to the right and left with his elbows as he passed, and planting himself before Van Winkle, with one arm akimbo, the other resting on his cane, his keen eyes and sharp hat penetrating, as it were, into his very soul, demanded in an austere tone, "what brought him to the election with a gun on his shoulder, and a mob at his heels, and whether he meant to breed a riot in the village?"—"Alas! gentlemen," cried Rip, somewhat dismayed, "I am a poor quiet man, a native of the place, and a loyal subject of the king, God bless him!"

Here a general shout burst from the by-standers—"A tory! a tory! a spy! a refugee! hustle him! away with him!" It was with great difficulty that the self-important man in the cocked hat restored order; and, having assumed a tenfold austerity of brow, demanded again of the unknown culprit, what he came there for, and whom he was seeking? The poor man humbly assured him that he meant no harm, but merely came there in search of some of his neighbors, who used to keep about the tavern.

"Well—who are they?—name them."

Rip bethought himself a moment, and inquired, "Where's Nicholas Vedder?"

There was a silence for a little while, when an old man replied, in a thin piping voice, "Nicholas Vedder! why, he is dead and gone these eighteen years! There was a wooden tombstone in the churchyard that used to tell all about him, but that's rotten and gone too."

"Where's Brom Dutcher?"

---

9. *Cf.* Genesis xi: 1–9. The "confusion of tongues" occurred at Babel.
1. The earliest American political parties—Federalist (Hamiltonian) and Democratic Republican (Jeffersonian).

"Oh, he went off to the army in the beginning of the war; some say he was killed at the storming of Stony Point [2]—others say he was drowned in a squall at the foot of Antony's Nose.[3] I don't know—he never came back again."

"Where's Van Bummel, the schoolmaster?"

"He went off to the wars too, was a great militia general, and is now in congress."

Rip's heart died away at hearing of these sad changes in his home and friends, and finding himself thus alone in the world. Every answer puzzled him too, by treating of such enormous lapses of time, and of matters which he could not understand: war—congress—Stony Point;—he had no courage to ask after any more friends, but cried out in despair, "Does nobody here know Rip Van Winkle?"

"Oh, Rip Van Winkle!" exclaimed two or three, "Oh, to be sure! that's Rip Van Winkle yonder, leaning against the tree."

Rip looked, and beheld a precise counterpart of himself, as he went up the mountain: apparently as lazy, and certainly as ragged. The poor fellow was now completely confounded. He doubted his own identity, and whether he was himself or another man. In the midst of his bewilderment, the man in the cocked hat demanded who he was, and what was his name?

"God knows," exclaimed he, at his wit's end; "I'm not myself—I'm somebody else—that's me yonder—no—that's somebody else got into my shoes—I was myself last night, but I fell asleep on the mountain, and they've changed my gun, and every thing's changed, and I'm changed, and I can't tell what's my name, or who I am!"

The by-standers began now to look at each other, nod, wink significantly, and tap their fingers against their foreheads. There was a whisper, also, about securing the gun, and keeping the old fellow from doing mischief, at the very suggestion of which the self-important man in the cocked hat retired with some precipitation. At this critical moment a fresh comely woman passed through the throng to get a peep at the gray-bearded man. She had a chubby child in her arms, which, frightened at his looks, began to cry. "Hush, Rip," cried she, "hush, you little fool; the old man won't hurt you." The name of the child, the air of the mother, the tone of her voice, all awakened a train of recollections in his mind. "What is your name, my good woman?" asked he.

"Judith Gardenier."

---

2. A strategic headland on the Hudson below West Point, captured by Mad Anthony Wayne, July 18, 1779, in one of the most daring and brilliant exploits of the Revolution.
3. Another fortified promontory on the Hudson, scene of a bloody contest in 1777.

"And your father's name?"

"Ah, poor man, Rip Van Winkle was his name, but it's twenty years since he went away from home with his gun, and never has been heard of since—his dog came home without him; but whether he shot himself, or was carried away by the Indians, nobody can tell. I was then but a little girl."

Rip had but one question more to ask; but he put it with a faltering voice:

"Where's your mother?"

"Oh, she too had died but a short time since; she broke a blood-vessel in a fit of passion at a New-England peddler."

There was a drop of comfort, at least, in this intelligence. The honest man could contain himself no longer. He caught his daughter and her child in his arms. "I am your father!" cried he—"Young Rip Van Winkle once—old Rip Van Winkle now!—Does nobody know poor Rip Van Winkle?"

All stood amazed, until an old woman, tottering out from among the crowd, put her hand to her brow, and peering under it in his face for a moment, exclaimed, "Sure enough! it is Rip Van Winkle —it is himself! Welcome home again, old neighbor—Why, where have you been these twenty long years?"

Rip's story was soon told, for the whole twenty years had been to him but as one night. The neighbors stared when they heard it; some were seen to wink at each other, and put their tongues in their cheeks: and the self-important man in the cocked hat, who, when the alarm was over, had returned to the field, screwed down the corners of his mouth, and shook his head—upon which there was a general shaking of the head throughout the assemblage.

It was determined, however, to take the opinion of old Peter Vanderdonk, who was seen slowly advancing up the road. He was a descendant of the historian [4] of that name, who wrote one of the earliest accounts of the province. Peter was the most ancient inhabitant of the village, and well versed in all the wonderful events and traditions of the neighborhood. He recollected Rip at once, and corroborated his story in the most satisfactory manner. He assured the company that it was a fact, handed down from his ancestor the historian, that the Kaatskill mountains had always been haunted by strange beings. That it was affirmed that the great Hendrick Hudson, the first discoverer of the river and country, kept a kind of vigil there every twenty years, with his crew of the Half-moon; being permitted in this way to revisit the scenes of his enterprise, and keep a guardian eye upon the river, and the great

4. Adriaen Van der Donck (*ca.* 1620–1655), Dutch lawyer and founder of Yonkers, wrote a description of New Netherland, published in Dutch (Amsterdam, 1655).

city called by his name.[5] That his father had once seen them in their old Dutch dresses playing at nine-pins in a hollow of the mountain; and that he himself had heard, one summer afternoon, the sound of their balls, like distant peals of thunder.

To make a long story short, the company broke up, and returned to the more important concerns of the election. Rip's daughter took him home to live with her; she had a snug, well-furnished house, and a stout cheery farmer for a husband, whom Rip recollected for one of the urchins that used to climb upon his back. As to Rip's son and heir, who was the ditto of himself, seen leaning against the tree, he was employed to work on the farm; but evinced an hereditary disposition to attend to any thing else but his business.

Rip now resumed his old walks and habits; he soon found many of his former cronies, though all rather the worse for the wear and tear of time; and preferred making friends among the rising generation, with whom he soon grew into great favor.

Having nothing to do at home, and being arrived at that happy age when a man can be idle with impunity, he took his place once more on the bench at the inn door, and was reverenced as one of the patriarchs of the village, and a chronicle of the old times "before the war." It was some time before he could get into the regular track of gossip, or could be made to comprehend the strange events that had taken place during his torpor. How that there had been a revolutionary war—that the country had thrown off the yoke of old England—and that, instead of being a subject of His Majesty George the Third, he was now a free citizen of the United States. Rip, in fact, was no politician; the changes of states and empires made but little impression on him; but there was one species of despotism under which he had long groaned, and that was—petticoat government. Happily that was at an end; he had got his neck out of the yoke of matrimony, and could go in and out whenever he pleased, without dreading the tyranny of Dame Van Winkle. Whenever her name was mentioned, however, he shook his head, shrugged his shoulders, and cast up his eyes; which might pass either for an expression of resignation to his fate, or joy at his deliverance.

He used to tell his story to every stranger that arrived at Mr. Doolittle's Hotel. He was observed, at first, to vary on some points every time he told it, which was, doubtless, owing to his having so recently awaked. It at last settled down precisely to the tale I have related, and not a man, woman, or child in the neighbor-

5. The town of Hudson handled a considerable shipping in Irving's youth. Henry (not Hendrick) Hudson, an English adventurer, discovered and explored the river for the East Indian Company in 1609; abandoned on Hudson Bay by mutineers in 1611, he passed from history into legend.

hood, but knew it by heart. Some always pretended to doubt the reality of it, and insisted that Rip had been out of his head, and that this was one point on which he always remained flighty. The old Dutch inhabitants, however, almost universally gave it full credit. Even to this day they never hear a thunderstorm of a summer afternoon about the Kaatskill, but they say Hendrick Hudson and his crew are at their game of nine-pins; and it is a common wish of all hen-pecked husbands in the neighborhood, when life hangs heavy on their hands, that they might have a quieting draught out of Rip Van Winkle's flagon.

1819, 1860–1861

From Tales of a Traveller

Adventure of the German Student [6]

On a stormy night, in the tempestuous times of the French revolution, a young German was returning to his lodgings, at a late hour, across the old part of Paris. The lightning gleamed, and the loud claps of thunder rattled through the lofty narrow streets —but I should first tell you something about this young German.

Gottfried Wolfgang was a young man of good family. He had studied for some time at Gottingen, but being of a visionary and enthusiastic character, he had wandered into those wild and speculative doctrines which have so often bewildered German students. His secluded life, his intense application, and the singular nature of his studies, had an effect on both mind and body. His health was impaired; his imagination diseased. He had been indulging in fanciful speculations on spiritual essences, until, like Swedenborg, he had an ideal world of his own around him. He took up a notion, I do not know from what cause, that there was an evil influence hanging over him; an evil genius or spirit seeking to ensnare him and ensure his perdition. Such an idea working on his melancholy temperament, produced the most gloomy effects. He became haggard and desponding. His friends discovered the mental malady preying upon him, and determined that the best cure was a change of scene; he was sent, therefore, to finish his studies amidst the splendors and gayeties of Paris.

6. The Gothic story, employing physical and psychological terror in a weird or mysterious setting, had enjoyed a vogue toward the end of the previous century, especially in German literature and among British writers from Walpole to Ann Radcliffe and "Monk" Lewis. An earlier American author, Charles Brockden Brown, had succeeded notably in this vein. Irving gave a humorously perverse twist to the Gothic tale; the present story, which appeared in *Tales of a Traveller,* is an excellent example of his success. This literary impulse later reached its American perfection in the psychological subtleties of Poe.

Wolfgang arrived at Paris at the breaking out of the revolution.[7] The popular delirium at first caught his enthusiastic mind, and he was captivated by the political and philosophical theories of the day: but the scenes of blood which followed shocked his sensitive nature, disgusted him with society and the world, and made him more than ever a recluse. He shut himself up in a solitary apartment in the *Pays Latin*,[8] the quarter of students. There, in a gloomy street not far from the monastic walls of the Sorbonne, he pursued his favorite speculations. Sometimes he spent hours together in the great libraries of Paris, those catacombs of departed authors, rummaging among their hoards of dusty and obsolete works in quest of food for his unhealthy appetite. He was, in a manner, a literary ghoul, feeding in the charnel-house of decayed literature.

Wolfgang, though solitary and recluse, was of an ardent temperament, but for a time it operated merely upon his imagination. He was too shy and ignorant of the world to make any advances to the fair, but he was a passionate admirer of female beauty, and in his lonely chamber would often lose himself in reveries on forms and faces which he had seen, and his fancy would deck out images of loveliness far surpassing the reality.

While his mind was in this excited and sublimated state, a dream produced an extraordinary effect upon him. It was of a female face of transcendent beauty. So strong was the impression made, that he dreamt of it again and again. It haunted his thoughts by day, his slumbers by night; in fine, he became passionately enamoured of this shadow of a dream. This lasted so long that it became one of those fixed ideas which haunt the minds of melancholy men, and are at times mistaken for madness.

Such was Gottfried Wolfgang, and such his situation at the time I mentioned. He was returning home late one stormy night, through some of the old and gloomy streets of the *Marais*, the ancient part of Paris. The loud claps of thunder rattled among the high houses of the narrow streets. He came to the *Place de Grève*, the square where public executions are performed. The lightning quivered about the pinnacles of the ancient *Hôtel de Ville*,[9] and shed flickering gleams over the open space in front. As Wolfgang was crossing the square, he shrank back with horror at finding himself close by the guillotine. It was the height of the reign of terror, when this dreadful instrument of death stood ever ready, and its scaffold was continually running with the blood of the virtuous and the brave. It had that very day been actively em-

---

7. The French Revolution is generally dated from 1789; the Republic was declared in 1792.
8. The Latin Quarter, adjacent to the University (*cf.* Sorbonne, below), occupied by students, artists, and bohemians.
9. City hall.

ployed in the work of carnage, and there it stood in grim array, amidst a silent and sleeping city, waiting for fresh victims.

Wolfgang's heart sickened within him, and he was turning shuddering from the horrible engine, when he beheld a shadowy form, cowering as it were at the foot of the steps which led up to the scaffold. A succession of vivid flashes of lightning revealed it more distinctly. It was a female figure, dressed in black. She was seated on one of the lower steps of the scaffold, leaning forward, her face hid in her lap; and her long dishevelled tresses hanging to the ground, streaming with the rain which fell in torrents. Wolfgang paused. There was something awful in this solitary monument of woe. The female had the appearance of being above the common order. He knew the times to be full of vicissitude, and that many a fair head, which had once been pillowed on down, now wandered houseless. Perhaps this was some poor mourner whom the dreadful axe had rendered desolate, and who sat here heartbroken on the strand of existence, from which all that was dear to her had been launched into eternity.

He approached, and addressed her in the accents of sympathy. She raised her head and gazed wildly at him. What was his astonishment at beholding, by the bright glare of the lightning, the very face which had haunted him in his dreams. It was pale and disconsolate, but ravishingly beautiful.

Trembling with violent and conflicting emotions, Wolfgang again accosted her. He spoke something of her being exposed at such an hour of the night, and to the fury of such a storm, and offered to conduct her to her friends. She pointed to the guillotine with a gesture of dreadful signification.

"I have no friend on earth!" said she.

"But you have a home," said Wolfgang.

"Yes—in the grave!"

The heart of the student melted at the words.

"If a stranger dare make an offer," said he, "without danger of being misunderstood, I would offer my humble dwelling as a shelter; myself as a devoted friend. I am friendless myself in Paris, and a stranger in the land; but if my life could be of service, it is at your disposal, and should be sacrificed before harm or indignity should come to you."

There was an honest earnestness in the young man's manner that had its effect. His foreign accent, too, was in his favor; it showed him not to be a hackneyed inhabitant of Paris. Indeed, there is an eloquence in true enthusiasm that is not to be doubted. The homeless stranger confided herself implicitly to the protection of the student.

He supported her faltering steps across the *Pont Neuf*, and by the place where the statue of Henry the Fourth had been over-thrown by the populace. The storm had abated, and the thunder rumbled at a distance. All Paris was quiet; that great volcano of human passion slumbered for a while, to gather fresh strength for the next day's eruption. The student conducted his charge through the ancient streets of the *Pays Latin,* and by the dusky walls of the Sorbonne, to the great dingy hotel which he inhabited. The old portress who admitted them stared with surprise at the un-usual sight of the melancholy Wolfgang with a female companion.

On entering his apartment, the student, for the first time, blushed at the scantiness and indifference of his dwelling. He had but one chamber—an old-fashioned saloon—heavily carved, and fantastically furnished with the remains of former magnificence, for it was one of those hotels in the quarter of the Luxembourg palace, which had once belonged to nobility. It was lumbered with books and papers, and all the usual apparatus of a student, and his bed stood in a recess at one end.

When lights were brought, and Wolfgang had a better oppor-tunity of contemplating the stranger, he was more than ever intoxi-cated by her beauty. Her face was pale, but of a dazzling fairness, set off by a profusion of raven hair that hung clustering about it. Her eyes were large and brilliant, with a singular expression ap-proaching almost to wildness. As far as her black dress permitted her shape to be seen, it was of perfect symmetry. Her whole appearance was highly striking, though she was dressed in the simplest style. The only thing approaching to an ornament which she wore, was a broad black band round her neck, clasped by dia-monds.

The perplexity now commenced with the student how to dispose of the helpless being thus thrown upon his protection. He thought of abandoning his chamber to her, and seeking shelter for himself elsewhere. Still he was so fascinated by her charms, there seemed to be such a spell upon his thoughts and senses, that he could not tear himself from her presence. Her manner, too, was singular and unaccountable. She spoke no more of the guillotine. Her grief had abated. The attentions of the student had first won her con-fidence, and then, apparently, her heart. She was evidently an enthusiast like himself, and enthusiasts soon understood each other.

In the infatuation of the moment, Wolfgang avowed his pas-sion for her. He told her the story of his mysterious dream, and how she had possessed his heart before he had ever seen her. She was strangely affected by his recital, and acknowledged to have felt an impulse towards him equally unaccountable. It was the time for wild theory and wild actions. Old prejudices and superstitions were done away; every thing was under the sway of the "Goddess of Reason." [1] Among other rubbish of the old times, the forms and ceremonies of marriage began to be considered superfluous bonds for honorable minds. Social compacts were the vogue. Wolfgang was too much of a theorist not to be tainted by the liberal doctrines of the day.

"Why should we separate?" said he: "our hearts are united; in the eye of reason and honor we are as one. What need is there of sordid forms to bind high souls together?"

The stranger listened with emotion: she had evidently received illumination at the same school.

"You have no home nor family," continued he; "let me be every thing to you, or rather let us be every thing to one another. If form is necessary, form shall be observed—there is my hand. I pledge myself to you for ever."

"For ever?" said the stranger, solemnly.

"For ever!" repeated Wolfgang.

The stranger clasped the hand extended to her: "then I am yours," murmured she, and sank upon his bosom.

The next morning the student left his bride sleeping, and sallied forth at an early hour to seek more spacious apartments suitable to the change in his situation. When he returned, he found the stranger lying with her head hanging over the bed, and one arm thrown over it. He spoke to her, but received no reply. He advanced to awaken her from her uneasy posture. On taking her hand, it was cold—there was no pulsation—her face was pallid and ghastly.—In a word she was a corpse.

Horrified and frantic, he alarmed the house. A scene of confusion ensued. The police was summoned. As the officer of police entered the room, he started back on beholding the corpse.

"Good heaven!" cried he, "how did this woman come here?"

"Do you know anything about her?" said Wolfgang, eagerly.

"Do I?" exclaimed the officer: "she was guillotined yesterday."

He stepped forward; undid the black collar round the neck of the corpse, and the head rolled on the floor!

The student burst into a frency. "The fiend! the fiend has gained possession of me!" shrieked he: "I am lost for ever."

They tried to soothe him, but in vain. He was possessed with the frightful belief that an evil spirit had reanimated the dead body to ensnare him. He went distracted, and died in a mad-house.

Here the old gentleman with the haunted head finished his narrative.

---

1. The "Goddess of Reason" had been literally enthroned, in recognition of the rationalistic program of the Revolution concerning government and social institutions, including marriage.

"And is this really a fact?" said the inquisitive gentleman.

"A fact not to be doubted," replied the other. "I had it from the best authority. The student told it me himself. I saw him in a mad-house in Paris."

1824, 1860–61

JAMES FENIMORE COOPER

(1789–1851)

Cooper was born at Burlington, New Jersey, September 15, 1789. The next year his father settled on the family estate, now Cooperstown, at the foot of Otsego Lake, in New York. There the family was dominant; Judge Cooper was by nature the landed proprietor. Young Cooper was privately tutored; then he attended Yale about three years, without achieving a degree. After a year at sea before the mast, he was commissioned a midshipman in the United States Navy in 1808. Three years later he married Susan Augusta DeLancey, daughter of a wealthy family in Mamaroneck, Westchester County, New York; he then resigned his commission and became the country gentleman, devoting himself to his family, and to agricultural, political, financial, and social interests in Cooperstown and in Westchester County.

According to a charming legend, Cooper's first novel (*Precaution*, 1820) was a response to his wife's challenge to improve on the current British society fiction, and the failure of this work turned him to historical novels. *The Spy* (1821), a novel of the Revolution, foreshadowed his typical hero in Harvey Birch, and launched his career as the American rival of Sir Walter Scott in the popular field of historical romance. In the remaining thirty years of his life, he poured out a staggering total of thirty-three novels, numerous volumes of social comment, a *History of the Navy*, and five volumes of travels.

In *The Leather-Stocking Tales* the American frontier hero first materialized, to run his limitless course to the present day, through the romance, dime novel, drama, movies, and television. Fearless and miraculously resourceful, he survives the rigors of nature and the villainy of man by superior strength and skill, and by the help of heaven, for he is always quaintly moral. In short, he is the knight of the Christian romances transplanted to the soil of democracy and the American forest and frontier. Cooper's Natty Bumppo appears in the five novels under various names which, like a knight of old, he has gained by his exploits. Deerslayer merges into Hawk-eye, Pathfinder, and Leather-Stocking.

Cooper did not plan these novels as a series, nor did he publish them in the chronological order of the events in their hero's life. In *The Pioneers* (1823), the author's third novel, Natty Bumppo first appeared, as a seasoned scout in advancing years, accompanied by the dying Chingachgook, the old Indian chief who has been his faithful comrade in adventure. *The Leather-Stocking Tales* are named below in the order of events in the life of Natty Bumppo: *The Deerslayer* (1841), early adventures with the hostile Hurons, on Lake Otsego, New York, in 1740–1745; *The Last of the Mohicans* (1826), an adventure of the French and Indian Wars, in the Lake George country in 1757; *The Pathfinder* (1840), continuing the same border warfare in 1760, in the St. Lawrence and Lake Ontario country; *The Pioneers* (1823), described above, taking place in 1793, as the eastern forest frontier begins to disappear and old Chingachgook dies; and *The Prairie* (1827), set in the new frontier of the western plains in 1804, where the aged Leather-Stocking, having assisted some white pioneers and the Pawnees against the Sioux, takes leave of life amid people who can still value his devotion to a dying chivalry.

Almost as popular in their own day as *The Leather-Stocking Tales* were Cooper's romances of seafaring and naval combat; of these *The Pilot* (1823) set the pattern and provided the typical heroes in Long Tom Coffin and the mysterious "Pilot," generally taken to represent the gallant John Paul Jones. Later novels of the sea included, notably, *The Red Rover* (1828), *The Water-Witch* (1830), *The*

Two Admirals (1842), and *The Wing-and-Wing* (1842).

Cooper's earnestness as a social critic was strongly evident in his novels based on European history. *The Bravo* (1831), *The Heidenmauer* (1832), and *The Headsman* (1833) are satires of European feudalism, but follow the conventional pattern which Scott had established for historical romance. From 1826 to 1833 Cooper lived observantly abroad, ostensibly as American consul at Lyon, but actually as a persistent traveler. His novels of foreign locale, as well as his travel books and volumes of social comment, reflect his continuous awareness of contrasts in society, behavior, and government between the United States and Europe, particularly Great Britain. Abroad he was regarded as a champion of American life; but at home, his comments ironically gained him a reputation as a defender of the aristocracy. His *Sketches of Switzerland* and *Gleanings in Europe*, published in five volumes between 1836 and 1838, are now regarded as genuine contributions to our literature of travel, but at the time they antagonized equalitarian democrats, and the breach was widened by such commentaries and novels as *A Letter to His Countrymen* (1834), and *Homeward Bound*, *Home as Found*, and *The American Democrat*, all published in 1838.

Among the best contributions of his prolific later years is a trilogy of novels, *Satanstoe* (1845), *The Chainbearer* (1845), and *The Redskins* (1846), in which the author employs the fiction of certain "Littlepage Manuscripts," purported to contain records of three generations of a great family of upstate New York landholders. The novels form a consecutive social history of three generations of Dutch patroon society in the Hudson Valley, ending with the Anti-Rent Wars of the 1840's, when the tenants successfully opposed the feudal leases and perpetual sovereignty of the lords of the manor. Thus was founded the family novel of several volumes. Uneven in quality, the *Littlepage Manuscripts* succeed by their fine sense of history and their narrative intensity, and they are the last of Cooper's works to do so.

The Leather-Stocking Tales have been reprinted many times but never critically edited prior to the forty-eight–volume edition of *The Works of James Fenimore Cooper* now being published by the State University of New York Press. The authoritative *Descriptive*

Bibliography of the Writings of James Fenimore Cooper, by Robert E. Spiller and P. C. Blackburn, 1934, is indispensable for serious study. The Author's Revised Edition appeared in 12 vols. in 1851, followed by an edition illustrated by F. O. C. Darley, 32 vols., 1859–1861. The Household Edition, 32 vols., 1876–1884, contains valuable introductory essays by Susan Fenimore Cooper, the novelist's daughter. The *Works,* 33 vols., 1895–1900, is still procurable. See also *Gleanings in Europe,* 2 vols., edited by Robert E. Spiller, 1928–1930, and *The American Democrat,* edited by H. L. Mencken, 1931. An excellent collection of the nonfiction is *Cooper: Representative Selections,* edited by Robret E. Spiller, American Writers Series, 1936. James F. Beard's *Letters and Journals of James Fenimore Cooper* comprises six volumes, 1960–1968. An earlier compilation of *The Correspondence,* 2 vols., by J. F. Cooper, 1922, is useful.

There is no definitive biography; but *Fenimore Cooper, Critic of His Times,* by Robert E. Spiller, 1931, is an authoritative and penetrating study, and may be supplemented by the same author's Introduction to the *Representative Selections* (listed above). The comments by Susan Fenimore Cooper in *The Cooper Gallery,* 1865, and T. R. Lounsbury's biography, 1882, are useful; so also are Donald A. Ringe, *James Fenimore Cooper,* 1962, and Warren S. Walker, *Leather-Stocking and the Critics,* 1965.

From The American Democrat

An Aristocrat and a Democrat

We live in an age when the words aristocrat and democrat are much used, without regard to the real significations. An aristocrat is one of a few who possess the political power of a country; a democrat, one of the many. The words are also properly applied to those who entertain notions favorable to aristocratical or democratical forms of government. Such persons are not necessarily either aristocrats or democrats in fact, but merely so in opinion. Thus a member of a democratical government may have an aristocratical bias, and vice versa.

To call a man who has the habits and opinions of a gentleman, an aristocrat from that fact alone, is an abuse of terms and betrays ignorance of the true principles of government, as well as of the world. It must be an equivocal freedom under which every one is not the master of his own innocent acts and associations; and he is a sneaking democrat indeed who will submit to be dictated to, in those habits over which neither law nor morality assumes a right of control.

Some men fancy that a democrat can only be one who seeks the level, social, mental and moral, of the majority, a rule that would at once exclude all men of refinement, education, and taste from the class. These persons are enemies of democracy, as they at once render it impracticable. They are usually great sticklers for their own associations and habits, too, though unable to comprehend any of a nature that are superior. They are, in truth, aristocrats in principle, though assuming a contrary pretension, the groundwork of all their feelings and arguments being self. Such is not the intention of liberty, whose aim is to leave every man to be the master of his own acts; denying hereditary honors, it is true, as unjust and unnecessary, but not denying the inevitable consequences of civilization.

The law of God is the only rule of conduct in this, as in other matters. Each man should do as he would be done by. Were the question put to the greatest advocate of indiscriminate association, whether he would submit to have his company and habits dictated to him, he would be one of the first to resist the tyranny; for they who are the most rigid in maintaining their own claims in such matters, are usually the loudest in decrying those whom they fancy to be better off than themselves. Indeed, it may be taken as a rule in social intercourse, that he who is the most apt to question the pretensions of others is the most conscious of the doubtful position he himself occupies; thus establishing the very claims he affects to deny, by letting his jealousy of it be seen. Manners, education, and refinement, are positive things, and they bring with them innocent tastes which are productive of high enjoyments; and it is as unjust to deny their possessors their indulgence as it would be to insist on the less fortunate's passing the time they would rather devote to athletic amusements, in listening to operas for which they have no relish, sung in a language they do not understand.

All that democracy means, is as equal a participation in rights as is practicable; and to pretend that social equality is a condition of popular institutions is to assume that the latter are destructive of civilization, for, as nothing is more self-evident than the impossibility of raising all men to the highest standard of tastes and refinement, the alternative would be to reduce the entire community to the lowest. The whole embarrassment on this point exists in the difficulty of making men comprehend qualities they do not themselves possess. We can all perceive the difference between ourselves and our inferiors, but when it comes to a question of the difference between us and our superiors, we fail to appreciate merits of which we have no proper conceptions. In face of this obvious difficulty, there is the safe and just governing rule, already mentioned, or that of permitting every one to be the undisturbed judge of his own habits and associations, so long as they are innocent and do not impair the rights of others to be equally judges for themselves. It follows, that social intercourse must regulate itself, independently of institutions, with the exception that the latter, while they withhold no natural, bestow no factitious advantages beyond those which are inseparable from the rights of property, and general civilization.

In a democracy, men are just as free to aim at the highest attainable places in society, as to attain the largest fortunes; and it would be clearly unworthy of all noble sentiment to say that the grovelling competition for money shall alone be free, while that which enlists all the liberal acquirements and elevated sentiments of the race, is denied the democrat. Such an avowal would be at once a declaration of the inferiority of the system, since nothing but ignorance and vulgarity could be its fruits.

The democratic gentleman must differ in many essential particulars from the aristocratical gentleman, though in their ordinary habits and tastes they are virtually identical. Their principles vary; and, to a slight degree, their deportment accordingly. The democrat, recognizing the right of all to participate in power, will be more liberal in his general sentiments, a quality of superiority in itself; but in conceding this much to his fellow man, he will proudly maintain his own independence of vulgar domination as indispensable to his personal habits. The same principles and manliness that would induce him to depose a royal despot would induce him to resist a vulgar tyrant.

There is no more capital, though more common error, than to suppose him an aristocrat who maintains his independence of habits; for democracy asserts the control of the majority, only in matters of law, and not in matters of custom. The very object of the institution is the utmost practicable personal liberty, and to affirm the contrary would be sacrificing the end to the means.

An aristocrat, therefore, is merely one who fortifies his exclusive privileges by positive institutions, and a democrat, one who is willing to admit of a free competition in all things. To say, however, that the last supposes this competition will lead to nothing is an assumption that means are employed without any reference to an end. He is the purest democrat who best maintains his rights, and no rights can be dearer to a man of cultivation than exemptions from unseasonable invasions on his time by the coarse minded and ignorant.

1838

From The Deerslayer, Chapter XXVII [1]

[*The Young Deerslayer*]

It was an imposing scene into which Deerslayer now found himself advancing. All the older warriors were seated on the trunk of the fallen tree, waiting his approach with grave decorum. On the right stood the young men, armed, while the left was occupied by the women and children. In the center was an open space of considerable extent, always canopied by leaves, but from which the underbrush, dead wood, and other obstacles had been carefully removed. The more open area had probably been much used by former parties, for this was the place where the appearance of a sward was the most decided. The arches of the woods, even at high noon, cast their somber shadows on the spot, which the brilliant rays of the sun that struggled through the leaves contributed to mellow, and, if such an expression can be used, to illuminate. It was probably from a similar scene that the mind of man first got its idea of the effects of Gothic tracery and churchly hues; this temple of nature producing some such effect, so far as light and shadows were concerned, as the well-known offspring of human invention.

As was not unusual among the tribes and wandering bands of the aborigines, two chiefs shared, in nearly equal degrees, the principal and primitive authority that was wielded over these children of the forest. * * * One was a senior, well known for eloquence in debate, wisdom in council, and prudence in measures; while his great competitor, if not his rival, was a brave, distinguished in war, notorious for ferocity, and remarkable, in the way of intellect, for nothing but the cunning and expedients of the warpath. The first was Rivenoak, who has already been introduced to the reader, while the last was called le Panthère, in the language of the Canadas; or the Panther, to resort to the vernacular of the English colonies. The appellation of the fighting chief was supposed to indicate the qualities of the warrior, agreeably to a practice of the red-man's nomenclature; ferocity, cunning, and treachery being, perhaps, the distinctive features of his character. The title had been received

1. This episode and the two which follow have been drawn from three different novels of the series of *Leather-Stocking Tales*. They present three characteristic pictures of the frontier hero Natty Bumppo: in his youth (*The Deerslayer*); in the period of his greatest exploits and usefulness (*The Last of the Mohicans*); and as the patriarch, dying along with an American legend and a way of life (*The Prairie*). The chapters have been printed in the chronological order of Natty's life.

In *The Deerslayer* young Natty is involved in the French and Indian Wars against the hostile Huron Indians (allies of the French) near Lake Otsego, New York. Earlier in the novel, he had been trained as a hunter by the friendly Delawares and had won the name of Deerslayer. Now, however, the Hurons have captured him. They have released him to accomplish a mission for them, but he is on his word of honor to return at an appointed hour. The mission has been unsuccessful; Chapter XXVII opens with Deerslayer's voluntary return to captivity—and probable death—in fulfillment of his pledge.

from the French, and was prized so much the more from that circumstance, the Indian submitting profoundly to the greater intelligence of his pale-face allies in most things of this nature. How well the *sobriquet* was merited, will be seen in the sequel.

Rivenoak and the Panther sat side by side, awaiting the approach of their prisoner, as Deerslayer put his moccasined foot on the stand; nor did either move, or utter a syllable, until the young man had advanced into the center of the area, and proclaimed his presence with his voice. This was done firmly, though in the simple manner that marked the character of the individual.

"Here I am, Mingos," [2] he said, in the dialect of the Delawares, a language that most present understood; "here I am, and there is the sun. One is not more true to the laws of natur', than the other has proved true to his word. I am your prisoner; do with me what you please. My business with man and 'arth is settled; nothing remains now but to meet the white man's God, accordin' to a white man's duties and gifts."

A murmur of approbation escaped even the women at this address, and, for an instant there was a strong and pretty general desire to adopt into the tribe one who owned so brave a spirit. Still there were dissenters from this wish, among the principal of whom might be classed the Panther, and his sister, le Sumach, so called from the number of her children, who was the widow of le Loup Cervier,[3] now known to have fallen by the hand of the captive. Native ferocity held one in subjection, while the corroding passion of revenge prevented the other from admitting any gentler feeling at the moment. Not so with Rivenoak. This chief arose, stretched his arm before him in a gesture of courtesy, and paid his compliments with an ease and dignity that a prince might have envied. As, in that band, his wisdom and eloquence were confessedly without rivals, he knew that on himself would properly fall the duty of first replying to the speech of the pale-face.

"Pale-face, you are honest," said the Huron orator. "My people are happy in having captured a man, and not a skulking fox. We now know you; we shall treat you like a brave. If you have slain one of our warriors, and helped to kill others, you have a life of your own ready to give away in return. Some of my young men thought that the blood of a pale-face was too thin; that it would refuse to run under the Huron knife. You will show them it is not so; your heart is stout as well as your body. It is a pleasure to make such a prisoner; should my warriors say that the death of le Loup Cervier ought not to be forgotten, and that he cannot travel towards the land of spirits alone, that his enemy must be sent to overtake him, they will remember that he fell by the hand of a brave, and send you after him

2. Familiar name for the Hurons.   3. French for "lynx."

with such signs of our friendship as shall not make him ashamed to keep your company. I have spoken; you know what I have said."

"True enough, Mingo, all true as the gospel," returned the simple-minded hunter; "you *have* spoken, and I *do* know not only what you have *said*, but, what is still more important, what you *mean*. I dare to say your warrior the Lynx, was a stouthearted brave, and worthy of your fri'ndship and respect, but I do not feel unworthy to keep his company without any passport from your hands. Nevertheless, here I am, ready to receive judgment from your council, if, indeed, the matter was not determined among you afore I got back."

"My old men would not sit in council over a pale-face until they saw him among them," answered Rivenoak, looking around him a little ironically; "they said it would be like sitting in council over the winds; they go where they will, and come back as they see fit, and not otherwise. There was one voice that spoke in your favor, Deerslayer, but it was alone, like the song of the wren whose mate has been struck by the hawk."

"I thank that voice, whos'ever it may have been, Mingo, and will say it was as true a voice as the rest were lying voices. A furlough is as binding on a pale-face, if he be honest, as it is on a red-skin; and was it not so, I would never bring disgrace on the Delawares, among whom I may be said to have received my edication. But words are useless and lead to braggin' feelin's; here I am; act your will on me."

Rivenoak made a sign of acquiescence, and then a short conference was privately held among the chiefs. As soon as the latter ended, three or four young men fell back from among the armed group, and disappeared. Then it was signified to the prisoner that he was at liberty to go at large on the point, until a council was held concerning his fate. * * *

In the meantime the business of the camp appeared to proceed in its regular train. The chiefs consulted apart, admitting no one but the Sumach to their councils; for she, the widow of the fallen warrior, had an exclusive right to be heard on such an occasion. The young men strolled about in indolent listlessness, awaiting the result with Indian patience, while the females prepared the feast that was to celebrate the termination of the affair, whether it proved fortunate, or otherwise, for our hero. No one betrayed feeling; and an indifferent observer, beyond the extreme watchfulness of the sentinels, would have detected no extraordinary movement or sensation to denote the real state of things. Two or three old women put their heads together, and, it appeared, unfavorably to the prospect of Deerslayer, by their scowling looks and angry gesture; but a group of Indian girls were evidently animated by a different impulse, as was apparent by stolen glances that expressed pity and regret. In this condition of the camp, an hour soon glided away.

Suspense is, perhaps, the feeling, of all others, that is most difficult to be supported. When Deerslayer landed, he fully, in the course of a few minutes, expected to undergo the tortures of an Indian revenge, and he was prepared to meet his fate manfully; but the delay proved far more trying than the nearer approach of suffering, and the intended victim began seriously to meditate some desperate effort at escape, as it might be from sheer anxiety to terminate the scene, when he was suddenly summoned to appear, once more, in front of his judges, who had already arranged the band in its former order, in readiness to receive him.

"Killer of the Deer," commenced Rivenoak, as soon as his captive stood before him, "my aged men have listened to wise words; they are ready to speak. You are a man whose fathers came from beyond the rising sun; we are children of the setting sun; we turn our faces towards the Great Sweet Lakes, when we look towards our villages. It may be a wise country and full of riches, towards the morning; but it is very pleasant towards the evening. We love most to look in that direction. When we gaze at the east, we feel afraid, canoe after canoe bringing more and more of your people in the track of the sun, as if their land was so full as to run over. The redmen are few already; they have need of help. One of our best lodges has lately been emptied by the death of its master; it will be a long time before his son can grow big enough to sit in his place. There is his widow; she will want venison to feed her and her children, for her sons are yet like the young of the robin before they quit the nest. By your hand has this great calamity befallen her. She has two duties; one to le Loup Cervier, and one to his children. Scalp for scalp, life for life, blood for blood, is one law; to feed her young, another. We know you, Killer of the Deer. You are honest; when you say a thing, it is so. You have but one tongue, and that is not forked, like a snake's. Your head is never hid in the grass; all can see it. What you say, that will you do. You are just. When you have done wrong, it is your wish to do right again, as soon as you can. Here is the Sumach; she is alone in her wigwam, with children crying around her for food; yonder is a rifle; it is loaded and ready to be fired. Take the gun; go forth and shoot a deer; bring the venison and lay it before the widow of le Loup Cervier; feed her children; call yourself her husband. After which, your heart will no longer be Delaware, but Huron; le Sumach's ears will not hear the cries of her children; my people will count the proper number of warriors."

"I feared this, Rivenoak," answered Deerslayer, when the other had ceased speaking; "yes, I did dread that it would come to this.

Hows'ever, the truth is soon told, and that will put an end to all expectations on this head. Mingo, I'm white, and Christian-born; 'twould ill become me to take a wife, under red-skin forms, from among heathen. That which I wouldn't do in peaceable times, and under a bright sun, still less would I do behind clouds, in order to save my life. I may never marry; most likely Providence, in putting me up here in the woods, has intended I should live single, and without a lodge of my own; but should such a thing come to pass, none but a woman of my own color and gifts shall darken the door of my wigwam. As for feeding the young of your dead warrior, I would do that cheerfully, could it be done without discredit; but it cannot, seeing that I can never live in a Huron village. Your own young men must find the Sumach in venison, and the next time she marries, let her take a husband whose legs are not long enough to overrun territory that don't belong to him. We fou't a fair battle, and he fell; in this there is nothin' but what a brave expects, and should be ready to meet. As for getting a Mingo heart, as well might you expect to see grey hairs on a boy, or the blackberry growing on the pine. No, no, Huron; my gifts are white, so far as wives are consarned; it is Delaware in all things touchin' Indians."

These words were scarcely out of the mouth of Deerslayer, before a common murmur betrayed the dissatisfaction with which they had been heard. The aged women, in particular, were loud in their expressions of disgust; and the gentle Sumach herself, a woman quite old enough to be our hero's mother, was not the least pacific in her denunciations. But all the other manifestations of disappointment and discontent were thrown into the background by the fierce resentment of the Panther. This grim chief had thought it a degradation to permit his sister to become the wife of a pale-face of the Yengeese [4] at all. * * * The animal from which he got his name does not glare on his intended prey with more frightful ferocity than his eyes gleamed on the captive; nor was his arm backward in seconding the fierce resentment that almost consumed his breast.

"Dog of the pale-faces!" he exclaimed, in Iroquois, "go yell among the curs of your own evil hunting-grounds!"

The denunciation was accompanied by an appropriate action. Even while speaking, his arm was lifted, and the tomahawk hurled. Luckily the loud tones of the speaker had drawn the eye of Deerslayer towards him, else would that moment have probably closed his career. So great was the dexterity with which this dangerous weapon was thrown, and so deadly the intent, that it would have riven the skull of the prisoner, had he not stretched forth an arm, and caught the handle in one of its turns, with a readiness quite as remarkable as the skill with which the missile had been hurled. The

4. Indian pronunciation of "English"; supposed source of "Yankee."

projectile force was so great, notwithstanding, that when Deer-slayer's arm was arrested, his hand was raised above and behind his own head, and in the very attitude necessary to return the attack. It is not certain whether the circumstance of finding himself unexpectedly in this menacing posture and armed, tempted the young man to retaliate, or whether sudden resentment overcame his forbearance and prudence. His eye kindled, however, and a small red spot appeared on each cheek, while he cast all his energy in the effort of his arm, and threw back the weapon at his assailant. The unexpectedness of this blow contributed to its success, the Panther neither raising an arm nor bending his head to avoid it. The keen little axe struck the victim in a perpendicular line with the nose, directly between the eyes, literally braining him on the spot. Sallying forward, as the serpent darts at his enemy even while receiving its own death-wound, this man of powerful frame fell his length into the open area formed by the circle, quivering in death. A common rush to his relief left the captive, for a single instant, quite without the crowd; and, willing to make one desperate effort for life he bounded off with the activity of a deer. There was but a breathless instant, when the whole band, old and young, women and children, abandoning the lifeless body of the Panther where it lay, raised the yell of alarm, and followed in pursuit.

Sudden as had been the event which induced Deerslayer to make this desperate trial of speed, his mind was not wholly unprepared for the fearful emergency. In the course of the past hour, he had pondered well on the chances of such an experiment, and had shrewdly calculated all the details of success and failure. At the first leap, therefore, his body was completely under the direction of an intelligence that turned all its efforts to the best account, and prevented everything like hesitation or indecision, at the important instant of the start. To this alone was he indebted for the first great advantage, that of getting through the line of sentinels unharmed. * * *

Several rifles were discharged at Deerslayer * * * as he came out into the comparative exposure of the clear forest. But the direction of his line of flight, which partially crossed that of the fire, the haste with which the weapons had been aimed, and the general confusion that prevailed in the camp, prevented any harm from being done. Bullets whistled past him, and many cut twigs from the branches at his side, but not one touched even his dress. The delay caused by these fruitless attempts was of great service to the fugitive, who had gained more than a hundred yards on even the leading men of the Hurons, ere something like concert and order had entered into the chase. To think of following with rifle in hand was out of the question; and after emptying their pieces in vague hopes of wounding their captive, the best runners of the Indians threw them aside, calling out to the women and boys to recover and load them again as soon as possible.

Deerslayer knew too well the desperate nature of the struggle in which he was engaged, to lose one of the precious moments. He also knew that his only hope was to run in a straight line, for as soon as he began to turn, or double, the greater number of his pursuers would put escape out of the question. He held his way, therefore, in a diagonal direction up the acclivity, which was neither very high nor very steep in this part of the mountain, but which was sufficiently toilsome for one contending for life, to render it painfully oppressive. There, however, he slackened his speed to recover breath, proceeding even at a quick walk or a slow trot, along the more difficult parts of the way. The Hurons were whooping and leaping behind him; but this he disregarded, well knowing they must overcome the difficulties he had surmounted ere they could reach the elevation to which he had attained. The summit of the first hill was now quite near him, and he saw, by the formation of the land, that a deep glen intervened, before the base of a second hill could be reached. Walking deliberately to the summit, he glanced eagerly about him in every direction, in quest of a cover. None offered in the ground; but a fallen tree lay near him, and desperate circumstances require desperate remedies. This tree lay in a line parallel to the glen, at the brow of the hill; to leap on it, and then to force his person as close as possible under its lower side, took but a moment. Previously to disappearing from his pursuers, however, Deerslayer stood on the height and gave a cry of triumph, as if exulting at the sight of the descent that lay before him.—In the next instant he was stretched beneath the tree.

No sooner was this expedient adopted, than the young man ascertained how desperate had been his own efforts, by the violence of the pulsations in his frame. He could hear his heart beat, and his breathing was like the action of a bellows in quick motion. Breath was gained, however, and the heart soon ceased to throb as if about to break through its confinement. The footsteps of those who toiled up the opposite side of the acclivity were now audible, and presently voices and treads announced the arrival of the pursuers. The foremost shouted as they reached the height; then, fearful that their enemy would escape under favor of the descent, each leaped upon the fallen tree, and plunged into the ravine, trusting to get a sight of the pursued ere he reached the bottom. In this manner, Huron followed Huron, until Natty began to hope the whole had passed. Others succeeded, however, until quite forty had leaped over the tree; and then he counted them, as the surest mode of ascertaining how many could be behind. Presently all were in the bottom of the glen, quite a hundred feet below him, and some had even ascended part of the opposite hill, when it became evident an inquiry was making as to the direction he had taken. This was the critical moment; and one of nerves less steady, or of a training that had been neglected, would have seized it to rise, and fly. Not so with Deerslayer. He still lay quiet, watching with jealous vigilance every movement below, and fast regaining his breath.

The Hurons now resembled a pack of hounds at fault. Little was said, but each man ran about, examining the dead leaves, as the hound hunts for the lost scent. The great number of moccasins that had passed made the examination difficult, though the in-toe of an Indian was easily to be distinguished from the freer and wider step of a white man. Believing that no more pursuers remained behind, and hoping to steal away unseen, Deerslayer suddenly threw himself over the tree, and fell on the upper side. This achievement appeared to be effected successfully, and hope beat high in the bosom of the fugitive. Rising to his hands and feet, after a moment lost in listening to the sounds in the glen, in order to ascertain if he had been seen, the young man next scrambled to the top of the hill, a distance of only ten yards, in the expectation of getting its brow between him and his pursuers, and himself so far under cover. Even this was effected, and he rose to his feet, walking swiftly but steadily along the summit, in a direction opposite to that in which he had first fled.[5] * * *

1841

From The Last of the Mohicans, Chapter XXXII [6]

[*The Hawk-eye of the Indian Wars*]

During the time Uncas [7] was making this disposition of his forces, the woods were as still, and, with the exception of those who had

5. After gaining more distance on the pursuing Indians, Deerslayer is sighted and pursued, but again he outwits them: lying flat in a canoe, he safely drifts out of sight down the lake.
6. In this novel, Natty Bumppo, a mature and seasoned scout, is known as Hawk-eye. The central event is the capture of the British Fort William Henry by the French and their Huron allies in 1757. The English commander's daughters, Cora and Alice Munro, have been guided through the forest by Magua, an Indian secret agent of the French, who hopes to gain possession of Cora by betraying the party to the French. Hawk-eye has foiled this plot, assisted by his faithful friends, the Delaware chieftain Chingachgook and his warrior son Uncas, and by

David Gamut, a wandering music master.

In the present chapter this party has left the fallen fort under safe conduct from the French, accompanied by Munro and by Major Duncan Heyward, the fiancé of Alice Munro. But Magua provokes an Indian attack, in which the girls are captured. Alice is gallantly rescued by her fiancé; but under tribal law the Delawares are obliged to permit Magua to depart with Cora, since she is his own captive. However, under the leadership of Uncas, they at once pursue the Hurons, among whom Magua has taken refuge.
7. The "Last of the Mohicans," who is killed in this chapter. Cooper has borrowed the name of a real chief of the Mohegans of early Massachusetts.

met in council, apparently, as much untenanted, as when they came fresh from the hands of their Almighty Creator. The eye could range, in every direction, through the long and shadowed vistas of the trees; but nowhere was any object to be seen, that did not properly belong to the peaceful and slumbering scenery. Here and there a bird was heard fluttering among the branches of the beeches, and occasionally a squirrel dropped a nut, drawing the startled looks of the party, for a moment, to the place; but the instant the casual interruption ceased, the passing air was heard murmuring above their heads, along that verdant and undulating surface of forest, which spread itself unbroken, unless by stream or lake, over such a vast region of country. Across the tract of wilderness, which lay between the Delawares and the village of their enemies, it seemed as if the foot of man had never trodden, so breathing and deep was the silence in which it lay. But Hawk-eye, whose duty led him foremost in the adventure, knew the character of those with whom he was about to contend, too well, to trust the treacherous quiet.

When he saw his little band again collected, the scout threw "kill-deer" [8] into the hollow of his arm, and making a silent signal that he would be followed, * * * turned, and perceived that his party had been followed thus far by the singing-master.

"Do you know, friend," asked the scout gravely, and perhaps with a little of the pride of conscious deserving in his manner, "that this is a band of rangers, chosen for the most desperate service, and put under the command of one, who, though another might say it with a better face, will not be apt to leave them idle. It may not be five, it cannot be thirty, minutes before we tread on the body of a Huron, living or dead."

"Though not admonished of your intentions in words," returned David, whose face was a little flushed, and whose ordinarily quiet and unmeaning eyes glimmered with an expression of unusual fire, "your men have reminded me of the children of Jacob going out to battle against the Shechemites, for wickedly aspiring to wedlock with a woman of a race that was favoured of the Lord.[9] Now, I have journeyed far, and sojourned much, in good and evil, with the maiden ye seek; and, though not a man of war, with my loins girded and my sword sharpened, yet would I gladly strike a blow in her behalf."

The scout hesitated, as if weighing the chances of such a strange enlistment in his mind before he answered—

"You know not the use of any we'pon. You carry no rifle; and believe me, what the Mingoes take they will freely give again."

---

8. His rifle, which had become legendary; *cf.* the swords of famous knights of romance.

9. *Cf.* Genesis xxxiv; Jacob slew the Shechemite for this violation.

"Though not a vaunting and bloodily disposed Goliath," returned David, drawing a sling from beneath his parti-coloured and uncouth attire, "I have not forgotten the example of the Jewish boy.[1] With this ancient instrument of war have I practised much in my youth, and peradventure the skill has not entirely departed from me."

"Ay!" said Hawk-eye, considering the deer-skin thong and apron, with a cold and discouraging eye; "the thing might do its work." * * * Pointing in the direction he wished to proceed, Hawk-eye advanced, the band breaking off in single files, and following so accurately in his footsteps, as to leave, if we except Heyward and David, the trail of but a single man.

The party was, however, scarcely uncovered, before a volley from a dozen rifles was heard in their rear, and a Delaware leaping high into the air, like a wounded deer, fell at his whole length, perfectly dead. * * *

Animating his followers by his voice, and his own example, Hawk-eye then gave the word to bear down upon their foes. The charge, in that rude species of warfare, consisted merely in pushing from cover to cover, nigher to the enemy, and in this manoeuvre he was instantly and successfully obeyed. The Hurons were compelled to withdraw, and the scene of the contest rapidly changed from the more open ground on which it had commenced, to a spot where the assailed found a thicket to rest upon. Here the struggle was protracted, arduous, and, seemingly, of doubtful issue. The Delawares, though none of them fell, beginning to bleed freely, in consequence of the disadvantage at which they were held. * * *

Then turning, with a prompt and decided air, * * * he called aloud to his Indians, in their own language. His words were answered by a shout, and at a given signal, each warrior made a swift movement around his particular tree. The sight of so many dark bodies, glancing before their eyes at the same instant, drew a hasty, and, consequently, an ineffectual fire from the Hurons. Then, without stopping to breathe, the Delawares leaped, in long bounds, towards the wood, like so many panthers springing upon their prey. Hawk-eye was in front, brandishing his terrible rifle, and animating his followers by his example. A few of the older and more cunning Hurons, who had not been deceived by the artifice which had been practised to draw their fire, now made a close and deadly discharge of their pieces, and justified the apprehensions of the scout, by felling three of his foremost warriors. But the shock was insufficient to repel their impetus of the charge. The Delawares broke into the cover, with the ferocity of their natures, and swept away every trace of resistance by the fury of the onset.

The combat endured only for an instant, hand to hand, and then

1. The boy David killed Goliath with a stone from a sling; *cf.* I Samuel xvii.

the assailed yielded ground rapidly, until they reached the opposite margin of the thicket, where they clung to their cover, with the sort of obstinacy that is so often witnessed in hunted brutes. At this critical moment, when the success of the struggle was again becoming doubtful, the crack of a rifle was heard behind the Hurons, and a bullet came whizzing from among some beaver lodges, which were situated in the clearing, in their rear, and was followed by the fierce and appalling yell of the war-whoop.

"There speaks the Sagamore!" [2] shouted Hawk-eye, answering the cry with his own stentorian voice; "we have them now in face and back!"

The effect on the Hurons was instantaneous. Discouraged by so unexpected an assault, from a quarter that left them no opportunity for cover, their warriors uttered a common yell of disappointment and despair, and breaking off in a body, they spread themselves across the opening, heedless of every other consideration but flight. Many fell, in making the experiment, under the bullets and the blows of the pursuing Delawares.

We shall not pause to detail the meeting between the scout and Chingachgook. * * *

At that instant the whoop was given, and a dozen Hurons fell by a discharge from Chingachgook and his band. The shout that followed, was answered by a single war-cry from the forest, and a yell passed through the air, that sounded as though a thousand throats were united in a common effort. The Hurons staggered, deserting the centre of their line, and Uncas issued through the opening they left, from the forest, at the head of a hundred warriors.

Waving his hands right and left, the young chief pointed out the enemy to his followers, who instantly separated in the pursuit. The war now divided, both wings of the broken Hurons seeking protection in the woods again, hotly pressed by the victorious warriors of the Lenape.[3] A minute might have passed, but the sounds were already receding in different directions, and gradually losing their distinctness beneath the echoing arches of the woods. One little knot of Hurons, however, had disdained to seek a cover, and were retiring, like lions at bay, slowly and sullenly up the acclivity. * * * Magua was conspicuous in this party, both by his fierce and savage mien, and by the air of haughty authority he yet maintained.

In his eagerness to expedite the pursuit, Uncas had left himself nearly alone; but the moment his eye caught the figure of le Subtil,[4] every other consideration was forgotten. Raising his cry of battle, which recalled some six or seven warriors, and reckless of the dis-

2. *I.e.*, the chief, Chingachgook.
3. The Lenni Lenape, another name for the Delawares.

4. "Le Renard Subtil" ("Crafty Fox") is the nickname given Magua by the French.

parity of their numbers, he rushed upon his enemy. Le Renard, who watched the movement, paused to receive him with secret joy. But at the moment when he thought the rashness of his impetuous young assailant had left him at his mercy, another shout was given, and la Longue Carabine [5] was seen rushing to the rescue, attended by all his white associates. The Huron instantly turned, and commenced a rapid retreat up the ascent.

There was no time for greetings or congratulations; for Uncas, though unconscious of the presence of his friends, continued the pursuit with the velocity of the wind. * * * Still Magua, though daring and much exposed, escaped from every effort against his life, with that sort of fabled protection, that was made to overlook the fortunes of favoured heroes in the legends of ancient poetry. Raising a yell that spoke volumes of anger and disappointment, the subtle chief, when he saw his comrades fallen, darted away from the place, attended by his two only surviving friends, leaving the Delawares engaged in stripping the dead of the bloody trophies of their victory.

But Uncas, who had vainly sought him in the mêlée, bounded forward in pursuit; Hawk-eye, Heyward, and David, still pressing on his footsteps. The utmost that the scout could effect, was to keep the muzzle of his rifle a little in advance of his friend, to whom, however, it answered every purpose of a charmed shield. Once Magua appeared disposed to make another and a final effort to revenge his losses; but abandoning his intentions so soon as demonstrated, he leaped into a thicket of bushes, through which he was followed by his enemies, and suddenly entered the mouth of the cave already known to the reader. Hawk-eye, who had only forborne to fire in tenderness to Uncas, raised a shout of success, and proclaimed aloud, that now they were certain of their game. The pursuers dashed into the long and narrow entrance, in time to catch a glimpse of the retreating forms of the Hurons. Their passage through the natural galleries and subterraneous apartments of the cavern was preceded by the shrieks and cries of hundreds of women and children. The place, seen by its dim and uncertain light, appeared like the shades of the infernal regions, across which unhappy ghosts and savage demons were flitting in multitudes.

Still Uncas kept his eye on Magua, as if life to him possessed but a single object. Heyward and the scout still pressed on his rear, actuated, though, possibly, in a less degree, by a common feeling. But their way was becoming intricate, in those dark and gloomy passages, and the glimpses of the retiring warriors less distinct and frequent; and for a moment the trace was believed to be lost, when a white robe was seen fluttering in the further extremity of a passage that seemed to lead up the mountain.

5. "The Long Rifle," as the French have nicknamed Hawk-eye.

" 'Tis Cora," exclaimed Heyward, in a voice in which horror and delight were wildly mingled.

"Cora! Cora!" echoed Uncas, bounding forward like a deer.

" 'Tis the maiden!" shouted the scout. "Courage, lady; we come —we come." * * *

"We must close!" said the scout, passing his friends by a desperate leap; "the knaves will pick us all off at this distance; and see; they hold the maiden so as to shield themselves!"

Though his words were unheeded, or rather unheard, his example was followed by his companions, who, by incredible exertions, got near enough to the fugitives to perceive that Cora was borne along between the two warriors, while Magua prescribed the direction and manner of their flight. At this moment the forms of all four were strongly drawn against an opening in the sky, and then they disappeared. Nearly frantic with disappointment, Uncas and Heyward increased efforts that already seemed superhuman, and they issued from the cavern on the side of the mountain, in time to note the route of the pursued. The course lay up the ascent, and still continued hazardous and laborious. * * * But the impetuous young men were rewarded, by finding that, encumbered with Cora, the Hurons were rapidly losing ground in the race.

"Stay; dog of the Wyandots!" exclaimed Uncas, shaking his bright tomahawk at Magua; "a Delaware girl calls stay!"

"I will go no farther," cried Cora, stopping unexpectedly on a ledge of rocks, that overhung a deep precipice, at no great distance from the summit of the mountain. "Kill me if thou wilt, detestable Huron, I will go no farther."

The supporters of the maiden raised their ready tomahawks with the impious joy that fiends are thought to take in mischief, but Magua suddenly stayed the uplifted arms. The Huron chief, after casting the weapons he had wrested from his companions over the rock, drew his knife, and turned to his captive, with a look in which conflicting passions fiercely contended.

"Woman," he said, "choose; the wigwam or the knife of le Subtil!"

Cora regarded him not; but dropping on her knees, with a rich glow suffusing itself over her features, she raised her eyes and stretched her arms towards Heaven, saying, in a meek and yet confiding voice—

"I am thine! do with me as thou seest best!"

"Woman," repeated Magua hoarsely, and endeavouring in vain to catch a glance from her serene and beaming eye, "choose."

But Cora neither heard nor heeded his demand. The form of the Huron trembled in every fibre, and he raised his arm on high, but dropped it again, with a bewildered air, like one who doubted. Once more he struggled with himself, and lifted the keen weapon again—but just then a piercing cry was heard above them, and Uncas appeared, leaping frantically, from a fearful height, upon the ledge. Magua recoiled a step, and one of his assistants, profiting by the chance, sheathed his own knife in the bosom of the maiden.

The Huron sprang like a tiger on his offending and already retreating countryman, but the falling form of Uncas separated the unnatural combatants. Diverted from his object by this interruption, and maddened by the murder he had just witnessed, Magua buried his weapon in the back of the prostrate Delaware, uttering an unearthly shout, as he committed the dastardly deed. But Uncas arose from the blow, as the wounded panther turns upon his foe, and struck the murderer of Cora to his feet, by an effort in which the last of his failing strength was expended. Then, with a stern and steady look, he turned to le Subtil, and indicated, by the expression of his eyes, all that he would do, had not the power deserted him. The latter seized the nerveless arm of the unresisting Delaware, and passed his knife into his bosom three several times, before his victim, still keeping his gaze riveted on his enemy with a look of inextinguishable scorn, fell dead at his feet.

"Mercy! mercy! Huron," cried Heyward, from above, in tones nearly choked by horror; "give mercy, and thou shalt receive it!"

Whirling the bloody knife up at the imploring youth, the victorious Magua uttered a cry so fierce, so wild, and yet so joyous, that it conveyed the sounds of savage triumph to the ears of those who fought in the valley, a thousand feet below. He was answered by an appalling burst from the lips of the scout, whose tall person was just then seen moving swiftly towards him, along those dangerous crags, with steps as bold and reckless, as if he possessed the power to move in middle air. But when the hunter reached the scene of the ruthless massacre, the ledge was tenanted only by the dead.

His keen eye took a single look at the victims, and then shot its fierce glances over the difficulties of the ascent in his front. A form stood at the brow of the mountain, on the very ledge of the giddy height, with uplifted arms, in an awful attitude of menace. Without stopping to consider his person, the rifle of Hawk-eye was raised, but a rock, which fell on the head of one of the fugitives below, exposed the indignant and glowing countenance of the honest Gamut. Then Magua issued from a crevice, and stepping with calm indifference over the body of the last of his associates, he leaped a wide fissure, and ascended the rocks at a point where the arm of David could not reach him. A single bound would carry him to the brow of the precipice, and assure his safety. Before taking the leap, however, the Huron paused, and shaking his hand at the scout, he shouted—

"The pale-faces are dogs! the Delawares women! Magua leaves them on the rocks, for the crows!"

Laughing hoarsely, he made a desperate leap, and fell short of his mark; though his hands grasped a shrub on the verge of the height. The form of Hawk-eye had crouched like a beast about to take its spring, and his frame trembled so violently with eagerness, that the muzzle of the half raised rifle played like a leaf fluttering in the wind. Without exhausting himself with fruitless efforts, the cunning Magua suffered his body to drop to the length of his arms, and found a fragment for his feet to rest on. Then summoning all his powers, he renewed the attempt, and so far succeeded, as to draw his knees on the edge of the mountain. It was now, when the body of his enemy was most collected together, that the agitated weapon of the scout was drawn to his shoulder. The surrounding rocks, themselves, were not steadier than the piece became for the single instant that it poured out its contents. The arms of the Huron relaxed, and his body fell back a little, while his knees still kept their position. Turning a relentless look on his enemy, he shook his hand at him, in grim defiance. But his hold loosened, and his dark person was seen cutting the air with its head downwards, for a fleeting instant, until it glided past the fringe of shrubbery which clung to the mountain, in its rapid flight to destruction.[6]

1826

From The Prairie, Chapter XXXIX[7]

[Death of a Hero]

Middleton gazed about him in growing concern, for no cry, no song, no shout welcomed him among a people, from whom he had so lately parted with regret. His uneasiness, not to say apprehensions, was shared by all his followers. Determination and stern resolution began to assume the place of anxiety in every eye, as each man silently felt for his arms, and assured himself that his several weapons were in a state for instant and desperate service. But there was no answering symptom of hostility on the part of their hosts.

6. After this adventure Hawk-eye returns to the forest, to become the Pathfinder of a later novel.
7. In *The Prairie* we find Natty Bumppo, or Leather-Stocking, nearly ninety at the time of his death in 1804. He has abandoned the dwindling forests of the East where, as he thinks, the new settlements have brought a kind of sophisticated softness; and he has followed the frontier to the Indian country of the great western plains. There in his old age his skill and bravery have won him the reverence due a "white sachem"

from the Pawnees, among whom he has settled down to meet his death, still "the trapper" with his hound Hector and the famous rifle, "kill-deer." Duncan Uncas Middleton, who is present at the death scene, is the grandson of Duncan Heyward and Alice Munro of *The Last of the Mohicans.* He and Leather-Stocking had shared some desperate adventures a few years earlier; now, learning of the old trapper's illness, Middleton has come out from the Army post to visit him.

Hard-Heart beckoned for Middleton and Paul to follow, leading the way towards the cluster of forms, that occupied the centre of the circle. Here the visitors found a solution of all the movements which had given them so much reason for apprehension.

The trapper was placed on a rude seat, which had been made with studied care, to support his frame in an upright and easy attitude. The first glance of the eye told his former friends, that the old man was at length called upon to pay the last tribute of nature. His eye was glazed and apparently as devoid of sight as of expression. His features were a little more sunken and strongly marked than formerly; but there, all change, so far as exterior was concerned, might be said to have ceased. His approaching end was not to be ascribed to any positive disease, but had been a gradual and mild decay of the physical powers. Life, it is true, still lingered in his system, but it was as though at times entirely ready to depart, and then it would appear to reanimate the sinking form, as if reluctant to give up the possession of a tenement, that had never been undermined by vice or corrupted by disease. It would have been no violent fancy to have imagined, that the spirit fluttered about the placid lips of the old woodsman, reluctant to depart from a shell, that had so long given it an honest and an honourable shelter.

His body was so placed as to let the light of the setting sun fall full upon the solemn features. His head was bare, the long, thin locks of gray fluttering lightly in the evening breeze. His rifle lay upon his knee, and the other accoutrements of the chase were placed at his side within reach of his hand. Between his feet lay the figure of a hound, with its head crouching to the earth as if it slumbered, and so perfectly easy and natural was its position, that a second glance was necessary to tell Middleton, he saw only the skin of Hector, stuffed, by Indian tenderness and ingenuity, in a manner to represent the living animal. * * *

When he had placed his guests in front of the dying man, Hard-Heart, after a pause, that proceeded as much from sorrow as decorum, leaned a little forward and demanded—

"Does my father hear the words of his son?"

"Speak," returned the trapper, in tones that issued from his inmost chest, but which were rendered awfully distinct by the death-like stillness, that reigned in the place. "I am about to depart from the village of the Loups, and shortly shall be beyond the reach of your voice."

"Let the wise chief have no cares for his journey," continued Hard-Heart with an earnest solicitude, that led him to forget, for the moment, that others were waiting to address his adopted parent; "a hundred Loups shall clear his path from briars."

"Pawnee, I die, as I have lived, a Christian man," resumed the trapper with a force of voice, that had the same startling effect on his hearers, as is produced by the trumpet, when its blast rises suddenly and freely on the air after its obstructed sounds have been heard struggling in the distance; "as I came into life, so will I leave it. Horses and arms are not needed to stand in the presence of the Great Spirit of my people. He knows my colour and according to my gifts will he judge my deeds."

"My father will tell my young men how many Mingoes he has struck and what acts of valour and justice he has done, that they may know how to imitate him."

"A boastful tongue is not heard in the heaven of a white man!" solemnly returned the old man. "What I have done He has seen. His eyes are always open. That which has been well done, he will remember; wherein I have been wrong will he not forget to chastise, though he will do the same in mercy. No, my son; a Pale-face may not sing his own praises, and hope to have them acceptable before his God!"

A little disappointed, the young partisan stepped modestly back, making way for the recent comers to approach. Middleton took one of the meagre hands of the trapper and struggling to command his voice, he succeeded in announcing his presence. The old man listened like one whose thoughts were dwelling on a very different subject, but when the other had succeeded in making him understand, that he was present, an expression of joyful recognition passed over his faded features—

"I hope you have not so soon forgotten those, whom you so materially served!" Middleton concluded. "It would pain me to think my hold on your memory was so light."

"Little that I have ever seen is forgotten," returned the trapper; "I am at the close of many weary days, but there is not one among them all, that I could wish to overlook. I remember you with the whole of your company; ay, and your gran'ther, that went before you. I am glad, that you have come back upon these plains, for I had need of one, who speaks the English, since little faith can be put in the traders of these regions. Will you do a favour, lad, to an old and dying man?"

"Name it," said Middleton; "it shall be done."

"It is a far journey to send such trifles," resumed the old man, who spoke at short intervals as strength and breath permitted; "A far and weary journey is the same; but kindnesses and friendships are things not to be forgotten. There is a settlement among the Otsego hills—"

"I know the place," interrupted Middleton, observing that he spoke with increasing difficulty; "proceed to tell me what you would have done."

"Take then this rifle, and pouch, and horn, and send them to the person, whose name is graven on the plates of the stock. A trader cut the letters with his knife, for it is long, that I have intended to send him such a token of my love!"

"It shall be so. Is there more that you could wish?"

"Little else have I to bestow. My traps I give to my Indian son; for honestly and kindly has he kept his faith. Let him stand before me."

Middleton explained to the chief, what the trapper had said, and relinquished his own place to the other.

"Pawnee," continued the old man, always changing his language to suit the person he addressed, and not unfrequently according to the ideas he expressed, "it is a custom of my people for the father to leave his blessing with the son, before he shuts his eyes forever. This blessing I give to you; take it, for the prayers of a Christian man will never make the path of a just warrior, to the blessed prairies, either longer or more tangled. May the God of a white man look on your deeds with friendly eyes, and may you never commit an act that shall cause him to darken his face. I know not whether we shall ever meet again. There are many traditions concerning the place of Good Spirits. It is not for one like me, old and experienced though I am, to set up my opinions against a nation's. You believe in the blessed prairies, and I have faith in the sayings of my fathers. If both are true, our parting will be final; but if it should prove, that the same meaning is hid under different words, we shall yet stand together, Pawnee, before the face of your Wahcondah, who will then be no other than my God. There is much to be said in favour of both religions, for each seems suited to its own people, and no doubt it was so intended. I fear I have not altogether followed the gifts of my colour, inasmuch as I find it a little painful to give up for ever the use of the rifle, and the comforts of the chase. But then the fault has been my own, seeing that it could not have been His. Ay, Hector," he continued, leaning forward a little, and feeling for the ears of the hound, "our parting has come at last, dog, and it will be a long hunt. You have been an honest, and a bold, and a faithful hound. Pawnee, you cannot slay the pup on my grave, for where a Christian dog falls, there he lies forever; but you can be kind to him, after I am gone for the love you bear his master."

"The words of my father, are in my ears," returned the young partisan, making a grave and respectfully gesture of assent. * * *

The old man made a long, and apparently a musing pause. At times he raised his eyes wistfully as if he would again address Middleton, but some innate feeling appeared always to suppress his words. The other, who observed his hesitation, enquired in a way most likely to encourage him to proceed, whether there was aught else, that he could wish to have done.

"I am without kith or kin in the wide world!" the trapper answered; "when I am gone, there will be an end of my race. We have never been chiefs, but honest, and useful in our way, I hope it cannot be denied, we have always proved ourselves. My father lies buried near the sea, and the bones of his son will whiten on the prairies—"

"Name the spot, and your remains shall be placed by the side of your father," interrupted Middleton.

"Not so, not so, Captain. Let me sleep, where I have lived, beyond the din of the settlements. Still I see no need, why the grave of an honest man should be hid, like a Red-skin in his ambushment. I paid a man in the settlements to make and put a graven stone at the head of my father's resting place. It was the value of twelve beaver-skins, and cunningly and curiously was it carved! Then it told to all comers that the body of such a Christian lay beneath; and it spoke of his manner of life, of his years, and of his honesty. When we had done with the Frenchers in the old war, I made a journey to the spot, in order to see that all was rightly performed, and glad I am to say the workman had not forgotten his faith."

"And such a stone you would have at your grave?"

"I! no, no, I have no son but Hard-Heart, and it is little, that an Indian knows of White fashions and usages. Besides I am his debtor, already, seeing it is so little I have done, since I have lived in his tribe. The rifle might bring the value of such a thing—but then I know, it will give the boy pleasure to hang the piece in his hall, for many is the deer and the bird that he has seen to destroy. No, no, the gun must be sent to him, whose name is graven on the lock!"

"But there is one, who would gladly prove his affection in the way you wish; he, who owes you not only his deliverance from so many dangers, but who inherits a heavy debt of gratitude from his ancestors. The stone shall be put at the head of your grave."

The old man extended his emaciated hand, and gave the other a squeeze of thanks.

"I thought, you might be willing to do it, but I was backward in asking the favour," he said, "seeing that you are not of my kin. Put no boastful words on the same, but just the name, the age and the time of the death, with something from the holy book; no more, no more. My name will then not be altogether lost on 'arth; I need no more." * * *

The trapper had remained nearly motionless for an hour. His eyes, alone, had occasionally opened and shut. When opened, his gaze seemed fastened on the clouds, which hung around the western horizon, reflecting the bright colours, and giving form and loveliness to the glorious tints of an American sunset. The hour—the calm beauty of the season—the occasion, all conspired to fill the spectators with solemn awe. Suddenly, while musing on the remarkable position, in which he was placed, Middleton felt the hand, which he held, grasp his own with incredible power, and the old man, supported on either side by his friends, rose upright to his feet. For a moment he looked about him, as if to invite all in presence to listen, (the lingering remnant of human frailty,) and then with a fine military elevation of the head, and with a voice that might be heard in every part of that numerous assembly, he pronounced the word— "Here!"

A movement so entirely unexpected, and the air of grandeur and humility, which were so remarkably united in the mien of the trapper, together with the clear and uncommon force of his utterance, produced a short period of confusion in the faculties of all present. When Middleton and Hard-Heart, who had each involuntarily extended a hand to support the form of the old man, turned to him again, they found, that the subject of their interest was removed forever beyond the necessity of their care. They mournfully placed the body in its seat, and Le Balafré arose to announce the termination of the scene to the tribe. The voice of the old Indian seemed a sort of echo from that invisible world, to which the meek spirit of the trapper had just departed.

"A valiant, a just and a wise warrior has gone on the path, which will lead him to the blessed grounds of his people!" he said. "When the voice of the Wahcondah called him, he was ready to answer. Go, my children; remember the just chief of the Pale-faces, and clear your own tracks from briars!"

The grave was made beneath the shade of some noble oaks. It has been carefully watched to the present hour by the Pawnees of the Loup, and is often shown to the traveller and the trader as a spot where a just White-man sleeps. In due time the stone was placed at its head, with the simple inscription, which the trapper had himself requested. The only liberty taken by Middleton was to add,—"May no wanton hand disturb his remains!"

1827

WILLIAM CULLEN BRYANT
(1794–1878)

William Cullen Bryant was one of the great personalities of his age, an individual whose force, courage, and dynamic liberalism as an editor provided effective leadership in American cultural and political life from the Age of Jackson through the Civil War and Reconstruction period. As poet and critic he gave an American formulation to the romantic movement; he provided an example of disciplined imagination and precise expression; he opposed to the usual insipid generalization about nature his close observation of the natural object; and finally, he encouraged American poets to seek cultural independence from Europe by writing of their own American experience. To be sure, Bryant inherited, with his American generation, a measure of neoclassical restraint and didacticism that troubles the reader of a later generation. Yet in spite of the vast changes in the sensibility of readers and the nature of modern experience, a few of his poems are timeless, while the reader who can recapture the sense of that older time will find in many others a moving inspiration and a genuine insight.

Born in Cummington, in the Berkshire foothills of western Massachusetts, a fine natural setting for the boyhood of a poet of nature, Bryant benefited also from the companionship of his father, Dr. Peter Bryant, an enthusiastic naturalist and a persistent walker in the woods. No wonder that he later remembered his reading, at the age of sixteen, the *Lyrical Ballads* of Wordsworth and Coleridge, when "a thousand springs seemed to gush up at once into my heart, and the face of nature, of a sudden, to change into a strange freshness." He was then at Williams College, where he remained only a year, but his reading had already included much beyond the elementary schooling provided at Cummington—he had access to his father's ample library and to those of two clergymen, one his uncle, who tutored him in classical languages and literature.

He had written verses from the age of nine; when he was only fourteen his father sent to a Boston publisher his satire, *The Embargo* (1808), which reflected the Federalist resentment against Jefferson's trade restrictions, intended to avert war with England. The next year a second volume of his juvenile poems appeared in Boston, and in 1811, after one year at college, he wrote the first draft of "Thanatopsis." These early poems reflected influences that he soon learned to absorb in his own independent style: the neoclassical forms of Addison, Pope, and Johnson; the attitudes of the "graveyard school," especially as represented by Blair, Thomson, Young, Gray, and Henry Kirke White; and finally, the mature romanticism of Scott, Cowper, Burns, Coleridge, and Wordsworth.

For a time, literature became secondary to the law. After four years of preparation, he was admitted to the bar, and practiced at Great Barrington from 1816 to 1825. In this interval he married, and held a political office, but the man of letters would not be suppressed. In 1817 his publication of "Thanatopsis" drew general attention to his genius; it was widely copied and became at once a familiar poem. He began to write sporadically for the magazines, and his essay on "Early American Verse" (1818) established him as a discerning critic. In 1821 he was called to read "The Ages" as the Phi Beta Kappa poem at Harvard. His first collected *Poems* appeared in Boston in 1821. In 1825 he accepted a minor editorial position in New York, and within a year he became assistant editor of the New York *Evening Post*.

In New York, to the end of his days, he was a dominant leader in literature and in public causes. He became the intimate of Cooper and of such Knickerbockers as Irving, Halleck, and Verplanck, and the friend, often the adviser, of later arrivals. In spite of the sometimes long intervals between volumes, he remained a familiar poet of the people; an illustrated edition of 1846 became a popular favorite, and his last approved collection, the Household Edition of 1876, remained in print into the present century. He made six extensive tours abroad and published two widely read volumes of *Letters of a Traveller*. In his declining years he furnished his countrymen with good poetic translations of the *Iliad* (1870) and the *Odyssey* (1871–1872). His *Library of Poetry and Song* (1871–1872) was the first great critical anthology in America. Meanwhile he had become editor in chief of the *Evening Post* (1829), which soon became his property, and, under his management, one of our first great national newspapers.

Bryant's persistent themes, besides religion and nature, dealt with humanitarian reform and national morality. Although his boyhood satire was leveled at Jefferson's embargo, he became a great leader of the northern Democrats; just as in religion, having rejected, in "Thanatopsis" the strict Calvinism of Cummington, he passed through a stage of Deism to become, in mature life, a prominent leader of the Unitarian movement. As a liberal Democrat he waged continual newspaper warfare for various freedoms—freedom of speech, of religion, and of labor association and collective bargaining, free trade, and the freedom of the masses from oppressive debtor laws and the exploitation of banking and currency regulations. In defense of one freedom he helped destroy the Democratic party, for he waged continuous warfare for free soil and, finally, the freedom of the slaves. As a poet he was able to express the common idealism of his countrymen at a level of propriety and dignity so high as to make him, for the time, their most revered spokesman.

The Poetical Works of William Cullen Bryant, Household Edition, 1876, is his final text and provides the basis for the text of poems reprinted below. *The Life and Works of William Cullen Bryant*, 6 vols., edited by Parke Godwin, 1883–1884, is the standard collection. The Roslyn Edition of the *Poetical Works*, edited by H. C. Sturges, 1903, is the best available one-volume edition, containing also a good bibliography. Tremaine McDowell's *Bryant: Representative Selections*, American Writers Series, 1935, is excellent in text, introduction, and notes.

Parke Godwin's *Biography* (1883) was authoritative. One-volume studies are John Bigelow, *William Cullen Bryant*, 1890; W. A. Bradley, *William Cullen Bryant*, 1905; H. H. Peckham, *Gotham Yankee*, 1950; Albert F. McLean, *William Cullen Bryant*, 1964; and Charles H. Brown, *William Cullen Bryant*, 1971. Allan Nevins, *The Evening Post: A Century of Journalism*, 1922, and Curtiss S. Johnson's *Politics and a Belly-Full: Journalistic Career of William Cullen Bryant * * *, 1962, provide new light on Bryant.

Blank verse

Thanatopsis [1]

To him who in the love of Nature holds
Communion with her visible forms, she speaks *descript. of Nature's language*
A various language; for his gayer hours
She has a voice of gladness, and a smile
And eloquence of beauty, and she glides   5
Into his darker musings, with a mild
And healing sympathy, that steals away
Their sharpness, ere he is aware. When thoughts
Of the last bitter hour come like a blight
Over thy spirit, and sad images   10
Of the stern agony, and shroud, and pall,
And breathless darkness, and the narrow house,
Make thee to shudder, and grow sick at heart,—
Go forth, under the open sky, and list
To Nature's teachings, while from all around—   15
Earth and her waters, and the depths of air,—
Comes a still voice—

               Yet a few days, and thee
The all-beholding sun shall see no more
In all his course; nor yet in the cold ground,
Where thy pale form was laid, with many tears,   20
Nor in the embrace of ocean, shall exist
Thy image. Earth, that nourished thee, shall claim
Thy growth, to be resolved to earth again,
And, lost each human trace, surrendering up
Thine individual being, shalt thou go   25
To mix forever with the elements,
To be a brother to the insensible rock
And to the sluggish clod, which the rude swain
Turns with his share,[2] and treads upon. The oak
Shall send his roots abroad, and pierce thy mould. 30

   Yet not to thine eternal resting-place
Shalt thou retire alone, nor couldst thou wish
Couch more magnificent. Thou shalt lie down
With patriarchs of the infant world, with kings,
The powerful of the earth, the wise, the good,   35

---

1. "Thanatopsis" (meaning "a meditation on death"), written in Bryant's seventeenth year (1811), was frequently revised, before and after its first publication (*North American Review*, September, 1817). It is still one of the most familiar of American poems. Recalling the British "graveyard school" in general, and specifically the poems of Henry Kirke White, Blair, Southey, and Cowper, it asserts its independence by its American largeness of landscape. It also expresses Bryant's early rejection of orthodox Calvinism—the young Deist stoically compares death with the crumbling of the insensible clod. In a few years he had swung to the Unitarian position (see "To a Waterfowl") and become a leader of Unitarian liberalism.
2. Plowshare.

Fair forms, and hoary seers of ages past,
All in one mighty sepulchre. The hills
Rock-ribbed and ancient as the sun, the vales
Stretching in pensive quietness between;
The venerable woods—rivers that move   40
In majesty, and the complaining brooks
That make the meadows green; and, poured round all,
Old Ocean's gray and melancholy waste,—
Are but the solemn decorations all
Of the great tomb of man. The golden sun,   45
The planets, all the infinite host of heaven,
Are shining on the sad abodes of death,
Through the still lapse of ages. All that tread
The globe are but a handful of the tribes
That slumber in its bosom.—Take the wings   50
Of morning, pierce the Barcan [3] wilderness,
Or lose thyself in the continuous woods
Where rolls the Oregon,[4] and hears no sound,
Save his own dashings—yet the dead are there:
And millions in those solitudes, since first   55
The flight of years began, have laid them down
In their last sleep—the dead reign there alone.
So shalt thou rest, and what if thou withdraw
In silence from the living, and no friend
Take note of thy departure? All that breathe   60
Will share thy destiny. The gay will laugh
When thou are gone, the solemn brood of care
Plod on, and each one as before will chase
His favorite phantom; yet all these shall leave
Their mirth and their employments, and shall come   65
And make their bed with thee. As the long train
Of ages glide away, the sons of men,
The youth in life's green spring, and he who goes
In the full strength of years, matron and maid,
The speechless babe, and the gray-headed man—   70
Shall one by one be gathered to thy side,
By those, who in their turn shall follow them.

So live, that when thy summons comes to join
The innumerable caravan, which moves
To that mysterious realm, where each shall take   *hope*   75
His chamber in the silent halls of death,   *no*
Thou go not, like the quarry-slave at night,

---

3. The desert of Barca (in Libya,
North Africa) is compared with the
"Great American Desert" then shown

on maps.
4. The Indian name; now the Columbia River.

Scourged to his dungeon, but, sustained and soothed
By an unfaltering trust, approach thy grave,
Like one who wraps the drapery of his couch   80
About him, and lies down to pleasant dreams.

1811   1817, 1821

The Yellow Violet

When beechen buds begin to swell,
    And woods the blue-bird's warble know,
The yellow violet's modest bell
    Peeps from the last year's leaves below.

Ere russet fields their green resume,   5
    Sweet flower, I love, in forest bare,
To meet thee, when thy faint perfume
    Alone is in the virgin air.

Of all her train, the hands of Spring
    First plant thee in the watery mould,   10
And I have seen thee blossoming
    Beside the snow-bank's edges cold.

Thy parent sun, who bade thee view
    Pale skies, and chilling moisture sip,
Has bathed thee in his own bright hue,   15
    And streaked with jet thy glowing lip.

Yet slight thy form, and low thy seat,
    And earthward bent thy gentle eye,
Unapt the passing view to meet
    When loftier flowers are flaunting nigh.   20

Oft, in the sunless April day,
    Thy early smile has stayed my walk;
But midst the gorgeous blooms of May,
    I passed thee on thy humble stalk.

So they, who climb to wealth, forget   25
    The friends in darker fortunes tried.
I copied them—but I regret
    That I should ape the ways of pride.

And when again the genial hour
    Awakes the painted tribes of light,   30
I'll not o'erlook the modest flower
    That made the woods of April bright.

1814   1821

To a Waterfowl

Whither, 'midst falling dew,
While glow the heavens with the last steps of day,
Far, through their rosy depths, dost thou pursue
    Thy solitary way?

Vainly the fowler's eye
Might mark thy distant flight, to do thee wrong,
As, darkly seen against the crimson sky,
    Thy figure floats along.

Seek'st thou the plashy brink
Of weedy lake, or marge of river wide,
Or where the rocking billows rise and sink
    On the chafed ocean side?

There is a Power, whose care
Teaches thy way along that pathless coast,—
The desert and illimitable air,
    Lone wandering, but not lost.

All day thy wings have fann'd,
At that far height, the cold thin atmosphere;
Yet stoop not, weary, to the welcome land,
    Though the dark night is near.

And soon that toil shall end,
Soon shalt thou find a summer home, and rest,
And scream among thy fellows; reeds shall bend,
    Soon, o'er thy sheltered nest.

Thou'rt gone, the abyss of heaven
Hath swallowed up thy form, yet, on my heart
Deeply hath sunk the lesson thou hast given,
    And shall not soon depart.

He, who, from zone to zone,
Guides through the boundless sky thy certain flight,
In the long way that I must trace alone,
    Will lead my steps aright.

1815   1818, 1821

A Forest Hymn

The groves were God's first temples. Ere man learned
To hew the shaft, and lay the architrave,
And spread the roof above them—ere he framed

The lofty vault, to gather and roll back
The sound of anthems; in the darkling wood,   5
Amid the cool and silence, he knelt down,
And offered to the Mightiest solemn thanks
And supplication. For his simple heart
Might not resist the sacred influences
Which, from the stilly twilight of the place,   10
And from the gray old trunks that high in heaven
Mingled their mossy boughs, and from the sound
Of the invisible breath that swayed at once
All their green tops, stole over him, and bowed
His spirit with the thought of boundless power   15
And inaccessible majesty. Ah, why
Should we, in the world's riper years, neglect
God's ancient sanctuaries, and adore
Only among the crowd, and under roofs
That our frail hands have raised? Let me, at least,   20
Here, in the shallow of this aged wood,
Offer one hymn—thrice happy, if it find
Acceptance in His ear.

                    Father, thy hand
Hath reared these venerable columns, thou
Didst weave this verdant roof. Thou didst look down   25
Upon the naked earth, and, forthwith, rose
All these fair ranks of trees. They, in thy sun,
Budded, and shook their green leaves in thy breeze,
And shot toward heaven. The century-living crow
Whose birth was in their tops, grew old and died   30
Among their branches, till, at last, they stood,
As now they stand, massy, and tall, and dark,
Fit shrine for humble worshipper to hold
Communion with his Maker. These dim vaults,
These winding aisles, of human pomp or pride   35
Report not. No fantastic carvings show
The boast of our vain race to change the form
Of thy fair works. But thou art here—thou fill'st
The solitude. Thou art in the soft winds
That run along the summit of these trees   40
In music; thou art in the cooler breath
That from the inmost darkness of the place
Comes, scarcely felt; the barky trunks, the ground,
The fresh moist ground, are all instinct with thee.
Here is continual worship;—Nature, here,   45
In the tranquillity that thou dost love,

Enjoys thy presence. Noiselessly, around,
From perch to perch, the solitary bird
Passes; and yon clear spring, that, midst its herbs,
Wells softly forth and wandering steeps the roots   50
Of half the mighty forest, tells no tale
Of all the good it does. Thou hast not left
Thyself without a witness, in the shades,
Of thy perfections. Grandeur, strength, and grace
Are here to speak of thee. This mighty oak—   55
By whose immovable stem I stand and seem
Almost annihilated—not a prince,
In all that proud old world beyond the deep,
E're wore his crown as loftily as he
Wears the green coronal of leaves with which   60
Thy hand had graced him. Nestled at his root
Is beauty, such as blooms not in the glare
Of the broad sun. That delicate forest flower,
With scented breath and look so like a smile,
Seems, as it issues from the shapeless mould,   65
An emanation of the indwelling Life.
A visible token of the upholding Love,
That are the soul of this great universe.

 My heart is awed within me when I think
Of the great miracle that still goes on,   70
In silence, round me—the perpetual work
Of thy creation, finished, yet renewed
Forever. Written on thy works I read
The lesson of thy own eternity.
Lo! all grow old and die—but see again,   75
How on the faltering footsteps of decay
Youth presses—ever gay and beautiful youth
In all its beautiful forms. These lofty trees
Wave not less proudly that their ancestors
Moulder beneath them. Oh, there is not lost   80
One of earth's charms: upon her bosom yet,
After the flight of untold centuries,
The freshness of her far beginning lies
And yet shall lie. Life mocks the idle hate
Of his arch-enemy Death—yea, seats himself   85
Upon the tyrant's throne—the sepulchre,
And of the triumphs of his ghastly foe
Makes his own nourishment. For he came forth
From thine own bosom, and shall have no end.

There have been holy men who hid themselves 90
Deep in the <u>woody wilderness,</u> and gave
Their lives to thought and prayer, till they outlived
The generation born with them, nor seemed
Less aged than the hoary trees and rocks
Around them;—and there have been holy men 95
Who deemed it were not well to pass life thus.
But let me often to these solitudes
Retire, and in thy presence reassure
My feeble virtue. Here its enemies,
The passions, at thy plainer footsteps shrink 100
And tremble and are still. O God! when thou
Dost scare the world with <u>tempests,</u> set on fire
The heavens with falling <u>thunderbolts,</u> or fill,
With all the waters of the firmament,
The swift dark <u>whirlwind</u> that uproots the woods 105
And drowns the villages; when, at thy call,
Uprises the great deep and throws himself
Upon the continent, and overwhelms
Its cities—who forgets not, at the sight
Of these tremendous tokens of thy power, 110
His pride, and lays his strifes and follies by?
Oh, from these sterner aspects of thy face
Spare me and mine, <u>nor let us need the wrath</u>
<u>Of the mad unchained elements to teach</u>
Who rules them. Be it ours to meditate, 115
In these calm shades, thy milder majesty,
And to the <u>beautiful order of thy works</u>
<u>Learn to conform the order of our lives.</u>

[handwritten marginalia: natural order gives rise to natural response]

1825, 1832

The Past

Thou unrelenting Past!
Strong are the barriers round thy dark domain,
    And fetters, sure and fast,
Hold all that enter thy unbreathing reign.

    Far in thy realm withdrawn, 5
Old empires sit in sullenness and gloom,
    And glorious ages gone
Lie deep within the shadow of thy womb.

    Childhood, with all its mirth,
Youth, Manhood, Age that draws us to the ground, 10

And last, Man's Life on earth,
Glide to thy dim dominions, and are bound.

Thou hast my better years;
Thou hast my earlier friends, the good, the kind,
Yielded to thee with tears—
The venerable form,[5] the exalted mind.

My spirit yearns to bring
The lost ones back—yearns with desire intense,
And struggles hard to wring
Thy bolts apart, and pluck thy captives thence.

In vain; thy gates deny
All passage save to those who hence depart;
Nor to the streaming eye
Thou giv'st them back—nor to the broken heart.

In the abysses hide
Beauty and excellence unknown; to thee
Earth's wonder and her pride
Are gathered, as the waters to the sea;

Labors of good to man,
Unpublished charity, unbroken faith,
Love, that midst grief began,
And grew with years, and faltered not in death.

Full many a mighty name
Lurks in thy depths, unuttered, unrevered;
With thee are silent fame,
Forgotten arts, and wisdom disappeared.

Thine for a space are they—
Yet shalt thou yield thy treasures up at last:
Thy gates shall yet give way,
Thy bolts shall fall, inexorable Past!

All that of good and fair
Has gone into thy womb from earliest time,
Shall then come forth to wear
The glory and the beauty of its prime.

They have not perished—no!
Kind words, remembered voices once so sweet,
Smiles, radiant long ago,
And features, the great soul's apparent seat.

---

5. Identified as his father, Dr. Peter Bryant, who died in 1820. *Cf.* the last stanza.

All shall come back; each tie
Of pure affection shall be knit again;   50
   Alone shall Evil die,
And Sorrow dwell a prisoner in thy reign.

And then shall I behold
Him, by whose kind paternal side I sprung,
   And her, who, still and cold,   55
Fills the next grave—the beautiful and young.[6]

1828, 1832

To the Fringed Gentian [7]

Thou blossom bright with autumn dew,
And colored with the heaven's own blue,
That openest when the quiet light
Succeeds the keen and frosty night—

Thou comest not when violets lean   5
O'er wandering brooks and springs unseen,
Or columbines, in purple dressed,
Nod o'er the ground-bird's hidden nest.

Thou waitest late and com'st alone,
When woods are bare and birds are flown,   10
And frosts and shortening days portend
The aged year is near his end.

Then doth thy sweet and quiet eye
Look through its fringes to the sky,
Blue—blue—as if that sky let fall   15
A flower from its cerulean wall.

I would that thus, when I shall see
The hour of death draw near to me,
Hope, blossoming within my heart,
May look to heaven as I depart.   20

1829   1832

6. His favorite sister, Mrs. Sarah Bryant Shaw, who died in 1824.
7. "Draw your own images, in describing nature, from what you observe around you," Bryant wrote his brother (Godwin, *Life,* Vol. I, p. 281). A botanist from youth, he took the lead in opposition to stereotyped references to nature. For a discussion of his successful realism in this direction see Norman Foerster, "Bryant," in his *Nature in American Literature* (1923).

The Prairies [8]

These are the gardens of the Desert, these
The unshorn fields, boundless and beautiful,
For which the speech of England has no name [9]—
The Prairies. I behold them for the first,
And my heart swells, while the dilated sight   5
Takes in the encircling vastness. Lo! they stretch
In airy undulations, far away,
As if the Ocean, in his gentlest swell,
Stood still, with all his rounded billows fixed,
And motionless forever. Motionless?—   10
No—they are all unchained again. The clouds
Sweep over with their shadows, and, beneath,
The surface rolls and fluctuates to the eye; [1]
Dark hollows seem to glide along and chase
The sunny ridges. Breezes of the South!   15
Who toss the golden and the flame-like flowers,
And pass the prairie-hawk that, poised on high,
Flaps his broad wings, yet moves not [2]—ye have played
Among the palms of Mexico and vines
Of Texas, and have crisped the limpid brooks   20
That from the fountains of Sonora [3] glide
Into the calm Pacific—have ye fanned
A nobler or a lovelier scene than this?
Man hath no part in all this glorious work:
The hand that built the firmament hath heaved   25
And smoothed these verdant swells, and sown their slopes
With herbage, planted them with island-groves,
And hedged them round with forests. Fitting floor
For this magnificent temple of the sky—
With flowers whose glory and whose multitude   30
Rival the constellations! The great heavens
Seem to stoop down upon the scene in love,—
A nearer vault, and of a tenderer blue,
Than that which bends above our Eastern hills.

As o'er the verdant waste I guide my steed,   35
Among the high rank grass that sweeps his sides
The hollow beating of his footstep seems

---

8. Written on the poet's first sight of the prairies, on a visit to his brothers in Illinois in 1832.
9. "Prairie," in the tongue of the French settlers, signified "meadow."
1. "* * * when the shadows of the clouds are passing rapidly over them, the face of the ground seems to fluctuate and toss like billows of the sea" [from Bryant's note].
2. "I have seen the prairie-hawk balancing himself in the air for hours together, apparently over the same spot, probably watching his prey" [Bryant's note].
3. State in northwest Mexico.

A sacrilegious sound. I think of those
Upon whose rest he tramples. Are they here—
The dead of other days?—and did the dust   40
Of these fair solitudes once stir with life
And burn with passion? Let the mighty mounds [4]
That overlook the rivers, or that rise
In the dim forest crowded with old oaks,
Answer. A race, that long has passed away,   45
Built them; a disciplined and populous race
Heaped, with long toil, the earth, while yet the Greek
Was hewing the Pentelicus [5] to forms
Of symmetry, and rearing on its rock
The glittering Parthenon. These ample fields   50
Nourished their harvests, here their herds were fed,
When haply by their stalls the bison lowed,
And bowed his manèd shoulder to the yoke.
All day this desert murmured with their toils,
Till twilight blushed, and lovers walked, and wooed   55
In a forgotten language, and old tunes,
From instruments of unremembered form,
Gave the soft winds a voice. The red-man came—
The roaming hunter-tribes, warlike and fierce,
And the mound-builders vanished from the earth.   60
The solitude of centuries untold
Has settled where they dwelt. The prairie-wolf
Hunts in their meadows, and his fresh-dug den
Yawns by my path. The gopher mines the ground
Where stood their swarming cities. All is gone;   65
All—save the piles of earth that hold their bones,
The platforms where they worshipped unknown gods,
The barriers which they builded from the soil
To keep the foe at bay—till o'er the walls
The wild beleaguerers broke, and, one by one,   70
The strongholds of the plain were forced, and heaped
With corpses. The brown vultures of the wood
Flocked to those vast uncovered sepulchres,
And sat, unscared and silent, at their feast.
Haply some solitary fugitive,   75
Lurking in marsh and forest, till the sense
Of desolation and of fear became
Bitterer than death, yielded himself to die.

4. Ascribed to the supposed ancient "Mound Builders"; now associated with Indian burials. See Bryant's earlier reference to former civilizations on this continent in "Thanatopsis," ll. 50–57.

5. Or Pentelikon, a Greek mountain; source of the fine marble of such ancient buildings in nearby Athens as the Parthenon (l. 50), celebrated temple of Athena.

Man's better nature triumphed then. Kind words
Welcomed and soothed him; the rude conquerors   80
Seated the captive with their chiefs; he chose
A bride among their maidens, and at length
Seemed to forget—yet ne'er forgot—the wife
Of his first love, and her sweet little ones,
Butchered, amid their shrieks, with all his race.   85

Thus change the forms of being. Thus arise
Races of living things, glorious in strength,
And perish, as the quickening breath of God
Fills them, or is withdrawn. The red-man, too,
Has left the blooming wilds he ranged so long,   90
And, nearer to the Rocky Mountains, sought
A wilder hunting-ground. The beaver builds
No longer by these streams, but far away,
On waters whose blue surface ne'er gave back
The white man's face—among Missouri's springs,   95
And pools whose issues swell the Oregon [6]—
He rears his little Venice. In these plains
The bison feeds no more. Twice twenty leagues
Beyond remotest smoke of hunter's camp,
Roams the majestic brute, in herds that shake   100
The earth with thundering steps—yet here I meet
His ancient footprints stamped beside the pool.

Still this great solitude is quick with life.
Myriads of insects, gaudy as the flowers
They flutter over, gentle quadrupeds,   105
And birds, that scarce have learned the fear of man,
Are here, and sliding reptiles of the ground,
Startlingly beautiful. The graceful deer
Bounds to the wood at my approach. The bee,
A more adventurous colonist than man,   110
With whom he came across the eastern deep,
Fills the savannas with his murmurings,
Within the hollow oak. I listen long
To his domestic hum, and think I hear
The sound of that advancing multitude   115
Which soon shall fill these deserts. From the ground
Comes up the laugh of children, the soft voice
Of maidens, and the sweet and solemn hymn
Of Sabbath worshippers. The low of herds   120
Blends with the rustling of the heavy grain

6. *Cf.* "Thanatopsis." Now the Columbia River.

Over the dark brown furrows. All at once
A fresher wind sweeps by, and breaks my dream,
And I am in the wilderness alone.

1832   1833, 1834

The Death of Lincoln [7]

Oh, slow to smite and swift to spare,
  Gentle and merciful and just!
Who, in the fear of God, didst bear
  The sword of power, a nation's trust!

In sorrow by thy bier we stand,   5
  Amid the awe that hushes all,
And speak the anguish of a land
  That shook with horror at thy fall.

Thy task is done; the bond are free:
  We bear thee to an honored grave,   10
Whose proudest monument shall be
  The broken fetters of the slave.

Pure was thy life; its bloody close
  Hath placed thee with the sons of light,
Among the noble host of those   15
  Who perished in the cause of Right.

1865   1866, 1871

The Flood of Years [8]

A mighty Hand, from an exhaustless Urn,
Pours forth the never-ending Flood of Years,
Among the nations. How the rushing waves
Bear all before them! On their foremost edge,
And there alone, is Life. The Present there   5
Tosses and foams, and fills the air with roar
Of mingled noises. There are they who toil,
And they who strive, and they who feast, and they
Who hurry to and fro. The sturdy swain—
Woodman and delver with the spade —is there,   10

7. Lincoln died by the assassin's bullet on April 15, 1865, and his funeral train at once started its long pilgrimage to Springfield, Illinois. According to Godwin, Bryant wrote his poem at the request of the Committee of Arrangements for the ceremony in the city of New York. As "Abraham Lincoln: Poetical Tribute to the Memory of Abraham Lincoln" the poem appeared in the *Atlantic Monthly* for January, 1866.

8. For the stages of Bryant's religious thought see the poems "Thanatopsis" and "To a Waterfowl." According to Godwin, when Bryant was questioned concerning the faith expressed in "The Flood of Years," he replied, "I believe in the everlasting life of the soul; and it seems to me that immortality would be but an imperfect gift without the recognition in the life to come of those who are dear to us."

And busy artisan beside his bench,
And pallid student with his written roll.
A moment on the mounting billow seen,
The flood sweeps over them and they are gone.
There groups of revellers whose brows are twined   15
With roses, ride the topmost swell awhile,
And as they raise their flowing cups and touch
The clinking brim to brim, are whirled beneath
The waves and disappear. I hear the jar
Of beaten drums, and thunders that break forth   20
From cannon, where the advancing billow sends
Up to the sight long files of armèd men,
That hurry to the charge through flame and smoke.
The torrent bears them under, whelmed and hid
Slayer and slain, in heaps of bloody foam.   25
Down go the steed and rider, the plumed chief
Sinks with his followers; the head that wears
The imperial diadem goes down beside
The felon's with cropped ear and branded cheek.
A funeral-train—the torrent sweeps away   30
Bearers and bier and mourners. By the bed
Of one who dies men gather sorrowing,
And women weep aloud; the flood rolls on;
The wail is stifled and the sobbing group
Borne under. Hark to that shrill, sudden shout,   35
The cry of an applauding multitude,
Swayed by some loud-voiced orator who wields
The living mass as if he were its soul!
The waters choke the shout and all is still.
Lo! next a kneeling crowd, and one who spreads   40
The hands in prayer, the engulfing wave o'ertakes
And swallows them and him. A sculptor wields
The chisel, and the stricken marble grows
To beauty; at his easel, eager-eyed,
A painter stands, and sunshine at his touch   45
Gathers upon his canvas, and life glows;
A poet, as he paces to and fro,
Murmurs his sounding lines. Awhile they ride
The advancing billow, till its tossing crest
Strikes them and flings them under, while their tasks   50
Are yet unfinished. See a mother smile
On her young babe that smiles to her again;
The torrent wrests it from her arms; she shrieks
And weeps, and amidst her tears is carried down.
A beam like that of moonlight turns the spray   55

To glistening pearls; two lovers, hand in hand,
Rise on the billowy swell and fondly look
Into each other's eyes. The rushing flood
Flings them apart: the youth goes down; the maid
With hands outstretched in vain, and streaming eyes,   60
Waits for the next high wave to follow him.
An aged man succeeds; his bending form
Sinks slowly. Mingling with the sullen stream
Gleam the white locks, and then are seen no more.
    Lo! wider grows the stream—a sea-like flood   65
Saps earth's walled cities; massive palaces
Crumble before it; fortresses and towers
Dissolve in the swift waters; populous realms
Swept by the torrent see their ancient tribes
Engulfed and lost; their very languages   70
Stifled, and never to be uttered more.
    I pause and turn my eyes, and looking back
Where that tumultuous flood has been, I see
The silent ocean of the Past, a waste
Of waters weltering over graves, its shores   75
Strewn with the wreck of fleets where mast and hull
Drop away piecemeal; battlemented walls
Frown idly, green with moss, and temples stand
Unroofed, forsaken by the worshipper.
There lie memorial stones, whence time has gnawed   80
The graven legends, thrones of kings o'erturned,
The broken altars of forgotten gods,
Foundations of old cities and long streets
Where never fall of human foot is heard,
On all the desolate pavement. I behold   85
Dim glimmerings of lost jewels, far within
The sleeping waters, diamond, sardonyx,
Ruby and topaz, pearl and chrysolite,
Once glittering at the banquet on fair brows
That long ago were dust, and all around   90
Strewn on the surface of that silent sea
Are withering bridal wreaths, and glossy locks
Shorn from dear brows, by loving hands, and scrolls
O'er written, haply with fond words of love
And vows of friendship, and fair pages flung   95
Fresh from the printer's engine. There they lie
A moment, and then sink away from sight.
    I looked, and the quick tears are in my eyes,
For I behold in every one of these
A blighted hope, a separate history   100

Of human sorrows, telling of dear ties
Suddenly broken, dreams of happiness
Dissolved in air, and happy days too brief
That sorrowfully ended, and I think
How painfully must the poor heart have beat   105
In bosoms without number, as the blow
Was struck that slew their hope and broke their peace.
   Sadly I turn and look before, where yet
The Flood must pass, and I behold a mist
Where swarm dissolving forms, the brood of Hope,   110
Divinely fair, that rest on banks of flowers,
Or wander among rainbows, fading soon
And reappearing, haply giving place
To forms of grisly aspect such as Fear
Shapes from the idle air—where serpents lift   115
The head to strike, and skeletons stretch forth
The bony arm in menace. Further on
A belt of darkness seems to bar the way
Long, low, and distant, where the Life to come
Touches the Life that is. The Flood of Years   120
Rolls toward it near and nearer. It must pass
That dismal barrier. What is there beyond?
Hear what the wise and good have said. Beyond
That belt of darkness, still the Years roll on
More gently, but with not less mighty sweep.   125
They gather up again and softly bear
All the sweet lives that late were overwhelmed
And lost to sight, all that in them was good,
Noble, and truly great, and worthy of love—
The lives of infants and ingenuous youths,   130
Sages and saintly women who have made
Their households happy; all are raised and borne
By that great current in its onward sweep,
Wandering and rippling with caressing waves
Around green islands fragrant with the breath   135
Of flowers that never wither. So they pass
From stage to stage along the shining course
Of that bright river, broadening like a sea.
As its smooth eddies curl along their way
They bring old friends together; hands are clasped   140
In joy unspeakable; the mother's arms
Again are folded round the child she loved
And lost. Old sorrows are forgotten now,
Or but remembered to make sweet the hour
That overpays them; wounded hearts that bled   145

Or broke are healed forever. In the room
Of this grief-shadowed present, there shall be
A Present in whose reign no grief shall gnaw
The heart, and never shall a tender tie
Be broken; in whose reign the eternal Change
That waits on growth and action shall proceed
With everlasting Concord hand in hand.

150

1876   1876

THE INDIAN HERITAGE

When the white man arrived in North America he was met by a people who had remained in a relatively stable relationship to their land and to each other for thousands of years. The individual tribes and tribal groups of the red men differed from one another in their cultural traditions and modes of existence. Nevertheless, from coast to coast and from the Tropic of Cancer to the Arctic Circle — Penobscot, Iroquois, Seminole, Pawnee, Navaho, Yaqui, Klamath, Squamish, Flathead, Ojibway, Cree, and Tlingit —they had more in common with one another than they did with the explorers, traders, and settlers who came one after another in waves that were soon to inundate them.

None of the tribes located in the area that was to become the United States possessed more than the rudiments of a written language. They could not have recorded their songs, stories, and poems in written form for posterity, even if it had appeared to them that such recording was desirable. This is not to say, however, that they did not value the lore of the past and the narrative and lyric inventions of the present—far from it. During centuries of stability each tribe had produced a body of oral tradition treasured and handed down from generation to generation through the minds and mouths of those individuals most gifted with clear memories and the power to sing and to recite the lore of the past in such a fashion that it remained eternally new. Time had done its winnowing, as it always does in the folk process. It was not necessary to lament the absence of accurate transcripts because it was difficult to imagine a time when there would be no one left to tell the old stories, or no audiences to tell them to.

That time has now long since arrived for some tribes, and for others it appears closer with each passing year. In some ways the situation is analogous to that presented to those who wish to study the beginnings of English literature: that which was recorded in writing in Anglo-Saxon and even in Middle English times and has made its way down to us through the vicissitudes of the years is but a fraction of the material that once existed (but for the chance preservation of one manuscript, we would have no *Beowulf*). In some very important ways, however, the analogy is flawed. The same white invasion that was to herald the end of the Indian way of life brought with it not only its own written languages but the tools to devise written records of the various Indian languages and dialects. Later came phonographs and tape recorders to record more accurately than could any written record the tonal nuances of Indian poetry and song.

One result is that anyone who wishes to commence a serious study of Indian tradition is confronted almost immediately with an immense body of material. The tales that Stith Thompson wrote of in the 1920's as "by far the most extensive body of tales representative of any primitive people" have been augmented by the efforts of two generations of field-workers since his time. The same holds true for songs, poems, and oratory. Despite the wealth of material that has been gathered, however, it would be difficult to argue that the white man has as yet done justice to the stories and images of the red man.

Language remains a serious obstacle to understanding. Poetry, particularly, resists translation, even when it is couched in a language not far removed linguistically from one's own. Indian poetry, especially, appears at times to depend so completely upon repetition of sound and rhythm that any translation must be in a sense a new poem. Tales and speeches suffer less in translation than do poems, but in these areas, too, the Indian has not fared well. Too often the anthropologists, ethnologists, clergymen, government clerks, and amateur literary men who have been responsible for most of the translations have had no great literary command of their own language. Often the best that one can hope for is a plodding literal accuracy.

Cultural differences have presented other obstacles. White men have been recording Indian material in North America for over three hundred years, but much of what they have written must be approached in a mood of healthy skepticism. Indians have not always revealed all that they knew, or told their stories to white men as they would tell them to other Indians. White recorders have not always perceived what was valuable, and they have sometimes altered what they received in order to shape it better to their own needs and prejudices or to those of their audience.

With the advent of Indian education and assimilation or partial assimilation into the white man's world, Indians have increasingly desired to correct the misunderstandings concerning their lore by re-creating it as essentially an Indian literature, written anew in English or translated from the traditional tales by Indians conversant in two tongues and two cultures. But Indian tradition still is largely confined to government and university archives, unread nineteenth-century tomes, and almost equally unread twentieth-century folklore and anthropological journals. It has had its greatest popularity at second hand, through its influence on writers as early as Longfellow and as recent as Gary Snyder and N. Scott Momaday. At first hand, and in its most enduring forms, it deserves an audience wider than any it has yet found.

The most extensive collections of Indian material are found in the *Annual Reports of the Bureau of American Ethnology*, 1881–1933, and in the *BAE Bulletin*, 1887–present. Excellent examples are Frances Densmore, "Papago Music," *Bulletin 90*, BAE, 1929, and Francis La Flesche, "The Osage Tribe," 36th, 39th, 43rd, and 45th *Annual Report*, BAE, 1921, 1925, 1928, and 1930. Important early nineteenth-century works include Albert Gallatin, "A Synopsis of the Indian Tribes of North America," *Transactions of the American Antiquarian Society*, Vol. II, 1836; Thomas L. McKenney and James Hall, *History of the Indian Tribes of North America*, 3 vols., 1837 (reprinted, edited by Frederick Webb Hodge, 3 vols., 1933–1934); Henry Rowe Schoolcraft, *Algic Researches*, 2 vols., 1839 (the principal source for Mentor L. Williams, *Schoolcraft's Indian Legends*, 1956); Schoolcraft, *The Red Race of America*, 1847; and Schoolcraft, *Information Respecting the History, Condition and Prospects of the Indian Tribes of the United States*, 6 vols., 1851–1857. General anthologies include Natalie Curtis, ed., *The Indians' Book*, 1907; Stith Thompson, ed., *Tales of the North American Indians*, 1929; Margot Astrov, ed., *The Winged Serpent: American Indian Prose and Poetry*, 1946; Charles Hamilton, ed., *Cry of the Thunderbird: The American Indian's Own Story*, 1950 (new edition, 1972); A. Grove Day, *The Sky Clears: Poetry of the American Indians*, 1951; and Thomas E. Sanders and Walter W. Peek, *Literature of the American Indian*, 1973.

Tales

The Chief's Daughters [1]

In the evening, in summer, upon a hot night two young girls, chief's daughters, lay on the ground outside their tents gazing at the sky. As the stars came out one of them said:—

"I wish I were away up there. Do you see where that dim star is? There is where I wish I might be." And she fixed her eyes upon the twinkling star that seemed to be vanishing behind the clouds.

The other girl said: "It is too dim. I wish I were up by that bright one, that large brilliant star," and she pointed to where a steady light glowed red.

Soon they were asleep and the brilliant lights in the blue above kept watch. In the night when they awoke each young girl found herself where she had wished to be. The one in the dim star was in the home of a brave young chief, and she became his bride and was happy. The beautiful star had appeared dim to her while she was yet upon the earth because it was so far, far away that she could not see its glorious light.

1. "The Chief's Daughters" is an example of a widespread tale commonly referred to as "The Star Husband." The source of the present text is George Truman Kercheval, "An Otoe and an Omaha Tale," *Journal of American Folk-Lore*, Vol. VI, 1893. The informant for this tale was identified by Kercheval as an Otoe woman from Nebraska.

The girl in the bright star found herself in a servant's home, and was obliged to do all manner of work and to become the servant's wife. This star had been nearer the earth, and so it had seemed to be the larger and brighter star. When this girl found that her friend had gone to a beautiful star and become the wife of a chief, with plenty of servants to wait upon her, and that she was never permitted to do any work, she cried and cried because the change in her own condition seemed more cruel, and she was even obliged to live with a servant.

The girls were still friends and often met in the clouds and went out to gather wild turnips, but the chief's wife could never dig, her friend was always obliged to serve her. Whenever they started out an old man would say to them:—

"When you dig a turnip, you must strike with the hoe once, then pull up the turnip. Never, by any means, strike twice." After going to gather turnips many times and receiving always this same instruction the chief's wife grew curious, and one day she said to her friend:

"Why is it, they tell us to strike but once? To-day when you dig that turnip I wish you to strike twice. Let us see why they allow us to strike but once."

The servant struck once with the hoe and took up the turnip, then, as commanded, she struck with her hoe again in the same place. Behold a hole! She leaned forward and looked down. She saw her home. She cried to her friend. "Look! I can see through the clouds. See! there is our home."

The chief's wife looked also, and she saw the village and her home. The girls sat looking through the hole, and they longed to go home, and they sat weeping. An old man chanced to pass by, and he saw them and stopped and asked:—

"What is the matter? What are you crying about?"

And they answered, "Because we can see our home. We are so far away, we wish to be there, but we can never get there."

The old man passed on. He went to the chief and he told him that the girls sat weeping because they could see their home, and they wanted to go back to the earth.

The chief then called all his people together, and he sent them away to find all the lariats that they could.

In the village, on the earth, every one had mourned for the chief's daughters, who had so strangely disappeared, and could not be found. It was a long time since they were lost; but the people still thought of them.

To-day in the village a great many people had come to see the boys and young men play. They used a ring and a long stick, round at one end. One person would throw the ring in the air and at the same time another would try to send his arrow through it;

the men would run swiftly and throw their sticks when they were near the ring, for the one who got most arrows through while the ring was still in the air was the winner. All the people were excited over the game and urging on the young men, when one of them happened to look up toward the sky.

"Why, look up," he called out, "something is coming down. Look! They are very large. Look at them!"

All who heard stopped and looked up, and others seeing them look, turned to see what it was. Many ran to the spot where these things were falling. Then the people found they were the lost girls.

The good chief in the dim star had ordered all the lariats knotted together and then he had wound them around the bodies of the two girls and dropped them gently through the hole in the sky to the earth, keeping tight the end of the rope until the girls reached the ground.

Joyfully the Indians ran before the girls to carry the news of their return to their sorrowful parents. One of the girls looked sad and pitiful, the other looked happy as though she had been in some beautiful place.

1893

Coyote and Bear [2]

Coyote was going along through the timber, when all at once a Bear jumped from the bushes and faced him. Coyote was scared nearly to death, and he said to himself: "What shall I do?" He took his bow in his hand, and beating upon it with his arrow he sang this song:

> I can still the rivers which flow and they stop.
> What shall I do with this rough-handed fellow standing
> before me?
> I can kill him with my bow and arrows.

At that time, it being hot weather, the waters had gone down and the bed of the river had become dry. Bear saw that the creek was nearly dry and he said to himself: "This must be a wonderful man who can make the rivers and streams run dry in this way." Then he listened again and heard another song. Old Coyote sang:

> I overturned even the timber
> That extended over yonder,
> Standing yonder, with my wonderful bow.

2. The trickster, in human or animal form, frequently provides subject matter for Indian tales. Sometimes his tricks succeed and sometimes, as in this instance, they fail. The source of the present text is G. A. Dorsey, *The* *Pawnee: Mythology*, Part I, 1906. Dorsey relates that "this story is told to the children to teach them that they must not make war on people who have greater powers than they themselves possess."

Bear looked around and saw great big trees down, with the roots turned up. A few days before there had been a cyclone, which had blown down the trees and turned up the roots, and Bear looked at the trees that were down, and said: "Why, this is a wonderful man if he can do all this." Then Coyote sang again:

> Even the hills yonder I killed,
> Yes, even the hills yonder.
> Then this rough-chapped, flat-footed one
> I could easily kill
> With my wonderful bow.

Bear looked over the prairies and saw that there were no hills and mountains, and he believed Coyote. The people had burned the grass from the prairies so that they looked level all over. Then Coyote sang:

> I killed even the waters that
> Flowed through the land
> With my wonderful bow.

They had bright sunlight when they first met, but Coyote had seen that a fog was rising. Bear said: "This is a wonderful man, for he can make the sun disappear." Bear became afraid of Coyote and said: "Well, grandson, let us travel together." Coyote said: "All right." In the evening they made a fire, and when they had made the fire, Coyote told Bear to cook the meat on hot coals. Bear cooked the meat, and when it was done he took it off, but had one eye on Coyote all the time. When he made a motion to reach out for something he noticed Coyote jump. Bear took the piece of meat and reached out to hand the meat over to Coyote and Coyote jumped. Bear said: "Oh, yes! you have been fooling me with your big talk," and he jumped towards Coyote and Coyote ran for his life, but Bear caught him and killed him.

1906

Oratory

Speech of Red Jacket [3]

FRIEND AND BROTHER: It was the will of the Great Spirit that we should meet together this day. He orders all things, and has given us a fine day for our Council. HE has taken his garment from before the sun, and caused it to shine with brightness upon

3. Red Jacket (*c.* 1752–1830), a Seneca chief, was one of the most famous of all Indian orators. The occasion for this speech was a meeting held in the summer of 1805 to set up a missionary station among the six nations of the Iroquois. The source of the present text is William L. Stone, *Life and Times of Sa-Go-Ye-Wat-Ha*, 1866.

us. Our eyes are opened, that we see clearly; our ears are unstopped, that we have been able to hear distinctly the words you have spoken. For all these favors we thank the Great Spirit; and HIM *only*.

BROTHER: This council fire was kindled by you. It was at your request that we came together at this time. We have listened with attention to what you have said. You requested us to speak our minds freely. This gives us great joy; for we now consider that we stand upright before you, and can speak what we think. All have heard your voice, and all speak to you now as one man. Our minds are agreed.

BROTHER: You say you want an answer to your talk before you leave this place. It is right you should have one, as you are a great distance from home, and we do not wish to detain you. But we will first look back a little, and tell you what our fathers have told us, and what we have heard from the white people.

BROTHER: Listen to what we say. There was a time when our forefathers owned this great island. Their seats extended from the rising to the setting sun. The Great Spirit had made it for the use of Indians. HE had created the buffalo, the deer, and other animals for food. HE had made the bear and the beaver. Their skins served us for clothing. HE had scattered them over the country, and taught us how to take them. HE had caused the earth to produce corn for bread. All this HE had done for his red children, because HE loved them. If we had some disputes about our hunting ground, they were generally settled without the shedding of much blood. But an evil day came upon us. Your forefathers crossed the great water and landed on this island. Their numbers were small. They found friends and not enemies. They told us they had fled from their own country for fear of wicked men, and had come here to enjoy their religion. They asked for a small seat. We took pity on them, granted their request; and they sat down amongst us. We gave them corn and meat; they gave us poison [4] in return.

The white people, BROTHER, had now found our country. Tidings were carried back, and more came amongst us. Yet we did not fear them. We took them to be friends. They called us brothers. We believed them and gave them a larger seat. At length their numbers had greatly increased. They wanted more land; they wanted our country. Our eyes were opened, and our minds became uneasy. Wars took place. Indians were hired to fight against Indians, and many of our people were destroyed. They also brought strong liquor amongst us. It was strong and powerful, and has slain thousands.

BROTHER: Our seats were once large and yours were small.

4. "Rum" [Stone's note].

You have now become a great people, and we have scarcely a place left to spread our blankets. You have got our country, but are not satisfied; you want to force your religion upon us.

BROTHER: Continue to listen. You say that you are sent to instruct us how to worship the Great Spirit agreeably to his mind, and, if we do not take hold of the religion which you white people teach, we shall be unhappy hereafter. You say that you are right and we are lost. How do we know this to be true? We understand that your religion is written in a book. If it was intended for us as well as you, why has not the Great Spirit given to us, and not only to us, but why did he not give to our forefathers, the knowledge of that book, with the means of understanding it rightly? We only know what you tell us about it. How shall we know when to believe, being so often deceived by the white people?

BROTHER: You say there is but one way to worship and serve the Great Spirit. If there is but one religion, why do you white people differ so much about it? Why not all agreed, as you can all read the book?

BROTHER: We do not understand these things. We are told that your religion was given to your forefathers, and has been handed down from father to son. We also have a religion, which was given to our forefathers, and has been handed down to us their children. We worship in that way. It teaches us to be thankful for all the favors we receive; to love each other, and to be united. We never quarrel about religion.

BROTHER: The Great Spirit has made us all, but HE has made a great difference between his white and red children. HE has given us different complexions and different customs. To you HE has given the arts. To these HE has not opened our eyes. We know these things to be true. Since HE has made so great a difference between us in other things, why may we not conclude that he has given us a different religion according to our understanding? The Great Spirit does right. HE knows what is best for his children; we are satisfied.

BROTHER: We do not wish to destroy your religion, or take it from you. We only want to enjoy our own.

BROTHER: You say you have not come to get our land or our money, but to enlighten our minds. I will now tell you that I have been at your meetings, and saw you collect money from the meeting. I cannot tell what this money was intended for, but suppose that it was for your minister, and if we should conform to your way of thinking, perhaps you may want some from us.[5]

---

5. "This paragraph is not contained in the first edition of the speech, as published by James D. Bemis, in 1811; but I find it in the speech as given by Drake, in his Book of the Indians, and also in Thatcher's Indian Biography. Still, it appears to me to be an interpolation" [Stone's note].

BROTHER: We are told that you have been preaching to the white people in this place. These people are our neighbors. We are acquainted with them. We will wait a little while, and see what effect your preaching has upon them. If we find it does them good, makes them honest and less disposed to cheat Indians, we will then consider again of what you have said.

BROTHER: You have now heard our answer to your talk, and this is all we have to say at present. As we are going to part, we will come and take you by the hand, and hope the Great Spirit will protect you on your journey, and return you safe to your friends.

1805   1811, 1866

Speech of Red Cloud [6]

My Brothers and my Friends who are before me today: God Almighty has made us all, and He is here to hear what I have to say to you today. The Great Spirit made us both. He gave us lands and He gave you lands. You came here and we received you as brothers. When the Almighty made you, He made you all white and clothed you. When He made us He made us with red skins and poor. When you first came we were very many and you were few. Now you are many and we are few. You do not know who appears before you to speak. He is a representative of the original American race, the first people of this continent. We are good, and not bad. The reports which you get about us are all on one side. You hear of us only as murderers and thieves. We are not so. If we had more lands to give to you we would give them, but we have no more. We are driven into a very little island, and we want you, our dear friends, to help us with the Government of the United States. The Great Spirit made us poor and ignorant. He made you rich and wise and skillful in things which we know nothing about. The good Father made you to eat tame game and us to eat wild game. Ask any one who has gone through to California. They will tell you we have treated them well. You have children. We, too, have children, and we wish to bring them up well. We ask you to help us do it. At the mouth of Horse Creek, in 1852, the Great Father made a treaty with us. We agreed to let him pass through our territory

6. Red Cloud (*c.* 1822–1909) was a chief of the Oglala Sioux, the Indians with whom Francis Parkman had spent three weeks in 1846. Relations with the white man since that time had worsened to the point where Parkman noted in the preface to the 1872 edition of *The Oregon Trail* that he had been informed "two or three years ago" that "the Indians with whom I had been domesticated, a band of the hated Sioux, had nearly all been killed * * * ." In 1870 Red Cloud went to Washington on a peace mission to President Grant. The present speech was delivered on June 16, 1870, a few days after leaving Washington, to a crowded audience at Cooper Institute in New York. The text is from *The New York Times*, June 17, 1870.

unharmed for fifty-five years. We kept our word. We committed no murders, no depredations, until the troops came there. When the troops were sent there trouble and disturbance arose. Since that time there have been various goods sent from time to time to us, but only once did they reach us, and soon the Great Father took away the only good man he had sent us, Col. Fitzpatrick.[7] The Great Father said we must go to farming, and some of our men went to farming near Fort Laramie, and were treated very badly indeed. We came to Washington to see our Great Father that peace might be continued. The Great Father that made us both wishes peace to be kept; we want to keep peace. Will you help us? In 1868 men came out and brought papers. We could not read them, and they did not tell us truly what was in them. We thought the treaty was to remove the forts and that we should then cease from fighting. But they wanted to send us traders on the Missouri. We did not want to go on the Missouri, but wanted traders where we were. When I reached Washington the Great Father explained to me what the treaty was, and showed me that the interpreters had deceived me. All I want is right and justice. I have tried to get from the Great Father what is right and just. I have not altogether succeeded. I want you to help me to get what is right and just. I represent the whole Sioux nation, and they will be bound by what I say. I am no Spotted Tail,[8] to say one thing one day and be bought for a pin the next. Look at me. I am poor and naked, but I am the Chief of the nation. We do not want riches, but we want to train our children right. Riches would do us no good. We could not take them with us to the other world. We do not want riches, we want peace and love.

The riches that we have in this world, Secretary Cox [9] said truly, we cannot take with us to the next world. Then I wish to know why Commissioners are sent out to us who do nothing but rob us and get the riches of this world away from us! I was brought up among the traders, and those who came out there in the early times treated me well and I had a good time with them. They taught us to wear clothes and to use tobacco and ammunition. But, by and by, the Great Father sent out a different kind of men; men who cheated and drank whisky; men who were so bad that the Great Father could not keep them at home and so sent them out there. I have sent a great many words to the Great Father but they never reached him. They were drowned on the way, and I was afraid the words I spoke lately to the Great Father would not reach you, so I came to speak to you myself; and now I

7. Perhaps John Fitzpatrick, Indian agent at Fort Laramie, *c.* 1853.
8. A chief of the Brulé band of Sioux and principal rival of Red Cloud.
9. J. D. Cox, Secretary of the Interior.

am going away to my home. I want to have men sent out to my people whom we know and can trust. I am glad I have come here. You belong in the East and I belong in the West, and I am glad I have come here and that we could understand one another. I am very much obliged to you for listening to me. I go home this afternoon. I hope you will think of what I have said to you. I bid you all an affectionate farewell.

1870

Poetry

Twelfth Song of the Thunder [1]

The voice that beautifies the land!
The voice above,
The voice of the thunder
Within the dark cloud
Again and again it sounds,   5
The voice that beautifies the land.

The voice that beautifies the land!
The voice below;
The voice of the grasshopper
Among the plants   10
Again and again it sounds,
The voice that beautifies the land.

Formula to Destroy Life [2]

Listen! Now I have come to step over your soul. You are of the —— clan. Your name is ——. Your spittle I have put at rest under the earth. Your soul I have put at rest under the earth. I have come to cover you over with the black rock. I have come to cover you over with the black cloth. I have come to cover you with the black slabs, never to reappear. Toward the black coffin of the upland in the Darkening Land your paths shall stretch out. So shall it be for you. The clay of the upland has come to cover you. Instantly the black clay has lodged there where it is at rest at the black houses in the Darkening Land. With the black coffin and with the black slabs I have come to cover you. Now your soul has faded away. It has become blue. When darkness comes your spirit shall grow less and dwindle away, never to reappear. Listen!

1. From Washington Matthews, *The Mountain Chant: A Navajo Ceremony*, 1887.
2. From James Mooney, *Sacred Formulas of the Cherokees*, 1891. The blanks are to be filled in by the shaman with the clan and name of the victim.

The Corn Grows Up [3]

The corn grows up.
The waters of the dark clouds drop, drop.
The rain descends.
The waters from the corn leaves drop, drop.
The rain descends.   5
The waters from the plants drop, drop.
The corn grows up.
The waters of the dark mists drop, drop.

Dramatic Situation: the deer's point of view

At the Time of the White Dawn [4]

At the time of the White Dawn;
   At the time of the White Dawn,
I arose and went away.
   At Blue Nightfall I went away.

I ate the thornapple leaves   5
   And the leaves made me dizzy.
I drank thornapple flowers
   And the drink made me stagger.

The hunter, Bow-remaining,
   He overtook and killed me,   10
Cut and threw my horns away.
   The hunter, Reed-remaining,
He overtook and killed me,
   Cut and threw my feet away.

Now the flies become crazy   15
   And they drop with flapping wings.
The drunken butterflies sit
   With opening and shutting wings.

Snake the Cause [5]

In the path he was coiled up.
On a long stick he was coiled up.
On the edge of the water he was coiled up.
Around a tree branch he was coiled, it was said.

3. From Washington Matthews, "Songs of Sequence of the Navajos," *The Journal of American Folk-Lore,* vol. VII, 1894.
4. From Frank Russell, *The Pima Indians,* 1908. The song is sung "to bring success when setting out on a deer hunt" [Russell].
5. From Frank G. Speck, *Ceremonial Songs of the Creek and Yuchi Indians,* 1911. The formula is intended to cure toothache by sympathetic magic based on the resemblance between the swollen cheeks of the snake and those of the sufferer. The medicine administered with the formula consists of twigs and dried leaves, representing the form and color of the snake, placed in water, "blown into, and given to the patient to drink" [Speck].

On a hollow tree he was coiled up. ·5
He hisses continuously.
Lying he made a noise.
Stone is in the grass
Here coiled up.
Lying he made a noise. 10
On a long stick.
Here coiled up.
Lying he made a noise.
In the sunny path.
Here coiled up. 15
Hiss!

Three Songs of Owl Woman [6]

I

Brown owls come here in the blue evening,
They are hooting about,
They are shaking their wings and hooting.

II

How shall I begin my song
In the blue night that is settling?
I will sit here and begin my song.

III

In the great night my heart will go out,
Toward me the darkness comes rattling,
In the great night my heart will go out.

The Weaver's Lamentation [7]

1

You have left me to linger in hopeless longing,
Your presence had ever made me feel no want,
You have left me to travel in sorrow.
Left me to travel in sorrow; Ah! the pain, the pain,
Your presence had ever made me feel no want, 5
You have left me to travel in sorrow; Ah! the pain,
Left me to travel in sorrow; Ah! the pain, the pain, the pain,

6. From Frances Densmore, *Papago Music*, 1929. Owl Woman was a Papago medicine woman, some of whose songs, she claimed, were given to her by the disembodied spirits of the dead.

7. From Francis La Flesche, *The Osage Tribe: Rite of the Wa-Xó-Be*, 1930. Son of an Omaha chief, La Flesche was educated as an ethnologist and has published widely in his field.

2

You have left me to linger in hopeless longing,
In your presence there was no sorrow,
You have gone and sorrow I shall feel, as I travel, Ah!
   the pain, the pain.   10
You have gone and sorrow I shall feel as I travel,
You have left me to linger in hopeless longing.
In your presence there was no sorrow,
You have gone and sorrow I shall feel as I travel; Ah!
   the pain, the pain, the pain,
Content with your presence, I wanted nothing more,   15
You have left me to travel in sorrow; Ah! the pain, the
   pain, the pain.

Symbolic and Ethical Idealism

NATHANIEL HAWTHORNE
(1804–1864)

To understand Hawthorne the reader must set aside an attractive legend. Only accidental circumstances support the tradition of the shy recluse, brooding in solitude upon the gloomier aspects of Puritan New England, whose writings are a kind of spiritual autobiography. Instead, during most of his life, Hawthorne was decidedly a public figure, capable, when necessary, of a certain urbanity. As a writer, he set out quite consciously to exploit his antiquarian enthusiasms and his understanding of the colonial history of New England. He was absorbed by the enigmas of evil and of moral responsibility, interwoven with man's destiny in nature and in eternity; but in this interest he was not unusual, for he shared it with such contemporaries as Poe, Emerson, and Melville, and with others more remote, such as Milton and Shakespeare.

It is true that for some years after his graduation from college he lived quietly in quiet Salem, but a young man engrossed in historical study and in learning the writer's craft is not notably queer if he does not seek society or marriage, especially if he is poor. In later years Hawthorne successfully managed his official duties, made a large circle of friends, and performed the extrovert functions of a foreign consul with competence, if without joy. The true Hawthorne is revealed just as much by "The Old Manse," an essay light-spirited and affectionate, as by "Rappaccini's Daughter," "Ethan Brand," or *The Scarlet Letter*. We understand better his full manliness and humanity now that Professor Randall Stewart has restored their pristine vigor to the gently henpecked texts that Mrs. Hawthorne published of his *Note-Books*.

Born in Salem, Massachusetts, July 4, 1804, Hawthorne was five generations removed from his Puritan American forebears. When the boy was twelve, his widowed mother took him to live with her brother in Maine, but old Salem had already enkindled his antiquarian inclination. To Salem he returned to prepare for college. At Bowdoin College (1821–1825), where he was, he said, "an idle student," but "always reading," he made a friend of Longfellow, his classmate, and lifetime intimates of Horatio Bridge and of Franklin Pierce, later president of the United States.

The next twelve years, of so-called "seclusion," in his mother's Salem home, were years of literary apprenticeship. He read widely, preparing himself to be the chronicler of the antiquities and the spiritual temper of colonial New England. His first novel, *Fanshawe* (1828), an abortive chronicle of Bowdoin life, was recalled and almost completely destroyed. He made observant walking trips about Massachusetts; remote portions of New England he frequently visited as the guest of his uncle, whose extensive stagecoach business provided the means. In 1832 there appeared in a gift book, *The Token*, his first published tales, including "The Gentle Boy." Other stories followed, in *The Token* and various magazines, to be collected in 1837 as *Twice-Told Tales* (enlarged in 1842), a volume of masterpieces, but only a few discerning critics, such as Poe, then understood what he was doing.

He had become secretly engaged to Sophia Peabody in 1838, and since his stories were not gaining popular support, he secured remunerative employment in the Boston Custom House. Seven months at Brook Farm, a socialistic co-operative, led him to abandon the idea of taking his bride there; on their marriage in 1842 they settled in Concord, at the Old Manse, Emerson's ancestral home. There he spent four idyllic years, during which the stories of *Mosses from an Old Manse* (1846) were published serially and as a volume.

His sales were still meager, and he returned to Salem as surveyor in the Custom House (1846–1849). He lost this position, with other Democrats, at the next election, but in 1850 he published *The Scarlet Letter*, which made his fame, changed his fortune, and gave to our literature its first symbolic novel, a year before the appearance of Melville's *Moby-Dick*. In this novel were concentrated the entire resources of Hawthorne's creative personality and experience.

After a short time in the Berkshires, Hawthorne settled in 1852 at the Wayside, Concord, which became his permanent home. He was at the height of his creative activity. *The House of the Seven Gables* (1851), a great novel of family decadence, was followed by *The Blithedale Romance* (1852), a minor novel on the Brook Farm experiment. Among the tales of *The Snow-Image* (1851), were "Ethan Brand" and "The Great Stone Face." A *Wonder Book* (1852) and *Tanglewood Tales* (1853) entered the literature of juvenile classics.

The *Life of Franklin Pierce* (1852) was recognized handsomely by the new president, who appointed his college friend as consul at Liverpool (1853–1857). Hawthorne faithfully performed the duties, which he found uncongenial, while seeing much of England and recording his impressions in the *English Note-Books* (published after his death) and *Our Old Home* (1863), a sheaf of essays. A long holiday on the Continent resulted in the *French and Italian Note-Books* (not published in his lifetime), and *The Marble Faun* (1860), a novel with an Italian setting, whose moral allegory, while not satisfactorily clarified, continues to interest the student of Hawthorne's thought. In 1860 Hawthorne brought his family back to the Wayside. He died on May 18, 1864, at Plymouth, New Hampshire, on a walking tour.

Although in many of his stories, and in the two great novels, Hawthorne created genuine characters and situations, he holds his permanent audience primarily by the interest and the consistent vitality of his criticism of life. Beyond his remarkable sense of the past, which gives a genuine ring to the historical reconstructions, beyond his precise and simple style, which is in the great tradition of familiar narrative, the principal appeal of his work is in the quality of its allegory, always richly ambivalent, providing enigmas which each reader solves in his own terms. Reference is made, in the stories below, to his discovery of the Puritan past of his family, the persecutors of Quakers and "witches"; but wherever his interest started, it led him to a long investiga-

tion of the problems of moral and social responsibility. His enemies are intolerance, the hypocrisy that hides the common sin, and the greed that refuses to share joy; he fears beyond everything withdrawal from mankind, the cynical suspicion, the arrogant perfectionism that cannot bide its mortal time—whatever divorces the pride-ridden intellect from the common heart of humanity. It is not enough to call him the critic of the Puritan; the Quaker or the transcendental extremist might be equally guilty; and Aylmer and Ethan Brand are not Puritans. His remedy is in nature and in the sweetness of a world freed not from sin, but from the corrosive sense of guilt.

In progress is the definitive *Centenary Edition of The Works of Nathaniel Hawthorne* (Ohio State), edited by William Charvat, Roy Harvey Pearce, Claude M. Simpson, and Matthew J. Bruccoli; Fredson Bowers, textual editor. An earlier edition is *The Complete Works * * *, 12 vols., edited by George P. Lathrop, 1883. *The Heart of Hawthorne's Journals* was edited by Newton Arvin, 1929. Randall Stewart edited *The American Notebooks of Nathaniel Hawthorne*, 1932, and *The English Notebooks*, 1941.

Recent revaluation began with *Nathaniel Hawthorne*, by Randall Stewart, 1948. George E. Woodberry's *Nathaniel Hawthorne*, 1902, is still not superseded for its scope and data. See also Julian Hawthorne, *Nathaniel Hawthorne and His Wife*, 2 vols., 1884; Mark Van Doren, *Nathaniel Hawthorne*, 1949; H. H. Waggoner, *Hawthorne, A Critical Study*, rev. ed., 1963; R. R. Male, *Hawthorne's Tragic Vision*, 1957; Harry Levin, *Power of Blackness*, 1960; H. H. Hoeltje, *Inward Sky * * *, 1962; Arlin Turner, *Nathaniel Hawthorne*, 1955; Terence Martin, *Nathaniel Hawthorne*, 1965; Richard Fogle, *Hawthorne's Fiction * * *, 1964; and Frederick C. Crews, *The Sins of the Fathers: Hawthorne's Psychological Themes*, 1966.

My Kinsman, Major Molineux [1]

After the kings of Great Britain had assumed the right of appointing the colonial governors, the measures of the latter seldom met with the ready and generous approbation which had been paid to those of their predecessors, under the original charters. The people looked with most jealous scrutiny to the exercise of power which did not emanate from themselves, and they usually rewarded their rulers with slender gratitude for the compliances by which, in softening their instructions from beyond the sea, they had incurred the reprehension of those who gave them. The annals of Massachusetts Bay will inform us, that of six governors in the space of about forty years from the surrender of the old charter, under James II., two were imprisoned by a popular insurrection; a third, as Hutchinson [2] inclines to believe, was driven from the province by the whizzing of a musket-ball; a fourth, in the opinion of the same historian, was hastened to his grave by continual bickerings with the House of Representatives; and the remaining two, as well as their successors, till the revolution, were favored with few and brief intervals of peaceful sway. The inferior members of the court party, in times of high political excitement, led scarcely a more desirable life. These remarks may serve as a preface to the following adventures, which chanced upon a summer night, not far from a hundred years ago. The reader, in order to avoid a long and dry detail of colonial affairs, is requested to dispense with an account of the train of circumstances that had caused much temporary inflammation of the popular mind.

It was near nine o'clock of a moonlight evening, when a boat crossed the ferry with a single passenger, who had obtained his conveyance at that unusual hour by the promise of an extra fare. While he stood on the landing-place, searching in either pocket for the means of fulfilling his agreement, the ferryman lifted a lantern, by the aid of which, and the newly risen moon, he took a very accurate survey of the stranger's figure. He was a youth of barely eighteen years, evidently country-bred, and now, as it should seem, upon his first visit to town. He was clad in a coarse gray

1. This story is one of the early narratives Hawthorne published in *The Token* for 1832. It was included twenty years later in *The Snow-Image*, the source of this text. As an allegory it is concerned with Hawthorne's familiar polarity of good and evil, of light and darkness, in the affairs of mankind. The effect is heightened, however, by the interest in character and action, in which the real and the fantastic are mingled. As in "Young Goodman Brown" or the

much later "Ethan Brand" the fantastic is associated with the actual—here with such elements of experience as the journey into life of an innocent lad, or, at the ideal level, with the conflict between the reactionary Crown authority and the rebellious democratic ideas of American colonials.
2. Thomas Hutchinson (1711–1780), royal governor of Massachusetts and historian of colonial New England.

coat, well worn, but in excellent repair; his under garments were durably constructed of leather, and fitted tight to a pair of service-able and well-shaped limbs; his stockings of blue yarn were the incontrovertible work of a mother or a sister; and on his head was a three-cornered hat, which in its better days had perhaps sheltered the graver brow of the lad's father. Under his left arm was a heavy cudgel formed of an oak sapling, and retaining a part of the hard-ened root; and his equipment was completed by a wallet, not so abundantly stocked as to incommode the vigorous shoulders on which it hung. Brown, curly hair, well-shaped features, and bright, cheerful eyes were nature's gifts, and worth all that art could have done for his adornment.

The youth, one of whose names was Robin, finally drew from his pocket the half of a little province bill of five shillings, which, in the depreciation in that sort of currency, did but satisfy the ferryman's demand, with the surplus of a sexangular piece of parchment, valued at three pence. He then walked forward into the town, with as light a step as if his day's journey had not already exceeded thirty miles, and with as eager an eye as if he were enter-ing London city, instead of the little metropolis of a New England colony. Before Robin had proceeded far, however, it occurred to him that he knew not whither to direct his steps; so he paused, and looked up and down the narrow street, scrutinizing the small and mean wooden buildings that were scattered on either side.

"This low hovel cannot be my kinsman's dwelling," thought he, "nor yonder old house, where the moonlight enters at the broken casement; and truly I see none hereabouts that might be worthy of him. It would have been wise to inquire my way of the ferry-man, and doubtless he would have gone with me, and earned a shilling from the Major for his pains. But the next man I meet will do as well."

He resumed his walk, and was glad to perceive that the street now became wider, and the houses more respectable in their ap-pearance. He soon discerned a figure moving on moderately in ad-vance, and hastened his steps to overtake it. As Robin drew nigh, he saw that the passenger was a man in years, with a full periwig of gray hair, a wide-skirted coat of dark cloth, and silk stockings rolled above his knees. He carried a long and polished cane, which he struck down perpendicularly before him at every step; and at regular intervals he uttered two successive hems, of a peculiarly solemn and sepulchral intonation. Having made these observa-tions, Robin laid hold of the skirt of the old man's coat, just when the light from the open door and windows of a barber's shop fell upon both their figures.

"Good evening to you, honored sir," said he, making a low bow, and still retaining his hold of the skirt. "I pray you tell me whereabouts is the dwelling of my kinsman, Major Molineux."

The youth's question was uttered very loudly; and one of the barbers, whose razor was descending on a well-soaped chin, and another who was dressing a Ramillies wig,[3] left their occupations, and came to the door. The citizen, in the mean time, turned a long-favored countenance upon Robin, and answered him in a tone of excessive anger and annoyance. His two sepulchral hems, however, broke into the very centre of his rebuke, with most singular effect, like a thought of the cold grave obtruding among wrathful passions.

"Let go my garment, fellow! I tell you, I know not the man you speak of. What! I have authority, I have—hem, hem—authority; and if this be the respect you show for your betters, your feet shall be brought acquainted with the stocks by daylight, tomorrow morning!"

Robin released the old man's skirt, and hastened away, pursued by an ill-mannered roar of laughter from the barber's shop. He was at first considerably surprised by the result of his question, but, being a shrewd youth, soon thought himself able to account for the mystery.

"This is some country representative," was his conclusion, "who has never seen the inside of my kinsman's door, and lacks the breeding to answer a stranger civilly. The man is old, or verily—I might be tempted to turn back and smite him on the nose. Ah, Robin, Robin! even the barber's boys laugh at you for choosing such a guide! You will be wiser in time, friend Robin."

He now became entangled in a succession of crooked and narrow streets, which crossed each other, and meandered at no great distance from the water-side. The smell of tar was obvious to his nostrils, the masts of vessels pierced the moonlight above the tops of the buildings, and the numerous signs, which Robin paused to read, informed him that he was near the centre of business. But the streets were empty, the shops were closed, and lights were visible only in the second stories of a few dwelling-houses. At length, on the corner of a narrow lane, through which he was passing, he beheld the broad countenance of a British hero swinging before the door of an inn, whence proceeded the voices of many guests. The casement of one of the lower windows was thrown back, and a very thin curtain permitted Robin to distinguish a party at supper, round a well-furnished table. The fragrance of the good cheer steamed forth into the outer air, and the youth could not fail to recollect that the last remnant of his

---

3. A wig with a plaited tail named in honor of British victory at Ramillies.

travelling stock of provision had yielded to his morning appetite, and that noon had found and left him dinnerless.

"Oh, that a parchment three-penny might give me a right to sit down at yonder table!" said Robin, with a sigh. "But the Major will make me welcome to the best of his victuals; so I will even step boldly in, and inquire my way to his dwelling."

He entered the tavern, and was guided by the murmur of voices and the fumes of tobacco to the public-room. It was a long and low apartment, with oaken walls, grown dark in the continual smoke, and a floor which was thickly sanded, but of no immaculate purity. A number of persons—the larger part of whom appeared to be mariners, or in some way connected with the sea—occupied the wooden benches, or leather-bottomed chairs, conversing on various matters, and occasionally lending their attention to some topic of general interest. Three or four little groups were draining as many bowls of punch, which the West India trade had long since made a familiar drink in the colony. Others, who had the appearance of men who lived by regular and laborious handicraft, preferred the insulated bliss of an unshared potation, and became more taciturn under its influence. Nearly all, in short, evinced a predilection for the Good Creature in some of its various shapes, for this is a vice to which, as Fast Day sermons of a hundred years ago will testify, we have a long hereditary claim. The only guests to whom Robin's sympathies inclined him were two or three sheepish countrymen, who were using the inn somewhat after the fashion of a Turkish caravansary; they had gotten themselves into the darkest corner of the room, and heedless of the Nicotian [4] atmosphere, were supping on the bread of their own ovens, and the bacon cured in their own chimney-smoke. But though Robin felt a sort of brotherhood with these strangers, his eyes were attracted from them to a person who stood near the door, holding whispered conversation with a group of ill-dressed associates. His features were separately striking almost to grotesqueness, and the whole face left a deep impression on the memory. The forehead bulged out into a double prominence, with a vale between; the nose came boldly forth in an irregular curve, and its bridge was of more than a finger's breadth; the eyebrows were deep and shaggy, and the eyes glowed beneath them like fire in a cave.

While Robin deliberated of whom to inquire respecting his kinsman's dwelling, he was accosted by the innkeeper, a little man in a stained white apron, who had come to pay his professional welcome to the stranger. Being in a second generation from a French

4. A reference to Nicosia, capital of Cyprus, where tobacco was processed.

Protestant, he seemed to have inherited the courtesy of his parent nation; but no variety of circumstances was ever known to change his voice from the one shrill note in which he now addressed Robin.

"From the country, I presume, sir?" said he, with a profound bow. "Beg leave to congratulate you on your arrival, and trust you intend a long stay with us. Fine town here, sir, beautiful buildings, and much that may interest a stranger. May I hope for the honor of your commands in respect to supper?"

"The man sees a family likeness! the rogue has guessed that I am related to the Major!" thought Robin, who had hitherto experienced little superfluous civility.

All eyes were now turned on the country lad, standing at the door, in his worn three-cornered hat, gray coat, leather breeches, and blue yarn stockings, leaning on an oaken cudgel, and bearing a wallet on his back.

Robin replied to the courteous innkeeper, with such an assumption of confidence as befitted the Major's relative. "My honest friend," he said, "I shall make it a point to patronize your house on some occasion, when"—here he could not help lowering his voice—"when I may have more than a parchment three-pence in my pocket. My present business," continued he, speaking with lofty confidence, "is merely to inquire my way to the dwelling of my kinsman, Major Molineux."

There was a sudden and general movement in the room, which Robin interpreted as expressing the eagerness of each individual to become his guide. But the innkeeper turned his eyes to a written paper on the wall, which he read, or seemed to read, with occasional recurrences to the young man's figure.

"What have we here?" said he, breaking his speech into little dry fragments. " 'Left the house of the subscriber, bounden servant, Hezekiah Mudge,—had on, when he went away, gray coat, leather breeches, master's third-best hat. One pound currency reward to whosoever shall lodge him in any jail in the providence.' Better trudge, boy; better trudge!"

Robin had begun to draw his hand towards the lighter end of the oak cudgel, but a strange hostility in every countenance induced him to relinquish his purpose of breaking the courteous innkeeper's head. As he turned to leave the room, he encountered a sneering glance from the bold-featured personage whom he had before noticed; and no sooner was he beyond the door, than he heard a general laugh, in which the innkeeper's voice might be distinguished, like the dropping of small stones into a kettle.

"Now, is it not strange," thought Robin, with his usual shrewdness,—"is it not strange that the confession of an empty pocket should outweigh the name of my kinsman, Major Molineux? Oh, if I had one of those grinning rascals in the woods, where I and my oak sapling grew up together, I would teach him that my arm is heavy though my purse be light!"

On turning the corner of the narrow lane, Robin found himself in a spacious street, with an unbroken line of lofty houses on each side, and a steepled building at the upper end, whence the ringing of a bell announced the hour of nine. The light of the moon, and the lamps from the numerous shop-windows, discovered people promenading on the pavement, and amongst them Robin had hoped to recognize his hitherto inscrutable relative. The result of his former inquiries made him unwilling to hazard another, in a scene of such publicity, and he determined to walk slowly and silently up the street, thrusting his face close to that of every elderly gentleman, in search of the Major's lineaments. In his progress, Robin encountered many gay and gallant figures. Embroidered garments of showy colors, enormous periwigs, gold-laced hats, and silver-hilted swords glided past him and dazzled his optics. Travelled youths, imitators of the European fine gentlemen of the period, trod jauntily along, half dancing to the fashionable tunes which they hummed, and making poor Robin ashamed of his quiet and natural gait. At length, after many pauses to examine the gorgeous display of goods in the shop-windows, and after suffering some rebukes for the impertinence of his scrutiny into people's faces, the Major's kinsman found himself near the steepled building, still unsuccessful in his search. As yet, however, he had seen only one side of the thronged street; so Robin crossed, and continued the same sort of inquisition down the opposite pavement, with stronger hopes than the philosopher seeking an honest man, but with no better fortune. He had arrived about midway towards the lower end, from which his course began, when he overheard the approach of some one who struck down a cane on the flagstones at every step, uttering at regular intervals, two sepulchral hems.

"Mercy on us!" quoth Robin, recognizing the sound.

Turning a corner, which chanced to be close at his right hand, he hastened to pursue his researches in some other part of the town. His patience now was wearing low, and he seemed to feel more fatigue from his rambles since he crossed the ferry, than from his journey of several days on the other side. Hunger also pleaded loudly with him, and Robin began to balance the propriety of demanding, violently, and with lifted cudgel, the necessary guidance from the first solitary passenger whom he should meet. While a resolution to this effect was gaining strength, he entered a street of mean appearance, on either side of which a row of ill-built houses was straggling towards the harbor. The moonlight fell upon no passenger along the whole extent, but in the third domicile which Robin passed there was a half-opened door, and his keen glance detected a woman's garment within.

"My luck may be better here," said he to himself.

Accordingly, he approached the door, and beheld it shut closer as he did so; yet an open space remained, sufficing for the fair occupant to observe the stranger, without a corresponding display on her part. All that Robin could discern was a strip of scarlet petticoat, and the occasional sparkle of an eye, as if the moonbeams were trembling on some bright thing.

"Pretty mistress," for I may call her so with a good conscience, thought the shrewd youth, since I know nothing to the contrary, —"my sweet pretty mistress, will you be kind enough to tell me whereabouts I must seek the dwelling of my kinsman, Major Molineux?"

Robin's voice was plaintive and winning, and the female, seeing nothing to be shunned in the handsome country youth, thrust open the door, and came forth into the moonlight. She was a dainty little figure, with a white neck, round arms, and a slender waist, at the extremity of which her scarlet petticoat jutted out over a hoop, as if she were standing in a balloon. Moreover, her face was oval and pretty, her hair dark beneath the little cap, and her bright eyes possessed a sly freedom, which triumphed over those of Robin.

"Major Molineux dwells here," said this fair woman.

Now, her voice was the sweetest Robin had heard that night, yet he could not help doubting whether that sweet voice spoke Gospel truth. He looked up and down the mean street, and then surveyed the house before which they stood. It was a small, dark edifice of two stories, the second of which projected over the lower floor, and the front apartment had the aspect of a shop for petty commodities.

"Now, truly, I am in luck," replied Robin, cunningly, "and so indeed is my kinsman, the Major, in having so pretty a housekeeper. But I prithee trouble him to step to the door; I will deliver him a message from his friends in the country, and then go back to my lodgings at the inn."

"Nay, the Major has been abed this hour or more," said the lady of the scarlet petticoat; "and it would be to little purpose to disturb him to-night, seeing his evening draught was of the strongest. But he is a kind-hearted man, and it would be as much as my life's worth to let a kinsman of his turn away from the door. You are the good old gentleman's very picture, and I could swear that was his rainy-weather hat. Also he has garments very much resembling those leather small-clothes. But come in, I pray, for I bid you hearty welcome in his name."

So saying, the fair and hospitable dame took our hero by the hand; and the touch was light, and the force was gentleness, and though Robin read in her eyes what he did not hear in her words, yet the slender-waisted woman in the scarlet petticoat proved stronger than the athletic country youth. She had drawn his half-willing footsteps nearly to the threshold, when the opening of a door in the neighborhood startled the Major's housekeeper, and, leaving the Major's kinsman, she vanished speedily into her own domocile. A heavy yawn preceded the appearance of a man, who, like the Moonshine of Pyramus and Thisbe,[5] carried a lantern, needlessly aiding his sister luminary in the heavens. As he walked sleepily up the street, he turned his broad, dull face on Robin, and displayed a long staff, spiked at the end.

"Home, vagabond, home!" said the watchman, in accents that seemed to fall asleep as soon as they were uttered. "Home, or we'll set you in the stocks by peep of day!"

"This is the second hint of this kind," thought Robin. "I wish they would end my difficulties, by setting me there to-night."

Nevertheless, the youth felt an instinctive antipathy towards the guardian of midnight order, which at first prevented him from asking his usual question. But just when the man was about to vanish behind the corner, Robin resolved not to lose the opportunity, and shouted lustily after him,—

"I say, friend! will you guide me to the house of my kinsman, Major Molineux?"

The watchman made no reply, but turned the corner and was gone; yet Robin seemed to hear the sound of drowsy laughter stealing along the solitary street. At that moment, also, a pleasant titter saluted him from the open window above his head; he looked up, and caught the sparkle of a saucy eye; a round arm beckoned to him, and next he heard light footsteps descending the staircase within. But Robin, being of the household of a New England clergyman, was a good youth, as well as a shrewd one; so he resisted temptation, and fled away.

He now roamed desperately, and at random, through the town, almost ready to believe that a spell was on him, like that by which a wizard of his country had once kept three pursuers wandering, a whole winter night, within twenty paces of the cottage which they sought. The streets lay before him, strange and desolate, and the lights were extinguished in almost every house. Twice, however, little parties of men, among whom Robin distinguished individuals in outlandish attire, came hurrying along; but, though on both occasions, they paused to address him, such intercourse did not at

5. Moonshine is a character in the Shakespearean version of Pyramus and Thisbe, *A Midsummer Night's Dream.*

all enlighten his perplexity. They did but utter a few words in some language of which Robin knew nothing, and perceiving his inability to answer, bestowed a curse upon him in plain English and hastened away. Finally, the lad determined to knock at the door of every mansion that might appear worthy to be occupied by his kinsman, trusting that perseverance would overcome the fatality that had hitherto thwarted him. Firm in this resolve, he was passing beneath the walls of a church, which formed the corner of two streets, when, as he turned into a shade of its steeple, he encountered a bulky stranger, muffled in a cloak. The man was proceeding with the speed of earnest business, but Robin planted himself full before him, holding the oak cudgel with both hands across his body as a bar to further passage.

"Halt, honest man, and answer me a question," said he, very resolutely. "Tell me, this instant, whereabouts is the dwelling of my kinsman, Major Molineux!"

"Keep your tongue between your teeth, fool, and let me pass!" said a deep, gruff voice, which Robin partly remembered. "Let me pass, or I'll strike you to the earth!"

"No, no, neighbor!" cried Robin, flourishing his cudgel, and then thrusting its larger end close to the man's muffled face. "No, no, I'm not the fool you take me for, nor do you pass till I have an answer to my question. Whereabouts is the dwelling of my kinsman, Major Molineux?"

The stranger, instead of attempting to force his passage, stepped back into the moonlight, unmuffled his face, and stared full into that of Robin.

"Watch here an hour, and Major Molineux will pass by," said he.

Robin gazed with dismay and astonishment on the unprecedented physiognomy of the speaker. The forehead with its double prominence, the broad ·hooked nose, the shaggy eyebrows, and fiery eyes were those which he had noticed at the inn, but the man's complexion had undergone a singular, or, more properly, a twofold change. One side of the face blazed an intense red, while the other was black as midnight, the division line being in the broad bridge of the nose; and a mouth which seemed to extend from ear to ear was black or red, in contrast to the color of the cheek. The effect was as if two individual devils, a fiend of fire and a fiend of darkness, had united themselves to form this infernal visage. The stranger grinned in Robin's face, muffled his party-colored features, and was out of sight in a moment.

"Strange things we travellers see!" ejaculated Robin.

He seated himself, however, upon the steps of the church-door, resolving to wait the appointed time for his kinsman. A few moments were consumed in philosophical speculations upon the species of man who had just left him; but having settled this point shrewdly, rationally, and satisfactorily, he was compelled to look elsewhere for his amusement. And first he threw his eyes along the street. It was of more respectable appearance than most of those into which he had wandered; and the moon, creating, like the imaginative power, a beautiful strangeness in familiar objects, gave something of romance to a scene that might not have possessed it in the light of day. The irregular and often quaint architecture of the houses, some of whose roofs were broken into numerous little peaks, while others ascended, steep and narrow, into a single point, and others again were square; the pure snow-white of some of their complexions, the aged darkness of others, and the thousand sparklings, reflected from bright substances in the walls of many; these matters engaged Robin's attention for a while, and then began to grow wearisome. Next he endeavored to define the forms of distant objects, starting away, with almost ghostly indistinctness, just as his eye appeared to grasp them; and finally he took a minute survey of an edifice which stood on the opposite side of the street, directly in front of the church-door, where he was stationed. It was a large, square mansion, distinguished from its neighbors by a balcony, which rested on tall pillars, and by an elaborate Gothic window, communicating therewith.

"Perhaps this is the very house I have been seeking," thought Robin.

Then he strove to speed away the time, by listening to a murmur which swept continually along the street, yet was scarcely audible, except to an unaccustomed ear like his; it was a low, dull, dreamy sound, compounded of many noises, each of which was at too great a distance to be separately heard. Robin marvelled at this snore of a sleeping town, and marvelled more whenever its continuity was broken by now and then a distant shout, apparently loud where it originated. But altogether it was a sleep-inspiring sound, and, to shake off its drowsy influence, Robin arose, and climbed a window-frame, that he might view the interior of the church. There the moonbeams came trembling in, and fell down upon the deserted pews, and extended along the quiet aisles. A fainter yet more awful radiance was hovering around the pulpit, and one solitary ray had dared to rest upon the open page of the great Bible. Had nature, in that deep hour, become a worshipper in the house which man had builded? Or was that heavenly light the visible sanctity of the place,—visible because no earthly and impure feet were within the walls? The scene made Robin's heart shiver with a sensation of loneliness stronger than he had ever felt in the remotest depths of his native woods; so he turned away and sat down again before the door. There were graves around the church, and now an uneasy thought obtruded into Robin's breast. What if the object of his search, which had been so often and so strangely thwarted, were all the time mouldering in his shroud? What if his kinsman should glide through yonder gate, and nod and smile to him in dimly passing by?

"Oh that any breathing thing were here with me!" said Robin.

Recalling his thoughts from the uncomfortable track, he sent them over forest, hill, and stream, and attempted to imagine how that evening of ambiguity and weariness had been spent by his father's household. He pictured them assembled at the door, beneath the tree, the great old tree, which had been spared for its huge twisted trunk and venerable shade, when a thousand leafy brethren fell. There, at the going down of the summer sun, it was his father's custom to perform domestic worship, that the neighbors might come and join with him like brothers of the family, and that the wayfaring man might pause to drink at the fountain, and keep his heart pure by freshening the memory of home. Robin distinguished the seat of every individual of the little audience; he saw the good man in the midst, holding the Scriptures in the golden light that fell from the western clouds; he beheld him close the book and all rise up to pray. He heard the old thanksgiving for daily mercies, the old supplications for their continuance, to which he had so often listened in weariness, but which were now among his dear remembrances. He perceived the slight inequality of his father's voice when he came to speak of the absent one; he noted how his mother turned her face to the broad and knotted trunk; how his elder brother scorned, because the beard was rough upon his upper lip, to permit his features to be moved; how the younger sister drew down a low hanging branch before her eyes; and how the little one of all, whose sports had hitherto broken the decorum of the scene, understood the prayer for her playmate, and burst into clamorous grief. Then he saw them go in at the door; and when Robin would have entered also, the latch tinkled into its place, and he was excluded from his home.

"Am I here, or there?" cried Robin, starting; for all at once, when his thoughts had become visible and audible in a dream, the long, wide, solitary street shone out before him.

He aroused himself, and endeavored to fix his attention steadily upon the large edifice which he had surveyed before. But still his mind kept vibrating between fancy and reality; by turns, the pillars of the balcony lengthened into the tall, bare stems of pines, dwindled down to human figures, settled again into their true shape and size, and then commenced a new succession of changes. For a single moment, when he deemed himself awake, he could have sworn that a visage—one which he seemed to remember, yet could not absolutely name as his kinsman's—was looking towards him from the Gothic window. A deeper sleep wrestled with and nearly overcame him, but fled at the sound of footsteps along the opposite pavement. Robin rubbed his eyes, discerned a man passing at the foot of the balcony, and addressed him in a loud, peevish, and lamentable cry.

"Hallo, friend! must I wait here all night for my kinsman, Major Molineux?"

The sleeping echoes awoke, and answered the voice; and the passenger, barely able to discern a figure sitting in the oblique shade of the steeple, traversed the street to obtain a nearer view. He was himself a gentleman in the prime, of open, intelligent, cheerful, and altogether prepossessing countenance. Perceiving a country youth, apparently homeless and without friends, he accosted him in a tone of real kindness, which had become strange to Robin's ears.

"Well, my good lad, why are you sitting here?" inquired he. "Can I be of service to you in any way?"

"I am afraid not, sir," replied Robin, despondingly; "yet I shall take it kindly, if you'll answer me a single question. I've been searching, half the night, for one Major Molineux; now, sir, is there really such a person in these parts, or am I dreaming?"

"Major Molineux! The name is not altogether strange to me," said the gentleman, smiling. "Have you any objection to telling me the nature of your business with him?"

Then Robin briefly related that his father was a clergyman, settled on a small salary, at a long distance back in the country, and that he and Major Molineux were brothers' children. The Major, having inherited riches, and acquired civil and military rank, had visited his cousin, in great pomp, a year or two before; had manifested much interest in Robin and an elder brother, and, being childless himself, had thrown out hints respecting the future establishment of one of them in life. The elder brother was destined to succeed to the farm which his father cultivated in the interval of sacred duties; it was therefore determined that Robin should profit by his kinsman's generous intentions, especially as he seemed to be rather the favorite, and was thought to possess other necessary endowments.

"For I have the name of being a shrewd youth," observed Robin, in this part of his story.

"I doubt not you deserve it," replied his new friend, good-naturedly; "but pray proceed."

"Well, sir, being nearly eighteen years old, and well grown, as you see," continued Robin, drawing himself up to his full height,

"I thought it high time to begin in the world. So my mother and sister put me in handsome trim, and my father gave me half the remnant of his last year's salary, and five days ago I started for this place, to pay the Major a visit. But, would you believe it, sir! I crossed the ferry a little after dark, and have yet found nobody that would show me the way to his dwelling; only, an hour or two since, I was told to wait here, and Major Molineux would pass by."

"Can you describe the man who told you this?" inquired the gentleman.

"Oh, he was a very ill-favored fellow, sir," replied Robin, "with two great bumps on his forehead, a hook nose, fiery eyes; and, what struck me as the strangest, his face was of two different colors. Do you happen to know such a man, sir?"

"Not intimately," answered the stranger, "but I chanced to meet him a little time previous to your stopping me. I believe you may trust his word, and that the Major will very shortly pass through this street. In the mean time, as I have a singular curiosity to witness your meeting, I will sit down here upon the steps and bear you company."

He seated himself accordingly, and soon engaged his companion in animated discourse. It was but of brief continuance, however, for a noise of shouting, which had long been remotely audible, drew so much nearer that Robin inquired its cause.

"What may be the meaning of this uproar?" asked he. "Truly, if your town be always as noisy, I shall find little sleep while I am an inhabitant."

"Why, indeed, friend Robin, there do appear to be three or four riotous fellows abroad to-night," replied the gentleman. "You must not expect all the stillness of your native woods here in our street. But the watch will shortly be at the heels of these lads and"—

"Ay, and set them in the stocks by peep of day," interrupted Robin, recollecting his own encounter with the drowsy lantern-bearer. "But, dear sir, if I may trust my ears, an army of watchmen would never make head against such a multitude of rioters. There were at least a thousand voices went up to make that one shout."

"May not a man have several voices, Robin, as well as two complexions?" said his friend.

"Perhaps a man may; but Heaven forbid that a woman should!" responded the shrewd youth, thinking of the seductive tones of the Major's housekeeper.

The sounds of a trumpet in some neighboring street now became so evident and continual, that Robin's curiosity was strongly excited. In addition to the shouts, he heard frequent bursts from many instruments of discord, and a wild and confused laughter filled up the intervals. Robin rose from the steps, and looked wistfully towards a point whither people seemed to be hastening.

"Surely some prodigious merry-making is going on," exclaimed he. "I have laughed very little since I left home, sir, and should be sorry to lose an opportunity. Shall we step round the corner by that darkish house, and take our share of the fun?"

"Sit down again, sit down, good Robin," replied the gentleman, laying his hand on the skirt of the gray coat. "You forget that we must wait here for your kinsman; and there is reason to believe that he will pass by, in the course of a very few moments."

The near approach of the uproar had now disturbed the neighborhood; windows flew open on all sides; and many heads, in the attire of the pillow, and confused by sleep suddenly broken, were protruded to the gaze of whoever had leisure to observe them. Eager voices hailed each other from house to house, all demanding the explanation, which not a soul could give. Half-dressed men hurried towards the unknown commotion, stumbling as they went over the stone steps that thrust themselves into the narrow footwalk. The shouts, the laughter, and the tuneless bray, the antipodes of music, came onwards with increasing din, till scattered individuals, and then denser bodies, began to appear round a corner at the distance of a hundred yards.

"Will you recognize your kinsman, if he passes in this crowd?" inquired the gentleman.

"Indeed, I can't warrant it, sir; but I'll take my stand here, and keep a bright lookout," answered Robin, descending to the outer edge of the pavement.

A mighty stream of people now emptied into the street, and came rolling slowly towards the church. A single horseman wheeled the corner in the midst of them, and close behind him came a band of fearful wind-instruments, sending forth a fresher discord now that no intervening buildings kept it from the ear. Then a redder light disturbed the moonbeams, and a dense multitude of torches shone along the street, concealing, by their glare, whatever object they illuminated. The single horseman, clad in a military dress, and bearing a drawn sword, rode onward as the leader, and, by his fierce and variegated countenance, appeared like war personified; the red of one cheek was an emblem of fire and sword; the blackness of the other betokened the mourning that attends them. In his train were wild figures in the Indian dress, and many fantastic shapes without a model, giving the whole march a visionary air, as if a dream had broken forth from some feverish brain, and were sweeping visibly through the midnight streets. A mass of people, inactive, except as applauding spectators, hemmed the procession in; and several women ran along the sidewalk, piercing the confusion of heavier sounds with their shrill voices of mirth or terror.

"The double-faced fellow has his eye upon me," muttered Robin, with an indefinite but an uncomfortable idea that he was himself to bear a part in the pageantry.

The leader turned himself in the saddle, and fixed his glance full upon the country youth, as the steed went slowly by. When Robin had freed his eyes from those fiery ones, the musicians were passing before him, and the torches were close at hand; but the unsteady brightness of the latter formed a veil which he could not penetrate. The rattling of wheels over the stones sometimes found its way to his ear, and confused traces of a human form appeared at intervals, and then melted into the vivid light. A moment more, and the leader thundered a command to halt: the trumpets vomited a horrid breath, and then held their peace; the shouts and laughter of the people died away, and there remained only a universal hum, allied to silence. Right before Robin's eyes was an uncovered cart. There the torches blazed the brightest, there the moon shouted out like day, and there, in tar-and-feathery dignity, sat his kinsman, Major Molineux!

He was an elderly man, of large and majestic person, and strong, square features, betokening a steady soul; but steady as it was his enemies had found means to shake it. His face was pale as death, and far more ghastly; the broad forehead was contracted in his agony, so that his eyebrows formed one grizzled line; his eyes were red and wild, and the foam hung white upon his quivering lip. His whole frame was agitated by a quick and continual tremor, which his pride strove to quell, even in those circumstances of overwhelming humiliation. But perhaps the bitterest pang of all was when his eyes met those of Robin; for he evidently knew him on the instant, as the youth stood witnessing the foul disgrace of a head grown gray in honor. They stared at each other in silence, and Robin's knees shook, and his hair bristled, with a mixture of pity and terror. Soon, however, a bewildering excitement began to seize upon his mind; the preceding adventures of the night, the unexpected appearance of the crowd, the torches, the confused din and the hush that followed, the spectre of his kinsman reviled by that great multitude,—all this, and, more than all, a perception of tremendous ridicule in the whole scene, affected him with a sort of mental inebriety. At that moment a voice of sluggish merriment saluted Robin's ears, he turned instinctively, and just behind the corner of the church stood the lantern-bearer, rubbing his eyes, and drowsily enjoying the lad's amazement. Then he heard a peal of laughter like the ringing of silvery bells; a woman twitched his arm, a saucy eye met his, and he saw the lady of the scarlet petti-coat. A sharp, dry cachinnation appealed to his memory, and standing on tiptoe in the crowd, with his white apron over his head, he beheld the courteous little innkeeper. And lastly, there sailed over the heads of the multitude a great, broad laugh, broken in the midst by two sepulchral hems, thus, "Haw, haw, haw,— hem, hem,—haw, haw, haw, haw!"

The sound proceeded from the balcony of the opposite edifice, and thither Robin turned his eyes. In front of the Gothic window stood the old citizen, wrapped in a wide gown, his gray periwig exchanged for a nightcap, which was thrust back from his fore-head, and his silk stockings hanging about his legs. He supported himself on his polished cane in a fit of convulsive merriment, which manifested itself on his solemn old features like a funny in-scription on a tombstone. Then Robin seemed to hear the voices of the barbers, of the guests of the inn, and of all who had made sport of him that night. The contagion was spreading among the multitude, when all at once, it seized upon Robin, and he sent forth a shout of laughter that echoed through the street,—every man shook his sides, every man emptied his lungs, but Robin's shout was the loudest there. The cloud-spirits peeped from their silvery islands, as the congregated mirth went roaring up the sky! The Man in the Moon heard the far bellow. "Oho," quoth he, "the old earth is frolicsome to-night!"

When there was a momentary calm in that tempestuous sea of sound, the leader gave the sign, the procession resumed its march. On they went, like fiends that throng in mockery around some dead potentate, mighty no more, but majestic still in his agony. On they went, in counterfeited pomp, in senseless uproar, in frenzied merriment, trampling all on an old man's heart. On swept the tumult, and left a silent street behind.

* * *

"Well, Robin, are you dreaming?" inquired the gentleman, lay-ing his hand on the youth's shoulder.

Robin started, and withdrew his arm from the stone post to which he had instinctively clung, as the living stream rolled by him. His cheek was somewhat pale, and his eye not quite as lively as in the earlier part of the evening.

"Will you be kind enough to show me the way to the ferry?" said he, after a moment's pause.

"You have, then, adopted a new subject of inquiry?" observed his companion, with a smile.

"Why, yes, sir," replied Robin, rather dryly. "Thanks to you, and to my other friends, I have at last met my kinsman, and he will scarce desire to see my face again. I begin to grow weary of a town life, sir. Will you show me the way to the ferry?"

"No, my good friend Robin—not to-night, at least," said the gentleman. "Some few days hence, if you wish it, I will speed you on your journey. Or, if you prefer to remain with us, perhaps, as you are a shrewd youth, you may rise in the world without the help of your kinsman, Major Molineux."

1832, 1851

Young Goodman Brown [6]

Young Goodman Brown came forth at sunset into the street at Salem village; but put his head back, after crossing the threshold, to exchange a parting kiss with his young wife. And Faith, as the wife was aptly named, thrust her own pretty head into the street, letting the wind play with the pink ribbons of her cap while she called to Goodman Brown.

"Dearest heart," whispered she, softly and rather sadly, when her lips were close to his ear, "prithee put off your journey until sunrise and sleep in your own bed to-night. A lone woman is troubled with such dreams and such thoughts that she's afeared of herself sometimes. Pray tarry with me this night, dear husband, of all nights in the year."

"My love and my Faith," replied young Goodman Brown, "of all nights in the year, this one night must I tarry away from thee. My journey, as thou callest it, forth and back again, must needs be done 'twixt now and sunrise. What, my sweet, pretty wife, dost thou doubt me already, and we but three months married?"

"Then God bless you!" said Faith, with the pink ribbons; "and may you find all well when you come back."

"Amen!" cried Goodman Brown. "Say thy prayers, dear Faith, and go to bed at dusk, and no harm will come to thee."

So they parted; and the young man pursued his way until, being about to turn the corner by the meeting-house, he looked back and saw the head of Faith still peeping after him with a melancholy air, in spite of her pink ribbons.

6. Medieval literature abounds in descriptions of the "Witches' Sabbath," a midnight orgy of evil rites at which Satan himself sometimes presided. Hawthorne was certainly familiar with Cotton Mather's description, in *The Wonders of the Invisible World* (1693), of such "Diabolical Sacraments" as taking place in Massachusetts. Hawthorne's story is a memorable portrayal of a Puritan community, but its theme is universal. The concept of mankind's natural depravity was a principal determinant in Puritan thought, but Goodman Brown's corruption through his loss of simple faith in the goodness of mankind represents a timeless tragedy. This story appeared in the *New England Magazine* for April, 1835, and was collected in *Mosses from an Old Manse* (1846).

"Poor little Faith!" thought he, for his heart smote him. "What a wretch am I to leave her on such an errand! She talks of dreams, too. Methought as she spoke there was trouble in her face, as if a dream had warned her what work is to be done to-night. But no, no; 't would kill her to think it. Well, she's a blessed angel on earth; and after this one night I'll cling to her skirts and follow her to heaven."

With this excellent resolve for the future, Goodman Brown felt himself justified in making more haste on his present evil purpose. He had taken a dreary road, darkened by all the gloomiest trees of the forest, which barely stood aside to let the narrow path creep through, and closed immediately behind. It was all as lonely as could be; and there is this peculiarity in such a solitude, that the traveller knows not who may be concealed by the innumerable trunks and the thick boughs overhead; so that with lonely footsteps he may yet be passing through an unseen multitude.

"There may be a devilish Indian behind every tree," said Goodman Brown to himself; and he glanced fearfully behind him as he added, "What if the devil himself should be at my very elbow!"

His head being turned back, he passed a crook of the road, and, looking forward again, beheld the figure of a man, in grave and decent attire, seated at the foot of an old tree. He arose at Goodman Brown's approach and walked onward side by side with him.

"You are late, Goodman Brown," said he. "The clock of the Old South [7] was striking as I came through Boston, and that is full fifteen minutes agone."

"Faith kept me back a while," replied the young man, with a tremor in his voice, caused by the sudden appearance of his companion, though not wholly unexpected.

It was now deep dusk in the forest, and deepest in that part of it where these two were journeying. As nearly as could be discerned, the second traveller was about fifty years old, apparently in the same rank of life as Goodman Brown, and bearing a considerable resemblance to him, though perhaps more in expression than features. Still they might have been taken for father and son. And yet, though the elder person was as simply clad as the younger, and as simple in manner too, he had an indescribable air of one who knew the world, and who would not have felt abashed at the governor's dinner table or in King William's court,[8] were it possible that his affairs should call him thither. But the only thing about him that could be fixed upon as remarkable was his staff, which bore the

---

7. *I.e.*, Old South Church, Boston, famous as the secret rendezvous of American patriots before the Revolution. However, the Church was erected in 1729, while the story seems to be set somewhat earlier, before 1702. See the reference to "King William's court," just below.

8. William III was King of England from 1689 to 1702.

likeness of a great black snake, so curiously wrought that it might almost be seen to twist and wriggle itself like a living serpent. This, of course, must have been an ocular deception, assisted by the uncertain light.

"Come, Goodman Brown," cried his fellow-traveller, "this is a dull pace for the beginning of a journey. Take my staff, if you are so soon weary."

"Friend," said the other, exchanging his slow pace for a full stop, "having kept covenant by meeting thee here, it is my purpose now to return whence I came. I have scruples touching the matter thou wot'st of."

"Sayest thou so?" replied he of the serpent, smiling apart. "Let us walk on, nevertheless, reasoning as we go; and if I convince thee not thou shalt turn back. We are but a little way in the forest yet."

"Too far! too far!" exclaimed the goodman, unconsciously resuming his walk. "My father never went into the woods on such an errand, nor his father before him. We have been a race of honest men and good Christians since the days of the martyrs; and shall I be the first of the name of Brown that ever took this path and kept"—

"Such company, thou wouldst say," observed the elder person, interpreting his pause. "Well said, Goodman Brown! I have been as well acquainted with your family as with ever a one among the Puritans; and that's no trifle to say. I helped your grandfather, the constable, when he lashed the Quaker woman so smartly through the streets of Salem; and it was I that brought your father a pitch-pine knot, kindled at my own hearth, to set fire to an Indian village, in King Philip's war.[9] They were my good friends, both; and many a pleasant walk have we had along this path, and returned merrily after midnight. I would fain be friends with you for their sake."

"If it be as thou sayest," replied Goodman Brown, "I marvel they never spoke of these matters; or, verily, I marvel not, seeing that the least rumor of the sort would have driven them from New England. We are a people of prayer, and good works to boot, and abide no such wickedness."

"Wickedness or not," said the traveller with the twisted staff, "I have a very general acquaintance here in New England. The deacons of many a church have drunk the communion wine with me; the selectmen of divers towns make me their chairman; and a majority of the Great and General Court are firm supporters of my interest. The governor and I, too—But these are state secrets."

"Can this be so?" cried Goodman Brown, with a stare of

9. King Philip, or Metacomet, was the last leader of Indian resistance in southern New England, which ended with his death in 1676.

amazement at his undisturbed companion. "Howbeit, I have nothing to do with the governor and council; they have their own ways, and are no rule for a simple husbandman [1] like me. But, were I to go on with thee, how should I meet the eye of that good old man, our minister, at Salem village? Oh, his voice would make me tremble both Sabbath day and lecture day." [2]

Thus far the elder traveller had listened with due gravity; but now burst into a fit of irrepressible mirth, shaking himself so violently that his snake-like staff actually seemed to wriggle in sympathy.

"Ha! ha! ha!" shouted he again and again; then composing himself, "Well, go on, Goodman Brown, go on; but, prithee, don't kill me with laughing."

"Well, then, to end the matter at once," said Goodman Brown, considerably nettled, "there is my wife, Faith. It would break her dear little heart; and I'd rather break my own."

"Nay, if that be the case," answered the other, "e'en go thy ways, Goodman Brown. I would not for twenty old women like the one hobbling before us that Faith should come to any harm."

As he spoke he pointed his staff at a female figure on the path, in whom Goodman Brown recognized a very pious and exemplary dame, who had taught him his catechism in youth, and was still his moral and spiritual adviser, jointly with the minister and Deacon Gookin.

"A marvel, truly, that Goody [3] Cloyse should be so far in the wilderness at nightfall," said he. "But with your leave, friend, I shall take a cut through the woods until we have left this Christian woman behind. Being a stranger to you, she might ask whom I was consorting with and whither I was going."

"Be it so," said his fellow-traveller. "Betake you to the woods, and let me keep the path."

Accordingly the young man turned aside, but took care to watch his companion, who advanced softly along the road until he had come within a staff's length of the old dame. She, meanwhile, was making the best of her way, with singular speed for so aged a woman, and mumbling some indistinct words—a prayer, doubtless—as she went. The traveller put forth his staff and touched her withered neck with what seemed the serpent's tail.

"The devil!" screamed the pious old lady.

---

1. Generally, "farmer," but then sometimes denoting any man of humble station, conventionally addressed as "Goodman."
2. The day of the midweek sermon, generally Thursday.
3. A contraction of "Goodwife," then a term of civility in addressing a wife of humble station (*cf.* "Goodman"). Goody Cloyse, like Goody Cory and Martha Carrier, who appear later, were among the "witches" of Salem sentenced in 1692 by the court of magistrates of which Hawthorne's forebear was a member.

"Then Goody Cloyse knows her old friend?" observed the traveller, confronting her and leaning on his writhing stick.

"Ah, forsooth, and is it your worship indeed?" cried the good dame. "Yea, truly is it, and in the very image of my old gossip, Goodman Brown, the grandfather of the silly fellow that now is. But—would your worship believe it?—my broomstick hath strangely disappeared, stolen, as I suspect, by that unhanged witch, Goody Cory, and that, too, when I was all anointed with the juice of smallage,[4] and cinquefoil, and wolf's bane"—

"Mingled with fine wheat and the fat of a new-born babe," said the shape of old Goodman Brown.

"Ah, your worship knows the recipe," cried the old lady, cackling aloud. "So, as I was saying, being all ready for the meeting, and no horse to ride on, I made up my mind to foot it; for they tell me there is a nice young man to be taken into communion to-night. But now your good worship will lend me your arm, and we shall be there in a twinkling."

"That can hardly be," answered her friend. "I may not spare you my arm, Goody Cloyse; but here is my staff, if you will."

So saying, he threw it down at her feet, where, perhaps, it assumed life, being one of the rods which its owner had formerly lent to the Egyptian magi. Of this fact, however, Goodman Brown could not take cognizance. He had cast up his eyes in astonishment, and, looking down again, beheld neither Goody Cloyse nor the serpentine staff, but his fellow-traveller alone, who waited for him as calmly as if nothing had happened.

"That old woman taught me my catechism," said the young man; and there was a world of meaning in this simple comment.

They continued to walk onward, while the elder traveller exhorted his companion to make good speed and persevere in the path, discoursing so aptly that his arguments seemed rather to spring up in the bosom of his auditor than to be suggested by himself. As they went, he plucked a branch of maple to serve for a walking stick, and began to strip it of the twigs and little boughs, which were wet with evening dew. The moment his fingers touched them they became strangely withered and dried up as with a week's sunshine. Thus the pair proceeded, at a good free pace, until suddenly, in a gloomy hollow of the road, Goodman Brown sat himself down on the stump of a tree and refused to go any farther.

"Friend," said he, stubbornly, "my mind is made up. Not another step will I budge on this errand. What if a wretched old woman do choose to go to the devil when I thought she was going to heaven: is that any reason why I should quit my dear Faith and go after her?"

4. Wild celery. In the literature of witchcraft a plant credited with magic powers.

"You will think better of this by and by," said his acquaintance, composedly. "Sit here and rest yourself a while; and when you feel like moving again, there is my staff to help you along."

Without more words, he threw his companion the maple stick, and was as speedily out of sight as if he had vanished into the deepening gloom. The young man sat a few moments by the roadside, applauding himself greatly, and thinking with how clear a conscience he should meet the minister in his morning walk, nor shrink from the eye of good old Deacon Gookin. And what calm sleep would be his that very night, which was to have been spent so wickedly, but so purely and sweetly now, in the arms of Faith! Amidst these pleasant and praiseworthy meditations, Goodman Brown heard the tramp of horses along the road, and deemed it advisable to conceal himself within the verge of the forest, conscious of the guilty purpose that had brought him thither, though now so happily turned from it.

On came the hoof tramps and the voices of the riders, two grave old voices, conversing soberly as they drew near. These mingled sounds appeared to pass along the road, within a few yards of the young man's hiding-place; but, owing doubtless to the depth of the gloom at that particular spot, neither the travellers nor their steeds were visible. Though their figures brushed the small boughs on the wayside, it could not be seen that they intercepted, even for a moment, the faint gleam from the strip of bright sky athwart which they must have passed. Goodman Brown alternately crouched and stood on tiptoe, pulling aside the branches and thrusting forth his head as far as he durst without discerning so much as a shadow. It vexed him the more, because he could have sworn, were such a thing possible, that he recognized the voices of the minister and Deacon Gookin, jogging along quietly, as they were wont to do, when bound to some ordination or ecclesiastical council. While yet within hearing, one of the riders stopped to pluck a switch.

"Of the two, reverend sir," said the voice like the deacon's, "I had rather miss an ordination dinner than to-night's meeting. They tell me that some of our community are to be here from Falmouth and beyond, and others from Connecticut and Rhode Island, besides several of the Indian powwows, who, after their fashion, know almost as much deviltry as the best of us. Moreover, there is a goodly young woman to be taken into communion."

"Mighty well, Deacon Gookin!" replied the solemn old tones of the minister. "Spur up, or we shall be late. Nothing can be done, you know, until I get on the ground."

The hoofs clattered again; and the voices, talking so strangely in the empty air, passed on through the forest, where no church had ever been gathered or solitary Christian prayed. Whither, then, could these holy men be journeying so deep into the heathen wilderness? Young Goodman Brown caught hold of a tree for support, being ready to sink down on the ground, faint and overburdened with the heavy sickness of his heart. He looked up to the sky, doubting whether there really was a heaven above him. Yet there was the blue arch, and the stars brightening in it.

"With heaven above and Faith below, I will yet stand firm against the devil!" cried Goodman Brown.

While he still gazed upward into the deep arch of the firmament and had lifted his hands to pray, a cloud, though no wind was stirring, hurried across the zenith and hid the brightening stars. The blue sky was still visible, except directly overhead, where this black mass of cloud was sweeping swiftly northward. Aloft in the air, as if from the depths of the cloud, came a confused and doubtful sound of voices. Once the listener fancied that he could distinguish the accents of towns-people of his own, men and women, both pious and ungodly, many of whom he had met at the communion table, and had seen others rioting at the tavern. The next moment, so indistinct were the sounds, he doubted whether he had heard aught but the murmur of the old forest, whispering without a wind. Then came a stronger swell of those familiar tones, heard daily in the sunshine at Salem village, but never until now from a cloud of night. There was one voice, of a young woman, uttering lamentations, yet with an uncertain sorrow, and entreating for some favor, which, perhaps, it would grieve her to obtain; and all the unseen multitude, both saints and sinners, seemed to encourage her onward.

"Faith!" shouted Goodman Brown, in a voice of agony and desperation; and the echoes of the forest mocked him, crying, "Faith! Faith!" as if bewildered wretches were seeking her all through the wilderness.

The cry of grief, rage, and terror was yet piercing the night, when the unhappy husband held his breath for a response. There was a scream, drowned immediately in a louder murmur of voices, fading into far-off laughter, as the dark cloud swept away, leaving the clear and silent sky above Goodman Brown. But something fluttered lightly down through the air and caught on the branch of a tree. The young man seized it, and beheld a pink ribbon.

"My Faith is gone!" cried he, after one stupefied moment. "There is no good on earth; and sin is but a name. Come, devil; for to thee is this world given."

And, maddened with despair, so that he laughed loud and long, did Goodman Brown grasp his staff and set forth again, at such a rate that he seemed to fly along the forest path rather than to walk or run. The road grew wilder and drearier and more faintly traced, and vanished at length, leaving him in the heart of the dark wilderness, still rushing onward with the instinct that guides mortal man to evil. The whole forest was peopled with frightful sounds—the creaking of the trees, the howling of wild beasts, and the yell of Indians; while sometimes the wind tolled like a distant church bell, and sometimes gave a broad roar around the traveller, as if all Nature were laughing him to scorn. But he was himself the chief horror of the scene, and shrank not from its other horrors.

"Ha! ha! ha!" roared Goodman Brown when the wind laughed at him. "Let us hear which will laugh loudest. Think not to frighten me with your deviltry. Come witch, come wizard, come Indian powwow, come devil himself, and here comes Goodman Brown. You may as well fear him as he fear you."

In truth, all through the haunted forest there could be nothing more frightful than the figure of Goodman Brown. On he flew among the black pines, brandishing his staff with frenzied gestures, now giving vent to an inspiration of horrid blasphemy, and now shouting forth such laughter as set all the echoes of the forest laughing like demons around him. The fiend in his own shape is less hideous than when he rages in the breast of man. Thus sped the demoniac on his course, until, quivering among the trees, he saw a red light before him, as when the felled trunks and branches of a clearing have been set on fire, and throw up their lurid blaze against the sky, at the hour of midnight. He paused, in a lull of the tempest that had driven him onward, and heard the swell of what seemed a hymn, rolling solemnly from a distance with the weight of many voices. He knew the tune; it was a familiar one in the choir of the village meeting-house. The verse died heavily away, and was lengthened by a chorus, not of human voices, but of all the sounds of the benighted wilderness pealing in awful harmony together. Goodman Brown cried out, and his cry was lost to his own ear by its unison with the cry of the desert.

In the interval of silence he stole forward until the light glared full upon his eyes. At one extremity of an open space, hemmed in by the dark wall of the forest, arose a rock, bearing some rude, natural resemblance either to an altar or a pulpit, and surrounded by four blazing pines, their tops aflame, their stems untouched, like candles at an evening meeting. The mass of foliage that had overgrown the summit of the rock was all on fire, blazing high into the night and fitfully illuminating the whole field. Each pendent twig and leafy festoon was in a blaze. As the red light arose and fell, a numerous congregation alternately shone forth, then disappeared in shadow, and again grew, as it were, out of the darkness, peopling the heart of the solitary woods at once.

"A grave and dark-clad company," quoth Goodman Brown.

In truth they were such. Among them, quivering to and fro between gloom and splendor, appeared faces that would be seen next day at the council board of the province, and others which, Sabbath after Sabbath, looked devoutly heavenward, and benignantly over the crowded pews, from the holiest pulpits in the land. Some affirm that the lady of the governor was there. At least there were high dames well known to her, and wives of honored husbands, and widows, a great multitude, and ancient maidens, all of excellent repute, and fair young girls, who trembled lest their mothers should espy them. Either the sudden gleams of light flashing over the obscure field bedazzled Goodman Brown, or he recognized a score of the church members of Salem village famous for their especial sanctity. Good old Deacon Gookin had arrived, and waited at the skirts of that venerable saint, his revered pastor. But, irreverently consorting with these grave, reputable, and pious people, these elders of the church, these chaste dames and dewy virgins, there were men of dissolute lives and women of spotted fame, wretches given over to all mean and filthy vice, and suspected even of horrid crimes. It was strange to see that the good shrank not from the wicked, nor were the sinners abashed by the saints. Scattered also among their pale-faced enemies were the Indian priests, or powwows, who had often scared their native forest with more hideous incantations than any known to English witchcraft.

"But where is Faith?" thought Goodman Brown; and, as hope came into his heart, he trembled.

Another verse of the hymn arose, a slow and mournful strain, such as the pious love, but joined to words which expressed all that our nature can conceive of sin, and darkly hinted at far more. Unfathomable to mere mortals is the lore of fiends. Verse after verse was sung; and still the chorus of the desert swelled between like the deepest tone of a mighty organ; and with the final peal of that dreadful anthem there came a sound, as if the roaring wind, the rushing streams, the howling beasts, and every other voice of the unconcerted wilderness were mingling and according with the voice of guilty man in homage to the prince of all. The four blazing pines threw up a loftier flame, and obscurely discovered shapes and visages of horror on the smoke wreaths above the impious assembly. At the same moment the fire on the rock shot redly forth and formed a glowing arch above its base, where now appeared a figure. With reverence be it spoken, the figure bore no slight similitude, both in garb and manner, to some grave divine of the New England churches.

"Bring forth the converts!" cried a voice that echoed through the field and rolled into the forest.

At the word, Goodman Brown stepped forth from the shadow of the trees and approached the congregation, with whom he felt a loathful brotherhood by the sympathy of all that was wicked in his heart. He could have well-nigh sworn that the shape of his own dead father beckoned him to advance, looking downward from a smoke wreath, while a woman, with dim features of despair, threw out her hand to warn him back. Was it his mother? But he had no power to retreat one step, nor to resist, even in thought, when the minister and good old Deacon Gookin seized his arms and led him to the blazing rock. Thither came also the slender form of a veiled female, led between Goody Cloyse, that pious teacher of the catechism, and Martha Carrier, who had received the devil's promise to be queen of hell. A rampant hag was she. And there stood the proselytes beneath the canopy of fire.

"Welcome, my children," said the dark figure, "to the communion of your race. Ye have found thus young your nature and your destiny. My children, look behind you!"

They turned; and flashing forth, as it were, in a sheet of flame, the fiend worshippers were seen; the smile of welcome gleamed darkly on every visage.

"There," resumed the sable form, "are all whom ye have reverenced from youth. Ye deemed them holier than yourselves and shrank from your own sin, contrasting it with their lives of righteousness and prayerful aspirations heavenward. Yet here are they all in my worshipping assembly. This night it shall be granted you to know their secret deeds: how hoary-bearded elders of the church have whispered wanton words to the young maids of their households; how many a woman, eager for widows' weeds, has given her husband a drink at bedtime and let him sleep his last sleep in her bosom; how beardless youths have made haste to inherit their fathers' wealth; and how fair damsels—blush not, sweet ones—have dug little graves in the garden, and bidden me, the sole guest, to an infant's funeral. By the sympathy of your human hearts for sin ye shall scent out all the places—whether in church, bedchamber, street, field, or forest—where crime has been committed, and shall exult to behold the whole earth one stain of guilt, one mighty blood spot. Far more than this. It shall be yours to penetrate, in every bosom, the deep mystery of sin, the fountain of all wicked arts, and which inexhaustibly supplies more evil impulses than human power—than my power at its utmost—can make manifest in deeds. And now, my children, look upon each other."

They did so; and, by the blaze of the hell-kindled torches, the wretched man beheld his Faith, and the wife her husband, trembling before that unhallowed altar.

"Lo, there ye stand, my children," said the figure, in a deep and solemn tone, almost sad with its despairing awfulness, as if his once angelic nature could yet mourn for our miserable race. "Depending upon one another's hearts, ye had still hoped that virtue were not all a dream. Now are ye undeceived. Evil is the nature of mankind. Evil must be your only happiness. Welcome again, my children, to the communion of your race."

"Welcome," repeated the fiend worshippers, in one cry of despair and triumph.

And there they stood, the only pair, as it seemed, who were yet hesitating on the verge of wickedness in this dark world. A basin was hollowed, naturally, in the rock. Did it contain water, reddened by the lurid light? or was it blood? or, perchance, a liquid flame? Herein did the shape of evil dip his hand and prepare to lay the mark of baptism upon their foreheads, that they might be partakers of the mystery of sin, more conscious of the secret guilt of others, both in deed and thought, than they could now be of their own. The husband cast one look at his pale wife, and Faith at him. What polluted wretches would the next glance show them to each other, shuddering alike at what they disclosed and what they saw!

"Faith! Faith!" cried the husband, "look up to heaven, and resist the wicked one."

Whether Faith obeyed he knew not. Hardly had he spoken when he found himself amid calm night and solitude, listening to a roar of the wind which died heavily away through the forest. He staggering against the rock, and felt it chill and damp; while a hanging twig, that had been all on fire, besprinkled his cheek with the coldest dew.

The next morning young Goodman Brown came slowly into the street of Salem village, staring around him like a bewildered man. The good old minister was taking a walk along the graveyard to get an appetite for breakfast and meditate his sermon, and bestowed a blessing, as he passed, on Goodman Brown. He shrank from the venerable saint as if to avoid an anathema. Old Deacon Gookin was at domestic worship, and the holy words of his prayer were heard through the open window. "What God doth the wizard pray to?" quoth Goodman Brown. Goody Cloyse, that excellent old Christian, stood in the early sunshine at her own lattice, catechizing a little girl who had brought her a pint of morning's milk. Goodman Brown snatched away the child as from the grasp of the fiend himself. Turning the corner by the meeting-house, he spied the head of Faith, with the pink ribbons, gazing anxiously forth, and bursting into such joy at sight of him that she skipped along the street and almost kissed her husband before the whole village. But Goodman Brown looked sternly and sadly into her face, and passed on without a greeting.

Had Goodman Brown fallen asleep in the forest and only dreamed a wild dream of a witch-meeting?

Be it so if you will; but, alas! it was a dream of evil omen for young Goodman Brown. A stern, a sad, a darkly meditative, a distrustful, if not a desperate man did he become from the night of that fearful dream. On the Sabbath day, when the congregation were singing a holy psalm, he could not listen because an anthem of sin rushed loudly upon his ear and drowned all the blessed strain. When the minister spoke from the pulpit with power and fervid eloquence, and, with his hand on the open Bible, of the sacred truths of our religion, and of saint-like lives and triumphant deaths, and of future bliss or misery unutterable, then did Goodman Brown turn pale, dreading lest the roof should thunder down upon the gray blasphemer and his hearers. Often, awaking suddenly at midnight, he shrank from the bosom of Faith; and at morning or eventide, when the family knelt down at prayer, he scowled and muttered to himself, and gazed sternly at his wife, and turned away. And when he had lived long, and was borne to his grave a hoary corpse, followed by Faith, an aged woman, and children and grandchildren, a goodly procession, besides neighbors not a few, they carved no hopeful verse upon his tombstone, for his dying hour was gloom.

1835, 1846

The Minister's Black Veil

A Parable [5]

The sexton stood in the porch of Milford meeting-house, pulling busily at the bell-rope. The old people of the village came stooping along the street. Children, with bright faces, tripped merrily be-

5. The interpretation of this parable has intrigued generations of readers. The dying speech of Parson Hooper connects the symbol of his black veil with the hypocritical secret sins of mankind. But see also Poe's interpretation in his review of Hawthorne's *Twice-Told Tales*. In this interpretation, the story is associated with *The Scarlet Letter* as much as with "Young Goodman Brown." A clue has also been sought in Hawthorne's footnote to the title of the story, which reads as follows: "Another clergyman in New England, Mr. Joseph Moody, of York, Maine, who died about eighty years since, made himself remarkable by the same eccentricity that is here related of the Reverend Mr. Hooper. In his case, however, the symbol had a different import. In early life he had accidentally killed a beloved friend; and from that day till the hour of his own death, he hid his face from men." Stewart suggests (*Nathaniel Hawthorne*, p. 257) that Hawthorne purposely refrained from emphasizing a single cause for the destructive estrangement of Hooper from mankind. The story first appeared in *The Token* for 1836, and was collected in *Twice-Told Tales* (1837).

side their parents, or mimicked a graver gait, in the conscious dignity of their Sunday clothes. Spruce bachelors looked sidelong at the pretty maidens, and fancied that the Sabbath sunshine made them prettier than on week days. When the throng had mostly streamed into the porch, the sexton began to toll the bell, keeping his eye on the Reverend Mr. Hooper's door. The first glimpse of the clergyman's figure was the signal for the bell to cease its summons.

"But what has good Parson Hooper got upon his face?" cried the sexton in astonishment.

All within hearing immediately turned about, and beheld the semblance of Mr. Hooper, pacing slowly his meditative way towards the meeting-house. With one accord they started, expressing more wonder than if some strange minister were coming to dust the cushions of Mr. Hooper's pulpit.

"Are you sure it is our parson?" inquired Goodman Gray of the sexton.

"Of a certainty it is good Mr. Hooper," replied the sexton. "He was to have exchanged pulpits with Parson Shute, of Westbury; but Parson Shute sent to excuse himself yesterday, being to preach a funeral sermon."

The cause of so much amazement may appear sufficiently slight. Mr. Hooper, a gentlemanly person, of about thirty, though still a bachelor, was dressed with due clerical neatness, as if a careful wife had starched his band, and brushed the weekly dust from his Sunday's garb. There was but one thing remarkable in his appearance. Swathed about his forehead, and hanging down over his face, so low as to be shaken by his breath, Mr. Hooper had on a black veil. On a nearer view it seemed to consist of two folds of crape, which entirely concealed his features, except the mouth and chin, but probably did not intercept his sight, further than to give a darkened aspect to all living and inanimate things. With this gloomy shade before him, good Mr. Hooper walked onward, at a slow and quiet pace, stooping somewhat, and looking on the ground, as is customary with abstracted men, yet nodding kindly to those of his parishioners who still waited on the meeting-house steps. But so wonder-struck were they that his greeting hardly met with a return.

"I can't really feel as if good Mr. Hooper's face was behind that piece of crape," said the sexton.

"I don't like it," muttered an old woman, as she hobbled into the meeting-house. "He has changed himself into something awful, only by hiding his face."

"Our parson has gone mad!" cried Goodman Gray, following him across the threshold.

A rumor of some unaccountable phenomenon had preceded Mr. Hooper into the meeting-house, and set all the congregation astir. Few could refrain from twisting their heads towards the door; many stood upright, and turned directly about; while several little boys clambered upon the seats, and came down again with a terrible racket. There was a general bustle, a rustling of the women's gowns and shuffling of the men's feet, greatly at variance with that hushed repose which should attend the entrance of the minister. But Mr. Hooper appeared not to notice the perturbation of his people. He entered with an almost noiseless step, bent his head mildly to the pews on each side, and bowed as he passed his oldest parishioner, a white-haired great-grandsire, who occupied an arm-chair in the centre of the aisle. It was strange to observe how slowly this venerable man became conscious of something singular in the appearance of his pastor. He seemed not fully to partake of the prevailing wonder, till Mr. Hooper had ascended the stairs, and showed himself in the pulpit, face to face with his congregation, except for the black veil. That mysterious emblem was never once withdrawn. It shook with his measured breath, as he gave out the psalm; it threw its obscurity between him and the holy page, as he read the Scriptures; and while he prayed, the veil lay heavily on his uplifted countenance. Did he seek to hide it from the dread Being whom he was addressing?

Such was the effect of this simple piece of crape, that more than one woman of delicate nerves was forced to leave the meeting-house. Yet perhaps the pale-faced congregation was almost as fearful a sight to the minister, as his black veil to them.

Mr. Hooper had the reputation of a good preacher, but not an energetic one: he strove to win his people heavenward by mild, persuasive influences, rather than to drive them thither by the thunders of the Word. The sermon which he now delivered was marked by the same characteristics of style and manner as the general series of his pulpit oratory. But there was something, either in the sentiment of the discourse itself, or in the imagination of the auditors, which made it greatly the most powerful effort that they had ever heard from their pastor's lips. It was tinged, rather more darkly than usual, with the gentle gloom of Mr. Hooper's temperament. The subject had reference to secret sin, and those sad mysteries which we hide from our nearest and dearest, and would fain conceal from our own consciousness, even forgetting that the Omniscient can detect them. A subtle power was breathed into his words. Each member of the congregation, the most innocent girl, and the man of hardened breast, felt as if the preacher had crept upon them, behind his awful veil, and discovered their hoarded iniquity of deed or thought. Many spread their clasped hands on their bosoms. There was nothing terrible in what Mr. Hooper said, at least, no violence; and yet, with every tremor of his melancholy voice, the hearers quaked. An unsought pathos came hand in hand with awe. So sensible were the audience of some unwonted attribute in their minister, that they longed for a breath of wind to blow aside the veil, almost believing that a stranger's visage would be discovered, though the form, gesture, and voice were those of Mr. Hooper.

At the close of the services, the people hurried out with indecorous confusion, eager to communicate their pent-up amazement, and conscious of lighter spirits the moment they lost sight of the black veil. Some gathered in little circles, huddled closely together, with their mouths all whispering in the centre; some went homeward alone, wrapt in silent meditation; some talked loudly, and profaned the Sabbath day with ostentatious laughter. A few shook their sagacious heads, intimating that they could penetrate the mystery; while one or two affirmed that there was no mystery at all, but only that Mr. Hooper's eyes were so weakened by the midnight lamp, as to require a shade. After a brief interval, forth came good Mr. Hooper also, in the rear of his flock. Turning his veiled face from one group to another, he paid due reverence to the hoary heads, saluted the middle aged with kind dignity as their friend and spiritual guide, greeted the young with mingled authority and love, and laid his hands on the little children's heads to bless them. Such was always his custom on the Sabbath day. Strange and bewildered looks repaid him for his courtesy. None, as on former occasions, aspired to the honor of walking by their pastor's side. Old Squire Saunders, doubtless by an accidental lapse of memory, neglected to invite Mr. Hooper to his table, where the good clergyman had been wont to bless the food, almost every Sunday since his settlement. He returned, therefore, to the parsonage, and, at the moment of closing the door, was observed to look back upon the people, all of whom had their eyes fixed upon the minister. A sad smile gleamed faintly from beneath the black veil, and flickered about his mouth, glimmering as he disappeared.

"How strange," said a lady, "that a simple black veil, such as any woman might wear on her bonnet, should become such a terrible thing on Mr. Hooper's face!"

"Something must surely be amiss with Mr. Hooper's intellects," observed her husband, the physician of the village. "But the strangest part of the affair is the effect of this vagary, even on a sober-minded man like myself. The black veil, though it covers only our pastor's face, throws its influence over his whole person, and makes him ghostlike from head to foot. Do you not feel it so?"

"Truly do I," replied the lady; "and I would not be alone with him for the world. I wonder he is not afraid to be alone with himself!"

"Men sometimes are so," said her husband.

The afternoon service was attended with similar circumstances. At its conclusion, the bell tolled for the funeral of a young lady. The relatives and friends were assembled in the house, and the more distant acquaintances stood about the door, speaking of the good qualities of the deceased, when their talk was interrupted by the appearance of Mr. Hooper, still covered with his black veil. It was now an appropriate emblem. The clergyman stepped into the room where the corpse was laid, and bent over the coffin, to take a last farewell of his deceased parishioner. As he stooped, the veil hung straight down from his forehead, so that, if her eyelids had not been closed forever, the dead maiden might have seen his face. Could Mr. Hooper be fearful of her glance, that he so hastily caught back the black veil? A person who watched the interview between the dead and living, scrupled not to affirm, that, at the instant when the clergyman's features were disclosed, the corpse had slightly shuddered, rustling the shroud and muslin cap, though the countenance retained the composure of death. A superstitious old woman was the only witness of this prodigy. From the coffin Mr. Hooper passed into the chamber of the mourners, and thence to the head of the staircase, to make the funeral prayer. It was a tender and heart-dissolving prayer, full of sorrow, yet so imbued with celestial hopes, that the music of a heavenly harp, swept by the fingers of the dead, seemed faintly to be heard among the saddest accents of the minister. The people trembled, though they but darkly understood him when he prayed that they, and himself, and all of mortal race, might be ready, as he trusted this young maiden had been, for the dreadful hour that should snatch the veil from their faces. The bearers went heavily forth, and the mourners followed, saddening all the street, with the dead before them, and Mr. Hooper in his black veil behind.

"Why do you look back?" said one in the procession to his partner.

"I had a fancy," replied she, "that the minister and the maiden's spirit were walking hand in hand."

"And so had I, at the same moment," said the other.

That night, the handsomest couple in Milford village were to be joined in wedlock. Though reckoned a melancholy man, Mr. Hooper had a placid cheerfulness for such occasions, which often excited a sympathetic smile where livelier merriment would have been thrown away. There was no quality of his disposition which made him more beloved than this. The company at the wedding awaited his arrival with impatience, trusting that the strange awe, which had gathered over him throughout the day, would now be dispelled. But such was not the result. When Mr. Hooper came, the first thing that their eyes rested on was the same horrible black veil, which had added deeper gloom to the funeral, and could portend nothing but evil to the wedding. Such was its immediate effect on the guests that a cloud seemed to have rolled duskily from beneath the black crape, and dimmed the light of the candles. The bridal pair stood up before the minister. But the bride's cold fingers quivered in the tremulous hand of the bridegroom, and her deathlike paleness caused a whisper that the maiden who had been buried a few hours before was come from her grave to be married. If ever another wedding were so dismal, it was that famous one where they tolled the wedding knell. After performing the ceremony, Mr. Hooper raised a glass of wine to his lips, wishing happiness to the new-married couple in a strain of mild pleasantry that ought to have brightened the features of the guests, like a cheerful gleam from the hearth. At that instant, catching a glimpse of his figure in the looking-glass, the black veil involved his own spirit in the horror with which it overwhelmed all others. His frame shuddered, his lips grew white, he spilt the untasted wine upon the carpet, and rushed forth into the darkness. For the Earth, too, had on her Black Veil.

The next day, the whole village of Milford talked of little else than Parson Hooper's black veil. That, and the mystery concealed behind it, supplied a topic for discussion between acquaintances meeting in the street, and good women gossiping at their open windows. It was the first item of news that the tavern-keeper told to his guests. The children babbled of it on their way to school. One imitative little imp covered his face with an old black handkerchief, thereby so affrighting his playmates that the panic seized himself, and he well-nigh lost his wits by his own waggery.

It was remarkable that of all the busybodies and impertinent people in the parish, not one ventured to put the plain question to Mr. Hooper, wherefore he did this thing. Hitherto, whenever there appeared the slightest call for such interference, he had never lacked advisers, nor shown himself averse to be guided by their judgment. If he erred at all, it was by so painful a degree of self-distrust, that even the mildest censure would lead him to consider an indifferent action as a crime. Yet, though so well acquainted with this amiable weakness, no individual among his parishioners chose to make the black veil a subject of friendly remonstrance. There was a feeling of dread, neither plainly confessed nor carefully concealed, which caused each to shift the responsibility upon another, till at length it was found expedient to send a deputation to the church, in order to deal with Mr.

Hooper about the mystery, before it should grow into a scandal. Never did an embassy so ill discharge its duties. The minister received them with friendly courtesy, but became silent, after they were seated, leaving to his visitors, the whole burden of introducing their important business. The topic, it might be supposed, was obvious enough. There was the black veil swathed round Mr. Hooper's forehead, and concealing every feature above his placid mouth, on which, at times, they could perceive the glimmering of a melancholy smile. But that piece of crape, to their imagination, seemed to hang down before his heart, the symbol of a fearful secret between him and them. Were the veil but cast aside, they might speak freely of it, but not till then. Thus they sat a considerable time, speechless, confused, and shrinking uneasily from Mr. Hooper's eye, which they felt to be fixed upon them with an invisible glance. Finally, the deputies returned abashed to their constituents, pronouncing the matter too weighty to be handled, except by a council of the churches, if, indeed, it might not require a general synod.

But there was one person in the village unappalled by the awe with which the black veil had impressed all beside herself. When the deputies returned without an explanation, or even venturing to demand one, she, with the calm energy of her character, determined to chase away the strange cloud that appeared to be settling round Mr. Hooper, every moment more darkly than before. As his plighted wife, it should be her privilege to know what the black veil concealed. At the minister's first visit, therefore, she entered upon the subject with a direct simplicity, which made the task easier both for him and her. After he had seated himself, she fixed her eyes steadfastly upon the veil, but could discern nothing of the dreadful gloom that had so overawed the multitude: it was but a double fold of crape, hanging down from his forehead to his mouth, and slightly stirring with his breath.

"No," she said aloud, and smiling, "there is nothing terrible in this piece of crape, except that it hides a face which I am always glad to look upon. Come, good sir, let the sun shine from behind the cloud. First lay aside your black veil: then tell me why you put it on."

Mr. Hooper's smile glimmered faintly.

"There is an hour to come," said he, "when all of us shall cast aside our veils. Take it not amiss, beloved friend, if I wear this piece of crape till then."

"Your words are a mystery, too," returned the young lady. "Take away the veil from them, at least."

"Elizabeth, I will," said he, "so far as my vow may suffer me. Know, then, this veil is a type and a symbol, and I am bound to wear it ever, both in light and darkness, in solitude and before the gaze of multitudes, and as with strangers, so with my familiar friends. No mortal eye will see it withdrawn. This dismal shade must separate me from the world: even you, Elizabeth, can never come behind it!"

"What grievous affliction hath befallen you," she earnestly inquired, "that you should thus darken your eyes forever?"

"If it be a sign of mourning," replied Mr. Hooper, "I, perhaps, like most other mortals, have sorrows dark enough to be typified by a black veil."

"But what if the world will not believe that it is the type of an innocent sorrow?" urged Elizabeth. "Beloved and respected as you are, there may be whispers that you hide your face under the consciousness of secret sin. For the sake of your holy office, do away this scandal!"

The color rose into her cheeks as she intimated the nature of the rumors that were already abroad in the village. But Mr. Hooper's mildness did not forsake him. He even smiled again—that same sad smile, which always appeared like a faint glimmering of light, proceeding from the obscurity beneath the veil.

"If I hide my face for sorrow, there is cause enough," he merely replied; "and if I cover it for secret sin, what mortal might not do the same?"

And with this gentle, but unconquerable obstinancy did he resist all her entreaties. At length Elizabeth sat silent. For a few moments she appeared lost in thought, considering, probably, what new methods might be tried to withdraw her lover from so dark a fantasy, which, if it had no other meaning, was perhaps a symptom of mental disease. Though of a firmer character than his own, the tears rolled down her cheeks. But, in an instant, as it were, a new feeling took the place of sorrow: her eyes were fixed insensibly on the black veil, when, like a sudden twilight in the air, its terrors fell around her. She arose, and stood trembling before him.

"And do you feel it then, at last?" said he mournfully.

She made no reply, but covered her eyes with her hand, and turned to leave the room. He rushed forward and caught her arm.

"Have patience with me, Elizabeth!" cried he, passionately. "Do not desert me, though this veil must be between us here on earth. Be mine, and hereafter there shall be no veil over my face, no darkness between our souls! It is but a mortal veil—it is not for eternity! O! you know not how lonely I am, and how frightened, to be alone behind my black veil. Do not leave me in this miserable obscurity forever!"

"Lift the veil but once, and look me in the face," said she.

"Never! It cannot be!" replied Mr. Hooper.

"Then farewell!" said Elizabeth.

She withdrew her arm from his grasp, and slowly departed, pausing at the door, to give one long shuddering gaze, that seemed almost to penetrate the mystery of the black veil. But, even amid his grief, Mr. Hooper smiled to think that only a material emblem had separated him from happiness, though the horrors, which it shadowed forth, must be drawn darkly between the fondest of lovers.

From that time no attempts were made to remove Mr. Hooper's black veil, or, by a direct appeal, to discover the secret which it was supposed to hide. By persons who claimed a superiority to popular prejudice, it was reckoned merely an eccentric whim, such as often mingles with the sober actions of men otherwise rational, and tinges them all with its own semblance of insanity. But with the multitude, good Mr. Hooper was irreparably a bugbear. He could not walk the street with any peace of mind, so conscious was he that the gentle and timid would turn aside to avoid him, and that others would make it a point of hardihood to throw themselves in his way. The impertinence of the latter class compelled him to give up his customary walk at sunset to the burial ground; for when he leaned pensively over the gate, there would always be faces behind the gravestones, peeping at his black veil. A fable went the rounds that the stare of the dead people drove him thence. It grieved him, to the very depth of his kind heart, to observe how the children fled from his approach, breaking up their merriest sports, while his melancholy figure was yet afar off. Their instinctive dread caused him to feel more strongly than aught else, that a preternatural horror was interwoven with the threads of the black crape. In truth, his own antipathy to the veil was known to be so great, that he never willingly passed before a mirror, nor stooped to drink at a still fountain, lest, in its peaceful bosom, he should be affrighted by himself. This was what gave plausibility to the whispers, that Mr. Hooper's conscience tortured him for some great crime too horrible to be entirely concealed, or otherwise than so obscurely intimated. Thus, from beneath the black veil, there rolled a cloud into the sunshine, an ambiguity of sin or sorrow, which enveloped the poor minister, so that love or sympathy could never reach him. It was said that ghost and fiend consorted with him there. With self-shudderings and outward terrors, he walked continually in its shadow, groping darkly within his own soul, or gazing through a medium that saddened the whole world. Even the lawless wind, it was believed, respected his dreadful secret, and never blew aside the veil. But still good Mr. Hooper sadly smiled at the pale visages of the worldly throng as he passed by.

Among all its bad influences, the black veil had one desirable effect, of making its wearer a very efficient clergyman. By the aid of his mysterious emblem—for there was no other apparent cause—he became a man of awful power over souls that were in agony for sin. His converts always regarded him with a dread peculiar to themselves, affirming, though but figuratively, that, before he brought them to celestial light, they had been with him behind the black veil. Its gloom, indeed, enabled him to sympathize with all dark affections. Dying sinners cried aloud for Mr. Hooper, and would not yield their breath till he appeared; though ever, as he stooped to whisper consolation, they shuddered at the veiled face so near their own. Such were the terrors of the black veil, even when Death had bared his visage! Strangers came long distances to attend service at his church, with the mere idle purpose of gazing at his figure, because it was forbidden them to behold his face. But many were made to quake ere they departed! Once, during Governor Belcher's[6] administration, Mr. Hooper was appointed to preach the election sermon. Covered with his black veil, he stood before the chief magistrate, the council, and the representatives, and wrought so deep an impression, that the legislative measures of that year were characterized by all the gloom and piety of our earliest ancestral sway.

In this manner Mr. Hooper spent a long life, irreproachable in outward act, yet shrouded in dismal suspicions; kind and loving, though unloved, and dimly feared; a man apart from men, shunned in their health and joy, but ever summoned to their aid in mortal anguish. As years wore on, shedding their snows above his sable veil, he acquired a name throughout the New England churches, and they called him Father Hooper. Nearly all his parishioners, who were of mature age when he was settled, had been borne away by many a funeral: he had one congregation in the church, and a more crowded one in the churchyard; and having wrought so late into the evening, and done his work so well, it was now good Father Hooper's turn to rest.

Several persons were visible by the shaded candle-light, in the death chamber of the old clergyman. Natural connections he had none. But there was the decorously grave, though unmoved physician, seeking only to mitigate the last pangs of the patient whom he could not save. There were the deacons, and other eminently pious members of his church. There, also, was the Reverend Mr.

---

6. Jonathan Belcher was governor of Massachusetts and New Hampshire from 1730 to 1741.

Clark, of Westbury, a young and zealous divine, who had ridden in haste to pray by the bedside of the expiring minister. There was the nurse, no hired handmaiden of death, but one whose calm affection had endured thus long in secrecy, in solitude, amid the chill of age, and would not perish, even at the dying hour. Who, but Elizabeth! And there lay the hoary head of good Father Hooper upon the death pillow, with the black veil still swathed about his brow, and reaching down over his face, so that each more difficult gasp of his faint breath caused it to stir. All through life that piece of crape had hung between him and the world: it had separated him from cheerful brotherhood and woman's love, and kept him in that saddest of all prisons, his own heart; and still it lay upon his face, as if to deepen the gloom of his darksome chamber, and shade him from the sunshine of eternity.

For some time previous, his mind had been confused, wavering doubtfully between the past and the present, and hovering forward, as it were, at intervals, into the indistinctness of the world to come. There had been feverish turns, which tossed him from side to side, and wore away what little strength he had. But in his most convulsive struggles, and in the wildest vagaries of his intellect, when no other thought retained its sober influence, he still showed an awful solicitude lest the black veil should slip aside. Even if his bewildered soul could have forgotten, there was a faithful woman at his pillow, who, with averted eyes, would have covered that aged face, which she had last beheld in the comeliness of manhood. At length the death-stricken old man lay quietly in the torpor of mental and bodily exhaustion, with an imperceptible pulse, and breath that grew fainter and fainter, except when a long, deep, and irregular inspiration seemed to prelude the flight of his spirit.

The minister of Westbury approached the bedside.

"Venerable Father Hooper," said he, "the moment of your release is at hand. Are you ready for the lifting of the veil that shuts in time from eternity?"

Father Hooper at first replied merely by a feeble motion of his head; then, apprehensive, perhaps, that his meaning might be doubtful, he exerted himself to speak.

"Yea," said he, in faint accents, "my soul hath a patient weariness until that veil be lifted."

"And is it fitting," resumed the Reverend Mr. Clark, "that a man so given to prayer, of such a blameless example, holy in deed and thought, so far as mortal judgment may pronounce; is it fitting that a father in the church should leave a shadow on his memory, that may seem to blacken a life so pure? I pray you, my venerable brother, let not this thing be! Suffer us to be gladdened by your triumphant aspect as you go to your reward. Before the veil of eternity be lifted, let me cast aside this black veil from your face!"

And thus speaking, the Reverend Mr. Clark bent forward to reveal the mystery of so many years. But, exerting a sudden energy, that made all the beholders stand aghast, Father Hooper snatched both his hands from beneath the bedclothes, and pressed them strongly on the black veil, resolute to struggle, if the minister of Westbury would contend with a dying man.

"Never!" cried the veiled clergyman. "On earth, never!"

"Dark old man!" exclaimed the affrighted minister, "with what horrible crime upon your soul are you now passing to the judgment?"

Father Hooper's breath heaved; it rattled in his throat; but, with a mighty effort, grasping forward with his hands, he caught hold of life, and held it back till he should speak. He even raised himself in bed; and there he sat, shivering with the arms of death around him, while the black veil hung down, awful, at that last moment, in the gathered terrors of a lifetime. And yet the faint, sad smile, so often there, now seemed to glimmer from its obscurity, and linger on Father Hooper's lips.

"Why do you tremble at me alone?" cried he, turning his veiled face round the circle of pale spectators. "Tremble also at each other! Have men avoided me, and women shown no pity, and children screamed and fled, only for my black veil? What, but the mystery which it obscurely typifies, has made this piece of crape so awful? When the friend shows his inmost heart to his friend; the lover to his best beloved; when man does not vainly shrink from the eye of his Creator, loathsomely treasuring up the secret of his sin; then deem me a monster, for the symbol beneath which I have lived, and die! I look around me, and lo! on every visage a Black Veil!"

While his auditors shrank from one another, in mutual affright, Father Hooper fell back upon his pillow, a veiled corpse, with a faint smile lingering on his lips. Still veiled, they laid him in his coffin, and a veiled corpse they bore him to the grave. The grass of many years has sprung up and withered on that grave; the burial stone is moss-grown, and good Mr. Hooper's face is dust; but awful is still the thought that it mouldered beneath the Black Veil!

1836, 1837

Rappaccini's Daughter [7]

A young man, named Giovanni Guasconti, came, very long ago, from the more southern region of Italy, to pursue his studies at the University of Padua. Giovanni, who had but a scanty supply of gold ducats in his pocket, took lodgings in a high and gloomy chamber of an old edifice which looked not unworthy to have been the palace of a Paduan noble, and which, in fact, exhibited over its entrance the armorial bearings of a family long since extinct. The young stranger, who was not unstudied in the great poem of his country, recollected that one of the ancestors of this family, and perhaps an occupant of this very mansion, had been pictured by Dante as a partaker of the immortal agonies of his Inferno. These reminiscences and associations, together with the tendency to heartbreak natural to a young man for the first time out of his native sphere, caused Giovanni to sigh heavily as he looked around the desolate and ill-furnished apartment.

"Holy Virgin, signor!" cried old Dame Lisabetta, who, won by the youth's remarkable beauty of person, was kindly endeavoring to give the chamber a habitable air, "what a sigh was that to come out of a young man's heart! Do you find this old mansion gloomy? For the love of Heaven, then, put your head out of the window, and you will see as bright sunshine as you have left in Naples."

Guasconti mechanically did as the old woman advised, but could not quite agree with her that the Paduan sunshine was as cheerful as that of southern Italy. Such as it was, however, it fell upon a garden beneath the window and expended its fostering influences on a variety of plants, which seemed to have been cultivated with exceeding care.

"Does this garden belong to the house?" asked Giovanni.

"Heaven forbid, signor, unless it were fruitful of better pot herbs than any that grow there now," answered old Lisabetta. "No; that garden is cultivated by the own hands of Signor Giacomo Rappaccini, the famous doctor, who, I warrant him, has been heard of as

7. It may be part of the perennial charm of this allegorical tale that there has been no general agreement as to its interpretation. In "Rappaccini's Daughter," the symbols and elements are complex, and seem at first to be contradictory. One notes the <u>theme of intellectual arrogance</u> again, in the figures of <u>Rappaccini and Baglioni</u>, reminiscent of such stories as "The Birthmark" and "Ethan Brand." As the consequence of Rappaccini's arrogance, there is the "awful doom" of Beatrice—<u>she is isolated from her kind</u>, as were Young Goodman Brown, Parson Hooper, and Wakefield, for their various mistakes. At the same time, one notes in the love story of Giovanni and Beatrice that Giovanni first saw the garden as an "Eden of poisonous flowers," replete with its "Adam," its particular "tree" (Beatrice's), and its reptile. Thus it forms <u>an association with</u> Hawthorne's <u>attack on the</u> puritanical <u>concept of original depravity</u> in *The Scarlet Letter*. "Rappaccini's Daughter" was first published in the *Democratic Review* for December, 1844, and was collected in *Mosses from an Old Manse* (1846).

far as Naples. It is said that he distils these plants into medicines that are as potent as a charm. Oftentimes you may see the signor doctor at work, and perchance the signora, his daughter, too, gathering the strange flowers that grow in the garden."

The old woman had now done what she could for the aspect of the chamber; and, commending the young man to the protection of the saints, took her departure.

Giovanni still found no better occupation than to look down into the garden beneath his window. From its appearance, he judged it to be one of those botanic gardens which were of earlier date in Padua than elsewhere in Italy or in the world. Or, not improbably, it might once have been the pleasure-place of an opulent family; for there was the ruin of a marble fountain, in the centre, sculptured with rare art, but so wofully shattered that it was impossible to trace the original design from the chaos of remaining fragments. The water, however, continued to gush and sparkle into the sunbeams as cheerfully as ever. A little gurgling sound ascended to the young man's window, and made him feel as if the fountain were an immortal spirit that sung its song unceasingly and without heeding the vicissitudes around it, while one century imbodied it in marble and another scattered the perishable garniture on the soil. All about the pool into which the water subsided grew various plants, that seemed to require a plentiful supply of moisture for the nourishment of gigantic leaves, and, in some instances, flowers gorgeously magnificent. There was one shrub in particular, set in a marble vase in the midst of the pool, that bore a profusion of purple blossoms, each of which had the lustre and richness of a gem; and the whole together made a show so resplendent that it seemed enough to illuminate the garden, even had there been no sunshine. Every portion of the soil was peopled with plants and herbs, which, if less beautiful, still bore tokens of assiduous care, as if all had their individual virtues, known to the scientific mind that fostered them. Some were placed in urns, rich with old carving, and others in common garden pots; some crept serpent-like along the ground or climbed on high, using whatever means of ascent was offered them. One plant had wreathed itself round a statue of Vertumnus,[8] which was thus quite veiled and shrouded in a drapery of hanging foliage, so happily arranged that it might have served a sculptor for a study.

While Giovanni stood at the window he heard a rustling behind a screen of leaves, and became aware that a person was at work in the garden. His figure soon emerged into view, and showed itself to be that of no common laborer, but a tall, emaciated, sallow, and

8. Roman deity of the gardens and orchards, who presided over the change of seasons.

sickly-looking man, dressed in a scholar's garb of black. He was beyond the middle term of life, with gray hair, a thin, gray beard, and a face singularly marked with intellect and cultivation, but which could never, even in his more youthful days, have expressed much warmth of heart.

Nothing could exceed the intentness with which this scientific gardener examined every shrub which grew in his path: it seemed as if he was looking into their inmost nature, making observations in regard to their creative essence, and discovering why one leaf grew in this shape and another in that, and wherefore such and such flowers differed among themselves in hue and perfume. Nevertheless, in spite of this deep intelligence on his part, there was no approach to intimacy between himself and these vegetable existences. On the contrary, he avoided their actual touch or the direct inhaling of their odors with a caution that impressed Giovanni most disagreeably; for the man's demeanor was that of one walking among malignant influences, such as savage beasts, or deadly snakes, or evil spirits, which, should he allow them one moment of license, would wreak upon him some terrible fatality. It was strangely frightful to the young man's imagination to see this air of insecurity in a person cultivating a garden, that most simple and innocent of human toils, and which had been alike the joy and labor of the unfallen parents of the race. Was this garden, then, the Eden of the present world? And this man, with such a perception of harm in what his own hands caused to grow,—was he the Adam?

The distrustful gardener, while plucking away the dead leaves or pruning the too luxuriant growth of the shrubs, defended his hands with a pair of thick gloves. Nor were these his only armor. When, in his walk through the garden, he came to the magnificent plant that hung its purple gems beside the marble fountain, he placed a kind of mask over his mouth and nostrils, as if all this beauty did but conceal a deadlier malice; but, finding his task still too dangerous, he drew back, removed the mask, and called loudly, but in the infirm voice of a person affected with inward disease,—

"Beatrice! Beatrice!"

"Here am I, my father. What would you?" cried a rich and youthful voice from the window of the opposite house—a voice as rich as a tropical sunset, and which made Giovanni, though he knew not why, think of deep hues of purple or crimson and of perfumes heavily delectable. "Are you in the garden?"

"Yes, Beatrice," answered the gardener, "and I need your help."

Soon there emerged from under a sculptured portal the figure of a young girl, arrayed with as much richness of taste as the most splendid of the flowers, beautiful as the day, and with a bloom so deep and vivid that one shade more would have been too much. She looked redundant with life, health, and energy; all of which attributes were bound down and compressed, as it were, and girdled tensely, in their luxuriance, by her virgin zone.[9] Yet Giovanni's fancy must have grown morbid while he looked down into the garden; for the impression which the fair stranger made upon him was as if here were another flower, the human sister of those vegetable ones, as beautiful as they, more beautiful than the richest of them, but still to be touched only with a glove, nor to be approached without a mask. As Beatrice came down the garden path, it was observable that she handled and inhaled the odor of several of the plants which her father had most sedulously avoided.

"Here, Beatrice," said the latter, "see how many needful offices require to be done to our chief treasure. Yet, shattered as I am, my life might pay the penalty of approaching it so closely as circumstances demand. Henceforth, I fear, this plant must be consigned to your sole charge."

"And gladly will I undertake it," cried again the rich tones of the young lady, as she bent towards the magnificent plant and opened her arms as if to embrace it. "Yes, my sister, my splendor, it shall be Beatrice's task to nurse and serve thee; and thou shalt reward her with thy kisses and perfumed breath, which to her is as the breath of life."

Then, with all the tenderness in her manner that was so strikingly expressed in her words, she busied herself with such attentions as the plant seemed to require; and Giovanni, at his lofty window, rubbed his eyes and almost doubted whether it were a girl tending her favorite flower, or one sister performing the duties of affection to another. The scene soon terminated. Whether Dr. Rappaccini had finished his labors in the garden, or that his watchful eye had caught the stranger's face, he now took his daughter's arm and retired. Night was already closing in; oppressive exhalations seemed to proceed from the plants and steal upward past the open window; and Giovanni, closing the lattice, went to his couch and dreamed of a rich flower and beautiful girl. Flower and maiden were different, and yet the same, and fraught with some strange peril in either shape.

But there is an influence in the light of morning that tends to rectify whatever errors of fancy, or even of judgment, we may have incurred during the sun's decline, or among the shadows of the night, or in the less wholesome glow of moonshine. Giovanni's first movement, on starting from sleep, was to throw open the window

---

9. Originally, a belt or girdle. In Mediterranean countries, unmarried women wore a distinctive variety of belt, hence a "virgin zone."

and gaze down into the garden which his dreams had made so fertile of mysteries. He was surprised and a little ashamed to find how real and matter-of-fact an affair it proved to be, in the first rays of the sun which gilded the dew-drops that hung upon leaf and blossom, and, while giving a brighter beauty to each rare flower, brought everything within the limits of ordinary experience. The young man rejoiced that, in the heart of the barren city, he had the privilege of overlooking this spot of lovely and luxuriant vegetation. It would serve, he said to himself, as a symbolic language to keep him in communion with Nature. Neither the sickly and thoughtworn Dr. Giocomo Rappaccini, it is true, nor his brilliant daughter, were now visible; so that Giovanni could not determine how much of the singularity which he attributed to both was due to their own qualities and how much to his wonder-working fancy; but he was inclined to take a most rational view of the whole matter.

In the course of the day he paid his respects to Signor Pietro Baglioni, professor of medicine in the university, a physician of eminent repute, to whom Giovanni had brought a letter of introduction. The professor was an elderly personage, apparently of genial nature, and habits that might almost be called jovial. He kept the young man to dinner, and made himself very agreeable by the freedom and liveliness of his conversation, especially when warmed by a flask or two of Tuscan wine. Giovanni, conceiving that men of science, inhabitants of the same city, must needs be on familiar terms with one another, took an opportunity to mention the name of Dr. Rappaccini. But the professor did not respond with so much cordiality as he had anticipated.

"Ill would it become a teacher of the divine art of medicine," said Professor Pietro Baglioni, in answer to a question of Giovanni, "to withhold due and well-considered praise of a physician so eminently skilled as Rappaccini; but, on the other hand, I should answer it but scantily to my conscience were I to permit a worthy youth like yourself, Signor Giovanni, the son of an ancient friend, to imbibe erroneous ideas respecting a man who might hereafter chance to hold your life and death in his hands. The truth is, our worshipful Dr. Rappaccini has as much science as any member of the faculty —with perhaps one single exception—in Padua, or all Italy; but there are certain grave objections to his professional character."

"And what are they?" asked the young man.

"Has my friend Giovanni any disease of body or heart, that he is so inquisitive about physicians?" said the professor, with a smile. "But as for Rappaccini, it is said of him—and I, who know the man well, can answer for its truth—that he cares infinitely more for science than for mankind. His patients are interesting to him only as subjects for some new experiment. He would sacrifice human life, his own among the rest, or whatever else was dearest to him, for the sake of adding so much as a grain of mustard seed to the great heap of his accumulated knowledge."

"Methinks he is an awful man indeed," remarked Guasconti, mentally recalling the cold and purely intellectual aspect of Rappaccini. "And yet, worshipful professor, is it not a noble spirit? Are there many men capable of so spiritual a love of science?"

"God forbid," answered the professor, somewhat testily; "at least, unless they take sounder views of the healing art than those adopted by Rappaccini. It is his theory that all medicinal virtues are comprised within those substances which we term vegetable poisons. These he cultivates with his own hands, and is said even to have produced new varieties of poison, more horribly deleterious than Nature, without the assistance of this learned person, would ever have plagued the world withal. That the signor doctor does less mischief than might be expected with such dangerous substances is undeniable. Now and then, it must be owned, he has effected, or seemed to effect, a marvellous cure; but, to tell you my private mind, Signor Giovanni, he should receive little credit for such instances of success,—they being probably the work of chance, —but should be held strictly accountable for his failures, which may justly be considered his own work."

The youth might have taken Baglioni's opinions with many grains of allowance had he known that there was a professional warfare of long continuance between him and Dr. Rappaccini, in which the latter was generally thought to have gained the advantage. If the reader be inclined to judge for himself, we refer him to certain black-letter tracts on both sides, preserved in the medical department of the University of Padua.

"I know not, most learned professor," returned Giovanni, after musing on what had been said of Rappaccini's exclusive zeal for science,—"I know not how dearly this physician may love his art; but surely there is one object more dear to him. He has a daughter."

"Aha!" cried the professor, with a laugh. "So now our friend Giovanni's secret is out. You have heard of this daughter, whom all the young men in Padua are wild about, though not half a dozen have ever had the good hap to see her face. I know little of the Signora Beatrice save that Rappaccini is said to have instructed her deeply in his science, and that, young and beautiful as fame reports her, she is already qualified to fill a professor's chair. Perchance her father destines her for mine! Other absurd rumors there be, not worth talking about or listening to. So now, Signor Giovanni, drink off your glass of lachryma." [1]

---

1. In full, Lachryma Christi (tears of Christ), an esteemed Italian wine from the Neapolitan area.

Guasconti returned to his lodgings somewhat heated with the wine he had quaffed, and which caused his brain to swim with strange fantasies in reference to Dr. Rappaccini and the beautiful Beatrice. On his way, happening to pass by a florist's, he bought a fresh bouquet of flowers.

Ascending to his chamber, he seated himself near the window, but within the shadow thrown by the depth of the wall, so that he could look down into the garden with little risk of being discovered. All beneath his eye was a solitude. The strange plants were basking in the sunshine, and now and then nodding gently to one another, as if in acknowledgment of sympathy and kindred. In the midst, by the shattered fountain, grew the magnificent shrub, with its purple gems clustering all over it; they glowed in the air, and gleamed back again out of the depths of the pool, which thus seemed to overflow with colored radiance from the rich reflection that was steeped in it. At first, as we have said, the garden was a solitude. Soon, however,—as Giovanni had half hoped, half feared, would be the case,—a figure appeared beneath the antique sculptured portal, and came down between the rows of plants, inhaling their various perfumes as if she were one of those beings of old classic fable that lived upon sweet odors. On again beholding Beatrice, the young man was even startled to perceive how much her beauty exceeded his recollection of it; so brilliant, so vivid, was its character, that she glowed amid the sunlight, and, as Giovanni whispered to himself, positively illuminated the more shadowy intervals of the garden path. Her face being now more revealed than on the former occasion, he was struck by its expression of simplicity and sweetness,—qualities that had not entered into his idea of her character, and which made him ask anew what manner of mortal she might be. Nor did he fail again to observe, or imagine, an analogy between the beautiful girl and the gorgeous shrub that hung its gemlike flowers over the fountain,—a resemblance which Beatrice seemed to have indulged a fantastic humor in heightening, both by the arrangement of her dress and the selection of its hues.

Approaching the shrub, she threw open her arms, as with a passionate ardor, and drew its branches into an intimate embrace—so intimate that her features were hidden in its leafy bosom and her glistening ringlets all intermingled with the flowers.

"Give me thy breath, my sister," exclaimed Beatrice; "for I am faint with common air. And give me this flower of thine, which I separate with gentlest fingers from the stem and place it close beside my heart."

With these words the beautiful daughter of Rappaccini plucked one of the richest blossoms of the shrub, and was about to fasten it in her bosom. But now, unless Giovanni's draughts of wine had bewildered his senses, a singular incident occurred. A small orange-colored reptile, of the lizard or chameleon species, chanced to be creeping along the path, just at the feet of Beatrice. It appeared to Giovanni,—but, at the distance from which he gazed, he could scarcely have seen anything so minute,—it appeared to him, however, that a drop or two of moisture from the broken stem of the flower descended upon the lizard's head. For an instant the reptile contorted itself violently, and then lay motionless in the sunshine.[2] Beatrice observed this remarkable phenomenon, and crossed herself, sadly, but without surprise; nor did she therefore hesitate to arrange the fatal flower in her bosom. There it blushed, and almost glimmered with the dazzling effect of a precious stone, adding to her dress and aspect the one appropriate charm which nothing else in the world could have supplied. But Giovanni, out of the shadow of his window, bent forward and shrank back, and murmured and trembled.

"Am I awake? Have I my senses?" said he to himself. "What is this being? Beautiful shall I call her, or inexpressibly terrible?"

Beatrice now strayed carelessly through the garden, approaching closer beneath Giovanni's window, so that he was compelled to thrust his head quite out of its concealment in order to gratify the intense and painful curiosity which she excited. At this moment there came a beautiful insect over the garden wall; it had, perhaps, wandered through the city, and found no flowers or verdure among those antique haunts of men until the heavy perfumes of Dr. Rappaccini's shrubs had lured it from afar. Without alighting on the flowers, this winged brightness seemed to be attracted by Beatrice, and lingered in the air and fluttered about her head. Now, here it could not be but that Giovanni Guasconti's eyes deceived him. Be that as it might, he fancied that, while Beatrice was gazing at the insect with childish delight, it grew faint and fell at her feet; its bright wings shivered; it was dead—from no cause that he could discern, unless it were the atmosphere of her breath. Again Beatrice crossed herself and sighed heavily as she bent over the dead insect.

An impulsive movement of Giovanni drew her eyes to the window. There she beheld the beautiful head of the young man—rather a Grecian than an Italian head, with fair, regular features, and a glistening of gold among his ringlets—gazing down upon her like a being that hovered in mid air. Scarcely knowing what he did, Giovanni threw down the bouquet which he had hitherto held in his hand.

2. The presence of the reptile in the garden reminds the reader that Giovanni's first sight of the place had suggested a Garden of Eden of which the Adam was Rappaccini. But here the reptile is a harmless lizard, and the fruit of Beatrice's particular "tree" has killed it.

"Signora," said he, "there are pure and healthful flowers. Wear them for the sake of Giovanni Guasconti."

"Thanks, signor," replied Beatrice, with her rich voice, that came forth as it were like a gush of music, and with a mirthful expression half childish and half woman-like. "I accept your gift, and would fain recompense it with this precious purple flower; but if I toss it into the air it will not reach you. So Signor Guasconti must even content himself with my thanks."

She lifted the bouquet from the ground, and then, as if inwardly ashamed at having stepped aside from her maidenly reserve to respond to a stranger's greeting, passed swiftly homeward through the garden. But few as the moments were, it seemed to Giovanni, when she was on the point of vanishing beneath the sculptured portal, that his beautiful bouquet was already beginning to wither in her grasp. It was an idle thought; there could be no possibility of distinguishing a faded flower from a fresh one at so great a distance.

For many days after this incident the young man avoided the window that looked into Dr. Rappaccini's garden, as if something ugly and monstrous would have blasted his eyesight had he been betrayed into a glance. He felt conscious of having put himself, to a certain extent, within the influence of an unintelligible power by the communication which he had opened with Beatrice. The wisest course would have been, if his heart were in any real danger, to quit his lodgings and Padua itself at once; the next wiser, to have accustomed himself, as far as possible, to the familiar and daylight view of Beatrice—thus bringing her rigidly and systematically within the limits of ordinary experience. Least of all, while avoiding her sight, ought Giovanni to have remained so near this extraordinary being that the proximity and possibility even of intercourse should give a kind of substance and reality to the wild vagaries which his imagination ran riot continually in producing. Guasconti had not a deep heart—or, at all events, its depths were not sounded now; but he had a quick fancy, and an ardent southern temperament, which rose every instant to a higher fever pitch. Whether or no Beatrice possessed those terrible attributes, that fatal breath, the affinity with those so beautiful and deadly flowers which were indicated by what Giovanni had witnessed, she had at least instilled a fierce and subtle poison into his system. It was not love, although her rich beauty was a madness to him; nor horror, even while he fancied her spirit to be imbued with the same baneful essence that seemed to pervade her physical frame; but a wild offspring of both love and horror that had each parent in it, and burned like one and shivered like the other. Giovanni knew not what to dread; still less did he know what to hope; yet hope and dread kept a continual warfare in his breast, alternately vanquishing one another and starting up afresh to renew the contest. Blessed are all simple emotions, be they dark or bright! It is the lurid intermixture of the two that produces the illuminating blaze of the infernal regions.

Sometimes he endeavored to assuage the fever of his spirit by a rapid walk through the streets of Padua or beyond its gates: his footsteps kept time with the throbbings of his brain, so that the walk was apt to accelerate itself to a race. One day he found himself arrested; his arm was seized by a portly personage, who had turned back on recognizing the young man and expended much breath in overtaking him.

"Signor Giovanni! Stay, my young friend!" cried he. "Have you forgotten me? That might well be the case if I were as much altered as yourself."

It was Baglioni, whom Giovanni had avoided ever since their first meeting, from a doubt that the professor's sagacity would look too deeply into his secrets. Endeavoring to recover himself, he stared forth wildly from his inner world into the outer one and spoke like a man in a dream.

"Yes; I am Giovanni Guasconti. You are Professor Pietro Baglioni. Now let me pass!"

"Not yet, not yet, Signor Giovanni Guasconti," said the professor, smiling, but at the same time scrutinizing the youth with an earnest glance. "What! did I grow up side by side with your father? and shall his son pass me like a stranger in these old streets of Padua? Stand still, Signor Giovanni; for we must have a word or two before we part."

"Speedily, then, most worshipful professor, speedily," said Giovanni, with feverish impatience. "Does not your worship see that I am in haste?"

Now, while he was speaking there came a man in black along the street, stooping and moving feebly like a person in inferior health. His face was all overspread with a most sickly and sallow hue, but yet so pervaded with an expression of piercing and active intellect that an observer might easily have overlooked the merely physical attributes and have seen only this wonderful energy. As he passed, this person exchanged a cold and distant salutation with Baglioni, but fixed his eyes upon Giovanni with an intentness that seemed to bring out whatever was within him worthy of notice. Nevertheless, there was a peculiar quietness in the look, as if taking merely a speculative, not a human, interest in the young man.

"It is Dr. Rappaccini!" whispered the professor when the stranger had passed. "Has he ever seen your face before?"

"Not that I know," answered Giovanni, starting at the name.

"He *has* seen you! he must have seen you!" said Baglioni, hastily. "For some purpose or other, this man of science is making a study of you. I know that look of his! It is the same that coldly illuminates his face as he bends over a bird, a mouse, or a butterfly, which, in pursuance of some experiment, he has killed by the perfume of a flower; a look as deep as Nature itself, but without Nature's warmth of love. Signor Giovanni, I will stake my life upon it, you are the subject of one of Rappaccini's experiments!"

"Will you make a fool of me?" cried Giovanni, passionately. "*That,* signor professor, were an untoward experiment."

"Patience! Patience!" replied the imperturbable professor. "I tell thee, my poor Giovanni, that Rappaccini has a scientific interest in thee. Thou hast fallen into fearful hands! And the Signora Beatrice, —what part does she act in this mystery?"

But Guasconti, finding Baglioni's pertinacity intolerable, here broke away, and was gone before the professor could again seize his arm. He looked after the young man intently and shook his head.

"This must not be," said Baglioni to himself. "The youth is the son of my old friend, and shall not come to any harm from which the arcana of medical science can preserve him. Besides, it is too insufferable an impertinence in Rappaccini, thus to snatch the lad out of my own hands, as I may say, and make use of him for his infernal experiments. This daughter of his! It shall be looked to. Perchance, most learned Rappaccini, I may foil you where you little dream of it!"

Meanwhile Giovanni had pursued a circuitous route, and at length found himself at the door of his lodgings. As he crossed the threshold he was met by old Lisabetta, who smirked and smiled, and was evidently desirous to attract his attention; vainly, however, as the ebullition of his feelings had momentarily subsided into a cold and dull vacuity. He turned his eyes full upon the withered face that was puckering itself into a smile, but seemed to behold it not. The old dame, therefore, laid her grasp upon his cloak.

"Signor! signor!" whispered she, still with a smile over the whole breadth of her visage, so that it looked not unlike a grotesque carving in wood, darkened by centuries. "Listen, signor! There is a private entrance into the garden!"

"What do you say?" exclaimed Giovanni, turning quickly about, as if an inanimate thing should start into feverish life. "A private entrance into Dr. Rappaccini's garden?"

"Hush! hush! not so loud!" whispered Lisabetta, putting her hand over his mouth. "Yes; into the worshipful doctor's garden, where you may see all his fine shrubbery. Many a young man in Padua would give gold to be admitted among those flowers."

Giovanni put a piece of gold into her hand.

"Show me the way," said he.

A surmise, probably excited by his conversation with Baglioni, crossed his mind, that this interposition of old Lisabetta might perchance be connected with the intrigue, whatever were its nature, in which the professor seemed to suppose that Dr. Rappaccini was involving him. But such a suspicion, though it disturbed Giovanni, was inadequate to restrain him. The instant that he was aware of the possibility of approaching Beatrice, it seemed an absolute necessity of his existence to do so. It mattered not whether she were angel or demon; he was irrevocably within her sphere, and must obey the law that whirled him onward, in ever-lessening circles, towards a result which he did not attempt to foreshadow; and yet, strange to say, there came across him a sudden doubt whether this intense interest on his part were not delusory; whether it were really of so deep and positive a nature as to justify him in now thrusting himself into an incalculable position; whether it were not merely the fantasy of a young man's brain, only slightly or not at all connected with his heart.

He paused, hesitated, turned half about, but again went on. His withered guide led him along several obscure passages, and finally undid a door, through which, as it was opened, there came the sight and sound of rustling leaves, with the broken sunshine glimmering among them. Giovanni stepped forth, and, forcing himself through the entanglement of a shrub that wreathed its tendrils over the hidden entrance, stood beneath his own window in the open area of Dr. Rappaccini's garden.

How often is it the case that, when impossibilities have come to pass and dreams have condensed their misty substance into tangible realities, we find ourselves calm, and even coldly self-possessed, amid circumstances which it would have been a delirium or joy or agony to anticipate! Fate delights to thwart us thus. Passion will choose his own time to rush upon the scene, and lingers sluggishly behind when an appropriate adjustment of events would seem to summon his appearance. So was it now with Giovanni. Day after day his pulses had throbbed with feverish blood at the improbable idea of an interview with Beatrice, and of standing with her, face to face, in this very garden, basking in the Oriental sunshine of her beauty, and snatching from her full gaze the mystery which he deemed the riddle of his own existence. But now there was a singular and untimely equanimity within his breast. He threw a glance around the garden to discover if Beatrice or her father were present, and, perceiving that he was alone, began a critical observation of the plants.

The aspect of one and all of them dissatisfied him; their gorgeousness seemed fierce, passionate, and even unnatural. There was hardly an individual shrub which a wanderer, straying by himself through a forest, would not have been startled to find growing wild, as if an unearthly face had glared at him out of the thicket. Several also would have shocked a delicate instinct by an appearance of artificialness indicating that there had been such commixture, and, as it were, adultery, of various vegetable species, that the production was no longer of God's making, but the monstrous offspring of man's depraved fancy, glowing with only an evil mockery of beauty. They were probably the result of experiment, which in one or two cases had succeeded in mingling plants individually lovely into a compound possessing the questionable and ominous character that distinguished the whole growth of the garden. In fine, Giovanni recognized but two or three plants in the collection, and those of a kind that he well knew to be poisonous. While busy with these contemplations he heard the rustling of a silken garment, and, turning, beheld Beatrice emerging from beneath the sculptured portal.

Giovanni had not considered with himself what should be his deportment; whether he should apologize for his intrusion into the garden, or assume that he was there with the privity at least, if not by the desire, of Dr. Rappaccini or his daughter; but Beatrice's manner placed him at his ease, though leaving him still in doubt by what agency he had gained admittance. She came lightly along the path and met him near the broken fountain. There was surprise in her face, but brightened by a simple and kind expression of pleasure.

"You are a connoisseur in flowers, signor," said Beatrice, with a smile, alluding to the bouquet, which he had flung her from the window. "It is no marvel, therefore, if the sight of my father's rare collection has tempted you to take a nearer view. If he were here, he could tell you many strange and interesting facts as to the nature and habits of these shrubs; for he has spent a lifetime in such studies, and this garden is his world."

"And yourself, lady," observed Giovanni, "if fame says true,—you likewise are deeply skilled in the virtues indicated by these rich blossoms and these spicy perfumes. Would you deign to be my instructress, I should prove an apter scholar than if taught by Signor Rappaccini himself."

"Are there such idle rumors?" asked Beatrice, with the music of a pleasant laugh. "Do people say that I am skilled in my father's science of plants? What a jest is there! No; though I have grown up among these flowers, I know no more of them than their hues and perfume; and sometimes methinks I would fain rid myself of even that small knowledge. There are many flowers here, and those not

the least brilliant, that shock and offend me when they meet my
eye. But pray, signor, do not believe these stories about my science. <u>Believe nothing of me save what you see with your own
eyes.</u>"

"And must I believe all that I have seen with my own eyes?"
asked Giovanni, pointedly, while the recollection of former scenes
made him shrink. "No, signora; you demand too little of me. Bid
me believe nothing save what comes from your own lips."

It would appear that Beatrice understood him. There came a
deep flush to her cheek; but she looked full into Giovanni's eyes,
and responded to his gaze of uneasy suspicion with a queenlike
haughtiness.

"I do so bid you, signor," she replied. "Forget whatever you
may have fancied in regard to me. If true to the outward senses,
still it may be false in its essence; but the words of Beatrice Rappaccini's lips are true from the depths of the heart outward. Those
you may believe."

A fervor glowed in her whole aspect and beamed upon Giovanni's consciousness like the light of truth itself; but while she
spoke there was a fragrance in the atmosphere around her, rich
and delightful, though evanescent, yet which the young man, from
an indefinable reluctance, scarcely dared to draw into his lungs. It
might be the odor of the flowers. Could it be Beatrice's breath
which thus embalmed her words with a strange richness, as if by
steeping them in her heart? A faintness passed like a shadow over
Giovanni and flitted away; he seemed to gaze through the beautiful
girl's eyes into her transparent soul, and felt no more doubt or
fear.

The tinge of passion that had colored Beatrice's manner vanished; she became gay, and appeared to derive a pure delight from
her communion with the youth not unlike what the maiden of a
lonely island might have felt conversing with a voyager from the
civilized world. Evidently her experience of life had been confined
within the limits of that garden. She talked now about matters as
simple as the daylight or summer clouds, and now asked questions
in reference to the city, or Giovanni's distant home, his friends,
his mother, and his sisters—questions indicating such seclusion,
and such lack of familiarity with modes and forms, that Giovanni
responded as if to an infant. Her spirit gushed out before him like a
fresh rill that was just catching its first glimpse of the sunlight and
wondering at the reflections of earth and sky which were flung into
its bosom. There came thoughts, too, from a deep source, and
fantasies of a gemlike brilliancy, as if diamonds and rubies sparkled upward among the bubbles of the fountain. Ever and anon
there gleamed across the young man's mind a sense of wonder

that he should be walking side by side with the being who had so wrought upon his imagination, whom he had idealized in such hues of terror, in whom he had positively witnessed such manifestations of dreadful attributes,—that he should be conversing with Beatrice like a brother, and should find her so human and so maidenlike. But such reflections were only momentary; the effect of her character was too real not to make itself familiar at once.

In this free intercourse they had strayed through the garden, and now, after many turns among its avenues, were come to the shattered fountain, beside which grew the magnificent shrub, with its treasury of glowing blossoms. A fragrance was diffused from it which Giovanni recognized as identical with that which he had attributed to Beatrice's breath, but incomparably more powerful. As her eyes fell upon it, Giovanni beheld her press her hand to her bosom as if her heart were throbbing suddenly and painfully.

"For the first time in my life," murmured she, addressing the shrub, "I have forgotten thee."

"I remember, signora," said Giovanni, "that you once promised to reward me with one of these living gems for the bouquet which I had the happy boldness to fling to your feet. Permit me now to pluck it as a memorial of this interview."

He made a step towards the shrub with extended hand; but Beatrice darted forward, uttering a shriek that went through his heart like a dagger. She caught his hand and drew it back with the whole force of her slender figure. Giovanni felt her touch thrilling through his fibres.

"Touch it not!" exclaimed she, in a voice of agony. "Not for thy life! It is fatal!"

Then, hiding her face, she fled from him and vanished beneath the sculptured portal. As Giovanni followed her with his eyes, he beheld the emaciated figure and pale intelligence of Dr. Rappaccini, who had been watching the scene, he knew not how long, within the shadow of the entrance.

No sooner was Guasconti alone in his chamber than the image of Beatrice came back to his passionate musings, invested with all the witchery that had been gathering around it ever since his first glimpse of her, and now likewise imbued with a tender warmth of girlish womanhood. She was human; her nature was endowed with all gentle and feminine qualities; she was worthiest to be worshipped; she was capable, surely, on her part, of the height and heroism of love. Those tokens which he had hitherto considered as proofs of a frightful peculiarity in her physical and moral system were now either forgotten, or, by the subtle sophistry of passion transmitted into a golden crown of enchantment, rendering Beatrice the more admirable by so much as she was the more unique.

Whatever had looked ugly was now beautiful; or, if incapable of such a change, it stole away and hid itself among those shapeless half ideas which throng the dim region beyond the daylight of our perfect consciousness. Thus did he spend the night, nor fell asleep until the dawn had begun to awake the slumbering flowers in Dr. Rappaccini's garden, whither Giovanni's dreams doubtless led him. Up rose the sun in his due season, and, flinging his beams upon the young man's eyelids, awoke him to a sense of pain. When thoroughly aroused, he became sensible of a burning and tingling agony in his hand—in his right hand—the very hand which Beatrice had grasped in her own when he was on the point of plucking one of the gemlike flowers. On the back of that hand there was now a purple print like that of four small fingers, and the likeness of a slender thumb upon his wrist.

Oh, how stubbornly does love,—or even that cunning semblance of love which flourishes in the imagination, but strikes no depth of root into the heart,—how stubbornly does it hold its faith until the moment comes when it is doomed to vanish into thin mist! Giovanni wrapped a handkerchief about his hand and wondered what evil thing had stung him, and soon forgot his pain in a reverie of Beatrice.

After the first interview, a second was in the inevitable course of what we call fate. A third; a fourth; and a meeting with Beatrice in the garden was no longer an incident in Giovanni's daily life, but the whole space in which he might be said to live; for the anticipation and memory of that ecstatic hour made up the remainder. Nor was it otherwise with the daughter of Rappaccini. She watched for the youth's appearance, and flew to his side with confidence as unreserved as if they had been playmates from early infancy—as if they were such playmates still. If, by any unwonted chance, he failed to come at the appointed moment, she stood beneath the window and sent up the rich sweetness of her tones to float around him in his chamber and echo and reverberate throughout his heart: "Giovanni! Giovanni! Why tarriest thou! Come down!" And down he hastened into that Eden of poisonous flowers.

But, with all this intimate familiarity, there was still a reserve in Beatrice's demeanor, so rigidly and invariably sustained that the idea of infringing it scarcely occurred to his imagination. By all appreciable signs, they loved; they had looked love with eyes that conveyed the holy secret from the depths of one soul into the depths of the other, as if it were too sacred to be whispered by the way; they had even spoken love in those gushes of passion when their spirits darted forth in articulated breath like tongues of long-hidden flame; and yet there had been no seal of lips, no clasp of hands, nor any slightest caress such as love claims and hallows. He had never touched one of the gleaming ringlets of her hair; her garment—so marked was the physical barrier between them—had never been waved against him by a breeze. On the few occasions when Giovanni had seemed tempted to overstep the limit, Beatrice grew so sad, so stern, and withal wore such a look of desolate separation, shuddering at itself, that not a spoken word was requisite to repel him. At such times he was startled at the horrible suspicions that rose, monster-like, out of the caverns of his heart and stared him in the face; his love grew thin and faint as the morning mist, his doubts alone had substance. But, when Beatrice's face brightened again after the momentary shadow, she was transformed at once from the mysterious, questionable being whom he had watched with so much awe and horror; she was now the beautiful and unsophisticated girl whom he felt his spirit knew with a certainty beyond all other knowledge.

A considerable time had now passed since Giovanni's last meeting with Baglioni. One morning, however, he was disagreeably surprised by a visit from the professor, whom he had scarcely thought of for whole weeks, and would willingly have forgotten still longer. Given up as he had long been to a pervading excitement, he could tolerate no companions except upon condition of their perfect sympathy with his present state of feeling. Such sympathy was not to be expected from Professor Baglioni.

The visitor chatted carelessly for a few moments about the gossip of the city and the university, and then took up another topic.

"I have been reading an old classic author lately," said he, "and met with a story that strangely interested me. Possibly you may remember it.[3] It is of an Indian prince, who sent a beautiful woman as a present to Alexander the Great. She was as lovely as the dawn and gorgeous as the sunset; but what especially distinguished her was a certain rich perfume in her breath—richer than a garden of Persian roses. Alexander, as was natural to a youthful conqueror, fell in love at first sight with this magnificent stranger; but a certain sage physician, happening to be present, discovered a terrible secret in regard to her."

"And what was that?" asked Giovanni, turning his eyes downward to avoid those of the professor.

"That this lovely woman," continued Baglioni, with emphasis, "had been nourished with poisons from her birth upward, until her

---

3. Baglioni's story finds its source in a passage copied by Hawthorne, in his *American Notebooks,* from Sir Thomas Browne's *Vulgar Errors* (1646), Book VII, Caption 17.

whole nature was so imbued with them that she herself had become the deadliest poison in existence. Poison was her element of life. With that rich perfume of her breath she blasted the very air. Her love would have been poison—her embrace death. Is not this a marvellous tale?"

"A childish fable," answered Giovanni, nervously starting from his chair. "I marvel how your worship finds time to read such nonsense among your graver studies."

"By and by," said the professor, looking uneasily about him, "what singular fragrance is this in your apartment? Is it the perfume of your gloves? It is faint, but delicious; and yet, after all, by no means agreeable. Were I to breathe it long, methinks it would make me ill. It is like the breath of a flower; but I see no flowers in the chamber."

"Nor are there any," replied Giovanni, who had turned pale as the professor spoke; "nor, I think, is there any fragrance except in your worship's imagination. Odors, being a sort of element combined of the sensual and the spiritual, are apt to deceive us in this manner. The recollection of a perfume, the bare idea of it, may easily be mistaken for a present reality."

"Ay; but my sober imagination does not often play such tricks," said Baglioni; "and, were I to fancy any kind of odor, it would be that of some vile apothecary drug, wherewith my fingers are likely enough to be imbued. Our worshipful friend Rappaccini, as I have heard, tinctures his medicaments with odors richer than those of Araby. Doubtless, likewise, the fair and learned Signora Beatrice would minister to her patients with draughts as sweet as a maiden's breath; but woe to him that sips them!"

Giovanni's face evinced many contending emotions. The tone in which the professor alluded to the pure and lovely daughter of Rappaccini was a torture to his soul; and yet the intimation of a view of her character, opposite to his own, gave instantaneous distinctness to a thousand dim suspicions, which now grinned at him like so many demons. But he strove hard to quell them and to respond to Baglioni with a true lover's perfect faith.

"Signor professor," said he, "you were my father's friend; perchance, too, it is your purpose to act a friendly part toward his son. I would fain feel nothing towards you save respect and deference; but I pray you to observe, signor, that there is one subject on which we must not speak. You know not the Signora Beatrice. You cannot, therefore, estimate the wrong—the blasphemy, I may even say—that is offered to her character by a light or injurious word."

"Giovanni! my poor Giovanni!" answered the professor, with a calm expression of pity. "I know this wretched girl far better than yourself. You shall hear the truth in respect to the poisoner Rap-

paccini and his poisonous daughter; yes, poisonous as she is beautiful. Listen; for, even should you do violence to my gray hairs, it
shall not silence me. That old fable of the Indian woman has become a truth by the deep and deadly science of Rappaccini and in
the person of the lovely Beatrice."

Giovanni groaned and hid his face.

"Her father," continued Baglioni, "was not restrained by natural
affection from offering up his child in this horrible manner as the
victim of his insane zeal for science; for, let us do him justice, he
is as true a man of science as ever distilled his own heart in an alembic. What, then, will be your fate? Beyond a doubt you are selected as the material of some new experiment. Perhaps the result
is to be death; perhaps a fate more awful still. Rappaccini, with
what he calls the interest of science before his eyes, will hesitate at
nothing."

"It is a dream," muttered Giovanni to himself; "surely it is a
dream."

"But," resumed the professor, "be of good cheer, son of my friend.
It is not yet too late for the rescue. Possibly we may even succeed
in bringing back this miserable child within the limits of ordinary
nature, from which her father's madness has estranged her. Behold
this little silver vase! It was wrought by the hands of the renowned
Benvenuto Cellini,[4] and is well worthy to be a love gift to the
fairest dame in Italy. But its contents are invaluable. One little sip
of this antidote would have rendered the most virulent poisons of
the Borgias[5] innocuous. Doubt not that it will be as efficacious
against those of Rappaccini. Bestow the vase, and the precious
liquid within it, on your Beatrice, and hopefully await the result."

Baglioni laid a small, exquisitely wrought silver vial on the table
and withdrew, leaving what he had said to produce its effect upon
the young man's mind.

"We will thwart Rappaccini yet," thought he, chuckling to himself, as he descended the stairs; "but, let us confess the truth of
him, he is a wonderful man—a wonderful man indeed; a vile empiric, however, in his practice, and therefore not to be tolerated by
those who respect the good old rules of the medical profession."

Throughout Giovanni's whole acquaintance with Beatrice, he
had occasionally, as we have said, been haunted by dark surmises
as to her character; yet so thoroughly had she made herself felt by
him as a simple, natural, most affectionate, and guileless creature,
that the image now held up by Professor Baglioni looked as strange

---

4. Benvenuto Cellini (1500–1571),
famous Italian sculptor, and perhaps the
greatest goldsmith of the Renaissance.
5. Italian family influential in the
papacy and politics (1455–1519),
charged with the poisoning of numerous
enemies.

and incredible as if it were not in accordance with his own original conception. True, there were ugly recollections connected with his first glimpses of the beautiful girl; he could not quite forget the bouquet that withered in her grasp, and the insect that perished amid the sunny air, by no ostensible agency save the fragrance of her breath. These incidents, however, dissolving in the pure light of her character, had no longer the efficacy of facts, but were acknowledged as mistaken fantasies, by whatever testimony of the senses they might appear to be substantiated. There is something truer and more real than what we can see with the eyes and touch with the finger. On such better evidence had Giovanni founded his confidence in Beatrice, though rather by the necessary force of her high attributes than by any deep and generous faith on his part. But now his spirit was incapable of sustaining itself at the height to which the early enthusiasm of passion had exalted it; he fell down, grovelling among earthly doubts, and defiled therewith the pure whiteness of Beatrice's image. Not that he gave her up; but he did distrust. He resolved to institute some decisive test that should satisfy him, once for all, whether there were those dreadful peculiarities in her physical nature which could not be supposed to exist without some corresponding monstrosity of soul. His eyes, gazing down afar, might have deceived him as to the lizard, the insect, and the flowers; but if he could witness, at the distance of a few paces, the sudden blight of one fresh and healthful flower in Beatrice's hand, there would be room for no further question. With this idea he hastened to the florist's and purchased a bouquet that was still gemmed with the morning dew-drops.

It was now the customary hour of his daily interview with Beatrice. Before descending into the garden, Giovanni failed not to look at his figure in the mirror,—a vanity to be expected in a beautiful young man, yet, as displaying itself at that troubled and feverish moment, the token of a certain shallowness of feeling and insincerity of character. He did gaze, however, and said to himself that his features had never before possessed so rich a grace, nor his eyes such vivacity, nor his cheeks so warm a hue of superabundant life.

"At least," thought he, "her poison has not yet insinuated itself into my system. I am no flower to perish in her grasp."

With that thought he turned his eyes on the bouquet, which he had never once laid aside from his hand. A thrill of indefinable horror shot through his frame on perceiving that those dewy flowers were already beginning to droop; they wore the aspect of things that had been fresh and lovely yesterday. Giovanni grew white as marble, and stood motionless before the mirror, staring at his own reflection there as at the likeness of something frightful. He remembered Baglioni's remark about the fragrance that seemed to pervade the chamber. It must have been the poison in his breath! Then he shuddered—shuddered at himself. Recovering from his stupor, he began to watch with curious eye a spider that was busily at work hanging its web from the antique cornice of the apartment, crossing and recrossing the artful system of interwoven lines—as vigorous and active a spider as ever dangled from an old ceiling. Giovanni bent towards the insect, and emitted a deep, long breath. The spider suddenly ceased its toil; the web vibrated with a tremor originating in the body of the small artisan. Again Giovanni sent forth a breath, deeper, longer, and imbued with a venomous feeling out of his heart: he knew not whether he were wicked, or only desperate. The spider made a convulsive gripe with his limbs and hung dead across the window.

"Accursed! accursed!" muttered Giovanni, addressing himself. "Hast thou grown so poisonous that this deadly insect perishes by thy breath?"

At that moment a rich, sweet voice came floating up from the garden.

"Giovanni! Giovanni! It is past the hour! Why tarriest thou? Come down!"

"Yes," muttered Giovanni again. "She is the only being whom my breath may not slay! Would that it might!"

He rushed down, and in an instant was standing before the bright and loving eyes of Beatrice. A moment ago his wrath and despair had been so fierce that he could have desired nothing so much as to wither her by a glance; but with her actual presence there came influences which had too real an existence to be at once shaken off: recollections of the delicate and benign power of her feminine nature, which had so often enveloped him in a religious calm; recollections of many a holy and passionate outgush of her heart, when the pure fountain had been unsealed from its depths and made visible in its transparency to his mental eye; recollections which, had Giovanni known how to estimate them, would have assured him that all this ugly mystery was but an earthly illusion, and that, whatever mist of evil might seem to have gathered over her, the real Beatrice was a heavenly angel. Incapable as he was of such high faith, still her presence had not utterly lost its magic. Giovanni's rage was quelled into an aspect of sullen insensibility. Beatrice, with a quick spiritual sense, immediately felt that there was a gulf of blackness between them which neither he nor she could pass. They walked on together, sad and silent, and came thus to the marble fountain and to its pool of water on the ground, in the midst of which grew the shrub that bore gem-like blossoms. Giovanni was affrighted at the eager enjoyment—the appetite, as it were—with which he found himself inhaling the fragrance of the flowers.

"Beatrice," asked he, abruptly, "whence came this shrub?"

"My father created it," answered she, with simplicity.

"Created it! created it!" repeated Giovanni. "What mean you, Beatrice?"

"He is a man fearfully acquainted with the secrets of Nature," replied Beatrice; "and, at the hour when I first drew breath, this plant sprang from the soil, the offspring of his science, of his intellect, while I was but his earthly child. Approach it not!" continued she, observing with terror that Giovanni was drawing nearer to the shrub. "It has qualities that you little dream of. But I, dearest Giovanni,—I grew up and blossomed with the plant and was nourished with its breath. It was my sister, and I loved it with a human affection; for, alas!—hast thou not suspected it?—there was an awful doom."

Here Giovanni frowned so darkly upon her that Beatrice paused and trembled. But her faith in his tenderness reassured her, and made her blush that she had doubted for an instant.

"There was an awful doom," she continued, "the effect of my father's fatal love of science, which estranged me from all society of my kind. Until Heaven sent thee, dearest Giovanni, oh, how lonely was thy poor Beatrice!"

"Was it a hard doom?" asked Giovanni, fixing his eyes upon her.

"Only of late have I known how hard it was," answered she, tenderly. "Oh, yes; but my heart was torpid, and therefore quiet."

Giovanni's rage broke forth from his sullen gloom like a lightning flash out of a dark cloud.

"Accursed one!" cried he, with venomous scorn and anger. "And, finding thy solitude wearisome, thou hast severed me likewise from all the warmth of life and enticed me into thy region of unspeakable horror!"

"Giovanni!" exclaimed Beatrice, turning her large bright eyes upon his face. The force of his words had not found its way into her mind; she was merely thunderstruck.

"Yes, poisonous thing!" repeated Giovanni, beside himself with passion. "Thou hast done it! Thou hast blasted me! Thou hast filled my veins with poison! Thou hast made me as hateful, as ugly, as loathsome and deadly a creature as thyself—a world's wonder of hideous monstrosity! Now, if our breath be happily as fatal to ourselves as to all others, let us join our lips in one kiss of unutterable hatred, and so die!"

"What has befallen me?" murmured Beatrice, with a low moan out of her heart. "Holy Virgin, pity me, a poor heartbroken child!"

"Thou,—dost thou pray?" cried Giovanni, still with the same

fiendish scorn. "Thy very prayers, as they come from thy lips, taint the atmosphere with death. Yes, yes; let us pray! Let us to church and dip our fingers in the holy water at the portal! They that come after us will perish as by a pestilence! Let us sign crosses in the air! It will be scattering curses abroad in the likeness of holy symbols!"

"Giovanni," said Beatrice, calmly, for her grief was beyond passion, "why dost thou join thyself with me thus in those terrible words? I, it is true, am the horrible thing thou namest me. But thou,—what hast thou to do, save with one other shudder at my hideous misery to go forth out of the garden and mingle with thy race, and forget that there ever crawled on earth such a monster as poor Beatrice?"

"Dost thou pretend ignorance?" asked Giovanni, scowling upon her. "Behold! this power have I gained from the pure daughter of Rappaccini."

There was a swarm of summer insects flitting through the air in search of the food promised by the flower odors of the fatal garden. They circled round Giovanni's head, and were evidently attracted towards him by the same influence which had drawn them for an instant within the sphere of several of the shrubs. He sent forth a breath among them, and smiled bitterly at Beatrice as at least a score of the insects fell dead upon the ground.

"It see it! I see it!" shrieked Beatrice. "It is my father's fatal science! No, no, Giovanni; it was not I! Never! never! I dreamed only to love thee and be with thee a little time, and so to let thee pass away, leaving but thine image in mine heart; for, Giovanni, believe it, though my body be nourished with poison, my spirit is God's creature, and craves love as its daily food. But my father,—he has united us in this fearful sympathy. Yes; spurn me, tread upon me, kill me! Oh, what is death after such words as thine? But it was not I. Not for a world of bliss would I have done it."

Giovanni's passion had exhausted itself in its outburst from his lips. There now came across him a sense, mournful, and not without tenderness, of the intimate and peculiar relationship between Beatrice and himself. They stood, as it were, in an utter solitude, *each alone* which would be made none the less solitary by the densest throng of human life. Ought not, then, the desert of humanity around them to press this insulated pair closer together? If they should be cruel to one another, who was there to be kind to them? Besides, thought Giovanni, might there not still be a hope of his returning within the limits of ordinary nature, and leading Beatrice, the redeemed Beatrice, by the hand? O, weak, and selfish, and unworthy spirit, that could dream of an earthly union and earthly happiness as possible, after such deep love had been so bitterly wronged as was Beatrice's love by Giovanni's blighting words! No, no; there could be no such hope. She must pass heavily, with that broken heart, across the borders of Time—she must bathe her hurts in some fount of paradise, and forget her grief in the light of immortality, and *there* be well.

But Giovanni did not know it.

"Dear Beatrice," said he, approaching her, while she shrank away as always at his approach, but now with different impulse, "dearest Beatrice, our fate is not yet so desperate. Behold! there is a medicine, potent, as a wise physician has assured me, and almost divine in its efficacy. It is composed of ingredients the most opposite to those by which thy awful father has brought this calamity upon thee and me. It is distilled of blessed herbs. Shall we not quaff it together, and thus be purified from evil?"

"Give it me!" said Beatrice, extending her hand to receive the little silver vial which Giovanni took from his bosom. She added, with a peculiar emphasis, "I will drink; but do thou await the result."

She put Baglioni's antidote to her lips; and, at the same moment, the figure of Rappaccini emerged from the portal and came slowly towards the marble fountain. As he drew near, the pale man of science seemed to gaze with a triumphant expression at the beautiful youth and maiden, as might an artist who should spend his life in achieving a picture or a group of statuary and finally be satisfied with his success. He paused; his bent form grew erect with conscious power; he spread out his hands over them in the attitude of a father imploring a blessing upon his children; but those were the same hands that had thrown poison into the stream of their lives. Giovanni trembled. Beatrice shuddered nervously, and pressed her hand upon her heart.

"My daughter," said Rappaccini, "thou art no longer lonely in the world. Pluck one of those precious gems from thy sister shrub and bid thy bridegroom wear it in his bosom. It will not harm him now. My science and the sympathy between thee and him have so wrought within his system that he now stands from common men, as thou dost, daughter of my pride and triumph, from ordinary women. Pass on, then, through the world, most dear to one another and dreadful to all besides!"

"My father," said Beatrice, feebly,—and still as she spoke she kept her hand upon her heart,—"wherefore didst thou inflict this miserable doom upon thy child?"

"Miserable!" exclaimed Rappaccini. "What mean you, foolish girl? Dost thou deem it misery to be endowed with marvellous gifts against which no power nor strength could avail an enemy—misery, to be able to quell the mightiest with a breath—misery, to be as terrible as thou art beautiful? Wouldst thou, then, have preferred the condition of a weak woman, exposed to all evil and capable of none?"

"I would fain have been loved, not feared," murmured Beatrice, sinking down upon the ground. "But now it matters not. I am going, father, where the evil which thou hast striven to mingle with my being will pass away like a dream—like the fragrance of these poisonous flowers, which will no longer taint my breath among the flowers of Eden. Farewell, Giovanni! Thy words of hatred are like lead within my heart; but they, too, will fall away as I ascend. Oh, was there not, from the first, more poison in thy nature than in mine?"

To Beatrice,—so radically had her earthly part been wrought upon by Rappaccini's skill,—as poison had been life, so the powerful antidote was death; and thus the poor victim of man's ingenuity and of thwarted nature, and of the fatality that attends all such efforts of perverted wisdom, perished there, at the feet of her father and Giovanni. Just at that moment Professor Pietro Baglioni looked forth from the window, and called loudly, in a tone of triumph mixed with horror, to the thunderstricken man of science,—

"Rappaccini! Rappaccini! and is *this* the upshot of your experiment!"

1844, 1846

Ethan Brand [6]

A Chapter from an Abortive Romance

Bartram the lime-burner, a rough, heavy-looking man, begrimed with charcoal, sat watching his kiln, at nightfall, while his little son played at building houses with the scattered fragments of marble, when, on the hillside below them, they heard a roar of laughter, not mirthful, but slow, and even solemn, like a wind shaking the boughs of the forest.

---

6. "Ethan Brand" represents the savage culmination of Hawthorne's recurrent theme, the awful consequences of intellectual withdrawal from humanity—the repudiation of involvement with the general heart of man. The germ of the story is found in a memorandum, dated 1844, in *The American Notebooks* (edited by Randall Stewart, p. 106): "The Unpardonable Sin might consist in a want of love and reverence for the Human Soul; in consequence of which, the investigator pried into its dark depths * * * from a cold philosophical curiosity,—content that it should be wicked in whatever kind or degree, and

only desiring to study it out. Would not this, in other words, be the separation of the intellect from the heart?" In the same source (pp. 36–67 *passim*) are detailed descriptions of the principal characters and scenes of this tale, including the lime-kiln; these were written during a holiday that Hawthorne spent near North Adams, Massachusetts, in the summer of 1838. "Ethan Brand" was first published in the *Boston Museum* for January 5, 1850, and was reprinted in the *Dollar Magazine* for May, 1850; it was collected in *The Snow-Image and Other Tales* (London, 1851, Boston, 1852).

"Father, what is that?" asked the little boy, leaving his play, and pressing betwixt his father's knees.

"Oh, some drunken man, I suppose," answered the lime-burner; "some merry fellow from the bar-room in the village, who dared not laugh loud enough within doors lest he should blow the roof of the house off. So here he is, shaking his jolly sides at the foot of Graylock." [7]

"But, father," said the child, more sensitive than the obtuse, middle-aged clown, "he does not laugh like a man that is glad. So the noise frightens me!"

"Don't be a fool, child!" cried his father, gruffly. "You will never make a man, I do believe; there is too much of your mother in you. I have known the rustling of a leaf startle you. Hark! Here comes the merry fellow now. You shall see that there is no harm in him."

Bartram and his little son, while they were talking thus, sat watching the same lime-kiln that had been the scene of Ethan Brand's solitary and meditative life, before he began his search for the Unpardonable Sin. Many years, as we have seen, had now elapsed, since that portentous night when the IDEA was first developed.[8] The kiln, however, on the mountain-side, stood unimpaired, and was in nothing changed since he had thrown his dark thoughts into the intense glow of its furnace, and melted them, as it were, into the one thought that took possession of his life. It was a rude, round, tower-like structure about twenty feet high, heavily built of rough stones, and with a hillock of earth heaped about the larger part of its circumference; so that the blocks and fragments of marble might be drawn by cart-loads, and thrown in at the top. There was an opening at the bottom of the tower, like an oven-mouth, but large enough to admit a man in a stooping posture, and provided with a massive iron door. With the smoke and jets of flame issuing from the chinks and crevices of this door, which seemed to give admittance into the hillside, it resembled nothing so much as the private entrance to the infernal regions, which the shepherds of the Delectable Mountains [9] were accustomed to show to pilgrims.

There are many such lime-kilns in that tract of country, for the purpose of burning the white marble which composes a large part of the substance of the hills. Some of them, built years ago, and long deserted, with weeds growing in the vacant round of the interior, which is open to the sky, and grass and wild-flowers rooting

7. The highest elevation in Massachusetts—Mount Greylock, in the Berkshires.
8. *Cf.* the subtitle of this story, declaring it to be "A Chapter from an Abortive Romance." Another vestige of the longer work survives in the reference to "the Esther of our tale," below.
9. A place of temptation for Christian in Bunyan's *Pilgrim's Progress* (Part II, 1684), which also permitted him to see, in the distance, the Celestial City.

themselves into the chinks of the stones, look already like relics of antiquity, and may yet be overspread with the lichens of centuries to come. Others, where the lime-burner still feeds his daily and night-long fire, afford points of interest to the wanderer among the hills, who seats himself on a log of wood or a fragment of marble, to hold a chat with the solitary man. It is a lonesome, and, when the character is inclined to thought, may be an intensely thought-ful occupation; as it proved in the case of Ethan Brand, who had mused to such strange purpose, in days gone by, while the fire in this very kiln was burning.

The man who now watched the fire was of a different order, and troubled himself with no thoughts save the very few that were requisite to his business. At frequent intervals, he flung back the clashing weight of the iron door, and, turning his face from the insufferable glare, thrust in huge logs of oak, or stirred the immense brands with a long pole. Within the furnace were seen the curling and riotous flames, and the burning marble, almost molten with the intensity of heat; while without, the reflection of the fire quiv-ered on the dark intricacy of the surrounding forest, and showed in the foreground a bright and ruddy little picture of the hut, the spring beside its door, the athletic and coal-begrimed figure of the lime-burner, and the half-frightened child, shrinking into the pro-tection of his father's shadow. And when again the iron door was closed, then reappeared the tender light of the half-full moon, which vainly strove to trace out the indistinct shapes of the neigh-boring mountains; and, in the upper sky, there was a flitting congregation of clouds, still faintly tinged with the rosy sunset, though thus far down into the valley the sunshine had vanished long and long ago.

The little boy now crept still closer to his father, as footsteps were heard ascending the hillside, and a human form thrust aside the bushes that clustered beneath the trees.

"Halloo! who is it?" cried the lime-burner, vexed at his son's timidity, yet half infected by it. "Come forward, and show your-self, like a man, or I'll fling this chunk of marble at your head!"

"You offer me a rough welcome," said a gloomy voice, as the unknown man drew nigh. "Yet I neither claim nor desire a kinder one, even at my own fireside."

To obtain a distincter view, Bartram threw open the iron door of the kiln, whence immediately issued a gush of fierce light, that smote full upon the stranger's face and figure. To a careless eye there appeared nothing very remarkable in his aspect, which was that of a man in a coarse, brown, country-made suit of clothes, tall and thin, with the staff and heavy shoes of a wayfarer. As he advanced, he fixed his eyes—which were very bright—intently upon the brightness of the furnace, as if he beheld, or expected to behold, some object worthy of note within it.

"Good evening, stranger," said the lime-burner; "whence come you, so late in the day?"

"I come from my search," answered the wayfarer; "for, at last, it is finished."

"Drunk!—or crazy!" muttered Bartram to himself. "I shall have trouble with the fellow. The sooner I drive him away, the better."

The little boy, all in a tremble, whispered to his father, and begged him to shut the door of the kiln, so that there might not be so much light; for that there was something in the man's face which he was afraid to look at, yet could not look away from. And, indeed, even the lime-burner's dull and torpid sense began to be impressed by an indescribable something in that thin, rugged, thoughtful visage, with the grizzled hair hanging wildly about it, and those deeply sunken eyes, which gleamed like fires within the entrance of a mysterious cavern. But, as he closed the door, the stranger turned towards him, and spoke in a quiet, familiar way, that made Bartram feel as if he were a sane and sensible man, after all.

"Your task draws to an end, I see," said he. "This marble has already been burning three days. A few hours more will convert the stone to lime."

"Why, who are you?" exclaimed the lime-burner. "You seem as well acquainted with my business as I am myself."

"And well I may be," said the stranger; "for I followed the same craft many a long year, and here, too, on this very spot. But you are a new-comer in these parts. Did you never hear of Ethan Brand?"

"The man that went in search of the Unpardonable Sin?" asked Bartram, with a laugh.

"The same," answered the stranger. "He has found what he sought, and therefore he comes back again."

"What! then you are Ethan Brand himself?" cried the lime-burner, in amazement. "I am a new-comer here, as you say, and they call it eighteen years since you left the foot of Graylock. But, I can tell you, the good folks still talk about Ethan Brand, in the village yonder, and what a strange errand took him away from his lime-kiln. Well, and so you have found the Unpardonable Sin?"

"Even so!" said the stranger, calmly.

"If the question is a fair one," proceeded Bartram, "where might it be?"

Ethan Brand laid his finger on his own heart.

"Here!" replied he.

And then, without mirth in his countenance, but as if moved by an involuntary recognition of the infinite absurdity of seeking throughout the world for what was the closest of all things to himself, and looking into every heart, save his own, for what was hidden in no other breast, he broke into a laugh of scorn. It was the same slow, heavy laugh, that had almost appalled the lime-burner when it heralded the wayfarer's approach.

The solitary mountain-side was made dismal by it. Laughter, when out of place, mistimed, or bursting forth from a disordered state of feeling, may be the most terrible modulation of the human voice. The laughter of one asleep, even if it be a little child,—the madman's laugh,—the wild, screaming laugh of a born idiot,— are sounds that we sometimes tremble to hear, and would always willingly forget. Poets have imagined no utterance of fiends or hobgoblins so fearfully appropriate as a laugh. And even the obtuse lime-burner felt his nerves shaken, as this strange man looked inward at his own heart, and burst into laughter that rolled away into the night, and was indistinctly reverberated among the hills.

"Joe," said he to his little son, "scamper down to the tavern in the village, and tell the jolly fellows there that Ethan Brand has come back, and that he has found the Unpardonable Sin!"

The boy darted away on his errand, to which Ethan Brand made no objection, nor seemed hardly to notice it. He sat on a log of wood, looking steadfastly at the iron door of the kiln. When the child was out of sight, and his swift and light footsteps ceased to be heard treading first on the fallen leaves and then on the rocky mountainpath, the lime-burner began to regret his departure. He felt that the little fellow's presence had been a barrier between his guest and himself, and that he must now deal, heart to heart, with a man who, on his own confession, had committed the one only crime for which Heaven could afford no mercy. That crime, in its indistinct blackness, seemed to overshadow him. The lime-burner's own sins rose up within him, and made his memory riotous with a throng of evil shapes that asserted their kindred with the Master Sin, whatever it might be, which it was within the scope of man's corrupted nature to conceive and cherish. They were all of one family; they went to and fro between his breast and Ethan Brand's, and carried dark greetings from one to the other.

Then Bartram remembered the stories which had grown traditionary in reference to this strange man, who had come upon him like a shadow of the night, and making himself at home in his old place, after so long absence that the dead people, dead and buried for years, would have had more right to be at home, in any familiar spot, than he. Ethan Brand, it was said, had conversed with Satan himself in the lurid blaze of this very kiln. The legend had been matter of mirth heretofore, but looked grisly now. According to this tale, before Ethan Brand departed on his search, he had been accustomed to evoke a fiend from the hot furnace of the lime-kiln, night after night, in order to confer with him about the Unpardonable Sin; the man and the fiend each laboring to frame the image of some mode of guilt which could neither be atoned for nor forgiven. And, with the first gleam of light upon the mountaintop, the fiend crept in at the iron door, there to abide the intensest element of fire, until again summoned forth to share in the dreadful task of extending man's possible guilt beyond the scope of Heaven's else infinite mercy.

While the lime-burner was struggling with the horror of these thoughts, Ethan Brand rose from the log, and flung open the door of the kiln. The action was in such accordance with the idea in Bartram's mind, that he almost expected to see the Evil One issue forth, red-hot from the raging furnace.

"Hold! hold!" cried he, with a tremulous attempt to laugh; for he was ashamed of his fears, although they overmastered him. "Don't, for mercy's sake, bring out your Devil now!"

"Man!" sternly replied Ethan Brand, "what need have I of the Devil? I have left him behind me, on my track. It is with such halfway sinners as you that he busies himself. Fear not, because I open the door. I do but act by old custom, and am going to trim your fire, like a lime-burner, as I was once."

He stirred the vast coals, thrust in more wood, and bent forward to gaze into the hollow prison-house of the fire, regardless of the fierce glow that reddened upon his face. The lime-burner sat watching him, and half suspected this strange guest of a purpose, if not to evoke a fiend, at least to plunge bodily into the flames, and thus vanish from the sight of man. Ethan Brand, however, drew quietly back, and closed the door of the kiln.

"I have looked," said he, "into many a human heart that was seven times hotter with sinful passions than yonder furnace is with fire. But I found not there what I sought. No, not the Unpardonable Sin!"

"What is the Unpardonable Sin?" asked the lime-burner; and then he shrank farther from his companion, trembling lest his question should be answered.

"It is a sin that grew within my own breast," replied Ethan Brand, standing erect, with a pride that distinguishes all enthusiasts of his stamp. "A sin that grew nowhere else! The sin of an intellect that triumphed over the sense of brotherhood with man and reverence for God, and sacrificed everything to its own mighty claims! The only sin that deserves a recompense of immortal agony! Freely, were it to do again, would I incur the guilt. Unshrinkingly I accept the retribution!"

"The man's head is turned," muttered the lime-burner to himself. "He may be a sinner like the rest of us,—nothing more likely, —but, I'll be sworn, he is a madman too."

Nevertheless, he felt uncomfortable at his situation, alone with Ethan Brand on the wild mountain-side, and was right glad to hear the rough murmur of tongues, and the footsteps of what seemed a pretty numerous party, stumbling over the stones and rustling through the underbrush. Soon appeared the whole lazy regiment that was wont to infest the village tavern, comprehending three or four individuals who had drunk flip beside the bar-room fire through all the winters, and smoked their pipes beneath the stoop through all the summers, since Ethan Brand's departure. Laughing boisterously, and mingling all their voices together in unceremonious talk, they now burst into the moonshine and narrow streaks of firelight that illuminated the open space before the lime-kiln. Bartram set the door ajar again, flooding the spot with light, that the whole company might get a fair view of Ethan Brand, and he of them.

There, among other old acquaintances, was a once ubiquitous man, now almost extinct, but whom we were formerly sure to encounter at the hotel of every thriving village throughout the country. It was the stage-agent. The present specimen of the genus was a wilted and smoke-dried man, wrinkled and red-nosed, in a smartly cut, brown, bob-tailed coat, with brass buttons, who, for a length of time unknown, had kept his desk and corner in the bar-room, and was now still puffing what seemed to be the same cigar that he had lighted twenty years before. He had great fame as a dry joker, though, perhaps, less on account of any intrinsic humor than from a certain flavor of brandy-toddy and tobacco-smoke, which impregnated all his ideas and expressions, as well as his person. Another well-remembered, though strangely altered, face was that of Lawyer Giles, as people still called him in courtesy; an elderly ragamuffin, in his soiled shirt-sleeves and tow-cloth trousers. This poor fellow had been an attorney, in what he called his better days, a sharp practitioner, and in great vogue among the village litigants; but flip, and sling, and toddy, and cocktails, imbibed at all hours, morning, noon, and night, had caused him to slide from intellectual to various kinds and degrees of bodily labor, till at last, to adopt his own phrase, he slid into a soap-vat. In other words, Giles was now a soap-boiler, in a small way. He had come to be but the fragment of a human being, a part of one foot having been chopped off by an axe, and an entire hand torn away by the devilish grip of a steam-engine. Yet, though the corporeal hand was gone, a spiritual member remained; for, stretching forth the stump, Giles steadfastly averred that he felt an invisible thumb and fingers with as vivid a sensation as before the real ones were amputated. A maimed and miserable wretch he was; but one, nevertheless, whom the world could not trample on, and had no right to scorn, either in this or any previous stage of his misfortunes, since he had still kept up the courage and spirit of a man, asked nothing in charity, and with his one hand—and that the left one—fought a stern battle against want and hostile circumstances.

Among the throng, too, came another personage, who, with certain points of similarity to Lawyer Giles, had many more of difference. It was the village doctor; a man of some fifty years, whom, at an earlier period of his life, we introduced as paying a professional visit to Ethan Brand during the latter's supposed insanity. He was now a purple-visaged, rude, and brutal, yet half-gentlemanly figure, with something wild, ruined, and desperate in his talk, and in all the details of his gesture and manners. Brandy possessed this man like an evil spirit, and made him as surly and savage as a wild beast, and as miserable as a lost soul; but there was supposed to be in him such wonderful skill, such native gifts of healing, beyond any which medical science could impart, that society caught hold of him, and would not let him sink out of its reach. So, swaying to and fro upon his horse, and grumbling thick accents at the bed-side, he visited all the sick-chambers for miles about among the mountain towns, and sometimes raised a dying man, as it were, by miracle, or quite as often, no doubt, sent his patient to a grave that was dug many a year too soon. The doctor had an everlasting pipe in his mouth, and, as somebody said, in allusion to his habit of swearing, it was always alight with hell-fire.

These three worthies pressed forward, and greeted Ethan Brand each after his own fashion, earnestly inviting him to partake of the contents of a certain black bottle, in which, as they averred, he would find something far better worth seeking for than the Unpardonable Sin. No mind, which has wrought itself by intense and solitary meditation into a high state of enthusiasm, can endure the kind of contact with low and vulgar modes of thought and feeling to which Ethan Brand was now subjected. It made him doubt—and, strange to say, it was a painful doubt—whether he had indeed found the Unpardonable Sin, and found it within himself. The whole question on which he had exhausted life, and more than life, looked like a delusion.

"Leave me," he said bitterly, "ye brute beasts, that have made yourselves so, shrivelling up your souls with fiery liquors! I have done with you. Years and years ago, I groped into your hearts, and found nothing there for my purpose. Get ye gone!"

"Why, you uncivil scoundrel," cried the fierce doctor, "is that the way you respond to the kindness of your best friends? Then let me tell you the truth. You have no more found the Unpardonable Sin than yonder boy Joe has. You are but a crazy fellow,—I told you so twenty years ago,—neither better nor worse than a crazy fellow, and the fit companion of old Humphrey, here!"

He pointed to an old man, shabbily dressed, with long white hair, thin visage, and unsteady eyes. For some years past this aged person had been wandering about among the hills, inquiring of all travellers whom he met for his daughter. The girl, it seemed, had gone off with a company of circus-performers; and occasionally tidings of her came to the village, and fine stories were told of her glittering appearance as she rode on horseback in the ring, or performed marvellous feats on the tight-rope.

The white-haired father now approached Ethan Brand, and gazed unsteadily into his face.

"They tell me you have been all over the earth," said he, wringing his hands with earnestness. "You must have seen my daughter, for she makes a grand figure in the world, and everybody goes to see her. Did she send any word to her old father, or say when she was coming back?"

Ethan Brand's eyes quailed beneath the old man's. That daughter, from whom he so earnestly desired a word of greeting, was the Esther of our tale, the very girl whom, with such cold and remorseless purpose, Ethan Brand had made the subject of a psychological experiment, and wasted, absorbed, and perhaps annihilated her soul, in the process.

"Yes," murmured he, turning away from the hoary wanderer; "it is no delusion. There is an Unpardonable Sin!"

While these things were passing, a merry scene was going forward in the area of cheerful light, beside the spring and before the door of the hut. A number of the youth of the village, young men and girls, had hurried up the hillside, impelled by curiosity to see Ethan Brand, the hero of so many a legend familiar to their childhood. Finding nothing, however, very remarkable in his aspect,— nothing but a sunburnt wayfarer in plain garb and dusty shoes, who sat looking into the fire as if he fancied pictures among the coals, —these young people speedily grew tired of observing him. As it happened, there was other amusement at hand. An old German Jew, travelling with a diorama [1] on his back, was passing down the mountain-road towards the village just as the party turned aside from it, and, in hopes of eking out the profits of the day, the showman had kept them company to the lime-kiln.

---

1. A box or chamber with a lens for viewing enlarged pictures, either transparencies or stereoscopic (three-dimensional) views.

"Come, old Dutchman," cried one of the young men, "let us see your pictures, if you can swear they are worth looking at!"

"Oh, yes, Captain," answered the Jew,—whether as a matter of courtesy or craft, he styled everybody Captain,—"I shall show you, indeed, some very superb pictures!"

So, placing his box in a proper position, he invited the young men and girls to look through the glass orifices of the machine, and proceeded to exhibit a series of the most outrageous scratchings and daubings, as specimens of the fine arts, that ever an itinerant showman had the face to impose upon his circle of spectators. The pictures were worn out, moreover, tattered, full of cracks and wrinkles, dingy with tobacco-smoke, and otherwise in a most pitiable condition. Some purported to be cities, public edifices, and ruined castles in Europe; others represented Napoleon's battles and Nelson's seafights; and in the midst of these would be seen a gigantic, brown, hairy hand,—which might have been mistaken for the Hand of Destiny, though, in truth, it was only the showman's, —pointing its forefinger to various scenes of the conflict, while its owner gave historical illustrations. When, with much merriment at its abominable deficiency of merit, the exhibition was concluded, the German bade little Joe put his head into the box. Viewed through the magnifying-glasses, the boy's round, rosy visage assumed the strangest imaginable aspect of an immense Titanic child, the mouth grinning broadly, and the eyes and every other feature overflowing with fun at the joke. Suddenly, however, that merry face turned pale, and its expression changed to horror, for this easily impressed and excitable child had become sensible that the eye of Ethan Brand was fixed upon him through the glass.

"You make the little man to be afraid, Captain," said the German Jew, turning up the dark and strong outline of his visage, from his stooping posture. "But look again, and, by chance, I shall cause you to see somewhat that is very fine, upon my word!"

Ethan Brand gazed into the box for an instant, and then starting back, looked fixedly at the German. What had he seen? Nothing, apparently; for a curious youth, who had peeped in almost at the same moment, beheld only a vacant space of canvas.

"I remember you now," muttered Ethan Brand to the showman.

"Ah, Captain," whispered the Jew of Nuremberg, with a dark smile, "I find it to be a heavy matter in my show-box,—this Unpardonable Sin! By my faith, Captain, it has wearied my shoulders, this long day, to carry it over the mountain."

"Peace," answered Ethan Brand, sternly, "or get thee into the furnace yonder!"

The Jew's exhibition had scarcely concluded, when a great, elderly dog—who seemed to be his own master, as no person in the company laid claim to him—saw fit to render himself the object of public notice. Hitherto, he had shown himself a very quiet, well-disposed old dog, going round from one to another, and, by way of being sociable, offering his rough head to be patted by any kindly hand that would take so much trouble. But now, all of a sudden, this grave and venerable quadruped, of his own mere motion, and without the slightest suggestion from anybody else, began to run round after his tail, which, to heighten the absurdity of the proceeding, was a great deal shorter than it should have been. Never was seen such headlong eagerness in pursuit of an object that could not possibly be attained; never was heard such a tremendous outbreak of growling, snarling, barking, and snapping,—as if one end of the ridiculous brute's body were at deadly and most unforgivable enmity with the other. Faster and faster, round about went the cur; and faster and still faster fled the unapproachable brevity of his tail; and louder and fiercer grew his yells of rage and animosity; until, utterly exhausted, and as far from the goal as ever, the foolish old dog ceased his performance as suddenly as he had begun it. The next moment he was as mild, quiet, sensible, and respectable in his deportment, as when he first scraped acquaintance with the company.

As may be supposed, the exhibition was greeted with universal laughter, clapping of hands, and shouts of encore, to which the canine performer responded by wagging all that there was to wag of his tail, but appeared totally unable to repeat his very successful effort to amuse the spectators.

Meanwhile, Ethan Brand had resumed his seat upon the log, and moved, it might be, by a perception of some remote analogy between his own case and that of this self-pursuing cur, he broke into the awful laugh, which, more than any other token, expressed the condition of his inward being. From that moment, the merriment of the party was at an end; they stood aghast, dreading lest the inauspicious sound should be reverberated around the horizon, and that mountain would thunder it to mountain, and so the horror be prolonged upon their ears. Then, whispering one to another that it was late,—that the moon was almost down,—that the August night was growing chill,—they hurried homewards, leaving the lime-burner and little Joe to deal as they might with their unwelcome guest. Save for these three human beings, the open space on the hillside was a solitude, set in a vast gloom of forest. Beyond that darksome verge, the firelight glimmered on the stately trunks and almost black foliage of pines, intermixed with the lighter verdure of sapling oaks, maples, and poplars, while here and there lay the gigantic corpses of dead trees, decaying on the leaf-strewn soil. And it seemed to little Joe—a timorous and imaginative child—that the silent forest was holding its breath until some fearful thing should happen.

Ethan Brand thrust more wood into the fire, and closed the door of the kiln; then looking over his shoulder at the lime-burner and his son, he bade, rather than advised, them to retire to rest.

"For myself, I cannot sleep," said he. "I have matters that it concerns me to meditate upon. I will watch the fire, as I used to do in the old time."

"And call the Devil out of the furnace to keep you company, I suppose," muttered Bertram, who had been making intimate acquaintance with the black bottle above mentioned. "But watch, if you like, and call as many devils as you like! For my part, I shall be all the better for a snooze. Come, Joe!"

As the boy followed his father into the hut, he looked back at the wayfarer, and the tears came into his eyes, for his tender spirit had an intuition of the bleak and terrible loneliness in which this man had enveloped himself.

When they had gone, Ethan Brand sat listening to the crackling of the kindled wood, and looking at the little spirts of fire that issued through the chinks of the door. These trifles, however, once so familiar, had but the slightest hold of his attention, while deep within his mind he was reviewing the gradual but marvellous change that had been wrought upon him by the search to which he had devoted himself. He remembered how the night dew had fallen upon him,—how the dark forest had whispered to him,—how the stars had gleamed upon him,—a simple and loving man, watching his fire in the years gone by, and ever musing as it burned. He remembered with what tenderness, with what love and sympathy for mankind, and what pity for human guilt and woe, he had first begun to contemplate those ideas which afterwards became the inspiration of his life; with what reverence he had then looked into the heart of man, viewing it as a temple originally divine, and, however desecrated, still to be held sacred by a brother; with what awful fear he had deprecated the success of his pursuit, and prayed that the Unpardonable Sin might never be revealed to him. Then ensued that vast intellectual development, which, in its progress, disturbed the counterpoise between his mind and heart. The Idea that possessed his life had operated as a means of education; it had gone on cultivating his powers to the highest point of which they were susceptible; it had raised him from the level of an unlettered laborer to stand on a starlit eminence; whither the philosophers of the earth, laden with the lore of universities, might vainly strive to clamber after him. So much for the intellect! But where was the heart? That, indeed, had withered, —had contracted,—had hardened,—had perished! It had ceased to partake of the universal throb. He had lost his hold of the magnetic chain of humanity. He was no longer a brother-man, opening the chambers or the dungeons of our common nature by the key of holy sympathy, which gave him a right to share in all its secrets; he was now a cold observer, looking on mankind as the subject of his experiment, and, at length, converting man and woman to be his puppets, and pulling the wires that moved them to such degrees of crime as were demanded for his study.

Thus Ethan Brand became a fiend. He began to be so from the moment that his moral nature had ceased to keep the pace of improvement with his intellect. And now, as his highest effort and inevitable development,—as the bright and gorgeous flower, and rich, delicious fruit of his life's labor,—he had produced the Unpardonable Sin!

"What more have I to seek? what more to achieve?" said Ethan Brand to himself. "My task is done, and well done!"

Starting from the log with a certain alacrity in his gait and ascending the hillock of earth that was raised against the stone circumference of the lime-kiln, he thus reached the top of the structure. It was a space of perhaps ten feet across, from edge to edge, presenting a view of the upper surface of the immense mass of broken marble with which the kiln was heaped. All these innumerable blocks and fragments of marble were red-hot and vividly on fire, sending up great spouts of blue flame, which quivered aloft and danced madly, as within a magic circle, and sank and rose again, with continual and multitudinous activity. As the lonely man bent forward over this terrible body of fire, the blasting heat smote up against his person with a breath that, it might be supposed, would have scorched and shrivelled him up in a moment.

Ethan Brand stood erect, and raised his arms on high. The blue flames played upon his face, and imparted the wild and ghastly light which alone could have suited its expression; it was that of a fiend on the verge of plunging into his gulf of intensest torment.

"O Mother Earth," cried he, "who are no more my Mother, and into whose bosom this frame shall never be resolved! O mankind, whose brotherhood I have cast off, and trampled thy great heart beneath my feet! O stars of heaven, that shone on me of old, as if to light me onward and upward!—farewell all, and forever. Come, deadly element of Fire,—henceforth my familiar frame! Embrace me, as I do thee!"

That night the sound of a fearful peal of laughter rolled heavily through the sleep of the lime-burner and his little son; dim shapes of horror and anguish haunted their dreams, and seemed still present in the rude hovel, when they opened their eyes to the daylight.

"Up, boy, up!" cried the lime-burner, staring about him. "Thank Heaven, the night is gone, at last; and rather than pass such another, I would watch my lime-kiln, wide awake, for a twelvemonth. This Ethan Brand, with his humbug of an Unpardonable Sin, has done me no such mighty favor, in taking my place!"

He issued from the hut, followed by little Joe, who kept fast hold of his father's hand. The early sunshine was already pouring its gold upon the mountain-tops, and though the valleys were still in shadow, they smiled cheerfully in the promise of the bright day that was hastening onward. The village, completely shut in by hills, which swelled away gently about it, looked as if it had rested peacefully in the hollow of the great hand of Providence. Every dwelling was distinctly visible; the little spires of the two churches pointed upwards, and caught a foreglimmering of brightness from the sun-gilt skies upon their gilded weathercocks. The tavern was astir, and the figure of the old, smoke-dried stage-agent, cigar in mouth, was seen beneath the stoop. Old Graylock was glorified with a golden cloud upon his head. Scattered likewise over the breasts of the surrounding mountains, there were heaps of hoary mist, in fantastic shapes, some of them far down into the valley, others high up towards the summits, and still others, of the same family of mist or cloud, hovering in the gold radiance of the upper atmosphere. Stepping from one to another of the clouds that rested on the hills, and thence to the loftier brotherhood that sailed in air, it seemed almost as if a mortal man might thus ascend into the heavenly regions. Earth was so mingled with sky that it was a day-dream to look at it.

To supply that charm of the familiar and homely, which Nature so readily adopts into a scene like this, the stage coach was rattling down the mountain-road, and the driver sounded his horn, while Echo caught up the notes, and intertwined them into a rich and varied and elaborate harmony, of which the original performer could lay claim to little share. The great hills played a concert among themselves, each contributing a strain of airy sweetness.

Little Joe's face brightened at once.

"Dear father," cried he, skipping cheerily to and fro, "that strange man is gone, and the sky and the mountains all seem glad of it!"

"Yes," growled the lime-burner, with an oath, "but he has let the fire go down, and no thanks to him if five hundred bushels of lime are not spoiled. If I catch the fellow hereabouts again, I shall feel like tossing him into the furnace!"

With his long pole in his hand, he ascended to the top of the kiln. After a moment's pause, he called to his son.

"Come up here, Joe!" said he.

So little Joe ran up the hillock, and stood by his father's side. The marble was all burnt into perfect, snow-white lime. But on its surface, in the midst of the circle,—snow-white too, and thoroughly converted into lime,—lay a human skeleton, in the attitude of a person who, after long toil, lies down to long repose. Within the ribs—strange to say—was the shape of a human heart.

"Was the fellow's heart made of marble?" cried Bartram, in some perplexity at this phenomenon. "At any rate, it is burnt into what looks like special good lime; and, taking all the bones together, my kiln is half a bushel the richer for him."

So saying, the rude lime-burner lifted his pole, and, letting it fall upon the skeleton, the relics of Ethan Brand were crumbled into fragments.

1850, 1851–1852

EDGAR ALLAN POE
(1809–1849)

A century and more after his death, Poe is still among the most popular of American authors. Cheap reprints of his stories and poems circulate even from newsstands, but unlike most authors of extreme popularity, Poe has also exerted a continuous influence on the most advanced writers and critics.

His works are directed toward universal human responses, which change very little, if at all, with the passing of time and events. He influenced the course of creative writing and criticism by emphasizing the art that appeals simultaneously to reason and to emotion, and by insisting that the work of art is not a fragment of the author's life, nor an adjunct to some didactic purpose, but an object created in the cause of beauty—which he defined in its largest spiritual implications. This creative act, according to Poe, involves the utmost concentration and unity, together with the most scrupulous use of words.

This definition of sensibility was directly opposed to the view implicit in the prevailing American literature of Poe's generation, as represented in general by the works of Emerson, Hawthorne, Longfellow, Whittier, and Holmes, all born in the years from 1803 to 1809. These others turned toward Wordsworth, while Poe took Coleridge as his lodestar in his search for a consistent theory of art. Hawthorne's symbolism links him with Poe, but Hawthorne's impulses were too often didactic, while Poe taught no moral lessons except the discipline of beauty. Only in Melville, among the authors before the Civil War, does one find the same sensibility for symbolic expression. The literary tradition of Poe, preserved by European symbolism, especially in France, played a considerable part in shaping the spirit of our twentieth-century literature, particularly in its demand for the intellectual analysis and controlled perception of emotional consciousness.

The familiar legend of Poe is at variance with his actual personality. Finding himself in conflict with the prevailing spirit of his age, he took refuge in the Byronic myth of the lonely and misunderstood artist. Indeed, his neurotic personality sometimes resembled that of his own fictional characters; it is much easier to see now, than it was then, how vastly sublimated are the actual events which first suggested "To Helen" or "Ligeia."

The son of itinerant actors, he was born in Boston, January 19, 1809. His father, David Poe, apparently deserted his wife and disappeared about eighteen months later. Elizabeth Arnold Poe, an English-born actress, died during a tour, in Richmond in 1811, and her infant son became the ward of the Allan family, although he was never legally adopted. John Allan was a substantial Scottish tobacco exporter; Mrs. Allan lavished on the young poet the erratic affections of the childless wife of a somewhat unfaithful husband. In time this situation led to tensions and jealousies which permanently estranged Poe from his foster father; but in youth he enjoyed the genteel and thorough education, with none of the worldly expectations, of a young Virginia gentleman.

Allan's business interests took him abroad, and Poe lived with the family in England and Scotland from 1815 to 1820, attending a fine classical preparatory school at Stoke Newington for three years. When he was eleven, the family returned to Richmond, where he continued his studies at a local academy. His precocious adoration of Jane Stith Stanard, the young mother of a schoolfellow, later inspired the lyric "To Helen," according to his own report. At this period he considered himself engaged to Sarah Elmira Royster. Her father's objections to a stripling with no prospects resulted in her engagement to another while Poe was at the University of Virginia in 1826. His gambling debts prompted Allan to remove him from the University within a year, in spite of his obvious academic competence.

Unable to come to terms with Allan, who wanted to employ him in the business, Poe ran away to Boston, where he published *Tamerlane and Other Poems* (1827), significantly signed "By a Bostonian"; then he disappeared into the army under the name of "Edgar A. Perry." The death of Mrs. Allan produced a temporary reconciliation with Allan, who offered to seek an appointment to West Point for the young sergeant major. Poe secured a discharge from the army, and published *Al Aaraaf, Tamerlane, and Minor Poems* (1829). Before entering West Point (July 1, 1830) he again had a violent disagreement with Allan, who still declined to assure his prospects. Finding himself unsuited to the life at the Academy, he provoked a dismissal by an infraction of duty, and left three weeks before March 6, 1831, when he was officially excluded. Allan, who had married again, refused to befriend him; two years later his death ended all expectations. Meanwhile, in New York, Poe had published *Poems* (1831), again without results that would suggest his ability to survive by writing.

From 1831 to 1835 Poe lived as a hack writer in Baltimore, with his aunt, the motherly Mrs. Maria Poe Clemm, whose daughter, Virginia, later became his wife. This period of poverty and struggle is almost a merciful blank on the record.

In 1832 the Philadelphia *Saturday Courier* published Poe's first five short stories, a part of the *Tales of the Folio Club*. In 1833 his first characteristic short story, combining pseudoscience and terror, won a prize of fifty dollars and publication in the *Baltimore Saturday Visitor*. "MS Found in a Bottle" appeared on October 12, heralding the success of the formula for popular fiction which Poe was slowly developing by a close study of periodical literature. The prize story won him friends, and ultimately an assistant editorship on the Richmond *Southern Literary Messenger* (1835–1837). In September, 1835, Poe secretly married his cousin, Virginia Clemm; the ceremony was repeated publicly in Richmond eight months later, when Virginia was not quite fourteen.

Poe's experience with the *Messenger* set a pattern which was to continue, with minor variations, in later editorial associations. He was a brilliant editor; he secured important contributors; he attracted attention by his own critical articles. He failed through personal instability. His devotion to Virginia was beset by some insecurity never satisfactorily explained; he had periods of quarrelsomeness which estranged him from his editorial associates. Apparently he left the *Messenger* of his own accord, but during a time of strained relations, with a project for a magazine of his own which he long cherished without result.

After a few months in New York, Poe settled down to his period of greatest accomplishment (1838–1844) in Philadelphia. There he was editor of, or associated with, *Burton's Gentleman's Magazine* (1839), *Graham's Magazine* (1841–1842), and *The Saturday Museum* (1843). He became well-known in literary circles as a result of the vitality of his critical articles, which were a by-product of his editorial functions, the publication of new poems and revised versions of others, and the appearance of some of his greatest stories in *Graham's*. He collected from earlier periodicals his *Tales of the Grotesque and Arabesque* (2 vols., 1840). His fame was assured by "The Gold Bug," which won the prize of one hundred dollars offered in 1843 by the Philadelphia *Dollar Newspaper*.

Unable to hold a permanent editorial connection in Philadelphia, Poe moved in 1844 to New York, where he found sporadic employment on the *Evening Mirror* and the *Broadway*

Journal. For some time it had been evident that Virginia must soon die of tuberculosis, and this apprehension, added to grueling poverty, had increased Poe's eccentricities. Even an occasional escape by alcohol could not go unnoticed in anyone for whom only a moderate indulgence was ruinous, and Poe's reputation, in these years, suffered in consequence. His candid reviews and critical articles increased the number of his enemies, who besmirched his reputation by gossip concerning a number of literary ladies with whom his relations were actually indiscreet but innocent. Yet in 1845 he climaxed his literary life. "The Raven" appeared in the *Mirror*, and in *The Raven and Other Poems*, his major volume of poems. His *Tales* also appeared in New York and London. The Poes found a little cottage at Fordham (now part of New York City) in 1846, and Virginia died there the following January. Poe was feverishly at work on *Eureka* (1848), then deemed the work of a demented mind, but now critically important as a "prose poem" in which he attempted to unify the laws of physical science with those of aesthetic reality.

His life ended, as it had been lived, in events so strange that he might have invented them. In 1849, learning that Sarah Elmira Royster, his childhood sweetheart, was a widow, he visited Richmond and secured her consent to marry him. About two months later he left for Philadelphia on a business engagement. Six days thereafter he was found unconscious on the streets of Baltimore, and he died in delirium after four days, on October 7, 1849.

During a short life of poverty, anxiety, and fantastic tragedy Poe achieved the establishment of a new symbolic poetry within the small compass of forty-eight poems; the formalization of the new short story; the invention of the story of detection and the broadening of science fiction; the foundation of a new fiction of psychological analysis and symbolism; and the slow development, in various stages, of an important critical theory and a discipline of analytical criticism.

Of the seven multivolume editions of the *Works*, only two are now in print. *Works of Edgar Allan Poe*, 10 vols., was edited by E. C. Stedman and G. E. Woodberry, 1894–1895, and reprinted in 1914. Unless otherwise noted, this is the source of the present texts. Also reliable is the Virginia Edition, 17 vols., edited by J. A. Harrison, 1902. *The Poems of Edgar Allan Poe*, edited by Killis Campbell, 1917, shows the evolution of the texts; the same editor published a scholarly edition of *Poe's Short Stories*, 1927. *The Complete Poems and Stories of Edgar Allan Poe*, edited by A. H. Quinn and E. H. O'Neill, 1 vol., 1946, is excellent. *Edgar Allan Poe: Representative Selections*, edited by M. Alterton and H. Craig, 1935, contains an excellent critical apparatus.

The standard scholarly biography is *Edgar Allan Poe*, by A. H. Quinn, 1941. Valuable for their critical quality are G. E. Woodberry, *The Life of Edgar Allan Poe, Personal and Literary*, 2 vols., 1885, rev. 1909; Hervey Allen, *Israfel—The Life and Times of Edgar Allan Poe*, 2 vols., 1926; Killis Campbell, *The Mind of Poe and Other Studies*, 1933; N. B. Fagin, *The Histrionic Mr. Poe*, 1949; E. Wagenknecht, *Edgar Allan Poe, The Man behind the Legend*, 1963; and S. P. Moss, *Poe's Literary Battles * * ***, 1963. Some recent criticism includes E. H. Davidson, *Poe, a Critical Study*, 1957; E. W. Parks, *Edgar Allan Poe*, 1964; and Daniel Hoffman, *Poe, Poe, Poe * * ***, 1972. *The Letters of Edgar Allan Poe*, 2 vols., were edited by J. W. Ostrom, 1948.

Romance

Romance, who loves to nod and sing,
With drowsy head and folded wing,
Among the green leaves as they shake
Far down within some shadowy lake,
To me a painted paroquet   5
Hath been—a most familiar bird—
Taught me my alphabet to say,
To lisp my very earliest word,
While in the wild wood I did lie,
A child—with a most knowing eye.   10

Of late, eternal Condor [1] years
So shake the very Heaven on high
With tumult as they thunder by,
I have no time for idle cares
Through gazing on the unquiet sky.   15
And when an hour with calmer wings
Its down upon my spirit flings—
That little time with lyre and rhyme
To while away—forbidden things!
My heart would feel to be a crime   20
Unless it trembled with the strings.

1829

Sonnet—To Science

Science! true daughter of Old Time thou art!
    Who alterest all things with thy peering eyes.
Why preyest thou thus upon the poet's heart,
    Vulture, whose wings are dull realities?
How should he love thee? or how deem thee wise?   5
    Who wouldst not leave him in his wandering
To seek for treasure in the jewelled skies,
    Albeit he soared with an undaunted wing?
Has thou not dragged Diana [2] from her car?
    And driven the Hamadryad from the wood   10
To seek a shelter in some happier star?
    Hast thou not torn the Naiad from her flood,

---

1. The Andean vulture, noted for courage and ruthlessness.
2. Roman goddess, whose "car" was the moon. She was revered for her chastity; cf. "Dian" in "Ulalume."

The Elfin from the green grass, and <u>from me</u> *sees himself as poet*
The summer dream beneath the tamarind [3] tree?

1829   1829, 1845

Lenore [4]

Ah, broken is the golden bowl! [5]—the spirit flown forever!
Let the bell toll!—a saintly soul floats on the Stygian [6] river:—
And, Guy De Vere, hast *thou* no tear?—weep now or never more!
See! on yon drear and rigid bier low lies thy love, Lenore!
Come, let the burial rite be read—the funeral song be sung!—   5
An anthem for the queenliest dead that ever died so young—
A dirge for her the doubly dead in that she died so young.

"Wretches! [7] ye loved her for her wealth, and ye hated her for her
    pride;
And, when she fell in feeble health, ye blessed her—that she
    died:—
How *shall* the ritual, then, be read—the requiem how be sung   10
By you—by yours, the evil eye,—by yours, the slanderous tongue
That did to death the innocence that died, and died so young?"

Peccavimus; [8] yet rave not thus! but let a Sabbath song
Go up to God so solemnly the dead may feel no wrong!
The sweet Lenore hath gone before, with Hope that flew beside,   15
Leaving thee wild for the dear child that should have been thy
    bride—
For her, the fair and debonair, that now so lowly lies,
The life upon her yellow hair, but not within her eyes—
The life still there upon her hair, the death upon her eyes.

"Avaunt!—avaunt! to friends from fiends the indignant ghost is
    riven—   20
From Hell unto a high estate within the utmost Heaven—
From moan and groan to a golden throne beside the King of
    Heaven:—
Let *no* bell toll, then, lest her soul, amid its hallowed mirth,

3. An oriental tree idealized in Eastern poetry.
4. "Lenore" first appeared as "A Pæan" in the 1831 volume, and was revised three times. The final form, given here, appeared in the *Richmond Whig*, September 18, 1849. Originally it was in short lines, indicated in general by the internal rimes in the present text. The dirge for the delicate girl killed by the cruelty or falseness of her family or lover was conventional in romantic poetry; but this poem recalls the poet's resentment at the marriage, which he ascribed to a cruel intrigue, of his sweetheart, Miss Royster, to an older man of wealth; and his grief at the death of his foster mother, Mrs. Allan.
5. *Cf.* Ecclesiastes xii: 6.
6. The river Styx, in Greek mythology, separates the world of the living from the Hades of death.
7. Stanzas 2 and 4, between quotation marks, are the lover's address to the "wretches," Lenore's false friends.
8. We have sinned.

Should catch the note as it doth float up from the damnèd Earth!
And I—to-night my heart is light:—no dirge will I upraise,   25
But waft the angel on her flight with a Pæan of old days!"

1831, 1849

The Sleeper [9]

At midnight, in the month of June,
I stand beneath the mystic moon.
An opiate vapor, dewy, dim,[1]
Exhales from out her golden rim,
And, softly dripping, drop by drop,   5
Upon the quiet mountain top,
Steals drowsily and musically
Into the universal valley.
The rosemary [2] nods upon the grave;
The lily lolls upon the wave;   10
Wrapping the fog about its breast,
The ruin moulders into rest;
Looking like Lethe,[3] see! the lake
A conscious slumber seems to take,
And would not, for the world, awake.   15
All Beauty sleeps!—and lo! where lies
(Her casement open to the skies)
Irene, with her Destinies!

Oh, lady bright! can it be right—
This window open to the night?   20
The wanton airs, from the tree-top,
Laughingly through the lattice drop—
The bodiless airs, a wizard rout,
Flit through thy chamber in and out,
And wave the curtain canopy   25
So fitfully—so carefully—
Above the closed and fringed lid
'Neath which thy slumb'ring soul lies hid,
That, o'er the floor and down the wall,
Like ghosts the shadows rise and fall!   30
Oh, lady dear, hast thou no fear?

9. As "Irene" in the 1831 volume, the poem contained only the substance of "The Sleeper," which emerged in the 1845 volume as given here, after several revisions.
1. The superstition that night air and moonlight had deadly effects, especially on delicate girls, outlived the century.
2. The flower of rosemary connotes fidelity or remembrance; *cf.* Ophelia in *Hamlet*, Act IV, Scene v, l. 174.
3. In Greek mythology, a river of Hades whose water provided forgetfulness.

Why and what art thou dreaming here?
Sure thou art come o'er far-off seas,
A wonder to these garden trees!
Strange is thy pallor! strange thy dress!   35
Strange, above all, thy length of tress,[4]
And this all solemn silentness!

The lady sleeps! Oh, may her sleep,
Which is enduring, so be deep!
Heaven have her in its sacred keep!   40
This chamber changed for one more holy,
This bed for one more melancholy,
I pray to God that she may lie
Forever with unopened eye,
While the dim sheeted ghosts go by!   45

My love, she sleeps! Oh, may her sleep,
As it is lasting, so be deep!
Soft may the worms about her creep![5]
Far in the forest, dim and old,
For her may some tall vault unfold—   50
Some vault that oft hath flung its black
And winged panels fluttering back,
Triumphant, o'er the crested palls,
Of her grand family funerals—

Some sepulchre, remote, alone,   55
Against whose portal she hath thrown,
In childhood, many an idle stone—
Some tomb from out whose sounding door
She ne'er shall force an echo more,
Thrilling to think, poor child of sin!   60
It was the dead who groaned within.

1831, 1845

Israfel [6]

In Heaven a spirit doth dwell
"Whose heart-strings are a lute";
None sing so wildly well

---

4. A familiar superstition held that the hair grew very rapidly just after death. 5. The good taste of this line has been called in question, but the figure was common to the romance of melancholy. Campbell (*The Poems of Edgar Allan Poe*, p. 213) cites Shelley (*Rosalind and Helen*, l. 345): "And the crawling worms were cradling her"; and Byron (*Giaour*, ll. 945–946): "It is as if the dead could feel / The icy worm around them steal * * *."

6. As in "Al Aaraaf," with which this may be compared, Poe here attempts to express a poetic creed, emphasized by the motto which he had printed, either above or below the text, in a number of editions: "And the angel Israfel, [whose

As the angel Israfel,
And the giddy stars (so legends tell)   5
Ceasing their hymns, attend the spell
    Of his voice, all mute.

Tottering above
    In her highest noon,
    The enamored moon   10
Blushes with love,
    While, to listen, the red levin [7]
    (With the rapid Pleiads, even,
    Which were seven) [8]
Pauses in Heaven.   15

And they say (the starry choir
    And the other listening things)
That Israfeli's fire   *Image of fire*
Is owing to that lyre
    By which he sits and sings— *aeolian Harp*   20
The trembling living wire
    Of those unusual strings.

But the skies that angel trod,
    Where deep thoughts are a duty—
Where Love's a grown-up God—   25
    Where the Houri [9] glances are
Imbued with all the beauty
    Which we worship in a star.

Therefore, thou art not wrong,
    Israfeli, who despisest
An unimpassioned song;   30
To thee the laurels belong,
    Best bard, because the wisest!
Merrily live, and long!

The ecstacies above   35
    With thy burning measures suit—

---

heart-strings are a lute,] and who has the sweetest voice of all God's creatures. —KORAN." Except for the phrase within brackets, this quotation was adapted from George Sale's translation of the Koran, Section IV (1734), in which Israfel is represented as one of the four angels beside the throne of God. In 1845 and subsequent editions, Poe interpolated the bracketed words, also the second line of his poem. Campbell (*The Poems of Edgar Allan Poe,* p. 203) finds the source of this line in De Béranger's "Le Refus" (ll. 41–42), which Poe used in 1839 as the motto for "The Fall of the House of Usher," as follows: "Son cœur est un luth suspendu; / Sitôt qu'on le touche il résonne" ("His heart is a suspended lute; Whenever one touches it, it resounds").

7. Lightning.

8. Classic myth saw this constellation as seven sisters, one lost or hidden.

9. A nymph of the Mohammedan paradise.

Thy grief, thy joy, thy hate, thy love,
    With the fervor of thy lute—
Well may the stars be mute!

Yes, Heaven is thine; but this   40
    Is a world of sweets and sours;
    Our flowers are merely—flowers,
And the shadow of thy perfect bliss
    Is the sunshine of ours.

If I could dwell   45
Where Israfel
    Hath dwelt, and he where I,
He might not sing so wildly well
    A mortal melody,
While a bolder note than this might swell   50
From my lyre within the sky.

one of the most perfect of Poe's poetry

1831, 1845

To Helen [1]

Helen, thy beauty is to me
    Like those Nicean [2] barks of yore,
That gently, o'er a perfumed sea,
    The weary, way-worn wanderer bore
To his own native shore.   5

On desperate seas long wont to roam,
    Thy hyacinth hair,[3] thy classic face,
Thy Naiad [4] airs have brought me home
    To the glory that was Greece
And the grandeur that was Rome.[5]   10

1. Poe traced the inspiration of this lyric to "the first purely ideal love of my soul," Mrs. Jane Stith Stanard, a young Richmond neighbor, who died in 1824. Poe approved Lowell's statement that he wrote the first draft a year earlier, at fourteen. It was rigorously revised; the personal element is almost wholly sublimated in the idealization of the tradition of pure beauty in art.

2. No wholly convincing identification has been made. Perhaps Poe used this word merely because it is musical and suggestive. All guesses have suggested Mediterranean and classical associations, referring to cultural pilgrimages of Catullus, Bacchus, or Ulysses, all conforming to the sense of the following three lines. The conjectures, with supporting references, are summarized in Campbell (*Poems*, p. 201); the Catullus theory is added by J. J. Jones in "Poe's 'Nicéan Barks'" (*American Literature*, II, 1931, 433–438).

3. In "Ligeia" (below), Poe associates "the Homeric epithet, 'hyacinthine'" with "raven-black * * * and naturally-curling tresses"; in another story, "The Assignation," a girl's hair resembles the "clustered curls" of "the young hyacinth"; and in classic myth, the flower preserved the memory of Apollo's love for the dead young Hyacinthus. *Cf.* the following phrase, "thy classic face."

4. The naiads of classical myth were nymphs associated with fresh water (lakes, rivers, fountains). *Cf.* "desperate seas," above.

5. Compare these perfect lines with those of the first version (*Poems*, 1831): "To the beauty of fair Greece, / And the grandeur of old Rome."

>   Lo! in yon brilliant window-niche
>   How statue-like I see thee stand!
>   The agate lamp within thy hand,[6]
>   Ah! Psyche, from the regions which
>   Are Holy Land!   15

1823   1831, 1845

The City in the Sea [7]

>   Lo! Death has reared himself a throne
>   In a strange city lying alone
>   Far down within the dim West,
>   Where the good and the bad and the worst and the best
>   Have gone to their eternal rest.   5
>   There shrines and palaces and towers
>   (Time-eaten towers that tremble not!)
>   Resemble nothing that is ours.
>   Around, by lifting winds forgot,
>   Resignedly beneath the sky   10
>   The melancholy waters lie.
>
>   No rays from the holy heaven come down
>   On the long night-time of that town;
>   But light from out the lurid sea
>   Streams up the turrets silently—   15
>   Gleams up the pinnacles far and free—
>   Up domes—up spires—up kingly halls—
>   Up fanes—up Babylon-like [8] walls—
>   Up shadowy long-forgotten bowers
>   Of sculptured ivy and stone flowers—   20
>   Up many and many a marvellous shrine
>   Whose wreathèd friezes intertwine
>   The viol, the violet, and the vine.
>
>   Resignedly beneath the sky
>   The melancholy waters lie.   25
>   So blend the turrets and shadows there

6. Byron's early influence has been perceived in these three lines (Campbell, *Poems,* p. 203); but it has not been recalled that Byron once emulated Leander, the legendary Greek lover, who nightly swam the Hellespont, guided to Hero's arms by her lamp, aloft on a tower. Bryon wrote passionately of these lovers, in *The Bride of Abydos,* II, stanza 1. Lamps and vessels were sometimes made of agate in antiquity, and the stone was a talismanic symbol of immortality.

7. The meanings of this poem are emphasized by its earlier titles: "The Doomed City" (1831); "The City of Sin" (1836). Parallels with Byron and Shelley are noted by Campbell (*Poems,* p. 208), but observe the prevalence, in Poe's poems and tales, of the theme of the dominion of evil.
8. Babylon, in Biblical literature, is the symbol of the wicked city doomed. See, for example, Revelation xvi: 18–19; and Isaiah xiv.

That all seem pendulous in air,
While from a proud tower in the town
Death looks gigantically down.

There open fanes and gaping graves   30
Yawn level with the luminous waves;
But not the riches there that lie
In each idol's diamond eye—
Not the gaily-jewelled dead
Tempt the waters from their bed;   35
For no ripples curl, alas!
Along that wilderness of glass—
No swellings tell that winds may be
Upon some far-off happier sea—
No heavings hint that winds have been   40
On seas less hideously serene.

But lo, a stir is in the air!
The wave—there is a movement there!
As if the towers had thrust aside,
In slightly sinking, the dull tide—   45
As if their tops had feebly given
A void within the filmy Heaven.
The waves have now a redder glow—
The hours are breathing faint and low—
And when, amid no earthly moans,   50
Down, down that town shall settle hence,
Hell, rising from a thousand thrones,
Shall do it reverence.

1831, 1845

The Coliseum [9]

Type of the antique Rome! Rich reliquary
Of lofty contemplation left to Time
By buried centuries of pomp and power!
At length—at length—after so many days
Of weary pilgrimage and burning thirst   5
(Thirst for the springs of lore that in thee lie),
I kneel, an altered and an humble man,
Amid thy shadows, and so drink within
My very soul thy grandeur, gloom, and glory!

9. This appeared, with many minor alterations, in five magazines before being
collected in the volume of 1845. While
Byron's feeling for antiquity is recalled
in several lines, the poem bears the
genuine stamp of Poe, and represents
his best blank verse.

Vastness! and Age! and Memories of Eld! 10
Silence! and Desolation! and dim Night!
I feel ye now—I feel ye in your strength—
O spells more sure than e'er Judæan king [1]
Taught in the gardens of Gethsemane!
O charms more potent than the rapt Chaldee [2] 15
Ever drew down from out the quiet stars!

Here, where a hero fell, a column falls!
Here, where a mimic eagle [3] glared in gold,
A midnight vigil holds the swarthy bat!
Here, where the dames of Rome their gilded hair 20
Waved to the wind, now wave the reed and thistle!
Here, where on golden throne the monarch lolled,
Glides, spectre-like, unto his marble home,
Lit by the wan light of the hornèd moon,
The swift and silent lizard of the stones! 25

But stay! these walls—these ivy-clad arcades—
These mouldering plinths—these sad and blackened shafts—
These vague entablatures—this crumbling frieze—
These shattered cornices—this wreck—this ruin—
These stones—alas! these gray stones—are they all— 30
All of the famed, and the colossal left
By the corrosive Hours to Fate and me?

"Not all"—the Echoes answer me—"not all!
Prophetic sounds and loud arise forever
From us, and from all Ruin, unto the wise, 35
As melody from Memnon [4] to the Sun.
We rule the hearts of mightiest men—we rule
With a despotic sway all giant minds.
We are not impotent—we pallid stones.
Not all our power is gone—not all our fame— 40
Not all the magic of our high renown—
Not all the wonder that encircles us—
Not all the mysteries that in us lie—
Not all the memories that hang upon
And cling around about us as a garment, 45
Clothing us in a robe of more than glory."

1833, 1845

1. Jesus Christ. Gethsemane (l. 14) was the scene of his agony and arrest. *Cf.* Matthew xxvi: 36.
2. The fabled astrologers of antiquity.
3. The image of an eagle in bronze was carried on a standard by the Roman legions.
4. Slain son of the Dawn, or Aurora; his statue on the Nile was said to respond with harp music at the first light of every dawn. *Cf.* Ovid, *Metamorphoses*, Book XIII, following l. 622; Pausanias, I, 42, Section 2.

To One in Paradise [5]

Thou wast all that to me, love,
   For which my soul did pine—
A green isle in the sea, love,
   A fountain and a shrine,
All wreathed with fairy fruits and flowers,   5
   And all the flowers were mine.

Ah, dream too bright to last!
   Ah, starry Hope! that didst arise
But to be overcast!
   A voice from out the Future cries,   10
"On! on!"—but o'er the Past
   (Dim gulf!) my spirit hovering lies
Mute, motionless, aghast!

For, alas! alas! with me
   The light of Life is o'er!   15
   No more—no more—no more—
(Such language holds the solemn sea
   To the sands upon the shore)
Shall bloom the thunder-blasted tree,
   Or the stricken eagle soar!   20

And all my days are trances,
   And all my nightly dreams
Are where thy dark eye glances,
   And where thy footstep gleams—
In what ethereal dances,   25
   By what eternal streams.

1834, 1845

Sonnet—Silence

There are some qualities—some incorporate things,
   That have a double life, which thus is made
A type of that twin entity which springs
   From matter and light, evinced in solid and shade.
There is a two-fold *Silence*—sea and shore—   5
   Body and soul. One dwells in lonely places,
   Newly with grass o'ergrown; some solemn graces,
Some human memories and tearful lore,
Render him terrorless: his name's "No More."

5. Poe's fondness for this dirge, which he published in six versions before the 1845 collection, supports the theory that it refers to Miss Royster, lost sweetheart of his youth, whom he regarded symbolically as dead.

He is the corporate Silence: dread him not!   10
  No power hath he of evil in himself;
But should some urgent fate (untimely lot!)
  Bring thee to meet his shadow (nameless elf,
That haunteth the lone regions where hath trod
No foot of man), commend thyself to God!   15

1840, 1845

Dream-Land

By a route obscure and lonely,
Haunted by ill angels only,
Where an Eidolon,[6] named NIGHT,
On a black throne reigns upright,
I have reached these lands but newly   5
From an ultimate dim Thule[7]—
From a wild weird clime that lieth, sublime,
    Out of SPACE—out of TIME.

Bottomless vales and boundless floods,
And chasms, and caves, and Titan woods,   10
With forms that no man can discover
For the tears that drip all over;
Mountains toppling evermore
Into seas without a shore;
Seas that restlessly aspire,   15
Surging, unto skies of fire;
Lakes that endlessly outspread
Their lone waters, lone and dead,—
Their still waters, still and chilly
With the snows of the lolling lily.   20

By the lakes that thus outspread
Their lone waters, lone and dead,—
Their sad waters, sad and chilly
With the snows of the lolling lily,—
By the mountains—near the river   25
Murmuring lowly, murmuring ever,—
By the grey woods,—by the swamp
Where the toad and the newt encamp,—
By the dismal tarns and pools
    Where dwell the Ghouls,—   30
By each spot the most unholy—

6. Literally, an image. *Cf.* "The Raven" (ll. 46–47), in which Night is also personified as a symbol of Death.

7. In antiquity, the farthest northern limits of the habitable world.

In each nook most melancholy,—
There the traveller meets, aghast,
Sheeted Memories of the Past—
Shrouded forms that start and sigh   35
As they pass the wanderer by—
White-robed forms of friends long given,
In agony, to the Earth—and Heaven.

For the heart whose woes are legion
'T is a peaceful, soothing region—   40
For the spirit that walks in shadow
'T is—oh, 't is an Eldorado! [8]
But the traveller, travelling through it,
May not—dare not openly view it;
Never its mysteries are exposed   45
To the weak human eye unclosed;
So wills its King, who hath forbid
The uplifting of the fringéd lid;
And thus the sad Soul that here passes
Beholds it but through darkened glasses.   50

By a route obscure and lonely,
Haunted by ill angels only,
Where an Eidolon, named NIGHT,
On a black throne reigns upright,
I have wandered home but newly   55
From this ultimate dim Thule.

                                        1844, 1845

The Raven [9]

Once upon a midnight dreary, while I pondered weak and weary,
Over many a quaint and curious volume of forgotten lore,
While I nodded, nearly napping, suddenly there came a tapping,
As of some one gently rapping, rapping at my chamber door.
" 'Tis some visitor," I muttered, "tapping at my chamber door—   5
     Only this and nothing more."

8. Literally, "The golden"; a legendary city of treasure in Spanish America, sought by explorers—hence, any unattainable, rich goal.
9. One complete autograph MS. survives, and variant readings appeared in the numerous magazine publications of "The Raven" before Poe's death. The 1845 *Poems* version is followed here. His recapitulation of its creation (see "The Philosophy of Composition") is an excellent example of analytical criticism, substantiating his assertion that he had carefully calculated this poem for popular appeal. Yet the "lost Lenore" is a central experience in Poe's life; the power of the poem depends in considerable degree upon the tension between calculated effect and genuine emotional experience. Lenore is variously identified as Miss Royster, a youthful sweetheart, and as Virginia, his wife, whose long and hopeless illness was ended by death in 1847.

Ah, distinctly I remember it was in the bleak December,
And each separate dying ember wrought its ghost upon the floor.
Eagerly I wished the morrow;—vainly I had sought to borrow
From my books surcease of sorrow—sorrow for the lost Lenore—   10
For the rare and radiant maiden whom the angels name Lenore—
       Nameless here for evermore.

And the silken sad uncertain rustling of each purple curtain
Thrilled me—filled me with fantastic terrors never felt before;
So that now, to still the beating of my heart, I stood repeating,   15
" 'Tis some visitor entreating entrance at my chamber door—
Some late visitor entreating entrance at my chamber door;—
      This it is and nothing more."

Presently my soul grew stronger; hesitating then no longer,
"Sir," said I, "or Madam, truly your forgiveness I implore;   20
But the fact is I was napping, and so gently you came rapping,
And so faintly you came tapping, tapping at my chamber door,
That I scarce was sure I heard you"—here I opened wide the
   door;—
      Darkness there, and nothing more.

Deep into that darkness peering, long I stood there wondering, fear-
   ing,   25
Doubting, dreaming dreams no mortals ever dared to dream before;
But the silence was unbroken, and the stillness gave no token,
And the only word there spoken was the whispered word, "Lenore!"
This I whispered, and an echo murmured back the word, "Le-
   nore!"—
      Merely this and nothing more.   30

Back into the chamber turning, all my soul within me burning,
Soon again I heard a tapping somewhat louder than before.
"Surely," said I, "surely that is something at my window lattice;
Let me see, then, what thereat is, and this mystery explore—
Let my heart be still a moment and this mystery explore;—   35
      'Tis the wind and nothing more."

Open here I flung the shutter, when, with many a flirt and flutter,
In there stepped a stately raven of the saintly days of yore;
Not the least obeisance made he; not a minute stopped or stayed he;
But, with mien of lord or lady, perched above my chamber door—   40
Perched upon a bust of Pallas [1] just above my chamber door—
      Perched, and sat, and nothing more.

1. Poe's conscious selection of Pallas Athena, goddess of wisdom, for the raven's perch, recalls his reported at-tempt, in an early draft, to have the bitter truth revealed by an owl, Athena's traditional bird of wisdom.

Then this ebony bird beguiling my sad fancy into smiling,
By the grave and stern decorum of the countenance it wore,
"Though thy crest be shorn and shaven, thou," I said, "art sure no
    craven,   45
Ghastly grim and ancient raven wandering from the Nightly
    shore—
Tell me what thy lordly name is on the Night's Plutonian
    shore!" [2]
                  Quoth the raven, "Nevermore."

Much I marvelled this ungainly fowl to hear discourse so plainly,
Though its answer little meaning—little relevancy bore;   50
For we cannot help agreeing that no living human being
Ever yet was blessed with seeing bird above his chamber door—
Bird or beast upon the sculptured bust above his chamber door,
          With such name as "Nevermore."

But the raven, sitting lonely on the placid bust, spoke only   55
That one word, as if his soul in that one word did he outpour.
Nothing farther then he uttered—not a feather then he fluttered—
Till I scarcely more than muttered, "Other friends have flown be-
    fore—
On the morrow *he* will leave me as my hopes have flown before."
          Then the bird said, "Nevermore."   60

Startled at the stillness broken by reply so aptly spoken,
"Doubtless," said I, "what it utters is its only stock and store,
Caught from some unhappy master whom unmerciful Disaster
Followed fast and followed faster till his songs one burden bore—
Till the dirges of his Hope that melancholy burden bore   65
          Of 'Never—nevermore.' "

But the raven still beguiling all my sad soul into smiling,
Straight I wheeled a cushioned seat in front of bird and bust and
    door;
There, upon the velvet sinking, I betook myself to linking
Fancy unto fancy, thinking what this ominous bird of yore—   70
What this grim, ungainly, ghastly, gaunt, and ominous bird of yore
          Meant in croaking "Nevermore."

This I sat engaged in guessing, but no syllable expressing
To the fowl whose fiery eyes now burned into my bosom's core;
This and more I sat divining, with my head at ease reclining   75
On the cushion's velvet lining that the lamplight gloated [3] o'er,

---

2. The infernal regions were ruled by
Pluto.
3. A double meaning is inherent in the

rare usage of the word "gloated" in the
sense of "to refract light from."

But whose velvet violet lining with the lamplight gloating o'er,
    She shall press, ah, nevermore!

Then, methought, the air grew denser, perfumed from an unseen
    censer
Swung by angels whose faint foot-falls tinkled on the tufted floor. 80
"Wretch," I cried, "thy God hath lent thee—by these angels he
    hath sent thee
Respite—respite and nepenthe [4] from thy memories of Lenore!
Quaff, oh quaff this kind nepenthe and forget this lost Lenore!"
    Quoth the raven, "Nevermore."

"Prophet!" said I, "thing of evil!—prophet still, if bird or devil!—
Whether Tempter sent, or whether tempest tossed thee here
    ashore,
Desolate, yet all undaunted, on this desert land enchanted—   87
On this home by Horror haunted,—tell me truly, I implore—
Is there—*is* there balm in Gilead? [5]—tell me—tell me, I im-
    plore!"
    Quoth the raven, "Nevermore."   90

"Prophet!" said I, "thing of evil!—prophet still, if bird or devil!
By that heaven that bends above us—by that God we both
    adore—
Tell this soul with sorrow laden if, within the distant Aidenn, [6]
It shall clasp a sainted maiden whom the angels name Lenore—
Clasp a rare and radiant maiden whom the angels name Lenore." 95
    Quoth the raven, "Nevermore."

"Be that word our sign of parting, bird or fiend!" I shrieked, up-
    starting—
"Get thee back into the tempest and the Night's Plutonian shore!
Leave no black plume as a token of that lie thy soul hath spoken!
Leave my loneliness unbroken!—quit the bust above my door! 100
Take thy beak from out my heart, and take thy form from off
    my door!"
    Quoth the raven, "Nevermore."

And the raven, never flitting, still is sitting, *still* is sitting
On the pallid bust of Pallas just above my chamber door;
And his eyes have all the seeming of a demon's that is dreaming, 105
And the lamp-light o'er him streaming throws his shadow on the
    floor;

---

4. In classical mythology, a potion ban-
ishing sorrow, as in the *Odyssey*, IV,
419–430.
5. *Cf.* Jeremiah viii: 22: "Is there no
balm in Gilead?"—a reference to an
esteemed medicinal herb from that region.
6. Variant spelling and pronunciation
for "Eden."

And my soul from out that shadow that lies floating on the floor
    Shall be lifted—nevermore!

1842–1844   1845

Ulalume [7]

The skies they were ashen and sober;
    The leaves they were crispèd and sere—
    The leaves they were withering and sere:
It was night, in the lonesome October
    Of my most immemorial [8] year: 5
It was hard by the dim lake of Auber,
    In the misty mid region of Weir [9]—
It was down by the dank tarn of Auber,
    In the ghoul-haunted woodland of Weir.

Here once, through an alley Titanic,[1]   10
    Of cypress, I roamed with my Soul—
    Of cypress, with Psyche,[2] my Soul.
These were days when my heart was volcanic
    As the scoriac [3] rivers that roll—
    As the lavas that restlessly roll   15
Their sulphurous currents down Yaanek [4]
    In the ultimate climes of the pole—
That groan as they roll down Mount Yaanek
    In the realms of the boreal pole.

Our talk had been serious and sober,   20
    But our thoughts they were palsied and sere—
    Our memories were treacherous and sere;
For we knew not the month was October,
    And we marked not the night of the year
    (Ah, night of all nights in the year!)—   25

7. "Ulalume" appears variously with and without the tenth stanza, given here. The poem appeared in four magazines during Poe's last years of life, 1847–1849. In one of these, the tenth stanza was dropped, as it was in Griswold's edition of Poe's *Works* the next year (1850). But, in the same year Griswold included the poem, *with* the tenth stanza, in the tenth edition of his *Poets and Poetry of America*. This text also agrees with the Ingram manuscript (J. P. Morgan Library, New York) that Poe wrote only a month before his death, except for a slight variant in line 28. We have here followed the Ingram reading, since that seems to have been Poe's last preference. Campbell (*The Poems of Edgar Allan Poe*, p. 273) suggests that Poe may have derived the name "Ulalume" from Latin *ululare*, "to wail."
8. Poe's invention of an intensive, meaning "most memorable." In the years 1846–1847, Poe's troubles reached their crisis in his illness, poverty, literary quarrels, and the increasing illness and death of Virginia.
9. Auber and Weir are poetic place names.
1. Implying both "enormous" and "primeval," since the Titans were the earliest race of Greek gods.
2. The Greek word meant "the soul," the spiritual personality. *Cf.* Psyche's speech, ll. 51–55.
3. A coinage. *Cf.* "scoria," meaning "slaggy lava."
4. An imaginary volcano.

We noted not the dim lake of Auber
   (Though once we had journeyed down here)—
We remembered not the dank tarn of Auber,
   Nor the ghoul-haunted woodland of Weir.

And now, as the night was senescent   30
   And star-dials pointed to morn—
   As the star-dials hinted of morn—
At the end of our path a liquescent
   And nebulous lustre was born,
Out of which a miraculous crescent   35
   Arose with a duplicate horn—
Astarte's [5] bediamonded crescent
   Distinct with its duplicate horn.

And I said: "She is warmer than Dian;
   She rolls through an ether of sighs—   40
   She revels in a region of sighs.
She has seen that the tears are not dry on
   These cheeks, where the worm never dies,[6]
And has come past the stars of the Lion,[7]
   To point us the path to the skies—   45
   To the Lethean peace of the skies [8]—
Come up, in despite of the Lion,
   To shine on us with her bright eyes—
Come up through the lair of the Lion,
   With love in her luminous eyes."   50

But Psyche, uplifting her finger,
   Said: "Sadly this star I mistrust—
   Her pallor I strangely mistrust:
Ah, hasten!—ah, let us not linger!
   Ah, fly!—let us fly!—for we must."   55
In terror she spoke, letting sink her
   Wings till they trailed in the dust—
In agony sobbed, letting sink her
   Plumes till they trailed in the dust—
   Till they sorrowfully trailed in the dust.   60

I replied: "This is nothing but dreaming:
   Let us on by this tremulous light!
   Let us bathe in this crystalline light!

---

5. The Phoenician goddess of fertility, and the Ashtoreth of the Old Testament, there condemned for her carnality. A moon goddess, she is here compared with Diana (Dian, l. 39), the Roman huntress of the moon, renowned for chastity.

6. *Cf.* Isaiah lxvi: 24.
7. The constellation Leo, here suggesting a danger in the Zodiac, through which Astarte has passed.
8. In classical mythology, the Lethe was the river of forgetfulness.

Its Sibyllic [9] splendor is beaming
  With Hope and in Beauty to-night:—   65
    See!—it flickers up the sky through the night!
Ah, we safely may trust to its gleaming,
  And be sure it will lead us aright—
We surely may trust to a gleaming,
  That cannot but guide us aright,   70
    Since it flickers up to Heaven through the night."

Thus I pacified Psyche and kissed her,
  And tempted her out of her gloom—
  And conquered her scruples and gloom;
And we passed to the end of the vista,   75
  But were stopped by the door of a tomb—
  By the door of a legended tomb;
And I said: "What is written, sweet sister,
  On the door of this legended tomb?"
She replied: "Ulalume—Ulalume—   80
  'Tis the vault of thy lost Ulalume!"

Then my heart it grew ashen and sober
  As the leaves that were crispèd and sere—
  As the leaves that were withering and sere;
And I cried: "It was surely October   85
  On *this* very night of last year
  That I journeyed—I journeyed down here!—
  That I brought a dread burden down here—
  On this night of all nights in the year,
  Ah, what demon has tempted me here?   90
Well I know, now, this dim lake of Auber—
  This misty mid region of Weir—
Well I know, now, this dank tarn of Auber,
  This ghoul-haunted woodland of Weir."

Said we, then—the two, then: "Ah, can it   95
  Have been that the woodlandish ghouls—
  The pitiful, the merciful ghouls—
To bar up our way and to ban it
  From the secret that lies in these wolds—
  From the thing that lies hidden in these wolds—   100
Have drawn up the spectre of a planet
  From the limbo of lunary souls—
This sinfully scintillant planet
  From the Hell of the planetary souls?"

1847, 1850

9. Usually, "Sibylline"; from "Sibyl," any one of several prophetesses of classic myth.

Annabel Lee[1]

It was many and many a year ago,
   In a kingdom by the sea,
That a maiden there lived whom you may know
   By the name of Annabel Lee;—
And this maiden she lived with no other thought
   Than to love and be loved by me.

She was a child and *I* was a child,
   In this kingdom by the sea,
But we loved with a love that was more than love—
   I and my Annabel Lee—   10
With a love that the wingéd seraphs of Heaven
   Coveted her and me.

And this was the reason that, long ago,
   In this kingdom by the sea,
A wind blew out of a cloud by night   15
   Chilling my Annabel Lee;
So that her highborn kinsmen came
   And bore her away from me,
To shut her up in a sepulchre
   In this kingdom by the sea.   20

The angels, not half so happy in Heaven,
   Went envying her and me:—
Yes! that was the reason (as all men know,
   In this kingdom by the sea)
That the wind came out of the cloud, chilling   25
   And killing my Annabel Lee.

But our love it was stronger by far than the love
   Of those who were older than we—
   Of many far wiser than we—
And neither the angels in Heaven above   30
   Nor the demons down under the sea,
Can ever dissever my soul from the soul
   Of the beautiful Annabel Lee:—

For the moon never beams without bringing me dreams
   Of the beautiful Annabel Lee;   35
And the stars never rise but I see the bright eyes
   Of the beautiful Annabel Lee;

[handwritten marginal note: Poe's fascenation w/ young girls.*]*

1. The text is that of first publication,
in the New York *Tribune* for October 9,
1849, two days after the poet's death.
The poem appeared in two other magazines within three months, and was collected in Griswold's edition of Poe's
Works (1850).

And so, all the night-tide, I lie down by the side
Of my darling, my darling, my life and my bride,
    In her sepulchre there by the sea—
    In her tomb by the side of the sea.   40

1849, 1850

Ligeia [2]

And the will therein lieth, which dieth not. Who knoweth the mysteries of the will, with its vigor? For God is but a great will pervading all things by nature of its intentness. Man doth not yield himself to the angels, nor unto death utterly, save only through the weakness of his feeble will.

—JOSEPH GLANVILL [3]

I cannot, for my soul, remember how, when, or even precisely where, I first became acquainted with the lady Ligeia. Long years have since elapsed, and my memory is feeble through much suffering. Or, perhaps, I cannot *now* bring these points to mind, because, in truth, the character of my beloved, her rare learning, her singular yet placid cast of beauty, and the thrilling and enthralling eloquence of her low musical language, made their way into my heart by paces so steadily and stealthily progressive that they have been unnoticed and unknown. Yet I believe that I met her first and most frequently in some large, old, decaying city near the Rhine. Of her family—I have surely heard her speak. That it is of a remotely ancient date cannot be doubted. Ligeia! Ligeia! Buried in studies of a nature more than all else adapted to deaden impressions of the outward world, it is by that sweet word alone—by Ligeia—that I bring before mine eyes in fancy the image of her who is no more. And now, while I write, a recollection flashes upon me that I have *never known* the paternal name of her who was my friend and my betrothed, and who became the partner of my studies, and finally the wife of my bosom. Was it a playful charge on the part of my Ligeia? or was it a test of my strength of affection, that I should institute no inquiries upon this point? or was it rather a caprice of my own—a wildly romantic offering on the shrine of the most passionate devotion? I but indistinctly recall the fact itself—what wonder that I have utterly forgotten the circumstances which originated or attended it. And, indeed, if ever

2. Poe once declared that "Ligeia" was his best tale. In his attraction to the theme of psychic survival, especially that of a beautiful woman, he employed reincarnation in "Legeia" and "Morella" and premature burial in "Berenice" and "The Fall of the House of Usher." In the poems, psychic survival is a persistent overtone. "Ligeia" first appeared in the *American Museum* for September, 1838, and was collected in Poe's *Tales of the Grotesque and Arabesque* (1840).

3. The source of this epigraph has never been discovered. If Poe invented it, he ascribed it to a likely author. Joseph Glanvill (1636–1680), an English ecclesiastical theorist, was associated with the Cambridge Platonists. Their intuitional idealism partly embraced cabbalism, an ancient Hebrew occultism emphasizing spiritualistic manifestations and the eternity of the soul.

that spirit which is entitled *Romance*—if ever she, the wan and the misty-winged *Ashtophet* [4] of idolatrous Egypt, presided, as they tell, over marriages ill-omened, then most surely she presided over mine.

There is one dear topic, however, on which my memory fails me not. It is the *person* of Ligeia. In stature she was tall, somewhat slender, and, in her latter days, even emaciated. I would in vain attempt to portray the majesty, the quiet ease, of her demeanor, or the incomprehensible lightness and elasticity of her footfall. She came and departed as a shadow. I was never made aware of her entrance into my closed study save by the dear music of her low sweet voice, as she placed her marble hand upon my shoulder. In beauty of face no maiden ever equalled her. It was the radiance of an opium dream—an airy and spirit-lifting vision more wildly divine than the phantasies which hovered about the slumbering souls of the daughters of Delos.[5] Yet her features were not of that regular mould which we have been falsely taught to worship in the classical labors of the heathen. "There is no exquisite beauty," says Bacon, Lord Verulam,[6] speaking truly of all the forms and *genera* of beauty, "without some *strangeness* in the proportion." Yet, although I saw that the features of Ligeia were not of a classic regularity—although I perceived that her loveliness was indeed "exquisite," and felt that there was much of "strangeness" pervading it, yet I have tried in vain to detect the irregularity and to trace home my own perception of "the strange." I examined the contour of the lofty and pale forehead—it was faultless—how cold indeed that word when applied to a majesty so divine!—the skin rivalling the purest ivory, the commanding extent and repose, the gentle prominence of the regions above the temples; and then the raven-black, the glossy, the luxuriant and naturally-curling tresses, setting forth the full force of the Homeric epithet, "hyacinthine!" [7] I looked at the delicate outlines of the nose—and nowhere but in the graceful medallions of the Hebrews had I beheld a similar perfection. There were the same luxurious smoothness of surface, the same scarcely perceptible tendency to the aquiline, the same harmoniously curved nostrils speaking the free spirit. I regarded the sweet mouth. Here was indeed the triumph of all things heavenly

4. T. O. Mabbott has identified Ashtophet as the principal goddess of Sidon—now Saida in modern Lebanon (not Egypt); there was, however, another Phoenician fertility goddess, known as Ashtoreth, who was also honored in Egypt.
5. Delos, a Greek island of the Cyclades, the mythological birthplace of the twins Apollo and Artemis, became a shrine. Artemis was attended by maidens sworn to chastity, perhaps Poe's "daughters of Delos." In Asia Minor, Ephesus, and Taurus, and in literature, Artemis as moon-goddess was confused with Astarte (Ashtoreth); *cf*. the name "Ashtophet," above, and stanza 4 of "Ulalume."
6. Francis Bacon, *Essayes* (1625), "Of Beauty." Bacon wrote "excellent beauty," not "exquisite."
7. *Cf*. "To Helen."

—the magnificent turn of the short upper lip—the soft, voluptu-ous slumber of the under—the dimples which sported, and the color which spoke—the teeth glancing back, with a brilliancy almost startling, every ray of the holy light which fell upon them in her serene and placid, yet most exultingly radiant of all smiles. I scrutinized the formation of the chin—and here, too, I found the gentleness of breadth, the softness and the majesty, the fullness and the spirituality, of the Greek—the contour which the god Apollo revealed but in a dream, to Cleomenes,[8] the son of the Athenian. And then I peered into the large eyes of Ligeia.

For eyes we have no models in the remotely antique. It might have been, too, that in these eyes of my beloved lay the secret to which Lord Verulam alludes. They were, I must believe, far larger than the ordinary eyes of our own race. They were even fuller than the fullest of the gazelle eyes of the tribe of the valley of Nourja-had.[9] Yet it was only at intervals—in moments of intense excite-ment—that peculiarity became more than slightly noticeable in Ligeia. And at such moments was her beauty—in my heated fancy thus it appeared perhaps—the beauty of beings either above or apart from the earth—the beauty of the fabulous Houri[1] of the Turk. The hue of the orbs was the most brilliant of black, and, far over them, hung jetty lashes of great length. The brows, slightly irregular in outline, had the same tint. The "strangeness," how-ever, which I found in the eyes, was of a nature distinct from the formation, or the color, or the brilliancy of the features, and must, after all, be referred to the *expression*. Ah, word of no meaning! behind whose vast latitude of mere sound we intrench our ignor-ance of so much of the spiritual. The expression of the eyes of Ligeia! How for long hours have I pondered upon it! How have I, through the whole of a midsummer night, struggled to fathom it! What was it—that something more profound than the well of Democritus[2]—which lay far within the pupils of my beloved? What *was* it? I was possessed with a passion to discover. Those eyes! those large, those shining, those divine orbs! they became to me twin stars of Leda,[3] and I to them devoutest of astrologers.

There is no point, among the many incomprehensible anomalies of the science of mind, more thrillingly exciting than the fact—

8. The Venus de' Medici bears the sig-nature of Cleomenes, possibly a late forgery; and Apollo, patron of the arts, is suggested by Poe as the source of the sculptor's inspiration.

9. *The History of Nourjahad* (1767), an oriental romance by Frances Sheridan (1724–1766), was still familiar.

1. A nymph of the Mohammedan para-dise.

2. Democritus, the Greek "laughing philosopher" of the fifth century B.C., one of whose surviving fragments is the source of the proverb, "Truth lies at the bottom of a well."

3. In the constellation Gemini, accord-ing to Greek myth, the two bright stars are Castor and Pollux, twin sons of the mortal Leda and the god Zeus, who visited her as a swan.

never, I believe, noticed in the schools—that, in our endeavors to recall to memory something long forgotten, we often find ourselves *upon the very verge* of remembrance, without being able, in the end, to remember. And thus how frequently, in my intense scrutiny of Ligeia's eyes, have I felt approaching the full knowledge of their expression—felt it approaching—yet not quite be mine—and so at length entirely depart! And (strange, oh strangest mystery of all!) I found, in the commonest objects of the universe, a circle of analogies to that expression. I mean to say that, subsequently to the period when Ligeia's beauty passed into my spirit, there dwelling as in a shrine, I derived, from many existences in the material world, a sentiment such as I felt always aroused within me by her large and luminous orbs. Yet not the more could I define that sentiment, or analyze, or even steadily view it. I recognized it, let me repeat, sometimes in the survey of a rapidly-growing vine—in the contemplation of a moth, a butterfly, a chrysalis, a stream of running water. I have felt it in the ocean; in the falling of a meteor. I have felt it in the glances of unusually aged people. And there are one or two stars in heaven (one especially, a star of the sixth magnitude, double and changeable, to be found near the large star in Lyra [4]) in a telescopic scrutiny of which I have been made aware of the feeling. I have been filled with it by certain sounds from stringed instruments, and not unfrequently by passages from books. Among innumerable other instances, I well remember something in a volume of Joseph Glanvill, which (perhaps merely from its quaintness—who shall say?) never failed to inspire me with the sentiment;—"And the will therein lieth, which dieth not. Who knoweth the mysteries of the will, with its vigor? For God is but a great will pervading all things by nature of its intentness. Man doth not yield him to the angels, nor unto death utterly, save only through the weakness of his feeble will."

Length of years, and subsequent reflection, have enabled me to trace, indeed, some remote connection between this passage in the English moralist and a portion of the character of Ligeia. An *intensity* in thought, action, or speech, was possibly, in her, a result, or at least an index, of that gigantic volition which, during our long intercourse, failed to give other and more immediate evidence of its existence. Of all the women whom I have ever known, she, the outwardly calm, the ever-placid Ligeia, was the most violently a prey to the tumultuous vultures of stern passion. And of such passion I could form no estimate, save by the miraculous expansion of those eyes which at once so delighted and appalled me—by the

4. The constellation contains two double stars. Poe's "large star" is Vega, or Alpha Lyrae, of the first magnitude. The other, lower and to the left, is Epsilon Lyrae, requiring a telescope, as he says, for observation.

almost magical melody, modulation, distinctness and placidity of her very low voice—and by the fierce energy (rendered doubly effective by contrast with her manner of utterance) of the wild words which she habitually uttered.

I have spoken of the learning of Ligeia: it was immense—such as I have never known in woman. In the classical tongues was she deeply proficient, and as far as my own acquaintance extended in regard to the modern dialects of Europe, I have never known her at fault. Indeed upon any theme of the most admired, because simply the most abstruse of the boasted erudition of the academy, have I *ever* found Ligeia at fault? How singularly—how thrillingly, this one point in the nature of my wife has forced itself, at this late period only, upon my attention! I said her knowledge was such as I have never known in woman—but where breathes the man who has traversed, and successfully, *all* the wide areas of moral, physical, and mathematical science? I saw not then what I now clearly perceive, that the acquisitions of Ligeia were gigantic, were astounding; yet I was sufficiently aware of her infinite supremacy to resign myself, with a child-like confidence, to her guidance through the chaotic world of metaphysical investigation at which I was most busily occupied during the earlier years of our marriage. With how vast a triumph—with how vivid a delight—with how much of all that is ethereal in hope—did I *feel*, as she bent over me in studies but little sought—but less known—that delicious vista by slow degrees expanding before me, down whose long, gorgeous, and all untrodden path, I might at length pass onward to the goal of a wisdom too divinely precious not to be forbidden!

How poignant, then, must have been the grief with which, after some years, I beheld my well-grounded expectations take wings to themselves and fly away! Without Ligeia I was but as a child groping benighted. Her presence, her readings alone, rendered vividly luminous the many mysteries of the transcendentalism in which we were immersed. Wanting the radiant lustre of her eyes, letters, lambent and golden, grew duller than Saturnian lead.[5] And now those eyes shone less and less frequently upon the pages over which I pored. Ligeia grew ill. The wild eyes blazed with a too—too glorious effulgence; the pale fingers became of the transparent waxen hue of the grave, and the blue veins upon the lofty forehead swelled and sank impetuously with the tides of the most gentle emotion. I saw that she must die—and I struggled desperately in spirit with the grim Azrael.[6] And the struggles of the passionate wife were, to my astonishment, even more energetic than my own.

5. In ancient alchemy and chemistry, lead bore the name of Saturn. *Cf.* "saturnine."

6. In Mohammedan and Hebrew mythology, the Angel of Death.

There had been much in her stern nature to impress me with the belief that, to her, death would have come without its terrors;— but not so. Words are impotent to convey any just idea of the fierceness of resistance with which she wrestled with the Shadow. I groaned in anguish at the pitiable spectacle. I would have soothed —I would have reasoned; but, in the intensity of her wild desire for life,—for life—*but* for life—solace and reason were alike the uttermost of folly. Yet not until the last instance, amid the most convulsive writhings of her fierce spirit, was shaken the external placidity of her demeanor. Her voice grew more gentle—grew more low—yet I would not wish to dwell upon the wild meaning of the quietly uttered words. My brain reeled as I hearkened entranced, to a melody more than mortal—to assumptions and aspirations which mortality had never before known.

That she loved me I should not have doubted; and I might have been easily aware that, in a bosom such as hers, love would have reigned no ordinary passion. But in death only, was I fearfully impressed with the strength of her affection. For long hours, detaining my hand, would she pour out before me the overflowing of a heart whose more than passionate devotion amounted to idolatry. How had I deserved to be so blessed by such confessions?—how had I deserved to be so cursed with the removal of my beloved in the hour of her making them? But upon this subject I cannot bear to dilate. Let me say only, that in Ligeia's more than womanly abandonment to a love, alas! all unmerited, all unworthily bestowed, I at length recognized the principle of her longing with so wildly earnest a desire for the life which was now fleeing so rapidly away. It is this wild longing—it is this eager vehemence of desire for life— *but* for life—that I have no power to portray—no utterance capable of expressing.

At high noon of the night in which she departed, beckoning me, peremptorily, to her side, she bade me repeat certain verses composed by herself not many days before. I obeyed her.—They were these: [7]

> Lo! 'tis a gala night
> Within the lonesome latter years!
> An angel throng, bewinged, bedight
> In veils, and drowned in tears,
> Sit in a theatre, to see
> A play of hopes and fears,
> While the orchestra breathes fitfully
> The music of the spheres.

7. This poem was not a part of the story as first published in 1838. Entitled "The Conqueror Worm," it appeared separately in *Graham's Magazine* for January, 1843; it was first incorporated in the version of the tale printed in the *Broadway Journal* for September 27, 1845.

> Mimes, in the form of God on high,
>> Mutter and mumble low,
> And hither and thither fly—
>> Mere puppets they, who come and go
> At bidding of vast formless things
>> That shift the scenery to and fro,
> Flapping from out their Condor wings
>> Invisible Wo!
>
> That motley drama!—oh, be sure
>> It shall not be forgot!
> With its Phantom chased forever more,
>> By a crowd that seize it not,
> Through a circle that ever returneth in
>> To the self-same spot,
> And much of Madness and more of Sin
>> And Horror the soul of the plot.
>
> But see, amid the mimic rout,
>> A crawling shape intrude!
> A blood-red thing that writhes from out
>> The scenic solitude!
> It writhes!—it writhes! with mortal pangs
>> The mimes become its food,
> And the seraphs sob at vermin fangs
>> In human gore imbued.
>
> Out—out are the lights—out all!
>> And over each quivering form,
> The curtain, a funeral pall,
>> Comes down with the rush of a storm,
> And the angels, all pallid and wan,
>> Uprising, unveiling, affirm
> That the play is the tragedy, "Man,"
>> And its hero the Conqueror Worm.

"O God!" half shrieked Ligeia, leaping to her feet and extending her arms aloft with a spasmodic movement, as I made an end of these lines—"O God! O Divine Father!—shall these things be undeviatingly so?—shall this Conqueror be not once conquered? Are we not part and parcel in Thee? Who—who knoweth the mysteries of the will with its vigor? Man doth not yield him to the angels, *nor unto death utterly*, save only through the weakness of his feeble will."

And now, as if exhausted with emotion, she suffered her white arms to fall, and returned solemnly to her bed of Death. And as she breathed her last sighs, there came mingled with them a low murmur from her lips. I bent to them my ear and distinguished, again, the concluding words of the passage in Glanvill—"*Man doth not yield him to the angels, nor unto death utterly, save only through the weakness of his feeble will.*"

She died;—and I, crushed into the very dust with sorrow, could no longer endure the lonely desolation of my dwelling in the dim and decaying city by the Rhine. I had no lack of what the world calls wealth. Ligeia had brought me far more, very far more than ordinarily falls to the lot of mortals. After a few months, therefore, of weary and aimless wandering, I purchased, and put in some repair, an abbey, which I shall not name, in one of the wildest and least frequented portions of fair England. The gloomy and dreary grandeur of the building, the almost savage aspect of the domain, the many melancholy and time-honored memories connected with both, had much in unison with the feelings of utter abandonment which had driven me into that remote and unsocial region of the country. Yet although the external abbey, with its verdant decay hanging about it, suffered but little alteration, I gave way, with a child-like perversity, and perchance with a faint hope of alleviating my sorrows, to a display of more than regal magnificence within.— For such follies, even in childhood, I had imbibed a taste and now they came back to me as if in the dotage of grief. Alas, I feel how much even of incipient madness might have been discovered in the gorgeous and fantastic draperies, in the solemn carvings of Egypt, in the wild cornices and furniture, in the Bedlam patterns of the carpets of tufted gold! I had become a bounden slave in the trammels of opium, and my labors and my orders had taken a coloring from my dreams. But these absurdities I must not pause to detail. Let me speak only of that one chamber, ever accursed, whither in a moment of mental alienation, I led from the altar as my bride—as the successor of the unforgotten Ligeia—the fair-haired and blue-eyed Lady Rowena Trevanion, of Tremaine.

There is no individual portion of the architecture and decoration of that bridal chamber which is not now visibly before me. Where were the souls of the haughty family of the bride, when, through thirst of gold, they permitted to pass the threshold of an apartment so bedecked, a maiden and a daughter so beloved? I have said that I minutely remember the details of the chamber—yet I am sadly forgetful on topics of deep moment—and here there was no system, no keeping, in the fantastic display, to take hold upon the memory. The room lay in a high turret of the castellated abbey, was pentagonal in shape, and of capacious size. Occupying the whole southern face of the pentagon was the sole window—an immense sheet of unbroken glass from Venice—a single pane, and tinted of a leaden hue, so that the rays of either the sun or moon, passing through it, fell with a ghastly lustre on the objects within. Over the upper portion of this huge window, extended the trellice-work of an aged vine, which clambered up the massy walls of the turret. The ceiling, of gloomy-looking oak, was excessively lofty, vaulted, and elaborately fretted with the wildest and most grotesque specimens of a semi-Gothic, semi-Druidical device. From out the most central recess of this melancholy vaulting, depended, by a single chain of gold with long links, a huge censer of the same metal, Saracenic in pattern, and with many perforations so contrived that there writhed in and out of them, as if endued with a serpent vitality, a continual succession of parti-colored fires.

Some few ottomans and golden candelabra, of Eastern figure, were in various stations about—and there was the couch, too—the bridal couch—of an Indian model, and low, and sculptured of solid ebony, with a pall-like canopy above. In each of the angles of the chamber stood on end a gigantic sarcophagus of black granite, from the tombs of the kings over against Luxor,[8] with their aged lids full of immemorial sculpture. But in the draping of the apartment lay, alas! the chief phantasy of all. The lofty walls, gigantic in height—even unproportionably so—were hung from summit to foot, in vast folds, with a heavy and massive-looking tapestry—tapestry of a material which was found alike as a carpet on the floor, as a covering for the ottomans and the ebony bed, as a canopy for the bed, and as the gorgeous volutes of the curtains which partially shaded the window. The material was the richest cloth of gold. It was spotted all over, at irregular intervals, with arabesque figures, about a foot in diameter, and wrought upon the cloth in patterns of the most jetty black. But these figures partook of the true character of the arabesque only when regarded from a single point of view. By a contrivance now common, and indeed traceable to a very remote period of antiquity, they were made changeable in aspect. To one entering the room, they bore the appearance of simple monstrosities; but upon a farther advance, this appearance gradually departed; and step by step, as the visitor moved his station in the chamber, he saw himself surrounded by an endless succession of the ghastly forms which belong to the superstition of the Norman, or arise in the guilty slumbers of the monk. The phantasmagoric effect was vastly heightened by the artificial introduction of a strong continual current of wind behind the draperies —giving a hideous and uneasy animation to the whole.

In halls such as these—in a bridal chamber such as this—I

8. The ancient site of Thebes, in middle Egypt, on the Nile. The fascination of Egypt for romantic writers reflected the remarkable development of Egyptology since Jean François Champollion began deciphering hieroglyphics early in the century.

passed, with the Lady of Tremaine, the unhallowed hours of the first month of our marriage—passed them with but little disquietude. That my wife dreaded the fierce moodiness of my temper —that she shunned me and loved me but little—I could not help perceiving; but it gave me rather pleasure than otherwise. I loathed her with a hatred belonging more to demon than to man. My memory flew back (oh, with what intensity of regret!) to Ligeia, the beloved, the august, the beautiful, the entombed. I revelled in recollections of her purity, of her wisdom, of her lofty, her ethereal nature, of her passionate, her idolatrous love. Now, then, did my spirit fully and freely burn with more than all the fires of her own. In the excitement of my opium dreams (for I was habitually fettered in the shackles of the drug) I would call aloud upon her name, during the silence of the night, or among the sheltered recesses of the glens by day, as if, through the wild eagerness, the solemn passion, the consuming ardor of my longing for the departed, I could restore her to the pathway she had abandoned—ah, *could* it be forever?—upon the earth.

About the commencement of the second month of the marriage, the Lady Rowena was attacked with sudden illness, from which her recovery was slow. The fever which consumed her rendered her nights uneasy; and in her perturbed state of half-slumber, she spoke of sounds, and of motions, in and about the chamber of the turret, which I concluded had no origin save in the distemper of her fancy, or perhaps in the phantasmagoric influence of the chamber itself. She became at length convalescent—finally well. Yet but a brief period elapsed, ere a second more violent disorder again threw her upon a bed of suffering; and from this attack her frame, at all times feeble, never altogether recovered. Her illnesses were, after this epoch, of alarming character, and of more alarming recurrence, defying alike the knowledge and the great exertions of her physicians. With the increase of the chronic disease which had thus, apparently, taken too sure hold upon her constitution to be eradicated by human means, I could not fail to observe a similar increase in the nervous irritation of her temperament, and in her excitability by trivial causes of fear. She spoke again, and now more frequently and pertinaciously, of the sounds—of the slight sounds— and of the unusual motions among the tapestries, to which she had formerly alluded.

One night, near the closing in of September, she pressed this distressing subject with more than usual emphasis upon my attention. She had just awakened from an unquiet slumber, and I had been watching, with feelings half of anxiety, half of a vague terror, the workings of her emaciated countenance. I sat by the side of her ebony bed, upon one of the ottomans of India. She partly arose, and spoke, in an earnest low whisper, of sounds which she *then* heard, but which I could not hear—of motions which she *then* saw, but which I could not perceive. The wind was rushing hurriedly behind the tapestries, and I wished to show her (what, let me confess it, I could not *all* believe) that those almost inarticulate breathings, of those very gentle variations of the figures upon the wall, were but the natural effects of that customary rushing of the wind. But a deadly pallor, overspreading her face, had proved to me that my exertions to reassure her would be fruitless. She appeared to be fainting, and no attendants were within call. I remembered where was deposited a decanter of light wine which had been ordered by her physicians, and hastened across the chamber to procure it. But, as I stepped beneath the light of the censer, two circumstances of a startling nature attracted my attention. I had felt that some palpable although invisible object had passed lightly by my person; and I saw that there lay upon the golden carpet, in the very middle of the rich lustre thrown from the censer, a shadow—a faint, indefinite shadow of angelic aspect—such as might be fancied for the shadow of a shade. But I was wild with the excitement of an immoderate dose of opium, and heeded these things but little, nor spoke of them to Rowena. Having found the wine, I recrossed the chamber, and poured out a goblet-ful, which I held to the lips of the fainting lady. She had now partially recovered, however, and took the vessel herself, while I sank upon an ottoman near me, with my eyes fastened upon her person. It was then that I became distinctly aware of a gentle foot-fall upon the carpet, and near the couch; and in a second thereafter, as Rowena was in the act of raising the wine to her lips, I saw, or may have dreamed that I saw, fall within the goblet, as if from some invisible spring in the atmosphere of the room, three or four large drops of a brilliant and ruby colored fluid. If this I saw—not so Rowena. She swallowed the wine unhesitatingly, and I forbore to speak to her of a circumstance which must, after all, I considered, have been but the suggestion of a vivid imagination, rendered morbidly active by the terror of the lady, by the opium, and by the hour.

Yet I cannot conceal it from my own perception that, immediately subsequent to the fall of the ruby-drops, a rapid change for the worse took place in the disorder of my wife; so that, on the third subsequent night, the hands of her menials prepared her for the tomb, and on the fourth, I sat alone, with her shrouded body, in that fantastic chamber which had received her as my bride.—Wild visions, opium-engendered, flitted, shadow-like, before me. I gazed with unquiet eyes upon the sarcophagi in the angles of the room, upon the varying figures of the drapery, and upon the writhing of the parti-colored fires in the censer overhead. My eyes then fell, as

I called to mind the circumstances of the former night, to the spot beneath the glare of the censer where I had seen the faint traces of the shadow. It was there, however, no longer; and breathing with greater freedom, I turned my glances to the pallid and rigid figure upon the bed. Then rushed upon me a thousand memories of Ligeia—and then came back upon my heart, with the turbulent violence of a flood, the whole of that unutterable woe with which I had regarded *her* thus enshrouded. The night waned; and still, with a bosom full of bitter thoughts of the one only and supremely beloved, I remained gazing upon the body of Rowena.

It might have been midnight, or perhaps earlier, or later, for I had taken no note of time, when a sob, low, gentle, but very distinct, startled me from my revery.—I *felt* that it came from the bed of ebony—the bed of death. I listened in an agony of superstitious terror—but there was no repetition of the sound. I strained my vision to detect any motion in the corpse—but there was not the slightest perceptible. Yet I could not have been deceived. I *had* heard the noise, however faint, and my soul was awakened within me. I resolutely and perseveringly kept my attention riveted upon the body. Many minutes elapsed before any circumstance occurred tending to throw light upon the mystery. At length it became evident that a slight, a very feeble, and barely noticeable tinge of color had flushed up within the cheeks, and along the sunken small veins of the eyelids. Through a species of unutterable horror and awe, for which the language of mortality has no sufficiently energetic expression, I felt my heart cease to beat, my limbs grow rigid where I sat. Yet a sense of duty finally operated to restore my self-possession. I could no longer doubt that we had been precipitate in our preparations—that Rowena still lived. It was necessary that some immediate exertion be made; yet the turret was altogether apart from the portion of the abbey tenanted by the servants—there were none within call—I had no means of summoning them to my aid without leaving the room for many minutes—and this I could not venture to do. I therefore struggled alone in my endeavors to call back the spirit still hovering. In a short period it was certain, however, that a relapse had taken place; the color disappeared from both eyelid and cheek, leaving a wanness even more than that of marble; the lips became doubly shrivelled and pinched up in the ghastly expression of death; a repulsive clamminess and coldness overspread rapidly the surface of the body; and all the usual rigorous stiffness immediately supervened. I fell back with a shudder upon the couch from which I had been so startlingly aroused, and again gave myself up to passionate waking visions of Ligeia.

An hour thus elapsed when (could it be possible?) I was a second time aware of some vague sound issuing from the region of the bed. I listened—in extremity of horror. The sound came again—it was a sigh. Rushing to the corpse, I saw—distinctly saw—a tremor upon the lips. In a minute afterward they relaxed, disclosing a bright line of the pearly teeth. Amazement now struggled in my bosom with the profound awe which had hitherto reigned there alone. I felt that my vision grew dim, that my reason wandered; and it was only by a violent effort that I at length succeeded in nerving myself to the task which duty thus once more had pointed out. There was now a partial glow upon the forehead and upon the cheek and throat; a perceptible warmth pervaded the whole frame; there was even a slight pulsation in the heart. The lady *lived*; and with redoubled ardor I betook myself to the task of restoration. I chafed and bathed the temples and the hands, and used every exertion which experience, and no little medical reading, could suggest. But in vain. Suddenly, the color fled, the pulsation ceased, the lips resumed the expression of the dead, and, in an instant afterward, the whole body took upon itself the icy chilliness, the livid hue, the intense rigidity, the sunken outline, and all the loathsome peculiarities of that which has been, for many days, a tenant of the tomb.

And again I sunk into visions of Ligeia—and again (what marvel that I shudder while I write?) *again* there reached my ears a low sob from the region of the ebony bed. But why shall I minutely detail the unspeakable horrors of that night? Why shall I pause to relate how, time after time, until near the period of the gray dawn, this hideous drama of revivification was repeated; how each terrific relapse was only into a sterner and apparently more irredeemable death; how each agony wore the aspect of a struggle with some invisible foe; and how each struggle was succeeded by I know not what of wild change in the personal appearance of the corpse? Let me hurry to a conclusion.

The greater part of the fearful night had worn away, and she who had been dead, once again stirred—and now more vigorously than hitherto, although arousing from a dissolution more appalling in its utter hopelessness than any. I had long ceased to struggle or to move, and remained sitting rigidly upon the ottoman, a helpless prey to a whirl of violent emotions, of which extreme awe was perhaps the least terrible, the least consuming. The corpse, I repeat, stirred, and now more vigorously than before. The hues of life flushed up with unwonted energy into the countenance—the limbs relaxed—and, save that the eyelids were yet pressed heavily together, and that the bandages and draperies of the grave still imparted their charnel character to the figure, I might have dreamed that Rowena had indeed shaken off, utterly, the fetters of

Death. But if this idea was not, even then, altogether adopted, I could at least doubt no longer, when, arising from the bed, tottering, with feeble steps, with closed eyes, and with the manner of one bewildered in a dream, the thing that was enshrouded advanced boldly and palpably into the middle of the apartment.

I trembled not—I stirred not—for a crowd of unutterable fancies connected with the air, the stature, the demeanor of the figure, rushing hurriedly through my brain, had paralyzed—had chilled me into stone. I stirred not—but gazed upon the apparition. There was a mad disorder in my thoughts—a tumult unappeasable. Could it, indeed, be the *living* Rowena who confronted me? Could it indeed be Rowena *at all*—the fair-haired, the blue-eyed Lady Rowena Trevanion of Tremaine? Why, *why* should I doubt it? The bandage lay heavily about the mouth—but then might it not be the mouth of the breathing Lady of Tremaine? And the cheeks —there were the roses as in her noon of life—yes, these might indeed be the fair cheeks of the living Lady of Tremaine. And the chin, with its dimples, as in health, might it not be hers?—but *had she then grown taller since her malady?* What inexpressible madness seized me with that thought? One bound, and I had reached her feet! Shrinking from my touch, she let fall from her head, unloosened, the ghastly cerements which had confined it, and there streamed forth, into the rushing atmosphere of the chamber, huge masses of long and dishevelled hair; *it was blacker than the raven wings of the midnight!* And now slowly opened *the eyes* of the figure which stood before me. "Here then, at least," I shrieked aloud, "can I never—can I never be mistaken—these are the full, and the black, and the wild eyes—of my lost love—of the lady—of the LADY LIGEIA!"

1838, 1840

The Fall of the House of Usher

Son cœur est un luth suspendu;
Sitôt qu'on le touche il résonne.
—DE BERANGER 9

During the whole of a dull, dark, and soundless day in the autumn of the year, when the clouds hung oppressively low in the heavens, I had been passing alone, on horseback, through a singularly dreary tract of country, and at length found myself, as the shades of the evening drew on, within view of the melancholy House of Usher. I know not how it was—but, with the first glimpse of the building, a sense of insufferable gloom pervaded my spirit. I

---

9. Pierre Jean de Béranger, from "Le Refus" (ll. 41–42); translated, "His heart is a suspended lute; Whenever one touches it, it resounds." *Cf.* "Israfel."

say insufferable; for the feeling was unrelieved by any of that half-pleasurable, because poetic, sentiment with which the mind usually receives even the sternest natural images of the desolate or terrible. I looked upon the scene before me—upon the mere house, and the simple landscape features of the domain—upon the bleak walls—upon the vacant eye-like windows—upon a few rank sedges—and upon a few white trunks of decayed trees—with an utter depression of soul which I can compare to no earthly sensation more properly than to the after-dream of the reveller upon opium— the bitter lapse into every-day life—the hideous dropping off of the veil. There was an iciness, a sinking, a sickening of the heart—an unredeemed dreariness of thought which no goading of the imagi- nation could torture into aught of the sublime. What was it—I paused to think—what was it that so unnerved me in the contem- plation of the House of Usher? It was a mystery all insoluble; nor could I grapple with the shadowy fancies that crowded upon me as I pondered. I was forced to fall back upon the unsatisfactory conclusion, that while, beyond doubt, there *are* combinations of very simple natural objects which have the power of thus affecting us, still the analysis of this power lies among considerations beyond our depth. It was possible, I reflected, that a mere different ar- rangement of the particulars of the scene, of the details of the pic- ture, would be sufficient to modify, or perhaps to annihilate its capacity for sorrowful impression; and, acting upon this idea, I reined my horse to the precipitous brink of a black and lurid tarn that lay in unruffled lustre by the dwelling, and gazed down—but with a shudder even more thrilling than before—upon the remod- elled and inverted images of the gray sedge, and the ghastly tree- stems, and the vacant and eye-like windows.

Nevertheless, in this mansion of gloom I now proposed to myself a sojourn of some weeks. Its proprietor, Roderick Usher, had been one of my boon companions in boyhood; but many years had elapsed since our last meeting. A letter, however, had lately reached me in a distant part of the country—a letter from him— which, in its wildly importunate nature, had admitted of no other than a personal reply. The MS. gave evidence of nervous agitation. The writer spoke of acute bodily illness—of a mental disorder which oppressed him—and of an earnest desire to see me, as his best and indeed his only personal friend, with a view of attempting, by the cheerfulness of my society, some alleviation of his malady. It was the manner in which all this, and much more, was said—it was the apparent *heart* that went with his request—which allowed me no room for hesitation; and I accordingly obeyed forthwith what I still considered a very singular summons.

Although, as boys, we had been even intimate associates, yet I really knew little of my friend. His reserve had been always excessive and habitual. I was aware, however, that his very ancient family had been noted, time out of mind, for a peculiar sensibility of temperament, displaying itself, through long ages, in many works of exalted art, and manifested, of late, in repeated deeds of munificent yet unobtrusive charity, as well as in a passionate devotion to the intricacies, perhaps even more than to the orthodox and easily recognizable beauties, of musical science. I had learned, too, the very remarkable fact, that the stem of the Usher race, all time-honored as it was, had put forth, at no period, any enduring branch; in other words, that the entire family lay in the direct line of descent, and had always, with very trifling and very temporary variation, so lain. It was this deficiency, I considered, while running over in thought the perfect keeping of the character of the premises with the accredited character of the people, and while speculating upon the possible influence which the one, in the long lapse of centuries, might have exercised upon the other—it was this deficiency, perhaps, of collateral issue, and the consequent undeviating transmission, from sire to son, of the patrimony with the name, which had, at length, so identified the two as to merge the original title of the estate in the quaint and equivocal appellation of the "House of Usher"—an appellation which seemed to include, in the minds of the peasantry who used it, both the family and the family mansion.

I have said that the sole effect of my somewhat childish experiment—that of looking down within the tarn—had been to deepen the first singular impression. There can be no doubt that the consciousness of the rapid increase of my superstition—for why should I not so term it?—served mainly to accelerate the increase itself. Such, I have long known, is the paradoxical law of all sentiments having terror as a basis. And it might have been for this reason only, that, when I again uplifted my eyes to the house itself, from its image in the pool, there grew in my mind a strange fancy—a fancy so ridiculous, indeed, that I but mention it to show the vivid force of the sensations which oppressed me. I had so worked upon my imagination as really to believe that about the whole mansion and domain there hung an atmosphere peculiar to themselves and their immediate vicinity—an atmosphere which had no affinity with the air of heaven, but which had reeked up from the decayed trees, and the gray wall, and the silent tarn—a pestilent and mystic vapor, dull, sluggish, faintly discernible, and leaden-hued.

Shaking off from my spirit what *must* have been a dream, I scanned more narrowly the real aspect of the building. Its principal feature seemed to be that of an excessive antiquity. The discoloration of ages had been great. Minute fungi overspread the whole exterior, hanging in a fine tangled web-work from the eaves. Yet all this was apart from any extraordinary dilapidation. No portion of the masonry had fallen; and there appeared to be a wild inconsistency between its still perfect adaptation of parts, and the crumbling condition of the individual stones. In this there was much that reminded me of the specious totality of old wood-work which has rotted for long years in some neglected vault, with no disturbance from the breath of the external air. Beyond this indication of extensive decay, however, the fabric gave little token of instability. Perhaps the eye of a scrutinizing observer might have discovered a barely perceptible fissure, which, extending from the roof of the building in front, made its way down the wall in a zigzag direction, until it became lost in the sullen waters of the tarn.

Noticing these things, I rode over a short causeway to the house. A servant in waiting took my horse, and I entered the Gothic archway of the hall. A valet, of stealthy step, thence conducted me, in silence, through many dark and intricate passages in my progress to the *studio* of his master. Much that I encountered on the way contributed, I know not how, to heighten the vague sentiments of which I have already spoken. While the objects around me—while the carvings of the ceilings, the sombre tapestries of the walls, the ebon blackness of the floors, and the phantasmagoric armorial trophies which rattled as I strode, were but matters to which, or to such as which, I had been accustomed from my infancy—while I hesitated not to acknowledge how familiar was all this—I still wondered to find how unfamiliar were the fancies which ordinary images were stirring up. On one of the staircases, I met the physician of the family. His countenance, I thought, wore a mingled expression of low cunning and perplexity. He accosted me with trepidation and passed on. The valet now threw open a door and ushered me into the presence of his master.

The room in which I found myself was very large and lofty. The windows were long, narrow, and pointed, and at so vast a distance from the black oaken floor as to be altogether inaccessible from within. Feeble gleams of encrimsoned light made their way through the trellised panes, and served to render sufficiently distinct the more prominent objects around; the eye, however, struggled in vain to reach the remoter angles of the chamber, or the recesses of the vaulted and fretted ceiling. Dark draperies hung upon the walls. The general furniture was profuse, comfortless, antique, and tattered. Many books and musical instruments lay scattered about, but failed to give any vitality to the scene. I felt that I breathed an atmosphere of sorrow. An air of stern, deep, and irredeemable gloom hung over and pervaded all.

Upon my entrance, Usher arose from a sofa on which he had

been lying at full length, and greeted me with a vivacious warmth which had much in it, I at first thought, of an overdone cordiality —of the constrained effect of the *ennuyé* [1] man of the world. A glance, however, at his countenance convinced me of his perfect sincerity. We sat down; and for some moments, while he spoke not, I gazed upon him with a feeling half of pity, half of awe. Surely, man had never before so terribly altered, in so brief a period, as had Roderick Usher! It was with difficulty that I could bring myself to admit the identity of the wan being before me with the companion of my early boyhood. Yet the character of his face had been at all times remarkable. [2] A cadaverousness of complexion; an eye large, liquid, and luminous beyond comparison; lips somewhat thin and very pallid, but of a surpassingly beautiful curve; a nose of a delicate Hebrew model, but with a breadth of nostril unusual in similar formations; a finely moulded chin, speaking, in its want of prominence, of a want of moral energy; hair of a more than web-like softness and tenuity;—these features, with an inordinate expansion above the regions of the temple, made up altogether a countenance not easily to be forgotten. And now in the mere exaggeration of the prevailing character of these features, and of the expression they were wont to convey, lay so much of change that I doubted to whom I spoke. The now ghastly pallor of the skin, and the now miraculous lustre of the eye, above all things startled and even awed me. The silken hair, too, had been suffered to grow all unheeded, and as, in its wild gossamer texture, it floated rather than fell about the face, I could not, even with effort, connect its Arabesque expression with any idea of simple humanity.

In the manner of my friend I was at once struck with an incoherence—an inconsistency; and I soon found this to arise from a series of feeble and futile struggles to overcome an habitual trepidancy— an excessive nervous agitation. For something of this nature I had indeed been prepared, no less by his letter, than by reminiscences of certain boyish traits, and by conclusions deduced [3] from his peculiar physical conformation and temperament. His action was alternately vivacious and sullen. His voice varied rapidly from a tremulous indecision (when the animal spirits seemed utterly in abeyance) to that species of energetic concision—that abrupt, weighty, unhurried, and hollow-sounding enunciation—that leaden, self-balanced, and perfectly modulated guttural utterance, which may be observed in the lost drunkard, or the irreclaimable eater of opium, during the periods of his most intense excitement.

It was thus that he spoke of the object of my visit, of his earnest

---

1. Bored.
2. Hervey Allen wrote: "The description of Roderick Usher is the most perfect pen-portrait of Poe himself."

3. Poe, like many intelligent contemporaries, trusted the phrenological deduction of character from external characteristics.

desire to see me, and of the solace he expected me to afford him. He entered, at some length, into what he conceived to be the nature of his malady. It was, he said, a constitutional and a family evil, and one for which he despaired to find a remedy—a mere nervous affection, he immediately added, which would undoubtedly soon pass off. It displayed itself in a host of unnatural sensations. Some of these, as he detailed them, interested and bewildered me; although, perhaps, the terms and the general manner of their narration had their weight. He suffered much from a morbid acuteness of the senses; the most insipid food was alone endurable; he could wear only garments of certain texture; the odors of all flowers were oppressive; his eyes were tortured by even a faint light; and there were but peculiar sounds, and these from stringed instruments, which did not inspire him with horror.

To an anomalous species of terror I found him a bounden slave. "I shall perish," said he, "I *must* perish in this deplorable folly. Thus, thus, and not otherwise, shall I be lost. I dread the events of the future, not in themselves, but in their results. I shudder at the thought of any, even the most trivial, incident, which may operate upon this intolerable agitation of soul. I have, indeed, no abhorrence of danger, except in its absolute effect—in terror. In this unnerved, in this pitiable, condition I feel that the period will sooner or later arrive when I must abandon life and reason together, in some struggle with the grim phantasm, FEAR."

I learned, moreover, at intervals, and through broken and equivocal hints, another singular feature of his mental condition. He was enchained by certain superstitious impressions in regard to the dwelling which he tenanted, and whence, for many years, he had never ventured forth—in regard to an influence whose supposititious force was conveyed in terms too shadowy here to be re-stated —an influence which some peculiarities in the mere form and substance of his family mansion had, by dint of long sufferance, he said, obtained over his spirit—an effect which the *physique* of the gray walls and turrets, and of the dim tarn into which they all looked down, had, at length, brought about upon the *morale* of his existence.

He admitted, however, although with hesitation, that much of the peculiar gloom which thus afflicted him could be traced to a more natural and far more palpable origin—to the severe and long-continued illness—indeed to the evidently approaching dissolution—of a tenderly beloved sister, his sole companion for long years, his last and only relative on earth. "Her decease," he said, with a bitterness which I can never forget, "would leave him (him, the hopeless and the frail) the last of the ancient race of the Ushers." While he spoke, the lady Madeline (for so was she called) passed through a remote portion of the apartment, and, without having noticed my presence, disappeared. I regarded her with an utter astonishment not unmingled with dread; and yet I found it impossible to account for such feelings. A sensation of stupor oppressed me as my eyes followed her retreating steps. When a door, at length, closed upon her, my glance sought instinctively and eagerly the countenance of the brother; but he had buried his face in his hands, and I could only perceive that a far more than ordinary wanness had overspread the emaciated fingers through which trickled many passionate tears.

The disease of the lady Madeline had long baffled the skill of her physicians. A settled apathy, a gradual wasting away of the person, and frequent although transient affections of a partially cataleptical character were the unusual diagnosis. · Hitherto she had steadily borne up against the pressure of her malady, and had not betaken herself finally to bed; but on the closing in of the evening of my arrival at the house, she succumbed (as her brother told me at night with inexpressible agitation) to the prostrating power of the destroyer; and I learned that the glimpse I had obtained of her person would thus probably be the last I should obtain——that the lady, at least while living, would be seen by me no more.

For several days ensuing, her name was unmentioned by either Usher or myself; and during this period I was busied in earnest endeavors to alleviate the melancholy of my friend. We painted and read together, or I listened, as if in a dream, to the wild improvisations of his speaking guitar. And thus, as a closer and still closer intimacy admitted me more unreservedly into the recesses of his spirit, the more bitterly did I perceive the futility in all attempt at cheering a mind from which darkness, as if an inherent positive quality, poured forth upon all objects of the moral and physical universe in one unceasing radiation of gloom.

I shall ever bear about me a memory of the many solemn hours I thus spent alone with the master of the House of Usher. Yet I should fail in any attempt to convey an idea of the exact character of the studies, or of the occupations, in which he involved me, or led me the way. An excited and highly distempered ideality threw a sulphureous lustre over all. His long improvised dirges will ring forever in my ears. Among other things, I hold painfully in mind a certain singular perversion and amplification of the wild air of the last waltz of Von Weber.[4] From the paintings over which his elaborate fancy brooded, and which grew, touch by touch, into vaguenesses at which I shuddered the more thrillingly, because I shuddered knowing not why——from these paintings (vivid as their

4. Karl Maria Von Weber (1786–1826), pioneer of German romantic opera, did not compose "The Last Waltz of Von Weber." It was one of the *Danses Brilliantes* (1822) by Karl Gottlieb Reissiger (1798–1859).

images now are before me) I would in vain endeavor to educe more than a small portion which should lie within the compass of merely written words. By the utter simplicity, by the nakedness of his designs, he arrested and overawed attention. If ever mortal painted an idea, that mortal was Roderick Usher. For me at least, in the circumstances then surrounding me, there arose out of the pure abstractions which the hypochondriac contrived to throw upon his canvas, an intensity of intolerable awe, no shadow of which felt I ever yet in the contemplation of the certainly glowing yet too concrete reveries of Fuseli.[5]

One of the phantasmagoric conceptions of my friend, partaking not so rigidly of the spirit of abstraction, may be shadowed forth, although feebly, in words. A small picture presented the interior of an immensely long and rectangular vault or tunnel, with low walls, smooth, white, and without interruption or device. Certain accessory points of the design served well to convey the idea that this excavation lay at an exceeding depth below the surface of the earth. No outlet was observed in any portion of its vast extent, and no torch or other artificial source of light was discernible; yet a flood of intense rays rolled throughout, and bathed the whole in a ghastly and inappropriate splendor.

I have just spoken of that morbid condition of the auditory nerve which rendered all music intolerable to the sufferer, with the exception of certain effects of stringed instruments. It was, perhaps, the narrow limits to which he thus confined himself upon the guitar which gave birth, in great measure, to the fantastic character of his performances. But the fervid *facility* of his *impromptus* could not be so accounted for. They must have been, and were, in the notes, as well as in the words of his wild fantasias (for he not unfrequently accompanied himself with rhymed verbal improvisations), the result of that intense mental collectedness and concentration to which I have previously alluded as observable only in particular moments of the highest artificial excitement. The words of one of these rhapsodies I have easily remembered. I was, perhaps, the more forcibly impressed with it as he gave it, because, in the under or mystic current of its meaning, I fancied that I perceived, and for the first time, a full consciousness on the part of Usher of the tottering of his lofty reason upon her throne. The verses, which were entitled "The Haunted Palace," [6] ran very nearly, if not accurately, thus:—

5. Swiss-born Johann Heinrich Füssli (1742–1825). As Henry Fuseli he became, in London, a romantic impressionist and illustrator of Shakespeare and Milton.

6. This poem was published in the *Baltimore Museum* for April, 1839, five months before it appeared as part of the present story.

I.

In the greenest of our valleys,
   By good angels tenanted,
Once a fair and stately palace—
   Radiant palace—reared its head.
In the monarch Thought's dominion—
   It stood there!
Never seraph spread a pinion
   Over fabric half so fair.

II.

Banners yellow, glorious, golden,
   On its roof did float and flow
(This—all this—was in the olden
   Time long ago);
And every gentle air that dallied,
   In that sweet day,
Along the ramparts plumed and pallid,
   A winged odor went away.

III.

Wanderers in that happy valley
   Through two luminous windows saw
Spirits moving musically
   To a lute's well-tunèd law;
Round about a throne, where sitting
   (Porphyrogene!)[7]
In state his glory well befitting,
   The ruler of the realm was seen.

IV.

And all with pearl and ruby glowing
   Was the fair palace door,
Through which came flowing, flowing, flowing
   And sparkling evermore,
A troop of Echoes whose sweet duty
   Was but to sing,
In voices of surpassing beauty,
   The wit and wisdom of their king.

V.

But evil things, in robes of sorrow,
   Assailed the monarch's high estate;
(Ah, let us mourn, for never morrow
   Shall dawn upon him, desolate!)
And, round about his home, the glory
   That blushed and bloomed

7. A Greek derivative; "born to the purple"—a mark of royalty.

Is but a dim-remembered story
Of the old time entombed.

VI.

And travellers now within that valley,
Through the red-litten windows see
Vast forms that move fantastically
To a discordant melody;
While, like a rapid ghastly river,
Through the pale door;
A hideous throng rush out forever,
And laugh—but smile no more.

I well remember that suggestions arising from this ballad led us into a train of thought wherein there became manifest an opinion of Usher's which I mention not so much on account of its novelty (for other men [8] have thought thus), as on account of the pertinacity with which he maintained it. This opinion, in its general form, was that of the sentience of all vegetable things. But, in his disordered fancy, the idea had assumed a more daring character, and trespassed, under certain conditions, upon the kingdom of inorganization. I lack words to express the full extent, or the earnest *abandon* of his persuasion. The belief, however, was connected (as I have previously hinted) with the gray stones of the home of his forefathers. The conditions of the sentience had been here, he imagined, fulfilled in the method of collocation of these stones—in the order of their arrangement, as well as in that of the many *fungi* which overspread them, and of the decayed trees which stood around—above all, in the long undisturbed endurance of this arrangement, and in its reduplication in the still waters of the tarn. Its evidence—the evidence of the sentience—was to be seen, he said (and I here started as he spoke), in the gradual yet certain condensation of an atmosphere of their own about the waters and the walls. The result was discoverable, he added, in that silent yet importunate and terrible influence which for centuries had moulded the destinies of his family, and which made *him* what I now saw him—what he was. Such opinions need no comment, and I will make none.

Our books [9]—the books, which, for years, had formed no small

8. "Watson, Dr. Percival, Spallanzani, and especially the Bishop of Llandaff.— See 'Chemical Essays,' vol. v" [Poe's note].

9. Usher's library is occult and fantastically learned, suggesting his own state of mind and foreshadowing the later burial and resurrection of his sister, Madeline. *Vert-Vert* and *Chartreuse,* by Jean Baptiste Gresset

(1709–1777), are lusty, anticlerical satires; in the novel of Machiavelli (1469–1527), an infernal demon visits the earth to prove that women are the damnation of men; in *Heaven and Hell* (1758), the mystical scientist Swedenborg argues the continuity of spiritual identity; while the following title, by Ludwig Holberg (1684–1754) again suggests a round trip into the

portion of the mental existence of the invalid—were, as might be supposed, in strict keeping with this character of phantasm. We pored together over such works as the *Ververt et Chartreuse* of Gresset; the *Belphegor* of Machiavelli; the *Heaven and Hell* of Swedenborg; the *Subterranean Voyage of Nicholas Klimm* of Holberg; the *Chiromancy* of Robert Flud, of Jean D'Indaginé, and of De la Chambre; the *Journey into the Blue Distance* of Tieck; and the *City of the Sun* of Campanella. One favorite volume was a small octavo edition of the *Directorium Inquisitorium*, by the Dominican Eymeric de Gironne; and there were passages in Pomponius Mela, about the old African Satyrs and Ægipans, over which Usher would sit dreaming for hours. His chief delight, however, was found in the perusal of an exceedingly rare and curious book in quarto Gothic—the manual of a forgotten church—the *Vigiliæ Mortuorum secundum Chorum Ecclesiæ Maguntinæ.*

I could not help thinking of the wild ritual of this work, and of its probable influence upon the hypochondriac, when, one evening, having informed me abruptly that the lady Madeline was no more, he stated his intention of preserving her corpse for a fortnight (previously to its final interment), in one of the numerous vaults within the main walls of the building. The worldly reason, however, assigned for this singular proceeding, was one which I did not feel at liberty to dispute. The brother had been led to his resolution (so he told me) by consideration of the unusual character of the malady of the deceased, of certain obtrusive and eager inquiries on the part of her medical men,[1] and of the remote and exposed situation of the burial-ground of the family. I will not deny that when I called to mind the sinister countenance of the person whom I met upon the staircase, on the day of my arrival at the house, I had no desire to oppose what I regarded as at best but a harmless, and by no means an unnatural, precaution.

At the request of Usher, I personally aided him in the arrangements for the temporary entombment. The body having been encoffined, we two alone bore it to its rest. The vault in which we

---

world of death. The next three writers are exponents of chiromancy, or occult divination by palmistry: Robert Flud (1574–1637), British Rosicrucian and pesudoscientist; and two Frenchmen— Jean D'Indaginé (*Chiromantia*, 1522), and Marin Cureau de la Chambre, (*Principes de la Chiromancie*, 1653). The next two titles again suggest the journey to another world. T. O. Mabbott states that Poe used the subtitle to refer to *Das Alte Buch* by Ludwig Tieck (1773–1853); the book by Tommaso Campanella (1568–1639), Italian philosopher, describes an ideal other world. *Inquisitorum Directorium* was an account of procedures and tortures, by Nicolas Eymeric de Girone (*ca.* 1320–1399), once inquisitor-general for Castile. Pomponius Mela was a Roman of the first century A.D., but his *Geography*, when printed at Milan in 1471, was still given credence for such wonders as the "Ægipans," reputed goatmen of Africa. The last title, translated as *The Vigils of the Dead* * * * , has not been identified; but there were many such titles in the Middle Ages.

1. The stealing of the bodies of the dead for medical students and scientists was then a common practice.

placed it (and which had been so long unopened that our torches, half smothered in its oppressive atmosphere, gave us little opportunity for investigation) was small, damp, and entirely without means of admission for light; lying, at great depth, immediately beneath that portion of the building in which was my own sleeping apartment. It had been used, apparently, in remote feudal times, for the worst purposes of a donjon-keep, and, in later days, as a place of deposit for powder, or some other highly combustible substance, as a portion of its floor, and the whole interior of a long archway through which we reached it, were carefully sheathed with copper. The door, of massive iron, had been, also, similarly protected. Its immense weight caused an unusually sharp, grating sound, as it moved upon its hinges.

Having deposited our mournful burden upon tressels within this region of horror, we partially turned aside the yet unscrewed lid of the coffin, and looked upon the face of the tenant. A striking similitude between the brother and sister now first arrested my attention; and Usher, divining, perhaps, my thoughts, murmured out some few words from which I learned that the deceased and himself had been twins, and that sympathies of a scarcely intelligible nature had always existed between them. Our glances, however, rested not long upon the dead—for we could not regard her unawed. The disease which had thus entombed the lady in the maturity of youth, had left, as usual in all maladies of a strictly cataleptical character, the mockery of a faint blush upon the bosom and the face, and that suspiciously lingering smile upon the lip which is so terrible in death. We replaced and screwed down the lid, and, having secured the door of iron, made our way, with toil, into the scarcely less gloomy apartments of the upper portion of the house.

And now, some days of bitter grief having elapsed, an observable change came over the features of the mental disorder of my friend. His ordinary manner had vanished. His ordinary occupations were neglected or forgotten. He roamed from chamber to chamber with hurried, unequal, and objectless step. The pallor of his countenance had assumed, if possible, a more ghastly hue—but the luminousness of his eye had utterly gone out. The once occasional huskiness of his tone was heard no more; and a tremulous quaver, as if of extreme terror, habitually characterized his utterance. There were times, indeed, when I thought his unceasingly agitated mind was laboring with some oppressive secret, to divulge which he struggled for the necessary courage. At times, again, I was obliged to resolve all into the mere inexplicable vagaries of madness, for I beheld him gazing upon vacancy for long hours, in an attitude of the profoundest attention, as if listening to some imaginary sound.

It was no wonder that his condition terrified—that it infected me. I felt creeping upon me, by slow yet certain degrees, the wild influences of his own fantastic yet impressive superstitions.

It was, especially, upon retiring to bed late in the night of the seventh or eighth day after the placing of the lady Madeline within the donjon, that I experienced the full power of such feelings. Sleep came not near my couch—while the hours waned and waned away. I struggled to reason off the nervousness which had dominion over me. I endeavored to believe that much, if not all of what I felt, was due to the bewildering influence of the gloomy furniture of the room—of the dark and tattered draperies, which, tortured into motion by the breath of a rising tempest, swayed fitfully to and fro upon the walls, and rustled uneasily about the decorations of the bed. But my efforts were fruitless. An irrepressible tremor gradually pervaded my frame; and, at length, there sat upon my very heart an incubus of utterly causeless alarm. Shaking this off with a gasp and a struggle, I uplifted myself upon the pillows, and, peering earnestly within the intense darkness of the chamber, hearkened—I know not why, except that an instinctive spirit prompted me—to certain low and indefinite sounds which came, through the pauses of the storm, at long intervals, I knew not whence. Overpowered by an intense sentiment of horror, unaccountable yet unendurable, I threw on my clothes with haste (for I felt that I should sleep no more during the night), and endeavored to arouse myself from the pitiable condition into which I had fallen, by pacing rapidly to and fro through the apartment.

I had taken but few turns in this manner, when a light step on an adjoining staircase arrested my attention. I presently recognized it as that of Usher. In an instant afterward he rapped, with a gentle touch, at my door, and entered, bearing a lamp. His countenance was, as usual, cadaverously wan—but, moreover, there was a species of mad hilarity in his eyes—an evidently restrained *hysteria* in his whole demeanor. His air appalled me—but any thing was preferable to the solitude which I had so long endured, and I even welcomed his presence as a relief.

"And you have not seen it?" he said abruptly, after having stared about him for some moments in silence—"you have not then seen it?—but, stay! you shall." Thus speaking, and having carefully shaded his lamp, he hurried to one of the casements, and threw it freely open to the storm.

The impetuous fury of the entering gust nearly lifted us from our feet. It was, indeed, a tempestuous yet sternly beautiful night, and one wildly singular in its terror and its beauty. A whirlwind had apparently collected its force in our vicinity; for there were frequent and violent alterations in the direction of the wind; and the exceeding density of the clouds (which hung so low as to press upon the turrets of the house) did not prevent our perceiving the life-like velocity with which they flew careering from all points against each other, without passing away into the distance. I say that even their exceeding density did not prevent our perceiving this—yet we had no glimpse of the moon or stars, nor was there any flashing forth of the lightning. But the under surfaces of the huge masses of agitated vapor, as well as all terrestrial objects immediately around us, were glowing in the unnatural light of a faintly luminous and distinctly visible gaseous exhalation which hung about and enshrouded the mansion.

"You must not—you shall not behold this!" said I, shuddering, to Usher, as I led him, with a gentle violence, from the window to a seat. "These appearances, which bewilder you, are merely electrical phenomena not uncommon—or it may be that they have their ghastly origin in the rank miasma of the tarn. Let us close this casement;—the air is chilling and dangerous to your frame. Here is one of your favorite romances. I will read, and you shall listen:— and so we will pass away this terrible night together."

The antique volume which I had taken up was the "Mad Trist" of Sir Launcelot Canning;[2] but I had called it a favorite of Usher's more in sad jest than in earnest; for, in truth, there is little in its uncouth and unimaginative prolixity which could have had interest for the lofty and spiritual ideality of my friend. It was, however, the only book immediately at hand; and I indulged a vague hope that the excitement which now agitated the hypochondriac, might find relief (for the history of mental disorders is full of similar anomalies) even in the extremeness of the folly which I should read. Could I have judged, indeed, by the wild overstrained air of vivacity with which he hearkened, or apparently hearkened, to the words of the tale, I might well have congratulated myself upon the success of my design.

I had arrived at that well-known portion of the story where Ethelred, the hero of the Trist, having sought in vain for peaceable admission into the dwelling of the hermit, proceeds to make good an entrance by force. Here, it will be remembered, the words of the narrative run thus:

"And Ethelred, who was by nature of a doughty heart, and who was now mighty withal, on account of the powerfulness of the wine which he had drunken, waited no longer to hold parley with the hermit, who, in sooth, was of an obstinate and maliceful turn, but, feeling the rain upon his shoulders, and fearing the rising of the tempest, uplifted his mace outright, and, with blows, made quickly room in the plankings of the door for his gauntleted hand; and

2. Not identified; possibly Poe invented the book and the author for his purpose.

now pulling therewith sturdily, he so cracked, and ripped, and tore all asunder, that the noise of the dry and hollow-sounding wood alarumed and reverberated throughout the forest."

At the termination of this sentence I started and, for a moment, paused; for it appeared to me (although I at once concluded that my excited fancy had deceived me)—it appeared to me that, from some very remote portion of the mansion, there came, indistinctly to my ears, what might have been, in its exact similarity of character, the echo (but a stifled and dull one certainly) of the very cracking and ripping sound which Sir Launcelot had so particularly described. It was, beyond doubt, the coincidence alone which had arrested my attention; for, amid the rattling of the sashes of the casements, and the ordinary commingled noises of the still increasing storm, the sound, in itself, had nothing, surely, which should have interested or disturbed me. I continued the story:

"But the good champion Ethelred, now entering within the door, was sore enraged and amazed to perceive no signal of the maliceful hermit; but, in the stead thereof, a dragon of a scaly and prodigious demeanor, and of a fiery tongue, which sate in guard before a palace of gold, with a floor of silver; and upon the wall there hung a shield of shining brass with this legend enwritten—

> Who entereth herein, a conqueror hath bin;
> Who slayeth the dragon, the shield he shall win.

And Ethelred uplifted his mace, and struck upon the head of the dragon, which fell before him, and gave up his pesty breath, with a shriek so horrid and harsh, and withal so piercing, that Ethelred had fain to close his ears with his hands against the dreadful noise of it, the like whereof was never before heard."

Here again I paused abruptly, and now with a feeling of wild amazement—for there could be no doubt whatever that, in this instance, I did actually hear (although from what direction it proceeded I found it impossible to say) a low and apparently distant, but harsh, protracted, and most unusual screaming or grating sound—the exact counterpart of what my fancy had already conjured up for the dragon's unnatural shriek as described by the romancer.

Oppressed, as I certainly was, upon the occurrence of this second and most extraordinary coincidence, by a thousand conflicting sensations, in which wonder and extreme terror were predominant, I still retained sufficient presence of mind to avoid exciting, by any observation, the sensitive nervousness of my companion. I was by no means certain that he had noticed the sounds in question; although, assuredly, a strange alteration had, during the last few minutes, taken place in his demeanor. From a position fronting my own, he had gradually brought round his chair, so as to sit with his face to the door of the chamber; and thus I could but partially perceive his features, although I saw that his lips trembled as if he were murmuring inaudibly. His head had dropped upon his breast —yet I knew that he was not asleep, from the wide and rigid opening of the eye as I caught a glance of it in profile. The motion of his body, too, was at variance with this idea—for he rocked from side to side with a gentle yet constant and uniform sway. Having rapidly taken notice of all this, I resumed the narrative of Sir Launcelot, which thus proceeded:

"And now, the champion, having escaped from the terrible fury of the dragon, bethinking himself of the brazen shield, and of the breaking up of the enchantment which was upon it, removed the carcass from out of the way before him, and approached valorously over the silver pavement of the castle to where the shield was upon the wall; which in sooth tarried not for his full coming, but fell down at his feet upon the silver floor, with a mighty great and terrible ringing sound."

No sooner had these syllables passed my lips, than—as if a shield of brass had indeed, at the moment, fallen heavily upon a floor of silver—I became aware of a distinct, hollow, metallic, and clangorous, yet apparently muffled, reverberation. Completely unnerved, I leaped to my feet; but the measured rocking movement of Usher was undisturbed. I rushed to the chair in which he sat. His eyes were bent fixedly before him, and throughout his whole countenance there reigned a stony rigidity. But, as I placed my hand upon his shoulder, there came a strong shudder over his whole person; a sickly smile quivered about his lips; and I saw that he spoke in a low, hurried, and gibbering murmur, as if unconscious of my presence. Bending closely over him, I at length drank in the hideous import of his words.

"Now hear it?—yes, I hear it, and *have* heard it. Long—long—long—many minutes, many hours, many days, have I heard it—yet I dared not—oh, pity me, miserable wretch that I am!—I dared not—I *dared* not speak! *We have put her living in the tomb!* Said I not that my senses were acute? I *now* tell you that I heard her feeble first movements in the hollow coffin. I heard them—many, many days ago—yet I dared not—*I dared not speak!* And now—to-night—Ethelred—ha! ha!—the breaking of the hermit's door, and the death-cry of the dragon, and the clangor of the shield—say, rather, the rending of her coffin, and the grating of the iron hinges of her prison, and her struggles within the coppered archway of the vault! Oh! whither shall I fly? Will she not be here anon? Is she not hurrying to upbraid me for my haste? Have I not heard her footstep on the stair? Do I not distinguish that heavy and horrible beating of her heart? Madman!" —here he sprang furiously to his feet, and shrieked out his syllables, as if in the effort he were giving up his soul—"MADMAN! I TELL YOU THAT SHE NOW STANDS WITHOUT THE DOOR!"

As if in the superhuman energy of his utterance there had been found the potency of a spell, the huge antique panels to which the speaker pointed threw slowly back, upon the instant, their ponderous and ebony jaws. It was the work of the rushing gust—but then without those doors there *did* stand the lofty and enshrouded figure of the lady Madeline of Usher. There was blood upon her white robes, and the evidence of some bitter struggle upon every portion of her emaciated frame. For a moment she remained trembling and reeling to and fro upon the threshold—then, with a low moaning cry, fell heavily inward upon the person of her brother, and in her violent and now final death-agonies, bore him to the floor a corpse, and a victim to the terrors he had anticipated.

From that chamber, and from that mansion, I fled aghast. The storm was still abroad in all its wrath as I found myself crossing the old causeway. Suddenly there shot along the path a wild light, and I turned to see whence a gleam so unusual could have issued; for the vast house and its shadows were alone behind me. The radiance was that of the full, setting, and blood-red moon, which now shone vividly through that once barely discernible fissure, of which I have before spoken as extending from the roof of the building, in a zigzag direction, to the base. While I gazed, this fissure rapidly widened—there came a fierce breath of the whirlwind—the entire orb of the satellite burst at once upon my sight —my brain reeled as I saw the mighty walls rushing asunder— there was a long tumultuous shouting sound like the voice of a thousand waters [3]—and the deep and dank tarn at my feet closed sullenly and silently over the fragments of the HOUSE OF USHER.

1839, 1840

The Purloined Letter [4]

Nil sapientiæ odibsius acumine nimio. [5]
—SENECA

At Paris, just after dark one gusty evening in the autumn of 18—, I was enjoying the twofold luxury of meditation and a meerschaum, in company with my friend C. Auguste Dupin, in his little back

---

3. *Cf.* Ezekiel xliii: 2: "[God's] voice was like a noise of many waters."
4. Written early in 1844, a shorter version of this story appeared in *Chambers' Edinburgh Journal* for November of that year, whether with Poe's consent is not known. In his *Tales* of 1845 he used the present text, which was first published in *The Gift* (1845). A. H. Quinn terms this narrative, of the three in which Dupin appears, "the most unified of the stories of ratiocination." One device which sets it apart from those of Poe's imitators is that his detective solves the case on the basis of what he knows of the *character* of the Minister D——.
5. "Nothing is more inimical to wisdom than too much subtlety."

library, or book-closet, *au troisième,*[6] No. 33, *Rue Dunôt, Faubourg St. Germain.* For one hour at least we had maintained a profound silence; while each, to any casual observer, might have seemed intently and exclusively occupied with the curling eddies of smoke that oppressed the atmosphere of the chamber. For myself, however, I was mentally discussing certain topics which had formed matter for conversation between us at an earlier period of the evening; I mean the affair of the Rue Morgue, and the mystery attending the murder of Marie Rogêt.[7] I looked upon it, therefore, as something of a coincidence, when the door of our apartment was thrown open and admitted our old acquaintance, Monsieur G——, the Prefect of the Parisian police.

We gave him a hearty welcome; for there was nearly half as much of the entertaining as of the contemptible about the man, and we had not seen him for several years. We had been sitting in the dark, and Dupin now arose for the purpose of lighting a lamp, but sat down again, without doing so, upon G.'s saying that he had called to consult us, or rather to ask the opinion of my friend, about some official business which had occasioned a great deal of trouble.

"If it is any point requiring reflection," observed Dupin, as he forebore to enkindle the wick, "we shall examine it to better purpose in the dark."

"That is another of your odd notions," said the Prefect, who had a fashion of calling every thing "odd" that was beyond his comprehension, and thus lived amid an absolute legion of "oddities."

"Very true," said Dupin, as he supplied his visitor with a pipe, and rolled towards him a comfortable chair.

"And what is the difficulty now?" I asked. "Nothing more in the assassination way, I hope?"

"Oh no; nothing of that nature. The fact is, the business is *very* simple indeed, and I make no doubt that we can manage it sufficiently well ourselves; but then I thought Dupin would like to hear the details of it, because it is so excessively *odd.*"

"Simple and odd," said Dupin.

"Why, yes; and not exactly that, either. The fact is, we have all been a good deal puzzled because the affair *is* so simple, and yet baffles us altogether."

"Perhaps it is the very simplicity of the thing which puts you at fault," said my friend.

"What nonsense you *do* talk!" replied the Prefect, laughing heartily.

"Perhaps the mystery is a little *too* plain," said Dupin.

"Oh, good heavens! who ever heard of such an idea?"

6. In a French dwelling, the fourth floor.

7. The first and second murders solved by Dupin in Poe's fiction.

"A little *too* self-evident."

"Ha! ha! ha!—ha! ha! ha!—ho! ho! ho!"—roared our visitor, profoundly amused, "oh, Dupin, you will be the death of me yet!"

"And what, after all, *is* the matter on hand?" I asked.

"Why, I will tell you," replied the Prefect, as he gave a long, steady, and contemplative puff, and settled himself in his chair. "I will tell you in a few words; but, before I begin, let me caution you that this is an affair demanding the greatest secrecy, and that I should most probably lose the position I now hold, were it known that I confided it to any one."

"Proceed," said I.

"Or not," said Dupin.

"Well, then; I have received personal information, from a very high quarter, that a certain document of the last importance has been purloined from the royal apartments. The individual who purloined it is known; this beyond a doubt; he was seen to take it. It is known, also, that it still remains in his possession."

"How is this known?" asked Dupin.

"It is clearly inferred," replied the Prefect, "from the nature of the document, and from the non-appearance of certain results which would at once arise from its passing *out* of the robber's possession;—that is to say, from his employing it as he must design in the end to employ it."

"Be a little more explicit," I said.

"Well, I may venture so far as to say that the paper gives its holder a certain power in a certain quarter where such power is immensely valuable." The Prefect was fond of the cant of diplomacy.

"Still I do not quite understand," said Dupin.

"No? Well; the disclosure of the document to a third person who shall be nameless would bring in question the honor of a personage of most exalted station; and this fact gives the holder of the document an ascendancy over the illustrious personage whose honor and peace are so jeopardized."

"But this ascendancy," I interposed, "would depend upon the robber's knowledge of the loser's knowledge of the robber. Who would dare——"

"The thief," said G——, "is the Minister D——, who dares all things, those unbecoming as well as those becoming a man. The method of the theft was not less ingenious than bold. The document in question—a letter, to be frank—had been received by the personage robbed while alone in the royal *boudoir*. During its perusal she was suddenly interrupted by the entrance of the other exalted personage from whom especially it was her wish to conceal it. After a hurried and vain endeavor to thrust it in a drawer, she was forced to place it, open as it was, upon a table. The address, however, was uppermost, and, the contents thus unexposed, the letter escaped notice. At this juncture enters the Minister D——. His lynx eye immediately perceives the paper, recognizes the hand-writing of the address, observes the confusion of the personage addressed, and fathoms her secret. After some business transactions, hurried through in his ordinary manner, he produces a letter some-what similar to the one in question, opens it, pretends to read it, and then places it in close juxtaposition to the other. Again he con-verses, for some fifteen minutes, upon the public affairs. At length, in taking leave, he takes also from the table the letter to which he had no claim. Its rightful owner saw, but, of course, dared not call attention to the act, in the presence of the third personage who stood at her elbow. The Minister decamped; leaving his own letter —one of no importance—upon the table."

"Here, then," said Dupin to me, "you have precisely what you demand to make the ascendancy complete—the robber's knowledge of the loser's knowledge of the robber."

"Yes," replied the Prefect; "and the power thus attained has, for some months past, been wielded, for political purposes, to a very dangerous extent. The personage robbed is more thoroughly con-vinced, every day, of the necessity of reclaiming her letter. But this, of course, cannot be done openly. In fine, driven to despair, she has committed the matter to me."

"Than whom," said Dupin, amid a perfect whirlwind of smoke, "no more sagacious agent could, I suppose, be desired, or even imagined."

"You flatter me," replied the Prefect; "but it is possible that some such opinion may have been entertained."

"It is clear," said I, "as you observe, that the letter is still in possession of the Minister; since it is this possession, and not any employment of the letter, which bestows the power. With the em-ployment the power departs."

"True," said G——; "and upon this conviction I proceeded. My first care was to make thorough search of the Minister's hôtel; [8] and here my chief embarrassment lay in the necessity of searching with-out his knowledge. Beyond all things, I have been warned of the danger which would result from giving him reason to suspect our design."

"But," said I, "you are quite *au fait* [9] in these investigations. The Parisian police have done this thing often before."

"Oh yes; and for this reason I did not despair. The habits of the Minister gave me, too, a great advantage. He is frequently absent from home all night. His servants are by no means numerous. They sleep at a distance from their master's apartment, and, being chiefly

8. Town house.   9. Skilled, expert.

Neapolitans, are readily made drunk. I have keys, as you know, with which I can open any chamber or cabinet in Paris. For three months a night has not passed, during the greater part of which I have not been engaged, personally, in ransacking the D—— Hôtel. My honor is interested, and, to mention a great secret, the reward is enormous. So I did not abandon the search until I had become fully satisfied that the thief is a more astute man than myself. I fancy that I have investigated every nook and corner of the premises in which it is possible that the paper can be concealed."

"But is it not possible," I suggested, "that although the letter may be in the possession of the Minister, as it unquestionably is, he may have concealed it elsewhere than upon his own premises?"

"This is barely possible," said Dupin. "The present peculiar condition of affairs at court, and especially of those intrigues in which D—— is known to be involved, would render the instant availability of the document—its susceptibility of being produced at a moment's notice—a point of nearly equal importance with its possession."

"Its susceptibility of being produced?" said I.

"That is to say, of being *destroyed*," said Dupin.

"True," I observed; "the paper is clearly then upon the premises. As for its being upon the person of the Minister, we may consider that as out of the question."

"Entirely," said the Prefect. "He has been twice waylaid, as if by footpads, and his person rigorously searched under my own inspection."

"You might have spared yourself this trouble," said Dupin. "D——, I presume, is not altogether a fool, and, if not, must have anticipated these waylayings, as a matter of course."

"Not *altogether* a fool," said G——, "but then he's a poet, which I take to be only one remove from a fool."

"True," said Dupin, after a long and thoughtful whiff from his meerschaum, "although I have been guilty of certain doggerel myself."

"Suppose you detail," said I, "the particulars of your search."

"Why the fact is, we took our time, and we searched *every where*. I have had long experience in these affairs. I took the entire building, room by room; devoting the nights of a whole week to each. We examined, first, the furniture of each apartment. We opened every possible drawer; and I presume you know that, to a properly trained police agent, such a thing as a *secret* drawer is impossible. Any man is a dolt who permits a 'secret' drawer to escape him in a search of this kind. The thing is *so* plain. There is a certain amount of bulk—a space—to be accounted for in every cabinet. Then we have accurate rules. The fiftieth part of a line could not escape us.

After the cabinets we took the chairs. The cushions we probed with the fine long needles you have seen me employ. From the tables we removed the tops."

"Why so?"

"Sometimes the top of a table, or other similarly arranged piece of furniture, is removed by the person wishing to conceal an article; then the leg is excavated, the article deposited within the cavity, and the top replaced. The bottoms and tops of bed-posts are employed in the same way."

"But could not the cavity be detected by sounding?" I asked.

"By no means, if, when the article is deposited, a sufficient wadding of cotton be placed around it. Besides, in our case, we were obliged to proceed without noise."

"But you could not have removed—you could not have taken to pieces *all* articles of furniture in which it would have been possible to make a deposit in the manner you mention. A letter may be compressed into a thin spiral roll, not differing much in shape or bulk from a large knitting-needle, and in this form it might be inserted into the rung of a chair, for example. You did not take to pieces all the chairs?"

"Certainly not; but we did better—we examined the rungs of every chair in the hôtel, and, indeed, the jointings of every description of furniture, by the aid of a most powerful microscope.[1] Had there been any traces of recent disturbance we should not have failed to detect it instantly. A single grain of gimlet-dust, for example, would have been as obvious as an apple. Any disorder in the glueing—any unusual gaping in the joints—would have sufficed to insure detection."

"I presume you looked to the mirrors, between the boards and the plates, and you probed the beds and the bed-clothes, as well as the curtains and carpets."

"That of course; and when we had absolutely completed every particle of the furniture in this way, then we examined the house itself. We divided its entire surface into compartments, which we numbered, so that none might be missed; then we scrutinized each individual square inch throughout the premises, including the two houses immediately adjoining, with the microscope, as before."

"The two houses adjoining!" I exclaimed; "you must have a great deal of trouble."

"We had; but the reward offered is prodigious."

"You include the *grounds* about the houses?"

"All the grounds are paved with brick. They gave us compara-

---

1. Probably a hand magnifying glass with a powerful lens. The term "microscope" long continued to be used for this instrument as well as for the compound microscope now used in scientific researches.

tively little trouble. We examined the moss between the bricks, and found it undisturbed."

"You looked among D——'s papers, of course, and into the books of the library?"

"Certainly; we opened every package and parcel; we not only opened every book, but we turned over every leaf in each volume, not contenting ourselves with a mere shake, according to the fashion of some of our police officers. We also measured the thickness of every book-*cover*, with the most accurate admeasurement, and applied to each the most jealous scrutiny of the microscope. Had any of the bindings been recently meddled with, it would have been utterly impossible that the fact should have escaped observation. Some five or six volumes, just from the hands of the binder, we carefully probed, longitudinally, with the needles."

"You explored the floors beneath the carpets?"

"Beyond doubt. We removed every carpet, and examined the boards with the microscope."

"And the paper on the walls?"

"Yes."

"You looked into the cellars?"

"We did."

"Then," I said, "you have been making a miscalculation, and the letter is *not* upon the premises, as you suppose."

"I fear you are right there," said the Prefect. "And now, Dupin, what would you advise me to do?"

"To make a thorough re-search of the premises."

"That is absolutely needless," replied G——. "I am not more sure that I breathe than I am that the letter is not at the Hôtel."

"I have no better advice to give you," said Dupin. "You have, of course, an accurate description of the letter?"

"Oh yes!"—And here the Prefect, producing a memorandum-book, proceeded to read aloud a minute account of the internal, and especially of the external appearance of the missing document. Soon after finishing the perusal of this description, he took his departure, more entirely depressed in spirits than I had ever known the good gentleman before.

In about a month afterwards he paid us another visit, and found us occupied very nearly as before. He took a pipe and a chair and entered into some ordinary conversation. At length I said,—

"Well, but G——, what of the purloined letter? I presume you have at last made up your mind that there is no such thing as over-reaching the Minister?"

"Confound him, say I—yes; I made the re-examination, however, as Dupin suggested—but it was all labor lost, as I knew it would be."

"How much was the reward offered, did you say?" asked Dupin.

"Why, a very great deal—a *very* liberal reward—I don't like to say how much, precisely; but one thing I *will* say, that I wouldn't mind giving my individual cheque for fifty thousand francs to any one who could obtain me that letter. The fact is, it is becoming of more and more importance every day; and the reward has been lately doubled. If it were trebled, however, I could do no more than I have done."

"Why, yes," said Dupin, drawlingly, between the whiffs of his meerschaum, "I really—think, G——, you have not exerted yourself—to the utmost in this matter. You might—do a little more, I think, eh?"

"How?—in what way?"

"Why—puff, puff—you might—puff, puff—employ counsel in the matter, eh?—puff, puff, puff. Do you remember the story they tell of Abernethy?"

"No; hang Abernethy!"

"To be sure! hang him and welcome. But, once upon a time, a certain rich miser conceived the design of sponging upon this Abernethy for a medical opinion. Getting up, for this purpose, an ordinary conversation in a private company, he insinuated his case to his physician, as that of an imaginary individual.

"'We will suppose,' said the miser, 'that his symptoms are such and such; now, doctor, what would *you* have directed him to take?'"

"'Take!' said Abernethy, 'why, take *advice*, to be sure.'"

"But," said the Prefect, a little discomposed, "I am *perfectly* willing to take advice, and to pay for it. I would *really* give fifty thousand francs to any one who would aid me in the matter."

"In that case," replied Dupin, opening a drawer, and producing a cheque-book, "you may as well fill me up a cheque for the amount mentioned. When you have signed it, I will hand you the letter."

"I was astounded. The Prefect appeared absolutely thunderstricken. For some minutes he remained speechless and motionless, looking incredulously at my friend with open mouth, and eyes that seemed starting from their sockets; then, apparently recovering himself in some measure, he seized a pen, and after several pauses and vacant stares, finally filled up and signed a cheque for fifty thousand francs, and handed it across the table to Dupin. The latter examined it carefully and deposited it in his pocket-book; then, unlocking an *escritoire*,[2] took thence a letter and gave it to the Prefect. This functionary grasped it in a perfect agony of joy, opened it with a trembling hand, cast a rapid glance at its contents, and then, scrambling and struggling to the door, rushed at length unceremoniously from the room and from the house, without having

2. Writing desk.

uttered a syllable since Dupin had requested him to fill up the cheque.

When he had gone, my friend entered into some explanations.

"The Parisian police," he said, "are exceedingly able in their way. They are persevering, ingenious, cunning, and thoroughly versed in the knowledge which their duties seem chiefly to demand. Thus, when G—— detailed to us his mode of searching the premises at the Hôtel D——, I felt entire confidence in his having made a satisfactory investigation—so far as his labors extended."

"So far as his labors extended?" said I.

"Yes," said Dupin. "The measures adopted were not only the best of their kind, but carried out to absolute perfection. Had the letter been deposited within the range of their search, these fellows would, beyond a question, have found it."

I merely laughed—but he seemed quite serious in all that he said.

"The measures, then," he continued, "were good in their kind, and well executed; their defect lay in their being inapplicable to the case, and to the man. A certain set of highly ingenious resources are, with the Prefect, a sort of Procrustean bed,[3] to which he forcibly adapts his designs. But he perpetually errs by being too deep or too shallow, for the matter in hand; and many a schoolboy is a better reasoner than he. I knew one about eight years of age, whose success at guessing in the game of 'even and odd' attracted universal admiration. This game is simple, and is played with marbles. One player holds in his hand a number of these toys, and demands of another whether that number is even or odd. If the guess is right, the guesser wins one; if wrong, he loses one. The boy to whom I allude won all the marbles of the school. Of course he had some principle of guessing; and this lay in mere observation and admeasurement of the astuteness of his opponents. For example, an arrant simpleton is his opponent, and, holding up his closed hand, asks, 'are they even or odd?' Our schoolboy replies, 'odd,' and loses; but upon the second trial he wins, for he then says to himself, 'the simpleton had them even upon the first trial, and his amount of cunning is just sufficient to make him have them odd upon the second; I will therefore guess odd';—he guesses odd, and wins. Now, with a simpleton a degree above the first, he would have reasoned thus: 'This fellow finds that in the first instance I guessed odd, and, in the second, he will propose to himself upon the first impulse, a simple variation from even to odd, as did the first simpleton; but then a second thought will suggest that this is too simple a variation, and finally he will decide upon putting it even as before. I will there-

---

3. Procrustes was a legendary Greek robber who bound his victims to a bed. If too short, they were stretched to fit it; if too long, parts of their legs were cut off.

fore guess even';—he guesses even, and wins. Now this mode of reasoning in the schoolboy, whom his fellows termed 'lucky,'—what, in its last analysis, is it?"

"It is merely," I said, "an identification of the reasoner's intellect with that of his opponent."

"It is," said Dupin; "and, upon inquiring of the boy by what means he effected the *thorough* identification in which his success consisted, I received answer as follows: 'When I wish to find out how wise, or how stupid, or how good, or how wicked is any one, or what are his thoughts at the moment, I fashion the expression on my face, as accurately as possible, in accordance with the expression of his, and then wait to see what thoughts or sentiments arise in my mind or heart, as if to match or correspond with the expression.' This response of the schoolboy lies at the bottom of all the spurious profundity which has been attributed to Rochefoucauld, to La Bougive, to Machiavelli, and to Campanella."

"And the identification," I said, "of the reasoner's intellect with that of his opponent, depends, if I understand you aright, upon the accuracy with which the opponent's intellect is admeasured."

"For its practical value it depends upon this," replied Dupin; "and the Prefect and his cohort fail so frequently, first, by default of this identification, and, secondly, by ill-admeasurement, or rather through non-admeasurement of the intellect with which they are engaged. They consider only their *own* ideas of ingenuity; and, in searching for anything hidden, advert only to the modes in which *they* would have hidden it. They are right in this much—that their own ingenuity is a faithful representative of that of *the mass*; but when the cunning of the individual felon is diverse in character from their own, the felon foils them, of course. This always happens when it is above their own, and very usually when it is below. They have no variation of principle in their investigations; at best, when urged by some unusual emergency—by some extraordinary reward —they extend or exaggerate their old modes of *practice*, without touching their principles. What, for example, in this case of D——, has been done to vary the principle of action? What is all this boring, and probing, and sounding, and scrutinizing with the microscope, and dividing the surface of the building into registered square inches—what is it all but an exaggeration *of the application* of the one principle or set of principles of search, which are based upon the one set of motions regarding human ingenuity, to which the Prefect, in the long routine of his duty, has been accustomed? Do you not see he has taken it for granted that *all* men proceed to conceal a letter—not exactly in a gimlet-hole bored in a chair-leg— but, at least, in *some* out-of-the-way hole or corner suggested by the same tenor of thought which would urge a man to secrete a letter in a gimlet-hole bored in a chair-leg? And do you not see also, that such *recherchés* [4] nooks for concealment are adapted only for ordinary occasions, and would be adopted only by ordinary intellects; for, in all cases of concealment, a disposal of the article concealed—a disposal of it in this *recherché* manner—is, in the very first instance, presumable and presumed; and thus its discovery depends, not at all upon the acumen, but altogether upon the mere care, patience, and determination of the seekers; and where the case is of importance—or, what amounts to the same thing in the policial eyes, when the reward is of magnitude,—the qualities in question have *never* been known to fail? You will now understand what I meant in suggesting that, had the purloined letter been hidden any where within the limits of the Prefect's examination—in other words, had the principle of its concealment been comprehended within the principles of the Prefect—its discovery would have been a matter altogether beyond question. This functionary, however, has been thoroughly mystified; and the remote source of his defeat lies in the supposition that the Minister is a fool, because he has acquired renown as a poet. All fools are poets; this the Prefect *feels*; and he is merely guilty of a *non distributio medii* [5] in thence inferring that all poets are fools."

"But is this really the poet?" I asked. "There are two brothers, I know; and both have attained reputation in letters. The Minister I believe has written learnedly on the Differential Calculus. He is a mathematician, and no poet."

"You are mistaken; I know him well; he is both. As poet *and* mathematician, he would reason well; as mere mathematician, he could not have reasoned at all, and thus would have been at the mercy of the Prefect."

"You surprise me," I said, "by these opinions, which have been contradicted by the voice of the world. You do not mean to set at naught the well-digested idea of centuries. The mathematical reason has long been regarded as *the* reason *par excellence*.

" '*Il y a à parier*,' " replied Dupin, quoting from Chamfort, " '*que toute idée publique, toute convention reçue, est une sottise, car elle a convenu au plus grand nombre.*' [6] The mathematicians, I grant you, have done their best to promulgate the popular error to which you allude, and which is none the less an error for its promulgation as truth. With an art worthy a better cause, for example, they have insinuated the term 'analysis' into application to algebra. The French are the originators of this particular deception; but if a term is of any importance—if words derive any value from applicability—then 'analysis' conveys 'algebra' about as much as, in

---

4. Choice, studied.
5. "Undistributed middle," as in a syllogism, which will lead to a false conclusion.

6. "The odds are that every idea which is widely accepted, every received convention, is a stupidity, since it is suitable to the masses."

Latin, '*ambitus*' implies 'ambition,' '*religio*' 'religion,' or '*homines. honesti*' a set of *honorable men*." [7]

"You have a quarrel on hand, I see," said I, "with some of the algebraists of Paris; but proceed."

"I dispute the availability, and thus the value, of that reason which is cultivated in any especial form other than the abstractly logical. I dispute, in particular, the reason educed by mathematical study. The mathematics are the science of form and quantity; mathematical reasoning is merely logic applied to observation upon form and quantity. The great error lies in supposing that even the truths of what is called *pure* algebra, are abstract or general truths. And this error is so egregious that I am confounded at the universality with which it has been received. Mathematical axioms are *not* axioms of general truth. What is true of *relation*—of form and quantity—is often grossly false in regard to morals, for example. In this latter science it is very usually *un*true that the aggregated parts are equal to the whole. In chemistry also the axiom fails. In the consideration of motive it fails; for two motives, each of a given value, have not, necessarily, a value when united, equal to the sum of their values apart. There are numerous other mathematical truths which are only truths within the limits of *relation*. But the mathematician argues, from his *finite truths*, through habit, as if they were of an absolutely general applicability—as the world indeed imagines them to be. Bryant, in his very learned 'Mythology,' mentions an analogous source of error, when he says that 'although the Pagan fables are not believed, yet we forget ourselves continually, and make inferences from them as existing realities.' With the algebraists, however, who are Pagans themselves, the 'Pagan fables' *are* believed, and the inferences are made, not so much through lapse of memory, as through an unaccountable addling of the brains. In short, I never yet encountered the mere mathematician who could be trusted out of equal roots, or one who did not clandestinely hold it as a point of his faith that $x^2 + px$ was absolutely and unconditionally equal to q. Say to one of these gentlemen, by way of experiment, if you please, that you believe occasions may occur where $x^2 + px$ is *not* altogether equal to q, and, having made him understand what you mean, get out of his reach as speedily as convenient, for beyond doubt, he will endeavor to knock you down.

"I mean to say," continued Dupin, while I merely laughed at his last observations, "that if the Minister had been no more than a mathematician, the Prefect would have been under no necessity of giving me this check. I knew him, however, as both mathematician and poet, and my measures were adapted to his capacity, with

7. Dupin's point is that a word's original meaning is not necessarily indicated by others which may have derived from it.

reference to the circumstances by which he was surrounded. I knew him as a courtier, too, and as a bold *intriguant*.[8] Such a man, I considered, could not fail to be aware of the ordinary policial modes of action. He could not have failed to anticipate—and events have proved that he did not fail to anticipate—the waylayings to which he was subjected. He must have foreseen, I reflected, the secret investigations of his premises. His frequent absences from home at night, which were hailed by the Prefect as certain aids to his success, I regarded only as *ruses*, to afford opportunity for thorough search to the police, and thus the sooner to impress them with the conviction to which G——, in fact, did finally arrive—the conviction that the letter was not upon the premises. I felt, also, that the whole train of thought, which I was at some pains in detailing to you just now, concerning the invariable principle of policial action in searches for articles concealed—I felt that this whole train of thought would necessarily pass through the mind of the Minister. It would imperatively lead him to despise all the ordinary *nooks* of concealment. *He* could not, I reflect, be so weak as not to see that the most intricate and remote recess of his hôtel would be as open as his commonest closets to the eyes, to the probes, to the gimlets, and to the microscopes of the Prefect. I saw, in fine, that he would be driven, as a matter of course, to *simplicity*, if not deliberately induced to it as a matter of choice. You will remember, perhaps, how desperately the Prefect laughed when I suggested, upon our first interview, that it was just possible this mystery troubled him so much on account of its being so *very* self-evident."

"Yes," said I, "I remember his merriment well. I really thought he would have fallen into convulsions."

"The material world," continued Dupin, "abounds with the very strict analogies to the immaterial; and thus some color of truth has been given to the rhetorical dogma, that metaphor, or simile, may be made to strengthen an argument, as well as to embellish a description. The principle of the *vis inertiæ*,[9] for example, seems to be identical in physics and metaphysics. It is not more true in the former, that a large body is with more difficulty set in motion than a smaller one, and that its subsequent *momentum* is commensurate with this difficulty, than it is, in the latter, that intellects of the vaster capacity, while more forcible, more constant, and more eventful in their movements than those of inferior grade, are yet the less readily moved, and more embarrassed and full of hesitation in the first few steps of their progress. Again: have you ever noticed which of the street signs, over the shop doors, are the most attractive of attention?"

"I have never given the matter a thought," I said.

8. Schemer.   9. Inertia.

"There is a game of puzzles," he resumed, "which is played upon a map. One party playing requires another to find a given word—the name of town, river, state or empire—any word, in short, upon the motley and perplexed surface of the chart. A novice in the game generally seeks to embarrass his opponents by giving them the most minutely lettered names; but the adept selects such words as stretch, in large characters, from one end of the chart to the other. These, like the over-largely lettered signs and placards of the street, escape observation by dint of being excessively obvious; and here the physical oversight is precisely analogous with the moral inapprehension by which the intellect suffers to pass unnoticed those considerations which are too obtrusively and too palpably self-evident. But this is a point, it appears, somewhat above or beneath the understanding of the Prefect. He never once thought it probable, or possible, that the Minister had deposited the letter immediately beneath the nose of the whole world, by way of best preventing any portion of that world from perceiving it.

"But the more I reflected upon the daring, dashing, and discriminating ingenuity of D——; upon the fact that the document must always have been *at hand*, if he intended to use it to good purpose; and upon the decisive evidence, obtained by the Prefect, that it was not hidden within the limits of that dignitary's ordinary search—the more satisfied I became that, to conceal this letter, the Minister had resorted to the comprehensive and sagacious expedient of not attempting to conceal it at all.

"Full of these ideas, I prepared myself with a pair of green spectacles, and called one fine morning, quite by accident, at the Ministerial hôtel. I found D—— at home, yawning, lounging, and dawdling, as usual, and pretending to be in the last extremity of *ennui*. He is, perhaps, the most really energetic human being now alive—but that is only when nobody sees him.

"To be even with him, I complained of my weak eyes, and lamented the necessity of the spectacles, under cover of which I cautiously and thoroughly surveyed the apartment, while seemingly intent only upon the conversation of my host.

"I paid especial attention to a large writing-table near which he sat, and upon which lay confusedly some miscellaneous letters and other papers, with one or two musical instruments and a few books. Here, however, after a long and very deliberate scrutiny, I saw nothing to excite particular suspicion.

"At length my eyes, in going the circuit of the room, fell upon a trumpery filigree card-rack of pasteboard, that hung dangling by a dirty blue ribbon, from a little brass knob just beneath the middle of the mantel-piece. In this rack, which had three or four compartments, were five or six visiting cards and a solitary letter. This last was much soiled and crumpled. It was torn nearly in two, across the middle—as if a design, in the first instance, to tear it entirely up as worthless, had been altered, or stayed, in the second. It had a large black seal, bearing the D—— cipher *very* conspicuously, and was addressed, in a diminutive female hand, to D——, the Minister, himself. It was thrust carelessly, and even, as it seemed, contemptuously, into one of the upper divisions of the rack.

"No sooner had I glanced at this letter, than I concluded it to be that of which I was in search. To be sure, it was, to all appearance, radically different from the one of which the Prefect had read us so minute a description. Here the seal was large and black, with the D—— cipher; there it was small and red, with the ducal arms of the S—— family. Here, the address, to the Minister, was diminutive and feminine; there the superscription, to a certain royal personage, was markedly bold and decided; the size alone formed a point of correspondence. But, then, the *radicalness* of these differences, which was excessive; the dirt; the soiled and torn condition of the paper, so inconsistent with the *true* methodical habits of D——, and so suggestive of a design to delude the beholder into an idea of the worthlessness of the document;—these things, together with the hyperobtrusive situation of this document, full in the view of every visitor, and thus exactly in accordance with the conclusions to which I had previously arrived; these things, I say, were strongly corroborative of suspicion, in one who came with the intention to suspect.

"I protracted my visit as long as possible, and, while I maintained a most animated discussion with the Minister, on a topic which I knew well had never failed to interest and excite him, I kept my attention really riveted upon the letter. In this examination, I committed to memory its external appearance and arrangement in the rack; and also fell, at length, upon a discovery which set at rest whatever trivial doubt I might have entertained. In scrutinizing the edges of the paper, I observed them to be more *chafed* than seemed necessary. They presented the *broken* appearance which is manifested when a stiff paper, having been once folded and pressed with a folder, is refolded in a reversed direction, in the same creases or edges which had formed the original fold. This discovery was sufficient. It was clear to me that the letter had been turned, as a glove, inside out, re-directed, and re-sealed. I bade the Minister good morning, and took my departure at once, leaving a gold snuff-box upon the table.

"The next morning I called for the snuff-box, when we resumed, quite eagerly, the conversation of the preceding day. While thus engaged, however, a loud report, as if of a pistol, was heard immediately beneath the windows of the hotel, and was succeeded by

a series of fearful screams, and the shoutings of a mob. D——
rushed to a casement, threw it open, and looked out. In the meantime, I stepped to the card-rack, took the letter, put it in my pocket,
and replaced it by a *fac-simile* (so far as regards externals), which
I had carefully prepared at my lodgings; imitating the D——
cipher, very readily, by means of a seal formed of bread.

"The disturbance in the street had been occasioned by the frantic behavior of a man with a musket. He had fired it among a crowd
of women and children. It proved, however, to have been without
ball, and the fellow was suffered to go his way as a lunatic or a
drunkard. When he had gone, D—— came from the window,
whither I had followed him immediately upon securing the object
in view. Soon afterwards I bade him farewell. The pretended lunatic was a man in my own pay."

"But what purpose had you," I asked, "in replacing the letter by
a *fac-simile?* Would it not have been better, at the first visit, to
have seized it openly, and departed?"

"D——," replied Dupin, "is a desperate man, and a man of
nerve. His hôtel, too, is not without attendants devoted to his interests. Had I made the wild attempt you suggest, I might never have
left the Ministerial presence alive. The good people of Paris might
have heard of me no more. But I had an object apart from these
considerations. You know my political prepossessions. In this matter, I act as a partisan of the lady concerned. For eighteen months
the Minister has had her in his power. She has now him in hers—
since, being unaware that the letter is not in his possession, he will
proceed with his exactions as if it was. Thus will he inevitably commit himself, at once, to his political destruction. His downfall, too,
will not be more precipitate than awkward. It is all very well to talk
about the *facilis descensus Averni*,[1] but in all kinds of climbing, as
Catalani said of singing, it is far more easy to get up than to come
down. In the present instance I have no sympathy—at least no pity
—for him who descends. He is that *monstrum horrendum*,[2] an unprincipled man of genius. I confess, however, that I should like
very well to know the precise character of his thoughts, when, being
defied by her whom the Prefect terms 'a certain personage,' he is
reduced to opening the letter which I left for him in the card-rack."

"How? did you put any thing particular in it?"

"Why—it did not seem altogether right to leave the interior
blank—that would have been insulting. D——, at Vienna once, did
me an evil turn, which I told him, quite good-humoredly, that I
should remember. So, as I knew he would feel some curiosity in
regard to the identity of the person who had outwitted him, I

---

1. "The easy descent to Avernus
[Hell]." Poe misquotes slightly from   Virgil's *Aeneid*, VI, 126.
2. Horrible monster.

thought it a pity not to give him a clue. He is well acquainted with my MS., and I just copied into the middle of the blank sheet the words—

> —*Un dessein si funeste,*
> *S'il n'est digne d' Atrée, est digne de Thyeste.*

They are to be found in Crébillon's 'Atrée.' " [3]

1844   1844, 1845

The Cask of Amontillado [4]

The thousand injuries of Fortunato I had borne as I best could; but when he ventured upon insult, I vowed revenge. You, who so well know the nature of my soul, will not suppose, however, that I gave utterance to a threat. At *length* I would be avenged; this was a point definitely settled—but the very definitiveness with which it was resolved precluded the idea of risk. I must not only punish, but punish with impunity. A wrong is unredressed when retribution overtakes its redresser. It is equally unredressed when the avenger fails to make himself felt as such to him who had done the wrong.

It must be understood, that neither by word nor deed had I given Fortunato cause to doubt my good-will. I continued, as was my wont, to smile in his face, and he did not perceive that my smile *now* was at the thought of his immolation.

He had a weak point—this Fortunato—although in other regards he was a man to be respected and even feared. He prided himself on his connoisseurship in wine. Few Italians have the true virtuoso spirit. For the most part their enthusiasm is adopted to suit the time and opportunity—to practise imposture upon the British and Austrian *millionnaires*. In painting and gemmary Fortunato, like his countrymen, was a quack—but in the matter of old wines he was sincere. In this respect I did not differ from him materially: I was skilful in the Italian vintages myself, and bought largely whenever I could.

3. "A design so deadly, even if not worthy of Atreus, is worthy of Thyestes." The quotation is from an eighteenth-century tragedy by the French dramatist Crébillon (pseudonym for Prosper Jolyot). The reference is to King Atreus of Mycenae, who murdered his nephews and served them to their father Thyestes at a feast. Thyestes had seduced the wife of Atreus and laid a curse on his house.
4. Originally published in *Godey's Lady's Book* for November, 1846, this story was first collected by Griswold in his edition of Poe's *Works* (1850). It is one of those later stories, written from 1841 on, in which Poe best exemplifies the principles of concentration and thematic totality which he enounced in 1842, in his review (reprinted in this volume) of Hawthorne's *Twice-told Tales*. It also illustrates his best command of dialogue, social situation, and the swift dramatic climax and shows him to be possessed of a sense of humor not always evident elsewhere in his works.

It was about dusk, one evening during the supreme madness of the carnival season, that I encountered my friend. He accosted me with excessive warmth, for he had been drinking much. The man wore motley. He had on a tight-fitting parti-striped dress, and his head was surmounted by the conical cap and bells. I was so pleased to see him, that I thought I should never have done wringing his hand.

I said to him: "My dear Fortunato, you are luckily met. How remarkably well you are looking to-day! But I have received a pipe [5] of what passes for Amontillado, [6] and I have my doubts."

"How?" said he. "Amontillado? A pipe? Impossible! And in the middle of the carnival!"

"I have my doubts," I replied; "and I was silly enough to pay the full Amontillado price without consulting you in the matter. You were not to be found, and I was fearful of losing a bargain."

"Amontillado!"

"I have my doubts."

"Amontillado!"

"And I must satisfy them."

"Amontillado!"

"As you are engaged, I am on my way to Luchesi. If any one has a critical turn, it is he. He will tell me——"

"Luchesi cannot tell Amontillado from Sherry."

"And yet some fools will have it that his taste is a match for your own."

"Come, let us go."

"Whither?"

"To your vaults."

"My friend, no; I will not impose upon your good nature. I perceive you have an engagement. Luchesi——"

"I have no engagement;—come."

"My friend, no. It is not the engagement, but the severe cold with which I perceive you are afflicted. The vaults are insufferably damp. They are encrusted with nitre."

"Let us go, nevertheless. The cold is merely nothing. Amontillado! You have been imposed upon. And as for Luchesi, he cannot distinguish Sherry from Amontillado."

Thus speaking, Fortunato possessed himself of my arm. Putting on a mask of black silk, and drawing a *roquelaire* [7] closely about my person, I suffered him to hurry me to my palazzo.

There were no attendants at home; they had absconded to make merry in honor of the time. I had told them that I should not re-

5. A French derivative; in England and the United States a large cask with the volume of two hogsheads.

6. A pale, dry sherry, much esteemed, originating in Montilla, Spain.

7. A short cloak.

turn until the morning, and had given them explicit orders not to stir from the house. These orders were sufficient, I well knew, to insure their immediate disappearance, one and all, as soon as my back was turned.

I took from their sconces two flambeaux, and giving one to Fortunato, bowed him through several suites of rooms to the archway that led into the vaults. I passed down a long and winding staircase, requesting him to be cautious as he followed. We came at length to the foot of the descent, and stood together on the damp ground of the catacombs of the Montresors.

The gait of my friend was unsteady, and the bells upon his cap jingled as he strode.

"The pipe?" said he.

"It is farther on," said I; "but observe the white web-work which gleams from these cavern walls."

He turned toward me, and looked into my eyes with two filmy orbs that distilled the rheum of intoxication.

"Nitre?" he asked, at length.

"Nitre," I replied. "How long have you had that cough?"

"Ugh! ugh! ugh!—ugh! ugh! ugh!—ugh! ugh! ugh!—ugh! ugh! ugh!— ugh! ugh! ugh!"

My poor friend found it impossible to reply for many minutes.

"It is nothing," he said, at last.

"Come," I said, with decision, "we will go back; your health is precious. You are rich, respected, admired, beloved; you are happy, as once I was. You are a man to be missed. For me it is no matter. We will go back; you will be ill, and I cannot be responsible. Besides, there is Luchesi——"

"Enough," he said; "the cough is a mere nothing; it will not kill me. I shall not die of a cough."

"True—true," I replied; "and, indeed, I had no intention of alarming you unnecessarily; but you should use all proper caution. A draught of this Medoc [8] will defend us from the damps."

Here I knocked off the neck of a bottle which I drew from a long row of its fellows that lay upon the mould.

"Drink," I said, presenting him the wine.

He raised it to his lips with a leer. He paused and nodded to me familiarly, while his bells jingled.

"I drink," he said, "to the buried that repose around us."

"And I to your long life."

He again took my arm, and we proceeded.

"These vaults," he said, "are extensive."

---

8. Correctly, "Médoc," a claret from the Médoc, near Bordeaux, France. Except for the varieties branded by certain vineyards, however, it is not a connoisseur's wine.

"The Montresors," I replied, "were a great and numerous family."

"I forget your arms."

"A huge human foot d'or, in a field azure; [9] the foot crushes a serpent rampant whose fangs are imbedded in the heel."

"And the motto?"

"*Nemo me impune lacessit.*" [1]

"Good!" he said.

The wine sparkled in his eyes and the bells jingled. My own fancy grew warm with the Medoc. We had passed through walls of piled bones, with casks and puncheons intermingling, into the inmost recesses of the catacombs. I paused again, and this time I made bold to seize Fortunato by an arm above the elbow.

"The nitre!" I said; "see, it increases. It hangs like moss upon the vaults. We are below the river's bed. The drops of moisture trickle among the bones. Come, we will go back ere it is too late. Your cough——"

"It is nothing," he said; "let us go on. But first, another draught of the Medoc."

I broke and reached him a flagon of De Grâve.[2] He emptied it at a breath. His eyes flashed with a fierce light. He laughed and threw the bottle upward with a gesticulation I did not understand.

I looked at him in surprise. He repeated the movement—a grotesque one.

"You do not comprehend?" he said.

"Not I," I replied.

"Then you are not of the brotherhood."

"How?"

"You are not of the masons." [3]

"Yes, yes," I said; "yes, yes."

"You? Impossible! A mason?"

"A mason," I replied.

"A sign," he said.

"It is this," I answered, producing a trowel from beneath the folds of my *roquelaire*.

"You jest," he exclaimed, recoiling a few paces. "But let us proceed to the Amontillado."

"Be it so," I said, replacing the tool beneath the cloak, and again offering him my arm. He leaned upon it heavily. We continued our route in search of the Amontillado. We passed through a range of

---

9. The coat of arms bore a golden foot on an azure field. "Rampant," in the following sentence, means "rearing up." Fortunato intended an insult in pretending to forget the coat of arms.

1. "No one attacks me with impunity." This is the legend of the royal arms of Scotland.

2. Correctly, "Graves," a light wine from the Bordeaux area.

3. Properly, "Masons"; an allusion to the secret society of Freemasons. The trowel, ironically shown by Montresor, is a symbol of their supposed origin as a guild of stoneworkers.

low arches, descended, passed on, and descending again, arrived at a deep crypt, in which the foulness of the air caused our flambeaux rather to glow than flame.

At the most remote end of the crypt there appeared another less spacious. Its walls had been lined with human remains, piled to the vault overhead, in the fashion of the great catacombs of Paris.[4] Three sides of this interior crypt were still ornamented in this manner. From the fourth the bones had been thrown down, and lay promiscuously upon the earth, forming at one point a mound of some size. Within the wall thus exposed by the displacing of the bones, we perceived a still interior recess, in depth about four feet, in width three, in height six or seven. It seemed to have been constructed for no especial use within itself, but formed merely the interval between two of the colossal supports of the roof of the catacombs, and was backed by one of the circumscribing walls of solid granite.

It was in vain that Fortunato, uplifting his dull torch, endeavored to pry into the depth of the recess. Its termination the feeble light did not enable us to see.

"Proceed," I said; "herein is the Amontillado. As for Luchesi ____"

"He is an ignoramus," interrupted my friend, as he stepped unsteadily forward, while I followed immediately at his heels. In an instant he had reached the extremity of the niche, and finding his progress arrested by the rock, stood stupidly bewildered. A moment more and I had fettered him to the granite. In its surface were two iron staples, distant from each other about two feet, horizontally. From one of these depended a short chain, from the other a padlock. Throwing the links about his waist, it was but the work of a few seconds to secure it. He was too much astounded to resist. Withdrawing the key I stepped back from the recess.

"Pass your hand," I said, "over the wall; you cannot help feeling the nitre. Indeed it is *very* damp. Once more let me *implore* you to return. No? Then I must positively leave you. But I must first render you all the little attentions in my power."

"The Amontillado!" ejaculated my friend, not yet recovered from his astonishment.

"True," I replied; "the Amontillado."

As I said these words I busied myself among the pile of bones of which I have before spoken. Throwing them aside, I soon uncovered a quantity of building stone and mortar. With these materials and with the aid of my trowel, I began vigorously to wall up the entrance of the niche.

I had scarcely laid the first tier of the masonry when I discovered that the intoxication of Fortunato had in a great measure worn off.

4. Like the earlier catacombs of Italy, those of Paris were subterranean galleries with recessed niches for burial vaults.

The earliest indication I had of this was a low moaning cry from the depth of the recess. It was *not* the cry of a drunken man. There was then a long and obstinate silence. I laid the second tier, and the third, and the fourth; and then I heard the furious vibrations of the chain. The noise lasted for several minutes, during which, that I might hearken to it with the more satisfaction, I ceased my labors and sat down upon the bones. When at last the clanking subsided, I resumed the trowel, and finished without interruption the fifth, the sixth, and the seventh tier. The wall was now nearly upon a level with my breast. I again paused, and holding the flambeaux over the masonwork, threw a few feeble rays upon the figure within.

A succession of loud and shrill screams, bursting suddenly from the throat of the chained form, seemed to thrust me violently back. For a brief moment I hesitated—I trembled. Unsheathing my rapier, I began to grope with it about the recess; but the thought of an instant reassured me. I placed my hand upon the solid fabric of the catacombs, and felt satisfied. I reapproached the wall. I replied to the yells of him who clamored. I re-echoed—I aided—I surpassed them in volume and in strength. I did this, and the clamorer grew still.

It was now midnight, and my task was drawing to a close. I had completed the eighth, the ninth, and the tenth tier. I had finished a portion of the last and the eleventh; there remained but a single stone to be fitted and plastered in. I struggled with its weight; I placed it partially in its destined position. But now there came from out the niche a low laugh that erected the hairs upon my head. It was succeeded by a sad voice, which I had difficulty in recognizing as that of the noble Fortunato. The voice said—

"Ha! ha! ha!—he! he!—a very good joke indeed—an excellent jest. We will have many a rich laugh about it at the palazzo—he! he! he!—over our wine—he! he! he!"

"The Amontillado!" I said.

"He! he! he!—he! he! he!—yes, the Amontillado. But is it not getting late? Will not they be awaiting us at the palazzo, the Lady Fortunato and the rest? Let us be gone."

"Yes," I said, "let us be gone."

"For the love of God, Montresor!"

"Yes," I said, "for the love of God!"

But to these words I hearkened in vain for a reply. I grew impatient. I called aloud:

"Fortunato!"

No answer. I called again:

"Fortunato!"

No answer still. I thrust a torch through the remaining aperture and let it fall within. There came forth in return only a jingling of the bells. My heart grew sick—on account of the dampness of the catacombs. I hastened to make an end of my labor. I forced the last stone into its position; I plastered it up. Against the new masonry I re-erected the old rampart of bones. For the half of a century no mortal has disturbed them. *In pace requiescat!*[5]

1846, 1850

Twice-Told Tales, by Nathaniel Hawthorne[6]
A Review

* * *

But it is of his tales that we desire principally to speak. The tale proper, in our opinion, affords unquestionably the fairest field for the exercise of the loftiest talent, which can be afforded by the wide domains of mere prose. Were we bidden to say how the highest genius could be more advantageously employed for the best display of its own powers, we should answer, without hesitation—in the composition of a rhymed poem, not to exceed in length what might be perused in an hour. Within this limit alone can the highest order of true poetry exist. We need only here say, upon this topic, that, in almost all classes of composition, the unity of effect or impression is a point of the greatest importance. It is clear, moreover, that this unity cannot be thoroughly preserved in productions whose perusal cannot be completed at one sitting. We may continue the reading of a prose composition, from the very nature of prose itself, much longer than we can persevere, to any good purpose, in the perusal of a poem. This latter, if truly fulfilling the demands of the poetic sentiment, induces an exaltation of the soul which cannot be long sustained. All high excitements are necessarily transient. Thus a long poem is a paradox. And, without unity of impression, the deepest effects cannot be brought about. Epics were the offspring of an imperfect sense of Art, and their reign is no more. A poem *too* brief may produce a vivid, but never an intense or enduring impression. Without a certain continuity of effort—without a certain duration or repetition of purpose—the soul is never deeply moved. There must be the dropping of the water upon the rock. De Béranger[7] has wrought brilliant things—pungent and spirit-stirring—but, like all immassive bodies, they lack *momentum*, and thus fail to satisfy the Poetic Sentiment. They sparkle and excite, but, from

---

5. May he rest in peace!
6. This is one of Poe's most important critical articles. In the fourth paragraph begins the famous formulation of the short story as a literary *genre*, which Poe was the first to define, and was already illustrating in his own stories, at the height of his maturity. Apart from this, of course, the essay is one of Poe's most characteristic critiques. It first ap-

peared in *Graham's Magazine* for May, 1842, although Poe had printed a brief notice of five paragraphs in the April issue (see his opening sentence).
7. *Cf.* "Israfel," epigraph to "The Fall of the House of Usher," and "The Poetic Principle" for other references to Pierre Jean de Béranger (1780–1857), French lyric poet.

want of continuity, fail deeply to impress. Extreme brevity will degenerate into epigrammatism; but the sin of extreme length is even more unpardonable. *In medio tutissimus ibis*.[8]

Were we called upon, however, to designate that class of composition which, next to such a poem as we have suggested, should best fulfil the demands of high genius—should offer it the most advantageous field of exertion—we should unhesitatingly speak of the prose tale, as Mr. Hawthorne has here exemplified it. We allude to the short prose narrative, requiring from a half-hour to one or two hours in its perusal. The ordinary novel is objectionable, from its length, for reasons already stated in substance. As it cannot be read at one sitting, it deprives itself, of course, of the immense force derivable from *totality*. Worldly interests intervening during the pauses of perusal, modify, annul, or counteract, in a greater or less degree, the impressions of the book. But simple cessation in reading would, of itself, be sufficient to destroy the true unity. In the brief tale, however, the author is enabled to carry out the fulness of his intention, be it what it may. During the hour of perusal the soul of the reader is at the writer's control. There are no external or extrinsic influences—resulting from weariness or interruption.

A skilful literary artist has constructed a tale. If wise, he has not fashioned his thoughts to accommodate his incidents; but having conceived, with deliberate care, a certain unique or single *effect* to be wrought out, he then invents such incidents—he then combines such events as may best aid him in establishing this preconceived effect. If his very initial sentence tend not to the outbringing of this effect, then he has failed in his first step. In the whole composition there should be no word written, of which the tendency, direct or indirect, is not to the one pre-established design. And by such means, with such care and skill, a picture is at length painted which leaves in the mind of him who contemplates it with a kindred art, a sense of the fullest satisfaction. The idea of the tale has been presented unblemished, because undisturbed; and this is an end unattainable by the novel. Undue brevity is just as exceptionable here as in the poem; but undue length is yet more to be avoided.

We have said that the tale has a point of superiority even over the poem. In fact, while the *rhythm* of this latter is an essential aid in the development of the poem's highest idea—the idea of the Beautiful—the artificialities of this rhythm are an inseparable bar to the development of all points of thought or expression which have their basis in *Truth*. But Truth is often, and in very great degree, the aim of the tale. Some of the finest tales are tales of ratiocination. Thus the field of this species of composition, if not in so elevated a region

8. "You travel most safely in the middle [moderate] course"; Ovid, in the *Metamorphoses;* the advice of Helios to his son Phaëthon, who insists on driving the chariot of the sun for a day, and nearly burns up the earth by neglecting his father's injunction.

on the mountain of Mind, is a table-land of far vaster extent than the domain of the mere poem. Its products are never so rich, but infinitely more numerous, and more appreciable by the mass of mankind. The writer of the prose tale, in short, may bring to his theme a vast variety of modes or inflections of thought and expression— (the ratiocinative, for example, the sarcastic, or the humorous) which are not only antagonistical to the nature of the poem, but absolutely forbidden by one of its most peculiar and indispensable adjuncts; we allude, of course, to rhythm. It may be added here, *par parenthèse*,[9] that the author who aims at the purely beautiful in a prose tale is laboring at a great disadvantage. For Beauty can be better treated in the poem. Not so with terror, or passion, or horror, or a multitude of such other points. And here it will be seen how full of prejudice are the usual animadversions against those *tales of effect*, many fine examples of which were found in the earlier numbers of *Blackwood*.[1] The impressions produced were wrought in a legitimate sphere of action, and constituted a legitimate although sometimes an exaggerated interest. They were relished by every man of genius: although there were found many men of genius who condemned them without just ground. The true critic will but demand that the design intended be accomplished, to the fullest extent, by the means most advantageously applicable.

We have very few American tales of real merit—we may say, indeed, none, with the exception of *The Tales of a Traveller* of Washington Irving, and these *Twice-Told Tales* of Mr. Hawthorne. Some of the pieces of Mr. John Neal[2] abound in vigor and originality; but, in general, his compositions of this class are excessively diffuse, extravagant, and indicative of an imperfect sentiment of Art. Articles at random are, now and then, met with in our periodicals which might be advantageously compared with the best effusions of the British Magazines; but, upon the whole, we are far behind our progenitors in this department of literature.

Of Mr. Hawthorne's tales we should say, emphatically, that they belong to the highest region of Art—an Art subservient to genius of a very lofty order. We had supposed, with good reason for so supposing, that he had been thrust into his present position by one of the impudent *cliques* which beset our literature, and whose pretensions it is our full purpose to expose at the earliest opportunity; but we have been most agreeably mistaken. We know of few compositions which the critic can more honestly commend than these *Twice-Told Tales*. As Americans, we feel proud of the book.

Mr. Hawthorne's distinctive trait is invention, creation, imagina-

---

9. Parenthetically.
1. The *Edinburgh Monthly Magazine* (1817) soon simply called *Blackwood's Magazine*, was noted from the beginning for fiction creating the mood of

"terror, or passion, or horror" that Poe here associates with "effect."
2. John Neal (1793–1876), voluminous American writer and journalist, had been a *Blackwood's* author.

tion, originality—a trait which, in the literature of fiction, is positively worth all the rest. But the nature of the originality, so far as regards its manifestation in letters, is but imperfectly understood. The inventive or original mind as frequently displays itself in novelty of *tone* as in novelty of matter. Mr. Hawthorne is original at *all* points. * * *

The Philosophy of Composition [3]

Charles Dickens, in a note now lying before me, alluding to an examination I once made of the mechanism of *Barnaby Rudge*,[4] says—"By the way, are you aware that Godwin wrote his *Caleb Williams* backward?[5] He first involved his hero in a web of difficulties, forming the second volume, and then, for the first, cast about him for some mode of accounting for what had been done."

I cannot think this the *precise* mode of procedure on the part of Godwin—and indeed what he himself acknowledges, is not altogether in accordance with Mr. Dickens's idea—but the author of *Caleb Williams* was too good an artist not to perceive the advantage derivable from at least a somewhat similar process. Nothing is more clear than that every plot, worth the name, must be elaborated to its *dénouement* [6] before anything be attempted with the pen. It is only with the *dénouement* constantly in view that we can give a plot its indispensable air of consequence, or causation, by making the incidents, and especially the tone at all points, tend to the development of the intention.

There is a radical error, I think, in the usual mode of constructing a story. Either history affords a thesis—or one is suggested by an incident of the day—or, at best, the author sets himself to work

3. This essay has survived endless discussions as to whether Poe actually composed "The Raven" in the manner described. It retains its fascination and its usefulness because it convincingly shows what elements, somehow or other, went into "The Raven," and what processes, at one time or another, occurred in the creative mind of the author during the four years in which he repeatedly returned to this work. If, in the limited scope of a lecture (for which the paper was probably intended), Poe distorted the time sequence or foreshortened the perspective of ideas concerned in the process, the critical truth of his "best specimen of analysis," as he called it, is not diminished. He was concerned to demonstrate that a poem, like any other work of art, is fabricated of materials selected for consciously determined purposes; that these plastic potentials are shaped by the creative intelligence to make them most useful in communicating the intended effect or idea. This concept, in accord with his theory of creation, which he believed valid for fiction as well as for poetry, was directly opposed to the romantic assumption that the artist is himself an instrument responding intuitively to pressures of inspiration. Thus the essay is a source of information concerning Poe's theories and practice, while providing, at the same time, a model of analytical criticism. It was first published in *Graham's Magazine* for April, 1846.
4. In 1841, while Dickens's *Barnaby Rudge* was appearing serially, Poe wrote a review in which he succeeded in naming the murderer, still supposedly shrouded in mystery.
5. See Godwin's Preface to *Caleb Williams* (1794) for confirmation.
6. Literally, the "untying"; hence, the "solution" of a fictional plot.

in the combination of striking events to form merely the basis of his narrative—designing, generally, to fill in with description, dialogue, or autorial [sic] comment, whatever crevices of fact, or action, may, from page to page, render themselves apparent.

I prefer commencing with the consideration of an *effect*. Keeping originality *always* in view—for he is false to himself who ventures to dispense with so obvious and so easily attainable a source of interest—I say to myself, in the first place, "Of the innumerable effects, or impressions, of which the heart, the intellect, or (more generally) the soul is susceptible, what one shall I, on the present occasion, select?" Having chosen a novel, first, and secondly a vivid effect, I consider whether it can be best wrought by incident or tone—whether by ordinary incidents and peculiar tone, or the converse, or by peculiarity both of incident and tone—afterward looking about me (or rather within) for such combinations of event, or tone, as shall best aid me in the construction of the effect.

I have often thought how interesting a magazine paper might be written by any author who would—that is to say who could—detail, step by step, the processes by which any one of his compositions attained its ultimate point of completion. Why such a paper has never been given to the world, I am much at a loss to say—but, perhaps, the autorial vanity has had more to do with the omission than any one other cause. Most writers—poets in especial—prefer having it understood that they compose by a species of fine frenzy—an ecstatic intuition—and would positively shudder at letting the public take a peep behind the scenes, at the elaborate and vacillating crudities of thought—at the true purposes seized only at the last moment—at the innumerable glimpses of idea that arrived not at the maturity of full view—at the fully matured fancies discarded in despair as unmanageable—at the cautious selections and rejections—at the painful erasures and interpolations—in a word, at the wheels and pinions—the tackle for scene-shifting—the step-ladders and demon-traps—the cock's feathers, the red paint, and the black patches, which, in ninety-nine cases out of the hundred, constitute the properties of the literary *histrio*.[7]

I am aware, on the other hand, that the case is by no means common, in which an author is at all in condition to retrace the steps by which his conclusions have been attained. In general, suggestions, having arisen pell-mell, are pursued and forgotten in a similar manner.

For my own part, I have neither sympathy with the repugnance alluded to, nor at any time the least difficulty in recalling to mind the progressive steps of any of my compositions; and, since the interest of an analysis, or reconstruction, such as I have considered a

7. Actor.

desideratum, is quite independent of any real or fancied interest in the thing analyzed, it will not be regarded as a breach of decorum on my part to show the *modus operandi* [8] by which some one of my own works was put together. I select *The Raven,* as most generally known. It is my design to render it manifest that no one point in its composition is referrible either to accident or intuition—that the work proceeded, step by step, to its completion with the precision and rigid consequence of a mathematical problem.

Let us dismiss, as irrelevant to the poem, *per se,* the circumstance —or say the necessity—which, in the first place, gave rise to the intention of composing *a* poem that should suit at once the popular and the critical taste.

We commence, then, with this intention.

The initial consideration was that of extent. If any literary work is too long to be read at one sitting, we must be content to dispense with the immensely important effect derivable from unity of impression—for, if two sittings be required, the affairs of the world interfere, and every thing like totality is at once destroyed. But since, *ceteris paribus,*[9] no poet can afford to dispense with *any thing* that may advance his design, it but remains to be seen whether there is, in extent, any advantage to counterbalance the loss of unity which attends it. Here I say no, at once. What we term a long poem is, in fact, merely a succession of brief ones—that is to say, of brief poetical effects. It is needless to demonstrate that a poem is such, only inasmuch as it intensely excites, by elevating, the soul; and all intense excitements are, through a psychal [1] necessity, brief. For this reason, at least one half of the *Paradise Lost* is essentially prose—a succession of poetical excitements interspersed, *inevitably,* with corresponding depressions—the whole being deprived, through the extremeness of its length, of the vastly important artistic element, totality, or unity, of effect.

It appears evident, then, that there is a distinct limit, as regards length, to all works of literary art—the limit of a single sitting— and that, although in certain classes of prose composition, such as *Robinson Crusoe* (demanding no unity) this limit may be advantageously overpassed, it can never properly be overpassed in a poem. Within this limit, the extent of a poem may be made to bear mathematical relation to its merit—in other words, to the excitement or elevation—again in other words, to the degree of the true poetical effect which it is capable of inducing; for it is clear that the brevity must be in direct ratio of the intensity of the intended effect:— this, with one proviso—that a certain degree of duration is absolutely requisite for the production of any effect at all.

8. Method of performance.   1. Psychological.
9. Other things being equal.

Holding in view these considerations, as well as that degree of excitement which I deemed not above the popular, while not below the critical, taste, I reached at once what I conceived the proper *length* for my intended poem—a length of about one hundred lines. It is, in fact, a hundred and eight.

My next thought concerned the choice of an impression, or effect, to be conveyed; and here I may as well observe that, throughout the construction, I kept steadily in view the design of rendering the work *universally* appreciable. I should be carried too far out of my immediate topic were I to demonstrate a point upon which I have repeatedly insisted, and which, with the poetical, stands not in the slightest need of demonstration—the point, I mean, that Beauty is the sole legitimate province of the poem. A few words, however, in elucidation of my real meaning, which some of my friends have evinced a disposition to misrepresent. That pleasure which is at once the most intense, the most elevating, and the most pure, is, I believe, found in the contemplation of the beautiful. When, indeed, men speak of Beauty, they mean, precisely, not a quality, as is supposed, but an effect—they refer, in short, just to that intense and pure elevation of *soul*—*not* of intellect, or of heart—upon which I have commented, and which is experienced in consequence of contemplating "the beautiful." Now I designate Beauty as the province of the poem, merely because it is an obvious rule of Art that effects should be made to spring from direct causes—that objects should be attained through means best adapted for their attainment—no one as yet having been weak enough to deny that the peculiar elevation alluded to is *most readily* attained in the poem. Now the object, Truth, or the satisfaction of the intellect, and the object Passion, or the excitement of the heart, are, although attainable, to a certain extent, in poetry, far more readily attainable in prose. Truth, in fact, demands a precision, and Passion a *homeliness* (the truly passionate will comprehend me) which are absolutely antagonistic to that Beauty which, I maintain, is the excitement, or pleasurable elevation, of the soul. It by no means follows from any thing here said, that passion, or even truth, may not be introduced, and even profitably introduced, into a poem—for they may serve in elucidation, or aid the general effect, as do discords in music, by contrast—but the true artist will always contrive, first, to tone them into proper subservience to the predominant aim, and, secondly, to enveil them, as far as possible, in that Beauty which is the atmosphere and the essence of the poem.

Regarding, then, Beauty as my province, my next question referred to the *tone* of its highest manifestation—and all experience has shown that this tone is one of *sadness*. Beauty of whatever kind, in its supreme development, invariably excites the sensitive soul to tears. Melancholy is thus the most legitimate of all the poetical tones.

The length, the province, and the tone, being thus determined, I betook myself to ordinary induction, with the view of obtaining some artistic piquancy which might serve me as a key-note in the construction of the poem—some pivot upon which the whole structure might turn. In carefully thinking over all the usual artistic effects—or more properly *points*, in the theatrical sense—I did not fail to perceive immediately that no one had been so universally employed as that of the *refrain*. The universality of its employment sufficed to assure me of its intrinsic value, and spared me the necessity of submitting it to analysis. I considered it, however, with regard to its susceptibility of improvement, and soon saw it to be in a primitive condition. As commonly used, the *refrain*, or burden, not only is limited to lyric verse, but depends for its impression upon the force of monotone—both in sound and thought. The pleasure is deduced solely from the sense of identity—of repetition. I resolved to diversify, and so heighten, the effect, by adhering, in general, to the monotone of sound, while I continually varied that of thought: that is to say, I determined to produce continuously novel effects, by the variation of the *application* of the refrain—the refrain itself remaining, for the most part, unvaried.

These points being settled, I next bethought me of the *nature* of my refrain. Since its application was to be repeatedly varied, it was clear that the refrain itself must be brief, for there would have been an insurmountable difficulty in frequent variations of application in any sentence of length. In proportion to the brevity of the sentence, would, of course, be the facility of the variation. This led me at once to a single word as the best refrain.

The question now arose as to the *character* of the word. Having made up my mind to a refrain, the division of the poem into stanzas was, of course, a corollary: the refrain forming the close of each stanza. That such a close, to have force, must be sonorous and susceptible of protracted emphasis, admitted no doubt; and these considerations inevitably led me to the long *o* as the most sonorous vowel, in connection with *r* as the most producible consonant.

The sound of the refrain being thus determined, it became necessary to select a word embodying this sound, and at the same time in the fullest possible keeping with that melancholy which I had predetermined as the tone of the poem. In such a search it would have been absolutely impossible to overlook the word "Nevermore." In fact, it was the very first which presented itself.

The next *desideratum* was a pretext for the continuous use of the one word "Nevermore." In observing the difficulty which I at once found in inventing a sufficiently plausible reason for its continuous repetition, I did not fail to perceive that this difficulty arose solely from the pre-assumption that the word was to be so continuously or monotonously spoken by a *human* being—I did not fail to perceive, in short, that the difficulty lay in the reconciliation of this monotony with the exercise of reason on the part of the creature repeating the word. Here, then, immediately arose the idea of a *non-reasoning* creature capable of speech; and, very naturally, a parrot, in the first instance, suggested itself, but was superseded forthwith by a Raven, as equally capable of speech, and infinitely more in keeping with the intended *tone*.

I had now gone so far as the conception of a Raven—the bird of ill omen—monotonously repeating the one word, "Nevermore" at the conclusion of each stanza, in a poem of melancholy tone, and in length about one hundred lines. Now, never losing sight of the object *supremeness*, or perfection, at all points, I asked myself—"Of all melancholy topics, what, according to the *universal* understanding of mankind, is the *most* melancholy?" "Death"—was the obvious reply. "And when," I said, "is this most melancholy of topics most poetical?" From what I have already explained at some length, the answer, here also, is obvious—"When it most closely allies itself to *Beauty*." The death, then, of a beautiful woman, is, unquestionably, the most poetical topic in the world—and equally is it beyond doubt that the lips best suited for such topic are those of a bereaved lover.

I had now to combine the two ideas, of a lover lamenting his deceased mistress, and a Raven continuously repeating the word "Nevermore." I had to combine these, bearing in mind my design of varying, at every turn, the *application* of the word repeated; but the only intelligible mode of such combination is that of imagining the Raven employing the word in answer to the queries of the lover. And here it was that I saw at once the opportunity afforded for the effect on which I had been depending—that is to say, the effect of the *variation of application*. I saw that I could make the first query propounded by the lover—the first query to which the Raven should reply "Nevermore"—that I could make this first query a commonplace one—the second less so—the third still less, and so on—until at length the lover, startled from his original *nonchalance* by the melancholy character of the word itself—by its frequent repetition—and by a consideration of the ominous reputation of the fowl that uttered it—is at length excited to superstition, and wildly propounds queries of a far different character—queries whose solution he has passionately at heart—propounds them half in superstition and half in that species of despair which delights in self-torture—propounds them not altogether because he believes in the prophetic or demoniac character of the bird (which, reason assures him, is merely repeating a lesson learned by rote) but because he experiences a phrenzied pleasure in so modeling his questions as to receive from the *expected* "Nevermore" the most delicious because the most intolerable of sorrow. Perceiving the opportunity thus afforded me—or, more strictly, thus forced upon me in the progress of the construction—I first established in mind the climax, or concluding query—that query to which "Nevermore" should be in the last place an answer—that in reply to which this word "Nevermore" should involve the utmost conceivable amount of sorrow and despair.

Here then the poem may be said to have its beginning—at the end, where all works of art should begin—for it was here, at this point of my preconsiderations, that I first put pen to paper in the composition of the stanza:

"Prophet," said I, "thing of evil! prophet still if bird or devil!
By that heaven that bends above us—by that God we both adore,
Tell this soul with sorrow laden, if within the distant Aidenn,
It shall clasp a sainted maiden whom the angels name Lenore—
Clasp a rare and radiant maiden whom the angels name Lenore."
Quoth the Raven, "Nevermore."

I composed this stanza, at this point, first, that by establishing the climax, I might the better vary and graduate, as regards serious- ness and importance, the proceding queries of the lover; and secondly, that I might definitely settle the rhythm, the meter, and the length and general arrangement of the stanza,—as well as graduate the stanzas which were to precede, so that none of them might surpass this in rhythmical effect. Had I been able, in the sub- sequent composition, to construct more vigorous stanzas, I should, without scruple, have purposely enfeebled them, so as not to inter- fere with the climacteric effect.

And here I may as well say a few words of the versification. My first object (as usual) was originality. The extent to which this has been neglected, in versification, is one of the most unaccountable things in the world. Admitting that there is little possibility of variety in mere *rhythm*, it is still clear that the possible varieties of meter and stanza are absolutely infinite—and yet, *for centuries, no man, in verse, has ever done, or ever seemed to think of doing, an original thing.* The fact is, that originality (unless in minds of very unusual force) is by no means a matter, as some suppose, of impulse or intuition. In general, to be found, it must be elaborately sought, and although a positive merit of the highest class, demands in its attainment less of invention than negation.

Of course, I pretend to no originality in either the rhythm or meter of *The Raven*. The former is trochaic—the latter is octameter acatalectic, alternating with heptameter catalectic repeated in the refrain of the fifth verse, and terminating with tetrameter catalectic. Less pedantically—the feet employed throughout (trochees) consist of a long syllable followed by a short: the first line of the stanza consists of eight of these feet—the second of seven and a half (in effect two-thirds)—the third of eight—the fourth of seven and a half—the fifth the same—the sixth three and a half. Now, each of these lines, taken individually, has been employed before; and what originality *The Raven* has, is in their *combination into stanza*; nothing even remotely approaching this combination has ever been attempted. The effect of this originality of combination is aided by other unusual, and some altogether novel effects, arising from an extension of the application of the principles of rhyme and alliteration.

The next point to be considered was the mode of bringing together the lover and the Raven—and the first branch of this consideration was the *locale*. For this the most natural suggestion might seem to be a forest, or the fields—but it has always appeared to me that a close *circumscription of space* is absolutely necessary to the effect of insulated incident:—it has the force of a frame to a picture. It has an indisputable moral power in keeping concentrated the attention, and, of course, must not be confounded with mere unity of place.

I determined, then, to place the lover in his chamber—in a chamber rendered sacred to him by memories of her who had frequented it. The room is represented as richly furnished—this in mere pursuance of the ideas I have already explained on the subject of Beauty, as the sole true poetical thesis.

The *locale* being thus determined, I had now to introduce the bird—and the thought of introducing him through the window, was inevitable. The idea of making the lover suppose, in the first instance, that the flapping of the wings of the bird against the shutter, is a "tapping" at the door, originated in a wish to increase, by prolonging, the reader's curiosity, and in a desire to admit the incidental effect arising from the lover's throwing open the door, finding all dark, and thence adopting the half-fancy that it was the spirit of his mistress that knocked.

I made the night tempestuous, first, to account for the Raven's seeking admission, and secondly, for the effect of contrast with the (physical) serenity within the chamber.

I made the bird alight on the bust of Pallas, also for the effect of contrast between the marble and the plumage—it being understood that the bust was absolutely *suggested* by the bird—the bust of *Pallas* being chosen, first, as most in keeping with the scholarship of the lover, and secondly, for the sonorousness of the word, *Pallas,* itself.

About the middle of the poem, also, I have availed myself of the force of contrast, with a view of deepening the ultimate impression. For example, an air of the fantastic—approaching as nearly to the ludicrous as was admissible—is given to the Raven's entrance. He comes in "with many a flirt and flutter."

Not the *least obeisance made he*—not a moment stopped or stayed he,
But with *mien of lord or lady*, perched above my chamber door.

In the two stanzas which follow, the design is more obviously carried out:—

Then this ebony bird beguiling my sad fancy into smiling
By the *grave and stern decorum of the countenance it wore*,
"Though thy *crest be shorn and shaven* thou," I said, "art sure no craven,
Ghastly grim and ancient Raven wandering from the nightly shore—
Tell me what thy lordly name is on the Night's Plutonian shore?"
　　　　　Quoth the Raven, "Nevermore."

Much I marvelled *this ungainly fowl* to hear discourse so plainly
Though its answer little meaning—little relevancy bore;
For we cannot help agreeing that no living human being
Ever yet was blessed with seeing bird above his chamber door—
Bird or beast upon the sculptured bust above his chamber door,
　　　　　With such name as "Nevermore."

The effect of the *dénouement* being thus provided for, I immediately drop the fantastic for a tone of the most profound seriousness—this tone commencing in the stanza directly following the one last quoted, with the line,

But the Raven, sitting lonely on that placid bust, spoke only, etc.

From this epoch the lover no longer jests—no longer sees any thing even of the fantastic in the Raven's demeanor. He speaks of him as a "grim, ungainly, ghastly, gaunt, and ominous bird of yore," and feels the "fiery eyes" burning into his "bosom's core." This revolution of thought, or fancy, on the lover's part, is intended to induce a similar one on the part of the reader—to bring the mind into a proper frame for the *dénouement*—which is now brought about as rapidly and as *directly* as possible.

With the *dénouement* proper—with the Raven's reply, "Nevermore," to the lover's final demand if he shall meet his mistress in another world—the poem, in its obvious phase, that of a simple narrative, may be said to have its completion. So far, every thing is within the limits of the unaccountable—of the real. A raven, having learned by rote the single word "Nevermore," and having escaped from the custody of its owner, is driven at midnight, through the violence of a storm, to seek admission at a window from which a light still gleams—the chamber-window of a student, occupied half in poring over a volume, half in dreaming of a beloved mistress deceased. The casement being thrown open at the fluttering of the bird's wings, the bird itself perches on the most convenient seat out of the immediate reach of the student, who, amused by the incident and the oddity of the visitor's demeanor, demands of it, in jest and without looking for a reply, its name. The raven addressed, answers with its customary word, "Nevermore"—a word which finds immediate echo in the melancholy heart of the student, who, giving utterance aloud to certain thoughts suggested by the occasion, is again startled by the fowl's repetition of "Nevermore." The student now guesses the state of the case, but is impelled, as I have before explained, by the human thirst for self-torture, and in part by superstition, to propound such queries to the bird as will bring him, the lover, the most of the luxury of sorrow, through the anticipated answer "Nevermore." With the indulgence, to the extreme, of this self-torture, the narration, in what I have termed its first or obvious phase, has a natural termination, and so far there has been no overstepping of the limits of the real.

But in subjects so handled, however skilfully, or with however vivid an array of incident, there is always a certain hardness or nakedness, which repels the artistical eye. Two things are invariably required—first, some amount of complexity, or more properly, adaptation; and, secondly, some amount of suggestiveness—some under-current, however indefinite, of meaning. It is this latter, in especial, which imparts to a work of art so much of that *richness* (to borrow from colloquy a forcible term) which we are too fond of confounding with *the ideal*. It is the *excess* of the suggested meaning—it is the rendering this the upper instead of the under current of the theme—which turns into prose (and that of the very flattest kind) the so-called poetry of the so-called transcendentalists.

Holding these opinions, I added the two concluding stanzas of the poem—their suggestiveness being thus made to pervade all the narrative which has preceded them. The undercurrent of meaning is rendered first apparent in the lines—

"Take thy beak from out *my heart*, and take thy form from off my
    door!"
        Quoth the Raven, "Nevermore!"

It will be observed that the words, "from out my heart," involve the first metaphorical expression in the poem. They, with the answer, "Nevermore," dispose the mind to seek a moral in all that has been previously narrated. The reader begins now to regard the Raven as emblematical—but it is not until the very last line of the very last stanza, that the intention of making him emblematical of *Mournful and Never-ending Remembrance* is permitted distinctly to be seen:

And the Raven, never flitting, still is sitting, still is sitting,
On the pallid bust of Pallas, just above my chamber door;
And his eyes have all the seeming of a demon's that is dreaming,
And the lamplight o'er him streaming throws his shadow on the
 floor;
And my soul *from out that shadow* that lies floating on the floor
   Shall be lifted—nevermore.

1846

HERMAN MELVILLE
(1819–1891)

Melville's parents were both of substantial New York families, but his father's bankruptcy, soon followed by his death, left the mother in financial difficulties when the boy was only twelve. She then settled near Albany, where Melville for a time attended the local academy. Following a brief career as a clerk in his brother's store and in a bank, he went to sea at the age of nineteen. His experiences as a merchant sailor on the *St. Lawrence* and ashore in the slums of Liverpool, later recalled in *Redburn*, awakened the abhorrence, expressed throughout his fiction, of the darkness of man's deeds, and the evil seemingly inherent in nature itself. After this first brief seafaring interlude, he taught school and began to write sporadically.

In 1841, he shipped once more before the mast, aboard a Fair Haven whaler, the *Acushnet*, bound for the Pacific. Altogether, it was nearly four years before he returned from the South Seas. After eighteen months he deserted the whaler, in company with a close friend, at Nukuhiva, in the Marquesas Islands. In *Typee*, these adventures are embellished by fictional license, but the author and "Toby" Green certainly spent at least a month among the handsome Marquesan Taipis, whose free and idyllic island life was flawed by their regrettable habit of eating their enemies. A passing whaler provided an "escape" to Tahiti. Melville soon shipped on another whaler, *Charles and Henry* of Nantucket, which carried him finally to the Hawaiian Islands. In Honolulu he enlisted for naval service, aboard the U.S.S. *United States*, and was discharged fourteen months later at Boston.

The youth had had a compelling personal experience, and being a natural writer, he at once set to work producing a fiction based in part on his own adventures, employing literary materials which he was the first American writer to exploit. *Typee* (London and New York, 1846) was the first modern novel of South Seas adventure, as the later *Moby-Dick* was the first literary classic of whaling. Indeed, his significant novels almost all reflect his experiences prior to his discharge from the Navy. His impulsive literary energies drove him steadily for eleven years, during which he was the author of ten major volumes; after 1857 he published no fiction, and his life fell into seeming confusion, producing an enigma endlessly intriguing to his critics.

In the beginning he was almost embarrassed by success. *Typee* was at once recognized for the merits which have made it a classic, but its author was notoriously identified as the character who had lived and eaten with cannibals, and loved the dusky Fayaway—an uncomfortable position for a young New Yorker just married to the daughter of a Boston chief justice. *Omoo* (1847), somewhat inferior to *Typee*, was also a successful novel of Pacific adventures. *Mardi* (1849) began to puzzle a public impatient of symbolic enigmas; but *Redburn* (1849) and *White-Jacket* (1850) were novels of exciting adventure, although the first, as has been suggested above, devotes much of its energy to so-

ciological satire, while the second emphasizes the floggings and other cruelties and degradations then imposed upon enlisted men in naval service and seamen generally.

In 1851, Melville's masterpiece, *Moby-Dick* was published. A robust and realistic novel of adventure, drawing upon the author's fascination with the whale and whaling, it achieves a compelling symbolism in the character of Captain Ahab, whose monomaniacal fury against the whale, or the evil it represents to him, sends him to his death. This book is now seen as one of a trilogy, including the earlier *Mardi* and *Pierre* (1852), but neither of the others is wholly comprehensible or successful. Together, however, they represent the struggle of man against his destiny at various levels of experience.

In 1850, Melville had established a residence at Arrowhead, a farm near Pittsfield, Massachusetts. There, completing *Moby-Dick*, with Hawthorne nearby, a stimulating new friend, he was at the height of his career. Yet he published but one more distinguished volume of fiction— *The Piazza Tales* (1856), a collection of such smaller masterpieces as "Benito Cereno," "Bartleby the Scrivener," and "The Encantadas." *Pierre* was denounced on moral grounds, and because there was marked confusion of narrative elements and symbolism in that strange novel of incest. *Israel Potter* (1855) and *The Confidence-Man* (1857) are now of some interest but were not then successful; they marked his last effort to make a career of literature. Readers in general did not understand the symbolic significance of his works, his sales were unsatisfactory, and when the plates of his volumes were destroyed in a publisher's fire, the books were not reprinted. Four volumes of poems, not then well received, have continued to be better appreciated in recent years.

After some hard and bitter years he settled down humbly in 1866 as a customs inspector in New York, at the foot of Gansevoort Street, which had been named for his mother's distinguished family. Before doing so, however, he launched himself on a pursuit of certainty, a tour to the Holy Land, that inspired *Clarel*. In this uneven poem there are profound spiritual discoveries and descriptive sketches or lyrics of power substantiating the lyric vision of his novels. His versification anticipated the twentieth-century techniques. The Civil War involved him deeply in a human cause and produced sensitive poetry in *Battle-Pieces and Aspects of the War* (1866). Besides *Clarel* (1867), two much smaller volumes of poetry were *John Marr and Other Sailors* (1888) and *Timoleon* (1891).

In *Billy Budd*, printed below, the novelist recaptured his highest powers during the very last years of his life. He worked on the novelette from November, 1888, until April, 1891, and the manuscript was not fully prepared for press when he died the following September 28 (see the first note to *Billy Budd*). The story is related to the author's earliest adventures at sea; its theme has obvious connection with that of *Moby-Dick*; yet the essential spirit of the work cancels the infuriated rebellion of Captain Ahab. In its reconciliation of the temporal with the eternal there is a sense of luminous peace and atonement.

Melville's greatness is something no commentator has quite explained. It shines above the stylistic awkwardness of many passages, the blurred outlines that result from the confusion of autobiography with invented action, the tendency of the author to lose control of his own symbols, or to set the metaphysical thunderbolt side by side with factual discussion or commonplace realism. Having survived the neglect of his contemporaries and the elaborate attentions of recent critics, he emerges secure in the power and influence of *Typee*, *Moby-Dick*, *The Piazza Tales*, *Billy Budd*, and a number of poems.

The Complete Writings of Herman Melville, The Northwestern-Newbury Editions is in progress at Northwestern University under the general editorship of Harrison Hayford, Hershel Parker, and George Thomas Tanselle. *The Works of Herman Melville*, 16 vols., London, 1922–1924, has been standard. A group of scholars has promoted good editions of *Collected Poems* (H. P. Vincent), 1945; *Piazza Tales* (E. S. Oliver), 1948; *Pierre* (H. S. Murray), 1949; *Moby-Dick* (L. S. Mansfield and H. P. Vincent), 1952; *Clarel* (W. E. Bezanson), 1960; and *The Confidence-Man* (E. S. Foster), 1954. A definitive text of *Moby-Dick* is *Moby-Dick: A Norton Critical Edition* (Harrison Hayford and Hershel Parker), 1967. A good edition of *Moby-Dick* is also edited by W. Thorp. 1947. Melville's journals appeared as *Journal of a Visit to London and the Continent* (Eleanor Melville Metcalf), 1948; and *Journal of a Visit to Europe and the Levant * * * * (H. C. Horsford), 1955.

R. M. Weaver, *Herman Melville: Mariner and Mystic*, 1921, was the first full-length biography. Later notable biographies and studies are John Freeman, *Herman Melville*, 1926; Lewis Mumford, *Herman Melville*, 1929, revised, 1963; Charles R. Anderson, *Melville in the South Seas*, 1939; William Braswell, *Melville's Religious Thought*, 1943; W. E. Sedgwick, *Herman Melville: The Tragedy of Mind*, 1944; H. P. Vincent, *The Trying Out of Moby Dick*, 1949, and *The Tailoring of Melville's White Jacket*, 1970; Leon Howard, *Herman Melville: A Biog-*raphy, 1951; Jay Leyda, *The Melville Log: A Documentary Life of Herman Melville*, 1951; Eleanor Melville Metcalf, *Herman Melville: Cycle and Epicycle*, 1953; E. H. Rosenberry, *Melville and the Comic Spirit*, 1955; James Baird, *Ishmael*, 1956; Perry Miller, *The Raven and the Whale * * * *, 1956; and Newton Arvin, *Herman Melville*, 1950, 1957. *The Letters * * * *, 1960, is a collection by Merrell R. Davis and W. H. Gilman.

From The Encantadas, or Enchanted Isles [1]

Sketch First: The Isles at Large

> —"*That may not be, said then the ferryman,*
> *Least we unweeting hap to be fordonne;*
> *For those same islands seeming now and than,*
> *Are not firme land, nor any certein wonne,*
> *But stragling plots which to and fro do ronne*
> *In the wide waters; therefore are they hight*
> *The Wandering Islands; therefore do them shonne;*
> *For they have oft drawne many a wandring wight*
> *Into most deadly daunger and distressed plight;*
> *For whosoever once hath fastened*
> *His foot thereon may never it secure*
> *But wandreth evermore uncertein and unsure.*"

• • • • • •

1. *The Encantadas* appeared as ten sketches in *Putnam's Monthly Magazine*, March, April, and May 1854. Along with "Benito Cereno" and "Bartleby the Scrivener" they were collected in the *Piazza Tales* of 1856.

Of these three masterpieces, *The Encantadas* has received perhaps the least attention. Yet it is one of the most pleasing of Melville's works in its reportage of the unfamiliar and in picturesque event and setting. Also in it Melville reveals his final understanding of the natural world that mankind is doomed to conquer or be conquered by. In the Encantadas, as a seaman long before, he had seen little "enchantment," but rather craggy and scoriac cinder heaps and antediluvian, mammoth tortoises that had given these islands their other Spanish name, Galápagos. These monsters, man's earliest living ancestors, quickened his imagination as they and other arrested species in these islands quickened the scientific insight of Darwin. But to different ends. Melville saw a fantastic creature with "'Memento [mori]' burning in live letters upon his back."

It has not been generally, or at least not sufficiently, noticed that the ten sketches are the orchestration of a single theme. Here the dark Melville speaks in his most reasoned voice, sustained by the actual data of nature. These islands, geologically speaking, represent the primitive substance, gushing molten from beneath the hardening crust of the earth, changeless since in the unchanging climate of the equator, tempered always by the surrounding sea. On these primordial, scarcely vegetated mountains of lava he resurrects a selection of the people whose adventures and fate on these islands are remembered in tradition or in chronicles.

In the four sketches that have been reprinted here, the editors believe that they have represented adequately the range and the excellence of *The Encantadas*. In "The Isles at Large" and "Rock Rodondo" Melville compacted the primitive natural setting of the islands. In "Norfolk Isle and the Chola Widow" a new Eden is destroyed by the fury of nature and the evil of mankind, yet it is one of the greatest stories of love and the only example of Melville's complete success with the theme. By contrast, in "Sketch Nine" the savage terrain meets its match in Hermit Oberlus, a combination of Caliban and Satan, yet completely realized as someone the reader may have known.

The text is that of Melville's edition of *The Piazza Tales* (1856). For identification of the epigraphs of the four sketches we are indebted to Leon Howard, "Melville and Spenser * * * ," *Modern Language Notes*, XLVI, 291–292; and to Russell Thomas, "Melville's use of Some Sources * * * ," *American Literature*, III, 432–456.

"Darke, dolefull, dreary, like a greedy grave,
That still for carrion carcasses doth crave;
On top whereof ay dwelt the ghastly owl,
Shrieking his balefull note, which ever drave
Far from that haunt all other cheerful fowl,
And all about it wandering ghosts did wayle and howl." 2

Take five-and-twenty heaps of cinders dumped here and there in an outside city lot; imagine some of them magnified into mountains, and the vacant lot the sea; and you will have a fit idea of the general aspect of the Encantadas, or Enchanted Isles. A group rather of extinct volcanoes than of isles; looking much as the world at large might after a penal conflagration.

It is to be doubted whether any spot of earth can, in desolateness, furnish a parallel to this group. Abandoned cemeteries of long ago, old cities by piecemeal tumbling to their ruin, these are melancholy enough; but, like all else which has but once been associated with humanity they still awaken in us some thoughts of sympathy, however sad. Hence, even the Dead Sea, along with whatever other emotions it may at times inspire, does not fail to touch in the pilgrim some of his less unpleasurable feelings.

And as for solitariness; the great forests of the north, the expanses of unnavigated waters, the Greenland ice-fields, are the profoundest of solitudes to a human observer; still the magic of their changeable tides and seasons mitigates their terror; because, though unvisited by men, those forests are visited by the May; the remotest seas reflect familiar stars even as Lake Erie does; and in the clear air of a fine Polar day, the irradiated, azure ice shows beautifully as malachite.

But the special curse, as one may call it, of the Encantadas, that which exalts them in desolation above Idumea 3 and the Pole, is that to them change never comes; neither the change of seasons nor of sorrows. Cut by the Equator, they know not autumn and they know not spring; while already reduced to the lees of fire, ruin itself can work little more upon them. The showers refresh the deserts, but in these isles, rain never falls. Like split Syrian gourds, left withering in the sun, they are cracked by an everlasting drought beneath a torrid sky. "Have mercy upon me," the wailing spirit of the Encantadas seems to cry, "and send Lazarus that he may dip the tip of his finger in water and cool my tongue for I am tormented in this flame." 4

Another feature in these isles is their emphatic uninhabitable-

2. The epigraph is drawn from Spenser's *The Faerie Queene;* the first section from Bk. II, xii, stanza 11 (entire) and stanza 12, last three lines. The second section is from Bk. I, ix, stanza 33.
3. Idumea, or Edom, was part of the wilderness in which the Israelites wandered, southeast of Palestine.
4. *Cf.* Luke xvi: 24—the parable of the beggar Lazarus and the rich man who later cries out these words from the flames of Hell.

ness. It is deemed to fit type of all-forsaken overthrow, that the jackal should den in the wastes of weedy Babylon; but the Encantadas refuse to harbour even the outcasts of the beasts. Man and wolf alike disown them. Little but reptile life is here found:—tortoises, lizards, immense spiders, snakes, and the strangest anomaly of outlandish Nature, the *aguano*. No voice, no low, no howl is heard; the chief sound of life here is a hiss.

On most of the isles where vegetation is found at all, it is more ungrateful than the blankness of Aracama.[5] Tangled thickets of wiry bushes, without fruit and without a name, springing up among deep fissures of calcined rock, and treacherously masking them; or a parched growth of distorted cactus trees.

In many places the coast is rock-bound, or more properly, clinker-bound; tumbled masses of blackish or greenish stuff like the dross of an iron-furnace, forming dark clefts and caves here and there, into which a ceaseless sea pours a fury of foam; overhanging them with a swirl of grey, haggard mist, amidst which sail screaming flights of unearthly birds heightening the dismal din. However calm the sea without, there is no rest for these swells and those rocks, they lash and are lashed, even when the outer ocean is most at peace with itself. On the oppressive, clouded days such as are peculiar to this part of the watery Equator, the dark vitrified masses, many of which raise themselves among white whirlpools and breakers in detached and perilous places off the shore, present a most Plutonian sight. In no world but a fallen one could such lands exist.

Those parts of the strand free from the marks of fire stretch away in wide level beaches of multitudinous dead shells, with here and there decayed bits of sugar-cane, bamboos, and cocoanuts, washed upon this other and darker world from the charming palm isles to the westward and southward; all the way from Paradise to Tartarus;[6] while mixed with the relics of distant beauty you will sometimes see fragments of charred wood and mouldering ribs of wrecks. Neither will any one be surprised at meeting these last, after observing the conflicting currents which eddy throughout nearly all the wide channels of the entire group. The capriciousness of the tides of air sympathizes with those of the sea. Nowhere is the wind so light, baffling, and every way unreliable, and so given to perplexing calms, as at the Encantadas. Nigh a month has been spent by a ship going from one isle to another, though but thirty miles between; for owing to the force of the current, the boats employed to tow barely suffice to keep the craft from sweeping upon the cliffs, but do nothing toward accelerating her voyage. Sometimes it is im-

5. *I.e.*, Atacama, the vast salt desert of Chile and Bolivia.

6. In classic myth a deep abyss in Hades; *cf.* above, "Plutonian."

possible for a vessel from afar to fetch up with the group itself, unless large allowances for prospective lee-way have been made ere its coming in sight. And yet, at other times, there is a mysterious indraft, which irresistibly draws a passing vessel among the isles, though not bound to them.

True, at one period, as to some extent at the present day, large fleets of whalemen cruised for Spermaceti [7] upon what some seamen call the Enchanted Ground. But this, as in due place will be described, was off the great outer isle of Albemarle, away from the intricacies of the smaller isles, where there is plenty of sea-room; and hence, to that vicinity, the above remarks do not altogether apply; though even there the current runs at times with singular force, shifting, too, with as singular a caprice. Indeed, there are seasons when currents quite unaccountable prevail for a great distance round about the total group, and are so strong and irregular as to change a vessel's course against the helm, though sailing at the rate of four or five miles the hour. The difference in the reckonings of navigators produced by these causes, along with the light and variable winds, long nourished a persuasion that there existed two distinct clusters of isles in the parallel of the Encantadas, about a hundred leagues apart. Such was the idea of their earlier visitors, the Buccaneers; and as late as 1750, the charts of that part of the Pacific accorded with the strange delusion. And this apparent fleetingness and unreality of the locality of the isles were most probably one reason for the Spaniards calling them the Encantada, or Enchanted Group.

But not uninfluenced by their character, as they now confessedly exist, the modern voyager will be inclined to fancy that the bestowal of this name might have in part originated in that air of spell-bound desertness which so significantly invests the isles. Nothing can better suggest the aspect of once living things malignly crumbled from ruddiness into ashes. Apples of Sodom,[8] after touching, seem these isles.

However wavering their place may seem by reason of the currents, they themselves, at least to one upon the shore, appear invariably the same: fixed, cast, glued into the very body of cadaverous death.

Nor would the appellation, enchanted, seem misapplied in still another sense. For concerning the peculiar reptile inhabitant of these wilds—whose presence gives the group its second Spanish name, Gallipagos—concerning the tortoises found here, most mariners have long cherished a superstition, not more frightful than grotesque. They earnestly believe that all wrecked sea-officers, more

---

7. Precious oil from the whale's head.
8. Not a real fruit but a symbol related to the story in Genesis of Sodom, a city so evil that God destroyed it.

especially commodores and captains, are at death (and in some cases, before death) transformed into tortoises; thenceforth dwelling upon these hot aridities, sole solitary Lords of Asphaltum.

Doubtless so quaintly dolorous a thought was originally inspired by the woe-begone landscape itself, but more particularly, perhaps, by the tortoises. For apart from their strictly physical features, there is something strangely self-condemned in the appearance of these creatures. Lasting sorrow and penal hopelessness are in no animal form so suppliantly expressed as in theirs; while the thought of their wonderful longevity does not fail to enhance the impression.

Nor even at the risk of meriting the charge of absurdly believing in enchantments, can I restrain the admission that sometimes, even now, when leaving the crowded city to wander out July and August among the Adirondack Mountains, far from the influences of towns and proportionally nigh to the mysterious ones of Nature; when at such times I sit me down in the mossy head of some deep-wooded gorge, surrounded by prostrate trunks of blasted pines, and recall, as in a dream, my other and far-distant rovings in the baked heart of the charmed isles; and remember the sudden glimpses of dusky shells, and long languid necks protruded from the leafless thickets; and again have beheld the vitreous inland rocks worn down and grooved into deep ruts by ages and ages of the slow draggings of tortoises in quest of pools of scanty water; I can hardly resist the feeling that in my time I have indeed slept upon evilly enchanted ground.

Nay, such is the vividness of my memory, or the magic of my fancy, that I know not whether I am not the occasional victim of optical delusion concerning the Gallipagos. For often in scenes of social merriment, and especially at revels held by candle light in old-fashioned mansions—when the shadows are thrown into the further recesses of an angular and spacious room, making them put on a look of haunted undergrowth of lonely woods—I have drawn the attention of my comrades by my fixed gaze and sudden change of air, as I have seemed to see, slowly emerging from those imagined solitudes, and heavily crawling along the floor, the ghost of a gigantic tortoise, with "Memento . . ." burning in live letters upon his back.

Sketch Third: Rock Rodondo

"For they this hight the Rock of vile Reproach,
A dangerous and dreadful place,
To which nor fish nor fowl did once approach,
But yelling meaws with sea-gulls hoars and bace
And cormoyrants with birds of ravenous race,
Which still sit waiting on that dreadful clift."

.   .   .   .   .

"With that the rolling sea resounding soft
In his big base them fitly answered,
And on the Rock, the waves breaking aloft,
A solemn meane unto them measured."

. . . . . .

"Then he the boteman bad row easily,
And let him heare some part of that rare melody."

. . . . . .

"Suddenly an innumerable flight
Of harmefull fowles about them fluttering cride,
And with their wicked wings them oft did smight
And sore annoyed, groping in that griesly night."

. . . . . .

"Even all the nation of unfortunate
And fatal birds about them flocked were." 9

To go up into a high stone tower is not only a very fine thing in itself; but the very best mode of gaining a comprehensive view of the region round about. It is all the better if this tower stand solitary and alone, like that mysterious Newport one,¹ or else be sole survivor of some perished castle.

Now, with reference to the Enchanted Isles, we are fortunately supplied with just such a noble point of observation in a remarkable rock, from its peculiar figure called of old by the Spaniards, Rock Rodondo, or Round Rock. Some two hundred and fifty feet high, rising straight from the sea ten miles from land, with the whole mountainous group to the south and east, Rock Rodondo occupies, on a large scale, very much the position which the famous Campanile or detached Bell Tower ² of Saint Mark does with respect to the tangled group of hoary edifices around it.

Ere ascending, however, to gaze abroad upon the Encantadas, this sea-tower itself claims attention. It is visible at the distance of thirty miles; and, fully participating in that enchantment which pervades the group, when first seen afar invariably is mistaken for a sail. Four leagues away, on a golden, hazy noon, it seems some Spanish Admiral's ship, stacked up with glittering canvas. Sail ho! Sail ho! Sail ho! from all three masts. But coming nigh, the enchanted frigate is transformed apace into a craggy keep.

My first visit to the spot was made in the grey of the morning. With a view of fishing, we had lowered three boats, and pulling some two miles from our vessel found ourselves, just before dawn of day, close under the moonshadow of Rodondo. Its aspect was

9. The epigraph is adapted from Spenser's *The Faerie Queene*, Bk. II, xii, stanzas 8, 33, 35, and 36.
1. At the time, antiquarians were arguing whether the ancient stone tower at Newport, R. I., was not actually constructed by Norse voyagers of the eleventh century.
2. In St. Mark's Square, Venice.

heightened, and yet softened, by the strange double twilight of the hour. The great full moon burned in the low west like a half-spent beacon casting a soft mellow tinge upon the sea, like that cast by a waning fire of embers upon a midnight hearth; while along the entire east the invisible sun sent pallid intimations of his coming. The wind was light; the waves languid; the stars twinkled with a faint effulgence; all nature seemed supine with the long night watch, and half-suspended in jaded expectation of the sun. This was the critical hour to catch Rodondo in his perfect mood. The twilight was just enough to reveal every striking point, without tearing away the dim investiture of wonder.

From a broken, stair-like base, washed, as the steps of a water-palace, by the waves, the tower rose in entablatures of strata to a shaven summit. These uniform layers which compose the mass form its most peculiar feature. For at their lines of junction they project flatly into encircling shelves, from top to bottom, rising one above another in graduated series. And as the eaves of any old barn or abbey are alive with swallows, so were all these rocky ledges with unnumbered sea-fowl. Eaves upon eaves, and nests upon nests. Here and there were long birdlime streaks of a ghostly white staining the tower from sea to air, readily accounting for its sail-like look afar. All would have been bewitchingly quiescent, were it not for the demoniac din created by the birds. Not only were the eaves rustling with them, but they flew densely overhead, spreading themselves into a winged and continually shifting canopy. The tower is the resort of aquatic birds for hundreds of leagues around. To the north, to the east, to the west, stretches nothing but eternal ocean; so that the man-of-war hawk coming from the coasts of North America, Polynesia, or Peru, makes his first land at Rodondo. And yet though Rodondo be terra-firma, no landbird ever lighted on it. Fancy a red-robin or a canary there! What a falling into the hands of the Philistines, when the poor warbler should be surrounded by such locust-flights of strong bandit birds, with long bills cruel as daggers.

I know not where one can better study the Natural History of strange sea-fowl than at Rodondo. It is the aviary of Ocean. Birds light here which never touched mast or tree; hermit-birds, which ever fly alone, cloud-birds, familiar with unpierced zones of air.

Let us first glance low down to the lowermost shelf of all, which is the widest too, and but a little space from highwater mark. What outlandish beings are these? Erect as men, but hardly as symmetrical, they stand all around the rock like sculptured caryatides, supporting the next range of eaves above. Their bodies are grotesquely misshapen; their bills short; their feet seemingly legless; while the members at their sides are neither fin, wing, nor arm. And truly neither fish, flesh nor fowl is the penguin; as an edible, pertaining neither to Carnival nor Lent; without exception the most ambiguous and least lovely creature yet discovered by man. Though dabbling in all three elements, and indeed possessing some rudimental claims to all, the penguin is at home in none. On land it stumps; afloat it sculls; in the air it flops. As if ashamed of her failure Nature keeps this ungainly child hidden away at the ends of the earth, in the Straits of Magellan and on the abased sea-story of Rodondo.

But look, what are yon woe-begone regiments drawn up on the next shelf above? What rank and file of large strange fowl? What sea Friars of Orders Grey? Pelicans. Their elongated bills, and heavy leathern pouches, suspended thereto, give them the most lugubrious expression. A pensive race, they stand for hours together without motion. Their dull, ashy plumage imparts an aspect as if they had been powdered over with cinders. A penitential bird indeed—fitly haunting the shores of the clinkered Encantadas—whereupon tormented Job himself might have well sat down and scraped himself with potsherds.

Higher up now we mark the gony, or grey albatross, anomalously so called, an unsightly unpoetic bird, unlike its storied kinsman, which is the snow-white ghost of the haunted Capes of Hope and Horn.

As we still ascend from shelf to shelf we find the tenants of the tower serially disposed in order of their magnitude—gannets, black and speckled haglets, jays, sea-hens, sperm-whalebirds, gulls of all varieties:—thrones, princedoms, powers, dominating one above another in senatorial array; while sprinkled over all, like an ever-repeated fly in a great piece of broidery, the stormy petrel or Mother Cary's chicken sounds his continual challenge and alarm. That this mysterious humming-bird of ocean, which had it but brilliancy of hue might from its evanescent liveliness be almost called its butterfly, yet whose chirrup under the stern is ominous to mariners as to the peasant the death-tick sounding from behind the chimney-jam—should have its special haunt at the Encantadas, contributes in the seaman's mind not a little to their dreary spell.

As day advances the dissonant din augments. With ear-splitting cries the wild birds celebrate their matins. Each moment, flights push from the tower, and join the aerial choir hovering overhead, while their places below are supplied by darting myriads. But down through all this discord of commotion I heard clear silver bugle-like notes unbrokenly falling, like oblique lines of swift slanting rain in a cascading shower. I gaze far up, and behold a snow-white angelic thing, with one long lance-like feather thrust out behind. It is the bright inspiring chanticleer of ocean, the beauteous bird, from its bestirring whistle of musical invocation, fitly styled the "Boatswain's Mate."

The winged life clouding Rodondo on that well-remembered morning, I saw had its full counterpart in the finny hosts which people the waters at its base. Below the waterline, the rock seemed one honey-comb of grottoes, affording labyrinthine lurking places for swarms of fairy fish. All were strange; many exceedingly beautiful; and would have well graced the costliest glass globes in which goldfish are kept for a show. Nothing was more striking then the complete novelty of many individuals of this multitude. Here hues were seen as yet unpainted, and figures which are unengraved.

To show the multitude, avidity, and nameless fearlessness and tameness of these fish, let me say that often marking through clear spaces of water—temporarily made so by the concentric dartings of the fish above the surface—certain larger and less unwary wights, which swam slow and deep, our anglers would cautiously essay to drop their lines down to these last. But in vain; there was no passing the uppermost zone. No sooner did the hook touch the sea than a hundred infatuates contended for the honour of capture. Poor fish of Rodondo! in your victimized confidence you are of the number of those who inconsiderately trust while they do not understand, human nature.

But the dawn is now fairly day. Band after band the seafowl sail away to forage the deep for their food. The tower is left solitary, save the fish caves at its base. Its birdlime gleams in the golden rays like the whitewash of a tall lighthouse, or the lofty sails of a cruiser. This moment, doubtless, while we know it to be a dead desert rock, other voyagers are taking oaths it is a glad populous ship.

But ropes now, and let us ascend. Yet soft, this is not so easy.

Sketch Eighth: Norfolk Isle and the Chola Widow

> "At last they in a island did espy
> A seemly woman sitting by the shore,
> That with great sorrow and sad agony
> Seemed some great misfortune to deplore,
> And loud to them for succor called evermore."

> "Black his eyes as the midnight sky,
> White his neck as the driven snow,
> Red his cheek as the morning light;—
> Cold he lies in the ground below.
>   My love is dead,
>   Gone to his death-bed,
> All under the cactus tree."

> "Each lonely scene shall thee restore,
> For thee the tear be duly shed;
> Belov'd till life can charm no more,
> And mourned till Pity's self be dead." [3]

3. The epigraph is adapted from Spenser's *The Faerie Queene*, Bk. II, xii, 27; from Chatterton's "The Mynstrelles Song," stanza 2; and from William Collins's "Dirge in Cymbelene." The last did not appear with this sketch in *Putnam's Monthly*; added in *Piazza Tales*.

Far to the northeast of Charles's Isle, sequestered from the rest, lies Norfolk Isle; and, however insignificant to most voyagers, to me, through sympathy, that lone island has become a spot made sacred by the strongest trials of humanity.

It was my first visit to the Encantadas. Two days had been spent ashore in hunting tortoises. There was not time to capture many; so on the third afternoon we loosed our sails. We were just in the act of getting under way, the uprooted anchor yet suspended and invisibly swaying beneath the wave, as the good ship gradually turned her heel to leave the isle behind, when the seaman who heaved with me at the windlass paused suddenly, and directed my attention to something moving on the land, not along the beach, but somewhat back, fluttering from a height.

In view of the sequel of this little story, be it here narrated how it came to pass, that an object which partly from its being so small was quite lost to every other man on board, still caught the eye of my handspike companion. The rest of the crew, myself included, merely stood up to our spikes in heaving; whereas, unwontedly exhilarated at every turn of the ponderous windlass, my belted comrade leaped atop of it, with might and main giving a downward, thewey, perpendicular heave, his raised eye bent in cheery animation upon the slowly receding shore. Being high lifted above all others was the reason he perceived the object, otherwise unperceivable; and this elevation of his eye was owing to the elevation of his spirits; and this again—for truth must out—to a dram of Peruvian pisco, in guerdon for some kindness done, secretly administered to him that morning by our mulatto steward. Now, certainly, pisco does a deal of mischief in the world; yet seeing that, in the present case, it was the means, though indirect, of rescuing a human being from the most dreadful fate, must we not also needs admit that sometimes pisco does a deal of good?

Glancing across the water in the direction pointed out, I saw some white thing hanging from an inland rock, perhaps half a mile from the sea.

"It is a bird; a white-winged bird; perhaps a—no; it is—it is a handkerchief!"

"Aye, a handkerchief!" echoed my comrade, and with a louder shout apprised the captain.

Quickly now—like the running out and training of a great gun —the long cabin spy-glass was thrust through the mizzen rigging from the high platform of the poop; whereupon a human figure was plainly seen upon the inland rock, eagerly waving towards us what seemed to be the handkerchief.

Our captain was a prompt, good fellow. Dropping the glass, he lustily ran forward, ordering the anchor to be dropped again; hands to stand by a boat, and lower away.

In a half-hour's time the swift boat returned. It went with six and came with seven; and the seventh was a woman.

It is not artistic heartlessness, but I wish I could but draw in crayons; for this woman was a most touching sight; and crayons, tracing softly melancholy lines, would best depict the mournful image of the dark-damasked Chola widow.

Her story was soon told, and though given in her own strange language was as quickly understood, for our captain from long trading on the Chilian coast was well versed in the Spanish. A *cholo*, or half-breed Indian woman of Payta in Peru, three years gone by, with her young new-wedded husband Felipe, of pure Castilian blood, and her one only Indian brother, Truxill, Hunilla had taken passage on the main in a French whaler, commanded by a joyous man; which vessel, bound to the cruising grounds beyond the Enchanted Isles, proposed passing close by their vicinity. The object of the little party was to procure tortoise oil, a fluid which for its great purity and delicacy is held in high estimation wherever known; and it is well known all along this part of the Pacific coast. With a chest of clothes, tools, cooking utensils, a rude apparatus for trying out the oil, some casks of biscuit, and other things, not omitting two favourite dogs, of which faithful animal all the Cholos are very fond, Hunilla and her companions were safely landed at their chosen place; the Frenchman, according to the contract made ere sailing, engaged to take them off upon returning from a four months' cruise in the westward seas; which interval the three adventurers deemed quite sufficient for their purposes.

On the isle's lone beach they paid him in silver for their passage out, the stranger having declined to carry them at all except upon that condition; though willing to take every means to insure the due fulfilment of his promise. Felipe had striven hard to have this payment put off to the period of the ship's return. But in vain. Still, they thought they had, in another way, ample pledge of the good faith of the Frenchman. It was arranged that the expenses of the passage home should not be payable in silver, but in tortoises; one hundred tortoises ready captured to the returning captain's hand. These the Cholos meant to secure after their own work was done, against the probable time of the Frenchman's coming back; and no doubt in prospect already felt, that in those hundred tortoises—now somewhere ranging in the isle's interior—they possessed one hundred hostages. Enough: the vessel sailed; the gazing three on shore answered the loud glee of the singing crew; and ere evening, the French craft was hull down in the distant sea, its masts three faintest lines which quickly faded from Hunilla's eye.

The stranger had given a blithesome promise, and had anchored it with oaths; but oaths and anchors equally will drag; nought else abides on fickle earth but unkept promises of joy. Contrary winds from out unstabled skies, or contrary moods of his more varying mind, or shipwreck and sudden death in solitary waves; whatever was the cause, the blithe stranger never was seen again.

Yet, however dire a calamity was here in store, misgivings of it ere due time never disturbed the Cholos's busy mind, now all intent upon the toilsome matter which had brought them hither. Nay, by swift doom coming like the thief at night, ere seven weeks went by, two of the little party were removed from all anxieties of land or sea. No more they sought to gaze with feverish fear, or still more feverish hope, beyond the present's horizon line; but into the furthest future their own silent spirits sailed. By persevering labour beneath that burning sun, Felipe and Truxill had brought down to their hut many scores of tortoises, and tried out the oil, when, elated with their good success, and to reward themselves for such hard work, they, too hastily, made a catamaran, or Indian raft, much used on the Spanish main, and merrily started a fishing trip just without a long reef with many jagged gaps, running parallel with the shore, about half a mile from it. By some bad tide or hap—or natural negligence of joyfulness (for though they could not be heard, yet by their gestures they seemed singing at the time), forced in deep water against that iron bar—the ill-made catamaran was overset, and came all to pieces; when, dashed by broad-chested swells between their broken logs and the sharp teeth of the reef, both adventurers perished before Hunilla's eyes.

Before Hunilla's eyes they sank. The real woe of this event passed before her sight as some sham tragedy on the stage. She was seated on a rude bower among the withered thickets, crowning a lofty cliff, a little back from the beach. The thickets were so disposed, that in looking upon the sea at large she peered out from among the branches as from the lattice of a high balcony. But, upon the day we speak of here, the better to watch the adventure of those two hearts she loved, Hunilla had withdrawn the branches to one side and held them so. They formed an oval frame through which the bluey boundless sea rolled like a painted one. And there, the invisible painter painted to her view the wave-tossed and disjointed raft, its once level logs slantingly upheaved, as raking masts, and the four struggling arms undistinguishable among them; and then all subsided into smooth-flowing creamy waters, slowly drifting the splintered wreck; while first and last, no sound of any sort was heard. Death in a silent picture; a dream of the eye; such vanishing shapes as the mirage shows.

So instant was the scene, so trance-like its mild pictorial effect, so distant from her blasted tower and her common sense of things, that Hunilla gazed and gazed, nor raised a finger or a wail. But as good to sit thus dumb, in stupor staring on that dumb show, for all that otherwise might be done. With half a mile of sea between, could her two enchanted arms aid those four fated ones? The distance long, the time one sand. After the lightning is beheld, what fool shall ever stay the thunderbolt? Felipe's body was washed ashore, but Truxill's never came; only his gay, braided hat of golden straw—that same sunflower thing he waved to her, pushing from the strand—and now, to the last gallant, it still saluted her. But Felipe's body floated to the marge, with one arm encirclingly outstretched. Lock-jawed in grim death, the lover-husband softly clasped his bride—true to her even in death's dream. Ah, Heaven, when man thus keeps his faith, wilt thou be faithless who created the faithful one? But they cannot break faith who never plighted it.

It needs not to be said what nameless misery now wrapped the lonely widow. In telling her own story she passed this almost entirely over, simply recounting the event. Construe the comment of her features as you might; from her mere words little would you have weened that Hunilla was herself the heroine of her tale. But not thus did she defraud us of our tears. All hearts bled that grief could be so brave.

She but showed us her soul's lid, and the strange ciphers thereon engraved; all within, with pride's timidity, was withheld. Yet was there one exception. Holding out her small olive hand before our captain, she said in mild and slowest Spanish, "Señor, I buried him;" then paused, struggled as against the writhed coilings of a snake, and cringing suddenly, leaped up, repeating in impassioned pain, "I buried him, my life, my soul!"

Doubtless it was by half-unconscious, automatic motions of her hands, that this heavy-hearted one performed the final offices for Felipe, and planted a rude cross of withered sticks—no green ones might be had—at the head of that lonely grave, where rested now in lasting uncomplaint and quiet haven he whom untranquil seas had overthrown.

But some dull sense of another body that should be interred, of another cross that should hallow another grave—unmade as yet; some dull anxiety and pain touching her undiscovered brother now haunted the oppressed Hunilla. Her hands fresh from the burial earth, she slowly went back to the beach, with unshaped purposes wandered there, her spellbound eye bent upon the incessant waves. But they bore nothing to her but a dirge, which maddened her to think that murderers should mourn. As time went by, and these things came less dreamingly to her mind, the strong persuasions of her Romish faith, which sets peculiar store by consecrated urns, prompted her to resume in waking earnest that pious search which had but been begun as in somnambulism. Day after day, week after week, she trod the cindery beach, till at length a double motive edged every eager glance. With equal longing she now looked for the living and the dead; the brother and the captain; alike vanished, never to return. Little accurate note of time had Hunilla taken under such emotions as were hers, and little, outside herself, served for calendar or dial. As to poor Crusoe in the self-same sea, no saint's bell pealed forth the lapse of week or month; each day went by unchallenged; no chanticleer announced those sultry dawns, no lowing herds those poisonous nights. All wonted and steadily recurring sounds, human or humanized by sweet fellowship with man, but one stirred that torrid trance,—the cry of dogs; save which nought but the rolling sea invaded it, an all pervading monotone; and to the widow that was the least loved voice she could have heard.

No wonder that as her thoughts now wandered to the unreturning ship, and were beaten back again, the hope against hope so struggled in her soul, that at length she desperately said, "Not yet, not yet; my foolish heart runs on too fast." She forced patience for some further weeks. But to those whom earth's sure indraft draws, patience or impatience is still the same.

Hunilla now sought to settle precisely in her mind, to an hour, how long it was since the ship had sailed; and then, with the same precision, how long a space remained to pass. But this proved impossible. What present day or month it was she could not say. Time was her labyrinth, in which Hunilla was entirely lost.

And now follows—

Against my own purposes a pause descends upon me here. One knows not whether nature doth not impose some secrecy upon him who has been privy to certain things. At least, it is to be doubted whether it be good to blazon such. If some books are deemed most baneful and their sale forbid, how then with deadlier facts, not dreams of doting men? Those whom books will hurt will not be proof against events. Events, not books, should be forbid. But in all things man sows upon the wind, which bloweth just there wither it listeth; for ill or good man cannot know. Often ill comes from the good, as good from ill.

When Hunilla—

Dire sight it is to see some silken beast long dally with a golden lizard ere she devour. More terrible, to see how feline Fate will sometimes dally with a human soul, and by a nameless magic make it repulse one sane despair with another which is but mad. Unwittingly I imp this cat-like thing, sporting with the heart of him who reads; for if he feel not, he does read in vain.

—"The ship sails this day, to-day," at last said Hunilla to herself; "this gives me certain time to stand on; without certainty I go mad. In loose ignorance I have hoped and hoped; now in firm knowledge I will but wait. Now I live and no longer perish in bewilderings. Holy Virgin, aid me! Thou wilt waft back the ship. Oh, past length of weary weeks—all to be dragged over—to buy the certainty of to-day, I freely give ye, though I tear ye from me!"

As mariners tossed in tempest on some desolate ledge patch them a boat out of the remnants of their vessel's wreck, and launch it in the self-same waves—see here Hunilla, this lone ship-wrecked soul, out of treachery invoking trust. Humanity, thou strong thing. I worship thee, not in the laurelled victor, but in this vanquished one.

Truly, Hunilla leaned upon a reed, a real one; no metaphor; a real Eastern reed. A piece of hollow cane, drifted from unknown isles, and found upon the beach, its once jagged ends rubbed smoothly even as by sand-paper; its golden glazing gone. Long ground between the sea and land, upper and nether stone, the unvarnished substance was filed bare, and wore another polish now, one with itself, the polish of its agony. Circular lines at intervals cut all round this surface, divided it into six panels of unequal length. In the first were scored the days, each tenth one marked by a longer and deeper notch; the second was scored for the number of sea-fowl eggs for sustenance, picked out from the rocky nests; the third, how many fish had been caught from the shore; the fourth, how many small tortoises found inland; the fifth, how many days of sun; the sixth, of clouds; which last, of the two, was the greater one. Long night of busy numbering, misery's mathematics, to weary her too-wakeful soul to sleep; yet sleep for that was none.

The panel of the days was deeply worn, the long tenth notches half effaced, as alphabets of the blind. Ten thousand times the longing widow had traced her finger over the bamboo—dull flute, which played on, gave no sound—as if counting birds flown by in air, would hasten tortoises creeping through the woods.

After the one hundred and eightieth day no further mark was seen; that last one was the faintest, as the first the deepest.

"There were more days," said our Captain; "many, many more; why did you not go on and notch them too, Hunilla?"

"Señor, ask me not."

"And meantime, did no other vessel pass the isle?"

"Nay, Señor;—but—"

"You do not speak; but *what*, Hunilla?"

"Ask me not, Señor."

"You saw ships pass, far away; you waved to them; they passed on;—was that it, Hunilla?"

"Señor, be it as you say."

Braced against her woe, Hunilla would not—durst not—trust the weakness of her tongue. Then when our Captain asked whether any whale-boats had——

But no, I will not file this thing complete for scoffing souls to quote, and call it firm proof upon their side. The half shall here remain untold. Those two unnamed events which befell Hunilla on this isle, let them abide between her and her God. In nature, as in law, it may be libellous to speak some truths.

Still, how it was that, although our vessel had lain three days anchored nigh the isle, its one human tenant should not have discovered us till just upon the point of sailing, never to revisit so lone and far a spot; this needs explaining ere the sequel come.

The place where the French captain had landed the little party was on the farther and opposite end of the isle. There too it was that they had afterwards built their hut. Nor did the widow in her solitude desert the spot where her loved ones had dwelt with her, and where the dearest of the twain now slept his last long sleep, and all her plaints awaked him not, and he of husbands the most faithful during life.

Now, high broken land rises between the opposite extremities of the isle. A ship anchored at one side is invisible from the other. Neither is the isle so small but a considerable company might wander for days through the wilderness of one side, and never be seen, or their halloos heard, by any stranger holding aloof on the other. Hence Hunilla, who naturally associated the possible coming of ships with her own part of the isle, might to the end have remained quite ignorant of the presence of our vessel, were it not for a mysterious presentiment, borne to her, so our mariners averred, by this isle's enchanted air. Nor did the widow's answer undo the thought.

"How did you come to cross the isle this morning then, Hunilla?" said our Captain.

"Señor, something came flitting by me. It touched my cheek, my heart, Señor."

"What do you say, Hunilla?"

"I have said, Señor; something came through the air."

It was a narrow chance. For when in crossing the isle Hunilla gained the high land in the centre, she must then for the first have perceived our masts, and also marked that their sails were being loosed, perhaps even heard the echoing chorus of the windlass song. The strange ship was about to sail, and she behind. With all haste she now descends the height on the hither side, but soon loses sight of the ship among the sunken jungles at the mountain's base. She struggles on through the withered branches, which seek at every step to bar her path, till she comes to the isolated rock, still some way from the water. This she climbs, to reassure herself. The ship is still in plainest sight. But now, worn out with over tension, Hunilla all but faints; she fears to step down from her giddy perch; she is feign to pause, there where she is, and as a last resort catches the turban from her head, unfurls and waves it over the jungles towards us.

During the telling of her story the mariners formed a voiceless circle round Hunilla and the Captain; and when at length the word was given to man the fastest boat, and pull round to the isle's thither side, to bring away Hunilla's chest and the tortoise-oil—such alacrity of both cheery and sad obedience seldom before was seen. Little ado was made. Already the anchor had been recommitted to the bottom and the ship swung calmly to it.

But Hunilla insisted upon accompanying the boat as indispensable pilot to her hidden hut. So, being refreshed with the best the steward could supply, she started with us. Nor did ever any wife of the most famous admiral in her husband's barge receive more silent reverence of respect, than poor Hunilla from this boat's crew.

Rounding many a vitreous cape and bluff, in two hours' time we shot inside the fatal reef; wound into a secret cove, looked up along a green many-gabled lava wall, and saw the island's solitary dwelling.

It hung upon an impending cliff, sheltered on two sides by tangled thickets, and half-screened from view in front by juttings of the rude stairway, which climbed the precipice from the sea. Built of canes, it was thatched with long, mildewed grass. It seemed an abandoned hayrick, whose haymakers were now no more. The roof inclined but one way; the eaves coming to within two feet of the ground. And here was a simple apparatus to collect the dews, or rather doubly-distilled and finest winnowed rains, which, in mercy or in mockery, the night skies sometimes drop upon these blighted Encantadas. All along beneath the eave, a spotted sheet, quite weather-stained, was spread, pinned to short, upright stakes, set in the shallow sand. A small clinker, thrown into the cloth, weighed its middle down, thereby straining all moisture into a calabash placed below. This vessel supplied each drop of water ever drunk upon the isle by the Cholos. Hunilla told us the calabash would sometimes, but not often, be half filled over-night. It held six quarts, perhaps. "But," said she, "we were used to thirst. At Sandy Payta, where I live, no shower from heaven ever fell; all the water there is brought on mules from the inland vales."

Tied among the thickets were some twenty moaning tortoises, supplying Hunilla's lonely larder; while hundreds of vast tableted black bucklers, like displaced, shattered tombstones of dark slate, were also scattered round. These were the skeleton backs of those great tortoises from which Felipe and Truxill had made their precious oil. Several large calabashes and two goodly kegs were filled with it. In a pot near by were the caked crusts of a quantity which had been permitted to evaporate. "They meant to have strained it off next day," said Hunilla, as she turned aside.

I forgot to mention the most singular sight of all, though the first that greeted us after landing; memory keeps not in all things to the order of occurrence.

Some ten small, soft-haired, ringleted dogs, of a beautiful breed, peculiar to Peru, set up a concert of glad welcomings when we gained the beach, which was responded to by Hunilla. Some of these dogs had, since her widowhood, been born upon the isle, the progeny of the two brought from Payta. Owing to the jagged steeps and pitfalls, tortuous thickets, sunken clefts and perilous intricacies of all sorts in the interior, Hunilla, admonished by the loss of one favourite among them, never allowed these delicate creatures to follow her in her occasional bird's-nest climbs and other wanderings; so that, through long habituation, they offered not to follow, when that morning she crossed the land; and her own soul was then too full of other things to heed their lingering behind. Yet, all along she had so clung to them, that, besides what moisture they lapped up at early daybreak from the small scoop-holes among the adjacent rocks, she had shared the dew of her calabash among them; never laying by any considerable store against those prolonged and utter droughts, which in some disastrous seasons warp these isles.

Having pointed out, at our desire, what few things she would like transported to the ship—her chest, the oil, not omitting the live tortoises which she intended for a grateful present to our Captain —we immediately set to work, carrying them to the boat down the long, sloping stair of deeply-shadowed rock. While my comrades were thus employed, I looked, and Hunilla had disappeared.

It was not curiosity alone, but, it seems to me, something different mingled with it, which prompted me to drop my tortoises and once more gaze slowly around. I remembered the husband buried by Hunilla's hands. A narrow pathway led into a dense part of the thickets. Following it through many mazes, I came out upon a small, round, open space, deeply chambered there.

The mound rose in the middle; a bare heap of finest sand, like that unverdured heap found at the bottom of an hour-glass run out. At its head stood the cross of withered sticks; the dry, peeled bark still fraying from it; its transverse limb tied up with rope, and forlornly adroop in the silent air.

Hunilla was partly prostrate upon the grave; her dark head bowed and lost in her long, loosened Indian hair; her hands extended to the cross-foot, with a little brass crucifix clasped between; a crucifix worn featureless, like an ancient graven knocker long plied in vain. She did not see me, and I made no noise but slid aside and left the spot.

A few moments, ere all was ready for our going, she reappeared among us. I looked into her eyes, but saw no tear. There was something which seemed strangely haughty in her air, and yet it was the air of woe. A Spanish and an Indian grief, which would not visibly lament. Pride's height in vain abased to proneness on the rock; nature's pride subduing nature's torture.

Like pages the small and silken dogs surrounded her, as she slowly descended towards the beach. She caught the two most eager creatures in her arms:—"Mia Teeta! Mia Tometeeta!" and fondling them, inquired how many could we take on board.

The mate commanded the boat's crew; not a hard-hearted man, but his way of life had been such that in most things, even in the smallest, simple utility was his leading motive.

"We cannot take them all, Hunilla; our supplies are short; the winds are unreliable; we may be a good many days going to Tombez. So take those you have, Hunilla; but no more."

She was in the boat; the oarsmen too were seated; all save one, who stood ready to push off and then spring himself. With the sagacity of their race, the dogs now seemed aware that they were in the very instant of being deserted upon a barren strand. The gunwales of the boat were high; its prow—presented inland—was lifted; so, owing to the water, which they seemed instinctively to shun, the dogs could not well leap into the little craft. But their busy paws had scraped the prow, as it had been some farmer's door shutting them out from shelter in a winter storm. A clamorous agony of alarm. They did not howl, or whine; they all but spoke.

"Push off! Give way!" cried the mate. The boat gave one heavy drag and lurch, and next moment shot swiftly from the beach, turned on her heel, and sped. The dogs ran howling along the water's marge; now pausing to gaze at the flying boat, then motioning as if to leap in chase, but mysteriously withheld themselves; and again ran howling along the beach. Had they been human beings hardly would they have more vividly inspired the sense of desolation. The oars were plied as confederate feathers of two wings. No one spoke. I looked back upon the beach, and then upon Hunilla, but her face was set in a stern dusky calm. The dogs crouching in her lap vainly licked her rigid hands. She never looked behind her; but sat motionless, till we turned a promontory of the coast and lost all sights and sounds astern. She seemed as one who, having experienced the sharpest of mortal pangs, was henceforth content to have all lesser heartstrings riven, one by one. To Hunilla, pain seemed so necessary, that pain in other beings—though by love and sympathy made her own—was unrepiningly to be borne. A heart of yearning in a frame of steel. A heart of earthly yearning, frozen by the frost which falleth from the sky.

The sequel is soon told. After a long passage, vexed by calms and baffling winds, we made the little port of Tombez in Peru, there to recruit the ship. Payta was not very distant. Our captain sold the tortoise oil to a Tombez merchant; and adding to the silver a contribution from all hands, gave it to our silent passenger, who knew not what the mariners had done.

The last seen of lone Hunilla she was passing into Payta town, riding upon a small gray ass; and before her on the ass's shoulders, she eyed the jointed workings of the beast's armorial cross.

Sketch Ninth: Hood's Isle and the Hermit Oberlus [4]

> *"That darkesome glen they enter, where they find*
> *That cursed man low sitting on the ground,*
> *Musing full sadly in his sullein mind;*
> *His griesly lockes long grouen and unbound,*
> *Disordered hong about his shoulders round,*
> *And hid his face, through which his hollow eyne*
> *Lookt deadly dull, and stared as astound;*
> *His raw-bone cheekes, through penurie and pine,*
> *Were shronke into the jawes, as he did never dine.*
> *His garments nought but many ragged clouts,*
> *With thornes together pind and patched reads,*
> *The which his naked sides he wrapt abouts."* [5]

Southeast of Crossman's Isle lies Hood's Isle, or McCain's Beclouded Isle; and upon its south side is a vitreous cove with a wide strand of dark pounded black lava, called Black Beach, or Oberlus's Landing. It might fitly have been styled Charon's.

It received its name from a wild white creature who spent many years here; in the person of a European bringing into this savage region qualities more diabolical than are to be found among any of the surrounding cannibals.

About half a century ago, Oberlus deserted at the above-named island, then, as now, a solitude. He built himself a den of lava and clinkers, about a mile from the Landing, subsequently called after him, in a vale, or expanded gulch, containing here and there among the rocks about two acres of soil capable of rude cultivation; the only place on the isle not too blasted for that purpose. Here he succeeded in raising a sort of degenerate potatoes and pumpkins, which from time to time he exchanged with needy whalemen passing, for spirits or dollars.

His appearance, from all accounts, was that of the victim of some malignant sorceress; he seemed to have drunk of Circe's cup; beast-like; rags insufficient to hide his nakedness; his befreckled skin blistered by continual exposure to the sun; nose flat; countenance contorted, heavy, earthy; hair and beard unshorn, profuse, and of a

---

4. Melville asserts that he had several authorities for this story in general and, specifically, Captain Horatio Porter's *Journal of a Cruise Made to the Pacific Islands* (1822), in which the exploits of one Patrick Watkins resemble the escapades of Oberlus (I, 131–135).
5. The epigraph is an adaptation from Spenser's *The Faerie Queene*, Bk. I, ix, 36.

fiery red. He struck strangers much as if he were a volcanic creature thrown up by the same convulsion which exploded into sight the isle. All bepatched and coiled asleep in his lonely lava den among the mountains, he looked, they say, as a heaped drift of withered leaves, torn from autumn trees, and so left in some hidden nook by the whirling halt for an instant of a fierce night-wind, which then ruthlessly sweeps on, somewhere else to repeat the capricious act. It is also reported to have been the strangest sight, this same Oberlus, of a sultry, cloudy morning, hidden under his shocking old black tarpaulin hat, hoeing potatoes among the lava. So warped and crooked was his strange nature, that the very handle of his hoe seemed gradually to have shrunk and twisted in his grasp, being a wretched bent stick, elbowed more like a savage's war-sickle than a civilized hoe-handle. It was his mysterious custom upon a first en-counter with a stranger ever to present his back; possibly, because that was his better side, since it revealed the least. If the encounter chanced in his garden, as it sometimes did—the new-landed stran-gers going from the sea-side straight through the gorge, to hunt up the queer green-grocer reported doing business here—Oberlus for a time hoed on, unmindful of all greeting, jovial or bland; as the curious stranger would turn to face him, the recluse, hoe in hand, as diligently would avert himself; bowed over, and sullenly revolv-ing round his murphy hill. Thus far for hoeing. When planting, his whole aspect and all his gestures were so malevolently and use-lessly sinister and secret, that he seemed rather in act of dropping poison into wells than potatoes into soil. But among his lesser and more harmless marvels was an idea he ever had, that his visitors came equally as well led by longings to behold the mighty hermit Oberlus in his royal state of solitude, as simply to obtain potatoes, or find whatever company might be upon a barren isle. It seems in-credible that such a being should possess such vanity; a misanthrope be conceited; but he really had his notion; and upon the strength of it, often gave himself amusing airs to captains. But after all, this is somewhat of a piece with the well-known eccentricity of some convicts, proud of that very hatefulness which makes them notori-ous. At other times, another unaccountable whim would seize him, and he would long dodge advancing strangers round the clinkered corners of his hut; sometimes like a stealthy bear, he would slink through the withered thickets up the mountains, and refuse to see the human face.

Except his occasional visitors from the sea—for a long period—the only companions of Oberlus were the crawling tortoises; and he seemed more than degraded to their level, having no desires for a time beyond theirs, unless it were for the stupor brought on by drunkenness. But sufficiently debased as he appeared, there yet lurked in him, only awaiting occasion for discovery, a still further proneness. Indeed the sole superiority of Oberlus over the tortoises was his possession of a larger capacity of degradation; and along with that, something like an intelligent will to it. Moreover, what is about to be revealed, perhaps will show, that selfish ambition, or the love of rule for its own sake, far from being the peculiar infirmity of noble minds, is shared by beings which have no mind at all. No creatures are so selfishly tyrannical as some brutes; as any one who has observed the tenants of the pasture must occasionally have observed.

"This island's mine by Sycorax my mother;" [6] said Oberlus to himself, glaring round upon his haggard solitude. By some means, barter or theft—for in those days ships at intervals still kept touching at his Landing—he obtained an old musket, with a few charges of powder and ball. Possessed of arms, he was stimulated to enterprise, as a tiger that first feels the coming of its claws. The long habit of sole dominion over every object round him, his almost unbroken solitude, his never encountering humanity except on terms of misanthropic independence, or mercantile craftiness, and even such encounters being comparatively but rare; all this must have gradually nourished in him a vast idea of his own importance, together with a pure animal sort of scorn for all the rest of the universe.

The unfortunate Creole, who enjoyed his brief term of royalty at Charles's Isle, was perhaps in some degree influenced by not unworthy motives; such as prompt other adventurous spirits to lead colonists into distant regions and assume political preeminence over them. His summary execution of many of his Peruvians is quite pardonable, considering the desperate characters he had to deal with; while his offering canine battle to the banded rebels seems under the circumstances altogether just.[7] But for this King Oberlus and what shortly follows, no shade of palliation can be given. He acted out of mere delight in tyranny and cruelty, by virtue of a quality in him inherited from Sycorax his mother. Armed now with that shocking blunderbuss, strong in the thought of being master of that horrid isle, he panted for a chance to prove his potency upon the first specimen of humanity which should fall unbefriended into his hands.

Nor was he long without it. One day he spied a boat upon the beach, with one man, a negro, standing by it. Some distance off was a ship, and Oberlus immediately knew how matters stood. The

---

6. Sycorax was the witch, the mother of Caliban, in Shakespeare's *The Tempest* (see especially I, ii, 258 ff).
7. In "Sketch Seventh: Charles's Isle and the Dog-King" a Creole soldier of fortune in Peru, given Charles's Isle for valor, enslaves his colonists with his pack of savage dogs. The colonists mutiny, exile him, and set up a refuge for desperadoes.

vessel had put in for wood, and the boat's crew had gone into the thickets for it. From a convenient spot he kept watch of the boat, till presently a straggling company appeared loaded with billets. Throwing these on the beach, they again went into the thickets, while the negro proceeded to load the boat.

Oberlus now makes all haste and accosts the negro, who, aghast at seeing any living being inhabiting such a solitude, and especially so horrific a one, immediately falls into a panic, not at all lessened by the ursine suavity of Oberlus, who begs the favour of assisting him in his labours. The negro stands with several billets on his shoulder, in act of shouldering others; and Oberlus, with a short cord concealed in his bosom, kindly proceeds to lift those other billets to their place. In so doing he persists in keeping behind the negro, who rightly suspicious of this, in vain dodges about to gain the front of Oberlus; but Oberlus dodges also; till at last, weary of this bootless attempt at treachery, or fearful of being surprised by the remainder of the party, Oberlus runs off a little space to a bush, and fetching his blunderbuss, savagely demands the negro to desist work and follow him. He refuses. Whereupon, presenting his piece, Oberlus snaps at him. Luckily the blunderbuss misses fire; but by this time, frightened out of his wits, the negro, upon a second intrepid summons, drops his billets, surrenders at discretion, and follows on. By a narrow defile familiar to him, Oberlus speedily removes out of sight of the water.

On their way up the mountains, he exultingly informs the negro, that henceforth he is to work for him, and be his slave, and that his treatment would entirely depend on his future conduct. But Oberlus, deceived by the first impulsive cowardice of the black, in an evil moment slackens his vigilance. Passing through a narrow way, and perceiving his leader quite off his guard, the negro, a powerful fellow, suddenly grasps him in his arms, throws him down, wrests his musketoon from him, ties his hands with the monster's own cord, shoulders him, and returns with him down to the boat. When the rest of the party arrive, Oberlus is carried on board the ship. This proved an Englishman and a smuggler—a sort of craft not apt to be over-charitable. Oberlus is severely whipped, then handcuffed, taken ashore, and compelled to make known his habitation and produce his property. His potatoes, pumpkins, and tortoises, with a pile of dollars he had hoarded from his mercantile operations, were secured on the spot. But while the too vindictive smugglers were busy destroying his hut and garden, Oberlus makes his escape into the mountains, and conceals himself there in impenetrable recesses, only known to himself, till the ship sails, when he ventures back, and by means of an old file which he sticks into a tree, contrives to free himself from his handcuffs.

Brooding among the ruins of his hut, and the desolate clinkers and extinct volcanoes of this outcast isle, the insulted misanthrope now meditates a signal revenge upon humanity, but conceals his purposes. Vessels still touch the Landing at times; and by and by Oberlus is enabled to supply them with some vegetables.

Warned by his former failure in kidnapping strangers, he now pursues a quite different plan. When seamen come ashore, he makes up to them like a free-and-easy comrade, invites them to his hut, and with whatever affability his red-haired grimness may assume, entreats them to drink his liquor and be merry. But his guests need little pressing; and so, soon as rendered insensible, are tied hand and foot, and pitched among the clinkers, are there concealed till the ship departs, when—finding themselves entirely dependent upon Oberlus, alarmed at his changed demeanour, his savage threats, and above all that shocking blunderbuss—they willingly enlist under him, becoming his humble slaves, and Oberlus the most incredible of tyrants. So much so, that two or three perish beneath his initiating process. He sets the remainder—four of them—to breaking the caked soil; transporting upon their backs loads of loamy earth, scooped up in moist clefts among the mountains; keeps them on the roughest fare; presents his piece at the slightest hint of insurrection; and in all respects converts them into reptiles at his feet; plebeian gartersnakes to this Lord Anaconda.

At last, Oberlus contrives to stock his arsenal with four rusty cutlasses, and an added supply of powder and ball intended for his blunderbuss. Remitting in good part the labour of his slaves, he now approves himself a man—or rather devil—of great abilities in the way of cajoling or coercing others into acquiescence with his own ulterior designs, however at first abhorrent to them. But indeed, prepared for almost any eventual evil by their previous lawless life, as a sort of ranging Cow-Boys of the sea, which had dissolved within them the whole moral man, so that they were ready to concrete in the first offered mould of baseness now; rotted down from manhood by their hopeless misery on the isle; wonted to cringe in all things to their lord, himself the worst of slaves; these wretches were now become wholly corrupted to his hands. He used them as creatures of an inferior race; in short, he gaffles his four animals, and makes murderers of them; out of cowards fitly manufacturing bravos.

Now, sword or dagger, human arms are but artificial claws and fangs, tied on like false spurs to the fighting cock. So, we repeat, Oberlus, czar of the isle, gaffles his four subjects; that is, with intent of glory, puts four rusty cutlasses into their hands. Like any other autocrat, he had a noble army now.

It might be thought a servile war would hereupon ensue. Arms in the hands of trodden slaves? how indiscreet of Emperor Oberlus! Nay, they had but cutlasses—sad old scythes enough—he a blunderbuss, which by its blind scatterings of all sorts of boulders, clinkers and other scoria would annihilate all four mutineers, like four pigeons at one shot. Besides, at first he did not sleep in his accustomed hut; every lurid sunset, for a time, he might have been seen wending his way among the riven mountains, there to secrete himself till dawn in some sulphurous pitfall, undiscoverable to his gang; but finding this at last too troublesome, he now each evening tied his slaves hand and foot, hid the cutlasses, and thrusting them into his barracks, shut to the door, and lying down before it, beneath a rude shed lately added, slept out the night, blunderbuss in hand.

It is supposed that not content with daily parading over a cindery solitude at the head of his fine army, Oberlus now meditated the most active mischief; his probable object being to surprise some passing ship touching at his dominions, massacre the crew, and run away with her to parts unknown. While these plans were simmering in his head, two ships touch in company at the isle, on the opposite side to his; when his designs undergo a sudden change.

The ships are in want of vegetables, which Oberlus promises in great abundance, provided they send their boats round to his landing, so that the crews may bring the vegetables from his garden; informing the two captains, at the same time, that his rascals—slaves and soldiers—had become so abominably lazy and good-for-nothing of late, that he could not make them work by ordinary inducements, and did not have the heart to be severe with them.

The arrangement was agreed to, and the boats were sent and hauled upon the beach. The crews went to the lava hut; but to their surprise nobody was there. After waiting till their patience was exhausted, they returned to the shore, when lo, some stranger—not the Good Samaritan either—seems to have very recently passed that way. Three of the boats were broken in a thousand pieces, and the fourth was missing. By hard toil over the mountains and through the clinkers, some of the strangers succeeded in returning to that side of the isle where the ships lay, when fresh boats are sent to the relief of the rest of the hapless party.

However, amazed at the treachery of Oberlus, the two captains, afraid of new and still more mysterious atrocities,—and indeed, half imputing such strange events to the enchantments associated with these isles,—perceive no security but an instant flight; leaving Oberlus and his army in quiet possession of the stolen boat.

On the eve of sailing they put a letter in a keg, giving the Pacific Ocean intelligence of the affair, and moored the keg in the bay. Some time subsequent, the keg was opened by another captain chancing to anchor there, but not until after he had dispatched a boat round to Oberlus's Landing. As may be readily surmised, he felt no little inquietude till the boat's return; when another letter was handed him, giving Oberlus's version of the affair. This precious document had been found pinned half-mildewed to the clinker wall of the sulphurous and deserted hut. It ran as follows; showing that Oberlus was at least an accomplished writer, and no mere boor; and what is more, was capable of the most tristful eloquence.

"Sir: I am the most unfortunate ill-treated gentleman that lives. I am a patriot, exiled from country by the cruel hand of tyranny.

"Banished to these Enchanted Isles, I have again and again besought captains of ships to sell me a boat, but always have been refused, though I offered the handsomest prices in Mexican dollars. At length an opportunity presented of possessing myself of one, and I did not let it slip.

"I have been long endeavouring by hard labour and much solitary suffering to accumulate something to make myself comfortable in a virtuous though unhappy old age; but at various times have been robbed and beaten by men professing to be Christians.

"To-day I sail from the Enchanted group in the good boat Charity bound to the Feejee Isles.

"Fatherless Oberlus.

"P.S.—Behind the clinkers, nigh the oven, you will find the old fowl. Do not kill it; be patient; I leave it setting; if it shall have any chicks, I hearby bequeathe them to you, whoever you may be. But don't count your chicks before they are hatched."

The fowl proved a starveling rooster, reduced to a sitting posture by sheer debility.

Oberlus declares that he was bound to the Feejee Isles; but this was only to throw pursuers on a false scent. For after a long time he arrived, alone in his open boat, at Guayaquil. As his miscreants were never again beheld on Hood's Isle, it is supposed, either that they perished for want of water on the passage to Guayaquil, or what is quite as probable, were thrown overboard by Oberlus, when he found the water growing scarce.

From Guayaquil Oberlus proceeded to Payta; and there, with that nameless witchery peculiar to some of the ugliest animals, wound himself into the affections of a tawny damsel; prevailing upon her to accompany him back to his Enchanted Isle; which doubtless he painted as a Paradise of flowers, not a Tartarus of clinkers.

But unfortunately for the colonization of Hood's Isle with a choice variety of animated nature, the extraordinary and devilish aspect of Oberlus made him to be regarded in Payta as a highly suspicious character. So that being found concealed one night, with matches in his pocket, under the hull of a small vessel just ready to be launched, he was seized and thrown into jail.

The jails in most South American towns are generally of the

least wholesome sort. Built of huge cakes of sunburnt brick, and containing but one room, without windows or yard, and but one door heavily grated with wooden bars, they present both within and without the grimmest aspect. As public edifices they conspicuously stand upon the hot and dusty Plaza, offering to view, through the gratings, their villainous and hopeless inmates, burrowing in all sorts of tragic squalor. And here, for a long time, Oberlus was seen; the central figure of a mongrel and assassin band; a creature whom it is religion to detest, since it is philanthropy to hate a misanthrope.[8]

1854, 1856

From JOHN MARR AND OTHER SAILORS

Old Counsel [9]

OF THE YOUNG MASTER OF A WRECKED CALIFORNIA CLIPPER

Come out of the Golden Gate,
Go round the Horn with streamers,[1]
Carry royals early and late;
But, brother, be not over-elate—
All hands save ship! has startled dreamers.   5

1888

The Tuft of Kelp

All dripping in tangles green,
Cast up by a lonely sea
If purer for that, O Weed,
Bitterer, too, are ye?

1888

8. "They who may be disposed to question the possibility of the character above depicted, are referred to the 2nd vol. of Porter's Voyage into the Pacific, where they will recognize many sentences, for expedition's sake derived verbatim from thence, and incorporated here; the main difference—save a few passing reflections—between the two accounts being, that the present writer had added to Porter's facts accessory ones picked up in the Pacific from reliable sources; and where facts conflict, has naturally preferred his own authorities to Porter's. As, for instance, *his* authorities place Oberlus on Hood's Isle; Porter's, on Charles's Isle. The letter found in the hut is also somewhat different, for while at the Encantadas he was informed that not only did it evince a certain clerkliness, but was full of the strangest satiric effrontery which does not adequately appear in Porter's version. I accordingly altered it to suit the general character of its author" [Melville's note].

9. This deft, articulate epigram ridicules simultaneously the uninformed escapism in the romantic idea of seafaring and by inference the similar attitude of adolescence toward the journey of life.

1. "Streamers," long narrow pennants, usually gay, were carried aloft on gala occasions or when a difficult passage had been accomplished, as around Cape Horn; so also "royals" or royal sails (next line), mounted high aloft, are only for fair weather.

Billy Budd [2]
Sailor

An Inside Narrative [3]

DEDICATED
TO
JACK CHASE
ENGLISHMAN

Wherever that great heart may now be
Here on Earth or harbored in Paradise

*reconciliation
of the temporal
and the eternal*

Captain of the Maintop
in the year 1843
in the U.S. Frigate
United States

1

In the time before steamships, or then more frequently than now, a stroller along the docks of any considerable seaport would occasionally have his attention arrested by a group of bronzed mariners, man-of-war's men or merchant sailors in holiday attire, ashore on liberty. In certain instances they would flank, or like a bodyguard quite surround, some superior figure of their own class, moving

---

2. *Billy Budd* is a great work on its own terms; it also is in sharp contrast, thematically, with *Moby-Dick* and so enlarges our understanding of Melville. From the moment of its dedicatory note, the author's private personality is intricately incorporated with his creative energy and narrative insight. Melville was a shipmate with Jack Chase on the "United States" (see Dedication), a young sailor experiencing the cruelties and hardships which he soon excoriated in *White-Jacket*, in which Jack Chase appears as a character. *Billy Budd*, Melville's testament of reconciliation, provides a clarifying contrast with the novels of the earlier period, with the young novelist's heartbreaking rebellion against the overwhelming capacity for evil in man and the universe, and the inescapable doom, as in *Moby-Dick*, of those who pit themselves against the implacable Leviathan. In *Billy Budd* the author is at least reconciled to the enigma that innocence must suffer because others represent the "depravity according to nature."

Billy Budd was not published until after Melville's death. The manuscript that he left has been described by Harrison Hayford and Merton M. Sealts, Jr., as "a semi-final draft, not a final fair copy ready for publication." Apparently Melville took the story through several stages of development from 1886 until he died in 1891 (these stages are shown in Hayford and Sealts's "Genetic Text"). The manuscript was first edited in 1924 and published as a supplement to *The Works* * * * (1922–24). It was edited again in 1948, and most recently by Hayford and Sealts in 1962. The Hayford and Sealts "Reading Text" is reprinted here. It "embodies the *wording* * * * that in [their] judgment most closely approximates Melville's final intention. * * * " The "Reading Text" standardizes the accidentals of the manuscript.

3. The phrase has evoked the puzzlement which was probably intended. The most cogent explanations are that this tale represents Melville's reconciliation to the necessary "depravity according to nature" (see ending, Ch. 11); or that it refers to the sensational Somers trial (1842)—his cousin Guert Gansevoort, presiding officer—which sent three Navy personnel to the yardarm for mutiny. Both of these may have influenced Melville.

along with them like Aldebaran [4] among the lesser lights of his constellation. That signal object was the "Handsome Sailor" of the less
prosaic time alike of the military and merchant navies. With no
perceptible trace of the vainglorious about him, rather with the
offhand unaffectedness of natural regality, he seemed to accept the
spontaneous homage of his shipmates.

A somewhat remarkable instance recurs to me. In Liverpool, now
half a century ago, I saw under the shadow of the great dingy street-
wall of Prince's Dock (an obstruction long since removed) a common sailor so intensely black that he must needs have been a native
African of the unadulterate blood of Ham—a symmetric figure
much above the average height. The two ends of a gay silk handkerchief thrown loose about the neck danced upon the displayed ebony
of his chest, in his ears were big hoops of gold, and a Highland bonnet with a tartan band set off his shapely head. It was a hot noon in
July; and his face, lustrous with perspiration, beamed with barbaric
good humor. In jovial sallies right and left, his white teeth flashing
into view, he rollicked along, the center of a company of his shipmates. These were made up of such an assortment of tribes and
complexions as would have well fitted them to be marched up by
Anacharsis Cloots [5] before the bar of the first French Assembly as
Representatives of the Human Race. At each spontaneous tribute
rendered by the wayfarers to this black pagod of a fellow—the
tribute of a pause and stare, and less frequently an exclamation—the
motley retinue showed that they took that sort of pride in the evoker
of it which the Assyrian priests doubtless showed for their grand
sculptured Bull when the faithful prostrated themselves.

To return. If in some cases a bit of a nautical Murat [6] in setting
forth his person ashore, the Handsome Sailor of the period in question evinced nothing of the dandified Billy-be-Dam, an amusing
character all but extinct now, but occasionally to be encountered,
and in a form yet more amusing than the original, at the tiller of
the boats on the tempestuous Erie Canal or, more likely, vaporing
in the groggeries along the towpath. Invariably a proficient in his
perilous calling, he was also more or less of a mighty boxer or
wrestler. It was strength and beauty. Tales of his prowess were recited. Ashore he was the champion; afloat the spokesman; on every
suitable occasion always foremost. Close-reefing topsails in a gale,
there he was, astride the weather yardarm-end, foot in the Flemish
horse as stirrup, both hands tugging at the earing as at a bridle, in

4. This large red star was regarded
by the ancients as the "eye" of the
Bull, the constellation Taurus.
5. The Baron de Cloots (1775–1794),
leading such a rabble, spoke for the
Rights of Man before the French Assembly. *Cf.* Carlyle, *The French*

Revolution.
6. Joachim Murat (1767?–1815);
French military adventurer and con-
spirator with Napoleon. As King of
Naples he was called "the Dandy
King."

very much the attitude of young Alexander curbing the fiery Buce-phalus.[7] A superb figure, tossed up as by the horns of Taurus [8] against the thunderous sky, cheerily hallooing to the strenuous file along the spar.

The moral nature was seldom out of keeping with the physical make. Indeed, except as toned by the former, the comeliness and power, always attractive in masculine conjunction, hardly could have drawn the sort of honest homage the Handsome Sailor in some examples received from his less gifted associates.

Such a cynosure, at least in aspect, and something such too in nature, though with important variations made apparent as the story proceeds, was welkin-eyed Billy Budd—or Baby Budd, as more familiarly, under circumstances hereafter to be given, he at last came to be called—aged twenty-one, a foretopman of the British fleet toward the close of the last decade of the eighteenth century. It was not very long prior to the time of the narration that follows that he had entered the King's service, having been impressed [9] on the Narrow Seas from a homeward-bound English merchantman into a seventy-four [1] outward bound, H.M.S. *Bellipotent*; which ship, as was not unusual in those hurried days, having been obliged to put to sea short of her proper complement of men. Plump upon Billy at first sight in the gangway the boarding officer, Lieutenant Rat-cliffe, pounced, even before the merchantman's crew was formally mustered on the quarter-deck for his deliberate inspection. And him only he elected. For whether it was because the other men when ranged before him showed to ill advantage after Billy, or whether he had some scruples in view of the merchantman's being rather short-handed, however it might be, the officer contented himself with his first spontaneous choice. To the surprise of the ship's company, though much to the lieutenant's satisfaction, Billy made no demur. But, indeed, any demur would have been as idle as the protest of a goldfinch popped into a cage.

Noting this uncomplaining acquiescence, all but cheerful, one might say, the shipmaster turned a surprised glance of silent re-proach at the sailor. The shipmaster was one of those worthy mortals found in every vocation, even the humbler ones—the sort of person whom everybody agrees in calling "a respectable man." And—nor so strange to report as it may appear to be—though a ploughman of the troubled waters, lifelong contending with the intractable ele-ments, there was nothing his honest soul at heart loved better than simple peace and quiet. For the rest, he was fifty or thereabouts, a little inclined to corpulence, a prepossessing face, unwhiskered, and

---

7. The famous war horse of Alexander the Great (356–323 B.C.).
8. *Cf.* Aldebaran, above.
9. British naval commanders were per-mitted to complete their crews by force.
1. *I.e.*, a ship carrying seventy-four guns.

of an agreeable color—a rather full face, humanely intelligent in expression. On a fair day with a fair wind and all going well, a certain musical chime in his voice seemed to be the veritable unobstructed outcome of the innermost man. He had much prudence, much conscientiousness, and there were occasions when these virtues were the cause of overmuch disquietude in him. On a passage, so long as his craft was in any proximity to land, no sleep for Captain Graveling. He took to heart those serious responsibilities not so heavily borne by some shipmasters.

Now while Billy Budd was down in the forecastle getting his kit together, the *Bellipotent's* lieutenant, burly and bluff, nowise disconcerted by Captain Graveling's omitting to proffer the customary hospitalities on an occasion so unwelcome to him, an omission simply caused by preoccupation of thought, unceremoniously invited himself into the cabin, and also to a flask from the spirit locker, a receptacle which his experienced eye instantly discovered. In fact he was one of those sea dogs in whom all the hardship and peril of naval life in the great prolonged wars of this time never impaired the natural instinct for sensuous enjoyment. His duty he always faithfully did; but duty is sometimes a dry obligation, and he was for irrigating its aridity, whenever possible, with a fertilizing decoction of strong waters. For the cabin's proprietor there was nothing left but to play the part of the enforced host with whatever grace and alacrity were practicable. As necessary adjuncts to the flask, he silently placed tumbler and water jug before the irrepressible guest. But excusing himself from partaking just then, he dismally watched the unembarrassed officer deliberately diluting his grog a little, then tossing it off in three swallows, pushing the empty tumbler away, yet not so far as to be beyond easy reach, at the same time settling himself in his seat and smacking his lips with high satisfaction, looking straight at the host.

These proceedings over, the master broke the silence; and there lurked a rueful reproach in the tone of his voice: "Lieutenant, you are going to take my best man from me, the jewel of 'em."

"Yes, I know," rejoined the other, immediately drawing back the tumbler preliminary to a replenishing. "Yes, I know. Sorry."

"Beg pardon, but you don't understand, Lieutenant. See here, now. Before I shipped that young fellow, my forecastle was a rat-pit of quarrels. It was black times, I tell you, aboard the *Rights* here. I was worried to that degree my pipe had no comfort for me. But Billy came; and it was like a Catholic priest striking peace in an Irish shindy. Not that he preached to them or said or did anything in particular; but a virtue went out of him, sugaring the sour ones. They took to him like hornets to treacle; all but the buffer of the gang, the big shaggy chap with the fire-red whiskers. He indeed, out of envy, perhaps, of the newcomer, and thinking such a "sweet and pleasant fellow," as he mockingly designated him to the others, could hardly have the spirit of a gamecock, must needs bestir himself in trying to get up an ugly row with him. Billy forebore with him and reasoned with him in a pleasant way—he is something like myself, Lieutenant, to whom aught like a quarrel is hateful—but nothing served. So, in the second dogwatch one day, the Red Whiskers in presence of the others, under pretense of showing Billy just whence a sirloin steak was cut—for the fellow had once been a butcher—insultingly gave him a dig under the ribs. Quick as lightning Billy let fly his arm. I dare say he never meant to do quite as much as he did, but anyhow he gave the burly fool a terrible drubbing. It took about half a minute, I should think. And, lord bless you, the lubber was astonished at the celerity. And will you believe it, Lieutenant, the Red Whiskers now really loves Billy—loves him, or is the biggest hypocrite that ever I heard of. But they all love him. Some of 'em do his washing, darn his old trousers for him; the carpenter is at odd times making a pretty little chest of drawers for him. Anybody will do anything for Billy Budd; and it's the happy family here. But now, Lieutenant, if that young fellow goes—I know how it will be aboard the *Rights*. Not again very soon shall I, coming up from dinner, lean over the capstan smoking a quiet pipe —no, not very soon again, I think. Ay, Lieutenant, you are going to take away the jewel of 'em; you are going to take away my peacemaker!" And with that the good soul had really some ado in checking a rising sob.

"Well," said the lieutenant, who had listened with amused interest to all this and now was waxing merry with his tipple; "well, blessed are the peacemakers, especially the fighting peacemakers. And such are the seventy-four beauties some of which you see poking their noses out of the portholes of yonder warship lying to for me," pointing through the cabin window at the *Bellipotent*. "But courage! Don't look so downhearted, man. Why, I pledge you in advance the royal approbation. Rest assured that His Majesty will be delighted to know that in a time when his hardtack is not sought for by sailors with such avidity as should be, a time also when some shipmasters privily resent the borrowing from them a tar or two for the service; His Majesty, I say, will be delighted to learn that *one* shipmaster at least cheerfully surrenders to the King the flower of his flock, a sailor who with equal loyalty makes no dissent.—But where's my beauty? Ah," looking through the cabin's open door, "here he comes; and, by Jove, lugging along his chest—Apollo with his portmanteau!—My man," stepping out to him, "you can't take that big box aboard a warship. The boxes there are mostly shot boxes. Put your duds in a bag, lad. Boot and saddle for the cavalryman, bag and hammock for the man-of-war's man."

The transfer from chest to bag was made. And, after seeing his man into the cutter and then following him down, the lieutenant pushed off from the *Rights-of-Man*.[2] That was the merchant ship's name, though by her master and crew abbreviated in sailor fashion into the *Rights*. The hardheaded Dundee owner was a staunch admirer of Thomas Paine, whose book in rejoinder to Burke's arraignment of the French Revolution had then been published for some time and had gone everywhere. In christening his vessel after the title of Paine's volume the man of Dundee was something like his contemporary shipowner, Stephen Girard[3] of Philadelphia, whose sympathies, alike with his native land and its liberal philosophers, he evinced by naming his ships after Voltaire, Diderot, and so forth.

But now, when the boat swept under the merchantman's stern, and officer and oarsmen were noting—some bitterly and others with a grin—the name emblazoned there; just then it was that the new recruit jumped up from the bow where the coxswain had directed him to sit, and waving hat to his silent shipmates sorrowfully looking over at him from the taffrail, bade the lads a genial good-bye. Then, making a salutation as to the ship herself, "And good-bye to you too, old *Rights-of-Man*."

"Down, sir!" roared the lieutenant, instantly assuming all the rigor of his rank, though with difficulty repressing a smile.

To be sure, Billy's action was a terrible breach of naval decorum. But in that decorum he had never been instructed; in consideration of which the lieutenant would hardly have been so energetic in reproof but for the concluding farewell to the ship. This he rather took as meant to convey a covert sally on the new recruit's part, a sly slur at impressment in general, and that of himself in especial. And yet, more likely, if satire it was in effect, it was hardly so by intention, for Billy, though happily endowed with the gaiety of high health, youth, and a free heart, was yet by no means of a satirical turn. The will to it and the sinister dexterity were alike wanting. To deal in double meanings and insinuations of any sort was quite foreign to his nature.

As to his enforced enlistment, that he seemed to take pretty much as he was wont to take any vicissitude of weather. Like the animals, though no philosopher, he was, without knowing it, practically a fatalist. And it may be that he rather liked this adventurous

2. Title of a work by Thomas Paine, discussed earlier in this volume.
3. Girard (1750–1831), the great Philadelphia merchant and banker, remained in his native France until he was twenty-seven and read widely among the liberal authors of that period.

turn in his affairs, which promised an opening into novel scenes and martial excitements.

Aboard the *Bellipotent* our merchant sailor was forthwith rated as an able seaman and assigned to the starboard watch of the foretop. He was soon at home in the service, not at all disliked for his unpretentious good looks and a sort of genial happy-go-lucky air. No merrier man in his mess: in marked contrast to certain other individuals included like himself among the impressed portion of the ship's company; for these when not actively employed were sometimes, and more particularly in the last dogwatch when the drawing near of twilight induced revery, apt to fall into a saddish mood which in some partook of sullenness. But they were not so young as our foretopman, and no few of them must have known a hearth of some sort, others may have had wives and children left, too probably, in uncertain circumstances, and hardly any but must have have had acknowledged kith and kin, while for Billy, as will shortly be seen, his entire family was practically invested in himself.

2

Though our new-made foretopman was well received in the top and on the gun decks, hardly here was he that cynosure he had previously been among those minor ship's companies of the merchant marine, with which companies only had he hitherto consorted.

He was young; and despite his all but fully developed frame, in aspect looked even younger than he really was, owing to a lingering adolescent expression in the as yet smooth face all but feminine in purity of natural complexion but where, thanks to his seagoing, the lily was quite suppressed and the rose had some ado visibly to flush through the tan.

To one essentially such a novice in the complexities of factitious life, the abrupt transition from his former and simpler sphere to the ampler and more knowing world of a great warship; this might well have abashed him had there been any conceit or vanity in his composition. Among her miscellaneous multitude, the *Bellipotent* mustered several individuals who however inferior in grade were of no common natural stamp, sailors more signally susceptive of that air which continuous martial discipline and repeated presence in battle can in some degree impart even to the average man. As the Handsome Sailor, Billy Budd's position aboard the seventy-four was something analogous to that of a rustic beauty transplanted from the provinces and brought into competition with the highborn dames of the court. But this change of circumstances he scarce noted. As little did he observe that something about him provoked an ambiguous smile in one or two harder faces among the bluejackets. Nor less unaware was he of the peculiar favorable effect his person and demeanor had upon the more intelligent gentlemen of the quarter-deck. Nor could this well have been otherwise. Cast in a mold peculiar to the finest physical examples of those Englishmen in whom the Saxon strain would seem not at all to partake of any Norman or other admixture, he showed in face that humane look of reposeful good nature which the Greek sculptor in some instances gave to his heroic strong man, Hercules. But this again was subtly modified by another and pervasive quality. The ear, small and shapely, the arch of the foot, the curve in mouth and nostril, even the indurated hand dyed to the orange-tawny of the toucan's [4] bill, a hand telling alike of the halyards and tar bucket; but, above all, something in the mobile expression, and every chance attitude and movement, something suggestive of a mother eminently favored by Love and the Graces; all this strangely indicated a lineage in direct contradiction to his lot. The mysteriousness here became less mysterious through a matter of fact elicited when Billy at the capstan was being formally mustered into the service. Asked by the officer, a small, brisk little gentleman as it chanced, among other questions, his place of birth, he replied, "Please, sir, I don't know."

"Don't know where you were born? Who was your father?"

"God knows, sir."

Struck by the straightforward simplicity of these replies, the officer next asked, "Do you know anything about your beginning?"

"No, sir. But I have heard that I was found in a pretty silk-lined basket hanging one morning from the knocker of a good man's door in Bristol."

"*Found,* say you? Well," throwing back his head and looking up and down the new recruit; "well, it turns out to have been a pretty good find. Hope they'll find some more like you, my man; the fleet sadly needs them."

Yes, Billy Budd was a foundling, a presumable by-blow,[5] and, evidently, no ignoble one. Noble descent was as evident in him as in a blood horse.

For the rest, with little or no sharpness of faculty or any trace of the wisdom of the serpent, nor yet quite a dove, he possessed that kind and degree of intelligence going along with the unconventional rectitude of a sound human creature, one to whom not yet has been proffered the questionable apple of knowledge. He was illiterate; he could not read, but he could sing, and like the illiterate nightingale was sometimes the composer of his own song.

---

4. Colorful bird of the American tropics, whose beak is conspicuously large.
5. An illegitimate child.

Of self-consciousness he seemed to have little or none, or about as much as we may reasonably impute to a dog of Saint Bernard's breed.

Habitually living with the elements and knowing little more of the land than as a beach, or rather, that portion of the terraqueous globe providentially set apart for dance-houses, doxies, and tapsters, in short what sailors call a "fiddler's green," his simple nature remained unsophisticated by those moral obliquities which are not in every case incompatible with that manufacturable thing known as respectability. But are sailors, frequenters of fiddlers' greens, without vices? No; but less often than with landsmen do their vices, so called, partake of crookedness of heart, seeming less to proceed from viciousness than exuberance of vitality after long constraint: frank manifestations in accordance with natural law. By his original constitution aided by the co-operating influences of his lot, Billy in many respects was little more than a sort of upright barbarian, much such perhaps as Adam presumably might have been ere the urbane Serpent wriggled himself into his company.

And here be it submitted that apparently going to corroborate the doctrine of man's Fall, a doctrine now popularly ignored, it is observable that where certain virtues pristine and unadulterate peculiarly characterize anybody in the external uniform of civilization, they will upon scrutiny seem not to be derived from custom or convention, but rather to be out of keeping with these, as if indeed exceptionally transmitted from a period prior to Cain's city and citified man. The character marked by such qualities has to an unvitiated taste an untampered-with flavor like that of berries, while the man thoroughly civilized, even in a fair specimen of the breed, has to the same moral palate a questionable smack as of a compounded wine. To any stray inheritor of these primitive qualities found, like Caspar Hauser,[6] wandering dazed in any Christian capital of our time, the good-natured poet's famous invocation, near two thousand years ago, of the good rustic out of his latitude in the Rome of the Caesars, still appropriately holds:

> Honest and poor, faithful in word and thought,
> What hath thee, Fabian, to the city brought?[7]

Though our Handsome Sailor has as much of masculine beauty as one can expect anywhere to see; nevertheless, like the beautiful woman in one of Hawthorne's minor tales,[8] there was just one thing amiss in him. No visible blemish indeed, as with the lady; no, but

6. Kaspar Hauser (1812?–1833) mysteriously appeared in 1828 in Nuremberg, Germany. Popularly imagined to be of noble birth, he aroused international attention, and was mysteriously assassinated.
7. Martial, *Epigrams*, Book IV, 5.
8. Apparently "The Birthmark"; *cf.* "blemish," below.

an occasional liability to a vocal defect. Though in the hour of elemental uproar or peril he was everything that a sailor should be, yet under sudden provocation of strong heart-feeling his voice, otherwise singularly musical, as if expressive of the harmony within, was apt to develop an organic hesitancy, in fact more or less of a stutter or even worse. In this particular Billy was a striking instance that the arch interferer, the envious marplot of Eden, still has more or less to do with every human consignment to this planet of Earth. In every case, one way or another he is sure to slip in his little card, as much as to remind us—I too have a hand here.

The avowal of such an imperfection in the Handsome Sailor should be evidence not alone that he is not presented as a conventional hero, but also that the story in which he is the main figure is no romance.

3

At the time of Billy Budd's arbitrary enlistment into the *Bellipotent* that ship was on her way to join the Mediterranean fleet. No long time elapsed before the junction was effected. As one of that fleet the seventy-four participated in its movements, though at times on account of her superior sailing qualities, in the absence of frigates, dispatched on separate duty as a scout and at times on less temporary service. But with all this the story has little concernment, restricted as it is to the inner life of one particular ship and the career of an individual sailor.

It was the summer of 1797. In the April of that year had occurred the commotion at Spithead followed in May by a second and yet more serious outbreak in the fleet of the Nore.[9] The latter is known, and without exaggeration in the epithet, as "the Great Mutiny." It was indeed a demonstration more menacing to England than the contemporary manifestoes and conquering and proselyting armies of the French Directory. To the British Empire the Nore Mutiny was what a strike in the fire brigade would be to London threatened by general arson. In a crisis when the kingdom might well have anticipated the famous signal that some years later published along the naval line of battle what it was that upon occasion England expected of Englishmen [1] *that* was the time when at the mastheads of the three-deckers and seventy-fours moored in her own roadstead— a fleet the right arm of a Power then all but the sole free conservative one of the Old World—the bluejackets, to be numbered by thousands, ran up with huzzas the British colors with the union and

9. Scene of a mutiny in the British Navy; occurred at the mouth of the Thames in 1797.

1. In 1805, in the naval battle against the French and Spanish off Trafalgar, where he was killed, Admiral Nelson ran up the famous signal "England expects every man to do his duty."

cross wiped out; by that cancellation transmuting the flag of founded law and freedom defined, into the enemy's red meteor of unbridled and unbounded revolt. Reasonable discontent growing out of practical grievances in the fleet had been ignited into irrational combustion as by live cinders blown across the Channel from France in flames.

The event converted into irony for a time those spirited strains of Dibdin [2]—as a song-writer no mean auxiliary to the English government at that European conjuncture—strains celebrating, among other things, the patriotic devotion of the British tar: "And as for my life, 'tis the King's!"

Such an episode in the Island's grand naval story her naval historians naturally abridge, one of them (William James) [3] candidly acknowledging that fain would he pass it over did not "impartiality forbid fastidiousness." And yet his mention is less a narration than a reference, having to do hardly at all with details. Nor are these readily to be found in the libraries. Like some other events in every age befalling states everywhere, including America, the Great Mutiny was of such character that national pride along with views of policy would fain shade it off into the historical background. Such events cannot be ignored, but there is a considerate way of historically treating them. If a well-constituted individual refrains from blazoning aught amiss or calamitious in his family, a nation in the like circumstance may without reproach be equally discreet.

Though after parleyings between government and the ringleaders, and concessions by the former as to some glaring abuses, the first uprising—that at Spithead—with difficulty was put down, or matters for the time pacified; yet at the Nore the unforeseen renewal of insurrection on a yet larger scale, and emphasized in the conferences that ensued by demands deemed by the authorities not only inadmissible but aggressively insolent, indicated—if the Red Flag did not sufficiently do so—what was the spirit animating the men. Final suppression, however, there was; but only made possible perhaps by the unswerving loyalty of the marine corps and a voluntary resumption of loyalty among influential sections of the crews.

To some extent the Nore Mutiny may be regarded as analogous to the distempering irruption of contagious fever in a frame constitutionally sound, and which anon throws it off.

At all events, of these thousands of mutineers were some of the tars who not so very long afterwards—whether wholly prompted thereto by patriotism, or pugnacious instinct, or by both—helped to win a coronet for Nelson at the Nile, and the naval crown of crowns

2. Charles Dibdin (1745–1814), an English dramatist, also remembered for ballads and chanteys, such as "Poor Jack," quoted below.

3. This entire sentence is a paraphrase of British historian William James's *The Naval History of Great Britain* (6 vols., London, 1860), II, 26.

for him at Trafalgar.[4] To the mutineers, those battles and especially Trafalgar were a plenary absolution and a grand one. For all that goes to make up scenic naval display and heroic magnificence in arms, those battles, especially Trafalgar, stand unmatched in human annals.

4

In this matter of writing, resolve as one may to keep to the main road, some bypaths have an enticement not readily to be withstood. I am going to err into such a bypath. If the reader will keep me company I shall be glad. At the least, we can promise ourselves that pleasure which is wickedly said to be in sinning, for a literary sin the divergence will be.

Very likely it is no new remark that the inventions of our time have at last brought about a change in sea warfare in degree corresponding to the revolution in all warfare effected by the original introduction from China into Europe of gunpowder. The first European firearm, a clumsy contrivance, was, as is well known, scouted by no few of the knights as a base implement, good enough peradventure for weavers too craven to stand up crossing steel with steel in frank fight. But as ashore knightly valor, though shorn of its blazonry, did not cease with the knights, neither on the seas—though nowadays in encounters there a certain kind of displayed gallantry be fallen out of date as hardly applicable under changed circumstances—did the nobler qualities of such naval magnates as Don John of Austria, Doria, Van Tromp, Jean Bart, the long line of British admirals, and the American Decaturs of 1812 become obsolete with their wooden walls.[5]

Nevertheless, to anybody who can hold the Present at its worth without being inappreciative of the Past, it may be forgiven, if to such an one the solitary old hulk at Portsmouth, Nelson's *Victory*, seems to float there, not alone as the decaying monument of a fame incorruptible, but also as a poetic reproach, softened by its picturesqueness, to the *Monitors* [6] and yet mightier hulls of the European ironclads. And this not altogether because such craft are unsightly,

4. For his victory at the Nile (1798), Nelson was made a baron; after Copenhagen (1801) a viscount; but he died in action at the victory off Trafalgar.
5. All famous "iron admirals" of the wooden ships. Don John of Austria commanded the fleet of the Holy League in the defeat of the Turks at Lepanto (1571); Andrea Doria (1468–1560), Genoese admiral, was the "Liberator of Genoa" from the Turks; Maarten Tromp (1597–1653) commanded the Dutch fleets in struggles for independence from Spain, Portugal, and Britain;

Jean Bart, famous French soldier of fortune, commanded privateers against the Dutch (1686–1697); and the American naval hero Stephen Decatur was renowned for daring exploits against the Tripoli pirates (1803–1804) and for victories over British ships in the War of 1812.
6. During the Civil War, the *Monitor*'s defeat of the southern *Merrimac* in Hampton Roads (March, 1862) ended the first engagement between ironclad ships.

unavoidably lacking the symmetry and grand lines of the old battle-ships, but equally for other reasons.

There are some, perhaps, who while not altogether inaccessible to that poetic reproach just alluded to, may yet on behalf of the new order be disposed to parry it; and this to the extent of iconoclasm, if need be. For example, prompted by the sight of the star inserted in the *Victory's* quarter-deck designating the spot where the Great Sailor fell, these martial utilitarians [7] may suggest considerations implying that Nelson's ornate publication of his person in battle was not only unnecessary, but not military, nay, savored of foolhardiness and vanity. They may add, too, that at Trafalgar it was in effect nothing less than a challenge to death; and death came; and that but for his bravado the victorious admiral might possibly have survived the battle, and so, instead of having his sagacious dying injunctions overruled by his immediate successor in command, he himself when the contest was decided might have brought his shattered fleet to anchor, a proceeding which might have averted the deplorable loss of life by shipwreck in the elemental tempest that followed the martial one.

Well, should we set aside the more than disputable point whether for various reasons it was possible to anchor the fleet, then plausibly enough the Benthamites of war may urge the above. But the *might-have-been* is but boggy ground to build on. And, certainly, in foresight as to the larger issue of an encounter, and anxious preparations for it—buoying the deadly way and mapping it out, as at Copenhagen—few commanders have been so painstakingly circumspect as this same reckless declarer of his person in fight.

Personal prudence, even when dictated by quite other than selfish considerations, surely is no special virtue in a military man; while an excessive love of glory, impassioning a less burning impulse, the honest sense of duty, is the first. If the name *Wellington* is not so much of a trumpet to the blood as the simpler name *Nelson*, the reason for this may perhaps be inferred from the above. Alfred [8] in his funeral ode on the victory of Waterloo ventures not to call him the greatest soldier of all time, though in the same ode he invokes Nelson as "the greatest sailor since our world began."

At Trafalgar Nelson on the brink of opening the fight sat down and wrote his last brief will and testament. If under the presentiment of the most magnificent of all victories to be crowned by his own glorious death, a sort of priestly motive led him to dress his person in the jewelled vouchers of his own shining deeds; if thus to have adorned himself for the altar and the sacrifice were indeed vainglory, then affectation and fustian is each more heroic line in

7. The English Utilitarians, followers of Jeremy Bentham (1748–1832), based their widespread reforms on the idea that the *useful* is the good. *Cf.* "Benthamites of war," below.
8. *I.e.,* Tennyson; the quoted line is from his "Ode on the Death of the Duke of Wellington" (1852).

the great epics and dramas, since in such lines the poet but embodies in verse those exaltations of sentiment that a nature like Nelson, the opportunity being given, vitalizes into acts.

5

Yes, the outbreak at the Nore was put down. But not every grievance was redressed. If the contractors, for example, were no longer permitted to ply some practices peculiar to their tribe everywhere, such as providing shoddy cloth, rations not sound, or false in the measure; not the less impressment, for one thing, went on. By custom sanctioned for centuries, and judicially maintained by a Lord Chancellor as late as Mansfield,[9] that mode of manning the fleet, a mode now fallen into a sort of abeyance but never formally renounced, it was not practicable to give up in those years. Its abrogation would have crippled the indispensable fleet, one wholly under canvas, no steam power, its innumerable sails and thousands of cannon, everything in short, worked by muscle alone; a fleet the more insatiate in demand for men, because then multiplying its ships of all grades against contingencies present and to come of the convulsed Continent.

Discontent foreran the Two Mutinies, and more or less it lurkingly survived them. Hence it was not unreasonable to apprehend some return of trouble sporadic or general. One instance of such apprehensions: In the same year with this story, Nelson, then Rear Admiral Sir Horatio, being with the fleet off the Spanish coast, was directed by the admiral in command to shift his pennant from the *Captain* to the *Theseus*; and for this reason: that the latter ship having newly arrived on the station from home, where it had taken part in the Great Mutiny, danger was apprehended from the temper of the men; and it was thought that an officer like Nelson was the one, not indeed to terrorize the crew into base subjection, but to win them, by force of his mere presence and heroic personality, back to an allegiance if not as enthusiastic as his own yet as true.

So it was that for a time, on more than one quarter-deck, anxiety did exist. At sea, precautionary vigilance was strained against relapse. At short notice an engagement might come on. When it did, the lieutenants assigned to batteries felt it incumbent on them, in some instances, to stand with drawn swords behind the men working the guns.

6

But on board the seventy-four in which Billy now swung his hammock, very little in the manner of the men and nothing obvious in the demeanor of the officers would have suggested to an ordinary

9. William Murray, Baron Mansfield, British parliamentarian, became lord chief justice in 1756 and was later a cabinet minister (1773–1788).

observer that the Great Mutiny was a recent event. In their general bearing and conduct the commissioned officers of a warship naturally take their tone from the commander, that is if he have that ascendancy of character that ought to be his.

Captain the Honorable Edward Fairfax Vere, to give his full title, was a bachelor of forty or thereabouts, a sailor of distinction even in a time prolific of renowned seamen. Though allied to the higher nobility, his advancement had not been altogether owing to influences connected with the circumstance. He had seen much service, been in various engagements, always acquitting himself as an officer mindful of the welfare of his men, but never tolerating an infraction of discipline; thoroughly versed in the science of his profession, and intrepid to the verge of temerity, though never injudiciously so. For his gallantry in the West Indian waters as flag lieutenant under Rodney in that admiral's crowning victory over De Grasse,[1] he was made a post captain.

Ashore, in the garb of a civilian, scarce anyone would have taken him for a sailor, more especially that he never garnished unprofessional talk with nautical terms, and grave in his bearing, evinced little appreciation of mere humor. It was not out of keeping with these traits that on a passage when nothing demanded his paramount action, he was the most undemonstrative of men. Any landsman observing this gentleman not conspicuous by his stature and wearing no pronounced insignia, emerging from his cabin to the open deck, and noting the silent deference of the officers retiring to leeward, might have taken him for the King's guest, a civilian aboard the King's ship, some highly honorable discreet envoy on his way to an important post. But in fact this unobtrusiveness of demeanor may have proceeded from a certain unaffected modesty of manhood sometimes accompanying a resolute nature, a modesty evinced at all times not calling for pronounced action, which shown in any rank of life suggests a virtue aristocratic in kind. As with some others engaged in various departments of the world's more heroic activities, Captain Vere though practical enough upon occasion would at times betray a certain dreaminess of mood. Standing alone on the weather side of the quarter-deck, one hand holding by the rigging, he would absently gaze off at the blank sea. At the presentation to him then of some minor matter interrupting the current of his thoughts, he would show more or less irascibility; but instantly he would control it.

In the navy he was popularly known by the appellation "Starry Vere." How such a designation happened to fall upon one who

---

1. The British admiral George Brydges, Baron Rodney (1719–1792), defeated the French admiral De Grasse in a naval engagement off Dominica, in the Leewards, in 1782.

whatever his sterling qualities was without any brilliant ones, was in this wise: A favorite kinsman, Lord Denton, a freehearted fellow, had been the first to meet and congratulate him upon his return to England from his West Indian cruise; and but the day previous turning over a copy of Andrew Marvell's [2] poems had lighted, not for the first time, however, upon the lines entitled "Appleton House," the name of one of the seats of their common ancestor, a hero in the German wars of the seventeenth century, in which poem occur the lines:

> This 'tis to have been from the first
> In a domestic heaven nursed,
> Under the discipline severe
> Of Fairfax and the starry Vere.

And so, upon embracing his cousin fresh from Rodney's great victory wherein he had played so gallant a part, brimming over with just family pride in the sailor of their house, he exuberantly exclaimed, "Give ye joy, Ed; give ye joy, my starry Vere!" This got currency, and the novel prefix serving in familiar parlance readily to distinguish the *Bellipotent*'s captain from another Vere his senior, a distant relative, an officer of like rank in the navy, it remained permanently attached to the surname.

7

In view of the part that the commander of the *Bellipotent* plays in scenes shortly to follow, it may be well to fill out that sketch of him outlined in the previous chapter.

Aside from his qualities as a sea officer Captain Vere was an exceptional character. Unlike no few of England's renowned sailors, long and arduous service with signal devotion to it had not resulted in absorbing and *salting* the entire man. He had a marked leaning toward everything intellectual. He loved books, never going to sea without a newly replenished library, compact but of the best. The isolated leisure, in some cases so wearisome, falling at intervals to commanders even during a war cruise, never was tedious to Captain Vere. With nothing of that literary taste which less heeds the thing conveyed than the vehicle, his bias was toward those books to which every serious mind of superior order occupying any active post of authority in the world naturally inclines: books treating of actual men and events no matter of what era—history, biography, and unconventional writers like Montaigne, who, free from cant and convention, honestly and in the spirit of common sense philosophize upon realities. In this line of reading he found confirmation of

2. Marvell was a British poet (1621–1678). "Appleton House" refers also to a Vere-Fairfax estate named "Denton"—hence Melville's "Lord Denton."

his own more reserved thoughts—confirmation which he had vainly sought in social converse, so that as touching most fundamental topics, there had got to be established in him some positive convictions which he forefelt would abide in him essentially unmodified so long as his intelligent part remained unimpaired. In view of the troubled period in which his lot was cast, this was well for him. His settled convictions were as a dike against those invading waters of novel opinion social, political, and otherwise, which carried away as in a torrent no few minds in those days, minds by nature not inferior to his own. While other members of that aristocracy to which by birth he belonged were incensed at the innovators mainly because their theories were inimical to the privileged classes, Captain Vere disinterestedly opposed them not alone because they seemed to him insusceptible of embodiment in lasting institutions, but at war with the peace of the world and the true welfare of mankind.

With minds less stored than his and less earnest, some officers of his rank, with whom at times he would necessarily consort, found him lacking in the companionable quality, a dry and bookish gentleman, as they deemed. Upon any chance withdrawal from their company one would be apt to say to another something like this: "Vere is a noble fellow, Starry Vere. 'Spite the gazettes, Sir Horatio" (meaning him who became Lord Nelson) "is at bottom scarce a better seaman or fighter. But between you and me now, don't you think there is a queer streak of the pedantic running through him? Yes, like the King's yarn in a coil of navy rope?"

Some apparent ground there was for this sort of confidential criticism; since not only did the captain's discourse never fall into the jocosely familiar, but in illustrating of any point touching the stirring personages and events of the time he would be as apt to cite some historic character or incident of antiquity as he would be to cite from the moderns. He seemed unmindful of the circumstance that to his bluff company such remote allusions, however pertinent they might really be, were altogether alien to men whose reading was mainly confined to the journals. But considerateness in such matters is not easy to natures constituted like Captain Vere's. Their honesty prescribes to them directness, sometimes far-reaching like that of a migratory fowl that in its flight never heeds when it crosses a frontier.

8

The lieutenants and other commissioned gentlemen forming Captain Vere's staff it is not necessary here to particularize, nor needs it to make any mention of any of the warrant officers. But among the petty officers was one who, having much to do with the story, may as well be forthwith introduced. His portrait I essay, but shall never hit it. This was John Claggart, the master-at-arms.³ But that sea title may to landsmen seem somewhat equivocal. Originally, doubtless, that petty officer's function was the instruction of the men in the use of arms, sword or cutlass. But very long ago, owing to the advance in gunnery making hand-to-hand encounters less frequent and giving to niter and sulphur the pre-eminence over steel, that function ceased; the master-at-arms of a great warship becoming a sort of chief of police charged among other matters with the duty of preserving order on the populous lower gun decks.

Claggart was a man about five-and-thirty, somewhat spare and tall, yet of no ill figure upon the whole. His hand was too small and shapely to have been accustomed to hard toil. The face was a notable one, the features all except the chin cleanly cut as those on a Greek medallion; yet the chin, beardless as Tecumseh's,⁴ had something of strange protuberant broadness in its make that recalled the prints of the Reverend Dr. Titus Oates, the historic deponent with the clerical drawl in the time of Charles II and the fraud of the alleged Popish Plot.⁵ It served Claggart in his office that his eye could cast a tutoring glance. His brow was of the sort phrenologically associated with more than average intellect; silken jet curls partly clustering over it, making a foil to the pallor below, a pallor tinged with a faint shade of amber akin to the hue of time-tinted marbles of old. This complexion, singularly contrasting with the red or deeply bronzed visages of the sailors, and in part the result of his official seclusion from the sunlight, though it was not exactly displeasing, nevertheless seemed to hint of something defective or abnormal in the constitution and blood. But his general aspect and manner were so suggestive of an education and career incongruous with his naval function that when not actively engaged in it he looked like a man of high quality, social and moral, who for reasons of his own was keeping incog.⁶ Nothing was known of his former life. It might be that he was an Englishman; and yet there lurked a bit of accent in his speech suggesting that possibly he was not such by birth, but through naturalization in early childhood. Among certain grizzled sea gossips of the gun decks and forecastle went a rumor perdue that the master-at-arms was a *chevalier* who had volunteered into the King's navy by way of compounding for some mysterious swindle whereof he had been arraigned at the King's Bench. The

3. *Cf. White-Jacket,* Chapter 6, describing the master-at-arms as a type, "whom all sailors hate, * * * the universal informer and hunter-up of delinquents. * * * It is a heartless * * * office."

4. Shawnee chieftain (1768?–1813), leader of a western Indian alliance;

hated for joining the British in the War of 1812.

5. Titus Oates (1649–1705) viciously fabricated the "evidence" in 1678 of the alleged "Popish Plot" to seize the English crown by regicide and terror.

6. Then a familiar abbreviation for *incognito,* with identity concealed.

fact that nobody could substantiate this report was, of course, nothing against its secret currency. Such a rumor once started on the gun decks in reference to almost anyone below the rank of a commissioned officer would, during the period assigned to this narrative, have seemed not altogether wanting in credibility to the tarry old wiseacres of a man-of-war crew. And indeed a man of Claggart's accomplishments, without prior nautical experience entering the navy at mature life, as he did, and necessarily allotted at the start to the lowest grade in it; a man too who never made allusion to his previous life ashore; these were circumstances which in the dearth of exact knowledge as to his true antecedents opened to the invidious a vague field for unfavorable surmise.

But the sailors' dogwatch gossip concerning him derived a vague plausibility from the fact that now for some period the British navy could so little afford to be squeamish in the matter of keeping up the muster rolls, that not only were press gangs notoriously abroad both afloat and ashore, but there was little or no secret about another matter, namely, that the London police were at liberty to capture any able-bodied suspect, any questionable fellow at large, and summarily ship him to the dockyard or fleet. Furthermore, even among voluntary enlistments there were instances where the motive thereto partook neither of patriotic impulse nor yet of a random desire to experience a bit of sea life and martial adventure. Insolvent debtors of minor grade, together with the promiscuous lame ducks of morality, found in the navy a convenient and secure refuge, secure because, once enlisted aboard a King's ship, they were as much in sanctuary as the transgressor of the Middle Ages harboring himself under the shadow of the altar. Such sanctioned irregularities, which for obvious reasons the government would hardly think to parade at the time and which consequently, and as affecting the least influential class of mankind, have all but dropped into oblivion, lend color to something for the truth whereof I do not vouch, and hence have some scruple in stating; something I remember having seen in print though the book I cannot recall; but the same thing was personally communicated to me now more than forty years ago by an old pensioner in a cocked hat with whom I had a most interesting talk on the terrace at Greenwich, a Baltimore Negro, a Trafalgar man.[7] It was to this effect: In the case of a warship short of hands whose speedy sailing was imperative, the deficient quota, in lack of any other way of making it good, would be eked out by drafts culled direct from the jails. For reasons previously suggested it would not perhaps be easy at the present day directly to prove or disprove the allegation. But allowed as a verity,

7. *I.e.*, one who had fought at the Battle of Trafalgar (1805), Nelson's fatal victory.

how significant would it be of England's straits at the time confronted by those wars which like a flight of harpies rose shrieking from the din and dust of the fallen Bastille. That era appears measurably clear to us who look back at it, and but read of it. But to the grandfathers of us graybeards, the more thoughtful of them, the genius of it presented an aspect like that of Camoëns' Spirit of the Cape,[8] an eclipsing menace mysterious and prodigious. Not America was exempt from apprehension. At the height of Napoleon's unexampled conquests, there were Americans who had fought at Bunker Hill who looked forward to the possibility that the Atlantic might prove no barrier against the ultimate schemes of this French portentous upstart from the revolutionary chaos who seemed in act of fulfilling judgment prefigured in the Apocalypse.

But the less credence was to be given to the gun-deck talk touching Claggart, seeing that no man holding his office in a man-of-war can ever hope to be popular with the crew. Besides, in derogatory comments upon anyone against whom they have a grudge, or for any reason or no reason mislike, sailors are much like landsmen: they are apt to exaggerate or romance it.

About as much was really known to the *Bellipotent*'s tars of the master-at-arms' career before entering the service as an astronomer knows about a comet's travels prior to its first observable appearance in the sky. The verdict of the sea quidnuncs[9] has been cited only by way of showing what sort of moral impression the man made upon rude uncultivated natures whose conceptions of human wickedness were necessarily of the narrowest, limited to ideas of vulgar rascality—a thief among the swinging hammocks during a night watch, or the man-brokers and land-sharks of the seaports.

It was no gossip, however, but fact that though, as before hinted, Claggart upon his entrance into the navy was, as a novice, assigned to the least honorable section of a man-of-war's crew, embracing the drudgery, he did not long remain there. The superior capacity he immediately evinced, his constitutional sobriety, an ingratiating deference to superiors, together with a peculiar ferreting genius manifested on a singular occasion; all this, capped by a certain austere patriotism, abruptly advanced him to the position of master-at-arms.

Of this maritime chief of police the ship's corporals, so called, were the immediate subordinates, and compliant ones; and this, as is to be noted in some business departments ashore, almost to a degree inconsistent with entire moral volition. His place put various converging wires of underground influence under the chief's con-

8. Camões (1524–1580), Portuguese poet. In his epic, the *Lusiads*, Vasco da Gama narrowly escaped this monster's ravage off the Cape of Good Hope on the first successful voyage around Africa to India.
9. Literally, "what now?" Hence, a busybody, a gossip.

trol, capable when astutely worked through his understrappers of operating to the mysterious discomfort, if nothing worse, of any of the sea commonalty.

9

Life in the foretop well agreed with Billy Budd. There, when not actually engaged on the yards yet higher aloft, the topmen, who as such had been picked out for youth and activity, constituted an aerial club lounging at ease against the smaller stun'sails rolled up into cushions, spinning yarns like the lazy gods, and frequently amused with what was going on in the busy world of the decks below. No wonder then that a young fellow of Billy's disposition was well content in such society. Giving no cause of offense to anybody, he was always alert at a call. So in the merchant service it had been with him. But now such a puctiliousness in duty was shown that his topmates would sometimes good-naturedly laugh at him for it. This heightened alacrity had its cause, namely, the impression made upon him by the first formal gangway-punishment he had ever witnessed, which befell the day following his impressment. It had been incurred by a little fellow, young, a novice afterguardsman absent from his assigned post when the ship was being put about; a dereliction resulting in a rather serious hitch to that maneuver, one demanding instantaneous promptitude in letting go and making fast. When Billy saw the culprit's naked back under the scourge, gridironed with red welts and worse, when he marked the dire expression in the liberated man's face as with his woolen shirt flung over him by the executioner he rushed forward from the spot to bury himself in the crowd, Billy was horrified. He resolved that never through remissness would he make himself liable to such a visitation or do or omit aught that might merit even verbal reproof. What then was his surprise and concern when ultimately he found himself getting into petty trouble occasionally about such matters as the stowage of his bag or something amiss in his hammock, matters under the police oversight of the ship's corporals of the lower decks, and which brought down on him a vague threat from one of them.

So heedful in all things as he was, how could this be? He could not understand it, and it more than vexed him. When he spoke to his young topmates about it they were either lightly incredulous or found something comical in his unconcealed anxiety. "Is it your bag, Billy?" said one. "Well, sew yourself up in it, bully boy, and then you'll be sure to know if anybody meddles with it."

Now there was a veteran aboard who because his years began to disqualify him for more active work had been recently assigned duty as mainmastman in his watch, looking to the gear belayed at the rail roundabout that great spar near the deck. At off-times the foretopman had picked up some acquaintance with him, and now in his trouble it occurred to him that he might be the sort of person to go to for wise counsel. He was an old Dansker long anglicized in the service, of few words, many wrinkles, and some honorable scars. His wizened face, time-tinted and weather-stained to the complexion of an antique parchment, was here and there peppered blue by the chance explosion of a gun cartridge in action.

He was an *Agamemnon* man, some two years prior to the time of this story having served under Nelson when still captain in that ship immortal in naval memory, which dismantled and in part broken up to her bare ribs is seen a grand skeleton in Haden's etching.[1] As one of a boarding party from the *Agamemnon* he had received a cut slantwise along one temple and cheek leaving a long pale scar like a streak of dawn's light falling athwart the dark visage. It was on account of that scar and the affair in which it was known that he had received it, as well as from his blue-peppered complexion, that the Dansker went among the *Bellipotent*'s crew by the name of "Board-Her-in-the-Smoke."

Now the first time that his small weasel eyes happened to light on Billy Budd, a certain grim internal merriment set all his ancient wrinkles into antic play. Was it that his eccentric unsentimental old sapience, primitive in its kind, saw or thought it saw something which in contrast with the warship's environment looked oddly incongruous in the Handsome Sailor? But after slyly studying him at intervals, the old Merlin's equivocal merriment was modified; for now when the twain would meet, it would start in his face a quizzing sort of look, but it would be but momentary and sometimes replaced by an expression of speculative query as to what might eventually befall a nature like that, dropped into a world not without some mantraps and against whose subtleties simple courage lacking experience and address, and without any touch of defensive ugliness, is of little avail; and where such innocence as man is capable of does yet in a moral emergency not always sharpen the faculties or enlighten the will.

However it was, the Dansker in his ascetic way rather took to Billy. Nor was this only because of a certain philosophic interest in such a character. There was another cause. While the old man's eccentricities, sometimes bordering on the ursine, repelled the juniors, Billy, undeterred thereby, revering him as a salt hero, would make advances, never passing the old *Agamemnon* man without a salutation marked by that respect which is seldom lost on the aged, however crabbed at times or whatever their station in life.

---

1. Francis Seymour Haden (1818– 1910), English surgeon, influential in the revival of etching. His "Breaking Up of the Agamemnon" (1870) won durable fame.

There was a vein of dry humor, or what not, in the mastman; and whether in freak or patriarchal irony touching Billy's youth and athletic frame, or for some other and more recondite reason, from the first in addressing him he always substituted *Baby* for Billy, the Dansker in fact being the originator of the name by which the foretopman eventually became known aboard ship.

Well then, in his mysterious little difficulty going in quest of the wrinkled one, Billy found him off duty in a dogwatch ruminating by himself, seated on a shot box of the upper gun deck, now and then surveying with a somewhat cynical regard certain of the more swaggering promenaders there. Billy recounted his trouble, again wondering how it all happened. The salt seer attentively listened, accompanying the foretopman's recital with queer twitchings of his wrinkles and problematical little sparkles of his small ferret eyes. Making an end of his story, the foretopman asked, "And now, Dansker, do tell me what you think of it."

The old man, shoving up the front of his tarpaulin and deliberately rubbing the long slant scar at the point where it entered the thin hair, laconically said, "Baby Budd, *Jemmy Legs*" [2] (meaning the master-at-arms) "is down on you."

"*Jemmy Legs!*" ejaculated Billy, his welkin eyes expanding. "What for? Why, he calls me 'the sweet and pleasant young fellow,' they tell me."

"Does he so?" grinned the grizzled one; then said, "Ay, Baby lad, a sweet voice has Jemmy Legs."

"No, not always. But to me he has. I seldom pass him but there comes a pleasant word."

"And that's because he's down upon you, Baby Budd."

Such reiteration, along with the manner of it, incomprehensible to a novice, disturbed Billy almost as much as the mystery for which he had sought explanation. Something less unpleasingly oracular he tried to extract; but the old sea Chiron,[3] thinking perhaps that for the nonce he had sufficiently instructed his young Achilles, pursed his lips, gathered all his wrinkles together, and would commit himself to nothing further.

Years, and those experiences which befall certain shrewder men subordinated lifelong to the will of superiors, all this had developed in the Dansker the pithy guarded cynicism that was his leading characteristic.

10

The next day an incident served to confirm Billy Budd in his incredulity as to the Dansker's strange summing up of the case sub-

---

2. "Jimmy Legs" is still a term of disparagement for the master-at-arms in the United States Navy.

3. In Greek myth, the wisest of the centaurs, skilled in healing, who befriended Achilles and other heroes.

mitted. The ship at noon, going large before the wind, was rolling on her course, and he below at dinner and engaged in some sportful talk with the members of his mess, chanced in a sudden lurch to spill the entire contents of his soup pan upon the new-scrubbed deck. Claggart, the master-at-arms, official rattan in hand, happened to be passing along the battery in a bay of which the mess was lodged, and the greasy liquid streamed just across his path. Stepping over it, he was proceeding on his way without comment, since the matter was nothing to take notice of under the circumstances, when he happened to observe who it was that had done the spilling. His countenance changed. Pausing, he was about to ejaculate something hasty at the sailor, but checked himself, and pointing down to the streaming soup, playfully tapped him from behind with his rattan, staying in a low musical voice peculiar to him at times, "Handsomely done, my lad! And handsome is as handsome did it, too!" And with that passed on. Not noted by Billy as not coming within his view was the involuntary smile, or rather grimace, that accompanied Claggart's equivocal words. Aridly it drew down the thin corners of his shapely mouth. But everybody taking his remark as meant for humorous, and at which therefore as coming from a superior they were bound to laugh "with counterfeited glee," [4] acted accordingly; and Billy, tickled, it may be, by the allusion to his being the Handsome Sailor, merrily joined in; then addressing his messmates exclaimed, "There now, who says that Jemmy Legs is down on me!"

"And who said he was, Beauty?" demanded one Donald with some surprise. Whereat the foretopman looked a little foolish, recalling that it was only one person, Board-Her-in-the-Smoke, who had suggested what to him was the smoky idea that his master-at-arms was in any peculiar way hostile to him. Meantime that functionary, resuming his path, must have momentarily worn some expression less guarded than that of the bitter smile, usurping the face from the heart—some distorting expression perhaps, for a drummer-boy heedlessly frolicking along from the opposite direction and chancing to come into light collision with his person was strangely disconcerted by his aspect. Nor was the impression lessened when the official, impetuously giving him a sharp cut with the rattan, vehemently exclaimed, "Look where you go!"

11

What was the matter with the master-at-arms? And, be the matter what it might, how could it have direct relation to Billy Budd, with whom prior to the affair of the spilled soup he had never come

4. *Cf.* Oliver Goldsmith, "The Deserted Village," l. 201, relating to the severe schoolmaster.

into any special contact official or otherwise? What indeed could the trouble have to do with one so little inclined to give offense as the merchant-ship's "peacemaker," even him who in Claggart's own phrase was "the sweet and pleasant young fellow"? Yes, why should Jemmy Legs, to borrow the Dansker's expression, be "down" on the Handsome Sailor? But, at heart and not for nothing, as the late chance encounter may indicate to the discerning, down on him, secretly down on him, he assuredly was.

Now to invent something touching the more private career of Claggart, something involving Billy Budd, of which something the latter should be wholly ignorant, some romantic incident implying that Claggart's knowledge of the young bluejacket began at some period anterior to catching sight of him on board the seventy-four —all this, not so difficult to do, might avail in a way more or less interesting to account for whatever of enigma may appear to lurk in the case. But in fact there was nothing of the sort. And yet the cause necessarily to be assumed as the sole one assignable is in its very realism as much charged with that prime element of Radcliffian romance, the mysterious, as any that the ingenuity of the author of *The Mysteries of Udolpho* [5] could devise. For what can more partake of the mysterious than an antipathy spontaneous and profound such as is evoked in certain exceptional mortals by the mere aspect of some other mortal, however harmless he may be, if not called forth by this very harmlessness itself?

Now there can exist no irritating juxtaposition of dissimilar personalities comparable to that which is possible aboard a great warship fully manned and at sea. There, every day among all ranks, almost every man comes into more or less of contact with almost every other man. Wholly there to avoid even the sight of an aggravating object one must needs give it Jonah's toss [6] or jump overboard himself. Imagine how all this might eventually operate on some peculiar human creature the direct reverse of a saint!

But for the adequate comprehending of Claggart by a normal nature these hints are insufficient. To pass from a normal nature to him one must cross "the deadly space between." And this is best done by indirection.

Long ago an honest scholar, my senior, said to me in reference to one who like himself is now no more, a man so unimpeachably respectable that against him nothing was ever openly said though among the few something was whispered, "Yes, X——is a nut not to be cracked by the tap of a lady's fan. You are aware that I am the adherent of no organized religion, much less of any philosophy built into a system. Well, for all that, I think that to try and get into

5. *The Mysteries of Udolpho* (1794), by Ann Radcliffe, was among the most popular of Gothic romances.

6. In the language of seafaring, the putting overboard of an unlucky person or object.

X——, enter his labyrinth and get out again, without a clue derived from some source other than what is known as 'knowledge of the world'—that were hardly possible, at least for me."

"Why," said I, "X——, however singular a study to some, is yet human, and knowledge of the world assuredly implies the knowledge of human nature, and in most of its varieties."

"Yes, but a superficial knowledge of it, serving ordinary purposes. But for anything deeper, I am not certain whether to know the world and to know human nature be not two distinct branches of knowledge, which while they may coexist in the same heart, yet either may exist with little or nothing of the other. Nay, in an average man of the world, his constant rubbing with it blunts that finer spiritual insight indispensable to the understanding of the essential in certain exceptional characters, whether evil ones or good. In a matter of some importance I have seen a girl wind an old lawyer about her little finger. Nor was it the dotage of senile love. Nothing of the sort. But he knew law better than he knew the girl's heart. Coke and Blackstone [7] hardly shed so much light into obscure spiritual places as the Hebrew prophets. And who were they? Mostly recluses."

At the time, my inexperience was such that I did not quite see the drift of all this. It may be that I see it now. And, indeed, if that lexicon which is based on Holy Writ were any longer popular, one might with less difficulty define and denominate certain phenomenal men. As it is, one must turn to some authority not liable to the charge of being tinctured with the biblical element.

In a list of definitions included in the authentic translation of Plato, a list attributed to him, occurs this: "Natural Depravity: a depravity according to nature," a definition which, though savoring of Calvinism, by no means involves Calvin's dogma as to total mankind. Evidently its intent makes it applicable but to individuals. Not many are the examples of this depravity which the gallows and jail supply. At any rate, for notable instances, since these have no vulgar alloy of the brute in them, but invariably are dominated by intellectuality, one must go elsewhere. Civilization, especially if of the austerer sort, is auspicious to it. It folds itself in the mantle of respectability. It has its certain negative virtues serving as silent auxiliaries. It never allows wine to get within its guard. It is not going too far to say that it is without vices or small sins. There is a phenomenal pride in it that exludes them. It is never mercenary or avaricious. In short, the depravity here meant partakes nothing of the sordid or sensual. It is serious, but free from acerbity. Though no flatterer of mankind it never speaks ill of it.

---

7. The *Reports* and the *Institutes* of Sir Edward Coke (1552–1634) and the *Commentaries* of Sir William Black- stone (1723–1780) were the foundations of modern British and American jurisprudence.

But the thing which in eminent instances signalizes so exceptional a nature is this: Though the man's even temper and discreet bearing would seem to intimate a mind peculiarly subject to the law of reason, not the less in heart he would seem to riot in complete exemption from that law, having apparently little to do with reason further than to employ it as an ambidexter implement for effecting the irrational. That is to say: Toward the accomplishment of an aim which in wantonness of atrocity would seem to partake of the insane, he will direct a cool judgment sagacious and sound. These men are madmen, and of the most dangerous sort, for their lunacy is not continuous, but occasional, evoked by some special object; it is protectively secretive, which is as much as to say it is self-contained, so that when, moreover, most active it is to the average mind not distinguishable from sanity, and for the reason above suggested: that whatever its aims may be—and the aim is never declared—the method and the outward proceeding are always perfectly rational.

Now something such an one was Claggart, in whom was the mania of an evil nature, not engendered by vicious training or corrupting books or licentious living, but born with him and innate, in short "a depravity according to nature."

Dark sayings are these, some will say. But why? Is it because they somewhat savor of Holy Writ in its phrase "mystery of iniquity"? [8] If they do, such savor was far enough from being intended, for little will it commend these pages to many a reader of today.

The point of the present story turning on the hidden nature of the master-at-arms has necessitated this chapter. With an added hint or two in connection with the incident at the mess, the resumed narrative must be left to vindicate, as it may, its own credibility.

12

That Claggart's figure was not amiss, and his face, save the chin, well molded, has already been said. Of these favorable points he seemed not insensible, for he was not only neat but careful in his dress. But the form of Billy Budd was heroic; and if his face was without the intellectual look of the pallid Claggart's, not the less was it lit, like his, from within, though from a different source. The bonfire in his heart made luminous the rose-tan in his cheek.

In view of the marked contrast between the persons of the twain, it is more than probable that when the master-at-arms in the scene last given applied to the sailor the proverb "Handsome is as hand-

8. *Cf.* II Thessalonians ii: 7: "For the mystery of iniquity doth already work"; the words that follow recognize a Satanic and active principle of evil in nature.

some does," he there let escape an ironic inkling, not caught by the young sailors who heard it, as to what it was that had first moved him against Billy, namely, his significant personal beauty.

Now envy and antipathy, passions irreconcilable in reason, nevertheless in fact may spring conjoined like Chang and Eng in one birth.[9] Is Envy then such a monster? Well, though many an arraigned mortal has in hopes of mitigated penalty pleaded guilty to horrible actions, did ever anybody seriously confess to envy? Something there is in it universally felt to be more shameful than even felonious crime. And not only does everybody disown it, but the better sort are inclined to incredulity when it is in earnest imputed to an intelligent man. But since its lodgment is in the heart not the brain, no degree of intellect supplies a guarantee against it. But Claggart's was no vulgar form of the passion. Nor, as directed toward Billy Budd, did it partake of that streak of apprehensive jealousy, that marred Saul's visage perturbedly brooding on the comely young David.[1] Claggart's envy struck deeper. If askance he eyed the good looks, cheery health, and frank enjoyment of young life in Billy Budd, it was because these went along with a nature that, as Claggart magnetically felt, had in its simplicity never willed malice or experienced the reactionary bite of that serpent. To him, the spirit lodged within Billy, and looking out from his welkin eyes as from windows, that ineffability it was which made the dimple in his dyed cheek, suppled his joints, and dancing in his yellow curls made him pre-eminently the Handsome Sailor. One person excepted, the master-at-arms was perhaps the only man in the ship intellectually capable of adequately appreciating the moral phenomenon presented in Billy Budd. And the insight but intensified his passion, which assuming various secret forms within him, at times assumed that of cynic disdain, disdain of innocence—to be nothing more than innocent! Yet in an aesthetic way he saw the charm of it, the courageous free-and-easy temper of it, and fain would have shared it, but he despaired of it.

With no power to annul the elemental evil in him, though readily enough he could hide it; apprehending the good, but powerless to be it; a nature like Claggart's, surcharged with energy as such natures almost invariably are, what recourse is left to it but to recoil upon itself and, like the scorpion for which the Creator alone is responsible, act out to the end the part allotted it.

<h2 style="text-align:center">13</h2>

Passion, and passion in its profoundest, is not a thing demanding a palatial stage whereon to play its part. Down among the ground-

9. The original Siamese twins (1811–1874), first exhibited in the United States in 1829.
1. *Cf.* I Samuel xviii: 5–12.

lings, among the beggars and rakers of the garbage, profound passion is enacted. And the circumstances that provoke it, however, trivial or mean, are no measure of its power. In the present instance the stage is a scrubbed gun deck, and one of the external provocations a man-of-war's man's spilled soup.

Now when the master-at-arms noticed whence came that greasy fluid streaming before his feet, he must have taken it—to some extent wilfully, perhaps—not for the mere accident it assuredly was, but for the sly escape of a spontaneous feeling on Billy's part more or less answering to the antipathy on his own. In effect a foolish demonstration, he must have thought, and very harmless, like the futile kick of a heifer, which yet were the heifer a shod stallion would not be so harmless. Even so was it that into the gall of Claggart's envy he infused the vitriol of his contempt. But the incident confirmed to him certain telltale reports purveyed to his ear by "Squeak," one of his more cunning corporals, a grizzled little man, so nicknamed by the sailors on account of his squeaky voice and sharp visage ferreting about the dark corners of the lower decks after interlopers, satirically suggesting to them the idea of a rat in a cellar.

From his chief's employing him as an implicit tool in laying little traps for the worriment of the foretopman—for it was from the master-at-arms that the petty persecutions heretofore adverted to had proceeded—the corporal, having naturally enough concluded that his master could have no love for the sailor, made it his business, faithful understrapper that he was, to foment the ill blood by perverting to his chief certain innocent frolics of the good-natured foretopman, besides inventing for his mouth sundry contumelious epithets he claimed to have overheard him let fall. The master-at-arms never suspected the veracity of these reports, more especially as to the epithets, for he well knew how secretly unpopular may become a master-at-arms, at least a master-at-arms of those days, zealous in his function, and how the bluejackets shoot at him in private their raillery and wit; the nickname by which he goes among them (Jemmy Legs) implying under the form of merriment their cherished disrespect and dislike. But in view of the greediness of hate for pabulum it hardly needed a purveyor to feed Claggart's passion.

An uncommon prudence is habitual with the subtler depravity, for it has everything to hide. And in case of an injury but suspected, its secretiveness voluntarily cuts it off from enlightenment or disillusion; and, not unreluctantly, action is taken upon surmise as upon certainty. And the retaliation is apt to be in monstrous disproportion to the supposed offense; for when in anybody was revenge in its exactions aught else but an inordinate usurer? But how with Claggart's conscience? For though consciences are unlike as foreheads, every intelligence, not excluding the scriptural devils who "believe and tremble," has one. But Claggart's conscience being but the lawyer to his will, made ogres of trifles, probably arguing that the motive imputed to Billy in spilling the soup just when he did, together with the epithets alleged, these, if nothing more, made a strong case against him; nay, justified animosity into a sort of retributive righteousness. The Pharisee is the Guy Fawkes [2] prowling in the hid chambers underlying some natures like Claggart's. And they can really form no conception of an unreciprocated malice. Probably the master-at-arms' clandestine persecution of Billy was started to try the temper of the man; but it had not developed any quality in him that enmity could make official use of or even pervert into plausible self-justification; so that the occurrence at the mess, petty if it were, was a welcome one to that peculiar conscience assigned to be the private mentor of Claggart; and, for the rest, not improbably it put him upon new experiments.

14

Not many days after the last incident narrated, something befell Billy Budd that more graveled him than aught that had previously occurred.

It was a warm night for the latitude; and the foretopman, whose watch at the time was properly below, was dozing on the uppermost deck whither he had ascended from his hot hammock, one of hundreds suspended so closely wedged together over a lower gun deck that there was little or no swing to them. He lay as in the shadow of a hillside, stretched under the lee of the booms, a piled ridge of spare spars amidships between foremast and mainmast among which the ship's largest boat, the launch, was stowed. Alongside of three other slumberers from below, he lay near that end of the booms which approaches the foremast; his station aloft on duty as a foretopman being just over the deck-station of the forecastlemen, entitling him according to usage to make himself more or less at home in that neighborhood.

Presently he was stirred into semiconsciousness by somebody, who must have previously sounded the sleep of the others, touching his shoulder, and then, as the foretopman raised his head, breathing into his ear in a quick whisper, "Slip into the lee forechains, Billy; there is something in the wind. Don't speak. Quick, I will meet you there," and disappearing.

Now Billy, like sundry other essentially good-natured ones, had

2. Principal conspirator in the Gunpowder Plot (1604–1605) to blow up the British Houses of Parliament.

some of the weaknesses inseparable from essential good nature; and among these was a reluctance, almost an incapacity of plumply saying *no* to an abrupt proposition not obviously absurd on the face of it, nor obviously unfriendly, nor iniquitous. And being of warm blood, he had not the phlegm tacitly to negative any proposition by unresponsive inaction. Like his sense of fear, his apprehension as to aught outside of the honest and natural was seldom very quick. Besides, upon the present occasion, the drowse from his sleep still hung upon him.

However it was, he mechanically rose and, sleepily wondering what could be in the wind, betook himself to the designated place, a narrow platform, one of six, outside of the high bulwarks and screened by the great deadeyes and multiple columned lanyards of the shrouds and backstays; and, in a great warship of that time, of dimensions commensurate to the hull's magnitude; a tarry balcony in short, overhanging the sea, and so secluded that one mariner of the *Bellipotent*, a Nonconformist old tar of a serious turn, made it even in daytime his private oratory.

In his retired nook the stranger soon joined Billy Budd. There was no moon as yet; a haze obscured the starlight. He could not distinctly see the stranger's face. Yet from something in the outline and carriage, Billy took him, and correctly, for one of the afterguard.

"Hist! Billy," said the man, in the same quick cautionary whisper as before. "You were impressed, weren't you? Well, so was I"; and he paused, as to mark the effect. But Billy, not knowing exactly what to make of this, said nothing. Then the other: "We are not the only impressed ones, Billy. There's a gang of us.—Couldn't you —help—at a pinch?"

"What do you mean?" demanded Billy, here thoroughly shaking off his drowse.

"Hist, hist!" the hurried whisper now growing husky. "See here," and the man held up two small objects faintly twinkling in the night-light; "see, they are yours, Billy, if you'll only——"

But Billy broke in, and in his resentful eagerness to deliver himself his vocal infirmity somewhat intruded. "D—d—damme, I don't know what you are d—d—driving at, or what you mean, but you had better g—g—go where you belong!" For the moment the fellow, as confounded, did not stir; and Billy, springing to his feet, said, "If you d—don't start, I'll t—t—toss you back over the r—rail!" There was no mistaking this, and the mysterious emissary decamped, disappearing in the direction of the mainmast in the shadow of the booms.

"Hallo, what's the matter?" here came growling from a forecastleman awakened from the deck-doze by Billy's raised voice. And as the foretopman reappeared and was recognized by him: "Ah,

Beauty, is it you? Well, something must have been the matter, for you st—st—stuttered."

"Oh," rejoined Billy, now mastering the impediment, "I found an afterguardsman in our part of the ship here, and I bid him be off where he belongs."

"And is that all you did about it, Foretopman?" gruffly demanded another, an irascible old fellow of brick-colored visage and hair who was known to his associate forecastlemen as "Red Pepper." "Such sneaks I should like to marry to the gunner's daughter!"—by that expression meaning that he would like to subject them to disciplinary castigation over a gun.

However, Billy's rendering of the matter satisfactorily accounted to these inquirers for the brief commotion, since of all the sections of a ship's company the forecastlemen, veterans for the most part and bigoted in their sea prejudices, are the most jealous in resenting territorial encroachments, especially on the part of any of the afterguard, of whom they have but a sorry opinion—chiefly landsmen, never going aloft except to reef or furl the mainsail, and in no wise competent to handle a marlinspike or turn in a deadeye, say.

15

This incident sorely puzzled Billy Budd. It was an entirely new experience, the first time in his life that he had ever been personally approached in underhand intriguing fashion. Prior to this encounter he had known nothing of the afterguardsman, the two men being stationed wide apart, one forward and aloft during his watch, the other on deck and aft.

What could it mean? And could they really be guineas, those two glittering objects the interloper had held up to his (Billy's) eyes? Where could the fellow get guineas? Why, even spare buttons are not so plentiful at sea. The more he turned the matter over, the more he was nonplussed, and made uneasy and discomfited. In his disgustful recoil from an overture which, though he but ill comprehended, he instictively knew must involve evil of some sort, Billy Budd was like a young horse fresh from the pasture suddenly inhaling a vile whiff from some chemical factory, and by repeated snortings trying to get it out of his nostrils and lungs. This frame of mind barred all desire of holding further parley with the fellow, even were it but for the purpose of gaining some enlightenment as to his design in approaching him. And yet he was not without natural curiosity to see how such a visitor in the dark would look in broad day.

He espied him the following afternoon in his first dogwatch below, one of the smokers on that forward part of the upper gun deck allotted to the pipe. He recognized him by his general cut and build more than by his round freckled face and glassy eyes of pale blue, veiled with lashes all but white. And yet Billy was a bit uncertain whether indeed it were he—yonder chap about his own age chatting and laughing in freehearted way, leaning against a gun; a genial young fellow enough to look at, and something of a rattlebrain, to all appearance. Rather chubby too for a sailor, even an afterguardsman. In short, the last man in the world, one would think, to be overburdened with thoughts, especially those perilous thoughts that must needs belong to a conspirator in any serious project, or even to the underling of such a conspirator.

Although Billy was not aware of it, the fellow, with a side long watchful glance, had perceived Billy first, and then noting that Billy was looking at him, thereupon nodded a familiar sort of friendly recognition as to an old acquaintance, without interrupting the talk he was engaged in with the group of smokers. A day or two afterwards, chancing in the evening promenade on a gun deck to pass Billy, he offered a flying word of good-fellowship, as it were, which by its unexpectedness, and equivocalness under the circumstances, so embarrassed Billy that he knew not how to respond to it, and let it go unnoticed.

Billy was now left more at a loss than before. The ineffectual speculations into which he was led were so disturbingly alien to him that he did his best to smother them. It never entered his mind that here was a matter which, from its extreme questionableness, it was his duty as a loyal bluejacket to report in the proper quarter. And, probably, had such a step been suggested to him, he would have been deterred from taking it by the thought, one of novice magnanimity, that it would savor overmuch of the dirty work of a telltale. He kept the thing to himself. Yet upon one occasion he could not forbear a little disburdening himself to the old Dansker, tempted thereto perhaps by the influence of a balmy night when the ship lay becalmed; the twain, silent for the most part, sitting together on deck, their heads propped against the bulwarks. But it was only a partial and anonymous account that Billy gave, the unfounded scruples above referred to preventing full disclosure to anybody. Upon hearing Billy's version, the sage Dansker seemed to divine more than he was told; and after a little meditation, during which his wrinkles were pursed as into a point, quite effacing for the time that quizzing expression his face sometimes wore: "Didn't I say so, Baby Budd?"

"Say what?" demanded Billy.

"Why, *Jemmy Legs* is *down* on you."

"And what," rejoined Billy in amazement, "has *Jemmy Legs* to do with that cracked afterguardsman?"

"Ho, it was an afterguardsman, then. A cat's-paw, a cat's-paw!"
And with that exclamation, whether it had reference to a light puff
of air just then coming over the calm sea, or a subtler relation to
the afterguardsman, there is no telling, the old Merlin gave a twisting wrench with his black teeth at his plug of tobacco, vouchsafing
no reply to Billy's impetuous question, though now repeated, for it
was his wont to relapse into grim silence when interrogated in
skeptical sort as to any of his sententious oracles, not always very
clear ones, rather partaking of that obscurity which invests most
Delphic deliverances from any quarter.

Long experience had very likely brought this old man to that
bitter prudence which never interferes in aught and never gives
advice.

16

Yes, despite the Dansker's pithy insistence as to the master-at-
arms being at the bottom of these strange experiences of Billy on
board the *Bellipotent*, the young sailor was ready to ascribe them to
almost anybody but the man who, to use Billy's own expression,
"always had a pleasant word for him." This is to be wondered at.
Yet not so much to be wondered at. In certain matters, some sailors
even in mature life remain unsophisticated enough. But a young
seafarer of the disposition of our athletic foretopman is much of a
child-man. And yet a child's utter innocence is but its blank ignorance, and the innocence more or less wanes as intelligence waxes.
But in Billy Budd intelligence, such as it was, had advanced while
yet his simple-mindedness remained for the most part unaffected.
Experience is a teacher indeed; yet did Billy's years make his experience small. Besides, he had none of that intuitive knowledge
of the bad which in natures not good or incompletely so foreruns
experience, and therefore may pertain, as in some instances it too
clearly does pertain, even to youth.

And what could Billy know of man except of man as a mere
sailor? And the old-fashioned sailor, the veritable man before the
mast, the sailor from boyhood up, he, though indeed of the same
species as a landsman, is in some respects singularly distinct from
him. The sailor is frankness, the landsman is finesse. Life is not a
game with the sailor, demanding the long head—no intricate game
of chess where few moves are made in straightforwardness and ends
are attained by indirection, an oblique, tedious, barren game hardly
worth that poor candle burnt out in playing it.[3]

Yes, as a class, sailors are in character a juvenile race. Even their
deviations are marked by juvenility, this more especially holding

3. *Cf.* Shakespeare, *Macbeth*, Act V, Scene 5, ll. 15–17.

true with the sailors of Billy's time. Then too, certain things which apply to all sailors do more pointedly operate here and there upon the junior one. Every sailor, too, is accustomed to obey orders without debating them; his life afloat is externally ruled for him; he is not brought into that promiscuous commerce with mankind where unobstructed free agency on equal terms—equal superficially, at least—soon teaches one that unless upon occasion he exercise a distrust keen in proportion to the fairness of the appearance, some foul turn may be served him. A ruled undemonstrative distrustfulness is so habitual, not with businessmen so much as with men who know their kind in less shallow relations than business, namely, certain men of the world, that they come at last to employ it all but unconsciously; and some of them would very likely feel real surprise at being charged with it as one of their general characteristics.

17

But after the little matter at the mess Billy Budd no more found himself in strange trouble at times about his hammock or his clothes bag or what not. As to that smile that occasionally sunned him, and the pleasant passing word, these were, if not more frequent, yet if anything more pronounced than before.

But for all that, there were certain other demonstrations now. When Claggart's unobserved glance happened to light on belted Billy rolling along the upper gun deck in the leisure of the second dogwatch, exchanging passing broadsides of fun with other young promenaders in the crowd, that glance would follow the cheerful sea Hyperion [4] with a settled meditative and melancholy expression, his eyes strangely suffused with incipient feverish tears. Then would Claggart look like a man of sorrows. Yes, and sometimes the melancholy expression would have in it a touch of soft yearning, as if Claggart could even have loved Billy but for fate and ban. But this was an evanescence, and quickly repented of, as it were, by an immitigable look, inching and shriveling the visage into the momentary semblance of a wrinkled walnut. But sometimes catching sight in advance of the foretopman coming in his direction, he would, upon their nearing, step aside a little to let him pass, dwelling upon Billy for the moment with the glittering dental satire of a Guise.[5] But upon any abrupt unforeseen encounter a red light would flash forth from his eye like a spark from an anvil in a dusk smithy. That

4. In early Greek myth, the Titan Helios, god of the sun; later identified with Apollo, god of manly youth and beauty.
5. The Guises, a powerful ducal family of France in the sixteenth and seventeenth centuries, engaged in violent intrigues attractive to romancers, for example Dumas. As for the "glittering dental satire," *cf.* Hamlet's discovery "that one may smile * * * and be a villain" (Act I, Scene 5, ll. 103–105).

quick, fierce light was a strange one, darted from orbs which in repose were of a color nearest approaching a deeper violet, the softest of shades.

Though some of these caprices of the pit could not but be observed by their object, yet were they beyond the construing of such a nature. And the thews of Billy were hardly compatible with that sort of sensitive spiritual organization which in some cases instinctively conveys to ignorant innocence an admonition of the proximity of the malign. He thought the master-at-arms acted in a manner rather queer at times. That was all. But the occasional frank air and pleasant word went for what they purported to be, the young sailor never having heard as yet of the "too fair-spoken man."

Had the foretopman been conscious of having done or said anything to provide the ill will of the official, it would have been different with him, and his sight might have been purged if not sharpened. As it was, innocence was his blinder.

So was it with him in yet another matter. Two minor officers, the armorer and captain of the hold, with whom he had never exchanged a word, his position in the ship not bringing him into contact with them, these men now for the first began to cast upon Billy, when they chanced to encounter him, that peculiar glance which evidences that the man from whom it comes has been some way tampered with, and to the prejudice of him upon whom the glance lights. Never did it occur to Billy as a thing to be noted or a thing suspicious, though he well knew the fact, that the armorer and captain of the hold, with the ship's yeoman, apothecary, and others of that grade, were by naval usage messmates of the master-at-arms, men with ears convenient to his confidential tongue.

But the general popularity that came from our Handsome Sailor's manly forwardness upon occasion and irresistible good nature, indicating no mental superiority tending to excite an invidious feeling, this good will on the part of most of his shipmates made him the less to concern himself about such mute aspects toward him as those whereto allusion has just been made, aspects he could not so fathom as to infer their whole import.

As to the afterguardsman, though Billy for reasons already given necessarily saw little of him, yet when the two did happen to meet, invariably came the fellow's offhand cheerful recognition, sometimes accompanied by a passing pleasant word or two. Whatever that equivocal young person's original design may really have been, or the design of which he might have been the deputy, certain it was from his manner upon these occasions that he had wholly dropped it.

It was as if his precocity of crookedness (and every vulgar villain is precocious) had for once deceived him, and the man he had sought to entrap as a simpleton had through his very simplicity ignominiously baffled him.

But shrewd ones may opine that it was hardly possible for Billy to refrain from going up to the afterguardsman and bluntly demanding to know his purpose in the initial interview so abruptly closed in the forechains. Shrewd ones may also think it but natural in Billy to set about sounding some of the other impressed men of the ship in order to discover what basis, if any, there was for the emissary's obscure suggestions as to plotting disaffection aboard. Yes, shrewd ones may so think. But something more, or rather something else than mere shrewdness is perhaps needful for the due understanding of such a character as Billy Budd's.

As to Claggart, the monomania in the man—if that indeed it were—as involuntarily disclosed by starts in the manifestations detailed, yet in general covered over by his self-contained and rational demeanor; this, like a subterranean fire, was eating its way deeper and deeper in him. Something decisive must come of it.

18

After the mysterious interview in the forechains, the one so abruptly ended there by Billy, nothing especially germane to the story occurred until the events now about to be narrated.

Elsewhere it has been said that in the lack of frigates (of course better sailers than line-of-battle ships) in the English squadron up the Straits at that period, the *Bellipotent* 74 was occasionally employed not only as an available substitute for a scout, but at times on detached service of more important kind. This was not alone because of her sailing qualities, not common in a ship of her rate, but quite as much, probably, that the character of her commander, it was thought, specially adapted him for any duty where under unforseen difficulties a prompt initiative might have to be taken in some matter demanding knowledge and ability in addition to those qualities implied in good seamanship. It was on an expedition of the latter sort, a somewhat distant one, and when the *Bellipotent* was almost at her furthest remove from the fleet, that in the latter part of an afternoon watch she unexpectedly came in sight of a ship of the enemy. It proved to be a frigate. The latter, perceiving through the glass that the weight of men and metal would be heavily against her, invoking her light heels crowded sail to get away. After a chase urged almost against hope and lasting until about the middle of the first dogwatch, she signally succeeded in effecting her escape.

Not long after the pursuit had been given up, and ere the excitement incident thereto had altogether waned away, the master-at-arms, ascending from his cavernous sphere, made his appearance cap in hand by the mainmast respectfully waiting the notice of Captain Vere, then solitary walking the weather side of the quarter-deck, doubtless somewhat chafed at the failure of the pursuit. The spot where Claggert stood was the place allotted to men of lesser grades seeking more particular interview either with the officer of the deck or the captain himself. But from the latter it was not often that a sailor or petty officer of those days would seek a hearing; only some exceptional cause would, according to established custom, have warranted that.

Presently, just as the commander, absorbed in his reflections, was on the point of turning aft in his promenade, he became sensible of Claggart's presence, and saw the doffed cap held in deferential expectancy. Here be it said that Captain Vere's personal knowledge of this petty officer had only begun at the time of the ship's last sailing from home, Claggart then for the first, in transfer from a ship detained for repairs, supplying on board the *Bellipotent* the place of a previous master-at-arms disabled and ashore.

No sooner did the commander observe who it was that now deferentially stood awaiting his notice than a peculiar expression came over him. It was not unlike that which uncontrollably will flit across the countenance of one at unawares encountering a person who, though known to him indeed, has hardly been long enough known for thorough knowledge, but something in whose aspect nevertheless now for the first provokes a vaguely repellent distaste. But coming to a stand and resuming much of his wonted official manner, save that a sort of impatience lurked in the intonation of the opening word, he said "Well? What is it, Master-at-arms?"

With the air of a subordinate grieved at the necessity of being a messenger of ill tidings, and while conscientiously determined to be frank yet equally resolved upon shunning overstatement, Claggart at this invitation, or rather summons to disburden, spoke up. What he said, conveyed in the language of no uneducated man, was to the effect following, if not altogether in these words, namely, that during the chase and preparations for the possible encounter he had seen enough to convince him that at least one sailor aboard was a dangerous character in a ship mustering some who not only had taken a guilty part in the late serious troubles, but others also who, like the man in question, had entered His Majesty's service under another form than enlistment.

At this point Captain Vere with some impatience interrupted him: "Be direct, man; say *impressed men*."

Claggart made a gesture of subservience, and proceeded. Quite lately he (Claggart) had begun to suspect that on the gun decks some sort of movement prompted by the sailor in question was covertly going on, but he had not thought himself warranted in reporting the suspicion so long as it remained indistinct. But from what he had that afternoon observed in the man referred to, the suspicion of something clandestine going on had advanced to a point less removed from certainty. He deeply felt, he added, the serious responsibility assumed in making a report involving such possible consequences to the individual mainly concerned, besides tending to augment those natural anxieties which every naval commander must feel in view of extraordinary outbreaks so recent as those which, he sorrowfully said it, it needed not to name.

Now at the first broaching of the matter Captain Vere, taken by surprise, could not wholly dissemble his disquietude. But as Claggart went on, the former's aspect changed into restiveness under something in the testifier's manner in giving his testimony. However, he refrained from interrupting him. And Claggart, continuing, concluded with this: "God forbid, your honor, that the *Bellipotent* should be the experience of the——"

"Never mind that!" here peremptorily broke in the superior, his face altering with anger, instinctively divining the ship that the other was about to name, one in which the Nore Mutiny had assumed a singularly tragical character that for a time jeopardized the life of its commander. Under the circumstances he was indignant at the purposed allusion. When the commissioned officers themselves were on all occasions very heedful how they referred to the recent events in the fleet, for a petty officer unnecessarily to allude to them in the presence of his captain, this struck him as a most immodest presumption. Besides, to his quick sense of self-respect it even looked under the circumstances something like an attempt to alarm him. Nor at first was he without some surprise that one who so far as he had hitherto come under his notice had shown considerable tact in his function should in this particular evince such lack of it.

But these thoughts and kindred dubious ones flitting across his mind were suddenly replaced by an intuitional surmise which, though as yet obscure in form, served practically to affect his reception of ill tidings. Certain it is that, long versed in everything pertaining to the complicated gun-deck life, which like every other form of life has its secret mines and dubious side, the side popularly disclaimed, Captain Vere did not permit himself to be unduly disturbed by the general tenor of his subordinate's report.

Furthermore, if in view of recent events prompt action should be taken at the first palpable sign of recurring insubordination, for all that, not judicious would it be, he thought, to keep the idea of lingering disaffection alive by undue forwardness in crediting an informer, even if his own subordinate and charged among other things with police surveillance of the crew. This feeling would not perhaps have so prevailed with him were it not that upon a prior occasion the patriotic zeal officially evinced by Claggert had somewhat irritated him as appearing rather supersensible and strained. Furthermore, something even in the official's self-possessed and somewhat ostentatious manner in making his specifications strangely reminded him of a bandsman, a perjurous witness in a capital case before a courtmartial ashore of which when a lieutenant he (Captain Vere) had been a member.

Now the peremptory check given to Claggart in the matter of the arrested allusion was quickly followed up by this: "You say that there is at least one dangerous man aboard. Name him."

"William Budd, a foretopman, your honor."

"William Budd!" repeated Captain Vere with unfeigned astonishment. "And mean you the man that Lieutenant Ratcliffe took from the merchantman not very long ago, the young fellow who seems to be so popular with the men—Billy, the Handsome Sailor, as they call him?"

"The same, your honor, but for all his youth and good looks, a deep one. Not for nothing does he insinuate himself into the good will of his shipmates, since at the least they will at a pinch say—all hands will—a good word for him, and at all hazards. Did Lieutenant Ratcliffe happen to tell your honor of that adroit fling of Budd's, jumping up in the cutter's bow under the merchantman's stern when he was being taken off? It is even masked by that sort of good-humored air that at heart he resents his impressment. You have but noted his fair cheek. A mantrap may be under the ruddy-tipped daisies."

Now the Handsome Sailor as a signal figure among the crew had naturally enough attracted the captain's attention from the first. Though in general not very demonstrative to his officers, he had congratulated Lieutenant Ratcliffe upon his good fortune in lighting on such a fine specimen of the *genus homo*, who in the nude might have posed for a statue of young Adam before the Fall. As to Billy's adieu to the ship *Rights-of-Man*, which the boarding lieutenant had indeed reported to him, but, in a deferential way, more as a good story than aught else, Captain Vere, though mistakenly understanding it as a satiric sally, had but thought so much the better of the impressed man for it; as a military sailor, admiring the spirit that could take an arbitrary enlistment so merrily and sensibly. The foretopman's conduct, too, so far as it had fallen under the captain's notice, had confirmed the first happy augury, while the new recruit's qualities as a "sailor-man" seemed to be such that he had thought of recommending him to the executive officer for promotion to a place that would more frequently bring him under his own observation, namely, the captaincy of the mizzentop, replacing there in the starboard watch a man not so young whom partly for that reason he deemed less fitted for the post. Be it parenthesized here that since the mizzentopmen have not to handle such breadths of heavy canvas as the lower sails on the mainmast and foremast, a young man if of the right stuff not only seems best adapted to duty there, but in fact is generally selected for the captaincy of that top, and the company under him are light hands and often but striplings. In sum, Captain Vere had from the beginning deemed Billy Budd to be what in the naval parlance of the time was called a "King's bargain": that is to say, for his Britannic Majesty's navy a capital investment at small outlay or none at all.

After a brief pause, during which the reminiscences above mentioned passed vividly through his mind and he weighed the import of Claggert's last suggestion conveyed in the phrase "mantrap under the daisies," and the more he weighed it the less reliance he felt in the informer's good faith, suddenly he turned upon him and in a low voice demanded: "Do you come to me, Master-at-arms, with so foggy a tale? As to Budd, cite me an act or spoken word of his confirmatory of what you in general charge against him. Stay," drawing nearer to him: "heed what you speak. Just now, and in a case like this, there is a yardarm-end for the false witness."

"Ah, your honor!" sighed Claggert, mildly shaking his shapely head as in sad deprecation of such unmerited severity of tone. Then, bridling—erecting himself as in virtuous self-assertion—he circumstantially alleged certain words and acts which collectively, if credited, led to presumptions mortally inculpating Budd. And for some of these averments, he added, substantiating proof was not far.

With gray eyes impatient and distrustful essaying to fathom to the bottom Claggert's calm violet ones, Captain Vere again heard him out; then for the moment stood ruminating. The mood he evinced, Claggart—himself for the time liberated from the other's scrutiny—steadily regarded with a look difficult to render: a look curious of the operation of his tactics, a look such as might have been that of the spokesman of the envious children of Jacob deceptively imposing upon the troubled patriarch the blood-dyed coat of young Joseph.[6]

Though something exceptional in the moral quality of Captain Vere made him, in earnest encounter with a fellow man, a veritable touchstone of that man's essential nature, yet now as to Claggart and what was really going on in him his feeling partook less of intuitional conviction than of strong suspicion clogged by strange dubieties. The perplexity he evinced proceeded less from aught touching the man informed against—as Claggart doubtless opined

6. Genesis xxxvii: 11–33.

—than from considerations how best to act in regard to the informer. At first, indeed, he was naturally for summoning that substantiation of his allegations which Claggart said was at hand. But such a proceeding would result in the matter at once getting abroad, which in the present stage of it, he thought, might undesirably affect the ship's company. If Claggart was a false witness—that closed the affair. And therefore, before trying the accusation, he would first practically test the accuser; and he thought this could be done in a quiet, undemonstrative way.

The measure he determined upon involved a shifting of the scene, a transfer to a place less exposed to observation than the broad quarter-deck. For although the few gun-room officers there at the time had, in due observance of naval etiquette, withdrawn to leeward the moment Captain Vere had begun his promenade on the deck's weather side; and though during the colloquy with Claggart they of course ventured not to diminish the distance; and though throughout the interview Captain Vere's voice was far from high, and Claggart's silvery and low; and the wind in the cordage and the wash of the sea helped the more to put them beyond ear-shot; nevertheless, the interview's continuance already had attracted observation from some topmen aloft and other sailors in the waist or further forward.

Having determined upon his measures, Captain Vere forthwith took action. Abruptly turning to Claggart, he asked, "Master-at-arms, is it now Budd's watch aloft?"

"No, your honor."

Whereupon, "Mr. Wilkes!" summoning the nearest midshipman. "Tell Albert to come to me." Albert was the captain's hammock-boy, a sort of sea valet in whose discretion and fidelity his master had much confidence. The lad appeared.

"You know Budd, the foretopman?"

"I do, sir."

"Go find him. It is his watch off. Manage to tell him out of earshot that he is wanted aft. Contrive it that he speaks to nobody. Keep him in talk yourself. And not till you get well aft here, not till then let him know that the place where he is wanted is my cabin. You understand. Go.—Master-at-arms, show yourself on the decks below, and when you think it time for Albert to be coming with his man, stand by quietly to follow the sailor in."

19

Now when the foretopman found himself in the cabin, closeted there, as it were, with the captain and Claggart, he was surprised enough. But it was a surprise unaccompanied by apprehension or distrust. To an immature nature essentially honest and humane, forewarning intimations of subtler danger from one's kind come tardily if at all. The only thing that took shape in the young sailor's mind was this: Yes, the captain, I have always thought, looks kindly upon me. Wonder if he's going to make me his coxswain. I should like that. And may be now he is going to ask the master-at-arms about me.

"Shut the door there, sentry," said the commander; "stand without, and let nobody come in.—Now, Master-at-arms, tell this man to his face what you told of him to me," and stood prepared to scrutinize the mutually confronting visages.

With the measured step and calm collected air of an asylum physician approaching in the public hall some patient beginning to show indications of a coming paroxysm, Claggart deliberately advanced within short range of Billy and, mesmerically looking him in the eye, briefly recapitulated the accusation.

Not at first did Billy take it in. When he did, the rose-tan of his cheek looked struck as by white leprosy. He stood like one impaled and gagged. Meanwhile the accuser's eyes, removing not as yet from the blue dilated ones, underwent a phenomenal change, their wonted rich violet color blurring into a muddy purple. Those lights of human intelligence, losing human expression, were gelidly protruding like the alien eyes of certain uncatalogued creatures of the deep. The first mesmeristic glance was one of serpent fascination; the last was as the paralyzing lurch of the torpedo fish.

"Speak, man!" said Captain Vere to the transfixed one, struck by his aspect even more than by Claggart's. "Speak! Defend yourself!" Which appeal caused but a strange dumb gesturing and gurgling in Billy; amazement at such an accusation so suddenly sprung on inexperienced nonage; this, and, it may be, horror of the accuser's eyes, serving to bring out his lurking defect and in this instance for the time intensifying it into a convulsed tongue-tie; while the intent head and entire form straining forward in an agony of ineffectual eagerness to obey the injunction to speak and defend himself, gave an expression to the face like that of a condemned vestal priestess in the moment of being buried alive, and in the first struggle against suffocation.

Though at the time Captain Vere was quite ignorant of Billy's liability to vocal impediment, he now immediately divined it, since vividly Billy's aspect recalled to him that of a bright young schoolmate of his whom he had once seen struck by much the same startling impotence in the act of eagerly rising in the class to be foremost in response to a testing question put to it by the master. Going close up to the young sailor, and laying a soothing hand on his shoulder, he said, "There is no hurry, my boy. Take your time, take your time." Contrary to the effect intended, these words so fatherly in tone, doubtless touching Billy's heart to the quick, prompted yet more violent efforts at utterance—efforts soon ending for the time in confirming the paralysis, and bringing to his face an expression which was as a crucifixion to behold. The next instant, quick as the flame from a discharged cannon at night, his right arm shot out, and Claggart dropped to the deck. Whether intentionally or but owing to the young athlete's superior height, the blow had taken effect full upon the forehead, so shapely and intellectual-looking a feature in the master-at-arms; so that the body fell over lengthwise, like heavy plank tilted from erectness. A gasp or two, and he lay motionless.

"Fated boy," breathed Captain Vere in tone so low as to be almost a whisper, "what have you done! But here, help me."

The twain raised the felled one from the loins up into a sitting position. The spare form flexibly acquiesced, but inertly. It was like handling a dead snake. They lowered it back. Regaining erectness, Captain Vere with one hand covering his face stood to all appearance as impassive as the object at his feet. Was he absorbed in taking in all the bearings of the event and what was best not only now at once to be done, but also in the sequel? Slowly he uncovered his face; and the effect was as if the moon emerging from eclipse should reappear with quite another aspect than that which had gone into hiding. The father in him, manifested towards Billy thus far in the scene, was replaced by the military disciplinarian. In his official tone he bade the foretopman retire to a stateroom aft (pointing it out), and there remain till thence summoned. This order Billy in silence mechanically obeyed. Then going to the cabin door where it opened on the quarter-deck, Captain Vere said to the sentry without, "Tell somebody to send Albert here." When the lad appeared, his master so contrived it that he should not catch sight of the prone one. "Albert," he said to him, "tell the surgeon I wish to see him. You need not come back till called."

When the surgeon entered—a self-poised character of that grave sense and experience that hardly anything could take him aback—Captain Vere advanced to meet him, thus unconsciously intercepting his view of Claggart, and, interrupting the other's wonted ceremonious salutation, said, "Nay. Tell me how it is with yonder man," directing his attention to the prostrate one.

The surgeon looked, and for all his self-command somewhat started at the abrupt revelation. On Claggart's always pallid complexion, thick black blood was now oozing from nostril and ear. To the gazer's professional eye it was unmistakably no living man that he saw.

"Is it so, then?" said Captain Vere, intently watching him. "I thought it. But verify it." Whereupon the customary tests confirmed the surgeon's first glance, who now, looking up in unfeigned concern, cast a look of intense inquisitiveness upon his superior. But Captain Vere, with one hand to his brow, was standing motionless. Suddenly, catching the surgeon's arm convulsively, he exclaimed, pointing to the body, "It is the divine judgment on Ananias! [7] Look!"

Disturbed by the excited manner he had never before observed in the *Bellipotent*'s captain, and as yet wholly ignorant of the affair, the prudent surgeon nevertheless held his peace, only again looking an earnest interrogatory as to what it was that had resulted in such a tragedy.

But Captain Vere was now again motionless, standing absorbed in thought. Again starting, he vehemently exclaimed, "Struck dead by an angel of God! Yet the angel must hang!"

At these passionate interjections, mere incoherences to the listener as yet unapprised of the antecedents, the surgeon was profoundly discomposed. But now, as recollecting himself, Captain Vere in less passionate tone briefly related the circumstances leading up to the event. "But come; we must dispatch," he added. "Help me to remove him" (meaning the body) "to yonder compartment," designating one opposite that where the foretopman remained immured. Anew disturbed by a request that, as implying a desire for secrecy, seemed unaccountably strange to him, there was nothing for the subordinate to do but comply.

"Go now," said Captain Vere with something of his wonted manner. "Go now. I presently shall call a drumhead court. Tell the lieutenants what has happened, and tell Mr. Mordant" (meaning the captain of marines), "and charge them to keep the matter to themselves."

20

Full of disquietude and misgiving, the surgeon left the cabin. Was Captain Vere suddenly affected in his mind, or was it but a transient excitement, brought about by so strange and extraordinary a tragedy? As to the drumhead court, it struck the surgeon as impolitic, if nothing more. The thing to do, he thought, was to place Billy Budd in confinement, and in a way dictated by usage, and postpone further action in so extraordinary a case to such time as they should rejoin the squadron, and then refer it to the admiral. He recalled the unwonted agitation of Captain Vere and his excited exclamations, so at variance with his normal manner. Was he unhinged?

7. Having lied, "not * * * unto men, but unto God," Ananias was stricken dead (Acts v: 1–5).

But assuming that he is, it is not so susceptible of proof. What then can the surgeon do? No more trying situation is conceivable than that of an officer subordinate under a captain whom he suspects to be not mad, indeed, but yet not quite unaffected in his intellects. To argue his order to him would be insolence. To resist him would be mutiny.

In obedience to Captain Vere, he communicated what had happened to the lieutenants and captain of marines, saying nothing as to the captain's state. They fully shared his own surprise and concern. Like him too, they seemed to think that such a matter should be referred to the admiral.

21

Who in the rainbow can draw the line where the violet tint ends and the orange tint begins? Distinctly we see the difference of the colors, but where exactly does the one first blendingly enter into the other? So with sanity and insanity. In pronounced cases there is no question about them. But in some supposed cases, in various degrees supposedly less pronounced, to draw the exact line of demarcation few will undertake, though for a fee becoming considerate some professional experts will. There is nothing namable but that some men will, or undertake to, do it for pay.

Whether Captain Vere, as the surgeon professionally and privately surmised, was really the sudden victim of any degree of aberration, every one must determine for himself by such light as this narrative may afford.

That the unhappy event which has been narrated could not have happened at a worse juncture was but too true. For it was close on the heel of the suppressed insurrections, an aftertime very critical to naval authority, demanding from every English sea commander two qualities not readily interfusable—prudence and rigor. Moreover, there was something crucial in the case.

In the jugglery of circumstances preceeding and attending the event on board the *Bellipotent,* and in the light of that martial code whereby it was formally to be judged, innocence and guilt personified in Claggart and Budd in effect changed places. In a legal view the apparent victim of the tragedy was he who had sought to victimize a man blameless; and the indisputable deed of the latter, navally regarded, constituted the most heinous of military crimes. Yet more. The essential right and wrong involved in the matter, the clearer that might be, so much the worse for the responsibility of a loyal sea commander, inasmuch as he was not authorized to determine the matter on that primitive basis.

Small wonder then that the *Bellipotent*'s captain, though in general a man of rapid decision, felt that circumspectness not less than promptitude was necessary. Until he could decide upon his course, and in each detail; and not only so, but until the concluding measure was upon the point of being enacted, he deemed it advisable, in view of all the circumstances, to guard as much as possible against publicity. Here he may or may not have erred. Certain it is, however, that subsequently in the confidential talk of more than one or two gun rooms and cabins he was not a little criticized by some officers, a fact imputed by his friends and vehemently by his cousin Jack Denton to professional jealousy of Starry Vere. Some imaginative ground for invidious comment there was. The maintenance of secrecy in the matter, the confining all knowledge of it for a time to the place where the homicide occurred, the quarter-deck cabin; in these particulars lurked some resemblance to the policy adopted in those tragedies of the palace which have occurred more -than once in the capital founded by Peter the Barbarian.[8]

The case indeed was such that fain would the *Bellipotent's* captain have deferred taking any action whatever respecting it further than to keep the foretopman a close prisoner till the ship rejoined the squadron and then submitting the matter to the judgment of his admiral.

But a true military officer is in one particular like a true monk. Not with more of self-abnegation will the latter keep his vows of monastic obedience than the former his vows of allegiance to martial duty.

Feeling that unless quick action was taken on it, the deed of the foretopman, so soon as it should be known on the gun decks, would tend to awaken any slumbering embers of the Nore among the crew, a sense of the urgency of the case overruled in Captain Vere every other consideration. But though a conscientious disciplinarian, he was no lover of authority for mere authority's sake. Very far was he from embracing opportunities for monopolizing to himself the perils of moral responsibility, none at least that could properly be referred to an official superior or shared with him by his official equals or even subordinates. So thinking, he was glad it would not be at variance with usage to turn the matter over to a summary court of his own officers, reserving to himself, as the one on whom the ultimate accountability would rest, the right of maintaining a supervision of it, or formally or informally interposing at need. Accordingly a drumhead court was summarily convened, he electing the individuals composing it: the first lieutenant, the captain of marines, and the sailing master.

In associating an officer of marines with the sea lieutenant and the sailing master in a case having to do with a sailor, the commander perhaps deviated from general custom. He was prompted

8. Peter I, Czar of Russia (1682–1725), founded St. Petersburg (1703).

thereto by the circumstance that he took that soldier to be a judicious person, thoughtful, and not altogether incapable of grappling with a difficult case unprecedented in his prior experience. Yet even as to him he was not without some latent misgiving, for withal he was an extremely good-natured man, an enjoyer of his dinner, a sound sleeper, and inclined to obesity—a man who though he would always maintain his manhood in battle might not prove altogether reliable in a moral dilemma involving aught of the tragic. As to the first lieutenant and the sailing master, Captain Vere could not but be aware that though honest natures, of approved gallantry upon occasion, their intelligence was mostly confined to the matter of active seamanship and the fighting demands of their profession.

The court was held in the same cabin where the unfortunate affair had taken place. This cabin, the commander's, embraced the entire area under the poop deck. Aft, and on either side, was a small stateroom, the one now temporarily a jail and the other a deadhouse, and a yet smaller compartment, leaving a space between expanding forward into a goodly oblong of length coinciding with the ship's beam. A skylight of moderate dimension was overhead, and at each end of the oblong space were two sashed porthole windows easily convertible back into embrasures for short carronades.

All being quickly in readiness, Billy Budd was arraigned, Captain Vere necessarily appearing as the sole witness in the case, and as such temporarily sinking his rank, though singularly maintaining it in a matter apparently trivial, namely, that he testified from the ship's weather side, with that object having caused the court to sit on the lee side. Concisely he narrated all that had led up to the catastrophe, omitting nothing in Claggart's accusation and deposing as to the manner in which the prisoner had received it. At this testimony the three officers glanced with no little surprise at Billy Budd, the last man they would have suspected either of the mutinous design alleged by Claggart or the undeniable deed he himself had done. The first lieutenant, taking judicial primacy and turning toward the prisoner, said, "Captain Vere has spoken. Is it or is it not as Captain Vere says?"

In response came syllables not so much impeded in the utterance as might have been anticipated. They were these: "Captain Vere tells the truth. It is just as Captain Vere says, but it is not as the master-at-arms said. I have eaten the King's bread and I am true to the King."

"I believe you, my man," said the witness, his voice indicating a suppressed emotion not otherwise betrayed.

"God will bless you for that, your honor!" not without stammering said Billy, and all but broke down. But immediately he was recalled to self-control by another question, to which with the same emotional difficulty of utterance he said, "No, there was no malice between us. I never bore malice against the master-at-arms. I am sorry that he is dead. I did not mean to kill him. Could I have used my tongue I would not have struck him. But he foully lied to my face and in presence of my captain, and I had to say something, and I could only say it with a blow, God help me!"

In the impulsive aboveboard manner of the frank one the court saw confirmed all that was implied in words that just previously had perplexed them, coming as they did from the testifier to the tragedy and promptly following Billy's impassioned disclaimer of mutinous intent—Captain Vere's words, "I believe you, my man."

Next it was asked of him whether he knew of or suspected aught savoring of incipient trouble (meaning mutiny, though the explicit term was avoided) going on in any section of the ship's company.

The reply lingered. This was naturally imputed by the court to the same vocal embarrassment which had retarded or obstructed previous answers. But in main it was otherwise here, the question immediately recalling to Billy's mind the interview with the after-guardsman in the forechains. But an innate repugnance to playing a part at all approaching that of an informer against one's own ship-mates—the same erring sense of uninstructed honor which had stood in the way of his reporting the matter at the time, though as a loyal man-of-war's man it was incumbent on him, and failure so to do, if charged against him and proven, would have subjected him to the heaviest of penalties; this, with the blind feeling now his that nothing really was being hatched, prevailed with him. When the answer came it was a negative.

"One question more," said the officer of marines, now first speaking and with a troubled earnestness. "You tell us that what the master-at-arms said against you was a lie. Now why should he have so lied, so maliciously lied, since you declare there was no malice between you?"

At that question, unintentionally touching on a spiritual sphere wholly obscure to Billy's thoughts, he was nonplussed, evincing a confusion indeed that some observers, such as can readily be imagined, would have construed into involuntary evidence of hidden guilt. Nevertheless, he strove some way to answer, but all at once relinquished the vain endeavor, at the same time turning an appealing glance towards Captain Vere as deeming him his best helper and friend. Captain Vere, who had been seated for a time, rose to his feet, addressing the interrogator. "The question you put to him comes naturally enough. But how can he rightly answer it?—or anybody else, unless indeed it be he who lies within there," designating the compartment where lay the corpse. "But the prone one there will not rise to our summons. In effect, though, as it seems to me, the point you make is hardly material. Quite aside from any conceivable motive actuating the master-at-arms, and irrespective of the provocation to the blow, a martial court must needs in the present case confine its attention to the blow's consequence, which consequence justly is to be deemed not otherwise than as the striker's deed."

This utterance, the full significance of which it was not at all likely that Billy took in, nevertheless caused him to turn a wistful interrogative look toward the speaker, a look in its dumb expressiveness not unlike that which a dog of generous breed might turn upon his master, seeking in his face some elucidation of a previous gesture ambiguous to the canine intelligence. Nor was the same utterance without marked effect upon the three officers, more especially the soldier. Couched in it seemed to them a meaning unanticipated, involving a prejudgment on the speaker's part. It served to augment a mental disturbance previously evident enough.

The soldier once more spoke, in a tone of suggestive dubiety addressing at once his associates and Captain Vere: "Nobody is present—none of the ship's company, I mean—who might shed lateral light, if any is to be had, upon what remains mysterious in this matter."

"That is thoughtfully put," said Captain Vere; "I see your drift. Ay, there is a mystery; but to use a scriptural phrase, it is a 'mystery of iniquity,' a matter for psychologic theologians to discuss. But what has a military court to do with it? Not to add that for us any possible investigation of it is cut off by the lasting tongue-tie of—him—in yonder," again designating the mortuary stateroom. "The prisoner's deed—with that alone we have to do."

To this, and particularly the closing reiteration, the marine soldier, knowing not how aptly to reply, sadly abstained from saying aught. The first lieutenant, who at the outset had not unnaturally assumed primacy in the court, now overrulingly instructed by a glance from Captain Vere, a glance more effective than words, resumed that primacy. Turning to the prisoner, "Budd," he said, and scarce in equable tones, "Budd," if you have aught further to say for yourself, say it now."

Upon this the young sailor turned another quick glance toward Captain Vere; then, as taking a hint from that aspect, a hint confirming his own instinct that silence was now best, replied to the lieutenant, "I have said all, sir."

The marine—the same who had been the sentinel without the cabin door at the time that the foretopman, followed by the master-at-arms, entered it—he, standing by the sailor throughout these judicial proceedings, was now directed to take him to the after compartment originally assigned to the prisoner and his custodian.

As the twain disappeared from view, the three officers, as partially liberated from some inward constraint associated with Billy's mere presence, simultaneously stirred in their seats. They exchanged looks of troubled indecision, yet feeling that decide they must and without long delay. For Captain Vere, he for the time stood—unconsciously with his back toward them, apparently in one of his absent fits—gazing out from a sashed porthole to windward upon the monotonous blank of the twilight sea. But the court's silence continuing, broken only at moments by brief consultations, in low earnest tones, this served to arouse him and energize him. Turning, he to-and-fro paced the cabin athwart; in the returning ascent to windward climbing the slant deck in the ship's lee roll, without knowing its symbolizing thus in his action a mind resolute to surmount difficulties even if against primitive instincts strong as the wind and the sea. Presently he came to a stand before the three. After scanning their faces he stood less as mustering his thoughts for expression than as one only deliberating how best to put them to well-meaning men not intellectually mature, men with whom it was necessary to demonstrate certain principles that were axioms to himself. Similar impatience as to talking is perhaps one reason that deters some minds from addressing any popular assemblies.

When speak he did, something, both in the substance of what he said and his manner of saying it, showed the influence of unshared studies modifying and tempering the practical training of an active career. This, along with his phraseology, now and then was suggestive of the grounds whereon rested that imputation of a certain pedantry socially alleged against him by certain naval men of wholly practical cast, captains who nevertheless would frankly concede that His Majesty's navy mustered no more efficient officer of their grade than Starry Vere.

What he said was to this effect: "Hitherto I have been but the witness, little more; and I should hardly think now to take another tone, that of your coadjutor for the time, did I not perceive in you —at the crisis too—a troubled hesitancy, proceeding, I doubt not, from the clash of military duty with moral scruple—scruple vitalized by compassion. For the compassion, how can I otherwise than share it? But, mindful of paramount obligations, I strive against scruples that may tend to enervate decision. Not, gentlemen, that I hide from myself that the case is an exceptional one. Speculatively regarded, it well might be referred to a jury of casuists. But for us here, acting not as casuists or moralists, it is a case practical, and under martial law practically to be dealt with.

"But your scruples: do they move as in a dusk? Challenge them. Make them advance and declare themselves. Come now; do they import something like this: If, mindless of palliating circumstances, we are bound to regard the death of the master-at-arms as the prisoner's deed, then does that deed constitute a capital crime whereof the penalty is a mortal one. But in natural justice is nothing but the prisoner's overt act to be considered? How can we adjudge to summary and shameful death a fellow creature innocent before God, and whom we feel to be so?—Does that state it aright? You sign sad assent. Well, I too feel that, the full force of that. It is Nature. But do these buttons that we wear attest that our allegiance is to Nature? No, to the King. Though the ocean, which is inviolate Nature primeval, though this be the element where we move and have our being as sailors, yet as the King's officers lies our duty in a sphere correspondingly natural? So little is that true, that in receiving our commissions we in the most important regards ceased to be natural free agents. When war is declared are we the commissioned fighters previously consulted? We fight at command. If our judgments approve the war, that is but coincidence. So in other particulars. So now. For suppose condemnation to follow these present proceedings. Would it be so much we ourselves that would condemn as it would be martial law operating through us? For that law and the rigor of it, we are not responsible. <u>Our vowed responsibility is in this: That however pitilessly that law may operate in any instances, we nevertheless adhere to it and administer it.</u>

"But the exceptional in the matter moves the hearts within you. Even so too is mine moved. But let not warm hearts betray heads that should be cool. Ashore in a criminal case, will an upright judge allow himself off the bench to be waylaid by some tender kinswoman of the accused seeking to touch him with her tearful plea? Well, the heart here, sometimes the feminine in man, is as that piteous woman, and hard though it be, she must here be ruled out."

He paused, earnestly studying them for a moment; then resumed.

"But something in your aspect seems to urge that it is not solely the heart that moves in you, but also the conscience, the private conscience. But tell me whether or not, occupying the position we do, private conscience should not yield to that imperial one formulated in the code under which alone we officially proceed?"

Here the three men moved in their seats, less convinced than agitated by the course of an argument troubling but the more the spontaneous conflict within.

Perceiving which, the speaker paused for a moment; then abruptly changing his tone, went on.

"To steady us a bit, let us recur to the facts.—In wartime at sea a man-of-war's man strikes his superior in grade, and the blow kills. Apart from its effect the blow itself is, according to the Articles of War, a capital crime. Furthermore——"

"Ay, sir," emotionally broke in the officer of marines, "in one sense it was. But surely Budd purposed neither mutiny nor homicide."

"Surely not, my good man. And before a court less arbitrary and more merciful than a martial one, that plea would largely extenuate. At the Last Assizes [9] it shall acquit. But how here? We proceed under the law of the Mutiny Act. In feature no child can resemble his father more than that Act resembles in spirit the thing from which it derives—War. In His Majesty's service—in this ship, indeed—there are Englishmen forced to fight for the King against their will. Against their conscience, for aught we know. Though as their fellow creatures some of us may appreciate their position, yet as navy officers what reck we of it? Still less recks the enemy. Our impressed men he would fain cut down in the same swath with our volunteers. As regards the enemy's naval conscripts, some of whom may even share our own abhorrence of the regicidal French Directory,[1] it is the same on our side. War looks but to the frontage, the appearance. And the Mutiny Act, War's child, takes after the father. Budd's intent or non-intent is nothing to the purpose.

"But while, put to it by those anxieties in you which I cannot but respect, I only repeat myself—while thus strangely we prolong proceedings that should be summary—the enemy may be sighted and an engagement result. We must do; and one of two things must we do—condemn or let go."

"Can we not convict and yet mitigate the penalty?" asked the sailing master, here speaking, and falteringly, for the first.

"Gentlemen, were that clearly lawful for us under the circumstances, consider the consequences of such clemency. The people" (meaning the ship's company) "have native sense; most of them are familiar with our naval usage and tradition; and how would they take it? Even could you explain to them—which our official position forbids—they, long molded by arbitrary discipline, have not that kind of intelligent responsiveness that might qualify them to comprehend and discriminate. No, to the people the foretopman's deed, however it be worded in the announcement, will be plain homicide committed in a flagrant act of mutiny. What penalty for that should follow, they know. But it does not follow. Why? they will ruminate. You know what sailors are. Will they not revert to

9. Assizes are the highest judicial courts of review of the British counties; here the term refers to the scriptural Judgment Day.
1. The executive council of the French

First Republic (1795–1799). This was the enemy against whom the British fleet was engaged in 1797, the year of this story.

the recent outbreak at the Nore? Ay. They know the well-founded alarm—the panic it struck throughout England. Your clement sentence they would account pusillanimous. They would think that we flinch, that we are afraid of them—afraid of practicing a lawful rigor singularly demanded at this juncture, lest it should provoke new troubles. What shame to us such a conjecture on their part, and how deadly to discipline. You see then, whither, prompted by duty and the law, I steadfastly drive. But I beseech you, my friends, do not take me amiss. I feel as you do for this unfortunate boy. But did he know our hearts, I take him to be of that generous nature that he would feel even for us on whom in this military necessity so heavy a compulsion is laid."

With that, crossing the deck he resumed his place by the sashed porthole, tactly leaving the three to come to a decision. On the cabin's opposite side the troubled court sat silent. Loyal lieges, plain and practical, though at bottom they dissented from some points Captain Vere had put to them, they were without the faculty, hardly had the inclination, to gainsay one whom they felt to be an earnest man, one too not less their superior in mind than in naval rank. But it is not improbable that even such of his words as were not without influence over them, less came home to them than his closing appeal to their instinct as sea officers: in the forethought he threw out as to the practical consequences to discipline, considering the unconfirmed tone of the fleet at the time, should a man-of-war's man's violent killing at sea of a superior in grade be allowed to pass for aught else than a capital crime demanding prompt infliction of the penalty.

Not unlikely they were brought to something more or less akin to that harassed frame of mind which in the year 1842 actuated the commander of the U.S. brig-of-war *Somers* to resolve, under the so-called Articles of War, Articles modeled upon the English Mutiny Act, to resolve upon the execution at sea of a midshipman and two sailors as mutineers designing the seizure of the brig. Which resolution was carried out though in a time of peace and within not many day's sail of home. An act vindicated by a naval court of inquiry subsequently convened ashore. History, and here cited without comment. True, the circumstances on board the *Somers* were different from those on board the *Bellipotent*. But the urgency felt, well-warranted or otherwise, was much the same.

Says a writer whom few know, "Forty years after a battle it is easy for a noncombatant to reason about how it ought to have been fought. It is another thing personally and under fire to have to direct the fighting while involved in the obscuring smoke of it. Much so with respect to other emergencies involving considerations both practical and moral, and when it is imperative promptly to act. The greater the fog the more it imperils the steamer, and speed is put on though at the hazard of running somebody down. Little ween the snug card players in the cabin of the responsibilities of the sleepless man on the bridge."

In brief, Billy Budd was formally convicted and sentenced to be hung at the yardarm in the early morning watch, it being now night. Otherwise, as is customary in such cases, the sentence would forthwith have been carried out. In wartime on the field or in the fleet, a mortal punishment decreed by a drumhead court—on the field sometimes decreed by but a nod from the general—follows without delay on the heel of conviction, without appeal.

22

It was Captain Vere himself who of his own motion communicated the finding of the court to the prisoner, for that purpose going to the compartment where he was in custody and bidding the marine there to withdraw for the time.

Beyond the communication of the sentence, what took place at this interview was never known. But in view of the character of the twain briefly closeted in that stateroom, each radically sharing in the rarer qualities of our nature—so rare indeed as to be all but incredible to average minds however much cultivated—some conjectures may be ventured.

It would have been in consonance with the spirit of Captain Vere should he on this occasion have concealed nothing from the condemned one—should he indeed have frankly disclosed to him the part he himself had played in bringing about the decision, at the same time revealing his actuating motives. On Billy's side it is not improbable that such a confession would have been received in much the same spirit that prompted it. Not without a sort of joy, indeed, he might have appreciated the brave opinion of him implied in his captain's making such a confidant of him. Nor, as to the sentence itself, could he have been insensible that it was imparted to him as to one not afraid to die. Even more may have been. Captain Vere in end may have developed the passion sometimes latent under an exterior stoical or indifferent. He was old enough to have been Billy's father. The austere devotee of military duty, letting himself melt back into what remains primeval in our formalized humanity, may in end have caught Billy to his heart, even as Abraham may have caught young Isaac on the brink of resolutely offering him up in obedience to the exacting behest.[2] But there is no telling the sacrament, seldom if in any case revealed to the gadding world, wherever under circumstances at all akin to those here attempted to be set forth two of great Nature's nobler order embrace. There is

2. *Cf.* Genesis xxii: 1–14.

privacy at the time, inviolable to the survivor; and holy oblivion, the sequel to each diviner magnanimity, providentially covers all at last.

The first to encounter Captain Vere in act of leaving the compartment was the senior lieutenant. The face he beheld, for the moment one expressive of the agony of the strong, was to that officer, though a man of fifty, a startling revelation. That the condemned one suffered less than he who mainly had effected the condemnation was apparently indicated by the former's exclamation in the scene soon perforce to be touched upon.

23

Of a series of incidents within a brief term rapidly following each other, the adequate narration may take up a term less brief, especially if explanation or comment here and there seem requisite to the better understanding of such incidents. Between the entrance into the cabin of him who never left it alive, and him who when he did leave it left it as one condemned to die; between this and the closeted interview just given, less than an hour and a half had elapsed. It was an interval long enough, however, to awaken speculations among no few of the ship's company as to what it was that could be detaining in the cabin the master-at-arms and the sailor; for a rumor that both of them had been seen to enter it and neither of them had been seen to emerge, this rumor had got abroad upon the gun decks and in the tops, the people of a great warship being in one respect like villagers, taking microscopic note of every outward movement or non-movement going on. When therefore, in weather not at all tempestuous, all hands were called in the second dogwatch, a summons under such circumstances not usual in those hours, the crew were not wholly unprepared for some announcement extraordinary, one having connection too with the continued absence of the two men from their wonted haunts.

There was a moderate sea at the time; and the moon, newly risen and near to being at its full, silvered the white spar deck wherever not blotted by the clear-cut shadows horizontally thrown of fixtures and moving men. On either side the quarterdeck the marine guard under arms was drawn up; and Captain Vere, standing in his place surrounded by all the wardroom officers, addressed his men. In so doing, his manner showed neither more nor less than that properly pertaining to his supreme position aboard his own ship. In clear terms and concise he told them what had taken place in the cabin: that the master-at-arms was dead, that he who had killed him had been already tried by a summary court and condemned to death, and that the execution would take place in the early morning watch. The word *mutiny* was not named in what he said. He refrained too from making the occasion an opportunity for any preachment as to the maintenance of discipline, thinking perhaps that under existing circumstances in the navy the consequence of violating discipline should be made to speak for itself.

Their captain's announcement was listened to by the throng of standing sailors in a dumbness like that of a seated congregation of believers in hell listening to the clergyman's announcement of his Calvinistic text.

At the close, however, a confused murmur went up. It began to wax. All but instantly, then, at a sign, it was pierced and suppressed by shrill whistles of the boatswain and his mates. The word was given to about ship.

To be prepared for burial Claggart's body was delivered to certain petty officers of his mess. And here, not to clog the sequel with lateral matters, it may be added that at a suitable hour, the master-at-arms was committed to the sea with every funeral honor properly belonging to his naval grade.

In this proceeding as in every public one growing out of the tragedy strict adherence to usage was observed. Nor in any point could it have been at all deviated from, either with respect to Claggart or Billy Budd, without begetting undesirable speculations in the ship's company, sailors, and more particularly men-of-war's men, being of all men the greatest sticklers for usage. For similar cause, all communication between Captain Vere and the condemned one ended with the closeted interview already given, the latter being now surrendered to the ordinary routine preliminary to the end. His transfer under guard from the captain's quarters was effected without unusual precautions—at least no visible ones. If possible, not to let the men so much as surmise that their officers anticipate aught amiss from them is the tacit rule in a military ship. And the more that some sort of trouble should really be apprehended, the more do the officers keep that apprehension to themselves, though not the less unostentatious vigilance may be augmented. In the present instance, the sentry placed over the prisoner had strict orders to let no one have communication with him but the chaplain. And certain unobtrusive measures were taken absolutely to insure this point.

24

In a seventy-four of the old order the deck known as the upper gun deck was the one covered over by the spar deck, which last, though not without its armament, was for the most part exposed to the weather. In general it was at all hours free from hammocks; those of the crew swinging on the lower gun deck and berth deck, the latter being not only a dormitory but also the place for the stowing of the sailors' bags, and on both sides lined with the large chests or movable pantries of the many messes of the men.

On the starboard side of the *Bellipotent's* upper gun deck, be-hold Billy Budd under sentry lying prone in irons in one of the bays formed by the regular spacing of the guns comprising the batteries on either side. All these pieces were of the heavier caliber of that period. Mounted on lumbering wooden carriages, they were hampered with cumbersome harness of breeching and strong side-tackles for running them out. Guns and carriages, together with the long rammers and shorter linstocks lodged in loops overhead—all these, as customary, were painted black; and the heavy hempen breechings, tarred to the same tint, wore the like livery of the un-dertakers. In contrast with the funereal hue of these surroundings, the prone sailor's exterior apparel, white jumper and white duck trousers, each more or less soiled, dimly glimmered in the obscure light of the bay like a patch of discolored snow in early April lin-gering at some upland cave's black mouth. In effect he is already in his shroud, or the garments that shall serve him in lieu of one. Over him but scarce illuminating him, two battle lanterns swing from two massive beams of the deck above. Fed with the oil sup-plied by the war contractors (whose gains, honest or otherwise, are in every land an anticipated portion of the harvest of death), with flickering splashes of dirty yellow light they pollute the pale moon-shine all but ineffectually struggling in obstructed flecks through the open ports from which the tampioned [3] cannon protrude. Other lanterns at intervals serve but to bring out somewhat the obscurer bays which, like small confessionals or side-chapels in a cathedral, branch from the long dim-vistaed broad aisle between the two bat-teries of that covered tier.

Such was the deck where now lay the Handsome Sailor. Through the rose-tan of his complexion no pallor could have shown. It would have taken days of sequestration from the winds and the sun to have brought about the effacement of that. But the skeleton in the cheekbone at the point of its angle was just beginning delicately to be defined under the warm-tinted skin. In fervid hearts self-con-tained, some brief experiences devour our human tissue as secret fire in a ship's hold consumes cotton in the bale.

But now lying between the two guns, as nipped in the vice of fate, Billy's agony, mainly proceeding from a generous young heart's virgin experience of the diabolical incarnate and effective in some men—the tension of that agony was over now. It survived not the something healing in the closeted interview with Captain Vere. Without movement, he lay as in a trance, that adolescent expres-sion previously noted as his taking on something akin to the look of a slumbering child in the cradle when the warm hearth-glow of the still chamber at night plays on the dimples that at whiles mys-

3. Plugged with a tampion, as the muzzle of a gun.

teriously form in the cheek, silently coming and going there. For now and then in the gyved one's trance a serene happy light born of some wandering reminiscence or dream would diffuse itself over his face, and then wane away only anew to return.

The chaplain, coming to see him and finding him thus, and perceiving no sign that he was conscious of his presence, attentively regarded him for a space, then slipping aside, withdrew for the time, peradventure feeling that even he, the minister of Christ though receiving his stipend from Mars, had no consolation to proffer which could result in a peace transcending that which he beheld. But in the small hours he came again. And the prisoner, now awake to his surroundings, noticed his approach, and civilly, all but cheerfully, welcomed him. But it was to little purpose that in the interview following, the good man sought to bring Billy Budd to some godly understanding that he must die, and at dawn. True, Billy himself freely referred to his death as a thing close at hand; but it was something in the way that children will refer to death in general, who yet among their other sports will play a funeral with hearse and mourners.

Not that like children Billy was incapable of conceiving what death really is. No, but he was wholly without irrational fear of it, a fear more prevalent in highly civilized communities than those so-called barbarous ones which in all respects stand nearer to unadulterate Nature. And, as elsewhere said, a barbarian Billy radically was—as much so, for all the costume, as his countrymen the British captives, living trophies, made to march in the Roman triumph of Germanicus.[4] Quite as much so as those later barbarians, young men probably, and picked specimens among the earlier British converts to Christianity, at least nominally such, taken to Rome (as today converts from lesser isles of the sea may be taken to London), of whom the Pope of that time, admiring the strangeness of their personal beauty so unlike the Italian stamp, their clear ruddy complexion and curled flaxen locks, exclaimed, "Angles" (meaning *English*, the modern derivative), "Angles, do you call them? And is it because they look so like angels?" Had it been later in time, one would think that the Pope had in mind Fra Angelico's [5] seraphs, some of whom, plucking apples in gardens of the Hesperides, have the faint rosebud complexion of the more beautiful English girls.

If in vain the good chaplain sought to impress the young barbarian with ideas of death akin to those conveyed in the skull, dial,

4. Germanicus Caesar (15 B.C.–A.D. 19), Roman general and conqueror, whose triumphs were spectacularly celebrated in Rome in A.D. 17.
5. Italian friar-painter of the fifteenth century, famous for his religious frescoes. The Hesperides, in classical myth, were fabulous gardens where grew golden apples, guarded by a dragon.

and crossbones on old tombstones, equally futile to all appearance were his efforts to bring home to him the thought of salvation and a Savior. Billy listened, but less out of awe or reverence, perhaps, than from a certain natural politeness, doubtless at bottom regarding all that in much the same way that most mariners of his class take any discourse abstract or out of the common tone of the workaday world. And this sailor way of taking clerical discourse is not wholly unlike the way in which the primer of Christianity, full of transcendent miracles, was received long ago on tropic isles by any superior *savage*, so called—a Tahitian, say of Captain Cook's time or shortly after that time.[6] Out of natural courtesy he received, but did not appropriate. It was like a gift placed in the palm of an outreached hand upon which the fingers do not close.

But the *Bellipotent*'s chaplain was a discreet man possessing the good sense of a good heart. So he insisted not in his vocation here. At the instance of Captain Vere, a lieutenant had apprised him of pretty much everything as to Billy; and since he felt that innocence was even a better thing than religion wherewith to go to Judgment, he reluctantly withdrew; but in his emotion not without first performing an act strange enough in an Englishman, and under the circumstances yet more so in any regular priest. Stooping over, he kissed on the fair cheek his fellow man, a felon in martial law, one whom though on the confines of death he felt he could never convert to a dogma; nor for all that did he fear for his future.

Marvel not that having been made acquainted with the young sailor's essential innocence the worthy man lifted not a finger to avert the doom of such a martyr to martial discipline. So to do would not only have been as idle as invoking the desert, but would also have been an audacious transgression of the bounds of his function, one as exactly prescribed to him by military law as that of the boatswain or any other naval officer. Bluntly put, a chaplain is the minister of the Prince of Peace serving in the host of the God of War—Mars. As such, he is as incongruous as a musket would be on the altar at Christmas. Why, then, is he there? Because he indirectly subserves the purpose attested by the cannon; because too he lends the sanction of the religion of the meek to that which practically is the abrogation of everything but brute Force.

25

The night so luminous on the spar deck, but otherwise on the cavernous ones below, levels so like the tiered galleries in a coal

---

6. Captain James Cook (1728–1779), British explorer, made remarkable discoveries in the Pacific, visiting the Marquesas Islands and Tahiti, where Melville adventured in 1842.

mine—the luminous night passed away. But like the prophet in the chariot disappearing in heaven and dropping his mantle to Elisha, the withdrawing night transferred its pale robe to the breaking day. A meek, shy light appeared in the East, where stretched a diaphanous fleece of white furrowed vapor. That light slowly waxed. Suddenly *eight bells* was struck aft, responded to by one louder metallic stroke from forward. It was four o'clock in the morning. Instantly the silver whistles were heard summoning all hands to witness punishment. Up through the great hatchways rimmed with racks of heavy shot the watch below came pouring, overspreading with the watch already on deck the space between the mainmast and foremast including that occupied by the capacious launch and the black booms tiered on either side of it, boat and booms making a summit of observation for the powder-boys and younger tars. A different group comprising one watch of topmen leaned over the rail of that sea balcony, no small one in a seventy-four, looking down on the crowd below. Man or boy, none spake but in whisper, and few spake at all. Captain Vere—as before, the central figure among the assembled commissioned officers—stood nigh the break of the poop deck facing forward. Just below him on the quarter-deck the marines in full equipment were drawn up much as at the scene of the promulgated sentence.

At sea in the old time, the execution by halter of a military sailor was generally from the foreyard. In the present instance, for special reasons the mainyard was assigned. Under an arm of that yard the prisoner was presently brought up, the chaplain attending him. It was noted at the time, and remarked upon afterwards, that in this final scene the good man evinced little or nothing of the perfunctory. Brief speech indeed he had with the condemned one, but the genuine Gospel was less on his tongue than in his aspect and manner towards him. The final preparations personal to the latter being speedily brought to an end by two boatswain's mates, the consummation impended. Billy stood facing aft. At the penultimate moment, his words, his only ones, words wholly unobstructed in the utterance, were these: "God bless Captain Vere!" Syllables so unanticipated coming from one with the ignominious hemp about his neck—a conventional felon's benediction directed aft towards the quarters of honor; syllables too delivered in the clear melody of a singing bird on the point of launching from the twig—had a phenomenal effect, not unenhanced by the rare personal beauty of the young sailor, spiritualized now through late experiences so poignantly profound.

Without volition, as it were, as if indeed the ship's populace were but the vehicles of some vocal current electric, with one voice from alow and aloft came a resonant sympathetic echo: "God bless Captain Vere!" And yet at that instant Billy alone must have been in their hearts, even as in their eyes.

At the pronounced words and the spontaneous echo that voluminously rebounded them, Captain Vere, either through stoic self-control or a sort of momentary paralysis induced by emotional shock, stood erectly rigid as a musket in the ship-armorer's rack.

The hull, deliberately recovering from the periodic roll to leeward, was just regaining an even keel when the last signal, a preconcerted dumb one, was given. At the same moment it chanced that the vapory fleece hanging low in the East was shot through with a soft glory as of the fleece of the Lamb of God seen in mystical vision, and simultaneously therewith, watched by the wedged mass of up-turned faces, Billy ascended; and, ascending, took the full rose of the dawn.

In the pinioned figure arrived at the yard-end, to the wonder of all no motion was apparent, none save that created by the slow roll of the hull in moderate weather, so majestic in a great ship ponderously cannoned.

26

When some days afterwards, in reference to the singularity just mentioned, the purser, a rather ruddy, rotund person more accurate as an accountant than profound as a philosopher, said at mess to the surgeon, "What testimony to the force lodged in will power," the latter, saturnine, spare, and tall, one in whom a discreet causticity went along with a manner less genial than polite, replied, "Your pardon, Mr. Purser. In a hanging scientifically conducted—and under special orders I myself directed how Budd's was to be effected —any movement following the completed suspension and originating in the body suspended, such movement indicates mechanical spasm in the muscular system. Hence the absence of that is no more attributable to will power, as you call it, than to horsepower— begging your pardon."

"But this muscular spasm you speak of, is not that in a degree more or less invariable in these cases?"

"Assuredly so, Mr. Purser."

"How then, my good sir, do you account for its absence in this instance?"

"Mr. Purser, it is clear that your sense of the singularity in this matter equals not mine. You account for it by what you call will power—a term not yet included in the lexicon of science. For me, I do not, with my present knowledge, pretend to account for it at all. Even should we assume the hypothesis that at the first touch of the halyards the action of Budd's heart, intensified by extraordinary emotion at its climax, abruptly stopped—much like a watch when in carelessly winding it up you strain at the finish, thus snapping the chain—even under that hypothesis how account for the phenomenon that followed?"

"You admit, then, that the absence of spasmodic movement was phenomenal."

"It was phenomenal, Mr. Purser, in the sense that it was an appearance the cause of which is not immediately to be assigned."

"But tell me, my dear sir," pertinaciously continued the other, "was the man's death effected by the halter, or was it a species of euthanasia?"

"*Euthanasia*, Mr. Purser, is something like your *will power:* I doubt its authenticity as a scientific term—begging your pardon again. It is at once imaginative and metaphysical—in short, Greek. —But," abruptly changing his tone, "there is a case in the sick bay that I do not care to leave to my assistants. Beg your pardon, but excuse me." And rising from the mess he formally withdrew.

27

The silence at the moment of execution and for a moment or two continuing thereafter, a silence but emphasized by the regular wash of the sea against the hull or the flutter of a sail caused by the helmsman's eyes being tempted astray, this emphasized silence was gradually disturbed by a sound not easily to be verbally rendered. Whoever has heard the freshet-wave of a torrent suddenly swelled by pouring showers in tropical mountains, showers not shared by the plain; whoever has heard the first muffled murmur of its sloping advance through precipitous woods may form some conception of the sound now heard. The seeming remoteness of its source was because of its murmurous indistinctness, since it came from close by, even from the men massed on the ship's open deck. Being inarticulate, it was dubious in significance further than it seemed to indicate some capricious revulsion of thought or feeling such as mobs ashore are liable to, in the present instance possibly implying a sullen revocation on the men's part of their involuntary echoing of Billy's benediction. But ere the murmur had time to wax into clamor it was met by a strategic command, the more telling that it came with abrupt unexpectedness: "Pipe down the starboard watch, Boatswain, and see that they go."

Shrill as the shriek of the sea hawk, the silver whistles of the boatswain and his mates pierced that ominous low sound, dissipating it; and yielding to the mechanism of discipline the throng was thinned by one-half. For the remainder, most of them were set to temporary employments connected with trimming the yards and so forth, business readily to be got up to serve occasion by any officer of the deck.

Now each proceeding that follows a mortal sentence pronounced at sea by a drumhead court is characterized by promptitude not perceptibly merging into hurry, though bordering that. The hammock, the one which had been Billy's bed when alive, having already been ballasted with shot and otherwise prepared to serve for his canvas coffin, the last offices of the sea undertakers, the sailmaker's mates, were now speedily completed. When everything was in readiness a second call for all hands, made necessary by the strategic movement before mentioned, was sounded, now to witness burial.

The details of this closing formality it needs not to give. But when the tilted plank let slide its freight into the sea, a second strange human murmur was heard, blended now with another inarticulate sound proceeding from certain larger seafowl who, their attention having been attracted by the peculiar commotion in the water resulting from the heavy sloped dive of the shotted hammock into the sea, flew screaming to the spot. So near the hull did they come, that the stridor or bony creak of their gaunt double-jointed pinions was audible. As the ship under light airs passed on, leaving the burial spot astern, they still kept circling it low down with the moving shadow of their outstretched wings and the croaked requiem of their cries.

Upon sailors as superstitious as those of the age preceding ours, men-of-war's men too who had just beheld the prodigy of repose in the form suspended in air, and now foundering in the deeps; to such mariners the action of the seafowl, though dictated by mere animal greed for prey, was big with no prosaic significance. An uncertain movement began among them, in which some encroachment was made. It was tolerated but for a moment. For suddenly the drum beat to quarters, which familiar sound happening at least twice every day, had upon the present occasion a signal peremptoriness in it. True martial discipline long continued superinduces in average man a sort of impulse whose operation at the official word of command much resembles in its promptitude the effect of an instinct.

The drumbeat dissolved the multitude, distributing most of them along the batteries of the two covered gun decks. There, as wonted, the guns' crews stood by their respective cannon erect and silent. In due course the first officer, sword under arm and standing in his place on the quarter-deck, formally received the successive reports of the sworded lieutenants commanding the sections of batteries below; the last of which reports being made, the summed report he delivered with the customary salute to the commander. All this occupied time, which in the present case was the object in beating to quarters at an hour prior to the customary one. That such variance from usage was authorized by an officer like Captain Vere, a martinet as some deemed him, was evidence of the necessity for unusual action implied in what he deemed to be temporarily the mood of his men. "With mankind," he would say, "forms, measured forms, are everything; and that is the import couched in the story of Orpheus with his lyre spellbinding the wild denizens of the wood." And this he once applied to the disruption of forms going on across the Channel and the consequences thereof.

At this unwonted muster at quarters, all proceeded as at the regular hour. The band on the quarter-deck played a sacred air, after which the chaplain went through the customary morning service. That done, the drum beat the retreat; and toned by music and religious rites subserving the discipline and purposes of war, the men in their wonted orderly manner dispersed to the places allotted them when not at the guns.

And now it was full day. The fleece of low-hanging vapor had vanished, licked up by the sun that late had so glorified it. And the circumambient air in the clearness of its serenity was like smooth white marble in the polished block not yet removed from the marble-dealer's yard.

28

The symmetry of form attainable in pure fiction cannot so readily be achieved in a narration essentially having less to do with fable than with fact. Truth uncompromisingly told will always have its ragged edges; hence the conclusion of such a narration is apt to be less finished than an architectural finial.

How it fared with the Handsome Sailor during the year of the Great Mutiny has been faithfully given. But though properly the story ends with his life, something in way of sequel will not be amiss. Three brief chapters will suffice.

In the general rechristening under the Directory of the craft originally forming the navy of the French monarchy, the *St. Louis* line-of-battle ship was named the *Athée* (the *Atheist*). Such a name, like some other substituted ones in the Revolutionary fleet, while proclaiming the infidel audacity of the ruling power, was yet, though not so intended to be, the aptest name, if one consider it, ever given to a warship; far more so indeed than the *Devastation*, the *Erebus* (the *Hell*), and similar names bestowed upon fighting ships.

On the return passage to the English fleet from the detached cruise during which occurred the events already recorded, the *Bellipotent* fell in with the *Athée*. An engagement ensued, during which Captain Vere, in the act of putting his ship alongside the enemy with a view of throwing his boarders across her bulwarks, was hit by a musket ball from a porthole of the enemy's main cabin. More than disabled, he dropped to the deck and was carried below to the same cockpit where some of his men already lay. The senior lieutenant took command. Under him the enemy was finally captured, and though much crippled was by rare good fortune successfully taken into Gibraltar, an English port not very distant from the scene of the fight. There, Captain Vere with the rest of the wounded was put ashore. He lingered for some days, but the end came. Unhappily he was cut off too early for the Nile and Trafalgar.[7] The spirit that 'spite its philosophic austerity may yet have indulged in the most secret of all passions, ambition, never attained to the fulness of fame.

Not long before death, while lying under the influence of that magical drug which, soothing the physical frame, mysteriously operates on the subtler element in man, he was heard to murmur words inexplicable to his attendant: "Billy Budd, Billy Budd." That these were not the accents of remorse would seem clear from what the attendant said to the *Bellipotent*'s senior officer of marines, who, as the most reluctant to condemn of the members of the drumhead court, too well knew, though here he kept the knowledge to himself, who Billy Budd was.

29

Some few weeks after the execution, among other matters under the head of "News from the Mediterranean," there appeared in a naval chronicle of the time, an authorized weekly publication, an account of the affair. It was doubtless for the most part written in good faith, though the medium, partly rumor, through which the facts must have reached the writer served to deflect and in part falsify them. The account was as follows:

"On the tenth of the last month a deplorable occurrence took place on board H.M.S. *Bellipotent*. John Claggart, the ship's master-at-arms, discovering that some sort of plot was incipient among an inferior section of the ship's company, and that the ringleader was one William Budd; he, Claggart, in the act of arraigning the man before the captain, was vindictively stabbed to the heart by the suddenly drawn sheath knife of Budd.

"The deed and the implement employed sufficiently suggest that though mustered into the service under an English name the assassin was no Englishman, but one of those aliens adopting Eng-

---

7. Admiral Nelson destroyed Napoleon's fleet at the Battle of the Nile (1798); at Trafalgar in 1805 he ended the French naval wars with victory and was himself killed.

lish cognomens whom the present extraordinary necessities of the service have caused to be admitted into it in considerable numbers.

"The enormity of the crime and the extreme depravity of the criminal appear the greater in view of the character of the victim, a middle-aged man respectable and discreet, belonging to that minor official grade, the petty officers, upon whom, as none know better than the commissioned gentlemen, the efficiency of His Majesty's navy so largely depends. His function was a responsible one, at once onerous and thankless; and his fidelity in it the greater because of his strong patriotic impulse. In this instance as in so many other instances in these days, the character of this unfortunate man signally refutes, if refutation were needed, that peevish saying attributed to the late Dr. Johnson, that patriotism is the last refuge of a scoundrel.

"The criminal paid the penalty of his crime. The promptitude of the punishment has proved salutary. Nothing amiss is now apprehended aboard H.M.S. *Bellipotent.*"

The above, appearing in a publication now long ago superannuated and forgotten, is all that hitherto has stood in human record to attest what manner of men respectively were John Claggart and Billy Budd.

30

Everything is for a term venerated in navies. Any tangible object associated with some striking incident of the service is converted into a monument. The spar from which the foretopman was suspended was for some few years kept trace of by the bluejackets. Their knowledges followed it from ship to dockyard and again from dockyard to ship, still pursuing it even when at last reduced to a mere dockyard boom. To them a chip of it was as a piece of the Cross. Ignorant though they were of the secret facts of the tragedy, and not thinking but that the penalty was somehow unavoidably inflicted from the naval point of view, for all that, they instinctively felt that Billy was a sort of man as incapable of mutiny as of wilful murder. They recalled the fresh young image of the Handsome Sailor, that face never deformed by a sneer or subtler vile freak of the heart within. This impression of him was doubtless deepened by the fact that he was gone, and in a measure mysteriously gone. On the gun decks of the *Bellipotent* the general estimate of his nature and its unconscious simplicity eventually found rude utterance from another foretopman, one of his own watch, gifted, as some sailors are, with an artless *poetic* temperament. The tarry hand made some lines which, after circulating among the shipboard crews for a while, finally got rudely printed at Portsmouth as a ballad. The title given to it was the sailor's.

Billy in the Darbies [8]

Good of the chaplain to enter Lone Bay
And down on his marrowbones here and pray
For the likes just o' me, Billy Budd.—But, look:
Through the port comes the moonshine astray!
It tips the guard's cutlass and silvers this nook;
But 'twill die in the dawning of Billy's last day.
A jewel-block they'll make of me tomorrow,
Pendant pearl from the yardarm-end
Like the eardrop I gave to Bristol Molly—
O, 'tis me, not the sentence they'll suspend.
Ay, ay, all is up; and I must up too,
Early in the morning, aloft from alow.
On an empty stomach now never it would do.
They'll give me a nibble—bit o' biscuit ere I go.
Sure, a messmate will reach me the last parting cup;
But, turning heads away from the hoist and the belay,
Heaven knows who will have the running of me up!
No pipe to those halyards.—But aren't it all sham?
A blur's in my eyes; it is dreaming that I am.
A hatchet to my hawser? All adrift to go?
The drum roll to grog, and Billy never know?
But Donald he has promised to stand by the plank;
So I'll shake a friendly hand ere I sink.
But—no! It is dead then I'll be, come to think.
I remember Taff the Welshman when he sank.
And his cheek it was like the budding pink.
But me they'll lash in hammock, drop me deep.
Fathoms down, fathoms down, how I'll dream fast asleep.
I feel it stealing now. Sentry, are you there?
Just ease these darbies at the wrist,
And roll me over fair!
I am sleepy, and the oozy weeds about me twist.

1886–1891   1924, 1948, 1962

8. Manacles or irons.

Transcendental Idealism

RALPH WALDO EMERSON
(1803–1882)

The durability of Emerson for the general reader is one measure of his genius. Now, a century and a half after his birth, the forum and the market place echo his words and ideas. As Ralph L. Rusk has suggested, this is partly because "he is wise man, wit, and poet, all three," and partly because his speculations proved prophetic, having as firm a practical relationship with the conditions of our present age as with the history of mankind before him. "His insatiable passion for unity resembles Einstein's" as much as Plato's; and this passion unites serenity and practicality, God and science, in a manner highly suggestive for those attempting to solve the twentieth-century dilemmas which have seemed most desperately urgent.

Emerson was born to the clerical tradition; his father was pastor of the First Unitarian Church of Boston, and successor to a line of nonconformist and Puritan clergymen. William Emerson died in 1811, when the boy was eight, leaving his widow to face poverty and to educate their five sons. At Boston Latin School, at the Latin school in Concord,

and at Harvard College (where from 1817 to 1821 he enjoyed a "scholarship" in return for services) young Emerson kindled no fires. His slow growth is recorded in his journal for the next eight years. He assisted at his brother William's Boston "School for Young Ladies" (1821–1825), conducting the enterprise alone the last year. In 1825 he entered Harvard Divinity School; in spite of an interval of illness, he was by 1829 associated with the powerful Henry Ware in the pulpit of the Second Unitarian Church of Boston. That year he married Ellen Tucker, whose death, less than two years later, acutely grieved him throughout his life.

In 1832, in the first flush of a genuine success in the pulpit, he resigned from the ministry. At the time, he told his congregation he could no longer find inherent grace in the observation of the Lord's Supper, and later he said that his ideas of self-reliance and the general divinity of man caused him to conclude that "in order to be a good minister it was necessary to leave the ministry." His decision was not the result of hasty judgment. These ideas (as

Rusk shows in his excellent *Life of Ralph Waldo Emerson*) had long been available to him in his study of such nonconformists as Fénelon, George Fox, Luther, and Carlyle. They were later made explicit also in his poem "The Problem," printed among the selections in this volume. Six years after his resignation from the ministry, in his "Divinity School Address" (1838), he clarified his position and made permanent his breach with the church. The transcendental law, Emerson believed, was the "moral law," through which man discovers the nature of God, a living spirit; yet it had been the practice of historical Christianity— "as if God were dead"—to formalize Him and to fundamentalize religion through fixed conventions of dogma and scripture. The true nature of life was energetic and fluid; its transcendental unity resulted from the convergence of all forces upon the energetic truth, the heart of the moral law.

Meanwhile, his personal affairs had taken shape again. After resigning his pulpit, he traveled (1832–1833) in France, Italy, and Great Britain, meeting such writers as Landor, Coleridge, Wordsworth, and Carlyle. All of these had been somewhat influenced by the idealism of recent German philosophy, but Carlyle alone was his contemporary, and the two became lasting friends. In 1833, Emerson launched himself upon the career of public lecturer, which thereafter gave him his modest livelihood, made him a familiar figure in many parts of the country, and supported one of his three trips abroad. In 1835,

he made a second marriage, notably successful, and soon settled in his own house, near the ancestral Old Manse in Concord, where his four children were born. The first-born, Waldo (1836), mitigated Emerson's loss of two younger and much-loved brothers in the two previous years; but Waldo, too, died in his sixth year, in the chain of bereavements that Emerson suffered.

The informal Transcendental Club began to meet at the Manse in 1836, including in its association a number of prominent writers of Boston, and others of Concord, such as Bronson Alcott and later, Thoreau, whom Emerson took for a time into his household. Margaret Fuller was selected as first editor of *The Dial*, their famous little magazine, and Emerson succeeded her for two years (1842–1844). He could not personally bring himself to join their co-operative Brook Farm community, although he supported its theory.

After 1850 he gave much of his thought to national politics, social reforms, and the growing contest over slavery. By this time, however, the bulk of his important work had been published, much of the prose resulting from lectures, sometimes rewritten or consolidated in larger forms. *Nature* (1836), his first book, was followed by his first *Essays*, (1841), *Essays: Second Series* (1844), and *Poems* (1847). Emerson wrote and published his poems sporadically, as though they were by-products, but actually they contain the core of his philosophy, which is essentially lyrical, and they are often its best expression. The criticism of the day neglected them, or disparaged them for their alleged formal irregularity in an age of metrical conformity. Today they are read in the light of rhythmic principles recovered by Whitman, whom Emerson first defended almost singlehanded; and their greatness is now evident to a generation newly awakened to the symbolism of ideas which is present in the long tradition from John Donne to T. S. Eliot. Emerson authorized a second volume, *May-Day and Other Poems*, in 1867 and a finally revised *Selected Poems* in 1876.

In 1845, Emerson gave the series of lectures published in 1850 as *Representative Men*. He took this series to England in 1847, and visited Paris again before returning to Concord. His later major works include the remarkable *Journals* and *Letters*, published after his death, the compilation, *Nature, Addresses, and Lectures* (1849), and the provocative essays of *English Traits* (1856) and *The Conduct of Life* (1860).

In 1871 there were evidences that the lofty intellect, now internationally recognized, was beginning to fail. In 1872 his house in Concord was damaged by fire and friends raised a fund to send him abroad and to repair the damage in his absence, but the trip was not sufficient to stem the failing tide of health and memory. He recovered his energies sporadically until 1877, and died in 1882.

It is a familiar truism that Emerson was not an original philosopher, and he fully recognized the fact. "I am too young yet by several ages," he wrote, "to compile a code." Yet confronted by his transcendent vision of the unity of life in the metaphysical Absolute, he declared, "I wish to know the laws of this wonderful power, that I may domesticate it." That he succeeded so well in this mission is the evidence of his true originality and his value for following generations of Americans. In the American soil, and in the common sense of his own mind, he "domesticated" the richest experience of many lands and cultures; he is indeed the "transparent eyeball" through which much of the best light of the ages is brought to a focus of usefulness for the present day.

The Complete Works, 12 vols., Centenary Edition, was published 1903–1904; see also *Uncollected Writings* * * * , edited by C. C. Bigelow, 1912; *The Journals of Ralph Waldo Emerson*, 10 vols., edited by E. W. Emerson and W. E. Forbes, 1909–1914; *The Heart of Emerson's Journals*, edited by Bliss Perry, 1926, 1959; *Uncollected Lectures*, edited by C. F. Gohdes, 1933; *Young Emerson Speaks* * * * , sermons, edited by A. C. McGiffert, 1938; *The Letters of Ralph Waldo Emerson*, 6 vols., edited by R. L. Rusk, 1939. Definitive editions are in progress. In print are *Ralph Waldo Emerson: Early Lectures*, edited by S. E. Whicher and R. E. Spiller, 1959; Vol. II, R. E. Spiller, 1964; Vol. III, R. E. Spiller and W. E. Williams, 1972; *Journals and Miscellaneous Notebooks*, edited by W. H. Gilman and others, 1961—; *The Collected Works* * * * , Vol. I, *Nature, Addresses, and Lectures*, R. E. Spiller and A. R. Ferguson, 1972 (a CEAA edition). One-volume selections are *The Complete Essays and Other Writings* * * * , edited by Brooks Atkinson, 1940; *Ralph Waldo Emerson: Representative Selections*, edited, with a good introduction, by F. J. Carpenter, 1934.

The definitive biography is R. L. Rusk, *The Life of Ralph Waldo Emerson*, 1949. See also G. W. Cooke, *Ralph Waldo Emerson* * * * , 1881; J. E. Cabot, *A Memoir of Ralph Waldo Emerson*, 2 vols., 1887; G. E. Woodbury, *Ralph Waldo Emerson*, 1907. Other special studies are V. C. Hopkins,

Spires of Form, 1951; S. Paul, *Emerson's Angle of Vision*, 1952; S. E. Whicher, *Freedom and Fate*, 1953; and F. J. Carpenter, *Emerson Handbook*, 1953.

The Transcendentalists: An Anthology, compiled by Perry Miller, 1950, is the best introduction to American transcendentalism as a whole and to its literature.

The texts of Emerson below are *Es-* *says: Second Series*, 1844; *Nature, Addresses, and Lectures*, edited by R. E. Spiller and A. R. Ferguson, 1972 (Vol. I of *The Collected Works of Ralph Waldo Emerson*, a CEEA edition) for "Nature," "The American Scholar" and "The Divinity School Address;" *Essays*, revised 1847 and 1850; *Representative Men*, first edition, 1850; *The Conduct of Life*, 1860; and *Selected Poems*, 1876.

Nature [1]

A subtle chain of countless rings
The next unto the farthest brings;
The eye reads omens where it goes,
And speaks all languages the rose;
And, striving to be man, the worm
Mounts through all the spires of form.

Introduction

Our age is retrospective. It builds the sepulchres of the fathers. It writes biographies, histories, and criticism. The foregoing generations beheld God and nature face to face; we, through their eyes. Why should not we also enjoy an original relation to the universe? Why should not we have a poetry and philosophy of insight and not of tradition, and a religion by revelation to us, and not the history of theirs? Embosomed for a season in nature, whose floods of life stream around and through us, and invite us by the powers they supply, to action proportioned to nature, why should we grope among the dry bones of the past, or put the living generation into masquerade out of its faded wardrobe? The sun shines to-day also. There is more wool and flax in the fields. There are new lands,

1. Emerson's first major work, *Nature*, was also the first comprehensive expression of American transcendentalism. For the student it provides a fresh and lyrical intimation of many of the leading ideas that Emerson developed in various later essays and poems. The author first mentioned this book in a diary entry made in 1833, on his return voyage from the first European visit, during which he had met a number of European writers, especially Carlyle. In 1834, when he settled in the Old Manse, his grandfather's home in Concord, he had already written five chapters. He completed the first draft of the volume there, in the very room in which Hawthorne later wrote his *Mosses from an Old Manse*. The small first edition of *Nature*, published anonymously in 1836, gained critical attention, but few general readers. It was not reprinted until 1849, when it was collected in *Nature, Addresses, and Lectures*. At that time Emerson substituted, as epigraph, the present poem, instead of the quotation from Plotinus which had introduced the first edition: "Nature is but an image or imitation of wisdom, the last thing of the soul; Nature being a thing which doth only do, but not know." The new epigraph supported the concept of evolution presented in *Nature*. Darwin's *Origin of Species* did not appear until 1859, but Emerson had seen the classification of species in 1833 at the Paris Jardin des Plantes, while Lamarck was anticipating Darwin, and Lyell's popular *Geology* emphasized fossil remains. The transcendentalists, and Emerson in particular, regarded theories of evolution as supporting a concept of progress and unity as ancient as the early Greek nature pholosophy. These ideas persist throughout *Nature*.

new men, new thoughts. Let us demand our own works and laws and worship.

Undoubtedly we have no questions to ask which are unanswerable. We must trust the perfection of the creation so far, as to believe that whatever curiosity the order of things has awakened in our minds, the order of things can satisfy. Every man's condition is a solution in hieroglyphic to those inquiries he would put. He acts it as life, before he apprehends it as truth. In like manner, nature is already, in its forms and tendencies, describing its own design. Let us interrogate the great apparition, that shines so peacefully around us. Let us inquire, to what end is nature?

All science has one aim, namely, to find a theory of nature. We have theories of races and of functions, but scarcely yet a remote approach to an idea of creation. We are now so far from the road to truth, that religious teachers dispute and hate each other, and speculative men are esteemed unsound and frivolous. But to a sound judgment, the most abstract truth is the most practical. Whenever a true theory appears, it will be its own evidence. Its test is, that it will explain all phenomena. Now many are thought not only unexplained but inexplicable; as language, sleep, madness, dreams, beasts, sex.

Philosophically considered, the universe is composed of Nature and the Soul. Strictly speaking, therefore, all that is separate from us, all which Philosophy distinguishes as the NOT ME, that is, both nature and art, all other men and my own body, must be ranked under this name, NATURE. In enumerating the values of nature and casting up their sum, I shall use the word in both senses;—in its common and in its philosophical import. In inquiries so general as our present one, the inaccuracy is not material; no confusion of thought will occur. *Nature,* in the common sense, refers to essences unchanged by man; space, the air, the river, the leaf. *Art* is applied to the mixture of his will with the same things, as in a house, a canal, a statue, a picture. But his operations taken together are so insignificant, a little chipping, baking, patching, and washing, that in an impression so grand as that of the world on the human mind, they do not vary the result.

Chapter I. Nature

To go into solitude, a man needs to retire as much from his chamber as from society. I am not solitary whilst I read and write, though nobody is with me. But if a man would be alone, let him look at the stars. The rays that come from those heavenly worlds, will separate between him and vulgar things. One might think the atmosphere was made transparent with this design, to give man, in the heavenly bodies, the perpetual presence of the sublime. Seen in the streets of cities, how great they are! If the stars should appear one night in a thousand years, how would men believe and adore; and preserve for many generations the remembrance of the city of God which had been shown! But every night come out these envoys of beauty, and light the universe with their admonishing smile.

The stars awaken a certain reverence, because though always present, they are always inaccessible; but all natural objects make a kindred impression, when the mind is open to their influence. Nature never wears a mean appearance. Neither does the wisest man extort all her secret, and lose his curiosity by finding out all her perfection. Nature never became a toy to a wise spirit. The flowers, the animals, the mountains, reflected all the wisdom of his best hour, as much as they had delighted the simplicity of his childhood.

When we speak of nature in this manner, we have a distinct but most poetical sense in the mind. We mean the integrity of impression made by manifold natural objects. It is this which distinguishes the stick of timber of the wood-cutter, from the tree of the poet. The charming landscape which I saw this morning, is indubitably made up of some twenty or thirty farms. Miller owns this field, Locke that, and Manning the woodland beyond. But none of them owns the landscape. There is a property in the horizon which no man has but he whose eye can integrate all the parts, that is, the poet. This is the best part of these men's farms, yet to this their warranty-deeds give no title.

To speak truly, few adult persons can see nature. Most persons do not see the sun. At least they have a very superficial seeing. The sun illuminates only the eye of the man, but shines into the eye and the heart of the child. The lover of nature is he whose inward and outward senses are still truly adjusted to each other; who has retained the spirit of infancy even into the era of manhood. His intercourse with heaven and earth, becomes part of his daily food. In the presence of nature, a wild delight runs through the man, in spite of real sorrows. Nature says,—he is my creature, and maugre [2] all his impertinent griefs, he shall be glad with me. Not the sun or the summer alone, but every hour and season yields its tribute of delight; for every hour and change corresponds to and authorizes a different state of the mind, from breathless noon to grimmest midnight. Nature is a setting that fits equally well a comic or a mourning piece. In good health, the air is a cordial of incredible virtue. Crossing a bare common, in snow puddles, at twilight, under a clouded sky, without having in my thoughts any occurrence of special good fortune, I have enjoyed a perfect exhilaration. Almost I fear to think how glad I am. In the woods too, a man casts off his

2. Despite.

years, as the snake his slough, and at what period soever of life, is always a child. In the woods, is perpetual youth. Within these plantations of God, a decorum and sanctity reign, a perennial festival is dressed, and the guest sees not how he should tire of them in a thousand years. In the woods, we return to reason and faith. There I feel that nothing can befal me in life,—no disgrace, no calamity, (leaving me my eyes,) which nature cannot repair. Standing on the bare ground,—my head bathed by the blithe air, and uplifted into infinite space,—all mean egotism vanishes. I become a transparent eye-ball. I am nothing. I see all. The currents of the Universal Being circulate through me; I am part or particle[3] of God. The name of the nearest friend sounds then foreign and accidental. To be brothers, to be acquaintances,—master or servant, is then a trifle and a disturbance. I am the lover of uncontained and immortal beauty. In the wilderness, I find something more dear and connate than in streets or villages. In the tranquil landscape, and especially in the distant line of the horizon, man beholds somewhat as beautiful as his own nature.

The greatest delight which the fields and woods minister, is the suggestion of an occult relation between man and the vegetable. I am not alone and unacknowledged. They nod to me and I to them. The waving of the boughs in the storm, is new to me and old. It takes me by surprise, and yet is not unknown. Its effect is like that of a higher thought or a better emotion coming over me, when I deemed I was thinking justly or doing right.

Yet it is certain that the power to produce this delight, does not reside in nature, but in man, or in a harmony of both. It is necessary to use these pleasures with great temperance. For, nature is not always tricked in holiday attire, but the same scene which yesterday breathed perfume and glittered as for the frolic of the nymphs, is overspread with melancholy today. Nature always wears the colors of the spirit. To a man laboring under calamity, the heat of his own fire hath sadness in it. Then, there is a kind of contempt of the landscape felt by him who has just lost by death a dear friend.[4] The sky is less grand as it shuts down over less worth in the population.

Chapter II. Commodity [5]

Whoever considers the final cause of the world, will discern a multitude of uses that enter as parts into that result. They all ad-

3. The Centenary Edition (1903) bases its reading, "parcel," on a manuscript variant.
4. Writing this at the age of thirty-two, Emerson already had "lost by death" his first wife, a bride of eighteen months; and, within the last two years, two brothers.
5. In a sense now unfamiliar, commodity is a physical good.

mit of being thrown into one of the following classes: Commodity; Beauty; Language; and Discipline.

Under the general name of Commodity, I rank all those advantages which our senses owe to nature. This, of course, is a benefit which is temporary and mediate, not ultimate, like its service to the soul. Yet although low, it is perfect in its kind, and is the only use of nature which all men apprehend. The misery of man appears like childish petulance, when we explore the steady and prodigal provision that has been made for his support and delight on this green ball which floats him through the heavens. What angels invented these splendid ornaments, these rich conveniences, this ocean of air above, this ocean of water beneath, this firmament of earth between? this zodiac of lights, this tent of dropping clouds, this striped coat of climates, this fourfold year? Beasts, fire, water, stones, and corn serve him. The field is at once his floor, his work-yard, his play-ground, his garden, and his bed.

> "More servants wait on man
> Than he'll take notice of."——[6]

Nature, in its ministry to man, is not only the material, but is also the process and the result. All the parts incessantly work into each other's hands for the profit of man. The wind sows the seed; the sun evaporates the sea; the wind blows the vapor to the field; the ice, on the other side of the planet, condenses rain on this; the rain feeds the plant; the plant feeds the animal; and thus the endless circulations of the divine charity nourish man.

The useful arts are but reproductions or new combinations by the wit of man, of the same natural benefactors. He no longer waits for favoring gales, but by means of steam, he realizes the fable of Æolus's bag,[7] and carries the two and thirty winds in the boiler of his boat. To diminish friction, he paves the road with iron bars, and, mounting a coach with a ship-load of men, animals, and merchandise behind him, he darts through the country, from town to town, like an eagle or a swallow through the air. By the aggregate of these aids, how is the face of the world changed, from the era of Noah to that of Napoleon! The private poor man hath cities, ships, canals, bridges, built for him. He goes to the post-office, and the human race run on his errands; to the book-shop, and the human race read and write of all that happens, for him; to the court-house, and nations repair his wrongs. He sets his house upon the road, and the human race go forth every morning, and shovel out the snow, and cut a path for him.

6. From "Man," by George Herbert (1593–1633). *Cf.* "Prospects," below.
7. In the *Odyssey*, Bk. X, Æolus gave Odysseus "a mighty bag, bottling storm winds," which his envious sailors opened, producing a tempest.

But there is no need of specifying particulars in this class of uses. The catalogue is endless, and the examples so obvious, that I shall leave them to the reader's reflection, with the general remark, that this mercenary benefit is one which has respect to a farther good. A man is fed, not that he may be fed, but that he may work.

Chapter III. Beauty

A nobler want of man is served by nature, namely, the love of Beauty.

The ancient Greeks called the world κόσμος,[8] beauty. Such is the constitution of all things, or such the plastic power of the human eye, that the primary forms, as the sky, the mountain, the tree, the animal, give us a delight *in and for themselves*; a pleasure arising from outline, color, motion, and grouping. This seems partly owing to the eye itself. The eye is the best of artists. By the mutual action of its structure and of the laws of light, perspective is produced, which integrates every mass of objects, of what character soever, into a well colored and shaded globe, so that where the particular objects are mean and unaffecting, the landscape which they compose, is round and symmetrical. And as the eye is the best composer, so light is the first of painters. There is no object so foul that intense light will not make beautiful. And the stimulus it affords to the sense, and a sort of infinitude which it hath, like space and time, makes all matter gay. Even the corpse hath its own beauty. But beside this general grace diffused over nature, almost all the individual forms are agreeable to the eye, as is proved by our endless imitations of some of them, as the acorn, the grape, the pine-cone, the wheat-ear, the egg, the wings and forms of most birds, the lion's claw, the serpent, the butterfly, sea-shells, flames, clouds, buds, leaves, and the forms of many trees, as the palm.

For better consideration, we may distribute the aspects of Beauty in a threefold manner.

1. First, the simple perception of natural forms is a delight. The influence of the forms and actions in nature, is so needful to man, that, in its lowest functions, it seems to lie on the confines of commodity and beauty. To the body and mind which have been cramped by noxious work or company, nature is medicinal and restores their tone. The tradesman, the attorney comes out of the din and craft of the street, and sees the sky and the woods, and is a man again. In their eternal calm, he finds himself. The health of the eye seems to demand a horizon. We are never tired, so long as we can see far enough.

---

8. *Kosmos* (cosmos). By this Greek word, meaning essentially "a universal order or harmony of parts," Emerson suggests his own conception of beauty.

But in other hours, Nature satisfies the soul purely by its love-liness, and without any mixture of corporeal benefit. I have seen the spectacle of morning from the hill-top over against my house, from day-break to sun-rise, with emotions which an angel might share. The long slender bars of cloud float like fishes in the sea of crimson light. From the earth, as a shore, I look out into that silent sea. I seem to partake its rapid transformations: the active enchantment reaches my dust, and I dilate and conspire with the morning wind. How does Nature deify us with a few and cheap elements! Give me health and a day, and I will make the pomp of emperors ridiculous. The dawn is my Assyria; [9] the sun-set and moon-rise my Paphos, [1] and unimaginable realms of faerie; broad noon shall be my Eng-land of the senses and the understanding; the night shall be my Germany [2] of mystic philosophy and dreams.

Not less excellent, except for our less susceptibility in the after-noon, was the charm, last evening, of a January sunset. The western clouds divided and subdivided themselves into pink flakes modu-lated with tints of unspeakable softness; and the air had so much life and sweetness, that it was a pain to come within doors. What was it that nature would say? Was there no meaning in the live re-pose of the valley behind the mill, and which Homer or Shakspeare could not re-form for me in words? The leafless trees become spires of flame in the sunset, with the blue east for the background, and the stars of the dead calices [3] of flowers, and every withered stem and stubble rimed with frost, contribute something to the mute music.

The inhabitants of cities suppose that the country landscape is pleasant only half the year. I please myself with observing the graces of the winter scenery, and believe that we are as much touched by it as by the genial influences of summer. To the atten-tive eye, each moment of the year has its own beauty, and in the same field, it beholds, every hour, a picture which was never seen before, and which shall never be seen again. The heavens change every moment, and reflect their glory or gloom on the plains be-neath. The state of the crop in the surrounding farms alters the ex-pression of the earth from week to week. The succession of native plants in the pastures and road-sides, which make the silent clock by which time tells the summer hours, will make even the divi-sions of the day sensible to a keen observer. The tribes of birds and insects, like the plants punctual to their time, follow each other,

9. Here emblematic of an early period of splendor.
1. Ancient city of Cyprus, noted for its worship of Aphrodite, Greek goddess of sensual love.
2. The rational empiricism of English thinkers, especially Hume and the Scot-tish "common-sense" school, is com-pared with German idealism, *e.g.*, Hegel and Kant.
3. Now usually "calyxes" or "calyces," plural of "calyx," the outer perianth of a flower.

and the year has room for all. By water-courses, the variety is greater. In July, the blue pontederia or pickerel-weed blooms in large beds in the shallow parts of our pleasant river,[4] and swarms with yellow butterflies in continual motion. Art cannot rival this pomp of purple and gold. Indeed the river is a perpetual gala, and boasts each month a new ornament.

But this beauty of Nature which is seen and felt as beauty, is the least part. The shows of day, the dewy morning, the rainbow, mountains, orchards in blossom, stars, moonlight, shadows in still water, and the like, if too eagerly hunted, become shows merely, and mock us with their unreality. Go out of the house to see the moon, and 't is mere tinsel; it will not please as when its light shines upon your necessary journey. The beauty that shimmers in the yellow afternoons of October, who ever could clutch it? Go forth to find it, and it is gone: 't is only a mirage as you look from the windows of diligence.

2. The presence of a higher, namely, of the spiritual element is essential to its perfection. The high and divine beauty which can be loved without effeminacy, is that which is found in combination with the human will, and never separate. Beauty is the mark God sets upon virtue. Every natural action is graceful. Every heroic act is also decent, and causes the place and the bystanders to shine. We are taught by great actions that the universe is the property of every individual in it. Every rational creature has all nature for his dowry and estate. It is his, if he will. He may divest himself of it; he may creep into a corner, and abdicate his kingdom, as most men do, but he is entitled to the world by his constitution. In proportion to the energy of his thought and will, he takes up the world into himself. "All those things for which men plough, build, or sail, obey virtue;" said an ancient historian.[5] "The winds and waves," said Gibbon,[6] "are always on the side of the ablest navigators." So are the sun and moon and all the stars of heaven. When a noble act is done,—perchance in a scene of great natural beauty; when Leonidas and his three hundred martyrs consume one day in dying, and the sun and moon come each and look at them once in the steep defile of Thermopylæ;[7] when Arnold Winkelried,[8] in the high Alps, under the shadow of the avalanche, gathers in his side a sheaf of Austrian spears to break the line for his com-

4. The Concord River, a meandering branch of the Merrimack.
5. Gaius Sallustius Crispus Sallust (86–34 B.C.), Roman historian; from *The Conspiracy of Cataline.*
6. Edward Gibbon (1737–1794); from *The History of the Decline and Fall of the Roman Empire* (1776–1788), Volume II, Chapter 68.
7. King Leonidas and his three hundred Spartans in 480 B.C. gave their lives in the defense of this pass against the entire Persian army.
8. The traditional hero of Swiss independence, Arnold von Winkelried, at the Battle of Sempach (1386), exposed himself to the volley of Austrian spears, thus providing a breach through which the ready Swiss rushed to victory.

rades; are not these heroes entitled to add the beauty of the scene to the beauty of the deed? When the bark of Columbus nears the shore of America;—before it, the beach lined with savages, fleeing out of all their huts of cane; the sea behind; and the purple mountains of the Indian Archipelago around, can we separate the man from the living picture? Does not the New World clothe his form with her palm-groves and savannahs as fit drapery? Ever does natural beauty steal in like air, and envelope great actions. When Sir Harry Vane [9] was dragged up the Tower-hill, sitting on a sled, to suffer death, as the champion of the English laws, one of the multitude cried out to him, "You never sate on so glorious a seat." Charles II., to intimidate the citizens of London, caused the patriot Lord Russell [1] to be drawn in an open coach, through the principal streets of the city, on his way to the scaffold. "But," to use the simple narrative of his biographer,[2] "the multitude imagined they saw liberty and virtue sitting by his side." In private places, among sordid objects, an act of truth or heroism seems at once to draw to itself the sky as its temple, the sun as its candle. Nature stretcheth out her arms to embrace man, only let his thoughts be of equal greatness. Willingly does she follow his steps with the rose and the violet, and bend her lines of grandeur and grace to the decoration of her darling child. Only let his thoughts be of equal scope, and the frame will suit the picture. A virtuous man is in unison with her works, and makes the central figure of the visible sphere. Homer, Pindar, Socrates, Phocion,[3] associate themselves fitly in our memory with the whole geography and climate of Greece. The visible heavens and earth sympathize with Jesus. And in common life, whosoever has seen a person of powerful character and happy genius, will have remarked how easily he took all things along with him,—the persons, the opinions, and the day, and nature became ancillary to a man.

3. There is still another aspect under which the beauty of the world may be viewed, namely, as it becomes an object of the intellect. Beside the relation of things to virtue, they have a relation to thought. The intellect searches out the absolute order of things as they stand in the mind of God, and without the colors of affection. The intellectual and the active powers seem to succeed each other

9. Puritan statesman, once colonial governor of Massachusetts, who opposed the restoration of Charles II (1660) and was executed for treason.
1. William, Lord Russell (1639–1683), strongly opposed the corrupt court and the Catholic party, and was executed for treason in 1683 on perjured testimony connecting him with the Rye House Plot.
2. The excellent *Life of William Lord Russell* (1819), by Lord John Russell,
was still current.
3. Ancient Greeks of "natural virtue:" Homer was traditionally regarded as the author of the heroic epics; Pindar was the great lyrist of heroic themes; Socrates brought philosophical inquiry into the streets, and died in defense of it; Phocion, general and statesman, long successfully negotiated Athenian nationalism during the Macedonian conquest, was at 85 wrongly charged and executed for treason.

in man, and the exclusive activity of the one, generates the exclusive activity of the other. There is something unfriendly in each to the other, but they are like the alternate periods of feeding and working in animals; each prepares and certainly will be followed by the other. Therefore does beauty, which, in relation to actions, as we have seen, comes unsought, and comes because it is unsought, remain for the apprehension and pursuit of the intellect; and then again, in its turn, of the active power. Nothing divine dies. All good is eternally reproductive. The beauty of nature reforms itself in the mind, and not for barren contemplation, but for new creation.

All men are in some degree impressed by the face of the world; some men even to delight. This love of beauty is Taste. Others have the same love in such excess, that, not content with admiring, they seek to embody it in new forms. The creation of beauty is Art.

The production of a work of art throws a light upon the mystery of humanity. A work of art is an abstract or epitome of the world. It is the result or expression of nature, in miniature. For although the works of nature are innumerable and all different, the result or the expression of them all is similar and single. Nature is a sea of forms radically alike and even unique. A leaf, a sun-beam, a landscape, the ocean, make an analogous impression on the mind. What is common to them all,—that perfectness and harmony, is beauty. Therefore the standard of beauty is the entire circuit of natural forms,—the totality of nature; which the Italians expressed by defining beauty "il piu nell' uno." [4] Nothing is quite beautiful alone: nothing but is beautiful in the whole. A single object is only so far beautiful as it suggests this universal grace. The poet, the painter, the sculptor, the musician, the architect, seek each to concentrate this radiance of the world on one point, and each in his several work to satisfy the love of beauty which stimulates him to produce. Thus is Art, a nature passed through the alembic of man. Thus in art, does nature work through the will of man filled with the beauty of her first works.

The world thus exists to the soul to satisfy the desire of beauty. Extend this element to the uttermost, and I call it an ultimate end. No reason can be asked or given why the soul seeks beauty. Beauty, in its largest and profoundest sense, is one expression for the universe. God is the all-fair. Truth, and goodness, and beauty, are but different faces of the same All. But beauty in nature is not ultimate. It is the herald of inward and eternal beauty, and is not alone a solid and satisfactory good. It must therefore stand as a part and not as yet the last or highest expression of the final cause of Nature.

4. "The many in one." *Cf.* the poem "Each and All," below.

Chapter IV. Language

A third use which Nature subserves to man is that of Language. Nature is the vehicle of thought, and in a simple, double, and three-fold degree.

1. Words are signs of natural facts.
2. Particular natural facts are symbols of particular spiritual facts.
3. Nature is the symbol of spirit.

1. Words are signs of natural facts. The use of natural history is to give us aid in supernatural history. The use of the outer creation is to give us language for the beings and changes of the inward creation. Every word which is used to express a moral or intellectual fact, if traced to its root, is found to be borrowed from some material appearance. *Right* [5] originally means *straight; wrong* means *twisted. Spirit* primarily means *wind; transgression,* the crossing of a *line; supercilious,* the *raising of the eye-brow.* We say the *heart* to express emotion, the *head* to denote thought; and *thought* and *emotion* are, in their turn, words borrowed from sensible things, and now appropriated to spiritual nature. Most of the process by which this transformation is made, is hidden from us in the remote time when language was framed; but the same tendency may be daily observed in children. Children and savages use only nouns or names of things, which they continually convert into verbs, and apply to analogous mental acts.

2. But this origin of all words that convey a spiritual import,— so conspicuous a fact in the history of language,—is our least debt to nature. It is not words only that are emblematic; it is things which are emblematic. Every natural fact is a symbol of some spiritual fact. Every appearance in nature corresponds to some state of the mind, and that state of the mind can only be described by presenting that natural appearance as its picture. An enraged man is a lion, a cunning man is a fox, a firm man is a rock, a learned man is a torch. A lamb is innocence; a snake is subtle spite; flowers express to us the delicate affections. Light and darkness are our familiar expression for knowledge and ignorance; and heat for love. Visible distance behind and before us, is respectively our image of memory and hope.

Who looks upon a river in a meditative hour, and is not reminded of the flux of all things? Throw a stone into the stream, and the circles that propagate themselves are the beautiful type of all influence. Man is conscious of a universal soul within or behind his individual life, wherein, as in a firmament, the natures of Jus-

5. The words in italics prove his proposition: the original root of each was determined by a "natural fact."

tice, Truth, Love, Freedom, arise and shine. This universal soul, he calls Reason: it is not mine or thine or his, but we are its; we are its property and men. And the blue sky in which the private earth is buried, the sky with its eternal calm, and full of everlasting orbs, is the type of Reason. That which, intellectually considered, we call Reason, considered in relation to nature, we call Spirit. Spirit is the Creator. Spirit hath life in itself. And man in all ages and countries, embodies it in his language, as the FATHER.

It is easily seen that there is nothing lucky or capricious in these analogies, but that they are constant, and pervade nature. These are not the dreams of a few poets, here and there, but man is an analogist, and studies relations in all objects. He is placed in the centre of beings, and a ray of relation passes from every other being to him. And neither can man be understood without these objects, nor these objects without man. All the facts in natural history taken by themselves, have no value, but are barren like a single sex. But marry it to human history, and it is full of life. Whole Floras, all Linnæus' and Buffon's [6] volumes, are but dry catalogues of facts; but the most trivial of these facts, the habit of a plant, the organs, or work, or noise of an insect, applied to the illustration of a fact in intellectual philosophy, or, in any way associated to human nature, affects us in the most lively and agreeable manner. The seed of a plant,—to what affecting analogies in the nature of man, is that little fruit made use of, in all discourse, up to the voice of Paul, who calls the human corpse a seed,[7]—"It is sown a natural body; it is raised a spiritual body." The motion of the earth round its axis, and round the sun, makes the day, and the year. These are certain amounts of brute light and heat. But is there no intent of an analogy between man's life and the seasons? And do the seasons gain no grandeur or pathos from that analogy? The instincts of the ant are very unimportant considered as the ant's; but the moment a ray of relation is seen to extend from it to man, and the little drudge is seen to be a monitor, a little body with a mighty heart, then all its habits, even that said to be recently observed, that it never sleeps, become sublime.

Because of this radical [8] correspondence between visible things and human thoughts, savages, who have only what is necessary, converse in figures. As we go back in history, language becomes more picturesque, until its infancy, when it is all poetry; or, all

6. Linnaeus (Carl von Linné, 1707–1778), Swedish botanist, founded the modern system of plant classification; Comte de Buffon (Georges Louis Le Clerc, 1707–1788), French naturalist, initiated and was an important collaborator on the forty-four-volume *Histoire Naturelle* (finished in 1804), a comprehensive formulation of the biological sciences.

7. *Cf.* I Corinthians xv: 42–44.

8. In the etymological sense: from the Latin *radix*, "a root."

spiritual facts are represented by natural symbols.[9] The same symbols are found to make the original elements of all languages. It has moreover been observed, that the idioms of all languages approach each other in passages of the greatest eloquence and power. And as this is the first language, so is it the last. This immediate dependence of language upon nature, this conversion of an outward phenomenon into a type of somewhat in human life, never loses its power to affect us. It is this which gives that piquancy to the conversation of a strong-natured farmer or back-woodsman, which all men relish.

Thus is nature an interpreter, by whose means man converses with his fellow men. A man's power to connect his thought with its proper symbol, and so to utter it, depends on the simplicity of his character, that is, upon his love of truth and his desire to communicate it without loss. The corruption of man is followed by the corruption of language. When simplicity of character and the sovereignty of ideas is broken up by the prevalence of secondary desires, the desire of riches, the desire of pleasure, the desire of power, the desire of praise,—and duplicity and falsehood take place of simplicity and truth, the power over nature as an interpreter of the will, is in a degree lost; new imagery ceases to be created, and old words are perverted to stand for things which are not; a paper currency is employed when there is no bullion in the vaults. In due time, the fraud is manifest, and words lose all power to stimulate the understanding or the affections. Hundreds of writers may be found in every long-civilized nation, who for a short time believe, and make others believe, that they see and utter truths, who do not of themselves clothe one thought in its natural garment, but who feed unconsciously upon the language created by the primary writers of the country, those, namely, who hold primarily on nature.

But wise men pierce this rotten diction and fasten words again to visible things; so that picturesque language is at once a commanding certificate that he who employs it, is a man in alliance with truth and God. The moment our discourse rises above the ground line of familiar facts, and is inflamed with passion or exalted by thought, it clothes itself in images. A man conversing in earnest, if he watch his intellectual processes, will find that always a material image, more or less luminous, arises in his mind, contemporaneous with every thought, which furnishes the vestment of the thought. Hence, good writing and brilliant discourse are perpetual allegories. This imagery is spontaneous. It is the blending of experience with the present action of the mind. It is proper

9. This romantic theory of primitive word symbolism, then accepted, has now been superseded.

creation. It is the working of the Original Cause through the instruments he has already made.

These facts may suggest the advantage which the country-life possesses for a powerful mind, over the artificial and curtailed life of cities. We know more from nature than we can at will communicate. Its light flows into the mind evermore, and we forget its presence. The poet, the orator, bred in the woods, whose senses have been nourished by their fair and appeasing changes, year after year, without design and without heed,—shall not lose their lesson altogether, in the roar of cities or the broil of politics. Long hereafter, amidst agitation and terror in national councils,—in the hour of revolution,—these solemn images shall reappear in their morning lustre, as fit symbols and words of the thoughts which the passing events shall awaken. At the call of a noble sentiment, again the woods wave, the pines murmur, the river rolls and shines, and the cattle low upon the mountains, as he saw and heard them in his infancy. And with these forms, the spells of persuasion, the keys of power are put into his hands.

3. We are thus assisted by natural objects in the expression of particular meanings. But how great a language to convey such peppercorn [1] informations! Did it need such noble races of creatures, this profusion of forms, this host of orbs in heaven, to furnish man with the dictionary and grammar of his municipal [2] speech? Whilst we use this grand cipher to expedite the affairs of our pot and kettle, we feel that we have not yet put it to its use, neither are able. We are like travellers using the cinders of a volcano to roast their eggs. Whilst we see that it always stands ready to clothe what we would say, we cannot avoid the question, whether the characters are not significant of themselves. Have mountains, and waves, and skies, no significance but what we consciously give them, when we employ them as emblems of our thoughts? The world is emblematic. Parts of speech are metaphors because the whole of nature is a metaphor of the human mind. The laws of moral nature answer to those of matter as face to face in a glass. "The visible world and the relation of its parts, is the dial plate of the invisible." The axioms of physics translate the laws of ethics. Thus, "the whole is greater than its part;" "reaction is equal to action;" "the smallest weight may be made to lift the greatest, the difference of weight being compensated by time;" and many the like propositions, which have an ethical as well as physical sense. These propositions have a much more extensive and universal sense when applied to human life, than when confined to technical use.

---

1. Petty; a meaning derived from the ancient use of a peppercorn for the nominal payment of an obligation.
2. In its earlier meaning, "local."

In like manner, the memorable words of history, and the proverbs of nations, consist usually of a natural fact, selected as a picture or parable of a moral truth. Thus; A rolling stone gathers no moss; A bird in the hand is worth two in the bush; A cripple in the right way, will beat a racer in the wrong; Make hay whilst the sun shines; 'T is hard to carry a full cup even; Vinegar is the son of wine; The last ounce broke the camel's back; Long-lived trees make roots first;—and the like. In their primary sense these are trivial facts, but we repeat them for the value of their analogical import. What is true of proverbs, is true of all fables, parables, and allegories.

This relation between the mind and matter is not fancied by some poet, but stands in the will of God, and so is free to be known by all men. It appears to men, or it does not appear. When in fortunate hours we ponder this miracle, the wise man doubts, if, at all other times, he is not blind and deaf;

> ———"Can these things be,
> And overcome us like a summer's cloud,
> Without our special wonder?" [3]

for the universe becomes transparent, and the light of higher laws than its own, shines through it. It is the standing problem which has exercised the wonder and the study of every fine genius since the world began; from the era of the Egyptians and the Brahmins, to that of Pythagoras, of Plato, of Bacon, of Leibnitz, of Swedenborg.[4] There sits the Sphinx at the road-side, and from age to age, as each prophet comes by, he tries his fortune at reading her riddle.[5] There seems to be a necessity in spirit to manifest itself in material forms; and day and night, river and storm, beast and bird, acid and alkali, preëxist in necessary Ideas in the mind of God, and are what they are by virtue of preceding affections, in the world of spirit. A Fact is the end or last issue of spirit. The visible creation is the terminus or the circumference of the invisible world. "Material objects," said a French philosopher, "are necessarily kinds of *scoriæ* [6] of the substantial thoughts of the Creator, which must

3. *Macbeth*, Act III, Scene iv, ll. 110–112. The first two editions read, erroneously, "Can these things be," for "Can such things be."

4. All these taught, in one way or another, a universe "transparent" in Emerson's meaning above. The Greek Pythagoras (sixth century B.C.), like the Egyptian and Brahmin mystics, taught the transmigration of souls; the Greek Plato (428–347 B.C.) was the father of western philosophical idealism; Francis Bacon (1561–1626), British founder of inductive science, was mystical in his religious philosophy;

the German Gottfried Wilhelm von Leibnitz (1646–1716) promulgated a philosophical optimism later satirized by such determinists as Voltaire; and Emanuel Swedenborg (1688–1772) was a Swedish religious thinker, who later became Emerson's example for "The Mystic" in *Representative Men.*

5. In classic myth, the Sphinx of Thebes slew all travelers unable to solve her riddle. At last Oedipus did so; whereupon, as predicted, she killed herself and he became king.

6. Slag from smelting lava.

always preserve an exact relation to their first origin; in other words, visible nature must have a spiritual and moral side."

This doctrine is abstruse, and though the images of "garment," "scoriæ," "mirror," &c., may stimulate the fancy, we must summon the aid of subtler and more vital expositors to make it plain. "Every scripture is to be interpreted by the same spirit which gave it forth,"—is the fundamental law of criticism. A life in harmony with nature, the love of truth and of virtue, will purge the eyes to understand her text. By degrees we may come to know the primitive sense of the permanent objects of nature, so that the world shall be to us an open book, and every form significant of its hidden life and final cause.

A new interest surprises us, whilst, under the view now suggested, we contemplate the fearful extent and multitude of objects; since "every object rightly seen, unlocks a new faculty of the soul." That which was unconscious truth, becomes, when interpreted and defined in an object, a part of the domain of knowledge,—a new weapon in the magazine of power.

Chapter V. Discipline

In view of this significance of nature, we arrive at once at a new fact, that nature is a discipline.[7] This use of the world includes the preceding uses, as parts of itself.

Space, time, society, labor, climate, food, locomotion, the animals, the mechanical forces, give us sincerest lessons, day by day, whose meaning is unlimited. They educate both the Understanding and the Reason. Every property of matter is a school for the understanding,—its solidity or resistance, its inertia, its extension, its figure, its divisibility. The understanding adds, divides, combines, measures, and finds everlasting nutriment and room for its activity in this worthy scene. Meantime, Reason transfers all these lessons into its own world of thought, by perceiving the analogy that marries Matter and Mind.

1. Nature is a discipline of the understanding in intellectual truths. Our dealing with sensible objects is a constant exercise in the necessary lessons of difference, of likeness, of order, of being and seeming, of progressive arrangement; of ascent from particular

7. Emerson's analysis of the proposition "nature is a discipline" shows the American transcendentalist's version of the then current Idealism—the romantic philosophy of German thinkers, of whom probably Hegel most influenced the Concord group. The aspects and the experience of nature, says Emerson, "educate both the Understanding and the Reason." The Understanding is concerned with the knowledge of the properties, behavior, and significance of material and social reality. This requires rationality. But Reason itself, as a faculty, is concerned with the intuition of Nature's truth. And in transcendental terms, there is the unity of the whole, involving Understanding and Reason simultaneously in the condition of knowing.

to general; of combination to one end of manifold forces. Proportioned to the importance of the organ to be formed, is the extreme care with which its tuition [8] is provided,—a care pretermitted in no single case. What tedious training, day after day, year after year, never ending, to form the common sense; what continual reproduction of annoyances, inconveniences, dilemmas; what rejoicing over us of little men; what disputing of prices, what reckonings of interest,—and all to form the Hand of the mind;—to instruct us that "good thoughts are no better than good dreams, unless they be executed!"

The same good office is performed by Property and its filial systems of debt and credit. Debt, grinding debt, whose iron face the widow, the orphan, and the sons of genius fear and hate;— debt, which consumes so much time, which so cripples and disheartens a great spirit with cares that seem so base, is a preceptor whose lessons cannot be foregone, and is needed most by those who suffer from it most. Moreover, property, which has been well compared to snow,—"if it fall level to-day, it will be blown into drifts to-morrow,"—is merely the surface action of internal machinery, like the index on the face of a clock. Whilst now it is the gymnastics of the understanding, it is hiving in the foresight of the spirit, experience in profounder laws.

The whole character and fortune of the individual are affected by the least inequalities in the culture of the understanding; for example, in the perception of differences. Therefore is Space, and therefore Time, that man may know that things are not huddled and lumped, but sundered and individual. A bell and a plough have each their use, and neither can do the office of the other. Water is good to drink, coal to burn, wool to wear; but wool cannot be drunk, nor water spun, nor coal eaten. The wise man shows his wisdom in separation, in gradation, and his scale of creatures and of merits, is as wide as nature. The foolish have no range in their scale, but suppose every man is as every other man. What is not good they call the worst, and what is not hateful, they call the best.

In like manner, what good heed, nature forms in us! She pardons no mistakes. Her yea is yea, and her nay, nay.

The first steps in Agriculture, Astronomy, Zoölogy, (those first steps which the farmer, the hunter, and the sailor take,) teach that nature's dice are always loaded; [9] that in her heaps and rubbish are concealed sure and useful results.

How calmly and genially the mind apprehends one after another the laws of physics! What noble emotions dilate the mortal as he

8. Here in its older sense of "guardianship," as well as "instruction."
9. E. W. Emerson found the source of this in Fragment 763, from a lost play by Sophocles: "The dice of Zeus ever fall aright" (Centenary Edition, I, 409).

enters into the counsels of the creation, and feels by knowledge the privilege to BE! His insight refines him. The beauty of nature shines in his own breast. Man is greater that [1] he can see this, and the universe less, because Time and Space relations vanish as laws are known.

Here again we are impressed and even daunted by the immense Universe to be explored. 'What we know, is a point to what we do not know.' Open any recent journal of science, and weigh the problems suggested concerning Light, Heat, Electricity, Magnetism, Physiology, Geology, and judge whether the interest of natural science is likely to be soon exhausted.

Passing by many particulars of the discipline of nature we must not omit to specify two.

The exercise of the Will or the lesson of power is taught in every event. From the child's successive possession of his several senses up to the hour when he saith, "thy will be done!" [2] he is learning the secret, that he can reduce under his will, not only particular events, but great classes, nay the whole series of events, and so conform all facts to his character. Nature is thoroughly mediate. It is made to serve. It receives the dominion of man as meekly as the ass on which the Saviour rode.[3] It offers all its kingdoms [4] to man as the raw material which he may mould into what is useful. Man is never weary of working it up. He forges the subtile and delicate air into wise and melodious words, and gives them wing as angels of persuasion and command. More and more, with every thought, does his kingdom stretch over things, until the world becomes, at last, only a realized will,—the double of the man.

2. Sensible objects conform to the premonitions of Reason and reflect the conscience. All things are moral; and in their boundless changes have an unceasing reference to spiritual nature. Therefore is nature glorious with form, color, and motion, that every globe in the remotest heaven; every chemical change from the rudest crystal up to the laws of life; every change of vegetation from the first principle of growth in the eye of a leaf, to the tropical forest and antediluvian, coal-mine; [5] every animal function from the sponge up to Hercules, shall hint or thunder to man the laws of right and wrong, and echo the Ten Commandments. Therefore is nature ever the ally of Religion: lends all her pomp and riches to the religious sentiment. Prophet and priest, David, Isaiah, Jesus, have drawn deeply from this source.

This ethical character so penetrates the bone and marrow of

1. Reads "than" in 1849; corrected in the Centenary Edition.
2. See the Lord's Prayer, Matthew vi: 9; and cf. Acts xxi: 14.
3. See John xii: 12–15; and cf. Zecha-riah ix: 9.
4. Cf. Matthew iv: 8.
5. I.e., coal results from the deep burial of forests by geomorphic up-heaval.

nature, as to seem the end for which it was made. Whatever private purpose is answered by any member or part, this is its public and universal function, and is never omitted. Nothing in nature is exhausted in its first use. When a thing has served an end to the uttermost, it is wholly new for an ulterior service. In God, every end is converted into a new means. Thus the use of Commodity, regarded by itself, is mean and squalid. But it is to the mind an education in the great doctrine of Use, namely, that a thing is good only so far as it serves; that a conspiring of parts and efforts to the production of an end, is essential to any being. The first and gross manifestation of this truth, is our inevitable and hated training in values and wants, in corn and meat.

It has already been illustrated, in treating of the significance of material things, that every natural process is but a version of a moral sentence. The moral laws lies at the centre of nature and radiates to the circumference. It is the pith and marrow of every substance, every relation, and every process. All things with which we deal, preach to us. What is a farm but a mute gospel? The chaff and the wheat, weeds and plants, blight, rain, insects, sun,—it is a sacred emblem from the first furrow of spring to the last stack which the snow of winter overtakes in the fields. But the sailor, the shepherd, the miner, the merchant, in their several resorts, have each an experience precisely parallel and leading to the same conclusion: because all organizations are radically alike. Nor can it be doubted that this moral sentiment which thus scents the air, and grows in the grain, and impregnates the waters of the world, is caught by man and sinks into his soul. The moral influence of nature upon every individual is that amount of truth which it illustrates to him. Who can estimate this? Who can guess how much firmness the sea-beaten rock has taught the fisherman? how much tranquillity has been reflected to man from the azure sky, over whose unspotted deeps the winds forevermore drive flocks of stormy clouds, and leave no wrinkle or stain? how much industry and providence and affection we have caught from the pantomine of brutes? What a searching preacher of self-command is the varying phenomenon of Health!

Herein is especially apprehended the Unity of Nature,—the Unity in Variety,—which meets us everywhere. All the endless variety of things make a unique, an identical impression. Xenophanes [6] complained in his old age, that, look where he would, all things hastened back to Unity. He was weary of seeing the same entity in the tedious variety of forms. The fable of Proteus [7] has a cordial truth.

6. Greek pre-Socratic philosopher (sixth century B.C.), who taught the unity of all existence—"All is one."

7. Proteus, in Greek fable, could elusively change his form.

Every particular in nature, a leaf, a drop, a crystal, a moment of time is related to the whole, and partakes of the perfection of the whole. Each particle is a microcosm, and faithfully renders the likeness of the world.[8]

Not only resemblances exist in things whose analogy is obvious, as when we detect the type of the human hand in the flipper of the fossil saurus,[9] but also in objects wherein there is great superficial unlikeness. Thus architecture is called "frozen music," by De Stael and Goethe.[1] Vitruvius [2] thought an architect should be a musician. "A Gothic church," said Coleridge,[3] "is a petrified religion." Michael Angelo maintained, that, to an architect, a knowledge of anatomy is essential. In Haydn's oratorios,[4] the notes present to the imagination not only motions, as, of the snake, the stag, and the elephant, but colors also; as the green grass. The law of harmonic sounds reappears in the harmonic colors. The granite is differenced in its laws only by the more or less of heat, from the river that wears it away. The river, as it flows, resembles the air that flows over it; the air resembles the light which traverses it with more subtle currents; the light resembles the heat which rides with it through Space. Each creature is only a modification of the other; the likeness in them is more than the difference, and their radical law is one and the same. Hence it is, that a rule of one art, or a law of one organization, holds true throughout nature. So intimate is this Unity, that, it is easily seen, it lies under the undermost garment of nature, and betrays its source in universal Spirit. For, it pervades Thought also. Every universal truth which we express in words, implies or supposes every other truth. *Omne verum vero consonat.*[5] It is like a great circle on a sphere, comprising all possible circles; which, however, may be drawn, and comprise it, in like manner. Every such truth is the absolute Ens [6] seen from one side. But it has innumerable sides.

The same central Unity is still more conspicuous in actions. Words are finite organs of the infinite mind. They cannot cover the dimensions of what is in truth. They break, chop, and impoverish

8. The idea that the microcosm recapitulates the universal macrocosm recurs throughout transcendentalism and in Emerson's writing; the pantheism of Xenophanes, just mentioned, suggests it here.

9. A suffix, used in paleontology, for names of various families of extinct reptilian mammoths.

1. Madame de Staël (1766–1817), see *Corinne ou l'Italie* (1807), Book IV, Chapter 3; Johann W. von Goethe (1749–1832), see *Conversations with Eckermann*, the passage dated March 23, 1829. *Cf.* Emerson's *Journals*, Vol. III, p. 363.

2. Marcus Vitruvius Pollio, Roman architect (first century B.C.), *De Architectura*, Book I, Chapter i, Section 8.

3. Samuel Taylor Coleridge, in "A Lecture on the General Characteristics of the Gothic Mind in the Middle Ages" (*Literary Remains*, 1836): "a Gothic cathedral is the petrification of our religion."

4. Joseph Haydn (1732–1809). His two greatest oratorios, *The Creation* and *The Seasons*, are especially rich in such natural description as Emerson suggests here.

5. Every truth harmonizes with all other truth.

6. "Being" in the most general sense of the term.

it. An action is the perfection and publication of thought. A right action seems to fill the eye, and to be related to all nature. "The wise man, in doing one thing, does all; or, in the one thing he does rightly, he sees the likeness of all which is done rightly."

Words and actions are not the attributes of mute and brute nature. They introduce us to the human form, of which all other organizations appear to be degradations. When this organization appears among so many that surround it, the spirit prefers it to all others. It says, 'From such as this, have I drawn joy and knowledge. In such as this, have I found and beheld myself. I will speak to it. It can speak again. It can yield me thought already formed and alive.' In fact, the eye,—the mind,—is always accompanied by these forms, male and female; and these are incomparably the richest informations of the power and order that lie at the heart of things. Unfortunately, every one of them bears the marks as of some injury; is marred and superficially defective. Nevertheless, far different from the deaf and dumb nature around them, these all rest like fountain-pipes on the unfathomed sea of thought and virtue whereto they alone, of all organizations, are the entrances.

It were a pleasant inquiry to follow into detail their ministry to our education, but where would it stop? We are associated in adolescent and adult life with some friends, who, like skies and waters, are coextensive with our idea; who, answering each to a certain affection of the soul, satisfy our desire on that side; whom we lack power to put at such focal distance from us, that we can mend or even analyze them. We cannot chuse but love them. When much intercourse with a friend has supplied us with a standard of excellence, and has increased our respect for the resources of God who thus sends a real person to outgo our ideal; when he has, moreover, become an object of thought, and, whilst his character retains all its unconscious effect, is converted in the mind into solid and sweet wisdom,—it is a sign to us that his office is closing, and he is commonly withdrawn from our sight in a short time.[7]

Chapter VI. Idealism

Thus is the unspeakable but intelligible and practicable meaning of the world conveyed to man, the immortal pupil, in every object of sense. To this one end of Discipline, all parts of nature conspire.

A noble doubt perpetually suggests itself, whether this end be not the Final Cause of the Universe; and whether nature outwardly exists. It is a sufficient account of that Appearance as we call the

7. According to E. W. Emerson (Centenary Edition, Vol. I, p. 410), this thought relates to the death, within the previous two years, of Emerson's brothers Edward and Charles, the latter of whom he called "a brother and a friend in one."

World, that God will teach a human mind, and so makes it the receiver of a certain number of congruent sensations, which we call sun and moon, man and woman, house and trade. In my utter impotence to test the authenticity of the report of my senses, to know whether the impressions they make on me correspond with outlying objects, what difference does it make, whether Orion is up there in heaven, or some god paints the image in the firmament of the soul? The relations of parts and the end of the whole remaining the same, what is the difference, whether land and sea interact, and worlds revolve and intermingle without number or end,— deep yawning under deep,[8] and galaxy balancing galaxy, throughout absolute space, or, whether, without relations of time and space, the same appearances are inscribed in the constant faith of man? Whether nature enjoy a substantial existence without, or is only in the apocalypse [9] of the mind, it is alike useful and alike venerable to me. Be it what it may, it is ideal to me, so long as I cannot try the accuracy of my senses.

The frivolous make themselves merry with the Ideal theory,[1] as if its consequences were burlesque; as if it affected the stability of nature. It surely does not. God never jests with us, and will not compromise the end of nature, by permitting any inconsequence in its procession. Any distrust of the permanence of laws, would paralyze the faculties of man. Their permanence is sacredly respected, and his faith therein is perfect. The wheels and springs of man are all set to the hypothesis of the permanence of nature. We are not built like a ship to be tossed, but like a house to stand. It is a natural consequence of this structure, that, so long as the active powers predominate over the reflective, we resist with indignation any hint that nature is more short-lived or mutable than spirit. The broker, the wheelwright, the carpenter, the toll-man, are much displeased at the intimation.

But whilst we acquiesce entirely in the permanence of natural laws, the question of the absolute existence of nature, still remains open. It is the uniform effect of culture on the human mind, not to shake our faith in the stability of particular phenomena, as of heat, water, azote; [2] but to lead us to regard nature as a phenomenon, not a substance; to attribute necessary existence to spirit; to esteem nature as an accident and an effect.

To the senses and the unrenewed understanding, belongs a sort of instinctive belief in the absolute existence of nature. In their view, man and nature are indissolubly joined. Things are ultimates, and they never look beyond their sphere. The presence of Reason

---

8. *Cf.* Psalms xlii: 7.
9. A prophetic revelation.
1. That is, they make a jest of the transcendental belief (suggested in the two previous paragraphs) that the essential reality of the thing inheres in the idea, to be sought in the mind.
2. Nitrogen.

mars this faith. The first effort of thought tends to relax this despotism of the senses, which binds us to nature as if we were a part of it, and shows us nature aloof, and, as it were, afloat. Until this higher agency intervened, the animal eye sees, with wonderful accuracy, sharp outlines and colored surfaces. When the eye of Reason opens, to outline and surface are at once added, grace and expression. These proceed from imagination and affection, and abate somewhat of the angular distinctness of objects. If the Reason be stimulated to more earnest vision, outlines and surfaces become transparent, and are no longer seen; causes and spirits are seen through them. The best, the happiest moments of life, are these delicious awakenings of the higher powers, and the reverential withdrawing of nature before its God.

Let us proceed to indicate the effects of culture. 1. Our first institution in the Ideal philosophy is a hint from nature herself.

Nature is made to conspire with spirit to emancipate us. Certain mechanical changes, a small alteration in our local position apprizes us of a dualism. We are strangely affected by seeing the shore from a moving ship, from a balloon, or through the tints of an unusual sky. The least change in our point of view, gives the whole world a pictorial air. A man who seldom rides, needs only to get into a coach and traverse his own town, to turn the street into a puppet-show. The men, the women,—talking, running, bartering, fighting, —the earnest mechanic, the lounger, the beggar, the boys, the dogs, are unrealized [3] at once, or, at least, wholly detached from all relation to the observer, and seen as apparent, not substantial beings. What new thoughts are suggested by seeing a face [4] of country quite familiar, in the rapid movement of the rail-road car! Nay, the most wonted objects, (make a very slight change in the point of vision,) please us most. In a camera obscura,[5] the butcher's cart, and the figure of one of our own family amuse us. So a portrait of a well-known face gratifies us. Turn the eyes upside down, by looking at the landscape through your legs, and how agreeable is the picture, though you have seen it any time these twenty years!

In these cases, by mechanical means, is suggested the difference between the observer and the spectacle,—between man and nature. Hence arises a pleasure mixed with awe; I may say, a low degree of the sublime is felt from the fact, probably, that man is hereby apprized, that, whilst the world is a spectacle, something in himself is stable.

2. In a higher manner, the poet communicates the same pleasure. By a few strokes he delineates, as on air, the sun, the mountain,

---

3. *I.e.*, deprived of reality.
4. In the archaic sense, meaning "view."

5. An optical instrument, the ancestor of the camera.

the camp, the city, the hero, the maiden, not different from what we know them, but only lifted from the ground and afloat before the eye. He unfixes the land and the sea, makes them revolve around the axis of his primary thought, and disposes them anew. Possessed himself by a heroic passion, he uses matter as symbols of it. The sensual man conforms thoughts to things; the poet conforms things to his thoughts. The one esteems nature as rooted and fast; the other, as fluid, and impresses his being thereon. To him, the refractory world is ductile and flexible; he invests dust and stones with humanity, and makes them the words of the Reason. The imagination may be defined to be, the use which the Reason makes of the material world. Shakspeare possesses the power of subordinating nature for the purposes of expression, beyond all poets. His imperial muse tosses the creation like a bauble from hand to hand, and uses it to embody any capricious shade of thought that is uppermost in his mind. The remotest spaces of nature are visited, and the farthest sundered things are brought together, by a subtle spiritual connexion. We are made aware that magnitude of material things is merely relative, and all objects shrink and expand to serve the passion of the poet. Thus, in his sonnets, the lays of birds, the scents and dyes of flowers, he finds to be the *shadow* of his beloved; [6] time, which keeps her from him, is his *chest*; [7] the suspicion she has awakened, is her *ornament*;

> The ornament of beauty is Suspect,
> A crow which flies in heaven's sweetest air.[8]

His passion is not the fruit of chance; it swells, as he speaks, to a city, or a state.

> No, it was builded far from accident;
> It suffers not in smiling pomp, nor falls
> Under the brow of thralling discontent;
> It fears not policy, that heretic,
> That works on leases of short numbered hours,
> But all alone stands hugely politic.[9]

In the strength of his constancy, the Pyramids [1] seem to him recent and transitory. And the freshness of youth and love dazzles him with its resemblance to morning.

> Take those lips away
> Which so sweetly were forsworn;

---

6. *Cf.* **Shakespeare, Sonnet XCVIII.**
7. *Cf.* Shakespeare, Sonnet LXV, l. 10.
8. Shakespeare, Sonnet LXX, ll. 3–4. For "which" read "that."

9. From Shakespeare, Sonnet CXXIV, with slight alteration.
1. *Cf.* Shakespeare, Sonnet CXXIII, l. 2.

> And those eyes,—the break of day,
> Lights that do mislead the morn.[2]

The wild beauty of this hyperbole, I may say, in passing, it would not be easy to match in literature.

This transfiguration which all material objects undergo through the passion of the poet,—this power which he exerts, at any moment, to magnify the small, to micrify the great,—might be illustrated by a thousand examples from his Plays. I have before me the Tempest, and will cite only these few lines.

> ARIEL. The strong based promontory
> Have I made shake, and by the spurs plucked up
> The pine and cedar.[3]

Prospero calls for music to sooth the frantic Alonzo, and his companions;

> A solemn air, and the best comforter
> To an unsettled fancy, cure thy brains
> Now useless, boiled within thy skull.[4]

Again;

> The charm dissolves apace
> And, as the morning steals upon the night,
> Melting the darkness, so their rising senses
> Begin to chase the ignorant fumes that mantle
> Their clearer reason.
> Their understanding
> Begins to swell: and the approaching tide
> Will shortly fill the reasonable shores
> That now lie foul and muddy.[5]

The perception of real affinities between events, (that is to say, of *ideal* affinities, for those only are real,) enables the poet thus to make free with the most imposing forms and phenomena of the world, and to assert the predominance of the soul.

3. Whilst thus the poet delights us by animating nature like a creator, with his own thoughts, he differs from the philosopher only herein, that the one proposes Beauty as his main end; the other Truth. But, the philosopher, not less than the poet, postpones the apparent order and relations of things to the empire of thought. "The problem of philosophy," according to Plato, "is, for all that

2. See Shakespeare's *Measure For Measure*, the song opening Act IV, Scene 1. Lines 1–4 are here slightly altered.
3. *The Tempest*, Act V, Scene 1, ll.

46–48; but the speaker is Prospero, not Ariel.
4. *Ibid*. Act V, Scene 1, ll. 58–60.
5. *Ibid*. Act V, Scene 1, ll. 64–68, 79–82.

exists conditionally, to find a ground unconditioned and absolute." [6]
It proceeds on the faith that a law determines all phenomena,
which being known, the phenomena can be predicted. That law,
when in the mind, is an idea. Its beauty is infinite. The true philosopher and the true poet are one, and a beauty, which is truth,
and a truth, which is beauty, is the aim of both. Is not the charm of
one of Plato's or Aristotle's definitions, strictly like that of the
Antigone of Sophocles? [7] It is, in both cases, that a spiritual life
has been imparted to nature; that the solid seeming block of matter has been pervaded and dissolved by a thought; that this feeble
human being has penetrated the vast masses of nature with an informing soul, and recognised itself in their harmony, that is, seized
their law. In physics, when this is attained, the memory disburth-
ens itself of its cumbrous catalogues of particulars, and carries
centuries of observation in a single formula.

Thus even in physics, the material is ever degraded before the
spiritual. The astronomer, the geometer, rely on their irrefragable
analysis, and disdain the results of observation. The sublime remark
of Euler [8] on his law of arches, "This will be found contrary to all
experience, yet is true;" had already transferred nature into the
mind, and left matter like an outcast corpse.

4. Intellectual science has been observed to beg invariably a
doubt of the existence of matter. Turgot [9] said, "He that has never
doubted the existence of matter, may be assured he has no aptitude
for metaphysical inquiries." It fastens the attention upon immortal
necessary uncreated natures, that is, upon Ideas; and in their beautiful and majestic presence, we feel that our outward being is a
dream and a shade. Whilst we wait in this Olympus of gods, we
think of nature as an appendix to the soul. We ascend into their
region, and know that these are the thoughts of the Supreme Being.
"These are they who were set up from everlasting, from the beginning, or ever the earth was. When he prepared the heavens, they
were there; when he established the clouds above, when he strengthened the fountains of the deep. Then they were by him, as one
brought up with him. Of them took he counsel." [1]

Their influence is proportionate. As objects of science, they are
accessible to few men. Yet all men are capable of being raised by
piety or by passion, into their region. And no man touches these
divine natures, without becoming, in some degree, himself divine.
Like a new soul, they renew the body. We become physically nimble and lightsome; we tread on air; life is no longer irksome, and

6. See *The Republic,* Book V.
7. Sophocles (496?–406 B.C.) produced in the *Antigone* one of the most
moving of the great Greek tragedies.
8. Leonhard Euler (1707–1783), Swiss
mathematician.

9. Anne Robert Jacques Turgot (1727–
1781), French liberal, statesman and
economist.
1. Condensed paraphrase of Proverbs
viii: 23, 27, 28, 30.

we think it will never be so. No man fears age or misfortune or death, in their serene company, for he is transported out of the district of change. Whilst we behold unveiled the nature of Justice and Truth, we learn the difference between the absolute and the conditional or relative. We apprehend the absolute. As it were, for the first time, *we exist*. We become immortal, for we learn that time and space are relations of matter; that, with a perception of truth, or a virtuous will, they have no affinity.

5. Finally, religion and ethics, which may be fitly called,—the practice of ideas, or the introduction of ideas into life,—have an analogous effect with all lower culture, in degrading nature and suggesting its dependence on spirit. Ethics and religion differ herein; that the one is the system of human duties commencing from man; the other, from God. Religion includes the personality of God; Ethics does not. They are one to our present design. They both put nature under foot. The first and last lesson of religion is, "The things that are seen, are temporal; the things that are unseen are eternal." [2] It puts an affront upon nature. It does that for the unschooled, which philosophy does for Berkeley and Viasa.[3] The uniform language that may be heard in the churches of the most ignorant sects, is,—'Contemn the unsubstantial shows of the world; they are vanities, dreams, shadows, unrealities; seek the realities of religion.' The devotee flouts nature. Some theosophists [4] have arrived at a certain hostility and indignation towards matter, as the Manichean [5] and Plotinus.[6] They distrusted in themselves any looking back to these flesh-pots of Egypt.[7] Plotinus was ashamed of his body. In short, they might all better say of matter, what Michael Angelo said of external beauty, "it is the frail and weary weed, in which God dresses the soul, which he has called into time."

It appears that motion, poetry, physical and intellectual science, and religion, all tend to affect our convictions of the reality of the external world. But I own there is something ungrateful in expanding too curiously the particulars of the general proposition, that all culture tends to imbue us with idealism. I have no hostility to nature, but a child's love to it. I expand and live in the warm day like corn and melons. Let us speak her fair. I do not wish to fling stones at my beautiful mother, nor soil my gentle nest. I only wish

---

2. *Cf.* II Corinthians iv: 18.

3. George Berkeley (1685–1753), English churchman and thinker, whose idealistic philosophy is here associated with the spirit of Viasa, a legendary Hindu personage credited with the authorship of a substantial part of the Sanskrit scriptures.

4. The term is here broadly applied to theologians who claim direct knowledge of God by mystical revelation.

5. An adherent to the doctrine of Mani, or Manes, a third century Persian sage who asserted that the body was produced by evil or darkness, but the soul streams from the principle of goodness or light.

6. Plotinus (204?–270? A.D.), a Roman Platonist of Egyptian origin, gave a mystical and symbolic interpretation to the doctrines of Plato.

7. *Cf.* Exodus xvi: 3.

to indicate the true position of nature in regard to man, wherein to establish man, all right education tends; as the ground which to attain is the object of human life, that is, of man's connexion with nature. Culture inverts the vulgar views of nature, and brings the mind to call that apparent, which it uses to call real, and that real, which it uses to call visionary. Children, it is true, believe in the external world. The belief that it appears only, is an afterthought, but with culture, this faith will as surely arise on the mind as did the first.

The advantage of the ideal theory over the popular faith, is this, that it presents the world in precisely that view which is most desirable to the mind. It is, in fact, the view which Reason, both speculative and practical,[8] that is, philosophy and virtue, take. For, seen in the light of thought, the world always is phenomenal; and virtue subordinates it to the mind. Idealism sees the world in God. It beholds the whole circle of persons and things, of actions and events, of country and religion, not as painfully accumulated, atom after atom, act after act, in an aged creeping Past, but as one vast picture, which God paints on the instant eternity, for the contemplation of the soul. Therefore the soul holds itself off from a too trivial and microscopic study of the universal tablet. It respects the end too much, to immerse itself in the means. It sees something more important in Christianity, than the scandals of ecclesiastical history or the niceties of criticism; and, very incurious concerning persons or miracles, and not at all disturbed by chasms of historical evidence, it accepts from God the phenomenon, as it finds it, as the pure and awful form of religion in the world. It is not hot and passionate at the appearance of what it calls its own good or bad fortune, at the union or opposition of other persons. No man is its enemy. It accepts whatsoever befals, as part of its lesson. It is a watcher more than a doer, and it is a doer, only that it may the better watch.

Chapter VII. Spirit

It is essential to a true theory of nature and of man, that it should contain somewhat progressive. Uses that are exhausted or that may be, and facts that end in the statement, cannot be all that is true of this brave lodging wherein man is harbored, and wherein all his faculties find appropriate and endless exercise. And all the uses of nature admit of being summed in one, which yields the activity of man an infinite scope. Through all its kingdoms, to the suburbs and outskirts of things, it is faithful to the cause whence it had its

8. Kant's distinction between the practical Reason (understanding), which regulates behavior, and speculative Reason, which supports metaphysical thought, was a familiar concept among transcendentalists.

origin. It always speaks of Spirit. It suggests the absolute. It is a perpetual effect. It is a great shadow pointing always to the sun behind us.

The aspect of nature is devout. Like the figure of Jesus, she stands with bended head, and hands folded upon the breast. The happiest man is he who learns from nature the lesson of worship.

Of that ineffable essence which we call Spirit, he that thinks most, will say least. We can foresee God in the course and, as it were, distant phenomena of matter; but when we try to define and describe himself, both language and thought desert us, and we are as helpless as fools and savages. That essence refuses to be recorded in propositions, but when man has worshipped him intellectually, the noblest ministry of nature is to stand as the apparition of God. It is the great organ through which the universal spirit speaks to the individual, and strives to lead back the individual to it.

When we consider Spirit, we see that the views already presented do not include the whole circumference of man. We must add some related thoughts.

Three problems are put by nature to the mind; What is matter? Whence is it? and Whereto? The first of these questions only, the ideal theory answers. Idealism saith: matter is a phenomenon, not a substance. Idealism acquaints us with the total disparity between the evidence of our own being, and the evidence of the world's being. The one is perfect; the other, incapable of any assurance; the mind is a part of the nature of things; the world is a divine dream, from which we may presently awake to the glories and certainties of day. Idealism is a hypothesis to account for nature by other principles than those of carpentry and chemistry. Yet, if it only deny the existence of matter, it does not satisfy the demands of the spirit. It leaves God out of me. It leaves me in the splendid labyrinth of my perceptions, to wander without end. Then the heart resists it, because it baulks the affections in denying substantive being to men and women. Nature is so pervaded with human life, that there is something of humanity in all, and in every particular. But this theory makes nature foreign to me, and does not account for that consanguinity which we acknowledge to it.

Let it stand then, in the present state of our knowledge, merely as a useful introductory hypothesis, serving to apprize us of the eternal distinction between the soul and the world.

But when, following the invisible steps of thought, we come to inquire, Whence is matter? and Whereto? many truths arise to us out of the recesses of consciousness. We learn that the highest is present to the soul of man, that the dread universal essence, which is not wisdom, or love, or beauty, or power, but all in one, and each entirely, is that for which all things exist, and that by which they are; that spirit creates; that behind nature, throughout nature, spirit is present; that spirit is one and not compound; that spirit does not act upon us from without, that is, in space and time, but spiritually, or through ourselves. Therefore, that spirit, that is, the Supreme Being, does not build up nature around us, but puts it forth through us, as the life of the tree puts forth new branches and leaves through the pores of the old. As a plant upon the earth, so a man rests upon the bosom of God; he is nourished by unfailing fountains, and draws, at his need, inexhaustible power. Who can set bounds to the possibilities of man? Once inhale the upper air, being admitted to behold the absolute natures of justice and truth, and we learn that man has access to the entire mind of the Creator, is himself the creator in the finite. This view, which admonishes me where the sources of wisdom and power lie, and points to virtue as to

> "The golden key
> Which opes the palace of eternity," [9]

carries upon its face the highest certificate of truth, because it animates me to create my own world through the purification of my soul.

The world proceeds from the same spirit as the body of man. It is a remoter and inferior incarnation of God, a projection of God in the unconscious. But it differs from the body in one important respect. It is not, like that, now subjected to the human will. Its serene order is inviolable by us. It is therefore, to us, the present expositor of the divine mind. It is a fixed point whereby we may measure our departure. As we degenerate, the contrast between us and our house is more evident. We are as much strangers in nature, as we are aliens from God. We do not understand the notes of birds. The fox and the deer run away from us; the bear and tiger rend us. We do not know the uses of more than a few plants, as corn and the apple, the potato and the vine. Is not the landscape, every glimpse of which hath a grandeur, a face of him? Yet this may show us what discord is between man and nature, for you cannot freely admire a noble landscape, if laborers are digging in the field hard by. The poet finds something ridiculous in his delight, until he is out of the sight of men.

Chapter VIII. Prospects

In inquiries respecting the laws of the world and the frame of things, the highest reason is always the truest. That which seems faintly possible—it is so refined, is often faint and dim because it is

---

9. John Milton, *Comus*, ll. 13–14.

deepest seated in the mind among the eternal verities. Empirical [1] science is apt to cloud the sight, and, by the very knowledge of functions and processes, to bereave the student of the manly contemplation of the whole. The savant [2] becomes unpoetic. But the best read naturalist who lends an entire and devout attention to truth, will see that there remains much to learn of his relation to the world, and that it is not to be learned by any addition or subtraction or other comparison of known quantities, but is arrived at by untaught sallies of the spirit, by a continual self-recovery, and by entire humility. He will perceive that there are far more excellent qualities in the student than preciseness and infallibility; that a guess is often more fruitful than an indisputable affirmation, and that a dream may let us deeper into the secret of nature than a hundred concerted experiments.

For, the problems to be solved are precisely those which the physiologist and the naturalist omit to state. It is not so pertinent to man to know all the individuals of the animal kingdom, as it is to know whence and whereto is this tyrannizing unity in his constitution, which evermore separates and classifies things, endeavoring to reduce the most diverse to one form. When I behold a rich landscape, it is less to my purpose to recite correctly the order and superposition of the strata, than to know why all thought of multitude is lost in a tranquil sense of unity. I cannot greatly honor minuteness in details, so long as there is no hint to explain the relation between things and thoughts; no ray upon the *metaphysics* of conchology, of botany, of the arts, to show the relation of the forms of flowers, shells, animals, architecture, to the mind, and build science upon ideas. In a cabinet of natural history,[3] we become sensible of a certain occult recognition and sympathy in regard to the most unwieldy and eccentric forms of beast, fish, and insect. The American who has been confined, in his own country, to the sight of buildings designed after foreign models, is surprised on entering York Minister [4] or St. Peter's at Rome,[5] by the feeling that these structures are imitations also,—faint copies of an invisible archetype. Nor has science sufficient humanity, so long as the naturalist overlooks that wonderful congruity which subsists between man and the world; of which he is lord, not because he is the most subtile inhabitant, but because he is its head and heart, and

1. Experimental, based on systematized observation, as contrasted with intuitive cognition.
2. By derivation, "one who knows," a scholar; but here suggesting a dogmatist.
3. The "cabinet," or display case of classified specimens, was then a principal pedagogical instrument for biological science.

4. The stately minster (cathedral) at York, England, replacing a church dating from 627, was under construction from 1230 to 1474.
5. Saint Peter's at Rome, like York Minster, was long under construction (1445–1626). It was the work of many creators, of whom Michelangelo was the most important.

finds something of himself in every great and small thing, in every mountain stratum, in every new law of color, fact of astronomy, or atmospheric influence which observation or analysis lay open. A perception of this mystery inspires the muse of George Herbert,[6] the beautiful psalmist of the seventeenth century. The following lines are part of his little poem on Man.

> "Man is all symmetry,
> Full of proportions, one limb to another,
> And to all the world besides.
> Each part may call the farthest, brother;
> For head with foot hath private amity,
> And both with moons and tides.
>
> "Nothing hath got so far
> But man hath caught and kept it as his prey;
> His eyes dismount the highest star;
> He is in little all the sphere.
> Herbs gladly cure our flesh, because that they
> Find their acquaintance there.
>
> "For us, the winds do blow,
> The earth doth rest, heaven move, and fountains flow:
> Nothing we see, but means our good,
> As our delight, or as our treasure;
> The whole is either our cupboard of food,
> Or cabinet of pleasure.
>
> "The stars have us to bed:
> Night draws the curtain; which the sun withdraws.
> Music and light attend our head.
> All things unto our flesh are kind,
> In their descent and being; to our mind,
> In their ascent and cause.
>
> "More servants wait on man
> Than he'll take notice of. In every path,
> He treads down that which doth befriend him
> When sickness makes him pale and wan.
> Oh mighty love! Man is one world, and hath
> Another to attend him."

The perception of this class of truths makes the eternal attraction which draws men to science, but the end is lost sight of in attention to the means. In view of this half-sight of science, we accept the sentence of Plato, that, "poetry comes nearer to vital truth than

6. British metaphysical poet (1593–1633). The lines quoted are from "Man," stanzas 3–6 and 8.

history." Every surmise and vaticination [7] of the mind is entitled to a certain respect, and we learn to prefer imperfect theories, and sentences, which contain glimpses of truth, to digested systems which have no one valuable suggestion. A wise writer will feel that the ends of study and composition are best answered by announcing undiscovered regions of thought, and so communicating, through hope, new activity to the torpid spirit.

I shall therefore conclude this essay with some traditions of man and nature, which a certain poet [8] sang to me; and which, as they have always been in the world, and perhaps reappear to every bard, may be both history and prophecy.

'The foundations of man are not in matter, but in spirit. But the element of spirit is eternity. To it, therefore, the longest series of events, the oldest chronologies are young and recent. In the cycle of the universal man, from whom the known individuals proceed, centuries are points, and all history is but the epoch of one degradation.

'We distrust and deny inwardly our sympathy with nature. We own and disown our relation to it, by turns. We are, like Nebuchadnezzar,[9] dethroned, bereft of reason, and eating grass like an ox. But who can set limits to the remedial force of spirit?

'A man is a god in ruins. When men are innocent, life shall be longer, and shall pass into the immortal, as gently as we awake from dreams. Now, the world would be insane and rabid, if these disorganizations should last for hundreds of years. It is kept in check by death and infancy. Infancy is the perpetual Messiah, which comes into the arms of fallen men, and pleads with them to return to paradise.

'Man is the dwarf of himself. Once he was permeated and dissolved by spirit. He filled nature with his overflowing currents. Out from him sprang the sun and moon; from man, the sun; from woman, the moon. The laws of his mind, the periods of his actions externized themselves into day and night, into the year and the seasons. But, having made for himself this huge shell, his waters retired; he no longer fills the veins and veinlets; he is shrunk to a drop. He sees, that the structure still fits him, but fits him colossally. Say, rather, once it fitted him, now it corresponds to him from far and on high. He adores timidly his own work. Now is man the follower of the sun, and woman the follower of the moon. Yet

---

7. Ordinarily, prophecy; here, as a mental process, revelation.
8. [Amos] Bronson Alcott (1799–1888), transcendentalist and educational pioneer, employed conversation as the medium for his philosophy. E. W. Emerson (Centenary Edition, Vol. I, p. 412) notes that his father here attempted to reproduce the style of Alcott's "conversations" (*cf.* "Orphic Sayings," *The Dial*, 1840). See Emerson's phrase "my Orphic poet." The rituals and songs of the cult of Orpheus were described as "mystic and oracular."
9. Daniel iv: 31–33.

sometimes he starts in his slumber, and wonders at himself and his house, and muses strangely at the resemblance betwixt him and it. He perceives that if his law is still paramount, if still he have elemental power, "if his word is sterling yet in nature," it is not conscious power, it is not inferior but superior to his will. It is Instinct.' Thus my Orphic poet sang.

At present, man applies to nature but half his force. He works on the world with his understanding alone. He lives in it, and masters it by a penny-wisdom; and he that works most in it, is but a half-man, and whilst his arms are strong and his digestion good, his mind is imbruted and he is a selfish savage. His relation to nature, his power over it, is through the understanding; as by manure; the economic use of fire, wind, water, and the mariner's needle; steam, coal, chemical agriculture; the repairs of the human body by the dentist and the surgeon. This is such a resumption of power, as if a banished king should buy his territories inch by inch, instead of vaulting at once into his throne. Meantime, in the thick darkness, there are not wanting gleams of a better light,—occasional examples of the action of man upon nature with his entire force,—with reason as well as understanding. Such examples are; the traditions of miracles in the earliest antiquity of all nations; the history of Jesus Christ; the achievements of a principle, as in religious and political revolutions, and in the abolition of the Slave-trade; the miracles of enthusiasm,[1] as those reported of Swedenborg, Hohenlohe, and the Shakers; many obscure and yet contested facts, now arranged under the name of Animal Magnetism; [2] prayer; eloquence; self-healing; and the wisdom of children. These are examples of Reason's momentary grasp of the sceptre; the exertions of a power which exists not in time or space, but an instantaneous in-streaming causing power. The difference between the actual and the ideal force of man is happily figured by the schoolmen, in saying, that the knowledge of man is an evening knowledge, *vespertina cognitio*, but that of God is a morning knowledge, *matutina cognitio*.[3]

The problem of restoring to the world original and eternal beauty, is solved by the redemption of the soul. The ruin or the blank, that we see when we look at nature, is in our own eye. The axis of vision is not coincident with the axis of things, and so they

1. In the historical sense, inspiration or possession by the god. Alexander Leopold, Prince of Hohenlohe (1794–1849), German Catholic priest, caused a sensational controversy by his "miracles"; the Shakers prophesied the millennium and exhibited hysterical manifestations of "possession."
2. The term given to hypnosis by the pioneer experimenter, Franz Anton Mesmer (1734–1815), Austrian physician. 3. These Latin phrases, translated in the sentence, belonged to the logic of the Schoolmen—the scholastic philosophers of the Middle Ages. See Centenary Edition, Vol. I, pp. 413–414, for particular reference to St. Augustine and St. Thomas Aquinas.

appear not transparent but opake.[4] The reason why the world lacks unity, and lies broken and in heaps, is, because man is disunited with himself. He cannot be a naturalist, until he satisfies all the demands of the spirit. Love is as much its demand, as perception. Indeed, neither can be perfect without the other. In the uttermost meaning of the words, thought is devout, and devotion is thought. Deep calls unto deep.[5] But in actual life, the marriage is not celebrated. There are innocent men who worship God after the tradition of their fathers, but their sense of duty has not yet extended to the use of all their faculties. And there are patient naturalists, but they freeze their subject under the wintry light of the understanding. Is not prayer also a study of truth,—a sally of the soul into the unfound infinite? No man ever prayed heartily, without learning something. But when a faithful thinker, resolute to detach every object from personal relations, and see it in the light of thought, shall, at the same time, kindle science with the fire of the holiest affections, then will God go forth anew into the creation.

It will not need, when the mind is prepared for study, to search for objects. The invariable mark of wisdom is to see the miraculous in the common. What is day? What is a year? What is summer? What is woman? What is a child? What is sleep? To our blindness, these things seem unaffecting. We make fables to hide the baldness of the fact and conform it, as we say, to the higher law of the mind. But when the fact is seen under the light of an idea, the gaudy fable fades and shrivels. We behold the real higher law. To the wise, therefore, a fact is true poetry, and the most beautiful of fables. These wonders are brought to our own door. You also are a man. Man and woman, and their social life, poverty, labor, sleep, fear, fortune, are known to you. Learn that none of these things is superficial, but that each phenomenon hath its roots in the faculties and affections of the mind. Whilst the abstract question occupies your intellect, nature brings it in the concrete to be solved by your hands. It were a wise inquiry for the closet, to compare, point by point, especially at remarkable crises in life, our daily history, with the rise and progress of ideas in the mind.

So shall we come to look at the world with new eyes. It shall answer the endless inquiry of the intellect,—What is truth? and of the affections,—What is good? by yielding itself passive to the educated Will. Then shall come to pass what my poet said; 'Nature is not fixed but fluid. Spirit alters, moulds, makes it. The immobility or bruteness of nature, is the absence of spirit; to pure spirit,

---

4. This is the 1849 reading. Later editions corrected the spelling to "opaque."

5. *Cf.* Psalms xlii: 7: "Deep calleth unto deep at the noise of thy waterspouts: all thy waves and thy billows are gone over me."

it is fluid, it is volatile, it is obedient. Every spirit builds itself a house; and beyond its house, a world; and beyond its world, a heaven. Know then, that the world exists for you. For you is the phenomenon perfect. What we are, that only can we see. All that Adam had, all that Cæsar could, you have and can do. Adam called his house, heaven and earth; Cæsar called his house, Rome; you perhaps call yours, a cobler's trade; a hundred acres of ploughed land; or a scholar's garret. Yet line for line and point for point, your dominion is as great as theirs, though without fine names. Build, therefore, your own world. As fast as you conform your life to the pure idea in your mind, that will unfold its great proportions. A correspondent revolution in things will attend the influx of the spirit. So fast will disagreeable appearances, swine, spiders, snakes, pests, mad-houses, prisons, enemies, vanish; they are temporary and shall be no more seen. The sordor and filths of nature, the sun shall dry up, and the wind exhale. As when the summer comes from the south, the snow-banks melt, and the face of the earth becomes green before it, so shall the advancing spirit create its ornaments along its path, and carry with it the beauty it visits, and the song which enchants it; it shall draw beautiful faces, and warm hearts, and wise discourse, and heroic acts, around its way, until evil is no more seen. The kingdom of man over nature, which cometh not with observation,—a dominion such as now is beyond his dream of God,—he shall enter without more wonder than the blind man feels who is gradually restored to perfect sight.'

1836

The American Scholar [6]

An Oration
Delivered Before the Phi Beta Kappa Society,
at Cambridge, August 31, 1837

MR. PRESIDENT, AND GENTLEMEN,

I greet you on the re-commencement of our literary year.[7] Our anniversary is one of hope, and, perhaps, not enough of labor. We

6. The Phi Beta Kappa address at Harvard College on August 31, 1837, like the guns of its author's "embattled farmers," was "heard round the world," the first clarion of an American literary renaissance. Emerson had no such heroic expectations; he had modestly recorded his compact with his destiny in his journal a month before: "If the All-wise would give me light, I should write for the Cambridge men a theory of the Scholar's office." But Lowell, remembering thirty-four years later the "enthusiasm of approval" (in "Thoreau," *My Study Windows*, 1871), saw the awakening of a spiritual epoch:

"The * * * Revolution [had made us] politically independent, but we were still socially and intellectually moved to English thought till Emerson cut the cable. * * * " Holmes's *obiter dictum*, "Our intellectual Declaration of Independence," however familiar, is still final. The address was published in 1837 and again in 1838; as *Man Thinking: An Oration*, in London in 1844; and as one of the essays in the collection, *Nature, Addresses, and Lectures* (1849).
7. *I.e.*, "our college year," then customarily beginning about September 1.

do not meet for games of strength or skill, for the recitation of histories, tragedies and odes, like the ancient Greeks; for parliaments of love and poesy, like the Troubadours; nor for the advancement of science,[8] like our cotemporaries[9] in the British and European capitals. Thus far, our holiday has been simply a friendly sign of the survival of the love of letters amongst a people too busy to give to letters any more. As such, it is precious as the sign of an indestructible instinct. Perhaps the time is already come, when it ought to be, and will be something else; when the sluggard intellect of this continent will look from under its iron lids and fill the postponed expectation of the world with something better than the exertions of mechanical skill. Our day of dependence, our long apprenticeship to the learning of other lands, draws to a close. The millions that around us are rushing into life, cannot always be fed on the sere remains of foreign harvests. Events, actions arise, that must be sung, that will sing themselves. Who can doubt that poetry will revive and lead in a new age, as the star in the constellation Harp[1] which now flames in our zenith, astronomers announce, shall one day be the pole-star for a thousand years?

In the light of this hope, I accept the topic which not only usage, but the nature of our association, seem to prescribe to this day,—the AMERICAN SCHOLAR. Year by year, we come up hither to read one more chapter of his biography. Let us inquire what light new days and events have thrown on his character, his duties and his hopes.

It is one of those fables, which out of an unknown antiquity, convey an unlooked-for wisdom, that the gods, in the beginning, divided Man into men, that he might be more helpful to himself;[2] just as the hand was divided into fingers, the better to answer its end.

The old fable covers a doctrine ever new and sublime; that there is One Man,—present to all particular men only partially, or through one faculty; and that you must take the whole society to find the whole man. Man is not a farmer, or a professor, or an engineer, but he is all. Man is priest, and scholar, and statesman, and producer, and solider. In the *divided* or social state, these functions are parcelled out to individuals, each of whom aims to do his stint of the joint work, whilst each other performs his. The fable implies that the individual to possess himself, must sometimes return

8. The development of learned associations abroad and the research of European universities had then no parallel in America.
9. The 1849 text read "co-temporaries"; corrected in later editions to "contemporaries."
1. The constellation Lyra, containing

Vega, the fourth brightest star of the heavens, to which Emerson refers.
2. Emerson was familiar with a version of this fable in Plato, the *Symposium;* and with another, "Of Brotherly Love," in Plutarch's *Morals* (E. W. Emerson, Centenary Edition, Vol. I, p. 417).

from his own labor to embrace all the other laborers. But unfortunately, this original unit, this fountain of power, has been so distributed to multitudes, has been so minutely subdivided and peddled out, that it is spilled into drops, and cannot be gathered. The state of society is one in which the members have suffered amputation from the trunk, and strut about so many walking monsters,— a good finger, a neck, a stomach, an elbow, but never a man.

Man is thus metamorphosed into a thing, into many things. The planter, who is Man sent out into the field to gather food, is seldom cheered by any idea of the true dignity of his ministry. He sees his bushel and his cart, and nothing beyond, and sinks into the farmer, instead of Man on the farm. The tradesman scarcely ever gives an ideal worth to his work, but is ridden by the routine of his craft, and the soul is subject to dollars. The priest becomes a form; the attorney, a statute-book; the mechanic, a machine; the sailor, a rope of a ship.

In this distribution of functions, the scholar is the delegated intellect. In the right state, he is, *Man Thinking*. In the degenerate state, when the victim of society, he tends to become a mere thinker, or, still worse, the parrot of other men's thinking.

In this view of him, as Man Thinking, the whole theory of his office is contained. Him nature solicits, with all her placid, all her monitory pictures. Him the past instructs. Him the future invites. Is not, indeed, every man a student, and do not all things exist for the student's behoof? And, finally, is not the true scholar the only true master? But, as the old oracle said, "All things have two handles. Beware of the wrong one." In life, too often, the scholar errs with mankind and forfeits his privilege. Let us see him in his school, and consider him in reference to the main influences he receives.

I. The first in time and the first in importance of the influences upon the mind is that of nature. Every day, the sun; and, after sunset, night and her stars. Ever the winds blow; ever the grass grows. Every day, men and women, conversing, beholding and beholden. The scholar must needs stand wistful and admiring before this great spectacle. He must settle its value in his mind. What is nature to him? There is never a beginning, there is never an end to the inexplicable continuity of this web of God, but always circular power returning into itself. Therein it resembles his own spirit, whose beginning, whose ending he never can find—so entire, so boundless. Far, too, as her splendors shine, system on system shooting like rays, upward, downward, without centre, without circumference,—in the mass and in the particle nature hastens to render account of herself to the mind. Classification begins. To the young mind, every thing is individual, stands by itself. By and by, it finds how to join two things, and see in them one nature; then three, then three thousand; and so, tyrannized over by its own unifying instinct, it goes on tying things together, diminishing anomalies, discovering roots running under ground, whereby contrary and remote things cohere, and flower out from one stem. It presently learns, that, since the dawn of history, there has been a constant accumulation and classifying of facts. But what is classification but the perceiving that these objects are not chaotic, and are not foreign, but have a law which is also a law of the human mind? The astronomer discovers that geometry, a pure abstraction of the human mind, is the measure of planetary motion. The chemist finds proportions and intelligible method throughout matter: and science is nothing but the finding of analogy, identity in the most remote parts. The ambitious soul sits down before each refractory fact; one after another, reduces all strange constitutions, all new powers, to their class and their law, and goes on forever to animate the last fibre of organization, the outskirts of nature, by insight.

Thus to him, to this school-boy under the bending dome of day, is suggested, that he and it proceed from one root; one is leaf and one is flower; relation, sympathy, stirring in every vein. And what is that Root? Is not that the soul of his soul?—A thought too bold —a dream too wild. Yet when this spiritual light shall have revealed the law of more earthly natures,—when he has learned to worship the soul, and to see that the natural philosophy that now is, is only the first gropings of its gigantic hand, he shall look forward to an ever expanding knowledge as to a becoming creator.[3] He shall see that nature is the opposite of the soul, answering to it part for part. One is seal, and one is print. Its beauty is the beauty of his own mind. Its laws are the laws of his own mind. Nature then becomes to him the measure of his attainments. So much of nature as he is ignorant of, so much of his own mind does he not yet possess. And, in fine, the ancient precept, "Know thyself," and the modern precept, "Study nature," becomes at last one maxim.

II. The next great influence[4] into the spirit of the scholar, is, the mind of the Past,—in whatever form, whether of literature, of art, of institutions, that mind is inscribed. Books are the best type of the influence of the past, and perhaps we shall get at the truth— learn the amount of this influence more conveniently—by considering their value alone.

The theory of books is noble. The scholar of the first age received into him the world around; brooded thereon; gave it the new

3. "Whether or no there be a God, it is certain that there will be." Translation in Emerson's *Journals* from a French source (Centenary Editions, Vol. I, p. 418).

4. As by Latin derivation, "inflowing."

arrangement of his own mind, and uttered it again. It came into him—life; it went out from him—truth. It came to him—short-lived actions; it went out from him—immortal thoughts. It came to him—business; it went from him—poetry. It was—dead fact; now, it is quick thought. It can stand, and it can go. It now endures, it now flies, it now inspires. Precisely in proportion to the depth of mind from which it issued, so high does it soar, so long does it sing.

Or, I might say, it depends on how far the process had gone, of transmuting life into truth. In proportion to the completeness of the distillation, so will the purity and imperishableness of the product be. But none is quite perfect. As no air-pump can by any means make a perfect vacuum, so neither can any artist entirely exclude the conventional, the local, the perishable from his book, or write a book of pure thought that shall be as efficient, in all respects, to a remote posterity, as to cotemporaries, or rather to the second age. Each age, it is found, must write its own books; or rather, each generation for the next succeeding. The books of an older period will not fit this.

Yet hence arises a grave mischief. The sacredness which attaches to the act of creation,—the act of thought,—is instantly transferred to the record. The poet chanting, was felt to be a divine man. Henceforth the chant is divine also. The writer was a just and wise spirit. Henceforward it is settled, the book is perfect; as love of the hero corrupts into worship of his statue. Instantly, the book becomes noxious. The guide is a tyrant. We sought a brother, and lo, a governor. The sluggish and perverted mind of the multitude, always slow to open to the incursions of Reason, having once so opened, having once received this book, stands upon it, and makes an outcry, if it is disparaged. Colleges are built on it. Books are written on it by thinkers, not by Man Thinking; by men of talent, that is, who start wrong, who set out from accepted dogmas, not from their own sight of principles. Meek young men grow up in libraries, believing it their duty to accept the views which Cicero, which Locke, which Bacon have given, forgetful that Cicero, Locke and Bacon [5] were only young men in libraries when they wrote these books.

Hence, instead of Man Thinking, we have the bookworm. Hence, the book-learned class, who value books, as such; not as related to nature and the human constitution, but as making a sort of Third

5. These were then standard authorities for the young student: Marcus Tullius Cicero (106–43 B.C.), both for his orations and his moral philosophy; John Locke (1632–1704), whose theory of knowledge dominated eighteenth-century thought; and Francis Bacon (1561–1626), British pioneer of inductive science.

Estate [6] with the world and the soul. Hence, the restorers of readings, the emendators, the bibliomaniacs of all degrees.

This is bad; this is worse than it seems. Books are the best of things, well used; abused, among the worst. What is the right use? What is the one end which all means go to effect? They are for nothing but to inspire. I had better never see a book than to be warped by its attraction clean out of my own orbit, and made a satellite instead of a system. The one thing in the world of value, is, the active soul,—the soul, free, sovereign, active. This every man is entitled to; this every man contains within him, although in almost all men, obstructed, and as yet unborn. The soul active sees absolute truth; and utters truth, or creates. In this action, it is genius; not the privilege of here and there a favorite, but the sound estate of every man. In its essence, it is progressive. The book, the college, the school of art, the institution of any kind, stop with some past utterance of genius. This is good, say they,—let us hold by this. They pin me down. The look backward and not forward. But genius always looks forward. The eyes of man are set in his forehead, not in his hindhead. Man hopes. Genius creates. To create,—to create,—is the proof of a divine presence. Whatever talents may be, if the man create not, the pure efflux [7] of the Deity is not his:—cinders and smoke, there may be, but not yet flame. There are creative manners, there are creative actions, and creative words; manners, actions, words, that is, indicative of no custom or authority, but springing spontaneous from the mind's own sense of good and fair.

On the other part, instead of being its own seer, let it receive always from another mind its truth, though it were in torrents of light, without periods of solitude, inquest and self-recovery, and a fatal disservice is done. Genius is always sufficiently the enemy of genius by over-influence. The literature of every nation bear me witness. The English dramatic poets have Shakspearized now for two hundred years.

Undoubtedly there is a right way of reading,—so it be sternly subordinated. Man Thinking must not be subdued by his instruments. Books are for the scholar's idle times. When he can read God directly, the hour is too precious to be wasted in other men's transcripts of their readings. But when the intervals of darkness come, as come they must,—when the soul seeth not, when the sun

6. Under the French monarchy, the "common" people; therefore, a term in bad odor with democrats (the clergy and nobles formed the first two estates).
7. "Outflowing," *cf.* "influence," above. Emerson may be alluding to the ancient theory of "effluxes" or "simulacra" propounded by Empedocles, which holds that only like perceives like. Here the interpretation would be that only the creative man understands the Deity.

is hid, and the stars withdraw their shining,—we repair to the lamps which were kindled by their ray to guide our steps to the East again, where the dawn is. We hear that we may speak. The Arabian proverb says, "A fig tree looking on a fig tree, becometh fruitful."

It is remarkable, the character of the pleasure we derive from the best books. They impress us ever with the conviction that one nature wrote and the same reads. We read the verses of one of the great English poets, of Chaucer, of Marvell, of Dryden, with the most modern joy,[8]—with a pleasure, I mean, which is in great part caused by the abstraction of all *time* from their verses. There is some awe mixed with the joy of our surprise, when this poet, who lived in some past world, two or three hundred years ago, says that which lies close to my own soul, that which I also had wellnigh thought and said. But for the evidence thence afforded to the philosophical doctrine of the identity of all minds, we should suppose some pre-established harmony, some foresight of souls that were to be, and some preparation of stores for their future wants, like the fact observed in insects, who lay up food before death for the young grub they shall never see.

I would not be hurried by any love of system, by any exaggeration of instincts, to underrate the Book. We all know, that as the human body can be nourished on any food, though it were boiled grass and the broth of shoes, so the human mind can be fed by any knowledge. And great and heroic men have existed, who had almost no other information than by the printed page. I only would say, that it needs a strong head to bear that diet. One must be an inventor to read well. As the proverb says, "He that would bring home the wealth of the Indies, must carry out the wealth of the Indies." [9] There is then creative reading, as well as creative writing. When the mind is braced by labor and invention, the page of whatever book we read becomes luminous with manifold allusion. Every sentence is doubly significant, and the sense of our author is as broad as the world.[1] We then see, what is always true, that as the seer's hour of vision is short and rare among heavy days and months, so is its record, perchance, the least part of his volume. The discerning will read in his Plato or Shakspeare, only that least part,—only the authentic utterances of the oracle,—and all the rest he rejects, were it never so many times Plato's and Shakspeare's.

Of course, there is a portion of reading quite indispensable to a

8. The timeless appeal of Chaucer and Dryden is self-evident, but a revival of interest in the poetry of Andrew Marvell (1621–1678) did not occur until the 1920's.
9. Boswell had reported Dr. Johnson as repeating this "Spanish" proverb in almost the same words and context (*Life of Dr. Johnson*, Everyman edition, Vol. II, p. 216).
1. Emerson had written the three previous sentences in his *Journal* ten months earlier (October 29, 1836; *Journals*, Vol. IV, p. 254).

wise man. History and exact science he must learn by laborious reading. Colleges, in like manner, have their indispensable office,—to teach elements. But they can only highly serve us, when they aim not to drill, but to create; when they gather from far every ray of various genius to their hospitable halls, and, by the concentrated fires, set the hearts of their youth on flame. Thought and knowledge are natures in which apparatus and pretension avail nothing. Gowns, and pecuniary foundations, though of towns of gold, can never countervail the least sentence or syllable of wit.[2] Forget this, and our American colleges will recede in their public importance whilst they grow richer every year.

III. There goes in the world a notion that the scholar should be a recluse, a valetudinarian,—as unfit for any handiwork or public labor, as a penknife for an axe. The so-called "practical men" sneer at speculative men, as if, because they speculate or *see*, they could do nothing. I have heard it said that the clergy,—who are always more universally than any other class, the scholars of their day,—are addressed as women: that the rough, spontaneous conversation of men they do not hear, but only a mincing and diluted speech. They are often virtually disfranchised; and, indeed, there are advocates for their celibacy. As far as this is true of the studious classes, it is not just and wise. Action is with the scholar subordinate, but it is essential. Without it, he is not yet man. Without it, thought can never ripen into truth. Whilst the world hangs before the eye as a cloud of beauty, we cannot even see its beauty. Inaction is cowardice, but there can be no scholar without the heroic mind. The preamble of thought, the transition through which it passes from the unconscious to the conscious, is action. Only so much do I know, as I have lived. Instantly we know whose words are loaded with life, and whose not.

The world,—this shadow of the soul, or *other me*, lies wide around. Its attractions are the keys which unlock my thoughts and make me acquainted with myself. I run eagerly into the resounding tumult. I grasp the hands of those next to me, and take my place in the ring to suffer and to work, taught by an instinct that so shall the dumb abyss be vocal with speech. I pierce its order; I dissipate its fear; I dispose of it within the circuit of my expanding life. So much only of life as I know by experience, so much of the wilderness have I vanquished and planted, or so far have I extended my being, my dominion. I do not see how any man can afford, for the sake of his nerves and his nap, to spare any action in which he can partake. It is pearls and rubies to his discourse. Drudgery, calamity, exasperation, want, are instructers in eloquence and wisdom. The

---

2. In the archaic but fundamental meaning: "knowledge," "intellect."

true scholar grudges every opportunity of action past by, as a loss of power.

It is the raw material out of which the intellect moulds her splendid products. A strange process too, this, by which experience is converted into thought, as a mulberry leaf is converted into satin.[3] The manufacture goes forward at all hours.

The actions and events of our childhood and youth are now matters of calmest observation. They lie like fair pictures in the air. Not so with our recent actions,—with the business which we now have in hand. On this we are quite unable to speculate. Our affections as yet circulate through it. We no more feel or know it, than we feel the feet, or the hand, or the brain of our body. The new deed is yet a part of life,—remains for a time immersed in our unconscious life. In some contemplative hour, it detaches itself from the life like a ripe fruit, to become a thought of the mind. Instantly, it is raised, transfigured; the corruptible has put on incorruption.[4] Always now it is an object of beauty, however, base its origin and neighborhood. Observe, too, the impossibility of antedating this act. In its grub state, it cannot fly, it cannot shine,—it is a dull grub. But suddenly, without observation, the selfsame thing unfurls beautiful wings, and is an angel of wisdom. So is there no fact, no event, in our private history, which shall not, sooner or later, lose its adhesive inert form, and astonish us by soaring from our body into the empyrean. Cradle and infancy, school and playground, the fear of boys, and dogs, and ferules, the love of little maids and berries, and many another fact that once filled the whole sky, are gone already; friend and relative, profession and party, town and country, nation and world, must also soar and sing.

Of course, he who has put forth his total strength in fit actions, has the richest return of wisdom. I will not shut myself out of this globe of action and transplant an oak into a flower pot, there to hunger and pine; nor trust the revenue of some single faculty, and exhaust one vein of thought, much like those Savoyards,[5] who, getting their livelihood by carving shepherds, shepherdesses, and smoking Dutchmen, for all Europe, went out one day to the mountain to find stock, and discovered that they had whittled up the last of their pine trees. Authors we have in numbers, who have written out their vein, and who, moved by a commendable prudence, sail for Greece or Palestine, follow the trapper into the prairie, or ramble round Algiers to replenish their merchantable stock.

If it were only for a vocabulary the scholar would be covetous of

---

3. *I.e.*, silkworms feed on mulberry leaves.
4. *Cf.* I Corinthians xv: 54.

5. Inhabitants of Savoy, now a province of southeast France, then still divided with Italy.

action. Life is our dictionary. Years are well spent in country labors; in town—in the insight into trades and manufactures; in frank intercourse with many men and women; in science; in art; to the one end of mastering in all their facts a language, by which to illustrate and embody our perceptions. I learn immediately from any speaker how much he has already lived, through the poverty or the splendor of his speech. Life lies behind us as the quarry from whence we get tiles and copestones for the masonry of to-day. This is the way to learn grammar. Colleges and books only copy the language which the field and the work-yard made.

But the final value of action, like that of books, and better than books, is, that it is a resource. That great principle of Undulation in nature, that shows itself in the inspiring and expiring of the breath; in desire and satiety; in the ebb and flow of the sea, in day and night, in heat and cold, and as yet more deeply ingrained in every atom and every fluid, is known to us under the name of Polarity,—these "fits of easy transmission and reflection," as Newton [6] called them, are the law of nature because they are the law of spirit.

The mind now thinks; now acts; and each fit reproduces the other. When the artist has exhausted his materials, when the fancy no longer paints, when thoughts are no longer apprehended, and books are a weariness,—he has always the resource *to live*. Character is higher than intellect. Thinking is the function. Living is the functionary. The stream retreats to its source. A great soul will be strong to live, as well as strong to think. Does he lack organ or medium to impart his truths? He can still fall back on this elemental force of living them. This is a total act. Thinking is a partial act. Let the grandeur of justice shine in his affairs. Let the beauty of affection cheer his lowly roof. Those "far from fame" who dwell and act with him, will feel the force of his constitution in the doings and passages of the day better than it can be measured by any public and designed display. Time shall teach him that the scholar loses no hour which the man lives. Herein he unfolds the sacred germ of his instinct, screened from influence. What is lost in seemliness is gained in strength. Not out of those on whom systems of education have exhausted their culture, comes the helpful giant to destroy the old or to build the new, but out of unhandselled [7] savage nature, out of terrible Druids and Berserkirs, come at last Alfred [8] and Shakspeare.

---

6. Sir Isaac Newton (1642–1727), English mathematician, the pioneer of modern physical science. The phrase is from *Optics* (1704), the summation of his researches in light.

7. A "handsel" was an inaugural gift for good luck. Here the word is used in its figurative meaning: "unencouraged,"

"unappreciated."

8. Druids were prehistoric Celtic priests; berserkers, incredibly savage warriors of Norse mythology. Alfred (849–899), greatest of the Saxon kings, was a patriot, lawgiver, and father of English prose.

I hear therefore with joy whatever is beginning to be said of the dignity and necessity of labor to every citizen. There is virtue yet in the hoe and the spade, for learned as well as for unlearned hands. And labor is every where welcome; always we are invited to work; only be this limitation observed, that a man shall not for the sake of wider activity sacrifice any opinion to the popular judgments and modes of action.

I have now spoken of the education of the scholar by nature, by books, and by action. It remains to say somewhat of his duties.

They are such as become Man Thinking. They may all be comprised in self-trust. The office of the scholar is to cheer, to raise, and to guide men by showing them facts amidst appearances. He plies the slow, unhonored, and unpaid task of observation. Flamsteed and Herschel,[9] in their glazed observatories, may catalogue the stars with the praise of all men, and, the results being splendid and useful, honor is sure. But he, in his private observatory, cataloguing obscure and nebulous stars of the human mind, which as yet no man has thought of as such,—watching days and months, sometimes, for a few facts; correcting still his old records;—must relinquish display and immediate fame. In the long period of his preparation, he must betray often an ignorance and shiftlessness in popular arts, incurring the disdain of the able who shoulder him aside. Long he must stammer in his speech; often forego the living for the dead. Worse yet, he must accept—how often! poverty and solitude. For the ease and pleasure of treading the old road, accepting the fashions, the education, the religion of society, he takes the cross of making his own, and, of course, the self-accusation, the faint heart, the frequent uncertainty and loss of time which are the nettles and tangling vines in the way of the self-relying and self-directed; and the state of virtual hostility in which he seems to stand to society, and especially to educated society. For all this loss and scorn, what offset? He is to find consolation in exercising the highest functions of human nature. He is one who raises himself from private considerations, and breathes and lives on public and illustrious thoughts. He is the world's eye. He is the world's heart. He is to resist the vulgar prosperity that retrogrades ever to barbarism, by preserving and communicating heroic sentiments, noble biographies, melodious verse, and the conclusions of history. Whatsoever oracles the human heart in all emergencies, in all solemn hours has uttered as its commentary on the world of actions,— these he shall receive and impart. And whatsoever new verdict Reason from her inviolable seat pronounces on the passing men and events of to-day,—this he shall hear and promulgate.

9. John Flamsteed (1646–1719), British astronomer; Sir [Frederick] William Herschel (1738–1822), his sister, Caroline, and his son, John Frederick William, were also astronomers, prominent during Emerson's lifetime.

These being his functions, it becomes him to feel all confidence in himself, and to defer never to the popular cry. He and he only knows the world. The world of any moment is the merest appearance. Some great decorum,[1] some fetish of a government, some ephemeral trade, or war, or man, is cried up by half mankind and cried down by the other half, as if all depended on this particular up or down. The odds are that the whole question is not worth the poorest thought which the scholar has lost in listening to the controversy. Let him not quit his belief that a popgun is a popgun, though the ancient and honorable of the earth affirm it to be the crack of doom. In silence, in steadiness, in severe abstraction, let him hold by himself; add observation to observation, patient of neglect, patient of reproach; and bide his own time,—happy enough if he can satisfy himself alone that this day he has seen something truly. Success treads on every right step. For the instinct is sure that prompts him to tell his brother what he thinks. He then learns that in going down into the secrets of his own mind, he has descended into the secrets of all minds. He learns that he who has mastered any law in his private thoughts, is master to that extent of all men whose language he speaks, and of all into whose language his own can be translated. The poet in utter solitude remembering his spontaneous thoughts and recording them, is found to have recorded that which men in crowded cities find true for them also. The orator distrusts at first the fitness of his frank confessions,—his want of knowledge of the persons he addresses,—until he finds that he is the complement of his hearers;—that they drink his words because he fulfils for them their own nature; the deeper he dives into his privatest secretest presentiment,—to his wonder he finds, this is the most acceptable, most public, and universally true. The people delight in it; the better part of every man feels, This is my music: this is myself.

In self-trust, all the virtues are comprehended. Free should the scholar be,—free and brave. Free even to the definition of freedom, "without any hindrance that does not arise out of his own constitution." Brave; for fear is a thing which a scholar by his very function puts behind him. Fear always springs from ignorance. It is a shame to him if his tranquillity, amid dangerous times, arise from the presumption that like children and women, his is a protected class; or if he seek a temporary peace by the diversion of his thoughts from politics or vexed questions, hiding his head like an ostrich in the flowering bushes, peeping into microscopes, and turning rhymes, as a boy whistles to keep his courage up. So is the danger a danger still: so is the fear worse. Manlike let him turn and face it. Let him look into its eye and search its nature, inspect its origin,—see the whelping of this lion,—which lies no great way

1. In the Latin sense: a critical code or standard.

back; he will then find in himself a perfect comprehension of its nature and extent; he will have made his hands meet on the other side, and can henceforth defy it, and pass on superior. The world is his who can see through its pretension. What deafness, what stone-blind custom, what overgrown error you behold, is there only by sufferance,—by your sufferance. See it to be a lie, and you have already dealt it its mortal blow.

Yes, we are the cowed,—we the trustless. It is a mischievous notion that we are come late into nature; that the world was finished a long time ago. As the world was plastic and fluid in the hands of God, so it is ever to so much of his attributes as we bring to it. To ignorance and sin, it is flint. They adapt themselves to it as they may; but in proportion as a man has anything in him divine, the firmament flows before him, and takes his signet and form. Not he is great who can alter matter, but he who can alter my state of mind. They are the kings of the world who give the color of their present thought to all nature and all art, and persuade men by the cheerful serenity of their carrying the matter, that this thing which they do, is the apple which the ages have desired to pluck, now at last ripe, and inviting nations to the harvest. The great man makes the great thing. Wherever Macdonald sits, there is the head of the table.[2] Linnæus makes botany the most alluring of studies and wins it from the farmer and the herb-woman. Davy, chemistry: and Cuvier, fossils.[3] The day is always his, who works in it with serenity and great aims. The unstable estimates of men crowd to him whose mind is filled with a truth, as the heaped waves of the Atlantic follow the moon.

For this self-trust, the reason is deeper than can be fathomed,—darker than can be enlightened. I might not carry with me the feeling of my audience in stating my own belief. But I have already shown the ground of my hope, in adverting to the doctrine that man is one. I believe man has been wronged: he has wronged himself. He has almost lost the light that can lead him back to his prerogatives. Men are become of no account. Men in history, men in the world of to-day are bugs, are spawn, and are called "the mass" and "the herd." In a century, in a millenium, one or two men; that is to say—one or two approximations to the right state of every man. All the rest behold in the hero or the poet their own green and crude being—ripened; yes, and are content to be less, so

2. The source is obscure, perhaps proverbial, since the same aphorism appears in Cervantes' *Don Quixote* (Part II, Chapter 31). There it is a boorish jest, not an epigram as here, and the character is not named MacDonald. "Donald" is by Gaelic derivation a "world ruler"; hence "MacDonald" in Scotland the son of a ruler or chief.

3. Sir Humphry Davy (1778–1829), English chemist, pioneer in electrolysis; Baron Georges Léopold Chrétien Frédéric Dagobert Cuvier (1769–1832), French naturalist, founder of comparative anatomy and paleontology.

that may attain to its full stature. What a testimony—full of grandeur, full of pity, is borne to the demands of his own nature, by the poor clansman, the poor partisan, who rejoices in the glory of his chief. The poor and the low find some amends to their immense moral capacity, for their acquiescence in a political and social inferiority. They are content to be brushed like flies from the path of a great person, so that justice shall be done by him to that common nature which it is the dearest desire of all to see enlarged and glorified. They sun themselves in the great man's light, and feel it to be their own element. They cast the dignity of man from their downtrod selves upon the shoulders of a hero, and will perish to add one drop of blood to make that great heart beat, those giant sinews combat and conquer. He lives for us, and we live in him.

Men such as they are, very naturally seek money or power; and power because it is as good as money,—the "spoils," so called, "of office." And why not? for they aspire to the highest, and this, in their sleep-walking, they dream is highest. Wake them, and they shall quit the false good and leap to the true, and leave governments to clerks and desks. This revolution is to be wrought by the gradual domestication of the idea of Culture. The main enterprise of the world for splendor, for extent, is the upbuilding of a man. Here are the materials strown along the ground. The private life of one man shall be a more illustrious monarchy,—more formidable to its enemy, more sweet and serene in its influence to its friend, than any kingdom in history. For a man, rightly viewed, comprehendeth the particular natures of all men. Each philosopher, each bard, each actor, has only done for me, as by a delegate, what one day I can do for myself. The books which once we valued more than the apple of the eye, we have quite exhausted. What is that but saying that we have come up with the point of view which the universal mind took through the eyes of that one scribe; we have been that man, and have passed on. First, one; then, another; we drain all cisterns, and waxing greater by all these supplies, we crave a better and more abundant food. The man has never lived that can feed us ever. The human mind cannot be enshrined in a person who shall set a barrier on any one side to this unbounded, unboundable empire. It is one central fire which flaming now out of the lips of Etna, lightens the capes of Sicily; and now out of the throat of Vesuvius, illuminates the towers and vineyards of Naples. It is one light which beams out of a thousand stars. It is one soul which animates all men.

But I have dwelt perhaps tediously upon this abstraction of the Scholar. I ought not to delay longer to add what I have to say, of nearer reference to the time and to this country.

Historically, there is thought to be a difference in the ideas which predominate over successive epochs, and there are data for marking the genius of the Classic, of the Romantic, and now of the Reflective or Philosophical age. With the views I have intimated of the oneness or the identity of the mind through all individuals, I do not much dwell on these differences. In fact, I believe each individual passes through all three. The boy is a Greek; the youth, romantic; the adult, reflective. I deny not, however, that a revolution in the leading idea may be distinctly enough traced.

Our age is bewailed as the age of Introversion. Must that needs be evil? We, it seems, are critical. We are embarrassed with second thoughts. We cannot enjoy any thing for hankering to know whereof the pleasure consists. We are lined with eyes. We see with our feet. The time is infected with Hamlet's unhappiness,—

"Sicklied o'er with the pale cast of thought." [4]

Is it so bad then? Sight is the last thing to be pitied. Would we be blind? Do we fear lest we should outsee nature and God, and drink truth dry? I look upon the discontent of the literary class as a mere announcement of the fact that they find themselves not in the state of mind of their fathers, and regret the coming state as untried; as a boy dreads the water before he has learned that he can swim. If there is any period one would desire to be born in,— is it not the age of Revolution; when the old and the new stand side by side, and admit of being compared; when the energies of all men are searched by fear and by hope; when the historic glories of the old, can be compensated by the rich possibilities of the new era? This time, like all times, is a very good one, if we but know what to do with it.

I read with joy some of the auspicious signs of the coming days as they glimmer already through poetry and art, through philosophy and science, through church and state.

One of these signs is the fact that the same movement which effected the elevation of what was called the lowest class in the state, assumed in literature a very marked and as benign an aspect. Instead of the sublime and beautiful, the near, the low, the common, was explored and poetized. That which had been negligently trodden under foot by those who were harnessing and provisioning themselves for long journeys into far countries, is suddenly found to be richer than all foreign parts. The literature of the poor, the feelings of the child, the philosophy of the street, the meaning of household life, are the topics of the time. It is a great stride. It is a sign—is it not? of new vigor, when the extremities are made active, when currents of warm life run into the hands and the feet. I ask not for the great, the remote, the romantic; what is doing in Italy

4. *Hamlet,* Act III, Scene i, l. 85.

or Arabia; what is Greek art, or Provencal Minstrelsy; [5] I embrace the common, I explore and sit at the feet of the familiar, the low. Give me insight into to-day, and you may have the antique and future worlds. What would we really know the meaning of? The meal in the firkin; the milk in the pan; the ballad in the street; the news of the boat; the glance of the eye; the form and the gait of the body;—show me the ultimate reason of these matters;—show me the sublime presence of the highest spiritual cause lurking, as always it does lurk, in these suburbs and extremities of nature; let me see every trifle bristling with the polarity that ranges it instantly on an eternal law; and the shop, the plough, and the leger, referred to the like cause by which light undulates and poets sing;—and the world lies no longer a dull miscellany and lumber room, but has form and order; there is no trifle; there is no puzzle; but one design unites and animates the farthest pinnacle and the lowest trench.

This idea has inspired the genius of Goldsmith, Burns, Cowper, and, in a newer time, of Goethe,[6] Wordsworth, and Carlyle. This idea they have differently followed and with various success. In contrast with their writing, the style of Pope, of Johnson, of Gibbon, looks cold and pedantic. This writing is blood-warm. Man is surprised to find that things near are not less beautiful and wondrous than things remote. The near explains the far. The drop is a small ocean. A man is related to all nature. This perception of the worth of the vulgar, is fruitful in discoveries. Goethe, in this very thing the most modern of the moderns, has shown us, as none ever did, the genius of the ancients.

There is one man of genius who has done much for this philosophy of life, whose literary value has never yet been rightly estimated;—I mean Emanuel Swedenborg. The most imaginative of men, yet writing with the precision of a mathematician, he endeavored to engraft a purely philosophical Ethics on the popular Christianity of his time. Such an attempt, of course, must have difficulty which no genius could surmount. But he saw and showed the connexion between nature and the affections of the soul. He pierced the emblematic or spiritual character of the visible, audible, tangible world. Especially did his shade-loving muse hover over and interpret the lower parts of nature; he showed the mysterious bond that allies moral evil to the foul material forms, and has given in epical parables a theory of insanity, of beasts, of unclean and fearful things.

Another sign of our times, also marked by an analogous political

5. Provence, ancient province in southeast France, was the cultural center of the troubadours, traveling minstrels (*fl.* 1200–1400).

6. Emerson used Goethe as his archetype for "The Writer" in *Representative Men.*

movement is, the new importance given to the single person. Every thing that tends to insulate the individual,—to surround him with barriers of natural respect, so that each man shall feel the world is his, and man shall treat with man as a sovereign state with a sovereign state;—tends to true union as well as greatness. "I learned," said the melancholy Pestalozzi,[7] "that no man in God's wide earth is either willing or able to help any other man." Help must come from the bosom alone. The scholar is that man who must take up into himself all the ability of the time, all the contributions of the past, all the hopes of the future. He must be an university of knowledges. If there be one lesson more than another which should pierce his ear, it is, The world is nothing, the man is all; in yourself is the law of all nature, and you know not yet how a globule of sap ascends; in yourself slumbers the whole of Reason; it is for you to know all, it is for you to dare all. Mr. President and Gentlemen, this confidence in the unsearched might of man, belongs by all motives, by all prophecy, by all preparation, to the American Scholar. We have listened too long to the courtly muses of Europe. The spirit of the American freeman is already suspected to be timid, imitative, tame. Public and private avarice make the air we breathe thick and fat. The scholar is decent, indolent, complaisant. See already the tragic consequence. The mind of this country taught to aim at low objects, eats upon itself. There is no work for any but the decorous and the complaisant. Young men of the fairest promise, who begin life upon our shores, inflated by the mountain winds, shined upon by all the stars of God, find the earth below not in unison with these,—but are hindered from action by the disgust which the principles on which business is managed inspire, and turn drudges, or die of disgust,— some of them suicides. What is the remedy? They did not yet see, and thousands of young men as hopeful now crowding to the barriers for the career, do not yet see, that if the single man plant himself indomitably on his instincts, and there abide, the huge world will come round to him. Patience—patience;—with the shades of all the good and great for company; and for solace, the perspective of your own infinite life; and for work, the study and the communication of principles, the making those instincts prevalent, the conversion of the world. Is it not the chief disgrace in the world, not to be an unit;—not to be reckoned one character;—not to yield that peculiar fruit which each man was created to bear, but to be reckoned in the gross, in the hundred, or the thousand, of the party, the section, to which we belong; and our opinion predicted geographically, as the north, or the south. Not so, brothers and friends,—please God, ours shall

7. Johann Heinrich Pestalozzi (1746–1827), Swiss educator, "melancholy" at the apparent failure of his theories, had a posthumous triumph. Bronson Alcott introduced his methods, hence Emerson's interest.

not be so. We will walk on our own feet; we will work with our own hands; we will speak our own minds. The study of letters shall be no longer a name for pity, for doubt, and for sensual indulgence. The dread of man and the love of man shall be a wall of defence and a wreath of joy around all. A nation of men will for the first time exist, because each believes himself inspired by the Divine Soul which also inspires all men.

1837

The Divinity School Address [8]

An Address
Delivered Before the Senior Class in Divinity College,
Cambridge, Sunday Evening, 15 July, 1838

In this refulgent summer it has been a luxury to draw the breath of life. The grass grows, the buds burst, the meadow is spotted with fire and gold in the tint of flowers. The air is full of birds, and sweet with the breath of the pine, the balm-of-Gilead, and the new hay. Night brings no gloom to the heart with its welcome shade. Through the transparent darkness the stars pour their almost spiritual rays. Man under them seems a young child, and his huge globe a toy. The cool night bathes the world as with a river, and prepares his eyes again for the crimson dawn. The mystery of nature was never displayed more happily. The corn and the wine have been freely dealt to all creatures, and the never-broken silence with which the old bounty goes forward, has not yielded yet one word of explanation. One is constrained to respect the perfection of this world, in which our senses converse. How wide; how rich; what invitation from every property it gives to every faculty of man! In its fruitful soils; in its navigable sea; in its mountains of metal and

---

8. It was at the request of the students themselves, not the faculty, that Emerson addressed the Harvard Senior Class in Divinity on Sunday evening, July 15, 1838. In his *Journal* during March he mentions his preoccupation with the desire to show these students how the "ugliness and unprofitableness" of the prevailing theology failed to represent "the glory and sweetness of the moral nature." The address offended conservative belief, thus arousing a minor controversy in the lay and religious press. In this Emerson himself took no part, referring to it as "a storm in a wash-bowl." However, he replied (October 8, 1838) to a letter from his predecessor as pastor at the Second Church of Boston, the Rev. Henry Ware, Jr., in a memorable statement of the transcendental method of knowing, in part as follows: "I have always been, from my very incapacity of methodical writing, 'a chartered libertine,' free to worship and free to rail; lucky when I could make myself understood, but never esteemed near enough to the institutions and mind of society to deserve the notice of the masters of literature and religion. * * * I could not give account of myself, if challenged. I could not possibly give you one of the 'arguments' you cruelly hint at, on which any doctrine of mine stands. For I do not know what arguments mean in reference to any expression of a thought. I delight in telling what I think, but if you ask how I dare say so, or why it is so, I am the most helpless of mortal men. I do not even see that either of these questions admits of an answer."

stone; in its forests of all woods; in its animals; in its chemical ingredients; in the powers and path of light, heat, attraction, and life, it is well worth the pith and heart of great men to subdue and enjoy it. The planters, the mechanics, the inventors, the astronomers, the builders of cities, and the captains, history delights to honor.

But the moment the mind opens, and reveals the laws which traverse the universe, and make things what they are, then shrinks the great world at once into a mere illustration and fable of this mind. What am I? and What is? asks the human spirit with a curiosity new-kindled, but never to be quenched. Behold these outrunning laws, which our imperfect apprehension can see tend this way and that, but not come full circle. Behold these infinite relations, so like, so unlike; many, yet one. I would study, I would know, I would admire forever. These works of thought have been the entertainments of the human spirit in all ages.

A more secret, sweet, and overpowering beauty appears to man when his heart and mind open to the sentiment of virtue. Then instantly he is instructed in what is above him. He learns that his being is without bound; that, to the good, to the perfect, he is born, low as he now lies in evil and weakness. That which he venerates is still his own, though he has not realized it yet. *He ought.* He knows the sense of that grand word, though his analysis fails entirely to render account of it. When in innocency, or when by intellectual perception, he attains to say,—'I love the Right; Truth is beautiful within and without, forevermore. Virtue, I am thine: save me: use me: thee will I serve, day and night, in great, in small, that I may be not virtuous, but virtue;'—then is the end of the creation answered, and God is well pleased.

The sentiment of virtue is a reverence and delight in the presence of certain divine laws. It perceives that this homely game of life we play, covers, under what seem foolish details, principles that astonish. The child amidst his baubles, is learning the action of light, motion, gravity, muscular force; and in the game of human life, love, fear, justice, appetite, man, and God, interact. These laws refuse to be adequately stated. They will not by us or for us be written out on paper, or spoken by the tongue. They elude, evade our persevering thought, and yet we read them hourly in each other's faces, in each other's actions, in our own remorse. The moral traits which are all globed into every virtuous act and thought,—in speech, we must sever, and describe or suggest by painful enumeration of many particulars. Yet, as this sentiment is the essence of all religion, let me guide your eye to the precise objects of the sentiment, by an enumeration of some of those classes of facts in which this element is conspicuous.

The intuition of the moral sentiment is an insight of the perfection of the laws of the soul. These laws execute themselves. They are out of time, out of space, and not subject to circumstance. Thus; in the soul of man there is a justice whose retributions are instant and entire. He who does a good deed, is instantly ennobled himself. He who does a mean deed, is by the action itself contracted. He who puts off impurity, thereby puts on purity. If a man is at heart just, then in so far is he God; the safety of God, the immortality of God, the majesty of God do enter into that man with justice. If a man dissemble, deceive, he deceives himself, and goes out of acquaintance with his own being. A man in the view of absolute goodness, adores, with total humility. Every step so downward, is a step upward. The man who renounces himself, comes to himself by so doing.

See how this rapid intrinsic energy worketh everywhere, righting wrongs, correcting appearances, and bringing up facts to a harmony with thoughts. Its operation in life, though slow to the senses, is, at last, as sure as in the soul. By it, a man is made the Providence to himself, dispensing good to his goodness, and evil to his sin. Character is always known. Thefts never enrich; alms never impoverish; murder will speak out of stone walls. The least admixture of a lie,—for example, the smallest mixture of vanity, the least attempt to make a good impression, a favorable appearance,—will instantly vitiate the effect. But speak the truth, and all nature and all spirits help you with unexpected furtherance. Speak the truth, and all things alive or brute are vouchers, and the very roots of the grass underground there, do seem to stir and move to bear you witness. See again the perfection of the Law as it applies itself to the affections, and becomes the law of society. As we are, so we associate. The good, by affinity, seek the good; the vile, by affinity, the vile. Thus of their own volition, souls proceed into heaven, into hell.

These facts have always suggested to man the sublime creed, that the world is not the product of manifold power, but of one will, of one mind; and that one mind is everywhere active, in each ray of the star, in each wavelet of the pool; and whatever opposes that will, is everywhere baulked and baffled, because things are made so, and not otherwise. Good is positive. Evil is merely privative, not absolute. It is like cold, which is the privation of heat. All evil is so much death or nonentity.[9] Benevolence is absolute and real. So much benevolence as a man hath, so much life hath he. For all things proceed out of this same spirit, which is differently named

9. In spite of statements often heard to the contrary, Emerson here plainly accepts the "odious fact" of evil. But evil is not, in the sense of logic, a "positive." Positives are absolute expressions of being, and "good" is one of them, a state of positive existence, to which "evil" is only a "privative," depriving good of some measure of its being. Good could be complete, but evil could not; if the deprivation (or evil) became complete, there would result "nonentity," neither good nor evil, but nothingness.

love, justice, temperance, in its different applications, just as the ocean receives different names on the several shores which it washes. All things proceed out of the same spirit, and all things conspire with it. Whilst a man seeks good ends, he is strong by the whole strength of nature. In so far as he roves from these ends, he bereaves himself of power, of auxiliaries; his being shrinks out of all remote channels, he becomes less and less, a mote, a point, until absolute badness is absolute death.

The perception of this law of laws always awakens in the mind a sentiment which we call the religious sentiment, and which makes our highest happiness. Wonderful is its power to charm and to command. It is a mountain air. It is the embalmer of the world. It is myrrh and storax, and chlorine and rosemary. It makes the sky and the hills sublime, and the silent song of the stars is it. By it, is the universe made safe and habitable, not by science or power. Thought may work cold and intransitive in things, and find no end or unity. But the dawn of the sentiment of virtue on the heart, gives and is the assurance that Law is sovereign over all natures; and the worlds, time, space, eternity, do seem to break out into joy.

This sentiment is divine and deifying. It is the beatitude of man. It makes him illimitable. Through it, the soul first knows itself. It corrects the capital mistake of the infant man, who seeks to be great by following the great, and hopes to derive advantages *from another*,—by showing the fountain of all good to be in himself, and that he, equally with every man, is an inlet into the deeps of Reason. When he says, "I ought;" when love warms him; when he chooses, warned from on high, the good and great deed; then, deep melodies wander through his soul from Supreme Wisdom. Then he can worship, and be enlarged by his worship; for he can never go behind this sentiment. In the sublimest flights of the soul, rectitude is never surmounted, love is never outgrown.

This sentiment lies at the foundation of society, and successively creates all forms of worship. The principle of veneration never dies out. Man fallen into superstition, into sensuality, is never wholly without the visions of the moral sentiment. In like manner, all the expressions of this sentiment are sacred and permanent in proportion to their purity. The expressions of this sentiment affect us deeper, greatlier, than all other compositions. The sentences of the oldest time, which ejaculate this piety, are still fresh and fragrant. This thought dwelled always deepest in the minds of men in the devout and contemplative East; not alone in Palestine, where it reached its purest expression, but in Egypt, in Persia, in India, in China. Europe has always owed to oriental genius, its divine impulses. What these holy bards said, all sane men found agreeable and true. And the unique impression of Jesus upon mankind, whose name is not so much written as ploughed into the history of this world, is proof of the subtle virtue of this infusion.

Meantime, whilst the doors of the temple stand open, night and day, before every man, and the oracles of this truth cease never, it is guarded by one stern condition; this, namely; It is an intuition. It cannot be received at second hand. Truly speaking, it is not instruction, but provocation, that I can receive from another soul. What he announces, I must find true in me, or wholly reject; and on his word, or as his second, be he who he may, I can accept nothing. On the contrary, the absence of this primary faith is the presence of degradation. As is the flood so is the ebb. Let this faith depart, and the very words it spake, and the things it made, become false and hurtful. Then falls the church, the state, art, letters, life. The doctrine of the divine nature being forgotten, a sickness infects and dwarfs the constitution. Once man was all; now he is an appendage, a nuisance. And because the indwelling Supreme Spirit cannot wholly be got rid of, the doctrine of it suffers this perversion, that the divine nature is attributed to one or two persons, and denied to all the rest, and denied with fury. The doctrine of inspiration is lost; the base doctrine of the majority of voices, usurps the place of the doctrine of the soul. Miracles, prophecy, poetry, the ideal life, the holy life, exist as ancient history merely; they are not in the belief, nor in the aspiration of society; but, when suggested, seem ridiculous. Life is comic or pitiful, as soon as the high ends of being fade out of sight, and man becomes near-sighted, and can only attend to what addresses the senses.

These general views, which, whilst they are general, none will contest, find abundant illustration in the history of religion, and especially in the history of the Christian church. In that, all of us have had our birth and nurture. The truth contained in that, you, my young friends, are now setting forth to teach. As the Cultus, or established worship of the civilized world, it has great historical interest for us. Of its blessed words, which have been the consolation of humanity, you need not that I should speak. I shall endeavor to discharge my duty to you, on this occasion, by pointing out two errors in its administration, which daily appear more gross from the point of view we have just now taken.

Jesus Christ belonged to the true race of prophets. He saw with open eye the mystery of the soul. Drawn by its severe harmony, ravished with its beauty, he lived in it, and had his being there. Alone in all history, he estimated the greatness of man. One man was true to what is in you and me. He saw that God incarnates himself in man, and evermore goes forth anew to take possession of his world. He said, in this jubilee of sublime emotion, 'I am divine. Through me, God acts; through me, speaks. Would you see God, see me; or, see thee, when thou also thinkest as I now think.' But what a distortion did his doctrine and memory suffer in the same, in the next, and the following ages! There is no doctrine of the Reason which will bear to be taught by the Understanding. The understanding caught this high chant from the poet's lips, and said, in the next age, 'This was Jehovah come down out of heaven. I will kill you, if you say he was a man.' The idioms of his language, and the figures of his rhetoric, have usurped the place of his truth; and churches are not built on his principles, but on his tropes. Christianity became a Mythus, as the poetic teaching of Greece and of Egypt, before. He spoke of miracles; for he felt that man's life was a miracle, and all that man doth, and he knew that this daily miracle shines, as the man is diviner. But the very word Miracle, as pronounced by Christian churches, gives a false impression; it is Monster. It is not one with the blowing clover and the falling rain.[1]

He felt respect for Moses and the prophets; but no unfit tenderness at postponing their initial revelations, to the hour and the man that now is; to the eternal revelation in the heart. Thus was he a true man. Having seen that the law in us is commanding, he would not suffer it to be commanded. Boldly, with hand, and heart, and life, he declared it was God. Thus was he a true man. Thus is he, as I think, the only soul in history who has appreciated the worth of a man.

1. In thus contemplating Jesus, we become very sensible of the first defect of historical Christianity. Historical Christianity has fallen into the error that corrupts all attempts to communicate religion. As it appears to us, and as it appeared for ages, it is not the doctrine of the soul, but an exaggeration of the personal, the positive, the ritual. It has dwelt, it dwells, with noxious exaggeration about the *person* of Jesus. The soul knows no persons. It invites every man to expand to the full circle of the universe, and will have no preferences but those of spontaneous love. But by this eastern monarchy of a Christianity, which indolence and fear have built, the friend of man is made the injurer of man. The manner in which his name is surrounded with expressions, which were once sallies of admiration and love, but are now petrified into official titles, kills all generous sympathy and liking. All who hear me, feel, that the

---

1. A denial of the miraculous and special divinity of Jesus Christ was the extreme limit of Emerson's radicalism. Beginning with the Unitarian "unity" of Father, Son, and Holy Spirit (as contrasted with the trinitarian view), he builds the syllogism early in this paragraph: Jesus Christ was God incarnate; the divine Jesus was also man; therefore another man, by being true to the God incarnate in him, may also be "divine" in the sense that Jesus was. The divinity of Christ was a miracle only as all things are—"the blowing clover and the falling rain." Later transcendentalists in many cases accepted Emerson's position. A few advanced clergymen "proclaimed the divinity of man"—the phrase appears on the tombstone of William Ellery Channing—but in 1838 it was a Unitarian "heresy."

language that describes Christ to Europe and America, is not the style of friendship and enthusiasm to a good and noble heart, but is appropriated and formal,—paints a demigod, as the Orientals or the Greeks would describe Osiris or Apollo. Accept the injurious impositions of our early catechetical instruction, and even honesty and self-denial were but splendid sins, if they did not wear the Christian name. One would rather be

'A pagan suckled in a creed outworn,'

than to be defrauded of his manly right in coming into nature, and finding not names and places, not land and professions, but even virtue and truth foreclosed and monopolized. You shall not be a man even. You shall not own the world; you shall not dare, and live after the infinite Law that is in you, and in company with the infinite Beauty which heaven and earth reflect to you in all lovely forms; but you must subordinate your nature to Christ's nature; you must accept our interpretations; and take his portrait as the vulgar draw it.

That is always best which gives me to myself. The sublime is excited in me by the great stoical doctrine, Obey thyself. That which shows God in me, fortifies me. That which shows God out of me, makes me a wart and a wen. There is no longer a necessary reason for my being. Already the long shadows of untimely oblivion creep over me, and I shall decease forever.

The divine bards are the friends of my virtue, of my intellect, of my strength. They admonish me, that the gleams which flash across my mind, are not mine, but God's; that they had the like, and were not disobedient to the heavenly vision. So I love them. Noble provocations go out from them, inviting me also to emancipate myself; to resist evil; to subdue the world; and to Be. And thus by his holy thoughts, Jesus serves us, and thus only. To aim to convert a man by miracles, is a profanation of the soul. A true conversion, a true Christ, is now, as always, to be made, by the reception of beautiful sentiments. It is true that a great and rich soul, like his, falling among the simple, does so preponderate, that, as his did, it names the world. The world seems to them to exist for him, and they have not yet drunk so deeply of his sense, as to see that only by coming again to themselves, or to God in themselves, can they grow forevermore. It is a low benefit to give me something; it is a high benefit to enable me to do somewhat of myself. The time is coming when all men will see, that the gift of God to the soul is not a vaunting, overpowering, excluding sanctity, but a sweet, natural goodness, a goodness like thine and mine, and that so invites thine and mine to be and to grow.

The injustice of the vulgar tone of preaching is not less flagrant to Jesus, than it is to the souls which it profanes. The preachers do not see that they make his gospel not glad, and shear him of the locks of beauty and the attributes of heaven. When I see a majestic Epaminondas,[2] or Washington; when I see among my contemporaries, a true orator, an upright judge, a dear friend; when I vibrate the melody and fancy of a poem; I see beauty that is to be desired. And so lovely, and with yet more entire consent of my human being, sounds in my ear the severe music of the bards that have sung of the true God in all ages. Now do not degrade the life and dialogues of Christ out of the circle of this charm, by insulation and peculiarity. Let them lie as they befel, alive and warm, part of human life, and of the landscape, and of the cheerful day.

2. The second defect of the traditionary and limited way of using the mind of Christ is a consequence of the first; this, namely; that the Moral Nature, that Law of laws, whose revelations introduce greatness,—yea, God himself, into the open soul, is not explored as the fountain of the established teaching in society. Men have come to speak of the revelation as somewhat long ago given and done, as if God were dead. The injury to faith throttles the preacher; and the goodliest of institutions becomes an uncertain and inarticulate voice.

It is very certain that it is the effect of conversation with the beauty of the soul, to beget a desire and need to impart to others the same knowledge and love. If utterance is denied, the thought lies like a burden on the man. Always the seer is a sayer. Somehow his dream is told. Somehow he publishes it with solemn joy. Sometimes with pencil on canvas; sometimes with chisel on stone; sometimes in towers and aisles of granite, his soul's worship is builded; sometimes in anthems of indefinite music; but clearest and most permanent, in words.

The man enamored of this excellency, becomes its priest or poet. The office is coeval with the world. But observe the condition, the spiritual limitation of the office. The spirit only can teach. Not any profane man, not any sensual, not any liar, not any slave can teach, but only he can give, who has; he only can create, who is. The man on whom the soul descends, through whom the soul speaks, alone can teach. Courage, piety, love, wisdom, can teach; and every man can open his door to these angels, and they shall bring him the gift of tongues. But the man who aims to speak as books enable, as synods use, as the fashion guides, and as interest commands, babbles. Let him hush.

To this holy office, you propose to devote yourselves. I wish you may feel your call in throbs of desire and hope. The office is the

---

2. Theban statesman and general (*ca.* 418–362 B.C.), famous for his integrity and leadership.

first in the world. It is of that reality, that it cannot suffer the deduction of any falsehood. And it is my duty to say to you, that the need was never greater of new revelation than now. From the views I have already expressed, you will infer the sad conviction, which I share, I believe, with numbers, of the universal decay and now almost death of faith in society. The soul is not preached. The Church seems to totter to its fall, almost all life extinct. On this occasion, any complaisance, would be criminal, which told you, whose hope and commission it is to preach the faith of Christ, that the faith of Christ is preached.

It is time that this ill-suppressed murmur of all thoughtful men against the famine of our churches; this moaning of the heart because it is bereaved of the consolation, the hope, the grandeur, that come alone out of the culture of the moral nature; should be heard through the sleep of indolence, and over the din of routine. This great and perpetual office of the preacher is not discharged. Preaching is the expression of the moral sentiment in application to the duties of life. In how many churches, by how many prophets, tell me, is man made sensible that he is an infinite Soul; that the earth and heavens are passing into his mind; that he is drinking forever the soul of God? Where now sounds the persuasion, that by its very melody imparadises my heart, and so affirms its own origin in heaven? Where shall I hear words such as in elder ages drew men to leave all and follow,—father and mother, house and land, wife and child? Where shall I hear these august laws of moral being so pronounced, as to fill my ear, and I feel ennobled by the offer of my uttermost action and passion? The test of the true faith, certainly, should be its power to charm and command the soul, as the laws of nature control the activity of the hands,—so commanding that we find pleasure and honor in obeying. The faith should blend with the light of rising and of setting suns, with the flying cloud, the singing bird, and the breath of flowers. But now the priest's Sabbath has lost the splendor of nature; it is unlovely; we are glad when it is done; we can make, we do make, even sitting in our pews, a far better, holier, sweeter, for ourselves.

Whenever the pulpit is usurped by a formalist, then is the worshipper defrauded and disconsolate. We shrink as soon as the prayers begin, which do not uplift, but smite and offend us. We are fain to wrap our cloaks about us, and secure, as best we can, a solitude that hears not. I once heard a preacher who sorely tempted me to say, I would go to church no more. Men go, thought I, where they are wont to go, else had no soul entered the temple in the afternoon. A snowstorm was falling around us. The snowstorm was real; the preacher merely spectral; and the eye felt the sad contrast in looking at him, and then out of the window behind him, into the beautiful meteor of the snow. He had lived in vain. He had no one word intimating that he had laughed or wept, was married or in love, had been commended, or cheated, or chagrined. If he had ever lived and acted, we were none the wiser for it. The capital secret of his profession, namely, to convert life into truth, he had not learned. Not one fact in all his experience, had he yet imported into his doctrine. This man had ploughed, and planted, and talked, and bought, and sold; he had read books; he had eaten and drunken; his head aches; his heart throbs; he smiles and suffers; yet was there not a surmise, a hint, in all the discourse, that he had ever lived at all. Not a line did he draw out of real history. The true preacher can always be known by this, that he deals out to the people his life,—life passed through the fire of thought. But of the bad preacher, it could not be told from his sermon, what age of the world he fell in; whether he had a father or a child; whether he was a freeholder or a pauper; whether he was a citizen or a countryman; or any other fact of his biography.

It seemed strange that the people should come to church. It seemed as if their houses were very unentertaining, that they should prefer this thoughtless clamor. It shows that there is a commanding attraction in the moral sentiment, that can lend a faint tint of light to dulness and ignorance, coming in its name and place. The good hearer is sure he has been touched sometimes; is sure there is somewhat to be reached, and some word that can reach it. When he listens to these vain words, he comforts himself by their relation to his remembrance of better hours, and so they clatter and echo unchallenged.

I am not ignorant that when we preach unworthily, it is not always quite in vain. There is a good ear, in some men, that draws supplies to virtue out of very indifferent nutriment. There is poetic truth concealed in all the common-places of prayer and of sermons, and though foolishly spoken, they may be wisely heard; for, each is some select expression that broke out in a moment of piety from some stricken or jubilant soul, and its excellency made it remembered. The prayers and even the dogmas of our church, are like the zodiac of Denderah,[3] and the astronomical monuments of the Hindoos, wholly insulated from anything now extant in the life and business of the people. They mark the height to which the waters once rose. But this docility is a check upon the mischief from the good and devout. In a large portion of the community, the religious service gives rise to quite other thoughts and emotions. We need not chide the negligent servant. We are struck with pity, rather, at the swift retribution of his sloth. Alas for the unhappy man that

3. Denderah (or Tentyra) was an ancient city in Egypt, dedicated to the worship of the goddess Hathor.

is called to stand in the pulpit, and *not* give bread of life. Everything that befals, accuses him. Would he ask contributions for the missions, foreign or domestic? Instantly his face is suffused with shame, to propose to his parish, that they should send money a hundred or a thousand miles, to furnish such poor fare as they have at home, and would do well to go the hundred or the thousand miles, to escape. Would he urge people to a godly way of living;— and can he ask a fellow creature to come to Sabbath meetings, when he and they all know what is the poor uttermost they can hope for therein? Will he invite them privately to the Lord's Supper? [4] He dares not. If no heart warm this rite, the hollow, dry creaking formality is too plain, than that he can face a man of wit and energy, and put the invitation without terror. In the street, what has he to say to the bold village blasphemer? The village blasphemer sees fear in the face, form, and gait of the minister.

Let me not taint the sincerity of this plea by any oversight of the claims of good men. I know and honor the purity and strict conscience of numbers of the clergy. What life the public worship retains, it owes to the scattered company of pious men, who minister here and there in the churches, and who, sometimes accepting with too great tenderness the tenet of the elders, have not accepted from others, but from their own heart, the genuine impulses of virtue, and so still command our love and awe, to the sanctity of character. Moreover, the exceptions are not so much to be found in a few eminent preachers, as in the better hours, the truer inspirations of all,—nay, in the sincere moments of every man. But with whatever exception, it is still true, that tradition characterizes the preaching of this country; that it comes out of the memory, and not out of the soul; that it aims at what is usual, and not at what is necessary and eternal; that thus, historical Christianity destroys the power of preaching, by withdrawing it from the exploration of the moral nature of man, where the sublime is, where are the resources of astonishment and power. What a cruel injustice it is to the Law, the joy of the whole earth, which alone can make thought dear and rich; that Law whose fatal sureness the astronomical orbits poorly emulate, that it is travestied and depreciated, that it is behooted and behowled, and not a trait, not a word of it articulated. The pulpit in losing sight of this Law, loses all its inspiration, and gropes after it knows not what. And for want of this culture, the soul of the community is sick and faithless. It wants nothing so much as a stern, high, stoical, Christian discipline, to make it know itself and the divinity that speaks through it. Now man is ashamed of him-

4. In 1832, when Emerson decided he must give up his ministry, he especially emphasized his inability to find any special grace or sanction in the Lord's Supper. Now he is associating this with all formalism—the giving the "bread" without the "life" of religion.

self; he skulks and sneaks through the world, to be tolerated, to be pitied, and scarcely in a thousand years does any man dare to be wise and good, and so draw after him the tears and blessings of his kind.

Certainly there have been periods when, from the inactivity of the intellect on certain truths, a greater faith was possible in names and persons. The Puritans in England and America, found in the Christ of the Catholic Church, and in the dogmas inherited from Rome, scope for their austere piety, and their longings for civil freedom. But their creed is passing away, and none arises in its room. I think no man can go with his thoughts about him, into one of our churches, without feeling that what hold the public worship had on men, is gone or going. It has lost its grasp on the affection of the good, and the fear of the bad. In the country,—neighborhoods, half parishes are *signing off*,—to use the local term. It is already beginning to indicate character and religion to withdraw from the religious meetings. I have heard a devout person, who prized the Sabbath, say in bitterness of heart, "On Sundays, it seems wicked to go to church." And the motive, that holds the best there, is now only a hope and a waiting. What was once a mere circumstance, that the best and the worst men in the parish, the poor and the rich, the learned and the ignorant, young and old, should meet one day as fellows in one house, in sign of an equal right in the soul,—has come to be a paramount motive for going thither.

My friends, in these two errors, I think, I find the causes of that calamity of a decaying church and a wasting unbelief, which are casting malignant influences around us, and making the hearts of good men sad. And what greater calamity can fall upon a nation, than the loss of worship? Then all things go to decay. Genius leaves the temple, to haunt the senate, or the market. Literature becomes frivolous. Science is cold. The eye of youth is not lighted by the hope of other worlds, and age is without honor. Society lives to trifles, and when men die, we do not mention them.

And now, my brothers, you will ask, What in these desponding days can be done by us? The remedy is already declared in the ground of our complaint of the Church. We have contrasted the Church with the Soul. In the soul, then, let the redemption be sought. In one soul, in your soul, there are resources for the world. Wherever a man comes, there comes revolution. The old is for slaves. When a man comes, all books are legible, all things transparent, all religions are forms. He is religious. Man is the wonderworker. He is seen amid miracles. All men bless and curse. He saith yea and nay, only. The stationariness of religion; the assumption that the age of inspiration is past, that the Bible is closed; the fear of degrading the character of Jesus by representing him as a man;

indicate with sufficient clearness the falsehood of our theology. It is the office of a true teacher to show us that God is, not was; that He speaketh, not spake. The true Christianity,—a faith like Christ's in the infinitude of man,—is lost. None believeth in the soul of man, but only in some man or person old and departed. Ah me! no man goeth alone. All men go in flocks to this saint or that poet, avoiding the God who seeth in secret. They cannot see in secret; they love to be blind in public. They think society wiser than their soul, and know not that one soul, and their soul, is wiser than the whole world. See how nations and races flit by on the sea of time, and leave no ripple to tell where they floated or sunk, and one good soul shall make the name of Moses, or of Zeno, or of Zoroaster,[5] reverend forever. None assayeth the stern ambition to be the Self of the nation, and of nature, but each would be an easy secondary to some Christian scheme, or sectarian connexion, or some eminent man. Once leave your own knowledge of God, your own sentiment, and take secondary knowledge, as St. Paul's, or George Fox's, or Swedenborg's,[6] and you get wide from God with every year this secondary form lasts, and if, as now, for centuries,—the chasm yawns to that breadth, that men can scarcely be convinced there is in them anything divine.

Let me admonish you, first of all, to go alone; to refuse the good models, even those most sacred in the imagination of men, and dare to love God without mediator or veil. Friends enough you shall find who will hold up to your emulation Wesleys and Oberlins,[7] Saints and Prophets. Thank God for these good men, but say, 'I also am a man.' Imitation cannot go above its model. The imitator dooms himself to hopeless mediocrity. The inventor did it, because it was natural to him, and so in him it has a charm. In the imitator, something else is natural, and he bereaves himself of his own beauty, to come short of another man's.

Yourself a newborn bard of the Holy Ghost,—cast behind you all conformity, and acquaint men at first hand with Deity. Be to them a man. Look to it first and only, that you are such; that fashion, custom, authority, pleasure, and money are nothing to you,—are not bandages over your eyes, that you cannot see,—but live with the privilege of the immeasurable mind. Not too anxious to

---

5. Zeno, Greek philosopher of the late fourth and early third centuries B.C., founded the Stoic school of philosophy; Zoroaster reputedly initiated and gave his name to the religion of the ancient Persians.

6. The teachings of Fox (1624–1691), founder of the Society of Friends, were developed largely as a protest against the Presbyterian system; Emmanuel Swedenborg (1688–1722) devoted much of his life to psychical and spiritual research and wrote works of Scriptural interpretation.

7. *I.e.*, men of the caliber of John Wesley (1703–1791), the evangelist and theologian who founded Methodism, or Jean Frédéric Oberlin (1740–1826), a Protestant clergyman famed for his improvements of education and morality in his Alsatian pastorate.

visit periodically all families and each family in your parish connexion,—when you meet one of these men or women, be to them a divine man; be to them thought and virtue; let their timid aspirations find in you a friend; let their trampled instincts be genially tempted out in your atmosphere; let their doubts know that you have doubted, and their wonder feel that you have wondered. By trusting your own soul, you shall gain a greater confidence in other men. For all our penny-wisdom, for all our soul-destroying slavery to habit, it is not to be doubted, that all men have sublime thoughts; that all men do value the few real hours of life; they love to be heard; they love to be caught up into the vision of principles. We mark with light in the memory the few interviews, we have had in the dreary years of routine and of sin, with souls that made our souls wiser; that spoke what we thought; that told us what we knew; that gave us leave to be what we inly were. Discharge to men the priestly office, and, present or absent, you shall be followed with their love as by an angel.

And, to this end, let us not aim at common degrees of merit. Can we not leave, to such as love it, the virtue that glitters for the commendation of society, and ourselves pierce the deep solitudes of absolute ability and worth? We easily come up to the standard of goodness in society. Society's praise can be cheaply secured, and almost all men are content with those easy merits; but the instant effect of conversing with God, will be, to put them away. There are sublime merits; persons who are not actors, not speakers, but influences; persons too great for fame, for display; who disdain eloquence; to whom all we call art and artist, seems too nearly allied to show and by-ends, to the exaggeration of the finite and selfish and loss of the universal. The orators, the poets, the commanders encroach on us only as fair women do, by our allowance and homage. Slight them by preoccupation of mind, slight them, as you can well afford to do, by high and universal aims, and they instantly feel that you have right, and that it is in lower places that they must shine. They also feel your right; for they with you are open to the influx of the all-knowing Spirit, which annihilates before its broad noon the little shades and gradations of intelligence in the compositions we call wiser and wisest.

In such high communion, let us study the grand strokes of rectitude: a bold benevolence, an independence of friends, so that not the unjust wishes of those who love us, shall impair our freedom, but we shall resist for truth's sake the freest flow of kindness, and appeal to sympathies far in advance; and,—what is the highest form in which we know this beautiful element,—a certain solidity of merit, that has nothing to do with opinion, and which is so essentially and mainfestly virtue, that it is taken for granted, that the right, the brave, the generous step will be taken by it, and nobody thinks of commending it. You would compliment a coxcomb doing a good act, but you would not praise an angel. The silence that accepts merit as the most natural thing in the world, is the highest applause. Such souls, when they appear, are the Imperial Guard of Virtue, the perpetual reserve, the dictators of fortune. One needs not praise their courage,—they are the heart and soul of nature. O my friends, there are resources in us on which we have not drawn. There are men who rise refreshed on hearing a threat; men to whom a crisis which intimidates and paralyzes the majority—demanding not the faculties of prudence and thrift, but comprehension, immovableness, the readiness of sacrifice,—comes graceful and beloved as a bride. Napoleon said of Massena, that he was not himself until the battle began to go against him; then, when the dead began to fall in ranks around him, awoke his powers of combination, and he put on terror and victory as a robe. So it is in rugged crises, in unweariable endurance, and in aims which put sympathy out of question, that the angel is shown. But these are heights that we can scarce remember and look up to, without contrition and shame. Let us thank God that such things exist.

And now let us do what we can to rekindle the smouldering, nigh quenched fire on the altar. The evils of the church that now is, are manifest. The question returns, What shall we do? I confess, all attempts to project and establish a Cultus with new rites and forms, seem to me vain. Faith makes us, and not we it, and faith makes its own forms. All attempts to contrive a system, are as cold as the new worship introduced by the French to the goddess of Reason,—to-day, pasteboard and fillagree, and ending to-morrow in madness and murder. Rather let the breath of new life be breathed by you through the forms already existing. For, if once you are alive, you shall find they shall become plastic and new. The remedy to their deformity is, first, soul, and second, soul, and evermore, soul. A whole popedom of forms, one pulsation of virtue can uplift and vivify. Two inestimable advantages Christianity has given us; first; the Sabbath, the jubilee of the whole world; whose light dawns welcome alike into the closet of the philosopher, into the garret of toil, and into prison cells, and everywhere suggests, even to the vile, a thought of the dignity of spiritual being. Let it stand forevermore, a temple, which new love, new faith, new sight shall restore to more than its first splendor to mankind. And secondly, the institution of preaching,—the speech of man to men,—essentially the most flexible of all organs, of all forms. What hinders that now, everywhere, in pulpits, in lecture-rooms, in houses, in fields, wherever the invitation of men or your own occasions lead you, you speak the very truth, as your life and conscience teach it, and cheer the waiting, fainting hearts of men with new hope and new revelation? I look for the hour when that supreme Beauty, which ravished the souls of those Eastern men, and chiefly of those Hebrews, and through their lips spoke oracles to all time, shall speak in the West also. The Hebrew and Greek Scriptures contain immortal sentences, that have been bread of life to millions. But they have no epical integrity; are fragmentary; are not shown in their order to the intellect. I look for the new Teacher, that shall follow so far those shining laws, that he shall see them come full circle; shall see their rounding complete grace; shall see the world to be the mirror of the soul; shall see the identity of the law of gravitation with purity of heart; and shall show that the Ought, that Duty, is one thing with Science, with Beauty, and with Joy.

1838   1838

Self-Reliance [8]

"Ne te quæsiveris extra."

"Man is his own star; and the soul that can
Render an honest and a perfect man
Commands all light, all influence, all fate;
Nothing to him falls early or too late.
Our acts our angels are, or good or ill,
Our fatal shadows that walk by us still."
—EPILOGUE TO BEAUMONT AND
FLETCHER'S HONEST MAN'S FORTUNE

Cast the bantling on the rocks,
Suckle him with the she-wolf's teat,
Wintered with the hawk and fox,
Power and speed be hands and feet.

I read the other day some verses written by an eminent painter [9] which were original and not conventional. The soul always hears an admonition in such lines, let the subject be what it may. The sentiment they instil is of more value than any thought they may con-

---

8. "Self-Reliance" is generally regarded as indispensable for the clear understanding of Emerson's matured philosophy of individualism. This individualism functions through the relations of the "self" with God, or the "Over-Soul" —which is another name for the moral law inherent in nature. But these relations are not automatic; the individual is accorded the responsibility of freedom of choice, guided by intuition and experience. Apart from its ideas, "Self-Reliance" is regarded by many as the high tide of Emerson's prose; it is compact and cogent in its logic, and its style is a perfect instrument for its emotional intensity and its wit. The ideas of this essay took shape over a long period. It contains a passage from a journal entry of 1832, and others from various lec-

tures delivered between 1836 and 1839 (Centenary Edition, Vol. II, pp. 389–390). It was first published in *Essays* [First Series] (1841), which Emerson revised for the edition of 1847, on which the present text is based.

The Latin epigraph reads "Do not seek [answers] outside yourself." The first edition of "Self-Reliance" bore all three epigraphs as printed here. Emerson composed the quatrain himself, and dropped it from the second edition (1847). It was restored by later editors of the essay and also appears in the *Poems* as "Power."

9. The painter-poet may be the American Washington Allston (1779–1843), or the English William Blake (1757–1827), according to E. W. Emerson (Centenary Edition, Vol. II, p. 390).

tain. To believe your own thought, to believe that what is true for you in your private heart is true for all men,—that is genius. Speak your latent conviction, and it shall be the universal sense; for the inmost in due time becomes the outmost,—and our first thought is rendered back to us by the trumpets of the Last Judgment. Familiar as the voice of the mind is to each, the highest merit we ascribe to Moses, Plato, and Milton is that they set at naught books and traditions, and spoke not what men, but what they thought. A man should learn to detect and watch that gleam of light which flashes across his mind from within, more than the lustre of the firmament of bards and sages. Yet he dismisses without notice his thought, because it is his. In every work of genius we recognize our own rejected thoughts: they come back to us with a certain alienated majesty. Great works of art have no more affecting lesson for us than this. They teach us to abide by our spontaneous impression with good-humored inflexibility then most when the whole cry of voices is on the other side. Else, to-morrow a stranger will say with masterly good sense precisely what we have thought and felt all the time, and we shall be forced to take with shame our own opinion from another.

There is a time in every man's education when he arrives at the conviction that envy is ignorance; that imitation is suicide; that he must take himself for better for worse as his portion; that though the wide universe is full of good, no kernel of nourishing corn can come to him but through his toil bestowed on that plot of ground which is given to him to till. The power which resides in him is new in nature, and none but he knows what that is which he can do, nor does he know until he has tried. Not for nothing one face, one character, one fact, makes much impression on him, and another none. This sculpture in the memory is not without preëstablished harmony. The eye was placed where one ray should fall, that it might testify of that particular ray. We but half express ourselves, and are ashamed of that divine idea which each of us represents. It may be safely trusted as proportionate and of good issues, so it be faithfully imparted, but God will not have his work made manifest by cowards. A man is relieved and gay when he has put his heart into his work and done his best; but what he has said or done otherwise shall give him no peace. It is a deliverance which does not deliver. In the attempt his genius deserts him; no muse befriends; no invention, no hope.

Trust thyself: every heart vibrates to that iron string. Accept the place the divine providence has found for you, the society of your contemporaries, the connection of events. Great men have always done so, and confided themselves childlike to the genius of their age, betraying their perception that the absolutely trustworthy was seated at their heart, working through their hands, predominating in all their being. And we are now men, and must accept in the highest mind the same transcendent destiny; and not minors and invalids in a protected corner, not cowards fleeing before a revolution, but guides, redeemers, and benefactors, obeying the Almighty effort, and advancing on Chaos and the Dark.[1]

What pretty oracles nature yields us on this text, in the face and behaviour of children, babes, and even brutes! That divided and rebel mind, that distrust of a sentiment because our arithmetic has computed the strength and means opposed to our purpose, these have not. Their mind being whole, their eye is as yet unconquered, and when we look in their faces, we are disconcerted. Infancy conforms to nobody: all conform to it, so that one babe commonly makes four or five out of the adults who prattle and play to it. So God has armed youth and puberty and manhood no less with its own piquancy and charm, and made it enviable and gracious and its claims not to be put by, if it will stand by itself. Do not think the youth has no force, because he cannot speak to you and me. Hark! in the next room his voice is sufficiently clear and emphatic. It seems he knows how to speak to his contemporaries. Bashful or bold, then, he will know how to make us seniors very unnecessary.

The nonchalance of boys who are sure of a dinner, and would disdain as much as a lord to do or say aught to conciliate one, is the healthy attitude of human nature. A boy is in the parlour what the pit [2] is in the playhouse; independent, irresponsible, looking out from his corner on such people and facts as pass by, he tries and sentences them on their merits, in the swift, summary ways of boys, as good, bad, interesting, silly, eloquent, troublesome. He cumbers himself never about consequences, about interests: he gives an independent, genuine verdict. You must court him: he does not court you. But the man is, as it were, clapped into jail by his consciousness. As soon as he has once acted or spoken with éclat, he is a committed person, watched by the sympathy or the hatred of hundreds, whose affections must now enter into his account. There is no Lethe [3] for this. Ah, that he could pass again into his neutrality! Who can thus avoid all pledges, and having observed, observe again from the same unaffected, unbiased, unbribable, unaffrighted innocence, must always be formidable. He would utter opinions on all passing affairs, which being seen to be not private, but necessary, would sink like darts into the ear of men, and put them in fear.

These are the voices which we hear in solitude, but they grow faint and inaudible as we enter into the world. Society everywhere

---

1. *Cf.* Milton, *Paradise Lost*, Book I, l. 453.
2. In old theaters, the cheaper seats behind the orchestra, below the level of the stage.
3. In Greek myth, a river of forgetfulness in the nether world.

is in conspiracy against the manhood of every one of its members. Society is a joint-stock company, in which the members agree, for the better securing of his bread to each shareholder, to surrender the liberty and culture of the eater. The virtue in most request is conformity. Self-reliance is its aversion. It loves not realities and creators, but names and customs.

Whoso would be a man, must be a nonconformist. He who would gather immortal palms must not be hindered by the name of goodness, but must explore if it be goodness. Nothing is at last sacred but the integrity of your own mind. Absolve you to yourself, and you shall have the suffrage of the world. I remember an answer which when quite young I was prompted to make to a valued adviser, who was wont to importune me with the dear old doctrines of the church. On my saying, What have I to do with the sacredness of traditions, if I live wholly from within? my friend suggested,—"But these impulses may be from below, not from above." I replied, "They do not seem to me to be such; but if I am the Devil's child, I will live then from the Devil." No law can be sacred to me but that of my nature. Good and bad are but names very readily transferable to that or this; the only right is what is after my constitution, the only wrong what is against it. A man is to carry himself in the presence of all opposition as if everything were titular and ephemeral but he. I am ashamed to think how easily we capitulate to badges and names, to large societies and dead institutions. Every decent and well-spoken individual affects and sways me more than is right. I ought to go upright and vital, and speak the rude truth in all ways. If malice and vanity wear the coat of philanthropy, shall that pass? If an angry bigot assumes this bountiful cause of Abolition, and comes to me with his last news from Barbadoes,[4] why should I not say to him, "Go love thy infant; love thy wood-chopper; be good-natured and modest: have that grace; and never varnish your hard, uncharitable ambition with this incredible tenderness for black folk a thousand miles off. Thy love afar is spite at home." Rough and graceless would be such greeting, but truth is handsomer than the affectation of love. Your goodness must have some edge to it,—else it is none. The doctrine of hatred must be preached as the counteraction of the doctrine of love when that pules and whines. I shun father and mother and wife and brother, when my genius calls me.[5] I would write on the lintels of the door-post, *Whim*.[6] I hope it is somewhat better than whim at last, but we cannot spend the day in explanation. Expect me not to show cause why I seek or why I exclude company. Then, again, do

4. British legislation abolished slavery in the West Indies, including Barbados, in 1833.
5. *Cf*. Matthew x: 34–37.

6. *Cf*. Exodus xii: 17. In Hebrew and other Eastern cultures, a mark on the lintel or doorframe characterized the resident.

not tell me, as a good man did to-day, of my obligation to put all poor men in good situations. Are they *my* poor? I tell thee, thou foolish philanthropist, that I grudge the dollar, the dime, the cent I give to such men as do not belong to me and to whom I do not belong. There is a class of persons to whom by all spiritual affinity I am bought and sold; for them I will go to prison, if need be; but your miscellaneous popular charities; the education at college of fools; the building of meeting-houses to the vain end to which many now stand; alms to sots; and the thousandfold Relief Societies;—though I confess with shame I sometimes succumb and give the dollar, it is a wicked dollar, which by and by I shall have the manhood to withhold.

Virtues are, in the popular estimate, rather the exception than the rule. There is the man *and* his virtues. Men do what is called a good action, as some piece of courage or charity, much as they would pay a fine in expiation of daily nonappearance on parade. Their works are done as an apology or extenuation of their living in the world,—as invalids and the insane pay a high board. Their virtues are penances. I do not wish to expiate, but to live. My life is for itself and not for a spectacle. I much prefer that it should be of a lower strain, so it be genuine and equal, than that it should be glittering and unsteady. I wish it to be sound and sweet, and not to need diet and bleeding. I ask primary evidence that you are a man, and refuse this appeal from the man to his actions. I know that for myself it makes no difference whether I do or forbear those actions which are reckoned excellent. I cannot consent to pay for a privilege where I have intrinsic right. Few and mean as my gifts may be, I actually am, and do not need for my own assurance or the assurance of my fellows any secondary testimony.

What I must do is all that concerns me, not what the people think. This rule, equally arduous in actual and in intellectual life, may serve for the whole distinction between greatness and meanness. It is the harder, because you will always find those who think they know what is your duty better than you know it. It is easy in the world to live after the world's opinion; it is easy in solitude to live after our own; but the great man is he who in the midst of the crowd keeps with perfect sweetness the independence of solitude.

The objection to conforming to usages that have become dead to you is, that it scatters your force. It loses your time and blurs the impression of your character. If you maintain a dead church, contribute to a dead Bible-society, vote with a great party either for the government or against it, spread your table like base house-keepers,—under all these screens I have difficulty to detect the precise man you are. And, of course, so much force is withdrawn from all your proper life. But do your work, and I shall know you. Do your work, and you shall reinforce yourself. A man must consider what a blind man's-buff is this game of conformity. If I know your sect, I anticipate your argument. I hear a preacher announce for his text and topic the expediency of one of the institutions of his church. Do I not know beforehand that not possibly can he say a new and spontaneous word? Do I not know that, with all this ostentation of examining the grounds of the institution, he will do no such thing? Do I not know that he is pledged to himself not to look but at one side,—the permitted side, not as a man, but as a parish minister? He is a retained attorney, and these airs of the bench are the emptiest affectation. Well, most men have bound their eyes with one or another handkerchief, and attached themselves to some one of these communities of opinion. This conformity makes them not false in a few particulars, authors of a few lies, but false in all particulars. Their every truth is not quite true. Their two is not the real two, their four not the real four; so that every word they say chagrins us, and we know not where to begin to set them right. Meantime nature is not slow to equip us in the prison-uniform of the party to which we adhere. We come to wear one cut of face and figure, and acquire by degrees the gentlest asinine expression. There is a mortifying experience in particular, which does not fail to wreak itself also in the general history; I mean "the foolish face of praise," [7] the forced smile which we put on in company where we do not feel at ease in answer to conversation which does not interest us. The muscles, not spontaneously moved, but moved by a low usurping wilfulness, grow tight about the outline of the face, with the most disagreeable sensation.

For nonconformity the world whips you with its displeasure. And therefore a man must know how to estimate a sour face. The bystanders look askance on him in the public street or in the friend's parlour. If this aversion had its origin in contempt and resistance like his own, he might well go home with a sad countenance; but the sour faces of the multitude, like their sweet faces, have no deep cause, but are put on and off as the wind blows and a newspaper directs. Yet is the discontent of the multitude more formidable than that of the senate and the college. It is easy enough for a firm man who knows the world to brook the rage of the cultivated classes. Their rage is decorous and prudent, for they are timid as being very vulnerable themselves. But when to their feminine rage the indignation of the people is added, when the ignorant and the poor are aroused, when the unintelligent brute force that lies at the bottom of society is made to growl and mow,[8] it needs the habit of magnanimity and religion to treat it godlike as a trifle of no concernment.

The other terror that scares us from self-trust is our consistency;

---

7. *Cf.* Alexander Pope, "Epistle to Dr. Arbuthnot," l. 212.   8. To mock or grimace.

a reverence for our past act or word, because the eyes of others have no other data for computing our orbit than our past acts, and we are loth to disappoint them.

But why should you keep your head over your shoulder? Why drag about this corpse of your memory, lest you contradict somewhat you have stated in this or that public place? Suppose you should contradict yourself; what then? It seems to be a rule of wisdom never to rely on your memory alone, scarcely even in acts of pure memory, but to bring the past for judgment into the thousand-eyed present, and live ever in a new day. In your metaphysics you have denied personality to the Deity: yet when the devout motions of the soul come, yield to them heart and life, though they should clothe God with shape and color. Leave your theory, as Joseph his coat in the hand of the harlot [9] and flee.

A foolish consistency is the hobgoblin of little minds, adored by little statesmen and philosophers and divines. With consistency a great soul has simply nothing to do. He may as well concern himself with his shadow on the wall. Speak what you think now in hard words, and to-morrow speak what to-morrow thinks in hard words again, though it contradict every thing you said to-day.—"Ah, so you shall be sure to be misunderstood."—Is it so bad, then, to be misunderstood? Pythagoras was misunderstood, and Socrates, and Jesus, and Luther, and Copernicus, and Galileo,[1] and Newton, and every pure and wise spirit that ever took flesh. To be great is to be misunderstood.

I suppose no man can violate his nature. All the sallies of his will are rounded in by the law of his being, as the inequalities of Andes and Himmaleh are insignificant in the curve of the sphere. Nor does it matter how you gauge and try him. A character is like an acrostic or Alexandrian stanza;[2] read it forward, backward, or across, it still spells the same thing. In this pleasing, contrite wood-life which God allows me, let me record day by day my honest thought without prospect or retrospect, and, I cannot doubt, it will be found symmetrical, though I mean it not, and see it not. My book should smell of pines and resound with the hum of insects. The swallow over my window should interweave that thread or straw he carries in his bill into my web also. We pass for what we are. Character teaches above our wills. Men imagine that they communicate

9. *Cf.* Joseph and Potiphar's wife, Genesis xxxix: 12.
1. Pythagoras, Greek thinker of the fifth century B.C., aroused controversy by his revolutionary ideas and mathematical discoveries; Copernicus (1473–1543) risked charges of impiety in promulgating the theory of the solar system now accepted; Galileo (1564–1642) was tried by the Inquisition and condemned to retirement for supporting the theories of Copernicus. The remainder of these names suggest familiar controversies.
2. An Alexandrian stanza is a palindrome, or an arrangement of words which read the same backward as forward.

their virtue or vice only by overt actions, and do not see that virtue or vice emit a breath every moment.

There will be an agreement in whatever variety of actions, so they be each honest and natural in their hour. For of one will, the actions will be harmonious, however unlike they seem. These varieties are lost sight of at a little distance, at a little height of thought. One tendency unites them all. The voyage of the best ship is a zigzag line of a hundred tacks. See the line from a sufficient distance, and it straightens itself to the average tendency. Your genuine action will explain itself, and will explain your other genuine actions. Your conformity explains nothing. Act singly, and what you have already done singly will justify you now. Greatness appeals to the future. If I can be firm enough to-day to do right, and scorn eyes, I must have done so much right before as to defend me now. Be it how it will, do right now. Always scorn appearances, and you always may. The force of character is cumulative. All the foregone days of virtue work their health into this. What makes the majesty of the heroes of the senate and the field, which so fills the imagination? The consciousness of a train of great days and victories behind. They shed a united light on the advancing actor. He is attended as by a visible escort of angels. That is it which throws thunder into Chatham's [3] voice, and dignity into Washington's port, and America into Adams's [4] eye. Honor is venerable to us because it is no ephemera. It is always ancient virtue. We worship it to-day because it is not of to-day. We love it and pay it homage, because it is not a trap for our love and homage, but is self-dependent, self-derived, and therefore of an old immaculate pedigree, even if shown in a young person.

I hope in these days we have heard the last of conformity and consistency. Let the words be gazetted [5] and ridiculous henceforward. Instead of the gong for dinner, let us hear a whistle from the Spartan fife.[6] Let us never bow and apologize more. A great man is coming to eat at my house. I do not wish to please him; I wish that he should wish to please me. I will stand here for humanity, and though I would make it kind, I would make it true. Let us affront and reprimand the smooth mediocrity and squalid contentment of the times, and hurl in the face of custom, and trade, and office, the fact which is the upshot of all history, that there is a great responsible Thinker and Actor working wherever a man works; that a true

---

3. The Earl of Chatham, William Pitt (1708–1778), greatest English orator of his day; he supported the American colonists in Parliament.
4. By 1841 there had been three Adamses to whom this reference might apply: Samuel, a leader of the Revolution; John, who became the second

president; and John Quincy, the sixth president.
5. *I.e.*, "dismissed." The British official "gazettes" announced dismissals, bankruptcies, and the like, as well as honors.
6. The strict discipline of Spartan life would preclude any but the most austere music.

man belongs to no other time or place, but is the centre of things. Where he is, there is nature. He measures you, and all men, and all events. Ordinarily, every body in society reminds us of somewhat else, or of some other person. Character, reality, reminds you of nothing else; it takes place of the whole creation. The man must be so much, that he must make all circumstances indifferent. Every true man is a cause, a country, and an age; requires infinite spaces and numbers and time fully to accomplish his design;—and posterity seem to follow his steps as a train of clients. A man Caesar is born, and for ages after we have a Roman Empire. Christ is born, and millions of minds so grow and cleave to his genius that he is confounded with virtue and the possible of man. An institution is the lengthened shadow of one man; as, Monachism, of the Hermit Anthony; [7] the Reformation, of Luther; Quakerism, of Fox; [8] Methodism, of Wesley; Abolition, of Clarkson.[9] Scipio, Milton called "the height of Rome;" [1] and all history resolves itself very easily into the biography of a few stout and earnest persons.

Let a man then know his worth, and keep things under his feet. Let him not peep or steal, or skulk up and down with the air of a charity-boy, a bastard, or an interloper, in the world which exists for him. But the man in the street, finding no worth in himself which corresponds to the force which built a tower or sculptured a marble god, feels poor when he looks on these. To him a palace, a statue, or a costly book have an alien and forbidding air, much like a gay equipage, and seem to say like that, "Who are you, Sir?" Yet they all are his, suitors for his notice, petitioners to his faculties that they will come out and take possession. The picture waits for my verdict: it is not to command me, but I am to settle its claims to praise. That popular fable [2] of the sot who was picked up dead drunk in the street, carried to the duke's house, washed and dressed and laid in the duke's bed, and, on his waking, treated with all obsequious ceremony like the duke, and assured that he had been insane, owes its popularity to the fact, that it symbolizes so well the state of man, who is in the world a sort of sot, but now and then wakes up, exercises his reason and finds himself a true prince.

Our reading is mendicant and sycophantic. In history, our imagination plays us false. Kingdom and lordship, power and estate, are a gaudier vocabulary than private John and Edward in a small house

7. The hermitages of St. Anthony (ca. 250–350) were the beginnings of Christian monasticism.
8. George Fox (1624–1691) founded the Society of Friends in England (1647).
9. Thomas Clarkson (1760–1846) was the pioneer of the British antislavery movement.

1. *Cf.* John Milton, *Paradise Lost*, Book IX, l. 510. Scipio Africanus "the Elder" (237–183 B.C.), conqueror of Hannibal, was the greatest Roman general before Julius Caesar.
2. *Cf.* the same story in Shakespeare's "Induction," *The Taming of the Shrew* (Centenary Edition, Vol. II, p. 392).

and common day's work; but the things of life are the same to both; the sum total of both is the same. Why all this deference to Alfred,[3] and Scanderbeg,[4] and Gustavus?[5] Suppose they were virtuous; did they wear out virtue? As great a stake depends on your private act to-day, as followed their public and renowned steps. When private men shall act with original views, the lustre will be transferred from the actions of kings to those of gentlemen.

The world has been instructed by its kings, who have so magnetized the eyes of nations. It has been taught by this colossal symbol the mutual reverence that is due from man to man. The joyful loyalty with which men have everywhere suffered the king, the noble, or the great proprietor to walk among them by a law of his own, make his own scale of men and things, and reverse theirs, pay for benefits not with money but with honor, and represent the law in his person, was the hieroglyphic by which they obscurely signified their consciousness of their own right and comeliness, the right of every man.

The magnetism which all original action exerts is explained when we inquire the reason of self-trust. Who is the Trustee? What is the aboriginal Self, on which a universal reliance may be grounded? What is the nature and power of that science-baffling star, without parallax,[6] without calculable elements, which shoots a ray of beauty even into trivial and impure actions, if the least mark of independence appear? The inquiry leads us to that source, at once the essence of genius, of virtue, and of life, which we call Spontaneity or Instinct. We denote this primary wisdom as Intuition, whilst all later teachings are tuitions. In that deep force, the last fact behind which analysis cannot go, all things find their common origin. For the sense of being which in calm hours rises, we know not how, in the soul, is not diverse from things, from space, from light, from time, from man, but one with them, and proceeds obviously from the same source whence their life and being also proceed. We first share the life by which things exist, and afterwards see them as appearances in nature, and forget that we have shared their cause. Here is the fountain of action and of thought. Here are the lungs of that inspiration which giveth man wisdom, and which cannot be denied without impiety and atheism. We lie in the lap of immense intelligence, which makes us receivers of its truth and organs of its activity. When we discern justice, when we discern

3. Alfred (849–899), called "the Great" among Saxon kings of Britain.
4. Scanderbeg (Turkish title, "Iskander Bey") was George Castriota (1403?–1468), national hero of the Albanians, whom he led against the Turks.
5. Sweden's King Gustavus I (Gustavus Vasa, 1496–1560) defeated the Danes, and proclaimed Christianity; Gustavus II (Gustavus Adolphus, 1594–1632) freed Swedish territories occupied by Denmark, Russia, and Poland.
6. *I.e.*, "incalculable."

truth, we do nothing of ourselves, but allow a passage to its beams. If we ask whence this comes, if we seek to pry into the soul that causes, all philosophy is at fault. Its presence or its absence is all we can affirm. Every man discriminates between the voluntary acts of his mind, and his involuntary perceptions, and knows that to his involuntary perceptions a perfect faith is due. He may err in the expression of them, but he knows that these things are so, like day and night, not to be disputed. My wilful actions and acquisitions are but roving;—the idlest reverie, the faintest native emotion, command my curiosity and respect. Thoughtless people contradict as readily the statement of perceptions as of opinions, or rather much more readily; for they do not distinguish between perception and notion. They fancy that I choose to see this or that thing. But perception is not whimsical, but fatal. If I see a trait, my children will see it after me, and in course of time, all mankind,—although it may chance that no one has seen it before me. For my perception of it is as much a fact as the sun.

The relations of the soul to the divine spirit are so pure, that it is profane to seek to interpose helps. It must be that when God speaketh he should communicate, not one thing, but all things; should fill the world with his voice; should scatter forth light, nature, time, souls, from the centre of the present thought; and new date and new create the whole. Whenever a mind is simple, and receives a divine wisdom, old things pass away,—means, teachers, texts, temples fall; it lives now, and absorbs past and future into the present hour. All things are made sacred by relation to it,—one as much as another. All things are dissolved to their centre by their cause, and, in the universal miracle, petty and particular miracles disappear. If, therefore, a man claims to know and speak of God, and carries you backward to the phraseology of some old mouldered nation in another country, in another world, believe him not. Is the acorn better than the oak which is its fulness and completion? Is the parent better than the child into whom he has cast his ripened being? Whence, then, this worship of the past? The centuries are conspirators against the sanity and authority of the soul. Time and space are but physiological colors which the eye makes, but the soul is light; where it is, is day; where it was, is night; and history is an impertinence and an injury, if it be anything more than a cheerful apologue or parable of my being and becoming.

Man is timid and apologetic; he is no longer upright; he dares not say "I think," "I am," but quotes some saint or sage. He is ashamed before the blade of grass or the blowing rose. These roses under my window make no reference to former roses or to better ones; they are for what they are; they exist with God to-day. There is no time to them. There is simply the rose; it is perfect in every moment of its existence. Before a leaf-bud has burst, its whole life acts; in the full-blown flower there is no more; in the leafless root there is no less. Its nature is satisfied, and it satisfies nature, in all moments alike. But man postpones or remembers; he does not live in the present, but with reverted eye laments the past, or, heedless of the riches that surround him, stands on tiptoe to foresee the future. He cannot be happy and strong until he too lives with nature in the present, above time.

This should be plain enough. Yet see what strong intellects dare not yet hear God himself, unless he speaks the phraseology of I know not what David, or Jeremiah, or Paul. We shall not always set so great a price on a few texts, on a few lives. We are like children who repeat by rote the sentences of grandames and tutors, and, as they grow older, of the men of talents and character they chance to see,—painfully recollecting the exact words they spoke; afterwards, when they come into the point of view which those had who uttered these sayings, they understand them, and are willing to let the words go; for, at any time, they can use words as good when occasion comes. If we live truly, we shall see truly. It is as easy for the strong man to be strong, as it is for the weak to be weak. When we have new perception, we shall gladly disburden the memory of its hoarded treasures as old rubbish. When a man lives with God, his voice shall be as sweet as the murmur of the brook and the rustle of the corn.

And now at last the highest truth of this subject remains unsaid; probably cannot be said; for all that we say is the far-off remembering of the intuition. That thought, by what I can now nearest approach to say it, is this. When good is near you, when you have life in yourself, it is not by any known or accustomed way; you shall not discern the foot-prints of any other; you shall not see the face of man; you shall not hear any name;—the way, the thought, the good, shall be wholly strange and new. It shall exclude example and experience. You take the way from man, not to man. All persons that ever existed are its forgotten ministers. Fear and hope are alike beneath it. There is somewhat low even in hope. In the hour of vision, there is nothing that can be called gratitude, nor properly joy. The soul raised over passion beholds identity and eternal causation, perceives the self-existence of Truth and Right, and calms itself with knowing that all things go well. Vast spaces of nature, the Atlantic Ocean, the South Sea,—long intervals of time, years, centuries,—are of no account. This which I think and feel underlay every former state of life and circumstances, as it does underlie my present, and what is called life, and what is called death.

Life only avails, not the having lived. Power ceases in the instant of repose; it resides in the moment of transition from a past to a new state, in the shooting of the gulf, in the darting to an aim. This one fact the world hates, that the soul *becomes*; for that forever degrades the past, turns all riches to poverty, all reputation to a shame, confounds the saint with the rogue, shoves Jesus and Judas equally aside. Why, then, do we prate of self-reliance? Inasmuch as the soul is present, there will be power not confident but agent. To talk of reliance is a poor external way of speaking. Speak rather of that which relies, because it works and is. Who has more obedience than I masters me, though he should not raise his finger. Round him I must revolve by the gravitation of spirits. We fancy it rhetoric, when we speak of eminent virtue. We do not yet see that virtue is Height, and that a man or a company of men, plastic and permeable to principles, by the law of nature must overpower and ride all cities, nations, kings, rich men, poets, who are not.

This is the ultimate fact which we so quickly reach on this, as on every topic, the resolution of all into the ever-blessed One. Self-existence is the attribute of the Supreme Cause, and it constitutes the measure of good by the degree in which it enters into all lower forms. All things real are so by so much virtue as they contain. Commerce, husbandry, hunting, whaling, war, eloquence, personal weight, are somewhat, and engage my respect as examples of its presence and impure action. I see the same law working in nature for conservation and growth. Power is in nature the essential measure of right. Nature suffers nothing to remain in her kingdoms which cannot help itself. The genesis and maturation of a planet, its poise and orbit, the bended tree recovering itself from the strong wind, the vital resources of every animal and vegetable, are demonstrations of the self-sufficing, and therefore self-relying soul.

Thus all concentrates: let us not rove; let us sit at home with the cause. Let us stun and astonish the intruding rabble of men and books and institutions, by a simple declaration of the divine fact. Bid the invaders take the shoes from off their feet, for God is here within.[7] Let our simplicity judge them, and our docility to our own law demonstrate the poverty of nature and fortune beside our native riches.

But now we are a mob. Man does not stand in awe of man, nor is his genius admonished to stay at home, to put itself in communication with the internal ocean, but it goes abroad to beg a cup of water of the urns of other men. We must go alone. I like the silent church before the service begins, better than any preaching. How far off, how cool, how chaste the persons look, begirt each one with a precinct or sanctuary! So let us always sit. Why should we assume

7. *Cf.* Joshua v: 15; Exodus iii: 5.

the faults of our friends, or wife, or father, or child, because they sit around our hearth, or are said to have the same blood? All men have my blood, and I all men's. Not for that will I adopt their petulance or folly, even to the extent of being ashamed of it. But your isolation must not be mechanical, but spiritual, that is, must be elevation. At times the whole world seems to be in conspiracy to importune you with emphatic trifles. Friend, client, child, sickness, fear, want, charity, all knock at once at thy closet door, and say,—"Come out unto us." But keep thy state; come not into their confusion. The power men possess to annoy me, I give them by a weak curiosity. No man can come near me but through my act. "What we love that we have, but by desire we bereave ourselves of the love."

If we cannot at once rise to the sanctities of obedience and faith, let us at least resist our temptations; let us enter into the state of war, and wake Thor [8] and Woden,[9] courage and constancy, in our Saxon breasts. This is to be done in our smooth times by speaking the truth. Check this lying hospitality and lying affection. Live no longer to the expectation of these deceived and deceiving people with whom we converse. Say to them, "O father, O mother, O wife, O brother, O friend, I have lived with you after appearances hitherto. Henceforward I am the truth's. Be it known unto you that henceforward I obey no laws less than the eternal law. I will have no covenants but proximities. I shall endeavor to nourish my parents, to support my family, to be the chaste husband of one wife,—but these relations I must fill after a new and unprecedented way. I appeal from your customs. I must be myself. I cannot break myself any longer for you, or you. If you can love me for what I am, we shall be the happier. If you cannot, I will still seek to deserve that you should. I will not hide my tastes or aversions. I will so trust that what is deep is holy, that I will do strongly before the sun and moon whatever inly rejoices me, and the heart appoints. If you are noble, I will love you; if you are not, I will not hurt you and myself by hypocritical attentions. If you are true, but not in the same truth with me, cleave to your companions; I will seek my own. I do this not selfishly but humbly and truly. It is alike your interest, and mine, and all men's, however long we have dwelt in lies, to live in truth. Does this sound harsh to-day? You will soon love what is dictated by your nature as well as mine, and if we follow the truth, it will bring us out safe at last."—But so you may give these friends pain. Yes, but I cannot sell my liberty and my power, to save their sensibility. Besides, all persons have their moments of reason, when

8. In Norse myth, "the Thunderer," god of war.
9. Anglo-Saxon form of the name of

Odin—in Teutonic myth the god of war but also the patron of the slain.

they look out into the region of absolute truth; then will they justify me, and do the same thing.

The populace think that your rejection of popular standards is a
rejection of all standard, and mere antinomianism;[1] and the bold
sensualist will use the name of philosophy to gild his crimes. But
the law of consciousness abides. There are two confessionals, in one
or the other of which we must be shriven. You may fulfil your
round of duties by clearing yourself in the *direct*, or in the *reflex*
way. Consider whether you have satisfied your relations to father,
mother, cousin, neighbour, town, cat and dog; whether any of these
can upbraid you. But I may also neglect this reflex standard, and
absolve me to myself. I have my own stern claims and perfect circle.
It denies the name of duty to many offices that are called duties.
But if I can discharge its debts, it enables me to dispense with the
popular code. If any one imagines that this law is lax, let him keep
its commandment one day.

And truly it demands something godlike in him who has cast off
the common motives of humanity, and has ventured to trust himself for a taskmaster. High be his heart, faithful his will, clear his
sight, that he may in good earnest be doctrine, society, law, to himself, that a simple purpose may be to him as strong as iron necessity
is to others!

If any man consider the present aspects of what is called by distinction *society*, he will see the need of these ethics. The sinew and
heart of man seem to be drawn out, and we are become timorous,
desponding whimperers. We are afraid of truth, afraid of fortune,
afraid of death, and afraid of each other. Our age yields no great
and perfect persons. We want men and women who shall renovate
life and our social state, but we see that most natures are insolvent,
cannot satisfy their own wants, have an ambition out of all proportion to their practical force and do lean and beg day and night continually. Our housekeeping is mendicant, our arts, our occupations,
our marriages, our religion, we have not chosen, but society has
chosen for us. We are parlour soldiers. We shun the rugged battle
of fate, where strength is born.

If our young men miscarry in their first enterprises, they lose all
heart. If the young merchant fails, men say he is *ruined*. If the finest genius studies at one of our colleges, and is not installed in an
office within one year afterwards in the cities or suburbs of Boston
or New York, it seems to his friends and to himself that he is right
in being disheartened, and in complaining the rest of his life. A
sturdy lad from New Hampshire or Vermont, who in turn tries all
the professions, who *teams it*, *farms it*, *peddles*, keeps a school,

---

1. The doctrine of salvation by faith alone, without reference to breaches of
the moral law.

preaches, edits a newspaper, goes to Congress, buys a township, and so forth, in successive years, and always, like a cat, falls on his feet, is worth a hundred of these city dolls. He walks abreast with his days, and feels no shame in not "studying a profession," for he does not postpone his life, but lives already. He has not one chance, but a hundred chances. Let a Stoic [2] open the resources of man, and tell men they are not leaning willows, but can and must detach themselves; that with the exercise of self-trust, new powers shall appear; that a man is the word made flesh,[3] born to shed healing to the nations, that he should be ashamed of our compassion, and that the moment he acts from himself, tossing the laws, the books, idolatries, and customs out of the window, we pity him no more, but thank and revere him,—and that teacher shall restore the life of man to splendor, and make his name dear to all history.

It is easy to see that a greater self-reliance must work a revolution in all the offices and relations of men; in their religion; in their education; in their pursuits; their modes of living; their association; in their property; in their speculative views.

1. In what prayers do men allow themselves! That which they call a holy office is not so much as brave and manly. Prayer looks abroad and asks for some foreign addition to come through some foreign virtue, and loses itself in endless mazes of natural and supernatural, and mediatorial and miraculous. Prayer that craves a particular commodity,—anything less than all good,—is vicious. Prayer is the contemplation of the facts of life from the highest point of view. It is the soliloquy of a beholding and jubilant soul. It is the spirit of God pronouncing his works good.[4] But prayer as a means to effect a private end is meanness and theft. It supposes dualism and not unity in nature and consciousness. As soon as the man is at one with God, he will not beg. He will then see prayer in all action. The prayer of the farmer kneeling in his field to weed it, the prayer of the rower kneeling with the stroke of his oar, are true prayers heard throughout nature, though for cheap ends. Caratach, in Fletcher's Bonduca,[5] when admonished to inquire the mind of the god Audate, replies,—

> "His hidden meaning lies in our endeavours;
> Our valors are our best gods."

Another sort of false prayers are our regrets. Discontent is the want of self-reliance: it is infirmity of will. Regret calamities, if you can thereby help the sufferer; if not, attend your own work, and al-

---

2. The original Stoics, led by Zeno of Athens after 300 B.C., taught passionless self-reliance and submission to natural law.
3. *Cf.* John i: 14.

4. *Cf.* Genesis i: 25.
5. The Elizabethan playwright John Fletcher wrote *Bonduca* (1618) perhaps in collaboration with Francis Beaumont.

ready the evil begins to be repaired. Our sympathy is just as base. We come to them who weep foolishly, and sit down and cry for company, instead of imparting to them truth and health in rough electric shocks, putting them once more in communication with their own reason. The secret of fortune is joy in our hands. Welcome evermore to gods and men is the self-helping man. For him all doors are flung wide: him all tongues greet, all honors crown, all eyes follow with desire. Our love goes out to him and embraces him, because he did not need it. We solicitously and apologetically caress and celebrate him, because he held on his way and scorned our disapprobation. The gods love him because men hated him. "To the persevering mortal," said Zoroaster,[6] "the blessed Immortals are swift."

As men's prayers are a disease of the will, so are their creeds a disease of the intellect. They say with those foolish Israelites, "Let not God speak to us, lest we die. Speak thou, speak any man with us, and we will obey." [7] Everywhere I am hindered of meeting God in my brother, because he has shut his own temple doors, and recites fables merely of his brother's, or his brother's brother's God. Every new mind is a new classification.[8] If it prove a mind of uncommon activity and power, a Locke, a Lavoisier, a Hutton, a Bentham, a Fourier, it imposes its classification on other men, and lo! a new system. In proportion to the depth of the thought, and so to the number of the objects it touches and brings within reach of the pupil, is his complacency. But chiefly is this apparent in creeds and churches, which are also classifications of some powerful mind acting on the elemental thought of duty, and man's relation to the Highest. Such is Calvinism, Quakerism, Swedenborgism. The pupil takes the same delight in subordinating every thing to the new terminology, as a girl who has just learned botany in seeing a new earth and new seasons thereby. It will happen for a time, that the pupil will find his intellectual power has grown by the study of his master's mind. But in all unbalanced minds, the classification is idolized, passes for the end, and not for a speedily exhaustible means, so that the walls of the system blend to their eye in the remote horizon with the walls of the universe; the luminaries of heaven seem to them hung on the arch their master built. They cannot imagine how you aliens have any right to see,—how you can see; "It must be somehow that you stole the light from us." They

6. Reputed founder (sixth century B.C.?) of ancient Persian religion, recorded in the Avesta, here quoted.
7. *Cf.* the words of the Israelites to Moses concerning the Ten Commandments: Exodus xx: 19.
8. Each of the following was a pioneer of the "systematic" science: John Locke (1632–1704) developed a theory of knowledge; Antoine Laurent Lavoisier (1743–1794) pioneered in chemistry and James Hutton (1726–1797) in geology; Jeremy Bentham (1748–1832) formulated utilitarian concepts of law and government; François Marie Charles Fourier (1772–1837) originated plans for the co-operative organization of society.

do not yet perceive that light, unsystematic, indomitable, will break into any cabin, even into theirs. Let them chirp awhile and call it their own. If they are honest and do well, presently their neat new pinfold will be too strait and low, will crack, will lean, will rot and vanish, and the immortal light, all young, and joyful, million-orbed, million-colored, will beam over the universe as on the first morning.

2. It is for want of self-culture that the superstition of Travelling, whose idols are Italy, England, Egypt, retains its fascination for all educated Americans. They who made England, Italy, or Greece venerable in the imagination did so by sticking fast where they were, like an axis of the earth. In manly hours, we feel that duty is our place. The soul is no traveller; the wise man stays at home, and when his necessities, his duties, on any occasion call him from his house, or into foreign lands, he is at home still, and shall make men sensible by the expression of his countenance, that he goes the missionary of wisdom and virtue, and visits cities and men like a sovereign, and not like an interloper or a valet.

I have no churlish objection to the circumnavigation of the globe, for the purposes of art, of study, and benevolence, so that the man is first domesticated, or does not go abroad with the hope of finding somewhat greater than he knows. He who travels to be amused, or to get somewhat which he does not carry, travels away from himself, and grows old even in youth among old things. In Thebes, in Palmyra, his will and mind have become old and dilapidated as they. He carries ruins to ruins.

Travelling is a fool's paradise. Our first journeys discover to us the indifference of places. At home I dream that at Naples, at Rome, I can be intoxicated with beauty, and lose my sadness. I pack my trunk, embrace my friends, embark on the sea and at last wake up in Naples, and there beside me is the stern fact, the sad self, unrelenting, identical, that I fled from. I seek the Vatican, and the palaces. I affect to be intoxicated with sights and suggestions, but I am not intoxicated. My giant goes with me wherever I go.

3. But the rage of travelling is a symptom of a deeper unsoundness affecting the whole intellectual action. The intellect is vagabond, and our system of education fosters restlessness. Our minds travel when our bodies are forced to stay at home. We imitate; and what is imitation but the travelling of the mind? Our houses are built with foreign taste; our shelves are garnished with foreign ornaments; our opinions, our tastes, our faculties, lean, and follow the Past and the Distant. The soul created the arts wherever they have flourished. It was in his own mind that the artist sought his model. It was an application of his own thought to the thing to be done and the conditions to be observed. And why need we copy the Doric or the Gothic model? Beauty, convenience, grandeur of

thought, and quaint expression are as near to us as to any, and if the American artist will study with hope and love the precise thing to be done by him, considering the climate, the soil, the length of the day, the wants of the people, the habit and form of the government, he will create a house in which all these will find themselves fitted, and taste and sentiment will be satisfied also.

Insist on yourself; never imitate. Your own gift you can present every moment with the cumulative force of a whole life's cultivation; but of the adopted talent of another, you have only an extemporaneous, half possession. That which each can do best, none but his Maker can teach him. No man yet knows what it is, nor can, till that person has exhibited it. Where is the master who could have taught Shakspeare? Where is the master who could have instructed Franklin, or Washington, or Bacon, or Newton? Every great man is a unique. The Scipionism of Scipio is precisely that part he could not borrow.[9] Shakspeare will never be made by the study of Shakspeare. Do that which is assigned you, and you cannot hope too much or dare too much. There is at this moment for you an utterance brave and grand as that of the colossal chisel of Phidias,[1] or trowel of the Egyptians, or the pen of Moses, or Dante, but different from all these. Not possibly will the soul, all rich, all eloquent, with thousand-cloven tongue, deign to repeat itself but if you can hear what these patriarchs say, surely you can reply to them in the same pitch of voice; for the ear and the tongue are two organs of one nature. Abide in the simple and noble regions of thy life, obey thy heart, and thou shall reproduce the Foreworld again.

4. As our Religion, our Education, our Art look abroad, so does our spirit of society. All men plume themselves on the improvement of society, and no man improves.

Society never advances. It recedes as fast on one side as it gains on the other. It undergoes continual changes; it is barbarous, it is civilized, it is christianized, it is rich, it is sicentific; but this change is not amelioration. For every thing that is given, something is taken. Society acquires new arts, and loses old instincts. What a contrast between the well-clad, reading, writing, thinking American, with a watch, a pencil, and a bill of exchange in his pocket, and the naked New Zealander, whose property is a club, a spear, a mat, and an undivided twentieth of a shed to sleep under! But compare the health of the two men, and you shall see that the white man has lost his aboriginal strength. If the traveller tells us truly, strike the savage with a broad-axe and in a day or two the flesh shall unite

9. The essay "Self-Reliance" originated as a development of the preceding portion of this paragraph, which formed an entry in Emerson's journal for 1832 (*cf*. Centenary Edition, Vol. II, p. 395).
1. The greatest of ancient Greek sculptors (*fl*. fifth century B.C.).

and heal as if you struck the blow into soft pitch, and the same blow shall send the white to his grave.

The civilized man has built a coach, but has lost the use of his feet. He is supported on crutches, but lacks so much support of muscle. He has a fine Geneva watch, but he fails of the skill to tell the hour by the sun. A Greenwich nautical almanac he has, and so being sure of the information when he wants it, the man in the street does not know a star in the sky. The solstice he does not observe; the equinox he knows as little; and the whole bright calendar of the year is without a dial in his mind. His note-books impair his memory; his libraries overload his wit; the insurance-office increases the number of accidents; and it may be a question whether machinery does not encumber; whether we have not lost by refinement some energy, by a Christianity, entrenched in establishments and forms, some vigor of wild virtue. For every Stoic was a Stoic; but in Christendom where is the Christian?

There is no more deviation in the moral standard than in the standard of height or bulk. No greater men are now than ever were. A singular equality may be observed between the great men of the first and of the last ages; nor can all the science, art, religion, and philosophy of the nineteenth century avail to educate greater men than Plutarch's [2] heroes, three or four and twenty centuries ago. Not in time is the race progressive. Phocion, Socrates, Anaxagoras, Diogenes, are great men, but they leave no class. He who is really of their class will not be called by their name, but will be his own man, and in his turn the founder of a sect. The arts and inventions of each period are only its costume, and do not invigorate men. The harm of the improved machinery may compensate its good. Hudson and Behring accomplished so much in their fishing-boats, as to astonish Parry and Franklin,[3] whose equipment exhausted the resources of science and art. Galileo, with an opera-glass,[4] discovered a more splendid series of celestial phenomena than any one since. Columbus found the New World in an undecked boat. It is curious to see the periodical disuse and perishing of means and machinery, which were introduced with loud laudation a few years or centuries before. The great genius returns to essential man. We reckoned the improvements of the art of war among the triumphs of science, and yet Napoleon conquered Europe by the bivouac, which consisted of falling back on naked valor, and disencumbering

2. Graeco-Roman biographer (46?–120?), whose *Lives* became a source book for Renaissance literature, especially the Elizabethan.

3. The earlier explorers, Henry Hudson (died 1611) and Vitus Bering (Behring) (1680–1741), left their names on the map of North America;

Sir William E. Parry, (1790–1855) and Sir John Franklin (1786–1847) were English Arctic explorers famous in Emerson's day.

4. The "opera-glass" of Galileo (1564–1642), Italian astronomer, was the first modern refracting telescope.

it of all aids. The Emperor held it impossible to make a perfect army, says Las Casas,[5] "without abolishing our arms, magazines, commissaries, and carriages, until, in imitation of the Roman custom, the soldier should receive his supply of corn, grind it in his handmill, and bake his bread himself."

Society is a wave. The wave moves onward, but the water of which it is composed does not. The same particle does not rise from the valley to the ridge. Its unity is only phenomenal. The persons who make up a nation to-day, next year die, and their experience dies with them.

And so the reliance on Property, including the reliance on governments which protect it, is the want of self-reliance. Men have looked away from themselves and at things so long, that they have come to esteem the religious, learned, and civil institutions as guards of property, and they deprecate assaults on these, because they feel them to be assaults on property. They measure their esteem of each other by what each has, and not by what each is. But a cultivated man becomes ashamed of his property, out of new respect for his nature. Especially he hates what he has, if he sees that it is accidental,—came to him by inheritance, or gift, or crime; then he feels that it is not having, it does not belong to him, has no root in him, and merely lies there, because no revolution or no robber takes it away. But that which a man is, does always by necessity acquire, and what the man acquires is living property, which does not wait the beck of rulers, or mobs, or revolutions, or fire, or storm, or bankruptcies, but perpetually renews itself whenever the man breathes. "Thy lot or portion of life," said the Caliph Ali,[6] "is seeking after thee; therefore be at rest from seeking after it." Our dependence on these foreign goods leads us to our slavish respect for numbers. The political parties meet in numerous conventions; the greater the concourse, and with each new uproar of announcement, The delegation from Essex! The Democrats from New Hampshire! The Whigs of Maine! the young patriot feels himself stronger than before by a new thousand of eyes and arms. In like manner the reformers summon conventions, and vote and resolve in multitude. Not so, O friends! will the God deign to enter and inhabit you, but by a method precisely the reverse. It is only as a man puts off all foreign support, and stands alone, that I see him to be strong and to prevail. He is weaker by every recruit to his

5. Properly Las Cases (Comte Emmanuel Augustin Dieudonné de, 1766–1842), Napoleon's secretary during his exile on St. Helena, who compiled from the Emperor's conversations the *Mémorial de Sante Hélène* (1818, revised 1823) which Emerson here paraphrases.
6. Ali ibn-abu-Talib (600?–661), the fourth Moslem Caliph and son-in-law of the Prophet; his reputed sayings, surviving as proverbs, had appeared in English translation (1832).

banner. Is not a man better than a town? Ask nothing of men, and, in the endless mutation, thou only firm column must presently appear the upholder of all that surrounds thee. He who knows that power is inborn, that he is weak because he has looked for good out of him and elsewhere, and so perceiving, throws himself unhesitatingly on his thought, instantly rights himself, stands in the erect position, commands his limbs, works miracles; just as a man who stands on his feet is stronger than a man who stands on his head.

So use all that is called Fortune. Most men gamble with her, and gain all, and lose all, as her wheel rolls.[7] But do thou leave as unlawful these winnings, and deal with Cause and Effect, the chancellors of God. In the Will work and acquire, and thou hast chained the wheel of Chance, and shalt sit hereafter out of fear from her rotations. A political victory, a rise of rents, the recovery of your sick, or the return of your absent friend, or some other favorable event, raises your spirits, and you think good days are preparing for you. Do not believe it. Nothing can bring you peace but yourself. Nothing can bring you peace but the triumph of principles.

1841

Fate [8]

Delicate omens traced in air,
To the lone bard true witness bare;
Birds with auguries on their wings
Chanted undeceiving things,
Him to beckon, him to warn;
Well might then the poet scorn
To learn of scribe or courier
Hints writ in vaster character;
And on his mind, at dawn of day,
Soft shadows of the evening lay.
For the prevision is allied
Unto the thing so signified;
Or say, the foresight that awaits
Is the same Genius that creates. [9]

It chanced during one winter a few years ago, that our cities were bent on discussing the theory of the Age. By an odd coincidence, four or five noted men were each reading a discourse to the citizens of Boston or New York, on the Spirit of the Times. It so happened

7. The ancients sometimes pictured Fortuna as dispensing her gifts at the whim of a wheel of chance.
8. "Fate" was first delivered as a lecture on December 22, 1851, in Boston as part of a series on "The Conduct of Life." Emerson continued to work on it somewhat after that date

and finally published it as the first essay in his last major book, *The Conduct of Life,* 1860.
9. Another version of the epigraph was published in the Centenary Edition, Vol. IX, 326. The last four lines were also used in the poem "Fate," Centenary Edition, Vol. IX, 197.

that the subject had the same prominence in some remarkable pamphlets and journals issued in London in the same season. To me, however, the question of the times resolved itself into a practical question of the conduct of life. How shall I live? We are incompent to solve the times. Our geometry cannot span the huge orbits of the prevailing ideas, behold their return and reconcile their opposition. We can only obey our own polarity. 'T is fine for us to speculate and elect our course, if we must accept an irresistible dictation.

In our first steps to gain our wishes we come upon immovable limitations. We are fired with the hope to reform men. After many experiments we find that we must begin earlier,—at school. But the boys and girls are not docile; we can make nothing of them. We decide that they are not of good stock. We must begin our reform earlier still,—at generation: that is to say, there is Fate, or laws of the world.

But if there be irresistible dictation, this dictation understands itself. If we must accept Fate, we are not less compelled to affirm liberty, the significance of the individual, the grandeur of duty, the power of character. This is true, and that other is true. But our geometry cannot span these extreme points and reconcile them. What to do? By obeying each thought frankly, by harping, or, if you will, pounding on each string, we learn at last its power. By the same obedience to other thoughts we learn theirs, and then comes some reasonable hope of harmonizing them. We are sure that, though we know not how, necessity does comport with liberty, the individual with the world, my polarity with the spirit of the times. The riddle of the age has for each a private solution. If one would study his own time, it must be by this method of taking up in turn each of the leading topics which belong to our scheme of human life, and by firmly stating all that is agreeable to experience on one, and doing the same justice to the opposing facts in the others, the true limitations will appear. Any excess of emphasis on one part would be corrected, and a just balance would be made.

But let us honestly state the facts. Our America has a bad name for superficialness. Great men, great nations, have not been boasters and buffoons, but perceivers of the terror of life, and have manned themselves to face it. The Spartan, embodying his religion in his country, dies before its majesty without a question. The Turk, who believes his doom is written on the iron leaf in the moment when he entered the world, rushes on the enemy's sabre with undivided will. The Turk, the Arab, the Persian, accepts the foreordained fate:—

"On two days, it steads not to run from thy grave,
  The appointed, and the unappointed day;
On the first, neither balm nor physician can save,
  Nor thee, on the second, the Universe slay."

The Hindoo under the wheel is as firm. Our Calvinists in the last generation had something of the same dignity. They felt that the weight of the Universe held them down to their place. What could *they* do? Wise men feel that there is something which cannot be talked or voted away,—a strap or belt which girds the world:—

"The Destinee, ministre general,
  That executeth in the world over al,
  The purveiance that God hath seen beforne,
  So strong it is, that though the world had sworne
  The contrary of a thing by yea or nay,
  Yet sometime it shall fallen on a day
  That falleth not oft in a thousand yeer;
  For certainly, our appetités here,
  Be it or warre, or pees, or hate, or love,
  All this is ruled by the sight above."

CHAUCER: *The Knighte's Tale*

The Greek Tragedy expressed the same sense. "Whatever is fated that will take place. The great immense mind of Jove is not to be transgressed."

Savages cling to a local god of one tribe or town. The broad ethics of Jesus were quickly narrowed to village theologies, which preach an election or favoritism. And now and then an amiable parson, like Jung Stilling[1] or Robert Huntington,[2] believes in a pistareen[3]-Providence, which, whenever the good man wants a dinner, makes that somebody shall knock at his door and leave a half-dollar. But Nature is no sentimentalist,—does not cosset or pamper us. We must see that the world is rough and surly, and will not mind drowning a man or a woman, but swallows your ship like a grain of dust. The cold, inconsiderate of persons, tingles your blood, benumbs your feet, freezes a man like an apple. The diseases, the elements, fortune, gravity, lightning, respect no persons. The way of Providence is a little rude. The habit of snake and spider, the snap of the tiger and other leapers and bloody jumpers, the crackle of the bones of his prey in the coil of the anaconda,—these are in the system, and our habits are like theirs. You

1. Johann H. Jung-Stilling (1740–1817), German mystic.
2. Robert Huntington (1636–1701),
English Orientalist.
3. A Spanish silver coin.

have just dined, and however scrupulously the slaughter-house is concealed in the graceful distance of miles, there is complicity, expensive races,—race living at the expense of race. The planet is liable to shocks from comets, perturbations from planets, rendings from earthquake and volcano, alterations of climate, precessions of equinoxes. Rivers dry up by opening of the forest. The sea changes its bed. Towns and counties fall into it. At Lisbon an earthquake killed men like flies. At Naples three years ago ten thousand persons were crushed in a few minutes. The scurvy at sea, the sword of the climate in the west of Africa, at Cayenne, at Panama, at New Orleans, cut off men like a massacre. Our western prairie shakes with fever and ague. The cholera, the small-pox, have proved as mortal to some tribes as a frost to the crickets, which, having filled the summer with noise, are silenced by a fall of the temperature of one night. Without uncovering what does not concern us, or counting how many species of parasites hang on a bombyx,[4] or groping after intestinal parasites or infusory biters, or the obscurities of alternate generation,—the forms of the shark, the *labrus*, the jaw of the sea-wolf paved with crushing teeth, the weapons of the grampus, and other warriors hidden in the sea, are hints of ferocity in the interiors of nature. Let us not deny it up and down. Providence has a wild, rough, incalculable road to its end, and it is of no use to try to whitewash its huge, mixed instrumentalities, or to dress up that terrific benefactor in a clean shirt and white neckcloth of a student in divinity.

Will you say, the disasters which threaten mankind are exceptional, and one need not lay his account for cataclysms every day? Aye, but what happens once may happen again, and so long as these strokes are not to be parried by us they must be feared.

But these shocks and ruins are less destructive to us than the stealthy power of other laws which act on us daily. An expense of ends to means is fate;—organization tyrannizing over character. The menagerie, or forms and powers of the spine, is a book of fate; the bill of the bird, the skull of the snake, determines tyrannically its limits. So is the scale of races, of temperaments; so is sex; so is climate; so is the reaction of talents imprisoning the vital power in certain directions. Every spirit makes its house; but afterwards the house confines the spirit.

The gross lines are legible to the dull; the cabman is phrenologist so far, he looks in your face to see if his shilling is sure. A dome of brow denotes one thing, a pot-belly another; a squint, a pug-nose, mats of hair, the pigment of the epidermis, betray character. People seem sheathed in their tough organization. Ask Spurz-

4. The silkworm moth.

heim,[5] ask the doctors, ask Quetelet [6] if temperaments decide nothing?—or if there be anything they do not decide? Read the description in medical books of the four temperaments and you will think you are reading your own thoughts which you had not yet told. Find the part which black eyes and which blue eyes play severally in the company. How shall a man escape from his ancestors, or draw off from his veins the black drop which he drew from his father's or his mother's life? It often appears in a family as if all the qualities of the progenitors were potted in several jars, —some ruling quality in each son or daughter of the house; and sometimes the unmixed temperament, the rank unmitigated elixir, the family vice is drawn off in a separate individual and the others are proportionally relieved. We sometimes see a change of expression in our companion and say his father or his mother comes to the windows of his eyes, and sometimes a remote relative. In different hours a man represents each of several of his ancestors, as if there were seven or eight of us rolled up in each man's skin,— seven or eight ancestors at least; and they constitute the variety of notes for that new piece of music which his life is. At the corner of the street you read the possibility of each passenger in the facial angle, in the complexion, in the depth of his eye. His parentage determines it. Men are what their mothers made them. You may as well ask a loom which weaves huckabuck [7] why it does not make cashmere, as expect poetry from this engineer, or a chemical discovery from that jobber. Ask the digger in the ditch to explain Newton's laws; the fine organs of his brain have been pinched by overwork and squalid poverty from father to son for a hundred years. When each comes forth from his mother's womb, the gate of gifts closes behind him. Let him value his hands and feet, he has but one pair. So he has but one future, and that is already predetermined in his lobes and described in that little fatty face, pig-eye, and squat form. All the privilege and all the legislation of the world cannot meddle or help to make a poet or a prince of him.

Jesus said, "When he looketh on her, he hath committed adultery." [8] But he is an adulterer before he has yet looked on the woman, by the superfluity of animal and the defect of thought in his constitution. Who meets him, or who meets her, in the street, sees that they are ripe to be each other's victim.

In certain men digestion and sex absorb the vital force, and the stronger these are, the individual is so much weaker. The more of these drones perish, the better for the hive. If, later, they give birth to some superior individual, with force enough to add to this

5. Johann Spurzheim (1776–1832), student of phrenology.
6. Lambert Quetelet (1796–1874), Belgian statistician.
7. A rough linen fabric.
8. *Cf.* Matthew 5:28.

animal a new aim and a complete apparatus to work it out, all the ancestors are gladly forgotten. Most men and most women are merely one couple more. Now and then one has a new cell or camarilla opened in his brain,—an architectural, a musical, or a philological knack; some stray taste or talent for flowers, or chemistry, or pigments, or story-telling; a good hand for drawing, a good foot for dancing, an athletic frame for wide journeying, etc.—which skill nowise alters rank in the scale of nature, but serves to pass the time; the life of sensation going on as before. At last these hints and tendencies are fixed in one or in a succession. Each absorbs so much food and force as to become itself a new centre. The new talent draws off so rapidly the vital force that not enough remains for the animal functions, hardly enough for health; so that in the second generation, if the like genius appear, the health is visibly deteriorated and the generative force impaired.

People are born with the moral or with the material bias;— uterine brothers with this diverging destination; and I suppose, with high magnifiers, Mr. Frauenhofer [9] or Dr. Carpenter [1] might come to distinguish in the embryo, at the fourth day,—this is a Whig, and that a Free-soiler.

It was a poetic attempt to lift this mountain of Fate, to reconcile this despotism of race with liberty, which led the Hindoos to say, "Fate is nothing but the deeds committed in a prior state of existence." I find the coincidence of the extremes of Eastern and Western speculation in the daring statement of Schelling,[2] "There is in every man a certain feeling that he has been what he is from all eternity, and by no means became such in time." To say it less sublimely,—in the history of the individual is always an account of his condition, and he knows himself to be a party to his present estate.

A good deal of our politics is physiological. Now and then a man of wealth in the heyday of youth adopts the tenet of broadest freedom. In England there is always some man of wealth and large connection, planting himself, during all his years of health, on the side of progress, who, as soon as he begins to die, checks his forward play, calls in his troops and becomes conservative. All conservatives are such from personal defects. They have been effeminated by position or nature, born halt and blind, through luxury of their parents, and can only, like invalids, act on the defensive. But strong natures, backwoodsmen, New Hampshire giants, Na-

9. Joseph von Frauenhofer, German astronomer.
1. William B. Carpenter, author of *The Microscope, Its Revelations and Uses.*
2. Friedrich von Schelling (1775–1854), German philosopher.

poleons, Burkes,[3] Broughams,[4] Websters,[5] Kossuths,[6] are inevitable patriots, until their life ebbs and their defects and gout, palsy and money, warp them.

The strongest idea incarnates itself in majorities and nations, in the healthiest and strongest. Probably the election goes by avoirdupois weight, and if you could weigh bodily the tonnage of any hundred of the Whig and the Democratic party in a town on the Dearborn balance, as they passed the hay-scales, you could predict with certainty which party would carry it. On the whole it would be rather the speediest way of deciding the vote, to put the selectmen or the mayor and aldermen at the hay-scales.

In science we have to consider two things: power and circumstance. All we know of the egg, from each successive discovery, is, *another vesicle*; and if, after five hundred years you get a better observer or a better glass, he finds, within the last observed, another. In vegetable and animal tissue it is just alike, and all that the primary power or spasm operates is still vesicles, vesicles. Yes, —but the tyrannical Circumstance! A vesicle in new circumstances, a vesicle lodged in darkness, Oken[7] thought, became animal; in light, a plant. Lodged in the parent animal, it suffers changes which end in unsheathing miraculous capability in the unaltered vesicle, and it unlocks itself to fish, bird, or quadruped, head and foot, eye and claw. The Circumstance is Nature. Nature is what you may do. There is much you may not. We have two things,—the circumstance, and the life. Once we thought positive power was all. Now we learn that negative power, or circumstance, is half. Nature is the tyrannous circumstance, the thick skull, the sheathed snake, the ponderous, rock-like jaw; necessitated activity; violent direction; the conditions of a tool, like the locomotive, strong enough on its track, but which can do nothing but mischief off of it; or skates, which are wings on the ice but fetters on the ground.

The book of Nature is the book of Fate. She turns the gigantic pages,—leaf after leaf,—never re-turning one. One leaf she lays down, a floor of granite; then a thousand ages, and a bed of slate; a thousand ages, and a measure of coal; a thousand ages, and a layer of marl and mud: vegetable forms appear; her first misshapen animals, zoöphyte, trilobium, fish; then, saurians,—rude forms, in which she has only blocked her future statue, concealing under these unwieldy monsters the fine type of her coming king. The face of

3. Edmund Burke (1729–1797), English statesman.
4. Henry Brougham (1778–1868), British political leader.
5. Daniel Webster (1782–1852), American statesman.
6. Louis Kossuth (1802–1894), Hungarian patriot.
7. Lorenz Oken (1779–1851), German naturalist.

the planet cools and dries, the races meliorate, and man is born. But when a race has lived its term, it comes no more again.

The population of the world is a conditional population; not the best, but the best that could live now; and the scale of tribes, and the steadiness with which victory adheres to one tribe and defeat to another, is as uniform as the superposition of strata. We know in history what weight belongs to race. We see the English, French, and Germans planting themselves on every shore and market of America and Australia, and monopolizing the commerce of these countries. We like the nervous and victorious habit of our own branch of the family. We follow the step of the Jew, of the Indian, of the Negro. We see how much will has been expended to extinguish the Jew, in vain. Look at the unpalatable conclusions of Knox,[8] in his Fragment of Races;—a rash and unsatisfactory writer, but charged with pungent and unforgetable truths. "Nature respects race, and not hybrids." "Every race has its own *habitat*." "Detach a colony from the race, and it deteriorates to the crab." See the shades of the picture. The German and Irish millions, like the Negro, have a great deal of guano in their destiny. They are ferried over the Atlantic and carted over America, to ditch and to drudge, to make corn cheap and then to lie down prematurely to make a spot of green grass on the prairie.

One more fagot of these adamantine bandages is the new science of Statistics. It is a rule that the most casual and extraordinary events, if the basis of population is broad enough, become matter of fixed calculation. It would not be safe to say when a captain like Bonaparte, a singer like Jenny Lind, or a navigator like Bowditch[9] would be born in Boston; but, on a population of twenty or two hundred millions, something like accuracy may be had.

'T is frivolous to fix pedantically the date of particular inventions. They have all been invented over and over fifty times. Man is the arch machine of which all these shifts drawn from himself are toy models. He helps himself on each emergency by copying or duplicating his own structure, just so far as the need is. 'T is hard to find the right Homer, Zoroaster, or Menu; harder still to find the Tubal Cain, or Vulcan, or Cadmus, or Copernicus, or Fust,[1] or Fulton; the indisputable inventor. There are scores and centuries of them. "The air is full of men." This kind of talent so abounds, this constructive tool-making efficiency, as if it adhered to the chemic atoms; as if the air he breathes were made of Vaucansons, Franklins, and Watts.

---

8. Robert Knox, in *The Races of Man* (1850), held races to be biologically distinct.

9. Nathaniel Bowditch (1773–1838).
1. Johann Fust, the fifteenth-century printer.

Doubtless in every million there will be an astronomer, a mathematician, a comic poet, a mystic. No one can read the history of astronomy without perceiving that Copernicus, Newton, Laplace, are not new men, or a new kind of men, but that Thales, Anaximenes, Hipparchus, Empedocles, Aristarchus, Pythagoras, Œnipodes, had anticipated them; each had the same tense geometrical brain, apt for the same vigorous computation and logic; a mind parallel to the movement of the world. The Roman mile probably rested on a measure of a degree of the meridian. Mahometan and Chinese know what we know of leap-year, of the Gregorian calendar, and of the precession of the equinoxes. As in every barrel of cowries brought to New Bedford there shall be one *orangia*,[2] so there will, in a dozen millions of Malays and Mahometans, be one or two astronomical skulls. In a large city, the most casual things, and things whose beauty lies in their casualty, are produced as punctually and to order as the baker's muffin for breakfast. Punch makes exactly one capital joke a week; and the journals contrive to furnish one good piece of news every day.

And not less work the laws of repression, the penalties of violated functions. Famine, typhus, frost, war, suicide and effete races must be reckoned calculable parts of the system of the world.

These are pebbles from the mountain, hints of the terms by which our life is walled up, and which show a kind of mechanical exactness, as of a loom or mill in what we call casual or fortuitous events.

The force with which we resist these torrents of tendency looks so ridiculously inadequate that it amounts to little more than a criticism or protest made by a minority of one, under compulsion of millions. I seemed in the height of a tempest to see men overboard struggling in the waves, and driven about here and there. They glanced intelligently at each other, but 't was little they could do for one another; 't was much if each could keep afloat alone. Well, they had a right to their eye-beams, and all the rest was Fate.

We cannot trifle with this reality, this cropping-out in our planted gardens of the core of the world. No picture of life can have any veracity that does not admit the odious facts. A man's power is hooped in by a necessity which, by many experiments, he touches on every side until he learns its arc.

The element running through entire nature, which we popularly call Fate, is known to us as limitation. Whatever limits us we call Fate. If we are brute and barbarous, the fate takes a brute and dreadful shape. As we refine, our checks become finer. If we rise

2. An especially valuable variety of cowrie (a South Pacific seashell).

to spiritual culture, the antagonism takes a spiritual form. In the Hindoo fables, Vishnu follows Maya through all her ascending changes, from insect and crawfish up to elephant; whatever form she took, he took the male form of that kind, until she became at last woman and goddess, and he a man and a god. The limitations refine as the soul purifies, but the ring of necessity is always perched at the top.

When the gods in the Norse heaven were unable to bind the Fenris Wolf [3] with steel or with weight of mountains,—the one he snapped and the other he spurned with his heel,—they put round his foot a limp band softer than silk or cobweb, and this held him; the more he spurned it the stiffer it drew. So soft and so stanch is the ring of Fate. Neither brandy, nor nectar, nor sulphuric ether, nor hell-fire, nor ichor, nor poetry, nor genius, can get rid of this limp band. For if we give it the high sense in which the poets use it, even thought itself is not above Fate; that too must act according to eternal laws, and all that is wilful and fantastic in it is in opposition to its fundamental essence.

And last of all, high over thought, in the world of morals, Fate appears as vindicator, levelling the high, lifting the low, requiring justice in man, and always striking soon or late when justice is not done. What is useful will last, what is hurtful will sink. "The doer must suffer," said the Greeks; "you would soothe a Deity not to be soothed." "God himself cannot procure good for the wicked," said the Welsh triad. "God may consent, but only for a time," said the bard of Spain. The limitation is impassable by any insight of man. In its last and loftiest ascensions, insight itself and the freedom of the will is one of its obedient members. But we must not run into generalizations too large, but show the natural bounds or essential distinctions, and seek to do justice to the other elements as well.

Thus we trace Fate in matter, mind, and morals; in race, in retardations of strata, and in thought and character as well. It is everywhere bound or limitation. But Fate has its lord; limitation its limits,—is different seen from above and from below, from within and from without. For though Fate is immense, so is Power, which is the other fact in the dual world, immense. If Fate follows and limits Power, Power attends and antagonizes Fate. We must respect Fate as natural history, but there is more than natural history. For who and what is this criticism that pries into the matter? Man is not order of nature, sack and sack, belly and members, link in a chain, nor any ignominious baggage; but a stupendous antagonism, a dragging together of the poles of the Universe. He

---

3. Associated with Loki, god of discord in Norse mythology.

betrays his relation to what is below him,—thick-skulled, small-brained, fishy, quadrumanous, quadruped ill-disguised, hardly escaped into biped,—and has paid for the new powers by loss of some of the old ones. But the lightning which explodes and fashions planets, maker of planets and suns, is in him. On one side elemental order, sandstone and granite, rock-ledges, peat-bog, forest, sea and shore; and on the other part thought, the spirit which composes and decomposes nature,—here they are, side by side, god and devil, mind and matter, king and conspirator, belt and spasm, riding peacefully together in the eye and brain of every man.

Nor can he blink the freewill. To hazard the contradiction,—freedom is necessary. If you please to plant yourself on the side of Fate, and say, Fate is all; then we say, a part of Fate is the freedom of man. Forever wells up the impulse of choosing and acting in the soul. Intellect annuls Fate. So far as a man thinks, he is free. And though nothing is more disgusting than the crowing about liberty by slaves, as most men are, and the flippant mistaking for freedom of some paper preamble like a Declaration of Independence or the statute right to vote, by those who have never dared to think or to act,—yet it is wholesome to man to look not at Fate, but the other way: the practical view is the other. His sound relation to these facts is to use and command, not to cringe to them. "Look not on Nature, for her name is fatal," said the oracle. The too much contemplation of these limits induces meanness. They who talk much of destiny, their birth-star, etc., are in a lower dangerous plane, and invite the evils they fear.

I cited the instinctive and heroic races as proud believers in Destiny. They conspire with it; a loving resignation is with the event. But the dogma makes a different impression when it is held by the weak and lazy. 'T is weak and vicious people who cast the blame on Fate. The right use of Fate is to bring up our conduct to the loftiness of nature. Rude and invincible except by themselves are the elements. So let man be. Let him empty his breast of his windy conceits, and show his lordship by manners and deeds on the scale of nature. Let him hold his purpose as with the tug of gravitation. No power, no persuasion, no bribe shall make him give up his point. A man ought to compare advantageously with a river, an oak, or a mountain. He shall have not less the flow, the expansion, and the resistance of these.

'T is the best use of Fate to teach a fatal courage. Go face the fire at sea, or the cholera in your friend's house, or the burglar in your own, or what danger lies in the way of duty,—knowing you are guarded by the cherubim of Destiny. If you believe in Fate to your harm, believe it at least for your good.

For if Fate is so prevailing, man also is part of it, and can confront fate with fate. If the Universe have these savage accidents, our atoms are as savage in resistance. We should be crushed by the atmosphere, but for the reaction of the air within the body. A tube made of a film of glass can resist the shock of the ocean if filled with the same water. If there be omnipotence in the stroke, there is omnipotence of recoil.

1. But Fate against Fate is only parrying and defence: there are also the noble creative forces. The revelation of Thought takes man out of servitude into freedom. We rightly say of ourselves, we were born and afterward we were born again, and many times. We have successive experiences so important that the new forgets the old, and hence the mythology of the seven or the nine heavens. The day of days, the great day of the feast of life, is that in which the inward eye opens to the Unity in things, to the omnipresence of law:—sees that what is must be and ought to be, or is the best. This beatitude dips from on high down on us and we see. It is not in us so much as we are in it. If the air come to our lungs, we breathe and live; if not, we die. If the light come to our eyes, we see; else not. And if truth come to our mind we suddenly expand to its dimensions, as if we grew to worlds. We are as lawgivers; we speak for Nature; we prophesy and divine.

This insight throws us on the party and interest of the Universe, against all and sundry; against ourselves as much as others. A man speaking from insight affirms of himself what is true of the mind: seeing its immortality, he says, I am immortal; seeing its invincibility, he says, I am strong. It is not in us, but we are in it. It is of the maker, not of what is made. All things are touched and changed by it. This uses and is not used. It distances those who share it from those who share it not. Those who share it not are flocks and herds. It dates from itself; not from former men or better men, gospel, or constitution, or college, or custom. Where it shines, Nature is no longer intrusive, but all things make a musical or pictorial impression. The world of men show like a comedy without laughter: populations, interests, government, history; 't is all toy figures in a toy house. It does not overvalue particular truths. We hear eagerly every thought and word quoted from an intellectual man. But in his presence our own mind is roused to activity, and we forget very fast what he says, much more interested in the new play of our own thought than in any thought of his. 'T is the majesty into which we have suddenly mounted, the impersonality, the scorn of egotisms, the sphere of laws, that engage us. Once we were stepping a little this way and a little that way; now we are as men in a balloon, and do not think so much of the point we have left, or the point we would make, as of the liberty and glory of the way.

Just as much intellect as you add, so much organic power. He who sees through the design, presides over it, and must will that which must be. We sit and rule, and, though we sleep, our dream will come to pass. Our thought, though it were only an hour old, affirms an oldest necessity, not to be separated from thought, and not to be separated from will. They must always have coexisted. It apprises us of its sovereignty and godhead, which refuse to be severed from it. It is not mine or thine, but the will of all mind. It is poured into the souls of all men, as the soul itself which constitutes them men. I know not whether there be, as is alleged, in the upper region of our atmosphere, a permanent westerly current which carries with it all atoms which rise to that height, but I see that when souls reach a certain clearness of perception they accept a knowledge and motive above selfishness. A breath of will blows eternally through the universe of souls in the direction of the Right and Necessary. It is the air which all intellects inhale and exhale, and it is the wind which blows the worlds into order and orbit.

Thought dissolves the material universe by carrying the mind up into a sphere where all is plastic. Of two men, each obeying his own thought, he whose thought is deepest will be the strongest character. Always one man more than another represents the will of Divine Providence to the period.

2. If thought makes free, so does the moral sentiment. The mixtures of spiritual chemistry refuse to be analyzed. Yet we can see that with the perception of truth is joined the desire that it shall prevail; that affection is essential to will. Moreover, when a strong will appears, it usually results from a certain unity of organization, as if the whole energy of body and mind flowed in one direction. All great force is real and elemental. There is no manufacturing a strong will. There must be a pound to balance a pound. Where power is shown in will, it must rest on the universal force. Alaric [4] and Bonaparte must believe they rest on a truth, or their will can be bought or bent. There is a bribe possible for any finite will. But the pure sympathy with universal ends is an infinite force, and cannot be bribed or bent. Whoever has had experience of the moral sentiment cannot choose but believe in unlimited power. Each pulse from that heart is an oath from the Most High. I know not what the word *sublime* means, if it be not the intimations, in this infant, of a terrific force. A text of heroism, a name and anecdote of courage, are not arguments but sallies of freedom. One of these is the verse of the Persian Hafiz,[5] "'T is written on the gate of Heaven, 'Woe unto him who suffers himself to be betrayed by Fate!'" Does the reading of history make us fatalists? What cour-

---

4. Fourth-century king of the Visigoths.   5. Fourteenth-century Persian poet.

age does not the opposite opinion show! A little whim of will to be free gallantly contending against the universe of chemistry.

But insight is not will, nor is affection will. Perception is cold, and goodness dies in wishes. As Voltaire said, 't is the misfortune of worthy people that they are cowards; "un des plus grands malheurs des honnêtes gens c'est qu'ils sont des lâches." There must be a fusion of these two to generate the energy of will. There can be no driving force except through the conversion of the man into his will, making him the will, and the will him. And one may say boldly that no man has a right perception of any truth who has not been reacted on by it so as to be ready to be its martyr.

The one serious and formidable thing in nature is a will. Society is servile from want of will, and therefore the world wants saviours and religions. One way is right to go; the hero sees it, and moves on that aim, and has the world under him for root and support. He is to others as the world. His approbation is honor; his dissent, infamy. The glance of his eye has the force of sunbeams. A personal influence towers up in memory only worthy, and we gladly forget numbers, money, climate, gravitation, and the rest of Fate.

We can afford to allow the limitation, if we know it is the meter of the growing man. We stand against Fate, as children stand up against the wall in their father's house and notch their height from year to year. But when the boy grows to man, and is master of the house, he pulls down that wall and builds a new and bigger. 'T is only a question of time. Every brave youth is in training to ride and rule this dragon. His science is to make weapons and wings of these passions and retarding forces. Now whether, seeing these two things, fate and power, we are permitted to believe in unity? The bulk of mankind believe in two gods. They are under one dominion here in the house, as friend and parent, in social circles, in letters, in art, in love, in religion; but in mechanics, in dealing with steam and climate, in trade, in politics, they think they come under another; and that it would be a practical blunder to transfer the method and way of working of one sphere into the other. What good, honest, generous men at home, will be wolves and foxes on 'Change! What pious men in the parlor will vote for what reprobates at the polls! To a certain point, they believe themselves the care of a Providence. But in a steamboat, in an epidemic, in war, they believe a malignant energy rules.

But relation and connection are not somewhere and sometimes, but everywhere and always. The divine order does not stop where their sight stops. The friendly power works on the same rules in the next farm and the next planet. But where they have not experience they run against it and hurt themselves. Fate then is a name for facts not yet passed under the fire of thought; for causes which are unpenetrated.

But every jet of chaos which threatens to exterminate us is convertible by intellect into wholesome force. Fate is unpenetrated causes. The water drowns ship and sailor like a grain of dust. But learn to swim, trim your bark, and the wave which drowned it will be cloven by it and carry it like its own foam, a plume and a power. The cold is inconsiderate of persons, tingles your blood, freezes a man like a dewdrop. But learn to skate, and the ice will give you a graceful, sweet, and poetic motion. The cold will brace your limbs and brain to genius, and make you foremost men of time. Cold and sea will train an imperial Saxon race, which nature cannot bear to lose, and after cooping it up for a thousand years in yonder England, gives a hundred Englands, a hundred Mexicos. All the bloods it shall absorb and domineer: and more than Mexicos, the secrets of water and steam, the spasms of electricity, the ductility of metals, the chariot of the air, the ruddered balloon are awaiting you.

The annual slaughter from typhus far exceeds that of war; but right drainage destroys typhus. The plague in the sea-service from scurvy is healed by lemon juice and other diets portable or procurable; the depopulation by cholera and small-pox is ended by drainage and vaccination; and every other pest is not less in the chain of cause and effect, and may be fought off. And whilst art draws out the venom, it commonly extorts some benefit from the vanquished enemy. The mischievous torrent is taught to drudge for man; the wild beasts he makes useful for food, or dress, or labor; the chemic explosions are controlled like his watch. These are now the steeds on which he rides. Man moves in all modes, by legs of horses, by wings of wind, by steam, by gas of balloon, by electricity, and stands on tiptoe threatening to hunt the eagle in his own element. There's nothing he will not make his carrier.

Steam was till the other day the devil which we dreaded. Every pot made by any human potter or brazier had a hole in its cover, to let off the enemy, lest he should lift pot and roof and carry the house away. But the Marquis of Worcester, Watt, and Fulton bethought themselves that where was power was not devil, but was God; that it must be availed of, and not by any means let off and wasted. Could he lift pots and roofs and houses so handily? He was the workman they were in search of. He could be used to lift away, chain and compel other devils far more reluctant and dangerous, namely, cubic miles of earth, mountains, weight or resistance of water, machinery, and the labors of all men in the world; and time he shall lengthen, and shorten space.

It has not fared much otherwise with higher kinds of steam. The opinion of the million was the terror of the world, and it was attempted either to dissipate it, by amusing nations, or to pile it over with strata of society,—a layer of soldiers, over that a layer of lords, and a king on the top; with clamps and hoops of castles, garrisons, and police. But sometimes the religious principle would get in and burst the hoops and rive every mountain laid on top of it. The Fultons and Watts of politics, believing in unity, saw that it was a power, and by satisfying it (as justice satisfies everybody), through a different disposition of society,—grouping it on a level instead of piling it into a mountain,—they have contrived to make of this terror the most harmless and energetic form of a State.

Very odious, I confess, are the lessons of Fate. Who likes to have a dapper phrenologist pronouncing on his fortunes? Who likes to believe that he has, hidden in his skull, spine, and pelvis, all the vices of a Saxon or Celtic race, which will be sure to pull him down,—with what grandeur of hope and resolve he is fired,—into a selfish, huckstering, servile, dodging animal? A learned physician tells us the fact is invariable with the Neapolitan, that when mature he assumes the forms of the unmistakable scoundrel. That is a little overstated,—but may pass.

But these are magazines and arsenals. A man must thank his defects, and stand in some terror of his talents. A transcendent talent draws so largely on his forces as to lame him; a defect pays him revenues on the other side. The sufferance which is the badge of the Jew, has made him, in these days, the ruler of the rulers of the earth. If Fate is ore and quarry, if evil is good in the making, if limitation is power that shall be, if calamities, oppositions, and weights are wings and means,—we are reconciled.

Fate involves the melioration. No statement of the Universe can have any soundness which does not admit its ascending effort. The direction of the whole and of the parts is toward benefit, and in proportion to the health. Behind every individual closes organization; before him opens liberty,—the Better, the Best. The first and worse races are dead. The second and imperfect races are dying out, or remain for the maturing of higher. In the latest race, in man, every generosity, every new perception, the love and praise he extorts from his fellows, are certificates of advance out of fate into freedom. Liberation of the will from the sheaths and clogs of organization which he has outgrown, is the end and aim of this world. Every calamity is a spur and valuable hint; and where his endeavors do not yet fully avail, they tell as tendency. The whole circle of animal life—tooth against tooth, devouring war, war for food, a yelp of pain and a grunt of triumph, until at last the whole menagerie, the whole chemical mass is mellowed and refined for higher use—pleases at a sufficient perspective.

But to see how fate slides into freedom and freedom into fate, observe how far the roots of every creature run, or find if you can a point where there is no thread of connection. Our life is consentaneous and far-related. This knot of nature is so well tied that nobody was ever cunning enough to find the two ends. Nature is intricate, overlapped, interweaved and endless. Christopher Wren [6] said of the beautiful King's College chapel, that "if anybody would tell him where to lay the first stone, he would build such another." But where shall we find the first atom in this house of man, which is all consent, inosculation and balance of parts?

The web of relation is shown in *habitat*, shown in hibernation. When hibernation was observed, it was found that whilst some animals became torpid in winter, others were torpid in summer: hibernation then was a false name. The *long sleep* is not an effect of cold, but is regulated by the supply of food proper to the animal. It becomes torpid when the fruit or prey it lives on is not in season, and regains its activity when its food is ready.

Eyes are found in light; ears in auricular air; feet on land; fins in water; wings in air; and each creature where it was meant to be, with a mutual fitness. Every zone has its own *Fauna*. There is adjustment between the animal and its food, its parasite, its enemy. Balances are kept. It is not allowed to diminish in numbers, nor to exceed. The like adjustments exist for man. His food is cooked when he arrives; his coal in the pit; the house ventilated; the mud of the deluge dried; his companions arrived at the same hour, and awaiting him with love, concert, laughter and tears. These are coarse adjustments, but the invisible are not less. There are more belongings to every creature than his air and his food. His instincts must be met, and he has predisposing power that bends and fits what is near him to his use. He is not possible until the invisible things are right for him, as well as the visible. Of what changes then in sky and earth, and in finer skies and earths, does the appearance of some Dante or Columbus apprise us!

How is this effected? Nature is no spendthrift, but takes the shortest way to her ends. As the general says to his soldiers, "If you want a fort, build a fort," so nature makes every creature do its own work and get its living,—is it planet, animal or tree. The planet makes itself. The animal cell makes itself;—then, what it wants. Every creature, wren or dragon, shall make its own lair. As soon as there is life, there is self-direction and absorbing and using of material. Life is freedom,—life in the direct ratio of its amount. You may be sure the new-born man is not inert. Life works both volun-

6. Noted English architect (1632–1723).

tarily and supernaturally in its neighborhood. Do you suppose he can be estimated by his weight in pounds, or that he is contained in his skin,—this reaching, radiating, jaculating[7] fellow? The smallest candle fills a mile with its rays, and the papillæ of a man run out to every star.

When there is something to be done, the world knows how to get it done. The vegetable eye makes leaf, pericarp, root, bark, or thorn, as the need is; the first cell converts itself into stomach, mouth, nose, or nail, according to the want; the world throws its life into a hero or a shepherd, and puts him where he is wanted. Dante and Columbus were Italians, in their time; they would be Russians or Americans to-day. Things ripen, new men come. The adaptation is not capricious. The ulterior aim, the purpose beyond itself, the correlation by which planets subside and crystallize, then animate beasts and men,—will not stop but will work into finer particulars, and from finer to finest.

The secret of the world is the tie between person and event. Person makes event, and event person. The "times," "the age," what is that but a few profound persons and a few active persons who epitomize the times?—Goethe, Hegel, Metternich, Adams, Calhoun, Guizot, Peel, Cobden, Kossuth, Rothschild, Astor, Brunel, and the rest. The same fitness must be presumed between a man and the time and event, as between the sexes, or between a race of animals and the food it eats, or the inferior races it uses. He thinks his fate alien, because the copula is hidden. But the soul contains the event that shall befall it; for the event is only the actualization of its thoughts, and what we pray to ourselves for is always granted. The event is the print of your form. It fits you like your skin. What each does is proper to him. Events are the children of his body and mind. We learn that the soul of Fate is the soul of us, as Hafiz sings,—

> "Alas! till now I had not known,
> My guide and fortune's guide are one."

All the toys that infatuate men and which they play for,—houses, land, money, luxury, power, fame, are the selfsame thing, with a new gauze or two of illusion overlaid. And of all the drums and rattles by which men are made willing to have their heads broke, and are led out solemnly every morning to parade,—the most admirable is this by which we are brought to believe that events are arbitrary and independent of actions. At the conjuror's, we detect the hair by which he moves his puppet, but we have not eyes sharp enough to descry the thread that ties cause and effect.

Nature magically suits the man to his fortunes, by making these

7. Darting to and fro.

the fruit of his character. Ducks take to the water, eagles to the sky, waders to the sea margin, hunters to the forest, clerks to counting-rooms, soldiers to the frontier. Thus events grow on the same stem with persons; are sub-persons. The pleasure of life is according to the man that lives it, and not according to the work or the place. Life is an ecstasy. We know what madness belongs to love,—what power to paint a vile object in hues of heaven. As insane persons are indifferent to their dress, diet, and other accommodations, and as we do in dreams, with equanimity, the most absurd acts, so a drop more of wine in our cup of life will reconcile us to strange company and work. Each creature puts forth from itself its own condition and sphere, as the slug sweats out its slimy house on the pear-leaf, and the woolly aphides on the apple perspire their own bed, and the fish its shell. In youth we clothe ourselves with rain-bows and go as brave as the zodiac. In age we put out another sort of perspiration,—gout, fever, rheumatism, caprice, doubt, fretting and avarice.

A man's fortunes are the fruit of his character. A man's friends are his magnetisms. We go to Herodotus and Plutarch for examples of Fate; but we are examples. *"Quisque suos patimur manes."* [8] The tendency of every man to enact all that is in his constitution is ex-pressed in the old belief that the efforts which we make to escape from our destiny only serve to lead us into it: and I have noticed a man likes better to be complimented on his position, as the proof of the last or total excellence, than on his merits.

A man will see his character emitted in the events that seem to meet, but which exude from and accompany him. Events expand with the character. As once he found himself among toys, so now he plays a part in colossal systems, and his growth is declared in his ambition, his companions and his performance. He looks like a piece of luck, but is a piece of causation; the mosaic, angulated and ground to fit into the gap he fills. Hence in each town there is some man who is, in his brain and performance, an explanation of the til-lage, production, factories, banks, churches, ways of living and society of that town. If you do not chance to meet him, all that you see will leave you a little puzzled; if you see him it will be-come plain. We know in Massachusetts who built New Bedford, who built Lynn, Lowell, Lawrence, Clinton, Fitchburg, Holyoke, Portland, and many another noisy mart. Each of these men, if they were transparent, would seem to you not so much men as walking cities, and wherever you put them they would build one.

History is the action and reaction of these two,—Nature and Thought; two boys pushing each other on the curbstone of the pavement. Everything is pusher or pushed; and matter and mind

8. "Each of us suffers his own genius," Virgil's *Aeneid*, VI, 743.

are in perpetual tilt and balance, so. Whilst the man is weak, the earth takes up him. He plants his brain and affections. By and by he will take up the earth, and have his gardens and vineyards in the beautiful order and productiveness of his thought. Every solid in the universe is ready to become fluid on the approach of the mind, and the power to flux it is the measure of the mind. If the wall remain adamant, it accuses the want of thought. To a subtle force it will stream into new forms, expressive of the character of the mind. What is the city in which we sit here, but an aggregate of incongruous materials which have obeyed the will of some man? The granite was reluctant, but his hands were stronger, and it came. Iron was deep in the ground and well combined with stone, but could not hide from his fires. Wood, lime, stuffs, fruits, gums, were dispersed over the earth and sea, in vain. Here they are, within reach of every man's day-labor,—what he wants of them. The whole world is the flux of matter over the wires of thought to the poles or points where it would build. The races of men rise out of the ground preoccupied with a thought which rules them, and divided into parties ready armed and angry to fight for this metaphysical abstraction. The quality of the thought differences the Egyptian and the Roman, the Austrian and the American. The men who come on the stage at one period are all found to be related to each other. Certain ideas are in the air. We are all impressionable, for we are made of them; all impressionable, but some more than others, and these first express them. This explains the curious contemporaneousness of inventions and discoveries. The truth is in the air, and the most impressionable brain will announce it first, but all will announce it a few minutes later. So women, as most susceptible, are the best index of the coming hour. So the great man, that is, the man most imbued with the spirit of the time, is the impressionable man;— of a fibre irritable and delicate, like iodine to light. He feels the infinitesimal attractions. His mind is righter than others because he yields to a current so feeble as can be felt only by a needle delicately poised.

The correlation is shown in defects. Möller, in his Essay on Architecture, taught that the building which was fitted accurately to answer its end would turn out to be beautiful though beauty had not been intended. I find the like unity in human structures rather virulent and pervasive; that a crudity in the blood will appear in the argument; a hump in the shoulder will appear in the speech and handiwork. If his mind could be seen, the hump would be seen. If a man has a see-saw in his voice, it will run into his sentences, into his poem, into the structure of his fable, into his speculation, into his charity. And as every man is hunted by his own dæmon, vexed by his own disease, this checks all his activity.

So each man, like each plant, has his parasites. A strong, astrin-gent, bilious nature has more truculent enemies than the slugs and moths that fret my leaves. Such an one has curculios, bores, knife-worms; a swindler ate him first, then a client, then a quack, then smooth, plausible gentlemen, bitter and selfish as Moloch.

This correlation really existing can be divined. If the threads are there, thought can follow and show them. Especially when a soul is quick and docile, as Chaucer sings:—

> "Or if the soule of proper kind
> Be so parfite as men find,
> That it wot what is to come,
> And that he warneth all and some
> Of everiche of hir aventures,
> By avisions or figures;
> But that our flesh hath no might
> To understand it aright
> For it is warned too derkely." [9]

Some people are made up of rhyme, coincidence, omen, periodicity, and presage: they meet the person they seek; what their compan-ion prepares to say to them, they first say to him; and a hundred signs apprise them of what is about to befall.

Wonderful intricacy in the web, wonderful constancy in the de-sign this vagabond life admits. We wonder how the fly finds its mate, and yet year after year, we find two men, two women, with-out legal or carnal tie, spend a great part of their best time within a few feet of each other. And the moral is that what we seek we shall find; what we flee from flees from us; as Goethe said, "what we wish for in youth, comes in heaps on us in old age," too often cursed with the granting of our prayer: and hence the high caution, that since we are sure of having what we wish, we beware to ask only for high things.

One key, one solution to the mysteries of human condition, one solution to the old knots of fate, freedom, and foreknowledge, ex-ists; the propounding, namely, of the double consciousness. A man must ride alternately on the horses of his private and his public nature, as the equestrians in the circus throw themselves nimbly from horse to horse, or plant one foot on the back of one and the other foot on the back of the other. So when a man is the victim of his fate, has sciatica in his loins and cramp in his mind; a club-foot and a club in his wit; a sour face and a selfish temper; a strut in his gait and a conceit in his affection; or is ground to powder by the vice of his race;—he is to rally on his relation to the Universe,

9. Proem, "The House of Fame."

which his ruin benefits. Leaving the dæmon who suffers, he is to take sides with the Deity who secures universal benefit by his pain.

To offset the drag of temperament and race, which pulls down, learn this lesson, namely, that by the cunning co-presence of two elements, which is throughout nature, whatever lames or paralyzes you draws in with it the divinity, in some form, to repay. A good intention clothes itself with sudden power. When a god wishes to ride, any chip or pebble will bud and shoot out winged feet and serve him for a horse.

Let us build altars to the Blessed Unity which holds nature and souls in perfect solution, and compels every atom to serve an universal end. I do not wonder at a snow-flake, a shell, a summer landscape, or the glory of the stars; but at the necessity of beauty under which the universe lies; that all is and must be pictorial; that the rainbow and the curve of the horizon and the arch of the blue vault are only results from the organism of the eye. There is no need for foolish amateurs to fetch me to admire a garden of flowers, or a sun-gilt cloud, or a waterfall, when I cannot look without seeing splendor and grace. How idle to choose a random sparkle here or there, when the indwelling necessity plants the rose of beauty on the brow of chaos, and discloses the central intention of Nature to be harmony and joy.

Let us build altars to the Beautiful Necessity. If we thought men were free in the sense that in a single exception one fantastical will could prevail over the law of things, it were all one as if a child's hand could pull down the sun. If in the least particular one could derange the order of nature,—who would accept the gift of life?

Let us build altars to the Beautiful Necessity, which secures that all is made of one piece; the plaintiff and defendant, friend and enemy, animal and planet, food and eater are of one kind. In astronomy is vast space but no foreign system; in geology, vast time but the same laws as to-day. Why should we be afraid of Nature, which is no other than "philosophy and theology embodied"? Why should we fear to be crushed by savage elements, we who are made up of the same elements? Let us build to the Beautiful Necessity, which makes man brave in believing that he cannot shun a danger that is appointed, nor incur one that is not; to the Necessity which rudely or softly educates him to the perception that there are no contingencies; that Law rules throughout existence; a Law which is not intelligent but intelligence;—not personal nor impersonal—it disdains words and passes understanding; it dissolves persons; it vivifies nature; yet solicits the pure in heart to draw on all its omnipotence.

Concord Hymn

SUNG AT THE COMPLETION OF THE BATTLE MONUMENT,[1]

JULY 4, 1837

By the rude bridge that arched the flood,
   Their flag to April's breeze unfurled,
Here once the embattled farmers stood
   And fired the shot heard round the world.

The foe long since in silence slept;   5
   Alike the conqueror silent sleeps;
And Time the ruined bridge has swept
   Down the dark stream which seaward creeps.

On this green bank, by this soft stream,
   We set to-day a votive stone;   10
That memory may their deed redeem,
   When, like our sires, our sons are gone.

Spirit, that made those heroes dare
   To die, and leave their children free,
Bid Time and Nature gently spare   15
   The shaft we raise to them and thee.

1837, 1876

Each and All [2]

Little thinks, in the field, yon red-cloaked clown
Of thee from the hill-top looking down;
The heifer that lows in the upland farm,
Far-heard, lows not thine ear to charm;
The sexton, tolling his bell at noon,
Deems not that great Napoleon   5
Stops his horse, and lists with delight,

1. The monument commemorates the battles of Lexington and Concord, April 19, 1775. At the dedication, this poem was distributed as a printed leaflet; it was not collected until the *Selected Poems* of 1876, for which Emerson made slight revisions, here retained. He also changed the title to "Concord Fight," and wrongly dated the commemoration as "April 19, 1836." The editors of the Centenary Edition restored the now familiar title, and corrected the date to July 4, 1837. We have followed them in these respects.
2. The transcendent unity of the many and the one, presented from various angles in the essays, from *Nature* to "Plato," here begets one of Emerson's most characteristic poems. At least the episode of the sea shells is actual; Emerson recorded it in his *Journal* for May 16, 1834. The poem appeared in the *Western Messenger* for February, 1839, and in the collections of 1847 and 1876.

Whilst his files sweep round yon Alpine height;
Nor knowest thou what argument
Thy life to thy neighbor's creed has lent.   10
All are needed by each one;
Nothing is fair or good alone.
I thought the sparrow's note from heaven,
Singing at dawn on the alder bough;
I brought him home, in his nest, at even;   15
He sings the song, but it cheers not now,
For I did not bring home the river and sky;—
He sang to my ear,—they sang to my eye.
The delicate shells lay on the shore;
The bubbles of the latest wave   20
Fresh pearls to their enamel gave,
And the bellowing of the savage sea
Greeted their safe escape to me.
I wiped away the weeds and foam,
I fetched my sea-born treasures home;   25
But the poor, unsightly, noisome things
Had left their beauty on the shore
With the sun and the sand and the wild uproar.
The lover watched his graceful maid,
As 'mid the virgin train she strayed,   30
Nor knew her beauty's best attire
Was woven still by the snow-white choir.
At last she came to his hermitage,
Like the bird from the woodlands to the cage:—
The gay enchantment was undone,   35
A gentle wife, but fairy none.
Then I said, "I covet truth;
Beauty is unripe childhood's cheat;
I leave it behind with the games of youth:"—
As I spoke, beneath my feet   40
The ground-pine curled its pretty wreath,
Running over the club-moss burrs;
I inhaled the violet's breath;
Around me stood the oaks and firs;
Pine-cones and acorns lay on the ground;   45
Over me soared the eternal sky,
Full of light and of deity;
Again I saw, again I heard,
The rolling river, the morning bird;—
Beauty through my senses stole;   50
I yielded myself to the perfect whole.

1839, 1847

The Rhodora:

ON BEING ASKED, WHENCE IS THE FLOWER? [3]

In May, when sea-winds pierced our solitudes,
I found the fresh Rhodora in the woods,
Spreading its leafless blooms in a damp nook,
To please the desert and the sluggish brook.
The purple petals, fallen in the pool,   5
Made the black water with their beauty gay;
Here might the red-bird come his plumes to cool,
And court the flower that cheapens his array.
Rhodora! if the sages ask thee why
This charm is wasted on the earth and sky,   10
Tell them, dear, that if eyes were made for seeing,
Then Beauty is its own excuse for being:
Why thou wert there, O rival of the rose!
I never thought to ask, I never knew;
But in my simple ignorance, suppose   15
The self-same Power that brought me there brought you.

a "silly" expression of transcendentalism

1834   1839, 1847

The Problem [4]

I like a church; I like a cowl;
I love a prophet of the soul;
And on my heart monastic aisles
Fall like sweet strains, or pensive smiles;
Yet not for all his faith can see   5
Would I that cowled churchman be.

Why should the vest on him allure,
Which I could not on me endure?

dramatic situation

Not from a vain or shallow thought
His awful Jove young Phidias [5] brought,   10

3. Like "Each and All," this is one of the four lyrics which, in 1839, were the first of Emerson's poems to be published in periodicals. "The Rhodora" first appeared in the *Western Messenger* for July, 1839 and was collected in the volumes of 1847 and 1876.
4. Soon after "The Divinity School Address," in his *Journal* for August 28, 1838, Emerson entered his objection to the "division of labor" that sets the clergyman apart from those who express in other ways the wholeness and holiness of the divine unity. In "The Problem," the artist, poet, thinker, prophet, all the genuine Makers among men, reaffirm the same Pentecost, as priests of the God made manifest in nature. First published in the *Dial* for July, 1840, the poem was collected in the volumes of 1847 and 1876.
5. Phidias was the great sculptor of Pericles' Athens. However, his masterpiece, the Zeus ("Jove") described by Pausanias, was in the temple at Olympia.

Never from lips of cunning fell
The thrilling Delphic oracle; [6]
Out from the heart of nature rolled
The burdens of the Bible old;
The litanies of nations came,   15
Like the volcano's tongue of flame,
Up from the burning core below,—
The canticles of love and woe;
The hand that rounded Peter's dome [7]
And groined the aisles of Christian Rome   20
Wrought in a sad sincerity;
Himself from God he could not free;
He builded better than he knew;—
The conscious stone to beauty grew.

Know'st thou what wove yon woodbird's nest   25
Of leaves, and feathers from her breast?
Or how the fish outbuilt her shell,
Painting with morn each annual cell?
Or how the sacred pine-tree adds
To her old leaves new myriads?   30
Such and so grew these holy piles,
Whilst love and terror laid the tiles.
Earth proudly wears the Parthenon, [8]
As the best gem upon her zone;
And Morning opes with haste her lids,   35
To gaze upon the Pyramids;
O'er England's abbeys bends the sky,
As on its friends, with kindred eye;
For out of Thought's interior sphere,
These wonders rose to upper air;   40
And Nature gladly gave them place,
Adopted them into her race,
And granted them an equal date
With Andes and with Ararat.

These temples grew as grows the grass;   45
Art might obey, but not surpass.
The passive Master lent his hand
To the vast soul that o'er him planned;
And the same power that reared the shrine

the artist

---

6. The Delphic oracle communicated
the revelations of Apollo, the loftiest
embodiment of the Greek mind and
creativeness.
7. Michelangelo designed and engi-
neered the great dome of St. Peter's
at Rome, nearly completed when he
died in 1564.
8. Greatest architectural monument of
Greek culture, it honored Athena, goddess of wisdom.

Bestrode the tribes that knelt within.   50
Ever the fiery Pentecost [9]
Girds with one flame the countless host,
Trances the heart through chanting choirs,
And through the priest the mind inspires.
The word unto the prophet spoken   55
Was writ on tables yet unbroken; [1]
The word by seers or sibyls told,
In groves of oak, or fanes of gold,
Still floats upon the morning wind,
Still whispers to the willing mind.   60
One accent of the Holy Ghost
The heedless world hath never lost.
I know what say the fathers wise,—
The Book itself before me lies,
Old Crysostom, [2] best Augustine, [3]   65
And he who blent both in his line,
The younger *Golden Lips* or mines,
Taylor, [4] the Shakspeare of divines.
His words are music in my ear,
I see his cowled portrait dear;   70
And yet, for all his faith could see,
I would not the good bishop be.

1839   1840, 1847

The Sphinx [5]

The Sphinx is drowsy,
  Her wings are furled;
Her ear is heavy,
  She broods on the world.
'Who'll tell me my secret,   5

9. The miraculous descent of the Holy Ghost upon the disciples of Jesus after his resurrection. *Cf.* Acts ii: 1–36.
1. *Cf.* Exodus xxxii: 19.
2. John of Antioch (347?–407), Greek Church Father and saint, later called Chrysostom ("Golden Mouth") in honor of his *Homilies*.
3. St. Augustine (354–430), whose *Confessions* Emerson once called "golden words" (*cf.* l. 67, and Centenary Edition, Vol. IX, p. 406).
4. Jeremy Taylor (1613–1667), English churchman, author of *Holy Living* and *Holy Dying*.
5. The Sphinx of Thebes was known in legend for her riddle, whose answer symbolized the rise and fall of man. The inscrutable Great Sphinx near the pyramids of Giza, Egypt, combines various animal and human characteristics. The association of these ideas is clarified by Emerson's note on the meaning of the poem, in his notebooks (1859): "The perception of identity unites all things and explains one by another, and the most rare and strange is equally facile as the most common. But if the mind live only in particulars, and see only differences (wanting the power to see the whole—all in each), then the world addresses to this mind a question it cannot answer, and each new fact tears it in pieces." The poem appeared in *The Dial* for January, 1841, and in the volumes of 1847 and 1876.

The ages have kept?—
I awaited the seer,
While they slumbered and slept;—

'The fate of the man-child;
The meaning of man;   10
Known fruit of the Unknown;
Daedalian [6] plan;
Out of sleeping a waking,
Out of waking a sleep;
Life death overtaking;   15
Deep underneath deep?

'Erect as a sunbeam,
Upspringeth the palm;
The elephant browses,
Undaunted and calm;   20
In beautiful motion
The thrush plies his wings;
Kind leaves of his covert
Your silence he sings.

'The waves, unashamed,   25
In difference sweet,
Play glad with the breezes,
Old playfellows meet;
The journeying atoms,
Primordial wholes,   30
Firmly draw, firmly drive,
By their animate poles.

'Sea, earth, air, sound, silence,
Plant, quadruped, bird,
By one music enchanted,   35
One deity stirred,—
Each the other adorning
Accompany still;
Night veileth the morning,
The vapor the hill.   40

'The babe by its mother
Lies bathed in joy;
Glide its hours uncounted,—
The sun is its toy;
Shines the peace of all being,   45

6. Daedalus, in Greek mythology, personified the development of craftsmanship
among mortals, and finally devised wings to escape the vengeance of a god.

Without cloud, in its eyes;
And the sum of the world
    In soft miniature lies.

'But man crouches and blushes,
    Absconds and conceals;
He creepeth and peepeth,
    He palters and steals;
Infirm, melancholy,
    Jealous glancing around,
An oaf, an accomplice,
    He poisons the ground.

'Out spoke the great mother,
    Beholding his fear;—
At the sound of her accents
    Cold shuddered the sphere:—
"Who has drugged my boy's cup?
    Who has mixed my boy's bread?
Who, with sadness and madness,
    Has turned my child's head?" '

I heard a poet answer
    Aloud and cheerfully,
'Say on, sweet Sphinx! thy dirges
    Are pleasant songs to me.
Deep love lieth under
    These pictures of time;
They fade in the light of
    Their meaning sublime.

'The fiend that man harries
    Is love of the Best;
Yawns the pit of the Dragon,[7]
    Lit by rays from the Blest.[8]
The Lethe of Nature
    Can't trance him again,
Whose soul sees the perfect,
    Which his eyes seek in vain.

'To vision profounder
    Man's spirit must dive;
His aye-rolling orb
    At no goal will arrive;
The heavens that now draw him

50

55

60

65

70

75

80

85

7. Where an angel chained "the dragon, that old serpent, which is the Devil"; *cf*. **Revelation xx: 1–3.**

8. General term in hymnology and Scripture for God's heaven of redemption.

With sweetness untold,
Once found,—for new heavens
   He spurneth the old.

'Pride ruined the angels,
   Their shame them restores;
And the joy that is sweetest
   Lurks in stings of remorse.[9]   90
Have I a lover
   Who is noble and free?—
I would he were nobler   95
   Than to love me.

'Eterne alternation
   Now follows, now flies;
And under pain, pleasure,—
   Under pleasure, pain lies.   100
Love works at the centre,
   Heart-heaving alway;
Forth speed the strong pulses
   To the borders of day.

'Dull Sphinx, Jove keep thy five wits: 105
   Thy sight is growing blear;
Rue, myrrh and cummin [1] for the Sphinx,—
   Her muddy eyes to clear!'—
The old Sphinx bit her thick lip,—
   Said, 'Who taught thee me to name?   110
I am thy spirit, yoke-fellow,
   Of thine eye I am eyebeam.[2]

'Thou art the unanswered question;
   Couldst see thy proper eye
Alway it asketh, asketh;   115
   And each answer is a lie.
So take thy quest through nature,
   It through thousand natures ply;
Ask on, thou clothed eternity;
   Time is the false reply.'   120

9. Ll. 91–92 were changed in the post-humous Centenary Edition to read: "Lurks the joy that is sweetest / In stings of remorse."
1. In the ancient tradition of the herbalist, rue was medicine for remorse (*cf.* l. 92); myrrh was the Hebrew aromatic for anointment or purification, brought to the infant Jesus by the Magi, and offered Him upon the Cross (*cf.* ll. 76–80); cummin was a Palestinian spice, a relish for food (*cf.* ll. 99–104).
2. Thus the poet is the prophet of the riddle of the Sphinx or of nature. See *Nature*, Chapter I, paragraph 4: "I become a transparent eyeball."

Uprose the merry Sphinx,
   And crouched no more in stone;
She melted into purple cloud,
   She silvered in the moon;
She spired into a yellow flame;   125
   She flowered in blossoms red;
She flowed into a foaming wave:
   She stood Monadnoc's ³ head.

Thorough a thousand voices
   Spoke the universal dame: 130
'Who telleth one of my meanings,
   Is master of all I am.'

                            1841, 1847

Compensation ⁴

I

The wings of Time are black and white,
Pied with morning and with night.
Mountain tall and ocean deep
Trembling balance duly keep.
In changing moon and tidal wave   5
Glows the feud of Want and Have.
Gauge of more and less through space,
Electric star or pencil plays,
The lonely Earth amid the balls
That hurry through the eternal halls,   10
A makeweight flying to the void,
Supplemental asteroid,
Or compensatory spark,
Shoots across the neutral Dark.

II

Man's the elm, and Wealth the vine;   15
Stanch and strong the tendrils twine:
Though the frail ringlets thee deceive,
None from its stock that vine can reave.
Fear not, then, thou child infirm,
There's no god dare wrong a worm;   20
Laurel crowns cleave to deserts,
And power to him who power exerts.
Hast not thy share? On winged feet,
Lo! it rushes thee to meet;

3. A peak that dominates the mountain scenery of southwest New Hampshire.
4. "Compensation" was Emerson's poetical motto for the essay of the same name, published in *Essays* [First Series] (1841). Together with other such "Elements and Mottoes" it was collected in *May-Day and Other Pieces* (1867).

And all that Nature made thy own,   25
Floating in air or pent in stone,
Will rive the hills, and swim the sea,
And, like thy shadow, follow thee.[5]

1841, 1867

Ode to Beauty [6]

Who gave thee, O Beauty,
The keys of this breast,—
Too credulous lover
Of blest and unblest?
Say, when in lapsed ages   5
Thee knew I of old?
Or what was the service
For which I was sold?
When first my eyes saw thee,
I found me thy thrall,   10
By magical drawings,
Sweet tyrant of all!
I drank at thy fountain
False waters of thirst;
Thou intimate stranger,   15
Thou latest and first!
Thy dangerous glances
Make women of men;
New-born, we are melting
Into nature again.   20

Lavish, lavish promiser,
Night persuading gods to err!
Guest of million painted forms,
Which in turn thy glory warms!
The frailest leaf, the mossy bark,   25
The acorn's cup, the rain-drop's arc,
The swinging spider's silver line,
The ruby of the drop of wine,
The shining pebble of the pond,
Thou inscribest with a bond,   30
In thy momentary play,
Would bankrupt nature to repay.

---

5. Ll. 23–28 are an enlarged paraphrase from "a noble sentence of Ali," cousin and son-in-law of Mohammed (Centenary Edition, Vol. IX, p. 494).
6. The "Ode to Beauty," distinguished among Emerson's poems for a lyric grace that responds to feeling more than to idea, was published in *The Dial* for October, 1843. It was revised slightly for the *Poems* (1847), and finally, for the *Selected Poems* (1876), as given here.

Ah, what avails it
To hide or to shun
Whom the Infinite One   35
Hath granted his throne?
The heaven high over
Is the deep's lover;
The sun and sea,
Informed by thee,   40
Before me run
And draw me on,
Yet fly me still,
As Fate refuses
To me the heart Fate for me chooses.   45
Is it that my opulent soul
Was mingled from the generous whole;
Sea-valleys and the deep of skies
Furnished several supplies;
And the sands whereof I'm made   50
Draw me to them, self-betrayed?
I turn the proud portfolio
Which holds the grand designs
Of Salvator, of Guercino,
And Piranesi's lines.[7]   55
I hear the lofty paeans
Of the masters of the shell,[8]
Who heard the starry music
And recount the numbers well;
Olympian bards who sung   60
Divine Ideas below,[9]
Which always find us young
And always keep us so.
Oft, in streets or humblest places,
I detect far-wandered graces,   65
Which, from Eden wide astray,
In lowly homes have lost their way.

Thee gliding through the sea of form,
Like the lightning through the storm,

---

7. According to Emerson's editors (Centenary Edition, Vol. IX, p. 432), Margaret Fuller had sent him the "portfolio" (l. 52). Salvator Rosa (1615–1673) was leader of the Neapolitan revival of landscape painting; Guercino (Giovanni Francesco Barbieri, 1591–1666) was a Bolognese eclectic painter; Giambattista Piranesi (1720–1778), Italian architect and painter, influenced both neoclassical architects and later romantic writers by his engravings of classical antiquity. 8. According to Greek myth, it was from a turtle shell that Apollo formed the lyre, instrument of the twin arts of music and poetry; hence poets are "masters of the shell." 9. The Greek gods, dwelling on Mount Olympus, heard daily the poetry of divine bards; Orpheus, a mortal, taught by Apollo, "sung / Divine ideas below."

Somewhat not to be possessed,   70
Somewhat not to be caressed,
No feet so fleet could ever find,
No perfect form could ever bind.
Thou eternal fugitive,
Hovering over all that live,   75
Quick and skilful to inspire
Sweet, extravagant desire,
Starry space and lily-bell
Filling with thy roseate smell,
Wilt not give the lips to taste   80
Of the nectar which thou hast.

All that's good and great with thee
Works in close conspiracy;
Thou hast bribed the dark and lonely
To report thy features only,   85
And the cold and purple morning
Itself with thoughts of thee adorning;
The leafy dell, the city mart,
Equal trophies of thine art;
E'en the flowing azure air   90
Thou hast touched for my despair;
And, if I languish into dreams,
Again I meet the ardent beams.
Queen of things! I dare not die
In Being's deeps past ear and eye;   95
Lest there I find the same deceiver
And be the sport of Fate forever.
Dread Power, but dear! if God thou be,
Unmake me quite, or give thyself to me!

1843, 1847

Hamatreya [1]

Bulkeley, Hunt, Willard, Hosmer, Meriam, Flint,[2]
Possessed the land which rendered to their toil
Hay, corn, roots, hemp, flax, apples, wool and wood.

1. In Emerson's journal (1845) appears a long passage from the Hindu *Vishnu Purana.* The gist of this poem is found in the following extract: "Kings who with perishable frames have possessed this ever-enduring world, and who * * * have indulged the feeling that suggests 'This earth is mine, —it is my son's,—it belongs to my dynasty,'—have all passed away. * * * Earth laughs, as if smiling with autumnal flowers to behold her kings unable to effect the subjugation of themselves." The song of the Earth (on which Emerson based the "Earth-Song" in this poem) is then recited to Maitreya, but Emerson rejected that name for his title in favor of the variant "Hamatreya." The poem was published in the *Poems* (1847) and in the *Selected Poems* (1876), as here printed.
2. Names of first settlers of Concord, Massachusetts, including Peter Bulkeley, an ancestor of Emerson.

Each of these landlords walked amidst his farm,
Saying, ' 'T is mine, my children's and my name's.   5
How sweet the west wind sounds in my own trees!
How graceful climb those shadows on my hill!
I fancy these pure waters and the flags
Know me, as does my dog: we sympathize;
And, I affirm, my actions smack of the soil.'   10

Where are these men? Asleep beneath their grounds:
And strangers, fond as they, their furrows plough.
Earth laughs in flowers, to see her boastful boys
Earth-proud, proud of the earth which is not theirs;
Who steer the plough, but cannot steer their feet   15
Clear of the grave.
They added ridge to valley, brook to pond,
And sighed for all that bounded their domain;
'This suits me for a pasture; that's my park;
We must have clay, lime, gravel, granite-ledge,   20
And misty lowland, where to go for peat.
The land is well,—lies fairly to the south.
'T is good, when you have crossed the sea and back,
To find the sitfast acres where you left them.'
Ah! the hot owner sees not Death, who adds   25
Him to his land, a lump of mould the more.
Hear what the Earth says:—

EARTH-SONG

Mine and yours;
Mine, not yours.
Earth endures;   30
Stars abide—
Shine down in the old sea;
Old are the shores;
But where are old men?
I who have seen much,   35
Such have I never seen.

The lawyer's deed
Ran sure,
In tail,[3]
To them, and to their heirs   40
Who shall succeed,
Without fail,
Forevermore.

3. *I.e.,* "entailed"; legal term applied to an estate irrevocably settled upon
designated descendants.

Here is the land,
Shaggy with wood,   45
With its old valley,
Mound and flood.
But the heritors?—
Fled like the flood's foam.
The lawyer, and the laws,   50
And the kingdom,
Clean swept herefrom.

They called me theirs,
Who so controlled me;
Yet every one   55
Wished to stay, and is gone,
How am I theirs,
If they cannot hold me,
But I hold them?

When I heard the Earth-song,   60
I was no longer brave;
My avarice cooled
Like lust in the chill of the grave.

1847

Give All to Love [4]

Give all to love;
Obey thy heart;
Friends, kindred, days,
Estate, good-fame,
Plans, credit and the Muse,—   5
Nothing refuse.

'T is a brave master;
Let it have scope:
Follow it utterly,
Hope beyond hope: 10
High and more high
It dives into noon,
With wing unspent,
Untold intent;
But it is a god,   15

4. "Give All to Love" is puzzling to readers who have not understood Emerson's toughness of mind in pushing his ideas to their logical limits of social application. If his theory of individualism is sound, it must function also between lovers. Thus he ends another poem, "The Initial Love": "So lovers melt their sundered selves, / Yet melted would be twain."

Knows its own path
And the outlets of the sky.

It was never for the mean;
It requiereth courage stout.
Souls above doubt,   20
Valor unbending,
It will reward,—
They shall return
More than they were,
And ever ascending.   25

Leave all for love;
Yet, hear me, yet,
One word more thy heart behoved,
One pulse more of firm endeavor,—
Keep thee to-day,   30
To-morrow, forever,
Free as an Arab
Of thy beloved.

Cling with life to the maid;
But when the surprise,   35
First vague shadow of surmise
Flits across her bosom young,
Of a joy apart from thee,
Free be she, fancy-free;
Nor thou detain her vesture's hem,   40
Nor the palest rose she flung
From her summer diadem.

Though thou loved her as thyself,
As a self of purer clay,
Though her parting dims the day,   45
Stealing grace from all alive;
Heartily know,
When half-gods go,
The gods arrive.

1847

Ode

INSCRIBED TO W. H. CHANNING [5]

Though loath to grieve
The evil time's sole patriot,
I cannot leave
My honied thought
For the priest's cant,   5
Or statesman's rant.

If I refuse
My study for their politique,
Which at the best is trick,
The angry Muse   10
Puts confusion in my brain.

But who is he that prates
Of the culture of mankind,
Of better arts and life?
Go, blindworm, go,   15
Behold the famous States
Harrying Mexico
With rifle and with knife!

Or who, with accent bolder,
Dare praise the freedom-loving mountaineer?   20
I found by thee, O rushing Contoocook! [6]
And in thy valleys, Agiochook! [7]
The jackals of the negro-holder. [8]

The God who made New Hampshire
Taunted the lofty land   25
With little men;—
Small bat and wren
House in the oak:—
If earth-fire cleave
The upheaved land, and bury the folk,   30

Emerson's voice

Emerson's thoughts give to W. H. Channing a voice in form of a relatta

---

5. The so-called Channing Ode was published in the *Poems* (1847), in the midst of the Mexican War, which Emerson had opposed both on pacific grounds and because the war was presumably fomented to achieve the extension of slave territory. Willian Henry Channing (1810–1884) was a Unitarian clergyman and active transcendentalist. Whether or not he had urged Emerson to give concrete support to the mounting abolition movement, Channing was so fully identified with such humanitarian causes that the poet was justified in using his friend's name to establish his argument, which strikingly illustrates the application of his philosophy to social action.

6. A branch of the Merrimack River in New Hampshire.

7. Indian name for the White Mountains of New Hampshire.

8. *I.e.*, those who hounded escaped slaves under sanction of the fugitive-slave laws; the jackal is a mean and cowardly wild dog.

The southern crocodile would grieve.
Virtue palters; Right is hence;
Freedom praised, but hid;
Funeral eloquence
Rattles the coffin-lid.   35

What boots thy zeal,
O glowing friend,
That would indignant rend
The northland from the south?
Wherefore? to what good end?   40
Boston Bay and Bunker Hill
Would serve things still;—
Things are of the snake.

The horseman serves the horse,
The neatherd serves the neat,[9]   45
The merchant serves the purse,
The eater serves his meat;
'T is the day of the chattel,
Web to weave, and corn to grind;
Things are in the saddle,   50
And ride mankind.

There are two laws discrete,
Not reconciled,—
Law for man, and law for things;
The last builds town and fleet,   55
But it runs wild,
And doth the man unking.

'T is fit the forest fall,
The steep be graded,
The mountain tunnelled,   60
The sand shaded,
The orchard planted,
The glebe tilled,
The prairie granted,
The steamer built.   65

Let man serve law for man;
Live for friendship, live for love,
For truth's and harmony's behoof;
The state may follow how it can,
As Olympus follows Jove.[1]   70

---

9. Obsolete term for oxen.   father-god of the Greek deities on
1. Jove (Jupiter, or Zeus) was the   Olympus.

Yet do not I implore
The wrinkled shopman to my sounding woods,
Nor did the unwilling senator
Ask votes of thrushes in the solitudes.
Every one to his chosen work;— 75
Foolish hands may mix and mar;
Wise and sure the issues are.
Round they roll till dark is light,
Sex to sex, and even to odd;—
The over-god 80
Who marries Right to Might,
Who peoples, unpeoples,—
He who exterminates
Races by stronger races,
Black by white faces,— 85
Knows to bring honey
Out of the lion; [2]
Grafts gentlest scion
On pirate and Turk.

The Cossack eats Poland,[3] 90
Like stolen fruit;
Her last noble is ruined,
Her last poet mute:
Straight, into double band
The victors divide; 95
Half for freedom strike and stand;—
The astonished Muse finds thousands at her side.

1847

Fable [4]

The mountain and the squirrel
Had a quarrel,
And the former called the latter "Little Prig;"
Bun replied,
"You are doubtless very big; 5
But all sorts of things and weather
Must be taken in together,
To make up a year
And a sphere.
And I think it no disgrace 10
To occupy my place.

---

2. *Cf.* Samson's exploit (Judges xiv: 9).
3. In spite of the Russian military despotism in Poland after the popular insurrections of 1830–1831, a new Polish generation was striking for liberty in 1846 (*cf.* ll. 94–96).
4. "Fable" first appeared in *The Diadem* in 1846, and was collected in the volumes of 1847 and 1876.

If I'm not so large as you,
You are not so small as I,
And not half so spry.
I'll not deny you make   15
A very pretty squirrel track;
Talents differ; all is well and wisely put;
If I cannot carry forests on my back,
Neither can you crack a nut."

1845   1846, 1847

Brahma [5]

If the red slayer think he slays,
  Or if the slain think he is slain,
They know not well the subtle ways
  I keep, and pass, and turn again.

Far or forgot to me is near;   5
  Shadow and sunlight are the same;
The vanished gods to me appear;
  And one to me are shame and fame.

They reckon ill who leave me out;
  When me they fly, I am the wings;   10
I am the doubter and the doubt,
  And I the hymn the Brahmin sings.

The strong gods pine for my abode,
  And pine in vain the sacred Seven, [6]
But thou, meek lover of the good!   15
  Find me, and turn thy back on heaven.

1856   1857, 1867

Days [7]

Daughters of Time, the hypocritic Days,
Muffled and dumb like barefoot dervishes,

5. Brahma is the Hindu supreme soul of the universe—an uncreated, illimitable, and timeless essence or being. Emerson, discussing with his daughter the perplexity into which his poem had thrown many, said "Tell them to say Jehovah instead of Brahma." The poem is an exposition of the erroneous relativity of human and temporal perception, as compared with the sublime harmony of cosmic divinity. The images of the poem are presumably based on certain extracts in Emerson's *Journals* from the *Vishnu Purana*, extensively discussed in the Centenary Edition (Vol. IX, pp. 464–467). "Brahma" was one of four poems by Emerson in the first number of the *Atlantic Monthly*, November, 1857; it then took its place in the volumes of 1867 and 1876.
6. The seven high saints of the Brahmin faith.
7. One of the most perfect of Emerson's lyrics, "Days" appeared with "Brahma" in the *Atlantic Monthly* for November, 1857 and in the volumes of 1867 and 1876.

And marching single in an endless file,
Bring diadems and fagots in their hands.
To each they offer gifts after his will,
Bread, kingdoms, stars, and sky that holds them all. 5
I, in my pleached garden,[8] watched the pomp,
Forgot my morning wishes, hastily
Took a few herbs and apples, and the Day
Turned and departed silent. I, too late, 10
Under her solemn fillet saw the scorn.

1857, 1867

Waldeinsamkeit[9]

I do not count the hours I spend
In wandering by the sea;
The forest is my loyal friend,
Like God it useth me.

In plains that room for shadows make 5
Of skirting hills to lie,
Bound in by streams which give and take
Their colors from the sky;

Or on the mountain-crest sublime,
Or down the oaken glade, 10
O what have I to do with time?
For this the day was made.

Cities of mortals woe-begone
Fantastic care derides,
But in the serious landscape lone 15
Stern benefit abides.

Sheen will tarnish, honey cloy,
And merry is only a mask of sad,
But, sober on a fund of joy,
The woods at heart are glad. 20

There the great Planter plants
Of fruitful worlds the grain,
And with a million spells enchants
The souls that walk in pain.

8. In which the branches of trees or shrubs are interwoven ("pleached"), making them flat—hence formal, artificial.

9. Emerson's son and editor translated this German title as "Forest Solitude," and associated it with the woods of Walden, Thoreau's hermitage.

Still on the seeds of all he made   25
The rose of beauty burns;
Through times that wear and forms that fade,
Immortal youth returns.

The black ducks mounting from the lake,
The pigeon in the pines,   30
The bittern's boom, a desert make
Which no false art refines.

Down in yon watery nook,
Where bearded mists divide,
The gray old gods whom Chaos knew,   35
The sires of Nature, hide.

Aloft, in secret veins of air,
Blows the sweet breath of song,
O, few to scale those uplands dare,
Though they to all belong!   40

See thou bring not to field or stone
The fancies found in books;
Leave authors' eyes, and fetch your own,
To brave the landscape's looks.

Oblivion here thy wisdom is,   45
Thy thrift, the sleep of cares;
For a proud idleness like this
Crowns all thy mean affairs.

1858, 1867

Terminus [1]

It is time to be old,
To take in sail:—
The god of bounds,
Who sets to seas a shore,
Came to me in his fatal rounds,   5
And said: 'No more!
No farther shoot
Thy broad ambitious branches, and thy root,
Fancy departs: no more invent,
Contract they firmament   10
To compass of a tent.

1. Terminus was the Roman deity of boundaries; the poem, of course, has autobiographical significance. It ap- peared in the *Atlantic Monthly* for January, 1867, and the same year in the *May-Day* volume.

There's not enough for this and that,
Make thy option which of two;
Economize the failing river,
Nor the less revere the Giver,   15
Leave the many and hold the few.
Timely wise accept the terms,
Soften the fall with wary foot;
A little while
Still plan and smile,   20
And, fault of novel germs,
Mature the unfallen fruit.
Curse, if thou wilt, thy sires,
Bad husbands of their fires,
Who, when they gave thee breath,   25
Failed to bequeath
The needful sinew stark as once,
The Baresark [2] marrow to thy bones,
But left a legacy of ebbing veins,
Inconstant heat and nerveless reins,—   30
Amid the Muses, left thee deaf and dumb,
Amid the gladiators, halt and numb.'

    As the bird trims her to the gale,
I trim myself to the storm of time,
I man the rudder, reef the sail,   35
Obey the voice at eve obeyed at prime:
'Lowly faithful, banish fear,
Right onward drive unharmed;
The port well worth the cruise, is near,
And every wave is charmed.'   40

1867

HENRY DAVID THOREAU

(1817–1862)

Thoreau died at forty-four, having published relatively little of what he had written. He expressed his characteristic dilemma when he declared: "My life has been the poem I would have writ, / But I could not both live and utter it." At his best, perhaps he succeeded in doing just that.

Thoreau's outward life reflected his inward stature as a small and quiet pond reflects the diminished outline of a moun-

---

2. *I.e.*, berserk ("bare of shirt"); said of the ancient Germanic warriors who fought without armor.

tain. Concord, the place where he lived and died, was tiny, but it was the center of an exciting intellectual world, and the poverty of his family did not prevent him from getting a good start in the classics at the local academy. At Harvard College in Cambridge, a few miles away, he maintained himself frugally with the help of his aunts and by doing chores and teaching during leisure hours and vacations. There he began his *Journals*, ultimately to become the largest of his works, a storehouse of his observations and ideas. Upon graduation he tried teaching, and for a time conducted a private school in Concord with his brother, John; but he had no inclination toward a career in the ordinary sense. Living was the object of life, and work was never an end in itself, but merely the self-respecting means by which one paid his way in the world. While he made his home with his father, he assisted him in his trade of pencil maker, but he lost interest as soon as they had learned to make the best pencil to be had. When he lived with Emerson (1841–1843 and 1847–1848) he did the chores, and he kept the house while Emerson was abroad. At the home of Emerson's brother William, on Staten Island in 1843, he tutored the children. In Concord village, he did odd jobs, hired himself out, and surveyed other men's lands without coveting them.

Meanwhile, his inward life, as recorded in the *Journals*, was vastly enriched by experience and steady reading. In the year of his graduation from Harvard (1837), his Concord neighbor, Emerson, made his address on *The American Scholar*, and both the man and the essay became Thoreau's early guide. The next year he delivered his first lecture, at the Concord Lyceum; he later gave lectures from Bangor, Maine, to Philadelphia, but never acquired Emerson's skill in communicating to his audience. On his journeys he made friends as various as Orestes Brownson, Horace Greeley, John Brown, and Walt Whitman; he and Emerson were the two who recognized Whitman's genius from the beginning. At home in Concord he attended Alcott's "conversations," and shared the intellectual excitements and stimulation of the informal Transcendental Club which met at Concord and Boston. The Club sponsored *The Dial* (1840–1844), to which he contributed essays drawn from his *Journals* and his study of natural history and philosophy.

A number of his best poems also appeared in *The Dial*. His later poems were often genuinely inspired and independent. Emerson meant only praise in declaring that "his biography is in his verses"; it is true that the same lyrical response to ideas pervades his poetry, his prose, and his life. Thoreau tacitly recognized this by incorporating much of his poetry in *A Week on the Concord and Merrimack Rivers* (1849) and *Walden* (1854), the two volumes that were published before his death. But it is a mistake to suppose that the serene individualism of his writings reflects only an unbroken serenity of life. Many Massachusetts neighbors, and even some transcendentalists, regarded Thoreau as an extremist, especially on public and economic issues. There were painful clashes of temperament with Emerson. In his personal life he suffered deep bereavements. His older brother, John, who was also his best friend, revealed his love for Ellen Sewall, the girl whom Henry hoped to marry; she refused them both. Two years later, John died of lockjaw at twenty-seven, first victim of the family frailty. The beloved sister Helen died at thirty-six, and Thoreau's death occurred after seven years of tuberculosis.

Two aspects of Thoreau's life provided the bulk of his literary materials: his active concern with social issues and his feeling for the unity of man and nature. He took an early interest in abolition, appearing as speaker at antislavery conventions, once in company with John Brown, whom he later publicly defended after the terrifying and bloody raid at Harpers Ferry. (See "Slavery in Massachusetts," 1854, and "A Plea for John Brown," 1859.) He was able also to associate his private rebellion with large social issues, as in his resistance to taxation. He refused to pay the church taxes (1838) because they were levied on all alike, as for an "established" church. In his refusal to pay the poll tax, which cost him a jail sentence (1845), he was resisting the "constitutional" concept which led Massachusetts to give support in Congress to southern leadership, as represented by the Mexican War and repugnant laws concerning slave "property."

Four years later he formalized his theory of social action in the essay "Civil Disobedience," the origin of the modern concept of pacific resistance as the final instrument of minority opinion, which found its spectacular demonstration in the life of Mahatma Gandhi of India.

Thoreau's works at all points reveal his economic and social individualism, but until recently his readers responded chiefly to his accurate and sympathetic reporting of nature, his interesting use of the stored learning of the past, and the wit, grace, and power of his style. His description of nature was based on his journals of his various "excursions," as he called them. *A Week on the Concord and Merrimack Rivers*, his first published volume, described a boat trip with his brother, John, in 1839. Other trips of literary significance were his explorations of the Penobscot forests of Maine (1846, 1853, and 1857) and his walking tours in Cape Cod (1840, 1850, 1855, and 1857) and in Canada. Certain essays on these adventures were published in magazines before his death; later his friends published *The Maine Woods* (1864), *Cape Cod* (1865), and *A Yankee in Canada* (1866), which resulted from a trip to Canada with W. E. Channing in 1850.

Almost all of the richness of Thoreau is in *Walden*. In his revelation of the simplicity and divine unity of nature, in his faith in man, in his own sturdy individualism, in his deep-rooted love for one place as an epitome of the universe, Thoreau reminds us of what we are and what we yet may be.

Posthumously collected volumes of Thoreau, in addition to those mentioned in the text, were *Excursions*, 1863, *Early Spring in Massachusetts*, 1881, *Summer*, 1884, *Winter*, 1888, *Autumn*, 1892, and *Poems of Nature*, 1895. A recent critical edition of the poems is *Collected Poems*, edited by Carl Bode, 1943, enlarged, 1966.

The Riverside Edition, 10 vols., 1894, is superseded by the Manuscript Edition and the standard Walden Edition (from the same plates), *The Writings * * *￼* , 20 vols., 1906. Letters are in *Familiar Letters * * *￼* , 1894, included as Vol. VI of the Walden Edition. *The Journals* (1837–1861), edited by Bradford Torrey, available as Vols. VII–XX of the Walden Edition, were newly edited by Francis H. Allen, 1949, and again in 2 vols. with a foreword by Walter Harding, 1963. *Consciousness in Concord: Thoreau's Lost Journal (1840–41)*, was published by Perry Miller, 1958. *The Heart of Thoreau's Journals* was edited by Odell Shepard, 1927. An available modern collection is *The Works of Thoreau*, Cambridge Edition, edited by H. S. Canby, 1947; standard selections are *Henry David*

Thoreau: Representative Selections, edited by B. V. Crawford, 1934. C. Bode and W. Harding edited *The Correspondence * * *￼* , 1958. Milton Meltzer, *Thoreau: People, Principles, and Politics*, 1963, is a good selection. A definitive edition of the *Works*, under the general editorship of Walter D. Harding, is in progress.

Standard biographies of Thoreau are those of F. B. Sanborn, 1882, H. S. Salt, 1896, and Mark Van Doren, 1916. Recent scholarship and criticism is reflected in J. B. Atkinson, *Henry Thoreau, the Cosmic Yankee*, 1927; H. S. Canby, *Thoreau*, 1939; J. W. Krutch, *Henry David Thoreau*, 1948; R. L. Cook, *Passage to Walden*, 1949; H. B. Hough, *Thoreau of Walden*, 1956; S. Paul, *The Shores of America*, 1958; W. Harding, *Thoreau: A Century of Criticism*, 1954; the *Thoreau Handbook*, 1959; and with M. Meltzer, *A Thoreau Profile*, 1962; and Stanley Cavell, *The Senses of Walden*, 1972. Harding published *The Days of Henry Thoreau*, 1965, a definitive biography; August Derleth published *Concord Rebel: A Life of Henry David Thoreau*, 1962.

The prose texts in this volume are those of first appearance in a book, unless otherwise noted. The poems are a collation of *Poems of Nature* with the excerpts in *Walden* and *A Week*.

From A Week on the Concord and Merrimack Rivers

[Nature, Poetry, and the Poet] [1]

If one doubts whether Grecian valor and patriotism are not a fiction of the poets, he may go to Athens and see still upon the walls of the temple of Minerva [2] the circular marks made by the shields taken from the enemy in the Persian war, which were suspended there. We have not far to seek for living and unquestionable evidence. The very dust takes shape and confirms some story which we had read. As Fuller said, commenting on the zeal

---

1. *A Week on the Concord and Merrimack Rivers* (1849) was Thoreau's first book, the miscellany of an already learned young poet and meditative thinker. While describing his "fluvial excursions" with his brother, John, on these rivers in 1839, he makes observant comments on nature, man, society, and literature, occasionally introducing a poem of his own. *Walden* has a more finished style, but *A Week * * *￼* is distinguished among Thoreau's works for

its unique morning-charm, as whimsical as the naming of chapters for days of the week. The scattered passages here assembled express a theory of art and poetry, transcendental in nature, which Thoreau consistently supported. A number of the poems of *A Week * * *￼* are also reprinted below, as noted.

2. Known to the Greeks as Athena, goddess of wisdom, protectress of Athens, to whom were dedicated the spoils of battle, as here mentioned.

of Camden,[3] "A broken urn is a whole evidence; or an old gate still surviving out of which the city is run out." When Solon [4] endeavored to prove that Salamis had formerly belonged to the Athenians, and not to the Megareans, he caused the tombs to be opened, and showed that the inhabitants of Salamis turned the faces of their dead to the same side with the Athenians, but the Megareans to the opposite side. There they were to be interrogated.

Some minds are as little logical or argumentative as nature; they can offer no reason or "guess," but they exhibit the solemn and incontrovertible fact. If a historical question arises, they cause the tombs to be opened. Their silent and practical logic convinces the reason and the understanding at the same time. Of such sort is always the only pertinent question and the only unanswerable reply.

Our own country furnishes antiquities as ancient and durable, and as useful, as any; rocks at least as well covered with moss, and a soil which if it is virgin, is but virgin mould, the very dust of nature. What if we cannot read Rome, or Greece, Etruria, or Carthage, or Egypt, or Bablyon, on these; are our cliffs bare? The lichen on the rocks is a rude and simple shield which beginning and imperfect Nature suspended there. Still hangs her wrinkled trophy. And here too the poet's eye may still detect the brazen nails which fastened Time's inscriptions, and if he has the gift, decipher them by this clue. The walls that fence our fields, as well as modern Rome, and not less the Parthenon itself, are all built of ruins. Here may be heard the din of rivers, and ancient winds which have long since lost their names sough through our woods;—the first faint sounds of spring, older than the summer of Athenian glory, the titmouse lisping in the wood, the jay's scream, and blue-bird's warble, and the hum of

> "bees that fly
> About the laughing blossoms of sallowy."

Here is the gray dawn for antiquity, and our to-morrow's future should be at least paulo-post [5] to theirs which we have put behind us. There are the red-maple and birchen leaves, old runes which are not yet deciphered; catkins, pine-cones, vines, oak-leaves, and acorns; the very things themselves, and not their forms in stone, —so much the more ancient and venerable. And even to the cur-

---

3. Thomas Fuller (1608–1661), churchman and writer, in his famous *History of the Worthies of England*, praised William Camden (1551–1623), a learned schoolmaster whose history, *Britannia*, treated British antiquities; but Thoreau, as he says in the following paragraphs, would rather draw the poet's attention to the antiquities of nature.
4. Greek statesman (638?–559? B.C.), called "the lawgiver," who made his advent as one of the Seven Wise Men of Greece by this recovery of Salamis.
5. Latin, "a little bit afterward"; hence, "at the least interval succeeding to theirs."

rent summer there has come down tradition of a hoary-headed master of all art, who once filled every field and grove with statues and god-like architecture, of every design which Greece has lately copied; whose ruins are now mingled with the dust, and not one block remains upon another. The century sun and unwearied rain have wasted them, till not one fragment from that quarry now exists; and poets perchance will feign that gods sent down the material from heaven.   *   *   *

Poetry is the mysticism of mankind.

The expressions of the poet cannot be analyzed; his sentence is one word, whose syllables are words. There are indeed no *words* quite worthy to be set to his music. But what matter if we do not hear the words always, if we hear the music?

Much verse fails of being poetry because it was not written exactly at the right crisis, though it may have been inconceivably near to it. It is only by a miracle that poetry is written at all. It is not recoverable thought, but a hue caught from a vaster receding thought.

A poem is one undivided, unimpeded expression fallen ripe into literature, and it is undividedly and unimpededly received by those for whom it was matured.

If you can speak what you will never hear,—if you can write what you will never read, you have done rare things.

There are two classes of men called poets. The one cultivates life, the other art,—one seeks food for nutriment, the other for flavor; one satisfies hunger, the other gratifies the palate. There are two kinds of writing, both great and rare; one that of genius, or the inspired, the other of intellect and taste, in the intervals of inspiration. The former is above criticism, always correct, giving the law to criticism. It vibrates and pulsates with life forever. It is sacred, and to be read with reverence, as the works of nature are studied. There are few instances of a sustained style of this kind; perhaps every man has spoken words, but the speaker is then careless of the record. Such a style removes us out of personal relations with its author, we do not take his words on our lips, but his sense into our hearts. It is the stream of inspiration, which bubbles out, now here, now there, now in this man, now in that. It matters not through what ice-crystals it is seen, now a fountain, now the ocean stream running under ground. It is in Shakespeare, Alpheus, in Burns, Arethuse,[6] but ever the same. —The other is self-possessed and wise. It is reverent of genius, and greedy of inspiration. It is conscious in the highest and the least de-

---

6. Alpheus, fabled god of a Greek river, pursued the nymph Arethusa, who was changed into a Sicilian fountain; but Alpheus followed her undersea in order to mingle their waters (see Thoreau's previous sentence).

gree. It consists with the most perfect command of the faculties. It dwells in a repose as of the desert, and objects are as distinct in it as oases or palms in the horizon of sand. The train of thought moves with subdued and measured step, like a caravan. But the pen is only an instrument in its hand, and not instinct with life, like a longer arm. It leaves a thin varnish or glaze over all its work. The works of Goethe furnish remarkable instances of the latter.

There is no just and serene criticism as yet. Nothing is considered simply as it lies in the lap of eternal beauty, but our thoughts, as well as our bodies, must be dressed after the latest fashions. Our taste is too delicate and particular. It says nay to the poet's work, but never yea to his hope. It invites him to adorn his deformities, and not to cast them off by expansion, as the tree its bark. We are a people who live in a bright light, in houses of pearl and porcelain, and drink only light wines, whose teeth are easily set on edge by the least natural sour. If we had been consulted, the backbone of the earth would have been made, not of granite, but of Bristol spar.[7] A modern author would have died in infancy in a ruder age. But the poet is something more than a scald,[8] "a smoother and polisher of language;" he is a Cincinnatus [9] in literature, and occupies no west end of the world. Like the sun, he will indifferently select his rhymes, and with a liberal taste weave into his verse the planet and the stubble.

In these old books the stucco has long since crumbled away, and we read what was sculptured in the granite. They are rude and massive in their proportions, rather than smooth and delicate in their finish. The workers in stone polish only their chimney ornaments, but their pyramids are roughly done. There is a soberness in a rough aspect, as of unhewn granite, which addresses a depth in us, but a polished surface hits only the ball of the eye. The true finish is the work of time and the use to which a thing is put. The elements are still polishing the pyramids. Art may varnish and gild, but it can do no more. A work of genius is roughhewn from the first, because it anticipates the lapse of time, and has an ingrained polish, which still appears when fragments are broken off, an essential quality of its substance. Its beauty is at the same time its strength, and it breaks with a lustre.

1839   1849

---

7. The spars are lustrous rocks, readily broken; granite, though less eye-catching, is hard and durable.
8. The ancient Norse *skald* generally recited poems already traditional.
9. Lucius Quintus Cincinnatus (519– 439? B.C.), legendary symbol of virtuous power, was twice appointed dictator of Rome in military crises, and promptly defeating his country's enemies, resigned his powers in favor of his farm.

Walden [1]

> I do not propose to write an ode to dejection, but to brag as lustily as chanticleer in the morning, standing on his roost, if only to wake my neighbors up.

Economy

When I wrote the following pages, or rather the bulk of them, I lived alone, in the woods, a mile from any neighbor, in a house which I had built myself, on the shore of Walden Pond, in Concord, Massachusetts, and earned my living by the labor of my hands only. I lived there two years and two months. At present I am a sojourner in civilized life again.

I should not obtrude my affairs so much on the notice of my readers if very particular inquiries had not been made by my townsmen concerning my mode of life, which some would call impertinent, though they do not appear to me at all impertinent, but, considering the circumstances, very natural and pertinent. Some have asked what I got to eat; if I did not feel lonesome; if I was not afraid; and the like. Others have been curious to learn what portion of my income I devoted to charitable purposes; and some, who have large families, how many poor children I maintained. I will therefore ask those of my readers who feel no particular interest in me to pardon me if I undertake to answer some of these questions in this book. In most books, the *I*, or first person, is omitted; in this it will be retained; that, in respect to egotism, is the main difference. We commonly do not remember that it is, after all, always the first person that is speaking. I should not talk so much about myself if there were any body else whom I knew as well. Unfortunately, I am confined to this theme by the

1. The earliest manuscript of this world-famous book, entitled "Walden, or Life in the Woods," was prepared, as Thoreau there states, "about 1846." It was later revised in the preparation of readings for meetings of the Concord Lyceum and again for publication as a volume in 1854, the source of the present text. As in previous issues, we have silently corrected Thoreau's printed text to conform with the few unmistakable verbal changes made in his hand on a "correction copy"; these were published in full by Reginald L. Cook (*Thoreau Society Bulletin*, Winter, 1953). A very few of Thoreau's glosses or marginal comments are represented in our footnotes but plainly ascribed to Thoreau. For a useful report on the variants published by Cook and on the textual scholarship relevant to *Walden*, see *Walden and Civil Disobedience: A Norton Critical Edition* edited by Owen Thomas, 1966, p. 222, and Preface, p. vi. The work is a masterpiece of human perception; in Thoreau's simple familiar style the mastery of the casual results from strict discipline. The book is unostentatiously learned because Thoreau's knowledge was a constant fact of his intellect, not the result of the mere memory of information. In fact, this book is a complex organization of themes related to the central concept of individualism: such as the economy of individualism (the experiment at Walden Pond); the spiritual and temporal values of individualism in society or in solitude; the survival of self-reliance amid depersonalizing social organizations; the related observation of animal and plant life; and the transcendental concept of the accomplished human personality, simultaneously aware of relations both with Time and the Timeless.

narrowness of my experience. Moreover, I, on my side, require of every writer, first or last, a simple and sincere account of his own life, and not merely what he has heard of other men's lives; some such account as he would send to his kindred from a distant land; for if he has lived sincerely, it must have been in a distant land to me. Perhaps these pages are more particularly addressed to poor students. As for the rest of my readers, they will accept such portions as apply to them. I trust that none will stretch the seams in putting on the coat, for it may do good service to him whom it fits.

I would fain say something, not so much concerning the Chinese and Sandwich Islanders as you who read these pages, who are said to live in New England; something about your condition, especially your outward condition or circumstances in this world, in this town, what it is, whether it is necessary that it be as bad as it is, whether it cannot be improved as well as not. I have travelled a good deal in Concord; and every where, in shops, and offices, and fields, the inhabitants have appeared to me to be doing penance in a thousand remarkable ways. What I have heard of Bramins [2] sitting exposed to four fires and looking in the face of the sun; or hanging suspended, with their heads downward, over flames; or looking at the heavens over their shoulders "until it becomes impossible for them to resume their natural position, while from the twist of the neck nothing but liquids can pass into the stomach;" or dwelling, chained for life, at the foot of a tree; or measuring with their bodies, like caterpillars, the breadth of vast empires; or standing on one leg on the tops of pillars,—even these forms of conscious penance are hardly more incredible and astonishing than the scenes which I daily witness. The twelve labors of Hercules [3] were trifling in comparison with those which my neighbors have undertaken; for they were only twelve, and had an end; but I could never see that these men slew or captured any monster or finished any labor. They have no friend Iolas to burn with a hot iron the root of the hydra's head, but as soon as one head is crushed, two spring up.

I see young men, my townsmen, whose misfortune it is to have inherited farms, houses, barns, cattle, and farming tools; for these are more easily acquired than got rid of. Better if they had been born in the open pasture and suckled by a wolf, that they might have seen with clearer eyes what field they were called to labor in. Who made them serfs of the soil? Why should they eat their

2. Usually Brahmin; of the highest Hindu caste. The unexpected propriety of the absurd comparison is vintage Thoreau.
3. Son of the Greek god Zeus, but born of a mortal; his twelve superhuman feats included one with human help—that of Iolas. At death, deified as an incarnation of manly strength, he married Hebe, goddess of youth.

sixty acres, when man is condemned to eat only his peck of dirt? Why should they begin digging their graves as soon as they are born? They have got to live a man's life, pushing all these things before them, and get on as well as they can. How many a poor immortal soul have I met well nigh crushed and smothered under its load, creeping down the road of life, pushing before it a barn seventy-five feet by forty, its Augean stables⁴ never cleansed, and one hundred acres of land, tillage, mowing, pasture, and wood-lot! The portionless, who struggle with no such unnecessary inherited encumbrances, find it labor enough to subdue and cultivate a few cubic feet of flesh.

But men labor under a mistake. The better part of the man is soon ploughed into the soil for compost. By a seeming fate, commonly called necessity, they are employed, as it says in an old book, laying up treasures which moth and rust will corrupt and thieves break through and steal.⁵ It is a fool's life, as they will find when they get to the end of it, if not before. It is said that Deucalion and Pyrrha⁶ created men by throwing stones over their heads behind them:—

> Inde genus durum sumus, experiensque laborum,
> Et documenta damus quâ simus origine nati.

Or, as Raleigh rhymes it in his sonorous way,—

> "From thence our kind hard-hearted is, enduring pain and
> care,
> Approving that our bodies of a stony nature are."

So much for a blind obedience to a blundering oracle, throwing the stones over their heads behind them, and not seeing where they fell.

Most men, even in this comparatively free country, through mere ignorance and mistake, are so occupied with the factitious cares and superfluously coarse labors of life that its finer fruits cannot be plucked by them. Their fingers, from excessive toil, are too clumsy and tremble too much for that. Actually, the laboring man has not leisure for a true integrity day by day; he cannot afford to sustain the manliest relations to men; his labor would be depreciated in the market. He has no time to be any thing but a machine. How can he remember well his ignorance—which his growth requires—who has so often to use his knowledge? We

---

4. The stables of Augeus housed 3,000 oxen and had not been cleaned for thirty years, but Hercules (see 3 above) accomplished this task in one day by making the Peneus and the Alpheus rivers flow through the stalls.
5. Matt. 6:19–20.

6. The survivors of the flood by which Zeus destroyed mankind. The Latin quotation is from Ovid's *Metamorphoses*, Book I, lines 414–415, the translation from Sir Walter Raleigh's *History of the World*. Cf. Thoreau's essay on Raleigh.

should feed and clothe him gratuitously sometimes, and recruit him with our cordials, before we judge of him. The finest qualities of our nature, like the bloom on fruits, can be preserved only by the most delicate handling. Yet we do not treat ourselves nor one another thus tenderly.

Some of you, we all know, are poor, find it hard to live, are sometimes, as it were, gasping for breath. I have no doubt that some of you who read this book are unable to pay for all the dinners which you have actually eaten, or for the coats and shoes which are fast wearing or are already worn out, and have come to this page to spend borrowed or stolen time, robbing your creditors of an hour. It is very evident what mean and sneaking lives many of you live, for my sight has been whetted by experience; always on the limits, trying to get into business and trying to get out of debt, a very ancient slough, called by the Latins *æs alienum*, another's brass, for some of their coins were made of brass; still living, and dying, and buried by this other's brass; always promising to pay, promising to pay, to-morrow, and dying to-day, insolvent; seeking to curry favor, to get custom, by how many modes, only not state-prison offences; lying, flattering, voting, contracting yourselves into a nutshell of civility, or dilating into an atmosphere of thin and vaporous generosity, that you may persuade your neighbor to let you make his shoes, or his hat, or his coat, or his carriage, or import his groceries for him; making yourselves sick, that you may lay up something against a sick day, something to be tucked away in an old chest, or in a stocking behind the plastering, or, more safely, in the brick bank; no matter where, no matter how much or how little.

I sometimes wonder that we can be so frivolous, I may almost say, as to attend to the gross but somewhat foreign form of servitude called Negro Slavery, there are so many keen and subtle masters that enslave both north and south. It is hard to have a southern overseer; it is worse to have a northern one; but worst of all when you are the slave-driver of yourself. Talk of a divinity in man! Look at the teamster on the highway, wending to market by day or night; does any divinity stir within him? His highest duty to fodder and water his horses! What is his destiny to him compared with the shipping interests? Does not he drive for Squire Make-a-stir? How godlike, how immortal, is he? See how he cowers and sneaks, how vaguely all the day he fears, not being immortal nor divine, but the slave and prisoner of his own opinion of himself, a fame won by his own deeds. Public opinion is a weak tyrant compared with our own private opinion. What a man thinks of himself, that it is which determines, or rather indicates, his fate. Self-emancipation even in the West Indian provinces of the fancy and imagination,—what Wilberforce [7] is there to bring that about? Think, also, of the ladies of the land weaving toilet cushions against the last day, not to betray too green an interest in their fates! As if you could kill time without injuring eternity.

The mass of men lead lives of quiet desperation. What is called resignation is confirmed desperation. From the desperate city you go into the desperate country, and have to console yourself with the bravery of minks and muskrats. A stereotyped but unconscious despair is concealed even under what are called the games and amusements of mankind. There is no play in them, for this comes after work. But it is a characteristic of wisdom not to do desperate things.

When we consider what, to use the words of the catechism, is the chief end of man,[8] and what are the true necessaries and means of life, it appears as if men had deliberately chosen the common mode of living because they preferred it to any other. Yet they honestly think there is no choice left. But alert and healthy natures remember that the sun rose clear. It is never too late to give up our prejudices. No way of thinking or doing, however ancient, can be trusted without proof. What every body echoes or in silence passes by as true to-day may turn out to be falsehood tomorrow, mere smoke of opinion, which some had trusted for a cloud that would sprinkle fertilizing rain on their fields. What old people say you cannot do you try and find that you can. Old deeds for old people, and new deeds for new. Old people did not know enough once, perchance, to fetch fresh fuel to keep the fire a-going; new people put a little dry wood under a pot, and are whirled round the globe with the speed of birds, in a way to kill old people, as the phrase is. Age is no better, hardly so well, qualified for an instructor as youth, for it has not profited so much as it has lost. One may almost doubt if the wisest man has learned any thing of absolute value by living. Practically, the old have no very important advice to give the young, their own experience has been so partial, and their lives have been such miserable failures, for private reasons, as they must believe; and it may be that they have some faith left which belies that experience, and they are only less young than they were. I have lived some thirty years on this planet, and I have yet to hear the first syllable of valuable or even earnest advice from my seniors. They have told me nothing, and probably cannot tell me any thing, to the purpose. Here is life, an experiment to a great extent untried by me; but it does not avail me that they have tried it. If I have any experience which

7. William Wilberforce (1759–1833), leader of the anti-slavery forces in England.

8. See response—"To glorify God, and to enjoy Him forever." *Westminster Shorter Catechism.*

I think valuable, I am sure to reflect that this my Mentors [9] said nothing about. * * *

In any weather, at any hour of the day or night, I have been anxious to improve the nick of time, and notch it on my stick too; to stand on the meeting of two eternities, the past and future, which is precisely the present moment; to toe that line. You will pardon some obscurities, for there are more secrets in my trade than in most men's, and yet not voluntarily kept, but inseparable from its very nature. I would gladly tell all that I know about it, and never paint "No Admittance" on my gate.

I long ago lost a hound, a bay horse, and a turtle-dove, and am still on their trail. Many are the travellers I have spoken concerning them, describing their tracks and what calls they answered to. I have met one or two who had heard the hound, and the tramp of the horse, and even seen the dove disappear behind a cloud, and they seemed as anxious to recover them as if they had lost them themselves.

To anticipate, not the sunrise and the dawn merely, but, if possible, Nature herself! How many mornings, summer and winter, before yet any neighbor was stirring about his business, have I been about mine! No doubt, many of my townsmen have met me returning from this enterprise, farmers starting for Boston in the twilight, or woodchoppers going to their work. It is true, I never assisted the sun materially in his rising, but, doubt not, it was of the last importance only to be present at it.

So many autumn, ay, and winter days, spent outside the town, trying to hear what was in the wind, to hear and carry it express! I well-nigh sunk all my capital in it, and lost my own breath into the bargain, running in the face of it. If it had concerned either of the political parties, depend upon it, it would have appeared in the Gazette with the earliest intelligence. At other times watching from the observatory of some cliff or tree, to telegraph any new arrival; or waiting at evening on the hill-tops for the sky to fall, that I might catch something, though I never caught much, and that, manna-wise, would dissolve again in the sun.

For a long time I was reporter to a journal,[1] of no very wide circulation, whose editor has never yet seen fit to print the bulk of my contributions, and, as is too common with writers, I got only my labor for my pains. However, in this case my pains were their own reward.

For many years I was self-appointed inspector of snow storms

---

9. Engaged in the siege of Troy, Odysseus chose Mentor as guardian for his son Telemachus; hence, "mentor" signifies a wise teacher. See Homer's *Odyssey*.

1. Speaking whimsically, he had "reported" to his own "journal" since his Harvard days; also to *The Dial* of the Transcendental Club (1840–1844).

and rain storms, and did my duty faithfully; surveyor, if not of highways, then of forest paths and all across-lot routes, keeping them open, and ravines bridged and passable at all seasons, where the public heel had testified to their utility.

I have looked after the wild stock of the town, which give a faithful herdsman a good deal of trouble by leaping fences; and I have had an eye to the unfrequented nooks and corners of the farm; though I did not always know whether Jonas or Solomon worked in a particular field to-day; that was none of my business. I have watered the red huckleberry, the sand cherry and the nettle tree, the red pine and the black ash, the white grape and the yellow violet, which might have withered else in dry seasons.

In short, I went on thus for a long time, I may say it without boasting, faithfully minding my business, till it became more and more evident that my townsmen would not after all admit me into the list of town officers, nor make my place a sinecure with a moderate allowance. My accounts, which I can swear to have kept faithfully, I have, indeed, never got audited, still less accepted, still less paid and settled. However, I have not set my heart on that. * * *

Near the end of March, 1845, I borrowed an axe and went down to the woods by Walden Pond, nearest to where I intended to build my house, and began to cut down some tall arrowy white pines, still in their youth, for timber. It is difficult to begin without borrowing, but perhaps it is the most generous course thus to permit your fellow-men to have an interest in your enterprise. The owner of the axe, as he released his hold on it, said that it was the apple of his eye; but I returned it sharper than I received it. It was a pleasant hillside where I worked, covered with pine woods, through which I looked out on the pond, and a small open field in the woods where pines and hickories were springing up. The ice in the pond was not yet dissolved, though there were some open spaces, and it was all dark colored and saturated with water. There were some slight flurries of snow during the days that I worked there; but for the most part when I came out on to the railroad, on my way home, its yellow sand heap stretched away gleaming in the hazy atmosphere, and the rails shone in the spring sun, and I heard the lark and pewee and other birds already come to commence another year with us. They were pleasant spring days, in which the winter of man's discontent [2] was thawing as well as the earth, and the life that had lain torpid began to stretch itself. One day, when my axe had come off and I had cut a green hickory for a wedge, driving it with a stone, and had placed the whole to soak

2. *Cf.* Shakespeare, *Richard III,* I, 1, line 1, "Now is the winter of our discontent / made glorious summer by this sun of York."

in a pond hole in order to swell the wood, I saw a striped snake run into the water, and he lay on the bottom, apparently without inconvenience, as long as I staid there, or more than a quarter of an hour; perhaps because he had not yet fairly come out of the torpid state. It appeared to me that for a like reason men remain in their present low and primitive condition; but if they should feel the influence of the spring of springs arousing them, they would of necessity rise to a higher and more ethereal life. I had previously seen the snakes in frosty mornings in my path with portions of their bodies still numb and inflexible, waiting for the sun to thaw them. On the 1st of April it rained and melted the ice, and in the early part of the day, which was very foggy, I heard a stray goose groping about over the pond and cackling as if lost, or like the spirit of the fog.

So I went on for some days cutting and hewing timber, and also studs and rafters, all with my narrow axe, not having many communicable or scholar-like thoughts, singing to myself,—

> Men say they know many things;
> But lo! they have taken wings,—
> The arts and sciences,
> And a thousand appliances;
> The wind that blows
> Is all that any body knows.

I hewed the main timbers six inches square, most of the studs on two sides only, and the rafters and floor timbers on one side, leaving the rest of the bark on, so that they were just as straight and much stronger than sawed ones. Each stick was carefully mortised or tenoned by its stump, for I had borrowed other tools by this time. My days in the woods were not very long ones; yet I usually carried my dinner of bread and butter, and read the newspaper in which it was wrapped, at noon, sitting amid the green pine boughs which I had cut off, and to my bread was imparted some of their fragrance, for my hands were covered with a thick coat of pitch. Before I had done I was more the friend than the foe of the pine tree, though I had cut down some of them, having become better acquainted with it. Sometimes a rambler in the wood was attracted by the sound of my axe, and we chatted pleasantly over the chips which I had made.

By the middle of April, for I made no haste in my work, but rather made the most of it, my house was framed and ready for the raising. I had already bought the shanty of James Collins, an Irishman who worked on the Fitchburg Railroad, for boards. James Collins' shanty was considered an uncommonly fine one. When I called to see it. he was not at home. I walked about the outside, at first unobserved from within, the window was so deep and high. It was of small dimensions, with a peaked cottage roof, and not much else to be seen, the dirt being raised five feet all around as if it were a compost heap. The roof was the soundest part, though a good deal warped and made brittle by the sun. Doorsill there was none, but a perennial passage for the hens under the door board. Mrs. C. came to the door and asked me to view it from the inside. The hens were driven in by my approach. It was dark, and had a dirt floor for the most part, dank, clammy, and aguish, only here a board and there a board which would not bear removal. She lighted a lamp to show me the inside of the roof and the walls, and also that the board floor extended under the bed, warning me not to step into the cellar, a sort of dust hole two feet deep. In her own words, they were "good boards overhead, good boards all around, and a good window,"—of two whole squares originally, only the cat had passed out that way lately. There was a stove, a bed, and a place to sit, an infant in the house where it was born, a silk parasol, gilt-framed looking-glass, and a patent new coffee mill nailed to an oak sapling, all told. The bargain was soon concluded, for James had in the mean while returned. I to pay four dollars and twenty-five cents to-night, he to vacate at five to-morrow morning, selling to nobody else meanwhile: I to take possession at six. It were well, he said, to be there early, and anticipate certain indistinct but wholly unjust claims on the score of ground rent and fuel. This he assured me was the only encumbrance. At six I passed him and his family on the road. One large bundle held their all,—bed, coffee-mill, looking-glass, hens, —all but the cat, she took to the woods and became a wild cat, and, as I learned afterward, trod in a trap set for woodchucks, and so became a dead cat at last.

I took down this dwelling the same morning, drawing the nails, and removed it to the pond side by small cartloads, spreading the boards on the grass there to bleach and warp back again in the sun. One early thrush gave me a note or two as I drove along the woodland path. I was informed treacherously by a young Patrick that neighbor Seeley, an Irishman, in the intervals of the carting, transferred the still tolerable, straight, and drivable nails, staples, and spikes to his pocket, and then stood when I came back to pass the time of day, and look freshly up, unconcerned, with spring thoughts, at the devastation; there being a dearth of work, as he said. He was there to represent spectatordom, and help make this seemingly insignificant event one with the removal of the gods of Troy.[3]

---

3. At the fall of Troy (*cf.* Homer's *Iliad*) the Greek conquerors, Ulysses and Diomede, carried off the images of the gods, including the Palladium. (Pallas was the patroness of Troy.)

I dug my cellar in the side of a hill sloping to the south, where a woodchuck had formerly dug his burrow, down through sumach and blackberry roots, and the lowest stain of vegetation, six feet square by seven deep, to a fine sand where potatoes would not freeze in any winter. The sides were left shelving, and not stoned; but the sun having never shone on them, the sand still keeps its place. It was but two hours' work. I took particular pleasure in this breaking of ground, for in almost all latitudes men dig into the earth for an equable temperature. Under the most splendid house in the city is still to be found the cellar where they store their roots as of old, and long after the superstructure has disappeared posterity remark its dent in the earth. The house is still but a sort of porch at the entrance of a burrow.

At length, in the beginning of May, with the help of some of my acquaintances, rather to improve so good an occasion for neighborliness than from any necessity, I set up the frame of my house. No man was ever more honored in the character of his raisers than I. They are destined, I trust, to assist at the raising of loftier structures one day.[4] I began to occupy my house on the 4th of July, as soon as it was boarded and roofed, for the boards were carefully feather-edged and lapped, so that it was perfectly impervious to rain; but before boarding I laid the foundation of a chimney at one end, bringing two cartloads of stones up the hill from the pond in my arms. I built the chimney after my hoeing in the fall, before a fire became necessary for warmth, doing my cooking in the mean while out of doors on the ground, early in the morning: which mode I still think is in some respects more convenient and agreeable than the usual one. When it stormed before my bread was baked, I fixed a few boards over the fire, and sat under them to watch my loaf, and passed some pleasant hours in that way. In those days, when my hands were much employed, I read but little, but the least scraps of paper which lay on the ground, my holder, or tablecloth, afforded me as much entertainment, in fact answered the same purpose as the Iliad. * * *

Before winter I built a chimney, and shingled the sides of my house, which were already impervious to rain, with imperfect and sappy shingles made of the first slice of the log, whose edges I was obliged to straighten with a plane.

I have thus a tight shingled and plastered house, ten feet wide by fifteen long, and eight-feet posts, with a garret and a closet, a large window on each side, two trap doors, one door at the end, and a brick fireplace opposite. The exact cost of my house, paying the usual price for such materials as I used, but not counting

---

4. According to tradition his house-raisers included Emerson, Alcott, and W. E. Channing.

the work, all of which was done by myself, was as follows; and I give the details because very few are able to tell exactly what their houses cost, and fewer still, if any, the separate cost of the various materials which compose them:—

Boards,	. . . .	$8 03½,	mostly shanty boards.
Refuse shingles for roof and sides,	. .	4 00	
Laths,	. . . .	1 25	
Two second-hand windows with glass,	.	2 43	
One thousand old brick,	. . . . .	4 00	
Two casks of lime,	. . . .	2 40	That was high.
Hair,	. . . .	0 31	More than I needed.
Mantle-tree iron,	. . . .	0 15	
Nails,	. . . .	3 90	
Hinges and screws,	. . . .	0 14	
Latch,	. . . .	0 10	
Chalk,	. . . .	0 01	
Transportation,	. . . .	1 40	} I carried a good part on my back.
In all,	. . . .	$28 12½	

These are all the materials excepting the timber, stones and sand, which I claimed by squatter's right. I have also a small wood-shed adjoining, made chiefly of the stuff which was left after building the house.

I intend to build me a house which will surpass any on the main street in Concord in grandeur and luxury, as soon as it pleases me as much and will cost me no more than my present one.

I thus found that the student who wishes for a shelter can obtain one for a lifetime at an expense not greater than the rent which he now pays annually. If I seem to boast more than is becoming, my excuse is that I brag for humanity rather than for myself; and my shortcomings and inconsistencies do not affect the truth of my statement. Notwithstanding much cant and hypocrisy, —chaff which I find it difficult to separate from my wheat, but for which I am as sorry as any man,—I will breathe freely and stretch myself in this respect, it is such a relief to both the moral and physical system; and I am resolved that I will not through humility become the devil's attorney. I will endeavor to speak a good word for the truth. At Cambridge College [5] the mere rent of a student's room, which is only a little larger than my own, is thirty dollars each year, though the corporation had the advantage of building thirty-two side by side and under one roof, and the occupant suffers the inconvenience of many and noisy neighbors, and perhaps a residence in the fourth story. I cannot but think

5. At Harvard College in Cambridge Thoreau had a small room on the fourth (top) floor of Hollis dormitory, worked part time for his expenses, and was dependent on relatives for additional assistance.

that if we had more true wisdom in these respects, not only less education would be needed, because, forsooth, more would already have been acquired, but the pecuniary expense of getting an education would in a great measure vanish. Those conveniences which the student requires at Cambridge or elsewhere cost him or somebody else ten times as great a sacrifice of life as they would with proper management on both sides. Those things for which the most money is demanded are never the things which the student most wants. Tuition, for instance, is an important item in the term bill, while for the far more valuable education which he gets by associating with the most cultivated of his contemporaries no charge is made. The mode of founding a college is, commonly, to get up a subscription of dollars and cents, and then following blindly the principles of a division of labor to its extreme, a principle which should never be followed but with circumspection,—to call in a contractor who makes this a subject of speculation, and he employs Irishmen or other operatives actually to lay the foundations, while the students that are to be are said to be fitting themselves for it; and for these oversights successive generations have to pay. I think that it would be *better than this*, for the students, or those who desire to be benefited by it, even to lay the foundation themselves. The student who secures his coveted leisure and retirement by systematically shirking any labor necessary to man obtains but an ignoble and unprofitable leisure, defrauding himself of the experience which alone can make leisure fruitful. "But," says one, "you do not mean that the students should go to work with their hands instead of their heads?" I do not mean that exactly, but I mean something which he might think a good deal like that; I mean that they should not *play* life, or *study* it merely, while the community supports them at this expensive game, but earnestly *live* it from beginning to end. How could youths better learn to live than by at once trying the experiment of living? Methinks this would exercise their minds as much as mathematics. If I wished a boy to know something about the arts and sciences, for instance, I would not pursue the common course, which is merely to send him into the neighborhood of some professor, where any thing is professed and practised but the art of life;—to survey the world through a telescope or a microscope, and never with the natural eye; to study chemistry, and not learn how his bread is made, or mechanics, and not learn how it is earned; to discover new satellites to Neptune, and not detect the motes in his eyes, or to what vagabond he is a satellite himself; or to be devoured by the monsters that swarm all around him, while contemplating the monsters in a drop of vinegar. Which would have advanced the most at the end of a month,—the boy who had made his own jackknife from the ore which he had dug and smelted, reading as much as would be necessary for this,—or the boy who had attended the lectures on metallurgy at the Institute in the mean while, and had received a Rogers' penknife [6] from his father? Which would be most likely to cut his fingers? . . . To my astonishment I was informed on leaving college that I had studied navigation!—why, if I had taken one turn down the harbor I should have known more about it. Even the *poor* student studies and is taught only *political* economy, while that economy of living which is synonymous with philosophy is not even sincerely professed in our colleges. The consequence is, that while he is reading Adam Smith, Ricardo, and Say,[7] he runs his father in debt irretrievably.

irony

As with our colleges, so with a hundred "modern improvements;" there is an illusion about them; there is not always a positive advance. The devil goes on exacting compound interest to the last for his early share and numerous succeeding investments in them. Our inventions are wont to be pretty toys, which distract our attention from serious things. They are but improved means to an unimproved end, an end which it was already but too easy to arrive at; as railroads lead to Boston or New York. We are in great haste to construct a magnetic telegraph from Maine to Texas; but Maine and Texas, it may be, have nothing important to communicate. Either is in such a predicament as the man who was earnest to be introduced to a distinguished deaf woman, but when he was presented, and one end of her ear trumpet was put into his hand, had nothing to say.[8] As if the main object were to talk fast and not to talk sensibly. We are eager to tunnel under the Atlantic and bring the old world some weeks nearer to the new; but perchance the first news that will leak through into the broad, flapping American ear will be that the Princess Adelaide [9] has the whooping cough. After all, the man whose horse trots a mile in a minute does not carry the most important messages; he is not an evangelist, nor does he come round eating locusts and wild honey.[1] I doubt if Flying Childers [2] ever carried a peck of corn to mill. * * *

For more than five years I maintained myself thus solely by the labor of my hands, and I found, that by working about six

---

6. An English knife of famous Sheffield steel.
7. The Scotsman Adam Smith (1723–1790) in *The Wealth of Nations* (1776) formulated the "classical" economics; the Englishman David Ricardo (1772–1823) and the Frenchman Jean Baptiste Say (1767–1832) both broadened its applications.
8. The story is told of Harriet Martineau, a distinguished novelist and

economist, who visited Concord in 1836.
9. When Thoreau was writing these passages in 1846 the newspapers were reporting the health of Adelaide, Princess of Orleans, sister of King Louis Philippe of France. She died the next year.
1. Referring to the evangelist, John the Baptist; *cf.* Matt. 3:1–4.
2. An English race horse who currently held the record for speed.

weeks in a year, I could meet all the expenses of living. The whole of my winters, as well as most of my summers, I had free and clear for study. I have thoroughly tried school-keeping, and found that my expenses were in proportion, or rather out of proportion, to my income, for I was obliged to dress and train, not to say think and believe, accordingly, and I lost my time into the bargain. As I did not teach for the good of my fellow-men, but simply for a livelihood, this was a failure. I have tried trade; but I found that it would take ten years to get under way in that, and that then I should probably be on my way to the devil. I was actually afraid that I might by that time be doing what is called a good business. When formerly I was looking about to see what I could do for a living, some sad experience in conforming to the wishes of friends being fresh in my mind to tax my ingenuity, I thought often and seriously of picking huckleberries; that surely I could do, and its small profits might suffice,—for my greatest skill has been to want but little,—so little capital it required, so little distraction from my wonted moods, I foolishly thought. While my acquaintances went unhesitatingly into trade or the professions, I contemplated this occupation as most like theirs; ranging the hills all summer to pick the berries which came in my way, and thereafter carelessly dispose of them; so, to keep the flocks of Admetus.[3] I also dreamed that I might gather the wild herbs, or carry evergreens to such villagers as loved to be reminded of the woods, even to the city, by hay-cart loads. But I have since learned that trade curses every thing it handles; and though you trade in messages from heaven, the whole curse of trade attaches to the business.

As I preferred some things to others, and especially valued my freedom, as I could fare hard and yet succeed well, I did not wish to spend my time in earning rich carpets or other fine furniture, or delicate cookery, or a house in the Grecian or the Gothic style just yet. If there are any to whom it is no interruption to acquire these things, and who know how to use them when acquired, I relinquish to them the pursuit. Some are "industrious," and appear to love labor for its own sake, or perhaps because it keeps them out of worse mischief; to such I have at present nothing to say. Those who would not know what to do with more leisure than they now enjoy, I might advise to work twice as hard as they do,— work till they pay for themselves, and get their free papers. For myself I found that the occupation of a day-laborer was the most independent of any, especially as it required only thirty to forty days in a year to support one. The laborer's day ends with the going down of the sun, and he is then free to devote himself to his

---

3. Mythical Greek king of Pherae in Thessaly, hence associated with pastoral themes.

chosen pursuit, independent of his labor; but his employer, who speculates from month to month, has no respite from one end of the year to the other.

In short, I am convinced, both by faith and experience, that to maintain one's self on this earth is not a hardship but a pastime,[4] if we will live simply and wisely; as the pursuits of the simpler nations are still the sports of the more artificial. It is not necessary that a man should earn his living by the sweat of his brow, unless he sweats easier than I do.

One young man of my acquaintance, who has inherited some acres, told me that he thought he should live as I did, *if he had the means.* I would not have any one adopt *my* mode of living on any account; for, beside that before he has fairly learned it I may have found out another for myself, I desire that there may be as many different persons in the world as possible; but I would have each one be very careful to find out and pursue *his own* way, and not his father's or his mother's or his neighbor's instead. The youth may build or plant or sail, only let him not be hindered from doing that which he tells me he would like to do. It is by a mathematical point only that we are wise, as the sailor or the fugitive slave keeps the polestar in his eye; but that is sufficient guidance for all our life. We may not arrive at our port within a calculable period, but we would preserve the true course.

Undoubtedly, in this case, what is true for one is truer still for a thousand, as a large house is not proportionally more expensive than a small one, since one roof may cover, one cellar underlie, and one wall separate several apartments. But for my part, I preferred the solitary dwelling. Moreover, it will commonly be cheaper to build the whole yourself than to convince another of the advantage of the common wall; and when you have done this, the common partition, to be much cheaper, must be a thin one, and that other may prove a bad neighbor, and also not keep his side in repair. The only coöperation which is commonly possible is exceedingly partial and superficial; and what little true coöperation there is, is as if it were not, being a harmony inaudible to men. If a man has faith he will coöperate with equal faith every where; if he has not faith, he will continue to live like the rest of the world, whatever company he is joined to. To coöperate, in the highest as well as the lowest sense, means *to get our living together.* I heard it proposed lately that two young men should travel together over the world, the one without money, earning his means as he went, before the mast and behind the plough, the

4. A familiar theory of Charles Fourier (1772–1837), French founder of the agrarian coöperatives later represented in the United States by Brook Farm and Fruitlands, projects of the transcendentalists.

other carrying a bill of exchange in his pocket. It was easy to see that they could not long be companions or coöperate, since one would not *operate* at all. They would part at the first interesting crisis in their adventures. Above all, as I have implied, the man who goes alone can start to-day; but he who travels with another must wait till that other is ready, and it may be a long time before they get off.

But all this is very selfish, I have heard some of my townsmen say. I confess that I have hitherto indulged very little in philanthropic enterprises. I have made some sacrifices to a sense of duty, and among others have sacrificed this pleasure also. There are those who have used all their arts to persuade me to undertake the support of some poor family in the town; and if I had nothing to do,—for the devil finds employment for the idle,[5]—I might try my hand at some such pastime as that. However, when I have thought to indulge myself in this respect, and lay their Heaven under an obligation by maintaining certain poor persons in all respects as comfortably as I maintain myself, and have even ventured so far as to make them the offer, they have one and all unhesitatingly preferred to remain poor. While my townsmen and women are devoted in so many ways to the good of their fellows, I trust that one at least may be spared to other and less humane pursuits. You must have a genius for charity as well as for any thing else. As for Doing-good, that is one of the professions which are full. Moreover, I have tried it fairly, and, strange as it may seem, am satisfied that it does not agree with my constitution. Probably I should not consciously and deliberately forsake my particular calling to do the good which society demands of me, to save the universe from annihilation; and I believe that a like but infinitely greater steadfastness elsewhere is all that now preserves it. But I would not stand between any man and his genius; and to him who does this work, which I decline, with his whole heart and soul and life, I would say, Persevere, even if the world call it doing evil, as it is most likely they will. * * *

There is no odor so bad as that which arises from goodness tainted. It is human, it is divine, carrion. If I knew for a certainty that a man was coming to my house with the conscious design of doing me good, I should run for my life, as from that dry and parching wind of the African deserts called the simoom, which fills the mouth and nose and ears and eyes with dust till you are suffocated, for fear that I should get some of his good done to me,—some of its virus mingled with my blood. No,—in this case

5. *Cf.* Isaac Watts, *Divine Songs*, XX, for the source of this quotation, popular in Thoreau's youth.

I would rather suffer evil the natural way. A man is not a good *man* to me because he will feed me if I should be starving, or warm me if I should be freezing, or pull me out of a ditch if I should ever fall into one. I can find you a Newfoundland dog that will do as much. Philanthropy is not love for one's fellow-man in the broadest sense. Howard [6] was no doubt an exceedingly kind and worthy man in his way, and has his reward; but, comparatively speaking, what are a hundred Howards to us, if their philanthropy do not help *us* in our best estate, when we are most worthy to be helped? I never heard a philanthropic meeting in which it was sincerely proposed to do any good to me, or the like of me. * * *

I believe that what so saddens the reformer is not his sympathy with his fellows in distress, but, though he be the holiest son of God, is his private ail. Let this be righted, let the spring come to him, the morning rise over his couch, and he will forsake his generous companions without apology. My excuse for not lecturing against the use of tobacco is, that I never chewed it; that is a penalty which reformed tobacco-chewers have to pay; though there are things enough I have chewed, which I could lecture against. If you should ever be betrayed into any of these philanthropies, do not let your left hand know what your right hand does,[7] for it is not worth knowing. Rescue the drowning and tie your shoe-strings. Take your time, and set about some free labor.

Our manners have been corrupted by communication with the saints. Our hymn-books resound with a melodious cursing of God and enduring him forever.[8] One would say that even the prophets and redeemers had rather consoled the fears than confirmed the hopes of man. There is nowhere recorded a simple and irrepressible satisfaction with the gift of life, any memorable praise of God. All health and success does me good, however far off and withdrawn it may appear; all disease and failure helps to make me sad and does me evil, however much sympathy it may have with me or I with it. If, then, we would indeed restore mankind by truly Indian, botanic, magnetic, or natural means, let us first be as simple and well as Nature ourselves, dispel the clouds which hang over our own brows, and take up a little life into our pores. Do not stay to be an overseer of the poor, but endeavor to become one of the worthies of the world.

I read in the Gulistan, or Flower Garden, of Sheik Sadi of Shiraz,[9] that "They asked a wise man, saying; Of the many celebrated trees which the Most High God has created lofty and umbrageous,

6. John Howard (1726–1790), English leader of prison reform.
7. *Cf.* Matt. 6:3.
8. *Cf. Westminster Shorter Catechism.*

9. Sadi (Muslih-ud-Din Saadi, 1184–1291), Persian poet; his *Gulistan* was well known to American and European writers of the romantic period.

they call none azad, or free, excepting the cypress, which bears no fruit; what mystery is there in this? He replied; Each has its appropriate produce, and appointed season, during the continuance of which it is fresh and blooming, and during their absence dry and withered; to neither of which states is the cypress exposed, being always flourishing; and of this nature are the azads, or religious independents.—Fix not thy heart on that which is transitory; for the Dijlah, or Tigris, will continue to flow through Bagdad after the race of caliphs [1] is extinct: if thy hand has plenty, be liberal as the date tree; but if it affords nothing to give away, be an azad, or free man, like the cypress." * * *

Where I Lived, and What I Lived for

* * * I do not propose to write an ode to dejection, but to brag as lustily as chanticleer in the morning, standing on his roost, if only to wake my neighbors up.

When first I took up my abode in the woods, that is, began to spend my nights as well as days there, which, by accident, was on Independence day, or the fourth of July, 1845, my house was not finished for winter, but was merely a defence against the rain, without plastering or chimney, the walls being of rough weather-stained boards, with wide chinks, which made it cool at night. The upright white hewn studs and freshly planed door and window casings gave it a clean and airy look, especially in the morning, when its timbers were saturated with dew, so that I fancied that by noon some sweet gum would exude from them. To my imagination it retained throughout the day more or less of this auroral character, reminding me of a certain house on a mountain which I had visited the year before. This was an airy and unplastered cabin, fit to entertain a travelling god, and where a goddess might trail her garments. The winds which passed over my dwelling were such as sweep over the ridges of mountains, bearing the broken strains, or celestial parts only, of terrestrial music. The morning wind forever blows, the poem of creation is uninterrupted; but few are the ears that hear it. Olympus is but the outside of the earth every where.

The only house I had been the owner of before, if I except a boat, was a tent, which I used occasionally when making excursions in the summer, and this is still rolled up in my garret; but the boat, after passing from hand to hand, has gone down the stream of time. With this more substantial shelter about me, I had made some progress toward settling in the world. This frame, so slightly clad, was a sort of crystallization around me, and reacted

1. Bagdad, on the Tigris River, modern capital of Iraq, was an ancient Moslem city ruled by a caliph.

on the builder. +he+ +tent+ It was suggestive somewhat as a picture in outlines. I did not need to go out doors to take the air, for the atmosphere within had lost none of its freshness. It was not so much within doors as behind a door where I sat, even in the rainiest weather. The Harivansa [2] says, "An abode without birds is like a meat without seasoning." Such was not my abode, for I found myself suddenly neighbor to the birds; not by having imprisoned one, but having caged myself near them. I was not only nearer to some of those which commonly frequent the garden and the orchard, but to those wilder and more thrilling songsters of the forest which never, or rarely, serenade a villager,—the wood-thrush, the veery, the scarlet tanger, the field-sparrow, the whippoorwill, and many others.

I was seated by the shore of a small pond, about a mile and a half south of the village of Concord and somewhat higher than it, in the midst of an extensive wood between that town and Lincoln, and about two miles south of that our only field known to fame, Concord Battle Ground; but I was so low in the woods that the opposite shore, half a mile off, like the rest, covered with wood, was my most distant horizon. For the first week, whenever I looked out on the pond it impressed me like a tarn high up on the side of a mountain, its bottom far above the surface of other lakes, and, as the sun arose, I saw it throwing off its nightly clothing of mist, and here and there, by degrees, its soft ripples or its smooth reflecting surface was revealed, while the mists, like ghosts, were stealthily withdrawing in every direction into the woods, as at the breaking up of some nocturnal conventicle. The very dew seemed to hang upon the trees later into the day than usual, as on the sides of mountains.

This small lake was of most value as a neighbor in the intervals of a gentle rain storm in August, when, both air and water being perfectly still, but the sky overcast, mid-afternoon had all the serenity of evening, and the wood-thrush sang around, and was heard from shore to shore. A lake like this is never smoother than at such a time; and the clear portion of the air above it being shallow and darkened by clouds, the water, full of light and reflections, becomes a lower heaven itself so much the more important. From a hill top near by, where the wood had been recently cut off, there was a pleasing vista southward across the pond, through a wide indentation in the hills which form the shore there, where their opposite sides sloping toward each other suggested a stream flowing out in that direction through a wooded valley, but stream there was none. That way I looked between and over the

2. A fifth-century Hindu epic of the deeds and teachings of Krishma, the reincarnation of the god Vishnu.

near green hills to some distant and higher ones in the horizon, tinged with blue. Indeed, by standing on tiptoe I could catch a glimpse of some of the peaks of the still bluer and more distant mountain ranges in the north-west, those true-blue coins from heaven's own mint, and also of some portion of the village. But in other directions, even from this point, I could not see over or beyond the woods which surrounded me. It is well to have some water in your neighborhood, to give buoyancy to and float the earth. One value even of the smallest well is, that when you look into it you see that earth is not continent but insular. This is as important as that it keeps butter cool. When I looked across the pond from this peak toward the Sudbury meadows, which in time of flood I distinguished elevated perhaps by a mirage in their seething valley, like a coin in a basin, all the earth beyond the pond appeared like a thin crust insulated and floated even by this small sheet of intervening water, and I was reminded that this on which I dwelt was but *dry land*. * * *

I went to the woods because I wished to live deliberately, to front only the essential facts of life, and see if I could not learn what it had to teach, and not, when I came to die, discover that I had not lived. I did not wish to live what was not life, living is so dear; nor did I wish to practise resignation, unless it was quite necessary. I wanted to live deep and suck out all the marrow of life, to live so sturdily and Spartan-like as to put to rout all that was not life, to cut a broad swath and shave close, to drive life into a corner, and reduce it to its lowest terms, and, if it proved to be mean, why then to get the whole and genuine meanness of it, and publish its meanness to the world; or if it were sublime, to know it by experience, and be able to give a true account of it in my next excursion. For most men, it appears to me, are in a strange uncertainty about it, whether it is of the devil or of God, and have *somewhat hastily* concluded that it is the chief end of man here to "glorify God and enjoy him forever." [3]

Still we live meanly, like ants; though the fable tells us that we were long ago changed into men; like pygmies we fight with cranes; [4] it is error upon error, and clout upon clout, and our best virtue has for its occasion a superfluous and evitable wretchedness. Our life is frittered away by detail. An honest man has hardly need to count more than his ten fingers, or in extreme cases he may add his ten toes, and lump the rest. Simplicity, simplicity, simplicity! I say, let your affairs be as two or three, and not a hundred or a thousand; instead of a million count half a dozen, and

---

3. In an earlier passage he satirized the creed (*Westminster Shorter Catechism*); here he quotes it straight but with evident disapprobation.

4. Homer, *Iliad*, Book III, 5, tells of pygmies so tiny that they were menaced by flights of cranes.

keep your accounts on your thumb nail. In the midst of this chopping sea of civilized life, such are the clouds and storms and quicksands and thousand-and-one items to be allowed for, that a man has to live, if he would not founder and go to the bottom and not make his port at all, by dead reckoning,[5] and he must be a great calculator indeed who succeeds. Simplify, simplify. Instead of three meals a day, if it be necessary eat but one; instead of a hundred dishes, five; and reduce other things in proportion. Our life is like a German Confederacy,[6] made up of petty states, with its boundary forever fluctuating, so that even a German cannot tell you how it is bounded at any moment. The nation itself, with all its so called internal improvements, which, by the way, are all external and superficial, is just such an unwieldy and overgrown establishment, cluttered with furniture and tripped up by its own traps, ruined by luxury and heedless expense, by want of calculation and a worthy aim, as the million households in the land; and the only cure for it as for them is in a rigid economy, a stern and more than Spartan simplicity of life and elevation of purpose. It lives too fast. Men think that it is essential that the *Nation* have commerce, and export ice, and talk through a telegraph, and ride thirty miles an hour, without a doubt, whether *they* do or not; but whether we should live like baboons or like men, is a little uncertain. If we do not get out sleepers,[7] and forge rails, and devote days and nights to the work, but go to tinkering upon our *lives* to improve *them*, who will build railroads? And if railroads are not built, how shall we get to heaven in season? But if we stay at home and mind our business, who will want railroads? We do not ride on the railroad; it rides upon us. Did you ever think what those sleepers are that underlie the railroad? Each one is a man, an Irishman, or a Yankee man. The rails are laid on them, and they are covered with sand, and the cars run smoothly over them. They are sound sleepers, I assure you. And every few years a new lot is laid down and run over; so that, if some have the pleasure of riding on a rail, others have the misfortune to be ridden upon. And when they run over a man that is walking in his sleep, a supernumerary sleeper in the wrong position, and wake him up, they suddenly stop the cars, and make a hue and cry about it, as if this were an exception. I am glad to know that it takes a gang of men for every five miles to keep the sleepers down and level in their beds as it is, for this is a sign that they may sometime get up again.

5. In navigation the calculation of a ship's position by distance, speed, and direction sailed, not by more accurate astronomical observation.

6. A confederation of German states, effected in 1815; was not consolidated until 1866, and became the German Empire under Bismark only in 1871.

7. Ties.

Why should we live with such hurry and waste of life? We are determined to be starved before we are hungry. Men say that a stitch in time saves nine, and so they take a thousand stitches to-day to save nine to-morrow. As for *work*, we haven't any of any consequence. We have the Saint Vitus' dance, and cannot possibly keep our heads still. If I should only give a few pulls at the parish bell-rope, as for a fire, that is, without setting the bell,[8] there is hardly a man on his farm in the outskirts of Concord, notwithstanding that press of engagements which was his excuse so many times this morning, nor a boy, nor a woman, I might almost say, but would forsake all and follow that sound, not mainly to save property from the flames, but, if we will confess the truth, much more to see it burn, since burn it must, and we, be it known, did not set it on fire,—or to see it put out, and have a hand in it, if that is done as handsomely; yes, even if it were the parish church itself. Hardly a man takes a half hour's nap after dinner, but when he wakes he holds up his head and asks, "What's the news?" as if the rest of mankind had stood his sentinels. Some give directions to be waked every half hour, doubtless for no other purpose; and then, to pay for it, they tell what they have dreamed. After a night's sleep the news is as indispensable as the breakfast. "Pray tell me any thing new that has happened to a man any where on this globe,"—and he reads it over his coffee and rolls, that a man has had his eyes gouged out this morning on the Wachito River;[9] never dreaming the while that he lives in the dark unfathomed mammoth cave of this world, and has but the rudiment of an eye himself.

For my part, I could easily do without the post-office. I think that there are very few important communications made through it. To speak critically, I never received more than one or two letters in my life—I wrote this some years ago—that were worth the postage. The penny-post is, commonly, an institution through which you seriously offer a man that penny for his thoughts which is so often safely offered in jest. And I am sure that I never read any memorable news in a newspaper. If we read of one man robbed, or murdered, or killed by accident, or one house burned, or one vessel wrecked, or one steamboat blown up, or one cow run over on the Western Railroad,[1] or one mad dog killed, or one lot of grasshoppers in the winter,—we never need read of another. One is enough. If you are acquainted with the principle, what do you care for a myriad instances and applications? To a philosopher all *news*, as it is called, is gossip, and they who edit and read it are

---

8. "Setting the bell" resulted from a complete rotation of the bell on its wheel.
9. Obviously at a great distance; the Ouachita begins in Arkansas and ends in Louisiana.
1. From Boston to Troy, N. Y.; later part of the Boston and Maine system.

old women over their tea. Yet not a few are greedy after this gossip. There was such a rush, as I hear, the other day at one of the offices to learn the foreign news by the last arrival, that several large squares of plate glass belonging to the establishment were broken by the pressure,—news which I seriously think a ready wit might write a twelvemonth or twelve years beforehand with sufficient accuracy. As for Spain, for instance, if you know how to throw in Don Carlos and the Infanta, and Don Pedro and Seville and Granada,[2] from time to time in the right proportions,—they may have changed the names a little since I saw the papers,—and serve up a bull-fight when other entertainments fail, it will be true to the letter, and give us as good an idea of the exact state or ruin of things in Spain as the most succinct and lucid reports under this head in the newspapers: and as for England, almost the last significant scrap of news from that quarter was the revolution of 1649; and if you have learned the history of her crops for an average year, you never need attend to that thing again, unless your speculations are of a merely pecuniary character. If one may judge who rarely looks into the newspapers, nothing new does ever happen in foreign parts, a French revolution not excepted.

What news! how much more important to know what that is which was never old! "Kieou-he-yu [3] (great dignitary of the state of Wei) sent a man to Khoung-tseu to know his news. Khoung-tseu caused the messenger to be seated near him, and questioned him in these terms: What is your master doing? The messenger answered with respect: My master desires to diminish the number of his faults, but he cannot accomplish it. The messenger being gone, the philosopher remarked: What a worthy messenger! What a worthy messenger!" The preacher, instead of vexing the ears of drowsy farmers on their day of rest at the end of the week,—for Sunday is the fit conclusion of an ill-spent week, and not the fresh and brave beginning of a new one,—with this one other draggle-tail of a sermon, should shout with thundering voice,—"Pause! Avast! Why so seeming fast, but deadly slow?"

Shams and delusions are esteemed for soundest truths, while reality is fabulous. If men would steadily observe realities only, and not allow themselves to be deluded, life, to compare it with such things as we know, would be like a fairy tale and the Arabian Nights' Entertainments. If we respected only what is inevitable and has a right to be, music and poetry would resound along the streets. When we are unhurried and wise, we perceive that only great and worthy things have any permanent and absolute exist-

2. The death of King Ferdinand in 1839 inspired two contenders, Don Carlos and Don Pedro; the Infanta, Princess Isabella, was proclaimed Queen in 1843.

3. *Cf.* Confucius, *Analects XIV*, 26, 1–2.

ence,—that petty fears and petty pleasures are but the shadow of the reality. This is always exhilarating and sublime. By closing the eyes and slumbering, and consenting to be deceived by shows, men establish and confirm their daily life of routine and habit every where, which still is built on purely illusory foundations. Children, who play life, discern its true law and relations more clearly than men, who fail to live it worthily, but who think that they are wiser by experience, that is, by failure. I have read in a Hindoo book, that "there was a king's son, who, being expelled in infancy from his native city, was brought up by a forester, and, growing up to maturity in that state, imagined himself to belong to the barbarous race with which he lived. One of his father's ministers having discovered him, revealed to him what he was, and the misconception of his character was removed, and he knew himself to be a prince. So soul," continues the Hindoo philosopher, "from the circumstances in which it is placed, mistakes its own character, until the truth is revealed to it by some holy teacher, and then it knows itself to be *Brahme*." [4] I perceive that we inhabitants of New England live this mean life that we do because our vision does not penetrate the surface of things. We think that that *is* which *appears* to be. If a man should walk through this town and see only the reality, where, think you, would the "Milldam" go to? If he should give us an account of the realities he beheld there, we should not recognize the place in his description. Look at a meeting-house, or a court-house, or a jail, or a shop, or a dwelling-house, and say what that thing really is before a true gaze, and they would all go to pieces in your account of them. Men esteem truth remote, in the outskirts of the system, behind the farthest star, before Adam and after the last man. In eternity there is indeed something true and sublime. But all these times and places and occasions are now and here. God himself culminates in the present moment, and will never be more divine in the lapse of all the ages. And we are enabled to apprehend at all what is sublime and noble only by the perpetual instilling and drenching of the reality that surrounds us. The universe constantly and obediently answers to our conceptions; whether we travel fast or slow, the track is laid for us. Let us spend our lives in conceiving then. The poet or the artist never yet had so fair and noble a design but some of his posterity at least could accomplish it.

Let us spend one day as deliberately as Nature, and not be thrown off the track by every nutshell and mosquito's wing that falls on the rails. Let us rise early and fast, or break fast, gently

<hr>

4. To the Hindu, God the Creator—but also the supreme essence or intelligence. *Cf.* the transcendental "Oversoul," Emerson's "Brahma," and notes above.

and without perturbation; let company come and let company go, let the bells ring and the children cry,—determined to make a day of it. Why should we knock under and go with the stream? Let us not be upset and overwhelmed in that terrible rapid and whirlpool called a dinner, situated in the meridian shallows. Weather this danger and you are safe, for the rest of the way is down hill. With unrelaxed nerves, with morning vigor, sail by it, looking another way, tied to the mast like Ulysses.[5] If the engine whistles, let it whistle till it is hoarse for its pains. If the bell rings, why should we run? We will consider what kind of music they are like. Let us settle ourselves, and work and wedge our feet downward through the mud and slush of opinion, and prejudice, and tradition, and delusion, and appearance, that alluvion which covers the globe, through Paris and London, through New York and Boston and Concord, through church and state, through poetry and philosophy and religion, till we come to a hard bottom and rocks in place, which we can call *reality*, and say, This is, and no mistake; and then begin, having a *point d'appui*,[6] below freshet and frost and fire, a place where you might found a wall or a state, or set a lamp-post safely, or perhaps a gauge, not a Nilometer,[7] but a Realo-meter, that future ages might know how deep a freshet of shams and appearances have gathered from time to time. If you stand right fronting and face to face to a fact, you will see the sun glimmer on both its surfaces, as if it were a cimeter, and feel its sweet edge dividing you through the heart and marrow, and so you will happily conclude your mortal career. Be it life or death, we crave only reality. If we are really dying, let us hear the rattle in our throats and feel cold in the extremities; if we are alive, let us go about our business.

Time is but the stream I go a-fishing in. I drink at it; but while I drink I see the sandy bottom and detect how shallow it is. Its thin current slides away, but eternity remains. I would drink deeper; fish in the sky, whose bottom is pebbly with stars. I cannot count one. I know not the first letter of the alphabet. I have always been regretting that I was not as wise as the day I was born. The intellect is a cleaver; it discerns and rifts its way into the secret of things. I do not wish to be any more busy with my hands than is necessary. My head is hands and feet. I feel all my best faculties concentrated in it. My instinct tells me that my head is an organ for burrowing, as some creatures use their snout and fore-paws, and with it I would mine and burrow my way through these

---

5. Mariners bewitched by the Sirens' songs often leaped to destruction, so Ulysses (Odysseus) has himself bound to the mast. He encounters the whirl-pool of Charybdis after passing the Sirens (*Odyssey*, Book XII).
6. A point of support.
7. An ancient instrument for recording the rise and fall of the Nile River.

hills. I think that the richest vein is somewhere hereabouts; so by the divining rod and thin rising vapors I judge; and here I will begin to mine.

Brute Neighbors

* * * The mice which haunted my house were not the common ones, which are said to have been introduced into the country, but a wild native kind (*mus leucopus*) not found in the village. I sent one to a distinguished naturalist, and it interested him much. When I was building, one of these had its nest underneath the house, and before I had laid the second floor, and swept out the shavings, would come out regularly at lunch time and pick up the crums at my feet. It probably had never seen a man before; and it soon became quite familiar, and would run over my shoes and up my clothes. It could readily ascend the sides of the room by short impulses, like a squirrel, which it resembled in its motions. At length, as I leaned with my elbow on the bench one day, it ran up my clothes, and along my sleeve, and round and round the paper which held my dinner, while I kept the latter close, and dodged and played at bo-peep with it; and when at last I held still a piece of cheese between my thumb and finger, it came and nibbled it, sitting in my hand, and afterward cleaned its face and paws, like a fly, and walked away.

A phœbe soon built in my shed, and a robin for protection in a pine which grew against the house. In June the partridge (*Tetrao umbellus,*) which is so shy a bird, led her brood past my windows, from the woods in the rear to the front of my house, clucking and calling to them like a hen, and in all her behavior proving herself the hen of the woods. The young suddenly disperse on your approach, at a signal from the mother, as if a whirlwind had swept them away, and they so exactly resemble the dried leaves and twigs that many a traveller has placed his foot in the midst of a brood, and heard the whir of the old bird as she flew off, and her anxious calls and mewing, or seen her trail her wings to attract his attention, without suspecting their neighborhood. The parent will sometimes roll and spin round before you in such a dishabille, that you cannot, for a few moments, detect what kind of creature it is. The young squat still and flat, often running their heads under a leaf, and mind only their mother's directions given from a distance, nor will your approach make them run again and betray themselves. You may even tread on them, or have your eyes on them for a minute, without discovering them. I have held them in my open hand at such a time, and still their only care, obedient to their mother and their instinct, was to squat there without fear or trembling. So perfect is this instinct, that once, when I had laid them on the leaves again, and one accidentally fell on its side, it was found with the rest in exactly the same position ten minutes afterward. They are not callow like the young of most birds, but more perfectly developed and precocious even than chickens. The remarkably adult yet innocent expression of their open and serene eyes is very memorable. All intelligence seems reflected in them. They suggest not merely the purity of infancy, but a wisdom clarified by experience. Such an eye was not born when the bird was, but is coeval with the sky it reflects. The woods do not yield another such a gem. The traveller does not often look into such a limpid well. The ignorant or reckless sportsman often shoots the parent at such a time, and leaves these innocents to fall a prey to some prowling beast or bird, or gradually mingle with the decaying leaves which they so much resemble. It is said that when hatched by a hen they will directly disperse on some alarm, and so are lost, for they never hear the mother's call which gathers them again. These were my hens and chickens.

It is remarkable how many creatures live wild and free though secret in the woods, and still sustain themselves in the neighborhood of towns, suspected by hunters only. How retired the otter manages to live here! He grows to be four feet long, as big as a small boy, perhaps without any human being getting a glimpse of him. I formerly saw the raccoon in the woods behind where my house is built, and probably still heard their whinnering at night. Commonly I rested an hour or two in the shade at noon, after planting, and ate my lunch, and read a little by a spring which was the source of a swamp and of a brook, oozing from under Brister's Hill, half a mile from my field. The approach to this was through a succession of descending grassy hollows, full of young pitch-pines, into a larger wood about the swamp. There, in a very secluded and shaded spot, under a spreading white-pine, *pastoral* there was yet a clean firm sward to sit on. I had dug out the spring and made a well of clear gray water, where I could dig up a pailful without rolling it, and thither I went for this purpose almost every day in midsummer, when the pond was warmest. Thither too the wood-cock led her brood, to probe the mud for worms, flying but a foot above them down the bank, while they ran in a troop beneath; but at last, spying me, she would leave her young and circle round and round me, nearer and nearer till within four or five feet, pretending broken wings and legs, to attract my attention, and get off her young, who would already have taken up their march with faint wiry peep, single file through the swamp, as she directed. Or I heard the peep of the young when I could not see the parent bird. There too the turtle-doves sat over the spring, or fluttered from bough to bough of the soft white-pines over my head; or the red squirrel, coursing down the nearest bough, was particularly familiar and inquisitive. You only need sit still long enough in some attractive spot in the woods that all its inhabitants may exhibit themselves to you by turns.

I was witness to events of a less peaceful character. One day when I went out to my wood-pile, or rather my pile of stumps, I observed two large ants, the one red, the other much larger, nearly half an inch long, and black, fiercely contending with one another. Having once got hold they never let go, but struggled and wrestled and rolled on the chips incessantly. Looking farther, I was surprised to find that the chips were covered with such combatants, that it was not a *duellum,* but a *bellum,*[8] a war between two races of ants, the red always pitted against the black, and frequently two red ones to one black. The legions of these Myrmidons[9] covered all the hills and vales in my wood-yard, and the ground was already strewn with the dead and dying, both red and black. It was the only battle which I have ever witnessed, the only battle-field I ever trod while the battle was raging; internecine war; the red republicans on the one hand, and the black imperialists on the other. On every side they were engaged in deadly combat, yet without any noise that I could hear, and human soldiers never fought so resolutely. I watched a couple that were fast locked in each other's embraces, in a little sunny valley amid the chips, now at noon-day prepared to fight till the sun went down, or life went out. The smaller red champion had fastened himself like a vice to his adversary's front, and through all the tumblings on that field never for an instant ceased to gnaw at one of his feelers near the root, having already caused the other to go by the board; while the stronger black one dashed him from side to side, and, as I saw on looking nearer, had already divested him of several of his members. They fought with more pertinacity than bull-dogs. Neither manifested the least disposition to retreat. It was evident that their battle-cry was Conquer or die. In the mean while there came along a single red ant on the hill-side of this valley, evidently full of excitement, who either had despatched his foe, or had not yet taken part in the battle; probably the latter, for he had lost none of his limbs; whose mother had charged him to return with his shield or upon it.[1] Or perchance he was some Achilles, who had nourished his wrath apart, and had

8. Not a duel but a war.
9. Soldiers who followed Achilles (*Iliad*). *Myrmes* is Greek for "ant."

1. The legendary command of the Spartan mothers to their warrior sons (*Iliad*).

now come to avenge or rescue his Patroclus.[2] He saw this unequal combat from afar,—for the blacks were nearly twice the size of the red,—he drew near with rapid pace till he stood on his guard within half an inch of the combatants; then, watching his opportunity, he sprang upon the black warrior, and commenced his operations near the root of his right fore-leg, leaving the foe to select among his own members; and so there were three united for life, as if a new kind of attraction had been invented which put all other locks and cements to shame. I should not have wondered by this time to find that they had their respective musical bands stationed on some eminent chip, and playing their national airs the while, to excite the slow and cheer the dying combatants. I was myself excited somewhat even as if they had been men. The more you think of it, the less the difference. And certainly there is not the fight recorded in Concord history, at least, if in the history of America, that will bear a moment's comparison with this, whether for the numbers engaged in it, or for the patriotism and heroism displayed. For numbers and for carnage it was an Austerlitz or Dresden.[3] Concord Fight! [4] Two killed on the patriots' side, and Luther Blanchard wounded! Why here every ant was a Buttrick,—"Fire! for God's sake fire!"—and thousands shared the fate of Davis and Hosmer. There was not one hireling there. I have no doubt that it was a principle they fought for, as much as our ancestors, and not to avoid a three-penny tax on their tea; and the results of this battle will be as important and memorable to those whom it concerns as those of the battle of Bunker Hill, at least.

I took up the chip on which the three I have particularly described were struggling, carried it into my house, and placed it under a tumbler on my window-sill, in order to see the issue. Holding a microscope to the first-mentioned red ant, I saw that, though he was assiduously gnawing at the near fore-leg of his enemy, having severed his remaining feeler, his own breast was all torn away, exposing what vitals he had there to the jaws of the black warrior, whose breast-plate was apparently too thick for him to pierce; and the dark carbuncles of the sufferer's eyes shone with ferocity such as war only could excite. They struggled half an hour longer under the tumbler, and when I looked again the black soldier had severed the heads of his foes from their bodies, and the still living heads were hanging on either side of him like

2. Achilles had withdrawn from the battle with the Trojans, sulking from a slight; at the death of his friend Patroclus, he leaped into the fray and killed the great Trojan Hector (*Iliad*).
3. Two bloody battles of the Napoleonic wars.

4. Major John Buttrick and 500 minutemen successfully repelled the British regulars and "hirelings" at Concord Bridge, April 19, 1775, the first battle of the American Revolution. Captain Isaac Davis and David Hosmer were the American dead.

ghastly trophies at his saddle-bow, still apparently as firmly fastened as ever, and he was endeavoring with feeble struggles, being without feelers and with only the remnant of a leg, and I
know not how many other wounds, to divest himself of them;
which at length, after half an hour more, he accomplished. I
raised the glass, and he went off over the window-sill in that crippled state. Whether he finally survived that combat, and spent
the remainder of his days in some Hotel des Invalides,[5] I do not
know; but I thought that his industry would not be worth much
thereafter. I never learned which party was victorious, nor the
cause of the war; but I felt for the rest of that day as if I had had
my feelings excited and harrowed by witnessing the struggle, the
ferocity and carnage, of a human battle before my door.

Kirby and Spence tell us that the battles of ants have long been
celebrated and the date of them recorded, though they say that
Huber [6] is the only modern author who appears to have witnessed
them. "Æneas Sylvius," [7] say they, "after giving a very circum-
stantial account of one contested with great obstinacy by a great
and small species on the trunk of a pear tree," adds that " 'This
action was fought in the pontificate of Eugenius the Fourth, in the
presence of Nicholas Pistoriensis, an eminent lawyer, who related
the whole history of the battle with the greatest fidelity.' A similar engagement between great and small ants is recorded by
Olaus Magnus,[8] in which the small ones, being victorious, are said
to have buried the bodies of their own soldiers, but left those of
their giant enemies a prey to the birds. This event happened previous to the expulsion of the tyrant Christiern the Second from
Sweden." The battle which I witnessed took place in the Presidency of Polk,[9] five years before the passage of Webster's Fugitive-Slave Bill. * * *

Conclusion

* * * I left the woods for as good a reason as I went there. Perhaps it seemed to me that I had several more lives to live, and could
not spare any more time for that one. It is remarkable how easily
and insensibly we fall into a particular route, and make a beaten
track for ourselves. I had not lived there a week before my feet
wore a path from my door to the pond-side; and though it is five

5. A veteran's hospital in Paris.
6. Standard authorities on entomology
were Kirby and Spence (cited above),
4 vols., 1815–1826, and François Huber
(1750–1831), partially blind from
youth, who "witnessed" insect behavior
with the aid of his wife and son.
7. The pen name of Pope Pius II
(1405–1464), poet and historian.

8. Swedish-born ecclesiastic (1490–
1558), entered a Roman monastery and
produced a standard history of Sweden.
9. James K. Polk was president from
1845 to 1849. Webster, representing
Northern liberals, supported the Con-
gressional "Compromises of 1850,"
thus reaffirming the validity of fugitive-
slave laws.

or six years since I trod it, it is still quite distinct. It is true, I fear that others may have fallen into it, and so helped to keep it open. The surface of the earth is soft and impressible by the feet of men; and so with the paths which the mind travels. How worn and dusty, then, must be the highways of the world, how deep the ruts of tradition and conformity! I did not wish to take a cabin passage, but rather to go before the mast and on the deck of the world, for there I could best see the moonlight amid the mountains. I do not wish to go below now.

I learned this, at least, by my experiment; that if one advances confidently in the direction of his dreams, and endeavors to live the life which he has imagined, he will meet with a success unexpected in common hours. He will put some things behind, will pass an invisible boundary; new, universal, and more liberal laws will begin to establish themselves around and within him; or the old laws be expanded, and interpreted in his favor in a more liberal sense, and he will live with the license of a higher order of beings. In proportion as he simplifies his life, the laws of the universe will appear less complex, and solitude will not be solitude, nor poverty poverty, nor weakness weakness. If you have built castles in the air, your work need not be lost; that is where they should be. Now put the foundations under them.

It is a ridiculous demand which England and America make, that you shall speak so that they can understand you. Neither men nor toad-stools grow so. As if that were important, and there were not enough to understand you without them. As if Nature could support but one order of understandings, could not sustain birds as well as quadrupeds, flying as well as creeping things, and *hush* and *who*, which Bright [1] can understand, were the best English. As if there were safety in stupidity alone. I fear chiefly lest my expression may not be *extra- vagant* enough, may not wander far enough beyond the narrow limits of my daily experience, so as to be adequate to the truth of which I have been convinced. *Extra vagance!* it depends on how you are yarded. The migrating buffalo, which seeks new pastures in another latitude, is not extravagant like the cow which kicks over the pail, leaps the cow-yard fence, and runs after her calf, in milking time. I desire to speak somewhere *without* bounds; like a man in a waking moment, to men in their waking moments; for I am convinced that I cannot exaggerate enough even to lay the foundation of a true expression. Who that has heard a strain of music feared then lest he should speak extravagantly any more forever? In view of the future or

1. General terms for driving horses or cattle are "hush" and "whoa." "Bright" is reported to have been a localism for the ox, then a draught animal in New England.

possible, we should live quite laxly and undefined in front, our outlines dim and misty on that side; as our shadows reveal an insensible perspiration toward the sun. The volatile truth of our words should continually betray the inadequacy of the residual statement. Their truth is instantly *translated*; its literal monument alone remains. The words which express our faith and piety are not definite; yet they are significant and fragrant like frankincense to superior natures.

Why level downward to our dullest perception always, and praise that as common sense? The commonest sense is the sense of men asleep, which they express by snoring. Sometimes we are inclined to class those who are once-and-a-half witted with the half-witted, because we appreciate only a third part of their wit. Some would find fault with the morning-red, if they ever got up early enough. "They pretend," as I hear, "that the verses of Kabir[2] have four different senses; illusion, spirit, intellect, and the exoteric doctrine of the Vedas;" but in this part of the world it is considered a ground for complaint if a man's writings admit of more than one interpretation. While England endeavors to cure the potato-rot, will not any endeavor to cure the brain-rot, which prevails so much more widely and fatally?

I do not suppose that I have attained to obscurity, but I should be proud if no more fatal fault were found with my pages on this score than was found with the Walden ice. Southern customers objected to its blue color, which is the evidence of its purity, as if it were muddy, and preferred the Cambridge ice, which is white, but tastes of weeds. The purity men love is like the mists which envelop the earth, and not like the azure ether beyond.

Some are dinning in our ears that we Americans, and moderns generally, are intellectual dwarfs compared with the ancients, or even the Elizabethan men. But what is that to the purpose? A living dog is better than a dead lion.[3] Shall a man go and hang himself because he belongs to the race of pygmies, and not be the biggest pygmy that he can? Let every one mind his own business, and endeavor to be what he was made.

Why should we be in such desperate haste to succeed, and in such desperate enterprises? If a man does not keep pace with his companions, perhaps it is because he hears a different drummer. Let him step to the music which he hears, however measured or far away. It is not important that he should mature as soon as an apple-tree or an oak. Shall he turn his spring into summer? If the condition of things which we were made for is not yet, what were any reality which we can substitute? We will not be ship-

---

2. Kabir (1450?–1518), Indian reformer who tried to unite Moslem and Hindu sects. Cf. Garcin de Tassy, *History of Hindu Literature* (1839).

3. Cf. Ecclesiastes ix: 4.

wrecked on a vain reality. Shall we with pains erect a heaven of blue glass over ourselves, though when it is done we shall be sure to gaze still at the true ethereal heaven far above, as if the former were not? * * *

I live in the angle of a leaden wall, into whose composition was poured a little alloy of bell metal. Often, in the repose of my mid-day, there reaches my ears a confused *tintinnabulum* [4] from without. It is the noise of my contemporaries. My neighbors tell me of their adventures with famous gentlemen and ladies, what notabilities they met at the dinner-table; but I am no more interested in such things than in the contents of the Daily Times. The interest and the conversation are about costume and manners chiefly; but a goose is a goose still, dress it as you will. They tell me of California and Texas, of England and the Indies, of the Hon. Mr. —— of Georgia or of Massachusetts, all transient and fleeting phenomena, till I am ready to leap from their court-yard like the Mameluke bey. [5] I delight to come to my bearings, —not walk in procession with pomp and parade, in a conspicu-ous place, but to walk even with the Builder of the universe, if I may,—not to live in this restless, nervous, bustling, trivial Nineteenth Century, but stand or sit thoughtfully while it goes by. What are men celebrating? They are all on a committee of arrangements, and hourly expect a speech from somebody. God is only the president of the day, and Webster is his orator. I love to weigh, to settle, to gravitate toward that which most strongly and rightfully attracts me;—not hang by the beam of the scale and try to weigh less,—not suppose a case, but take the case that is; to travel the only path I can, and that on which no power can resist me. It affords me no satisfaction to commence to spring an arch before I have got a solid foundation. Let us not play at kittlybenders. [6] There is a solid bottom every where. We read that the traveller asked the boy if the swamp before him had a hard bottom. The boy replied that it had. But presently the traveller's horse sank in up to the girths, and he observed to the boy, "I thought you said that this bog had a hard bottom." "So it has," answered the latter, "but you have not got half way to it yet." So it is with the bogs and quicksands of society; but he is an old boy that knows it. * * *

The life in us is like the water in the river. It may rise this year higher than man has ever known it, and flood the parched uplands; even this may be the eventful year, which will drown out all our muskrats. It was not always dry land where we dwell. I see far inland the banks which the stream anciently washed,

4. Latin: a small tinkling bell.
5. According to legend, one of the vic-tims escaped the Massacre of the Mamelukes in 1811 in Egypt by leaping to his horse from a wall.
6. A child's dare game of skating on thin ice.

before science began to record its freshets. Every one has heard the story which has gone the rounds of New England, of a strong and beautiful bug which came out of the dry leaf of an old table of apple-tree wood, which had stood in a farmer's kitchen for sixty years, first in Connecticut, and afterward in Massachusetts,— from an egg deposited in the living tree many years earlier still, as appeared by counting the annual layers beyond it; which was heard gnawing out for several weeks, hatched perchance by the heat of an urn. Who does not feel his faith in a resurrection and immortality strengthened by hearing of this? Who knows what beautiful and winged life, whose egg has been buried for ages under many concentric layers of woodenness in the dead dry life of society, deposited at first in the alburnum of the green and living tree, which has been gradually converted into the semblance of its well-seasoned tomb,—heard perchance gnawing out now for years by the astonished family of man, as they sat round the festive board,—may unexpectedly come forth from amidst society's most trivial and handselled furniture, to enjoy its perfect summer life at last!

I do not say that John or Jonathan [7] will realize all this; but such is the character of that morrow which mere lapse of time can never make to dawn. The light which puts out our eyes is darkness to us. Only that day dawns to which we are awake. There is more day to dawn. The sun is but a morning star.

1846   1854

Civil Disobedience [8]

I heartily accept the motto,—"That government is best which governs least;" [9] and I should like to see it acted up to more rapidly and systematically. Carried out, it finally amounts to this,

7. "John Bull" and "Brother Jonathan" were then the familiar personifications of the common man in England and the United States.
8. "Civil Disobedience" was neglected for more than half a century, although it formulates democratic ideas inherent in *Walden*. Thoreau believed, and demonstrated by example, that if government, responding to expediency or majority pressures, infringes upon the fundamental freedom of thought or choice of moral alternatives of the individual or the minority, the remedy is nonviolent, or pacific, resistance. Recently these ideas have had increasing attention wherever rising population and industrial pressures endanger the preservation of democratic individualism. More strikingly, through

its acknowledged influence on Mahatma Gandhi, the essay became associated with a movement of incalculable significance for Asia and the world. This essay first appeared in the anthology *Aesthetic Essays* (1849), edited by Elizabeth Palmer Peabody, transcendentalist bookseller in Boston. There it was entitled "Resistance to Civil Government." Under its present title it appeared in the posthumous collections *A Yankee in Canada* (1866) and *Miscellanies* (1893).
9. These words echo Paine and Jefferson; the belief that government was a social contract sanctioned only by necessity was an active influence during the Revolution and the Constitutional Convention.

which also I believe,—"That government is best which governs not at all;" and when men are prepared for it, that will be the kind of government which they will have. Government is at best but an expedient; but most governments are usually, and all governments are sometimes, inexpedient. The objections which have been brought against a standing army, and they are many and weighty, and deserve to prevail, may also at last be brought against a standing government. The standing army is only an arm of the standing government. The government itself, which is only the mode which the people have chosen to execute their will, is equally liable to be abused and perverted before the people can act through it. Witness the present Mexican war, the work of comparatively a few individuals [1] using the standing government as their tool; for, in the outset, the people would not have consented to this measure.

This American government,—what is it but a tradition, though a recent one, endeavoring to transmit itself unimpaired to posterity, but each instant losing some of its integrity? It has not the vitality and force of a single living man; for a single man can bend it to his will. It is a sort of wooden gun to the people themselves. But it is not the less necessary for this; for the people must have some complicated machinery or other, and hear its din, to satisfy that idea of government which they have. Governments show thus how successfully men can be imposed on, even impose on themselves, for their own advantage. It is excellent, we must all allow. Yet this government never of itself furthered any enterprise, but by the alacrity with which it got out of its way. *It* does not keep the country free. *It* does not settle the West. *It* does not educate. The character inherent in the American people has done all that has been accomplished; and it would have done somewhat more, if the government had not sometimes got in its way. For government is an expedient by which men would fain succeed in letting one another alone; and, as has been said, when it is most expedient, the governed are most let alone by it. Trade and commerce, if they were not made of india-rubber, would never manage to bounce over the obstacles which legislators are continually putting in their way; and, if one were to judge these men wholly by the effects of their actions and not partly by their intentions, they would deserve to be classed and punished with those mischievous persons who put obstructions on the railroads.

But, to speak practically and as a citizen, unlike those who call themselves no-government men, I ask for, not at once no govern-

---

1. The war was regarded by northern reformers as resulting primarily from the selfish interest of southern politicians and northern cotton merchants in extending slave territory.

ment, but *at once* a better government. Let every man make known what kind of government would command his respect, and that will be one step toward obtaining it.

After all, the practical reason why, when the power is once in the hands of the people, a majority are permitted, and for a long period continue, to rule is not because they are most likely to be in the right, nor because this seems fairest to the minority, but because they are physically the strongest. But a government in which the majority rule in all cases cannot be based on justice, even as far as men understand it. Can there not be a government in which majorities do not virtually decide right and wrong, but conscience? [2]—in which majorities decide only those questions to which the rule of expediency is applicable? Must the citizen ever for a moment, or in the least degree, resign his conscience to the legislator? Why has every man a conscience, then? I think that we should be men first, and subjects afterward. It is not desirable to cultivate a respect for the law, so much as for the right. The only obligation which I have a right to assume is to do at any time what I think right. It is truly enough said that a corporation has no conscience; but a corporation of conscientious men is a corporation *with* a conscience. Law never made men a whit more just; and, by means of their respect for it, even the well-disposed are daily made the agents of injustice. A common and natural result of an undue respect for law is, that you may see a file of soldiers, colonel, captain, corporal, privates, powder-monkeys, and all, marching in admirable order over hill and dale to the wars, against their wills, ay, against their common sense and consciences, which makes it very steep marching indeed, and produces a palpitation of the heart. They have no doubt that it is damnable business in which they are concerned; they are all peaceably inclined. Now, what are they? Men at all? or small movable forts and magazines, at the service of some unscrupulous man in power? Visit the Navy-Yard, and behold a marine, such a man as an American government can make, or such as it can make a man with its black arts,—a mere shadow and reminiscence of humanity, a man laid out alive and standing, and already, as one may say, buried under arms with funeral accompaniments, though it may be,—

> "Not a drum was heard, not a funeral note,
>   As his corse to the rampart we hurried;
> Not a soldier discharged his farewell shot
>   O'er the grave where our hero we buried." [3]

---

2. Recalling a principal controversy of the Constitutional Convention, where the conservative minority, represented by Hamilton and Adams, were overcome by the Jeffersonians, who favored majority rule.

3. Charles Wolfe (1791–1823), Irish clergyman who died at thirty-two, won several decades of remembrance by his "Burial of Sir John Moore at Coruna" (1817), of which this is the opening.

The mass of men serve the state thus, not as men mainly, but as machines, with their bodies. They are the standing army, and the militia, jailers, constables, *posse comitatus*,[4] etc. In most cases there is no free exercise whatever of the judgment or of the moral sense; but they put themselves on a level with wood and earth and stones; and wooden men can perhaps be manufactured that will serve the purpose as well. Such command no more respect than men of straw or a lump of dirt. They have the same sort of worth only as horses and dogs. Yet such as these even are commonly esteemed good citizens. Others—as most legislators, politicians, lawyers, ministers, and office-holders—serve the state chiefly with their heads; and, as they rarely make any moral distinctions, they are as likely to serve the devil, without *intending* it, as God. A very few,—as heroes, patriots, martyrs, reformers in the great sense, and *men*—serve the state with their consciences also, and so necessarily resist it for the most part; and they are commonly treated as enemies by it. A wise man will only be useful as a man, and will not submit to be "clay," and "stop a hole to keep the wind away," [5] but leave that office to his dust at least:—

> "I am too high-born to be propertied,
> To be a secondary at control,
> Or useful serving-man and instrument
> To any sovereign state throughout the world." [6]

He who gives himself entirely to his fellow-men appears to them useless and selfish; but he who gives himself partially to them is pronounced a benefactor and philanthropist.

How does it become a man to behave toward this American government to-day? I answer, that he cannot without disgrace be associated with it.[7] I cannot for an instant recognize that political organization as *my* government which is the *slave's* government also.

All men recognize the right of revolution; that is, the right to refuse allegiance to, and to resist, the government, when its tyranny or its inefficiency are great and unendurable. But almost all say that such is not the case now. But such was the case, they think, in the Revolution of '75. If one were to tell me that this was a bad government because it taxed certain foreign commodities brought to its ports, it is most probable that I should not make an ado about it, for I can do without them. All machines have their friction; and possibly this does enough good to counterbalance the evil. At any rate, it is a great evil to make a stir about

4. Legal Latin, meaning "having the authority of the county"; *cf.* the sheriff's "posse."
5. *Cf.* Shakespeare, *Hamlet*, Act V, Scene 1, ll. 236–237.
6. *Cf.* Shakespeare, *King John*, Act V, Scene 2, ll. 79–82.
7. Many accused Polk's administration (1845–1849) of strengthening slavery through fugitive-slave laws and the Mexican War.

it. But when the friction comes to have its machine, and oppression and robbery are organized, I say, let us not have such a machine any longer. In other words, when a sixth of the population of a nation which has undertaken to be the refuge of liberty are slaves, and a whole country [8] is unjustly overrun and conquered by a foreign army, and subjected to military law, I think that it is not too soon for honest men to rebel and revolutionize. What makes this duty the more urgent is the fact that the country so overrun is not our own, but ours is the invading army.

Paley,[9] a common authority with many on moral questions, in his chapter on the "Duty of Submission to Civil Government," resolves all civil obligation into expediency; and he proceeds to say "that so long as the interest of the whole society requires it, that is, so long as the established government cannot be resisted or changed without public inconveniency, it is the will of God . . . that the established government be obeyed,—and no longer. This principle being admitted, the justice of every particular case of resistance is reduced to a computation of the quantity of the danger and grievance on the one side, and of the probability and expense of redressing it on the other." Of this, he says, every man shall judge for himself. But Paley appears never to have contemplated those cases to which the rule of expediency does not apply, in which a people, as well as an individual, must do justice, cost what it may. If I have unjustly wrested a plank from a drowning man, I must restore it to him though I drown myself. This, according to Paley, would be inconvenient. But he that would save his life, in such a case, shall lose it.[1] This people must cease to hold slaves, and to make war on Mexico, though it cost them their existence as a people.

In their practice, nations agree with Paley; but does any one think that Massachusetts does exactly what is right at the present crisis?

> "A drab of state, a cloth-o'-silver slut,
> To have her train borne up, and her soul trail in the dirt."

Practically speaking, the opponents to a reform in Massachusetts are not a hundred thousand politicians at the South, but a hundred thousand merchants and farmers here, who are more interested in commerce and agriculture than they are in humanity, and are not prepared to do justice to the slave and to Mexico, *cost what it may*. I quarrel not with far-off foes, but with those who, near at home, coöperate with, and do the bidding of, those

8. Mexico.
9. William Paley (1743–1805), British thinker, whose utilitarianism motivates this quotation from his *Principles of Moral and Political Philosophy* (1785).
1. *Cf.* Luke ix: 24.

far away, and without whom the latter would be harmless. We are accustomed to say, that the mass of men are unprepared; but improvement is slow, because the few are not materially wiser or better than the many. It is not so important that many should be as good as you, as that there be some absolute goodness somewhere; for that will leaven the whole lump.[2] There are thousands who are *in opinion* opposed to slavery and to the war, who yet in effect do nothing to put an end to them; who, esteeming themselves children of Washington and Franklin, sit down with their hands in their pockets, and say that they know not what to do, and do nothing; who even postpone the question of freedom to the question of free trade, and quietly read the prices-current along with the latest advices from Mexico, after dinner, and, it may be, fall asleep over them both. What is the price-current of an honest man and patriot to-day? They hesitate, and they regret, and sometimes they petition; but they do nothing in earnest and with effect. They will wait, well disposed, for others to remedy the evil, that they may no longer have it to regret. At most, they give only a cheap vote, and a feeble countenance and God-speed, to the right, as it goes by them. There are nine hundred and ninety-nine patrons of virtue to one virtuous man. But it is easier to deal with the real possessor of a thing than with the temporary guardian of it.

All voting is a sort of gaming, like checkers or backgammon, with a slight moral tinge to it, a playing with right and wrong, with moral questions; and betting naturally accompanies it. The character of the voters is not staked. I cast my vote, perchance, as I think right; but I am not vitally concerned that that right should prevail. I am willing to leave it to the majority. Its obligation, therefore, never exceeds that of expediency. Even voting *for the right* is *doing* nothing for it. It is only expressing to men feebly your desire that it should prevail. A wise man will not leave the right to the mercy of chance, nor wish it to prevail through the power of the majority. There is but little virtue in the action of masses of men. When the majority shall at length vote for the abolition of slavery, it will be because they are indifferent to slavery, or because there is but little slavery left to be abolished by their vote. *They* will then be the only slaves. Only *his* vote can hasten the abolition of slavery who asserts his own freedom by his vote.

I hear of a convention to be held at Baltimore,[3] or elsewhere, for the selection of a candidate for the Presidency, made up chiefly

2. *Cf.* I Corinthians v: 6.
3. The Democratic convention at Baltimore, in May, 1848, fulfilled Thoreau's prediction of expediency in its platform, and in its man, Lewis Cass, "a northern man with southern principles."

of editors, and men who are politicians by profession; but I think, what is it to any independent, intelligent, and respectable man what decision they may come to? Shall we not have the advantage of his wisdom and honesty, nevertheless? Can we not count upon some independent votes? Are there not many individuals in the country who do not attend conventions? But no: I find that the respectable man, so called, has immediately drifted from his position, and despairs of his country, when his country has more reason to despair of him. He forthwith adopts one of the candidates thus selected as the only *available* one, thus proving that he is himself *available* for any purposes of the demagogue. His vote is of not more worth than that of any unprincipled foreigner or hireling native, who may have been bought. O for a man who is a *man*, and, as my neighbor says, has a bone in his back which you cannot pass your hand through! Our statistics are at fault: the population has been returned too large. How many *men* are there to a square thousand miles in this country? Hardly one. Does not America offer any inducement for men to settle here? The American has dwindled into an Odd Fellow,[4]—one who may be known by the development of his organ of gregariousness, and a manifest lack of intellect and cheerful self-reliance; whose first and chief concern, on coming into the world, is to see that the almshouses are in good repair; and, before yet he has lawfully donned the virile garb,[5] to collect a fund for the support of the widows and orphans that may be; who, in short, ventures to live only by the aid of the Mutual Insurance company, which has promised to bury him decently.

It is not a man's duty, as a matter of course, to devote himself to the eradication of any, even the most enormous, wrong; he may still properly have other concerns to engage him; but it is his duty, at least, to wash his hands of it, and, if he gives it no thought longer, not to give it practically his support. If I devote myself to other pursuits and contemplations, I must first see, at least, that I do not pursue them sitting upon another man's shoulders. I must get off him first, that he may pursue his contemplations too. See what gross inconsistency is tolerated. I have heard some of my townsmen say, "I should like to have them order me out to help put down an insurrection of the slaves, or to march to Mexico;—see if I would go;" and yet these very men have each, directly by their allegiance, and so indirectly, at least, by their money, furnished a substitute. The soldier is applauded who refuses to serve in an unjust war by those who do not refuse to sustain the

4. The Independent Order of Odd Fellows, one of numerous secret fraternal societies then being developed for social diversion and mutual insurance.

5. *Cf.* the *toga virilis*, which the Roman boy was permitted to wear on attaining the age of fourteen.

unjust government which makes the war; is applauded by those whose own act and authority he disregards and sets at naught; as if the state were penitent to that degree that it hired one to scourge it while it sinned, but not to that degree that it left off sinning for a moment. Thus, under the name of Order and Civil Government, we are all made at last to pay homage to and support our own meanness. After the first blush of sin comes its indifference; and from immoral it becomes, as it were, *un*moral, and not quite unnecessary to that life which we have made.

The broadest and most prevalent error requires the most disinterested virtue to sustain it. The slight reproach to which the virtue of patriotism is commonly liable, the noble are most likely to incur. Those who, while they disapprove of the character and measures of a government, yield to it their allegiance and support, are undoubtedly its most conscientious supporters, and so frequently the most serious obstacles to reform. Some are petitioning the State to dissolve the Union, to disregard the requisitions of the President. Why do they not dissolve it themselves,—the union between themselves and the State,—and refuse to pay their quota into its treasury? Do not they stand in the same relation to the State that the State does to the Union? And have not the same reasons prevented the State from resisting the Union which have prevented them from resisting the State?

How can a man be satisfied to entertain an opinion merely, and enjoy *it*? Is there any enjoyment in it, if his opinion is that he is aggrieved? If you are cheated out of a single dollar by your neighbor, you do not rest satisfied with knowing that you are cheated, or with saying that you are cheated, or even with petitioning him to pay you your due; but you take effectual steps at once to obtain the full amount, and see that you are never cheated again. Action from principle, the perception and the performance of right, changes things and relations; it is essentially revolutionary, and does not consist wholly with anything which was. It not only divides States and churches, it divides families; ay, it divides the *individual*, separating the diabolical in him from the divine.

Unjust laws exist: shall we be content to obey them, or shall we endeavor to amend them, and obey them until we have succeeded, or shall we transgress them at once? Men generally, under such a government as this, think that they ought to wait until they have persuaded the majority to alter them. They think that, if they should resist, the remedy would be worse than the evil. But it is the fault of the government itself that the remedy *is* worse than the evil. *It* makes it worse. Why is it not more apt to anticipate and provide for reform? Why does it not cherish its wise minority? Why does it cry and resist before it is hurt? Why does it not encourage its citizens to be on the alert to point out its faults, and *do* better than it would have them? Why does it always crucify Christ, and excommunicate Copernicus and Luther,[6] and pronounce Washington and Franklin rebels?

One would think, that a deliberate and practical denial of its authority was the only offense never contemplated by government; else, why has it not assigned its definite, its suitable and proportionate penalty? If a man who has no property refuses but once to earn nine shillings for the State, he is put in prison for a period unlimited by any law that I know, and determined only by the discretion of those who placed him there; but if he should steal ninety times nine shillings from the State, he is soon permitted to go at large again.

If the injustice is part of the necessary friction of the machine of government, let it go, let it go: perchance it will wear smooth, —certainly the machine will wear out. If the injustice has a spring, or a pulley, or a rope, or a crank, exclusively for itself, then perhaps you may consider whether the remedy will not be worse than the evil; but if it is of such a nature that it requires you to be the agent of injustice to another, then, I say, break the law. Let your life be a counter friction to stop the machine. What I have to do is to see, at any rate, that I do not lend myself to the wrong which I condemn.

As for adopting the ways which the State has provided for remedying the evil, I know not of such ways. They take too much time, and a man's life will be gone. I have other affairs to attend to. I came into this world, not chiefly to make this a good place to live in, but to live in it, be it good or bad. A man has not everything to do, but something; and because he cannot do *everything*, it is not necessary that he should do *something* wrong. It is not my business to be petitioning the Governor or the Legislature any more than it is theirs to petition me; and if they should not hear my petition, what should I do then? But in this case the State has provided no way: its very Constitution is the evil. This may seem to be harsh and stubborn and unconciliatory; but it is to treat with the utmost kindness and consideration the only spirit that can appreciate or deserves it. So is all change for the better, like birth and death, which convulse the body.

I do not hesitate to say, that those who call themselves Abolitionists should at once effectually withdraw their support, both in person and property, from the government of Massachusetts, and not wait till they constitute a majority of one, before they

6. Copernicus was on his deathbed (1543) when his description of the solar system was published, later to come under the ban of the Church; but Luther, the founder of the German Reformation, was officially excommunicated in 1521, twenty-five years before his death.

suffer the right to prevail through them. I think that it is enough if they have God on their side, without waiting for that other one.[7] Moreover, any man more right than his neighbors constitutes a majority of one already.

I meet this American government, or its representative, the State government, directly, and face to face, once a year—no more —in the person of its tax-gatherer; this is the only mode in which a man situated as I am necessarily meets it; and it then says distinctly, Recognize me; and the simplest, the most effectual, and, in the present posture of affairs, the indispensablest mode of treating with it on this head, of expressing your little satisfaction with and love for it, is to deny it then. My civil neighbor, the tax-gatherer, is the very man I have to deal with,—for it is, after all, with men and not with parchment that I quarrel,—and he has voluntarily chosen to be an agent of the government. How shall he ever know well what he is and does as an officer of the government, or as a man, until he is obliged to consider whether he shall treat me, his neighbor, for whom he has respect, as a neighbor and well-disposed man, or as a maniac and disturber of the peace, and see if he can get over this obstruction to his neighborliness without a ruder and more impetuous thought or speech corresponding with his action. I know this well, that if one thousand, if one hundred, if ten men whom I could name,—if ten *honest* men only,—ay, if *one* HONEST man, in this State of Massachusetts, *ceasing to hold slaves*, were actually to withdraw from this co-partnership, and be locked up in the county jail therefor, it would be the abolition of slavery in America.[8] For it matters not how small the beginning may seem to be: what is once well done is done forever. But we love better to talk about it: that we say is our mission. Reform keeps many scores of newspapers in its service, but not one man. If my esteemed neighbor, the State's ambassador,[9] who will devote his days to the settlement of the question of human rights in the Council Chamber, instead of being threatened with the prisons of Carolina, were to sit down the prisoner of Massachusetts, that State which is so anxious to foist the sin of slavery upon her sister,—though at present she can discover only an act of inhospitality to be the ground of a quarrel with her, —the Legislature would not wholly waive the subject the following winter.

7. *Cf.* the proverb "One on God's side is a majority."
8. An example of the operation of passive resistance, the doctrine for which Gandhi acknowledged indebtedness to Thoreau.
9. Samuel Hoar (1778–1856), distinguished Concord lawyer and congressman, was officially delegated to South Carolina to test certain laws denying the ports to Negro seamen on Massachusetts ships, under penalty of arrest and possible enslavement. Hoar was forcibly expelled from South Carolina by action of the legislature.

Under a government which imprisons any unjustly, the true place for a just man is also a prison. The proper place to-day, the only place which Massachusetts has provided for her freer and less desponding spirits, is in her prisons, to be put out and locked out of the State by her own act, as they have already put themselves out by their principles. It is there that the fugitive slave, and the Mexican prisoner on parole, and the Indian come to plead the wrongs of his race should find them; on that separate, but more free and honorable ground, where the State places those who are not *with* her, but *against* her,—the only house in a slave State in which a free man can abide with honor. If any think that their influence would be lost there, and their voices no longer afflict the ear of the State, that they would not be as an enemy within its walls, they do not know by how much truth is stronger than error, nor how much more eloquently and effectively he can combat injustice who has experienced a little in his own person. Cast your whole vote, not a strip of paper merely, but your whole influence. A minority is powerless while it conforms to the majority; it is not even a minority then; but it is irresistible when it clogs by its whole weight. If the alternative is to keep all just men in prison, or give up war and slavery, the State will not hesitate which to choose. If a thousand men were not to pay their tax-bills this year, that would not be a violent and bloody measure, as it would be to pay them, and enable the State to commit violence and shed innocent blood. This is, in fact, the definition of a peaceable revolution, if any such is possible. If the tax-gatherer, or any other public officer, asks me, as one has done, "But what shall I do?" my answer is, "If you really wish to do anything, resign your office." When the subject has refused allegiance, and the officer has resigned his office, then the revolution is accomplished. But even suppose blood should flow. Is there not a sort of blood shed when the conscience is wounded? Through this wound a man's real manhood and immortality flow out, and he bleeds to an everlasting death. I see this blood flowing now.

I have contemplated the imprisonment of the offender, rather than the seizure of his goods,—though both will serve the same purpose,—because they who assert the purest right, and consequently are most dangerous to a corrupt State, commonly have not spent much time in accumulating property. To such the State renders comparatively small service, and a slight tax is wont to appear exorbitant, particularly if they are obliged to earn it by special labor [1] with their hands. If there were one who lived wholly without the use of money, the State itself would hesitate to de-

---

1. Referring to his stand against the Massachusetts church tax and poll tax, assessed against all males.

mand it of him. But the rich man—not to make any invidious comparison—is always sold to the institution which makes him rich. Absolutely speaking, the more money, the less virtue; for money comes between a man and his objects, and obtains them for him; and it was certainly no great virtue to obtain it. It puts to rest many questions which he would otherwise be taxed to answer; while the only new question which it puts is the hard but superfluous one, how to spend it. Thus his moral ground is taken from under his feet. The opportunities of living are diminished in proportion as what are called the "means" are increased. The best thing a man can do for his culture when he is rich is to endeavor to carry out those schemes which he entertained when he was poor. Christ answered the Herodians according to their condition. "Show me the tribute-money," said he;—and took one penny out of his pocket;—if you use money which has the image of Caesar on it and which he has made current and valuable, that is, *if you are men of the State*, and gladly enjoy the advantages of Caesar's government, then pay him back some of his own when he demands it. "Render therefore to Caesar that which is Caesar's, and to God those things which are God's," [2]—leaving them no wiser than before as to which was which; for they did not wish to know.

When I converse with the freest of my neighbors, I perceive that, whatever they may say about the magnitude and seriousness of the question, and their regard for the public tranquillity, the long and the short of the matter is, that they cannot spare the protection of the existing government, and they dread the consequences to their property and families of disobedience to it. For my own part, I should not like to think that I ever rely on the protection of the State. But, if I deny the authority of the State when it presents its tax-bill, it will soon take and waste all my property, and so harass me and my children without end. This is hard. This makes it impossible for a man to live honestly, and at the same time comfortably, in outward respects. It will not be worth the while to accumulate property; that would be sure to go again. You must hire or squat somewhere, and raise but a small crop, and eat that soon. You must live within yourself, and depend upon yourself always tucked up and ready for a start, and not have many affairs. A man may grow rich in Turkey even, if he will be in all respects a good subject of the Turkish government. Confucius [3] said: "If a state is governed by the principles of reason, poverty and misery are subjects of shame; if a state is not

2. *Cf.* Matthew xxii: 16–21.
3. Confucius (551?–479? B.C.) was primarily a utilitarian and social philosopher; his formulation of Chinese "wisdom," preserved in the *Analects*, was familiar in translation to the Transcendentalists.

governed by the principles of reason, riches and honors are the subjects of shame." No: until I want the protection of Massachusetts to be extended to me in some distant Southern port, where my liberty is endangered, or until I am bent solely on building up an estate at home by peaceful enterprise, I can afford to refuse allegiance to Massachusetts, and her right to my property and life. It costs me less in every sense to incur the penalty of disobedience to the State than it would to obey. I should feel as if I were worth less in that case.

Some years ago, the State met me in behalf of the Church, and commanded me to pay a certain sum toward the support of a clergyman whose preaching my father attended, but never I myself. "Pay," it said, "or be locked up in the jail."[4] I declined to pay. But, unfortunately, another man saw fit to pay it. I did not see why the schoolmaster should be taxed to support the priest, and not the priest the schoolmaster; for I was not the State's schoolmaster, but I supported myself by voluntary subscription. I did not see why the lyceum should not present its tax-bill, and have the State to back its demand, as well as the Church. However, at the request of the select men, I condescended to make some such statement as this in writing:—"Know all men by these presents, that I, Henry Thoreau, do not wish to be regarded as a member of any incorporated society which I have not joined." This I gave to the town clerk; and he has it. The State, having thus learned that I did not wish to be regarded as a member of that church, has never made a like demand on me since; though it said that it must adhere to its original presumption that time. If I had known how to name them, I should then have signed off in detail from all the societies which I never signed on to; but I did not know where to find a complete list.

I have paid no poll-tax for six years. I was put into a jail once on this account, for one night;[5] and, as I stood considering the walls of solid stone, two or three feet thick, the door of wood and iron, a foot thick, and the iron grating which strained the light, I could not help being struck with the foolishness of that institution which treated me as if I were mere flesh and blood and bones, to be locked up. I wondered that it should have concluded at length that this was the best use it could put me to, and had never thought to avail itself of my services in some way. I saw that, if there was a wall of stone between me and my townsmen, there

4. Thoreau's resistance to compulsory church taxes occurred in 1838, and he was not jailed. The failure to comply with the poll tax probably began in 1840 (see the next paragraph).
5. Bronson Alcott had resisted the tax and been jailed for one night in 1843.

The fundamental reason for resistance, for both men, was repugnance at supporting a state that recognized slavery, as Massachusetts still did in legal fact. H. S. Canby in his *Thoreau* (p. 473) dates Thoreau's experience in jail as July 23 or 24, 1846.

was a still more difficult one to climb or break through before they could get to be as free as I was. I did not for a moment feel confined, and the walls seemed a great waste of stone and mortar. I felt as if I alone of all my townsmen had paid my tax. They plainly did not know how to treat me, but behaved like persons who are underbred. In every threat and in every compliment there was a blunder; for they thought that my chief desire was to stand the other side of that stone wall. I could not but smile to see how industriously they locked the door on my meditations, which followed them out again without let or hindrance, and *they* were really all that was dangerous. As they could not reach me, they had resolved to punish my body; just as boys, if they cannot come at some person against whom they have a spite, will abuse his dog. I saw that the State was half-witted, that it was timid as a lone woman with her silver spoons, and that it did not know its friends from its foes, and I lost all my remaining respect for it, and pitied it.

Thus the State never intentionally confronts a man's sense, intellectual or moral, but only his body, his senses. It is not armed with superior wit or honesty, but with superior physical strength. I was not born to be forced. I will breathe after my own fashion. Let us see who is the strongest. What force has a multitude? They only can force me who obey a higher law than I. They force me to become like themselves. I do not hear of *men* being *forced* to live this way or that by masses of men. What sort of life were that to live? When I meet a government which says to me, "Your money or your life," why should I be in haste to give it my money? It may be in a great strait, and not know what to do: I cannot help that. It must help itself; do as I do. It is not worth the while to snivel about it. I am not responsible for the successful working of the machinery of society. I am not the son of the engineer. I perceive that, when an acorn and a chestnut fall side by side, the one does not remain inert to make way for the other, but both obey their own laws, and spring and grow and flourish as best they can, till one, perchance, overshadows and destroys the other. If a plant cannot live according to its nature, it dies; and so a man.

The night in prison was novel and interesting enough. The prisoners in their shirt-sleeves were enjoying a chat and the evening air in the doorway, when I entered. But the jailer said, "Come, boys, it is time to lock up;" and so they dispersed, and I heard the sound of their steps returning into the hollow apartments. My room-mate was introduced to me by the jailer as "a first-rate fellow and a clever[6] man." When the door was locked, he showed me where to hang my hat, and how he managed matters there.

6. American dialect for "honest," "kind."

The rooms were white-washed once a month; and this one, at least, was the whitest, most simply furnished, and probably the neatest apartment in the town. He naturally wanted to know where I came from, and what brought me there; and, when I had told him, I asked him in my turn how he came there, presuming him to be an honest man, of course; and, as the world goes, I believe he was. "Why," said he, "they accuse me of burning a barn; but I never did it." As near as I could discover, he had probably gone to bed in a barn when drunk, and smoked his pipe there; and so a barn was burnt. He had the reputation of being a clever man, had been there some three months waiting for his trial to come on, and would have to wait as much longer; but he was quite domesticated and contented, since he got his board for nothing, and thought that he was well treated.

He occupied one window, and I the other; and I saw that if one stayed there long, his principal business would be to look out the window. I had soon read all the tracts that were left there, and examined where former prisoners had broken out, and where a grate had been sawed off, and heard the history of the various occupants of that room; for I found that even here there was a history and a gossip which never circulated beyond the walls of the jail. Probably this is the only house in the town where verses are composed, which are afterward printed in circular form, but not published. I was shown quite a long list of verses which were composed by some young men who had been detected in an attempt to escape, who avenged themselves by singing them.

I pumped my fellow-prisoner as dry as I could, for fear I should never see him again; but at length he showed me which was my bed, and left me to blow out the lamp.

It was like traveling into a far country, such as I had never expected to behold, to lie there for one night. It seemed to me that I never had heard the town clock strike before, nor the evening sounds of the village; for we slept with the windows open, which were inside the grating. It was to see my native village in the light of the Middle Ages, and our Concord was turned into a Rhine stream, and visions of knights and castles passed before me. They were the voices of old burghers that I heard in the streets. I was an involuntary spectator and auditor of whatever was done and said in the kitchen of the adjacent village-inn,—a wholly new and rare experience to me. It was a closer view of my native town. I was fairly inside of it. I never had seen its institutions before. That is one of the peculiar institutions; for it is a shire town. I began to comprehend what its inhabitants were about.

In the morning, our breakfasts were put through the hole in

the door, in small oblong-square tin pans, made to fit, and holding a pint of chocolate, with brown bread, and an iron spoon. When they called for the vessels again, I was green enough to return what bread I had left; but my comrade seized it, and said that I should lay that up for lunch or dinner. Soon after he was let out to work at haying in a neighboring field, whither he went every day, and would not be back till noon; so he bade me good-day, saying that he doubted if he should see me again.

When I came out of prison,—for some one interfered, and paid that tax,[7]—I did not perceive that great changes had taken place on the common, such as he observed who went in a youth and emerged a tottering and gray-headed man; and yet a change had to my eyes come over the scene,—the town, and State, and country,—greater than any that mere time could effect. I saw yet more distinctly the State in which I lived. I saw to what extent the people among whom I lived could be trusted as good neighbors and friends; that their friendship was for summer weather only; that they did not greatly propose to do right; that they were a distinct race from me by their prejudices and superstitions, as the Chinamen and Malays are; that in their sacrifices to humanity they ran no risks, not even to their property; that after all they were not so noble but they treated the thief as he had treated them, and hoped, by a certain outward observance and a few prayers, and by walking in a particular straight though useless path from time to time, to save their souls. This may be to judge my neighbors harshly; for I believe that many of them are not aware that they have such an institution as the jail in their village.

It was formerly the custom in our village, when a poor debtor came out of jail, for his acquaintances to salute him, looking through their fingers, which were crossed to represent the grating of a jail window, "How do ye do?" My neighbors did not thus salute me, but first looked at me, and then at one another, as if I had returned from a long journey. I was put into jail as I was going to the shoemaker's to get a shoe which was mended. When I was let out the next morning, I proceeded to finish my errand, and, having put on my mended shoe, joined a huckleberry party, who were impatient to put themselves under my conduct; and in half an hour,—for the horse was soon tackled,—was in the midst of a huckleberry field, on one of our highest hills, two miles off, and then the State was nowhere to be seen.

This is the whole history of "My Prisons."[8]

---

7. It is legendary but unlikely that Emerson paid the tax. Family reminiscence ascribed the deed to his Aunt Maria.

8. English translation of the title *Le Mie Prigioni* (1832), a record of his years of hard labor in Austrian prisons by Silvio Pellico (1789–1854), Italian poet, playwright, and patriot.

I have never declined paying the highway tax, because I am as desirous of being a good neighbor as I am of being a bad subject; and as for supporting schools, I am doing my part to educate my fellow-countrymen now. It is for no particular item in the tax-bill that I refuse to pay it. I simply wish to refuse allegiance to the State, to withdraw and stand aloof from it effectually. I do not care to trace the course of my dollar, if I could, till it buys a man or a musket to shoot one with,—the dollar is innocent,—but I am concerned to trace the effects of my allegiance. In fact, I quietly declare war with the State, after my fashion, though I will still make what use and get what advantage of her I can, as is usual in such cases.

If others pay the tax which is demanded of me, from a sympathy with the State, they do but what they have already done in their own case, or rather they abet injustice to a greater extent than the State requires. If they pay the tax from a mistaken interest in the individual taxed, to save his property, or prevent his going to jail, it is because they have not considered wisely how far they let their private feelings interfere with the public good.

This, then, is my position at present. But one cannot be too much on his guard in such a case, lest his action be biased by obstinacy or an undue regard for the opinions of men. Let him see that he does only what belongs to himself and to the hour.

I think sometimes, Why, this people mean well, they are only ignorant; they would do better if they knew how: why give your neighbors this pain to treat you as they are not inclined to? But I think again, This is no reason why I should do as they do, or permit others to suffer much greater pain of a different kind. Again, I sometimes say to myself, When many millions of men, without heat, without ill will, without personal feeling of any kind, demand of you a few shillings only, without the possibility, such is their constitution, of retracting or altering their present demand, and without the possibility, on your side, of appeal to any other millions, why expose yourself to this overwhelming brute force? You do not resist cold and hunger, the winds and the waves, thus obstinately; you quietly submit to a thousand similar necessities. You do not put your head into the fire. But just in proportion as I regard this as not wholly a brute force, but partly a human force, and consider that I have relations to those millions as to so many millions of men, and not of mere brute or inanimate things, I see that appeal is possible, first and instantaneously, from them to the Maker of them, and, secondly, from them to themselves. But if I put my head deliberately into the fire, there is no appeal to fire or to the Maker of fire, and I have only myself to blame. If I could convince myself that I had any right to be satisfied with men as they are, and to treat them accordingly, and not according, in some respects, to my requisitions and expectations of what they and I ought to be, then, like a good Mussulman and fatalist, I should endeavor to be satisfied with things as they are, and say it is the will of God. And, above all, there is this difference between resisting this and a purely brute or natural force, that I can resist this with some effect; but I cannot expect, like Orpheus,[9] to change the nature of the rocks and trees and beasts.

I do not wish to quarrel with any man or nation. I do not wish to split hairs, to make fine distinctions, or set myself up as better than my neighbors. I seek rather, I may say, even an excuse for conforming to the laws of the land. I am but too ready to conform to them. Indeed, I have reason to suspect myself on this head; and each year, as the tax-gatherer comes round, I find myself disposed to review the acts and position of the general and State governments, and the spirit of the people, to discover a pretext for conformity.

> "We must affect our country as our parents,
> And if at any time we alienate
> Our love or industry from doing it honor,
> We must respect effects and teach the soul
> Matter of conscience and religion,
> And not desire of rule or benefit."

I believe that the State will soon be able to take all my work of this sort out of my hands, and then I shall be no better a patriot than my fellow-countrymen. Seen from a lower point of view, the Constitution, with all its faults, is very good; the law and the courts are very respectable; even the State and this American government are, in many respects, very admirable, and rare things, to be thankful for, such as a great many have described them; but seen from a point of view a little higher, they are what I have described them; seen from a higher still, and the highest, who shall say what they are, or that they are worth looking at or thinking of at all?

However, the government does not concern me much, and I shall bestow the fewest possible thoughts on it. It is not many moments that I live under a government, even in this world. If a man is thought-free, fancy-free, imagination-free, that which *is not* never for a long time appearing *to be* to him, unwise rulers or reformers cannot fatally interrupt him.

I know that most men think differently from myself; but those whose lives are by profession devoted to the study of these or

9. Orpheus, a mythical Greek poet-musician, caused "rocks and trees and beasts" to follow the music of his lute.

kindred subjects content me as little as any. Statesmen and legislators, standing so completely within the institution, never distinctly and nakedly behold it. They speak of moving society, but
have no resting-place without it. They may be men of a certain
experience and discrimination, and have no doubt invented ingenious and even useful systems, for which we sincerely thank them;
but all their wit and usefulness lie within certain not very wide
limits. They are wont to forget that the world is not governed by
policy and expediency. Webster [1] never goes behind government,
and so cannot speak with authority about it. His words are wisdom
to those legislators who contemplate no essential reform in the
existing government; but for thinkers, and those who legislate for
all time, he never once glances at the subject. I know of those
whose serene and wise speculations on this theme would soon reveal the limits of his mind's range and hospitality. Yet, compared
with the cheap professions of most reformers, and the still cheaper
wisdom and eloquence of politicians in general, his are almost the
only sensible and valuable words, and we thank Heaven for him.
Comparatively, he is always strong, original, and, above all, practical. Still, his quality is not wisdom, but prudence. The lawyer's
truth is not Truth, but consistency or a consistent expediency.
Truth is always in harmony with herself, and is not concerned
chiefly to reveal the justice that may consist with wrong-doing.
He well deserves to be called, as he has been called, the Defender
of the Constitution. There are really no blows to be given by him
but defensive ones. He is not a leader, but a follower. His leaders
are the men of '87.[2] "I have never made an effort," he says, "and
never propose to make an effort; I have never countenanced an
effort, and never mean to countenance an effort, to disturb the
arrangement as originally made, by which the various States came
into the Union." Still thinking of the sanction which the Constitution gives to slavery, he says, "Because it was a part of the
original compact,—let it stand." Notwithstanding his special acuteness and ability, he is unable to take a fact out of its merely
political relations, and behold it as it lies absolutely to be disposed of by the intellect,—what, for instance, it behooves a man
to do here in America to-day with regard to slavery,—but ventures, or is driven, to make some such desperate answer as the
following, while professing to speak absolutely, and as a private
man,—from which what new and singular code of social duties
might be inferred? "The manner," says he, "in which the gov-

---

1. Daniel Webster's respect for authority won him the title (mentioned later
in this paragraph) "Defender of the
Constitution"; he was therefore willing
to compromise about slavery while it
was "constitutional," thus losing many
northern supporters.
2. *I.e.*, the framers of the Constitution,
which was sent to the states for ratification in 1787.

ernments of those States where slavery exists are to regulate it is for their own consideration, under their responsibility to their constituents, to the general laws of propriety, humanity, and justice, and to God. Associations formed elsewhere, springing from a feeling of humanity, or any other cause, have nothing whatever to do with it. They have never received any encouragement from me, and they never will."

They who know of no purer sources of truth, who have traced up its stream no higher, stand, and wisely stand, by the Bible and the Constitution, and drink at it there with reverence and humility; but they who behold where it comes trickling into this lake or that pool, gird up their loins once more, and continue their pilgrimage toward its fountain-head.

No man with a genius for legislation has appeared in America. They are rare in the history of the world. There are orators, politicians, and eloquent men, by the thousand; but the speaker has not yet opened his mouth to speak who is capable of settling the much-vexed questions of the day. We love eloquence for its own sake, and not for any truth which it may utter, or any heroism it may inspire. Our legislators have not yet learned the comparative value of free trade and of freedom, of union, and of rectitude, to a nation. They have no genius or talent for comparatively humble questions of taxation and finance, commerce and manufactures and agriculture. If we were left solely to the wordy wit of legislators in Congress for our guidance, uncorrected by the seasonable experience and the effectual complaints of the people, America would not long retain her rank among the nations. For eighteen hundred years, though perchance I have no right to say it, the New Testament has been written; yet where is the legislator who has wisdom and practical talent enough to avail himself of the light which it sheds on the science of legislation?

The authority of government, even such as I am willing to submit to,—for I will cheerfully obey those who know and can do better than I, and in many things even those who neither know nor can do so well,—is still an impure one; to be strictly just, it must have the sanction and consent of the governed. It can have no pure right over my person and property but what I concede to it. The progress from an absolute to a limited monarchy, from a limited monarchy to a democracy, is a progress toward a true respect for the individual. Even the Chinese philosopher was wise enough to regard the individual as the basis of the empire. Is a democracy, such as we know it, the last improvement possible in government? Is it not possible to take a step further towards recognizing and organizing the rights of man? There will never be a really free and enlightened State until the State comes to recognize the individual as a higher and independent power, from which all its own power and authority are derived, and treats him accordingly. I please myself with imagining a State at last which can afford to be just to all men, and to treat the individual with respect as a neighbor; which even would not think it inconsistent with its own repose if a few were to live aloof from it, not meddling with it, nor embraced by it, who fulfilled all the duties of neighbors and fellow-men. A State which bore this kind of fruit, and suffered it to drop off as fast as it ripened, would prepare the way for a still more perfect and glorious State, which also I have imagined, but not yet anywhere seen.

1848   1849, 1866

My Prayer [3]

Great God, I ask thee for no meaner pelf
Than that I may not disappoint myself;
That in my action I may soar as high
As I can now discern with this clear eye.

And next in value, which thy kindness lends,   5
That I may greatly disappoint my friends,
Howe'er they think or hope that it may be,
They may not dream how thou'st distinguished me;

That my weak hand may equal my firm faith,
And my life practice more than my tongue saith;   10
    That my low conduct may not show,
        Nor my relenting lines,
    That I thy purpose did not know,
        Or overrated thy designs.

1842, 1866

Rumors from an Aeolian Harp [4]

There is a vale which none hath seen,
Where foot of man has never been,

3. The first appearance of this poem was its quotation, without title, in an article, "Prayers," by Emerson in *The Dial* for July, 1842. It reappeared in periodicals as "A Prayer" and "My Prayer" before Thoreau's death, and was first collected in the posthumous *A Yankee in Canada* (1866) as "Prayer." The following is the text from *Poems of Nature* (1895).
4. In the Greek myth, Aeolus possessed a harp played by the movement of the winds of heaven, over which the gods had granted him dominion. The symbolic idea—that nature is the source of the artist's inspiration, is recalled in Thoreau's introductory comment for the poem: "Music is the sound of the universal laws promulgated. It is the only assured tone" ("Monday," in *A Week on the Concord and Merrimack Rivers,* 1849). The poem first appeared, without the comment, in *The Dial* for October, 1842. The text is identical in *Poems of Nature* (1895) and *A Week * * * ,* as given here.

Such as here lives with toil and strife,
An anxious and a sinful life.

There every virtue has its birth,   5
Ere it descends upon the earth,
And thither every deed returns,
Which in the generous bosom burns.

There love is warm, and youth is young,
And poetry is yet unsung,   10
For Virtue still adventures there,
And freely breathes her native air.

And ever, if you hearken well,
You still may hear its vesper bell,
And tread of high-souled men go by,   15
Their thoughts conversing with the sky.

1842, 1849

The Inward Morning [5]

Packed in my mind lie all the clothes
    Which outward nature wears,
And in its fashion's hourly change
    It all things else repairs.

In vain I look for change abroad,   5
    And can no difference find,
Till some new ray of peace uncalled
    Illumes my inmost mind.

What is it gilds the trees and clouds,
    And paints the heavens so gay,   10
But yonder fast-abiding light
    With its unchanging ray?

Lo, when the sun streams through the wood,
    Upon a winter's morn,
Where'er his silent beams intrude   15
    The murky night is gone.

How could the patient pine have known
    The morning breeze would come,
Or humble flowers anticipate
    The insect's noonday hum,—   20

Till the new light with morning cheer
    From far streamed through the aisles,

5. First published in *The Dial* for October, 1842, and reprinted in Thoreau's "Wednesday" chapter of *A Week on the Concord and Merrimack Rivers* (1849), where the text is identical with that of *Poems of Nature* (1895) and that given here.

And nimbly told the forest trees
    For many stretching miles?

I've heard within my inmost soul   25
    Such cheerful morning news,
In the horizon of my mind
    Have seen such orient hues,

As in the twilight of the dawn,
    When the first birds awake,   30
Are heard within some silent wood,
    Where they the small twigs break,

Or in the eastern skies are seen,
    Before the sun appears,
The harbingers of summer heats   35
    Which from afar he bears.

1842, 1849

Smoke [6]

Light-winged Smoke, Icarian bird,[7]
Melting thy pinions in thy upward flight;
Lark without song, and messenger of dawn,
Circling above the hamlets as they nest;
Or else, departing dream, and shadowy form   5
Of midnight vision, gathering up thy skirts;
By night star-veiling, and by day
Darkening the light and blotting out the sun;
Go thou my incense upward from this hearth,
And ask the gods to pardon this clear flame.   10

1843, 1854

6. One of the vignettes captioned "Orphics" published in *The Dial* for April, 1843, this was reprinted in "House-warming" in *Walden* (1854), following the sentence: "When the villagers were lighting their fires beyond the horizon, I too gave notice to the various wild inhabitants of Walden vale, by a smoky streamer from my chimney, that I was awake." The *Walden* text is identical with that of *Poems of Nature*, except for a comma at the end of l. 2.
7. Daedalus, mythical artisan of the Greeks, escaped his enemies on wings made of feathers, and wax, but Icarus, his son, melted his by flying too near the sun, and plunged to his death.

The Humanitarian and Critical Temper

HENRY WADSWORTH LONGFELLOW
(1807–1882)

Longfellow was one of the most serious writers of his age, and although a poet, enormously popular. He combined considerable learning with an enlightened understanding of the people, and he expressed the lives and ideals of humbler Americans in poems that they could not forget. Amid the rising democracy of his day, Longfellow became the national bard. His more popular poems strongly reflected the optimistic sentiment and the love of a good lesson that characterized the humanitarian spirit of the people. Unfortunately for his reputation in the twentieth century, the surviving picture has been that of the gray old poet of "The Children's Hour," seated by the fireside in the armchair made from "the spreading chestnut tree," a present from the children of Cambridge. Recent criticism has again emphasized the other Longfellow, well known to more discerning readers of his own day as the poet of "The Saga of King Olaf" and *Christus*, the author of great ballads and of many sonnets and reflective lyrics remarkable for imaginative propriety and constructive skill. To be sure, the familiar spirit is always present in his work, and this is not the tradition admired today, but it too contributes to what in his writing is genuine, large, and enduring.

Longfellow was born in Portland, Maine, on February 27, 1807, into a family of established tradition and moderate means. He attended Portland Academy and was tutored for admission to nearby Bowdoin College, which he entered in the sophomore class, a fellow student of Hawthorne. Having published his first poem at thirteen, two years earlier, he dreamed of "future eminence in literature." Upon his graduation in 1825, he accepted a professorship of foreign languages at Bowdoin, which included a provision for further preparatory study abroad. He visited France, Spain, Italy, and Germany, returning to Bowdoin in the autumn of 1829.

There he taught for six years, edited textbooks, and wrote articles on European literatures in the tradition of his profession. His reward was the offer of the Smith professorship at Harvard, which George Ticknor was vacating; and a leave of absence for further study of German. Meanwhile, he had married (1831), and published in the *New England Magazine* the travel sketches which appeared as his first volume, *Outre Mer*, in 1835. The twenty months abroad (1835–1836), increased Longfellow's knowledge of Germanic and Scandinavian literatures, soon to become a deep influence upon his writing.

His young wife died during the journey, in November, 1835. With renewed dedication to the combined responsibilities of teacher and creative writer, at the dawn of the well-named "flowering of New England," Longfellow soon became a leading figure among the writers and scholars of that region. Hawthorne was now an intimate friend. Within three years he entered upon the decade of remarkable production (1839–1849) which gave him national prominence and the affection of his countrymen.

Hyperion, a prose romance, and *Voices of the Night*, his first collection of poems, both appeared in 1839. *Ballads and Other Poems* (December, 1841, dated 1842), containing "The Skeleton in Armor," "The Wreck of the Hesperus," and "The Village Blacksmith," exactly expressed the popular spirit of the day. *Poems on Slavery* (1842) was followed by *The Spanish Student* (1843), his first large treatment of a foreign theme.

Of more importance was *The Belfry of Bruges and Other Poems* (1845, dated 1846). Such poems as "Nuremberg" illustrate how the poet familiarized untraveled Americans with the European scene and culture. At the same time he was acquainting his countrymen with themselves in such poems as "The Arsenal at Springfield," "The Old Clock on the Stairs," and "The Arrow and the Song." His contribution to the epic of his country found its first large expression in *Evangeline* (1847), which aroused national enthusiasm for its pictorial vividness and narrative skill. *The Seaside and the Fireside* (1849, dated 1850) contained "The Building of the Ship," a powerful plea for national unity in the face of the mounting crises before the Civil War. Minor works of this period include a prose tale, *Kavanagh* (1849), and several anthologies of poetry and criticism.

After two decades of conflict between the writer and the teacher, he resigned his Harvard professorship to James Russell Lowell in 1854. But Craigie House, his home in Cambridge, remained no less a sort of literary capitol. Longfellow had lodged there on first going to Harvard, and it became his as a gift from Nathan Appleton, the Lowell industrialist whose daughter the poet had married in 1843.

In 1855, he published *The Song of Hiawatha*, based on American Indian legends, and in 1858 *The Courtship of Miles Standish*, which popularized the legend of Plymouth Colony. These poems gave him an impregnable position in the affections of his countrymen, and increased his already wide recognition abroad. It is to be remembered that his appeal for the common reader in England was as great as at home, and rivaled that of Tennyson; a bust of Longfellow occupies a niche near the memorial to T. S. Eliot (who became a British citizen) in Westminster Abbey's Poets' Corner. They are the only Americans so honored.

In 1861, his beloved Frances Appleton, reputed heroine of *Hyperion* and eighteen years his wife, was burned to death. His deep religious feeling and his reflective spirit, present in his work from the beginning, now became dominant. He bent his energies upon two large works, earlier begun and laid aside. To the translation of Dante's *Divine Comedy* he brought both a scholar's love and religious devotion. It appeared in three volumes (1865–1867), principally in unrimed triplets, and it long remained a useful translation, although in most respects not an inspired one. However, *Christus, A Mystery* (1872) reveals at many points his highest inspiration. *The Golden Legend*, a cycle of religious miracle plays, ultimately Part II of *Christus*, had appeared in 1851. He now added Part III, *The New England Tragedies* (1868), two fine closet dramas dealing with the Puritan themes of "John Endicott" and "Giles Corey." Part I, published in 1871 as *The Divine Tragedy*, dealt with Christ's life and Passion.

During these last twenty years the poet published several additional volumes, containing many of his most mature reflective lyrics. When *Tales of a Wayside Inn* appeared in 1863, his publishers prepared an unprecedented first edition of fifteen thousand copies. A second group of the *Tales* appeared in *Three Books of Song* (1872), and a third in *Aftermath* (1873). These famous *Tales* ranged from the level of "Paul Revere's Ride" to "The Saga of King Olaf," a high point of accomplishment. Among other volumes were *Flower-de-Luce* (1867), in which the sonnets "Divina Commedia" appeared as a sequence; *The Masque of Pandora* (1875); *Kéramos and Other Poems* (1878); *Ultima Thule* (1880); and *In the Harbor*, published in 1882, the year of his death.

Longfellow's lapses into didacticism and sentimentality reflected the flabbier romanticism of his age, but he has remained in the tradition and memory of the American people. Admiration for Longfellow today rests on his gift for narrative and his daring experiments in narrative verse, on his balladry, his popularization of the national epic, his naturalization of foreign themes and poetic forms, his ability to bring his erudition within the range of general understanding, his versatile and sensitive craftsmanship, and, perhaps beyond all else, on the large and endearing qualities of the man himself.

The standard text is the Riverside Edition of the *Complete Poetical and Prose Works*, 11 vols., edited by H. E. Scudder, 1886, with valuable notes, based in part on Samuel Longfellow's *Life.* The one-volume *Complete Poetical Works*, Cambridge Edition, 1893, is excellent, and available.

The Life of Henry Wadsworth Longfellow, 2 vols., 1886, by the poet's brother, Samuel Longfellow, was for years the standard work, still serviceable. The same author added a third volume, *Final Memorials*, in 1887. A recent definitive work is Newton Arvin's *Longfellow: His Life and Work*, 1963. The best shorter biographies are T. W. Higginson, *Henry Wadsworth Longfellow*, American Men of Letters Series, 1902; James T. Hatfield, *New Light on Longfellow*, 1933; Lawrence Thompson, *Young Longfellow*, 1938; and Edward Wagenknecht, *Henry Wadsworth Longfellow * * *, 1966.

Hymn to the Night [1]

'Ασπασίη, τρίλλιστος

I heard the trailing garments of the Night
  Sweep through her marble halls!
I saw her sable skirts all fringed with light
  From the celestial walls!

I felt her presence, by its spell of might,   5
  Stoop o'er me from above;
The calm, majestic presence of the Night,
  As of the one I love.

I heard the sounds of sorrow and delight,
  The manifold, soft chimes,   10
That fill the haunted chambers of the Night,
  Like some old poet's rhymes.

From the cool cisterns of the midnight air
  My spirit drank repose;
The fountain of perpetual peace flows there,—   15
  From those deep cisterns flows.

O holy Night! from thee I learn to bear
  What man has borne before!
Thou layest thy finger on the lips of Care,
  And they complain no more.   20

Peace! Peace! Orestes-like [2] I breathe this prayer!
  Descend with broad-winged flight,
The welcome, the thrice-prayed for, the most fair,
  The best-beloved Night!

1839   1839

1. Written "in the summer of 1839," and published in December as the leading poem of the poet's first volume, *Voices of the Night*. The epigraph, translated "Welcome, thrice prayed for" (*cf.* l. 23), is from Homer's *Iliad*, Book VIII, l. 488.
2. Orestes was pursued by the Furies for having killed his mother to avenge his father's murder. His discovery of "peace" is the subject of Aeschylus' *Eumenides*.

The Skeleton in Armor [3]

"Speak! speak! thou fearful guest
Who, with thy hollow breast
Still in rude armor drest,
   Comest to daunt me!
Wrapt not in Eastern balms,   5
But with thy fleshless palms
Stretched, as if asking alms,
   Why dost thou haunt me?"

Then, from those cavernous eyes
Pale flashes seemed to rise,   10
As when the Northern skies
   Gleam in December;
And, like the water's flow
Under December's snow,
Came a dull voice of woe   15
   From the heart's chamber.

"I was a Viking old!
My deeds, though manifold,
No Skald in song has told,
   No Saga taught thee!   20
Take heed, that in thy verse
Thou dost the tale rehearse,
Else dread a dead man's curse;
   For this I sought thee.

"Far in the Northern Land,   25
By the wild Baltic's strand,
I, with my childish hand,
   Tamed the gerfalcon; [4]
And, with my skates fast-bound,
Skimmed the half-frozen Sound,   30
That the poor whimpering hound
   Trembled to walk on.

"Oft to his frozen lair
Tracked I the grisly bear,

---

3. This, like "The Wreck of the Hesperus," is an experiment in balladry. Its sources are older, representing the rough, two-beat measures of the verse of the Old English, Icelandic, and Norse skalds, or poets (*cf.* l. 19), which Longfellow had been studying, and used again in "The Saga of King Olaf." The story was Longfellow's response to the debated theories that an ancient stone tower in Newport, and an "armored" skeleton unearthed and destroyed at Fall River, were relics of prehistoric Scandinavian settlement. Written in 1840, the poem appeared in the *Knickerbocker Magazine* for January, 1841, before being collected in *Ballads and Other Poems* that year.
4. A large Arctic Falcon used in hunting.

While from my path the hare   35
  Fled like a shadow;
Oft through the forest dark
Followed the were-wolf's bark,
Until the soaring lark
  Sang from the meadow.   40

"But when I older grew,
Joining a corsair's crew,
O'er the dark sea I flew
  With the marauders.
Wild was the life we led;   45
Many the souls that sped,
Many the hearts that bled,
  By our stern orders.

"Many a wassail-bout
Wore the long Winter out;   50
Often our midnight shout
  Set the cocks crowing,
As we the Berserk's [5] tale
Measured in cups of ale,
Draining the oaken pail,   55
  Filled to o'erflowing.

"Once as I told in glee
Tales of the stormy sea,
Soft eyes did gaze on me,
  Burning yet tender;   60
And as the white stars shine
On the dark Norway pine,
On that dark heart of mine
  Fell their soft splendor.

"I wooed the blue-eyed maid,   65
Yielding, yet half afraid,
And in the forest's shade
  Our vows were plighted.
Under its loosened vest
Fluttered her little breast,   70
Like birds within their nest
  By the hawk frighted.

"Bright in her father's hall
Shields gleamed upon the wall,

5. Berserkers were legendary Norse warriors of invulnerable fury in battle.

Loud sang the minstrels all,   75
    Chanting his glory;
When of old Hildebrand
I asked his daughter's hand,
Mute did the minstrels stand.
    To hear my story.   80

"While the brown ale he quaffed,
Loud then the champion laughed,
And as the wind-gusts waft
    The sea-foam brightly,
So the loud laugh of scorn,   85
Out of those lips unshorn,
From the deep drinking-horn
    Blew the foam lightly.

"She was a Prince's child,
I but a Viking wild,   90
And though she blushed and smiled,
    I was discarded!
Should not the dove so white
Follow the sea-mew's [6] flight,
Why did they leave that night   95
    Her nest unguarded?

"Scarce had I put to sea,
Bearing the maid with me,
Fairest of all was she
    Among the Norsemen!   100
When on the white sea-strand,
Waving his armèd hand,
Saw we old Hildebrand,
    With twenty horsemen.

"Then launched they to the blast,   105
Bent like a reed each mast,
Yet we were gaining fast,
    When the wind failed us;
And with a sudden flaw
Came round the gusty Skaw,[7]   110
So that our foe we saw
    Laugh as he hailed us.

"And as to catch the gale
Round veered the flapping sail,

6. A species of European sea gull.   7. The northernmost cape of Jutland, Denmark.

'Death!' was the helmsman's hail,   115
  'Death without quarter!'
Mid-ships with iron keel
Struck we her ribs of steel;
Down her black hulk did reel
  Through the black water!   120

"As with his wings aslant,
Sails the fierce cormorant,
Seeking some rocky haunt,
  With his prey laden,—
So toward the open main,   125
Beating to sea again,
Through the wild hurricane,
  Bore I the maiden.

"Three weeks we westward bore,
And when the storm was o'er   130
Cloud-like we saw the shore
  Stretching to leeward;
There for my lady's bower
Built I the lofty tower,[8]
Which, to this very hour,   135
  Stands looking seaward.

"There lived we many years;
Time dried the maiden's tears;
She had forgot her fears,
  She was a mother;   140
Death closed her mild blue eyes,
Under that tower she lies;
Ne'er shall the sun arise
  On such another!

"Still grew my bosom then,   145
Still as a stagnant fen!
Hateful to me were men,
  The sunlight hateful!
In the vast forest here,
Clad in my warlike gear,   150
Fell I upon my spear,
  Oh, death was grateful!

"Thus, seamed with many scars,
Bursting these prison bars,

8. *I.e.,* the Newport tower.

Up to its native stars   155
  My soul ascended!
There from the flowing bowl
Deep drinks the warrior's soul,
Skoal! [9] to the Northland! *skoal!"*
  Thus the tale ended.   160

1840   1841

Serenade [1]

Stars of the summer night!
  Far in yon azure deeps,
Hide, hide your golden light!
    She sleeps!
  My lady sleeps!   5
    Sleeps!

Moon of the summer night!
  Far down yon western steeps,
Sink, sink in silver light!
    She sleeps!   10
  My lady sleeps!
    Sleeps!

Wind of the summer night!
  Where yonder woodbine creeps,
Fold, fold thy pinions light!   15
    She sleeps!
  My lady sleeps!
    Sleeps!

Dreams of the summer night!
  Tell her, her lover keeps   20
Watch! while in slumbers light
    She sleeps!
  My lady sleeps!
    Sleeps!

1840   1842, 1843

9. "In Scandinavia, this is the customary salutation when drinking a health.
* * * " [Longfellow's note].
1. This famous song, written in 1840,
was published in September, 1842, in
Graham's Magazine, and in 1843 as
part of the drama *The Spanish Student*
(Act I, Scene 3, ll. 8 ff.), where it is
sung below the bedroom balcony of
Preciosa, by her lover, Victorian.

Mezzo Cammin [2]

WRITTEN AT BOPPARD ON THE RHINE AUGUST 25, 1842, JUST
BEFORE LEAVING FOR HOME

Half of my life is gone, and I have let
   The years slip from me and have not fulfilled
   The aspiration of my youth, to build
   Some tower of song with lofty parapet.
Not indolence, nor pleasure, nor the fret   5
   Of restless passions that would not be stilled,
   But sorrow, and a care that almost killed,[3]
   Kept me from what I may accomplish yet;
Though, half-way up the hill, I see the Past
   Lying beneath me with its sounds and sights,—   10
   A city in the twilight dim and vast,
With smoking roofs, soft bells, and gleaming lights,—
   And hear above me on the autumnal blast
The cataract of Death far thundering from the heights.

1842   [1845] 1846

The Arsenal at Springfield [4]

This is the Arsenal. From floor to ceiling,
   Like a huge organ, rise the burnished arms;
But from their silent pipes no anthem pealing
   Startles the villages with strange alarms.

Ah! what a sound will rise, how wild and dreary,   5
   When the death-angel touches those swift keys!
What loud lament and dismal Miserere [5]
   Will mingle with their awful symphonies!

2. Among Longfellow's sonnets, this is notable for the effective irregularity of its extended last line. The words of the title appear in the first line of Dante's *Divine Comedy: Nel mezzo del cammin di nostra vita,* translated, "Midway upon the journey of our life." Like Dante when he wrote these lines, Longfellow had reached the mid-point of the biblical three score and ten years. The poem was collected in *The Belfry of Bruges,* dated 1846, but published on December 23, 1845.
3. Longfellow's first wife had died in 1835, during his previous trip abroad.
4. Longfellow and his second wife on their wedding journey in 1843 visited Springfield, Massachusetts, where the rows of guns on the walls of the arsenal suggested to the bride the organ pipes of death. The first International Peace Conference was meeting in London that year, and the next, 1844, saw the birth of the *Christian Citizen,* the first periodical devoted to the cause of peace. Longfellow responded with this poem in *Graham's Magazine,* April, 1844, and the next year collected it in *The Belfry of Bruges.*
5. A lyrical supplication for mercy; specifically, the first line of Psalm L, in the Latin Vulgate, used in the Catholic service: *Miserere mei Domine* ("Have mercy on me, Lord").

I hear even now the infinite fierce chorus,
    The cries of agony, the endless groan,   10
Which, through the ages that have gone before us,
    In long reverberations reach our own.

On helm and harness rings the Saxon hammer,
    Through Cimbric [6] forest roars the Norseman's song,
And loud, amid the universal clamor,   15
    O'er distant deserts sounds the Tartar gong.

I hear the Florentine, who from his palace
    Wheels out his battle-bell with dreadful din,
And Aztec priests upon their teocallis [7]
    Beat the wild war-drums made of serpent's skin;   20

The tumult of each sacked and burning village;
    The shout that every prayer for mercy drowns;
The soldiers' revels in the midst of pillage;
    The wail of famine in beleaguered towns;

The bursting shell, the gateway wrenched asunder,   25
    The rattling musketry, the clashing blade;
And ever and anon, in tones of thunder,
    The diapason of the cannonade.

Is it, O man, with such discordant noises,
    With such accursed instruments as these,   30
Thou drownest Nature's sweet and kindly voices,
    And jarrest the celestial harmonies?

Were half the power that fills the world with terror,
    Were half the wealth bestowed on camps and courts,
Given to redeem the human mind from error,   35
    There were no need of arsenals or forts:

The warrior's name would be a name abhorrèd!
    And every nation, that should lift again
Its hand against a brother, on its forehead
    Would wear forevermore the curse of Cain!   40

Down the dark future, through long generations,
    The echoing sounds grow fainter and then cease;
And like a bell, with solemn, sweet vibrations,
    I hear once more the voice of Christ say, "Peace!"

---

6. The Cimbri, originally Danish, long opposed the Roman Empire.

7. Places of worship of Mexican and Central American Indians, the temple surmounting a truncated pyramidal mound.

Peace! and no longer from its brazen portals 45
  The blast of War's great organ shakes the skies!
But beautiful as songs of the immortals,
  The holy melodies of love arise.

1844   1844, [1845] 1846

The Building of the Ship[8]

"Build me straight, O worthy Master!
  Stanch and strong, a goodly vessel,
That shall laugh at all disaster,
  And with wave and whirlwind wrestle!"

The merchant's word 5
Delighted the Master heard;
For his heart was in his work, and the heart
Giveth grace unto every Art.
A quiet smile played round his lips,
As the eddies and dimples of the tide 10
Play round the bows of ships,
That steadily at anchor ride.
And with a voice that was full of glee,
He answered, "Erelong we will launch
A vessel as goodly, and strong, and stanch, 15
As ever weathered a wintry sea!"
And first with nicest skill and art,
Perfect and finished in every part,
A little model the Master wrought,
Which should be to the larger plan 20
What the child is to the man,
Its counterpart in miniature;
That with a hand more swift and sure

8. In November, 1849, "The Building of the Ship" appeared as the "leading piece" in *The Seaside and Fireside* (dated 1850). It was at once recognized as relating to the national disunity that had just reached its crisis with the Mexican War. The Compromise of 1850 had not yet effected an uneasy truce between the factions of North and South when the great Fanny Kemble read the poem, on February 12, to an audience "of more than than three thousand" in Boston. It swept the country and remained an eloquent plea for the preservation of the Union. On a dark day of the Civil War, when Noah Brooks read it to President Lincoln, "his eyes filled with tears, and * * * he did not speak for some minutes, but finally said, with simplicity: 'It is a wonderful gift to be able to stir men like that.'" During World War II, Winston Churchill, in a speech referring to Allied unity, quoted part of the famous closing section. Longfellow acknowledged the inspiration of Schiller's *The Song of the Bell* for the form of this poem; certainly he was also inspired by his love of craftsmanship, and especially by his observation of the craft of the shipbuilder in the Portland Harbor of his boyhood.

The greater labor might be brought
To answer to his inward thought. 25
And as he labored, his mind ran o'er
The various ships that were built of yore,
And above them all, and strangest of all
Towered the Great Harry,⁹ crank and tall,
Whose picture was hanging on the wall, 30
With bows and stern raised high in air,
And balconies hanging here and there,
And signal lanterns and flags afloat,
And eight round towers, like those that frown
From some old castle, looking down 35
Upon the drawbridge and the moat.
And he said with a smile, "Our ship, I wis,
Shall be of another form than this!"
It was of another form, indeed;
Built for freight, and yet for speed, 40
A beautiful and gallant craft;
Broad in the beam, that the stress of the blast,
Pressing down upon sail and mast,
Might not the sharp bows overwhelm;
Broad in the beam, but sloping aft 45
With graceful curve and slow degrees,
That she might be docile to the helm,
And that the currents of parted seas,
Closing behind, with mighty force,
Might aid and not impede her course. 50

In the ship-yard stood the Master,
With the model of the vessel,
That should laugh at all disaster,
And with wave and whirlwind wrestle!

Covering many a rood of ground, 55
Lay the timber piled around;
Timber of chestnut, and elm, and oak,
And scattered here and there, with these,
The knarred ¹ and crooked cedar knees;
Brought from regions far away, 60
From Pascagoula's sunny bay,²
And the banks of the roaring Roanoke! ³

---

9. Famous war vessel, built in 1488 by
Henry VII, first Tudor King of England (1485–1509), whose marriage in
1486 united the warring Houses of Lan-
caster and York.
1. Gnarled, knotty.

2. Mouth of the Pascagoula River, at
the eastern extremity of the gulf coast
of Mississippi.
3. The Roanoke flows through Virginia
and northern North Carolina, emptying
in Albemarle Sound.

Ah! what a wondrous thing it is
To note how many wheels of toil
One thought, one word, can set in motion! 65
There's not a ship that sails the ocean,
But every climate, every soil,
Must bring its tribute, great or small,
And help to build the wooden wall!

The sun was rising o'er the sea, 70
And long the level shadows lay,
As if they, too, the beams would be
Of some great, airy argosy,
Framed and launched in a single day.
That silent architect, the sun, 75
Had hewn and laid them every one,
Ere the work of man was yet begun.
Beside the Master, when he spoke,
A youth, against an anchor leaning,
Listened, to catch his slightest meaning, 80
Only the long waves, as they broke
In ripples on the pebbly beach,
Interrupted the old man's speech.

Beautiful they were, in sooth,
The old man and the fiery youth! 85
The old man, in whose busy brain
Many a ship that sailed the main
Was modelled o'er and o'er again;—
The fiery youth, who was to be
The heir of his dexterity, 90
The heir of his house, and his daughter's hand,
When he had built and launched from land
What the elder head had planned.

"Thus," said he, "will we build this ship!
Lay square the blocks upon the slip, 95
And follow well this plan of mine.
Choose the timbers with greatest care;
Of all that is unsound beware;
For only what is sound and strong
To this vessel shall belong. 100
Cedar of Maine and Georgia pine
Here together shall combine.
A goodly frame, and a goodly fame,
And the UNION be her name!
For the day that gives her to the sea 105

Shall give my daughter unto thee!"

The Master's word
Enraptured the young man heard;
And as he turned his face aside,
With a look of joy and a thrill of pride   110
Standing before
Her father's door,
He saw the form of his promised bride.
The sun shone on her golden hair,
And her cheek was glowing fresh and fair,   115
With the breath of morn and the soft sea air.
Like a beauteous barge was she,
Still at rest on the sandy beach,
Just beyond the billow's reach;
But he   120
Was the restless, seething, stormy sea!
Ah, how skilful grows the hand
That obeyeth Love's command!
It is the heart, and not the brain,
That to the highest doth attain,   125
And he who followeth Love's behest
Far excelleth all the rest!
Thus with the rising of the sun
Was the noble task begun,
And soon throughout the ship-yard's bounds   130
Were heard the intermingled sounds
Of axes and of mallets, plied
With vigorous arms on every side;
Plied so deftly and so well,
That, ere the shadows of evening fell,   135
The keel of oak for a noble ship,
Scarfed [4] and bolted, straight and strong,
Was lying ready, and stretched along
The blocks, well placed upon the slip.
Happy, thrice happy, every one   140
Who sees his labor well begun,
And not perplexed and multiplied,
By idly waiting for time and tide!

And when the hot, long day was o'er,
The young man at the Master's door   145
Sat with the maiden calm and still,
And within the porch, a little more

---

4. Jointed. Two timbers bearing weight in a continuous line, as in a keel, are scarfed by halved and overlapped ends spliced together by bolts.

Removed beyond the evening chill,
The father sat, and told them tales
Of wrecks in the great September gales, 150
Of pirates crossing the Spanish Main,
And ships that never came back again,
The chance and change of a sailor's life,
Want and plenty, rest and strife,
His roving fancy, like the wind, 155
That nothing can stay and nothing can bind,
And the magic charm of foreign lands,
With shadows of palms, and shining sands,
Where the tumbling surf,
O'er the coral reefs of Madagascar, 160
Washes the feet of the swarthy Lascar,
As he lies alone and asleep on the turf,
And the trembling maiden held her breath
At the tales of that awful, pitiless sea,
With all its terror and mystery, 165
The dim, dark sea, so like unto Death,
That divides and yet unites mankind!
And whenever the old man paused, a gleam
From the bowl of his pipe would awhile illume
The silent group in the twilight gloom, 170
And thoughtful faces, as in a dream;
And for a moment one might mark
What had been hidden by the dark,
That the head of the maiden lay at rest,
Tenderly, on the young man's breast! 175
Day by day the vessel grew,
With timbers fashioned strong and true,
Stemson and keelson and sternson-knee,[5]
Till, framed with perfect symmetry,
A skeleton ship rose up to view! 180
And around the bows and along the side
The heavy hammers and mallets plied,
Till after many a week, at length,
Wonderful for form and strength,
Sublime in its enormous bulk, 185
Loomed aloft the shadowy hulk!
And around it columns of smoke, upwreathing,
Rose from the boiling, bubbling, seething

5. In the fundamental "frame" of a ship, the keelson (kelson) is the principal longitudinal supporting member of the keel; the stemson is the upright support of the timbers at the bow; the sternson-knee is the after end (rear) of the keelson, fitted to support the upright sternpost.

Caldron, that glowed
And overflowed   190
With the black tar, heated for the sheathing.
And amid the clamors
Of clattering hammers,
He who listened heard now and then
The song of the Master and his men:—   195

"Build me straight, O worthy Master,
    Stanch and strong, a goodly vessel,
That shall laugh at all disaster,
    And with wave and whirlwind wrestle!

With oaken brace and copper band,   200
Lay the rudder on the sand,
That, like a thought, should have control
Over the movement of the whole;
And near it the anchor, whose giant hand
Would reach down and grapple with the land,   205
And immovable and fast
Hold the great ship against the bellowing blast!
And at the bows an image stood,
By a cunning artist carved in wood,
With robes of white, that far behind   210
Seemed to be fluttering in the wind.
It was not shaped in a classic mould,
Not like a Nymph or Goddess of old,
Or Naiad rising from the water,
But modelled from the Master's daughter!   215
On many a dreary and misty night,
'Twill be seen by the rays of the signal light,
Speeding along through the rain and the dark,
Like a ghost in its snow-white sark,[6]
The pilot of some phantom bark,   220
Guiding the vessel, in its flight,
By a path none other knows aright!
Behold, at last,
Each tall and tapering mast
Is swung into its place;   225
Shrouds and stays
Holding it firm and fast![7]

6. Shirt.
7. Longfellow carefully notes "that sometimes * * * vessels are launched fully sparred and rigged * * * in order to save time, and to make a show." He begs the exception "as better suited to my purpose than the general rule," citing instances in New York, and in Maine at Portland and Ellsworth.

Long ago,
In the deer-haunted forests of Maine,
When upon mountain and plain   230
Lay the snow,
They fell,—those lordly pines!
Those grand, majestic pines!
'Mid shouts and cheers
The jaded steers,   235
Panting beneath the goad,
Dragged down the weary, winding road
Those captive kings so straight and tall,
To be shorn of their streaming hair,
And naked and bare,   240
To feel the stress and the strain
Of the wind and the reeling main,
Whose roar
Would remind them forevermore
Of their native forests they should not see again.   245

And everywhere
The slender, graceful spars
Poise aloft in the air,
And at the mast-head,
White, blue, and red,   250
A flag unrolls the stripes and stars.
Ah! when the wanderer, lonely, friendless,
In foreign harbors shall behold
That flag unrolled,
'Twill be as a friendly hand   255
Stretched out from his native land,
Filling his heart with memories sweet and endless!

All is finished! and at length
Has come the bridal day
Of beauty and strength.   260
Today the vessel shall be launched!
With fleecy clouds the sky is blanched,
And o'er the bay,
Slowly, in all his splendors dight,
The great sun rises to behold the sight.   265
The ocean old,
Centuries old,
Strong as youth, and as uncontrolled,
Paces restless to and fro,
Up and down the sands of gold.   270

His beating heart is not at rest;
And far and wide,
With ceaseless flow,
His beard of snow
Heaves with the heaving of his breast.   275
He waits impatient for his bride.
There she stands,
With her foot upon the sands,
Decked with flags and streamers gay,
In honor of her marriage day,   280
Her snow-white signals fluttering, blending,
Round her like a veil descending,
Ready to be
The bride of the gray old sea.

On the deck another bride   285
Is standing by her lover's side.
Shadows from the flag and shrouds,
Like the shadows cast by clouds,
Broken by many a sudden fleck,
Fall around them on the deck.   290

The prayer is said,
The service read,
The joyous bridegroom bows his head;
And in tears the good old Master
Shakes the brown hand of his son,   295
Kisses his daughter's glowing cheek
In silence, for he cannot speak,
And ever faster
Down his own the tears begin to run.
The worthy pastor—   300
The shepherd of that wandering flock,
That has the ocean for its wold,
That has the vessel for its fold,
Leaping ever from rock to rock—
Spake, with accents mild and clear,   305
Words of warning, words of cheer,
But tedious to the bridegroom's ear.
He knew the chart
Of the sailor's heart,
All its pleasures and its griefs,   310
All its shallows and rocky reefs,
All those secret currents, that flow
With such resistless undertow,

And lift and drift, with terrible force,
The will from its moorings and its course.   315
Therefore he spake, and thus [8] said he:—
"Like unto ships far off at sea,
Outward or homeward bound, are we.

Before, behind, and all around,
Floats and swings the horizon's bound,   320
Seems at its distant rim to rise
And climb the crystal wall of the skies,
And then again to turn and sink,
As if we could slide from its outer brink.
Ah! it is not the sea,   325
It is not the sea that sinks and shelves,
But ourselves
That rock and rise
With endless and uneasy motion,
Now touching the very skies,   330
Now sinking into the depths of ocean.
Ah! if our souls but poise and swing
Like the compass in its brazen ring,
Ever level and ever true
To the toil of the task we have to do,   335
We shall sail securely, and safely reach
The Fortunate Isles,[9] on whose shining beach
The sights we see, and the sounds we hear,
Will be those of joy and not of fear!"

Then the Master,   340
With a gesture of command,
Waved his hand;
And at the word,
Loud and sudden there was heard,
All around them and below,   345
The sound of hammers, blow on blow,
Knocking away the shores and spurs.[1]
And see! she stirs!
She starts,—she moves,—she seems to feel
The thrill of life along her keel,   350
And, spurning with her foot the ground,
With one exulting, joyous bound,

---

8. Pastors of sailors' churches, endeared in the tradition of New England wooden ships and whaling, are typified by the famous Father Taylor of the Seamen's Bethel of Boston, whose sea-savored sermons are recalled in that below, as also in that of Melville's Father Mapple (*Moby Dick*, Chapter 9).

9. Established by Virgil's "fortunate isle" as journey's end, or paradise; *cf. Aeneid*, Book VI, l. 639.

1. Carpenter's terms for the props and braces that hold the vessel in the slip.

She leaps into the ocean's arms!
And lo! from the assembled crowd
There rose a shout, prolonged and loud,   355
That to the ocean seemed to say,
"Take her, O bridegroom, old and gray,
Take her to thy protecting arms,
With all her youth and all her charms!"

How beautiful she is! How fair   360
She lies within those arms, that press
Her form with many a soft caress
Of tenderness and watchful care!
Sail forth into the sea, O ship!
Through wind and wave, right onward steer!   365
The moistened eye, the trembling lip,
Are not the signs of doubt or fear.
Sail forth into the sea of life,
O gentle, loving, trusting wife,
And safe from all adversity   370
Upon the bosom of that sea
Thy comings and thy goings be!
For gentleness and love and trust
Prevail o'er angry wave and gust;
And in the wreck of noble lives   375
Something immortal still survives!

Thou, too, sail on, O Ship of State!
Sail on, O UNION, strong and great!
Humanity with all its fears,
With all the hopes of future years,   380
Is hanging breathless on thy fate!
We know what Master laid thy keel,
What Workmen wrought thy ribs of steel,
Who made each mast, and sail, and rope,
What anvils rang, what hammers beat,   385
In what a forge and what a heat
Were shaped the anchors of thy hope!
Fear not each sudden sound and shock,
'Tis of the wave and not the rock;
'Tis but the flapping of the sail,   390
And not a rent made by the gale!
In spite of rock and tempest's roar,
In spite of false lights on the shore,
Sail on, nor fear to breast the sea!
Our hearts, our hopes, are all with thee,   395
Our hearts, our hopes, our prayers, our tears,

Our faith triumphant o'er our fears,
Are all with thee,—are all with thee!

1849   [1849] 1850

The Jewish Cemetery at Newport[2]

How strange it seems! These Hebrews in their graves,
    Close by the street of this fair seaport town,
Silent beside the never-silent waves,
    At rest in all this moving up and down!

The trees are white with dust, that o'er their sleep   5
    Wave their broad curtains in the southwind's breath,
While underneath these leafy tents they keep
    The long, mysterious Exodus of Death.[3]

And these sepulchral stones, so old and brown,
    That pave with level flags their burial-place,   10
Seem like the tablets of the Law, thrown down
    And broken by Moses at the mountain's base.[4]

The very names recorded here are strange,
    Of foreign accent, and of different climes;
Alvares and Rivera[5] interchange   15
    With Abraham and Jacob of old times.

"Blessed be God! for he created Death!"
    The mourners said, "and Death is rest and peace;"
Then added, in the certainty of faith,
    "And giveth life that nevermore shall cease."   20

Closed are the portals of their Synagogue,
    No Psalms of David now the silence break,
No Rabbi reads the ancient Decalogue
    In the grand dialect the Prophets spake.

2. In his diary for July 9, 1852, at Newport, Rhode Island, the poet wrote: "Went this morning into the Jewish burying-ground * * * There are few graves; nearly all are low tombstones of marble with Hebrew inscriptions, and a few words added in English or Portuguese. * * * It is a shady nook, at the corner of two dusty, frequented streets, with an iron fence and a granite gateway * * * " The poem was written in the difficult stanza of Gray's "Elegy Written in a Country Church-yard." Longfellow's poem appeared in *Putnam's Monthly Magazine* for July, 1854, and was included in the "Birds of Passage" section of *The Courtship of Miles Standish* (1858).
3. Exodus, second book of the Old Testament, records the migration of the Israelites from Egypt under Moses.
4. *Cf.* Exodus xxxii: 19.
5. The majority of the colonial Jewish families of New England were traders from Portugal or Spain.

Gone are the living, but the dead remain,   25
    And not neglected; for a hand unseen,
Scattering its bounty, like a summer rain,
    Still keeps their graves and their remembrance green.

How came they here? What burst of Christian hate,
    What persecution, merciless and blind,   30
Drove o'er the sea—that desert desolate—
    These Ishmaels and Hagars of mankind? [6]

They lived in narrow streets and lanes obscure,
    Ghetto and Judenstrass,[7] in mirk and mire;
Taught in the school of patience to endure   35
    The life of anguish and the death of fire.

All their lives long, with the unleavened bread
    And bitter herbs of exile and its fears,
The wasting famine of the heart they fed,
    And slaked its thirst with marah [8] of their tears.   40

Anathema maranatha! [9] was the cry
    That rang from town to town, from street to street;
At every gate the accursed Mordecai [1]
    Was mocked and jeered, and spurned by Christian feet.

Pride and humiliation hand in hand   45
    Walked with them through the world where'er they went;
Trampled and beaten were they as the sand,
    And yet unshaken as the continent.

For in the background figures vague and vast
    Of patriarchs and of prophets rose sublime,   50
And all the great traditions of the Past
    They saw reflected in the coming time.

And thus forever with reverted look
    The mystic volume of the world they read,
Spelling it backward like a Hebrew book,   55
    Till life became a Legend of the Dead.

6. Abraham's concubine, Hagar, and her son, Ishmael, were exiled when his aged wife, Sarah, bore Isaac (Genesis xvi and xxi).
7. Ghetto and Judenstrass (German, correctly *Judenstrasse,* "street of Jews") refer to restricted urban areas designated for Jews.
8. Hebrew, "bitterness." Marah was a spring of bitter, undrinkable water found by the famishing Israelites in the wilderness. *Cf.* Exodus xv: 23–26.
9. *Cf.* I Corinthians xvi: 22. St. Paul's terms, *Anathema* (Greek, "devoted to destruction") *Maran 'atha* (Aramaic, "at the coming of the Lord"), were applied to all those who "love not the Lord Jesus Christ"; later they were applied specifically to the Jews.
1. Haman and his friends, jealous of the advancement of the Jew Mordecai, attempted to obtain a decree for the destruction of all Jews in the realm of the Persian king, Ahasuerus. See Esther iii.

But ah! what once has been shall be no more!
The groaning earth in travail and in pain
Brings forth its races, but does not restore,
And the dead nations never rise again.   60

1852   1854, 1858

My Lost Youth [2]

Often I think of the beautiful town
  That is seated by the sea; [3]
Often in thought go up and down
The pleasant streets of that dear old town,
  And my youth comes back to me.   5
    And a verse of a Lapland song
    Is haunting my memory still:
    "A boy's will is the wind's will,
And the thoughts of youth are long, long thoughts." [4]

I can see the shadowy lines of its trees,   10
  And catch, in sudden gleams,
The sheen of the far-surrounding seas,
And islands that were the Hesperides [5]
  Of all my boyish dreams.
    And the burden of that old song,   15
    It murmurs and whispers still:
    "A boy's will is the wind's will,
And the thoughts of youth are long, long thoughts."

I remember the black wharves and the slips,
  And the sea-tides tossing free;   20
And Spanish sailors with bearded lips,
And the beauty and mystery of the ships,

2. Like "The Building of the Ship," this poem contains "a memory of Portland,—my native town, the city by the sea," as Longfellow noted in his diary on March 29, 1855. The next day, he continued, "Wrote the poem; and am rather pleased with it, and with the bringing in of the two lines of the old Lapland song." He was referring to the two-line refrain ending each stanza. These words became so familiar that, as late as 1913, Robert Frost could call his first volume *A Boy's Will,* and be understood. Longfellow's poem appeared in *Putnam's Monthly Magazine* for August, 1855, and was included among the "other poems" of *The Courtship of Miles Standish* volume (1858).

3. In his diary Longfellow associates these words with those of Francesca in Dante's *Inferno,* v, 97–98: "Sieda la terra dove nato fui / Sulla marina." (The city where I was born is situated on the seashore.)
4. The Cambridge *Complete Poetical Works* reports the source of this refrain as John Scheffer's *History of Lapland* (Oxford, 1674), where occur the lines: "A Youth's desire is the desire of the wind, / All his essaies / Are long delaies, / No issue can they find."
5. The mythical garden of the golden apples which Ge (the earth) gave Hera, queen of the gods, on her marriage to Zeus.

And the magic of the sea.
    And the voice of that wayward song
    Is singing and saying still: 25
    "A boy's will is the wind's will,
And the thoughts of youth are long, long thoughts."

I remember the bulwarks by the shore,
    And the fort upon the hill; [6]
The sunrise gun, with its hollow roar,   30
The drum-beat repeated o'er and o'er,
    And the bugle wild and shrill.
    And the music of that old song
    Throbs in my memory still:
    "A boy's will is the wind's will,   35
And the thoughts of youth are long, long thoughts."

I remember the sea-fight far away, [7]
    How it thundered o'er the tide!
And the dead captains, as they lay
In their graves, o'erlooking the tranquil bay   40
    Where they in battle died.
    And the sound of that mournful song
    Goes through me with a thrill:
    "A boy's will is the wind's will,
And the thoughts of youth are long, long thoughts."   45

I can see the breezy dome of groves,
    The shadows of Deering's Woods;
And the friendships old and the early loves
Come back with a Sabbath sound, as of doves
    In quiet neighborhoods.   50
    And the verse of that sweet old song,
    It flutters and murmurs still:
    "A boy's will is the wind's will,
And the thoughts of youth are long, long thoughts."

I remember the gleams and glooms that dart   55
    Across the school-boy's brain;
The song and the silence in the heart,

6. Years before, in 1846, Longfellow noted in his diary a walk around "Munjoy's Hill and Fort St. Lawrence." There he "lay down in one of the embrasures and listened to the lashing, lulling sound of the sea just at my feet * * * the harbor was full of white sails * * * Meditated a poem on the old Fort." But no poem resulted at that time.

7. "This was the engagement between the [American] *Enterprise* and [British] *Boxer* off the harbor of Portland, in which both captains were slain. They were buried side by side in the cemetery on Mountjoy [Munjoy Hill]" [Longfellow's note]. The *Enterprise* won this battle (1813), which Longfellow, a boy of six, may have seen; he is reported as witnessing the burial of the captains.

That in part are prophecies, and in part
  Are longings wild and vain.
    And the voice of that fitful song   60
    Sings on, and is never still:
    "A boy's will is the wind's will,
And the thoughts of youth are long, long thoughts."

There are things of which I may not speak;
  There are dreams that cannot die;   65
There are thoughts that make the strong heart weak,
And bring a pallor into the cheek,
  And a mist before the eye.
    And the words of that fatal song
    Come over me like a chill: 70
    "A boy's will is the wind's will,
And the thoughts of youth are long, long thoughts."

Strange to me now are the forms I meet
  When I visit the dear old town;
But the native air is pure and sweet,   75
And the trees that o'ershadow each well-known street,
  As they balance up and down,
    Are singing the beautiful song,
    Are sighing and whispering still:
    "A boy's will is the wind's will,   80
And the thoughts of youth are long, long thoughts."

And Deering's Woods are fresh and fair,
  And with joy that is almost pain
My heart goes back to wander there,
And among the dreams of the days that were,   85
  I find my lost youth again.
    And the strange and beautiful song,
    The groves are repeating it still:
    "A boy's will is the wind's will,
And the thoughts of youth are long, long thoughts."   90

1855   1855, 1858

Divina Commedia [8]

I

Oft have I seen at some cathedral door
  A laborer, pausing in the dust and heat,

8. After his second wife was burned to death in 1861, Longfellow found relief in his translation of Dante's *Divine Comedy*. Volume I, *Inferno*, appeared in 1865, introduced by the first two sonnets. In the complete translation (1867), the six sonnets were distributed as introductory pieces, two for each

Lay down his burden, and with reverent feet
Enter, and cross himself, and on the floor
Kneel to repeat his paternoster [9] o'er;   5
   Far off the noises of the world retreat;
   The loud vociferations of the street
Become an undistinguishable roar.
So, as I enter here from day to day,
   And leave my burden at this minster gate,   10
   Kneeling in prayer, and not ashamed to pray,
The tumult of the time disconsolate
   To inarticulate murmurs dies away,
   While the eternal ages watch and wait.

II

How strange the sculptures that adorn these towers!
   This crowd of statues, in whose folded sleeves
   Birds build their nests; while canopied with leaves
Parvis [1] and portal bloom like trellised bowers,
And the vast minster seems a cross of flowers!   5
   But fiends and dragons on the gargoyled eaves [2]
   Watch the dead Christ between the living thieves, [3]
And, underneath, the traitor Judas lowers!
Ah! from what agonies of heart and brain,
   What exultations trampling on despair,   10
   What tenderness, what tears, what hate of wrong,
What passionate outcry of a soul in pain,
   Uprose this poem of the earth and air,
   This mediæval miracle of song!

III

I enter, and I see thee in the gloom
   Of the long aisles, O poet saturnine! [4]
   And strive to make my steps keep pace with thine.
The air is filled with some unknown perfume;
The congregation of the dead make room   5
   For thee to pass; the votive tapers shine;
   Like rooks that haunt Ravenna's [5] groves of pine

---

volume. They appeared first, however, in the *Atlantic Monthly* for December, 1864 and November, 1866. As a sequence of sonnets they were first published in the volume *Flower-de-Luce* (1867). In these masterpieces of sonnet literature, the poet's experience of Dante and his great religious poem is identified with the personal tragedy of his wife's death in the flames.
9. Translated "Our Father"; *i.e.*, the Lord's Prayer.

1. A court, or a single portico, before a church.
2. The grotesques in Dante's *Inferno* are in this passage compared with those of cathedral sculpture.
3. Christ was crucified between two thieves, and was declared dead before they.
4. Referring to the grave and solemn tone of Dante.
5. Dante often expressed fondness for Ravenna, where he was buried.

The hovering echoes fly from tomb to tomb.
From the confessionals I hear arise
  Rehearsals of forgotten tragedies,   10
  And lamentations from the crypts below;
And then a voice celestial that begins
  With the pathetic words, "Although your sins
  As scarlet be," and ends with "as the snow." [6]

IV

With snow-white veil and garments as of flame,
  She stands before thee, who so long ago
  Filled thy young heart with passion and woe
From which thy song and all its splendors came; [7]
And while with stern rebuke she speaks thy name,   5
  The ice about thy heart melts as the snow
  On mountain heights, and in swift overflow
  Comes gushing from thy lips in sobs of shame.
Thou makest full confession; and a gleam,
  As of the dawn on some dark forest cast,   10
  Seems on thy lifted forehead to increase;
Lethe and Eunoë [8]—the remembered dream
  And the forgotten sorrow—bring at last
  That perfect pardon which is perfect peace.

V

I lift mine eyes, and all the windows blaze
  With forms of Saints and holy men who died,
  Here martyred and hereafter glorified;
And the great Rose [9] upon its leaves displays
Christ's Triumph, and the angelic roundelays,   5
  With splendor upon splendor multiplied;
  And Beatrice again at Dante's side
  No more rebukes, but smiles her words of praise. [1]
And then the organ sounds, and unseen choirs
  Sing the old Latin hymns of peace and love   10
  And benedictions of the Holy Ghost;
And the melodious bells among the spires
  O'er all the house-tops and through heaven above
  Proclaim the elevation of the Host! [2]

6. *Cf.* Isaiah i: 18, and Dante, *Purgatorio*, xxxi, 98.
7. Dante experiences visionary union with the dead Beatrice in both the *Purgatorio* and the *Paradiso*.
8. In the *Purgatorio*, Dante drinks the waters of two rivers: Lethe, providing forgetfulness; and Eunoë, giving memory of the good.
9. In the *Paradiso*, xxxi, Dante's pilgrimage ends with his vision of the *rosa sempeterna*, in which the Virgin and the Trinity appear, surrounded by the saints in a paradise shaped like the petals of a great rose.
1. *Cf. Paradiso*, xxx.
2. The consecrated bread of the sacrament of the Lord's Supper (Eucharist), held up or "elevated" at the climax of this ritual.

VI

O star of morning and of liberty![3]
 O bringer of the light, whose splendor shines
 Above the darkness of the Apennines,
 Forerunner of the day that is to be!
The voices of the city and the sea,   5
 The voices of the mountains and the pines,
 Repeat thy song, till the familiar lines
 Are footpaths for the thought of Italy!
Thy flame is blown abroad from all heights,
 Through all the nations, and a sound is heard,   10
 As of a mighty wind, and men devout,
Strangers of Rome, and the new proselytes,
 In their own language hear thy wondrous word,
 And many are amazed and many doubt.

1864–1867   1865–1867

Chaucer

An old man in a lodge within a park;
 The chamber walls depicted all around
 With portraitures of huntsman, hawk, and hound,
 And the hurt deer. He listeneth to the lark,
Whose song comes with the sunshine through the dark   5
 Of painted glass in leaden lattice bound;
 He listeneth and he laugheth at the sound,
 Then writeth in a book like any clerk[4]
He is the poet of the dawn, who wrote
 The Canterbury Tales, and his old age   10
 Made beautiful with song; and as I read
I hear the crowing cock, I hear the note
 Of lark and linnet, and from every page
 Rise odors of ploughed field or flowery mead.

1873   1875

Keats

The young Endymion sleeps Endymion's sleep;[5]
The shepherd-boy whose tale was left half told!

3. The familiar concept of Dante as morning star of a new democratic freedom, especially for Italy.
4. A scholar. *Cf.* Chaucer's "Clerk of Oxenford," one of the most appealing characters of the *Canterbury Tales.*
5. Longfellow suggests the analogy of the tragically brief life of John Keats with the theme of the Romantic poet's most ambitious poem, *Endymion* (1818). The youth, in search of eternal beauty personified in a visionary goddess, discovers her to be the goddess of the moon, who rewards his love with immortality and eternal sleep.

The solemn grove uplifts its shield of gold
To the red rising moon, and loud and deep
The nightingale is singing from the steep;   5
    It is midsummer, but the air is cold;
    Can it be death? Alas, beside the fold
A shepherd's pipe lies shattered near his sheep.
Lo! in the moonlight gleams a marble white,
    On which I read: "Here lieth one whose name   10
    Was writ in water." [6] And was this the meed
Of his sweet singing? Rather let me write:
    "The smoking flax before it burst to flame
    Was quenched by death, and broken the bruised reed." [7]

1873   1875

Nature [8]

As a fond mother, when the day is o'er,
    Leads by the hand her little child to bed,
    Half willing, half reluctant to be led,
And leave his broken playthings on the floor,
Still gazing at them through the open door,   5
    Nor wholly reassured and comforted
    By promises of others in their stead,
    Which, though more splendid, may not please him more;
So Nature deals with us, and takes away
    Our playthings one by one, and by the hand   10
    Leads us to rest so gently, that we go
Scarce knowing if we wish to go or stay,
    Being too full of sleep to understand
    How far the unknown transcends the what we know.

1875

The Tide Rises, the Tide Falls

The tide rises, the tide falls,
The twilight darkens, the curlew calls; [9]

6. Keats composed this as his own epitaph (writing "lies," not "lieth"), and directed that it be inscribed on his tombstone.
7. "A bruised reed shall he not break, and the smoking flax shall he not quench" (Isaiah xlii: 3).
8. This sonnet, famous for its fusion of simplicity with profound sentiment, appeared in the volume *The Masque of Pandora* (1875).

9. The cry of the curlew along the shore must suggest evening for anyone with a seashore boyhood. This allegory of the evening of life, simple, yet strong, and deeply felt, stands high among Longfellow's many treatments of the theme at this time, such as "Morituri Salutamus," "Nature," and the two poems that follow. Appropriately, this poem appeared in the volume *Ultima Thule* (1880).

Along the sea-sands damp and brown
The traveller hastens toward the town,
    And the tide rises, the tide falls.   5

Darkness settles on roofs and walls,
But the sea, the sea in the darkness calls;
The little waves, with their soft, white hands,
Efface the footprints in the sands,
    And the tide rises, the tide falls.   10

The morning breaks; the steeds in their stalls
Stamp and neigh, as the hostler calls;
The day returns, but nevermore
Returns the traveller to the shore,
    And the tide rises, the tide falls.   15

1879   1880

Ultima Thule

DEDICATION: TO G. W. G. [1]

With favoring winds, o'er sunlit seas,
We sailed for the Hesperides,[2]
The land where golden apples grow;
But that, ah! that was long ago.

How far since then the ocean streams   5
Have swept us from the land of dreams,
That land of fiction and of truth,
The lost Atlantis [3] of our youth!

Whither, ah, whither? are not these
The tempest-haunted Orcades,[4]   10
Where sea-gulls scream, and breakers roar,
And wreck and sea-weed line the shore?

Ultima Thule! Utmost Isle!
Here in thy harbors for awhile

1. The volume *Ultima Thule* (1880), was dedicated, in this poem, to George Washington Greene, a friend with whom, in young manhood, Longfellow had shared confessions of goals and aspirations in life. Ultima Thule, to ancient navigators, suggested the northernmost limits of the habitable world, the ultimate journey's end.
2. The Hesperides were the "blessed Isles" of Greek myth, where the golden apples grew which Ge (the earth) gave to Hera as a wedding gift.
3. A fabulous land of wealth and happiness which, the ancients believed, had sunk into the sea.
4. A variant text gives "Hebrides"; like the Orcades these are islands off the Scottish coast, and were, to the ancient Greeks, "tempest-haunted."

We lower our sails, awhile we rest   15
From the unending endless quest.

1879   1880

JOHN GREENLEAF WHITTIER
(1807–1892)

Longfellow became a poet of the people by choice and by nature, but Whittier was fitted for that rôle also by all the circumstances of his early experience and family tradition. The Whittiers had farmed along the Merrimack, almost within sight of the sea, since the days of Thomas Whittier, who in 1648 cleared the farmstead near Haverhill, Massachusetts, where the poet was born in 1807. The family immortalized in *Snow-Bound* was frugal by necessity, but also by conviction, for the Quaker way of life, to which the Whittiers were devoted, was one of simplicity, piety, and social responsibility. Although Whittier's opportunities were severely limited, the responsibility for study and expression was a Quaker tradition; the imagination of the young poet was nourished on the impassioned mysticism and moral earnestness of the classic journals of early Friends, on the Bible and *Pilgrim's Progress*, and on the few books that chance brought to a country farmhouse. Less by chance than by destiny, as it seems, the schoolmaster, Joshua Coffin, lent the boy the poetry of Robert Burns.

At nineteen he had a poem accepted for publication. The Newburyport *Press*, in which it appeared, was edited by William Lloyd Garrison, soon to become the editor of the *Liberator*, the foremost journal of abolitionism. Garrison, who became Whittier's lifelong friend and associate in emancipation propaganda, encouraged the lad to think of himself as a writer. He abandoned the trade of cobbler, which he was learning, and returned to school. He spent a year at Haverhill Academy, taught school, worked for a Boston publisher, and held obscure editorial positions while his articles and poems appeared with increasing frequency in a variety of publications. His first volume, *Legends of New England* (1831), was prose; a poem published the next year, *Moll Pitcher*, had a story with some elements of interest, but after revising it for the volume of 1840 the poet wisely excluded it from further collections. This was the fate of a large proportion of his early poems.

Meanwhile his general activities had given him a position, if not actual prominence, in the journalism of reform. *Justice and Expediency* (1833) was a notable antislavery tract, coinciding with his election as delegate to the National Anti-Slavery Convention in Philadelphia. Such participation led to his election, in 1835, to the Massachusetts legislature, where he served one term, while drawing a small additional income as editor of the Haverhill *Gazette*. In 1836 he moved down the Merrimack to nearby Amesbury, where, in 1840, he chose the permanent residence which has become a shrine to his memory. Meanwhile his best energies and writing had been devoted to the antislavery cause. In 1835, he and the British abolitionist, George Thompson, mobbed on a lecture tour in Concord, New Hampshire, drove their carriage through a hail of bullets, miraculously escaping with their lives. In 1837 he went to Philadelphia to write for an abolition paper, which he edited as *The Pennsylvania Freeman* for two years before returning to Amesbury.

In this quiet town the remainder of his life was centered. He maintained intermittent editorial connections with the local *Transcript,* and was contributing editor for several more distant publications, notably the antislavery *National Era* in Washington. He continued, for the next quarter of a century, to be more generally known as a propagandist of reform than as a poet, although actually he had now found his own independent voice. A new Whittier, master of a firm and simple eloquence, appeared with increasing frequency in such volumes as *Ballads and Other Poems* (1844), *Voices of Freedom* (1846), *Songs of Labor* (1850), *The Chapel of the Hermits and Other Poems* (1853), *The Panorama and Other Poems* (1856),

and *Home Ballads and Poems* (1860).

His fellow literary men recognized his maturity in this period, and he was inevitably included in the group associated with Lowell, Holmes, and others, in the founding of the *Atlantic Monthly* in 1857. But although his poems were published in a collected edition in London (1850) and in Boston (1857), it was not until his masterpiece, *Snow-Bound,* appeared in 1866 that his countrymen at large recognized his value, and rewarded him with a sufficient sale to make his situation comfortable.

His personal life was now beset by problems, reflected in the increasing religious fervor and thoughtfulness of his lyrics. He had never married, devoting his slender means to his family at Amesbury, and the death of his mother and two sisters occurred between 1857 and 1864. His health, which had never been vigorous, was in steady decline after a severe illness during the winter of 1867–1868. Emancipation, together with the success of other reforms, suddenly canceled his old incentives. His seventieth birthday, in 1877, was celebrated at the famous dinner given him by the *Atlantic Monthly,* which was attended by almost every living American author of note from the generation of Bryant to that of Mark Twain and received much public attention both here and abroad. His eightieth birthday was marked by a national celebration.

It would be injudicious to

rank Whittier among the great poets, yet it is certain that his genuine values will survive the neglect of recent decades.

The standard edition is *The Writings of John Greenleaf Whittier*, Riverside Edition, 7 vols., 1888–1889; reissued, enlarged, as the Standard Library Edition, 7 vols., 1894. The complete one-volume Cambridge Edition. *The Complete Poetical Works of John Greenleaf Whittier*, 1894, is still the best generally available edition.

The standard biography is Samuel T. Pickard, *Life and Letters of John Greenleaf Whittier*, 2 vols., 1894, revised 1907. The same author published *Whittier-Land*, a useful study, in 1904. G. R. Carpenter's *Whittier*, American Men of Letters Series, 1903, is a good introduction. More recent studies of value are Whitman Bennett, *Whittier: Bard of Freedom*, 1941; John A. Pollard, *John Greenleaf Whittier * * ***, 1949; Lewis Leary, *John Greenleaf Whittier*, 1961; John B. Pickard, *John Greenleaf Whittier * * ***, 1961; and Edward Wagenknecht, *John Greenleaf Whittier * * ***, 1967.

Ichabod [1]

So fallen! so lost! the light withdrawn
    Which once he wore!
The glory from his gray hairs gone
    Forevermore!

Revile him not, the Tempter hath   5
    A snare for all;
And pitying tears, not scorn and wrath,
    Befit his fall!

Oh, dumb be passion's stormy rage,
    When he who might   10
Have lighted up and led his age,
    Falls back in night.

Scorn! would the angels laugh, to mark
    A bright soul driven,
Fiend-goaded, down the endless dark,   15
    From hope and heaven!

Let not the land once proud of him
    Insult him now,
Nor brand with deeper shame his dim,
    Dishonored brow.   20

1. Hebrew, "without glory"; see I Samuel iv: 21. The poet wrote the following note for the collected *Writings* (1888): "This poem was the outcome of the surprise and grief and forecast of evil consequences which I felt on reading the seventh of March speech of Daniel Webster in support of the 'compromise' and the Fugitive Slave Bill. No partisan or personal enmity dictated it. On the contrary my admiration of the splendid personality and intellectual power of the great Senator was never stronger than when I laid down his speech, and, in one of the saddest moments of my life, penned my protest." Many then agreed with Whittier that the greatly beloved statesman had fallen from glory. However, his compromise with the moderate slavery views of Clay, in order to defeat the radical Calhoun, is sympathetically viewed by many later historians. Webster died in 1852. Thirty years later, in "The Lost Occasion," Whittier admitted that Webster erred on the side of logic. "Ichabod" first appeared in *The National Era* for May 2, 1850, was collected the same year in *Songs of Labor*, and was retained in later collections.

But let its humbled sons, instead,
    From sea to lake,
A long lament, as for the dead,
    In sadness make.

Of all we loved and honored, naught
    Save power remains;   25
A fallen angel's pride of thought,
    Still strong in chains.

All else is gone; from those great eyes
    The soul has fled;   30
When faith is lost, when honor dies,
    The man is dead!

Then pay the reverence of old days
    To his dead fame;
Walk backward, with averted gaze,
    And hide the shame!   35

1850

First-Day Thoughts [2]

In calm and cool and silence, once again
    I find my old accustomed place among
My brethren,[3] where, perchance, no human tongue
Shall utter words; where never hymn is sung,
Nor deep-toned organ blown, nor censer swung,   5
Nor dim light falling through the pictured pane!
There, syllabled by silence, let me hear
The still small voice which reached the prophet's ear;
Read in my heart a still diviner law
Than Israel's leader [4] on his tables saw!   10
There let me strive with each besetting sin,
    Recall my wandering fancies, and restrain
    The sore disquiet of a restless brain;
    And, as the path of duty is made plain,
May grace be given that I may walk therein,   15
    Not like the hireling, for his selfish gain,
With backward glances and reluctant tread,

2. "First Day" is Sunday. The Quakers designated the days of the week by number, to avoid reference to the pagan gods for which the days are named. "First-Day Thoughts" was originally published in *The Chapel of the Hermits and Other Poems* (1853).
3. Friends' worship emphasized fellowship, and utilized communal silence instead of music, hymns, images, and stained glass (ll. 3–6). The object of worship was the direct revelation of God to the individual—the perception of the "inward light" (ll. 7–10).
4. Moses. For the "tables" of the laws, *cf.* Exodus xxxi: 18, and xx, *passim*.

Making a merit of his coward dread,
  But, cheerful, in the light around me thrown,
  Walking as one to pleasant service led;   20
  Doing God's will as if it were my own,
Yet trusting not in mine, but in his strength alone!

1853

Skipper Ireson's Ride [5]

Of all the rides since the birth of time,
Told in story or sung in rhyme,—
On Apuleius's [6] Golden Ass,
Or one-eyed Calender's [7] horse of brass,
Witch astride of a human back,   5
Islam's prophet [8] on Al-Borák,—
The strangest ride that ever was sped
Was Ireson's, out from Marblehead!
  Old Floyd Ireson, for his hard heart,
    Tarred and feathered and carried in a cart   10
  By the women of Marblehead!

Body of turkey, head of owl,
Wings a-droop like a rained-on fowl,
Feathered and ruffled in every part,
Skipper Ireson stood in the cart.   15
Scores of women, old and young,

5. Whittier declared that this ballad "was founded solely on a fragment of rhyme which I heard from one of my early schoolmates, a native of Marblehead." The "fragment" was the refrain sung by the women; and there was a story current about Skipper Ireson which, Whittier supposed, "dated back at least a century." The poet wrote a rough draft in 1828, nearly thirty years before he published the poem. However, his record of the events was "pure fancy," as he took pains to declare in his note for his edition of 1888. There he approves the recent *History of Marblehead*, by Samuel Roads (1879), which places the incident in 1808, names the historical Ireson "Benjamin," not "Floyd," and asserts that Ireson was not responsible for neglecting "a sinking wreck." His guilty crew, by false accusations, diverted the consequences from themselves to Ireson. Roads says that the victim, contrary to legend, was carried in a dory, not a cart, and that men, not women, were the principal avengers. The poem appeared in the *Atlantic Monthly*, in December, 1857. Lowell, the first editor of the *Atlantic Monthly*, "familiar with Marblehead and its dialect," suggested changes making the "burthen" more "provincial" (letter to Whittier, Nov. 4, 1857; in Pickard, *Life and Letters*, Vol. II, pp. 406–407). It was collected in *Home Ballads and Poems* (1860).

6. Second-century Roman rhetorician; in his *Golden Ass* (or *Metamorphoses*) the transformation of a man to an ass is made the vehicle for comic criticism.

7. A calender is a mendicant dervish, or friar. In the *Arabian Nights* tale ("The Story of the Third Calendar," called "The Story of the Third Royal Mendicant" in later translations), he did not ride the "horse of brass" whose rider he killed, but his consequent enchanted journey cost him his eye.

8. Mohammed. In one legend, he was conveyed to the highest heaven by a supernatural winged creature named Al-Borák.

Strong of muscle, and glib of tongue,
Pushed and pulled up the rocky lane,
Shouting and singing the shrill refrain:
   "Here's Flud Oirson, fur his horrd horrt,
   Torr'd an' futherr'd an' corr'd in a corrt
      By the women o' Morble'ead!" [9]   20

Wrinkled scolds with hands on hips,
Girls in bloom of cheek and lips,
Wild-eyed, free-limbed, such as chase   25
Bacchus [1] round some antique vase,
Brief of skirt, with ankles bare,
Loose of kerchief and loose of hair,
With conch-shells blowing and fish-horns' twang,
Over and over the Maenads sang: 30
   "Here's Flud Oirson, fur his horrd horrt,
   Torr'd an' futherr'd an' corr'd in a corrt
      By the women o' Morble'ead!"

Small pity for him!—He sailed away
From a leaking ship in Chaleur Bay,[2]—   35
Sailed away from a sinking wreck,
With his own town's-people on her deck!
"Lay by! lay by!" they called to him.
Back he answered, "Sink or swim!
Brag of your catch of fish again!"   40
And off he sailed through the fog and rain!
   Old Floyd Ireson, for his hard heart,
   Tarred and feathered and carried in a cart
      By the women of Marblehead!

Fathoms deep in dark Chaleur   45
That wreck shall lie forevermore.
Mother and sister, wife and maid,
Looked from the rocks of Marblehead
Over the moaning and rainy sea,—
Looked for the coming that might not be!   50
What did the winds and the sea-birds say
Of the cruel captain who sailed away—?
   Old Floyd Ireson, for his hard heart,
   Tarred and feathered and carried in a cart
      By the women of Marblehead!   55

9. Following the advice of Lowell, his editor, Whittier used the Marblehead dialect for the refrain in stanzas 2, 3, 6, and 7, after establishing the standard English in stanza 1.

1. Roman god of wine generally shown as attended by wild, frenetic girls called Bacchantes or Maenads (l. 30).
2. In the Gulf of St. Lawrence.

Through the street, on either side,
Up flew windows, doors swung wide;
Sharp-tongued spinsters, old wives gray,
Treble lent the fish-horn's bray.
Sea-worn grandsires, cripple-bound,   60
Hulks of old sailors run aground,
Shook head, and fist, and hat, and cane,
And cracked with curses the hoarse refrain:
   "Here's Flud Oirson, fur his horrd horrt,
    Torr'd an' futherr'd an' corr'd in a corrt   65
     By the women o' Morble'ead!"

Sweetly along the Salem road
Bloom of orchard and lilac showed.
Little the wicked skipper knew
Of the fields so green and the sky so blue.   70
Riding there in his sorry trim,
Like an Indian idol glum and grim,
Scarcely he seemed the sound to hear
Of voices shouting, far and near:
   "Here's Flud Oirson, fur his horrd horrt,   75
    Torr'd an' futherr'd an' corr'd in a corrt
     By the women o' Morble'ead!"

"Hear me, neighbors!" at last he cried,—
"What to me is this noisy ride?
What is the shame that clothes the skin   80
To the nameless horror that lives within?
Waking or sleeping, I see a wreck,
And hear a cry from a reeling deck!
Hate me and curse me,—I only dread
The hand of God and the face of the dead!"   85
   Said old Floyd Ireson, for his hard heart,
    Tarred and feathered and carried in a cart
     By the women of Marblehead!

Then the wife of the skipper lost at sea
Said, "God has touched him! why should we!"   90
Said an old wife mourning her only son,
"Cut the rogue's tether and let him run!"
So with soft relentings, and rude excuse,
Half scorn, half pity, they cut him loose,
And gave him a cloak to hide him in,   95
And left him alone with his shame and sin.
   Poor Floyd Ireson, for his hard heart,

Tarred and feathered and carried in a cart
By the women of Marblehead!

1857, 1860

Telling the Bees [3]

Here is the place; right over the hill
  Runs the path I took;
You can see the gap in the old wall still,
  And the stepping-stones in the shallow brook.

There is the house, with the gate red-barred,   5
  And the poplars tall;
And the barn's brown length, and the cattle-yard,
  And the white horns tossing above the wall.

There are the beehives ranged in the sun;
  And down by the brink   10
Of the brook are her poor flowers, weed-o'errun,
  Pansy and daffodil, rose and pink.

A year has gone, as the tortoise goes,
  Heavy and slow;
And the same rose blows, and the same sun glows,   15
  And the same brook sings of a year ago.

There's the same sweet clover-smell in the breeze;
  And the June sun warm
Tangles his wings of fire in the trees,
  Setting, as then, over Fernside farm.   20

I mind me how with a lover's care
  From my Sunday coat
I brushed off the burrs, and smoothed my hair,
  And cooled at the brookside my brow and throat.

Since we parted, a month had passed,—   25
  To love, a year;

3. First collected in *Home Ballads and Other Poems* (1860) after appearing in the *Atlantic Monthly* for April, 1858. On submitting it to Lowell, Whittier admitted the fear that its "simplicity" might occasion disparagement. Actually, it is his purest ballad, free of didacticism, and simply faithful to the Whittier homestead, "Fernside farm." However, it was not his sister Mary who had died there the year before, but his mother. In the volume, the poet added the following explanatory note: "A remarkable custom, brought from the Old Country, formerly prevailed in the rural districts of New England. On the death of a member of the family, the bees were at once informed of the event, and their hives dressed in mourning. This ceremonial was supposed to be necessary to prevent the swarms from leaving their hives and seeking a new home."

Down through the beeches I looked at last
　　On the little red gate and the well-sweep near.

I can see it all now,—the slantwise rain
　　Of light through the leaves,
The sundown's blaze on her window-pane,　　　　　　　30
　　The bloom of her roses under the eaves.

Just the same as a month before,—
　　The house and the trees,
The barn's brown gable, the vine by the door,—　　　35
　　Nothing changed but the hives of bees.

Before them, under the garden wall,
　　Forward and back,
Went drearily singing the chore-girl small,
　　Draping each hive with a shred of black.　　　　　40

Trembling, I listened: the summer sun
　　Had the chill of snow;
For I knew she was telling the bees of one
　　Gone on the journey we all must go!

Then I said to myself, "My Mary weeps　　　　　　　45
　　For the dead to-day:
Haply her blind old grandsire sleeps
　　The fret and the pain of his age away."

But her dog whined low; on the doorway sill,
　　With his cane to his chin,　　　　　　　　　　　50
The old man sat; and the chore-girl still
　　Sung to the bees stealing out and in.

And the song she was singing ever since
　　In my ear sounds on:—
"Stay at home, pretty bees, fly not hence!　　　　　55
　　Mistress Mary is dead and gone!"

　　　　　　　　　　　　　　　　　　　　1858, 1860

Laus Deo [4]

It is done!
Clang of bell and roar of gun
How the belfries rock and reel!

4. The title, familiar in the Latin Vulgate Bible, is translated as "Praise be to God." The prefatory note, as amplified in the collected *Writings* of 1888, reads as follows: "On hearing the bells ring on the passage of the constitutional amendment abolishing slavery. The resolution was adopted by Congress, January 31, 1865. The ratification by the requisite number of states was announced December 18, 1865."

How the great guns, peal on peal,   5
Fling the joy from town to town! [5]

Send the tidings up and down.
          Ring, O bells!
     Every stroke exulting tells
Of the burial hour of crime.
     Loud and long, that all may hear,   10
     Ring for every listening ear
Of Eternity and Time!

          Let us kneel:
     God's own voice is in that peal,
And this spot is holy ground. [6]   15
     Lord, forgive us! What are we,
     That our eyes this glory see,
That our ears have heard this sound!

          For the Lord
     On the whirlwind is abroad;   20
In the earthquake He has spoken:
     He has smitten with His thunder [7]
     The iron walls asunder,
And the gates of brass are broken!

          Loud and long   25
     Lift the old exulting song;
Sing with Miriam by the sea,
     He has cast the mighty down;
     Horse and rider sink and drown;
'He hath triumphed gloriously!' [8]   30

          Did we dare,
     In our agony of prayer, [9]
Ask for more than He has done?
     When was ever his right hand
     Over any time or land   35
Stretched as now beneath the sun? [1]

          How they pale,
     Ancient myth and song and tale,
In this wonder of our days,

5. Whittier "sat in the Friends' meet-ing-house in Amesbury, and listened to the bells and cannon." As he later told Lucy Larcom, the poem "wrote itself, or rather sang itself, while the bells rang" (Pickard, *Life and Letters*, Vol. II, pp. 488–489).
6. *Cf.* Exodus iii: 3–6.
7. *Cf.* Job xxxvii: 2–12.
8. *Cf.* Exodus xv: 21–22.
9. *Cf.* Luke xxii: 39–44.
1. Isaiah repeatedly used this figure, for both God's wrath and God's mercy. Compare Isaiah v: 25 with xiv: 27, and see ix: 12–13 and x: 4.

When the cruel rod of war   40
Blossoms white with righteous law,[2]
And the wrath of man is praise!

Blotted out!
All within and all about
Shall a fresher life begin;   45
Freer breathe the universe
As it rolls its heavy curse
On the dead and buried sin!

It is done!
In the circuit of the sun   50
Shall the sound thereof go forth.
It shall bid the sad rejoice,
It shall give the dumb a voice,
It shall belt with joy the earth![3]

Ring and swing,   55
Bells of joy! On morning's wing
Sound the song of praise abroad!
With a sound of broken chains
Tell the nations that He reigns,
Who alone is Lord and God![4]   60

1865

OLIVER WENDELL HOLMES

(1809–1894)

Holmes's reading made a full man; his sense of responsibility made a man ever ready for the play of ideas which he regarded as inseparable from living; his scientific training made him an exact and formidable opponent; his wit was at once an instrument and a recreation; his sense of humor and love of fun gave a kindly and human dimension to his criticism of life.

These characteristics of his personality and his writing were a natural reflection of the New England "renaissance," of the highly cultured society into which he was born, in Cambridge, Massachusetts, in 1809. He was graduated from Harvard with the class of 1829, which he later celebrated annually for many years, in the best poems ever lavished upon such a subject. In 1830, while studying law at Harvard, he initiated the effective movement to prevent the scrapping of the gallant ship *Constitution*, by composing his famous poem "Old Ironsides,"

2. A double reference to Aaron's rod: of war (*cf.* Exodus vii: 8–17), and of law (*cf.* Numbers xvii: 8–10).

3. *Cf.* Isaiah xxxv: 4–8.
4. *Cf.* Psalms xlvi, echoed in this stanza.

written impromptu with the competence of the born writer. In the next two years, magazine readers saw the first two of his *Autocrat* papers, thereafter not to be resumed for a quarter of a century although he frequently contributed to the periodicals during his busy years of professional activity.

That profession was medicine, which he began to study in 1830 in Boston. In 1833 he went to Paris, where the new emphasis on experimental techniques was revolutionizing medical science. Here Holmes laid the foundations for his later pioneering in microscopy, but his devotion to science was not so great as to prevent him from spending holidays on long rambles about Europe. He returned to Harvard in 1836 to take his degree in medicine, and that year he also published *Poems*, his first volume.

Although he acknowledged that he had "a right to be grateful to his ancestors," what he inherited was a tradition, not a fortune. He soon found that he was not happy in the practice of medicine, and turned to the teaching of medical science. After serving as professor of anatomy at Dartmouth (1838–1840), he returned to general practice in Boston upon his marriage in 1840; but in 1847 he found his true vocation in the appointment as Parkman Professor of Anatomy and Physiology in Harvard Medical School. Among his scientific publications, the most notable had been an analysis of the shortcomings of homeopathy, and, in 1843, a study of "The Contagiousness of Puerperal Fever," a contribution to the reduction of the fearful mortality rate then connected with childbirth. However, his professional reputation was won not by research, of which he did his share, but by his high accomplishments as a clinician and a medical educator. He was dean of Harvard Medical School from 1847 to 1853, and until his retirement, as emeritus professor, in 1882, he continued to contribute to the broad development of medical education.

Literature, however, remained his avocation. His periodical contributions were included, along with new poems, in the *Poems* of 1846 and 1849, the former published in London, where he began to be recognized for his light verse. In 1852 he first collected his *Poetical Works*. In 1854 he published the *Songs of the Class of 1829*, to be reissued with additions for many years.

In 1857, he, and other members of the Saturday Club, founded the *Atlantic Monthly*, which he named. His famous *Autocrat of the Breakfast-Table* appeared in it serially, beginning with the first number, and established the familiar tone which that justly celebrated magazine preserved for many years. The *Autocrat* was published as a volume in 1858. Thereafter this wise and whimsical table talk, which ranks with the best "conversations" of literature, continued to appear in the *Atlantic*, and was collected in *The Professor at the Breakfast-Table* (1860), *The Poet at the Breakfast-Table* (1872), and *Over the Teacups* (1891).

By contrast, the novels of

Holmes are unimpressive, especially as narratives. Yet many readers have found compensation in the witty commentary, the sociological criticism, and the psychological explication of *Elsie Venner* (1861), *The Guardian Angel* (1867), and *A Mortal Antipathy* (1885). For all their shortcomings in fictional technique, these were pioneering experiments in the analysis of elements then becoming familiar to the clinicians of mental science, such as prenatal influence, hereditary traits, and mental trauma or fixations, in their relations to the problems of moral responsibility. Here Holmes arrayed the resources of his science against the Calvinistic orthodoxy that he attacked on various levels—including the ridiculous, in "The Deacon's Masterpiece."

Meanwhile many of his poems were published, chiefly in the *Atlantic*, and later in the volumes of 1862, 1875, 1880, 1883 (a collected *Poetical Works*), and 1888. In spite of the real merit of some of his reflective lyrics, his recognition as a poet, here and abroad, was based on the unquestioned success of his comic verse, his gracious occasional poems, his urbane and witty light verse and *vers de société*. By its nature, humorous and light verse must seem casual and easy, and in view of its relative impermanence as compared with serious poetry, the survival of Holmes's work with the best of this *genre* is evidence of his genius.

No short sketch can do justice to the many-sided activities of this small dynamo. He was scientist and teacher, poet, essayist, and novelist. He could have had a career as a serious lecturer; he became a favorite after-dinner speaker. He wrote three biographical volumes—*Motley* (1879); *Emerson*, for the American Men of Letters series (1885); and *Henry Jacob Biglow* (1891). He gave numerous professional lectures, assisted in founding the American Medical Association, and wrote his quota of medical articles and books. Retired from his professorship at seventy-three, he at once undertook the three-year task of revising and annotating his works. He turned the observations of a foreign journey into *Our Hundred Days in Europe* (1887). If he was conservative with respect to the humanitarian cultural tradition, he was also a radical and courageous opponent of all meaningless survivals or current shams. He broke with both the Calvinistic and Unitarian traditions of New England. Within his Brahmin "caste," as he called it, he attacked the snobbish respect for wealth, privilege, and idleness. In his novels he employed a new frankness which only his adroit expression made acceptable to his time. While laughing at feminism, he supported the admission of women to medical schools. He advocated such unpopular advances in medical practice as anesthesia and antisepsis. He energetically and cheerfully outlived the entire illustrious generation of his contemporary authors, and died in 1894, just past eighty-five.

The standard text is the Riverside Edition, *The Writings of Oliver Wendell Holmes*, 13 vols., 1891–1892, reproduced in the Standard Library Edition, 1892, to which were added in 1896 the two volumes of Morse's *Life and Letters* (listed below). The poems below are taken from *The Complete Poetical Works of Oliver Wendell Holmes,* Cambridge Edition, 1 vol., edited by H. E. Scudder, 1895, still available, and the best text. The notes by Holmes reproduced in this volume are from his revised *Poetical Works* of 1883. *The Autocrat of the Breakfast-Table,* often reprinted, was critically edited by Franklin T. Baker, 1928. *Oliver Wen-*

dell Holmes: Representative Selections, edited by S. I. Hayakawa and H. M. Jones, American Writers Series, 1939, is excellent for its selections, introduction, and bibliography.

For biography and criticism, see J. T. Morse, *Life and Letters of Oliver Wendell Holmes,* 2 vols., 1896; M. A. DeWolfe Howe, *Holmes of the Breakfast-Table,* 1939; Eleanor M. Tilton, *Amiable Autocrat,* 1947; and the introduction to the volume of *Representative Selections* edited by Hayakawa and Jones (listed above).

Old Ironsides [1]

Ay, tear her tattered ensign down!
   Long has it waved on high,
And many an eye has danced to see
   That banner in the sky;
Beneath it rung the battle shout,   5
   And burst the cannon's roar;—
The meteor of the ocean air
   Shall sweep the clouds no more.

Her deck, once red with heroes' blood,
   Where knelt the vanquished foe,   10
Where winds were hurrying o'er the flood,
   And waves were white below,
No more shall feel the victor's tread,
   Or know the conquered knee;—
The harpies of the shore shall pluck   15
   The eagle of the sea!

Oh, better that her shattered hulk
   Should sink beneath the wave;
Her thunders shook the mighty deep,
   And there should be her grave;   20
Nail to the mast her holy flag,
   Set every threadbare sail,

1. In 1830, just graduated from Harvard and re-enrolled as a law student, Holmes saw in the Boston *Daily Advertiser* the announcement that the frigate *Constitution* was to be demolished. "Old Ironsides," then lying in Boston's Charlestown Navy Yard, a veteran of Decatur's fleet in the Barbary Wars, had decisively vanquished the renowned British *Guerrière* (August 19, 1812) in the last British war, and was an object of national reverence. Holmes's stirring poem appeared in the *Advertiser* two days later (September 16, 1830), was widely reprinted, and circulated in broadside form in Washington. The poem is credited with having saved the ship, which was reconditioned; it certainly established young Holmes as a writer, and became part of the literature of the schoolroom for a century. In *Poems,* 1836, the author's first collection, the poem appeared as part of "Poetry: A Metrical Essay," which he had just read before the Harvard Phi Beta Kappa; after several reprintings it appeared independently, with its present title, in *Poems,* 1862.

And give her to the god of storms,
  The lightning and the gale!

1830, 1836

My Aunt[2]

My aunt! my dear unmarried aunt!
  Long years have o'er her flown;
Yet still she strains the aching clasp
  That binds her virgin zone;[3]
I know it hurts her,—though she looks   5
  As cheerful as she can;
Her waist is ampler than her life,
  For life is but a span.

My aunt! my poor deluded aunt!
  Her hair is almost gray;   10
Why will she train that winter curl
  In such a spring-like way?
How can she lay her glasses down,
  And say she reads as well,
When through a double convex lens   15
  She just makes out to spell?

Her father—grandpapa! forgive
  This erring lip its smiles—
Vowed she should make the finest girl
  Within a hundred miles;   20
He sent her to a stylish school;
  'T was in her thirteenth June;
And with her, as the rules required,
  "Two towels and a spoon."

They braced my aunt against a board,   25
  To make her straight and tall;
They laced her up, they starved her down,
  To make her light and small;
They pinched her feet, they singed her hair,
  They screwed it up with pins;—   30
Oh, never mortal suffered more
  In penance for her sins.

2. Published in the *New England Magazine* for October, 1831; reprinted in the *Harbinger* volume of 1833; collected in *Poems*, 1836.
3. A broad ornamental girdle or belt.

So, when my precious aunt was done,
    My grandsire brought her back
(By daylight, lest some rabid youth   35
    Might follow on the track);
"Ah!" said my grandsire, as he shook
    Some powder in his pan,[4]
"What could this lovely creature do
    Against a desperate man!"   40

Alas! nor chariot, nor barouche,[5]
    Nor bandit cavalcade,
Tore from the trembling father's arms
    His all-accomplished maid.
For her how happy had it been!   45
    And Heaven had spared to me
To see one sad, ungathered rose
    On my ancestral tree.

                                1831, 1836

The Chambered Nautilus [6]

This is the ship of pearl, which, poets feign,
    Sails the unshadowed main,—
    The venturous bark that flings
On the sweet summer wind its purpled wings
In gulfs enchanted, where the Siren sings,   5
    And coral reefs lie bare,
Where the cold sea-maids rise to sun their streaming hair.

Its webs of living gauze no more unfurl;
    Wrecked is the ship of pearl!
    And every chambered cell,   10
Where its dim dreaming life was wont to dwell,

4. In ancient breech-loading muskets and pistols, the hollow in the lock that received the priming powder.
5. Types of four-wheeled carriages then fashionable: the chariot light and open; the barouche with a folding top, facing seats, and a driver's seat in front.
6. The pearly nautilus is a cephalopod of the South Pacific and Indian oceans, which builds a spiral shell, adding a chamber each year, and was thought by the Greeks to be capable of sailing by erecting a membrane (ll. 3–5). Of this poem, Holmes wrote George Ticknor (Morse, *Life and Letters,* Vol. II, p. 278), "I am as willing to submit this to criticism as any I have written, in form as well as in substance, and I have not seen any English verse of just the same pattern." In substance, it develops a religious idea persistent in his revolt against such concepts as original depravity, predestination, and grace, in the Calvinist tradition. Here the lowly shellfish and man are bound, by the same law of progress, to strive for constantly higher attainments. *Cf.* the anti-Calvinism of "The Living Temple" and "The Deacon's Masterpiece." This poem was part of *The Autocrat of the Breakfast-Table,* first published in the February, 1858 installment in the *Atlantic Monthly* and in the volume of the *Autocrat* later in that year. It was collected in *Songs in Many Keys* (1862).

As the frail tenant shaped his growing shell,
   Before thee lies revealed,—
Its irised ceiling rent, its sunless crypt unsealed!

Year after year beheld the silent toil   15
    That spreads his lustrous coil;
      Still, as the spiral grew,
He left the past year's dwelling for the new,
Stole with soft step its shining archway through,
    Built up its idle door,   20
Stretched in his last-found home, and knew the old no more.

Thanks for the heavenly message brought by thee,
    Child of the wandering sea,
    Cast from her lap, forlorn!
From thy dead lips a clearer note is born   25
Than ever Triton blew from wreathèd horn! [7]
    While on mine ear it rings,
Through the deep caves of thought I hear a voice that sings:—

Build thee more stately mansions, O my soul,
    As the swift seasons roll!   30
    Leave thy low-vaulted past!
Let each new temple, nobler than the last,
Shut thee from heaven with a dome more vast,
    Till thou at length art free,
Leaving thine outgrown shell by life's unresting sea!   35

1858

The Living Temple [8]

    Not in the world of light alone,
    Where God has built his blazing throne
    Nor yet alone in earth below,
    With belted seas that come and go,
    And endless isles of sunlit green,   5
    Is all thy Maker's glory seen:
    Look in upon thy wondrous frame,—
    Eternal wisdom still the same!

7. *Cf.* Wordsworth's sonnet "The World Is Too Much with Us," l. 14: "Or hear old Triton blow his wreathèd horn."

8. "The Living Temple," which Holmes calls "an anatomist's hymn" in the *Autocrat*, represents another phase of his revolt against Puritanism, which defamed the body as the vessel of man's corruption. Note how the poet's imagination transforms the otherwise gruesome discoveries of the anatomist's scalpel. The poem was published in the volume of *The Autocrat of the Breakfast-Table* (1858), after appearing in the *Atlantic Monthly* installment of the *Autocrat* for May, 1858. It appeared separately among the poems of *Songs in Many Keys* (1862).

The smooth, soft air with pulse-like waves
Flows murmuring through its hidden caves,   10
Whose streams of brightening purple rush,
Fired with a new and livelier blush,
While all their burden of decay
The ebbing current steals away,
And red with Nature's flame they start   15
From the warm fountains of the heart.

No rest that throbbing slave may ask,
Forever quivering o'er his task,
While far and wide a crimson jet
Leaps forth to fill the woven net   20
Which in unnumbered crossing tides
The flood of burning life divides,
Then, kindling each decaying part,
Creeps back to find the throbbing heart.

But warmed with that unchanging flame   25
Behold the outward moving frame,
Its living marbles jointed strong
With glistening band and silvery thong,
And linked to reason's guiding reins
By myriad rings in trembling chains,   30
Each graven with the threaded zone
Which claims it as the master's own.

See how yon beam of seeming white
Is braided out of seven-hued light,[9]
Yet in those lucid globes no ray   35
By any chance shall break astray.
Hark how the rolling surge of sound,
Arches and spirals circling round,
Wakes the hushed spirit through thine ear
With music it is heaven to hear.   40

Then mark the cloven sphere that holds
All thought in its mysterious folds;
That feels sensation's faintest thrill,
And flashes forth the sovereign will;
Think on the stormy world that dwells   45
Locked in its dim and clustering cells!
The lightning gleams of power it sheds
Along its hollow glassy threads!

---

9. *I.e.,* the seven colors of the visible spectrum into which white light is dispersed in a rainbow or a crystal.

O Father! grant thy love divine
To make these mystic temples thine!   50
When wasting age and wearying strife
Have sapped the leaning walls of life,
When darkness gathers over all,
And the last tottering pillars fall,
Take the poor dust thy mercy warms,   55
And mould it into heavenly forms!

1858

The Deacon's Masterpiece

OR, THE WONDERFUL "ONE-HOSS SHAY" [1]
A LOGICAL STORY

Have you heard of the wonderful one-hoss shay,
That was built in such a logical way
It ran a hundred years to a day,
And then, of a sudden, it—ah, but stay,
I'll tell you what happened without delay,   5
Scaring the parson into fits,
Frightening people out of their wits,—
Have you ever heard of that, I say?

Seventeen hundred and fifty-five.
Georgius Secundus [2] was then alive,—   10
Snuffy old drone from the German hive.
That was the year when Lisbon-town
Saw the earth open and gulp her down, [3]
And Braddock's [4] army was done so brown,
Left without a scalp to its crown.   15
It was on the terrible Earthquake-day
That the Deacon finished the one-hoss shay. [5]

1. It is probably to the credit of this poem that many have read it as an amusing story, without reference to its underlying satirical allegory. Against the Calvinist theology, surviving from the Puritan past in New England, Holmes arrayed the arguments of rationalism and scientific empiricism, in literature ranging from the present comic burlesque to his serious novels and his essay, in 1880, on Jonathan Edwards. Edwards, in *The Freedom of the Will* (1754), had produced a masterpiece of Puritan logic. Holmes's thesis in this comic ballad is that a system of logic, however perfect, must collapse if its premises are false. The poem was part of *The Autocrat of the Breakfast-Table* (1858) first appearing in the installment published in the *Atlantic Monthly* for September, 1858, and later included with the poems of successive collections.
2. George II, king of England from 1727 to 1760, was German-born.
3. The devastating earthquake in Lisbon in 1755 evoked theological argument concerning God's agency.
4. General Edward Braddock (1695–1755), British commander in the last of the French and Indian Wars, was killed in action.
5. Actually it was in 1754, not 1755, that Edwards published *The Freedom of the Will*.

Now in building of chaises, I tell you what,
There is always *somewhere* a weakest spot,—
In hub, tire, felloe,[6] in spring or thill,[7]   20
In panel, or crossbar, or floor, or sill,
In screw, bolt, thoroughbrace,[8]—lurking still,
Find it somewhere you must and will,—
Above or below, or within or without,—
And that's the reason, beyond a doubt,   25
That a chaise *breaks down*, but doesn't *wear out*.

But the Deacon swore (as deacons do,
With an "I dew vum," or an "I tell *yeou*")
He would build one shay to beat the taown
'N' the keounty 'n' all the kentry raoun';   30
It should be so built that it *could n'* break daown:
"Fur," said the Deacon, " 't 's mighty plain
Thut the weakes' place mus' stan' the strain;
'N' the way t' fix it, uz I maintain,
                                    Is only jest   35
T' make that place uz strong uz the rest."

So the Deacon inquired of the village folk
Where he could find the strongest oak,
That couldn't be split nor bent nor broke,—
That was for spokes and floor and sills;   40
He sent for lancewood to make the thills;
The crossbars were ash, from the straightest trees,
The panels of white-wood, that cuts like cheese,
But lasts like iron for things like these;
The hubs of logs from the "Settler's ellum,"—   45
Last of its timber,—they couldn't sell 'em,
Never an axe had seen their chips,
And the wedges flew from between their lips,
Their blunt ends frizzled like celery-tips;
Step and prop-iron, bolt and screw,   50
Spring, tire, axle, and linchpin[9] too,
Steel of the finest, bright and blue;
Thoroughbrace bison-skin, thick and wide;
Boot, top, dasher, from tough old hide
Found in the pit when the tanner died.   55
That was the way he "put her through."
"There!" said the Deacon, "naow she'll dew!"

6. The exterior wooden rim of a wheel.
7. The thills of a carriage are the two slender shafts between which the horse is harnessed.
8. A stout leather support by which the body of the carriage was slung to the springs.
9. A linchpin, like a modern cotter pin, was inserted through the end of the axletree to retain the wheel on its bearing.

Do! I tell you, I rather guess
She was a wonder, and nothing less!
Colts grew horses, beards turned gray, 60
Deacon and deaconess dropped away,
Children and grandchildren—where were they?
But there stood the stout old one-hoss shay
As fresh as on Lisbon-earthquake-day!

EIGHTEEN HUNDRED;—it came and found 65
The Deacon's masterpiece strong and sound.
Eighteen hundred increased by ten;—
"Hahnsum kerridge" they called it then.
Eighteen hundred and twenty came;—
Running as usual; much the same. 70
Thirty and forty at last arrive,
And then come fifty, and FIFTY-FIVE.

Little of all we value here
Wakes on the morn of its hundredth year
Without both feeling and looking queer. 75
In fact, there's nothing that keeps its youth,
So far as I know, but a tree and truth.
(This is a moral that runs at large;
Take it.—You're welcome.—No extra charge.)

FIRST OF NOVEMBER,—the earthquake-day,— 80
There are traces of age in the one-hoss shay,
A general flavor of mild decay,
But nothing local, as one may say.
There couldn't be,—for the Deacon's art
Had made it so like in every part 85
That there wasn't a chance for one to start.
For the wheels were just as strong as the thills,
And the floor was just as strong as the sills,
And the panels just as strong as the floor,
And the whipple-tree [1] neither less nor more, 90
And the back crossbar as strong as the fore,
And spring and axle and hub *encore*.
And yet, *as a whole*, it is past a doubt
In another hour it will be *worn out!*

First of November, 'Fifty-five! 95
This morning the parson takes a drive.
Now, small boys, get out of the way!
Here comes the wonderful one-hoss shay,

---

1. A bar pivoted on the frame behind the horse, to which the traces, or side harness, are fastened.

Drawn by a rat-tailed, ewe-necked bay.
"Huddup!" said the parson.—Off went they.   100
The parson was working his Sunday's text,—
Had got to *fifthly*, and stopped perplexed
At what the—Moses—was coming next.
All at once the horse stood still,
Close by the meet'n'-house on the hill.   105
First a shiver, and then a thrill,
Then something decidedly like a spill,—
And the parson was sitting upon a rock,
At half past nine by the meet'n'-house clock,—
Just the hour of the Earthquake shock!   110
What do you think the parson found,
When he got up and stared around?
The poor old chaise in a heap or mound,
As if it had been to the mill and ground!
You see, of course, if you're not a dunce   115
How it went to pieces all at once,—
All at once, and nothing first,—
Just as bubbles do when they burst.

End of the wonderful one-hoss shay.
Logic is logic. That's all I say.   120

1858

Dorothy Q.[2]

A FAMILY PORTRAIT

Grandmother's mother: her age, I guess,
Thirteen summers, or something less;
Girlish bust, but womanly air;
Smooth, square forehead with uprolled hair;
Lips that lover has never kissed;   5
Taper fingers and slender wrist;
Hanging sleeves of stiff brocade;
So they painted the little maid.

On her hand a parrot green
Sits unmoving and broods serene.   10
Hold up the canvas full in view,—

2. "Dorothy was the daughter of Judge Edmund Quincy, and the niece of Josiah Quincy, junior, the young poet and orator who died just before the American Revolution, of which he was one of the most eloquent and effective promoters" [Holmes's note]. This Dorothy was the poet's maternal great-grandmother; her girlish portrait was associated with his childhood interest in the legends of his family. The poem appeared in the *Atlantic Monthly* for January, 1871, and was collected in *Songs of Many Seasons* (1875).

Look! there's a rent the light shines through,
Dark with a century's fringe of dust,—
That was a Red-Coat's rapier-thrust! [3]
Such is the tale the lady old,   15
Dorothy's daughter's daughter, told.

Who the painter was none may tell,—
One whose best was not over well;
Hard and dry, it must be confessed,
Flat as a rose that has long been pressed;   20
Yet in her cheek the hues are bright,
Dainty colors of red and white,
And in her slender shape are seen
Hint and promise of stately mien.

Look not on her with eyes of scorn,—   25
Dorothy Q. was a lady born!
Ay! since the galloping Normans came,
England's annals have known her name; [4]
And still to the three-hilled rebel town [5]
Dear is that ancient name's renown,   30
For many a civic wreath they won,
The youthful sire and the gray-haired son.

O Damsel Dorothy! Dorothy Q.!
Strange is the gift that I owe to you;
Such a gift as never a king   35
Save to daughter or son might bring,—
All my tenure of heart and hand,
All my title to house and land;
Mother and sister and child and wife   40
And joy and sorrow and death and life!

What if a hundred years ago
Those close-shut lips had answered No,
When forth the tremulous question came
That cost the maiden her Norman name,
And under the folds that look so still   45
The bodice swelled with the bosom's thrill?
Should I be I, or would it be
One tenth another, to nine tenths me?

3. "The British officer had aimed at the right eye and just missed it" [unpublished manuscript note, Tilton, *Amiable Autocrat*, p. 6].
4. The Norman invasion (1066) brought such French names as Quincy into English genealogies.
5. Colonial Boston was built on three hills; Tremont Street preserves that memory in its name, once given to the city itself.

Soft is the breath of a maiden's YES:
Not the light gossamer stirs with less;   50
But never a cable that holds so fast
Through all the battles of wave and blast,
And never an echo of speech or song
That lives in the babbling air so long!
There were tones in the voice that whispered then   55
You may hear to-day in a hundred men.

O lady and lover, how faint and far
Your images hover,—and here we are,
Solid and stirring in flesh and bone,—
Edward's and Dorothy's—all their own,—   60
A goodly record for Time to show
Of a syllable spoken so long ago!—
Shall I bless you, Dorothy, or forgive
For the tender whisper that bade me live?

It shall be a blessing, my little maid!   65
I will heal the stab of the Red-Coat's blade,[6]
And freshen the gold of the tarnished frame,
And gild with a rhyme your household name;
So you shall smile on us brave and bright
As first you greeted the morning's light,   70
And live untroubled by woes and fears
Through a second youth of a hundred years.

1871, 1875

From The Autocrat of the Breakfast-Table[7]

I

I was just going to say, when I was interrupted,[8] that one of the many ways of classifying minds is under the heads of arithmetical and algebraical intellects. All economical and practical wisdom is

6. "The canvas of the painting was so much decayed that it had to be replaced by a new one, in doing which the rapier thrust was of course filled up" [Holmes's note].
7. *The Autocrat of the Breakfast-Table* resulted from Lowell's insistence that, if he undertook the editorship of the projected *Atlantic Monthly*, Holmes would agree to become a regular contributor. Installments of the *Autocrat* began with the first number of the magazine, November, 1857, and concluded with the issue for October, 1858. These were a mature development of the "table-talk" that Holmes had long before published under the same title in the *New England Magazine* (November, 1831, January, 1832). The *Autocrat* and succeeding collections represent at its best the patrician cultivation and Augustan wit that flourished with the New England renaissance, and perpetuated a long tradition in the "genteel" culture of the United States.
8. *I.e.*, twenty-five years ago, when he published the early *Autocrat* essays in the *New England Magazine*.

an extension or variation of the following arithmetical formula: $2 + 2 = 4$. Every philosophical proposition has the more general character of the expression $a + b = c$. We are mere operatives, empirics, and egotists, until we learn to think in letters instead of figures.

They all stared. There is a divinity student lately come among us to whom I commonly address remarks like the above, allowing him to take a certain share in the conversation, so far as assent or pertinent questions are involved. He abused his liberty on this occasion by presuming to say that Leibnitz [9] had the same observation.— No, sir, I replied, he has not. But he said a mighty good thing about mathematics, that sounds something like it, and you found it, *not in the original*, but quoted by Dr. Thomas Reid.[1] I will tell the company what he did say, one of these days.

—If I belong to a Society of Mutual Admiration?—I blush to say that I do not at this present moment. I once did, however. It was the first association to which I ever heard the term applied; a body of scientific young men in a great foreign city [2] who admired their teacher, and to some extent each other. Many of them deserved it; they have become famous since. It amuses me to hear the talk of one of those beings described by Thackeray—

"Letters four do form his name" [3]—

about a social development which belongs to the very noblest stage of civilization. All generous companies of artists, authors, philanthropists, men of science, are, or ought to be, Societies of Mutual Admiration. A man of genius, or any kind of superiority, is not

9. Gottfried Wilhelm von Leibnitz (1646–1716), German philosopher and mathematician. He contributed to the science of calculus, hence the appropriateness of this allusion.
1. Founder of the Scottish school of "common-sense," optimistic toward the self-determining powers of the human mind.
2. "The 'body of scientific young men in a great foreign city" was the Société d'Observation Médicale, of Paris, of which M. Louis was president, and MM. Barth, Grisotte, and our own Dr. Bowditch were members. They agreed in admiring their justly-honored president, and thought highly of some of their associates, who have since made good their promise of distinction.

"About the time when these papers were published, the Saturday Club was founded, or, rather, found itself in existence, without any organization, almost without parentage. It was natural enough that such men as Emerson, Longfellow, Agassiz, Peirce, with Hawthorne, Motley, Sumner, when within reach, and others who would be good company for them, should meet and dine together * * * If some of them had not admired each other they would have been exceptions in the world of letters and science. The club deserves being remembered for having no constitution or by-laws, for making no speeches, coming and going at will without remark, and acting out, though it did not proclaim the motto, 'Shall I not take mine ease in mine inn?' There was and is nothing of the Bohemian element about this club, but it has had many good times and not a little good talking" [Holmes's note].
3. Consider "snob" as the four-letter word in this context (Thackeray wrote *The Book of Snobs*). The line of verse, however, is quoted from Coleridge's "Fire, Famine, and Slaughter" (1798), a satire on Sir William Pitt, prime minister of England, whose name has four letters.

debarred from admiring the same quality in another, nor the other from returning his admiration. They may even associate together and continue to think highly of each other. * * *

If the Mutuals have really nothing among them worth admiring, that alters the question. But if they are men with noble powers and qualities, let me tell you that, next to youthful love and family affections, there is no human sentiment better than that which unites the Societies of Mutual Admiration. And what would literature or art be without such associations? Who can tell what we owe to the Mutual Admiration Society of which Shakespeare, and Ben Jonson, and Beaumont and Fletcher were members?[4] Or to that of which Addison and Steele formed the centre,[5] and which gave us the Spectator? Or to that where Johnson,[6] and Goldsmith, and Burke, and Reynolds, and Beauclerk, and Boswell, most admiring among all admirers, met together? Was there any great harm in the fact that the Irvings and Paulding[7] wrote in company? or any unpardonable cabal in the literary union of Verplanck and Bryant and Sands,[8] and as many more as they chose to associate with them? * * *

This business of conversation is a very serious matter. There are men whom it weakens one to talk with an hour more than a day's fasting would do. Mark this which I am going to say, for it is as good as a working professional man's advice, and costs you nothing: It is better to lose a pint of blood from your veins than to have a nerve tapped. Nobody measures your nervous force as it runs away, nor bandages your brain and marrow after the operation.

There are men of *esprit*[9] who are excessively exhausting to some people. They are the talkers who have what may be called *jerky* minds. Their thoughts do not run in the natural order of sequence. They say bright things on all possible subjects, but their zigzags rack you to death. After a jolting half-hour with one of these jerky companions, talking with a dull friend affords great relief. It is like taking the cat in your lap after holding a squirrel.

What a comfort a dull but kindly person is, to be sure, at times! A ground-glass shade over a gas-lamp does not bring more solace to our dazzled eyes than such a one to our minds. * * *

—Little localized powers, and little narrow streaks of specialized

4. This group met for fellowship in the Mermaid Tavern, London.
5. Joseph Addison (1672–1719) and Sir Richard Steele (1672–1729), great English essayists of the *Spectator* papers, together with Swift and other London wits were associated in the Kit-Cat Club.
6. Samuel Johnson (1709–1784) was the center of this coterie, known as "The Club"; *cf.* Boswell's *Johnson*.

7. Washington Irving collaborated with his older brothers, Peter and William, and with James K. Paulding in the *Salmagundi* essays, earliest work of the "Knickerbocker" coterie of New Yorkers.
8. The poet Bryant collaborated with Gulian Verplanck and Robert C. Sands, fellow "Knickerbockers," in *The Talisman* (1827–1830), a gift book.
9. French, meaning "spirited wit."

knowledge, are things men are very apt to be conceited about. Nature is very wise; but for this encouraging principle how many small talents and little accomplishments would be neglected! Talk about conceit as much as you like, it is to human character what salt is to the ocean; it keeps it sweet, and renders it endurable. Say rather it is like the natural unguent of the sea-fowl's plumage, which enables him to shed the rain that falls on him and the wave in which he dips. When one has had *all* his conceit taken out of him, when he has lost *all* his illusions, his feathers will soon soak through, and he will fly no more.

"So you admire conceited people, do you?" said the young lady who has come to the city to be finished off for—the duties of life.

I am afraid you do not study logic at your school, my dear. It does not follow that I wish to be pickled in brine because I like a salt-water plunge at Nahant.[1] I say that conceit is just as natural a thing to human minds as a centre is to a circle. But little-minded people's thoughts move in such small circles that five minutes' conversation gives you an arc long enough to determine their whole curve. An arc in the movement of a large intellect does not sensibly differ from a straight line. Even if it have the third vowel as its centre, it does not soon betray it. The highest thought, that is, is the most seemingly impersonal; it does not obviously imply any individual centre.

Audacious self-esteem, with good ground for it, is always imposing. What resplendent beauty that must have been which could have authorized Phryne to "peel"[2] in the way she did! What fine speech are those two: "*Non omnis moriar*,"[3] and "I have taken all knowledge to be my province"![4] Even in common people, conceit has the virtue of making them cheerful; the man who thinks his wife, his baby, his house, his horse, his dog, and himself severally unequalled, is almost sure to be a good-humored person, though liable to be tedious at times.

—What are the great faults of conversation? Want of ideas, want of words, want of manners, are the principal ones, I suppose you think. I don't doubt it, but I will tell you what I have found spoil more good talks than anything else;—long arguments on special points between people who differ on the fundamental principles upon which these points depend. No men can have satisfactory relations with each other until they have agreed on certain *ultimata* of belief not to be disturbed in ordinary conversation, and unless they

1. On the seashore near Boston.
2. Phryne, a fourth century Athenian courtesan of fabulous beauty, the reputed model for Praxiteles' "Aphrodite"; during a festival for Poseidon, god of the Mediterranean, she publicly disrobed and entered the sea.
3. *Cf.* Horace, *Odes*, III, xxx, l. 6: "I shall not altogether die."
4. From a letter written by Francis Bacon to Lord Burghley in 1592.

have sense enough to trace the secondary questions depending upon these ultimate beliefs to their source. In short, just as a written constitution is essential to the best social order, so a code of finalities is a necessary condition of profitable talk between two persons. Talking is like playing on the harp; there is as much in laying the hand on the strings to stop their vibrations as in twanging them to bring out their music.

—Do you mean to say the pun-question [5] is not clearly settled in your minds? Let me lay down the law upon the subject. Life and language are alike sacred. Homicide and *verbicide*—that is, violent treatment of a word with fatal results to its legitimate meaning, which is its life—are alike forbidden. Manslaughter, which is the meaning of the one, is the same as man's laughter, which is the end of the other. A pun is *primâ facie* [6] an insult to the person you are talking with. It implies utter indifference to or sublime contempt for his remarks, no matter how serious. I speak of total depravity, and one says all that is written on the subject is deep raving. I have committed my self-respect by talking with such a person. I should like to commit him, but cannot, because he is a nuisance. Or I speak of geological convulsions, and he asks me what was the cosine of Noah's ark; also, whether the Deluge was not a deal huger than any modern inundation.

A pun does not commonly justify a blow in return. But if a blow were given for such a cause, and death ensued, the jury would be judges both of the facts and of the pun, and might, if the latter were of an aggravated character, return a verdict of justifiable homicide. Thus, in a case lately decided before Miller, J., [7] Doe presented Roe a subscription paper, and urged the claims of suffering humanity. Roe replied by asking, When charity was like a top? It was in evidence that Doe preserved a dignified silence. Roe then said, "When it begins to hum." Doe then—and not till then—struck Roe, and his head happening to hit a bound volume of the Monthly Rag-Bag and Stolen Miscellany, intense mortification ensued with a fatal result. The chief laid down his notions of the law to his brother justices, who unanimously replied, "Jest so." The chief rejoined, that no man should jest so without being punished for it, and charged for the prisoner, who was acquitted, and the pun ordered to be burned by the sheriff. The bound volume was forfeited as a deodand, [8] but not claimed.

People that make puns are like wanton boys that put coppers on

5. In the following paragraphs, Holmes's argument against puns is punctured by his own.
6. On first appearance; *i.e.*, by nature.
7. In legal parlance, "Miller, Judge"; but Holmes refers also to Joe Miller (1684–1738), famous English come-

dian, whose popular survival was occasioned by successive editions of *Joe Miller's Jest-Book*.
8. Literally, "given to God"; a forfeit to the crown or church for charitable use.

the railroad tracks. They amuse themselves and other children, but their little trick may upset a freight train of conversation for the sake of a battered witticism.

I will thank you, B. F., to bring down two books, of which I will mark the places on this slip of paper. (While he is gone, I may say that this boy, our landlady's youngest, is called BENJAMIN FRANKLIN, after the celebrated philosopher of that name. A highly merited compliment.)

I wished to refer to two eminent authorities. Now be so good as to listen. The great moralist [9] says: "To trifle with the vocabulary which is the vehicle of social intercourse is to tamper with the currency of human intelligence. He who would violate the sanctities of his mother tongue would invade the recesses of the paternal till without remorse, and repeat the banquet of Saturn [1] without an indigestion."

And, once more, listen to the historian.[2] "The Puritans hated puns. The Bishops were notoriously addicted to them. The Lords Temporal carried them to the verge of license. Majesty itself must have its Royal quibble. 'Ye be burly, my Lord of Burleigh,' said Queen Elizabeth, 'but ye shall make less stir in our realm than my Lord of Leicester.' The gravest wisdom and the highest breeding lent their sanction to the practice. Lord Bacon playfully declared himself a descendant of 'Og, the King of Bashan.[3] Sir Philip Sidney, with his last breath, reproached the soldier who brought him water, for wasting a casque full upon a dying man. A courtier, who saw Othello performed at the Globe Theatre, remarked, that the blackamoor was a brute, and not a man. 'Thou hast reason,' replied a great Lord, 'according to Plato [4] his saying; for this be a two-legged animal *with* feathers.' The fatal habit became universal. The langauge was corrupted. The infection spread to the national conscience. Political double-dealings naturally grew out of verbal double meanings. The teeth of the new dragon were sown by the Cadmus [5] who introduced the alphabet of equivocation. What was levity in the time of the Tudors grew to regicide and revolution in the age of the Stuarts." * * *

—What if, instead of talking this morning, I should read you a copy of verses, with critical remarks by the author? Any of the company can retire like that.

---

9. Several critics have detected a parody of Dr. Samuel Johnson in the following pretended quotation.
1. One of the myths of Saturn has him consuming all but one of his children.
2. As above, what follows is a parody, this time of the historian T. B. Macaulay (cf. the following paragraph).
3. Cf. Deuteronomy iii: 1.

4. Diogenes Laeritus said: "Plato * * * defined man to be a two-legged animal without feathers"; but here Othello is ridiculously endowed *with* feathers, since he smothered Desdemona in her bed.
5. The Cadmus of Greek myth killed a dragon and sowed its teeth, reaping a crop of warriors who slew each other.

ALBUM VERSES

When Eve had led her lord away,
  And Cain had killed his brother,
The stars and flowers, the poets say,
  Agreed with one another,

To cheat the cunning tempter's art,
  And teach the race its duty,
By keeping on its wicked heart
  Their eyes of light and beauty.

A million sleepless lids, they say,
  Will be at least a warning;
And so the flowers would watch by day,
  The stars from eve to morning.

On hill and prairie, field and lawn,
  Their dewy eyes upturning,
The flowers still watch from reddening dawn
  Till western skies are burning.

Alas! each hour of daylight tells
  A tale of shame so crushing,
That some turn white as sea-bleached shells,
  And some are always blushing.

But when the patient stars look down
  On all their light discovers,
The traitor's smile, the murderer's frown,
  The lips of lying lovers,

They try to shut their saddening eyes,
  And in the vain endeavor
We see them twinkling in the skies,
  And so they wink forever.

What do *you* think of these verses, my friends?—Is that piece
an impromptu? said my landlady's daughter. (Aet. 19 +. Tender-
eyed blonde. Long ringlets. Cameo pin. Gold pencil-case on a
chain. Locket. Bracelet. Album. Autograph book. Accordeon. Reads
Byron, Tupper, and Sylvanus Cobb, Junior,[6] while her mother
makes the puddings. Says "Yes?" when you tell her anything.)—
Oui et non, ma petite,—Yes and no, my child. Five of the seven
verses were written off-hand; the other two took a week,—that is,

---

6. Martin Farquhar Tupper (1810–
1889) published many editions of his
versified moral maxims, *Proverbial Phi-*
losophy (1838); Sylvanus Cobb, Jr.
(1823–1887) is credited with literally
thousands of sentimental stories.

were hanging round the desk in a ragged, forlorn, unrhymed condition as long as that. All poets will tell you just such stories. *C'est le* DERNIER *pas qui coute.*[7] Don't you know how hard it is for some people to get out of a room after their visit is really over? They want to be off, and you want to have them off, but they don't know how to manage it. One would think they had been built in your parlor or study, and were waiting to be launched. I have contrived a sort of ceremonial inclined plane for such visitors, which being lubricated with certain smooth phrases, I back them down, metaphorically speaking, stern-foremost, into their "native element," the great ocean of outdoors. Well, now, there are poems as hard to get rid of as these rural visitors. They come in glibly, use up all the serviceable rhymes, *day, ray, beauty, duty, skies, eyes, other, brother, mountain, fountain,* and the like; and so they go on until you think it is time for the wind-up, and the wind-up won't come on any terms. So they lie about until you get sick of the sight of them, and end by thrusting some cold scrap of a final couplet upon them, and turning them out of doors. I suspect a good many "impromptus" could tell just such a story as the above.—Here turning to our landlady, I used an illustration which pleased the company much at the time, and has since been highly commended. "Madam," I said, "you can pour three gills and three quarters of honey from that pint jug, if it is full, in less than one minute; but Madam, you could not empty that last quarter of a gill, though you were turned into a marble Hebe,[8] and held the vessel upside down for a thousand years."

One gets tired to death of the old, old rhymes, such as you see in that copy of verses,—which I don't mean to abuse, or to praise either. I always feel as if I were a cobbler, putting new top-leathers to an old pair of bootsoles and bodies, when I am fitting sentiments to these venerable jingles.

.   .   .   .   .   . youth
.   .   .   .   .   . morning
.   .   .   .   .   . truth
.   .   .   .   .   . warning.

Nine tenths of the "Juvenile Poems" written spring out of the above musical and suggestive coincidences.

"Yes?" said our landlady's daughter. * * *

—Self-made men?—Well, yes. Of course every body likes and respects self-made men. It is a great deal better to be made in that way than not to be made at all. Are any of you younger people old

---

7. Usually, in the French proverb, "it is the *first* step that costs"; Holmes makes it the *last.*
8. Mythological cupbearer to the gods.

enough to remember that Irishman's house on the marsh at Cambridgeport, which house he built from drain to chimney-top with his own hands? It took him a good many years to build it, and one could see that it was a little out of plumb, and a little wavy in outline, and a little queer and uncertain in general aspect. A regular hand could certainly have built a better house; but it was a very good house for a "self-made" carpenter's house, and people praised it, and said how remarkably well the Irishman had succeeded. They never thought of praising the fine blocks of houses a little farther on.

Your self-made man, whittled into shape with his own jack-knife, deserves more credit, if that is all, than the regular engine-turned article, shaped by the most approved pattern, and French-polished by society and travel. But as to saying that one is every way the equal of the other, that is another matter. The right of strict social discrimination of all things and persons, according to their merits, native or acquired, is one of the most precious republican privileges. I take the liberty to exercise it when I say that, *other things being equal,* in most relations of life I prefer a man of family.

What do I mean by a man of family?—O, I'll give you a general idea of what I mean. Let us give him a first-rate fit out; it costs us nothing.

Four or five generations of gentlemen and gentlewomen; among them a member of his Majesty's Council for the Province, a Governor or so, one or two Doctors of Divinity, a member of Congress, not later than the time of long boots with tassels. * * *

No, my friends, I go (always, other things being equal) for the man who inherits family traditions and the cumulative humanities of at least four or five generations. Above all things, as a child, he should have tumbled about in a library. All men are afraid of books, who have not handled them from infancy. Do you suppose our dear *didascalos* [9] over there ever read *Poli Synopsis,* or consulted *Castelli Lexicon,* [1] while he was growing up to their stature? Not he; but virtue passed through the hem of their parchment and leather garments whenever he touched them, [2] as the precious drugs sweated through the bat's handle in the Arabian story. I tell you he is at home wherever he smells the invigorating fragrance of Russia leather. [3] No self-made man feels so. One may, it is true, have all the antecedents I have spoken of, and yet be a boor or a shabby fellow. One may have none of them, and yet be fit for

9. " 'Our dear *didascalos*' [teacher] was meant for Professor James Russell Lowell, now Minister to England. It requires the union of exceptional native gifts and generations of training to bring the 'natural man' of New England to the completeness of scholarly manhood, such as that which adds new distinction to the name he bears, already remarkable * * * " [Holmes's note].
1. Matther Poole (1625–1679) published in Latin the scholarly *Synopses of Sacred Scriptures* * * * (London, 1669–1676). Another standard scholarly work was Bartolommeo Castelli's *Lexicon of Graeco-Roman Medicine* (1713).
2. *Cf.* Luke vi: 17–19; Mark v: 25–30.
3. *I.e.,* fine bindings.

councils and courts. Then let them change places. Our social arrangement has this great beauty, that its strata shift up and down as they change specific gravity, without being clogged by layers of prescription. But I still insist on my democratic liberty of choice, and I go for the man with the gallery of family portraits against the one with the twenty-five cent daguerreotype, unless I find out that the last is the better of the two. * * *

1857, 1858

JAMES RUSSELL LOWELL

(1819–1891)

James Russell Lowell conscientiously represented the patrician ideal of those who demand responsible leadership in return for democracy's highest benefits. As a spokesman for this tradition, he was less the Brahmin than Holmes, and had higher expectations of the people as a whole. Elmwood, his birthplace, the ancestral home in Cambridge, Massachusetts, remained throughout his life the hub of his versatile activities. Gifted, tireless, and by temperament both the humanitarian and the humanist, he gave himself zealously to social reform and the antislavery movement; he made a career as poet, critic, editor, and Harvard professor; and without seeking office, he participated in public leadership from the level of local politics to that of the national party councils and foreign diplomacy. Small wonder if his literary critics have been unable to discover a convincing unity in the brilliant but disparate accomplishments of his pen.

The son of a Unitarian clergyman of old family but somewhat limited means, Lowell was graduated in 1838 from Harvard College, and in 1840 from the Law School. The year before, he had sold his first poem, and he soon found the magazines, especially the popular *Graham's*, friendly to his verse and critical articles. Within two years he had collected the poems of *A Years Life* (1841), and left the practice of law in favor of literature.

In 1843, with Robert Carter, he established and edited *The Pioneer*. Reflecting its founder's belief that a periodical of high literary quality could survive without concessions to mass appeal, the magazine lived only three months, but it foreshadowed the famous *Atlantic Monthly*, of which Lowell became the first editor in 1857. His second collection, *Poems*, appeared in 1844. That year he married Maria White, whose devotion to abolition and to humanitarian causes perhaps strengthened his own. They settled in Philadelphia, where Lowell had been called as editorial writer for *The Pennsylvania Freeman*, an antislavery periodical. He began also to contribute articles against slavery to the *National Anti-Slavery Standard* and other periodicals, including the London *Daily News*. A collection of his literary essays, *Conversations on Some of the Old Poets,* appeared in 1845, and was reprinted in London.

Now well established as a writer, he returned to Elmwood in 1846, to experience a virtual triumph that summer when the first of *The Biglow Papers* appeared in the Boston *Courier* (June 17, 1846). The series grew to nine numbers, and gained enormous popularity for its audacious opposition to the Mexican War, which free-soil readers regarded as an elaborate conspiracy among southern politicians for the extension of slave territory by conquest. The success of these letters was as much literary as political. Hosea Biglow's shrewd and homespun wit was enormously amusing, and his "letters" represented the first successful effort to employ the Yankee dialect and humor—an established comic tradition—in satirical poetry of genuine excellence. The series was issued as a volume in 1848, at the conclusion of the war. In 1862, at a moment of northern despondency in the Civil War, Hosea Biglow again appeared, now as a stalwart defender of northern policy and a sharp-witted satirist of the Confederacy.

The year 1848 was truly Lowell's *annus mirabilis.* Then only twenty-nine, he collected his two-volume *Poems: Second Series,* and published *The Biglow Papers* and two new masterpieces, *The Vision of Sir Launfal* and *A Fable for Critics.* The former marks the high point of Lowell's earlier romanticism. An ethical romance inspired by the Arthurian legends, it taught that Holiness and the Grail do not wait at the end of chivalric adventure, but are found in the heart and in the wooden cup of charity. The poem remained a favorite for nearly a century, and its "Prelude" is still one of the most familiar of American poems of nature. *A Fable for Critics* was a daring publication for a young author, impishly dissecting the leading authors of the day, including reverend seniors such as Bryant and Cooper. Only an accepted member of the family, and one armed with Lowell's wit, urbane good nature, and sense of justice, could have accomplished it without disaster. Disarmingly and shrewdly, he hung up his own portrait as one "who's striving Parnassus to climb / With a whole bale of *isms*" on his back. Many of his comments still have value as impressionistic sketches, and their wit, at least, remains untarnished.

When his literary fame was at its greatest, Lowell reached a crucial turning point of his life. Between 1847 and 1853, death took three of his four children, and in 1853, the beloved and frail Maria White. He published travel sketches resulting from a trip abroad in 1851–1852 and gave a few lectures, but the creative fire was banked for a time.

In 1855, he was appointed to succeed Longfellow as Smith Professor of Modern Languages at Harvard, and he served with distinction in this capacity, particularly as a brilliant lecturer, until 1872. He joined with the founders of the *Atlantic Monthly* in 1857, and as editor during its first five years, he helped to shape its policy. This activity, and his remarriage in

1857, brought again a widening of his circle of literary association and interest. The events of the Civil War restored him to literary prominence with the resumption of *The Biglow Papers* which appeared at intervals in the *Atlantic Monthly* between January, 1862, and May, 1866, and were published as a collected *Second Series* in 1867.

In 1864 he became joint editor, with Charles E. Norton, of the *North American Review*, and he maintained this distinguished connection until he resigned his professorship at Harvard. At this time he made his reputation as a memorial poet, delivering, on public occasions, such lofty and stirring odes as the "Commemoration Ode" (1865), and, in 1875, the "Concord Centennial Ode" and "Under the Old Elm." His poetry was becoming noticeably more restrained and formal in spirit, but also more thoughtful. During this period, he published two volumes of poems—*Under the Willows* (1869) and *The Cathedral* (1869, dated 1870)— and collections of his critical and familiar essays—*Among My Books* (1870; *Second Series*, 1876), and *My Study Windows* (1871). His literary criticism was now recognized at home and abroad, and on his trip to England (1872–1874) he was widely celebrated, and awarded honorary degrees at Oxford and Cambridge.

On his return, Lowell again took an active part in politics, particularly as a public speaker. He was a delegate to the Republican national convention in 1876, and sailed as American ambassador to Spain in July,

1877. In 1880 he became ambassador to Great Britain, where, as a cultural representative of the United States, his services were widely recognized. Among the several important speeches during his five years in this post, the most notable was "Democracy," delivered at Birmingham in 1884.

In the six years following his retirement from diplomacy, Lowell lived quietly at Elmwood, except for brief trips abroad in 1888 and 1889. He collected his essays and speeches: *Democracy and Other Addresses* (1887), *Political Essays* (1888), and *Latest Literary Essays* (1891). *The Old English Dramatists* was posthumously published in 1892. He collected the poems of *Heartsease and Rue* (1888). He edited his collected works in ten volumes. On August 21, 1891, he died at Elmwood. He was enormously gifted, but his meteoric writings do not suggest the inward order of a great author. However, the selections below are still alive, and lively records of the culture that produced them.

The standard text is the Riverside Edition, on which the selections in this volume are based. It was published as *The Writings of James Russell Lowell*, 10 vols., edited by James Russell Lowell, 1890. To this were added Vol. XI, *Latest Literary Essays and Addresses* * * *, 1891, and Vol. XII, *The Old English Dramatists*, 1892. The *Letters* * * * , 2 vols., edited by Charles E. Norton, appeared in 1894; and the *Life*, 2 vols., by H. E. Scudder, in 1901; the texts of the Riverside Edition, together with these supplementary volumes, were reprinted under the editorial supervision of Charles E. Norton as the Elmwood Edition, 16 vols., 1904, Norton's *Letters* * * * was extended to 3 vols. in 1904. The best one-volume collection is *The Complete Poetical Works of James Russell Lowell*, Cambridge Edition, edited by H. E. Scudder, 1897, with valuable notes. A good one-volume selection of the prose and poetry, in the American Writers Series, was edited by H. H. Clark and Norman Foerster, 1949. M. A. DeWolfe Howe edited *New Letters of James Russell Lowell*, 1932. Thelma M. Smith edited *The Uncollected Poetry of James Russell Lowell*, 1950.

The standard early biography is H. E. Scudder, *James Russell Lowell: A Biography*, 2 vols., 1901, included in the Elmwood Edition. The definitive modern biography is Martin Duberman, *James Russell Lowell*, 1966. Also useful are E. E. Hale, Jr., *James Russell Lowell and His Friends*, 1899; Ferris Greenslet, *James Russell Lowell: His Life and Work*, 1905; Richmond C. Beatty, *James Russell Lowell*, 1942; Leon Howard, *Victorian Knight-Errant*, 1952; and Edward Wagenknecht, *James Russell Lowell * * ** , 1971.

From A Fable for Critics [1]

READER! *walk up at once* (*it will soon be too late*) *and buy at a perfectly ruinous rate*

A

FABLE FOR CRITICS;

OR, BETTER,

(*I like, as a thing that the reader's first fancy may strike,*
an old-fashioned title-page,
such as presents a tabular view of the volume's contents,)

A GLANCE

AT A FEW OF OUR LITERARY PROGENIES

(*Mrs. Malaprop's word*) [2]

FROM

THE TUB OF DIOGENES; [3]

A VOCAL AND MUSICAL MEDLEY,

THAT IS,

A SERIES OF JOKES

BY A WONDERFUL QUIZ

who accompanies himself with a rub-a-dub-dub, full of spirit and grace, on the top of the tub.

Set forth in October, the 21st day, In the year '48, G. P. Putnam, Broadway.

* * *

1. Lowell's delight in this *jeu d'esprit*, as he termed it, has been shared by his readers since it first appeared in 1848. Loosely modeled after other critical essays in verse (Alexander Pope's *Dunciad*, Leigh Hunt's *Feast of the Poets*), the *Fable* avoids extravagant satire or praise, aiming rather at witty criticism of contemporary American writers. The setting of the title page, and the preface "To the Reader," were carefully designed by Lowell to disguise the fact that they, too, are verse, suggesting the tone of casual humor of the entire book. Speaking of its composition several years later, Lowell said that the *Fable* was extemporized and sent off in daily installments to his friend Charles F. Briggs in New York, to whom he dedicated and gave the book. However, from letters passing between him and Briggs, it appears that he sent off some six hundred lines in the fall, and followed them with successive installments over a period of months, until August, 1848. The title page of the first edition gave the date as "October, the 21st day, in the year '48"; but the book actually came from the press on the twenty-fifth of the month.

2. Mrs. Malaprop, in Sheridan's *The Rivals* (1775), had a genius for misusing words.

3. Diogenes (412?–323 B.C.), Greek Cynic philosopher, according to tradition, lived in a tub, and from there ridiculed conventional society.

"There comes Emerson first, whose rich words, every one,
Are like gold nails [4] in temples to hang trophies on,
Whose prose is grand verse, while his verse, the Lord knows,
Is some of it pr—No, 'tis not even prose;
I'm speaking of metres; some poems have welled   5
From those rare depths of soul that have ne'er been excelled;
They're not epics, but that doesn't matter a pin,
In creating, the only hard thing's to begin;
A grass-blade's no easier to make than an oak;
If you've once found the way, you've achieved the grand stroke;   10
In the worst of his poems are mines of rich matter,
But thrown in a heap with a crash and a clatter;
Now it is not one thing nor another alone
Makes a poem, but rather the general tone,
The something pervading, uniting the whole,   15
The before unconceived, unconceivable soul,
So that just in removing this trifle or that, you
Take away, as it were, a chief limb of the statue;
Roots, wood, bark, and leaves singly perfect may be,
But, clapt hodge-podge together, they don't make a tree.   20

"But, to come back to Emerson (whom, by the way,
I believe we left waiting),—he is, we may say,
A Greek head on right Yankee shoulders, whose range
Has Olympus for one pole, for t'other the Exchange; [5]
He seems, to my thinking (although I'm afraid   25
The comparison must, long ere this, have been made),
A Plotinus-Montaigne,[6] where the Egyptian's gold mist
And the Gascon's shrewd wit cheek-by-jowl coexist;
All admire, and yet scarcely six converts he's got
To I don't (nor they either) exactly know what;   30
For though he builds glorious temples, 'tis odd
He leaves never a doorway to get in a god.
'Tis refreshing to old-fashioned people like me
To meet such a primitive Pagan as he,
In whose mind all creation is duly respected   35
As parts of himself—just a little projected;
And who's willing to worship the stars and the sun,
A convert to—nothing but Emerson.
So perfect a balance there is in his head,

---

4. *Cf.* Ecclesiastes xii: 11; "The words of the wise are * * * as nails fastened by the masters of assemblies."
5. The contrast between the practical and the idealistic aspects of Emerson's nature is suggested by these opposites—the home of the gods of Greece and the stock exchange.
6. Plotinus (205–270), a Roman Neoplatonic philosopher born in Egypt; Michel Eyquem de Montaigne (1533–1592), French essayist, known for his skeptical and sophisticated wit.

That he talks of things sometimes as if they were dead; 40
Life, nature, love, God, and affairs of that sort,
He looks at as merely ideas; in short,
As if they were fossils stuck round in a cabinet,
Of such vast extent that our earth's a mere dab in it;
Composed just as he is inclined to conjecture her, 45
Namely, one part pure earth, ninety-nine parts pure lecturer;
You are filled with delight at his clear demonstration,
Each figure, word, gesture, just fits the occasion,
With the quiet precision of science he'll sort 'em,
But you can't help suspecting the whole a *post mortem*. 50

"There are persons, mole-blind to the soul's make and style,
Who insist on a likeness 'twixt him and Carlyle; [7]
To compare him with Plato [8] would be vastly fairer,
Carlyle's the more burly, but E. is the rarer;
He sees fewer objects, but clearlier, truelier, 55
If C.'s as original, E.'s more peculiar;
That he's more of a man you might say of the one,
Of the other he's more of an Emerson;
C.'s the Titan, as shaggy of mind as of limb,—
E. the clear-eyed Olympian, rapid and slim; 60
The one's two thirds Norseman, the other half Greek,
Where the one's most abounding, the other's to seek;
C.'s generals require to be seen in the mass,—
E.'s specialties gain if enlarged by the glass;
C. gives nature and God his own fits of the blues, 65
And rims common-sense things with mystical hues,—
E. sits in a mystery calm and intense,
And looks coolly around him with sharp common-sense;
C. shows you how every-day matters unite
With the dim transdiurnal recesses of night,— 70
While E., in a plain, preternatural way,
Makes mysteries matters of mere every day;
C. draws all his characters quite *à la* Fuseli,[9]—
Not sketching their bundles of muscles and thews illy,
He paints with a brush so untamed and profuse 75
They seem nothing but bundles of muscles and thews;
E. is rather like Flaxman,[1] lines strait and severe,
And a colorless outline, but full, round, and clear;—

7. Thomas Carlyle (1795–1881), English essayist and historian.
8. Plato (427–347 B.C.), Greek philosopher.
9. Johann Heinrich Füssli (1742–1825), German-Swiss engraver and painter, whose illustrations for Milton's *Paradise Lost* are extravagant in anatomical detail.
1. John Flaxman (1755–1826), English sculptor and draftsman, whose drawings illustrating Homer's and Dante's works are in the classic pattern.

To the men he thinks worthy he frankly accords
The design of a white marble statue in words.   80
C. labors to get at the centre, and then
Take a reckoning from there of his actions and men;
E. calmly assumes the said centre as granted,
And, given himself, has whatever is wanted.

"He has imitators in scores, who omit   85
No part of the man but his wisdom and wit,—
Who go carefully o'er the sky-blue of his brain,
And when he has skimmed it once, skim it again;
If at all they resemble him, you may be sure it is
Because their shoals mirror his mists and obscurities,   90
As a mud-puddle seems deep as heaven for a minute,
While a cloud that floats o'er is reflected within it.

* * *

"There is Bryant, as quiet, as cool, and as dignified,
As a smooth, silent iceberg, that never is ignified,
Save when by reflection 'tis kindled o' nights   95
With a semblance of flame by the chill Northern Lights.
He may rank (Griswold [2] says so) first bard of your nation
(There's no doubt that he stands in supreme iceolation),
Your topmost Parnassus [3] he may set his heel on,
But no warm applauses come, peal following peal on,—   100
He's too smooth and too polished to hang any zeal on:
Unqualified merits, I'll grant, if you choose, he has 'em,
But he lacks the one merit of kindling enthusiasm;
If he stir you at all, it is just, on my soul,
Like being stirred up with the very North Pole.   105

"He is very nice reading in summer, but *inter
Nos*,[4] we don't want *extra* freezing in winter;
Take him up in the depth of July, my advice is,
When you feel an Egyptian devotion to ices.[5]
But, deduct all you can, there's enough that's right good in him,
He has a true soul for field, river, and wood in him;   111
And his heart, in the midst of brick walls, or where'er it is,
Glows, softens, and thrills with the tenderest charities—
To you mortals that delve in this trade-ridden planet?
No, to old Berkshire's hills, with their limestone and granite.   115

2. Rufus Wilmot Griswold (1815–1857), editor of the then popular *Poets and Poetry of America* (1842).
3. Parnassus, mountain in Greece, sacred to Apollo, the god of music and poetry, according to Greek myth was the one mountain whose summit reached above the waves in the Flood.
4. Latin, meaning "among ourselves," or "between us." Lowell makes a play on this and *extra* [*nos*].
5. A play on the name of Isis, Egyptian goddess.

If you're one who *in loco* (add *foco* here) *desipis*,[6]
You will get of his outermost heart (as I guess) a piece;
But you'd get deeper down if you came as a precipice,
And would break the last seal of its inwardest fountain,
If you only could palm yourself off for a mountain.   120
Mr. Quivis,[7] or somebody quite as discerning,
Some scholar who's hourly expecting his learning,
Calls B. the American Wordsworth; but Wordsworth
May be rated at more than your whole tuneful herd's worth.
No, don't be absurd, he's an excellent Bryant;   125
But, my friends, you'll endanger the life of your client,
By attempting to stretch him up into a giant:
If you choose to compare him, I think there are two per-
-sons fit for a parallel—Thomson and Cowper;[8]
I don't mean exactly,—there's something of each,   130
There's T.'s love of nature, C.'s penchant to preach;
Just mix up their minds so that C.'s spice of craziness
Shall balance and neutralize T.'s turn for laziness,
And it gives you a brain cool, quite frictionless, quiet,
Whose internal police nips the buds of all riot,—   135
A brain like a permanent strait-jacket put on
The heart that strives vainly to burst off a button,—
A brain which, without being slow or mechanic,
Does more than a larger less drilled, more volcanic;
He's a Cowper condensed, with no craziness bitten,   140
And the advantage that Wordsworth before him had written.

"But, my dear little bardlings, don't prick up your ears
Nor suppose I would rank you and Bryant as peers;
If I call him an iceberg, I don't mean to say
There is nothing in that which is grand in its way;   145
He is almost the one of your poets that knows
How much grace, strength, and dignity lie in Repose;
If he sometimes fall short, he is too wise to mar
His thought's modest fulness by going too far;
'Twould be well if your authors should all make a trial   150
Of what virtue there is in severe self-denial,

---

6. *Cf.* Horace, *Odes* IV.xii.28: *"dulce est desipere in loco"* ("It's fun at times to engage in trifling"). *Foco* adds a pun on a New York Democratic faction whose members brought matches to a party caucus in case their opponents turned off the gaslights.
7. "Mr. Anyone" or "Whoever-he-is."
8. James Thomson (1700–1748), author of *The Seasons* (1730), graphic in its description of nature, and *The Castle of Indolence* (1748); William Cowper (1731–1800), author of *Olney Hymns* (1779) and *The Task* (1785), and mentally unstable. Lowell added the following note: "To demonstrate quickly and easily how per-/-versely absurd 'tis to sound this name Cowper, / As people in general call him named *super*, / I remark that he rhymes it himself with horse-trooper."

And measure their writings by Hesiod's [9] staff,
Which teaches that all has less value than half.

"There is Whittier, whose swelling and vehement heart
Strains that strait-breasted drab of the Quaker apart,   155
And reveals the live Man, still supreme and erect,
Underneath the bemummying wrappers of sect;
There was ne'er a man born who had more of the swing
Of the true lyric bard and all that kind of thing;
And his failures arise (though he seem not to know it)   160
From the very same cause that has made him a poet,—
A fervor of mind which knows no separation
'Twixt simple excitement and pure inspiration,
As my Pythoness [1] erst sometimes erred from not knowing
If 'twere I or mere wind through her tripod was blowing;   165
Let his mind once get head in its favorite direction
And the torrent of verse bursts the dams of reflection,
While, borne with the rush of the metre along,
The poet may chance to go right or go wrong,
Content with the whirl and delirium of song;   170
Then his grammar's not always correct, nor his rhymes,
And he's prone to repeat his own lyrics sometimes,
Not his best, though, for those are struck off at white-heats
When the heart in his breast like a trip-hammer beats,
And can ne'er be repeated again any more   175
Than they could have been carefully plotted before:
Like old what's-his-name [2] there at the battle of Hastings
(Who, however, gave more than mere rhythmical bastings),
Our Quaker leads off metaphorical fights
For reform and whatever they call human rights,   180
Both singing and striking in front of the war,
And hitting his foes with the mallet of Thor;
Anne haec, one exclaims, on beholding his knocks,
Vestis filii tun, [3] O leather-clad Fox? [4]
Can that be thy son, in the battle's mid din,   185
Preaching brotherly love and then driving it in
To the brain of the tough old Goliath [5] of sin,

9. Greek didactic poet of the eighth
century B.C.
1. The priestess of the oracle at Delphi,
named the Pythia, inhaled the vapors of
the chasm while seated on a tripod (l.
165) and uttered the supposedly inspired prophecies.
2. Taillefer, an armed and mounted
minstrel, who led the charge of William's Norman horsemen at the battle
of Hastings (October 14, 1066), singing the *Song of Roland,* and fell before

the English forces.
3. *Anne haec * * * Vestis filii tui. Cf.*
Genesis xxxvii: 32: "Is this thy son's
coat, or not," asked by Joseph's
brothers of his father Jacob.
4. George Fox (1624–1691), founder
of the Society of Friends, was famous
for his leather breeches.
5. The Philistine giant, slain by a stone
from David's slingshot. *Cf.* I Samuel
xvii: 49.

With the smoothest of pebbles from Castaly's spring [6]
Impressed on his hard moral sense with a sling?

* * *

"There comes Poe, with his raven, like Barnaby Rudge,[7] 190
Three-fifths of him genius and two-fifths sheer fudge,
Who talks like a book of iambs and pentameters,
In a way to make people of common sense damn metres,
Who has written some things quite the best of their kind,
But the heart somehow seems all squeezed out by the mind, 195
Who—But hey-day! What's this? Messieurs Mathews [8] and Poe,
You mustn't fling mud-balls at Longfellow so,
Does it make a man worse that his character's such
As to make his friends love him (as you think) too much?
Why, there is not a bard at this moment alive 200
More willing than he that his fellows should thrive;
While you are abusing him thus, even now
He would help either one of you out of a slough;
You may say that he's smooth and all that till you're hoarse,
But remember that elegance also is force; 205
After polishing granite as much as you will,
The heart keeps its tough old persistency still;
Deduct all you can, *that* still keeps you at bay;
Why, he'll live till men weary of Collins and Gray.[9]
I'm not over-fond of Greek metres in English,[1] 210
To me rhyme's a gain, so it be not too jinglish,
And your modern hexameter verses are no more
Like Greek ones than sleek Mr. Pope [2] is like Homer;
As the roar of the sea to the coo of a pigeon is,
So, compared to your moderns, sounds old Melesigenes;[3] 215
I may be too partial, the reason, perhaps, o't is
That I've heard the old blind man [4] recite his own rhapsodies,
And my ear with that music impregnate may be,
Like the poor exiled shell with the soul of the sea,
Or as one can't bear Strauss [5] when his nature is cloven 220

6. A fountain on Mount Parnassus, sacred to Apollo, god of poetry and music.
7. The central character in Dickens's *Barnaby Rudge* (1841) owned a raven.
8. Cornelius Mathews (1817–1889), editor, novelist, and magazine writer who, like Poe, criticized Longfellow's poetic form and subject matter.
9. William Collins (1721–1759), author of odes and elegies; Thomas Gray (1716–1771), author of "Elegy Written in a Country Churchyard" (1751).

1. Referring to Longfellow's use of the hexameter in *Evangeline*.
2. Alexander Pope (1688–1744) used the heroic couplet in his translation of the *Iliad* (1715–1720), achieving the spirit more of eighteenth-century terseness than of Homeric grandeur.
3. *I.e.*, Melos-born, referring to Homer; his birthplace is actually uncertain.
4. Homer.
5. Johann Strauss (1804–1849), composer of waltzes and polkas.

To its deeps within deeps by the stroke of Beethoven; [6]
But, set that aside, and 'tis truth that I speak,
Had Theocritus [7] written in English, not Greek,
I believe that his exquisite sense would scarce change a line
In that rare, tender, virgin-like pastoral Evangeline.   225
That's not ancient nor modern, its place is apart
Where time has no sway, in the realm of pure Art,
'Tis a shrine of retreat from Earth's hubbub and strife
As quiet and chaste as the author's own life.

* * *

"There is Lowell, who's striving Parnassus to climb   230
With a whole bale of *isms* tied together with rhyme,
He might get on alone, spite of brambles and boulders,
But he can't with that bundle he has on his shoulders,
The top of the hill he will ne'er come nigh reaching
Till he learns the distinction 'twix singing and preaching;   235
His lyre has some chords that would ring pretty well,
But he'd rather by half make a drum of the shell,
And rattle away till he's old as Methusalem, [8]
At the head of a march to the last new Jerusalem."

* * *

1848

From The Biglow Papers, First Series [9]

No. I: A Letter

FROM MR. EZEKIEL BIGLOW OF JAALAM TO THE HON. JOSEPH T.
BUCKINGHAM, EDITOR OF THE BOSTON COURIER, ENCLOSING A
POEM OF HIS SON, MR. HOSEA BIGLOW

6. Ludwig van Beethoven (1770–1827), composer of symphonies and concertos.
7. Greek pastoral poet (third century B.C.).
8. *Cf.* Genesis v: 27; "And all the days of Methuselah were nine hundred sixty and nine years * * * "
9. On June 17, 1846, in the Boston *Courier,* there appeared a letter to the editor, supposedly from an up-country farmer, enclosing a poem written by his son after a disturbing trip to Boston. In so unassuming and disguised a manner, Lowell began *The Biglow Papers,* unsurpassed in American literature for political and social satire, the authentic use of Yankee idiom, and the skillful blending of sincerity and broad humor. Provoked by the poet's belief that the Mexican War was a threat to domestic unity and a political maneuver to extend slave territory, the poems appeared in the Boston *Courier* and the *National Anti-Slavery Standard* before their publication as *The Biglow Papers* in 1848. "Edited" by the pedantic "Rev. Homer Wilbur," who blithely wrote his own press notices, affixed a scholarly title page, and strewed Latin quotations through the volume, the poems indicate the New England character of Hosea Biglow—"homely common-sense vivified and heated by conscience"— and of Birdofredum Sawin, the "un-moral" foil for Hosea, not here represented.

The early years of the Civil War brought Biglow and Sawin into print again, as staunch and caustic supporters of the Union, in the *Atlantic Monthly,* and in 1862 *The Biglow Papers, Second*

JAYLEM, june 1846.

MISTER EDDYTER:—

Our Hosea wuz down to Boston last week, and he see a cruetin Sarjunt [1] a struttin round as popler as a hen with 1 chicking, with 2 fellers a drummin and fifin arter him like all nater. the sarjunt he thout Hosea hed n't gut his i teeth cut cos he looked a kindo's though he'd jest com down,[2] so he cal'lated to hook him in, but Hosy wood n't take none o' his sarse [3] for all he hed much as 20 Rooster's tales stuck onto his hat and eenamost enuf brass a-bobbin up and down on his shoulders and figureed onto his coat and trousis, let alone wut nater hed sot in his featers, to make a 6 pounder out on.

wal, Hosea he com home considerabal riled, and arter I'd gone to bed I heern Him a-thrashin round like a short-tailed Bull in fli-time. The old Woman ses she to me ses she, Zekle, ses she, our Hosee's gut the chollery or suthin anuther ses she, don't you Bee skeered, ses I, he's oney amakin pottery [4] ses i, he's ollers on hand at that ere busynes like Da & martin,[5] and shure enuf, cum mornin, Hosy he cum down stares full chizzle,[6] hare on eend and cote tales flyin, and sot rite of to go reed his varses to Parson Wilbur bein he hain't aney grate shows o' book larnin himself, bimeby he cum back and sed the parson wuz dreffle tickled with 'em as i hoop you will Be, and said they wuz True grit.

Hosea ses 't ain't hardly fair to call 'em his'n now, cos the parson kind o' slicked off sum o' the last varses, but he told Hosee he did n't want to put his ore in to tetch to the Rest on 'em, bein they wuz verry well As thay wuz, and then Hosy ses he sed suthin anuther about Simplex Mundishes [7] or sum sech feller, but I guess Hosea kind o' did n't hear him, for I never hearn o' nobody o' that name in this villadge, and I've lived here man and boy 76 year cum next tater diggin, and thair ain't no wheres a kitting spryer 'n I be.

If you print 'em I wish you'd jest let folks know who hosy's father is, cos my ant Keziah used to say it's nater to be curus ses she, she ain't livin though and he's a likely kind o' lad.

                                                    EZEKIEL BIGLOW.

Series was published in England. In the introduction to the American edition of 1867, Lowell described the genesis of the *Papers,* adding a masterly defense and explanation of the Yankee dialect. The notes signed "H.W." are those of the supposititious editor, "Homer Wilbur."

1. President Polk authorized by an act of May 13, 1846, called out fifty thousand volunteers, and in Massachusetts, as elsewhere, the recruiting sergeants used every inducement to meet their quotas.

2. *I.e.,* "just come down from the country."

3. *"sarse:* abuse, impertinence" [Lowell's note; like other definitions that follow, this is taken from the glossary of the 1848 edition].

4. *"Aut insanit, aut versos facit.—* H.W." ["Either he is mad, or he is making poetry."]

5. Makers of shoe blacking, Day and Martin advertised their product in verse.

6. *I.e.,* full of grit; determined.

7. Hosea's misunderstanding of the parson's criticism: *simplex mundis,* "simpleton of the world."

THRASH away, you'll *hev* to rattle
　　On them kittle-drums o' yourn,—
't ain't a knowin' kind o' cattle
　　Thet is ketched with mouldy corn;
Put in stiff, you fifer feller,　　　　　　　　　　5
　　Let folks see how spry you be,—
Guess you'll toot till you are yeller
　　'fore you git ahold o' me!

Thet air flag's a leetle rotten,
　　Hope it ain't your Sunday's best;　　　　　10
Fact! it takes a sight o' cotton [8]
　　To stuff out a soger's [9] chest:
Sence we farmers hev to pay fer 't,
　　Ef you must wear humps like these,
S'posin you should try salt hay fer 't,　　　　15
　　It would du ez slick ez grease.

'T would n't suit them Southun fellers,
　　They're a dreffle graspin' set,
We must ollers blow the bellers
　　Wen they want their irons het;　　　　　20
May be it's all right ez preachin',
　　But *my* narves it kind o' grates,
Wen I see the overreachin'
　　O' them nigger-drivin' States.

Them thet rule us, them slave-traders,　　　25
　　Hain't they cut a thunderin' swarth
(Helped by Yankee renegaders),
　　Thru the vartu o' the North!
We begin to think it's nater
　　To take sarse an' not be riled;—　　　　30
Who 'd expect to see a tater
　　All on eend at bein' biled?

Ez fer war, I call it murder,—
　　There you hev it plain an' flat;
I don't want to go no furder　　　　　　　　　35
　　Than my Testyment fer that;
God hez sed so plump an' fairly,
　　It's ez long ez it is broad,
An' you've gut to git up airly
　　Ef you want to take in God.　　　　　　　40

'T ain't your eppyletts an' feathers

---

8. A reference to the staple of southern economy.
9. "*sogerin*', soldiering: a barbarous amusement common among men in the savage state" [Lowell's note].

Make the thing a grain more right;
    't ain't afollerin' your bell-wethers [1]
Will excuse ye in His sight;
Ef you take a sword an' dror it,   45
    An' go stick a feller thru,
Guv'ment ain't to answer for it,
    God'll send the bill to you.

Wut's the use o' meetin'-goin'
    Every Sabbath, wet or dry,   50
Ef it's right to go amowin'
    Feller-men like oats an' rye?
I dunno but wut it's pooty
    Trainin' round in bobtail coats,—
But it's curus Christian dooty   55
    This 'ere cuttin' folk's throats.

They may talk o' Freedom's airy [2]
    Tell they're pupple in the face,—
It's a grand gret cemetary
    Fer the barthrights of our race;   60
They jest want this Californy
    So's to lug new slave-states in [3]
To abuse ye, an' to scorn ye,
    An' to plunder ye like sin.

Ain't it cute to see a Yankee   65
    Take sech everlastin' pains,
All to git the Devil's thankee
    Helpin' on 'em weld their chains?
Wy, it's jest ez clear ez figgers,
    Clear ez one an' one make two,   70
Chaps thet make black slaves o' niggers
    Want to make wite slaves o' you.

Tell ye jest the eend I've come to
    Arter cipherin' plaguy smart,
An' it makes a handy sum, tu,
    Any gump [4] could larn by heart;   75
Laborin' man an' laborin' woman
    Hev one glory an' one shame.
Ev'ythin' thet's done inhuman
    Injers all on 'em the same.   80

'T aint by turnin' out to hack folks

---

1. The male sheep with a bell on his neck, leading the flock.
2. *"airy:* area" [Lowell's note].
3. The Compromise of 1850 settled the doubt as to California's status by admitting her as a free state.
4. *"gump:* a foolish fellow, a dullard" [Lowell's note].

You're agoin' to git your right,
　Nor by lookin' down on black folks
　　Coz you're put upon by wite;
　Slavery ain't o' nary color,　　　　　　　　　85
　　't ain't the hide thet makes it wus;
　All it keers fer in a feller
　　's jest to make him fill its pus.⁵

Want to tackle *me* in, du ye?
　I expect you'll hev to wait;　　　　　　　　90
Wen cold lead puts daylight thru ye
　You'll begin to kal'late; ⁶
S'pose the crows wun't fall to pickin'
　All the carkiss from your bones,
Coz you helped to give a lickin'　　　　　　95
　To them poor half-Spanish drones?

Jest go home an' ask our Nancy
　Wether I'd be sech a goose
Ez to jine ye,—guess you'd fancy
　The etarnal bung wuz loose!　　　　　　100
She wants me fer home consumption,
　Let alone the hay's to mow,—
Ef you're arter folks o' gumption,
　You've a darned long row to hoe.

Take them editors thet's crowin'　　　　　105
　Like a cockerel three months old,—
Don't ketch any on 'em going',
　Though they *be* so blasted bold;
Ain't they a prime lot o' fellers?
　'Fore they think on 't guess they'll sprout　110
(Like a peach thet's got the yellers),⁷
　With the meanness bustin' out.

Wal, go 'long to help 'em stealin'
　Bigger pens to cram with slaves,
Help the men thet's ollers dealin'　　　　115
　Insults on your fathers' graves;
Help the strong to grind the feeble,
　Help the many agin' the few,
Help the men thet call your people
　Witewashed slaves an' peddlin' crew!　　120

Massachusetts, God forgive her,

5. "*pus:* purse" [Lowell's note].
6. Calculate; *i.e.,* consider.

7. A disease of peach trees resulting in
no fruit.

She's akneelin' with the rest,[8]
She, thet ough' to ha' clung ferever
   In her grand old eagle-nest;
She thet ough' to stand so fearless   125
   W'ile the wracks are round her hurled,
Holdin' up a beacon peerless
   To the oppressed of all the world!

Hain't they sold your colored seamen?
   Hain't they made your env'ys w'iz? [9]   130
Wut'll make ye act like freemen?
   Wut'll git your dander riz?
Come, I'll tell ye wut I'm thinkin'
   Is our dooty in this fix,
They'd ha' done 't ez quick ez winkin'   135
   In the days o' seventy-six.

Clang the bells in every steeple,
   Call all true men to disown
The tradoocers of our people,
   The enslavers o' their own;   140
Let our dear old Bay State proudly
   Put the trumpet to her mouth,
Let her ring this messidge loudly
   In the ears of all the South:—

"I'll return ye good fer evil   145
   Much ez we frail mortils can,
But I wun't go help the Devil
   Makin' man the cus o' man;
Call me coward, call me traitor,
   Jest ez suits your mean idees,—   150
Here I stand a tyrant-hater,
   An' the friend o' God an' Peace!"

Ef I'd *my* way I hed ruther
   We should go to work an' part,
They take one way, we take t'other,   155
   Guess it would n't break my heart;
Man hed ough' to put asunder
   Them thet God has noways jined;
An' I should n't gretly wonder
   Ef there's thousands o' my mind.   160

8. The seven representatives from Massachusetts had voted for the bill recognizing a state of war with Mexico on May 11, 1846, and allocating funds for military use.
9. Samuel Hoar and George Hubbard had been sent south to protest the capture and sale of free colored citizens of Massachusetts; as "env'ys," or envoys, they had been made to "w'iz" (whiz), *i.e.*, to leave the South.

From The Biglow Papers, Second Series

From the *Introduction*

THE COURTIN' [1]

God makes sech nights, all white an' still
  Fur'z you can look or listen,
Moonshine an' snow on field an' hill,
  All silence an' all glisten.

Zekle crep' up quite unbeknown   5
  An' peeked in thru' the winder,
An' there sot Huldy all alone,
  'ith no one nigh to hender.

A fireplace filled the room's one side
  With half a cord o' wood in—   10
There warn't no stoves (tell comfort died)
  To bake ye to a puddin'.

The wa'nut logs shot sparkles out
  Towards the pootiest, bless her,
An' leetle flames danced all about   15
  The chiny on the dresser.

Agin the chimbley crook-necks [2] hung,
  An' in amongst 'em rusted
The ole queen's-arm [3] thet gran'ther Young
  Fetched back f'om Concord busted.   20

The very room, coz she was in,
  Seemed warm f'om floor to ceilin',
An' she looked full ez rosy agin
  Ez the apples she was peelin'.

---

1. Originally a poem of only forty-four lines in *The Biglow Papers, First Series* (1848), it was extended as Lowell here explains in the introduction to the *Second Series* (1867): "The only attempt I had ever made at anything like a pastoral (if that may be called an attempt which was the result almost of pure accident) was in 'The Courtin'.' While the Introduction to the First Series was going through the press, I received word from the printer that there was a blank page left which must be filled. I sat down at once and improvised another fictitious 'notice of the press,' in which, because verse would fill up space more cheaply than prose, I inserted an extract from a supposed ballad of Mr. Biglow. I kept no copy of it, and the printer, as directed, cut it off when the gap was filled. Presently I began to receive letters asking for the rest of it, sometimes for the *balance* of it. I had none, but to answer such demands, I patched a conclusion upon it in a later edition. Those who had only the first continued to importune me. Afterward, being asked to write it out as an autograph for the Baltimore Sanitary Commission Fair, I added other verses, into some of which I infused a little more sentiment in a homely way, and after a fashion completed it by sketching in the characters and making a connected story. Most likely I have spoiled it, but I shall put it at the end of this Introduction, to answer once for all those kindly importunings."
2. Gourds.
3. Revolutionary musket.

'Twas kin' o' kingdom-come to look 25
   On sech a blessed cretur,
A dogrose blushin' to a brook
   Ain't modester nor sweeter.

He was six foot o' man, A 1,
   Clear grit an' human natur'. 30
None couldn't quicker pitch a ton
   Nor dror a furrer straighter.

He'd sparked it with full twenty gals,
   Hed squired 'em, danced 'em, druv 'em,
Fust this one, an' then thet, by spells— 35
   All is, he couldn't love 'em.

But long o' her his veins 'ould run
   All crinkly like curled maple,
The side she breshed felt full o' sun
   Ez a south slope in Ap'il. 40

She thought no v'ice hed sech a swing
   Ez hisn in the choir;
My! when he made Ole Hunderd [4] ring,
   She *knowed* the Lord was nigher.

An' she'd blush scarlit, right in prayer, 45
   When her new meetin'-bunnet
Felt somehow thru' its crown a pair
   O' blue eyes sot upun it.

Thet night, I tell ye, she looked *some!*
   She seemed to 've gut a new soul, 50
For she felt sartin-sure he'd come,
   Down to her very shoe-sole.

She heered a foot, an' knowed it tu,
   A-raspin' on the scraper,—
All ways to once her feelin's flew 55
   Like sparks in burnt-up paper.

He kin' o' l'itered on the mat,
   Some doubtfle o' the sekle,[5]
His heart kep' goin' pity-pat,
   But hern went pity Zekle. 60

An' yit she gin her cheer a jerk
   Ez though she wished him furder,
An' on her apples kep' to work,
   Parin' away like murder.

4. A psalm tune named from its use
with the One Hundredth Psalm.
5. Sequel, or outcome of his visit.

"You want to see my Pa, I s'pose?"   65
    "Wal . . . no . . . I come dasignin' "—
"To see my Ma? She's sprinklin' clo'es
    Agin to-morrer's i'nin'."

To say why gals acts so or so,
    Or don't, 'ould be persumin';   70
Mebby to mean *yes* an' say *no*
    Comes nateral to women.

He stood a spell on one foot fust,
    Then stood a spell on t'other,
An' on which one he felt the wust   75
    He couldn't ha' told ye nuther.

Says he, "I'd better call agin!"
Says she, "Think likely, Mister:"
Thet last word pricked him like a pin,
    An' . . . Wal, he up an' kist her.   80

When Ma bimeby upon 'em slips,
    Huldy sot pale ez ashes,
All kin' o' smily roun' the lips
    An' teary roun' the lashes.

For she was jes' the quiet kind   85
    Whose naturs never vary,
Like streams that keep a summer mind
    Snowhid in Jenooary.

The blood clost roun' her heart felt glued
    Too tight for all expressin',   90
Tell mother see how metters stood,
    An' gin 'em both her blessin'.

Then her red come back like the tide
    Down to the Bay o' Fundy,
An' all I know is they was cried   95
    In meetin' [6] come nex' Sunday.

From No. II: *Mason and Slidell: A Yankee Idyll* [7]
JONATHAN TO JOHN

It don't seem hardly right, John
    When both my hands was full,

---

6. The wedding banns were "cried" or announced in church.
7. The *Trent* affair, the occasion of the first threat of European intervention in the Civil War, involved two Confederate agents, James M. Mason and John Slidell, who were forcibly removed from the British ship *Trent* on November 8, 1861, by Charles Wilkes, Union captain of the U.S.S. *San Jacinto*, to prevent them from accomplishing their diplomatic mission to London. Only

To stump me to a fight, John,—
  Your cousin, tu, John Bull!
    Ole Uncle S. sez he, "I guess   5
    We know it now," sez he
"The lion's paw is all the law,
    Accordin' to J.B.,
    Thet's fit for you an' me!"

You wonder why we're hot, John?   10
  Your mark wuz on the guns,
The neutral guns, thet shot, John,
  Our brothers an' our sons:
    Ole Uncle S. sez he, "I guess
    There's human blood," sez he,   15
"By fits an' starts, in Yankee hearts,
    Though 't may surprise J. B.
    More'n it would you an' me."

Ef *I* turned mad dogs loose, John,
  On *your* front-parlor stairs,   20
Would it jest meet your views, John,
  To wait an' sue their heirs?
    Ole Uncle S. sez he, "I guess,
    I on'y guess," sez he,
"Thet ef Vattel [8] on *his* toes fell,   25
    'T would kind o' rile J. B.,
    Ez wal ez you an' me!"

Who made the law thet hurts, John,
  Heads I win,—ditto tails?
"*J.B.*" was on his shirts, John,   30
  Onless my memory fails.
    Ole Uncle S. sez he, "I guess,
    (I'm good at thet)," sez he,
"Thet sauce for goose ain't *jest* the juice
    For ganders with J.B.,   35
    No more 'n with you or me!"

---

the efforts of English and Union statesmen kept the furor in the press from erupting into a declaration of war over this breach of international neutrality. President Lincoln was persuaded to release the prisoners, who were sent on to their destination. The event actually served to strengthen English determination to remain neutral.

In his letter to the editors of the *Atlantic Monthly*, where the poem first appeared in February, 1862, Homer Wilbur sets forth the American distress over the affair, followed by a poem of Hosea's in the form of an allegory between Concord Bridge (representing anger at England) and the Bunker Hill Monument (representing conciliation toward England), and then concludes with "Jonathan to John" (America to England), given here. The entire work was first separately reprinted in Boston (1862), and was included in *The Biglow Papers, Second Series* (1867).

8. Emmerich von Vattel (1714–1767), Swiss jurist whose *Droit des Gens* * * * (1758) argued that natural law was above legislation, providing a justification for liberal revolution.

When your rights was our wrongs, John,
  You did n't stop for fuss,—
Britanny's trident prongs, John,
   Was good 'nough law for us.[9]   40
    Ole Uncle S. sez he, "I guess,
     Though physic's good," sez he,
"It doesn't foller thet he can swaller
    Prescriptions signed 'J. B.,'
     Put up by you an' me!"   45

We own the ocean, tu, John:
  You mus' n' take it hard,
Ef we can't think with you, John,
  It's jest your own back-yard.
    Ole Uncle S. sez he, "I guess,   50
     Ef *thet* 's his claim," sez he,
"The fencin'-stuff'll cost enough
    To bust up friend J. B.,
     Ez wal ez you an' me!"

Why talk so dreffle big, John,   55
  Of honor when it meant
You didn't care a fig, John,
  But jest for *ten per cent?* [1]
    Ole Uncle S. sez he, "I guess
     He's like the rest," sez he: 60
"When all is done, it's number one
    Thet's nearest to J. B.,
     Ez wal ez t' you an' me!"

We give the critters back, John,
  Cos Abram thought 't was right; [2]   65
It warn't your bullyin' clack, John,
  Provokin' us to fight.
    Ole Uncle S. sez he, "I guess
     We've a hard row," sez he,
"To hoe jest now; but thet, somehow,   70
    May happen to J. B.,
     Ez wal ez you an' me!"

We ain't so weak an' poor, John,
  With twenty million people,

9. A reference to the incident of the British seizure of the American *Caroline* in the Canadian insurrection of 1837. The American ship, in defiance of President Van Buren's insistence on neutrality, was used to convey armed American sympathizers across the Niagara River; English forces fired the ship in American waters, but five years later, in the Webster-Ashburton Treaty (1842), Britain made amends for the incident. The "trident prongs" here denote British naval law.
1. *I.e.*, the presumed English profit from selling war materiel to the South.
2. The "critters" are Mason and Slidell; "Abram" is Abraham Lincoln.

An' close to every door, John,   75
   A school-house an' a steeple.
      Ole Uncle S. sez he, "I guess
      It is a fact," sez he,
"The surest plan to make a Man
      Is, think him so, J. B.,   80
      Ez much ez you or me!"

Our folks believe in Law, John;
   An' it's for her sake, now,
They've left the axe an' saw, John,
   The anvil an' the plough.   85
      Ole Uncle S. sez he, "I guess,
      Ef 't warn't for law," sez he,
"There 'd be one shindy from here to Indy;
      An' thet don't suit J. B.
      (When 't ain't 'twix you an' me!)"   90

We know we've got a cause, John,
   Thet's honest, just, an' true;
We thought 't would win applause, John,
   Ef nowheres else, from you.
      Ole Uncle S. sez he, "I guess   95
      His love of right," sez he,
"Hangs by a rotten fibre o' cotton:
      There's natur' in J. B.,
      Ez wal 'z you an' me!"

The South says, "*Poor folks down!*" John,   100
   An' "*All men up!*" say we,—
White, yaller, black, an' brown, John:
   Now which is your idee?
      Ole Uncle S. sez he, "I guess,
      John preaches wal," sez he;   105
"But, sermon thru, an' come to *du*,
      "Why, there's the old J. B.
      A crowdin' you an' me!"

Shall it be love, or hate, John?
   It's you thet's to decide;   110
Ain't *your* bonds held by Fate, John,
   Like all the world's beside?
      Ole Uncle S. sez he, "I guess
      Wise men forgive," sez he,
"But not forgit; an' some time yit   115
      Thet truth may strike J. B.,
      Ez wal ez you an' me!"

God means to make this land, John,
  Clear thru, from sea to sea,
Believe and understand, John,   120
  The *wuth* o' bein' free.
    Ole Uncle S. sez he, "I guess,
      God's price is high," sez he;
    "But nothin' else than wut He sells
      Wears long, an thet J. B.   125
    May larn, like you an' me!"

1867

Ode Recited at the Harvard Commemoration[3]

JULY 21, 1865

I

Weak-winged is song,
Nor aims at that clear-ethered height
Whither the brave deeds climbs for light:
  We seem to do them wrong,
Bringing our robin's-leaf to deck their hearse   5
Who in warm life-blood wrote their nobler verse,
Our trivial song to honor those who come
With ears attuned to strenuous trump and drum,
And shaped in squadron-strophes their desire,
Live battle-odes whose lines were steel and fire: 10
  Yet sometimes feathered words are strong,
A gracious memory to buoy up and save
From Lethe's[4] dreamless ooze, the common grave
  Of the unventurous throng.

II

Today our Reverend Mother[5] welcomes back   15

3. Lowell read this poem to a group of friends and alumni of Harvard College on July 21, 1865, to honor the Harvard men, living and dead, who had fought in the recently concluded Civil War. Three of his nephews had died in the conflict, and his personal involvement had been intensified by his hatred of war, evident in *The Biglow Papers, First Series*, and his resentment of slavery, reflected in the *Second Series*. In this poem he finds some consolation in the sober joy of peace and victory: "O Beautiful! my Country! ours once more!" He wrote to a friend: "The poem was written with a vehement speed, which I thought I had lost in the skirts of my professor's gown. Till within two days of the celebration I was hopelessly dumb, and then it all came with a rush, literally making me lean * * * and so nervous that I was weeks in getting over it." The form of the poem, which is a so-called Cowleyan ode, was chosen by the poet because of the suitability of the varied verse structure for reading aloud. The sixth strophe, on Lincoln, not in the original reading, was added immediately afterward. Privately printed at Cambridge in 1865, the poem appeared in the *Atlantic Monthly* for September, 1865, and was reprinted in *Harvard Memorial Biographies* (1866), *Under the Willows* (1869), and *Three Memorial Poems* (1877).

4. A river of Hades whose waters when drunk provided forgetfulness of the past life.

5. *I.e.*, Harvard College, their Alma Mater.

Her wisest Scholars, those who understood a
The deeper teaching of her mystic tome, b
  And offered their fresh lives to make it good: a
      No lore of Greece or Rome, b
No science peddling with the names of things, c   20
Or reading stars to find inglorious fates, d
      Can lift our life with wings c
Far from Death's idle gulf that for the many waits, d
      And lengthen out our dates d
With that clear fame whose memory sings c   25
In manly hearts to come, and nerves them and dilates: d
Nor such thy teaching, Mother of us all! e
      Not such the trumpet-call e
      Of thy diviner mood, f
      That could thy sons entice g   30
From happy homes and toils, the fruitful nest h
Of those half-virtues which the world calls best, h
      Into War's tumult rude; f
      But rather far that stern device g
The sponsors chose that round thy cradle stood i   35
      In the dim, unventured wood, i
    The VERITAS [6] that lurks beneath j
    The letter's unprolific sheath, j
Life of whate'er makes life worth living, k
Seed-grain of high emprise, immortal food, i   40
  One heavenly thing whereof earth hath the giving. k

III

Many loved Truth, and lavished life's best oil
  Amid the dust of books to find her,
Content at last, for guerdon of their toil,
  With the cast mantle she hath left behind her.   45
    Many in sad faith sought for her,
    Many with crossed hands sighed for her;
    But these, our brothers, fought for her,
    At life's dear peril wrought for her,
    So loved her that they died for her,   50
    Tasting the raptured fleetness
    Of her divine completeness:
    Their higher instinct knew
Those love her best who to themselves are true,
And what they dare to dream of, dare to do;   55
    They followed her and found her
    Where all may hope to find,
Not in the ashes of the burnt-out mind,

6. "Veritas" ("Truth") on the seal of Harvard College.

But beautiful, with danger's sweetness round her.
   Where faith made whole with deed 60
    Breathes its awakening breath
    Into the lifeless creed,
    They saw her plumed and mailed,
    With sweet, stern face unveiled,
And all-repaying eyes, look proud on them in death. 65

IV

Our slender life runs rippling by, and glides
   Into the silent hollow of the past;
    What is there that abides
    To make the next age better for the last?
    Is earth too poor to give us 70
   Something to live for here that shall outlive us?
    Some more substantial boon
Than such as flows and ebbs with Fortune's fickle moon?
    The little that we see
    From doubt is never free; 75
    The little that we do
    Is but half-nobly true;
    With our laborious hiving
What men call treasure, and the gods call dross,
   Life seems a jest of Fate's contriving, 80
   Only secure in every one's conniving,
A long account of nothings paid with loss,
Where we poor puppets, jerked by unseen wires,
   After our little hour of strut and rave,
With all our pasteboard passions and desires, 85
Loves, hates, ambitions, and immortal fires,
   Are tossed pell-mell together in the grave.
   But stay! no age was e'er degenerate,
   Unless men held it at too cheap a rate,
   For in our likeness still we shape our fate. 90
    Ah, there is something here
   Unfathomed by the cynic's sneer,
   Something that gives our feeble light
   A high immunity from Night,
   Something that leaps life's narrow bars 95
To claim its birthright with the hosts of heaven;
   A seed of sunshine that can leaven
   Our earthly dullness with the beams of stars,
    And glorify our clay
With light from fountains elder than the Day; 100
    A conscience more divine than we,
    A gladness fed with secret tears,

A vexing, forward-reaching sense
Of some more noble permanence;
A light across the sea,   105
Which haunts the soul and will not let it be,
Still beaconing from the heights of undegenerate years.

V

Whither leads the path
To ampler fates that leads?
Not down through flowery meads,   110
To reap an aftermath
Of youth's vainglorious weeds,
But up the steep, amid the wrath
And shock of deadly-hostile creeds,
Where the world's best hope and stay   115
By battle's flashes gropes a desperate way,
And every turf the fierce foot clings to bleeds.
Peace hath her not ignoble wreath,
Ere yet the sharp, decisive word
Light the black lips of cannon, and the sword   120
Dreams in its easeful sheath;
But some day the live coal behind the thought,
Whether from Baäl's stone [7] obscene,
Or from the shrine serene
Of God's pure altar brought,   125
Bursts up in flame; the war of tongue and pen
Learns with what deadly purpose it was fraught,
And, helpless in the fiery passion caught,
Shakes all the pillared state with shock of men:
Some day the soft Ideal that we wooed   130
Confronts us fiercely, foe-beset, pursued,
And cries reproachful: "Was it, then, my praise,
And not myself was loved? Prove now thy truth;
I claim of thee the promise of thy youth;
Give me thy life, or cower in empty phrase,   135
The victim of thy genius, not its mate!"
Life may be given in many ways,
And loyalty to Truth be sealed
As bravely in the closet as the field,
So bountiful is Fate;   140
But then to stand beside her,
When craven churls deride her,
To front a lie in arms and not to yield,
This shows, methinks, God's plan

7. *Cf.* I Kings xviii for the contest between Elijah and the idolatrous priests of
the pagan deity Baäl.

And measure of a stalwart man,   145
    Limbed like the old heroic breeds,
    Who stands self-poised on manhood's solid earth,
  Not forced to frame excuses for his birth,
Fed from within with all the strength he needs.

VI

Such was he, our Martyr-Chief,[8]   150
    Whom late the Nation he had led,
    With ashes on her head,
Wept with the passion of an angry grief:
Forgive me, if from present things I turn
To speak what in my heart will beat and burn,   155
And hang my wreath on his world-honored urn.
    Nature, they say, doth dote,
    And cannot make a man
    Save on some worn-out plan,
    Repeating us by rote: 160
For him her Old-World moulds aside she threw,
    And choosing sweet clay from the breast
    Of the unexhausted West,
With stuff untainted shaped a hero new,
Wise, steadfast in the strength of God, and true.   165
    How beautiful to see
Once more a shepherd of mankind indeed,
Who loved his charge, but never loved to lead;
One whose meek flock the people joyed to be,
    Not lured by any cheat of birth,   170
    But by his clear-grained human worth,
And brave old wisdom of sincerity!
    They knew that outward grace is dust;
    They could not choose but trust
In that sure-footed mind's unfaltering skill,   175
    And supple-tempered will
That bent like perfect steel to spring again and thrust.
    His was no lonely mountain-peak of mind,
    Thrusting to thin air o'er our cloudy bars,
    A sea-mark now, now lost in vapors blind;   180
    Broad prairie rather, genial, level-lined,
    Fruitful and friendly for all human kind,
Yet also nigh to heaven and loved of loftiest stars.
        Nothing of Europe here,
Or, then, of Europe fronting mornward still,   185
    Ere any names of Serf and Peer
    Could Nature's equal scheme deface

8. Lincoln.

And thwart her genial will;
Here was a type of the true elder race,
And one of Plutarch's men [9] talked with us face to face.   190
I praise him not; it were too late;
And some innative weakness there must be
In him who condescends to victory
Such as the Present gives, and cannot wait,
Safe in himself as in a fate.   195
So always firmly he:
He knew to bide his time,
And can his fame abide,
Still patient in his simple faith sublime,
Till the wise years decide.   200
Great captains, with their guns and drums,
Disturb our judgment for the hour,
But at last silence comes;
These all are gone, and, standing like a tower,
Our children shall behold his fame.   205
The kindly-earnest, brave, foreseeing man,
Sagacious, patient, dreading praise, not blame,
New birth of our new soil, the first American.

VII

Long as man's hope insatiate can discern
Or only guess some more inspiring goal   210
Outside of Self, enduring as the pole,
Along whose course the flying axles burn
Of spirits bravely-pitched, earth's manlier brood;
Long as below we cannot find
The meed that stills the inexorable mind;   215
So long this faith to some ideal Good,
Under whatever mortal names it masks,
Freedom, Law, Country, this ethereal mood
That thanks the Fates for their severer tasks,
Feeling its challenged pulses leap,   220
While others skulk in subterfuges cheap,
And, set in Danger's van, has all the boon it asks,
Shall win man's praise and woman's love,
Shall be a wisdom that we set above
All other skills and gifts to culture dear,   225
A virtue round whose forehead we inwreathe
Laurels that with a living passion breathe
When other crowns grow, while we twine them, sear.
What brings us thronging these high rites to pay,

9. Lowell compares Lincoln to one of the heroes of ancient history memorialized
by Plutarch (46?–120) in his *Parallel Lives*.

And seal these hours the noblest of our year,   230
 Save that our brothers found this better way?

VIII

 We sit here in the Promised Land
 That flows with Freedom's honey and milk; [1]
 But 'twas they won it, sword in hand,
Making the nettle danger soft for us as silk.   235
 We welcome back our bravest and our best;—
 Ah me! not all! some come not with the rest,
Who went forth brave and bright as any here!
I strive to mix some gladness with my strain,
   But the sad strings complain,   240
   And will not please the ear:
I sweep them for a pæan, but they wane
   Again and yet again
Into a dirge, and die away, in pain.
In these brave ranks I only see the gaps,   245
Thinking of dear ones whom the dumb turf wraps,
Dark to the triumph which they died to gain:
  Fitlier may others greet the living,
  For me the past is unforgiving;
   I with uncovered head   250
   Salute the sacred dead,
Who went, and who return not.—Say not so!
'Tis not the grapes of Canaan [2] that repay,
But the high faith that failed not by the way;
Virtue treads paths that end not in the grave;   255
No ban of endless night exiles the brave;
   And to the saner mind
We rather seem the dead that stayed behind.
Blow, trumpets, all your exultations blow!
For never shall their aureoled presence lack: 260
I see them muster in a gleaming row,
With ever-youthful brows that nobler show;
We find in our dull road their shining track;
   In every nobler mood
We feel the orient of their spirit glow,   265
Part of our life's unalterable good,
Of all our saintlier aspiration;
  They come transfigured back,
Secure from change in their high-hearted ways,
Beautiful evermore, and with the rays   270
Of morn on their white Shields of Expectation!

---

1. *Cf.* Exodus iii: 8.   2. *Cf.* Numbers xiii: 23–27.

IX

But is there hope to save
Even this ethereal essence from the grave?
What ever 'scaped Oblivion's subtle wrong
Save a few clarion names, or golden threads of song?   275
  Before my musing eye
  The mighty ones of old sweep by,
Disvoicèd now and insubstantial things,
As noisy once as we; poor ghosts of kings,
Shadows of empire wholly gone to dust,   280
And many races, nameless long ago,
To darkness driven by that imperious gust
Of ever-rushing Time that here doth blow:
O visionary world, condition strange,
Where naught abiding is but only Change,   285
Where the deep-bolted stars themselves still shift and range!
Shall we to more continuance make pretence?
Renown builds tombs; a life-estate is Wit;
  And, bit by bit,
The cunning years steal all from us but woe;   290
Leaves are we, whose decays no harvest sow.
  But, when we vanish hence,
Shall they lie forceless in the dark below,
Save to make green their little length of sods,
Or deepen pansies for a year or two,   295
Who now to us are shining-sweet as gods?
Was dying all they had the skill to do?
That were not fruitless; but the Soul resents
Such short-lived service, as if blind events
Ruled without her, or earth could so endure;   300
She claims a more divine investiture
Of longer tenure than Fame's airy rents;
Whate'er she touches doth her nature share;
Her inspiration haunts the ennobled air,
  Gives eyes to mountains blind,   305
Ears to the deaf earth, voices to the wind,
And her clear trump sings succor everywhere
By lonely bivouacs to the wakeful mind;
For soul inherits all that soul could dare:
  Yea, Manhood hath a wider span   310
And larger privilege of life than man.
The single deed, the private sacrifice,
So radiant now through proudly-hidden tears,
Is covered up erelong from mortal eyes

With thoughtless drift of the deciduous years;   315
But that high privilege that makes all men peers,
That leap of heart whereby a people rise
    Up to a noble anger's height,
And, flamed on by the Fates, not shrink, but grow more bright,
  That swift validity in noble veins,   320
    Of choosing danger and disdaining shame,
      Of being set on flame
    By the pure fire that flies all contact base
But wraps its chosen with angelic might,
    These are imperishable gains,   325
  Sure as the sun, medicinal as light,
  These hold great futures in their lusty reins
And certify to earth a new imperial race.

X

    Who now shall sneer?
    Who dare again to say we trace   330
    Our lines to a plebeian race?
    Roundhead and Cavalier! [3]
Dumb are those names erewhile in battle loud;
Dream-footed as the shadow of a cloud,
    They flit across the ear: 335
That is best blood that hath most iron in 't,
To edge resolve with, pouring without stint
    For what makes manhood dear.
    Tell us not of Plantagenets,
Hapsburgs, and Guelfs,[4] whose thin bloods crawl   340
Down from some victor in a border-brawl!
    How poor their outworn coronets,
Matched with one leaf of that plain civic wreath
Our brave for honor's blazon shall bequeath,
    Through whose desert a rescued Nation sets   345
Her heel on treason, and the trumpet hears
Shout victory, tingling Europe's sullen ears
    With vain resentments and more vain regrets!

XI

    Not in anger, not in pride,
    Pure from passion's mixture rude   350
    Ever to base earth allied,

---

3. Roundheads were Puritan followers of Cromwell in the English civil war, founders of Massachusetts; and Cavaliers were supporters of Charles I, representative of the early settlers of Virginia.
4. Plantagenets, the ruling house of England (1154–1399); Hapsburgs, the rulers of the Holy Roman Empire from the middle of the fifteenth to the eighteenth centuries; Guelphs, the papal party in Italy in the thirteenth and fourteenth centuries; all here symbols of the intrigue and the disastrous wars that left Europe in political chaos.

But with far-heard gratitude,
Still with heart and voice renewed,
To heroes living and dear martyrs dead,
The strain should close that consecrates our brave.   355
Lift the heart and lift the head!
Lofty be its mood and grave,
Not without a martial ring,
Not without a prouder tread
And a peal of exultation: 360
Little right has he to sing
Through whose heart in such an hour
Beats no march of conscious power,
Sweeps no tumult of elation!
'Tis no Man we celebrate,   365
By his country's victories great,
A hero half, and half the whim of Fate,
But the pith and marrow of a Nation
Drawing force from all her men,
Highest, humblest, weakest, all,   370
For her time of need, and then
Pulsing it again through them,
Till the basest can no longer cower,
Feeling his soul spring up divinely tall,
Touched but in passing by her mantle-hem.   375
Come back, then, noble pride, for 'tis her dower!
How could poet ever tower,
If his passions, hopes, and fears,
If his triumphs and his tears,
Kept not measure with his people?   380
Boom, cannon, boom to all the winds and waves!
Clash out, glad bells, from every rocking steeple!
Banners, advance with triumph, bend your staves!
And from every mountain-peak
Let beacon-fire to answering beacon speak,   385
Katahdin tell Monadnock, Whiteface [5] he,
And so leap on in light from sea to sea,
Till the glad news be sent
Across a kindling continent,
Making earth feel more firm and air breathe braver: 390
"Be proud! for she is saved, and all have helped to save her!
She that lifts up the manhood of the poor,
She of the open soul and open door,
With room about her hearth for all mankind!
The fire is dreadful in her eyes no more;   395

5. Mountains in Maine, New Hampshire, and New York.

From her bold front the helm she doth unbind,
Sends all her handmaid armies back to spin,
And bids her navies, that so lately hurled
Their crashing battle, hold their thunders in,
Swimming like birds of calm along the unharmful shore.   400
No challenge sends she to the elder world,
That looked askance and hated; [6] a light scorn
Plays o'er her mouth, as round her mighty knees
She calls her children back, and waits the morn
Of nobler day, enthroned between her subject seas."   405

XII

Bow down, dear Land, for thou hast found release!
Thy God, in these distempered days,
Hath taught thee the sure wisdom of His ways,
And through thine enemies hath wrought thy peace!
Bow down in prayer and praise!   410
No poorest in thy borders but may now
Lift to the juster skies a man's enfranchised brow.
O Beautiful! my Country! ours once more!
Smoothing thy gold of war-dishevelled hair
O'er such sweet brows as never other wore,   415
And letting thy set lips,
Freed from wrath's pale eclipse,
The rosy edges of their smiles lay bare,
What words divine of lover or of poet
Could tell our love and make thee know it,   420
Among the Nations bright beyond compare?
What were our lives without thee?
What all our lives to save thee?
We reck not what we gave thee;
We will not dare to doubt thee,   425
But ask whatever else, and we will dare!

1865   1865

FREDERICK DOUGLASS
(1817?–1895)

Frederick Douglass was born into slavery on Maryland's Eastern Shore, the son of a Negro slave and a white man. He never knew for certain the identity of his father and saw his mother but a few times after he was taken from her as an infant. At twenty-one he escaped and settled with his wife, who was free, in New Bedford, Massachusetts, changing his original name,

6. A reference to the unpopularity of the Union cause in some circles in England and France.

Frederick Bailey, to Frederick Douglass in order to avoid pursuit. Without formal education, he had taught himself to read and write and had perhaps already developed something of the speaking skill for which he soon became famous.

Given a subscription to William Lloyd Garrison's *Liberator,* he found himself drawn quickly into the abolition movement. Despite the obvious danger to an American Negro who advertised himself as an escaped slave, he spent three years lecturing in that capacity in the pay of the anti-slavery forces before he sat down to write his first book. When the *Narrative of the Life of Frederick Douglass* (1845) appeared, it had the advantage of a preface by William Lloyd Garrison and a prefatory letter by Wendell Phillips. More important to posterity, however, was the fact that it was written by a man with a sharp memory for details, a good, plain style, thoroughly tested on the lecture platform, and a vivid sense of the importance of his story.

In some ways the 1845 *Narrative* remains his most interesting work even though he twice expanded it, in *My Bondage and My Freedom* (1855) and *Life and Times of Frederick Douglass* (1881), in order to accommodate later experiences and changing perspectives. Douglass went on to a distinguished career as a newspaper publisher in Rochester, New York, a United States Marshal and Recorder of Deeds in Washington, D.C., and eventually Consul-General to the Republic of Haiti. Along the way he helped enlist Negro troops for the Union cause, spoke on behalf of women's rights, and shocked a good many of his friends and associates by taking a white woman as his second wife. Because he was always a prolific writer of letters, speeches, editorials, and magazine articles, his published works in addition to his autobiographies fill four volumes. For all the fascination and success of his later life, however, never again did he attain the power of expression of the young man only eight years away from slavery who sat down to write the *Narrative.*

The versions of Douglass's autobiography are *Narrative of the Life of Frederick Douglass, An American Slave,* 1845, the source of the present selections; *My Bondage and My Freedom,* 1855; and *Life and Times of Frederick Douglass,* 1881 (revised edition, 1892). *Narrative* has been edited with an introduction by Benjamin Quarles, 1960. Douglass's other writings are collected in *The Life and Writings of Frederick Douglass,* edited by Philip Foner, 4 vols., 1950–1955. Early biographies are Frederic May Holland, *Frederick Douglass: The Colored Orator,* 1891, and Booker T. Washington, *Frederick Douglass,* 1906. More recent studies are Benjamin Quarles, *Frederick Douglass,* 1948; Philip Foner, *Frederick Douglass, a Biography,* 1964; and Arna Bontemps, *Free at Last: the Life of Frederick Douglass,* 1971.

From Narrative of the Life of Frederick Douglass

Chapter I

I was born in Tuckahoe, near Hillsborough, and about twelve miles from Easton, in Talbot county, Maryland. I have no accurate knowledge of my age, never having seen any authentic record containing it. By far the larger part of the slaves know as little of their ages as horses know of theirs, and it is the wish of most masters within my knowledge to keep their slaves thus ignorant. I do not remember to have ever met a slave who could tell of his birthday. They seldom come nearer to it than planting-time, harvest-time, cherry-time, spring-time, or fall-time. A want of information concerning my own was a source of unhappiness to me even during childhood. The white children could tell their ages. I could not tell why I ought to be deprived of the same privilege. I was not allowed to make any inquiries of my master concerning it. He deemed all such inquiries on the part of a slave improper and impertinent, and evidence of a restless spirit. The nearest estimate I can give makes me now between twenty-seven and twenty-eight years of age. I come to this, from hearing my master say, some time during 1835, I was about seventeen years old.

My mother was named Harriet Bailey. She was the daughter of Isaac and Betsey Bailey, both colored, and quite dark. My mother was of a darker complexion than either my grandmother or grandfather.

My father was a white man. He was admitted to be such by all I ever heard speak of my parentage. The opinion was also whispered that my master was my father; but of the correctness of this opinion, I know nothing; the means of knowing was withheld from me. My mother and I were separated when I was but an infant—before I knew her as my mother. It is a common custom, in the part of Maryland from which I ran away, to part children from their mothers at a very early age. Frequently, before the child has reached its twelfth month, its mother is taken from it, and hired out on some farm a considerable distance off, and the child is placed under the care of an old woman, too old for field labor. For what this separation is done, I do not know, unless it be to hinder the development of the child's affection toward its mother, and to blunt and destroy the natural affection of the mother for the child. This is the inevitable result.

I never saw my mother, to know her as such, more than four or five times in my life; and each of these times was very short in duration, and at night. She was hired by a Mr. Stewart, who lived about twelve miles from my home. She made her journeys to see me in the night, travelling the whole distance on foot, after the performance of her day's work. She was a field hand, and a whipping is the penalty of not being in the field at sunrise, unless a slave has special permission from his or her master to the contrary —a permission which they seldom get, and one that gives to him that gives it the proud name of being a kind master. I do not recollect of ever seeing my mother by the light of day. She was with me in the night. She would lie down with me, and get me to sleep, but long before I waked she was gone. Very little communication ever took place between us. Death soon ended what little we could have while she lived, and with it her hardships and suffering. She died when I was about seven years old, on one of my master's farms, near Lee's Mill. I was not allowed to be present during her illness, at her death, or burial. She was gone long before I knew any thing about it. Never having enjoyed, to any considerable extent, her soothing presence, her tender and watchful care, I received the tidings of her death with much the same emotions I should have probably felt at the death of a stranger.

Called thus suddenly away, she left me without the slightest intimation of who my father was. The whisper that my master was my father, may or may not be true; and, true or false, it is of but little consequence to my purpose whilst the fact remains, in all its glaring odiousness, that slaveholders have ordained, and by law established, that the children of slave women shall in all cases follow the condition of their mothers; and this is done too obviously to administer to their own lusts, and make a gratification of their wicked desires profitable as well as pleasurable; for by this cunning arrangement, the slaveholder, in cases not a few, sustains to his slaves the double relation of master and father.

I know of such cases; and it is worthy of remark that such slaves invariably suffer greater hardships, and have more to contend with, than others. They are, in the first place, a constant offence to their mistress. She is ever disposed to find fault with them; they can seldom do any thing to please her; she is never better pleased than when she sees them under the lash, especially when she suspects her husband of showing to his mulatto children favors which he withholds from his black slaves. The master is frequently compelled to sell this class of his slaves, out of deference to the feelings of his white wife; and, cruel as the deed may strike any one to be, for a man to sell his own children to human flesh-mongers, it is often the dictate of humanity for him to do so; for, unless he does this, he must not only whip them himself, but must stand by and see one white son tie up his brother, of but few shades darker complexion than himself, and ply the gory lash to his naked back; and if he lisp one word of disapproval, it is set down to his parental partiality, and only makes a bad matter worse, both for himself and the slave whom he would protect and defend.

Every year brings with it multitudes of this class of slaves. It was doubtless in consequence of a knowledge of this fact, that one great statesman of the south predicted the downfall of slavery by the inevitable laws of population. Whether this prophecy is ever fulfilled or not, it is nevertheless plain that a very different-looking class of people are springing up at the south, and are now held in slavery, from those originally brought to this country from Africa; and if their increase will do no other good, it will do away the force of the argument, that God cursed Ham,[1] and therefore American slavery is right. If the lineal descendants of Ham are alone to be scripturally enslaved, it is certain that slavery at the south must soon become unscriptural; for thousands are ushered into the world, annually, who, like myself, owe their existence to white fathers, and those fathers most frequently their own masters.

Chapter X

I left Master Thomas's house, and went to live with Mr. Covey, on the 1st of January, 1833.[2] I was now, for the first time in my life, a field hand. In my new employment, I found myself even more awkward than a country boy appeared to be in a large city. I had been at my new home but one week before Mr. Covey gave me a very severe whipping, cutting my back, causing the blood to run, and raising ridges on my flesh as large as my little finger. The details of this affair are as follows: Mr. Covey sent me, very early in the morning of one of our coldest days in the month of January, to the woods, to get a load of wood. He gave me a team of unbroken oxen. He told me which was the in-hand ox, and which the off-hand one. He then tied the end of a large rope around the horns of the in-hand ox, and gave me the other end of it, and told me, if the oxen started to run, that I must hold on upon the rope. I had never driven oxen before, and of course I was very awkward. I, however, succeeded in getting to the edge of the woods with little difficulty; but I had got a very few rods into the woods, when the oxen took fright, and started full tilt, carrying the cart against trees, and over stumps, in the most frightful manner. I expected every moment that my brains would be dashed out against the trees. After running thus for a considerable distance, they finally upset the cart, dashing it with great force against a tree, and threw themselves into a dense thicket. How I escaped death, I do not know. There I was, entirely alone, in a thick wood, in a place new to me. My cart was upset and shattered, my oxen were entangled among the young trees, and there was none to help me. After a long spell of effort, I succeeded in getting my cart righted, my oxen disentangled, and again yoked to the cart. I now proceeded with my team to the place where

---

1. The second son of Noah. Ham was traditionally held to be the ancestor of African peoples.

2. As becomes clear later, Douglass was at this time about sixteen years old. His owner had leased him to Mr. Covey for a year.

I had, the day before, been chopping wood, and loaded my cart pretty heavily, thinking in this way to tame my oxen. I then proceeded on my way home. I had now consumed one half of the day. I got out of the woods safely, and now felt out of danger. I stopped my oxen to open the woods gate; and just as I did so, before I could get hold of my ox-rope, the oxen again started, rushed through the gate, catching it between the wheel and the body of the cart, tearing it to pieces, and coming within a few inches of crushing me against the gate-post. Thus twice, in one short day, I escaped death by the merest chance. On my return, I told Mr. Covey what had happened, and how it happened. He ordered me to return to the woods again immediately. I did so, and he followed on after me. Just as I got into the woods, he came up and told me to stop my cart, and that he would teach me how to trifle away my time, and break gates. He then went to a large gum-tree, and with his axe cut three large switches, and, after trimming them up neatly with his pocket-knife, he ordered me to take off my clothes. I made him no answer, but stood with my clothes on. He repeated his order. I still made him no answer, nor did I move to strip myself. Upon this he rushed at me with the fierceness of a tiger, tore off my clothes, and lashed me till he had worn out his switches, cutting me so savagely as to leave the marks visible for a long time after. This whipping was the first of a number just like it, and for similar offences.

I lived with Mr. Covey one year. During the first six months, of that year, scarce a week passed without his whipping me. I was seldom free from a sore back. My awkwardness was almost always his excuse for whipping me. We were worked fully up to the point of endurance. Long before day we were up, our horses fed, and by the first approach of day we were off to the field with our hoes and ploughing teams. Mr. Covey gave us enough to eat, but scarce time to eat it. We were often less than five minutes taking our meals. We were often in the field from the first approach of day till its last lingering ray had left us; and at saving-fodder time, midnight often caught us in the field binding blades.

Covey would be out with us. The way he used to stand it, was this. He would spend the most of his afternoons in bed. He would then come out fresh in the evening, ready to urge us on with his words, example, and frequently with the whip. Mr. Covey was one of the few slaveholders who could and did work with his hands. He was a hard-working man. He knew by himself just what a man or a boy could do. There was no deceiving him. His work went on in his absence almost as well as in his presence; and he had the faculty of making us feel that he was ever present with us. This he did by surprising us. He seldom approached the spot where we were at work openly, if he could do it secretly. He always aimed at taking us by surprise. Such was his cunning, that we used to call him, among ourselves, "the snake." When we were at work in the cornfield, he would sometimes crawl on his hands and knees to avoid detection, and all at once he would rise nearly in our midst, and scream out, "Ha, ha! Come, come! Dash on, dash on!" This being his mode of attack, it was never safe to stop a single minute. His comings were like a thief in the night. He appeared to us as being ever at hand. He was under every tree, behind every stump, in every bush, and at every window, on the plantation. He would sometimes mount his horse, as if bound to St. Michael's, a distance of seven miles, and in half an hour afterwards you would see him coiled up in the corner of the wood-fence, watching every motion of the slaves. He would, for this purpose, leave his horse tied up in the woods. Again, he would sometimes walk up to us, and give us orders as though he was upon the point of starting on a long journey, turn his back upon us, and make as though he was going to the house to get ready; and, before he would get half way thither, he would turn short and crawl into a fence-corner, or behind some tree, and there watch us till the going down of the sun.

Mr. Covey's *forte* consisted in his power to deceive. His life was devoted to planning and perpetrating the grossest deceptions. Every thing he possessed in the shape of learning or religion, he made conform to his disposition to deceive. He seemed to think himself equal to deceiving the Almighty. He would make a short prayer in the morning, and a long prayer at night; and, strange as it may seem, few men would at times appear more devotional than he. The exercises of his family devotions were always commenced with singing; and, as he was a very poor singer himself, the duty of raising the hymn generally came upon me. He would read his hymn, and nod at me to commence. I would at times do so; at others, I would not. My non-compliance would almost always produce much confusion. To show himself independent of me, he would start and stagger through with his hymn in the most discordant manner. In this state of mind, he prayed with more than ordinary spirit. Poor man! such was his disposition, and success at deceiving, I do verily believe that he sometimes deceived himself into the solemn belief, that he was a sincere worshipper of the most high God; and this, too, at a time when he may be said to have been guilty of compelling his woman slave to commit the sin of adultery. The facts in the case are these: Mr. Covey was a poor man; he was just commencing in life; he was only able to buy one slave; and, shocking as is the fact, he bought her, as he said, for *a breeder*. This woman was named Caroline. Mr. Covey bought her from Mr. Thomas Lowe, about six miles from St. Michael's. She was a large, able-bodied woman, about twenty years old. She had already given birth to one child, which proved her to be just what he wanted. After buying her, he hired a married man of Mr. Samuel Harrison, to live with him one year; and him he used to fasten up with her every night! The result was, that, at the end of the year, the miserable woman gave birth to twins. At this result Mr. Covey seemed to be highly pleased, both with the man and the wretched woman. Such was his joy, and that of his wife, that nothing they could do for Caroline during her confinement was too good, or too hard, to be done. The children were regarded as being quite an addition to his wealth.

If at any one time of my life more than another, I was made to drink the bitterest dregs of slavery, that time was during the first six months of my stay with Mr. Covey. We were worked in all weathers. It was never too hot or too cold; it could never rain, blow, hail, or snow, too hard for us to work in the field. Work, work, work, was scarcely more the order of the day than of the night. The longest days were too short for him, and the shortest nights too long for him. I was somewhat unmanageable when I first went there, but a few months of this discipline tamed me. Mr. Covey succeeded in breaking me. I was broken in body, soul, and spirit. My natural elasticity was crushed, my intellect languished, the disposition to read departed, the cheerful spark that lingered about my eye died; the dark night of slavery closed in upon me; and behold a man transformed into a brute!

Sunday was my only leisure time. I spent this in a sort of beast-like stupor, between sleep and wake, under some large tree. At times I would rise up, a flash of energetic freedom would dart through my soul, accompanied with a faint beam of hope, that flickered for a moment, and then vanished. I sank down again, mourning over my wretched condition. I was sometimes prompted to take my life, and that of Covey, but was prevented by a combination of hope and fear. My sufferings on this plantation seem now like a dream rather than a stern reality.

Our house stood within a few rods of the Chesapeake Bay, whose broad bosom was ever white with sails from every quarter of the habitable globe. Those beautiful vessels, robed in purest white, so delightful to the eye of freemen, were to me so many shrouded ghosts, to terrify and torment me with thoughts of my wretched condition. I have often, in the deep stillness of a summer's Sabbath, stood all alone upon the lofty banks of that noble bay, and traced, with saddened heart and tearful eye, the countless number of sails moving off to the mighty ocean. The sight of these always affected me powerfully. My thoughts would compel utterance;

and there, with no audience but the Almighty, I would pour out my soul's complaint, in my rude way, with an apostrophe to the moving multitude of ships:—

"You are loosed from your moorings, and are free; I am fast in my chains, and am a slave! You move merrily before the gentle gale, and I sadly before the bloody whip! You are freedom's swift-winged angels, that fly round the world; I am confined in bands of iron! O that I were free! O, that I were on one of your gallant decks, and under your protecting wing! Alas! betwixt me and you, the turbid waters roll. Go on, go on. O that I could also go! Could I but swim! If I could fly! O, why was I born a man, of whom to make a brute! The glad ship is gone; she hides in the dim distance. I am left in the hottest hell of unending slavery. O God, save me! God, deliver me! Let me be free! Is there any God? Why am I a slave? I will run away. I will not stand it. Get caught, or get clear, I'll try it. I had as well die with ague as the fever. I have only one life to lose. I had as well be killed running as die standing. Only think of it; one hundred miles straight north, and I am free! Try it? Yes! God helping me, I will. It cannot be that I shall live and die a slave. I will take to the water. This very bay shall yet bear me into freedom. The steamboats steered in a north-east course from North Point. I will do the same; and when I get to the head of the bay, I will turn my canoe adrift, and walk straight through Delaware into Pennsylvania. When I get there, I shall not be required to have a pass; I can travel without being disturbed. Let but the first opportunity offer, and, come what will, I am off. Meanwhile, I will try to bear up under the yoke. I am not the only slave in the world. Why should I fret? I can bear as much as any of them. Besides, I am but a boy, and all boys are bound to some one. It may be that my misery in slavery will only increase my happiness when I get free. There is a better day coming."

Thus I used to think, and thus I used to speak to myself; goaded almost to madness at one moment, and at the next reconciling myself to my wretched lot.

I have already intimated that my condition was much worse, during the first six months of my stay at Mr. Covey's, than in the last six. The circumstances leading to the change in Mr. Covey's course toward me form an epoch in my humble history. You have seen how a man was made a slave; you shall see how a slave was made a man. On one of the hottest days of the month of August, 1833, Bill Smith, William Hughes, a slave named Eli, and myself, were engaged in fanning wheat. Hughes was clearing the fanned wheat from before the fan, Eli was turning, Smith was feeding, and I was carrying wheat to the fan. The work was simple, requiring strength rather than intellect; yet, to one entirely unused to such work, it came very hard. About three o'clock of that day, I broke down; my strength failed me; I was seized with a violent aching of the head, attended with extreme dizziness; I trembled in every limb. Finding what was coming, I nerved myself up, feeling it would never do to stop work. I stood as long as I could stagger to the hopper with grain. When I could stand no longer, I fell, and felt as if held down by an immense weight. The fan of course stopped; every one had his own work to do; and no one could do the work of the other, and have his own go on at the same time.

Mr. Covey was at the house, about one hundred yards from the treading-yard where we were fanning. On hearing the fan stop, he left immediately, and came to the spot where we were. He hastily inquired what the matter was. Bill answered that I was sick, and there was no one to bring wheat to the fan. I had by this time crawled away under the side of the post and rail-fence by which the yard was enclosed, hoping to find relief by getting out of the sun. He then asked where I was. He was told by one of the hands. He came to the spot, and, after looking at me awhile, asked me what was the matter. I told him as well as I could, for I scarce had strength to speak. He then gave me a savage kick in the side, and told me to get up. I tried to do so, but fell back in the attempt. He gave me another kick, and again told me to rise. I again tried, and succeeded in gaining my feet; but, stooping to get the tub with which I was feeding the fan, I again staggered and fell. While down in this situation, Mr. Covey took up the hickory slat with which Hughes had been striking off the half-bushel measure, and with it gave me a heavy blow upon the head, making a large wound, and the blood ran freely; and with this again told me to get up. I made no effort to comply, having now made up my mind to let him do his worst. In a short time after receiving this blow, my head grew better. Mr. Covey had now left me to my fate. At this moment I resolved, for the first time, to go to my master, enter a complaint, and ask his protection. In order to this, I must that afternoon walk seven miles; and this, under the circumstances, was truly a severe undertaking. I was exceedingly feeble; made so as much by the kicks and blows which I received, as by the severe fit of sickness to which I had been subjected. I, however, watched my chance, while Covey was looking in an opposite direction, and started for St. Michael's. I succeeded in getting a considerable distance on my way to the woods, when Covey discovered me, and called after me to come back, threatening what he would do if I did not come. I disregarded both his calls and his threats, and made my way to the woods as fast as my feeble state would allow; and thinking I might be overhauled by him if I kept the road, I walked through the woods, keeping far enough from the road to avoid detection, and near enough to prevent losing my way. I had not gone far before my little strength again failed me. I could go no farther. I fell down, and lay for a considerable time. The blood was yet oozing from the wound on my head. For a time I thought I should bleed to death; and think now that I should have done so, but that the blood so matted my hair as to stop the wound. After lying there about three quarters of an hour, I nerved myself up again, and started on my way, through bogs and briers, barefooted and bareheaded, tearing my feet sometimes at nearly every step; and after a journey of about seven miles, occupying some five hours to perform it, I arrived at master's store. I then presented an appearance enough to affect any but a heart of iron. From the crown of my head to my feet, I was covered with blood. My hair was all clotted with dust and blood; my shirt was stiff with blood. My legs and feet were torn in sundry places with briers and thorns, and were also covered with blood. I suppose I looked like a man who had escaped a den of wild beasts, and barely escaped them. In this state I appeared before my master, humbly entreating him to interpose his authority for my protection. I told him all the circumstances as well as I could, and it seemed, as I spoke, at times to affect him. He would then walk the floor, and seek to justify Covey by saying he expected I deserved it. He asked me what I wanted. I told him, to let me get a new home; that as sure as I lived with Mr. Covey again, I should live with but to die with him; that Covey would surely kill me; he was in a fair way for it. Master Thomas ridiculed the idea that there was any danger of Mr. Covey's killing me, and said that he knew Mr. Covey; that he was a good man, and that he could not think of taking me from him; that, should he do so, he would lose the whole year's wages; that I belonged to Mr. Covey for one year, and that I must go back to him, come what might; and that I must not trouble him with any more stories, or that he would himself *get hold of me.* After threatening me thus, he gave me a very large dose of salts, telling me that I might remain in St. Michael's that night, (it being quite late,) but that I must be off back to Mr. Covey's early in the morning; and that if I did not, he would *get hold of me,* which meant that he would whip me. I remained all night, and, according to his orders, I started off to Covey's in the morning, (Saturday morning,) wearied in body and broken in spirit. I got no supper that night, or breakfast that morning. I reached Covey's about nine o'clock; and just as I was getting over the fence that divided Mrs.

Kemp's fields from ours, out ran Covey with his cowskin, to give me another whipping. Before he could reach me, I succeeded in getting to the cornfield; and as the corn was very high, it afforded me the means of hiding. He seemed very angry, and searched for me a long time. My behavior was altogether unaccountable. He finally gave up the chase, thinking, I suppose, that I must come home for something to eat; he would give himself no further trouble in looking for me. I spent that day mostly in the woods, having the alternative before me,—to go home and be whipped to death, or stay in the woods and be starved to death. That night, I fell in with Sandy Jenkins, a slave with whom I was somewhat acquainted. Sandy had a free wife who lived about four miles from Mr. Covey's; and it being Saturday, he was on his way to see her. I told him my circumstances, and he very kindly invited me to go home with him. I went home with him, and talked this whole matter over, and got his advice as to what course it was best for me to pursue. I found Sandy an old adviser. He told me, with great solemnity, I must go back to Covey; but that before I went, I must go with him into another part of the woods, where there was a certain *root*, which, if I would take some of it with me, carrying it *always on my right side*, would render it impossible for Mr. Covey, or any other white man, to whip me. He said he had carried it for years; and since he had done so, he had never received a blow, and never expected to while he carried it. I at first rejected the idea, that the simple carrying of a root in my pocket would have any such effect as he had said, and was not disposed to take it; but Sandy impressed the necessity with much earnestness, telling me it could do no harm, if it did no good. To please him, I at length took the root, and, according to his direction, carried it upon my right side. This was Sunday morning. I immediately started for home; and upon entering the yard gate, out came Mr. Covey on his way to meeting. He spoke to me very kindly, bade me drive the pigs from a lot near by, and passed on towards the church. Now, this singular conduct of Mr. Covey really made me begin to think that there was something in the *root* which Sandy had given me; and had it been on any other day than Sunday, I could have attributed the conduct to no other cause than the influence of that root; and as it was, I was half inclined to think the *root* to be something more than I at first had taken it to be. All went well till Monday morning. On this morning, the virtue of the *root* was fully tested. Long before daylight, I was called to go and rub, curry, and feed, the horses. I obeyed, and was glad to obey. But whilst thus engaged, whilst in the act of throwing down some blades from the loft, Mr. Covey entered the stable with a long rope; and just as I was half out of the loft, he caught hold of my legs, and was about tying me. As soon as I found what he was up to, I gave a sudden spring, and as I did so, he holding to my legs, I was brought sprawling on the stable floor. Mr. Covey seemed now to think he had me, and could do what he pleased; but at this moment—from whence came the spirit I don't know—I resolved to fight; and, suiting my action to the resolution, I seized Covey hard by the throat; and as I did so, I rose. He held on to me, and I to him. My resistance was so entirely unexpected, that Covey seemed taken all aback. He trembled like a leaf. This gave me assurance, and I held him uneasy, causing the blood to run where I touched him with the ends of my fingers. Mr. Covey soon called out to Hughes for help. Hughes came, and, while Covey held me, attempted to tie my right hand. While he was in the act of doing so, I watched my chance, and gave him a heavy kick close under the ribs. This kick fairly sickened Hughes, so that he left me in the hands of Mr. Covey. This kick had the effect of not only weakening Hughes, but Covey also. When he saw Hughes bending over with pain, his courage quailed. He asked me if I meant to persist in my resistance. I told him I did, come what might; that he had used me like a brute for six months, and that I was determined to be used so no longer. With that, he strove to drag me to a stick that was lying just out of the stable door. He meant to knock me down. But just as he was leaning over to get the stick, I seized him with both hands by his collar, and brought him by a sudden snatch to the ground. By this time, Bill came. Covey called upon him for assistance. Bill wanted to know what he could do. Covey said, "Take hold of him, take hold of him!" Bill said his master hired him out to work, and not to help to whip me; so he left Covey and myself to fight our own battle out. We were at it for nearly two hours. Covey at length let me go, puffing and blowing at a great rate, saying that if I had not resisted, he would not have whipped me half so much. The truth was, that he had not whipped me at all. I considered him as getting entirely the worst end of the bargain; for he had drawn no blood from me, but I had from him. The whole six months afterwards, that I spent with Mr. Covey, he never laid the weight of his finger upon me in anger. He would occasionally say, he didn't want to get hold of me again. "No," thought I, "you need not; for you will come off worse than you did before."

This battle with Mr. Covey was the turning-point in my career as a slave. It rekindled the few expiring embers of freedom, and revived within me a sense of my own manhood. It recalled the departed self-confidence, and inspired me again with a determination to be free. The gratification afforded by the triumph was a full compensation for whatever else might follow, even death itself. He only can understand the deep satisfaction which I experienced, who has himself repelled by force the bloody arm of slavery. I felt as I never felt before. It was a glorious resurrection, from the tomb of slavery, to the heaven of freedom. My long-crushed spirit rose, cowardice departed, bold defiance took its place; and I now resolved that, however long I might remain a slave in form, the day had passed forever when I could be a slave in fact. I did not hesitate to let it be known of me, that the white man who expected to succeed in whipping, must also succeed in killing me.

From this time I was never again what might be called fairly whipped, though I remained a slave four years afterwards. I had several fights, but was never whipped.

It was for a long time a matter of surprise to me why Mr. Covey did not immediately have me taken by the constable to the whipping-post, and there regularly whipped for the crime of raising my hand against a white man in defence of myself. And the only explanation I can now think of does not entirely satisfy me; but such as it is, I will give it. Mr. Covey enjoyed the most unbounded reputation for being a first-rate overseer and negro-breaker. It was of considerable importance to him. That reputation was at stake; and had he sent me—a boy about sixteen years old—to the public whipping-post, his reputation would have been lost; so, to save his reputation, he suffered me to go unpunished.

1845

ABRAHAM LINCOLN
(1809–1865)

In the affections of his countrymen, Lincoln has become a legend, and the actual events of his life are also common knowledge. His parents, Thomas and Nancy Hanks Lincoln, were virtually illiterate pioneers, and their child of destiny was born, on February 12, 1809, in a backwoods log cabin in Hardin County, Kentucky. Two years later, the Lincolns were tilling thirty acres of cleared land in the forest at Knob Creek, below Louisville. When the boy was only seven, the family trekked north across the Ohio into southern Indiana, taking squatter-rights on woodland again. There young Lincoln grew to manhood. His mother, a mystical and sensitive woman who influenced him deeply, died when he was nine. Her place was soon taken by Sarah Bush, practical and courageous, who encouraged his innate genius and ambition. Educational opportunities were limited—the boy spent no more than a year altogether in several schoolhouses—but he read and reread the few good books that he could obtain, such as the Bible and *Pilgrim's Progress*, *Robinson Crusoe*, Aesop's *Fables*, Weems's *Washington*, and Grimshaw's *History of the United States*. At nineteen he worked his way to New Orleans on a Mississippi flatboat.

When Lincoln was twenty-one, he accompanied the still-impoverished family westward, to Decatur, Illinois; but when, the next spring, Tom Lincoln decided upon a further move, to Coles County, the young frontiersman decided that he must strike out for himself. He agreed to take a flatboat loaded with merchandise to New Orleans. Returning, Abe Lincoln brought history to the Sangamon country by settling at New Salem, near Springfield, Illinois. There the force of his homespun integrity gradually brought him into local prominence. From hired hand and rail splitter he rose to be storekeeper and postmaster of New Salem. He read whatever he could find, and studied law. An unsuccessful candidate in 1832 for election to the legislature, he went off to the five-weeks' Black Hawk War with a company of volunteers who elected him as captain.

In 1834, running as a Whig, he won the election and went to Vandalia, then the capital, on borrowed money, wearing a pair of new blue jeans. There his political moderation began to take form. He supported the opposition of his party to Jackson's financial policies, and he agreed with free-soilers that the federal authority legally extended to the control of slavery in the territories; however, on constitutional grounds, he had to oppose abolition in the states. But abolition was not yet a genuine political issue, and he held office for four consecutive terms (1834–1842). In 1837 he opened a law office in Springfield, the new capital. There, in 1842, he returned to private practice, and married Mary Todd.

During the next few years, as a circuit-riding lawyer, he won a modest prosperity and a considerable reputation. In 1847 the Illinois Whigs sent him to Congress, just as the brief Mexican War drew to its close. The question of slavery in the newly won territories divided the Whigs in such border states as Illinois. Lincoln consistently opposed the extension of slavery, and joined those who sought to embarrass Polk, the Democratic president, as instigator of a slave-state war. Lincoln knew at the time that by taking this stand he would alienate voters of all parties in Illinois, and he was not nominated in 1849.

Again in private practice in Springfield, this time with William H. Herndon as his partner, he enjoyed great success as a lawyer, and continued to participate in politics, though apparently with no high ambitions. In 1854 he was again elected to the state legislature, but his opposition to the principle of squatter sovereignty embodied in Douglas's Kansas-Nebraska Bill sent him stump speaking, and he resigned from the legislature in 1855 to run for the Senate. He was defeated, but threw the votes of his supporters in such a manner as to elect an opponent of Douglas.

In 1856, after the disruption

of the southern Whigs by these controversies, Lincoln joined the newly formed Republican party, and in 1858 he was the candidate for the Senate against the Democrat, Stephen A. Douglas. At the party convention he made the famous declaration that "A house divided against itself cannot stand," in a speech which, then and later, was heard through the land. In his seven debates with Douglas during the campaign, he demonstrated his cool logic, his devastating humor, and his firm moderation as an enemy of slavery who opposed both the abolition and the extension of slavery on consistent constitutional principles, Although he lost the election, he was clearly a man who might lead the Republicans to national victory; yet it seems that he then had no such idea himself.

In the speech at Cooper Union in 1860 he repeated more formally the principles which he had developed in the heat of the debates. Now that secession was openly advocated in the South, the preservation of the Union was the paramount issue; and this, he thought, could best be assured by strict adherence to the provisions of the Constitution, in respect to both the states and the territorial areas. Three months later the Republican party named him as their candidate. He defeated the candidates of the split Democratic party in November and was inaugurated on March 4, 1861.

The remainder of Lincoln's history is that of the Civil War. A few of the events which best reveal him are reflected in the selections in this volume. Unprepared by previous experience,

he became, within two years, the master of complex and gigantic events, the principal strategist of the northern cause, and, as it seemed, the tragic embodiment of the nation's suffering, North and South. His second inauguration occurred on March 4, 1865. On April 9, Lee surrendered the remnant of the Army of Virginia to Grant at Appomattox. On the night of Good Friday, April 14, just six weeks after his inauguration, Lincoln was assassinated by John Wilkes Booth in Ford's Theatre, Washington. He died early the next morning.

Much might be said of Lincoln's place in literature, but that seems unnecessary. He spoke always from the heart of the people, with speech at once lofty and common; what he had to say seems to embody the best that they have learned of human compassion and nobility; and his words have been received and treasured around the earth as the language of humanity itself.

Among the collections of Lincoln's writings the most comprehensive is *The Collected Works of Abraham Lincoln*, 9 vols., edited by Roy P. Basler and others, 1953. Standard, though less comprehensive, is *The Complete Works of Abraham Lincoln*, 2 vols., edited by John G. Nicolay and John Hay, 1894; enlarged, 12 vols., 1905. One-volume selections are *Abraham Lincoln: His Speeches and Writings*, edited by Roy P. Basler, 1946, containing an excellent critical introduction; *Selections from Lincoln*, 1927; and Richard N. Current, *The Political Thought of Abraham Lincoln*, 1967.

John G. Nicolay and John Hay wrote the comprehensive biography, *Abraham Lincoln: A History*, 10 vols., 1890. Carl Sandburg's *Abraham Lincoln: The Prairie Years*, 2 vols., 1926, and *Abraham Lincoln: The War Years*, 4 vols., 1939, are classics. Satisfactory one-volume biographies are those by Lord Charnwood, 1917; Albert J. Beveridge, 1928; and David Flowden, 1969. Paul M. Angle compiled *The Lincoln Reader*, 1947, comprising selections from various biographies, chronologically arranged. See also James G. Randall, *Lincoln the President*, 4 vols.,

1945–1955; and Benjamin P. Thomas, *Abraham Lincoln*, 1952, the best brief account.

Reply to Horace Greeley[1]

EXECUTIVE MANSION,
WASHINGTON, August 22, 1862

HON. HORACE GREELEY.

DEAR SIR:—I have just read yours of the 19th, addressed to myself through the New York *Tribune*. If there be in it any statements or assumptions of fact which I may know to be erroneous, I do not, now and here, controvert them.[2] If there be in it any inferences which I may believe to be falsely drawn, I do not, now and here, argue against them. If there be perceptible in it an impatient and dictatorial tone, I waive it in deference to an old friend, whose heart I have always supposed to be right.

As to the policy I "seem to be pursuing," as you say, I have not meant to leave any one in doubt.

I would save the Union. I would save it the shortest way under the Constitution. The sooner the national authority can be restored, the nearer the Union will be "the Union as it was." If there be those who would not save the Union unless they could at the same time save slavery, I do not agree with them. If there be those who would not save the Union unless they could at the same time destroy slavery, I do not agree with them. My paramount object in this struggle is to save the Union, and is not either to save or to destroy slavery. If I could save the Union without freeing any slave, I would do it; and if I could save it by freeing all the slaves, I would do it; and if I could save it by freeing some and leaving others alone, I would also do that. What I do about slavery and the colored race, I do because I believe it helps to save the Union; and what I forbear, I forbear because I do not believe it would help to save the Union. I shall do less whenever I shall believe what I am doing hurts the cause; and I shall do more whenever I shall

1. Horace Greeley (1811–1872), the powerful editor of the New York *Tribune*, an ardent free-soiler and abolitionist, had supported Lincoln from the beginning, and sponsored his appearance in New York for the address at Cooper Union. However, in the summer of 1862 he shared the opinion of many northerners who criticized Lincoln's hesitation to emancipate the slaves—an act which he long postponed in accordance with the spirit of his first-inaugural message. Greeley's open letter to Lincoln, entitled "A Prayer of Twenty Millions," appeared in the *Tribune* on August 19, 1862. A month earlier, on July 22, Lincoln had already shown his cabinet a first draft of the Emancipation Proclamation, but he was withholding it until a decisive improvement in the military fortunes of the North might give it proper emphasis. Meanwhile he replied to Greeley as here shown; the letter appeared in the *National Intelligencer* for August 23, 1862. A month later, on September 22, 1862, after Lee's army had been forced to withdraw at Antietam (September 17), Lincoln issued his famous Proclamation. 2. *I.e.*, public policy forbade his revealing that he had already written the Emancipation Proclamation.

believe doing more will help the cause. I shall try to correct errors when shown to be errors, and I shall adopt new views so fast as they shall appear to be true views. I have here stated my purpose according to my view of official duty, and I intend no modification of my oft-expressed personal wish that all men, everywhere, could be free.

Yours,

A. LINCOLN.

Letter to General Joseph Hooker [3]

January 26, 1863

MAJOR-GENERAL HOOKER.

GENERAL. I have placed you at the head of the Army of the Potomac. Of course I have done this upon what appear to me to be sufficient reasons, and yet I think it best for you to know that there are some things in regard to which I am not quite satisfied with you. I believe you to be a brave and skillful soldier, which of course I like. I also believe you do not mix politics with your profession, in which you are right. You have confidence in yourself, which is a valuable if not an indispensable quality. You are ambitious, which, within reasonable bounds, does good rather than harm; but I think that during General Burnside's command of the army you have taken counsel of your ambition and thwarted him as much as you could, in which you did a great wrong to the country and to a most meritorious and honorable brother officer. I have heard, in such a way as to believe it, of your recently saying that both the army and the government needed a dictator. Of course it was not for this, but in spite of it, that I have given you the command. Only those generals who gain success can set up dictators. What I now ask of you is military success, and I will risk the dictatorship. The government will support you to the utmost of its ability, which is neither more nor less than it has done and will do for all commanders. I much fear that the spirit which you have aided to infuse into the army, of criticizing their commander and withholding confidence from him, will now turn upon you. I shall

3. Lincoln's letter to Hooker reflects the darkest Union crisis in the Civil War. During 1862, the inactivity of General McClellan, commanding the major Army of the Potomac, stretched northern nerves to the limit. He was succeeded by Burnside, who combined a gallant aggressiveness with dangerous recklessness. The battle at Fredericksburg, December 13, resulting in disastrous carnage, aggravated the wave of despair and criticism, in which subordinate generals participated. General Hooker, after Fredericksburg, had openly advocated a "dictatorship." Lincoln also knew that he talked too much, drank heavily, and resisted authority; but he had justly earned in combat the nickname of Fighting Joe, he was a good strategist, and the troops idolized him. In elevating him to chief command, Lincoln handed him this frank letter, one of the most remarkable in military annals. Later, failing to defeat Lee at Chancellorsville (May 4, 1863), Hooker gallantly resigned his command, and was succeeded by Meade.

assist you as far as I can to put it down. Neither you nor Napoleon, if he were alive again, could get any good out of any army while such a spirit prevails in it; and now beware of rashness. Beware of rashness, but with energy and sleepless vigilance go forward and give us victories.

Yours very truly,

A. LINCOLN.

Letter to General U. S. Grant [4]

July 13, 1863

MAJOR-GENERAL U. S. GRANT.

MY DEAR GENERAL: I do not remember that you and I ever met personally. I write this now as a grateful acknowledgment for the almost inestimable service you have done the country. I wish to say a word further. When you first reached the vicinity of Vicksburg, I thought you should do what you finally did—march the troops across the neck, run the batteries with the transports, and thus go below; and I never had any faith, except a general hope that you knew better than I, that the Yazoo Pass expedition and the like could succeed. When you got below and took Port Gibson, Grand Gulf and vicinity, I thought you should go down the river and join General Banks, and when you turned northward, east of the Big Black, I feared it was a mistake. I now wish to make the personal acknowledgment that you were right and I was wrong.

Yours,

A. LINCOLN.

Address at the Dedication of the Gettysburg National Cemetery [5]

Four score and seven years ago our fathers brought forth on this continent, a new nation, conceived in Liberty, and dedicated to the proposition that all men are created equal.

Now we are engaged in a great civil war; testing whether that

---

4. On July 4, 1863, Grant, who had risen from obscurity, forced the surrender of Vicksburg and its thirty thousand defenders, gaining control of the lower Mississippi after two months of strategic maneuvers and engagements on incredibly difficult terrain. On the same day, the Battle of Gettysburg had ended Lee's penetration of the northern heartland, but Lincoln was bitterly disappointed because Meade, having made a last-ditch if courageous defense in a battle forced upon him, had then failed to pursue and destroy Lee's broken but gallant army in retreat. Grant, by contrast, had for months steadily seized the initiative and had now virtually divided the Confederate territory. A few months after this letter, Lincoln appointed Grant as commander in chief of all the Armies, including Meade's.

5. The thousands of dead were hastily buried at Gettysburg, but part of the battlefield was at once set apart as a national memorial where the slain could be reverently enshrined. Within three months, dedication ceremonies were announced, and numerous government dignitaries invited to attend. Edward Everett, honored statesman and orator, was chosen as the speaker. Although Lincoln had been invited to say a few appropriate words, it was not supposed that he could spare the time from his

nation, or any nation so conceived and so dedicated, can long endure. We are met on a great battlefield of that war. We have come to dedicate a portion of that field as a final resting-place for those who here gave their lives that that nation might live. It is altogether fitting and proper that we should do this.

But, in a larger sense, we cannot dedicate—we cannot consecrate—we cannot hallow—this ground. The brave men, living and dead, who struggled here have consecrated it, far above our poor power to add or detract. The world will little note, nor long remember, what we say here, but it can never forget what they did here. It is for us the living, rather, to be dedicated here to the unfinished work which they who fought here have thus far so nobly advanced. It is rather for us to be here dedicated to the great task remaining before us—that from these honored dead we take increased devotion to that cause for which they gave the last full measure of devotion; that we here highly resolve that these dead shall not have died in vain; that this nation, under God,[6] shall have a new birth of freedom; and that government of the people, by the people, for the people,[7] shall not perish from the earth.

Second Inaugural Address [8]

FELLOW-COUNTRYMEN:

At this second appearing to take the oath of the presidential office, there is less occasion for an extended address than there was at the first. Then a statement, somewhat in detail, of a course to

---

duties as president and commander in chief. Yet he had privately wanted such an opportunity to tell the plain people, simply, what was the true spiritual and democratic meaning of the war. Belatedly he accepted, and had the opportunity to compose only a first draft of his remarks before leaving Washington. The next morning in Gettysburg, he made a revised draft. On November 19, 1863, at least fifteen thousand people listened while Everett recited, for two hours, a memorized address, a fine example of the formal oratory of his day. Then Lincoln stood before the throng, and in two minutes, scarcely glancing at the single page in his hand, spoke the two hundred and sixty words which succeeding generations were to repeat as their own rededication to the democratic love of mankind.

6. The words "under God," not in the earlier manuscript, came to Lincoln's lips as he spoke, and were included in copies of the speech that he later made (See Thomas, *Abraham Lincoln*, p. 402).

7. Whether Lincoln knew it or not. Theodore Parker, Boston clergyman and abolition leader, in an antislavery address in 1850 had characterized democracy as "a government of all the people, by all the people, for all the people."

8. At Lincoln's second inaugural, on March 4, 1865, the defeat of the Confederacy was assured. Within the previous six months, Sherman had swept victoriously from Atlanta to the sea and northward again, Sheridan had cleared the Shenandoah and Thomas the Tennessee country, Grant had the remnant of the Army of Virginia cornered in the defense of Richmond, and Lincoln had received the first Confederate peace delegation. These events were reflected in the words of the grave leader, haggard and careworn at the virtual moment of triumph, as he stood in a portico of the Capitol to deliver his inaugural address, the bronze statue of Freedom, which had been prone four years before, now mounted on the completed dome above his head. To the throng that surrounded him he uttered, in his noble last sentence, the words of forgiveness and love toward the vanquished that have re-echoed around the world, and may live forever. Six weeks later, on Easter eve, he lay dead of the assassin's bullet.

be pursued, seemed fitting and proper. Now, at the expiration of four years, during which public declarations have been constantly called forth on every point and phase of the great contest which still absorbs the attention and engrosses the energies of the nation, little that is new could be presented. The progress of our arms, upon which all else chiefly depends, is as well known to the public as to myself; and it is, I trust, reasonably satisfactory and encouraging to all. With high hope for the future, no prediction in regard to it is ventured.

On the occasion corresponding to this four years ago, all thoughts were anxiously directed to an impending civil war. All dreaded it —all sought to avert it. While the inaugural address was being delivered from this place, devoted altogether to saving the Union without war, insurgent agents were in the city seeking to destroy it without war—seeking to dissolve the Union, and divide effects, by negotiation. Both parties deprecated war; but one of them would make war rather than let the nation survive; and the other would accept war rather than let it perish. And the war came.

One-eighth of the whole population were colored slaves, not distributed generally over the Union, but localized in the Southern part of it. These slaves constituted a peculiar and powerful interest. All knew that this interest was, somehow, the cause of the war. To strengthen, perpetuate, and extend this interest was the object for which the insurgents would rend the Union, even by war; while the government claimed no right to do more than to restrict the territorial enlargement of it.

Neither party expected for the war the magnitude or the duration which it has already attained. Neither anticipated that the cause of the conflict might cease with, or even before, the conflict itself should cease.[9] Each looked for an easier triumph, and a result less fundamental and astounding. Both read the same Bible, and pray to the same God; and each invokes his aid against the other. It may seem strange that any men should dare to ask a just God's assistance in wringing their bread from the sweat of other men's faces; but let us judge not, that we be not judged.[1] The prayers of both could not be answered—that of neither has been answered fully.

The Almighty has his own purposes. "Woe unto the world because of offences! for it must needs be that offences come; but woe to that man by whom the offence cometh." [2] If we shall suppose that American slavery is one of those offences which, in the providence of God, must needs come, but which, having continued

9. *I.e.*, that the slaves would already have been freed, by the Emancipation Proclamation, effective January 1, 1863.

1. *Cf.* Matthew vii: 1.
2. *Cf.* Matthew xviii: 7.

through his appointed time, he now wills to remove, and that he gives to both North and South this terrible war, as the woe due to those by whom the offence came, shall we discern therein any departure from those divine attributes which the believers in a living God always ascribe to him? Fondly do we hope—fervently do we pray—that this mighty scourge of war may speedily pass away. Yet, if God wills that it continue until all the wealth piled by the bondman's two hundred and fifty years of unrequited toil shall be sunk, and until every drop of blood drawn with the lash shall be paid by another drawn with the sword, as was said three thousand years ago, so still it must be said, "The judgments of the Lord are true and righteous altogether." [3]

With malice toward none; with charity for all; with firmness in the right, as God gives us to see the right, let us strive on to finish the work we are in; to bind up the nation's wounds; to care for him who shall have borne the battle, and for his widow, and his orphan—to do all which may achieve and cherish a just and lasting peace among ourselves, and with all nations.

3. *Cf.* Psalms xix: 9.

The Emergence of Modern American Literature

1865-1920

The half century from the Civil War to the First World War was an epoch of dynamic change in American life, and of corresponding developments in literature. During this period the nation consolidated its continental domain, absorbed a host of immigrants, developed its potential as the most rescurceful industrial powerhouse in the world, and moved toward a genuine hegemony in world affairs. The young nation finally put off its country ways and assumed the character of an urban civilization, while grappling, with uneven success, with the many responsibilities, political problems, and social disorders accompanying changes so fundamental and gigantic.

The conquered Southland, at the beginning of this era, was fully occupied with the problems of reconstruction and survival, but the industrial machine of the North, geared to a new high by the recent demands of the war, soon attained an unprecedented productive capacity. Immigrants thronged into the industrial centers, or joined the march of older Americans to the West, where the last frontiers gave way before the growth of railroads, the improvement of farm machinery, and expanding markets. Within a few years even the South, having survived military occupation, exploitation by carpetbaggers and scalawags, and political reprisals from Washington, had developed a new economy of small farmsteads and sharecroppers, with a newborn retail market at the crossroads and a revived urban prosperity responding to the mounting demand for staple crops. As a whole, the period immediately succeeding the Civil War was marked by the restless expansion of new lands and new wealth, by an increasing solidarity among the various sections of the country, by the discovery and exploitation of new natural resources, by the development of revolutionary inventions, new technologies, and new industries, by great accumulations of capital, and by a spirit of optimism and speculation so overwhelming that only the most serious gave attention to the

873

burgeoning economic atrocities and delinquencies that are now associated with the period of Grant's presidency.

By the 1880's, however, the growing pains of rapid expansion, and the consequent social dislocations, were everywhere acutely evident. The agrarian interests, the still-feeble labor movement, and the underprivileged urban masses found common cause against the industrial giant and his financial overlords. Reform movements and labor unrest appeared in successive waves of protest, while financial crises, and the exposure of governmental and private schemes to exploit the economy, only accentuated the widening gap between the privileged or ruthless few and the great majority who did not seem to share proportionately in the prosperity of the world's richest nation. Confronted with the *laissez-faire* economics of the Gospel of Wealth, serious reform thinkers in the eighties and nineties viewed the existing order with increasing distaste and pessimism. Their concern was heightened by government acts of intervention and so-called financial "imperialism" overseas, of which the Spanish-American War of 1898 caused the most violent reactions among the liberals. By this time, however, the reform and labor movements, which had seemed so abortive only two decades earlier, had begun to consolidate and to exert strong political pressure, while new social and economic legislation improved the prospects of the average citizen. For more than a decade before the end of this period in 1914, the American scene was marked by relative domestic peace and orderly economic development, as though in preparation for the ordeals of world war which lay ahead.

FROM ROMANTICISM TO REALISM

American writers and thinkers, attempting to express the shifting tensions and complexities of these strenuous decades, moved steadily from romanticism toward increasingly realistic objectives and literary forms, and toward pragmatic, instrumental, or naturalistic interpretations of man and his destiny. The process was gradual, reflecting the periodic fluctuations in the history of American society. During this period, however, literature became a genuine instrument of evaluation and expression in American life; it found for the first time a vast and general audience representing the people as a whole; it ultimately produced a highly critical realistic movement whose characteristic works were quite clearly the product of a different world from that which, in the previous generation, had been represented by the romantic idealism of Cooper and Irving, Emerson, Hawthorne, and Longfellow.

In this process, the Civil War provided a dramatic point of cleavage. As Mark Twain shrewdly observed in writing *The Gilded Age:* "The eight years in America from 1860 to 1868 uprooted institutions that were centuries old, changed the politics of a people, transformed the social life of half the country, and wrought so profoundly upon the entire national character that the influence cannot be measured." For literature one measure of the change is to compare the popular and typical works of the five years before the war with those of the same period succeeding the struggle. The accepted tradition of our literature in the years from 1855 to 1861 was represented in the publication of Longfellow's *The Song of Hiawatha* and *The Courtship of Miles Standish*, Emerson's *English Traits* and *The Conduct of Life*, Simms's romances—*The Forayers* and *Eutaw*—Irving's *Life of Washington*, Hawthorne's *The Marble Faun*, Holmes's *Autocrat* papers, and Whittier's *Home Ballads*. By contrast, directly after the war, during the years from 1867 to 1872, the country heard for the first time the genuine voice of the new West, in such stories by Bret Harte as "The Luck of Roaring Camp"; in Mark Twain's earliest successes—*The Celebrated Jumping Frog of Calaveras County and Other Sketches*, *The Innocents Abroad*, and *Roughing It*; in John Hay's *Pike County Ballads* and Joaquin Miller's *Songs of the Sierras*. During the same years a new standard of reality in the portrayal of contemporary life was evident in such works as John W. De Forest's *Miss Ravenel's Conversion from Secession to Loyalty*, Thomas Bailey Aldrich's *The Story of a Bad Boy*, and Edward Eggleston's *The Hoosier Schoolmaster*. Above all, Henry James and William Dean Howells, who were destined to take their places beside Mark Twain as the great figures of the realistic movement, made

their first important contributions: James in 1871, when he published "A Passionate Pilgrim" in a periodical, and Howells in his first novel, *Their Wedding Journey* (1872).

Yet the older voices were not stilled. Many romantic authors no longer living, such as Cooper, Irving, Poe, and Hawthorne, continued to grow in popularity; and new publications by such earlier writers as Emerson, Longfellow, Lowell, and Holmes continued to exert an influence. For two decades, beginning authors in this age of transition were caught between the ideals of the older world and those of a new age that was struggling to find its voice. It is no wonder that many young writers, especially among the pioneers of realism, were not able to be faithful to its demands. This was especially true of the early regionalists. Such writers as Harte, Cable, and Harris realistically depicted the daily and common actualities and dialects of their localities; they sought to identify characters with their surroundings, and sometimes achieved psychological penetration in this respect. In general, however, the regionalists exaggerated the picturesque, the charming, or the bizarre to create what came to be known as "local color"; and they all to some degree surrendered to the didactic impulse, and sentimentalized their characters in support of some predetermined moral judgment or ideal, as Bret Harte did in his picture of Poker Flat, with its outcasts and fallen women. In addition, the rise of realism was strenuously opposed by certain authors who, combining serious purpose with superior talents, regarded themselves as defenders of ideality, of aesthetic purity, or of certain fixed standards of propriety or morality. Even Howells, a vigorous defender of "decency" in literature, was criticized, because of his preference for the commonplace, as one who "copied life"—a familiar false charge—or built in paving blocks instead of Pentelican marble.

To be sure, the defenders of ideality found strenuous opponents. Even before the war, Whitman was attacking the code of chivalry, the wasted life of the sheltered female, and the unreality of the standards of fictional romance and Byronic poetry. He was soon assisted by younger authors, especially those of the western frontiers. Bret Harte's *Condensed Novels*, published in 1867, contained irresistible parodies of Dumas, Dickens, Cooper, and others; Mark Twain irreverently lampooned Scott for engendering the "Sir Walter Disease," and Cooper for his incredible Indians and his ignorance of the real frontier. Yet romanticism was not really vanquished at the popular level. The sentimental domestic novel continued to flourish, and the cheaper magazines, responding to a surge of newly won respectability among the middle class, still dripped with the didactic sentiment that had been established, principally by lady poets and novelists, before the war. Finally, the historical and regional romance, always widely read, reached new heights of popularity by the end of the century.

A comparatively few authors, with a more limited audience, became the pioneers of the literature now recognized as "modern" in spirit and in form. In the largest sense, this realistic modernity in a work of literature results from several factors: the author's insistence upon strict analytical observation of the subject, and his determination to portray it exactly; an increased awareness of psychological phenomena, which enlarges the writer's franchise and the reader's tolerance in the selection of materials that might once have been rejected as too commonplace or as actually sordid; and the full recognition of the writer's social function as the critic and interpreter of life. These factors, or a significant portion of them, were present in the best efforts of the memorable writers of the realistic movement in the nineteenth century, and taken as a whole, they may serve as a description, if not a definition, of the realistic impulse.

Three of the earliest poets to respond to the new spirit were actually rooted very deeply in the romantic idealism of the waning epoch, but because of particular gifts of character or fortune, Walt Whitman, Emily Dickinson, and Sidney Lanier each spoke with a new voice combining noble and enduring elements from both ages, the old and the new. Whitman, born the same year as Lowell, but slower in finding his subject, stood apart from the romantics even in 1855, when the first small edition of *Leaves of Grass* was an ugly duckling, while Longfellow's *Hiawatha* paddled approved down the mainstream of literature. Yet Whitman's vision of America was based on the idealism of the past—on the individualism of Jefferson and Tom Paine; on the intuitional faith of Emerson and on transcendental humanitarianism; on the reform movements and proletarian idealism that had accompanied the rise of the common man in the Age of Jackson. At the same time, Whitman produced a verse that was destined to revolutionize the form of modern poetry; his psychological realism, coupled with his interest in science, enabled him to transfigure "forbidden" subjects; and no later realist ever looked more sharply than he, or with more gusto, at the commonplace object or the lowly person. Emily Dickinson was a product of Amherst village, where colonial America lingered in puritan overtones. She inherited the tradition of the romantic nature poets; but her realism and psychological truth made her seem contemporary to a much later generation. Sidney Lanier, a Georgia regionalist bred in the old South, infused his nature poetry with the southern economics of corn and cotton, with incisive criticism of the growing abuses of the industrial and mercantile systems, and with a stirring sense of the complexities of individual responsibility.

REGIONALISM

Mark Twain, the earliest gigantic figure among the regionalists, was indebted, like Harte and Cable and other contemporaries, to progenitors among the humbler comic journalists. From the Age of Jackson onward, they had inundated the popular press with anecdotes and fiction drawn from sources deep in the common life of America. In this literature, most of it decidedly regional in character, the humorous anecdote mingled with white and Negro folklore, with frontier tall tales and hunting stories, and with folk song and balladry. The best of the regional literature, serious and comic, ultimately provided a better understanding of the United States as a whole. Whitman and Mark Twain both asserted that the great writer must "absorb" his country, but amid the swift changes of American life, the "great American novel" which critics had been demanding could not be written. However, as Eggleston remarked in 1892, looking back upon the regional movement, the great American novel appeared "in sections"— in the matured realism of Twain and Howells, in the novels of such lesser writers as Eggleston himself and De Forest, and in the stories of Cable and Harris, Aldrich, Mary E. Wilkins Freeman, Sarah Orne Jewett, Garland, and Crane. A movement that had begun in broad humor and in the wider horizons of the West and Southwest produced also, particularly among the women writers and the New Englanders, the accurate depiction of the domestic scene, the narrow life, the individual character, caught in some humble light that reminds the reader of the work of the *genre* painters of the Flemish school, at once highly individuated and intensely national. In fiction thus motivated, the increasing consciousness of the influence of environment on character and fate prepared the way for the growing spirit of naturalistic and sociological determinism.

THE GILDED AGE

This awareness of American social and economic life was characteristic of the later literature of the realistic movement. By 1870 the country had already begun to experience the abuses and dislocations that accompany a rapid change in the character of civilization, and by 1875 the public and private morality of the land had reached its lowest ebb, in the period called by Mark Twain "the Gilded Age," and by others "the Tragic Era" or "the Great Barbecue." Within a decade industrial production had tripled, and railroads spanning the continent had brought the shrinking frontiers into a national economy. The enlarged demand for labor had attracted immigrants in such numbers that there were nearly seven and a half million foreign born in a population of about forty million. The new Atlantic cable and the expansion of practicable telegraphic communications further augmented the great strides of American commerce and domestic trade. In the older cities, crowded with newcomers, fortunes were quickly made and lost amid a general atmosphere of speculation and chicanery, and the mansions of the new millionaires burgeoned in contrast with the poverty of the new slums. The endless drive to the West was not continued by a host of homesteading farmers and immigrants from northern Europe; they suffered the privations and poverty of a new soil, but by 1880 they had brought into cultivation twenty million acres of virgin land and founded an agricultural economy which reached from the grain and cattle ranches of the Midwest to the orchards in the fertile valleys of the Pacific coast. In this West, with its limitless opportunities, its violent contrasts, and its seething mixture of old American settlers with immigrants from many lands, a social democracy developed that was new in the history of mankind.

However, the gap between the rich and the poor had actually widened in the industrial centers, and the vast numbers of workers, augmented by the hordes of underprivileged immigrants, began to form a working class in the European sense. Working conditions were still almost unregulated; a working day of from ten to twelve hours prevailed; and labor organizations were in the embryonic stage. Meanwhile, the operations of the "robber barons" of industry and finance, having gained their first real headway amid the scandals during Grant's administration, had risen to proportions justifying the unlovely epithets by which this age has been designated. Parrington, in *The Beginnings of Critical Realism in America*, says of the audacious leaders of the day that "they fought their way encased in rhinoceros hides"—the gamblers of Wall Street, the Drews, the Vanderbilts, Jim Fiske, Jay Gould, "blackguards for the most part, railway wreckers, cheaters and swindlers"; they were assisted by treasury-looting, vote-selling political bosses such as Tweed, Wood, and Cameron; they were supported by "professional keepers of the public morals" such as Comstock and Beecher; while the public in general seemed to take for granted the gaudy extravagance and "humbuggery" of an age in which Barnum was the predestined showman. A series of panics and depressions, beginning in 1873, increased the burdens and the discontent of the poor. A stouthearted believer in his country, Walt Whitman, excoriating his age with whiplash words in *Democratic Vistas* (1871), could only conclude that "the problem of the future of America is in certain respects as dark as it is vast."

This is not to assert that the realists at once devoted themselves primarily to the social and economic problem novel, although by 1890 many of them were doing so. The realists of the 1870's were sternly aware of the social problem, but their emphasis was on the character of the individual confronted by hardships or moral dilemmas. That the best of realism was not then a literature of reform is evident in the best work of the regionalists in general, and of Mark Twain, Howells, and Henry James, among the masters. For two decades Howells, who was chiefly distinguished for his novels of character, remained the spokesman of realism by virtue of his ability to communicate its spirit in fiction and essay, and to disseminate his *obiter dicta* from the editor's chair of the *Atlantic*, and later *Harper's Magazine*. Many other realists imposed fewer restrictions as to

propriety, and thus ranged over wider areas of life, but no other was more genuinely respected as an artist or more widely heard than Howells. Whether in his early comedies of manners, in his portrayals of the contrasts of international society, or in such novels concerning the business world as *The Rise of Silas Lapham* (1885), his emphasis was on character—until his declining years, after 1890, when his problem novels were written.

The greatest of the realists, Henry James, was the master of profundity and of a psychological subtlety more suited to the understanding of the present age than his own; his great novels are studies of character first of all, and the rise or ruin of his notable characters is predetermined at the very roots of existence or experience.

The work of the later American realists was both substantiated and strengthened by the new vogue of European realists, who had been disparaged by earlier readers on moral grounds—such Russians as Dostoevski, Turgenev, and Tolstoi, and the French naturalists, especially Zola, Flaubert, and Maupassant. The same sources may have strengthened the note of pessimistic determinism that steadily increased down into the nineties, when a full-fledged American naturalism developed. Mark Twain, however, came to this position independently. This gloomy attitude may be the necessary frame of reference for the great humorist; in the case of Twain, in any event, it dominated his genius. Even his earliest comic sketches are overshadowed by the same specter of mankind's cruelty, greed, and stupidity that lurks in such later masterpieces as "The Man That Corrupted Hadleyburg" (1900) and *The Mysterious Stranger* (1916).

The social problems of the country grew in size with its industrial and financial development, and it seemed that the American experiment, undertaken by Europeans to secure liberty, was doomed to produce for the masses only unrewarding poverty. During the later eighties the preoccupation of the national thought with social and economic problems was reflected in a swelling tide of literature. Conservative economic ideas were championed by many, such as William Graham Sumner, who, in *What Social Classes Owe to Each Other* (1883), defended capitalism as the operation of a benign natural selection of those fit to survive. Andrew Carnegie's *Triumphant Democracy* (1886) sounded much the same note. Meanwhile the collectivists gained their widest audience in a long succession of utopian novels, of which Edward Bellamy's *Looking Backward* (1888) was the most influential. Howells, who by this time was a Christian socialist in theory, became the critic of economic society in *A Hazard of New Fortunes* (1890), the first of his economic novels, and in 1894 enriched the utopian movement by publishing *A Traveler from Altruria*. Actually, in retrospect the social advances of those years are seen to be considerable. They were the climax to a titanic economic development which had produced many social problems, but the gains were being consolidated, and were soon to be felt in permanent improvements in the economic welfare of Americans in general. The Populist movement, begun in 1891, never won an election, but the members of that shifting coalition of farm- and labor-reform groups—chiefly sustained by the mounting democracy of the West—under the leadership of Bryan saw most of their objectives enormously advanced in little more than a decade. Theodore Roosevelt, in liberal reforms from 1901 to 1909, curbed the monopolies and "the malefactors of great wealth," instituted a sound policy to conserve the national resources for the people, and became the first president to make the welfare of "the little man" a powerful political issue. However, our literature had long before this developed, during the nineties, a naturalistic tendency which has survived well into the present troubled century.

SPIRITUAL UNREST

Strict naturalism in the European sense did not at first flourish widely in this country, where it was understood that social remedies were available even if sometimes opposed or postponed. After 1880, however, a growing spirit of skepticism, of spiritual unrest and disturbed religious faith, was reflected in the changing economic thought and morality of America and in the deterministic attitudes of intellectuals and writers. When Darwin published *The Origin of Species* in 1859 it was still possible for Whitman to regard the book as an optimistic confirmation of the ancient belief in man's progress and gradual betterment. John Fiske, like lesser early popularizers of evolutionary science, expounded its theories in the light of theistic faith, and rejoiced that God was revealed in biology as in Scripture. However, it was soon evident that pessimistic determinism was inherent in the new biology, anthropology, and geology, as well as in the recent experiences of economic man. The theory that the human individual, as much as any creature of a lower order, is determined by accidents of heredity, environment, and natural selection, seemed to deprive him of that special place among the creatures of God that had been the comfort of his religion, and of that necessary exercise of individual responsibility which had been common to democratic idealism and the Christian ethic. Herbert Spencer's sociology utilized the biological theory of the survival of the fittest in support of competition as an agency which prevented "the artificial preservation of those least able to take care of themselves." Rugged individualists—*laissez-faire* economists such as Sumner or industrialists such as Carnegie —could take comfort, but many others watched the struggling industrial masses, still poverty-stricken amid plenty, and wondered whether these were really the ways of God.

The literary reactions were variously expressed by such thinkers as William James, Santayana, and Henry Adams, by poets like Moody, Lodge, and Robinson, by such social critics as Veblen and Steffens, and by the later realistic and naturalistic novelists, influenced, as they were, by the writings of the Russian and French naturalists. American philosophy, represented by William James, Santayana, and Dewey, tended toward instrumentalism and rationalism, in contrast with the intuitional idealism of the nineteenth century. If the thinkers of this period evaded outright pessimism, it was by some dualistic resolution of their systems of thought. From his researches in psychology, James drew his "radical empiricism" in *The Will to Believe* (1897)—a defense of the acceptance of metaphysical concepts on the evidence of faith alone. In *Pragmatism* (1907) he gave a name to his new philosophy, which asserts that the value of an idea is tested by its consequences in terms of satisfaction and behavior. John Dewey's instrumentalism was a projection of pragmatism in the evaluation of experience, education, and social instruments in an age of change. Santayana's complex and voluminous system cannot be recapitulated with any simplicity. Its dualism differentiates between the material universe—the reality that man can apprehend only through reason—and the "essences" of higher reality and supernal value in the "realms" of faith. Henry Adams suggested a correspondence between the science and the philosophy of the day in his dynamic theory of history. Accepting the Spencerian hypothesis that history is evolutionary, he sought its laws by analogy with the principle of thermodynamics that energy tends constantly to be dispersed from a center. In *Mont-Saint-Michel and Chartres* (1904) he depicted medieval Christianity as a "universe." By contrast, the contemporary world, depicted in *The Education of Henry Adams* (1907), was a "multiverse" whose symbol was the dynamo, dissipating its energies outward toward diverse poles, with consequent loss of emphasis on individual and social spiritual value.

NATURALISM

It was against this background of troubled thought that the first American naturalistic writers emerged in the 1890's, but they were by no means simply the product of philosophic thought. Artists first of all, and realists in their aims, they were in general impressed by the artistic success of European naturalists and by the resources of the empirical description of experience as a means for securing the realistic portrayal of life.

The typical American naturalists were generally concerned with concrete factors in character and environment. The short-lived and able Frank Norris, in such novels as *Moran of the Lady Letty* (1898) and *McTeague* (1899), explored the personality with naturalistic fervor and only incidental social connotations; but in *The Octopus* (1901), his best-known work, he made a telling attack upon the ramified system of monopolistic financial and railroad power that for a time exploited and often ruined the farmers of the West. In *The Pit* (1903) he examined the drive for economic power in an analysis of the grain monopoly. Stephen Crane found vent for his naturalism in studies of the eastern slums, of the meanness of small-town life, and of the natural depravity of man. Hamlin Garland's conception of strict, delineative realism, which he called "veritism," was in fact naturalistic both in method and materials; his sketches in *Main-Travelled Roads* (1891) deal with characters whose choices are effectively canceled by circumstances or by the conditions of nature. Theodore Dreiser, who also belongs to this generation by date of birth, was the purest naturalist among American writers. Circumstances postponed the creation of *Sister Carrie* (1900), his first work, until he was nearly thirty; and the smothering of that book by unofficial censorship further delayed his active career as a novelist. Carrie Meeber conquers the nearly impossible conditions of poverty only by the animal law of survival, of which she takes advantage with intelligence, ruthlessness, and calm disregard of conventional moral restrictions.

Dreiser alone of these early naturalists and dissenters inherited the literary world after 1915, for which their generation had prepared the way. Garland in later years devoted himself for the most part to more popular forms of fiction. Norris and Crane both died at thirty. But younger authors continued the social dissent, the most important novelists among them being Upton Sinclair and Jack London, who both wrote with tempered naturalism. *The Jungle* (1906) grew out of Sinclair's investigation of the stockyards and packing industry, and brought results in the form of pure-food legislation; but its fictional interest is the story of Jurgis, the Slavic workman, trapped by the brutality, poverty, and disease in which he lives, until bereft of wife and family, brought to the brink of crime, he becomes a socialist agitator. Jack London, unlike Sinclair, remained throughout his career a naturalist and radical socialist. Typical are *The Call of the Wild* (1903), a study of the law of survival in the life of a wild dog; *The Sea-Wolf* (1904), in which the same motivations are transferred to the whaling Captain, Wolf Larsen, a ruthless superman; and *The Iron Heel* (1907), a novel of class warfare. In a sense the short-story formula that O. Henry employed to portray his children of chance—typically in *The Four Million* (1906)—is a satiric response to a naturalistic predisposition.

It is evident that there is no clear cleavage between the nineteenth and the twentieth century in American literature. Victorian acceptances and compromises, genteel survivals, lingered on until 1910 and beyond; but the modern temper which about 1915 produced the "twentieth-century renaissance" originated in the intellectual life of the previous century. The emerging modern American literature, which began with the optimistic voice of Whitman, closed the first decade of the twentieth century with social and economic protest. The one nation, strong and unified, which Lincoln had envisioned, had become an actuality. Urban industrialism posed still-imponderable questions of slum clearance, social welfare, and labor practices. The romantic idealism of 1865 had given way to the realism of Howells, to the psychological penetration of James, to the naturalism of Crane, Norris, and Dreiser. Yet our literature continued to reflect the survival in American life of those youthful virtues that remind us of what we have been and what we should ever strive to be.

Pioneers of a New Poetry

WALT WHITMAN
(1819–1892)

Walt Whitman is important to our literature first of all because he was a great poet. "When Lilacs Last in the Dooryard Bloom'd" or "Out of the Cradle Endlessly Rocking," or "Crossing Brooklyn Ferry"—to name only a few—would be masterpieces in any literature. Second, as an artist he had the kind of courage and vision upon which new epochs are founded. In 1855 he was the first voice of the revolution which after 1870 swept over European literature, and much later reached the United States.

That kind of genius which is uncommon sense made him know that the time had come for many barriers to fall—barriers to the welfare and the expression of the individual, which he valued above all else. Thus, in advance of the "new" psychology he insisted on the unity of the personality and the significant importance of all experience. He extolled the values of the common, the miracle of the mouse, the wholesome soundness of the calloused hand, the body's sweat. He attempted "to make illustrious" the "procrea-

tive urge of the universe," or of sex in man.

Whitman's free verse provided an example that slowly communicated itself to later poets who likewise sought to refresh their art. His use of rhythm as a fluid instrument of verse demonstrated a range of possibilities beyond that of conventional meter. He wrote symphonically, associating themes and melodies with great freedom and suggestiveness; he abandoned conventional and hackneyed poetic figures and drew his symbolism freshly from experience. He remains one of our most important poets because he announced and instructed a new age; but he is equally important as a defender of the central American idealism of the past. Spiritually he sprang from the tradition that Emerson represented—his was the transcendental or intuitional temperament that trusts the innate spiritual intimations of the individual and makes him responsible to them. On the plane of political thought he was also an apostle of individualism, and represented the nineteenth-century projection of Jeffersonian idealism.

Walter Whitman was born on a farm on Long Island, then rural countryside, on May 31, 1819; his father was of British, his mother of Dutch, ancestry. Walter Whitman senior, a carpenter as well as a farmer, twice in Walt's youth tried his fortune at housebuilding in Brooklyn, at that time not quite a city in size. Thus the young poet experienced a vital cross section of American common life: about the island the farmers and fishermen, the sailors and clammers, and the hamlets in which they lived; the nascent urban community of Brooklyn, where a boy could still catch fish in a nearby pond; the great harbor with its ships, and across the water the spires of Manhattan, visited by means of the exciting ferryboats, and later to become for the poet always "my city." As a boy he had five years of common schooling in Brooklyn, then in 1830 began work as an office boy. But by natural instinct he turned to the printing offices. Until the early fifties he worked as a journalist, attaining a considerable position as editor of the Brooklyn *Eagle* (1846–1848). On the way up he was an apprentice on the Long Island *Patriot* (1832) and a journeyman printer in New York. Then, after teaching in various country schools on Long Island while contributing to local newspapers, he founded at Huntington his own weekly newspaper, the *Long Islander*, in 1838. In 1839 he was a compositor on the Long Island *Democrat*, and in 1840, at twenty-one, he stumped the Is-

land for Van Buren during the presidential campaign. During the next six years he was in New York, as newspaperman and as editor of the *Aurora*, the *Tatler*, and the New York *Democrat*. When he took over the *Eagle* in Brooklyn in 1846 he was seasoned in his profession, and he gained recognition in the New York area during his editorship. He resigned in 1848 because the backers of the paper, faced with the split in the Democratic party caused by the Mexican War, found it expedient to support compromise with the southern Democrats, while their editor was an unswerving free-soil Democrat. Probably for adventure's sake, Whitman then took the editorship of the New Orleans *Crescent*, traveling southward partly by Mississippi steamboat with his brother Jeff; he returned in six months to edit the Brooklyn *Freeman*.

But now he had in mind his great project. Shaken by the ominous shadows that gathered over the country as "the irrepressible conflict" took shape in the Mexican War, he had conceived of a book to interpret American democratic idealism as he had experienced it. It was to be a poem in a new form with which he had been experimenting since perhaps 1847. He gave up his newspaper work, and living with his parents in Brooklyn, worked as part-time carpenter while writing *Leaves of Grass*. The first edition went on sale in New York probably on July 4, 1855. It had been privately printed, as were all but two of the first seven editions. The frankness of *Leaves of*

Grass, together with its revolutionary form, precluded the possibility of wide reception. It was simply about sixty years ahead of its time, and Whitman, realizing this, accepted the situation with equanimity, knowing "the amplitude of time." There was a dribble of orders for each successive edition, most of them sold from his home, wherever it then might be.

But it is a mistake to suppose that the author was neglected. Emerson wrote his famous message, "I greet you at the beginning of a great career," less than three weeks after Whitman sent him a copy. Within the year Thoreau and Bronson Alcott had ferreted out the author's dwelling in Brooklyn, and Emerson himself soon paid a visit. So through the years, leaders of thought saw the greatness of what he was doing. By 1868 the young John Burroughs had written a book on Whitman and William Michael Rossetti had responded to a growing interest among English intellectuals by publishing an English edition. During the 1870's Whitman's name began to be mentioned by German critics, and within another decade translations of his poems in German and French made him famous on the Continent. Still most Americans ignored his work, and he lived in poverty all his life.

From 1855 until 1862 he subsisted by literary hack work and journalism in Brooklyn, meanwhile enlarging his poems for the second edition of 1856 and the fundamental edition of 1860. There the poems began to fall into position as parts of a single "poem," as the author

said. It was to represent life in terms of one life, which had to be seen through the poet's eyes, yet he would be reporting only what seemed true and important to everyone.

In 1862, his brother George was wounded, and Whitman went to the war front in Virginia. Finding his brother's condition not serious, he remained in Washington as a volunteer war nurse, visiting hospitals for a part of every day, and supporting himself by part-time work in the Army paymaster's office. This was the experience which led to the poems of *Drum-Taps* (1865). "When Lilacs Last in the Dooryard Bloom'd," written for the second issue of this book, after the assassination of Lincoln that April, provided a passionate climax for the theme of the entire volume in its veneration of the President, who represented for Whitman a shining example of democratic comradeship and love for man.

In 1865, Whitman was appointed clerk in the Bureau of Indian Affairs only to be discharged in six months by Secretary Harlan because of the unsavory reputation of his book. At once appointed to the attorney general's office he rather gained by the experience because his eloquent friend William Douglas O'Connor, in his fiery pamphlet *The Good Gray Poet* (1866), published a fine vindication of Whitman's work.

The poet held his position in Washington until 1874, and during that time published, again at his own expense, two more editions of *Leaves of Grass*. In 1873, at fifty-four, he suffered a severe stroke of paralysis, and soon was an invalid at the home of his brother George in Camden, New Jersey. He never again recovered his full vitality, although he was well enough, on occasion, to give a public reading or lecture nearby, or to visit Burroughs, now an established naturalist, at his Hudson River farm. In 1879 he made his long-anticipated trans-continental journey, as far west as Nevada.

In 1881 *Leaves of Grass* found a publisher in Osgood and Company of Boston, and sold well until the District Attorney classified it as "obscene literature" and ordered the cancellation of "A Woman Waits for Me," "To a Common Prostitute," and certain isolated phrases. Whitman refused to comply. He took the plates to Rees Welsh, later David McKay, in Philadelphia, where his works were published for many years thereafter. In 1882 he published his best prose essays as *Specimen Days and Collect*. For the first time his volumes had a considerable sale. He was able to buy his own little house, now famous, in Mickle Street, Camden, and in the last decade of his life it became a place of pilgrimage for many American and British visitors. Until his death in 1892 he was never far from the edge of poverty, but as he said, in his own time he had "really arrived." The 1892 edition of

Leaves of Grass, which he signed on his deathbed, is one of America's great books, and it has had world-wide influence.

Whitman's writings were collected as *The Complete Writings of Walt Whitman,* 10 vols., edited by R. M. Bucke and others, 1902, a limited edition long out of print. There are many editions of *Leaves of Grass* and the major prose essays, generally derived from the 1902 edition. Long the standard scholarly one-volume 1902 text is *Leaves of Grass,* inclusive edition, edited by Emory Holloway, 1924, 1954, containing prefaces by Whitman and the variorum readings by O. L. Triggs. Gay W. Allen and Sculley Bradley are general editors of the collaborative edition in progress, *The Collected Writings of Walt Whitman* (18 vols.), of which the nine published volumes include *Correspondence, Major Prose, Early Poetry and Prose,* and the *Reader's Edition of "Leaves of Grass"* (a textual variorum is in progress).

Gay W. Allen's *Walt Whitman Handbook,* 1946, 1957, was the beginning of a new era in Whitman scholarship and a summation of the abundant criticism and biography already in print. It has been superseded by Allen's *A Reader's Guide to Walt Whitman,* 1970. Of the many earlier biographies, those still in use include Emory Holloway, *Whitman, an Interpretation in Narrative,* 1926; Newton Arvin, *Whitman,* 1938; H. S. Canby, *Walt Whitman, An American,* 1943; Frederick Schyberg, *Walt Whitman,* translated from the Danish by Evie Allen, 1951; Gay W. Allen, *The Solitary Singer: Walt Whitman,* 1955; 3rd ed., revised, 1967, thoroughly dependable and a bibliographical source as well; and a distinguished critical biography, Roger Asselineau, *The Evolution of Walt Whitman,* 2 vols., translated from the French, Cambridge, Mass., 1960, 1962.

The following texts of *Leaves of Grass* are those of the last authorized edition, Philadelphia, 1891–1892; "Democratic Vistas" and "Specimen Days" follow the complete text of *Specimen Days and Collect,* 1882.

Preface to the 1855 Edition of Leaves of Grass [1]

America does not repel the past or what it has produced under its forms or amid other politics or the idea of castes or the old

1. The first-edition text is important primarily because Whitman's reprints in prose collections in 1882 and 1892 show this essay decimated by the transfer of many of the prose phrases and sentences into eight poems which survived in

religions . . . . accepts the lesson with calmness . . . is not so impatient as has been supposed that the slough still sticks to opinions and manners and literature while the life which served its requirements has passed into the new life of the new forms . . . perceives that the corpse is slowly borne from the eating and sleeping rooms of the house . . . perceives that it waits a little while in the door . . . that it was fittest for its days . . . that its action has descended to the stalwart and wellshaped heir who approaches . . . and that he shall be fittest for his days.

The Americans of all nations at any time upon the earth have probably the fullest poetical nature. The United States themselves are essentially the greatest poem. In the history of the earth hitherto the largest and most stirring appear tame and orderly to their ampler largeness and stir. Here at last is something in the doings of man that corresponds with the broadcast doings of the day and night. Here is not merely a nation but a teeming nation of nations. Here is action untied from strings necessarily blind to particulars and details magnificently moving in vast masses. Here is the hospitality which forever indicates heroes. . . . Here are the roughs and beards and space and ruggedness and nonchalance that the soul loves. Here the performance disdaining the trivial unapproached in the tremendous audacity of its crowds and groupings and the push of its perspective spreads with crampless and flowing breadth and showers its prolific and splendid extravagance. One sees it must indeed own the riches of the summer and winter, and need never be bankrupt while corn grows from the ground or the orchards drop apples or the bays contain fish or men beget children upon women.

Other states indicate themselves in their deputies . . . . but the genius of the United States is not best or most in its executives or legislatures, nor in its ambassadors or authors or colleges or churches or parlors, nor even in its newspapers or inventors . . . but always most in the common people. Their manners speech dress friendships—the freshness and candor of their physiognomy —the picturesque looseness of their carriage . . . their deathless attachment to freedom—their aversion to anything indecorous or soft or mean—the practical acknowledgment of the citizens of one state by the citizens of all other states—the fierceness of their roused resentment—their curiosity and welcome of novelty —their self-esteem and wonderful sympathy—their susceptibility to a slight—the air they have of persons who never knew how

---

Leaves of Grass; but the most fully affected were the three major poems, "By Blue Ontario's Shore," "Song of Prudence," and "Song of the Answerer." In this essay, the power of his prose is commensurate with his poetry. As an important expression of a theory of American literature it has continued to influence modern literature in general.

it felt to stand in the presence of superiors—the fluency of their speech—their delight in music, the sure symptom of manly tenderness and native elegance of soul . . . their good temper and openhandedness—the terrible significance of their elections—the President's taking off his hat to them not they to him—these too are unrhymed poetry. It awaits the gigantic and generous treatment worth of it.

The largeness of nature or the nation were monstrous without a corresponding largeness and generosity of the spirit of the citizen. Not nature nor swarming states nor streets and steamships nor prosperous business nor farms nor capital nor learning may suffice for the ideal of man . . . nor suffice the poet. No reminiscences may suffice either. A live nation can always cut a deep mark and can have the best authority the cheapest . . . namely from its own soul. This is the sum of the profitable uses of individuals or states and of present action and grandeur and of the subjects of poets.—As if it were necessary to trot back generation after generation to the eastern records! As if the beauty and sacredness of the demonstrable must fall behind that of the mythical! As if men do not make their mark out of any times! As if the opening of the western continent by discovery and what has transpired since in North and South America were less than the small theatre of the antique or the aimless sleepwalking of the middle ages! The pride of the United States leaves the wealth and finesse of the cities and all returns of commerce and agriculture and all the magnitude of geography or shows of exterior victory to enjoy the breed of fullsized men or one fullsized man unconquerable and simple.

The American poets are to enclose old and new for America is the race of races. Of them a bard is to be commensurate with a people. To him the other continents arrive as contributions . . . he gives them reception for their sake and his own sake. His spirit responds to his country's spirit . . . he incarnates its geography and natural life and rivers and lakes. Mississippi with annual freshets and changing chutes, Missouri and Columbia and Ohio and Saint Lawrence with the falls and beautiful masculine Hudson, do not embouchure where they spend themselves more than they embouchure into him. The blue breadth over the inland sea of Virginia and Maryland and the sea off Massachusetts and Maine and over Manhattan bay and over Champlain and Erie and over Ontario and Huron and Michigan and Superior, and over the Texan and Mexican and Floridian and Cuban seas and over the seas off California and Oregon, is not tallied by the blue breadth of the waters below more than the breadth of above and below is tallied by him. When the long Atlantic coast stretches longer and the Pacific coast stretches longer he easily stretches with them north or south. He spans between them also from east to west and reflects what is between them. On him rise solid growths that offset the growths of pine and cedar and hemlock and liveoak and locust and chestnut and cypress and hickory and limetree and cottonwood and tuliptree and cactus and wildvine and tamarind and persimmon . . . . and tangles as tangled as any canebrake or swamp . . . . and forests coated with transparent ice and icicles hanging from the boughs and crackling in the wind . . . . and sides and peaks of mountains . . . . and pasturage sweet and free as savannah or upland or prairie . . . . with flights and songs and screams that answer those of the wildpigeon and high-hold and orchard oriole and coot and surf-duck and red-shouldered-hawk and fish-hawk and white-ibis and indian-hen and cat-owl and water-pheasant and qua-bird and pied-sheldrake and blackbird and mockingbird and buzzard and condor and night-heron and eagle. To him the hereditary countenance descends both mother's and father's. To him enter the essences of the real things and past and present events—of the enormous diversity of temperature and agriculture and mines—the tribes of red aborigines—the weatherbeaten vessels entering new ports or making landings on rocky coasts—the first settlements north or south—the rapid stature and muscle—the haughty defiance of '76, and the war and peace and formation of the constituion . . . . the union always surrounded by blatherers and always calm and impregnable—the perpetual coming of immigrants—the wharf hem'd cities and superior marine—the unsurveyed interior—the loghouses and clearings and wild animals and hunters and trappers . . . . the free commerce—the fisheries and whaling and golddigging—the endless gestation of new states—the convening of Congress every December, the members duly coming up from all climates and the uttermost parts . . . . the noble character of the young mechanics and of all free American workmen and workwomen . . . . the general ardor and friendliness and enterprise—the perfect equality of the female with the male . . . . the long amativeness—the fluid movement of the population—the factories and mercantile life and laborsaving machinery—the Yankee swap—the New-York firemen and the target excursion—the southern plantation life—the character of the northeast and of the northwest and southwest—slavery and the tremulous spreading of hands to protect it, and the stern opposition to it which shall never cease till it ceases or the speaking of tongues and the moving of lips cease. For such the expression of the American poet is to be transcendent and new. It is to be indirect and not direct or descriptive or epic. Its quality goes through these to much more. Let the age and wars of other nations be chanted and their eras and characters be illustrated and that finish the verse. Not so the great psalm of the republic. Here the theme is creative and has vista. Here comes one among the wellbeloved stonecutters and plans with decision and science and sees the solid and beautiful forms of the future where there are now no solid forms.

Of all nations the United States with veins full of poetical stuff most need poets and will doubtless have the greatest and use them the greatest. Their Presidents shall not be their common referee so much as their poets shall. Of all mankind the great poet is the equable man. Not in him but off from him things are grotesque or eccentric or fail of their sanity. Nothing out of its place is good and nothing in its place is bad. He bestows on every object or quality its fit proportions neither more nor less. He is the arbiter of the diverse and he is the key. He is the equalizer of his age and land . . . . he supplies what wants supplying and checks what wants checking. If peace is the routine out of him speaks the spirit of peace, large, rich, thrifty, building vast and populous cities, encouraging agriculture and the arts and commerce—lighting the study of man, the soul, immortality—federal, state or municipal government, marriage, health, freetrade, intertravel by land and sea . . . . nothing too close, nothing too far off . . . the stars not too far off. In war he is the most deadly force of the war. Who recruits him recruits horse and foot . . . he fetches parks of artillery the best that engineer ever knew. If the time becomes slothful and heavy he knows how to arouse it . . . he can make every word he speaks draw blood. Whatever stagnates in the flat of custom or obedience or legislation he never stagnates. Obedience does not master him, he masters it. High up out of reach he stands turning a concentrated light . . . he turns the pivot with his finger . . . he baffles the swiftest runners as he stands and easily overtakes and envelops them. The time straying toward infidelity and confections and persiflage he withholds by his steady faith . . . he spreads out his dishes . . . he offers the sweet firmfibered meat that grows men and women. His brain is the ultimate brain. He is no arguer . . . he is judgment. He judges not as the judge judges but as the sun falling around a helpless thing. As he sees the farthest he has the most faith. His thoughts are the hymns of the praise of things. In the talk on the soul and eternity and God off of his equal plane he is silent. He sees eternity less like a play with a prologue and denouement . . . . he sees eternity in men and women . . . he does not see men and women as dreams or dots. Faith is the antiseptic of the soul . . . it pervades the com-

mon people and preserves them . . . they never give up believing
and expecting and trusting. There is that indescribable freshness
and unconsciousness about an illiterate person that humbles and
mocks the power of the noblest expressive genius. The poet sees for
a certainty how one not a great artist may be just as sacred and
perfect as the greatest artist. . . . The power to destroy or re-
mould is freely used by him but never the power of attack. What
is past is past. If he does not expose superior models and prove
himself by every step he takes he is not what is wanted. The
presence of the greatest poet conquers . . . not parleying or struggling or any prepared attempts. Now he has passed that way see
after him! there is not left any vestige of despair or misanthropy
or cunning or exclusiveness or the ignominy of a nativity or color
or delusion of hell or the necessity of hell . . . . and no man
thenceforward shall be degraded for ignorance or weakness or sin.

The greatest poet hardly knows pettiness or triviality. If he
breathes into any thing that was before thought small it dilates
with the grandeur and life of the universe. He is a seer . . . . he
is individual . . . he is complete in himself . . . . the others are
as good as he, only he sees it and they do not. He is not one of the
chorus . . . . he does not stop for any regulation . . . he is the
president of regulation. What the eyesight does to the rest he
does to the rest. Who knows the curious mystery of the eyesight?
The other senses corroborate themselves, but this is removed
from any proof but its own and foreruns the identities of the
spiritual world. A single glance of it mocks all the investigations
of man and all the instruments and books of the earth and all
reasoning. What is marvellous? what is unlikely? what is impossible or baseless or vague? after you have once just opened the
space of a peachpit and given audience to far and near and to
the sunset and had all things enter with electric swiftness softly
and duly without confusion or jostling or jam.

The land and sea, the animals fishes and birds, the sky of
heaven and the orbs, the forests mountains and rivers, are not
small themes . . . but folks expect of the poet to indicate more
than the beauty and dignity which always attach to dumb real
objects . . . . they expect him to indicate the path between reality
and their souls. Men and women perceive the beauty well enough
. . . probably as well as he. The passionate tenacity of hunters,
woodmen, early risers, cultivators of gardens and orchards and
fields, the love of healthy women for the manly form, seafaring
persons, drivers of horses, the passion for light and the open air,
all is an old varied sign of the unfailing perception of beauty and
of a residence of the poetic in outdoor people. They can never
be assisted by poets to perceive . . . some may but they never

can. The poetic quality is not marshalled in rhyme or uniformity or abstract addresses to things nor in melancholy complaints or good precepts, but is the life of these and much else and is in the soul. The profit of rhyme is that it drops seeds of a sweeter and more luxuriant rhyme, and of uniformity that it conveys itself into its own roots in the ground out of sight. The rhyme and uniformity of perfect poems show the free growth of metrical laws and bud from them as unerringly and loosely as lilacs or roses on a bush, and take shapes as compact as the shapes of chestnuts and oranges and melons and pears, and shed the perfume impalpable to form. The fluency and ornaments of the finest poems or music or orations or recitations are not independent but dependent. All beauty comes from beautiful blood and a beautiful brain. If the greatnesses are in conjunction in a man or woman it is enough . . . . the fact will prevail through the universe . . . . but the gaggery and gilt of a million years will not prevail. Who troubles himself about his ornaments or fluency is lost. This is what you shall do: Love the earth and sun and the animals, despise riches, give alms to every one that asks, stand up for the stupid and crazy, devote your income and labor to others, hate tyrants, argue not concerning God, have patience and indulgence toward the people, take off your hat to nothing known or unknown or to any man or number of men, go freely with powerful uneducated persons and with the young and with the mothers of families, read these leaves in the open air every season of every year of your life, re-examine all you have been told at school or church or in any book, dismiss whatever insults your own soul, and your very flesh shall be a great poem and have the richest fluency not only in its words but in the silent lines of its lips and face and between the lashes of your eyes and in every motion and joint of your body. . . . . The poet shall not spend his time in unneeded work. He shall know that the ground is always ready ploughed and manured . . . . others may not know it but he shall. He shall go directly to the creation. His trust shall master the trust of everything he touches . . . . and shall master all attachment.

The known universe has one complete lover and that is the greatest poet. He consumes an eternal passion and is indifferent which chance happens and which possible contingency of fortune or misfortune and persuades daily and hourly his delicious pay. What balks or breaks others is fuel for his burning progress to contact and amorous joy. Other proportions of the reception of pleasure dwindle to nothing to his proportions. All expected from heaven or from the highest he is rapport with in the sight of the daybreak or a scene of the winter woods or the presence of children playing or with his arm round the neck of a man or woman. His love above all love has leisure and expanse . . . he leaves room ahead of himself. He is no irresolute or suspicious lover . . . he is sure . . . he scorns intervals. His experience and the showers and thrills are not for nothing. Nothing can jar him . . . . suffering and darkness cannot—death and fear cannot. To him complaint and jealousy and envy are corpses buried and rotten in the earth . . . . he saw them buried. The sea is not surer of the shore or the shore of the sea than he is of the fruition of his love and of all perfection and beauty.

The fruition of beauty is no chance of hit or miss . . . it is inevitable as life . . . . it is exact and plumb as gravitation. From the eyesight proceeds another eyesight and from the hearing proceeds another hearing and from the voice proceeds another voice eternally curious of the harmony of things with man. To these respond perfections not only in the committees that were supposed to stand for the rest but in the rest themselves just the same. These understand the law of perfection in masses and floods . . . that its finish is to each for itself and onward from itself . . . that it is profuse and impartial . . . that there is not a minute of the light or dark nor an acre of the earth or sea without it—nor any direction of the sky nor any trade or employment nor any turn of events. This is the reason that about the proper expression of beauty there is precision and balance . . . one part does not need to be thrust above another. The best singer is not the one who has the most lithe and powerful organ . . . the pleasure of poems is not in them that take the handsomest measure and similes and sound.

Without effort and without exposing in the least how it is done the greatest poet brings the spirit of any or all events and passions and scenes and persons some more and some less to bear on your individual character as you hear or read. To do this well is to compete with the laws that pursue and follow time. What is the purpose must surely be there and the clue of it must be there . . . . and the faintest indication is the indication of the best and then becomes the clearest indication. Past and present and future are not disjoined but joined. The greatest poet forms the consistence of what is to be from what has been and is. He drags the dead out of their coffins and stands them again on their feet . . . . he says to the past, Rise and walk before me that I may realize you. He learns the lesson . . . . he places himself where the future becomes present. The greatest poet does not only dazzle his rays over character and scenes and passions . . . he finally ascends and finishes all . . . he exhibits the pinnacles that no man can tell what they are for or what is beyond . . . . he glows a moment on the extremest verge. He is most wonderful in his last half-hidden smile or frown . . . by that flash of the moment of parting the one that sees it shall be encouraged or terrified afterwards for many years. The greatest poet does not moralize or make applications of morals . . . he knows the soul. The soul has that measureless pride which consists in never acknowledging any lessons but its own. But it has sympathy as measureless as its pride and the one balances the other and neither can stretch too far while it stretches in company with the other. The inmost secrets of art sleep with the twain. The greatest poet has lain close betwixt both and they are vital in his style and thoughts.

The art of art, the glory of expression and the sunshine of the light of letters is simplicity. Nothing is better than simplicity . . . . nothing can make up for excess or for the lack of definiteness. To carry on the heave of impulse and pierce intellectual depths and give all subjects their articulations are powers neither common nor very uncommon. But to speak in literature with the perfect rectitude and insouciance of the movements of animals and the unimpeachableness of the sentiment of trees in the woods and grass by the roadside is the flawless triumph of art. If you have looked on him who has achieved it you have looked on one of the masters of the artists of all nations and times. You shall not contemplate the flight of the graygull over the bay or the mettlesome action of the blood horse or the tall leaning of sunflowers on their stalk or the appearance of the sun journeying through heaven or the appearance of the moon afterward with any more satisfaction than you shall contemplate him. The greatest poet has less a marked style and is more the channel of thoughts and things without increase or diminution, and is the free channel of himself. He swears to his art, I will not be meddlesome, I will not have in my writing any elegance or effect or originality to hang in the way between me and the rest like curtains. I will have nothing hang in the way, not the richest curtains. What I tell I tell for precisely what it is. Let who may exalt or startle or fascinate or soothe I will have purposes as health or heat or snow has and be as regardless of observation. What I experience or portray shall go from my composition without a shred of my composition. You shall stand by my side and look in the mirror with me.

The old red blood and stainless gentility of great poets will be proved by their unconstraint. A heroic person walks at his ease through and out of that custom or precedent or authority that suits him not. Of the traits of the brotherhood of writers savans musicians inventors and artists nothing is finer than silent defiance advancing from new free forms. In the need of poems philosophy politics mechanism science behaviour, the craft of art, an appropriate native grand-opera, shipcraft, or any craft, he is greatest forever and forever who contributes the greatest original practical example. The cleanest expression is that which finds no sphere worthy of itself and makes one.

The messages of great poets to each man and woman are, Come to us on equal terms, Only then can you understand us, We are no better than you, What we enclose you enclose, What we enjoy you may enjoy. Did you suppose there could be only one Supreme? We affirm there can be unnumbered Supremes, and that one does not countervail another any more than one eyesight countervails another . . . and that men can be good or grand only of the consciousness of their supremacy within them. What do you think is the grandeur of storms and dismemberments and the deadliest battles and wrecks and the wildest fury of the elements and the power of the sea and the motion of nature and of the throes of human desires and dignity and hate and love? It is that something in the soul which says, Rage on, Whirl on, I tread master here and everywhere, Master of the spasms of the sky and of the shatter of the sea, Master of nature and passion and death, And of all terror and all pain.

The American bards shall be marked for generosity and affection and for encouraging competitors . . . They shall be kosmos . . . without monopoly and secrecy . . . glad to pass any thing to any one . . . hungry for equals night and day. They shall not be careful of riches and privilege . . . . they shall be riches and privilege . . . they shall perceive who the most affluent man is. The most affluent man is he that confronts all the shows he sees by equivalents out of the stronger wealth of himself. The American bard shall delineate no class of persons nor one or two out of the strata of interests nor love most nor truth most nor the soul most nor the body most . . . . and not be for the eastern states more than the western or the northern states more than the southern.

Exact science and its practical movements are no checks on the greatest poet but always his encouragement and support. The outset and remembrance are there . . . there the arms that lifted him first and brace him best . . . . there he returns after all his goings and comings. The sailor and traveler . . . the anatomist chemist astronomer geologist phrenologist spiritualist mathematician historian and lexicographer are not poets, but they are the lawgivers of poets and their construction underlies the structure of every perfect poem. No matter what rises or is uttered they sent the seed of the conception of it . . . of them and by them stand the visible proofs of souls . . . . always of their fatherstuff

must be begotten the sinewy races of bards. If there shall be love
and content between the father and the son and if the greatness of
the son is the exuding of the greatness of the father there shall
be love between the poet and the man of demonstrable science.
In the beauty of poems are the tuft and final applause of science.

Great is the faith of the flush of knowledge and of the investigation of the depths of qualities and things. Cleaving and circling
here swells the soul of the poet yet is president of itself always.
The depths are fathomless and therefore calm. The innocence and
nakedness are resumed . . . they are neither modest nor immodest. The whole theory of the special and supernatural and
all that was twined with it or educed out of it departs as a dream.
What has ever happened . . . . what happens and whatever may
or shall happen, the vital laws enclose all . . . . they are sufficient
for any case and for all cases . . . none to be hurried or retarded . . . . any miracle of affairs or persons inadmissible in the
vast clear scheme where every motion and every spear of grass and
the frames and spirits of men and women and all that concerns
them are unspeakably perfect miracles all referring to all and each
distinct and in its place. It is also not consistent with the reality
of the soul to admit that there is anything in the known universe
more divine than men and women.

Men and women and the earth and all upon it are simply to
be taken as they are, and the investigation of their past and
present and future shall be unintermitted and shall be done with
perfect candor. Upon this basis philosophy speculates ever looking
toward the poet, ever regarding the eternal tendencies of all toward happiness never inconsistent with what is clear to the senses
and to the soul. For the eternal tendencies of all toward happiness
make the only point of sane philophy. Whatever comprehends
less than that . . . whatever is less than the laws of light and of
astronomical motion . . . or less than the laws that follow the
thief the liar the glutton and the drunkard through this life and
doubtless afterward . . . . . . or less than vast stretches of time or
the slow formation of density or the patient upheaving of strata—is
of no account. Whatever would put God in a poem or system of
philosophy as contending against some being or influence is also
of no account. Sanity and ensemble characterise the great master
. . . spoilt in one principle all is spoilt. The great master has
nothing to do with miracles. He sees health for himself in being
one of the mass . . . . he sees the hiatus in singular eminence. To
the perfect shape comes common ground. To be under the general
law is great for that is to correspond with it. The master knows
that he is unspeakably great and that all are unspeakably great

. . . . that nothing for instance is greater than to conceive children and bring them up well . . . that to be is just as great as to perceive or tell.

In the make of the great masters the idea of political liberty is indispensible. Liberty takes the adherence of heroes wherever men and women exist . . . . but never takes any adherence or welcome from the rest more than from poets. They are the voice and exposition of liberty. They out of ages are worthy the grand idea . . . . to them it is confided and they must sustain it. Nothing has precedence of it and nothing can warp or degrade it. The attitude of great poets is to cheer up slaves and horrify despots. The turn of their necks, the sound of their feet, the motions of their wrists, are full of hazard to the one and hope to the other. Come nigh them awhile and though they neither speak or advise you shall learn the faithful American lesson. Liberty is poorly served by men whose good intent is quelled from one failure or two failures or any number of failures, or from the casual indifference or ingratitude of the people, or from the sharp show of the tushes of power, or the bringing to bear soldiers and cannon or any penal statutes. Liberty relies upon itself, invites no one, promises nothing, sits in calmness and light, is positive and composed, and knows no discouragement. The battle rages with many a loud alarm and frequent advance and retreat . . . . the enemy triumphs . . . . the prison, the handcuffs, the iron necklace and anklet, the scaffold, garrote and leadballs do their work . . . . the cause is asleep . . . . the strong throats are choked with their own blood . . . . the young men drop their eyelashes toward the ground when they pass each other . . . . and is liberty gone out of that place? No never. When liberty goes it is not the first to go nor the second or third to go . . . it waits for all the rest to go . . . it is the last . . . When the memories of the old martyrs are faded utterly away . . . . when the large names of patriots are laughed at in the public halls from the lips of the orators . . . . when the boys are no more christened after the same but christened after tyrants and traitors instead . . . . when the laws of the free are grudgingly permitted and laws for informers and blood-money are sweet to the taste of the people . . . . when I and you walk abroad upon the earth stung with compassion at the sight of numberless brothers answering our equal friendship and calling no man master—and when we are elated with noble joy at the sight of slaves . . . . when the soul retires in the cool communion of the night and surveys its experience and has much extasy over the word and deed that put back a helpless innocent person into the gripe of the gripers or into any cruel inferiority . . . . when those in all parts of these states who could easier realize the true

American character but do not yet—when the swarms of cringers, suckers, doughfaces, lice of politics, planners of sly involutions for their own preferment to city offices or state legislatures or the judiciary or congress or the presidency, obtain a response of love and natural deference from the people whether they get the offices or no . . . . when it is better to be a bound booby and rogue in office at a high salary than the poorest free mechanic or farmer with his hat unmoved from his head and firm eyes and a candid and generous heart . . . . and when servility by town or state or the federal government or any oppression on a large scale or small scale can be tried on without its own punishment following duly after in exact proportion against the smallest chance of escape . . . . or rather when all life and all the souls of men and women are discharged from any part of the earth—then only shall the instinct of liberty be discharged from that part of the earth.

As the attributes of the poets of the kosmos concentre in the real body and soul and in the pleasure of things they possess the superiority of genuineness over all fiction and romance. As they emit themselves facts are showered over with light . . . . the daylight is lit with more volatile light . . . . also the deep between the setting and rising sun goes deeper many fold. Each precise object or condition or combination or process exhibits a beauty . . . . the multiplication table its—old age its—the carpenter's trade its—the grand-opera its . . . . the hugehulled cleanshaped New-York clipper at sea under steam or full sail gleams with unmatched beauty . . . . the American circles and large harmonies of government gleam with theirs . . . . and the commonest definite intentions and actions with theirs. The poets of the kosmos advance through all interpositions and coverings and turmoils and stratagems to first principles. They are of use . . . . they dissolve poverty from its need and riches from its conceit. You large proprietor they say shall not realize or perceive more than any one else. The owner of the library is not he who holds a legal title to it having bought and paid for it. Any one and every one is owner of the library who can read the same through all the varieties of tongues and subjects and styles, and in whom they enter with ease and take residence and force toward paternity and maternity, and make supple and powerful and rich and large. . . . . These American states strong and healthy and accomplished shall receive no pleasure from violations of natural models and must not permit them. In paintings or mouldings or carvings in mineral or wood, or in the illustrations of books or newspapers, or in any comic or tragic prints, or in the patterns of woven stuffs or any thing to beautify rooms or furniture or costumes, or to put upon cornices or monuments or on the prows or sterns of ships, or to put anywhere before the human eye indoors or out, that which distorts honest shapes or which creates unearthly beings or places or contingencies is a nuisance and revolt. Of the human form especially it is so great it must never be made ridiculous. Of ornaments to a work nothing outre can be allowed . . but those ornaments can be allowed that conform to the perfect facts of the open air and that flow out of the nature of the work and come irrepressibly from it and are necessary to the completion of the work. Most works are most beautiful without ornament . . . Exaggerations will be revenged in human physiology. Clean and vigorous children are jetted and conceived only in those communities where the models of natural forms are public every day. . . . . Great genius and the people of these states must never be demeaned to romances. As soon as histories are properly told there is no more need of romances.

The great poets are also to be known by the absence in them of tricks and by the justification of perfect personal candor. Then folks echo a new cheap joy and a divine voice leaping from their brains: How beautiful is candor! All faults may be forgiven of him who has perfect candor. Henceforth let no man of us lie, for we have seen that openness wins the inner and outer world and that there is no single exception, and that never since our earth gathered itself in a mass have deceit or subterfuge or prevarication attracted its smallest particle or the faintest tinge of a shade— and that through the enveloping wealth and rank of a state or the whole republic of states a sneak or sly person shall be discovered and despised . . . . and that the soul has never been once fooled and never can be fooled . . . . and thrift without the loving nod of the soul is only a fœtid puff . . . . and there never grew up in any of the continents of the globe nor upon any planet or satellite or star, nor upon the asteroids, nor in any part of ethereal space, nor in the midst of density, nor under the fluid wet of the sea, nor in that condition which precedes the birth of babes, nor at any time during the changes of life, nor in that condition that follows what we term death, nor in any stretch of abeyance or action afterward of vitality, nor in any process of formation or reformation anywhere, a being whose instinct hated the truth.

Extreme caution or prudence, the soundest organic health, large hope and comparison and fondness for women and children, large alimentiveness and destructiveness and causality, with a perfect sense of the oneness of nature and the propriety of the same spirit applied to human affairs . . . these are called up of the float of the brain of the world to be parts of the greatest poet from his birth out of his mother's womb and from her birth out of her mother's. Caution seldom goes far enough. It has been thought that the prudent citizen was the citizen who applied himself to solid gains and did well for himself and his family and completed a lawful life without debt or crime. The greatest poet sees and admits these economies as he sees the economies of food and sleep, but has higher notions of prudence than to think he gives much when he gives a few slight attentions at the latch of the gate. The premises of the prudence of life are not the hospitality of it or the ripeness and harvest of it. Beyond the independence of a little sum laid aside for burial-money, and of a few clapboards around and shingles overhead on a lot of American soil owned, and the easy dollars that supply the year's plain clothing and meals, the melancholy prudence of the abandonment of such a great being as a man is to the toss and pallor of years of moneymaking with all their scorching days and icy nights and all their stifling deceits and underhanded dodgings, or infinitessimals of parlors, or shameless stuffing while others starve . . and all the loss of the bloom and odor of the earth and of the flowers and atmosphere and of the sea and of the true taste of the women and men you pass or have to do with in youth or middle age, and the issuing sickness and desperate revolt at the close of a life without elevation or naivete, and the ghastly chatter of a death without serenity or majesty, is the great fraud upon modern civilization and forethought, blotching the surface and system which civilization undeniably drafts, and moistening with tears the immense features it spreads and spreads with such velocity before the reached kisses of the soul . . . Still the right explanation remains to be made about prudence. The prudence of the mere wealth and respectability of the most esteemed life appears too faint for the eye to observe at all when little and large alike drop quietly aside at the thought of the prudence suitable for immortality. What is wisdom that fills the thinness of a year or seventy or eighty years to wisdom spaced out by ages and coming back at a certain time with strong reinforcements and rich presents and the clear faces of wedding-guests as far as you can look in every direction running gaily toward you? Only the soul is of itself . . . . all else has reference to what ensues. All that a person does or thinks is of consequence. Not a move can a man or woman make that affects him or her in a day or a month or any part of the direct lifetime or the hour of death but the same affects him or her onward afterward through the indirect lifetime. The indirect is always as great and real as the direct. The spirit receives from the body just as much as it gives to the body. Not one name of word or deed . . not of venereal sores or discolorations . . not the privacy of the onanist . . not of the putrid veins of gluttons or rumdrinkers . . not peculation or cunning or be-

trayal or murder . . no serpentine poison of those that seduce
women . . not the foolish yielding of women . . not prostitution . . not of any depravity of young men . . not of the attainment of gain by discreditable means . . not any nastiness
of appetite . . not any harshness of officers to men or judges
to prisoners or fathers to sons or sons to fathers or husbands to
wives or bosses to their boys . . not of greedy looks or malignant wishes . . . nor any of the wiles practised by people upon
themselves . . . ever is or ever can be stamped on the programme
but it is duly realized and returned, and that returned in further
performances . . . and they returned again. Nor can the push of
charity or personal force ever be anything else than the profoundest
reason, whether it brings arguments to hand or no. No specification is necessary . . to add or subtract or divide is in vain.
Little or big, learned or unlearned, white or black, legal or illegal,
sick or well, from the first inspiration down the windpipe to the
last expiration out of it, all that a male or female does that is
vigorous and benevolent and clean is so much sure profit to him
or her in the unshakable order of the universe and through the
whole scope of it forever. If the savage or felon is wise it is well
. . . . if the greatest poet or savan is wise it is simply the same
. . if the President or chief justice is wise it is the same . . .
if the young mechanic or farmer is wise it is no more or less . .
if the prostitute is wise it is no more nor less. The interest will
come round . . all will come round. All the best actions of
war and peace . . . all help given to relatives and strangers and
the poor and old and sorrowful and young children and widows and
the sick, and to all shunned persons . . all furtherance of fugitives and of the escape of slaves . . all the self-denial that stood
steady and aloof on wrecks and saw others take the seats of the
boat . . . all offering of substance or life for the good old cause,
or for a friend's sake or opinion's sake . . . all pains of enthusiasts
scoffed at by their neighbors . . all the vast sweet love and
precious suffering of mothers . . . all honest men baffled in strifes
recorded or unrecorded . . . . all the grandeur and good of the few
ancient nations whose fragments of annals we inherit . . and all
the good of the hundreds of far mightier and more ancient nations
unknown to us by name or date or location . . . . all that was ever
manfully begun, whether it succeeded or not . . . . all that has at
any time been well suggested out of the divine heart of man or
by the divinity of his mouth or by the shaping of his great hands
. . and all that is well thought or done this day on any part of
the surface of the globe . . or on any of the wandering stars or
fixed stars by those there as we are here . . or that is henceforth to be well thought or done by you whoever you are, or by

any one—these singly and wholly inured at their time and inure now and will inure always to the identities from which they sprung or shall spring . . . . Did you guess any of them lived only its moment? The world does not so exist . . no parts palpable or impalpable so exist . . no result exists now without being from its long antecedent result, and that from its antecedent, and so backward without the farthest mentionable spot coming a bit nearer the beginning than any other spot. . . . . . . Whatever satisfies the soul is truth. The prudence of the greatest poet answers at last the craving and glut of the soul, is not contemptuous of less ways of prudence if they conform to its ways, puts off nothing, permits no let-up for its own case or any case, has no particular sabbath or judgment-day, divides not the living from the dead or the righteous from the unrighteous, is satisfied with the present, matches every thought or act by its correlative, knows no possible forgiveness or deputed atonement . . knows that the young man who composedly periled his life and lost it has done exceeding well for himself, while the man who has not periled his life and retains it to old age in riches and ease has perhaps achieved nothing for himself worth mentioning . . and that only that person has no great prudence to learn who has learnt to prefer real long-lived things, and favors body and soul the same, and perceives the indirect assuredly following the direct, and what evil or good he does leaping onward and waiting to meet him again—and who in his spirit in any emergency whatever neither hurries or avoids death.

The direct trial of him who would be the greatest poet is today. If he does not flood himself with the immediate age as with vast oceanic tides . . . . . and if he does not attract his own land body and soul to himself and hang on its neck with incomparable love and plunge his semitic muscle into its merits and demerits . . . and if he be not himself the age transfigured . . . . and if to him is not opened the eternity which gives similitude to all periods and locations and processes and animate and inanimate forms, and which is the bond of time, and rises up from its inconceivable vagueness and infiniteness in the swimming shape of today, and is held by the ductile anchors of life, and makes the present spot the passage from what was to what shall be, and commits itself to the representation of this wave of an hour and this one of the sixty beautiful children of the wave—let him merge in the general run and wait his development. . . . . . . Still the final test of poems or any character or work remains. The prescient poet projects himself centuries ahead and judges performer or performance after the changes of time. Does it live through them? Does it still hold on untired? Will the same style and the direction of genius to

similar points be satisfactory now? Has no new discovery in
science or arrival at superior planes of thought and judgment and
behaviour fixed him or his so that either can be looked down
upon? Have the marches of tens and hundreds and thousands of
years made willing detours to the right hand and the left hand for
his sake? Is he beloved long and long after he is buried? Does the
young man think often of him? and the young woman think
often of him? and do the middleaged and the old think of him?

A great poem is for ages and ages in common and for all degrees
and complexions and all departments and sects and for a woman
as much as a man and a man as much as a woman. A great poem
is no finish to a man or woman but rather a beginning. Has any
one fancied he could sit at last under some due authority and rest
satisfied with explanations and realize and be content and full?
To no such terminus does the greatest poet bring . . . he brings
neither cessation or sheltered fatness and ease. The touch of him
tells in action. Whom he takes he takes with firm sure grasp
into live regions previously unattained . . . . thenceforward is no
rest . . . . they see the space and ineffable sheen that turn the
old spots and lights into dead vacuums. The companion of him
beholds the birth and progress of stars and learns one of the
meanings. Now there shall be a man cohered out of tumult
and chaos . . . . the elder encourages the younger and shows him
how . . . they two shall launch off fearlessly together till the new
world fits an orbit for itself and looks unabashed on the lesser
orbits of the stars and sweeps through the ceaseless rings and
shall never be quiet again.

There will soon be no more priests. Their work is done. They
may wait awhile . . perhaps a generation or two . . dropping
off by degrees. A superior breed shall take their place . . . . the
gangs of kosmos and prophets en masse shall take their place. A new
order shall arise and they shall be the priests of man, and every
man shall be his own priest. The churches built under their
umbrage shall be the churches of men and women. Through
the divinity of themselves shall the kosmos and the new breed of
poets be interpreters of men and women and of all events and
things. They shall find their inspiration in real objects today,
symptoms of the past and future. . . . . They shall not deign to
defend immortality or God or the perfection of things or liberty
or the exquisite beauty and reality of the soul. They shall arise in
America and be responded to from the remainder of the earth.

The English language befriends the grand American expression
. . . . it is brawny enough and limber and full enough. On the
tough stock of a race who through all change of circumstances
was never without the idea of political liberty, which is the animus

of all liberty, it has attracted the terms of daintier and gayer and subtler and more elegant tongues. It is the powerful language of resistance . . . it is the dialect of common sense. It is the speech of the proud and melancholy races and of all who aspire. It is the chosen tongue to express growth faith self-esteem freedom justice equality friendliness amplitude prudence decision and courage. It is the medium that shall well nigh express the inexpressible.

No great literature nor any like style of behaviour or oratory or social intercourse or household arrangements or public institutions or the treatment by bosses of employed people, nor executive detail or detail of the army or navy, nor spirit of legislation or courts or police or tuition or architecture or songs or amusements or the costumes of young men, can long elude the jealous and passionate instinct of American standards. Whether or no the sign appears from the mouths of the people, it throbs a live interrogation in every freeman's and freewoman's heart after that which passes by, or this built to remain. Is it uniform with my country? Are its disposals without ignominious distinctions? Is it for the evergrowing communes of brothers and lovers, large, well-united, proud beyond the old models, generous beyond all models? Is it something grown fresh out of the fields or drawn from the sea for use to me today here? I know that what answers for me an American must answer for any individual or nation that serves for a part of my materials. Does this answer? or is it without reference to universal needs? or sprung of the needs of the less developed society of special ranks? or old needs of pleasure overlaid by modern science and forms? Does this acknowledge liberty with audible and absolute acknowledgement, and set slavery at nought for life and death? Will it help breed one goodshaped and wellhung man, and a woman to be his perfect and independent mate? Does it improve manners? Is it for the nursing of the young of the republic? Does it solve readily with the sweet milk of the nipples of the breasts of the mother of many children? Has it too the old ever-fresh forbearance and impartiality? Does it look with the same love on the last born and on those hardening toward stature, and on the errant, and on those who disdain all strength of assault outside of their own?

The poems distilled from other poems will probably pass away. The coward will surely pass away. The expectation of the vital and great can only be satisfied by the demeanor of the vital and great. The swarms of the polished deprecating and reflectors and the polite float off and leave no remembrance. America prepares with composure and goodwill for the visitors that have sent word. It is not intellect that is to be their warrant and welcome. The talented, the artist, the ingenious, the editor, the statesman, the erudite . . they are not unappreciated . . they fall in their place and do their work. The soul of the nation also does its work. No disguise can pass on it . . no disguise can conceal from it. It rejects none, it permits all. Only toward as good as itself and toward the like of itself will it advance half-way. An individual is as superb as a nation when he has the qualities which make a superb nation. The soul of the largest and wealthiest and proudest nation may well go half-way to meet that of its poets. The signs are effectual. There is no fear of mistake. If the one is true the other is true. The proof of a poet is that his country absorbs him as affectionately as he has absorbed it.

1855

Song of Myself [2]

1

I celebrate myself, and sing myself,
And what I assume you shall assume,
For every atom belonging to me as good belongs to you.

I loafe and invite my soul,
I lean and loafe at my ease observing a spear of summer grass.   5

My tongue, every atom of my blood, form'd from this soil, this air,
Born here of parents born here from parents the same, and their
    parents the same,
I, now thirty-seven years old in perfect health begin,
Hoping to cease not till death.

Creeds and schools in abeyance,   10
Retiring back a while sufficed at what they are, but never forgotten,
I harbor for good or bad, I permit to speak at every hazard,
Nature without check with original energy.

2

Houses and rooms are full or perfumes, the shelves are crowded with
    perfumes,
I breathe the fragrance myself and know it and like it,   15
The distillation would intoxicate me also, but I shall not let it.

The atmosphere is not a perfume, it has no taste of the distillation,
    it is odorless,
It is for my mouth forever, I am in love with it,
I will go to the bank by the wood and become undisguised and
    naked,

2. This poem was untitled in the first edition of *Leaves of Grass;* in the second edition it was called "Poem of Walt Whitman, an American"; and finally, in 1881–1882, it became "Song of Myself." The "I" or "myself" in the poem, though sometimes personal, is more often generic and cosmic.

I am mad for it to be in contact with me.   20
The smoke of my own breath,
Echoes, ripples, buzz'd whispers, love-root, silk-thread, crotch and
    vine,
My respiration and inspiration, the beating of my heart, the passing
    of blood and air through my lungs,
The sniff of green leaves and dry leaves, and of the shore and dark-
    color'd sea-rocks, and of hay in the barn,
The sound of the belch'd words of my voice loos'd to the eddies of
    the wind,   25
A few light kisses, a few embraces, a reaching around of arms,
The play of shine and shade on the trees as the supple boughs wag,
The delight alone or in the rush of the streets, or along the fields
    and hill-sides,
The feeling of health, the full-noon trill, the song of me rising from
    bed and meeting the sun.

Have you reckon'd a thousand acres much? have you reckon'd the
    earth much?   30
Have you practis'd so long to learn to read?
Have you felt so proud to get at the meaning of poems?

Stop this day and night with me and you shall possess the origin of
    all poems,
You shall possess the good of the earth and sun, (there are millions
    of suns left,)
You shall no longer take things at second or third hand, nor look
    through the eyes of the dead, nor feed on the spectres in
    books,   35
You shall not look through my eyes either, nor take things from me,
You shall listen to all sides and filter them from your self.

3

I have heard what the talkers were talking, the talk of the beginning
    and the end,
But I do not talk of the beginning or the end.

There was never any more inception than there is now,   40
Nor any more youth or age than there is now,
And will never be any more perfection than there is now,
Nor any more heaven or hell than there is now.

Urge and urge and urge,
Always the procreant urge of the world.   45

Out of the dimness opposite equals advance, always substance and
    increase, always sex,
Always a knit of identity, always distinction, always a breed of life.

To elaborate is no avail, learn'd and unlearn'd feel that it is so.

Sure as the most certain sure, plumb in the uprights, well
    entretied,[3] braced in the beams,
Stout as a horse, affectionate, haughty, electrical,   50
I and this mystery here we stand.

Clear and sweet is my soul, and clear and sweet is all that is not my
    soul.

Lack one lacks both, and the unseen is proved by the seen,
Till that becomes unseen and receives proof in its turn.

Showing the best and dividing it from the worst age vexes age,   55
Knowing the perfect fitness and equanimity of things, while they
    discuss I am silent, and go bathe and admire myself.

Welcome is every organ and attribute of me, and of any man hearty
    and clean,
Not an inch nor a particle of an inch is vile, and none shall be less
    familiar than the rest.

I am satisfied—I see, dance, laugh, sing;
As the hugging and loving bed-fellow [4] sleeps at my side through the
    night, and withdraws at the peep of the day with stealthy
    tread,   60
Leaving me baskets cover'd with white towels swelling the house
    with their plenty,
Shall I postpone my acceptation and realization and scream at my
    eyes,
That they turn from gazing after and down the road,
And forthwith cipher and show me to a cent,
Exactly the value of one and exactly the value of two, and which is
    ahead?   65

4

Trippers and askers surround me,
People I meet, the effect upon me of my early life or the ward
    and city I live in, or the nation,
The latest dates, discoveries, inventions, societies, authors old and
    new,
My dinner, dress, associates, looks, compliments, dues,
The real or fancied indifference of some man or woman I love,   70
The sickness of one of my folks or of myself, or ill-doing or loss or
    lack of money, or depressions or exaltations;

3. Carpenter's term for "cross-braced,"   4. In 1855 read, "As God comes a
as between two joists.   loving bed-fellow."

Battles, the horrors of fratricidal war, the fever of doubtful news,
 the fitful events;
These come to me days and night and go from me again,
But they are not the Me myself.

Apart from the pulling and hauling stands what I am,   75
Stands amused, complacent, compassionating, idle, unitary,
Looks down, is erect, or bends an arm on an impalpable certain
 rest,
Looking with side-curved head curious what will come next,
Both in and out of the game and watching and wondering at it.

Backward I see in my own days where I sweated through fog with
 linguists and contenders,
I have no mockings or arguments, I witness and wait.   80

5

I believe in you my soul,[5] the other I am must not abase itself to
 you,
And you must not be abased to the other.

Loafe with me on the grass, loose the stop from your throat,
Not words, not music or rhyme I want, not custom or lecture, not
 even the best,   85
Only the lull I like, the hum of your valvèd voice.

I mind how once we lay such a transparent summer morning,
How you settled your head athwart my hips and gently turn'd
 over upon me,
And parted the shirt from my bosom-bone, and plunged your
 tongue to my bare-stript heart,
And reach'd till you felt my beard, and reach'd till you held my
 feet.   90

Swiftly arose and spread around me the peace and knowledge
 that pass all the argument of the earth,
And I know that the hand of God is the promise of my own,
And I know that the spirit of God is the brother of my own,
And that all the men ever born are also my brothers, and the
 women my sisters and lovers,
And that a kelson of the creation is love,   95
And limitless are leaves stiff or drooping in the fields,
And brown ants in the little wells beneath them,
And mossy scabs of the worm fence, heap'd stones, elder, mullein
 and poke-weed.

---

5. In medieval poetry the debate or dialogue between the body and soul was a conventional device, but it lacked the erotic language employed here.

6

A child said *What is the grass?* fetching it to me with full hands;
How could I answer the child? I do not know what it is any more
    than he.   100

I guess it must be the flag of my disposition, out of hopeful green
    stuff woven.

Or I guess it is the handkerchief of the Lord,
A scented gift and remembrancer designedly dropt,
Bearing the owner's name someway in the corners, that we may
    see and remark, and say *Whose?*

Or I guess the grass is itself a child, the produced babe of the
    vegetation.   105

Or I guess it is a uniform hieroglyphic,
And it means, Sprouting alike in broad zones and narrow zones,
Growing among black folks as among white,
Kanuck, Tuckahoe, Congressman, Cuff,[6] I give them the same, I
    receive them the same.

And now it seems to me the beautiful uncut hair of graves.   110

Tenderly will I use you curling grass,
It may be you transpire from the breasts of young men,
It may be if I had known them I would have loved them,
It may be you are from old people, or from offspring taken soon
    out of their mothers' laps,
And here you are the mothers' laps.   115

This grass is very dark to be from the white heads of old mothers,
Darker than the colorless beards of old men,
Dark to come from under the faint red roofs of mouths.

O I perceive after all so many uttering tongues,
And I perceive they do not come from the roofs of mouths for
    nothing.   120

I wish I could translate the hints about the dead young men and
    women,
And the hints about old men and mothers, and the offspring
    taken soon out of their laps.

What do you think has become of the young and old men?
And what do you think has become of the women and children?

6. "Kanuck" denotes a French Cana- region and ate tuckahoe, a fungus;
dian; "Tuckahoe," a Virginian who and "Cuff," a Negro.
lived on poor lands in the tidewater

They are alive and well somewhere,   125
The smallest sprout shows there is really no death,
And if ever there was it led forward life, and does not wait at the
     end to arrest it,
And ceas'd the moment life appear'd.

All goes onward and outward, nothing collapses,
And to die is different from what any one supposed, and luckier.   130

7

Has any one supposed it lucky to be born?
I hasten to inform him or her it is just as lucky to die, and I
     know it.

I pass death with the dying and birth with the new-wash'd babe,
     and am not contain'd between my hat and boots,
And peruse manifold objects, no two alike and every one good,
The earth good and the stars good, and their adjuncts all good.   135

I am not an earth nor an adjunct of an earth,
I am the mate and companion of people, all just as immortal
     and fathomless as myself,
(They do not know how immortal, but I know.)

Every kind for itself and its own, for me mine male and female,
For me those that have been boys and that love women,   140
For me the man that is proud and feels how it stings to be
     slighted,
For me the sweet-heart and the old maid, for me mothers and the
     mothers of mothers,
For me lips that have smiled, eyes that have shed tears,
For me children and the begetters of children.

Undrape! you are not guilty to me, nor stale nor discarded,   145
I see through the broadcloth and gingham whether or no,
And am around, tenacious, acquisitive, tireless, and cannot be
     shaken away.

8

The little one sleeps in its cradle,
I lift the gauze and look a long time, and silently brush away flies
     with my hand.

The youngster and the red-faced girl turn aside up the bushy
     hill,
I peeringly view them from the top.   150

The suicide sprawls on the bloody floor of the bedroom,
I witness the corpse with its dabbled hair, I note where the pistol
     has fallen.

The blab of the pave, tires of carts, sluff of boot-soles, talk of the
    promenaders,
The heavy omnibus, the driver with his interrogating thumb, the
    clank of the shod horses on the granite floor,   155
The snow-sleighs, clinking, shouted jokes, pelts of snow-balls,
The hurrahs for popular favorites, the fury of rous'd mobs,
The flap of the curtain'd litter, a sick man inside borne to the
    hospital,
The meeting of enemies, the sudden oath, the blows and fall,
The excited crowd, the policeman with his star quickly working
    his passage to the centre of the crowd,   160
The impassive stones that receive and return so many echoes,
What groans of over-fed or half-starv'd who fall sunstruck or in fits,
What exclamations of women taken suddenly who hurry home
    and give birth to babes,
What living and buried speech is always vibrating here, what howls
    restrain'd by decorum,
Arrests of criminals, slights, adulterous offers made, acceptances,
    rejections with convex lips,   165
I mind them or the show or resonance of them—I come and I
    depart.

                                9
The big doors of the country barn stand open and ready,
The dried grass of the harvest-time loads the slow-drawn wagon,
The clear light plays on the brown gray and green intertinged,
The armfuls are pack'd to the sagging mow.   170

I am there, I help, I came stretch'd atop of the load,
I felt its soft jolts, one leg reclined on the other,
I jump from the cross-beams and seize the clover and timothy,
And roll head over heels and tangle my hair full of wisps.

                               10
Alone far in the wilds and mountains I hunt,   175
Wandering amazed at my own lightness and glee,
In the late afternoon choosing a safe spot to pass the night,
Kindling a fire and broiling the fresh-kill'd game,
Falling asleep on the gather'd leaves with my dog and gun by my
    side.

The Yankee clipper is under her sky-sails, she cuts the sparkle and
    scud,   180
My eyes settle the land, I bend at her prow or shout joyously from
    the deck.

The boatmen and clam-diggers arose early and stopt for me,

I tuck'd my trowser-ends in my boots and went and had a good
time;
You should have been with us that day round the chowder-kettle.

I saw the marriage of the trapper in the open air in the far west,
the bride was a red girl,   185
Her father and his friends sat near cross-legged and dumbly smoking, they had moccasins to their feet and large thick blankets hanging from their shoulders,
On a bank lounged the trapper, he was drest mostly in skins, his
luxuriant beard and curls protected his neck, he held his
bride by the hand,
She had long eyelashes, her head was bare, her coarse straight
locks descended upon her voluptuous limbs and reach'd to
her feet.

The runaway slave came to my house and stopt outside,
I heard his motions crackling the twigs of the woodpile,   190
Through the swung half-door of the kitchen I saw him limpsy and
weak,
And went where he sat on a log and led him in and assured him,
And brought water and fill'd a tub for his sweated body and
bruis'd feet,
And gave him a room that enter'd from my own, and gave him
some coarse clean clothes,
And remember perfectly well his revolving eyes and his awk-
wardness,   195
And remember putting plasters on the galls of his neck and
ankles;
He staid with me a week before he was recuperated and pass'd
north,
I had him sit next to me at table, my fire-lock lean'd in the corner.

11

Twenty-eight young men bathe by the shore,
Twenty-eight young men and all so friendly;   200
Twenty-eight years of womanly life and all so lonesome.

She owns the fine house by the rise of the bank,
She hides handsome and richly drest aft the blinds of the window.

Which of the young men does she like the best?
Ah the homeliest of them is beautiful to her.   205

Where are you off to, lady? for I see you,
You splash in the water there, yet stay stock still in your room.

Dancing and laughing along the beach came the twenty-ninth
bather,

The rest did not see her, but she saw them and loved them.

The beards of the young men glisten'd with wet, it ran from their
    long hair,   210
Little streams pass'd all over their bodies.

An unseen hand also pass'd over their bodies,
It descended trembling from their temples and ribs.

The young men float on their backs, their white bellies bulge to
    the sun, they do not ask who seizes fast to them,
They do not know who puffs and declines with pendant and bend-
    ing arch,   215
They do not think whom they souse with spray.

12

The butcher-boy puts off his killing-clothes, or sharpens his knife
    at the stall in the market,
I loiter enjoying his repartee and his shuffle [7] and break-down.

Blacksmiths with grimed and hairy chests environ the anvil,
Each has his main-sledge, they are all out, there is a great heat in
    the fire.   220

From the cinder-strew'd threshold I follow their movements,
The lithe sheer of their waists plays even with their massive arms,
Overhand the hammers swing, overhand so slow, overhand so sure,
They do not hasten, each man hits in his place.

13

The negro holds firmly the reins of his four horses, the block
    swags underneath on its tied-over chain,   225
The negro that drives the long dray of the stone-yard, steady and
    tall he stands pois'd on one leg on the string-piece,
His blue shirt exposes his ample neck and breast and loosens over
    his hip-band,
His glance is calm and commanding, he tosses the slouch of his
    hat away from his forehead,
The sun falls on his crispy hair and mustache, falls on the black
    of his polish'd and perfect limbs.

I behold the picturesque giant and love him, and I do not stop
    there,   230
I go with the team also.

In me the caresser of life wherever moving, backward as well as
    forward sluing,

---

7. A lazy dance, with sliding and tapping of the feet; a break-down is a rollicking,
noisy dance.

To niches aside and junior bending, not a person or object missing,
Absorbing all to myself and for this song.

Oxen that rattle the yoke and chain or halt in the leafy shade,
what is that you express in your eyes?   235
It seems to me more than all the print I have read in my life.

My tread scares the wood-drake and wood-duck on my distant
and day-long ramble,
They rise together, they slowly circle around.

I believe in those wing'd purposes,
And acknowledge red, yellow, white, playing within me,   240
And consider green and violet and the tufted crown intentional,
And do not call the tortoise unworthy because she is not some-
thing else,   ,
And the jay in the woods never studied the gamut, yet trills
pretty well to me,
And the look of the bay mare shames silliness out of me.

14

The wild gander leads his flock through the cool night,   245
Ya-honk he says, and sounds it down to me like an invitation,
The pert may suppose it meaningless, but I listening close,
Find its purpose and place up there toward the wintry sky.

The sharp-hoof'd moose of the north, the cat on the house-sill,
the chickadee, the prairie-dog,
The litter of the grunting sow as they tug at her teats,   250
The brood of the turkey-hen and she with her half-spread wings,
I see in them and myself the same old law.

The press of my foot to the earth springs a hundred affections,
They scorn the best I can do to relate them.

I am enamour'd of growing out-doors,   255
Of men that live among cattle or taste of the ocean or woods,
Of the builders and steerers of ships and the wielders of axes and
mauls, and the drivers of horses,
I can eat and sleep with them week in and week out.

What is commonest, cheapest, nearest, easiest, is Me,
Me going in for my chances, spending for vast returns,   260
Adorning myself to bestow myself on the first that will take me,
Not asking the sky to come down to my good will,
Scattering it freely forever.

15

The pure contralto sings in the organ loft,

The carpenter dresses his plank, the tongue of his foreplane whistles its wild ascending lisp,   265
The married and unmarried children ride home to their Thanksgiving dinner,
The pilot seizes the king-pin,[8] he heaves down with a strong arm,
The mate stands braced in the whale-boat, lance and harpoon are ready,
The duck-shooter walks by silent and cautious stretches,
The deacons are ordain'd with cross'd hands at the altar,   270
The spinning-girl retreats and advances to the hum of the big wheel,
The farmer stops by the bars as he walks on a First-day[9] loafe and looks at the oats and rye,
The lunatic is carried at last to the asylum a confirm'd case,
(He will never sleep any more as he did in the cot in his mother's bedroom;)
The jour printer[1] with gray head and gaunt jaws works at his case,   275
He turns his quid of tobacco while his eyes blurr with the manuscript;
The malform'd limbs are tied to the surgeon's table,
What is removed drops horribly in a pail;
The quadroon girl is sold at the auction-stand, the drunkard nods by the bar-room stove,
The machinist rolls up his sleeves, the policeman travels his beat, the gate-keeper marks who pass,   280
The young fellow drives the express-wagon, (I love him, though I do not know him;)
The half-breed straps on his light boots to compete in the race,
The western turkey-shooting draws old and young, some lean on their rifles, some sit on logs,
Out from the crowd steps the marksman, takes his position, levels his piece;
The groups of newly-come immigrants cover the wharf or levee,   285
As the woolly-pates hoe in the sugar-field, the overseer views them from his saddle,
The bugle calls in the ball-room, the gentlemen run for their partners, the dancers bow to each other,
The youth lies awake in the cedar-roof'd garret and harks to the musical rain,
The Wolverine[2] sets traps on the creek that helps fill the Huron,

8. An extended spoke of the wheel.
9. Quaker designation for Sunday.
1. Colloquial for journeyman printer, *i.e.*, one who has learned his trade but is not yet a master printer. His "case" is the box that holds his type.
2. Native of Michigan.

The squaw wrapt in her yellow-hemm'd cloth is offering moccasins and bead-bags for sale,   290
The connoisseur peers along the exhibition-gallery with half-shut
eyes bent sideways,
As the deck-hands make fast the steamboat the plank is thrown
for the shore-going passengers,
The young sister holds out the skein while the elder sister winds
it off in a ball, and stops now and then for the knots,
The one-year wife is recovering and happy having a week ago
borne her first child,
The clean-hair'd Yankee girl works with her sewing-machine or in
the factory or mill,   295
The paving-man leans on his two-handed rammer, the reporter's
lead flies swiftly over the note-book, the sign-painter is let-
tering with blue and gold,
The canal boy trots on the tow-path, the book-keeper counts at
his desk, the shoemaker waxes his thread,
The conductor beats time for the band and all the performers
follow him,
The child is baptized, the convert is making his first professions,
The regatta is spread on the bay, the race is begun, (how the
white sails sparkle!)   300
The drover watching his drove sings out to them that would stray,
The pedler sweats with his pack on his back, (the purchaser hig-
gling about the odd cent;)
The bride unrumples her white dress, the minute-hand of the
clock moves slowly,
The opium-eater reclines with rigid head and just-open'd lips,
The prostitute draggles her shawl, her bonnet bobs on her tipsy
and pimpled neck,   305
The crowd laugh at her blackguard oaths, the men jeer and wink
to each other,
(Miserable! I do not laugh at your oaths nor jeer you;)
The President holding a cabinet council is surrounded by the
great Secretaries,
On the piazza walk three matrons stately and friendly with twined
arms,
The crew of the fish-smack pack repeated layers of halibut in the
hold,   310
The Missourian crosses the plains toting his wares and his cattle,
As the fare-collector goes through the train he gives notice by the
jingling of loose change,
The floor-men are laying the floor, the tinners are tinning the
roof, the masons are calling for mortar,

In single file each shouldering his hod pass onward the laborers;
Seasons pursuing each other the indescribable crowd is gather'd,
    it is the fourth of Seventh-month,[3] (what salutes of cannon
    and small arms!)   315
Seasons pursuing each other the plougher ploughs, the mower
    mows, and the winter-grain falls in the ground;
Off on the lakes the pike-fisher watches and waits by the hole in
    the frozen surface,
The stumps stand thick round the clearing, the squatter strikes
    deep with his axe,
Flatboatmen make fast towards dusk near the cotton-wood or pe-
    can-trees,
Coon-seekers go through the regions of the Red river or through
    those drain'd by the Tennessee, or through those of the
    Arkansas,   320
Torches shine in the dark that hangs on the Chattahooche or Alta-
    mahaw,
Patriarchs sit at supper with sons and grandsons and great-grand-
    sons around them,
In walls of adobie, in canvas tents, rest hunters and trappers
    after their day's sport,
The city sleeps and the country sleeps,
The living sleep for their time, the dead sleep for their time,   325
The old husband sleeps by his wife and the young husband sleeps
    by his wife;
And these tend inward to me, and I tend outward to them,
And such as it is to be of these more or less I am,
And of these one and all I weave the song of myself.

16

I am of old and young, of the foolish as much as the wise,   330
Regardless of others, ever regardful of others,
Maternal as well as paternal, a child as well as a man,
Stuff'd with the stuff that is coarse and stuff'd with the stuff that
    is fine,
One of the Nation of many nations, the smallest the same and
    the largest the same,
A Southerner soon as a Northerner, a planter nonchalant and hos-
    pitable down by the Oconee I live,   335
A Yankee bound my own way ready for trade, my joints the
    limberest joints on earth and the sternest joints on earth,
A Kentuckian walking the vale of the Elkhorn in my deer-skin
    leggings, a Louisianian or Georgian,

3. Fourth of July. Such Quaker designations for months and days of the week
avoided pagan implications.

A boatman over lakes or bays or along coasts, a Hoosier, Badger,
Buckeye; [4]
At home on Kanadian snow-shoes or up in the bush, or with
fishermen off Newfoundland,
At home in the fleet of ice-boats, sailing with the rest and tack-
ing,
At home on the hills of Vermont or in the woods of Maine, or 340
the Texan ranch,
Comrade of Californians, comrade of free North-Westerners, (lov-
ing their big proportions,)
Comrade of raftsmen and coalmen, comrade of all who shake
hands and welcome to drink and meat,
A learner with the simplest, a teacher of the thoughtfullest,
A novice beginning yet experient of myriads of seasons, 345
Of every hue and caste am I, of every rank and religion,
A farmer, mechanic, artist, gentleman, sailor, quaker,
Prisoner, fancy-man, rowdy, lawyer, physician, priest.

I resist any thing better than my own diversity,
Breathe the air but leave plenty after me, 350
And am not stuck up, and am in my place.

(The moth and the fish-eggs are in their place,
The bright suns I see and the dark suns I cannot see are in their
place,
The palpable is in its place and the impalpable is in its place.)

17

These are really the thoughts of all men in all ages and lands, they
are not original with me,
If they are not yours as much as mine they are nothing, or next to 355
nothing,
If they are not the riddle and the untying of the riddle they are
nothing,
If they are not just as close as they are distant they are nothing.

This is the grass that grows wherever the land is and the water is,
This is the common air that bathes the globe. 360

18

With music strong I come, with my cornets and my drums,
I play not marches for accepted victors only, I play marches for
conquer'd and slain persons.

Have you heard that it was good to gain the day?
I also say it is good to fall, battles are lost in the same spirit in
which they are won.

4. Nicknames for people from Indiana, Wisconsin, and Ohio, respectively.

I beat and pound for the dead, 365
I blow through my embouchures [5] my loudest and gayest for them.

Vivas to those who have fail'd!
And to those whose war-vessels sank in the sea!
And to those themselves who sank in the sea!
And to all generals that lost engagements, and all overcome
    heroes!
And the numberless unknown heroes equal to the greatest heroes
    known! 371

19

This is the meal equally set, this the meat for natural hunger,
It is for the wicked just the same as the righteous, I make appoint-
    ments with all,
I will not have a single person slighted or left away,
The kept-woman, sponger, thief, are hereby invited, 375
The heavy-lipp'd slave is invited, the venerealee is invited;
There shall be no difference between them and the rest.

This is the press of a bashful hand, this the float and odor of hair,
This the touch of my lips to yours, this the murmur of yearning,
This the far-off depth and height reflecting my own face, 380
This the thoughtful merge of myself, and the outlet again.

Do you guess I have some intricate purpose?
Well I have, for the Fourth-month showers have, and the mica on
    the side of a rock has.

Do you take it I would astonish?
Does the daylight astonish? does the early redstart twittering
    through the woods? 385
Do I astonish more than they?

This hour I tell things in confidence,
I might not tell everybody, but I will tell you.

20

Who goes there? hankering, gross, mystical, nude;
How is it I extract strength from the beef I eat? 390

What is a man anyhow? what am I? what are you?

All I mark as my own you shall offset it with your own,
Else it were time lost listening to me.

I do not snivel that snivel the world over,
That months are vacuums and the ground but wallow and filth. 395

5. Mouthpieces of musical instruments.

Whimpering and truckling fold with powders [6] for invalids, conformity goes to the fourth-remov'd,
I wear my hat as I please indoors or out.

Why should I pray? why should I venerate and be ceremonious?

Having pried through the strata, analyzed to a hair, counsel'd with doctors and calculated close,
I find no sweeter fat than sticks to my own bones.   400

In all people I see myself, none more and not one a barley-corn less,
And the good or bad I say of myself I say of them.

I know I am solid and sound,
To me the converging objects of the universe perpetually flow,
All are written to me, and I must get what the writing means.   405

I know I am deathless,
I know this orbit of mine cannot be swept by a carpenter's compass,
I know I shall not pass like a child's carlacue [7] cut with a burnt stick at night.

I know I am august,
I do not trouble my spirit to vindicate itself or be understood,   410
I see that the elementary laws never apologize,
(I reckon I behave no prouder than the level I plant my house by, after all.)

I exist as I am, that is enough,
If no other in the world be aware I sit content,
And if each and all be aware I sit content.   415

One world is aware and by far the largest to me, and that is myself,
And whether I come to my own to-day or in ten thousand or ten million years,
I can cheerfully take it now, or with equal cheerfulness I can wait.

My foothold is tenon'd and mortis'd in granite, [8]
I laugh at what you call dissolution,   420
And I know the amplitude of time.

21

I am the poet of the Body and I am the poet of the Soul,
The pleasures of heaven are with me and the pains of hell are with me,

6. Each dose of powdered medicine was separately wrapped.
7. *Cf.* "curlicue."
8. The tenon-and-mortise joint is noted for strength.

The first I graft and increase upon myself, the latter I translate
    into a new tongue.

I am the poet of the woman the same as the man,   425
And I say it is as great to be a woman as to be a man,
And I say there is nothing greater than the mother of men.

I chant the chant of dilation or pride,
We have had ducking and deprecating about enough,
I show that size is only development.   430

Have you outstript the rest? are you the President?
It is a trifle, they will more than arrive there every one, and still
    pass on.

I am he that walks with the tender and growing night,
I call to the earth and sea half-held by the night.

Press close bare-bosom'd night—press close magnetic nourishing
    night!   435
Night of south winds—night of the large few stars!
Still nodding night—mad naked summer night.

Smile O voluptuous cool-breath'd earth!
Earth of the slumbering and liquid trees!
Earth of departed sunset—earth of the mountains misty-topt!   440
Earth of the vitreous pour of the full moon just tinged with blue!
Earth of shine and dark mottling the tide of the river!
Earth of the limpid gray of clouds brighter and clearer for my sake!
Far-swooping elbow'd earth—rich apple-blossom'd earth!
Smile, for your lover comes.   445

Prodigal, you have given me love—therefore I to you give love!
O unspeakable passionate love.

22

You sea! I resign myself to you also—I guess what you mean,
I behold from the beach your crooked inviting fingers,
I believe you refuse to go back without feeling of me,   450
We must have a turn together, I undress, hurry me out of sight
    of the land,
Cushion me soft, rock me in billowy drowse,
Dash me with amorous wet, I can repay you.

Sea of stretch'd ground-swells,
Sea breathing broad and convulsive breaths,   455
Sea of the brine of life and of unshovell'd yet always-ready graves,
Howler and scooper of storms, capricious and dainty sea,
I am integral with you, I too am of one phase and of all phases.

Partaker of influx and efflux I, extoller of hate and conciliation,
Extoller of amies and those that sleep in each others' arms.   460

I am he attesting sympathy,
(Shall I make my list of things in the house and skip the house
    that supports them?)

I am not the poet of goodness only, I do not decline to be the
    poet of wickedness also.

What blurt is this about virtue and about vice?
Evil propels me and reform of evil propels me, I stand indifferent,
My gait is no fault-finder's or rejecter's gait,   466
I moisten the roots of all that has grown.

Did you fear some scrofula out of the unflagging pregnancy?
Did you guess the celestial laws are yet to be work'd over and
    rectified?

I find one side a balance and the antipodal side a balance,   470
Soft doctrine as steady help as stable doctrine,
Thoughts and deeds of the present our rouse and early start.

This minute that comes to me over the past decillions,
There is no better than it and now.

What behaved well in the past or behaves well to-day is not such
    a wonder,   475
The wonder is always and always how there can be a mean man
    or an infidel.

23

Endless unfolding of words of ages!
And mine a word of the modern, the word En-Masse.

A word of the faith that never balks,
Here or henceforward it is all the same to me, I accept Time ab-
    solutely.   480

It alone is without flaw, it alone rounds and completes all,
That mystic baffling wonder alone completes all.

I accept Reality and dare not question it,
Materialism first and last imbuing.

Hurrah for positive science! long live exact demonstration!   485
Fetch stonecrop [9] mixt with cedar and branches of lilac,
This is the lexicographer, this the chemist, this made a grammar
    of the old cartouches,

9. A hardy serum then esteemed for healing: *cf.* "cedar" and "lilac" following.

These mariners put the ship through dangerous unknown seas,
This is the geologist, this works with the scalpel, and this is a
mathematician.

Gentlemen, to you the first honors always! 490
Your facts are useful, and yet they are not my dwelling,
I but enter by them to an area of my dwelling.

Less the reminders of properties told my words,
And more the reminders they of life untold, and of freedom and
extrication,
And make short account of neuters and geldings, and favor men
and women fully equipt, 495
And beat the gong of revolt, and stop with fugitives and them
that plot and conspire.

24

Walt Whitman, a kosmos,[1] of Manhattan the son,
Turbulent, fleshly, sensual, eating, drinking and breeding,
No sentimentalist, no stander above men and women or apart
from them,
No more modest than immodest. 500

Unscrew the locks from the doors!
Unscrew the doors themselves from their jambs!

Whoever degrades another degrades me,
And whatever is done or said returns at last to me.

Through me the afflatus[2] surging and surging, through me the
current and index. 505

I speak the pass-word primeval, I give the sign of democracy,
By God! I will accept nothing which all cannot have their counterpart of on the same terms.

Through me many long dumb voices,
Voices of the interminable generations of prisoners and slaves,
Voices of the diseas'd and despairing and of thieves and dwarfs, 510
Voices of cycles of preparation and accretion,
And of the threads that connect the stars, and of wombs and of
the father-stuff,
And of the rights of them the others are down upon,
Of the deform'd, trivial, flat, foolish, despised,
Fog in the air, beetles rolling balls of dung. 515

Through me forbidden voices,
Voices of sexes and lusts, voices veil'd and I remove the veil,
Voices indecent by me clarified and transfigur'd.

---

1. German transcendental idealism,
which influenced Whitman, stressed
the relations between the individual
microcosm and the universal macrocosm.
2. Latin, a string wind or blast, figuratively "inspiration."

I do not press my fingers across my mouth,
I keep as delicate around the bowels as around the head and heart,
Copulation is no more rank to me than death is.   521

I believe in the flesh and the appetites,
Seeing, hearing, feeling, are miracles, and each part and tag of me
    is a miracle.

Divine am I inside and out, and I make holy whatever I touch or
    am touch'd from,
The scent of these arm-pits aroma finer than prayer,   525
This head more than churches, bibles, and all the creeds.

If I worship one thing more than another it shall be the spread
    of my own body, or any part of it,
Translucent mould of me it shall be you!
Shaded ledges and rests it shall be you!
Firm masculine colter [3] it shall be you!   530
Whatever goes to the tilth [4] of me it shall be you!
You my rich blood! your milky stream pale strippings of my life!
Breast that presses against other breasts it shall be you!
My brain it shall be your occult convolutions!
Root of wash'd sweet-flag! timorous pond-snipe! nest of guarded
    duplicate eggs! it shall be you!   535
Mix'd tussled hay of head, beard, brawn, it shall be you!
Trickling sap of maple, fibre of manly wheat, it shall be you!
Suns so generous it shall be you!
Vapors lighting and shading my face it shall be you!
You sweaty brooks and dews it shall be you!   540
Winds whose soft-tickling genitals rub against me it shall be you!
Broad muscular fields, branches of live oak, loving lounger in my
    winding paths, it shall be you!
Hands I have taken, face I have kiss'd, mortal I have ever touch'd,
    it shall be you.

I dote on myself, there is that lot of me and all so luscious,
Each moment and whatever happens thrills me with joy,   545
I cannot tell how my ankles bend, nor whence the cause of my
    faintest wish,
Nor the cause of the friendship I emit, nor the cause of the friend-
    ship I take again.

That I walk up my stoop, I pause to consider if it really be,

---

3. Sharp blade attached to a plow to cut the ground in advance of the plow-share.

4. Act of cultivation or tillage of the soil.

A morning-glory at my window satisfies me more than the metaphysics of books.

To behold the day-break!   550
The little light fades the immense and diaphanous shadows,
The air tastes good to my palate.

Hefts of the moving world at innocent gambols silently rising,
freshly exuding,
Scooting obliquely high and low.

Something I cannot see puts upward libidinous prongs,   555
Seas of bright juice suffuse heaven.

The earth by the sky staid with, the daily close of their junction,
The heav'd challenge from the east that moment over my head,
The mocking taunt, See then whether you shall be master!

25

Dazzling and tremendous how quick the sun-rise would kill me,   560
If I could not now and always send sun-rise out of me.

We also ascend dazzling and tremendous as the sun,
We found our own O my soul in the calm and cool of the day-
break.

My voice goes after what my eyes cannot reach,
With the twirl of my tongue I encompass worlds and volumes of
worlds.   565

Speech is the twin of my vision, it is unequal to measure itself,
It provokes me forever, it says sarcastically,
Walt you contain enough, why don't you let it out then?

Come now I will not be tantalized, you conceive too much of
articulation,
Do you not know O speech how the buds beneath you are folded?
Waiting in gloom, protected by frost,   571
The dirt receding before my prophetical screams,
I underlying causes to balance them at last,
My knowledge my live parts, it keeping tally with the meaning
of all things,
Happiness, (which whoever hears me let him or her set out in
search of this day.)   575

My final merit I refuse you, I refuse putting from me what I really
am,
Encompass worlds, but never try to encompass me,
I crowd your sleekest and best by simply looking toward you.

Writing and talk do not prove me,
I carry the plenum [5] of proof and every thing else in my face,   580
With the hush of my lips, I wholly confound the skeptic.

26

Now I will do nothing but listen,
To accrue what I hear into this song, to let sounds contribute
     toward it.

I hear bravuras of birds, bustle of growing wheat, gossip of flames,
     clack of sticks cooking my meals.
I hear the sound I love, the sound of the human voice,   585
I hear all sounds running together, combined, fused or following,
Sounds of the city and sounds out of the city, sounds of the day
     and night,
Talkative young ones to those that like them, the loud laugh of
     work-people at their meals,
The angry base of disjointed friendship, the faint tones of the sick,
The judge with hands tight to the desk, his pallid lips pronounc-
     ing a death-sentence,
The heave'e'yo of stevedores unlading ships by the wharves, the   590
     refrain of the anchor-lifters,
The ring of alarm-bells, the cry of fire, the whirr of swift-streak-
     ing engines and hose-carts with premonitory tinkles and
     color'd lights,
The steam-whistle, the solid roll of the train of approaching cars,
The slow march play'd at the head of the association marching
     two and two,
(They go to guard some corpse, the flag-tops are draped with black
     muslin.)   595

I hear the violoncello, ('tis the young man's heart's complaint,)
I hear the key'd cornet, it glides quickly in through my ears,
It shakes mad-sweet pangs through my belly and breast.

I hear the chorus, it is a grand opera,
Ah this indeed is music—this suits me.   600

A tenor large and fresh as the creation fills me,
The orbic flex of his mouth is pouring and filling me full.

I hear the train'd soprano (what work with hers is this?)
The orchestra whirls me wider than Uranus [6] flies.
It wrenches such ardors from me I did not know I possess'd them,
It sails me, I dab with bare feet, they are lick'd by the indolent
     waves,   606

5. Fullness.
6. The seventh major planet; in Greek mythology the personification of Heaven.

I am cut by bitter and angry hail, I lose my breath,
Steep'd amid honey'd morphine, my windpipe throttled in fakes [7]
    of death,
At length let up again to feel the puzzle of puzzles,
And that we call Being.   610

27

To be in any form, what is that?
(Round and round we go, all of us, and ever come back thither,)
If nothing lay more develop'd the quahaug [8] in its callous shell
    were enough.

Mine is no callous shell,
I have instant conductors all over me whether I pass or stop,   615
They seize every object and lead it harmlessly through me.

I merely stir, press, feel with my fingers, and am happy,
To touch my person to some one else's is about as much as I can
    stand.

28

Is this then a touch? quivering me to a new identity,
Flames and ether making a rush for my veins,   620
Treacherous tip of me reaching and crowding to help them,
My flesh and blood playing out lightning to strike what is hardly
    different from myself,
On all sides prurient provokers stiffening my limbs,
Straining the udder of my heart for its withheld drip,
Behaving licentious toward me, taking no denial,   625
Depriving me of my best as for a purpose,
Unbuttoning my clothes, holding me by the bare waist,
Deluding my confusion with the calm of the sunlight and pas-
    ture-fields,
Immodestly sliding the fellow-senses away,
They bribed to swap off with touch and go and graze at the edges
    of me,   630
No consideration, no regard for my draining strength or my anger,
Fetching the rest of the herd around to enjoy them a while,
Then all uniting to stand on a headland and worry me.
The sentries desert every other part of me,
They have left me helpless to a red marauder,   635
They all come to the headland to witness and assist against me.

I am given up by traitors,
I talk wildly, I have lost my wits, I and nobody else am the
    greatest traitor,

---

7. A nautical term for the windings of   8. An edible Atlantic-coast clam.
a coiled cable or hawser.

I went myself first to the headland, my own hands carried me there.

You villain touch! what are you doing? my breath is tight in its throat,
Unclench your floodgates, you are too much for me.   640

29

Blind loving wrestling touch, sheath'd hooded sharp-tooth'd touch!
Did it make you ache so, leaving me?

Parting track'd by arriving, perpetual payment of perpetual loan,
Rich showering rain, and recompense richer afterward.   645

Sprouts take and accumulate, stand by the curb prolific and vital,
Landscapes projected masculine, full-sized and golden.

30

All truths wait in all things,
They neither hasten their own delivery nor resist it,
They do not need the obstetric forceps of the surgeon,   650
The insignificant is as big to me as any,
(What is less or more than a touch?)

Logic and sermons never convince,
The damp of the night drives deeper into my soul.

(Only what proves itself to every man and woman is so,   655
Only what nobody denies is so.)

A minute and a drop of me settle my brain,
I believe the soggy clods shall become lovers and lamps,
And a compend of compends is the meat of a man or woman,
And a summit and flower there is the feeling they have for each other,   660
And they are to branch boundlessly out of that lesson until it becomes omnific,
And until one and all shall delight us, and we them.

31

I believe a leaf of grass is no less than the journey-work of the stars,
And the pismire [9] is equally perfect, and a grain of sand, and the egg of the wren,
And the tree-toad is a chef-d'œuvre for the highest,   665
And the running blackberry would adorn the parlors of heaven,
And the narrowest hinge in my hand puts to scorn all machinery,
And the cow crunching with depress'd head surpasses any statue,
And a mouse is miracle enough to stagger sextillions of infidels.

9. An ant.

I find I incorporate gneiss, coal, long-threaded moss, fruits, grains,
esculent roots,   670
And am stucco'd with quadrupeds and birds all over,
And have distanced what is behind me for good reasons,
But call any thing back again when I desire it.

In vain the speeding or shyness,
In vain the plutonic [1] rocks send their old heat against my approach,
In vain the mastodon retreats beneath its own powder'd bones,   676
In vain objects stand leagues off and assume manifold shapes,
In vain the ocean settling in hollows and the great monsters lying
low,
In vain the buzzard houses herself with the sky,
In vain the snake slides through the creepers and logs,   680
In vain the elk takes to the inner passes of the woods,
In vain the razor-bill'd auk sails far north to Labrador,
I follow quickly, I ascend to the nest in the fissure of the cliff.

32
I think I could turn and live with animals, they are so placid and
self-contain'd,
I stand and look at them long and long.   685

They do not sweat and whine about their condition,
They do not lie awake in the dark and weep for their sins,
They do not make me sick discussing their duty to God,
Not one is dissatisfied, not one is demented with the mania of
owning things,
Not one kneels to another, nor to his kind that lived thousands of
years ago,   690
Not one is respectable or unhappy over the whole earth.

So they show their relations to me and I accept them,
They bring me tokens of myself, they evince them plainly in
their possession.

I wonder where they get those tokens,
Did I pass that way huge times ago and negligently drop them?   695

Myself moving forward then and now and forever,
Gathering and showing more always and with velocity,
Infinite and omnigenous, and the like of these among them,
Not too exclusive toward the reachers of my remembrancers,
Picking out here one that I love, and now go with him on broth-
erly terms.   700

A gigantic beauty of a stallion, fresh and responsive to my caresses,

1. Molten conglomerate associated with the earliest earth-age (Archeozoic).

Head high in the forehead, wide between the ears,
Limbs glossy and supple, tail dusting the ground,
Eyes full of sparkling wickedness, ears finely cut, flexibly moving.

His nostrils dilate as my heels embrace him,   705
His well-built limbs tremble with pleasure as we race around and
    return.
I but use you a minute, then I resign you, stallion,
Why do I need your paces when I myself out-gallop them?
Even as I sand or sit passing faster than you.

33

Space and Time! now I see it is true, what I guess'd at,   710
What I guess'd when I loaf'd on the grass,
What I guess'd while I lay alone in my bed,
And again as I walk'd the beach under the paling stars of the
    morning.

My ties and ballasts leave me, my elbows rest in sea-gaps,
I skirt sierras, my palms cover continents,   715
I am afoot with my vision.

By the city's quadrangular houses—in log huts, camping with
    lumbermen,
Along the ruts of the turnpike, along the dry gulch and rivulet
    bed,
Weeding my onion-patch or hoeing rows of carrots and parsnips,
    crossing savannas, trailing in forests,
Prospecting, gold-digging, girdling the trees of a new purchase,   720
Scorch'd ankle-deep by the hot sand, hauling my boat down the
    shallow river,
Where the panther walks to and fro on a limb overhead, where
    the buck turns furiously at the hunter,
Where the rattlesnake suns his flabby length on a rock, where the
    otter is feeding on fish,
Where the alligator in his tough pimples sleeps by the bayou,
Where the black bear is searching for roots or honey, where the
    beaver pats the mud with his paddle-shaped tail;   725
Over the growing sugar, over the yellow-flower'd cotton plant,
    over the rice in its low moist field,
Over the sharp-peak'd farm house, with its scallop'd scum and
    slender shoots from the gutters,
Over the western persimmon, over the long-leav'd corn, over the
    delicate blue-flower flax,
Over the white and brown buckwheat, a hummer and buzzer
    there with the rest,

Over the dusky green of the rye as it ripples and shades in the
    breeze;   730
Scaling mountains, pulling myself cautiously up, holding on by
    low scragged limbs,
Walking the path worn in the grass and beat through the leaves of
    the brush,
Where the quail is whistling betwixt the woods and the wheat-lot,
Where the bat flies in the Seventh-month eve, where the great
    gold-bug drops through the dark,
Where the brook puts out of the roots of the old tree and flows
    to the meadow,   735
Where cattle stand and shake away flies with the tremulous shud-
    dering of their hides,
Where the cheese-cloth hangs in the kitchen, where andirons
    straddle the hearth-slab, where cobwebs fall in festoons from
    the rafters;
Where trip-hammers crash, where the press is whirling its cylin-
    ders,
Where the human heart beats with terrible throes under its ribs,
Where the pear-shaped balloon is floating aloft, (floating in it my-
    self and looking composedly down,)   740
Where the life-car [2] is drawn on the slip-noose, where the heat
    hatches pale-green eggs in the dented sand.
Where the she-whale swims with her calf and never forsakes it,
Where the steam-ship trails hind-ways its long pennant of smoke,
Where the fin of the shark cuts like a black chip out of the water,
Where the half-burn'd brig is riding on unknown currents,   745
Where shells grow to her slimy deck, where the dead are corrupt-
    ing below;
Where the dense-starr'd flag is borne at the head of the regiments,
Approaching Manhattan up by the long-stretching island,
Under Niagara, the cataract falling like a veil over my counte-
    nance,
Upon a door-step, upon the horse-block of hard wood outside,   750
Upon the race-course, or enjoying picnics or jigs or a good game
    of base-ball,
At he-festivals, with blackguard gibes, ironical license, bull-
    dances,[3] drinking, laughter,
At the cider-mill tasting the sweets of the brown mash, sucking
    the juice through a straw,
At apple-peelings wanting kisses for all the red fruit I find,
At musters, beach-parties, friendly bees, huskings, house-raisings;

---

2. Watertight vessel moved by ropes
to rescue people from wrecked ships.

3. Slang, derived from "buffalo
dance," originally danced by Indians.

Where the mocking-bird sounds his delicious gurgles, cackles, screams, weeps,

Where the hay-rick stands in the barn-yard, where the dry-stalks are scatter'd, where the brood-cow waits in the hovel, ⁷⁵⁵

Where the bull advances to do his masculine work, where the stud to the mare, where the cock is treading the hen,

Where the heifers browse, where geese nip their food with short jerks,

Where sun-down shadows lengthen over the limitless and lonesome prairie,

Where herds of buffalo make a crawling spread of the square miles far and near, ⁷⁶⁰

Where the humming-bird shimmers, where the neck of the long-lived swan is curving and winding,

Where the laughing-gull scoots by the shore, where she laughs her near-human laugh,

Where bee-hives range on a gray bench in the garden half hid by the high weeds,

Where band-neck'd partridges roost in a ring on the ground with their heads out, ⁷⁶⁵

Where burial coaches enter the arch'd gates of a cemetery,

Where winter wolves bark amid wastes of snow and icicled trees,

Where the yellow-crown'd heron comes to the edge of the marsh at night and feeds upon small crabs,

Where the splash of swimmers and divers cools the warm noon,

Where the katy-did works her chromatic reed on the walnut-tree over the well, ⁷⁷⁰

Through patches of citrons and cucumbers with silver-wired leaves,

Through the salt-lick or orange glade, or under conical firs,

Through the gymnasium, through the curtain'd saloon, through the office or public hall;

Pleas'd with the native and pleas'd with the foreign, pleas'd with the new and old,

Pleas'd with the homely woman as well as the handsome, ⁷⁷⁵

Pleas'd with the quakeress as she puts off her bonnet and talks melodiously,

Pleas'd with the tune of the choir of the whitewash'd church,

Pleas'd with the earnest words of the sweating Methodist preacher, impress'd seriously at the camp-meeting;

Looking in at the shop windows of Broadway the whole forenoon, flatting the flesh of my nose on the thick plate glass,

Wandering the same afternoon with my face turn'd up to the clouds, or down a lane or along the beach, ⁷⁸⁰

My right and left arms round the sides of two friends, and I in
    the middle;
Coming home with the silent and dark-cheek'd bush-boy, (behind
    me he rides at the drape of the day,)
Far from the settlements studying the print of animals' feet, or
    the moccasin print,
By the cot in the hospital reaching lemonade to a feverish patient,
Nigh the coffin'd corpse when all is still, examining with a candle;
Voyaging to every port to dicker and adventure,   786
Hurrying with the modern crowd as eager and fickle as any,
Hot toward one I hate, ready in my madness to knife him,
Solitary at midnight in my back yard, my thoughts gone from me
    a long while,
Walking the old hills of Judæa with the beautiful gentle God by
    my side,   790
Speeding through space, speeding through heaven and the stars,
Speeding amid the seven satellites and the broad ring, and the
    diameter of eighty thousand miles,
Speeding with tail'd meteors, throwing fire-balls like the rest,
Carrying the crescent child that carries its own full mother in its
    belly,
Storming, enjoying, planning, loving, cautioning,   795
Backing and filling, appearing and disappearing,
I tread day and night such roads.

I visit the orchards of spheres and look at the product,
And look at quintillions ripen'd and look at quintillions green.

I fly those flights of a fluid and swallowing soul,   800
My course runs below the soundings of plummets.

I help myself to material and immaterial,
No guard can shut me off, no law prevent me.

I anchor my ship for a little while only,
My messengers continually cruise away or bring their returns to
    me.   805

I go hunting polar furs and the seal, leaping chasms with a pike-
    pointed staff, clinging to topples of brittle and blue.

I ascend to the foretruck,
I take my place late at night in the crow's-nest,
We sail the arctic sea, it is plenty light enough,
Through the clear atmosphere I stretch around on the wonderful
    beauty,   810

The enormous masses of ice pass me and I pass them, the scenery
    is plain in all directions,
The white-topt mountains show in the distance, I fling out my
    fancies toward them,
We are approaching some great battle-field in which we are soon
    to be engaged,
We pass the colossal outposts of the encampment, we pass with
    still feet and caution,
Or we are entering by the suburbs some vast and ruin'd city, 815
The blocks and fallen architecture more than all the living cities
    of the globe.

I am a free companion, I bivouac by invading watchfires,
I turn the bridegroom out of bed and stay with the bride myself,
I tighten her all night to my thighs and lips.

My voice is the wife's voice, the screech by the rail of the stairs, 820
They fetch my man's body up dripping and drown'd.

I understand the large hearts of heroes,
The courage of present times and all times,
How the skipper saw the crowded and rudderless wreck [4] of the
    steam-ship, and Death chasing it up and down the storm,
How he knuckled tight and gave not back an inch, and was faith-
    ful of days and faithful of nights,
And chalk'd in large letters on a board, *Be of good cheer, we will* 825
    not desert you;
How he follow'd with them and tack'd with them three days
    and would not give it up,
How he saved the drifting company at last,
How the lank loose-gown'd women look'd when boated from the
    side of their prepared graves,
How the silent old-faced infants and the lifted sick, and the sharp-
    lipp'd unshaven men; 830
All this I swallow, it tastes good, I like it well, it becomes mine,
I am the man, I suffer'd, I was there.

The disdain and calmness of martyrs,
The mother of old, condemn'd for a witch, burnt with dry wood,
    her children gazing on,
The hounded slave that flags in the race, leans by the fence,
    blowing, cover'd with sweat, 835
The twinges that sting like needles his legs and neck, the mur-
    derous buckshot and the bullets,
All these I feel or am.

4. Whitman describes the wreck and rescue of the *San Francisco* three hundred
miles out of New York harbor, December 23–24, 1853.

I am the hounded slave, I wince at the bite of the dogs,
Hell and despair are upon me, crack and again crack the marks-
    men,
I clutch the rails of the fence, my gore dribs, thinn'd with the
    ooze of my skin,   840
I fall on the weeds and stones,
The riders spur their unwilling horses, haul close,
Taunt my dizzy ears and beat me violently over the head with
    whipstocks.

Agonies are one of my changes of garments,
I do not ask the wounded person how he feels, I myself become
    the wounded person,   845
My hurts turn livid upon me as I lean on a cane and observe.

I am the mash'd fireman with breast-bone broken,
Tumbling walls buried me in their debris,
Heat and smoke I inspired, I heard the yelling shouts of my
    comrades,
I heard the distant click of their picks and shovels,   850
They have clear'd the beams away, they tenderly lift me forth.

I lie in the night air in my red shirt, the pervading hush is for my
    sake,
Painless after all I lie exhausted but not so unhappy,
White and beautiful are the faces around me, the heads are bared
    of their fire-caps,
The kneeling crowd fades with the light of the torches.   855

Distant and dead resuscitate,
They show as the dial or move as the hands of me, I am the clock
    myself.

I am an old artillerist, I tell of my fort's bombardment,
I am there again.

Again the long roll of the drummers,   860
Again the attacking cannon, mortars,
Again to my listening ears the cannon responsive.

I take part, I see and hear the whole,
The cries, curses, roar, the plaudits for well-aim'd shots,
The ambulanza [5] slowly passing trailing its red drip,   865
Workmen searching after damages, making indispensable repairs,
The fall of grenades through the rent roof, the fan-shaped ex-
    plosion,

---

5. Properly, in Spanish, "ambulancia."

The whizz of limbs, heads, stone, wood, iron, high in the air.

Again gurgles the mouth of my dying general, he furiously waves
 with his hand,
He gasps through the clot *Mind not me—mind—the entrench-
 ments.* 870

34

Now I tell what I know in Texas in my early youth,
(I tell not the fall of Alamo,[6]
Not one escaped to tell the fall of Alamo,
The hundred and fifty are dumb yet at Alamo,)
'Tis the tale of the murder in cold blood of four hundred and
 twelve young men.[7] 875

Retreating they had form'd in a hollow square with their baggage
 for breastworks,
Nine hundred lives out of the surrounding enemy's, nine times
 their number, was the price they took in advance,
Their colonel was wounded and their ammunition gone,
They treated for an honorable capitulation, receiv'd writing and
 seal, gave up their arms and march'd back prisoners of war.

They were the glory of the race of rangers, 880
Matchless with horse, rifle, song, supper, courtship,
Large, turbulent, generous, handsome, proud, and affectionate,
Bearded, sunburnt, drest in the free costume of hunters,
Not a single one over thirty years of age.

The second First-day morning they were brought out in squads
 and massacred, it was beautiful early summer, 885
The work commenced about five o'clock and was over by eight.

None obey'd the command to kneel,
Some made a mad and helpless rush, some stood stark and
 straight,
A few fell at once, shot in the temple or heart, the living and
 dead lay together,
The maim'd and mangled dug in the dirt, the new-comers saw
 them there, 890
Some half-kill'd attempted to crawl away,
These were despatch'd with bayonets or batter'd with the blunts
 of muskets.

---

6. A mission converted into a fort at
San Antonio, where the Texas garrison
of 180 was annihilated by four thousand Mexicans (March 6, 1836).
7. The massacre of Colonel James W.
Fannin and his troops at Goliad on
March 27, 1836. "Goliad" like "the
Alamo" became a rallying cry for Texans in their fight for independence.

A youth not seventeen years old seiz'd his assassin till two more
    came to release him,
The three were all torn and cover'd with the boy's blood.

At eleven o'clock began the burning of the bodies;   895
That is the tale of the murder of the four hundred and twelve
    young men.

35

Would you hear of an old-time sea-fight?
Would you learn who won by the light of the moon and stars?
List to the yarn, as my grandmother's father the sailor told it to
    me.[8]

Our foe was no skulk in his ship I tell you, (said he,)   900
His was the surly English pluck, and there is no tougher or truer,
    and never was, and never will be;
Along the lower'd eve he came horribly raking us.

We closed with him, the yards entangled, the cannon touch'd,
My captain lash'd fast with his own hands.

We had receiv'd some eighteen pound shots under the water,   905
On our lower-gun-deck two large pieces had burst at the first fire,
    killing all around and blowing up overhead.

Fighting at sun-down, fighting at dark,
Ten o'clock at night, the full moon well up, our leaks on the gain,
    and five feet of water reported,
The master-at-arms loosing the prisoners confined in the after-
    hold to give them a chance for themselves.

The transit to and from the magazine is now stopt by the sen-
    tinels,   910
They see so many strange faces they do not know whom to trust.

Our frigate takes fire,
The other asks if we demand quarter?
If our colors are struck and the fighting done?

Now I laugh content, for I hear the voice of my little captain,   915
We have not struck, he composedly cries, *we have just begun our
    part of the fighting.*

Only three guns are in use,
One is directed by the captain himself against the enemy's main-
    mast,

---

8. The victory of John Paul Jones, commanding the *Bonhomme Richard*, over the British frigate *Serapis* in the North Sea during the American Revolution (September 23, 1779).

Two well serv'd with grape and canister silence his musketry and
   clear his decks.

The tops alone second the fire of this little battery, especially the
   main-top,   920
They hold out bravely during the whole of the action.

Not a moment's cease,
The leaks gain fast on the pumps, the fire eats toward the powder-
   magazine.

One of the pumps has been shot away, it is generally thought we
   are sinking.

Serene stands the little captain,   925
He is not hurried, his voice is neither high nor low,
His eyes give more light to us than our battle-lanterns.

Toward twelve there in the beams of the moon they surrender to
   us.

36

Stretch'd and still lies the midnight,
Two great hulls motionless on the breast of the darkness,   930
Our vessel riddled and slowly sinking, preparations to pass to the
   one we have conquer'd,
The captain on the quarter-deck coldly giving his orders through
   a countenance white as a sheet,
Near by the corpse of the child that serv'd in the cabin,
The dead face of an old salt with long white hair and carefully
   curl'd whiskers,
The flames spite of all that can be done flickering aloft and below,
The husky voices of the two or three officers yet fit for duty,   936
Formless stacks of bodies and bodies by themselves, dabs of flesh
   upon the masts and spars,
Cut of cordage, dangle of rigging, light shock of the soothe of
   waves,
Black and impassive guns, litter of powder-parcels, strong scent,
A few large stars overhead, silent and mournful shining,   940
Delicate sniffs of sea-breeze, smells of sedgy grass and fields by the
   shore, death-messages given in charge to survivors,
The hiss of the surgeon's knife, the gnawing teeth of his saw,
Wheeze, cluck, swash of falling blood, short wild scream, and
   long, dull, tapering groan,
These so, these irretrievable.

37

You laggards there on guard! look to your arms!   945
In at the conquer'd doors they crowd! I am possess'd!

Embody all presences outlaw'd or suffering,
See myself in prison shaped like another man,
And feel the dull unintermitted pain.

For me the keepers of convicts shoulder their carbines and keep
    watch,   950
It is I let out in the morning and barr'd at night.

Not a muntineer walks handcuff'd to jail but I am handcuff'd to
    him and walk by his side,
(I am less the jolly one there, and more the silent one with sweat
    on my twitching lips.)

Not a youngster is taken for larceny but I go up too, and am tried
    and sentenced.

Not a cholera patient lies at the last gasp but I also lie at the last
    gasp,   955
My face is ash-color'd, my sinews gnarl, away from me people
    retreat.

Askers embody themselves in me and I am embodied in them,
I project my hat, sit shame-faced, and beg.

38

Enough! enough! enough!
Somehow I have been stunn'd. Stand back!   960
Give me a little time beyond my cuff'd head, slumbers, dreams,
    gaping,
I discover myself on the verge of a usual mistake.

That I could forget the mockers and insults!
That I could forget the trickling tears and the blows of the bludg-
    eons and hammers!
That I could look with a separate look on my own crucifixion and
    bloody crowning!   965

I remember now,
I resume the overstaid fraction,
The grave of rock multiplies what has been confided to it, or to
    any graves,
Corpses rise, gashes heal, fastenings roll from me.

I troop forth replenish'd with supreme power, one of an average
    unending procession,
        970
Inland and sea-coast we go, and pass all boundary lines,
Our swift ordinances on their way over the whole earth,
The blossoms we wear in our hats the growth of thousands of
    years.

Eleves, I salute you! come forward!
Continue your annotations, continue your questionings.   975

39

The friendly and flowing savage, who is he?
Is he waiting for civilization, or past it and mastering it?

Is he some Southwesterner rais'd out-doors? is he Kanadian?
Is he from the Mississippi country? Iowa, Oregon, California?
The mountains? prairie-life, bush-life? or sailor from the sea?   980

Wherever he goes men and women accept and desire him,
They desire he should like them, touch them, speak to them, stay
     with them.

Behavior lawless as snow-flakes, words simple as grass, uncomb'd
     head, laughter, and naiveté,
Slow-stepping feet, common features, common modes and emana-
     tions,
They descend in new forms from the tips of his fingers,   985
They are wafted with the odor of his body or breath, they fly out
     of the glance of his eye

40

Flaunt of the sunshine I need not your bask—lie over!
You light surfaces only, I force surfaces and depths also.

Earth! you seem to look for something at my hands,
Say, old top-knot,[9] what do you want?   990

Man or woman, I might tell how I like you, but cannot,
And might tell what it is in me and what it is in you, but cannot,
And might tell that pining I have, that pulse of my nights and
     days.

Behold, I do not give lectures or a little charity,
When I give I give myself.   995

You there, impotent, loose in the knees,
Open your scarf'd chops till I blow grit within you,
Spread your palms and lift the flaps of your pockets,
I am not to be denied, I compel, I have stores plenty and to spare,
And any thing I have I bestow.   1000

I do not ask who you are, that is not important to me,
You can do nothing and be nothing but what I will infold you.

To cotton-field drudge or cleaner of privies I lean,
On his right cheek I put the family kiss,

9. Then a term of comic familiarity; originally applied to the Indians of the
midwest.

And in my soul I swear I never will deny him. 1005

On women fit for conception I start bigger and nimbler babes,
(This day I am jetting the stuff of far more arrogant republics.)

To any one dying, thither I speed and twist the knob of the door,
Turn the bed-clothes toward the foot of the bed,
Let the physician and the priest go home. 1010

I seize the descending man and raise him with resistless will,
O despairer, here is my neck,
By God, you shall not go down! hang your whole weight upon me.

I dilate you with tremendous breath, I buoy you up,
Every room of the house do I fill with an arm'd force, 1015
Lovers of me, bafflers of graves.

Sleep—I and they keep guard all night,
Not doubt, not decease shall dare to lay finger upon you,
I have embraced you, and henceforth possess you to myself,
And when you rise in the morning you will find what I tell you is
    so. 1020

41

I am he bringing help for the sick as they pant on their backs,
And for strong upright men I bring yet more needed help.

I heard what was said of the universe,
Heard it and heard it of several thousand years;
It is middling well as far as it goes—but is that all? 1025

Magnifying and applying come I,
Outbidding at the start the old cautious hucksters,[1]
Taking myself the exact dimensions of Jehovah,
Lithographing Kronos, Zeus his son, and Hercules his grandson,
Buying drafts of Osiris, Isis, Belus, Brahma, Buddha, 1030
In my portfolio placing Manito loose, Allah on a leaf, the crucifix
    engraved,
With Odin and the hideous-faced Mexitli and every idol and
    image,[2]
Taking them all for what they are worth and not a cent more,
Admitting they were alive and did the work of their days,
(They bore mites as for unfledg'd birds who have now to rise and
    fly and sing for themselves,) 1035

---

1. Peddler, small tradesman.
2. Whitman hoped for a universal religion, embracing aspects of all faiths. In these lines he has listed deities from various religions and mythologies: Hebraic (Jehovah), Greek (Kronos, Zeus, Hercules), Egyptian (Osiris, Isis), Babylonian (Belus), Hindu (Brahma), Buddhist (Buddha), American Indian (Manito), Islamic (Allah), Norse (Odin), and Aztec (Mexitli).

Accepting the rough deific sketches to fill out better in myself, bestowing them freely on each man and woman I see,
Discovering as much or more in a framer framing a house,
Putting higher claims for him there with his roll'd-up sleeves
  driving the mallet and chisel,
Not objecting to special revelations, considering a curl of smoke or
  a hair on the back of my hand just as curious as any revelation,
Lads ahold of fire-engines and hook-and-ladder ropes no less to me
  than the gods of the antique wars,   1040
Minding their voices peal through the crash of destruction,
Their brawny limbs passing safe over charr'd laths, their white
  foreheads whole and unhurt out of the flames;
By the mechanic's wife with her babe at her nipple interceding
  for every person born,
Three scythes at harvest whizzing in a row from three lusty angels
  with shirts bagg'd out at their waists,
The snag-tooth'd hostler with red hair redeeming sins past and to
  come,   1045
Selling all he possesses, traveling on foot to fee lawyers for his
  brother and sit by him while he is tried for forgery;
What was strewn in the amplest strewing the square rod about
  me, and not filling the square rod then,
The bull and the bug never worshipp'd half enough,
Dung and dirt more admirable than was dream'd,
The supernatural of no account, myself waiting my time to be
  one of the supremes,   1050
The day getting ready for me when I shall do as much good as
  the best, and be as prodigious;
By my life-lumps! becoming already a creator,
Putting myself here and now to the ambush'd womb of the
  shadows.

42

A call in the midst of the crowd,
My own voice, orotund sweeping and final.   1055

Come my children,
Come my boys and girls, my women, household and intimates,
Now the performer launches his nerve, he has pass'd his prelude
  on the reeds within.

Easily written loose-finger'd chords—I feel the thrum of your climax and close.

My head slues round on my neck,   1060
Music rolls, but not from the organ,

Folks are around me, but they are no household of mine.

Ever the hard unsunk ground,
Ever the eaters and drinkers, ever the upward and downward sun,
 ever the air and the ceaseless tides,
Ever myself and my neighbors, refreshing, wicked, real,   1065
Ever the old inexplicable query, ever that thorn'd thumb, that
 breath of itches and thirsts,
Ever the vexer's *hoot! hoot!* till we find where the sly one hides
 and bring him forth,
Ever love, ever the sobbing liquid of life,
Ever the bandage under the chin, ever the trestles of death.

Here and there with dimes on the eyes walking,   1070
To feed the greed of the belly the brains liberally spooning,
Tickets buying, taking, selling, but in to the feast never once going,
Many sweating, ploughing, thrashing, and then the chaff for pay-
 ment receiving,
A few idly owning, and they the wheat continually claiming.

This is the city and I am one of the citizens,   1075
Whatever interests the rest interests me, politics, wars, markets,
 newspapers, schools,
The mayor and councils, banks, tariffs, steamships, factories,
 stocks, stores, real estate and personal estate.

The little plentiful manikins skipping around in collars and tail'd
 coats,
I am aware who they are, (they are positively not worms or fleas,)
I acknowledge the duplicates of myself, the weakest and shallow-
 est is deathless with me,   1080
What I do and say the same waits for them,
Every thought that flounders in me the same flounders in them.

I know perfectly well my own egotism,
Know my omnivorous lines and must not write any less,
And would fetch you whoever you are flush with myself.   1085

Not words of routine this song of mine,
But abruptly to question, to leap beyond yet nearer bring;
This printed and bound book—but the printer and the printing-
 office boy?
The well-taken photographs—but your wife or friend close and
 solid in your arms?
The black ship mail'd with iron, her mighty guns in her turrets—
 but the pluck of the captain and engineers?   1090
In the houses the dishes and fare and furniture—but the host and
 hostess, and the look out of their eyes?

The sky up there—yet here or next door, or across the way?
The saints and sages in history—but you yourself?
Sermons, creeds, theology—but the fathomless human brain,
And what is reason? and what is love? and what is life?   1095

43

I do not despise you priests, all time, the world over,
My faith is the greatest of faiths and the least of faiths,
Enclosing worship ancient and modern and all between ancient
    and modern,
Believing I shall come again upon the earth after five thousand
    years,
Waiting responses from oracles, honoring the gods, saluting the
    sun,
Making a fetich of the first rock or stump, powowing with sticks
    in the circle of obis,[3]   1101
Helping the lama or brahmin as he trims the lamps of the idols,
Dancing yet through the streets in a phallic procession, rapt and
    austere in the woods a gymnosophist,
Drinking mead from the skull-cup, to Shastas and Vedas [4] admi-
    rant, minding the Koran,
Walking the teokallis,[5] spotted with gore from the stone and
    knife, beating the serpent-skin drum,
Accepting the Gospels, accepting him that was crucified, knowing   1105
    assuredly that he is divine,
To the mass kneeling or the puritan's prayer rising, or sitting
    patiently in a pew,
Ranting and frothing in my insane crisis, or waiting dead-like till
    my spirit arouses me,
Looking forth on pavement and land, or outside of pavement and
    land,
Belonging to the winders of the circuit of circuits.   1110

One of that centripetal and centrifugal gang I turn and talk like a
    man leaving charges before a journey.

Down-hearted doubters dull and excluded,
Frivolous, sullen, moping, angry, affected, disheartern'd, atheistical,
I know every one of you, I know the sea of torment, doubt, de-
    spair and unbelief.

3. Properly, "obi" or "obeah," African sorcery brought by slaves to the southern states.
4. Shastas (properly "shastras") are the books of instructions, the Vedas, the most ancient sacred writings, of Hindu religion.
5. Teocallis, ancient Aztec temples situated on terraced pyramids, up which the human sacrifices climbed to their doom.

How the flukes splash! 1115
How they contort rapid as lightning, with spasms and spouts of
  blood!

Be at peace bloody flukes of doubters and sullen mopers,
I take my place among you as much as among any,
The past is the push of you, me, all, precisely the same,
And what is yet untried and afterward is for you, me, all, precisely
  the same. 1120

I do not know what is untried and afterward,
But I know it will in its turn prove sufficient, and cannot fail.

Each who passes is consider'd, each who stops is consider'd, not a
  single one can it fail.

It cannot fail the young man who died and was buried,
Nor the young woman who died and was put by his side, 1125
Nor the little child that peep'd in at the door, and then drew
  back and was never seen again,
Nor the old man who has lived without purpose, and feels it with
  bitterness worse than gall,
Nor him in the poor house tubercled by rum and the bad disorder,
Nor the numberless slaughter'd and wreck'd, nor the brutish ko-
  boo [6] call'd the ordure of humanity, 1129

Nor the sacs merely floating with open mouths for food to slip in,
Nor any thing in the earth, or down in the oldest graves of the
  earth,
Nor any thing in the myriads of spheres, nor the myriads of
  myriads that inhabit them,
Nor the present, nor the least wisp that is known.

44

It is time to explain myself—let us stand up.

What is known I strip away, 1135
I launch all men and women forward with me into the Unknown.

The clock indicates the moment—but what does eternity indicate?

We have thus far exhausted trillions of winters and summers,
There are trillions ahead, and trillions ahead of them.

Births have brought us richness and variety, 1140
And other births will bring us richness and variety.

6. A native of Palembang, east coast of Sumatra (T. O. Mabbott, *Explicator*
XI, 34).

I do not call one greater and one smaller,
That which fills its period and place is equal to any.

Were mankind murderous or jealous upon you, my brother, my
    sister?
I am sorry for you, they are not murderous or jealous upon me,   1145
All has been gentle with me, I keep no account with lamentation,
(What have I to do with lamentation?)

I am an acme of things accomplish'd, and I an encloser of things
    to be.

My feet strike an apex of the apices of the stairs,
On every step bunches of ages, and larger bunches between the
    steps,   1150
All below duly travel'd, and still I mount and mount.

Rise after rise bow the phantoms behind me,
Afar down I see the huge first Nothing, I know I was even there,
I waited unseen and always, and slept through the lethargic mist,
And took my time, and took no hurt from the fetid carbon.   1155

Long I was hugg'd close—long and long.

Immense have been the preparations for me,
Faithful and friendly the arms that have helped me.

Cycles ferried my cradle, rowing and rowing like cheerful boat-
    men,
For room to me stars kept aside in their own rings,   1160
They sent influences to look after what was to hold me.

Before I was born out of my mother generations guided me,
My embryo has never been torpid, nothing could overlay it.

For it the nebula cohered to an orb,
The long slow strata piled to rest it on,   1165
Vast vegetables gave it sustenance,
Monstrous sauroids transported it in their mouths and deposited
    it with care.[7]

All forces have been steadily employ'd to complete and delight
    me,
Now on this spot I stand with my robust soul.

45

O span of youth! ever-push'd elasticity!   1170
O manhood, balanced, florid and full.

My lovers suffocate me,

---

7. *I.e.,* "Sauria"; mammoth reptiles, generally prehistoric. The idea that snakes
carry their eggs in their mouths occurs in folklore.

Crowding my lips, thick in the pores of my skin,
Jostling me through streets and public halls, coming naked to me
    at night,
Crying by day *Ahoy!* from the rocks of the river, swinging and
    chirping over my head,   1175
Calling my name from flower-beds, vines, tangled underbrush,
Lighting on every moment of my life,
Bussing my body with soft balsamic busses,
Noiselessly passing handfuls out of their hearts and giving them
    to be mine.

Old age superbly rising! O welcome, ineffable grace of dying days!

Every condition promulges not only itself, it promulges what
    grows after and out of itself,   1181
And the dark hush promulges [8] as much as any.

I open my scuttle at night and see the far-sprinkled systems,
And all I see multiplied as high as I can cipher edge but the rim
    of the farther systems.

Wider and wider they spread, expanding, always expanding, 1185
Outward and outward and forever outward.

My sun has his sun and round him obediently wheels,
He joins with his partners a group of superior circuit,
And greater sets follow, making specks of the greatest inside them.

There is no stoppage and never can be stoppage,   1190
If I, you, and the worlds, and all beneath or upon their surfaces,
    were this moment reduced back to a pallid float, it would
    not avail in the long run,
We should surely bring up again where we now stand,
And surely go as much farther, and then farther and farther.

A few quadrillions of eras, a few octillions of cubic leagues, do not
    hazard the span or make it impatient,
They are but parts, any thing is but a part.   1195

See ever so far, there is limitless space outside of that,
Count ever so much, there is limitless time around that.

My rendezvous is appointed, it is certain,
The Lord will be there and wait till I come on perfect terms,
The great Camerado, the lover true for whom I pine will be there.

                          46
I know I have the best of time and space, and was never measured
    and never will be measured.   1201

8. Archaic: promulgates.

I tramp a perpetual journey, (come listen all!)
My signs are a rain-proof coat, good shoes, and a staff cut from the
woods,
No friend of mine takes his ease in my chair,
I have no chair, no church, no philosophy,   1205
I lead no man to a dinner-table, library, exchange,
But each man and each woman of you I lead upon a knoll,
My left hand hooking you round the waist,
My right hand pointing to landscapes of continents and the pub-
lic road.

Not I, not any one else can travel that road for you,   1210
You must travel it for yourself.

It is not far, it is within reach,
Perhaps you have been on it since you were born and did not
know,
Perhaps it is everywhere on water and on land.

Shoulder your duds dear son, and I will mine, and let us hasten
forth,
                                                                        1215
Wonderful cities and free nations we shall fetch as we go.

If you tire, give my both burdens, and rest the chuff⁹ of your
hand on my hip,

And in due time you shall repay the same service to me,
For after we start we never lie by again.

This day before dawn I ascended a hill and look'd at the crowded
heaven,
                                                                        1220
And I said to my spirit *When we become the enfolders of those
orbs, and the pleasure and knowledge of every thing in them,
shall we be fill'd and satisfied then?*
And my spirit said *No, we but level that lift to pass and continue
beyond.*

You are also asking me questions and I hear you,
I answer that I cannot answer, you must find out for yourself.

Sit a while dear son,   1225
Here are biscuits to eat and here is milk to drink,
But as soon as you sleep and renew yourself in sweet clothes, I kiss
you with a good-by kiss and open the gate for your egress hence.

Long enough have you dream'd contemptible dreams,
Now I wash the gum from your eyes,

9. English dial. for "chubby"; here, "the weight."

You must habit yourself to the dazzle of the light and of every
    moment of your life.   1230

Long have you timidly waded holding a plank by the shore,
Now I will you to be a bold swimmer,
To jump off in the midst of the sea, rise again, nod to me, shout,
    and laughingly dash with your hair.

47

I am the teacher of athletes,
He that by me spreads a wider breast than my own proves the
    width of my own,   1235
He most honors my style who learns under it to destroy the
    teacher.

The boy I love, the same becomes a man not through derived
    power, but in his own right,
Wicked rather than virtuous out of conformity or fear,
Fond of his sweetheart, relishing well his steak,
Unrequited love or a slight cutting him worse than sharp steel
    cuts,
First-rate to ride, to fight, to hit the bull's eye, to sail a skiff, to
    sing a song or play on the banjo,   1241
Preferring scars and the beard and faces pitted with small-pox
    over all latherers,
And those well-tann'd to those that keep out of the sun.

I teach straying from me, yet who can stray from me?
I follow you whoever you are from the present hour,   1245
My words itch at your ears till you understand them.

I do not say these things for a dollar or to fill up the time while I
    wait for a boat,
(It is you talking just as much as myself, I act as the tongue of
    you,
Tied in your mouth, in mine it begins to be loosen'd.)

I swear I will never again mention love or death inside a house,   1250
And I swear I will never translate myself at all, only to him or
    her who privately stays with me in the open air.

If you would understand me go to the heights or water-shore,
The nearest gnat is an explanation, and a drop or motion of
    waves a key,
The maul, the oar, the hand-saw, second my words.

No shutter'd room or school can commune with me,   1255
But roughs and little children better than they.

The young mechanic is closest to me, he knows me well,
The woodman that takes his axe and jug with him shall take me
with him all day,
The farm-boy ploughing in the field feels good at the sound of
my voice,
In vessels that sail my words sail, I go with fishermen and seamen
and love them.   1260

The soldier camp'd or upon the march is mine,
On the night ere the pending battle many seek me, and I do not fail
them,
On that solemn night (it may be their last) those that know me
seek me.

My face rubs to the hunter's face when he lies down alone in his
blanket,
The driver thinking of me does not mind the jolt of his wagon,   1265
The young mother and old mother comprehend me,
The girl and the wife rest the needle a moment and forget where
they are,
They and all would resume what I have told them.

48

I have said that the soul is not more than the body,
And I have said that the body is not more than the soul,   1270
And nothing, not God, is greater to one than one's self is,
And whoever walks a furlong without sympathy walks to his own
funeral drest in his shroud,
And I or you pocketless of a dime may purchase the pick of the
earth,
And to glance with an eye or show a bean in its pod confounds the
learning of all times,
And there is no trade or employment but the young man following
it may become a hero,   1275
And there is no object so soft but it makes a hub for the wheel'd
universe,
And I say to any man or woman, Let your soul stand cool and composed before a million universes.

And I say to mankind, Be not curious about God,
For I who am curious about each am not curious about God,
(No array of terms can say how much I am at peace about God and
about death.)   1280

I hear and behold God in every object, yet understand God not
in the least,
Nor do I understand who there can be more wonderful than myself.

Why should I wish to see God better than this day?
I see something of God each hour of the twenty-four, and each
    moment then,
In the faces of men and women I see God, and in my own face in
    the glass,   1285
I find letters from God dropt in the street, and every one is sign'd
    by God's name,
And I leave them where they are, for I know that wheresoe'er I go
Others will punctually come for ever and ever.

49

And as to you Death, and you bitter hug of mortality, it is idle to
    try to alarm me.

To his work without flinching the accoucheur [1] comes,   1290
I see the elder-hand pressing receiving supporting,
I recline by the sills of the exquisite flexible doors,
And mark the outlet, and mark the relief and escape.

And as to you Corpse I think you are good manure, but that does
    not offend me,
I smell the white roses sweet-scented and growing.   1295
I reach to the leafy lips, I reach to the polish'd breasts of melons.

And as to you Life I reckon you are the leavings of many deaths,
(No doubt I have died myself ten thousand times before.)

I hear you whispering there O stars of heaven,
O suns—O grass of graves—O perpetual transfers and promo-
    tions,   1300
If you do not say any thing how can I say any thing?

Of the turbid pool that lies in the autumn forest,
Of the moon that descends the steeps of the soughing twilight,
Toss, sparkles of day and dusk—toss on the black stems that decay
    in the muck,
Toss to the moaning gibberish of the dry limbs.   1305

I ascend from the moon, I ascend from the night,
I perceive that the ghastly glimmer is noonday sunbeams reflected,
And debouch [2] to the steady and central from the offspring great or
    small.

50

There is that in me—I do not know what it is—but I know it is in
    me.

Wrench'd and sweaty—calm and cool then my body becomes,   1310

---

1. Obstetrician, midwife.   mouth, and note, l. 1292, "the ex-
2. Emerge. *Cf.* French "bouche," a   quisite, flexible doors."

I sleep—I sleep long.

I do not know it—it is without name—it is a word unsaid,
It is not in any dictionary, utterance, symbol.

Something it swings on more than the earth I swing on,
To it the creation is the friend whose embracing awakes me.   1315

Perhaps I might tell more. Outlines! I plead for my brothers and
sisters.

Do you see O my brothers and sisters?
It is not chaos or death—it is form, union, plan—it is eternal life
—it is Happiness.

51

The past and present wilt—I have fill'd them, emptied them,
And proceed to fill my next fold of the future.   1320

Listener up there! what have you to confide to me?
Look in my face while I snuff the sidle of evening,[3]
(Talk honestly, no one else hears you, and I stay only a minute
longer.)

Do I contradict myself?
Very well then I contradict myself,   1325
(I am large, I contain multitudes.)

I concentrate toward them that are nigh, I wait on the door-slab.

Who has done his day's work? who will soonest be through with his
supper?
Who wishes to walk with me?

Will you speak before I am gone? will you prove already too late?

52

The spotted hawk swoops by and accuses me, he complains of my
gab and my loitering.   1331

I too am not a bit tamed, I too am untranslatable,
I sound my barbaric yawp over the roofs of the world.

The last scud of day holds back for me,
It flings my likeness after the rest and true as any on the shadow'd
wilds,   1335
It coaxes me to the vapor and the dusk.

I depart as air, I shake my white locks at the runaway sun,
I effuse my flesh in eddies, and drift it in lacy jags.

---

3. "Snuff," colloq. for "snuff-out"; "slide"; derived from the "side-light," or
porthole window, of a ship.

I bequeath myself to the dirt to grow from the grass I love,
If you want me again look for me under your boot-soles.   1340

You will hardly know who I am or what I mean,
But I shall be good health to you nevertheless,
And filter and fibre your blood.

Failing to fetch me at first keep encouraged,
Missing me one place search another,   1345
I stop somewhere waiting for you.

1855, 1881–1882

From CHILDREN OF ADAM
Out of the Rolling Ocean the Crowd

Out of the rolling ocean the crowd came a drop gently to me,
Whispering *I love you, before long I die,*
I have travel'd a long way merely to look on you to touch you.
For I could not die till I once look'd on you,
For I fear'd I might afterward lose you.   5

Now we have met, we have look'd, we are safe,
Return in peace to the ocean my love,
I too am part of that ocean my love, we are not so much separated,
Behold the great rondure, the cohesion of all, how perfect!
But as for me, for you, the irresistible sea is to separate us,   10
As for an hour carrying us diverse, yet cannot carry us diverse
    forever;
Be not impatient—a little space—know you I salute the air, the
    ocean and the land,
Every day at sundown for your dear sake my love.

1865, 1867

Once I Pass'd Through a Populous City

Once I pass'd through a populous city imprinting my brain for
    future use with its shows, architecture, customs, traditions,
Yet now of all that city I remember only a woman [4] I casually met
    there who detain'd me for love of me,
Day by day and night by night we were together—all else has long
    been forgotten by me,
I remember I say only that woman who passionately clung to me,

4. An early MS. of this poem shows "man" stricken out and "woman" substituted.
Line 4 reads, in part, "only one rude and ignorant man."

Again we wander, we love, we separate again,   5
Again she holds me by the hand, I must not go,
I see her close beside me with silent lips sad and tremulous.

1860, 1867

Facing West from California's Shores

Facing west from California's shores,
Inquiring, tireless, seeking what is yet unfound,
I, a child, very old, over waves, towards the house of maternity,
   the land of migrations, look afar,
Look off the shores of my Western sea, the circle almost circled;
For starting westward from Hindustan, from the vales of Kash-
   mere,   5
From Asia, from the north, from the God, the sage, and the hero,
From the south, from the flowery peninsulas and the spice islands,
Long having wander'd since, round the earth having wander'd,
Now I face home again, very pleas'd and joyous,
(But where is what I started for so long ago?   10
And why is it yet unfound?)

1860, 1867

As Adam Early in the Morning

As Adam early in the morning,
Walking forth from the bower refresh'd with sleep,
Behold me where I pass, hear my voice, approach,
Touch me, touch the palm of your hand to my body as I pass,
Be not afraid of my body.   5

1861, 1867

From CALAMUS [6]

For You O Democracy

Come, I will make the continent indissoluble,
I will make the most splendid race the sun ever shone upon,
I will make divine magnetic lands,
      With the love of comrades,
      With the life-long love of comrades.   5

5. Asia interested Whitman as the supposed birthplace of the human race.
6. The "Calamus" poems first appeared
in the third edition of *Leaves of Grass*

(1860). The calamus, a species of water
reed, sometimes appears in myth and
literature, as it does here, as a symbol
of male comradeship.

I will plant companionship thick as trees along all the rivers of
America, and along the shores of the great lakes, and all over
the prairies,
I will make inseparable cities with their arms about each other's
necks,
> By the love of comrades,
> By the manly love of comrades.

For you these from me, O Democracy, to serve you ma femme!   10
For you, for you I am trilling these songs.

1860, 1881–1882

I Saw in Louisiana a Live-oak Growing

I saw in Louisiana a live-oak growing,
All alone stood it and the moss hung down from the branches,
Without any companion it grew there uttering joyous leaves of
dark green,
And its look, rude, unbending, lusty, made me think of myself,
But I wonder'd how it could utter joyous leaves standing alone
there without its friend near, for I knew I could not,   5
And I broke off a twig with a certain number of leaves upon it, and
twined around it a little moss,
And brought it away, and I have placed it in sight in my room,
It is not needed to remind me as of my own dear friends,
(For I believe lately I think of little else than of them,)
Yet it remains to me a curious token, it makes me think of manly
love;   10
For all that, and though the live-oak glistens there in Louisiana
solitary in a wide flat space,
Uttering joyous leaves all its life without a friend a lover near,
I know very well I could not.

1860, 1867

Crossing Brooklyn Ferry [7]

1

Flood-tide below me! I see you face to face!
Clouds of the west—sun there half an hour high—I see you also
face to face.

Crowds of men and women attired in the usual costumes, how
curious you are to me!

7. First called "Sun-Down Poem" in the second edition of *Leaves of Grass*
(1856). This lyric was a favorite with Thoreau.

On the ferry-boats the hundreds and hundreds that cross, returning home, are more curious to me than you suppose,
And you that shall cross from shore to shore years hence are more
 to me, and more in my meditations, than you might suppose. 5

2

The impalpable sustenance of me from all things at all hours of the
 day,
The simple, compact, well-join'd scheme, myself disintegrated,
 every one disintegrated yet part of the scheme,
The similitudes of the past and those of the future, *moves toward transcendence of time*
The glories strung like beads on my smallest sights and hearings,
 on the walk in the street and the passage over the river,
The current rushing so swiftly and swimming with me far away, 10
The others that are to follow me, the ties between me and them,
The certainty of others, the life, love, sight, hearing of others.

Others will enter the gates of the ferry and cross from shore to
 shore,
Others will watch the run of the flood-tide,
Others will see the shipping of Manhattan north and west, and
 the heights of Brooklyn to the south and east,
Others will see the islands large and small; 15
Fifty years hence, others will see them as they cross, the sun half
 an hour high,
A hundred years hence, or ever so many hundred years hence,
 others will see them,
Will enjoy the sunset, the pouring-in of the flood-tide, the falling-
 back to the sea of the ebb-tide.

3

It avails not, time nor place—distance avails not, 20
I am with you, you men and women of a generation, or ever so
 many generations hence, *Shared senses*
Just as you feel when you look on the river and sky, so I felt,
Just as any of you is one of a living crowd, I was one of a crowd,
Just as you are refresh'd by the gladness of the river and the bright
 flow, I was refresh'd,
Just as you stand and lean on the rail, yet hurry with the swift cur-
 rent, I stood yet was hurried, 25
Just as you look on the numberless masts of ships and the thick-
 stemm'd pipes of steamboats, I look'd.

I too many and many a time cross'd the river of old,
Watched the Twelfth-month sea-gulls, saw them high in the air
 floating with motionless wings, oscillating their bodies,
Saw how the glistening yellow lit up parts of their bodies and left
 the rest in strong shadow,

Saw the slow-wheeling circles and the gradual edging toward the
  south,   30
Saw the reflection of the summer sky in the water,
Had my eyes dazzled by the shimmering track of beams,
Look'd at the fine centrifugal spokes of light round the shape of
  my head in the sunlit water,
Look'd on the haze on the hills southward and south-westward,
Look'd on the vapor as it flew in fleeces tinged with violet,   35
Look'd toward the lower bay to notice the vessels arriving,
Saw their approach, saw aboard those that were near me,
Saw the white sails of schooners and sloops, saw the ships at anchor,
The sailors at work in the rigging or out astride the spars,
The round masts, the swinging motion of the hulls, the slender
  serpentine pennants,   40
The large and small steamers in motion, the pilots in their pilot-
  houses,
The white wake left by the passage, the quick tremulous whirl of
  the wheels,
The flags of all nations, the falling of them at sunset,
The scallop-edged waves in the twilight, the ladled cups, the
  frolicsome crests and glistening,
The stretch afar growing dimmer and dimmer, the gray walls of the
  granite storehouses by the docks,   45
On the river the shadowy group, the big steam-tug closely flank'd
  on each side by the barges, the hay-boat, the belated lighter,
On the neighboring shore the fires from the foundry chimneys
  burning high and glaringly into the night,
Casting their flicker of black contrasted with wild red and yellow
  light over the tops of houses, and down into the clefts of streets.

4

These and all else were to me the same as they are to you,
I loved well those cities, loved well the stately and rapid river,   50
The men and women I saw were all near to me,
Others the same—others who look back on me because I look'd
  forward to them,
(The time will come, though I stop here to-day and to-night.)

5

What is it then between us?
What is the count of the scores or hundreds of years between us?   55

Whatever it is, it avails not—distance avails not, and place avails
  not,
I too lived, Brooklyn of ample hills was mine,
I too walk'd the streets of Manhattan island, and bathed in the
  waters around it,
I too felt the curious abrupt questionings stir within me,

In the day among crowds of people sometimes they came upon
    me, 60
In my walks home late at night or as I lay in my bed they came
    upon me,
I too had been struck from the float forever held in solution, *receives*
I too had receiv'd identity by my body, *individual Soul (of Oversoul) receives Nothing.*
That I was I knew was of my body, and what I should be I knew I
    should be of my body.

6

It is not upon you alone the dark patches fall, 65
The dark threw its patches down upon me also,
The best I had done seem'd to me blank and suspicious,
My great thoughts as I supposed them, were they not in reality
    meagre?
Nor is it you alone who know what it is to be evil,
I am he who knew what it was to be evil, 70
I too knitted the old knot of contrariety,
Blabb'd, blush'd, resented, lied, stole, grudg'd,
Had guile, anger, lust, hot wishes I dared not speak,
Was wayward, vain, greedy, shallow, sly, cowardly, malignant,
The wolf, the snake, the hog, not wanting in me, 75
The cheating look, the frivolous word, the adulterous wish, not
    wanting,
Refusals, hates, postponements, meanness, laziness, none of these
    wanting,
Was one with the rest, the days and haps of the rest,
Was call'd by my nighest name by clear loud voices of young men
    as they saw me approaching or passing,
Felt their arms on my neck as I stood, or the negligent leaning of
    their flesh against me as I sat, 80
Saw many I loved in the street or ferry-boat or public assembly, yet
    never told them a word,
Lived the same life with the rest, the same old laughing, gnawing,
    sleeping,
Play'd the part that still looks back on the actor or actress,
The same old role, the role that is what we make it, as great as we
    like,
Or as small as we like, or both great and small. 85

7

Closer yet I approach you,
What thought you have of me now, I had as much of you—I laid
    in my stores in advance,
I consider'd long and seriously of you before you were born.

Who was to know what should come home to me?
Who knows but I am enjoying this? 90

Who knows, for all the distance, but I am as good as looking at
    you now, for all you cannot see me?

8

Ah, what can ever be more stately and admirable to me than mast-
    hemm'd Manhattan?
River and sunset and scallop-edg'd waves of flood-tide?
The sea-gulls oscillating their bodies, the hay-boat in the twilight,
    and the belated lighter?
What gods can exceed these that clasp me by the hand, and with
    voices I love call me promptly and loudly by my nighest name
    as I approach?   95
What is more subtle than this which ties me to the woman or man
    that looks in my face?
Which fuses me into you now, and pours my meaning into you?

We understand then do we not?
What I promis'd without mentioning it, have you not accepted?
What the study could not teach—what the preaching could not
    accomplish is accomplish'd, is it not?   100

9

Flow on, river! flow with the flood-tide, and ebb with the ebb-
    tide!
Frolic on, crested and scallop-edg'd waves!
Gorgeous clouds of the sunset! drench with your splendor me, or
    the men and women generations after me!
Cross from shore to shore, countless crowds of passengers!
Stand up, tall masts of Mannahatta! [8] stand up, beautiful hills of
    Brooklyn!   105
Throb, baffled and curious brain! throw out questions and answers!
Suspend here and everywhere, eternal float of solution!
Gaze, loving and thirsting eyes, in the house or street or public
    assembly!
Sound out, voices of young men! loudly and musically call me by
    my nighest name!
Live, old life! play the part that looks back on the actor or actress! 110
Play the old role, the role that is great or small according as one
    makes it!
Consider, you who peruse me, whether I may not in unknown
    ways be looking upon you;
Be firm, rail over the river, to support those who lean idly, yet
    haste with the hasting current;
Fly on, sea-birds! fly sideways, or wheel in large circles high in the
    air;

8. The original Indian names of this locality delighted Whitman: "Manna-hatta," the dwelling of the God Manito; and "Paumanok" for fish-shaped Long Island.

Receive the summer sky, you water, and faithfully hold it till all
    downcast eyes have time to take it from you!   115
Diverge, fine spokes of light, from the shape of my head, or any
    one's head, in the sunlit water!
Come on, ships from the lower bay! pass up or down, white-sail'd
    schooners, sloops, lighters!
Flaunt away, flags of all nations! be duly lower'd at sunset!
Burn high your fires, foundry chimneys! cast black shadows at
    nightfall! cast red and yellow light over the tops of the houses!
Appearances, now or henceforth, indicate what you are,   120
You necessary film, continue to envelop the soul,
About my body for me, and your body for you, be hung our di-
    vinest aromas,
Thrive, cities—bring your freight, bring your shows, ample and
    sufficient rivers,
Expand, being than which none else is perhaps more spiritual,
Keep your places, objects than which none else is more lasting.   125

You have waited, you always wait, you dumb, beautiful ministers,
We receive you with free sense at last, and are insatiate hence-
    forward,
Not you any more shall be able to foil us, or withhold yourselves
    from us,
We use you, and do not cast you aside—we plant you permanent-
    ly within us,
We fathom you not—we love you—there is perfection in you
    also,   130
You furnish your parts toward eternity,
Great or small, you furnish your parts toward the soul.

1856, 1881–1882

From Sea-Drift

Out of the Cradle Endlessly Rocking [9]

Out of the cradle endlessly rocking,
Out of the mocking-bird's throat, the musical shuttle,
Out of the Ninth-month [1] midnight,
Over the sterile sands and the fields beyond, where the child leav-
    ing his bed wander'd alone, bareheaded, barefoot,

9. "Out of the Cradle Endlessly Rocking" became the first poem in a section
entitled "Sea-Drift" in the 1881 edition
of *Leaves of Grass*. In the 1871 edition
this section was entitled "Sea-Shore
Memories." The sea provided inspiration for Whitman, who in these poems
hints at some of the major crises of his
life.
1. The Quaker designation for September may here also suggest the human
cycle of fertility and birth, in contrast
with "sterile sands" in the next line.

Down from the shower'd halo,   5
Up from the mystic play of shadows twining and twisting as if
    they were alive,
Out from the patches of briers and blackberries,
From the memories of the bird that chanted to me,
From your memories sad brother, from the fitful risings and fallings
    I heard,
From under that yellow half-moon late-risen and swollen as if
    with tears,   10
From those beginning notes of yearning and love there in the
    mist,
From the thousand responses of my heart never to cease,
From the myriad thence-arous'd words,
From the word stronger and more delicious than any,
From such as now they start the scene revisiting,   15
As a flock, twittering, rising, or overhead passing,
Borne hither, ere all eludes me, hurriedly,
A man, yet by these tears a little boy again,
Throwing myself on the sand, confronting the waves,
I, chanter of pains and joys, uniter of here and hereafter,   20
Taking all hints to use them, but swiftly leaping beyond them,
A reminiscence sing.

Once Paumanok,[2]
When the lilac-scent was in the air and Fifth-month grass was
    growing,
Up this seashore in some briers,   25
Two feather'd guests from Alabama, two together,
And their nest, and four light-green eggs spotted with brown,
And every day the he-bird to and fro near at hand,
And every day the she-bird crouch'd on her nest, silent, with bright
    eyes,
And every day I, a curious boy, never too close, never disturbing
    them,   30
Cautiously peering, absorbing, translating.

Shine! shine! shine!
Pour down your warmth, great sun!
While we bask, we two together.

Two together!   35
Winds blow south, or winds blow north,
Day come white, or night come black,
Home, or rivers and mountains from home,

---

2. Whitman liked the Indian name for Long Island ("a fish" or "fish-shaped").
This poem, like "starting from Paumanok," deals with the genesis of his life.

Singing all time, minding no time,
While we two keep together.[3]   40

Till of a sudden,
May-be kill'd, unknown to her mate,
One forenoon the she-bird crouch'd not on the nest,
Nor return'd that afternoon, nor the next,
Nor ever appear'd again.   45

And thenceforward all summer in the sound of the sea,
And at night under the full of the moon in calmer weather,
Over the hoarse surging of the sea,
Or flitting from brier to brier by day,
I saw, I heard at intervals the remaining one, the he-bird,   50
The solitary guest from Alabama.

Blow! blow! blow!
Blow up sea-winds along Paumanok's shore;
I wait and I wait till you blow my mate to me.

Yes, when the stars glisten'd,   55
All night long on the prong of a moss-scallop'd stake,
Down almost amid the slapping waves,
Sat the lone singer wonderful causing tears.

He call'd on his mate,
He pour'd forth the meaning which I of all men know.   60

Yes my brother I know,
The rest might not, but I have treasur'd every note,
For more than once dimly down to the beach gliding,
Silent, avoiding the moonbeams, blending myself with the shad-
    ows,
Recalling now the obscure shapes, the echoes, the sounds and
    sights after their sorts,   65
The white arms out in the breakers tirelessly tossing,
I, with bare feet, a child, the wind wafting my hair,
Listen'd long and long.

Listen'd to keep, to sing, now translating the notes,
Following you my brother.   70

Soothe! soothe! soothe!
Close on its wave soothes the wave behind,

---

3. The mockingbird songs were altered for rhythmic verisimilitude in several editions subsequent to the magazine publication of 1859. Whitman, himself an ornithologist, had also the advice of his friend John Burroughs, the talented naturalist. Note the characteristic re-iteration and the staccato twittering (*e.g.* lines 80, 91–92, 111).

And again another behind embracing and lapping, every one close,
But my love soothes not me, not me.

Low hangs the moon, it rose late,   75
It is lagging—O I think it is heavy with love, with love.

O madly the sea pushes upon the land,
With love, with love.

O night! do I not see my love fluttering out among the breakers?
What is that little black thing I see there in the white?   80

Loud! loud! loud!
Loud I call to you, my love!

High and clear I shoot my voice over the waves,
Surely you must know who is here, is here,
You must know who I am, my love.   85

Low-hanging moon!
What is that dusky spot in your brown yellow?
O it is the shape, the shape of my mate!
O moon do not keep her from me any longer.

Land! land! O land!   90
Whichever way I turn, O I think you could give me my mate back
      again if you only would,
For I am almost sure I see her dimly whichever way I look.

O rising stars!
Perhaps the one I want so much will rise, will rise with some of you.

O throat! O trembling throat!   95
Sound clearer through the atmosphere!
Pierce the woods, the earth,
Somewhere listening to catch you must be the one I want.

Shake out carols!
Solitary here, the night's carols!
Carols of lonesome love! death's carols!   100
Carols under that lagging, yellow, waning moon!
O under that moon where she droops almost down into the sea!
O reckless despairing carols.

But soft! sink low!   105
Soft! let me just murmur,
And do you wait a moment you husky-nois'd sea,
For somewhere I believe I heard my mate responding to me,
So faint, I must be still, be still to listen,

But not altogether still, for then she might not come immediately
    to me.   110

Hither my love!
Here I am! here!
With this just-sustain'd note I announce myself to you,
This gentle call is for you my love, for you.

Do not be decoy'd elsewhere,   115
That is the whistle of the wind, it is not my voice,
That is the fluttering, the fluttering of the spray,
Those are the shadows of leaves.

O darkness! O in vain!
O I am very sick and sorrowful.   120
O brown halo in the sky near the moon, drooping upon the sea!
O troubled reflection in the sea!
O throat! O throbbing heart!
And I singing uselessly, uselessly all the night.

O past! O happy life! O songs of joy!   125
In the air, in the woods, over fields,
Loved! loved! loved! loved! loved!
But my mate no more, no more with me!
We two together no more.

The aria sinking,[4]   130
All else continuing, the stars shining,
The winds blowing, the notes of the bird continuous echoing,
With angry moans the fierce old mother incessantly moaning,
On the sands of Paumanok's shore gray and rustling,
The yellow half-moon enlarged, sagging down, drooping, the face
    of the sea almost touching,   135
The boy ecstatic, with his bare feet the waves, with his hair the at-
    mosphere dallying,
The love in the heart long pent, now loose, now at last tumultu-
    ously bursting,
The aria's meaning, the ears, the soul, swiftly depositing,
The strange tears down the cheeks coursing,
The colloquy there, the trio, each uttering,   140
The undertone, the savage old mother incessantly crying,
To the boy's soul's questions sullenly timing, some drown'd secret
    hissing,
To the outsetting bard.

4. Robert D. Faner, in *Whitman and the Opera*, 1951, shows Whitman's indebtedness to the aria and other operatic forms of lyric.

Demon or bird! (said the boy's soul,)
Is it indeed toward your mate you sing? or is it really to me? 145
For I, that was a child, my tongue's use sleeping, now I have heard
    you,
Now in a moment I know what I am for, I awake,
And already a thousand singers, a thousand songs, clearer, louder
    and more sorrowful than yours,
A thousand warbling echoes have started to life within me, never
    to die.

O you singer solitary, singing by yourself, projecting me, 150
O solitary me listening, never more shall I cease perpetuating you,
Never more shall I escape, never more the reverberations,
Never more the cries of unsatisfied love be absent from me,
Never again leave me to be the peaceful child I was before what
    there in the night,
By the sea under the yellow and sagging moon, 155
The messenger there arous'd, the fire, the sweet hell within,
The unknown want, the destiny of me. *to find expression*

O give me the clew! (it lurks in the night here somewhere,)
O if I am to have so much, let me have more!

A word then, (for I will conquer it,) 160
The word final, superior to all,
Subtle, sent up—what is it?—I listen;
Are you whispering it, and have been all the time, you sea-waves?
Is that it from your liquid rims and wet sands?

Whereto answering, the sea, 165
Delaying not, hurrying not,
Whisper'd me through the night, and very plainly before day-
    break,
Lisp'd to me the low and delicious word death,
And again death, death, death, death,
Hissing melodious, neither like the bird nor like my arous'd
    child's heart, 170
But edging near as privately for me rustling at my feet,
Creeping thence steadily up to my ears and laving me softly all
    over,
Death, death, death, death, death.

Which I do not forget,
But fuse the song of my dusky demon and brother, 175
That he sang to me in the moonlight on Paumanok's gray beach,
With the thousand responsive songs at random,
My own songs awaked from that hour,

And with them the key, the word up from the waves,
The word of the sweetest song and all songs,   180
That strong and delicious word which, creeping to my feet,
(Or like some old crone rocking the cradle, swathed in sweet gar-
      ments, bending aside,)
The sea whisper'd me.

                                        1859, 1881–1882

To the Man-of-War-Bird [5]

Thou who has slept all night upon the storm,
Waking renew'd on thy prodigious pinions,
(Burst the wild storm? above it thou ascended'st,
And rested on the sky, thy slave that cradled thee,)
Now a blue point, far, far in heaven floating,   5
As to the light emerging here on deck I watch thee,
(Myself a speck, a point on the world's floating vast.)

Far, far at sea,
After the night's fierce drifts have strewn the shore with wrecks,
With re-appearing day as now so happy and serene,   10
The rosy and elastic dawn, the flashing sun,
The limpid spread of air cerulean,
Thou also re-appearest.

Thou born to match the gale, (thou art all wings,)
To cope with heaven and earth and sea and hurricane,   15
Thou ship of air that never furl'st thy sails,
Days, even weeks untired and onward, through spaces, realms gy-
      rating,
At dusk that look'st on Senegal,[6] at morn America,
That sport'st amid the lightning-flash and thunder-cloud,
In them, in thy experiences, had'st thou my soul,   20
What joys! what joys were thine! [7]

                                        1876, 1881–1882

---

5. This poem is based on a French poem by Jules Michelet; it was one of twenty new poems added in the seventh edition of *Leaves of Grass* (1881–1882).

6. A republic in French West Africa.
7. *Cf.* the thirteenth stanza of Shelley's "To a Skylark," a poem well known to Whitman, for a reversal of the sentiment of these lines.

From BY THE ROADSIDE

Gods

Lover divine and perfect Comrade,
Waiting content, invisible yet, but certain,
Be thou my God.

Thou, thou, the Ideal Man,
Fair, able, beautiful, content, and loving,   5
Complete in body and dilate in spirit,
Be thou my God.

O Death, (for Life has served its turn,)
Opener and usher to the heavenly mansion,
Be thou my God.   10

Aught, aught of mightiest, best I see, conceive, or know,
(To break the stagnant tie—thee, thee to free, O soul,)
Be thou my God.

All great ideas, the races' aspirations,
All heroisms, deeds of rapt enthusiasts,   15
Be ye my Gods.

Or Time and Space,
Or shape of Earth divine and wondrous,
Or some fair shape I viewing, worship,
Or lustrous orb of sun or star by night,   20
Be ye my Gods.

                                              1871, 1881–1882

The Dalliance of the Eagles [8]

Skirting the river road, (my forenoon walk, my rest,)
Skyward in air a sudden muffled sound, the dalliance of the eagles,
The rushing amorous contact high in space together,
The clinching interlocking claws, a living, fierce, gyrating wheel,
Four beating wings, two beaks, a swirling mass tight grappling,   5
In tumbling turning clustering loops, straight downward falling,
Till o'er the river pois'd, the twain yet one, a moment's lull,
A motionless still balance in the air, then parting, talons loosing,
Upward again on slow-firm pinions slanting, their separate diverse
     flight,
She hers, he his, pursuing.   10

                                              1880, 1881–1882

8. This poem was written from an ac-   edition of *Leaves of Grass* (1881–
count furnished the poet by John Bur-   1882).
roughs. It was included in the seventh

From DRUM-TAPS [9]

Cavalry Crossing a Ford [1]

A line in long array where they wind betwixt green islands,
They take a serpentine course, their arms flash in the sun—hark to
the musical clank,
Behold the silvery river, in it the splashing horses loitering stop to
drink,
Behold the brown-faced men, each group, each person a picture,
the negligent rest on the saddles,
Some emerge on the opposite bank, others are just entering the
ford—while,   5
Scarlet and blue and snowy white,
The guidon flags flutter gayly in the wind.

                                                    1865, 1871

Vigil Strange I Kept on the Field One Night

Vigil strange I kept on the field one night;
When you my son and my comrade dropt at my side that day,
One look I but gave which your dear eyes return'd with a look I
shall never forget,
One touch of your hand to mine O boy, reach'd up as you lay on
the ground,
Then onward I sped in the battle, the even-contested battle,   5
Till late in the night reliev'd to the place at last again I made my
way,
Found you in death so cold dear comrade, found your body son of
responding kisses, (never again on earth responding,)
Bared your face in the starlight, curious the scene, cool blew the
moderate night-wind,
Long there and then in vigil I stood, dimly around me the battle-
field spreading,
Vigil wondrous and vigil sweet there in the fragrant silent night,   10
But not a tear fell, not even a long-drawn sigh, long, long I gazed,
Then on the earth partially reclining sat by your side leaning my
chin in my hands,
Passing sweet hours, immortal and mystic hours with you dearest
comrade—not a tear, not a word,

9. *Drum-Taps* (1865) contained fifty-
three poems, some of them written at
or near the battle front in Virginia.
These poems were later given a central
position in *Leaves of Grass*, as representing a crucial experience of democracy and the poet.

1. In *American Renaissance*, 1941,
F. O. Matthiessen likens many of Whitman's poems to "genre painting" of the
Flemish school—homely, quiet life arrested, suggesting perhaps a story. See,
following this, five other such "genre
paintings."

Vigil of silence, love and death, vigil for you my son and my soldier,
As onward silently stars aloft, eastward new ones upward stole,   15
Vigil final for you brave boy, (I could not save you, swift was your
   death,
I faithfully loved you and cared for you living, I think we shall
   surely meet again,)
Till at latest lingering of the night, indeed just as the dawn
   appear'd,
My comrade I wrapt in his blanket, envelop'd well his form,
Folded the blanket well, tucking it carefully over head and care-
   fully under feet,   20
And there and then and bathed by the rising sun, my son in his
   grave, in his rude-dug grave I deposited,
Ending my vigil strange with that, vigil of night and battle-field dim,
Vigil for boy of responding kisses, (never again on earth responding,)
Vigil for comrade swiftly slain, vigil I never forget, how as day
   brighten'd,
I rose from the chill ground and folded my soldier well in his
   blanket,   25
And buried him where he fell.

                                        1865, 1867

A Sight in Camp in the Daybreak Gray and Dim [2]

A sight in camp in the daybreak gray and dim,
As from my tent I emerge so early sleepless,
As slow I walk in the cool fresh air the path near by the hospital
   tent,
Three forms I see on stretchers lying, brought out there untended
   lying,
Over each the blanket spread, ample brownish woolen blanket,   5
Gray and heavy blanket, folding, covering all.

Curious I halt and silent stand,
Then with light fingers I from the face of the nearest the first just
   lift the blanket;
Who are you elderly man so gaunt and grim, with well-gray'd hair,
   and flesh all sunken about the eyes?
Who are you my dear comrade?   10

Then to the second I step—and who are you my child and darling?
Who are you sweet boy with cheeks yet blooming?

---

2. Whitman's notebook at the front, dated 1862–1863, records his awe at lifting
the blanket and seeing the calm and beautiful face.

Then to the third—a face nor child nor old, very calm, as of beautiful yellow-white ivory;
Young man I think I know you—I think this face is the face of the Christ himself,
Dead and divine and brother of all, and here again he lies.   15

1865, 1867

The Wound-Dresser

1

An old man bending I come among new faces,
Years looking backward resuming in answer to children,
Come tell us old man, as from young men and maidens that love me,
(Arous'd and angry, I'd thought to beat the alarum, and urge relentless war,
But soon my fingers fail'd me, my face droop'd and I resign'd myself,   5
To sit by the wounded and soothe them, or silently watch the dead;)
Years hence of these scenes, of these furious passions, these chances,
Of unsurpass'd heroes, (was one side so brave? the other was equally brave;)
Now be witness again, paint the mightiest armies of earth,
Of those armies so rapid so wondrous what saw you to tell us?   10
What stays with you latest and deepest? of curious panics,
Of hard-fought engagements or sieges tremendous what deepest remains?

2

O maidens and young men I love and that love me,
What you ask of my days those the strangest and sudden your talking recalls,   14
Soldier alert I arrive after a long march cover'd with sweat and dust,
In the nick of time I come, plunge in the fight, loudly shout in the rush of successful charge,
Enter the captur'd works—yet lo, like a swift-running river they fade,
Pass and are gone they fade—I dwell not on soldiers' perils or soldiers' joys,
(Both I remember well—many the hardships, few the joys, yet I was content.)

But in silence, in dreams' projections,   20
While the world of gain and appearance and mirth goes on,

So soon what is over forgotten, and waves wash the imprints off
the sand,
With hinged knees returning I enter the doors, (while for you
up there,
Whoever you are, follow without noise and be of strong heart.)

Bearing the bandages, water and sponge,   25
Straight and swift to my wounded I go,
Where they lie on the ground after the battle brought in,
Where their priceless blood reddens the grass the ground,
Or to the rows of the hospital tent, or under the roof'd hospital,
To the long rows of cots up and down each side I return,   30
To each and all one after another I draw near, not one do I miss,
An attendant follows holding a tray, he carries a refuse pail,
Soon to be fill'd with clotted rags and blood, emptied, and fill'd
again.

I onward go, I stop,
With hinged knees and steady hand to dress wounds,   35
I am firm with each, the pangs are sharp yet unavoidable,
One turns to me his appealing eyes—poor boy! I never knew you,
Yet I think I could not refuse this moment to die for you, if that
would save you.

3

On, on I go, (open doors of time! open hospital doors!)
The crush'd head I dress, (poor crazed hand tear not the bandage
away,)   40
The neck of the cavalry-man with the bullet through and through
I examine,
Hard the breathing rattles, quite glazed already the eye, yet life
struggles hard,
(Come sweet death! be persuaded O beautiful death!
In mercy come quickly.)

From the stump of the arm, the amputated hand,   45
I undo the clotted lint, remove the slough, wash off the matter
and blood,
Back on his pillow the soldier bends with curv'd neck and side-
falling head,
His eyes are closed, his face is pale, he dares not look on the
bloody stump,
And has not yet look'd on it.

I dress a wound in the side, deep, deep,   50
But a day or two more, for see the frame all wasted and sinking,
And the yellow-blue countenance see.

I dress the perforated shoulder, the foot with the bullet-wound,
Cleanse the one with a gnawing and putrid gangrene, so sickening, so offensive,
While the attendant stands behind aside me holding the tray and
  pail.   55

I am faithful, I do not give out,
The fractur'd thigh, the knee, the wound in the abdomen,
These and more I dress with impassive hand, (yet deep in my
  breast a fire, a burning flame.)

4

Thus in silence in dreams' projections,
Returning, resuming, I thread my way through the hospitals,   60
The hurt and wounded I pacify with soothing hand,
I sit by the restless all the dark night, some are so young,
Some suffer so much, I recall the experience sweet and sad,
(Many a soldier's loving arms about this neck have cross'd and
  rested,
Many a soldier's kiss dwells on these bearded lips.)   65

1865   1881

Look Down Fair Moon

Look down fair moon and bathe this scene,
Pour softly down night's nimbus floods on faces ghastly, swollen,
  purple,
On the dead on their backs with arms toss'd wide,
Pour down your unstinted nimbus sacred moon.

1865, 1867

Reconciliation

Word over all, beautiful as the sky,
Beautiful that war and all its deeds of carnage must in time be
  utterly lost,
That the hands of the sisters Death and Night incessantly softly
  wash again, and ever again, this soil'd world;
For my enemy is dead, a man divine as myself is dead,
I look where he lies white-faced and still in the coffin—I draw
  near,   5
Bend down and touch lightly with my lips the white face in the
  coffin.

1865–1866, 1881–1882

When Lilacs Last in the Dooryard Bloom'd [3]

1

When lilacs [4] last in the dooryard bloom'd,
And the great star early droop'd in the western sky in the night,
I mourn'd, and yet shall mourn with ever-returning spring.

Ever-returning spring, trinity sure to me you bring,
Lilac blooming perennial and drooping star in the west,   5
And thought of him I love.

2

O powerful western fallen star!
O shades of night—O moody, tearful night!
O great star disappear'd—O the black murk that hides the star!
O cruel hands that hold me powerless—O helpless soul of me!   10
O harsh surrounding cloud that will not free my soul.

3

In the dooryard fronting an old farm-house near the white-wash'd
    palings,
Stands the lilac-bush tall-growing with heart-shaped leaves of rich
    green,
With many a pointed blossom rising delicate, with the perfume
    strong I love,
With every leaf a miracle—and from this bush in the dooryard,   15
With delicate-color'd blossoms and heart-shaped leaves of rich
    green,
A sprig with its flower I break.

4

In the swamp in secluded recesses,
A shy and hidden bird is warbling a song.

Solitary the thrush,   20
The hermit withdrawn to himself, avoiding the settlements,
Sings by himself a song.

Song of the bleeding throat,
Death's outlet song of life, (for well dear brother I know,
If thou wast not granted to sing thou would'st surely die.)   25

3. "When Lilacs Last in the Dooryard
Bloom'd" is one of four elegies entitled
"Memories of President Lincoln," which
were added, after Lincoln's death, to
later issues of *Drum-Taps* (1865). It
is generally regarded as one of Whitman's greatest poems. The bard of
American democratic comradeship saw,
in the life and death of Lincoln, the
human symbol of his theme, and in the
Drum-Taps volume, the keystone of the
arch of his *Leaves of Grass*.
4. The lilac, which may be Persian in
its origin, had, in Eastern symbolism, a
connection with manly love. Other symbols in this poem are the hermit thrush
and its song and the evening star. See
1. 205.

5

Over the breast of the spring, the land, amid cities,
Amid lanes and through old woods, where lately the violets peep'd
    from the ground, spotting the gray debris,
Amid the grass in the fields each side of the lanes, passing the end-
    less grass,
Passing the yellow-spear'd wheat, every grain from its shroud in
    the dark-brown fields uprisen,
Passing the apple-tree blows of white and pink in the orchards,   30
Carrying a corpse to where it shall rest in the grave,
Night and day journeys a coffin.

6

Coffin that passes through lanes and streets,[5]
Through day and night with the great cloud darkening the land,
With the pomp of the inloop'd flags with the cities draped in black,
With the show of the States themselves as of crape-veil'd women
    standing,   36
With processions long and winding and the flambeaus of the night,
With the countless torches lit, with the silent sea of faces and the
    unbared heads,
With the waiting depot, the arriving coffin, and the sombre faces,
With dirges through the night, with the thousand voices rising
    strong and solemn,   40
With all the mournful voices of the dirges pour'd around the
    coffin,
The dim-lit churches and the shuddering organs—where amid
    these you journey,
With the tolling tolling bells' perpetual clang,
Here, coffin that slowly passes,
I give you my sprig of lilac.   45

7

(Nor for you, for one alone,
Blossoms and branches green to coffins all I bring,
For fresh as the morning, thus would I chant a song for you O
    sane and sacred death.

All over bouquets of roses,
O death, I cover you over with roses and early lilies,   50
But mostly and now the lilac that blooms the first,
Copious I break, I break the sprigs from the bushes,

5. The funeral train of Abraham Lincoln passed, amid multitudes of mourners, through Maryland, Pennsylvania, New Jersey, New York, Ohio, and Indiana, on its way to Springfield, Illinois, where the martyred President was buried.

With loaded arms I come, pouring for you,
For you and the coffins all of you O death.)

8

O western orb sailing the heaven,   55
Now I know what you must have meant as a month since I walk'd,
As I walk'd in silence the transparent shadowy night,
As I saw you had something to tell as you bent to me night after
    night,
As you droop'd from the sky low down as if to my side, (while
    the other stars all look'd on,)
As we wander'd together the solemn night, (for something I know
    not what kept me from sleep,)   60
As the night advanced, and I saw on the rim of the west how full
    you were of woe,
As I stood on the rising ground in the breeze in the cool trans-
    parent night,
As I watch'd where you pass'd and was lost in the netherward black
    of the night,
As my soul in its trouble dissatisfied sank, as where you sad orb,
Concluded, dropt in the night, and was gone.   65

9

Sing on there in the swamp,
O singer bashful and tender, I hear your notes, I hear your call,
I hear, I come presently, I understand you,
But a moment I linger, for the lustrous star has detain'd me,
The star my departing comrade holds and detains me.   70

10

O how shall I warble myself for the dead one there I loved?
And how shall I deck my song for the large sweet soul that has
    gone?
And what shall my perfume be for the grave of him I love?

Sea-winds blown from east and west,
Blown from the Eastern sea and blown from the Western sea, till
    there on the prairies meeting,   75
These and with these and the breath of my chant,
I'll perfume the grave of him I love.

11

O what shall I hang on the chamber walls?
And what shall the pictures be that I hang on the walls,
To adorn the burial-house of him I love?   80

Pictures of growing spring and farms and homes,
With the Fourth-month eve at sundown, and the gray smoke lucid
    and bright,

With floods of the yellow gold of the gorgeous, indolent, sinking
    sun, burning, expanding the air,
With the fresh sweet herbage under foot, and the pale green leaves
    of the trees prolific,
In the distance the flowing glaze, the breast of the river, with a
    wind-dapple here and there,   85
With ranging hills on the banks, with many a line against the sky,
    and shadows,
And the city at hand with dwellings so dense, and stacks of
    chimneys,
And all the scenes of life and the workshops, and the workmen
    homeward returning.

12

Lo, body and soul—this land,
My own Manhattan with spires, and the sparkling and hurrying
    tides, and the ships,   90
The varied and ample land, the South and the North in the light,
    Ohio's shores and flashing Missouri,
And ever the far-spreading prairies cover'd with grass and corn.

Lo, the most excellent sun so calm and haughty,
The violet and purple morn with just-felt breezes,
The gentle soft-born measureless light,   95
The miracle spreading, bathing all, the fulfill'd noon,
The coming eve delicious, the welcome night and the stars,
Over my cities shining all, enveloping man and land.

13

Sing on, sing on you gray-brown bird,
Sing from the swamps, the recesses, pour your chant from the
    bushes,   100
Limitless out of the dusk, out of the cedars and pines.

Sing on dearest brother, warble your reedy song,
Loud human song, with voice of uttermost woe.

O liquid and free and tender!
O wild and loose to my soul—O wondrous singer!   105
You only I hear—yet the star holds me, (but will soon depart,)
Yet the lilac with mastering odor holds me.

14

Now while I sat in the day and look'd forth,
In the close of the day with its light and the fields of spring, and
    the farmers preparing their crops,
In the large unconscious scenery of my land with its lakes and for-
    ests,   110

In the heavenly aerial beauty, (after the perturb'd winds and the
  storms,)
Under the arching heavens of the afternoon swift passing, and the
  voices of children and women,
The many-moving sea-tides, and I saw the ships how they sail'd,
And the summer approaching with richness, and the fields all
  busy with labor,
And the infinite separate houses, how they all went on, each with
  its meals and minutia of daily usages,   115
And the streets how their throbbings throbb'd, and the cities
  pent—lo, then and there.
Falling upon them all and among them all, enveloping me with
  the rest,
Appear'd the cloud, appear'd the long black trail,
And I knew death, its thought, and the sacred knowledge of death.

Then with the knowledge of death as walking one side of me,   120
And the thought of death close-walking the other side of me,
And I in the middle as with companions, and as holding the hands
  of companions,
I fled forth to the hiding receiving night that talks not,
Down to the shores of the water, the path by the swamp in the
  dimness,
To the solemn shadowly cedars and ghostly pines so still.   125

And the singer so shy to the rest receiv'd me,
The gray-brown bird I know receiv'd us comrades three,
And he sang the carol of death, and a verse for him I love.

From deep secluded recesses,
From the fragrant cedars and the ghostly pines so still,   130
Came the carol of the bird.

And the charm of the carol rapt me,
As I held as if by their hands my comrades in the night,
And the voice of my spirit tallied the song of the bird.

Come lovely and soothing death,[6]   135
Undulate round the world, serenely arriving, arriving,
In the day, in the night, to all, to each,
Sooner or later delicate death.

Prais'd be the fathomless universe,
For life and joy, and for objects and knowledge curious,   141

---

6. Compare the song of the bird in this poem with the lyric songs of the bird in
"Out of the Cradle Endlessly Rocking."

And for love, sweet love—but praise! praise! praise!
For the sure-enwinding arms of cool-enfolding death.

Dark mother always gliding near with soft feet,
Have none chanted for thee a chant of fullest welcome?
Then I chant it for thee, I glorify thee above all,   145
I bring thee a song that when thou must indeed come, come un-
falteringly.

Approach strong deliveress,
When it is so, when thou hast taken them I joyously sing the dead,
Lost in the loving floating ocean of thee,
Laved in the flood of thy bliss O death.   150

From me to thee glad serenades,
Dances for thee I propose saluting thee, adornments and feast-
ings for thee,
And the sights of the open landscape and the high-spread sky are
fitting,
And life and the fields, and the huge and thoughtful night.

The night in silence under many a star,   155
The ocean shore and the husky whispering wave whose voice I
know,
And the soul turning to thee O vast and well-veil'd death,
And the body gratefully nestling close to thee.

Over the tree-tops I float thee a song,
Over the rising and sinking waves, over the myriad fields and the
prairies wide,   160
Over the dense-pack'd cities all and the teeming wharves and ways,
I float this carol with joy, with joy to thee O death.

15

To the tally of my soul,
Loud and strong kept up the gray-brown bird,
With pure deliberate notes spreading filling the night.   165

Loud in the pines and cedars dim,
Clear in the freshness moist and the swamp-perfume,
And I with my comrades there in the night.

While my sight that was bound in my eyes unclosed,
As to long panoramas of visions.   170

And I saw askant the armies,
I saw as in noiseless dreams hundreds of battle-flags,
Borne through the smoke of the battles and pierc'd with missiles
I saw them,

And carried hither and yon through the smoke, and torn and
    bloody,
And at last but a few shreds left on the staffs, (and all in silence,)
And the staffs all splinter'd and broken.   176

I saw battle-corpses, myriads of them,
And the white skeletons of young men, I saw them,
I saw the debris and debris of all the slain soldiers of the war,
But I saw they were not as was thought,   180
They themselves were fully at rest, they suffer'd not,
The living remain'd and suffer'd, the mother suffer'd,
And the wife and the child and the musing comrade suffer'd,
And the armies that remain'd suffer'd.

16

Passing the visions, passing the night,   185
Passing, unloosing the hold of my comrades' hands,
Passing the song of the hermit bird and the tallying song of my
    soul,
Victorious song, death's outlet song, yet varying ever-altering song,
As low and wailing, yet clear the notes, rising and falling, flooding
    the night,
Sadly sinking and fainting, as warning and warning, and yet again
    bursting with joy,   190
Covering the earth and filling the spread of the heaven,
As that powerful psalm in the night I heard from recesses,
Passing, I leave thee lilac with heart-shaped leaves,
I leave thee there in the door-yard, blooming, returning with
    spring.

I cease from my song for thee,   195
From my gaze on thee in the west, fronting the west, communing
    with thee,
O comrade lustrous with silver face in the night.

Yet each to keep and all, retrievements out of the night,
The song, the wondrous chant of the gray-brown bird,
And the tallying chant, the echo arous'd in my soul,   200
With the lustrous and drooping star with the countenance full of
    woe,
With the holders holding my hand nearing the call of the bird,
Comrades mine and I in the midst, and their memory ever to
    keep, for the dead I loved so well,
For the sweetest, wisest soul of all my days and lands—and this
    for his dear sake,
Lilac and star and bird twined with the chant of my soul,   205
There in the fragrant pines and the cedars dusk and dim.

                                  1865, 1881

From AUTUMN RIVULETS [7]

There Was a Child Went Forth

There was a child went forth every day,
And the first object he look'd upon, that object he became,
And that object became part of him for the day or a certain part
of the day,
Or for many years or stretching cycles of years.

The early lilacs became part of this child,   5
And grass and white and red morning-glories, and white and red
clover, and the song of the phœbe-bird,
And the Third-month lambs and the sow's pink-faint litter, and
the mare's foal and the cow's calf,
And the noisy brood of the barnyard or by the mire of the pond-
side,
And the fish suspending themselves so curiously below there,
and the beautiful curious liquid,
And the water-plants with their graceful flat heads, all became
part of him.   10

The field-sprouts of Fourth-month and Fifth-month became part
of him,
Winter-grain sprouts and those of the light-yellow corn, and the
esculent roots of the garden,
And the apple-trees cover'd with blossoms and the fruit afterward,
and wood-berries, and the commonest weeds by the road,
And the old drunkard staggering home from the outhouse of the
tavern whence he had lately risen,
And the schoolmistress that pass'd on her way to the school,   15
And the friendly boys that pass'd, and the quarrelsome boys,
And the tidy and fresh-cheek'd girls, and the barefoot negro boy
and girl,
And all the changes of city and country wherever he went.

His own parents, he that had father'd him and she that had con-
ceiv'd him in her womb and birth'd him,
They gave this child more of themselves than that,   20
They gave him afterward every day, they became part of him.

The mother at home quietly placing the dishes on the supper-
table,
The mother with mild words, clean her cap and gown, a whole-

---

7. The title "Autumn Rivulets" does not
refer in particular to the poet's later
years, but in its imagery implies a "sea
of time" to which the "wayward rivulets" of individual life flow. "Autumn
Rivulets" as a group title first appeared
in the seventh edition of *Leaves of
Grass* (1881).

some odor falling off her person and clothes as she walks by.
The father, strong, self-sufficient, manly, mean, anger'd, unjust,
The blow, the quick loud word, the tight bargain, the crafty lure,
The family usages, the language, the company, the furniture, the
yearning and swelling heart,   25
Affection that will not be gainsay'd, the sense of what is real, the
thought if after all it should prove unreal,
The doubts of day-time and the doubts of night-time, the curious
whether and how,
Whether that which appears so is so, or is it all flashes and specks?
Men and women crowding fast in the streets, if they are not
flashes and specks what are they?   30
The streets themselves and the façades of houses, and goods in
the windows,
Vehicles, teams, the heavy-plank'd wharves, the huge crossing at
the ferries,
The village on the highland seen from afar at sunset, the river
between,
Shadows, aureola and mist, the light falling on roofs and gables of
white or brown two miles off,
The schooner near by sleepily dropping down the tide, the little
boat slack-tow'd astern,   35
The hurrying tumbling waves, quick-broken crests, slapping,
The strata of color'd clouds, the long bar of maroon-tint away solitary by itself, the spread of purity it lies motionless in,
The horizon's edge, the flying sea-crow, the fragrance of salt marsh
and shore mud,
These became part of that child who went forth every day, and
who now goes, and will always go forth every day.

1855, 1871

To a Common Prostitute [8]

Be composed—be at ease with me—I am Walt Whitman, liberal
and lusty as Nature,
Not till the sun excludes you do I exclude you,
Not till the waters refuse to glisten for you and the leaves to rustle
for you, do my words refuse to glisten and rustle for you.

My girl I appoint with you an appointment, and I charge you that
you make preparation to be worthy to meet me,
And I charge you that you be patient and perfect till I come.   5

---

8. Whitman told William Sloane Kennedy that this poem was inspired by
"the beautiful little idyl of the New
Testament concerning the woman taken
in adultery." *Cf.* John viii: 3–11.

Till then I salute you with a significant look that you do not forget me.

1860

Prayer of Columbus [9]

A batter'd, wreck'd old man,
Thrown on this savage shore, far, far from home,
Pent by the sea and dark rebellious brows, twelve dreary months,
Sore, stiff with many toils, sicken'd and nigh to death,
I take my way along the island's edge,   5
Venting a heavy heart.

I am too full of woe!
Haply I may not live another day;
I cannot rest O God, I cannot eat or drink or sleep,
Till I put forth myself, my prayer, once more to Thee,   10
Breathe, bathe myself once more in Thee, commune with Thee,
Report myself once more to Thee.

Thou knowest my years entire, my life,
My long and crowded life of active work, not adoration merely;
Thou knowest the prayers and vigils of my youth,   15
Thou knowest my manhood's solemn and visionary meditations,
Thou knowest how before I commenced I devoted all to come to
      Thee,
Thou knowest I have in age ratified all those vows and strictly
      kept them,
Thou knowest I have not once lost nor faith nor ecstasy in Thee,
In shackles, prison'd, in disgrace, repining not,   20
Accepting all from Thee, as duly come from Thee.

All my emprises have been fill'd with Thee,
My speculations, plans, begun and carried on in thought of Thee,
Sailing the deep or journeying the land for Thee;
Intentions, purports, aspirations mine, leaving results to Thee. 25

O I am sure they really came from Thee,
The urge, the ardor, the unconquerable will,
The potent, felt, interior command, stronger than words,
A message from the Heavens whispering to me even in sleep,
These sped me on.   30

By me and these the work so far accomplish'd,
By me earth's elder cloy'd and stifled lands uncloy'd, unloos'd,

9. "Prayer of Columbus" was written
in 1874, when Whitman had little hope
of recovering from his first severe stroke
of paralysis. He often referred to his
poems as a kind of exploration: *cf.
Passage to India.*

By me the hemispheres rounded and tied, the unknown to the
known.

The end I know not, it is all in Thee,
Or small or great I know not—happy what broad fields, what
lands,   35
Haply the brutish measureless human undergrowth I know,
Transplanted there may rise to stature, knowledge worthy Thee,
Haply the swords I know may there indeed be turn'd to reaping-
tools,
Haply the lifeless cross I know, Europe's dead cross, may bud and
blossom there.

One effort more, my altar this bleak sand;   40
That Thou O God my life hast lighted,
With ray of light, steady, ineffable, vouchsafed of Thee,
Light rare untellable, lighting the very light,
Beyond all signs, descriptions, languages;
For that O God, be it my latest word, here on my knees   45
Old, poor, and paralyzed, I thank Thee.

My terminus near,
The clouds already closing in upon me,
The voyage balk'd, the course disputed, lost,
I yield my ships to Thee.   50

My hands, my limbs grow nerveless,
My brain feels rack'd, bewilder'd,
Let the old timbers part, I will not part,
I will cling fast to Thee, O God, though the waves buffet me,
Thee, Thee at least I know.   55

Is it the prophet's thought I speak, or am I raving?
What do I know of life? what of myself?
I know not even my own work past or present,
Dim ever-shifting guesses of it spread before me,
Of newer better worlds, their mighty parturition,   60
Mocking, perplexing me.

And these things I see suddenly, what mean they?
As if some miracle, some hand divine unseal'd my eyes,
Shadowy vast shapes smile through the air and sky,
And on the distant waves sail countless ships,   65
And anthems in new tongues I hear saluting me.

                                                            1874, 1881–1882

The Sleepers [1]

1

I wander all night in my vision,
Stepping with light feet, swiftly and noiselessly stepping and
   stopping,
Bending with open eyes over the shut eyes of sleepers,
Wandering and confused, lost to myself, ill-assorted, contradic-
   tory,
Pausing, gazing, bending, and stopping.   5

How solemn they look there, stretch'd and still,
How quiet they breathe, the little children in their cradles.

The wretched features of ennuyés, the white features of corpses,
   the livid faces of drunkards, the sick-gray faces of onanists,
The gash'd bodies on battle-fields, the insane in their strong-door'd
   rooms, the sacred idiots, the new-born emerging from
   gates, and the dying emerging from gates,
The night pervades them and infolds them.   10

The married couple sleep calmly in their bed, he with his palm on
   the hip of the wife, and she with her palm on the hip of
   the husband,
The sisters sleep lovingly side by side in their bed,
The men sleep lovingly side by side in theirs,
And the mother sleeps with her little child carefully wrapt.

The blind sleep, and the deaf and dumb sleep,   15
The prisoner sleeps well in the prison, the runaway son sleeps,
The murderer that is to be hung next day, how does he sleep?
And the murder'd person, how does he sleep?

The female that loves unrequited sleeps,   20
And the male that loves unrequited sleeps,
The head of the money-maker that plotted all day sleeps,
And the enraged and treacherous dispositions, all, all sleep.

I stand in the dark with drooping eyes by the worst-suffering and
   the most restless,
I pass my hands soothingly to and fro a few inches from them,
The restless sink in their beds, they fitfully sleep.   25

1. Out of the twelve poems constituting the first *Leaves of Grass* edition, 1855, eleven survived in the canon poems of 1881, but only the "Song of Myself" and "The Sleepers" were destined to represent its core. Like galvanic poles, these two draw from the mass two different kinds of poems, unlike in their sensibility. The "Song of Myself" gathers together poems of conscious vitality in which the physical and spiritual identity and individualism are paramount. "The Sleepers" associates those poems that deal most purely with the consciousness, with the existential condition and, hence, also with the subconscious, as a condition of being. This was a radical, unprecedented direction of sensibility. "The Sleepers" has been called "the only surrealist American poem of the nineteenth century." Recognizably related to it are "Out of the Cradle, Endlessly Rocking," "Proud Music of the Storm," and "Crossing Brooklyn Ferry."

Now I pierce the darkness, new beings appear,
The earth recedes from me into the night,
I saw that it was beautiful, and I see that what is not the earth is
beautiful.

I go from bedside to bedside, I sleep close with the other sleepers
each in turn,
I dream in my dream all the dreams of the other dreamers,   30
And I become the other dreamers.

I am a dance—play up there! the fit is whirling me fast!

I am the ever-laughing—it is new moon and twilight,
I see the hiding of douceurs,[2] I see nimble ghosts whichever way
I look,
Cache [3] and cache again deep in the ground and sea, and where it
is neither ground nor sea.   35

Well do they do their jobs those journeymen divine,
Only from me can they hide nothing, and would not if they could,
I reckon I am their boss and they make me a pet besides,
And surround me and lead me and run ahead when I walk,
To lift their cunning [4] covers to signify me with stretch'd arms, and
resume the way;   40
Onward we move, a gay gang of blackguards! with mirth-shouting
music and wild-flapping pennants of joy!

I am the actor, the actress, the voter, the politician,
The emigrant and the exile, the criminal that stood in the box,
He who has been famous and he who shall be famous after to-day,
The stammerer, the well-form'd person, the wasted or feeble
person.   45

I am she [5] who adorn'd herself and folded her hair expectantly,
My truant lover has come, and it is dark.

Double yourself and receive me darkness,
Receive me and my lover too, he will not let me go without
him.

I roll myself upon you as upon a bed, I resign myself to the dusk.   50

He whom I call answers me and takes the place of my lover,
He rises with me silently from the bed.

Darkness, you are gentler than my lover, his flesh was sweaty and
panting,
I feel the hot moisture yet that he left me.

---

2. French: "sweets," here rather "delights"; see the progression of erotic
experience to line 41.
3. French: "hide."
4. Here in the colloquial sense of
"quaint," "charming," "attractive"

(Eric Partridge, *A Dictionary of Slang*,
1961).
5. In the remainder of this section, of
the three identities, one seems to be the
darkness itself, regarded as a profound,
generative force.

My hands are spread forth, I pass them in all directions,   55
I would sound up the shadowy shore to which you are journeying.

Be careful darkness! already what was it touch'd me?
I thought my lover had gone, else darkness and he are one,
I hear the heart-beat, I follow, I fade away.

2

I descend [6] my western course, my sinews are flaccid,   60
Perfume and youth course through me and I am their wake.

It is my face yellow and wrinkled instead of the old woman's,
I sit low in a straw-bottom chair and carefully darn my grandson's
stockings.

It is I too, the sleepless widow looking out on the winter midnight,
I see the sparkles of starshine on the icy and pallid earth.   65

A shroud I see and I am the shroud, I wrap a body and lie in the
coffin,
It is dark here under ground, it is not evil or pain here, it is blank
here, for reasons.

(It seems to me that every thing in the light and air ought to be
happy,
Whoever is not in his coffin and the dark grave let him know he
has enough.)

3

I see a beautiful gigantic swimmer swimming naked through the
eddies of the sea,   70
His brown hair lies close and even to his head, he strikes out with
courageous arms, he urges himself with his legs,
I see his white body, I see his undaunted eyes,
I hate the swift-running eddies that would dash him head-fore-
most on the rocks.

What are you doing you ruffianly red-trickled waves?
Will you kill the courageous giant? will you kill him in the prime
of his middle age?   75

Steady and long he struggles,
He is baffled, bang'd, bruis'd, he holds out while his strength holds
out,
The slapping eddies are spotted with his blood, they bear him
away, they roll him, swing him, turn him,
His beautiful body is borne in the circling eddies, it is continually
bruis'd on rocks,
Swiftly and out of sight is borne the brave corpse.   80

6. Of the six episodes following, with
which the poet identifies, all are of loss
or death, and three are from actuality—
the battle of Brooklyn Heights, August
27, 1776 (Washington escaped with only
a remnant of his troops), Washington's
farewell to his troops, and the visit of
the Indian squaw to the Whitman (or
Van Velsov) homestead.

4

I turn but do not extricate myself,
Confused, a past-reading, another, but with darkness yet.

The beach is cut by the razory ice-wind, the wreck-guns sound,
The tempest lulls, the moon comes floundering through the drifts.

I look where the ship helplessly heads end on, I hear the burst as
 she strikes, I hear the howls of dismay, they grow fainter
 and fainter.   85

I cannot aid with my wringing fingers,
I can but rush to the surf and let it drench me and freeze
 upon me.

I search with the crowd, not one of the company is wash'd to us
 alive,
In the morning I help pick up the dead and lay them in rows in
 a barn.

5

Now of the older war-days, the defeat at Brooklyn,   90
Washington stands inside the lines, he stands on the intrench'd
 hills amid a crowd of officers,
His face is cold and damp, he cannot repress the weeping drops,
He lifts the glass perpetually to his eyes, the color is blanch'd from
 his cheeks,
He sees the slaughter of the southern braves confided to him by
 their parents.

The same at last and at last when peace is declared,   95
He stands in the room of the old tavern, the well-belov'd soldiers
 all pass through,
The officers speechless and slow draw near in their turns,
The chief encircles their necks with his arm and kisses them on
 the cheek,
He kisses lightly the wet cheeks one after another, he shakes
 hands and bids good-by to the army.

6

Now what my mother told me one day as we sat at dinner
 together,   100
Of when she was a nearly grown girl living home with her parents
 on the old homestead.

A red squaw came one breakfast-time to the old homestead,
On her back she carried a bundle of rushes for rush-bottoming
 chairs,
Her hair, straight, shiny, coarse, black, profuse, half-envelop'd her
 face,
Her step was free and elastic, and her voice sounded exquisitely
 as she spoke.   105

My mother look'd in delight and amazement at the stranger,
She look'd at the freshness of her tall-borne face and full and
    pliant limbs.
The more she look'd upon her she loved her,
Never before had she seen such wonderful beauty and purity,
She made her sit on a bench by the jamb of the fireplace, she
    cook'd food for her.   110
She had no work to give her, but she gave her remembrance and
    fondness.

The red squaw staid all the forenoon and toward the middle of
    the afternoon she went away,
O my mother was loth to have her go away,
All the week she thought of her, she watch'd for her many a
    month,
She remember'd her many a winter and many a summer,   115
But the red squaw never came nor was heard of there again.

7

A show of the summer softness—a contact of something unseen
    —an amour of the light and air,
I am jealous and overwhelm'd with friendliness,
And will go gallivant with the light and air myself.

O love and summer, you are in the dreams and in me,   120
Autumn and winter are in the dreams, the farmer goes with his
    thrift,
The droves and crops increase, the barns are well-fill'd.

Elements merge in the night, ships make tacks in the dreams,
The sailor sails, the exile returns home,
The fugitive returns unharm'd, the immigrant is back beyond
    months and years,   125
The poor Irishman lives in the simple house of his childhood
    with the well-known neighbors and faces,
They warmly welcome him, he is barefoot again, he forgets he is
    well off,
The Dutchman voyages home, and the Scotchman and Welshman
    voyage home, and the native of the Mediterranean voyages
    home,
To every port of England, France, Spain, enter well-fill'd ships,
The Swiss foots it toward his hills, the Prussian goes his way, the
    Hungarian his way, and the Pole his way,   130
The Swede returns, and the Dane and Norwegian return.

The homeward bound and the outward bound,
The beautiful lost swimmer, the ennuyé, the onanist, the female
    that loves unrequited, the money-maker,
The actor and actress, those through with their parts and those
    waiting to commence,

The affectionate boy, the husband and wife, the voter, the nominee
    that is chosen and the nominee that has fail'd,   135
The great already known and the great any time after to-day,
The stammerer, the sick, the perfect-form'd, the homely,
The criminal that stood in the box, the judge that sat and sen-
    tenced him, the fluent lawyers, the jury, the audience,
The laugher and weeper, the dancer, the midnight widow, the red
    squaw,
The consumptive, the erysipalite, the idiot, he that is wrong'd,   140
The antipodes, and every one between this and them in the dark,
I swear they are averaged now—one is no better than the other,
The night and sleep have liken'd them and restored them.

I swear they are all beautiful,
Every one that sleeps is beautiful, every thing in the dim light is
    beautiful,   145
The wildest and bloodiest is over, and all is peace.

Peace is always beautiful,
The myth of heaven indicates peace and night.

The myth of heaven indicates the soul,
The soul is always beautiful, it appears more or it appears less, it
    comes or it lags behind,   150
It comes from its embower'd garden and looks pleasantly on
    itself and encloses the world,
Perfect and clean the genitals previously jetting, and perfect and
    clean the womb cohering,
The head well-grown proportion'd and plumb, and the bowels and
    joints proportion'd and plumb.

The soul is always beautiful,
The universe is duly in order, every thing is in its place,   155
What has arrived is in its place and what waits shall be in its place,
The twisted skull waits, the watery or rotten blood waits,
The child of the glutton or venerealee waits long, and the child
    of the drunkard waits long, and the drunkard himself waits
    long,
The sleepers that lived and died wait, the far advanced are to go on
    in their turns, and the far behind are to come on in
    their turns,
The diverse shall be no less diverse, but they shall flow and unite
    —they unite now.   160

8

The sleepers are very beautiful as they lie unclothed,
They flow hand in hand over the whole earth from east to west as
    they lie unclothed,
The Asiatic and African are hand in hand, the European and
    American are hand in hand,
Learn'd and unlearn'd are hand in hand, and male and female are
    hand in hand,

The bare arm of the girl crosses the bare breast of her lover, they
    press close without lust, his lips press her neck,   165
The father holds his grown or ungrown son in his arms with
    measureless love, and the son holds the father in his arms
    with measureless love,
The white hair of the mother shines on the white wrist of the
    daughter,
The breath of the boy goes with the breath of the man, friend is
    inarm'd by friend,
The scholar kisses the teacher and the teacher kisses the scholar,
    the wrong'd is made right,
The call of the slave is one with the master's call, and the master
    salutes the slave,   170
The felon steps forth from the prison, the insane becomes sane,
    the suffering of sick persons is reliev'd,
The sweatings and fevers stop, the throat that was unsound is
    sound, the lungs of the consumptive are resumed, the poor
    distress'd head is free,
The joints of the rheumatic move as smoothly as ever, and
    smoother than ever,
Stiflings and passages open, the paralyzed become supple,
The swell'd and convuls'd and congested awake to themselves
    in condition,   175
They pass the invigoration of the night and the chemistry of the
    night, and awake.

I too pass from the night,
I stay a while away O night, but I return to you again and love you.

Why should I be afraid to trust myself to you?
I am not afraid, I have been well brought forward by you,   180
I love the rich running day, but I do not desert her in whom I lay
    so long,
I know not how I came of you and I know not where I go with
    you, but I know I came well and shall go well.

I will stop only a time with the night, and rise betimes,
I will duly pass the day O my mother, and duly return to you.

1855   1881

From WHISPERS OF HEAVENLY DEATH

Darest Thou Now O Soul

Darest thou now O soul,
Walk out with me toward the unknown region,
Where neither ground is for the feet nor any path to follow?

No map there, nor guide,
Nor voice sounding, nor touch of human hand,   5

Nor face with blooming flesh, nor lips, nor eyes, are in that land.

I know it not O soul,
Nor dost thou, all is a blank before us,
All waits undream'd of in that region, that inaccessible land.

Till when the ties loosen,   10
All but the ties eternal, Time and Space,
Nor darkness, gravitation, sense, nor any bounds bounding us.

Then we burst forth, we float,
In Time and Space O soul, prepared for them,
Equal equipt at last, (O joy! O fruit of all!) them to fulfil O soul.   15

1868, 1881

Whispers of Heavenly Death [7]

Whispers of heavenly death murmur'd I hear,
Labial gossip of night, sibilant chorals,
Footsteps gently ascending, mystical breezes wafted soft and low,
Ripples of unseen rivers, tides of a current flowing, forever flowing,
(Or is it the plashing of tears? the measureless waters of human
     tears?)   5

I see, just see skyward, great cloud-masses,
Mournfully slowly they roll, silently swelling and mixing,
With at times a half-dimm'd sadden'd far-off star,
Appearing and disappearing.

(Some parturition rather, some solemn immortal birth;   10
On the frontiers to eyes impenetrable,
Some soul is passing over.)

1868, 1871

Chanting the Square Deific [8]

Chanting the square deific, out of the One advancing, out of the
     sides,
Out of the old and new, out of the square entirely divine,
Solid, four-sided, (all the sides needed,) from this side Jehovah am
     I,
Old Brahm I, and I Saturnius am; [9]
Not Time affects me—I am Time, old, modern as any,   5

7. "Whispers of Heavenly Death" is
the title poem of a new section added
to Leaves of Grass in 1871.
8. In analyzing the religious experience
of mankind, Whitman follows trinitarian orthodoxy in his references to God
the Father, or creator; God the Son, or

intercessor; and God the Holy Ghost,
or the intuitive revelation. But note
that in stanza 3 Whitman also places
Satan among the "deific" experiences.
9. Supreme gods of the Hebrew, Hindu,
and Roman religions.

Unpersuadable, relentless, executing righteous judgments,
As the Earth, the Father, the brown old Kronos,[1] with laws,
Aged beyond computation, yet ever new, ever with those mighty
 laws rolling,
Relentless I forgive no man—whoever sins dies—I will have that
 man's life;
Therefore let none expect mercy—have the seasons, gravitation, the
 appointed days, mercy? no more have I,   10
But as the seasons and gravitation, and as all the appointed days that
 forgive not,
I dispense from this side judgments inexorable without the least
 remorse.

2

Consolator most mild, the promis'd one advancing,
With gentle hand extended, the mightier God am I,
Foretold by prophets and poets in their most rapt prophecies and
 poems,   15
From this side, lo! the Lord Christ gazes—lo! Hermes [2] I—lo! mine
 is Hercules' [3] face,
All sorrow, labor, suffering, I, tallying it, absorb in myself,
Many times have I been rejected, taunted, put in prison, and cruci-
 fied, and many times shall be again,
All the world have I given up for my dear brothers' and sisters' sake,
 for the soul's sake,
Wending my way through the homes of men, rich or poor, with
 the kiss of affection,   20
For I am affection, I am the cheer-bringing God, with hope and all-
 enclosing charity,
With indulgent words as to children, with fresh and sane words,
 mine only,
Young and strong I pass knowing well I am destin'd myself to an
 early death;
But my charity has no death—my wisdom dies not, neither early
 nor late,
And my sweet love bequeath'd here and elsewhere never dies.   25

3

Aloof, dissatisfied, plotting revolt,
Comrade of criminals, brother of slaves,
Crafty, despised, a drudge, ignorant,
With sudra [4] face and worn brow, black, but in the depths of my
 heart, proud as any,
Lifted now and always against whoever scorning assumes to rule
 me,   30

---

1. The Greek god, more primitive than Zeus, whose name, "Time," suggests an origin before creation.
2. Messenger for the gods on Olympus.
3. The most celebrated hero of classical mythology, son of Zeus and a mortal woman, worshiped for his many benefits to mankind.
4. Among the Hindu castes of India, the Sudra is the lowest, the caste of the untouchables.

Morose, full of guile, full of reminiscences, brooding, with many wiles,
(Though it was thought I was baffled and dispel'd, and my wiles done, but that will never be,)
Defiant, I, Satan, still live, still utter words, in new lands duly appearing, (and old ones also,)
Permanent here from my side, warlike, equal with any, real as any,
Nor time nor change shall ever change me or my words.   35

4

Santa Spirita,[5] breather, life,
Beyond the light, lighter than light,
Beyond the flames of hell, joyous, leaping easily above hell,
Beyond Paradise, perfumed solely with mine own perfume,
Including all life on earth, touching, including God, including Saviour and Satan,   40
Ethereal, pervading all (for without me what were all? what were God?)
Essence of forms, life of the real identities, permanent, positive, (namely the unseen,)
Life of the great round world, the sun and stars, and of man, I, the general soul,
Here the square finishing, the solid, I the most solid,
Breathe my breath also through these songs.   45

1865–1866, 1881–1882

A Noiseless Patient Spider

A noiseless patient spider,
I mark'd where on a little promontory it stood isolated,
Mark'd how to explore the vacant vast surrounding,
It launch'd forth filament, filament, filament, out of itself,
Ever unreeling them, ever tirelessly speeding them.   5

And you O my soul where you stand,
Surrounded, detached, in measureless oceans of space,
Ceaselessly musing, venturing, throwing, seeking the spheres to connect them,
Till the bridge you will need be form'd, till the ductile anchor hold,
Till the gossamer thread you fling catch somewhere, O my soul.   10

1868   1881

5. Holy Spirit. *Cf.* John xiv: 16–17.

From FROM NOON TO STARRY NIGHT [6]

To a Locomotive in Winter

Thee for my recitative,
Thee in the driving storm even as now, the snow, the winter-day
    declining,
Thee in thy panoply, thy measur'd dual throbbing and thy beat
    convulsive,
Thy black cylindric body, golden brass and silvery steel,
Thy ponderous side-bars, parallel and connecting rods, gyrating,
    shuttling at thy sides,   5
Thy metrical, now swelling pant and roar, now tapering in the
    distance,
Thy great protruding head-light fix'd in front,
Thy long, pale, floating vapor-pennants, tinged with delicate purple,
The dense and murky clouds out-belching from thy smoke-stack,
Thy knitted frame, thy springs and valves, the tremulous twinkle of
    thy wheels,   10
Thy train of cars behind, obedient, merrily following,
Through gale or calm, now swift, now slack, yet steadily careering;
Type of the modern—emblem of motion and power—pulse of the
    continent,
For once come serve the Muse and merge in verse, even as here I
    see thee,
With storm and buffeting gusts of wind and falling snow,   15
By day thy warning ringing bell to sound its notes,
By night thy silent signal lamps to swing.

Fierce-throated beauty!
Roll through my chant with all thy lawless music, thy swinging
    lamps at night,
Thy madly-whistled laughter, echoing, rumbling like an earthquake,
    rousing all,   20
Law of thyself complete, thine own track firmly holding,
(No sweetness debonair of tearful harp or glib piano thine,)
Thy trills of shrieks by rocks and hills return'd,
Launch'd o'er the prairies wide, across the lakes,
To the free skies unpent and glad and strong.   25

1876, 1881

By Broad Potomac's Shore

By broad Potomac's shore, again old tongue,
(Still uttering, still ejaculating, canst never cease this babble?)

---

6. Whitman first grouped a number of
poems (some of them previously published) under the title "From Noon to
Starry Night" in the seventh edition of
Leaves of Grass (1881–1882).

Again old heart so gay, again to you, your sense, the full flush spring
  returning,
Again the freshness and the odors, again Virginia's summer sky,
  pellucid blue and silver,
Again the forenoon purple of the hills,   5
Again the deathless grass, so noiseless soft and green,
Again the blood-red roses blooming.

Perfume this book of mine O blood-red roses!
Lave subtly with your waters every line Potomac!
Give me of you O spring, before I close, to put between its pages!   10
O forenoon purple of the hills, before I close, of you!
O deathless grass, of you!

                                                              1872, 1881

From Democratic Vistas [7]

  I say that democracy can never prove itself beyond cavil, until
it founds and luxuriantly grows its own forms of art, poems,
schools, theology, displacing all that exists, or that has been produced anywhere in the past, under opposite influences. It is curious
to me that while so many voices, pens, minds, in the press, lecture
rooms, in our Congress, etc., are discussing intellectual topics,
pecuniary dangers, legislative problems, the suffrage, tariff and
labor questions, and the various business and benevolent needs of
America, with propositions, remedies, often worth deep attention,
there is one need, a hiatus the profoundest, that no eye seems to
perceive, no voice to state. Our fundamental want today in the
United States, with closest, amplest reference to present conditions, and to the future, is of a class, and the clear idea of a class,
of native authors, literatuses, far different, far higher in grade,
than any yet known, sacerdotal, modern, fit to cope with our occasions, lands, permeating the whole mass of American mentality,
taste, belief, breathing into it a new breath of life, giving it decision, affecting politics far more than the popular superficial
suffrage, with results inside and underneath the elections of Presidents or Congresses—radiating, begetting appropriate teachers,
schools, manners, and, as its grandest result, accomplishing (what
neither the schools nor the churches and their clergy have hitherto
accomplish'd, and without which this nation will no more stand,

7. After the ordeal of the Civil War,
Whitman wrote two essays analyzing
and criticizing the condition of democracy in the United States. "Democracy"
appeared in the *Galaxy*, December,
1867, and "Personalism" in the same
periodical in May, 1868. In 1871 the
two essays were consolidated in the
volume, *Democratic Vistas*.

permanently, soundly, than a house will stand without a sub-stra-
tum), a religious and moral character beneath the political and
productive and intellectual bases of the States. For know you not,
dear, earnest reader, that the people of our land may all read and
write, and may all possess the right to vote—and yet the main
things may be entirely lacking?—(and this to suggest them).

View'd, today, from a point of view sufficiently over-arching,
the problem of humanity all over the civilized world is social and
religious, and is to be finally met and treated by literature. The
priest departs, the divine literatus comes. Never was anything
more wanted than, today, and here in the States, the poet of the
modern is wanted, or the great literatus of the modern. At all
times, perhaps, the central point in any nation, and that whence
it is itself really sway'd the most, and whence it sways others, is
its national literature, especially its archetypal poems. Above all
previous lands, a great original literature is surely to become the
justification and reliance (in some respects the sole reliance of
American democracy).

Few are aware how the great literature penetrates all, gives hue
to all, shapes aggregates and individuals, and, after subtle ways,
with irresistible power, constructs, sustains, demolishes at will.
Why tower, in reminiscence, above all the nations of the earth,
two special lands, petty in themselves, yet inexpressibly gigantic,
beautiful, columnar? Immortal Judah lives, and Greece immortal
lives, in a couple of poems.

* * *

It may be claim'd (and I admit the weight of the claim) that
common and general worldly prosperity, and a populace well-to-
do, and with all life's material comforts, is the main thing, and is
enough. It may be argued that our republic is, in performance,
really enacting today the grandest arts, poems, etc., by beating up
the wilderness into fertile farms, and in her railroads, ships, machinery, etc. And it may be ask'd, Are these not better, indeed,
for America, than any utterances even of greatest rhapsode, artist,
or literatus?

I too hail those achievements with pride and joy: then answer
that the soul of man will not with such only—nay, not with such
at all—be finally satisfied; but needs what, (standing on these
and on all things, as the feet stand on the ground), is addressed
to the loftiest, to itself alone.

Out of such considerations, such truths, arises for treatment in
these Vistas the important question of character, of an American
stock-personality, with literatures and arts for outlets and return-

expressions, and, of course, to correspond, within outlines common to all. To these, the main affair, the thinkers of the United States, in general so acute, have either given feeblest attention, or have remain'd, and remain, in a state of somnolence.

For my part, I would alarm and caution even the political and business reader, and to the utmost extent, against the prevailing delusion that the establishment of free political institutions, and plentiful intellectual smartness, with general good order, physical plenty, industry, etc. (desirable and precious advantages as they all are), do, of themselves, determine and yield to our experiment of democracy the fruitage of success. With such advantages at present fully, or almost fully, possess'd—the Union just issued, victorious, from the struggle with the only foes it need ever fear (namely, those within itself, the interior ones), and with unprecedented materialistic advancement—society, in these States, is canker'd, crude, superstitious and rotten. Political, or law-made society is, and private, or voluntary society, is also. In any vigor, the element of the moral conscience, the most important, the verteber to State or man, seems to me either entirely lacking, or seriously enfeebled or ungrown.

I say we had best look our times and lands searchingly in the face, like a physician diagnosing some deep disease. Never was there, perhaps, more hollowness at heart than at present, and here in the United States. Genuine belief seems to have left us. The underlying principles of the States are not honestly believ'd in (for all this hectic glow, and these melodramatic screamings), nor is humanity itself believ'd in. What penetrating eye does not everywhere see through the mask? The spectacle is appalling. We live in an atmosphere of hypocrisy throughout. The men believe not in the women, nor the women in the men. A scornful superciliousness rules in literature. The aim of all the *littérateurs* is to find something to make fun of. A lot of churches, sects, etc., the most dismal phantasms I know, usurp the name of religion. Conversation is a mass of badinage. From deceit in the spirit, the mother of all false deeds, the offspring is already incalculable. An acute and candid person, in the revenue department in Washington, who is led by the course of his employment to regularly visit the cities, north, south, and west, to investigate frauds, has talked much with me about his discoveries. The depravity of the business classes of our country is not less than has been supposed, but infinitely greater. The official services of America, national, state, and municipal, in all their branches and departments, except the judiciary, are saturated in corruption, bribery, falsehood, maladministration; and the judiciary is tainted. The great cities reek with respectable as much as non-respectable robbery and scoundrelism. In fashionable life, flippancy, tepid amours, weak infidelism, small aims, or no aims at all, only to kill time. In business (this all-devouring modern word, business), the one sole object is, by any means, pecuniary gain. The magician's serpent in the fable ate up all the other serpents; and moneymaking is our magician's serpent, remaining today sole master of the field. The best class we show, is but a mob of fashionably dress'd speculators and vulgarians. True, indeed, behind this fantastic farce, enacted on the visible stage of society, solid things and stupendous labors are to be discover'd, existing crudely and going on in the background, to advance and tell themselves in time. Yet the truths are none the less terrible. I say that our New World democracy, however great a success in uplifting the masses out of their sloughs, in materialistic development, products, and in a certain highly deceptive superficial popular intellectuality, is, so far, an almost complete **fail**ure in its social aspects, and in really grand religious, moral, literary, and æsthetic results. In vain do we march with unprecedented strides to empire so colossal, outvying the antique, beyond Alexander's, beyond the proudest sway of Rome. In vain have we annex'd Texas, California, Alaska, and reach north for Canada and south for Cuba. It is as if we were somehow being endow'd with a vast and more and more thoroughly appointed body, and then left with little or no soul.

* * *

But sternly discarding, shutting our eyes to the glow and grandeur of the general superficial effect, coming down to what is of the only real importance, Personalities, and examining minutely, we question, we ask, Are there, indeed, *men* here worthy the name? Are there athletes? Are there perfect women, to match the generous material luxuriance? Is there a pervading atmosphere of beautiful manners? Are there crops of fine youths, and majestic old persons? Are there arts worthy freedom and a rich people? Is there a great moral and religious civilization—the only justification of a great material one? Confess that to severe eyes, using the moral microscope upon humanity, a sort of dry and flat Sahara appears, these cities, crowded with petty grotesques, malformations, phantoms, playing meaningless antics. Confess that everywhere, in shop, street, church, theatre, barroom, official chair, are pervading flippancy and vulgarity, low cunning, infidelity—everywhere the youth puny, impudent, foppish, prematurely ripe—everywhere an abnormal libidinousness, unhealthy forms, male, female, painted, padded, dyed, chignon'd, muddy complexions, bad blood, the capacity for good motherhood decreasing or decreas'd, shallow notions of beauty, with a range of manners, or rather lack of manners (considering the advantages enjoy'd), probably the meanest to be seen in the world.

Of all this, and these lamentable conditions, to breathe into them the breath recuperative of sane and heroic life, I say a new-founded literature, not merely to copy and reflect existing surfaces, or pander to what is called taste—not only to amuse, pass away time, celebrate the beautiful, the refined, the past, or exhibit technical, rhythmic, or grammatical dexterity—but a literature underlying life, religious, consistent with science, handling the elements and forces with competent power, teaching and training men—and, as perhaps the most precious of its results, achieving the entire redemption of woman out of these incredible holds and webs of silliness, millinery, and every kind of dyspeptic depletion —and thus insuring to the States a strong and sweet Female Race, a race of perfect Mothers—is what is needed.

* * *

For after the rest is said—after the many time-honor'd and really true things for subordination, experience, rights of property, etc., have been listen'd to and acquiesced in—after the valuable and well-settled statement of our duties and relations in society is thoroughly conn'd over and exhausted—it remains to bring forward and modify everything else with the idea of that Something a man is (last precious consolation of the drudging poor), standing apart from all else, divine in his own right, and a woman in hers, sole and untouchable by any canons of authority, or any rule derived from precedent, state-safety, the acts of legislatures, or even from what is called religion, modesty, or art. The radiation of this truth is the key of the most significant doing of our immediately preceding three centuries, and has been the political genesis and life of America. Advancing visibly, it still more advances invisibly. Underneath the fluctuations of the expressions of society, as well as the movements of the politics of the leading nations of the world, we see steadily pressing ahead and strengthening itself, even in the midst of immense tendencies toward aggregation, this image of completeness in separation, of individual personal dignity, of a single person, either male or female, characterized in the main, not from extrinsic acquirements or position, but in the pride of himself or herself alone; and as an eventual conclusion and summing up (or else the entire scheme of things is aimless, a cheat, a crash), the simple idea that the last, best dependence is to be upon humanity itself, and its own inherent, normal, full-grown qualities without any superstitious support whatever. This idea of perfect individualism it is indeed that deepest tinges and gives character to the idea of the aggregate. * * *

I submit, therefore, that the fruition of democracy, on aught like a grand scale, resides altogether in the future. As, under any profound and comprehensive view of the gorgeous-composite feudal world, we see in it, through the long ages and cycles of ages, the results of a deep, integral, human and divine principle, or fountain, from which issued laws, ecclesia, manners, institutes, costumes, personalities, poems (hitherto unequal'd), faithfully partaking of their source, and indeed only arising either to betoken it, or to furnish parts of that varied-flowing display, whose center was one and absolute—so, long ages hence, shall the due historian or critic make at least an equal retrospect, an equal history for the democratic principle. It too must be adorn'd, credited with its results—then, when it, with imperial power, through amplest time, has dominated mankind—has been the source and test of all the moral, æsthetic, social, political, and religious expressions and institutes of the civilized world—has begotten them in spirit and in form, and has carried them to its own unprecedented heights—has had (it is possible) monastics and ascetics, more numerous, more devout than the monks and priests of all previous creeds—has sway'd the ages with a breadth and rectitude tallying Nature's own—has fashion'd, systematized, and triumphantly finish'd and carried out, in its own interest, and with unparallel'd success, a new earth and a new man.

Thus we presume to write, as it were, upon things that exist not, and travel by maps yet unmade, and a blank. But the throes of birth are upon us; and we have something of this advantage in seasons of strong formations, doubts, suspense—for then the afflatus of such themes haply may fall upon us, more or less; and then, hot from surrounding war and revolution, our speech, though without polish'd coherence, and a failure by the standard called criticism, comes forth, real at least as the lightnings.

And maybe we, these days, have, too, our own reward—(for there are yet some, in all lands, worthy to be so encouraged). Though not for us the joy of entering at the last the conquered city—not ours the chance ever to see with our own eyes the peerless power and splendid *éclat* of the democratic principle, arriv'd at meridian, filling the world with effulgence and majesty far beyond those of past history's kings, or all dynastic sway—there is yet, to whoever is eligible among us, the prophetic vision, the joy of being toss'd in the brave turmoil of these times—the promulgation and the path, obedient, lowly reverent to the voice, the gesture of the god, or holy ghost, which others see not, hear not —with the proud consciousness that amid whatever clouds, seductions, or heart-wearying postponements, we have never deserted, never despair'd, never abandon'd the faith.

So much contributed, to the conn'd well, to help prepare and brace our edifice, our plann'd Idea—we still proceed to give it in another of its aspects—perhaps the main, the high façade of all. For to democracy, the leveler, the unyielding principle of the average, surely join'd another principle, equally unyielding, closely tracking the first, indispensable to it, opposite (as the sexes are opposite), and whose existence, confronting and ever modifying the other, often clashing, paradoxical, yet neither of highest avail without the other, plainly supplies to these grand cosmic politics of ours, and to the launch'd forth mortal dangers of republicanism, today, or any day, the counterpart and offset whereby Nature restrains the deadly original relentlessness of all her first-class laws. This second principle is individuality, the pride and centripetal isolation of a human being in himself—identity—personalism. Whatever the name, its acceptance and thorough infusions through the organizations of political commonalty now shooting Aurora-like about the world, are of utmost importance, as the principle itself is needed for very life's sake. It forms, in a sort, or is to form, the compensating balance-wheel of the successful working machinery of aggregate America.

And, if we think of it, what does civilization itself rest upon—and what object has it, what its religions, arts, schools, etc., but rich, luxuriant, varied personalism? To that, all bends; and it is because toward such result democracy alone, on anything like Nature's scale, breaks up the limitless fallows of human-kind, and plants the seed, and gives fair play, that its claims now precede the rest. The literature, songs, æsthetics, etc., of a country are of importance principally because they furnish the materials and suggestions of personality for the women and men of that country, and enforce them in a thousand effective ways.[8] As the topmost

8. "After the rest is satiated, all interest culminates in the field of persons, and never flags there. Accordingly in this field have the great poets and literatuses signally toiled. They too, in all ages, all lands, have been creators, fashioning, making types of men and women, as Adam and Eve are made in the divine fable. Behold, shaped, bred by orientalism, feudalism, through their long growth and culmination, and breeding back in return—(when shall we have an equal series, typical of democracy?)—behold, commencing in primal Asia (apparently formulated, in what beginning we know, in the gods of the mythologies, and coming down thence), a few samples out of the countless product, bequeath'd to the moderns, bequeath'd to America as studies. For the men, Yudishtura, Rama, Arjuna, Solomon, most of the Old and New Testament characters; Achilles, Ulysses, Theseus, Prometheus, Hercules, Aeneas, Plutarch's heroes; the Merlin of Celtic bards; the Cid, Arthur and his knights, Siegfried and Hagen in the Nibelungen; Roland and Oliver; Roustam in the Shah-Nemah; and so on to Milton's Satan, Cervantes' Don Quixote, Shakespeare's Hamlet, Richard II, Lear, Marc Antony, etc., and the modern Faust. These, I say, are models, combined, adjusted to other standards than

claim of a strong consolidating of the nationality of these States is, that only by such powerful compaction can the separate States secure that full and free swing within their spheres, which is becoming to them, each after its kind, so will individuality, and unimpeded branchings, flourish best under imperial republican forms.

Assuming Democracy to be at present in its embryo condition, and that the only large and satisfactory justification of it resides in the future, mainly through the copious production of perfect characters among the people, and through the advent of a sane and pervading religiousness, it is with regard to the atmosphere and spaciousness fit for such characters, and of certain nutriment and cartoon-draftings proper for them, and indicating them for New World purposes, that I continue the present statement—an exploration, as of new ground, wherein, like other primitive surveyors, I must do the best I can, leaving it to those who come after me to do much better. (The service, in fact, if any, must be to break a sort of first path or track, no matter how rude and ungeometrical.) * * *

There is, in sanest hours, a consciousness, a thought that rises, independent, lifted out from all else, calm, like the stars, shining eternal. This is the thought of identity—yours for you, whoever you are, as mine for me. Miracle of miracles, beyond statement, most spiritual and vaguest of earth's dreams, yet hardest basic fact, and only entrance to all facts. In such devout hours, in the midst of the significant wonders of heaven and earth (significant only because of the Me in the center), creeds, conventions, fall away and become of no account before this simple idea. Under the luminousness of real vision, it alone takes possession, takes value. Like the shadowy dwarf in the fable, once liberated and look'd upon, it expands over the whole earth, and spreads to the roof of heaven.

The quality of Being, in the object's self, according to its own central idea and purpose, and of growing therefrom and thereto—not criticism by other standards, and adjustments thereto—is the lesson of Nature. True, the full man wisely gathers, culls, absorbs; but if, engaged disproportionately in that, he slights or overlays the precious idiocrasy and special nativity and intention that he is, the man's self, the main thing, is a failure, however wide his gen-

America's, but of priceless value to her and hers.

Among women, the goddesses of the Egyptian, Indian, and Greek mythologies, certain Bible characters, especially the Holy Mother; Cleopatra, Penelope; the portraits of Brunhelde and Chriem- hilde in the Nibelungen; Oriana, Una, etc.; the modern Consuelo, Walter Scott's Jeanie and Effie Deans, etc., etc. (Yet woman portrayed or outlin'd at her best, or as perfect human mother, does not hitherto, it seems to me, fully appear in literature.)" [Whitman's note].

eral cultivation. Thus, in our times, refinement and delicatesse [9] are not only attended to sufficiently, but threaten to eat us up, like a cancer. Already, the democratic genius watches, ill-pleased, these tendencies. Provision for a little healthy rudeness, savage virtue, justification of what one has in one's self, whatever it is, is demanded. Negative qualities, even deficiencies, would be a relief. Singleness and normal simplicity and separation, amid this more and more complex, more and more artificialized state of society —how pensively we yearn for them! how we would welcome their return!

In some such direction, then—at any rate enough to preserve the balance—we feel called upon to throw what weight we can, not for absolute reasons, but current ones. To prune, gather, trim, conform, and ever cram and stuff, and be genteel and proper, is the pressure of our days. While aware that much can be said even in behalf of all this, we perceive that we have not now to consider the question of what is demanded to serve a half-starved and barbarous nation, or set of nations, but what is most applicable, most pertinent, for numerous congeries of conventional, over-corpulent societies, already becoming stifled and rotten with flatulent, infidelistic literature, and polite conformity and art. In addition to establish'd sciences, we suggest a science as it were of healthy average personalism, on original-universal grounds, the object of which should be to raise up and supply through the States a copious race of superb American men and women, cheerful, religious, ahead of any yet known.

America has yet morally and artistically originated nothing. She seems singularly unaware that the models of persons, books, manners, etc., appropriate for former conditions and for European lands, are but exiles and exotics here. No current of her life, as shown on the surfaces of what is authoritatively called her society, accepts or runs into social or æsthetic democracy; but all the currents set squarely against it. Never, in the Old World, was thoroughly upholster'd exterior appearance and show, mental and other, built entirely on the idea of caste, and on the sufficiency of mere outside acquisition—never were glibness, verbal intellect more the test, the emulation—more loftily elevated as head and sample—than they are on the surface of our republican States this day. The writers of a time hint the mottoes of its gods. The word of the modern, say these voices, in the word Culture.

We find ourselves abruptly in close quarters with the enemy. This word Culture, or what it has come to represent, involves, by contrast, our whole theme, and has been, indeed, the spur, urg-

9. Borrowed from the French and used by Whitman to mean "fastidiousness to the point of squeamishness."

ing us to engagement. Certain questions arise. As now taught, accepted and carried out, are not the processes of culture rapidly creating a class of supercilious infidels, who believe in nothing? Shall a man lose himself in countless masses of adjustments, and be so shaped with reference to this, that, and the other, that the simply good and healthy and brave parts of him are reduced and clipp'd away, like the bordering of box in a garden? You can cultivate corn and roses and orchards—but who shall cultivate the mountain peaks, the ocean, and the tumbling gorgeousness of the clouds? Lastly—is the readily given reply that culture only seeks to help, systematize, and put in attitude, the elements of fertility and power, a conclusive reply?

I do not so much object to the name, or word, but I should certainly insist, for the purposes of these States, on a radical change of category, in the distribution of precedence. I should demand a programme of culture, drawn out, not for a single class alone, or for the parlors or lecture rooms, but with an eye to practical life, the west, the workingmen, the facts of farms and jackplanes and engineers, and of the broad range of the women also of the middle and working strata, and with reference to the perfect equality of women, and of a grand and powerful motherhood. I should demand of this programme or theory a scope generous enough to include the widest human area. It must have for its spinal meaning the formation of a typical personality of character, eligible to the uses of the high average of men—and *not* restricted by conditions ineligible to the masses. The best culture will always be that of the manly and courageous instincts, and loving perceptions, and of self-respect—aiming to form, over this continent, an idiocrasy of universalism, which, true child of America, will bring joy to its mother, returning to her in her own spirit, recruiting myriads of offspring, able, natural, perceptive, tolerant, devout believers in her, America, and with some definite instinct why and for what she has arisen, most vast, most formidable of historic births, and is, now and here, with wonderful step, journeying through Time.

The problem, as it seems to me, presented to the New World, is, under permanent law and order, and after preserving cohesion (ensemble-Individuality), at all hazards, to vitalize man's free play of special Personalism,[1] recognizing in it something that calls ever more to be consider'd, fed, and adopted as the substratum for the

---

1. It seems likely that Whitman first introduced the term "Personalism" to designate the fusion between the independent individual and the ideal democratic society. It was already an established term in German transcendentalism (in Schleiermacher's *Discourses,* not then translated). Bronson Alcott got it from Whitman; through the St. Louis transcendentalists it then passed into the general literature of American philosophy.

best that belongs to us (government indeed is for it), including the new æsthetics of our future.

To formulate beyond this present vagueness—to help line and put before us the species, or a specimen of the species, of the democratic ethnology of the future, is a work toward which the genius of our land, with peculiar encouragement, invites her well-wishers. Already certain limnings, more or less grotesque, more or less fading and watery, have appear'd. We too (repressing doubts and qualms) will try our hand.

Attempting, then, however crudely, a basic model or portrait of personality for general use for the manliness of the State (and doubtless that is most useful which is most simple and comprehensive for all, and toned low enough), we should prepare the canvas well beforehand. Parentage must consider itself in advance. (Will the time hasten when fatherhood and motherhood shall become a science—and the noblest science?) To our model, a clear-blooded, strong-fibered physique is indispensable; the questions of food, drink, air, exercise, assimilation, digestion, can never be intermitted. Out of these we descry a well-begotten selfhood—in youth, fresh, ardent, emotional, aspiring, full of adventure; at maturity, brave, perceptive, under control, neither too talkative nor too reticent, neither flippant nor somber; of the bodily figure, the movements easy, the complexion showing the best blood, somewhat flush'd, breast expanded, an erect attitude, a voice whose sound outvies music, eyes of calm and steady gaze, yet capable also of flashing—and a general presence that holds its own in the company of the highest. (For it is native personality, and that alone, that endows a man to stand before presidents or generals, or in any distinguished collection, with *aplomb*—and *not* culture, or any knowledge or intellect whatever.)

* * *

Leaving still unspecified several sterling parts of any model fit for the future personality of America, I must not fail, again and ever, to pronounce myself on one, probably the least attended to in modern times—a hiatus, indeed, threatening its gloomiest consequences after us. I mean the simple, unsophisticated Conscience, the primary moral element. If I were asked to specify in what quarter lie the grounds of darkest dread, respecting the America of our hopes, I should have to point to this particular. I should demand the invariable application to individuality, this day and any day, of the old, ever-true plumb-rule of persons, eras, nations. Our triumphant modern civilizee,[2] with his all-schooling and

---

2. Whitman's coinage: one civilized to the point of weakness.

his wondrous appliances, will still show himself but an amputation while this deficiency remains. Beyond (assuming a more hopeful tone), the vertebration of the manly and womanly personalism of our Western world, can only be, and is, indeed, to be (I hope), its all penetrating Religiousness.

The ripeness of Religion is doubtless to be looked for in this field of individuality, and is a result that no organization or church can ever achieve. As history is poorly retain'd by what the technists call history, and is not given out from their pages, except the learner has in himself the sense of the well-wrapt, never yet written, perhaps impossible to be written, history—so Religion, although casually arrested, and, after a fashion preserv'd in the churches and creeds, does not depend at all upon them, but is a part of the identified soul, which, when greatest, knows not bibles in the old way, but in new ways—the identified soul, which can really confront Religion when it extricates itself entirely from the churches, and not before.

Personalism fuses this, and favors it. I should say, indeed, that only in the perfect uncontamination and solitariness of individuality may the spirituality of religion positively come forth at all. Only here, and on such terms, the meditation, the devout ecstasy, the soaring flight. Only here, communion with the mysteries, the eternal problems, whence? whither? Alone, and identity, and the mood—and the soul emerges, and all statements, churches, sermons, melt away like vapors. Alone, and silent thought and awe, and aspiration—and then the interior consciousness, like a hitherto unseen inscription, in magic ink, beams out its wondrous lines to the sense. Bibles may convey, and priests expound, but it is exclusively for the noiseless operation of one's isolated Self, to enter the pure ether of veneration, reach the divine levels, and commune with the unutterable. * * *

1867–1868, 1871

SIDNEY LANIER

(1842–1881)

Sidney Lanier was born in Macon, Georgia, on February 3, 1842, and he received his education at Oglethorpe University. When the Civil War started, Lanier enlisted as a Confederate private, serving actively until captured four months before the end of the conflict. In the Federal prison at Point Lookout, Maryland, he developed tuberculosis, and the remainder of his life became a fight against poor health and poverty. His first published book was a novel, *Tiger-Lilies* (1867), based upon his experiences in the Civil War.

Though Lanier constantly devoted himself to poetry, it was not until the publication of "Corn" (1875) in *Lippincott's* that he received recognition. This poem and "The Symphony" (1875), which followed, were both timely in subject matter, the first touching on the plight of penniless farmers, the latter attacking the evils of commercialism. His cantata, *The Centennial Meditation of Columbia, 1776–1876*, was performed at the opening of the Centennial Exhibition in Philadelphia and was well received when sung by a large chorus, but when published, without Dudley Buck's music, it was harshly criticized. In these works he was attempting a resolution between the rhythms of poetry and those of music, which he had studied all his life; but like Whitman he discovered that the majority of readers, accustomed to the established meters, were deaf to the new rhythms that he provided in such poems as "The Symphony" and "The Marshes of Glynn" (1878).

A volume of verse, *Poems* (1877), did not sell, and soon Lanier was forced into hack work to earn a living, made more difficult by ill health. A winter spent in San Antonio (1872) where he enjoyed the German choral societies, had been followed by his engagement in 1873 as flutist in the Peabody Orchestra in Baltimore. In 1878, still intent upon exploring the relations between poetry and music, he settled once more in

Baltimore, where he again had the opportunity to serve as flutist in the Peabody Symphony Orchestra. There he added to his small earnings by lecturing on English literature and versification at the Johns Hopkins University in 1879. The same year he edited *The Boy's Froissart*, following it with his best-selling book, *The Boy's King Arthur* (1880). His lectures on versification, published as *The Science of English Verse* (1880), presented his thesis that poetry and music are governed by the same artistic laws. Though his study of prosody is no longer considered important, the book is nonetheless an interesting early advocacy of fluid verse form. Lanier hoped it would bring him a professorship in the university, but critical reception was indifferent, and no professional advancement resulted. His final years were spent in gathering materials for his lectures and in writing some of his best poetry. He died when only forty years old, leaving a sufficient number of fine poems to suggest an even greater potentiality. Lanier's widow edited *Poems of Sidney Lanier* (1884), and some of his lectures at Johns Hopkins were later published as *The English Novel* (1883) and *Shakespeare and His Forerunners* (1902).

Though a southerner by tradition and chivalrous by nature, Lanier was never one to dwell on the dead past. In his social and economic criticism he was ahead of his times, and his dialect poems, with their mild humor, gave Lanier a place in the vanguard of regional realism.

A full critical edition of Lanier's writings is *The Centennial Edition of Sidney Lanier*, 10 vols., under the general editorship of Charles R. Anderson, 1945. Morgan Callaway, Jr., edited *Select Poems of Sidney Lanier*, 1895, with a scholarly introduction, notes, and bibliography. Henry W. Lanier edited *Selections from Sidney Lanier: Prose and Verse*, 1916; *Selected Poems of Sidney Lanier*, edited by Stark Young, 1947, contains some less accessible poems. *The Letters of Sidney Lanier, 1866–1881*, were edited by Henry Lanier, 1899.

Studies of Lanier's life and work are: Edwin Mims, *Sidney Lanier*, 1905; Aubrey H. Starke, *Sidney Lanier: A Biographical and Critical Study*, 1933; Lincoln Lorenz, *The Life of Sidney Lanier*, 1935; and Jack De Bellis, *Sidney Lanier*, 1972. A good study of Lanier's versification is Gay W. Allen's "Sidney Lanier," in his *American Prosody*, 1935, pp. 277–306. Philip Graham and Joseph Jones compiled *A Concordance to the Poems of Sidney Lanier*, 1939. Our text is based on the editions of 1877 and 1884.

The Symphony [1]

'O Trade! O Trade! would thou wert dead!
The Time needs heart—'tis tired of head:
We're all for love,' the violins said.
'Of what avail the rigorous tale [2]
Of bill for coin and box for bale?   5
Grant thee, O Trade! thine uttermost hope:
Level red gold with blue sky-slope,
And base it deep as devils grope:
When all's done, what hast thou won
Of the only sweet that's under the sun?   10
Ay, canst thou buy a single sigh
Of true love's least, least ecstasy?'
Then, with a bridegroom's heart-beats trembling,
All the mightier strings assembling
Ranged them on the violins' side   15
As when the bridegroom leads the bride,
And, heart in voice, together cried:
'Yea, what avail the endless tale
Of gain by cunning and plus by sale?
Look up the land, look down the land,   20
The poor, the poor, the poor, they stand
Wedged by the pressing of Trade's hand
Against an inward-opening door
That pressure tightens evermore:
They sigh a monstrous foul-air sigh   25
For the outside leagues of liberty,

1. "The Symphony" was written in Baltimore in March, 1875, and published in *Lippincott's* for June of that year; it was reprinted with revisions in *Poems* (1877) and with further revisions in *Poems of Sidney Lanier* (1884). Lanier's devotion to music, his strong belief that commercialism was destroying spiritual values, and his hope for a society based on harmony and love, are three persistent themes in all his writing. These lines offer a remarkable demonstration of his theory of the resemblances between music and poetry. See also the musical cadences of "The Marshes of Glynn."
2. A just count; a reckoning by number; also, of course, a "story."

Where Art, sweet lark, translates the sky
Into a heavenly melody.
"Each day, all day" (these poor folks say),
"In the same old year-long, drear-long way,   30
We weave in the mills and heave in the kilns,
We sieve mine-meshes under the hills,
And thieve much gold from the Devil's bank tills,
To relieve, O God, what manner of ills?—
The beasts, they hunger, and eat, and die;   35
And so do we, and the world's a sty;
Hush, fellow-swine: why nuzzle and cry?
Swinehood hath no remedy
Say many men, and hasten by,
Clamping the nose and blinking the eye.   40
But who said once, in the lordly tone,
Man shall not live by bread alone
But all that cometh from the Throne? [3]
    Hath God said so?
    But Trade saith No: 45
And the kilns and the curt-tongued mills say Go!
There's plenty that can, if you can't: we know.
Move out, if you think you're underpaid.
The poor are prolific; we're not afraid;
"Trade is trade." '   50
Thereat this passionate protesting
Meekly changed, and softened till
It sank to sad requesting
And suggesting sadder still:
'And oh, if men might some time see   55
How piteous-false the poor decree
That trade no more than trade must be!
Does business mean, *Die, you—live, I?*
Then "Trade is trade" but sings a lie;
'Tis only war grown miserly.   60
If business is battle, name it so:
War-crimes less will shame it so,
And widows less will blame it so.
Alas, for the poor to have some part
In yon sweet living lands of Art,   65
Makes problem not for head, but heart.
Vainly might Plato's brain revolve it:
Plainly the heart of a child could solve it.'

And then, as when from words that seem but rude

3. *Cf.* Luke iv: 4.

We pass to silent pain that sits abrood 70
Back in our heart's great dark and solitude,
So sank the strings to gentle throbbing
Of long chords change-marked with sobbing—
Motherly sobbing, not distinctlier heard
Than half wing-openings of the sleeping bird, 75
Some dream of danger to her young hath stirred.
Then stirring and demurring ceased, and lo!
Every least ripple of the strings' song-flow
Died to a level with each level bow
And made a great chord tranquil-surfaced so, 80
As a brook beneath his curving bank doth go
To linger in the sacred dark and green
Where many boughs the still pool overlean
And many leaves make shadow with their sheen.
    But presently 85
A velvet flute-note fell down pleasantly
Upon the bosom of that harmony,
And sailed and sailed incessantly,
As if a petal from a wild-rose blown
Had fluttered down upon that pool of tone 90
And boatwise dropped o' the convex side
And floated down the glassy tide
And clarified and glorified
The solemn spaces where the shadows bide.
From the warm concave of that fluted note 95
Somewhat, half song, half odor, forth did float,
As if a rose might somehow be a throat:
'When Nature from her far-off glen
Flutes her soft messages to men,
    The flute can say them o'er again; 100
    Yea, Nature, singing sweet and lone,
Breathes through life's strident polyphone [4]
The flute-voice in the world of tone.
    Sweet friends,
    Man's love ascends 105
To finer and diviner ends
Than man's mere thought e'er comprehends,
For I, e'en I,
As here I lie,
A petal on a harmony, 110
Demand of Science whence and why
Man's tender pain, man's inward cry,
When he doth gaze on earth and sky?

4. *Cf.* "polyphony," the multiplicity of sounds.

I am not overbold:
    I hold
Full powers from Nature manifold.   115
I speak for each no-tonguèd tree
That, spring by spring, doth nobler be,
And dumbly and most wistfully
His mighty prayerful arms outspreads   120
Above men's oft-unheeding heads,
And his big blessing downward sheds.
I speak for all-shaped blooms and leaves,
Lichens on stones and moss on eaves,
Grasses and grains in ranks and sheaves;   125
Broad-fronded ferns and keen-leaved canes,
And briery mazes bounding lanes,
And marsh-plants, thirsty-cupped for rains,
And milky stems and sugary veins;
For every long-armed woman-vine   130
That round a piteous tree doth twine;
For passionate odors, and divine
Pistils, and petals crystalline;
All purities of shady springs,
All shynesses of film-winged things   135
That fly from tree-trunks and bark-rings;
All modesties of mountain-fawns
That leap to covert from wild lawns,
And tremble if the day but dawns;
All sparklings of small beady eyes   140
Of birds, and sidelong glances wise
Wherewith the jay hints tragedies;
All piquancies of prickly burs,
And smoothnesses of downs and furs,
Of eiders [5] and of minivers; [6]   145
All limpid honeys that do lie
At stamen-bases, nor deny
The humming-birds' fine roguery,
Bee-thighs, nor any butterfly;
All gracious curves of slender wings,   150
Bark-mottlings, fibre-spiralings,
Fern-wavings and leaf-flickerings;
Each dial-marked leaf and flower-bell
Wherewith in every lonesome dell
Time to himself his hours doth tell;   155
All tree-sounds, rustlings of pine-cones,

5. Very soft feathers from the eider duck, hence eider down.

6. A white fur valued highly for court costumes in the Middle Ages.

Wind-sighings, doves' melodious moans,
And night's unearthly under-tones;
All placid lakes and waveless deeps,
All cool reposing mountain-steeps, 160
Vale-calms and tranquil lotos-sleeps;—
Yea, all fair forms, and sounds, and lights,
And warmths, and mysteries, and mights,
Of Nature's utmost depths and heights.
—These doth my timid tongue present, 165
Their mouthpiece and leal [7] instrument
And servant, all love-eloquent.
I head, when *All for love* the violins cried:
So, Nature calls through all her system wide,
Give me thy love, O man, so long denied. 170
Much time is run, and man hath changed his ways,
Since Nature, in the antique fable-days,
Was hid from man's true love by proxy fays,
False fauns and rascal gods that stole her praise.
The nymphs, cold creatures of man's colder brain, 175
Chilled Nature's streams till man's warm heart was fain
Never to lave its love in them again.
Later, a sweet Voice *Love thy neighbor* said; [8]
Then first the bounds of neighborhood outspread
Beyond all confines of old ethnic dread. 180
Vainly the Jew might wag his covenant head:
All men are neighbors, so the sweet Voice said.
So, when man's arms had circled all man's race,
The liberal compass of his warm embrace
Stretched bigger yet in the dark bounds of space; 185
With hands a-grope he felt smooth Nature's grace,
Drew her to breast and kissed her sweetheart face:
Yea, man found neighbors in great hills and trees
And streams and clouds and suns and birds and bees,
And throbbed with neighbor-loves in loving these. 190
But oh, the poor! the poor! the poor!
That stand by the inward-opening door
Trade's hand doth tighten ever more,
And sigh their monstrous foul-air sigh
For the outside hills of liberty, 195
Where Nature spreads her wild blue sky
For Art to make into melody!
Thou Trade! thou king of the modern days!
　　　Change thy ways,
　　　Change thy ways; 200

7. Loyal.　　　　　8. *Cf.* Matthew xxii: 39.

Let the sweaty laborers file
    A little while,
    A little while,
Where Art and Nature sing and smile.
Trade! is thy heart all dead, all dead?   205
And hast thou nothing but a head?
I'm all for heart,' the flute-voice said,
And into sudden silence fled,
Like as a blush that while 'tis red
Dies to a still, still white instead.   210

    Thereto a thrilling calm succeeds,
Till presently the silence breeds
A little breeze among the reeds [9]
That seems to blow by sea-marsh weeds:
Then from the gentle stir and fret   215
Sings out the melting clarionet,
Like as a lady sings while yet
Her eyes with salty tears are wet.
'O Trade! O Trade!' the Lady said,
'I too will wish thee utterly dead   220
If all thy heart is in thy head.
For O my God! and O my God!
What shameful ways have women trod
At beckoning of Trade's golden rod!
Alas when sighs are traders' lies,   225
And heart's-ease eyes and violet eyes
    Are merchandise!
O purchased lips that kiss with pain!
O cheeks coin-spotted with smirch and stain!
O trafficked hearts that break in twain!   230
—And yet what wonder at my sisters' crime?
So hath Trade withered up Love's sinewy prime,
Men love not women as in olden time.
Ah, not in these cold merchantable days
Deem men their life an opal gray, where plays   235
The one red Sweet of gracious ladies'-praise.
Now, comes a suitor with sharp prying eye—
Says, *Here, you Lady, if you'll sell, I'll buy:
Come, heart for heart—a trade? What! weeping? why?*
Shame on such wooers' dapper mercery! [1]   240
I would my lover kneeling at my feet
In humble manliness should cry, O *sweet!*

9. Orchestral instruments with reeds for producing sound.

1. The wares of a mercer (dealer in textiles); also, mercenariness.

I know not if thy heart my heart will greet:
I ask not if thy love my love can meet:
Whate'er thy worshipful soft tongue shall say,   245
I'll kiss thine answer, be it yea or nay:
I do but know I love thee, and I pray
To be thy knight until my dying day.[2]
Woe him that cunning trades in hearts contrives!
Base love good women to base loving drives   250
If men loved larger, larger were our lives;
And wooed they nobler, won they nobler wives.'

There thrust the bold straightforward horn
To battle for that lady lorn,
With heartsome voice of mellow scorn,   255
Like any knight in knighthood's morn.
   'Now comfort thee,' said he,
     'Fair Lady.
For God shall right thy grievous wrong,
And man shall sing thee a true-love song.   260
Voiced in act his whole life long,
   Yea, all thy sweet life long,
     Fair Lady.
Where's he that craftily hath said,
The day of chivalry is dead?   265
I'll prove that lie upon his head,
   Or I will die instead,
     Fair Lady.
Is Honor gone into his grave?
Hath Faith become a caitiff knave,   270
And Selfhood turned into a slave
   To work in Mammon's cave,[3]
     Fair Lady?
Will Truth's long blade ne'er gleam again?
Hath Giant Trade in dungeons slain   275
All great contempts of mean-got gain
   And hates of inward stain,
     Fair Lady?
For aye shall name and fame be sold,
And place be hugged for the sake of gold,   280

2. In ll. 253–323, this idea is developed in the song of the Knight to the Lady, a reconstruction of a lyric form familiar in the medieval literature of chivalry. This remarkable lyric is in conformity with Lanier's social and artistic motivation as a writer, and with the southern tradition of which he was a creative spokesman.

3. Mammon personifies selfish devotion to riches. In Edmund Spenser's *Faërie Queene*, Book II, Canto vii, Sir Guyon (Temperance) visits Mammon's cave of worldly wealth but does not succumb to greed.

And smirch-robed Justice feebly scold
  At Crime all money-bold,
      Fair Lady?
Shall self-wrapt husbands aye forget
Kiss-pardons for the daily fret   285
Wherewith sweet wifely eyes are wet—
  Blind to lips kiss-wise set—
      Fair Lady?
Shall lovers higgle, heart for heart,
Till wooing grows a trading mart   290
Where much for little, and all for part,
  Make love a cheapening art,
      Fair Lady?
Shall woman scorch for a single sin
That her betrayer may revel in,   295
And she be burnt, and he but grin
  When that the flames begin,
      Fair Lady?
Shall ne'er prevail the woman's plea,
We maids would far, far whiter be   300
If that our eyes might sometimes see
  Men maids in purity,
      Fair Lady?
Shall Trade aye salve his conscience-aches
With jibes at Chivalry's old mistakes— 305
The wars that o'erhot knighthood makes
  For Christ's and ladies' sakes,
      Fair Lady?
Now by each knight that e'er hath prayed
To fight like a man and love like a maid, 310
Since Pembroke's [4] life, as Pembroke's blade,
  I' the scabbard, death, was laid,
      Fair Lady,
I dare avouch my faith is bright
That God doth right and God hath might. 315
Nor time hath changed His hair to white,
  Nor His dear love to spite,
      Fair Lady.
I doubt no doubts: I strive, and shrive my clay,
And fight my fight in the patient modern way 320
For true love and for thee—ah me! and pray
  To be thy knight until my dying day,
      Fair Lady.'

---

4. William Herbert, third Earl of Pembroke, nephew of Sir Philip Sidney; the first folio of Shakespeare's plays was dedicated to him and his brother.

Made end that knightly horn, and spurred away
Into the thick of the melodious fray.   325

And then the hautboy [5] played and smiled,
And sang like any large-eyed child,
Cool-hearted and all undefiled.
      'Huge Trade!' he said,
'Would thou wouldst lift me on thy head   330
And run where'er my finger led!
Once said a Man—and wise was He—
Never shalt thou the heavens see,
Save as a little child thou be.' [6]
Then o'er sea-lashings of commingling tunes   335
The ancient wise bassoons,
            Like weird,
            Gray-beard
Old harpers sitting on the high sea-dunes,
            Chanted runes:[7]   340
'Bright-waved gain, gray-waved loss,
The sea of all doth lash and toss,
One wave forward and one across:
But now 'twas trough, now 'tis crest,
And worst doth foam and flash to best,   345
            And curst to blest.
'Life! Life! thou sea-fugue,[8] writ from east to west,
            Love, Love alone can pore
            On thy dissolving score
            Of harsh half-phrasings,   350
               Blotted ere writ,
            And double erasings
               Of chords most fit.
Yea, Love, sole music-master blest,
May read thy weltering palimpsest.[9]   355
To follow Time's dying melodies through,
And never to lose the old in the new,
And ever to solve the discords true—
            Love alone can do.
And ever Love hears the poor-folks' crying,   360
And ever Love hears the women's sighing,
And ever sweet knighthood's death-defying,

5. Oboe; a slender wood-wind instrument with a plaintive tone.
6. *Cf.* Matthew xix: 14, and Mark x:
15.
7. Poems; originally runes were verses
written in ancient characters used by
the Norsemen.

8. Fugue: a musical composition generally having several themes, enunci-
ated in turn, and gradually reaching
a marked climax at the end.
9. A parchment from which writing has
been erased to make space for another
text.

And ever wise childhood's deep implying,
But never a trader's glozing and lying.

'And yet shall Love himself be heard,   365
Though long deferred, though long deferred:
O'er the modern waste a dove [1] hath whirred:
Music is Love in search of a word.'

1875, 1877

Song of the Chattahoochee [2]

Out of the hills of Habersham,
    Down the valleys of Hall,[3]
I hurry amain to reach the plain,
Run the rapid and leap the fall,
Split at the rock and together again,   5
Accept my bed, or narrow or wide,
And flee from folly on every side
With a lover's pain to attain the plain
        Far from the hills of Habersham,
        Far from the valleys of Hall.   10

All down the hills of Habersham,
    All through the valleys of Hall,
The rushes cried *Abide, abide,*
The willful waterweeds held me thrall,
The laving laurel turned my tide,   15
The ferns and the fondling grass said *Stay,*
The dewberry dipped for to work delay,
And the little reeds sighed *Abide, abide,*
        Here in the hills of Habersham,
        Here in the valleys of Hall.   20

High o'er the hills of Habersham,
    Veiling the valleys of Hall,
The hickory told me manifold
Fair tales of shade, the poplar tall
Wrought me her shadowy self to hold,   25
The chestnut, the oak, the walnut, the pine,

1. During the flood Noah sent the dove from the ark, seeking land. On the seventh day the dove returned with an olive leaf (Genesis viii: 8–11).
2. The Chattahoochee is a small river in Lanier's native Georgia. The poet considered music and poetry to be a single and natural expression of his ideal theory of unity. He conceived of nature, society, and moral obligation as being unified by a single compul-sion, as is the river, personified in its life-giving journey from its source to the great sea of eternity. This poem was published in the *Independent* for December 20, 1883, and reprinted with emendations in *Poems of Sidney Lanier* (1884).
3. Habersham is a county in the northeastern section of Georgia; Hall County is slightly to the southwest of it.

Overleaning, with flickering meaning and sign,
Said, *Pass not, so cold, these manifold*
    Deep shades of the hills of Habersham,
    These glades in the valleys of Hall.   30

And oft in the hills of Habersham,
    And oft in the valleys of Hall,
The white quartz shone, and the smooth brook-stone
Did bar me of passage with friendly brawl,
And many a luminous jewel lone   35
—Crystals clear or a-cloud with mist,
Ruby, garnet and amethyst—
Made lures with the lights of streaming stone
    In the clefts of the hills of Habersham,
    In the beds of the valleys of Hall.   40

But oh, not the hills of Habersham,
    And oh, not the valleys of Hall
Avail: I am fain for to water the plain.
Downward the voices of Duty call—
Downward, to toil and be mixed with the main,   45
The dry fields burn, and the mills are to turn,
And a myriad flowers mortally yearn,
And the lordly main from beyond the plain
    Calls o'er the hills of Habersham,
    Calls through the valleys of Hall.   50

1877   1883, 1884

EMILY DICKINSON
(1830–1886)

Emily Dickinson was born on December 10, 1830, in Amherst, Massachusetts, where her grandfather had been a leader in founding Amherst College. Her father, Edward Dickinson, a successful lawyer who became a member of Congress, served the college as a trustee, and was its treasurer for forty years. Though reported a stern and authoritarian moralist, he was perhaps no more patriarchal than other fathers of his time; but when he spoke, his timid wife "trembled, obeyed, and was silent." The conservative Amherst of that day, in which the church wielded the highest authority, was a small and rigid world, ideally constructed to provoke the rebelliousness latent in Emily Dickinson's spirit. Like her sister Lavinia, Emily never married; Austin, her lawyer brother, having surrendered to his father's opposition to his going west, opposed him by marrying Susan Gilbert, a "worldly" New Yorker, who became Emily's confidante.

In her poems Emily Dickinson constructed her own world—of the garden and the beautiful Connecticut valley scenery; of the books, many of them forbidden, smuggled in by her brother; of her private and quite startling thoughts; for a time, of her few congenial friends at Amherst Academy. For less than a year (1847) she went over the hills to South Hadley Female Seminary (Mount Holyoke), but failing to respond to the academic severity of the famous Mary Lyon, she returned to Amherst, which she never again left, except for brief visits to Washington, Philadelphia, and Boston in the earlier years.

On her return from South Hadley, Emily may have fallen in love with young Ben Newton, who in 1848 was living with her family as her father's law apprentice. He was a brilliant free-thinker, and introduced her to a new world of ideas; but he was too poor to marry, even if her father could conceivably have given approval. He died of tuberculosis five years later, having begun his practice in another town some distance away. In such poems as "My life closed twice before its close," however, Emily Dickinson acknowledges at least two persons in that complex and passionate world that her imagination created, perhaps to fill the void of not-having. According to the family tradition she met the Reverend Charles Wadsworth in Philadelphia in 1854, on one of her rare journeys, when she was on the way to visit her father, then in Washington for his term in Congress. Since Ben Newton had just died, and Emily was seeking spiritual assurance, it may have been Wadsworth who "tried to teach me immortality," as she wrote of someone not named, who afterward "left the land." Although married, Wadsworth continued to visit Emily in Amherst until 1862, when he accepted a call to California. The poet's family and friends as biographers supported the Amherst legend that Emily spent her middle years as a white-clad recluse. However, new evidence continues to indicate that the poet's human associations were more continuous and varied than was before supposed, substantiating the passionate impulsiveness which animated her poetry as a whole. In her writing she was encouraged by her girlhood friend Helen Hunt Jackson, famous author of *Ramona*; and after 1862 by Thomas Wentworth Higginson, a literary friend of the family, who tried unsuccessfully to "improve" her unconventional style; she had the advice of Samuel Bowles, editor of the famous *Springfield Republican*, but probably no more than seven of her poems slipped into print during her lifetime. It was probably just as well. Readers of the twentieth century would understand her better, for it was their idiom that she spoke.

From 1884 until her death on May 16, 1886, Emily Dickinson was a semi-invalid, in a condition of mental decline. Three posthumous collections between 1890 and 1896 won her the reputation of a powerful eccentric; later collections of her poems, beginning in 1914, established her recognition as a major poet and her immediate influence upon those young writers who were then creating the radical poetry of the present century. By the instinct of the artist she had found her own way, in the 1860's, toward forms of expression which only became naturalized in the iconoclastic 1920's. Her style was simple yet passionate, and marked by economy and concentration. Like the later generation she discovered that the sharp, intense image is the poet's best instrument. She anticipated the modern enlargement of melody by assonance, dissonance, and "off-rhyme"; she discovered, as twentieth-century poets later did, the utility of the ellipsis of thought and the verbal ambiguity. Her ideas were witty, rebellious, and original, yet she confined her materials to the world of her small village, her domestic circle, her garden, and a few good books. She possessed the most acute awareness of sensory experience and psychological actualities, and she expressed radical discoveries in these areas with frankness and force. Confronted with the question of how, in her narrow life, she came by these instruments and this knowledge, one can only conclude that it was by sheer genius. She remains incomparable because her originality sets her apart from all others, but her poems shed the unmistakable light of greatness.

Excepting seven poems that appeared in periodicals, Emily Dickinson's poetry was published posthumously. The definitive edition is *The Poems of Emily Dickinson*, edited by Thomas H. Johnson, 3 vols., 1955, which includes variant readings critically compared with all known manuscripts. The present edition follows Johnson's chronology and adopts his numbering of the poems, and the text used is that established by Johnson.

Thomas H. Johnson has edited *Letters of Emily Dickinson*, 3 vols., 1958; and *Emily Dickinson: Selected Letters*, 1971. For excellent accounts of Emily Dickinson's life see George F. Whicher, *This Was a Poet*, 1938; and Thomas H. Johnson, *Emily Dickinson: An Interpretive Biography*, 1955. Genevieve Taggard, *The Life and Mind of Emily Dickinson*, 1930, is a sound study. Millicent T. Bingham, *Ancestors' Brocades*, 1945, gives intimate revelations of the Dickinson family. Good critical interpretations are Richard Chase, *Emily Dickinson*, American Men of Letters Series, 1951; Henry W. Wells, *Introduction to Emily Dickinson*, 1947; Charles R. Anderson, *Emily Dickinson's Poetry: Stairway to Surprise*, 1960; Jay Leyda, *The Years and Hours of Emily Dickinson*, 1960; Richard Sewall, *Emily Dickinson: A Collection of Critical Essays*, 1963; Caesar Blake and Carlton Wells, *The Recognition of Emily Dickinson* * * *, 1964; Clark Griffith, *The Long Shadow: Emily Dickinson's Tragic Poetry*, 1964; Douglas Duncan, *Emily Dickinson*, 1965; Albert Gelpi, *Emily Dickinson, The Mind of the Poet*, 1965; David T. Porter, *The Art of Emily Dickinson's Early Poetry*, 1966; David Higgins, *Portrait of Emily Dickinson*, 1967; John B. Pickard, *Emily Dickinson: An Introduction and Interpretation*, 1967; Brita Lindberg-Seyersted, *The Voice of the Poet: Aspects of Style* * * *, 1968; Ruth Miller, *The Poetry of Emily Dickinson*, 1968; William R. Sherwood, *Stages in the Mind and Art* * * *, 1968; John Cody, *The Inner Life of Emily Dickinson*, 1971; and John Evangelist Walsh, *The Hidden Life of Emily Dickinson*, 1971. S. P. Rosenbaum edited *A Concordance to the Poems of Emily Dickinson*, 1964.

J. 49

I never lost as much but twice,
And that was in the sod.
Twice have I stood a beggar
Before the door of God!

Angels—twice descending   5
Reimbursed my store—
Burglar! Banker—Father!
I am poor once more!

c. 1858   1890

#'s keyed to Johnson's (Thomas edition of E. Dickinson's poems © 1955

J. 67

Success is counted sweetest
By those who ne'er succeed.
To comprehend a nectar
Requires sorest need.

Not one of all the purple Host
Who took the Flag today   6
Can tell the definition
So clear of Victory

As he defeated—dying—
On whose forbidden ear   10
The distant strains of triumph
Burst agonized and clear!
c. 1859   1878, 1890

J. 76

Exultation is the going
Of an inland soul to sea,
Past the houses—past the head-
          lands—
Into deep Eternity—

Bred as we, among the moun-
          tains,   5
Can the sailor understand
The divine intoxication
Of the first league out from
          land?
c. 1859   1890

J. 130

These are the days when Birds
          come back—
A very few—a Bird or two—
To take a backward look.

These are the days when skies
          resume
The old—old sophistries of
          June—   5
A blue and gold mistake.

Oh fraud that cannot cheat the
          Bee—
Almost thy plausibility
Induces my belief.

Till ranks of seeds their witness
          bear—   10
And softly thro' the altered air
Hurries a timid leaf.

Oh Sacrament of summer days,
Oh Last Communion in the
          Haze—
Permit a child to join.   15

Thy sacred emblems to
          partake—
Thy consecrated bread to take
And thine immortal wine!
c. 1859   1890

J. 148

All overgrown by cunning
          moss,
All interspersed with weed,
The little cage of "Currer Bell" [1]
In quiet "Haworth" laid.

Gathered from many
          wanderings—   5
Gethsemane [2] can tell
Thro' what transporting anguish
She reached the Asphodel! [3]

Soft fall the sounds of Eden
Upon her puzzled ear—   10
Oh what an afternoon for
          Heaven,
When "Bronte" entered there!
c. 1859   1896

1. Charlotte Brontë, British novelist (1816–1855), wrote under the name of "Currer Bell." She lived in Haworth, Yorkshire (see next line).
2. A garden outside Jerusalem, where Christ suffered agony before his betrayal and arrest (Matthew xxvi: 36).
3. In Greek mythology the flower of the Elysian Fields, where the worthy dead enjoy complete happiness.

J. 160

Just lost, when I was saved!
Just felt the world go by!
Just girt me for the onset with
    Eternity,
When breath blew back,
And on the other side   5
I heard recede the disappointed
    tide!

Therefore, as One returned, I
    feel
Odd secrets of the line to tell!
Some Sailor, skirting foreign
    shores—
Some pale Reporter, from the
    awful doors   10
Before the Seal!

Next time, to stay!
Next time, the things to see
By Ear unheard,
Unscrutinized by Eye—   15

Next time, to tarry,
While the Ages steal—
Slow tramp the Centuries,
And the Cycles wheel!
c. 1860   1891

J. 162

My River runs to thee—
Blue Sea! Wilt welcome me?
My River waits reply—
Oh Sea—look graciously—
I'll fetch thee Brooks   5
From spotted nooks—
Say—Sea—Take *Me*!
c. 1860   1890

J. 182

If I shouldn't be alive
When the Robins come,

Give the one in Red Cravat,
A Memorial crumb.

If I couldn't thank you,   5
Being fast asleep,
You will know I'm trying
With my Granite lip!
c. 1860   1890

J. 214

I taste a liquor never brewed—
From Tankards scooped in
    Pearl—
Not all the Vats upon the
    Rhine
Yield such an Alcohol!

Inebriate of Air—am I—   *Romantic*
And Debauchee of Dew—
Reeling—thro endless summer
    days—
From inns of Molten Blue—

When "Landlords" turn the
    drunken Bee
Out of the Foxglove's door—   10
When Butterflies—renounce
    their "drams"—
I shall but drink the more!

Till Seraphs swing their snowy
    Hats—
And Saints—to windows run—
To see the little Tippler   15
Leaning against the—Sun—
c. 1860   1861, 1890

J. 241

I like a look of Agony,
Because I know it's true—
Men do not sham Convulsion,
Nor simulate, a Throe—

The Eyes glaze once—and that
    is Death—   5
Impossible to feign

The Beads upon the Forehead
By homely Anguish strung.
c. 1861   1890

J. 252

I can wade Grief—
Whole Pools of it—
I'm used to that—
But the least push of Joy
Breaks up my feet—   5
And I tip—drunken—
Let no Pebble—smile—
'Twas the New Liquor—
That was all!

Power is only Pain—   10
Stranded, thro' Discipline,
Till Weights—will hang—
Give Balm—to Giants—
And they'll wilt, like Men—
Give Himmaleh [4]—   15
They'll Carry—Him!
c. 1861   1891

J. 258

There's a certain Slant of light,
Winter Afternoons—
That oppresses, like the Heft
Of Cathedral Tunes—

Heavenly Hurt, it gives us—   5
We can find no scar,
But internal difference,
Where the Meanings, are—

None may teach it—Any—
'Tis the Seal Despair—   10
An imperial affliction
Sent us of the Air—

When it comes, the Land-
scape listens—

4. A personification of the Himalayas,
mountains in India, imagined as a god
in Hindu mythology.

Shadows—hold their breath—
When it goes, 'tis like the
Distance   15
On the look of Death—
c. 1861   1890

J. 285

The Robin's my Criterion for
Tune—
Because I grow—where
Robins do—
But, were I Cuckoo born—
I'd swear by him—
The ode familiar—rules the
Noon—   5
The Buttercup's, my Whim
for Bloom—
Because, we're Orchard
sprung—
But, were I Britain born,
I'd Daisies spurn—
None but the Nut—October
fit—   10
Because, through dropping it,
The Seasons flit—I'm taught—
Without the Snow's Tableau
Winter, were lie—to me—
Because I see—New
Englandly—   15
The Queen, discerns like me—
Provincially—
c. 1861   1929

J. 288

I'm Nobody! Who are you?
Are you—Nobody—Too?
Then there's a pair of us?
Don't tell! they'd advertise—
you know!

How dreary—to be—
Somebody!   5
How public—like a Frog—

To tell one's name—the
    livelong June—
To an admiring Bog!
c. 1861   1891

J. 290

Of Bronze—and Blaze—
The North—Tonight—
So adequate—it forms—
So preconcerted with itself—
So distant—to alarms—   5
An Unconcern so sovereign
To Universe, or me—
Infects my simple spirit
With Taints of Majesty—
Till I take vaster attitudes— 10
And strut upon my stem—
Disdaining Men, and Oxygen,
For Arrogance of them—

My Splendors, are Menagerie—
But their Competeless Show 15
Will entertain the Centuries
When I, am long ago,
An Island in dishonored
    Grass—
Whom none but Beetles—
    know.
c. 1861   1896

J. 303

The Soul selects her own
    Society—
Then—shuts the Door—
To her divine Majority—
Present no more—

Unmoved—she notes the
    Chariots—pausing   5
At her low Gate—
Unmoved—an Emperor be
    kneeling
Upon her Mat—

I've known her—from an
    ample nation—
Choose One—   10
Then—close the Valves of her
    attention—
Like Stone—
c. 1862   1890

J. 318

I'll tell you how the Sun rose—
A Ribbon at a time—
The Steeples swam in
    Amethyst—
The news, like Squirrels, ran—
The Hills untied their
    Bonnets—   5
The Bobolinks—begun—
Then I said softly to myself—
"That must have been the
    Sun"!
But how he set—I know not—
There seemed a purple stile 10
That little Yellow boys and
    girls
Were climbing all the while—
Till when they reached the
    other side,
A Dominie [5] in Gray—
Put gently up the evening
    Bars—   15
And led the flock away—
c. 1860   1890

J. 320

We play at Paste—
Till qualified, for Pearl—
Then, drop the Paste—
And deem ourself a fool—

The Shapes—though—were
    similar—   5
And our new Hands

5. A pastor or clergyman.

Learned *Gem*-Tactics—
Practicing *Sands*—
c. 1862   1891

J. 322

There came a Day at
    Summer's full,
Entirely for me—
I thought that such were for
    the Saints,
Where Resurrections—be—

The Sun, as common, went
    abroad,   5
The flowers, accustomed, blew,
As if no soul the solstice passed
That maketh all things new—

The time was scarce profaned,
    by speech—
The symbol of a word—   10
Was needless, as at Sacrament,
The Wardrobe—of our Lord—

Each was to each The
    Sealed Church,
Permitted to commune this—
    time—
Lest we too awkward show   15
At Supper of the Lamb.

The Hours slid fast—as
    Hours will,
Clutched tight, by greedy
    hands—
So faces on two Decks, look
    back,
Bound to opposing lands—   20

And so when all the time had
    leaked,
Without external sound
Each bound the Other's
    Crucifix—
We gave no other Bond—

Sufficient troth, that we shall
    rise—   25

Deposed—at length, the
    Grave—
To that new Marriage,
Justified—through Calvaries of
    Love—
c. 1861   1890

J. 324

Some keep the Sabbath going
    to Church—
I keep it, staying at Home—
With a Bobolink for a
    Chorister—
And an Orchard, for a Dome—

Some keep the Sabbath in
    Surplice—   5
I just wear my Wings—
And instead of tolling the Bell,
    for Church,
Our little Sexton—sings.

God preaches, a noted
    Clergyman—   9
And the sermon is never long,
So instead of getting to Heaven,
    at last—
I'm going, all along.
c. 1860   1864

J. 328

A Bird came down the Walk—
He did not know I saw—
He bit an Angleworm in
    halves
And ate the fellow, raw,

And then he drank a Dew   5
From a convenient Grass—
And then hopped sidewise to
    the Wall
To let a Beetle pass—

He glanced with rapid eyes
That hurried all around—   10

They looked like frightened
   Beads, I thought—
He stirred his Velvet Head

Like one in danger, Cautious,
I offered him a Crumb
And he unrolled his feathers   15
And rowed him softer home—

Than Oars divide the Ocean,
Too silver for a seam—
Or Butterflies, off Banks
   of Noon
Leap, plashless as they swim.   20
c. 1862   1891

J. 333

The Grass so little has to do—
A Sphere of simple Green—
With only Butterflies to brood
And Bees to entertain—

And stir all day to pretty Tunes
The Breezes fetch along—
And hold the Sunshine in its
   lap
And blow to everything—

And thread the Dews, all night,
   like Pearls—
And make itself so fine   10
A Duchess were too common
For such a noticing—

And even when it dies—to pass
In Odors so divine—
Like Lowly spices, lain to
   sleep—   15
Or Spikenards, perishing—

And then, in Sovereign Barns
   to dwell—
And dream the Days away,
The Grass so little has to do
I wish I were a Hay—   20
c. 1862   1890

J. 341

After great pain, a formal
   feeling comes—
The Nerves sit ceremonious,
   like Tombs—
The stiff Heart questions was
   it He, that bore,
And Yesterday, or Centuries
   before?

The Feet, mechanical, go
   round—   5
Of Ground, or Air, or
   Ought [6]—
A Wooden way
Regardless grown,
A Quartz contentment, like a
   stone—

This is the Hour of Lead—   10
Remembered, if outlived,
As Freezing persons, recollect
   the Snow—
First—Chill—then Stupor—
   then the letting go—
c. 1862   1929

J. 401

What Soft—Cherubic
   Creatures—
These Gentlewomen are—
One would as soon assault a
   Plush—
Or violate a Star—

Such Dimity Convictions—   5
A Horror so refined
Of freckled Human Nature—
Of Deity—ashamed—

It's such a common—Glory—
A Fisherman's—Degree—   10

6. **Nothing.**

Redemption—Brittle Lady—
Be so—ashamed of Thee—
c. 1862   1896

J. 435

Much Madness is divinest
        Sense—
To a discerning Eye—
Much Sense—the starkest
        Madness—
'Tis the Majority
In this, as All, prevail—   5
Assent—and you are sane—
Demur—you're straightway
        dangerous—
And handled with a Chain—
c. 1862   1890

J. 441

This is my letter to the World
That never wrote to Me—
The simple News that Nature
        told—
With tender Majesty

Her Message is committed   5
To Hands I cannot see—
For love of Her—Sweet—
        countrymen—
Judge tenderly—of Me
c. 1862   1890

J. 449

I died for Beauty—but was
        scarce
Adjusted in the Tomb
When One who died for
        Truth, was lain
In an adjoining Room—

He questioned softly "Why
        I failed"?   5

"For Beauty", I replied—
"And I—for Truth—Themself
        Are One—
We Brethren, are", He said—

And so, as Kinsmen, met a
        Night—
We talked between the
        Rooms—
Until the Moss had reached   10
        our lips—
And covered up—our names—
c. 1862   1890

J. 465

I heard a Fly buzz—when I
        died—
The Stillness in the Room
Was like the Stillness in the
        Air—
Between the Heaves of
        Storm—

The Eyes around—had wrung
        them dry—   5
And Breaths were gathering
        firm
For that last Onset—when
        the King
Be witnessed—in the Room—

I willed my Keepsakes—
        Signed away
What portion of me be   10
Assignable—and then it was
There interposed a Fly—

With Blue—uncertain
        stumbling Buzz—
Between the light—and me—
And then the Windows
        failed—and then   15
I could not see to see—
c. 1862   1896

J. 478

I had no time to Hate—
Because
The Grave would hinder Me—
And Life was not so
Ample I   5
Could finish—Enmity—

Nor had I time to Love—
But since
Some Industry must be—
The little Toil of Love—   10
I thought—
Be large enough for Me—
c. 1862   1896

J. 511

If you [7] were coming in the
     Fall,
I'd brush the Summer by
With half a smile, and half
     a spurn,
As Housewives do, a Fly.

If I could see you in a year,   5
I'd wind the months in balls—
And put them each in separate
     Drawers,
For fear the numbers fuse—

If only Centuries, delayed,
I'd count them on my Hand,   10
Subtracting, till my fingers
     dropped
Into Van Dieman's Land.[8]

If certain, when this life was
     out—
That yours and mine, should be
I'd toss it yonder, like a Rind,
And take Eternity—

---

7. A possible reference to Charles
Wadsworth, who had moved to California.
8. Tasmania, an island off southeastern
Australia, was then being settled, and
was regarded as being extremely remote.

But, now, uncertain of the
     length
Of this, that is between,
It goads me, like the
     Goblin Bee—
That will not state—its sting.
c. 1862   1890

J. 526

To hear an Oriole sing
May be a common thing—
Or only a divine.

It is not of the Bird
Who sings the same, unheard,
As unto Crowd—

The Fashion of the Ear
Attireth that it hear
In Dun, or fair—

So whether it be Rune,   10
Or whether it be none
Is of within.

The "Tune is in the Tree—"
The Skeptic—showeth me—
"No Sir! In Thee!"   15
c. 1862   1891

J. 528

Mine—by the Right of the
     White Election!
Mine—by the Royal Seal!
Mine—by the Sign in the
     Scarlet prison—
Bars—cannot conceal!

Mine—here—in Vision—
     and in Veto!   5
Mine—by the Grave's
     Repeal—
Titled—Confirmed—
Delirious Charter!
Mine—long as Ages steal!
c. 1862   1890

J. 547

I've seen a Dying Eye
Run round and round a
    Room—
In search of Something—as
    it seemed—
Then Cloudier become—
And then—obscure with Fog—
And then—be soldered down
Without disclosing what it be
'Twere blessed to have seen—
c. 1862   1890

J. 556

The Brain, within its Groove
Runs evenly—and true—
But let a Splinter swerve—
'Twere easier for You—

To put a Current back—   5
When Floods have slit the
    Hills—
And scooped a Turnpike for
    Themselves—
And trodden out the Mills—
c. 1862   1890

J. 579

I had been hungry, all the
    Years—
My Noon had Come—to
    dine—
I trembling drew the Table
    near—
And touched the Curious
    Wine—

'Twas this on Tables I had
    seen—   5
When turning, hungry, Home
I looked in Windows, for the
    Wealth
I could not hope—for Mine—

I did not know the ample
    Bread—   10
'Twas so unlike the Crumb
The Birds and I, had often
    shared
In Nature's—Dining Room—

The Plenty hurt me—'twas
    so new—
Myself felt ill—and odd—
As Berry—of a Mountain
    Bush—   15
Transplanted—to the Road—

Nor was I hungry—so I found
That Hunger—was a way
Of Persons outside Windows—
The Entering—takes away—   20
c. 1862   1891

J. 581

I found the words to every
    thought
I ever had—but One—
And that—defies me—
As a Hand did try to chalk
    the Sun

To Races—nurtured in the
    Dark—   5
How would your own—begin?
Can Blaze be shown in
    Cochineal [9]—
Or Noon—in Mazarin? [1]
c. 1862   1891

J. 585

I like to see it lap the Miles—
And lick the Valleys up—
And stop to feed itself at
    Tanks—
And then—prodigious step

9. A red dye.
1. Reddish-blue.

Around a Pile of Mountains—
And supercilious peer
In Shanties—by the sides
    of Roads—
And then a Quarry pare

To fit its Ribs
And crawl between   10
Complaining all the while
In horrid—hooting stanza—
Then chase itself down Hill—

And neigh like Boanerges [2]—
Then—punctual as a Star   15
Stop—docile and omnipotent
At its own stable door—
c. 1862   1891

J. 636

The Way I read a Letter's—
    this—
'Tis first—I lock the Door—
And push it with my fingers—
    next—
For transport it be sure—

And then I go the furthest off
To counteract a knock—
Then draw my little Letter
    forth
And slowly pick the lock—

Then—glancing narrow, at
    the Wall—
And narrow at the floor   10
For firm Conviction of a Mouse
Not exorcised before—

Peruse how infinite I am
To no one that You—know—
And sigh for lack of Heaven—
    but not   15
The Heaven God bestow—
c. 1862   1891

J. 640

I cannot live with You [3]—
It would be Life—
And Life is over there—
Behind the Shelf

The Sexton keeps the Key to—
Putting up
Our Life—His Porcelain—
Like a Cup—

Discarded of the Housewife—
Quaint—or Broke—   10
A newer Sevres [4] pleases—
Old Ones crack—

I could not die—with You—
For One must wait
To shut the Other's Gaze
    down—   15
You—could not—

And I—Could I stand by
And see You—freeze—
Without my Right of Frost—
Death's privilege?   20

Nor could I rise—with You—
Because Your Face
Would put out Jesus'—
That New Grace

Glow plain—and foreign   25
On my homesick Eye—
Except that You than He
Shone closer by—

They'd judge Us—How—
For You—served Heaven—
    You know,   30
Or sought to—
I could not—

Because You saturated Sight—

---

2. A surname meaning "sons of thunder," given by Christ to James and
John (Mark iii: 17).

3. The references to Christian ministry
associate this poem with Wadsworth.
4. A fine porcelain made in the French
town of that name.

And I had no more Eyes
For sordid excellence   35
As Paradise

And were You lost, I
    would be—
Though My Name
Rang loudest
On the Heavenly fame—   40

And were You—saved—
And I—condemned to be
Where You were not—
That self—were Hell to Me—

So We must meet apart—   45
You there—I—here—
With just the Door ajar
That Oceans are—and Prayer—
And that White Sustenance—
Despair—   50
c. 1862   1890

J. 650

Pain—has an Element of
    Blank—
It cannot recollect
When it begun—or if
    there were
A time when it was not—

It has no Future—but itself—
Its Infinite contain   6
Its Past—enlightened to
    perceive
New Periods—of Pain.
c. 1862   1890

J. 701

A Thought went up my mind
    today—
That I have had before—
But did not finish—some way
    back—
I could not fix the Year—

Nor where it went—nor
    why it came   5
The second time to me—
Nor definitely, what it was—
Have I the Art to say—

But somewhere—in my Soul—
    I know—
I've met the Thing before—   10
It just reminded me—'twas
    all—
And came my way no more—
c. 1863   1891

J. 712

Because I could not stop for
    Death—
He kindly stopped for me—
The Carriage held but just
    Ourselves—
And Immortality.

We slowly drove—He knew
    no haste   5
And I had put away
My labor and my leisure too,
For His Civility—

We passed the School, where
    Children strove
At Recess—in the Ring—   10
We passed the Fields of
    Gazing Grain—
We passed the Setting Sun—

Or rather—He passed Us—
The Dews drew quivering and
    chill—   14
For only Gossamer, my Gown—
My Tippet—only Tulle—

We paused before a House
    that seemed
A Swelling of the Ground—   18
The Roof was scarcely visible—
The Cornice—in the Ground—

Since then—'tis Centuries—
   and yet
Feels shorter than the Day
I first surmised the Horses'
   Heads
Were toward Eternity—
c. 1863   1890

[handwritten: Were they headed toward Eternity or Death that She doesn't answer question]

J. 732

She rose to His Requirement—
   dropt
The Playthings of Her Life
To take the honorable Work
Of Woman, and of Wife—

If ought She missed in Her
   new Day,   5
Of Amplitude, or Awe—
Or first Prospective—Or the
   Gold
In using, wear away,

It lay unmentioned—as the Sea
Develop Pearl, and Weed,   10
But only to Himself—
   be known
The Fathoms they abide—
c. 1863   1890

J. 816

A Death blow is a Life blow
   to Some
Who till they died, did not
   alive become—
Who had they lived, had
   died but when
They died, Vitality begun.
c. 1864   1891

J. 823

Not what We did, shall be
   the test
When Act and Will are done

But what Our Lord infers We
   would
Had We diviner been—
c. 1864   1929

J. 986

A narrow Fellow in the Grass
Occasionally rides—
You may have met Him—
   did you not
His notice sudden is—

The Grass divides as with
   a Comb—   5
A spotted shaft is seen—
And then it closes at your feet
And opens further on—

He likes a Boggy Acre
A Floor too cool for Corn— 10
Yet when a Boy, and
   Barefoot—
I more than once at Noon

Have passed, I thought, a
   Whip lash
Unbraiding in the Sun
When stooping to secure it 15
It wrinkled, and was gone—

Several of Nature's People
I know, and they know me—
I feel for them a transport
Of cordiality—   20

But never met this Fellow
Attended, or alone
Without a tighter breathing
And Zero at the Bone—
c. 1865   1866, 1891

J. 1052

I never saw a Moor—
I never saw the Sea—
Yet know I how the Heather
   looks

And what a Billow be.

I never spoke with God   5
Nor visited in Heaven—
Yet certain am I of the spot
As if the Checks were given—
c. 1865   1890

J. 1078

The Bustle in a House
The Morning after Death
Is solemnest of industries
Enacted upon Earth—

The Sweeping up the Heart   5
And putting Love away
We shall not want to use again
Until Eternity.
c. 1866   1890

J. 1082

Revolution is the Pod
Systems rattle from
When the Winds of Will are
    stirred
Excellent is Bloom

But except its Russet Base   5
Every Summer be
The Entomber of itself,
So of Liberty—

Left inactive on the Stalk
All its Purple fled   10
Revolution shakes it for
Test if it be dead.
c. 1866   1929

J. 1100

The last Night that She lived [5]
It was a Common Night

5. "On Thursday, 3 May 1866, Laura
Dickey (Mrs. Frank W.) of Michigan,
youngest daughter of Mr. and Mrs. L.
M. Hills, died at her parents' home in
Amherst. The Hills land lay next to the
Dickinsons on the East" [Johnson's
note].

Except the Dying—this to Us
Made Nature different

We noticed smallest things—   5
Things overlooked before
By this great light upon our
    Minds
Italicized—as 'twere.

As We went out and in
Between Her final Room   10
And Rooms where Those
    to be alive
Tomorrow were, a Blame

That Others could exist
While She must finish quite
A Jealousy for Her arose   15
So nearly infinite—

We waited while She passed—
It was a narrow time—
Too jostled were Our Souls
    to speak
At length the notice came.   20

She mentioned, and forgot—
Then lightly as a Reed
Bent to the Water,
    struggled scarce—
Consented, and was dead—

And We—We placed the
    Hair—   25
And drew the Head erect—
And then an awful leisure was
Belief to regulate—
c. 1866   1890

J. 1176

We never know how high
    we are
Till we are asked to rise
And then if we are true to plan
Our statures touch the skies—

The Heroism we recite   5
Would be a normal thing

Did not ourselves the
    Cubits warp
For fear to be a King—
c. 1870   1896

J. 1207

He preached upon "Breadth"
    till it argued him narrow—
The Broad are too broad to
    define
And of "Truth" until it
    proclaimed him a Liar—
The Truth never flaunted a
    Sign—

Simplicity fled from his
    counterfeit presence   5
As Gold the Pyrites [6] would
    shun—
What confusion would cover
    the innocent Jesus
To meet so enabled a Man!
c. 1872   1891

J. 1263

There is no Frigate like a Book
To take us Lands away
Nor any Coursers like a Page
Of prancing Poetry—

This Traverse may the
    poorest take   5
Without oppress of Toll—
How frugal is the Chariot
That bears the Human soul.
c. 1873   1894

J. 1304

Not with a Club, the
    Heart is broken

Nor with a Stone—
A Whip so small you could
    not see it
I've known

To lash the Magic Creature   5
Till it fell,
Yet that Whip's Name
Too noble then to tell.

Magnanimous as Bird
By Boy descried—   10
Singing unto the Stone
Of which it died—

Shame need not crouch
In such an Earth as Ours—
Shame—stand erect—   15
The Universe is yours.
c. 1874   1896

J. 1332

Pink—small—and punctual [7]—
Aromatic—low—
Covert—in April—
Candid—in May—
Dear to the Moss—   5
Known to the Knoll—
Next to the Robin
In every human Soul—
Bold little Beauty
Bedecked with thee   10
Nature forswears
Antiquity—
c. 1875   1890

J. 1463

A Route of Evanescence
With a revolving Wheel—
A Resonance of Emerald—
A Rush of Cochineal [8]—

6. Iron pyrites, sometimes mistaken for gold, and known as "fool's gold."

7. "(With the first Arbutus.)" [Dickinson's note].

8. A red dye.

And every Blossom on the
   Bush   5
Adjusts its tumbled Head—
The mail from Tunis, probably,
An easy Morning's Ride—
c. 1879   1891

J. 1465

Before you thought of Spring
Except as a Surmise
You see—God bless his
   suddenness—
A Fellow in the Skies
Of independent Hues   5
A little weather worn
Inspiriting habiliments
Of Indigo and Brown—
With specimens of Song
As if for you to choose—   10
Discretion in the interval
With gay delays he goes
To some superior Tree
Without a single Leaf
And shouts for joy to Nobody
But his seraphic self—
c. 1871   1891

J. 1510

How happy is the little Stone
That rambles in the Road
   alone,
And doesn't care about Careers
And Exigencies never fears—
Whose Coat of elemental
   Brown   5
A passing Universe put on,
And independent as the Sun
Associates or glows alone,
Fulfilling absolute Decree
In casual simplicity [9]—   10
c. 1881   1891

9. In a letter, probably to her sister-in-
law, Emily Dickinson adds beneath the

J. 1540

As imperceptibly as Grief
The Summer lapsed away—
Too imperceptible at last
To seem like Perfidy—
A Quietness distilled   5
As Twilight long begun,
Or Nature spending with
   herself
Sequestered Afternoon—
The Dusk drew earlier in—
The Morning foreign shone— 10
A courteous, yet harrowing
   Grace,
As Guest, that would be gone—
And thus, without a Wing
Or service of a Keel
Our Summer made her light
   escape   15
Into the Beautiful.
c. 1865   1891

J. 1587

He ate and drank the precious
   Words—
His Spirit grew robust—
He knew no more that he
   was poor,
Nor that his frame was Dust—

He danced along the dingy
   Days   5
And this Bequest of Wings
Was but a Book—What
   Liberty
A loosened spirit brings—
c. 1883   1890

poem: "Heaven the Balm of a surly
Technicality!" In a letter to T. W. Higginson she adds the separate quatrain
(J. 1543): "Obtaining but our own Extent / In whatsoever Realm— / 'Twas
Christ's own personal Expanse / That
bore him from the Tomb—." Johnson
notes that "the thought seems to be a
reflection on the Calvinist orthodoxy
that only the 'saved' get into heaven."

J. 1624

Apparently with no surprise
To any happy Flower
The Frost beheads it at its
    play—
In accidental power—
The blonde Assassin passes
    on—   5
The Sun proceeds unmoved
To measure off another Day
For an Approving God.
c. 1884   1890

J. 1732

My life closed twice before
    its close—
It yet remains to see
If Immortality unveil
A third event to me

So huge, so hopeless to
    conceive   5
As these that twice befell.
Parting is all we know of
    heaven,
And all we need of hell.
?   1896

J. 1760

Elysium[1] is as far as to
The very nearest Room
If in that Room a Friend await
Felicity or Doom—

What fortitude the Soul
    contains,   5
That it can so endure
The accent of a coming Foot—
The opening of a Door—
c. 1882   1890

1. Paradise.

The Regional Realists

SAMUEL LANGHORNE CLEMENS

(1835–1910)

The pattern of the life of Samuel Langhorne Clemens, or "Mark Twain," for seventy-five years was the pattern of America—from frontier community to industrial urbanity, from river boats to railroads, from an aggressive, bumptious adolescence toward a troubled and powerful maturity. His intuitive and romantic response to that life was colored simultaneously by healthy skepticism, and a strong suspicion that the geography and citizens of America were not conforming to scriptural patterns of the Promised Land. This discrepancy between the American expectation and the disturbing reality, to which many writers have reacted with bitterness, or with gloomy acceptance and alarms, provoked Mark Twain to adopt the critical weapons of the humorist.

The inheritor of an indigenous tradition of humor compounded of Indian and Negro legend, New England wryness and dryness, and frontier extravagance, Mark Twain spent his early years in an ideal location for such influences to mold his life and his writing. Hannibal, Missouri, strategically placed on the banks of the Mississippi, in the period before the Civil War saw the commerce and travelers of a nation pass its wharfs and look westward from its streets. For a perceptive boy, such experiences were not to be forgotten, and later he preserved them in books that are world classics of the remembrance of a lost and happy time. His youth was typical of life in a fluid, diverse, yet morally exacting community in a chaotic period. His schooling was brief, and at eighteen he went to Philadelphia, New York, and Washington, doing itinerant newspaper work and sending his first travel letters to his brother Orion, who published them in his Muscatine *Journal*. He followed his brother to Keokuk, then moved on to Cincinnati, and from there embarked on an intended journey to South America, with the amusing results recounted in *Life on the Mississippi*. Once he was on the river, his boyhood ambition to be a pilot returned, and discarding all thoughts of the Amazon, he persuaded Horace Bixby, a famous pilot, to school him in the intricate art of Mississippi navigation. After less than two years as a "cub," Twain received his pilot's license; the Civil War then put an end to piloting, but his nostalgic love of the river life was forever fixed in his pseudonym, "Mark Twain," the leadsman's cry meaning a two-fathom sounding, or "safe water."

The Civil War brought change and tension to the Clemens family who were, like so many, divided in their loyalty and allegiance. Orion Clemens, a strong Union man, campaigned for Lincoln and was appointed secretary of the Nevada Territory. Troubled by his brother's inclination toward the southern tradition of the family, Orion persuaded him, rather easily, to go west as his assistant, although he did not need one. In 1861 they traveled by stagecoach across the plains to Carson City, a journey described with hilarious half-truth and half-fiction in *Roughing It*. Neither the political job nor subsequent ventures in mining were profitable, and Twain began contributing letters, signed "Josh," to the Virginia City *Territorial Enterprise*, which led to his joining its staff in 1862. From that time he was to remain a writer, although he occasionally lectured and ventured into business on the side. The "Jumping Frog" story, now famous as "The Notorious Jumping Frog of Calaveras County," published in the New York *Saturday Press* in 1865, brought him national attention; on the West Coast he was already well known as a journal-

istic associate of Bret Harte and Artemus Ward, remembered for his humorous sketches in various papers and for a successful reportorial trip to Hawaii. A commission from the *Alta California* to write a series of travel letters now enabled him for the first time to go to Europe.

Twain's excursion on the *Quaker City* to Europe and the Holy Land resulted in *The Innocents Abroad* (1869), a best seller, followed by an equally successful lecture tour. In 1870, he married Olivia Langdon and settled down as editor of the Buffalo *Express*, but he soon moved to Hartford. His first effort at a novel, *The Gilded Age* (1873), written in collaboration with Charles Dudley Warner, was a bitter yet amusing narrative of post-Civil War political and business corruption, and offers interesting parallels with *A Connecticut Yankee in King Arthur's Court* (1889), a comic critique of society in a fantastic vein. These books, with their quizzical and detached humor, suggest Twain's ability to view his age with qualified affection while satirizing the economic and spiritual disorders, the narrow insularity, of mid-nineteenth-century America. Yet that American provincialism, exploited for comic effect in *The Innocents Abroad* and in the later travel books, *A Tramp Abroad* (1880) and the classic *Life on the Mississippi* (1883), never overshadowed his love of the American land and its people. That love, intensified by childhood memories, evoked his two unquestioned masterpieces. *Tom Sawyer* (1876) and

Huckleberry Finn (1885) combine recollections of Hannibal in Twain's youth, the spell of a great river, and the intangible quality of an art that relies on simplicity for its greatest effect. On one level, the nostalgic account of childhood, on another, the social and moral record and judgment of an epoch in American history, the two books have attained the position of classics in the world's literature. They were followed by lesser works, such as *The American Claimant* (1892), *The £1,000,000 Bank-Note* (1893), *The Tragedy of Pudd'nhead Wilson* (1894), *Personal Recollections of Joan of Arc* (1896), and *Following the Equator* (1897), the last of the travel volumes. *Tom Sawyer Abroad* (1894) and *Tom Sawyer, Detective* (1896) ended Twain's employment of Huck and Tom in fiction.

The tradition of American humor, from colonial folk myth and *Poor Richard's Almanack*, to the Yankee wit of Lowell's *Biglow Papers*, spreading through the national press from Josh Billings, John Phoenix, Artemus Ward, and unnumbered, forgotten local humorists, followed the pattern of any folk literature in its immediate and intuitive response to cultural and social patterns. Mark Twain is America's greatest humorist not only because of his unsurpassed mastery of that essential pattern but because his humor served to point up errors in American life —its gaucheries, pretenses, and political debilities—and at the same time expressed a faith in the American dream, optimistic and unquenchable.

The discrepancy between that dream and its questionable fulfillment, so obvious to the writers of the twentieth century, found expression also in Mark Twain's personal life. His literary successes and popularity in America and abroad were contrasted with emotional complexities, tragic losses, and business disappointments; his later writings evidence a skepticism saved from petulance by a great artist's sincerity. *The Man That Corrupted Hadleyburg* (1900), reprinted below, and *The Mysterious Stranger* (1916) are indictments of more than national cupidity and hypocrisy; they are troubled inquiries into the nature of man himself. And they appear to be at strange variance with such books as *Tom Sawyer* unless the reader recognizes in Twain the dichotomy of personality that William Dean Howells may have had in mind when he called him "the Lincoln of our literature."

Several complete editions of Mark Twain have been published, of which the best are the Author's National Edition, in 25 vols., 1907–1918, and the rare but excellent *The Writings of Mark Twain*, 37 vols., edited by Albert Bigelow Paine, 1922–1925. A good one-volume collection is *The Portable Mark Twain*, edited by Bernard De Voto, 1946. A definitive edition of the works is planned jointly by the University of Iowa and the University of California, and a documentary collection of *Mark Twain Papers* is in progress at the University of California. Both are CEAA sponsored.

The Autobiography of Mark Twain, edited by Charles Neider, 1959, includes material not in the 1924 edition by Albert Bigelow Paine, nor in *Mark Twain in Eruption*, edited by Bernard De Voto, 1940. The authorized life by Albert Bigelow Paine, *Mark Twain, A Biography*, 3 vols., 1912, was reissued in 1935. This is supplemented by DeLancey Ferguson, *Mark*

Twain, Man and Legend, 1943; by Bernard De Voto, *Mark Twain's America,* 1932; by Dixon Wecter's *Sam Clemens of Hannibal,* 1952; and by Justin Kaplan's excellent *Mr. Clemens and Mark Twain,* 1966. Important collections of correspondence are *Mark Twain's Letters,* 2 vols., edited by Albert Bigelow Paine, 1917; *The Love Letters of Mark Twain,* edited by Dixon Wecter, 1949; *Mark Twain–Howells Letters,* 2 vols., edited by Henry Nash Smith and William M. Gibson, 1960; and *Mark Twain's Letters from Hawaii,* edited by A. Grove Day, 1966. Charles Neider edited *The Complete Short Stories,* 1957, *The Complete Essays,* 1963, and *The Complete Travel Books,* 2 vols., 1967. *Letters from the Earth,* miscellaneous sketches, were edited by Bernard De Voto in 1939 and published in 1962. A sound critical study is Edward Wagenknecht, *Mark Twain: The Man and His Work,* 1935 (revised, 1967). E. Hudson Long, *Mark Twain Handbook,* 1958, is useful. See also K. A. Lynn, *Mark Twain and Southwestern Humor,* 1959; W. Blair, *Mark Twain and Huck Finn,* 1960; R. B. Salomon, *Twain and the Image of History,* 1961; A. E. Stone, Jr., *The Innocent Eye * * *,* 1961; Douglas Grant, *Mark Twain,* 1963; H. N. Smith, *Mark Twain: The Development of a Writer,* 1962; Louis Budd, *Mark Twain: Social Philosopher,* 1962; Pascal Covico, *Mark Twain's Humor: The Image of a World,* 1962; Robert Wiggins, *Mark Twain: Jackleg Novelist,* 1964; Margaret Duckett, *Mark Twain and Bret Harte,* 1965; James M. Cox, *Mark Twain: The Fate of Humor,* 1966; Robert Regan, *Unpromising Heroes: Mark Twain and His Characters,* 1966; Fred W. Lorch, *The Trouble Begins at Eight: Mark Twain's Lecture Tours,* 1968; and Maxwell Geismar, *Mark Twain: An American Prophet,* 1970.

From Roughing It [1]

[When the Buffalo Climbed a Tree]

Next morning just before dawn, when about five hundred and fifty miles from St. Joseph,[2] our mud-wagon [3] broke down. We were to be delayed five or six hours, and therefore we took horses, by invitation, and joined a party who were just starting on a buffalo hunt. It was noble sport galloping over the plain in the dewy freshness of the morning, but our part of the hunt ended in disaster and disgrace, for a wounded buffalo bull chased the passenger Bemis nearly two miles, and then he forsook his horse and took to a lone tree. He was very sullen about the matter for some twenty-four hours, but at last he began to soften little by little, and finally he said:

"Well, it was not funny, and there was no sense in those gawks making themselves so facetious over it. I tell you I was angry in earnest for awhile. I should have shot that long gangly lubber they called Hank, if I could have done it without crippling six or seven other people—but of course I couldn't, the old 'Allen' [4] 's so confounded comprehensive. I wish those loafers had been up in the

1. The sketches in *Roughing It* were based on Twain's memories, generously intermingled with elements of the tall tale, of his overland trip to Nevada in 1861 in company with his brother Orion, who had been appointed secretary of the Nevada Territory. Orion kept a journal which Mark drew on for certain facts. The present text of *Roughing It* is based on the first edition of 1872.
2. The Missouri gateway to the frontier, from which the overland stages started westward.
3. A less comfortable type of stagecoach, with open sides and simple benches.
4. A revolver named after its inventor, often called a "pepperbox" because it had six barrels.

tree; they wouldn't have wanted to laugh so. If I had had a horse worth a cent—but no, the minute he saw that buffalo bull wheel on him and give a bellow, he raised straight up in the air and stood on his heels. The saddle began to slip, and I took him round the neck and laid close to him, and began to pray. Then he came down and stood up on the other end awhile, and the bull actually stopped pawing sand and bellowing to contemplate the inhuman spectacle. Then the bull made a pass at him and uttered a bellow that sounded perfectly frightful, it was so close to me, and that seemed to literally prostrate my horse's reason, and make a raving distracted maniac of him, and I wish I may die if he didn't stand on his head for a quarter of a minute and shed tears. He was absolutely out of his mind—he was, as sure as truth itself, and he really didn't know what he was doing. Then the bull came charging at us, and my horse dropped down on all fours and took a fresh start—and then for the next ten minutes he would actually throw one hand-spring after another so fast that the bull began to get unsettled, too, and didn't know where to start in—and so he stood there sneezing, and shoveling dust over his back, and bellowing every now and then, and thinking he had got a fifteen-hundred dollar circus horse for breakfast, certain. Well, I was first out on his neck —the horse's, not the bull's—and then underneath, and next on his rump, and sometimes head up, and sometimes heels—but I tell you it seemed solemn and awful to be ripping and tearing and carrying on so in the presence of death, as you might say. Pretty soon the bull made a snatch for us and brought away some of my horse's tail (I suppose, but do not know, being pretty busy at the time), but *something* made him hungry for solitude and suggested to him to get up and hunt for it. And then you ought to have seen that spider-legged old skeleton go! and you ought to have seen the bull cut out after him, too—head down, tongue out, tail up, bellowing like everything, and actually mowing down the weeds, and tearing up the earth, and boosting up the sand like a whirlwind! By George, it was a hot race! I and the saddle were back on the rump, and I had the bridle in my teeth and holding on to the pommel with both hands. First we left the dogs behind; then we passed a jackass rabbit;[5] then we overtook a cayote,[6] and were gaining on an antelope when the rotten girths let go and threw me about thirty yards off to the left, and as the saddle went down over the horse's rump he gave it a lift with his heels that sent it more than four hundred yards up in the air, I wish I may die in a minute if he didn't. I fell at the foot of the only solitary tree there was in nine counties adjacent (as any creature could see with

5. A large rabbit indigenous to the West, jokingly said to resemble a miniature donkey.

6. Twain's spelling for "coyote," a prairie wolf.

the naked eye), and the next second I had hold of the bark with four sets of nails and my teeth, and the next second after that I was astraddle of the main limb and blaspheming my luck in a way that made my breath smell of brimstone. I *had* the bull, now, if he did not think of *one* thing. But that one thing I dreaded. I dreaded it very seriously. There was a possibility that the bull might not think of it, but there were greater chances that he would. I made up my mind what I would do in case he did. It was a little over forty feet to the ground from where I sat. I cautiously unwound the lariat from the pommel of my saddle—"

"Your *saddle?* Did you take your saddle up in the tree with you?"

"Take it up in the tree with me? Why, how you talk. Of course I didn't. No man could do that. It *fell* in the tree when it came down."

"Oh—exactly."

"Certainly. I unwound the lariat, and fastened one end of it to the limb. It was the very best green raw-hide, and capable of sustaining tons. I made a slip-noose in the other end, and then hung it down to see the length. It reached down twenty-two feet—half way to the ground. I then loaded every barrel of the Allen with a double charge. I felt satisfied. I said to myself, if he never thinks of that one thing that I dread, all right—but if he does, all right anyhow—I am fixed for him. But don't you know that the very thing a man dreads is the thing that always happens? Indeed it is so. I watched the bull, now, with anxiety—anxiety which no one can conceive of who has not been in such a situation and felt that at any moment death might come. Presently a thought came into the bull's eye. I knew it! said I—if my nerve fails now, I am lost. Sure enough, it was just as I had dreaded, he started in to climb the tree—"

"What, the bull?"

"Of course—who else?"

"But a bull can't climb a tree."

"He can't, can't he? Since you know so much about it, did you ever see a bull try?"

"No! I never dreamt of such a thing."

"Well, then, what is the use of your talking that way, then? Because you never saw a thing done, is that any reason why it can't be done?"

"Well, all right—go on. What did you do?"

"The bull started up, and got along well for about ten feet, then slipped and slid back. I breathed easier. He tried it again—got up a little higher—slipped again. But he came at it once more, and this time he was careful. He got gradually higher and higher, and my spirits went down more and more. Up he came—an inch at a time—with his eyes hot, and his tongue hanging out. Higher and higher—hitched his foot over the stump of a limb, and looked up, as much as to say, 'You are my meat, friend.' Up again—higher and higher, and getting more excited the closer he got. He was within ten feet of me! I took a long breath,—and then said I, 'It is now or never.' I had the coil of the lariat all ready; I paid it out slowly, till it hung right over his head; all of a sudden I let go of the slack, and the slipnoose fell fairly round his neck! Quicker than lightning I out with the Allen and let him have it in the face. It was an awful roar, and must have scared the bull out of his senses. When the smoke cleared away, there he was, dangling in the air, twenty foot from the ground, and going out of one convulsion into another faster than you could count! I didn't stop to count, any-how—I shinned down the tree and shot for home."

"Bemis, is all that true, just as you have stated it?"

"I wish I may rot in my tracks and die the death of a dog if it isn't."

"Well, we can't refuse to believe it, and we don't. But if there were some proofs—"

"Proofs! Did I bring back my lariat?"

"No."

"Did I bring back my horse?"

"No."

"Did you ever see the bull again?"

"No."

"Well, then, what more do you want? I never saw anybody as particular as you are about a little thing like that."

I made up my mind that if this man was not a liar he only missed it by the skin of his teeth.

1872

From Life on the Mississippi [7]

The Boys' Ambition [8]

When I was a boy, there was but one permanent ambition among my comrades in our village [9] on the west bank of the Mis-

---

7. *Life on the Mississippi* (1883) is perhaps the finest literary treatment of a trade; it is also a poetic narrative in praise of the mighty Mississippi. The first half of the book—by far the better—is a nostalgic account of a boy's ambition to become a pilot and his experiences as a "cub" in the pilot house. The second half is a report of the author's recent journey on the river and of a visit to his old home. The Reverend Joseph Twichell, a lifelong friend, first suggested to Twain that his cub-pilot reminiscences would make

wonderful reading matter, and in-spired with the idea, he immediately began "Old Times on the Mississippi" (Chapters IV–XVII of *Life on the Mississippi*), which appeared in the *Atlantic Monthly* in 1875. These selec-tions are reprinted from the first edi-tion of the book.
8. This is Chapter IV of *Life on the Mississippi*, and the first chapter of "Old Times on the Mississippi," pub-lished in the *Atlantic Monthly* in 1875.
9. "Hannibal, Missouri" [Twain's note].

sissippi River. That was, to be a steamboatman. We had transient ambitions of other sorts, but they were only transient. When a circus came and went, it left us all burning to become clowns; the first negro minstrel show that ever came to our section left us all suffering to try that kind of life; now and then we had a hope that, if we lived and were good, God would permit us to be pirates. These ambitions faded out, each in its turn; but the ambition to be a steamboatman always remained.

Once a day a cheap, gaudy packet arrived upward from St. Louis, and another downward from Keokuk.[1] Before these events, the day was glorious with expectancy; after them, the day was a dead and empty thing. Not only the boys, but the whole village, felt this. After all these years I can picture that old time to myself now, just as it was then: the white town drowsing in the sunshine of a summer's morning; the streets empty, or pretty nearly so; one or two clerks sitting in front of the Water Street stores, with their splint-bottomed chairs tilted back against the walls, chins on breasts, hats slouched over their faces, asleep—with shingle-shavings enough around to show what broke them down; a sow and a litter of pigs loafing along the sidewalk, doing a good business in watermelon rinds and seeds; two or three lonely little freight piles scattered about the "levee"; a pile of "skids" on the slope of the stone-paved wharf, and the fragrant town drunkard alseep in the shadow of them; two or three wood flats at the head of the wharf, but nobody to listen to the peaceful lapping of the wavelets against them; the great Mississippi, the majestic, the magnificent Mississippi, rolling its mile-wide tide along, shining in the sun; the dense forest away on the other side; the "point" above the town, and the "point" below, bounding the river-glimpse and turning it into a sort of sea, and withal a very still and brilliant and lonely one. Presently a film of dark smoke appears above one of those remote "points"; instantly a negro drayman, famous for his quick eye and prodigious voice, lifts up the cry, "S-t-e-a-m-boat a-comin'!" and the scene changes! The town drunkard stirs, the clerks wake up, a furious clatter of drays follows, every house and store pours out a human contribution, and all in a twinkling the dead town is alive and moving. Drays, carts, men, boys, all go hurrying from many quarters to a common center, the wharf. Assembled there, the people fasten their eyes upon the coming boat as upon a wonder they are seeing for the first time. And the boat *is* rather a handsome sight, too. She is long and sharp and trim and pretty; she has two tall, fancy-topped chimneys, with a gilded device of some kind swung between them; a fanciful pilot-house, all glass and "gingerbread," perched on top of the "texas" deck [2] behind them;

1. In southeastern Iowa.
2. The officers' quarters, largest on the boat, were called the "texas," and the deck just over them the "texas deck."

the paddle-boxes are gorgeous with a picture or with gilded rays above the boat's name; the boiler-deck, the hurricane-deck, and the texas deck are fenced and ornamented with clean white railings; there is a flag gallantly flying from the jack-staff; the furnace doors are open and the fires glaring bravely; the upper decks are black with passengers; the captain stands by the big bell, calm, imposing, the envy of all; great volumes of the blackest smoke are rolling and tumbling out of the chimneys—a husbanded grandeur created with a bit of pitch-pine just before arriving at a town; the crew are grouped on the forecastle; the broad stage is run far out over the port bow, and an envied deck-hand stands picturesquely on the end of it with a coil of rope in his hand; the pent steam is screaming through the gauge-cocks; the captain lifts his hand, a bell rings, the wheels stop; then they turn back, churning the water to foam, and the steamer is at rest. Then such a scramble as there is to get aboard, and to get ashore, and to take in freight and to discharge freight, all at one and the same time; and such a yelling and cursing as the mates facilitate it all with! Ten minutes later the steamer is under way again, with no flag on the jack-staff and no black smoke issuing from the chimneys. After ten more minutes the town is dead again, and the town drunkard alseep by the skids once more.

My father was a justice of the peace, and I supposed he possessed the power of life and death over all men, and could hang anybody that offended him. This was distinction enough for me as a general thing; but the desire to be a steamboatman kept intruding, nevertheless. I first wanted to be a cabin-boy, so that I could come out with a white apron on and shake a table-cloth over the side, where all my old comrades could see me; later I thought I would rather be the deck-hand who stood on the end of the stage-plank with the coil of rope in his hand, because he was particularly conspicuous. But these were only day-dreams—they were too heavenly to be contemplated as real possibilities. By and by one of our boys went away. He was not heard of for a long time. At last he turned up as apprentice engineer or "striker" on a steamboat. This thing shook the bottom out of all my Sunday-school teachings. That boy had been notoriously worldly, and I just the reverse; yet he was exalted to this eminence, and I left in obscurity and misery. There was nothing generous about this fellow in his greatness. He would always manage to have a rusty bolt to scrub while his boat tarried at our town, and he would sit on the inside guard and scrub it, where we all could see him and envy him and loathe him. And whenever his boat was laid up he would come home and swell around the town in his blackest and greasiest clothes, so that nobody could help remembering that he was a steamboatman; and he used all sorts of steamboat technicalities in his talk, as if he were so used to them that he forgot common people could not understand them. He would speak of the "labboard" side of a horse in an easy, natural way that would make one wish he was dead. And he was always talking about "St. Looy" like an old citizen; he would refer casually to occasions when he was "coming down Fourth Street," or when he was "passing by the Planter's House," or when there was a fire and he took a turn on the brakes of "the old Big Missouri"; and then he would go on and lie about how many towns the size of ours were burned down there that day. Two or three of the boys had long been persons of consideration among us because they had been to St. Louis once and had a vague general knowledge of its wonders, but the day of their glory was over now. They lapsed into a humble silence, and learned to disappear when the ruthless "cub"-engineer approached. This fellow had money, too, and hair-oil. Also an ignorant silver watch and a showy brass watch-chain. He wore a leather belt and used no suspenders. If ever a youth was cordially admired and hated by his comrades, this one was. No girl could withstand his charms. He "cut out" every boy in the village. When his boat blew up at last, it diffused a tranquil contentment among us such as we had not known for months. But when he came home the next week, alive, renowned, and appeared in church all battered up and bandaged, a shining hero, stared at and wondered over by everybody, it seemed to us that the partiality of Providence for an undeserving reptile had reached a point where it was open to criticism.

This creature's career could produce but one result, and it speedily followed. Boy after boy managed to get on the river. The minister's son became an engineer. The doctor's and the postmaster's sons became "mud clerks"; the wholesale liquor dealer's son became a barkeeper on a boat; four sons of the chief merchant, and two sons of the county judge, became pilots. Pilot was the grandest position of all. The pilot, even in those days of trivial wages, had a princely salary—from a hundred and fifty to two hundred and fifty dollars a month, and no board to pay. Two months of his wages would pay a preacher's salary for a year. Now some of us were left disconsolate. We could not get on the river— at least our parents would not let us.

So, by and by, I ran away. I said I would never come home again till I was a pilot and could come in glory. But somehow I could not manage it. I went meekly aboard a few of the boats that lay packed together like sardines at the long St. Louis wharf, and humbly inquired for the pilots, but got only a cold shoulder and short words from mates and clerks. I had to make the best of this sort of treatment for the time being, but I had comforting daydreams of a future when I should be a great and honored pilot, with plenty of money, and could kill some of these mates and clerks and pay for them.

[A *Mississippi Cub-Pilot*] [3]

The boat backed out from New Orleans at four in the afternoon, and it was "our watch" until eight. Mr. Bixby, my chief, "straightened her up," plowed her along past the sterns of the other boats that lay at the Levee, and then said, "Here take her; shave those steamships as close as you'd peel an apple." I took the wheel, and my heartbeat fluttered up into the hundreds; for it seemed to me that we were about to scrape the side off every ship in the line, we were so close. I held my breath and began to claw the boat away from the danger; and I had my own opinion of the pilot who had known no better than to get us into such peril, but I was too wise to express it. In half a minute I had a wide margin of safety intervening between the *Paul Jones* and the ships; and within ten seconds more I was set aside in disgrace, and Mr. Bixby was going into danger again and flaying me alive with abuse of my cowardice. I was stung, but I was obliged to admire the easy confidence with which my chief loafed from side to side of his wheel, and trimmed the ships so closely that disaster seemed ceaselessly imminent. When he had cooled a little he told me that the easy water was close ashore and the current outside, and therefore we must hug the bank, up-stream, to get the benefit of the former, and stay well out, down-stream, to take advantage of the latter. In my own mind I resolved to be a down-stream pilot and leave the up-streaming to people dead to prudence.

Now and then Mr. Bixby called my attention to certain things. Said he, "This is Six-Mile Point." I assented. It was pleasant enough information, but I could not see the bearing of it. I was not conscious that it was a matter of any interest to me. Another time he said, "This is Nine-Mile Point." Later he said, "This is Twelve-Mile Point." They were all about level with the water's edge; they all looked about alike to me; they were monotonously unpicturesque. I hoped Mr. Bixby would change the subject. But no; he would crowd up around a point, hugging the shore with affection, and then say: "The slack water ends here, abreast this bunch of China trees; now we cross over." So he crossed over. He gave me the wheel once or twice, but I had no luck. I either came near chipping off the edge of a sugar-plantation, or I yawed too far from shore, and so dropped back into disgrace again and got abused.

The watch was ended at last, and we took supper and went to bed. At midnight the glare of a lantern shone in my eyes, and the night watchman said:

3. From *Life on the Mississippi*, Chapters VI and VII.

"Come, turn out!"

And then he left. I could not understand this extraordinary procedure; so I presently gave up trying to, and dozed off to sleep. Pretty soon the watchman was back again, and this time he was gruff. I was annoyed. I said:

"What do you want to come bothering around here in the middle of the night for? Now, as like as not, I'll not get to sleep again tonight."

The watchman said:

"Well, if this ain't good, I'm blessed."

The "off-watch" was just turning in, and I heard some brutal laughter from them, and such remarks as "Hello, watchman! ain't the new cub turned out yet? He's delicate, likely. Give him some sugar in a rag, and send for the chambermaid to sing 'Rock-a-by Baby,' to him."

About this time Mr. Bixby appeared on the scene. Something like a minute later I was climbing the pilot-house steps with some of my clothes on and the rest in my arms. Mr. Bixby was close behind, commenting. Here was something fresh—this thing of getting up in the middle of the night to go to work. It was a detail in piloting that had never occurred to me at all. I knew that boats ran all night, but somehow I had never happened to reflect that somebody had to get up out of a warm bed to run them. I began to fear that piloting was not quite so romantic as I had imagined it was; there was something very real and worklike about this new phase of it.

It was a rather dingy night, although a fair number of stars were out. The big mate was at the wheel, and he had the old tub pointed at a star and was holding her straight up the middle of the river. The shores on either hand were not much more than half a mile apart, but they seemed wonderfully far away and ever so vague and indistinct. The mate said:

"We've got to land at Jones's plantation, sir."

The vengeful spirit in me exulted. I said to myself, "I wish you joy of your job, Mr. Bixby; you'll have a good time finding Mr. Jones's plantation such a night as this; and I hope you never *will* find it as long as you live."

Mr. Bixby said to the mate:

"Upper end of the plantation, or the lower?"

"Upper."

"I can't do it. The stumps there are out of water at this stage. It's no great distance to the lower, and you'll have to get along with that."

"All right, sir. If Jones don't like it, he'll have to lump it, I reckon."

And then the mate left. My exultation began to cool and my

wonder to come up. Here was a man who not only proposed to find this plantation on such a night, but to find either end of it you preferred. I dreadfully wanted to ask a question, but I was carrying about as many short answers as my cargo-room would admit of, so I held my peace. All I desired to ask Mr. Bixby was the simple question whether he was ass enough to really imagine he was going to find that plantation on a night when all plantations were exactly alike and all of the same color. But I held in. I used to have fine inspirations of prudence in those days.

Mr. Bixby made for the shore and soon was scraping it, just the same as if it had been daylight. And not only that, but singing:

> "Father in heaven, the day is declining," etc.

It seemed to me that I had put my life in the keeping of a peculiarly reckless outcast. Presently he turned on me and said:

"What's the name of the first point above New Orleans?"

I was gratified to be able to answer promptly, and I did. I said I didn't know.

"Don't *know*?"

This manner jolted me. I was down at the foot again, in a moment. But I had to say just what I had said before.

"Well, you're a smart one!" said Mr. Bixby. "What's the name of the *next* point?"

Once more I didn't know.

"Well, this beats anything. Tell me the name of *any* point or place I told you."

I studied awhile and decided that I couldn't.

"Look here! What do you start out from, above Twelve-Mile Point, to cross over?"

"I—I—don't know."

"You—you—don't know?" mimicking my drawling manner of speech. "What *do* you know?"

"I—I—nothing, for certain."

"By the great Cæsar's ghost, I believe you! You're the stupidest dunderhead I ever saw or ever heard of, so help me Moses! The idea of *you* being a pilot—*you!* Why, you don't know enough to pilot a cow down a lane."

Oh, but his wrath was up! He was a nervous man, and he shuffled from one side of his wheel to the other as if the floor was hot. He would boil awhile to himself, and then overflow and scald me again.

"Look here! What do you suppose I told you the names of those points for?"

I tremblingly considered a moment, and then the devil of temptation provoked me to say:

"Well to—to—be entertaining, I thought."

This was a red rag to the bull. He raged and stormed so (he was crossing the river at the time) that I judged it made him blind, because he ran over the steering-oar of a trading-scow. Of course the traders sent up a volley of red-hot profanity. Never was a man so grateful as Mr. Bixby was; because he was brimful, and here were subjects who could *talk back.* He threw open a window, thrust his head out, and such an irruption followed as I never had heard before. The fainter and farther away the scowmen's curses drifted, the higher Mr. Bixby lifted his voice and the weightier his adjectives grew. When he closed the window he was empty. You could have drawn a seine through his system and not caught curses enough to disturb your mother with. Presently he said to me in the gentlest way:

"My boy, you must get a little memorandum-book; and every time I tell you a thing, put it down right away. There's only one way to be a pilot, and that is to get this entire river by heart. You have to know it just like A B C."

That was a dismal revelation to me; for my memory was never loaded with anything but blank cartridges. However, I did not feel discouraged long. I judged that it was best to make some allowances, for doubtless Mr. Bixby was "stretching." Presently he pulled a rope and struck a few strokes on the big bell. The stars were all gone now, and the night was as black as ink. I could hear the wheels churn along the bank, but I was not entirely certain that I could see the shore. The voice of the invisible watchman called up from the hurricane-deck:

"What's this, sir?"

"Jones's plantation."

I said to myself, "I wish I might venture to offer a small bet that it isn't." But I did not chirp. I only waited to see. Mr. Bixby handled the engine-bells, and in due time the boat's nose came to the land, a torch glowed from the forecastle, a man skipped ashore, a darky's voice on the bank said: "Gimme de k'yarpet-bag, Mass' Jones," and the next moment we were standing up the river again, all serene. I reflected deeply awhile, and then said—but not aloud —"Well, the finding of that plantation was the luckiest accident that ever happened; but it couldn't happen again in a hundred years." And I fully believed it *was* an accident, too.[4]

* * * The thing that was running in my mind was, "Now, if

---

4. Several pages of expository matter have been omitted at this point. The young pilot has gained some confidence in the seven hundred miles of up-stream navigation. At St. Louis, Mr. Bixby abandons the *Paul Jones* for "a big New Orleans boat * * * a grand affair," and takes his apprentice pilot with him. Now they are headed down-stream, at a low and dangerous stage of the river, with several unemployed pilots.

my ears hear aright, I have not only to get the names of all the towns and islands and bends, and so on, by heart, but I must even get up a warm personal acquaintanceship with every old snag and one-limbed cottonwood and obscure wood-pile that ornaments the banks of this river for twelve hundred miles; and more than that, I must actually know where these things are in the dark, unless these guests are gifted with eyes that can pierce through two miles of solid blackness. I wish the piloting business was in Jericho and I had never thought of it."

At dusk Mr. Bixby tapped the big bell three times (the signal to land), and the captain emerged from his drawing-room in the forward end of the "texas," and looked up inquiringly. Mr. Bixby said:

"We will lay up here all night, captain."

"Very well, sir."

That was all. The boat came to shore and was tied up for the night. It seemed to me a fine thing that the pilot could do as he pleased, without asking so grand a captain's permission. I took my supper and went immediately to bed, discouraged by my day's observations and experiences. My late voyage's note-booking was but a confusion of meaningless names. It had tangled me all up in a knot every time I had looked at it in the daytime. I now hoped for respite in sleep; but no, it reveled all through my head till sunrise again, a frantic and tireless nightmare.

Next morning I felt pretty rusty and low-spirited. We went booming along, taking a good many chances, for we were anxious to "get out of the river" (as getting out to Cairo was called) before night should overtake us. But Mr. Bixby's partner, the other pilot, presently grounded the boat, and we lost so much time getting her off that it was plain the darkness would overtake us a good long way above the mouth. This was a great misfortune, especially to certain of our visiting pilots, whose boats would have to wait for their return, no matter how long that might be. It sobered the pilot-house talk a good deal. Coming up-stream, pilots did not mind low water or any kind of darkness; nothing stopped them but fog. But down-stream work was different; a boat was too nearly helpless, with a stiff current pushing behind her; so it was not customary to run down-stream at night in low water.

There seemed to be one small hope, however: if we could get through the intricate and dangerous Hat Island crossing before night, we could venture the rest, for we would have plainer sailing and better water. But it would be insanity to attempt Hat Island at night. So there was a deal of looking at watches all the rest of the day, and a constant ciphering upon the speed we were making; Hat Island was the eternal subject; sometimes hope was high and sometimes we were delayed in a bad crossing, and down it went again. For hours all hands lay under the burden of this suppressed excitement; it was even communicated to me, and I got to feeling so solicitous about Hat Island, and under such an awful pressure of responsibility, that I wished I might have five minutes on shore to draw a good, full, relieving breath, and start over again. We were standing no regular watches. Each of our pilots ran such portions of the river as he had run when coming up-stream, because of his greater familiarity with it; but both remained in the pilot-house constantly.

An hour before sunset Mr. Bixby took the wheel, and Mr. W. stepped aside. For the next thirty minutes every man held his watch in his hand and was restless, silent, and uneasy. At last somebody said, with a doomful sigh:

"Well, yonder's Hat Island—and we can't make it."

All the watches closed with a snap, everybody sighed and muttered something about its being "too bad, too bad—ah, if we could *only* have got here half an hour sooner!" and the place was thick with the atmosphere of disappointment. Some started to go out, but loitered, hearing no bell-tap to land. The sun dipped behind the horizon, the boat went on. Inquiring looks passed from one guest to another; and one who had his hand on the door-knob and had turned it, waited, then presently took away his hand and let the knob turn back again. We bore steadily down the bend. More looks were exchanged, and nods of surprised admiration—but no words. Insensibly the men drew together behind Mr. Bixby, as the sky darkened and one or two dim stars came out. The dead silence and sense of waiting became oppressive. Mr. Bixby pulled the cord, and two deep, mellow tones from the big bell floated off on the night. Then a pause, and one more note was struck. The watchman's voice followed, from the hurricane-deck:

"Labboard lead, there! Stabboard lead!"

The cries of the leadsmen began to rise out of the distance, and were gruffly repeated by the word-passers on the hurricane-deck.

"M-a-r-k three! M-a-r-k three! Quarter-less-three! Half twain! Quarter twain! M-a-r-k twain! Quarter-less—"

Mr. Bixby pulled two bell-ropes, and was answered by faint jinglings far below in the engine-room, and our speed slackened. The steam began to whistle through the gauge-cocks. The cries of the leadsmen went on—and it is a weird sound, always, in the night. Every pilot in the lot was watching now, with fixed eyes, and talking under his breath. Nobody was calm and easy but Mr. Bixby. He would put his wheel down and stand on a spoke, and

as the steamer swung into her (to me) utterly invisible marks—
for we seemed to be in the midst of a wide and gloomy sea—he
would meet and fasten her there. Out of the murmur of half-
audible talk, one caught a coherent sentence now and then—such
as:

"There; she's over the first reef all right!"

After a pause, another subdued voice:

"Her stern's coming down just *exactly* right, by *George!*"

"Now she's in the marks; over she goes!"

Somebody else muttered:

"Oh, it was done beautiful—*beautiful!*"

Now the engines were stopped altogether, and we drifted with
the current. Not that I could see the boat drift, for I could not,
the stars being all gone by this time. This drifting was the dis-
malest work; it held one's heart still. Presently I discovered a
blacker gloom than that which surrounded us. It was the head of
the island. We were closing right down upon it. We entered its
deeper shadow, and so imminent seemed the peril that I was
likely to suffocate; and I had the strongest impulse to do *something*, anything, to save the vessel. But still Mr. Bixby stood by
his wheel, silent, intent as a cat, and all the pilots stood shoulder
to shoulder at his back.

"She'll not make it!" somebody whispered.

The water grew shoaler and shoaler, by the leadsman's cries, till
it was down to:

"Eight-and-a-half! E-i-g-h-t feet! E-i-g-h-t feet! Seven-and—"

Mr. Bixby said warningly through his speaking-tube to the engineer:

"Stand by, now!"

"Ay, ay, sir!"

"Seven-and-a-half! Seven feet! Six-and—"

We touched bottom! Instantly Mr. Bixby set a lot of bells ringing, shouted through the tube, "*Now*, let her have it—every
ounce you've got!" then to his partner, "Put her hard down!
snatch her! snatch her!" The boat rasped and ground her way
through the sand, hung upon the apex of disaster a single tremendous instant, and then over she went! And such a shout as
went up at Mr. Bixby's back never loosened the roof of a pilot-
house before!

There was no more trouble after that. Mr. Bixby was a hero that
night; and it was some little time, too, before his exploit ceased to
be talked about by river-men.

Fully to realize the marvelous precision required in laying the
great steamer in her marks in that murky waste of water, one should

know that not only must she pick her intricate way through snags
and blind reefs, and then shave the head of the island so closely as
to brush the overhanging foliage with her stern, but at one place
she must pass almost within arm's reach of a sunken and invisible
wreck that would snatch the hull timbers from under her if she
should strike it, and destroy a quarter of a million dollars' worth of
steamboat and cargo in five minutes, and maybe a hundred and
fifty human lives into the bargain.

The last remark I heard that night was a compliment to Mr.
Bixby, uttered in soliloquy and with unction by one of our guests.
He said:

"By the Shadow of Death, but he's a lightning pilot!"

1874   1875, 1883

The Man That Corrupted Hadleyburg [5]

I

It was many years ago. Hadleyburg was the most honest and upright town in all the region round about. It had kept that reputation unsmirched during three generations, and was prouder of it
than of any other of its possessions. It was so proud of it, and so
anxious to insure its perpetuation, that it began to teach the principles of honest dealing to its babies in the cradle, and make the
like teachings the staple of their culture thenceforward through
all the years devoted to their education. Also, throughout the
formative years temptations were kept out of the way of the young
people, so that their honesty could have every chance to harden
and solidify, and become a part of their very bone. The neighboring towns were jealous of this honorable supremacy, and affected
to sneer at Hadleyburg's pride in it and call it vanity; but all the
same they were obliged to acknowledge that Hadleyburg was in
reality an incorruptible town; and if pressed they would also acknowledge that the mere fact that a young man hailed from Hadleyburg was all the recommendation he needed when he went
forth from his natal town to seek for responsible employment.

But at last, in the drift of time, Hadleyburg had the ill luck to
offend a passing stranger—possibly without knowing it, certainly
without caring, for Hadleyburg was sufficient unto itself, and cared
not a rap for strangers or their opinions. Still, it would have been

5. This story was first published in *Harper's Magazine* for December, 1899, and then collected in *The Man That* *Corrupted Hadleyburg and Other Stories and Essays* (1900), which the present text follows.

well to make an exception in this one's case, for he was a bitter man and revengeful. All through his wanderings during a whole year he kept his injury in mind, and gave all his leisure moments to trying to invent a compensating satisfaction for it. He contrived many plans, and all of them were good, but none of them was quite sweeping enough; the poorest of them would hurt a great many individuals, but what he wanted was a plan which would comprehend the entire town, and not let so much as one person escape unhurt. At last he had a fortunate idea, and when it fell into his brain it lit up his whole head with an evil joy. He began to form a plan at once, saying to himself, "That is the thing to do—I will corrupt the town."

Six months later he went to Hadleyburg, and arrived in a buggy at the house of the old cashier of the bank about ten at night. He got a sack out of the buggy, shouldered it, and staggered with it through the cottage yard, and knocked at the door. A woman's voice said "Come in," and he entered, and set his sack behind the stove in the parlor, saying politely to the old lady who sat reading the *Missionary Herald* by the lamp:

"Pray keep your seat, madam, I will not disturb you. There— now it is pretty well concealed; one would hardly know it was there. Can I see your husband a moment, madam?"

No, he was gone to Brixton, and might not return before morning.

"Very well, madam, it is no matter. I merely wanted to leave that sack in his care, to be delivered to the rightful owner when he shall be found. I am a stranger; he does not know me; I am merely passing through the town tonight to discharge a matter which has been long in my mind. My errand is now completed, and I go pleased and a little proud, and you will never see me again. There is a paper attached to the sack which will explain everything. Good-night, madam."

The old lady was afraid of the mysterious big stranger, and was glad to see him go. But her curiosity was roused, and she went straight to the sack and brought away the paper. It began as follows:

"TO BE PUBLISHED; *or, the right man sought out by private inquiry—either will answer. This sack contains gold coin weighing a hundred and sixty pounds four ounces—*"

"Mercy on us, and the door not locked!"

Mrs. Richards flew to it all in a tremble and locked it, then pulled down the window-shades and stood frightened, worried, and wondering if there was anything else she could do toward making herself and the money more safe. She listened awhile for burglars, then surrendered to curiosity and went back to the lamp and finished reading the paper:

"*I am a foreigner, and am presently going back to my own country, to remain there permanently. I am grateful to America for what I have received at her hands during my stay under her flag; and to one of her citizens—a citizen of Hadleyburg—I am especially grateful for a great kindness done me a year or two ago. Two great kindnesses; in fact. I will explain. I was a gambler. I say I WAS. I was a ruined gambler. I arrived in this village at night, hungry and without a penny. I asked for help—in the dark; I was ashamed to beg in the light. I begged of the right man. He gave me twenty dollars—that is to say, he gave me life, as I considered it. He also gave me fortune; for out of that money I have made myself rich at the gaming-table. And finally, a remark which he made to me has remained with me to this day, and has at last conquered me; and in conquering has saved the remnant of my morals; I shall gamble no more. Now I have no idea who that man was, but I want him found, and I want him to have this money, to give away, throw away or keep, as he pleases. It is merely my way of testifying my gratitude to him. If I could stay, I would find him myself; but no matter, he will be found. This is an honest town, an incorruptible town, and I know I can trust it without fear. This man can be identified by the remark which he made to me; I feel persuaded that he will remember it.*

"*And now my plan is this: If you prefer to conduct the inquiry privately, do so. Tell the contents of this present writing to any one who is likely to be the right man. If he shall answer, 'I am the man; the remark I made was so-and-so,' apply the test—to wit: open the sack, and in it you will find a sealed envelope containing that remark. If the remark mentioned by the candidate tallies with it, give him the money, and ask no further questions, for he is certainly the right man.*

"*But if you shall prefer a public inquiry, then publish this present writing in the local paper—with these instructions added, to wit: Thirty days from now, let the candidate appear at the town-hall at eight in the evening (Friday), and hand his remark, in a sealed envelope, to the Rev. Mr. Burgess (if he will be kind enough to act); and let Mr. Burgess there and then destroy the seals on the sack, open it, and see if the remark is correct; if correct, let the money be delivered, with my sincere gratitude, to my benefactor thus identified.*"

Mrs. Richards sat down, gently, quivering with excitement, and was soon lost in thinking—after this pattern: "What a strange thing it is! . . . And what a fortune for that kind man who set his bread afloat upon the waters! . . . If he had only been my husband that did it!—for we are so poor, so old and poor! . . ." Then, with a sigh—"But it was not my Edward; no, it was not he that gave the stranger twenty dollars. It is a pity too; I see it now. . . ." Then, with a shudder—"But it is *gambler's* money! the wages of sin: we couldn't take it; we couldn't touch it. I don't like to be near it; it seems a defilement." She moved to a farther chair. . . . "I wish Edward would come, and take it to the bank; a burglar might come at any moment; it is dreadful to be here all alone with it."

At eleven Mr. Richards arrived, and while his wife was saying, "I am *so* glad you've come!" he was saying, "I'm so tired—tired clear out; it is dreadful to be poor, and have to make these dismal journeys at my time of life. Always at the grind, grind, grind, on a salary—another man's slave, and he sitting at home in his slippers, rich and comfortable."

"I am so sorry for you, Edward, you know that; but be comforted; we have our livelihood; we have our good name—"

"Yes, Mary, and that is everything. Don't mind my talk—it's just a moment's irritation and doesn't mean anything. Kiss me—there, it's all gone now, and I am not complaining any more. What have you been getting? What's in the sack?"

Then his wife told him the great secret. It dazed him for a moment; then he said:

"It weighs a hundred and sixty pounds? Why, Mary, it's for-ty thou-sand dollars—think of it—a whole fortune! Not ten men in this village are worth that much. Give me the paper."

He skimmed through it and said:

"Isn't it an adventure! Why, it's a romance; it's like the impossible things one reads about in books, and never sees in life." He was well stirred up now; cheerful, even gleeful. He tapped his old wife on the cheek, and said, humorously, "Why, we're rich, Mary, rich; all we've got to do is to bury the money and burn the papers. If the gambler ever comes to inquire, we'll merely look coldly upon him and say: 'What is this nonsense you are talking? We have never heard of you and your sack of gold before;' and then he would look foolish, and—"

"And in the mean time, while you are running on with your jokes, the money is still here, and it is fast getting along toward burglar-time."

"True. Very well, what shall we do—make the inquiry private? No, not that: it would spoil the romance. The public method is better. Think what a noise it will make! And it will make all the other towns jealous; for no stranger would trust such a thing to any town but Hadleyburg, and they know it. It's a great card for us. I must get to the printing-office now, or I shall be too late."

"But stop—stop—don't leave me here alone with it, Edward!"

But he was gone. For only a little while, however. Not far from his own house he met the editor-proprietor of the paper, and gave him the document, and said, "Here is a good thing for you, Cox— put it in."

"It may be too late, Mr. Richards, but I'll see."

At home again he and his wife sat down to talk the charming mystery over; they were in no condition for sleep. The first question was, Who could the citizen have been who gave the stranger the twenty dollars? It seemed a simple one; both answered it in the same breath—

"Barclay Goodson."

"Yes," said Richards, "he could have done it, and it would have been like him, but there's not another in the town."

"Everybody will grant that, Edward—grant it privately, anyway. For six months, now, the village has been its own proper self once more—honest, narrow, self-righteous and stingy."

"It is what he always called it, to the day of his death—said it right out publicly, too."

"Yes, and he was hated for it."

"Oh, of course; but he didn't care. I reckon he was the best-hated man among us, except the Reverend Burgess."

"Well, Burgess deserves it—he will never get another congregation here. Mean as the town is, it knows how to estimate *him*. Edward, doesn't it seem odd that the stranger should appoint Burgess to deliver the money?"

"Well, yes—it does. That is—that is—"

"Why so much that-*is*-ing? Would *you* select him?"

"Mary, maybe the stranger knows him better than this village does."

"Much *that* would help Burgess!"

The husband seemed perplexed for an answer; the wife kept a steady eye upon him, and waited. Finally Richards said, with the hesitancy of one who is making a statement which is likely to encounter doubt:

"Mary, Burgess is not a bad man."

His wife was certainly surprised.

"Nonsense!" she exclaimed.

"He is not a bad man. I know. The whole of his unpopularity had its foundation in that one thing—the thing that made so much noise."

"That 'one thing,' indeed! As if that 'one thing' wasn't enough, all by itself."

"Plenty. Plenty. Only he wasn't guilty of it."

"How you talk! Not guilty of it! Everybody knows he *was* guilty."

"Mary, I give you my word—he was innocent."

"I can't believe it, and I don't. How do you know?"

"It is a confession. I am ashamed, but I will make it. I was the only man who knew he was innocent. I could have saved him, and —and—well, you know how the town was wrought up—I hadn't the pluck to do it. It would have turned everybody against me. I felt mean, ever so mean; but I didn't dare; I hadn't the manliness to face that."

Mary looked troubled, and for a while was silent. Then she said, stammeringly:

"I—I don't think it would have done for you to—to—One mustn't—er—public opinion—one has to be so careful—so—" It was a difficult road, and she got mired; but after a little she got started again. "It was a great pity, but—Why, we couldn't afford it, Edward—we couldn't indeed. Oh, I wouldn't have had you do it for anything!"

"It would have lost us the good-will of so many people, Mary; and then—and then—"

"What troubles me now is, what *he* thinks of us, Edward."

"He? *He* doesn't suspect that I could have saved him."

"Oh," exclaimed the wife, in a tone of relief, "I am glad of that. As long as he doesn't know that you could have saved him, he— he—well, that makes it a great deal better. Why, I might have known he didn't know, because he is always trying to be friendly with us, as little encouragement as we give him. More than once people have twitted me with it. There's the Wilsons, and the Wilcoxes, and the Harknesses, they take a mean pleasure in saying, '*Your friend* Burgess,' because they know it pesters me. I wish he wouldn't persist in liking us so; I can't think why he keeps it up."

"I can explain it. It's another confession. When the thing was new and hot, and the town made a plan to ride him on a rail, my conscience hurt me so that I couldn't stand it, and I went privately and gave him notice, and he got out of the town and staid out till it was safe to come back."

"Edward! If the town had found it out—"

"*Don't!* It scares me yet, to think of it. I repented of it the minute it was done; and I was even afraid to tell you, lest your face might betray it to somebody. I didn't sleep any that night, for worrying. But after a few days I saw that no one was going to suspect me, and after that I got to feeling glad I did it. And I feel glad yet, Mary—glad through and through."

"So do I, now, for it would have been a dreadful way to treat him. Yes, I'm glad; for really you did owe him that, you know. But, Edward, suppose it should come out yet, some day!"

"It won't."

"Why!"

"Because everybody thinks it was Goodson."

"Of course they would!"

"Certainly. And of course *he* didn't care. They persuaded poor old Sawlsberry to go and charge it on him, and he went blustering over there and did it. Goodson looked him over, like as if he was hunting for a place on him that he could despise the most, then he says, 'So you are the Committee of Inquiry, are you?' Sawlsberry said that was about what he was. 'Hm. Do they require particulars, or do you reckon a kind of a *general* answer will do?' 'If they require particulars, I will come back, Mr. Goodson; I will take the general answer first.' 'Very well, then, tell them to go to hell—I reckon that's general enough. And I'll give you some advice, Sawlsberry; when you come back for the particulars, fetch a basket to carry the relics of yourself home in.' "

"Just like Goodson; it's got all the marks. He had only vanity; he thought he could give advice better than any other person."

"It settled the business, and saved us, Mary. The subject was dropped."

"Bless you, I'm not doubting *that*."

Then they took up the gold-sack mystery again, with some interest. Soon the conversation began to suffer breaks—interruptions caused by absorbed thinkings. The breaks grew more and more frequent. At last Richards lost himself wholly in thought. He sat long, gazing vacantly at the floor, and by-and-by he began to punctuate his thoughts with little nervous movements of his hands that seemed to indicate vexation. Meantime his wife too had relapsed into a thoughtful silence, and her movements were beginning to show a troubled discomfort. Finally Richards got up and strode aimlessly about the room, ploughing his hands through his hair, much as a somnambulist might do who was having a bad dream. Then he seemed to arrive at a definite purpose; and without a word he put on his hat and passed quickly out of the house. His wife sat brooding, with a drawn face, and did not seem to be aware that she was alone. Now and then she murmured, "Lead us not into t . . . but—but—we are so poor, so poor! . . . Lead us not into . . . Ah, who would be hurt by it?—and no one would ever know. . . . Lead us . . . ." The voice died out in mumblings. After a little she glanced up and muttered in a half frightened, half-glad way—

"He is gone! But, oh dear, he may be too late—too late. . . . Maybe not—maybe there is still time." She rose and stood thinking, nervously clasping and unclasping her hands. A slight shudder shook her frame, and she said, out of a dry throat, "God forgive me—it's awful to think such things—but . . . Lord, how we are made—how strangely we are made!"

She turned the light low, and slipped steathily over and kneeled down by the sack and felt of its ridgy sides with her hands, and fondled them lovingly; and there was a gloating light in her poor old eyes. She fell into fits of absence; and came half out of them at times to mutter, "If we had only waited!—oh, if we had only waited a little, and not been in such a hurry!"

Meantime Cox had gone home from his office and told his wife all about the strange thing that had happened, and they had talked it over eagerly, and guessed that the late Goodson was the only man in the town who could have helped a suffering stranger with so noble a sum as twenty dollars. Then there was a pause, and the two became thoughtful and silent. And by-and-by nervous and fidgety. At last the wife said, as if to herself:

"Nobody knows this secret but the Richardses . . . and us . . . nobody."

The husband came out of his thinkings with a slight start, and gazed wistfully at his wife, whose face was become very pale; then he hesitatingly rose, and glanced furtively at his hat, then at his wife—a sort of mute inquiry. Mrs. Cox swallowed once or twice, with her hand at her throat, then in place of speech she nodded her head. In a moment she was alone, and mumbling to herself.

And now Richards and Cox were hurrying through the deserted streets, from opposite dirctions. They met, panting, at the foot of the printing-office stairs; by the night-light there they read each other's face. Cox whispered:

"Nobody knows about this but us?"

The whispered answer was,

"Not a soul—on honor, not a soul!"

"If it isn't too late to—"

The men were starting up-stairs; at this moment they were over-taken by a boy, and Cox asked:

"Is that you, Johnny?"

"Yes, sir."

"You needn't ship the early mail—nor *any* mail; wait till I tell you."

"It's already gone, sir."

"*Gone?*" It had the sound of an unspeakable disappointment in it.

"Yes, sir. Time-table for Brixton and all the towns beyond changed to-day, sir—had to get the papers in twenty minutes earlier than common. I had to rush; if I had been two minutes later—"

The men turned and walked slowly away, not waiting to hear the rest. Neither of them spoke during ten minutes; then Cox said, in a vexed tone:

"What possessed you to be in such a hurry, I can't make out."

The answer was humble enough:

"I see it now, but somehow I never thought, you know, until it was too late. But the next time—"

"Next time be hanged! It won't come in a thousand years."

Then the friends separated without a good-night, and dragged themselves home with the gait of mortally stricken men. At their homes their wives sprang up with an eager "Well?"—then saw the answer with their eyes and sank down sorrowing, without waiting for it to come in words. In both houses a discussion followed of a heated sort—a new thing; there had been discussions before, but not heated ones, not ungentle ones. The discussions to-night were a sort of seeming plagiarisms of each other. Mrs. Richards said,

"If you had only waited, Edward—if you had only stopped to think; but no, you must run straight to the printing-office and spread it all over the world."

"It *said* publish it."

"That is nothing; it also said do it privately, if you liked. There, now—is that true, or not?"

"Why, yes—yes, it is true; but when I thought what a stir it would make, and what a compliment it was to Hadleyburg that a stranger should trust it so—"

"Oh, certainly, I know all that; but if you had only stopped to think, you would have seen that you *couldn't* find the right man, because he is in his grave, and hasn't left chick nor child nor relation behind him; and as long as the money went to somebody that awfully needed it, and nobody would be hurt by it, and—and—"

She broke down, crying. Her husband tried to think of some comforting thing to say, and presently came out with this:

"But after all, Mary, it must be for the best—it *must* be; we know that. And we must remember that it was so ordered—"

"Ordered! Oh, everything's *ordered*, when a person has to find some way out when he has been stupid. Just the same, it was *ordered* that the money should come to us in this special way, and it was you that must take it on yourself to go meddling with the designs of Providence—and who gave you the right? It was wicked, that is what it was—just blasphemous presumption, and no more becoming to a meek and humble professor of—"

"But, Mary, you know how we have been trained all our lives long, like the whole village, till it is absolutely second nature to us to stop not a single moment to think when there's an honest thing to be done—"

"Oh, I know it, I know it—it's been one everlasting training and training and training in honesty—honesty shielded, from the very cradle, against every possible temptation, and so it's *artificial* honesty, and weak as water when temptation comes, as we have seen this night. God knows I never had shade nor shadow of a doubt of my petrified and indestructible honesty until now—and now, under the very first big and real temptation, I—Edward, it is my belief that this town's honesty is as rotten as mine is; as rotten as yours is. It is a mean town, a hard, stingy town, and hasn't a virtue in the world but this honesty it is so celebrated for and so conceited about; and so help me, I do believe that if ever the day comes that its honesty falls under great temptation, its grand reputation will go to ruin like a house of cards. There, now, I've made confession, and I feel better; I am a humbug, and I've been one all my life, without knowing it. Let no man call me honest again—I will not have it."

"I—Well, Mary, I feel a good deal as you do; I certainly do. It seems strange, too, so strange. I never could have believed it—never."

A long silence followed; both were sunk in thought. At last the wife looked up and said:

"I know what you are thinking, Edward."

Richards had the embarrassed look of a person who is caught.

"I am ashamed to confess it, Mary, but—"

"It's no matter, Edward, I was thinking the same question myself."

"I hope so. State it."

"You were thinking, if a body could only guess out *what the remark was* that Goodson made to the stranger."

"It's perfectly true. I feel guilty and ashamed. And you?"

"I'm past it. Let us make a pallet here; we've got to stand watch till the bank vault opens in the morning and admits the sack. . . . Oh, dear, oh, dear—if we hadn't made the mistake!"

The pallet was made, and Mary said:

"The open sesame—what could it have been? I do wonder what that remark could have been? But come; we will get to bed now."

"And sleep?"

"No; think."

"Yes, think."

By this time the Coxes too had completed their spat and their reconciliation, and were turning in—to think, to think, and toss, and fret, and worry over what the remark could possibly have been which Goodson made to the stranded derelict: that golden remark; that remark worth forty thousand dollars, cash.

The reason that the village telegraph-office was open later than usual that night was this: The foreman of Cox's paper was the local representative of the Associated Press. One might say its honorary representative, for it wasn't four times a year that he could furnish thirty words that would be accepted. But this time it was different. His despatch stating what he had caught got an instant answer:

"*Send the whole thing—all the details—twelve hundred words.*"

A colossal order! The foreman filled the bill; and he was the proudest man in the State. By breakfast-time the next morning the name of Hadleyburg the Incorruptible was on every lip in America, from Montreal to the Gulf, from the glaciers of Alaska to the orange-groves of Florida; and millions and millions of people were discussing the stranger and his money-sack, and wondering if the right man would be found, and hoping some more news about the matter would come soon—right away.

II

Hadleyburg village woke up world-celebrated—astonished—happy—vain. Vain beyond imagination. Its nineteen principal citizens and their wives went about shaking hands with each other, and beaming, and smiling, and congratulating, and saying *this* thing adds a new word to the dictionary—*Hadleyburg*, synonym for *incorruptible*—destined to live in dictionaries forever! And the minor and unimportant citizens and their wives went around acting in much the same way. Everybody ran to the bank to see the gold-sack; and before noon grieved and envious crowds began to flock in from Brixton and all the neighboring towns; and that afternoon and next day reporters began to arrive from everywhere to verify the sack and its history and write the whole thing up anew, and make dashing free-hand pictures of the sack and of Richards's house, and the bank, and the Presbyterian church, and the Baptist church, and the public square, and the town-hall where the test would be applied and the money delivered; and damnable portraits of the Richardses, and Pinkerton the banker, and Cox, and the foreman, and Reverend Burgess, and the postmaster—and even of Jack Halliday, who was the loafing, good-natured, no-account, irreverent fisherman, hunter, boys' friend, stray-dog's friend, typical "Sam Lawson" [6] of the town. The little mean, smirking, oily Pinkerton showed the sack to all comers, and rubbed his sleek palms together pleasantly, and enlarged upon the town's fine old reputation for honesty and upon this wonderful endorsement of it, and hoped and believed that the example would now spread far and wide over the American world, and be epoch-making in the matter of moral regeneration. And so on, and so on.

By the end of a week things had quieted down again; the wild intoxication of pride and joy had sobered to a soft, sweet, silent

6. A lazy humorous Yankee character who appears in Harriet Beecher Stowe's *Oldtown Folks* (1869) and *Sam Lawson's Oldtown Fireside Stories* (1872).

delight—a sort of deep, nameless, unutterable content. All faces bore a look of peaceful, holy happiness.

Then a change came. It was a gradual change: so gradual that its beginnings were hardly noticed; maybe were not noticed at all, except by Jack Halliday, who always noticed everything; and always made fun of it, too, no matter what it was. He began to throw out chaffing remarks about people not looking quite so happy as they did a day or two ago; and next he claimed that the new aspect was deepening to positive sadness; next, that it was taking on a sick look; and finally he said that everybody was become so moody, thoughtful, and absent-minded that he could rob the meanest man in town of a cent out of the bottom of his breeches pocket and not disturb his revery.

At this stage—or at about this stage—a saying like this was dropped at bedtime—with a sigh, usually—by the head of each of the nineteen principal households: "Ah, what *could* have been the remark that Goodson made!"

And straightway—with a shudder—came this, from the man's wife:

"Oh, *don't!* What horrible thing are you mulling in your mind? Put it away from you, for God's sake!"

But that question was wrung from those men again the next night—and got the same retort. But weaker.

And the third night the men uttered the question yet again—with anguish, and absently. This time—and the following night—the wives fidgeted feebly, and tried to say something. But didn't.

And the night after that they found their tongues and responded—longingly,

"Oh, if we *could* only guess!"

Halliday's comments grew daily more and more sparklingly disagreeable and disparaging. He went diligently about, laughing at the town, individually and in mass. But his laugh was the only one left in the village: it fell upon a hollow and mournful vacancy and emptiness. Not even a smile was findable anywhere. Halliday carried a cigar-box around on a tripod, playing that it was a camera, and halted all passers and aimed the thing and said, "Ready!—now look pleasant, please," but not even this capital joke could surprise the dreary faces into any softening.

So three weeks passed—one week was left. It was Saturday evening—after supper. Instead of the aforetime Saturday-evening flutter and bustle and shopping and larking, the streets were empty and desolate. Richards and his old wife sat apart in their little parlor—miserable and thinking. This was become their evening habit now: the life-long habit which had preceded it, of reading, knitting, and contented chat, or receiving or paying neighborly calls, was dead and gone and forgotten, ages ago—two or three weeks ago; nobody talked now, nobody read, nobody visited—the whole village sat at home, sighing, worrying, silent. Trying to guess out that remark.

The postman left a letter. Richards glanced listlessly at the superscription and the post-mark—unfamiliar, both—and tossed the letter on the table and resumed his might-have-beens and his hopeless dull miseries where he had left them off. Two or three hours later his wife got wearily up and was going away to bed without a good-night—custom now—but she stopped near the letter and eyed it awhile with a dead interest, then broke it open, and began to skim it over. Richards, sitting there with his chair tilted back against the wall and his chin between his knees, heard something fall. It was his wife. He sprang to her side, but she cried out:

"Leave me alone, I am too happy. Read the letter—read it!"

He did. He devoured it, his brain reeling. The letter was from a distant State, and it said:

"*I am a stranger to you, but no matter: I have something to tell. I have just arrived home from Mexico, and learned about that episode. Of course you do not know who made that remark, but I know, and I am the only person living who does know. It was* GOODSON. *I knew him well, many years ago. I passed through your village that very night, and was his guest till the midnight train came along. I overheard him make that remark to the stranger in the dark—it was in Hale Alley. He and I talked of it the rest of the way home, and while smoking in his house. He mentioned many of your villagers in the course of his talk—most of them in a very uncomplimentary way, but two or three favorably: among these latter yourself. I say 'favorably'—nothing stronger. I remember his saying he did not actually* LIKE *any person in the town—not one; but that you—I* THINK *he said you—am almost sure, had done him a very great service once, possibly without knowing the full value of it, and he wished he had a fortune, he would leave it to you when he died, and a curse apiece for the rest of the citizens. Now, then, if it was you that did him that service, you are his legitimate heir, and entitled to the sack of gold. I know that I can trust to your honor and honesty, for in a citizen of Hadleyburg these virtues are an unfailing inheritance, and so I am going to reveal to you the remark, well satisfied that if you are not the right man you will seek and find the right one and see that poor Goodson's debt of gratitude for the service referred to is paid. This is the remark:* 'YOU ARE FAR FROM BEING A BAD MAN: GO, AND RE-FORM.'*

"HOWARD L. STEPHENSON"

"Oh, Edward, the money is ours, and I am so grateful, *oh*, so grateful—kiss me, dear, it's forever since we kissed—and we needed it so—the money—and now you are free of Pinkerton and his bank, and nobody's slave any more; it seems to me I could fly for joy."

It was a happy half-hour that the couple spent there on the settee caressing each other; it was the old days come again—days that had begun with their courtship and lasted without a break till the stranger brought the deadly money. By-and-by the wife said:

"Oh, Edward, how lucky it was you did him that grand service, poor Goodson! I never liked him, but I love him now. And it was fine and beautiful of you never to mention it or brag about it." Then, with a touch of reproach, "But you ought to have told *me*, Edward, you ought to have told your wife, you know."

"Well, I—er—well, Mary, you see——"

"Now stop hemming and hawing, and tell me about it, Edward. I always loved you, and now I'm proud of you. Everybody believes there was only one good generous soul in this village, and now it turns out that you—Edward, why don't you tell me?"

"Well—er—er— Why, Mary, I can't!"

"You *can't? Why* can't you?"

"You see, he—well, he—he made me promise I wouldn't."

The wife looked him over, and said, very slowly,

"Made—you—promise? Edward, what do you tell me that for?"

"Mary, do you think I would lie?"

She was troubled and silent for a moment, then she laid her hand within his and said:

"No . . . no. We have wandered far enough from our bearings —God spare us that! In all your life you have never uttered a lie. But now—now that the foundations of things seem to be crumbling from under us, we—we——" She lost her voice for a moment, then said, brokenly, "Lead us not into temptation. . . . I think you made the promise, Edward. Let it rest so. Let us keep away from that ground. Now—that is all gone by; let us be happy again; it is no time for clouds."

Edward found it something of an effort to comply, for his mind kept wandering—trying to remember what the service was that he had done Goodson.

The couple lay awake the most of the night, Mary happy and busy, Edward busy, but not so happy. Mary was planning what she would do with the money. Edward was trying to recall that service. At first his conscience was sore on account of the lie he had told Mary—if it was a lie. After much reflection—suppose it *was* a lie?

What then? Was it such a great matter? Aren't we always *acting* lies? Then why not *tell* them? Look at Mary—look what she had done. While he was hurrying off on his honest errand, what was she doing? Lamenting because the papers hadn't been destroyed and the money kept! Is theft better than lying?

That point lost its sting—the lie dropped into the background and left comfort behind it. The next point came to the front: *had* he rendered that service? Well, here was Goodson's own evidence as reported in Stephenson's letter; there could be no better evidence than that—it was even *proof* that he had rendered it. Of course. So that point was settled. . . . No, not quite. He recalled with a wince that this unknown Mr. Stephenson was just a trifle unsure as to whether the performer of it was Richards or some other—and, oh dear, he had to put Richards on his honor! He must himself decide whither that money must go—and Mr. Stephenson was not doubting that if he was the wrong man he would go honorably and find the right one. Oh, it was odious to put a man in such a situation—ah, why couldn't Stephenson have left out that doubt! What did he want to intrude that for?

Further reflection. How did it happen that *Richards's* name remained in Stephenson's mind as indicating the right man, and not some other man's name? That looked good. Yes, that looked very good. In fact, it went on looking better and better, straight along— until by-and-by it grew into positive *proof*. And then Richards put the matter at once out of his mind, for he had a private instinct that a proof once established is better left so.

He was feeling reasonably comfortable now, but there was still one other detail that kept pushing itself on his notice: of course he had done that service—that was settled; but what *was* that service? He must recall it—he would not go to sleep till he had recalled it; it would make his peace of mind perfect. And so he thought and thought. He thought of a dozen things—possible services, even probable services—but none of them seemed adequate, none of them seemed large enough, none of them seemed worth the money—worth the fortune Goodson had wished he could leave in his will. And besides, he couldn't remember having done them, anyway. Now, then—now, then—what *kind* of a service would it be that would make a man so inordinately grateful? Ah—the saving of his soul! That must be it. Yes, he could remember, now, how he once set himself the task of converting Goodson, and labored at it as much as—he was going to say three months; but upon closer examination it shrunk to a month, then to a week, then to a day, then to nothing. Yes, he remembered now, and with unwelcome vividness, that Goodson had told him to go to thunder and mind his own business—*he* wasn't hankering to follow Hadleyburg to heaven!

So that solution was a failure—he hadn't saved Goodson's soul. Richards was discouraged. Then after a little came another idea: had he saved Goodson's property? No, that wouldn't do—he hadn't any. His life? This is it! Of course. Why, he might have thought of it before. This time he was on the right track, sure. His imagination was hard at work in a minute, now.

Thereafter during a stretch of two exhausting hours he was busy saving Goodson's life. He saved it in all kinds of difficult and perilous ways. In every case he got it saved satisfactorily up to a certain point; then, just as he was beginning to get well persuaded that it had really happened, a troublesome detail would turn up which made the whole thing impossible. As in the matter of drowning, for instance. In that case he had swum out and tugged Goodson ashore in an unconscious state with a great crowd looking on and applauding, but when he had got it all thought out and was just beginning to remember all about it a whole swarm of disqualifying details arrived on the ground: the town would have known of it, it would glare like a limelight in his own memory instead of being an inconspicuous service which he had possibly rendered "without knowing its full value." And at this point he remembered that he couldn't swim, anyway.

Ah—*there* was a point which he had been overlooking from the start: it had to be a service which he had rendered "possibly without knowing the full value of it." Why, really, that ought to be an easy hunt—much easier than those others. And sure enough, by-and-by he found it. Goodson, years and years ago, came near marrying a very sweet and pretty girl, named Nancy Hewitt, but in some way or other the match had been broken off; the girl died, Goodson remained a bachelor, and by-and-by became a soured one and a frank despiser of the human species. Soon after the girl's death the village found out, or thought it had found out, that she carried a spoonful of negro blood in her veins. Richards worked at these details a good while, and in the end he thought he remembered things concerning them which must have gotten mislaid in his memory through long neglect. He seemed to dimly remember that it was *he* that found out about the negro blood; that it was he that told the village; that the village told Goodson where they got it; that he thus saved Goodson from marrying the tainted girl; that he had done him this great service "without knowing the full value of it," in fact without knowing that he *was* doing it; but that Goodson knew the value of it, and what a narrow escape he had had, and so went to his grave grateful to his benefactor and wishing he had a fortune to leave him. It was all clear and simple now, and the more he went over it the more luminous and certain it grew; and at last, when he nestled to sleep satisfied and happy, he remembered the whole thing just as if it had been yesterday. In fact, he dimly remembered Goodson's *telling* him his gratitude once. Meantime Mary had spent six thousand dollars on a new house for herself and a pair of slippers for her pastor, and then had fallen peacefully to rest.

That same Saturday evening the postman had delivered a letter to each of the other principal citizens—nineteen letters in all. No two of the envelopes were alike, and no two of the superscriptions were in the same hand, but the letters inside were just like each other in every detail but one. They were exact copies of the letter received by Richards—handwriting and all—and were all signed by Stephenson, but in place of Richards's name each receiver's own name appeared.

All night long eighteen principal citizens did what their caste-brother Richards was doing at the same time—they put in their energies trying to remember what notable service it was that they had unconsciously done Barclay Goodson. In no case was it a holiday job; still they succeeded.

And while they were at this work, which was difficult, their wives put in the night spending the money, which was easy. During that one night the nineteen wives spent an average of seven thousand dollars each out of the forty thousand in the sack—a hundred and thirty-three thousand altogether.

Next day there was a surprise for Jack Halliday. He noticed that the faces of the nineteen chief citizens and their wives bore that expression of peaceful and holy happiness again. He could not understand it, neither was he able to invent any remarks about it that could damage it or disturb it. And so it was his turn to be dissatisfied with life. His private guesses at the reasons for the happiness failed in all instances, upon examination. When he met Mrs. Wilcox and noticed the placid ecstasy in her face, he said to himself, "Her cat has had kittens"—and went and asked the cook; it was not so; the cook had detected the happiness, but did not know the cause. When Halliday found the duplicate ecstasy in the face of "Shadbelly" Billson (village nickname), he was sure some neighbor of Billson's had broken his leg, but inquiry showed that this had not happened. The subdued ecstasy in Gregory Yates's face could mean but one thing—he was a mother-in-law short; it was another mistake. "And Pinkerton—Pinkerton—he had collected ten cents that he thought he was going to lose." And so on, and so on. In some cases the guesses had to remain in doubt, in the others they proved distinct errors. In the end Halliday said to himself, "Anyway, it foots up that there's nineteen Hadleyburg families temporarily in heaven: I don't know how it happened; I only know Providence is off duty to-day."

An architect and builder from the next State had lately ventured to set up a small business in this unpromising village, and his sign had now been hanging out a week. Not a customer yet; he was a discouraged man, and sorry he had come. But his weather changed suddenly now. First one and then another chief citizen's wife said to him privately:

"Come to my house Monday week—but say nothing about it for the present. We think of building."

He got eleven invitations that day. That night he wrote his daughter and broke off her match with her student. He said she could marry a mile higher than that.

Pinkerton the banker and two or three other well-to-do men planned country-seats—but waited. That kind don't count their chickens until they are hatched.

The Wilsons devised a grand new thing—a fancy-dress ball. They made no actual promises, but told all their acquaintanceship in confidence that they were thinking the matter over and thought they should give it—"and if we do, you will be invited, of course." People were surprised, and said, one to another, "Why, they are crazy, those poor Wilsons, they can't afford it." Several among the nineteen said privately to their husbands, "It is a good idea, we will keep still till their cheap thing is over, then *we* will give one that will make it sick."

The days drifted along, and the bill of future squanderings rose higher and higher, wilder and wilder, more and more foolish and reckless. It began to look as if every member of the nineteen would not only spend his whole forty thousand dollars before receiving-day, but be actually in debt by the time he got the money. In some cases light-headed people did not stop with planning to spend, they really spent—on credit. They bought land, mortgages, farms, speculative stocks, fine clothes, horses, and various other things, paid down the bonus, and made themselves liable for the rest—at ten days. Presently the sober second thought came, and Halliday noticed that a ghastly anxiety was beginning to show up in a good many faces. Again he was puzzled, and didn't know what to make of it. "The Wilcox kittens aren't dead, for they weren't born; nobody's broken a leg; there's no shrinkage in mother-in-laws; *nothing* has happened—it is an insolvable mystery."

There was another puzzled man, too—the Rev. Mr. Burgess. For days, wherever he went, people seemed to follow him or to be watching out for him; and if he ever found himself in a retired spot, a member of the nineteen would be sure to appear, thrust an envelope privately into his hand, whisper "To be opened at the town-hall Friday evening," then vanish away like a guilty thing. He was expecting that there might be one claimant for the sack—doubtful, however, Goodson being dead—but it never occurred to him that all this crowd might be claimants. When the great Friday came at last, he found that he had nineteen envelopes.

III

The town-hall had never looked finer. The platform at the end of it was backed by a showy draping of flags; at intervals along the walls were festoons of flags; the gallery fronts were clothed in flags; the supporting columns were swathed in flags; all this was to impress the stranger, for he would be there in considerable force, and in a large degree he would be connected with the press. The house was full. The 412 fixed seats were occupied; also the 68 extra chairs which had been packed into the aisles; the steps of the platform were occupied; some distinguished strangers were given seats on the platform; at the horseshoe of tables which fenced the front and sides of the platform sat a strong force of special correspondents who had come from everywhere. It was the best-dressed house the town had ever produced. There were some tolerably expensive toilets there, and in several cases the ladies who wore them had the look of being unfamiliar with that kind of clothes. At least the town thought they had that look, but the notion could have arisen from the town's knowledge of the fact that these ladies had never inhabited such clothes before.

The gold-sack stood on a little table at the front of the platform where all the house could see it. The bulk of the house gazed at it with a burning interest, a mouth-watering interest, a wistful and pathetic interest; a minority of nineteen couples gazed at it tenderly, lovingly, proprietarily, and the male half of this minority kept saying over to themselves the moving little impromptu speeches of thankfulness for the audience's applause and congratulations which they were presently going to get up and deliver. Every now and then one of these got a piece of paper out of his vest pocket and privately glanced at it to refresh his memory.

Of course there was a buzz of conversation going on—there always is; but at last when the Rev. Mr. Burgess rose and laid his hand on the sack he could hear his microbes gnaw, the place was so still. He related the curious history of the sack, then went on to speak in warm terms of Hadleyburg's old and well-earned reputation for spotless honesty, and of the town's just pride in this reputation. He said that this reputation was a treasure of priceless value; that under Providence its value had now become inestimably enhanced, for the recent episode had spread this fame far and wide, and thus had focussed the eyes of the American world upon this village, and made its name for all time, as he hoped and believed, a synonym for commercial incorruptibility. [*Applause.*] "And who is to be the guardian of this noble treasure—the community as a whole? No! The responsibility is individual, not communal. From this day forth each and every one of you is in his own person its special guardian and individually responsible that no harm shall come to it. Do you—does each of you—accept this great trust? [*Tumultuous assent.*] Then all is well. Transmit it to your children and to your children's children. To-day your purity is beyond reproach—see to it that it shall remain so. To-day there is not a person in your community who could be beguiled to touch a penny not his own—see to it that you abide in this grace. ["*We will! we will!*"] This is not the place to make comparisons between ourselves and other communities—some of them ungracious toward us; they have their ways, we have ours; let us be content. [*Applause.*] I am done. Under my hand, my friends, rests a stranger's eloquent recognition of what we are: through him the world will always henceforth know what we are. We do not know who he is, but in your name I utter your gratitude, and ask you to raise your voices in endorsement."

The house rose in a body and made the walls quake with the thunders of its thankfulness for the space of a long minute. Then it sat down, and Mr. Burgess took an envelope out of his pocket. The house held its breath while he slit the envelope open and took from it a slip of paper. He read its contents—slowly and impressively—the audience listening with tranced attention to this magic document, each of whose words stood for an ingot of gold:

" '*The remark which I made to the distressed stranger was this:* "*You are very far from being a bad man; go, and reform.*" ' "
Then he continued: "We shall know in a moment now whether the remark here quoted corresponds with the one concealed in the sack; and if that shall prove to be so—and it undoubtedly will—this sack of gold belongs to a fellow-citizen who will henceforth stand before the nation as the symbol of the special virtue which has made our town famous throughout the land—Mr. Billson!"

The house had gotten itself all ready to burst into a proper tornado of applause; but instead of doing it, it seemed stricken with a paralysis; there was a deep hush for a moment or two, then a wave of whispered murmurs swept the place—of about this tenor: "*Billson!* oh, come, this is *too* thin! Twenty dollars to a stranger—or *anybody—Billson!* Tell it to the marines!" And now at this point the house caught its breath all of a sudden in a new access of astonishment, for it discovered that whereas in one part of the hall Deacon Billson was standing up with his head meekly bowed, in another part of it Lawyer Wilson was doing the same. There was a wondering silence now for a while. Everybody was puzzled, and nineteen couples were surprised and indignant.

Billson and Wilson turned and stared at each other. Billson asked, bitingly,

"Why do *you* rise, Mr. Wilson?"

"Because I have a right to. Perhaps you will be good enough to explain to the house why *you* rise?"

"With great pleasure. Because I wrote that paper."

"It is an impudent falsity! I wrote it myself."

It was Burgess's turn to be paralyzed. He stood looking vacantly at first one of the men and then the other, and did not seem to know what to do. The house was stupefied. Lawyer Wilson spoke up, now, and said,

"I ask the Chair to read the name signed to that paper."

That brought the Chair to itself, and it read out the name,

" 'John Wharton *Billson*.' "

"There!" shouted Billson, "what have you got to say for yourself, now? And what kind of apology are you going to make to me and to this insulted house for the imposture which you have attempted to play here?"

"No apologies are due, sir; and as for the rest of it, I publicly charge you with pilfering my note from Mr. Burgess and substituting a copy of it signed with your own name. There is no other way by which you could have gotten hold of the test-remark; I alone, of living men, possessed the secret of its wording."

There was likely to be a scandalous state of things if this went on; everybody noticed with distress that the short-hand scribes were scribbling like mad; many people were crying "Chair, Chair! Order! order!" Burgess rapped with his gavel, and said:

"Let us not forget the proprieties due. There has evidently been a mistake somewhere, but surely that is all. If Mr. Wilson gave me an envelope—and I remember now that he did—I still have it."

He took one out of his pocket, opened it, glanced at it, looked surprised and worried, and stood silent a few moments. Then he waved his hand in a wandering and mechanical way, and made an effort or two to say something, then gave it up, despondently. Several voices cried out:

"Read it! read it! What is it?"

So he began in a dazed and sleep-walker fashion:

" '*The remark which I made to the unhappy stranger was this:* "*You are far from being a bad man.* [The house gazed at him, marvelling.] *Go, and reform."* ' [*Murmurs:* "Amazing! what can this mean?"] This one," said the Chair, "is signed Thurlow G. Wilson."

"There!" cried Wilson, "I reckon that settles it! I knew perfectly well my note was purloined."

"Purloined!" retorted Billson. "I'll let you know that neither you nor any man of your kidney must venture to—"

The Chair. "Order, gentlemen, order! Take your seats, both of you, please."

They obeyed, shaking their heads and grumbling angrily. The house was profoundly puzzled; it did not know what to do with this curious emergency. Presently Thompson got up. Thompson was the hatter. He would have liked to be a Nineteener; but such was not for him; his stock of hats was not considerable enough for the position. He said:

"Mr. Chairman, if I may be permitted to make a suggestion, can both of these gentlemen be right? I put it to you, sir, can both have happened to say the very same words to the stranger? It seems to me—"

The tanner got up and interrupted him. The tanner was a disgruntled man; he believed himself entitled to be a Nineteener, but he couldn't get recognition. It made him a little unpleasant in his ways and speech. Said he:

"Sho, *that's* not the point! *That* could happen—twice in a hundred years—but not the other thing. *Neither* of them gave the twenty dollars!" [*A ripple of applause.*]

Billson. "I did!"

Wilson. "I did!"

Then each accused the other of pilfering.

The Chair. "Order! Sit down, if you please—both of you. Neither of the notes has been out of my possession at any moment."

A Voice. "Good—that settles *that!*"

The Tanner. "Mr. Chairman, one thing is now plain: one of these men has been eavesdropping under the other one's bed, and filching family secrets. If it is not unparliamentary to suggest it, I will remark that both are equal to it. [*The Chair.* "Order! order!"] I withdraw the remark, sir, and will confine myself to suggesting that *if* one of them has overheard the other reveal the test-remark to his wife, we shall catch him now."

A Voice. "How?"

The Tanner. "Easily. The two have not quoted the remark in exactly the same words. You would have noticed that, if there hadn't been a considerable stretch of time and an exciting quarrel inserted between the two readings."

A Voice. "Name the difference."

The Tanner. "The word *very* is in Billson's note, and not in the other."

Many Voices. "That's so—he's right."

The Tanner. "And so, if the Chair will examine the test-remark in the sack, we shall know which of these two frauds—[*The Chair.* "Order!"]—which of these two adventurers—[*The Chair.* "Order! order!"]—which of these two gentlemen—[*laughter and applause*]—is entitled to wear the belt as being the first dishonest blatherskite ever bred in this town—which he has dishonored, and which will be a sultry place for him from now out!" [*Vigorous applause.*]

Many Voices. "Open it!—open the sack!"

Mr. Burgess made a slit in the sack, slid his hand in and brought out an envelope. In it were a couple of folded notes. He said:

"One of these is marked, 'Not to be examined until all written communications which have been addressed to the Chair—if any—shall have been read.' The other is marked '*The Test.*' Allow me. It is worded—to wit:

" 'I do not require that the first half of the remark which was made to me by my benefactor shall be quoted with exactness, for it was not striking, and could be forgotten; but its closing fifteen words are quite striking, and I think easily rememberable; unless *these* shall be accurately reproduced, let the applicant be regarded as an imposter. My benefactor began by saying he seldom gave advice to any one, but that it always bore the hall-mark [7] of high value when he did give it. Then he said this—and it has never faded from my memory: "*You are far from being a bad man—*" ' "

Fifty Voices. "That settles it—the money's Wilson's! Wilson! Wilson! Speech! Speech!"

People jumped up and crowded around Wilson, wringing his hand and congratulating fervently—meantime the Chair was hammering with the gavel and shouting:

"Order, gentlemen! Order! Order! Let me finish reading, please." When quiet was restored, the reading was resumed—as follows:

" ' "Go, *and reform—or, mark my words—some day, for your sins, you will die and go to hell or Hadleyburg—*TRY AND MAKE IT THE FORMER." ' "

A ghastly silence followed. First an angry cloud began to settle darkly upon the faces of the citizenship; after a pause the cloud began to rise, and a tickled expression tried to take its place; tried so hard that it was only kept under with great and painful difficulty;

7. *I.e.*, the mark of truth, from the official mark of the Goldsmiths' Company in London, guaranteeing the purity of an object for sale at the Goldsmiths' Hall.

the reporters, the Brixtonites, and other strangers bent their heads down and shielded their faces with their hands, and managed to hold in by main strength and heroic courtesy. At this most inopportune time burst upon the stillness the roar of a solitary voice—Jack Halliday's:

"*That's* got the hall-mark on it!"

Then the house let go, strangers and all. Even Mr. Burgess's gravity broke down presently, then the audience considered itself officially absolved from all restraint, and it made the most of its privilege. It was a good long laugh, and a tempestuously wholehearted one, but it ceased at last—long enough for Mr. Burgess to try to resume, and for the people to get their eyes partially wiped; then it broke out again; and afterward yet again; then at last Burgess was able to get out these serious words:

"It is useless to try to disguise the fact—we find ourselves in the presence of a matter of grave import. It involves the honor of your town, it strikes at the town's good name. The difference of a single word between the test-remarks offered by Mr. Wilson and Mr. Billson was itself a serious thing, since it indicated that one or the other of these gentlemen had committed a theft—"

The two men were sitting limp, nerveless, crushed; but at these words both were electrified into movement, and started to get up—

"Sit down!" said the Chair, sharply, and they obeyed. "That, as I have said, was a serious thing. And it was—but for only one of them. But the matter has become graver; for the honor of *both* is now in formidable peril. Shall I go even further, and say in inextricable peril? *Both* left out the crucial fifteen words." He paused. During several moments he allowed the pervading stillness to gather and deepen its impressive effects, then added: "There would seem to be but one way whereby this could happen. I ask these gentlemen—Was there *collusion?—agreement?*"

A low murmur sifted through the house; its import was, "He's got them both."

Billson was not used to emergencies; he sat in a helpless collapse. But Wilson was a lawyer. He struggled to his feet, pale and worried, and said:

"I ask the indulgence of the house while I explain this most painful matter. I am sorry to say what I am about to say, since it must inflict irreparable injury upon Mr. Billson, whom I have always esteemed and respected until now, and in whose invulnerability to temptation I entirely believed—as did you all. But for the preservation of my own honor I must speak—and with frankness. I confess with shame—and I now beseech your pardon for it —that I said to the ruined stranger all of the words contained in the test-remark, including the disparaging fifteen. [*Sensation.*] When the late publication was made I recalled them, and I resolved to claim the sack of coin, for by every right I was entitled to it. Now I will ask you to consider this point, and weigh it well: that stranger's gratitude to me that night knew no bounds; he said himself that he could find no words for it that were adequate, and that if he should ever be able he would repay me a thousandfold. Now, then, I ask you this: could I expect—could I believe—could I even remotely imagine—that, feeling as he did, he would do so ungrateful a thing as to add those quite unnecessary fifteen words to his test?—set a trap for me?—expose me as a slanderer of my own town before my own people assembled in a public hall? It was preposterous; it was impossible. His test would contain only the kindly opening clause of my remark. Of that I had no shadow of doubt. You would have thought as I did. You would not have expected a base betrayal from one whom you had befriended and against whom you had committed no offence. And so, with perfect confidence, perfect trust, I wrote on a piece of paper the opening words—ending with 'Go, and reform,'—and signed it. When I was about to put it in an envelope I was called into my back office, and without thinking I left the paper lying open on my desk." He stopped, turned his head slowly toward Billson, waited a moment, then added: "I ask you to note this: when I returned, a little later, Mr. Billson was retiring by my street door." (*Sensation.*)

In a moment Billson was on his feet and shouting:

"It's a lie! It's an infamous lie!"

The Chair. "Be seated, sir! Mr. Wilson has the floor."

Billson's friends pulled him into his seat and quieted him, and Wilson went on:

"Those are the simple facts. My note was now lying in a different place on the table from where I had left it. I noticed that, but attached no importance to it, thinking a draught had blown it there. That Mr. Billson would read a private paper was a thing which could not occur to me; he was an honorable man, and he would be above that. If you will allow me to say it, I think his extra word '*very*' stands explained; it is attributable to a defect of memory. I was the only man in the world who could furnish here any detail of the test-mark—by *honorable* means. I have finished."

There is nothing in the world like a persuasive speech to fuddle the mental apparatus and upset the convictions and debauch the emotions of an audience not practised in the tricks and delusions of oratory. Wilson sat down victorious. The house submerged him in tides of approving applause; friends swarmed to him and shook him by the hand and congratulated him, and Billson was shouted down and not allowed to say a word. The Chair hammered and hammered with its gavel, and kept shouting:

"But let us proceed, gentlemen, let us proceed!"

At last there was a measurable degree of quiet, and the hatter said:

"But what is there to proceed with, sir, but to deliver the money?"

Voices. "That's it! That's it! Come forward, Wilson!"

The Hatter. "I move three cheers for Mr. Wilson, Symbol of the special virtue which—"

The cheers burst forth before he could finish; and in the midst of them—and in the midst of the clamor of the gavel also—some enthusiasts mounted Wilson on a big friend's shoulder and were going to fetch him in triumph to the platform. The Chair's voice now rose above the noise—

"Order! To your places! You forget that there is still a document to be read." When quiet had been restored he took up the document, and was going to read it, but laid it down again, saying, "I forgot; this is not to be read until all written communications received by me have first been read." He took an envelope out of his pocket, removed its enclosure, glanced at it—seemed astonished—held it out and gazed at it—stared at it.

Twenty or thirty voices cried out:

"What is it? Read it! read it!"

And he did—slowly, and wondering:

" 'The remark which I made to the stranger—[*Voices.* "Hello! how's this?"]—was this: "You are far from being a bad man. [*Voices.* "Great Scott!"] Go, and reform." ' [*Voice.* "Oh, saw my leg off!"] Signed by Mr. Pinkerton the banker.' "

The pandemonium of delight which turned itself loose now was of a sort to make the judicious weep. Those whose withers were unwrung laughed till the tears ran down; the reporters, in throes of laughter, set down disordered pothooks which would never in the world be decipherable; and a sleeping dog jumped up, scared out of its wits, and barked itself crazy at the turmoil. All manner of cries were scattered through the din: "We're getting rich—*two* Symbols of Incorruptibility!—without counting Billson!" "*Three!* —count Shadbelly in—we can't have too many!" "All right— Billson's elected!" "Alas, poor Wilson—victim of *two* thieves!"

A Powerful Voice. "Silence! The Chair's fished up something more out of its pocket."

Voices. "Hurrah! Is it something fresh? Read it! read! read!"

The Chair [*reading*]. " 'The remark which I made,' etc. 'You are far from being a bad man. Go,' etc. Signed, 'Gregory Yates.' "

Tornado of Voices. "Four Symbols!" " 'Rah for Yates!" "Fish again!"

The house was in a roaring humor now, and ready to get all the fun out of the occasion that might be in it. Several Nineteeners, looking pale and distressed, got up and began to work their way toward the aisles, but a score of shouts went up:

"The doors, the doors—close the doors; no Incorruptible shall leave this place! Sit down, everybody!"

The mandate was obeyed.

"Fish again! Read! read!"

The Chair fished again, and once more the familiar words began to fall from its lips—" 'You are far from being a bad man—' "

"Name! name! What's his name?"

" 'L. Ingoldsby Sargent.' "

"Five elected! Pile up the Symbols! Go on, go on!"

" 'You are far from being a bad—' "

"Name! name!"

" 'Nicholas Whitworth.' "

"Hooray! hooray! it's a symbolical day!"

Somebody wailed in, and began to sing this rhyme (leaving out "it's") to the lovely "Mikado" tune of "When a man's afraid, a beautiful maid—"; [8] the audience joined in, with joy; then, just in time, somebody contributed another line—

"And don't you this forget——"

The house roared it out. A third line was at once furnished—

"Corruptibles far from Hadleyburg are——"

The house roared that one too. As the last note died, Jack Halliday's voice rose high and clear, freighted with a final line—

"But the Symbols are here, you bet!"

That was sung, with booming enthusiasm. Then the happy house started in at the beginning and sang the four lines through twice, with immense swing and dash, and finished up with a crashing three-times-three and a tiger for "Hadleyburg the Incorruptible and all Symbols of it which we shall find worth to receive the hallmark to-night."

Then the shoutings at the Chair began again, all over the place:

"Go on! go on! Read! read some more! Read all you've got!"

"That's it—go on! We are winning eternal celebrity!"

A dozen men got up now and began to protest. They said that this farce was the work of some abandoned joker, and was an insult to the whole community. Without a doubt these signatures were all forgeries—

---

8. "When a man's afraid, / A beautiful maid / Is a cheering sight to see" (*The Mikado*, Act II).

"Sit down! sit down! Shut up! You are confessing. We'll find *your* names in the lot."

"Mr. Chairman, how many of those envelopes have you got?"

The Chair counted.

"Together with those that have been already examined, there are nineteen."

A storm of derisive applause broke out.

"Perhaps they all contain the secret. I move that you open them all and read every signature that is attached to a note of that sort —and read also the first eight words of the note."

"Second the motion!"

It was put and carried—uproariously. Then poor old Richards got up, and his wife rose and stood at his side. Her head was bent down, so that none might see that she was crying. Her husband gave her his arm, and so supporting her, he began to speak in a quavering voice:

"My friends, you have known us two—Mary and me—all our lives, and I think you have liked us and respected us—"

The Chair interrupted him:

"Allow me. It is quite true—that which you are saying, Mr. Richards; this town *does* know you two; it *does* like you; it *does* respect you; more—it honors you and *loves* you—"

Halliday's voice rang out:

"That's the hall-marked truth, too! If the Chair is right, let the house speak up and say it. Rise! Now, then—hip! hip! hip!—all together!"

The house rose in mass, faced toward the old couple eagerly, filled the air with a snowstorm of waving handkerchiefs, and delivered the cheers with all its affectionate heart.

The Chair then continued:

"What I was going to say is this: We know your good heart, Mr. Richards, but this is not a time for the exercise of charity toward offenders. [Shouts of "Right! right!"] I see your generous purpose in your face, but I cannot allow you to plead for these men—"

"But I was going to—"

"Please take your seat, Mr. Richards. We must examine the rest of these notes—simple fairness to the men who have already been exposed requires this. As soon as that has been done—I give you my word for this—you shall be heard."

Many Voices. "Right!—the Chair is right—no interruption can be permitted at this stage! Go on!—the names! the names!—according to the terms of the motion!"

The old couple sat reluctantly down, and the husband whispered to the wife, "It is pitifully hard to have to wait; the shame will be greater than ever when they find we were only going to plead for *ourselves.*"

Straightway the jollity broke loose again with the reading of the names.

" 'You are far from being a bad man—' Signature, 'Robert J. Titmarsh.'

" 'You are far from being a bad man—' Signature, 'Eliphalet Weeks.'

" 'You are far from being a bad man—' Signature, 'Oscar B. Wilder.' "

At this point the house lit upon the idea of taking the eight words out of the Chairman's hands. He was not unthankful for that. Thenceforward he held up each note in its turn, and waited. The house droned out the eight words in a massed and measured and musical deep volume of sound (with a daringly close resemblance to a well-known church chant)—" 'You are f-a-r from being a b-a-a-a-d man.' " Then the Chair said, "Signature, 'Archibald Wilcox.' " And so on, and so on, name after name, and everybody had an increasingly and gloriously good time except the wretched Nineteen. Now and then, when a particularly shining name was called, the house made the Chair wait while it chanted the whole of the test-remark from the beginning to the closing words, "And go to hell or Hadleyburg—try and make it the for-or-m-e-r!" and in these special cases they added a grand and agonized and imposing "A-a-a-a-*men!*"

The list dwindled, dwindled, dwindled, poor old Richards keeping tally of the count, wincing when a name resembling his own was pronounced, and waiting in miserable suspense for the time to come when it would be his humiliating privilege to rise with Mary and finish his plea, which he was intending to word thus: ". . . for until now we have never done any wrong thing, but have gone our humble way unreproached. We are very poor, we are old, and have no chick nor child to help us; we were sorely tempted, and we fell. It was my purpose when I got up before to make confession and beg that my name might not be read out in this public place, for it seemed to us that we could not bear it; but I was prevented. It was just; it was our place to suffer with the rest. It has been hard for us. It is the first time we have ever heard our name fall from any one's lips—sullied. Be merciful—for the sake of the better days; make our shame as light to bear as in your charity you can." At this point in his revery Mary nudged him, perceiving that his mind was absent. The house was chanting. "You are f-a-r," etc.

"Be ready," Mary whispered. "Your name comes now; he has read eighteen."

The chant ended.

"Next! next! next!" came volleying from all over the house.

Burgess put his hand into his pocket. The old couple, trembling, began to rise, Burgess fumbled a moment, then said,

"I find I have read them all."

Faint with joy and surprise, the couple sank into their seats, and Mary whispered:

"Oh, bless God, we are saved!—he has lost ours—I wouldn't give this for a hundred of those sacks!"

The house burst out with its "Mikado" travesty, and sang it three times with ever-increasing enthusiasm, rising to its feet when it reached for the third time the closing line—

> "But the Symbols are here, you bet!"

and finishing up with cheers and a tiger for "Hadleyburg purity and our eighteen immortal representatives of it."

Then Wingate, the saddler, got up and proposed cheers "for the cleanest man in town, the one solitary important citizen in it who didn't try to steal that money—Edward Richards."

They were given with great and moving heartiness; then somebody proposed that Richards be elected sole Guardian and Symbol of the now Sacred Hadleyburg Tradition, with power and right to stand up and look the whole sarcastic world in the face.

Passed, by acclamation; then they sang the "Mikado" again, and ended it with,

> "And there's *one* Symbol left, you bet!"

There was a pause; then—

A Voice. "Now, then, who's to get the sack?"

The Tanner (with bitter sarcasm). "That's easy. The money has to be divided among the eighteen Incorruptibles. They gave the suffering stranger twenty dollars apiece—and that remark—each in his turn—it took twenty-two minutes for the procession to move past. Staked the stranger—total contribution, $360. All they want is just the loan back—and interest—forty thousand dollars altogether."

Many voices [derisively]. "That's it! Divvy! divvy! Be kind to the poor—don't keep them waiting!"

The Chair. "Order! I now offer the stranger's remaining document. It says: 'If no claimant shall appear [*grand chorus of groans*], I desire that you open the sack and count out the money to the principal citizens of your town, they to take it in trust [*Cries of "Oh! Oh! Oh!"*], and use it in such ways as to them shall seem best for the propagation and preservation of your community's noble reputation for incorruptible honesty [*more cries*]—a reputation to which their names and their efforts will add a new and far-reaching lustre.' [*Enthusiastic outburst of sarcastic applause.*] That seems to be all. No—here is a postscript:

" 'P. S.—CITIZENS OF HADLEYBURG: There *is* no test-remark—nobody made one. [*Great sensation.*] There wasn't any pauper stranger, nor any twenty-dollar contribution, nor any accompanying benediction and compliment—these are all inventions. [*General buzz and hum of astonishment and delight.*] Allow me to tell my story—it will take but a word or two. I passed through your town at a certain time, and received a deep offense which I had not earned. Any other man would have been content to kill one or two of you and call it square, but to me that would have been a trivial revenge, and inadequate; for the dead do not *suffer*. Besides, I could not kill you all—and, anyway, made as I am, even that would not have satisfied me. I wanted to damage every man in the place, and every woman—and not in their bodies or in their estate, but in their vanity—the place where feeble and foolish people are most vulnerable. So I disguised myself and came back and studied you. You were easy game. You had an old and lofty reputation for honesty, and naturally you were proud of it —it was your treasure of treasures, the very apple of your eye. As soon as I found out that you carefully and vigilantly kept yourselves and your children *out of temptation*, I knew how to proceed. Why, you simple creatures, the weakest of all weak things is a virtue which has not been tested in the fire. I laid a plan, and gathered a list of names. My project was to corrupt Hadleyburg the incorruptible. My idea was to make liars and thieves of nearly half a hundred smirchless men and women who had never in their lives uttered a lie or stolen a penny. I was afraid of Goodson. He was neither born nor reared in Hadleyburg. I was afraid that if I started to operate my scheme by getting my letter laid before you, you would say to yourselves. "Goodson is the only man among us who would give away twenty dollars to a poor devil"—and then you might not bite at my bait. But Heaven took Goodson; then I knew I was safe, and I set my trap and baited it. It may be that I shall not catch all the men to whom I mailed the pretended test secret, but I shall catch the most of them, if I know Hadleyburg nature. [*Voices.* "Right—he got every last one of them."] I believe they will even steal ostensible *gamble*-money, rather than miss, poor, tempted, and mistrained fellows. I am hoping to eternally and everlastingly squelch your vanity and give Hadleyburg a new renown—one that will *stick*—and spread far. If I have succeeded, open the sack and summon the Committee on Propagation and Preservation of the Hadleyburg Reputation.' "

A Cyclone of Voices. "Open it! Open it! The Eighteen to the front! Committee on Propagation of the Tradition! Forward—the Incorruptibles!"

The Chair ripped the sack wide, and gathered up a handful of bright, broad, yellow coins, shook them together, then examined them—

"Friends, they are only gilded disks of lead!"

There was a crashing outbreak of delight over this news, and when the noise had subsided, the tanner called out:

"By right of apparent seniority in this business, Mr. Wilson is Chairman of the Committee on Propagation of the Tradition. I suggest that he step forward on behalf of his pals, and receive in trust the money."

A Hundred Voices. "Wilson! Wilson! Wilson! Speech! Speech!"

Wilson [*in a voice trembling with anger*]. "You will allow me to say, without apologies for my language, *damn* the money!"

A Voice. "Oh, and him a Baptist!"

A Voice. "Seventeen Symbols left! Step up, gentlemen, and assume your trust!"

There was a pause—no response.

The Saddler. "Mr. Chairman, we've got *one* clean man left, anyway, out of the late aristocracy; and he needs money, and deserves it. I move that you appoint Jack Halliday to get up there and auction off that sack of gilt twenty-dollar pieces, and give the result to the right man—the man whom Hadleyburg delights to honor—Edward Richards."

This was received with great enthusiasm, the dog taking a hand again; the saddler started the bids at a dollar, the Brixton folk and Barnum's representative fought hard for it, the people cheered every jump that the bids made, the excitement climbed moment by moment higher and higher, the bidders got on their mettle and grew steadily more and more daring, more and more determined, the jumps went from a dollar up to five, then to ten, then to twenty, then fifty, then to a hundred, then—

At the beginning of the auction Richards whispered in distress to his wife: "Oh, Mary, can we allow it? It—it—you see, it is an honor-reward, a testimonial to purity of character, and—and—can we allow it? Hadn't I better get up and—Oh, Mary, what ought we to do?—what do you think we—" [*Halliday's voice.* "Fifteen I'm bid!—fifteen for the sack!—twenty!—ah, thanks!—thirty—thanks again! Thirty, thirty, thirty!—do I hear forty?—forty it is! Keep the ball rolling, gentlemen, keep it rolling!—fifty!—thanks, noble Roman!—going at fifty, fifty, fifty!—seventy!—ninety!—splendid!—a hundred!—pile it up, pile it up!—hundred and twenty—forty!—just in time!—hundred and fifty—TWO hun-*

dred!—superb! Do I hear two h— thanks!—two hundred and fifty!——"]

"It is another temptation, Edward—I'm all in a tremble—but, oh, we've escaped one temptation, and that ought to warn us, to— [*"Six did I hear?—thanks!—six fifty, six f—SEVEN hundred!"*] And yet, Edward, when you think—nobody susp—[*"Eight hundred dollars!—hurrah!—make it nine!—Mr. Parsons, did I hear you say—thanks!—nine!—this noble sack of virgin lead going at only nine hundred dollars, gilding and all—come! do I hear—a thousand!—gratefully yours!—did some one say eleven?—a sack which is going to be the most celebrated in the whole Uni——"*] Oh, Edward" (*beginning to sob*), "we are so poor!—but—but—do as you think best—do as you think best."

Edward fell—that is, he sat still; sat with a conscience which was not satisfied, but which was overpowered by circumstances.

Meanwhile a stranger, who looked like an amateur detective gotten up as an impossible English earl, had been watching the evening's proceedings with manifest interest, and with a contented expression in his face; and he had been privately commenting to himself. He was now soliloquizing somewhat like this: "None of the Eighteen are bidding; that is not satisfactory; I must change that—the dramatic unities require it; they must buy the sack they tried to steal; they must pay a heavy price, too—some of them are rich. And another thing, when I make a mistake in Hadleyburg nature the man that puts that error upon me is entitled to a high honorarium, and some one must pay it. The poor old Richards has brought my judgment to shame; he is an honest man;—I don't understand it, but I acknowledge it. Yes, he saw my deuces— *and* with a straight flush, and by rights the pot is his. And it shall be a jackpot, too, if I can manage it. He disappointed me, but let that pass."

He was watching the bidding. At a thousand, the market broke; the prices tumbled swiftly. He waited—and still watched. One competitor dropped out; then another, and another. He put in a bid or two, now. When the bids had sunk to ten dollars, he added a five; some one raised him a three; he waited a moment, then flung in a fifty-dollar jump, and the sack was his—at $1,282. The house broke out in cheers—then stopped; for he was on his feet and had lifted his hand. He began to speak.

"I desire to say a word, and ask a favor. I am a speculator in rarities, and I have dealings with persons interested in numismatics all over the world. I can make a profit on this purchase, just as it stands; but there is a way, if I can get your approval, whereby I can make every one of these leaden twenty-dollar pieces worth its face in gold, and perhaps more. Grant me that approval, and I will give part of my gains to your Mr. Richards, whose invulnerable probity you have so justly and so cordially recognized to-night; his share shall be ten thousand dollars, and I will hand him the money to-morrow. [*Great applause from the house.* But the "invulnerable probity" made the Richardses blush prettily; however, it went for modesty, and did no harm.] If you will pass my proposition by a good majority—I would like a two-thirds vote—I will regard that as the town's consent, and that is all I ask. Rarities are always helped by any device which will rouse curiosity and compel remark. Now if I may have your permission to stamp upon the faces of each of these ostensible coins the names of the eighteen gentlemen who——"

Nine-tenths of the audience were on their feet in a moment—dog and all—and the proposition was carried with a whirlwind of approving applause and laughter.

They sat down, and all the Symbols except "Dr." Clay Harkness got up, violently protesting against the proposed outrage, and threatening to——

"I beg you not to threaten me," said the stranger, calmly. "I know my legal rights, and am not accustomed to being frightened at bluster." [*Applause.*] He sat down. "Dr." Harkness saw an opportunity here. He was one of the two very rich men of the place, and Pinkerton was the other. Harkness was proprietor of a mint; that is to say, a popular patent medicine. He was running for the Legislature on one ticket, and Pinkerton on the other. It was a close race and a hot one, and getting hotter every day. Both had strong appetites for money; each had bought a great tract of land, with a purpose; there was going to be a new railway, and each wanted to be in the Legislature and help locate the route to his own advantage; a single vote might make the decision, and with it two or three fortunes. The stake was large, and Harkness was a daring speculator. He was sitting close to the stranger. He leaned over while one or another of the other Symbols was entertaining the house with protests and appeals, and asked, in a whisper,

"What is your price for the sack?"

"Forty thousand dollars."

"I'll give you twenty."

"No."

"Twenty-five."

"No."

"Say thirty."

"The price is forty thousand dollars; not a penny less."

"All right, I'll give it. I will come to the hotel at ten in the morning. I don't want it known; will see you privately."

"Very good." Then the stranger got up and said to the house: "I find it late. The speeches of these gentlemen are not without merit, not without interest, not without grace; yet if I may be excused I will take my leave. I thank you for the great favor which you have shown me in granting my petition. I ask the Chair to keep the sack for me until to-morrow, and to hand these three five-hundred-dollar notes to Mr. Richards." They were passed up to the Chair. "At nine I will call for the sack, and at eleven will deliver the rest of the ten thousand to Mr. Richards in person, at his home. Good-night."

Then he slipped out, and left the audience making a vast noise, which was composed of a mixture of cheers, the "Mikado" song, dog-disapproval, and chant, "you are f-a-r from being a b-a-a-d man—a-a-a-a-men!"

IV

At home the Richardses had to endure congratulations and compliments until midnight. Then they were left to themselves. They looked a little sad, and they sat silent and thinking. Finally Mary sighed and said,

"Do you think we are to blame, Edward—*much* to blame?" and her eyes wandered to the accusing triplet of big bank-notes lying on the table, where the congratulators had been gloating over them and reverently fingering them. Edward did not answer at once; then he brought out a sigh and said, hesitatingly:

"We—we couldn't help it, Mary. It—well, it was ordered. *All* things are."

Mary glanced up and looked at him steadily, but he didn't return the look. Presently she said:

"I thought congratulations and praises always tasted good. But —it seems to me, now—Edward?"

"Well?"

"Are you going to stay in the bank?"

"N-no."

"Resign?"

"In the morning—by note."

"It does seem best."

Richards bowed his head in his hands and muttered:

"Before, I was not afraid to let oceans of people's money pour through my hands, but—Mary, I am so tired, so tired—"

"We will go to bed."

At nine in the morning the stranger called for the sack and took it to the hotel in a cab. At ten Harkness had a talk with him privately. The stranger asked for and got five checks on a metropolitan bank—drawn to "Bearer,"—four for $1,500 each, and one for $34,000. He put one of the former in his pocket-book, and the remainder, representing $38,500, he put in an envelope, and with these he added a note, which he wrote after Harkness was gone. At eleven he called at the Richards house and knocked. Mrs. Richards peeped through the shutters, then went and received the envelope, and the stranger disappeared without a word. She came back flushed and a little unsteady on her legs, and gasped out:

"I am sure I recognized him! Last night it seemed to me that maybe I had seen him somewhere before."

"He is the man that brought the sack here?"

"I am almost sure of it."

"Then he is the ostensible Stephenson too, and sold every important citizen in this town with his bogus secret. Now if he has sent checks instead of money, we are sold too, after we thought we had escaped. I was beginning to feel fairly comfortable once more, after my night's rest, but the look of that envelope makes me sick. It isn't fat enough; $8,500 in even the largest bank-notes makes more bulk than that."

"Edward, why do you object to checks?"

"Checks signed by Stephenson! I am resigned to take the $8,500 if it could come in bank-notes—for it does seem that it was so ordered, Mary—but I have never had much courage, and I have not the pluck to try to market a check signed with that disastrous name. It would be a trap. That man tried to catch me; we escaped somehow or other; and now he is trying a new way. If it is checks—"

"Oh, Edward, it is *too* bad!" and she held up the checks and began to cry.

"Put them in the fire! quick! we mustn't be tempted. If it is a trick to make the world laugh at *us*, along with the rest, and— Give them to *me*, since you can't do it!" He snatched them and tried to hold his grip till he could get to the stove; but he was human, he was a cashier, and he stopped a moment to make sure of the signature. Then he came near to fainting.

"Fan me, Mary, fan me! They are the same as gold!"

"Oh, how lovely, Edward! Why?"

"Signed by Harkness. What can the mystery of that be, Mary?"

"Edward, do you think——"

"Look here—look at this! Fifteen—fifteen—fifteen—thirty-four. Thirty-eight thousand five hundred! Mary, the sack isn't worth twelve dollars, and Harkness—apparently—has paid about par for it."

"And does it all come to us, do you think—instead of the ten thousand?"

"Why, it looks like it. And the checks are made to 'Bearer,' too."

"Is that good, Edward? What is it for?"

"A hint to collect them at some distant bank, I reckon. Perhaps Harkness doesn't want the matter known. What is that—a note?"

"Yes. It was with the checks."

It was in the "Stephenson" handwriting, but there was no signature. It said:

"I am a disappointed man. Your honesty is beyond the reach of temptation. I had a different idea about it, but I wronged you in that, and I beg pardon, and do it sincerely. I honor you—and that is sincere, too. This town is not worthy to kiss the hem of your garment. Dear sir, I made a square bet with myself that there were nineteen debauchable men in your self-righteous community. I have lost. Take the whole pot, you are entitled to it."

Richards drew a deep sigh, and said:
"It seems written with fire—it burns so. Mary—I am miserable again."

"I, too. Ah, dear, I wish——"

"To think, Mary—he *believes* in me."

"Oh, don't, Edward—I can't bear it."

"If those beautiful words were deserved, Mary—and God knows I believed I deserved them once—I think I could give the forty thousand dollars for them. And I would put that paper away, as representing more than gold and jewels, and keep it always. But now—We could not live in the shadow of its accusing presence, Mary."

He put it in the fire.

A messenger arrived and delivered an envelope. Richards took from it a note and read it; it was from Burgess.

"You saved me, in a difficult time. I saved you last night. It was at cost of a lie, but I made the sacrifice freely, and out of a grateful heart. None in this village knows so well as I know how brave and good and noble you are. At bottom you cannot respect me, knowing as you do of that matter of which I am accused, and by the general voice condemned; but I beg that you will at least believe that I am a grateful man; it will help me to bear my burden.

[Signed] "BURGESS."

"Saved, once more. And on such terms!" He put the note in the fire. "I—I wish I were dead, Mary, I wish I were out of it all."

"Oh, these are bitter, bitter days, Edward. The stabs, through their very generosity, are so deep—and they come so fast!"

Three days before the election each of two thousand voters suddenly found himself in possession of a prized memento—one of the renowned bogus double-eagles. Around one of its faces was stamped these words: "THE REMARK I MADE TO THE POOR STRANGER WAS—" Around the other face was stamped these: "GO, AND REFORM. [SIGNED] PINKERTON." Thus the entire remaining refuse of the renowned joke was emptied upon a single head, and with calamitous effect. It revived the recent vast laugh and concentrated it upon Pinkerton; and Harkness's election was a walkover.

Within twenty-four hours after the Richardses had received their checks their consciences were quieting down, discouraged; the old couple were learning to reconcile themselves to the sin which they had committed. But they were to learn, now, that a sin takes on new and real terrors when there seems a chance that it is going to be found out. This gives it a fresh and most substantial and important aspect. At church the morning sermon was of the usual pattern; it was the same old things said in the same old way; they had heard them a thousand times and found them innocuous, next to meaningless, and easy to sleep under; but now it was different: the sermon seemed to bristle with accusations; it seemed aimed straight and specially at people who were concealing deadly sins. After church they got away from the mob of congratulators as soon as they could, and hurried homeward, chilled to the bone at they did not know what—vague, shadowy, indefinite fears. And by chance they caught a glimpse of Mr. Burgess as he turned a corner. He paid no attention to their nod of recognition! He hadn't seen it; but they did not know that. What could his conduct mean? It might mean—it might mean—oh, a dozen dreadful things. Was it possible that he knew that Richards could have cleared him of guilt in that bygone time, and had been silently waiting for a chance to even up accounts? At home, in their distress they got to imagining that their servant might have been in the next room listening when Richards revealed the secret to his wife that he knew of Burgess's innocence; next, Richards began to imagine that he had heard the swish of a gown in there at that time; next, he was sure he *had* heard it. They would call Sarah in, on a pretext, and watch her face: if she had been betraying them to Mr. Burgess, it would show in her manner. They asked her some questions—questions which were so random and incoherent and seemingly purposeless that the girl felt sure that the old people's minds had been affected by their sudden good fortune; the sharp and watchful gaze which they bent upon her frightened her, and that completed the business. She blushed, she became nervous and confused, and to the old people these were plain signs of guilt —guilt of some fearful sort or other—without doubt she was a spy and a traitor. When they were alone again they began to piece many unrelated things together and get horrible results out of the combination. When things had got about to the worst, Richards was delivered of a sudden gasp, and his wife asked:

"Oh, what is it?—what is it?"

"The note—Burgess's note! Its language was sarcastic, I see it now." He quoted: " 'At bottom you cannot respect me, *knowing*, as you do, of *that matter* of which I am accused'—oh, it is perfectly plain, now, God help me! He knows that I know! You see the ingenuity of the phrasing. It was a trap—and like a fool, I walked into it. And Mary—?"

"Oh, it is dreadful—I know what you are going to say—he didn't return your transcript of the pretended test-remark."

"No—kept it to destroy us with. Mary, he has exposed us to some already. I know it—I know it well. I saw it in a dozen faces after church. Ah, he wouldn't answer our nod of recognition—*he* knew what he had been doing!"

In the night the doctor was called. The news went around in the morning that the old couple were rather seriously ill—prostrated by the exhausting excitement growing out of their great windfall, the congratulations, and the late hours, the doctor said. The town was sincerely distressed; for these old people were about all it had left to be proud of, now.

Two days later the news was worse. The old couple were delirious, and were doing strange things. By witness of the nurses, Richards had exhibited checks—for $8,500? No—for an amazing sum— $38,500! What could be the explanation of this gigantic piece of luck?

The following day the nurses had more news—and wonderful. They had concluded to hide the checks, lest harm come to them; but when they searched they were gone from under the patient's pillow—vanished away. The patient said:

"Let the pillow alone; what do you want?"

"We thought it best that the checks——"

"You will never see them again—they are destroyed. They came from Satan. I saw the hell-brand on them, and I knew they were sent to betray me to sin." Then he fell to gabbling strange and dreadful things which were not clearly understandable, and which the doctor admonished them to keep to themselves.

Richards was right; the checks were never seen again.

A nurse must have talked in her sleep, for within two days the forbidden gabblings were the property of the town; and they were of a surprising sort. They seemed to indicate that Richards had been a claimant for the sack himself, and that Burgess had concealed that fact and then maliciously betrayed it.

Burgess was taxed with this and stoutly denied it. And he said it was not fair to attach weight to the chatter of a sick old man who was out of his mind. Still, suspicion was in the air, and there was much talk.

After a day or two it was reported that Mrs. Richards's delirious deliveries were getting to be duplicates of her husband's. Suspicion flamed up into conviction, now, and the town's pride in the purity of its one undiscredited important citizen began to dim down and flicker toward extinction.

Six days passed, then came more news. The old couple were dying. Richards's mind cleared in his latest hour, and he sent for Burgess. Burgess said:

"Let the room be cleared. I think he wishes to say something in privacy."

"No!" said Richards; "I want witnesses. I want you all to hear my confession, so that I may die a man, and not a dog. I was clean —artificially—like the rest; and like the rest I fell when temptation came. I signed a lie, and claimed the miserable sack. Mr. Burgess remembered that I had done him a service, and in gratitude (and ignorance) he suppressed my claim and saved me. You know the thing that was charged against Burgess years ago. My testimony, and mine alone, could have cleared him, and I was a coward, and left him to suffer disgrace—"

"No—no—Mr. Richards, you—"

"My servant betrayed my secret to him—"

"No one has betrayed anything to me—"

—"and then he did a natural and justifiable thing, he repented of the saving kindness which he had done me, and he *exposed* me— as I deserved—"

"Never!—I make oath—"

"Out of my heart I forgive him."

Burgess's impassioned protestations fell upon deaf ears; the dying man passed away without knowing that once more he had done poor Burgess a wrong. The old wife died that night.

The last of the sacred Nineteen had fallen a prey to the fiendish sack; the town was stripped of the last rag of its ancient glory. Its mourning was not showy, but it was deep.

By act of the Legislature—upon prayer and petition—Hadleyburg was allowed to change its name to (never mind what—I will not give it away), and leave one word out of the motto that for many generations had graced the town's official seal.

It is an honest town once more, and the man will have to rise early that catches it napping again.

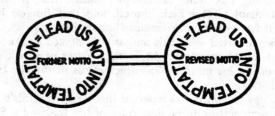

1899, 1900

From Letters from the Earth [9]

Letter II: Satan to Michael and Gabriel

* * * Now then, you have the facts. You know what the human race enjoys, and what it doesn't enjoy. It has invented a heaven, out of its own head, all by itself: guess what it is like! In fifteen hundred eternities you couldn't do it. The ablest mind known to you or me in fifty million aeons couldn't do it. Very well, I will tell you about it.

1. First of all, I recall to your attention the extraordinary fact with which I began. To wit, that the human being, like the immortals, naturally places sexual intercourse far and away above all other joys—yet he has left it out of his heaven! The very thought of it excites him; opportunity sets him wild; in this state he will risk life, reputation, everything—even his queer heaven itself—to make good that opportunity and ride it to the overwhelming climax. From youth to middle age all men and all women prize copulation above all other pleasures combined, yet it is actually as I have said: it is not in their heaven; prayer takes its place.

* * *

2. In man's heaven *everybody sings!* The man who did not sing on earth sings there; the man who could not sing on earth is able to do it there. This universal singing is not casual, not occasional, not relieved by intervals of quiet; it goes on, all day long, and every day, during a stretch of twelve hours. And *everybody stays;* whereas in the earth the place would be empty in two hours. The singing is of hymns alone. Nay, it is of *one* hymn alone. The words are always the same, in number they are only about a dozen, there is no rhyme, there is no poetry: "Hosannah, hosannah, hosannah, Lord God of Sabaoth, 'rah! 'rah! 'rah! siss!—boom! . . . a-a-ah!"

3. Meantime, every person is playing on a harp—those millions and millions!—whereas not more than twenty in the thousand of them could play an instrument in the earth, or ever wanted to.

Consider the deafening hurricane of sound—millions and millions of voices screaming at once and millions and millions of harps gritting their teeth at the same time! I ask you: is it hideous, is it odious, is it horrible?

Consider further: it is a *praise* service; a service of compliment,

---

1. *Letters from the Earth* (1962) is a volume of sketches Clemens wrote "at intervals over four decades" but did not complete or publish. There is evidence, however, that he intended them for posterity. Amusingly expressed, they still represent a dark distrust in and disaffection toward humanity en masse.

These materials were edited by Bernard De Voto in 1936 but not published at that time.

In "Letter II" the archangel Satan, exiled to the earth, tries to communicate the unbelievable absurdity of mankind to his respectable colleagues in heaven, Gabriel and Michael.

of flattery, of adulation! Do you ask who it is that is willing to endure this strange compliment, this insane compliment; and who not only endures it, but takes it, enjoys it, requires it, *commands* it? Hold your breath!

It is God! This race's God, I mean. He sits on his throne, attended by his four and twenty elders and some other dignitaries pertaining to his court, and looks out over his miles and miles of tempestuous worshippers, and smiles, and purrs, and nods his satisfaction northward, eastward, southward; as quaint and naïve a spectacle as has yet been imagined in this universe, I have it.

It is easy to see that the inventor of the heaven did not originate the idea, but copied it from the show-ceremonies of some sorry little sovereign State up in the back settlements of the Orient somewhere.

All sane white people hate noise; yet they have tranquilly accepted this kind of a heaven—without thinking, without reflection, without examination—and they actually want to go to it! Profoundly devout old gray-headed men put in a large part of their time dreaming of the happy day when they will lay down the cares of this life and enter into the joys of that place. Yet you can see how unreal it is to them, and how little it takes a grip upon them as being fact, for they make no practical preparation for the great change: you never see one of them with a harp, you never hear one of them sing.

As you have seen, that singular show is a service of praise: praise by hymn, praise by prostration. It takes the place of "church." Now then, in the earth these people cannot stand much church—an hour and a quarter is the limit, and they draw the line at once a week. That is to say, Sunday. One day in seven; and even then they do not look forward to it with longing. And so— consider what their heaven provides for them: "church" that lasts forever, and a Sabbath that has no end! They quickly weary of this brief hebdomadal [1] Sabbath here, yet they long for that eternal one; they dream of it, they talk about it, they *think* they think they are going to enjoy it—with all their simple hearts they think they think they are going to be happy in it!

It is because they do not think at all; they only think they think. Whereas they can't think; not two human beings in ten thousand have anything to think with. And as to imagination—oh, well, look at their heaven! They accept it, they approve it, they admire it. That gives you their intellectual measure.

4. The inventor of their heaven empties into it all the nations of the earth, in one common jumble. All are on an equality abso-

1. Weekly; at seven-day intervals.

lute, no one of them ranking another; they have to be "brothers"; they have to mix together, pray together, harp together, hosannah together—whites, niggers, Jews, everybody—there's no distinction. Here in the earth all nations hate each other, and every one of them hates the Jews. Yet every pious person adores that heaven and wants to get into it. He really does. And when he is in a holy rapture he thinks he thinks that if he were only there he would take all the populace to his heart, and hug, and hug, and hug!

He is a marvel—man is! I would I knew who invented him.

5. Every man in the earth possesses some share of intellect, large or small; and be it large or be it small he takes a pride in it. Also his heart swells at mention of the names of the majestic intellectual chiefs of his race, and he loves the tale of their splendid achievements. For he is of their blood, and in honoring themselves they have honored him. Lo, what the mind of man can do! he cries; and calls the roll of the illustrious of all the ages; and points to the imperishable literatures they have given to the world, and the mechanical wonders they have invented, and the glories wherewith they have clothed science and the arts; and to them he uncovers, as to kings, and gives to them the profoundest homage, and the sincerest, his exultant heart can furnish—thus exalting intellect above all things else in his world, and enthroning it there under the arching skies in a supremacy unapproachable. And then he contrives a heaven that hasn't a rag of intellectuality in it anywhere!

Is it odd, is it curious, is it puzzling? It is exactly as I have said, incredible as it may sound. This sincere adorer of intellect and prodigal rewarder of its mighty services here in the earth has invented a religion and a heaven which pay no compliments to intellect, offer it no distinctions, fling to it no largess: in fact, never even mention it.

By this time you will have noticed that the human being's heaven has been thought out and constructed upon an absolutely definite plan; and that this plan is, that it shall contain, in labored detail, each and every imaginable thing that is repulsive to a man, and not a single thing he likes!

Very well, the further we proceed the more will this curious fact be apparent.

Make a note of it: in man's heaven there are no exercises for the intellect, nothing for it to live upon. It would rot there in a year —rot and stink. Rot and stink—and at that stage become holy. A blessed thing: for only the holy can stand the joys of that bedlam.

BRET HARTE

(1836–1902)

Through the dramatic, romantic, and humorous use of regional material from the gold camps of the Sierras, Bret Harte brought the heady smells of pines and campfires, the raucous sounds of Poker Flat and other ephemeral mining towns, and the hilarious contrast of westerner and eastern dude to the fascinated attention of the eastern states and England. He was born in Albany, New York. At the age of eighteen he accompanied his widowed mother to California, where he became a compositor on a small Humboldt County newspaper, the *Northern California*. Moving to San Francisco as typesetter on the *Golden Era*, he soon became its editor, and later was editor of the *Californian*. In 1864 he was appointed secretary to the California Mint, a sinecure leaving him free to write.

He published a volume of poems and a book of sketches in 1867 and then, as editor of the *Overland Monthly*—the *Atlantic Monthly* of the Pacific slope—he wrote a story which carried the name of Bret Harte across the continent, "The Luck of Roaring Camp" (August, 1868). Five months later came "The Outcasts of Poker Flat" (January, 1869), and then a humorous poem, "Plain Language from Truthful James" (September, 1870), each acclaimed on both seaboards. The poem, popularly called "The Heathen Chinee," was approvingly reprinted by American newspapers, and swept on to England. Abandoning California, refusing offers from Chicago, Harte chose Boston; there, feted by the Saturday Club, he became a contributing editor of the *Atlantic Monthly* with a stipend of ten thousand dollars for which he was to supply twelve selections.

Harte disappointed the editors of the *Atlantic* by his decline in effort and performance. Though popularity lingered through the appearance of several volumes of short stories, he could not repeat his first success. His ambition for worldly recognition caused him to seek an appointment in the diplomatic service. He served as United States consul at Crefeld, Germany, in 1878, and at Glasgow from 1880 to 1885. He collected his journalistic work into numerous books: *Tales of the Argonauts* (1875), *A Sappho of Green Springs* (1891), *Colonel Starbottle's Client* (1892), *A Protégée of Jack Hamlin's* (1894), *The Bell-Ringer of Angel's* (1894), *Mr. Jack Hamlin's Meditation* (1899), and *Condensed Novels* (1902). Harte also wrote several novels and novelettes, of which *M'liss: An Idyll of Red Mountain* (1873) and *Gabriel Conroy* (1876) continue to have some appeal. He tried his hand at the drama, collaborating with Mark Twain upon an unsuccessful play, *Ah Sin* (1877). The phenomenal success of his early work in England was largely responsible for his decision to remain there at the conclusion of his diplomatic service.

His work was often sentimental, melodramatic, and mawkish; yet in his best fiction and in his collected *Poems* (1871) he succeeded in catching the flavor of a time and place in American history.

There are several collected editions of Bret Harte. Two of the best are *The Writings of Bret Harte*, 19 vols., 1896–1914; and *The Works of Bret Harte*, 25 vols., 1914. A standard biography is George R. Stewart, Jr., *Bret Harte: Argonaut and Exile*, 1931. Richard O'Connor's *Bret Harte*, 1966, emphasizes his picturesque foibles. Good volumes of selections are *Tales of the Gold Rush*, with introduction by Oscar Lewis, 1944, and *Bret Harte: Representative Selections*, edited by Joseph B. Harrison, American Writers Series, 1941. See also Margaret Duckett, *Mark Twain and Bret Harte*, 1964.

Important critical estimates are made by Fred Lewis Pattee, *The Development of the American Short Story*, 1923, pp. 220–244; and by Arthur H. Quinn, *American Fiction*, 1936, pp. 232–242.

The Angelus [1]

(HEARD AT THE MISSION, DOLORES, 1868)

Bells of the Past, whose long-forgotten music
    Still fills the wide expanse,
Tingeing the sober twilight of the Present
    With color of romance!

I hear your call, and see the sun descending,   5
    On rock and wave and sand,
As down the coast the Mission voices, blending,
    Girdle the heathen land.

Within the circle of your incantation
    No blight nor mildew falls;   10
Nor fierce unrest, nor lust, nor low ambition
    Passes those airy walls.

Borne on the swell of your long waves receding,
    I touch the farther Past;
I see the dying glow of Spanish glory,   15
    The sunset dream and last!

Before me rise the dome-shaped Mission towers,
    The white Presidio;
The swart commander in his leathern jerkin,
    The priest in stole of snow.   20

Once more I see Portolá's [2] cross uplifting
    Above the setting sun;

1. Bret Harte was inspired to write "The Angelus" upon hearing the bells of the old Spanish mission Dolores in San Francisco. Originally published in the *Overland Monthly* for October, 1868, it was collected in *Poems* (1871). The text follows the 1871 edition.
2. Don Gaspar de Portolá, Spanish governor of Lower California, discovered San Francisco Bay in 1769.

And past the headland, northward, slowly drifting
  The freighted galleon.

O solemn bells! whose consecrated masses   25
  Recall the faith of old;
O tinkling bells! that lulled with twilight music
  The spiritual fold!

Your voices break and falter in the darkness,—
  Break, falter, and are still;   30
And veiled and mystic, like the Host descending,
  The sun sinks from the hill!

                                          1868, 1871

The Society Upon the Stanislaus [3]

I reside at Table Mountain, and my name is Truthful James;
I am not up to small deceit or any sinful games;
And I'll tell in simple language what I know about the row
That broke up our Society [4] upon the Stanislow.[5]

But first I would remark, that it is not a proper plan   5
For any scientific gent to whale his fellow-man,
And, if a member don't agree with his peculiar whim,
To lay for that same member for to "put a head" on him.

Now nothing could be finer or more beautiful to see
Than the first six months' proceedings of that same Society, 10
Till Brown of Calaveras [6] brought a lot of fossil bones
That he found within a tunnel near the tenement of Jones.

Then Brown he read a paper, and he reconstructed there,
From those same bones, an animal that was extremely rare;
And Jones then asked the Chair for a suspension of the rules, 15
Till he could prove that those same bones was one of his lost mules.

Then Brown he smiled a bitter smile, and said he was at fault.
It seemed he had been trespassing on Jones's family vault;
He was a most sarcastic man, this quiet Mr. Brown,
And on several occasions he had cleaned out the town.   20

3. First published in the *San Francisco News Letter* * * *, in 1868, as "Proceedings of the Academy of Natural Sciences at Smith's Crossing, Tuolumne County"; then collected in *Poems* (1871) as "The Society Upon the Stanislaus." The present text is based on the latter edition.
4. The persistent outbreak of literary and scientific societies in western mining towns and frontier outposts was a phenomenon frequently satirized at the time. Harte here burlesques the California Academy of Natural Science, San Francisco.
5. Stanislaus Peak in northeastern California.
6. Calaveras County, east of San Francisco. *Cf.* Harte's story "Brown of Calaveras" (1870), and Mark Twain's "The Notorious Jumping Frog of Calaveras County."

Now I hold it is not decent for a scientific gent
To say another is an ass,—at least, to all intent;
Nor should the individual who happens to be meant
Reply by having rocks at him, to any great extent.

Then Abner Dean of Angel's [7] raised a point of order, when   25
A chunk of old red sandstone took him in the abdomen,
And he smiled a kind of sickly smile, and curled up on the floor,
And the subsequent proceedings interested him no more.

For, in less time than I write it, every member did engage
In a warfare with the remnants of a palæozoic age;   30
And the way they heaved those fossils in their anger was a sin,
Till the skull of an old mammoth caved the head of Thompson in.

And this is all I have to say of these improper games,
For I live at Table Mountain, and my name is Truthful James;
And I've told in simple language what I know about the row   35
That broke up our Society upon the Stanislow.

1868, 1871

The Outcasts of Poker Flat [8]

As Mr. John Oakhurst, gambler, stepped into the main street of
Poker Flat on the morning of the 23d of November, 1850, he was
conscious of a change in its moral atmosphere since the preceding
night. Two or three men, conversing earnestly together, ceased as
he approached, and exchanged significant glances. There was a Sabbath lull in the air, which, in a settlement unused to Sabbath influences, looked ominous.

Mr. Oakhurst's calm, handsome face betrayed small concern in
these indications. Whether he was conscious of any predisposing
cause, was another question. "I reckon they're after somebody," he
reflected; "likely it's me." He returned to his pocket the handkerchief with which he had been whipping away the red dust of Poker
Flat from his neat boots, and quietly discharged his mind of any
further conjecture.

In point of fact, Poker Flat was "after somebody." It had lately
suffered the loss of several thousand dollars, two valuable horses,
and a prominent citizen. It was experiencing a spasm of virtuous
reaction, quite as lawless and ungovernable as any of the acts that
had provoked it. A secret committee [9] had determined to rid the

7. Now Angels Camp, a mining town
in northeastern California.
8. First published in the *Overland
Monthly* for January, 1869, and collected in *The Luck of Roaring Camp*
and Other Sketches (1870), which the
present text follows.
9. Vigilance committees were often organized in the West for the protection
of life and property.

town of all improper persons. This was done permanently in regard of two men who were then hanging from the boughs of a sycamore in the gulch, and temporarily in the banishment of certain other objectionable characters. I regret to say that some of these were ladies. It is but due to the sex, however, to state that their impropriety was professional, and it was only in such easily established standards of evil that Poker Flat ventured to sit in judgment.

Mr. Oakhurst was right in supposing that he was included in this category. A few of the committee had urged hanging him as a possible example, and a sure method of reimbursing themselves from his pockets of the sums he had won from them. "It's agin justice," said Jim Wheeler, "to let this yer young man from Roaring Camp—an entire stranger—carry away our money." But a crude sentiment of equity residing in the breasts of those who had been fortunate enough to win from Mr. Oakhurst overruled this narrower local prejudice.

Mr. Oakhurst received his sentence with philosophic calmness, none the less coolly that he was aware of the hesitation of his judges. He was too much of a gambler not to accept fate. With him life was at best an uncertain game, and he recognized the usual percentage in favor of the dealer.

A body of armed men accompanied the deported wickedness of Poker Flat to the outskirts of the settlement. Besides Mr. Oakhurst, who was known to be a coolly desperate man, and for whose intimidation the armed escort was intended, the expatriated party consisted of a young woman familiarly known as "The Duchess"; another, who had won the title of "Mother Shipton"; and "Uncle Billy," a suspected sluice-robber[1] and confirmed drunkard. The cavalcade provoked no comments from the spectators, nor was any word uttered by the escort. Only when the gulch which marked the uttermost limit of Poker Flat was reached, the leader spoke briefly and to the point. The exiles were forbidden to return at the peril of their lives.

As the escort disappeared, their pent-up feelings found vent in a few hysterical tears from the Duchess, some bad language from Mother Shipton, and a Parthian[2] volley of expletives from Uncle Billy. The philosophic Oakhurst alone remained silent. He listened calmly to Mother Shipton's desire to cut somebody's heart out, to the repeated statements of the Duchess that she would die in the road, and to the alarming oaths that seemed to be bumped out of Uncle Billy as he rode forward. With the easy good humor charac-

---

1. In gold mining, the sluice was a trough or series of boxes through which gold was washed from gravel and sand. 2. The Parthians, Asians of the first century B.C., would counterfeit wild flight from their enemies, and then wheel, catching them off guard with a quick volley.

teristic of his class, he insisted upon exchanging his own riding-horse, "Five-Spot," for the sorry mule which the Duchess rode. But even this act did not draw the party into any closer sympathy. The young woman readjusted her somewhat draggled plumes with a feeble, faded coquetry; Mother Shipton eyed the possessor of "Five-Spot" with malevolence, and Uncle Billy included the whole party in one sweeping anathema.

The road to Sandy Bar—a camp that, not having as yet experienced the regenerating influences of Poker Flat, consequently seemed to offer some invitation to the emigrants—lay over a steep mountain range. It was distant a day's severe travel. In that advanced season, the party soon passed out of the moist, temperate regions of the foothills into the dry, cold, bracing air of the Sierras. The trail was narrow and difficult. At noon the Duchess, rolling out of her saddle upon the ground, declared her intention of going no farther, and the party halted.

The spot was singularly wild and impressive. A wooded amphitheatre, surrounded on three sides by precipitous cliffs of naked granite, sloped gently toward the crest of another precipice that overlooked the valley. It was, undoubtedly, the most suitable spot for a camp, had camping been advisable. But Mr. Oakhurst knew that scarcely half the journey to Sandy Bar was accomplished, and the party were not equipped or provisioned for delay. This fact he pointed out to his companions curtly, with a philosophic commentary on the folly of "throwing up their hand before the game was played out." But they were furnished with liquor, which in this emergency stood them in place of food, fuel, rest, and prescience. In spite of his remonstrances, it was not long before they were more or less under its influence. Uncle Billy passed rapidly from a bellicose state into one of stupor, the Duchess became maudlin, and Mother Shipton snored. Mr. Oakhurst alone remained erect, leaning against a rock, calmly surveying them.

Mr. Oakhurst did not drink. It interfered with a profession which required coolness, impassiveness, and presence of mind, and, in his own language, he "couldn't afford it." As he gazed at his recumbent fellow exiles, the loneliness begotten of his pariah trade, his habits of life, his very vices, for the first time seriously oppressed him. He bestirred himself in dusting his black clothes, washing his hands and face, and other acts characteristic of his studiously neat habits, and for a moment forgot his annoyance. The thought of deserting his weaker and more pitiable companions never perhaps occurred to him. Yet he could not help feeling the want of that excitement which, singularly enough, was most conducive to that calm equanimity for which he was notorious. He looked at the gloomy walls that rose a thousand feet sheer above the circling pines around him, at the sky ominously clouded, at the valley below, already deepening into shadow; and, doing so, suddenly he heard his own name called.

A horseman slowly ascended the trail. In the fresh, open face of the newcomer Mr. Oakhurst recognized Tom Simson, otherwise known as "The Innocent," of Sandy Bar. He had met him some months before over a "little game," and had, with perfect equanimity, won the entire fortune—amounting to some forty dollars—of that guileless youth. After the game was finished, Mr. Oakhurst drew the youthful speculator behind the door and thus addressed him: "Tommy, you're a good little man, but you can't gamble worth a cent. Don't try it over again." He then handed him his money back, pushed him gently from the room, and so made a devoted slave of Tom Simson.

There was a remembrance of this in his boyish and enthusiastic greeting of Mr. Oakhurst. He had started, he said, to go to Poker Flat to seek his fortune. "Alone?" No, not exactly alone; in fact (a giggle), he had run away with Piney Woods. Didn't Mr. Oakhurst remember Piney? She that used to wait on the table at the Temperance House? They had been engaged a long time, but old Jake Woods had objected, and so they had run away, and were going to Poker Flat to be married, and here they were. And they were tired out, and how lucky it was they had found a place to camp, and company. All this the Innocent delivered rapidly, while Piney, a stout, comely damsel of fifteen, emerged from behind the pine-tree, where she had been blushing unseen, and rode to the side of her lover.

Mr. Oakhurst seldom troubled himself with sentiment, still less with propriety; but he had a vague idea that the situation was not fortunate. He retained, however, his presence of mind sufficiently to kick Uncle Billy, who was about to say something, and Uncle Billy was sober enough to recognize in Mr. Oakhurst's kick a superior power that would not bear trifling. He then endeavored to dissuade Tom Simson from delaying further, but in vain. He even pointed out the fact that there was no provision, nor means of making a camp. But, unluckily, the Innocent met this objection by assuring the party that he was provided with an extra mule loaded with provisions, and by the discovery of a rude attempt at a log house near the trail. "Piney can stay with Mrs. Oakhurst," said the Innocent, pointing to the Duchess, "and I can shift for myself."

Nothing but Mr. Oakhurst's admonishing foot saved Uncle Billy from bursting into a roar of laughter. As it was, he felt compelled to retire up the cañon until he could recover his gravity. There he confided the joke to the tall pine-trees, with many slaps of his leg, contortions of his face, and the usual profanity. But when he returned to the party, he found them seated by a fire—for the air had grown strangely chill and the sky overcast—in apparently amicable conversation. Piney was actually talking in an impulsive girlish fashion to the Duchess, who was listening with an interest and animation she had not shown for many days. The Innocent was holding forth, apparently with equal effect, to Mr. Oakhurst and Mother Shipton, who was actually relaxing into amiability. "Is this yer a d——d picnic?" said Uncle Billy, with inward scorn, as he surveyed the sylvan group, the glancing firelight, and the tethered animals in the foreground. Suddenly an idea mingled with the alcoholic fumes that disturbed his brain. It was apparently of a jocular nature, for he felt impelled to slap his leg again and cram his fist into his mouth.

As the shadows crept slowly up the mountain, a slight breeze rocked the tops of the pine-trees and moaned through their long and gloomy aisles. The ruined cabin, patched and covered with pine bows, was set apart for the ladies. As the lovers parted, they unaffectedly exchanged a kiss, so honest and sincere that it might have been heard above the swaying pines. The frail Duchess and the malevolent Mother Shipton were probably too stunned to remark upon this last evidence of simplicity, and so turned without a word to the hut. The fire was replenished, the men lay down before the door, and in a few minutes were asleep.

Mr. Oakhurst was a light sleeper. Toward morning he awoke benumbed and cold. As he stirred the dying fire, the wind, which was now blowing strongly, brought to his cheek that which caused the blood to leave it,—snow!

He started to his feet with the intention of awakening the sleepers, for there was no time to lose. But turning to where Uncle Billy had been lying, he found him gone. A suspicion leaped to his brain, and a curse to his lips. He ran to the spot where the mules had been tethered—they were no longer there. The tracks were already rapidly disappearing in the snow.

The momentary excitement brought Mr. Oakhurst back to the fire with his usual calm. He did not waken the sleepers. The Innocent slumbered peacefully, with a smile on his good-humored, freckled face; the virgin Piney slept beside her frailer sisters as sweetly as though attended by celestial guardians; and Mr. Oakhurst, drawing his blanket over his shoulders, stroked his mustaches and waited for the dawn. It came slowly in a whirling mist of snowflakes that dazzled and confused the eye. What could be seen of the landscape appeared magically changed. He looked over the valley, and summed up the present and future in two words, "Snowed in!"

A careful inventory of the provisions, which, fortunately for the party, had been stored within the hut, and so escaped the felonious fingers of Uncle Billy, disclosed the fact that with care and prudence they might last ten days longer. "That is," said Mr. Oakhurt *sotto voce* [3] to the Innocent, "if you're willing to board us. If you ain't—and perhaps you'd better not—you can wait till Uncle Billy gets back with provisions." For some occult reason, Mr. Oakhurst could not bring himself to disclose Uncle Billy's rascality, and so offered the hypothesis that he had wandered from the camp and had accidentally stampeded the animals. He dropped a warning to the Duchess and Mother Shipton, who of course knew the facts of their associate's defection. "They'll find out the truth about us *all* when they find out anything," he added significantly, "and there's no good frightening them now."

Tom Simson not only put all his worldly store at the disposal of Mr. Oakhurst, but seemed to enjoy the prospect of their enforced seclusion. "We'll have a good camp for a week, and then the snow'll melt, and we'll all go back together." The cheerful gayety of the young man and Mr. Oakhurst's calm infected the others. The Innocent, with the aid of pine boughs, extemporized a thatch for the roofless cabin, and the Duchess directed Piney in the rearrangement of the interior with a taste and tact that opened the blue eyes of that provincial maiden to their fullest extent. "I reckon now you're used to fine things at Poker Flat," said Piney. The Duchess turned away sharply to conceal something that reddened her cheeks through their professional tint, and Mother Shipton requested Piney not to "chatter." But when Mr. Oakhurst returned from a weary search for the trail, he heard the sound of happy laughter echoed from the rocks. He stopped in some alarm, and his thoughts first naturally reverted to the whiskey, which he had prudently cachéd. "And yet it don't somehow sound like whiskey," said the gambler. It was not until he caught sight of the blazing fire through the still blinding storm, and the group around it, that he settled to the conviction that it was "square fun."

Whether Mr. Oakhurst had cachéd his cards with the whiskey as something debarred the free access of the community, I cannot say. It was certain that, in Mother Shipton's words, he "didn't say 'cards' once" during that evening. Haply the time was beguiled by an accordion, produced somewhat ostentatiously by Tom Simson from his pack. Notwithstanding some difficulties attending the manipulation of this instrument, Piney Woods managed to pluck several reluctant melodies from its keys, to an accompaniment by the Innocent on a pair of bone castanets. But the crowning festivity of the evening was reached in a rude camp-meeting hymn, which

3. In a low tone.

the lovers, joining hands, sang with great earnestness and vocifera-
tion. I fear that a certain defiant tone and Covenanter's [4] swing
to its chorus, rather than any devotional quality, caused it speedily
to infect the others, who at last joined in the refrain:

> "I'm proud to live in the service of the Lord,
> And I'm bound to die in His army." [5]

The pines rocked, the storm eddied and whirled above the miserable group, and the flames of their altar leaped heavenward, as if
in token of the vow.

At midnight the storm abated, the rolling clouds parted, and the
stars glittered keenly above the sleeping camp. Mr. Oakhurst,
whose professional habits had enabled him to live on the smallest
possible amount of sleep, in dividing the watch with Tom Simson
somehow managed to take upon himself the greater part of that
duty. He excused himself to the Innocent by saying that he had
"often been a week without sleep." "Doing what?" asked Tom.
"Poker!" replied Oakhurst sententiously. "When a man gets a
streak of luck,—nigger-luck [6]—he don't get tired. The luck gives in
first. Luck," continued the gambler reflectively, "is a mighty queer
thing. All you know about it for certain is that it's bound to change.
And it's finding out when it's going to change that makes you.
We've had a streak of bad luck since we left Poker Flat,—you come
along, and slap you get into it, too. If you can hold your cards right
along you're all right. For," added the gambler, with cheerful ir-
relevance—

> " 'I'm proud to live in the service of the Lord,
> And I'm bound to die in His army.' "

The third day came, and the sun, looking through the white-
curtained valley, saw the outcasts divide their slowly decreasing
store of provisions for the morning meal. It was one of the peculiarities of that mountain climate that its rays diffused a kindly
warmth over the wintry landscape, as if in regretful commiseration
of the past. But it revealed drift on drift of snow piled high
around the hut,—a hopeless, uncharted, trackless sea of white
lying below the rocky shores to which the castaways still clung.
Through the marvelously clear air the smoke of the pastoral village
of Poker Flat rose miles away. Mother Shipton saw it, and from a
remote pinnacle of her rocky fastness hurled in that direction a
final malediction. It was her last vituperative attempt, and perhaps

4. *I.e.,* the martial beat of the songs of
the Scottish Covenanters, who militantly
supported their claim for separation
from the Church of England in the
seventeenth century.
5. Refrain of an early American spiritual, "Service of the Lord."
6. Unexpected good luck.

for that reason was invested with a certain degree of sublimity. It did her good, she privately informed the Duchess. "Just you go out there and cuss, and see." She then set herself to the task of amusing "the child," as she and the Duchess were pleased to call Piney. Piney was no chicken, but it was a soothing and original theory of the pair thus to account for the fact that she didn't swear and wasn't improper.

When night crept up again through the gorges, the reedy notes of the accordion rose and fell in fitful spasms and long-drawn gasps by the flickering campfire. But music failed to fill entirely the aching void left by insufficient food, and a new diversion was proposed by Piney—story-telling. Neither Mr. Oakhurst nor his female companions caring to relate their personal experiences, this plan would have failed too, but for the Innocent. Some months before he had chanced upon a stray copy of Mr. Pope's ingenious translation of the Iliad. He now proposed to narrate the principal incidents of that poem—having thoroughly mastered the argument and fairly forgotten the words—in the current vernacular of Sandy Bar. And so for the rest of that night the Homeric demigods again walked the earth. Trojan bully and wily Greek wrestled in the winds, and the great pines in the cañon seemed to bow to the wrath of the son of Peleus.[7] Mr. Oakhurst listened with quiet satisfaction. Most especially was he interested in the fate of "Ashheels,"[8] as the Innocent persisted in denominating the "swift-footed Achilles."

So, with small food and much of Homer and the accordion, a week passed over the heads of the outcasts. The sun again forsook them, and again from leaden skies the snowflakes were sifted over the land. Day by day closer around them drew the snowy circle, until at last they looked from their prison over drifted walls of dazzling white, that towered twenty feet above their heads. It became more and more difficult to replenish their fires, even from the fallen trees beside them, now half hidden in the drifts. And yet no one complained. The lovers turned from the dreary prospect and looked into each other's eyes and were happy. Mr. Oakhurst settled himself coolly to the losing game before him. The Duchess, more cheerful than she had been, assumed the care of Piney. Only Mother Shipton—once the strongest of the party— seemed to sicken and fade. At midnight on the tenth day she called Oakhurst to her side. "I'm going," she said, in a voice of querulous weakness, "but don't say anything about it. Don't waken the kids. Take the bundle from under my head, and open it." Mr. Oakhurst did so. It contained Mother Shipton's rations for the last week, untouched. "Give 'em to the child," she said, pointing

7. Achilles.
8. The mispronunciation is reinforced by the fact that Achilles could be wounded only in the heel.

to the sleeping Piney. "You've starved yourself," said the gambler. "That's what they call it," said the woman querulously, as she lay down again, and, turning her face to the wall, passed quietly away.

The accordion and the bones were put aside that day, and Homer was forgotten. When the body of Mother Shipton had been committed to the snow, Mr. Oakhurst took the Innocent aside, and showed him a pair of snowshoes, which he had fashioned from the old pack-saddle. "There's one chance in a hundred to save her yet," he said, pointing to Piney; "but it's there," he added, pointing toward Poker Flat. "If you can reach there in two days she's safe." "And you?" asked Tom Simson. "I'll stay here," was the curt reply.

The lovers parted with a long embrace. "You are not going, too?" said the Duchess, as she saw Mr. Oakhurst apparently waiting to accompany him. "As far as the cañon," he replied. He turned suddenly and kissed the Duchess, leaving her pallid face aflame, and her trembling limbs rigid with amazement.

Night came, but not Mr. Oakhurst. It brought the storm again and the whirling snow. Then the Duchess, feeding the fire, found that some one had quietly piled beside the hut enough fuel to last a few days longer. The tears rose to her eyes, but she hid them from Piney.

The women slept but little. In the morning, looking into each other's faces, they read their fate. Neither spoke, but Piney, accepting the position of the stronger, drew near and placed her arm around the Duchess's waist. They kept this attitude for the rest of the day. That night the storm reached its greatest fury, and, rending asunder the protecting pines, invaded the very hut.

Toward morning they found themselves unable to feed the fire, which gradually died away. As the embers slowly blackened, the Duchess crept closer to Piney, and broke the silence of many hours: "Piney, can you pray?" "No, dear," said Piney simply. The Duchess, without knowing exactly why, felt relieved, and putting her head upon Piney's shoulder, spoke no more. And so reclining, the younger and purer pillowing the head of her soiled sister upon her virgin breast, they fell asleep.

The wind lulled as if it feared to waken them. Feathery drifts of snow, shaken from the long pine boughs, flew like white-winged birds, and settled about them as they slept. The moon through the rifted clouds looked down upon what had been the camp. But all human stain, all trace of earthly travail, was hidden beneath the spotless mantle mercifully flung from above.

They slept all that day and the next, nor did they wake when voices and footsteps broke the silence of the camp. And when pitying fingers brushed the snow from their wan faces, you could scarcely have told, from the equal peace that dwelt upon them, which was she that had sinned. Even the law of Poker Flat recognized this, and turned away, leaving them still locked in each other's arms.

But at the head of the gulch, on one of the largest pinetrees, they found the deuce of clubs pinned to the bark with a bowie-knife. It bore the following, written in pencil in a firm hand:

†

BENEATH THIS TREE

LIES THE BODY

OF

JOHN OAKHURST,

WHO STRUCK A STREAK OF BAD LUCK

ON THE 23D OF NOVEMBER, 1850,

AND

HANDED IN HIS CHECKS

ON THE 7TH DECEMBER, 1850

†

And pulseless and cold, with a Derringer [9] by his side and a bullet in his heart, though still calm as in life, beneath the snow lay he who was at once the strongest and yet the weakest of the outcasts of Poker Flat.

1869, 1870

9. A small pistol of large caliber.

Masters of Critical Realism

WILLIAM DEAN HOWELLS

(1837–1920)

At the height of his career, about 1890, Howells was firmly established in serious literary opinion as the foremost man of letters of his generation in America. Today both Mark Twain and Henry James are considered greater authors than Howells. Yet his best writing is marked by truth and power; he is large both in the scope of his themes and in the volume and quality of his output. Perhaps ten of his novels have held their appeal, and four—*A Modern Instance, The Rise of Silas Lapham, Indian Summer,* and *A Hazard of New Fortunes*—are familiar classics of American fiction. He revitalized the realism of the day and opposed the prevalent sentimentality and idealization. As a critic he enthusiastically supported such younger radicals as Hamlin Garland and Stephen Crane, Frank Norris and the "questionable" dramatic realist, James A. Herne. He helped to establish the literary respectability in the East of that wild son of Missouri, Mark Twain. His criticism exerted a strong influence on his age. In his plays as in his fiction he advanced the comic criticism of society, and

broadened it to include the international contrast of manners. He wrote a number of notable books of travel, and his autobiographical sketches are distinguished.

From boyhood William Dean Howells smelled of printer's ink and manifested the instincts of the journalist. He was born on March 1, 1837, at Martin's Ferry, Ohio. His father, a country printer and newspaper publisher of roving disposition and literary inclinations, moved when the boy was three to Hamilton, twenty miles from Cincinnati, where he edited the Whig paper. There, by the age of nine, young Howells was setting type in his father's shop and listening to his Swedenborgian mysticism and literary idealism. His formal schooling was negligible, but he read unceasingly, and his natural gifts were such that at twenty-nine he became the assistant editor of the *Atlantic Monthly;* in his forties he was offered, and declined, professorships at Johns Hopkins and Harvard. In *A Boy's Town* (1890), Howells recorded his early adventures. When the boy was twelve his father bought an ill-fated newspaper at Dayton; the next year they moved to the Little Miami River, where they experienced the primitive life described in *My Year in a Log Cabin* (1893). After several moves with the family paper, Howells struck out at nineteen as a newspaperman in Cincinnati and in Columbus, where he became editor of the *Ohio State Journal*; meanwhile his mammoth appetite for books led him deep into the literature reflected in *My Literary Passions* (1895). With a fellow journalist, John J. Piatt, he composed *Poems of Two Friends* (1860); the same year his biography of the Republican presidential candidate, Lincoln, provided him with funds for his long-awaited literary pilgrimage to the East, where he met Lowell, Holmes, Emerson, Hawthorne, and Whitman, as recounted in *Literary Friends and Acquaintance* (1900).

The Lincoln biography also won the young journalist an appointment as consul to Venice (1861–1865), and provided four years of relative leisure. He gathered material for such early travel books as *Venetian Life* (1866) and *Italian Journeys* (1867), and for the Italian scenes of three of his minor novels. In 1865 he returned to Boston to join the editorial staff of the *Nation*. Within the year he was assistant editor of the *Atlantic Monthly*, whose first editor, James Russell Lowell, had nine years earlier launched it with the distinction that Howells later maintained as editor, between 1871 and 1881. During this busy decade Howells published six novels; his seventh,

A Modern Instance (1882), although it is imperfect in construction, represents the first perfection of his characteristic quality. In portraying the disintegration of Bartley Hubbard's career and marriage, Howells for the first time fully demonstrated a realism that was primarily concerned, not with praise or blame, but with observing in human destinies the natural consequences of character.

Leaving the *Atlantic*, Howells spent four years abroad (1881–1885) in travel and study, and in 1885 published his best-known work, *The Rise of Silas Lapham*. In this novel of Boston life Howells contrasts the Corys of Beacon Hill with the Laphams, whose enterprising development of a paint factory on their Vermont farm has led to the founding of a Boston industry and a new fortune. Silas Lapham, who comes to terms with himself at the cost of his fortune, is a character not soon forgotten.

After 1886 Howells was closely associated with *Harper's Magazine*. In his column, "The Editor's Study," appeared much of his criticism of fiction, collected in 1891 as *Criticism and Fiction*. After 1900 he was the familiar essayist of "The Easy Chair," in which his *obiter dicta* became widely familiar. During this New York period he was captivated by Tolstoi, whose Christian socialism motivated several of his novels, of which *A Hazard of New Fortunes* (1890) and *A Traveler from Altruria* (1894), a utopian novel, are the best known. Among his novels of manners of this period, his masterpiece is *Indian Summer* (1886), a story of the second blooming of love in middle life. Charming, witty, and mature, it represents his best use of the Italian scene as well as his closest approach to the style and content of his friend Henry James.

The close student of the period may take issue with Howells's contention that "the smiling aspects" of American life were the most prevalent and the most typical, and that American life was such that the novelist could confine himself to what would not offend the innocence of a young girl, and should therefore do so. But Howells perceptively explored the areas to which he limited himself, and within those limits his characters and their dialogue frequently attain a high degree of subtlety. In the psychological study of character and in his fascination with the dark or profound recesses of the human consciousness he acknowledged the inspiration of Hawthorne. The results in his writing, however, are independent of Hawthorne in both method and motivation. The best of his fiction stems from his analysis of character in social situations, from his abiding sense of the responsibility that people have for each other, and from his deft and witty revelation of the motives of men and women. Yet this high ability was increasingly diluted by his fictional propaganda for social and economic improvement. In addition he wrote too much, and sometimes for an immediate public—more

than thirty novels or novelettes, several volumes of short stories, and thirty-one dramas (chiefly one-act social comedies), as well as the sketches and travels. The best of his fiction, that dealing with character, like much of his autobiographical writing, continues to appeal with the freshness and power that belong to a master of literature.

The writings of Howells have not been collected, but editions of his more famous works are still in print. Henry Steele Commager edited *Selected Writings of William Dean Howells*, 1950, containing *The Rise of Silas Lapham, A Modern Instance, A Boy's Town*, and *My Mark Twain*. W. J. Meserve edited *Complete Plays of W. D. Howells*, 1960. A CEAA *Selected Edition of W. D. Howells*, 41 vols., is in process at Indiana University Press. O. W. Firkins wrote a critical biography, *William Dean Howells*, 1924. Mildred Howells edited *Life in Letters of William Dean Howells*, 2 vols., 1928. An indispensable study is the introduction by Clara and Rudolph Kirk to *William Dean Howells: Representative Selections*, American Writers Series, 1950. A large-scale critical study is Everett Carter, *Howells and the Age of Realism*, 1954. Edwin H. Cady, *The Road to Realism*, 1956, and *The Realist at War*, 1958, comprise studies of 1837–1885 and 1885–1920. Recent evaluations are Olov W. Fryckstedt, *In Quest of America: A Study of Howells' Early Development as a Novelist*, 1958; Van Wyck Brooks, *Howells: His Life and Work*, 1959; R. L. Hough, *Quiet Rebel*, 1959; George N. Bennett, *William Dean Howells: The Development of a Novelist*, 1959, and *The Realism of William Dean Howells, 1889–1920*, 1973; Clara M. Kirk, *W. D. Howells and Art in His Time*, 1965; George Carrington, *The Immense Complex Drama*, 1966; Kermit Vanderbilt, *The Achievement of William Dean Howells*, 1968; Edward Wagenknecht, *William Dean Howells: The Friendly Eye*, 1969; and Kenneth Lynn, *William Dean Howells: An American Life*, 1971. Howells' autobiographical reminiscences will be found in *A Boy's Town*, 1890; *My Year in a Log Cabin*, 1893; *My Literary Passions*, 1895; *Impressions and Experiences*, 1896; *Literary Friends and Acquaintance*, 1900; and *Years of My Youth*, 1916.

From Criticism and Fiction [1]

Chapter II

* * * Mr. Burke's Essay on the Sublime and the Beautiful [is] a singularly modern book, considering how long ago it was wrote (as the great Mr. Steele [2] would have written the participle a little longer ago), and full of a certain well-mannered and agreeable instruction. * * * "As for those called critics," the author says, "they have generally sought the rule of the arts in the wrong place; they have sought among poems, pictures, engravings, statues, and buildings; but art can never give the rules that make an art. This is, I believe, the reason why artists in general, and poets principally, have been confined in so narrow a circle; they have been rather imitators of one another than of nature. Critics follow them, and therefore can do little as guides. I can judge but poorly of anything while I measure it by no other standard than itself. The true standard of the arts is in every man's power; and an easy observation of the most common, sometimes of the meanest things, in nature will give the truest lights, where the greatest sagacity and industry that slights such observation must leave us in the dark, or, what is worse, amuse and mislead us by false lights."

* * * The time is coming, I hope, when each new author, each new artist, will be considered, not in his proportion to any other author or artist, but in his relation to the human nature, known to us all, which it is his privilege, his high duty, to interpret. "The true standard of the artist is in every man's power" already, as Burke says; Michelangelo's "light of the piazza," the glance of the common eye, is and always was the best light on a statue; Goethe's "boys and blackbirds" have in all ages been the real connoisseurs of berries; but hitherto the mass of common men have been afraid to apply their own simplicity, naturalness, and honesty to the appreciation of the beautiful. They have always cast about for the instruction of some one who professed to know better, and who brow-

---

1. *Criticism and Fiction* (1891) was the author's formulation, in one volume, of essays that first appeared from 1886 to 1891 in his influential column "The Editor's Study," a regular feature of *Harper's Magazine*. The locations in the volume are shown by the chapter numbers. These selections represent Howells's definition of the new realism that he practiced, "classic" in the sense that its object was a balanced interpretation of the common life of man in the United States; with this he contrasts the emergent naturalism, flourishing particularly in France and Russia, in which he detected a preference, or indeed a necessity, for specialized situations and characters pessimistically predetermined. Among the qualities that made these essays memorable, besides their literary merits, is Howells's concept that the reality of fiction bears a direct relationship to its cultural environment; secondly, that cultural change in the United States has since caused both the classic and the naturalistic fiction to survive.

2. Sir Richard Steele, dramatist, creative stylist of the 18th century periodicals, *The Tatler* and *The Spectator*, died in 1729, the year of the birth of Edmund Burke, the Irish statesman.

beat wholesome common-sense into the self-distrust that ends in sophistication. They have fallen generally to the worst of this bad species, and have been "amused and misled" (how pretty that quaint old use of amuse is!) "by the false lights" of critical vanity and self-righteousness. They have been taught to compare what they see and what they read, not with the things that they have observed and known, but with the things that some other artist or writer has done. Especially if they have themselves the artistic impulse in any direction they are taught to form themselves, not upon life, but upon the masters who became masters only by forming themselves upon life. The seeds of death are planted in them, and they can produce only the still-born, the academic. They are not told to take their work into the public square and see if it seems true to the chance passer, but to test it by the work of the very men who refused and decried any other test of their own work. The young writer who attempts to report the phrase and carriage of every-day life, who tries to tell just how he has heard men talk and seen them look, is made to feel guilty of something low and unworthy by the stupid people who would like to have him show how Shakespeare's men talked and looked, or Scott's, or Thackeray's, or Balzac's, or Hawthorne's, or Dickens's; he is instructed to idealize his personages, that is, to take the life-likeness out of them, and put the book-likeness into them. He is approached in the spirit of the wretched pedantry into which learning, much or little, always decays when it withdraws itself and stands apart from experience in an attitude of imagined superiority, and which would say with the same confidence to the scientist: "I see that you are looking at a grasshopper there which you have found in the grass, and I suppose you intend to describe it. Now don't waste your time and sin against culture in that way. I've got a grasshopper here, which has been evolved at considerable pains and expense out of the grasshopper in general; in fact, it's a type. It's made up of wire and card-board, very prettily painted in a conventional tint, and it's perfectly indestructible. It isn't very much like a real grasshopper, but it's a great deal nicer, and it's served to represent the notion of a grasshopper ever since man emerged from barbarism. You may say that it's artificial. Well, it is artificial; but then it's ideal too; and what you want to do is to cultivate the ideal. You'll find the books full of my kind of grasshopper, and scarcely a trace of yours in any of them. The thing that you are proposing to do is commonplace; but if you say that it isn't commonplace, for the very reason that it hasn't been done before, you'll have to admit that it's photographic."

As I said, I hope the time is coming when not only the artist, but the common, average man, who always "has the standard of

grasshopper! / metaphor / of the / ideal

the arts in his power," will have also the courage to apply it, and will reject the ideal grasshopper wherever he finds it, in science, in literature, in art, because it is not "simple, natural, and honest," because it is not like a real grasshopper. But I will own that I think the time is yet far off, and that the people who have been brought up on the ideal grasshopper, the heroic grasshopper, the impassioned grasshopper, the self-devoted, adventureful, good old romantic cardboard grasshopper, must die out before the simple, honest, and natural grasshopper can have a fair field. I am in no haste to compass the end of these good people, whom I find in the meantime very amusing. It is delightful to meet one of them, either in print or out of it—some sweet elderly lady or excellent gentleman whose youth was pastured on the literature of thirty or forty years ago—and to witness the confidence with which they preach their favorite authors as all the law and the prophets. They have commonly read little or nothing since or, if they have, they have judged it by a standard taken from these authors, and never dreamed of judging it by nature; they are destitute of the documents in the case of the later writers; they suppose that Balzac was the beginning of realism, and that Zola is its wicked end; they are quite ignorant, but they are ready to talk you down, if you differ from them, with an assumption of knowledge sufficient for any occasion. The horror, the resentment, with which they receive any question of their literary saints is genuine; you descend at once very far in the moral and social scale, and anything short of offensive personality is too good for you; it is expressed to you that you are one to be avoided, and put down even a little lower than you have naturally fallen.

* * *

Those good people, those curious and interesting if somewhat musty back-numbers, must always have a hero, an idol of some sort, and it is droll to find Balzac, who suffered from their sort such bitter scorn and hate for his realism while he was alive, now become a fetich in his turn, to be shaken in the faces of those who will not blindly worship him. But it is no new thing in the history of literature: whatever is established is sacred with those who do not think. At the beginning of the century, when romance was making the same fight against effete classicism which realism is making today against effete romanticism, the Italian poet Monti [3] declared that "the romantic was the cold grave of the Beautiful," just as the realistic is now supposed to be. The romantic of that day and the real of this are in certain degree the same. Romanticism

---

3. Vincenzo Monti (1754–1828), neoclassical poet.

then sought, as realism seeks now, to widen the bounds of sympathy, to level every barrier against aesthetic freedom, to escape from the paralysis of tradition. It exhausted itself in this impulse; and it remained for realism to assert that fidelity to experience and probability of motive are essential conditions of a great imaginative literature. It is not a new theory, but it has never before universally characterized literary endeavor. When realism becomes false to itself, when it heaps up facts merely, and maps life instead of picturing it, realism will perish too. Every true realist instinctively knows this, and it is perhaps the reason why he is careful of every fact, and feels himself bound to express or to indicate its meaning at the risk of over-moralizing. In life he finds nothing insignificant; all tells for destiny and character; nothing that God has made is contemptible. He cannot look upon human life and declare this thing or that thing unworthy of notice, any more than the scientist can declare a fact of the material world beneath the dignity of his inquiry. He feels in every nerve the equality of things and the unity of men; his soul is exalted, not by vain shows and shadows and ideals, but by realities, in which alone the truth lives. * * *

Chapter XIII

In fine, I would beseech the literary critics of our country to disabuse themselves of the mischievous notion that they are essential to the progress of literature in the way critics have vainly imagined. Canon Farrar [4] confesses that with the best will in the world to profit by the many criticisms of his books, he has never profited in the least by any of them; and this is almost the universal experience of authors. It is not always the fault of the critics. They sometimes deal honestly and fairly by a book, and not so often they deal adequately. But in making a book, if it is at all a good book, the author has learned all that is knowable about it, and every strong point and every weak point in it, far more accurately than any one else can possibly learn them. He has learned to do better than well for the future; but if his book is bad, he cannot be taught anything about it from the outside. It will perish; and if he has not the root of literature in him, he will perish as an author with it.

But what is it that gives tendency in art, then? What is it makes people like this at one time, and that at another? Above all, what makes a better fashion change for a worse; how can the ugly come to be preferred to the beautiful; in other words, how can an art decay?

4. Frederick W. Farrar (1831–1903), British clergyman and writer.

This question came up in my mind lately with regard to English fiction and its form, or rather its formlessness. How, for instance, could people who had once known the simple verity, the refined perfection of Miss Austen,[5] enjoy anything less refined and less perfect?

With her example before them, why should not English novelists have gone on writing simply, honestly, artistically, ever after? One would think it must have been impossible for them to do otherwise, if one did not remember, say, the lamentable behavior of the actors who support Mr. Jefferson, and their theatricality in the very presence of his beautiful naturalness. It is very difficult, that simplicity, and nothing is so hard as to be honest, as the reader, if he has ever happened to try it, must know. "The big bow-wow I can do myself, like any one going," said Scott, but he owned that the exquisite touch of Miss Austen was denied him; and it seems certainly to have been denied in greater or less measure to all her successors. But though reading and writing come by nature, as Dogberry [6] justly said, taste in them may be cultivated, or once cultivated, it may be preserved; and why was it not so among those poor islanders? * * *

Señor Valdés [7] is a realist, but a realist according to his own conception of realism; and he has some words of just censure for the French naturalists, whom he finds unnecessarily, and suspects of being sometimes even mercenarily, nasty. He sees the wide difference that passes between this naturalism and the realism of the English and Spanish; and he goes somewhat further than I should go in condemning it. "The French naturalism represents only a moment, and an insignificant part of life . . . It is characterized by sadness and narrowness. The prototype of this literature is the Madame Bovary of Flaubert. I am an admirer of this novelist, and especially of this novel; but often in thinking of it I have said, How dreary would literature be if it were no more than this! There is something antipathetic and gloomy and limited in it, as there is in modern French life;" but this seems to me exactly the best possible reason for its being. I believe with Señor Valdés that "no literature can live long without joy," not because of its mistaken aesthetics, however, but because no civilization can live long without joy. The expression of French life will change when French life changes; and French naturalism is better at its worst than French unnaturalism at its best. * * *

5. Jane Austen (1775–1817), British novelist.
6. Dogberry, a smug constable and misuser of words in Shakespeare's *Much Ado about Nothing.*
7. Armando Palacio Valdés (1853–

1938), Spanish critic and realistic novelist. His introduction to the English translation of his novel *Sister St. Sulpice* (1889) is the source of Howells's quotations. The novel was very popular in the United States.

Chapter XXI [8]

It is the difference of the American novelist's ideals from those of the English novelist that gives him his advantage, and seems to promise him the future. The love of the passionate and the heroic, as the Englishman has it, is such a crude and unwholesome thing, so deaf and blind to all the most delicate and important facts of art and life, so insensible to the subtle values in either that its presence or absence makes the whole difference, and enables one who is not obsessed by it to thank Heaven that he is not as that other man is.

There can be little question that many refinements of thought and spirit which every American is sensible of in the fiction of this continent, are necessarily lost upon our good kin beyond seas, whose thumb-fingered apprehension requires something gross and palpable for its assurance of reality. This is not their fault, and I am not sure that it is wholly their misfortune; they are made so as not to miss what they do not find, and they are simply content without those subtleties of life and character which it gives us so keen a pleasure to have noted in literature. If they perceive them at all it is as something vague and diaphanous, something that filmily wavers before their sense and teases them, much as the beings of an invisible world might mock one of our material frame by intimations of their presence. It is with reason, therefore, on the part of an Englishman, that Mr. Henley [9] complains of our fiction as a shadow-land, though we find more and more in it the faithful report of our life, its motives and emotions, and all the comparatively etherealized passions and ideals that influence it.

In fact, the American who chooses to enjoy his birthright to the full, lives in a world wholly different from the Englishman's, and speaks (too often through his nose) another language: he breathes a rarefied and nimble air full of shining possibilities and radiant promises which the fog-and-soot-clogged lungs of those less-favored islanders struggle in vain to fill themselves with. But he ought to be modest in his advantage, and patient with the coughing and sputtering of his cousin who complains of finding himself in an exhausted receiver on plunging into one of our novels. To be quite just to the poor fellow, I have had some such experience as that myself in the atmosphere of some of our more attenuated romances.

Yet every now and then I read a book with perfect comfort and much exhilaration, whose scenes the average Englishman would

8. This selection was first printed in *Harper's* in slightly different form, the final part appearing in September, 1886, and the first in October, 1890. It was incorporated into Chapter XXI of *Criticism and Fiction* (1891), which the present text follows.
9. William Ernest Henley (1849–1903), English poet, critic, and editor.

gasp in. Nothing happens; that is, nobody murders or debauches anybody else; there is no arson or pillage of any sort; there is not a ghost, or a ravening beast, or a hair-breadth escape, or a shipwreck, or a monster of self-sacrifice, or a lady five thousand years old in the whole course of the story; "no promenade, no band of music, nossing!" as Mr. Du Maurier's [1] Frenchman said of the meet for a fox-hunt. Yet it is all alive with the keenest interest for those who enjoy the study of individual traits and general conditions as they make themselves known to American experience.

These conditions have been so favorable hitherto (though they are becoming always less so) that they easily account for the optimistic faith of our novel which Mr. Hughes [2] notices. It used to be one of the disadvantages of the practice of romance in America, which Hawthorne more or less whimsically lamented, that there were so few shadows and inequalities in our broad level of prosperity; and it is one of the reflections suggested by Dostoïevsky's [3] novel, The Crime and the Punishment, that whoever struck a note so profoundly tragic in American fiction would do a false and mistaken thing—as false and as mistaken in its way as dealing in American fiction with certain nudities which the Latin peoples seem to find edifying. Whatever their deserts, very few American novelists have been led out to be shot, or finally exiled to the rigors of a winter at Duluth; [4] and in a land where journeymen carpenters and plumbers strike for four dollars a day the sum of hunger and cold is comparatively small, and the wrong from class to class has been almost inappreciable, though all this is changing for the worse. Our novelists, therefore, concern themselves with the more smiling aspects of life, which are the more American, and seek the universal in the individual rather than the social interests. It is worth while, even at the risk of being called commonplace, to be true to our well-to-do actualities; the very passions themselves seem to be softened and modified by conditions which formerly at least could not be said to wrong any one, to cramp endeavor, or to cross lawful desire. Sin and suffering and shame there must always be in the world, I suppose, but I believe that in this new world of ours it is still mainly from one to another one, and oftener still from one to one's self. We have death too in America, and a great deal of disagreeable and painful disease, which the multiplicity of our patent medicines does not seem to cure; but this is

1. George du Maurier (1834–1896), English author born in Paris, best known as the author of the popular novel *Trilby* (1894).
2. An English journalist, E. Hughes, who had commented on the differences between English and American novels.
3. Fëdor Dostoevski (1821–1881), great Russian novelist whose work Howells helped introduce to American readers.
4. Dostoevski himself was exiled to the Siberian mines.

tragedy that comes in the very nature of things, and is not peculiarly American, as the large, cheerful average of health and success and happy life is. It will not do to boast, but it is well to be true to the facts, and to see that, apart from these purely mortal troubles, the race here has enjoyed conditions in which most of the ills that have darkened its annals might be averted by honest work and unselfish behavior.

Chapter XXIV

One of the great newspapers the other day invited the prominent American authors to speak their minds upon a point in the theory and practice of fiction which had already vexed some of them. It was the question of how much or how little the American novel ought to deal with certain facts of life which are not usually talked of before young people, and especially young ladies. Of course the question was not decided, and I forget just how far the balance inclined to favor of a larger freedom in the matter. But it certainly inclined that way; one or two writers of the sex which is somehow supposed to have purity in its keeping (as if purity were a thing that did not practically concern the other sex, preoccupied with serious affairs) gave it a rather vigorous tilt to that side. In view of this fact it would not be the part of prudence to make an effort to dress the balance; and indeed I do not know that I was going to make any such effort. But there are some things to say, around and about the subject, which I should like to have some one else say, and which I may myself possibly be safe in suggesting.

One of the first of these is the fact, generally lost sight of by those who censure the Anglo-Saxon novel for its prudishness, that it is really not such a prude after all; and that if it is sometimes apparently anxious to avoid those experiences of life not spoken of before young people, this may be an appearance only. Sometimes a novel which has this shuffling air, this effect of truckling to propriety, might defend itself, if it could speak for itself, by saying that such experiences happened not to come within its scheme, and that, so far from maiming or mutilating itself in ignoring them, it was all the more faithfully representative of the tone of modern life in dealing with love that was chaste, and with passion so honest that it could be openly spoken of before the tenderest society bud at dinner. It might say that the guilty intrigue, the betrayal, the extreme flirtation even, was the exceptional thing in life, and unless the scheme of the story necessarily involved it, that it would be bad art to lug it in, and as bad taste as to introduce such topics in a mixed company. It could say very justly that the novel in our civilization now always addresses a mixed company, and that the vast majority of the company are ladies, and that very many, if not most, of these ladies are young girls. If the novel were written for men and for married women alone, as in continental Europe, it might be altogether different. But the simple fact is that it is not written for them alone among us, and it is a question of writing, under cover of our universal acceptance, things for young girls to read which you would be put out-of-doors for saying to them; or of frankly giving notice of your intention, and so cutting yourself off from the pleasure—and it is a very high and sweet one—of appealing to these vivid, responsive intelligences, which are none the less brilliant and admirable because they are innocent.

One day a novelist who liked, after the manner of other men, to repine at his hard fate, complained to his friend, a critic, that he was tired of the restriction he had put upon himself in this regard; for it is a mistake, as can be readily shown, to suppose that others impose it. "See how free those French fellows are!" he rebelled. "Shall we always be shut up to our tradition of decency?"

"Do you think it's much worse than being shut up to their tradition of indecency?" said his friend.

Then that novelist began to reflect, and he remembered how sick the invariable motive of the French novel made him. He perceived finally that, convention for convention, ours was not only more tolerable, but on the whole was truer to life, not only to its complexion, but also to its texture. No one will pretend that there is not vicious love beneath the surface of our society; if he did, the fetid explosions of the divorce trials would refute him; but if he pretended that it was in any just sense characteristic of our society, he could be still more easily refuted. Yet it exists, and it is unquestionably the material of tragedy, the stuff from which intense effects are wrought. The question, after owning this fact, is whether these intense effects are not rather cheap effects. I incline to think they are, and I will try to say why I think so, if I may do so without offence. The material itself, the mere mention of it, has an instant fascination; it arrests, it detains, till the last word is said, and while there is anything to be hinted. This is what makes a love intrigue of some sort all but essential to the popularity of any fiction. Without such an intrigue the intellectual equipment of the author must be of the highest, and then he will succeed only with the highest class of readers. But any author who will deal with a guilty love intrigue holds all readers in his hand, the highest with the lowest, as long as he hints the slightest hope of the smallest potential naughtiness. He need not at all be a great author; he may be a very shabby wretch, if he has but the courage or the trick of that sort of thing. The critics will call him "virile" and "passionate;" decent people will be ashamed to have been limed by him; but the low average will only ask another chance of flocking into his net. If he happens to be an able writer, his really fine and costly work will be unheeded, and the lure to the appetite will be chiefly remembered. There may be other qualities which make reputations for other men, but in his case they will count for nothing. He pays this penalty for his success in that kind; and every one pays some such penalty who deals with some such material. It attaches in like manner to the triumphs of the writers who now almost form a school among us, and who may be said to have established themselves in an easy popularity simply by the study of erotic shivers and fervors. They may find their account in the popularity, or they may not; there is no question of the popularity.

But I do not mean to imply that his case covers the whole ground. So far as it goes, though, it ought to stop the mouths of those who complain that fiction is enslaved to propriety among us. It appears that of a certain kind of impropriety it is free to give us all it will, and more. But this is not what serious men and women writing fiction mean when they rebel against the limitations of their art in our civilization. They have no desire to deal with nakedness, as painters and sculptors freely do in the worship of beauty; or with certain facts of life, as the stage does, in the service of sensation. But they ask why, when the conventions of the plastic and histrionic arts liberate their followers to the portrayal of almost any phase of the physical or of the emotional nature, an American novelist may not write a story on the lines of Anna Karenina or Madame Bovary. Sappho [5] they put aside, and from Zola's work they avert their eyes. They do not condemn him or Daudet, necessarily, or accuse their motives; they leave them out of the question; they do not want to do that kind of thing. But they do sometimes wish to do another kind, to touch one of the most serious and sorrowful problems of life in the spirit of Tolstoï and Flaubert, and then ask why they may not. At one time, they remind us, the Anglo-Saxon novelist did deal with such problems —De Foe in his spirit, Richardson in his, Goldsmith in his.[6] At what moment did our fiction lose this privilege? In what fatal hour did the Young Girl arise and seal the lips of Fiction, with a touch of her finger, to some of the most vital interests of life?

Whether I wished to oppose them in their aspirations for

---

5. Flaubert's *Madame Bovary* details the sordid plight of a weak woman lost in desolate love affairs; Tolstoi's *Anna Karenina* traces the tragedy of an illicit love which leads to death. Daudet's *Sappho* deals with a prostitute.
6. Daniel Defoe (1660–1731) treated illicit passion in *Moll Flanders* and *Roxana;* Samuel Richardson (1689–1761) wrote *Clarissa Harlowe,* in which the heroine dies of shame; and Oliver Goldsmith (1728–1774) dealt with seduction and desertion in *The Vicar of Wakefield.*

greater freedom, or whether I wished to encourage them, I should begin to answer them by saying that the Young Girl has never done anything of the kind. The manners of the novel have been improving with those of its readers; that is all. Gentlemen no longer swear or fall drunk under the table, or abduct young ladies and shut them up in lonely country-houses, or so habitually set about the ruin of their neighbors' wives, as they once did. Generally, people now call a spade an agricultural implement; they have not grown decent without having also grown a little squeamish, but they have grown comparatively decent; there is no doubt about that. They require of a novelist whom they respect unquestionable proof of his seriousness, if he proposes to deal with certain phases of life; they require a sort of scientific decorum. He can no longer expect to be received on the ground of entertainment only; he assumes a higher function, something like that of a physician or a priest, and they expect him to be bound by laws as sacred as those of such professions; they hold him solemnly pledged not to betray them or abuse their confidence. If he will accept the conditions, they give him their confidence, and he may then treat to his greater honor, and not at all to his disadvantage, of such experiences, such relations of men and women as George Eliot treats in Adam Bede, in Daniel Deronda, in Romola, in almost all her books; such as Hawthorne treats in The Scarlet Letter; such as Dickens treats in David Copperfield; such as Thackeray treats in Pendennis, and glances at in every one of his fictions; such as most of the masters of English fiction have at some time treated more or less openly. It is quite false or quite mistaken to suppose that our novels have left untouched these most important realities of life. They have only not made them their stock in trade; they have kept a true perspective in regard to them; they have relegated them in their pictures of life to the space and place they occupy in life itself, as we know it in England and America. They have kept a correct proportion, knowing perfectly well that unless the novel is to be a map, with everything scrupulously laid down in it, a faithful record of life in far the greater extent could be made to the exclusion of guilty love and all its circumstances and consequences.

I justify them in this view not only because I hate what is cheap and meretricious, and hold in peculiar loathing the cant of the critics who require "passion" as something in itself admirable and desirable in a novel, but because I prize fidelity in the historian of feeling and character. Most of these critics who demand "passion" would seem to have no conception of any passion but one. Yet there are several other passions: the passion of grief, the passion of avarice, the passion of pity, the passion of ambition, the passion of hate, the passion of envy, the passion of devotion, the passion of friendship; and all these have a greater part in the drama of life than the passion of love, and infinitely greater than the passion of guilty love. Wittingly or unwittingly, English fiction and American fiction have recognized this truth, not fully, not in the measure it merits, but in greater degree than most other fiction.

1891

Editha [7]

The air was thick with the war feeling, like the electricity of a storm which has not yet burst. Editha sat looking out into the hot spring afternoon, with her lips parted, and panting with the intensity of the question whether she could let him go. She had decided that she could not let him stay, when she saw him at the end of the still leafless avenue, making slowly up toward the house, with his head down, and his figure relaxed. She ran impatiently out on the veranda, to the edge of the steps, and imperatively demanded greater haste of him with her will before she called aloud to him, "George!"

He had quickened his pace in mystical response to her mystical urgence, before he could have heard her; now he looked up and answered "Well?"

"Oh, how united we are!" she exulted, and then she swooped down the steps to him. "What is it?" she cried.

"It's war," he said, and he pulled her up to him, and kissed her.

She kissed him back intensely, but irrelevantly, as to their passion, and uttered from deep in her throat, "How glorious!"

"It's war," he repeated, without consenting to her sense of it; and she did not know just what to think at first. She never knew what to think of him; that made his mystery, his charm. All through their courtship, which was contemporaneous with the growth of the war feeling, she had been puzzled by his want of seriousness about it. He seemed to despise it even more than he abhorred it. She could have understood his abhorring any sort of bloodshed; that would have been a survival of his old life when he thought he would be a minister, and before he changed and took up the law. But making light of a cause so high and noble seemed

7. "Editha," like Howells's most successful novels, combines a human situation with a concrete social or moral problem—in this case the problem of war—and he supports his social purpose without sacrificing the reality of his characters. The war in the story resembles the brief Spanish-American engagement of 1898.

"Editha" was first published in *Harper's Monthly Magazine* in January, 1905, collected in *Between the Dark and the Daylight* (1907).

to show a want of earnestness at the core of his being. Not but that she felt herself able to cope with a congenital defect of that sort, and make his love for her save him from himself. Now perhaps the miracle was already wrought in him. In the presence of the tremendous fact that he announced, all triviality seemed to have gone out of him; she began to feel that. He sank down on the top step, and wiped his forehead with his handkerchief, while she poured out upon him her question of the origin and authenticity of his news.

All the while, in her duplex emotioning, she was aware that now at the very beginning she must put a guard upon herself against urging him, by any word or act, to take the part that her whole soul willed him to take, for the completion of her ideal of him. He was very nearly perfect as he was, and he must be allowed to perfect himself. But he was peculiar, and he might very well be reasoned out of his peculiarity. Before her reasoning went her emotioning: her nature pulling upon his nature, her womanhood upon his manhood, without her knowing the means she was using to the end she was willing. She had always supposed that the man who won her would have done something to win her; she did not know what, but something. George Gearson had simply asked her for her love, on the way home from a concert, and she gave her love to him, without, as it were, thinking. But now, it flashed upon her, if he could do something worthy to *have* won her—be a hero, *her* hero—it would be even better than if he had done it before asking her; it would be grander. Besides, she had believed in the war from the beginning.

"But don't you see, dearest," she said, "that it wouldn't have come to this, if it hadn't been in the order of Providence? And I call any war glorious that is for the liberation of people who have been struggling for years against the cruelest oppression. Don't you think so too?"

"I suppose so," he returned, languidly. "But war! Is it glorious to break the peace of the world?"

"That ignoble peace! It was no peace at all, with that crime and shame at our very gates." She was conscious of parroting the current phrases of the newspapers, but it was no time to pick and choose her words. She must sacrifice anything to the high ideal she had for him, and after a good deal of rapid argument she ended with the climax: "But now it doesn't matter about the how or why. Since the war has come, all that is gone. There are no two sides, any more. There is nothing now but our country."

He sat with his eyes closed and his head leant back against the veranda, and he said with a vague smile, as if musing aloud, "Our country—right or wrong."

"Yes, right or wrong!" she returned fervidly. "I'll go and get you some lemonade." She rose rustling, and whisked away; when she came back with two tall glasses of clouded liquid, on a tray, and the ice clucking in them, he still sat as she had left him, and she said as if there had been no interruption: "But there is no question of wrong in this case. I call it a sacred war. A war for liberty, and humanity, if ever there was one. And I know you will see it just as I do, yet."

He took half the lemonade at a gulp, and he answered as he set the glass down: "I know you always have the highest idea. When I differ from you, I ought to doubt myself."

A generous sob rose in Editha's throat for the humility of a man, so very nearly perfect, who was willing to put himself below her.

Besides, she felt, more subliminally, that he was never so near slipping through her fingers as when he took that meek way.

"You shall not say that! Only, for once I happen to be right." She seized his hand in her two hands, and poured her soul from her eyes into his. "Don't you think so?" she entreated him.

He released his hand and drank the rest of his lemonade, and she added, "Have mine, too," but he shook his head in answering, "I've no business to think so, unless I act so, too."

Her heart stopped a beat before it pulsed on with leaps that she felt in her neck. She had noticed that strange thing in men; they seemed to feel bound to do what they believed, and not think a thing was finished when they said it, as girls did. She knew what was in his mind, but she pretended not, and she said, "Oh, I am not sure," and then faltered.

He went on as if to himself without apparently heeding her, "There's only one way of proving one's faith in a thing like this."

She could not say that she understood, but she did understand.

He went on again. "If I believed—if I felt as you do about this war—Do you wish me to feel as you do?"

Now she was really not sure; so she said, "George, I don't know what you mean."

He seemed to muse away from her as before. "There is a sort of fascination in it. I suppose that at the bottom of his heart every man would like at times to have his courage tested; to see how he would act."

"How can you talk in that ghastly way?"

"It *is* rather morbid. Still, that's what it comes to, unless you're swept away by ambition, or driven by conviction. I haven't the conviction or the ambition, and the other thing is what it comes to with me. I ought to have been a preacher, after all; then I couldn't have asked it of myself, as I must, now I'm a lawyer. And you believe it's a holy war, Editha?" he suddenly addressed her. "Or, I know you do! But you wish me to believe so, too?"

She hardly knew whether he was mocking or not, in the ironical way he always had with her plainer mind. But the only thing was to be outspoken with him.

"George, I wish you to believe whatever you think is true, at any and every cost. If I've tried to talk you into anything, I take it all back."

"Oh, I know that, Editha. I know how sincere you are, and how —I wish I had your undoubting spirit! I'll think it over; I'd like to believe as you do. But I don't, now; I don't, indeed. It isn't this war alone; though this seems peculiarly wanton and needless; but it's every war—so stupid; it makes me sick. Why shouldn't this thing have been settled reasonably?"

"Because," she said, very throatily again, "God meant it to be war."

"You think it was God? Yes, I suppose that is what people will say."

"Do you suppose it would have been war if God hadn't meant it?"

"I don't know. Sometimes it seems as if God had put this world into men's keeping to work it as they pleased."

"Now, George, that is blasphemy."

"Well, I won't blaspheme. I'll try to believe in your pocket Providence," he said, and then he rose to go.

"Why don't you stay to dinner?" Dinner at Balcom's Works was at one o'clock.

"I'll come back to supper, if you'll let me. Perhaps I shall bring you a convert."

"Well, you may come back, on that condition."

"All right. If I don't come, you'll understand."

He went away without kissing her, and she felt it a suspension of their engagement. It all interested her intensely; she was undergoing a tremendous experience, and she was being equal to it. While she stood looking after him, her mother came out through one of the long windows, on to the veranda, with a catlike softness and vagueness.

"Why didn't he stay to dinner?"

"Because—because—war has been declared," Editha pronounced, without turning.

Her mother said, "Oh, my!" and then said nothing more until she had sat down in one of the large Shaker chairs, and rocked herself for some time. Then she closed whatever tacit passage of thought there had been in her mind with the spoken words, "Well, I hope *he* won't go."

"And I hope he *will*," the girl said, and confronted her mother with a stormy exultation that would have frightened any creature less unimpressionable than a cat.

Her mother rocked herself again for an interval of cogitation. What she arrived at in speech was, "Well, I guess you've done a wicked thing, Editha Balcom."

The girl said, as she passed indoors through the same window her mother had come out by, "I haven't done anything—yet."

In her room, she put together all her letters and gifts from Gearson, down to the withered petals of the first flower he had offered, with that timidity of his veiled in that irony of his. In the heart of the packet she enshrined her engagement ring which she had restored to the pretty box he had brought it her in. Then she sat down, if not calmly yet strongly, and wrote:

"George: I understood—when you left me. But I think we had better emphasize your meaning that if we cannot be one in everything we had better be one in nothing. So I am sending these things for your keeping till you have made up your mind.

"I shall always love you, and therefore I shall never marry any one else. But the man I marry must love his country first of all, and be able to say to me,

> 'I could not love thee, dear, so much,
> Loved I not honor more.'

"There is no honor above America with me. In this great hour there is no other honor.

"Your heart will make my words clear to you. I have never expected to say so much, but it has come upon me that I must say the utmost.

Editha."

She thought she had worded her letter well, worded it in a way that could not be bettered; all had been implied and nothing expressed.

She had it ready to send with the packet she had tied with red, white, and blue ribbon, when it occurred to her that she was not just to him, that she was not giving him a fair chance. He had said he would go and think it over, and she was not waiting. She was pushing, threatening, compelling. That was not a woman's part. She must leave him free, free, free. She could not accept for her country or herself a forced sacrifice.

In writing her letter she had satisfied the impulse from which it sprang; she could well afford to wait till he had thought it over. She put the packet and the letter by, and rested serene in the consciousness of having done what was laid upon her by her love itself to do, and yet used patience, mercy, justice.

She had her reward. Gearson did not come to tea, but she had given him till morning, when, late at night there came up from the village the sound of a fife and drum with a tumult of voices, in shouting, singing, and laughing. The noise drew nearer and nearer; it reached the street end of the avenue; there it silenced itself, and one voice, the voice she knew best, rose over the silence. It fell; the air was filled with cheers; the fife and drum struck up, with the shouting, singing, and laughing again, but now retreating; and a single figure came hurrying up the avenue.

She ran down to meet her lover and clung to him. He was very gay, and he put his arm round her with a boisterous laugh. "Well, you must call me Captain, now; or Cap, if you prefer; that's what the boys call me. Yes, we've had a meeting at the town hall, and everybody has volunteered; and they selected me for captain, and I'm going to the war, the big war, the glorious war, the holy war ordained by the pocket Providence that blesses butchery. Come along; let's tell the whole family about it. Call them from their downy beds, father, mother, Aunt Hitty, and all the folks!"

But when they mounted the veranda steps he did not wait for a larger audience; he poured the story out upon Editha alone.

"There was a lot of speaking, and then some of the fools set up a shout for me. It was all going one way, and I thought it would be a good joke to sprinkle a little cold water on them. But you can't do that with a crowd that adores you. The first thing I knew I was sprinkling hell-fire on them. 'Cry havoc, and let slip the dogs of war.' That was the style. Now that it had come to the fight, there were no two parties; there was one country, and the thing was to fight the fight to a finish as quick as possible. I suggested volunteering then and there, and I wrote my name first of all on the roster. Then they elected me—that's all. I wish I had some ice-water!"

She left him walking up and down the veranda, while she ran for the ice-pitcher and a goblet, and when she came back he was still walking up and down, shouting the story he had told her to her father and mother, who had come out more sketchily dressed than they commonly were by day. He drank goblet after goblet of the ice-water without noticing who was giving it, and kept on talking, and laughing through his talk wildly. "It's astonishing," he said, "how well the worse reason looks when you try to make it appear the better. Why, I believe I was the first convert to the war in that crowd to-night! I never thought I should like to kill a man; but now, I shouldn't care; and the smokeless powder lets you see the man drop that you kill. It's all for the country! What a thing it is to have a country that *can't* be wrong, but if it is, is right anyway!"

Editha had a great, vital thought, an inspiration. She set down the ice-pitcher on the veranda floor, and ran up-stairs and got the letter she had written him. When at last he noisily bade her father and mother, "Well, good night. I forgot I woke you up; I shan't want any sleep myself," she followed him down the avenue to the gate. There, after the whirling words that seemed to fly away from her thoughts and refuse to serve them, she made a last effort to solemnize the moment that seemed so crazy, and pressed the letter she had written upon him.

"What's this?" he said, "Want me to mail it?"

"No, no. It's for you. I wrote it after you went this morning. Keep it—keep it—and read it sometime—" She thought, and then her inspiration came: "Read it if ever you doubt what you've done, or fear that I regret your having done it. Read it after you've started."

They strained each other in embraces that seemed as ineffective as their words, and he kissed her face with quick, hot breaths that were so unlike him, that made her feel as if she had lost her old lover and found a stranger in his place. The stranger said, "What a gorgeous flower you are, with your red hair, and your blue eyes that look black now, and your face with the color painted out by the white moonshine! Let me hold you under my chin, to see whether I love blood, you tiger-lily!" Then he laughed Gearson's laugh, and released her, scared and giddy. Within her wilfulness she had been frightened by a sense of subtler force in him, and mystically mastered as she had never been before.

She ran all the way back to the house, and mounted the steps panting. Her mother and father were talking of the great affair. Her mother said: "Wa'n't Mr. Gearson in rather of an excited state of mind? Didn't you think he acted curious?"

"Well, not for a man who'd just been elected captain and had to set 'em up for the whole of Company A," her father chuckled back.

"What in the world do you mean, Mr. Balcom? Oh! There's Editha!" She offered to follow the girl indoors.

"Don't come, mother!" Editha called, vanishing.

Mrs. Balcom remained to reproach her husband. "I don't see much of anything to laugh at."

"Well, it's catching. Caught it from Gearson. I guess it won't be much of a war, and I guess Gearson don't think so, either. The other fellows will back down as soon as they see we mean it. I wouldn't lose any sleep over it. I'm going back to bed, myself."

Gearson came again next afternoon, looking pale, and rather

sick, but quite himself even to his languid irony. "I guess I'd better tell you, Editha, that I consecrated myself to your god of battles last night by pouring too many libations to him down my own throat. But I'm all right, now. One has to carry off the excitement, somehow."

"Promise me," she commanded, "that you'll never touch it again!"

"What! Not let the cannikin clink? Not let the soldier drink? Well, I promise."

"You don't belong to yourself now; you don't even belong to *me*. You belong to your country, and you have a sacred charge to keep yourself strong and well for your country's sake. I have been thinking, thinking all night and all day long."

"You look as if you had been crying a little, too," he said with his queer smile.

"That's all past. I've been thinking, and worshipping *you*. Don't you suppose I know all that you've been through, to come to this? I've followed you every step from your old theories and opinions."

"Well, you've had a long row to hoe."

"And I know you've done this from the highest motives—"

"Oh, there won't be much pettifogging to do till this cruel war is—"

"And you haven't simply done it for my sake. I couldn't respect you if you had."

"Well, then we'll say I haven't. A man that hasn't got his own respect intact wants the respect of all the other people he can corner. But we won't go into that. I'm in for the thing now, and we've got to face our future. My idea is that this isn't going to be a very protracted struggle; we shall just scare the enemy to death before it comes to a fight at all. But we must provide for contingencies, Editha. If anything happens to me—"

"Oh, George!" She clung to him sobbing.

"I don't want you to feel foolishly bound to my memory. I should hate that, wherever I happened to be."

"I am yours, for time and eternity—time and eternity." She liked the words; they satisfied her famine for phrases.

"Well, say eternity; that's all right; but time's another thing; and I'm talking about time. But there is something! My mother! If anything happens—"

She winced, and he laughed. "You're not the bold soldier-girl of yesterday!" Then he sobered. "If anything happens, I want you to help my mother out. She won't like my doing this thing. She brought me up to think war a fool thing as well as a bad thing. My father was in the civil war; all through it; lost his arm in it."

She thrilled with the sense of the arm round her; what if that should be lost? He laughed as if divining her: "Oh, it doesn't run in the family, as far as I know!" Then he added, gravely, "He came home with misgivings about war, and they grew on him. I guess he and mother agreed between them that I was to be brought up in his final mind about it; but that was before my time. I only knew him from my mother's report of him and his opinions; I don't know whether they were hers first; but they were hers last. This will be a blow to her. I shall have to write and tell her—"

He stopped, and she asked, "Would you like me to write too, George?"

"I don't believe that would do. No, I'll do the writing. She'll understand a little if I say that I thought the way to minimize it was to make war on the largest possible scale at once—that I felt I must have been helping on the war somehow if I hadn't helped keep it from coming, and I knew I hadn't; when it came, I had no right to stay out of it."

Whether his sophistries satisfied him or not, they satisfied her. She clung to his breast, and whispered, with closed eyes and quivering lips, "Yes, yes, yes!"

"But if anything should happen, you might go to her, and see what you could do for her. You know? It's rather far off; she can't leave her chair—"

"Oh, I'll go, if it's the ends of the earth! But nothing will happen! Nothing *can!* I—"

She felt herself lifted with his rising, and Gearson was saying, with his arm still around her, to her father: "Well, we're off at once, Mr. Balcom. We're to be formally accepted at the capital, and then bunched up with the rest somehow, and sent into camp somewhere, and got to the front as soon as possible. We all want to be in the van, of course; we're the first company to report to the Governor. I came to tell Editha, but I hadn't got round to it."

She saw him again for a moment at the capital, in the station, just before the train started southward with his regiment. He looked well, in his uniform, and very soldierly, but somehow girlish, too, with his clean-shaven face and slim figure. The manly eyes and the strong voice satisfied her, and his preoccupation with some unexpected details of duty flattered her. Other girls were weeping and bemoaning themselves, but she felt a sort of noble distinction in the abstraction, the almost unconsciousness, with which they parted. Only at the last moment he said, "Don't forget my mother. It mayn't be such a walkover as I supposed," and he laughed at the notion.

He waved his hand to her, as the train moved off—she knew it among a score of hands that were waved to other girls from the platform of the car, for it held a letter which she knew was hers. Then he went inside the car to read it, doubtless, and she did not see him again. But she felt safe for him through the strength of what she called her love. What she called her God, always speaking the name in a deep voice and with the implication of a mutual understanding, would watch over him and keep him and bring him back to her. If with an empty sleeve, then he should have three arms instead of two, for both of hers should be his for life. She did not see, though, why she should always be thinking of the arm his father had lost.

There were not many letters from him, but they were such as she could have wished, and she put her whole strength into making hers such as she imagined he could have wished, glorifying and supporting him. She wrote to his mother glorifying him as their hero, but the brief answer she got was merely to the effect that Mrs. Gearson was not well enough to write herself, and thanking her for her letter by the hand of some one who called herself "Yrs truly, Mrs. W. J. Andrews."

Editha determined not to be hurt, but to write again quite as if the answer had been all she expected. But before it seemed as if she could have written, there came news of the first skirmish, and in the list of the killed which was telegraphed as a trifling loss on our side, was Gearson's name. There was a frantic time of trying to make out that it might be, must be, some other Gearson; but the name, and the company and the regiment, and the State were too definitely given.

Then there was a lapse into depths out of which it seemed as if she could never rise again; then a lift into clouds far above all grief, black clouds, that blotted out the sun, but where she soared with him, with George, George! She had the fever that she expected of herself, but she did not die in it; she was not even delirious, and it did not last long. When she was well enough to leave her bed, her one thought was of George's mother, of his strangely worded wish that she should go to her and see what she could do for her. In the exultation of the duty laid upon her— it buoyed her up instead of burdening her—she rapidly recovered.

Her father went with her on the long railroad journey from northern New York to western Iowa; he had business out at Davenport, and he said he could just as well go then as any other time; and he went with her to the little country town where George's mother lived in a little house on the edge of illimitable corn-fields, under trees pushed to a top of the rolling prairie. George's father had settled there after the civil war, as so many other old soldiers had done; but they were Eastern people, and Editha fancied touches of the East in the June rose overhanging the front door, and the garden with early summer flowers stretching from the gate of the paling fence.

It was very low inside the house, and so dim, with the closed blinds, that they could scarcely see one another: Editha tall and black in her crapes which filled the air with the smell of their dyes; her father standing decorously apart with his hat on his forearm, as at funerals; a woman rested in a deep armchair, and the woman who had let the strangers in stood behind the chair.

The seated woman turned her head round and up, and asked the woman behind her chair, "*Who* did you say?"

Editha, if she had done what she expected of herself, would have gone down on her knees at the feet of the seated figure and said, "I am George's Editha," for answer.

But instead of her own voice she heard that other woman's voice, saying, "Well, I don't know as I *did* get the name just right. I guess I'll have to make a little more light in here," and she went and pushed two of the shutters ajar.

Then Editha's father said in his public will-now-address-a-few-remarks tone, "My name is Balcom, ma'am; Junius H. Balcom, of Balcom's Works, New York; my daughter—"

"Oh!" The seated woman broke in, with a powerful voice, the voice that always surprised Editha from Gearson's slender frame. "Let me see you! Stand round where the light can strike on your face," and Editha dumbly obeyed. "So, you're Editha Balcom," she sighed.

"Yes," Editha said, more like a culprit than a comforter.

"What did you come for?" Mrs. Gearson asked.

Editha's face quivered, and her knees shook. "I came—because—because George—" She could go no farther.

"Yes," the mother said, "he told me he had asked you to come if he got killed. You didn't expect that, I suppose, when you sent him."

"I would rather have died myself than done it!" Editha said with more truth in her deep voice than she ordinarily found in it. "I tried to leave him free—"

"Yes, that letter of yours, that came back with his other things, left him free."

Editha saw now where George's irony came from.

"It was not to be read before—unless—until—I told him so," she faltered.

"Of course, he wouldn't read a letter of yours, under the circumstances, till he thought you wanted him to. Been sick?" the woman abruptly demanded.

"Very sick," Editha said, with self-pity.

"Daughter's life," her father interposed, "was almost despaired of, at one time."

Mrs. Gearson gave him no heed. "I suppose you would have been glad to die, such a brave person as you! I don't believe *he* was glad to die. He was always a timid boy, that way; he was afraid of a good many things; but if he was afraid he did what he made up his mind to. I suppose he made up his mind to go, but I knew what it cost him, by what it cost me when I heard of it. I had been through *one* war before. When you sent him you didn't expect he would get killed."

The voice seemed to compassionate Editha, and it was time. "No," she huskily murmured.

"No, girls don't; women don't, when they give their men up to their country. They think they'll come marching back, somehow, just as gay as they went, or if it's an empty sleeve, or even an empty pantaloon, it's all the more glory, and they're so much the prouder of them, poor things."

The tears began to run down Editha's face; she had not wept till then; but it was now such a relief to be understood that the tears came.

"No, you didn't expect him to get killed," Mrs. Gearson repeated in a voice which was startlingly like George's again. "You just expected him to kill some one else, some of those foreigners, that weren't there because they had any say about it, but because they had to be there, poor wretches—conscripts, or whatever they call 'em. You thought it would be all right for my George, *your* George, to kill the sons of those miserable mothers and the husbands of those girls that you would never see the faces of." The woman lifted her powerful voice in a psalmlike note. "I thank my God he didn't live to do it! I thank my God they killed him first, and that he ain't livin' with their blood on his hands!" She dropped her eyes which she had raised with her voice, and glared at Editha. "What you got that black on for?" She lifted herself by her powerful arms so high that her helpless body seemed to hang limp its full length. "Take it off, take it off, before I tear it from your back!"

The lady who was passing the summer near Balcom's Works was sketching Editha's beauty, which lent itself wonderfully to the effects of a colorist. It had come to that confidence which is rather apt to grow between artist and sitter, and Editha had told her everything.

"To think of your having such a tragedy in your life!" the lady said. She added: "I suppose there are people who feel that way about war. But when you consider the good this war has done—

how much it has done for the country! I can't understand such people, for my part. And when you had come all the way out there to console her—got up out of a sick bed! Well!"

"I think," Editha said, magnanimously, "she wasn't quite in her right mind; and so did papa."

"Yes," the lady said, looking at Editha's lips in nature and then at her lips in art, and giving an empirical touch to them in the picture. "But how dreadful of her! How perfectly—excuse me —how *vulgar!*"

A light broke upon Editha in the darkness which she felt had been without a gleam of brightness for weeks and months. The mystery that had bewildered her was solved by the word; and from that moment she rose from grovelling in shame and self-pity, and began to live again in the ideal.

1905, 1907

HENRY JAMES
(1843–1916)

Born in New York City on April 15, 1843, the brother of the philosopher-scientist William James, Henry James was influenced by the patrician attitudes of his father, who combined an interest in philosophy and theology with full enjoyment of the cultural life of his own city and of the world. The James children were privately tutored in New York, and received special schooling abroad between 1855 and 1860, when the family lived in London, Switzerland, France, and Germany—everywhere at a level of intense intellectual activity. Henry James studied painting briefly; but at the age of nineteen was admitted to Harvard Law School. Two years later he had plunged into authorship, and he won his way into the best literary magazines. Two long trips abroad are reflected in his *Atlantic* story "A Passionate Pilgrim" (1871), motivated by the cultural attraction and repulsion between England and America. The year before, Mary Temple, James's beloved cousin, had died; by 1876 he was settled in London, and thereafter made his home in England. In 1915, impatient at America's aloofness from World War I, he became a British citizen.

In 1875 he published his first collection of stories, *A Passionate Pilgrim and Other Tales*, and the *Atlantic* serialized his first novel of consequence, *Roderick Hudson*, in which a talented young American sculptor is transplanted to Florence for study, only to be crushed and destroyed by the artifice and materialistic cynicism of international society. These works established the theme and the techniques of his first period.

Spending much time in Paris, he came to know Flaubert and Turgenev. The French and Russian realists and naturalists influenced his style, which became increasingly "chiseled," in Flaubert's sense. He accepted also the naturalists' concept of the novelist as the clinical researcher into life, but did not follow their unselective zeal to report everything observed; he admitted a measure of determinism, but rejected the pessimistic extreme according to which human character becomes the waif of chance.

Among other fine works, *The American* appeared in 1877, *Daisy Miller* in 1879, *The Portrait of a Lady,* his greatest novel of this period, in 1881, and *The Princess Casamassima* in 1886. In the first, a young American, having won a fortune in manufacturing and speculation, seeks abroad the development of cultural satisfactions. In this he succeeds, but he is wretchedly defeated in a genuine love affair by the rigid convention and ingrained evil of French Bourbon aristocracy. Equally striking in its contrasts of social values is the story of Daisy, a hoydenish, healthy, and wholly lovable American girl of small-town wealth who in Rome runs afoul of the European codes of the cloistered woman. Isabel Archer, the "Lady" of the third novel, another American girl, triumphs over the rigidities of both British and Italian society and survives the bad marriage into which she has been tricked by a cynical fortune hunter and his worldly mistress, to arrive at a kind of austere selfhood and

mastery of the Paris social world. In *The Princess Casamassima* James resumes the adventures of the pathetic heroine of *Roderick Hudson* and the cynical society she represents, but he also for once turns his mirror in the opposite direction, catching the social issues inherent in the lives of London's lower orders and the ominous premonitory specter of a social revolution.

From *The Tragic Muse* (1890) to the end of his career in fiction more than fifteen years later, James developed an increasingly complex style, marked by meaningful ambiguities and ellipses in the dialogue together with convoluted and modifier-ridden exposition. Thus the functions of prose rhythm were enlarged as by no other author in English fiction before Joyce. At the same time, the psychological motivations of his characters became more intense and more frequently abnormal, while the social situations possessed increasing subtlety. The earliest of the principal novels of this so-called "major phase" was *The Spoils of Poynton* (1897), in which the possession of a house and its *objets d'art* corrupts certain members of a family and their associates, and produces spiritual ruin and psychological disorder. *What Maisie Knew* (1897) uses the innocence of a little girl as the center of revelation for the idle and destructive amours of her divorced parents, with whom she lives alternately. *The Turn of the Screw* (1898) is superficially a story of the supernatural, involving two children and their governess in an ancient British country house, but fundamentally it studies the pathological effects of an ambiguous evil influence upon the innocence of the children. *The Awkward Age* (1899) follows the emotional life of Nanda Brookenham from the innocence of girlhood seclusion into her mother's sophisticated and selfish social world, through the period of matrimonial barter into a kind of detached acceptance. *The Sacred Fount* (1901), one of James's most baffling studies in ambiguity, explores the relationships that may or may not be taking place during a weekend at an English country house. *The Wings of the Dove* (1902) studies the victimization of the dying Milly Theale by the affair carried on between her suitor and her fortune-hunting best friend, and her innocent revenge on their amorality. *The Ambassadors* (1903) is a brilliantly tragic account of an emissary who attempts to persuade an American heir to leave Paris to take charge of his profitable business interests in Massachusetts, only to have the ambassador himself converted as a result of the expansion of his consciousness in Paris. In *The Golden Bowl* (1904) the admirable Maggie Verver is confronted with a continuing liaison between her husband and her father's young wife, a situation created at least partially by the strength of the attachment between father and daughter. Her love and tact, together with her father's sensitive maturity, save them all.

The short stories and the novelettes of James are not minor works except in their length. In general they follow the patterns that have been suggested above for the novels. The critical writings of James, even excluding the penetrating essays with which he prefaced the New York Edition of the novels, would have given him a position as a major critic if he had not made his reputation as a novelist. His several dramas were not acceptable to the stage, in contrast with some of his novels recently staged or filmed with success: *Washington Square* (as *The Heiress*), *The Turn of the Screw* (as *The Innocents*), *The Portrait of a Lady*, *The Aspern Papers*, *The Spoils of Poynton*, and *The Golden Bowl*.

James's belief that prose was as subject as poetry to intensification and to investment with symbolic value has been profoundly influential on the generations since his death. He was a pioneer in utilizing psychological devices which communicated a more intense realization of character and situation. By transferring his center of "consciousness" to the awakening mind of an innocent child, or to the confessional pages of a diary, for example, he implicated the reader in the analytic process and in the story itself, foreshadowing such psychological instruments as stream of consciousness. By experimenting with various technical effects achieved through the adoption of severely limited points of view—ranging from the objectivity of the dramatic method through the extreme subjectivity of the unreliable narrator—he influenced the shape of the twentieth-century novel in the hands even of writers whose talents were vastly dissimilar to his own.

Among the authors he influenced were Lawrence, Joyce, Conrad, Edith Wharton, Virginia Woolf, Willa Cather, and T. S. Eliot. Perhaps more indirectly, Fitzgerald, Hemingway, and Faulkner are also his descendants. In contrast with the European naturalists whose tutelage he acknowledged, he rebelled against the materialistic interpetation of human destiny, and struggled with the problem of undeniable evil as desperately as Hawthorne, whom, among earlier Americans, he most admired. He offset his portrayals of the evil tendencies of life toward greed, treachery, and pathological dualism by the constant representation of innocence, lofty choices, and moral idealism. His experience of life may seem limited and specialized, but he employed it for great and far-reaching ends.

The standard edition of James's works, containing his last revised texts and valuable prefaces, is *The Novels and Tales of Henry James*, 26 vols., 1907–1917, known as the New York Edition (reissued, 1962–1965). There is also a good English edition, *The Novels and Stories of Henry James*, 35 vols., 1921–1923. Philip Rahv edited *The Great Short Novels of Henry James*, 1944; Clifton Fadiman edited *The Short Stories of Henry James*, 1945; and F. O. Matthiessen edited *The American Novels and Stories of Henry James*, 1947. Other recent compilations are *Stories of Writers*

and Artists, edited, with an introduction, by F. O. Matthiessen, 1944; *The Scenic Art,* edited by Allan Wade, 1948; and *The Ghostly Tales of Henry James,* with an introduction by Leon Edel, 1948 (reissued, with a new introduction, as *Henry James: Stories of the Supernatural,* 1970). Leon Edel also edited *The Complete Plays of Henry James,* 1949, and the definitive 8-vol. edition of James's *Complete Tales,* 1964. Percy Lubbock selected and edited *Letters of Henry James,* 2 vols., 1920. Also important is *The Selected Letters of Henry James,* edited by Leon Edel, 1955. R. P. Blackmur edited *The Art of the Novel: Critical Prefaces,* 1943. *The Notebooks of Henry James,* 1947, was edited by F. O. Matthiessen and K. B. Murdock.

Important are F. W. Dupee's *Henry James,* revised, 1956, and his edition of the *Autobiography,* 1956. A complete biography is Pelham Edgar, *Henry James: Man and Author,* 1927. A partial study is H. Montgomery Hyde, *Henry James at Home,* 1969. Leon Edel has written a comprehensive biography, *Henry James,* 5 vols., 1953–1972. Other important volumes are J. W. Beach, *The Method of Henry James,* revised, 1954; and F. O. Matthiessen, *Henry James, The Major Phase,* 1944. Leon Edel and Dan H. Laurence compiled *A Bibliography of Henry James,* 1957.

Recent important critical work includes Dorothea Krook, *The Ordeal of Consciousness in Henry James,* 1962; Maxwell Geismar, *Henry James and the Jacobites,* 1963; Millicent Bell, *Edith Wharton and Henry James: The Story of a Friendship,* 1965; S. Gorley Putt, *Henry James: A Reader's Guide,* 1966; Walter Isle, *Experiments in Form: Henry James's Novels, 1896–1901,* 1968; Christof Wegelin, *The Image of Europe in Henry James,* 1968; Sallie Sears, *The Negative Imagination: Form and Perspective in the Novels of Henry James,* 1969; Ora Segal, *The Lucid Reflector: The Observer in Henry James' Fiction,* 1969; Peter Buitenhuis, *The Grasping Imagination: The American Writings of Henry James,* 1970; and Philip M. Weinstein, *Henry James and the Requirements of the Imagination,* 1971.

The Real Thing [1]

I

When the porter's wife, who used to answer the house-bell, announced "A gentleman and a lady, sir," I had, as I often had in

---

1. "* * * my much-loved friend George du Maurier had spoken to me of a call from a strange and striking couple desirous to propose themselves as artist's models for his weekly 'social' illustrations to 'Punch,' and the acceptance of whose services would have entailed the dismissal of an undistinguished but highly expert pair, also husband and wife, who had come to him from far

those days—the wish being father to the thought—an immediate vision of sitters. Sitters my visitors in this case proved to be; but not in the sense I should have preferred. There was nothing at first however to indicate that they mightn't have come for a portrait. The gentleman, a man of fifty, very high and very straight, with a moustache slightly grizzled and a dark grey walking-coat admirably fitted, both of which I noted professionally—I don't mean as a barber or yet as a tailor—would have struck me as a celebrity if celebrities often were striking. It was a truth of which I had for some time been conscious that a figure with a good deal of frontage was, as one might say, almost never a public institution. A glance at the lady helped to remind me of this paradoxical law: she also looked too distinguished to be a "personality." Moreover one would scarcely come across two variations together.

Neither of the pair immediately spoke—they only prolonged the preliminary gaze suggesting that each wished to give the other a chance. They were visibly shy; they stood there letting me take them in—which, as I afterwards perceived, was the most practical thing they could have done. In this way their embarrassment served their cause. I had seen people painfully reluctant to mention that they desired anything so gross as to be represented on canvas; but the scruples of my new friends appeared almost insurmountable. Yet the gentleman might have said "I should like a portrait of my wife," and the lady might have said "I should like a portrait of my husband." Perhaps they weren't husband and wife —this naturally would make the matter more delicate. Perhaps they wished to be done together—in which case they ought to have brought a third person to break the news.

"We come from Mr. Rivet," the lady finally said with a dim smile that had the effect of a moist sponge passed over a "sunk" piece of painting, as well as of a vague allusion to vanished beauty. She was as tall and straight, in her degree, as her companion, and

---

back on the irregular day and whom, thanks to a happy, and to that extent lucrative, appearance of 'type' on the part of each, he had reproduced, to the best effect, in a thousand drawing-room attitudes and combinations. Exceedingly modest members of society, they earned their bread by looking and, with the aid of supplied toggery, dressing, greater favourites of fortune to the life; or, otherwise expressed, by skilfully feigning a virtue not in the least native to them. Here meanwhile were their so handsome proposed, so anxious, so almost haggard competitors, originally, by every sign, of the best condition and estate, but overtaken by reverses even while conforming impeccably to the standard of superficial 'smartness' and pleading with well-bred ease and the right light tone, not to say with feverish gaiety, that (as in the interest of art itself) *they* at least shouldn't have to 'make believe.' The question thus thrown up by the two friendly critics of the rather lurid little passage was of whether their not having to make believe *would* in fact serve them, and above all serve their interpreter as well as the borrowed graces of the comparatively sordid professionals who had had, for dear life, to *know how* (which was to have learnt how) to do something. The question, I recall, struck me as exquisite, and out of a momentary fond consideration of it 'The Real Thing' sprang at a bound" [James's introduction]. *The Real Thing and Other Tales* appeared in 1893. The present text is based on the New York Edition (Vol. XVIII, 1909).

with ten years less to carry. She looked as sad as a woman could look whose face was not charged with expression; that is, her tinted oval mask showed waste as an exposed surface shows friction. The hand of time had played over her freely, but to an effect of elimination. She was slim and stiff, and so well-dressed, in dark blue cloth, with lappets and pockets and buttons, that it was clear she employed the same tailor as her husband. The couple had an indefinable air of prosperous thrift—they evidently got a good deal of luxury for their money. If I was to be one of their luxuries it would behove me to consider my terms.

"Ah, Claude Rivet recommended me?" I echoed; and I added that it was very kind of him, though I could reflect that, as he only painted landscape, this wasn't a sacrifice.

The lady looked very hard at the gentleman, and the gentleman looked round the room. Then staring at the floor a moment and stroking his moustache, he rested his pleasant eyes on me with the remark: "He said you were the right one."

"I try to be, when people want to sit."

"Yes, we should like to," said the lady anxiously.

"Do you mean together?"

My visitors exchanged a glance. "If you could do anything with *me* I suppose it would be double," the gentleman stammered.

"Oh yes, there's naturally a higher charge for two figures than for one."

"We should like to make it pay," the husband confessed.

"That's very good of you," I returned, appreciating so unwonted a sympathy—for I supposed he meant pay the artist.

A sense of strangeness seemed to dawn on the lady. "We mean for the illustrations—Mr. Rivet said you might put one in."

"Put in—an illustration?" I was equally confused.

"Sketch her off, you know," said the gentleman, colouring.

It was only then that I understood the service Claude Rivet had rendered me; he had told them how I worked in black-and-white, for magazines, for storybooks, for sketches of contemporary life, and consequently had copious employment for models. These things were true, but it was not less true—I may confess it now; whether because the aspiration was to lead to everything or to nothing I leave the reader to guess—that I couldn't get the honours, to say nothing of the emoluments, of a great painter of portraits out of my head. My "illustrations" were my pot-boilers; I looked to a different branch of art—far and away the most interesting it had always seemed to me—to perpetuate my fame. There was no shame in looking to it also to make my fortune; but that fortune was by so much further from being made from the moment my visitors wished to be "done" for nothing. I was disappointed; for in the pictorial sense I had immediately *seen* them.

I had seized their type—I had already settled what I would do with it. Something that wouldn't absolutely have pleased them, I afterwards reflected.

"Ah you're—you're—a—?" I began as soon as I had mastered my surprise. I couldn't bring out the dingy word "models": it seemed so little to fit the case.

"We haven't had much practice," said the lady.

"We've got to *do* something, and we've thought that an artist in your line might perhaps make something of us," her husband threw off. He further mentioned that they didn't know many artists and that they had gone first, on the off-chance—he painted views of course, but sometimes put in figures; perhaps I remembered—to Mr. Rivet, whom they had met a few years before at a place in Norfolk where he was sketching.

"We used to sketch a little ourselves," the lady hinted.

"It's very awkward, but we absolutely *must* do something," her husband went on.

"Of course we're not so *very* young," she admitted with a wan smile.

With the remark that I might as well know something more about them the husband had handed me a card extracted from a neat new pocket-book—their appurtenances were all of the freshest—and inscribed with the words "Major Monarch." Impressive as these words were they didn't carry my knowledge much further; but my visitor presently added: "I've left the army and we've had the misfortune to lose our money. In fact our means are dreadfully small."

"It's awfully trying—a regular strain," said Mrs. Monarch.

They evidently wished to be discreet—to take care not to swagger because they were gentlefolk. I felt them willing to recognise this as something of a drawback, at the same time that I guessed at an underlying sense—their consolation in adversity—that they *had* their points. They certainly had; but these advantages struck me as preponderantly social; such for instance as would help to make a drawing-room look well. However, a drawing-room was always, or ought to be, a picture.

In consequence of his wife's allusion to their age Major Monarch observed: "Naturally it's more for the figure that we thought of going in. We can still hold ourselves up." On the instant I saw that the figure was indeed their strong point. His "naturally" didn't sound vain, but it lighted up the question. "*She* has the best one," he continued, nodding at his wife with a pleasant after-dinner absence of circumlocution. I could only reply, as if we were in fact sitting over our wine, that this didn't prevent his own from being very good; which led him in turn to make answer: "We thought that if you ever have to do people like us we might be something like it. *She* particularly—for a lady in a book, you know."

I was so amused by them that, to get more of it, I did my best to take their point of view; and though it was an embarrassment to find myself appraising physically, as if they were animals on hire or useful blacks, a pair whom I should have expected to meet only in one of the relations in which criticism is tacit, I looked at Mrs. Monarch judicially enough to be able to exclaim after a moment with conviction: "Oh yes, a lady in a book!" She was singularly like a bad illustration.

"We'll stand up, if you like," said the Major; and he raised himself before me with a really grand air.

I could take his measure at a glance—he was six feet two and a perfect gentleman. It would have paid any club in process of formation and in want of a stamp to engage him at a salary to stand in the principal window. What struck me at once was that in coming to me they had rather missed their vocation; they could surely have been turned to better account for advertising purposes. I couldn't of course see the thing in detail, but I could see them make somebody's fortune—I don't mean their own. There was something in them for a waistcoat-maker, an hotel-keeper or a soap-vendor. I could imagine "We always use it" pinned on their bosoms with the greatest effect; I had a vision of the brilliancy with which they would launch a table d'hôte.

Mrs. Monarch sat still, not from pride but from shyness, and presently her husband said to her: "Get up, my dear, and show how smart you are." She obeyed, but she had no need to get up to show it. She walked to the end of the studio and then came back blushing, her fluttered eyes on the partner of her appeal. I was reminded of an incident I had accidentally had a glimpse of in Paris—being with a friend there, a dramatist about to produce a play, when an actress came to him to ask to be entrusted with a part. She went through her paces before him, walked up and down as Mrs. Monarch was doing. Mrs. Monarch did it quite as well, but I abstained from applauding. It was very odd to see such people apply for such poor pay. She looked as if she had ten thousand a year. Her husband had used the word that described her: she was in the London current jargon essentially and typically "smart." Her figure was, in the same order of ideas, conspicuously and irreproachably "good." For a woman of her age her waist was surprisingly small; her elbow moreover had the orthodox crook. She held her head at the conventional angle, but why did she come to *me*? She ought to have tried on jackets at a big shop. I feared my visitors were not only destitute but "artistic"—which would be a great complication. When she sat down again I thanked her, observing that what a draughtsman most valued in his model was the faculty of keeping quiet.

"Oh *she* can keep quiet," said Major Monarch. Then he added jocosely: "I've always kept her quiet."

"I'm not a nasty fidget, am I?" It was going to wring tears from me, I felt, the way she hid her head, ostrich-like, in the other broad bosom.

The owner of this expanse addressed his answer to me. "Perhaps it isn't out of place to mention—because we ought to be quite business-like, oughtn't we?—that when I married her she was known as the Beautiful Statue."

"Oh dear!" said Mrs. Monarch ruefully.

"Of course I should want a certain amount of expression," I rejoined.

"Of *course!*"—and I had never heard such unanimity.

"And then I suppose you know that you'll get awfully tired."

"Oh we *never* get tired!" they eagerly cried.

"Have you had any kind of practice?"

They hesitated—they looked at each other. "We've been photographed—*immensely*," said Mrs. Monarch.

"She means the fellows have asked us themselves," added the Major.

"I see—because you're so good-looking."

"I don't know what they thought, but they were always after us."

"We always got our photographs for nothing," smiled Mrs. Monarch.

"We might have brought some, my dear," her husband remarked.

"I'm not sure we have any left. We've given quantities away," she explained to me.

"With our autographs and that sort of thing," said the Major.

"Are they to be got in the shops?" I enquired as a harmless pleasantry.

"Oh yes, *hers*—they used to be."

"Not now," said Mrs. Monarch with her eyes on the floor.

II

I could fancy the "sort of thing" they put on the presentation copies of their photographs, and I was sure they wrote a beautiful hand. It was odd how quickly I was sure of everything that concerned them. If they were now so poor as to have to earn shillings and pence they could never have had much of a margin. Their good looks had been their capital, and they had good-humouredly made the most of the career that this resource marked out for them. It was in their faces, the blankness, the deep intellectual repose of the twenty years of country-house visiting that had given them pleasant intonations. I could see the sunny drawing-rooms, sprinkled with periodicals she didn't read, in which Mrs. Monarch had continuously sat; I could see the wet shrubberies in which she had walked, equipped to admiration for either exercise. I could see the rich covers the Major had helped to shoot and the wonderful garments in which, late at night, he repaired to the smoking-room to talk about them. I could imagine their leggings and waterproofs, their knowing tweeds and rugs, their rolls of sticks and cases of tackle and neat umbrellas; and I could evoke the exact appearance of their servants and the compact variety of their luggage on the platforms of country stations.

They gave small tips, but they were liked; they didn't do anything themselves, but they were welcome. They looked so well everywhere; they gratified the general relish for stature, complexion and "form." They knew it without fatuity or vulgarity, and they respected themselves in consequence. They weren't superficial; they were thorough and kept themselves up—it had been their line. People with such a taste for activity had to have some line. I could feel how even in a dull house they could have been counted on for the joy of life. At present something had happened—it didn't matter what, their little income had grown less, it had grown least—and they had to do something for pocket-money. Their friends could like them, I made out, without liking to support them. There was something about them that represented credit—their clothes, their manners, their type; but if credit is a large empty pocket in which an occasional chink reverberates, the chink at least must be audible. What they wanted of me was to help to make it so. Fortunately they had no children—I soon divined that. They would also perhaps wish our relations to be kept secret: this was why it was "for the figure"—the reproduction of the face would betray them.

I liked them—I felt, quite as their friends must have done—they were so simple; and I had no objection to them if they would suit. But somehow with all their perfections I didn't easily believe in them. After all they were amateurs, and the ruling passion of my life was the detestation of the amateur. Combined with this was another perversity—an innate preference for the represented subject over the real one: the defect of the real one was so apt to be a lack of representation. I liked things that appeared; then one was sure. Whether they *were* or not was a subordinate and almost always a profitless question. There were other considerations, the first of which was that I already had two or three recruits in use, notably a young person with big feet, in alpaca, from Kilburn, who for a couple of years had come to me regularly for my illustrations and with whom I was still—perhaps ignobly—satisfied. I frankly explained to my visitors how the case stood, but they had taken more precautions than I supposed. They had reasoned out their opportunity, for Claude Rivet had told them of the projected *édition de luxe* of one of the writers of our day—the rarest of the novelists—who, long neglected by the multitudinous vulgar and dearly prized by the attentive (need I mention Philip Vincent?) had had the happy fortune of seeing, late in life, the dawn and then the full light of a higher criticism; an estimate in which on the part of the public there was something really of expiation. The edition preparing, planned by a publisher of taste, was practically an act of high reparation; the wood-cuts with which it was to be enriched were the homage of English art to one of the most independent representatives of English letters. Major and Mrs. Monarch confessed to me they had hoped I might be able to work *them* into my branch of the enterprise. They knew I was to do the first of the books, "Rutland Ramsay," but I had to make clear to them that my participation in the rest of the affair—this first book was to be a test—must depend on the satisfaction I should give. If this should be limited my employers would drop me with scarce common forms. It was therefore a crisis for me, and naturally I was making special preparations, looking about for new people, should they be necessary, and securing the best types. I admitted however that I should like to settle down to two or three good models who would do for everything.

"Should we have often to—a—put on special clothes?" Mrs. Monarch timidly demanded.

"Dear yes—that's half the business."

"And should we be expected to supply our own costumes?"

"Oh no; I've got a lot of things. A painter's models put on—or put off—anything he likes."

"And you mean—a—the same?"

"The same?"

Mrs. Monarch looked at her husband again.

"Oh she was just wondering," he explained, "if the costumes are in *general* use." I had to confess that they were, and I mentioned further that some of them—I had a lot of genuine greasy last-century things—had served their time, a hundred years ago, on living world-stained men and women; on figures not perhaps so far removed, in that vanished world, from *their* type, the Monarchs', *quoi!* of a breeched and bewigged age. "We'll put on anything that *fits*," said the Major.

"Oh I arrange that—they fit in the pictures."

"I'm afraid I should do better for the modern books. I'd come as you like," said Mrs. Monarch.

"She has got a lot of clothes at home: they might do for contemporary life," her husband continued.

"Oh I can fancy scenes in which you'd be quite natural." And indeed I could see the slipshod rearrangements of stale properties —the stories I tried to produce pictures for without the exasperation of reading them—whose sandy tracts the good lady might help to people. But I had to return to the fact that for this sort of work—the daily mechanical grind—I was already equipped: the people I was working with were fully adequate.

"We only thought we might be more like *some* characters," said Mrs. Monarch mildly, getting up.

Her husband also rose; he stood looking at me with a dim wistfulness that was touching in so fine a man. "Wouldn't it be rather a pull sometimes to have—a—to have—?" He hung fire; he wanted me to help him by phrasing what he meant. But I couldn't —I didn't know. So he brought it out awkwardly: "The *real* thing; a gentleman, you know, or a lady." I was quite ready to give a general assent—I admitted that there was a great deal in that. This encouraged Major Monarch to say, following up his appeal with an unacted gulp: "It's awfully hard—we've tried everything." The gulp was communicative; it proved too much for his wife. Before I knew it Mrs. Monarch had dropped again upon a divan and burst into tears. Her husband sat down beside her, holding one of her hands; whereupon she quickly dried her eyes with the other, while I felt embarrassed as she looked up at me. "There isn't a confounded job I haven't applied for—waited for—prayed for. You can fancy we'd be pretty bad first. Secretaryships and that sort of thing? You might as well ask for a peerage. I'd be *anything*—I'm strong; a messenger or a coalheaver. I'd put on a gold-laced cap and open carriage-doors in front of the haberdasher's; I'd hang about a station to carry portmanteaux; I'd be a postman. But they won't *look* at you; there are thousands as good as yourself already on the ground. *Gentlemen,* poor beggars, who've drunk their wine, who've kept their hunters!"

I was as reassuring as I knew how to be, and my visitors were presently on their feet again while, for the experiment, we agreed on an hour. We were discussing it when the door opened and Miss Churm came in with a wet umbrella. Miss Churm had to take the omnibus to Maida Vale and then walk half a mile. She looked a trifle blowsy and slightly splashed. I scarcely ever saw her come in without thinking afresh how odd it was that, being so little in herself, she should yet be so much in others. She was a meagre little Miss Churm, but was such an ample heroine of romance. She was only a freckled cockney,[2] but she could represent everything, from a fine lady to a shepherdess; she had the faculty as she might have had a fine voice or long hair. She couldn't spell and she loved beer,

---

2. A native of London's East End slums.

but she had two or three "points," and practice, and a knack, and mother-wit, and a whimsical sensibility, and a love of the theatre, and seven sisters, and not an ounce of respect, especially for the *h*. The first thing my visitors saw was that her umbrella was wet, and in their spotless perfection they visibly winced at it. The rain had come on since their arrival.

"I'm all in a soak; there *was* a mess of people in the 'bus. I wish you lived near a stytion," said Miss Churm. I requested her to get ready as quickly as possible, and she passed into the room in which she always changed her dress. But before going out she asked me what she was to get into this time.

"It's the Russian princess, don't you know?" I answered; "the one with the 'golden eyes,' in black velvet, for the long thing in the *Cheapside*."

"Golden eyes? I *say!*" cried Miss Churm, while my companions watched her with intensity as she withdrew. She always arranged herself, when she was late, before I could turn round; and I kept my visitors a little on purpose, so that they might get an idea, from seeing her, what would be expected of themselves. I mentioned that she was quite my notion of an excellent model—she was really very clever.

"Do you think she looks like a Russian princess?" Major Monarch asked with lurking alarm.

"When I make her, yes."

"Oh if you have to *make* her—!" he reasoned, not without point.

"That's the most you can ask. There are so many who are not makeable."

"Well now, *here's* a lady"—and with a persuasive smile he passed his arm into his wife's—"who's already made!"

"Oh I'm not a Russian princess," Mrs. Monarch protested a little coldly. I could see she had known some and didn't like them. There at once was a complication of a kind I never had to fear with Miss Churm.

This young lady came back in black velvet—the gown was rather rusty and very low on her lean shoulders—and with a Japanese fan in her red hands. I reminded her that in the scene I was doing she had to look over some one's head. "I forget whose it is; but it doesn't matter. Just look over a head."

"I'd rather look over a stove," said Miss Churm; and she took her station near the fire. She fell into position, settled herself into a tall attitude, gave a certain backward inclination to her head and a certain forward droop to her fan, and looked, at least to my prejudiced sense, distinguished and charming, foreign and dangerous. We left her looking so while I went downstairs with Major and Mrs. Monarch.

"I believe I could come about as near it as that," said Mrs. Monarch.

"Oh you think she's shabby, but you must allow for the alchemy of art."

However, they went off with an evident increase of comfort founded on their demonstrable advantage in being the real thing. I could fancy them shuddering over Miss Churm. She was very droll about them when I went back, for I told her what they wanted.

"Well, if *she* can sit I'll tyke to book-keeping," said my model.

"She's very ladylike," I replied as an innocent form of aggravation.

"So much the worse for *you*. That means she can't turn round."

"She'll do for the fashionable novels."

"Oh yes, she'll *do* for them!" my model humorously declared. "Ain't they bad enough without her?" I had often sociably denounced them to Miss Churm.

III

It was for the elucidation of a mystery in one of these works that I first tried Mrs. Monarch. Her husband came with her, to be useful if necessary—it was sufficiently clear that as a general thing he would prefer to come with her. At first I wondered if this were for "propriety's" sake—if he were going to be jealous and meddling. The idea was too tiresome, and if it had been confirmed it would speedily have brought our acquaintance to a close. But I soon saw there was nothing in it and that if he accompanied Mrs. Monarch it was—in addition to the chance of being wanted—simply because he had nothing else to do. When they were separate his occupation was gone and they never *had* been separate. I judged rightly that in their awkward situation their close union was their main comfort and that this union had no weak spot. It was a real marriage, an encouragement to the hesitating, a nut for pessimists to crack. Their address was humble—I remember afterwards thinking it had been the only thing about them that was really professional— and I could fancy the lamentable lodgings in which the Major would have been left alone. He could sit there more or less grimly with his wife—he couldn't sit there anyhow without her.

He had too much tact to try and make himself agreeable when he couldn't be useful; so when I was too absorbed in my work to talk he simply sat and waited. But I liked to hear him talk—it made my work, when not interrupting it, less mechanical, less special. To listen to him was to combine the excitement of going out with the economy of staying at home. There was only one hindrance—that I seemed not to know any of the people this brilliant couple had known. I think he wondered extremely, during the term of our intercourse, whom the deuce I *did* know. He hadn't a stray sixpence of an idea to fumble for, so we didn't spin it very fine; we confined ourselves to questions of leather and even of liquor—saddlers and breeches-makers and how to get excellent claret cheap—and matters like "good trains" and the habits of small game. His lore on these last subjects was astonishing—he managed to interweave the station-master with the ornithologist. When he couldn't talk about greater things he could talk cheerfully about smaller, and since I couldn't accompany him into reminiscences of the fashionable world he could lower the conversation without a visible effort to my level.

So earnest a desire to please was touching in a man who could so easily have knocked one down. He looked after the fire and had an opinion on the draught of the stove without my asking him, and I could see that he thought many of my arrangements not half knowing. I remember telling him that if I were only rich I'd offer him a salary to come and teach me how to live. Sometimes he gave a random sigh of which the essence might have been: "Give me even such a bare old barrack as *this*, and I'd do something with it!" When I wanted to use him he came alone; which was an illustration of the superior courage of women. His wife could bear her solitary second floor, and she was in general more discreet; showing by various small reserves that she was alive to the propriety of keeping our relations markedly professional—not letting them slide into sociability. She wished it to remain clear that she and the Major were employed, not cultivated, and if she approved of me as a superior, who could be kept in his place, she never thought me quite good enough for an equal.

She sat with great intensity, giving the whole of her mind to it, and was capable of remaining for an hour almost as motionless as before a photographer's lens. I could see she had been photographed often, but somehow the very habit that made her good for that purpose unfitted her for mine. At first I was extremely pleased with her ladylike air, and it was a satisfaction, on coming to follow her lines, to see how good they were and how far they could lead the pencil. But after a little skirmishing I began to find her too insurmountably stiff; do what I would with it my drawing looked like a photograph or a copy of a photograph. Her figure had no variety of expression—she herself had no sense of variety. You may say that this was my business and was only a question of placing her. Yet I placed her in every conceivable position and she managed to obliterate their differences. She was always a lady certainly, and into the bargain was always the same lady. She was the real thing, but always the same thing. There were moments when I rather writhed under the serenity of her confidence that she *was* the real thing. All her dealings with me and all her husband's were an implication that this was lucky for *me*. Meanwhile I found myself trying to invent types that approached her own, instead of making her own transform itself—in the clever way that was not impossible for instance to poor Miss Churm. Arrange as I would and take the precautions I would, she always came out, in my pictures, too tall —landing me in the dilemma of having represented a fascinating woman as seven feet high, which (out of respect perhaps to my own very much scantier inches) was far from my idea of such a personage.

The case was worse with the Major—nothing I could do would keep *him* down, so that he became useful only for the representation of brawny giants. I adored variety and range, I cherished human accidents, the illustrative note; I wanted to characterise closely, and the thing in the world I most hated was the danger of being ridden by a type. I had quarrelled with some of my friends about it: I had parted company with them for maintaining that one *had* to be, and that if the type was beautiful—witness Raphael and Leonardo—the servitude was only a gain. I was neither Leonardo nor Raphael—I might only be a presumptuous young modern searcher; but I held that everything was to be sacrificed sooner than character. When they claimed that the obsessional form could easily *be* character I retorted, perhaps superficially, "Whose?" It couldn't be everybody's—it might end in being nobody's.

After I had drawn Mrs. Monarch a dozen times I felt surer even than before that the value of such a model as Miss Churm resided precisely in the fact that she had no positive stamp, combined of course with the other fact that what she did have was a curious and inexplicable talent for imitation. Her usual appearance was like a curtain which she could draw up at request for a capital performance. This performance was simply suggestive; but it was a word to the wise—it was vivid and pretty. Sometimes even I thought it, though she was plain herself, too insipidly pretty; I made it a reproach to her that the figures drawn from her were monotonously (*bêtement*,[3] as we used to say) graceful. Nothing made her more angry; it was so much her pride to feel she could sit for characters that had nothing in common with each other. She would accuse me at such moments of taking away her "reputytion."

It suffered a certain shrinkage, this queer quantity, from the repeated visits of my new friends. Miss Churm was greatly in demand, never in want of employment, so I had no scruple in putting her off occasionally, to try them more at my ease. It was certainly amusing at first to do the real thing—it was amusing to do Major Monarch's trousers. They *were* the real thing, even if he did come out colossal. It was amusing to do his wife's black hair—it was so

3. Foolishly.

mathematically neat—and the particular "smart" tension of her tight stays. She lent herself especially to positions in which the face was somewhat averted or blurred; she abounded in ladylike back views and *profils perdus*.[4] When she stood erect she took naturally one of the attitudes in which court-painters represent queens and princesses; so that I found myself wondering whether, to draw out this accomplishment, I couldn't get the editor of the *Cheapside* to publish a really royal romance, "A Tale of Buckingham Palace." Sometimes however the real thing and the make-believe came into contact; by which I mean that Miss Churm, keeping an appointment or coming to make one on days when I had much work in hand, encountered her invidious rivals. The encounter was not on their part, for they noticed her no more than if she had been the housemaid; not from intentional loftiness, but simply because as yet, professionally, they didn't know how to fraternise, as I could imagine they would have liked—or at least that the Major would. They couldn't talk about the omnibus—they always walked; and they didn't know what else to try—she wasn't interested in good trains or cheap claret. Besides, they must have felt—in the air— that she was amused at them, secretly derisive of their ever knowing how. She wasn't a person to conceal the limits of her faith if she had had a chance to show them. On the other hand Mrs. Monarch didn't think her tidy; for why else did she take pains to say to me—it was going out of the way, for Mrs. Monarch—that she didn't like dirty women?

One day when my young lady happened to be present with my other sitters—she even dropped in, when it was convenient, for a chat—I asked her to be so good as to lend a hand in getting tea, a service with which she was familiar and which was one of a class that, living as I did in a small way, with slender domestic resources, I often appealed to my models to render. They liked to lay hands on my property, to break the sitting, and sometimes the china—it made them feel Bohemian. The next time I saw Miss Churm after this incident she surprised me greatly by making a scene about it— she accused me of having wished to humiliate her. She hadn't resented the outrage at the time, but had seemed obliging and amused, enjoying the comedy of asking Mrs. Monarch, who sat vague and silent, whether she would have cream and sugar, and putting an exaggerated simper into the question. She had tried intonations—as if she too wished to pass for the real thing—till I was afraid my other visitors would take offence.

Oh, they were determined not to do this, and their touching patience was the measure of their great need. They would sit by the hour, uncomplaining, till I was ready to use them; they would come back on the chance of being wanted and would walk away cheer-

4. Half-rear views "losing" most of the profile.

fully if it failed. I used to go to the door with them to see in what magnificent order they retreated. I tried to find other employment for them—I introduced them to several artists. But they didn't "take," for reasons I could appreciate, and I became rather anxiously aware that after such disappointments they fell back upon me with a heavier weight. They did me the honour to think me most *their* form. They weren't romantic enough for the painters, and in those days there were few serious workers in black-and-white. Besides, they had an eye to the great job I had mentioned to them—they had secretly set their hearts on supplying the right essence for my pictorial vindication of our fine novelist. They knew that for this undertaking I should want no costume-effects, none of the frippery of past ages—that it was a case in which everything would be contemporary and satirical and presumably genteel. If I could work them into it their future would be assured, for the labour would of course be long and the occupation steady.

One day Mrs. Monarch came without her husband—she explained his absence by his having had to go the City. While she sat there in her usual relaxed majesty there came at the door a knock which I immediately recognised as the subdued appeal of a model out of work. It was followed by the entrance of a young man whom I at once saw to be a foreigner and who proved in fact an Italian acquainted with no English word but my name, which he uttered in a way that made it seem to include all others. I hadn't then visited his country, nor was I proficient in his tongue; but as he was not so meanly constituted—what Italian is?—as to depend only on that member for expression he conveyed to me, in familiar but graceful mimicry, that he was in search of exactly the employment in which the lady before me was engaged. I was not struck with him at first, and while I continued to draw I dropped few signs of interest or encouragement. He stood his ground however —not importunely, but with a dumb dog-like fidelity in his eyes that amounted to innocent impudence, the manner of a devoted servant—he might have been in the house for years—unjustly suspected. Suddenly it struck me that this very attitude and expression made a picture; whereupon I told him to sit down and wait till I should be free. There was another picture in the way he obeyed me, and I observed as I worked that there were others still in the way he looked wonderingly, with his head thrown back, about the high studio. He might have been crossing himself in Saint Peter's. Before I finished I said to myself "The fellow's a bankrupt orange-monger, but a treasure."

When Mrs. Monarch withdrew he passed across the room like a flash to open the door for her, standing there with the rapt pure gaze of the young Dante spellbound by the young Beatrice. As I never insisted, in such situations, on the blankness of the British domestic, I reflected that he had the making of a servant—and I needed one, but couldn't pay him to be only that—as well as of a model; in short I resolved to adopt my bright adventurer if he would agree to officiate in the double capacity. He jumped at my offer, and in the event my rashness—for I had really known nothing about him—wasn't brought home to me. He proved a sympathetic though a desultory ministrant, and had in a wonderful degree the *sentiment de la pose*.[5] It was uncultivated, instinctive, a part of the happy instinct that had guided him to my door and helped him to spell out my name on the card nailed to it. He had had no other introduction to me than a guess, from the shape of my high north window, seen outside, that my place was a studio and that as a studio it would contain an artist. He had wandered to England in search of fortune, like other itinerants, and had embarked, with a partner and a small green hand-cart, on the sale of penny ices. The ices had melted away and the partner had dissolved in their train. My young man wore tight yellow trousers with reddish stripes and his name was Oronte. He was sallow but fair, and when I put him into some old clothes of my own he looked like an Englishman. He was as good as Miss Churm, who could look, when requested, like an Italian.

IV

I thought Mrs. Monarch's face slightly convulsed when, on her coming back with her husband, she found Oronte installed. It was strange to have to recognise in a scrap of a lazzarone a competitor to her magnificent Major. It was she who scented danger first, for the Major was anecdotically unconscious. But Oronte gave us tea, with a hundred eager confusions—he had never been concerned in so queer a process—and I think she thought better of me for having at last an "establishment." They saw a couple of drawings that I had made of the establishment, and Mrs. Monarch hinted that it never would have struck her he had sat for them. "Now the drawings you make from *us,* they look exactly like us," she reminded me, smiling in triumph; and I recognised that this was indeed just their defect. When I drew the Monarchs I couldn't anyhow get away from them—get into the character I wanted to represent; and I hadn't the least desire my model should be discoverable in my picture. Miss Churm never was, and Mrs. Monarch thought I hid her, very properly, because she was vulgar; whereas if she was lost it was only as the dead who go to heaven are lost—in the gain of an angel the more.

By this time I had got a certain start with "Rutland Ramsay," the first novel in the great projected series; that is I had produced a dozen drawings, several with the help of the Major and his wife, and I had sent them in for approval. My understanding with the

5. Instinct for correct posing.

publishers, as I have already hinted, had been that I was to be left to do my work, in this particular case, as I liked, with the whole book committed to me; but my connexion with the rest of the series was only contingent. There were moments when, frankly, it *was* a comfort to have the real thing under one's hand; for there were characters in "Rutland Ramsay" that were very much like it. There were people presumably as erect as the Major and women of as good a fashion as Mrs. Monarch. There was a great deal of country-house life—treated, it is true, in a fine fanciful ironical generalised way—and there was a considerable implication of knickerbockers and kilts. There were certain things I had to settle at the outset; such things for instance as the exact appearance of the hero and the particular bloom and figure of the heroine. The author of course gave me a lead, but there was a margin for interpretation. I took the Monarchs into my confidence, I told them frankly what I was about, I mentioned my embarrassments and alternatives. "Oh take *him!*" Mrs. Monarch murmured sweetly, looking at her husband; and "What could you want better than my wife?" the Major enquired with the comfortable candour that now prevailed between us.

I wasn't obliged to answer these remarks—I was only obliged to place my sitters. I wasn't easy in mind, and I postponed a little timidly perhaps the solving of my question. The book was a large canvas, the other figures were numerous, and I worked off at first some of the episodes in which the hero and the heroine were not concerned. When once I had set *them* up I should have to stick to them—I couldn't make my young man seven feet high in one place and five feet nine in another. I inclined on the whole to the latter measurement, though the Major more than once reminded me that *he* looked about as young as any one. It was indeed quite possible to arrange him, for the figure, so that it would have been difficult to detect his age. After the spontaneous Oronte had been with me a month, and after I had given him to understand several times over that his native exuberance would presently constitute an insurmountable barrier to our further intercourse, I waked to a sense of his heroic capacity. He was only five feet seven, but the remaining inches were latent. I tried him almost secretly at first, for I was really rather afraid of the judgment my other models would pass on such a choice. If they regarded Miss Churm as little better than a snare what would they think of the representation by a person so little the real thing as an Italian street-vendor of a protagonist formed by a public school?

If I went a little in fear of them it wasn't because they bullied me, because they had got an oppressive foothold, but because in their really pathetic decorum and mysteriously permanent newness they counted on me so intensely. I was therefore very glad when Jack Hawley came home: he was always of such good counsel. He painted badly himself, but there was no one like him for putting his finger on the place. He had been absent from England for a year; he had been somewhere—I don't remember where—to get a fresh eye. I was in a good deal of dread of any such organ, but we were old friends; he had been away for months and a sense of emptiness was creeping into my life. I hadn't dodged a missile for a year.

He came back with a fresh eye, but with the same old black velvet blouse, and the first evening he spent in my studio we smoked cigarettes till the small hours. He had done no work himself, he had only got the eye; so the field was clear for the production of my little things. He wanted to see what I had produced for the *Cheapside*, but he was disappointed in the exhibition. That at least seemed the meaning of two or three comprehensive groans which, as he lounged on my big divan, his leg folded under him, looking at my latest drawings, issued from his lips with the smoke of the cigarette.

"What's the matter with you?" I asked.

"What's the matter with *you?*"

"Nothing save that I'm mystified."

"You are indeed. You're quite off the hinge. What's the meaning of this new fad?" And he tossed me, with visible irreverence, a drawing in which I happened to have depicted both my elegant models. I asked if he didn't think it good, and he replied that it struck him as execrable, given the sort of thing I had always represented myself to him as wishing to arrive at; but I let that pass—I was so anxious to see exactly what he meant. The two figures in the picture looked colossal, but I supposed this was *not* what he meant, inasmuch as, for aught he knew to the contrary, I might have been trying for some such effect. I maintained that I was working exactly in the same way as when he last had done me the honour to tell me I might do something some day. "Well, there's a screw loose somewhere," he answered; "wait a bit and I'll discover it." I depended upon him to do so: where else was the fresh eye? But he produced at last nothing more luminous than "I don't know—I don't like your types." This was lame for a critic who had never consented to discuss with me anything but the question of execution, the direction of strokes and the mystery of values.

"In the drawings you've been looking at I think my types are very handsome."

"Oh they won't do!"

"I've been working with new models."

"I see you have. *They* won't do."

"Are you very sure of that?"

"Absolutely—they're stupid."

"You mean *I* am—for I ought to get round that."

"You *can't*—with such people. Who are they?"

I told him, so far as was necessary, and he concluded heartlessly: "*Ce sont des gens qu'il faut mettre à la porte.*" [6]

"You've never seen them; they're awfully good"—I flew to their defence.

"Not seen them? Why all this recent work of yours drops to pieces with them. It's all I want to see of them."

"No one else has said anything against it—the *Cheapside* people are pleased."

"Every one else is an ass, and the *Cheapside* people the biggest asses of all. Come, don't pretend at this time of day to have pretty illusions about the public, especially about publishers and editors. It's not for *such* animals you work—it's for those who know, *color che sanno;* [7] so keep straight for *me* if you can't keep straight for yourself. There was a certain sort of thing you used to try for— and a very good thing it was. But this twaddle isn't *in* it." When I talked with Hawley later about "Rutland Ramsay" and its possible successors he declared that I must get back into my boat again or I should go to the bottom. His voice in short was the voice of warning.

I noted the warning, but I didn't turn my friends out of doors. They bored me a good deal; but the very fact that they bored me admonished me not to sacrifice them—if there was anything to be done with them—simply to irritation. As I look back at this phase they seem to me to have pervaded my life not a little. I have a vision of them as most of the time in my studio, seated against the wall on an old velvet bench to be out of the way, and resembling the while a pair of patient courtiers in a royal ante-chamber. I'm convinced that during the coldest weeks of the winter they held their ground because it saved them fire. Their newness was losing its gloss, and it was impossible not to feel them objects of charity. Whenever Miss Churm arrived they went away, and after I was fairly launched in "Rutland Ramsay" Miss Churm arrived pretty often. They managed to express to me tacitly that they supposed I wanted her for the low life of the book, and I let them suppose it, since they had attempted to study the work—it was lying about the studio—without discovering that it dealt only with the highest circles. They had dipped into the most brilliant of our novelists without deciphering many passages. I still took an hour from them, now and again, in spite of Jack Hawley's warning:

6. "They are the kind of people one must get rid of."

7. Dante's reference to Aristotle: "*Vidi il Maestro di color che sanno*" ["I saw the master of those who know"], *Inferno*, iv, 131.

it would be time enough to dismiss them, if dismissal should be necessary, when the rigour of the season was over. Hawley had made their acquaintance—he had met them at my fireside—and thought them a ridiculous pair. Learning that he was a painter they tried to approach him, to show him too that they were the real thing; but he looked at them, across the big room, as if they were miles away: they were a compendium of everything he most objected to in the social system of his country. Such people as that, all convention and patent-leather, with ejaculations that stopped conversation, had no business in a studio. A studio was a place to learn to see, and how could you see through a pair of feather-beds?

The main inconvenience I suffered at their hands was that at first I was shy of letting it break upon them that my artful little servant had begun to sit to me for "Rutland Ramsay." They knew I had been odd enough—they were prepared by this time to allow oddity to artists—to pick a foreign vagabond out of the streets when I might have had a person with whiskers and credentials; but it was some time before they learned how high I rated his accomplishments. They found him in an attitude more than once, but they never doubted I was doing him as an organ-grinder. There were several things they never guessed, and one of them was that for a striking scene in the novel, in which a footman briefly figured, it occurred to me to make use of Major Monarch as the menial. I kept putting this off, I didn't like to ask him to don the livery— besides the difficulty of finding a livery to fit him. At last, one day late in the winter, when I was at work on the despised Oronte, who caught one's idea on the wing, and was in the glow of feeling myself go very straight, they came in, the Major and his wife, with their society laugh about nothing (there was less and less to laugh at); came in like country-callers—they always reminded me of that— who have walked across the park after church and are presently persuaded to stay to luncheon. Luncheon was over, but they could stay to tea—I knew they wanted it. The fit was on me, however, and I couldn't let my ardour cool and my work wait, with the fading daylight, while my model prepared it. So I asked Mrs. Monarch if she would mind laying it out—a request which for an instant brought all the blood to her face. Her eyes were on her husband's for a second, and some mute telegraphy passed between them. Their folly was over the next instant; his cheerful shrewdness put an end to it. So far from pitying their wounded pride, I must add, I was moved to give it as complete a lesson as I could. They bustled about together and got out the cups and saucers and made the kettle boil. I know they felt as if they were waiting on my servant, and when the tea was prepared I said: "He'll have a cup, please— he's tired." Mrs. Monarch brought him one where he stood, and he took it from her as if he had been a gentleman at a party squeezing a crush-hat with an elbow.

Then it came over me that she had made a great effort for me—made it with a kind of nobleness—and that I owed her a compensation. Each time I saw her after this I wondered what the compensation could be. I couldn't go on doing the wrong thing to oblige them. Oh it *was* the wrong thing, the stamp of the work for which they sat—Hawley was not the only person to say it now. I sent in a large number of the drawings I had made for "Rutland Ramsay," and I received a warning that was more to the point than Hawley's. The artistic adviser of the house for which I was working was of opinion that many of my illustrations were not what had been looked for. Most of these illustrations were the subjects in which the Monarchs had figured. Without going into the question of what *had* been looked for, I had to face the fact that at this rate I shouldn't get the other books to do. I hurled myself in despair on Miss Churm—I put her through all her paces. I not only adopted Oronte publicly as my hero, but one morning when the Major looked in to see if I didn't require him to finish a *Cheapside* figure for which he had begun to sit the week before, I told him I had changed my mind—I'd do the drawing from my man. At this my visitor turned pale and stood looking at me. "Is *he* your idea of an English gentleman?" he asked.

I was disappointed, I was nervous, I wanted to get on with my work; so I replied with irritation: "Oh my dear Major—I can't be ruined for *you!*"

It was a horrid speech, but he stood another moment—after which, without a word, he quitted the studio. I drew a long breath, for I said to myself that I shouldn't see him again. I hadn't told him definitely that I was in danger of having my work rejected, but I was vexed at his not having felt the catastrophe in the air, read with me the moral of our fruitless collaboration, the lesson that in the deceptive atmosphere of art even the highest respectability may fail of being plastic.

I didn't owe my friends money, but I did see them again. They reappeared together three days later, and, given all the other facts, there was something tragic in that one. It was a clear proof they could find nothing else in life to do. They had threshed the matter out in a dismal conference—they had digested the bad news that they were not in for the series. If they weren't useful to me even for the *Cheapside* their function seemed difficult to determine, and I could only judge at first that they had come, forgivingly, decorously, to take a last leave. This made me rejoice in secret that I had little leisure for a scene; for I had placed both my other models in position together and I was pegging away at a drawing from which I hoped to derive glory. It had been suggested by the passage in which Rutland Ramsay, drawing up a chair to Artemisia's piano-stool, says extraordinary things to her while she ostensibly fingers out a difficult piece of music. I had done Miss Churm at the piano before—it was an attitude in which she knew how to take on an absolutely poetic grace. I wished the two figures to "compose" together with intensity, and my little Italian had entered perfectly into my conception. The pair were vividly before me, the piano had been pulled out; it was a charming show of blended youth and murmured love, which I had only to catch and keep. My visitors stood and looked at it, and I was friendly to them over my shoulder.

They made no response, but I was used to silent company and went on with my work, only a little disconcerted—even though exhilarated by the sense that *this* was at least the ideal thing—at not having got rid of them after all. Presently I heard Mrs. Monarch's sweet voice beside or rather above me: "I wish her hair were a little better done." I looked up and she was staring with a strange fixedness at Miss Churm, whose back was turned to her. "Do you mind my just touching it?" she went on—a question which made me spring up for an instant as with the instinctive fear that she might do the young lady a harm. But she quieted me with a glance I shall never forget—I confess I should like to have been able to paint *that*—and went for a moment to my model. She spoke to her softly, laying a hand on her shoulder and bending over her; and as the girl, understanding, gratefully assented, she disposed her rough curls, with a few quick passes, in such a way as to make Miss Churm's head twice as charming. It was one of the most heroic personal services I've ever seen rendered. Then Mrs. Monarch turned away with a low sigh, and, looking about her as if for something to do, stooped to the floor with a noble humility and picked up a dirty rag that had dropped out of my paint-box.

The Major meanwhile had also been looking for something to do, and, wandering to the other end of the studio, saw before him my breakfast-things neglected, unremoved. "I say, can't I be useful *here?*" he called out to me with an irrepressible quaver. I assented with a laugh that I fear was awkward, and for the next ten minutes, while I worked, I heard the light clatter of china and the tinkle of spoons and glass. Mrs. Monarch assisted her husband—they washed up my crockery, they put it away. They wandered off into my little scullery, and I afterwards found that they had cleaned my knives and that my slender stock of plate had an unprecedented surface. When it came over me, the latent eloquence of what they were doing, I confess that my drawing was blurred for a moment—the picture swam. They had accepted their failure, but they couldn't accept their fate. They had bowed their heads in bewilderment to the perverse and cruel law in virtue of which the real thing could be so much less precious than the unreal; but they didn't want to starve. If my servants were my models, then my models might be my servants. They would reverse the parts—the others would sit for the ladies and gentlemen and *they* would do the work. They would still be in the studio—it was an intense dumb appeal to me not to turn them out. "Take us on," they wanted to say— "we'll do *anything*."

My pencil dropped from my hand; my sitting was spoiled and I got rid of my sitters, who were also evidently rather mystified and awestruck. Then, alone with the Major and his wife I had a most uncomfortable moment. He put their prayer into a single sentence: "I say, you know—just let *us* do for you, can't you?" I couldn't—it was dreadful to see them emptying my slops; but I pretended I could, to oblige them, for about a week. Then I gave them a sum of money to go away, and I never saw them again. I obtained the remaining books, but my friend Hawley repeats that Major and Mrs. Monarch did me a permanent harm, got me into false ways. If it be true I'm content to have paid the price—for the memory.

1893, 1909

The Beast in the Jungle [8]

I

What determined the speech that startled him in the course of their encounter scarcely matters, being probably but some words

8. Among the selections in this volume, "The Beast in the Jungle" represents the vintage James, with the highest complexity of symbolism and, at the same time, the greatest clarity of motivation. He wrote the story in 1901, immediately after completing *The Ambassadors*—to James' mind his most finished product—and it would seem that this story owes much to that novel for its motivation. Like Strether in *The Ambassadors*, John Marcher spends his life in the shadow of the more vivid experiences of others. Both lives are tragic because the means of escape lie at hand, ready for the grasping. By comparison, the force of this story is heightened because Marcher's predicament is recognized by only one individual, May Bartram, and she alone could have saved him.

In his preface to the story published in the New York Edition of his collected works, James describes his "poor gentleman" as having "the conviction,

lodged in his brain, part and parcel of his imagination from far back, that experience would be marked for him, and whether for good or for ill, by some rare distinction, some incalculable violence or unprecedented stroke. * * * Therefore as each item of experience comes, with its possibilities, into view, he can but dismiss it under this sterilising habit of the failure to find it good enough and thence to appropriate it. * * * He is afraid to recognise what he incidentally misses, since what his high belief amounts to is not that he shall have felt and vibrated less than any one else, but that he shall have felt and vibrated more; which no acknowledgment of the minor loss must conflict with." This fear James symbolizes as the threatened leap of the beast.

So Marcher moves on through his detached life, the jungle of his own egoism and fear of experience. In "The Art of Fiction" James defines experi-

spoken by himself quite without intention—spoken as they lingered and slowly moved together after their renewal of acquaintance. He had been conveyed by friends an hour or two before to the house at which she was staying; the party of visitors at the other house, of whom he was one, and thanks to whom it was his theory, as always, that he was lost in the crowd, had been invited over to luncheon. There had been after luncheon much dispersal, all in the interest of the original motive, a view of Weatherend itself [9] and the fine things, intrinsic features, pictures, heirlooms, treasures of all the arts, that made the place almost famous; and the great rooms were so numerous that guests could wander at their will, hang back from the principal group and in cases where they took such matters with the last seriousness give themselves up to mysterious appreciations and measurements. There were persons to be observed, singly or in couples, bending toward objects in out-of-the-way corners with their hands on their knees and their heads nodding quite as with the emphasis of an excited sense of smell. When they were two they either mingled their sounds of ecstasy or melted into silences of even deeper import, so that there were aspects of the occasion that gave it for Marcher much the air of the "look round," previous to a sale highly advertised, that excites or quenches, as may be, the dream of acquisition. The dream of acquisition at Weatherend would have had to be wild indeed, and John Marcher found himself, among such suggestions, disconcerted almost equally by the presence of those who knew too much and by that of those who knew nothing. The great rooms caused so much poetry and history to press upon him that he needed some straying apart to feel in a proper relation with them, though this impulse was not, as happened, like the gloating of some of his companions, to be compared to the movements of a dog sniffing a cupboard. It had an issue promptly enough in a direction that was not to have been calculated.

It led, briefly, in the course of the October afternoon, to his closer meeting with May Bartram, whose face, a reminder, yet not quite a remembrance, as they sat much separated at a very

ence as being never limited and never complete—"it is an immense sensibility." His fatal lack in this capacity prevents Marcher from comprehending his long awaited "rare and strange" fate to be simply that nothing will ever happen to him, that he is to be a man without being human. The figurative beast strikes when Marcher discovers, too late, that the springs of life were in May Bartram's more acute and suffering sensibility.

The story appears in a volume of stories, *The Better Sort* (1903), and was finally collected with tales of the "quasi-supernatural" in *The Altar of the Dead* in the New York Edition (Vol. XVII, 1909), the source of this text.

9. As Leon Edel suggests in his introduction to *Henry James: Selected Fiction*, the author sets the tone early in the story by the uncomplicated symbolism of Weatherend's name, "suggesting temporal changes and the seasons" and the comparison in the names of May and Marcher.

long table, had begun merely by troubling him rather pleasantly. It affected him as the sequel of something of which he had lost the beginning. He knew it, and for the time quite welcomed it, as a continuation, but didn't know what it continued, which was an interest or an amusement the greater as he was also somehow aware—yet without a direct sign from her—that the young woman herself hadn't lost the thread. She hadn't lost it, but she wouldn't give it back to him, he saw, without some putting forth of his hand for it; and he not only saw that, but saw several things more, things odd enough in the light of the fact that at the moment some accident of grouping brought them face to face he was still merely fumbling with the idea that any contact between them in the past would have had no importance. If it had had no importance he scarcely knew why his actual impression of her should so seem to have so much; the answer to which, however, was that in such a life as they all appeared to be leading for the moment one could but take things as they came. He was satisfied, without in the least being able to say why, that this young lady might roughly have ranked in the house as a poor relation; satisfied also that she was not there on a brief visit, but was more or less a part of the establishment—almost a working, a remunerated part. Didn't she enjoy at periods a protection that she paid for by helping, among other services, to show the place and explain it, deal with the tiresome people, answer questions about the dates of the building, the styles of the furniture, the authorship of the pictures, the favourite haunts of the ghost? It wasn't that she looked as if you could have given her shillings—it was impossible to look less so. Yet when she finally drifted toward him, distinctly handsome, though ever so much older—older than when he had seen her before—it might have been as an effect of her guessing that he had, within the couple of hours, devoted more imagination to her than to all the others put together, and had thereby penetrated to a kind of truth that the others were too stupid for. She *was* there on harder terms than any one; she was there as a consequence of things suffered, one way and another, in the interval of years; and she remembered him very much as she was remembered—only a good deal better.

By the time they at last thus came to speech they were alone in one of the rooms—remarkable for a fine portrait over the chimney-place—out of which their friends had passed, and the charm of it was that even before they had spoken they had practically arranged with each other to stay behind for talk. The charm, happily, was in other things too—partly in there being scarce a spot at Weatherend without something to stay behind for. It was in the way the autumn day looked into the high windows as it waned; the way the red light, breaking at the close from under a low sombre sky, reached out in a long shaft and played over old wainscots, old tapestry, old gold, old colour. It was most of all perhaps in the way she came to him as if, since she had been turned on to deal with the simpler sort, he might, should he choose to keep the whole thing down, just take her mild attention for a part of her general business. As soon as he heard her voice, however, the gap was filled up and the missing link supplied; the slight irony he divined in her attitude lost its advantage. He almost jumped at it to get there before her. "I met you years and years ago in Rome. I remember all about it." She confessed to disappointment—she had been so sure he didn't; and to prove how well he did he began to pour forth the particular recollections that popped up as he called for them. Her face and her voice, all at his service now, worked the miracle—the impression operating like the torch of a lamplighter who touches into flame, one by one, a long row of gas-jets. Marcher flattered himself the illumination was brilliant, yet he was really still more pleased on her showing him, with amusement, that in his haste to make everything right he had got most things rather wrong. It hadn't been at Rome—it had been at Naples; and it hadn't been eight years before—it had been more nearly ten. She hadn't been, either, with her uncle and aunt, but with her mother and her brother; in addition to which it was not with the Pembles *he* had been, but with the Boyers, coming down in their company from Rome—a point on which she insisted, a little to his confusion, and as to which she had her evidence in hand. The Boyers she had known, but didn't know the Pembles, though she had heard of them, and it was the people he was with who had made them acquainted. The incident of the thunderstorm that had raged round them with such violence as to drive them for refuge into an excavation—this incident had not occurred at the Palace of the Cæsars, but at Pompeii, on an occasion when they had been present there at an important find.

He accepted her amendments, he enjoyed her corrections, though the moral of them was, she pointed out, that he *really* didn't remember the least thing about her;[1] and he only felt it as a drawback that when all was made strictly historic there didn't appear much of anything left. They lingered together still, she neglecting her office—for from the moment he was so clever she had no proper right to him—and both neglecting the house, just waiting as to see if a memory or two more wouldn't again breathe on them. It hadn't taken them many minutes, after all, to put down on the table, like the cards of a pack, those that constituted

1. A portent of their different degrees of awareness of life; the difference becomes more evident as their relationship grows.

their respective hands; only what came out was that the pack was unfortunately not perfect—that the past, invoked, invited, encouraged, could give them, naturally, no more than it had. It had made them anciently meet—her at twenty, him at twenty-five; but nothing was so strange, they seemed to say to each other, as that, while so occupied, it hadn't done a little more for them. They looked at each other as with the feeling of an occasion missed; the present would have been so much better if the other, in the far distance, in the foreign land, hadn't been so stupidly meagre. There weren't apparently, all counted, more than a dozen little old things that had succeeded in coming to pass between them; trivialities of youth, simplicities of freshness, stupidities of ignorance, small possible germs, but too deeply buried—too deeply (didn't it seem?) to sprout after so many years. Marcher could only feel he ought to have rendered her some service—saved her from a capsized boat in the Bay or at least recovered her dressing-bag, filched from her cab in the streets of Naples by a lazzarone with a stiletto. Or it would have been nice if he could have been taken with fever all alone at his hotel, and she could have come to look after him, to write to his people, to drive him out in convalescence. *Then* they would be in possession of the something or other that their actual show seemed to lack. It yet somehow presented itself, this show, as too good to be spoiled; so that they were reduced for a few minutes more to wondering a little helplessly why—since they seemed to know a certain number of the same people—their reunion had been so long averted. They didn't use that name for it, but their delay from minute to minute to join the others was a kind of confession that they didn't quite want it to be a failure. Their attempted supposition of reasons for their not having met but showed how little they knew of each other. There came in fact a moment when Marcher felt a positive pang. It was vain to pretend she was an old friend, for all the communities were wanting, in spite of which it was as an old friend that he saw she would have suited him. He had new ones enough—was surrounded with them for instance on the stage of the other house; as a new one he probably wouldn't have so much as noticed her. He would have liked to invent something, get her to make-believe with him that some passage of a romantic or critical kind *had* originally occurred. He was really almost reaching out in imagination—as against time—for something that would do, and saying to himself that if it didn't come this sketch of a fresh start would show for quite awkwardly bungled. They would separate, and now for no second or no third chance. They would have tried and not succeeded. Then it was, just at the turn, as he afterwards made it out to himself, that, everything else failing, she herself decided to take up the case and, as it were, save the situation. He felt as soon as she spoke that she had been consciously keeping back what she said and hoping to get on without it; a scruple in her that immensely touched him when, by the end of three or four minutes more, he was able to measure it. What she brought out, at any rate, quite cleared the air and supplied the link—the link it was so odd he should frivolously have managed to lose.

"You know you told me something I've never forgotten and that again and again has made me think of you since; it was that tremendously hot day when we went to Sorrento, across the bay, for the breeze. What I allude to was what you said to me, on the way back, as we sat under the awning of the boat enjoying the cool. Have you forgotten?"

He had forgotten and was even more surprised than ashamed. But the great thing was that he saw in this no vulgar reminder of any "sweet" speech. The vanity of women had long memories, but she was making no claim on him of a compliment or a mistake. With another woman, a totally different one, he might have feared the recall possibly even of some imbecile "offer." So, in having to say that he had indeed forgotten, he was conscious rather of a loss than of a gain; he already saw an interest in the matter of her mention. "I try to think—but I give it up. Yet I remember the Sorrento day."

"I'm not very sure you do," May Bartram after a moment said; "and I'm not very sure I ought to want you to. It's dreadful to bring a person back at any time to what he was ten years before. If you've lived away from it," she smiled, "so much the better."

"Ah if *you* haven't why should I?" he asked.

"Lived away, you mean, from what I myself was?"

"From what *I* was. I was of course an ass," Marcher went on; "but I would rather know from you just the sort of ass I was than —from the moment you have something in your mind—not know anything."

Still, however, she hesitated. "But if you've completely ceased to be that sort—?"

"Why I can then all the more bear to know. Besides, perhaps I haven't."

"Perhaps. Yet if you haven't," she added, "I should suppose you'd remember. Not indeed that *I* in the least connect with my impression the invidious name you use. If I had only thought you foolish," she explained, "the thing I speak of wouldn't so have remained with me. It was about yourself." She waited as if it might come to him; but as, only meeting her eyes in wonder, he gave no sign, she burnt her ships. "Has it ever happened?"

Then it was that, while he continued to stare, a light broke for him and the blood slowly came to his face, which began to burn with recognition. "Do you mean I told you——?" But he faltered, lest what came to him shouldn't be right, lest he should only give himself away.

"It was something about yourself that it was natural one shouldn't forget—that is if one remembered you at all. That's why I ask you," she smiled, "if the thing you then spoke of has ever come to pass?"

Oh then he saw, but he was lost in wonder and found himself embarrassed. This, he also saw, made her sorry for him, as if her allusion had been a mistake. It took him but a moment, however, to feel it hadn't been, much as it had been a surprise. After the first little shock of it her knowledge on the contrary began, even if rather strangely, to taste sweet to him. She was the only other person in the world then who would have it, and she had had it all these years, while the fact of his having so breathed his secret had unaccountably faded from him. No wonder they couldn't have met as if nothing had happened. "I judge," he finally said, "that I know what you mean. Only I had strangely enough lost any sense of having taken you so far into my confidence."

"Is it because you've taken so many others as well?"

"I've taken nobody. Not a creature since then."

"So that I'm the only person who knows?"

"The only person in the world."

"Well," she quickly replied, "I myself have never spoken. I've never, never repeated of you what you told me." She looked at him so that he perfectly believed her. Their eyes met over it in such a way that he was without a doubt. "And I never will."

She spoke with an earnestness that, as if almost excessive, put him at ease about her possible derision. Somehow the whole question was a new luxury to him—that is from the moment she was in possession. If she didn't take the sarcastic view she clearly took the sympathetic, and that was what he had had, in all the long time, from no one whomsoever. What he felt was that he couldn't at present have begun to tell her, and yet could profit perhaps exquisitely by the accident of having done so of old. "Please don't then. We're just right as it is."

"Oh I am," she laughed, "if you are!" To which she added: "Then you do still feel in the same way?"

It was impossible he shouldn't take to himself that she was really interested, though it all kept coming as a perfect surprise. He had thought of himself so long as abominably alone, and lo he wasn't alone a bit. He hadn't been, it appeared, for an hour—since those moments on the Sorrento boat. It was *she* who had been, he seemed to see as he looked at her—she who had been made so by the graceless fact of his lapse of fidelity. To tell her what he had told her—what had it been but to ask something of her? something that she had given, in her charity, without his having, by a remembrance, by a return of the spirit, failing another encounter, so much as thanked her. What he had asked of her had been simply at first not to laugh at him. She had beautifully not done so for ten years, and she was not doing so now. So he had endless gratitude to make up. Only for that he must see just how he had figured to her. "What, exactly, was the account I gave—?"

"Of the way you did feel? Well, it was very simple. You said you had had from your earliest time, as the deepest thing within you, the sense of being kept for something rare and strange, possibly prodigious and terrible, that was sooner or later to happen to you, that you had in your bones the foreboding and the conviction of, and that would perhaps overwhelm you."

"Do you call that very simple?" John Marcher asked.

She thought a moment. "It was perhaps because I seemed, as you spoke, to understand it."

"You do understand it?" he eagerly asked.

Again she kept her kind eyes on him. "You still have the belief?"

"Oh!" he exclaimed helplessly. There was too much to say.

"Whatever it's to be," she clearly made out, "it hasn't yet come."

He shook his head in complete surrender now. "It hasn't yet come. Only, you know, it isn't anything I'm to *do*, to achieve in the world, to be distinguished or admired for. I'm not such an ass as *that*. It would be much better, no doubt, if I were."

"It's to be something you're merely to suffer?"

"Well, say to wait for—to have to meet, to face, to see suddenly break out in my life; possibly destroying all further consciousness, possibly annihilating me; possibly, on the other hand, only altering everything, striking at the root of all my world and leaving me to the consequences, however they shape themselves."

She took this in, but the light in her eyes continued for him not to be that of mockery. "Isn't what you describe perhaps but the expectation—or at any rate the sense of danger, familiar to so many people—of falling in love?"

John Marcher wondered. "Did you ask me that before?"

"No—I wasn't so free-and-easy then. But it's what strikes me now."

"Of course," he said after a moment, "it strikes you. Of course it strikes *me*. Of course what's in store for me may be no more than that. The only thing is," he went on, "that I think if it had been that I should by this time know."

"Do you mean because you've *been* in love?" And then as he but looked at her in silence: "You've been in love, and it hasn't meant such a cataclysm, hasn't proved the great affair?"

"Here I am, you see. It hasn't been overwhelming."

"Then it hasn't been love," said May Bartram.[2]

"Well, I at least thought it was. I took it for that—I've taken it till now. It was agreeable, it was delightful, it was miserable," he explained. "But it wasn't strange. It wasn't what *my* affair's to be."

"You want something all to yourself—something that nobody else knows or *has* known?"

"It isn't a question of what I 'want'—God knows I don't want anything. It's only a question of the apprehension that haunts me— that I live with day by day."

He said this so lucidly and consistently that he could see it further impose itself. If she hadn't been interested before she'd have been interested now. "Is it a sense of coming violence?"

Evidently now too again he liked to talk of it. "I don't think of it as—when it does come—necessarily violent. I only think of it as natural and as of course above all unmistakeable. I think of it simply as *the* thing. *The* thing will of itself appear natural."

"Then how will it appear strange?"

Marcher bethought himself. "It won't—to *me*."

"To whom then?"

"Well," he replied, smiling at last, "say to you."

"Oh then I'm to be present?"

"Why you *are* present—since you know."

"I see." She turned it over. "But I mean at the catastrophe."

At this, for a minute, their lightness gave way to their gravity; it was as if the long look they exchanged held them together. "It will only depend on yourself—if you'll watch with me."

"Are you afraid?" she asked.

"Don't leave me *now*," he went on.

"Are you afraid?" she repeated.

"Do you think me simply out of my mind?" he pursued instead of answering. "Do I merely strike you as a harmless lunatic?"

"No," said May Bartram. "I understand you. I believe you."

"You mean you feel how my obsession—poor old thing!—may correspond to some possible reality?"

"To some possible reality."

"Then you *will* watch with me?"

She hesitated, then for the third time put her question. "Are you afraid?"

2. May's comment, relating both to Marcher's experiences in general and to his failure in participation, even in love, lights up the entire situation but leaves Marcher in the shadow.

"Did I tell you I was—at Naples?"

"No, you said nothing about it."

"Then I don't know. And I should *like* to know," said John Marcher. "You'll tell me yourself whether you think so. If you'll watch with me you'll see."

"Very good then." They had been moving by this time across the room, and at the door, before passing out, they paused as for the full wind-up of their understanding. "I'll watch with you," said May Bartram.

II

The fact that she "knew"—knew and yet neither chaffed him nor betrayed him—had in a short time begun to constitute between them a goodly bond, which became more marked when, within the year that followed their afternoon at Weatherend, the opportunities for meeting multiplied. The event that thus promoted these occasions was the death of the ancient lady her great-aunt, under whose wing, since losing her mother, she had to such an extent found shelter, and who, though but the widowed mother of the new successor to the property, had succeeded—thanks to a high tone and a high temper—in not forfeiting the supreme position at the great house. The deposition of this personage arrived but with her death, which, followed by many changes, made in particular a difference for the young woman in whom Marcher's expert attention had recognised from the first a dependent with a pride that might ache though it didn't bristle. Nothing for a long time had made him easier than the thought that the aching must have been much soothed by Miss Bartram's now finding herself able to set up a small home in London. She had acquired property, to an amount that made that luxury just possible, under her aunt's extremely complicated will, and when the whole matter began to be straightened out, which indeed took time, she let him know that the happy issue was at last in view.[3] He had seen her again before that day, both because she had more than once accompanied the ancient lady to town and because he had paid another visit to the friends who so conveniently made of Weatherend one of the charms of their own hospitality. These friends had taken him back there; he had achieved there again with Miss Bartram some quiet detachment; and he had in London succeeded in persuading her to more than one brief absence from her aunt. They went together, on these latter occasions, to the National Gallery and the South Kensington Museum, where, among vivid reminders, they talked of Italy at large—not now attempting to recover, as at first, the taste of their youth and their ignorance.

---

3. James's persistent preference for the financial independence of his characters did not result from any contempt of an earned salary, but from his wish to have characters "free" for the interplay of situation and response.

That recovery, the first day at Weatherend, had served its purpose well, had given them quite enough; so that they were, to Marcher's sense, no longer hovering about the headwaters of their stream, but had felt their boat pushed sharply off and down the current.

They were literally afloat together; for our gentleman this was marked, quite as marked as that the fortunate cause of it was just the buried treasure of her knowledge. He had with his own hands dug up this little hoard, brought to light—that is to within reach of the dim day constituted by their discretions and privacies—the object of value the hiding-place of which he had, after putting it into the ground himself, so strangely, so long forgotten. The rare luck of his having again just tumbled on the spot made him indifferent to any other question; he would doubtless have devoted more time to the odd accident of his lapse of memory if he hadn't been moved to devote so much to the sweetness, the comfort, as he felt, for the future, that this accident itself had helped to keep fresh. It had never entered into his plan that any one should "know," and mainly for the reason that it wasn't in him to tell any one. That would have been impossible, for nothing but the amusement of a cold world would have waited on it. Since, however, a mysterious fate had opened his mouth betimes, in spite of him, he would count that a compensation and profit by it to the utmost. That the right person *should* know tempered the asperity of his secret more even than his shyness had permitted him to imagine; and May Bartram was clearly right, because—well, because there she was. Her knowledge simply settled it; he would have been sure enough by this time had she been wrong. There was that in his situation, no doubt, that disposed him too much to see her as a mere confidant, taking all her light for him from the fact—the fact only—of her interest in his predicament; from her mercy, sympathy, seriousness, her consent not to regard him as the funniest of the funny. Aware, in fine, that her price for him was just in her giving him this constant sense of his being admirably spared, he was careful to remember that she had also a life of her own, with things that might happen to *her*, things that in friendship one should likewise take account of. Something fairly remarkable came to pass with him, for that matter, in this connexion—something represented by a certain passage of his consciousness, in the suddenest way, from one extreme to the other.

He had thought himself, so long as nobody knew, the most disinterested person in the world, carrying his concentrated burden, his perpetual suspense, ever so quietly, holding his tongue about it, giving others no glimpse of it nor of its effect upon his life, asking of them no allowance and only making on his side all those that were asked. He hadn't disturbed people with the queerness of their having to know a haunted man, though he had had moments of rather special temptation on hearing them say they were forsooth "unsettled." If they were as unsettled as he was—he who had never been settled for an hour in his life—they would know what it meant. Yet it wasn't, all the same, for him to make them, and he listened to them civilly enough. This was why he had such good—though possibly such rather colourless—manners; this was why, above all, he could regard himself, in a greedy world, as decently—as in fact perhaps even a little sublimely—unselfish. Our point is accordingly that he valued this character quite sufficiently to measure his present danger of letting it lapse, against which he promised himself to be much on his guard. He was quite ready, none the less, to be selfish just a little, since surely no more charming occasion for it had come to him. "Just a little," in a word, was just as much as Miss Bartram, taking one day with another, would let him. He never would be in the least coercive, and would keep well before him the lines on which consideration for her—the very highest—ought to proceed. He would thoroughly establish the heads under which her affairs, her requirements, her peculiarities—he went so far as to give them the latitude of that name—would come into their intercourse. All this naturally was a sign of how much he took the intercourse itself for granted. There was nothing more to be done about *that*. It simply existed; had sprung into being with her first penetrating question to him in the autumn light there at Weatherend. The real form it should have taken on the basis that stood out large was the form of their marrying. But the devil in this was that the very basis itself put marrying out of the question. His conviction, his apprehension, his obsession, in short, wasn't a privilege he could invite a woman to share; and that consequence of it was precisely what was the matter with him. Something or other lay in wait for him, amid the twists and the turns of the months and the years, like a crouching beast in the jungle. It signified little whether the crouching beast were destined to slay him or to be slain. The definite point was the inevitable spring of the creature; and the definite lesson from that was that a man of feeling didn't cause himself to be accompanied by a lady on a tiger-hunt. Such was the image under which he had ended by figuring his life.

They had at first, none the less, in the scattered hours spent together, made no allusion to that view of it; which was a sign he was handsomely alert to give that he didn't expect, that he in fact didn't care, always to be talking about it. Such a feature in one's outlook was really like a hump on one's back. The difference it made every minute of the day existed quite independently of discussion. One discussed of course *like* a hunchback, for there was always, if nothing else, the hunchback face. That remained, and she was watching him; but people watched best, as a general thing, in silence, so that such would be predominantly the manner of their vigil. Yet he didn't want, at the same time, to be tense and solemn; tense and solemn was what he imagined he too much showed for with other people. The thing to be, with the one person who knew, was easy and natural—to make the reference rather than be seeming to avoid it, to avoid it rather than be seeming to make it, and to keep it, in any case, familiar, facetious even, rather than pedantic and portentous. Some such consideration as the latter was doubtless in his mind for instance when he wrote pleasantly to Miss Bartram that perhaps the great thing he had so long felt as in the lap of the gods was no more than this circumstance, which touched him so nearly, of her acquiring a house in London. It was the first allusion they had yet again made, needing any other hitherto so little; but when she replied, after having given him the news, that she was by no means satisfied with such a trifle as the climax to so special a suspense, she almost set him wondering if she hadn't even a larger conception of singularity for him than he had for himself. He was at all events destined to become aware little by little, as time went by, that she was all the while looking at his life, judging it, measuring it, in the light of the thing she knew, which grew to be at last, with the consecration of the years, never mentioned between them save as "the real truth" about him. That had always been his own form of reference to it, but she adopted the form so quietly that, looking back at the end of a period, he knew there was no moment at which it was traceable that she had, as he might say, got inside his idea, or exchanged the attitude of beautifully indulging for that of still more beautifully believing him.

It was always open to him to accuse her of seeing him but as the most harmless of maniacs, and this, in the long run—since it covered so much ground—was his easiest description of their friendship. He had a screw loose for her, but she liked him in spite of it and was practically, against the rest of the world, his kind wise keeper, unremunerated but fairly amused and, in the absence of other near ties, not disreputably occupied. The rest of the world of course thought him queer, but she, she only, knew how, and above all why, queer; which was precisely what enabled her to dispose the concealing veil in the right folds. She took his gaiety from him—since it had to pass with them for gaiety—as she took everything else; but she certainly so far justified by her unerring touch his finer sense of the degree to which he had ended by convincing her. *She* at least never spoke of the secret of his life except as "the real truth about you," and she had in fact a wonderful way of making it seem, as such, the secret of her own life too. That was in fine how he so constantly felt her as allowing for him; he couldn't on the whole call it anything else. He allowed for himself, but she, exactly, allowed still more; partly because, better placed for a sight of the matter, she traced his unhappy perversion through reaches of its course into which he could scarce follow it. He knew how he felt, but, besides knowing that, she knew how he *looked* as well; he knew each of the things of importance he was insidiously kept from doing, but she could add up the amount they made, understand how much, with a lighter weight on his spirit, he might have done, and thereby establish how, clever as he was, he fell short. Above all she was in the secret of the difference between the forms he went through—those of his little office under Government, those of caring for his modest patrimony, for his library, for his garden in the country, for the people in London whose invitations he accepted and repaid—and the detachment that reigned beneath them and that made of all behaviour, all that could in the least be called behaviour, a long act of dissimulation. What it had come to was that he wore a mask painted with the social simper, out of the eye-holes of which there looked eyes of an expression not in the least matching the other features. This the stupid world, even after years, had never more than half-discovered. It was only May Bartram who had, and she achieved, by an art indescribable, the feat of at once—or perhaps it was only alternately—meeting the eyes from in front and mingling her own vision, as from over his shoulder, with their peep through the apertures.

So while they grew older together she did watch with him, and so she let this association give shape and colour to her own existence. Beneath *her* forms as well detachment had learned to sit, and behaviour had become for her, in the social sense, a false account of herself. There was but one account of her that would have been true all the while and that she could give straight to nobody, least of all to John Marcher. Her whole attitude was a virtual statement, but the perception of that only seemed called to take its place for him as one of the many things necessarily crowded out of his consciousness. If she had moreover, like himself, to make sacrifices to their real truth, it was to be granted that her compensation might have affected her as more prompt and more natural. They had long periods, in this London time, during which, when they were together, a stranger might have listened to them without in the least pricking up his ears; on the other hand the real truth was equally liable at any moment to rise to the surface, and the auditor would then have wondered indeed what they were talking about. They had from an early hour made up their mind that society was, luckily, unintelligent, and the margin allowed them by this had fairly become one of their commonplaces. Yet there were still moments when the situation turned almost fresh—usually under the effect of some expression drawn from herself. Her expressions doubtless repeated themselves, but her intervals were generous. "What saves us, you know, is that we answer so completely to so usual an appearance: that of the man and woman whose friendship has become such a daily habit—or almost—as to be at last indispensable." That for instance was a remark she had frequently enough had occasion to make, though she had given it at different times different developments. What we are especially concerned with is the turn it happened to take from her one afternoon when he had come to see her in honour of her birthday. This anniversary had fallen on a Sunday, at a season of thick fog and general outward gloom; but he had brought her his customary offering, having known her now long enough to have established a hundred small traditions. It was one of his proofs to himself, the present he made her on her birthday, that he hadn't sunk into real selfishness.[4] It was mostly nothing more than a small trinket, but it was always fine of its kind, and he was regularly careful to pay for it more than he thought he could afford. "Our habit saves you at least, don't you see? because it makes you, after all, for the vulgar, indistinguishable from other men. What's the most inveterate mark of men in general? Why the capacity to spend endless time with dull women—to spend it I won't say without being bored, but without minding that they are, without being driven off at a tangent by it; which comes to the same thing. I'm your dull woman, a part of the daily bread for which you pray at church. That covers your tracks more than anything."

"And what covers yours?" asked Marcher, whom his dull woman could most to this extent amuse. "I see of course what you mean by your saving me, in this way and that, so far as other people are concerned—I've seen it all along. Only what is it that saves *you?* I often think, you know, of that."

She looked as if she sometimes thought of that too, but rather in a different way. "Where other people, you mean, are concerned?"

"Well, you're really so in with me, you know—as a sort of result of my being so in with yourself. I mean of my having such an immense regard for you, being so tremendously mindful of all you've done for me. I sometimes ask myself if it's quite fair. Fair I mean to have so involved and—since one may say it—interested you. I almost feel as if you hadn't really had time to do anything else."

4. James makes use of smaller incidents to reveal Marcher's gift for deluding himself, on which the principal issue of the story depends.

"Anything else but be interested?" she asked. "Ah what else does one ever want to be? If I've been 'watching' with you, as we long ago agreed I was to do, watching's always in itself an absorption."

"Oh certainly," John Marcher said, "if you hadn't had your curiosity—! Only doesn't it sometimes come to you as time goes on that your curiosity isn't being particularly repaid?"

May Bartram had a pause. "Do you ask that, by any chance, because you feel at all that yours isn't? I mean because you have to wait so long."

Oh he understood what she meant! "For the thing to happen that never does happen? For the beast to jump out? No, I'm just where I was about it. It isn't a matter as to which I can *choose*, I can decide for a change. It isn't one as to which there *can* be a change. It's in the lap of the gods. One's in the hands of one's law —there one is. As to the form the law will take, the way it will operate, that's its own affair."

"Yes," Miss Bartram replied; "of course one's fate's coming, of course it *has* come in its own form and its own way, all the while. Only, you know, the form and the way in your case were to have been—well, something so exceptional and, as one may say, so particularly *your* own."

Something in this made him look at her with suspicion. "You say 'were to *have* been,' as if in your heart you had begun to doubt."

"Oh!" she vaguely protested.

"As if you believe," he went on, "that nothing will now take place."

She shook her head slowly but rather inscrutably. "You're far from my thought."

He continued to look at her. "What then is the matter with you?"

"Well," she said after another wait, "the matter with me is simply that I'm more sure than ever my curiosity, as you call it, will be but too well repaid."

They were frankly grave now; he had got up from his seat, had turned once more about the little drawing-room to which, year after year, he brought his inevitable topic; in which he had, as he might have said, tasted their intimate community with every sauce, where every object was as familiar to him as the things of his own house and the very carpets were worn with his fitful walk very much as the desks in old counting-houses are worn by the elbows of generations of clerks. The generations of his nervous moods had been at work there, and the place was the written history of his whole middle life. Under the impression of what his friend had just said he knew himself, for some reason, more aware of these things; which made him, after a moment, stop again before her. "Is it possibly that you've grown afraid?"

"Afraid?" He thought, as she repeated the word, that his question had made her, a little, change colour; so that, lest he should have touched on a truth, he explained very kindly: "You remember that that was what you asked *me* long ago—that first day at Weatherend."

"Oh yes, and you told me you didn't know—that I was to see for myself. We've said little about it since, even in so long a time."

"Precisely," Marcher interposed—"quite as if it were too delicate a matter for us to make free with. Quite as if we might find, on pressure, that I *am* afraid. For then," he said, "we shouldn't, should we? quite know what to do."

She had for the time no answer to this question. "There have been days when I thought you were. Only, of course," she added, "there have been days when we have thought almost anything."

"Everything. Oh!" Marcher softly groaned as with a gasp, half-spent, at the face, more uncovered just then than it had been for a long while, of the imagination always with them. It had always had its incalculable moments of glaring out, quite as with the very eyes of the very Beast, and, used as he was to them, they could still draw from him the tribute of a sigh that rose from the depths of his being. All they had thought, first and last, rolled over him; the past seemed to have been reduced to mere barren speculation. This in fact was what the place had just struck him as so full of—the simplification of everything but the state of suspense. That remained only by seeming to hang in the void surrounding it. Even his original fear, if fear it had been, had lost itself in the desert. "I judge, however," he continued, "that you see I'm not afraid now."

"What I see, as I make it out, is that you've achieved something almost unprecedented in the way of getting used to danger. Living with it so long and so closely you've lost your sense of it; you know it's there, but you're indifferent, and you cease even, as of old, to have to whistle in the dark. Considering what the danger is," May Bartram wound up, "I'm bound to say I don't think your attitude could well be surpassed."

John Marcher faintly smiled. "It's heroic?"

"Certainly—call it that."

It was what he would have liked indeed to call it. "I *am* then a man of courage?"

"That's what you were to show me."

He still, however, wondered. "But doesn't the man of courage know what he's afraid of—or *not* afraid of? I don't know *that*, you see. I don't focus it. I can't name it. I only know I'm exposed."

"Yes, but exposed—how shall I say?—so directly. So intimately. That's surely enough."

"Enough to make you feel then—as what we may call the end and the upshot of our watch—that I'm not afraid?"

"You're not afraid. But it isn't," she said, "the end of our watch. That is it isn't the end of yours. You've everything still to see."

"Then why haven't *you*?" he asked. He had had, all along, today, the sense of her keeping something back, and still had it. As this was his first impression of that it quite made a date. The case was the more marked as she didn't at first answer; which in turn made him go on. "You know something I don't." Then his voice, for that of a man of courage trembled a little. "You know what's to happen." Her silence, with the face she showed, was almost a confession—it made him sure. "You know, and you're afraid to tell me. It's so bad that you're afraid I'll find out."

All this might be true, for she did look as if, unexpectedly to her, he had crossed some mystic line that she had secretly drawn round her. Yet she might, after all, not have worried; and the real climax was that he himself, at all events, needn't. "You'll never find out." [5]

III

It was all to have made, none the less, as I have said, a date; which came out in the fact that again and again, even after long intervals, other things that passed between them wore in relation to this hour but the character of recalls and results. Its immediate effect had been indeed rather to lighten insistence—almost to provoke a reaction; as if their topic had dropped by its own weight and as if moreover, for that matter, Marcher had been visited by one of his occasional warnings against egotism. He had kept up, he felt, and very decently on the whole, his consciousness of the importance of not being selfish, and it was true that he had never sinned in that direction without promptly enough trying to press the scales the other way. He often repaired his fault, the season permitting, by inviting his friend to accompany him to the opera; and it not infrequently thus happened that, to show he didn't wish her to have but one sort of food for her mind, he was the cause of her appearing there with him a dozen nights in the month. It even happened that, seeing her home at such times, he occasionally went in with her to finish, as he called it, the evening, and, the better to make his point, sat down to the frugal but always careful little supper that awaited his pleasure. His point was made, he thought, by his not eternally insisting with her on himself; made

5. From this point, their relationship undergoes a subtle change. Marcher is aware that May knows the root of his predicament, while she, by her admission of this knowledge, may assume in his eyes a superiority incompatible with his thinking of their marriage.

for instance, at such hours, when it befell that, her piano at hand and each of them familiar with it, they went over passages of the opera together. It chanced to be on one of these occasions, however, that he reminded her of her not having answered a certain question he had put to her during the talk that had taken place between them on her last birthday. "What is it that saves *you?*" —saved her, he meant, from that appearance of variation from the usual human type. If he had practically escaped remark, as she pretended, by doing, in the most important particular, what most men do—find the answer to life in patching up an alliance of a sort with a woman no better than himself—how had she escaped it, and how could the alliance, such as it was, since they must suppose it had been more or less noticed, have failed to make her rather positively talked about?

"I never said," May Bartram replied, "that it hadn't made me a good deal talked about."

"Ah well then you're not 'saved.' "

"It hasn't been a question for me. If you've had your woman I've had," she said, "my man."

"And you mean that makes you all right?"

Oh it was always as if there were so much to say! "I don't know why it shouldn't make me—humanly, which is what we're speaking of—as right as it makes you."

"I see," Marcher returned. " 'Humanly,' no doubt, as showing that you're living for something. Not, that is, just for me and my secret."

May Bartram smiled. "I don't pretend it exactly shows that I'm not living for you. It's my intimacy with you that's in question."

He laughed as he saw what she meant. "Yes, but since, as you say, I'm only, so far as people make out, ordinary, you're—aren't you?—no more than ordinary either. You help me to pass for a man like another. So if I *am,* as I understand you, you're not compromised. Is that it?"

She had another of her waits, but she spoke clearly enough. "That's it. It's all that concerns me—to help you to pass for a man like another."

He was careful to acknowledge the remark handsomely. "How kind, how beautiful, you are to me! How shall I ever repay you?"

She had her last grave pause, as if there might be a choice of ways. But she chose. "By going on as you are."

It was into this going on as he was that they relapsed, and really for so long a time that the day inevitably came for a further sounding of their depths. These depths, constantly bridged over by a structure firm enough in spite of its lightness and of its occasional oscillation in the somewhat vertiginous air, invited on occasion, in the interest of their nerves, a dropping of the plummet and a measurement of the abyss. A difference had been made moreover, once for all, by the fact that she had all the while not appeared to feel the need of rebutting his charge of an idea within her that she didn't dare to express—a charge uttered just before one of the fullest of their later discussions ended. It had come up for him then that she "knew" something and that what she knew was bad—too bad to tell him. When he had spoken of it as visibly so bad that she was afraid he might find it out, her reply had left the matter too equivocal to be let alone and yet, for Marcher's special sensibility, almost too formidable again to touch. He circled about it at a distance that alternately narrowed and widened and that still wasn't much affected by the consciousness in him that there was nothing she could "know," after all, any better than he did. She had no source of knowledge he hadn't equally—except of course that she might have finer nerves. That was what women had where they were interested; they made out things, where people were concerned, that the people often couldn't have made out for themselves. Their nerves, their sensibility, their imagination, were conductors and revealers, and the beauty of May Bartram was in particular that she had given herself so to his case. He felt in these days what, oddly enough, he had never felt before, the growth of a dread of losing her by some catastrophe—some catastrophe that yet wouldn't at all be *the* catastrophe partly because she had almost of a sudden begun to strike him as more useful to him than ever yet, and partly by reason of an appearance of uncertainty in her health, coincident and equally new. It was characteristic of the inner detachment he had hitherto so successfully cultivated and to which our whole account of him is a reference, it was characteristic that his complications, such as they were, had never yet seemed so as at this crisis to thicken about him, even to the point of making him ask himself if he were, by any chance, of a truth, within sight or sound, within touch or reach, within the immediate jurisdiction, of the thing that waited.

When the day came, as come it had to, that his friend confessed to him her fear of a deep disorder in her blood, he felt somehow the shadow of a change and the chill of a shock. He immediately began to imagine aggravations and disasters, and above all to think of her peril as the direct menace for himself of personal privation. This indeed gave him one of those partial recoveries of equanimity that were agreeable to him—it showed him that what was still first in his mind was the loss she herself might suffer. "What if she should have to die before knowing, before seeing—?" It would have been brutal, in the early stages of her trouble, to put that question to her; but it had immediately sounded for him to his

own concern, and the possibility was what most made him sorry
for her. If she did "know," moreover, in the sense of her having
had some—what should he think?—mystical irresistible light, this
would make the matter not better, but worse, inasmuch as her
original adoption of his own curiosity had quite become the basis
of her life. She had been living to see what would *be* to be seen,
and it would quite lacerate her to have to give up before the accomplishment of the vision. These reflections, as I say, quickened his
generosity; yet, make them as he might, he saw himself, with the
lapse of the period, more and more disconcerted. It lapsed for him
with a strange steady sweep, and the oddest oddity was that it gave
him, independently of the threat of much inconvenience, almost
the only positive surprise his career, if career it could be called,
had yet offered him. She kept the house as she had never done; he
had to go to her to see her—she could meet him nowhere now,
though there was scarce a corner of their loved old London in
which she hadn't in the past, at one time or another, done so; and
he found her always seated by her fire in the deep old-fashioned
chair she was less and less able to leave. He had been struck one
day, after an absence exceeding his usual measure, with her suddenly looking much older to him than he had ever thought of her
being; then he recognised that the suddenness was all on his side
—he had just simply and suddenly noticed. She looked older because inevitably, after so many years, she *was* old, or almost; which
was of course true in still greater measure of her companion. If
she was old, or almost, John Marcher assuredly was, and yet it was
her showing of the lesson, not his own, that brought the truth
home to him.[6] His surprises began here; when once they had
begun they multiplied; they came rather with a rush: it was as if,
in the oddest way in the world, they had all been kept back,
sown in a thick cluster, for the late afternoon of life, the time at
which for people in general the unexpected has died out.

One of them was that he should have caught himself—for he
had so done—*really* wondering if the great accident would take
form now as nothing more than his being condemned to see this
charming woman, this admirable friend, pass away from him. He
had never so unreservedly qualified her as while confronted in
thought with such a possibility; in spite of which there was small
doubt for him that as an answer to his long riddle the mere effacement of even so fine a feature of his situation would be an abject
anti-climax. It would represent, as connected with his past attitude, a drop of dignity under the shadow of which his existence

---

6. Marcher's sudden recognition of
May's aging, in connection with her
obviously serious illness, shatters his
unawareness of his own age. The shock
induces the notion that his encounter
with destiny is to be, not spectacular,
but too late.

could only become the most grotesque of failures. He had been far from holding it a failure—long as he had waited for the appearance that was to make it a success. He had waited for quite another thing, not for such a thing as that. The breath of his good faith came short, however, as he recognised how long he had waited, or how long at least his companion had. That she, at all events, might be recorded as having waited in vain—this affected him sharply, and all the more because of his at first having done little more than amuse himself with the idea. It grew more grave as the gravity of her condition grew, and the state of mind it produced in him, which he himself ended by watching as if it had been some definite disfigurement of his outer person, may pass for another of his surprises. This conjoined itself still with another, the really stupefying consciousness of a question that he would have allowed to shape itself had he dared. What did everything mean—what, that is, did *she* mean, she and her vain waiting and her probable death and the soundless admonition of it all—unless that, at this time of day, it was simply, it was overwhelmingly too late? He had never at any stage of his queer consciousness admitted the whisper of such a correction; he had never till within these last few months been so false to his conviction as not to hold that what was to come to him had time, whether *he* struck himself as having it or not. That at last, at last, he certainly hadn't it, to speak of, or had it but in the scantiest measure—such, soon enough, as things went with him, became the inference with which his old obsession had to reckon: and this it was not helped to do by the more and more confirmed appearance that the great vagueness casting the long shadow in which he had lived had, to attest itself, almost no margin left. Since it was in Time that he was to have met his fate, so it was in Time that his fate was to have acted; and as he waked up to the sense of no longer being young, which was exactly the sense of being stale, just as that, in turn, was the sense of being weak, he waked up to another matter beside. It all hung together; they were subject, he and the great vagueness, to an equal and indivisible law. When the possibilities themselves had accordingly turned stale, when the secret of the gods had grown faint, had perhaps even quite evaporated, that, and that only, was failure. It wouldn't have been failure to be bankrupt, dishonoured, pilloried, hanged; it was failure not to be anything.[7] And so, in the dark valley into which his path had taken its unlooked-for twist, he wondered not a little as he groped. He didn't care what awful crash might overtake him, with what ignominy or what monstrosity he might yet be associated—since he wasn't

7. By his own failure to give love, and his consequent incapacity to receive it, Marcher invites the first stirring of the beast. The lair is time itself, a jungle to Marcher because he has wastefully stumbled through it.

after all too utterly old to suffer—if it would only be decently proportionate to the posture he had kept, all his life, in the threatened presence of it. He had but one desire left—that he shouldn't have been "sold."

IV

Then it was that, one afternoon, while the spring of the year was young and new she met all in her own way his frankest betrayal of these alarms. He had gone in late to see her, but evening hadn't settled and she was presented to him in that long fresh light of waning April days which affects us often with a sadness sharper than the greyest hours of autumn. The week had been warm, the spring was supposed to have begun early, and May Bartram sat, for the first time in the year, without a fire; a fact that, to Marcher's sense, gave the scene of which she formed part a smooth and ultimate look, an air of knowing, in its immaculate order and cold meaningless cheer, that it would never see a fire again. Her own aspect—he could scarce have said why—intensified this note. Almost as white as wax, with the marks and signs in her face as numerous and as fine as if they had been etched by a needle, with soft white draperies relieved by a faded green scarf on the delicate tone of which the years had further refined, she was the picture of a serene and exquisite but impenetrable sphinx, whose head, or indeed all whose person, might have been powdered with silver. She was a sphinx, yet with her white petals and green fronds she might have been a lily too—only an artificial lily, wonderfully imitated and constantly kept, without dust or stain, though not exempt from a slight droop and a complexity of faint creases, under some clear glass bell. The perfection of household care, of high polish and finish, always reigned in her rooms, but they now looked most as if everything had been wound up, tucked in, put away, so that she might sit with folded hands and with nothing more to do. She was "out of it," to Marcher's vision; her work was over; she communicated with him as across some gulf or from some island of rest that she had already reached, and it made him feel strangely abandoned. Was it—or rather wasn't it— that if for so long she had been watching with him the answer to their question must have swum into her ken and taken on its name, so that her occupation was verily gone? He had as much as charged her with this in saying to her, many months before, that she even then knew something she was keeping from him. It was a point he had never since ventured to press, vaguely fearing as he did that it might become a difference, perhaps a disagreement, between them. He had in this later time turned nervous, which was what he in all the other years had never been; and the oddity was that his nervousness should have waited till he had begun to doubt, should have held off so long as he was sure. There was something, it seemed to him, that the wrong word would bring down on his head, something that would so at least ease off his tension. But he wanted not to speak the wrong word; that would make everything ugly. He wanted the knowledge he lacked to drop on him, if drop it could, by its own august weight. If she was to forsake him it was surely for her to take leave. This was why he didn't directly ask her again what she knew; but it was also why, approaching the matter from another side, he said to her in the course of his visit: "What do you regard as the very worst that at this time of day *can* happen to me?"

He had asked her that in the past often enough; they had, with the odd irregular rhythm of their intensities and avoidances, exchanged ideas about it and then had seen the ideas washed away by cool intervals, washed like figures traced in sea-sand. It had ever been the mark of their talk that the oldest allusions in it required but a little dismissal and reaction to come out again, sounding for the hour as new. She could thus at present meet his enquiry quite freshly and patiently. "Oh yes, I've repeatedly thought, only it always seemed to me of old that I couldn't quite make up my mind. I thought of dreadful things, between which it was difficult to choose; and so must you have done."

"Rather! I feel now as if I had scarce done anything else. I appear to myself to have spent my life in thinking of nothing *but* dreadful things. A great many of them I've at different times named to you, but there were others I couldn't name."

"They were too, too dreadful?"

"Too, too dreadful—some of them."

She looked at him a minute, and there came to him as he met it an inconsequent sense that her eyes, when one got their full clearness, were still as beautiful as they had been in youth, only beautiful with a strange cold light—a light that somehow was a part of the effect, if it wasn't rather a part of the cause, of the pale hard sweetness of the season and the hour. "And yet," she said at last, "there are horrors we've mentioned."

It deepened the strangeness to see her, as such a figure in such a picture, talk of "horrors," but she was to do in a few minutes something stranger yet—though even of this he was to take the full measure but afterwards—and the note of it already trembled. It was, for the matter of that, one of the signs that her eyes were having again the high flicker of their prime. He had to admit, however, what she said. "Oh yes, there were times when we did go far." He caught himself in the act of speaking as if it all were over. Well, he wished it were; and the consummation depended for him clearly and more and more on his friend.

But she had now a soft smile. "Oh far—!"

It was oddly ironic. "Do you mean you're prepared to go further?"

She was frail and ancient and charming as she continued to look at him, yet it was rather as if she had lost the thread. "Do you consider that we went far?"

"Why I thought it the point you were just making—that we *had* looked most things in the face."

"Including each other?" She still smiled. "But you're quite right. We've had together great imaginations, often great fears; but some of them have been unspoken."

"Then the worst—we haven't faced that. I *could* face it, I believe, if I knew what you think it. I feel," he explained, "as if I had lost my power to conceive such things." And he wondered if he looked as blank as he sounded. "It's spent."

"Then why do you assume," she asked, "that mine isn't?"

"Because you've given me signs to the contrary. It isn't a question for you of conceiving, imagining, comparing. It isn't a question now of choosing." At last he came out with it. "You know something I don't. You've shown me that before."

These last words had affected her, he made out in a moment, exceedingly, and she spoke with firmness. "I've shown you, my dear, nothing."

He shook his head. "You can't hide it."

"Oh, oh!" May Bartram sounded over what she couldn't hide. It was almost a smothered groan.

"You admitted it months ago, when I spoke of it to you as of something you were afraid I should find out. Your answer was that I couldn't, that I wouldn't, and I don't pretend I have. But you had something therefore in mind, and I now see how it must have been, how it still is, the possibility that, of all possibilities, has settled itself for you as the worst. This," he went on, "is why I appeal to you. I'm only afraid of ignorance to-day—I'm not afraid of knowledge." And then as for a while she said nothing: "What makes me sure is that I see in your face and feel here, in this air and amid these appearances, that you're out of it. You've done. You've had your experience. You leave me to my fate."

Well, she listened, motionless and white in her chair, as on a decision to be made, so that her manner was fairly an avowal, though still, with a small fine inner stiffness, an imperfect surrender. "It *would* be the worst," she finally let herself say. "I mean the thing I've never said."

It hushed him a moment. "More monstrous than all the monstrosities we've named?"

"More monstrous. Isn't that what you sufficiently express," she asked, "in calling it the worst?"

Marcher thought. "Assuredly—if you mean, as I do, something that includes all the loss and all the shame that are thinkable."

"It would if it *should* happen," said May Bartram. "What we're speaking of, remember, is only my idea."

"It's your belief," Marcher returned. "That's enough for me. I feel your beliefs are right. Therefore if, having this one, you give me no more light on it, you abandon me."

"No, no!" she repeated. "I'm with you—don't you see?—still." And as to make it more vivid to him she rose from her chair—a movement she seldom risked in these days—and showed herself, all draped and all soft, in her fairness and slimness. "I haven't forsaken you."

It was really, in its effort against weakness, a generous assurance, and had the success of the impulse not, happily, been great, it would have touched him to pain more than to pleasure. But the cold charm in her eyes had spread, as she hovered before him, to all the rest of her person, so that it was for the minute almost a recovery of youth. He couldn't pity her for that; he could only take her as she showed—as capable even yet of helping him. It was as if, at the same time, her light might at any instant go out; wherefore he must make the most of it. There passed before him with intensity the three or four things he wanted most to know; but the question that came of itself to his lips really covered the others. "Then tell me if I shall consciously suffer."

She promptly shook her head. "Never!"

It confirmed the authority he imputed to her, and it produced on him an extraordinary effect. "Well, what's better than that? Do you call that the worst?"

"You think nothing is better?" she asked.

She seemed to mean something so special that he again sharply wondered, though still with the dawn of a prospect of relief. "Why not, if one doesn't *know?*" After which, as their eyes, over his question, met in a silence, the dawn deepened and something to his purpose came prodigiously out of her very face. His own, as he took it in, suddenly flushed to the forehead, and he gasped with the force of a perception to which, on the instant, everything fitted. The sound of his gasp filled the air; then he became articulate. "I see—if I don't suffer!"

In her own look, however, was doubt. "You see what?"

"Why what you mean—what you've always meant."

She again shook her head. "What I mean isn't what I've always meant. It's different."

"It's something new?"

She hung back from it a little. "Something new. It's not what you think. I see what you think."

His divination drew breath then; only her correction might be wrong. "It isn't that I *am* a blockhead?" he asked between faintness and grimness. "It isn't that it's all a mistake?"

"A mistake?" she pityingly echoed. *That* possibility, for her, he saw, would be monstrous; and if she guaranteed him the immunity from pain it would accordingly not be what she had in mind. "Oh no," she declared; "it's nothing of that sort. You've been right."

Yet he couldn't help asking himself if she weren't, thus pressed, speaking but to save him. It seemed to him he should be most in a hole if its history should prove all a platitude. "Are you telling me the truth, so that I shan't have been a bigger idiot than I can bear to know? I *haven't* lived with a vain imagination, in the most besotted illusion? I haven't waited but to see the door shut in my face?"

She shook her head again. "However the case stands *that* isn't the truth. Whatever the reality, it *is* a reality. The door isn't shut. The door's open," said May Bartram.

"Then something's to come?"

She waited once again, always with her cold sweet eyes on him. "It's never too late." She had, with her gliding step, diminished the distance between them, and she stood nearer to him, close to him, a minute, as if still charged with the unspoken. Her movement might have been for some finer emphasis of what she was at once hesitating and deciding to say. He had been standing by the chimney-piece, fireless and sparely adorned, a small perfect old French clock and two morsels of rosy Dresden constituting all its furniture; and her hand grasped the shelf while she kept him waiting, grasped it a little as for support and encouragement. She only kept him waiting, however; that is he only waited. It had become suddenly, from her movement and attitude, beautiful and vivid to him that she had something more to give him; her wasted face delicately shone with it—it glittered almost as with the white lustre of silver in her expression. She was right, incontestably, for what he saw in her face was the truth, and strangely, without consequence, while their talk of it as dreadful was still in the air, she appeared to present it as inordinately soft. This, prompting bewilderment, made him but gape the more gratefully for her revelation, so that they continued for some minutes silent, her face shining at him, her contact imponderably pressing, and his stare all kind but all expectant. The end, none the less, was that what he had expected failed to come to him. Something else took place instead, which seemed to consist at first in the mere closing of her eyes. She gave way at the same instant to a slow fine shudder, and though he remained staring—though he stared in fact but the harder—turned off and regained her chair. It was the end of what she had been intending, but it left him thinking only of that.

"Well, you don't say—?"

She had touched in her passage a bell near the chimney and had sunk back strangely pale. "I'm afraid I'm too ill."

"Too ill to tell me?" It sprang up sharp to him, and almost to his lips, the fear she might die without giving him light. He checked himself in time from so expressing his question, but she answered as if she had heard the words.

"Don't you know—now?"

" 'Now'—?" She had spoken as if some difference had been made within the moment. But her maid, quickly obedient to her bell, was already with them. "I know nothing." And he was afterwards to say to himself that he must have spoken with odious impatience, such an impatience as to show that, supremely disconcerted, he washed his hands of the whole question.

"Oh!" said May Bartram.

"Are you in pain?" he asked as the woman went to her.

"No," said May Bartram.

Her maid, who had put an arm round her as if to take her to her room, fixed on him eyes that appealingly contradicted her; in spite of which, however, he showed once more his mystification. "What then has happened?"

She was once more, with her companion's help, on her feet, and, feeling withdrawal imposed on him, he had blankly found his hat and gloves and had reached the door. Yet he waited for her answer. "What *was* to," she said.

V

He came back the next day, but she was then unable to see him, and as it was literally the first time this had occurred in the long stretch of their acquaintance he turned away, defeated and sore, almost angry—or feeling at least that such a break in their custom was really the beginning of the end—and wandered alone with his thoughts, especially with the one he was least able to keep down. She was dying and he would lose her; she was dying and his life would end. He stopped in the Park, into which he had passed, and stared before him at his recurrent doubt. Away from her the doubt pressed again; in her presence he had believed her, but as he felt his forlornness he threw himself into the explanation that, nearest at hand, had most of a miserable warmth for him and least of a cold torment. She had deceived him to save him—to put him off with something in which he should be able to rest. What could the thing that was to happen to him be, after all, but just this thing that had begun to happen? Her dying, her death, his consequent solitude—*that* was what he had figured as the Beast in the Jungle, that was what had been in the lap of the gods. He had had her word for it as he left her—what else on earth could she have meant? It wasn't a thing of a monstrous order; not a fate rare and distinguished; not a stroke of fortune that overwhelmed and immortalised; it had only the stamp of the common doom. But poor Marcher at this hour judged the common doom sufficient. It would serve his turn, and even as the consummation of infinite waiting he would bend his pride to accept it. He sat down on a bench in the twilight. He hadn't been a fool. Something had *been,* as she had said, to come. Before he rose indeed it had quite struck him that the final fact really matched with the long avenue through which he had had to reach it. As sharing his suspense and as giving herself all, giving her life, to bring it to an end, she had come with him every step of the way. He had lived by her aid, and to leave her behind would be cruelly, damnably to miss her. What could be more overwhelming than that?

Well, he was to know within the week, for though she kept him a while at bay, left him restless and wretched during a series of days on each of which he asked about her only again to have to turn away, she ended his trial by receiving him where she had always received him. Yet she had been brought out at some hazard into the presence of so many of the things that were, consciously, vainly, half their past, and there was scant service left in the gentleness of her mere desire, all too visible, to check his obsession and wind up his long trouble. That was clearly what she wanted, the one thing more for her own peace while she could still put out her hand. He was so affected by her state that, once seated by her chair, he was moved to let everything go; it was she herself therefore who brought him back, took up again, before she dismissed him, her last words of the other time. She showed how she wished to leave their business in order. "I'm not sure you understood. You've nothing to wait for more. It *has* come."

Oh how he looked at her! "Really?"

"Really."

"The thing that, as you said, *was* to?"

"The thing that we began in our youth to watch for."

Face to face with her once more he believed her; it was a claim to which he had so abjectly little to oppose. "You mean that it has come as a positive definite occurrence, with a name and a date?"

"Positive. Definite. I don't know about the 'name,' but oh with a date!"

He found himself again too helplessly at sea. "But come in the night—come and passed me by?"

May Bartram had her strange faint smile. "Oh no, it hasn't passed you by!"

"But if I haven't been aware of it and it hasn't touched me—?"

"Ah your not being aware of it"—and she seemed to hesitate an instant to deal with this—"your not being aware of it is the strangeness *in* the strangeness. It's the wonder *of* the wonder." She spoke as with the softness almost of a sick child, yet now at last, at the end of all, with the perfect straightness of a sibyl. She visibly knew that she knew, and the effect on him was of something co-ordinate, in its high character, with the law that had ruled him. It was the true voice of the law; so on her lips would the law itself have sounded. "It *has* touched you," she went on. "It has done its office. It has made you all its own."

"So utterly without my knowing it?"

"So utterly without your knowing it." His hand, as he leaned to her, was on the arm of her chair, and, dimly smiling always now, she placed her own on it. "It's enough if *I* know it."

"Oh!" he confusedly breathed, as she herself of late so often had done.

"What I long ago said is true. You'll never know now, and I think you ought to be content. You've *had* it," said May Bartram.

"But had what?"

"Why what was to have marked you out. The proof of your law. It has acted. I'm too glad," she then bravely added, "to have been able to see what it's *not*."

He continued to attach his eyes to her, and with the sense that it was all beyond him, and that *she* was too, he would still have sharply challenged her hadn't he so felt it an abuse of her weakness to do more than take devoutly what she gave him, take it hushed as to a revelation. If he did speak, it was out of the fore-knowledge of his loneliness to come. "If you're glad of what it's 'not' it might then have been worse?"

She turned her eyes away, she looked straight before her; with which after a moment: "Well, you know our fears."

He wondered. "It's something then we never feared?"

On this slowly she turned to him. "Did we ever dream, with all our dreams, that we should sit and talk of it thus?"

He tried for a little to make out that they had; but it was as if their dreams, numberless enough, were in solution in some thick cold mist through which thought lost itself. "It might have been that we couldn't talk?"

"Well"—she did her best for him—"not from this side. This, you see," she said, "is the *other* side."

"I think," poor Marcher returned, "that all sides are the same to me." Then, however, as she gently shook her head in correction: "We mightn't, as it were, have got across——?"

"To where we are—no. We're *here*"—she made her weak emphasis.

"And much good does it do us!" was her friend's frank comment.

"It does us the good it can. It does us the good that *it* isn't here. It's past. It's behind," said May Bartram. "Before——" but her voice dropped.

He had got up, not to tire her, but it was hard to combat his yearning. She after all told him nothing but that his light had failed—which he knew well enough without her. "Before——?" he blankly echoed.

"Before, you see, it was always to *come*. That kept it present."

"Oh I don't care what comes now! Besides," Marcher added, "it seems to me I liked it better present, as you say, than I can like it absent with *your* absence."

"Oh mine!"—and her pale hands made light of it.

"With the absence of everything." He had a dreadful sense of standing there before her for—so far as anything but this proved, this bottomless drop was concerned—the last time of their life. It rested on him with a weight he felt he could scarce bear, and this weight it apparently was that still pressed out what remained in him of speakable protest. "I believe you; but I can't begin to pretend I understand. *Nothing*, for me, is past; nothing *will* pass till I pass myself, which I pray my stars may be as soon as possible. Say, however," he added, "that I've eaten my cake, as you contend, to the last crumb—how can the thing I've never felt at all be the thing I was marked out to feel?"

She met him perhaps less directly, but she met him unperturbed. "You take your 'feelings' for granted. You were to suffer your fate. That was not necessarily to know it."

"How in the world—when what is such knowledge but suffering?"

She looked up at him a while in silence. "No—you don't understand."

"I suffer," said John Marcher.

"Don't, don't!"

"How can I help at least *that?*"

"*Don't!*" May Bartram repeated.

She spoke it in a tone so special, in spite of her weakness, that he stared an instant—stared as if some light, hitherto hidden, had shimmered across his vision. Darkness again closed over it, but the gleam had already become for him an idea. "Because I haven't the right——?"

"Don't *know*—when you needn't," she mercifully urged. "You needn't—for we shouldn't."

"Shouldn't?" If he could but know what she meant!

"No—it's too much."

"Too much?" he still asked but, with a mystification that was the next moment of a sudden to give way. Her words, if they meant something, affected him in this light—the light also of her wasted face—as meaning *all*, and the sense of what knowledge had been for herself came over him with a rush which broke through into a question. "Is it of that then you're dying?"

She but watched him, gravely at first, as to see, with this, where he was, and she might have seen something or feared something that moved her sympathy. "I would live for you still—if I could." Her eyes closed for a little, as if, withdrawn into herself, she were for a last time trying. "But I can't!" she said as she raised them again to take leave of him.

She couldn't indeed, as but too promptly and sharply appeared, and he had no vision of her after this that was anything but darkness and doom. They had parted for ever in that strange talk; access to her chamber of pain, rigidly guarded, was almost wholly forbidden him; he was feeling now moreover, in the face of doctors, nurses, the two or three relatives attracted doubtless by the presumption of what she had to "leave," how few were the rights, as they were called in such cases, that he had to put forward, and how odd it might even seem that their intimacy shouldn't have given him more of them. The stupidest fourth cousin had more, even though she had been nothing in such a person's life. She had been a feature of features in *his*, for what else was it to have been so indispensable? Strange beyond saying were the ways of existence, baffling for him the anomaly of his lack, as he felt it to be, of producible claim. A woman might have been, as it were, everything to him, and it might yet present him in no connexion that any one seemed held to recognise. If this was the case in these closing weeks it was the case more sharply on the occasion of the last offices rendered, in the great grey London cemetery, to what had been mortal, to what had been precious, in his friend. The concourse at her grave was not numerous, but he saw himself treated as scarce more nearly concerned with it than if there had been a thousand others. He was in short from this moment face to face with the fact that he was to profit extraordinarily little by the interest May Bartram had taken in him. He couldn't quite have said what he expected, but he hadn't surely expected this approach to a double privation. Not only had her interest failed him, but he seemed to feel himself unattended—and for a reason he couldn't seize—by the distinction, the dignity, the propriety, if nothing else, of the man markedly bereaved. It was as if in the view of society he had not *been* markedly bereaved, as if there still failed some sign or proof of it, and as if none the less his character could never be affirmed nor the deficiency ever made up. There were moments as the weeks went by when he would have liked, by some almost aggressive act, to take his stand on the intimacy of his loss, in order that it *might* be questioned and his retort, to the relief of his spirit, so recorded; but the moments of an irritation more helpless followed fast on these, the moments during which, turning things over with a good conscience but with a bare horizon, he found himself wondering if he oughtn't to have begun, so to speak, further back.

He found himself wondering indeed at many things, and this last speculation had others to keep it company. What could he have done, after all, in her lifetime, without giving them both, as it were, away? He couldn't have made known she was watching him, for that would have published the superstition of the Beast. This was what closed his mouth now—now that the Jungle had been threshed to vacancy and that the Beast had stolen away. It sounded too foolish and too flat; the difference for him in this particular, the extinction in his life of the element of suspense, was such as in fact to surprise him. He could scarce have said what the effect resembled; the abrupt cessation, the positive prohibition, of music perhaps, more than anything else, in some place all adjusted and all accustomed to sonority and to attention. If he could at any rate have conceived lifting the veil from his image at some moment of the past (what had he done, after all, if not lift it to *her?*) so to do this to-day, to talk to people at large of the Jungle cleared and confide to them that he now felt it as safe, would have been not only to see them listen as to a goodwife's tale, but really to hear himself tell one. What it presently came to in truth was that poor Marcher waded through his beaten grass, where no life stirred, where no breath sounded, where no evil eye seemed to gleam from a possible lair, very much as if vaguely looking for the Beast, and still more as if acutely missing it. He walked about in an existence that had grown strangely more spacious and, stopping fitfully in places where the undergrowth of life struck him as closer, asked himself yearningly, wondered secretly and sorely, if it would have lurked here or there. It would have at all events *sprung;* what was at least complete was his belief in the truth itself of the assurance given him. The change from his old sense to his new was absolute and final: what was to happen *had* so absolutely and finally happened that he was as little able to know a fear for his future as to know a hope; so absent in short was any question of anything still to come. He was to live entirely with the other question, that of his unidentified past, that of his having to see his fortune impenetrably muffled and masked.

The torment of this vision became then his occupation; he couldn't perhaps have consented to live but for the possibility of guessing. She had told him, his friend, not to guess; she had forbidden him, so far as he might, to know, and she had even in a sort denied the power in him to learn: which were so many things, precisely, to deprive him of rest. It wasn't that he wanted, he argued for fairness, that anything past and done should repeat itself; it was only that he shouldn't, as an anticlimax, have been taken sleeping so sound as not to be able to win back by an effort of thought the lost stuff of consciousness. He declared to himself at moments that he would either win it back or have done with consciousness for ever; he made this idea his one motive in fine, made it so much his passion that none other, to compare with it, seemed ever to have touched him. The lost stuff of consciousness became thus for him as a strayed or stolen child to an unappeasable father; he hunted it up and down very much as if he were knocking at doors and enquiring of the police. This was the spirit in which, inevitably, he set himself to travel; he started on a journey that was to be as long as he could make it; it danced before him that, as the other side of the globe couldn't possibly have less to say to him, it might, by a possibility of suggestion, have more. Before he quitted London, however, he made a pilgrimage to May Bartram's grave, took his way to it through the endless avenues of the grim suburban metropolis, sought it out in the wilderness of tombs, and, though he had come but for the renewal of the act of farewell, found himself, when he had at last stood by it, beguiled into long intensities. He stood for an hour, powerless to turn away and yet powerless to penetrate the darkness of death; fixing with his eyes her inscribed name and date, beating his forehead against the fact of the secret they kept, drawing his breath, while he waited, as if some sense would in pity of him rise from the stones. He kneeled on the stones, however, in vain; they kept what they concealed; and if the face of the tomb did become a face for him it was because her two names became a pair of eyes that didn't know him. He gave them a last long look, but no palest light broke.

VI

He stayed away, after this, for a year; he visited the depths of Asia, spending himself on scenes of romantic interest, of superlative sanctity; but what was present to him everywhere was that for a man who had known what *he* had known the world was vulgar and vain. The state of mind in which he had lived for so many years shone out to him, in reflexion, as a light that coloured and refined, a light beside which the glow of the East was garish, cheap and thin. The terrible truth was that he had lost—with everything else—a distinction as well; the things he saw couldn't help being common when he had become common to look at them. He was simply now one of them himself—he was in the dust, without a peg for the sense of difference; and there were hours when, before the temples of gods and the sepulchres of kings, his spirit turned for nobleness of association to the barely discriminated slab in the London suburb. That had become for him, and more intensely with time and distance, his one witness of a past glory. It was all that was left to him for proof or pride, yet the past glories of Pharaohs were nothing to him as he thought of it. Small wonder then that he came back to it on the morrow of his return. He was drawn there this time as irresistibly as the other, yet with a confidence, almost, that was doubtless the effect of the many months that had elapsed. He had lived, in spite of himself, into his change of feeling, and in wandering over the earth had wandered, as might be said, from the circumference to the centre of his desert. He had settled to his safety and accepted perforce his extinction; figuring to himself, with some colour, in the likeness of certain little old men he remembered to have seen, of whom, all meagre and wizened as they might look, it was related that they had in their time fought twenty duels or been loved by ten princesses. They indeed had been wondrous for others while he was but wondrous for himself; which, however, was exactly the cause of his haste to renew the wonder by getting back, as he might put it, into his own presence. That had quickened his steps and checked his delay. If his visit was prompt it was because he had been separated so long from the part of himself that alone he now valued.

It's accordingly not false to say that he reached his goal with a certain elation and stood there again with a certain assurance. The creature beneath the sod *knew* of his rare experience, so that, strangely now, the place had lost for him its mere blankness of expression. It met him in mildness—not, as before, in mockery; it wore for him the air of conscious greeting that we find, after absence, in things that have closely belonged to us and which seem to confess of themselves to the connexion. The plot of ground, the graven tablet, the tended flowers affected him so as belonging to him that he resembled for the hour a contented landlord reviewing a piece of property. Whatever had happened—well, had happened. He had not come back this time with the vanity of that question, his former worrying "what, *what?*" now practically so spent. Yet he would none the less never again so cut himself off from the spot; he would come back to it every month, for if he did nothing else by its aid he at least held up his head. It thus grew for him, in the oddest way, a positive resource; he carried out his idea of periodical returns, which took their place at last among the most inveterate of his habits. What it all amounted to, oddly enough, was that in his finally so simplified world this garden of death gave him the few square feet of earth on which he could still most live. It was as if, being nothing anywhere else for any one, nothing even for himself, he were just everything here, and if not for a crowd of witnesses or indeed for any witness but John Marcher, then by clear right of the register that he could scan like an open page. The open page was the tomb of his friend, and *there* were the facts of the past, there the truth of his life, there the backward reaches in which he could lose himself. He did this from time to time with such effect that he seemed to wander through the old years with his hand in the arm of a companion who was, in the most extraordinary manner, his other, his younger self; and to wander, which was more extraordinary yet, round and round a third presence—not wandering she, but stationary, still, whose eyes, turning with his revolution, never ceased to follow him, and whose seat was his point, so to speak, of orientation. Thus in short he settled to live—feeding all on the sense that he once *had* lived, and dependent on it not alone for a support but for an identity.

It sufficed him in its way for months and the year elapsed; it would doubtless even have carried him further but for an accident, superficially slight, which moved him, quite in another direction, with a force beyond any of his impressions of Egypt or of India. It was a thing of the merest chance—the turn, as he afterwards felt, of a hair, though he was indeed to live to believe that if light hadn't come to him in this particular fashion it would still have come in another. He was to live to believe this, I say, though he was not to live, I may not less definitely mention, to do much else. We allow him at any rate the benefit of the conviction, struggling up for him at the end, that, whatever might have happened or not happened, he would have come round of himself to the light. The incident of an autumn day had put the match to the train laid from of old by his misery. With the light before him he knew that even of late his ache had only been smothered. It was strangely drugged, but it throbbed; at the touch it began to bleed. And the touch, in the event, was the face of a fellow mortal. This face, one grey afternoon when the leaves were thick in the alleys, looked into Marcher's own, at the cemetery, with an expression like the cut of a blade. He felt it, that is, so deep down that he winced at the steady thrust. The person who so mutely assaulted him was a figure he had noticed, on reaching his own goal, absorbed by a grave a short distance away, a grave apparently fresh, so that the emotion of the visitor would probably match it for frankness. This fact alone forbade further attention, though during the time he stayed he remained vaguely conscious of his neighbour, a middle-aged man apparently, in mourning, whose bowed back, among the clustered monuments and mortuary yews, was constantly presented. Marcher's theory that these were elements in contact with which he himself revived, had suffered, on this occasion, it may be granted, a marked, an excessive check. The autumn day was dire for him as none had recently been, and he rested with a heaviness he had not yet known on the low stone table that bore May Bartram's name. He rested without power to move, as if some spring in him, some spell vouchsafed, had suddenly been broken for ever. If he could have done that moment as he wanted he would simply have stretched himself on the slab that was ready to take him, treating it as a place prepared to receive his last sleep. What in all the wide world had he now to keep awake for? He stared before him with the question, and it was then that, as one of the cemetery walks passed near him, he caught the shock of the face.

His neighbour at the other grave had withdrawn, as he himself, with force enough in him, would have done by now, and was advancing along the path on his way to one of the gates. This brought him close, and his pace was slow, so that—and all the more as there was a kind of hunger in his look—the two men were for a minute directly confronted. Marcher knew him at once for one of the deeply stricken—a perception so sharp that nothing else in the picture comparatively lived, neither his dress, his age, nor his presumable character and class; nothing lived but the deep ravage of the features he showed. He *showed* them—that was the point; he was moved, as he passed, by some impulse that was either a signal for sympathy or, more possibly, a challenge to an opposed sorrow. He might already have been aware of our friend, might at some previous hour have noticed in him the smooth habit of the scene, with which the state of his own senses so scantly consorted, and might thereby have been stirred as by an overt discord. What Marcher was at all events conscious of was in the first place that the image of scarred passion presented to him was conscious too—of something that profaned the air; and in the second that, roused, startled, shocked, he was yet the next moment looking after it, as it went, with envy. The most extraordinary thing that had happened to him—though he had given that name to other matters as well—took place, after his immediate vague stare, as a consequence of this impression. The stranger passed, but the raw glare of his grief remained, making our friend wonder in pity what wrong, what wound it expressed, what injury not to be healed. What had the man *had*, to make him by the loss of it so bleed and yet live?

Something—and this reached him with a pang—that *he*, John

Marcher, hadn't; the proof of which was precisely John Marcher's arid end. No passion had ever touched him, for this was what passion meant; he had survived and maundered and pined, but where had been *his* deep ravage? The extraordinary thing we speak of was the sudden rush of the result of this question. The sight that had just met his eyes named to him, as in letters of quick flame, something he had utterly, insanely missed, and what he had missed made these things a train of fire, made them mark themselves in an anguish of inward throbs. He had seen *outside* of his life, not learned it within, the way a woman was mourned when she had been loved for herself: such was the force of his conviction of the meaning of the stranger's face, which still flared for him as a smoky torch. It hadn't come to him, the knowledge, on the wings of experience; it had brushed him, jostled him, upset him, with the disrespect of chance, the insolence of accident. Now that the illumination had begun, however, it blazed to the zenith, and what he presently stood there gazing at was the sounded void of his life. He gazed, he drew breath, in pain; he turned in his dismay, and, turning, he had before him in sharper incision than ever the open page of his story. The name on the table smote him as the passage of his neighbour had done, and what it said to him, full in the face, was that *she* was what he had missed. This was the awful thought, the answer to all the past, the vision at the dread clearness of which he grew as cold as the stone beneath him. Everything fell together, confessed, explained, overwhelmed; leaving him most of all stupefied at the blindness he had cherished. The fate he had been marked for he had met with a vengeance—he had emptied the cup to the lees; he had been the man of his time, *the* man, to whom nothing on earth was to have happened. That was the rare stroke—that was his visitation. So he saw it, as we say, in pale horror, while the pieces fitted and fitted. So *she* had seen it while he didn't, and so she served at this hour to drive the truth home. It was the truth, vivid and monstrous, that all the while he had waited the wait was itself his portion. This the companion of his vigil had at a given moment made out, and she had then offered him the chance to baffle his doom. One's doom, however, was never baffled, and on the day she told him his own had come down she had seen him but stupidly stare at the escape she offered him.

The escape would have been to love her; then, *then* he would have lived. *She* had lived—who could say now with what passion? —since she had loved him for himself; whereas he had never thought of her (ah how it hugely glared at him!) but in the chill of his egotism and the light of her use. Her spoken words came back to him—the chain stretched and stretched. The Beast had lurked indeed, and the Beast, at its hour, had sprung; [8] it had sprung in that twilight of the cold April when, pale, ill, wasted, but all beautiful, and perhaps even then recoverable, she had risen from her chair to stand before him and let him imaginably guess. It had sprung as he didn't guess; it had sprung as she hopelessly turned from him, and the mark, by the time he left her, had fallen where it *was* to fall. He had justified his fear and achieved his fate; he had failed, with the last exactitude, of all he was to fail of; and a moan now rose to his lips as he remembered she had prayed he mightn't know. This horror of waking—*this* was knowledge, knowledge under the breath of which the very tears in his eyes seemed to freeze. Through them, none the less, he tried to fix it and hold it; he kept it there before him so that he might feel the pain. That at least, belated and bitter, had something of the taste of life. But the bitterness suddenly sickened him, and it was as if, horribly, he saw, in the truth, in the cruelty of his image, what had been appointed and done. He saw the Jungle of his life and saw the lurking Beast; then, while he looked, perceived it, as by a stir of the air, rise, huge and hideous, for the leap that was to settle him. His eyes darkened—it was close; and, instinctively turning, in his hallucination, to avoid it, he flung himself, face down, on the tomb.

1901   1903, 1909

The Jolly Corner [9]

I

"Every one asks me what I 'think' of everything," said Spencer Brydon; "and I make answer as I can—begging or dodging the

---

8. "She had loved him. With his base safety and shrinkage he never knew. *That* was what might have happened, and what *has* happened is that it didn't" (From a passage in James's notebooks on "The Beast in the Jungle").

9. Among the James stories here, "The Jolly Corner" invites comparison with "The Beast in the Jungle" (*q.v.*, above). Of the earlier story James observed (see preface, New York Edition, Vol. XVII) that the protagonist, John Marcher, "burns" through life obsessed by an early intimation that, "for good or ill," his fate was to be marked by "rare distinction, some incalculable violence." Hence Marcher ignored common experiences mankind share in various degrees, only to discover his obtuseness too late, when already he had become "the man in the world to whom nothing whatever was to happen." By contrast with this negative

destiny, Spencer Brydon returns to his "Jolly Corner" in New York, having already made good his early robust and positive choice to abandon his native New York to live abroad.

The gothic and supernatural elements in this story resemble a popular genre, of which James's "The Turn of the Screw" (1898) is the greatest example and in which Howells comes closest to James in power and verisimilitude. Loosely classed as "ghost stories" they transcended this popular form by the force of their dependence on valid psychic or psychological experience and on perceptions beyond sensory verification. James remarked, in the preface to this story, that "the idea entertained [was] the strange and sinister embroidered on the very type of the normal, * * * an analysis of some of the conceivably rarest and intensest grounds for * * * a *malaise* so incongruous * * * as to be almost compromising. Spencer Brydon's

question, putting them off with any nonsense. It wouldn't matter to any of them really," he went on, "for, even were it possible to meet in that stand-and-deliver way so silly a demand on so big a subject, my 'thoughts' would still be almost altogether about something that concerns only myself." He was talking to Miss Staverton, with whom for a couple of months now he had availed himself of every possible occasion to talk; this disposition and this resource, this comfort and support, as the situation in fact presented itself, having promptly enough taken the first place in the considerable array of rather unattenuated surprises attending his so strangely belated return to America. Everything was somehow a surprise; and that might be natural when one had so long and so consistently neglected everything, taken pains to give surprises so much margin for play. He had given them more than thirty years—thirty-three, to be exact; and they now seemed to him to have organised their performance quite on the scale of that licence. He had been twenty-three on leaving New York—he was fifty-six today: unless indeed he were to reckon as he had sometimes, since his repatriation, found himself feeling; in which case he would have lived longer than is often allotted to man. It would have taken a century, he repeatedly said to himself, and said also to Alice Staverton, it would have taken a longer absence and a more averted mind than those even of which he had been guilty, to pile up the differences, the newnesses, the queernesses, above all the bignesses, for the better or the worse, that at present assaulted his vision wherever he looked.

The great fact all the while however had been the incalculability; since he *had* supposed himself, from decade to decade, to be allowing, and in the most liberal and intelligent manner, for brilliancy of change. He actually saw that he had allowed for nothing; he missed what he would have been sure of finding, he found what he would never have imagined. Proportions and values were upside-down; the ugly things he had expected, the ugly things of his far-away youth, when he had too promptly waked up to a sense of the ugly—these uncanny phenomena placed him rather, as it happened, under the charm; whereas the "swagger" things, the modern, the monstrous, the famous things, those he had more particularly, like thousands of ingenuous enquirers every year, come over to see, were exactly his sources of dismay. They were as so many set traps for displeasure, above all for reaction, of which his restless tread was constantly pressing the spring. It was inter-

adventure, however, is one of those finished fantasies that, achieving sense or not, speak best even to the critical sense for themselves." "The Jolly Corner" appeared first in *The English Review*, December, 1908. Our text is the New York Edition (Vol. XVII, 1909).

esting, doubtless, the whole show, but it would have been too disconcerting hadn't a certain finer truth saved the situation. He had distinctly not, in this steadier light, come over *all* for the monstrosities; he had come, not only in the last analysis but quite on the face of the act, under an impulse with which they had nothing to do. He had come—putting the thing pompously—to look at his "property," which he had thus for a third of a century not been within four thousand miles of; or, expressing it less sordidly, he had yielded to the humour of seeing again his house on the jolly corner, as he usually, and quite fondly, described it—the one in which he had first seen the light, in which various members of his family had lived and had died, in which the holidays of his over-schooled boyhood had been passed and the few social flowers of his chilled adolescence gathered, and which, alienated then for so long a period, had, through the successive deaths of his two brothers and the termination of old arrangements, come wholly into his hands. He was the owner of another, not quite so "good" —the jolly corner having been, from far back, superlatively extended and consecrated; and the value of the pair represented his main capital, with an income consisting, in these later years, of their respective rents which (thanks precisely to their original excellent type) had never been depressingly low. He could live in "Europe," as he had been in the habit of living, on the product of these flourishing New York leases, and all the better since, that of the second structure, the mere number in its long row, having within a twelvemonth fallen in, renovation at a high advance had proved beautifully possible.

These were items of property indeed, but he had found himself since his arrival distinguishing more than ever between them. The house within the street, two bristling blocks westward, was already in course of reconstruction as a tall mass of flats; he had acceded, some time before, to overtures for this conversion—in which, now that it was going forward, it had been not the least of his astonishments to find himself able, on the spot, and though without a previous ounce of such experience, to participate with a certain intelligence, almost with a certain authority. He had lived his life with his back so turned to such concerns and his face addressed to those of so different an order that he scarce knew what to make of this lively stir, in a compartment of his mind never yet penetrated, of a capacity for business and a sense for construction. These virtues, so common all round him now, had been dormant in his own organism—where it might be said of them perhaps that they had slept the sleep of the just. At present, in the splendid autumn weather—the autumn at least was a pure boon in the terrible place—he loafed about his "work" undeterred,

secretly agitated; not in the least "minding" that the whole proposition, as they said, was vulgar and sordid, and ready to climb
ladders, to walk the plank, to handle materials and look wise
about them, to ask questions, in fine, and challenge explanations
and really "go into" figures.

It amused, it verily quite charmed him; and by the same stroke,
it amused, and even more, Alice Staverton, though perhaps charming her perceptibly less. She wasn't however going to be better-off
for it, as *he* was—and so astonishingly much: nothing was now
likely, he knew, ever to make her better-off than she found herself,
in the afternoon of life, as the delicately frugal possessor and tenant of the small house in Irving Place to which she had subtly
managed to cling through her almost unbroken New York career.
If he knew the way to it now better than to any other address
among the dreadful multiplied numberings which seemed to him
to reduce the whole place to some vast ledger-page, overgrown,
fantastic, of ruled and criss-crossed lines and figures—if he had
formed, for his consolation, that habit, it was really not a little
because of the charm of his having encountered and recognised,
in the vast wilderness of the wholesale, breaking through the
mere gross generalisation of wealth and force and success, a small
still scene where items and shades, all delicate things, kept the
sharpness of the notes of a high voice perfectly trained, and where
economy hung about like the scent of a garden. His old friend
lived with one maid and herself dusted her relics and trimmed
her lamps and polished her silver; she stood off, in the awful modern crush, when she could, but she sallied forth and did battle
when the challenge was really to "spirit," the spirit she after all
confessed to, proudly and a little shyly, as to that of the better
time, that of *their* common, their quite far-away and antediluvian
social period and order. She made use of the street-cars when need
be, the terrible things that people scrambled for as the panic-
stricken at sea scramble for the boats; she affronted, inscrutably,
under stress, all the public concussions and ordeals; and yet, with
that slim mystifying grace of her appearance, which defied you to
say if she were a fair young woman who looked older through
trouble, or a fine smooth older one who looked young through
successful indifference; with her precious reference, above all, to
memories and histories into which he could enter, she was as exquisite for him as some pale pressed flower (a rarity to begin with),
and, failing other sweetnesses, she was a sufficient reward of his
effort. They had communities of knowledge, "their" knowledge
(this discriminating possessive was always on her lips) of presences
of the other age, presences all overlaid, in his case, by the experience of a man and the freedom of a wanderer, overlaid by plea-

sure, by infidelity, by passages of life that were strange and dim to her, just by "Europe" in short, but still unobscured, still exposed and cherished, under that pious visitation of the spirit from which she had never been diverted.

She had come with him one day to see how his "apartment-house" was rising; he had helped her over gaps and explained to her plans, and while they were there had happened to have, before her, a brief but lively discussion with the man in charge, the representative of the building-firm that had undertaken his work. He had found himself quite "standing-up" to this personage over a failure on the latter's part to observe some detail of one of their noted conditions, and had so lucidly urged his case that, besides ever so prettily flushing, at the time, for sympathy in his triumph, she had afterwards said to him (though to a slightly greater effect of irony) that he had clearly for too many years neglected a real gift. If he had but stayed at home he would have anticipated the inventor of the sky-scraper. If he had but stayed at home he would have discovered his genius in time really to start some new variety of awful architectural hare and run it till it burrowed in a gold-mine. He was to remember these words, while the weeks elapsed, for the small silver ring they had sounded over the queerest and deepest of his own lately most disguised and most muffled vibrations.

It had begun to be present to him after the first fortnight, it had broken out with the oddest abruptness, this particular wanton wonderment: it met him there—and this was the image under which he himself judged the matter, or at least, not a little, thrilled and flushed with it—very much as he might have been met by some strange figure, some unexpected occupant, at a turn of one of the dim passages of an empty house. The quaint analogy quite hauntingly remained with him, when he didn't indeed rather improve it by a still intenser form: that of his opening a door behind which he would have made sure of finding nothing, a door into a room shuttered and void, and yet so coming, with a great suppressed start, on some quite erect confronting presence, something planted in the middle of the place and facing him through the dusk. After that visit to the house in construction he walked with his companion to see the other and always so much the better one, which in the eastward direction formed one of the corners, the "jolly" one precisely, of the street now so generally dishonoured and disfigured in its westward reaches, and of the comparatively conservative Avenue. The Avenue still had pretensions, as Miss Staverton said, to decency; the old people had mostly gone, the old names were unknown, and here and there an old association seemed to stray, all vaguely, like some very aged person, out too late, whom you might meet and feel the impulse to watch or follow, in kindness, for safe restoration to shelter.

They went in together, our friends; he admitted himself with his key, as he kept no one there, he explained, preferring, for his reasons, to leave the place empty, under a simple arrangement with a good woman living in the neighbourhood and who came for a daily hour to open windows and dust and sweep. Spencer Brydon had his reasons and was growing aware of them; they seemed to him better each time he was there, though he didn't name them all to his companion, any more than he told her as yet how often, how quite absurdly often, he himself came. He only let her see for the present, while they walked through the great blank rooms, that absolute vacancy reigned and that, from top to bottom, there was nothing but Mrs. Muldoon's broomstick, in a corner, to tempt the burglar. Mrs. Muldoon was then on the premises, and she loquaciously attended the visitors, preceding them from room to room and pushing back shutters and throwing up sashes—all to show them, as she remarked, how little there was to see. There was little indeed to see in the great gaunt shell where the main dispositions and the general apportionment of space, the style of an age of ampler allowances, had nevertheless for its master their honest pleading message, affecting him as some good old servant's, some lifelong retainer's appeal for a character, or even for a retiring-pension; yet it was also a remark of Mrs. Muldoon's that, glad as she was to oblige him by her noonday round, there was a request she greatly hoped he would never make of her. If he should wish her for any reason to come in after dark she would just tell him, if he "plased," that he must ask it of somebody else.

The fact that there was nothing to see didn't militate for the worthy woman against what one *might* see, and she put it frankly to Miss Staverton that no lady could be expected to like, could she? "craping up to thim top storeys in the ayvil hours." The gas and electric light were off the house, and she fairly evoked a gruesome vision of her march through the great grey rooms—so many of them as there were too!—with her glimmering taper. Miss Staverton met her honest glare with a smile and the profession that she herself certainly would recoil from such an adventure. Spencer Brydon meanwhile held his peace—for the moment; the question of the "evil" hours in his old home had already become too grave for him. He had begun some time since to "crape," and he knew just why a packet of candles addressed to that pursuit had been stowed by his own hand, three weeks before, at the back of a drawer of the fine old sideboard that occupied, as a "fixture," the deep recess in the dining-room. Just now he laughed at his companions—quickly however changing the subject; for the reason

that, in the first place, his laugh struck him even at that moment
as starting the odd echo, the conscious human resonance (he scarce
knew how to qualify it) that sounds made while he was there alone
sent back to his ear or his fancy; and that, in the second, he imagined Alice Staverton for the instant on the point of asking him,
with a divination, if he ever so prowled. There were divinations
he was unprepared for, and he had at all events averted enquiry by
the time Mrs. Muldoon had left them, passing on to other parts.

There was happily enough to say, on so consecrated a spot, that
could be said freely and fairly; so that a whole train of declarations was precipitated by his friend's having herself broken out,
after a yearning look round: "But I hope you don't mean they
want you to pull *this* to pieces!" His answer came, promptly,
with his re-awakened wrath: it was of course exactly what they
wanted, and what they were "at" him for, daily, with the iteration
of people who couldn't for their life understand a man's liability
to decent feelings. He had found the place, just as it stood and
beyond what he could express, an interest and a joy. There were
values other than the beastly rent-values, and in short, in short—!
But it was thus Miss Staverton took him up. "In short you're to
make so good a thing of your sky-scraper that, living in luxury on
those ill-gotten gains, you can afford for a while to be sentimental
here!" Her smile had for him, with the words, the particular mild
irony with which he found half her talk suffused; an irony without bitterness and that came, exactly, from her having so much
imagination—not, like the cheap sarcasms with which one heard
most people, about the world of "society," bid for the reputation
of cleverness, from nobody's really having any. It was agreeable to
him at this very moment to be sure that when he had answered,
after a brief demur, "Well yes: so, precisely, you may put it!" her
imagination would still do him justice. He explained that even if
never a dollar were to come to him from the other house he would
nevertheless cherish this one; and he dwelt, further, while they
lingered and wandered, on the fact of the stupefaction he was already exciting, the positive mystification he felt himself create.

He spoke of the value of all he read into it, into the mere sight
of the walls, mere shapes of the rooms, mere sound of the floors,
mere feel, in his hand, of the old silver-plated knobs of the several
mahogany doors, which suggested the pressure of the palms of
the dead; the seventy years of the past in fine that these things represented, the annals of nearly three generations, counting his
grandfather's, the one that had ended there, and the impalpable
ashes of his long-extinct youth, afloat in the very air like microscopic motes. She listened to everything; she was a woman who
answered intimately but who utterly didn't chatter. She scattered

abroad therefore no cloud of words; she could assent, she could agree, above all she could encourage, without doing that. Only at the last she went a little further than he had done himself. "And then how do you know? You may still, after all, want to live here." It rather indeed pulled him up, for it wasn't what he had been thinking, at least in her sense of the words. "You mean I may decide to stay on for the sake of it?"

"Well, *with* such a home—!" But, quite beautifully, she had too much tact to dot so monstrous an *i*, and it was precisely an illustration of the way she didn't rattle. How could any one—of any wit—insist on any one else's "wanting" to live in New York?

"Oh," he said, "I *might* have lived here (since I had my opportunity early in life); I might have put in here all these years. Then everything would have been different enough—and, I dare say, 'funny' enough. But that's another matter. And then the beauty of it—I mean of my perversity, of my refusal to agree to a 'deal'—is just in the total absence of a reason. Don't you see that if I had a reason about the matter at all it would *have* to be the other way, and would then be inevitably a reason of dollars? There are no reasons here *but* of dollars. Let us therefore have none whatever—not the ghost of one."

They were back in the hall then for departure, but from where they stood the vista was large, through an open door, into the great square main saloon, with its almost antique felicity of brave spaces between windows. Her eyes came back from that reach and met his own a moment. "Are you very sure the 'ghost' of one doesn't, much rather, serve—?"

He had a positive sense of turning pale. But it was as near as they were then to come. For he made answer, he believed, between a glare and a grin: "O ghosts—of course the place must swarm with them! I should be ashamed of it if it didn't. Poor Mrs. Muldoon's right, and it's why I haven't asked her to do more than look in."

Miss Staverton's gaze again lost itself, and things she didn't utter, it was clear, came and went in her mind. She might even for the minute, off there in the fine room, have imagined some element dimly gathering. Simplified like the death-mask of a handsome face, it perhaps produced for her just then an effect akin to the stir of an expression in the "set" commemorative plaster. Yet whatever her impression may have been she produced instead a vague platitude. "Well, if it were only furnished and lived in—!"

She appeared to imply that in case of its being still furnished he might have been a little less opposed to the idea of a return. But she passed straight into the vestibule, as if to leave her words behind her, and the next moment he had opened the house-door and was standing with her on the steps. He closed the door and, while he re-pocketed his key, looking up and down, they took in the comparatively harsh actuality of the Avenue, which reminded him of the assault of the outer light of the Desert on the traveller emerging from an Egyptian tomb. But he risked before they stepped into the street his gathered answer to her speech. "For me it *is* lived in. For me it *is* finished." At which it was easy to her to sigh "Ah yes—!" all vaguely and discreetly; since his parents and his favourite sister, to say nothing of other kin, in numbers, had run their course and met their end there. That represented, within the walls, ineffaceable life.

It was a few days after this that, during an hour passed with her again, he had expressed his impatience of the too flattering curiosity—among the people he met—about his appreciation of New York. He had arrived at none at all that was socially producible, and as for that matter of his "thinking" (thinking the better or the worse of anything there) he was wholly taken up with one subject of thought. It was mere vain egoism, and it was moreover, if she liked, a morbid obsession. He found all things come back to the question of what he personally might have been, how he might have led his life and "turned out," if he had not so, at the outset, given it up. And confessing for the first time to the intensity within him of his absurd speculation—which but proved also, no doubt, the habit of too selfishly thinking—he affirmed the impotence there of any other source of interest, any other native appeal. "What would it have made of me, what would it have made of me? I keep for ever wondering, all idiotically; as if I could possibly know! I see what it has made of dozens of others, those I meet, and it positively aches within me, to the point of exasperation, that it would have made something of me as well. Only I can't make out *what*, and the worry of it, the small rage of curiosity never to be satisfied, brings back what I remember to have felt, once or twice, after judging best, for reasons, to burn some important letter unopened. I've been sorry, I've hated it—I've never known what was in the letter. You may of course say it's a trifle—!"

"I don't say it's a trifle," Miss Staverton gravely interrupted.

She was seated by her fire, and before her, on his feet and restless, he turned to and fro between this intensity of his idea and a fitful and unseeing inspection, through his single eye-glass, of the dear little old objects on her chimney-piece. Her interruption made him for an instant look at her harder. "I shouldn't care if you did!" he laughed, however; "and it's only a figure, at any rate, for the way I now feel. *Not* to have followed my perverse young course—and almost in the teeth of my father's curse, as I may say; not to have kept it up, so, 'over there,' from that day to this, without a doubt or a pang; not, above all, to have liked it, to have loved it, so much, loved it, no doubt, with such an abysmal conceit of my own preference: some variation from *that*, I say, must have produced some different effect for my life and for my 'form.' I should have stuck here—if it had been possible; and I was too young, at twenty-three, to judge, *pour deux sous*,[1] whether it *were* possible. If I had waited I might have seen it was, and then I might have been, by staying here, something nearer to one of these types who have been hammered so hard and made so keen by their conditions. It isn't that I admire them so much—the question of any charm in them, or of any charm, beyond that of the rank money-passion, exerted by their conditions *for* them, has nothing to do with the matter: it's only a question of what fantastic, yet perfectly possible, development of my own nature I mayn't have missed. It comes over me that I had then a strange *alter ego* deep down somewhere within me, as the full-blown flower is in the small tight bud, and that I just took the course, I just transferred him to the climate, that blighted him for once and for ever."

"And you wonder about the flower," Miss Staverton said. "So do I, if you want to know; and so I've been wondering these several weeks. I believe in the flower," she continued, "I feel it would have been quite splendid, quite huge and monstrous."

"Monstrous above all!" her visitor echoed; "and I imagine, by the same stroke, quite hideous and offensive."

"You don't believe that," she returned; "if you did you wouldn't wonder. You'd know, and that would be enough for you. What you feel—and what I feel *for* you—is that you'd have had power."

"You'd have liked me that way?" he asked.

She barely hung fire. "How should I not have liked you?"

"I see. You'd have liked me, have preferred me, a billionaire!"

"How should I not have liked you?" she simply again asked.

He stood before her still—her question kept him motionless. He took it in, so much there was of it; and indeed his not otherwise meeting it testified to that. "I know at least what I am," he simply went on; "the other side of the medal's clear enough. I've not been edifying—I believe I'm thought in a hundred quarters to have been barely decent. I've followed strange paths and worshipped strange gods; it must have come to you again and again—in fact you've admitted to me as much—that I was leading, at any time these thirty years, a selfish frivolous scandalous life. And you see what it has made of me."

She just waited, smiling at him. "You see what it has made of *me*."

"Oh you're a person whom nothing can have altered. You

1. For two cents.

were born to be what you are, anywhere, anyway: you've the perfection nothing else could have blighted. And don't you see how, without my exile, I shouldn't have been waiting till now—?" But he pulled up for the strange pang.

"The great thing to see," she presently said, "seems to me to be that it has spoiled nothing. It hasn't spoiled your being here at last. It hasn't spoiled this. It hasn't spoiled your speaking—" She also however faltered.

He wondered at everything her controlled emotion might mean "Do you believe then—too dreadfully!—that I *am* as good as I might ever have been?"

"Oh no! Far from it!" With which she got up from her chair and was nearer to him. "But I don't care," she smiled.

"You mean I'm good enough?"

She considered a little. "Will you believe it if I say so? I mean will you let that settle your question for you?" And then as if making out in his face that he drew back from this, that he had some idea which, however absurd, he couldn't yet bargain away: "Oh you don't care either—but very differently: you don't care for anything but yourself."

Spencer Brydon recognised it—it was in fact what he had absolutely professed. Yet he importantly qualified. "*He* isn't myself. He's the just so totally other person. But I do want to see him," he added. "And I can. And I shall."

Their eyes met for a minute while he guessed from something in hers that she divined his strange sense. But neither of them otherwise expressed it, and her apparent understanding, with no protesting shock, no easy derision, touched him more deeply than anything yet, constituting for his stifled perversity, on the spot, an element that was like breatheable air. What she said however was unexpected. "Well, *I've* seen him."

"You—?"

"I've seen him in a dream."

"Oh a 'dream'—!" It let him down.

"But twice over," she continued. "I saw him as I see you now."

"You've dreamed the same dream—?"

"Twice over," she repeated. "The very same."

This did somehow a little speak to him, as it also gratified him. "You dream about me at that rate?"

"Ah about *him!*" she smiled.

His eyes again sounded her. "Then you know all about him." And as she said nothing more: "What's the wretch like?"

She hesitated, and it was as if he were pressing her so hard that, resisting for reasons of her own, she had to turn away. "I'll tell you some other time!"

II

It was after this that there was most of a virtue for him, most of a cultivated charm, most of a preposterous secret thrill, in the particular form of surrender to his obsession and of address to what he more and more believed to be his privilege. It was what in these weeks he was living for—since he really felt life to begin but after Mrs. Muldoon had retired from the scene and, visiting the ample house from attic to cellar, making sure he was alone, he knew himself in safe possession and, as he tacitly expressed it, let himself go. He sometimes came twice in the twenty-four hours; the moments he liked best were those of gathering dusk, of the short autumn twilight; this was the time of which, again and again, he found himself hoping most. Then he could, as seemed to him, most intimately wander and wait, linger and listen, feel his fine attention, never in his life before so fine, on the pulse of the great vague place: he preferred the lampless hour and only wished he might have prolonged each day the deep crepuscular spell. Later —rarely much before midnight, but then for a considerable vigil —he watched with his glimmering light; moving slowly, holding it high, playing it far, rejoicing above all, as much as he might, in open vistas, reaches of communication between rooms and by passages; the long straight chance or show, as he would have called it, for the revelation he pretended to invite. It was practice he found he could perfectly "work" without exciting remark; no one was in the least the wiser for it; even Alice Staverton, who was moreover a well of discretion, didn't quite fully imagine.

He let himself in and let himself out with the assurance of calm proprietorship; and accident so far favoured him that, if a fat Avenue "officer" had happened on occasion to see him entering at eleven-thirty, he had never yet, to the best of his belief, been noticed as emerging at two. He walked there on the crisp November nights, arrived regularly at the evening's end; it was as easy to do this after dining out as to take his way to a club or to his hotel. When he left his club, if he hadn't been dining out, it was ostensibly to go to his hotel; and when he left his hotel, if he had spent a part of the evening there, it was ostensibly to go to his club. Everything was easy in fine; everything conspired and promoted: there was truly even in the strain of his experience something that glossed over, something that salved and simplified, all the rest of consciousness. He circulated, talked, renewed, loosely and pleasantly, old relations—met indeed, so far as he could, new expectations and seemed to make out on the whole that in spite of the career, of such different contacts, which he had spoken of to Miss Staverton as ministering so little, for those who might have watched it, to edification, he was positively rather liked

than not. He was a dim secondary social success—and all with people who had truly not an idea of him. It was all mere surface
sound, this murmur of their welcome, this popping of their corks
—just as his gestures of response were the extravagant shadows,
emphatic in proportion as they meant little, of some game of
ombres chinoises.[2] He projected himself all day, in thought,
straight over the bristling line of hard unconscious heads and into
the other, the real, the waiting life; the life that, as soon as he had
heard behind him the click of his great house-door, began for him,
on the jolly corner, as beguilingly as the slow opening bars of some
rich music follows the tap of the conductor's wand.

He always caught the first effect of the steel point of his stick on
the old marble of the hall pavement, large black-and-white
squares that he remembered as the admiration of his childhood
and that had then made in him, as he now saw, for the growth of
an early conception of style. This effect was the dim reverberating
tinkle as of some far-off bell hung who should say where?—in the
depths of the house, of the past, of that mystical other world that
might have flourished for him had he not, for weal or woe, abandoned it. On this impression he did ever the same thing; he put
his stick noiselessly away in a corner—feeling the place once more
in the likeness of some great glass bowl, all precious concave crystal, set delicately humming by the play of a moist finger round its
edge. The concave crystal held, as it were, this mystical other
world, and the indescribably fine murmur of its rim was the sigh
there, the scarce audible pathetic wail to his strained ear, of all
the old baffled forsworn possibilities. What he did therefore by
this appeal of his hushed presence was to wake them into such
measure of ghostly life as they might still enjoy. They were shy, all
but unappeasably shy, but they weren't really sinister; at least
they weren't as he had hitherto felt them—before they had taken
the Form he so yearned to make them take, the Form he at moments saw himself in the light of fairly hunting on tiptoe, the
points of his evening-shoes, from room to room and from storey to
storey.

That was the essence of his vision—which was all rank folly, if
one would, while he was out of the house and otherwise occupied,
but which took on the last verisimilitude as soon as he was placed
and posted. He knew what he meant and what he wanted; it was
so clear as the figure on a cheque presented in demand for cash.
His *alter ego* "walked"—that was the note of his image of him,
while his image of his motive for his own odd pastime was the
desire to waylay him and meet him. He roamed, slowly, warily,
but all restlessly, he himself did—Mrs. Muldoon had been right,

2. Shadow theater.

absolutely, with her figure of their "craping"; and the presence he watched for would roam restlessly too. But it would be as cautious and as shifty; the conviction of its probable, in fact its already quite sensible, quite audible evasion of pursuit grew for him from night to night, laying on him finally a rigour to which nothing in his life had been comparable. It had been the theory of many superficially-judging persons, he knew, that he was wasting that life in a surrender to sensations, but he had tasted of no pleasure so fine as his actual tension, had been introduced to no sport that demanded at once the patience and the nerve of this stalking of a creature more subtle, yet at bay perhaps more formidable, than any beast of the forest. The terms, the comparisons, the very practices of the chase positively came again into play; there were even moments when passages of his occasional experience as a sportsman, stirred memories, from his younger time, of moor and mountain and desert, revived for him—and to the increase of his keenness—by the tremendous force of analogy. He found himself at moments—once he had placed his single light on some mantel-shelf or in some recess—stepping back into shelter or shade, effacing himself behind a door or in an embrasure, as he had sought of old the vantage of rack and tree; he found himself holding his breath and living in the joy of the instant supreme suspense created by big game alone.

He wasn't afraid (though putting himself the question as he believed gentlemen on Bengal tiger-shoots or in close quarters with the great bear of the Rockies had been known to confess to having put it); and this indeed—since here at least he might be frank!—because of the impression, so intimate and so strange, that he himself produced as yet a dread, produced certainly a strain, beyond the liveliest he was likely to feel. They fell for him into categories, they fairly became familiar, the signs, for his own perception, of the alarm his presence and his vigilance created; though leaving him always to remark, portentously, on his probably having formed a relation, his probably enjoying a consciousness, unique in the experience of man. People enough, first and last, had been in terror of apparitions, but who had ever before so turned the tables and become himself, in the apparitional world, an incalculable terror? He might have found this sublime and he quite dared to think of it; but he didn't too much insist, truly, on that side of his privilege. With habit and repetition he gained to an extraordinary degree the power to penetrate the dusk of distances and the darkness of corners, to resolve back into their innocence the treacheries of uncertain light, the evil-looking forms taken in the gloom by mere shadows, by accidents of the air, by shifting effects of perspective; putting down his dim luminary he could still wander on without it, pass into other rooms and, only knowing it was there behind him in case of need, see his way about, visually project for his purpose a comparative clearness. It made him feel, this acquired faculty, like some monstrous stealthy cat; he wondered if he would have glared at these moments with large shining yellow eyes, and what it mightn't verily be, for the poor hard-pressed *alter ego*, to be confronted with such a type.

He liked however the open shutters; he opened everywhere those Mrs. Muldoon had closed, closing them as carefully afterwards, so that she shouldn't notice: he liked—oh this he did like, and above all in the upper rooms!—the sense of the hard silver of the autumn stars through the window-panes, and scarcely less the flare of the street-lamps below, the white electric lustre which it would have taken curtains to keep out. This was human actual social; this was of the world he had lived in, and he was more at his ease certainly for the countenance, coldly general and impersonal, that all the while and in spite of his detachment it seemed to give him. He had support of course mostly in the rooms at the wide front and the prolonged side; it failed him considerably in the central shades and the parts at the back. But if he sometimes, on his rounds, was glad of his optical reach, so none the less often the rear of the house affected him as the very jungle of his prey. The place was there more subdivided; a large "extension" in particular, where small rooms for servants had been multiplied, abounded in nooks and corners, in closets and passages, in the ramifications especially of an ample back staircase over which he leaned, many a time, to look far down—not deterred from his gravity even while aware that he might, for a spectator, have figured some solemn simpleton playing at hide-and-seek. Outside in fact he might himself make the ironic *rapprochement*; but within the walls, and in spite of the clear windows, his consistency was proof against the cynical light of New York.

It had belonged to that idea of the exasperated consciousness of his victim to become a real test for him; since he had quite put it to himself from the first that, oh distinctly! he could "cultivate" his whole perception. He had felt it as above all open to cultivation —which indeed was but another name for his manner of spending his time. He was bringing it on, bringing it to perfection, by practice; in consequence of which it had grown so fine that he was now aware of impressions, attestations of his general postulate, that couldn't have broken upon him at once. This was the case more specifically with a phenomenon at last quite frequent for him in the upper rooms, the recognition—absolutely unmistakeable, and by a turn dating from a particular hour, his resumption of his campaign after a diplomatic drop, a calculated absence of three nights—of his being definitely followed, tracked at a distance carefully taken and to the express end that he should the less confidently, less arrogantly, appear to himself merely to pursue. It worried, it finally quite broke him up, for it proved, of all the conceivable impressions, the one least suited to his book. He was kept in sight while remaining himself—as regards the essence of his position—sightless, and his only recourse then was in abrupt turns, rapid recoveries of ground. He wheeled about, retracing his steps, as if he might so catch in his face at least the stirred air of some other quick revolution. It was indeed true that his fully dislocalised thought of these manœuvres recalled to him Pantaloon,[3] at the Christmas farce, buffeted and tricked from behind by ubiquitous Harlequin; but it left intact the influence of the conditions themselves each time he was re-exposed to them, so that in fact this association, had he suffered it to become constant, would on a certain side have but ministered to his intenser gravity. He had made, as I have said, to create on the premises the baseless sense of a reprieve, his three absences; and the result of the third was to confirm the after-effect of the second.

On his return, that night—the night succeeding his last intermission—he stood in the hall and looked up the staircase with a certainty more intimate than any he had yet known. "He's *there*, at the top, and waiting—not, as in general, falling back for disappearance. He's holding his ground, and it's the first time—which is a proof, isn't it? that something has happened for him." So Brydon argued with his hand on the banister and his foot on the lowest stair; in which position he felt as never before the air chilled by his logic. He himself turned cold in it, for he seemed of a sudden to know what now was involved. "Harder pressed?—yes, he takes it in, with its thus making clear to him that I've come, as they say, 'to stay.' He finally doesn't like and can't bear it, in the sense, I mean, that his wrath, his menaced interest, now balances with his dread. I've hunted him till he has 'turned': that, up there, is what has happened—he's the fanged or the antlered animal brought at last to bay." There came to him, as I say—but determined by an influence beyond my notation!—the acuteness of this certainty; under which however the next moment he had broken into a sweat that he would as little have consented to attribute to fear as he would have dared immediately to act upon it for enterprise. It marked none the less a prodigious thrill, a thrill that represented sudden dismay, no doubt, but also represented,

3. Pantaloon is traditionally an absurd old man on whom Harlequin, a clown, plays tricks.

and with the selfsame throb, the strangest, the most joyous, possibly the next minute almost the proudest, duplication of consciousness.

"He has been dodging, retreating, hiding, but now, worked up to anger, he'll fight!"—this intense impression made a single mouthful, as it were, of terror and applause. But what was wondrous was that the applause, for the felt fact, was so eager, since, if it was his other self he was running to earth, this ineffable identity was thus in the last resort not unworthy of him. It bristled there—somewhere near at hand, however unseen still—as the hunted thing, even as the trodden worm of the adage *must* at last bristle; and Brydon at this instant tasted probably of a sensation more complex than had ever before found itself consistent with sanity. It was as if it would have shamed him that a character so associated with his own should triumphantly succeed in just skulking, should to the end not risk the open; so that the drop of this danger was, on the spot, a great lift of the whole situation. Yet with another rare shift of the same subtlety he was already trying to measure by how much more he himself might now be in peril of fear; so rejoicing that he could, in another form, actively inspire that fear, and simultaneously quaking for the form in which he might passively know it.

The apprehension of knowing it must after a little have grown in him, and the strangest moment of his adventure perhaps, the most memorable or really most interesting, afterwards, of his crisis, was the lapse of certain instants of concentrated conscious *combat*, the sense of a need to hold on to something, even after the manner of a man slipping and slipping on some awful incline; the vivid impulse, above all, to move, to act, to charge, somehow and upon something—to show himself, in a word, that he wasn't afraid. The state of "holding-on" was thus the state to which he was momentarily reduced: if there had been anything, in the great vacancy, to seize, he would presently have been aware of having clutched it as he might under a shock at home have clutched the nearest chair-back. He had been surprised at any rate—of this he *was* aware—into something unprecedented since his original appropriation of the place; he had closed his eyes, held them tight, for a long minute, as with that instinct of dismay and that terror of vision. When he opened them the room, the other contiguous rooms, extraordinarily, seemed lighter—so light, almost, that at first he took the change for day. He stood firm, however that might be, just where he had paused; his resistance had helped him—it was as if there were something he had tided over. He knew after a little what this was—it had been in the imminent danger of flight. He had stiffened his will against going; without this he would have made for the stairs, and it seemed to him that, still with his eyes closed, he would have descended them, would have known how, straight and swiftly, to the bottom.

Well, as he had held out, here he was—still at the top, among the more intricate upper rooms and with the gauntlet of the others, of all the rest of the house, still to run when it should be his time to go. He would go at his time—only at his time: didn't he go every night very much at the same hour? He took out his watch—there was light for that: it was scarcely a quarter past one, and he had never withdrawn so soon. He reached his lodgings for the most part at two—with his walk of a quarter of an hour. He would wait for the last quarter—he wouldn't stir till then; and he kept his watch there with his eyes on it, reflecting while he held it that this deliberate wait, a wait with an effort, which he recognised, would serve perfectly for the attestation he desired to make. It would prove his courage—unless indeed the latter might most be proved by his budging at last from his place. What he mainly felt now was that, since he hadn't originally scuttled, he had his dignities—which had never in his life seemed so many—all to preserve and to carry aloft. This was before him in truth as a physical image, an image almost worthy of an age of greater romance. That remark indeed glimmered for him only to glow the next instant with a finer light; since what age of romance, after all, could have matched either the state of his mind or, "objectively," as they said, the wonder of his situation? The only difference would have been that, brandishing his dignities over his head as in a parchment scroll, he might then—that is in the heroic time—have proceeded downstairs with a drawn sword in his other grasp.

At present, really, the light he had set down on the mantel of the next room would have to figure his sword; which utensil, in the course of a minute, he had taken the requisite number of steps to possess himself of. The door between the rooms was open, and from the second another door opened to a third. These rooms, as he remembered, gave all three upon a common corridor as well, but there was a fourth, beyond them, without issue save through the preceding. To have moved, to have heard his step again, was appreciably a help; though even in recognising this he lingered once more a little by the chimney-piece on which his light had rested. When he next moved, just hesitating where to turn, he found himself considering a circumstance that, after his first and comparatively vague apprehension of it, produced in him the start that often attends some pang of recollection, the violent shock of having ceased happily to forget. He had come into sight of the door in which the brief chain of communication ended and which he now surveyed from the nearer threshold, the one not directly facing it. Placed at some distance to the left of this point, it would have admitted him to the last room of the four, the room without other approach or egress, had it not, to his intimate conviction, been closed *since* his former visitation, the matter probably of a quarter of an hour before. He stared with all his eyes at the wonder of the fact, arrested again where he stood and again holding his breath while he sounded its sense. Surely it had been *subsequently* closed—that is it had been on his previous passage indubitably open!

He took it full in the face that something had happened between—that he couldn't not have noticed before (by which he meant on his original tour of all the rooms that evening) that such a barrier had exceptionally presented itself. He had indeed since that moment undergone an agitation so extraordinary that it might have muddled for him any earlier view; and he tried to convince himself that he might perhaps then have gone into the room and, inadvertently, automatically, on coming out, have drawn the door after him. The difficulty was that this exactly was what he never did; it was against his whole policy, as he might have said, the essence of which was to keep vistas clear. He had them from the first, as he was well aware, quite on the brain: the strange apparition, at the far end of one of them, of his baffled "prey" (which had become by so sharp an irony so little the term now to apply!) was the form of success his imagination had most cherished, projecting into it always a refinement of beauty. He had known fifty times the start of perception that had afterwards dropped; had fifty times gasped to himself "There!" under some fond brief hallucination. The house, as the case stood, admirably lent itself; he might wonder at the taste, the native architecture of the particular time, which could rejoice so in the multiplication of doors—the opposite extreme to the modern, the actual almost complete proscription of them; but it had fairly contributed to provoke this obsession of the presence encountered telescopically, as he might say, focussed and studied in diminishing perspective and as by a rest for the elbow.

It was with these considerations that his present attention was charged—they perfectly availed to make what he saw portentous. He *couldn't*, by any lapse, have blocked that aperture; and if he hadn't, if it was unthinkable, why what else was clear but that there had been another agent? Another agent?—he had been catching, as he felt, a moment back, the very breath of him; but when had he been so close as in this simple, this logical, this completely personal act? It was so logical, that is, that one might have *taken* it for personal; yet for what did Brydon take it, he asked himself, while, softly panting, he felt his eyes almost leave their

sockets. Ah this time at last they *were*, the two, the opposed projections of him, in presence; and this time, as much as one would,
the question of danger loomed. With it rose, as not before, the
question of courage—for what he knew the blank face of the door
to say to him was "Show us how much you have!" It stared, it
glared back at him with that challenge; it put to him the two alternatives: should he just push it open or not? Oh to have this
consciousness was to *think*—and to think, Brydon knew, as he
stood there, was, with the lapsing moments, not to have acted!
Not to have acted—that was the misery and the pang—was even
still not to act; was in fact *all* to feel the thing in another, in a
new and terrible way. How long did he pause and how long did he
debate? There was presently nothing to measure it; for his vibration had already changed—as just by the effect of its intensity.
Shut up there, at bay, defiant, and with the prodigy of the thing
palpably proveably *done*, thus giving notice like some stark signboard—under that accession of accent the situation itself had
turned; and Brydon at last remarkably made up his mind on what
it had turned to.

It had turned altogether to a different admonition; to a supreme
hint, for him, of the value of Discretion! This slowly dawned, no
doubt—for it could take its time; so perfectly, on his threshold,
had he been stayed, so little as yet had he either advanced or
retreated. It was the strangest of all things that now when, by his
taking ten steps and applying his hand to a latch, or even his
shoulder and his knee, if necessary, to a panel, all the hunger of
his prime need might have been met, his high curiosity crowned,
his unrest assuaged—it was amazing, but it was also exquisite and
rare, that insistence should have, at a touch, quite dropped from
him. Discretion—he jumped at that; and yet not, verily, at such a
pitch, because it saved his nerves or his skin, but because, much
more valuably, it saved the situation. When I say he "jumped" at
it I feel the consonance of this term with the fact that—at the end
indeed of I know not how long—he did move again, he crossed
straight to the door. He wouldn't touch it—it seemed now that
he might *if* he would: he would only just wait there a little, to
show, to prove, that he wouldn't. He had thus another station,
close to the thin partition by which revelation was denied him;
but with his eyes bent and his hands held off in a mere intensity
of stillness. He listened as if there had been something to hear, but
this attitude, while it lasted, was his own communication. "If you
won't then—good: I spare you and I give up. You affect me as by
the appeal positively for pity: you convince me that for reasons
rigid and sublime—what do I know?—we both of us should have
suffered. I respect them then, and, though moved and privileged

as, I believe, it has never been given to man, I retire, I renounce
—never, on my honour, to try again. So rest for ever—and let
me!"

That, for Brydon was the deep sense of this last demonstration
—solemn, measured, directed, as he felt it to be. He brought it to
a close, he turned away; and now verily he knew how deeply he
had been stirred. He retraced his steps, taking up his candle,
burnt, he observed, well-nigh to the socket, and marking again,
lighten it as he would, the distinctness of his footfall; after which,
in a moment, he knew himself at the other side of the house. He
did here what he had not yet done at these hours—he opened half
a casement, one of those in the front, and let in the air of the
night; a thing he would have taken at any time previous for a
sharp rupture of his spell. His spell was broken now, and it didn't
matter—broken by his concession and his surrender, which made
it idle henceforth that he should ever come back. The empty street
—its other life so marked even by the great lamplit vacancy—
was within call, within touch; he stayed there as to be in it again,
high above it though he was still perched; he watched as for some
comforting common fact, some vulgar human note, the passage of
a scavenger or a thief, some night-bird however base. He would
have blessed that sign of life; he would have welcomed positively
the slow approach of his friend the policeman, whom he had hitherto only sought to avoid, and was not sure that if the patrol had
come into sight he mightn't have felt the impulse to get into
relation with it, to hail it, on some pretext, from his fourth floor.
The pretext that wouldn't have been too silly or too compromising, the explanation that would have saved his dignity and kept
his name, in such a case, out of the papers, was not definite to
him: he was so occupied with the thought of recording his Discretion—as an effect of the vow he had just uttered to his intimate
adversary—that the importance of this loomed large and something had overtaken all ironically his sense of proportion. If there
had been a ladder applied to the front of the house, even one of
the vertiginous perpendiculars employed by painters and roofers
and sometimes left standing overnight, he would have managed
somehow, astride of the window-sill, to compass by outstretched
leg and arm that mode of descent. If there had been some such
uncanny thing as he had found in his room at hotels, a workable
fire-escape in the form of notched cable or a canvas shoot, he
would have availed himself of it as a proof—well, of his present
delicacy. He nursed the sentiment, as the question stood, a little
in vain, and even—at the end of he scarce knew, once more, how
long—found it, as by the action of his mind of the failure of
response of the outer world, sinking back to vague anguish. It

seemed to him he had waited an age for some stir of the great grim hush; the life of the town was itself under a spell—so un-naturally, up and down the whole prospect of known and rather ugly objects, the blankness and the silence lasted. Had they ever, he asked himself, the hard-faced houses, which had begun to look livid in the dim dawn, had they ever spoken so little to any need of his spirit? Great built voids, great crowded stillnesses put on, often, in the heart of cities, for the small hours, a sort of sinister mask, and it was of this large collective negation that Brydon pres-ently became conscious—all the more that the break of day was, almost incredibly, now at hand, proving to him what a night he had made of it.

He looked again at his watch, saw what had become of his time-values (he had taken hours for minutes—not, as in other tense sit-uations, minutes for hours) and the strange air of the streets was but the weak, the sullen flush of a dawn in which everything was still locked up. His choked appeal from his own open window had been the sole note of life, and he could but break off at last as for a worse despair. Yet while so deeply demoralised he was ca-pable again of an impulse denoting—at least by his present mea-sure—extraordinary resolution; of retracing his steps to the spot where he had turned cold with the extinction of his last pulse of doubt as to there being in the place another presence than his own. This required an effort strong enough to sicken him; but he had his reason, which over-mastered for the moment everything else. There was the whole of the rest of the house to traverse, and how should he screw himself to that if the door he had seen closed were at present open? He could hold to the idea that the closing had practically been for him an act of mercy, a chance offered him to descend, depart, get off the ground and never again profane it. This conception held together, it worked; but what it meant for him depended now clearly on the amount of forbearance his recent action, or rather his recent inaction, had engendered. The image of the "presence," whatever it was, waiting there for him to go—this image had not yet been so concrete for his nerves as when he stopped short of the point at which certainty would have come to him. For, with all his resolution, or more exactly with all his dread, he did stop short—he hung back from really seeing. The risk was too great and his fear too definite: it took at this moment an awful specific form.

He knew—yes, as he had never known anything—that, *should* he see the door open, it would all too abjectly be the end of him. It would mean that the agent of his shame—for his shame was the deep abjection—was once more at large and in general possession; and what glared him thus in the face was the act that this would determine for him. It would send him straight about to the window he had left open, and by that window; be long ladder and dangling rope as absent as they would, he saw himself uncontrollably insanely fatally take his way to the street. The hideous chance of this he at least could avert; but he could only avert it by recoiling in time from assurance. He had the whole house to deal with, this fact was still there; only he now knew that uncertainty alone could start him. He stole back from where he had checked himself —merely to do so was suddenly like safety—and, making blindly for the greater staircase, left gaping rooms and sounding passages behind. Here was the top of the stairs, with a fine large dim descent and three spacious landings to mark off. His instinct was all for mildness, but his feet were harsh on the floors, and, strangely, when he had in a couple of minutes become aware of this, it counted somehow for help. He couldn't have spoken, the tone of his voice would have scared him, and the common conceit or resource of "whistling in the dark" (whether literally or figuratively) have appeared basely vulgar; yet he liked none the less to hear himself go, and when he had reached his first landing—taking it all with no rush, but quite steadily—that stage of success drew from him a gasp of relief.

The house, withal, seemed immense, the scale of space again inordinate; the open rooms to no one of which his eyes deflected, gloomed in their shuttered state like mouths of caverns; only the high skylight that formed the crown of the deep well created for him a medium in which he could advance, but which might have been, for queerness of colour, some watery under-world. He tried to think of something noble, as that his property was really grand, a splendid possession; but this nobleness took the form too of the clear delight with which he was finally to sacrifice it. They might come in now, the builders, the destroyers—they might come as soon as they would. At the end of two flights he had dropped to another zone, and from the middle of the third, with only one more left, he recognised the influence of the lower windows, of half-drawn blinds, of the occasional gleam of street-lamps, of the glazed spaces of the vestibule. This was the bottom of the sea, which showed an illumination of its own and which he even saw paved—when at a given moment he drew up to sink a long look over the banisters—with the marble squares of his childhood. By that time indubitably he felt, as he might have said in a commoner cause, better; it had allowed him to stop and draw breath, and the ease increased with the sight of the old black-and-white slabs. But what he most felt was that now surely, with the element of impunity pulling him as by hard firm hands, the case was settled for what he might have seen above had he dared that last look. The closed door, blessedly remote now, was still closed—and he had only in short to reach that of the house.

He came down further, he crossed the passage forming the access to the last flight; and if here again he stopped an instant it was almost for the sharpness of the thrill of assured escape. It made him shut his eyes—which opened again to the straight slope of the remainder of the stairs. Here was impunity still, but impunity almost excessive; inasmuch as the side-lights and the high fan-tracery of the entrance were glimmering straight into the hall; an appearance produced, he the next instant saw, by the fact that the vestibule gaped wide, that the hinged halves of the inner door had been thrown far back. Out of that again the *question* sprang at him, making his eyes, as he felt, half-start from his head, as they had done, at the top of the house, before the sign of the other door. If he had left that one open, hadn't he left this one closed, and wasn't he now in *most* immediate presence of some inconceivable occult activity? It was as sharp, the question, as a knife in his side, but the answer hung fire still and seemed to lose itself in the vague darkness to which the thin admitted dawn, glimmering archwise over the whole outer door, made a semicircular margin, a cold silvery nimbus that seemed to play a little as he looked—to shift and expand and contract.

It was as if there had been something within it, protected by indistinctness and corresponding in extent with the opaque surface behind, the painted panels of the last barrier to his escape, of which the key was in his pocket. The indistinctness mocked him even while he stared, affected him as somehow shrouding or challenging certitude, so that after faltering an instant on his step he let himself go with the sense that here *was* at last something to meet, to touch, to take, to know—something all unnatural and dreadful, but to advance upon which was the condition for him either of liberation or of supreme defeat. The penumbra, dense and dark, was the virtual screen of a figure which stood in it as still as some image erect in a niche or as some black-vizored sentinel guarding a treasure. Brydon was to know afterwards, was to recall and make out, the particular thing he had believed during the rest of his descent. He saw, in its great grey glimmering margin, the central vagueness diminish, and he felt it to be taking the very form toward which, for so many days, the passion of his curiosity had yearned. It gloomed, it loomed, it was something, it was somebody, the prodigy of a personal presence.

Rigid and conscious, spectral yet human, a man of his own substance and stature waited there to measure himself with his power to dismay. This only could it be—this only till he recognised, with his advance, that what made the face dim was the pair of raised hands that covered it and in which, so far from being offered in defiance, it was buried as for dark deprecation. So Brydon, before him, took him in; with every fact of him now, in the higher light, hard and acute—his planted stillness, his vivid truth, his grizzled bent head and white masking hands, his queer actuality of evening-dress, of dangling double eye-glass, of gleaming silk lappet and white linen, of pearl button and gold watch-guard and polished shoe. No portrait by a great modern master could have presented him with more intensity, thrust him out of his frame with more art, as if there had been "treatment," of the consummate sort, in his every shade and salience. The revulsion, for our friend, had become, before he knew it, immense—this drop, in the act of apprehension, to the sense of his adversary's inscrutable manoeuvre. That meaning at least, while he gaped, it offered him; for he could but gape at his other self in this other anguish, gape as a proof that *he*, standing there for the achieved, the enjoyed, the triumphant life, couldn't be faced in its triumph. Wasn't the proof in the splendid covering hands, strong and completely spread?—so spread and so intentional that, in spite of a special verity that surpassed every other, the fact that one of these hands had lost two fingers, which were reduced to stumps, as if accidentally shot away, the face was effectually guarded and saved.

"Saved," though, *would* it be?—Brydon breathed his wonder till the very impunity of his attitude and the very insistence of his eyes produced, as he felt, a sudden stir which showed the next instant as a deeper portent, while the head raised itself, the betrayal of a braver purpose. The hands, as he looked, began to move, to open; then, as if deciding in a flash, dropped from the face and left it uncovered and presented. Horror, with the sight, had leaped into Brydon's throat, gasping there in a sound he couldn't utter; for the bared identity was too hideous as *his*, and his glare was the passion of his protest. The face, *that* face, Spencer Brydon's? —he searched it still, but looking away from it in dismay and denial, falling straight from his height of sublimity. It was unknown, inconceivable, awful, disconnected from any possibility—! He had been "sold," he inwardly moaned, stalking such game as this: the presence before him was a presence, the horror within him a horror, but the waste of his nights had been only grotesque and the success of his adventure an irony. Such an identity fitted his at *no* point, made its alternative monstrous. A thousand times yes, as it came upon him nearer now—the face was the face of a stranger. It came upon him nearer now, quite as one of those expanding fantastic images projected by the magic lantern of childhood; for the stranger, whoever he might be, evil, odious, blatant, vulgar, had advanced as for aggression, and he knew himself give ground. Then harder pressed still, sick with the force of his shock, and falling back as under the hot breath and the roused passion of a life larger than his own, a rage of personality before which his own collapsed, he felt the whole vision turn to darkness and his very feet give way. His head went round; he was going; he had gone.

III

What had next brought him back, clearly—though after how long?—was Mrs. Muldoon's voice, coming to him from quite near, from so near that he seemed presently to see her as kneeling on the ground before him while he lay looking up at her; himself not wholly on the ground, but half-raised and upheld—conscious, yes, of tenderness of support and, more particularly, of a head pillowed in extraordinary softness and faintly refreshing fragrance. He considered, he wondered, his wit but half at his service; then another face intervened, bending more directly over him, and he finally knew that Alice Staverton had made her lap an ample and perfect cushion to him, and that she had to this end seated herself on the lowest degree of the staircase, the rest of his long person remaining stretched on his old black-and-white slabs. They were cold, these marble squares of his youth; but *he* somehow was not, in this rich return of consciousness—the most wonderful hour, little by little, that he had ever known, leaving him, as it did, so gratefully, so abysmally passive, and yet as with a treasure of intelligence waiting all round him for quiet appropriation; dissolved, he might call it, in the air of the place and producing the golden glow of a late autumn afternoon. He had come back, yes—come back from further away than any man but himself had ever travelled; but it was strange how with this sense what he had come back *to* seemed really the great thing, and as if his prodigious journey had been all for the sake of it. Slowly but surely his consciousness grew, his vision of his state thus completing itself: he had been miraculously *carried* back—lifted and carefully borne as from where he had been picked up, the uttermost end of an interminable grey passage. Even with this he was suffered to rest, and what had now brought him to knowledge was the break in the long mild motion.

It had brought him to knowledge, to knowledge—yes, this was the beauty of his state; which came to resemble more and more that of a man who has gone to sleep on some news of a great inheritance, and then, after dreaming it away, after profaning it with matters strange to it, has waked up again to serenity of certitude and has only to lie and watch it grow. This was the drift of his patience—that he had only to let it shine on him. He must moreover, with intermissions, still have been lifted and borne; since why and how else should he have known himself, later on, with the afternoon glow intenser, no longer at the foot of his stairs—situated as these now seemed at the dark other end of his tunnel—

but on a deep window-bench of his high saloon, over which had been spread, couch-fashion, a mantle of soft stuff lined with grey fur that was familiar to his eyes and that one of his hands kept fondly feeling as for its pledge of truth. Mrs. Muldoon's face had gone, but the other, the second he had recognised, hung over him in a way that showed how he was still propped and pillowed. He took it all in, and the more he took it the more it seemed to suffice: he was as much at peace as if he had had food and drink. It was the two women who had found him, on Mrs. Muldoon's having plied, at her usual hour, her latch-key—and on her having above all arrived while Miss Staverton still lingered near the house. She had been turning away, all anxiety, from worrying the vain bell-handle—her calculation having been of the hour of the good woman's visit; but the latter, blessedly, had come up while she was still there, and they had entered together. He had then lain, beyond the vestibule, very much as he was lying now—quite, that is, as he appeared to have fallen, but all so wondrously without bruise or gash; only in a depth of stupor. What he most took in, however, at present, with the steadier clearance, was that Alice Staverton had for a long unspeakable moment not doubted he was dead.

"It must have been that I *was*." He made it out as she held him. "Yes—I can only have died. You brought me literally to life. Only," he wondered, his eyes rising to her, "only, in the name of all the benedictions, how?"

It took her but an instant to bend her face and kiss him, and something in the manner of it, and in the way her hands clasped and locked his head while he felt the cool charity and virtue of her lips, something in all this beatitude somehow answered everything. "And now I keep you," she said.

"Oh keep me, keep me!" he pleaded while her face still hung over him: in response to which it dropped again and stayed close, clingingly close. It was the seal of their situation—of which he tasted the impress for a long blissful moment in silence. But he came back. "Yet how did you know—?"

"I was uneasy. You were to have come, you remember—and you had sent no word."

"Yes, I remember—I was to have gone to you at one today." It caught on to their "old" life and relation—which were so near and so far. "I was still out there in my strange darkness—where was it, what was it? I must have stayed there so long." He could but wonder at the depth and the duration of his swoon.

"Since last night?" she asked with a shade of fear for her possible indiscretion.

"Since this morning—it must have been: the cold dim dawn of

today. Where have I been," he vaguely wailed, "where have I been?" He felt her hold him close, and it was as if this helped him now to make in all security his mild moan. "What a long dark day!"

All in her tenderness she had waited a moment. "In the cold dim dawn?" she quavered.

But he had already gone on piecing together the parts of the whole prodigy. "As I didn't turn up you came straight—?"

She barely cast about. "I went first to your hotel—where they told me of your absence. You had dined out last evening and hadn't been back since. But they appeared to know you had been at your club."

"So you had the idea of *this*—?"

"Of what?" she asked in a moment.

"Well—of what has happened."

"I believed at least you'd have been here. I've known, all along," she said, "that you've been coming."

" 'Known' it—?"

"Well, I've believed it. I said nothing to you after that ta.k we had a month ago—but I felt sure. I knew you *would*," she declared.

"That I'd persist, you mean?"

"That you'd see him."

"Ah but I didn't!" cried Brydon with his long wail. "There's somebody—an awful beast; whom I brought, too horribly, to bay. But it's not me."

At this she bent over him again, and her eyes were in his eyes. "No—it's not you." And it was as if, while her face hovered, he might have made out in it, hadn't it been so near, some particular meaning blurred by a smile. "No, thank heaven," she repeated— "it's not you! Of course it wasn't to have been."

"Ah but it *was*," he gently insisted. And he stared before him now as he had been staring for so many weeks. "I was to have known myself."

"You couldn't!" she returned consolingly. And then reverting, and as if to account further for what she had herself done, "But it wasn't only *that*, that you hadn't been at home," she went on. "I waited till the hour at which we had found Mrs. Muldoon that day of my going with you; and she arrived, as I've told you, while, failing to bring any one to the door, I lingered in my despair on the steps. After a little, if she hadn't come, by such a mercy, I should have found means to hunt her up. But it wasn't," said Alice Staverton, as if once more with her fine intention—"it wasn't only that."

His eyes, as he lay, turned back to her. "What more then?"

She met it, the wonder she had stirred. "In the cold dim dawn, you say? Well, in the cold dim dawn of this morning I too saw you."

"Saw *me*—?"

"Saw *him*," said Alice Staverton. "It must have been at the same moment."

He lay an instant taking it in—as if he wished to be quite reasonable. "At the same moment?"

"Yes—in my dream again, the same one I've named to you. He came back to me. Then I knew it for a sign. He had come to you."

At this Brydon raised himself; he had to see her better. She helped him when she understood his movement, and he sat up, steadying himself beside her there on the window-bench and with his right hand grasping her left. "*He* didn't come to me."

"You came to yourself," she beautifully smiled.

"Ah I've come to myself now—thanks to you, dearest. But this brute, with his awful face—this brute's a black stranger. He's none of *me*, even as I *might* have been," Brydon sturdily declared.

But she kept the clearness that was like the breath of infallibility. "Isn't the whole point that you'd have been different?"

He almost scowled for it. "As different as *that*—?"

Her look again was more beautiful to him than the things of this world. "Haven't you exactly wanted to know *how* different? So this morning," she said, "you appeared to me."

"Like *him*?"

"A black stranger!"

"Then how did you know it was I?"

"Because, as I told you weeks ago, my mind, my imagination, had worked so over what you might, what you mightn't have been —to show you, you see, how I've thought of you. In the midst of that you came to me—that my wonder might be answered. So I knew," she went on; "and believed that, since the question held you too so fast, as you told me that day, you too would see for yourself. And when this morning I again saw I knew it would be because you had—and also then, from the first moment, because you somehow wanted me. *He* seemed to tell me of that. So why," she strangely smiled, "shouldn't I like him?"

It brought Spencer Brydon to his feet. "You 'like' that horror—?"

"I *could* have liked him. And to me," she said, "he was no horror. I had accepted him."

" 'Accepted'—?" Brydon oddly sounded.

"Before, for the interest of his difference—yes. And as *I* didn't disown him, as *I* knew him—which you at last, confronted with him in his difference, so cruelly didn't, my dear—well, he must have been, you see, less dreadful to me. And it may have pleased him that I pitied him."

She was beside him on her feet, but still holding his hand— still with her arm supporting him. But though it all brought for him thus a dim light, "You 'pitied' him?" he grudgingly, resentfully asked.

"He has been unhappy, he has been ravaged," she said.

"And haven't I been unhappy? Am not I—you've only to look at me!—ravaged?"

"Ah I don't say I like him *better*," she granted after a thought. "But he's grim, he's worn—and things have happened to him. He doesn't make shift, for sight, with your charming monocle."

"No"—it struck Brydon: "I couldn't have sported mine 'downtown.' They'd have guyed me there."

"His great convex pince-nez—I saw it, I recognised the kind —is for his poor ruined sight. And his poor right hand—!"

"Ah!" Brydon winced—whether for his proved identity or for his lost fingers. Then, "He has a million a year," he lucidly added. "But he hasn't you."

"And he isn't—no, he isn't—*you!*" she murmured as he drew her to his breast.

1908, 1909

The Art of Fiction [4]

I should not have affixed so comprehensive a title to these few remarks, necessarily wanting in any completeness upon a subject the full consideration of which would carry us far, did I not seem to discover a pretext for my temerity in the interesting pamphlet lately published under this name by Mr. Walter Besant.[5] Mr. Besant's lecture at the Royal Institution—the original form of his pamphlet—appears to indicate that many persons are interested in the art of fiction, and are not indifferent to such remarks, as those who practice it may attempt to make about it. I am therefore anxious not to lose the benefit of this favorable association, and to edge in a few words under cover of the attention which Mr. Besant is sure to have excited. There is something very encouraging in his having put into form certain of his ideas on the mystery of storytelling.

It is a proof of life and curiosity—curiosity on the part of the brotherhood of novelists as well as on the part of their readers.

4. Originally published in *Longman's Magazine* for September, 1884; included in *Partial Portraits* (1888), the source of the present text.
5. English novelist and critic (1836–1901).

Only a short time ago it might have been supposed that the English novel was not what the French call *discutable*.[6] It had no air
of having a theory, a conviction, a consciousness of itself behind
it—of being the expression of an artistic faith, the result of choice
and comparison. I do not say it was necessarily the worse for that:
it would take much more courage than I possess to intimate that
the form of the novel as Dickens and Thackeray (for instance) saw
it had any taint of incompleteness. It was, however, *naïf* (if I may
help myself out with another French word); and evidently if it be
destined to suffer in any way for having lost its *naïveté* it has now
an idea of making sure of the corresponding advantages. During
the period I have alluded to there was a comfortable, good-humored feeling abroad that a novel is a novel, as a pudding is a
pudding, and that our only business with it could be to swallow it.
But within a year or two, for some reason or other, there have been
signs of returning animation—the era of discussion would appear
to have been to a certain extent opened. Art lives upon discussion,
upon experiment, upon curiosity, upon variety of attempt, upon
the exchange of views and the comparison of standpoints; and
there is a presumption that those times when no one has anything
particular to say about it, and has no reason to give for practice or
preference, though they may be times of honor, are not times of
development—are times, possibly even, a little of dullness. The
successful application of any art is a delightful spectacle, but the
theory too is interesting; and though there is a great deal of the
latter without the former I suspect there has never been a genuine success that has not had a latent core of conviction. Discussion, suggestion, formulation, these things are fertilizing when
they are frank and sincere. Mr. Besant has set an excellent example
in saying what he thinks, for his part, about the way in which fiction should be written, as well as about the way in which it should
be published; for his view of the "art," carried on into an appendix, covers that too. Other laborers in the same field will doubtless take up the argument, they will give it the light of their experience, and the effect will surely be to make our interest in the
novel a little more what it had for some time threatened to fail to
be—a serious, active, inquiring interest, under protection of which
this delightful study may, in moments of confidence, venture to say
a little more what it thinks of itself.

It must take itself seriously for the public to take it so. The old
superstition about fiction being "wicked" has doubtless died out
in England; but the spirit of it lingers in a certain oblique regard
directed toward any story which does not more or less admit that
it is only a joke. Even the most jocular novel feels in some degree

6. Discussable.

the weight of the proscription that was formerly directed against literary levity: the jocularity does not always succeed in passing for orthodoxy. It is still expected, though perhaps people are ashamed to say it, that a production which is after all only a "make-believe" (for what else is a "story"?) shall be in some degree apologetic— shall renounce the pretension of attempting really to represent life. This, of course, any sensible, wide-awake story declines to do, for it quickly perceives that the tolerance granted to it on such a condition is only an attempt to stifle it disguised in the form of generosity. The old evangelical hostility to the novel, which was as explicit as it was narrow, and which regarded it as little less favorable to our immortal part than a stage play, was in reality far less insulting. The only reason for the existence of a novel is that it does attempt to represent life. When it relinquishes this attempt, the same attempt that we see on the canvas of the painter, it will have arrived at a very strange pass. It is not expected of the picture that it will make itself humble in order to be forgiven; and the analogy between the art of the painter and the art of the novelist is, so far as I am able to see, complete. Their inspiration is the same, their process (allowing for the different quality of the vehicle) is the same, their success is the same. They may learn from each other, they may explain and sustain each other. Their cause is the same, and the honor of one is the honor of another. The Mahometans think a picture an unholy thing, but it is a long time since any Christian did, and it is therefore the more odd that in the Christian mind the traces (dissimulated though they may be) of a suspicion of the sister art should linger to this day. The only effectual way to lay it to rest is to emphasize the analogy to which I just alluded—to insist on the fact that as the picture is reality, so the novel is history. That is the only general description (which does it justice) that we may give of the novel. But history also is allowed to represent life; it is not, any more than painting, expected to apologize. The subject matter of fiction is stored up likewise in documents and records, and if it will not give itself away, as they say in California, it must speak with assurance, with the tone of the historian. Certain accomplished novelists have a habit of giving themselves away which must often bring tears to the eyes of people who take their fiction seriously. I was lately struck, in reading over many pages of Anthony Trollope,[7] with his want of discretion in this particular. In a digression, a parenthesis or an aside, he concedes to the reader that he and this trusting friend are only "making believe." He admits that the events he narrates have not really happened, and that he can give his narrative any turn the reader may like best. Such a betrayal of a sacred

7. English novelist (1815–1882).

office seems to me, I confess, a terrible crime; it is what I mean by the attitude of apology, and it shocks me every whit as much in Trollope as it would have shocked me in Gibbon or Macaulay.[8] It implies that the novelist is less occupied in looking for the truth (the truth, of course I mean, that he assumes, the premises that we must grant him, whatever they may be) than the historian, and in doing so it deprives him at a stroke of all his standing room. To represent and illustrate the past, the actions of men, is the task of either writer, and the only difference that I can see is, in proportion as he succeeds, to the honor of the novelist, consisting as it does in his having more difficulty in collecting his evidence, which is so far from being purely literary. It seems to me to give him a great character, the fact that he has at once so much in common with the philosopher and the painter; this double analogy is a magnificent heritage.

It is of all this evidently that Mr. Besant is full when he insists upon the fact that fiction is one of the *fine* arts, deserving in its turn of all the honors and emoluments that have hitherto been reserved for the successful profession of music, poetry, painting, architecture. It is impossible to insist too much on so important a truth, and the place that Mr. Besant demands for the work of the novelist may be represented, a trifle less abstractly, by saying that he demands not only that it shall be reputed artistic, but that it shall be reputed very artistic indeed. It is excellent that he should have struck this note, for his doing so indicates that there was need of it, that his proposition may be to many people a novelty. One rubs one's eyes at the thought; but the rest of Mr. Besant's essay confirms the revelation. I suspect in truth that it would be possible to confirm it still further, and that one would not be far wrong in saying that in addition to the people to whom it has never occurred that a novel ought to be artistic, there are a great many others who, if this principle were urged upon them, would be filled with an indefinable mistrust. They would find it difficult to explain their repugnance, but it would operate strongly to put them on their guard. "Art," in our Protestant communities, where so many things have got so strangely twisted about, is supposed in certain circles to have some vaguely injurious effect upon those who make it an important consideration, who let it weigh in the balance. It is assumed to be opposed in some mysterious manner to morality, to amusement, to instruction. When it is embodied in the work of the painter (the sculptor is another affair!) you know what it is: it stands there before you, in the honesty of pink and green and a gilt frame; you can see the worst of it at a glance, and you can be on your *guard*. But when it is introduced into lit-

8. English historians.

erature it becomes more insidious—there is danger of its hurting you before you know it. Literature should be either instructive or amusing, and there is in many minds an impression that these artistic preoccupations, the search for form, contribute to neither end, interfere indeed with both. They are too frivolous to be edifying, and too serious to be diverting; and they are moreover priggish and paradoxical and superfluous. That, I think, represents the manner in which the latent thought of many people who read novels as an exercise in skipping would explain itself if it were to become articulate. They would argue, of course, that a novel ought to be "good," but they would interpret this term in a fashion of their own, which indeed would vary considerably from one critic to another. One would say that being good means representing virtuous and aspiring characters, placed in prominent positions; another would say that it depends on a "happy ending," on a distribution at the last of prizes, pensions, husbands, wives, babies, millions, appended paragraphs, and cheerful remarks. Another still would say that it means being full of incident and movement, so that we shall wish to jump ahead, to see who was the mysterious stranger, and if the stolen will was ever found, and shall not be distracted from this pleasure by any tiresome analysis or "description." But they would all agree that the "artistic" idea would spoil some of their fun. One would hold it accountable for all the description, another would see it revealed in the absence of sympathy. Its hostility to a happy ending would be evident, and it might even in some cases render any ending at all impossible. The "ending" of a novel is, for many persons, like that of a good dinner, a course of dessert and ices, and the artist in fiction is regarded as a sort of meddlesome doctor who forbids agreeable aftertastes. It is therefore true that this conception of Mr. Besant's of the novel as a superior form encounters not only a negative but a positive indifference. It matters little that as a work of art it should really be as little or as much of its essence to supply happy endings, sympathetic characters, and an objective tone, as if it were a work of mechanics: the association of ideas, however incongruous, might easily be too much for it if an eloquent voice were not sometimes raised to call attention to the fact that it is at once as free and as serious a branch of literature as any other.

Certainly this might sometimes be doubted in presence of the enormous number of works of fiction that appeal to the credulity of our generation, for it might easily seem that there could be no great character in a commodity so quickly and easily produced. It must be admitted that good novels are much compromised by bad ones, and that the field at large suffers discredit from overcrowding. I think, however, that this injury is only superficial, and that the superabundance of written fiction proves nothing against the principle itself. It has been vulgarized, like all other kinds of literature, like everything else today, and it has proved more than some kinds accessible to vulgarization. But there is as much difference as there ever was between a good novel and a bad one: the bad is swept with all the daubed canvases and spoiled marble into some unvisited limbo, or infinite rubbish yard beneath the back windows of the world, and the good subsists and emits its light and stimulates our desire for perfection. As I shall take the liberty of making but a single criticism of Mr. Besant, whose tone is so full of the love of his art, I may as well have done with it at once. He seems to me to mistake in attempting to say so definitely beforehand what sort of an affair the good novel will be. To indicate the danger of such an error as that has been the purpose of these few pages; to suggest that certain traditions on the subject, applied *a priori*, have already had much to answer for, and that the good health of an art which undertakes so immediately to reproduce life must demand that it be perfectly free. It lives upon exercise, and the very meaning of exercise is freedom. The only obligation to which in advance we may hold a novel, without incurring the accusation of being arbitrary, is that it be interesting. That general responsibility rests upon it, but it is the only one I can think of. The ways in which it is at liberty to accomplish this result (of interesting us) strike me as innumerable, and such as can only suffer from being marked out or fenced in by prescription. They are as various as the temperament of man, and they are successful in proportion as they reveal a particular mind, different from others. A novel is in its broadest definition a personal, a direct impression of life: that, to begin with, constitutes its value, which is greater or less according to the intensity of the impression. But there will be no intensity at all, and therefore no value, unless there is freedom to feel and say. The tracing of a line to be followed, of a tone to be taken, of a form to be filled out, is a limitation of that freedom and a suppression of the very thing that we are most curious about. The form, it seems to me, is to be appreciated after the fact: then the author's choice has been made, his standard has been indicated; then we can follow lines and directions and compare tones and resemblances. Then in a word we can enjoy one of the most charming of pleasures, we can estimate quality, we can apply the test of execution. The execution belongs to the author alone; it is what is most personal to him, and we measure him by that. The advantage, the luxury, as well as the torment and responsibility of the novelist, is that there is no limit to what he may attempt as an executant—no limit to his possible experiments, efforts, discoveries, successes. Here it is especially that he works, step by step, like his brother of the brush, of whom we may always say that he has painted his picture in a manner best known to himself. His manner is his secret, not necessarily a jealous one. He cannot disclose it as a general thing if he would; he would be at a loss to teach it to others. I say this with a due recollection of having insisted on the community of method of the artist who paints a picture and the artist who writes a novel. The painter *is* able to teach the rudiments of his practice, and it is possible, from the study of good work (granted the aptitude), both to learn how to paint and to learn how to write. Yet it remains true, without injury to the *rapprochement*,[9] that the literary artist would be obliged to say to his pupil much more than the other, "Ah, well, you must do it as you can!" It is a question of degree, a matter of delicacy. If there are exact sciences, there are also exact arts, and the grammar of painting is so much more definite that it makes the difference.

I ought to add, however, that if Mr. Besant says at the beginning of his essay that the "laws of fiction may be laid down and taught with as much precision and exactness as the laws of harmony, perspective, and proportion," he mitigates what might appear to be an extravagance by applying his remark to "general" laws, and by expressing most of these rules in a manner with which it would certainly be unaccommodating to disagree. That the novelist must write from his experience, that his "characters must be real and such as might be met with in actual life"; that "a young lady brought up in a quiet country village should avoid descriptions of garrison life," and "a writer whose friends and personal experiences belong to the lower middle class should carefully avoid introducing his characters into society"; that one should enter one's notes in a common-place book; that one's figures should be clear in outline; that making them clear by some trick of speech or of carriage is a bad method, and "describing them at length" is a worse one; that English fiction should have a "conscious moral purpose"; that "it is almost impossible to estimate too highly the value of careful workmanship—that is, of style"; that "the most important point of all is the story," that "the story is everything": these are principles with most of which it is surely impossible not to sympathize. That remark about the lower middle-class writer and his knowing his place is perhaps rather chilling; but for the rest I should find it difficult to dissent from any one of these recommendations. At the same time, I should find it difficult positively to assent to them, with the exception, perhaps, of the injunction as to entering one's notes in a common-place book. They scarcely seem to me to have the quality that Mr. Besant attributes to the rules of the

9. **Analogy.**

novelist—the "precision and exactness" of "the laws of harmony, perspective, and proportion." They are suggestive, they are even inspiring, but they are not exact, though they are doubtless as much so as the case admits of: which is a proof of that liberty of interpretation for which I just contended. For the value of these different injunctions—so beautiful and so vague—is wholly in the meaning one attaches to them. The characters, the situation, which strike one as real will be those that touch and interest one most, but the measure of reality is very difficult to fix. The reality of Don Quixote or of Mr. Micawber [1] is a very delicate shade; it is a reality so colored by the author's vision that, vivid as it may be, one would hesitate to propose it as a model: one would expose one's self to some very embarrassing questions on the part of a pupil. It goes without saying that you will not write a good novel unless you possess the sense of reality; but it will be difficult to give you a recipe for calling that sense into being. Humanity is immense, and reality has a myriad forms; the most one can affirm is that some of the flowers of fiction have the odor of it, and others have not; as for telling you in advance how your nosegay should be composed, that is another affair. It is equally excellent and inconclusive to say that one must write from experience; to our supposititious aspirant such a declaration might savor of mockery. What kind of experience is intended, and where does it begin and end? Experience is never limited, and it is never complete; it is an immense sensibility, a kind of huge spiderweb of the finest silken threads suspended in the chamber of consciousness, and catching every air-borne particle in its tissue. It is the very atmosphere of the mind; and when the mind is imaginative—much more when it happens to be that of a man of genius—it takes to itself the faintest hints of life, it converts the very pulses of the air into revelations. The young lady living in a village has only to be a damsel upon whom nothing is lost to make it quite unfair (as it seems to me) to declare to her that she shall have nothing to say about the military. Greater miracles have been seen than that, imagination assisting, she should speak the truth about some of these gentlemen. I remember an English novelist, a woman of genius, telling me that she was much commended for the impression she had managed to give in one of her tales of the nature and way of life of the French Protestant youth. She had been asked where she learned so much about this recondite being, she had been congratulated on her peculiar opportunities. These opportunities consisted in her having once, in Paris, as she ascended a staircase, passed an open door where, in the household of a *pasteur*,[2]

1. Character in Dickens's *David Cop-* 2. Pastor.
perfield.

some of the young Protestants were seated at table round a finished meal. The glimpse made a picture; it lasted only a moment, but that moment was experience. She had got her direct personal impression, and she turned out her type. She knew what youth was, and what Protestantism; she also had the advantage of having seen what it was to be French, so that she converted these ideas into a concrete image and produced a reality. Above all, however, she was blessed with the faculty which when you give it an inch takes an ell, and which for the artist is a much greater source of strength than any accident of residence or of place in the social scale. The power to guess the unseen from the seen, to trace the implication of things, to judge the whole piece by the pattern, the condition of feeling life in general so completely that you are well on your way to knowing any particular corner of it—this cluster of gifts may almost be said to constitute experience, and they occur in country and in town, and in the most differing stages of education. If experience consists of impressions, it may be said that impressions *are* experience, just as (have we not seen it?) they are the very air we breathe. Therefore, if I should certainly say to a novice, "Write from experience and experience only," I should feel that this was rather a tantalizing monition if I were not careful immediately to add, "Try to be one of the people on whom nothing is lost!"

I am far from intending by this to minimize the importance of exactness—of truth of detail. One can speak best from one's own taste, and I may therefore venture to say that the air of reality (solidity of specification) seems to me to be the supreme virtue of a novel—the merit on which all its other merits (including that conscious moral purpose of which Mr. Besant speaks) helplessly and submissively depend. If it be not there, they are all as nothing, and if these be there, they owe their effect to the success with which the author has produced the illusion of life. The cultivation of this success, the study of this exquisite process, form, to my taste, the beginning and the end of the art of the novelist. They are his inspiration, his despair, his reward, his torment, his delight. It is here in very truth that he competes with life; it is here that he competes with his brother the painter in *his* attempt to render the look of things, the look that conveys their meaning, to catch the color, the relief, the expression, the surface, the substance of the human spectacle. It is in regard to this that Mr. Besant is well inspired when he bids him take notes. He cannot possibly take too many, he cannot possibly take enough. All life solicits him, and to "render" the simplest surface, to produce the most momentary illusion, is a very complicated business. His case would be easier, and the rule would be more exact, if Mr. Besant had been able to tell him what notes to take. But this, I fear, he can never learn in any manual; it is the business of his life. He has to take a great many in order to select a few, he has to work them up as he can, and even the guides and philosophers who might have most to say to him must leave him alone when it comes to the application of precepts, as we leave the painter in communion with his palette. That his characters "must be clear in outline," as Mr. Besant says—he feels that down to his boots; but how he shall make them so is a secret between his good angel and himself. It would be absurdly simple if he could be taught that a great deal of "description" would make them so, or that on the contrary the absence of description and the cultivation of dialogue, or the absence of dialogue and the multiplication of "incident," would rescue him from his difficulties. Nothing, for instance, is more possible than that he be of a turn of mind for which this odd, literal opposition of description and dialogue, incident and description, has little meaning and light. People often talk of these things as if they had a kind of internecine distinctness, instead of melting into each other at every breath, and being intimately associated parts of one general effort of expression. I cannot imagine composition existing in a series of blocks, nor conceive, in any novel worth discussing at all, of a passage of description that is not in its intention narrative, a passage of dialogue that is not in its intention descriptive, a touch of truth of any sort that does not partake of the nature of incident, or an incident that derives its interest from any other source than the general and only source of the success of a work of art—that of being illustrative. A novel is a living thing, all one and continuous, like any other organism, and in proportion as it lives will it be found, I think, that in each of the parts there is something of each of the other parts. The critic who over the close texture of a finished work shall pretend to trace a geography of items will mark some frontiers as artificial, I fear, as any that have been known to history. There is an old-fashioned distinction between the novel of character and the novel of incident which must have cost many a smile to the intending fabulist who was keen about his work. It appears to me as little to the point as the equally celebrated distinction between the novel and the romance—to answer as little to any reality. There are bad novels and good novels, as there are bad pictures and good pictures; but that is the only distinction in which I see any meaning, and I can as little imagine speaking of a novel of character as I can imagine speaking of a picture of character. When one says picture one says of character, when one says novel one says of incident, and the terms may be transposed at will. What is character but the determination of incident? What is incident but the illustration of character? What is either a picture or a novel that is *not* of character? What else do we seek in it and find in it? It is an incident for a woman to stand up with her hand resting on a table and look out at you in a certain way; or if it be not an incident I think it will be hard to say what it is. At the same time it is an expression of character. If you say you don't see it (character in *that—allons donc!* [3]), this is exactly what the artist who has reasons of his own for thinking he *does* see it undertakes to show you. When a young man makes up his mind that he has not faith enough after all to enter the church as he intended, that is an incident, though you may not hurry to the end of the chapter to see whether perhaps he doesn't change once more. I do not say that these are extraordinary or startling incidents. I do not pretend to estimate the degree of interest proceeding from them, for this will depend upon the skill of the painter. It sounds almost puerile to say that some incidents are intrinsically much more important than others, and I need not take this precaution after having professed my sympathy for the major ones in remarking that the only classification of the novel that I can understand is into that which has life and that which has it not.

The novel and the romance, the novel of incident and that of character—these clumsy separations appear to me to have been made by critics and readers for their own convenience, and to help them out of some of their occasional queer predicaments, but to have little reality or interest for the producer, from whose point of view it is of course that we are attempting to consider the art of fiction. The case is the same with another shadowy category which Mr. Besant apparently is disposed to set up—that of the "modern English novel"; unless indeed it be that in this matter he has fallen into an accidental confusion of standpoints. It is not quite clear whether he intends the remarks in which he alludes to it to be didactic or historical. It is as difficult to suppose a person intending to write a modern English as to suppose him writing an ancient English novel: that is a label which begs the question. One writes the novel, one paints the picture, of one's language and of one's time, and calling it modern English will not, alas! make the difficult task any easier. No more, unfortunately, will calling this or that work of one's fellow artist a romance—unless it be, of course, simply for the pleasantness of the thing, as for instance when Hawthorne gave this heading to his story of *Blithedale*.[4] The French, who have brought the theory of fiction to remarkable completeness, have but one name for the novel, and have not attempted smaller things in it, that I can see, for that. I can think of no obligation to which the "romancer" would not be held equally with the novelist;

3. Come now!   4. *The Blithedale Romance.*

the standard of execution is equally high for each. Of course it is of
execution that we are talking—that being the only point of a
novel that is open to contention. This is perhaps too often lost
sight of, only to produce interminable confusions and cross purposes. We must grant the artist his subject, his idea, his *donnée*: [5]
our criticism is applied only to what he makes of it. Naturally I do
not mean that we are bound to like it or find it interesting: in
case we do not, our course is perfectly simple—to let it alone. We
may believe that of a certain idea even the most sincere novelist
can make nothing at all, and the event may perfectly justify our
belief; but the failure will have been a failure to execute, and it is
in the execution that the fatal weakness is recorded. If we pretend
to respect the artist at all, we must allow him his freedom of
choice, in the fact, in particular cases, of innumerable presumptions
that the choice will not fructify. Art derives a considerable part of
its beneficial exercise from flying in the face of presumptions, and
some of the most interesting experiments of which it is capable
are hidden in the bosom of common things. Gustave Flaubert has
written a story [6] about the devotion of a servant girl to a parrot,
and the production, highly finished as it is, cannot on the whole be
called a success. We are perfectly free to find it flat, but I think it
might have been interesting; and I, for my part, am extremely
glad he should have written it; it is a contribution to our knowledge
of what can be done—or what cannot. Ivan Turgénieff has written
a tale [7] about a deaf and dumb serf and a lap dog, and the thing
is touching, loving, a little masterpiece. He struck the note of
life where Gustave Flaubert missed it—he flew in the face of a
presumption and achieved a victory.

Nothing, of course, will ever take the place of the good old fashion of "liking" a work of art or of not liking it: the most improved
criticism will not abolish that primitive, that ultimate test. I mention this to guard myself from the accusation of intimating that
the idea, the subject, of a novel or a picture, does not matter. It
matters, to my sense, in the highest degree, and if I might put up
a prayer it would be that artists should select none but the richest. Some, as I have already hastened to admit, are much more
remunerative than others, and it would be a world happily arranged
in which persons intending to treat them should be exempt from
confusions and mistakes. This fortunate condition will arrive only,
I fear, on the same day that critics become purged from error.
Meanwhile, I repeat, we do not judge the artist with fairness unless
we say to him, "Oh, I grant you your starting point, because if I
did not I should seem to prescribe to you, and heaven forbid I

should take that responsibility. If I pretend to tell you what you must not take, you will call upon me to tell you then what you must take; in which case I shall be prettily caught. Moreover, it isn't till I have accepted your data that I can begin to measure you. I have the standard, the pitch; I have no right to tamper with your flute and then criticize your music. Of course I may not care for your idea at all; I may think it silly, or stale, or unclean; in which case I wash my hands of you altogether. I may content myself with believing that you will not have succeeded in being interesting, but I shall, of course, not attempt to demonstrate it, and you will be as indifferent to me as I am to you. I needn't remind you that there are all sorts of tastes: who can know it better? Some people, for excellent reasons, don't like to read about carpenters; others, for reasons even better, don't like to read about courtesans. Many object to Americans. Others (I believe they are mainly editors and publishers) won't look at Italians. Some readers don't like quiet subjects; others don't like bustling ones. Some enjoy a complete illusion, others the consciousness of large concessions. They choose their novels accordingly, and if they don't care about your idea they won't, *a fortiori*,[8] care about your treatment."

So that it comes back very quickly, as I have said, to the liking: in spite of M. Zola,[9] who reasons less powerfully than he represents, and who will not reconcile himself to this absoluteness of taste, thinking that there are certain things that people ought to like, and that they can be made to like. I am quite at a loss to imagine anything (at any rate in this matter of fiction) that people *ought* to like or to dislike. Selection will be sure to take care of itself, for it has a constant motive behind it. That motive is simply experience. As people feel life, so they will feel the art that is most closely related to it. This closeness of relation is what we should never forget in talking of the effort of the novel. Many people speak of it as a factitious, artificial form, a product of ingenuity, the business of which is to alter and arrange the things that surround us, to translate them into conventional, traditional molds. This, however, is a view of the matter which carries us but a very short way, condemns the art to an eternal repetition of a few familiar *clichés*, cuts short its development, and leads us straight up to a dead wall. Catching the very note and trick, the strange irregular rhythm of life, that is the attempt whose strenuous force keeps Fiction upon her feet. In proportion as in what she offers us we see life *without* rearrangement do we feel that we are touching the truth; in proportion as we see it *with* rearrangement do we

8. All the more.
9. Émile Zola (1840–1902), novelist and author of *Le roman expérimental*, which explains his theories of fiction.

feel that we are being put off with a substitute, a compromise and convention. It is not uncommon to hear an extraordinary assurance of remark in regard to this matter of rearranging, which is often spoken of as if it were the last word of art. Mr. Besant seems to me in danger of falling into the great error with his rather unguarded talk about "selection." Art is essentially selection, but it is a selection whose main care is to be typical, to be inclusive. For many people art means rose-colored window-panes, and selection means picking a bouquet for Mrs. Grundy.[1] They will tell you glibly that artistic considerations have nothing to do with the disagreeable, with the ugly; they will rattle off shallow commonplaces about the province of art and the limits of art till you are moved to some wonder in return as to the province and the limits of ignorance. It appears to me that no one can ever have made a seriously artistic attempt without becoming conscious of an immense increase—a kind of revelation—of freedom. One perceives in that case—by the light of a heavenly ray—that the province of art is all life, all feeling, all observation, all vision. As Mr. Besant so justly intimates, it is all experience. That is a sufficient answer to those who maintain that it must not touch the sad things of life, who stick into its divine unconscious bosom little prohibitory inscriptions on the end of sticks, such as we see in public gardens —"It is forbidden to walk on the grass; it is forbidden to touch the flowers; it is not allowed to introduce dogs or to remain after dark; it is requested to keep to the right." The young aspirant in the line of fiction whom we continue to imagine will do nothing without taste, for in that case his freedom would be of little use to him; but the first advantage of his taste will be to reveal to him the absurdity of the little sticks and tickets. If he have taste, I must add, of course he will have ingenuity, and my disrespectful reference to that quality just now was not meant to imply that it is useless in fiction. But it is only a secondary aid; the first is a capacity for receiving straight impressions.

Mr. Besant has some remarks on the question of "the story" which I shall not attempt to criticize, though they seem to me to contain a singular ambiguity, because I do not think I understand them. I cannot see what is meant by talking as if there were a part of a novel which is the story and part of it which for mystical reasons is not—unless indeed the distinction be made in a sense in which it is difficult to suppose that anyone should attempt to convey anything. "The story," if it represents anything, represents the subject, the idea, the *donnée* of the novel; and there is surely no "school"—Mr. Besant speaks of a school—which urges that a novel

should be all treatment and no subject. There must assuredly be
something to treat; every school is intimately conscious of that.
This sense of the story being the idea, the starting point, of the
novel, is the only one that I see in which it can be spoken of as
something different from its organic whole; and since in proportion
as the work is successful the idea permeates and penetrates it, informs and animates it, so that every word and every punctuation
point contribute directly to the expression, in that proportion do
we lose our sense of the story being a blade which may be drawn
more or less out of its sheath. The story and the novel, the idea
and the form, are the needle and thread, and I never heard of a
guild of tailors who recommended the use of thread without the
needle, or the needle without the thread. Mr. Besant is not the
only critic who may be observed to have spoken as if there were
certain things in life which constitute stories, and certain others
which do not. I find the same odd implications in an entertaining
article in the *Pall Mall Gazette*, devoted, as it happens, to Mr.
Besant's lecture. "The story is the thing!" says this graceful writer,
as if with a tone of opposition to some other idea. I should think it
was, as every painter who, as the time for "sending in" his picture
looms in the distance, finds himself still in quest of a subject—as
every belated artist not fixed about his theme will heartily agree.
There are some subjects which speak to us and others which do
not, but he would be a clever man who should undertake to give a
rule—an index expurgatorius [2]—by which the story and the no-
story should be known apart. It is impossible (to me at least) to
imagine any such rule which shall not be altogether arbitrary. The
writer in the *Pall Mall* opposes the delightful (as I suppose) novel
of *Margot la Balafrée* [3] to certain tales in which "Bostonian
nymphs" appear to have "rejected English dukes for psychological
reasons." [4] I am not acquainted with the romance just designated,
and can scarcely forgive the *Pall Mall* critic for not mentioning
the name of the author, but the title appears to refer to a lady
who may have received a scar [5] in some heroic adventure. I am
inconsolable at not being acquainted with this episode, but am utterly at a loss to see why it is a story when the rejection (or
acceptance) of a duke is not, and why a reason, psychological or
other, is not a subject when a cicatrix [6] is. They are all particles of
the multitudinous life with which the novel deals, and surely no
dogma which pretends to make it lawful to touch the one and unlawful to touch the other will stand for a moment on its feet. It is

2. The allusion is to the Catholic "Index" of forbidden books.
3. A novel, published in 1884, by For-
tuné Du Boisgobey.
4. James is defending himself. *Cf. An*
International Episode (1879) and *The*
Portrait of a Lady (1881).
5. *Balafrée* means "lady with a scar."
6. Scar.

the special picture that must stand or fall, according as it seem to possess truth or to lack it. Mr. Besant does not, to my sense, light up the subject by intimating that a story must, under penalty of not being a story, consist of "adventures." Why of adventures more than of green spectacles? [7] He mentions a category of impossible things, and among them he places "fiction without adventure." Why without adventure, more than without matrimony, or celibacy, or parturition, or cholera, or hydropathy,[8] or Jansenism? [9] This seems to me to bring the novel back to the hapless little role of being an artificial, ingenious thing—bring it down from its large, free character of an immense and exquisite correspondence with life. And what *is* adventure, when it comes to that, and by what sign is the listening pupil to recognize it? It is an adventure—an immense one—for me to write this little article; and for a Bostonian nymph to reject an English duke is an adventure only less stirring, I should say, than for an English duke to be rejected by a Bostonian nymph. I see dramas within dramas in that, and innumerable points of view. A psychological reason is, to my imagination, an object adorably pictorial; to catch the tint of its complexion—I feel as if that idea might inspire one to Titianesque [1] efforts. There are few things more exciting to me, in short, than a psychological reason, and yet I protest, the novel seems to me the most magnificent form of art. I have just been reading, at the same time, the delightful story of *Treasure Island,* by Mr. Robert Louis Stevenson and, in a manner less consecutive, the last tale from M. Edmond de Goncourt, which is entitled *Chérie.* One of these works treats of murders, mysteries, islands of dreadful renown, hairbreadth escapes, miraculous coincidences, and buried doubloons. The other treats of a little French girl who lived in a fine house in Paris, and died of wounded sensibility because no one would marry her. I call *Treasure Island* delightful because it appears to me to have succeeded wonderfully in what it attempts; and I venture to bestow no epithet upon *Chérie,* which strikes me as having failed deplorably in what it attempts—that is, in tracing the development of the moral consciousness of a child. But one of these productions strikes me as exactly as much of a novel as the other, and as having a "story" quite as much. The moral consciousness of a child is as much a part of life as the islands of the Spanish Main, and the one sort of geography seems to me to have those "surprises" of which Mr. Besant speaks quite as much as the other. For myself (since it comes back in the last resort, as I say, to the preference of the individual), the picture of the child's

7. *Cf.* Oliver Goldsmith, *The Vicar of Wakefield.*
8. Water therapy.
9. Heretical doctrines of Cornelius Jansen (1585–1638), Catholic bishop of Ypres.
1. The allusion is to the sixteenth-century Venetian painter.

experience has the advantage that I can at successive steps (an immense luxury, near to the "sensual pleasure" of which Mr. Besant's critic in the *Pall Mall* speaks) say Yes or No, as it may be, to what the artist puts before me. I have been a child in fact, but I have been on a quest for a buried treasure only in supposition, and it is a simple accident that with M. de Goncourt I should have for the most part to say No. With George Eliot, when she painted [2] that country with a far other intelligence, I always said Yes.

The most interesting part of Mr. Besant's lecture is unfortunately the briefest passage—his very cursory allusion to the "conscious moral purpose" of the novel. Here again it is not very clear whether he be recording a fact or laying down a principle; it is a great pity that in the latter case he should not have developed his idea. This branch of the subject is of immense importance, and Mr. Besant's few words point to considerations of the widest reach, not to be lightly disposed of. He will have treated the art of fiction but superficially who is not prepared to go every inch of the way that these considerations will carry him. It is for this reason that at the beginning of these remarks I was careful to notify the reader that my reflections on so large a theme have no pretension to be exhaustive. Like Mr. Besant, I have left the question of the morality of the novel till the last, and at the last I find I have used up my space. It is a question surrounded with difficulties, as witness the very first that meets us, in the form of a definite question, on the threshold. Vagueness, in such a discussion, is fatal, and what is the meaning of your morality and your conscious moral purpose? Will you not define your terms and explain how (a novel being a picture) a picture can be either moral or immoral? You wish to paint a moral picture or carve a moral statue: will you not tell us how you would set about it? We are discussing the Art of Fiction; questions of art are questions (in the widest sense) of execution; questions of morality are quite another affair, and will you not let us see how it is that you find it so easy to mix them up? These things are so clear to Mr. Besant that he has deduced from them a law which he sees embodied in English fiction, and which is "a truly admirable thing and a great cause for congratulation." It is a great cause for congratulation indeed when such thorny problems become as smooth as silk. I may add that in so far as Mr. Besant perceives that in point of fact English fiction has addressed itself preponderantly to these delicate questions he will appear to many people to have made a vain discovery. They will have been positively struck, on the contrary, with the moral timidity of the usual English novelist; with his (or with her) aversion to face the diffi-

2. *Cf. Silas Marner.*

culties with which on every side the treatment of reality bristles. He is apt to be extremely shy (whereas the picture that Mr. Besant draws is a picture of boldness), and the sign of his work, for the most part, is a cautious silence on certain subjects. In the English novel (by which of course I mean the American as well), more than in any other, there is a traditional difference between that which people know and that which they agree to admit that they know, that which they see and that which they speak of, that which they feel to be a part of life and that which they allow to enter into literature. There is the great difference, in short, between what they talk of in conversation and what they talk of in print. The essence of moral energy is to survey the whole field, and I should directly reverse Mr. Besant's remark and say not that the English novel has a purpose, but that it has a diffidence. To what degree a purpose in a work of art is a source of corruption I shall not attempt to inquire; the one that seems to me least dangerous is the purpose of making a perfect work. As for our novel, I may say lastly on this score that as we find it in England today it strikes me as addressed in a large degree to "young people," and that this in itself constitutes a presumption that it will be rather shy. There are certain things which it is generally agreed not to discuss, not even to mention, before young people. That is very well, but the absence of discussion is not a symptom of the moral passion. The purpose of the English novel—"a truly admirable thing, and a great cause for congratulation"—strikes me therefore as rather negative.

There is one point at which the moral sense and the artistic sense lie very near together; that is in the light of the very obvious truth that the deepest quality of a work of art will always be the quality of the mind of the producer. In proportion as that intelligence is fine will the novel, the picture, the statue partake of the substance of beauty and truth. To be constituted of such elements is, to my vision, to have purpose enough. No good novel will ever proceed from a superficial mind; that seems to me an axiom which, for the artist in fiction, will cover all needful moral ground: if the youthful aspirant take it to heart it will illuminate for him many of the mysteries of "purpose." There are many other useful things that might be said to him, but I have come to the end of my article, and can only touch them as I pass. The critic in the *Pall Mall Gazette*, whom I have already quoted, draws attention to the danger, in speaking of the art of fiction, of generalizing. The danger that he has in mind is rather, I imagine, that of particularizing, for there are some comprehensive remarks which, in addition to those embodied in Mr. Besant's suggestive lecture, might without fear of misleading him be addressed to the ingenuous student.

I should remind him first of the magnificence of the form that is open to him, which offers to sight so few restrictions and such innumerable opportunities. The other arts, in comparison, appear confined and hampered; the various conditions under which they are exercised are so rigid and definite. But the only condition that I can think of attaching to the composition of the novel is, as I have already said, that it be sincere. This freedom is a splendid privilege, and the first lesson of the young novelist is to learn to be worthy of it. "Enjoy it as it deserves," I should say to him; "take possession of it, explore it to its utmost extent, publish it, rejoice in it. All life belongs to you, and do not listen either to those who would shut you up into corners of it and tell you that it is only here and there that art inhabits, or to those who would persuade you that this heavenly messenger wings her way outside of life altogether, breathing a superfine air, and turning away her head from the truth of things. There is no impression of life, no manner of seeing it and feeling it, to which the plan of the novelist may not offer a place; you have only to remember that talents so dissimilar as those of Alexandre Dumas and Jane Austen, Charles Dickens and Gustave Flaubert have worked in this field with equal glory. Do not think too much about optimism and pessimism; try and catch the color of life itself. In France today we see a prodigious effort (that of Emile Zola,[3] to whose solid and serious work no explorer of the capacity of the novel can allude without respect), we see an extraordinary effort vitiated by a spirit of pessimism on a narrow basis. M. Zola is magnificent, but he strikes an English reader as ignorant; he has an air of working in the dark; if he had as much light as energy, his results would be of the highest value. As for the aberrations of a shallow optimism, the ground (of English fiction especially) is strewn with their brittle particles as with broken glass. If you must indulge in conclusions, let them have the taste of a wide knowledge. Remember that your first duty is to be as complete as possible—to make as perfect a work. Be generous and delicate and pursue the prize."

1884, 1888

3. *Cf.* James's study of Zola in *Notes on Novelists* (1914), pp. 26–64.

Literary Expression of Social Thought: The Turn of the Century

HENRY ADAMS

(1838–1918)

From childhood Henry Adams bore the responsibility of living up to the greatness of his fore-bears. During the summers he was usually sent from Boston—where he was born on February 16, 1838—to nearby Quincy, where his grandfather, John Quincy Adams, still wielded the national influence and authority that duly follows a former president of the United States. Nearby in Quincy stood the home of John Adams, his great-grandfather. In Quincy young Adams could see famous visiting persons and hear scraps of conversation, often of international import. At home in Boston it was much the same, for his father, Charles Francis Adams, was already taking his independent place in the world as a man of power, preparing himself for national service as a member of Congress, and later, during the Civil War, as minister to Eng-land, where his brilliant diplomacy was a factor in the success of the northern cause.

Later, in *The Education of Henry Adams* (1907), the author adopted the attitude of one whose education had been useless for dealing with the rapidly changing pattern of his age, but he had the best that Boston could offer—the well-stored libraries of his father and grandfather, and private instruction there, followed by Harvard University and the study of law at the University of Berlin. Travel on the Continent proved more attractive than German scholarship to the young man; he sought first-hand knowledge of music and art and the majestic cathedrals. Adams then settled in Washington as secretary to his father, recently elected to Congress, and when Charles Francis Adams became minister to England a short time later, he took his son with him, still as secretary. From London young Adams became a lively contributor to Boston and New York newspapers and to the *North American Review,* disturbing conservatives with an energetic debunking of historical legends—such as that of Pocahontas and Captain John Smith—and upsetting fundamentalists with his insistence on the importance of evolution in the history of civilization.

On his return to Washington in 1868, Adams found himself completely at odds with Reconstruction politics and with the Gilded Age in general; after writing a number of critical articles he accepted an appointment at Harvard, where he taught history (1870–1877). His courses reflected his growing interest in the Middle Ages, which later bore fruit in his writing, but he also kept in touch with the present as editor of the *North American Review.* His "dynamic theory of history" as a science began to take shape, but it was not until later that he found what was for him the answer in the laws of physical science.

In 1872 Adams married Marian Hooper, the attractive daughter of a prominent Boston physician, and heiress to a fortune; after a year in Europe they returned to Harvard, where he taught until 1877. He next settled in Washington, apparently fascinated again by history in the making, becoming as he said, "stable-companion to statesmen," among whom William Evarts and John Hay were his intimates. His interest in important associates of Thomas Jefferson produced his collection of *The Writings of Albert Gallatin* (1879) and a biography of Gallatin the same year. His anonymous novel, *Democracy* (1880), a satire upon corruption in national government and social life, was followed by a biography, *John Randolph* (1882). Many of Adams's own critical ideas appear in his novel *Esther* (1884), in which his wife probably served as model for the heroine; the significance of this is heightened by the suicide of Mrs. Adams in 1885, a crushing tragedy from which he never fully recovered. He first sought escape in a long journey through the Orient, then resumed his monumental undertaking, not completed until 1891, *The History of the United States during the Administrations of Jefferson and Madison,* in nine volumes. Thereafter Adams continued his writing through restless wanderings; *Historical Essays* (1891) and *Memoirs of Marau Taaroa, Last Queen of Tahiti* (1893) resulted from travel and research. More and more he saw history in terms of energy and force; he sought analogues in the physical sciences and consulted the scientists who were his friends. As he later explained in *The Education of Henry Adams,* and especially in the chapter entitled "The Dynamo and the Virgin," the scientific exhibits at the expositions in Chicago in 1893, and at Paris in 1900, were a concrete revelation of what he sought to know. The huge electro-dynamos became a symbol of the dawning age, in which "the human race may commit suicide by blowing up the world," as he prophetically foresaw in the *Education*. He now began to regard human thought, and hence the currents of history, as energetic forces, comparable to those physical energies described by the laws of thermodynamics, responding to similar laws of attraction and repulsion, acceleration, and dissipation. The significance of his theory for historians he succinctly expressed in "A Letter to American Teachers of History" (1910), reprinted by his brother, Brooks Adams, in *The Degradation of the Democratic Dogma* (1919).

The earliest literary fruit of Adams's theory was a masterpiece, *Mont-Saint-Michel and Chartres* (1904), which he called "A study of thirteenth-century unity," by contrast with his own age to be revealed in the *Education*—"A study of twentieth-century multiplicity." The power of the earlier age was the spiritual unity of philosophy, art, and vision that built the cathedrals, symbols of the Virgin; his own age presented no unity save the still-unsolved enigma of the atom. Never popular, Henry Adams was a sound scholar and a sincere artist, one whose message may be reconsidered today in the light of events not foreseen by his contemporaries.

There is no collected edition of Henry Adams. His most important works are *Democracy: An American Novel*, 1880, reprinted 1952; *Esther: A Novel*, 1884, reprinted with an introduction by Robert E. Spiller, 1938; *History of the United States of America during the Administration of Thomas Jefferson*, 1884–1885, and *History of the United States of America during the Administration of James Madison*, 1888–1889, both privately printed, published in 9 vols., 1889–1891, reprinted in 4 vols., with an introduction by Henry S. Commager, 1930, and condensed by Herbert Agar as *The Formative Years*, 1947; *Mont-Saint-Michel and Chartres*, 1904, reprinted 1936; *The Education of Henry Adams: An Autobiography*, privately printed 1907, published 1918, reprinted frequently; *The Degradation of the Democratic Dogma*, 1919, reprinted 1949; *Travels in Tahiti*, edited by Robert E. Spiller, 1947. Worthington C. Ford edited *A Cycle of Adams Letters, 1861–1865*, 2 vols., 1920, *Letters of Henry Adams, 1858–1891*, 1930, and *Letters of Henry Adams, 1892–1918*, 1938; Harold D. Cater edited *Henry Adams and His Friends: A Collection of His Unpublished Letters*, 1947. Newton Arvin edited *The Selected Letters of Henry Adams*, 1951.

Biographies are James Truslow Adams, *Henry Adams*, 1933; Ernest Samuels, *The Young Henry Adams*, 1948; *Henry Adams: The Middle Years, 1877–1891*, 1958; and *Henry Adams: The Major Phase*, 1964. See also Robert A. Hume, *Runaway Star: An Appreciation of Henry Adams*, 1951; Elizabeth Stevenson, *Henry Adams, A Biography*, 1955; J. C. Levenson, *The Mind and Art of Henry Adams*, 1957; George Hochfield, *Henry Adams: An Interpretation and Introduction*, 1962; Vern Wagner, *The Suspension of Henry Adams: A Study of Manner and Matter*, 1969; John Condor, *A Formula of His Own: Henry Adams's Literary Experiment*, 1970; and Melvin Lyon, *Symbol and Idea in Henry Adams*, 1970.

The Dynamo and the Virgin [1]

Until the Great Exposition of 1900 [2] closed its doors in November, Adams haunted it, aching to absorb knowledge, and helpless to find it. He would have liked to know how much of it could

1. Chapter 25 of *The Education of Henry Adams*, written after Adams had seen the dynamos at the Paris Exposition of 1900. Like Eugene O'Neill, who later treated a similar theme dramatically in *Dynamo*, Adams saw physical power replacing the spiritual idealism symbolized for the Middle Ages in the power of the Virgin. Hence the chapter is one expression of the author's "dynamic theory of history," which attempts to explain history as the power of ideas functioning as force, controlled by laws analogous to the physical laws of thermodynamics.
2. Held in Paris.

have been grasped by the best-informed man in the world. While he was thus meditating chaos, Langley [3] came by, and showed it to him. At Langley's behest, the Exhibition dropped its superfluous rags and stripped itself to the skin, for Langley knew what to study, and why, and how; while Adams might as well have stood outside in the night, staring at the Milky Way. Yet Langley said nothing new, and taught nothing that one might not have learned from Lord Bacon,[4] three hundred years before; but though one should have known the *Advancement of Science* [5] as well as one knew the *Comedy of Errors*, the literary knowledge counted for nothing until some teacher should show how to apply it. Bacon took a vast deal of trouble in teaching King James I and his subjects, American or other, towards the year 1620,[6] that true science was the development or economy of forces; yet an elderly American in 1900 knew neither the formula nor the forces; or even so much as to say to himself that his historical business in the Exposition concerned only the economies or developments of force since 1893; when he began the study at Chicago.[7]

Nothing in education is so astonishing as the amount of ignorance it accumulates in the form of inert facts. Adams had looked at most of the accumulations of art in the storehouses called Art Museums; yet he did not know how to look at the art exhibits of 1900. He had studied Karl Marx and his doctrines of history [8] with profound attention, yet he could not apply them at Paris. Langley, with the ease of a great master of experiment, threw out of the field every exhibit that did not reveal a new application of force, and naturally threw out, to begin with, almost the whole art exhibit. Equally, he ignored almost the whole industrial exhibit. He led his pupil directly to the forces. His chief interest was in new motors to make his airship feasible, and he taught Adams the astonishing complexities of the Daimler [9] motor, and of the automobile, which, since 1893, had become a nightmare at a hundred kilometres an hour, almost as destructive as the electric tram which was only ten years older; and threatening to become as terrible as the locomotive steam-engine itself, which was almost exactly Adams's own age.

Then he showed his scholar the great hall of dynamos, and ex-

3. Samuel Pierpont Langley (1834–1906), American physicist, who made important investigations in aeronautics and in the exploration of the solar spectrum.
4. Francis Bacon (1561–1626), British statesman and philosopher, a pioneer of modern inductive science.
5. Adams has in mind Bacon's *The Advancement of Learning* (1605).
6. Date of Bacon's *Novum Organum*.
7. The Columbian Exposition at Chicago (1893), where large technological exhibits were displayed.
8. Karl Marx (1818–1883), German economist who promulgated doctrines basic to modern Communism. *Das Kapital* is his classic expression of socialist economics and "doctrines of history" based on materialistic forces.
9. Gottlieb Daimler (1834–1900), German inventor of a high-speed internal-combustion engine.

plained how little he knew about electricity or force of any kind, even of his own special sun, which spouted heat in inconceivable volume, but which, as far as he knew, might spout less or more, at any time, for all the certainty he felt in it. To him, the dynamo itself was but an ingenious channel for conveying somewhere the heat latent in a few tons of poor coal hidden in a dirty engine-house carefully kept out of sight; but to Adams the dynamo became a symbol of infinity. As he grew accustomed to the great gallery of machines, he began to feel the forty-foot dynamos as a moral force, much as the early Christians felt the Cross. The planet itself seemed less impressive, in its old-fashioned, deliberate, annual or daily revolution, than this huge wheel, revolving within arm's-length at some vertiginous speed, and barely murmuring—scarcely humming an audible warning to stand a hair's-breadth further for respect of power—while it would not wake the baby lying close against its frame. Before the end, one began to pray to it; inherited instinct taught the natural expression of man before silent and infinite force. Among the thousand symbols of ultimate energy, the dynamo was not so human as some, but it was the most expressive.

Yet the dynamo, next to the steam-engine, was the most familiar of exhibits. For Adams's objects its value lay chiefly in its occult mechanism. Between the dynamo in the gallery of machines and the engine-house outside, the break of continuity amounted to abysmal fracture for a historian's objects. No more relation could he discover between the steam and the electric current than between the Cross and the cathedral. The forces were interchangeable if not reversible, but he could see only an absolute *fiat* in electricity as in faith. Langley could not help him. Indeed, Langley seemed to be worried by the same trouble, for he constantly repeated that the new forces were anarchical, and especially that he was not responsible for the new rays, that were little short of parricidal in their wicked spirit towards science. His own rays, with which he had doubled the solar spectrum, were altogether harmless and beneficent; but Radium denied its God [1]—or what was to Langley the same thing, denied the truths of his Science. The force was wholly new.

A historian who asked only to learn enough to be as futile as Langley or Kelvin,[2] made rapid progress under this teaching, and mixed himself up in the tangle of ideas until he achieved a sort of Paradise of ignorance vastly consoling to his fatigued senses. He wrapped himself in vibrations and rays which were new, and he

1. Research in radium, with its "rays," was the first source of knowledge of the disintegration of atoms.
2. William Thomson, Lord Kelvin (1824–1907), British physicist who made important contributions to electrodynamics and transatlantic telegraphy.

would have hugged Marconi [3] and Branly [4] had he met them, as he hugged the dynamo; while he lost his arithmetic in trying to figure out the equation between the discoveries and the economies of force. The economies, like the discoveries, were absolute, supersensual, occult; incapable of expression in horse-power. What mathematical equivalent could he suggest as the value of a Branly coherer? Frozen air, or the electric furnace, had some scale of measurement, no doubt, if somebody could invent a thermometer adequate to the purpose; but X-rays had played no part whatever in man's consciousness, and the atom itself had figured only as a fiction of thought. In these seven years man had translated himself into a new universe which had no common scale of measurement with the old. He had entered a supersensual world, in which he could measure nothing except by chance collisions of movements imperceptible to his senses, perhaps even imperceptible to his instruments, but perceptible to each other, and so to some known ray at the end of the scale. Langley seemed prepared for anything, even for an indeterminable number of universes interfused—physics stark mad in metaphysics.

Historians undertake to arrange sequences,—called stories, or histories—assuming in silence a relation of cause and effect. These assumptions, hidden in the depths of dusty libraries, have been astounding, but commonly unconscious and childlike; so much so, that if any captious critic were to drag them to light, historians would probably reply, with one voice, that they had never supposed themselves required to know what they were talking about. Adams, for one, had toiled in vain to find out what he meant. He had even published a dozen volumes of American history for no other purpose than to satisfy himself whether, by the severest process of stating, with the least possible comment, such facts as seemed sure, in such order as seemed rigorously consequent, he could fix for a familiar moment a necessary sequence of human movement. The result had satisfied him as little as at Harvard College. Where he saw sequence, other men saw something quite different, and no one saw the same unit of measure. He cared little about his experiments and less about his statesmen, who seemed to him quite as ignorant as himself and, as a rule, no more honest; but he insisted on a relation of sequence, and if he could not reach it by one method, he would try as many methods as science knew. Satisfied that the sequence of men led to nothing and that the sequence of their society could lead no further, while the mere sequence of time was artificial, and the sequence of thought was chaos, he

---

3. Marchese Guglielmo Marconi (1874–1937), Italian inventor of the wireless telegraph.

4. Edouard Branly (1846–1940), French inventor of the first practical detector for wireless waves.

turned at last to the sequence of force; and thus it happened that, after ten years' pursuit, he found himself lying in the Gallery of Machines at the Great Exposition of 1900, his historical neck broken by the sudden irruption of forces totally new.

Since no one else showed much concern, an elderly person without other cares had no need to betray alarm. The year 1900 was not the first to upset schoolmasters. Copernicus and Galileo [5] had broken many professional necks about 1600; Columbus had stood the world on its head towards 1500; but the nearest approach to the revolution of 1900 was that of 310, when Constantine [6] set up the Cross. The rays that Langley disowned, as well as those which he fathered, were occult, supersensual, irrational; they were a revelation of mysterious energy like that of the Cross; they were what, in terms of mediæval science, were called immediate modes of the divine substance.

The historian was thus reduced to his last resources. Clearly if he was bound to reduce all these forces to a common value, this common value could have no measure but that of their attraction on his own mind. He must treat them as they had been felt; as convertible, reversible, interchangeable attractions on thought. He made up his mind to venture it; he would risk translating rays into faith. Such a reversible process would vastly amuse a chemist, but the chemist could not deny that he, or some of his fellow physicists, could feel the force of both. When Adams was a boy in Boston, the best chemist in the place had probably never heard of Venus except by way of scandal, or of the Virgin except as idolatry; neither had he heard of dynamos or automobiles or radium; yet his mind was ready to feel the force of all, though the rays were unborn and the women were dead.

Here opened another totally new education, which promised to be by far the most hazardous of all. The knife-edge along which he must crawl, like Sir Lancelot in the twelfth century,[7] divided two kingdoms of force which had nothing in common but attraction. They were as different as a magnet is from gravitation, supposing one knew what a magnet was, or gravitation, or love. The force of the Virgin was still felt at Lourdes,[8] and seemed to be as potent

5. Copernicus (1473–1543), Polish astronomer who promulgated the theory that the earth rotates in an orbit around the sun; Galileo (1564–1642), Italian astronomer and physicist, reaffirmed the Copernican system, although required to recant by the Inquisition.
6. According to legend, the Roman emperor Constantine (280?–337) saw a vision of the Cross, bearing the words, "In this sign conquer," and proclaimed Christianity throughout the Roman world.
7. Thus Lancelot freed Guinevere imprisoned in a castle, in Chrétien de Troyes' *Chevalier de la Charratte*.
8. A French town at the foot of the Pyrenees, visited by pilgrims for its spring of healing waters, where a peasant girl, Bernadette Soubirous, had a vision of the Virgin Mary.

as X-rays; but in America neither Venus nor Virgin ever had value as force—at most as sentiment. No American had ever been truly afraid of either.

This problem in dynamics gravely perplexed an American historian. The Woman had once been supreme; in France she still seemed potent, not merely as a sentiment, but as a force. Why was she unknown in America? For evidently America was ashamed of her, and she was ashamed herself, otherwise they would not have strewn fig-leaves so profusely all over her. When she was a true force, she was ignorant of fig-leaves, but the monthly-magazine-made American female had not a feature that would have been recognized by Adam. The trait was notorious, and often humorous, but any one brought up among Puritans knew that sex was sin. In any previous age, sex was strength. Neither art nor beauty was needed. Every one, even among Puritans, knew that neither Diana of the Ephesians nor any of the Oriental goddesses was worshipped for her beauty. She was goddess because of her force; she was the animated dynamo; she was reproduction—the greatest and most mysterious of all energies; all she needed was to be fecund. Singularly enough, not one of Adams's many schools of education had ever drawn his attention to the opening lines of Lucretius, though they were perhaps the finest in all Latin Literature, where the poet invoked Venus exactly as Dante invoked the Virgin:—

'Quæ quoniam rerum naturam *sola* gubernas.' [9]

The Venus of Epicurean philosophy survived in the Virgin of the Schools:

'Donna, sei tanto grande, e tanto vali,
Che qual vuol grazia, e a te non ricorre,
Sua disianza vuol volar senz' ali.' [1]

All this was to American thought as though it had never existed. The true American knew something of the facts, but nothing of the feelings; he read the letter, but he never felt the law. Before this historical chasm, a mind like that of Adams felt itself helpless; he turned from the Virgin to the Dynamo as though he were a Branly coherer. On one side, at the Louvre and at Chartres, as he

9. "Thou, since thou alone dost govern the nature of things" (*De Rerum Natura*, Book I, 21, by Lucretius, 95–51? B.C., Roman poet and Epicurean philosopher).

1. "Lady, thou art so great in all things / That he who wishes grace, and seeks not thee, / Would have his wish fly upwards without wings" (Dante, *Paradiso*, xxxiii, 13–15).

knew by the record of work actually done and still before his eyes, was the highest energy ever known to man, the creator of four-fifths of his noblest art, exercising vastly more attraction over the human mind than all the steam-engines and dynamos ever dreamed of; and yet this energy was unknown to the American mind. An American Virgin would never dare command; an American Venus would never dare exist.

The question, which to any plain American of the nineteenth century seemed as remote as it did to Adams, drew him almost violently to study, once it was posed; and on this point Langleys were as useless as though they were Herbert Spencers [2] or dynamos. The idea survived only as art. There one turned as naturally as though the artist were himself a woman. Adams began to ponder, asking himself whether he knew of any American artist who had ever insisted on the power of sex, as every classic had always done; but he could think only of Walt Whitman; Bret Harte, as far as the magazines would let him venture; and one or two painters, for the flesh-tones. All the rest had used sex for sentiment, never for force; to them, Eve was a tender flower, and Herodias [3] an unfeminine horror. American art, like the American language and American education, was as far as possible sexless. Society regarded this victory over sex as its greatest triumph, and the historian readily admitted it, since the moral issue, for the moment, did not concern one who was studying the relations of unmoral force. He cared nothing for the sex of the dynamo until he could measure its energy.

Vaguely seeking a clue, he wandered through the art exhibit, and, in his stroll, stopped almost every day before Saint-Gaudens's General Sherman,[4] which had been given the central post of honor. Saint-Gaudens himself was in Paris, putting on the work his usual interminable last touches, and listening to the usual contradictory suggestions of brother sculptors. Of all the American artists who gave to American art whatever life it breathed in the seventies, Saint-Gaudens was perhaps the most sympathetic, but certainly the most inarticulate. General Grant or Don Cameron [5] had scarcely less instinct of rhetoric than he. All the others—the Hunts, Richardson, John La Farge, Stanford White [6]—were ex-

---

2. Herbert Spencer (1820–1903), English thinker, welcomed Darwinism and coined the phrase "survival of the fittest."
3. Lustful wife of King Herod, responsible for the death of John the Baptist. *Cf.* Mark vi: 17–28.
4. Augustus Saint-Gaudens (1848–1907), Irish-born American sculptor; he created the memorial in Rock Creek Cemetery, Washington, D. C., which Henry Adams erected to his wife. The

Sherman statue on the Fifth Avenue Plaza in New York commemorates General William T. Sherman of Civil War fame.
5. James Donald Cameron (1833–1918), secretary of war in Grant's cabinet.
6. William Morris Hunt (1824–1879), Vermont painter, and his brother Richard Morris Hunt (1828–1895), architect; Henry Hobson Richardson (1838–1886), New York architect; John La

uberant; only Saint-Gaudens could never discuss or dilate on an emotion, or suggest artistic arguments for giving to his work the forms that he felt. He never laid down the law, or affected the despot, or became brutalized like Whistler [7] by the brutalities of his world. He required no incense; he was no egoist; his simplicity of thought was excessive; he could not imitate, or give any form but his own to the creations of his hand. No one felt more strongly than he the strength of other men, but the idea that they could affect him never stirred an image in his mind.

This summer his health was poor and his spirits were low. For such a temper, Adams was not the best companion, since his own gaiety was not *folle*; but he risked going now and then to the studio on Mont Parnasse to draw him out for a stroll in the Bois de Boulogne, or dinner as pleased his moods, and in return Saint-Gaudens sometimes let Adams go about in his company.

Once Saint-Gaudens took him down to Amiens, with a party of Frenchmen, to see the cathedral. Not until they found themselves actually studying the sculpture of the western portal, did it dawn on Adams's mind that, for his purposes, Saint-Gaudens on that spot had more interest to him than the cathedral itself. Great men before great monuments express great truths, provided they are not taken too solemnly. Adams never tired of quoting the supreme phrase of his idol Gibbon,[8] before the Gothic cathedrals: "I darted a contemptuous look on the stately monuments of superstition." Even in the footnotes of his history, Gibbon had never inserted a bit of humor more human than this, and one would have paid largely for a photograph of the fat little historian, on the background of Notre Dame of Amiens, trying to persuade his readers —perhaps himself—that he was darting a contemptuous look on the stately monument, for which he felt in fact the respect which every man of his vast study and active mind always feels before objects worthy of it; but besides the humor, one felt also the relation. Gibbon ignored the Virgin, because in 1789 religious monuments were out of fashion. In 1900 his remark sounded fresh and simple as the green fields to ears that had heard a hundred years of other remarks, mostly no more fresh and certainly less simple. Without malice, one might find it more instructive than a whole lecture of Ruskin.[9] One sees what one brings, and at that moment Gibbon brought the French Revolution. Ruskin brought

---

Farge (1835–1910), New York artist and author, who accompanied Adams to the South Seas in 1886; Stanford White (1853–1906), New York architect.
7. James Abbott McNeill Whistler (1834–1903), American portrait and landscape painter.

8. Edward Gibbon (1737–1794), English historian, author of *The History of the Decline and Fall of the Roman Empire*.
9. John Ruskin (1819–1900), English author who wrote on architecture and painting.

reaction against the Revolution. Saint-Gaudens had passed beyond all. He liked the stately monuments much more than he liked Gibbon or Ruskin; he loved their dignity; their unity; their scale; their lines; their lights and shadows; their decorative sculpture; but he was even less conscious than they of the force that creates it all—the Virgin, the Woman—by whose genius "the stately monuments of superstition" were built, through which she was expressed. He would have seen more meaning in Isis [1] with the cow's horns, at Edfoo,[2] who expressed the same thought. The art remained, but the energy was lost even upon the artist.

Yet in mind and person Saint-Gaudens was a survival of the 1500; he bore the stamp of the Renaissance, and should have carried an image of the Virgin round his neck, or stuck in his hat, like Louis XI.[3] In mere time he was a lost soul that had strayed by chance into the twentieth century, and forgotten where it came from. He writhed and cursed at his ignorance, much as Adams did at his own, but in the opposite sense. Saint-Gaudens was a child of Benvenuto Cellini,[4] smothered in an American cradle. Adams was a quintessence of Boston, devoured by curiosity to think like Benvenuto. Saint-Gaudens's art was starved from birth, and Adams's instinct was blighted from babyhood. Each had but half of a nature, and when they came together before the Virgin of Amiens they ought both to have felt in her the force that made them one; but it was not so. To Adams she became more than ever a channel of force; to Saint-Gaudens she remained as before a channel of taste.

For a symbol of power, Saint-Gaudens instinctively preferred the horse, as was plain in his horse and Victory of the Sherman monument. Doubtless Sherman also felt it so. The attitude was so American that, for at least forty years, Adams had never realized that any other could be in sound taste. How many years had he taken to admit a notion of what Michaelangelo and Rubens [5] were driving at? He could not say; but he knew that only since 1895 had he begun to feel the Virgin or Venus as force, and not everywhere even so. At Chartres—perhaps at Lourdes—possibly at Cnidos if one could still find there the divinely naked Aphrodite of Praxiteles [6]—but otherwise one must look for force to the goddesses of Indian mythology. The idea died out long ago in the German and English stock. Saint-Gaudens at Amiens was hardly less sensitive

1. Egyptian nature goddess.
2. Edfu, city on the upper Nile.
3. French king (1423–1483), who prayed fervently and resorted to astrologers and physicians for guidance during his final years.
4. Florentine goldsmith and sculptor (1500–1571); his *Autobiography* cele-brates a sexual dynamism.
5. Peter Paul Rubens (1577–1640), great painter of the Flemish school.
6. Greek sculptor (fourth century B.C.), whose statue of Aphrodite was placed in the temple at Cnidos in Asia Minor.

to the force of the female energy than Matthew Arnold at the Grand Chartreuse.[7] Neither of them felt goddesses as power—only as reflected emotion, human expression, beauty, purity, taste, scarcely even as sympathy. They felt a railway train as power; yet they, and all other artists, constantly complained that the power embodied in a railway train could never be embodied in art. All the steam in the world could not, like the Virgin, build Chartres.

Yet in mechanics, whatever the mechanicians might think, both energies acted as interchangeable forces on man, and by action on man all known force may be measured. Indeed, few men of science measured force in any other way. After once admitting that a straight line was the shortest distance between two points, no serious mathematician cared to deny anything that suited his convenience, and rejected no symbol, unproved or unproveable, that helped him to accomplish work. The symbol was force, as a compass-needle or a triangle was force, as the mechanist might prove by losing it, and nothing could be gained by ignoring their value. Symbol or energy, the Virgin had acted as the greatest force the Western world ever felt, and had drawn man's activities to herself more strongly than any other power, natural or super-natural, had ever done; the historian's business was to follow the track of the energy; to find where it came from and where it went to; its complex source and shifting channels; its values, equivalents, conversions. It could scarcely be more complex than radium; it could hardly be deflected, diverted, polarized, absorbed more perplexingly than other radiant matter. Adams knew nothing about any of them, but as a mathematical problem of influence on human progress, though all were occult, all reacted on his mind, and he rather inclined to think the Virgin easiest to handle.

The pursuit turned out to be long and tortuous, leading at last into the vast forests of scholastic science. From Zeno to Descartes, hand in hand with Thomas Aquinas, Montaigne, and Pascal,[8] one stumbled as stupidly as though one were still a German student of 1860. Only with the instinct of despair could one force one's self into this old thicket of ignorance after having been repulsed at a score of entrances more promising and more popular. Thus far, no path had led anywhere, unless perhaps to an exceedingly modest living. Forty-five years of study had proved to be quite futile for

---

7. English Victorian poet (1822–1888), who wrote of La Grande Chartreuse, the chief home of the Carthusian order until 1903. There Arnold felt himself, "Wandering between two worlds, one dead,/ The other powerless to be born" ("Stanzas from the Grande Chartreuse," 1855).
8. Zeno of Elea (fifth century B.C.), Greek philosopher whose paradoxes stimulated dialectics; René Descartes (1596–1650), French philosopher and mathematician, father of modern philosophy; St. Thomas Aquinas (1225?–1274), Italian philosopher and theologian; Michel de Montaigne (1533–1592), French essayist and liberal thinker; Blaise Pascal (1623–1662) French mathematician, physicist, and moralist.

the pursuit of power; one controlled no more force in 1900 than in 1850, although the amount of force controlled by society had enormously increased. The secret of education still hid itself somewhere behind ignorance, and one fumbled over it as feebly as ever. In such labyrinths, the staff is a force almost more necessary than the legs; the pen becomes a sort of blind-man's dog, to keep him from falling into the gutters. The pen works for itself, and acts like a hand, modelling the plastic material over and over again to the form that suits it best. The form is never arbitrary, but is a sort of growth like crystallization, as any artist knows too well; for often the pencil or pen runs into side-paths and shapelessness, loses its relations, stops or is bogged. Then it has to return on its trail, and recover, if it can, its line of force. The result of a year's work depends more on what is struck out than on what is left in; on the sequence of the main lines of thought, than on their play or variety. Compelled once more to lean heavily on this support, Adams covered more thousands of pages with figures as formal as though they were algebra, laboriously striking out, altering, burning, experimenting, until the year had expired, the Exposition had long been closed, and winter drawing to its end before he sailed from Cherbourg, on January 19, 1901 for home.

1907

WILLIAM VAUGHN MOODY

(1869–1910)

Moody's birth in 1869 coincided with that of Edwin Arlington Robinson and Edgar Lee Masters. Only one or two years their junior were Stephen Crane and Theodore Dreiser. Together with the older Hamlin Garland, these may be regarded as the literary generation which first broke the established pattern of the nineteenth century. They were a transitional generation, and the public mind was not yet ready to receive them. Crane died at twenty-nine and Moody at forty-one, but even those who lived experienced the postponement of recognition until after 1910. Moody might later have stood beside his friend Robinson in the poetry of the twentieth century; yet even with his maturity unfulfilled, he holds a permanent place in our literature because from the beginning his poetry was genuine, original, and representative of the problems of the age.

Born in Spencer, Indiana, the son of a steamboat pilot, he was of New England stock, and represents the cultural flux from East to West that characterized his age. The early death of his father threw family responsibilities upon him, and he helped support the family while intermittently attending school. But he was genuinely precocious, eager for books, especially literature, and filled with the "back-trailing" yearning for the East that then manifested itself in the life of the West, and in the adventures of such authors as Twain, Howells, Garland, and Dreiser. When at nineteen he came to New York State to teach in a college-preparatory school, he had already taught for three winters in the high school at Spencer. On a scholarship and borrowed funds he entered Harvard at twenty, finished the course brilliantly in three years, and was permitted to spend the fourth as a traveling tutor for two boys who visited Greece and the eastern Mediterranean area. In Moody were equally blended the Puritan orthodoxy of his American ancestors and the pagan spirit of Greek beauty; in addition he was deeply concerned with the social and philosophical issues of his age.

Returning from the Mediterranean countries by way of Switerzland and Germany, he received his A.B. from Harvard in 1893, and continued in graduate study. He became an instructor in English in 1894, and the next year accepted a call to join the new and vital English department at the University of Chicago. There he established himself in his profession, published studies of English authors, especially Milton, and wrote, with Robert Morss Lovett, an excellent history of English literature. He published a notable edition of Milton's poems, and also edited a volume of Homer and classroom selections of Scott and De Quincey. Meanwhile his poems were appearing in periodicals, representing a sensibility strongly divergent from that prevailing in the period. Although he was an exquisite lyrist, the critical spirit was also very active in his work, whether directed at social problems, as in "Gloucester Moors," or at the contemporary perplexity evoked by new scientific concepts, as in "The Menagerie"; or expressed through a new critical symbolism, which became prevalent only much later, as in "Thammuz." The utilization of myth and anthropology in that poem and others foreshadowed the complex poems of a period that had not yet dawned. On another level he was a brilliant satirist of public affairs, as shown in such poems as "Ode in Time of Hesitation" and "On a Soldier Fallen in the Philippines."

In 1900 his philosophical speculation culminated in a poetic drama, *The Masque of Judgment*; in 1901 he published his first collection of *Poems*; in 1903 he ventured to support himself by his pen alone, actuated by the compulsions of new inspiration and by the encouragement of a few friends—Robinson and Percy MacKaye, Josephine Preston Peabody, and others of their New York circle, with whom he spent holidays whenever he could be free to visit the new literary capital which was forming in Greenwich Village. During the remainder of his brief life he brought two plays to successful production—*A Sabine Woman* (1906, revised as *The Great Divide* 1909) and *The Faith Healer* (1909); he revised his lyrics and extended his *Masque of Judgment* into a trilogy. In this poetic drama, as in his popular prose plays, Moody attacked the ancient concept of a God of Wrath and the puritanical belief in man's original depravity, which, as he believed, resulted in a burden of guilt wholly inconsistent with the modern personality and knowledge; he substituted the authority of nature as the source of man's moral sense. His psychological and cultural concept of the centrality of woman, influenced by the pagan survival in Greek literature and Genesis, also provided a link between Whitman and twentieth-century literature. This theme permeated his larger works—the stage plays and the Miltonic *Masque of Judgment*.

John M. Manly edited *The Poems and Plays of William Vaughn Moody*, 1912; Daniel G. Mason edited *Some Letters of William Vaughn Moody*, 1913. A good edition of Moody's best poems is *Selected Poems of William Vaughn Moody*, edited by Robert Morss Lovett, 1931.

A thorough critical biography is Maurice F. Brown, *Estranging Dawn: The Life and Works of William Vaughn Moody*, 1973. Good general studies are David D. Henry, *William Vaughn Moody: A Study*, 1934, and Martin Halpern, *William Vaughn Moody*, 1964. The fullest treatment of Moody as a dramatist is Arthur H. Quinn, *A History of the American Drama from the Civil War to the Present Day*, revised edition, 1936, Vol. II, pp. 1–26. See also, Sculley Bradley, "The Emergence of the Modern Drama," in *Literary History of the United States*, edited by Robert E. Spiller, Willard Thorp, Thomas H. Johnson, and Henry Seidel Canby, 1948, Vol. II, pp. 1013–1015.

Gloucester Moors [1]

A mile behind is Gloucester town
Where the fishing fleets put in,
A mile ahead the land dips down
And the woods and farms begin.
Here, where the moors stretch free   5
In the high blue afternoon,
Are the marching sun and talking sea,
And the racing winds that wheel and flee
On the flying heels of June.

Jill-o'er-the-ground is purple blue,   10
Blue is the quaker-maid,
The wild geranium holds its dew
Long in the boulder's shade.
Wax-red hangs the cup
From the huckleberry boughs,   15

1. According to Robert Morss Lovett, the poet's friend (*Selected Poems of William Vaughn Moody*, p. 206), this poem had its inception during the summer of 1900, when Moody spent a vacation on Cape Ann, Massachusetts. He was fresh, as he said, from "the heart of the debtor's country," Chicago, where he had been teaching. This is the best known of the poems reflecting his literary connection with social protest and the reform movement. It was published in *Scribner's* for December, 1900, and collected in *Poems* (1901), which the present text follows.

In barberry bells the grey moths sup
Or where the choke-cherry lifts high up
Sweet bowls for their carouse.

Over the shelf of the sandy cove
Beach-peas blossom late.   20
By copse and cliff the swallows rove
Each calling to his mate.
Seaward the sea-gulls go,
And the land-birds all are here;
That green-gold flash was a vireo,   25
And yonder flame where the marsh-flags grow
Was a scarlet tanager.

This earth is not the steadfast place
We landsmen build upon;
From deep to deep she varies pace,   30
And while she comes is gone.
Beneath my feet I feel
Her smooth bulk heave and dip;
With velvet plunge and soft upreel
She swings and steadies to her keel   35
Like a gallant, gallant ship.

These summer clouds she sets for sail,
The sun is her masthead light,
She tows the moon like a pinnace [2] frail
Where her phosphor wake churns bright.   40
Now hid, now looming clear,
On the face of the dangerous blue
The star fleets tack and wheel and veer,
But on, but on does the old earth steer
As if her port she knew.   45

God, dear God! Does she know her port,
Though she goes so far about?
Or blind astray, does she make her sport
To brazen and chance it out?
I watched when her captains passed: 50
She were better captainless.
Men in the cabin, before the mast,
But some were reckless and some aghast,
And some sat gorged at mess.

By her battened hatch I leaned and caught   55
Sounds from the noisome hold,—

2. Small boat, accessory to a larger vessel, often towed behind.

Cursing and sighing of souls distraught
And cries too sad to be told.
Then I strove to go down and see;
But they said, "Thou art not of us!" 60
I turned to those on the deck with me
And cried, "Give help!" But they said, "Let be:
Our ship sails faster thus."

Jill-o'er-the-ground is purple blue,
Blue is the quaker-maid, 65
The alder-clump where the brook comes through
Breeds cresses in its shade.
To be out of the moiling street
With its swelter and its sin!
Who has given to me this sweet, 70
And given my brother dust to eat?
And when will his wage come in?

Scattering wide or blown in ranks,
Yellow and white and brown,
Boats and boats from the fishing banks 75
Come home to Gloucester town.
There is cash to purse and spend,
There are wives to be embraced,
Hearts to borrow and hearts to lend,
And hearts to take and keep to the end,— 80
O little sails, make haste!

But thou, vast outbound ship of souls,
What harbor town for thee?
What shapes, when thy arriving tolls,
Shall crowd the banks to see? 85
Shall all the happy shipmates then
Stand singing brotherly?
Or shall a haggard ruthless few
Warp [3] her over and bring her to,
While the many broken souls of men 90
Fester down in the slaver's pen,
And nothing to say or do?

1900, 1901

3. To move a vessel by hauling on a line attached to a buoy or some other fixed object.

The Menagerie [4]

Thank God my brain is not inclined to cut
Such capers every day! I'm just about
Mellow, but then—There goes the tent-flap shut.
Rain's in the wind. I thought so: every snout
Was twitching when the keeper turned me out.   5

That screaming parrot makes my blood run cold.
Gabriel's trump! [5] the big bull elephant
Squeals 'Rain!' to the parched herd. The monkeys scold,
And jabber that it's rain water they want.
(It makes me sick to see a monkey pant.)   10

I'll foot it home, to try and make believe
I'm sober. After this I stick to beer,
And drop the circus when the sane folks leave.
A man's a fool to look at things too near:
They look back, and begin to cut up queer.   15

Beasts do, at any rate; especially
Wild devils caged. They have the coolest way
Of being something else than what you see:
You pass a sleek young zebra nosing hay,
A nylghau [6] looking bored and distingué,—   20

And think you've seen a donkey and a bird.
Not on your life! Just glance back, if you dare.
The zebra chews, the nylghau hasn't stirred;
But something's happened, Heaven knows what or where
To freeze your scalp and pompadour your hair.   25

I'm not precisely an æolian lute [7]
Hung in the wandering winds of sentiment,
But drown me if the ugliest, meanest brute
Grunting and fretting in that sultry tent
Didn't just floor me with embarrassment!   30

---

4. Moody resisted the pessimistic determinism of his generation, which reflected the materialistic interpretation of Darwinian evolution, both in smaller poems and on the larger scale of the dramas *The Great Divide* and *The Faith Healer*. In his poetic trilogy, *The Masque of Judgment*, he extended his attack to include the older Christian fundamentalist orthodoxy with its deterministic dogma of original sin. "The Menagerie" first appeared in *Poems* (1901), from which the present text is taken.
5. The trumpet of the last resurrection (Isaiah xxvii: 13). Gabriel, an archangel, usually a herald or divine messenger, became associated with this trumpet in the Jewish and Christian traditions.
6. The large Indian antelope.
7. Usually, "aeolian harp"; a stringed musical instrument producing tones when the wind blows across it.

'Twas like a thunder-clap from out the clear,—
One minute they were circus beasts, some grand,
Some ugly, some amusing, and some queer:
Rival attractions to the hobo band,
The flying jenny,[8] and the peanut stand.   35

Next minute they were old hearth-mates of mine!
Lost people, eyeing me with such a stare!
Patient, satiric, devilish, divine;
A gaze of hopeless envy, squalid care,
Hatred, and thwarted love, and dim despair.   40

Within my blood my ancient kindred spoke,—
Grotesque and monstrous voices, heard afar
Down ocean caves when behemoth [9] awoke,
Or through fern forests roared the plesiosaur [1]
Locked with the giant-bat in ghastly war.   45

And suddenly, as in a flash of light,
I saw great Nature working out her plan;
Through all her shapes from mastodon to mite
Forever groping, testing, passing on
To find at last the shape and soul of Man.   50

Till in the fullness of accomplished time,
Comes brother Forepaugh,[2] upon business bent,
Tracks her through frozen and through torrid clime,
And shows us, neatly labeled in a tent,
The stages of her huge experiment;   55

Blabbing aloud her shy and reticent hours;
Dragging to light her blinking, slothful moods;
Publishing fretful seasons when her powers
Worked wild and sullen in her solitudes,
Or when her mordant laughter shook the woods.   60

Here, round about me, were her vagrant births;
Sick dreams she had, fierce projects she essayed;
Her qualms, her fiery prides, her crazy mirths;
The troublings of her spirit as she strayed,
Cringed, gloated, mocked, was lordly, was afraid,   65

---

8. A small merry-go-round.
9. See Job xl: 15, where the behemoth is represented as a sort of colossal hippopotamus.
1. The plesiosaurus was a marine reptile of the age of dinosaurs, having a very long neck, small head, and limbs developed as paddles for swimming.
2. Adam Forepaugh was proprietor of a traveling circus and menagerie, popular in the nineties.

On that long road she went to seek mankind;
Here were the darkling coverts that she beat
To find the Hider she was sent to find;
Here the distracted footprints of her feet
Whereby her soul's Desire she came to greet.   70

But why should they, her botch-work, turn about
And stare disdain at me, her finished job?
Why was the place one vast suspended shout
Of laughter? Why did all the daylight throb
With soundless guffaw and dumb-stricken sob?   75

Helpless I stood among those awful cages;
The beasts were walking loose, and I was bagged!
I, I, last product of the toiling ages,
Goal of heroic feet that never lagged,—
A little man in trousers, slightly jagged.[3]   80

Deliver me from such another jury!
The Judgment Day will be a picnic to't.
Their satire was more dreadful than their fury,
And worst of all was just a kind of brute
Disgust, and giving up, and sinking mute.   85

Survival of the fittest, adaptation,
And all their other evolution terms,
Seem to omit one small consideration,
To wit, that tumblebugs and angleworms
Have souls: there's soul in everything that squirms.   90

And souls are restless, plagued, impatient things,
All dream and unaccountable desire;
Crawling, but pestered with the thought of wings;
Spreading through every inch of earth's old mire
Mystical hanker after something higher.   95

Wishes *are* horses, as I understand.
I guess a wistful polyp that has strokes
Of feeling faint to gallivant on land
Will come to be a scandal to his folks;
Legs he will sprout, in spite of threats and jokes.   100

And at the core of every life that crawls,
Or runs or flies or swims or vegetates—
Churning the mammoth's heart-blood, in the galls

3. A slang expression then current for "intoxicated."

Of shark and tiger planting gorgeous hates,
Lighting the love of eagles for their mates;   105

Yes, in the dim brain of the jellied fish
That is and is not living—moved and stirred
From the beginning a mysterious wish,
A vision, a command, a fatal Word:
The name of Man was uttered, and they heard.   110

Upward along the æons of old war
They sought him: wing and shank-bone, claw and bill
Were fashioned and rejected; wide and far
They roamed the twilight jungles of their will;
But still they sought him, and desired him still.   115

Man they desired, but mind you, Perfect Man,
The radiant and the loving, yet to be!
I hardly wonder, when they came to scan
The upshot of their strenuosity,
They gazed with mixed emotions upon *me*.   120

Well, my advice to you is, Face the creatures,
Or spot them sideways with your weather eye,
Just to keep tab on their expansive features;
It isn't pleasant when you're stepping high
To catch a giraffe smiling on the sly.   125

If nature made you graceful, don't get gay
Back-to before the hippopotamus;
If meek and godly, find some place to play
Besides right where three mad hyenas fuss:
You may hear language that we won't discuss.   130

If you're a sweet thing in a flower-bed hat,
Or her best fellow with your tie tucked in,
Don't squander love's bright springtime girding at
An old chimpanzee with an Irish chin:
There may be hidden meaning in his grin.   135

1901

On a Soldier Fallen in the Philippines [4]

Streets of the roaring town,
Hush for him, hush, be still!
He comes, who was stricken down

4. Cuba's conflict with Spain (1896–
1901) over independence was supported
by American liberals who believed in
self-determination. However, the war in
the Philippines reflected escalation of
"manifest destiny" into Pacific areas;

Doing the word of our will.
Hush! Let him have his state, 5
Give him his soldier's crown.
The grists of trade can wait
Their grinding at the mill,
But he cannot wait for his honor, now the trumpet has been blown;
Wreathe pride now for his granite brow, lay love on his breast
of stone. 10

Toll! Let the great bells toll
Till the clashing air is dim.
Did we wrong this parted soul?
We will make up it to him.
Toll! Let him never guess 15
What work we set him to.
Laurel, laurel, yes;
He did what we bade him do.
Praise, and never a whispered hint but the fight he fought was good;
Never a word that the blood on his sword was his country's own
heart's-blood. 20

A flag for the soldier's bier
Who dies that his land may live;
O, banners, banners here,
That he doubt not nor misgive!
That he heed not from the tomb 25
The evil days draw near
When the nation, robed in gloom,
With its faithless past shall strive.
Let him never dream that his bullet's scream went wide of its
island mark,
Home to the heart of his darling land where she stumbled and
sinned in the dark. 30

1901, 1912

---

the result of Admiral Dewey's victory at Manila was American occupation of the Philippines. American liberals also were concerned about the fate of the Filipino Emilio Aguinaldo, who had succeeded in establishing a popular government two years before the fall of the flimsy Spanish power in 1898 and who continued to maintain his government, as elected president, in spite of harassment by American-supported guerrillas. Moody represented the outraged liberal opinion in two poems still well known. In "An Ode in Time of Hesitation" (*Atlantic Monthly*, May, 1900) satire was derived from the image of the Saint-Gaudens statue in Boston of a Civil War colonel, Robert Gould Shaw. Shaw had recruited the first Negro regiment for the Northern army, which he led until he was killed in action at Ft. Wagner, S. C. (1863), and was buried in one grave with his comrades. The companion poem printed below, "On a Soldier Fallen in the Philippines" (*Atlantic Monthly*, February, 1901) reverses the image—the soldier was fighting against freedom, not for it. President Aguinaldo had been captured and was in American custody only one month later. The text is that of *The Poems and Plays*, 1912.

Realism and Naturalism: The Turn of the Century

STEPHEN CRANE

(1871–1900)

Among the *avant-garde* writers of the 1890's, Crane was most clearly the herald of the twentieth-century revolution in literature. Had he written *Maggie: A Girl of the Streets* (1893) or *The Red Badge of Courage* (1895) twenty-five years later, he would still have been as much a pioneer as Sherwood Anderson then was. Even more than Garland, Norris, Dreiser, or Robinson—his contemporaries—he made a clean break with the past in his selection of material, his craftsmanship, and his point of view. It was his nature to be experimental. At twenty he wrote *Maggie*, our first completely naturalistic novel. By the age of twenty-four he had produced, in his earliest short stories and his masterpiece, *The Red Badge of Courage*, the first examples of modern American impressionism. That year, in his collected poems, he was the first to respond to the radical genius of Emily Dickinson, and the re-sult was a volume of imagist impressionism twenty years in advance of the official imagists. He was in every respect phenomenal. At twenty-two, a failure in newspaper reporting, he was living from hand to mouth and borrowing money to have *Maggie* printed; at twenty-four he was the author of a classic that was then, and still is, a best seller; at twenty-five he was a star feature writer for a great syndicate; and before he reached his twenty-ninth birthday he was dead, leaving writings that filled twelve volumes in a collected edition.

The fourteenth and youngest child of a Methodist minister, Stephen Crane was born on November 1, 1871, in Newark, New Jersey. During his first ten years the family lived in Jersey City, Bloomington, and Paterson, New Jersey and finally in Port Jervis, New York, giving him the experience of small-city and small-town life which he utilized in his *Whilomville Stories*. In 1880 his father died, and after several removals the family settled in 1882 at Asbury Park, a New Jersey resort town. There an older brother, Townley Crane, ran a news-reporting agency, and gave Stephen Crane his first newspaper experience, as a reporter of vacation news. He attended school at nearby Pennington Academy and later at the Hudson River Institute, a military academy at Claverock, New York. His abilities were then chiefly observable on the baseball diamond, and his apprenticeship on small-town sand lots and at preparatory school led, in college, to brief athletic distinction. After a term each at Lafayette and at Syracuse (1890–1891) he brought his college days to an end, and relieved his family of a financial burden that they could not sustain.

Crane was apparently a born writer, and he turned to newspaper work as the natural and expedient means to earn a living. While in college he had sold sketches to the Detroit *Free Press* and during the summers he had written news for his brother. However, in the three years from 1892 until the publication of *The Red Badge of Courage* he experienced professional difficulty and economic hardship. He was simply not adapted to doing the factual reporting of routine assignments then required of the cub newsman. While still in college, during "two days before Christmas," 1891, he had written the first draft of *Maggie*, but newspaper reporting was something else. Editors were not impressed by news stories in which sense impressions and atmospheric touches triumphed over factual detail. He was reduced to hack writing "on space," placing feature stories individually wherever he could, principally in the New York *Tribune*. In this free-lance experience he came to know the mean streets and the poverty-ridden slums of New York and the adjacent New Jersey cities; indeed, himself very poor, he lived for several years in such places. He had not found a publisher for *Maggie*, now rewritten, and in 1893 he borrowed seven hundred dollars from his brother and paid for a private printing. In yellow paper wrappers, under the pseudonym of "Johnston Smith" it appeared that year as *Maggie: A Girl of the Streets*, and it did not sell. But it was noticed by Hamlin Garland, who became the friend of the younger man, helped him to find markets for his sketches, and called the attention of Howells to the serial publication of *The Red Badge of Courage* in 1894. *Maggie* was regularly published in 1896. Crane's professional worries were over, for his high abilities as a feature writer and special correspondent needed only initial recognition to secure him a position in journalism.

Crane's first two novels, and the short stories that he was already writing, were faithful to an expressed creed which, if it came more directly from good journalism than from close study of the European naturalists, produced much the same results in practice. He was convinced that if a story is transcribed in its actuality, as it appeared to occur in life, it will convey its own emotional weight without sentimental heightening, moralizing, or even interpretive comment. This view coincided with what he knew of the objective method by which the French naturalists achieved a correspondence between their style and their materials; and he was initially in agreement with the naturalistic belief that the destiny of human beings, like the biological fate of other creatures, is so much determined by factors beyond the control of individual will or choice that ethical judgment or moral comment by the author is irrelevant or impertinent. His example, however, found little response until the next century, when Dreiser and Sherwood Anderson, Hemingway, Dos Passos, and many others were illustrating the same viewpoint.

Maggie is not a great book, but its terrifying picture of brutality and degradation in the New York slums was unique for its time. *The Red Badge of Courage* employs the same technique to show the actualities of war, in this case, the Battle of Chancellorsville. Written by a man who had had no battle experience but whose imagination quickly absorbed the tales of Civil War veterans and the dramatic reality of Matthew Brady's photographs of combat, the story has continued to convince veterans of two world wars. First appearing in the Philadelphia

Press in 1894, the following year, with the help of Howells, it was published in book form and was immediately successful. Crane's subsequent experience reporting the Spanish-American and Graeco-Turkish wars for American and British newspapers resulted in such fine volumes as *The Little Regiment* (1896), *The Open Boat and other Tales of Adventure* (1898), and *Wounds in the Rain: War Stories* (1900). His tour of the West and Mexico in 1895 resulted in such famous western stories as "The Blue Hotel" and "The Bride Comes to Yellow Sky." His other major volumes include *George's Mother* (1896), *The Monster and Other Stories* (1899), *Whilomville Stories* (1900)—the last two being collections of short stories—and his poems: *The Black Riders and Other Lines* (1895), and *War is Kind* (1899).

Threatened with tuberculosis, he settled for a time in England, where he became the friend of Conrad, James, Barrie, Wells, and others, but his ill health demanded further seclusion and he went to Germany, where he died at Badenweiler on June 5, 1900.

The earlier standard editions—*The Works of Stephen Crane*, 12 vols., 1925–1927, and *The Collected Poems of Stephen Crane*, 1930, both edited by Wilson Follett—are now being superseded by the CEAA *University of Virginia Edition of the Works of Stephen Crane*, 10 vols., in progress. Robert W. Stallman has edited *Stephen Crane: An Omnibus*, 1952. Olov W. Fryckstedt edited *Stephen Crane: Uncollected Writings*, 1963, and Thomas Gullason has edited the *Complete Short Stories and Sketches*, 1963 and *The Complete Novels*, 1967. *The Sullivan*

County Sketches of Stephen Crane was edited by Melvin Schoberlin, 1949, and *Stephen Crane Letters*, 1960, were edited by R. W. Stallman and Lillian Gilkes. R. W. Stallman edited *Stephen Crane: Sullivan County Tales and Sketches*, 1968. Joseph Katz edited *The Poems of Stephen Crane: A Critical Edition*, 1966. The most exhaustive biography is R. W. Stallman, *Stephen Crane: A Biography*, 1968. Other biographies are Thomas Beer, *Stephen Crane: A Study in American Letters*, 1923, and John Berryman, *Stephen Crane*, 1950. E. H. Cady edited C. K. Linson's reminiscences, *My Stephen Crane*, 1958, and wrote the biography *Stephen Crane*, 1962. Daniel G. Hoffman gives a critical evaluation in *The Poetry of Stephen Crane*, 1957. Eric Solomon's *Stephen Crane in England: A Portrait of the Artist*, appeared in 1965, and his *Stephen Crane: From Parody to Realism* in 1966. A. W. Williams and Vincent Starrett edited *Stephen Crane: A Bibliography*, 1948. Recent studies include Eric Solomon, *Stephen Crane: From Parody to Realism*, 1966; Jean Cazemajou, *Stephen Crane: Ecrivain-journaliste, 1871–1900*, 1969; Marston LaFrance, *A Reading of Stephen Crane*, 1971; and Milne Holton, *The Fiction and Journalistic Writing of Stephen Crane*, 1972.

The Bride Comes to Yellow Sky [1]

I

The great Pullman was whirling onward with such dignity of motion that a glance from the window seemed simply to prove that the plains of Texas were pouring eastward. Vast flats of green grass, dull-hued spaces of mesquit and cactus, little groups of frame houses, woods of light and tender trees, all were sweeping into the east, sweeping over the horizon, a precipice.

A newly married pair had boarded this coach at San Antonio. The man's face was reddened from many days in the wind and sun, and a direct result of his new black clothes was that his brick-coloured hands were constantly performing in a most conscious fashion. From time to time he looked down respectfully at his attire. He sat with a hand on each knee, like a man waiting in a barber's shop. The glances he devoted to other passengers were furtive and shy.

The bride was not pretty, nor was she very young. She wore a dress of blue cashmere, with small reservations of velvet here and there, and with steel buttons abounding. She continually twisted her head to regard her puff sleeves, very stiff, straight, and high. They embarrassed her. It was quite apparent that she had cooked, and that she expected to cook, dutifully. The blushes caused by

1. In January, 1895, Crane went west for a four-month tour as a roving correspondent for Irving Bacheller's syndicate, which was successfully serializing the first publication of *The Red Badge of Courage*. From Nebraska through Texas to Mexico, he experienced and mentally photographed the last of the authentic and turbulent West, soon to pass into the folk myth of the nation. In that brief period, he absorbed the evanescent and pervasive qualities of the human encounter with a primitive environment and reported it with an exuberant fidelity matched only by such pictorial artists as Frederic Remington or Charles Graham. From the western trip came such classics as "The Blue Hotel," "Horses—One Dash," and the present selection which first appeared in *McClure's Magazine*, X, 4 (February, 1898) and was collected in *The Open Boat and Other Tales of Adventure*, New York, 1898.

the careless scrutiny of some passengers as she had entered the car were strange to see upon this plain, under-class countenance, which was drawn in placid, almost emotionless lines.

They were evidently very happy. "Ever been in a parlour-car before?" he asked, smiling with delight.

"No," she answered; "I never was. It's fine, ain't it?"

"Great! And then after a while we'll go forward to the diner, and get a big lay-out. Finest meal in the world. Charge a dollar."

"Oh, do they?" cried the bride. "Charge a dollar? Why, that's too much—for us—ain't it, Jack?"

"Not this trip, anyhow," he answered bravely. "We're going to go the whole thing."

Later he explained to her about the trains. "You see, it's a thousand miles from one end of Texas to the other; and this train runs right across it, and never stops but four times." He had the pride of an owner. He pointed out to her the dazzling fittings of the coach; and in truth her eyes opened wider as she contemplated the sea-green figured velvet, the shining brass, silver, and glass, the wood that gleamed as darkly brilliant as the surface of a pool of oil. At one end a bronze figure sturdily held a support for a separated chamber, and at convenient places on the ceiling were frescos in olive and silver.

To the minds of the pair, their surroundings reflected the glory of their marriage that morning in San Antonio; this was the environment of their new estate; and the man's face in particular beamed with an elation that made him appear ridiculous to the Negro porter. This individual at times surveyed them from afar with an amused and superior grin. On other occasions he bullied them with skill in ways that did not make it exactly plain to them that they were being bullied. He subtly used all the manners of the most unconquerable kind of snobbery. He oppressed them; but of this oppression they had small knowledge, and they speedily forgot that infrequently a number of travellers covered them with stares of derisive enjoyment. Historically there was supposed to be something infinitely humorous in their situation.

"We are due in Yellow Sky at 3:42," he said, looking tenderly into her eyes.

"Oh, are we?" she said, as if she had not been aware of it. To evince surprise at her husband's statement was part of her wifely amiability. She took from a pocket a little silver watch; and as she held it before her, and stared at it with a frown of attention, the new husband's face shone.

"I bought it in San Anton' from a friend of mine," he told her gleefully.

"It's seventeen minutes past twelve," she said, looking up at him with a kind of shy and clumsy coquetry. A passenger, noting this play, grew excessively sardonic, and winked at himself in one of the numerous mirrors.

At last they went to the dining-car. Two rows of Negro waiters, in glowing white suits, surveyed their entrance with the interest, and also the equanimity, of men who had been forewarned. The pair fell to the lot of a waiter who happened to feel pleasure in steering them through their meal. He viewed them with the manner of a fatherly pilot, his countenance radiant with benevolence. The patronage, entwined with the ordinary deference, was not plain to them. And yet, as they returned to their coach, they showed in their faces a sense of escape.

To the left, miles down a long purple slope, was a little ribbon of mist where moved the keening Rio Grande. The train was approaching it at an angle, and the apex was Yellow Sky. Presently it was apparent that, as the distance from Yellow Sky grew shorter, the husband became commensurately restless. His brick-red hands were more insistent in their prominence. Occasionally he was even rather absent-minded and far-away when the bride leaned forward and addressed him.

As a matter of truth, Jack Potter was beginning to find the shadow of a deed weigh upon him like a leaden slab. He, the town marshal of Yellow Sky, a man known, liked, and feared in his corner, a prominent person, had gone to San Antonio to meet a girl he believed he loved, and there, after the usual prayers, had actually induced her to marry him, without consulting Yellow Sky for any part of the transaction. He was now bringing his bride before an innocent and unsuspecting community.

Of course people in Yellow Sky married as it pleased them, in accordance with a general custom; but such was Potter's thought of his duty to his friends, or of their idea of his duty, or of an unspoken form which does not control men in these matters, that he felt he was heinous. He had committed an extraordinary crime. Face to face with this girl in San Antonio, and spurred by his sharp impulse, he had gone headlong over all the social hedges. At San Antonio he was like a man hidden in the dark. A knife to sever any friendly duty, any form, was easy to his hand in that remote city. But the hour of Yellow Sky—the hour of daylight—was approaching.

He knew full well that his marriage was an important thing to his town. It could only be exceeded by the burning of the new hotel. His friends could not forgive him. Frequently he had reflected on the advisability of telling them by telegraph, but a new cowardice had been upon him. He feared to do it. And now the train was hurrying him toward a scene of amazement, glee, and reproach. He glanced out of the window at the line of haze swinging slowly in toward the train.

Yellow Sky had a kind of brass band, which played painfully, to the delight of the populace. He laughed without heart as he thought of it. If the citizens could dream of his prospective arrival with his bride, they would parade the band at the station and escort them, amid cheers and laughing congratulations, to his adobe home.

He resolved that he would use all the devices of speed and plainscraft in making the journey from the station to his house. Once within that safe citadel, he could issue some sort of vocal bulletin, and then not go among the citizens until they had time to wear off a little of their enthusiasm.

The bride looked anxiously at him. "What's worrying you, Jack?"

He laughed again. "I'm not worrying, girl; I'm only thinking of Yellow Sky."

She flushed in comprehension.

A sense of mutual guilt invaded their minds and developed a finer tenderness. They looked at each other with eyes softly aglow. But Potter often laughed the same nervous laugh; the flush upon the bride's face seemed quite permanent.

The traitor to the feelings of Yellow Sky narrowly watched the speeding landscape. "We're nearly there," he said.

Presently the porter came and announced the proximity of Potter's home. He held a brush in his hand, and, with all his airy superiority gone, he brushed Potter's new clothes as the latter slowly turned this way and that way. Potter fumbled out a coin and gave it to the porter, as he had seen others do. It was a heavy and muscle-bound business, as that of a man shoeing his first horse.

The porter took their bag, and as the train began to slow they moved forward to the hooded platform of the car. Presently the two engines and their long string of coaches rushed into the station of Yellow Sky.

"They have to take water here," said Potter, from a constricted throat and in mournful cadence, as one announcing death. Before the train stopped his eye had swept the length of the platform, and he was glad and astonished to see there was none upon it but the station-agent, who, with a slightly hurried and anxious air, was walking toward the water-tanks. When the train had halted, the porter alighted first, and placed in position a little temporary step.

"Come on, girl," said Potter, hoarsely. As he helped her down they each laughed on a false note. He took the bag from the Negro, and bade his wife cling to his arm. As they slunk rapidly away, his hang-dog glance perceived that they were unloading the two trunks, and also that the station-agent, far ahead near the baggage-car, had turned and was running toward him, making gestures. He laughed, and groaned as he laughed, when he noted the first effect of his marital bliss upon Yellow Sky. He gripped his wife's arm firmly to his side, and they fled. Behind them the porter stood, chuckling fatuously.

II

The California express on the Southern Railway was due at Yellow Sky in twenty-one minutes. There were six men at the bar of the Weary Gentleman saloon. One was a drummer who talked a great deal and rapidly; three were Texans who did not care to talk at that time; and two were Mexican sheepherders, who did not talk as a general practice in the Weary Gentleman saloon. The barkeeper's dog lay on the board walk that crossed in front of the door. His head was on his paws, and he glanced drowsily here and there with the constant vigilance of a dog that is kicked on occasion. Across the sandy street were some vivid green grass-plots, so wonderful in appearance, amid the sands that burned near them in a blazing sun, that they caused a doubt in the mind. They exactly resembled the grass mats used to represent lawns on the stage. At the cooler end of the railway station, a man without a coat sat in a tilted chair and smoked his pipe. The fresh-cut bank of the Rio Grande circled near the town, and there could be seen beyond it a great plum-coloured plain of mesquit.

Save for the busy drummer and his companions in the saloon, Yellow Sky was dozing. The new-comer leaned gracefully upon the bar, and recited many tales with the confidence of a bard who has come upon a new field.

"—and at the moment that the old man fell downstairs with the bureau in his arms, the old woman was coming up with two scuttles of coal, and of course—"

The drummer's tale was interrupted by a young man who suddenly appeared in the open door. He cried: "Scratchy Wilson's drunk, and has turned loose with both hands." The two Mexicans at once set down their glasses and faded out of the rear entrance of the saloon.

The drummer, innocent and jocular, answered: "All right, old man. S'pose he has? Come in and have a drink, anyhow."

But the information had made such an obvious cleft in every skull in the room that the drummer was obliged to see its importance. All had become instantly solemn. "Say," said he, mystified, "what is this?" His three companions made the introductory gesture of eloquent speech; but the young man at the door forestalled them.

"It means, my friend," he answered, as he came into the saloon, "that for the next two hours this town won't be a health resort."

The barkeeper went to the door, and locked and barred it; reaching out of the window, he pulled in heavy wooden shutters, and barred them. Immediately a solemn, chapel-like gloom was upon the place. The drummer was looking from one to another.

"But say," he cried, "what is this, anyhow? You don't mean there is going to be a gun-fight?"

"Don't know whether there'll be a fight or not," answered one man grimly; "but there'll be some shootin'—some good shootin'."

The young man who had warned them waved his hand. "Oh, there'll be a fight fast enough, if any one wants it. Anybody can get a fight out there in the street. There's a fight just waiting."

The drummer seemed to be swayed between the interest of a foreigner and a perception of personal danger.

"What did you say his name was?" he asked.

"Scratchy Wilson," they answered in chorus.

"And will he kill anybody? What are you going to do? Does this happen often? Does he rampage around like this once a week or so? Can he break in that door?"

"No; he can't break down that door," replied the barkeeper. "He's tried it three times. But when he comes you'd better lay down on the floor, stranger. He's dead sure to shoot at it, and a bullet may come through."

Thereafter the drummer kept a strict eye upon the door. The time had not yet been called for him to hug the floor, but, as a minor precaution, he sidled near to the wall. "Will he kill anybody?" he said again.

The men laughed low and scornfully at the question.

"He's out to shoot, and he's out for trouble. Don't see any good in experimentin' with him."

"But what do you do in a case like this? What do you do?"

A man responded: "Why, he and Jack Potter—"

"But," in chorus the other men interrupted, "Jack Potter's in San Anton'."

"Well, who is he? What's he got to do with it?"

"Oh, he's the town marshal. He goes out and fights Scratchy when he gets on one of these tears."

"Wow!" said the drummer, mopping his brow. "Nice job he's got."

The voices had toned away to mere whisperings. The drummer wished to ask further questions, which were born of an increasing anxiety and bewilderment; but when he attempted them, the men merely looked at him in irritation and motioned him to remain silent. A tense waiting hush was upon them. In the deep shadows of the room their eyes shone as they listened for sounds from the street. One man made three gestures at the barkeeper; and the latter, moving like a ghost, handed him a glass and a bottle. The man poured a full glass of whisky, and set down the bottle noiselessly. He gulped the whisky in a swallow, and turned again toward the door in immovable silence. The drummer saw that the barkeeper, without a sound, had taken a Winchester from beneath the bar. Later he saw this individual beckoning to him, so he tiptoed across the room.

"You better come with me back of the bar."

"No, thanks," said the drummer, perspiring; "I'd rather be where I can make a break for the back door."

Whereupon the man of bottles made a kindly but peremptory gesture. The drummer obeyed it, and, finding himself seated on a box with his head below the level of the bar, balm was laid upon his soul at sight of various zinc and copper fittings that bore a resemblance to armour-plate. The barkeeper took a seat comfortably upon an adjacent box.

"You see," he whispered, "this here Scratchy Wilson is a wonder with a gun—a perfect wonder; and when he goes on the war-trail, we hunt our holes—naturally. He's about the last one of the old gang that used to hang out along the river here. He's a terror when he's drunk. When he's sober he's all right—kind of simple —wouldn't hurt a fly—nicest fellow in town. But when he's drunk —whoo!"

There were periods of stillness. "I wish Jack Potter was back from San Anton'," said the barkeeper. "He shot Wilson up once—in the leg—and he would sail in and pull out the kinks in this thing."

Presently they heard from a distance the sound of a shot, followed by three wild yowls. It instantly removed a bond from the men in the darkened saloon. There was a shuffling of feet. They looked at each other. "Here he comes," they said.

III

A man in a maroon-coloured flannel shirt, which had been purchased for purposes of decoration, and made principally by some Jewish women on the East Side of New York, rounded a corner and walked into the middle of the main street of Yellow Sky. In either hand the man held a long, heavy, blue-black revolver. Often he yelled, and these cries rang through a semblance of a deserted village, shrilly flying over the roofs in a volume that seemed to have no relation to the ordinary vocal strength of a man. It was as if the surrounding stillness formed the arch of a tomb over him. These cries of ferocious challenge rang against walls of silence. And his boots had red tops with gilded imprints, of the kind beloved in winter by little sledding boys on the hillsides of New England.

The man's face flamed in a rage begot of whisky. His eyes,

rolling, and yet keen for ambush, hunted the still doorways and windows. He walked with the creeping movement of the midnight cat. As it occurred to him, he roared menacing information. The long revolvers in his hands were as easy as straws; they were moved with an electric swiftness. The little fingers of each hand played sometimes in a musician's way. Plain from the low collar of the shirt, the cords of his neck straightened and sank, straightened and sank, as passion moved him. The only sounds were his terrible invitations. The calm adobes preserved their demeanour at the passing of this small thing in the middle of the street.

There was no offer of fight—no offer of fight. The man called to the sky. There were no attractions. He bellowed and fumed and swayed his revolvers here and everywhere.

The dog of the barkeeper of the Weary Gentleman saloon had not appreciated the advance of events. He yet lay dozing in front of his master's door. At sight of the dog, the man paused and raised his revolver humorously. At sight of the man, the dog sprang up and walked diagonally away, with a sullen head, and growling. The man yelled, and the dog broke into a gallop. As it was about to enter an alley, there was a loud noise, a whistling, and something spat the ground directly before it. The dog screamed, and, wheeling in terror, galloped headlong in a new direction. Again there was a noise, a whistling, and sand was kicked viciously before it. Fear-stricken, the dog turned and flurried like an animal in a pen. The man stood laughing, his weapons at his hips.

Ultimately the man was attracted by the closed door of the Weary Gentleman saloon. He went to it and, hammering with a revolver, demanded drink.

The door remaining imperturbable, he picked a bit of paper from the walk, and nailed it to the framework with a knife. He then turned his back contemptuously upon this popular resort and, walking to the opposite side of the street and spinning there on his heel quickly and lithely, fired at the bit of paper. He missed it by a half-inch. He swore at himself, and went away. Later he comfortably fusilladed the windows of his most intimate friend. The man was playing with this town; it was a toy for him.

But still there was no offer of fight. The name of Jack Potter, his ancient antagonist, entered his mind, and he concluded that it would be a glad thing if he should go to Potter's house, and by bombardment induce him to come out and fight. He moved in the direction of his desire, chanting Apache scalp-music.

When he arrived at it, Potter's house presented the same still front as had the other adobes. Taking up a strategic position, the man howled a challenge. But this house regarded him as might a great stone god. It gave no sign. After a decent wait, the man howled further challenges, mingling with them wonderful epithets.

Presently there came the spectacle of a man churning himself into deepest rage over the immobility of a house. He fumed at it as the winter wind attacks a prairie cabin in the North. To the distance there should have gone the sound of a tumult like the fighting of two hundred Mexicans. As necessity bade him, he paused for breath or to reload his revolvers.

IV

Potter and his bride walked sheepishly and with speed. Sometimes they laughed together shamefacedly and low.

"Next corner, dear," he said finally.

They put forth the efforts of a pair walking bowed against a strong wind. Potter was about to raise a finger to point the first appearance of the new home when, as they circled the corner, they came face to face with a man in a maroon-coloured shirt, who was feverishly pushing cartridges into a large revolver. Upon the instant the man dropped his revolver to the ground and, like lightning, whipped another from its holster. The second weapon was aimed at the bridegroom's chest.

There was a silence. Potter's mouth seemed to be merely a grave for his tongue. He exhibited an instinct to at once loosen his arm from the woman's grip, and he dropped the bag to the sand. As for the bride, her face had gone as yellow as old cloth. She was a slave to hideous rites, gazing at the apparitional snake.

The two men faced each other at a distance of three paces. He of the revolver smiled with a new and quiet ferocity.

"Tried to sneak up on me," he said. "Tried to sneak up on me!" His eyes grew more baleful. As Potter made a slight movement, the man thrust his revolver venomously forward. "No; don't you do it, Jack Potter. Don't you move a finger toward a gun just yet. Don't you move an eyelash. The time has come for me to settle with you, and I'm goin' to do it my own way, and loaf along with no interferin'. So if you don't want a gun bent on you, just mind what I tell you."

Potter looked at his enemy. "I ain't got a gun on me Scratchy," he said. "Honest, I ain't." He was stiffening and steadying, but yet somewhere at the back of his mind a vision of the Pullman floated: the sea-green figured velvet, the shining brass, silver, and glass, the wood that gleamed as darkly brilliant as the surface of a pool on oil—all the glory of the marriage, the environment of the new estate. "You know I fight when it comes to fighting, Scratchy Wilson; but I ain't got a gun on me. You'll have to do all the shootin' yourself."

His enemy's face went livid. He stepped forward, and lashed his weapon to and fro before Potter's chest. "Don't you tell me you ain't got no gun on you, you whelp. Don't tell me no lie like that. There ain't a man in Texas ever seen you without no gun. Don't take me for no kid." His eyes blazed with light, and his throat worked like a pump.

"I ain't takin' you for no kid," answered Potter. His heels had not moved an inch backward. "I'm takin' you for a damn fool. I tell you I ain't got a gun, and I ain't. If you're goin' to shoot me up, you better begin now; you'll never get a chance like this again."

So much enforced reasoning had told on Wilson's rage; he was calmer. "If you ain't got a gun, why ain't you got a gun?" he sneered. "Been to Sunday-school?"

"I ain't got a gun because I've just come from San Anton' with my wife. I'm married," said Potter. "And if I'd thought there was going to be any galoots like you prowling around when I brought my wife home, I'd had a gun, and don't you forget it."

"Married!" said Scratchy, not at all comprehending.

"Yes, married. I'm married," said Potter, distinctly.

"Married?" said Scratchy. Seemingly for the first time, he saw the drooping, drowning woman at the other man's side. "No!" he said. He was like a creature allowed a glimpse of another world. He moved a pace backward, and his arm, with the revolver, dropped to his side. "Is this the lady?" he asked.

"Yes; this is the lady," answered Potter.

There was another period of silence.

"Well," said Wilson at last, slowly, "I s'pose it's all off now."

"It's all off if you say so, Scratchy. You know I didn't make the trouble." Potter lifted his valise.

"Well, I 'low it's off, Jack," said Wilson. He was looking at the ground. "Married!" He was not a student of chivalry; it was merely that in the presence of this foreign condition he was a simple child of the earlier plains. He picked up his starboard revolver, and, placing both weapons in their holsters, he went away. His feet made funnel-shaped tracks in the heavy sand.

1898

THEODORE DREISER

(1871–1945)

Often termed the pioneer of naturalism in American letters, Theodore Dreiser equally deserves a place in our literature for his vigorous attack on the genteel tradition and his long and active interest in American social problems. His naturalism, different from Stephen Crane's, reflects a mechanistic concept of life; yet his portrayal of character shows the realization that human aspirations reflect spiritual sources which are gravely thwarted by the impulse to survive and by the consequent goals of economic society. In his compassion Dreiser is closer to Thomas Hardy's naturalism than to Zola's, his reputed archetype. These contrasting elements are present in all his fiction, from *Sister Carrie* (1900) to *The Bulwark* (1946).

Exceptionally responsive to environment, Dreiser found more than the usual stimulus for his writing in the disparity between the rich and the poor, the cultured sophisticate and the provincial, and the powerful and the weak members of society. The shattering effect of nineteenth-century science on traditional religious and social patterns, the emergence of new power groups, and the development of new theories in economics and political science vitally affected his writing.

One of several children of German immigrant parents, Dreiser was born in Terre Haute, Indiana, and his early years were a series of exposures to poverty, emotional instability, and religious bigotry in the home, and of frequent moves dictated by financial necessity. By the time he entered Indiana University, which he attended for one year, the young man was understandably in a state of bewilderment and rebellion that made him eager for independence and financial success. The newspaper world offered an avenue of escape that led from the St. Louis *Globe-Democrat* to

Chicago and Pittsburgh. He learned the profession of journalism, by which he later earned a living, from several magazines, notably the Butterick publications and the brilliant, satirical *American Spectator* (1932–1937), in association with such younger stars as G. J. Nathan, Ernest Boyd, Cabell, O'Neill, and Sherwood Anderson.

It is difficult for present-day readers to understand why *Sister Carrie* should have encountered difficulties in publication in 1900. Well-known naturalistic European novels were bolder and more explicit in depicting immorality and spiritual decay. But Dreiser dared write what people had often observed but did not wish to admit explicitly: that men and women do not always suffer in this life for transgressions of the social and moral code. The same circumstances that leave Carrie apparently untouched send Hurstwood to destruction; later Lester Kane in *Jennie Gerhardt* escapes, while Jennie suffers from their relationship.

This apparent helplessness in the face of inscrutable laws of fate and nature is the most obvious characteristic of Dreiser's fiction, but the years that followed the publication of *Jennie Gerhardt* in 1911 saw the development of other aspects of his philosophy as well. In the Cowperwood trilogy—*The Financier* (1912), *The Titan* (1914), and the posthumously published *The Stoic* (1947)—all based on the life of Charles T. Yerkes, he explored the emotional and social ambitions of one of America's most startling financial buccaneers. The trilogy continues to impress successive generations as a great creative work and a magnificent literary reconstruction of modern economic society, sustained as it is by the amoral combination of financial and political power epitomized in the ruthless tactics of a man who had few illusions and deliberately set out to conquer life with the weapons of cleverness, dishonesty, and ambition. The autobiographical volumes, *A Book About Myself* —retitled *Newspaper Days*— (1922) and *Dawn* (1931), reveal the author's early confusions, his struggles to find a successful pattern for life, and his groping for an explanation of the disparity between man's desires and his ultimate accomplishment. *The "Genius"* (1915), an account of an artist's life, is useful for its thinly disguised autobiographical descriptions of Dreiser's efforts to gain a literary foothold in New York.

In 1925 he published his best-known volume, *An American Tragedy*, an impressive work which became for a generation of Americans a synonym for literary naturalism. Dreiser utilized an actual murder as the basis of an exhaustive portrayal of a young man's tragic attempt to make a place for himself in a world whose demands he was incapable of meeting. The resolution—showing that Clyde Griffiths' crime was the result of environmental factors over which his weak nature had little control, and that society, with its aggressive materialism, was at the bar of judgment along with the criminal—was a powerful fictional appraisal of fundamental modern dilemmas.

While charges of verboseness and lack of integration of characters can be made against Dreiser, these defects result from his photographic realism. His insistence that the writer, as clinician of the forces of nature, must report life as he sees it, and therefore must have freedom to do so, has had an immeasurable influence on younger writers and an even greater though less tangible impact on American life.

Dreiser's works, in addition to the novels mentioned above, include the accounts of his travels in the United States and Russia, *A Traveller at Forty*, 1913; *A Hoosier Holiday*, 1916; and *Dreiser Looks at Russia*, 1928. Borden Deal has edited *The Tobacco Man: A Novel Based on Notes by Theodore Dreiser and Hy Kraft*, 1965. His plays were collected in *Plays of the Natural and the Supernatural*, 1916; and *The Hand of the Potter*, 1918. His short stories appeared in *Free and Other Stories*, 1918; and *Chains*, 1927. *Twelve Men*, 1919, is a series of sketches of friends and acquaintances; and *A Gallery of Women*, 1929, is a semifictional account of the personalities of various women. *Hey Rub-a-Dub-Dub*, 1920, is a series of philosophical essays. His poems appeared as *Moods, Cadenced and Declaimed*, 1926. Robert Palmer Saalbach edited *Selected Poems*, 1969. Other less important volumes are *The Color of a Great City*, 1923; *My City*, 1929; *The Aspirant*, 1929; *Epitaph*, 1929; *Fine Furniture*, 1930; and *Tragic America*, 1931.

Critical biographies are Robert H. Elias, *Theodore Dreiser: Apostle of Nature*, 1949, F. O. Matthiessen, *Theodore Dreiser*, 1951, and W. A. Swanberg's *Dreiser*, 1965. Of biographical interest is Helen Dreiser, *My Life With Dreiser*, 1951, and Marguerite Tjader, *Theodore Dreiser: A New Dimension*, 1965, also reminiscences. Robert H. Elias has edited *Letters of Theodore Dreiser*, 3 vols., 1959. Recent critical studies include John J. McAleer, *Theodore Dreiser: An Introduction and Interpretation*, 1968; Richard Lehan, *Theodore Dreiser: His World and His Novels*, 1969; Ellen Moers, *Two Dreisers*, 1969; and Robert Penn Warren, *Homage to Theodore Dreiser*, 1971.

The Second Choice [1]

SHIRLEY DEAR:

You don't want the letters. There are only six of them, anyhow, and think, they're all I have of you to cheer me on my travels. What good would they be to you—little bits of notes telling me you're sure to meet me—but me—think of me! If I send them to you, you'll tear them up, whereas if you leave them with me I can dab them with musk and ambergris and keep them in a little silver box, always beside me.

Ah, Shirley dear, you really don't know how sweet I think you are, how dear! There isn't a thing we have ever done together that isn't as clear in my mind as this great big skyscraper over the way here in Pittsburgh, and far more pleasing. In fact, my thoughts of you are the most precious and delicious things I have, Shirley.

But I'm too young to marry now. You know that, Shirley, don't you? I haven't placed myself in any way yet, and I'm so restless that I don't know whether I ever will, really. Only yesterday, old Roxbaum—that's my new employer here—came to me and wanted to know if I would like an assistant overseership on one of his coffee plantations in Java, said there would not be much money in it for a year or two, a bare living, but later there would be more—and I jumped at it. Just the thought of Java and going there did that, although I knew I could make more staying right here. Can't you see how it is with me, Shirl? I'm too restless and too young. I couldn't take care of you right, and you wouldn't like me after a while if I didn't.

But ah, Shirley sweet, I think the dearest things of you! There isn't an hour, it seems, but some little bit of you comes back— a dear, sweet bit—the night we sat on the grass in Tregore Park and counted the stars through the trees; that first evening at Sparrows Point when we missed the last train and had to walk to Langley. Remember the tree-toads, Shirl? And then that warm April Sunday in Atholby woods! Ah, Shirley, you don't want the six notes! Let me keep them. But think of me, will you, sweet, wherever you go and whatever you do? I'll always think of you, and wish that you had met a better, saner man than me, and that I really could have married you and been all you wanted me to be. By-by, sweet. I may start for Java within the month. If so, and you would want them, I'll send you some cards from there— if they have any.

Your worthless,

ARTHUR.

1. First printed in *Cosmopolitan* magazine, February 1918, this story was collected in *Free and Other Stories*, 1918.

She sat and turned the letter in her hand, dumb with despair. It was the very last letter she would ever get from him. Of that she was certain. He was gone now, once and for all. She had written him only once, not making an open plea but asking him to return her letters, and then there had come this tender but evasive reply, saying nothing of a possible return but desiring to keep her letters for old times' sake—the happy hours they had spent together.

The happy hours! Oh, yes, yes, yes—the happy hours!

In her memory now, as she sat here in her home after the day's work, meditating on all that had been in the few short months since he had come and gone, was a world of color and light—a color and a light so transfiguring as to seem celestial, but now, alas, wholly dissipated. It had contained so much of all she had desired —love, romance, amusement, laughter. He had been so gay and thoughtless, or headstrong, so youthfully romantic, and with such a love of play and change and to be saying and doing anything and everything. Arthur could dance in a gay way, whistle, sing after a fashion, play. He could play cards and do tricks, and he had such a superior air, so genial and brisk, with a kind of innate courtesy in it and yet an intolerance for slowness and stodginess or anything dull or dingy, such as characterized— But here her thoughts fled from him. She refused to think of any one but Arthur.

Sitting in her little bedroom now, off the parlor on the ground floor in her home in Bethune Street, and looking out over the Kessels' yard, and beyond that—there being no fences in Bethune Street—over the "yards" or lawns of the Pollards, Bakers, Cryders, and others, she thought of how dull it must all have seemed to him, with his fine imaginative mind and experiences, his love of change and gayety, his atmosphere of something better than she had ever known. How little she had been fitted, perhaps, by beauty or temperament to overcome this—the something—dullness in her work or her home, which possibly had driven him away. For, although many had admired her to date, and she was young and pretty in her simple way and constantly receiving suggestions that her beauty was disturbing to some, still, he had not cared for her —he had gone.

And now, as she meditated, it seemed that this scene, and all that it stood for—her parents, her work, her daily shuttling to and fro between the drug company for which she worked and this street and house—was typical of her life and what she was destined to endure always. Some girls were so much more fortunate. They had fine clothes, fine homes, a world of pleasure and opportunity in which to move. They did not have to scrimp and save and work to pay their own way. And yet she had always been compelled to do it, but had never complained until now—or until he came, and after. Bethune Street, with its commonplace front yards and houses nearly all alike, and this house, so like the others, room for room and porch for porch, and her parents, too, really like all the others, had seemed good enough, quite satisfactory, indeed, until then. But now, now!

Here, in their kitchen, was her mother, a thin, pale, but kindly woman, peeling potatoes and washing lettuce, and putting a bit of steak or a chop or a piece of liver in a frying-pan day after day, morning and evening, month after month, year after year. And next door was Mrs. Kessel doing the same thing. And next door Mrs. Cryder, And next door Mrs. Pollard. But, until now, she had not thought it so bad. But now—now—oh! And on all the porches or lawns all along this street were the husbands and fathers, mostly middle-aged or old men like her father, reading their papers or cutting the grass before dinner, or smoking and meditating afterward. Her father was out in front now, a stooped, forbearing, meditative soul, who had rarely anything to say—leaving it all to his wife, her mother, but who was fond of her in his dull, quiet way. He was a pattern-maker by trade, and had come into possession of this small, ordinary home via years of toil and saving, her mother helping him. They had no particular religion, as he often said, thinking reasonably human conduct a sufficient passport to heaven, but they had gone occasionally to the Methodist Church over in Nicholas Street, and she had once joined it. But of late she had not gone, weaned away by the other commonplace pleasures of her world.

And then in the midst of it, the dull drift of things, as she now saw them to be, he had come—Arthur Bristow—young, energetic, good-looking, ambitious, dreamful, and instanter, and with her never knowing quite how, the whole thing had been changed. He had appeared so swiftly—out of nothing, as it were.

Previous to him had been Barton Williams, stout, phlegmatic, good-natured, well-meaning, who was, or had been before Arthur came, asking her to marry him, and whom she allowed to half assume that she would. She had liked him in a feeble, albeit, as she thought, tender way, thinking him the kind, according to the logic of her neighborhood, who would make her a good husband, and, until Arthur appeared on the scene, had really intended to marry him. It was not really a love-match, as she saw now, but she thought it was, which was much the same thing, perhaps. But, as she now recalled, when Arthur came, how the scales fell from her eyes! In a trice, as it were, nearly, there was a new heaven and a new earth. Arthur had arrived, and with him a sense of something different.

Mabel Gove had asked her to come over to her house in West-leigh, the adjoining suburb, for Thanksgiving eve and day, and without a thought of anything, and because Barton was busy handling a part of the work in the despatcher's office of the Great Eastern and could not see her, she had gone. And then, to her surprise and strange, almost ineffable delight, the moment she had seen him, he was there—Arthur, with his slim, straight figure and dark hair and eyes and clean-cut features, as clean and attractive as those of a coin. And as he had looked at her and smiled and narrated humorous bits of things that had happened to him, something had come over her—a spell—and after dinner they had all gone round to Edith Barringer's to dance, and there as she had danced with him, somehow, without any seeming boldness on his part, he had taken possession of her, as it were, drawn her close, and told her she had beautiful eyes and hair and such a delicately rounded chin, and that he thought she danced gracefully and was sweet. She had nearly fainted with delight.

"Do you like me?" he had asked in one place in the dance, and, in spite of herself, she had looked up into his eyes, and from that moment she was almost mad over him, could think of nothing else but his hair and eyes and his smile and his graceful figure.

Mabel Gove had seen it all, in spite of her determination that no one should, and on their going to bed later, back at Mabel's home, she had whispered:

"Ah, Shirley, I saw. You like Arthur, don't you?"

"I think he's very nice," Shirley recalled replying, for Mabel knew of her affair with Barton and liked him, "but I'm not crazy over him." And for this bit of treason she had sighed in her dreams nearly all night.

And the next day, true to a request and a promise made by him, Arthur had called again at Mabel's to take her and Mabel to a "movie" which was not so far away, and from there they had gone to an ice-cream parlor, and during it all, when Mabel was not looking, he had squeezed her arm and hand and kissed her neck, and she had held her breath, and her heart had seemed to stop.

"And now you're going to let me come out to your place to see you, aren't you?" he had whispered.

And she had replied, "Wednesday evening," and then written the address on a little piece of paper and given it to him.

But now it was all gone, gone!

This house, which now looked so dreary—how romantic it had seemed that first night *he* called—the front room with its commonplace furniture, and later in the spring, the veranda, with its vines just sprouting, and the moon in May. Oh, the moon in May, and June and July, when he was here! How she had lied to Barton to make evenings for Arthur, and occasionally to Arthur to keep him from contact with Barton. She had not even mentioned Barton to Arthur because—because—well, because Arthur was so much better, and somehow (she admitted it to herself now) she had not been sure that Arthur would care for her long, if at all, and then—well, and then, to be quite frank, Barton might be good enough. She did not exactly hate him because she had found Arthur—not at all. She still liked him in a way—he was so kind and faithful, so very dull and straightforward and thoughtful of her, which Arthur was certainly not. Before Arthur had appeared, as she well remembered, Barton had seemed to be plenty good enough—in fact, all that she desired in a pleasant, companionable way, calling for her, taking her places, bringing her flowers and candy, which Arthur rarely did, and for that, if nothing more, she could not help continuing to like him and to feel sorry for him, and besides, as she had admitted to herself before, if Arthur had left her—. . . . . Weren't his parents better off than hers—and hadn't he a good position for such a man as he—one hundred and fifty dollars a month and the certainty of more later on? A little while before meeting Arthur, she had thought this very good, enough for two to live on at least, and she had thought some of trying it at some time or other—but now—now——

And that first night he had called—how well she remembered it—how it had transfigured the parlor next this in which she was now, filling it with something it had never had before, and the porch outside, too, for that matter, with its gaunt, leafless vine, and this street, too, even—dull, commonplace Bethune Street. There had been a flurry of snow during the afternoon while she was working at the store, and the ground was white with it. All the neighboring homes seemed to look sweeter and happier and more inviting than ever they had as she came past them, with their lights peeping from under curtains and drawn shades. She had hurried into hers and lighted the big red-shaded parlor lamp, her one artistic treasure, as she thought, and put it near the piano, between it and the window, and arranged the chairs, and then bustled to the task of making herself as pleasing as she might. For him she had gotten out her one best filmy house dress and done up her hair in the fashion she thought most becoming—and that he had not seen before—and powdered her cheeks and nose and darkened her eyelashes, as some of the girls at the store did, and put on her new gray satin slippers, and then, being so arrayed, waited nervously, unable to eat anything or to think of anything but him.

And at last, just when she had begun to think he might not be coming, he had appeared with that arch smile and a "Hello! It's here you live, is it? I was wondering. George, but you're twice as sweet as I thought you were, aren't you?" And then, in the little entryway, behind the closed door, he had held her and kissed her on the mouth a dozen times while she pretended to push against his coat and struggle and say that her parents might hear.

And, oh, the room afterward, with him in it in the red glow of the lamp, and with his pale handsome face made handsomer thereby, as she thought! He had made her sit near him and had held her hands and told her about his work and his dreams—all that he expected to do in the future—and then she had found herself wishing intensely to share just such a life—his life—anything that he might wish to do; only, she kept wondering, with a slight pain, whether he would want her to—he was so young, dreamful, ambitious, much younger and more dreamful than herself, although, in reality, he was several years older.

And then followed that glorious period from December to this late September, in which everything which was worth happening in love had happened. Oh, those wondrous days the following spring, when, with the first burst of buds and leaves, he had taken her one Sunday to Atholby, where all the great woods were, and they had hunted spring beauties in the grass, and sat on a slope and looked at the river below and watched some boys fixing up a sailboat and setting forth in it quite as she wished she and Arthur might be doing—going somewhere together—far, far away from all commonplace things and life! And then he had slipped his arm about her and kissed her cheek and neck, and tweaked her ear and smoothed her hair—and oh, there on the grass, with the spring flowers about her and a canopy of small green leaves above, the perfection of love had come—love so wonderful that the mere thought of it made her eyes brim now! And then had been days, Saturday afternoons and Sundays, at Atholby and Sparrows Point, where the great beach was, and in lovely Tregore Park, a mile or two from her home, where they could go of an evening and sit in or near the pavilion and have ice-cream and dance or watch the dancers. Oh, the stars, the winds, the summer breath of those days! Ah, me! Ah, me!

Naturally, her parents had wondered from the first about her and Arthur, and her and Barton, since Barton had already assumed a proprietary interest in her and she had seemed to like him. But then she was an only child and a pet, and used to presuming on that, and they could not think of saying anything to her. After all, she was young and pretty and was entitled to change her mind; only, only—she had had to indulge in a career of lying and subterfuge in connection with Barton, since Arthur was headstrong and wanted every evening that he chose—to call for her at the store and keep her down-town to dinner and a show.

Arthur had never been like Barton, shy, phlegmatic, obedient, waiting long and patiently for each little favor, but, instead, masterful and eager, rifling her of kisses and caresses and every delight of love, and teasing and playing with her as a cat would a mouse. She could never resist him. He demanded of her her time and her affection without let or hindrance. He was not exactly selfish or cruel, as some might have been, but gay and unthinking at times, unconsciously so, and yet loving and tender at others—nearly always so. But always he would talk of things in the future as if they really did not include her—and this troubled her greatly—of places he might go, things he might do, which, somehow, he seemed to think or assume that she could not or would not do with him. He was always going to Australia sometime, he thought, in a business way, or to South Africa, or possibly to India. He never seemed to have any fixed clear future for himself in mind.

A dreadful sense of helplessness and of impending disaster came over her at these times, of being involved in some predicament over which she had no control, and which would lead her on to some sad end. Arthur, although plainly in love, as she thought, and apparently delighted with her, might not always love her. She began, timidly at first (and always, for that matter), to ask him pretty, seeking questions about himself and her, whether their future was certain to be together, whether he really wanted her— loved her—whether he might not want to marry some one else or just her, and whether she wouldn't look nice in a pearl satin wedding-dress with a long creamy veil and satin slippers and a bouquet of bridal-wreath. She had been so slowly but surely saving to that end, even before he came, in connection with Barton; only, after *he* came, all thought of the import of it had been transferred to him. But now, also, she was beginning to ask herself sadly, "Would it ever be?" He was so airy, so inconsequential, so ready to say: "Yes, yes," and "Sure, sure! That's right! Yes, indeedy; you bet! Say, kiddie, but you'll look sweet!" But, somehow, it had always seemed as if this whole thing were a glorious interlude and that it could not last. Arthur was too gay and ethereal and too little settled in his own mind. His ideas of travel and living in different cities, finally winding up in New York or San Francisco, but never with her exactly until she asked him, was too ominous, although he always reassured her gaily: "Of course! Of course!" But somehow she could never believe it really, and it made her intensely sad at times, horribly gloomy. So often she wanted to cry, and she could scarcely tell why.

And then, because of her intense affection for him, she had finally quarreled with Barton, or nearly that, if one could say that one ever really quarreled with him. It had been because of a certain Thursday evening a few weeks before about which she had disap-

pointed him. In a fit of generosity, knowing that Arthur was coming Wednesday, and because Barton had stopped in at the store to
see her, she had told him that he might come, having regretted it
afterward, so enamored was she of Arthur. And then when Wednesday came, Arthur had changed his mind, telling her he would come
Friday instead, but on Thursday evening he had stopped in at the
store and asked her to go to Sparrows Point, with the result that
she had no time to notify Barton. He had gone to the house and
sat with her parents until ten-thirty, and then, a few days later, although she had written him offering an excuse, had called at the
store to complain slightly.

"Do you think you did just right, Shirley? You might have sent
word, mightn't you? Who was it—the new fellow you won't tell
me about?"

Shirley flared on the instant.

"Supposing it was? What's it to you? I don't belong to you yet,
do I? I told you there wasn't any one, and I wish you'd let me
alone about that. I couldn't help it last Thursday—that's all—and
I don't want you to be fussing with me—that's all. If you don't
want to, you needn't come any more, anyhow."

"Don't say that, Shirley," pleaded Barton. "You don't mean
that. I won't bother you, though, if you don't want me any more."

And because Shirley sulked, not knowing what else to do, he
had gone and she had not seen him since.

And then sometime later when she had thus broken with Barton, avoiding the railway station where he worked, Arthur had
failed to come at his appointed time, sending no word until the
next day, when a note came to the store saying that he had been
out of town for his firm over Sunday and had not been able to
notify her, but that he would call Tuesday. It was an awful blow.
At the time, Shirley had a vision of what was to follow. It seemed
for the moment as if the whole world had suddenly been reduced
to ashes, that there was nothing but black charred cinders anywhere—she felt that about all life. Yet it all came to her clearly
then that this was but the beginning of just such days and just
such excuses, and that soon, soon, he would come no more. He was
beginning to be tired of her and soon he would not even make
excuses. She felt it, and it froze and terrified her.

And then, soon after, the indifference which she feared did
follow—almost created by her own thoughts, as it were. First, it
was a meeting he had to attend somewhere on Wednesday night
when he was to have come for her. Then he was going out of town
again, over Sunday. Then he was going away for a whole week—it
was absolutely unavoidable, he said, his commercial duties were increasing—and once he had casually remarked that nothing could

stand in the way where she was concerned—never! She did not think of reproaching him with this; she was too proud. If he was going, he must go. She would not be willing to say to herself that she had never attempted to hold any man. But, just the same, she was agonized by the thought. When he was with her, he seemed tender enough; only, at times, his eyes wandered and he seemed slightly bored. Other girls, particularly pretty ones, seemed to interest him as much as she did.

And the agony of the long days when he did not come any more for a week or two at a time! The waiting, the brooding, the wondering, at the store and here in her home—in the former place making mistakes at times because she could not get her mind off him and being reminded of them, and here at her own home at nights, being so absent-minded that her parents remarked on it. She felt sure that her parents must be noticing that Arthur was not coming any more, or as much as he had—for she pretended to be going out with him, going to Mabel Gove's instead—and that Barton had deserted her too, he having been driven off by her indifference, never to come any more, perhaps, unless she sought him out.

And then it was that the thought of saving her own face by taking up with Barton once more occurred to her, of using him and his affections and faithfulness and dulness, if you will, to cover up her own dilemma. Only, this ruse was not to be tried until she had written Arthur this one letter—a pretext merely to see if there was a single ray of hope, a letter to be written in a gentle-enough way and asking for the return of the few notes she had written him. She had not seen him now in nearly a month, and the last time she had, he had said he might soon be compelled to leave her awhile—to go to Pittsburgh to work. And it was his reply to this that she now held in her hand—from Pittsburgh! It was frightful! The future without him!

But Barton would never know really what had transpired, if she went back to him. In spite of all her delicious hours with Arthur, she could call him back, she felt sure. She had never really entirely dropped him, and he knew it. He had bored her dreadfully on occasion, arriving on off days when Arthur was not about, with flowers or candy, or both, and sitting on the porch steps and talking of the railroad business and of the whereabouts and doings of some of their old friends. It was shameful, she had thought at times, to see a man so patient, so hopeful, so good-natured as Barton, deceived in this way, and by her, who was so miserable over another. Her parents must see and know, she had thought at these times, but still, what else was she to do?

"I'm a bad girl," she kept telling herself. "I'm all wrong. What right have I to offer Barton what is left?" But still, somehow, she realized that Barton, if she chose to favor him, would only to be too grateful for even the leavings of others where she was concerned, and that even yet, if she but designed to crook a finger, she could have him. He was so simple, so good-natured, so stolid and matter of fact, so different to Arthur whom (she could not help smiling at the thought of it) she was loving now about as Barton loved her— slavishly, hopelessly.

And then, as the days passed and Arthur did not write any more —just this one brief note—she at first grieved horribly, and then in a fit of numb despair attempted, bravely enough from one point of view, to adjust herself to the new situation. Why should she despair? Why die of agony where there were plenty who would still sigh for her—Barton among others? She was young, pretty, very—many told her so. She could, if she chose, achieve a vivacity which she did not feel. Why should she brook this unkindness without a thought of retaliation? Why shouldn't she enter upon a gay and heartless career, indulging in a dozen flirtations at once— dancing and kill all thoughts of Arthur in a round of frivolities? There were many who beckoned to her. She stood at her counter in the drug store on many a day and brooded over this, but at the thought of which one to begin with, she faltered. After her late love, all were so tame, for the present anyhow.

And then—and then—always there was Barton, the humble or faithful, to whom she had been so unkind and whom she had used and whom she still really liked. So often self-reproaching thoughts in connection with him crept over her. He must have known, must have seen how badly she was using him all this while, and yet he had not failed to come and come, until she had actually quarreled with him, and any one would have seen that it was literally hopeless. She could not help remembering, especially now in her pain, that he adored her. He was not calling on her now at all—by her indifference she had finally driven him away—but a word, a word—She waited for days, weeks, hoping against hope, and then——

The office of Barton's superior in the Great Eastern terminal had always made him an easy object for her blandishments, coming and going, as she frequently did, via this very station. He was in the office of the assistant train-despatcher on the ground floor, where passing to and from the local, which, at times, was quicker than a street-car, she could easily see him by peering in; only, she had carefully avoided him for nearly a year. If she chose now, and would call for a message-blank at the adjacent telegraph-window which was a part of his room, and raised her voice as she often had in the past, he could scarcely fail to hear, if he did not see her.

And if he did, he would rise and come over—of that she was sure, for he never could resist her. It had been a wile of hers in the old days to do this or to make her presence felt by idling outside. After a month of brooding, she felt that she must act—her position as a deserted girl was too much. She could not stand it any longer really—the eyes of her mother, for one.

It was six-fifteen one evening when, coming out of the store in which she worked, she turned her step disconsolately homeward. Her heart was heavy, her face rather pale and drawn. She had stopped in the store's retiring-room before coming out to add to her charms as much as possible by a little powder and rouge and to smooth her hair. It would not take much to reallure her former sweetheart, she felt sure—and yet it might not be so easy after all. Suppose he had found another? But she could not believe that. It had scarcely been long enough since he had last attempted to see her, and he was really so very, very fond of her and so faithful. He was too slow and certain in his choosing—he had been so with her. Still, who knows? With this thought, she went forward in the evening, feeling for the first time the shame and pain that comes of deception, the agony of having to relinquish an ideal and the feeling of despair that comes to those who find themselves in the position of suppliants, stooping to something which in better days and better fortune they would not know. Arthur was the cause of this.

When she reached the station, the crowd that usually filled it at this hour was swarming. There were so many pairs like Arthur and herself laughing and hurrying away or so she felt. First glancing in the small mirror of a weighing scale to see if she were still of her former charm, she stopped thoughtfully at a little flower stand which stood outside, and for a few pennies purchased a tiny bunch of violets. She then went inside and stood near the window, peering first furtively to see if he were present. He was. Bent over his work, a green shade over his eyes, she could see his stolid, genial figure at a table. Stepping back a moment to ponder, she finally went forward and, in a clear voice, asked,

"May I have a blank, please?"

The infatuation of the discarded Barton was such that it brought him instantly to his feet. In his stodgy, stocky way he rose, his eyes glowing with a friendly hope, his mouth wreathed in smiles, and came over. At the sight of her, pale, but pretty—paler and prettier, really, than he had ever seen her—he thrilled dumbly.

"How are you, Shirley?" he asked sweetly, as he drew near, his eyes searching her face hopefully. He had not seen her for so long that he was intensely hungry, and her paler beauty appealed to him more than ever. Why wouldn't she have him? he was asking himself. Why wouldn't his persistent love yet win her? Perhaps it might. "I haven't seen you in a month of Sundays, it seems. How are the folks?"

"They're all right, Bart," she smiled archly, "and so am I. How have you been? It has been a long time since I've seen you. I've been wondering how you were. Have you been all right? I was just going to send a message."

As he had approached, Shirley had pretended at first not to see him, a moment later to affect surprise, although she was really suppressing a heavy sigh. The sight of him, after Arthur, was not reassuring. Could she really interest herself in him any more? Could she?

"Sure, sure," he replied genially; "I'm always all right. You couldn't kill me, you know. Not going away, are you, Shirl?" he queried interestedly.

"No; I'm just telegraphing to Mabel. She promised to meet me to-morrow, and I want to be sure she will."

"You don't come past here as often as you did, Shirley," he complained tenderly. "At least, I don't seem to see you so often," he added with a smile. "It isn't anything I have done, is it?" he queried, and then, when she protested quickly, added: "What's the trouble, Shirl? Haven't been sick, have you?"

She affected all her old gaiety and ease, feeling as though she would like to cry.

"Oh, no," she returned; "I've been all right. I've been going through the other door, I suppose, or coming in and going out on the Langdon Avenue car." (This was true, because she had been wanting to avoid him.) "I've been in such a hurry, most nights, that I haven't had time to stop, Bart. You know how late the store keeps us at times."

He remembered, too, that in the old days she had made time to stop or meet him occasionally.

"Yes, I know," he said tactfully. "But you haven't been to any of our old card-parties either of late, have you? At least, I haven't seen you. I've gone to two or three, thinking you might be there."

That was another thing Arthur had done—broken up her interest in these old store and neighborhood parties and a banjo-and-mandolin club to which she had once belonged. They had all seemed so pleasing and amusing in the old days—but now— . . . . In those days Bart had been her usual companion when his work permitted.

"No," she replied evasively, but with a forced air of pleasant remembrance; "I have often thought of how much fun we had at those, though. It was a shame to drop them. You haven't seen Harry

Stull or Trina Task recently, have you?" she inquired, more to be saying something than for any interest she felt.

He shook his head negatively, then added:

"Yes, I did, too; here in the waiting-room a few nights ago. They were coming down-town to a theater, I suppose."

His face fell slightly as he recalled how it had been their custom to do this, and what their one quarrel had been about. Shirley noticed it. She felt the least bit sorry for him, but much more for herself, coming back so disconsolately to all this.

"Well, you're looking as pretty as ever, Shirley," he continued, noting that she had not written the telegram and that there was something wistful in her glance. "Prettier, I think," and she smiled sadly. Every word that she tolerated from him was as so much gold to him, so much of dead ashes to her. "You wouldn't like to come down some evening this week and see 'The Mouse-Trap,' would you? We haven't been to a theater together in I don't know when." His eyes sought hers in a hopeful, doglike way.

So—she could have him again—that was the pity of it! To have what she really did not want, did not care for! At the least nod now he would come, and this very devotion made it all but worthless, and so sad. She ought to marry him now for certain, if she began in this way, and could in a month's time if she chose, but oh, oh—could she? For the moment she decided that she could not, would not. If he had only repulsed her—told her to go—ignored her—but no; it was her fate to be loved by him in this moving, pleading way, and hers not to love him as she wished to love—to be loved. Plainly, he needed some one like her, whereas she, she——She turned a little sick, a sense of the sacrilege of gaiety at this time creeping into her voice, and exclaimed:

"No, no!" Then seeing his face change, a heavy sadness come over it, "Not this week, anyhow, I mean" ("Not so soon," she had almost said). "I have several engagements this week and I'm not feeling well. But"—seeing his face change, and the thought of her own state returning—"you might come out to the house some evening instead, and then we can go some other time."

His face brightened intensely. It was wonderful how he longed to be with her, how the least favor from her comforted and lifted him up. She could see also now, however, how little it meant to her, how little it could ever mean, even if to him it was heaven. The old relationship would have to be resumed in toto, once and for all, but did she want it that way now that she was feeling so miserable about this other affair? As she meditated, these various moods racing to and fro in her mind, Barton seemed to notice, and now it occurred to him that perhaps he had not pursued her enough—was too easily put off. She probably did like him yet. This evening, her present visit, seemed to prove it.

"Sure, sure!" he agreed. "I'd like that. I'll come out Sunday, if you say. We can go any time to the play. I'm sorry, Shirley, if you're not feeling well. I've thought of you a lot these days. I'll come out Wednesday, if you don't mind."

She smiled a wan smile. It was all so much easier than she had expected—her triumph—and so ashenlike in consequence, a flavor of dead-sea fruit and defeat about it all, that it was pathetic. How could she, after Arthur? How could he, really?

"Make it Sunday," she pleaded, naming the farthest day off, and then hurried out.

Her faithful lover gazed after her, while she suffered an intense nausea. To think—to think—it should all be coming to this! She had not used her telegraph-blank, and now had forgotten all about it. It was not the simple trickery that discouraged her, but her own future which could find no better outlet than this, could not rise above it apparently, or that she had no heart to make it rise above it. Why couldn't she interest herself in some one different to Barton? Why did she have to return to him? Why not wait and meet some other—ignore him as before? But no, no; nothing mattered now—no one—it might as well be Barton really as any one, and she would at least make him happy and at the same time solve her own problem. She went out into the trainshed and climbed into her train. Slowly, after the usual pushing and jostling of a crowd, it drew out toward Latonia, that suburban region in which her home lay. As she rode, she thought.

"What have I just done? What am I doing?" she kept asking herself as the clacking wheels on the rails fell into a rhythmic dance and the houses of the brown, dry, endless city fled past in a maze. "Severing myself decisively from the past—the happy past—for supposing, once I am married, Arthur should return and want me again—suppose! Suppose!"

Below at one place, under a shed, were some market-gardeners disposing of the last remnants of their day's wares—a sickly, dull life, she thought. Here was Rutgers Avenue, with its line of red street-cars, many wagons and tracks and counter-streams of automobiles—how often had she passed it morning and evening in a shuttle-like way, and how often would, unless she got married! And here, now, was the river flowing smoothly between its banks lined with coal-pockets and wharves—away, away to the huge deep sea which she and Arthur had enjoyed so much. Oh, to be in a small boat and drift out, out into the endless, restless, pathless deep! Somehow the sight of this water, to-night and every night, brought back those evenings in the open with Arthur at Sparrows

Point, the long line of dancers in Eckert's Pavilion, the woods at Atholby, the park, with the dancers in the pavilion—she choked back a sob. Once Arthur had come this way with her on just such an evening as this, pressing her hand and saying how wonderful she was. Oh, Arthur! Arthur! And now Barton was to take his old place again—forever, no doubt. She could not trifle with her life longer in this foolish way, or his. What was the use? But think of it!

Yes, it must be—forever now, she told herself. She must marry. Time would be slipping by and she would become too old. It was her only future—marriage. It was the only future she had ever contemplated really, a home, children, the love of some man whom she could love as she loved Arthur. Ah, what a happy home that would have been for her! But now, now—

But there must be no turning back now, either. There was no other way. If Arthur ever came back—but fear not, he wouldn't! She had risked so much and lost—lost him. Her little venture into true love had been such a failure. Before Arthur had come all had been well enough. Barton, stout and simple and frank and direct, had in some way—how, she could scarcely realize now—offered sufficient of a future. But now, now! He had enough money, she knew, to build a cottage for the two of them. He had told her so. He would do his best always to make her happy, she was sure of that. They could live in about the state her parents were living in or a little better, not much—and would never want. No doubt there would be children, because he craved them—several of them —and that would take up her time, long years of it—the sad, gray years! But then Arthur, whose children she would have thrilled to bear, would be no more, a mere memory—think of that!—and Barton, the dull, the commonplace, would have achieved his finest dream—and why?

Because love was a failure for her—that was why—and in her life there could be no more true love. She would never love any one again as she had Arthur. It could not be, she was sure of it. He was too fascinating, too wonderful. Always, always, wherever she might be, whoever she might marry, he would be coming back, intruding between her and any possible love, receiving any possible kiss. It would be Arthur she would be loving or kissing. She dabbed at her eyes with a tiny handkerchief, turned her face close to the window and stared out, and then as the environs of Latonia came into view, wondered (so deep is romance): What if Arthur should come back at some time—or now! Supposing he should be here at the station now, accidentally or on purpose, to welcome her, to soothe her weary heart. He had met her here before. How she would fly to him, lay her head on his shoulder, forget that Barton ever was, that they had ever separated for an hour. Oh, Arthur! Arthur!

But no, no; here was Latonia—here the viaduct over her train, the long business street and the cars marked "Center" and "Langdon Avenue" running back into the great city. A few blocks away in tree-shaded Bethune Street, duller and plainer than ever, was her parents' cottage and the routine of that old life which was now, she felt, more fully fastened upon her than ever before—the lawnmowers, the lawns, the front porches all alike. Now would come the going to and fro of Barton to business as her father and she now went to business, her keeping house, cooking, washing, ironing, sewing for Barton as her mother now did these things for her father and herself. And she would not be in love really, as she wanted to be. Oh, dreadful! She could never escape it really, now that she could endure it less, scarcely for another hour. And yet she must, must, for the sake of—for the sake of—she closed her eyes and dreamed.

She walked up the street under the trees, past the houses and lawns all alike to her own, and found her father on their veranda reading the evening paper. She sighed at the sight.

"Back, daughter?" he called pleasantly.

"Yes."

"Your mother is wondering if you would like steak or liver for dinner. Better tell her."

"Oh, it doesn't matter."

She hurried into her bedroom, threw down her hat and gloves, and herself on the bed to rest silently, and groaned in her soul. To think that it had all come to this!—Never to see him any more!— To see only Barton, and marry him and live in such a street, have four or five children, forget all her youthful companionships—and all to save her face before her parents, and her future. Why must it be? Should it be, really? She choked and stifled. After a little time her mother, hearing her come in, came to the door—thin, practical, affectionate, conventional.

"What's wrong, honey? Aren't you feeling well tonight? Have you a headache? Let me feel."

Her thin cool fingers crept over her temples and hair. She suggested something to eat or a headache powder right away.

"I'm all right, mother. I'm just not feeling well now. Don't bother. I'll get up soon. Please don't."

"Would you rather have liver or steak to-night, dear?"

"Oh, anything—nothing—please don't bother—steak will do— anything"—if only she could get rid of her and be at rest!

Her mother looked at her and shook her head sympathetically, then retreated quietly, saying no more. Lying so, she thought and thought—grinding, destroying thoughts about the beauty of the past, the darkness of the future—until able to endure them no longer she got up and, looking distractedly out of the window into the yard and the house next door, stared at her future fixedly. What should she do? What should she really do? There was Mrs. Kessel in her kitchen getting her dinner as usual, just as her own mother was now, and Mr. Kessel out on the front porch in his shirt-sleeves reading the evening paper. Beyond was Mr. Pollard in his yard, cutting the grass. All along Bethune Street were such houses and such people—simple, commonplace souls all—clerks, managers, fairly successful craftsmen, like her father and Barton, excellent in their way but not like Arthur the beloved, the lost— and here was she, perforce, or by decision of necessity, soon to be one of them, in some such street, as this no doubt, forever and— For the moment it choked and stifled her.

She decided that she would not. No, no, no! There must be some other way—many ways. She did not have to do this unless she really wished to—would not—only—Then going to the mirror she looked at her face and smoothed her hair.

"But what's the use?" she asked of herself wearily and resignedly after a time. "Why should I cry? Why shouldn't I marry Barton? I don't amount to anything, anyhow. Arthur wouldn't have me. I wanted him, and I am compelled to take some one else —or no one—what difference does it really make who? My dreams are too high, that's all. I wanted Arthur, and he wouldn't have me. I don't want Barton, and he crawls at my feet. I'm a failure, that's what's the matter with me."

And then, turning up her sleeves and removing a fichu which stood out too prominently from her breast, she went into the kitchen and, looking about for an apron, observed:

"Can't I help? Where's the tablecloth?" and finding it among napkins and silverware in a drawer in the adjoining room, proceeded to set the table.

1918

The Twentieth Century: Literary Renaissance and Social Challenge

Twentieth-century spiritual unrest and skepticism were deeply rooted in nineteenth-century thought. The great English Victorians, from Matthew Arnold to Thomas Hardy, contributed to its growth, while in the United States it was transmitted to the twentieth century by such writers as William James, Santayana, Henry Adams, Garland, Dreiser, Moody, and Robinson. Similarly, the spirit of economic and social revolt can be traced without interruption from the later works of Twain and Howells to those of Sherwood Anderson, Sandburg, and Lewis. Twentieth-century realism and naturalism, as well as new experiments in literary form, continued to draw inspiration from such nineteenth-century masters as Dostoevski and Turgenev, Balzac, Zola, Flaubert, and the French symbolists; and from such transitional European writers as Hardy and George Moore, Ibsen and Shaw, Gide, Yeats, and Synge. Romanticism became a mere genteel survival; Poe and Melville were more highly esteemed than Irving or Longfellow; Whitman, largely neglected by Americans during his life, exerted a powerful influence; Emily Dickinson, posthumously published in 1890, became a living force after 1914; and Henry James, an exotic to his American contemporaries, entered the midstream of twentieth-century literature.

TWENTIETH-CENTURY RENAISSANCE

By 1920, directly after the First World War, it was evident that a new age of literary expression was already well advanced. The volume of American literary activity, the large number of new authors, the high level of their powers, the originality, daring, and general success of many new forms of expression, and the absorbed response of a reading public larger and more critical than ever before, produced a new national literature at least as brilliant as the regional flowering of New England nearly a century earlier. The widely used phrase "twentieth-century renaissance" seems scarcely too pretentious.

Actually, however, the nature of this twentieth-century renaissance had already been established during the second decade of the century; the temporary absorption of the country in the World War from 1917 to 1919 barely interrupted the tide of new literature, although it provided fresh themes and focused even more sharply the spiritual problems and disillusionments of this critical generation of writers. If the war is regarded as a point of intellectual intensification and broadening experience, there may be some usefulness in the historical identification of the years before the war as a "little renaissance," distinguishing them from the full tide of accomplishment after 1920, when writers already established shared with younger newcomers in the expression of the mingled malaise, desire for social experiment, and tempered hope of the postwar generation. However, the years from about 1910 to the present may be viewed as a single literary period, punctuated and modified by World War I; by the financial crash of 1929 and the ensuing depression; by the "New Deal" recovery after 1933; and by World War II. The dominant character of this literature is its intensity and the almost scientific candor of its explorations into the spiritual nature of man and the value of his society and institutions.

By 1910 the nature of the new age was suggested in recent works of such writers as Henry James, William James, Henry Adams, Moody, Robinson, Gertrude Stein, Norris, London, Upton Sinclair, and Steffens. In 1911 Dreiser published *Jennie Gerhardt*, his first novel since 1900. In rapid succession appeared *The Financier* (1912), *The Titan* (1914), and *The "Genius"* (1915), establishing him as the great realist of his generation, and giving encouragement to the nascent naturalism of younger authors. In 1911 Edith Wharton produced in *Ethan Frome* a small naturalistic masterpiece of immediate influence. Ellen Glasgow in the same year published *The Miller of Old Church*, her first realistic novel of the soil.

It was also in 1911 that Ezra Pound, who had published his first *Personae* in 1909 in London, joined forces with T. E. Hulme, a young British thinker, in giving direction to the youthful group of American and British poets in London who soon were known as the imagists. They inaugurated the "new poetry" movement, published aesthetic manifestoes, attracted such American poets as "H.D.," William Carlos Williams, and Amy Lowell, and collected their poems in imagist anthologies. Their poems stimulated the development of free verse and other experimental forms. They contributed to the success of *Poetry: A Magazine of Verse*, founded in Chicago in 1912, destined to become an important vehicle. During this period Robinson reached the height of his poetic power with *The Man*

Against the Sky (1916) and *Merlin* (1917). Frost published his first volume in 1913; by 1923, when his fourth volume appeared, the world had seen the bulk of his best-known poems. A midwestern balladist, Vachel Lindsay, won a meteoric fame in three volumes between 1913 and 1917. The vital poetic criticism of midwestern life began with Masters's *Spoon River Anthology* in 1915; but even more impressive was the poetry of Sandburg who, in three volumes between 1916 and 1920, explored the lives of his midwestern commoners in a powerful free verse at once coarse and tender. Edna St. Vincent Millay published her first book of poems in 1917; T. S. Eliot, in two volumes published by 1920, appeared at once in his mature character.

In this period a vigorous criticism was fostered by such writers as More, Babbitt, Huneker, Spingarn, Van Wyck Brooks, and Mencken. The last had begun his crusade before 1910, and he reached the height of his satirical effectiveness as editor of the *American Mercury* after 1924. Essentially a conservative individualist, he waged unceasing war on the mass mind. He was a liberator: he directed his eloquent wrath against well-paid guardians of other people's morals, against the defenders of official "decency." He championed such "immoral" authors as Dreiser, Cabell, and Sherwood Anderson.

Cabell and Anderson were only two of many new experimentalists in fiction who had commanded attention before 1920. In a number of novels, of which *Jurgen* (1919) was best known, Cabell daringly infused medieval romance with somewhat too obvious sexual symbolism. The same year, in *Winesburg, Ohio,* Sherwood Anderson first exerted his influence as a pessimistic social critic and the subtle master of intense psychological motivations. Upton Sinclair, who had begun his attack on industrial capitalism in *The Jungle* (1906), was now publishing such books as *King Coal* (1917) and *The Brass Check* (1919). Ernest Poole, in *The Harbor* (1915), studied the degradation of the dock workers; Winston Churchill gained popular following with such liberal ethical novels as *The Inside of the Cup* (1913) and *A Far Country* (1915). Willa Cather produced *O Pioneers!* (1913), her first novel of the Nebraska frontier and the new immigrant Americans who enriched it with their lives. She returned to this theme in *My Ántonia* (1918), but meanwhile she had combined it, in *The Song of the Lark* (1915), with her discovery of the desert civilization of the Southwest, on which she later based her masterpiece, *Death Comes for the Archbishop* (1927).

Thus, by the time the Treaty of Versailles ended World War I, many of the powerful authors of this century had already created a new literature of enduring merit, characterized by aesthetic originality and rebellion, by the determination to shatter conventional taboos in their expression of physical and psychological actuality, by a mystical hunger for spiritual enlightenment which attracted them toward symbolic or primitivistic expression, and by a growing sense of responsibility for their fellow human beings, expressed in the directness of their attack upon the contemporary social order. Their target was the total society and its fundamental institutions; they were dedicated to the task of confirming the dignity and value of man in the face of complex new forces and ideas that threatened to dehumanize him. Authors in the generations younger than Dreiser, who had published many of his important works by 1915, had not adhered so rigorously to the formula of the naturalist Zola, yet our literature has continued to be preoccupied with the question of the extent of man's opportunity to escape the determination of his fate by blind laws of heredity, environment, and survival. Characteristic influences of naturalism are apparent in the "hard-boiled" style of Hemingway's early work and that of many successors; naturalism is mingled with primitivism in the novels of Steinbeck and Faulkner, and with primitivistic and Freudian elements in Jeffers, Caldwell, and O'Neill; it is reflected in the presentation of the strict relations between environment and fate illustrated by the *Studs Lonigan* trilogy (1932–1935) of Farrell, and in the Marxist criticism of history best exemplified by Dos Passos in *U.S.A.* (1930–1936). Indeed, the events of the First World War and its aftermath only strengthened the growing belief that history is a mechanism responding to the obdurate dynamics of force and mass.

WORLD WAR I

To the authors of the 1920's, the stupendous totality and horror of a world war was an inescapable demonstration of this mechanistic theory of history and human life. The human personality was dwarfed as much by the dehumanizing magnitude of modern events as by the obdurate tendency of natural laws to deny mankind a special destiny. The diminishment of individual identity has been intensified ever since.

The authors who faced the world of the 1920's had a more immediate cause of disillusionment. Since the armistice of November 11, 1918, they had witnessed the tragic failure of the Versailles Treaty and the League of Nations—after a war which liberals and writers, as well as the American masses, had supported as a crusade to "end war." Wilson's Fourteen Points in 1918 sincerely represented this idealism, yet the European statesmen who accepted his preliminary conditions for a peace conference had already made secret agreements to promote French and British imperialism, and to perpetuate the explosive dangers in European life. The isolationist fears and selfish provinciality which obstructed President Wilson's idealism at home contributed to the success of his diplomatic enemies abroad, and although many historians now view these events in a different perspective, the important fact for literary history is the vast disillusionment of American liberals and writers, which coincided with the national extravagances, corruptions, and social decadence of the so-called Jazz Age, during the 1920's.

The earliest literary manifestations of this age recorded the revolt of youth, but the large body of writings attesting the condition of "flaming youth" or the delinquency of the "flapper" has left for posterity only the wit and daring of Edna Millay's earlier poems and the first novels of F. Scott Fitzgerald. However, it would be a mistake to ignore the revolt, for to some degree it expressed the same attitudes that Mencken was displaying, and in the same disguise of meaningful badinage and uproar it revealed the spiritual perturbations which the greatest of our authors soon embodied in more enduring works. Youth was repelled by the reactionary sham and hypocrisy on every hand; by the "Red scares," witch-hunting and prohibition fostered by one-hundred-percent patriots and the new "puritans." However disorderly its noisy mixture of Byronism, Bohemianism, and gaiety, its object was the destruction of unhealthy psychological taboos.

The general disenchantment of serious writers after the war was only increased by the shocking prevalence of corruption and irresponsibility both in government and in private enterprise. In the years that followed, the European economies were crushed, while the United States became the economic capital of the world. But amid soaring prices, production, and profits, there was a brooding discontent among labor. The notorious scandals of the Harding administration (1920–1923) recalled the Gilded Age, while organized crime, thriving on the violation of the unpopular prohibition laws and the venality of officials, produced an era of violence, terror, and moral delinquency. In spite of the conservative policies of Coolidge (1923–1929) the tide of inflation and expansion swept on until 1929, when the country plunged into its greatest financial depression.

Yet this decade, from 1919 to 1929, produced the greatest body of our twentieth-century literature. The new authors of the period responded to the social and moral confusions that have been described. Expatriation was an early symptom of their restlessness. Such authors as Pound, Eliot, MacLeish, Hemingway, and Edmund Wilson, thronging in the literary "colonies" of London or Paris, or in Italy or elsewhere, were not "a lost generation" as Gertrude Stein in Paris asserted, for they ultimately promoted the absorption of reinvigorating European influences into contemporary American writing. The war itself provided a vital subject for many new authors. It inspired the first novel of Dos Passos, but he did not win attention until 1921 with *Three Soldiers.* Eliot was already well known when he published *The Waste Land* (1922), but it established his greatness and dramatically advanced the pessimistic conclusion that the war was a final evidence of the collapse of Western civilization.

Hemingway drew directly upon the spiritual consequences of the war in his early masterpieces, *In Our Time* (1924), *The Sun Also Rises* (1926), and *A Farewell to Arms* (1929), contrasting the hard and wounded gallantry of individuals with the soft decadence of society. Faulkner's first major work was a war novel, *Soldiers' Pay*, in 1926.

Other authors, responding to a variety of influences, gained prominence in other areas of literary revolt. Lewis, in *Main Street* (1920) and *Babbitt* (1922), appeared as the satirist of the patterned dullness of bourgeois success and the small-town mentality, while in 1925 Dreiser, in *An American Tragedy*, and Dos Passos, in *Manhattan Transfer*, pursued the theme of materialism in novels both naturalistic and tragic. Fitzgerald, in his masterpiece, *The Great Gatsby*, showed its consequences in terms of the fabulous high living, wild speculation, and organized criminality of the period.

The psychological probing of the spiritual personality, still continued by such earlier authors as Sherwood Anderson, Robinson, and Willa Cather, was augmented by the work of powerful new recruits. One was the brilliant Eugene O'Neill, who between 1919 and 1922 founded a new theater of spiritual symbolism, with such plays as *Anna Christie, Beyond the Horizon, The Emperor Jones,* and *The Hairy Ape*. Freudian conclusions appeared in the poems of Jeffers, beginning with *Tamar* (1924) and *Roan Stallion* (1925), and in the later

novels of Faulkner, beginning with *The Sound and the Fury* (1929).

In the same year the powerful young voice of Thomas Wolfe was heard in *Look Homeward, Angel,* the first of the succession of novels in which he reflected the search of a spiritually homeless younger generation for a sense of unity with a world apparently so vast, complex, and impersonal. Wolfe's vitality and natural optimism were in contrast with the mood then possessing Archibald MacLeish, who embodied the darkness of youth in such poems as *The Hamlet of A. MacLeish* (1928).

POETRY AND DRAMA
BETWEEN THE WARS

One of the most noteworthy phenomena of this literary revival was the opulence, power, and popularity of poetry and drama. The imagist and free-verse movements lost their momentum during the war, but such poets as Eliot, Jeffers, and MacLeish gave new directions and new strength to American poetry.

In general our poetry in this century, until the time of the Second World War, became increasingly subtle in its symbolism, more reliant upon allusions to earlier literary works or to suggestions of mythological meaning, and more inclined toward intellectual depth or brilliance. The imagists and Pound had found inspiration in the French symbolists, the classics, the troubadour poets, the Italian Renaissance, and ancient Chinese and Japanese forms. The erudition of Eliot emphasized also the inspiration of philosophy, religious thought, Eastern mysticism, and anthropological lore. Eliot and others rediscovered not only the Elizabethan poets and dramatists but also the English metaphysical poets of the Jacobean period.

The intense and often violent metaphysical image heightened the intellectual tension and symbolic range of poetry, making it more difficult, but also more capable as an instrument for representing by abstraction the emotional significance of ideas. Metaphysical tendencies characterized the poetry of MacLeish, Stevens, Williams, Marianne Moore, Cummings, Crane, and the Nashville "Fugitives," principally Ransom and Tate.

American drama between the two wars became for the first time a widely recognized instrument of national expression. During the first two decades of the century our theater, while flourishing, had relied principally on the long-established conventions of the drama. Slowly, however, it responded to the experimental, symbolic, and critical drama from abroad, to the influence of such dramatists as Ibsen, Strindberg, Hauptmann, Shaw, Galsworthy, and Maeterlinck.

Popular interest in the theater was quickened by the visits of companies from the experimental "art" theaters abroad, and soon the little-theater movement was represented in the United States by many urban professional groups and by community or regional companies. O'Neill, as the earliest liberator, was the leading experimentalist of the Provincetown group in

1916. By 1925, he had achieved the dominant stature he retained during the following decade. Each of his plays was a new experiment in form, but his emphasis was always on the psychological analysis and symbolic representation of character. Later Maxwell Anderson attained a position second only to that of O'Neill. His many dramas included social comedies, character problem plays, and dramas of social protest, tragedies in classical form, and experiments in the poetic drama. The little theaters developed regional writers, while the metropolitan theater brought to prominence scores of brilliant new authors and actors and sent an abundance of new plays touring the country.

Social and domestic comedy and the character problem play attained especial brilliance in the hands of Rachel Crothers, Barry, Kelly, Kaufman, Connelly, Wilder, Sidney Howard, Behrman, and Sherwood. In the area of social protest and propaganda the name of Elmer Rice was perhaps most prominent, although such others as Odets and Kingsley are well remembered. The element of social protest was also strong in the work of O'Neill, Maxwell Anderson, Barry, Kaufman, and others.

PRIMITIVISM

In connection with all forms of literature in the present century, the presence in certain authors of Freudian or primitivistic tendencies has been noted. If the author's techniques involved the artistic analysis of psychological motivation, he was here provided with an instrument which he could employ in support of a naturalistic or deterministic interpretation of life. Also, Freudian techniques authorized the use of materials which had been taboo, a use dramatically illustrated by Joyce's *Ulysses*, which reveals the aberrant and violent images present in the stream of consciousness of the central character. O'Neill, Faulkner, and Jeffers are only the three most successful of the many American authors who have analyzed the subconscious for characterization.

Similarly, primitivism, often supported by the premises of Freudian psychology, assumes that basic truths of human behavior are best observed where conditions are least inhibited by refinements or sophistication. The combination of the primitive with the picturesque provides the simple charm of balladry and other folk arts. However, violence is also primitive, and so is the untrammeled manifestation of sex, as these appear in works of London and Frank Norris, Faulkner, Hemingway, Steinbeck, and Jeffers; and it is assumed that refined persons can learn by observing the inhabitants of Tobacco Road or God's Little Acre.

DEPRESSION AND TOTALITARIAN MENACE

The era of the 1920's ended with the Great Depression, following the financial crash of 1929. Paralleling the rise of Hitler and Mussolini abroad, the depression period brought economic distress, ideological unrest, and a general reappraisal of American values. Many writers discovered the depths of their loyalty to traditional American idealism. MacLeish published *New Found Land* (1930) and *Conquistador* (1932), and gave himself for a decade to the writing of democratic propaganda. Sandburg, who had begun his career with collectivist sympathies, now wrote lovingly of *The People, Yes* (1936) and turned to the completion of his mammoth study of Lincoln.

The utopian promise of Marxism and various forms of state collectivism was reflected by numerous authors. Liberals such as Dos Passos and Hemingway were drawn temporarily to the left by sympathy for the loyalists in the Spanish civil war in 1936.

However, Marxist theory in the United States, largely academic, was soon defeated by the hard facts of Marxist history current; totalitarian dictatorships suppressed the individual in moral anarchy and with ruthless barbarity; Mussolini took Italy in 1922; Hitler usurped the German chancellorship for Fascism in 1933 and declared the Rome-Berlin axis in 1936; he took the Sudetenland, invaded Poland, and silenced Austria, 1938–1939; he led the chorus proclaming the "master race" and spheres of influence, while totalitarianism took over in Spain and Japan. Literary renaissance was ended in the United States, where fear grew that we should be engulfed in war.

ARMAGEDDON AND AFTER (1945–   )

The response of art and letters to the Second World War was slow and somber as compared with the spectacular renaissance of literature following the First

World War. Noteworthy experimental literature had gained attention before 1915, when the First World War began in Europe. That war delayed the "new" literature but later provided tragic inspiration for a generation of writers of great power. The Second World War (1939–1945) was entirely different in kind. It represented a crude barbarism that mankind had rejected ages before; it was the explosion of vengeance so long brooded upon that the recently defeated aggressor was willing to risk the survival of its national culture to follow a madman in a war shamefully intent on complete annihilation. Perhaps by some natural law of degradation the United States and its allies were swept for some unforgotten hours into a similar desperation at Hiroshima and Nagasaki.

Probably the common man realized that thirty years of war and disasters, related like a chain reaction, had occurred without his having much to do with it and had concluded only in an armed truce between two ideas, democracy and communism. He had seen the high hopes of the League of Nations vanish, and now the United Nations proved unable to prevent a cold war in which Russian communism took over Hungary, Rumania, Poland, Czechoslovakia, and East Germany between 1947 and 1949. Continuous insecurities in the relations between nations were made all the more menacing by the unrest in Africa and Asia. The rapid refinements of nuclear research, the development of the hydrogen bomb, and the excitements and mystery of space exploration all tended to dwarf the average man.

Although the danger of thermonuclear annihilation was the principal source of the insecurity of people in general, there was the consciousness also of the international condition of debility among the natural allies of the United States, no longer able to influence the stability of areas where they recently were powerful; and of the very limited success of the regional associations for collective security. What often seemed the failure of American policy was evident even nearby, in Latin America and Cuba. While apparently the communist dogma affected only an insignificant fraction of Americans, confidence was shaken in the adequacy of a fully democratic system to determine and to maintain a good society. While wage, price, and tax schedules supported a continuing inflation, American poverty cried out for help in the midst of plenty. As the predicted population "explosion" found the nation unprepared, the terrific pace of automation rapidly urbanized the landscape, while the "natural" life on the land almost disappeared. Such factors tended to separate man from the natural sources of his being, while high mobility destroyed the individual's relationship with a stable community. Both the war and industralism affected the large centers of Negro population, rural and urban, bringing belatedly into public view the long-neglected problems of race and civil rights.

For this younger generation the first law of life—survival—functioned in entirely new circumstances, because failure was no longer an individual matter—not death but annihilation, nothingness. The artist will not seek social remedies or found systems —these are within neither his competence nor his ordained function. The writers of interest here turned to the perception of life itself, and to the condition of being alive, and to the definition of the human personality. They sought new forms, found some, but for the most part carried to further limits the impulses begun by the generation of the first war, particularly in seeking language that best mediates between vernacular speech and the creative writer's need to instrument his motivations. Fiction, drama, and poetry continue to employ expressionism by means of verbal or metaphoric instruments that probe the motivating forces of human nature and behavior, particularly the nonrational, with directness and economy and violence.

RECENT FICTION AND DRAMA

In *After the Lost Generation* (1951) John Aldridge commented that young writers of fiction who appeared during the Second World War period did not show the inspiration and depth of the First World War generation. That evaluation begins to look prophetic. In fact, the fiction of the second war period was deeply affected by the changes in the human viewpoint which, for a time at least, involved a loss of faith in life itself, cynicism about human values, a failure to achieve personal identity, and dwarfing by contrast with the massive power of nonhuman things.

Even before the declared war in Europe, the Spanish Civil War (1936–1939) brought a number of American novels and plays into being, but only Hemingway's *For Whom the Bell Tolls* (1940) is remembered. During the European war, Faulkner wrote some of his greatest novels, including the Snopes trilogy; Hemingway, Steinbeck, Dos Passos, and Farrell continued to write, with less power but the same commitment, about man, scarred by the betrayals of a million years, yet generally able to remember who he was. Not so the lost, unidentified people of numerous novels during the war period and afterward. This phenomenon of personality is prevalent in the Second World War fiction.

Of the books dealing with the war itself probably the most interesting stories are about the American occupation forces. James Jones's *From Here to Eternity* (1951) was an enormous narrative of life in an army post and war between the sexes, a book almost as tedious as the life it so honestly depicted. The self-taught author learned to structure a novel better in three later war novels, especially *Some Come Running* (1958) and *The Thin Red Line* (1962).

In 1948 Norman Mailer, another war veteran, revealed an original genius in his over-long and violent *The Naked and the Dead*. His four subsequent novels are all experimental and relatively plotless. *An American Dream* (1965) is convincing revelation of his evident perception of deep changes in the tradition of moral responsibility and the presumed survival of an undersexed puritanism, but the unrelieved violence of the narrative symbols defeats the reader's belief.

Mailer's essay on Jack Kerouac's *On the Road* (1957) shows an affiliation with the "beat" author, but Mailer is not himself qualified for the "beat" position which, as Kerouac's classic shows, requires that the irresponsibility must be so much a natural and unavoidable condition that it is inherently comical. The members of the beat generation, however, with the exception of Kerouac, Allen Ginsberg, and perhaps Gary Snyder, were more important for their influence on later writers than for the intrinsic merit of their works.

A small group of new writers has emerged since 1945 as normally affected members of the war generation. These have taken up the "business-as-usual" of the novel. They write of whatever places and people their minds embrace most knowingly, with a surprising variety of techniques. Wright Morris, who published his first novel in 1942, carries his native Nebraska as Willa Cather did, in heart and mind, although both lived there steadily for only a short time. His best of many novels include *Man and Boy* (1951), *The Huge Season* (1955), and *Ceremony in Lone Tree* (1960); also *The Field of Vision* (1956), a highly successful experiment in fiction, whose method brings together a number of Nebraskan

exiles and by multiple exposures compares their sense of experiences long ago shared, when we see the alienation of each from any fixed identity and from each other.

Canadian-born Saul Bellow has long been associated with Chicago. His six novels since 1944 are all good, particularly *The Adventures of Augie March* (1953), *Henderson the Rain King* (1959), and *Mr. Sammler's Planet* (1970). The books are complex and various, but the dominant theme is the character in search of himself.

Bernard Malamud has been deeply identified with the Brooklyn of his childhood, and with the recent immigrant stocks, principally Jewish and Italian, in both Brooklyn and New York. Malamud is a master of the short-story form. Of his novels *The Assistant* (1952) is most praised, and it shows his controlled management of character and setting. Kiev in 1911 is the setting of his fourth novel, *The Fixer* (1966). This may be little less than a great novel on the theme of the innocent person destroyed by evil authority. His sources are fully studied, then transmuted by a mind at once learned and philosophical.

Russian-born Vladimir Nabokov did not receive serious critical attention in the United States until late in life, after the New York publication of *Lolita* in 1958. Now a resident of Switzerland, Nabokov has resisted easy categorization in his novels as in his life. In his own mind he was in 1966 "an American writer who has once been a Russian one."

John Updike, J. D. Salinger, and Truman Capote are all brilliant and possessed of a public, but each is to some degree committed to a distinctive style that is not flexible enough, and each is hampered by early associations which became a public image. Salinger, after a brilliant beginning, turned in upon himself and fell silent. Capote turned from fiction to the "non-fiction novel" in *In Cold Blood* (1966). Updike's *Rabbit, Run* (1960) is a remarkable novel, but its sequel, *Rabbit Redux* (1971), is not so successful. Nevertheless, Updike's continuing high level of accomplishment in his many novels and short stories places him in the front rank of our authors.

Besides Capote, southern writers have been numerous and valuable. Robert Penn Warren, youngest poet of the "Fugitives," survives as a master novelist whose subjects range from history and politics to human chivalry and faith. William Styron is also impressive in the scope and quality of his four novels (1951–1967). Caroline Gordon and Katherine Anne Porter are belletristic short story writers of exquisite excellence who made their reputations before the Second World War, but Miss Porter's *Ship of Fools* (1962) is a post-war contribution. Eudora Welty's, Flannery O'Connor's, and Peter Taylor's short stories are deservedly cherished. Carson McCullers' novels of penetrating psychological vision reached a climax of acceptance in 1946 with *The Member of the Wedding*. In the early 1960's two fine careers began

with the publication of Walker Percy's *The Moviegoer* (1961) and Reynolds Price's *A Long and Happy Life* (1962).

Since Richard Wright there has been a continuous succession of brilliant Negro writers in many fields, but among novelists and thinkers Ralph Ellison and James Baldwin have been preeminent and have established reputations in accord with their merit. Among lesser known writers of fiction Ann Petry and William Melvin Kelley should be noted. Gwendolyn Brooks, Robert Hayden, and Imamu Amiri Baraka (LeRoi Jones) have each published fine volumes of verse. More recently, Ishmael Reed has begun to emerge as a poet and novelist with a voice distinctly his own.

Recently, such novelists as John Barth, Joseph Heller, and Thomas Pynchon have experimented with a fiction loosely termed "black comedy" or "the novel of the absurd." Their heroes are "anti-heroes," against forces of "right" that are now only forces of "might." The conflict is not a new one, but the authors' attitude is: the more socially outrageous or subterranean the conflict, the funnier it should be. Pynchon's *V* (1963) was one of the most impressive works of its decade and his *Gravity's Rainbow* (1973) was welcomed with an immediate critical enthusiasm accorded few novels. Barth's reputation built slowly, climaxing with *Giles Goat-Boy* (1966). Heller's *Catch-22* (1961), although extraordinarily popular, was less impressive. Because of the success of such novels, the terms "black comedy" and "novel of the absurd" have become too-convenient catchalls used to describe the many books that in recent years have resulted from an impatience with older novelistic conventions of form and content, but that are often in other ways distinctive efforts, spawned by individual talents. Writers and individual novels that seem most worthy of mention include Jerzy Kosinski, *The Painted Bird* (1965); Donald Barthelme, *Snow White* (1967); and Robert Coover, *The Universal Baseball Association, Inc., J. Henry Waugh, Prop.* (1968).

Many of the writers mentioned above also wrote excellent short stories during the two decades of the 1950's and 1960's that witnessed a production that in combined quantity and quality had not previously been matched in any similar period in the nation's history. Besides those southern writers discussed earlier, whose talents appeared particularly suited to the short story form, a good many authors did their best writing in works of restricted scope. The title story of Tillie Olsen's *Tell Me a Riddle* (1961) was a classic in the form, though she has published little else, as was the title story of William Gass's *In the Heart of the Heart of the Country* (1968), which also demonstrated something of the elasticity of the genre. John O'Hara, who had long been known as a novelist, published after 1956 a half-dozen volumes of excellent stories. Philip Roth's *Goodbye, Columbus* (1959) set a standard he has seldom equaled in his longer works. John

Cheever's inventiveness and capacity for growth began to appear almost limitless with the appearance of his sixth collection, *The World of Apples,* in 1973. Joyce Carol Oates, best known for a series of sensational novels, was better still in the superbly sustained authority of her finest short stories.

The energies of the theater noticeably waned during World War II, and they cannot be said to have recovered in the decades following. The theater of Broadway today is marked by a dreary caution resulting from high production costs and the competition of mass vehicles of entertainment. Tennessee Williams has written dramas set in the South, rich in mood, notably *The Glass Menagerie* (1944), *A Streetcar Named Desire* (1947), and *Cat on a Hot Tin Roof* (1954). Arthur Miller contributed to the postwar stage perhaps its greatest play, *Death of a Salesman* (1949), a moving study of the "tragedy of the common man." Neither has contributed much in recent years. Among younger dramatists only Edward Albee seems to approach the power of Williams and Miller. After the considerable success of such early works as *The Zoo Story* (1960) and *Who's Afraid of Virginia Woolf* (1962), however, his work appears to have fallen off.

Elsewhere in America there is much interest in performed theater—"Off-Broadway," on college campuses, and in civic theaters supported by many communities. Few genuine new playwrights have yet emerged from these centers; several have experimented with "improvisational" and other kinds of non-literary theater. Some of the more recent poets represented in this volume—particularly Robert Lowell, who "imitated" American short stories in *The Old Glory* (1964), and Imamu Amiri Baraka—have, however, experimented with dramatic forms.

RECENT POETRY

By contrast with fiction, poetry was refreshed by a group of poets who grew up between the wars. These poets have explored the common anxiety for the lost self or personal identity, a quest that was common to American and English mid-century poets (*cf.* Auden). Muriel Rukeyser, who expressed a moving affirmative in the "Elegies," earlier found inspiration in primitive life and religion. John Holmes speaks for all in saying that his poems were "an effort to find himself."

The extraordinary power of Theodore Roethke and Robert Lowell has already given them the stature of "standard" poets. Each has the past in his bones: for Roethke the "usable past" was the biological inheritance. He found identification and the general meaning of being human by observing the life force in the behavior of animals, plants, and even inanimate creation. Lowell's usable and oft-pondered past with which, somehow, he must relate, was a complex family, social, and cultural tradition.

Richard Wilbur and Richard Eberhart also have much in common. Both have written remarkable poems of nature; in their mastery of the social situation both are abetted by innate wit and by their mastery of a precise and economical style. Each has written longer poems of deep purport heightened by subtle, vigorous imagery. Other poets born in the second decade of the twentieth century had careers marked by extremes of brilliant success and intolerable frustration and self-defeat, ended in some instances by early death or suicide. In one memorable sequence in *The Dream Songs* (1969) John Berryman calls the roll of individuals, like Delmore Schwartz and Randall Jarrell, whose fine promise ended prematurely.

The genuine inheritors of the experience of the Second World War were poets, most of whom were born after 1920, although a few, such as William Stafford, are older. They are not themselves "dehumanized" by automation, regimentation and the mass-culture, although some have been "alienated" by the inhumanity of man or by failures of democracy to realize its potential. Most do not worry about identifying. But they do realize that these conditions exist for mankind in general and their poems—like genuine literature in any age—bear the stamp of the poet's knowledge of the present human dilemma.

We have selected eleven poets to stand for this generation that has attempted to find what realities exist and to create something therefrom. They write for a new human personality not yet defined, and they squarely face psychological realities not so well understood before the wars as now—especially the realities of interpersonal relations. Some, such as James Dickey, Robert Bly, and Sylvia Plath, are so clearly individualistic that it is difficult to write of them collectively except in the most general terms. Most, however, share the rejection of materialism and the fears for the future quality of life voiced so stridently by Allen Ginsberg, so quietly by Gary Snyder. Few write their best poems directly on social issues, although most are strongly moved by injustice.

Perhaps the most striking and permanent accomplishment of the recent poets is their mastery of a new speech, a precise and often beautiful American vernacular, a corresponding directness in figurative equivalents, and a controlled but flexible rhythm, the sound of our live speech made illustrious. This inspiration is generally and variously from Whitman, Eliot, Stevens, Williams, from Roethke and Lowell—or from life.

American Revaluations

EDWIN ARLINGTON ROBINSON
(1869–1935)

Among the most gifted of his country's poets, Edwin Arlington Robinson is also notable for the scale and versatility of his work. Yet it is not easy to recall a poem, large or small, that does not illustrate his painstaking zeal for perfection even in the last detail of structure or phrasing. His perfectionism is not mere fussiness, but an intrinsic discipline of form and meaning. Robinson is truly philosophical, profound in thought and expression, and given to probing the subtlest areas of human psychology.

Robinson was descended through his mother from Anne Bradstreet, New England's first Colonial poet. He was born at Head Tide, Maine, on December 22, 1869. His father, aged fifty, had just then retired from business, and the family at once moved twelve miles down the Kennebec, to Gardiner, the "Tilbury Town" of his poems.

The presumed unhappiness of Robinson's boyhood has been exaggerated, but it is true that he had more than the usual handicaps to overcome. Late-born into his family, he was made conscious, as he grew up, of the example of his materially successful brothers in a community where such success was taken for granted. After graduation from high school he spent four difficult years in apparent idleness while reading extensively and laboring steadily at his verse, which editors as steadily declined to publish.

At the age of twenty-two he entered Harvard University, and he remained for two years as a special student, principally of philosophy, literature, and languages. The death of his father in 1893 caused his withdrawal, and inaugurated a period of mental depression. A chronic abscess of his ear for several years kept him in pain, and he feared he would lose his mind. The family inheritance was greatly reduced by the panic of 1893. Both his brothers, who had begun so brilliantly, proved unstable and then died within a few years, while his mother went into a long and harrowing illness. Just before his mother's death, the serious love affair of his youth was terminated in sorrow. Thereafter he shyly avoided such entanglements; in any case not until he was fifty could he have married on his income as a poet.

His mother's death relieved him of family responsibility. In 1896 he settled in New York, and unable to find a publisher, he had *The Torrent and the Night Before* printed at his own expense. The February, 1897, *Bookman* observed that his verse had the "true fire," but that "the world is not beautiful to him, but a prison house." Robinson's letter of reply, in the March number, contained a now-famous appraisal of his view of life. "The world is not a 'prison house,'" he said, "but a kind of spiritual kindergarten where millions of bewildered infants are trying to spell 'God' with the wrong blocks." The next year he included most of these poems in his second volume, *The Children of the Night* (1897), again defraying the costs of publication. These volumes ushered into the world such "bewildered infants," now famous, as Aaron Stark, with "eyes like little dollars," and Richard Cory, for whom a bullet was medicine, and Luke Havergal, caught in the web of fate.

After a year in New York he accepted an appointment at Harvard as office secretary to the president, but proved wholly unfit for such routine. Back in New York, while not gregarious, he was far from being such a recluse as is often imagined. According to Fullerton Waldo, he loved the bustling life of the streets as "Charles Lamb loved the tidal fullness along the Strand." For years he lived in Greenwich Village, in the then Bohemian area near Wash-

ington Square. There he had as intimates such writers and staunch friends as Josephine Preston Peabody and William Vaughn Moody, whom he had known at Harvard, and E. C. Stedman, Percy Mackaye, Hermann Hagedorn, Ridgely Torrence, and Daniel Gregory Mason, the composer, who taught music at Columbia. When *Captain Craig* finally secured a publisher in 1902, the poet was for a time spared the knowledge that it had been subsidized, secretly, by Gardiner friends. The revelation of this, together with the small sale of the volume, increased his desperation during 1903–1904, when he worked as a subway-construction inspector. Creative work under these circumstances was nearly impossible.

In March of 1905, he received his first check in ten years for writing accepted by a magazine, and within a week there arrived a letter from the President of the United States. Kermit Roosevelt, whose master at Groton was a Gardiner friend of the poet's, had sent his father a copy of *The Children of the Night*, which the President had much admired. Now, learning of the poet's plight, he had him appointed to a clerkship in the United States Custom House at New York. The salary was small, but Robinson had once again the time and energy for poetry. By the end of Roosevelt's term he had prepared the volume *The Town Down the River* (1910), and the President's influence had secured its publication by Scribner's.

Although it is reported that for years this notable poet depended in part upon the unobtrusive benefactions of his admirers, he was never again forced to waste his limited strength to obtain mere subsistence. A studio was provided for him in New York. After 1911 he spent many summers at the MacDowell Colony at Peterborough, New Hampshire, a retreat for artists, established in memory of Edward MacDowell. There, through succeeding summers, he completed the longer works of his second period.

In the Arthurian poems, each the size of a separate volume, Robinson developed a highly individualized blank verse, lofty in character yet modern in its speech rhythms, equally adaptable for sustained narrative, dialogue, and dramatic effects, and for the poet's characteristic discussion of ideas. His wit is nowhere seen to better advantage than in his long narratives. It is not dependent upon what is comic in the ordinary sense, but springs from the recognition of essential incongruities at the core of reality, and rewards only those who can follow the poet's fundamental thinking. The Arthurian poems are faithful to the sources—Malory and such continental chroniclers as Wolfram —but the characters have been reinterpreted in modern terms. The world of Arthur, in chaos as a result of the greed and faithlessness of its leadership, corresponded, it seemed to Robinson, to the condition of things at the time of the First World War. *Merlin* appeared in 1917, *Lancelot* in 1920, and *Tristram* in 1927.

The poet's financial rewards increased very slowly, but his first *Collected Poems* (1921) was awarded the Pulitzer Prize, and so was *The Man Who Died Twice* (1924), a major narrative of fantastic design but great power and moral significance, on the theme' of regeneration. *Tristram* also won the Pulitzer Prize, and as a selection of the Literary Guild, a book club, it gave the poet his first large sale. During the remaining nine years of his life, Robinson's financial worries were ended.

In his last years Robinson created several long narratives of modern life, beginning with *Cavender's House* (1929). These are psychological studies of character, all dealing, in various lights, with the nature of human guilt or fidelity, with the destructiveness of the desire for power or for possession. *The Glory of the Nightingales* (1930) and *Matthias at the Door* (1931) are the climax of Robinson's criticism of modern life, and subtly incorporate the constant symbols of light, darkness, regeneration, and responsibility that prevail in his poetry from the beginning and reach their highest tragic synthesis in *Tristram*. *Talifer* (1933) is a social comedy of subtlety and brilliant wit, in a vein of meaningful worldliness. *King Jasper* (1935), although it shows traces of the fatigue of a dying man, is a cleverly managed allegory, and is interesting as revealing the final phase of the poet's developing concept of patrician responsibility in democratic leadership.

The standard edition is *Collected Poems of Edwin Arlington Robinson*, 1921; enlarged editions appeared periodically through 1937. Collections of letters are *Selected Letters,* compiled by Ridgely Torrence, 1940; *Untriangulated Stars: Letters of Edwin Arlington Robinson to Harry de Forest Smith, 1890–1905,* edited by Denham Sutcliffe, 1947; and *Edwin Arlington Robinson's Letters to Edith Brower,* edited by Richard Cary, 1968. Standard biographies were published by Hermann Hagedorn, 1938; and Emory Neff, 1948.

Memoirs and critical studies are Lloyd Morris, *The Poetry of Edwin Arlington Robinson,* 1923; Mark Van Doren, *Edwin Arlington Robinson,* 1927; L. M. Beebe, *Edwin Arlington Robinson and the Arthurian Legend,* 1927; Charles Cestre, *An Introduction to Edwin Arlington Robinson,* 1930; R. W. Brown, *Next Door to a Poet,* 1937; E. Kaplan, *Philosophy in the Poetry of Edwin Arlington Robinson,* 1940; Yvor Winters, *Edwin Arlington Robinson,* 1946; Edwin G. Fussell, *Edwin Arlington Robinson,* 1954; Louis Untermeyer, *Edwin Arlington Robinson: A Reappraisal,* 1963; Chard P. Smith, *Where the Light Falls: A Portrait of Edwin Arlington Robinson,* 1965; Hoyt C. Franchere, *Edwin Arlington Robinson,* 1968; and Louis Coxe, *Edwin Arlington Robinson: The Life of Poetry,* 1969. Richard Cary edited *Appreciation of Edwin Arlington Robinson,* 1969.

Luke Havergal

Go to the western gate, Luke Havergal,
There where the vines cling crimson on the wall,
And in the twilight wait for what will come.
The leaves will whisper there of her, and some,
Like flying words, will strike you as they fall;   5
But go, and if you listen she will call.
Go to the western gate, Luke Havergal—
Luke Havergal.

No, there is not a dawn in eastern skies
To rift the fiery night that's in your eyes;   10
But there, where western glooms are gathering,
The dark will end the dark, if anything:
God slays Himself with every leaf that flies,
And hell is more than half of paradise.
No, there is not a dawn in eastern skies—   15
In eastern skies.

Out of a grave I come to tell you this,
Out of a grave I come to quench the kiss
That flames upon your forehead with a glow
That blinds you to the way that you must go.   20
Yes, there is yet one way to where she is,
Bitter, but one that faith may never miss.
Out of a grave I come to tell you this—
To tell you this.

There is the western gate, Luke Havergal,   25
There are the crimson leaves upon the wall.
Go, for the winds are tearing them away,—
Nor think to riddle the dead words they say,
Nor any more to feel them as they fall;

But go, and if you trust her she will call.   30
There is the western gate, Luke Havergal—
Luke Havergal.

1896

Richard Cory

Whenever Richard Cory went down town,
We people on the pavement looked at him:
He was a gentleman from sole to crown,
Clean favored, and imperially slim.

And he was always quietly arrayed,   5
And he was always human when he talked;
But still he fluttered pulses when he said,
'Good-morning,' and he glittered when he walked.

And he was rich—yes, richer than a king—
And admirably schooled in every grace: 10
In fine, we thought that he was everything
To make us wish that we were in his place.

So on we worked, and waited for the light,
And went without the meat, and cursed the bread;
And Richard Cory, one calm summer night,   15
Went home and put a bullet through his head.

1897

Miniver Cheevy

Miniver Cheevy, child of scorn,
  Grew lean while he assailed the seasons;
He wept that he was ever born,
  And he had reasons.

Miniver loved the days of old   5
  When swords were bright and steeds were prancing;
The vision of a warrior bold
  Would set him dancing.

Miniver sighed for what was not,
  And dreamed, and rested from his labors;   10
He dreamed of Thebes [1] and Camelot,[2]
  And Priam's [3] neighbors.

1. Ancient Greek city, prominent in Greek history and legend.
2. Legendary site of King Arthur's court in the Arthurian romances.
3. King of Troy and the father of the heroes Paris and Hector.

Miniver mourned the ripe renown
  That made so many a name so fragrant;
He mourned Romance, now on the town,   15
  And Art, a vagrant.

Miniver loved the Medici,[4]
  Albeit he had never seen one;
He would have sinned incessantly
  Could he have been one.   20

Miniver cursed the commonplace
  And eyed a khaki suit with loathing;
He missed the medieval grace
  Of iron clothing.

Miniver scorned the gold he sought,   25
  But sore annoyed was he without it;
Miniver thought, and thought, and thought,
  And thought about it.

Miniver Cheevy, born too late,
  Scratched his head and kept on thinking;   30
Miniver coughed, and called it fate,
  And kept on drinking.

       1910

Leonora

They have made for Leonora this low dwelling in the ground,
And with cedar they have woven the four walls round.
Like a little dryad hiding she'll be wrapped all in green,
Better kept and longer valued than by ways that would have been.

They will come with many roses in the early afternoon,   5
They will come with pinks and lilies and with Leonora soon;
And as long as beauty's garments over beauty's limbs are thrown,
There'll be lilies that are liars, and the rose will have its own.

There will be a wondrous quiet in the house that they have made,
And to-night will be a darkness in the place where she'll be laid;   10
But the builders, looking forward into time, could only see
Darker nights for Leonora than to-night shall ever be.

       1910

---

4. Renaissance merchant-princes, rulers of Florence for nearly two centuries, noted equally for their cruelties and for their benefactions to learning and art.

Bewick Finzer

Time was when his half million drew
    The breath of six per cent;
But soon the worm of what-was-not
    Fed hard on his content;
And something crumbled in his brain   5
    When his half million went.

Time passed, and filled along with his
    The place of many more;
Time came, and hardly one of us
    Had credence to restore,   10
From what appeared one day, the man
    Whom we had known before.

The broken voice, the withered neck,
    The coat worn out with care,
The cleanliness of indigence,   15
    The brilliance of despair,
The fond imponderable dreams
    Of affluence,—all were there.

Poor Finzer, with his dreams and schemes,
    Faces hard now in the race,
With heart and eye that have a task   20
    When he looks in the face
Of one who might so easily
    Have been in Finzer's place.

He comes unfailing for the loan   25
    We give and then forget;
He comes, and probably for years
    Will he be coming yet,—
Familiar as an old mistake,
    And futile as regret.   30

1916

Cassandra [5]

I heard one who said: "Verily,
    What word have I for children here?
Your Dollar is your only Word,[6]
    The wrath of it your only fear.

5. In the *Iliad*, Cassandra, daughter of King Priam, was enabled to prophesy by Apollo; when she refused to submit to his desires, he obtained that no one should believe her prophecies.
6. *Cf.* "Word," in John i: 1; and see the recurrence of "Dollar" as part of the unholy Trinity, in ll. 29–30.

"You build it altars tall enough
    To make you see, but you are blind;
You cannot leave it long enough
    To look before you or behind.

"When Reason beckons you to pause,
    You laugh and say that you know best;
But what it is you know, you keep
    As dark as ingots in a chest.

"You laugh and answer, 'We are young;
    O leave us now, and let us grow.'—
Not asking how much more of this
    Will Time endure or Fate bestow.

"Because a few complacent years
    Have made your peril of your pride,
Think you that you are to go on
    Forever pampered and untried?

"What lost eclipse of history,
    What bivouac of the marching stars,
Has given the sign for you to see
    Millenniums and last great wars?

"What unrecorded overthrow
    Of all the world has ever known,
Or ever been, has made itself
    So plain to you, and you alone?

"Your Dollar, Dove and Eagle make
    A Trinity that even you
Rate higher than you rate yourselves;
    It pays, it flatters, and it's new.[7]

"And though your very flesh and blood
    Be what your Eagle eats and drinks,
You'll praise him for the best of birds,
    Not knowing what the Eagle thinks.

"The power is yours, but not the sight;
    You see not upon what you tread;
You have the ages for your guide,
    But not the wisdom to be led.

"Think you to tread forever down
    The merciless old verities?

7. Robinson opposed "dollar diplomacy," the policy of protection for American investments in Latin America, which Wilson (1913) inherited.

And are you never to have eyes
    To see the world for what it is?

"Are you to pay for what you have   45
    With all you are?"—No other word
We caught, but with a laughing crowd
    Moved on. None heeded, and few heard.

1916

Old King Cole

In Tilbury Town did Old King Cole
    A wise old age anticipate,
Desiring, with his pipe and bowl,
    No Khan's extravagant estate.
No crown annoyed his honest head,   5
    No fiddlers three were called or needed;
For two disastrous heirs instead
    Made music more than ever three did.

Bereft of her with whom his life
    Was harmony without a flaw,   10
He took no other for a wife,
    Nor sighed for any that he saw;
And if he doubted his two sons,
    And heirs, Alexis and Evander,
He might have been as doubtful once   15
    Of Robert Burns and Alexander.

Alexis, in his early youth,
    Began to steal—from old and young.
Likewise Evander, and the truth
    Was like a bad taste on his tongue.   20
Born thieves and liars, their affair
    Seemed only to be tarred with evil—
The most insufferable pair
    Of scamps that ever cheered the devil.

The world went on, their fame went on,   25
    And they went on—from bad to worse;
Till, goaded hot with nothing done,
    And each accoutred with a curse,
The friends of Old King Cole, by twos,
    And fours, and sevens, and elevens,   30
Pronounced unalterable views
    Of doings that were not of heaven's.

And having learned again whereby
Their baleful zeal had come about,
King Cole met many a wrathful eye   35
So kindly that its wrath went out—
Or partly out. Say what they would,
He seemed the more to court their candor;
But never told what kind of good
Was in Alexis and Evander.   40

And Old King Cole, with many a puff
That haloed his urbanity,
Would smoke till he had smoked enough,
And listen most attentively.
He beamed as with an inward light   45
That had the Lord's assurance in it;
And once a man was there all night,
Expecting something every minute.

But whether from too little thought,
Or too much fealty to the bowl,   50
A dim reward was all he got
For sitting up with Old King Cole.
"Though mine," the father mused aloud,
"Are not the sons I would have chosen,
Shall I, less evilly endowed,   55
By their infirmity be frozen?

"They'll have a bad end, I'll agree,
But I was never born to groan;
For I can see what I can see,
And I'm accordingly alone.   60
With open heart and open door,
I love my friends, I like my neighbors;
But if I try to tell you more,
Your doubts will overmatch my labors.

"This pipe would never make me calm,   65
This bowl my grief would never drown.
For grief like mine there is no balm
In Gilead,[8] or in Tilbury Town.
And if I see what I can see,
I know not any way to blind it;   70
Nor more if any way may be
For you to grope or fly to find it.

8. *Cf.* Jeremiah viii: 22.

"There may be room for ruin yet,
And ashes for a wasted love;
Or, like One whom you may forget,   75
I may have meat you know not of.[9]
And if I'd rather live than weep
Meanwhile, do you find that surprising?
Why, bless my soul, the man's asleep!
That's good. The sun will soon be rising."   80

1916

Mr. Flood's Party

Old Eben Flood, climbing alone one night
Over the hill between the town below
And the forsaken upland hermitage
That held as much as he should ever know
On earth again of home, passed warily.   5
The road was his with not a native near;
And Eben, having leisure, said aloud;
For no man else in Tilbury Town to hear:

"Well, Mr. Flood, we have the harvest moon
Again, and we may not have many more;   10
The bird is on the wing, the poet says,
And you and I have said it here before.
Drink to the bird." [1] He raised up to the light
The jug that he had gone so far to fill,
And answered huskily: "Well, Mr. Flood,   15
Since you propose it, I believe I will."

Alone, as if enduring to the end
A valiant armor of scarred hopes outworn,
He stood there in the middle of the road
Like Roland's ghost winding a silent horn.[2]   20
Below him, in the town among the trees,
Where friends of other days had honored him,
A phantom salutation of the dead
Rang thinly till old Eben's eyes were dim.

Then, as a mother lays her sleeping child   25
Down tenderly, fearing it may awake,
He set the jug down slowly at his feet

---

9. *Cf.* John iv: 32. With these words
Jesus answered his disciples' invitation
to eat, having just converted the
Samaritan woman at Jacob's Well.
1. *Cf.* Edward FitzGerald, *The Rubái-
yát of Omar Khayyám*, ll. 25–28:
"Come, fill the Cup, and in the fire
of Spring / Your Winter-garment of
Repentance fling: / The Bird of Time
has but a little way / To flutter and
the Bird is on the Wing."
2. At Roncesvalles (A.D. 778), when
the battle became hopeless, Roland at
last blew his horn for help and died.

With trembling care, knowing that most things break;
And only when assured that on firm earth
It stood, as the uncertain lives of men   30
Assuredly did not, he paced away,
And with his hand extended paused again:

"Well, Mr. Flood, we have not met like this
In a long time; and many a change has come
To both of us, I fear, since last it was   35
We had a drop together. Welcome home!"
Convivially returning with himself,
Again he raised the jug up to the light;
And with an acquiescent quaver said:
"Well, Mr. Flood, if you insist I might.   40

"Only a very little, Mr. Flood—
For auld lang syne. No more, sir; that will do."
So, for the time, apparently it did,
And Eben evidently thought so too;
For soon amid the silver loneliness   45
Of night he lifted up his voice and sang,
Secure, with only two moons listening,
Until the whole harmonious landscape rang—

"For auld lang syne." The weary throat gave out,
The last word wavered; and the song being done,   50
He raised again the jug regretfully
And shook his head, and was again alone.
There was not much that was ahead of him,
And there was nothing in the town below—
Where strangers would have shut the many doors   55
That many friends had opened long ago.

1920

The Mill

The miller's wife had waited long,
    The tea was cold, the fire was dead;
And there might yet be nothing wrong
    In how he went and what he said:
"There are no millers any more,"   5
    Was all that she had heard him say;
And he had lingered at the door
    So long that it seemed yesterday.

Sick with a fear that had no form
    She knew that she was there at last;   10
And in the mill there was a warm
    And mealy fragrance of the past.
What else there was would only seem
    To say again what he had meant;
And what was hanging from a beam   15
    Would not have heeded where she went.

And if she thought it followed her,
    She may have reasoned in the dark
That one way of the few there were
    Would hide her and would leave no mark: 20
Black water, smooth above the weir
    Like starry velvet in the night,
Though ruffled once, would soon appear
    The same as ever to the sight.

1920

Firelight

Ten years together without yet a cloud,
They seek each other's eyes at intervals
Of gratefulness to firelight and four walls
For love's obliteration of the crowd.
Serenely and perennially endowed   5
And bowered as few may be, their joy recalls
No snake, no sword; and over them there falls
The blessing of what neither says aloud.

Wiser for silence, they were not so glad
Were she to read the graven tale of lines
On the wan face of one somewhere alone;   10
Nor were they more content could he have had
Her thoughts a moment since of one who shines
Apart, and would be hers if he had known.

1920

The Tree in Pamela's Garden

Pamela was too gentle to deceive
Her roses. "Let the men stay where they are,"
She said, "and if Apollo's avatar [3]

---

3. Embodiment. Apollo, smitten by
Cupid's golden arrow, fell in love with
Daphne, whom the prankish Cupid had
struck with the leaden arrow of reluctance. Daphne was saved from Apollo's
pursuit by being changed into a laurel
tree. *Cf.* the reference to Eve in l. 8,
recalling another tree in another garden.

Be one of them, I shall not have to grieve."
And so she made all Tilbury Town believe   5
She sighed a little more for the North Star
Than over men, and only in so far
As she was in a garden was like Eve.

Her neighbors—doing all that neighbors can
To make romance of reticence meanwhile—   10
Seeing that she had never loved a man,
Wished Pamela had a cat, or a small bird,
And only would have wondered at her smile
Could they have seen that she had overheard.

1921

New England [4]

Here where the wind is always north-north-east
And children learn to walk on frozen toes,
Wonder begets an envy of all those
Who boil elsewhere with such a lyric yeast
Of love that you will hear them at a feast   5
Where demons would appeal for some repose,
Still clamoring where the chalice overflows
And crying wildest who have drunk the least.

Passion is here a soilure of the wits,
We're told, and Love a cross for them to bear;   10
Joy shivers in the corner where she knits
And Conscience always has the rocking-chair,
Cheerful as when she tortured into fits
The first cat that was ever killed by Care.

1925

ROBERT FROST
(1874[1]–1963)

Among the American poets of stature since Whitman, Robert Frost is the most universal in his appeal. His art is an act of clarification, an act which, without simplifying the truth, renders it in some degree accessible to everyone. Frost found his poetry in the familiar objects and character of New England, but people who have never seen New Hampshire or Vermont, reading

4. In a Gardiner paper Robinson defended this sonnet as "an oblique attack" on those ridiculing the "alleged emotional and moral frigidity" of New England.
1. Not 1875 as often given.

his poems in California or Virginia, experience their revelation.

It is therefore not surprising that this poet of New England was first recognized in old England and that his boyhood was passed in California. His father, a journalist of southern extraction, left New Hampshire during the Civil War, and his professional engagements led him to California. There the poet was born on March 26, 1874, and was named Robert Lee in memory of the Old Dominion. He was eleven when his father died and his mother returned to her people in Lawrence, Massachusetts, and Amherst, New Hampshire.

Life with relatives proved difficult, so his mother went to teach school in Salem, New Hampshire. Frost later attended Lawrence High School. On graduation in 1892 he was one of two valedictorians; the other was Elinor White, whom he married three years later. Reluctant to accept his grandfather's support at Dartmouth College, Frost did not finish the first semester. Instead he tried himself out on a country paper, then turned to teaching school. He sent out his verses in quantity after 1890, but only a negligible few were accepted before 1913. Like Robinson he was much ahead of his time.

Faced with disappointment as a poet, his family growing, the young Frost accepted his grandfather's assistance, and studied at Harvard for two years (1897–1899), but he concluded that formal study was not the way for him. His good foundation in

the classics is apparent in his extraordinary word sense, in the disciplined forms of his poetry, and in his pagan delight in nature. His reading of science and philosophy has been influential throughout his poetry. But he had a deep-rooted fear: "They would have made me into a professor, or into a professional," he once said.

In 1900, with his grandfather's help, he procured a farm at Derry, New Hampshire, supporting his family, including four children, by a combination of farming and teaching. From 1900 to 1911 he taught English at Pinkerton Academy, Derry. In 1911–1912 he conducted a course in psychology at the State Normal School in Plymouth, nearby. Still he received from American editors the same heartbreaking refusals.

Elinor Frost, a steady source of inspiration, encouraged his instinct for a desperate remedy. They sold the farm in 1912 and on the small proceeds went to England, where the first stirrings of a new poetry movement had been noted. Wishing, as he says, to live "beneath a thatched roof" they moved to a small farmstead in the country. There Wilfred W. Gibson and Lascelles Abercrombie were neighbors, and others of the so-called "Georgians," Edward Thomas and Rupert Brooke, came as guests. Soon *A Boy's Will* (1913) was hailed in England as a work of genuine merit. It was followed in 1914 by *North of Boston*, one of the great volumes of this century. Both books were republished in the United States within the year.

At this point, according to a friend, Frost said to his wife, "My book has gone home; we must go too." In 1915 they were settled again on a New Hampshire farm, near Franconia, which suggested the title of *Mountain Interval* (1916).

In 1916 he read "The Ax-Helve" as the Phi Beta Kappa poem at Harvard University. Frost had magnificent qualities as a public reader; his reading tours during many years made him and his poetry household property and stimulated a popular interest in poetry. Also in 1916, Frost became "poet in residence" at Amherst College, where he returned for a time each winter for four years. At various times he served as lecturer or fellow at Wesleyan, Michigan, Dartmouth, Yale, and Harvard. In 1920 he participated in the founding of the Bread Loaf School of English (Middlebury College, Vermont), and he lectured there many summers. He lived nearby on his own land at Ripton.

Frost's later publications appeared at rather long intervals, yet almost every poem, large or small, is unforgettable. His *Selected Poems* (1923, revised 1928) was followed by *New Hampshire* (1923), which won the Pulitzer Prize. This is one of his longest poems, but one of his most witty and wise, an anecdotal discussion of the values of life and character, flavored with New England examples. In 1928 he published *West-Running Brook*, its title poem a complex masterpiece. *Collected Poems* first appeared in 1930, and won him his second Pulitzer Prize.

A Further Range (1936) also was awarded the Pulitzer Prize. His later volumes of lyrics are *A Witness Tree* (1942) and *Steeple Bush* (1947). *A Masque of Reason* (1945) and *A Masque of Mercy* (1947) are dramatic dialogues—discussions of religious insights and contemporary society.

Few major poets have shown such remarkable consistency as Robert Frost—the whole poet is the whole man, and he captures the reader as much by the grandeur of his personality (despite the sometimes difficult personal relations of his frustrating early years) as by impeccable rightness of form and phrase. "Art strips life to form," he has said, and the substance and the words of his poems coexist in one identity. In language, he sought to catch what he called the "tones of speech," but even more successfully than Wordsworth he pruned the "language really used by men" to achieve a propriety that spontaneous speech cannot attain.

For all his descriptive realism, Frost was temperamentally a poet of meditative sobriety. The truths he sought were innate in the heart of man and in common objects. But people forget, and poetry, he said, "makes you remember what you didn't know you knew." A poem is not didactic, but provides an immediate experience which "begins in delight, and ends in wisdom"; and it provides at least "a momentary stay against confusion." Of man alone or man in society Frost demands a responsible individualism controlled by an inner mandate, and thus his views remind us of the transcendentalism of earlier New Englanders.

The standard edition of Robert Frost is *The Poetry of Robert Frost,* edited by Edward Connery Lathem, 1969. *Selected Prose of Robert Frost* was edited by Hyde Cox and E. C. Lathem, 1966.

Early biographical and critical studies are G. B. Munson, *Robert Frost: A Study in Sensibility and Good Sense,* 1927; Sidney Cox, *Robert Frost: Original "Ordinary Man,"* 1929; Caroline Ford, *The Less Traveled Road: A Study of Robert Frost,* 1935; Lawrance R. Thompson, *Fire and Ice: The Art and Thought of Robert Frost,* 1942; Sidney Cox, *Swinger of Birches,* 1957; Reginald L. Cook, *The Dimensions of Robert Frost,* 1958; and a complete biography by Elizabeth S. Sergeant, *Robert Frost: The Trial By Existence,* 1960. Lawrance Thompson, *Robert Frost: The Early Years, 1874–1915,* 1966; and *Robert Frost: The Years of Triumph, 1915–1938,* 1970, are the first two volumes of a definitive life by Frost's designated biographer. See also Jean Gould, *Robert Frost * * *,* 1964; Louis Mertins, *Robert Frost * * *,* 1965; and *The Letters of Robert Frost to Louis Untermeyer,* edited by Untermeyer in 1963. Some new critical work is: J. F. Lynan, *The Pastoral Art of Robert Frost,* 1964; Reuben Brower, *The Poetry of Robert Frost * * *,* 1963; Radcliffe Squires, *The Major Themes of Robert Frost,* 1963; and Philip L. Gerber, *Robert Frost,* 1966. Lawrance R. Thompson edited *Selected Letters,* 1964; and Arnold Grade edited *Family Letters of Robert and Elinor Frost,* 1972. A volume of reminiscences is Louis Mertins, *Robert Frost: Life and Talks-Walking,* 1965. E. C. Lathem edited *Interviews with Robert Frost,* 1966; and *A Concordance to the Poetry of Robert Frost,* 1971. *Frost: A Time to Talk: Conversations and Indiscretions,* 1972, was compiled by Robert Frances. Elaine Barry edited *Robert Frost on Writing,* 1973.

The Wood-Pile

Out walking in the frozen swamp one gray day,
I paused and said, 'I will turn back from here.
No, I will go on farther—and we shall see.'
The hard snow held me, save where now and then
One foot went through. The view was all in lines   5
Straight up and down of tall slim trees
Too much alike to mark or name a place by
So as to say for certain I was here
Or somewhere else: I was just far from home.
A small bird flew before me. He was careful   10
To put a tree between us when he lighted,
And say no word to tell me who he was
Who was so foolish as to think what *he* thought.
He thought that I was after him for a feather—
The white one in his tail; like one who takes   15
Everything said as personal to himself.
One flight out sideways would have undeceived him.
And then there was a pile of wood for which
I forgot him and let his little fear
Carry him off the way I might have gone,   20
Without so much as wishing him good-night.
He went behind it to make his last stand.
It was a cord of maple, cut and split
And piled—and measured, four by four by eight.

And not another like it could I see.   25
No runner tracks in this year's snow looped near it.
And it was older sure than this year's cutting,
Or even last year's or the year's before.
The wood was gray and the bark warping off it
And the pile somewhat sunken. Clematis   30
Had wound strings round and round it like a bundle.
What held it though on one side was a tree
Still growing, and on one a stake and prop,
These latter about to fall. I thought that only
Someone who lived in turning to fresh tasks   35
Could so forget his handiwork on which
He spent himself, the labor of his ax,
And leave it there far from a useful fireplace
To warm the frozen swamp as best it could
With the slow smokeless burning of decay.   40

1914

After Apple-Picking

My long two-pointed ladder's sticking through a tree
Toward heaven still,
And there's a barrel that I didn't fill
Beside it, and there may be two or three
Apples I didn't pick upon some bough.   5
But I am done with apple-picking now.
Essence of winter sleep is on the night,
The scent of apples: I am drowsing off.
I cannot rub the strangeness from my sight
I got from looking through a pane of glass   10
I skimmed this morning from the drinking trough
And held against the world of hoary grass.
It melted, and I let it fall and break.
But I was well
Upon my way to sleep before it fell,   15
And I could tell
What form my dreaming was about to take.
Magnified apples appear and disappear,
Stem end and blossom end,
And every fleck of russet showing clear.   20
My instep arch not only keeps the ache,
It keeps the pressure of a ladder-round.
I feel the ladder sway as the boughs bend.

And I keep hearing from the cellar bin
The rumbling sound
Of load on load of apples coming in. 25
For I have had too much
Of apple-picking: I am overtired
Of the great harvest I myself desired.
There were ten thousand thousand fruit to touch, 30
Cherish in hand, lift down, and not let fall.
For all
That struck the earth,
No matter if not bruised or spiked with stubble,
Went surely to the cider-apple heap 35
As of no worth.
One can see what will trouble
This sleep of mine, whatever sleep it is.
Were he not gone,
The woodchuck could say whether it's like his 40
Long sleep, as I describe its coming on,
Or just some human sleep.

1914

Home Burial [2]

He saw her from the bottom of the stairs
Before she saw him. She was starting down,
Looking back over her shoulder at some fear.
She took a doubtful step and then undid it
To raise herself and look again. He spoke 5
Advancing toward her: "What is it you see
From up there always—for I want to know."
She turned and sank upon her skirts at that,
And her face changed from terrified to dull.
He said to gain time: "What is it you see," 10
Mounting until she cowered under him.
"I will find out now—you must tell me, dear."
She, in her place, refused him any help
With the least stiffening of her neck and silence.
She let him look, sure that he wouldn't see, 15
Blind creature; and a while he didn't see.
But at last he murmured, "Oh," and again, "Oh."

2. The family burial ground near the farmhouse can still be seen in remoter parts
of New England and other eastern areas.

"What is it—what?" she said.

                    "Just that I see."

"You don't," she challenged. "Tell me what it is."

"The wonder is I didn't see at once.   20
I never noticed it from here before.
I must be wonted to it—that's the reason.
The little graveyard where my people are!
So small the window frames the whole of it.
Not so much larger than a bedroom, is it?   25
There are three stones of slate and one of marble,
Broad-shouldered little slabs there in the sunlight
On the sidehill. We haven't to mind *those*.
But I understand: it is not the stones,
But the child's mound—"

           "Don't, don't, don't, don't," she cried.   30

She withdrew, shrinking from beneath his arm
That rested on the banister, and slid downstairs;
And turned on him with such a daunting look,
He said twice over before he knew himself:
"Can't a man speak of his own child he's lost?"   35

"Not you!—Oh, where's my hat? Oh, I don't need it!
I must get out of here. I must get air.—
I don't know rightly whether any man can."

"Amy! Don't go to someone else this time.
Listen to me. I won't come down the stairs."   40
He sat and fixed his chin between his fists.
"There's something I should like to ask you, dear."

"You don't know how to ask it."

                  "Help me, then."
Her fingers moved the latch for all reply.

"My words are nearly always an offense.   45
I don't know how to speak of anything
So as to please you. But I might be taught,
I should suppose. I can't say I see how.
A man must partly give up being a man
With womenfolk. We could have some arrangement   50
By which I'd bind myself to keep hands off
Anything special you're a-mind to name.
Though I don't like such things 'twixt those that love.

Two that don't love can't live together without them.
But two that do can't live together with them."   55
She moved the latch in a little. "Don't—don't go.
Don't carry it to someone else this time.
Tell me about it if it's something human.
Let me into your grief. I'm not so much
Unlike other folks as your standing there   60
Apart would make me out. Give me my chance.
I do think, though, you overdo it a little.
What was it brought you up to think it the thing
To take your mother-loss of a first child
So inconsolably—in the face of love.   65
You'd think his memory might be satisfied—"

"There you go sneering now!"

       "I'm not, I'm not!
You make me angry. I'll come down to you.
God, what a woman! And it's come to this,
A man can't speak of his own child that's dead."   70

"You can't because you don't know how to speak.
If you had any feelings, you that dug
With your own hand—how could you?—his little grave;
I saw you from that very window there,
Making the gravel leap and leap in air,   75
Leap up, like that, like that, and land so lightly
And roll back down the mound beside the hole.
I thought, Who is that man? I didn't know you.
And I crept down the stairs and up the stairs
To look again, and still your spade kept lifting.   80
Then you came in. I heard your rumbling voice
Out in the kitchen, and I don't know why,
But I went near to see with my own eyes.
You could sit there with the stains on your shoes
Of the fresh earth from your own baby's grave   85
And talk about your everyday concerns.
You had stood the spade up against the wall
Outside there in the entry, for I saw it."

"I shall laugh the worst laugh I ever laughed.
I'm cursed. God, if I don't believe I'm cursed."   90

"I can repeat the very words you were saying.
'Three foggy mornings and one rainy day
Will rot the best birch fence a man can build.'
Think of it, talk like that at such a time!

What had how long it takes a birch to rot   95
To do with what was in the darkened parlour.
You *couldn't* care! The nearest friends can go
With anyone to death, comes so far short
They might as well not try to go at all.
No, from the time when one is sick to death,   100
One is alone, and he dies more alone.
Friends make pretense of following to the grave,
But before one is in it, their minds are turned
And making the best of their way back to life
And living people, and things they understand.   105
But the world's evil. I won't have grief so
If I can change it. Oh, I won't, I won't!"

"There, you have said it all and you feel better.
You won't go now. You're crying. Close the door.
The heart's gone out of it: why keep it up?   110
Amy! There's someone coming down the road!"

"*You*—oh, you think the talk is all. I must go—
Somewhere out of this house. How can I make you—"

"If—you—do!" She was opening the door wider.
"Where do you mean to go? First tell me that.   115
I'll follow and bring you back by force. I *will!*—"

1914

Blueberries

"You ought to have seen what I saw on my way
To the village, through Patterson's pasture to-day:
Blueberries as big as the end of your thumb,
Real sky-blue, and heavy, and ready to drum
In the cavernous pail of the first one to come!   5
And all ripe together, not some of them green
And some of them ripe! You ought to have seen!"
"I don't know what part of the pasture you mean."

"You know where they cut off the woods—let me see—
It was two years ago—or no!—can it be   10
No longer than that?—and the following fall
The fire ran and burned it all up but the wall."

"Why, there hasn't been time for the bushes to grow.
That's always the way with the blueberries, though:
There may not have been the ghost of a sign   15

Of them anywhere under the shade of the pine,
But get the pine out of the way, you may burn
The pasture all over until not a fern
Or grass-blade is left, not to mention a stick,
And presto, they're up all around you as thick   20
And hard to explain as a conjuror's trick."

"It must be on charcoal they fatten their fruit.
I taste in them sometimes the flavor of soot.
And after all really they're ebony skinned:
The blue's but a mist from the breath of the wind,   25
A tarnish that goes at a touch of the hand,
And less than the tan with which pickers are tanned."

"Does Patterson know what he has, do you think?"

"He may and not care, and so leave the chewink
To gather them for him—you know what he is.   30
He won't make the fact that they're rightfully his
An excuse for keeping us other folk out."

"I wonder you didn't see Loren about."

"The best of it was that I did. Do you know,
I was just getting through what the field had to show   35
And over the wall and into the road,
When who should come by, with a democrat-load
Of all the young chattering Lorens alive,
But Loren, the fatherly, out for a drive."

"He saw you, then? What did he do? Did he frown?"   40

"He just kept nodding his head up and down.
You know how politely he always goes by.
But he thought a big thought—I could tell by his eye—
Which being expressed, might be this in effect:
'I have left those there berries, I shrewdly suspect,   45
To ripen too long. I am greatly to blame.' "

"He's a thriftier person than some I could name."

"He seems to be thrifty; and hasn't he need,
With the mouths of all those young Lorens to feed?
He has brought them all up on wild berries, they say,   50
Like birds. They store a great many away.
They eat them the year round, and those they don't eat
They sell in the store and buy shoes for their feet."

"Who cares what they say? It's a nice way to live,

Just taking what Nature is willing to give,   55
Not forcing her hand with harrow and plow."

"I wish you had seen his perpetual bow—
And the air of the youngsters! Not one of them turned,
And they looked so solemn-absurdly concerned."

"I wish I knew half what the flock of them know   60
Of where all the berries and other things grow,
Cranberries in bogs and raspberries on top
Of the boulder-strewn mountain, and when they will crop.
I met them one day and each had a flower
Stuck into his berries as fresh as a shower;   65
Some strange kind—they told me it hadn't a name."

"I've told you how once not long after we came,
I almost provoked poor Loren to mirth
By going to him of all people on earth
To ask if he knew any fruit to be had   70
For the picking. The rascal, he said he'd be glad
To tell if he knew. But the year had been bad.
There *had* been some berries—but those were all gone.
He didn't say where they had been. He went on:
'I'm sure—I'm sure'—as polite as could be.   75
He spoke to his wife in the door, 'Let me see,
Mame, *we* don't know any good berrying place?'
It was all he could do to keep a straight face."

"If he thinks all the fruit that grows wild is for him,
He'll find he's mistaken. See here, for a whim,   80
We'll pick in the Pattersons' pasture this year.
We'll go in the morning, that is, if it's clear,
And the sun shines out warm: the vines must be wet.
It's so long since I picked I almost forget
How we used to pick berries: we took one look round,   85
Then sank out of sight like trolls underground,
And saw nothing more of each other, or heard,
Unless when you said I was keeping a bird
Away from its nest, and I said it was you.
'Well, one of us is.' For complaining it flew   90
Around and around us. And then for a while
We picked, till I feared you had wandered a mile,
And I thought I had lost you. I lifted a shout
Too loud for the distance you were, it turned out,
For when you made answer, your voice was as low   95

As talking—you stood up beside me, you know."

"We sha'nt have the place to ourselves to enjoy—
Not likely, when all the young Lorens deploy.
They'll be there tomorrow, or even tonight.
They won't be too friendly—they may be polite—   100
To people they look on as having no right
To pick where they're picking. But we won't complain.
You ought to have seen how it looked in the rain,
The fruit mixed with water in layers of leaves,
Like two kinds of jewels, a vision for thieves."   105

1914

✓ Birches

When I see birches bend to left and right
Across the lines of straighter darker trees,
I like to think some boy's been swinging them.
But swinging doesn't bend them down to stay
As ice storms do. Often you must have seen them   5
Loaded with ice a sunny winter morning
After a rain. They click upon themselves
As the breeze rises, and turn many-colored
As the stir cracks and crazes their enamel.
Soon the sun's warmth makes them shed crystal shells   10
Shattering and avalanching on the snow-crust—
Such heaps of broken glass to sweep away
You'd think the inner dome of heaven had fallen.
They are dragged to the withered bracken by the load,
And they seem not to break; though once they are bowed   15
So low for long, they never right themselves:
You may see their trunks arching in the woods
Years afterwards, trailing their leaves on the ground
Like girls on hands and knees that throw their hair
Before them over their heads to dry in the sun.   20
But I was going to say when Truth broke in
With all her matter of fact about the ice storm
I should prefer to have some boy bend them
As he went out and in to fetch the cows—
Some boy too far from town to learn baseball,   25
Whose only play was what he found himself,
Summer or winter, and could play alone.
One by one he subdued his father's trees

By riding them down over and over again
Until he took the stiffness out of them, 30
And not one but hung limp, not one was left
For him to conquer. He learned all there was
To learn about not launching out too soon
And so not carrying the tree away
Clear to the ground. He always kept his poise 35
To the top branches, climbing carefully
With the same pains you use to fill a cup
Up to the brim, and even above the brim.
Then he flung outward, feet first, with a swish,
Kicking his way down through the air to the ground. 40
So was I once myself a swinger of birches.
And so I dream of going back to be.
It's when I'm weary of considerations,
And life is too much like a pathless wood
Where your face burns and tickles with the cobwebs 45
Broken across it, and one eye is weeping
From a twig's having lashed across it open.
I'd like to get away from earth awhile
And then come back to it and begin over.
May no fate willfully misunderstand me 50
And half grant what I wish and snatch me away
Not to return. Earth's the right place for love:
I don't know where it's likely to go better.
I'd like to go by climbing a birch tree,
And climb black branches up a snow-white trunk 55
Toward heaven, till the tree could bear no more,
But dipped its top and set me down again.
That would be good both going and coming back.
One could do worse than be a swinger of birches.

1916

Brown's Descent

Brown lived at such a lofty farm
    That everyone for miles could see
His lantern when he did his chores
    In winter after half-past three.

And many must have seen him make 5
    His wild descent from there one night,
'Cross lots, 'cross walls, 'cross everything,
    Describing rings of lantern light.

Between the house and barn the gale
   Got him by something he had on 10
And blew him out on the icy crust
   That cased the world, and he was gone!

Walls were all buried, trees were few:
   He saw no stay unless he stove
A hole in somewhere with his heel. 15
   But though repeatedly he strove

And stamped and said things to himself,
   And sometimes something seemed to yield,
He gained no foothold, but pursued
   His journey down from field to field. 20

Sometimes he came with arms outspread
   Like wings, revolving in the scene
Upon his longer axis, and
   With no small dignity of mien.

Faster or slower as he chanced, 25
   Sitting or standing as he chose,
According as he feared to risk
   His neck, or thought to spare his clothes.

He never let the lantern drop.
   And some exclaimed who saw afar 30
The figures he described with it,
   "I wonder what those signals are

Brown makes at such an hour of night!
   He's celebrating something strange.
I wonder if he's sold his farm, 35
   Or been made Master of the Grange."

He reeled, he lurched, he bobbed, he checked;
   He fell and made the lantern rattle
(But saved the light from going out.)
   So halfway down he fought the battle, 40

Incredulous of his own bad luck.
   And then becoming reconciled
To everything, he gave it up
   And came down like a coasting child.

"Well—I—be—" that was all he said, 45
   As standing in the river road,

He looked back up the slippery slope
   (Two miles it was) to his abode.

Sometimes as an authority
   On motorcars, I'm asked if I   50
Should say our stock was petered out,
   And this is my sincere reply:

Yankees are what they always were.
   Don't think Brown ever gave up hope
Of getting home again because   55
   He couldn't climb that slippery slope;

Or even thought of standing there
   Until the January thaw
Should take the polish off the crust.
   He bowed with grace to natural law,   60

And then went round it on his feet,
   After the manner of our stock;
Not much concerned for those to whom,
   At that particular time o'clock,

It must have looked as if the course   65
   He steered was really straight away
From that which he was headed for—
   Not much concerned for them, I say;

No more so than became a man—
   And politician at odd seasons.   70
I've kept Brown standing in the cold
   While I invested him with reasons;

But now he snapped his eyes three times;
   Then shook his lantern, saying, "Ile's
'Bout out!" [3] and took the long way home   75
   By road, a matter of several miles.

          1916

Nothing Gold Can Stay

   Nature's first green [4] is gold,
   Her hardest hue to hold.

3. The oil is about out.
4. In Old English, "green" signified "growth" as well as a color. This poem contains several dual references; for example, the Hebrew word "Eden" means "delight," and is here contrasted with "grief."

Her early leaf's a flower;
But only so an hour.
Then leaf subsides to leaf.   5
So Eden sank to grief,
So dawn goes down to day.
Nothing gold can stay.

1923

✓ Fire and Ice

Some say the world will end in fire,
Some say in ice.
From what I've tasted of desire
I hold with those who favor fire.
But if it had to perish twice,   5
I think I know enough of hate
To say that for destruction ice
Is also great
And would suffice.

1923

✓ Stopping by Woods on a Snowy Evening

Whose woods these are I think I know
His house is in the village though;
He will not see me stopping here
To watch his woods fill up with snow.

My little horse must think it queer   5
To stop without a farmhouse near
Between the woods and frozen lake
The darkest evening of the year.

He gives his harness bells a shake
To ask if there is some mistake.   10
The only other sound's the sweep
Of easy wind and downy flake.

The woods are lovely, dark and deep.
But I have promises to keep,
And miles to go before I sleep,   15
And miles to go before I sleep.

1923

The Ax-Helve

I've known ere now an interfering branch
Of alder catch my lifted ax behind me.
But that was in the woods, to hold my hand
From striking at another alder's roots,
And that was, as I say, an alder branch.   5
This was a man, Baptiste, who stole one day
Behind me on the snow in my own yard
Where I was working at the chopping-block,
And cutting nothing not cut down already.
He caught my ax expertly on the rise,   10
When all my strength put forth was in his favor,
Held it a moment where it was, to calm me,
Then took it from me—and I let him take it.
I didn't know him well enough to know
What it was all about. There might be something   15
He had in mind to say to a bad neighbor
He might prefer to say to him disarmed.
But all he had to tell me in French-English
Was what he thought of—not me, but my ax,
Me only as I took my ax to heart.   20
It was the bad ax-helve some one had sold me—
"Made on machine," he said, plowing the grain
With a thick thumbnail to show how it ran
Across the handle's long drawn serpentine,
Like the two strokes across a dollar sign.   25
"You give her one good crack, she's snap raght off.
Den where's your hax-ead flying t'rough de hair?"
Admitted; and yet, what was that to him?

"Come on my house and I put you one in
What's las' awhile—good hick'ry what's grow crooked,   30
De second growt' I cut myself—tough, tough!"

Something to sell? That wasn't how it sounded.

"Den when you say you come? It's cost you nothing.
To-naght?"

        As well tonight as any night.

Beyond an over-warmth of kitchen stove   35
My welcome differed from no other welcome.
Baptiste knew best why I was where I was.
So long as he would leave enough unsaid,

I shouldn't mind his being overjoyed
(If overjoyed he was) at having got me 40
Where I must judge if what he knew about an ax
That not everybody else knew was to count
For nothing in the measure of a neighbor.
Hard if, though cast away for life with Yankees,
A Frenchman couldn't get his human rating! 45

Mrs. Baptiste came in and rocked a chair
That had as many motions as the world:
One back and forward, in and out of shadow,
That got her nowhere; one more gradual,
Sideways, that would have run her on the stove 50
In time, had she not realized her danger
And caught herself up bodily, chair and all,
And set herself back where she started from.
"She ain't spick too much Henglish—dat's too bad."
I was afraid, in brightening first on me, 55
Then on Baptiste, as if she understood
What passed between us, she was only feigning.
Baptiste was anxious for her; but no more
Than for himself, so placed he couldn't hope
To keep his bargain of the morning with me 60
In time to keep me from suspecting him
Of really never having meant to keep it.

Needlessly soon he had his ax-helves out,
A quiverful to choose from, since he wished me
To have the best he had, or had to spare— 65
Not for me to ask which, when what he took
Had beauties he had to point me out at length
To insure their not being wasted on me.
He liked to have it slender as a whipstock,
Free from the least knot, equal to the strain 70
Of bending like a sword across the knee.
He showed me that the lines of a good helve
Were native to the grain before the knife
Expressed them, and its curves were no false curves
Put on it from without. And there its strength lay 75
For the hard work. He chafed its long white body
From end to end with his rough hand shut round it.
He tried it at the eyehole in the ax-head.
"Hahn, hahn," he mused, "don't need much taking down."
Baptiste knew how to make a short job long 80
For love of it, and yet not waste time either.

Do you know, what we talked about was knowledge?

Baptiste on his defense about the children
He kept from school, or did his best to keep—
Whatever school and children and our doubts 85
Of laid-on education had to do
With the curves of his ax-helves and his having
Used these unscrupulously to bring me
To see for once the inside of his house.
Was I desired in friendship, partly as some one 90
To leave it to, whether the right to hold
Such doubts of education should depend
Upon the education of those who held them?

But now he brushed the shavings from his knee
And stood the ax there on its horse's hoof, 95
Erect, but not without its waves, as when
The snake stood up for evil in the Garden,—
Top-heavy with a heaviness his short,
Thick hand made light of, steel-blue chin drawn down
And in a little—a French touch in that. 100
Baptiste drew back and squinted at it, pleased:
"See how she's cock her head!"

1923

The Grindstone

Having a wheel and four legs of its own
Has never availed the cumbersome grindstone
To get it anywhere that I can see.
These hands have helped it go, and even race;
Not all the motion, though, they ever lent, 5
Not all the miles it may have thought it went,
Have got it one step from the starting place.
It stands beside the same old apple tree.
The shadow of the apple tree is thin
Upon it now; its feet are fast in snow. 10
All other farm machinery's gone in,
And some of it on no more legs and wheel
Than the grindstone can boast to stand or go.
(I'm thinking chiefly of the wheelbarrow.)
For months it hasn't known the taste of steel 15
Washed down with rusty water in a tin.
But standing outdoors hungry, in the cold,
Except in towns at night, is not a sin.
And, anyway, its standing in the yard
Under a ruinous live apple tree 20

Has nothing any more to do with me,
Except that I remember how of old
One summer day, all day I drove it hard,
And someone mounted on it rode it hard,
And he and I between us ground a blade.   25

I gave it the preliminary spin,
And poured on water (tears it might have been);
And when it almost gaily jumped and flowed,
A Father-Time-like man got on and rode,
Armed with a scythe and spectacles that glowed.   30
He turned on willpower to increase the load
And slow me down—and I abruptly slowed,
Like coming to a sudden railroad station.
I changed from hand to hand in desperation.
I wondered what machine of ages gone   35
This represented an improvement on.
For all I knew it may have sharpened spears
And arrowheads itself. Much use for years
Had gradually worn it an oblate
Spheroid that kicked and struggled in its gait,   40
Appearing to return me hate for hate
(But I forgive it now as easily
As any other boyhood enemy
Whose pride has failed to get him anywhere).
I wondered who it was the man thought ground—   45
The one who held the wheel back or the one
Who gave his life to keep it going round?
I wondered if he really thought it fair
For him to have the say when we were done.
Such were the bitter thoughts to which I turned.   50

Not for myself was I so much concerned.
Oh no!—although, of course, I could have found
A better way to pass the afternoon
Than grinding discord out of a grindstone,
And beating insects at their gritty tune.   55
Nor was I for the man so much concerned.
Once when the grindstone almost jumped its bearing
It looked as if he might be badly thrown
And wounded on his blade. So far from caring,
I laughed inside, and only cranked the faster   60
(It ran as if it wasn't greased but glued);
I'd welcome any moderate disaster
That might be calculated to postpone
What evidently nothing could conclude.

The thing that made me more and more afraid 65
Was that we'd ground it sharp and hadn't known,
And now were only wasting precious blade.
And when he raised it dripping once and tried
The creepy edge of it with wary touch,
And viewed it over his glasses funny-eyed, 70
Only disinterestedly to decide
It needed a turn more, I could have cried
Wasn't there danger of a turn too much?
Mightn't we make it worse instead of better?
I was for leaving something to the whetter. 75
What if it wasn't all it should be? I'd
Be satisfied if he'd be satisfied.

1923

Two Look at Two

Love and forgetting might have carried them
A little further up the mountainside
With night so near, but not much further up.
They must have halted soon in any case
With thoughts of the path back, how rough it was 5
With rock and washout, and unsafe in darkness;
When they were halted by a tumbled wall
With barbed-wire binding. They stood facing this,
Spending what onward impulse they still had
In one last look the way they must not go, 10
On up the failing path, where, if a stone
Or earthslide moved at night, it moved itself;
No footstep moved it. "This is all," they sighed,
"Good-night to woods." But not so; there was more.
A doe from round a spruce stood looking at them 15
Across the wall, as near the wall as they.
She saw them in their field, they her in hers.
The difficulty of seeing what stood still,
Like some up-ended boulder split in two,
Was in her clouded eyes: they saw no fear there. 20
She seemed to think that, two thus, they were safe.
Then, as if they were something that, though strange,
She could not trouble her mind with too long,
She sighed and passed unscared along the wall.
"*This*, then, is all. What more is there to ask?" 25
But no, not yet. A snort to bid them wait.
A buck from round the spruce stood looking at them
Across the wall, as near the wall as they.

This was an antlered buck of lusty nostril,
Not the same doe come back into her place. 30
He viewed them quizzically with jerks of head,
As if to ask, "Why don't you make some motion?
Or give some sign of life? Because you can't.
I doubt if you're as living as you look."
Thus till he had them almost feeling dared 35
To stretch a proffering hand—and a spell-breaking.
Then he too passed unscared along the wall.
Two had seen two, whichever side you spoke from.
"This *must* be all." It was all. Still they stood,
A great wave from it going over them, 40
As if the earth in one unlooked-for favor
Had made them certain earth returned their love.

1923

Paul's Wife

To drive Paul [5] out of any lumber camp
All that was needed was to say to him,
"How is the wife, Paul?"—and he'd disappear.
Some said it was because he had no wife,
And hated to be twitted on the subject; 5
Others because he'd come within a day
Or so of having one, and then been jilted.
Others because he'd had one once, a good one,
Who'd run away with some one else and left him;
And others still because he had one now 10
He only had to be reminded of—
He was all duty to her in a minute:
He had to run right off to look her up,
As if to say, "That's so, how is my wife?
I hope she isn't getting into mischief." 15
No one was anxious to get rid of Paul.
He'd been the hero of the mountain camps
Ever since, just to show them, he had slipped
The bark of a whole tamarack off whole,
As clean as boys do off a willow twig 20
To make a willow whistle on a Sunday
In April by subsiding meadow brooks.
They seemed to ask him just to see him go,
"How is the wife, Paul?" and he always went.

5. The origin of the Paul Bunyan stories, considered as legends of the timber country, is still controversial. Frost's story has legendary flavor and the atmosphere of the French-Canadian border.

He never stopped to murder anyone 25
Who asked the question. He just disappeared—
Nobody knew in what direction,
Although it wasn't usually long
Before they heard of him in some new camp,
The same Paul at the same old feats of logging. 30
The question everywhere was why should Paul
Object to being asked a civil question—
A man you could say almost anything to
Short of a fighting word. You have the answers.
And there was one more not so fair to Paul: 35
That Paul had married a wife not his equal.
Paul was ashamed of her. To match a hero,
She would have had to be a heroine;
Instead of which she was some half-breed squaw.
But if the story Murphy told was true, 40
She wasn't anything to be ashamed of.

You know Paul could do wonders. Everyone's
Heard how he thrashed the horses on a load
That wouldn't budge until they simply stretched
Their rawhide harness from the load to camp. 45
Paul told the boss the load would be all right,
"The sun will bring your load in"—and it did—
By shrinking the rawhide to natural length.
That's what is called a stretcher. But I guess
The one about his jumping so's to land 50
With both his feet at once against the ceiling,
And then land safely right side up again,
Back on the floor, is fact or pretty near fact.
Well, this is such a yarn. Paul sawed his wife
Out of a white-pine log. Murphy was there 55
And, as you might say, saw the lady born.
Paul worked at anything in lumbering.
He'd been hard at it taking boards away
For—I forget—the last ambitious sawyer
To want to find out if he couldn't pile 60
The lumber on Paul till Paul begged for mercy.
They'd sliced the first slab off a big butt log,
And the sawyer had slammed the carriage back
To slam end-on again against the saw teeth.
To judge them by the way they caught themselves 65
When they saw what had happened to the log,
They must have had a guilty expectation

Something was going to go with their slambanging.
Something had left a broad black streak of grease
On the new wood the whole length of the log   70
Except, perhaps, a foot at either end.
But when Paul put his finger in the grease,
It wasn't grease at all, but a long slot.
The log was hollow. They were sawing pine.
"First time I ever saw a hollow pine.   75
That comes of having Paul around the place.
Take it to hell for me," the sawyer said.
Everyone had to have a look at it,
And tell Paul what he ought to do about it.
(They treated it as his.) "You take a jackknife,   80
And spread the opening, and you've got a dugout
All dug to go a-fishing in." To Paul
The hollow looked too sound and clean and empty
Ever to have housed birds or beasts or bees.
There was no entrance for them to get in by.   85
It looked to him like some new kind of hollow
He thought he'd *better* take his jackknife to.
So after work that evening he came back
And let enough light into it by cutting
To see if it was empty. He made out in there   90
A slender length of pith, or was it pith?
It might have been the skin a snake had cast
And left stood up on end inside the tree
The hundred years the tree must have been growing.
More cutting and he had this in both hands,   95
And looking from it to the pond near by,
Paul wondered how it would respond to water.
Not a breeze stirred, but just the breath of air
He made in walking slowly to the beach
Blew it once off his hands and almost broke it.   100
He laid it at the edge where it could drink.
At the first drink it rustled and grew limp.
At the next drink it grew invisible.
Paul dragged the shallows for it with his fingers,
And thought it must have melted. It was gone.   105
And then beyond the open water, dim with midges,
Where the log drive lay pressed against the boom,
It slowly rose a person, rose a girl,[6]
Her wet hair heavy on her like a helmet,
Who, leaning on a log, looked back at Paul.   110

---

6. Note the analogy with the nymphs and dryads of classical mythology.

And that made Paul in turn look back
To see if it was anyone behind him
That she was looking at instead of him.
(Murphy had been there watching all the time,
But from a shed where neither of them could see him.) 115
There was a moment of suspense in birth
When the girl seemed too waterlogged to live,
Before she caught her first breath with a gasp
And laughed. Then she climbed slowly to her feet,
And walked off, talking to herself or Paul, 120
Across the logs like backs of alligators,
Paul taking after her around the pond.

Next evening Murphy and some other fellows
Got drunk, and tracked the pair up Catamount,
From the bare top of which there is a view 125
To other hills across a kettle valley.
And there, well after dark, let Murphy tell it,
They saw Paul and his creature keeping house.
It was the only glimpse that anyone
Has had of Paul and her since Murphy saw them 130
Falling in love across the twilight millpond.
More than a mile across the wilderness
They sat together halfway up a cliff
In a small niche let into it, the girl
Brightly, as if a star played on the place, 135
Paul darkly, like her shadow. All the light
Was from the girl herself, though, not from a star,
As was apparent from what happened next.
All those great ruffians put their throats together,
And let out a loud yell, and threw a bottle, 140
As a brute tribute of respect to beauty.
Of course the bottle fell short by a mile,
But the shout reached the girl and put her light out.
She went out like a firefly, and that was all.

So there were witnesses that Paul was married, 145
And not to anyone to be ashamed of.
Everyone had been wrong in judging Paul.
Murphy told me Paul put on all those airs
About his wife to keep her to himself.
Paul was what's called a terrible possessor. 150
Owning a wife with him meant owning her.
She wasn't anybody else's business,
Either to praise her or so much as name her,
And he'd thank people not to think of her.

Murphy's idea was that a man like Paul   155
Wouldn't be spoken to about a wife
In any way the world knew how to speak.

1923

West-Running Brook

"Fred, where is north?"

"North? Nothing is there, my love.

The brook runs west."

"West-Running Brook then call it."
(West-Running Brook men call it to this day.)
"What does it think it's doing running west
When all the other country brooks flow east   5
To reach the ocean? It must be the brook
Can trust itself to go by contraries
The way I can with you—and you with me—
Because we're—we're—I don't know what we are.
What are we?"

"Young or new?"

"We must be something.   10
We've said we two. Let's change that to we three.
As you and I are married to each other,
We'll both be married to the brook. We'll build
Our bridge across it, and the bridge shall be
Our arm thrown over it asleep beside it.   15
Look, look, it's waving to us with a wave
To let us know it hears me."

"Why, my dear,
That wave's been standing off this jut of shore—"
(The black stream, catching on a sunken rock,
Flung backward on itself in one white wave,   20
And the white water rode the black forever,
Not gaining but not losing, like a bird
White feathers from the struggle of whose breast
Flecked the dark stream and flecked the darker pool
Below the point, and were at last driven wrinkled   25
In a white scarf against the far-shore alders.)
"That wave's been standing off this jut of shore
Ever since rivers, I was going to say,
Were made in heaven. It wasn't waved to us."

"It wasn't, yet it was. If not to you   30
It was to me—in an annunciation."

"Oh, if you take it off to lady-land,
As't were the country of the Amazons
We men must see you to the confines of
And leave you there, ourselves forbid to enter,—   35
It is your brook! I have no more to say."

"Yes, you have, too. Go on. You thought of something."

'Speaking of contraries, see how the brook
In that white wave runs counter to itself.
It is from that in water we were from   40
Long, long before we were from any creature.
Here we, in our impatience of the steps,
Get back to the beginning of beginnings,
The stream of everything that runs away.[7]
Some say existence like a Pirouot   45
And Pirouette, forever in one place,
Stands still and dances, but it runs away;
It seriously, sadly, runs away
To fill the abyss's void with emptiness.
It flows beside us in this water brook,   50
But it flows over us. It flows between us
To separate us for a panic moment.
It flows between us, over us, and *with* us.
And it is time, strength, tone, light, life and love—
And even substance lapsing unsubstantial;   55
The universal cataract of death
That spends to nothingness—and unresisted,
Save by some strange resistance in itself,
Not just a swerving, but a throwing back,
As if regret were in it and were sacred.   60
It has this throwing backward on itself
So that the fall of most of it is always
Raising a little, sending up a little.
Our life runs down in sending up the clock.
The brook runs down in sending up our life.   65
The sun runs down in sending up the brook.
And there is something sending up the sun.
It is this backward motion toward the source,
Against the stream, that most we see ourselves in,
The tribute of the current to the source.   70

7. A reference to Lucretius' *De Rerum Natura*, the stream of atoms, the swerving away from which produces all reality man can know.

It is from this in nature we are from.
It is most us."

"Today will be the day

You said so."
"No, today will be the day
You said the brook was called West-Running Brook."

"Today will be the day of what we both said." 75

1928

Tree at My Window

Tree at my window, window tree,
My sash is lowered when night comes on;
But let there never be curtain drawn
Between you and me.

Vague dream-head lifted out of the ground, 5
And thing next most diffuse to cloud,
Not all your light tongues talking aloud
Could be profound.

But, tree, I have seen you taken and tossed,
And if you have seen me when I slept, 10
You have seen me when I was taken and swept
And all but lost.

That day she put our heads together,
Fate had her imagination about her,
Your head so much concerned with outer, 15
Mine with inner, weather.

1928

Departmental

An ant on the table cloth
Ran into a dormant moth
Of many times his size.
He showed not the least surprise.
His business wasn't with such. 5
He gave it scarcely a touch,
And was off on his duty run.
Yet if he encountered one
Of the hive's enquiry squad
Whose work is to find out God 10

And the nature of time and space,
He would put him onto the case.
Ants are a curious race;
One crossing with hurried tread
The body of one of their dead   15
Isn't given a moment's arrest—
Seems not even impressed.
But he no doubt reports to any
With whom he crosses antennae,
And they no doubt report   20
To the higher-up at court.
Then word goes forth in Formic: [8]
"Death's come to Jerry McCormic,
Our selfless forager Jerry.
Will the special Janizary [9]   25
Whose office it is to bury
The dead of the commissary
Go bring him home to his people.
Lay him in state on a sepal.
Wrap him for shroud in a petal.   30
Embalm him with ichor of nettle.
This is the word of your Queen."
And presently on the scene
Appears a solemn mortician;
And taking formal position   35
With feelers calmly atwiddle,
Seizes the dead by the middle,
And heaving him high in air,
Carries him out of there.
No one stands round to stare.   40
It is nobody else's affair.

It couldn't be called ungentle.
But how thoroughly departmental.

1936

Come In

As I came to the edge of the woods,
Thrush music—hark!
Now if it was dusk outside,
Inside it was dark.

8. The family of ants is called the *Formicidae;* hence, "ant language."   9. A member of the special troops assigned to Turkish sovereigns.

Too dark in the woods for a bird   5
By sleight of wing
To better its perch for the night,
Though it still could sing.

The last of the light of the sun
That had died in the west   10
Still lived for one song more
In a thrush's breast.

Far in the pillared dark
Thrush music went—
Almost like a call to come in   15
To the dark and lament.

But no, I was out for stars:
I would not come in.
I meant not even if asked,
And I hadn't been.   20

1942

✓ Directive

Back out of all this now too much for us,
Back in a time made simple by the loss
Of detail, burned, dissolved, and broken off
Like graveyard marble sculpture in the weather,
There is a house that is no more a house   5
Upon a farm that is no more a farm
And in a town that is no more a town.
The road there, if you'll let a guide direct you
Who only has at heart your getting lost,
May seem as if it should have been a quarry—   10
Great monolithic knees the former town
Long since gave up pretense of keeping covered.
And there's a story in a book about it:
Besides the wear of iron wagon wheels
The ledges show lines ruled southeast-northwest,   15
The chisel work of an enormous Glacier
That graced his feet against the Arctic Pole.
You must not mind a certain coolness from him
Still said to haunt this side of Panther Mountain.
Nor need you mind the serial ordeal   20
Of being watched from forty cellar holes
As if by eye pairs out of forty firkins.
As for the woods' excitement over you

That sends light rustle rushes to their leaves,
Charge that to upstart inexperience. 25
Where were they all not twenty years ago?
They think too much of having shaded out
A few old pecker-fretted apple trees.
Make yourself up a cheering song of how
Someone's road home from work this once was, 30
Who may be just ahead of you on foot
Or creaking with a buggy load of grain.
The height of the adventure is the height
Of country where two village cultures faded
Into each other. Both of them are lost. 35
And if you're lost enough to find yourself
By now, pull in your ladder road behind you
And put a sign up CLOSED to all but me.
Then make yourself at home. The only field
Now left's no bigger than a harness gall. 40
First there's the children's house of make-believe,
Some shattered dishes underneath a pine,
The playthings in the playhouse of the children.
Weep for what little things could make them glad.
Then for the house that is no more a house, 45
But only a belilaced cellar hole,
Now slowly closing like a dent in dough.
This was no playhouse but a house in earnest.
Your destination and your destiny's
A brook that was the water of the house, 50
Cold as a spring as yet so near its source,
Too lofty and original to rage.
(We know the valley streams that when aroused
Will leave their tatters hung on barb and thorn.)
I have kept hidden in the instep arch 55
Of an old cedar at the waterside
A broken drinking goblet like the Grail
Under a spell so the wrong ones can't find it,
So can't get saved, as Saint Mark says they mustn't.
(I stole the goblet from the children's playhouse.) 60
Here are your waters and your watering place.
Drink and be whole again beyond confusion.

1947

Take Something Like a Star [1]

O Star (the fairest one in sight),
We grant your loftiness the right
To some obscurity of cloud—
It will not do to say of night,
Since dark is what brings out your light.　　　　5
Some mystery becomes the proud.
But to be wholly taciturn
In your reserve is not allowed.
Say something to us we can learn
By heart and when alone repeat.　　　　10
Say something! And it says "I burn."
But say with what degree of heat.
Talk Fahrenheit, talk Centigrade.
Use language we can comprehend.
Tell us what elements you blend.　　　　15
It gives us strangely little aid,
But does tell something in the end.
And steadfast as Keats' Eremite,[2]
Not even stooping from its sphere,
It asks a little of us here.　　　　20
It asks of us a certain height,
So when at times the mob is swayed
To carry praise or blame too far,
We may take something like a star
To stay our minds on and be staid.　　　　25

1943

CARL SANDBURG

(1878–1967)

Carl Sandburg's parents were Swedish immigrants, living at Galesburg, Illinois, when the boy was born on January 6, 1878. The father was then working on a railroad construction crew. They were a healthy and affectionate family, though very poor. At thirteen, Sandburg was obliged to leave school and go to work. For a time he found employment in Galesburg; then

1. First published in Frost's *Come In and Other Poems,* compiled by Louis Untermeyer, 1943, with the title "Choose Something Like a Star." "Take" was substituted in the title and in line 24 in *Selected Poems,* 1963. In Frost's *Complete Poems,* 1949, the poem was placed in a section titled "An Afterword," a position given to it also in *The Poetry of Robert Frost,* edited by Edward Connery Lathem, 1969.
2. *Cf.* Keats's sonnet "Bright Star! Would I Were Steadfast As Thou Art."

he became a migratory laborer, roaming from job to job in Kansas, Nebraska, and Colorado. He was at various times a milkman, a harvest hand, a hotel dishwasher, a barbershop porter, a stage hand, a brickmaker, and a sign painter. For a while he was a salesman of stereoscopes and the popular stereoscopic views of the day—a profitable employment and a good education for a poet of the people. In 1898, at the age of twenty, he settled again in Galesburg to follow the trade of house painter, but the Spanish-American War excited his interest and he enlisted in the Army. During active service in Puerto Rico he functioned as correspondent for the Galesburg *Evening Mail*, his first newspaper connection.

In eight months he was back in Galesburg, determined to secure a higher education. He had been reading hard with this in view, and he was provisionally admitted at Lombard College, although he might have preferred Knox, across town, where Lincoln had met Douglas in one of the famous debates of 1858. Young Sandburg had a good scholastic record, made a serious beginning with his writing, and became a local celebrity at basketball, but he did not graduate. A few weeks before the end of his senior year, in 1902, with all his record clear, he simply disappeared from the scene. For several years he lived as a roving newspaper reporter. In 1907 he secured an editorial position on a small Chicago paper, and made a connection which led him to Wisconsin as political organizer for the Social Democrats, a reform party, in 1908.

That year he married Lillian Steichen, sister of the famous artist-photographer Edward Steichen (of whom the poet published a pleasing biography in 1929). The young writer, aged thirty, now sought to establish the more settled pattern that befits a well-married man. In 1910 he secured appointment as secretary to the mayor of Milwaukee, and served for two years. But he was not interested in a political career. He was a writer, already the master of his trade as a journalist, although his few poems, published here and there in newspapers, did not suggest that he had found a subject or a satisfactory poetic form. He served for a year on the editorial staff of the liberal Milwaukee *Leader*. The next year, in 1913, he went to Chicago on an editorial engagement, and soon he became illustrious among the writers who were fostering a new literature in that city.

The first of Sandburg's poems in his characteristic and now familiar style was "Chicago," which appeared, in 1914, in *Poetry: A Magazine of Verse*. The *Chicago Poems* of 1916 was followed by *Cornhuskers* in 1918. That year Sandburg spent some months in Sweden as correspondent for a Chicago newspaper syndicate, and returned as editorial writer on the Chicago *Daily News*, a paper of national prominence. He remained with that paper for fifteen years as editorialist, feature writer, and columnist, retiring in 1933 under pressure of his private literary interests.

By 1920, when the "renaissance" of American literature was gaining momentum, Sandburg had reached the maturity of his power as a poet. He had twice been recognized by national awards, and his next volume, *Smoke and Steel* (1920), confirmed his position as the poet of the common man confronted with the complexities of the new industrial civilization. He began to give frequent public readings of his own poems, and soon emerged as the foremost minstrel of his time by adding to his programs the performance of American folk songs which he had long been collecting in his journeys about the country. He popularized the folk ballad before the radio became an important medium for his successors. His collection, *The American Songbag* (1927, revised and enlarged 1950), the first popular compilation of the sort, was enriched by his instinct for the genuine and his scholarly knowledge of this field. These qualities passed into his own poems, from *Slabs of the Sunburnt West* (1922) to *The People, Yes* (1936). The latter is a very knowing arrangement of American folk speech, folkways, and customs, interpreted in language that sensitively combines the flavor of the original with Sandburg's poetic perceptions.

Two other aspects of his career are noteworthy. His books for children began with *Rootabaga Stories* (1922), to be followed in 1923 by *Rootabaga Pigeons* and in 1930 by *Potato Face* and *Early Moon*. The prose stories in these collections are at a high level, but the poems especially take their place in the distinguished literature of childhood. More important is his

Abraham Lincoln: The Prairie Years (1926), a classic of biography both for its style, and for the literary tact which enabled him to remain faithful to the historical record of Lincoln without losing the American significance of the legendary Lincoln. During the next thirteen years, much of his spare time was devoted to the historical study that prepared him to complete his task in 1939, in the four volumes of *Abraham Lincoln: The War Years*, which was awarded the Pulitzer Prize. He concentrated his knowledge of the subject in the one-volume *Abraham Lincoln* of 1954, an authoritative and powerful study.

Sandburg has also published several books of a topical nature. He is author or coauthor of three volumes of Lincoln studies. During the Second World War, he published his commentary on events of the time in *Storm over the Land* (1942), and *Home Front Memo* (1943). His one novel, *Remembrance Rock* (1950), is a fictional survey of American history from the colonial period. His considerable influence on the national culture has been recognized by the award of many honorary degrees and the accolades of learned and literary academies.

His *Complete Poems*, published in 1950, gave perspective to an accomplishment of great spiritual value to his generation. When he first became known, he was hailed as an interesting and vigorous curiosity, a journalist of poetry, the form of his verse being regarded as at most an external device. Now he can be seen as a truly gifted poet who gave shape and permanence to the phrases, rhythms, and symbols of the American popular idiom, while embodying the common idealism of the people in forms often of notable subtlety. He has fulfilled Whitman's prescription for the poet—"that his country absorbs him as affectionately as he has absorbed it."

There is no complete collection of Sandburg's work. The standard text of the poems is *The Complete Poems of Carl Sandburg*, 1950; revised and expanded, 1970. The earlier volumes have been named in the text above. The *Selected Poems of Carl Sandburg*, edited by Rebecca West in 1926, contains a good selection to that date and a valuable critical introduction by the editor. Herbert Mitgang edited *The Letters of Carl Sandburg*, 1968.

Karl Detzer's *Carl Sandburg: A Study in Personality and Background*, 1941, is informative and critically sound. More recent is North Callahan, *Carl Sandburg: Lincoln of our Literature*, 1969. Carl Sandburg's autobiographical account, *Always the Young Strangers*, 1952, is of course authoritative in respect to biographical data as far as it goes, and illuminating for the student of Sandburg's personality. See also Richard Crowder, *Carl Sandburg*, 1963; and Hazell Durnell, *The America of Carl Sandburg*, 1965.

Nocturne in a Deserted Brickyard

Stuff of the moon
Runs on the lapping sand
Out to the longest shadows.
Under the curving willows,
And round the creep of the wave line,   5
Fluxions of yellow and dusk on the waters
Make a wide dreaming pansy of an old pond in the night.

(Imagist tendency)

1916

Monotone

The monotone of the rain is beautiful,
And the sudden rise and slow relapse
Of the long multitudinous rain.

The sun on the hills is beautiful,
Or a captured sunset sea-flung,   5
Bannered with fire and gold.

A face I know is beautiful—
With fire and gold of sky and sea,
And the peace of long warm rain.

1910   1916

Gone

Everybody loved Chick Lorimer in our town.
Far off
Everybody loved her.

So we all love a wild girl keeping a hold
      On a dream she wants.   5
Nobody knows now where Chick Lorimer went.
Nobody knows why she packed her trunk . . . a few old things
And is gone,
           Gone with her little chin
           Thrust ahead of her   10
           And her soft hair blowing careless
           From under a wide hat,
Dancer, singer, a laughing passionate lover.

Were there ten men or a hundred hunting Chick?
Were there five men or fifty with aching hearts?   15
      Everybody loved Chick Lorimer.
           Nobody knows where she's gone.

                          1916

A Fence

Now the stone house on the lake front is finished and the workmen
    are beginning the fence.
The palings are made of iron bars with steel points that can stab the
    life out of any man who falls on them.
As a fence, it is a masterpiece, and will shut off the rabble and all
    vagabonds and hungry men and all wandering children looking
    for a place to play.
Passing through the bars and over the steel points will go nothing
    except Death and the Rain and To-morrow.

1913   1916

Grass

    Pile the bodies high at Austerlitz [1] and Waterloo.
    Shovel them under and let me work—
        I am the grass; I cover all.

    And pile them high at Gettysburg
    And pile them high at Ypres and Verdun.   5
    Shovel them under and let me work.

    Two years, ten years, and passengers ask the conductor:
        What place is this?
        Where are we now?

1. The places named in the poem were all scenes of great battles in major wars:
the Napoleonic Wars, the Civil War, and World War I.

I am the grass.   10
Let me work.

                                                        1918

Southern Pacific

Huntington [2] sleeps in a house six feet long.
Huntington dreams of railroads he built and owned.
Huntington dreams of ten thousand men saying: Yes, sir.

Blithery sleeps in a house six feet long.
Blithery dreams of rails and ties he laid.   5
Blithery dreams of saying to Huntington: Yes, sir.

Huntington,
Blithery, sleep in houses six feet long.

                                                        1918

Washerwoman

The washerwoman is a member of the Salvation Army.
And over the tub of suds rubbing underwear clean
She sings that Jesus will wash her sins away
And the red wrongs she has done God and man
Shall be white as driven snow.   5
Rubbing underwear she sings of the Last Great Washday.

                                                        1918

Stars, Songs, Faces

Gather the stars if you wish it so.
Gather the songs and keep them.
Gather the faces of women.
Gather for keeping years and years.
        And then . . .   5
Loosen your hands, let go and say good-by.
    Let the stars and songs go.
    Let the faces and years go.
    Loosen your hands and say good-by.

                                                        1920

2. Collis P. Huntington, (1821–1900), early California financier, promoter and later president (1890) of the Southern Pacific and Central Pacific railroads.

On a Railroad Right of Way

Stream, go hide yourself.
In the tall grass, in the cat-tails,
In the browns of autumn, the last purple asters, the yellow
    whispers.
On the moss rock levels leave the marks of your wave-lengths.
Sing in your gravel, in your clean gully.   5
Let the moaning railroad trains go by.
Till they stop you, go on with your song.

The minnies [3] spin in the water gravel,
In the spears of the early autumn sun.
There must be winter fish.   10
Babies, you will be jumping fish
In the first snow month.

          1928

Waiting for the Chariot

(*Mrs. Peter Cartwright*)[4]

Can bare fact make the cloth of a shining poem?
In Sangamon County, Illinois, they remembered how
The aged widow walked a mile from home to Bethel Chapel
Where she heard the services and was called on
"To give her testimony," rising to speak freely, ending: 5
    "The past three weeks have been the happiest
  of all my life; I am waiting for the chariot."
The pastor spoke the benediction; the members rose and moved
Into the aisles toward the door, and looking back
They saw the widow of the famous circuit rider   10
Sitting quiet and pale in an inviolable dignity
And they heard the pastor: "The chariot has arrived."

          1960

3. Minnows.
4. Peter Cartwright (1785–1872), Methodist frontier evangelist in Kentucky and Illinois, ran against Lincoln in Illinois in 1846 for Congress and lost.

The Attack on Convention

H. L. MENCKEN
(1880–1956)

H. L. Mencken was the earliest of the iconoclasts of the 1920's —the most irreverent, clamorous, and resourceful leader of the crusade which crumbled the cherished idols and stereotypes of a surviving Victorian gentility. In his newspaper column (after 1910), in his editorials, and in his collections of essays, he made a battlefield of the entire terrain of contemporary life, attacking with equal agility and skill wherever he found what he regarded as entrenched stupidity or ignorance or hypocrisy—in literary standards, government, politics, economic life, foreign relations, and the manners or morals of his fellow Americans. He excoriated all official and professional defenders of the stereotype, especially the "professors," who, he believed, extended the dead hand of mere authority from universities moribund in traditionalism and intellectual timidity. An irony of his situation, which he no doubt enjoyed, was that his detractors regarded him as a dangerous radical, while actually he was, and is today considered, a conservative force. Henry Louis Mencken was

born in 1880 in Baltimore, Maryland, of mixed German and Irish stock, and was brought up in a family tradition that exalted learning and fostered a speculative originality of mind. His father conducted a successful tobacco business, and Mencken was early familiar with the concept that economic responsibility and intellectual leadership are properly combined in one person.

At the age of sixteen he was graduated from Baltimore Polytechnic Institute, and chose to study privately instead of going to college. Since his writings show a genuinely learned man, he evidently proceeded successfully with his self-discipline. At nineteen, having determined on a career in journalism, he joined the Baltimore *Morning Herald*. Later he became an editor for the Sun Syndicate, first on the *Evening Herald* (1905) and then on the Baltimore *Sun* (1906). He continued an association with these Baltimore papers as late as 1941, in addition to his many other editorial connections. In 1914 he and George Jean Nathan became co-editors

1369

of *The Smart Set,* for which Mencken had done book reviews from 1908 and Nathan had written dramatic criticism since 1909. In 1917 he began a long association as literary adviser to Alfred A. Knopf, then notable among the imaginative younger publishers. His trips abroad included service as correspondent in Germany in the winter of 1916–1917. Meanwhile his *Sun* column, "The Free Lance" (1910–1916), with its famous battles for individualism and freedom of public expression, had established his character as a controversialist. A *Book of Prefaces* (1917) was the first of his most characteristic critical volumes. In 1919 appeared *Prejudices: First Series,* and he continued to add other volumes of his collected critical essays until the *Sixth Series* of 1927. He winnowed the best of these for *Selected Prejudices* (1926) and *Selected Prejudices: Second Series* (1927). *The American Credo* (1920), a collaboration with Nathan, is associated in spirit with the *Prejudices.*

One of the most exciting periodicals of this period was *The American Mercury,* founded by Mencken and Nathan in 1923–1924, and edited by Mencken until 1933. Its policy was to satirize the stupidity of the mass mind and such typical manifestations of the period as prohibition; to expose, in a "spirit of boisterous scepticism," the "gaudy, gorgeous American scene"; and to support authors associated with this crusade of liberation, among whom were Dreiser, Sherwood Anderson, Sandburg, Edgar Lee Masters, Carl Van Vechten, Eugene O'-Neill, and Sinclair Lewis. During this whole period Mencken was also active as a contributing editor of the *Nation.*

In 1919 this versatile author and prodigious worker had published the first edition of a book which has permanently influenced our cultural history. This was *The American Language* (revised and enlarged 1921, 1923, 1936; *Supplement One,* 1945; *Supplement Two,* 1948). At first this work was ridiculed by the same reactionary authoritarians who had disapproved of the gusty, indigenous language that Mencken employed in his own writing. Yet it is now regarded as the sound beginning of a new functional approach in scholarly linguistics.

Later works of Mencken include, most importantly, his classic autobiographical series: *Happy Days, 1880–1892* (1940); *Newspaper Days, 1899–1906* (1941); and *Heathen Days, 1890–1936* (1943). His *Treatise on the Gods* appeared in 1930, the *Treatise on Right and Wrong* in 1934, and *A Mencken Chrestomathy,* a general anthology, in 1949.

In addition to the volumes mentioned above, there are *A Carnival of Buncombe,* 1956, edited by Malcolm Moos; *Minority Report: H. L. Mencken's Notebooks,* 1956; *Prejudices: A Selection,* 1958, edited by James T. Farrell; *The Bathtub Hoax and Other Blasts and Bravos from the Chicago Tribune,* 1958, collected by Robert McHugh; *H. L. Mencken: The American Scene,* 1965, edited by Huntington Cairns; and *H. L. Mencken's Smart Set Criticism,* 1968, edited by William H. Nolte. For biography, see the autobiographical volumes listed above, and Ernest A. Boyd, *H. L. Mencken,* 1925; Isaac Goldberg, *The Man Mencken,* 1925; Walter Lippmann, *H. L. Mencken,* 1926; Edgar Kemler, *The Irreverent*

Mr. Mencken, 1950; William Manchester, Disturber of the Peace, 1951; Sara Mayfield, The Constant Circle: H. L. Mencken and His Friends, 1968; Carl Bode, Mencken, 1969; and Douglas C. Stenerson, H. L. Mencken: Iconoclast from Baltimore, 1971.

See also M. K. Singleton, H. L.

Mencken and The American Mercury Adventure, 1962. William H. Nolte, H. L. Mencken, Literary Critic, 1966, is a comprehensive study of the earlier period. A permanent catalogue of Mencken items and bibliography is kept on cards at the Peabody Library in Baltimore.

From American Culture [1]

The capital defect in the culture of These States [2] is the lack of a civilized aristocracy, secure in its position, animated by an intelligent curiosity, skeptical of all facile generalizations, superior to the sentimentality of the mob, and delighting in the battle of ideas for its own sake. The word I use, despite the qualifying adjective, has got itself meanings, of course, that I by no means intend to convey. Any mention of an aristocracy, to a public fed upon democratic fustian, is bound to bring up images of stockbrokers' wives lolling obscenely in opera boxes, or of haughty Englishmen slaughtering whole generations of grouse in an inordinate and incomprehensible manner, or of bogus counts coming over to work their magic upon the daughters of breakfast-food and bathtub kings. This misconception belongs to the general American tradition. Its depth and extent are constantly revealed by the naïve assumption that the so-called fashionable folk of the large cities—chiefly wealthy industrials in the interior-decorator and country-club stage of culture—constitute an aristocracy, and by the scarcely less remarkable assumption that the peerage of England is identical with the gentry—that is, that such men as Lord Northcliffe,[3] Lord Riddel and even Lord Reading were English gentlemen.

Here, as always, the worshiper is the father of the gods, and no less when they are evil than when they are benign. The inferior man must find himself superiors, that he may marvel at his political equality with them, and in the presence of recognizable superiors de facto he creates superiors de jure.[4] The sublime principle of one man, one vote must be translated into terms of dollars,

1. First published in the Yale Review for June, 1920, this essay subsequently appeared in the section headed "The National Letters," in Prejudices: Second Series (1920). It was reprinted in A Mencken Chrestomathy (1949).
2. "These States" was a favorite and characteristic phrase of Walt Whitman's.
3. Lord Northcliffe, born Alfred C. W. Harmsworth, was descended from an ancient and influential family. He became a baron in 1905, and developed several London newspapers, including the Times. He was the recognized spokesman of the conservatives. Baron Riddell (not "Riddel") was in youth a Welsh barrister and also became a leader in conservative journalism, although less of a luminary than Lord Northcliffe. The Marquis of Reading, born Rufus Daniel Isaacs, won distinction by his gifted statesmanship, was created lord chief justice of England in 1913, and became viceroy and governor general of India in 1921.
4. That is, not finding superiors in actuality, he creates them by law.

diamonds, fashionable intelligence; the equality of all men before the law must have clear and dramatic proofs. Sometimes, perhaps, the thing goes further and is more subtle. The inferior man needs an aristocracy to demonstrate, not only his mere equality, but also his actual superiority. The society columns in the newspapers may have some such origin. They may visualize once more the accomplished journalist's understanding of the mob mind that he plays upon so skillfully, as upon some immense and cacophonous organ, always going *fortissimo*. What the inferior man and his wife see in the sinister revels of those brummagem [5] first families, I suspect, is often a massive witness to their own higher rectitude —in brief, to their firmer grasp upon the immutable axioms of Christian virtue, the one sound boast of the nether nine-tenths of humanity in every land under the cross.

But this bugaboo aristocracy is actually bogus, and the evidence of its bogusness lies in the fact that it is insecure. One gets into it only onerously, but out of it very easily. Entrance is effected by dint of a long and bitter struggle, and the chief accidents of that struggle are almost intolerable humiliations. The aspirant must school and steel himself to sniffs and sneers; he must see the door slammed upon him a hundred times before ever it is thrown open to him. To get in at all he must show a talent for abasement— and abasement makes him timorous. Worse, that timorousness is not cured when he succeeds at last. On the contrary, it is made even more tremulous, for what he faces within the gates is a scheme of things made up almost wholly of harsh and often unintelligible taboos, and the penalty for violating even the least of them is swift and disastrous. He must exhibit exactly the right social habits, appetites and prejudices, public and private. He must harbor exactly the right enthusiasms and indignations. He must have a hearty taste for exactly the right sports and games. His attitude toward the fine arts must be properly tolerant and yet not a shade too eager. He must read and like exactly the right books, pamphlets and public journals. He must put up at the right hotels when he travels. His wife must patronize the right milliners. He himself must stick to the right haberdashery. He must live in the right neighborhood. He must even embrace the right doctrines of religion. It would ruin him, for all society column purposes, to move to Union Hill, N.J., or to drink coffee from his saucer, or to marry a chambermaid with a gold tooth, or to join the Seventh Day Adventists. Within the boundaries of his curious order he is worse fettered than a monk in a cell. Its obscure conception of propriety, its nebulous notion that this or that is

5. British slang, a word derived from the name of the city of Birmingham, where, supposedly, trashy but showy wares were manufactured.

honorable, hampers him in every direction, and very narrowly. What he resigns when he enters, even when he makes his first deprecating knock at the door, is every right to attack the ideas that happen to prevail within. Such as they are, he must accept them without question. And as they shift and change he must shift and change with them, silently and quickly.

Obviously, that order cannot constitute a genuine aristocracy, in any rational sense. A genuine aristocracy is grounded upon very much different principles. Its first and most salient character is its interior security, and the chief visible evidence of that security is the freedom that goes with it—not only freedom in act, the divine right of the aristocrat to do what he damn well pleases, so long as he does not violate the primary guarantees and obligations of his class, but also and more importantly freedom in thought, the liberty to try and err, the right to be his own man. It is the instinct of a true aristocracy, not to punish eccentricity by expulsion, but to throw a mantle of protection about it—to safeguard it from the suspicions and resentments of the lower orders. Those lower orders are inert, timid, inhospitable to ideas, hostile to changes, faithful to a few maudlin superstitions. All progress goes on on the higher levels. It is there that salient personalities, made secure by artificial immunities, may oscillate most widely from the normal track. It is within that entrenched fold, out of reach of the immemorial certainties of the mob, that extraordinary men of the lower orders may find their city of refuge, and breathe a clear air. This, indeed, is at once the hall-mark and the justification of a genuine aristocracy— that it is beyond responsibility to the general masses of men, and hence superior to both their degraded longings and their no less degraded aversions. It is nothing if it is not autonomous, curious, venturesome, courageous, and everything if it is. It is the custodian of the qualities that make for change and experiment; it is the class that organizes danger to the service of the race; it pays for its high prerogatives by standing in the forefront of the fray.

No such aristocracy, it must be plain, is now on view in the United States. The makings of one were visible in the Virginia of the Eighteenth Century, but with Jefferson and Washington the promise died. In New England, it seems to me, there was never anything of the sort, either in being or in nascency: there was only a theocracy that degenerated very quickly into a plutocracy on the one hand and a caste of sterile pedants on the other—the passion for God splitting into a lust for dollars and a weakness for mere words. Despite the common notion to the contrary—a notion generated by confusing literacy with intelligence—the New England of the great days never showed any genuine enthusiasm for ideas. It began its history as a slaughter-house of ideas, and it is today not easily distinguishable from a cold-storage plant. Its celebrated adventures in mysticism, once apparently so bold and significant, are now seen to have been little more than an elaborate hocus-pocus—respectable Unitarians shocking the peasantry and scaring the horned cattle in the fields by masquerading in the robes of Rosicrucians. The notions that it embraced in those austere and far-off days were stale, and when it had finished with them they were dead. So in politics. Since the Civil War it has produced fewer political ideas, as political ideas run in the Republic, than any average county in Kansas or Nebraska. Appomattox seemed to be a victory for New England idealism. It was actually a victory for the New England plutocracy, and that plutocracy has dominated thought above the Housatonic [6] ever since. The sect of professional idealists has so far dwindled that it has ceased to be of any importance, even as an opposition. When the plutocracy is challenged now, it is challenged by the proletariat.

Well, what is on view in New England is on view in all other parts of the nation, sometimes with ameliorations, but usually with the colors merely exaggerated. What one beholds, sweeping the eye over the land, is a culture that, like the national literature, is in three layers—the plutocracy on top, a vast mass of undifferentiated human blanks bossed by demagogues at the bottom, and a forlorn *intelligentsia* gasping out a precarious life between. I need not set out at any length, I hope, the intellectual deficiencies of the plutocracy—its utter failure to show anything even remotely resembling the makings of an aristocracy. It is badly educated, it is stupid, it is full of low-caste superstitions and indignations, it is without decent traditions or informing vision; above all, it is extraordinarily lacking in the most elemental independence and courage. Out of this class comes the grotesque fashionable society of our big towns, already described. It shows all the stigmata of inferiority—moral certainty, cruelty, suspicion of ideas, fear. Never does it function more revealingly than in the recurrent *pogroms* against radicalism, *i.e.*, against humorless persons who, like Andrew Jackson, take the platitudes of democracy seriously. And what is the theory at the bottom of all these proceedings? So far as it can be reduced to comprehensible terms it is much less a theory than a fear—a shivering, idiotic, discreditable fear of a mere banshee [7]—an overpowering, paralyzing dread that some extra-eloquent Red, permitted to emit his balderdash unwhipped, may eventually convert a couple of courageous men, and that the courageous men, filled with indignation against the plutocracy, may take to the high-road, burn down a nail-factory or two, and slit the throat of some virtuous profiteer.

Obviously, it is out of reason to look for any hospitality to ideas in a class so extravagantly fearful of even the most palpably absurd of them. Its philosophy is firmly grounded upon the thesis that the existing order must stand forever free from attack, and not only from attack, but also from the mere academic criticism, and its ethics are firmly grounded upon the thesis that every attempt at any such criticism is a proof of moral turpitude. Within its own ranks, protected by what may be regarded as the privilege of the order, there is nothing to take the place of this criticism. In other countries the plutocracy has often produced men of reflective and analytical habit, eager to rationalize its instincts and to bring it into some sort of relationship to the main streams of human thought. The case of David Ricardo at once comes to mind, and there have been many others: John Bright, Richard Cobden, George Grote.[8] But in the United States no such phenomenon has been visible. Nor has the plutocracy ever fostered an inquiring spirit among its intellectual valets and footmen, which is to say, among the gentlemen who compose headlines and leading articles for its newspapers. What chiefly distinguishes the daily press of the United States from the press of all other countries pretending to culture is not its lack of truthfulness or even its lack of dignity and honor, for these deficiencies are common to newspapers everywhere, but its incurable fear of ideas, its constant effort to evade the discussion of fundamentals by translating all issues into a few elemental fears, its incessant reduction of all reflection to mere emotion. It is, in the true sense, never well-informed. It is seldom intelligent, save in the arts of the mob-master. It is never courageously honest. Held harshly to a rigid correctness of opinion, it sinks rapidly into formalism and feebleness. Its yellow section is perhaps its best section, for there the only vestige of the old free journalist survives. In the more respectable papers one finds only a timid and petulant animosity to all questioning of the existing order, however urbane and sincere—a pervasive and ill-concealed dread that the mob now heated up against the orthodox hobgoblins may suddenly begin to unearth hobgoblins of its own, and so run amok. * * *

1920

8. These were British thinkers and social reformers, yet also members of the "plutocracy." The economist, David Ricardo (1772–1823) was a successful broker; John Bright (1811–1889) and Richard Cobden (1804–1865), the reformers, were industrialists; the historian, George Grote (1794–1871) was a banker.

SHERWOOD ANDERSON
(1876–1941)

To the writers of the 1920's, Sherwood Anderson was a force and a pioneer, and he exercised an indirect influence on the literature of two decades. His unblemished powers are recognized today in a handful of magnificent short stories, in his perceptive and passionate letters, and in three "autobiographies" whose legendary character is frankly acknowledged. His other books, particularly his novels, are confused in purpose and uneven in performance. Yet in whatever he wrote there is always the fascination of his personality, complex and brooding, groping for answers to the riddles of the individual being, and desperately aware that to find answers for others, he must overcome the disunity in his own experience. He is one of the most genuinely subjective of our story tellers, at his best in such narrative episodes as involve his own experience and perplexities.

Although largely self-educated, Anderson was a serious thinker, and he read widely. He was among the earliest to respond to the new Freudian psychology, and was convinced that much of human behavior is a reaction to subconscious realities and to experiences hidden in the forgotten past of the individual. His characters grope unsuccessfully to discover the reality within themselves, while with equal frustration they confront the complexities of the machine age and the conventionality of urban and small-town life. If they escape at all, even briefly, it may be through the experience of sex, although this escape also is often blocked by brutalizing debasements. Another resolution is sometimes found, as in *Dark Laughter* (1925), when man is able to identify himself simply with the primitive forces of nature.

Anderson was raised in Clyde, Ohio, the fourth of seven children of a harness-maker, the "Windy" of his first novel, *Windy McPherson's Son* (1916). His schooling was sporadic, owing to his mother's need for help in supporting the family. What he learned working on farms, in shops, and especially in livery and racing stables later appeared in short stories that dealt generally with the emotional problems of boyhood. These are some of his most mature writings, reflecting the early conflict of his creative impulse with the spiritual poverty of small-town life and intimating the gradual alienation of his father which was a source of his chronic emotional disunity.

His mother died when Anderson was nineteen and the family fell apart. In 1896 he worked in Chicago. He enlisted for service in the Spanish-American War; after being discharged he spent the winter of 1899 in Springfield, Ohio, as a senior at Wittenberg Academy. In Chicago again, he became successful as an advertising writer and married in 1904. Moving to Cleveland in 1906, he acquired an interest in a factory in Elyria, Ohio, where he lived for five years. There he prospered financially, combining manufacturing with advertising while compensating for an inward revolt by writing drafts of three novels, including materials later published. In 1912 a nervous collapse required hospitalization. Now fully realizing his intense vocation for literature he terminated his business connections and the first of his four marriages.

In 1913 he started afresh in Chicago, writing advertising while giving his genuine efforts to fiction. "The little renaissance" in Chicago provided a favorable *avant-garde* climate; Sandburg, Lindsay, and Masters were "new voices," and many "little magazines" were eager to give scope to original talent. In 1919 his fourth book, *Winesburg, Ohio*, a short-story collection, won international attention with its intense psychological studies of trapped and warped personalities and its pity and tenderness. In 1921, in Europe, he met and was influenced by James Joyce and Gertrude Stein; in New Orleans, the next winter, he met and influenced William Faulkner.

In *Dark Laughter* (1925), his best and only popular novel, Anderson satirizes the arid pseudosophisticated intellectuals, particularly in their neurotic debasement of sex, in contrast to the carefree and uncorrupted sensuality of the Negro characters in the story. But his novels are unsatisfactory as wholes, though they have pages of brilliance and even of sheer genius.

After 1925, Anderson's growing interest was in proletarian movements and his novels declined. He now went to live near Marion, Virginia; in 1927, having bought two newspapers to edit there, he made Marion his permanent home. In 1941, at the start of a tour to South America, he died at Colon, Panama. His autobiographical reminiscences are excellent reading but so impressionistic that biographers have had to seek other sources.

Volumes of Anderson's short stories are *Winesburg, Ohio*, 1919; *The Triumph of the Egg*, 1921; *Horses and Men*, 1923; *Death in the Woods*, 1933. Anderson's novels are *Windy McPherson's Son*, 1916; *Marching Men*, 1917; *Poor White*, 1920; *Many Marriages*, 1923; *Dark Laughter*, 1925; *Beyond Desire*, 1932; *Kit Brandon*, 1936. His plays are collected in *Winesburg and Others*, 1937; his poems in *Mid-American Chants*, 1918; and *A New Testament*, 1927. Collections of essays are *The Modern Writer*, 1925; *Sherwood Anderson's Notebook*, 1926; *Hello Towns!* 1929; *Perhaps Women*, 1931; *No Swank*, 1934; *Puzzled America*, 1935. Autobiographical volumes are *A Story Teller's Story*, 1924; *Tar: A Midwest Childhood*, 1926; *Sherwood Anderson's Memoirs*, 1942. Correspondence on writing was collected in *Letters * * **, edited by H. M. Jones and W. B. Rideout, 1953. Ray Lewis White has edited critical editions of *A Story Teller's Story*, 1968; and *Tar*, 1969; as well as newspaper writings in *Return to Winesburg*, 1967; and correspondence in *Sherwood Anderson / Gertrude Stein*, 1972.

Studies are: I. Howe, *Sherwood Anderson*, 1951; J. Schevill, *Sherwood Anderson, His Life and Work*, 1951; R. Burbank, *Sherwood Anderson*, 1964; and David Anderson, *Sherwood Anderson: An Introduction and Interpretation*, 1967.

I Want to Know Why [1]

We got up at four in the morning, that first day in the east. On the evening before we had climbed off a freight train at the edge of town, and with the true instinct of Kentucky boys had found our way across town and to the race track and the stables at once. Then we knew we were all right. Hanley Turner right away found a nigger we knew. It was Bildad Johnson who in the winter works at Ed Becker's livery barn in our home town, Beckersville. Bildad is a good cook as almost all our niggers are and of course he, like everyone in our part of Kentucky who is anyone at all, likes the horses. In the spring Bildad begins to scratch around. A nigger from our country can flatter and wheedle anyone into letting him do most anything he wants. Bildad wheedles the stable men and the trainers from the horse farms in our country around Lexington. The trainers come into town in the evening to stand around and talk and maybe get into a poker game. Bildad gets in with them. He is always doing little favors and telling about things to eat, chicken browned in a pan, and how is the best way to cook sweet potatoes and corn bread. It makes your mouth water to hear him.

When the racing season comes on and the horses go to the races and there is all the talk on the streets in the evenings about the new colts, and everyone says when they are going over to Lexington or to the spring meeting at Churchill Downs or to Latonia, and the horsemen that have been down to New Orleans or maybe at the winter meeting at Havana in Cuba come home to spend a week before they start out again, at such a time when everything talked about in Beckersville is just horses and nothing else and the outfits start out and horse racing is in every breath of air you breathe, Bildad shows up with a job as cook for some outfit. Often when I think about it, his always going all season to the races and working in the livery barn in the winter where horses are and where men like to come and talk about horses, I wish I was a nigger. It's a foolish thing to say, but that's the way I am about being around horses, just crazy. I can't help it.

Well, I must tell you about what we did and let you in on what I'm talking about. Four of us boys from Beckersville, all whites and sons of men who live in Beckersville regular, made up our minds we were going to the races, not just to Lexington or Louisville, I don't mean, but to the big eastern track we were always hearing our Beckersville men talk about, to Saratoga. We were all pretty young then. I was just turned fifteen and I was the oldest of the four. It was my scheme. I admit that and I talked the others into trying it.

---

1. First published in *The Smart Set* for November, 1918, and collected in *The Triumph of the Egg* (1921).

There was Hanley Turner and Henry Rieback and Tom Tumberton and myself. I had thirty-seven dollars I had earned during the winter working nights and Saturdays in Enoch Myer's grocery. Henry Rieback had eleven dollars and the others, Hanley and Tom, had only a dollar or two each. We fixed it all up and laid low until the Kentucky spring meetings were over and some of our men, the sportiest ones, the ones we envied the most, had cut out—then we cut out too.

I won't tell you the trouble we had beating our way on freights and all. We went through Cleveland and Buffalo and other cities and saw Niagara Falls. We bought things there, souvenirs and spoons and cards and shells with pictures of the falls on them for our sisters and mothers, but thought we had better not send any of the things home. We didn't want to put the folks on our trail and maybe be nabbed.

We got into Saratoga as I said at night and went to the track. Bildad fed us up. He showed us a place to sleep in hay over a shed and promised to keep still. Niggers are all right about things like that. They won't squeal on you. Often a white man you might meet, when you had run away from home like that, might appear to be all right and give you a quarter or a half-dollar or something, and then go right and give you away. White men will do that, but not a nigger. You can trust them. They are squarer with kids. I don't know why.

At the Saratoga meeting that year there were a lot of men from home. Dave Williams and Arthur Mulford and Jerry Myers and others. Then there was a lot from Louisville and Lexington Henry Rieback knew but I didn't. They were professional gamblers and Henry Rieback's father is one too. He is what is called a sheet writer and goes away most of the year to tracks. In the winter when he is home in Beckersville he don't stay there much but goes away to cities and deals faro. He is a nice man and generous, is always sending Henry presents, a bicycle and a gold watch and a boy scout suit of clothes and things like that.

My own father is a lawyer. He's all right, but don't make much money and can't buy me things and anyway I'm getting so old now I don't expect it. He never said nothing to me against Henry, but Hanley Turner and Tom Tumberton's fathers did. They said to their boys that money so come by is no good and they didn't want their boys brought up to hear gamblers' talk and be thinking about such things and maybe embrace them.

That's all right and I guess the men know what they are talking about, but I don't see what it's got to do with Henry or with horses either. That's what I'm writing this story about. I'm puzzled. I'm getting to be a man and want to think straight and be O. K., and there's something I saw at the race meeting at the eastern track I can't figure out.

I can't help it, I'm crazy about thoroughbred horses. I've always been that way. When I was ten years old and saw I was growing to be big and couldn't be a rider I was so sorry I nearly died. Harry Hellinfinger in Beckersville, whose father is Postmaster, is grown up and too lazy to work, but likes to stand around in the street and get up jokes on boys like sending them to a hardware store for a gimlet to bore square holes and other jokes like that. He played one on me. He told me that if I would eat a half a cigar I would be stunted and not grow any more and maybe could be a rider. I did it. When father wasn't looking I took a cigar out of his pocket and gagged it down some way. It made me awful sick and the doctor had to be sent for, and then it did no good. I kept right on growing. It was a joke. When I told what I had done and why most fathers would have whipped me but mine didn't.

Well, I didn't get stunted and didn't die. It serves Harry Hellinfinger right. Then I made up my mind I would like to be a stable boy, but had to give that up too. Mostly niggers do that work and I knew father wouldn't let me go into it. No use to ask him.

If you've never been crazy about thoroughbreds it's because you've never been around where they are much and don't know any better. They're beautiful. There isn't anything so lovely and clean and full of spunk and honest and everything as some race horses. On the big horse farms that are all around our town Beckersville there are tracks and the horses run in the early morning. More than a thousand times I've got out of bed before daylight and walked two or three miles to the tracks. Mother wouldn't of let me go but father always says, "Let him alone." So I got some bread out of the bread box and some butter and jam, gobbled it and lit out.

At the tracks you sit on the fence with men, whites and niggers, and they chew tobacco and talk, and then the colts are brought out. It's early and the grass is covered with shiny dew and in another field a man is plowing and they are frying things in a shed where the track niggers sleep, and you know how a nigger can giggle and laugh and say things that make you laugh. A white man can't do it and some niggers can't but a track nigger can every time.

And so the colts are brought out and some are just galloped by stable boys, but almost every morning on a big track owned by a rich man who lives maybe in New York, there are always, nearly every morning, a few colts and some of the old race horses and geldings and mares that are cut loose.

It brings a lump up into my throat when a horse runs. I don't mean all horses but some. I can pick them nearly every time. It's in my blood like in the blood of race track niggers and trainers.

Even when they just go slob-jogging along with a little nigger on their backs I can tell a winner. If my throat hurts and it's hard for me to swallow, that's him. He'll run like Sam Hill when you let him out. If he don't win every time it'll be a wonder and because they've got him in a pocket behind another or he was pulled or got off bad at the post or something. If I wanted to be a gambler like Henry Rieback's father I could get rich. I know I could and Henry says so, too. All I would have to do is to wait 'til that hurt comes when I see a horse and then bet every cent. That's what I would do if I wanted to be a gambler, but I don't.

When you're at the tracks in the morning—not the race tracks but the training tracks around Beckersville—you don't see a horse, the kind I've been talking about, very often, but it's nice anyway. Any thoroughbred, that is sired right and out of a good mare and trained by a man that knows how, can run. If he couldn't what would he be there for and not pulling a plow?

Well, out of the stables they come and the boys are on their backs and it's lovely to be there. You hunch down on top of the fence and itch inside you. Over in the sheds the niggers giggle and sing. Bacon is being fried and coffee made. Everything smells lovely. Nothing smells better than coffee and manure and horses and niggers and bacon frying and pipes being smoked out of doors on a morning like that. It just gets you, that's what it does.

But about Saratoga. We was there six days and not a soul from home seen us and everything came off just as we wanted it to, fine weather and horses and races and all. We beat our way home and Bildad gave us a basket with fried chicken and bread and other eatables in, and I had eighteen dollars when we got back to Beckersville. Mother jawed and cried but Pop didn't say much. I told everything we done except one thing. I did and saw that alone. That's what I'm writing about. It got me upset. I think about it at night. Here it is.

At Saratoga we laid up nights in the hay in the shed Bildad had showed us and ate with the niggers early and at night when the race people had all gone away. The men from home stayed mostly in the grandstand and betting field, and didn't come out around the places where the horses are kept except to the paddocks just before a race when the horses are saddled. At Saratoga they don't have paddocks under an open shed as at Lexington and Churchill Downs and other tracks down in our country, but saddle the horses right out in an open place under trees on a lawn as smooth and nice as Banker Bohon's front yard here in Beckersville. It's lovely. The horses are sweaty and nervous and shine and the men come out and smoke cigars and look at them and the trainers are there and the owners, and your heart thumps so you can hardly breathe.

Then the bugle blows for post and the boys that ride come running out with their silk clothes on and you run to get a place by the fence with the niggers.

I always am wanting to be a trainer or owner, and at the risk of being seen and caught and sent home I went to the paddocks before every race. The other boys didn't but I did.

We got to Saratoga on a Friday and on Wednesday the next week the big Mullford Handicap was to be run. Middlestride was in it and Sunstreak. The weather was fine and the track fast. I couldn't sleep the night before.

What had happened was that both these horses are the kind it makes my throat hurt to see. Middlestride is long and looks awkward and is a gelding. He belongs to Joe Thompson, a little owner from home who only has a half-dozen horses. The Mullford Handicap is for a mile and Middlestride can't untrack fast. He goes away slow and is always way back at the half, then he begins to run and if the race is a mile and a quarter he'll just eat up everything and get there.

Sunstreak is different. He is a stallion and nervous and belongs on the biggest farm we've got in our country, the Van Riddle place that belongs to Mr. Van Riddle of New York. Sunstreak is like a girl you think about sometimes but never see. He is hard all over and lovely too. When you look at his head you want to kiss him. He is trained by Jerry Tillford who knows me and has been good to me lots of times, lets me walk into a horse's stall to look at him close and other things. There isn't anything as sweet as that horse. He stands at the post quiet and not letting on, but he is just burning up inside. Then when the barrier goes up he is off like his name, Sunstreak. It makes you ache to see him. It hurts you. He just lays down and runs like a bird dog. There can't anything I ever see run like him except Middlestride when he gets untracked and stretches himself.

Gee! I ached to see that race and those two horses run, ached and dreaded it too. I didn't want to see either of our horses beaten. We had never sent a pair like that to the races before. Old men in Beckersville said so and the niggers said so. It was a fact.

Before the race I went over to the paddocks to see. I looked a last look at Middlestride, who isn't such a much standing in a paddock that way, then I went to Sunstreak.

It was his day. I knew when I see him. I forgot all about being seen myself and walked right up. All the men from Beckersville were there and no one noticed me except Jerry Tillford. He saw me and something happened. I'll tell you about that.

I was standing looking at that horse and aching. In some way, I can't tell how, I knew just how Sunstreak felt inside. He was quiet and letting the niggers rub his legs and Mr. Van Riddle himself put the saddle on, but he was just a raging torrent inside. He was like the water in the river at Niagara Falls just before it goes plunk down. That horse wasn't thinking about running. He don't have to think about that. He was just thinking about holding himself back 'til the time for the running came. I knew that. I could just in a way see right inside him. He was going to do some awful running and I knew it. He wasn't bragging or letting on much or prancing or making a fuss, but just waiting. I knew it and Jerry Tillford his trainer knew. I looked up and then that man and I looked into each other's eyes. Something happened to me. I guess I loved the man as much as I did the horse because he knew what I knew. Seemed to me there wasn't anything in the world but that man and the horse and me. I cried and Jerry Tillford had a shine in his eyes. Then I came away to the fence to wait for the race. The horse was better than me, more steadier, and now I know better than Jerry. He was the quietest and he had to do the running.

Sunstreak ran first of course and he busted the world's record for a mile. I've seen that if I never see anything more. Everything came out just as I expected. Middlestride got left at the post and was way back and closed up to be second, just as I knew he would. He'll get a world's record too some day. They can't skin the Beckersville country on horses.

I watched the race calm because I knew what would happen. I was sure. Hanley Turner and Henry Rieback and Tom Tumberton were all more excited than me.

A funny thing had happened to me. I was thinking about Jerry Tillford the trainer and how happy he was all through the race. I liked him that afternoon even more than I ever liked my own father. I almost forgot the horses thinking that way about him. It was because of what I had seen in his eyes as he stood in the paddocks beside Sunstreak before the race started. I knew he had been watching and working with Sunstreak since the horse was a baby colt, had taught him to run and be patient and when to let himself out and not to quit, never. I knew that for him it was like a mother seeing her child do something brave or wonderful. It was the first time I ever felt for a man like that.

After the race that night I cut out from Tom and Hanley and Henry. I wanted to be by myself and I wanted to be near Jerry Tillford if I could work it. Here is what happened.

The track in Saratoga is near the edge of town. It is all polished up and trees around, the evergreen kind, and grass and everything painted and nice. If you go past the track you get to a hard road made of asphalt for automobiles, and if you go along this for a few miles there is a road turns off to a little rummy-looking farm house set in a yard.

That night after the race I went along that road because I had seen Jerry and some other men go that way in an automobile. I didn't expect to find them. I walked for a ways and then sat down by a fence to think. It was the direction they went in. I wanted to be as near Jerry as I could. I felt close to him. Pretty soon I went up the side road—I don't know why—and came to the rummy farm house. I was just lonesome to see Jerry, like wanting to see your father at night when you are a young kid. Just then an automobile came along and turned in. Jerry was in it and Henry Rieback's father, and Arthur Bedford from home, and Dave Williams and two other men I didn't know. They got out of the car and went into the house, all but Henry Rieback's father who quarreled with them and said he wouldn't go. It was only about nine o'clock, but they were all drunk and the rummy-looking farm house was a place for bad women to stay in. That's what it was. I crept up along a fence and looked through a window and saw.

It's what give me the fantods. I can't make it out. The women in the house were all ugly mean-looking women, not nice to look at or be near. They were homely too, except one who was tall and looked a little like the gelding Middlestride, but not clean like him, but with a hard ugly mouth. She had red hair. I saw everything plain. I got up by an old rose bush by an open window and looked. The women had on loose dresses and sat around in chairs. The men came in and some sat on the women's laps. The place smelled rotten and there was rotten talk, the kind a kid hears around a livery stable in a town like Beckersville in the winter but don't ever expect to hear talked when there are women around. It was rotten. A nigger wouldn't go into such a place.

I looked at Jerry Tillford. I've told you how I had been feeling about him on account of his knowing what was going on inside of Sunstreak in the minute before he went to the post for the race in which he made a world's record.

Jerry bragged in that bad woman house as I know Sunstreak wouldn't never have bragged. He said that he made that horse, that it was him that won the race and made the record. He lied and bragged like a fool. I never heard such silly talk.

And then, what do you suppose he did! He looked at the woman in there, the one that was lean and hard-mouthed and looked a little like the gelding Middlestride, but not clean like him, and his eyes began to shine just as they did when he looked at me and at Sunstreak in the paddocks at the track in the afternoon. I stood there by the window—gee!—but I wished I hadn't gone away from the tracks, but had stayed with the boys and the niggers and the horses. The tall rotten-looking woman was between us just as Sunstreak was in the paddocks in the afternoon.

Then, all of a sudden, I began to hate that man. I wanted to scream and rush in the room and kill him. I never had such a feeling before. I was so mad clean through that I cried and my fists were doubled up so my finger nails cut my hands.

And Jerry's eyes kept shining and he waved back and forth, and then he went and kissed that woman and I crept away and went back to the tracks and to bed and didn't sleep hardly any, and then next day I got the other kids to start home with me and never told them anything I seen.

I been thinking about it ever since. I can't make it out. Spring has come again and I'm nearly sixteen and go to the tracks mornings same as always, and I see Sunstreak and Middlestride and a new colt named Strident I'll bet will lay them all out, but no one thinks so but me and two or three niggers.

But things are different. At the tracks the air don't taste as good or smell as good. It's because a man like Jerry Tillford, who knows what he does, could see a horse like Sunstreak run, and kiss a woman like that the same day. I can't make it out. Darn him, what did he want to do like that for? I keep thinking about it and it spoils looking at horses and smelling things and hearing niggers laugh and everything. Sometimes I'm so mad about it I want to fight someone. It gives me the fantods. What did he do it for? I want to know why.

1918, 1921

EDNA ST. VINCENT MILLAY

(1892–1950)

Edna St. Vincent Millay's early appearances on the literary scene were all spectacular, and it was some time before the reading public adjusted itself to her kaleidoscopic transformations. In 1912, at the age of twenty, she was the unknown girl of Camden, Maine, whose "Renascence," a reflective poem of remarkable spiritual penetration and lyric beauty, became celebrated at once because the *Lyric Year* gave its annual award to an established author, while a number of prominent critics enthusiastically preferred the work of the girl poet. It is still, in fact, one of the favorite poems of its period. In 1917, somewhat revised, it became the title poem of her first volume, comprising poems written while she was a Vassar undergraduate. In 1920 A *Few Figs from Thistles* revealed another transformation. That year, when F. Scott Fitzgerald in *This Side of*

Paradise drew the fictional portrait of youth in the jazz age, Edna St. Vincent Millay temporarily became the lyric voice of that rebellious generation. With impudent irreverence she attacked the citadel of conventionalized feminine virtue, in poems that sang gaily of going "back and forth all night on the ferry," or cavalierly accepted a broken love, as in "Passer Mortuus Est," or cynically pretended forgetfulness of "What Lips My Lips Have Kissed."

Three years and two volumes of poetry later, *The Harp-Weaver and Other Poems* (1923) revealed the poet matured. The daring of *A Few Figs from Thistles* had now become a fine spiritual independence and vitality. The insight and emotional propriety of "Renascence" had acquired depth; she had thoroughly absorbed her principal literary inheritance, from the Elizabethan and Cavalier lyrists of England; she showed her mastery of the sonnet; and in "The Ballad of the Harp-Weaver" she caught the simplicity of the ballad form.

Born in Rockland, Maine, in 1892, Edna St. Vincent Millay grew up in that city and in nearby Camden. She lacked the financial means to attend college, but a friend of the family offered assistance. She enrolled at Barnard at twenty-one, but soon transferred to Vassar and was graduated in 1917. During her next few years, in Greenwich Village, she was able to support herself by sales of magazine verse and stories, and such satirical sketches as appeared in *Distressing Dialogues*

(1924) under the pseudonym of Nancy Boyd. While living in the village, she was associated with the Provincetown Players, with whom Eugene O'Neill's first success was won, and she wrote several poetic dramas which have been frequently performed by little-theater groups. One, *The King's Henchman* (1927), was the libretto for a Deems Taylor opera produced in 1927 by the Metropolitan Opera Company.

Following the appearance of *The Harp-Weaver and Other Poems,* her major volumes included *The Buck in the Snow and Other Poems* (1928); *Fatal Interview* (1931), a sequence of sonnets recording a love affair, of great psychological interest and lyric excellence; *Wine from These Grapes* (1934); and *Conversation at Midnight* (1937).

With Archibald MacLeish, Stephen Vincent Benét, and many others, she joined those who called upon writers to oppose the growing tyranny manifested in European affairs. The works evoked by these concerns were sincere and journalistically effective, as was *The Murder of Lidice* (1942). Other volumes of this latest period include *Huntsman, What Quarry?* (1939), *Make Bright the Arrows* (1940), and *"There Are No Islands, Any More"* (1940). During the last decade of her life, Miss Millay published much less frequently in magazines and made no new collections of her poems.

Collected Poems, 1956, was edited by Norma Millay. A major portion of her best work may be found in *Collected Sonnets,* 1941, and *Collected Lyrics,* 1943. A posthumous "collection of new poems," edited by Norma Millay, was entitled *Mine the Harvest*, 1954. The *Letters of Edna St. Vincent Millay*, edited by Allan Ross Macdougall, appeared in 1952.

Biographical studies are Elizabeth Atkins, *Edna St. Vincent Millay and Her Times*, 1936; Vincent Sheean, *The Indigo Bunting: A Memoir of Edna St.*

Vincent Millay, 1951; Toby Shafter, *Edna St. Vincent Millay, America's Best-loved Poet*, 1957; Miriam Gurko, *Restless Spirit: The Life of Edna St. Vincent Millay*, 1962; Norman A. Brittin, *Edna St. Vincent Millay*, 1967; and Jean Gould, *The Poet and Her Book: A Biography of Edna St. Vincent Millay*, 1969.

Passer Mortuus Est [1]

Death devours all lovely things;
   Lesbia with her sparrow
Shares the darkness,—presently
   Every bed is narrow.

Unremembered as old rain   5
   Dries the sheer libation,[2]
And the little petulant hand
   Is an annotation.

After all, my erstwhile dear,
   My no longer cherished,   10
Need we say it was not love,
   Now that love has perished?

1920, 1921

Justice Denied in Massachusetts [3]

Let us abandon then our gardens and go home
And sit in the sitting-room.
Shall the larkspur blossom or the corn grow under this cloud?
Sour to the fruitful seed
Is the cold earth under this cloud,   5
Fostering quack and weed, we have marched upon but cannot
   conquer;
We have bent the blades of our hoes against the stalks of them.

Let us go home, and sit in the sitting-room.
Not in our day
Shall the cloud go over and the sun rise as before,   10

1. Latin, "The sparrow is dead." Catullus, in *Carmine*, III, l. 3, uses these words in lamenting the death of a sparrow belonging to his mistress, "Lesbia," whose name Millay introduces in l. 2. The first line of the present poem also echoes Catullus' poem, ll. 13 and 14: "Accursed shades of Orcus [Death], / That devour all lovely things."
2. *I.e.*, the wine poured in honor of the dead.

3. Referring to the execution, on August 23, 1927, of Nicola Sacco and Bartolomeo Vanzetti, after nearly seven years of litigation. Many liberals rallied to their defense, claiming that these two "radicals" had not been proved guilty of the payroll robbery and murder for which they were convicted, but were victims of a hysterical conservative reaction. See also Dos Passos.

Beneficent upon us
Out of the glittering bay,
And the warm winds be blown inward from the sea
Moving the blades of corn
With a peaceful sound.   15
Forlorn, forlorn,
Stands the blue hay-rack by the empty mow.
And the petals drop to the ground,
Leaving the tree unfruited.
The sun that warmed our stooping backs and withered the weed
    uprooted—   20
We shall not feel it again.
We shall die in darkness, and be buried in the rain.

What from the splendid dead
We have inherited—
Furrows sweet to the grain, and the weed subdued—   25
See now the slug and the mildew plunder.
Evil does overwhelm
The larkspur and the corn;
We have seen them go under.

Let us sit here, sit still,   30
Here in the sitting-room until we die;
At the step of Death on the walk, rise and go;
Leaving to our children's children this beautiful doorway,
And this elm,
And a blighted earth to till   35
With a broken hoe.

1928

I Shall Go Back Again to the Bleak Shore [4]

I shall go back again to the bleak shore
And build a little shanty on the sand,
In such a way that the extremest band
Of brittle seaweed will escape my door
But by a yard or two; and nevermore   5
Shall I return to take you by the hand;
I shall be gone to what I understand,
And happier than I ever was before.
The love that stood a moment in your eyes,
The words that lay a moment on your tongue,   10

4. The following sonnets are among the many published individually in such volumes as *The Harp-Weaver* (1923), *Fatal Interview* (1931), and *Mine the Harvest* (1954). The texts are from *Collected Poems*, 1956.

Are one with all that in a moment dies,
A little under-said and over-sung.
But I shall find the sullen rocks and skies
Unchanged from what they were when I was young.

1923

Oh, Sleep Forever in the Latmian Cave

Oh, sleep forever in the Latmian cave,
Mortal Endymion, darling of the Moon! [5]
Her silver garments by the senseless wave
Shouldered and dropped and on the shingle strewn,
Her fluttering hand against her forehead pressed,   5
Her scattered looks that trouble all the sky,
Her rapid footsteps running down the west—
Of all her altered state, oblivious lie!
Whom earthen you, by deathless lips adored,
Wild-eyed and stammering to the grasses thrust,   10
And deep into her crystal body poured
The hot and sorrowful sweetness of the dust:
Whereof she wanders mad, being all unfit
For mortal love, that might not die of it.

1931

Those Hours When Happy Hours Were My Estate

Those hours when happy hours were my estate,—
Entailed, as proper, for the next in line,
Yet mine the harvest, and the title mine—
Those acres, fertile, and the furrow straight,
From which the lark would rise—all of my late   5
Enchantments, still, in brilliant colours, shine,
But striped with black, the tulip, lawn and vine,
Like gardens looked at through an iron gate.
Yet not as one who never sojourned there
I view the lovely segments of a past   10
I lived with all my senses, well aware
That this was perfect, and it would not last:
I smell the flower, though vacuum-still the air;
I feel its texture, though the gate is fast.

1954

5. In classic myth the Greek Artemis, or Roman Diana, goddess of the moon, fell in love with Endymion, a mortal youth of surpassing beauty. The goddess was thus drawn down from heaven, wooed the youth, and sacrificed the chastity that was one of her divine attributes. For this impiety, Jupiter doomed Endymion to sleep forever in beauty on Mount Latmos, where the grieving goddess visited him and took care of his flocks. See Ovid, *Ars Amatoria*, III: 83; and the poem *Endymion* by John Keats.

E. E. CUMMINGS

(1894–1963)

E. E. Cummings, whose first volume of poems, *Tulips and Chimneys*, appeared in 1923, remained a controversial but always prominent poet. Cummings produced a large volume of quite individualistic lyrics and exercised an exciting and probably a lasting influence on readers and on other poets. He was the moralist with an almost pagan dedication to the free expression of nature, both in the forms and the language of his art, and in human patterns of behavior. His joyful exploitation of the animal instincts, his love of untrammeled youth, his unabashed employment of the sexual experience—including the comic —and his insistence on the passionate character of genuine love, were so ingenuously and earnestly managed that they appeared free from offense or salaciousness if not even a step in advance of predictable changes in social attitudes. Also liberating was the dextrous novelty of his versification. Although more partial to traditional forms and meters than most twentieth-century poets, he often employed an accentual measure of great flexibility, freed from the traditional bondage of syllable-counting. Like both Pound and Sandburg before him, he experimented with the "rhythm of the phrase" characteristic of our ancestral English, which Walt Whitman rediscovered and for which William Carlos Williams at last found the name—"the variable foot." Like these predecessors also, he employed in many lyrics a line broken by the cadence of the phrases, thus heightening and distributing the emphasis and reducing the dependence on end-rhyme to the advantage of the melody of the verse as a whole. These efforts were assisted in many of his poems, particularly the earlier ones, by a fondness for typographical experimentation that betrayed a concern for design not surprising in a poet who was also a professional painter. In the later poems the experimentation tended less to the graphic and more to the playful disregard of the normal rules of syntax.

Edward Estlin Cummings was born on October 14, 1894, in Cambridge, Massachusetts. His father, then a member of the English department at Harvard, later served as pastor of the famous Old South Church in Boston, from 1905 to 1926. Cummings was graduated from Harvard in 1915 and remained to take his M.A. in 1916. In World War I, he enlisted in the Norton Harjes Ambulance Corps and was sent to France for active duty. A censor's mistake produced an uncomfortable comedy of errors which led to his spending three months in a French detention camp, charged with treasonable correspondence. This experience provided the material for *The Enormous Room* (1922), one of the memorable literary records of that war. Upon his release he at once volunteered for service in the United States Army. After the war, Cummings went to Paris for training in painting, to which he devoted himself professionally, first in Paris and later in New York.

The experimental nature of Cummings' poems is evident first in their mechanics—in the reduction of capital letters, purposeful underpunctuation, and the dissociation of phrases from logical relationships. More essential is his use of the stream-of-consciousness technique. His words or phrases may be symbolic objects representing the simultaneous presence in the mind of meaningful but illogical associations. Finally, his subjects or intended effects often involved allegedly "forbidden" areas of the mind or human behavior, or the language of violent or vulgar experience.

At his best he was an exquisite lyrist. In his love poems and poems of nature he conveyed an intense passion in forms of controlled beauty and propriety. He was a master of satire, armed with sparkling wit, or, when necessary, the heavy club of irony and invective, as in his attacks on advertisers, Babbitts, and super-patriots. And in those of his poems not consciously raucous for satirical effect, he united great melodic power with verbal precision and clarity.

Complete Poems, 1913–1962 appeared in 1973. An earlier *Complete Poems* was published in 2 vols. in 1968. *Poems 1923–1954*, 1954, is a comprehensive collection to that date; later volumes are *95 Poems*, 1958; *100 Selected Poems*, 1959; and *50 Poems*, 1960. Critical prose pieces are contained in *e. e. cummings: A Miscellany*, 1958 (revised, 1965), edited by George J. Firmage. F. W. Dupee and George Stade edited *Selected Letters of E. E. Cummings*, 1969.

The Magic Maker: E. E. Cummings, rev. ed., 1965, is an authorized critical biography by Charles Norman. Also of critical interest are Robert Wegner, *The Poetry and Prose of E. E. Cummings*, 1965; Norman Friedman, *e. e. cummings: The Growth of a Writer*, 1964; and S. V. Baum, ed., *Cummings and the Critics: Collection of Critical Articles*, 1960.

George Firmage edited *E. E. Cummings: A Bibliography*, 1964.

Thy Fingers Make Early Flowers

Thy fingers make early flowers of
all things.
thy hair mostly the hours love:
a smoothness which
sings, saying   5
(though love be a day)
do not fear, we will go amaying.

thy whitest feet crisply are straying.
Always
thy moist eyes are at kisses playing,   10
whose strangeness much
says; singing
(though love be a day)
for which girl art thou flowers bringing?

To be thy lips is a sweet thing   15
and small.

Death, Thee i call rich beyond wishing
if this thou catch,
else missing.
(though love be a day   20
and life be nothing, it shall not stop kissing).

1923

In Just-

in Just-
spring   when the world is mud-
luscious the little
lame balloonman

whistles   far   and wee   5

and eddieandbill come
running from marbles and
piracies and it's
spring

when the world is puddle-wonderful   10

the queer
old balloonman whistles
far   and   wee
and bettyandisbel come dancing

from hop-scotch and jump-rope and   15

it's
spring
and
    the

              goat-footed   20

balloonMan   whistles
far
and
wee

1923

When God Lets My Body Be

when god lets my body be

From each brave eye shall sprout a tree
fruit that dangles therefrom

the purpled world will dance upon
Between my lips which did sing   5

a rose shall beget the spring
that maidens whom passion wastes

will lay between their little breasts
My strong fingers beneath the snow

Into strenuous birds shall go
my love walking in the grass   10

their wings will touch with her face
and all the while shall my heart be

With the bulge and nuzzle of the sea

                                        1923

Buffalo Bill's Defunct

Buffalo Bill's
defunct
          who used to
          ride a watersmooth-silver
                              stallion   5
and break onetwothreefourfive pigeonsjustlikethat
                              Jesus

he was a handsome man
                    and what i want to know is
how do you like your blueeyed boy   10
Mister Death

                                        1923

O Thou to Whom the Musical White Spring

O Thou to whom the musical white spring

offers her lily inextinguishable,
taught by thy tremulous grace bravely to fling

Implacable death's mysteriously sable
robe from her redolent shoulders,
                    Thou from whose   5
feet reincarnate song suddenly leaping
flameflung, mounts, inimitably to lose
herself where the wet stars softly are keeping

their exquisite dreams—O Love! upon thy dim
shrine of intangible commemoration,   10
(from whose faint close as some grave languorous hymn

pledged to illimitable dissipation
unhurried clouds of incense fleetly roll)

i spill my bright incalculable soul.

                                        1925

My Sweet Old Etcetera

my sweet old etcetera
aunt lucy during the recent

war could and what
is more did tell you just
what everybody was fighting   5

for,
my sister

isabel created hundreds
(and
hundreds) of socks not to   10
mention shirts fleaproof earwarmers

etcetera wristers etcetera, my
mother hoped that

i would die etcetera
bravely of course my father used   15
to become hoarse talking about how it was
a privilege and if only he
could meanwhile my

self etcetera lay quietly
in the deep mud et   20

cetera
(dreaming,
et
      cetera, of
Your smile   25
eyes knees and of your Etcetera)

                                                          1926

Somewhere I Have Never Travelled, Gladly Beyond

somewhere i have never travelled,gladly beyond
any experience,your eyes have their silence:
in your most frail gesture are things which enclose me,
or which i cannot touch because they are too near

your slightest look easily will unclose me   5
though i have closed myself as fingers,
you open always petal by petal myself as Spring opens
(touching skilfully,mysteriously) her first rose

or if your wish be to close me,i and
my life will shut very beautifully,suddenly,   10
as when the heart of this flower imagines
the snow carefully everywhere descending;

nothing which we are to perceive in this world equals
the power of your intense fragility:whose texture
compels me with the colour of its countries,   15
rendering death and forever with each breathing

(i do not know what it is about you that closes
and opens;only something in me understands
the voice of your eyes is deeper than all roses)
nobody,not even the rain,has such small hands   20

1931

I Sing of Olaf Glad and Big

i sing of Olaf glad and big
whose warmest heart recoiled at war:
a conscientious object-or

his wellbelovéd colonel(trig
westpointer most succinctly bred)   5
took erring Olaf soon in hand;
but—though an host of overjoyed
noncoms(first knocking on the head
him)do through icy waters roll
that helplessness which others stroke   10
with brushes recently employed
anent this muddy toiletbowl,
while kindred intellects evoke
allegiance per blunt instruments—
Olaf(being to all intents   15
a corpse and wanting any rag
upon what God unto him gave)
responds,without getting annoyed
"I will not kiss your f.ing flag"

straightway the silver bird looked grave   20
(departing hurriedly to shave)

but—though all kinds of officers
(a yearning nation's blueeyed pride)
their passive prey did kick and curse
until for wear their clarion   25
voices and boots were much the worse,
and egged the firstclassprivates on
his rectum wickedly to tease
by means of skilfully applied
bayonets roasted hot with heat—   30
Olaf(upon what were once knees)
does almost ceaselessly repeat
"there is some s. I will not eat"

our president,being of which
assertions duly notified   35

threw the yellowsonofabitch
into a dungeon,where he died

Christ(of His mercy infinite)
i pray to see;and Olaf,too

preponderatingly because   40
unless statistics lie he was
more brave than me:more blond than you.

                                                              1931

If There Are Any Heavens

if there are any heavens my mother will(all by herself)have
one.   It will not be a pansy heaven nor
a fragile heaven of lilies-of-the-valley but
it will be a heaven of blackred roses

my father will be(deep like a rose   5
tall like a rose)

standing near my

(swaying over her
silent)
with eyes which are really petals and see   10

nothing with the face of a poet really which
is a flower and not a face with
hands
which whisper
This is my beloved my   15

                    (suddenly in sunlight
he will bow,

& the whole garden will bow)

                                                              1931

My Father Moved Through Dooms of Love

my father moved through dooms of love
through sames of am through haves of give,
singing each morning out of each night
my father moved through depths of height

this motionless forgetful where   5
turned at his glance to shining here;
that if(so timid air is firm)
under his eyes would stir and squirm

newly as from unburied which
floats the first who,his april touch   10

drove sleeping selves to swarm their fates
woke dreamers to their ghostly roots

and should some why completely weep
my father's fingers brought her sleep:
vainly no smallest voice might cry   15
for he could feel the mountains grow.

Lifting the valleys of the sea
my father moved through griefs of joy;
praising a forehead called the moon
singing desire into begin   20

joy was his song and joy so pure
a heart of star by him could steer
and pure so now and now so yes
the wrists of twilight would rejoice

keen as midsummer's keen beyond   25
conceiving mind of sun will stand,
so strictly(over utmost him
so hugely)stood my father's dream

his flesh was flesh his blood was blood:
no hungry man but wished him food;   30
no cripple wouldn't creep one mile
uphill to only see him smile.

Scorning the pomp of must and shall
my father moved through dooms of feel;
his anger was as right as rain   35
his pity was as green as grain

septembering arms of year extend
less humbly wealth to foe and friend
than he to foolish and to wise
offered immeasurable is   40

proudly and(by octobering flame
beckoned)as earth will downward climb,
so naked for immortal work
his shoulders marched against the dark

his sorrow was as true as bread: 45
no liar looked him in the head;
if every friend became his foe
he'd laugh and build a world with snow.

My father moved through theys of we,
singing each new leaf out of each tree   50
(and every child was sure that spring
danced when she heard my father sing)

then let men kill which cannot share,
let blood and flesh be mud and mire,

scheming imagine,passion willed,   55
freedom a drug that's bought and sold

giving to steal and cruel kind,
a heart to fear,to doubt a mind,
to differ a disease of same,
conform the pinnacle of am   60

though dull were all we taste as bright,
bitter all utterly things sweet,
maggoty minus and dumb death
all we inherit,all bequeath

and nothing quite so least as truth   65
—i say though hate were why men breathe—
because my father lived his soul
love is the whole and more than all

                                                                    1940

Anyone Lived in a Pretty How Town

anyone lived in a pretty how town
(with up so floating many bells down)
spring summer autumn winter
he sang his didn't he danced his did.

Women and men(both little and small)   5
cared for anyone not at all
they sowed their isn't they reaped their same
sun moon stars rain

children guessed(but only a few
and down they forgot as up they grew   10
autumn winter spring summer)
that noone loved him more by more

when by now and tree by leaf
she laughed his joy she cried his grief
bird by snow and stir by still   15
anyone's any was all to her

someones married their everyones
laughed their cryings and did their dance
(sleep wake hope and then)they
said their nerves they slept their dream   20

stars rain sun moon
(and only the snow can begin to explain
how children are apt to forget to remember
with up so floating many bells down)

one day anyone died i guess   25
(and noone stooped to kiss his face)

busy folk buried them side by side
little by little and was by was

all by all and deep by deep
· and more by more they dream their sleep   30
noone and anyone earth by april
wish by spirit and if by yes.

Woman and men(both dong and ding)
summer autumn winter spring
reaped their sowing and went their came   35
sun moon stars rain

1940

Up into the Silence the Green

up into the silence the green
silence with a white earth in it

you will(kiss me)go

out into the morning the young
morning with a warm world in it   5

(kiss me)you will go

on into the sunlight the fine
sunlight with a firm day in it

you will go(kiss me

down into your memory and   10
a memory and memory

i)kiss me(will go)

1940

Plato Told

plato told

him:he couldn't
believe it(jesus

told him;he
wouldn't believe   5
it)lao

tsze
certainly told
him,and general
(yes   10

mam)
sherman;
and even
(believe it
or   15

not)you
told him:i told
him;we told him
(he didn't believe it,no

sir)it took   20
a nipponized bit of
the old sixth

avenue
el;in the top of his head:to tell

him   25

1944

When Serpents Bargain for the Right to Squirm

when serpents bargain for the right to squirm
and the sun strikes to gain a living wage—
when thorns regard their roses with alarm
and rainbows are insured against old age

when every thrush may sing no new moon in   5
if all screech-owls have not okayed his voice
—and any wave signs on the dotted line
or else an ocean is compelled to close

when the oak begs permission of the birch
to make an acorn—valleys accuse their   10
mountains of having altitude—and march
denounces april as a saboteur

then we'll believe in that incredible
unanimal mankind(and not until)

1950

I Thank You God

i thank You God for most this amazing
day:for the leaping greenly spirits of trees
and a blue true dream of sky;and for everything
which is natural which is infinite which is yes

(i who have died am alive again today,   5
and this is the sun's birthday;this is the birth

Poets in Waste Land

EZRA POUND

(1885–1972)

Ezra Loomis Pound was born in Hailey, Idaho, on October 30, 1885. He attended the University of Pennsylvania and then Hamilton College, from which he was graduated in 1905. He returned to the University of Pennsylvania for graduate study in romance languages. He took an M.A. in 1906, spent the summer abroad, and returned to Pennsylvania on a fellowship for another year of study in Renaissance literature. In 1908 he again went abroad, and by 1920 regarded himself as a permanent expatriate.

By 1912, he was the author of seven volumes which identified him as a distinct poetic personality, who combined a command of the older tradition with impressive and often daring originality. When Harriet Monroe in 1912 issued from Chicago the prospectus for her new magazine, *Poetry: A Magazine of Verse*, Pound characteristically proposed himself as its foreign correspondent.

He was a prolific essayist for the little magazines of New York, London, and Paris, which then constituted a large and ex-citing literary world. He unselfishly and persistently championed the experimental and often unpopular artists whom he approved—Antheil, the musician; Gaudier-Brzeska, pioneer abstractionist sculptor, killed in World War I; and James Joyce, among others. Most important of all, perhaps, was the advice and encouragement which he gave to T. S. Eliot, who has candidly acknowledged the value of Pound's assistance in the final revison of *The Waste Land* and in connection with other poems of that period. Both poets of independent power and interests, they became the early leaders in restoring to poetry the use of literary reference as an imaginative instrument. Such referential figures of speech assume that the poet and his readers share a common cultural inheritance. In the present age of increasing complexity, diffuseness, and specialization of knowledge, both Pound and Eliot required of their readers a familiarity with the classics, the productions of the Italian and English Renaissance, and specialized areas of Continental literature, including the works of the French symbolists. After *The Waste Land* (1922), Eliot's poetry became somewhat less difficult in this respect, while Pound's continued to draw fundamentally upon his formidably recondite culture. A large part of his work consists of "reconstructions" in modern English of poems from earlier literatures, chiefly Greek, Latin, Italian, Provençal, and Chinese. Among his reconstructions, his *Homage to Sextus Propertius* is a masterpiece. He called the often-expanded volume of his poems his *Personae,* or "masks," referring to the conventionalized masks of the Greek drama.

A final obstacle for the reader is the violence of Pound's distrust of capitalism and his allegiance to the utopian concept of "social credit." Nevertheless, *Hugh Selwyn Mauberley* (1920), considered as a satire of the materialistic forces involved in World War I, is a masterpiece. In *The Cantos,* begun in 1917, the satire became intensified. The progressive series, exceeding the proposed limit of one hundred poems, are loosely connected cantos, like Dante's *Divina Commedia* in three sections, but representing a comedy human, not divine, dealing with the wreck of civilizations by reason of the infidelity of mankind in the three epochs—the ancient world, the Renaissance, and the modern period. With *The Pisan Cantos* of 1948 and *Section: Rock Drill* (1956), Cantos I to XCV had all been published except for two. By 1960 they numbered CIX, badly needing explication. A considerable number ber contain lyrical passages of

genuine power; they are in places supremely witty, and many of their topical references are shrewd and valuable. But their complexity renders them controversial. Somewhat resembling *Finnegans Wake* in structure, Pound's vast poem now has a position similar to that of Joyce's novel before critical scholarship provided its explication. Pound's critics have developed a voluminous commentary concerning *The Cantos,* which, like Joyce's work, employs the complex association of scholarly lore, anthropology, modern history and personages, private history and witticisms, and obscure literary interpolations in various languages, including Chinese ideograms.

In 1924 Pound left Paris for Rapallo, Italy, attracted by Mussolini's faithless promises of democratic state socialism. During World War II, Pound, on behalf of the Italian government, conducted radio broadcasts beamed at the American troops. He was returned to the United States as a citizen accused of treason, but on examination he was declared insane. After the treason charges were dismissed in 1958, Pound returned to Italy, where he died in 1972.

Principal earlier poetry volumes are *A Lume Spento,* 1908; *A Quinzaine for This Yule,* 1908; *Personae,* 1909, reprinted and enlarged, 1913 to 1926; *Exultations,* 1909; *Provença,* 1910, selected poems; *Canzoni,* 1911; *The Sonnets and Ballate of Guido Cavalcanti,* 1912; *Ripostes,* London, 1912, Boston, 1913, new edition, London, 1915; *Personae and Exultations,* 1913; *Cathay,* 1915; *Lustra,* London, 1916, New York, 1917; *Quia Pauper Amavi,* undated, *ca.* 1919, containing "Homage to Sextus Propertius" and *Cantos I–III; Hugh Selwyn Mauberley,* 1920;

Umbra, 1920, a collection from previous volumes; *Poems 1918–1921,* 1921; *Personae: The Collected Poems,* 1926; and *Homage to Sextus Propertius,* new edition, 1934. T. S. Eliot first edited a *Selected Poems* in 1928, of which the newest edition is 1959; a New York *Selected Poems* was issued in 1949 and 1957.

Publication of *The Cantos* began when *Poetry: A Magazine of Verse* printed one in each of three issues, June to August, 1917, collected as "Three Cantos" in the New York edition of *Lustra,* 1917. Their number was gradually increased, with revision and rearrangement, in several volumes: *The Pisan Cantos, LXXI to LXXXV,* 1948, the collection of the eighty-five in *The Cantos of Ezra Pound,* 1948, and *Cantos,* 1954. *Section: Rock Drill,* 1956, brought the number to ninety-five, and *Throne,* 1959, to one hundred and nine, collected in *The Cantos,* 1964. Pound's translation of *Sophokles' Women of Trachis* appeared in 1957. See also *The Translations of Ezra Pound,* ed. by Hugh Kenner (parallel texts), 1954, 1963. *Drafts and Fragments of Cantos CX–CXVII* appeared in 1969, and *Selected Cantos* in 1970.

Pound's voluminous prose contains some stimulating critical work. Typical volumes are *Gaudier-Brzeska,* 1910, a biography; *Pavannes and Divisions,* 1918; *Instigations,* 1920; *Indiscretions* (autobiographical), 1923; *The ABC of Reading,* 1934; *Culture,* 1938; *Money Pamphlets by Pound,* 1950–1952; *Pavannes and Divagations,* 1958; and *The Literary Essays of Ezra Pound,* 1954, edited by T. S. Eliot. *The Letters of Ezra Pound, 1907–1941* was edited by D. D. Paige in 1950. *Pound / Joyce: Letters and Essays* was edited by Forrest Read in 1967. Two of Pound's translations have bearing on the orientalism of *The Cantos: Confucian Analects * * * ,* 1950, and *Shih Ching, The Classic Anthology defined by Confucius.*

Critical studies include T. S. Eliot's introduction to the *Selected Poems,* 1928, and the same author's unsigned volume, *Ezra Pound: His Metric and Poetry,* 1917. A fundamental study is R. P. Blackmur, "Masks of Ezra Pound," reprinted from *Hound and Horn* (March, 1934) as a chapter of Blackmur's *The Double Agent,* 1935. Alice Admur published *The Poetry of Ezra Pound,* 1936. Explication or discussion of *The Cantos* may profitably be sought in the following: H. H. Watts, *Ezra Pound and "The Cantos,"* London, 1951; George Dekker, *The Cantos of Ezra Pound: A Critical Study,* 1963; Noel Stock, *Reading The Cantos,* 1967; and Daniel P. Pearlman, *The Barb of Time,* 1970. John H. Edwards and William Vasse, Jr., compiled an *Annotated Index to the Cantos of Ezra Pound,* 1957. See also J. J. Espey, *Ezra Pound's Mauberley,* 1955; Hugh Kenner, *The Poetry of Ezra Pound,* 1951; Donald Davie, *Ezra Pound: Poet as Sculptor,* 1963; L. S. Dembo, *The Confucian Odes * * * A Critical Study,* 1963; Noel Stock, *Poet in Exile: Ezra Pound,* 1964; Walter Sutton, ed., *Ezra Pound: A Collection of Critical Essays,* 1963; K. L. Goodwin, *The Influence of Ezra Pound,* 1966; N. Christoph de Nagy, *Ezra's Pound's Poetics and Literary Tradition,* 1966; Thomas H. Jackson, *The Early Poetry of Ezra Pound,* 1968; Eva Hesse, ed., *New Approaches to Ezra Pound,* 1969; Wai-Lim Yip, *Ezra Pound's Cathay,* 1969; Christine Brooke-Rose, *A ZBC of Ezra Pound,* 1971; and Hugh Kenner, *The Pound Era,* 1972. Major biographies are Charles Norman, *Ezra Pound,* 1960 (revised, 1969); and Noel Stock, *The Life of Ezra Pound,* 1970. See also Harry M. Meacham, *The Caged Panther: Ezra Pound at St. Elizabeths,* 1967; and Michael Reck, *Ezra Pound: A Close-Up,* 1967. A memoir by Pound's daughter is Mary de Rachewiltz, *Discretions,* 1971. Donald Gallup edited *A Bibliography of Ezra Pound,* 1963; and Gary Lane edited *A Concordance to Personae: The Shorter Poems of Ezra Pound,* 1972.

A Virginal

No, no! Go from me. I have left her lately.
I will not spoil my sheath with lesser brightness,
For my surrounding air has a new lightness;
Slight are her arms, yet they have bound me straitly
And left me cloaked as with a gauze of æther;
As with sweet leaves; as with a subtle clearness.   5
Oh, I have picked up magic in her nearness
To sheathe me half in half the things that sheathe her.
No, no! Go from me. I have still the flavor,

Soft as spring wind that's come from birchen bowers.   10
Green come the shoots, aye April in the branches,
As winter's wound with her sleight hand she staunches,
Hath of the trees a likeness of the savor:
As white their bark, so white this lady's hours.

1909

Portrait d'une Femme

Your mind and you are our Sargasso Sea,
London has swept about you this score years
And bright ships left you this or that in fee:
Ideas, old gossip, oddments of all things,
Strange spars of knowledge and dimmed wares of price.   5
Great minds have sought you—lacking someone else.
You have been second always. Tragical?
No. You preferred it to the usual thing:
One dull man, dulling and uxorious,
One average mind—with one thought less, each year.   10
Oh, you are patient, I have seen you sit
Hours, where something might have floated up.
And now you pay one. Yes, you richly pay.
You are a person of some interest, one comes to you
And takes strange gain away: 15
Trophies fished up; some curious suggestion;
Fact that leads nowhere; and a tale or two,
Pregnant with mandrakes,[1] or with something else
That might prove useful and yet never proves,
That never fits a corner or shows use,   20
Or finds its hour upon the loom of days:
The tarnished, gaudy, wonderful old work;
Idols and ambergris and rare inlays,
These are your riches, your great store; and yet
For all this sea-hoard of deciduous things,   25
Strange woods half sodden, and new brighter stuff:
In the slow float of different light and deep,
No! there is nothing! In the whole and all,
Nothing that's quite your own.
                    Yet this is you.   30

1912

---

1. Popular name of the mandragora. The shape of root in magic suggested a man; it yielded a narcotic.

Hugh Selwyn Mauberley [2]

LIFE AND CONTACTS

Vocat Æstus in Umbram [3]

—NEMESIANUS EC. IV.

E. P.
Ode pour L'Election de son Sépulchre [4]

I

For three years, out of key with his time,
He strove to resuscitate the dead art
Of poetry; to maintain "The sublime" [5]
In the old sense. Wrong from the start—

No hardly, but, seeing he had been born   5
In a half-savage country, out of date;
Bent resolutely on wringing lilies from the acorn;

2. Eliot called this "a document of an epoch"; it is also, in part, a summation of Ezra Pound's experience with the epoch climaxed by the First World War. The thirteen satiric lyrics of this poem reflects his alienation against the crass tendencies of the American *fin de siècle* and English Victorianism—especially its prudential morality in support of material "progress." He sought the creative freedom of the artist and originality, with due respect for the accumulated culture, both Western and Oriental. A good analysis of this poem in detail is John J. Espey, *Ezra Pound's Mauberley*, Berkeley, 1955. As Pound told Felix Schelling in a letter to this favorite teacher at Pennsylvania, "I'm no more Mauberley than Eliot is Prufrock. 'Mauberley' is a mere surface, * * * an attempt to condense the James novel." The five short lyrics of the 1920 "Mauberley" are less impressive than this first cycle. Several of the same motivations are carried over, but the action is reversed, since Mauberley, unlike Pound, is early done to death by age. The present poem, "Hugh Selwyn Mauberley: Life and Contacts," achieves independent unity for its purpose in the carefully ordered sequence of "contacts."

The text here reproduced is that of the first edition: The Ovid Press, 43 Belsege Street, London, 1920. This appeared in two hundred copies and in two forms with identical texts (confirmed by comparing one of each form in the Library of the University of Pennsylvania). Our footnotes show both the original text and the few revisions Pound authorized. For commentary on the text see, besides Espey, *Modern Poetry*, edited by Kimon Friar and J. M. Brinnin (1951): "Pound's Notes on 'Mauberley.'"

3. Latin, meaning "Heat summons us unto the shadow." Of Nemesianus (*fl.* A.D. 283), the Roman author of this line, little survives except his four *Eclogues*. This epigraph was omitted in *Pound's Selected Poems*, 1949.

4. "E. P. Ode on the Choice of His Tomb." *Cf.* Pierre de Ronsard, *Odes*, Book IV, *L'Election de son sépulchre.* Ronsard's cool detachment and perspective were attractive to Pound. *Cf.* also Stéphane Mallarmé's "Le Tombeau d'Edgar Poe." But obviously, Pound's initials also are "E.P."; and in this first-edition text he printed them conspicuously on a line alone and off center to emphasize, as it were, that the letters just below each, in the title line, gave the "E. P." signature in lower case. Espey (see note 2) argues convincingly from textual evidence (pp. 16–20) that Pound himself is the subject *only* in the first poem, headed, "*Ode*": that the "*Ode*," written ironically in the third person as the age's judgment of Pound, ends with his literary death. *Cf.* ll. 18–19 and footnote. Mallarmé's poem contains the line, *Donner un sens plus pur aux mots de la tribu,* which Eliot paraphrased, in *Little Gidding,* as, "To purify the dialect of the tribe." Pound shared this aim and gave expression to it in the first two sections of "Hugh Selwyn Mauberley."

5. Achievement of "the sublime" (*cf.* Longinus or Kant) involved a choice of literary materials and style of exalted spiritual significance.

Capaneus; [6] trout for factitious bait;

"Ιδμεν γάρ τοι πάνθ', ὅσ' ἐνὶ Τροίῃ [7]
Caught in the unstopped ear;   10
Giving the rocks small lee-way [8]
The chopped seas held him, therefore, that year.

His true Penelope was Flaubert, [9]
He fished by obstinate isles;
Observed the elegance of Circe's [1] hair   15
Rather than the mottoes on sun-dials. [2]

Unaffected by "the march of events,"
He passed from men's memory in *l'an trentiesme*
De son eage; [3] the case presents
No adjunct to the Muses' diadem.   20

II

The age demanded an image
Of its accelerated grimace,
Something for the modern stage,
Not, at any rate, an Attic grace;

Not, not certainly, the obscure reveries   25
Of the inward gaze;
Better mendacities
Than the classics in paraphrase!

The "age demanded" chiefly a mould in plaster,
Made with no loss of time,   30
A prose kinema, [4] not, assuredly, alabaster
Or the "sculpture" of rhyme.

III

The tea-rose tea-gown, etc.
Supplants the mousseline of Cos, [5]

6. Capaneus of Argos, in Aeschylus' *The Seven Against Thebes,* swore he would force entrance into Thebes in spite of Jove himself. The god, for this impiety, struck him dead with a thunderbolt.
7. The Greek line, sung by the Sirens in Homer's *Odyssey,* Book XII, l. 189, has here been slightly altered to read: "For we know all the things that are in Troy." Odysseus plugged his sailors' ears with wax, so that they would not leap overboard when they heard the Sirens. The "unstopped ear" mentioned in the next line was that of Odysseus, who had had himself bound to the mast for safety. The references to Odysseus' hazardous journey homeward continue to the end of the next stanza.
8. Scylla, which with the whirlpool Charybdis, formed a dangerous strait that Odysseus escaped only with the loss of six men.
9. Penelope, Odysseus' wife, clung faithfully to the hope of his return for many years, in spite of the importunities and plots of powerful suitors. Gustave Flaubert (1821–1880), "father of French realism," whose painstaking concern for "the exact word" caused critics to refer to his style as "chiseled" or "sculptured." See l. 32, below.
1. Circe, a beautiful sorceress, ruled a domain devoted to sloth and carnal appetite, where Odysseus lingered unduly, although his men were transformed into swine.
2. Sundials usually bear inscriptions referring ominously to the flight of time.
3. *Cf.* François Villon (1431–?); the first line of his *Grand Testament* reads: "In the thirtieth year of my life." Pound has changed "my" to "his." The phrase was re-echoed by a number of others—*e.g.,* Eliot and MacLeish.
4. Greek, meaning "motion"; *cf.* "cinema" for "motion picture."
5. Cos, an Aegean island and ancient cultural center, famous under Roman influence for its exquisite wares.

The pianola "replaces"   35
Sappho's barbitos.[6]

Christ follows Dionysus,
Phallic [7] and ambrosial
Made way for macerations;
Caliban casts out Ariel.[8]   40

All things are a flowing,
Sage Heracleitus [9] says:
But a tawdry cheapness
Shall outlast our days.[1]

Even the Christian beauty   45
Defects—after Samothrace; [2]
We see τὸ καλόν [3]
Decreed in the market place.

Faun's flesh is not to us,
Nor the saint's vision.   50
We have the press for wafer,[4]
Franchise for circumcision.

All men, in law, are equals.
Free of Peisistratus,[5]
We choose a knave or an eunuch   55
To rule over us.

O bright Apollo,
τίν' ἄνδρα, τίν' ἥρωα, τίνα θεὸν [6]
What god, man, or hero
Shall I place a tin wreath upon!   60

IV

These fought, in any case,
and some believing, pro domo,[7] in any case . . .

Some quick to arm,
some for adventure,   65
some from fear of weakness,

6. From the Greek *barbiton*, "a lyre,"
here associated with the poet Sappho.
The "pianola" is a mechanical player-
piano.
7. The Greek worship of Dionysus involved phallic rituals in contrast with
ritualistic "macerations"—that is, fasting.
8. In *The Tempest*, Shakespeare contrasts these two fantastic characters:
Caliban—enormous, earthy, and stupid;
and the sprite Ariel—ethereal and
beautiful.
9. The Greek philosopher Heraclitus
(*fl.* 550 B.C.) emphasized the concept
of "flux," or change: see "fragments"
recovered from his lost writings in
Eliot's epigraph to *Burnt Norton*,
below.

1. The 1920 "Mauberley" read: "reign
throughout our days."
2. The Greek island of Samothrace was
the supposed seat of the Cabiri, occult
pre-Hellenic divinities regarded by the
later Greeks as an attractive mystery.
3. "The beautiful," a common expression in the literature of philosophy.
4. Sacrificial bread of religious ritual;
specifically, of the Christian Eucharist.
5. Pisistratus (died 527 B.C.), thrice
the dictator of the Athenian state.
6. Pindar's Second Olympian Ode, l.
2, reads, in the reverse of this order,
"What God, what hero, what man shall
we loudly praise?"
7. The Latin phrase, "for home," anticipates ll. 71–72.

some from fear of censure,
some for love of slaughter, in imagination,
learning later . . .

some in fear, learning love of slaughter; 70
Died some, pro patria,
　　　　non "dulce" non "et decor" [8] . . .

walked eye-deep in hell
believing in old men's lies, then unbelieving
came home, home to a lie, 75
home to many deceits,
home to old lies and new infamy;

usury age-old and age-thick
and liars in public places.

Daring as never before, wastage as never before. 80
Young blood and high blood,
fair cheeks, and fine bodies;

fortitude as never before

frankness as never before,
disillusions as never told in the old days, 85
hysterias, trench confessions,
laughter out of dead bellies.

V [9]

There died a myriad,
And of the best, among them,
For an old bitch gone in the teeth, 90
For a botched civilization,

Charm, smiling at the good mouth,
Quick eyes gone under earth's lid,

For two gross of broken statues,
For a few thousand battered books.[1] 95

Yeux glauques [2]

Gladstone was still respected,
When John Ruskin produced

---

8. *Cf.* Horace, *Odes*, III, ii. l. 13: *Dulce et decorum est pro patria mori* ["It is sweet and appropriate to die for one's country"].
9. In the first edition, the four poems following are introduced by titles without the numerals VI to IX.
1. The climax of the poem is reached with the sacrifice of life "for a botched civilization" in the World War. In succeeding sections the poet re-examines the spiritual causes of collapse, each in some action or metaphor: in "Yeux glauques" the weight of a moral establishment, the reprobation of intellectual or creative originality, and in "*Siena mi fe'*" the resultant collapse or mediocrity of creativeness; Brennenbaum erases all his inherited traditions by his elegant conformity; Mr. Nixon advises the writer to sell himself to popular literature; the writer who will not do so lives in a leaky hovel; a gentlewoman is possessed of a sterile tradition, perhaps Milesian pottery; the author of the present poem (in XII) discovers that he is dwelling in a cultural and social vacuum and wryly bows out in his "Envoi, 1919," composed of remnants of literature that he knows to be genuine (see Espey, p. 15).
2. Glaucous eyes, dense blue-green; characterizing glaucoma, an illness causing gradual blindness.

"Kings Treasuries"; Swinburne
And Rossetti still abused.[3]

Fœtid Buchanan lifted up his voice   100
When that faun's head of hers
Became a pastime for
Painters and adulterers.[4]

The Burne-Jones cartons [5]
Have preserved her eyes;   105
Still, at the Tate, they teach
Cophetua to rhapsodize; [6]

Thin like brook-water,
With a vacant gaze.
The English Rubaiyat was still-born   110
In those days.[7]

The thin, clear gaze, the same
Still darts out faun-like from the half-ruin'd face
Questing and passive. . . .
"Ah, poor Jenny's case" . . .   115

Bewildered that a world
Shows no surprise
At her last maquero's [8]
Adulteries.

"Siena Mi Fe'; Disfecemi Maremma" [9]

Among the pickled fœtuses and bottled bones,   120
Engaged in perfecting the catalogue,
I found the last scion of the

3. William E. Gladstone (1809–1898) member of Parliament sixty-three years and four times Prime Minister, epitomizes the Victorian establishment. John Ruskin nearly coevally created a brilliant, eloquent critique of art and culture, with excursions into ethical and social betterment often sentimentalized, as was *Sesame and Lilies* (1865), which contained "Of Kings' Treasuries" (*cf.* l. 98). Dante Gabriel Rossetti, successful and controversial, was exceeded by Swinburne among the Pre-Raphaelites in breadth and in provocatively daring "fleshliness." (See Buchanan, note 4.)
4. Robert Williams Buchanan (1841–1901), prolific writer, attacked the Pre-Raphaelites in "The Fleshy School of Poetry" (1871) and especially Rossetti's "Jenny," a poem on the fate of a prostitute. Allusively and without authority Pound connects "Jenny's case" with Rossetti's wife, Elizabeth Siddal, who had been a popular model for these artists, and who becomes the central figure in "Yeux glauques"—see the following stanzas, alluding to her

eyes.
5. The translation to English, "cartoons," in some reprints, is not authorized.
6. Sir Edward Burne-Jones began painting with Rossetti in 1856, and it is likely that his early sketches ("cartons") show Elizabeth Siddal's eyes from the life. He did not complete his painting of the ballad-story "King Cophetua and the Beggar Maid" until 1884. Her eyes are "still, at the Tate," museum in London.
7. Referring to the failure of Fitz-Gerald's translation to win attention until Rossetti praised it.
8. In Spanish, one who lacquers (refinishes) pictures; but also, as in French *"maquereau,"* a pimp.
9. "Siena made me, Maremma undid me" (Dante, *Purgatory*, V, 135), spoken by the spirit of Pia de' Tolornei of Siena, whose husband sent her to Maremma to be murdered. Here the idea is comically applied since Verog's prototype fared very well as an immigrant to England.

Senatorial families of Strasbourg, Monsieur Verog.[1]

For two hours he talked of Gallifet; [2]
Of Dowson; of the Rhymers' Club;   125
Told me how Johnson (Lionel) died
By falling from a high stool in a pub . . .

But showed no trace of alcohol
At the autopsy, privately performed—
Tissue preserved—the pure mind   130
Arose toward Newman as the whiskey warmed.[3]

Dowson found harlots cheaper than hotels;
Headlam for uplift; [4] Image impartially imbued
With raptures for Bacchus, Terpsichore and the Church.
So spoke the author of "The Dorian Mood," [5]   135

M. Verog, out of step with the decade,
Detached from his contemporaries,
Neglected by the young,
Because of these reveries.

Brennbaum

The sky-like limpid eyes,   140
The circular infant's face,
The stiffness from spats to collar
Never relaxing into grace;

The heavy memories of Horeb, Sinai and the forty years,[6]
Showed only when the daylight fell   145
Level across the face
Of Brennbaum "The Impeccable."

Mr. Nixon [7]

In the cream gilded cabin of his steam yacht
Mr. Nixon advised me kindly, to advance with fewer
Dangers of delay. "Consider   150
        "Carefully the reviewer.

---

1. In real life, Victor Gustave Plarr
(1863–1929), whose family emigrated
from Strasbourg after the Franco-Prussian war. He was Dowson's biographer
and Librarian of the Royal College of
Surgeons (see l. 120, "pickled foetuses
and bottled bones"). He had been a
member of The Rhymers' Club; Pound
bases much of this poem on Plarr's
recollections (see Espey, pp. 91–96).
2. Properly, Galliffet, Gaston Alexandre
August, Marquis de (1830–1909), who
led the unsupported cavalry charge at
Sedan.
3. Ernest Dowson (1876–1900) was a
"decadent" poet; the Rhymers' Club included many prominent writers, the
greatest being Yeats; Lionel Johnson

(1867–1902), poet and critic, died from
a fall on the street, not in a pub, and
the reference to Cardinal Newman relates to Johnson's ardent Catholicism.
4. Rev. Stewart Headlam, churchman
and *bon vivant*, Dowson's friend.
5. That is, "Verog," or Plarr, whose
volume of poems should be properly entitled *In the Dorian Mood* (1896).
6. Horeb, the mountain of God, where
the angel of the Lord appeared to
Moses; on Mt. Sinai Moses received the
Commandments; and he led the Israelites for forty years in the desert.
7. Pound, in his Notes for Friar (see
Modern Poetry, edited by Friar and
Brinnin), says that Nixon "is a fictitious name for a real person."

"I was as poor as you are;
"When I began I got, of course,
"Advance on royalties, fifty at first," said Mr. Nixon,
"Follow me, and take a column,   155
"Even if you have to work free.

"Butter reviewers. From fifty to three hundred
"I rose in eighteen months;
"The hardest nut I had to crack
"Was Dr. Dundas.   160

"I never mentioned a man but with the view
"Of selling my own works.
"The tip's a good one, as for literature
"It gives no man a sinecure.

"And no one knows, at sight, a masterpiece.   165
"And give up verse, my boy,
"There's nothing in it."

                    .   .   .   .

Likewise a friend of Bloughram's [8] once advised me:
Don't kick against the pricks,
Accept opinion. The "Nineties" tried your game   170
And died, there's nothing in it.

X

Beneath the sagging roof
The stylist has taken shelter,
Unpaid, uncelebrated,
At last from the world's welter   175

Nature receives him;
With a placid and uneducated mistress
He exercises his talents
And the soil meets his distress.

The haven from sophistications and contentions   180
Leaks through its thatch;
He offers succulent cooking;
The door has a creaking latch.

XI

"Conservatrix of Milésien" [9]
Habits of mind and feeling,   185
Possibly. But in Ealing

---

8. "Bloughram * * * reference to Browning's Bishop, allegoric" wrote Pound. (See *Modern Poetry* by Friar and Brinnin.) In Browning's "Bishop Blougram's [*sic*] Apology," the Bishop is also a "practical man," expert at compromise. Espey reports (p. 24) that Pound would not agree to drop the "h" in "Bloughram."

9. Miletus, the most important and oldest of the twelve Ionian cities, became known by archaeological explorations to have had a high culture in very ancient times.

With the most bank-clerkly of Englishmen?

No, "Milésien" [1] is an exaggeration.
No instinct has survived in her
Older than those her grandmother   190
Told her would fit her station.

XII

"Daphne with her thighs in bark
Stretches toward me her leafy hands,"— [2]
Subjectively. In the stuffed-satin drawing-room
I await The Lady Valentine's commands,   195

Knowing my coat has never been
Of precisely the fashion
To stimulate, in her,
A durable passion;

Doubtful, somewhat, of the value   200
Of well-gowned approbation
Of literary effort,
But never of The Lady Valentine's vocation:

Poetry, her border of ideas,
The edge, uncertain, but a means of blending   205
With other strata
Where the lower and higher have ending;

A hook to catch the Lady Jane's attention,
A modulation toward the theatre,
Also, in the case of revolution,   210
A possible friend and comforter.

．　　．　　．　　．

Conduct, on the other hand, the soul
"Which the highest cultures have nourished"
To Fleet St. where
Dr. Johnson flourished;   215

Beside this thoroughfare
The sale of half-hose has
Long since superseded the cultivation
Of Pierian roses.[3]

1919   1920

---

1. Pound wrote "Milesian" in the 1949 edition but retained the French form in l. 184.
2. In Greek myth, a nymph, Daphne, praying for deliverance from the pursuit of Apollo, was turned into a laurel tree. Here it appears that the nymph is part of the decor of the drawing room. The first two lines of the poem are directly translated from *Le Château du souvenir* by Théophile Gautier, whose poetry was an early influence on Pound.
3. Pierian roses, in the sense of "poetry," derive from one of Sappho's fragments. Sappho's flower is the rose and Pieria is associated with worship of the Muses (see Espey, p. 98).

Envoi [4]

HUGH SELWYN MAUBERLEY (1919)

Go, dumb-born book,   220
Tell her that sang me once that song of Lawes: [5]
Hadst thou but song
As thou hast subjects known,
Then were there cause in thee that should condone
Even my faults that heavy upon me lie,   225
And build her glories their longevity.

Tell her that sheds
Such treasure in the air,
Recking naught else but that her graces give
Life to the moment,   230
I would bid them live
As roses might, in magic amber laid,
Red overwrought with orange and all made
One substance and one colour
Braving time.   235

Tell her that goes
With song upon her lips
But sings not out the song, nor knows
The maker of it, some other mouth,
May be as fair as hers,   240
Might, in new ages, gain her worshippers,
When our two dusts with Waller's shall be laid,
Siftings on siftings in oblivion,
Till change hath broken down
All things save Beauty alone.   245

1920

From Homage to Sextus Propertius [6]

[*The Cynthia Epistles*]

ELEGY V: 2

Yet you ask on what account I write so many love-lyrics
And whence this soft book comes into my mouth.

---

4. See the familiar "Go, Lovely Rose," by Edmund Waller (1606–1687).
5. Henry Lawes (1596–1662), well known as a composer, set to music many poems of his day. He was a friend of Milton, who praised him in a sonnet.
6. Roman elegaic poet, born in Umbria about 51 B.C. His poetry won the attention and patronage of Maecenas, benefactor of Virgil and Horace. Pound found the experimental and difficult poet irresistibly attractive and pro-
duced creative translations of twelve elegaic lyrics as imaginative as the original. The work was completed in 1917; sections were published in 1919 in *Poetry* and *The New Age;* it was fully printed the same year in *Quia Pauper Amavi.* There were later authorized textual and spelling changes, reflected in the following text; see J. P. Sullivan, *Ezra Pound and Sextus Propertius*, 1964, for a detailed discussion. Pound himself and numerous

Neither Calliope nor Apollo sung these things into my ear,
    My genius is no more than a girl.

If she with ivory fingers drive a tune through the lyre,   5
    We look at the process.
How easy the moving fingers; if hair is mussed on her forehead,
If she goes in a gleam of Cos,[7] in a slither of dyed stuff,
There is a volume in the matter; if her eyelids sink into sleep,
There are new jobs for the author;   10
And if she plays with me with her shirt off,
    We shall construct many Iliads.
And whatever she does or says
    We shall spin long yarns out of nothing.

Thus much the fates have allotted me, and if, Maecenas,   15
I were able to lead heroes into armour, I would not,
Neither would I warble of Titans, nor of Ossa
              spiked onto Olympus,
Nor of causeways over Pelion,[8]
Nor of Thebes in its ancient respectability,   20
    nor of Homer's reputation in Pergamus,
Nor of Xerxes' two-barreled kingdom,[9] nor of
    Remus and his royal family,
Nor of dignified Carthaginian characters,
Nor of Welsh mines and the profit Marus[1] had out of them.   25
I should remember Caesar's affairs . . .
              for a background,
Although Callimachus[2] did without them,
            and without Theseus,
Without an inferno, without Achilles attended of gods,   30
Without Ixion, and without the sons of Menoetius and the
    Argo and without Jove's grave and the Titans.

And my ventricles do not palpitate to Caesarial *ore rotundos,*[3]
Nor to the tune of the Phrygian fathers.[4]
Sailor, of winds; a plowman, concerning his oxen;

---

critics have observed a general resemblance in mood and situation between his *Propertius* and *Mauberley,* written a year later. While they represent different civilizations and disparate authors, "both * * * are works of self-justification concerned with the fate of an author in an age unsympathetic to his art," as John Espey remarks (*Ezra Pound's Mauberley,* 1955, Chapter 7), citing numerous parallels.

7. See *"Ode,"* l. 34.
8. In the war with the gods, the Titans attempted to pile the mountains Ossa and Pelion upon Mt. Olympus in order to scale heaven.
9. The Persian king (c. 519–465 B.C.) added Egypt to his dominion by subjugation but failed to conquer Greece,

480–479 B.C.
1. In the original, the line reads: *Cimbrorumque minas et benefacta Mari,* "The threats of the Cimbri and the great deeds of Marius," referring to the defeat of the Celtic invaders of Gaul by the Roman general Caius Marius in 102 B.C. Pound's reading is imaginative but far afield.
2. Callimachus does not need the inspiration of Caesar because the Alexandrian is already two centuries dead; the extension of this idea in the case of the lovelorn Propertius is a typical extravagance of Roman social verse.
3. Oratory.
4. Trojan heroes; the Roman poets frequently employed "Phrygian" for "Trojan."

Soldier, the enumeration of wounds; the sheep-feeder, of ewes; 35
We, in our narrow bed, turning aside from battles:
Each man where he can, wearing out the day in his manner.

3

It is noble to die of love, and honourable to remain
                            uncuckolded for a season.
And she speaks ill of light women,   40
                    and will not praise Homer
Because Helen's conduct is "unsuitable." 5

ELEGY VI

When, when, and whenever death closes our eyelids,

Moving naked over Acheron 6
            Upon the one raft, victor and conquered together,
Marius and Jugurtha 7 together,
                        one tangle of shadows.   5

Caesar plots against India,
Tigris and Euphrates shall, from now on, flow at his bidding,
Tibet shall be full of Roman policemen,
The Parthians shall get used to our statuary
                    and acquire a Roman religion;   10
One raft on the veiled flood of Acheron,
            Marius and Jugurtha together.

Nor at my funeral either will there be any long trail,
                    bearing ancestral lares and images;
No trumpets filled with my emptiness,   15
Nor shall it be on an Atalic 8 bed;
            The perfumed cloths will be absent.
A small plebeian procession.
            Enough, enough and in plenty
There will be three books at my obsequies   20
Which I take, my not unworthy gift, to Persephone.9

You will follow the bare scarified beast
Nor will you be weary of calling my name, nor too weary
            To place the last kiss on my lips
When the Syrian onyx 1 is broken.   25

5. See below, VII, l. 14.
6. Acheron, one of the rivers of the nether world the dead must cross.
7. Caius Marius (see l. 25) defeated the Numideans and in 104 B.C. took their captured king, Jugurtha, to Rome, where he soon died in a dungeon.
8. Properly, "Attalic," a jocose term for "grossly ornate," "luxurious"; with reference to the Attalids, rulers of Pergamum, whose privileged aristocracy ended with Attalus III, a debauched dilettante, who gave the kingdom to Rome at his death (133 B.C.).
9. Persephone, wife of Pluto, was queen of shades in the nether world; it was both pious and prudent for the dead to take gifts to her.
1. Line 25 is cryptic; the original line of Propertius is ironic: literally, "when enough onyx will be supplied to ransom Syria." Syria had been impoverished by her own rulers, then by the Romans—she could be bought cheap. Onyx receptacles were used to contain unguents and perfumes to anoint the dead. Pound's line assumes that these oils will be thrown into the funeral pyre; hence the onyx will be "broken."

"He who is now vacant dust
"Was once the slave of one passion";

Give that much inscription
       "Death why tardily come?"
You, sometimes, will lament a lost friend,   30
    For it is a custom:
That care for past men,

Since Adonis was gored in Idalia,[2] and the Cytherean
Ran crying with out-spread hair,
    In vain, you call back the shade,   35
In vain, Cynthia. Vain call to unanswering shadow,
    Small talk comes from small bones.

ELEGY VII

Me happy, night, night full of brightness;
Oh couch made happy by my long delectations;
How many words talked out with abundant candles;
Struggles when the lights were taken away;
Now with bared breasts she wrestled against me,   5
    Tunic spread in delay;
And she then opening my eyelids fallen in sleep,
Her lips upon them; and it was her mouth saying:
    Sluggard!

In how many varied embraces, our changing arms,   10
Her kisses, how many, lingering on my lips.
"Turn not Venus into a blinded motion,
    Eyes are the guides of love,
Paris took Helen naked coming from the bed of Menelaus,
Endymion's naked body, bright bait for Diana,"   15
    —such at least is the story.[3]

While our fates twine together, sate we our eyes with love:
For long night comes upon you
    and a day when no day returns.
Let the gods lay chains upon us   20
    so that no day shall unbind them.
Fool who would set a term to love's madness,
For the sun shall drive with black horses,
    earth shall bring wheat from barley,
The flood shall move toward the fountain   25
    Ere love know moderations,
    The fish shall swim in dry streams.

No, now while it may be, let not the fruit of life cease.

---

2. Idalia (usually Idalium), a town on Cyprus, an island dedicated to the worship of "the Cytherean" (Venus) who weeps because her lover, Adonis, was killed by a boar.
3. Endymion was sleeping on Mount Latmos in the moonlight, when Diana came down and lay beside him.

Dry wreaths drop their petals,
      their stalks are woven in baskets,   30
To-day we take the great breath of lovers,
      to-morrow fate shuts us in.

Though you give all your kisses
      you give but few.

Nor can I shift my pains to other,   35
  Hers will I be dead,
If she confers such nights upon me,
      long is my life, long in years,
If she give me many,
      God am I for the time.   40

1919

THOMAS STEARNS ELIOT
(1888–1965)

As compared with other major poets, T. S. Eliot published relatively little, but his excellence has been generally recognized ever since his first major poem, *The Waste Land*, appeared in 1922. However, he always remained a controversial figure. He was regarded almost with reverence by a coterie of critics; his own literary criticism has been influential, especially in its support of that form of poetry which employs intellectual discipline and cultural memory in preference to more accessible and more sensuous images and emotional suggestions. Eliot has been criticized for "unnecessary obscurity" or for "authoritarian severity"; but numerous other genuine poets of idea are instrumentally more complex, and his intellectual severity draws interest by its systematic traditionalism. Of his craftsmanship, his integrity, and his power, however, there has been little doubt.

Thomas Stearns Eliot was born in St. Louis, Missouri, on September 26, 1888, of New England stock, his Eliot grandfather having gone west as a Unitarian minister. He studied at private academies, entered Harvard at eighteen, and there attained the M.A. degree in 1910. A student of languages and belles-lettres, especially the writings of the Elizabethans and the metaphysical poets and the literature of the Italian Renaissance, he was also attracted to the study of philosophy, taught at Harvard by such men as Irving Babbitt and George Santayana. In the winter of 1910 he went to the University of Paris, where he was influenced by the lectures of the philosopher Henri Bergson. Again at Harvard (1911–1914), he studied Sanskrit and Oriental philosophy in the graduate school, was an assistant in the philosophy department, and in 1914 was awarded a traveling fellowship for study in Germany.

At Merton College, Oxford, in 1915, he again studied philosophy. That year he married the daughter of a British artist. For two years he taught in English academies, while bringing to fruition his first book of poems. In 1917, he published *Prufrock and Other Observations*. Few poets in their first book have so prophetically suggested the direction and power of what was to follow. "The Love Song of J. Alfred Prufrock" still holds its place in the development of Eliot's poetry as a whole; like much of his later work it concerns various aspects of the frustration and enfeeblement of individual character as seen in perspective with the decay of states, peoples, and religious faith.

From 1918 to 1924 Eliot was in the service of Lloyd's Bank in London. In 1920 his fourth volume, *Poems*, with "Gerontion" as its leading poem, again developed the same general pattern of ideas. It is remarkable that he excluded almost no poem of his early volumes from his later collected works. In 1920 also appeared *The Sacred Wood*, containing, among other essays, "Tradition and the Individual Talent," the earliest statement of his aesthetics. The aesthetic principle which he first elaborated in this essay provided a useful instrument for modern criticism. It relates primarily to the individual work of art, the poem conceived as a made object, an organic thing in itself, whose concrete elements are true correlatives of the artist's imagination and experience with respect to that poem. The degree to which fusion and concentration of intellect, feeling, and experience were achieved was Eliot's criterion for judging the poem. Such ideas he developed in other essays which have been influential in promoting the intrinsic analysis of poetry.

Also in 1920, Eliot began *The Waste Land*, one of the major works of modern literature. Its subject, the apparent failure of Western civilization which World War I seemed to demonstrate, set the tone of his poetry until 1930. Such poems as "Prufrock" and "Gerontion" had suggested the spiritual debility of the modern individual and his culture while in satirical counterpoint his Sweeney poems had symbolized the rising tide of anticultural infidelity and human baseness. It is likely that in his abundant use of literary reference in *The Waste Land* he was influenced by Pound, a close friend whose advice, as Eliot declared, he followed strictly in cutting and concentrating the poem. *The Waste Land* is the acknowledged masterpiece of its sort. It also introduced a form —the orchestration of related themes in successive movements —which he used again in "The Hollow Men" (1925), *Ash-Wednesday* (1930), and his later masterpieces, *Four Quartets* (1936–1942; 1943).

The Waste Land appeared as a volume in New York and London in 1922, but it had been published earlier that year in *The Criterion*, an influential London literary quarterly which Eliot edited from 1922 through 1939. His second volume of criticism, *Homage to John Dryden*

(1924) was much admired for its critical method. In 1925 Eliot became a member of the board of the publishing firm now known as Faber and Faber, and he was long in that association. He collected *Poems, 1909–1925* (1925). In 1927 he was confirmed in the Anglican Church and became a British subject.

A year later, in connection with the publication of the critical volume *For Lancelot Andrewes* (1928), he described himself as "a royalist in politics, a classicist in literature, and an Anglo-Catholic in religion"; and he has manifested an increasing reliance upon authority and tradition. His later poetry took a positive turn toward faith in life, in strong contrast with the desperation of *The Waste Land*. This was demonstrated by *Ash-Wednesday*, a poem of mystical conflict between faith and doubt, beautiful in its language if difficult in its symbolism. In 1932, in *Sweeney Agonistes*, he brought Sweeney to a deserved and gruesome death in a strange play that fascinates the attention by mingling penitence with musical comedy. In "The Hollow Men" he satirized the straw men, the Guy Fawkes men, whose world would end "not with a bang, but a whimper"; also in this period he produced the "Ariel Poems," including the exquisite and tender "Marina" (1930). *Murder in the Cathedral* (1935), a poetic tragedy on the betrayal of Thomas à Becket, has been successfully performed, and is a drama of impressive spiritual power. His *Collected Poems, 1909–1935* (1936), and the collected *Essays, Ancient and Modern*, which in the same year gave perspective to his criticism, brought to an end this first period of spiritual exploration.

Eliot's next major accomplishment, the *Four Quartets*, originated during his visit to the United States (1932–1934), his first return to his native country in seventeen years. During this period he wrote the small "Landscapes," some of them drawn from American scenes, which are spiritually connected with the theme of the *Quartets*. His lectures at Harvard University in 1932 resulted in the influential volume *The Uses of Poetry and the Uses of Criticism* (1933). In 1934 he lectured at the University of Virginia, and produced the study of orthodoxy and faith entitled *After Strange Gods, A Primer of Modern Heresy*. Presumably it was during this year that he conceived the subject of "Burnt Norton," the first of the *Quartets*.

The four poems that eventually resulted provide a reasoned philosophical discussion of the foundations of Christian faith, involving the nature of time, the significance of history, the religious psychology of man, and the nature of his experience; most importantly, perhaps, they attempt, by means of lofty poetic feeling and metaphysical insight, to suggest the actuality and meaning of such Christian mysteries as Incarnation and Pentecost. To some readers, these poems have seemed deficient in breadth, based as they are upon an authoritarian tradition of Christian philosophy; but they have been of unusual interest for an age desperately seeking to resolve the conflict between spiritual and material reality. The four poems, which had all been previously published, were brought together in *Four Quartets* (1943).

Eliot dramatized domestic life in terms of his philosophy. *The Family Reunion* (1939) was not generally considered successful as drama. *The Cocktail Party* (1949), *The Confidential Clerk* (1953), and *The Elder Statesman* (1958) created interest as experimental theater.

Few men of letters have been more fully honored in their own day than T. S. Eliot, and even those who strongly disagree with him seemed content with his selection for the Nobel Prize in 1948. *The Complete Poems and Plays* (1952) is a relatively small volume, but it represents an artist whose ideas are large, whose craftsmanship is the expression of artistic responsibility, and whose poems represent the progressive refinement and illustration of his aesthetics.

The Complete Poems and Plays of T. S. Eliot, 1952, contains in one volume everything of importance except *The Confidential Clerk,* 1954, and *The Elder Statesman,* 1958. This supersedes the earlier collections. Separate volumes of poetry and criticism are mentioned in the note above. Recent is *Collected Poems, 1909–1962,* 1963. *Poems Written in Early Youth,* 1967, was compiled by John Hayward. Valerie Eliot edited *The Waste Land: A Facsimile and Transcript of the Original Draft,* 1971. No comprehensive edition of his essays has been prepared: the principal collections are *Selected Essays, 1917–1932,* 1932; *Essays, Ancient and Modern,* 1936; *Selected Essays,* new edition,

1950; *Essays on Elizabethan Drama,* 1956; *On Poetry and Poets,* 1957; and *To Criticize the Critic and Other Writings,* 1965. Recent volumes of critical importance are *The Idea of a Christian Society,* 1940; *The Music of Poetry,* 1942; *Notes toward the Definition of Culture,* 1948; *The Three Voices of Poetry,* 1953; and *The Frontiers of Criticism,* 1956.

F. O. Matthiessen, *The Achievement of T. S. Eliot,* third edition, 1958, remains a fine introduction. *T. S. Eliot: A Selected Critique,* edited by Leonard Unger, 1948, is a well-selected collection of major essays interpreting Eliot; as is Allen Tate, ed., *T. S. Eliot: The Man and His Work,* 1966; and see Leonard Unger's *The Art of T. S. Eliot,* 1949. Other useful studies are in George Williamson, *The Talent of T. S. Eliot,* 1929; Edmund Wilson, *Axel's Castle,* 1931; F. R. Leavis, *New Bearings in English Poetry,* 1932; R. P. Blackmur, *The Double Agent,* 1935; Allen Tate, *Reactionary Essays on Poetry and Ideas,*. 1936; Cleanth Brooks, *Modern Poetry and the Tradition,* 1930; Clive Sansom, *The Poetry of T. S. Eliot,* 1947; Elizabeth A. Drew, *T. S. Eliot: The Design of His Poetry,* 1949; George Williamson, *A Reader's Guide to T. S. Eliot,* 1953; Grover Smith, Jr., *T. S. Eliot's Poetry and Plays: A Study in Sources and Meaning,* 1956; and Hugh Kenner, *Invisible Poet: T. S. Eliot,* 1959. More recent studies include Northrop Frye, *T. S. Eliot* (Writers and Critics, Series), 1963; Eric Thompson, *T. S. Eliot: The Metaphysical Perspective,* 1963; and Genesius Jones, *Approach to the Purpose: A Study of the Poetry of T. S. Eliot,* 1965; Leonard Unger, *T. S. Eliot: Moments and Patterns,* 1966; Fei-Pai Lu, *T. S. Eliot: The Dialectical Structure of His Theory of Poetry,* 1966; Harry Blamires, *Word Unheard: A Guide through Eliot's Four Quartets,* 1969; E. Martin Browne, *The Making of T. S. Eliot's Plays,* 1969; Marion Montgomery, *T. S. Eliot: An Essay on the American Magus,* 1969; Russell Kirk, *Eliot and His Age,* 1971; and Roger Kojecky, *T. S. Eliot's Social Criticism,* 1971. A critical biography is Bernard Bergonzi, *T. S. Eliot,* 1971. Memoirs are William Turner Levy and Victor Scherle, *Affectionately, T. S. Eliot: The Story of a Friendship, 1947–1965,* 1968; and Robert Sencourt, *T. S. Eliot: A Memoir,* 1971.

Tradition and the Individual Talent [1]

I

In English writing we seldom speak of tradition though we occasionally apply its name in deploring its absence. We cannot refer to 'the tradition' or to 'a tradition'; at most, we employ the adjective in saying that the poetry of So-and-so is 'traditional' or even 'too traditional.' Seldom, perhaps, does the word appear except in a phrase of censure. If otherwise, it is vaguely approbative, with the implication, as to the work approved, of some pleasing archæological reconstruction. You can hardly make the word agreeable to English ears without this comfortable reference to the reassuring science of archæology.

Certainly the word is not likely to appear in our appreciations of living or dead writers. Every nation, every race, has not only its own creative, but its own critical turn of mind; and is even more oblivious of the shortcomings and limitations of its critical habits than of those of its creative genius. We know, or think we know, from the enormous mass of critical writing that has appeared in the French language, the critical method or habit of the French; we only conclude (we are such unconscious people) that the French are 'more critical' than we, and sometimes even plume ourselves a little with the fact, as if the French were the less spontaneous. Perhaps they are; but we might remind ourselves that criticism is as inevitable as breathing, and that we should be none the worse for articulating what passes in our minds when we read a book and feel an emotion about it, for criticizing our own minds in their work of criticism. One of the facts that might come to light in this process is our tendency to insist, when we praise a poet, upon those aspects of his work in which he least resembles anyone else. In these aspects or parts of his work we pretend to find what is individual, what is the peculiar essence of the man. We dwell with satisfaction upon the poet's difference from his predecessors, especially his immediate predecessors; we endeavour to find something that can be isolated in order to be enjoyed. Whereas if we approach a poet without this prejudice we shall often find that not only the best, but the most individual parts of his work may be those in which the dead poets, his ancestors, assert their immortality most vigorously. And I do not mean the impressionable period of adolescence, but the period of full maturity.

Yet if the only form of tradition, of handing down, consisted in following the ways of the immediate generation before us in

1. Published early in his career, in *The Sacred Wood* (1920), this essay defines a primary critical position from which Eliot's subsequent ideas have developed.

a blind or timid adherence to its success, 'tradition' should positively be discouraged. We have seen many simple currents soon lost in the sand; and novelty is better than repetition. Tradition is a matter of much wider significance. It cannot be inherited, and if you want it you must obtain it by great labour. It involves, in the first place, the historical sense, which we may call nearly indispensable to anyone who would continue to be a poet beyond his twenty-fifth year; and the historical sense involves a perception, not only of the pastness of the past, but of its presence; the historical sense compels a man to write not merely with his own generation in his bones, but with a feeling that the whole of the literature of Europe from Homer and within it the whole of the literature of his own country has a simultaneous existence and composes a simultaneous order. This historical sense, which is a sense of the timeless as well as of the temporal and of the timeless and of the temporal together, is what makes a writer traditional. And it is at the same time what makes a writer most acutely conscious of his place in time, of his own contemporaneity.

No poet, no artist of any art, has his complete meaning alone. His significance, his appreciation is the appreciation of his relation to the dead poets and artists. You cannot value him alone; you must set him, for contrast and comparison, among the dead. I mean this as a principle of æsthetic, not merely historical, criticism. The necessity that he shall conform, that he shall cohere, is not onesided; what happens when a new work of art is created is something that happens simultaneously to all the works of art which preceded it. The existing monuments form an ideal order among themselves, which is modified by the introduction of the new (the really new) work of art among them. The existing order is complete before the new work arrives; for order to persist after the supervention of novelty, the *whole* existing order must be, if ever so slightly, altered; and so the relations, proportions, values of each work of art toward the whole are readjusted; and this is conformity between the old and the new. Whoever has approved this idea of order, of the form of European, of English literature will not find it preposterous that the past should be altered by the present as much as the present is directed by the past. And the poet who is aware of this will be aware of great difficulties and responsibilities.

In a peculiar sense he will be aware also that he must inevitably be judged by the standards of the past. I say judged, not amputated, by them; not judged to be as good as, or worse or better than, the dead; and certainly not judged by the canons of dead critics. It is a judgment, a comparison, in which two things are measured by each other. To conform merely would be for the new work not really to conform at all; it would not be new, and would therefore not be a work of art. And we do not quite say that the new is more valuable because it fits in; but its fitting in is a test of its value—a test, it is true, which can only be slowly and cautiously applied, for we are none of us infallible judges of conformity. We say: it appears to conform, and is perhaps individual, or it appears individual, and may conform; but we are hardly likely to find that it is one and not the other.

To proceed to a more intelligible exposition of the relation of the poet to the past: he can neither take the past as a lump, an indiscriminate bolus, nor can he form himself wholly on one or two private admirations, nor can he form himself wholly upon one preferred period. The first course is inadmissable, the second is an important experience of youth, and the third is a pleasant and highly desirable supplement. The poet must be very conscious of the main current, which does not at all flow invariably through the most distinguished reputations. He must be quite aware of the obvious fact that art never improves, but that the material of art is never quite the same. He must be aware that the mind of Europe—the mind of his own country—a mind which he learns in time to be much more important than his own private mind—is a mind which changes, and that this change is a development which abandons nothing *en route*, which does not superannuate either Shakespeare, or Homer, or the rock drawing of the Magdalenian draughtsmen.[2] That this development, refinement perhaps, complication certainly, is not, from the point of view of the artist, any improvement. Perhaps not even an improvement from the point of view of the psychologist or not to the extent which we imagine; perhaps only in the end based upon a complication in economics and machinery. But the difference between the present and the past is that the conscious present is an awareness of the past in a way and to an extent which the past's awareness of itself cannot show.

Someone said: 'The dead writers are remote from us because we *know* so much more than they did.' Precisely, and they are that which we know.

I am alive to a usual objection to what is clearly part of my programme for the *métier*[3] of poetry. The objection is that the doctrine requires a ridiculous amount of erudition (pedantry), a claim which can be rejected by appeal to the lives of poets in any pantheon. It will even be affirmed that much learning deadens or perverts poetic sensibility. While, however, we persist in believ-

2. In the rock shelters of La Madeleine (in southwest France) appear the first paleolithic cave drawings to be studied by modern scholars. The animal sketches particularly show an advanced art.

3. Craft; *i.e.*, art.

ing that a poet ought to know as much as will not encroach upon his necessary receptivity and necessary laziness, it is not desirable to confine knowledge to whatever can be put into a useful shape for examinations, drawing-rooms, or the still more pretentious modes of publicity. Some can absorb knowledge, the more tardy must sweat for it. Shakespeare acquired more essential history from Plutarch than most men could from the whole British Museum. What is to be insisted upon is that the poet must develop or procure the consciousness of the past and that he should continue to develop this consciousness throughout his career.

What happens is a continual surrender of himself as he is at the moment to something which is more valuable. The progress of an artist is a continual self-sacrifice, a continual extinction of personality.

There remains to define this process of depersonalization and its relation to the sense of tradition. It is in this depersonalization that art may be said to approach the condition of science. I therefore invite you to consider, as a suggestive analogy, the action which takes place when a bit of finely filiated platinum is introduced into a chamber containing oxygen and sulphur dioxide.[4]

II

Honest criticism and sensitive appreciation is directed not upon the poet but upon the poetry. If we attend to the confused cries of the newspaper critics and the *susurrus*[5] of popular repetition that follows, we shall hear the names of poets in great numbers; if we seek not Blue-book knowledge but the enjoyment of poetry, and ask for a poem, we shall seldom find it. I have tried to point out the importance of the relation of the poem to other poems by other authors, and suggested the conception of poetry as a living whole of all the poetry that has ever been written. The other aspect of this Impersonal theory of poetry is the relation of the poem to its author. And I hinted, by an analogy, that the mind of the mature poet differs from that of the immature one not precisely in any valuation of 'personality,' not being necessarily more interesting, or having 'more to say,' but rather by being a more finely perfected medium in which special, or very varied, feelings are at liberty to enter into new combinations.

The analogy was that of the catalyst. When the two gases previously mentioned are mixed in the presence of a filament of platinum, they form sulphurous acid. This combination takes place only if the platinum is present; nevertheless the newly formed acid contains no trace of platinum, and the platinum itself is ap-

4. As a catalyst; see the second paragraph below.   5. Latin for "murmuring."

parently unaffected: has remained inert, neutral, and unchanged. The mind of the poet is the shred of platinum. It may partly or exclusively operate upon the experience of the man himself; but, the more perfect the artist, the more completely separate in him will be the man who suffers and the mind which creates; the more perfectly will the mind digest and transmute the passions which are its material.[6]

The experience, you will notice, the elements which enter the presence of the transforming catalyst, are of two kinds: emotions and feelings. The effect of a work of art upon the person who enjoys it is an experience different in kind from any experience not of art. It may be formed out of one emotion, or may be a combination of several; and various feelings, inhering for the writer in particular words or phrases or images, may be added to compose the final result. Or great poetry may be made without the direct use of any emotion whatever: composed out of feelings solely. Canto XV of the *Inferno* (Brunetto Latini)[7] is a working up of the emotion evident in the situation; but the effect, though single as that of any work of art, is obtained by considerable complexity of detail. The last quatrain gives an image, a feeling attaching to an image, which 'came,' which did not develop simply out of what precedes, but which was probably in suspension in the poet's mind until the proper combination arrived for it to add itself to.[8] The poet's mind is in fact a receptacle for seizing and storing up numberless feelings, phrases, images, which remain there until all the particles which can unite to form a new compound are present together.

If you compare several representative passages of the greatest poetry you see how great is the variety of types of combination, and also how completely any semi-ethical criterion of 'sublimity' misses the mark. For it is not the 'greatness,' the intensity, of the emotions, the components, but the intensity of the artistic process, the pressure, so to speak, under which the fusion takes place, that counts. The episode of Paolo and Francesca employs a definite emotion, but the intensity of the poetry is something quite different from whatever intensity in the supposed experience it may give the impression of.[9] It is no more intense, furthermore, than

6. The concept of the poem itself as the sole object of the reader's attention has become a principal tenet of recent criticism.

7. In this canto, Dante records his meeting in Hell with the Florentine philosopher Brunetto Latini (1212?–1294?).

8. Brunetto, condemned, for "unnatural lust," never to "stop one instant," walks with Dante in grave discourse;

then must dash "like a racer" to regain his sordid companions, thus providing Eliot's catalysis of "feeling" with the "emotional image."

9. The lovers Paolo and Francesca, immortalized in Canto v of Dante's *Inferno*, had been slain by Francesca's jealous husband. Eliot distinguishes between the emotion of the lovers and Dante's fusion of various emotions in his narrative.

Canto XXVI, the voyage of Ulysses,[1] which has not the direct dependence upon an emotion. Great variety is possible in the process of transmutation of emotion: the murder of Agamemnon,[2] or the agony of Othello, gives an artistic effect apparently closer to a possible original than the scenes from Dante. In the *Agamemnon*, the artistic emotion approximates to the emotion of an actual spectator; in *Othello* to the emotion of the protagonist himself. But the difference between art and the event is always absolute; the combination which is the murder of Agamemnon is probably as complex as that which is the voyage of Ulysses. In either case there has been a fusion of elements. The ode of Keats contains a number of feelings which have nothing particular to do with the nightingale, but which the nightingale, partly perhaps because of its attractive name, and partly because of its reputation, served to bring together.

The point of view which I am struggling to attack is perhaps related to the metaphysical theory of the substantial unity of the soul: for my meaning is, that the poet has, not a 'personality' to express, but a particular medium, which is only a medium and not a personality, in which impressions and experiences combine in peculiar and unexpected ways. Impressions and experiences which are important for the man may take no place in the poetry, and those which become important in the poetry may play quite a negligible part in the man, the personality.

I will quote a passage [3] which is unfamiliar enough to be regarded with fresh attention in the light—or darkness—of these observations:

> And now methinks I could e'en chide myself
> For doating on her beauty, though her death
> Shall be revenged after no common action.
> Does the silkworm expend her yellow labours
> For thee? For thee does she undo herself?
> Are lordships sold to maintain ladyships
> For the poor benefit of a bewildering minute?
> Why does yon fellow falsify highways,
> And put his life between the judge's lips,
> To refine such a thing—keeps horse and men
> To beat their valours for her? . . .

---

1. Ulysses' straightforward account (in Dante's *Inferno*, xxvi) of his last voyage into the unknown sea, and his death by shipwreck, does not agree with Homer's *Odyssey*, and is thought to be Dante's invention.
2. In the *Agamemnon* by Aeschylus.

Eliot refers to the murder of Agamemnon by his wife's lover in the closing lines of "Sweeney among the Nightingales."
3. Act III, Scene 5, ll. 71–82, of *The Revenger's Tragedy* (1607), by Cyril Tourneur (*ca.* 1575–1626).

In this passage (as is evident if it is taken in its context) there is a combination of positive and negative emotions: an intensely strong attraction toward beauty and an equally intense fascination by the ugliness which is contrasted with it and which destroys it. This balance of contrasted emotion is in the dramatic situation to which the speech is pertinent, but that situation alone is inadequate to it. This is, so to speak, the structural emotion, provided by the drama. But the whole effect, the dominant tone, is due to the fact that a number of floating feelings, having an affinity to this emotion by no means superficially evident, have combined with it to give us a new art emotion.

It is not in his personal emotions, the emotions provoked by particular events in his life, that the poet is in any way remarkable or interesting. His particular emotions may be simple, or crude, or flat. The emotion in his poetry will be a very complex thing, but not with the complexity of the emotions of people who have very complex or unusual emotions in life. One error, in fact, of eccentricity in poetry is to seek for new human emotions to express; and in this search for novelty in the wrong place it discovers the perverse. The business of the poet is not to find new emotions, but to use the ordinary ones and, in working them up into poetry, to express feelings which are not in actual emotions at all. And emotions which he has never experienced will serve his turn as well as those familiar to him. Consequently, we must believe that 'emotion recollected in tranquillity' [4] is in an inexact formula. For it is neither emotion, nor recollection, nor, without distortion of meaning, tranquillity. It is a concentration, and a new thing resulting from the concentration, of a very great number of experiences which to the practical and active person would not seem to be experiences at all; it is a concentration which does not happen consciously or of deliberation. These experiences are not 'recollected,' and they finally unite in an atmosphere which is 'tranquil' only in that it is a passive attending upon the event. Of course this is not quite the whole story. There is a great deal, in the writing of poetry, which must be conscious and deliberate. In fact, the bad poet is usually unconscious where he ought to be conscious, and conscious where he ought to be unconscious. Both errors tend to make him 'personal.' Poetry is not a turning loose of emotion, but an escape from emotion; it is not the expression of personality, but an escape from personality. But, of course, only those who have personality and emotions know what it means to want to escape from these things.

---

4. Wordsworth, in the Preface to the second edition of *Lyrical Ballads* (1800), said that poetry "takes its origin from emotion recollected in tranquillity."

III

ὁ δὲ νοῦς ἴσως θειότερόν τι καὶ ἀπαθές ἐστιν.[5]

This essay proposes to halt at the frontier of metaphysics or mysticism, and confine itself to such practical conclusions as can be applied by the responsible person interested in poetry. To divert interest from the poet to the poetry is a laudable aim: for it would conduce to a juster estimation of actual poetry, good and bad. There are many people who appreciate the expression of sincere emotion in verse, and there is a smaller number of people who can appreciate technical excellence. But very few know when there is an expression of *significant* emotion, emotion which has its life in the poem and not in the history of the poet. The emotion of art is impersonal. And the poet cannot reach this impersonality without surrendering himself wholly to the work to be done. And he is not likely to know what is to be done unless he lives in what is not merely the present, but the present moment of the past, unless he is conscious, not of what is dead, but of what is already living.

1920

The Love Song of J. Alfred Prufrock

*S'io credessi che mia risposta fosse
a persona che mai tornasse al mondo,
questa fiamma staria senza più scosse.
Ma per ciò che giammai di questo fondo
non tornò vivo alcun, s'i'odo il vero,
senza tema d'infamia ti rispondo.*[6]

Let us go then, you and I,
When the evening is spread out against the sky
Like a patient etherised upon a table;
Let us go, through certain half-deserted streets,
The muttering retreats   5
Of restless nights in one-night cheap hotels
And sawdust restaurants with oyster-shells:
Streets that follow like a tedious argument
Of insidious intent
To lead you to an overwhelming question. . .   10
Oh, do not ask, 'What is it?'

5. "Perhaps the Mind is something divine, and [therefore] unaffected [by impressions from without]." The quotation is from Aristotle, *On the Soul* (*De Anima*), Chapter 4.
6. "If I believed my answer were being made to one who could ever return to the world, this flame would gleam [*i.e.*, this spirit would speak] no more; but since, if what I hear is true, never from this abyss did living man return, I answer thee without fear of infamy" (Dante, *Inferno*, xxvii, 61–66). The speaker, Guido da Montefeltro, promised absolution by Pope Boniface VIII, advised that prelate how to betray and destroy the Colonna family of Palestrina, and died unrepentant.

Let us go and make our visit.

In the room the women come and go
Talking of Michelangelo.[7]

The yellow fog [8] that rubs its back upon the window-panes,   15
The yellow smoke that rubs its muzzle on the window-panes,
Licked its tongue into the corners of the evening,
Lingered upon the pools that stand in drains,
Let fall upon its back the soot that falls from chimneys,
Slipped by the terrace, made a sudden leap,   20
And seeing that it was a soft October night,
Curled once about the house, and fell asleep.

And indeed there will be time
For the yellow smoke that slides along the street,
Rubbing its back upon the window-panes;   25
There will be time, there will be time
To prepare a face to meet the faces that you meet;
There will be time to murder and create,
And time for all the works and days [9] of hands
That lift and drop a question on your plate;   30
Time for you and time for me,
And time yet for a hundred indecisions,
And for a hundred visions and revisions,
Before the taking of a toast and tea.

In the room the women come and go   35
Talking of Michelangelo.

And indeed there will be time
To wonder, 'Do I dare?' and, 'Do I dare?'
Time to turn back and descend the stair,[1]
With a bald spot in the middle of my hair—   40
(They will say: 'How his hair is growing thin!')
My morning coat, my collar mounting firmly to the chin,
My necktie rich and modest, but asserted by a simple pin—
(They will say: 'But how his arms and legs are thin!')
Do I dare   45
Disturb the universe?
In a minute there is time

7. The lines suggest the futility of "arty" talk by dilettantes.
8. The yellow (or brown) fog of the sordid city was a familiar detail in French symbolism. See *The Waste Land*, ll. 60–61, with Eliot's note, there referring to Baudelaire.
9. *Works and Days*, by Hesiod (eighth century B.C.), "father of Greek didactic poetry," was an account of daily life and husbandry, intermingled with moral precepts.
1. Dante's figure of the stairway from Hell to Heaven (*Purgatorio*, xxvi, ll. 145–148) recurs in Eliot's poems; see, for example, l. 428 of *The Waste Land*, and *Ash-Wednesday*, Part III.

For decisions and revisions which a minute will reverse.

For I have known them all already, known them all—[2]
Have known the evenings, mornings, afternoons,　　　　　50
I have measured out my life with coffee spoons;
I know the voices dying with a dying fall [3]
Beneath the music from a farther room.
　　So how should I presume?

And I have known the eyes already, known them all—　　55
The eyes that fix you in a formulated phrase,
And when I am formulated, sprawling on a pin,
When I am pinned and wriggling on the wall,
Then how should I begin
To spit out all the butt-ends of my days and ways?　　60
　　And how should I presume?

And I have known the arms already, known them all—
Arms that are braceleted and white and bare
(But in the lamplight, downed with light brown hair!)
Is it perfume from a dress　　　　　65
That makes me so digress?
Arms that lie along a table, or wrap about a shawl.
　　And should I then presume?
　　And how should I begin?

　　　　·　　·　　·　　·　　·

Shall I say, I have gone at dusk through narrow streets　70
And watched the smoke that rises from the pipes
Of lonely men in shirt-sleeves, leaning out of windows? . . .

I should have been a pair of ragged claws
Scuttling across the floors of silent seas.

　　　　·　　·　　·　　·

And the afternoon, the evening, sleeps so peacefully!　75
Smoothed by long fingers,
Asleep . . . tired . . . or it malingers,
Stretched on the floor, here beside you and me.
Should I, after tea and cakes and ices,
Have the strength to force the moment to its crisis?　　80
But though I have wept and fasted, wept and prayed,
Though I have seen my head (grown slightly bald) brought in
　　upon a platter,

---

2. Echoes Laforgue's *Le Concile féerique* (*cf*. ll. 54 and 62).
3. *Cf*. Shakespeare, *Twelfth Night*, Act I, Scene 1, ll. 1–4: "If music be the food of love, play on; / Give me excess of it, that, surfeiting / The appetite may sicken, and so die. / That strain again! it had a dying fall."

I am no prophet [4]—and here's no great matter;
I have seen the moment of my greatness flicker,
And I have seen the eternal Footman hold my coat, and snicker,
And in short, I was afraid.   86

And would it have been worth it, after all,
After the cups, the marmalade, the tea,
Among the porcelain, among some talk of you and me,
Would it have been worth while,   90
To have bitten off the matter with a smile,
To have squeezed the universe into a ball
To roll it toward some overwhelming question,
To say: 'I am Lazarus, come from the dead,
Come back to tell you all,[5] I shall tell you all'—   95
If one, settling a pillow by her head,
   Should say: 'That is not what I meant at all,
   That is not it, at all.'

And would it have been worth it, after all,
Would it have been worth while,   100
After the sunsets and the dooryards and the sprinkled streets,
After the novels, after the teacups, after the skirts that trail along
     the floor—
And this, and so much more?—
It is impossible to say just what I mean!
But as if a magic lantern threw the nerves in patterns on a screen:
Would it have been worth while   106
If one, settling a pillow or throwing off a shawl,
And turning toward the window, should say:
   'That is not it at all,
   That is not what I meant, at all.'   110

                    ·   ·   ·   ·   ·

No! I am not Prince Hamlet,[6] nor was meant to be;
Am an attendant lord, one that will do
To swell a progress, start a scene or two,

4. *Cf.* Matthew xiv: 3–11. The head of
John the Baptist was brought to Queen
Herodias on a "charger." Prufrock is
"bald," quite unlike John the Baptist as
represented in Richard Strauss's opera
Salome (1905) or Oscar Wilde's play
(1894) on which it was based, both
emphasizing the passion of Herodias
for the prophet.
5. For the resurrection of Lazarus see
John xi: 1–44. *Cf.* the note on the
epigraph to this poem.
6. In the following passage (to l. 119)
the speaker, Prufrock, indicates his own
futility by comparing himself with
Hamlet and a number of other literary
characters. The "attendant lord" might
be Polonius, or Rosencrantz or
Guildenstern, in *Hamlet*. Chaucer, in
the *Canterbury Tales*, ll. 303–306, describes the speech of the Clerk as
terse, and "full of high sentence" (*i.e.*,
pithy wisdom). Eliot (l. 117) employs
the phrase differently, with the implication of empty pompousness. The court
"Fool" (l. 119) was a conventional
fixture of Elizabethan drama.

Advise the prince; no doubt, an easy tool,
Deferential, glad to be of use,   115
Politic, cautious, and meticulous;
Full of high sentence, but a bit obtuse;
At times, indeed, almost ridiculous—
Almost, at times, the Fool.

I grow old . . . I grow old . . .   120
I shall wear the bottoms of my trousers rolled.

Shall I part my hair behind? Do I dare to eat a peach?
I shall wear white flannel trousers, and walk upon the beach.
I have heard the mermaids singing, each to each.

I do not think that they will sing to me.   125

I have seen them riding seaward on the waves
Combing the white hair of the waves blown back
When the wind blows the water white and black.

We have lingered in the chambers of the sea
By sea-girls wreathed with seaweed red and brown   130
Till human voices wake us, and we drown.[7]

1917

Gerontion [8]

Thou hast nor youth nor age
But as it were an after dinner sleep
Dreaming of both.

Here I am, an old man in a dry month,
Being read to by a boy, waiting for rain.[9]
I was neither at the hot gates [1]
Nor fought in the warm rain
Nor knee deep in the salt marsh, heaving a cutlass,   5
Bitten by flies, fought.
My house is a decayed house,
And the Jew squats on the window sill, the owner,
Spawned in some estaminet of Antwerp,

---

7. According to legend, the sirens had the power to lure men to visit them in caves beneath the sea; but when their singing stopped the spell was broken, and the men would drown.
8. A coined word, from the Greek *geron*, "an old man." The epigraph is from Shakespeare, *Measure for Measure*, Act III, Scene 1, ll. 32–34. The poem is related in theme with *The Waste Land*, for which Eliot at first

intended it to appear as an introduction (Pound's *Letters*, 169–172).
9. Water (or rain) is here used as symbol of fertility or rebirth; see "Prufrock," ll. 124–131, and *The Waste Land, passim*.
1. A literal translation of the Greek word *Thermopylae*, the name of the pass where three hundred Spartans under Leonidas defeated the Persian host of Xerxes (480 B.C.).

Blistered in Brussels, patched and peeled in London.[2]   10
The goat coughs at night in the field overhead;
Rocks, moss, stonecrop, iron, merds.[3]
The woman keeps the kitchen, makes tea,
Sneezes at evening, poking the peevish gutter.

               I an old man,   15
A dull head among windy spaces.

Signs are taken from wonders. "We would see a sign!" [4]
The word within a word,[5] unable to speak a word,
Swaddled with darkness. In the juvescence of the year
Came Christ the tiger [6]   20

In depraved May,[7] dogwood and chestnut, flowering judas,
To be eaten, to be divided, to be drunk
Among whispers; by Mr. Silvero
With caressing hands, at Limoges
Who walked all night in the next room;   25

By Hakagawa, bowing among the Titians;
By Madame de Tornquist, in the dark room
Shifting the candles; Fräulein von Kulp
Who turned in the hall, one hand on the door.
Vacant shuttles
Weave the wind. I have no ghosts,   30
An old man in a draughty house

2. The "Jew" (l. 8) then frequently symbolized the merchant class, or trade in general, long disdained by British society as a vulgarity basely born "in some estaminet" (shady tavern) of a continental city, and there disgraced ("Blistered"); but now being made acceptable ("patched and peeled") in London.
3. French for "dung."
4. In John iv: 48, Jesus said to the nobleman whose son he healed: "Except ye see signs and wonders, ye will not believe"; and see in Matthew xii: 38, the Pharisaic demand: "Master, we would see a sign from thee."
5. See John i: 1: "In the beginning was the Word, and the Word was with God, and the Word was God." For "Swaddled with darkness," in the next line, see Luke ii: 12, "Ye shall find the babe [Jesus] wrapped in swaddling clothes, lying in a manger"; see also Job xxxviii: 2, 9. The theme of the lost primordial Word recurs in *Ash-Wednesday, The Waste Land,* and *Four Quartets.*
6. "Christ the tiger" suggests the bibli-

cal language of prophecy. In Revelation v: 5, Christ is called "the Lion of the tribe of Judah." The latter was that son of whom Jacob, in blessing, declared "Judah is a lion's whelp"; he further prophesied that Judah's descendants should inherit this power "until Shiloh [the Messiah] come" (Genesis xlix: 9–10). Finally, Eliot's "Christ the tiger" and the two following lines suggest the Eucharist—the transubstantiation of the bread and wine of the Sacrament into the body and blood of Christ —and remind us that Samson, finding "honey in the carcase of the lion," propounded the prophetic riddle, "Out of the eater came forth meat * * * " (*cf.* Judges xiv: 8–14).
7. *Cf. The Waste Land,* ll. 1–2: "April is the cruellest month, breeding / Lilacs out of the dead land." In the present passage (ll. 19–29), the offense of spring is identified with the betrayal of Christ (*cf.* "flowering judas," and Matthew xxvi: 14–16, 47–49). The poet has invented the names of the persons in this passage.

Under a windy knob.

After such knowledge, what forgiveness? Think now
History has much cunning passages, contrived corridors   35
And issues, deceives with whispering ambitions,
Guides us by vanities. Think now
She gives when our attention is distracted
And what she gives, gives with such supple confusions
That the giving famishes the craving. Gives too late   40
What's not believed in, or if still believed,
In memory only, reconsidered passion. Gives too soon
Into weak hands, what's thought can be dispensed with
Till the refusal propagates a fear. Think
Neither fear nor courage saves us. Unnatural vices   45
Are fathered by our heroism. Virtues
Are forced upon us by our impudent crimes.
These tears are shaken from the wrath-bearing tree.[8]
The tiger springs in the new year. Us he devours.[9] Think at last
We have not reached conclusion, when I   50
Stiffen in a rented house.[1] Think at last
I have not made this show purposelessly
And it is not by any concitation [2]
Of the backward devils.
I would meet you upon this honestly.   55
I that was near your heart was removed therefrom
To lose beauty in terror, terror in inquisition.
I have lost my passion: why should I need to keep it
Since what is kept must be adulterated?
I have lost my sight, smell, hearing, taste and touch: 60
How should I use it for your closer contact?

These with a thousand small deliberations
Protract the profit of their chilled delirium,
Excite the membrane, when the sense has cooled,
With pungent sauces, multiply variety   65
In a wilderness of mirrors. What will the spider do,
Suspend its operations, will the weevil
Delay? De Bailhache, Fresca, Mrs. Cammel,[3] whirled
Beyond the circuit of the shuddering Bear
In fractured atoms. Gull against the wind, in the windy straits   70

8. The tree of the Garden of Eden; see Genesis ii: 16–17, and iii: 1–19.
9. *Cf.* ll. 20–23. There the "tiger" was the bread and wine; now He is the avenger of the Judgment.
1. *Cf.* l. 7 and l. 74; the "house" is perhaps Gerontion's body.

2. Concerted action, excitation.
3. Unidentified persons, all to be "whirled / Beyond * * * the shuddering Bear" (l. 68), hence beyond the polestar, the northernmost star in the two constellations of the Bear.

Of Belle Isle, or running on the Horn,[4]
White feathers in the snow, the Gulf claims,
And an old man driven by the Trades
To a sleepy corner.

              Tenants of the house,   75
Thoughts of a dry brain in a dry season.

                                   1920

Sweeney Erect

And the trees about me,
Let them be dry and leafless; let the rocks
Groan with continual surges; and behind me
Make all a desolation. Look, look, wenches! [5]

Paint me a cavenous waste shore
   Cast in the unstilled Cyclades,[6]
Paint me the bold anfractuous rocks
   Faced by the snarled and yelping seas.

Display me Aeolus [7] above   5
   Reviewing the insurgent gales
Which tangle Ariadne's hair
   And swell with haste the perjured sails.

Morning stirs the feet and hands
   (Nausicaa and Polypheme),[8]   10
Gesture of orang-outang
   Rises from the sheets in steam.

This withered root of knots of hair
   Slitted below and gashed with eyes,

---

4. Belle Isle Straits are far north, between Labrador and Newfoundland; the Horn is the southern tip of South America.
5. *The Maid's Tragedy,* Act II, Scene 2, ll. 74–77, by Francis Beaumont and John Fletcher, late Elizabethan dramatists. In the play, Queen Aspatia, forsaken by her lover, asks her maid to weave her picture into a tapestry in the character of Ariadne. In the words here quoted she is describing the appropriate scenery for the tapestry. Eliot continues this description, and the traditional Ariadne story, in his first two stanzas.
6. *Cf.* Catullus, *Carmine,* LXIV. Ariadne saved the life of Theseus, who then accepted her love. He later deserted her on a wild coast in the Cy-

clades, and sailed for home. Ariadne's plight aroused Jupiter, who prevented Theseus from changing his sails from black to white—his signal to his father, King Aegeus, that he had survived. The stricken father killed himself on seeing the black sails afar off. (See "perjured sails," l. 8).
7. Ruler of the winds in classic myth.
8. See Homer, *Odyssey,* Books VIII and IX. Nausicaä was princess of Phaeacia; she rescued and befriended the shipwrecked Ulysses, loved him hopelessly, and sent him on his way in a ship supplied by her father. By contrast, Polyphemus was a one-eyed, man-eating giant, master of the Cyclops, whom Ulysses escaped by burning out his eye.

This oval O cropped out with teeth: 15
   The sickle motion from the thighs

Jackknifes upward at the knees
   Then straightens out from heel to hip
Pushing the framework of the bed
   And clawing at the pillow slip.   20

Sweeney [9] addressed full length to shave
   Broadbottomed, pink from nape to base,
Knows the female temperament
   And wipes the suds around his face.

(The lengthened shadow of a man   25
   Is history, said Emerson [1]
Who had not seen the silhouette
   Of Sweeney straddled in the sun.)

Tests the razor on his leg
   Waiting until the shriek subsides.   30
The epileptic on the bed
   Curves backward, clutching at her sides.

The ladies of the corridor
   Find themselves involved, disgraced,
Call witness to their principles   35
   And deprecate the lack of taste

Observing that hysteria
   Might easily be misunderstood;
Mrs. Turner intimates
   It does the house no sort of good.   40

But Doris,[2] towelled from the bath,
   Enters padding on broad feet,
Bringing sal volatile
   And a glass of brandy neat.

1920

---

9. The character of Sweeney appears in several of Eliot's poems, always associated with the degradation and vulgarization of life. See also "Mr. Eliot's Sunday Morning Service," "Sweeney among the Nightingales," and *The Waste Land*, l. 198. In *Sweeney Agonistes* (1932), an "unfinished" drama, he meets his predestined death as a murderer. In the present poem, the "orang-outang" of l. 11 recalls the phrase "Ape-neck Sweeney" in "Sweeney among the Nightingales." The title, "Sweeney Erect," suggests *Pithecanthropus erectus* (literally, "ape-man erect"), the fossil Java Man, earlier than *Homo sapiens*.

1. *Cf.* "Self-Reliance," paragraph 17: "An institution is the lengthened shadow of one man * * * and all history resolves itself very easily into the biography of a few stout and earnest perseons."

2. In *Sweeney Agonistes* Doris reappears in the same rôle. Sweeney offers to take her "to a cannibal isle" where there is only "birth, copulation, and death." Doris replies, "I'd be bored."

A Cooking Egg [3]

En l'an trentiesme de mon aage,
Que toutes mes hontes j'ay beues . . .[4]

Pipit sate upright in her chair
　　Some distance from where I was sitting;
Views of the Oxford Colleges
　　Lay on the table, with the knitting.

Daguerreotypes and silhouettes,　　　　　　　　　5
　　Her grandfather and great great aunts,
Supported on the mantelpiece
　　An *Invitation to the Dance*.[5]

　　　　·　　·　　　·　　　·

I shall not want Honour in Heaven
　　For I shall meet Sir Philip Sidney [6]　　　　10
And have talk with Coriolanus [7]
　　And other heroes of that kidney.[8]

I shall not want Capital in Heaven
　　For I shall meet Sir Alfred Mond.[9]
We two shall lie together, lapt　　　　　　　　15
　　In a five per cent. Exchequer Bond.

I shall not want Society in Heaven,
　　Lucretia Borgia shall be my Bride;
Her anecdotes will be more amusing
　　Than Pipit's experience could provide.　　　20

I shall not want Pipit in Heaven:
　　Madame Blavatsky [1] will instruct me

---

3. An egg for use in cooking only, as compared with one "strictly fresh"; its age is against it.
4. "In the thirtieth year of my life, / How I have drunken deep of all my shames . . . " (*Le Grand Testament*, 1461, François Villon, ll. 1–2). Reference to this climacteric of Villon's became a melancholy cliché among the poets of Eliot's generation.
5. This now-forgotten picture, along with books of *Views* (l. 3) and the family photographs, was once a conventional part of a somewhat prim domestic *décor*.
6. Gallant Elizabethan gentleman and good poet, of irreproachable family connections, Sir Philip Sidney chose for the "mistress" of his sonnets the

daughter of an earl.
7. A legendary Roman patrician leader. *Cf. The Waste Land*, l. 417, and Eliot's later "Coriolan" poems.
8. *Cf.* Plato, *Apology*, 41: "I myself, too, shall have a wonderful interest in there meeting and conversing with Palmedes, and Ajax the son of Telamon, and any other ancient hero who has suffered death through an unjust judgment * * * "
9. Sir Alfred Mond (died 1930) was a famous British financier and industrialist.
1. Elena Petrovna Blavatsky (died 1891), an internationally famous writer on the occult, worker of "miracles," and founder of the Theosophical Society.

In the Seven Sacred Trances;
　Piccarda de Donati [2] will conduct me.

.　　.　　.　　.　　.

But where is the penny world I bought　　25
To eat with Pipit behind the screen?
The red-eyed scavengers are creeping
　From Kentish Town and Golder's Green; [3]

Where are the eagles and the trumpets?

　Buried beneath some snow-deep Alps.　　30
Over buttered scones and crumpets
　Weeping, weeping multitudes
Droop in a hundred A.B.C.'s.[4]

1920

Mr. Eliot's Sunday Morning Service [5]

Look, look, master, here comes two religious caterpillars.
　　　　　　　　　　　　　　—THE JEW OF MALTA

Polyphiloprogenitive [6]
The sapient sutlers [7] of the Lord
Drift across the window-panes.
In the beginning was the Word.[8]

In the beginning was the Word.　　5
Superfetation of τὸ ἕν,[9]

2. See Dante, *Purgatorio,* xxiv, 10–15. In Purgatory, Dante inquires about the immortal destiny of Piccarda, who like his own wife was of the great Donati family. She was both "beautiful and good," and already "wears her glad crown" in Paradise. *Cf. Paradiso,* III, ll. 35 ff.
3. The "penny world" of innocence (l. 25) is compared with "Kentish Town" and "Golder's Green" of suburban London, then the habitats of upstart ambition.
4. The Aerated Bread Corporation, a chain of restaurants called the "A.B.C.'s," where "scones and crumpets," popular British pastries, are consumed in the ritual of afternoon tea.
5. The epigraph is from Christopher Marlow's *Jew of Malta,* Act IV, Scene 1, l. 21. This passage in the play attacks the corruption and carnality of the clergy. This idea is reflected at once in the extraordinary first line of the poem. Subsequent stanzas explore the relationship of the fertility impulse to sexual conduct, nature, and God; and its rôle in philosophy, religion, and

ritual. The speculation ends only in confusion, in the amusing last stanza, which confirms the suggestion that this meditation occurred in a bathtub beside a garden window, and shows "Sweeney" as part of everyone's nature (*cf.* "Sweeney Erect").
6. *Cf.* "philoprogenitive," designating a person possessed with desire for offspring. The masterful prefix "poly" adds the idea of promiscuity.
7. From the Early Dutch *soeteler,* "one who undertakes a humble employment." *Cf.* ll. 25–28. In modern parlance, the sutler is one who follows an army, selling provisions, liquor, and so on to the soldiers.
8. John i: 1. *Cf.* "Gerontion," l. 18, and observe the shift here from "Word" as spirit to "Word" as fertility (ll. 5 and 6 of this poem).
9. The Greek phrase, literally "the One," in Greek metaphysics came to mean "the unity of Being." Hence, in ll. 5 and 6, "the Word" implies a "superfetation"—sublime and universal pregnancy—within "being," or the Godhead.

And at the mensual [1] turn of time
Produced enervate Origen. [2]

A painter of the Umbrian school
Designed upon a gesso ground 10
The nimbus of the Baptized God. [3]
The wilderness is cracked and browned

But through the water pale and thin
Still shine the unoffending feet
And there above the painter set 15
The Father and the Paraclete. [4]

. . . . .

The sable presbyters [5] approach
The avenue of penitence;
The young are red and pustular
Clutching piaculative pence. 20

Under the penitential gates
Sustained by staring Seraphim
Where the souls of the devout
Burn invisible and dim.

Along the garden-wall the bees 25
With hairy bellies pass between
The staminate and pistilate,
Blest office of the epicene. [6]

Sweeney shifts from ham to ham
Stirring the water in his bath. [7] 30
The masters of the subtle schools
Are controversial, polymath. [8]

1920

---

1. Monthly.
2. Origen (died *ca.* 254 A.D.), a Father
of the Greek Church, was the first to
establish a synthesis of Hebrew Scripture and Greek philosophy. Although
his doctrines were later declared heretical, Eliot's "enervate" may refer also
to Origen's literal application of Matthew xix: 12, " * * * there be eunuchs,
which have made themselves eunuchs
for the kingdom of heaven's sake."
3. At the baptism of Jesus in the
wilderness by John the Baptist (*cf.*
Matthew iii: 11–17), "the heavens
were opened," but the "nimbus of the
Baptized God" also suggests the pagan
divinities in certain Eastern legends.
Since the painting is on "gesso"
(plaster), the "wilderness is cracked."
The phrase "unoffending feet" (l. 14)
recalls that when later Jesus was crucified, his feet were nailed to the cross.

4. Specifically, the Holy Spirit, which
descended "like a dove" at the baptism
(*cf.* Matthew iii: 16, Mark i: 10, Luke
iii: 22, and John i: 32).
5. Presbyters were Elders of the early
church, later traditionally clad in black
("sable"); here the reference is to ants
or other insects, whose "red" young
bring (l. 20) "piaculative [expiatory]
pence" (*cf.* "penance")—presumably
pollen, in this context. *Cf.* the bees (l.
25).
6. The bees are "epicene" (performing
the functions of both sexes) in carrying pollen from stamens to pistils (ll.
26–27).
7. See "Sweeney Erect." The presence
of Sweeney in "Mr. Eliot's" devotional
service comically suggests the relations
between animal man and spiritual man.
8. Variously or diversely learned.

The Waste Land [9]

"*Nam Sibyllam quidem Cumis ego ipse oculis meis vidi in ampulla pendere, et cum illi pueri dicerent: Σίβυλλα τί θέλεις; respondebat illa: ἀποθανεῖν θέλω.*" [1]

FOR EZRA POUND
il miglior fabbro [2]

I. The Burial of the Dead

April is the cruellest month, breeding
Lilacs out of the dead land,[3] mixing
Memory and desire, stirring
Dull roots with spring rain.
Winter kept us warm, covering   5
Earth in forgetful snow, feeding
A little life with dried tubers.

---

9. *The Waste Land* appeared in *The Criterion* (London) in October, 1922; in *The Dial* (New York) in November, 1922; and almost simultaneously as a book (New York, 1922). To many writers of the period following World War I, Western civilization seemed hopelessly bankrupt. While Eliot supported this view in his poem, the work was also a testament of faith in the Christian and classical traditions, threatened by infidelity. In his general note Eliot said, "Not only the title, but the plan and a good deal of the incidental symbolism of the poem was suggested by Miss Jessie L. Weston's book on the Grail Legend: *From Ritual to Romance*" (1920). He also acknowledged the influence of Sir James Frazer's *The Golden Bough* (12 volumes, 1890–1915), "especially the two volumes *Adonis, Attis, Osiris.*" These parts of Frazer's work deal in particular with ancient vegetation ceremonies and fertility legends. Similarly, Jessie L. Weston, in her study, found certain sources of the Holy Grail legends in pre-Christian myths, legends, and rituals concerning fertility. These primitive materials, reshaped by Christian influence, appeared as symbolic elements in the later stories of the Grail and of Arthur's knights. Eliot was particularly indebted to Miss Weston for the North European myth of the Fisher King, ruler of a Waste Land blighted by an evil spell which also rendered the King impotent. The salvation of King and country awaited the advent of a knight of fabulous virtue and courage, whose ordeals would provide answers for certain magical questions symbolic at once of religious purity and fertility. In connection with the Fisher King, Miss Weston emphasized the use of the fish as a symbol in early Christianity; the title "fishers of men," bestowed by Christ on his apostles; and the immemorial connection of the fish symbol with pagan fertility deities and their rituals. References to the ordeals of the Christian knights of later legends are mingled in Eliot's poem with pagan echoes and with a literary symbolism involving allusions or quotations relating to thirty-five authors, in several languages.

1. The epigraph is translated: "For I myself, with my own eyes, saw the Sibyl of Cumae hanging caged in a bottle, and when the boys said to her: 'Sibyl, what do you want'; she answered: 'I want to die' " (Petronius, *Satyricon*, Chapter 48). The Cumaean Sibyl, once beloved of Apollo, and the guide and counselor of Aeneas on his descent to Avernus, was the most famous and trusted prophetess of Greece. Apollo had granted her as many years of life as she could hold grains of dust in her hand, but she neglected to ask to remain young, and her authority had declined as she aged.

2. The Italian inscription to Ezra Pound reads "the better artisan" or "poet." The quoted phrase was taken from Dante, *Purgatorio*, xxvi, 117, where it was used by a poet in pointing out the renowned Arnaut Daniel, a troubadour. Eliot has acknowledged his indebtedness to Pound, especially in the final revisions of *The Waste Land*.

3. *Cf.* "depraved May" in "Gerontion," l. 21. In Oriental literature the lilac occurs in sexual symbolism. The title "The Burial of the Dead" suggests the mythical and ritualistic burial and resurrection of gods; note also its relationship to the theme of Part IV.

Summer surprised us, coming over the Starnbergersee [4]
With a shower of rain; we stopped in the colonnade,
And went on in sunlight, into the Hofgarten,[5]   10
And drank coffee, and talked for an hour.
Bin gar keine Russin, stamm' aus Litauen, echt deutsch.[6]
And when we were children, staying at the arch-duke's,
My cousin's, he took me out on a sled,
And I was frightened. He said, Marie,[7]   15
Marie, hold on tight. And down we went.
In the mountains, there you feel free.
I read, much of the night, and go south in the winter.

What are the roots that clutch, what branches grow
Out of this stony rubbish? Son of man,[8]   20
You cannot say, or guess, for you know only
A heap of broken images, where the sun beats,
And the dead tree gives no shelter, the cricket [9] no relief,
And the dry stone no sound of water. Only
There is shadow under this red rock,   25
(Come in under the shadow of this red rock),[1]
And I will show you something different from either
Your shadow at morning striding behind you
Or your shadow at evening rising to meet you;
I will show you fear in a handful of dust.[2]   30

> *Frisch weht der Wind*[3]
> *Der Heimat zu,*

4. A fashionable lake resort near Munich.
5. German term for an outdoor café; here presumably the famous one in Munich, in a public park containing a zoo.
6. "Indeed I am not Russian, I come from Litau, true German." (Lithuania had been frequently flooded by colonizing Germans.)
7. *Cf.* Eliot's statement, in his note to l. 218, that "all the women are one woman." By this comment Eliot relates Marie to "the hyacinth girl" (l. 36) and "the lady of situations" (l. 50), who reappears in Part II, "A Game of Chess."
8. "*Cf.* Ezekiel ii, 1" [Eliot's note]. Here God addresses Ezekiel, as usual, "Son of man" And in the third verse God continues: "I send thee to * * * a rebellious nation * * * : they and their fathers have transgressed against me."
9. "*Cf.* Ecclesiastes xii, 5" [Eliot's note]. In this and the following verse, the Preacher paints a desolate waste

land crushed by sin, when "the grass-hopper shall be a burden, * * * the wheel broken at the cistern."
1. Isaiah (xxxii: 2) prophesied the coming of a Messiah who "shall be * * * as rivers of water in a dry place, as the shadow of a great rock in a weary land."
2. Ecclesiastes (see l. 23) continues, in xii: 7, "Then shall the dust return to the earth as it was." *Cf.* the Sibyl's handful of dust, in the note to the epigraph of this poem.
3. "V. Tristan und Isolde, I, verses 5–8" [Eliot's note]. Ll. 31–42 represent three contrasted experiences of love: (1) a light love, here suggested by a lyric quoted from Wagner's opera, in which a carefree young sailor on Tristan's ship celebrates his beloved in Ireland: "Fresh wafts the wind / To the Homeland, / My Irish sweetheart [literally, "child"], / Where are you waiting?"; (2) the failure of love in the hyacinth garden (ll. 35–41); and finally, (3) Tristan's high but unhappy love for Isolde (l. 42).

Mein Irisch Kind,
Wo weilest du?

'You gave me hyacinths first a year ago;   35
'They called me the hyacinth girl.'
—Yet when we came back, late, from the Hyacinth garden,[4]
Your arms full, and your hair wet, I could not
Speak, and my eyes failed, I was neither
Living nor dead, and I knew nothing,   40
Looking into the heart of light, the silence.
Oed' und leer das Meer.[5]

Madame Sosostris, famous clairvoyante,
Had a bad cold, nevertheless
Is known to be the wisest woman in Europe,   45
With a wicked pack of cards.[6] Here, said she,
Is your card, the drowned Phoenician Sailor,
(Those are pearls that were his eyes.[7] Look!)
Here is Belladonna, the Lady of the Rocks,[8]
The lady of situations.   50
Here is the man with three staves, and here the Wheel,

4. The Greek *Hyacinthia*, an outdoor May festival, commemorated the mythical Hyacinthus, a boy beloved by Apollo and slain by the jealous act of Zephyrus (Ovid, *Metamorphoses*, X). Water again appears ("your hair wet") as a fertility symbol, while the phrase "I was neither living nor dead" echoes Dante, in the tremendous cold of the last circle of Hell, confronting Satan (*Inferno*, xxxiv, 25).
5. Eliot locates this line in Wagner's *Tristan und Isolde*, III, verse 24. Tristan, dying of a wound at his remote castle, awaits the ship of Isolde, who has fled from her husband, King Mark. Meanwhile a shepherd, appointed to watch for a sail, mournfully reports, in the words here quoted: "Desolate and deserted the sea."
6. The reference in ll. 46–56 is to the Tarot deck of cards, once honored in Eastern magic, now employed by a vulgar fortuneteller. In his note Eliot identifies certain of the cards: "I am not familiar with the exact constitution of the Tarot pack of cards, from which I have obviously departed to suit my own convenience. The Hanged Man, a member of the traditional pack, fits my purpose in two ways: because he is associated in my mind with the Hanged God of Frazer, and because I associate with him the hooded figure in the passage of the disciples to Emmaus in Part V. The Phoenician Sailor and the Merchant appear later; also

the 'crowds of people,' and Death by Water is executed in Part IV. The Man with Three Staves (an authentic member of the Tarot pack) I associate, quite arbitrarily, with the Fisher King himself."
7. Shakespeare, *The Tempest*, Act I, Scene 2, l. 398; from Ariel's song ("Full fathom five thy father lies") to the shipwrecked Ferdinand, "Sitting on a bank / Weeping again the King my father's wreck, / This music crept by me upon the waters." Ariel leads Ferdinand to Miranda, whose father, Prospero, has cast a magic blessing on their love. Actually, Ferdinand's father has escaped from the wreck, but the theme of the dead or betrayed father (or culture) persists in *The Waste Land*. The present reference is also associated with "the drowned Phoenician Sailor" (l. 47) and the Phlebas of Part IV, ll. 312–321.
8. The plant belladonna is the "deadly" nightshade. Here the capitalization of the word (literally, "beautiful lady") makes it suggestive of Italian epithets for the Virgin. One of the most beloved paintings of the Virgin is Leonardo's "Virgin of the Rocks" (here, "Lady of the Rocks"); in the next line, the "lady of situations" obviously is the lady of the intrigue in Part II, whose "vials" of cosmetics might include the drug belladonna, employed to brighten the eyes.

And here is the one-eyed merchant, and this card,
Which is blank, is something he carries on his back,[9]
Which I am forbidden to see. I do not find
The Hanged Man. Fear death by water.   55
I see crowds of people, walking round in a ring.
Thank you. If you see dear Mrs. Equitone,
Tell her I bring the horoscope myself:
One must be so careful these days.

Unreal City,[1]   60
Under the brown fog of a winter dawn,
A crowd flowed over London Bridge, so many,
I had not thought death had undone so many.[2]
Sighs, short and infrequent, were exhaled,[3]
And each man fixed his eyes before his feet.   65
Flowed up the hill and down King William Street,
To where Saint Mary Woolnoth kept the hours
With a dead sound on the final stroke of nine.[4]
There I saw one I knew, and stopped him, crying: 'Stetson!
'You who were with me in the ships at Mylae![5]   70
'That corpse you planted last year in your garden,[6]
'Has it begun to sprout? Will it bloom this year?
'Or has the sudden frost disturbed its bed?
'O keep the Dog far hence, that's friend to men,

9. *Cf.* "Mr. Eugenides, the Smyrna merchant" (ll. 209–214), who apparently "carries on his back" a burden of irregularities.

1. "*Cf.* Baudelaire: *'Fourmillante cité, cité pleine de rêves, / Où le spectre en plein jour raccroche le passant'*" [Eliot's note]; the opening lines of Poem 93, in *Fleurs du Mal*, translated as "Swarming city, city filled with dreams, / Where the ghost in full daylight hails the passerby." Baudelaire referred to Paris.

2. "*Cf. Inferno*, III, 55–57" [Eliot's note]. Just inside the gate of Hell, inscribed, "Abandon all hope, ye who enter here," Dante found those who "from cowardice had made the great refusal" to choose either good or evil, intent only on themselves, and now unacceptable both to Heaven and to Hell. The lines cited by Eliot are translated: "So long a train of people; I never should have believed Death had undone so many."

3. "*Cf. Inferno*, IV, 25–27" [Eliot's note]. Eliot cites Dante's lines concerning the virtuous heathen who never heard the Gospel; they were condemned to Limbo, without pain but

without hope of salvation, uttering "sighs, which caused the eternal air to tremble."

4. This London church was rebuilt under the influence of Sir Christopher Wren in the early eighteenth century. The significance of the "dead sound" of its ninth stroke ("a phenomenon," says Eliot's note, "which I have often noticed.") is controversial. In Matthew xxvii: 46, it was "about the ninth hour" on the cross that "Jesus cried with a loud voice * * * 'My God, My God, why hast thou forsaken me?'" And consider the ninth month in terms of fertility, a principal theme of this poem.

5. In the *Inferno*, Dante from time to time recognizes friends in the crowd of spirits. So in modern London, the speaker hails an acquaintance, "Stetson." But "Mylae" was a naval battle of the Punic War (260 B.C.), not of the World War in which "Stetson" presumably fought. Hence all wars are compared.

6. In its last episode, this section turns the reader's attention back to its title, "The Burial of the Dead."

'Or with his nails he'll dig it up again![7] 75
'You! hypocrite lecteur!—mon semblable,—mon frère! [8]

II. A Game of Chess [9]

The Chair she sat in, like a burnished throne,[1]
Glowed on the marble, where the glass
Held up by standards wrought with fruited vines
From which a golden Cupidon peeped out 80
(Another hid his eyes behind his wing)
Doubled the flames of sevenbranched candelabra
Reflecting light upon the table as
The glitter of her jewels rose to meet it,
From satin cases poured in rich profusion. 85
In vials of ivory and coloured glass
Unstoppered, lurked her strange synthetic perfumes,
Unguent, powdered, or liquid—troubled, confused
And drowned the sense in odours; stirred by the air
That freshened from the window, these ascended 90
In fattening the prolonged candle-flames,
Flung their smoke into the laquearia,[2]
Stirring the pattern on the coffered ceiling.
Huge sea-wood fed with copper
Burned green and orange, framed by the coloured stone, 95
In which sad light a carvèd dolphin swam.
Above the antique mantel was displayed
As though a window gave upon the sylvan scene [3]

7. Eliot's note refers to "the dirge in [John] Webster's *White Devil*." Act V, Scene 4, ll. 97–98, of that play reads: "But keep the wolf far thence, that's foe to men, / For with his nails he'll dig them up again." The lines are part of a song sung by a demented mother, whose son is burying the brother he slew. Eliot changes "foe" to "friend," and "wolf" to "Dog"—capitalized because it here means "Dog Star." Sirius, the Dog Star, faithfully follows his slain master, Orion, across the heavens; also, according to Frazer, in Eastern myth, Sirius was regarded as responsible for the annual rising of the waters of the Nile, an event associated with fertility and resurrection.
8. "V. Baudelaire, Preface to *Fleurs du Mal*" [Eliot's note]. The passage is translated, "hypocritical reader!—my double,—my brother!"
9. Thomas Middleton, in *A Game at Chesse* (1624), satirized a marriage based on political expediency. See also the note to l. 138.
1. "*Cf. Antony and Cleopatra*, II, ii,

l. 190" [Eliot's note]. Eliot's language here recalls the passage in Shakespeare, describing the regal splendor of the barge in which Cleopatra rode to her first meeting with Antony. Eliot's significant alteration of "barge" to read "Chair" suggests the seven stars of the Chair of Cassiopeia; this constellation was named for a mythical queen of Ethiopia so vain that she likened her beauty to that of the Nereids, thus causing the wrathful gods to visit her country with ravaging floods and monsters.
2. "Laquearia. V. *Aeneid*, I, 726; *dependent lychni laquearibus incensi, et noctem flammis funalia vincunt*" [Eliot's note]. The passage may be translated: "Lighted lamps hang from the golden laquearia (fretted ceiling), and flaming torches dispel the night." The scene is the feast given by Dido for Aeneas when the hero arrived at Carthage. When he departed, the Queen, smitten by passion, killed herself.
3. "Sylvan scene. V. Milton, *Paradise Lost*, IV, 140" [Eliot's note]. The

The change of Philomel,[4] by the barbarous king
So rudely forced; yet there the nightingale   100
Filled all the desert with inviolable voice
And still she cried, and still the world pursues,
'Jug Jug' to dirty ears.[5]
And other withered stumps of time
Were told upon the walls; staring forms   105
Leaned out, leaning, hushing the room enclosed.
Footsteps shuffled on the stair.
Under the firelight, under the brush, her hair
Spread out in fiery points
Glowed into words, then would be savagely still.   110

'My nerves are bad to-night. Yes, bad. Stay with me.
'Speak to me. Why do you never speak. Speak.
    'What are you thinking of? What thinking? What?
'I never know what you are thinking. Think.'

I think we are in rats' alley [6]   115
Where the dead men lost their bones.

'What is that noise?'
                        The wind under the door.[7]
'What is that noise now? What is the wind doing?'
                        Nothing again nothing.   120
                                        'Do
'You know nothing? Do you see nothing? Do you remember
'Nothing?'

    I remember
Those are pearls that were his eyes.[8]   125

---

phrase is associated with Milton's description of the first Eden, a place of innocent love. But here, see the next lines.
4. "*Cf.* Ovid, *Metamorphoses*, VI, Philomela" [Eliot's note]. King Tereus raped Philomela, sister of his wife, Procne, and cut out her tongue to silence her. Procne, for revenge, killed his son and served his heart for the King to eat. The gods, to save the sisters, turned them into birds: Philomela became the nightingale, and Procne, the swallow.
5. Eliot's note for this passage calls attention to his elaboration of the nightingale's song (vulgarized to "Jug Jug" for "dirty ears"), l. 204.
6. "*Cf.* Part III, l. 195" [Eliot's note].
7. "*Cf.* Webster: 'Is the wind in that door still?'" [Eliot's note]. In John Webster's *The Devil's Law Case*

(1623), Romelio, to hasten the death of Duke Contarino, who has willed him some money, stabs the Duke again through the wound of which he is dying. The consequent release of pus saves the Duke; when the surgeon finds him breathing, he exclaims, "Is the wind in that doore still?" The following passage in Eliot (ll. 119–124), again probably refers to Webster's *The White Devil* (see l. 75), in which a murderer asks his bound victim, "What dost thou think on?" and the victim replies, "Nothing; of nothing: * * * I remember nothing" (Act V, Scene 6, ll. 203–205).
8. "*Cf.* Part I, ll. 37, 48" [Eliot's note]. Thus the innocent love of Ferdinand and Miranda in *The Tempest* is compared with the episode in the hyacinth garden (l. 37) and with the present guilty episode.

'Are you alive, or not? Is there nothing in your head?'
               But

O O O O that Shakespeherian Rag—[9]
It's so elegant
So intelligent   130
'What shall I do now? What shall I do?'
'I shall rush out as I am, and walk the street
'With my hair down, so. What shall we do tomorrow?
'What shall we ever do?'
              The hot water at ten.   135
And if it rains, a closed car at four.
And we shall play a game of chess.
Pressing lidless eyes and waiting for a knock upon the door.[1]

When Lil's husband got demobbed,[2] I said—
I didn't mince my words, I said to her myself,   140
HURRY UP PLEASE ITS TIME [3]
Now Albert's coming back, make yourself a bit smart.
He'll want to know what you done with that money he gave you
To get yourself some teeth. He did, I was there.
You have them all out, Lil, and get a nice set,   145
He said, I swear, I can't bear to look at you.
And no more can't I, I said, and think of poor Albert,
He's been in the army four years, he wants a good time,
And if you don't give it him, there's others will, I said.
Oh is there, she said. Something o' that, I said.   150
Then I'll know who to thank, she said, and give me a straight look.
HURRY UP PLEASE ITS TIME
If you don't like it you can get on with it, I said.
Others can pick and choose if you can't.
But if Albert makes off, it won't be for lack of telling.   155
You ought to be ashamed, I said, to look so antique.
(And her only thirty-one.)
I can't help it, she said, pulling a long face,
It's them pills I took, to bring it off, she said.
(She's had five already, and nearly died of young George.)   160

9. A piece of ragtime music was then current containing a jazz refrain almost identical with ll. 128–130.
1. "*Cf.* the game of chess in [Thomas] Middleton's *Women Beware Women* [Eliot's note]. In Act II, Scene 2, of this play (dated 1657) a mother is kept engaged in a chess game while her daughter-in-law is being seduced in another room, on the stage balcony visible to the audience. The dramatist contrived that the accomplice should checkmate the mother at the moment when the daughter-in-law surrendered to the seducer.
2. British slang of the period for "demobilized" from the army.
3. The ominous suggestion of l. 138— "waiting for a knock upon the door"— is grotesquely projected into this warning of the British bartender that it is nearly legal closing time; this line, in turn, is reiterated as a grim refrain throughout the remainder of the scene.

The chemist [4] said it would be all right, but I've never been the
    same.
You *are* a proper fool, I said.
Well, if Albert won't leave you alone, there it is, I said,
What you get married for if you don't want children?
HURRY UP PLEASE ITS TIME   165
Well, that Sunday Albert was home, they had a hot gammon,[5]
And they asked me in to dinner, to get the beauty of it hot—
HURRY UP PLEASE ITS TIME
HURRY UP PLEASE ITS TIME
Goonight Bill. Goonight Lou. Goonight May. Goonight.   170
Ta ta. Goonight. Goonight.
Good night, ladies, good night, sweet ladies, good night, good
    night.[6]

III. *The Fire Sermon* [7]

The river's tent is broken; the last fingers of leaf
Clutch and sink into the wet bank. The wind
Crosses the brown land, unheard. The nymphs are departed.   175
Sweet Thames, run softly, till I end my song.[8]
The river bears no empty bottles, sandwich papers,
Silk handkerchiefs, cardboard boxes, cigarette ends
Or other testimony of summer nights. The nymphs are departed.
And their friends, the loitering heirs of city directors;   180
Departed, have left no addresses.
By the waters of Leman I sat down and wept [9] . . .
Sweet Thames, run softly till I end my song,
Sweet Thames, run softly, for I speak not loud or long.
But at my back in a cold blast I hear [1]   185
The rattle of the bones, and chuckle spread from ear to ear.

A rat crept softly through the vegetation
Dragging its slimy belly on the bank

---

4. British for "druggist."
5. British for "ham" or "bacon"; in dialect, also "thigh"; *cf.* American "gam."
6. *Cf. Hamlet*, Act IV, Scene 5. These were Ophelia's words, concluding the scene of her madness caused by her hopeless love for Hamlet and the murder of her father.
7. See the note to l. 308, in which the poet explains this title.
8. "V. Spenser, *Prothalamion*" [Eliot's note]. Eliot's l. 176 is the refrain of Spenser's "bridal song," published in 1596, a pastoral poem of supassing innocence depicting a wedding festival of water nymphs on the Thames. But *cf.* ll. 177–181, which give a suggestion

of life along the Thames in 1922.
9. *Cf.* Psalms cxxxvii: 1, 4. The exiled Jews wept "by the rivers of Babylon," unable to "sing the Lord's song in a strange land." The meaning of "Leman" here can only be conjectured. Lake Leman, the Swiss name for Lake Geneva, had been frequently mentioned in nineteenth-century poetry celebrating natural beauty. As late as Shakespeare, the common noun "leman" meant "mistress." In Old English, it was derived from roots meaning "dear man" or "dear mankind," a fact which strengthens the multiple association of this word in the context.
1. See the note to l. 196.

While I was fishing in the dull canal
On a winter evening round behind the gashouse [2]   190
Musing upon the king my brother's wreck
And on the king my father's death before him. [3]
White bodies naked on the low damp ground
And bones cast in a little low dry garret,
Rattled by the rat's foot only, year to year.   195
But at my back from time to time I hear [4]
The sound of horns [5] and motors, which shall bring
Sweeney to Mrs. Porter in the spring.
O the moon shone bright on Mrs. Porter [6]
And on her daughter   200
They wash their feet in soda water
Et O ces voix d'enfants, chantant dans la coupole! [7]

Twit twit twit
Jug jug jug jug jug jug [8]
So rudely forc'd.   205
Tereu

Unreal City
Under the brown fog of a winter noon
Mr. Eugenides, the Smyrna merchant
Unshaven, with a pocket full of currants   210

2. *Cf.* the theme of the Fisher King. The "gashouse" district of a town is often the tenderloin section.
3. "*Cf. The Tempest*, I, ii" [Eliot's note]. See l. 48.
4. "*Cf.* Marvell, *To His Coy Mistress*" [Eliot's note]. In that poem, ll. 21–22 read: "But at my back I always hear / Time's winged chariot hurrying near."
5. "*Cf.* Day, *Parliament of Bees:* When of the sudden, listening, you shall hear, / A noise of horns and hunting, which shall bring / Actaeon to Diana in the spring, / Where all shall see her naked skin. . . ." [Eliot's note]. The chaste Diana, bathing naked, was spied upon by Actaeon, whereupon he was turned into a stag and killed by his own hunting dogs. But (next line), Sweeney was going to see Mrs. Porter.
6. "I do not know the origin of the ballad from which these lines are taken: it was reported to me from Sydney, Australia" [Eliot's note]. In a ragtime song, "Redwing," popular in the United States (1910–1915), the refrain began, "Oh, the moon shone bright on pretty Redwing" (an American Indian maid). Among the parodies of the song known to soldiers in World War I, was an indecent version dealing with a Mrs. Porter, who kept a brothel in Cairo.
7. "V. Verlaine, *Parsifal*" [Eliot's note]. The line is translated: "And O those children's voices, singing from the cupola" (or choir loft). In order to attain the Holy Grail, Parsifal resisted the seduction of Kundry, a temptress; his ordeals accomplished, Kundry humbly washed his feet, an act reminiscent of the adulteress who washed the feet of Christ (Luke vii: 37–38), and in contrast with the practices of Mrs. Porter and her daughter.
8. *Cf.* ll. 99–103. In old legends, the nightingale sang "Tereu" in plaintive memory of Tereus. In Elizabethan poetry the word "jug" was added, as Eliot says (l. 103), for "dirty ears." The word "jug," derived from "juggler" was then a vulgarism indecently suggestive; see Shakespeare's *Henry VI, Part I*, Act V, Scene 4, l. 63: "She and the Dauphin have been juggling." Perhaps the most familiar poem employing the two words together is "Spring's Welcome," by John Lyly (1553–1606); ll. 2–3 read: "O 'tis the ravish'd nightingale. / Jug, jug, jug, jug, tereu! she cries * * * "

1450 · *Thomas Stearns Eliot*

C.i.f. London; documents at sight,[9]
Asked me in demotic [1] French
To luncheon at the Cannon Street Hotel
Followed by a weekend at the Metropole.

At the violet hour, when the eyes and back   215
Turn upward from the desk, when the human engine waits
Like a taxi throbbing waiting,
I Tiresias,[2] though blind, throbbing between two lives,
Old man with wrinkled female breasts, can see
At the violet hour, the evening hour that strives   220
Homeward, and brings the sailor home from sea,[3]
The typist home at teatime, clears her breakfast, lights
Her stove, and lays out food in tins.
Out of the window perilously spread
Her drying combinations touched by the sun's last rays,   225
On the divan are piled (at night her bed)
Stockings, slippers, camisoles, and stays.
I Tiresias, old man with wrinkled dugs
Perceived the scene, and foretold the rest—
I too awaited the expected guest.   230

9. "The currants were quoted at a price 'carriage and insurance free to London'; and the Bill of Lading, etc., were to be handed to the buyer upon payment of the sight draft" [Eliot's note].
1. "Vulgar," such French as a commercial traveler picks up. Compare Mr. Eugenides with "the one-eyed merchant" of the Tarot cards (l. 52), who carried a pack of forbidden mysteries. (*Cf.* the note to l. 218).
2. "Tiresias, although a mere spectator and not indeed a 'character,' is yet the most important personage in the poem, uniting all the rest. Just as the one-eyed merchant, seller of currants, melts into the Phoenician Sailor, and the latter is not wholly distinct from Ferdinand Prince of Naples [in *The Tempest*], so all the women are one woman, and the two sexes meet in Tiresias. The whole passage from Ovid is of great anthropological interest" [Eliot's note]. Eliot then quotes the Latin text of *Metamorphoses*, III, 320–338. In this tale, Tiresias "struck violently with his staff two great serpents who were coupling in the forest"; he was immediately transformed into a woman. Eight years later he found the same serpents, and repeated the blow in order to reverse his fate; he at once recovered his manhood. Later, Jove was bantering Juno, jesting that those of her sex gained more pleasure from the act of love than the male gods. The controversy was referred to Tiresias, since he knew the pleasures of love "on both sides." When Tiresias "confirmed the dictum of Jove," the hypersensitive goddess "condemned him to eternal blindness." "Since no god is permitted to undo the work of another, the omnipotent father" compensated Tiresias with the power to foretell the future. In other legends his fame as a soothsayer became universal; even in Hades his shade gave advice to Ulysses (*Odyssey*, Book XI). Hence Eliot employs Tiresias as the all-experienced interpreter of the human misadventures represented in *The Waste Land*.
3. "This may not appear as exact as Sappho's lines, but I had in mind the 'longshore' or 'dory' fisherman, who returns at nightfall" [Eliot's note]. "Sappho's lines" are probably the fragment No. CXLIX, addressed to the Evening Star, "which summons back all that the light Dawn scattered —the sheep, the goat, the child to its mother." Eliot also echoes Stevenson's "Requiem": "Home is the sailor, home from the sea." Since blue and violet are traditionally "Mary's colors," the "violet hour" (l. 220) contrasts ironically with the cheap intrigue that follows.

He, the young man carbuncular, arrives,
A small house agent's clerk, with one bold stare,
One of the low on whom assurance sits
As a silk hat on a Bradford millionaire.[4]
The time is now propitious, as he guesses,   235
The meal is ended, she is bored and tired,
Endeavours to engage her in caresses
Which still are unreproved, if undesired.
Flushed and decided, he assaults at once;
Exploring hands encounter no defence;   240
His vanity requires no response,
And makes a welcome of indifference.
(And I Tiresias have foresuffered all
Enacted on this same divan or bed;
I who have sat by Thebes below the wall   245
And walked among the lowest of the dead.[5])
Bestows one final patronising kiss,
And gropes his way, finding the stairs unlit . . .

She turns and looks a moment in the glass,
Hardly aware of her departed lover;   250
Her brain allows one half-formed thought to pass:
'Well now that's done: and I'm glad it's over.'
When lovely woman stoops to folly [6] and
Paces about her room again, alone,
She smoothes her hair with automatic hand,   255
And puts a record on the gramophone.

'This music crept by me upon the waters' [7]
And along the Strand, up Queen Victoria Street.
O City city, I can sometimes hear
Beside a public bar in Lower Thames Street,   260
The pleasant whining of mandoline
And a clatter and a chatter from within
Where fishmen lounge at noon: where the walls
Of Magnus Martyr hold [8]

4. Bradford, in West Yorkshire, near Leeds, had enjoyed an industrial boom, and hence is here associated with the newly rich upstart.
5. Tiresias prophesied in the market place by the wall of Thebes for several generations before he was killed at the destruction of the city; afterward he prophesied in Hades, where Ulysses went to consult him.
6. "V. Goldsmith, the song in *The Vicar of Wakefield*" [Eliot's note]. The song in Oliver Goldsmith's novel, published in 1766, begins, "When lovely woman stoops to folly," and asserts that if the betrayed maiden wishes to "wash her guilt away," her only remedy "is to die."
7. "V. *The Tempest,* as above [l. 48]" [Eliot's note].
8. "The interior of St. Magnus Martyr is to my mind one of the finest among Wren's interiors, * * * " [Eliot's note]. Its lofty steeple (1676), one of Sir Christopher Wren's masterpieces, rises amid the varied hubbub of lowly life and fishhouse gossip along lower Thames Street near London Bridge, as Eliot significantly remarks.

Inexplicable splendour of Ionian white and gold.   265

      The river sweats [9]
      Oil and tar
      The barges drift
      With the turning tide
      Red sails   270
      Wide
      To leeward, swing on the heavy spar.
      The barges wash
      Drifting logs
      Down Greenwich reach   275
      Past the Isle of Dogs.[1]
            Weialala leia
            Wallala leialala

      Elizabeth and Leicester [2]
      Beating oars   280
      The stern was formed
      A gilded shell
      Red and gold
      The brisk swell
      Rippled both shores [3]   285
      Southwest wind
      Carried down stream
      The peal of bells
      White towers
            Weialala leia   290
            Wallala leialala

'Trams and dusty trees.
Highbury bore me. Richmond and Kew

9. "The Song of the (three) Thames-daughters begins here. From line 292 to 306 inclusive they speak in turn. V. *Götterdämmerung*, III, i: the Rhine-daughters" [Eliot's note]. In Wagner's opera the Rhine-daughters lament that the gold of the Nibelungs, which they guarded, has been stolen, and with it has gone their joy, and the beauty of the river. They implore the hero, Siegfried, to retrieve the treasure. Eliot imitates the rhythms of Wagner's lyrics, and also borrows the exact words of the refrain (ll. 277–278).

1. These place names associated with the modern port of London suggest the contrast between the Thames of the industrial present and Spenser's idyllic picture of the Thames of the past (*cf.* ll. 173–184).

2. The early love of Queen Eliza-beth for the Earl of Leicester (Sir Robert Dudley) is recalled by Eliot's note: "V. Froude, *Elizabeth*, Vol. I, ch. iv, letter of De Quadra to Philip of Spain: 'In the afternoon we were in a barge, watching games on the river. (The queen) was alone with Lord Robert and myself on the poop, when they began to talk nonsense, and went so far that Lord Robert at last said, as I was on the spot there was no reason why they should not be married if the queen pleased.' "

3. In the six previous lines, Eliot suggests the phrases which Shakespeare employed to describe Cleopatra's barge (*cf.* l. 77). The courtly dalliance of Elizabeth and Leicester, and the heroic passion of Antony and Cleopatra, are thus associated with the two following episodes of contemporary life.

Undid me. By Richmond I raised my knees [4]
Supine on the floor of a narrow canoe.'   295

'My feet are at Moorgate,[5] and my heart
Under my feet. After the event
He wept. He promised "a new start."
I made no comment. What should I resent?'

'On Margate Sands.[6]   300
I can connect
Nothing with nothing.
The broken fingernails of dirty hands.
My people humble people who expect
Nothing.'   305
            la la

To Carthage then I came [7]

Burning burning burning burning [8]
O Lord Thou pluckest me out [9]
O Lord Thou pluckest   310

burning

4. "*Cf. Purgatorio*, V, 133: *Ricorditi di me, che son la Pia; / Siena mi fé, disfecemi Maremma*" [Eliot's note]. Translate: "Remember me, who am la Pia, / Siena made me, Maremma unmade me." The second line earlier provided Pound with the title of the sordid seventh poem of *Mauberley*. Dante met Pia de' Tolomei of Siena, whose husband had murdered her in his castle at Maremma. By contrast, Eliot presents a girl from undistinguished Highbury in London. Richmond, the place of her undoing, like Kew, is a popular pleasure resort on the Thames River.

5. Moorgate, once the name of a gate of the London Wall, now designates a slum area in the same locality. The speaker is the second Thames-daughter.

6. Margate, a favorite seaside resort for London excursionists, in Kent, northeast of Dover; the place of seduction for the third Thames-daughter.

7. "V. St. Augustine's *Confessions:* 'to Carthage then I came, where a cauldron of unholy loves sang all about mine ears' " [Eliot's note]. From *Confessions*, III, i; pagan Carthage was considered to be a place of great licentiousness. In this passage, Augustine confesses that, famished for love but not yet knowing the love of God, he "defiled the waters of friendship with the filth of uncleanliness, and soiled its purity with * * * lustfulness."

8. "The complete text of the Buddha's Fire Sermon (which corresponds in importance to the Sermon on the Mount) from which these words are taken, will be found translated in the late Henry Clarke Warren's *Buddhism in Translation* (Harvard Oriental Series)" [Eliot's note]. In his sermon, the Buddha warned against surrender to the senses, which are "on fire. With passion, . . . hatred, . . . infatuation, . . . birth, . . . old age, . . . death, . . . sorrow, . . . grief, . . . and despair are they on fire. [When the disciple] becomes purged of passion, * * * he becomes free; * * * he knows that rebirth is accomplished." For Christ's Sermon on the Mount, containing the most comprehensive account of His teaching, see Matthew v–vii.

9. "From St. Augustine's *Confessions* again. The collocation of these two representatives of eastern and western asceticism [Buddha and St. Augustine], as the culmination of this part of the poem, is not an accident" [Eliot's note]. St. Augustine's complete sentence was: "O Lord Thou pluckest me out of the burning." *Cf.* Zechariah iii: 1–2, "Joshua * * * a brand plucked out of the fire."

IV. *Death by Water* [1]

Phlebas the Phoenician, a fortnight dead,
Forgot the cry of gulls, and the deep sea swell
And the profit and loss.
                    A current under sea   315
Picked his bones in whispers. As he rose and fell
He passed the stages of his age and youth
Entering the whirlpool.
                    Gentile or Jew
O you who turn the wheel [2] and look to windward,   320
Consider Phlebas, who was once handsome and tall as you.

V. *What the Thunder Said* [3]

After the torchlight red on sweaty faces
After the frosty silence in the gardens [4]
After the agony in stony places
The shouting and the crying   325
Prison and palace and reverberation
Of thunder of spring over distant mountains
He who was living is now dead

1. The title "Death by Water," suggests also the "living water" (John iv: 5–14), a principal subject in Part V. Water was a pagan symbol of fertility, with ritualistic functions in the worship of Tammuz, Adonis, and Siva (see Frazer, *The Golden Bough,* which Eliot noted as a source). The god was immersed in the rivers to promote the fertility of land and people, or was given water burial in winter and resurrected in the spring. The intention of Eliot's lyric is made evident by its history: he wrote it first in French as a conclusion for the poem, "Dans le Restaurant" (*Poems,* 1920), a disgusted excoriation of an old waiter who gloats obscenely over his senile memory of an attempt, at the age of seven, to violate a little girl "under the wet willows." In the present work, Eliot has already associated Phlebas the Phoenician with Ferdinand (ll. 47–48). He seems to be associated too with the merchant, Eugenides (ll. 52 and 209); also in the French version Phlebas is a merchant sailor from Cornwall, absorbed in "the profits and losses and the cargoes of tin." The ancient Phoenicians were great Mediterranean traders; hence Phlebas in part symbolizes materialistic mercantilism.
2. Literally, the wheel of the helmsman, but note also the "wheel" of the whirlpool (ll. 315–318). Eliot places "the Wheel" in the Tarot pack (l. 51). The Tarot Wheel is depicted as responding to two competing forces—on the one hand, Anubis, an Egyptian divinity who conducts and watches over the dead; on the other, the Greek Typhon (Typhoeus), an all-devouring monster of evil—and thus it symbolizes the nature of man's fate in eternity.
3. "In the first part of Part V three themes are employed: the journey to Emmaus, the approach to the Chapel Perilous (see Miss Weston's book), and the present decay of eastern Europe" [Eliot's note]. On the journey to Emmaus, on the third day after He was crucified, Christ first proved His resurrection to His disciples by appearing to two of them; the Chapel Perilous was the place of the Christian knight's final ordeal in quest of the Grail, the symbol of faith; and the decay of civilization is evidence of infidelity to Christian revelation.
4. Of "the gardens," one was Gethsemane, the scene of Christ's final temptation, prayer, and dedication (see Matthew xxvi: 36–45); the other was a garden on Golgotha, the hill of the Crucifixion, where the disciples buried Him in a new tomb (see John xix: 41–42). This passage (ll. 322–330) recapitulates the events of Christ's Passion: the agony of Gethsemane, the betrayal, imprisonment, trial, crucifixion, and burial.

We who were living are now dying
With a little patience   330

Here is no water but only rock [5]
Rock and no water and the sandy road
The road winding above among the mountains
Which are mountains of rock without water
If there were water we should stop and drink   335
Amongst the rock one cannot stop or think
Sweat is dry and feet are in the sand
If there were only water amongst the rock
Dead mountain mouth of carious teeth that cannot spit
Here one can neither stand nor lie nor sit   340
There is not even silence in the mountains
But dry sterile thunder without rain
There is not even solitude in the mountains
But red sullen faces sneer and snarl
From doors of mudcracked houses   345
                                    If there were water
     And no rock
     If there were rock
     And also water
     And water   350
     A spring
     A pool among the rock
      If there were the sound of water only
     Not the cicada
     And dry grass singing   355
     But sound of water over a rock
     Where the hermit-thrush sings in the pine trees
     Drip drop drip drop drop drop drop [6]
     But there is no water

Who is the third who walks always beside you? [7]   360

5. The following thirty-six lines deal with the journey to Emmaus. But the country traversed by the bereft and grieving disciples recalls another "waste land" described by Ezekiel and Ecclesiastes (see Part I, ll. 19–30) as resulting from human infidelity to God.
6. Eliot's note refers to the "water-dripping song" of the hermit thrush, "which I have heard in Quebec Province."
7. "The following lines were stimulated by the account of one of the Antarctic expeditions (I forgot which, but I think one of Shackleton's): it was related that the party of explorers, at the extremity of their strength, had the constant delusion that there was *one more member* than could actually be counted" [Eliot's note]. On the journey to Emmaus, the two disciples, in desperation and grief at the death of Jesus, were joined by a wayfarer whom they were not permitted to recognize. This companion argued from Scripture that their dead Lord was indeed the foretold Messiah. Later, as he blessed the bread at the inn, "they knew him; and he vanished out of their sight." See Luke xxiv: 13–34.

When I count, there are only you and I together
But when I look ahead up the white road
There is always another one walking beside you
Gliding wrapt in a brown mantle, hooded
I do not know whether a man or a woman   365
—But who is that on the other side of you?

What is that sound high in the air [8]
Murmur of maternal lamentation
Who are those hooded hordes swarming
Over endless plains, stumbling in cracked earth   370
Ringed by the flat horizon only
What is the city over the mountains
Cracks and reforms and bursts in the violet air
Falling towers
Jerusalem Athens Alexandria   375
Vienna London
Unreal

A woman drew her long black hair out tight
And fiddled whisper music on those strings
And bats with baby faces in the violet light   380
Whistled, and beat their wings
And crawled head downward down a blackened wall
And upside down in air were towers
Tolling reminiscent bells, that kept the hours
And voices singing out of empty cisterns and exhausted wells.   385

In this decayed hole among the mountains
In the faint moonlight, the grass is singing
Over the tumbled graves, about the chapel [9]
There is the empty chapel, only the wind's home.
It has no windows, and the door swings,   390
Dry bones can harm no one.
Only a cock stood on the rooftree
Co co rico co co rico [1]

---

8. Ll. 367–377 express forebodings concerning the Russian Revolution, begun in 1917. Eliot quotes a passage from the German text of Hermann Hesse, *Blick ins Chaos* (1920), here translated in part: "Already half of Europe, or surely at least half of Eastern Europe, is on the way to chaos, traveling drunken, wtih a kind of sanctified ecstasy, headlong toward the abyss, and singing the while, singing drunken hymns, as Dmitri Karamazov sang." *Cf.* Dostoevski, *The*

Brothers Karamazov.
9. The Chapel Perilous of the Grail legends, where, if the knight endured his terrible last ordeals, he might hope to gain the Grail the next day. He has traversed a world grown utterly fantastic in its disorder (ll. 377–385) only to find the Chapel ruined and empty.
1. Peter three times denied his Master, and "immediately the cock crew," as Jesus had predicted (Matthew xxvi: 34 and 74).

In a flash of lightning. Then a damp gust
Bringing rain   395

Ganga ² was sunken, and the limp leaves
Waited for rain, while the black clouds
Gathered far distant, over Himavant.
The jungle crouched, humped in silence.
Then spoke the thunder   400
DA
Datta: what have we given? ³
My friend, blood shaking my heart
The awful daring of a moment's surrender
Which an age of prudence can never retract   405
By this, and this only, we have existed
Which is not to be found in our obituaries
Or in memories draped by the beneficent spider ⁴
Or under seals broken by the lean solicitor
In our empty rooms   410
DA
Dayadhvam: I have heard the key ⁵
Turn in the door once and turn once only
We think of the key, each in his prison ⁶
Thinking of the key, each confirms a prison   415
Only a nightfall, aethereal rumours

2. The ancient Sanskrit name for the river Ganges, in India. The Himalaya Mountains ("Himavant" in l. 398), were regarded as a deity, the mother of Devi, who was the consort of Siva; Devi and Siva were, among other things, goddess and god of fertility. The Ganges River, taking its source in the Himalayas, was worshiped as the sacred disseminator of fertility. At the spring festivals, maidens cast images of Siva into its waters; the ashes of devout Hindus are still returned to this source.
3. " 'Datta, dayadhvam, damyata' (Give, sympathize, control). The fable of the meaning of the Thunder is found in the *Brihadaranyaka-Upanishad*, 5, I. A translation is found in Deussen's *Sechzig Upanishads des Veda*, p. 489" [Eliot's note]. Eliot's choice of these words suggests the continuity of Western religious experience. This is emphasized by the words in Sanskrit, the hypothetical parent of the languages of Western culture.
4. "*Cf*. Webster, *The White Devil*, V, vi: '. . . they'll remarry / Ere the worm pierce your winding-sheet, ere the spider / Make a thin curtain for

your epitaphs' " [Eliot's note].
5. "*Cf. Inferno*, XXXIII, 46: *ed io sentii chiavar l'uscio di sotto / all' orrible torre*" [Eliot's note]. These lines are translated: "And I heard being locked below me the door of the horrible tower." They are part of the story told to Dante, in one of the innermost circles of Hell, by the traitor Count Ugolino of Pisa, who with Archbishop Ruggieri plotted the ruin of his grandson. But Ugolino was in turn imprisoned by Ruggieri, with his four sons, and starved to death. Dante finds the Count in Hell, gnawing upon the head of the traitorous Archbishop.
6. Referring to the Dante passage above, Eliot cites F. H. Bradley, *Appearance and Reality* (1893), p. 346: "My external sensations are no less private to myself than are my thoughts or my feelings. In either case my experience falls within my own circle, a circle closed on the outside; and with all its elements alike, every sphere is opaque to the others which surround it. . . . In brief, regarded as an existence which appears in a soul, the whole world for each is peculiar and private to that soul."

Revive for a moment a broken Coriolanus [7]

DA

Damyata: The boat responded
Gaily, to the hand expert with sail and oar   420
The sea was calm, your heart would have responded
Gaily, when invited, beating obedient
To controlling hands [8]

                I sat upon the shore
Fishing,[9] with the arid plain behind me   425
Shall I at least set my lands in order? [1]
London Bridge is falling down falling down falling down
Poi s'ascose nel foco che gli affina [2]
Quando fiam uti chelidon [3]—O swallow swallow
Le Prince d'Aquitaine à la tour abolie [4]   430
These fragments I have shored against my ruins
Why then Ile fit you. Hieronymo's mad againe.[5]

7. Gnaeus Marcius Coriolanus (fifth century B.C.). Shakespeare in *Coriolanus* followed the legendary account in Plutarch's *Lives*. During a disturbance by the starving plebeians, this patrician leader was exiled for proposing that the poor be fed from the public Roman store only in return for the dissolution of their tribunate. In exile he became a great leader of the Volscians, but they executed him when he spared Rome, his native city. See also Eliot's two "Coriolan" poems, and "A Cooking Egg," l. 11.
8. *Cf.* Part IV, "Death by Water."
9. "V. Weston: *From Ritual to Romance*, chapter on the Fisher King" [Eliot's note]. Consider the symbolic relations of the fish, water, and fertility. The fish also became an early Christian symbol—the letters of the Greek *ichthys* ("fish") were the initial letters of the Greek words for "Jesus Christ, of God the Son, Saviour." *Cf.* "fishing in the dull canal," l. 189.
1. Isaiah xxxviii: 1: "Thus saith the Lord, Set thine house in order: for thou shalt die, and not live."
2. The last line of a passage which Eliot quotes in his footnote: "V. *Purgatorio* XXVI, 148. '*Ara vos prec per aquella valor / que vos guida al som de l'escalina, / sovegna vos a temps de ma dolor.' / Poi s'ascose nel foco che gli affina.*" In these lines the twelfth-century Provençal poet Arnaut Daniel, remembering his early lustfulness, for which he was condemned, addresses Dante: "I pray you now, by the Goodness that guides you to the summit of this staircase, bethink you

in due season of my suffering." Then (as asserted in the line Eliot quotes in l. 428), "he disappeared into the flame that refines them." In 1919, Eliot had entitled a small volume *Ara Vos Prec.* In 1930 he introduced the exclamation *sovegna vos* in *Ash-Wednesday*, and he separately published the "staircase" section of that work (Part III) as "Som de l'Escalina." Evidently this passage from Dante had great meaning for him.
3. "V. *Pervigilium Veneris. Cf.* Philomela in Parts II and III" [Eliot's note]. The Latin phrase in the text means: "When shall I be like the swallow"; it is followed in the original Latin poem by the phrase, "and be free from dumb distress"—recalling Arnaut Daniel's hope of redemption. *Pervigilium Veneris*, an anonymous poem supposed to have been written in the second century A.D., celebrates the joy of all nature at the festival of Venus.
4. "V. Gerard de Nerval, Sonnet *El Desdichado*" [Eliot's note]. The French line is translated: "The Prince of Aquitaine at the ruined tower." One of the group of de Nerval's selections entitled *The Chimeras* (*Les Chimères*), this poem represents the speaker as "shadow shrouded, the widower, the unconsolable."
5. "V. Kyd's *Spanish Tragedy*" [Eliot's note]. Subtitled "Hieronymo Is Mad Again," Thomas Kyd's play (1594) is one of the most violent Elizabethan tragedies in the Senecan tradition. Hieronymo, requested by the King to write an entertainment for the court, replied, "Why, then

Datta. Dayadhvam. Damyata.
    Shantih   shantih   shantih [6]

1922

Marina [7]

Quis his locus, quae regio, quae mundi plaga? [8]

What seas what shores what grey rocks and what islands
What water lapping the bow
And scent of pine and the woodthrush singing through the fog
What images return
O my daughter.   5

Those who sharpen the tooth of the dog, meaning
Death
Those who glitter with the glory of the hummingbird, meaning
Death
Those who sit in the sty of contentment meaning   10
Death
Those who suffer the ecstasy of animals,[9] meaning
Death

Ile fit you!" (*i.e.,* "accommodate you"). He wrote a play in which he, as an actor, was able to kill the murderers of his son. He then killed himself.

6. "Shantih. Repeated as here, a formal ending to an Upanishad. 'The Peace which passeth understanding' is our equivalent to this word" [Eliot's note]. The Upanishads are treatises on theology, part of the Vedas, the ancient Hindu sacred literature. Eliot's translation of the Sanskrit *shantih* recalls various benedictions and salutations of Paul in his Epistles, particularly Philippians iv: 7: "And the peace of God, which passeth all understanding, shall keep your hearts and minds through Christ Jesus."

7. To *Pericles, Prince of Tyre* (1608?), Shakespeare contributed the last two acts, initiating, in the story of Marina, the theme of the idealized daughter which persisted during his last period, notably in *The Tempest.* In Act V, Scene 1, Pericles miraculously finds again his daughter, Marina, so called because she was born in a storm at sea. A second storm in her babyhood had bereft the sailor-prince of both wife and daughter. During years of roving adventure, Prince Pericles steadfastly loved his daughter, presumably dead. He finds her an escaped slave, grown to lovely

girlhood, and by saving her from further danger gains his place in her love. In Eliot's poem such a father, after years of seeking, re-enacts in reverie the pilgrimage of his past in the cathedral light of rediscovered passion and purity. Eliot, says F. O. Matthiessen (*The Achievement of T. S. Eliot,* p. 150) "recognizes a vision of idealized loveliness in the first adolescent awakening," and "the loss of such loveliness in the failure of actual sexual experience * * *. Regaining the purified vision in later life is the theme * * * of 'Marina.'"

8. "What place is this; what region; what quarter of the universe?" (Seneca, *Hercules Furens,* l. 1138). In Seneca's tragedy, Hercules, driven mad by the jealous Hera (Juno), kills his wife and children; but Minerva, goddess of wisdom, takes him in charge and brings him to his senses in a strange place, whereupon he utters the words of the epigraph. In contrast with that of Hercules, the feeling of guilt experienced by Pericles arises only from a belated sense of responsibility for the loss of his wife and daughter.

9. In the play *Pericles,* Marina first introduces herself to her unsuspecting father by singing a song beginning: "Amongst the harlots foul I walk, / Yet harlot none am I."

Are become unsubstantial, reduced by a wind,
A breath of pine, and the woodsong fog   15
By this grace dissolved in place

What is this face, less clear and clearer
The pulse in the arm, less strong and stronger—
Given or lent? more distant than stars and nearer than the eye

Whispers and small laughter between leaves and hurrying feet
Under sleep, where all the waters meet.   21

Bowsprit cracked with ice and paint cracked with heat.
I made this, I have forgotten
And remember.
The rigging weak and the canvas rotten   25
Between one June and another September.[1]
Made this unknowing, half conscious, unknown, my own.
The garboard strake [2] leaks, the seams need caulking.
This form, this face, this life
Living to live in a world of time beyond me; let me   30
Resign my life for this life, my speech for that unspoken,
The awakened, lips parted, the hope, the new ships.

What seas what shores what granite islands towards my timbers
And woodthrush calling through the fog
My daughter.   35

1930

Burnt Norton [3]

τοῦ λόγου δ'ἐόντος ξυνοῦ ζώουσιν οἱ πολλοί
ὡς ἰδίαν ἔχοντες φρόνησιν.—I. p. 77. Fr. 2.

ὁδὸς ἄνω κάτω μία καὶ ωὑτή.—I. p. 89. Fr. 60.

DIELS: DIE FRAGMENTE DER VORSOKRATIKER (HERAKLEITOS)

I

Time present and time past
Are both perhaps present in time future,

1. That is, not the *next* September, but the previous one, marking an interval of nine months. The associated figures of child and ship are simultaneously presented in ll. 22–29.
2. The planking next to the keel of any boat, hence the most vital spot.
3. "Burnt Norton" was written in 1934, in association with five small "Landscapes." It was included among the *Collected Poems* of 1936. In 1943 it appeared as the first of the *Four Quartets*, a unified work. There is a symphonic development and accumulation of themes throughout the four poems, while the last, "Little Gidding," is a resolution of the whole. Like *The Waste Land*, each "Quartet" has five parts, and comparable parts have a similar form and function in each of the four poems. The analogy of this organization with musical

And time future contained in time past.
If all time is eternally present
All time is unredeemable.[4]   5
What might have been is an abstraction
Remaining a perpetual possibility
Only in a world of speculation.
What might have been and what has been
Point to one end, which is always present.   10
Footfalls echo in the memory
Down the passage which we did not take
Towards the door we never opened
Into the rose-garden.[5] My words echo

structure, particularly that of the
sonata or of Beethoven's later quartets, is worthy of study.

The *Four Quartets* are an extended
meditation on the religious concept
of immortality, and a reasoned analysis of the Christian mysticism. In
"Burnt Norton" and "East Coker"
the poet makes symbolic use of "pure"
concepts of science—of such "abso-
lutes" as infinity and dynamic compensation ("At the still point of the
turning world"); these are contrasted
with human consciousness and historical experience. In "The Dry Sal-
vages" and "Little Gidding" the poet
assumes these arguments as contributing to our understanding of revelation, particularly such Christian revelations as the mystical experience in
which "the saint" is enabled "to apprehend / The point of intersection of
the timeless / With time." Such pure
revelation is accepted as an absolute,
confirming the doctrine of immortal
salvation by God's Grace, extended
through man's faith in the Annunciation and the Incarnation of Jesus
Christ, and the descent of the Holy
Spirit upon the apostles at the Pentecost. The continuing Grace of this
supernal union—the overarching theme
of the *Quartets*—Eliot found in those
later Christian mystics who had described a state of exalted contemplation in which it was granted them to
realize an absorption, untranslatable
in physical terms, in the Eternal Goodness, still and timeless. In these poems
Eliot was chiefly indebted to St. John
of the Cross (1542–1591), a Spanish
mystic who reported his experience in
The Dark Night of the Soul and *The
Ascent of Mt. Carmel.*

In "Burnt Norton," Eliot bases the
pyramid of the *Four Quartets* on a contrast of the relativity of mortal consciousness, time, and memory with the
absolute reality of the Timeless Eternal;
and he suggests, in Part V, a new

semantics (or perhaps a very old one)
for translating the symbols of human
experience into immortal terms.

Burnt Norton is identified as a
manor in Gloucestershire near which
Eliot has resided.

The Greek epigraphs are translated:
"But although the Word [*logos*] is
common to all, the majority of people
live as though they had each an understanding peculiarly their own"; and
"The way up and way down is one and
the same." Heraclitus (Herakleitos),
Greek philosopher (540?–475? B.C.),
emphasized two concepts: unity ("all
things come out of the One, and the
One out of all things"), and flux ("you
cannot step twice into the same river,
for fresh waters are ever flowing in
upon you"). Since Eliot has associated
Heraclitus with the *Quartets*, it is
also of interest that he attended the
lectures of Henri Bergson (1859–
1941) at the Sorbonne in 1911. Bergson was concerned with time and consciousness, and found their reality to
lie in their mobility, in the infinite flux,
not in the particular moment (*cf.* ll.
85–89).

4. See Ecclesiastes iii: 14–15: " * * *
whatsoever God doeth, it shall be for
ever * * * That which hath been is
now; and that which is to be hath already been; and God requireth that
which is past."

5. The persons in the rose-garden are
identified as children (l. 40 and ll.
172–173). The revelation simultaneously of sexual and spiritual significance is experienced by children
at play in a garden several times in
Eliot's poems. In "New Hampshire,"
written just before "Burnt Norton," a
boy and girl play in an apple orchard
visited by a bird. In the present passage (ll. 13–43) the bird reappears
as a thrush, while the rose-garden contains "echoes" (l. 17) recalling "our
first world" (ll. 21–22)—the garden
of Eden (*cf.* Genesis iii: 2–5). Thus

Thus, in your mind.
                    But to what purpose   15
Disturbing the dust on a bowl of rose-leaves
I do not know.
                    Other echoes
Inhabit the garden. Shall we follow?
Quick, said the bird, find them, find them,
Round the corner. Through the first gate,   20
Into our first world, shall we follow
The deception of the thrush? Into our first world.
There they were, dignified, invisible,
Moving without pressure, over the dead leaves,
In the autumn heat, through the vibrant air,   25
And the bird called, in response to
The unheard music hidden in the shrubbery,
And the unseen eyebeam crossed,[6] for the roses
Had the look of flowers that are looked at.
There they were as our guests, accepted and accepting.   30
So we moved, and they, in a formal pattern,
Along the empty alley, into the box circle,
To look down into the drained pool.
Dry the pool, dry concrete, brown edged,
And the pool was filled with water out of sunlight,   35
And the lotos rose, quietly, quietly,
The surface glittered out of heart of light,[7]
And they were behind us, reflected in the pool.
Then a cloud passed, and the pool was empty.
Go, said the bird, for the leaves were full of children,   40
Hidden excitedly, containing laughter.
Go, go, go, said the bird: human kind
Cannot bear very much reality.
Time past and time future
What might have been and what has been   45
Point to one end, which is always present.

"time present and time past" (l. 1) are made to correspond. The rose, persisting through the *Quartets* into their very last line, is an established symbol of love or sex, but often of a spiritually sublimated kind. Dante (*Paradiso*, xxiii, 73–74) saw the Virgin Mary in heaven as "the Rose, wherein the Word of God / Made itself flesh"; and he depicted the highest heaven (*Paradiso*, xxx) as a great white rose of supernal light (*rosa sempiterna*), to which Eliot alludes here (l. 16), and in the last "Quartet."

6. *Cf.* John Donne, "The Ecstasy": "Our eye-beams twisted"; the intensity of the passion is carried forward to the roses, in the next line.
7. Having traversed Paradise through lower levels of increasing brightness, Dante is permitted to glimpse the blinding supernal radiance of Father, Son, and Holy Spirit in threefold unity (*Paradiso*, xxxiii). Thus his phrase "heart of light" (l. 37) lends innocence to the preceding sexual imagery (ll. 28–36). But note the threatened fall of man from this "reality" (l. 43).

II

Garlic and sapphires in the mud [8]
Clot the bedded axle-tree.
The trilling wire in the blood
Sings below inveterate scars   50
Appeasing long forgotten wars.
The dance along the artery
The circulation of the lymph
Are figured in the drift of stars
Ascend to summer in the tree   55
We move above the moving tree
In light upon the figured leaf
And hear upon the sodden floor
Below, the boarhound and the boar
Pursue their pattern as before   60
But reconciled among the stars.

At the still point of the turning world.[9] Neither flesh nor fleshless;
Neither from nor towards; at the still point, there the dance is,
But neither arrest nor movement. And do not call it fixity,
Where past and future are gathered. Neither movement from nor
            towards,   65
Neither ascent nor decline. Except for the point, the still point,
There would be no dance, and there is only the dance.[1]
I can only say, *there* we have been: but I cannot say where.
And I cannot say, how long, for that is to place it in time.

The inner freedom from the practical desire,   70
The release from action and suffering, release from the inner
And the outer compulsion, yet surrounded
By a grace of sense, a white light still and moving,[2]   *Contrast release*
Erhebung [3] without motion, concentration   *between release and restraint*

8. In a sonnet by the French symbolist Stéphane Mallarmé, beginning, *"M'introduire dans ton histoire,"* l. 10 reads, *"Tonnerre et rubis aux moyeux"* ["Thunder and rubies at the hubs"]. Mallarmé further speaks of riding the sky in "chariots [poems] with fire-pierced wheels, the only vesperal of the * * * dying evening." Eliot's chariot is imbedded in "mud" (*cf.* the sound of *moyeux*), where the beauty of sapphires mingles with garlic (*cf. tonnerre,* "thunder." *Herbe du tonnerre,* "herb of thunder," is French for the house-leek; this plant is popularly confused with the leek, a close relative of garlic, whose name is derived from Old English *gar,* "lance," plus *leac,* "leek.")
9. Eliot used this phrase before, in "Triumphal March" (1931), one of the

"Coriolan" poems. Noting this, Matthiessen observes (*The Achievement of T. S. Eliot,* p. 184): "This notion of 'a mathematically pure point' (as Philip Wheelright called it) seems to be Eliot's poetic equivalent in our cosmology for Dante's 'unmoved mover'" (*i.e.,* the eternal Being).
1. *Cf.* G. W. F. Hegel, *The Phenomenology of Mind:* "The truth is thus the bacchanalian revel, where not a member is sober; and because every member no sooner becomes detached than it *eo ipso* collapses straightway, the revel is just as much a state of transparent unbroken calm."
2. *Cf.* Dante's vision of the eternal Light (*Paradiso,* xxxiii, 76–135).
3. German for "exaltation," "loftiness."

Without elimination, both a new world   75
And the old made explicit, understood
In the completion of its partial ecstasy,
The resolution of its partial horror.[4]
Yet the enchainment past and future
Woven in the weakness of the changing body,   80
Protects mankind from heaven and damnation
Which flesh cannot endure.

                    Time past and time future
Allow but a little consciousness.
To be conscious is not to be in time [5]   85
But only in time can the moment in the rose-garden,
The moment in the arbour where the rain beat,
The moment in the draughty church at smokefall
Be remembered; [6] involved with past and future.
Only through time time is conquered.   90

III

Here is a place of disaffection
Time before and time after
In a dim light: neither daylight
Investing form with lucid stillness
Turning shadow into transient beauty   95
With slow rotation suggesting permanence
Nor darkness to purify the soul
Emptying the sensual with deprivation
Cleansing affection from the temporal.[7]
Neither plenitude nor vacancy. Only a flicker   100
Over the strained time-ridden faces
Distracted from distraction by distraction
Filled with fancies and empty of meaning
Tumid apathy with no concentration
Men and bits of paper, whirled by the cold wind   105
That blows before and after time,
Wind in and out of unwholesome lungs
Time before and time after.
Eructation [8] of unhealthy souls
Into the faded air, the torpid   110

4. St. John of the Cross, in *The Dark Night of the Soul*, represents the condition that Eliot describes (ll. 70–82) as being the last stage of the mystic's preparation for unity with God. In that condition he has attained passivity in submissive contemplation of the will and majesty of God.
5. *Cf.* Bergson, *Time and Free Will:* "Pure duration is the form which our conscious states assume when our ego lets itself *live*, when it refrains from separating its present state from its former states."
6. *Cf.* Bergson, *Matter and Memory:* "Memory is just the intersection of mind and matter."
7. *Cf.* I John ii: 15–17: "Love not the world, neither the things that are in the world. * * * For all that is in the world * * * passeth away * * * but he that doeth the will of God abideth for ever."
8. *I.e.*, the belching forth.

Driven on the wind that sweeps the gloomy hills of London,
Hampstead and Clerkenwell, Campden and Putney,
Highgate, Primrose and Ludgate. Not here
Not here the darkness, in this twittering world.

Descend lower, descend only   115
Into the world of perpetual solitude,
World not world, but that which is not world,
Internal darkness, deprivation
And destitution of all property,
Desiccation of the world of sense,   120
Evacuation of the world of fancy,
Inoperancy of the world of spirit;
This is the one way, and the other
Is the same, not in movement
But abstention from movement; while the world moves   125
In appetency, on its metalled ways
Of time past and time future.

IV

Time and the bell have buried the day,
The black cloud carries the sun away.
Will the sunflower turn to us, will the clematis   130
Stray down, bend to us; tendril and spray
Clutch and cling?
Chill
Fingers of yew [9] be curled
Down on us? After the kingfisher's [1] wing   135
Has answered light to light,[2] and is silent, the light is still
At the still point of the turning world.

V

Words move, music moves
Only in time; but that which is only living
Can only die. Words, after speech, reach   140
Into the silence. Only by the form, the pattern,
Can words or music reach
The stillness, as a Chinese jar still
Moves perpetually in its stillness.
Not the stillness of the violin, while the note lasts,   145

---

9. The names of the flowers and tree in this lyric all have double meanings. The sunflower is of course the flower of light; clematis is popularly called "virgin's-bower"; the yew, a tree or shrub, has been traditionally associated with death and immortality.
1. *Cf.* the Fisher King of *The Waste Land,* associated in the Christian romances with Christ, who called his apostles "fishers of men" (Matthew iv: 18–19).
2. *Cf.* Dante, *Paradiso,* xxxiii, 109–120. The triune, supernal radiance of Dante's vision of the Godhead "answered light to light": he saw, "as rainbow upon rainbow," three circles "each an equal whole," forming "one sole aspect of divine essence."

Not that only, but the co-existence,
Or say that the end precedes the beginning,
And the end and the beginning were always there
Before the beginning and after the end.
And all is always now. Words strain,   150
Crack and sometimes break, under the burden,
Under the tension, slip, slide, perish,
Decay with imprecision, will not stay in place,
Will not stay still. Shrieking voices
Scolding, mocking, or merely chattering,   155
Always assail them. The Word in the desert
Is most attacked by voices of temptation,[3]
The crying shadow in the funeral dance,
The loud lament of the disconsolate chimera.

The detail of the pattern is movement,   160
As in the figure of the ten stairs.[4]
Desire itself is movement
Not in itself desirable;
Love is itself unmoving,
Only the cause and end of movement.   165
Timeless, and undesiring
Except in the aspect of time
Caught in the form of limitation
Between un-being and being.
Sudden in a shaft of sunlight   170
Even while the dust moves
There rises the hidden laughter
Of children in the foliage
Quick now, here, now, always—
Ridiculous the waste sad time   175
Stretching before and after.

1934   1936, 1943

3. *Cf.* the temptation of Christ in the wilderness (Luke iv: 1–4).
4. Eliot has identified "the ten stairs" as referring to the "Mystical Ladder of Divine Love," described by St. John of the Cross as having ten steps up which the soul of an individual rises, in ten stages of love for God. On the final step, "the soul becomes wholly assimilated into God in the beatific vision, * * * being perfectly purified by love." Eliot's lines (ll. 160–161) imply both a constant condition, which is the unchanging and perfect love of God ("the pattern"), and the "detail of the pattern," which is the "movement" of the mortal soul through the stages of realization of this love.

ROBINSON JEFFERS
(1887–1962)

John Robinson Jeffers was born on January 10, 1887, in Pittsburgh, Pennsylvania, where his father was professor of biblical languages and literature in Western Theological Seminary. In his early youth he was rigorously disciplined by his father in the classics and languages, attended schools in Switzerland and Germany, and traveled widely on the Continent and in England with his family. With advanced standing he entered the University of Pittsburgh (as it is now called), but on the removal of his family to California transferred to Occidental College, from which he was graduated at the precocious age of eighteen. After a term at the University of Zurich, he returned to the United States, and obtained his M.A. in literature at the University of Southern California. Although he had read widely in the classics and in German and French literature, and felt the desire to write, he had not found his subject. Meanwhile his profound interest in science drew him to the School of Medicine at the University of Southern California, which he attended for three years before transferring to the University of Washington to study forestry. In 1912, however, when a modest inheritance assured him an income, he turned again to writing, and published *Flagons and Apples*, a volume of love poems which shows little promise of his later originality.

In 1913 Una Call, whom he had met seven years earlier, was free to marry, and they settled at Carmel, California, before that wild and beautiful shore was surrounded first by an artists' colony and later by war industry. There on the cliffs facing the sea, he built Hawk Tower and Tor House from sea-cobbles, and secured seclusion by surrounding them with a small forest. There he lived in studious and creative privacy all his life. This is also the early Steinbeck country; Jeffers, like Steinbeck, became interested in the primitive life of the older generation of hill people and herders and in the survivals of Indian and Spanish culture mingled in their folkways. Their tragedies and their emotional attitudes seemed to accord at once with the primitive elements of Greek literature and with the understanding of the subconscious which he had derived from his reading of Freudian psychology. A third and harmonious factor was what Una Jeffers once described as "the spirit of this place."

Jeffers developed a style of great flexibility and lyric beauty, something between blank verse and free verse, in which the tones of colloquial speech are reproduced without weakening the poet's formal control of the line. In his narratives the lines are of unusual length, providing amplitude and luxuriance, but he has accomplished in his lyrics comparable rhythmic freedom for shorter lines in stanzaic composition. This highly individualistic style is heightened by the poet's musical sense and the semantic precision of his diction.

Jeffers's style is most effective in the tragic narratives, and especially in those with the greatest dramatic quality. These are in fact his unique contribution to our literature: *Tamar, Roan Stallion, The Tower Beyond Tragedy, Cawdor, The Loving Shepherdess, Thurso's Landing*, and *Give Your Heart to the Hawks*. Jeffers might have given us a genuine revival of the poetic drama, had the times been propitious. *The Tower Beyond Tragedy*, published in *Tamar and Other Poems* (1924), is a presentation of the Agamemnon story in dialogue form, with emphasis on the incest, madness, and return to sanity of Orestes —a reconstruction of the original that gives scope to the author's psychological analysis of the disease of humanity. Judith Anderson appeared briefly in a nonprofessional performance of this work and also acted in the author's reconstruction of the *Medea* (1946), which brought the spirit of Euripides alive on the American stage in one of the most memorable produc-

tions of its time. At least in this play this notable poet again recaptured the power of his earlier work. *The Cretan Woman*, a tragedy on the Phædra story, based on Euripides and Seneca, was produced in 1954.

There is no collected edition of the poetry of Jeffers, but the *Selected Poetry of Robinson Jeffers*, 1938, provides a cross section. The principal individual volumes are *Californians*, 1916; *Tamar and Other Poems*, 1924; *Roan Stallion, Tamar, and Other Poems*, 1925; *The Women at Point Sur*, 1927; *Cawdor and Other Poems*, 1928; *Dear Judas and Other Poems*, 1929; *Descent to the Dead*, 1931; *Thurso's Landing and Other Poems*, 1932; *Give Your Heart to the Hawks and Other Poems*, 1933; *Solstice and Other Poems*, 1935; *Such Counsels You Gave to Me and Other Poems*, 1937; *Be Angry at the Sun*, 1941; *Medea*, 1946; *The Double Axe*, 1948; *Hungerfield and Other Poems*, 1953; and *The Beginning and the End, and other Poems*, 1963. Ann N. Ridgeway edited *The Selected Letters of Robinson Jeffers, 1897–1962*, 1968.

Critical and biographical studies are George Sterling, *Robinson Jeffers*, 1926; Louis Adamic, *Robinson Jeffers*, 1929; L. C. Powell, *Robinson Jeffers: The Man and His Work*, revised 1940, with a bibliography of first editions; R. Squires, *Loyalties of Robinson Jeffers*, 1956; M. C. Monjian, *Robinson Jeffers*, 1958; Melba Bennett, *The Stone Mason of Tor House: The Life and Work of Robinson Jeffers*, 1966; Brother Antoninus, *Robinson Jeffers: Fragments of an Older Fury*, 1968; and Arthur B. Coffin, *Robinson Jeffers: Poet of Inhumanism*, 1970.

Boats in a Fog

Sports and gallantries, the stage, the arts, the antics of dancers,
The exuberant voices of music,
Have charm for children but lack nobility; it is bitter earnestness
That makes beauty; the mind
Knows, grown adult.

     A sudden fog-drift muffled the ocean,
A throbbing of engines moved in it,
At length, a stone's throw out, between the rocks and the vapor,

One by one moved shadows
Out of the mystery, shadows, fishing-boats, trailing each other,
Following the cliff for guidance,   10
Holding a difficult path between the peril of the sea-fog.
And the foam on the shore granite.
One by one, trailing their leader, six crept by me,
Out of the vapor and into it,
The throb of their engines subdued by the fog, patient and
     cautious,   15
Coasting all round the peninsula
Back to the buoys in Monterey harbor.[1] A flight of pelicans
Is nothing lovelier to look at;
The flight of the planets is nothing nobler; all the arts lose virtue
Against the essential reality   20
Of creatures going about their business among the equally
Earnest elements of nature.

                                                              1924

Shine, Perishing Republic

While this America settles in the mold of its vulgarity, heavily
     thickening to empire,
And protest, only a bubble in the molten mass, pops and sighs
     out, and the mass hardens,

I sadly smiling remember that the flower fades to make fruit, the
     fruit rots to make earth.
Out of the mother; and through the spring exultances, ripeness
     and decadence; and home to the mother.

You making haste haste on decay: not blameworthy; life is good,
     be it stubbornly long or suddenly   5
A mortal splendor: meteors are not needed less than mountains:
     shine, perishing republic.

But for my children, I would have them keep their distance from
     the thickening center; corruption
Never has been compulsory, when the cities lie at the monster's
     feet there are left the mountains.

And boys, be in nothing so moderate as in love of man, a clever
     servant, insufferable master.

---

1. Monterey, California, is the northern   prevalent fogs and by dangerous shoals
limit of the Jeffers country. The coastal   of rock.
waters are rendered hazardous by the

There is the trap that catches noblest spirits, that caught—they
    say—God, when he walked on earth.[2]

          10

1924

Granite and Cypress

White-maned, wide-throated, the heavy-shouldered children of the
    wind leap at the sea-cliff.
The invisible falcon [3]
Brooded on water, and bred them in wide waste places, in a bride-
    chamber wide to the stars' eyes
In the center of the ocean,
Where no prows pass nor island is lifted . . . the sea beyond
    Lobos [4] is whitened with the falcon's   5
Passage, he is here now,
The sky is one cloud, his wing-feathers hiss in the white grass, my
    sapling cypresses writhing
In the fury of his passage
Dare not dream of their centuries of future endurance of tempest.
    (I have granite and cypress,   10
Both long-lasting,
Planted in the earth; but the granite sea-boulders are prey to no
    hawk's wing, they have taken worse pounding,
Like me they remember
Old wars and are quiet; for we think that the future is one piece
    with the past, we wonder why tree-tops
And people are so shaken.)   15

1924

To the Stone-Cutters

Stone-cutters fighting time with marble, you foredefeated
Challengers of oblivion
Eat cynical earnings, knowing rock splits, records fall down,
The square-limbed Roman letters
Scale in the thaws, wear in the rain.   5
    The poet as well
Builds his monument mockingly;
For man will be blotted out, the blithe earth die, the brave sun
Die blind, his heart blackening:

2. Christ, of whom it was said (John
1: xiv), "And the Word [God] was
made flesh, and dwelt among us."
3. In this poem "the invisible falcon"
bred "the white maned * * * children
of the wind"; in the chivalric literature of falconry the achial falcon was
sometimes called "the master of the
wind."
4. A coastal headland near the poet's
home at Carmel, California.

Yet stones have stood for a thousand years, and pained thoughts
    found
The honey peace in old poems.   10

                                  1925

ARCHIBALD MACLEISH

(1892–   )

Archibald MacLeish was born on May 7, 1892, at Glencoe, a Chicago suburb. In due course he went to Hotchkiss School and Yale University, from which he was graduated in 1915. While a student at Harvard Law School he published two volumes of verse. Although he had married the previous year, he enlisted as a private in 1917. He saw service in France, and had reached the rank of artillery captain by the time he was discharged. For three years he practiced law in Boston, but the restlessness of the born writer was uppermost, and in 1923 he settled in Paris with his family and devoted himself to study and writing. His studies were reflected in his early poems in echoes of the Elizabethans, the French symbolists, and Pound and Eliot, but it was not long before he had developed an independent style.

His early volumes were so much overshadowed by his later work that they have suffered undeserved neglect. There is a morning light and some emotional insight in *The Happy Marriage* (1924). *The Pot of Earth* (1925), a modern story symbolizing woman as the earth-mother, reflects the influence that the republication of Frazer's *The Golden Bough* had on many writers of the time. *The*

Hamlet of A. MacLeish (1928) was his fifth and last volume of poems written abroad. In its wrestling with the spiritual defeatism to which the expatriate American writers in general succumbed, it has significance beyond its considerable merits as a poem. In "American Letter," which he wrote as he determined to return to the United States in 1928, he completed his break with the expatriates of Paris.

Stimulated by his new interest in the nature of society, MacLeish determined to write an epic which should utilize modern psychology and anthropological knowledge in describing the crisis of some great civilization. He chose the attempted conquest of the Mexican Aztecs by the Spanish Cortés, ending with the defeat of the Spaniards at the defense of Mexico City in 1520 by Montezuma, in which the great Indian ruler met his death. The account in his poem is fictional, but MacLeish did make substantial use of the chronicle of one of the participants, Bernál Díaz, and he retraced and studied the route of Cortés and his men across Mexico. *Conquistador* (1932) won the Pulitzer Prize, and took its place among the few enduring epics of modern literature.

By this time, however, Mac-

Leish was greatly disturbed by the unrest of the masses in the great depression and equally by what seemed to be an irresponsible selfishness and lack of concern among the successful. From 1929 until about 1937 he was on the staff of *Fortune* magazine, preparing the articles later published as *Housing in America, Jews in America,* and *Background of War.* His awakened social consciousness is reflected in the poems of *New Found Land* (1930) and is apparent again in the stirring satires of *Frescoes for Mr. Rockefeller's City* (1933), in *Panic* (1935), a verse play on financial irresponsibility, and in *Public Speech* (1936), in which satires on the same theme are mingled with sharp pictures of man under dictatorship, and warnings of the iron heels. *The Fall of the City* (1937) and *Air Raid* (1938) were successful radio plays in verse on similar themes, motivated by concern over the spread of fascism, which had recently precipitated civil war in Spain.

In 1939, President Franklin D. Roosevelt appointed MacLeish Librarian of Congress. While in this position, which he held until 1944, he continued, by lectures, broadcasts, and articles, to contribute to an awakened public spirit. Among collections of these writings, the most important are *The Irresponsibles* (1940); *A Time to Speak* (1941); *A Time to Act* (1943); and *American Story* (1944), ten dramatized broadcasts interpreting democratic idealism by episodes of American history. MacLeish served as assistant director of the Office of War Information and for a year directed the Office of Facts and Figures, both important propaganda agencies; he also served the President twice as diplomatic envoy abroad. In 1944–1945 he was assistant secretary of state, and in 1946 he went to Paris as chairman of the American delegation to UNESCO. In 1948 he resumed the role of gifted poet in the publication of *Actfive,* of which the title poem views with optimism the ultimate destiny of mankind. *Songs for Eve* (1954), a lyric sequence of passionate truth, revived popular interest in MacLeish, intensified by the appearance in 1958 of *JB: A Play in Verse,* which both delighted and mystified. A reviewer wrote: "If MacLeish has recourse to human integrity and human love for the answer to JB's need, it is because the Biblical Job offers him nothing beyond an arbitrary and heartless Cosmic Power." The play won the Pulitzer Prize in 1959. Since 1949, as Boylston Professor at Harvard, he has taught creative writing. His *Poetry and Experience* (1961) analyzes the poet's craft and the ultimate functions of the poem and the word.

Definitive to date is *Collected Poems, 1917–1952,* 1952. The poems of MacLeish's earlier period are well represented in the collection *Poems, 1924–1933,* 1933. A recent selection is *The Human Season: Selected Poems 1926–1972,* 1972. Prose is collected in *A Continuing Journey: Essays and Addresses,* 1968.

A critical study in Signi L. Falk, *Archibald MacLeish,* 1966. Other large-scale critical estimates will be found in Cleanth Brooks, *Modern Poetry and the Tradition,* 1939, pp. 110–135; and Oscar Cargill, *Intellectual America: Ideas on the March,* 1941, pp. 281–293. Also of interest is Warren Bush, *The Dialogues of Archibald MacLeish and Mark Van Doren,* 1964.

You, Andrew Marvell [1]

And here face down beneath the sun
And her upon earth's noonward height
To feel the always coming on
The always rising of the night

To feel creep up the curving east　　　　　5
The earthy chill of dusk and slow
Upon those under lands the vast
And ever climbing shadow grow

And strange at Ecbatan [2] the trees
Take leaf by leaf the evening strange　　　　10
The flooding dark about their knees
The mountains over Persia change

And now at Kermanshah the gate
Dark empty and the withered grass
And through the twilight now the late　　　　15
Few travelers in the westward pass

And Baghdad darken and the bridge
Across the silent river gone
And through Arabia the edge
Of evening widen and steal on　　　　20

And deepen on Palmyra's street
The wheel rut in the ruined stone
And Lebanon fade out and Crete
High through the clouds and overblown

And over Sicily the air　　　　25
Still flashing with the landward gulls
And loom and slowly disappear
The sails over the shadowy hulls

And Spain go under and the shore
Of Africa the gilded sand　　　　30
And evening vanish and no more
The low pale light across that land

---

1. An English poet (1621–1678), whose "To His Coy Mistress" contains the lines: "But at my back I always hear / Time's winged chariot hurrying near." See Eliot, *The Waste Land,* III, l. 185, for another use of Marvell's observation.
2. Beginning with Ecbatana, once the capital of Media Magna (part of Persia), the poet's thoughts move westward with the sun—to Kermanshah, Baghdad, Palmyra, Sicily, and so on. Thus the sense of time is related to the decay of civilizations. See Oswald Spengler, *The Decline of the West* (1918–1922), which influenced both MacLeish and Eliot.

Nor now the long light on the sea:

And here face downward in the sun
To feel how swift how secretly   35
The shadow of the night comes on. . . .

                                                                1930

American Letter [3]

FOR GERALD MURPHY

The wind is east but the hot weather continues,
Blue and no clouds, the sound of the leaves thin,
Dry like the rustling of paper, scored across
With the slate-shrill screech of the locusts.

                              The tossing of
Pines is the low sound. In the wind's running   5
The wild carrots smell of the burning sun.
Why should I think of the dolphins at Capo di Mele? [4]
Why should I see in my mind the taut sail
And the hill over St.-Tropez and your hand on the tiller?
Why should my heart be troubled with palms still?   10
I am neither a sold boy nor a Chinese official
Sent to sicken in Pa for some Lo-Yang dish.
This is my own land, my sky, my mountain:
This—not the humming pines and the surf and the sound
At the Ferme Blanche, nor Port Cros in the dusk and the harbor 15
Floating the motionless ship and the sea-drowned star.
I am neither Po Chüi [5] nor another after
Far from home, in a strange land, daft
For the talk of his own sort and the taste of his lettuces.
This land is my native land. And yet   20
I am sick for home for the red roofs and the olives,
And the foreign words and the smell of the sea fall.
How can a wise man have two countries?
How can a man have the earth and the wind and want
A land far off, alien, smelling of palm-trees
And the yellow gorse [6] at noon in the long calms?   25

3. The literary and artistic exiles of MacLeish's generation had turned to the cultural inheritance of Europe in revolt against the supposed aridity of American life. MacLeish suggests his rededication in the title of *New Found Land* (1930), the volume in which he first collected this poem, soon after returning from a long residence abroad.
4. The poet is remembering spots along the Mediterranean coast: Capo di Mele in Italy, and in later lines such French towns as St.-Tropez, Ferme Blanche, Port Cros, and Cette (now Sète).
5. Chinese poet (died 846 A.D.), whose lyrics celebrating his homeland were written far from his native place.
6. A European wild shrub, of wide distribution, which flourishes on uncultivated land.

It is a strange thing—to be an American.
Neither an old house it is with the air
Tasting of hung herbs and the sun returning
Year after year to the same door and the churn
Making the same sound in the cool of the kitchen   30
Mother to son's wife, and the place to sit
Marked in the dusk by the worn stone and the wellhead—
That—nor the eyes like each other's eyes and the skull
Shaped to the same fault and the hands' sameness.
Neither a place it is nor a blood name.   35
America is West and the wind blowing.
America is a great word and the snow,
A way, a white bird, the rain falling,
A shining thing in the mind and the gulls' call.
America is neither a land nor a people,   40
A word's shape it is, a wind's sweep—
America is alone: many together,
Many of one mouth, of one breath,
Dressed as one—and none brothers among them:
Only the taught speech and the aped tongue.   45
America is alone and the gulls calling.

It is a strange thing to be an American.
It is strange to live on the high world in the stare
Of the naked sun and the stars as our bones live.
Men in the old lands housed by their rivers.   50
They built their towns in the vales in the earth's ehelter.
We first inhabit the world. We dwell
On the half earth, on the open curve of a continent.
Sea is divided from sea by the day-fall. The dawn
Rides the low east with us many hours;   55
First are the capes, then are the shorelands, now
The blue Appalachians faint at the day rise;
The willows shudder with light on the long Ohio:
The Lakes scatter the low sun: the prairies
Slide out of the dark: in the eddy of clean air   60
The smoke goes up from the high plains of Wyoming:
The steep Sierras arise: the struck foam
Flames at the wind's heel on the far Pacific.
Already the moon leans to the eastern cliff:
The elms darken the door and the dust-heavy lilacs.   65

It is strange to sleep in the bare stars and to die
On an open land where few bury before us:
(From the new earth the dead return no more.)
It is strange to be born of no race and no people.
In the old lands they are many together. They keep   70

The wise past and the words spoken in common.
They remember the dead with their hands, their mouths dumb.
They answer each other with two words in their meeting.
They live together in small things. They eat
The same dish, their drink is the same and their proverbs. 75
Their youth is like. They are like in their ways of love.
They are many men. There are always others beside them.
Here it is one man and another and wide
On the darkening hills the faint smoke of the houses.
Here it is one man and the wind in the boughs. 80

Therefore our hearts are sick for the south water.
The smell of the gorse comes back to our night thought.
We are sick at heart for the red roofs and the olives;
We are sick at heart for the voice and the foot fall . . .

Therefore we will not go though the sea call us. 85

This, this is our land, this is our people,
This that is neither a land nor a race. We must reap
The wind here in the grass for our soul's harvest:
Here we must eat our salt or our bones starve.
Here we must live or live only as shadows. 90
This is our race, we that have none, that have had
Neither the old walls nor the voices around us,
This is our land, this is our ancient ground—
The raw earth, the mixed bloods and the strangers,
The different eyes, the wind, and the heart's change. 95
These we will not leave though the old call us.
This is our country-earth, our blood, our kind.
Here we will live our years till the earth blind us—

The wind blows from the east. The leaves fall.
Far off in the pines a jay rises. 100
The wind smells of haze and the wild ripe apples.

I think of the masts at Cette and the sweet rain.

1930

HART CRANE

(1899–1932)

The thirty-three years of Hart Crane's dark and troubled life were not sufficient to develop the genius that was in him, but when he put an end to his life he left a small collection of lyric masterpieces and an American epic of major stature, *The Bridge.* His emotional disintegration resulted from psychological disturbances probably personal in origin rather than reflections of the spiritual disillusionment which prevailed among the literary generation of the First World War. He was only fifteen when the war began in Europe; and when he planned *The Bridge*, it was with the expressed determination to celebrate the unbroken stream of humanistic idealism that he saw in the American historical experience, in contrast with Eliot's obituary for Western culture in *The Waste Land*.

Harold Hart Crane was born on July 21, 1899, in Garettsville, Ohio, but spent his boyhood in Cleveland. There his father prospered as a manufacturer of candies, and was determined to prepare the youth for a business career. Young Crane, who had begun writing poetry as a boy, and first published at fifteen, was equally determined to become a writer. He was emotionally disturbed by this breach with his father; soon a separation between his parents subjected him, as he said, to "the curse of sundered parenthood." At sixteen he refreshed childhood memories of Caribbean waters by visiting his mother at Isle of Pines, Cuba, where her relatives had sugar plantations. Like Gauguin, Crane was influenced emotionally by the tropics, which lent an exotic flavor to his work. On an early trip abroad he formed a deep attachment for Paris; later he was fascinated by New York, where he made long visits with relatives.

Soon Crane struck out for himself, and worked in various places as mechanic, clerk, salesman, and reporter. By 1922 he was settled in New York, living from hand to mouth, sporadically employed as a writer of advertising copy. He studied other writers—T. S. Eliot, Donne and the Elizabethans, and modern continental novelists. Occasionally he was able to publish a poem or two and these won him literary friends, notably Margaret Anderson and the New York coterie then writing for her *Little Review*. His first volume, *White Buildings* (1926), established his reputation as a poet's poet—not the same thing as winning an audience. He wrote slowly, a perfectionist painfully conscious of his relative lack of formal preparation for his task.

He was also spending much of his energy in developing the American materials and myth for *The Bridge*. Waldo Frank reports that the idea of taking Brooklyn Bridge as his basic symbol was suggested by the accident of his residence on Brooklyn Heights, in a mean room which nevertheless commanded a view of the great span from land to land, with the tides of humanity water-borne beneath it and flowing across it in ceaseless traffic. This conception of unity in diversity has obvious connections with American myth, and it occurs so often in Crane's lyrics as to suggest that it had in addition a private emotional significance for him. The sea and the city also persist as symbols of unity—the sea, which merges the individual identity in the universal solution; the city, an aggregate of individuals coming together in meaningful relationships. With these, in *The Bridge*, he associated the stream of history and the stream of time.

The benevolence of Otto Kahn enabled him to complete *The Bridge* in 1930, when it won the annual award of *Poetry* and recognition as a unique achievement. The plan of the poem is simple: in a succession of cantos we follow the westward thrust of the bridge—our history and time-stream—into the body of America, the body of Pocahontas, twin symbol with the bridge of "the flesh our feet have moved upon." "Powhatan's Daughter," the second poem, establishes the fertility myth; and a poem of Pocahontas, printed as a marginal gloss throughout the epic, is an idea in counterpoint to each successive theme. In "Van Winkle" (see below) Pocahontas "like Memory * * * is time's truant" among the shades of our history and its myth. In the fourth canto, "The River" (see below), Pocahontas merges with "the din and slogans" of modern America, and takes us backward through time, down the rails, trails, and rivers to the first explorers and their legends. In the fifth canto, a wild and beautiful Indian dance-phantasy, the continental nature myth emerges, and the final canto of this sequence, "Indiana," is the idyl of the settled land of homes, farms, town, and families. *The Bridge* acknowledges Man the creator, generic, anonymous, and, in the American experience, master of a wild continent, architect of its dream.

In 1931, Crane was awarded a Guggenheim Fellowship to be used in Mexico, where he proposed to write a long poem employing Mexican history. Failing to accomplish his object, and apparently suffering from the obsession that by the irregularities of his personal life he had squandered his power as an artist, on April 27, 1932, he disappeared into the sea from the stern of the vessel on which he was returning to New York.

The Complete Poems and Selected Letters and Prose of Hart Crane, 1966, was edited by Brom Weber. Hart Crane's *Collected Poems*, edited by Waldo Frank, appeared in 1933. For biography and criticism see Brom Weber, ed., *The Letters of Hart Crane*, 1952; Philip Horton, *Hart Crane * * *, 1937, 1957; Brom Weber, *Hart Crane*, 1948; Susan Jenkins Brown, *Robber Rocks: Letters and Memories of Hart Crane, 1923–1932*, 1969; and John Unterecker, *Voyager: A Life of Hart Crane*, 1969. Among earlier critical works see especially R. P. Blackmur, *The Double Agent*, 1935; and Allen Tate, *Reactionary Essays*, 1936. H. D. Howe compiled *Hart Crane: A Bibliography*, 1955.

More recent criticism includes L. S. Dembo, *Hart Crane's Sanskrit Charge: A Study of the Bridge*, 1960; Samuel Hazo, *Hart Crane: An Introduction and Interpretation*, 1963; Hunce Voelcker, *The Hart Crane Voyages*, 1967; R. W. B. Lewis, *The Poetry of Hart Crane*, 1967; Herbert A. Leibowitz, *Hart Crane: An Introduction to the Poetry*, 1968; and R. W. Butterfield, *The Broken Arc: A Study of Hart Crane*, 1969. H. D. Howe compiled *Hart Crane: A Bibliography*, 1955. Gary Lane edited *A Concordance to the Poems of Hart Crane*, 1972.

From The Bridge

Proem: To Brooklyn Bridge

How many dawns, chill from his rippling rest
The seagull's wings shall dip and pivot him,
Shedding white rings of tumult, building high
Over the chained bay waters Liberty—

Then, with inviolate curve, forsake our eyes   5
As apparitional as sails that cross
Some page of figures to be filed away;
—Till elevators drop us from our day . . .

I think of cinemas,[1] panoramic sleights
With multitudes bent toward some flashing scene   10
Never disclosed, but hastened to again,
Foretold to other eyes on the same screen;

And Thee,[2] across the harbor, silver-paced
As though the sun took step of thee, yet left
Some motion ever unspent in thy stride,—   15
Implicitly thy freedom staying thee!

Out of some subway scuttle, cell or loft
A bedlamite speeds to thy parapets,
Tilting there momently, shrill shirt ballooning,[3]
A jest falls from the speechless caravan.   20

Down Wall, from girder into street noon leaks,
A rip-tooth of the sky's acetylene; [4]
All afternoon the cloud-flown derricks turn . . .
Thy cables breathe the North Atlantic still.

And obscure as that heaven of the Jews,   25
Thy guerdon . . . Accolade thou dost bestow
Of anonymity time cannot raise:
Vibrant reprieve and pardon thou dost show.

O harp and altar, of the fury fused,
(How could mere toil align thy choiring strings!)   30
Terrific threshold of the prophet's pledge,
Prayer of pariah, and the lover's cry,—

Again the traffic lights that skim thy swift
Unfractioned idiom, immaculate sigh of stars,
Beading thy path—condense eternity: 35
And we have seen night lifted in thine arms.

Under thy shadow by the piers I waited;
Only in darkness is thy shadow clear.
The City's fiery parcels all undone,
Already snow submerges an iron year . . .   40

1. The prevailing term in Europe for "motion pictures"; but here note that the Greek word signifies "motion."
2. Brooklyn Bridge.
3. Some notoriety seekers (*e.g.*, Steve Brody) and many suicides have plunged from Brooklyn Bridge.
4. The fuel used to produce the white heat of the torches employed to cut and weld hard metals. Wall Street (*cf.* l. 21), near the bridge, was then visible from its summit.

O Sleepless as the river under thee,
Vaulting the sea, the prairies' dreaming sod,
Unto us lowliest sometime sweep, descend
And of the curveship lend a myth to God. .

*   *   *

Van Winkle

Macadam, gun-gray as the tunny's [5] belt,
Leaps from Far Rockaway [6] to Golden Gate:
Listen! the miles a hurdy-gurdy grinds—
Down gold arpéggios mile on mile unwinds.

Times earlier, when you hurried off to school,   5
—It is the same hour though a later day—
You walked with Pizarro in a copybook,
And Cortes rode up, reining tautly in—
Firmly as coffee grips the taste,—and away!

There was Priscilla's [7] cheek close in the wind,   10
And Captain Smith, all beard and certainty,
And Rip Van Winkle, bowing by the way,—
"Is this Sleepy Hollow, friend—?" And he—

And Rip forgot the office hours,
                    and he forgot the pay;   15
      Van Winkle sweeps a tenement
                    down town on Avenue A,—

The grind-organ says . . . Remember, remember
The cinder pile at the end of the backyard
Where we stoned the family of young
Garter snakes under . . . And the monoplanes   20
We launched—with paper wings and twisted
Rubber bands. . . . Recall—recall

                                   the rapid tongues
That flittered from under the ash heap day   25
After day whenever your stick discovered
Some sunning inch of unsuspecting fiber—
It flashed back at your thrust, as clean as fire.

And Rip was slowly made aware
            that he, Van Winkle, was not here
                                                   30

---

5. Any fish of the tuna family.
6. Far Rockaway is on the Atlantic
coast of Long Island; "to Golden
Gate," therefore, would be the span of
the continent from the Atlantic to the
Pacific.
7. Priscilla Alden, made familiar to
those who "hurried off to school" by
Longfellow's poem *The Courtship of
Miles Standish*.

> *nor there. He woke and swore he'd seen Broadway*
> *a Catskill daisy chain in May—*

So memory, that strikes a rhyme out of a box,
Or splits a random smell of flowers through glass—
Is it the whip stripped from the lilac tree   35
One day in spring my father took to me,
Or is it the Sabbatical, unconscious smile
My mother almost brought me once from church
And once only, as I recall—?

It flickered through the snow screen, blindly   40
It forsook her at the doorway; it was gone
Before I had left the window. It
Did not return with the kiss in the hall.

Macadam, gun-gray as the tunny's belt,
Leaps from Far Rockaway to Golden Gate . . .   45
Keep hold of that nickel for car-change, Rip,—
Have you got your paper—?
And hurry along, Van Winkle—it's getting late!

The River

Stick your patent name on a signboard [8]
brother—all over—going west—young man
Tintex—Japalac—Certain-teed Overalls ads
and lands sakes! under the new playbill ripped
in the guaranteed corner—see Bert Williams [9] what?   5
Minstrels when you steal a chicken just
save me the wing, for if it isn't
Erie it ain't for miles around a
Mazda—and the telegraphic night coming on Thomas

a Ediford—and whistling down the tracks   10
a headlight rushing with the sound—can you
imagine—while an EXPRESS makes time like
SCIENCE—COMMERCE and the HOLYGHOST
RADIO ROARS IN EVERY HOME WE HAVE THE NORTHPOLE
WALLSTREET AND VIRGINBIRTH WITHOUT STONES OR   15

---

8. In ll. 1–20 of this section the poet creates an impression of materialistic confusion by the free association of the slogans, events, and advertising of the period: among others "Japalac," a varnish; the Erie Railroad; the combination of Edison and Ford (Ediford); and the Twentieth Century Limited. Compare the similar devices used by Dos Passos in *U.S.A.*, the first part of which appeared at about the same time as this poem.
9. One of the most talented Negro comedians of this century; flourished from about 1895 until his death in 1922.

WIRES OR EVEN RUNning brooks [1] connecting ears
and no more sermons windows flashing roar
Breathtaking—as you like it . . . eh?

        So the 20th Century—so
whizzed the Limited—roared by and left   20
three men, still hungry on the tracks, ploddingly
watching the tail lights wizen and converge,
slipping gimleted and neatly out of sight.

      .   .   .

The last bear, shot drinking in the Dakotas,
Loped under wires that span the mountain stream.   25
Keen instruments, strung to a vast precision
Bind town to town and dream to ticking dream.
But some men take their liquor slow—and count—
Though they'll confess no rosary nor clue—
The river's minute by the far brook's year.   30
Under a world of whistles, wires and steam
Caboose-like they go ruminating through
Ohio, Indiana—blind baggage—
To Cheyenne tagging . . . Maybe Kalamazoo.

Time's renderings, time's blendings they construe   35
As final reckonings of fire and snow;
Strange bird-wit, like the elemental gist
Of unwalled winds they offer, singing low
My Old Kentucky Home and *Casey Jones,*
Some Sunny Day. I heard a road-gang chanting so.   40
And afterwards, who had a colt's eyes—one said,
"Jesus! Oh I remember watermelon days!" And sped
High in a cloud of merriment, recalled
"—And when my Aunt Sally Simpson smiled," he drawled—
"It was almost Louisiana, long ago."   45

"There's no place like Booneville though, Buddy,"
One said, excising a last burr from his vest,
"—For early trouting." Then peering in the can,
"—But I kept on the tracks." Possessed, resigned,
He trod the fire down pensively and grinned,   50
Spreading dry shingles of a beard. . . .

              Behind
My father's cannery works I used to see
Rail-squatters ranged in nomad raillery,

---

1. *Cf.* Shakespeare, *As You Like It,* Act II, Scene 1, ll. 16–17: "books in the
running brooks, / Sermons in stones," and so on.

The ancient men—wifeless or runaway   55
Hobo-trekkers that forever search
An empire wilderness of freight and rails.
Each seemed a child, like me, on a loose perch,
Holding to childhood like some termless play.
John, Jake, or Charley, hopping the slow freight   60
—Memphis to Tallahassee—riding the rods,
Blind fists of nothing, humpty-dumpty clods.

Yet they touch something like a key perhaps.
From pole to pole across the hills, the states
—They know a body under the wide rain;   65
Youngsters with eyes like fjords, old reprobates
With racetrack jargon,—dotting immensity
They lurk across her, knowing her yonder breast
Snow-silvered, sumac-stained or smoky blue,
Is past the valley-sleepers, south or west.   70
—As I have trod the rumorous midnights, too.

And past the circuit of the lamp's thin flame
(O Nights that brought me to her body bare!)
Have dreamed beyond the print that bound her name.
Trains sounding the long blizzards out—I heard   75
Wail into distances I knew were hers.
Papooses crying on the wind's long mane
Screamed redskin dynasties that fled the brain,
—Dead echoes! But I knew her body there,
Time like a serpent down her shoulder dark   80
And space, an eaglet's wing, laid on her hair.

Under the Ozarks, domed by Iron Mountain,
The old gods of the rain lie wrapped in pools
Where eyeless fish curvet a sunken fountain
And re-descend with corn from querulous crows.   85
Such pilferings make up their timeless eatage,
Propitiate them for their timber torn
By iron, iron—always the iron dealt cleavage!
They doze now, below axe and powder horn.

And Pullman breakfasters glide glistening steel   90
From tunnel into field—iron strides the dew—
Straddles the hill, a dance of wheel on wheel.
You have a half-hour's wait at Siskiyou,
Or stay the night and take the next train through.
Southward, near Cairo passing, you can see   95
The Ohio merging,—borne down Tennessee;
And if it's summer and the sun's in dusk

Maybe the breeze will lift the River's musk
—As though the waters breathed that you might know
Memphis Johnny, Steamboat Bill, Missouri Joe.[2]   100
Oh, lean from the window, if the train slows down,
As though you touched hands with some ancient clown,
—A little while gaze absently below
And hum *Deep River* with them while they go.

Yes, turn again and sniff once more—look see,   105
O Sheriff, Brakeman and Authority—
Hitch up your pants and crunch another quid,
For you, too, feed the River timelessly.
And few evade full measure of their fate;
Always they smile out eerily what they seem.   110
I could believe he joked at heaven's gate—
Dan Midland [3]—jolted from the cold brake-beam.

Down, down—born pioneers in time's despite,
Grimed tributaries to an ancient flow—
They win no frontier by their wayward plight,   115
But drift in stillness, as from Jordan's brow.

You will not hear it as the sea; even stone
Is not more hushed by gravity . . . But slow,
As loth to take more tribute—sliding prone
Like one whose eyes were buried long ago   120

The River, spreading, flows—and spends your dream.
What are you, lost within this tideless spell?
You are your father's father, and the stream—
A liquid theme that floating niggers swell.

Damp tonnage and alluvial march of days—   125
Nights turbid, vascular with silted shale
And roots surrendered down of moraine clays:
The Mississippi drinks the farthest dale.

O quarrying passion, undertowed sunlight!
The basalt surface drags a jungle grace   130
Ochreous and lynx-barred in lengthening might;
Patience! and you shall reach the biding place!

Over De Soto's bones the freighted floors

---

2. Old Mississippi folk songs. "Deep
River" (l. 104), a magnificent Negro
spiritual, is also a Mississippi River
song.
3. A storied hobo who fell from the
brake beam while "riding the rods."

Throb past the City storied of three thrones.[4]
Down two more turns the Mississippi pours   135
(Anon tall ironsides up from salt lagoons)

And flows within itself, heaps itself free.
All fades but one thin skyline 'round . . . Ahead
No embrace opens but the stinging sea;
The River lifts itself from its long bed.   140

Poised wholly on its dream, a mustard glow,
Tortured with history, its one will—flow!
—The Passion spreads in wide tongues, choked and slow,
Meeting the Gulf, hosannas silently below.[5]

1930

Voyages: II

—And yet this great wink of eternity,
Of rimless floods, unfettered leewardings,
Samite sheeted and processioned where
Her undinal vast belly moonward bends,[6]
Laughing the wrapt inflections of our love;   5

Take this Sea,[7] whose diapason knells
On scrolls of silver snowy sentences,
The sceptered terror of whose session rends
As her demeanors motion well or ill,
All but the pieties of lovers' hands.   10

And onward, as bells off San Salvador
Salute the crocus lusters of the stars,
In these poinsettia meadows of her tides,—
Adagios [8] of islands, O my Prodigal,
Complete the dark confessions her veins spell.   15

Mark how her turning shoulders wind the hours,[9]
And hasten while her penniless rich palms
Pass superscription of bent foam and wave,—

4. To prevent hostile Indians from discovering the death of Hernando De-Soto, his men buried him in the waters of the Mississippi, near the later site of New Orleans, whose history involved the "three thrones" of Spain, France, and England.
5. This canto, "The River," has identified the stream of men with that of history and with the history-haunted river; the leap of the Mississippi into the Gulf is a fundamental theme of *The Bridge* in its entirety.
6. The fact of the moon's influence on the tides is combined here with the myth of Undine's yearning for a mortal lover.
7. The Caribbean.
8. In music and the dance, a slow, graceful movement.
9. The tides are a clock for simple people living close to the shore.

Hasten, while they are true,—sleep, death, desire,
Close round one instant in one floating flower.   20

Bind us in time, O seasons clear, and awe.
O minstrel galleons of Carib fire,
Bequeath us to no earthly shore until
Is answered in the vortex of our grave
The seal's wide spindrift gaze toward paradise.   25

1926

Royal Palm

Green rustlings, more-than-regal charities
Drift coolly from that tower of whispered light.
Amid the noontide's blazed asperities
I watched the sun's most gracious anchorite [1]

Climb up as by communings, year on year   5
Uneaten of the earth or aught earth holds,
And the gray trunk, that's elephantine, rear
Its frondings sighing in aetherial folds.

Forever fruitless, and beyond that yield
Of sweat the jungle presses with hot love   10
And tendril till our deathward breath is sealed—
It grazes the horizons, launched above

Mortality—ascending emerald-bright,
A fountain at salute, a crown in view—
Unshackled, casual of its azured height,
As though it soared suchwise through heaven too.

1933

1. The ideas of chastity and fruitlessness (implied in "anchorite") are identified with the regal aloofness of the royal palm.

Fiction in Search of Reality

KATHERINE ANNE PORTER
(1890–   )

The reputation of Katherine Anne Porter in contemporary literature probably has no parallel. All her published fiction comprises but one novel, five novelettes, and three volumes of short stories. She has never had a popular following; yet nearly all discriminating readers are acquainted with her work, and she has exercised a considerable influence on many serious younger writers. Like Katherine Mansfield, whose inspiration she has recognized, she has attempted to achieve a style strictly objective without sacrificing sensitivity, and she has succeeded by such careful selection and combination of character, situation, and action that the resulting story is self-motivated, without the author's overt presence.

Miss Porter's preparation was long and careful. Although she had written stories almost from infancy, she did not satisfy her own standards sufficiently to attempt publication until she was thirty. She was born at Indian Creek, Texas, on May 15, 1890, and got her early education at various convent schools in Texas

and Louisiana. In 1920 she went to New York, where she made her home until 1937. During this period she also spent time in Europe and Mexico. She has written a study of the arts and crafts of the latter country, and she has published translations of Spanish, Latin-American, and French fiction. She was a newspaper reporter intermittently and later held an editorial post for a while.

After 1924 her stories began to appear both in standard literary magazines and in those of more experimental inclination. They were at once noticed, and when she collected only six of them in a limited edition, entitled *Flowering Judas* (1930), her reputation with the literary coterie was confirmed. The next year a Guggenheim Fellowship provided the opportunity for travel and writing in Europe.

Again in New York she published an enlarged edition of *Flowering Judas* (1935). Her first short novel, *Hacienda*, had appeared in 1924; her second novelette, *Noon Wine*, was published in 1937. The next year, again on a Guggenheim Fellowship, she went South. In 1939 appeared *Pale Horse, Pale Rider*, consisting of the title novelette, *Old Mortality*, and the previously published *Noon Wine*.

She has lived in Washington, D.C., since 1960. No *Safe Harbor* (1941) is a novelette; *The Leaning Tower* (1944), a collection of later stories. In 1952 she published *The Days Before*, an impressive collection of essays. The title of her long-awaited novel, *Ship of Fools* (1962), recalls the satirical *Das Narrenschiff* (1494), but she depicts a cruise in 1931 in which a large cast allegorically reflects the contemporary life of western man.

The Collected Stories of Katherine Anne Porter appeared in 1965 (revised, 1967). *The Collected Essays and Occasional Writings* appeared in 1970. Other volumes, besides those mentioned above, include *Outline of Mexican Popular Arts and Crafts*, 1922; *French Song Book*, 1933, translations; *The Itching Parrot*, 1942, translation from Spanish; *A Defense of Circe*, 1954.

Criticism includes H. J. Mooney, *Fiction and Criticism of Katherine Anne Porter*, 1957; William L. Nance, *Katherine Anne Porter and the Art of Rejection*, 1964; George Hendrick, *Katherine Anne Porter*, 1965; Lodwick Hartley and George Corey, eds., *Katherine Anne Porter: A Critical Symposium*, 1969; and M. M. Liberman, *Katherine Anne Porter's Fiction*, 1971.

The Jilting of Granny Weatherall [1]

She flicked her wrist neatly out of Doctor Harry's pudgy careful fingers and pulled the sheet up to her chin. The brat ought to be in knee breeches. Doctoring around the country with spectacles on his nose! "Get along now, take your schoolbooks and go. There's nothing wrong with me."

Doctor Harry spread a warm paw like a cushion on her forehead where the forked green vein danced and made her eyelids twitch. "Now, now, be a good girl, and we'll have you up in no time."

"That's no way to speak to a woman nearly eighty years old just because she's down. I'd have you respect your elders, young man."

"Well, Missy, excuse me." Doctor Harry patted her cheek. "But I've got to warn you, haven't I? You're a marvel, but you must be careful or you're going to be good and sorry."

"Don't tell me what I'm going to be. I'm on my feet now, morally speaking. It's Cornelia. I had to go to bed to get rid of her."

Her bones felt loose, and floated around in her skin, and Doctor Harry floated like a balloon around the foot of the bed. He floated and pulled down his waistcoat and swung his glasses on a cord. "Well, stay where you are, it certainly can't hurt you."

"Get along and doctor your sick," said Granny Weatherall. "Leave a well woman alone. I'll call for you when I want you. . . . Where were you forty years ago when I pulled through milk-leg

---

1. "The Jilting of Granny Weatherall" was collected in the author's first volume, *Flowering Judas and Other Stories* (1930). It was first published in *transition* for February, 1929.

and double pneumonia? You weren't even born. Don't let Cornelia lead you on," she shouted, because Doctor Harry appeared to float up to the ceiling and out. "I pay my own bills, and I don't throw my money away on nonsense!"

She meant to wave good-by, but it was too much trouble. Her eyes closed of themselves, it was like a dark curtain drawn around the bed. The pillow rose and floated under her, pleasant as a hammock in a light wind. She listened to the leaves rustling outside the window. No, somebody was swishing newspapers: no, Cornelia and Doctor Harry were whispering together. She leaped broad awake, thinking they whispered in her ear.

"She was never like this, *never* like this!" "Well, what can we expect?" "Yes, eighty years old. . . ."

Well, and what if she was? She still had ears. It was like Cornelia to whisper around doors. She always kept things secret in such a public way. She was always being tactful and kind. Cornelia was dutiful; that was the trouble with her. Dutiful and good: "So good and dutiful," said Granny, "that I'd like to spank her." She saw herself spanking Cornelia and making a fine job of it.

"What'd you say, Mother?"

Granny felt her face tying up in hard knots.

"Can't a body think, I'd like to know?"

"I thought you might want something."

"I do. I want a lot of things. First off, go away and don't whisper."

She lay and drowsed, hoping in her sleep that the children would keep out and let her rest a minute. It had been a long day. Not that she was tired. It was always pleasant to snatch a minute now and then. There was always so much to be done, let me see: tomorrow.

Tomorrow was far away and there was nothing to trouble about. Things were finished somehow when the time came; thank God there was always a little margin over for peace: then a person could spread out the plan of life and tuck in the edges orderly. It was good to have everything clean and folded away, with the hair brushes and tonic bottles sitting straight on the white embroidered linen: the day started without fuss and the pantry shelves laid out with rows of jelly glasses and brown jugs and white stone-china jars with blue whirligigs and words painted on them: coffee, tea, sugar, ginger, cinnamon, allspice: and the bronze clock with the lion on top nicely dusted off. The dust that lion could collect in twenty-four hours! The box in the attic with all those letters tied up, well, she'd have to go through that tomorrow. All those letters—George's letters and John's letters and her letters to them both—lying around for the children to find afterwards made her uneasy. Yes, that would be tomorrow's business. No use to let them know how silly she had been once.

While she was rummaging around she found death in her mind and it felt clammy and unfamiliar. She had spent so much time preparing for death there was no need for bringing it up again. Let it take care of itself now. When she was sixty she had felt very old, finished, and went around making farewell trips to see her children and grandchildren, with a secret in her mind: This is the very last of your mother, children! Then she made her will and came down with a long fever. That was all just a notion like a lot of other things, but it was lucky too, for she had once for all got over the idea of dying for a long time. Now she couldn't be worried. She hoped she had better sense now. Her father had lived to be one hundred and two years old and had drunk a noggin of strong hot toddy on his last birthday. He told the reporters it was his daily habit, and he owed his long life to that. He had made quite a scandal and was very pleased about it. She believed she'd just plague Cornelia a little.

"Cornelia! Cornelia!" No footsteps, but a sudden hand on her cheek. "Bless you, where have you been?"

"Here, mother."

"Well, Cornelia, I want a noggin of hot toddy."

"Are you cold, darling?"

"I'm chilly, Cornelia. Lying in bed stops the circulation. I must have told you that a thousand times."

Well, she could just hear Cornelia telling her husband that Mother was getting a little childish and they'd have to humor her. The thing that most annoyed her was that Cornelia thought she was deaf, dumb, and blind. Little hasty glances and tiny gestures tossed around her and over her head saying, "Don't cross her, let her have her way, she's eighty years old," and she sitting there as if she lived in a thin glass cage. Sometimes Granny almost made up her mind to pack up and move back to her own house where nobody could remind her every minute that she was old. Wait, wait, Cornelia, till your own children whisper behind your back!

In her day she had kept a better house and had got more work done. She wasn't too old yet for Lydia to be driving eighty miles for advice when one of the children jumped the track, and Jimmy still dropped in and talked things over: "Now, Mammy, you've a good business head, I want to know what you think about this? . . ." Old. Cornelia couldn't change the furniture around without asking. Little things, little things! They had been so sweet when they were little. Granny wished the old days were back again with the children young and everything to be done over. It had been a hard pull, but not too much for her. When she thought of all the food she had cooked, and all the clothes she had cut and sewed, and all the gardens she had made—well, the children showed it. There they were, made out of her, and they couldn't get away from that. Sometimes she wanted to see John again and point to them and say, Well, I didn't do so badly, did I? But that would have to wait. That was for tomorrow. She used to think of him as a man, but now all the children were older than their father, and he would be a child beside her if she saw him now. It seemed strange and there was something wrong in the idea. Why, he couldn't possibly recognize her. She had fenced in a hundred acres once, digging the post holes herself and clamping the wires with just a negro boy to help. That changed a woman. John would be looking for a young woman with the peaked Spanish comb in her hair and the painted fan. Digging post holes changed a woman. Riding country roads in the winter when women had their babies was another thing: sitting up nights with sick horses and sick negroes and sick children and hardly ever losing one. John, I hardly ever lost one of them! John would see that in a minute, that would be something he could understand, she wouldn't have to explain anything!

It made her feel like rolling up her sleeves and putting the whole place to rights again. No matter if Cornelia was determined to be everywhere at once, there were a great many things left undone on this place. She would start tomorrow and do them. It was good to be strong enough for everything, even if all you made melted and changed and slipped under your hands, so that by the time you finished you almost forgot what you were looking for. What was it I set out to do? she asked herself intently, but she could not remember. A fog rose over the valley, she saw it marching across the creek swallowing the trees and moving up the hill like an army of ghosts. Soon it would be at the near edge of the orchard, and then it was time to go in and light the lamps. Come in, children, don't stay out in the night air.

Lighting the lamps had been beautiful. The children huddled up to her and breathed like little calves waiting at the bars in the twilight. Their eyes followed the match and watched the flame rise and settle in a blue curve, then they moved away from her. The lamp was lit, they didn't have to be scared and hang on to mother any more. Never, never, never more. God, for all my life I thank Thee. Without Thee, my God, I could never have done it. Hail, Mary, full of grace.

I want you to pick all the fruit this year and see that nothing is wasted. There's always someone who can use it. Don't let good things rot for want of using. You waste life when you waste good food. Don't let things get lost. It's bitter to lose things. Now, don't let me get to thinking, not when I am tired and taking a little nap before supper. . . .

The pillow rose about her shoulders and pressed against her heart and the memory was being squeezed out of it: oh, push down the pillow, somebody: it would smother her if she tried to hold it. Such a fresh breeze blowing and such a green day with no threats in it. But he had not come, just the same. What does a woman do when she has put on the white veil and set out the white cake for a man and he doesn't come? She tried to remember. No, I swear he never harmed me but in that. He never harmed me but in that . . . and what if he did? There was the day, the day, but a whirl of dark smoke rose and covered it, crept up and over into the bright field where everything was planted so carefully in orderly rows. That was hell, she knew hell when she saw it. For sixty years she had prayed against remembering him and against losing her soul in the deep pit of hell, and now the two things were mingled in one and the thought of him was a smoky cloud from hell that moved and crept in her head when she had just got rid of Doctor Harry and was trying to rest a minute. Wounded vanity, Ellen, said a sharp voice in the top of her mind. Don't let your wounded vanity get the upper hand of you. Plenty of girls get jilted. You were jilted, weren't you? Then stand up to it. Her eyelids wavered and let in streamers of blue-gray light like tissue-paper over her eyes. She must get up and pull the shades down or she'd never sleep. She was in bed again and the shades were not drawn. How could that happen? Better turn over, hide from the light, sleeping in the light gave you nightmares. "Mother, how do you feel now?" and a stinging wetness on her forehead. But I don't like having my face washed in cold water!

Hapsy? George? Lydia? Jimmy? No, Cornelia, and her features were swollen and full of little puddles. "They're coming, darling, they'll all be here soon." Go wash your face, child, you look funny.

Instead of obeying, Cornelia knelt down and put her head on the pillow. She seemed to be talking but there was no sound. "Well, are you tongue-tied? Whose birthday is it? Are you going to give a party?"

Cornelia's mouth moved urgently in strange shapes. "Don't do that, you bother me, daughter."

"Oh, no, Mother. Oh, no. . . ."

Nonsense. It was strange about children. They disputed your every word. "No what, Cornelia?"

"Here's Doctor Harry."

"I won't see that boy again. He just left five minutes ago."

"That was this morning, Mother. It's night now. Here's the nurse."

"This is Doctor Harry, Mrs. Weatherall. I never saw you look so young and happy!"

"Ah, I'll never be young again—but I'd be happy if they'd let me lie in peace and get rested."

She thought she spoke up loudly, but no one answered. A warm weight on her forehead, a warm bracelet on her wrist, and a breeze went on whispering, trying to tell her something. A shuffle of leaves in the everlasting hand of God. He blew on them and they danced and rattled. "Mother, don't mind, we're going to give you a little hypodermic." "Look here, daughter, how do ants get in this bed? I saw sugar ants yesterday." Did you send for Hapsy too?

It was Hapsy she really wanted. She had to go a long way back through a great many rooms to find Hapsy standing with a baby on her arm. She seemed to herself to be Hapsy also, and the baby on Hapsy's arm was Hapsy and himself and herself, all at once, and there was no surprise in the meeting. Then Hapsy melted from within and turned flimsy as gray gauze and the baby was a gauzy shadow, and Hapsy came up close and said, "I thought you'd never come," and looked at her very searchingly and said, "You haven't changed a bit!" They leaned forward to kiss, when Cornelia began whispering from a long way off, "Oh, is there anything you want to tell me? Is there anything I can do for you?"

Yes, she had changed her mind after sixty years and she would like to see George. I want you to find George. Find him and be sure to tell him I forgot him. I want him to know I had my husband just the same and my children and my house like any other woman. A good house too and a good husband that I loved and fine children out of him. Better than I hoped for even. Tell him I was given back everything he took away and more. Oh, no, oh, God, no, there was something else besides the house and the man and the children. Oh, surely they were not all? What was it? Something not given back. . . . Her breath crowded down under her ribs and grew into a monstrous frightening shape with cutting edges; it bored up into her head, and the agony was unbelievable: Yes, John, get the Doctor now, no more talk, my time has come.

When this one was born it should be the last. The last. It should have been born first, for it was the one she had truly wanted. Everything came in good time. Nothing left out, left over. She was strong, in three days she would be as well as ever. Better. A woman needed milk in her to have her full health.

"Mother, do you hear me?"

"I've been telling you—"

"Mother, Father Connolly's here."

"I went to Holy Communion only last week. Tell him I'm not so sinful as all that."

"Father just wants to speak to you."

He could speak as much as he pleased. It was like him to drop in and inquire about her soul as if it were a teething baby, and then stay on for a cup of tea and a round of cards and gossip. He always had a funny story of some sort, usually about an Irishman who made his little mistakes and confessed them, and the point lay in some absurd thing he would blurt out in the confessional showing his struggles between native piety and original sin. Granny felt easy about her soul. Cornelia, where are your manners? Give Father Connolly a chair. She had her secret comfortable understanding with a few favorite aunts who cleared a straight road to God for her. All as surely signed and sealed as the papers for the new Forty Acres. Forever . . . heirs and assigns forever. Since the day the wedding cake was not cut, but thrown out and wasted. The whole bottom dropped out of the world, and there she was blind and sweating with nothing under her feet and the walls falling away. His hand had caught her under the breast, she had not fallen, there was the freshly polished floor with the green rug on it, just as before. He had cursed like a sailor's parrot and said, "I'll kill him for you." Don't lay a hand on him, for my sake leave something to God. "Now, Ellen, you must believe what I tell you. . . ."

So there was nothing, nothing to worry about any more, except sometimes in the night one of the children screamed in a nightmare, and they both hustled out shaking and hunting for the matches and calling, "There, wait a minute, here we are!" John, get the doctor now, Hapsy's time has come. But there was Hapsy standing by the bed in a white cap. "Cornelia, tell Hapsy to take off her cap. I can't see her plain."

Her eyes opened very wide and the room stood out like a picture she had seen somewhere. Dark colors with the shadows rising towards the ceiling in long angles. The tall black dresser gleamed with nothing on it but John's picture, enlarged from a little one, with John's very black eyes when they should have been blue. You never saw him, so how do you know how he looked? But the man insisted the copy was perfect, it was very rich and handsome. For a picture, yes, but it's not my husband. The table by the bed had a linen cover and a candle and a crucifix. The light was blue from Cornelia's silk lampshades. No sort of light at all, just frippery. You had to live forty years with kerosene lamps to appreciate honest electricity. She felt very strong and she saw Doctor Harry with a rosy nimbus around him.

"You look like a saint, Doctor Harry, and I vow that's as near as you'll ever come to it."

"She's saying something."

"I heard you, Cornelia. What's all this carrying-on?"

"Father Connolly's saying—"

Cornelia's voice staggered and bumped like a cart in a bad road. It rounded corners and turned back again and arrived nowhere. Granny stepped up in the cart very lightly and reached for the reins, but a man sat beside her and she knew him by his hands, driving the cart. She did not look in his face, for she knew without seeing, but looked instead down the road where the trees leaned over and bowed to each other and a thousand birds were singing a Mass. She felt like singing too, but she put her hand in the bosom of her dress and pulled out a rosary, and Father Connolly murmured Latin in a very solemn voice and tickled her feet. My God, will you stop that nonsense? I'm a married woman. What if he did run away and leave me to face the priest by myself? I found another a whole world better. I wouldn't have exchanged my husband for anybody except St. Michael himself, and you may tell him that for me with a thank you in the bargain.

Light flashed on her closed eyelids, and a deep roaring shook her. Cornelia, is that lightning? I hear thunder. There's going to be a storm. Close all the windows. Call the children in. . . . "Mother, here we are, all of us." "Is that you, Hapsy?" "Oh, no, I'm Lydia. We drove as fast as we could." Their faces drifted above her, drifted away. The rosary fell out of her hands and Lydia put it back. Jimmy tried to help, their hands fumbled together, Granny closed two fingers around Jimmy's thumb. Beads wouldn't do, it must be something alive. She was so amazed her thoughts ran round and round. So, my dear Lord, this is my death and I wasn't even thinking about it. My children have come to see me die. But I can't, it's not time. Oh, I always hated surprises. I wanted to give Cornelia the amethyst set—Cornelia, you're to have the amethyst set, but Hapsy's to wear it when she wants, and, Doctor Harry, do shut up. Nobody sent for you. Oh, my dear Lord, do wait a minute. I meant to do something about the Forty Acres, Jimmy doesn't need it and Lydia will later on, with that worthless husband of hers. I meant to finish the altar cloth and send six bottles of wine to Sister Borgia for her dyspepsia. I want to send six bottles of wine to Sister Borgia, Father Connolly, now don't let me forget.

Cornelia's voice made short turns and tilted over and crashed. "Oh, Mother, oh, Mother, oh, Mother. . . ."

"I'm not going, Cornelia. I'm taken by surprise. I can't go."

You'll see Hapsy again. What about her? "I thought you'd never come." Granny made a long journey outward, looking for Hapsy. What if I don't find her? What then? Her heart sank down and down, there was no bottom to death, she couldn't come to the end of it. The blue light from Cornelia's lampshade drew into a tiny point in the center of her brain, it flickered and winked like an eye, quietly it fluttered and dwindled. Granny lay curled down within herself, amazed and watchful, staring at the point of light that was herself; her body was now only a deeper mass of shadow in an endless darkness and this darkness would curl around the light and swallow it up. God, give a sign!

For the second time there was no sign. Again no bridegroom and the priest in the house.[2] She could not remember any other sorrow because this grief wiped them all away. Oh, no, there's nothing more cruel than this—I'll never forgive it. She stretched herself with a deep breath and blew out the light.

1929, 1930

F. SCOTT FITZGERALD
(1896–1940)

When F. Scott Fitzgerald died, at the age of forty-four, he was regarded as the lingering symbol of the Jazz Age, which he had named and had depicted with sentimental brilliance. In the three years from 1920 to 1922, he had established his position as historian of the younger generation by what seemed an avalanche of four books: two novels —*This Side of Paradise* (1920) and *The Beautiful and Damned* (1922)—and two collections of high-strung and arresting stories —*Flappers and Philosophers* (1920) and *Tales of the Jazz Age* (1922).

By the time of Fitzgerald's death in 1940 the Jazz Age, with all its "sad young men," its John Held flappers, and its adolescent Byronism, had been buried along with prohibition and tawdry night clubs under the rubble of the great depression of the thirties. Fitzgerald saw that the epoch with which he was identified had ended in 1929, and that a new generation, characterized by social responsibility and experimentation, had taken the citadel of the literary world. He was never able to get fully in step with this new generation. He had been taken captive by his own early success with a type of magazine story which was soon so profitable that he could not abandon it even though it became a stereotype. When the market for his magazine fiction began to wane, there was still the demand for fripperies in Hollywood. Meanwhile, it was barely recognized that he was, at his best, a genuine artist, having demonstrated his mastery in his second novel, *The Beautiful and*

---

2. *Cf.* Christ's parable of the bridegroom (Matthew xxv: 1–13).

Damned, and again in *The Great Gatsby* (1925), perhaps the most striking fictional analysis of the age of the gang barons and of the social conditions that produced them. No novelist of his time had better understood the nature of this joy-riding, extravagant, and irresponsible society, and the spiritual desperation and sterility that it represented. Evidently he was himself deeply involved in it, and only occasionally was he able to write at the top level of his powers. His two later novels are also of enduring interest, although each is marred by some fault of construction. *Tender Is the Night* (1934) is the more admired, but *The Last Tycoon* (1941), an unfinished posthumously published study of a Hollywood mogul, also contains the stamp of truth and critical penetration in its delineation of character and social situations.

Francis Scott Key Fitzgerald was born in St. Paul, Minnesota, on September 26, 1896. He had the early advantages of considerable travel and social life, although he looked with reluctant eye on the proffered benefits of formal education. He later said that it was only the presence of the Triangle Club at Princeton that induced him to go to college. At Princeton he collaborated on Triangle shows with his fellow student Edmund Wilson, and he retained throughout life his infatuation with the stage and musical-comedy world. In 1917 he left college and enlisted in the wartime army, serving as a lieutenant at a staff headquarters. The war terminated before he received an assignment abroad, and in the tedium of camp life he had meanwhile written a novel.

Unable to get his book published, he obtained work in 1919 as an advertising writer, and continued to send out stories and sketches to the magazines. Within a year he had found a magazine market and finished *This Side of Paradise.* That year he married and settled on Long Island. Later on, he acquired an estate in North Carolina, and lived variously in New York, Paris, and Hollywood; wherever he went, his habits were characterized by an extravagance which put upon him the strain of continuous and popular production.

His two later collections of short stories preserved what he considered genuine, and they are indeed so good that one realizes what was probably sacrificed by the tragic waste of his life. *All the Sad Young Men* (1926) reveals in its title his sense of his age, and a desperation which in his earlier period he too often cloaked in cynicism. His last collection, published in 1935, announces by the title, *Taps at Reveille,* his own feeling of impending personal disaster. He died in 1940 after a period of spectacular decline which justified his old friend, Edmund Wilson, in choosing *The Crack-Up* as the title for the posthumous edition of essays, letters, and notes.

There is no collected edition of Fitzgerald's works. His novels are *This Side of Paradise,* 1920; *The Beautiful and Damned,* 1922; *The Great Gatsby,* 1925; *Tender Is the Night,* 1934, revised edition posthumously published in 1951; and *The Last Tycoon,* posthumously published in 1941. The collections of short stories are *Flappers and Phi-*

losophers, 1920; *Tales of the Jazz Age*, 1922; *All the Sad Young Men*, 1926; and *Taps at Reveille*, 1935. *The Vegetable; or, From President to Postman*, 1923, is a satirical play. Andrew Turnbull has edited *The Letters of F. Scott Fitzgerald*, 1963, and *Scott Fitzgerald: Letters to His Daughter*, 1965. John Kuehl and Jackson Bryer edited *Dear Max: The Fitzgerald-Perkins Correspondence*, 1971. Matthew J. Bruccoli and Jennifer McCabe Atkinson edited *As Ever, Scott Fitz—*, 1972, letters between Fitzgerald and Harold Ober, his agent. John Kuehl edited *Thoughtbook of Francis Scott Key Fitzgerald*, 1965; and *The Apprentice Fiction of F. Scott Fitzgerald 1909–1917*, 1965. Matthew J. Bruccoli and Jackson Bryer edited *F. Scott Fitzgerald in His Own Time: A Miscellany*, 1971. Selections are *The Portable F. Scott Fitzgerald*, 1945, edited by Dorothy Parker; *The Stories * * * *, 1951, edited by Malcolm Cowley; *Afternoon of an Author*, 1957, introduction by Arthur Mizener, a volume of hitherto uncollected stories and essays; and Mizener, *The Fitzgerald Reader*, 1963.

Biographical and critical commentary will be found in *The Crack-Up*, 1945. Sheilah Graham, *Beloved Infidel*, 1958, is a book of reminiscences, as is *College of One*, 1967. There are two excellent biographies: Arthur Mizener, *The Far Side of Paradise*, 1951, rev. 1965; and Andrew Turnbull, *Scott Fitzgerald*, 1962. Other studies of interest include Nancy Milford, *Zelda*, 1970; Aaron Latham, *Crazy Sundays: F. Scott Fitzgerald in Hollywood*, 1971; and Sara Mayfield, *Exiles from Paradise: Zelda and Scott Fitzgerald*, 1971. *The Fictional Technique of F. Scott Fitzgerald* by James E. Miller, 1957, analyzes the first three novels. Alfred Kazin collected critical essays, *F. Scott Fitzgerald: The Man and His Work*, 1951; see also K. G. W. Cross, *F. Scott Fitzgerald*, 1964; James E. Miller, *F. Scott Fitzgerald, His Art and His Technique*, 1964; Sergio Perosa, *The Art of F. Scott Fitzgerald*, 1965; Henry D. Piper, *F. Scott Fitzgerald, a Critical Portrait*, 1965; Richard Lehan, *F. Scott Fitzgerald and the Craft of Fiction*, 1966; Jackson Bryer, *The Critical Reputation of F. Scott Fitzgerald: A Bibliographical Study*, 1967; Robert Sklar, *F. Scott Fitzgerald, The Last Laocoön*, 1967; and Milton R. Stern, *The Golden Moment: The Novels of F. Scott Fitzgerald*, 1970.

Babylon Revisited [1]

"And where's Mr. Campbell?" Charlie asked.

"Gone to Switzerland. Mr. Campbell's a pretty sick man, Mr. Wales."

"I'm sorry to hear that. And George Hardt?" Charlie inquired.

"Back in America, gone to work."

"And where is the Snow Bird?" [2]

"He was in here last week. Anyway, his friend, Mr. Schaeffer, is in Paris."

Two familiar names from the long list of a year and a half ago. Charlie scribbled an address in his notebook and tore out the page.

"If you see Mr. Schaeffer, give him this," he said. "It's my brother-in-law's address. I haven't settled on a hotel yet."

He was not really disappointed to find Paris so empty. But the stillness in the Ritz bar was strange and portentous. It was not an American bar any more—he felt polite in it, and not as if he owned it. It had gone back into France. He felt the stillness from

1. First published in the *Saturday Evening Post* for February 21, 1931, and collected in *Taps at Reveille* (1935), the last of the author's volumes to appear before his death. The story represents the final stage of his criticism of the generation of which he had become a symbol.
2. Slang for one addicted to (or sometimes peddling) "snow," *i.e.*, cocaine or heroin.

the moment he got out of the taxi and saw the doorman, usually in a frenzy of activity at this hour, gossiping with a *chasseur* [3] by the servants' entrance.

Passing through the corridor, he heard only a single, bored voice in the once-clamorous women's room. When he turned into the bar he travelled the twenty feet of green carpet with his eyes fixed straight ahead by old habit; and then, with his foot firmly on the rail, he turned and surveyed the room, encountering only a single pair of eyes that fluttered up from a newspaper in the corner. Charlie asked for the head barman, Paul, who in the latter days of the bull market had come to work in his own custom-built car—disembarking, however, with due nicety at the nearest corner. But Paul was at his country house today and Alix giving him information.

"No, no more," Charlie said. "I'm going slow these days."

Alix congratulated him: "You were going pretty strong a couple of years ago."

"I'll stick to it all right," Charlie assured him. "I've stuck to it for over a year and a half now."

"How do you find conditions in America?"

"I haven't been to America for months. I'm in business in Prague, representing a couple of concerns there. They don't know about me down there."

Alix smiled.

"Remember the night of George Hardt's bachelor dinner here?" said Charlie. "By the way, what's become of Claude Fessenden?"

Alix lowered his voice confidentially: "He's in Paris, but he doesn't come here any more. Paul doesn't allow it. He ran up a bill of thirty thousand francs, charging all his drinks and his lunches, and usually his dinner, for more than a year. And when Paul finally told him he had to pay, he gave him a bad check."

Alix shook his head sadly.

"I don't understand it, such a dandy fellow. Now he's all bloated up—" He made a plump apple of his hands.

Charlie watched a group of strident queens installing themselves in a corner.

"Nothing affects them," he thought. "Stocks rise and fall, people loaf or work, but they go on forever." The place oppressed him. He called for the dice and shook with Alix for the drink.

"Here for long, Mr. Wales?"

"I'm here for four or five days to see my little girl."

"Oh-h! You have a little girl?"

Outside, the fire-red, gas-blue, ghost-green signs shone smokily through the tranquil rain. It was late afternoon and the streets were in movement; the *bistros* gleamed. At the corner of the

3. Liveried footman or porter.

Boulevard des Capucines he took a taxi. The Place de la Concorde moved by in pink majesty; they crossed the logical Seine, and Charlie felt the sudden provincial quality of the left bank.

Charlie directed his taxi to the Avenue de l'Opéra, which was out of his way. But he wanted to see the blue hour spread over the magnificent façade, and imagine that the cab horns, playing endlessly the first few bars of *La Plus que Lente*,[4] were the trumpets of the Second Empire. They were closing the iron grill in front of Brentano's Bookstore, and people were already at dinner behind the trim little bourgeois hedge of Duval's. He had never eaten at a really cheap restaurant in Paris. Five-course dinner, four francs fifty, eighteen cents, wine included. For some odd reason he wished that he had.

As they rolled on to the Left Bank and he felt its sudden provincialism, he thought, "I spoiled this city for myself. I didn't realize it, but the days came along one after another, and then two years were gone, and everything was gone, and I was gone."

He was thirty-five, and good to look at. The Irish mobility of his face was sobered by a deep wrinkle between his eyes. As he rang his brother-in-law's bell in the Rue Palatine, the wrinkle deepened till it pulled down his brows; he felt a cramping sensation in his belly. From behind the maid who opened the door darted a lovely little girl of nine, who shrieked "Daddy!" and flew up, struggling like a fish, into his arms. She pulled his head around by one ear and set her cheek against his.

"My old pie," he said.

"Oh, daddy, daddy, daddy, daddy, dads, dads, dads!"

She drew him into the salon, where the family waited, a boy and girl his daughter's age, his sister-in-law and her husband. He greeted Marion with his voice pitched carefully to avoid either feigned enthusiasm or dislike, but her response was more frankly tepid, though she minimized her expression of unalterable distrust by directing her regard toward his child. The two men clasped hands in a friendly way and Lincoln Peters rested his for a moment on Charlie's shoulder.

The room was warm and comfortably American. The three children moved intimately about, playing through the yellow oblongs that led to other rooms; the cheer of six o'clock spoke in the eager smacks of the fire and the sounds of French activity in the kitchen. But Charlie did not relax; his heart sat up rigidly in his body and he drew confidence from his daughter, who from time to time came close to him, holding in her arms the doll he had brought.

"Really extremely well," he declared in answer to Lincoln's ques-

---

4. A slow waltz by Debussy. It was a fad for taxicabs to carry horns playing scraps of familiar music.

tion. "There's a lot of business there that isn't moving at all, but we're doing even better than ever. In fact, damn well. I'm bringing my sister over from America next month to keep house for me. My income last year was bigger than it was when I had money. You see, the Czechs——"

His boasting was for a specific purpose; but after a moment, seeing a faint restiveness in Lincoln's eyes, he changed the subject:

"Those are fine children of yours, well brought up, good manners."

"We think Honoria's a great little girl too."

Marion Peters came back from the kitchen. She was a tall woman with worried eyes, who had once possessed a fresh American loveliness. Charlie had never been sensitive to it and was always surprised when people spoke of how pretty she had been. From the first there had been an instinctive antipathy between them.

"Well, how do you find Honoria?" she asked.

"Wonderful. I was astonished how much she's grown in ten months. All the children are looking well."

"We haven't had a doctor for a year. How do you like being back in Paris?"

"It seems very funny to see so few Americans around."

"I'm delighted," Marion said vehemently. "Now at least you can go into the store without their assuming you're a millionaire. We've suffered like everybody, but on the whole it's a good deal pleasanter." [5]

"But it was nice while it lasted," said Charlie. "We were a sort of royalty, almost infallible, with a sort of magic around us. In the bar this afternoon"—he stumbled, seeing his mistake—"there wasn't a man I knew."

She looked at him keenly. "I should think you'd have had enough of bars."

"I only stayed a minute. I take one drink every afternoon, and no more."

"Don't you want a cocktail before dinner?" Lincoln asked.

"I take only one drink every afternoon, and I've had that."

"I hope you keep to it," said Marion.

Her dislike was evident in the coldness with which she spoke, but Charlie only smiled; he had larger plans. Her very aggressiveness gave him an advantage, and he knew enough to wait. He wanted them to initiate the discussion of what they knew had brought him to Paris.

At dinner he couldn't decide whether Honoria was most like him or her mother. Fortunate if she didn't combine the traits of

5. The American stock market crashed in 1929; when depression hit Paris, about two years later, the large American colony had vanished.

both that had brought them to disaster. A great wave of protectiveness went over him. He thought he knew what to do for her. He believed in character; he wanted to jump back a whole generation and trust in character again as the eternally valuable element. Everything else wore out.

He left soon after dinner, but not to go home. He was curious to see Paris by night with clearer and more judicious eyes than those of other days. He bought a *strapontin* [6] for the Casino and watched Josephine Baker [7] go through her chocolate arabesques.

After an hour he left and strolled toward Montmartre, up the Rue Pigalle into the Place Blanche. The rain had stopped and there were a few people in evening clothes disembarking from taxis in front of cabarets, and *cocottes* [8] prowling singly or in pairs, and many Negroes. He passed a lighted door from which issued music, and stopped with the sense of familiarity; it was Bricktop's, where he had parted with so many hours and so much money. A few doors farther on he found another ancient rendezvous and incautiously put his head inside. Immediately an eager orchestra burst into sound, a pair of professional dancers leaped to their feet and a maître d'hôtel [9] swooped toward him, crying, "Crowd just arriving, sir!" But he withdrew quickly.

"You have to be damn drunk," he thought.

Zelli's was closed, the bleak and sinister cheap hotels surrounding it were dark; up in the Rue Blanche there was more light and a local, colloquial French crowd. The Poet's Cave [1] had disappeared, but the two great mouths of the Café of Heaven and the Café of Hell still yawned—even devoured, as he watched, the meager contents of a tourist bus—a German, a Japanese, and an American couple who glanced at him with frightened eyes.

So much for the effort and ingenuity of Montmartre.[2] All the catering to vice and waste was on an utterly childish scale, and he suddenly realized the meaning of the word "dissipate"—to dissipate into thin air; to make nothing out of something. In the little hours of the night every move from place to place was an enormous human jump, an increase of paying for the privilege of slower and slower motion.

He remembered thousand-franc notes given to an orchestra for playing a single number, hundred-franc notes tossed to a doorman for calling a cab.

But it hadn't been given for nothing.

6. A low-priced jump seat that opens down into the aisle.
7. Josephine Baker, talented American Negro entertainer, became a spectacular feature of Parisian night life in the late twenties.
8. Prostitutes.

9. Headwaiter.
1. In Paris, *cave* (literally, "wine vault") was widely used to designate a cabaret below the sidewalk level.
2. During the twenties Montmartre, a quarter of Paris, had become the international center of Bohemianism.

It had been given, even the most wildly squandered sum, as an offering to destiny that he might not remember the things most worth remembering, the things that now he would always remember—his child taken from his control, his wife escaped to a grave in Vermont.

In the glare of a *brasserie* a woman spoke to him. He bought her some eggs and coffee, and then, eluding her encouraging stare, gave her a twenty-note franc and took a taxi to his hotel.

II

He woke up on a fine fall day—football weather. The depression of yesterday was gone and he liked the people on the streets. At noon he sat opposite Honoria at Le Grand Vatel, the only restaurant he could think of not reminiscent of champagne dinners and long luncheons that began at two and ended in a blurred and vague twilight.

"Now, how about vegetables? Oughtn't you to have some vegetables?"

"Well, yes."

"Here's *épinards* and *chou-fleur* and carrots and *haricots*." [3]

"I'd like *chou-fleur*."

"Wouldn't you like to have two vegetables?"

"I usually have only one at lunch."

The waiter was pretending to be inordinately fond of children. "*Qu'elle est mignonne, la petite! Elle parle exactement comme une française.*" [4]

"How about dessert? Shall we wait and see?"

The waiter disappeared. Honoria looked at her father expectantly.

"What are we going to do?"

"First, we're going to that toy store in the Rue Saint-Honoré and buy you anything you like. And then we're going to the vaudeville at the Empire."

She hesitated. "I like it about the vaudeville, but not the toy store."

"Why not?"

"Well, you brought me this doll." She had it with her. "And I've got lots of things. And we're not rich any more, are we?"

"We never were. But today you are to have anything you want."

"All right," she agreed resignedly.

When there had been her mother and a French nurse he had been inclined to be strict; now he extended himself, reached out for a new tolerance; he must be both parents to her and not shut any of her out of communication.

3. The French words mean "spinach," "cauliflower," "beans." 4. "She is charming, the little one! She speaks precisely like a French girl."

"I want to get to know you," he said gravely. "First let me introduce myself. My name is Charles J. Wales, of Prague."

"Oh, daddy!" her voice cracked with laughter.

"And who are you, please?" he persisted, and she accepted a rôle immediately: "Honoria Wales, Rue Palatine, Paris."

"Married or single?"

"No, not married. Single."

He indicated the doll. "But I see you have a child, madame."

Unwilling to disinherit it, she took it to her heart and thought quickly: "Yes, I've been married, but I'm not married now. My husband is dead."

He went on quickly, "And the child's name?"

"Simone. That's after my best friend at school."

"I'm very pleased that you're doing so well at school."

"I'm third this month," she boasted. "Elsie"—that was her cousin—"is only about eighteenth, and Richard is about at the bottom."

"You like Richard and Elsie, don't you?"

"Oh, yes. I like them all right."

Cautiously and casually he asked: "And Aunt Marion and Uncle Lincoln—which do you like best?"

"Oh, Uncle Lincoln, I guess."

He was increasingly aware of her presence. As they came in, a murmur of ". . . adorable" followed them, and now the people at the next table bent all their silences upon her, staring as if she were something no more conscious than a flower.

"Why don't I live with you?" she asked suddenly. "Because mamma's dead?"

"You must stay here and learn more French. It would have been hard for daddy to take care of you so well."

"I don't really need much taking care of any more. I do everything for myself."

Going out of the restaurant, a man and a woman unexpectedly hailed him.

"Well, the old Wales!"

"Hello there, Lorraine . . . Dunc."

Sudden ghosts out of the past: Duncan Schaeffer, a friend from college. Lorraine Quarles, a lovely, pale blonde of thirty; one of a crowd who had helped them make months into days in the lavish times of three years ago.

"My husband couldn't come this year," she said, in answer to his question. "We're poor as hell. So he gave me two hundred a month, and told me I could do my worst on that. . . . This your little girl?"

"What about coming back and sitting down?" Duncan asked.

"Can't do it." He was glad for an excuse. As always, he felt

Lorraine's passionate, provocative attraction, but his own rhythm was different now.

"Well, how about dinner?" she asked.

"I'm not free. Give me your address and let me call you."

"Charlie, I believe you're sober," she said judicially. "I honestly believe he's sober, Dunc. Pinch him and see if he's sober."

Charlie indicated Honoria with his head. They both laughed.

"What's your address?" said Duncan skeptically.

He hesitated, unwilling to give the name of his hotel.

"I'm not settled yet. I'd better call you. We're going to see the vaudeville at the Empire."

"There! That's what I want to do," Lorraine said. "I want to see some clowns and acrobats and jugglers. That's just what we'll do, Dunc."

"We've got to do an errand first," said Charlie. "Perhaps we'll see you there."

"All right, you snob. . . . Good-by, beautiful little girl."

"Good-by."

Honoria bobbed politely.

Somehow, an unwelcome encounter. They liked him because he was functioning, because he was serious; they wanted to see him, because he was stronger than they were now, because they wanted to draw a certain sustenance from his strength.

At the Empire, Honoria proudly refused to sit upon her father's folded coat. She was already an individual with a code of her own, and Charlie was more and more absorbed by the desire of putting a little of himself into her before she crystallized utterly. It was hopeless to try to know her in so short a time.

Between the acts they came upon Duncan and Lorraine in the lobby where the band was playing.

"Have a drink?"

"All right, but not up at the bar. We'll take a table."

"The perfect father."

Listening abstractedly to Lorraine, Charlie watched Honoria's eyes leave their table, and he followed them wistfully about the room, wondering what they saw. He met her glance and she smiled.

"I liked that lemonade," she said.

What had she said? What had he expected? Going home in a taxi afterward, he pulled her over until her head rested against his chest.

"Darling, do you ever think about your mother?"

"Yes, sometimes," she answered vaguely.

"I don't want you to forget her. Have you got a picture of her?"

"Yes, I think so. Anyhow, Aunt Marion has. Why don't you want me to forget her?"

"She loved you very much."

"I loved her too."

They were silent for a moment.

"Daddy, I want to come and live with you," she said suddenly. His heart leaped; he had wanted it to come like this.

"Aren't you perfectly happy?"

"Yes, but I love you better than anybody. And you love me better than anybody, don't you, now that mummy's dead?"

"Of course I do. But you won't always like me best, honey. You'll grow up and meet somebody your own age and go marry him and forget you ever had a daddy."

"Yes, that's true," she agreed tranquilly.

He didn't go in. He was coming back at nine o'clock and he wanted to keep himself fresh and new for the thing he must say then.

"When you're safe inside, just show yourself in that window."

"All right. Good-by, dads, dads, dads, dads."

He waited in the dark street until she appeared, all warm and glowing, in the window above and kissed her fingers out into the night.

III

They were waiting. Marion sat behind the coffee service in a dignified black dinner dress that just faintly suggested mourning. Lincoln was walking up and down with the animation of one who had already been talking. They were as anxious as he was to get into the question. He opened it almost immediately:

"I suppose you know what I want to see you about—why I really came to Paris."

Marion played with the black stars on her necklace and frowned.

"I'm awfully anxious to have a home," he continued. "And I'm awfully anxious to have Honoria in it. I appreciate your taking in Honoria for her mother's sake, but things have changed now"— he hesitated and then continued more forcibly—"changed radically with me, and I want to ask you to reconsider the matter. It would be silly for me to deny that about three years ago I was acting badly—"

Marion looked up at him with hard eyes.

"—But all that's over. As I told you, I haven't had more than a drink a day for over a year, and I take that drink deliberately, so that the idea of alcohol won't get too big in my imagination. You see the idea?"

"No," said Marion succinctly.

"It's a sort of stunt I set myself. It keeps the matter in proportion."

"I get you," said Lincoln. "You don't want to admit it's got any attraction for you."

"Something like that. Sometimes I forget and don't take it. But I try to take it. Anyhow, I couldn't afford to drink in my position. The people I represent are more than satisfied with what I've done, and I'm bringing my sister over from Burlington to keep house for me, and I want awfully to have Honoria too. You know that even when her mother and I weren't getting along well we never let anything that happened touch Honoria. I know she's fond of me and I know I'm able to take care of her—well, there you are. How do you feel about it?"

He knew that now he would have to take a beating. It would last an hour or two hours, and it would be difficult, but if he modulated his inevitable resentment to the chastened attitude of the reformed sinner, he might win his point in the end.

Keep your temper, he told himself. You don't want to be justified. You want Honoria.

Lincoln spoke first: "We've been talking it over ever since we got your letter last month. We're happy to have Honoria here. She's a dear little thing, and we're glad to be able to help her, but of course that isn't the question—"

Marion interrupted suddenly. "How long are you going to stay sober, Charlie?" she asked.

"Permanently, I hope."

"How can anybody count on that?"

"You know I never did drink heavily until I gave up business and came over here with nothing to do. Then Helen and I began to run around with—"

"Please leave Helen out of it. I can't bear to hear you talk about her like that."

He stared at her grimly; he had never been certain how fond of each other the sisters were in life.

"My drinking only lasted about a year and a half—from the time we came over until I—collapsed."

"It was time enough."

"It was time enough," he agreed.

"My duty is entirely to Helen," she said. "I try to think what she would have wanted me to do. Frankly, from the night you did that terrible thing you haven't really existed for me. I can't help that. She was my sister."

"Yes."

"When she was dying she asked me to look out for Honoria. If you hadn't been in a sanitarium then, it might have helped matters."

He had no answer.

"I'll never in my life be able to forget the morning when Helen knocked at my door, soaked to the skin and shivering, and said you'd locked her out."

Charlie gripped the sides of the chair. This was more difficult than he expected: he wanted to launch out into a long expostulation and explanation, but he only said: "The night I locked her out—" and she interrupted, "I don't feel up to going over that again."

After a moment's silence Lincoln said: "We're getting off the subject. You want Marion to set aside her legal guardianship and give you Honoria. I think the main point for her is whether she has confidence in you or not."

"I don't blame Marion," Charlie said slowly, "but I think she can have entire confidence in me. I had a good record up to three years ago. Of course, it's within human possibilities I may go wrong again. But if we wait much longer I'll lose Honoria's childhood and my chance for a home." He shook his head. "I'll simply lose her, don't you see?"

"Yes, I see," said Lincoln.

"Why didn't you think of all this before?" Marion asked.

"I suppose I did, from time to time, but Helen and I were getting along badly. When I consented to the guardianship, I was flat on my back in a sanitarium, and the market had cleaned me out. I knew I'd acted badly, and I thought if it would bring any peace to Helen, I'd agree to anything. But now it's different. I'm functioning, I'm behaving damn well, so far as—"

"Please don't swear at me," Marion said.

He looked at her, startled. With each remark the force of her dislike became more and more apparent. She had built up all her fear of life into one wall and faced it toward him. This trivial reproof was possibly the result of some trouble with the cook several hours before. Charlie became increasingly alarmed at leaving Honoria in this atmosphere of hostility against himself; sooner or later it would come out, in a word here, a shake of the head there, and some of that distrust would be irrevocably implanted in Honoria. But he pulled his temper down out of his face and shut it up inside him; he had won a point, for Lincoln realized the absurdity of Marion's remark, and asked her lightly since when she had objected to the word "damn."

"Another thing," Charlie said: "I'm able to give her certain advantages now. I'm going to take a French governess to Prague with me. I've got a lease on a new apartment—"

He stopped, realizing that he was blundering. They couldn't be expected to accept with equanimity the fact that his income was again twice as large as their own.

"I suppose you can give her more luxuries than we can," said Marion. "When you were throwing away money we were living along watching every ten francs. . . . I suppose you'll start doing it again."

"Oh, no," he said. "I've learned. I worked hard for ten years, you know—until I got lucky in the market, like so many people. Terribly lucky. It didn't seem any use working any more, so I quit. It won't happen again."

There was a long silence. All of them felt their nerves straining, and for the first time in a year Charlie wanted a drink. He was sure now that Lincoln Peters wanted him to have his child.

Marion shuddered suddenly; part of her saw that Charlie's feet were planted on the earth now, and her own maternal feeling recognized the naturalness of his desire; but she had lived for a long time with a prejudice—a prejudice founded on a curious disbelief in her sister's happiness, which, in the shock of one terrible night, had turned to hatred for him. It had all happened at a point in her life where the discouragement of ill health and adverse circumstances made it necessary for her to believe in tangible villainy and a tangible villain.

"I can't help what I think!" she cried out suddenly. "How much you were responsible for Helen's death, I don't know. It's something you'll have to square with your own conscience."

An electric current of agony surged through him; for a moment he was almost on his feet, an unuttered sound echoing in his throat. He hung on to himself for a moment, another moment.

"Hold on there," said Lincoln uncomfortably. "I never thought you were responsible for that."

"Helen died of heart trouble," Charlie said dully.

"Yes, heart trouble." Marion spoke as if the phrase had another meaning for her.

Then, in the flatness that followed her outburst, she saw him plainly and she knew he had somehow arrived at control over the situation. Glancing at her husband, she found no help from him, and as abruptly as if it were a matter of no importance, she threw up the sponge.

"Do what you like!" she cried, springing up from her chair. "She's your child. I'm not the person to stand in your way. I think if it were my child I'd rather see her—" She managed to check herself. "You two decide it. I can't stand this. I'm sick. I'm going to bed."

She hurried from the room; after a moment Lincoln said:

"This has been a hard day for her. You know how strongly she feels—" His voice was almost apologetic: "When a woman gets an idea in her head."

"Of course."

"It's going to be all right. I think she sees now that you—can provide for the child, and so we can't very well stand in your way or Honoria's way."

"Thank you, Lincoln."

"I'd better go along and see how she is."

"I'm going."

He was still trembling when he reached the street, but a walk down the Rue Bonaparte to the quais set him up, and as he crossed the Seine, fresh and new by the quai lamps, he felt exultant. But back in his room he couldn't sleep. The image of Helen haunted him. Helen whom he had loved so until they had senselessly begun to abuse each other's love, tear it into shreds. On that terrible February night that Marion remembered so vividly, a slow quarrel had gone on for hours. There was a scene at the Florida, and then he attempted to take her home, and then she kissed young Webb at a table; after that there was what she had hysterically said. When he arrived home alone he turned the key in the lock in wild anger. How could he know she would arrive an hour later alone, that there would be a snowstorm in which she wandered about in slippers, too confused to find a taxi? Then the aftermath, her escaping pneumonia by a miracle, and all the attendant horror. They were "reconciled," but that was the beginning of the end, and Marion, who had seen with her own eyes and who imagined it to be one of many scenes from her sister's martyrdom, never forgot.

Going over it again brought Helen nearer, and in the white, soft light that steals upon half sleep near morning he found himself talking to her again. She said that he was perfectly right about Honoria and that she wanted Honoria to be with him. She said she was glad he was being good and doing better. She said a lot of other things—very friendly things—but she was in a swing in a white dress, and swinging faster and faster all the time, so that at the end he could not hear clearly all that she said.

IV

He woke up feeling happy. The door of the world was open again. He made plans, vistas, futures for Honoria and himself, but suddenly he grew sad, remembering all the plans he and Helen had made. She had not planned to die. The present was the thing—work to do, and some one to love. But not to love too much, for he knew the injury that a father can do to a daughter or a mother to a son by attaching them too closely; afterward, out in the world, the child would seek in the marriage partner the same blind tenderness and, failing probably to find it, turn against love and life.

It was another bright, crisp day. He called Lincoln Peters at the bank where he worked and asked if he could count on taking Honoria when he left for Prague. Lincoln agreed that there was no reason for delay. One thing—the legal guardianship. Marion wanted to·retain that a while longer. She was upset by the whole matter, and it would oil things if she felt that the situation was still in her control for another year. Charlie agreed, wanting only the tangible, visible child.

Then the question of a governess. Charlie sat in a gloomy agency and talked to a cross Bernaise and to a buxom Breton peasant, neither of whom he could have endured. There were others whom he would see tomorrow.

He lunched with Lincoln Peters at Griffons, trying to keep down his exultation.

"There's nothing quite like your own child," Lincoln said. "But you understand how Marion feels too."

"She's forgotten how hard I worked for seven years there," Charlie said. "She just remembers one night."

"There's another thing," Lincoln hesitated. "While you and Helen were tearing around Europe throwing money away, we were just getting along. I didn't touch any of the prosperity be- cause I never got ahead enough to carry anything but my insur- ance. I think Marion felt there was some kind of injustice in it— you not even working toward the end, and getting richer and richer."

"It went just as quick as it came," said Charlie.

"Yes, a lot of it stayed in the hands of *chasseurs* and saxophone players and maîtres d'hôtel—well, the big party's over now. I just said that to explain Marion's feeling about those crazy years. If you drop in about six o'clock tonight before Marion's too tired, we'll settle the details on the spot."

Back at his hotel, Charlie found a *pneumatique* [5] that had been redirected from the Ritz bar where Charlie had left his address for the purpose of finding a certain man.

DEAR CHARLIE: You were so strange when we saw you the other day that I wondered if I did something to offend you. If so, I'm not conscious of it. In fact, I have thought about you too much for the last year, and it's always been in the back of my mind that I might see you if I came over here. We *did* have such good times that crazy spring, like the night you and I stole the butcher's tricycle, and the time we tried to call on the presi- dent and you had the old derby rim and the wire cane. Everybody seems so old lately, but I don't feel old a bit. Couldn't we get together some time today for old time's sake? I've got a vile hang-over for the moment, but will be feeling better this afternoon and will look for you about five in the sweet-shop at the Ritz.

Always devotedly,
LORRAINE.

5. A message; originally one delivered by pneumatic tube.

His first feeling was one of awe that he had actually, in his mature years, stolen a tricycle and pedalled Lorraine all over the Étoile [6] between the small hours and dawn. In retrospect it was a nightmare. Locking out Helen didn't fit in with any other act of his life, but the tricycle incident did—it was one of many. How many weeks or months of dissipation to arrive at that condition of utter irresponsibility?

He tried to picture how Lorraine had appeared to him then—very attractive; Helen was unhappy about it, though she said nothing. Yesterday, in the restaurant, Lorraine had seemed trite, blurred, worn away. He emphatically did not want to see her, and he was glad Alix had not given away his hotel address. It was a relief to think, instead, of Honoria, to think of Sundays spent with her and of saying good morning to her and of knowing she was there in his house at night, drawing her breath in the darkness.

At five he took a taxi and bought presents for all the Peters—a piquant cloth doll, a box of Roman soldiers, flowers for Marion, big linen handkerchiefs for Lincoln.

He saw, when he arrived in the apartment, that Marion had accepted the inevitable. She greeted him now as though he were a recalcitrant member of the family, rather than a menacing outsider. Honoria had been told she was going; Charlie was glad to see that her tact made her conceal her excessive happiness. Only on his lap did she whisper her delight and the question "When?" before she slipped away with the other children.

He and Marion were alone for a minute in the room, and on an impulse he spoke out boldly:

"Family quarrels are bitter things. They don't go according to any rules. They're not like aches or wounds; they're more like splits in the skin that won't heal because there's not enough material. I wish you and I could be on better terms."

"Some things are hard to forget," she answered. "It's a question of confidence." There was no answer to this and presently she asked, "When do you propose to take her?"

"As soon as I can get a governess. I hoped the day after tomorrow."

"That's impossible. I've got to get her things in shape. Not before Saturday."

He yielded. Coming back into the room, Lincoln offered him a drink.

"I'll take my daily whisky," he said.

It was warm here, it was a home, people together by a fire. The children felt very safe and important; the mother and father were

6. An open square in Paris, site of the Arc de Triomphe.

serious, watchful. They had things to do for the children more important than his visit here. A spoonful of medicine was, after all, more important than the strained relations between Marion and himself. They were not dull people, but they were very much in the grip of life and circumstances. He wondered if he couldn't do something to get Lincoln out of his rut at the bank.

A long peal at the door-bell; the *bonne à tout faire* [7] passed through and went down the corridor. The door opened upon another long ring, and then voices, and the three in the salon looked up expectantly; Richard moved to bring the corridor within his range of vision, and Marion rose. Then the maid came back along the corridor, closely followed by the voices, which developed under the light into Duncan Schaeffer and Lorraine Quarles.

They were gay, they were hilarious, they were roaring with laughter. For a moment Charlie was astounded; unable to understand how they had ferreted out the Peters' address.

"Ah-h-h!" Duncan wagged his finger roguishly at Charlie. "Ah-h-h!"

They both slid down another cascade of laughter. Anxious and at a loss, Charlie shook hands with them quickly and presented them to Lincoln and Marion. Marion nodded, scarcely speaking. She had drawn back a step toward the fire; her little girl stood beside her, and Marion put an arm about her shoulder.

With growing annoyance at the intrusion, Charlie waited for them to explain themselves. After some concentration Duncan said:

"We came to invite you out to dinner. Lorraine and I insist that all this shishi business 'bout your address got to stop."

Charlie came closer to them, as if to force them backward down the corridor.

"Sorry, but I can't. Tell me where you'll be and I'll phone you in half an hour."

This made no impression. Lorraine sat down suddenly on the side of a chair, and focussing her eyes on Richard, cried, "Oh, what a nice little boy! Come here, little boy." Richard glanced at his mother, but did not move. With a perceptible shrug of her shoulders, Lorraine turned back to Charlie:

"Come and dine. Sure your cousins won' mine. See you so sel'om. Or solemn."

"I can't," said Charlie sharply. "You two have dinner and I'll phone you."

Her voice became suddenly unpleasant. "All right, we'll go. But I remember once when you hammered on my door at four A.M. I was enough of a good sport to give you a drink. Come on, Dunc."

7. Maid of all work.

Still in slow motion, with blurred, angry faces, with uncertain feet, they retired along the corridor.

"Good night," Charlie said.

"Good night!" responded Lorraine emphatically.

When he went back into the salon Marion had not moved, only now her son was standing in the circle of her other arm. Lincoln was still swinging Honoria back and forth like a pendulum from side to side.

"What an outrage!" Charlie broke out. "What an absolute outrage!"

Neither of them answered. Charlie dropped into an armchair, picked up his drink, set it down again and said:

"People I haven't seen for two years having the colossal nerve—"

He broke off. Marion had made the sound "Oh!" in one swift, furious breath, turned her body from him with a jerk and left the room.

Lincoln set down Honoria carefully.

"You children go in and start your soup," he said, and when they obeyed, he said to Charlie:

"Marion's not well and she can't stand shocks. That kind of people make her really physically sick."

"I didn't tell them to come here. They wormed your name out of somebody. They deliberately—"

"Well, it's too bad. It doesn't help matters. Excuse me a minute."

Left alone, Charlie sat tense in his chair. In the next room he could hear the children eating, talking in monosyllables, already oblivious to the scene between their elders. He heard a murmur of conversation from a farther room and then the ticking bell of a telephone receiver picked up, and in a panic he moved to the other side of the room and out of earshot.

In a minute Lincoln came back. "Look here, Charlie. I think we'd better call off dinner for tonight. Marion's in bad shape."

"Is she angry with me?"

"Sort of," he said, almost roughly. "She's not strong and—"

"You mean she's changed her mind about Honoria."

"She's pretty bitter right now. I don't know. You phone me at the bank tomorrow."

"I wish you'd explain to her I never dreamed these people would come here. I'm just as sore as you are."

"I couldn't explain anything to her now."

Charlie got up. He took his coat and hat and started down the corridor. Then he opened the door of the dining room and said in a strange voice, "Good night, children."

Honoria rose and ran around the table to hug him.

"Good night, sweetheart," he said vaguely, and then trying to make his voice more tender, trying to conciliate something, "Good night, dear children."

V

Charlie went directly to the Ritz bar with the furious idea of finding Lorraine and Duncan, but they were not there, and he realized that in any case there was nothing he could do. He had not touched his drink at the Peters', and now he ordered a whisky-and-soda. Paul came over to say hello.

"It's a great change," he said sadly. "We do about half the business we did. So many fellows I hear about back in the States lost everything, maybe not in the first crash, but then in the second. Your friend George Hardt lost every cent, I hear. Are you back in the States?"

"No. I'm in business in Prague."

"I heard that you lost a lot in the crash."

"I did," and he added grimly, "but I lost everything I wanted in the boom."

"Selling short?"

"Something like that."

Again the memory of those days swept over him like a nightmare —the people they had met travelling; the people who couldn't add a row of figures or speak a coherent sentence. The little man Helen had consented to dance with at the ship's party, who had insulted her ten feet from the table; the women and girls carried screaming with drink or drugs out of public places . . . the men who locked their wives out in the snow, because the snow of '29 wasn't real snow. If you didn't want it to be snow, you just paid some money.

He went to the phone and called the Peters apartment; Lincoln answered.

"I called up because this thing is on my mind. Has Marion said anything definite?"

"Marion's sick," Lincoln answered shortly. "I know this thing isn't altogether your fault, but I can't have her go to pieces about it. I'm afraid we'll have to let it slide for six months; I can't take the chance of working her up to this state again."

"I see."

"I'm sorry, Charlie."

He went back to his table. His whisky glass was empty, but he shook his head when Alix looked at it questioningly. There wasn't much he could do now except send Honoria some things; he would send her a lot of things tomorrow. He thought rather angrily that this was just money—he had given so many people money. . . .

"No, no more," he said to another waiter. "What do I owe you?"

He would come back some day; they couldn't make him pay forever. But he wanted his child, and nothing was much good now, beside that fact. He wasn't young any more, with a lot of nice thoughts and dreams to have by himself. He was absolutely sure Helen wouldn't have wanted him to be so alone.

1931, 1935

WILLIAM FAULKNER
(1897–1962)

In creative genius, in the ability to construct a world of the imagination in which reality is more accessible than it is in the everyday actualities of life, William Faulkner has few peers in modern literature. This fact was only tardily recognized. His writing is difficult, obscure, and so often seemed disagreeable that many of his works were not widely read, and the recognition of his highest powers was attainable only in perspective. There was an ironical appropriateness in the fact that the Nobel committee, although for reasons not immediately connected with Faulkner's merits, was unable to reach a decision at the appointed time, and awarded him the 1949 Prize for literature a year late. Faulkner's full stature cannot be measured in any single work; however good in itself, the novel or story is usually integrated in a larger pattern with characters and events from other writings.

Faulkner regarded his major works as a "saga," a reconstruction of the life of Yoknapatawpha County, his fictional name for Lafayette County in northern Mississippi, where he lived at Oxford (the "Jefferson" of his novels). The documentary sources of his stories are family papers and county records extending back to the first settlements among the Indians. Yet if these are the materials of local social history, he also thought that he should find in them the semblance of the human spirit anywhere. He emphasized this central purpose in his address in acceptance of the Nobel Prize, in which he told younger writers that the only subject "worth the agony and sweat" of the artist is "the human heart in conflict with itself."

After about 1925, Faulkner lived quietly in Oxford, Mississippi, in the seclusion of the old house with its columned portico, belatedly depicted in popular media. Later on, as university writer in residence and public figure, his personal influence was forceful. He was born on September 25, 1897, in New Albany, Mississippi, but the family soon moved to Oxford, the seat of the University of Mississippi. His great-grandfather, William Falkner, had written a popular southern romance, but the boy was not literary in a marked way, and did not finish high school. In 1918, at the age of twenty-one, he enlisted in the Canadian Royal Flying Corps, but in about a year he returned to Oxford, where he next attended the University for two years. In 1922 he took a position as postmaster at the University; but in 1924 he went to New Orleans with newspaper work in mind. There he became a friend of Sherwood Anderson, then completing *Dark Laughter;* through him Faulkner became one of those associated with *The Double-Dealer,* an experimental magazine, in which he published verse and criticism. That year he prepared a collection of poems entitled *The Marble Faun* (1924). In New Orleans he wrote two novels, neither of ultimate consequence.

In 1925 he was again settled at Oxford. It has been reported that he worked as carpenter and farmer to provide for the publication of his first two novels. In 1929 he was able to publish two more, the beginning of his significant and mature work: *Sartoris,* which initiated the Yoknapatawpha cycle with a study of the Sartoris family; and *The Sound and the Fury,* which introduced the Compsons, a related family, and gave the world its first experience of this author's combination of experimental techniques and psychological violence. The novels of the cycle move on several planes of southern society. There are the old clans of Sartoris, Compson, Sutpen, McCaslin, de Spain, and others, some of them now in a condition of decadence, and others just as significantly readjusted to new social conditions. There are the older townspeople, generally substantial in character, in contrast with the Snopes clan, of whom Faulkner and his Oxford cronies made almost an oral legend before the sketches were published in magazines. Three novels chronicle

Flem Snopes, leader of rapacious kindred who emerge from backwoods burrows like rodents, to gnaw the props from under the old order. Flem grabs political and financial control; he uses a pretty wife to disgrace and depose the highborn Mayor, de Spain. He acquires the de Spain mansion, only to be destroyed, ironically by a Snopes whom he had betrayed. The early serial stories were reconstructed as *The Hamlet* (1940); *The Town* (1957) and *The Mansion* (1959) complete this very great comic epic. The older families hold in recollection the pioneers who first conquered the land, the "old people," as a heritage that they share with such woodsmen, part Indian, as Sam Fathers and Boon Hogganbeck in the stories of *Go Down, Moses* (1942). Curiously too, the Negroes have withstood better than the white people the shifting ordeals of history. There are scamps among them, but Faulkner emphasizes the strength of such Negroes as Dilsey in *The Sound and the Fury* and Lucas Beauchamp, last seen in *Intruder in the Dust* (1948). In the Yoknapatawpha group, *Light in August* (1932), *Absalom, Absalom!* (1936), and *The Unvanquished* (1938) are significant works. As *I Lay Dying* (1930) utilizes a folk tale concerning a delayed burial in a psychological study of the degenerated "poor whites." *Sanctuary* (1931) is a classic of horror and degradation representing the corruption of smalltown youth and the power of criminality in the age of jazz and prohibition. Its later sequel is *Requiem for a Nun* (1951). *The Wild Palms* (1939) and its twin, the popular *Old Man*, counterpoint a theme: in one, two lovers are destroyed by passionate violence; in the latter, a derelict convict and a lost woman, in the violence of an "Old Man" Mississippi flood, experience love and birth. A *Fable* (1954) is a retelling of the events of Holy Week, with the time and place shifted to World War I in France.

Faulkner's complex style may be regarded as consistent with his difficult objective—to keep continuously in focus the immediate character, "the human heart in conflict," while evoking that past which is always present with us. His style observes the conventions of a new prose, no more strict or unnatural than the conventions of poetry, and similarly intended to engage the imaginative participation of the reader and to provide a language more subjective and flexible than ordinary prose. This rhetorical convention—the dislocation of logical construction in the free association of images, often apparently, but only apparently, irrelevant to each other—facilitates Faulkner's psychological approach, the projection of events through the memory or consciousness of the character in the form of "interior monologue." No doubt Faulkner's style puts a burden on the reader, but whether or not he carries it further than may be necessary for his purposes, it has the effect of music and poetry in requiring active correspondence between the artist and the audience.

In 1950 Faulkner received the Nobel Prize, and, at home, the National Book Award for his *Collected Stories*. The conse-

quent reconsideration of Faulkner's work as a whole after such honors, unsought and long overdue, brought about, before his death, his general recognition as one of the greatest imaginative writers of the western world during his half century.

Besides those mentioned above, Faulkner's novels, not yet collected, are *Soldier's Pay*, 1926; *Mosquitoes*, 1927; *Pylon*, 1935; and *The Reivers*, 1962. *Flags in the Dust*, posthumously published in 1973, is an original, longer version of *Sartoris*. Volumes of short stories are *Idyll in the Desert*, 1931; *These 13: Stories*, 1931; *Miss Zilphia Gant*, 1932; *Doctor Martino and Other Stories*, 1934; *Go Down, Moses, and Other Stories*, 1942; *Knight's Gambit*, 1949; *Notes on a Horse Thief*, 1950; *Collected Stories of William Faulkner*, 1950; and *Big Woods*, 1955. Faulkner's poems appear in *The Marble Faun*, 1924; *Salmagundi*, 1932; *This Earth*, 1932; *A Green Bough*, 1933. Carvel Collins edited *New Orleans Sketches*, 1958, and *Early Prose and Poetry*, 1962. *Essays, Speeches and Public Letters of William Faulkner* was edited by James Meriwether, 1965. *The Faulkner-Cowley File: Letters and Memories 1944–1962*, was edited by Malcolm Cowley, 1966. *The Portable Faulkner*, 1946, is a good selection.

Biographical information is available in memoirs by two brothers: John Faulkner, *My Brother Bill: An Affectionate Memoir*, 1963; and Murry C. Falkner, *The Falkners of Mississippi*, 1967. See also James W. Webb and A. Wigfall Green, *William Faulkner of Oxford*, 1965; and Michael Millgate, *The Achievement of William Faulkner*, 1966.

Early critical studies are H. M. Campbell and R. E. Foster, *William Faulkner: A Critical Appraisal*, 1951; *William Faulkner: Two Decades of Criticism*, edited by F. J. Hoffman and O. W. Vickery, 1951 (and *Three Decades of Criticism*, 1960); Irving Howe, *William Faulkner: A Critical Study*, 1952; William V. O'Connor, *The Tangled Fire of William Faulkner*, 1954; and W. L. Miner, *The World of William Faulkner*, 1952.

More recent studies include Hyatt Waggoner, *William Faulkner, From Jefferson to the World*, 1960; Warren Beck, *Man in Motion* (the Snopes Trilogy), 1963; John W. Hunt, *William Faulkner: Art in Theological Tension*, 1965; Olga Vickery, *The Novels * * * A Critical Interpreta-*

tion, 1964; Cleanth Brooks, *William Faulkner: The Yoknapatawpha Country*, 1963; L. Thompson, *Faulkner: An Introduction and Interpretation*, 1963; R. P. Warren, ed., *Faulkner: A Collection of Critical Essays*, 1966; R. P. Adams, *Faulkner: Myth and Motion*, 1968; Walter Brylowski, *Faulkner's Olympian Laugh: Myth in the Novels*, 1968; H. Edward Richardson, *William Faulkner: The Journey to Self-Discovery*, 1969; and Linda Wagner, ed., *William Faulkner: Four Decades of Criticism*, 1973.

Spotted Horses [1]

Yes, sir. Flem Snopes has filled that whole country full of spotted horses. You can hear folks running them all day and all night, whooping and hollering, and the horses running back and forth across them little wooden bridges ever now and then kind of like thunder. Here I was this morning pretty near half way to town, with the team ambling along and me setting in the buckboard about half asleep, when all of a sudden something come swurging up outen the bushes and jumped the road clean, without touching hoof to it. It flew right over my team, big as a billboard and flying through the air like a hawk. It taken me thirty minutes to stop my team and untangle the harness and the buckboard and hitch them up again.

That Flem Snopes. I be dog if he ain't a case, now. One morning about ten years ago, the boys was just getting settled down on Varner's porch for a little talk and tobacco, when here come Flem out from behind the counter, with his coat off and his hair all parted, like he might have been clerking for Varner for ten years already. Folks all knowed him; it was a big family of them about five miles down the bottom. That year, at least. Share-cropping. They never stayed on any place over a year. Then they would move on to another place, with the chap or maybe the twins of that year's litter. It was a regular nest of them. But Flem. The rest of them stayed tenant farmers, moving ever year, but here come Flem one day, walking out from behind Jody Varner's counter like he owned it. And he wasn't there but a year or two before folks knowed that, if him and Jody was both still in that store in ten years more, it would be Jody clerking for Flem Snopes. Why, that fellow could make a nickel where it wasn't but four cents to begin with. He skun me in two trades, myself, and the fellow that can do that, I just hope he'll get rich before I do; that's all.

All right. So here Flem was, clerking at Varner's, making a nickel here and there and not telling nobody about it. No, sir.

1. "Spotted Horses" was first published in *Scribner's Magazine* for June, 1931, the source of the present text. Faulkner later expanded it in Book Four of *The Hamlet* (1940). In the context of the novel the longer version achieves a subtlety and a complexity not apparent in the earlier treatment. The magazine version is, as Faulkner noted in a letter to Malcolm Cowley, "shorter and more economical."

Folks never knowed when Flem got the better of somebody lessen
the fellow he beat told it. He'd just set there in the store-chair,
chewing his tobacco and keeping his own business to hisself, until
about a week later we'd find out it was somebody else's business he
was keeping to hisself—provided the fellow he trimmed was mad
enough to tell it. That's Flem.

We give him ten years to own ever thing Jody Varner had. But
he never waited no ten years. I reckon you-all know that gal of
Uncle Billy Varner's, the youngest one; Eula. Jody's sister. Ever
Sunday ever yellow-wheeled buggy and curried riding horse in that
country would be hitched to Bill Varner's fence, and the young
bucks setting on the porch, swarming around Eula like bees around
a honey pot. One of these here kind of big, soft-looking gals that
could giggle richer than plowed new-ground. Wouldn't none of
them leave before the others, and so they would set there on the
porch until time to go home, with some of them with nine and ten
miles to ride and then get up tomorrow and go back to the field.
So they would all leave together and they would ride in a clump
down to the creek ford and hitch them curried horses and yellow-
wheeled buggies and get out and fight one another. Then they
would get in the buggies again and go on home.

Well, one day about a year ago, one of them yellow-wheeled buggies and one of them curried saddle-horses quit this country. We
heard they was heading for Texas. The next day Uncle Billy and
Eula and Flem come in to town in Uncle Bill's surrey, and when
they come back, Flem and Eula was married. And on the next
day we heard that two more of them yellow-wheeled buggies had
left the country. They mought have gone to Texas, too. It's a big
place.

Anyway, about a month after the wedding, Flem and Eula went
to Texas, too. They was gone pretty near a year. Then one day last
month, Eula come back, with a baby. We figgered up, and we
decided that it was as well-growed a three-months-old baby as we
ever see. It can already pull up on a chair. I reckon Texas makes
big men quick, being a big place. Anyway, if it keeps on like it
started, it'll be chewing tobacco and voting time it's eight years
old.

And so last Friday here come Flem himself. He was on a wagon
with another fellow. The other fellow had one of these two-gallon
hats and a ivory-handled pistol and a box of ginger snaps sticking
out of his hind pocket, and tied to the tail-gate of the wagon was
about two dozen of them Texas ponies, hitched to one another
with barbed wire. They was colored like parrots and they was quiet
as doves, and ere a one of them would kill you quick as a rattlesnake. Nere a one of them had two eyes the same color, and nere a

one of them had ever see a bridle, I reckon; and when that Texas man got down offen the wagon and walked up to them to show how gentle they was, one of them cut his vest clean offen him, same as with a razor.

Flem had done already disappeared; he had went on to see his wife, I reckon, and to see if that ere baby had done gone on to the field to help Uncle Billy plow, maybe. It was the Texas man that taken the horses on to Mrs. Littlejohn's lot. He had a little trouble at first, when they come to the gate, because they hadn't never see a fence before, and when he finally got them in and taken a pair of wire cutters and unhitched them and got them into the barn and poured some shell corn into the trough, they durn nigh tore down the barn. I reckon they thought that shell corn was bugs, maybe. So he left them in the lot and he announced that the auction would begin at sunup to-morrow.

That night we was setting on Mrs. Littlejohn's porch. You-all mind the moon was nigh full that night, and we could watch them spotted varmints swirling along the fence and back and forth across the lot same as minnows in a pond. And then now and then they would all kind of huddle up against the barn and rest themselves by biting and kicking one another. We would hear a squeal, and then a set of hoofs would go Bam! against the barn, like a pistol. It sounded just like a fellow with a pistol, in a nest of cattymounts, taking his time.

II

It wasn't ere a man knowed yet if Flem owned them things or not. They just knowed one thing: that they wasn't never going to know for sho if Flem did or not, or if maybe he didn't just get on that wagon at the edge of town, for the ride or not. Even Eck Snopes didn't know, Flem's own cousin. But wasn't nobody surprised at that. We knowed that Flem would skin Eck quick as he would ere a one of us.

They was there by sunup next morning, some of them come twelve and sixteen miles, with seed-money tied up in tobacco sacks in their overalls, standing along the fence, when the Texas man come out of Mrs. Littlejohn's after breakfast and clumb onto the gate post with that ere white pistol butt sticking outen his hind pocket. He taken a new box of gingersnaps outen his pocket and bit the end offen it like a cigar and spit out the paper, and said the auction was open. And still they was coming up in wagons and a horse- and mule-back and hitching the teams across the road and coming to the fence. Flem wasn't nowhere in sight.

But he couldn't get them started. He begun to work on Eck, because Eck holp him last night to get them into the barn and feed them that shell corn. Eck got out just in time. He come outen that barn like a chip on the crest of a busted dam of water, and clumb into the wagon just in time.

He was working on Eck when Henry Armstid come up in his wagon. Eck was saying he was skeered to bid on one of them, because he might get it, and the Texas man says, "Them ponies? Them little horses?" He clumb down offen the gate post and went toward the horses. They broke and run, and him following them, kind of chirping to them, with his hand out like he was fixing to catch a fly, until he got three or four of them cornered. Then he jumped into them, and then we couldn't see nothing for a while because of the dust. It was a big cloud of it, and them blare-eyed, spotted things swoaring outen it twenty foot to a jump, in forty directions without counting up. Then the dust settled and there they was, that Texas man and the horse. He had its head twisted clean around like a owl's head. Its legs was braced and it was trembling like a new bride and groaning like a saw mill, and him holding its head wrung clean around on its neck so it was snuffing sky. "Look it over," he says, with his heels dug too and that white pistol sticking outen his pocket and his neck swole up like a spreading adder's until you could just tell what he was saying, cussing the horse and talking to us all at once: "Look him over, the fiddle-headed son of fourteen fathers. Try him, buy him; you will get the best—" Then it was all dust again, and we couldn't see nothing but spotted hide and mane, and that ere Texas man's boot-heels like a couple of walnuts on two strings, and after a while that two-gallon hat come sailing out like a fat old hen crossing a fence.

When the dust settled again, he was just getting outen the far fence corner, brushing himself off. He come and got his hat and brushed it off and come and clumb onto the gate post again. He was breathing hard. He taken the gingersnap box outen his pocket and et one, breathing hard. The hammer-head horse was still running round and round the lot like a merry-go-round at a fair. That was when Henry Armstid come shoving up to the gate in them patched overalls and one of them dangle-armed shirts of hisn. Hadn't nobody noticed him until then. We was all watching the Texas man and the horses. Even Mrs. Littlejohn; she had done come out and built a fire under the wash-pot in her back yard, and she would stand at the fence a while and then go back into the house and come out again with a arm full of wash and stand at the fence again. Well, here come Henry shoving up, and then we see Mrs. Armstid right behind him, in that ere faded wrapper and sunbonnet and them tennis shoes. "Git on back to that wagon," Henry says.

"Henry," she says.

"Here, boys," the Texas man says; "make room for missus to git up and see. Come on, Henry," he says; "here's your chance to buy that saddle-horse missus has been wanting. What about ten dollars, Henry?"

"Henry," Mrs. Armstid says. She put her hand on Henry's arm. Henry knocked her hand down.

"Git on back to that wagon, like I told you," he says.

Mrs. Armstid never moved. She stood behind Henry, with her hands rolled into her dress, not looking at nothing. "He hain't no more despair than to buy one of them things," she says. "And us not five dollars ahead of the pore house, he hain't no more despair." It was the truth, too. They ain't never made more than a bare living offen that place of theirs, and them with four chaps and the very clothes they wears she earns by weaving by the firelight at night while Henry's asleep.

"Shut your mouth and git on back to that wagon," Henry says. "Do you want I taken a wagon stake to you here in the big road?"

Well, that Texas man taken one look at her. Then he begun on Eck again, like Henry wasn't even there. But Eck was skeered. "I can git me a snapping turtle or a water moccasin for nothing. I ain't going to buy none."

So the Texas man said he would give Eck a horse. "To start the auction, and because you holp me last night. If you'll start the bidding on the next horse," he says, "I'll give you that fiddle-head horse."

I wish you could have seen them, standing there with their seed-money in their pockets, watching that Texas man give Eck Snopes a live horse, all fixed to call him a fool if he taken it or not. Finally Eck says he'll take it. "Only I just starts the bidding," he says. "I don't have to buy the next one lessen I ain't over-topped." The Texas man said all right, and Eck bid a dollar on the next one, with Henry Armstid standing there with his mouth already open, watching Eck and the Texas man like a mad-dog or something. "A dollar," Eck says.

The Texas man looked at Eck. His mouth was already open too, like he had started to say something and what he was going to say had up and died on him. "A dollar?" he says. "One dollar? You mean, *one* dollar, Eck?"

"Durn it," Eck says; "two dollars, then."

Well, sir, I wish you could a seen that Texas man. He taken out that gingersnap box and held it up and looked into it, careful, like it might have been a diamond ring in it, or a spider. Then he throwed it away and wiped his face with a bandanna. "Well," he says. "Well. Two dollars. Two dollars. Is your pulse all right, Eck?" he says. "Do you have ager-sweats at night, maybe?" he says. "Well," he says, "I got to take it. But are you boys going to stand there and see Eck get two horses at a dollar a head?"

That done it. I be dog if he wasn't nigh as smart as Flem Snopes.

He hadn't no more than got the words outen his mouth before here was Henry Armstid, waving his hand. "Three dollars," Henry says. Mrs. Armstid tried to hold him again. He knocked her hand off, shoving up to the gate post.

"Mister," Mrs. Armstid says, "we got chaps in the house and not corn to feed the stock. We got five dollars I earned my chaps a-weaving after dark, and him snoring in the bed. And he hain't no more despair."

"Henry bids three dollars," the Texas man says. "Raise him a dollar, Eck, and the horse is yours."

"Henry," Mrs. Armstid says.

"Raise him, Eck," the Texas man says.

"Four dollars," Eck says.

"Five dollars," Henry says, shaking his fist. He shoved up right under the gate post. Mrs. Armstid was looking at the Texas man too.

"Mister," she says, "if you take that five dollars I earned my chaps a-weaving for one of them things, it'll be a curse onto you and yourn during all the time of man."

But it wasn't no stopping Henry. He had shoved up, waving his fist at the Texas man. He opened it; the money was in nickels and quarters, and one dollar bill that looked like a cow's cud. "Five dollars," he says. "And the man that raises it'll have to beat my head off, or I'll beat hisn."

"All right," the Texas man says. "Five dollars is bid. But don't you shake your hand at me."

III

It taken till nigh sundown before the last one was sold. He got them hotted up once and the bidding got up to seven dollars and a quarter, but most of them went around three or four dollars, him setting on the gate post and picking the horses out one at a time by mouth-word, and Mrs. Littlejohn pumping up and down at the tub and stopping and coming to the fence for a while and going back to the tub again. She had done got done too, and the wash was hung on the line in the back yard, and we could smell supper cooking. Finally they was all sold; he swapped the last two and the wagon for a buckboard.

We was all kind of tired, but Henry Armstid looked more like a mad-dog than ever. When he bought, Mrs. Armstid had went back to the wagon, setting in it behind them two rabbit-sized, bone-pore mules, and the wagon itself looking like it would fall all to pieces soon as the mules moved. Henry hadn't even waited to pull it outen the road; it was still in the middle of the road and her setting in it, not looking at nothing, ever since this morning.

Henry was right up against the gate. He went up to the Texas man. "I bought a horse and I paid cash," Henry says. "And yet you expect me to stand around here until they are all sold before I can get my horse. I'm going to take my horse outen that lot."

The Texas man looked at Henry. He talked like he might have been asking for a cup of coffee at the table. "Take your horse," he says.

Then Henry quit looking at the Texas man. He begun to swallow, holding onto the gate. "Ain't you going to help me?" he says.

"It ain't my horse," the Texas man says.

Henry never looked at the Texas man again, he never looked at nobody. "Who'll help me catch my horse?" he says. Never nobody said nothing. "Bring the plowline," Henry says. Mrs. Armstid got outen the wagon and brought the plowline. The Texas man got down offen the post. The woman made to pass him, carrying the rope.

"Don't you go in there, missus," the Texas man says.

Henry opened the gate. He didn't look back. "Come on here," he says.

"Don't you go in there, missus," the Texas man says.

Mrs. Armstid wasn't looking at nobody, neither, with her hands across her middle, holding the rope. "I reckon I better," she says. Her and Henry went into the lot. The horses broke and run. Henry and Mrs. Armstid followed.

"Get him into the corner," Henry says. They got Henry's horse cornered finally, and Henry taken the rope, but Mrs. Armstid let the horse get out. They hemmed it up again, but Mrs. Armstid let it get out again, and Henry turned and hit her with the rope. "Why didn't you head him back?" Henry says. He hit her again. "Why didn't you?" It was about that time I looked around and see Flem Snopes standing there.

It was the Texas man that done something. He moved fast for a big man. He caught the rope before Henry could hit the third time, and Henry whirled and made like he would jump at the Texas man. But he never jumped. The Texas man went and taken Henry's arm and led him outen the lot. Mrs. Armstid come behind them and the Texas man taken some money outen his pocket and he give it into Mrs. Armstid's hand. "Get him into the wagon and take him on home," the Texas man says, like he might have been telling them he enjoyed his supper.

Then here come Flem. "What's that for, Buck?" Flem says.

"Thinks he bought one of them ponies," the Texas man says. "Get him on away, missus."

But Henry wouldn't go. "Give him back that money," he says. "I bought that horse and I aim to have him if I have to shoot him."

And there was Flem, standing there with his hands in his pockets, chewing, like he had just happened to be passing.

"You take your money and I take my horse," Henry says. "Give it back to him," he says to Mrs. Armstid.

"You don't own no horse of mine," the Texas man says. "Get him on home, missus."

Then Henry seen Flem. "You got something to do with these horses," he says. "I bought one. Here's the money for it." He taken the bill outen Mrs. Armstid's hand. He offered it to Flem. "I bought one. Ask him. Here. Here's the money," he says, giving the bill to Flem.

When Flem taken the money, the Texas man dropped the rope he had snatched outen Henry's hand. He had done sent Eck Snopes's boy up to the store for another box of gingersnaps, and he taken the box outen his pocket and looked into it. It was empty and he dropped it on the ground. "Mr. Snopes will have your money for you to-morrow," he says to Mrs. Armstid. "You can get it from him to-morrow. He don't own no horse. You get him into the wagon and get him on home." Mrs. Armstid went back to the wagon and got in. "Where's that ere buckboard I bought?" the Texas man says. It was after sundown then. And then Mrs. Littlejohn come out on the porch and rung the supper bell.

IV

I come on in and et supper. Mrs. Littlejohn would bring in a pan of bread or something, then she would go out to the porch a minute and come back and tell us. The Texas man had hitched his team to the buckboard he had swapped them last two horses for, and him and Flem had gone, and then she told that the rest of them that never had ropes had went back to the store with I.O. Snopes to get some ropes, and wasn't nobody at the gate but Henry Armstid, and Mrs. Armstid setting in the wagon in the road, and Eck Snopes and that boy of hisn. "I don't care how many of them fool men gets killed by them things," Mrs. Littlejohn says, "but I ain't going to let Eck Snopes take that boy into that lot again." So she went down to the gate, but she come back without the boy or Eck neither.

"It ain't no need to worry about that boy," I says. "He's charmed." He was right behind Eck last night when Eck went to help feed them. The whole drove of them jumped clean over that boy's head and never touched him. It was Eck that touched him. Eck snatched him into the wagon and taken a rope and frailed the tar outen him.

So I had done et and went to my room and was undressing, long as I had a long trip to make next day; I was trying to sell a machine to Mrs. Bundren up past Whiteleaf; when Henry Armstid opened that gate and went in by hisself. They couldn't make him wait for the balance of them to get back with their ropes. Eck Snopes said he tried to make Henry wait, but Henry wouldn't do it. Eck said Henry walked right up to them and that when they broke, they run clean over Henry like a hay-mow breaking down. Eck said he snatched that boy of hisn out of the way just in time and that them things went through that gate like a creek flood and into the wagons and teams hitched side the road, busting wagon tongues and snapping harness like it was fishing-line, with Mrs. Armstid still setting in their wagon in the middle of it like something carved outen wood. Then they scattered, wild horses and tame mules with pieces of harness and single trees dangling offen them, both ways up and down the road.

"There goes ourn, paw!" Eck says his boy said. "There it goes, into Mrs. Littlejohn's house." Eck says it run right up the steps and into the house like a boarder late for supper. I reckon so. Anyway, I was in my room, in my underclothes, with one sock on and one sock in my hand, leaning out the window when the commotion busted out, when I heard something run into the melodeon in the hall; it sounded like a railroad engine. Then the door to my room come sailing in like when you throw a tin bucket top into the wind and I looked over my shoulder and see something that looked like a fourteen-foot pinwheel a-blaring its eyes at me. It had to blare them fast, because I was already done jumped out the window.

I reckon it was anxious, too. I reckon it hadn't never seen barbed wire or shell corn before, but I know it hadn't never seen underclothes before, or maybe it was a sewing-machine agent it hadn't never seen. Anyway, it swirled and turned to run back up the hall and outen the house, when it met Eck Snopes and that boy just coming in, carrying a rope. It swirled again and run down the hall and out the back door just in time to meet Mrs. Littlejohn. She had just gathered up the clothes she had washed, and she was coming onto the back porch with a armful of washing in one hand and a scrubbing-board in the other, when the horse skidded up to her, trying to stop and swirl again. It never taken Mrs. Littlejohn no time a-tall.

"Git outen here, you son," she says. She hit it across the face with the scrubbing-board; that ere scrubbing-board split as neat as ere a axe could have done it, and when the horse swirled to run back up the hall, she hit it again with what was left of the scrubbing-board, not on the head this time. "And stay out," she says.

Eck and that boy was half-way down the hall by this time. I reckon that horse looked like a pinwheel to Eck too. "Git to hell outen here, Ad!" Eck says. Only there wasn't time. Eck dropped flat on his face, but the boy never moved. The boy was about a yard tall maybe, in overhalls just like Eck's; that horse swoared over his head without touching a hair. I saw that, because I was just coming back up the front steps, still carrying that ere sock and still in my underclothes, when the horse come onto the porch again. It taken one look at me and swirled again and run to the end of the porch and jumped the banisters and the lot fence like a hen-hawk and lit in the lot running and went out the gate again and jumped eight or ten upside-down wagons and went on down the road. It was a full moon then. Mrs. Armstid was still setting in the wagon like she had done been carved outen wood and left there and forgot.

That horse. It ain't never missed a lick. It was going about forty miles a hour when it come to the bridge over the creek. It would have had a clear road, but it so happened that Vernon Tull was already using the bridge when it got there. He was coming back from town; he hadn't heard about the auction; him and his wife and three daughters and Mrs. Tull's aunt, all setting in chairs in the wagon bed, and all asleep, including the mules. They waked up when the horse hit the bridge one time, but Tull said the first he knew was when the mules tried to turn the wagon around in the middle of the bridge and he seen that spotted varmint run right twixt the mules and run up the wagon tongue like a squirrel. He said he just had time to hit it across the face with his whip-stock, because about that time the mules turned the wagon around on that ere one-way bridge and that horse clumb across one of the mules and jumped down onto the bridge again and went on, with Vernon standing up in the wagon and kicking at it.

Tull said the mules turned in the harness and clumb back into the wagon too, with Tull trying to beat them out again, with the reins wrapped around his wrist. After that he says all he seen was overturned chairs and womenfolks' legs and white drawers shining in the moonlight, and his mules and that spotted horse going on up the road like a ghost.

The mules jerked Tull outen the wagon and drug him a spell on the bridge before the reins broke. They thought at first that he was dead, and while they was kneeling around him, picking the bridge splinters outen him, here come Eck and that boy, still carrying the rope. They was running and breathing a little hard. "Where'd he go?" Eck says.

V

I went back and got my pants and shirt and shoes on just in time to go and help get Henry Armstid outen the trash in the lot. I be dog if he didn't look like he was dead, with his head hanging back and his teeth showing in the moonlight, and a little rim of white under his eyelids. We could still hear them horses, here and there; hadn't none of them got more than four—five miles away yet, not knowing the country, I reckon. So we could hear them and folks yelling now and then: "Whooey. Head him!"

We toted Henry into Mrs. Littlejohn's. She was in the hall; she hadn't put down the armful of clothes. She taken one look at us, and she laid down the busted scrubbing-board and taken up the lamp and opened a empty door. "Bring him in here," she says.

We toted him in and laid him on the bed. Mrs. Littlejohn set the lamp on the dresser, still carrying the clothes. "I'll declare, you men," she says. Our shadows was way up the wall, tiptoeing too; we could hear ourselves breathing. "Better get his wife," Mrs. Littlejohn says. She went out, carrying the clothes.

"I reckon we had," Quick says. "Go get her, somebody."

"Whyn't you go?" Winterbottom says.

"Let Ernest git her," Durley says. "He lives neighbors with them."

Ernest went to fetch her. I be dog if Henry didn't look like he was dead. Mrs. Littlejohn come back, with a kettle and some towels. She went to work on Henry, and then Mrs. Armstid and Ernest come in. Mrs. Armstid come to the foot of the bed and stood there, with her hands rolled into her apron, watching what Mrs. Littlejohn was doing, I reckon.

"You men get outen the way," Mrs. Littlejohn says. "Git outside," she says. "See if you can't find something else to play with that will kill some more of you."

"Is he dead?" Winterbottom says.

"It ain't your fault if he ain't," Mrs. Littlejohn says. "Go tell Will Varner to come up here. I reckon a man ain't so different from a mule, come long come short. Except maybe a mule's got more sense."

We went to get Uncle Billy. It was a full moon. We could hear them, now and then, four mile away: "Whooey. Head him." The country was full of them, one on ever wooden bridge in the land, running across it like thunder: "Whooey. There he goes. Head him."

We hadn't got far before Henry begun to scream. I reckon Mrs. Littlejohn's water had brung him to; anyway, he wasn't dead. We went on to Uncle Billy's. The house was dark. We called to him, and after a while the window opened and Uncle Billy put his head out, peart as a peckerwood, listening. "Are they still trying to catch them durn rabbits?" he says.

He come down, with his britches on over his night-shirt and his suspenders dangling, carrying his horse-doctoring grip. "Yes, sir," he says, cocking his head like a woodpecker; "they're still a-try-ing."

We could hear Henry before we reached Mrs. Littlejohn's. He was going Ah-Ah-Ah. We stopped in the yard. Uncle Billy went on in. We could hear Henry. We stood in the yard, hearing them on the bridges, this-a-way and that: "Whooey. Whooey."

"Eck Snopes ought to caught hisn," Ernest says.

"Looks like he ought," Winterbottom said.

Henry was going Ah-Ah-Ah steady in the house; then he begun to scream. "Uncle Billy's started," Quick says. We looked into the hall. We could see the light where the door was. Then Mrs. Little-john come out.

"Will needs some help," she says. "You, Ernest. You'll do." Ernest went into the house.

"Hear them?" Quick said. "That one was on Four Mile bridge." We could hear them; it sounded like thunder a long way off; it didn't last long:

"Whooey."

We could hear Henry: "Ah-Ah-Ah-Ah-Ah."

"They are both started now," Winterbottom says. "Ernest too."

That was early in the night. Which was a good thing, because it taken a long night for folks to chase them things right and for Henry to lay there and holler, being as Uncle Billy never had none of this here chloryfoam to set Henry's leg with. So it was consid-erate in Flem to get them started early. And what do you reckon Flem's com-ment was?

That's right. Nothing. Because he wasn't there. Hadn't nobody see him since that Texas man left.

VI

That was Saturday night. I reckon Mrs. Armstid got home about daylight, to see about the chaps. I don't know where they thought her and Henry was. But lucky the oldest one was a gal, about twelve, big enough to take care of the little ones. Which she did for the next two days. Mrs. Armstid would nurse Henry all night and work in the kitchen for hern and Henry's keep, and in the afternoon she would drive home (it was about four miles) to see to the chaps. She would cook up a pot of victuals and leave it on the stove, and the gal would bar the house and keep the little ones quiet. I would hear Mrs. Littlejohn and Mrs. Armstid talking in the kitchen. "How are the chaps making out?" Mrs. Littlejohn says.

"All right," Mrs. Armstid says.

"Don't they git skeered at night?" Mrs. Littlejohn says.

"Ina May bars the door when I leave," Mrs. Armstid says. "She's got the axe in bed with her. I reckon she can make out."

I reckon they did. And I reckon Mrs. Armstid was waiting for Flem to come back to town; hadn't nobody seen him until this morning; to get her money the Texas man said Flem was keeping for her. Sho. I reckon she was.

Anyway, I heard Mrs. Armstid and Mrs. Littlejohn talking in the kitchen this morning while I was eating breakfast. Mrs. Littlejohn had just told Mrs. Armstid that Flem was in town. "You can ask him for that five dollars," Mrs. Littlejohn says.

"You reckon he'll give it to me?" Mrs. Armstid says.

Mrs. Littlejohn was washing dishes, washing them like a man, like they was made out of iron. "No," she says. "But asking him won't do no hurt. It might shame him. I don't reckon it will, but it might."

"If he wouldn't give it back, it ain't no use to ask," Mrs. Armstid says.

"Suit yourself," Mrs. Littlejohn says. "It's your money."

I could hear the dishes.

"Do you reckon he might give it back to me?" Mrs. Armstid says. "That Texas man said he would. He said I could get it from Mr. Snopes later."

"Then go and ask him for it," Mrs. Littlejohn says.

I could hear the dishes.

"He won't give it back to me," Mrs. Armstid says.

"All right," Mrs. Littlejohn says. "Don't ask him for it, then."

I could hear the dishes; Mrs. Armstid was helping. "You don't reckon he would, do you?" she says. Mrs. Littlejohn never said nothing. It sounded like she was throwing the dishes at one another. "Maybe I better go and talk to Henry about it," Mrs. Armstid says.

"I would," Mrs. Littlejohn says. I be dog if it didn't sound like she had two plates in her hands, beating them together. "Then Henry can buy another five-dollar horse with it. Maybe he'll buy one next time that will out and out kill him. If I thought that, I'd give you back the money, myself."

"I reckon I better talk to him first," Mrs. Armstid said. Then it sounded like Mrs. Littlejohn taken up all the dishes and throwed them at the cook-stove, and I come away.

That was this morning. I had been up to Bundren's and back, and I thought that things would have kind of settled down. So after breakfast, I went up to the store. And there was Flem, setting in the store chair and whittling, like he might not have ever moved since he come to clerk for Jody Varner. I. O. was leaning in the door, in his shirt sleeves and with his hair parted too, same as Flem was before he turned the clerking job over to I. O. It's a funny thing about them Snopes: they all looks alike, yet there ain't ere a two of them that claims brothers. They're always just cousins, like Flem and Eck and Flem and I. O. Eck was there too, squatting against the wall, him and that boy, eating cheese and crackers outen a sack; they told me that Eck hadn't been home a-tall. And that Lon Quick hadn't got back to town, even. He followed his horse clean down to Samson's Bridge, with a wagon and a camp outfit. Eck finally caught one of hisn. It run into a blind lane at Freeman's and Eck and the boy taken and tied their rope across the end of the lane, about three foot high. The horse come to the end of the lane and whirled and run back without ever stopping. Eck says it never seen the rope a-tall. He says it looked just like one of these here Christmas pinwheels. "Didn't it try to run again?" I says.

"No," Eck says, eating a bite of cheese offen his knife blade. "Just kicked some."

"Kicked some?" I says.

"It broke its neck," Eck says.

Well, they was squatting there, about six of them, talking, talking at Flem; never nobody knowed yet if Flem had ere a interest in them horses or not. So finally I come right out and asked him. "Flem's done skun all of us so much," I says, "that we're proud of him. Come on, Flem," I says, "how much did you and that Texas man make offen them horses? You can tell us. Ain't nobody here but Eck that bought one of them; the others ain't got back to town yet, and Eck's your own cousin; he'll be proud to hear, too. How much did you-all make?"

They was all whittling, not looking at Flem, making like they was studying. But you could a heard a pin drop. And I. O. He had been rubbing his back up and down on the door, but he stopped now, watching Flem like a pointing dog. Flem finished cutting the sliver offen his stick. He spit across the porch, into the road. "'Twarn't none of my horses," he says.

I. O. cackled, like a hen, slapping his legs with both hands. "You boys might just as well quit trying to get ahead of Flem," he said.

Well, about that time I see Mrs. Armstid come outen Mrs. Littlejohn's gate, coming up the road. I never said nothing. I says, "Well, if a man can't take care of himself in a trade, he can't blame the man that trims him."

Flem never said nothing, trimming at the stick. He hadn't seen Mrs. Armstid. "Yes, sir," I says. "A fellow like Henry Armstid ain't got nobody but hisself to blame."

"Course he ain't," I. O. says. He ain't seen her, neither. "Henry Armstid's a born fool. Always is been. If Flem hadn't a got his money, somebody else would."

We looked at Flem. He never moved. Mrs. Armstid come on up the road.

"That's right," I says. "But, come to think of it, Henry never bought no horse." We looked at Flem; you could a heard a match drop. "That Texas man told her to get that five dollars back from Flem next day. I reckon Flem's done already taken that money to Mrs. Littlejohn's and give it to Mrs. Armstid."

We watched Flem. I. O. quit rubbing his back against the door again. After a while Flem raised his head and spit across the porch, into the dust. I. O. cackled, just like a hen. "Ain't he a beating fellow, now?" I. O. says.

Mrs. Armstid was getting closer, so I kept on talking, watching to see if Flem would look up and see her. But he never looked up. I went on talking about Tull, about how he was going to sue Flem, and Flem setting there, whittling his stick, not saying nothing else after he said they wasn't none of his horses.

Then I. O. happened to look around. He seen Mrs. Armstid. "Psssst!" he says. Flem looked up. "Here she comes!" I. O says. "Go out the back. I'll tell her you done went in to town to-day."

But Flem never moved. He just set there, whittling, and we watched Mrs. Armstid come up onto the porch, in that ere faded sunbonnet and wrapper and them tennis shoes that made a kind of hissing noise on the porch. She come onto the porch and stopped, her hands rolled into her dress in front, not looking at nothing.

"He said Saturday," she says, "that he wouldn't sell Henry no horse. He said I could get the money from you."

Flem looked up. The knife never stopped. It went on trimming off a sliver same as if he was watching it. "He taken that money off with him when he left," Flem says.

Mrs. Armstid never looked at nothing. We never looked at her, neither, except that boy of Eck's. He had a half-et cracker in his hand, watching her, chewing.

"He said Henry hadn't bought no horse," Mrs. Armstid says. "He said for me to get the money from you today."

"I reckon he forgot about it," Flem said. "He taken that money off with him Saturday." He whittled again. I. O. kept on rubbing his back, slow. He licked his lips. After a while the woman looked up the road, where it went on up the hill, toward the graveyard. She looked up that way for a while, with that boy of Eck's watching her and I. O. rubbing his back slow against the door. Then she turned back toward the steps.

"I reckon it's time to get dinner started," she says.

"How's Henry this morning, Mrs. Armstid?" Winterbottom says.

She looked at Winterbottom; she almost stopped. "He's resting, I thank you kindly," she says.

Flem got up, outen the chair, putting his knife away. He spit across the porch. "Wait a minute, Mrs. Armstid," he says. She stopped again. She didn't look at him. Flem went on into the store, with I. O. done quit rubbing his back now, with his head craned after Flem, and Mrs. Armstid standing there with her hands rolled into her dress, not looking at nothing. A wagon come up the road and passed; it was Freeman, on the way to town. Then Flem come out again, with I. O. still watching him. Flem had one of these little striped sacks of Jody Varner's candy; I bet he still owns Jody that nickel, too. He put the sack into Mrs. Armstid's hand, like he would have put it into a hollow stump. He spit again across the porch. "A little sweetening for the chaps," he says.

"You're right kind," Mrs. Armstid says. She held the sack of candy in her hand, not looking at nothing. Eck's boy was watching the sack, the half-et cracker in his hand; he wasn't chewing now. He watched Mrs. Armstid roll the sack into her apron. "I reckon I better get on back and help with dinner," she says. She turned and went back across the porch. Flem set down in the chair again and opened his knife. He spit across the porch again, past Mrs. Armstid where she hadn't went down the steps yet. Then she went on, in that ere sunbonnet and wrapper all the same color, back down the road toward Mrs. Littlejohn's. You couldn't see her dress move, like a natural woman walking. She looked like a old snag still standing up and moving along on a high water. We watched her turn in at Mrs. Littlejohn's and go outen sight. Flem was whittling. I. O. begun to rub his back on the door. Then he begun to cackle, just like a durn hen.

"You boys might just as well quit trying," I. O. says. "You can't git ahead of Flem. You can't touch him. Ain't he a sight, now?"

I be dog if he ain't. If I had brung a herd of wild cattymounts into town and sold them to my neighbors and kinfolks, they would have lynched me. Yes, sir.

1931, 1940

A Justice [2]

I

Until Grandfather died, we would go out to the farm every Saturday afternoon. We would leave home right after dinner in the surrey, I in front with Roskus, and Grandfather and Caddy and Jason in the back. Grandfather and Roskus would talk, with the

---

2. Quentin Compson, the narrator of "A Justice" and "That Evening Sun," is also a major character in *The Sound and the Fury* (1929) and in *Absalom, Absalom!* (1936). He is supposed to have been born about 1890 and died by suicide in 1910. "A Justice" was published in *These 13*, 1931. The present text is from *Collected Stories*.

horses going fast, because it was the best team in the county. They would carry the surrey fast along the levels and up some of the hills even. But this was in north Mississippi, and on some of the hills Roskus and I could smell Grandfather's cigar.

The farm was four miles away. There was a long, low house in the grove, not painted but kept whole and sound by a clever carpenter from the quarters named Sam Fathers,[3] and behind it the barns and smokehouses, and further still, the quarters themselves, also kept whole and sound by Sam Fathers. He did nothing else, and they said he was almost a hundred years old. He lived with the Negroes and they—the white people; the Negroes called him a blue-gum—called him a Negro. But he wasn't a Negro. That's what I'm going to tell about.

When we got there, Mr. Stokes, the manager, would send a Negro boy with Caddy and Jason to the creek to fish, because Caddy was a girl and Jason was too little, but I wouldn't go with them. I would go to Sam Fathers' shop, where he would be making breast-yokes or wagon wheels, and I would always bring him some tobacco. Then he would stop working and he would fill his pipe—he made them himself, out of creek clay with a reed stem—and he would tell me about the old days. He talked like a nigger—that is, he said his words like niggers do, but he didn't say the same words—and his hair was nigger hair. But his skin wasn't quite the color of a light nigger and his nose and his mouth and chin were not nigger nose and mouth and chin. And his shape was not like the shape of a nigger when he gets old. He was straight in the back, not tall, a little broad, and his face was still all the time, like he might be somewhere else all the while he was working or when people, even white people, talked to him, or while he talked to me. It was just the same all the time, like he might be away up on a roof by himself, driving nails. Sometimes he would quit work with something half-finished on the bench, and sit down and smoke. And he wouldn't jump up and go back to work when Mr. Stokes or even Grandfather came along.

So I would give him the tobacco and he would stop work and sit down and fill his pipe and talk to me.

"These niggers," he said. "They call me Uncle Blue-Gum. And the white folks, they call me Sam Fathers."

"Isn't that your name?" I said.

---

3. Part Indian and part Negro, Sam Fathers earned his name in the manner narrated in this story, the main events of which take place *ca.* 1810–1820. In "The Bear" Sam Fathers dies in 1883. When Malcolm Cowley pointed out some of the inconsistencies he discovered while planning *The Portable Faulkner* (1946), Faulkner replied, "I realised some time ago you would get into this inconsistency and pitied you. I suggest you make dates, when you state them, as vague as possible. Say, in these Indian pieces, when you state a date, call it '18—' or 'ante 1840.'"

"No. Not in the old days. I remember. I remember how I never saw but one white man until I was a boy big as you are; a whisky trader that came every summer to the Plantation. It was the Man himself that named me. He didn't name me Sam Fathers though."

"The Man?" I said.

"He owned the Plantation, the Negroes, my mammy too. He owned all the land that I knew of until I was grown. He was a Choctaw chief. He sold my mammy to your great-grandpappy. He said I didn't have to go unless I wanted to, because I was a warrior too then. He was the one who named me Had-Two-Fathers."

"Had-Two-Fathers?" I said. "That's not a name. That's not anything."

"It was my name once. Listen."

II

This is how Herman Basket told it when I was big enough to hear talk. He said that when Doom came back from New Orleans, he brought this woman with him. He brought six black people, though Herman Basket said they already had more black people in the Plantation than they could find use for. Sometimes they would run the black men with dogs, like you would a fox or a cat or a coon. And then Doom brought six more when he came home from New Orleans. He said he won them on the steamboat, and so he had to take them. He got off the steamboat with the six black people, Herman Basket said, and a big box in which something was alive, and the gold box of New Orleans salt about the size of a gold watch. And Herman Basket told how Doom took a puppy out out of the box in which something was alive, and how he made a bullet of bread and a pinch of the salt in the gold box, and put the bullet into the puppy and the puppy died.

That was the kind of a man that Doom was, Herman Basket said. He told how, when Doom got off the steamboat that night, he wore a coat with gold all over it, and he had three gold watches, but Herman Basket said that even after seven years, Doom's eyes had not changed. He said that Doom's eyes were just the same as before he went away, before his name was Doom, and he and Herman Basket and my pappy were sleeping on the same pallet and talking at night, as boys will.

Doom's name was Ikkemotubbe then, and he was not born to be the Man, because Doom's mother's brother was the Man, and the Man had a son of his own, as well as a brother. But even then, and Doom no bigger than you are, Herman Basket said that sometimes the Man would look at Doom and he would say: "O Sister's Son, your eye is a bad eye, like the eye of a bad horse."

So the Man was not sorry when Doom got to be a young man

and said that he would go to New Orleans, Herman Basket said. The Man was getting old then. He used to like to play mumble-peg and to pitch horseshoes both, but now he just liked mumble-peg. So he was not sorry when Doom went away, though he didn't forget about Doom. Herman Basket said that each summer when the whisky-trader came, the Man would ask him about Doom. "He calls himself David Callicoat now," the Man would say. "But his name is Ikkemotubbe. You haven't heard maybe of a David Callicoat getting drowned in the Big River, or killed in the white man's fight at New Orleans?"

But Herman Basket said they didn't hear from Doom at all until he had been gone seven years. Then one day Herman Basket and my pappy got a written stick from Doom to meet him at the Big River. Because the steamboat didn't come up our river any more then. The steamboat was still in our river, but it didn't go anywhere any more. Herman Basket told how one day during the high water, about three years after Doom went away, the steamboat came and crawled up on a sand-bar and died.

That was how Doom got his second name, the one before Doom. Herman Basket told how four times a year the steamboat would come up our river, and how the People would go to the river and camp and wait to see the steamboat pass, and he said that the white man who told the steamboat where to swim was named David Callicoat. So when Doom told Herman Basket and pappy that he was going to New Orleans, he said, "And I'll tell you something else. From now on, my name is not Ikkemotubbe. It's David Callicoat. And some day I'm going to own a steamboat, too." That was the kind of man that Doom was, Herman Basket said.

So after seven years he sent them the written stick and Herman Basket and pappy took the wagon and went to meet Doom at the Big River, and Doom got off the steamboat with the six black people. "I won them on the steamboat," Doom said. "You and Crawford (my pappy's name was Crawfish-ford, but usually it was Craw-ford) can divide them."

"I don't want them," Herman Basket said that pappy said.

"Then Herman can have them all," Doom said.

"I don't want them either," Herman Basket said.

"All right," Doom said. Then Herman Basket said he asked Doom if his name was still David Callicoat, but instead of answering, Doom told one of the black people something in the white man's talk, and the black man lit a pine knot. Then Herman Basket said they were watching Doom take the puppy from the box and make the bullet of bread and the New Orleans salt which Doom had in the little gold box, when he said that pappy said:

"I believe you said that Herman and I were to divide these black people."

Then Herman Basket said he saw that one of the black people was a woman.

"You and Herman don't want them," Doom said.

"I wasn't thinking when I said that," pappy said. "I will take the lot with the woman in it. Herman can have the other three."

"I don't want them," Herman Basket said.

"You can have four, then," pappy said. "I will take the woman and one other."

"I don't want them," Herman Basket said.

"I will take only the woman," pappy said. "You can have the other five."

"I don't want them," Herman Basket said.

"You don't want them, either," Doom said to pappy. "You said so yourself."

Then Herman Basket said that the puppy was dead. "You didn't tell us your new name," he said to Doom.

"My name is Doom now," Doom said. "It was given me by a French chief in New Orleans. In French talking, Doo-um; [4] in our talking, Doom."

"What does it mean?" Herman Basket said.

He said how Doom looked at him for a while. "It means the Man," Doom said.

Herman Basket told how they thought about that. He said they stood there in the dark, with the other puppies in the box, the ones that Doom hadn't used, whimpering and scuffing, and the light of the pine knot shining on the eyeballs of the black people and on Doom's gold coat and on the puppy that had died.

"You cannot be the Man," Herman Basket said. "You are only on the sister's side. And the Man has a brother and a son."

"That's right," Doom said. "But if I were the Man, I would give Craw-ford those black people. I would give Herman something, too. For every black man I gave Craw-ford, I would give Herman a horse, if I were the Man."

"Craw-ford only wants this woman," Herman Basket said.

"I would give Herman six horses, anyway," Doom said. "But maybe the Man has already given Herman a horse."

"No," Herman Basket said. "My ghost is still walking."

It took them three days to reach the Plantation. They camped on the road at night. Herman Basket said that they did not talk.

They reached the Plantation on the third day. He said that the

---

4. Originally Faulkner conceived the name as "du homme." It was emended to " 'l'Homme' (and sometimes 'de l'Homme')" in the Appendix to *The Sound of the Fury*, first published in *The Portable Faulkner*, 1946.

Man was not very glad to see Doom, even though Doom brought a present of candy for the Man's son. Doom had something for all his kinsfolk, even for the Man's brother. The Man's brother lived by himself in a cabin by the creek. His name was Sometimes-Wakeup. Sometimes the People took him food. The rest of the time they didn't see him. Herman Basket told how he and pappy went with Doom to visit Sometimes-Wakeup in his cabin. It was at night, and Doom told Herman Basket to close the door. Then Doom took the puppy from pappy and set it on the floor and made a bullet of bread and the New Orleans salt for Sometimes-Wakeup to see how it worked. When they left, Herman Basket said how Sometimes-Wakeup burned a stick and covered his head with the blanket.

That was the first night that Doom was at home. On the next day Herman Basket told how the Man began to act strange at his food, and died before the doctor could get there and burn sticks. When the Willow-Bearer went to fetch the Man's son to be the Man, they found that he had acted strange and then died too.

"Now Sometimes-Wakeup will have to be the Man," pappy said.

So the Willow-Bearer went to fetch Sometimes-Wakeup to come and be the Man. The Willow-Bearer came back soon. "Sometimes-Wakeup does not want to be the Man," the Willow-Bearer said. "He is sitting in his cabin with his head in his blanket."

"Then Ikkemotubbe will have to be the Man," pappy said.

So Doom was the Man. But Herman Basket said that pappy's ghost would not be easy. Herman Basket said he told pappy to give Doom a little time. "I am still walking," Herman Basket said.

"But this is a serious matter with me," pappy said.

He said that at last pappy went to Doom, before the Man and his son had entered the earth, before the eating and the horse-racing were over. "What woman?" Doom said.

"You said that when you were the Man," pappy said. Herman Basket said that Doom looked at pappy but that pappy was not looking at Doom.

"I think you don't trust me," Doom said. Herman Basket said how pappy did not look at Doom. "I think you still believe that that puppy was sick," Doom said. "Think about it."

Herman Basket said that pappy thought.

"What do you think now?" Doom said.

But Herman Basket said that pappy still did not look at Doom. "I think it was a well dog," pappy said.

III

At last the eating and the horse-racing were over and the Man and his son had entered the earth. Then Doom said, "Tomorrow we will go and fetch the steamboat." Herman Basket told how Doom had been talking about the steamboat ever since he became the Man, and about how the House was not big enough. So that evening Doom said, "Tomorrow we will go and fetch the steamboat that died in the river."

Herman Basket said how the steamboat was twelve miles away, and that it could not even swim in the water. So the next morning there was no one in the Plantation except Doom and the black people. He told how it took Doom all that day to find the People. Doom used the dogs, and he found some of the People in hollow logs in the creek bottom. That night he made all the men sleep in the House. He kept the dogs in the House, too.

Herman Basket told how he heard Doom and pappy talking in the dark. "I don't think you trust me," Doom said.

"I trust you," pappy said.

"That is what I would advise," Doom said.

"I wish you could advise that to my ghost," pappy said.

The next morning they went to the steamboat. The women and the black people walked. The men rode in the wagons, with Doom following behind with the dogs.

The steamboat was lying on its side on the sand-bar. When they came to it, there were three white men on it. "Now we can go back home," pappy said.

But Doom talked to the white men. "Does this steamboat belong to you?" Doom said.

"It does not belong to you," the white men said. And though they had guns, Herman Basket said they did not look like men who would own a boat.

"Shall we kill them?" he said to Doom. But he said that Doom was still talking to the men on the steamboat.

"What will you take for it?" Doom said.

"What will you give for it?" the white men said.

"It is dead," Doom said. "It's not worth much."

"Will you give ten black people?" the white men said.

"All right," Doom said. "Let the black people who came with me from the Big River come forward." They came forward, the five men and the woman. "Let four more black people come forward." Four more came forward. "You are now to eat of the corn of those white men yonder," Doom said. "May it nourish you." The white men went away, the ten black people following them. "Now," Doom said, "let us make the steamboat get up and walk."

Herman Basket said that he and pappy did not go into the river with the others, because pappy said to go aside and talk. They went aside. Pappy talked, but Herman Basket said that he said he did not think it was right to kill white men, but pappy said how they could fill the white men with rocks and sink them in the river and nobody would find them. So Herman Basket said they overtook the three white men and the ten black people, then they turned back toward the boat. Just before they came to the steamboat, pappy said to the black men: "Go on to the Man. Go and help make the steamboat get up and walk. I will take this woman on home."

"This woman is my wife," one of the black men said. "I want her to stay with me."

"Do you want to be arranged in the river with rocks in your inside too?" pappy said to the black man.

"Do you want to be arranged in the river yourself?" the black man said to pappy. "There are two of you, and nine of us."

Herman Basket said that pappy thought. Then pappy said, "Let us go to the steamboat and help the Man."

They went to the steamboat. But Herman Basket said that Doom did not notice the ten black people until it was time to return to the Plantation. Herman Basket told how Doom looked at the black people, then looked at pappy. "It seems that the white men did not want these black people," Doom said.

"So it seems," pappy said.

"The white men went away, did they?" Doom said.

"So it seems," pappy said.

Herman Basket told how every night Doom would make all the men sleep in the House, with the dogs in the House too, and how each morning they would return to the steamboat in the wagons. The wagons would not hold everybody, so after the second day the women stayed at home. But it was three days before Doom noticed that pappy was staying at home too. Herman Basket said that the woman's husband may have told Doom. "Craw-ford hurt his back lifting the steamboat," Herman Basket said he told Doom. "He said he would stay at the Plantation and sit with his feet in the Hot Spring so that the sickness in his back could return to the earth."

"That is a good idea," Doom said. "He has been doing this for three days, has he? Then the sickness should be down in his legs by now."

When they returned to the Plantation that night, Doom sent for pappy. He asked pappy if the sickness had moved. Pappy said how the sickness moved very slow. "You must sit in the Spring more," Doom said.

"That is what I think," pappy said.

"Suppose you sit in the Spring at night too," Doom said.

"The night air will make it worse," pappy said.

"Not with a fire there," Doom said. "I will send one of the black people with you to keep the fire burning."

"Which one of the black people?" pappy said.

"The husband of the woman which I won on the steamboat," Doom said.

"I think my back is better," pappy said.

"Let us try it," Doom said.

"I know my back is better," pappy said.

"Let us try it, anyway," Doom said. Just before dark Doom sent four of the People to fix pappy and the black man at the Spring. Herman Basket said the People returned quickly. He said that as they entered the House, pappy entered also.

"The sickness began to move suddenly," pappy said. "It has reached my feet since noon today."

"Do you think it will be gone by morning?" Doom said.

"I think so," pappy said.

"Perhaps you had better sit in the Spring tonight and make sure," Doom said.

"I know it will be gone by morning," pappy said.

IV

When it got to be summer, Herman Basket said that the steamboat was out of the river bottom. It had taken them five months to get it out of the bottom, because they had to cut down the trees to make a path for it. But now he said the steamboat could walk faster on the logs. He told how pappy helped. Pappy had a certain place on one of the ropes near the steamboat that nobody was allowed to take, Herman Basket said. It was just under the front porch of the steamboat where Doom sat in his chair, with a boy with a branch to shade him and another boy with a branch to drive away the flying beasts. The dogs rode on the boat too.

In the summer, while the steamboat was still walking, Herman Basket told how the husband of the woman came to Doom again. "I have done what I could for you," Doom said. "Why don't you go to Craw-ford and adjust this matter yourself?"

The black man said that he had done that. He said that pappy said to adjust it by a cock-fight, pappy's cock against the black man's, the winner to have the woman, the one who refused to fight to lose by default. The black man said he told pappy he did not have a cock, and that pappy said that in that case the black man lost by default and that the woman belonged to pappy. "And what am I to do?" the black man said.

Doom thought. Then Herman Basket said that Doom called to him and asked him which was pappy's best cock and Herman Basket told Doom that pappy had only one. "That black one?" Doom said. Herman Basket said he told Doom that was the one. "Ah," Doom said. Herman Basket told how Doom sat in his chair on the porch of the steamboat while it walked, looking down at the People and the black men pulling the ropes, making the steamboat walk. "Go and tell Craw-ford you have a cock," Doom said to the black man. "Just tell him you will have a cock in the pit. Let it be tomorrow morning. We will let the steamboat sit down and rest." The black man went away. Then Herman Basket said that Doom was looking at him, and that he did not look at Doom. Because he said there was but one better cock in the Plantation than pappy's, and that one belonged to Doom. "I think that that puppy was not sick," Doom said. "What do you think?"

Herman Basket said that he did not look at Doom. "That is what I think," he said.

"That is what I would advise," Doom said.

Herman Basket told how the next day the steamboat sat and rested. The pit was in the stable. The People and the black people were there. Pappy had his cock in the pit. Then the black man put his cock into the pit. Herman Basket said that pappy looked at the black man's cock.

"This cock belongs to Ikkemotubbe," pappy said.

"It is his," the People told pappy. "Ikkemotubbe gave it to him with all to witness."

Herman Basket said that pappy had already picked up his cock. "This is not right," pappy said. "We ought not to let him risk his wife on a cock-fight."

"Then you withdraw?" the black man said.

"Let me think," pappy said. He thought. The People watched. The black man reminded pappy of what he had said about defaulting. Pappy said he did not mean to say that and that he withdrew it. The People told him that he could only withdraw by forfeiting the match. Herman Basket said that pappy thought again. The People watched. "All right," pappy said. "But I am being taken advantage of."

The cocks fought. Pappy's cock fell. Pappy took it up quickly. Herman Basket said it was like pappy had been waiting for his cock to fall so he could pick it quickly up. "Wait," he said. He looked at the People. "Now they have fought. Isn't that true?" The People said that it was true. "So that settles what I said about forfeiting."

Herman Basket said that pappy began to get out of the pit.

"Aren't you going to fight?" the black man said.

"I don't think this will settle anything," pappy said. "Do you?"

Herman Basket told how the black man looked at pappy. Then he quit looking at pappy. He was squatting. Herman Basket said the People looked at the black man looking at the earth between his feet. They watched him take up a clod of dirt, and then they watched the dust come out between the black man's fingers. "Do you think that this will settle anything?" pappy said.

"No," the black man said. Herman Basket said that the People could not hear him very good. But he said that pappy could hear him.

"Neither do I," pappy said. "It would not be right to risk your wife on a cock-fight."

Herman Basket told how the black man looked up, with the dry dust about the fingers of his hand. He said the black man's eyes looked red in the dark pit, like the eyes of a fox. "Will you let the cocks fight again?" the black man said.

"Do you agree that it doesn't settle anything?" pappy said.

"Yes," the black man said.

Pappy put his cock back into the ring. Herman Basket said that pappy's cock was dead before it had time to act strange, even. The black man's cock stood upon it and started to crow, but the black man struck the live cock away and he jumped up and down on the dead cock until it did not look like a cock at all, Herman Basket said.

Then it was fall, and Herman Basket told how the steamboat came to the Plantation and stopped beside the House and died again. He said that for two months they had been in sight of the Plantation, making the steamboat walk on the logs, but now the steamboat was beside the House and the House was big enough to please Doom. He gave an eating. It lasted a week. When it was over, Herman Basket told how the black man came to Doom a third time. Herman Basket said that the black man's eyes were red again, like those of a fox, and that they could hear his breathing in the room. "Come to my cabin," he said to Doom. "I have something to show you."

"I thought it was about that time," Doom said. He looked about the room, but Herman Basket told Doom that pappy had just stepped out. "Tell him to come also," Doom said. When they came to the black man's cabin, Doom sent two of the People to fetch pappy. Then they entered the cabin. What the black man wanted to show Doom was a new man.

"Look," the black man said. "You are the Man. You are to see justice done."

"What is wrong with this man?" Doom said.

"Look at the color of him," the black man said. He began to look around the cabin. Herman Basket said that his eyes went red and then brown and then red, like those of a fox. He said they could hear the black man's breathing. "Do I get justice?" the black man said. "You are the Man."

"You should be proud of a fine yellow man like this," Doom said. He looked at the new man. "I don't see that justice can darken him any," Doom said. He looked about the cabin also. "Come forward, Craw-ford," he said. "This is a man, not a copper snake; he will not harm you." But Herman Basket said that pappy would not come forward. He said the black man's eyes went red and then brown and then red when he breathed. "Yao," Doom said, "this is not right. Any man is entitled to have his melon patch protected from these wild bucks of the woods. But first let us name this man." Doom thought. Herman Basket said the black man's eyes went quieter now, and his breath went quieter too. "We will call him Had-Two-Fathers," Doom said.

V

Sam Fathers lit his pipe again. He did it deliberately, rising and lifting between thumb and forefinger from his forge a coal of fire. Then he came back and sat down. It was getting late. Caddy and Jason had come back from the creek, and I could see Grandfather and Mr. Stokes talking beside the carriage, and at that moment, as though he had felt my gaze, Grandfather turned and called my name.

"What did your pappy do then?" I said.

"He and Herman Basket built the fence," Sam Fathers said. "Herman Basket told how Doom made them set two posts into the ground, with a sapling across the top of them. The nigger and pappy were there. Doom had not told them about the fence then. Herman Basket said it was just like when he and pappy and Doom were boys, sleeping on the same pallet, and Doom would wake them at night and make them get up and go hunting with him, or when he would make them stand up with him and fight with their fists, just for fun, until Herman Basket and pappy would hide from Doom.

"They fixed the sapling across the two posts and Doom said to the nigger: 'This is a fence. Can you climb it?'

"Herman Basket said the nigger put his hand on the sapling and sailed over it like a bird.

"Then Doom said to pappy: 'Climb this fence.'

" 'This fence is too high to climb,' pappy said.

" 'Climb this fence, and I will give you the woman,' Doom said.

"Herman Basket said pappy looked at the fence a while. 'Let me go under this fence,' he said.

"No,' Doom said.

"Herman Basket told me how pappy began to sit down on the ground. 'It's not that I don't trust you,' pappy said.

" 'We will build the fence this high,' Doom said.

" 'What fence?' Herman Basket said.

" 'The fence around the cabin of this black man,' Doom said.

" 'I can't build a fence I couldn't climb,' pappy said.

" 'Herman will help you,' Doom said.

"Herman Basket said it was just like when Doom used to wake them and make them go hunting. He said the dogs found him and pappy about noon the next day, and that they began the fence that afternoon. He told me how they had to cut the saplings in the creek bottom and drag them in by hand, because Doom would not let them use the wagon. So sometimes one post would take them three or four days. 'Never mind,' Doom said. 'You have plenty of time. And the exercise will make Craw-ford sleep at night.'

"He told me how they worked on the fence all that winter and all the next summer, until after the whisky trader had come and gone. Then it was finished. He said that on the day they set the last post, the nigger came out of the cabin and put his hand on the top of a post (it was a palisade fence, the posts set upright in the ground) and flew out like a bird. 'This is a good fence,' the nigger said. 'Wait,' he said. 'I have something to show you.' Herman Basket said he flew back over the fence again and went into the cabin and came back. Herman Basket said that he was carrying a new man and that he held the new man up so they could see it above the fence. 'What do you think about this for color?' he said."

Grandfather called me again. This time I got up. The sun was already down beyond the peach orchard. I was just twelve then, and to me the story did not seem to have got anywhere, to have had point or end. Yet I obeyed Grandfather's voice, not that I was tired of Sam Fathers' talking, but with that immediacy of children with which they flee temporarily something which they do not quite understand; that, and the instinctive promptness with which we all obeyed Grandfather, not from concern of impatience or reprimand, but because we all believed that he did fine things, that his waking life passed from one fine (if faintly grandiose) picture to another.

They were in the surrey, waiting for me. I got in; the horses moved at once, impatient too for the stable. Caddy had one fish, about the size of a chip, and she was wet to the waist. We drove on, the team already trotting. When we passed Mr. Stokes' kitchen we could smell ham cooking. The smell followed us on to the gate. When we turned onto the road home it was almost sundown. Then we couldn't smell the cooking ham any more. "What were you and Sam talking about?" Grandfather said.

We went on, in that strange, faintly sinister suspension of twilight in which I believed that I could still see Sam Fathers back there, sitting on his wooden block, definite, immobile, and complete, like something looked upon after a long time in a preservative bath in a museum. That was it. I was just twelve then, and I would have to wait until I had passed on and through and beyond the suspension of twilight. Then I knew that I would know. But then Sam Fathers would be dead.

"Nothing, sir," I said. "We were just talking."

1931

That Evening Sun [5]

Monday is no different from any other weekday in Jefferson now. The streets are paved now, and the telephone and electric companies are cutting down more and more of the shade trees—the water oaks, the maples and locusts and elms—to make room for iron poles bearing clusters of bloated and ghostly and bloodless grapes, and we have a city laundry which makes the rounds on Monday morning, gathering the bundles of clothes into bright-colored, specially-made motor cars: the soiled wearing of a whole week now flees apparitionlike behind alert and irritable electric horns, with a long diminishing noise of rubber and asphalt like tearing silk, and even the Negro women who still take in white people's washing after the old custom, fetch and deliver it in automobiles.

But fifteen years ago, on Monday morning the quiet, dusty, shady streets would be full of Negro women with, balanced on their steady, turbaned heads, bundles of clothes tied up in sheets, almost as large as cotton bales, carried so without touch of hand between the kitchen door of the white house and the blackened washpot beside a cabin door in Negro Hollow.

Nancy would set her bundle on the top of her head, then upon the bundle in turn she would set the black straw sailor hat which she wore winter and summer. She was tall, with a high, sad face sunken a little where her teeth were missing. Sometimes we would go a part of the way down the lane and across the pasture with her, to watch the balanced bundle and the hat that never bobbed nor wavered, even when she walked down into the ditch and up the other side and stooped through the fence. She would go down on her hands and knees and crawl through the gap, her head rigid, up-tilted, the bundle steady as a rock or a balloon, and rise to her feet again and go on.

Sometimes the husbands of the washing women would fetch and deliver the clothes, but Jesus never did that for Nancy, even before father told him to stay away from our house, even when Dilsey was sick and Nancy would come to cook for us.

5. First published in *The American Mercury* for March, 1931, "That Evening Sun" was collected in *These 13*, 1931. The present text is from *Collected Stories*.

And then about half the time we'd have to go down the lane to Nancy's cabin and tell her to come on and cook breakfast. We would stop at the ditch, because father told us to not have anything to do with Jesus—he was a short black man, with a razor scar down his face—and we would throw rocks at Nancy's house until she came to the door, leaning her head around it without any clothes on.

"What yawl mean, chunking my house?" Nancy said. "What you little devils mean?"

"Father says for you to come on and get breakfast," Caddy said. "Father says it's over a half an hour now, and you've got to come this minute."

"I aint studying no breakfast," Nancy said. "I going to get my sleep out."

"I bet you're drunk," Jason said. "Father says you're drunk. Are you drunk, Nancy?"

"Who says I is?" Nancy said. "I got to get my sleep out. I aint studying no breakfast."

So after a while we quit chunking the cabin and went back home. When she finally came, it was too late for me to go to school. So we thought it was whisky until that day they arrested her again and they were taking her to jail and they passed Mr Stovall. He was the cashier in the bank and a deacon in the Baptist church, and Nancy began to say:

"When you going to pay me, white man? When you going to pay me, white man? It's been three times now since you paid me a cent—" Mr Stovall knocked her down, but she kept on saying, "When you going to pay me, white man? It's been three times now since—" until Mr Stovall kicked her in the mouth with his heel and the marshal caught Mr Stovall back, and Nancy lying in the street, laughing. She turned her head and spat out some blood and teeth and said, "It's been three times now since he paid me a cent."

That was how she lost her teeth, and all that day they told about Nancy and Mr Stovall, and all that night the ones that passed the jail could hear Nancy singing and yelling. They could see her hands holding to the window bars, and a lot of them stopped along the fence, listening to her and to the jailer trying to make her stop. She didn't shut up until almost daylight, when the jailer began to hear a bumping and scraping upstairs and he went up there and found Nancy hanging from the window bar. He said that it was cocaine and not whisky, because no nigger would try to commit suicide unless he was full of cocaine, because a nigger full of cocaine wasn't a nigger any longer.

The jailer cut her down and revived her; then he beat her,

whipped her. She had hung herself with her dress. She had fixed it all right, but when they arrested her she didn't have on anything except a dress and so she didn't have anything to tie her hands with and she couldn't make her hands let go of the window ledge. So the jailer heard the noise and ran up there and found Nancy hanging from the window, stark naked, her belly already swelling out a little, like a little balloon.

When Dilsey was sick in her cabin and Nancy was cooking for us, we could see her apron swelling out; that was before father told Jesus to stay away from the house. Jesus was in the kitchen, sitting behind the stove, with his razor scar on his black face like a piece of dirty string. He said it was a watermelon that Nancy had under her dress.

"It never come off of your vine, though," Nancy said.

"Off of what vine?" Caddy said.

"I can cut down the vine it did come off of," Jesus said.

"What makes you want to talk like that before these chillen?" Nancy said. "Whyn't you go on to work? You done et. You want Mr. Jason to catch you hanging around his kitchen, talking that way before these chillen?"

"Talking what way?" Caddy said. "What vine?"

"I cant hang around white man's kitchen," Jesus said. "But white man can hang around mine. White man can come in my house, but I cant stop him. When white man want to come in my house, I aint got no house. I cant stop him, but he cant kick me outen it. He cant do that."

Dilsey was still sick in her cabin. Father told Jesus to stay off our place. Dilsey was still sick. It was a long time. We were in the library after supper.

"Isn't Nancy through in the kitchen yet?" mother said. "It seems to me that she has had plenty of time to have finished the dishes."

"Let Quentin go and see," father said. "Go and see if Nancy is through, Quentin. Tell her she can go on home."

I went to the kitchen. Nancy was through. The dishes were put away and the fire was out. Nancy was sitting in a chair, close to the cold stove. She looked at me.

"Mother wants to know if you are through," I said.

"Yes," Nancy said. She looked at me. "I done finished." She looked at me.

"What is it?" I said. "What is it?"

"I aint nothing but a nigger," Nancy said. "It aint none of my fault."

She looked at me, sitting in the chair before the cold stove, the sailor hat on her head. I went through to the library. It was the cold stove and all, when you think of a kitchen being warm and busy and cheerful. And with a cold stove and the dishes all put away, and nobody wanting to eat at that hour.

"Is she through?" mother said.

"Yessum," I said.

"What is she doing?" mother said.

"She's not doing anything. She's through."

"I'll go and see," father said.

"Maybe she's waiting for Jesus to come and take her home," Caddy said.

"Jesus is gone," I said. Nancy told us how one morning she woke up and Jesus was gone.

"He quit me," Nancy said. "Done gone to Memphis, I reckon. Dodging them city *po*-lice for a while, I reckon."

"And a good riddance," father said. "I hope he stays there."

"Nancy's scaired of the dark," Jason said.

"So are you," Caddy said.

"I'm not," Jason said.

"Scairy cat," Caddy said.

"I'm not," Jason said.

"You, Candace!" mother said. Father came back.

"I am going to walk down the lane with Nancy," he said. "She says that Jesus is back."

"Has she seen him?" mother said.

"No. Some Negro sent her word that he was back in town. I wont be long."

"You'll leave me alone, to take Nancy home?" mother said. "Is her safety more precious to you than mine?"

"I wont be long," father said.

"You'll leave these children unprotected, with that Negro about?"

"I'm going too," Caddy said. "Let me go, Father."

"What would he do with them, if he were unfortunate enough to have them?" father said.

"I want to go, too," Jason said.

"Jason!" mother said. She was speaking to father. You could tell that by the way she said the name. Like she believed that all day father had been trying to think of doing the thing she wouldn't like the most, and that she knew all the time that after a while he would think of it. I stayed quiet, because father and I both knew that mother would want him to make me stay with her if she just thought of it in time. So father didn't look at me. I was the oldest. I was nine and Caddy was seven and Jason was five.

"Nonsense," father said. "We wont be long."

Nancy had her hat on. We came to the lane. "Jesus always been good to me," Nancy said. "Whenever he had two dollars, one of them was mine." We walked in the lane. "If I can just get through the lane," Nancy said, "I be all right then."

The lane was always dark. "This is where Jason got scared on Hallowe'en," Caddy said.

"I didn't," Jason said.

"Cant Aunt Rachel do anything with him?" father said. Aunt Rachel was old. She lived in a cabin beyond Nancy's, by herself. She had white hair and she smoked a pipe in the door, all day long; she didn't work any more. They said she was Jesus' mother. Sometimes she said she was and sometimes she said she wasn't any kin to Jesus.

"Yes, you did," Caddy said. "You were scairder than Frony. You were scairder than T.P. even. Scairder than niggers."

"Cant nobody do nothing with him," Nancy said. "He say I done woke up the devil in him and aint but one thing going to lay it down again."

"Well, he's gone now," father said. "There's nothing for you to be afraid of now. And if you'd just let white men alone."

"Let what white men alone?" Caddy said. "How let them alone?"

"He aint gone nowhere," Nancy said. "I can feel him. I can feel him now, in this lane. He hearing us talk, every word, hid somewhere, waiting. I aint seen him, and I aint going to see him again but once more, with that razor in his mouth. That razor on that string down his back, inside his shirt. And then I aint going to be even surprised."

"I wasn't scaired," Jason said.

"If you'd behave yourself, you'd have kept out of this," father said. "But it's all right now. He's probably in St. Louis now. Probably got another wife by now and forgot all about you."

"If he has, I better not find out about it," Nancy said. "I'd stand there right over them, and every time he wropped her, I'd cut that arm off. I'd cut his head off and I'd slit her belly and I'd shove—"

"Hush," father said.

"Slit whose belly, Nancy?" Caddy said.

"I wasn't scaired," Jason said. "I'd walk right down this lane by myself."

"Yah," Caddy said. "You wouldn't dare to put your foot down in it if we were not here too."

II

Dilsey was still sick, so we took Nancy home every night until mother said, "How much longer is this going on? I to be left alone in this big house while you take home a frightened Negro?"

We fixed a pallet in the kitchen for Nancy. One night we waked up, hearing the sound. It was not singing and it was not crying, coming up the dark stairs. There was a light in mother's room and we heard father going down the hall, down the back stairs, and Caddy and I went into the hall. The floor was cold. Our toes curled away from it while we listened to the sound. It was like singing and it wasn't like singing, like the sounds that Negroes make.

Then it stopped and we heard father going down the back stairs, and we went to the head of the stairs. Then the sound began again, in the stairway, not loud, and we could see Nancy's eyes halfway up the stairs, against the wall. They looked like cat's eyes do, like a big cat against the wall, watching us. When we came down the steps to where she was, she quit making the sound again, and we stood there until father came back up from the kitchen, with his pistol in his hand. He went back down with Nancy and they came back with Nancy's pallet.

We spread the pallet in our room. After the light in mother's room went off, we could see Nancy's eyes again. "Nancy," Caddy whispered, "are you asleep, Nancy?"

Nancy whispered something. It was oh or no, I dont know which. Like nobody had made it, like it came from nowhere and went nowhere, until it was like Nancy was not there at all; that I had looked so hard at her eyes on the stairs that they had got printed on my eyeballs, like the sun does when you have closed your eyes and there is no sun. "Jesus," Nancy whispered, "Jesus."

"Was it Jesus?" Caddy said. "Did he try to come into the kitchen?"

"Jesus," Nancy said. Like this: Jeeeeeeeeeeeeeeeesus, until the sound went out, like a match or a candle does.

"It's the other Jesus she means," I said.

"Can you see us, Nancy?" Caddy whispered. "Can you see our eyes too?"

"I aint nothing but a nigger," Nancy said. "God knows. God knows."

"What did you see down there in the kitchen?" Caddy whispered. "What tried to get in?"

"God knows," Nancy said. We could see her eyes. "God knows."

Dilsey got well. She cooked dinner. "You'd better stay in bed a day or two longer," father said.

"What for?" Dilsey said. "If I had been a day later, this place would be to rack and ruin. Get out of here now, and let me get my kitchen straight again."

Dilsey cooked supper too. And that night, just before dark, Nancy came into the kitchen.

"How do you know he's back?" Dilsey said. "You aint seen him."

"Jesus is a nigger," Jason said.

"I can feel him," Nancy said. "I can feel him laying yonder in the ditch."

"Tonight?" Dilsey said. "Is he there tonight?"

"Dilsey's a nigger too," Jason said.

"You try to eat something," Dilsey said.

"I dont want nothing," Nancy said.

"I aint a nigger," Jason said.

"Drink some coffee," Dilsey said. She poured a cup of coffee for Nancy. "Do you know he's out there tonight? How come you know it's tonight?"

"I know," Nancy said. "He's there, waiting. I know. I done lived with him too long. I know what he is fixing to do fore he know it himself."

"Drink some coffee," Dilsey said. Nancy held the cup to her mouth and blew into the cup. Her mouth pursed out like a spreading adder's, like a rubber mouth, like she had blown all the color out of her lips with blowing the coffee.

"I aint a nigger," Jason said. "Are you a nigger, Nancy?"

"I hellborn, child," Nancy said. "I wont be nothing soon. I going back where I come from soon."

III

She began to drink the coffee. While she was drinking, holding the cup in both hands, she began to make the sound again. She made the sound into the cup and the coffee sploshed out onto her hands and her dress. Her eyes looked at us and she sat there, her elbows on her knees, holding the cup in both hands, looking at us across the wet cup, making the sound. "Look at Nancy," Jason said. "Nancy cant cook for us now. Dilsey's got well now."

"You hush up," Dilsey said. Nancy held the cup in both hands, looking at us, making the sound, like there were two of them: one looking at us and the other making the sound. "Whyn't you let Mr Jason telefoam the marshal?" Dilsey said. Nancy stopped then, holding the cup in her long brown hands. She tried to drink some coffee again, but it sploshed out of the cup, onto her hands and her dress, and she put the cup down. Jason watched her.

"I cant swallow it," Nancy said. "I swallows but it wont go down me."

"You go down to the cabin," Dilsey said. "Frony will fix you a pallet and I'll be there soon."

"Wont no nigger stop him," Nancy said.

"I aint a nigger," Jason said. "Am I, Dilsey?"

"I reckon not," Dilsey said. She looked at Nancy. "I dont reckon so. What you going to do, then?"

Nancy looked at us. Her eyes went fast, like she was afraid there wasn't time to look, without hardly moving at all. She looked at us, at all three of us at one time. "You member that night I stayed in yawls' room?" she said. She told about how we waked up early the next morning, and played. We had to play quiet, on her pallet, until father woke up and it was time to get breakfast. "Go and ask your maw to let me stay here tonight," Nancy said. "I wont need no pallet. We can play some more."

Caddy asked mother. Jason went too. "I cant have Negroes sleeping in the bedrooms," mother said. Jason cried. He cried until mother said he couldn't have any dessert for three days if he didn't stop. Then Jason said he would stop if Dilsey would make a chocolate cake. Father was there.

"Why dont you do something about it?" mother said. "What do we have officers for?"

"Why is Nancy afraid of Jesus?" Caddy said. "Are you afraid of father, mother?"

"What could the officers do?" father said. "If Nancy hasn't seen him, how could the officers find him?"

"Then why is she afraid?" mother said.

"She says he is there. She says she knows he is there tonight."

"Yet we pay taxes," mother said. "I must wait here alone in this big house while you take a Negro woman home."

"You know that I am not lying outside with a razor," father said.

"I'll stop if Dilsey will make a chocolate cake," Jason said. Mother told us to go out and father said he didn't know if Jason would get a chocolate cake or not, but he knew what Jason was going to get in about a minute. We went back to the kitchen and told Nancy.

"Father said for you to go home and lock the door, and you'll be all right," Caddy said. "All right from what, Nancy? Is Jesus mad at you?" Nancy was holding the coffee cup in her hands again, her elbows on her knees and her hands holding the cup between her knees. She was looking into the cup. "What have you done that made Jesus mad?" Caddy said. Nancy let the cup go. It didn't break on the floor, but the coffee spilled out, and Nancy sat there with her hands still making the shape of the cup. She began to make the sound again, not loud. Not singing and not unsinging. We watched her.

"Here," Dilsey said. "You quit that, now. You get aholt of yourself. You wait here. I going to get Versh to walk home with you." Dilsey went out.

We looked at Nancy. Her shoulders kept shaking, but she quit making the sound. We watched her. "What's Jesus going to do to you?" Caddy said. "He went away."

Nancy looked at us. "We had fun that night I stayed in yawls' room, didn't we?"

"I didn't," Jason said. "I didn't have any fun."

"You were asleep in mother's room," Caddy said. "You were not there."

"Let's go down to my house and have some more fun," Nancy said.

"Mother wont let us," I said. "It's too late now."

"Dont bother her," Nancy said. "We can tell her in the morning. She wont mind."

"She wouldn't let us," I said.

"Dont ask her now," Nancy said. "Dont bother her now."

"She didn't say we couldn't go," Caddy said.

"We didn't ask," I said.

"If you go, I'll tell," Jason said.

"We'll have fun," Nancy said. "They won't mind, just to my house. I been working for yawl a long time. They won't mind."

"I'm not afraid to go," Caddy said. "Jason is the one that's afraid. He'll tell."

"I'm not," Jason said.

"Yes, you are," Caddy said. "You'll tell."

"I won't tell," Jason said. "I'm not afraid."

"Jason ain't afraid to go with me," Nancy said. "Is you, Jason?"

"Jason is going to tell," Caddy said. The lane was dark. We passed the pasture gate. "I bet if something was to jump out from behind that gate, Jason would holler."

"I wouldn't," Jason said. We walked down the lane. Nancy was talking loud.

"What are you talking so loud, for, Nancy?" Caddy said.

"Who; me?" Nancy said. "Listen at Quentin and Caddy and Jason saying I'm talking loud."

"You talk like there was five of us here," Caddy said. "You talk like father was here too."

"Who; me talking loud, Mr Jason?" Nancy said.

"Nancy called Jason 'Mister,'" Caddy said.

"Listen how Caddy and Quentin and Jason talk," Nancy said.

"We're not talking loud," Caddy said. "You're the one that's talking like father—"

"Hush," Nancy said; "hush, Mr Jason."

"Nancy called Jason 'Mister' aguh—"

"Hush," Nancy said. She was talking loud when we crossed the ditch and stooped through the fence where she used to stoop through with the clothes on her head. Then we came to her house. We were going fast then. She opened the door. The smell of the house was like the lamp and the smell of Nancy was like the wick, like they were waiting for one another to begin to smell. She lit the lamp and closed the door and put the bar up. Then she quit talking loud, looking at us.

"What're we going to do?" Caddy said.

"What do yawl want to do?" Nancy said.

"You said we would have some fun," Caddy said.

There was something about Nancy's house; something you could smell besides Nancy and the house. Jason smelled it, even. "I don't want to stay here," he said. "I want to go home."

"Go home, then," Caddy said.

"I don't want to go by myself," Jason said.

"We're going to have some fun," Nancy said.

"How?" Caddy said.

Nancy stood by the door. She was looking at us, only it was like she had emptied her eyes, like she had quit using them. "What do you want to do?" she said.

"Tell us a story," Caddy said. "Can you tell a story?"

"Yes," Nancy said.

"Tell it," Caddy said. We looked at Nancy. "You don't know any stories."

"Yes," Nancy said. "Yes, I do."

She came and sat in a chair before the hearth. There was a little fire there. Nancy built it up, when it was already hot inside. She built a good blaze. She told a story. She talked like her eyes looked, like her eyes watching us and her voice talking to us did not belong to her. Like she was living somewhere else, waiting somewhere else. She was outside the cabin. Her voice was inside and the shape of her, the Nancy that could stoop under a barbed wire fence with a bundle of clothes balanced on her head as though without weight, like a balloon, was there. But that was all. "And so this here queen come walking up to the ditch, where that bad man was hiding. She was walking up to the ditch, and she say, 'If I can just get past this here ditch,' was what she say . . ."

"What ditch?" Caddy said. "A ditch like the one out there? Why did a queen want to go into a ditch?"

"To get to her house," Nancy said. She looked at us. "She had to cross the ditch to get into her house quick and bar the door."

"Why did she want to go home and bar the door?" Caddy said.

IV

Nancy looked at us. She quit talking. She looked at us. Jason's legs stuck straight out of his pants where he sat on Nancy's lap. "I don't think that's a good story," he said. "I want to go home."

"Maybe we had better," Caddy said. She got up from the floor.

"I bet they are looking for us right now." She went toward the door.

"No," Nancy said. "Don't open it." She got up quick and passed Caddy. She didn't touch the door, the wooden bar.

"Why not," Caddy said.

"Come back to the lamp," Nancy said. "We'll have fun. You don't have to go."

"We ought to go," Caddy said. "Unless we have a lot of fun." She and Nancy came back to the fire, the lamp.

"I want to go home," Jason said. "I'm going to tell."

"I know another story," Nancy said. She stood close to the lamp. She looked at Caddy, like when your eyes look up at a stick balanced on your nose. She had to look down to see Caddy, but her eyes looked like that, like when you are balancing a stick.

"I won't listen to it," Jason said. "I'll bang on the floor."

"It's a good one," Nancy said. "It's better than the other one."

"What's it about?" Caddy said. Nancy was standing by the lamp. Her hand was on the lamp, against the light, long and brown.

"Your hand is on that hot globe," Caddy said. "Don't it feel hot to your hand?"

Nancy looked at her hand on the lamp chimney. She took her hand away, slow. She stood there, looking at Caddy, wringing her long hand as though it were tied to her wrist with a string.

"Let's do something else," Caddy said.

"I want to go home," Jason said.

"I got some popcorn," Nancy said. She looked at Caddy and then at Jason and then at me and then at Caddy again. "I got some popcorn."

"I don't like popcorn," Jason said. "I'd rather have candy."

Nancy looked at Jason. "You can hold the popper." She was still wringing her hand; it was long and limp and brown.

"All right," Jason said. "I'll stay a while if I can do that. Caddy can't hold it. I'll want to go home again if Caddy holds the popper."

Nancy built up the fire. "Look at Nancy putting her hands in the fire," Caddy said. "What's the matter with you, Nancy?"

"I got popcorn," Nancy said. "I got some." She took the popper from under the bed. It was broken. Jason began to cry.

"Now we can't have any popcorn," he said.

"We ought to go home, anyway," Caddy said, "Come on, Quentin."

"Wait," Nancy said; "wait. I can fix it. Don't you want to help me fix it?"

"I don't think I want any," Caddy said. "It's too late now."

"You help me, Jason," Nancy said. "Don't you want to help me?"

"No," Jason said. "I want to go home."

"Hush," Nancy said; "hush. Watch. Watch me. I can fix it so Jason can hold it and pop the corn." She got a piece of wire and fixed the popper.

"It won't hold good," Caddy said.

"Yes, it will," Nancy said. "Yawl watch. Yawl help me shell some corn."

The popcorn was under the bed too. We shelled it into the popper and Nancy helped Jason hold the popper over the fire.

"It's not popping," Jason said. "I want to go home."

"You wait," Nancy said. "It'll begin to pop. We'll have fun then." She was sitting close to the fire. The lamp was turned up so high it was beginning to smoke.

"Why don't you turn it down some?" I said.

"It's all right," Nancy said. "I'll clean it. Yawl wait. The popcorn will start in a minute."

"I don't believe it's going to start," Caddy said. "We ought to start home, anyway. They'll be worried."

"No," Nancy said. "It's going to pop. Dilsey will tell um yawl with me. I been working for yawl long time. They won't mind if yawl at my house. You wait, now. It'll start popping any minute now."

Then Jason got some smoke in his eyes and he began to cry. He dropped the popper into the fire. Nancy got a wet rag and wiped Jason's face, but he didn't stop crying.

"Hush," she said. "Hush." But he didn't hush. Caddy took the popper out of the fire.

"It's burned up," she said. "You'll have to get some more popcorn, Nancy."

"Did you put all of it in?" Nancy said.

"Yes," Caddy said. Nancy looked at Caddy. Then she took the popper and opened it and poured the cinders into her apron and began to sort the grains, her hands long and brown, and we watching her.

"Haven't you got any more?" Caddy said.

"Yes," Nancy said; "yes. Look. This here ain't burnt. All we need to do is—"

"I want to go home," Jason said. "I'm going to tell."

"Hush," Caddy said. We all listened. Nancy's head was already turned toward the barred door, her eyes filled with red lamplight. "Somebody is coming," Caddy said.

Then Nancy began to make that sound again, not loud, sitting there above the fire, her long hands dangling between her knees; all of a sudden water began to come out of her face in big drops, running down her face, carrying in each one a little turning ball of firelight like a spark until it dropped off her chin. "She's not crying," I said.

"I ain't crying," Nancy said. Her eyes were closed. "I ain't crying. Who is it?"

"I don't know," Caddy said. She went to the door and looked out. "We've got to go now," she said. "Here comes father."

"I'm going to tell," Jason said. "Yawl made me come."

The water still ran down Nancy's face. She turned in her chair. "Listen. Tell him. Tell him we going to have fun. Tell him I take good care of yawl until in the morning. Tell him to let me come home with yawl and sleep on the floor. Tell him I won't need no pallet. We'll have fun. You member last time how we had so much fun?"

"I didn't have any fun," Jason said. "You hurt me. You put smoke in my eyes. I'm going to tell."

V

Father came in. He looked at us. Nancy did not get up.

"Tell him," she said.

"Caddy made us come down here," Jason said. "I didn't want to."

Father came to the fire. Nancy looked up at him. "Can't you go to Aunt Rachel's and stay?" he said. Nancy looked up at father, her hands between her knees. "He's not here," father said. "I would have seen him. There's not a soul in sight."

"He in the ditch," Nancy said. "He waiting in the ditch yonder."

"Nonsense," father said. He looked at Nancy. "Do you know he's there?"

"I got the sign," Nancy said.

"What sign?"

"I got it. It was on the table when I come in. It was a hogbone, with blood meat still on it, laying by the lamp. He's out there. When yawl walk out that door, I gone."

"Gone where, Nancy?" Caddy said.

"I'm not a tattletale," Jason said.

"Nonsense," father said.

"He out there," Nancy said. "He looking through that window this minute, waiting for yawl to go. Then I gone."

"Nonsense," father said. "Lock up your house and we'll take you on to Aunt Rachel's."

"'Twont do no good," Nancy said. She didn't look at father now, but he looked down at her, at her long, limp, moving hands. "Putting it off wont do no good."

"Then what do you want to do?" father said.

"I don't know," Nancy said. "I can't do nothing. Just put it off. And that don't do no good. I reckon it belong to me. I reckon what I going to get ain't no more than mine."

"Get what?" Caddy said. "What's yours?"

"Nothing," father said. "You all must get to bed."

"Caddy made me come," Jason said.

"Go on to Aunt Rachel's," father said.

"It won't do no good," Nancy said. She sat before the fire, her elbows on her knees, her long hands between her knees. "When even your own kitchen wouldn't do no good. When even if I was sleeping on the floor in the room with your chillen, and the next morning there I am, and blood—"

"Hush," father said. "Lock the door and put out the lamp and go to bed."

"I scared of the dark," Nancy said. "I scared for it to happen in the dark."

"You mean you're going to sit right here with the lamp lighted?" father said. Then Nancy began to make the sound again, sitting before the fire, her long hands between her knees. "Ah, damnation," father said. "Come along, chillen. It's past bedtime."

"When yawl go home, I gone," Nancy said. She talked quieter now, and her face looked quiet, like her hands. "Anyway, I got my coffin money saved up with Mr. Lovelady." Mr. Lovelady was a short, dirty man who collected the Negro insurance, coming around to the cabins or the kitchens every Saturday morning, to collect fifteen cents. He and his wife lived at the hotel. One morning his wife committed suicide. They had a child, a little girl. He and the child went away. After a week or two he came back alone. We would see him going along the lanes and the back streets on Saturday mornings.

"Nonsense," father said. "You'll be the first thing I'll see in the kitchen tomorrow morning."

"You'll see what you'll see, I reckon," Nancy said. "But it will take the Lord to say what that will be."

VI

We left her sitting before the fire.

"Come and put the bar up," father said. But she didn't move. She didn't look at us again, sitting quietly there between the lamp and the fire. From some distance down the lane we could look back and see her through the open door.

"What, Father?" Caddy said. "What's going to happen?"

"Nothing," father said. Jason was on father's back, so Jason was the tallest of all of us. We went down into the ditch. I looked at it, quiet. I couldn't see much where the moonlight and the shadows tangled.

"If Jesus is hid here, he can see us, cant he?" Caddy said.

"He's not there," father said. "He went away a long time ago."

"You made me come," Jason said, high; against the sky it looked like father had two heads, a little one and a big one. "I didn't want to."

We went up out of the ditch. We could still see Nancy's house and the open door, but we couldn't see Nancy now, sitting before the fire with the door open, because she was tired. "I just done got tired," she said. "I just a nigger. It ain't no fault of mine."

But we could hear her, because she began just after we came up out of the ditch, the sound that was not singing and not unsinging. "Who will do our washing now, Father?" I said.

"I'm not a nigger," Jason said, high and close above father's head.

"You're worse," Caddy said, "you are a tattletale. If something was to jump out, you'd be scairder than a nigger."

"I wouldn't," Jason said.

"You'd cry," Caddy said.

"Caddy," father said.

"I wouldn't!" Jason said.

"Scairy cat," Caddy said.

"Candace!" father said.

1931, 1931

ERNEST HEMINGWAY
(1898–1961)

Hemingway's compelling inspiration was war, both as a personal and symbolic experience and as a continuing condition of mankind. New readers of the Second World War and beyond still found inspiration in his symbolic ritualism dedicated to the survival of selfhood in the midst of chaos. Hemingway also created a revolution in language which influenced the narrative and dialogue of two generations of novelists. During the last twenty years of his life he published little; as adventurer, hunter, and journalist he sometimes seemed to resemble one of his own created characters. When in 1952 he got it again "the way it was" in *The Old Man and the Sea*, a nearly flawless short novel, he was awarded the Pulitzer Prize (1953) and the Nobel Prize (1954) with a promptness that suggested an overdue recognition.

Born in Oak Park, near Chicago, on July 21, 1898, Ernest Miller Hemingway was the son of a physician who initiated him into the rituals of hunting and fishing in the Michigan north woods; he also gained an early proficiency in football and boxing. Graduated from high school he became a reporter for the Kansas City *Star* in 1917. Within the year he was in volunteer war service with an American ambulance unit in France, gained transfer to combat duty in the Italian Arditi (volunteer infantry) on the Italian front, and was seriously wounded. After the Armistice, with Italian decorations for valor, he returned to newspaper work. In 1920 he covered the Graeco-Turkish war and was appointed a Paris correspondent.

Post-war Paris was thronged with young artists. Intellectual ferment and artistic accomplishment expressed the same spiritual defeat that other expatriate intellectuals sought in escape. In his first novel, *The Sun Also Rises* (1926), with Gertrude Stein's remark, "You are all a lost generation," as epigraph, such characters as Lady Brett and Jake Barnes, the journalist unmanned by war wounds, expressed in another form the sterile wasteland of Eliot's poem of 1922. His first major book, *In Our Time* (1925), was a collection of stories in which Nick Adams is a sort of *alter ego* for the young Hemingway. Hemingway's psychological penetration and originality in plot and dialogue reawakened interest in the short story; at his unsurpassed best over limited stretches, he wrote some of the finest short stories of his time.

Two war novels and two uniquely interesting topical books brought Hemingway to the end of his major accomplishment in 1940. A *Farewell to Arms* (1929), based on his Italian service, is a distinguished war novel, although lingering sentiment breaks through the taut economy of the stylized language. Here he rejected the classic tragic unity in the catastrophic defeat of the lovers, who have hazardously escaped to safe harbor, only to face the cruel futility of Catherine's fatal accident in childbirth. Dying, she murmurs to Frederic, "I'm not a bit afraid. It's just a dirty trick." The author's naturalistic reinterpretation of fate was consistent. Robert Jordan, in *For Whom the Bell Tolls* (1940), loses his life for a cause already lost, and in fact not even a genuine cause. All causes in Hemingway's tragic vision are already lost, because that is nature and the way things are; but the losers need not be lost. What distinguished man and gave him salvation was his faithfulness in the ordeal which all are called upon to face—as Macomber must meet the buffalo—and if by some dirty trick he dies anyway, "we owe God a death"; but we can keep the rendezvous like men. Lady Brett knew the code: "It's sort of what we have *instead* of God."

In *For Whom the Bell Tolls*, his best novel, again love is found, and lost, as it seems, by the callous futility of nature. This episode of the Spanish Revolution is also an unforgettable revelation of the Spanish earth and its people. Spain and the bullfight had appeared in his first novel; later, in *Death in the Afternoon* (1932), he gave an interpretation of the bull-fight as ordeal and ritual, "very moral to me because I feel very fine while it is going on and have a feeling of life and death and mortality." The hunt is a comparable ordeal and ritual in *The Green Hills of Africa* (1935).

Like Stephen Crane, whom he admired as the pioneer of the naturalistic war novel, Hemingway embraced the cult of experience. Note his journalistic engagements on behalf of the Spanish loyalists between 1936 and 1940; or again on behalf of liberal causes in the war-torn 40's, as correspondent in China, and in the air over France, and on the Normandy beach. Crane's thirst for life was fatal and Hemingway's nearly as compelling. Always his writing had its roots in his experience. When he was unable to meet his own high standards he did not publish; nevertheless there are some extraordinarily fine passages in his posthumously published *Islands in the Stream* (1970). In *The Green Hills* he asserted his creed "to write as well as I can and learn as I go along. At the same time I have my life * * * which is a damned good life." You could only write "what you truly felt" and never "when there is no water in the well." Of the bullfight he remarked, "I was trying to learn to write, commencing with the simplest things, and one of the simplest things and the most fundamental is violent death." Death became, in his fiction, the extreme limit of experience and the final test of the genuine ordeal. Death

appears in his writing in violent forms, or understated as "bad luck," or symbolically projected as mutilation or sterility in Jake Barnes, Nick Adams, and the protagonists of *To Have and Have Not* (1937) and *Across the River and Into the Trees* (1950), his two so-called failures.

Hemingway left his Cuban estate in November, 1960, for a new "last home" in a remote spot near Ketchum, Idaho. During the next eight months he suffered two long illnesses requiring hospitalization. In the early morning of July 2, 1961, standing beside his beloved gun-rack in his home, he died of head wounds resulting from the discharge of his favorite shotgun, in his own hands.

Most of Hemingway's novels and topical volumes are mentioned above. *The Fifth Column and the First Forty-nine Stories*, 1938, contains all the stories of *In Our Time*, New York, 1925; *Men Without Women*, 1927; and *Winner Take Nothing*, 1933; some previously uncollected stories, and a play. *Torrents of Spring*, 1926, is a parody of Sherwood Anderson. The posthumous *A Moveable Feast* (1964) is a memoir of Paris life. Two early volumes are *Three Stones and Ten Poems*, 1923; and *in our time*, Paris, 1924. Recent collections include *By-Line: Ernest Hemingway: Selected Articles and Dispatches of Four Decades*, edited by William White, 1967; *The Fifth Column and Four Stories of the Spanish Civil War*, 1969; and *The Nick Adams Stories*, 1972.

Early studies are Carlos Baker, *Hemingway: The Writer As Artist*, 1952, revised 1956; Philip Young, *Ernest Hemingway*, 1952 (revised as *Ernest Hemingway: A Reconsideration*, 1966); and Charles A. Fenton, *The Apprenticeship of Ernest Hemingway: The Early Years*, 1954. See also Leicester Hemingway, *My Brother Ernest Hemingway*, 1962, and Lillian Ross, *Portrait of Hemingway*, 1962.

A solid biography is Carlos Baker, *Ernest Hemingway: A Life Story*, 1969.

Recent memoirs include L. R. Arnold, *High on the Wild with Hemingway,* 1968; A. E. Hotchner, *Papa Hemingway,* 1969; James McLendon, *Papa: Hemingway at Key West,* 1972; and Vernon Klimo and Will Oursler, *Hemingway and Jake,* 1972. Recent criticism includes Constance Cappel Montgomery, *Hemingway in Michigan,* 1966; Sheridan Baker, *Ernest Hemingway: An Introduction and Interpretation,* 1967; Leo Gurko, *Ernest Hemingway and the Pursuit of Heroism,* 1968; Richard B. Hovey, *Hemingway: The Inward Terrain,* 1968; Robert O. Stephens, *Hemingway's Nonfiction: The Public Voice,* 1968; Jackson J. Benson, *Hemingway: The Writer's Art of Self-Defense,* 1969; Emily Watts, *Ernest Hemingway and the Arts,* 1971; Arthur Waldhorn, *A Reader's Guide to Ernest Hemingway,* 1972; and Sheldon N. Grebstein, *Hemingway's Craft,* 1973. Audrey Hanneman compiled *Ernest Hemingway: A Comprehensive Bibliography,* 1967.

The Short Happy Life of Francis Macomber [1]

It was now lunch time and they were all sitting under the double green fly of the dining tent pretending that nothing had happened.

"Will you have lime juice or lemon squash?" Macomber asked.

"I'll have a gimlet," [2] Robert Wilson told him.

"I'll have a gimlet too. I need something," Macomber's wife said.

"I suppose it's the thing to do," Macomber agreed. "Tell him to make three gimlets."

The mess boy had started them already, lifting the bottles out of the canvas cooling bags that sweated wet in the wind that blew through the trees that shaded the tents.

"What had I ought to give them?" Macomber asked.

"A quid [3] would be plenty," Wilson told him. "You don't want to spoil them."

"Will the headman distribute it?"

"Absolutely."

Francis Macomber had, half an hour before, been carried to his tent from the edge of the camp in triumph on the arms and shoulders of the cook, the personal boys, the skinner and the porters. The gun-bearers had taken no part in the demonstration. When the native boys put him down at the door of his tent, he had shaken all their hands, received their congratulations, and then gone into the tent and sat on the bed until his wife came in. She did not speak to him when she came in and he left the tent at once to wash his face and hands in the portable wash basin outside and go over to the dining tent to sit in a comfortable canvas chair in the breeze and the shade.

"You've got your lion," Robert Wilson said to him, "and a damned fine one too."

1. *Cosmopolitan,* September, 1936; *The Fifth Column and the First Forty-nine Stories* (1938).

2. A drink (gin and lime juice).
3. British slang for one pound in currency.

Mrs. Macomber looked at Wilson quickly. She was an extremely handsome and well-kept woman of the beauty and social position which had, five years before, commanded five thousand dollars as the price of endorsing, with photographs, a beauty product which she had never used. She had been married to Francis Macomber for eleven years.

"He is a good lion, isn't he?" Macomber said. His wife looked at him now. She looked at both these men as though she had never seen them before.

One, Wilson, the white hunter, she knew she had never truly seen before. He was about middle height with sandy hair, a stubby mustache, a very red face and extremely cold blue eyes with faint white wrinkles at the corners that grooved merrily when he smiled. He smiled at her now and she looked away from his face at the way his shoulders sloped in the loose tunic he wore with the four big cartridges held in loops where the left breast pocket should have been, at his big brown hands, his old slacks, his very dirty boots and back to his red face again. She noticed where the baked red of his face stopped in a white line that marked the circle left by his Stetson hat that hung now from one of the pegs of the tent pole.

"Well, here's to the lion," Robert Wilson said. He smiled at her again and, not smiling, she looked curiously at her husband.

Francis Macomber was very tall, very well built if you did not mind that length of bone, dark, his hair cropped like an oarsman, rather thin-lipped, and was considered handsome. He was dressed in the same sort of safari clothes that Wilson wore except that his were new, he was thirty-five years old, kept himself very fit, was good at court games, had a number of big-game fishing records, and had just shown himself, very publicly, to be a coward.

"Here's to the lion," he said. "I can't ever thank you for what you did."

Margaret, his wife, looked away from him and back to Wilson.

"Let's not talk about the lion," she said.

Wilson looked over at her without smiling and now she smiled at him.

"It's been a very strange day," she said. "Hadn't you ought to put your hat on even under the canvas at noon? You told me that, you know."

"Might put it on," said Wilson.

"You know you have a very red face, Mr. Wilson," she told him and smiled again.

"Drink," said Wilson.

"I don't think so," she said. "Francis drinks a great deal, but his face is never red."

"It's red today," Macomber tried a joke.

"No," said Margaret. "It's mine that's red today. But Mr. Wilson's is always red."

"Must be racial," said Wilson. "I say, you wouldn't like to drop my beauty as a topic, would you?"

"I've just started on it."

"Let's chuck it," said Wilson.

"Conversation is going to be so difficult," Margaret said.

"Don't be silly, Margot," her husband said.

"No difficulty," Wilson said. "Got a damn fine lion."

Margot looked at them both and they both saw that she was going to cry. Wilson had seen it coming for a long time and he dreaded it. Macomber was past dreading it.

"I wish it hadn't happened. Oh, I wish it hadn't happened," she said and started for her tent. She made no noise of crying but they could see that her shoulders were shaking under the rose-colored, sun-proofed shirt she wore.

"Women upset," said Wilson to the tall man. "Amounts to nothing. Strain on the nerves and one thing'n another."

"No," said Macomber. "I suppose that I rate that for the rest of my life now."

"Nonsense. Let's have a spot of the giant killer," said Wilson. "Forget the whole thing. Nothing to it anyway."

"We might try," said Macomber. "I won't forget what you did for me though."

"Nothing," said Wilson. "All nonsense."

So they sat there in the shade where the camp was pitched under some wide-topped acacia trees with a boulder-strewn cliff behind them, and a stretch of grass that ran to the bank of a boulder-filled stream in front with forest beyond it, and drank their just-cool lime drinks and avoided one another's eyes while the boys set the table for lunch. Wilson could tell that the boys all knew about it now and when he saw Macomber's personal boy looking curiously at his master while he was putting dishes on the table he snapped at him in Swahili. The boy turned away with his face blank.

"What were you telling him?" Macomber asked.

"Nothing. Told him to look alive or I'd see he got about fifteen of the best."

"What's that? Lashes?"

"It's quite illegal," Wilson said. "You're supposed to fine them."

"Do you still have them whipped?"

"Oh, yes. They could raise a row if they chose to complain. But they don't. They prefer it to the fines."

"How strange!" said Macomber.

"Not strange, really," Wilson said. "Which would you rather do? Take a good birching or lose your pay?"

Then he felt embarrassed at asking it and before Macomber could answer he went on, "We all take a beating every day, you know, one way or another."

This was no better. "Good God," he thought. "I am a diplomat, aren't I?"

"Yes, we take a beating," said Macomber, still not looking at him. "I'm awfully sorry about the lion business. It doesn't have to go any further, does it? I mean no one will hear about it, will they?"

"You mean will I tell it at the Mathaiga Club?" Wilson looked at him now coldly. He had not expected this. So he's a bloody four-letter man as well as a bloody coward, he thought. I rather liked him too until today. But how is one to know about an American?

"No," said Wilson. "I'm a professional hunter. We never talk about our clients. You can be quite easy on that. It's supposed to be bad form to ask us not to talk though."

He had decided now that to break would be much easier. He would eat, then, by himself and could read a book with his meals. They would eat by themselves. He would see them through the safari [4] on a very formal basis—what was it the French called it? Distinguished consideration—and it would be a damn sight easier than having to go through this emotional trash. He'd insult him and make a good clean break. Then he could read a book with his meals and he'd still be drinking their whisky. That was the phrase for it when a safari went bad. You ran into another white hunter and you asked, "How is everything going?" and he answered, "Oh, I'm still drinking their whisky," and you knew everything had gone to pot.

"I'm sorry," Macomber said and looked at him with his American face that would stay adolescent until it became middle-aged, and Wilson noted his crew-cropped hair, fine eyes only faintly shifty, good nose, thin lips and handsome jaw. "I'm sorry I didn't realize that. There are lots of things I don't know."

So what could he do, Wilson thought. He was all ready to break it off quickly and neatly and here the beggar was apologizing after he had just insulted him. He made one more attempt. "Don't worry about me talking," he said. "I have a living to make. You know in Africa no woman ever misses her lion and no white man ever bolts."

4. From the Arabic, originally meaning "journey," but now usually designating a hunting expedition.

"I bolted like a rabbit," Macomber said.

Now what in hell were you going to do about a man who talked like that, Wilson wondered.

Wilson looked at Macomber with his flat, blue, machine-gunner's eyes and the other smiled back at him. He had a pleasant smile if you did not notice how his eyes showed when he was hurt.

"Maybe I can fix it up on buffalo," he said. "We're after them next, aren't we?"

"In the morning if you like," Wilson told him. Perhaps he had been wrong. This was certainly the way to take it. You most certainly could not tell a damned thing about an American. He was all for Macomber again. If you could forget the morning. But, of course, you couldn't. The morning had been about as bad as they come.

"Here comes the Memsahib," [5] he said. She was walking over from her tent looking refreshed and cheerful and quite lovely. She had a very perfect oval face, so perfect that you expected her to be stupid. But she wasn't stupid, Wilson thought, no, not stupid.

"How is the beautiful red-faced Mr. Wilson? Are you feeling better, Francis, my pearl?"

"Oh, much," said Macomber.

"I've dropped the whole thing," she said, sitting down at the table. "What importance is there to whether Francis is any good at killing lions? That's not his trade. That's Mr. Wilson's trade. Mr. Wilson is really very impressive killing anything. You do kill anything, don't you?"

"Oh, anything," said Wilson. "Simply anything." They are, he thought, the hardest in the world; the hardest, the cruelest, the most predatory and the most attractive and their men have softened or gone to pieces nervously as they have hardened. Or is it that they pick men they can handle? They can't know that much at the age they marry, he thought. He was grateful that he had gone through his education on American women before now because this was a very attractive one.

"We're going after buff [6] in the morning," he told her.

"I'm coming," she said.

"No, you're not."

"Oh, yes, I am. Mayn't I, Francis?"

"Why not stay in camp?"

"Not for anything," she said. "I wouldn't miss something like today for anything."

When she left, Wilson was thinking, when she went off to cry,

5. The native term of respect in India for addressing a European woman. British colonials carried it to Africa.
6. Buffalo.

she seemed a hell of a fine woman. She seemed to understand, to realize, to be hurt for him and for herself and to know how things really stood. She is away for twenty minutes and now she is back, simply enamelled in that American female cruelty. They are the damnedest women. Really the damnedest.

"We'll put on another show for you tomorrow," Francis Macomber said.

"You're not coming," Wilson said.

"You're very mistaken," she told him. "And I want *so* to see you perform again. You were lovely this morning. That is if blowing things' heads off is lovely."

"Here's the lunch," said Wilson. "You're very merry, aren't you?"

"Why not? I didn't come out here to be dull."

"Well, it hasn't been dull," Wilson said. He could see the boulders in the river and the high bank beyond with the trees and he remembered the morning.

"Oh, no," she said. "It's been charming. And tomorrow. You don't know how I look forward to tomorrow."

"That's eland he's offering you," Wilson said.

"They're the big cowy things that jump like hares, aren't they?"

"I suppose that describes them," Wilson said.

"It's very good meat," Macomber said.

"Did you shoot it, Francis?" she asked.

"Yes."

"They're not dangerous, are they?"

"Only if they fall on you," Wilson told her.

"I'm so glad."

"Why not let up on the bitchery just a little, Margot," Macomber said, cutting the eland steak and putting some mashed potato, gravy and carrot on the down-turned fork that tined through the piece of meat.

"I suppose I could," she said, "since you put it so prettily."

"Tonight we'll have champagne for the lion," Wilson said. "It's a bit too hot at noon."

"Oh, the lion," Margot said. "I'd forgotten the lion!"

So, Robert Wilson thought to himself, she *is* giving him a ride, isn't she? Or do you suppose that's her idea of putting up a good show? How should a woman act when she discovers her husband is a bloody coward? She's damn cruel but they're all cruel. They govern, of course, and to govern one has to be cruel sometimes. Still, I've seen enough of their damn terrorism.

"Have some more eland," he said to her politely.

That afternoon, late, Wilson and Macomber went out in the

motor car with the native driver and the two gun-bearers. Mrs. Macomber stayed in the camp. It was too hot to go out, she said, and she was going with them in the early morning. As they drove off Wilson saw her standing under the big tree, looking pretty rather than beautiful in her faintly rosy khaki, her dark hair drawn back off her forehead and gathered in a knot low on her neck, her face as fresh, he thought, as though she were in England. She waved to them as the car went off through the swale of high grass and curved around through the trees into the small hills of orchard bush.

In the orchard bush they found a herd of impala, and leaving the car they stalked one old ram with long, wide-spread horns and Macomber killed it with a very creditable shot that knocked the buck down at a good two hundred yards and sent the herd off bounding wildly and leaping over one another's backs in long, leg-drawn-up leaps as unbelievable and as floating as those one makes sometimes in dreams.

"That was a good shot," Wilson said. "They're a small target."

"Is it a worth-while head?" Macomber asked.

"It's excellent," Wilson told him. "You shoot like that and you'll have no trouble."

"Do you think we'll find buffalo tomorrow?"

"There's a good chance of it. They feed out early in the morning and with luck we may catch them in the open."

"I'd like to clear away that lion business," Macomber said. "It's not very pleasant to have your wife see you do something like that."

I should think it would be even more unpleasant to do it, Wilson thought, wife or no wife, or to talk about it having done it. But he said, "I wouldn't think about that any more. Any one could be upset by his first lion. That's all over."

But that night after dinner and a whisky and soda by the fire before going to bed, as Francis Macomber lay on his cot with the mosquito bar over him and listened to the night noises it was not all over. It was neither all over nor was it beginning. It was there exactly as it happened with some parts of it indelibly emphasized and he was miserably ashamed at it. But more than shame he felt cold, hollow fear in him. The fear was still there like a cold slimy hollow in all the emptiness where once his confidence had been and it made him feel sick. It was still there with him now.

It had started the night before when he had wakened and heard the lion roaring somewhere up along the river. It was a deep sound and at the end there were sort of coughing grunts that made him seem just outside the tent, and when Francis Macomber woke in the night to hear it he was afraid. He could hear his wife breathing quietly, asleep. There was no one to tell he was afraid, nor to be afraid with him, and, lying alone, he did not know the Somali [7] proverb that says a brave man is always frightened three times by a lion; when he first sees his track, when he first hears him roar and when he first confronts him. Then while they were eating breakfast by lantern light out in the dining tent, before the sun was up, the lion roared again and Francis thought he was just at the edge of camp.

"Sounds like an old-timer," Robert Wilson said, looking up from his kippers and coffee. "Listen to him cough."

"Is he very close?"

"A mile or so up the stream."

"Will we see him?"

"We'll have a look."

"Does his roaring carry that far? It sounds as though he were right in camp."

"Carries a hell of a long way," said Robert Wilson. "It's strange the way it carries. Hope he's a shootable cat. The boys said there was a very big one about here."

"If I get a shot, where should I hit him," Macomber asked, "to stop him?"

"In the shoulders," Wilson said. "In the neck if you can make it. Shoot for bone. Break him down."

"I hope I can place it properly," Macomber said.

"You shoot very well," Wilson told him. "Take your time. Make sure of him. The first one in is the one that counts."

"What range will it be?"

"Can't tell. Lion has something to say about that. Won't shoot unless it's close enough so you can make sure."

"At under a hundred yards?" Macomber asked.

Wilson looked at him quickly.

"Hundred's about right. Might have to take him a bit under. Shouldn't chance a shot at much over that. A hundred's a decent range. You can hit him wherever you want at that. Here comes the Memsahib."

"Good morning," she said. "Are we going after that lion?"

"As soon as you deal with your breakfast," Wilson said. "How are you feeling?"

"Marvellous," she said. "I'm very excited."

"I'll just go and see that everything is ready," Wilson went off. As he left the lion roared again.

"Noisy beggar," Wilson said. "We'll put a stop to that."

"What's the matter, Francis?" his wife asked him.

"Nothing," Macomber said.

"Yes, there is," she said. "What are you upset about?"

7. Of Somaliland, the eastern extremity of Africa, south of the Gulf of Aden.

"Nothing," he said.

"Tell me," she looked at him. "Don't you feel well?"

"It's that damned roaring," he said. "It's been going on all night, you know."

"Why didn't you wake me," she said. "I'd love to have heard it."

"I've got to kill the damned thing," Macomber said, miserably.

"Well, that's what you're out here for, isn't it?"

"Yes. But I'm nervous. Hearing the thing roar gets on my nerves."

"Well then, as Wilson said, kill him and stop his roaring."

"Yes, darling," said Francis Macomber. "It sounds easy, doesn't it?"

"You're not afraid, are you?"

"Of course not. But I'm nervous from hearing him roar all night."

"You'll kill him marvellously," she said. "I know you will. I'm awfully anxious to see it."

"Finish your breakfast and we'll be starting."

"It's not light yet," she said. "This is a ridiculous hour."

Just then the lion roared in a deep-chested moaning, suddenly guttural, ascending vibration that seemed to shake the air and ended in a sigh and a heavy, deep-chested grunt.

"He sounds almost here," Macomber's wife said.

"My God," said Macomber. "I hate that damned noise."

"It's very impressive."

"Impressive. It's frightful."

Robert Wilson came up then carrying his short, ugly, shockingly big-bored .505 Gibbs and grinning.

"Come on," he said. "Your gun-bearer has your Springfield and the big gun. Everything's in the car. Have you solids?" [8]

"Yes."

"I'm ready," Mrs. Macomber said.

"Must make him stop that racket," Wilson said. "You get in front. The Memsahib can sit back here with me."

They climbed into the motor car and, in the gray first daylight, moved off up the river through the trees. Macomber opened the breech of his rifle and saw he had metal-cased bullets, shut the bolt and put the rifle on safety. He saw his hand was trembling. He felt in his pocket for more cartridges and moved his fingers over the cartridges in the loops of his tunic front. He turned back to where Wilson sat in the rear seat of the doorless, box-bodied motor car beside his wife, them both grinning with excitement, and Wilson leaned forward and whispered,

"See the birds dropping. Means the old boy has left his kill."

8. Solid, jacketed bullets.

On the far bank of the stream Macomber could see, above the trees, vultures circling and plummeting down.

"Chances are he'll come to drink along here," Wilson whispered. "Before he goes to lay up. Keep an eye out."

They were driving slowly along the high bank of the stream which here cut deeply to its boulder-filled bed, and they wound in and out through big trees as they drove. Macomber was watching the opposite bank when he felt Wilson take hold of his arm. The car stopped.

"There he is," he heard the whisper. "Ahead and to the right. Get out and take him. He's a marvellous lion."

Macomber saw the lion now. He was standing almost broadside, his great head up and turned toward them. The early morning breeze that blew toward them was just stirring his dark mane, and the lion looked huge, silhouetted on the rise of bank in the gray morning light, his shoulders heavy, his barrel of a body bulking smoothly.

"How far is he?" asked Macomber, raising his rifle.

"About seventy-five. Get out and take him."

"Why not shoot from where I am?"

"You don't shoot them from cars," he heard Wilson saying in his ear. "Get out. He's not going to stay there all day."

Macomber stepped out of the curved opening at the side of the front seat, onto the step and down onto the ground. The lion still stood looking majestically and coolly toward this object that his eyes only showed in silhouette, bulking like some super-rhino. There was no man smell carried toward him and he watched the object, moving his great head a little from side to side. Then watching the object, not afraid, but hesitating before going down the bank to drink with such a thing opposite him, he saw a man figure detach itself from it and he turned his heavy head and swung away toward the cover of the trees as he heard a cracking crash and felt the slam of a .30–06 220-grain solid bullet that bit his flank and ripped in sudden hot scalding nausea through his stomach. He trotted, heavy, big-footed, swinging wounded full-bellied, through the trees toward the tall grass and cover, and the crash came again to go past him ripping the air apart. Then it crashed again and he felt the blow as it hit his lower ribs and ripped on through, blood sudden hot and frothy in his mouth, and he galloped toward the high grass where he could crouch and not be seen and make them bring the crashing thing close enough so he could make a rush and get the man that held it.

Macomber had not thought how the lion felt as he got out of the car. He only knew his hands were shaking and as he walked away from the car it was almost impossible for him to make his legs move. They were stiff in the thighs, but he could feel the muscles fluttering. He raised the rifle, sighted on the junction of the lion's head and shoulders and pulled the trigger. Nothing happened though he pulled until he thought his finger would break. Then he knew he had the safety on and as he lowered the rifle to move the safety over he moved another frozen pace forward, and the lion seeing his silhouette now clear of the silhouette of the car, turned and started off at a trot, and, as Macomber fired, he heard a whunk that meant that the bullet was home; but the lion kept on going. Macomber shot again and every one saw the bullet throw a spout of dirt beyond the trotting lion. He shot again, remembering to lower his aim, and they all heard the bullet hit, and the lion went into a gallop and was in the tall grass before he had the bolt pushed forward.

Macomber stood there feeling sick at his stomach, his hands that held the Springfield still cocked, shaking, and his wife and Robert Wilson were standing by him. Beside him too were the two gun-bearers chattering in Wakamba.[9]

"I hit him," Macomber said. "I hit him twice."

"You gut-shot him and you hit him somewhere forward," Wilson said without enthusiasm. The gun-bearers looked very grave. They were silent now.

"You may have killed him," Wilson went on. "We'll have to wait a while before we go in to find out."

"What do you mean?"

"Let him get sick before we follow him up."

"Oh," said Macomber.

"He's a hell of a fine lion," Wilson said cheerfully. "He's gotten into a bad place though."

"Why is it bad?"

"Can't see him until you're on him."

"Oh," said Macomber.

"Come on," said Wilson. "The Memsahib can stay here in the car. We'll go to have a look at the blood spoor."[1]

"Stay here, Margot," Macomber said to his wife. His mouth was very dry and it was hard for him to talk.

"Why?" she asked.

"Wilson says to."

"We're going to have a look," Wilson said. "You stay here. You can see even better from here."

"All right."

---

9. The dialect of their tribe. In other incidents, the Swahili dialect is mentioned, that being generally understood by all tribesmen and most whites.
1. The track of a wild animal.

Wilson spoke in Swahili to the driver. He nodded and said, "Yes, Bwana." [2]

Then they went down the steep bank and across the stream, climbing over and around the boulders and up the other bank, pulling up by some projecting roots, and along it until they found where the lion had been trotting when Macomber first shot. There was dark blood on the short grass that the gun-bearers pointed out with grass stems, and that ran away behind the river bank trees.

"What do we do?" asked Macomber.

"Not much choice," said Wilson. "We can't bring the car over. Bank's too steep. We'll let him stiffen up a bit and then you and I'll go in and have a look for him."

"Can't we set the grass on fire?" Macomber asked.

"Too green."

"Can't we send beaters?"

Wilson looked at him appraisingly. "Of course we can," he said. "But it's just a touch murderous. You see we know the lion's wounded. You can drive an unwounded lion—he'll move on ahead of a noise—but a wounded lion's going to charge. You can't see him until you're right on him. He'll make himself perfectly flat in cover you wouldn't think would hide a hare. You can't very well send boys in there to that sort of a show. Somebody bound to get mauled."

"What about the gun-bearers?"

"Oh, they'll go with us. It's their *shauri*.[3] You see, they signed on for it. They don't look too happy though, do they?"

"I don't want to go in there," said Macomber. It was out before he knew he'd said it.

"Neither do I," said Wilson very cheerily. "Really no choice though." Then, as an afterthought, he glanced at Macomber and saw suddenly how he was trembling and the pitiful look on his face.

"You don't have to go in, of course," he said. "That's what I'm hired for, you know. That's why I'm so expensive."

"You mean you'd go in by yourself? Why not leave him there?"

Robert Wilson, whose entire occupation had been with the lion and the problem he presented, and who had not been thinking about Macomber except to note that he was rather windy, suddenly felt as though he had opened the wrong door in a hotel and seen something shameful.

"What do you mean?"

"Why not just leave him?"

2. In African lingua franca, a respectful term of address to a man.
3. An East African word from the Arabic, originally meaning "negotiation," but in the vernacular, "business" or "predicament."

"You mean pretend to ourselves he hasn't been hit?"

"No. Just drop it."

"It isn't done."

"Why not?"

"For one thing, he's certain to be suffering. For another, some one else might run onto him."

"I see."

"But you don't have to have anything to do with it."

"I'd like to," Macomber said. "I'm just scared, you know."

"I'll go ahead when we go in," Wilson said, "with Kongoni tracking. You keep behind me and a little to one side. Chances are we'll hear him growl. If we see him we'll both shoot. Don't worry about anything. I'll keep you backed up. As a matter of fact, you know, perhaps you'd better not go. It might be much better. Why don't you go over and join the Memsahib while I just get it over with?"

"No, I want to go."

"All right," said Wilson. "But don't go in if you don't want to. This is my *shauri* now, you know."

"I want to go," said Macomber.

They sat under a tree and smoked.

"Want to go back and speak to the Memsahib while we're waiting?" Wilson asked.

"No."

"I'll just step back and tell her to be patient."

"Good," said Macomber. He sat there, sweating under his arms, his mouth dry, his stomach hollow feeling, wanting to find courage to tell Wilson to go on and finish off the lion without him. He could not know that Wilson was furious because he had not noticed the state he was in earlier and sent him back to his wife. While he sat there Wilson came up. "I have your big gun," he said. "Take it. We've given him time, I think. Come on."

Macomber took the big gun and Wilson said:

"Keep behind me and about five yards to the right and do exactly as I tell you." Then he spoke in Swahili to the two gun-bearers who looked the picture of gloom.

"Let's go," he said.

"Could I have a drink of water?" Macomber asked. Wilson spoke to the older gun-bearer, who wore a canteen on his belt, and the man unbuckled it, unscrewed the top and handed it to Macomber, who took it noticing how heavy it seemed and how hairy and shoddy the felt covering was in his hand. He raised it to drink and looked ahead at the high grass with the flat-topped trees behind it. A breeze was blowing toward them and the grass rippled gently in the wind. He looked at the gun-bearer and he could see the gun-bearer was suffering too with fear.

Thirty-five yards into the grass the big lion lay flattened out along the ground. His ears were back and his only movement was a slight twitching up and down of his long, black-tufted tail. He had turned at bay as soon as he had reached this cover and he was sick with the wound through his full belly, and weakening with the wound through his lungs that brought a thin foamy red to his mouth each time he breathed. His flanks were wet and hot and flies were on the little openings the solid bullets had made in his tawny hide, and his big yellow eyes, narrowed with hate, looked straight ahead, only blinking when the pain came as he breathed, and his claws dug in the soft baked earth. All of him, pain, sickness, hatred and all of his remaining strength, was tightening into an absolute concentration for a rush. He could hear the men talking and he waited, gathering all of himself into this preparation for a charge as soon as the men would come into the grass. As he heard their voices his tail stiffened to twitch up and down, and, as they came into the edge of the grass, he made a coughing grunt and charged.

Kongoni, the old gun-bearer, in the lead watching the blood spoor, Wilson watching the grass for any movement, his big gun ready, the second gun-bearer looking ahead and listening, Macomber close to Wilson, his rifle cocked, they had just moved into the grass when Macomber heard the blood-choked coughing grunt, and saw the swishing rush in the grass. The next thing he knew he was running; running wildly, in panic in the open, running toward the stream.

He heard the *ca-ra-wong!* of Wilson's big rifle, and again in a second crashing *carawong!* and turning saw the lion, horrible-looking now, with half his head seeming to be gone, crawling toward Wilson in the edge of the tall grass while the red-faced man worked the bolt on the short ugly rifle and aimed carefully as another blasting *carawong!* came from the muzzle, and the crawling, heavy, yellow bulk of the lion stiffened and the huge, mutilated head slid forward and Macomber, standing by himself in the clearing where he had run, holding a loaded rifle, while two black men and a white man looked back at him in contempt, knew the lion dead. He came toward Wilson, his tallness all seeming a naked reproach, and Wilson looked at him and said:

"Want to take pictures?"

"No," he said.

That was all any one had said until they reached the motor car. Then Wilson had said:

"Hell of a fine lion. Boys will skin him out. We might as well stay here in the shade."

Macomber's wife had not looked at him nor he at her and he had sat by her in the back seat with Wilson sitting in the front seat. Once he had reached over and taken his wife's hand without looking at her and she had removed her hand from his. Looking across the stream to where the gun-bearers were skinning out the lion he could see that she had been able to see the whole thing. While they sat there his wife had reached forward and put her hand on Wilson's shoulder. He turned and she had leaned forward over the low seat and kissed him on the mouth.

"Oh, I say," said Wilson, going redder than his natural baked color.

"Mr. Robert Wilson," she said. "The beautiful red-faced Mr. Robert Wilson."

Then she sat down beside Macomber again and looked away across the stream to where the lion lay, with uplifted, white-muscled, tendon-marked naked forearms, and white bloating belly, as the black men fleshed away the skin. Finally the gun-bearers bought the skin over, wet and heavy, and climbed in behind with it, rolling it up before they got in, and the motor car started. No one had said anything more until they were back in camp.

That was the story of the lion. Macomber did not know how the lion had felt before he started his rush, nor during it when the unbelievable smash of the .505 with a muzzle velocity of two tons had hit him in the mouth, nor what kept him coming after that, when the second ripping crash had smashed his hind quarters and he had come crawling on toward the crashing, blasting thing that had destroyed him. Wilson knew something about it and only expressed it by saying, "Damned fine lion," but Macomber did not know how Wilson felt about things either. He did not know how his wife felt except that she was through with him.

His wife had been through with him before but it never lasted. He was very wealthy, and would be much wealthier, and he knew she would not leave him ever now. That was one of the few things that he really knew. He knew about that, about motor cycles—that was earliest—about motor cars, about duck-shooting, about fishing, trout, salmon and big-sea, about sex in books, many books, too many books, abut all court games, about dogs, not much about horses, about hanging on to his money, about most of the other things his world dealt in, and about his wife not leaving him. His wife had been a great beauty and she was still a great beauty in Africa, but she was not a great enough beauty any more at home to be able to leave him and better herself and she knew it and he knew it. She had missed the chance to leave him and he knew it. If he had been better with women she would probably have started to worry about him getting another new, beautiful wife; but she knew too much about him to worry about him either. Also, he had always had a great tolerance which seemed the nicest thing about him if it were not the most sinister.

All in all they were known as a comparatively happily married couple, one of those whose disruption is often rumored but never occurs, and as the society columnist put it, they were adding more than a spice of *adventure* to their much envied and ever-enduring *Romance* by a *Safari* in what was known as *Darkest Africa* until the Martin Johnsons [4] lighted it on so many silver screens where they were pushing *Old Simba* the lion, the buffalo, *Tembo* the elephant and as well collecting specimens for the Museum of Natural History. This same columnist had reported them *on the verge* at least three times in the past and they had been. But they always made it up. They had a sound basis of union. Margot was too beautiful for Macomber to divorce her and Macomber had too much money for Margot ever to leave him.

It was now about three o'clock in the morning and Francis Macomber, who had been asleep a little while after he had stopped thinking about the lion, wakened and then slept again, woke suddenly, frightened in a dream of the bloody-headed lion standing over him, and listening while his heart pounded, he realized that his wife was not in the other cot in the tent. He lay awake with that knowledge for two hours.

At the end of that time his wife came into the tent, lifted her mosquito bar and crawled cozily into bed.

"Where have you been?" Macomber asked in the darkness.

"Hello," she said. "Are you awake?"

"Where have you been?"

"I just went out to get a breath of air."

"You did, like hell."

"What do you want me to say, darling?"

"Where have you been?"

"Out to get a breath of air."

"That's a new name for it. You *are* a bitch."

"Well, you're a coward."

"All right," he said. "What of it?"

"Nothing as far as I'm concerned. But please let's not talk, darling, because I'm very sleepy."

"You think that I'll take anything."

"I know you will, sweet."

---

4. Martin E. Johnson (1884–1937), explorer and adventurer, attained popular fame by his books and motion pictures of African wild life in the twenties; his wife appeared with him in the films.

"Well, I won't."

"Please, darling, let's not talk. I'm so very sleepy."

"There wasn't going to be any of that. You promised there wouldn't be."

"Well, there is now," she said sweetly.

"You said if we made this trip that there would be none of that. You promised."

"Yes, darling. That's the way I meant it to be. But the trip was spoiled yesterday. We don't have to talk about it, do we?"

"You don't wait long when you have an advantage, do you?"

"Please let's not talk. I'm so sleepy, darling."

"I'm going to talk."

"Don't mind me then, because I'm going to sleep." And she did.

At breakfast they were all three at the table before daylight and Francis Macomber found that, of all the many men that he had hated, he hated Robert Wilson the most.

"Sleep well?" Wilson asked in his throaty voice, filling a pipe.

"Did you?"

"Topping," the white hunter told him.

You bastard, thought Macomber, you insolent bastard.

So she woke him when she came in, Wilson thought, looking at them both with his flat, cold eyes. Well, why doesn't he keep his wife where she belongs? What does he think I am, a bloody plaster saint? Let him keep her where she belongs. It's his own fault.

"Do you think we'll find buffalo?" Margot asked, pushing away a dish of apricots.

"Chance of it," Wilson said and smiled at her. "Why don't you stay in camp?"

"Not for anything," she told him.

"Why not order her to stay in camp?" Wilson said to Macomber.

"You order her," said Macomber coldly.

"Let's not have any ordering, nor," turning to Macomber, "any silliness, Francis," Margot said quite pleasantly.

"Are you ready to start?" Macomber asked.

"Any time," Wilson told him. "Do you want the Memsahib to go?"

"Does it make any difference whether I do or not?"

The hell with it, thought Robert Wilson. The utter complete hell with it. So this is what it's going to be like. Well, this is what it's going to be like, then.

"Makes no difference," he said.

"You're sure you wouldn't like to stay in camp with her yourself and let me go out and hunt the buffalo?" Macomber asked.

"Can't do that," said Wilson. "Wouldn't talk rot if I were you."

"I'm not talking rot. I'm disgusted."

"Bad word, disgusted."

"Francis, will you please try to speak sensibly?" his wife said.

"I speak too damned sensibly," Macomber said. "Did you ever eat such filthy food?"

"Something wrong with the food?" asked Wilson quietly.

"No more than with everything else."

"I'd pull yourself together, laddybuck," Wilson said very quietly. "There's a boy waits at table that understands a little English."

"The hell with him."

Wilson stood up and puffing on his pipe strolled away, speaking a few words in Swahili to once of the gun-bearers who was standing waiting for him. Macomber and his wife sat on at the table. He was staring at his coffee cup.

"If you make a scene I'll leave you, darling," Margot said quietly.

"No, you won't."

"You can try it and see."

"You won't leave me."

"No," she said. "I won't leave you and you'll behave yourself."

"Behave myself? That's a way to talk. Behave myself."

"Yes. Behave yourself."

"Why don't *you* try behaving?"

"I've tried it so long. So very long."

"I hate that red-faced swine," Macomber said. "I loathe the sight of him."

"He's really *very* nice."

"Oh, *shut up*," Macomber almost shouted. Just then the car came up and stopped in front of the dining tent and the driver and the two gun-bearers got out. Wilson walked over and looked at the husband and wife sitting there at the table.

"Going shooting?" he asked.

"Yes," said Macomber, standing up. "Yes."

"Better bring a woolly. It will be cool in the car," Wilson said.

"I'll get my leather jacket," Margot said.

"The boy has it," Wilson told her. He climbed into the front with the driver and Francis Macomber and his wife, not speaking, in the back seat.

Hope the silly beggar doesn't take a notion to blow the back of my head off, Wilson thought to himself. Women *are* a nuisance on safari.

The car was grinding down to cross the river at a pebbly ford in the gray daylight and then climbed, angling up the steep bank, where Wilson had ordered a way shovelled out the day before so they could reach the parklike wooded rolling country on the far side.

It was a good morning, Wilson thought. There was a heavy dew and as the wheels went through the grass and low bushes he could smell the odor of the crushed fronds. It was an odor like verbena and he liked this early morning smell of the dew, the crushed bracken and the look of the tree trunks showing black through the early morning mist, as the car made its way through the untracked, parklike country. He had put the two in the back seat out of his mind now and was thinking about buffalo. The buffalo that he was after stayed in the daytime in a thick swamp where it was impossible to get a shot, but in the night they fed out into an open stretch of country and if he could come between them and their swamp with the car, Macomber would have a good chance at them in the open. He did not want to hunt buff with Macomber in thick cover. He did not want to hunt buff or anything else with Macomber at all, but he was a professional hunter and he had hunted with some rare ones in his time. If they got buff today there would only be rhino to come and the poor man would have gone through his dangerous game and things might pick up. He'd have nothing more to do with the woman and Macomber would get over that too. He must have gone through plenty of that before by the look of things. Poor beggar. He must have a way of getting over it. Well, it was the poor sod's own bloody fault.

He, Robert Wilson, carried a double size cot on safari to accommodate any windfalls he might receive. He had hunted for a certain clientele, the international, fast, sporting set, where the women did not feel they were getting their money's worth unless they had shared that cot with the white hunter. He despised them when he was away from them although he liked some of them well enough at the time, but he made his living by them; and their standards were his standards as long as they were hiring him.

They were his standards in all except the shooting. He had his own standards about the killing and they could live up to them or get some one else to hunt them. He knew, too, that they all respected him for this. This Macomber was an odd one though. Damned if he wasn't. Now the wife. Well, the wife. Yes, the wife. Hm, the wife. Well he'd dropped all that. He looked around at them. Macomber sat grim and furious. Margot smiled at him. She looked younger today, more innocent and fresher and not so professionally beautiful. What's in her heart God knows, Wilson thought. She hadn't talked much last night. At that it was a pleasure to see her.

The motor car climbed up a slight rise and went on through the trees and then out into a grassy prairie-like opening and kept in the shelter of the trees along the edge, the driver going slowly and Wilson looking carefully out across the prairie and all along its far side. He stopped the car and studied the opening with his field glasses. Then he motioned to the driver to go on and the car moved slowly along, the driver avoiding wart-hog holes and driving around the mud castles ants had built. Then, looking across the opening, Wilson suddenly turned and said,

"By God, there they are!"

And looking where he pointed, while the car jumped forward and Wilson spoke in rapid Swahili to the driver, Macomber saw three huge, black animals looking almost cylindrical in their long heaviness, like big black tank cars, moving at a gallop across the far edge of the open prairie. They moved at a stiff-necked, stiff bodied gallop and he could see the upswept wide black horns on their heads as they galloped heads out; the heads not moving.

"They're three old bulls," Wilson said. "We'll cut them off before they get to the swamp."

The car was going a wild forty-five miles an hour across the open and as Macomber watched, the buffalo got bigger and bigger until he could see the gray, hairless, scabby look of one huge bull and how his neck was a part of his shoulders and the shiny black of his horns as he galloped a little behind the others that were strung out in that steady plunging gait; and then, the car swaying as though it had just jumped a road, they drew up close and he could see the plunging hugeness of the bull, and the dust in his sparsely haired hide, the wide boss of horn and his outstretched, wide-nostrilled muzzle, and he was raising his rifle when Wilson shouted, "Not from the car, you fool!" and he had no fear, only hatred of Wilson, while the brakes clamped on and the car skidded, plowing sideways to an almost stop and Wilson was out on one side and he on the other, stumbling as his feet hit the still speeding-by of the earth, and then he was shooting at the bull as he moved away, hearing the bullets whunk into him, emptying his rifle at him as he moved steadily away, finally remembering to get his shots forward into the shoulder, and as he fumbled to re-load, he saw the bull was down. Down on his knees, his big head tossing, and seeing the other two still galloping he shot at the leader and hit him. He shot again and missed and he heard the *carawonging* roar as Wilson shot and saw the leading bull slide forward onto his nose.

"Get that other," Wilson said. "Now you're shooting!"

But the other bull was moving steadily at the same gallop and he missed, throwing a spout of dirt, and Wilson missed and the dust rose in a cloud and Wilson shouted, "Come on. He's too far!" and grabbed his arm and they were in the car again, Macomber and Wilson hanging on the sides and rocketing swayingly over the uneven ground, drawing up on the steady, plunging, heavy-necked, straight-moving gallop of the bull.

They were behind him and Macomber was filling his rifle, dropping shells onto the ground, jamming it, clearing the jam, then they were almost up with the bull when Wilson yelled "Stop," and the car skidded so that it almost swung over and Macomber fell forward onto his feet, slammed his bolt forward and fired as far forward as he could aim into the galloping, rounded black back, aimed and shot again, then again, then again, and the bullets, all of them hitting, had no effect on the buffalo that he could see. Then Wilson shot, the roar deafening him, and he could see the bull stagger. Macomber shot again, aiming carefully, and down he came, onto his knees.

"All right," Wilson said. "Nice work. That's the three."

Macomber felt a drunken elation.

"How many times did you shoot?" he asked.

"Just three," Wilson said. "You killed the first bull. The biggest one. I helped you finish the other two. Afraid they might have got into cover. You had them killed. I was just mopping up a little. You shot damn well."

"Let's go to the car," said Macomber. "I want a drink."

"Got to finish off that buff first," Wilson told him. The buffalo was on his knees and he jerked his head furiously and bellowed in pig-eyed, roaring rage as they came toward him.

"Watch he doesn't get up," Wilson said. Then, "Get a little broadside and take him in the neck just behind the ear."

Macomber aimed carefully at the center of the huge, jerking, rage-driven neck and shot. At the shot the head dropped forward.

"That does it," said Wilson. "Got the spine. They're a hell of a looking thing, aren't they?"

"Let's get the drink," said Macomber. In his life he had never felt so good.

In the car Macomber's wife sat very white faced. "You were marvellous, darling," she said to Macomber. "What a ride."

"Was it rough?" Wilson asked.

"It was frightful. I've never been more frightened in my life."

"Let's all have a drink," Macomber said.

"By all means," said Wilson. "Give it to the Memsahib." She drank the neat whisky from the flask and shuddered a little when she swallowed. She handed the flask to Macomber who handed it to Wilson.

"It was frightfully exciting," she said. "It's given me a dreadful headache. I didn't know you were allowed to shoot them from cars though."

"No one shot from cars," said Wilson coldly.

"I mean chase them from cars."

"Wouldn't ordinarily," Wilson said. "Seemed sporting enough to me though while we were doing it. Taking more chance driving that way across the plain full of holes and one thing and another than hunting on foot. Buffalo could have charged us each time we shot if he liked. Gave him every chance. Wouldn't mention it to any one, though. It's illegal if that's what you mean."

"It seemed very unfair to me," Margot said, "chasing those big helpless things in a motor car."

"Did it?" said Wilson.

"What would happen if they heard about it in Nairobi?" [5]

"I'd lose my licence for one thing. Other unpleasantnesses," Wilson said, taking a drink from the flask. "I'd be out of business."

"Really?"

"Yes, really."

"Well," said Macomber, and he smiled for the first time all day. "Now she has something on you."

"You have such a pretty way of putting things, Francis," Margot Macomber said. Wilson looked at them both. If a four-letter man marries a five-letter woman, he was thinking, what number of letters would their children be? What he said was, "We lost a gun-bearer. Did you notice it?"

"My God, no," Macomber said.

"Here he comes," Wilson said. "He's all right. He must have fallen off when we left the first bull."

Approaching them was the middle-aged gun-bearer, limping along in his knitted cap, khaki tunic, shorts and rubber sandals, gloomy-faced and disgusted looking. As he came up he called out to Wilson in Swahili and they all saw the change in the white hunter's face.

"What does he say?" asked Margot.

"He says the first bull got up and went into the bush," Wilson said with no expression in his voice.

"Oh," said Macomber blankly.

"Then it's going to be just like the lion," said Margot, full of anticipation.

"It's not going to be just like the lion," Wilson told her. "Did you want another drink, Macomber?"

"Thanks, yes," Macomber said. He expected the feeling he had had about the lion to come back but it did not. For the first time in his life he really felt wholly without fear. Instead of fear he had a feeling of definite elation.

"We'll go and have a look at the second bull," Wilson said. "I'll tell the driver to put the car in the shade."

"What are you going to do?" asked Margaret Macomber.

"Take a look at the buff," Wilson said.

5. Capital of Kenya, British East Africa colony and protectorate, which is the scene of this story, and now a nation.

"I'll come."

"Come along."

The three of them walked over to where the second buffalo bulked blackly in the open, head forward on the grass, the massive horns swung wide.

"He's a very good head," Wilson said. "That's close to a fifty-inch spread."

Macomber was looking at him with delight.

"He's hateful looking," said Margot. "Can't we go into the shade?"

"Of course," Wilson said. "Look," he said to Macomber, and pointed. "See that patch of bush?"

"Yes."

"That's where the first bull went in. The gun-bearer said when he fell off the bull was down. He was watching us helling along and the other two buff galloping. When he looked up there was the bull up and looking at him. Gun-bearer ran like hell and the bull went off slowly into that bush."

"Can we go in after him now?" asked Macomber eagerly.

Wilson looked at him appraisingly. Damned if this isn't a strange one, he thought. Yesterday he's scared sick and today he's a ruddy fire eater.

"No, we'll give him a while."

"Let's please go into the shade," Margot said. Her face was white and she looked ill.

They made their way to the car where it stood under a single, wide-spreading tree and all climbed in.

"Chances are he's dead in there," Wilson remarked. "After a little we'll have a look."

Macomber felt a wild unreasonable happiness that he had never known before.

"By God, that was a chase," he said. "I've never felt any such feeling. Wasn't it marvellous, Margot?"

"I hated it."

"Why?"

"I hated it," she said bitterly. "I loathed it."

"You know I don't think I'd ever be afraid of anything again," Macomber said to Wilson. "Something happened in me after we first saw the buff and started after him. Like a dam bursting. It was pure excitement."

"Cleans out your liver," said Wilson. "Damn funny things happen to people."

Macomber's face was shining. "You know something did happen to me," he said. "I feel absolutely different."

His wife said nothing and eyed him strangely. She was sitting far back in the seat and Macomber was sitting forward talking to Wilson who turned sideways talking over the back of the front seat.

"You know, I'd like to try another lion," Macomber said. "I'm really not afraid of them now. After all, what can they do to you?"

"That's it," said Wilson. "Worst one can do is kill you. How does it go? Shakespeare. Damned good. See if I can remember. Oh, damned good. Used to quote it to myself at one time. Let's see. 'By my troth, I care not; a man can die but once; we owe God a death and let it go which way it will he that dies this year is quit for the next.' Damned fine, eh?"

He was very embarrassed, having brought out this thing he had lived by, but he had seen men come of age before and it always moved him. It was not a matter of their twenty-first birthday.

It had taken a strange chance of hunting, a sudden precipitation into action without opportunity for worrying beforehand, to bring this about with Macomber, but regardless of how it had happened it had most certainly happened. Look at the beggar now, Wilson thought. It's that some of them stay little boys so long, Wilson thought. Sometimes all their lives. Their figures stay boyish when they're fifty. The great American boy-men. Damned strange people. But he liked this Macomber now. Damned strange fellow. Probably meant the end of cuckoldry too. Well, that would be a damned good thing. Damned good thing. Beggar had probably been afraid all his life. Don't know what started it. But over now. Hadn't had time to be afraid with the buff. That and being angry too. Motor car too. Motor cars made it familiar. Be a damn fire eater now. He'd seen it in the war work the same way. More of a change than any loss of virginity. Fear gone like an operation. Something else grew in its place. Main thing a man had. Made him into a man. Women knew it too. No bloody fear.

From the far corner of the seat Margaret Macomber looked at the two of them. There was no change in Wilson. She saw Wilson as she had seen him the day before when she had first realized what his great talent was. But she saw the change in Francis Macomber now.

"Do you have that feeling of happiness about what's going to happen?" Macomber asked, still exploring his new wealth.

"You're not supposed to mention it," Wilson said, looking in the other's face. "Much more fashionable to say you're scared. Mind you, you'll be scared too, plenty of times."

"But you *have* a feeling of happiness about action to come?"

"Yes," said Wilson. "There's that. Doesn't do to talk too much about all this. Talk the whole thing away. No pleasure in anything if you mouth it up too much."

"You're both talking rot," said Margot. "Just because you've chased some helpless animals in a motor car you talk like heroes."

"Sorry," said Wilson. "I have been gassing too much." She's worried about it already, he thought.

"If you don't know what we're talking about why not keep out of it?" Macomber asked his wife.

"You've gotten awfully brave, awfully suddenly," his wife said contemptuously, but her contempt was not secure. She was very afraid of something.

Macomber laughed, a very natural hearty laugh. "You know I *have*," he said. "I really have."

"Isn't it sort of late?" Margot said bitterly. Because she had done the best she could for many years back and the way they were together now was no one person's fault.

"Not for me," said Macomber.

Margot said nothing but sat back in the corner of the seat.

"Do you think we've given him time enough?" Macomber asked Wilson cheerfully.

"We might have a look," Wilson said. "Have you any solids left?"

"The gun-bearer has some."

Wilson called in Swahili and the older gun-bearer, who was skinning out one of the heads, straightened up, pulled a box of solids out of his pocket and brought them over to Macomber, who filled his magazine and put the remaining shells in his pocket.

"You might as well shoot the Springfield," Wilson said. "You're used to it. We'll leave the Mannlicher in the car with the Memsahib. Your gun-bearer can carry your heavy gun. I've this damned cannon. Now let me tell you about them." He had saved this until the last because he did not want to worry Macomber. "When a buff comes he comes with his head high and thrust straight out. The boss of the horns covers any sort of a brain shot. The only shot is straight into the nose. The only other shot is into his chest or, if you're to one side, into the neck or the shoulders. After they've been hit once they take a hell of a lot of killing. Don't try anything fancy. Take the easiest shot there is. They've finished skinning out that head now. Should we get started?"

He called to the gun-bearers, who came up wiping their hands, and the older one got into the back.

"I'll only take Kongoni," Wilson said. "The other can watch to keep the birds away."

As the car moved slowly across the open space toward the island of brushy trees that ran in a tongue of foliage along a dry water course that cut the open swale, Macomber felt his heart pounding and his mouth was dry again, but it was excitement, not fear.

"Here's where he went in," Wilson said. Then to the gun-bearer in Swahili, "Take the blood spoor."

The car was parallel to the patch of bush. Macomber, Wilson and the gun-bearer got down. Macomber, looking back, saw his wife, with the rifle by her side, looking at him. He waved to her and she did not wave back.

The brush was very thick ahead and the ground was dry. The middle-aged gun-bearer was sweating heavily and Wilson had his hat down over his eyes and his red neck showed just ahead of Macomber. Suddenly the gun-bearer said something in Swahili to Wilson and ran forward.

"He's dead in there," Wilson said. "Good work," and he turned to grip Macomber's hand and as they shook hands, grinning at each other, the gun-bearer shouted wildly and they saw him coming out of the bush sideways, fast as a crab, and the bull coming, nose out, mouth tight closed, blood dripping, massive head straight out, coming in a charge, his little pig eyes bloodshot as he looked at them. Wilson, who was ahead was kneeling shooting, and Macomber, as he fired, unhearing his shot in the roaring of Wilson's gun, saw fragments like slate burst from the huge boss of the horns, and the head jerked, he shot again at the wide nostrils and saw the horns jolt again and fragments fly, and he did not see Wilson now and, aiming carefully, shot again with the buffalo's huge bulk almost on him and his rifle almost level with the on-coming head, nose out, and he could see the little wicked eyes and the head start to lower and he felt a sudden white-hot, blinding flash explode inside his head and that was all he ever felt.

Wilson had ducked to one side to get in a shoulder shot. Macomber had stood solid and shot for the nose, shooting a touch high each time and hitting the heavy horns, splintering and chipping them like hitting a slate roof, and Mrs. Macomber, in the car, had shot at the buffalo with the 6.5 Mannlicher as it seemed about to gore Macomber and had hit her husband about two inches up and a little to one side of the base of his skull.

Francis Macomber lay now, face down, not two yards from where the buffalo lay on his side and his wife knelt over him with Wilson beside her.

"I wouldn't turn him over," Wilson said.

The woman was crying hysterically.

"I'd get back in the car," Wilson said. "Where's the rifle?"

She shook her head, her face contorted. The gun-bearer picked up the rifle.

"Leave it as it is," said Wilson. Then, "Go get Abdulla so that he may witness the manner of the accident."

He knelt down, took a handkerchief from his pocket, and spread it over Francis Macomber's crew-cropped head where it lay. The blood sank into the dry, loose earth.

Wilson stood up and saw the buffalo on his side, his legs out, his thinly-haired belly crawling with ticks. "Hell of a good bull," his brain registered automatically. "A good fifty inches, or better. Better." He called to the driver and told him to spread a blanket over the body and stay by it. Then he walked over to the motor car where the woman sat crying in the corner.

"That was a pretty thing to do," he said in a toneless voice. "He *would* have left you too."

"Stop it," she said.

"Of course it's an accident," he said. "I know that."

"Stop it," she said.

"Don't worry," he said. "There will be a certain amount of unpleasantness but I will have some photographs taken that will be very useful at the inquest. There's the testimony of the gun-bearers and the driver too. You're perfectly all right."

"Stop it," she said.

"There's a hell of a lot to be done," he said. "And I'll have to send a truck off to the lake to wireless for a plane to take the three of us into Nairobi. Why didn't you poison him? That's what they do in England."

"Stop it. Stop it. Stop it," the woman cried.

Wilson looked at her with his flat blue eyes.

"I'm through now," he said. "I was a little angry. I'd begun to like your husband."

"Oh, please stop it," she said. "Please, please stop it."

"That's better," Wilson said. "Please is much better. Now I'll stop."

1935   1936, 1938

THOMAS WOLFE
(1900–1938)

When Thomas Wolfe died, at the age of thirty-eight, he left four large novels, two of them not then published, besides numerous stories and miscellaneous writings. Both the man and his work were in certain respects unprecedented. The novels were not experimental in the formal sense; they used established methods of objective narration; yet, especially in the first two, the presence of the author himself was almost overwhelming. It became evident that Wolfe was his own character, whether Eugene Gant or George Webber, in all four books; and that he was producing a kind of domestic *roman à clef* in which the identifiable characters were not historical figures, but his own family and associates, depicted in scenes and situations which corresponded with those of his own life, whether in his native Asheville, North Carolina—which he called Altamont—or at the university, or in New York.

This was not the autobiographical novel as Dickens, for example, wrote it in *David Copperfield*, by inventing new events and characters to be placed within the chronological framework of his own life. Wolfe did not "invent" his important characters in the usual sense of the word; he discovered them. What he invented was a method of analyzing experience that did not need to be invented—his own. What he attempted was a new novel of spiritual exploration, and his *terra incognita* was composed of the people and the experience which he had absorbed as a result of his insatiable appetite for life.

That life began on October 3, 1900, at Asheville, then primarily a resort town, situated in the western North Carolina highlands. His father, the Oliver Gant of the novels, was a stonecutter, and his mother, portrayed as Eliza Gant, managed a residential boardinghouse in real life also. Like Eugene Gant in *Look Homeward, Angel*, Tom Wolfe did odd jobs, sold papers and magazines, and wondered about his father, who, like Oliver in "An Angel on the Porch," combined earthiness with quixotic sentiment and the habit of reciting poetry to any who would listen.

Huge in frame and abounding in energy, young Wolfe went down to the University of North Carolina in 1916 with his voracious appetence for life, knowledge, experience, food, smells, sensation, and in fact the world. There he read widely, began to write, and studied the theater in courses under the talented Frederick Koch, founder of the famous Carolina Playmakers. For them the young student wrote two plays, one later published in a collection by Professor Koch. Upon his graduation in 1920 Wolfe enrolled at Harvard, where he was a student in the "47 Workshop" of George Pierce Baker, and took his M.A. It was inevitable that he should bring with him a manuscript play when he went to New York in 1922, but producers were not impressed with this or later attempts, and Wolfe cherished for years his defeated first love for the theater. In the meantime, he supported himself by teaching composition at New York University while pouring out the stored material of his first novel, and until 1930 he continued to teach there intermittently.

Maxwell Perkins, a talented editor of the staff of Charles Scribner's Sons, has minimized the exaggerated legend that he was primarily responsible for Wolfe's first two novels. It is certain, however, that Wolfe had an enormous manuscript, whose bulk obscured the organic organization of a novel, and that after other editors had declined it, Perkins recognized his opportunity and obligation. He suggested the means by which the author could set aside certain materials for possible future use and could concentrate and give more formal order to the manuscript, which appeared as *Look Homeward, Angel* in 1929.

It was a distinguished success, and Wolfe's proposal for foreign travel to provide background for his novels won him a Guggenheim Fellowship which took him in 1930–1931 to Europe. He was particularly interested in Germany, where his visit provided fundamental materials for his last two novels, and laid the foundations for his quite considerable foreign recognition. The remainder of his short life was given to the prodigious literary re-creation of an accumulation of experience which he himself recognized as "gargantuan." His twice-renewed love affair with a famous and talented artist and designer both harrowed and enriched his spirit. His second novel, *Of Time and the River*, appeared in 1935, and his collection of short stories, *From Death to Morning*, also was published in that year. Still the furious fever of life and composition continued to drive him. By May of 1938 he had finished a third novel, and he had also placed in his publisher's hands the outline of a fourth, together with manuscript material including the entire text but still needing final pruning and organization. In July he was stricken by influenza, and pneumonia threatened. The febrile excitement of his creative life may at last have worn down his gigantic strength; at any rate, while recovering he contracted a cerebral infection, which caused his death on September 15, 1938.

The Web and the Rock ap-

peared posthumously in 1939, and *You Can't Go Home Again* in 1940. The protagonist in these works is George Webber, not Eugene Gant, but both are exaggerations, simplifications, and explanations of Thomas Wolfe himself. The fact that they are also the universal youth in quest of spiritual security and selfhood is what raises the novels above the literature of "confessions" into the realm of creative originality.

Wolfe matured rapidly. His prose was lyrical, befitting the subjective nature of his novels, and it was steadily enriched by his unusual sense of verbal associations and by his mammoth literary memory. The range of his imagination, like that of Whitman, at last embodied the myth of his country: her great cities interlaced by railroads no less than the continental immensity of her natural domain were symbols of the amplitude and creative energies of mankind, the final object of his study.

There is no collected edition of Wolfe's writings. In addition to the major titles named in the text above are the following: *The Story of a Novel*, 1936, Wolfe's revealing comment upon his personality and his work; *The Hills Beyond*, 1941, short stories; *Mannerhouse, A Play*, 1948; and *The Mountains*, edited by Pat M. Ryan, 1970, an early play; *The Letters of Thomas Wolfe*, 1956, edited by Elizabeth Nowell; *The Letters of Thomas Wolfe to His Mother*, edited by C. Hugh Holman and Sue F. Ross, 1968; and *The Notebooks of Thomas Wolfe*, edited by R. S. Kennedy and P. Reeves, 2 vols., 1970.

Full-length biographies are Elizabeth Nowell, *Thomas Wolfe*, 1960; and Andrew Turnbull, *Thomas Wolfe*, 1967. Other biographical and critical appraisals are: E. C. Aswell, "A Note on Thomas Wolfe," prefatory to *The*

Hills Beyond; H. J. Muller, *Thomas Wolfe,* 1947; Pamela H. Johnson, *Hungry Gulliver: An English Critical Appraisal of Thomas Wolfe,* 1948; Louis D. Rubin, *Thomas Wolfe, The Weather of His Youth,* 1955; and Floyd D. Watkins, *Thomas Wolfe's Characters,* 1957. Two volumes covering Wolfe's years at New York University are T. C. Pollock and Oscar Cargill, *Thomas Wolfe at Washington Square,* 1954; and *The Correspondence of Thomas Wolfe and Homer Andrew Watt,* edited by T. C. Pollock and Oscar Cargill, 1954. More recent studies include Richard Walsen, *Thomas Wolfe,* 1962; Richard S. Kennedy, *The Window of Memory: The Literary Career of Thomas Wolfe,* 1962; Richard Walser, *Thomas Wolfe: An Introduction and Interpretation,* 1967; and Leslie A. Field, ed., *Thomas Wolfe: Three Decades of Criticism,* 1968.

An Angel on the Porch [1]

Late on an afternoon in young summer Queen Elizabeth came quickly up into the square past Gant's marbleshop. Surrounded by the stones, the slabs, the cold carved lambs of death, the stone-cutter leaned upon the rail and talked with Jannadeau, the faithful burly Swiss who, fenced in a little rented place among Gant's marbles, was probing with delicate monocled intentness into the entrails of a watch.

"There goes the Queen," said Gant, stopping for a moment their debate.

"A smart woman. A pippin as sure as you're born," he added with relish.

He bowed gallantly with a sweeping flourish of his great-boned frame of six feet five. "Good evening, madam."

She replied with a bright smile of friendliness which may have had in it the flicker of old memory, including Jannadeau with a cheerful impersonal nod. For just a moment more she paused, turning her candid stare upon smooth granite slabs of death, carved lambs and cherubim within the shop, and finally on an angel stationed beside the door upon Gant's little porch. Then, with her brisk, firm tread, she passed the shop, untroubled by the jeweller's heavy stare of wounded virtue, as he glowered up from his dirty littered desk, following her vanishing form with a guttural mutter of distaste.

They resumed their debate:

"And you may mark my words," proceeded Gant, wetting his big thumb, as if he had never been interrupted, and continuing his attack upon the Democratic party, and all the bad weather, fire, famine, and pestilence that attended its administration, "if they get in again we'll have soup-kitchens, the banks will go to the

---

1. "An Angel on the Porch," the first piece of major fiction published by Thomas Wolfe, appeared as a short story in *Scribner's Magazine* for August, 1929. The same year it appeared again as Chapter 19 of Wolfe's first novel, *Look Homeward, Angel.* Soon after the author's death, his publishers reprinted this, his first story, side by side with his last story, "The Party at Jack's," in *Scribner's Magazine* for May, 1939.

wall, and your guts will grease your backbone before another winter's over."

The Swiss thrust out a dirty hand toward the library he consulted in all disputed areas—a greasy edition of "The World Almanac," three years old—saying triumphantly, after a moment of dirty thumbing, in strange wrenched accent: "Ah—just as I thought: the muni-*cip*-al taxation of Milwaukee under De*moc*-ratic administration in 1905 was two dollars and twenty-five cents the hundred, the lowest it had been in years. I cannot ima-*gine* why the total revenue is not given."

Judiciously reasonable, statistically argumentative, the Swiss argued with animation against his Titan, picking his nose with blunt black fingers, his broad yellow face breaking into flaccid creases, as he laughed gutturally at Gant's unreason, and at the rolling periods of his rhetoric.

Thus they talked in the shadow of the big angel that stood just beyond the door upon Gant's porch, leering down upon their debate with a smile of idiot benevolence. Thus they talked, while Elizabeth passed by, in the cool damp of Gant's fantastical brick shack, surrounded by the stones, the slabs, the cold carved lambs of death. And as they talked the gray and furtive eyes of the stone-cutter, which darkened so seldom now with the shade of the old hunger—for stone and the cold wrought face of an angel—looked out into the square at all the little pullulation of the town, touched, as that woman passed his door with gallant tread, by a memory he thought had died forever. The lost words. The forgotten faces. Where? When?

He was getting on to sixty-five, his long, erect body had settled, he stooped a little. He spoke of old age often, and he wept in his tirades now because of his great right hand, stiffened by rheumatism, which once had carved so cunningly the dove, the lamb, the cold joined hands of death (but never the soft stone face of an angel). Soaked in pity, he referred to himself as "The poor old cripple who has to provide for the whole family."

That proud and sensual flesh was on its way to dust.

The indolence of age and disintegration was creeping over him. He rose now a full hour later, he came to his shop punctually, but he spent long hours of the day extended on the worn leather couch of his office, or in gossip with Jannadeau, bawdy old Liddell, Cardiac, his doctor, and Fagg Sluder, who had salted away his fortune in two big buildings on the square, and was at the present moment tilted comfortably in a chair before the fire department, gossiping eagerly with members of the ball club, whose chief support he was. It was after five o'clock, the game was over.

Negro laborers, grisly with a white coating of cement, sloped down past the shop on their way home. The draymen dispersed slowly, a slouchy policeman loafed down the steps of the city hall picking his teeth, and on the market side, from high grilled windows, there came the occasional howls of a drunken negress. Life buzzed slowly like a fly.

The sun had reddened slightly, there was a cool flowing breath from the hills, a freshening relaxation over the tired earth, the hope, the ecstasy, of evening in the air. In slow pulses the thick plume of fountain rose, fell upon itself, and slapped the pool in lazy rhythms. A wagon rattled leanly over the big cobbles; beyond the firemen, the grocer Bradly wound up his awning with slow, creaking revolutions.

Across the square at its other edge the young virgins of the eastern part of town walked lightly home in chattering groups. They came to town at four o'clock in the afternoon, walked up and down the little avenue several times, entered a shop to purchase small justifications, and finally went into the chief drugstore, where the bucks of the town loafed and drawled in lazy, alert groups. It was their club, their brasserie, the forum of the sexes. With confident smiles the young men detached themselves from their group and strolled back to booth and table.

"Hey theah! Wheahd you come from?"

"Move ovah theah, lady. I want to tawk to you."

Gant looked and saw. His thin mouth was tickled by a faint sly smile. He wet his big thumb quickly.

While his fugitive eyes roved over the east end of the square, Gant talked with Jannadeau. Before the shop the comely matrons of the town came up from the market. From time to time they smiled, seeing him, and he bowed sweepingly. Such lovely manners!

"The king of England," he observed, "is only a figurehead. He doesn't begin to have the power of the President of the United States."

"His power is severely li*mi*ted," said Jannadeau gutturally, "by custom but not by statute. In actua*lity* he is still one of the most powerful monarchs in the world." His thick black fingers probed carefully into the viscera of a watch.

"The late King Edward, for all his faults," said Gant, wetting his thumb, "was a smart man. This fellow they've got now is a nonentity and a nincompoop." He grinned faintly, with pleasure, at this ghost of his old rhetoric, glancing furtively at the Swiss to see if the big words told.

His uneasy eyes followed carefully the stylish carriage of Queen Elizabeth's well-clad figure as she came down by the shop again.

She smiled pleasantly, bound homeward for her latticed terrace. He bowed elaborately.

"Good evening, madam," he said.

She disappeared. In a moment she came back decisively and mounted the broad steps. He watched her approach with quickened pulses. Twelve years.

"How's the madam?" he said gallantly as she crossed the porch. "Elizabeth, I was just telling Jannadeau you were the most stylish woman in town."

"Well, that's mighty sweet of you, Mr. Gant," she said in her cool, poised voice. "You've got a good word for every one."

She gave a bright, pleasant nod to Jannadeau, who swung his huge scowling head ponderously around and muttered at her.

"Why, Elizabeth," said Gant, "you haven't changed an inch in fifteen years. I don't believe you're a day older."

She was thirty-eight and cheerfully aware of it.

"Oh, yes," she said laughing. "You're only saying that to make me feel good. I'm no chicken any more."

She had a pale, clear skin, pleasantly freckled, carrot-colored hair, and a thin mouth live with humor. Her figure was trim and strong—no longer young. She had a great deal of energy, distinction, and elegance in her manner.

"How are all the girls, Elizabeth?" he asked kindly.

Her face grew sad. She began to pull her gloves off.

"That's what I came in to see you about," she said. "I lost one of them last week."

"Yes," said Gant gravely. "I was sorry to hear of that."

"She was the best girl I had," said Elizabeth. "I'd have done anything in the world for her. We did everything we could," she added. "I've no regrets on that score. I had a doctor and two trained nurses by her all the time."

She opened her black leather handbag. thrust her gloves into it, and pulling out a small blue-bordered handkerchief began to weep quietly.

"Huh-huh-huh-huh-huh," said Gant, shaking his head. "Too bad, too bad, too bad. Come back to my office," he said. They went back to the dusty little room and sat down. Elizabeth dried her eyes.

"What was her name?" he asked.

"We called her Lily—her full name was Lilian Reed."

"Why, I knew that girl," he exclaimed. "I spoke to her not over two weeks ago." He convinced himself permanently that this was true.

"Yes," said Elizabeth, "she went like that—one hemorrhage right after another. Nobody ever knew she was sick until last Wednesday. Friday she was gone." She wept again.

"T-t-t-t-t-t," he clucked regretfully. "Too bad, too bad. She was pretty as a picture."

"I couldn't have loved her more, Mr. Gant," said Elizabeth, "if she had been my own daughter."

"How old was she?" he asked.

"Twenty-two," said Elizabeth, beginning to weep again.

"What a pity! What a pity!" he agreed. "Did she have any people?"

"No one who would do anything for her," Elizabeth said. "Her mother died when she was thirteen—she was born out here on the Beetree Fork—and her father," she added indignantly, "is a mean old devil who's never done anything for her or any one else. He didn't even come to her funeral."

"He will be punished," said Gant darkly.

"As sure as there's a God in heaven," Elizabeth agreed, "he'll get what's coming to him in hell. The dirty old crook!" she continued virtuously, "I hope he rots!"

"You can depend upon it," he said grimly. "He will. Ah, Lord." He was silent a moment while he shook his head with slow regret.

"A pity, a pity," he muttered. "So young." He had the moment of triumph all men have when they hear some one has died. A moment, too, of grisly fear—sixty-four.

"I couldn't have loved her more," said Elizabeth, "if she'd been one of my own. A young girl like that with all her life before her."

"It's pretty sad when you come to think of it," he said. "By God it is!"

"And she was such a fine girl, Mr. Gant," said Elizabeth, weeping softly. "She had such a bright future before her. She had more opportunities than I ever had, and I suppose you know"—she spoke modestly—"what I've done."

"Why," he exclaimed, startled, "you're a rich woman, Elizabeth —damned if I don't believe you are. You own property all over town."

"I wouldn't say that," she answered, "but I've got enough to live on without ever doing another lick of work. I've had to work hard all my life. From now on I don't intend to turn my hand over."

She looked at him with a shy, pleased smile, and touched a coil of her fine hair with a small competent hand. He looked at her attentively, noting with pleasure her firm uncorseted hips, moulded compactly into her tailored suit, and her cocked comely legs tapering to graceful feet, shod in neat little slippers of tan. She was firm, strong, washed, and elegant—a faint scent of lilac hovered over her. He looked at her candid eyes, lucently gray, and saw that she was quite a great lady.

"By God, Elizabeth," he said, "you're a fine-looking woman!"

"I've had a good life," she said. "I've taken care of myself."

They had always known each other—since first they met. They had no excuses, no questions, no replies. The world fell away from them. In the silence they heard the pulsing slap of the fountain, the high laughter of bawdry in the square. He took a book of models from the desk and began to turn its slick pages. They showed modest blocks of Georgia marble and Vermont granite.

"I don't want any of these," she said impatiently. "I've already made up my mind. I know what I want."

He looked up surprised. "What is it?"

"I want the angel out front."

His face was startled and unwilling. He gnawed the corner of his thin lip. No one knew how fond he was of the angel. Publicly he called it his white elephant. He cursed it and said he had been a fool to order it. For six years it had stood on the porch weathering in all the wind and rain. It was now brown and fly-specked. But it had come from Carrara in Italy, and it held a stone lily delicately in one hand. The other hand was lifted in benediction, it was poised clumsily upon the ball of one phthisic foot, and its stupid white face wore a smile of soft stone idiocy.

In his rages Gant sometimes directed vast climaxes of abuse at the angel. "Fiend out of hell," he roared, "you have impoverished me, you have ruined me, you have cursed my declining years, and now you will crush me to death—fearful, awful, and unnatural monster that you are."

But sometimes when he was drunk he fell weeping on his knees before it, called it Cynthia, the name of his first wife, and entreated its love, forgiveness, and blessing for its sinful but repentant boy. There was from the square laughter.

"What's the matter?" said Elizabeth. "Don't you want to sell it?"

"It will cost you a good deal, Elizabeth," he said evasively.

"I don't care," she answered positively. "I've got the money. How much do you want?"

He was silent, thinking for a moment of the place where the angel stood. He knew he had nothing to cover or obliterate that place—it left a barren crater in his heart.

"All right," he said finally. "You can have it for what I paid for it—four hundred and twenty dollars."

She took a thick sheaf of bank notes from her purse and counted the money out for him. He pushed it back.

"No. Pay me when the job's finished and it has been set up. You want some sort of inscription, don't you?"

"Yes. There's her full name, age, place of birth, and so on," she said, giving him a scrawled envelope. "I want some poetry, too—something that suits a young girl taken off like this."

He pulled his tattered little book of inscriptions from a pigeon-hole and thumbed its pages, reading her a quatrain here and there. To each she shook her head. Finally he said:

"How's this one, Elizabeth?" He read:

> " 'She went away in beauty's flower,
> Before her youth was spent,
> Ere life and love had lived its hour
> God called her, and she went.
>
> Yet whispers Faith upon the wind:
> No grief to *her* was given.
> She left *your* love and went to find
> A greater one in heaven.' "

"Oh, that's lovely—lovely!" she said. "I want that one."

"Yes," he agreed. "I think that's the best one."

In the musty, cool smell of his little office they got up. Her gallant figure reached his shoulder. She buttoned her kid gloves over the small pink haunch of her palms and glanced about her. His battered sofa filled one wall, the line of his long body was printed in the leather. She looked up at him. His face was sad and grave. They remembered.

"It's a long time, Elizabeth," he said.

They walked slowly to the front through aisled marbles. Sentinelled just beyond the wooden doors the angel leered vacantly down. Jannadeau drew his great head turtlewise a little farther into the protective hunch of his burly shoulders. They went out into the porch.

The moon stood already like its own phantom in the clear-washed skies of evening. A little boy with an empty paper delivery-bag swung lithely by, his freckled nostrils dilating pleasantly with hunger and the fancied smell of supper. He passed, and for a moment, as they stood at the porch edge, all life seemed frozen in a picture: the firemen and Fagg Sluder had seen Gant, whispered, and were now looking toward him; a policeman, at the high side-porch of the police court, leaned on the rail and stared; at the near edge of the central plot below the fountain a farmer bent for water at a bubbling jet, rose dripping, and stared; from the tax collector's office, city hall, up-stairs, Yancy, huge, meaty, shirt-sleeved, stared.

And in that second the slow pulse of the fountain was suspended, life was held, like an arrested gesture, in photographic abeyance, and Gant felt himself alone move deathward in a world of seemings as, in 1910, a man might find himself again in a picture taken on the grounds of the Chicago Fair, when he was thirty, and his moustache black; and, noting the bustled ladies and the derbied men fixed in the second's pullulation, remember the dead instant, seek beyond the borders for what (he knew) was there. Or as a veteran who finds himself upon his elbow near Ulysses Grant, before the march, in pictures of the Civil War, and sees a dead man on a horse. Or I should say, like some completed Don, who finds himself again before a tent in Scotland in his youth, and notes a cricket-bat long lost and long forgotten; the face of a poet who had died, and young men and the tutor as they looked that Long Vacation when they read nine hours a day for greats.

Where now? Where after? Where then?

1929

The Poetry of Idea and Order

WALLACE STEVENS

(1879–1955)

Wallace Stevens created his poetry as a gifted nonprofessional, less concerned about promoting his literary reputation than about perfecting what he wrote. This passion for perfection is apparent in his disciplined thought, his intense and brilliant craftsmanship, and the meticulous propriety of his language, upon which he imposed the double burden of his wit and his faith that the clarification of the inner significance of an idea is a high function. What makes the poet potent, he said, "is that he creates the world to which we turn incessantly * * * and that he gives to life the supreme fictions without which we are unable to conceive of it." His work is primarily motivated by the belief that "ideas of order," that is, true ideas, correspond with an innate order in nature and the universe, and that it is the high privilege of individuals and mankind to discover this correspondence. Hence, many of his best poems derive their emotional power from reasoned revelation.

This philosophical intention is supported by the titles Stevens gave to his volumes—for example, *Harmonium, Ideas of Order*, and *Parts of a World*.

Wallace Stevens was certainly not an alienated escapist in his personal life. A successful lawyer and corporation executive, he became a discriminating enthusiast of the arts and of the sophisticated expressions of the good life which he found at home and abroad. Stevens was born in Reading, Pennsylvania, on October 2, 1879. He prepared for a career in law at Harvard University and at New York University Law School. Admitted to the bar in 1904, he engaged in general practice in New York City until 1916, when he became associated with the Hartford Accident and Indemnity Company. In 1934 he became vice-president of this insurance company, and he continued in its service until his retirement. Although he did not collect a volume of his poems until 1923, when he was already forty-four, he was actually one of the older generation of the "new" poets, who, after 1910, appeared in the flourishing little magazines, especially *Poetry: A Magazine of Verse. Harmonium* (1923) established his stature among the few poets of ideas.

Harmonium was revised and somewhat enlarged in 1931; meanwhile Stevens's accumulation of new poems, while slow, was steady, and the occasional appearance of one of them in a magazine gave evidence of his continued absorption with ideas of increasing subtlety. He perfected a style that brilliantly embodied his extraordinary wit in corresponding rhythmic and tonal effects, and in his ability to recall simultaneously the essential meaning and the connotative suggestions of a particular word. Twelve years elapsed without the appearance of a new volume, but from 1935 to 1937 there were three, each of considerable size, including his much admired *Man with the Blue Guitar.* Thereafter Stevens's volumes appeared at shorter intervals, and he assumed a position of foremost authority among the poets of the advanced and difficult form which he practiced. He won the Bollingen Poetry Prize for 1949.

The Collected Poems of Wallace Stevens was published in 1954. Other volumes are *Harmonium,* 1923, revised and enlarged 1931, 1937; *Ideas of Order,* 1935; *Owl's Clover,* 1936; *The Man with the Blue Guitar,* 1937; *Parts of a World,* 1942, revised, 1951; *Notes Toward a Supreme Fiction,* 1942; *Esthétique du Mal,* 1944; *Transport to Summer,* 1947; *Three Academic Pieces,* 1947; *A Primitive Like an Orb,* 1948; *The Auroras of Autumn,* 1950; *The Man with the Blue Guitar* and *Ideas of Order,* combined edition, 1952; *Selected Poems,* 1953; and *Opus Posthumous,* 1957, edited by S. F. Morse. *The Necessary Angel * * * ,* 1951, expounds Stevens's theory of poetry. Holly Stevens edited *Letters of Wallace Stevens,* 1966; and *The Palm at the End of the Mind: Selected Poems and a Play,* 1971.

Samuel F. Morse, *Wallace Stevens: Poetry as Life,* 1970, is a critical biography. Early critical studies are W. V. O'Connor, *The Shaping Spirit * * * ,* 1950; S. F. Morse, *Wallace Stevens,* 1950; R. Pack, *Wallace Stevens * * * ,* 1958; Daniel Fuchs, *The Comic Spirit of Wallace Stevens,* 1963; Eugene P. Nassar, *Wallace Stevens: An Anatomy of Figuration,* 1965; John J. Enck, *Wallace Stevens: Images and judgments,* 1964; Joseph Riddle, *The Clairvoyant Eye: The Poetry and Poetics of Wallace Stevens,* 1965. Frank Doggett, *Stevens' Poetry of Thought,* 1966, is a study of the influence of contemporary thinkers; *The Act of the Mind: Essays on the Poetry of Wallace Stevens,* edited by R. H. Pearce and J. H. Miller, 1966, contains twelve essays on this poet's ideas. Also see S. F. Morse, Jackson Bryer, and Joseph Riddle, *Wallace Stevens: Checklist and Bibliography of Stevens Criticism,* 1964.

Recent criticism includes Robert Buttel, *Wallace Stevens: The Making of Harmonium,* 1967; Ronald Sukenick, *Musing the Obscure,* 1967, a "reader's guide" to 47 poems; James Baird, *The Dome and the Rock: Structure in the Poetry of Wallace Stevens,* 1968; William Burney, *Wallace Stevens,* 1968; Helen Vendler, *On Extended Wings: Wallace Stevens' Longer Poems,* 1969; Richard A. Blessing, *Wallace Stevens' "Whole Harmonium,"* 1970; Edward Kessler, *Images of Wallace Stevens,* 1972; and A. Walton Litz, *Introspective Voyager: The Poetic Development of Wallace Stevens,* 1972.

Peter Quince at the Clavier [1]

I

Just as my fingers on these keys
Make music, so the self-same sounds
On my spirit make a music, too.

1. That is, Peter Quince at the keyboard, here presumably that of a harmonium, since the poem was collected in the poet's first volume, *Harmonium* (1923). In Shakespeare's *A Midsummer-Night's Dream,* Act I,

Music is feeling, then, not sound;
And thus it is that what I feel,   5
Here in this room, desiring you,

Thinking of your blue-shadowed silk,
Is music. It is like the strain
Waked in the elders by Susanna.[2]

Of a green evening, clear and warm,   10
She bathed in her still garden, while
The red-eyed elders watching, felt

The basses of their beings throb
In witching chords, and their thin blood
Pulse pizzicati of Hosanna.[3]   15

II

In the green water, clear and warm,
Susanna lay.
She searched
The touch of springs,   20
And found
Concealed imaginings.
She sighed,
For so much melody.

Upon the bank, she stood
In the cool   25
Of spent emotions.
She felt, among the leaves,
The dew
Of old devotions.

She walked upon the grass,   30
Still quavering.
The winds were like her maids,
On timid feet,
Fetching her woven scarves,
Yet wavering.   35

Scene 2. Peter Quince appears as director of an "interlude before the duke and the duchess, on his wedding day at night." Performed by such actors as Bottom, a weaver, the interlude degenerates into a madcap farce, although it portrays the "most cruel death of Pyramus and Thisby" (*cf.* Ovid, "Pyramus and Thisbe," *Metamorphoses,* Book IV). In presenting his story, Stevens follows the advice that Bottom gave Quince ll. 8–10: "First, good Peter Quince, say what the play treats on, then read the names of the actors, and so grow on to a point"; that is, he employed something analogous to the musical form of the sonata, with its exposition, development, recapitulation, and coda. The text given here is that of *The Collected Poems of Wallace Stevens* (1954).

2. See the History of Susanna, a book of the Old Testament Apocrypha. Certain Hebrew elders attempted the seduction of the beautiful and virtuous Susanna, wife of Joachim. Susanna accused them; they counter-charged that she had enticed them. Daniel proved her innocence and the elders were executed.

3. Pizzicati notes, produced by plucking the strings of an instrument instead of bowing, are thin and tinkling and associated with the dance; by contrast, a Hosanna is a hymn in praise of God.

A breath upon her hand
Muted the night.
She turned—
A cymbal crashed,
And roaring horns.   40

III

Soon, with a noise like tambourines.[4]
Came her attendant Byzantines.[5]

They wondered why Susanna cried
Against the elders by her side;

And as they whispered, the refrain   45
Was like a willow swept by rain.

Anon, their lamps' uplifted flame
Revealed Susanna and her shame.

And then, the simpering Byzantines
Fled, with a noise like tambourines.   50

IV

Beauty is momentary in the mind—
The fitful tracing of a portal;
But in the flesh it is immortal.

The body dies; the body's beauty lives.
So evenings die, in their green going,   55
A wave, interminably flowing.
So gardens die, their meek breath scenting
The cowl of winter, done repenting.
So maidens die, to the auroral
Celebration of a maiden's choral.   60

Susanna's music touched the bawdy strings
Of those white elders; but, escaping,
Left only Death's ironic scraping.
Now, in its immortality, it plays
On the clear viol of her memory,   65
And makes a constant sacrament of praise.

1915, 1923

Sunday Morning [6]

I

Complacencies of the peignoir, and late
Coffee and oranges in a sunny chair,

---

4. The swish and tinkle of women's garments and metal ornaments.
5. From Byzantium, later Constantinople, now Istanbul. At the time of Susanna, in the sixth century B.C., Byzantium was a Greek city, often plundered by enemy invaders, who took slaves as spoil.
6. In "Sunday Morning," one of Ste-

vens's greatest poems, he portrays the perturbation and consequent seeking of "everyman" who "feels the dark / Encroachment of that old catastrophe." Like Robinson (*cf.* "The Man Against the Sky") and many other poets, Stevens leaves the question beyond the reach of reason.

And the green freedom of a cockatoo
Upon a rug mingle to dissipate
The holy hush of ancient sacrifice.   5
She dreams a little, and she feels the dark
Encroachment of that old catastrophe,
As a calm darkens among water-lights.
The pungent oranges and bright, green wings
Seem things in some procession of the dead,   10
Winding across wide water, without sound.
The day is like wide water, without sound,
Stilled for the passing of her dreaming feet
Over the seas, to silent Palestine,
Dominion of the blood and sepulchre.   15

II

Why should she give her bounty to the dead?
What is divinity if it can come
Only in silent shadows and in dreams?
Shall she not find in comforts of the sun,
In pungent fruit and bright, green wings, or else   20
In any balm or beauty of the earth,
Things to be cherished like the thought of heaven?
Divinity must live within herself:
Passions of rain, or moods in falling snow;
Grievings in loneliness, or unsubdued   25
Elations when the forest blooms; gusty
Emotions on wet roads on autumn nights;
All pleasures and all pains, remembering
The bough of summer and the winter branch.
These are the measures destined for her soul.   30

III

Jove in the clouds had his inhuman birth.
No mother suckled him, no sweet land gave
Large-mannered motions to his mythy mind
He moved among us, as a muttering king,
Magnificent, would move among his hinds,   35
Until our blood, commingling, virginal,
With heaven, brought such requital to desire
The very hinds discerned it, in a star.
Shall our blood fail? Or shall it come to be
The blood of paradise? And shall the earth   40
Seem all of paradise that we shall know?
The sky will be much friendlier then than now,
A part of labor and a part of pain,
And next in glory to enduring love,
Not this dividing and indifferent blue.   45

IV

She says, "I am content when wakened birds,
Before they fly, test the reality
Of misty fields, by their sweet questionings;
But when the birds are gone, and their warm fields

Return no more, where, then, is paradise?" 50
There is not any haunt of prophecy,
Nor any old chimera of the grave,
Neither the golden underground, nor isle
Melodious, where spirits gat them home,
Nor visionary south, nor cloudy palm 55
Remote on heaven's hill, that has endured
As April's green endures; or will endure
Like her remembrance of awakened birds,
Or her desire for June and evening, tipped
By the consummation of the swallow's wings. 60

V

She says, "But in contentment I still feel
The need of some imperishable bliss."
Death is the mother of beauty; hence from her,
Alone, shall come fulfilment to our dreams
And our desires. Although she strews the leaves 65
Of sure obliteration on our paths,
The path sick sorrow took, the many paths
Where triumph rang its brassy phrase, or love
Whispered a little out of tenderness,
She makes the willow shiver in the sun 70
For maidens who were wont to sit and gaze
Upon the grass, relinquished to their feet.
She causes boys to pile new plums and pears
On disregarded plate. The maidens taste
And stray impassioned in the littering leaves. 75

VI

Is there no change of death in paradise?
Does ripe fruit never fall? Or do the boughs
Hang always heavy in that perfect sky,
Unchanging, yet so like our perishing earth,
With rivers like our own that seek for seas 80
They never find, the same receding shores
That never touch with inarticulate pang?
Why set the pear upon those river-banks
Or spice the shores with odors of the plum?
Alas, that they should wear our colors there, 85
The silken weavings of our afternoons,
And pick the strings of our insipid lutes!
Death is the mother of beauty, mystical,
Within whose burning bosom we devise
Our earthly mothers waiting, sleeplessly. 90

VII

Supple and turbulent, a ring of men
Shall chant in orgy on a summer morn
Their boisterous devotion to the sun,
Not as a god, but as a god might be,
Naked among them, like a savage source. 95
Their chant shall be a chant of paradise,

Out of their blood, returning to the sky;
And in their chant shall enter, voice by voice,
The windy lake wherein their lord delights,
The trees, like serafin, and echoing hills,   100
That choir among themselves long afterward.
They shall know well the heavenly fellowship
Of men that perish and of summer morn.
And whence they came and whither they shall go
The dew upon their feet shall manifest.   105

VIII

She hears, upon that water without sound,
A voice that cries, "The tomb in Palestine
Is not the porch of spirits lingering.
It is the grave of Jesus, where he lay."
We live in an old chaos of the sun,   110
Or old dependency of day and night,
Or island solitude, unsponsored, free,
Of that wide water, inescapable.
Deer walk upon our mountains, and the quail
Whistle about us their spontaneous cries;   115
Sweet berries ripen in the wilderness;
And, in the isolation of the sky,
At evening, casual flocks of pigeons make
Ambiguous undulations as they sink,
Downward to darkness, on extended wings.   120

1915, 1923

Anecdote of the Jar

I placed a jar in Tennessee,
And round it was, upon a hill.
It made the slovenly wilderness
Surround that hill.

The wilderness rose up to it,   5
And sprawled around, no longer wild.
The jar was round upon the ground
And tall and of a port in air.

It took dominion everywhere.
The jar was gray and bare.   10
It did not give of bird or bush,
Like nothing else in Tennessee.

1919, 1923

The Snow Man

One must have a mind of winter
To regard the frost and the boughs
Of the pine-trees crusted with snow;

And have been cold a long time
To behold the junipers shagged with ice,   5
The spruces rough in the distant glitter

Of the January sun; and not to think
Of any misery in the sound of the wind,
In the sound of a few leaves,

Which is the sound of the land   10
Full of the same wind
That is blowing in the same bare place

For the listener, who listens in the snow,
And, nothing himself, beholds
Nothing that is not there and the nothing that is.   15

1921, 1923

Bantams in Pine-Woods [7]

Chieftain Iffucan of Azcan in caftan [8]
Of tan with henna hackles, halt!

Damned universal cock, as if the sun
Was blackamoor to bear your blazing tail.

Fat! Fat! Fat! Fat! I am the personal.   5
Your world is you. I am my world.

You ten-foot poet among inchlings. Fat!
Begone! An inchling bristles in these pines,

Bristles, and points their Appalachian tangs.[9]
And fears not portly Azcan nor his hoos.   10

1922, 1923

A High-Toned Old Christian Woman

Poetry is the supreme fiction,[1] madame.
Take the moral law and make a nave of it
And from the nave [2] build haunted heaven. Thus,
The conscience is converted into palms,

7. Stevens's remarkable use of sound as secondary imagery is characteristic of this entire poem, especially of the first two lines. He ridicules the pretentiousness of the bantam chieftain (or poet) by naming him "Iffucan of Azcan"—certainly a disparaging pun —which is followed in line 2 by the suggestion of a cackling hen.
8. A colorful robe with girdle, worn in the Eastern Mediterranean areas.
9. The tang is a projecting shank, tongue, or the like; here, the cones of the pine, which the bristling inchling "points" at "portly Azcan."
1. Twenty-two years later, Stevens still attached cryptic importance to this phrase. See the poem "Notes Toward a Supreme Fiction" (1945), collected in *Transport to Summer* (1947).
2. The principal part of a church, for the congregation. The nave generally is lighted by clerestory windows (*cf.* "heaven").

Like windy citherns hankering for hymns.   5
We agree in principle. That's clear. But take
The opposing law and make a peristyle,[3]
And from the peristyle project a masque [4]
Beyond the planets. Thus, our bawdiness,[5]
Unpurged by epitaph, indulged at last,   10
Is equally converted into palms,[6]
Squiggling like saxophones. And palm for palm,
Madame, we are where we began. Allow,
Therefore, that in the planetary scene
Your disaffected flagellants,[7] well studied,   15
Smacking their muzzy [8] bellies in parade,
Proud of such novelties of the sublime,
Such tink and tank and tunk-a-tunk-tunk,
May, merely may, madame, whip from themselves
A jovial hullabaloo among the spheres.   20
This will make widows wince: But fictive things [9]
Wink as they will. Wink most when widows wince.

1922, 1923

The Emperor of Ice-Cream [1]

Call the roller of big cigars,
The muscular one, and bid him whip
In kitchen cups concupiscent curds.
Let the wenches dawdle in such dress
As they are used to wear, and let the boys   5
Bring flowers in last month's newspapers.
Let be be finale of seem.
The only emperor is the emperor of ice-cream.

Take from the dresser of deal,
Lacking the three glass knobs, that sheet   10
On which she embroidered fantails once
And spread it so as to cover her face.
If her horny feet protrude, they come
To show how cold she is, and dumb.

3. A system of columns surrounding a building or court; sometimes the space thus enclosed. Here it is compared with "nave," which, by contrast, exerts a more obvious upward thrust. Observe that the peristyle is usually associated with pagan (Greek) temples, the nave with Christian churches and cathedrals.
4. A festive dance, or revels, generally employing worldly masquerades.
5. In its original sense: boldness.
6. *Cf.* l. 4. Palm leaves associate equally with pagan, Christian, and quite worldly processionals. Here they suggest saxophones, contrasted with citherns (l. 5).

7. The practice of piety has frequently been accompanied by flagellation.
8. Muddled.
9. That is, things created by imaginative power.
1. The antithesis between the ineffectual domain of death and the domain of luxuries (big cigars) and commodities (ice cream) is the fulcrum of the idea in this poem. Over three hundred years ago, John Donne, in his sonnet "Death be not proud," saw the empery of death defeated by God's rule of immortal life. Donne's faith then found significant approval. Compare with the present allegory.

Let the lamp affix its beam.   15
The only emperor is the emperor of ice-cream.

                                                        1922, 1923

To the One of Fictive Music [2]

Sister and mother and diviner love,
And of the sisterhood of the living dead
Most near, most clear, and of the clearest bloom,
And of the fragrant mothers the most dear
And queen, and of diviner love the day   5
And flame and summer and sweet fire, no thread
Of cloudy silver sprinkles in your gown
Its venom of renown, and on your head
No crown is simpler than the simple hair.

Now, of the music summoned by the birth   10
That separates us from the wind and sea,
Yet leaves us in them, until earth becomes,
By being so much of the things we are,
Gross effigy and simulacrum, none
Gives motion to perfection more serene   15
Than yours, out of our imperfections wrought,
Most rare, or ever of more kindred air
In the laborious weaving that you wear.

For so retentive of themselves are men
That music is intensest which proclaims   20
The near, the clear, and vaunts the clearest bloom,
And of all vigils musing the obscure,
That apprehends the most which sees and names,
As in your name, an image that is sure,
Among the arrant spices of the sun,   25
O bough and bush and scented vine, in whom
We give ourselves our likest issuance.

Yet not too like, yet not so like to be
To near, too clear, saving a little to endow
Our feigning with the strange unlike, whence
            springs   30
The difference that heavenly pity brings.

2. A great love poem, magically cadenced and rich in tonality, this address
of the poet to his muse speaks eloquently for itself. However, one should
remember Stevens's special and repeated
use of the word "fictive" as "a thing
made" or "shaped" or "imagined."
The first line of "A High-Toned Old
Christian Woman" (1922) begins:
"Poetry is the supreme fiction"—a
concept twice demonstrated in the
poem itself. In the early "Anecdote of
the Jar" (1919), he exemplified the
meaning of the title of the last poem
in his final *Collected Poems:* "Not
Ideas about the Thing but the Thing
Itself." Along the way he tried to
formulate the principles in three poem-
essays: "The Comedian As the Letter
C," "The Man with the Blue Guitar,"
and, finally, "Notes Toward a Supreme
Fiction" in 1947.

For this, musician, in your girdle fixed
Bear other perfumes. On your pale head wear
A band entwining, set with fatal stones.
Unreal, give back to us what once you gave: 35
The imagination that we spurned and crave.

1922, 1923

The Idea of Order at Key West

She sang beyond the genius of the sea.
The water never formed to mind or voice,
Like a body wholly body, fluttering
Its empty sleeves; and yet its mimic motion
Made constant cry, caused constantly a cry,   5
That was not ours although we understood,
Inhuman, of the veritable ocean.

The sea was not a mask. No more was she.
The song and water were not medleyed sound
Even if what she sang was what she heard,   10
Since what she sang was uttered word by word.
It may be that in all her phrases stirred
The grinding water and the gasping wind;
But it was she and not the sea we heard.

For she was the maker of the song she sang.   15
The ever-hooded, tragic-gestured sea
Was merely a place by which she walked to sing.
Whose spirit is this? we said, because we knew
It was the spirit that we sought and knew
That we should ask this often as she sang.   20

If it was only the dark voice of the sea
That rose, or even colored by many waves;
If it was only the outer voice of sky
And cloud, of the sunken coral water-walled,
However clear, it would have been deep air,   25
The heaving speech of air, a summer sound
Repeated in a summer without end
And sound alone. But it was more than that,
More even than her voice, and ours, among
The meaningless plungings of water and the wind, 30
Theatrical d stances, bronze shadows heaped
On high horizons, mountainous atmospheres
Of sky and sea.

        It was her voice that made
The sky acutest at its vanishing.   35
She measured to the hour its solitude.
She was the single artificer of the world

In which she sang. And when she sang, the sea,
Whatever self it had, became the self
That was her song, for she was the maker. Then we,   40
As we beheld her striding there alone,
Knew that there never was a world for her
Except the one she sang and, singing, made.

Ramon Fernandez,[3] tell me, if you know,
Why, when the singing ended and we turned   45
Toward the town, tell why the glassy lights,
The lights in the fishing boats at anchor there,
As the night descended, tilting in the air,
Mastered the night and portioned out the sea,
Fixing emblazoned zones and fiery poles,   50
Arranging, deepening, enchanting night.

Oh! Blessed rage for order, pale Ramon,
The maker's rage to order words of the sea,
Words of the fragrant portals, dimly-starred,
And of ourselves and of our origins,   55
In ghostlier demarcations, keener sounds.

1934, 1935

The Candle A Saint

Green is the night, green kindled and apparelled.
It is she that walks among astronomers.

She strides above the rabbit and the cat,
Like a noble figure, out of the sky.

Moving among the sleepers, the men,   5
Those that lie chanting *green is the night*.

Green is the night and out of madness woven,
The self-same madness of the astronomers

And of him that sees, beyond the astronomers,
The topaz rabbit and the emerald cat,   10

That sees above them, that sees rise up above them,
The noble figure, the essential shadow,

Moving and being, the image at its source,
The abstract, the archaic queen. Green is the night.

1942

3. According to Stevens he invented   Ramon Fernandez (1894–1944) was
the name for the poem, though it   a French literary critic.
"turned out to be an actual name."

WILLIAM CARLOS WILLIAMS
(1883–1963)

The physician as man of letters, whether Rabelais or Dr. Oliver Wendell Holmes, has characteristically shown a special knowledge of humanity, a diagnostic reserve toward its frailty or strength, and enough humor to preserve his sanity. These characteristics all appeared strongly in the work of Dr. William Carlos Williams. He displayed a probing and clinical realism, as one taught by science to seek beauty and truth in the vulgar or the common as much as in the uncommon. Wallace Stevens once called his friend's materials "antipoetic": Dr. Williams writes of "the plums that were in the icebox"; of "a red wheelbarrow * * * beside the white chickens"; of weeds on the sour land "by the contagious hospital." Like Stevens he is a poet of ideas; but he could not, like Stevens, rely on "the *metaphysica*" to "crash in the mind" (see "A Glass of Water"). His poems were the investiture in the inevitable words of the "experience recollected." This investiture of the apt words appears in such poems as "Tract," or in "Queen-Ann's-Lace," or in "The Pause."

Williams's early interest in painting and the influence of two of his friends, the artists Charles Sheeler and Charles Demuth, is reflected in his sharp and graphic figures and in his feeling for form, texture, and color. Just as his material experiences and their metaphors were rooted in the common American soil, so also the language of Williams's poems—vocabulary, "measures," and rhythm—were inherent in the natural and common American speech. "The American idiom," he wrote, "is the language we use in the United States, * * * the language which governed Walt Whitman in his choice of words. * * * Measure in verse is inescapable. * * * To the fixed foot of the ancient line, including the Elizabethan, we must have a reply: it is the variable foot which we are beginning to discover after Whitman's advent." By "the variable foot," Williams meant a "measure" or foot not regulated by the number of syllables or by their distinction as "long" or "short." English formal poetry had been committed to syllable counting since the fourteenth century. The Old English meter had been accentual, not syllabic; popular balladry had remained accentual and so had the common English and American speech, but only Whitman had taken the hint for poetry before Williams.

William Carlos Williams was born in Rutherford, New Jersey, on September 17, 1883. After attending preparatory schools in New York and in Switzerland, he began his medical training at the University of Pennsylvania. There he gave serious attention to his poems and found another poet and friend in Pound, a student in the graduate school. After his graduation in 1906, Williams went to Leipzig for work in pediatrics. He renewed his friendship with Pound, then in London and a leader among the young experimental poets of imagism and other *avant-garde* writing. Although Pound included work by Williams in the first imagist anthology, the young physician was an individualist always.

Williams soon returned to his birthplace, Rutherford, where in 1910 he began his engrossing medical practice and, in spite of its exactions, produced more than twenty-five volumes of fiction and poetry. In many of his poems, and in the prose essays that often appeared in the same volumes, he kept up a running fire of commentary on his age, its foibles, and its art. He won his *alma mater*'s laurels for medical practice while deriving from that practice the knowledge of people and of a community history and life that inspired the best of his poems, his stories and sketches of life along the Passaic, and his epic *Paterson*, in five books, 1946–1958 (fragments of a sixth book were posthumously published in 1963). *Paterson*, perhaps his major accomplishment, shows the hand of the gifted writer, a knowledge of life at once humane and disciplined, disillusioned, witty, and yet compassionate. The work incorporates the history, the characters, and the myths of Paterson from its Indian origins to its industrial present. The lively *Autobiography* (1951) shows the surprising range of his association with the *avant garde* of American letters, especially during the critical period from 1910 to 1930. Williams received the Dial Award for Services to American Literature in 1926, the Guarantors Prize awarded by *Poetry: A*

Magazine of Verse in 1931, the Lomes Award in 1948, and the National Book Award for *Paterson* in 1949. *Journey to Love* (1955)—see "The Ivy Crown" (below) and *Paterson* V (1958) show an actual advance, after several years of declining health, in power and formal invention, including the "three-stress line." His acceptance of life, too often before muted, now speaks almost joyfully, as in the opening of *Paterson* V, "In old age/ the mind/ casts off/ rebelliously/ an eagle/ from its crag/." He died on March 4, 1963.

The following collections provide a cross-section of his best work: *Collected Poems, 1921–1931,* 1934; *Complete Collected Poems, 1906–1938,* 1938; *Selected Poems,* 1949; *Collected Later Poetry of William Carlos Williams,* 1950; *Collected Earlier Poems of William Carlos Williams,* 1951; *Paterson,* 4 vols., 1946–1951, collected in one volume, 1951; *The Desert Music and Other Poems,* 1954; and *Journey to Love,* 1955. *Paterson, Book V* appeared in 1958 and *Pictures from Brueghel* in 1962. *Paterson* (Books I–V, with fragments of VI) was published in 1963. Short stories include *The Knife of the Times,* 1932; *Life Along the Passaic River,* 1938; *Make Light of It,* 1950. His novels are *A Voyage to Pagany,* 1928; *White Mule,* 1937; *In the Money,* 1940; and *The Build-Up,* 1952. Collections of his essays are *The Great American Novel,* 1923; *In the American Grain,* 1925, reissued 1940; and *Selected Essays of William Carlos Williams,* 1954. *Many Loves,* a play, was produced in 1958. *The Selected Letters of William Carlos Williams,* 1957, was edited by J. C. Thirlwall. *Imaginations: Collected Early Prose,* 1970, was edited by Webster Schott.

The Autobiography of William Carlos Williams appeared in 1951. Williams dictated his recollections of many of his books in bibliographical order in *I Wanted to Write a Poem,* edited by Edith Heal, 1958. Emily M. Wallace compiled *A Bibliography of William Carlos Williams,* 1968.

Critical and biographical studies include Vivienne Koch, *William Carlos Williams,* 1950; Linda W. Wagner, *The Poems of William Carlos Williams,* 1964, and *The Prose of William Carlos*

Williams, 1970; James Guimond, *The Art of William Carlos Williams*, 1968; Sherman Paul, *The Music of Survival: A Biography of a Poem by William Carlos Williams*, 1968; Thomas R. Whitaker, *William Carlos Williams*, 1968; Bram Dijkstra, *The Hieroglyphics of a New Speech: Cubism, Stieglitz, and the Early Poetry of William Carlos Williams*, 1969; James E. Breslin, *William Carlos Williams: An American Artist*, 1970; Joel Conarroe, *William Carlos Williams' Paterson*, 1970; Benjamin Sankey, *A Companion to William Carlos Williams's Paterson*, 1971; and Mike Weaver, *William Carlos Williams: The American Background*, 1971.

To Mark Anthony in Heaven

This quiet morning light
reflected, how many times
from grass and trees and clouds
enters my north room
touching the walls with   5
grass and clouds and trees.
Anthony,
trees and grass and clouds.
Why did you follow
that beloved body   10
with your ships at Actium? [1]
I hope it was because
you knew her inch by inch
from slanting feet upward
to the roots of her hair   15
and down again and that
you saw her
above the battle's fury—
clouds and trees and grass—

For then you are   20
listening in heaven.

1913

Portrait of a Lady

Your thighs are appletrees
whose blossoms touch the sky.
Which sky? The sky
where Watteau [2] hung a lady's
slipper. Your knees   5
are a southern breeze—or
a gust of snow. Agh! what
sort of man was Fragonard? [3]

1. This refers to the story that Cleopatra betrayed her lover Anthony by withdrawing her navy from the crucial battle of Actium (31 B.C.); that in Alexandria she drove Anthony to suicide by pretending to be dead; and that her suicide resulted from these events.
2. Jean Antoine Watteau (1684–1721), French painter celebrated for romantic, idealized outdoor scenes. See Fragonard, below.
3. Jean Honoré Fragonard (1732–1806), French court painter of scenes of love and gallantry. His familiar painting, "The Swing," with a girl who has just kicked her shoe in air, is suggestive. Ascribing this gay jest to Watteau may have been intentional, since Fragonard did paint scenes regarded as salacious.

—as if that answered
anything. Ah, yes—below   10
the knees, since the tune
drops that way, it is
one of those white summer days,
the tall grass of your ankles
flickers upon the shore—   15
Which shore?—
the sand clings to my lips—
Which shore?
Agh, petals maybe. How
should I know?   20
Which shore? Which shore?
I said petals from an appletree.

1915

Tract

I will teach you my townspeople
how to perform a funeral—
for you have it over a troop
of artists—
unless one should scour the world—   5
you have the ground sense necessary.

See! the hearse leads.
I begin with a design for a hearse.
For Christ's sake not black [4]—
nor white either—and not polished!   10
Let it be weathered—like a farm wagon—
with gilt wheels (this could be
applied fresh at small expense)
or no wheels at all:
a rough dray to drag over the ground.   15

Knock the glass out!
My God—glass, my townspeople!
For what purpose? Is it for the dead
to look out or for us to see
how well he is housed or to see   20
the flowers or the lack of them—
or what?
To keep the rain and snow from him?
He will have a heavier rain soon:
pebbles and dirt and what not.   25
Let there be no glass—
and no upholstery! phew!

4. *Cf.* the persistent biblical concept of
God as immortal Light, and the identification of Christ with the Light in the
Gospels, especially John i: 1–9; and
iii: 19.

and no little brass rollers
and small easy wheels on the bottom—
my townspeople what are you thinking of!   30

A rough plain hearse then
with gilt wheels and no top at all.
On this the coffin lies
by its own weight.

          No wreaths please—   35
especially no hot-house flowers.
Some common memento is better,
something he prized and is known by:
his old clothes—a few books perhaps—
God knows what! You realize   40
how we are about these things,
my townspeople—
something will be found—anything—
even flowers if he had come to that.
So much for the hearse.   45

For heaven's sake though see to the driver!
Take off the silk hat! In fact
that's no place at all for him
up there unceremoniously
dragging our friend out of his own dignity!   50
Bring him down—bring him down!
Low and inconspicuous! I'd not have him ride
on the wagon at all—damn him—
the undertaker's understrapper!
Let him hold the reins   55
and walk at the side
and inconspicuously too!

Then briefly as to yourselves:
Walk behind—as they do in France,
seventh class, or if you ride   60
Hell take curtains! Go with some show
of inconvenience; sit openly—
to the weather as to grief.
Or do you think you can shut grief in?
What—from us? We who have perhaps   65
nothing to lose? Share with us
share with us—it will be money
in your pockets.
          Go now
I think you are ready.

1917

The Young Housewife

At ten A.M. the young housewife
moves about in negligée behind
the wooden walls of her husband's house.
I pass solitary in my car.

Then again she comes to the curb   5
to call the ice-man, fish-man, and stands
shy, uncorseted, tucking in
stray ends of hair, and I compare her
to a fallen leaf.

The noiseless wheels of my car   10
rush with a crackling sound over
dried leaves as I bow and pass smiling.

                                                        1917

Queen-Ann's-Lace

Her body is not so white as
anemone petals nor so smooth—nor
so remote a thing. It is a field
of the wild carrot taking
the field by force; the grass   5
does not raise above it.
Here is no question of whiteness,
white as can be, with a purple mole [5]
at the center of each flower.
Each flower is a hand's span   10
of her whiteness. Wherever
his hand has lain there is
a tiny purple blemish. Each part
is a blossom under his touch
to which the fibers of her being   15
stem one by one, each to its end,
until the whole field is a
white desire, empty, a single stem,
a cluster, flower by flower,
a pious wish to whiteness gone over—   20
or nothing.

                                                        1921

This Is Just to Say

I have eaten
the plums
that were in
the icebox

5. A single purple blossom in the center
of the flower Queen Anne's lace, or
wild carrot. Actually, the "flower" is
an umbel composed of a multitude of
tiny blossoms, all white except this
one, and all joined downward to the
top of the main stalk by an intricate
system of tiny stems (*cf.* ll. 15–16).

and which   5
you were probably
saving
for breakfast

Forgive me
they were delicious   10
so sweet
and so cold

1934

The Bull

It is in captivity—
ringed, haltered, chained
to a drag
the bull is godlike

Unlike the cows   5
he lives alone, nozzles
the sweet grass gingerly
to pass the time away

He kneels, lies down
and stretching out   10
a foreleg licks himself
about the hoof

then stays
with half-closed eyes,
Olympian commentary on   15
the bright passage of days.

—The round sun
smooths his lacquer
through
the glossy pinetrees   20

his substance hard
as ivory or glass—
through which the wind
yet plays—
          Milkless

he nods   25
the hair between his horns
and eyes matted
with hyacinthine curls

1934

A Sort of a Song

Let the snake wait under
his weed
and the writing
be of words, slow and quick, sharp
to strike, quiet to wait,   5
sleepless.

—through metaphor to reconcile
the people and the stones.
Compose. (No ideas
but in things) Invent!   10
Saxifrage [6] is my flower that splits
the rocks.

1944

The Dance [7]

In Breughel's great picture, The Kermess,
the dancers go round, they go round and
around, the squeal and the blare and the
tweedle of bagpipes, a bugle and fiddles
tipping their bellies (round as the thick-   5
sided glasses whose wash they impound)
their hips and their bellies off balance
to turn them. Kicking and rolling about
the Fair Grounds, swinging their butts, those
shanks must be sound to bear up under such   10
rollicking measures, prance as they dance
in Breughel's great picture, The Kermess.

1944

Raleigh Was Right [8]

We cannot go to the country
for the country will bring us no peace
What can the small violets tell us
that grow on furry stems in
the long grass among lance shaped leaves?   5

6. By derivation, "rock-breaker"; the saxifrage is a family of plants that characteristically grow in the clefts of rocks.
7. Pieter Brueghel (active 1551–died 1569), Flemish artist especially known for paintings of peasant life and the countryside. He was a favorite of Williams, who named one of his volumes *Pictures from Brueghel.* "The Kermess" is most exactly reproduced in the poet's words. Kermess has come to mean "fair" or "dance." It was originally in the Low Countries an outdoor festival celebrating the local saint's day.
8. Compare Christopher Marlowe's famous poem, "The Passionate Shepherd to His Love" ("Come live with me and be my love") and Sir Walter Raleigh's amusing rejoinder, "The Nymph's Reply to the Shepherd," which Williams skillfully represents in language wry, modern, and original.

Though you praise us
and call to mind the poets
who sung of our loveliness
it was long ago!
long ago! when country people   10
would plough and sow with
flowering minds and pockets at ease—
if ever this were true.

Not now. Love itself a flower
with roots in a parched ground.   15
Empty pockets make empty heads.
Cure it if you can but
do not believe that we can live
today in the country
for the country will bring us no peace.   20

1944

From Paterson, Book II

Sunday in the Park [9]

Outside

            outside myself

                        there is a world,

he rumbled, subject to my incursions
—a world   5

              (to me) at rest,

                  which I approach

concretely—

          The scene's the Park
          upon the rock,
          female to the city   10

—upon whose body Paterson instructs his thoughts
(concretely)

             —late spring,
        a Sunday afternoon!   15

9. This poem marks the author's literary command of the vulgate American, and in its meter it demonstrates his mastery of the musical phrasing and cadence of what he called the "variable foot." *Paterson* is in the long tradition of the "comic" epic: the heroic is rejected in favor of the common, modern, and urban interpretation of the history and myth of a city and the common speech of the people. In publishing Book III (1949) Williams was able to prepare a descriptive analysis of the four volumes, in which he emphasized the questions of language and the city suggested above. As for the modern mind and the city, his epigraph—quoted from Santayana, *The Last Puritan*—gives the meaning: "cities are a second body for the human mind, a second organism, more rational, permanent, and decorative * * * ; a work of natural yet moral art, where the soul sets up her trophies." The narrator of *Paterson*, "Dr. Paterson," the poet's *alter ego*, incorporates the Paterson myths centered on its "mountain," its river (the Passaic) with its falls and final plunge to the sea. This Williams makes explicit: "Paterson is a man (since I am

—and goes by the footpath to the cliff (counting:
the proof)

            himself among the others,
—treads there the same stones
on which their feet slip as they climb,
paced by their dogs!   20

laughing, calling to each other—

                Wait for me!

                 * * *

Walking —

      he leaves the path, finds hard going   25
across-field, stubble and matted brambles
seeming a pasture—but no pasture
—old furrows, to say labor sweated or
had sweated here

                          a flame,   30
spent.

         The file-sharp grass

When! from before his feet, half tripping,
picking a way, there starts   .
            a flight of empurpled wings!   35
—invisibly created (their
jackets dust-grey) from the dust kindled
to sudden ardor!

             They fly away, churring! until
their strength spent they plunge   40
to the coarse cover again and disappear
—but leave, livening the mind, a flashing
of wings and a churring song

AND a grasshopper of red basalt, boot-long,
tumbles from the core of his mind,   45
a rubble-bank disintegrating beneath a
tropic downpour

Chapultepec! grasshopper hill!

---

a man) who dives from cliffs and the
edges of waterfalls, to his death—
finally. But for all that he is a woman
* * * who *is* the cliff and the waterfall
* * * But he escapes in the end
* * * As he dies the rocks fission gradually into wild flowers the better to
express their sorrow, a language that
would have liberated them * * * had
they but known it in time to prevent
catastrophe. The brunt of the four
books of *Paterson* * * * is a search for
the redeeming language by which a
man's premature death * * * might
have been prevented." (See *Paterson
V* comment, end of the biographical
note on Williams.)

—a matt stone solicitously instructed
to bear away some rumor   50
of the living presence that has preceded
it, out-precedented its breath   .

These wings do not unfold for flight—
no need!
the weight (to the hand) finding   55
a counter-weight or counter buoyancy
by the mind's wings
He is afraid! What then?

Before his feet, at each step, the flight
is renewed. A burst of wings, a quick   60
churring sound

       couriers to the ceremonial of love!

—aflame in flight!
        —aflame only in flight!

           No flesh but the caress!   65

He is led forward by their announcing wings.

        * * *

Without invention nothing is well spaced,
unless the mind change, unless
the stars are new measured, according
to their relative positions, the   70
line will not change, the necessity
will not matriculate: unless there is
a new mind there cannot be a new
line, the old will go on
repeating itself with recurring   75
deadliness: without invention
nothing lies under the witch-hazel
bush, the alder does not grow from among
the hummocks margining the all
but spent channel of the old swale,   80
the small foot-prints
of the mice under the overhanging
tufts of the bunch-grass will not
appear: without invention the line
will never again take on its ancient   85
divisions when the word, a supple word,
lived in it, crumbled now to chalk.

Under the bush they lie protected
from the offending sun—
11 o'clock   90
      They seem to talk

—a park, devoted to pleasure : devoted to . grasshoppers!

3 colored girls, of age! stroll by
—their color flagrant,
                    their voices vagrant
their laughter wild, flagellant, dissociated
from the fixed scene   .

But the white girl, her head
upon an arm, a butt between her fingers
lies under the bush   .   .

Semi-naked, facing her, a sunshade
over his eyes,
he talks with her

—the jalopy half hid
behind them in the trees—
I bought a new bathing suit, just

pants and a brassier   :
the breasts and
the pudenda covered—beneath

the sun in frank vulgarity.
Minds beaten thin
by waste—among

the working classes SOME sort
of breakdown
has occurred. Semi-roused

they lie upon their blanket
face to face,
mottled by the shadow of the leaves

upon them, unannoyed,
at least here unchallenged.
Not undignified.   .   .

talking, flagrant beyond all talk
in perfect domesticity—
And having bathed

and having eaten (a few
sandwiches)
their pitiful thoughts do meet

in the flesh—surrounded
by churring loves! Gay wings
to bear them (in sleep)

—their thoughts alight,
away
    .   .   among the grass

95

100

105

110

115

120

125

130

Walking —

                        * * *
                    Sunday in the park,   135
limited by the escarpment, eastward; to
the west abutting on the old road: recreation
with a view! the binoculars chained
to anchored stanchions along the east wall—
        beyond which, a hawk   140
                        soars!

—a trumpet sounds fitfully.

Stand at the rampart (use a metronome
if your ear is deficient, one made in Hungary
if you prefer)   145
and look away north by east where the church
spires still spend their wits against
the sky   .   to the ball-park
in the hollow with its minute figures running
—beyond the gap where the river   150
plunges into the narrow gorge, unseen

—and the imagination soars, as a voice
beckons, a thundrous voice, endless
—as sleep: the voice
that has ineluctably called them—   155
                    that unmoving roar!
churches and factories
                    (at a price)
together, summoned them from the pit   .

—his voice, one among many (unheard)   160
moving under all.
                    The mountain quivers.
Time! Count! Sever and mark time!

So during the early afternoon, from place
to place he moves,
his voice mingling with other voices   165
—the voice in his voice
opening his old throat, blowing out his lips,
kindling his mind (more
than his mind will kindle)   170

            —following the hikers.

At last he comes to the idlers' favorite
haunts, the picturesque summit, where
the blue-stone (rust-red where exposed)
has been faulted at various levels   175
            (ferns rife among the stones)

into rough terraces and partly closed in
dens of sweet grass, the ground gently sloping.

* * *

1948, 1951

The Pause

Values are split, summer, the fierce
jet an axe would not sever, spreads out
at length, of its own weight, a rainbow
over the lake of memory—the hard
stem of pure speed broken. Autumn   5
comes, fruit of many contours, that
glistening tegument painters love hiding
the soft pulp of the insidious reason,
dormant, for worm to nibble or for woman.
But there, within the seed, shaken by   10
fear as by a sea, it wakes again! to
drive upward, presently, from that soft
belly such a stem as will crack quartz.

1950

The Ivy Crown

The whole process is a lie,
            unless,
                        crowned by excess,
it break forcefully,
            one way or another,   5
                        from its confinement—
or find a deeper well.
            Antony and Cleopatra
                        were right;
they have shown   10
            the way. I love you
                        or I do not live
at all.

Daffodil time
            is past. This is   15
                        summer, summer!
the heart says,
            and not even the full of it.
                        No doubts
are permitted—   20
            though they will come
                        and may
before our time
            overwhelm us.
                        We are only mortal   25

but being mortal
   can defy our fate.
      We may
by an outside chance
   even win! We do not   30
      look to see
jonquils and violets
   come again
      but there are,
still,   35
   the roses!

Romance has no part in it.
   The business of love is
      cruelty *which*,
by our wills,   40
   we transform
      to live together.
It has its seasons,
   for and against,
      whatever the heart   45
fumbles in the dark
   to assert
      toward the end of May.
Just as the nature of briars
   is to tear flesh,   50
      I have proceeded
through them.
   Keep
      the briars out,
they say.   55
   You cannot live
      and keep free of
briars.
Children pick flowers.
   Let them.   60
      Though having them
in hand
   they have no further use for them
      but leave them crumpled
at the curb's edge.   65

At our age the imagination
   across the sorry facts
      lifts us
to make roses
   stand before thorns.   70
      Sure
love is cruel
   and selfish
      and totally obtuse—

at least, blinded by the light,   75
    young love is.
        But we are older,
I to love
    and you to be loved,
        we have,   80
no matter how,
    by our wills survived
        to keep
the jeweled prize
    always   85
        at our finger tips.
We will it so
    and so it is
        past all accident.

                1955

MARIANNE MOORE

(1887–1972)

Marianne Moore's earliest poems appeared in 1915 in *Poetry: A Magazine of Verse* and in *The Egotist* (London). She was then recognized as a poet of genuine power but her reception was distinctly limited until the *Selected Poems* appeared in 1935. In 1951 the *Collected Poems* won the Bollingen Prize, the National Book Award, and the Pulitzer Prize. Then a burst of critical enthusiasm recapitulated the persistent, slow accumulation of her remarkable poetry during thirty-five years.

As Eliot wrote in 1935, her poems are "part of the body of durable poetry written in our time, in which an original sensibility and an alert intelligence and deep feeling have been engaged in maintaining the life of the English language." Her most disciplined poems have been compared with the metaphysical satires of John Donne; in them the initial idea, generally simple, has been extended by metaphoric devices to a new dimension of wit, expressed in language that is all sinew, severe and pure. In self-criticism she observed that her work could not be poetry unless "there is no other category in which to put it," because "poetry is a peerless proficiency of the imagination." If satiric, her writing is dedicatedly humane, corresponding with her generalization that "poetry watches life with affection," and she recalls a dictum of Confucius that "if there be a knife of resentment in the heart, the mind will not attain precision."

The alleged obscurity of this poetry will not exist for the reader who brings to it the willing correspondence of intellect and imagination; it is "difficult" only because of these requirements. Miss Moore perceptively observed of any poetry that its "metaphor substitutes compactness for confusion."

Initial unfamiliarity characterizes Miss Moore's versification also, but the informed reader soon discovers that she has used the old forms of poetry in a new way. The apparent unevenness of her lines results from the careful syllable count which sets the stanzaic pattern for each poem. The deceptively free rhythms which arise from her lack of attention to stress conform flexibly with changes of meaning and with prose phrases lifted bodily from various writings—science, history, reference books, current topical works—but seldom from literary sources, a fact in itself significant. While she is among the most daringly original of recent poets she also remains among the most conservative.

Marianne Craig Moore was born in 1887 at Kirkwood, near St. Louis, Missouri. After her graduation from Bryn Mawr College (1909) she studied business science at a Carlisle, Pennsylvania, school and headed the Commercial Department of the Carlisle Indian School (1911–1915). Her early poems in 1915 having won serious attention and publication, she became a professional writer, living for a time in Chatham, New Jersey. In New York City after 1920, she held an appointment as branch librarian of the New York Public Library (1921–1925). Her *Ob-servations* (1924) won her the *Dial* Award and appointment as a member of the staff of the *Dial*, prominent periodical devoted to the arts, where she remained until it failed in 1929. Her national awards included the Pulitzer Prize, the National Book Award, and the Bollingen Award.

The *Achievement of Marianne Moore: A Bibliography, 1907–1957*, compiled by E. P. Sheehy and A. Lohf, 1958, contains a comprehensive list of critical articles and reviews of her works extant to that date in periodicals or books. The same volume contains an excellent descriptive bibliography of Miss Moore's books and periodical writings. B. F. Engel's *Marianne Moore*, 1963, is a useful introductory study. Besides the major collections of her poems mentioned in the headnote, Miss Moore has published the following small volumes of new poems: *Poems*, 1921; *Marriage*, 1923; *The Pangolin and Other Verse*, 1936; *What Are Years*, 1941; *Nevertheless*, 1944; *A Face*, 1949; *Like a Bulwark*, 1956; *O To Be a Dragon*, 1959; and *Tell Me, Tell Me: Granite, Steel, and Other Topics*, 1966. A selection of her critical articles appeared as *Predilections*, 1955. *Poetry and Criticism* was published in 1965. *The Fables of La Fontaine*, 1954, and *Selected Fables*, 1955, are translations. A single volume of her poems was published as *Collected Poems*, 1951. *A Marianne Moore Reader*, 1961, contains prose and verse selected by the author. *The Complete Poems of Marianne Moore* was published in 1967.

Biographical and critical studies are A. Kingsley Weatherhead, *The Edge of the Image: Marianne Moore, William Carlos Williams and Some Other Poets*, 1967; George W. Nitchie, *Marianne Moore: An Introduction to the Poetry*, 1969; and Donald Hall, *Marianne Moore: The Cage and the Animal*, 1970. Gary Lane edited *A Concordance to the Poems of Marianne Moore*, 1972.

In the Days of Prismatic Colour [1]

not in the days of Adam and Eve, but when Adam
was alone; when there was no smoke and colour was

1. First published in *Contact* for January, 1921; included in *Observations* (1924) and all later collections. One of Miss Moore's early explorations of the relations between art and idea, contrasting the "murkiness" of extended complexity and sophistication with the naturalness of "the initial great truths," with respect to both form and substance.

fine, not with the refinement
    of early civilization art, but because
of its originality; [2] with nothing to modify it but the   5

mist that went up, obliqueness was a varia-
    tion of the perpendicular, plain to see and
to account for: it is no
    longer that; nor did the blue-red-yellow band
of incandescence that was colour keep its stripe: it also is   10
        one of

those things into which much that is peculiar can be
    read; complexity is not a crime, but carry
it to the point of murki-
    ness and nothing is plain. Complexity,   15
moreover, that has been committed to darkness, instead of
        granting it-

self to be the pestilence that it is, moves all a-
    bout as if to bewilder us with the dismal
fallacy that insistence   20
    is the measure of achievement and that all
truth must be dark. Principally throat, sophistication is as
        it al-

ways has been—at the antipodes from the init-
    ial great truths. "Part of it was crawling, part of it   25
was about to crawl, the rest
    was torpid in its lair." [3] In the short-legged, fit-
ful advance, the gurgling and all the minutiae—we have
        the classic

multitude of feet. To what purpose! Truth is no Apollo   30
    Belvedere,[4] no formal thing. The wave may go over it if
        it likes.
Know that it will be there when it says,
    "I shall be there when the wave has gone by."

                                                        1921, 1951

An Egyptian Pulled Glass Bottle
in the Shape of a Fish [5]

Here we have thirst
And patience, from the first,

2. Because of having been original with
nature (*cf.* ll. 1 and 2); *e.g.*, the
natural sunlight refracted into color by
a "prismatic" crystal rock or by mist.
3. "Nestor: *Greek Anthology*, Loeb
Classical Library, III, 129" [Miss
Moore's note]. This quotation and the
remainder of the poem refer primarily
to art form, as the earlier stanzas referred to ideas.
4. The most celebrated statue of Apol-

lo. The early Roman copy in marble of
the Greek original, now in the Vatican,
shows the highest formal perfection of
sculptural art.
5. First published in *Observations*
(1924). The association of several related impressions with a single, sharp
image suggests the author's early command of the techniques of the imagist
poets.

And art, as in a wave held up for us to see
    In its essential perpendicularity;

Not brittle but   5
Intense—the spectrum, that
Spectacular and nimble animal the fish,
Whose scales turn aside the sun's sword with their polish.

                                    1924, 1951

No Swan So Fine [6]

[handwritten marginalia: Paradox: contrast / the creation of / Louis XV / and his death. / art lives—Life dies]

"No water so still as the
    dead fountains of Versailles." [7] No swan,
with swart blind look askance
and gondoliering legs,[8] so fine
    as the chintz china one with fawn-   5
brown eyes and toothed gold
collar on to show whose bird it was.[9]

Lodged in the Louis Fifteenth
    candelabrum-tree [1] of cockscomb-
tinted buttons, dahlias,   10
sea-urchins, and everlastings,
    it perches on the branching foam
of polished sculptured
flowers—at ease and tall. The king is dead.

                                      1932, 1951

The Pangolin [2]

Another armoured animal—scale
    lapping scale with spruce-cone regularity until they
form the uninterrupted central

6. First published in *Poetry: A Magazine of Verse* for October, 1932, and first collected in *Selected Poems* (1935), this poem was retained in the *Collected Poems* (1951).

7. The author's note states that the source of this striking figure is an unnamed article by Percy Phillips in the *New York Times Magazine,* May 10, 1931. The live swans that used to adorn these "dead fountains" mediate between the dead fountains and the china swan.

8. The Italian gondolier propels his craft by paddling from the stern.

9. "A pair of Louis XV candelabra with Dresden figures of swans belonging to Lord Balfour" [Miss Moore's note]. In the sophisticated period of Louis's reign the swan's collar might actually have shown armorial identification.

1. The age of Louis XV, king of France from 1715 to 1774, was noted for opulent and luxurious art such as the rococo style here depicted, which in spite of profuse ornament sometimes achieved delicacy.

2. Published as the title poem of a volume in 1936, "The Pangolin" was included in *What Are Years* (1941) and *Collected Poems* (1951). Among the poet's celebrations of "impressive" creatures "of whom we seldom hear," this scaly anteater enthralls attention because of the animal's physical adaptation to survive deadly adversities by means of the evolved contrivances of his armor and by his own frugal rectitude, and also because he shares "certain postures" with man (*cf.* l. 86 *et seq.*).

tail-row! This near artichoke [3] with head and legs and
      grit-equipped gizzard,   5
the night miniature artist engineer is
    Leonardo's—da Vinci's replica [4]—
        impressive animal and toiler of whom we seldom
        hear.
    Armour seems extra. But for him,   10
      the closing ear-ridge [5]—
        or bare ear lacking even this small
        eminence and similarly safe

contracting nose and eye apertures   15
    impenetrably closable, are not;—a true ant-eater,
not cockroach-eater, who endures
    exhausting solitary trips through unfamiliar ground at
      night,
    returning before sunrise; stepping in the moonlight,
      on the moonlight peculiarly, that the outside   20
        edges of his hands may bear the weight and save
        the claws
    for digging. Serpentined about
      the tree, he draws
        away from danger unpugnaciously,   25
        with no sound but a harmless hiss; keeping

the fragile grace of the Thomas-
    of-Leighton Buzzard Westminster Abbey wrought-
      iron vine,[6] or
rolls himself into a ball that has   30
    power to defy all effort to unroll it; strongly intailed,
      neat
    head for core, on neck not breaking off, with curled-in
      feet.
    Nevertheless he has sting-proof scales; and nest   35
      of rocks closed with earth from inside, which he
      can thus darken
    Sun and moon and day and night and man and beast
      each with a splendour
        which man in all his vileness cannot   40
        set aside; each with an excellence!

"Fearful yet to be feared," the armoured
    ant-eater met by the driver-ant does not turn back, but
engulfs what he can, the flattened sword-

---

3. The artichoke is encased in concentric rings of scalelike leaves.
4. The reference to Leonardo da Vinci (1452–1519) recalls his accomplishments as gifted artist, inventor, and engineer.
5. "The 'closing ear-ridge,' and certain other detail, from *Pangolins* by Robert T. Hatt; *Natural History*, December, 1935" [Miss Moore's note].
6. "Thomas of Leighton Buzzard's vine: a fragment of ironwork in Westminster Abbey" [Miss Moore's note].

edged leafpoints on the tail and artichoke set leg- and 45
      body-plates
quivering violently when it retaliates
    and swarms on him. Compact like the furled
        fringed frill
          on the hat-brim of Gargallo's [7] hollow iron head 50
            of a
matador, he will drop and will
      then walk away
        unhurt, although if unintruded on,
          he cautiously works down the tree, helped 55

by his tail. The giant-pangolin-
    tail, graceful tool, as prop or hand or broom or axe,
        tipped like
the elephant's trunk with special skin,
    is not lost on the ant- and stone-swallowing uninjurable 60
artichoke which simpletons thought a living fable
      whom the stones had nourished, whereas ants had
        done
          so. Pangolins are not aggressive animals; between
          dusk and day they have the not unchain-like machine- 65
            like
        form and frictionless creep of a thing
        made graceful by adversities, con-
versities. To explain grace requires
    a curious hand. If that which is at all were not forever, 70
why would those who graced the spires
    with animals and gathered there to rest, on cold luxurious
low stone seats—a monk and monk and monk—between
        the thus
          ingenious roof-supports,[8] have slaved to confuse 75
          grace with a kindly manner, time in which to pay
            a debt,
        the cure for sins, a graceful use
        of what are yet
          approved stone mullions [9] branching out across 80
          the perpendiculars? A sailboat

was the first machine.[1] Pangolins, made
    for moving quietly also, are models of exactness,

---

7. Pablo Gargallo (1881–1934), Spanish painter and sculptor.
8. The grotesque but permanent figures of animals adorning the architectural members of ancient ecclesiastical buildings are compared with the living pangolin.
9. "Mullions" are the bars that subdivide the lights of a window. The "stone," and the "stone seats" of l. 73, suggest an ecclesiastical cloister or court.
1. "See F. L. Morse: *Power: Its Application from the 17th Dynasty to the 20th Century*" [Miss Moore's note]. The comparison of animal with man rises steadily to a crescendo in the next lines.

on four legs; or hind feet plantigrade,
 with certain postures of a man.[2] Beneath sun and moon, 85
  man slaving
to make his life more sweet, leaves half the flowers
  worth having,
   needing to choose wisely how to use the strength;
    a paper-maker like the wasp; a tractor of food- 90
    stuffs,
  like the ant; spidering a length
  of web from bluffs
   above a stream; in fighting, mechanicked
   like the pangolin; capsizing in 95

disheartenment. Bedizened or stark
 naked, man, the self, the being we call human, writing-
master to this world, griffons a dark
"Like does not like like that is obnoxious"; and writes
  error with four 100
r's. Among animals, one has a sense of humour.[3]
  Humour saves a few steps, it saves years. Un-
  ignorant,
  modest and unemotional, and all emotion,
  he has everlasting vigour, 105
   power to grow,
    though there are few creatures who can make one
    breathe faster and make one erecter.
Not afraid of anything is he,
 and then goes cowering forth, tread paced to meet an 110
  obstacle
at every step. Consistent with the
 formula—warm blood, no gills, two pairs of hands and
  a few hairs—that
is a mammal; there he sits in his own habitat, 115
  serge-clad, strong-shod. The prey of fear, he, always
   curtailed, extinguished, thwarted by the dusk,
    work partly done,
  says to the alternating blaze,
   "Again the sun! 120
    anew each day; and new and new and new,
    that comes into and steadies my soul."

1936, 1951

---

2. The pangolin is a plantigrade, an animal that resembles man by walking with heel and toe both touching ground. In the succeeding passages, man's behavior and "inventions" are compared with those of the pangolin and other animals. *Cf.* note 2 below.
3. The dualism of man-animal was noted in the previous stanza. Just above,

note the word "griffons": the name for a mythological hybrid of lion and eagle or for a breed of dog, here used as a verb. Hence a "griffoned" sentence would be growled out, as would the "error with four r's"; *cf.* the quoted sentence concerning man's humorless dislike of "obnoxious" kindred.

Rigorists [4]

"We saw reindeer
browsing," a friend who'd been in Lapland, said:
"finding their own food; they are adapted

    to scant *reino* [5]
or pasture, yet they can run eleven   5
miles in fifty minutes; the feet spread when

    the snow is soft,
and act as snow-shoes. They are rigorists,
however handsomely cutwork artists

    of Lapland and   10
Siberia elaborate the trace
or saddle-girth with saw-tooth leather lace. [6]

    One looked at us
with its firm face part brown, part white,—a queen
of alpine flowers. Santa Claus' reindeer, seen   15

    at last, had grey-
brown fur, with a neck like edelweiss or
lion's foot,—*leontopodium* more

    exactly." And
this candelabrum-headed ornament   20
for a place where ornaments are scarce, sent

    to Alaska,
was a gift preventing the extinction
of the Esquimo. The battle was won

    by a quiet man,   25
Sheldon Jackson, evangel to that race
whose reprieve he read in the reindeer's face.

                    1940, 1951

JOHN CROWE RANSOM
(1888–   )

John Crowe Ransom was born in Pulaski, Tennessee, on April 30, 1888, the son of a Methodist clergyman. He attended school in Nashville before entering Vanderbilt University, from

4. First published in *Life and Letters Today* (1940) and collected in the 1941 volume, *What Are Years*. In her notes the author quotes an 1895 report by Sheldon Jackson, U. S. Agent for Education for Alaska, describing the relief of hardship among the Alaskan Eskimo by introducing the reindeer from Siberia beginning in 1891.
5. The word *reino* is "pasture" in Lapp, conjecturally identified with the first

syllable of "reindeer," a word which also originated in Lapland.
6. The Lapland domesticated reindeer were those of the German Christmas legend of St. Niklaus (*cf.* "Santa Claus," l. 15). In this simple poem reminiscent of childhood, the author admires the adaptations of this deer, at once the rigorist, the savior, and the ornament.

which he was graduated in 1909. The following year he was appointed a Rhodes scholar and enrolled at Christ Church College, Oxford. He received the B.A. in 1913, having taken the "Greats," or classical course. After a year's teaching in a Mississippi secondary school he was appointed a member of the Vanderbilt English department. In 1922 he was one of the founders of the magazine *The Fugitive*, published at the University, with which such young authors as Allen Tate and Robert Penn Warren were also connected. Except for two years' service in the field artillery during World War I and a year's leave as a Guggenheim Fellow during 1931–1932, he remained a professor at Vanderbilt until 1937, resigning in that year to accept the position of Carnegie Professor of English at Kenyon College and to found and edit the *Kenyon Review*.

Ransom's career as a poet defined itself in large measure during his stay at Vanderbilt, although after he went to Kenyon he took a decided turn in a direction which had not been dominant before—that of literary criticism. *Poems About God* appeared in 1919, *Chills and Fever* in 1924, and *Two Gentlemen in Bonds* in 1926. The characteristic of his poetry most often noticed by critics is the skillful combination of wit and irony. The emotions are played down. "Assuredly I have a grief," he writes in the epigraph to one volume, "and I am shaken, but not as a leaf." His is a guarded style which suppresses any trace of sentimentality. It might be termed a semiclassical, mockingly pedantic treatment of romantic subjects. Despite some use of local detail, he cannot be classified as a local colorist.

Ransom's interests by 1930 had shifted toward social criticism. That year appeared *God Without Thunder*, the thesis of which is that Western man has suffered a tragic loss or defeat in surrendering to the modern deity, Science. Through this surrender God has been deprived of his Thunder, which is his Mystery. Also in 1930 the volume *I'll Take My Stand* was published "by Twelve Southerners," of whom Ransom was one. This was a collection of essays in defense of agrarian as opposed to industrial society.

Ransom's interest in literary criticism is evident in the pages of the *Kenyon Review*. He has also written two volumes important in revealing his conception of what the best poetry should be like. In 1938 was published *The World's Body*, in which he argues that it is the function of poetry to represent the fullness, or "body," of experience, something which science, with its concern for the abstract, is incapable of doing. Another collection of essays, *The New Criticism* (1941) examines and undertakes to evaluate the achievement of four contemporaries: I. A. Richards, T. S. Eliot, Yvor Winters, and William Empson. It concludes with Ransom's own statement of preference: "Wanted: An Ontological Critic." In 1945 he published his rigidly chosen *Selected*

Poems. Nothing from *Poems About God* was reprinted. *Poems and Essays* appeared in 1955.

Ransom's *Selected Poems* was revised and enlarged in the third edition, 1969. Prose is collected in *Beating the Bushes: Selected Essays, 1941–1970,* 1972. Critical studies include Louise Cowan, *The Fugitive Group: A Lit-* *erary History,* 1959; John L. Stewart, *The Burden of Time: The Fugitives and Agrarians,* 1965; Robert Buffington, *The Equilibrist: A Study of John Crowe Ransom's Poems, 1916–1963,* 1967; Thomas Daniel Young, ed., *John Crowe Ransom: Critical Essays and a Bibliography,* 1968; Thornton H. Parsons, *John Crowe Ransom,* 1969; and Miller Williams, *The Poetry of John Crowe Ransom,* 1972.

Bells for John Whiteside's Daughter

There was such speed in her little body,
And such lightness in her footfall,
It is no wonder that her brown study [1]
Astonishes us all.

Her wars were bruited in our high window.   5
We looked among orchard trees and beyond,
Where she took arms against her shadow,
Or harried unto the pond

The lazy geese, like a snow cloud
Dripping their snow on the green grass,   10
Tricking and stopping, sleepy and proud,
Who cried in goose, Alas,

For the tireless heart within the little
Lady with rod that made them rise
From their noon apple-dreams, and scuttle   15
Goose-fashion under the skies!

But now go the bells, and we are ready;
In one house we are sternly stopped
To say we are vexed at her brown study,
Lying so primly propped.   20

1924

The Equilibrists [2]

Full of her long white arms and milky skin
He had a thousand times remembered sin.
Alone in the press of people traveled he,
Minding her jacinth, and myrrh, and ivory.

1. Reverie or daydream.
2. Ordinarily the word signifies acrobats who perform feats of balancing. Here the lovers are attempting an equilibrium between two different ideals of love. The poet in the first four stanzas utilizes a traditional language of passion (*cf.* the Song of Solomon i: 13–14; iv: 1–7). Succeeding stanzas employ the Christian idealization of chastity, drawing upon the Arthurian romances and Dante.

Mouth he remembered: the quaint orifice   5
From which came heat that flamed upon the kiss,
Till cold words came down spiral from the head,
Grey doves from the officious tower illsped.

Body: it was a white field ready for love,
On her body's field, with the gaunt tower above,   10
The lilies grew, beseeching him to take,
If he would pluck and wear them, bruise and break.

Eyes talking: Never mind the cruel words,
Embrace my flowers, but not embrace the swords.
But what they said, the doves came straightway flying   15
And unsaid: Honor, Honor, they came crying.

Importunate her doves. Too pure, too wise,
Clambering on his shoulder, saying, Arise,
Leave me now, and never let us meet,
Eternal distance now command thy feet.   20

Predicament indeed, which thus discovers
Honor among thieves, Honor between lovers.
O such a little word is Honor, they feel!
But the grey word is between them cold as steel.[3]

At length I saw these lovers fully were come   25
Into their torture of equilibrium;
Dreadfully had forsworn each other, and yet
They were bound each to each, and they did not forget.

And rigid as two painful stars, and twirled
About the clustered night their prison world,   30
They burned with fierce love always to come near,
But Honor beat them back and kept them clear.

Ah, the strict lovers, they are ruined now!
I cried in anger. But with puddled brow
Devising for those gibbeted and brave   35
Came I descanting: Man, what would you have?

For spin your period out, and draw your breath,
A kinder saeculum [4] begins with Death.
Would you ascend to Heaven and bodiless dwell?
Or take your bodies honorless to Hell?   40

In Heaven you have heard no marriage is,[5]
No white flesh tinder to your lecheries,

---

3. In the medieval romances of chivalry it was a sword, not a "word," of "steel" that separated lovers. See, for example, the sword with its cruciform hilt that lay between Iseult and Tristram at night on their journey (*The Romance of Tristan and Iseult*, edited by Joseph Bédier).
4. Latin *saeculum* signifies a "cycle," "age," "period of time."
5. *Cf.* Matthew xxii: 30.

Your male and female tissue sweetly shaped
Sublimed away, and furious blood escaped.

Great lovers lie in Hell, the stubborn ones   45
Infatuate of the flesh upon the bones;
Stuprate [6] they rend each other when they kiss,
The pieces kiss again, no end to this.

But still I watched them spinning, orbited nice.
Their flames were not more radiant than their ice.   50
I dug in the quiet earth and wrought the tomb
And made these lines to memorize their doom:—

Epitaph

Equilibrists lie here; stranger, tread light;
Close, but untouching in each other's sight;
Mouldered the lips and ashy the tall skull,   55
Let them lie perilous and beautiful.

1927

6. Adjective from the Latin *stuprare,*
"to ravish." *Cf.* stanzas 7 and 8:
the entire effect suggests an *inverted*
image of Paolo and Francesca, love-
tormented but bodiless spirits (Dante,
Inferno V).

Literary Expression of Social Thought: The 1930's and 1940's

JOHN DOS PASSOS

(1896–1970)

Many writers have depended upon social history as a frame for their narratives; but John Dos Passos, in the three novels of *U.S.A.*, invented a new form, in which social history itself became the dynamic drive and motivation of a cycle of novels. His real protagonist in these volumes is American life from just before the First World War until the period of the great depression in the early thirties. His writing since the completion of the trilogy in 1936 did not continue on the same level of imagination and excellence, but the four chief works of that earlier period are sufficient to establish him as one of the most important of our recent writers.

John Dos Passos was born in Chicago on January 14, 1896. After preparation at private school, he entered Harvard, and he graduated with distinction in 1916. He had already begun to write, and like many privileged young idealists of his generation, he was persuaded that the machine age somehow necessarily debased and enslaved mankind. From this position to proletarian sympathies and a Marxist philosophy was but a short and natural step for the intellectuals of his period.

However, in 1916 Dos Passos went to Spain, intending to study architecture in Europe. The growing seriousness of the war changed his plans. He served first with a French ambulance unit, then with the Red Cross in Italy, and finally as a private in the medical corps of the United States Army. He then entered journalism, and spent several years as a foreign correspondent. His social idealism and his disillusion are reflected in his two war-inspired novels, *One Man's Initiation—1917* (1920) and *Three Soldiers* (1921). The latter may still rank as a fine book, although as a war novel it suffers by comparison with Hemingway's.

Three volumes of no permanent importance, one a novel, intervened before Dos Passos emerged as a writer of unique originality and force in *Manhattan Transfer* (1925). Here for the first time he employed kaleidoscopic organization—the chronological narrative is abandoned in favor of shifting scenes and episodes, at first apparently not connected, in which, however, the reappearance of certain characters in various associations produces a cross-sectional view of New York life.

An interval of playwriting followed, during which he planned and prepared materials for his trilogy, *U.S.A.* The first volume, *The 42nd Parallel*, appeared in 1930. This was followed by *1919* (1932) and *The Big Money* (1936). Each novel is an entity, but the three are unified by continuity of social motivation and fictional characters. The kaleidoscopic technique is retained from *Manhattan Transfer*, but the social scene is broadened. Side by side with the narrative concerning the fictional characters are the profiles or brief biographies of American leaders at every level, ranging from Ford and Morgan to Debs and to Valentino. The "newsreels" provide the setting—headlines, songs, and snatches from news articles, slogans, and advertisements are juxtaposed to define the social atmosphere at a given

time. The "camera eye" represents the author's stream of consciousness at the time of the action of his story.

As various forms of collectivist dictatorship bred their inevitable human tragedy in the period of World War II, the various topical volumes and essays of Dos Passos took a sharp turn to the right. *The Ground We Stand On* (1941) is a collection of essays on American leaders of the past, starting in colonial times, with emphasis on democratic individualists like Roger Williams, Jefferson, and Franklin, who stood for freedom of conscience, civil rights, and economic liberty. His reawakened admiration for Jefferson resulted in the study *The Head and Heart of Thomas Jefferson* (1953).

In his later work, Dos Passos still wrestles with the American problem of bigness, but is no more apprehensive of "big capital" than of "big labor." His later novels, reflecting his changes in viewpoint, are effective, but not really comparable in either power or originality with his earlier work, even though they are more judicious. They are *Adventures of a Young Man* (1939); *Number One* (1943), the portrait of an American demagogue and a satirical inquiry into the offenses of political demagoguery against the people; *The Grand Design* (1948), on the "New Deal" years of Franklin Roosevelt's administration; and *Most Likely To Succeed* (1954), a study of Communist "intellectuals." *Adventures of a Young*

Man, Number One, and The Grand Design were collected as a trilogy entitled *District of Columbia* (1953). Few experimental techniques appear in these novels or in *The Great Days* (1958), but *Midcentury* (1961) marks a return to the methods of *U.S.A.*

U.S.A. was first published under one cover in 1938. Other fiction is *Streets of Night*, 1923; and *Orient Express*, 1927. His early poems were collected in *A Pushcart at the Curb*, 1922. *Rosinante to the Road Again*, 1922, is a group of early travel essays on Spanish art and culture; later essays on his travels and observations, good journalistic reporting, are collected in *In All Countries*, 1934; *Journeys Between Wars*, 1938; *State of the Nation*, 1944; *Tour of Duty*, 1946, reporting his observations on World War II. Recent are *Brazil on the Move*, 1963; *Occasions and Protests*, 1964; *The Portugal Story*, 1969; and *Easter Island*, 1971. *The Best Times: An Informal Memoir*, 1966, is autobiographical. Kenneth S. Lynn edited *World in a Glass: A View of Our Century Selected from the Novels of John Dos Passos*, 1966. Townsend Ludington edited *The Fourteenth Chronicle: Letters and Diaries of John Dos Passos*, 1973.

The first full-length study is Georges-Albert Astre, *Thèmes et structures dans l'œuvre de John Dos Passos*, Paris, 1956. More recent are John H. Wrenn, *John Dos Passos*, 1961; Allen Belkind, ed., *Dos Passos, the Critics, and the Writer's Intention*, 1971; and Melvin Landsberg, *Dos Passos' Path to U.S.A.* 1972.

From U.S.A.[1]

From The 42nd Parallel

Proteus[2]

Steinmetz was a hunchback,
son of a hunchback lithographer.
He was born in Breslau in eighteen sixtyfive, graduated with

1. The selections from Dos Passos given here, all from *U.S.A.* (1938), were sufficiently independent in construction to win separate prepublication in various periodicals; each one illustrates a characteristic technical experiment of this novelist; and collectively considered they span the period of social history represented in the three novels, while developing, in continuous sequence, a major theme in the motivation of the trilogy. In this study of American industrial civilization, ending with the depression of the early thirties, the author stresses, on the one hand, the consolidation of large capital enterprise, the development of inventive genius, the scientific advances, and the increases in technological efficiency and in labor controls; in strong contrast, he also reveals the worker—his lack of security, his rootlessness—the organized opposition to the labor movement and the attacks on it as "radicalism," and the inroads of war and depression on common people. Prepublication of these sketches occurred as follows: "Big Bill" and "Proteus" (from *The 42nd Parallel*, 1930) and "The House of Morgan" and "The Body of an American" (from *1919*, 1932) were all among the pieces that the author contributed to the *New Masses* during the period 1930–1932. Of the selections from *The Big Money* (1936), "The American Plan" appeared in *Esquire* for January, 1934; "Newsreel LXVI" and "The Camera Eye (50)" were printed together in *Common Sense* for February, 1936; and "Vag" appeared in the *New Republic* for July 22, 1936.

2. Karl August Rudolf Steinmetz (1865–1923), German-born electrical engineer and inventor, left Germany, as described in this selection, a socialist fugitive. Then twenty-three, he changed his given names to "Charles Proteus." The Proteus of Greek legend was a prophetic old man of the sea, able to alter his shape to escape persecutors who wished to compel him to prophesy. The protean quality is recalled in Dos Passos' sketch.

highest honors at seventeen from the Breslau Gymnasium,[3] went to the University of Breslau to study mathematics;

mathematics to Steinmetz was muscular strength and long walks over the hills and the kiss of a girl in love and big evenings spent swilling beer with your friends;

on his broken back he felt the topheavy weight of society the way workingmen felt it on their straight backs, the way poor students felt it, was a member of a socialist club, editor of a paper called *The People's Voice.*

Bismarck [4] was sitting in Berlin like a big paperweight to keep the new Germany feudal, to hold down the empire for his bosses the Hohenzollerns.

Steinmetz had to run off to Zurich for fear of going to jail; at Zurich his mathematics woke up all the professors at the Polytechnic;

but Europe in the eighties was no place for a penniless German student with a broken back and a big head filled with symbolic calculus and wonder about electricity that is mathematics made power

and a socialist at that.

With a Danish friend he sailed for America steerage on an old French line boat *La Champagne,*

lived in Brooklyn at first and commuted to Yonkers where he had a twelvedollar a week job and Rudolph Eichemeyer [5] who was a German exile from fortyeight an inventor and electrician and owner of a factory where he made hatmaking machinery and electrical generators.

In Yonkers he [6] worked out the theory of the Third Harmonics and the law of hysteresis which states in a formula the hundredfold relations between the metallic heat, density, frequency when the poles change places in the core of a magnet under an alternating current.

It is Steinmetz's law of hysteresis that makes possible all the transformers that crouch in little boxes and gableroofed houses in all the hightension lines all over everywhere. The mathematical symbols of Steinmetz's law are the patterns of all transformers everywhere.

In eighteen ninetytwo when Eichemeyer sold out to the corporation that was to form General Electric, Steinmetz was entered in

3. In Germany, a type of secondary school preparing students for the university.

4. Otto Eduard Leopold von Bismarck (1815–1898), "the Iron Chancellor," had during the youth of Steinmetz been unifying Germany by his policy of "blood and iron." The Hohenzollerns (below) were the reigning royal family dur'ng this period.

5. Rudolf Eickemeyer (1831–1895), who came to the United States from Bavaria in 1850, by his 150 inventions fostered basic improvements in many industrial fields.

6. *I.e.*, Steinmetz.

the contract along with other valuable apparatus. All his life Steinmetz was a piece of apparatus belonging to General Electric.

First his laboratory was at Lynn, then it was moved and the little hunchback with it to Schenectady, the electric city.

General Electric humored him, let him be a socialist, let him
keep a greenhouseful of cactuses lit up by mercury lights, let him
have alligators, talking crows and a gila monster for pets and the
publicity department talked up the wizard, the medicine man who
knew the symbols that opened up the doors of Ali Baba's cave.[7]

Steinmetz jotted a formula on his cuff and next morning a thousand new powerplants had sprung up and the dynamos sang dollars and the silence of the transformers was all dollars,

and the publicity department poured oily stories into the ears
of the American public every Sunday and Steinmetz became the
little parlor magician,

who made a toy thunderstorm in his laboratory and made all the
toy trains run on time and the meat stay cold in the icebox and the
lamp in the parlor and the great lighthouses and the searchlights
and the revolving beams of light that guide airplanes at night towards Chicago, New York, St. Louis, Los Angeles,

and they let him be a socialist and believe that human society
could be improved the way you can improve a dynamo and they let
him be pro-German and write a letter offering his services to Lenin
because mathematicians are so impractical who make up formulas
by which you can build powerplants, factories, subway systems,
light, heat, air, sunshine but not human relations that affect the
stockholders' money and the directors' salaries.

Steinmetz was a famous magician and he talked to Edison tapping with the Morse code on Edison's knee
    because Edison was so very deaf
    and he went out West
    to make speeches that nobody understood
    and he talked to Bryan about God on a railroad train
    and all the reporters stood round while he and Einstein
    met face to face,
    but they couldn't catch what they said
    and Steinmetz was the most valuable piece of apparatus General
Electric had
    until he wore out and died.

1930

---

7. In the *Arabian Nights*, Ali Baba was
a woodcutter who learned the magic
password, *sesame*, that opened the
doors to the cave containing the treasure of the Forty Thieves.

From 1919

The House of Morgan

I commit my soul into the hands of my savior, wrote John Pierpont Morgan in his will, *in full confidence that having redeemed it and washed it in His most precious blood, He will present it faultless before my heavenly father, and I intreat my children to maintain and defend at all hazard and at any cost of personal sacrifice the blessed doctrine of complete atonement for sin through the blood of Jesus Christ once offered and through that alone,*

and into the hands of the House of Morgan represented by his son,

he committed,

when he died in Rome in 1913,

the control of the Morgan interests in New York, Paris and London, four national banks, three trust companies, three life insurance companies, ten railroad systems, three street railway companies, an express company, the International Mercantile Marine,

power,

on the cantilever principle, through interlocking directorates

over eighteen other railroads, U.S. Steel, General Electric, American Tel and Tel, five major industries;

the interwoven cables of the Morgan Stillman Baker combination held credit up like a suspension bridge, thirteen percent of the banking resources of the world.

The first Morgan to make a pool was Joseph Morgan, a hotelkeeper in Hartford Connecticut who organized stagecoach lines and bought up Ætna Life Insurance stock in a time of panic caused by one of the big New York fires in the 1830's;

his son Junius followed in his footsteps, first in the drygoods business, and then as a partner to George Peabody, a Massachusetts banker who built up an enormous underwriting and mercantile business in London and became a friend of Queen Victoria;

Junius married the daughter of John Pierpont, a Boston preacher, poet, eccentric, and abolitionist; and their eldest son,

John Pierpont Morgan

arrived in New York to make his fortune

after being trained in England, going to school at Vevey, proving himself a crack mathematician at the University of Göttingen,

a lanky morose young man of twenty,

just in time for the panic of '57.

(war and panics on the stock exchange, bankruptcies, warloans, good growing weather for the House of Morgan.)

When the guns started booming at Fort Sumter,[8] young Morgan turned some money over reselling condemned muskets to the U.S. army and began to make himself felt in the gold room in downtown New York; there was more in trading in gold than in trading in muskets; so much for the Civil War.

During the Franco-Prussian war [9] Junius Morgan floated a huge bond issue for the French government at Tours.

At the same time young Morgan was fighting Jay Cooke [1] and the German-Jew bankers in Frankfort over the funding of the American war debt (he never did like the Germans or the Jews).

The panic of '75 ruined Jay Cooke and made J. Pierpont Morgan the boss croupier of Wall Street; he united with the Philadelphia Drexels and built the Drexel building where for thirty years he sat in his glassedin office, redfaced and insolent, writing at his desk, smoking great black cigars, or, if important issues were involved, playing solitaire in his inner office; he was famous for his few words, Yes or No, and for his way of suddenly blowing up in a visitor's face and for that special gesture of the arm that meant, *What do I get out of it?*

In '77 Junius Morgan retired; J. Pierpont got himself made a member of the board of directors of the New York Central railroad and launched the first *Corsair*. He liked yachting and to have pretty actresses call him Commodore.

He founded the Lying-in Hospital on Stuyvesant Square, and was fond of going into St. George's church and singing a hymn all alone in the afternoon quiet.

In the panic of '93
at no inconsiderable profit to himself
Morgan saved the U.S. Treasury; gold was draining out, the country was ruined, the farmers were howling for a silver standard, Grover Cleveland and his cabinet were walking up and down in the blue room at the White House without being able to come to a decision, in Congress they were making speeches while the gold reserves melted at the Subtreasuries; poor people were starving; Coxey's army [2] was marching to Washington; for a long time Grover Cleveland couldn't bring himself to call in the representative of the Wall Street moneymasters; Morgan sat in his suite at the Arlington

---

8. The first military engagement of the Civil War (April 8, 1861).
9. In 1870–1871; a war promoted by Bismarck in his plan to unify the German states while crushing the regime of Emperor Napoleon III of France.
1. Jay Cooke (1821–1905) built his huge financial enterprises on his position as financial agent for the United States Treasury under his friend Salmon

P. Chase during the Civil War. "The panic of '75" actually began in 1873, with Cooke's failure through overexpansion.
2. Jacob Sechler Coxey, Pennsylvania businessman, in 1894 (and again in 1914) led an "army" of unemployed to Washington in support of his proposal for federal make-work projects to relieve unemployment in times of depression.

smoking cigars and quietly playing solitaire until at last the president sent for him;

he had a plan all ready for stopping the gold hemorrhage.

After that what Morgan said went; when Carnegie sold out he built the Steel Trust.

J. Pierpont Morgan was a bullnecked irascible man with small black magpie's eyes and a growth on his nose; he let his partners work themselves to death over the detailed routine of banking, and sat in his back office smoking black cigars; when there was something to be decided he said Yes or No or just turned his back and went back to his solitaire.

Every Christmas his librarian read him Dickens' A *Christmas Carol* from the original manuscript.

He was fond of canarybirds and pekinese dogs and liked to take pretty actresses yachting. Each *Corsair* was a finer vessel than the last.

When he dined with King Edward he sat at His Majesty's right; he ate with the Kaiser tête-à-tête; he liked talking to cardinals or the pope, and never missed a conference of Episcopal bishops;

Rome was his favorite city.

He liked choice cookery and old wines and pretty women and yachting, and going over his collections, now and then picking up a jewelled snuffbox and staring at it with his magpie's eyes.

He made a collection of the autographs of the rulers of France, owned glass cases full of Babylonian tablets, seals, signets, statuettes, busts,

Gallo-Roman bronzes,

Merovingian jewels, miniatures, watches, tapestries, porcelains, cuneiform inscriptions, paintings by all the old masters, Dutch, Italian, Flemish, Spanish,

manuscripts of the gospels and the Apocalypse,

a collection of the works of Jean-Jacques Rousseau,

and the letters of Pliny the Younger.

His collectors bought anything that was expessive or rare or had the glint of empire on it, and he had it brought to him and stared hard at it with his magpie's eyes. Then it was put in a glass case.

The last year of his life he went up the Nile on a dahabiyeh [3] and spent a long time staring at the great columns of the Temple of Karnak.

The panic of 1907 and the death of Harriman, his great opponent in railroad financing, in 1909, had left him the undisputed ruler of Wall Street, most powerful private citizen in the world;

---

3. A long, low houseboat, propelled by sail, used only on the Nile River.

an old man tired of the purple, suffering from gout, he had deigned to go to Washington to answer the questions of the Pujo Committee during the Money Trust Investigation: [4] Yes, I did what seemed to me to be for the best interests of the country.

So admirably was his empire built that his death in 1913 hardly caused a ripple in the exchanges of the world: the purple descended to his son, J. P. Morgan,

who had been trained at Groton and Harvard and by associating with the British ruling class

to be a more constitutional monarch: *J. P. Morgan suggests* . . .

By 1917 the Allies had borrowed one billion, nine hundred million dollars through the House of Morgan: we went overseas for democracy and the flag;

and by the end of the Peace Conference the phrase *J. P. Morgan suggests* had compulsion over a power of seventyfour billion dollars.

J. P. Morgan is a silent man, not given to public utterances, but during the great steel strike, he wrote Gary: [5] *Heartfelt congratulations on your stand for the open shop, with which I am, as you know, absolutely in accord. I believe American principles of liberty are deeply involved, and must win if we stand firm.*

(Wars and panics on the stock exchange,
machinegunfire and arson,
bankruptcies, warloans,
starvation, lice, cholera and typhus:
good growing weather for the House of Morgan.)

1932

From The Big Money

Newsreel LXVI

HOLMES DENIES STAY

A better world's in birth [6]

Tiny Wasps Imported From Korea In Battle To Death With Asiatic beetle

BOY CARRIED MILE DOWN SEWER; SHOT OUT ALIVE

4. The "Money Trust" was an alleged concentration of credit in the hands of a few financiers, supposedly responsible for such panics as that of 1907. Representative A. P. Pujo headed the House committee to investigate the matter in 1912.

5. Elbert H. Gary (1846–1927), an associate of Morgan, and the steel magnate who built Gary, Indiana, as a "company town," was an archfoe of labor. The strike here mentioned occurred in the fall of 1919, and resulted from Gary's stern resistance to the closed shop.

6. The centered lines of italics in this "newsreel" are verses from "The Internationale," a Communist song.

CHICAGO BARS MEETINGS

For justice thunders condemnation

Washington Keeps Eye On Radicals

Arise rejected of the earth

PARIS BRUSSELS MOSCOW GENEVA ADD THEIR VOICES

It is the final conflict
Let each stand in his place

Geologist Lost In Cave Six Days

The International Party

SACCO AND VANZETTI MUST DIE [7]

Shall be the human race.

Much I thought of you when I was lying in the death house—
the singing, the kind tender voices of the children from the play-
ground where there was all the life and the joy of liberty—just
one step from the wall that contains the buried agony of three
buried souls. It would remind me so often of you and of your
sister and I wish I could see you every moment, but I feel better
that you will not come to the death house so that you could not
see the horrible picture of three living in agony waiting to be
electrocuted.[8]

1936

The Camera Eye (50)

they have clubbed us off the streets   they are stronger   they
are rich   they hire and fire the politicians the newspapereditors
the old judges the small men with reputations the collegepresidents
the wardheelers   (listen businessmen collegepresidents judges
America will not forget her betrayers)   they hire the men with
guns   the uniforms the policecars the patrolwagons
    all right you have won   you will kill the brave men our friends
tonight
    there is nothing left to do   we are beaten   we the beaten
crowd together in these old dingy schoolrooms on Salem Street

7. The crux of this "newsreel" and of
the following "camera eye" is the case
of Nicola Sacco and Bartolomeo Vanzetti, convicted of murder in 1921 in
connection with a payroll robbery in
Massachusetts. They were tried amid
the tensions of a conservative reaction.
The convicted men freely professed adherence to the anarchist ideology, but
liberal opinion asserted that they also
had the reputation of being honest and
quiet workmen, and that there was no
real evidence of their connection with
the crime. Appeals of the case delayed
their execution, which finally occurred
in 1927.
8. This passage in italics is adapted
from Vanzetti's prison letters.

shuffle up and down the gritty creaking stairs sit hunched with bowed heads on benches and hear the old words of the haters of oppression   made new in sweat and agony tonight

our work is over   the scribbled phrases   the nights typing releases the smell of the printshop the sharp reek of newsprinted leaflets the rush for Western Union   stringing words into wires the search for stinging words to make you feel who are your oppressors America

America our nation has been beaten by strangers who have turned our language inside out who have taken the clean words our fathers spoke and made them slimy and foul

their hired men sit on the judge's bench they sit back with their feet on the tables under the dome of the State House they are ignorant of our beliefs they have the dollars the guns the armed forces the powerplants

they have built the electricchair and hired the executioner to throw the switch

all right we are two nations

America our nation has been beaten by strangers who have bought the laws and fenced off the meadows and cut down the woods for pulp and turned our pleasant cities into slums and sweated the wealth out of our people and when they want to they hire the executioner to throw the switch

but do they know that the old words of the immigrants are being renewed in blood and agony tonight do they know that the old American speech of the haters of oppression is new tonight in the mouth of an old woman from Pittsburgh of a husky boilermaker from Frisco who hopped freights clear from the Coast to come here in the mouth of a Back Bay socialworker in the mouth of an Italian printer of a hobo from Arkansas   the language of the beaten nation is not forgotten in our ears tonight

the men in the deathhouse made the old words new before they died

If it had not been for these things, I might have lived out my life talking at streetcorners to scorning men. I might have died unknown, unmarked, a failure. This is our career and our triumph. Never in our full life can we hope to do such work for tolerance, for justice, for man's understanding of man as now we do by an accident [9]

now their work is over   the immigrants haters of oppression lie quiet in black suits in the little undertaking parlor in the North End   the city is quiet   the men of the conquering nation are not to be seen on the streets

9. This passage in italics is from Vanzetti's prison letters.

they have won why are they scared to be seen on the streets? on the streets you see only the downcast faces of the beaten the streets belong to the beaten nation all the way to the cemetery where the bodies of the immigrants are to be burned we line the curbs in the drizzling rain we crowd the wet sidewalks elbow to elbow silent pale looking with scared eyes at the coffins

we stand defeated America

1936

Vag [1]

The young man waits at the edge of the concrete, with one hand he grips a rubbed suitcase of phony leather, the other hand almost making a fist, thumb up

that moves in ever so slight an arc when a car slithers past, a truck roars clatters; the wind of cars passing ruffles his hair, slaps grit in his face.

Head swims, hunger has twisted the belly tight,

he has skinned a heel through the torn sock, feet ache in the broken shoes, under the threadbare suit carefully brushed off with the hand, the torn drawers have a crummy feel, the feel of having slept in your clothes; in the nostrils lingers the staleness of discouraged carcasses crowded into a transient camp, the carbolic stench of the jail, on the taut cheeks the shamed flush from the boring eyes of cops and deputies, railroadbulls (they eat three squares a day, they are buttoned into well-made clothes, they have wives to sleep with, kids to play with after supper, they work for the big men who buy their way, they stick their chests out with the sureness of power behind their backs). Git the hell out, scram. Know what's good for you, you'll make yourself scarce. Gittin' tough, eh? Think you kin take it, eh?

The punch in the jaw, the slam on the head with the nightstick, the wrist grabbed and twisted behind the back, the big knee brought up sharp into the crotch,

the walk out of town with sore feet to stand and wait at the edge of the hissing speeding string of cars where the reek of ether and lead and gas melts into the silent grassy smell of the earth.

Eyes black with want seek out the eyes of the drivers, a hitch, a hundred miles down the road.

Overhead in the blue a plane drones. Eyes follow the silver Douglas that flashes once in the sun and bores its smooth way out of sight into the blue.

1. "Vag" concludes the novel *The Big Money*, and thus also the trilogy, *U.S.A.*, bringing the period of its history down to the great depression of the thirties. The "vag" (vagabond) then was a familiar sight, as throngs of the homeless unemployed roamed the streets or took to the road as migatory workers.

(The transcontinental passengers sit pretty, big men with bank-accounts, highlypaid jobs, who are saluted by doormen; telephone-girls say goodmorning to them. Last night after a fine dinner, drinks with friends, they left Newark. Roar of climbing motors slanting up into the inky haze. Lights drop away. An hour staring along a silvery wing at a big lonesome moon hurrying west through curdling scum. Beacons flash in a line across Ohio.

At Cleveland the plane drops banking in a smooth spiral, the string of lights along the lake swings in a circle. Climbing roar of the motors again; slumped in the soft seat drowsing through the flat moonlight night.

Chi. A glimpse of the dipper. Another spiral swoop from cool into hot air thick with dust and the reek of burnt prairies.

Beyond the Mississippi dawn creeps up behind through the murk over the great plains. Puddles of mist go white in the Iowa hills, farms, fences, silos, steel glint from a river. The blinking eyes of the beacons reddening into day. Watercourses vein the eroded hills.

Omaha. Great cumulus clouds, from coppery churning to creamy to silvery white, trail brown skirts of rain over the hot plains. Red and yellow badlands, tiny horned shapes of cattle.

Cheyenne. The cool high air smells of sweetgrass.

The tightbaled clouds to westward burst and scatter in tatters over the strawcolored hills. Indigo mountains jut rimrock. The plane breasts a huge crumbling cloudbank and toboggans over bumpy air across green and crimson slopes into the sunny dazzle of Salt Lake.

The transcontinental passenger thinks contracts, profits, vacation-trips, mighty continent between Atlantic and Pacific, power, wires humming dollars, cities jammed, hills empty, the indiantrail leading into the wagonroad, the macadamed pike, the concrete skyway; trains, planes: history the billiondollar speedup,

and in the bumpy air over the desert ranges towards Las Vegas

sickens and vomits into the carton container the steak and mushrooms he ate in New York. No matter, silver in the pocket, greenbacks in the wallet, drafts, certified checks, plenty restaurants in L. A.)

The young man waits on the side of the road; the plane has gone; thumb moves in a small arc when a car tears hissing past. Eyes seek the driver's eyes. A hundred miles down the road. Head swims, belly tightens, wants crawl over his skin like ants:

went to school, books said opportunity, ads promised speed, own your home, shine bigger than your neighbor, the radiocrooner whispered girls, ghosts of platinum girls coaxed from the screen; millions in winnings were chalked up on the boards in the offices, paychecks were for hands willing to work, the cleared desk of an executive with three telephones on it;

waits with swimming head, needs knot the belly, idle hands numb, beside the speeding traffic.

A hundred miles down the road.

1936

LANGSTON HUGHES
(1902–1967)

The enrollment of Langston Hughes as a student at Columbia University in 1922 brought to New York a man who was to display one of the surest and most long-lasting talents to be revealed in that cultural phenomenon during the 1920's that has come to be known as the Harlem Renaissance. Born in Joplin, Missouri, Hughes spent many of his early years with a grandmother in Lawrence, Kansas, but lived also in Topeka and in Lincoln, Illinois, before moving to Cleveland, Ohio, at fourteen. Residing in Cleveland with his mother and stepfather, but spending some of his summers with his father in Mexico, Hughes had begun to write and publish before he arrived in New York. Leaving Columbia after a year, he worked his way on shipboard to Africa and Europe, found employment as a cook and a busboy in Paris and in Washington, D.C., and continued to publish in New York magazines the poems that, together with his wanderings, were slowly creating a legend around him. About the time of the appearance of his first books of poetry, *The Weary Blues* (1926) and *Fine Clothes to the Jew* (1927), he ceased his other employment

to become the professional man of letters that he remained for the rest of his life. In the words of Arna Bontemps, "He has been a minstrel and a troubadour in the classic sense. He has had no other vocation * * * ."

There is scarcely a literary genre that he did not try. In the 1920's he was primarily a poet; later he continued to write poetry but turned increasingly to fiction, autobiographies, and children's books. Sometimes working alone and sometimes with Arna Bontemps, he edited a series of anthologies such as *The Poetry of the Negro, 1746–1949* (1949) and *An African Treasury* (1960) that helped to widen the bounds of sympathy and understanding for black literature.

Although there were from the beginning few who doubted Hughes' literary skill, at first some readers wished his portraits were more flattering to their subjects. Defending himself, he once wrote, "I knew only the people I had grown up with, and they weren't people whose shoes were always shined, who had been to Harvard, or who had heard of Bach." A factor contributing to his early success was the 1920's hunger for primitivism that readers found satisfied by Hughes's use of blues rhythms, and although critics have been at times ambivalent, the poems that use those rhythms continue to rank among his most successful. Similarly, although Hughes wrote excellent short stories in which he did not appear, Simple remains on the whole his finest fictional creation.

The source of the poetry selections below is *Montage of a Dream Deferred*, 1951. A convenient gathering is *Selected Poems of Langston Hughes*, 1965. *Not Without Laughter*, 1930, is a novel. *The Best of Simple*, 1961, the source of the sketches below, includes selections from three previous volumes and should be supplemented by *Simple's Uncle Sam*, 1965. Short story collections are *The Ways of White Folks*, 1934; *Laughing to Keep from Crying*, 1952; and *Something in Common and Other Stories*, 1963, which includes selections from the earlier volumes. *The Langston Hughes Reader* appeared in 1966. Studies include Donald C. Dickinson, *A Bio-bibliography of Langston Hughes*, 1967; James A. Emanuel, *Langston Hughes*, 1967; and Milton Meltzer, *Langston Hughes: A Biography*, 1968.

From Montage of a Dream Deferred

Dream Boogie

Good morning, daddy!
Ain't you heard
The boogie-woogie rumble
Of a dream deferred?

Listen closely: 5
You'll hear their feet
Beating out and beating out a—

    *You think
    It's a happy beat?*

Listen to it closely: 10
Ain't you heard
something underneath
like a—

    What did I say?

Sure,   15
I'm happy!
Take it away!

    *Hey, pop!
    Re-bop!
    Mop!*   20

    Y-e-a-h!

Theme for English B

The instructor said,

    *Go home and write
    a page tonight.*

> *And let that page come out of you—*
> *Then, it will be true.*   5

I wonder if it's that simple?

I am twenty-two, colored, born in Winston-Salem.
I went to school there, then Durham, then here
to this college on the hill above Harlem.
I am the only colored student in my class.   10
The steps from the hill lead down into Harlem,
through a park, then I cross St. Nicholas,
Eighth Avenue, Seventh, and I come to the Y,
the Harlem Branch Y, where I take the elevator
up to my room, sit down, and write this page: 15

It's not easy to know what is true for you or me
at twenty-two, my age. But I guess I'm what
I feel and see and hear, Harlem, I hear you:
hear you, hear me—we two—you, me, talk on this page.
(I hear New York, too.) Me—who?   20

Well, I like to eat, sleep, drink, and be in love.
I like to work, read, learn, and understand life.
I like a pipe for a Christmas present,
or records—Bessie, bop, or Bach.
I guess being colored doesn't make me *not* like   25
the same things other folks like who are other races.
So will my page be colored that I write?
Being me, it will not be white.
But it will be
a part of you, instructor.   30
You are white—
yet a part of me, as I am a part of you.
That's American.
Sometimes perhaps you don't want to be a part of me.
Nor do I often want to be a part of you.   35
But we are, that's true!
As I learn from you,
I guess you learn from me—
although you're older—and white—
and somewhat more free.   40

This is my page for English B.

Harlem

What happens to a dream deferred?

> Does it dry up
> like a raisin in the sun?
> Or fester like a sore—
> And then run?   5

Does it stink like rotten meat?
Or crust and sugar over—
like a syrupy sweet?

Maybe it just sags
like a heavy load.   10

Or does it explode?

1951

Feet Live Their Own Life

"If you want to know about my life," said Simple as he blew
the foam from the top of the newly filled glass the bartender put
before him, "don't look at my face, don't look at my hands. Look
at my feet and see if you can tell how long I been standing on
them."

"I cannot see your feet through your shoes," I said.

"You do not need to see through my shoes," said Simple. "Can't
you tell by the shoes I wear—not pointed, not rocking-chair, not
French-toed, not nothing but big, long, broad, and flat—that I
been standing on these feet a long time and carrying some heavy
burdens? They ain't flat from standing at no bar, neither, because
I always sets at a bar. Can't you tell that? You know I do not
hang out in a bar unless it has stools, don't you?"

"That I have observed," I said, "but I did not connect it with
your past life."

"Everything I do is connected up with my past life," said Simple. "From Virginia to Joyce, from my wife to Zarita, from my
mother's milk to this glass of beer, everything is connected up."

"I trust you will connect up with that dollar I just loaned you
when you get paid," I said. "And who is Virginia? You never
told me about her."

"Virginia is where I was borned," said Simple. "I *would* be
borned in a state named after a woman. From that day on,
women never give me no peace."

"You, I fear, are boasting. If the women were running after you
as much as you run after them, you would not be able to sit here
on this bar stool in peace. I don't see any women coming to
call you out to go home, as some of these fellows' wives do around
here."

"Joyce better not come in no bar looking for me," said Simple.
"That is why me and my wife busted up—one reason. I do not
like to be called out of no bar by a female. It's a man's prerogative to just set and drink sometimes."

"How do you connect that prerogative with your past?" I asked.

"When I was a wee small child," said Simple, "I had no place to set and think in, being as how I was raised up with three brothers, two sisters, seven cousins, one married aunt, a common-law uncle, and the minister's grandchild—and the house only had four rooms. I never had a place just to set and think. Neither to set and drink—not even much my milk before some hongry child snatched it out of my hand. I were not the youngest, neither a girl, nor the cutest. I don't know why, but I don't think nobody liked me much. Which is why I was afraid to like anybody for a long time myself. When I did like somebody, I was full-grown and then I picked out the wrong woman because I had no practice in liking anybody before that. We did not get along."

"Is that when you took to drink?"

"Drink took to me," said Simple. "Whiskey just naturally likes me but beer likes me better. By the time I got married I had got to the point where a cold bottle was almost as good as a warm bed, especially when the bottle could not talk and the bed-warmer could. I do not like a woman to talk to me too much—I mean about me. Which is why I like Joyce. Joyce most in generally talks about herself."

"I am still looking at your feet," I said, "and I swear they do not reveal your life to me. Your feet are no open book."

"You have eyes but you see not," said Simple. "These feet have stood on every rock from the Rock of Ages to 135th and Lenox. These feet have supported everything from a cotton bale to a hongry woman. These feet have walked ten thousand miles working for white folks and another ten thousand keeping up with colored. These feet have stood at altars, crap tables, free lunches, bars, graves, kitchen doors, betting windows, hospital clinics, WPA desks, social security railings, and in all kinds of lines from soup lines to the draft. If I just had four feet, I could have stood in more places longer. As it is, I done wore out seven hundred pairs of shoes, eighty-nine tennis shoes, twelve summer sandals, also six loafers. The socks that these feet have bought could build a knitting mill. The corns I've cut away would dull a German razor. The bunions I forgot would make you ache from now till Judgment Day. If anybody was to write the history of my life, they should start with my feet."

"Your feet are not all that extraordinary," I said. "Besides, everything you are saying is general. Tell me specifically some one thing your feet have done that makes them different from any other feet in the world, just one."

"Do you see that window in that white man's store across the street?" asked Simple. "Well, this right foot of mine broke out that window in the Harlem riots right smack in the middle. Didn't no other foot in the world break that window but mine. And this left foot carried me off running as soon as my right foot came down. Nobody else's feet saved me from the cops that night but these *two* feet right here. Don't tell me these feet ain't had a life of their own."

"For shame," I said, "going around kicking out windows. Why?"

"Why?" said Simple. "You have to ask my great-great-grandpa why. He must of been simple—else why did he let them capture him in Africa and sell him for a slave to breed my great-grandpa in slavery to breed my grandpa in slavery to breed my pa to breed me to look at that window and say, 'It ain't mine! Bam-mmm-mm-m!' and kick it out?"

"This bar glass is not yours either," I said. "Why don't you smash it?"

"It's got my beer in it," said Simple.

Just then Zarita came in wearing her Thursday-night rabbit-skin coat. She didn't stop at the bar, being dressed up, but went straight back to a booth. Simple's hand went up, his beer went down, and the glass back to its wet spot on the bar.

"Excuse me a minute," he said, sliding off the stool.

Just to give him pause, the dozens, that old verbal game of maligning a friend's female relatives, came to mind. "Wait," I said. "You have told me about what to ask your great-great-grandpa. But I want to know what to ask your great-great-grand*ma*."

"I don't play the dozens that far back," said Simple, following Zarita into the smoky juke-box blue of the back room.

1950

JAMES T. FARRELL

(1904–   )

James Thomas Farrell was born on February 27, 1904, in Chicago and was graduated from St. Cyril High School; he published sketches in the magazine —the earliest significantly entitled "Danny's Uncle." He did not live in the immediate neighborhood of his famous fictional characters, Danny and Studs; as he says, "the South Side was miles big," but his early fiction shows his intimate acquaintance with most of it. He loved to rove, and was then less interested in books than in baseball, of which he has written with enthusiasm, beginning with one of the pieces at St. Cyril. His first job, with an express company, is memorably reflected in his early fiction. In 1925 he enrolled as a full-time student at the University of Chicago, where his talented teacher, James Weber Linn, in 1927 accepted his class themes for publication in his newspaper column. In the same year he left the university to risk writing on his own time, although he returned intermittently as a student until 1930, when his germinal story, "Studs," appeared in *This Quarter*.

In 1927 Farrell found work in New York for a time. Again in Chicago, he supported himself by various employments and literary work until 1931 when, with *Young Lonigan* shaping up, he terminated his residence in Chicago and settled in New York City. *Young Lonigan* (1932) was an artistic success, and the completion of the Lonigan trilogy gained its author a place at the forefront of his generation. *The Young Manhood of Studs Lonigan* (1934) and *Judgment Day* (1935) brought the life of Studs to a tragic end, to which flaws in his soul and the limitations of a world in depression both contributed. Danny O'Neill was a character in *Young Lonigan, Gas-House McGinty* (1933), and a story, "Helen I Love You," before he appeared as the protagonist of *A World I Never Made* (1936), the first of the five novels of the O'Neill cycle (see bibliography). Before completing this cycle, in 1953, Farrell had also published the Bernard Carr cycle and at least twelve volumes of collected short stories.

The subtitle of his first novel, "A Boyhood on the Chicago Streets," drew disproportionate attention to this writer's awareness of social problems. However, Farrell has in fact and consciously dedicated his powers to the intense observation and fictional creation of human character. Studs Lonigan and Danny O'Neill were inspired by his knowledge of the city neighborhoods of middle-class solidarity common before World War I,

and by his close observation of boyhood friends and relatives, but the novels were neither autobiography nor *roman à clef*. The families of these boys and their friends—these artisans, salesmen, expressmen, schoolmates playing in yards or the park, all the variegated life of an established city neighborhood of the time—have been created, not merely transcribed. The Farrell character is the fictional statement of a human life, in which fate is a function of character, not of sociology. *Ellen Rogers* (1941), one of the author's most successful creations, represents a much more sophisticated social environment, but it was certainly the characters, not the social issue, that Thomas Mann had in mind when he praised it as "the best modern love story" that he had read. And it was the conflict of character with circumstance that John Dewey called "classic" in *Tommy Gallagher's Crusade*.

Few authors have been able to maintain so successfully as Farrell the point of view of the boy, and few have surpassed him in the power to portray the world of childhood and youth. At forty-five he wrote "The Fastest Runner on Sixty-first Street." Similarly, Ellen Rogers is only one of many women characters of all ages, including a childhood sweetheart of Studs, who remain in the reader's memory as persons known in actuality.

The Bernard Carr cycle of novels (after 1945), also many of the later short stories and volumes of nonfiction, reflect the author's enlarging contacts with life and ideas, his observation of new scenes, his life in Paris and elsewhere abroad, and his life in New York. Increasingly after World War II, he depicted with fidelity a more sophisticated environment, and the emerging groups of writers seeking to discover personal or social meaning amid the welter of shifting ideas. As a novelist he continued to explore human rather than social issues, but his nonfictional works during this period proclaim his interest, from early life, in social and political experiment and action, and in advanced ideas. "I still respect Marx," he says, referring to his essays on Marxian literature in A Note on Literary Criticism (1936). "Nietzsche and Freud were early influences too"; but he could add, "I was never a Social Darwinist," because his fiction does not conform to any social thesis. "I have always believed," he writes, "in freedom and dignity and have fought certain tendencies here as well as fascism and communism here and abroad"; but "my books are not problem solvers."

Farrell is one of the most interesting of modern stylists; his writing has an organic quality adapting readily to the subject at hand. Beach praised his Chicago novels as "the plainest, soberest, most straightforward, of any living novelist." However, the later novels and short stories, with their great range of subject matter, show a flexible prose conforming with the novelist's expressed aim to "write so that life may speak for itself."

Studs Lonigan appears in *Young Lonigan: A Boyhood on the Chicago Streets*, 1932; *The Young Manhood of Studs Lonigan*, 1934; and *Judgment Day*, 1935: in one volume, *Studs Lonigan: A Trilogy*, 1935. Danny O'Neill is a character in *Gas-House McGinty*, 1933. He becomes the dominant figure in the cycle including *A World I Never Made*, 1936; *No Star Is Lost*, 1938; *Father and Son*, 1940; *My Days of Anger*, 1943; and (the earliest in relation to Danny's life) *The Face of Time*, 1953. *Bernard Clare* (alias "Carr"), 1946, introduces the title character, protagonist also of *The Road Between*, 1949, and *Yet Other Waters*, 1952. Novels outside the cycles include *Ellen Rogers*, 1941; *This Man and This Woman*, 1951; and *Boarding House Blues*, 1961. Novels in his latest cycle, *A Universe of Time*, are *The Silence of History*, 1963; *What Time Collects*, 1964; *When Time Was Born*, 1966; *Lonely for the Future*, 1966; *A Brand New Life*, 1968; *Judith*, 1969; and *Invisible Swords*, 1970. A recent non-cycle novel is *New Year's Eve, 1929*, 1967.

Volumes of short stories include *Calico Shoes*, 1934; *Guillotine Party*, 1935; *Can All This Grandeur Perish?*, 1937; *$1000 a Week*, 1942; *To Whom It May Concern*, 1944; *When Boyhood Dreams Come True*, 1946; *The Life Adventurous*, 1947; *An American Dream Girl and Other Stories*, 1950; *French Girls Are Vicious*, 1955; *An Omnibus of Short Stories*, 1956—a collection of three previous volumes; *The Name is Fogarty* (humorous sketches) 1950; *A Dangerous Woman, and Other Stories*, 1957; *Side Street * * *, 1961; *Sound of a City*, 1962; *Childhood Is Not Forever and Other Stories*, 1969; and *Judith and Other Stories*, 1973.

Essays are in *A Note on Literary Criticism*, 1936; *The League of Frightened Philistines*, 1945; *Literature and Morality*, 1947. *Selected Essays* appeared in 1964, and *Collected Poems* in 1965.

A full-length study is Edgar M. Branch, *James T. Farrell*, 1971. Other critical accounts are Joseph Warren Beach, *American Fiction, 1920–1940*, 1941, and Oscar Cargill, *Intellectual America*, 1941. Autobiographical essays and reminiscent studies include *Reflections at Fifty*, 1954; *My Baseball Diary*, 1957; and *It Has Come to Pass*, 1958 (Israel). *A Bibliography* was edited by Edgar Branch, 1959.

The Fastest Runner on Sixty-first Street [1]

Morty Aiken liked to run and to skate. He liked running games and races. He liked running so much that sometimes he'd go over to Washington Park all by himself and run just for the fun of it. He got a kick out of running, and he had raced every kid he could get to run against him. His love of racing and running had even become a joke among many of the boys he knew. But even when they gave him the horse laugh it was done in a good-natured way, because he was a very popular boy. Older fellows liked him, and when they would see him, they'd say, there's a damn good kid and a damned fast runner.

When he passed his fourteenth birthday, Morty was a trifle smaller than most boys of his own age. But he was well known, and, in a way, almost famous in his own neighborhood. He lived at Sixty-first and Eberhardt, but kids in the whole area had heard of him, and many of them would speak of what a runner and what a skater Morty Aiken was.

He won medals in playground tournaments, and, in fact, he was the only lad from his school who had ever won medals in these tournaments. In these events he became the champion in the fifty- and hundred-yard dash, and with this he gained the reputation of being the best runner, for his age, on the South Side of Chicago.

He was as good a skater as he was a runner. In winter, he was to be seen regularly almost every day on the ice at the Washington Park lagoon or over on the Midway. He had a pair of Johnson racers which his father had given him, and he treasured these more than any other possession. His mother knitted him red socks and a red stocking cap for skating, and he had a red-and-white sweater. When he skated, he was like a streak of red. His form was excellent, and his sense of himself and of his body on the ice was sure and right. Almost every day there would be a game of I-Got-It. The skater who was *it* would skate in a wide circle, chased by the pack until he was caught. Morty loved to play I-Got-It, and on many a day this boy in short pants, wearing the red stocking cap, the red-and-white sweater, and the thick, knitted red woolen socks coming above the black shoes of his Johnson racers, would lead the pack, circling around and around and around, his head forward, his upper torso bent forward, his hands behind his back, his legs working with grace and giving him a speed that sometimes seemed miraculous. And in February, 1919, Morty competed in an ice derby, conducted under the auspices of the Chicago *Clarion*. He won two gold medals. His picture was on the first page of the sports section of the Sunday *Clarion*. All in all, he was a famous and cele-

---

1. From *An American Dream Girl and Other Stories* (1950).

brated lad. His father and mother were proud of him. His teacher and Mrs. Bixby, the principal of the school, were proud of him. Merchants on Sixty-first Street were proud of him. There was not a lad in the neighborhood who was greeted on the street by strangers as often as Morty.

Although he was outwardly modest, Morty had his dreams. He was graduated from grammar school in 1919, and was planning to go to Park High in the fall. He was impatient to go to high school and to get into high-school track meets. He'd never been coached, and yet look how good he was! Think of how good he would be when he had some coaching! He'd be a streak of lightning, if ever there was one. He dreamed that he would be called the Human Streak of Lightning. And after high school there would be college, college track meets, and the Big Ten championship, and after that he would join an athletic club and run in track meets, and he would win a place on the Olympic team, and somewhere, in Paris or Rome or some European city, he would beat the best runners in the world, and, like Ty Cobb [2] in baseball and Jess Willard [3] in prize fighting, he'd be the world's greatest runner.

And girls would all like him, and the most beautiful girl in the world would marry him. He liked girls, but girls liked him even more than he liked them. In May, a little while before his graduation, the class had a picnic, and they played post office. The post office was behind a clump of bushes in Jackson Park. He was called to the post office more than any other of the boys. There was giggling and talking and teasing, but it hadn't bothered him, especially because he knew that the other fellows liked and kind of envied him. To Morty, this was only natural. He accepted it. He accepted the fact that he was a streak of lightning on his feet and on the ice, and that this made him feel somehow different from other boys and very important. Even Tony Rabuski looked at him in this way, and if any kid would have picked on him, Tony would have piled into that kid. Tony was the toughest boy in school, and he was also considered to be the dumbest. He was also the poorest. He would often come to school wearing a black shirt, because a black shirt didn't show the dirt the way that other shirts did, and his parents couldn't afford to buy him many shirts. One day Tony was walking away from school with Morty, and Tony said:

"Kid, you run de fastest, I fight de best in de whole school. We make a crack-up team. We're pals. Shake, kid, we're pals."

Morty shook Tony's hand. For a fourteen-year-old boy, Tony had very big and strong hands. The other kids sometimes called them "meat hooks."

2. Tyrus Raymond Cobb (1886–1961), famous for his batting and base-stealing. 3. Jess Willard (1883–1968), heavyweight champion from 1915 to 1919.

Morty looked on this handshake as a pledge. He and Tony became friends, and they were often together. Morty had Tony come over to his house to play, and sometimes Tony stayed for a meal. Tony ate voraciously and wolfishly. When Morty's parents spoke of the way Tony ate and of the quantity of food he ate, Morty would reply by telling them that Tony was his friend.

Because he was poor and somewhat stupid, a dull and fierce resentment smoldered in Tony. Other boys out-talked him, and they were often able to plague and annoy him, and then outrun him because he was heavy footed. The kids used to laugh at Tony because they said he had lead, iron, and bricks in his big feet. After Morty and Tony had shaken hands and become pals, Morty never would join the other boys in razzing Tony. And he and Tony doped out a way that would permit Tony to get even with kids who tried to torment him. If some of the boys made game of Tony until he was confused and enraged and went for them, Morty would chase the boys. He had no difficulty in catching one of them. When he caught any of the boys who'd been teasing and annoying Tony, he'd usually manage to hold the boy until Tony would lumber up and exact his punishment and revenge. Sometimes Tony would be cruel, and on a couple of occasions when Tony, in a dull and stupefied rage, was sitting on a hurt, screaming boy and pounding him, Morty ordered Tony to lay off. Tony did so instantly. Morty didn't want Tony to be too cruel. He had come to like Tony and to look on him as a big brother. He'd always wanted a brother, and sometimes he would imagine how wonderful it would be if Tony could even come to live at his house.

The system Morty and Tony worked out, with Morty chasing and catching one of the boys who ragged Tony, worked out well. Soon the kids stopped ragging Tony. Because of their fear, and because they liked and respected Morty and wanted him to play with them, they began to accept Tony. And Tony began to change. Once accepted, so that he was no longer the butt of jokes, he looked on all the boys in Morty's gang as his pals. He would protect them as he would protect Morty. Tony then stopped scowling and making fierce and funny faces and acting in many odd little ways. After he became accepted, as a result of being Morty's pal, his behavior changed, and because he was strong and could fight, the boys began to admire him. At times he really hoped for strange boys to come around the neighborhood and act like bullies so he could beat them up. He wanted to fight and punch because he could feel powerful and would be praised and admired.

II

Ever since he had been a little fellow, Tony had often been called a "Polack" or a "dirty Polack." After he became one of the gang or group around Morty, some of the boys would tell him that he was a "white Polack." In his slow way, he thought about these words and what they meant. When you were called certain words, you were laughed at, you were looked at as if something were wrong with you. If you were a Polack, many girls didn't want to have anything to do with you. The boys and girls who weren't Polacks had fun together that Polacks couldn't have. Being a Polack and being called a Polack was like being called a sonofabitch. It was a name. When you were called a name like this, you were looked at as a different kind of kid from one who wasn't called a name. Morty Aiken wasn't called names. Tony didn't want to be called names. And if he fought and beat up those who called him names, they would be afraid of him. He wanted that. But he also wanted to have as much fun as the kids had who weren't called these names. And he worked it out that these kids felt better when they called other kids names. He could fight and he could call names, and if he called a kid a name, and that kid got tough, he could beat him up. He began to call names. And there was a name even worse than Polack—"nigger." If Tony didn't like a kid, he called him a "nigger." And he talked about the "niggers." He felt as good as he guessed these other kids did when he talked about the "niggers." And they could be beat up. They weren't supposed to go to Washington Park because that was a park for the whites. That was what he had often heard.

He heard it said so much that he believed it. He sometimes got a gang of the boys together and they would roam Washington Park, looking for colored boys to beat up. Morty went with them. He didn't particularly like to beat up anyone, but when they saw a colored kid and chased him, he would always be at the head, and he would be the one who caught the colored boy. He could grab or tackle him, and by that time the others would catch up. He worked the same plan that he and Tony had worked against the other boys. And after they caught and beat up a colored boy, they would all talk and shout and brag about what they had done, and talk about how they had each gotten in their licks and punches and kicks, and how fast Morty had run to catch that shine, and what a sock Tony had given him, and, talking all together and strutting and bragging, they felt good and proud of themselves, and they talked about how the Sixty-first Street boys would see to it that Washington Park would stay a white man's park.

And this became more and more important to Tony. There were those names, "Polack," "dirty Polack," "white Polack." If you could be called a "Polack," you weren't considered white. Well, when he beat them up, was he or wasn't he white? They knew. After the way he clouted these black ones, how could the other kids not say that Tony Rabuski wasn't white? That showed them all.

That showed he was a hero. He was a hero as much as Morty Aiken was.

III

Morty was a proud boy on the night he graduated from grammar school in June, 1919. When he received his diploma, there was more applause in the auditorium than there was for any other member of the class. He felt good when he heard this clapping, but, then, he expected it. He lived in a world where he was somebody, and he was going into a bigger world where he would still be somebody. He was a fine, clean-looking lad, with dark hair, frank blue eyes, regular and friendly features. He was thin but strong. He wore a blue serge suit with short trousers and a belted jacket, and a white shirt with a white bow tie. His class colors, orange and black ribbons, were pinned on the lapel of his coat. He was scrubbed and washed and combed. And he was in the midst of an atmosphere of gaiety and friendliness. The teachers were happy. There were proud and happy parents and aunts and uncles and older sisters. The local alderman made a speech praising everybody, and speaking of the graduating boys and girls as fine future Americans. And he declared that in their midst there were many promising lads and lassies who would live to enjoy great esteem and success. He also said that among this group there was also one who not only promised to become a stellar athlete but who had already won gold medals and honors.

And on that night, Morty's father and mother were very happy. They kept beaming with proud smiles. Morty was their only son. Mr. Aiken was a carpenter. He worked steadily, and he had saved his money so that the house he owned was now paid for. He and his wife were quiet-living people who minded their own business. Mr. Aiken was tall and rugged, with swarthy skin, a rough-hewn face, and the look and manner of a workman. He was a gentle but firm man, and was inarticulate with his son. He believed that a boy should have a good time in sports, should fight his own battles, and that boyhood—the best time of one's life—should be filled with happy memories.

The mother was faded and maternal. She usually had little to say; her life was dedicated to caring for her son and her husband and to keeping their home clean and orderly. She was especially happy to know that Morty liked running and skating, because these were not dangerous.

After the graduation ceremonies the father and mother took Morty home where they had cake and ice cream. The three of them sat together eating these refreshments, quiet but happy. The two parents were deeply moved. They were filled with gratification because of the applause given their son when he had walked forward on the stage to receive his diploma. They were raising a fine boy, and they could look people in the neighborhood in the eye and know that they had done their duty as parents. The father was putting money by for Morty's college education and hoped that, besides becoming a famous runner, Morty would become a professional man. He talked of this to the son and the mother over their ice cream and cake, and the boy seemed to accept his father's plans. And as the father gazed shyly at Morty he thought of his own boyhood on a Wisconsin farm, and of long summer days there. Morty had the whole summer before him. He would play and grow and enjoy himself. He was not a bad boy, he had never gotten into trouble, he wasn't the kind of boy who caused worry. It was fine. In August there would be his vacation, and they would all go to Wisconsin, and he would go fishing with the boy.

That evening Morty's parents went to bed feeling that this was the happiest day of their lives.

And Morty went to bed, a happy, light-hearted boy, thinking of the summer vacation which had now begun.

IV

The days passed. Some days were better than others. Some days there was little to do, and on other days there was a lot to do. Morty guessed that this was turning out to be as good as any summer he could remember.

Tony Rabuski was working, delivering flowers for a flower merchant, but he sometimes came around after supper, and the kids sat talking or playing on the steps of Morty's house or of another house in the neighborhood. Morty liked to play Run, Sheep, Run, because it gave him a chance to run, and he also liked hiding and searching and hearing the signals called out, and the excitement and tingling and fun when he'd be hiding, perhaps under some porch, and the other side would be near, maybe even passing right by, and he, and the other kids with him, would have to be so still, and he'd even try to hold his breath, and then finally, the signal for which he had been waiting—Run, Sheep, Run—and the race, setting off, tearing away along sidewalks and across streets, running like hell and like a streak of lightning, and feeling your speed in your legs and muscles and getting to the goal first.

The summer was going by, and it was fun. There wasn't anything to worry about and there were dreams. Edna Purcell, who had been in his class, seemed sweet on him, and she was a wonderful girl. One night she and some other girls came around, and they sat on the steps of Morty's house and played Tin-Tin. Morty had to kiss her. He did, with the kids laughing, and it seemed that something happened to him. He hadn't been shy when he was with girls, but now, when Edna was around, he would be shy. She was wonderful. She was more than wonderful. When he did have the courage to talk to her, he talked about running and iceskating. She told him she knew what a runner and skater he was. A fast skater, such as he was, wouldn't want to think of skating with someone like her. He said that he would, and that next winter he would teach her to skate better. Immediately, he found himself wishing it were next winter already, and he would imagine himself skating with her, and he could see them walking over to the Washington Park lagoon and coming home again. He would carry her skates, and when they breathed they would be able to see their breaths, and the weather would be cold and sharp and would make her red cheeks redder, and they would be alone, walking home, with the snow packed on the park, alone, the two of them walking in the park, with it quiet, so quiet that you would hear nothing, and it would be like they were in another world, and then, there in the quiet park, with white snow all over it, he would kiss Edna Purcell. He had kissed Edna when they'd played Tin-Tin, and Post Office, but he looked forward to the day that he got from her the kiss that would mean that she was his girl, his sweetheart, and the girl who would one day be his wife just like his mother was his father's wife. Everything he dreamed of doing, all the honors he would get, all the medals and cups he dreamed of winning—now all of this would be for Edna. And she was also going to Park High. He would walk to school with her, eat lunch with her, walk her home from school. When he ran in high-school track meets for Park High, Edna would be in the stands. He would give her his medals. He wanted to give her one of his gold skating medals, but he didn't know how to go about asking her to accept it.

No matter what Morty thought about, he thought about Edna at the same time. He thought about her every time he dreamed. When he walked on streets in the neighborhood, he thought of her. When he went to Washington Park or swimming, he thought of Edna. Edna, just to think of her, Edna made everything in the world wonderfully wonderful.

And thus the summer of 1919 was passing for Morty.

V

Morty sat on the curb with a group of boys, and they were bored and restless. They couldn't agree about what game to play, where to go, what to do to amuse themselves. A couple of them started to play Knife but gave it up. Morty suggested a race, but no one would race him. They couldn't agree on playing ball. One boy suggested swimming, but no one would go with him. Several of the boys wrestled, and a fight almost started. Morty sat by himself and thought about Edna. He guessed that he'd rather be with her than with the kids. He didn't know where she was. If he knew that she'd gone swimming, he'd go swimming. He didn't know what to do with himself. If he only could find Edna and if they would do something together, or go somewhere, like Jackson Park Beach, just the two of them, why, then, he knew that today would be the day that he would find a way of giving her one of his *Clarion* gold medals. But he didn't know where she was.

Tony Rabuski came around with four tough-looking kids. Tony had lost his job, and he said that the niggers had jumped him when he was delivering flowers down around Forty-seventh Street, and he wanted his pals to stick by him. He told them what had happened, but they didn't get it, because Tony couldn't tell a story straight. Tony asked them didn't they know what was happening? There were race riots, and the beaches and Washington Park and the whole South Side were full of dark clouds, and over on Wentworth Avenue the big guys were fighting, and the dark clouds were out after whites. They didn't believe Tony. But Morty said it was in the newspapers, and that there were race riots. The bored boys became excited. They bragged about what they would do if the jigs came over to their neighborhood. Tony said they had to get some before they got this far. When asked where they were, Tony said all over. Finally, they went over to Washington Park, picking up sticks and clubs and rocks on the way. The park was calm. A few adults were walking and strolling about. A lad of eighteen or nineteen lay under a tree with his head in the lap of a girl who was stroking his hair. Some of the kids smirked and leered as they passed the couple. Morty thought of Edna and wished he could take her to Washington Park and kiss her. There were seven or eight rowboats on the lagoon, but all of the occupants were white. The park sheep were grazing. Tony threw a rock at them, frightening the sheep, and they all ran, but no cop was around to shag them. They passed the boathouse, talking and bragging. They now believed the rumors which they themselves had made up. White girls and women were in danger, and anything might happen. A tall lad sat in the grass with a nursemaid. A baby carriage was near them. The lad called them over and asked them what they were doing with their clubs and rocks. Tony said they were looking for niggers. The lad said that he'd seen two near the goldfish pond and urged the boys to go and get the sonsofbitches. Screaming and shouting, they ran to the goldfish pond. Suddenly, Tony shouted:

"Dark clouds."

VI

They ran. Two Negro boys, near the goldfish pond, heard Tony's cry, and then the others' cry, and they ran. The mob of boys chased them. Morty was in the lead. Running at the head of the screaming, angry pack of boys, he forgot everything except how well and how fast he was running, and images of Edna flashed in and out of his mind. If she could see him running! He was running beautifully. He'd catch them. He was gaining. The colored boys ran in a northwest direction. They crossed the drive which flanked the southern end of the Washington Park ball field. Morty was stopped by a funeral procession. The other boys caught up with him. When the funeral procession passed, it was too late to try and catch the colored boys they had been chasing. Angry, bragging, they crossed over to the ball field and marched across it, shouting and yelling. They picked up about eight boys of their own age and three older lads of seventeen or eighteen. The older lads said they knew where they'd find some shines. Now was the time to teach them their place once and for all. Led by the older boys, they emerged from the north end of Washington Park and marched down Grand Boulevard, still picking up men and boys as they went along. One of the men who joined them had a gun. They screamed, looked in doorways for Negroes, believed everything anyone said about Negroes, and kept boasting about what they would do when they found some.

"Dark clouds," Tony boomed.

The mob let out. They crossed to the other side of Grand Boulevard and ran cursing and shouting after a Negro. Morty was in the lead. He was outrunning the men and the older fellows. He heard them shouting behind him. He was running. He was running like the playground hundred-yard champion of the South Side of Chicago. He was running like the future Olympic champion. He was running like he'd run for Edna. He was tearing along, pivoting out of the way of shocked, surprised pedestrians, running, really running. He was running like a streak of lightning.

The Negro turned east on Forty-eighth Street. He had a start of a block. But Morty would catch him. He turned into Forty-eighth Street. He tore along the center of the street. He began to breathe heavily. But he couldn't stop running now. He was outdistancing the gang, and he was racing his own gang and the Negro he was chasing. Down the center of the street and about half a block ahead of him, the Negro was tearing away for dear life. But Morty was gaining on him. Gaining. He was now about a half a block ahead of his own gang. They screamed murderously behind him. And they encouraged him. He heard shouts of encouragement.

"Catch 'em, Morty boy!"

"Thata boy, Morty boy!"

He heard Tony's voice. He ran.

The Negro turned into an alley just east of Forestville. Morty ran. He turned into the alley just in time to see the fleeing Negro spurt into a yard in the center of the block. He'd gained more. He was way ahead of the white mob. Somewhere behind him they were coming and yelling. He tore on. He had gained his second wind. He felt himself running, felt the movement of his legs and muscles, felt his arms, felt the sensation of his whole body as he raced down the alley. Never had he run so swiftly. Suddenly Negroes jumped out of yards. He was caught and pinioned. His only thought was one of surprise. Before he even realized what had happened, his throat was slashed. He fell, bleeding. Feebly, he mumbled just once:

"Mother!"

The Negroes disappeared.

He lay bleeding in the center of the dirty alley, and when the gang of whites caught up with him they found him dead in dirt and his own blood in the center of the alley. No Negroes were in sight. The whites surrounded his body. The boys trembled with fear. Some of them cried. One wet his pants. Then they became maddened. And they stood in impotent rage around the bleeding, limp body of Morty Aiken, the fastest runner on Sixty-first Street.

1950

RICHARD WRIGHT
(1908–1960)

In his autobiographical *Black Boy* (1945) Richard Wright recounts a childhood and adolescence marked by violence and terror. It is a strong book, perhaps his masterpiece. The prose is straightforward, leaving the events to speak for themselves. There are fewer sociological asides, fewer literary posturings than appear in some of his other works. When he wrote it he was at the height of his powers, far removed in time both from the black boy whose story he tells and the proletarian writer he had become in the 1930's.

Wright was the son of a tenant farmer, born on a plantation near Natchez, Mississippi. He spent a migratory childhood in Tennessee, Arkansas, and Mississippi, left often to his own devices while his mother worked as a cook or a maid. Seldom in any single school for as much as a year, he left home after graduating from the ninth grade and after a short stay in Memphis made his way to Chicago in 1927. Here *Black Boy* ends. In the last chapters Wright tells how a chance encounter with the works of Mencken led him to Sinclair Lewis and Theodore Dreiser. "All my life had shaped me for the realism, the naturalism of the modern novel, and I could not read enough of them." Like many of the writers of the 1930's, however, Wright came to believe that all writing is propaganda, that art must be subordinated to the class struggle. Devoting much of his energy to writing for *New Masses* and

The Daily Worker, he still managed to produce a respectable volume of short stories, *Uncle Tom's Children* (1938), and the novel *Native Son* (1940) before his break with the Communist party. Disillusioned with the party and with his life in the United States, he moved to France in 1947 and there produced his last books, none of which has achieved the reputation in the United States of *Native Son* and *Black Boy.* His last collection of stories, *Eight Men* (1961), was posthumously published and contained stories ranging in time from the begin-

ning until the end of his literary career.

Besides the volumes listed above, Wright's fictional works include *The Outsider,* 1953; *The Long Dream,* 1958; *Lawd Today,* 1963; and *Savage Holiday,* 1965. His nonfiction includes *Twelve Million Black Voices: A Folk History of the Negro in the U.S.,* 1941; *Black Power,* 1945; *The Color Curtain,* 1956; *Pagan Spain,* 1957; and *White Man, Listen!,* 1957. *Eight Men,* 1961, is the source of the story below. Thomas Knipp edited *Richard Wright: Letters to Joe C. Brown,* 1968. Biographical and critical studies are Constance Webb, *Richard Wright: A Biography,* 1968; Dan McCall, *The Example of Richard Wright,* 1969; Edward Margolies, *The Art of Richard Wright,* 1969; Russell Carl Brignano, *Richard Wright: An Introduction * * *,* 1970; and Michel Fabre, *The Unfinished Quest of Richard Wright,* 1973.

Big Black Good Man

Through the open window Olaf Jenson could smell the sea and hear the occasional foghorn of a freighter; outside, rain pelted down through an August night, drumming softly upon the pavements of Copenhagen, inducing drowsiness, bringing dreamy memory, relaxing the tired muscles of his work-wracked body. He sat slumped in a swivel chair with his legs outstretched and his feet propped atop an edge of his desk. An inch of white ash tipped the end of his brown cigar and now and then he inserted the end of the stogie into his mouth and drew gently upon it, letting wisps of blue smoke eddy from the corners of his wide, thin lips. The watery gray irises behind the thick lenses of his eyeglasses gave him a look of abstraction, of absent-mindedness, of an almost genial idiocy. He sighed, reached for his half-empty bottle of beer, and drained it into his glass and downed it with a long slow gulp, then licked his lips. Replacing the cigar, he slapped his right palm against his thigh and said half aloud:

"Well, I'll be sixty tomorrow. I'm not rich, but I'm not poor either . . . Really, I can't complain. Got good health. Traveled all over the world and had my share of the girls when I was young . . . And my Karen's a good wife. I own my home. Got no debts. And I love digging in my garden in the spring . . . Grew the biggest carrots of anybody last year. Ain't saved much money, but what the hell . . . Money ain't everything. Got a good job. Night portering ain't too bad." He shook his head and yawned. "Karen and I could of had some children, though. Would of been good company . . . 'Specially for Karen. And I could of taught 'em languages . . . English, French, German, Danish, Dutch, Swedish, Norwegian, and Spanish . . ." He took the cigar out of his mouth and eyed the white ash critically. "Hell of a lot of good language learning did me . . . Never got anything out of it. But those ten years in New York were fun . . . Maybe I could of got rich if I'd stayed in America . . . Maybe. But I'm satisfied. You can't have everything."

Behind him the office door opened and a young man, a medical student occupying room number nine, entered.

"Good evening," the student said.

"Good evening," Olaf said, turning.

The student went to the keyboard and took hold of the round, brown knob that anchored his key.

"Rain, rain, rain," the student said.

"That's Denmark for you," Olaf smiled at him.

"This dampness keeps me clogged up like a drainpipe," the student complained.

"That's Denmark for you," Olaf repeated with a smile.

"Good night," the student said.

"Good night, son," Olaf sighed, watching the door close.

Well, my tenants are my children, Olaf told himself. Almost all of his children were in their rooms now . . . Only seventy-two and forty-four were missing . . . Seventy-two might've gone to Sweden . . . And forty-four was maybe staying at his girl's place tonight, like he sometimes did . . . He studied the pear-shaped blobs of hard rubber, reddish brown like ripe fruit, that hung from the keyboard, then glanced at his watch. Only room thirty, eighty-one, and one hundred and one were empty . . . And it was almost midnight. In a few moments he could take a nap. Nobody hardly ever came looking for accommodations after midnight, unless a stray freighter came in, bringing thirsty, women-hungry sailors. Olaf chuckled softly. Why in hell was I ever a sailor? The whole time I was at sea I was thinking and dreaming about women. Then why didn't I stay on land where women could be had? Hunh? Sailors are crazy . . .

But he liked sailors. They reminded him of his youth, and there was something so direct, simple, and childlike about them. They always said straight out what they wanted, and what they wanted was almost always women and whisky . . . "Well, there's no harm in that . . . Nothing could be more natural," Olaf sighed, looking thirstily at his empty beer bottle. No; he'd not drink any more tonight; he'd had enough; he'd go to sleep . . .

He was bending forward and loosening his shoelaces when he heard the office door crack open. He lifted his eyes, then sucked in his breath. He did not straighten; he just stared up and around at

the huge black thing that filled the doorway. His reflexes refused
to function; it was not fear; it was just simple astonishment. He
was staring at the biggest, strangest, and blackest man he'd ever
seen in all his life.

"Good evening," the black giant said in a voice that filled the
small office. "Say, you got a room?"

Olaf sat up slowly, not to answer but to look at this brooding
black vision; it towered darkly some six and a half feet into the air,
almost touching the ceiling; and its skin was so black that it had a
bluish tint. And the sheer bulk of the man! . . . His chest bulged
like a barrel; his rocklike and humped shoulders hinted of mountain ridges; the stomach ballooned like a threatening stone; and
the legs were like telephone poles . . . The big black cloud of a
man now lumbered into the office, bending to get its buffalolike
head under the door frame, then advanced slowly upon Olaf, like
a stormy sky descending.

"You got a room?" the big black man asked again in a resounding voice.

Olaf now noticed that the ebony giant was well dressed, carried
a wonderful new suitcase, and wore black shoes that gleamed despite the raindrops that peppered their toes.

"You're American?" Olaf asked him.

"Yeah, man; sure," the black giant answered.

"Sailor?"

"Yeah. American Continental Lines."

Olaf had not answered the black man's question. It was not that
the hotel did not admit men of color; Olaf took in all comers—
blacks, yellows, whites, and browns . . . To Olaf, men were men,
and in his day, he'd worked and eaten and slept and fought with all
kinds of men. But this particular black man . . . Well, he didn't
seem human. Too big, too black, too loud, too direct, and probably too violent to boot . . . Olaf's five feet seven inches scarcely
reached the black giant's shoulder and his frail body weighed less,
perhaps, than one of the man's gigantic legs . . . There was something about the man's intense blackness and ungamely bigness that
frightened and insulted Olaf; he felt as though this man had
come here expressly to remind him how puny, how tiny, and how
weak and how white he was. Olaf knew, while registering his reactions, that he was being irrational and foolish; yet, for the first time
in his life, he was emotionally determined to refuse a man a room
solely on the basis of the man's size and color . . . Olaf's lips
parted as he groped for the right words in which to couch his refusal, but the black giant bent forward and boomed:

"I asked you if you got a room. I got to put up somewhere to-
night, man."

"Yes, we got a room," Olaf murmured.

And at once he was ashamed and confused. Sheer fear had made him yield. And he seethed against himself for his involuntary weakness. Well, he'd look over his book and pretend that he'd made a mistake; he'd tell this hunk of blackness that there was really no free room in the hotel, and that he was so sorry . . . Then, just as he took out the hotel register to make believe that he was poring over it, a thick roll of American bank notes, crisp and green, was thrust under his nose.

"Keep this for me, will you?" the black giant commanded. " 'Cause I'm gonna get drunk tonight and I don't wanna lose it."

Olaf stared at the roll; it was huge, in denominations of fifties and hundreds. Olaf's eyes widened.

"How much is there?" he asked.

"Two thousand six hundred," the giant said. "Just put it into an envelope and write 'Jim' on it and lock it in your safe, hunh?"

The black mass of man had spoken in a manner that indicated that it was taking it for granted that Olaf would obey. Olaf was licked. Resentment clogged the pores of his wrinkled white skin. His hands trembled as he picked up the money. No; he couldn't refuse this man . . . The impulse to deny him was strong, but each time he was about to act upon it something thwarted him, made him shy off. He clutched about desperately for an idea. Oh, yes, he could say that if he planned to stay for only one night, then he could not have the room, for it was against the policy of the hotel to rent rooms for only one night . . .

"How long are you staying? Just tonight?" Olaf asked.

"Naw. I'll be here for five or six days, I reckon," the giant answered offhandedly.

"You take room number thirty," Olaf heard himself saying. "It's forty kronor a day."

"That's all right with me," the giant said.

With slow, stiff movements, Olaf put the money in the safe and then turned and stared helplessly up into the living, breathing blackness looming above him. Suddenly he became conscious of the outstretched palm of the black giant; he was silently demanding the key to the room. His eyes downcast, Olaf surrendered the key, marveling at the black man's tremendous hands . . . He could kill me with one blow, Olaf told himself in fear.

Feeling himself beaten, Olaf reached for the suitcase, but the black hand of the giant whisked it out of his grasp.

"That's too heavy for you, big boy; I'll take it," the giant said.

Olaf let him. He thinks I'm nothing . . . He led the way down the corridor, sensing the giant's lumbering presence behind him. Olaf opened the door of number thirty and stood politely to one side, allowing the black giant to enter. At once the room seemed like a doll's house, so dwarfed and filled and tiny it was with a great living blackness . . . Flinging his suitcase upon a chair, the giant turned. The two men looked directly at each other now. Olaf saw that the giant's eyes were tiny and red, buried, it seemed, in muscle and fat. Black cheeks spread, flat and broad, topping the wide and flaring nostrils. The mouth was the biggest that Olaf had ever seen on a human face; the lips were thick, pursed, parted, showing snow-white teeth. The black neck was like a bull's . . . The giant advanced upon Olaf and stood over him.

"I want a bottle of whisky and a woman," he said. "Can you fix me up?"

"Yes," Olaf whispered, wild with anger and insult.

But what was he angry about? He'd had requests like this every night from all sorts of men and he was used to fulfilling them; he was a night porter in a cheap, water-front Copenhagen hotel that catered to sailors and students. Yes, men needed women, but this man, Olaf felt, ought to have a special sort of woman. He felt a deep and strange reluctance to phone any of the women whom he habitually sent to men. Yet he had promised. Could he lie and say that none was available? No. That sounded too fishy. The black giant sat upon the bed, staring straight before him. Olaf moved about quickly, pulling down the window shades, taking the pink coverlet off the bed, nudging the giant with his elbow to make him move as he did so . . . That's the way to treat 'im . . . Show 'im I ain't scared of 'im . . . But he was still seeking for an excuse to refuse. And he could think of nothing. He felt hypnotized, mentally immobilized. He stood hesitantly at the door.

"You send the whisky and the woman quick, pal?" the black giant asked, rousing himself from a brooding stare.

"Yes," Olaf grunted, shutting the door.

Goddamn, Olaf sighed. He sat in his office at his desk before the phone. Why did *he* have to come here? . . . I'm not pre-judiced . . . No, not at all . . . But . . . He couldn't think any more. God oughtn't make men as big and black as that . . . But what the hell was he worrying about? He'd sent women of all races to men of all colors . . . So why not a woman to the black giant? Oh, only if the man were small, brown, and intelligent-looking . . . Olaf felt trapped.

With a reflex movement of his hand, he picked up the phone and dialed Lena. She was big and strong and always cut him in for fifteen per cent instead of the usual ten per cent. Lena had four small children to feed and clothe. Lena was willing; she was, she said, coming over right now. She didn't give a good goddamn about how big and black the man was . . .

"Why you ask me that?" Lena wanted to know over the phone. "You never asked that before . . ."

"But this one is *big*," Olaf found himself saying.

"He's just a man," Lena told him, her voice singing stridently, laughingly over the wire. "You just leave that to me. You don't have to do anything. *I'll* handle 'im."

Lena had a key to the hotel door downstairs, but tonight Olaf stayed awake. He wanted to see her. Why? He didn't know. He stretched out on the sofa in his office, but sleep was far from him. When Lena arrived, he told her again how big and black the man was.

"You told me that over the phone," Lena reminded him.

Olaf said nothing. Lena flounced off on her errand of mercy. Olaf shut the office door, then opened it and left it ajar. But why? He didn't know. He lay upon the sofa and stared at the ceiling. He glanced at his watch; it was almost two o'clock . . . She's staying in there a long time . . . Ah, God, but he could do with a drink . . . Why was he so damned worked up and nervous about a nigger and a white whore? . . . He'd never been so upset in all his life. Before he knew it, he had drifted off to sleep. Then he heard the office door swinging creakingly open on its rusty hinges. Lena stood in it, grim and businesslike, her face scrubbed free of powder and rouge. Olaf scrambled to his feet, adjusting his eyeglasses, blinking.

"How was it?" he asked her in a confidential whisper.

Lena's eyes blazed.

"What the hell's that to you?" she snapped. "There's your cut," she said, flinging him his money, tossing it upon the covers of the sofa. "You're sure nosy tonight. You wanna take over my work?"

Olaf's pasty cheeks burned red.

"You go to hell," he said, slamming the door.

"I'll meet you there!" Lena's shouting voice reached him dimly.

He was being a fool; there was no doubt about it. But, try as he might, he could not shake off a primitive hate for that black mountain of energy, of muscle, of bone; he envied the easy manner in which it moved with such a creeping and powerful motion; he winced at the booming and commanding voice that came to him when the tiny little eyes were not even looking at him; he shivered at the sight of those vast and clawlike hands that seemed always to hint of death . . .

Olaf kept his counsel. He never spoke to Karen about the sordid doings at the hotel. Such things were not for women like Karen. He knew instinctively that Karen would have been amazed had he told her that he was worried sick about a nigger and a blonde whore . . . No; he couldn't talk to anybody about it, not even the hard-bitten old bitch who owned the hotel. She was concerned only about money; she didn't give a damn about how big and black a client was as long as he paid his room rent.

Next evening, when Olaf arrived for duty, there was no sight or sound of the black giant. A little later after one o'clock in the morning he appeared, left his key, and went out wordlessly. A few moments past two the giant returned, took his key from the board, and paused.

"I want that Lena again tonight. And another bottle of whisky," he said boomingly.

"I'll call her and see if she's in," Olaf said.

"Do that," the black giant said and was gone.

He thinks he's God, Olaf fumed. He picked up the phone and ordered Lena and a bottle of whisky, and there was a taste of ashes in his mouth. On the third night came the same request: Lena and whisky. When the black giant appeared on the fifth night, Olaf was about to make a sarcastic remark to the effect that maybe he ought to marry Lena, but he checked it in time . . . After all, he could kill me with one hand, he told himself.

Olaf was nervous and angry with himself for being nervous. Other black sailors came and asked for girls and Olaf sent them, but with none of the fear and loathing that he sent Lena and a bottle of whisky to the giant . . . All right, the black giant's stay was almost up. He'd said that he was staying for five or six nights; tomorrow night was the sixth night and that ought to be the end of this nameless terror.

On the sixth night Olaf sat in his swivel chair with his bottle of beer and waited, his teeth on edge, his fingers drumming the desk. But what the hell am I fretting for? . . . The hell with 'im . . . Olaf sat and dozed. Occasionally he'd awaken and listen to the foghorns of freighters sounding as ships came and went in the misty Copenhagen harbor. He was half asleep when he felt a rough hand on his shoulder. He blinked his eyes open. The giant, black and vast and powerful, all but blotted out his vision.

"What I owe you, man?" the giant demanded. "And I want my money."

"Sure," Olaf said, relieved, but filled as always with fear of this living wall of black flesh.

With fumbling hands, he made out the bill and received payment, then gave the giant his roll of money, laying it on the desk so as not to let his hands touch the flesh of the black mountain. Well, his ordeal was over. It was past two o'clock in the morning. Olaf even managed a wry smile and muttered a guttural "Thanks" for the generous tip that the giant tossed him.

Then a strange tension entered the office. The office door was shut and Olaf was alone with the black mass of power, yearning for it to leave. But the black mass of power stood still, immobile, looking down at Olaf. And Olaf could not, for the life of him, guess at what was transpiring in that mysterious black mind. The two of them simply stared at each other for a full two minutes, the giant's tiny little beady eyes blinking slowly as they seemed to measure and search Olaf's face. Olaf's vision dimmed for a second as terror seized him and he could feel a flush of heat overspread his body. Then Olaf sucked in his breath as the devil of blackness commanded:

"Stand up!"

Olaf was paralyzed. Sweat broke on his face. His worst premonitions about this black beast were coming true. This evil blackness was about to attack him, maybe kill him . . . Slowly Olaf shook his head, his terror permitting him to breathe:

"What're you talking about?"

"Stand up, I say!" the black giant bellowed.

As though hypnotized, Olaf tried to rise; then he felt the black paw of the beast helping him roughly to his feet.

They stood an inch apart. Olaf's pasty-white features were lifted to the giant's swollen black face. The ebony ensemble of eyes and nose and mouth and cheeks looked down at Olaf, silently; then, with a slow and deliberate movement of his gorillalike arms, he lifted his mammoth hands to Olaf's throat. Olaf had long known and felt that this dreadful moment was coming; he felt trapped in a nightmare. He could not move. He wanted to scream, but could find no words. His lips refused to open; his tongue felt icy and inert. Then he knew that his end had come when the giant's black fingers slowly, softly encircled his throat while a horrible grin of delight broke out on the sooty face . . . Olaf lost control of the reflexes of his body and he felt a hot stickiness flooding his underwear . . . He stared without breathing, gazing into the grinning blackness of the face that was bent over him, feeling the black fingers caressing his throat and waiting to feel the sharp, stinging ache and pain of the bones in his neck being snapped, crushed . . . He knew all along that I hated 'im . . . Yes, and now he's going to kill me for it, Olaf told himself with despair.

The black fingers still circled Olaf's neck, not closing, but gently massaging it, as it were, moving to and fro, while the obscene face grinned into his. Olaf could feel the giant's warm breath blowing on his eyelashes and he felt like a chicken about to have its neck wrung and its body tossed to flip and flap dyingly in the dust of the barnyard . . . Then suddenly the black giant withdrew his fingers from Olaf's neck and stepped back a pace, still grinning. Olaf sighed, trembling, his body seeming to shrink; he waited. Shame sheeted him for the hot wetness that was in his trousers. Oh, God, he's teasing me . . . He's showing me how easily he can kill me . . . He swallowed, waiting, his eyes stones of gray.

The giant's barrel-like chest gave forth a low, rumbling chuckle of delight.

"You laugh?" Olaf asked whimperingly.

"Sure I laugh," the giant shouted.

"Please don't hurt me," Olaf managed to say.

"I wouldn't hurt you, boy," the giant said in a tone of mockery. "So long."

And he was gone. Olaf fell limply into the swivel chair and fought off losing consciousness. Then he wept. *He was showing me how easily he could kill me . . . He made me shake with terror and then laughed and left . . .* Slowly, Olaf recovered, stood, then gave vent to a string of curses:

"Goddamn 'im! My gun's right there in the desk drawer; I should of shot 'im. Jesus, I hope the ship he's on sinks . . . I hope he drowns and the sharks eat 'im . . ."

Later, he thought of going to the police, but sheer shame kept him back; and, anyway, the giant was probably on board his ship by now. And he had to get home and clean himself. Oh, Lord, what could he tell Karen? Yes, he would say that his stomach had been upset . . . He'd change clothes and return to work. He phoned the hotel owner that he was ill and wanted an hour off; the old bitch said that she was coming right over and that poor Olaf could have the evening off.

Olaf went home and lied to Karen. Then he lay awake the rest of the night dreaming of revenge. He saw that freighter on which the giant was sailing; he saw it springing a dangerous leak and saw a torrent of sea water flooding, gushing into all the compartments of the ship until it found the bunk in which the black giant slept. Ah, yes, the foamy, surging waters would surprise that sleeping black bastard of a giant and he would drown, gasping and choking like a trapped rat, his tiny eyes bulging until they glittered red, the bitter water of the sea pounding his lungs until they ached and finally burst . . . The ship would sink slowly to the bottom of the cold, black, silent depths of the sea and a shark, a *white* one, would glide aimlessly about the shut portholes until it found an open one and it would slither inside and nose about until it found that swollen, rotting, stinking carcass of the black beast and it would then begin to nibble at the decomposing mass of tarlike flesh, eating the bones clean . . . Olaf always pictured the giant's bones as being jet black and shining.

Once or twice, during these fantasies of cannibalistic revenge, Olaf felt a little guilty about all the many innocent people, women and children, all white and blonde, who would have to go down into watery graves in order that that white shark could devour the evil giant's black flesh . . . But, despite feelings of remorse, the fantasy lived persistently on, and when Olaf found himself alone, it would crowd and cloud his mind to the exclusion of all else, affording him the only revenge he knew. To make me suffer just for the pleasure of it, he fumed. Just to show me how strong he was . . . Olaf learned how to hate, and got pleasure out of it.

Summer fled on wings of rain. Autumn flooded Denmark with color. Winter made rain and snow fall on Copenhagen. Finally spring came, bringing violets and roses. Olaf kept to his job. For many months he feared the return of the black giant. But when a year had passed and the giant had not put in an appearance, Olaf allowed his revenge fantasy to peter out, indulging in it only when recalling the shame that the black monster had made him feel.

Then one rainy August night, a year later, Olaf sat drowsing at his desk, his bottle of beer before him, tilting back in his swivel chair, his feet resting atop a corner of his desk, his mind mulling over the more pleasant aspects of his life. The office door cracked open. Olaf glanced boredly up and around. His heart jumped and skipped a beat. The black nightmare of terror and shame that he had hoped that he had lost forever was again upon him . . . Resplendently dressed, suitcase in hand, the black looming mountain filled the doorway. Olaf's thin lips parted and a silent moan, half a curse, escaped them.

"Hy," the black giant boomed from the doorway.

Olaf could not reply. But a sudden resolve swept him: this time he would even the score. If this black beast came within so much as three feet of him, he would snatch his gun out of the drawer and shoot him dead, so help him God . . .

"No rooms tonight," Olaf heard himself announcing in a determined voice.

The black giant grinned; it was the same infernal grimace of delight and triumph that he had had when his damnable black fingers had been around his throat . . .

"Don't want no room tonight," the giant announced.

"Then what are you doing here?" Olaf asked in a loud but tremulous voice.

The giant swept toward Olaf and stood over him; and Olaf could not move, despite his oath to kill him . . .

"What do you want then?" Olaf demanded once more, ashamed that he could not lift his voice above a whisper.

The giant still grinned, then tossed what seemed the same suitcase upon Olaf's sofa and bent over it; he zippered it open with a sweep of his clawlike hand and rummaged in it, drawing forth a flat, gleaming white object done up in glowing cellophane. Olaf watched with lowered lids, wondering what trick was now being played on him. Then, before he could defend himself, the giant had whirled and again long, black, snakelike fingers were encircling Olaf's throat . . . Olaf stiffened, his right hand clawing blindly for the drawer where the gun was kept. But the giant was quick.

"Wait," he bellowed, pushing Olaf back from the desk.

The giant turned quickly to the sofa and, still holding his fingers in a wide circle that seemed a noose for Olaf's neck, he inserted the rounded fingers into the top of the flat, gleaming object. Olaf had the drawer open and his sweaty fingers were now touching his gun, but something made him freeze. The flat, gleaming object was a shirt and the black giant's circled fingers were fitting themselves into its neck . . .

"A perfect fit!" the giant shouted.

Olaf stared, trying to understand. His fingers loosened about the gun. A mixture of a laugh and a curse struggled in him. He watched the giant plunge his hands into the suitcase and pull out other flat, gleaming shirts.

"One, two, three, four, five, six," the black giant intoned, his voice crisp and businesslike. "Six nylon shirts. And they're all yours. One shirt for each time Lena came . . . See, Daddy-O?"

The black, cupped hands, filled with billowing nylon whiteness, were extended under Olaf's nose. Olaf eased his damp fingers from his gun and pushed the drawer closed, staring at the shirts and then at the black giant's grinning face.

"Don't you like 'em?" the giant asked.

Olaf began to laugh hysterically, then suddenly he was crying, his eyes so flooded with tears that the pile of dazzling nylon looked like snow in the dead of winter. Was this true? Could he believe it? Maybe this too was a trick? But, no. There were six shirts, all nylon, and the black giant had had Lena six nights.

"What's the matter with you, Daddy-O?" the giant asked. "You blowing your top? Laughing and crying . . ."

Olaf swallowed, dabbed his withered fists at his dimmed eyes; then he realized that he had his glasses on. He took them off and dried his eyes and sat up. He sighed, the tension and shame and fear and haunting dread of his fantasy went from him, and he leaned limply back in his chair . . .

"Try one on," the giant ordered.

Olaf fumbled with the buttons of his shirt, let down his suspenders, and pulled the shirt off. He donned a gleaming nylon one and the giant began buttoning it for him.

"Perfect, Daddy-O," the giant said.

His spectacled face framed in sparkling nylon, Olaf sat with trembling lips. So he'd not been trying to kill me after all.

"You want Lena, don't you?" he asked the giant in a soft whisper. "But I don't know where she is. She never came back here after you left—"

"I know where Lena is," the giant told him. "We been writing to each other. I'm going to her house. And, Daddy-O, I'm late." The giant zippered the suitcase shut and stood a moment gazing down at Olaf, his tiny little red eyes blinking slowly. Then Olaf realized that there was a compassion in that stare that he had never seen before.

"And I thought you wanted to kill me," Olaf told him. "I was scared of you . . ."

"Me? Kill you?" the giant blinked. "When?"

"That night when you put your fingers about my throat—"

"What?" the giant asked, then roared with laughter. "Daddy-O, you're a funny little man. I wouldn't hurt you. I like you. You a *good* man. You helped me."

Olaf smiled, clutching the pile of nylon shirts in his arms.

"You're a good man too," Olaf murmured. Then loudly: "You're a big black good man."

"Daddy-O, you're crazy," the giant said.

He swept his suitcase from the sofa, spun on his heel, and was at the door in one stride.

"Thanks!" Olaf cried after him.

The black giant paused, turned his vast black head, and flashed a grin.

"Daddy-O, drop dead," he said and was gone.

1957, 1961

Twentieth-Century Drama

TENNESSEE WILLIAMS

(1911–   )

Thomas Lanier Williams was born in Columbus, Mississippi, and lived in Nashville, Tennessee, and in various towns in Mississippi before his family settled in St. Louis in 1918. The atmosphere of his early years was that of the various Episcopal rectories where he, his mother, and his sister Rose lived with his clergyman grandfather prior to the move to St. Louis to join the father, a sales manager for a shoe company. If his early life was unsettled, it was at least sheltered; the years in St. Louis were marked by family problems, by Rose's gradual withdrawal into her own inner world, and by Williams's abortive attempts to launch his literary career. At sixteen he won a prize in a national writing contest and at seventeen he saw his first short story in print in *Weird Tales*. After three years at the University of Missouri, however, he was forced to leave school to spend three years in the "living death" of a shoe factory. Briefly a student at Washington University, he finally secured his A.B. from the University of Iowa in 1938. By this time he had seen his

plays in local productions in Memphis, in Webster Groves, Missouri, and in St. Louis, and two years later *Battle of Angels* (1940) opened in Boston under the auspices of the Theatre Guild, but failed to make it to New York.

The arrival of *The Glass Menagerie* in New York in 1945 was a major theatrical event. It signaled the emergence from obscurity of a playwright whose talent, together with that of Arthur Miller, was to dominate the American theater for the next two decades. More prolific than Miller, and a prodigious rewriter of his earlier efforts, Williams for years averaged at least one play on Broadway every two years. With rare exceptions, his plays have been huge successes on both critical and commercial terms; not since the heyday of Eugene O'Neill has an American playwright written so much, so successfully, so well. Frequently the best of his efforts have become major Hollywood films, with Williams demonstrating his versatility by his work on the film scripts.

The success of the film versions of so many of his plays underscores the fluidity of his stage management. Rarely is the action in a Williams play confined to one moment of time or one corner of physical space throughout a scene of any great duration. Rather the dialogue of the characters dwells continually on another time or another place. Intrusions from without—street cries, songs heard in the distance, the arrival of unexpected guests—serve as reminders of action past, and yet to come. More than some other playwrights (and in this respect following the strong lead of O'Neill), Williams makes use of the technical possibilities of the twentieth-century stage. Sets dissolve, walls fade away, lights bring one part of the stage into the foreground, while the rest recedes in darkness. A novelist, short story writer, and poet, as well as a playwright, Williams is at his best when he is writing for the theater, but he does not allow himself to be hampered by any of its conventions or by the expectations of his audience.

"I write from my own tensions," Williams once said. "For me, this is a form of therapy." His work has a quality of obsession about it. Much of it is clearly, in origin, autobiographical, but whether the core of observed fact is large, as it is in *The Glass Menagerie*, or considerably smaller, as it appears to be in A *Streetcar Named Desire* (1947) or *Suddenly Last Summer* (1958), that core is relatively unimportant when measured against the drive toward

metaphor and symbol that characterizes the work as a whole. At times, as in its indifferent reaction to *Camino Real* (1953), the theater-going public has not been completely willing to accept Williams's frequent disregard for the usual conventions of theatrical verisimilitude. On the whole, however, it has accepted from him a language that is often poetic in its intensity, situations more marked by distortions than faithfulness to actuality, and characters and themes that appear to strike at the truth through the sidelong routes of dream, myth, and nightmare.

The major plays, with dates of first production, include *Battle of Angels*, 1940; *The Glass Menagerie*, 1944; *Summer and Smoke*, 1947; *A Streetcar Named Desire*, 1947; *The Rose Tattoo*, 1951; *Camino Real*, 1953; *Cat on a Hot Tin Roof*, 1955; *Orpheus Descending*, 1957; *Suddenly Last Summer*, 1958; *Sweet Bird of Youth*, 1959; *Period of Adjustment*, 1959; *The Night of the Iguana*, 1961; and *The Milk Train Doesn't Stop Here Anymore*, 1962. All, except *The Milk Train * * * *, are included in *The Theatre of Tennessee Williams*, 4 vols., 1971, which includes also *The Eccentricities of a Nightingale*. Short plays are collected in *27 Wagons Full of Cotton and Other One-Act Plays*, 1946 (revised, 1953). A novel is *The Roman Spring of Mrs. Stone*, 1950. Short story collections are *One Arm and Other Stories*, 1948; *Hard Candy: A Book of Stories*, 1954; and *The Knightly Quest*, 1967 (revised, 1968). A book of verse is *In the Winter of Cities*, 1956 (revised, 1964).

Biographical and critical studies include Signi Falk, *Tennessee Williams*, 1961; Nancy M. Tischler, *Tennessee Williams: Rebellious Puritan*, 1961; Edwina D. Williams, *Remember Me to Tom*, 1963; Gilbert Maxwell, *Tennessee Williams and Friends: An Informal Biography*, 1965; and Esther M. Jackson, *The Broken World of Tennessee Williams*, 1966. Mike Steen edited *A Look at Tennessee Williams*, 1969.

The Glass Menagerie

Nobody, not even the rain, has such small hands.

E. E. CUMMINGS

SCENE: *An Alley in St. Louis*

Part I. Preparation for a Gentleman Caller.
Part II. The Gentleman calls.

Time: Now and the Past.

THE CHARACTERS

AMANDA WINGFIELD (*the mother*)
A little woman of great but confused vitality clinging frantically to another time and place. Her characterization must be carefully created, not copied from type. She is not paranoiac, but her life is paranoia. There is much to admire in Amanda, and as much to love and pity as there is to laugh at. Certainly she has endurance and a kind of heroism, and though her foolishness makes her unwittingly cruel at times, there is tenderness in her slight person.

LAURA WINGFIELD (*her daughter*)
Amanda, having failed to establish contact with reality, continues to live vitally in her illusions, but Laura's situation is even graver. A childhood illness has left her crippled, one leg slightly shorter than the other, and held in a brace. This defect need not be more than suggested on the stage. Stemming from this, Laura's separation increases till she is like a piece of her own glass collection, too exquisitely fragile to move from the shelf.

TOM WINGFIELD (*her son*)
And the narrator of the play. A poet with a job in a warehouse. His nature is not remorseless, but to escape from a trap he has to act without pity.

JIM O'CONNOR (*the gentleman caller*)
A nice, ordinary, young man.

Scene I

The Wingfield apartment is in the rear of the building, one of those vast hive-like conglomerations of cellular living-units that flower as warty growths in overcrowded urban centers of lower middle-class population and are symptomatic of the impulse of this largest and fundamentally enslaved section of American society to avoid fluidity and differentiation and to exist and function as one interfused mass of automatism.

The apartment faces an alley and is entered by a fire escape, a structure whose name is a touch of accidental poetic truth, for all of these huge buildings are always burning with the slow and implacable fires of human desperation. The fire escape is part of what we see—that is, the landing of it and steps descending from it.

The scene is memory and is therefore nonrealistic. Memory takes a lot of poetic license. It omits some details; others are exaggerated, according to the emotional value of the articles it touches, for memory is seated predominantly in the heart. The interior is therefore rather dim and poetic.

At the rise of the curtain, the audience is faced with the dark, grim rear wall of the Wingfield tenement. This building is flanked on both sides by dark, narrow alleys which run into murky canyons of tangled clotheslines, garbage cans, and the sinister latticework of neighboring fire escapes. It is up and down these side alleys that exterior entrances and exits are made during the play. At the end of Tom's opening commentary, the dark tenement wall slowly becomes transparent and reveals the interior of the ground-floor Wingfield apartment.

Nearest the audience is the living room, which also serves as a sleeping room for Laura, the sofa unfolding to make her bed. Just beyond, separated from the living room by a wide arch or second proscenium with transparent faded portieres (or second curtain), is the dining room. In an old-fashioned whatnot in the living room are seen scores of transparent glass animals. A blown-up photograph of the father hangs on the wall of the living room, to the left of the archway. It is the face of a very handsome young man in a doughboy's First World War cap. He is gallantly smiling, ineluctably smiling, as if to say "I will be smiling forever."

Also hanging on the wall, near the photograph, are a typewriter keyboard chart and a Gregg shorthand diagram. An upright typewriter on a small table stands beneath the charts.

The audience hears and sees the opening scene in the dining room through both the transparent fourth wall of the building and the transparent gauze portieres of the dining-room arch. It is during this revealing scene that the fourth wall slowly ascends, out of sight. This transparent exterior wall is not brought down again until the very end of the play, during Tom's final speech.

The narrator is an undisguised convention of the play. He takes whatever license with dramatic convention is convenient to his purposes.

Tom enters, dressed as a merchant sailor, and strolls across to the fire escape. There he stops and lights a cigarette. He addresses the audience.

TOM. Yes, I have tricks in my pocket, I have things up my sleeve. But I am the opposite of a stage magician. He gives you illusion that has the appearance of truth. I give you truth in the pleasant disguise of illusion.

To begin with, I turn back time. I reverse it to that quaint period, the thirties, when the huge middle class of America was matriculating in a school for the blind. Their eyes had failed them, or they had failed their eyes, and so they were having their fingers pressed forcibly down on the fiery Braille alphabet of a dissolving economy.

In Spain there was revolution. Here there was only shouting and confusion. In Spain there was Guernica. Here there were disturbances of labor, sometimes pretty violent, in otherwise peaceful cities such as Chicago, Cleveland, Saint Louis . . .

This is the social background of the play.

[*Music begins to play.*]

The play is memory. Being a memory play, it is dimly lighted, it is sentimental, it is not realistic. In memory everything seems to happen to music. That explains the fiddle in the wings.

I am the narrator of the play, and also a character in it. The other characters are my mother, Amanda, my sister, Laura, and a gentleman caller who appears in the final scenes. He is the most realistic character in the play, being an emissary from a world of reality that we were somehow set apart from. But since I have a poet's weakness for symbols, I am using this character also as a symbol; he is the long-delayed but always expected something that we live for.

There is a fifth character in the play who doesn't appear except in this larger-than-life-size photograph over the mantel. This is our father who left us a long time ago. He was a telephone man who fell in love with long distances; he gave up his job with the telephone company and skipped the light fantastic out of town . . .

The last we heard of him was a picture postcard from Mazatlan, on the Pacific coast of Mexico, containing a message of two words: "Hello—Goodbye!" and no address.

I think the rest of the play will explain itself. . . .

[*Amanda's voice becomes audible through the portieres.*]

[*Legend on screen: "Où sont les neiges." [1]*]

[*Tom divides the portieres and enters the dining room. Amanda and Laura are seated at a drop-leaf table. Eating is indicated by gestures without food or utensils. Amanda faces the audience. Tom and Laura are seated in profile. The interior has lit up softly*]

---

1. A partial quotation of the refrain, "Mais où sont les neiges d'antan?" ("But where are the snows of yesteryear?") from the "Ballade des dames du temps jadis" ("Ballade of the Ladies of Bygone Times" by François Villon (1431–?).

and through the scrim we see Amanda and Laura seated at the table.]

AMANDA. [*Calling.*] Tom?

TOM. Yes, Mother.

AMANDA. We can't say grace until you come to the table!

TOM. Coming, Mother. [*He bows slightly and withdraws, reappearing a few moments later in his place at the table.*]

AMANDA. [*To her son.*] Honey, don't *push* with your *fingers*. If you have to push with something, the thing to push with is a crust of bread. And chew—chew! Animals have secretions in their stomachs which enable them to digest food without mastication, but human beings are supposed to chew their food before they swallow it down. Eat food leisurely, son, and really enjoy it. A well-cooked meal has lots of delicious flavors that have to be held in the mouth for appreciation. So chew your food and give your salivary glands a chance to function!

[*Tom deliberately lays his imaginary fork down and pushes his chair back from the table.*]

TOM. I haven't enjoyed one bite of this dinner because of your constant directions on how to eat it. It's you that make me rush through meals with your hawklike attention to every bite I take. Sickening—spoils my appetite—all this discussion of—animals' secretion—salivary glands—mastication!

AMANDA. [*Lightly.*] Temperament like a Metropolitan star!

[*Tom rises and walks toward the living room.*]

You're not excused from the table.

TOM. I'm getting a cigarette.

AMANDA. You smoke too much.

[*Laura rises.*]

LAURA. I'll bring in the blanc mange.

[*Tom remains standing with his cigarette by the portieres.*]

AMANDA. [*Rising.*] No, sister, no, sister—you be the lady this time and I'll be the darky.

LAURA. I'm already up.

AMANDA. Resume your seat, little sister—I want you to stay fresh and pretty—for gentlemen callers!

LAURA. [*Sitting down.*] I'm not expecting any gentlemen callers.

AMANDA. [*Crossing out to the kitchenette, airily.*] Sometimes they come when they are least expected! Why, I remember one Sunday afternoon in Blue Mountain—

[*She enters the kitchenette.*]

TOM. I know what's coming!

LAURA. Yes. But let her tell it.

TOM. Again?

LAURA. She loves to tell it.

[*Amanda returns with a bowl of dessert.*]

AMANDA. One Sunday afternoon in Blue Mountain—your mother received—*seventeen!*—gentlemen callers! Why, sometimes there weren't chairs enough to accommodate them all. We had to send the nigger over to bring in folding chairs from the parish house.

TOM. [*Remaining at the portieres.*] How did you entertain those gentlemen callers?

AMANDA. I understood the art of conversation!

TOM. I bet you could talk.

AMANDA. Girls in those days *knew* how to talk, I can tell you.

TOM. Yes?

[*Image on screen*: Amanda as a girl on a porch, greeting callers.]

AMANDA. They knew how to entertain their gentlemen callers. It wasn't enough for a girl to be possessed of a pretty face and a graceful figure—although I wasn't slighted in either respect. She also needed to have a nimble wit and a tongue to meet all occasions.

TOM. What did you talk about?

AMANDA. Things of importance going on in the world! Never anything coarse or common or vulgar.

[*She addresses Tom as though he were seated in the vacant chair at the table though he remains by the portieres. He plays this scene as though reading from a script.*]

My callers were gentlemen—all! Among my callers were some of the most prominent young planters of the Mississippi Delta—planters and sons of planters!

[*Tom motions for music and a spot of light on Amanda. Her eyes lift, her face glows, her voice becomes rich and elegiac.*]

[*Screen legend:* "Ou sont les neiges d'antan?"]

There was young Champ Laughlin who later became vice-president of the Delta Planters Bank. Hadley Stevenson who was drowned in Moon Lake and left his widow one hundred and fifty thousand in Government bonds. There were the Cutrere brothers, Wesley and Bates. Bates was one of my bright particular beaux! He got in a quarrel with that wild Wainwright boy. They shot it out on the floor of Moon Lake Casino. Bates was shot through the stomach. Died in the ambulance on his way to Memphis. His widow was also well provided-for, came into eight or ten thousand acres, that's all. She married him on the rebound—never loved her—carried my picture on him the night he died! And there was that boy that every girl in the Delta had set her cap for! That beautiful, brilliant young Fitzhugh boy from Greene County!

TOM. What did he leave his widow?

AMANDA. He never married! Gracious, you talk as though all of my old admirers had turned up their toes to the daisies!

TOM. Isn't this the first you've mentioned that still survives?

AMANDA. That Fitzhugh boy went North and made a fortune—came to be known as the Wolf of Wall Street! He had the Midas touch, whatever he touched turned to gold! And I could have been Mrs. Duncan J. Fitzhugh, mind you! But—I picked your *father!*

LAURA. [*Rising.*] Mother, let me clear the table.

AMANDA. No, dear, you go in front and study your typewriter chart. Or practice your shorthand a little. Stay fresh and pretty!—It's almost time for our gentlemen callers to start arriving. [*She flounces girlishly toward the kitchenette.*] How many do you suppose we're going to entertain this afternoon?

[*Tom throws down the paper and jumps up with a groan.*]

LAURA. [*Alone in the dining room.*] I don't believe we're going to receive any, Mother.

AMANDA. [*Reappearing, airily.*] What? No one—not one? You must be joking!

[*Laura nervously echoes her laugh. She slips in a fugitive manner through the half-open portieres and draws them gently behind her. A shaft of very clear light is thrown on her face against the faded tapestry of the curtains. Faintly the music of "The Glass Menagerie" is heard as she continues, lightly.*]

Not one gentleman caller? It can't be true! There must be a flood, there must have been a tornado!

LAURA. It isn't a flood, it's not a tornado, Mother. I'm just not popular like you were in Blue Mountain. . . .

[*Tom utters another groan. Laura glances at him with a faint, apologetic smile. Her voice catches a little.*]

Mother's afraid I'm going to be an old maid.

[*The scene dims out with the "Glass Menagerie" music.*]

Scene II

On the dark stage the screen is lighted with the image of blue roses. Gradually Laura's figure becomes apparent and the screen goes out. The music subsides.

Laura is seated in the delicate ivory chair at the small claw-foot table. She wears a dress of soft violet material for a kimono—her hair is tied back from her forehead with a ribbon. She is washing and polishing her collection of glass. Amanda appears on the fire escape steps. At the sound of her ascent, Laura catches her breath, thrusts the bowl of ornaments away, and seats herself stiffly before the diagram of the typewriter keyboard as though it held her spellbound. Something has happened to Amanda. It is written in her face as she climbs to the landing: a look that is grim and hopeless and a little absurd. She has on one of those cheap or imitation velvety-looking cloth coats with imitation fur collar. Her hat is five or six years old, one of those dreadful cloche hats that were worn in the late Twenties, and she is clutching an enormous black patent-leather pocketbook with nickel clasps and initials. This is her full-dress outfit, the one she usually wears to the D.A.R. Before entering she looks through the door. She purses her lips, opens her eyes very wide, rolls them upward and shakes her head. Then she slowly lets herself in the door. Seeing her mother's expression Laura touchs her lips with a nervous gesture.

LAURA. Hello, Mother, I was— [*She makes a nervous gesture toward the chart on the wall. Amanda leans against the shut door and stares at Laura with a martyred look.*]

AMANDA. Deception? Deception? [*She slowly removes her hat and gloves, continuing the sweet suffering stare. She lets the hat and gloves fall on the floor—a bit of acting.*]

LAURA. [*Shakily.*] How was the D.A.R. meeting?

[*Amanda slowly opens her purse and removes a dainty white handkerchief which she shakes out delicately and delicately touches to her lips and nostrils.*]

Didn't you go to the D.A.R. meeting, Mother?

AMANDA. [*Faintly, almost inaudibly.*] —No.—No. [*Then more forcibly.*] I did not have the strength—to go to the D.A.R. In fact, I did not have the courage! I wanted to find a hole in the ground and hide myself in it forever! [*She crosses slowly to the wall and removes the diagram of the typewriter keyboard. She holds it in front of her for a second, staring at it sweetly and sorrowfully —then bites her lips and tears it in two pieces.*]

LAURA. [*Faintly.*] Why did you do that, Mother?

[*Amanda repeats the same procedure with the chart of the Gregg Alphabet.*]

Why are you—

AMANDA. Why? Why? How old are you, Laura?

LAURA. Mother, you know my age.

AMANDA. I thought that you were an adult; it seems that I was mistaken. [*She crosses slowly to the sofa and sinks down and stares at Laura.*]

LAURA. Please don't stare at me, Mother.

[*Amanda closes her eyes and lowers her head. There is a ten-second pause.*]

AMANDA. What are we going to do, what is going to become of us, what is the future?

[*There is another pause.*]

LAURA. Has something happened, Mother?

[*Amanda draws a long breath, takes out the handkerchief again, goes through the dabbing process.*]

Mother, has—something happened?

AMANDA. I'll be all right in a minute, I'm just bewildered— [*She hesitates.*] —by life. . . .

LAURA. Mother, I wish that you would tell me what's happened!

AMANDA. As you know, I was supposed to be inducted into my office at the D.A.R. this afternoon.

[*Screen image*: A swarm of typewriters.]

But I stopped off at Rubicam's Business College to speak to your teachers about your having a cold and ask them what progress they thought you were making down there.

LAURA. Oh. . . .

AMANDA. I went to the typing instructor and introduced myself as your mother. She didn't know who you were. "Wingfield," she said, "We don't have any such student enrolled at the school!"

I assured her she did, that you had been going to classes since early in January.

"I wonder," she said, "If you could be talking about that terribly shy little girl who dropped out of school after only a few days' attendance?"

"No," I said, "Laura, my daughter, has been going to school every day for the past six weeks!"

"Excuse me," she said. She took the attendance book out and there was your name, unmistakably printed, and all the dates you were absent until they decided that you had dropped out of school.

I still said, "No, there must have been some mistake! There must have been some mix-up in the records!"

And she said, "No—I remember her perfectly now. Her hands shook so that she couldn't hit the right keys! The first time we gave a speed test, she broke down completely—was sick at the stomach and almost had to be carried into the wash room! After that morning she never showed up any more. We phoned the house but never got any answer"—While I was working at Famous–Barr, I suppose, demonstrating those—

[*She indicates a brassiere with her hands.*]

Oh! I felt so weak I could barely keep on my feet! I had to sit down while they got me a glass of water! Fifty dollars' tuition, all of our plans—my hopes and ambitions for you—just gone up the spout, just gone up the spout like that.

[*Laura draws a long breath and gets awkwardly to her feet. She crosses to the Victrola and winds it up.*]

What are you doing?

LAURA. Oh! [*She releases the handle and returns to her seat.*]

AMANDA. Laura, where have you been going when you've gone out pretending that you were going to business college?

LAURA. I've just been going out walking.

AMANDA. That's not true.

LAURA. It is. I just went walking.

AMANDA. Walking? Walking? In winter? Deliberately courting pneumonia in that light coat? Where did you walk to, Laura?

LAURA. All sorts of places—mostly in the park.

AMANDA. Even after you'd started catching that cold?

LAURA. It was the lesser of two evils, Mother.

[*Screen image*: Winter scene in a park.]

I couldn't go back there. I—threw up—on the floor!

AMANDA. From half past seven till after five every day you mean to tell me you walked around in the park, because you wanted to make me think that you were still going to Rubicam's Business College?

LAURA. It wasn't as bad as it sounds. I went inside places to get warmed up.

AMANDA. Inside where?

LAURA. I went in the art museum and the bird houses at the Zoo. I visited the penguins every day! Sometimes I did without lunch and went to the movies. Lately I've been spending most of my afternoons in the Jewel Box, that big glass house where they raise the tropical flowers.

AMANDA. You did all this to deceive me, just for deception? [*Laura looks down.*] Why?

LAURA. Mother, when you're disappointed, you get that awful suffering look on your face, like the picture of Jesus' mother in the museum!

AMANDA. Hush!

LAURA. I couldn't face it.

[*There is a pause. A whisper of strings is heard. Legend on screen*: "The Crust of Humility."]

AMANDA. [*Hopelessly fingering the huge pocketbook.*] So what are we going to do the rest of our lives? Stay home and watch the parades go by? Amuse ourselves with the glass menagerie, darling? Eternally play those worn-out phonograph records your father left as a painful reminder of him? We won't have a business career— we've given that up because it gave us nervous indigestion! [*She laughs wearily.*] What is there left but dependency all our lives? I know so well what becomes of unmarried women who aren't prepared to occupy a position. I've seen such pitiful cases in the South—barely tolerated spinsters living upon the grudging patronage of sister's husband or brother's wife!—stuck away in some little mousetrap of a room—encouraged by one in-law to visit another— little birdlike women without any nest—eating the crust of humility all their life!

Is that the future that we've mapped out for ourselves? I swear it's the only alternative I can think of! [*She pauses.*] It isn't a very pleasant alternative, is it? [*She pauses again.*] Of course—some girls *do marry.*

[*Laura twists her hands nervously.*]

Haven't you ever liked some boy?

LAURA. Yes. I liked one once. [*She rises.*] I came across his picture a while ago.

AMANDA. [*With some interest.*] He gave you his picture?

LAURA. No, it's in the yearbook.

AMANDA. [*Disappointed.*] Oh—a high school boy.

[*Screen image*: Jim as the high school hero bearing a silver cup.]

LAURA. Yes. His name was Jim. [*She lifts the heavy annual from the claw-foot table.*] Here he is in *The Pirates of Penzance.*

AMANDA. [*Absently.*] The what?

LAURA. The operetta the senior class put on. He had a wonderful voice and we sat across the aisle from each other Mondays, Wednesdays and Fridays in the Aud. Here he is with the silver cup for debating! See his grin?

AMANDA. [*Absently.*] He must have had a jolly disposition.

LAURA. He used to call me—Blue Roses.

[*Screen image*: Blue roses.]

AMANDA. Why did he call you such a name as that?

LAURA. When I had that attack of pleurosis—he asked me what was the matter when I came back. I said pleurosis—he thought that I said Blue Roses! So that's what he always called me after that. Whenever he saw me, he'd holler, "Hello, Blue Roses!" I didn't care for the girl that he went out with. Emily Meisenbach. Emily was the best-dressed girl at Soldan. She never struck me, though, as being sincere . . . It says in the Personal Section— they're engaged. That's—six years ago! They must be married by now.

AMANDA. Girls that aren't cut out for business careers usually wind up married to some nice man. [*She gets up with a spark of revival.*] Sister, that's what you'll do!

[*Laura utters a startled, doubtful laugh. She reaches quickly for a piece of glass.*]

LAURA. But, Mother—

AMANDA. Yes? [*She goes over to the photograph.*]

LAURA. [*In a tone of frightened apology.*] I'm—crippled!

AMANDA. Nonsense! Laura, I've told you never, never to use that word. Why, you're not crippled, you just have a little defect— hardly noticeable, even! When people have some slight disadvantage like that, they cultivate other things to make up for it— develop charm—and vivacity—and—*charm!* That's all you have to do! [*She turns again to the photograph.*] One thing your father had *plenty of*—was *charm!*

[*The scene fades out with music.*]

Scene III

Legend on screen: "After the fiasco—"
Tom speaks from the fire escape landing.

TOM. After the fiasco at Rubicam's Business College, the idea of getting a gentleman caller for Laura began to play a more and more important part in Mother's calculations. It became an obsession. Like some archetype of the universal unconscious, the image of the gentleman caller haunted our small apartment. . . .

[*Screen image*: A young man at the door of a house with flowers.]

An evening at home rarely passed without some allusion to this image, this specter, this hope. . . . Even when he wasn't mentioned, his presence hung in Mother's preoccupied look and in my sister's frightened, apologetic manner—hung like a sentence passed upon the Wingfields!

Mother was a woman of action as well as words. She began to take logical steps in the planned direction. Late that winter and in the early spring—realizing that extra money would be needed to properly feather the nest and plume the bird—she conducted a vigorous campaign on the telephone, roping in subscribers to one of those magazines for matrons called *The Homemaker's Companion*, the type of journal that features the serialized sublimations of ladies of letters who think in terms of delicate cuplike breasts, slim, tapering waists, rich, creamy thighs, eyes like wood smoke in autumn, fingers that soothe and caress like strains of music, bodies as powerful as Etruscan sculpture.

[*Screen image*: The cover of a glamor magazine.]

[*Amanda enters with the telephone on a long extension cord. She is spotlighted in the dim stage.*]

AMANDA. Ida Scott? This is Amanda Wingfield! We *missed* you at the D.A.R. last Monday! I said to myself: She's probably suffering with that sinus condition! How is that sinus condition? Horrors! Heaven have mercy!—You're a Christian martyr, yes, that's what you are, a Christian martyr!

Well, I just now happened to notice that your subscription to the *Companion*'s about to expire! Yes, it expires with the next issue, honey!—just when that wonderful new serial by Bessie Mae Hopper is getting off to such an exciting start. Oh, honey, it's something that you can't miss! You remember how *Gone with the Wind* took everybody by storm? You simply couldn't go out if you hadn't read it. All everybody *talked* was Scarlett O'Hara. Well, this is a book that critics already compare to *Gone with the Wind*. It's the *Gone with the Wind* of the post-World-War generation!—What?— Burning?—Oh, honey, don't let them burn, go take a look in the oven and I'll hold the wire! Heavens—I think she's hung up!

[*The scene dims out.*]

[*Legend on screen:* "You think I'm in love with Continental Shoemakers?"]

[*Before the lights come up again, the violent voices of Tom and Amanda are heard. They are quarreling behind the portieres. In front of them stands Laura with clenched hands and panicky expression. A clear pool of light on her figure throughout this scene.*]

TOM. What in Christ's name am I—

AMANDA. [*Shrilly.*] Don't you use that—

TOM. —supposed to do?

AMANDA. —expression! Not in my—

TOM. Ohhh!

AMANDA. —presence! Have you gone out of your senses?

TOM. I have, that's true, *driven* out!

AMANDA. What is the matter with you, you—big—big—IDIOT!

TOM. Look!—I've got *no thing*, no single thing—

AMANDA. Lower your voice!

TOM. —in my life here that I can call my OWN! Everything is—

AMANDA. Stop that shouting!

TOM. Yesterday you confiscated my books! You had the nerve to—

AMANDA. I took that horrible novel back to the library—yes! That hideous book by that insane Mr. Lawrence.

[*Tom laughs wildly.*]

I cannot control the output of diseased minds or people who cater to them—

[*Tom laughs still more wildly.*]

BUT I WON'T ALLOW SUCH FILTH BROUGHT INTO MY HOUSE! No, no, no, no, no!

TOM. House, house! Who pays rent on it, who makes a slave of himself to—

AMANDA. [*Fairly screeching.*] Don't you DARE to—

TOM. No, no, I mustn't say things! I've got to just—

AMANDA. Let me tell you—

TOM. I don't want to hear any more!

[*He tears the portieres open. The dining-room area is lit with a turgid smoky red glow. Now we see Amanda; her hair is in metal curlers and she is wearing a very old bathrobe, much too large for her slight figure, a relic of the faithless Mr. Wingfield. The upright typewriter now stands on the drop-leaf table, along with a wild disarray of manuscripts. The quarrel was probably precipitated by Amanda's interruption of Tom's creative labor. A chair lies overthrown on the floor. Their gesticulating shadows are cast on the ceiling by the fiery glow.*]

AMANDA. You *will* hear more, you—

TOM. No, I won't hear more, I'm going out!

AMANDA. You come right back in—

TOM. Out, out, out! Because I'm—

AMANDA. Come back here, Tom Wingfield! I'm not through talking to you!

TOM. Oh, go—

LAURA. [*Desperately.*] —Tom!

AMANDA. You're going to listen, and no more insolence from you! I'm at the end of my patience!

[*He comes back toward her.*]

TOM. What do you think I'm at? Aren't I supposed to have any patience to reach the end of, Mother? I know, I know. It seems unimportant to you, what I'm *doing*—what I *want* to do—having a little *difference* between them! You don't think that—

AMANDA. I think you've been doing things that you're ashamed of. That's why you act like this. I don't believe that you go every night to the movies. Nobody goes to the movies night after night. Nobody in their right mind goes to the movies as often as you pretend to. People don't go to the movies at nearly midnight, and movies don't let out at two A.M. Come in stumbling. Muttering to yourself like a maniac! You get three hours' sleep and then go to work. Oh, I can picture the way you're doing down there. Moping, doping, because you're in no condition.

TOM. [*Wildly.*] No, I'm in no condition!

AMANDA. What right have you got to jeopardize your job? Jeopardize the security of us all? How do you think we'd manage if you were—

TOM. Listen! You think I'm crazy about the *warehouse?* [*He bends fiercely toward her slight figure.*] You think I'm in love with the Continental Shoemakers? You think I want to spend fifty-five *years* down there in that—*celotex interior!* with—*fluorescent—tubes!* Look! I'd rather somebody picked up a crowbar and battered out my brains—than go back mornings! I *go!* Every time you come in yelling that Goddamn "Rise and Shine!" "Rise and Shine!" I say to myself, "How *lucky dead* people are!" But I get up. I *go!* For sixty-five dollars a month I give up all that I dream of doing and being *ever!* And you say self—*self's* all I ever think of. Why, listen, if self is what I thought of, Mother, I'd be where he is—GONE! [*He points to his father's picture.*] As far as the system of transportation reaches! [*He starts past her. She grabs his arm.*] Don't grab at me, Mother!

AMANDA. Where are you going?

TOM. I'm going to the *movies!*

AMANDA. I don't believe that lie!

[*Tom crouches toward her, overtowering her tiny figure. She backs away, gasping.*]

TOM. I'm going to opium dens! Yes, opium dens, dens of vice and criminals' hangouts, Mother. I've joined the Hogan Gang, I'm a hired assassin, I carry a tommy gun in a violin case! I run a string of cat houses in the Valley! They call me Killer, Killer Wingfield, I'm leading a double-life, a simple, honest warehouse worker by day, by night a dynamic *czar* of the *underworld, Mother.* I go to gambling casinos, I spin away fortunes on the roulette table! I wear a patch over one eye and a false mustache, sometimes I put on green whiskers. On those occasions they call me—*El Diablo!* Oh, I could tell you many things to make you sleepless! My enemies plan to dynamite this place. They're going to blow us all sky-high some night! I'll be glad, very happy, and so will you! You'll go up, up on a broomstick, over Blue Mountain with seventeen gentlemen callers! You ugly—babbling old—*witch.* . . . [*He goes through a series of violent, clumsy movements, seizing his overcoat, lunging to the door, pulling it fiercely open. The women watch him, aghast. His arm catches in the sleeve of the coat as he struggles to pull it on. For a moment he is pinioned by the bulky garment. With an outraged groan he tears the coat off again, splitting the shoulder of it, and hurls it across the room. It strikes against the shelf of Laura's glass collection, and there is a tinkle of shattering glass. Laura cries out as if wounded.*]

[*Music.*]

[*Screen legend:* "The Glass Menagerie."]

LAURA. [*Shrilly.*] My glass!—menagerie. . . . [*She covers her face and turns away.*]

[*But Amanda is still stunned and stupefied by the "ugly witch" so that she barely notices this occurrence. Now she recovers her speech.*]

AMANDA. [*In an awful voice.*] I won't speak to you—until you apologize!

[*She crosses through the portieres and draws them together behind her. Tom is left with Laura. Laura clings weakly to the mantel with her face averted. Tom stares at her stupidly for a moment. Then he crosses to the shelf. He drops awkwardly on his knees to collect the fallen glass, glancing at Laura as if he would speak but couldn't.*]

["*The Glass Menagerie*" *music steals in as the scene dims out.*]

Scene IV

The interior of the apartment is dark. There is a faint light in the alley. A deep-voiced bell in a church is tolling the hour of five.

Tom appears at the top of the alley. After each solemn boom of the bell in the tower, he shakes a little noisemaker or rattle as if to express the tiny spasm of man in contrast to the sustained power and dignity of the Almighty. This and the unsteadiness of his advance make it evident that he has been drinking. As he climbs the few steps to the fire escape landing light steals up inside. Laura appears in the front room in a nightdress. She notices that Tom's bed is empty. Tom fishes in his pockets for his door key, removing a motley assortment of articles in the search, including a shower of movie ticket stubs and an empty bottle. At last he finds the key, but just as he is about to insert it, it slips from his fingers. He strikes a match and crouches below the door.

TOM. [*Bitterly.*] One crack—and it falls through!

[LAURA *opens the door.*]

LAURA. Tom! Tom, what are you doing?

TOM. Looking for a door key.

LAURA. Where have you been all this time?

TOM. I have been to the movies.

LAURA. All this time at the movies?

TOM. There was a very long program. There was a Garbo picture and a Mickey Mouse and a travelogue and a newsreel and a preview of coming attractions. And there was an organ solo and a collection for the Milk Fund—simultaneously—which ended up in a terrible fight between a fat lady and an usher!

LAURA. [*Innocently.*] Did you have to stay through everything?

TOM. Of course! And, oh, I forgot! There was a big stage show! The headliner on this stage show was Malvolio the Magician. He performed wonderful tricks, many of them, such as pouring water back and forth between pitchers. First it turned to wine and then it turned to beer and then it turned to whisky. I know it was whisky it finally turned into because he needed somebody to come up out of the audience to help him, and I came up—both shows! It was Kentucky Straight Bourbon. A very generous fellow, he gave souvenirs. [*He pulls from his back pocket a shimmering rainbow-colored scarf.*] He gave me this. This is his magic scarf. You can have it, Laura. You wave it over a canary cage and you get a bowl of goldfish. You wave it over the goldfish bowl and they fly away canaries. . . . But the wonderfullest trick of all was the coffin trick. We nailed him into a coffin and he got out of the coffin without removing one nail. [*He has come inside.*] There is a trick that would come in handy for me—get me out of this two-by-four situation! [*He flops onto the bed and starts removing his shoes.*]

LAURA. Tom—shhh!

TOM. What're you shushing me for?

LAURA. You'll wake up Mother.

TOM. Goody, goody! Pay 'er back for all those "Rise an' Shines."

[*He lies down, groaning.*] You know it don't take much intelligence to get yourself into a nailed-up coffin, Laura. But who in hell ever got himself out of one without removing one nail?

[*As if in answer, the father's grinning photograph lights up. The scene dims out.*]

[*Immediately following, the church bell is heard striking six. At the sixth stroke the alarm clock goes off in Amanda's room, and after a few moments we hear her calling: "Rise and Shine! Rise and Shine! Laura, go tell your brother to rise and shine!"*]

TOM. [*Sitting up slowly.*] I'll rise—but I won't shine.

[*The light increases.*]

AMANDA. Laura, tell your brother his coffee is ready.

[*Laura slips into the front room.*]

LAURA. Tom!—It's nearly seven. Don't make Mother nervous.

[*He stares at her stupidly.*]

[*Beseechingly.*] Tom, speak to Mother this morning. Make up with her, apologize, speak to her!

TOM. She won't to me. It's her that started not speaking.

LAURA. If you just say you're sorry she'll start speaking.

TOM. Her not speaking—is that such a tragedy?

LAURA. Please—please!

AMANDA. [*Calling from the kitchenette.*] Laura, are you going to do what I asked you to do, or do I have to get dressed and go out myself?

LAURA. Going, going—soon as I get on my coat!

[*She pulls on a shapeless felt hat with a nervous, jerky movement, pleadingly glancing at Tom. She rushes awkwardly for her coat. The coat is one of Amanda's, inaccurately made-over, the sleeves too short for Laura.*]

Butter and what else?

AMANDA. [*Entering from the kitchenette.*] Just butter. Tell them to charge it.

LAURA. Mother, they make such faces when I do that.

AMANDA. Sticks and stones can break our bones, but the expression on Mr. Garfinkel's face won't harm us! Tell your brother his coffee is getting cold.

LAURA. [*At the door.*] Do what I asked you, will you, will you, Tom?

[*He looks sullenly away.*]

AMANDA. Laura, go now or just don't go at all!

LAURA. [*Rushing out.*] Going—going!

[*A second later she cries out. Tom springs up and crosses to the door. Tom opens the door.*]

TOM. Laura?

LAURA. I'm all right. I slipped, but I'm all right.

AMANDA. [*Peering anxiously after her.*] If anyone breaks a leg on those fire-escape steps, the landlord ought to be sued for every cent he possesses! [*She shuts the door. Now she remembers she isn't speaking to Tom and returns to the other room.*]

[*As Tom comes listlessly for his coffee, she turns her back to him and stands rigidly facing the window on the gloomy gray vault of the areaway. Its light on her face with its aged but childish features is cruelly sharp, satirical as a Daumier print.*]

[*The music of "Ave Maria," is heard softly.*]

[*Tom glances sheepishly but sullenly at her averted figure and slumps at the table. The coffee is scalding hot; he sips it and gasps and spits it back in the cup. At his gasp, Amanda catches her breath and half turns. Then she catches herself and turns back to the window. Tom blows on his coffee, glancing sidewise at his mother. She clears her throat. Tom clears his. He starts to rise, sinks back down again, scratches his head, clears his throat again. Amanda coughs. Tom raises his cup in both hands to blow on it, his eyes staring over the rim of it at his mother for several moments. Then he slowly sets the cup down and awkwardly and hesitantly rises from the chair.*]

TOM. [*Hoarsely.*] Mother. I—I apologize, Mother.

[*Amanda draws a quick, shuddering breath. Her face works grotesquely. She breaks into childlike tears.*]

I'm sorry for what I said, for everything that I said, I didn't mean it.

AMANDA. [*Sobbingly.*] My devotion has made me a witch and so I make myself hateful to my children!

TOM. No, you *don't*.

AMANDA. I worry so much, don't sleep, it makes me nervous!

TOM. [*Gently.*] I understand that.

AMANDA. I've had to put up a solitary battle all these years. But you're my right-hand bower! Don't fall down, don't fail!

TOM. [*Gently.*] I try, Mother.

AMANDA. [*With great enthusiasm.*] Try and you will *succeed!* [*The notion makes her breathless.*] Why, you—you're just *full* of natural endowments! Both of my children—they're *unusual* children! Don't you think I know it? I'm so—*proud!* Happy and— feel I've—so much to be thankful for but—promise me one thing, son!

TOM. What, Mother?

AMANDA. Promise, son, you'll—never be a drunkard!

TOM. [*Turns to her grinning.*] I will never be a drunkard, Mother.

AMANDA. That's what frightened me so, that you'd be drinking! Eat a bowl of Purina!

TOM. Just coffee, Mother.

AMANDA. Shredded wheat biscuit?

TOM. No. No, Mother, just coffee.

AMANDA. You can't put in a day's work on an empty stomach. You've got ten minutes—don't gulp! Drinking too-hot liquids makes cancer of the stomach. . . . Put cream in.

TOM. No, thank you.

AMANDA. To cool it.

TOM. No! No, thank you, I want it black.

AMANDA. I know, but it's not good for you. We have to do all that we can do to build ourselves up. In these trying times we live in, all that we have to cling to is—each other. . . . That's why it's so important to— Tom, I— I sent out your sister so I could discuss something with you. If you hadn't spoken I would have spoken to you. [*She sits down.*]

TOM. [*Gently.*] What is it, Mother, that you want to discuss?

AMANDA. *Laura!*

[*Tom puts his cup down slowly.*]

[*Legend on screen:* "Laura." *Music:* "The Glass Menagerie."]

TOM. —Oh.—Laura . . .

AMANDA. [*Touching his sleeve.*] You know how Laura is. So quiet but—still water runs deep! She notices things and I think she—broods about them.

[*Tom looks up.*]

A few days ago I came in and she was crying.

TOM. What about?

AMANDA. You.

TOM. Me?

AMANDA. She has an idea that you're not happy here.

TOM. What gave her that idea?

AMANDA. What gives her any idea? However, you do act strangely. I—I'm not criticizing, understand *that!* I know your ambitions do not lie in the warehouse, that like everybody in the whole wide world—you've had to—make sacrifices, but—Tom—Tom—life's not easy, it calls for—Spartan endurance! There's so many things in my heart that I cannot describe to you! I've never told you but I—*loved* your father. . . .

TOM. [*Gently.*] I know that, Mother.

AMANDA. And you—when I see you taking after his ways! Staying out late—and—well, you *had* been drinking the night you were in that—terrifying condition! Laura says that you hate the apartment and that you go out nights to get away from it! Is that true, Tom?

TOM. No. You say there's so much in your heart that you can't describe to me. That's true of me, too. There's so much in my heart that I can't describe to *you!* So let's respect each other's—

AMANDA. But, why—*why,* Tom—are you always so *restless?* Where do you *go* to, nights?

TOM. I—go to the movies.

AMANDA. Why do you go to the movies so much, Tom?

TOM. I go to the movies because—I like adventure. Adventure is something I don't have much of at work, so I go to the movies.

AMANDA. But, Tom, you go to the movies *entirely* too *much!*

TOM. I like a lot of adventure.

[*Amanda looks baffled, then hurt. As the familiar inquisition resumes, Tom becomes hard and impatient again. Amanda slips back into her querulous attitude toward him.*]

[*Image on screen: A sailing vessel with Jolly Roger.*]

AMANDA. Most young men find adventure in their careers.

TOM. Then most young men are not employed in a warehouse.

AMANDA. The world is full of young men employed in warehouses and offices and factories.

TOM. Do all of them find adventure in their careers?

AMANDA. They do or they do without it! Not everybody has a craze for adventure.

TOM. Man is by instinct a lover, a hunter, a fighter, and none of those instincts are given much play at the warehouse!

AMANDA. Man is by instinct! Don't quote instinct to me! Instinct is something that people have got away from! It belongs to animals! Christian adults don't want it!

TOM. What do Christian adults want, then, Mother?

AMANDA. Superior things! Things of the mind and the spirit! Only animals have to satisfy instincts! Surely your aims are somewhat higher than theirs! Than monkeys—pigs—

TOM. I reckon they're not.

AMANDA. You're joking. However, that isn't what I wanted to discuss.

TOM. [*Rising.*] I haven't much time.

AMANDA. [*Pushing his shoulders.*] Sit down.

TOM. You want me to punch in red at the warehouse, Mother?

AMANDA. You have five minutes. I want to talk about Laura.

[*Screen legend:* "Plans and Provisions."]

TOM. All right! What about Laura?

AMANDA. We have to be making some plans and provisions for her. She's older than you, two years, and nothing has happened. She just drifts along doing nothing. It frightens me terribly how she just drifts along.

TOM. I guess she's the type that people call home girls.

AMANDA. There's no such type, and if there is, it's a pity! That is unless the home is hers, with a husband!

TOM. What?

AMANDA. Oh, I can see the handwriting on the wall as plain as I see the nose in front of my face! It's terrifying! More and more you remind me of your father! He was out all hours without explanation!—Then *left! Goodbye!* And me with the bag to hold. I saw that letter you got from the Merchant Marine. I know what you're dreaming of. I'm not standing here blindfolded. [*She pauses.*] Very well, then. Then *do* it! But not till there's somebody to take your place.

TOM. What do you mean?

AMANDA. I mean that as soon as Laura has got somebody to take care of her, married, a home of her own, independent—why, then you'll be free to go wherever you please, on land, on sea, whichever way the wind blows you! But until that time you've got to look out for your sister. I don't say me because I'm old and don't matter! I say for your sister because she's young and dependent.

I put her in business college—a dismal failure! Frightened her so it made her sick at the stomach. I took her over to the Young People's League at the church. Another fiasco. She spoke to nobody, nobody spoke to her. Now all she does is fool with those pieces of glass and play those worn-out records. What kind of a life is that for a girl to lead?

TOM. What can I do about it?

AMANDA. Overcome selfishness! Self, self, self is all that you think of!

[*Tom springs up and crosses to get his coat. It is ugly and bulky. He pulls on a cap with earmuffs.*]

Where is your muffler? Put your wool muffler on!

[*He snatches it angrily from the closet, tosses it around his neck and pulls both ends tight.*]

Tom! I haven't said what I had in mind to ask you.

TOM. I'm too late to—

AMANDA. [*Catching his arm—very importunately; then shyly.*] Down at the warehouse, aren't there some—nice young men?

TOM. No!

AMANDA. There *must* be—*some* . . .

TOM. Mother—[*He gestures.*]

AMANDA. Find out one that's clean-living—doesn't drink and ask him out for sister!

TOM. What?

AMANDA. For *sister!* To *meet!* Get *acquainted!*

TOM. [*Stamping to the door.*] Oh, my *go-osh!*

AMANDA. Will you?

[*He opens the door. She says, imploringly.*]

Will you?

[*He starts down the fire escape.*]

Will you? *Will* you, dear?

TOM. [*Calling back.*] Yes!

[*Amanda closes the door hesitantly and with a troubled but faintly hopeful expression.*]
[*Screen image:* The cover of a glamor magazine.]
[*The spotlight picks up Amanda at the phone.*]

AMANDA. Ella Cartwright? This is Amanda Wingfield! How are you, honey?
How is that kidney condition?

[*There is a five-second pause.*]
Horrors!

[*There is another pause.*]

You're a Christian martyr, yes, honey, that's what you are, a Christian martyr! Well, I just now happened to notice in my little red book that your subscription to the *Companion* has just run out! I knew that you wouldn't want to miss out on the wonderful serial starting in this new issue. It's by Bessie Mae Hopper, the first thing she's written since *Honeymoon for Three.* Wasn't that a strange and interesting story? Well, this one is even lovelier, I believe. It has a sophisticated, society background. It's all about the horsey set on Long Island!

[*The light fades out.*]

Scene V

Legend on the screen: "Annunciation."
Music is heard as the light slowly comes on.

It is early dusk of a spring evening. Supper has just been finished in the Wingfield apartment. Amanda and Laura, in light-colored dresses, are removing dishes from the table in the dining room, which is shadowy, their movements formalized almost as a dance or ritual, their moving forms as pale and silent as moths. Tom, in white shirt and trousers, rises from the table and crosses toward the fire escape.

AMANDA. [*As he passes her.*] Son, will you do me a favor?
TOM. What?
AMANDA. Comb your hair! You look so pretty when your hair is combed!

[*Tom slouches on the sofa with the evening paper. Its enormous headline reads: "Franco Triumphs."*]

There is only one respect in which I would like you to emulate your father.
TOM. What respect is that?
AMANDA. The care he always took of his appearance. He never allowed himself to look untidy.

[*He throws down the paper and crosses to the fire escape.*]

Where are you going?

TOM. I'm going out to smoke.

AMANDA. You smoke too much. A pack a day at fifteen cents a pack. How much would that amount to in a month? Thirty times fifteen is how much, Tom? Figure it out and you will be astounded at what you could save. Enough to give you a night-school course in accounting at Washington U.! Just think what a wonderful thing that would be for you, son!

[*Tom is unmoved by the thought.*]

TOM. I'd rather smoke. [*He steps out on the landing, letting the screen door slam.*]

AMANDA. [*Sharply.*] I know! That's the tragedy of it. . . . [*Alone, she turns to look at her husband's picture.*]

[*Dance music: "The World Is Waiting for the Sunrise!"*]

TOM. [*To the audience.*] Across the alley from us was the Paradise Dance Hall. On evenings in spring the windows and doors were open and the music came outdoors. Sometimes the lights were turned out except for a large glass sphere that hung from the ceiling. It would turn slowly about and filter the dusk with delicate rainbow colors. Then the orchestra played a waltz or a tango, something that had a slow and sensuous rhythm. Couples would come outside, to the relative privacy of the alley. You could see them kissing behind ash pits and telephone poles. This was the compensation for lives that passed like mine, without any change or adventure. Adventure and change were imminent in this year. They were waiting around the corner for all these kids. Suspended in the mist over Berchtesgaden, caught in the folds of Chamberlain's umbrella. In Spain there was Guernica! But here there was only hot swing music and liquor, dance halls, bars, and movies, and sex that hung in the gloom like a chandelier and flooded the world with brief, deceptive rainbows. . . . All the world was waiting for bombardments!

[*Amanda turns from the picture and comes outside.*]

AMANDA. [*Sighing.*] A fire escape landing's a poor excuse for a porch. [*She spreads a newspaper on a step and sits down, gracefully and demurely as if she were settling into a swing on a Mississippi veranda.*] What are you looking at?

TOM. The moon.

AMANDA. Is there a moon this evening?

TOM. It's rising over Garfinkel's Delicatessen.

AMANDA. So it is! A little silver slipper of a moon. Have you made a wish on it yet?

TOM. Um-hum.

AMANDA. What did you wish for?

TOM. That's a secret.

AMANDA. A secret, huh? Well, I won't tell mine either. I will be just as mysterious as you.

TOM. I bet I can guess what yours is.

AMANDA. Is my head so transparent?

TOM. You're not a sphinx.

AMANDA. No, I don't have secrets. I'll tell you what I wished for on the moon. Success and happiness for my precious children! I wish for that whenever there's a moon, and when there isn't a moon, I wish for it, too.

TOM. I thought perhaps you wished for a gentleman caller.

AMANDA. Why do you say that?

TOM. Don't you remember asking me to fetch one?

AMANDA. I remember suggesting that it would be nice for your sister if you brought home some nice young man from the warehouse. I think that I've made that suggestion more than once.

TOM. Yes, you have made it repeatedly.

AMANDA. Well?

TOM. We are going to have one.

AMANDA. What?

TOM. A gentleman caller!

[*The annunciation is celebrated with music.*]

[*Amanda rises.*]

[*Image on screen*: A caller with a bouquet.]

AMANDA. You mean you have asked some nice young man to come over?

TOM. Yep. I've asked him to dinner.

AMANDA. You really did?

TOM. I did!

AMANDA. You did, and did he—*accept?*

TOM. He did!

AMANDA. Well, well—well, well! That's—lovely!

TOM. I thought that you would be pleased.

AMANDA. It's definite then?

TOM. Very definite.

AMANDA. Soon?

TOM. Very soon.

AMANDA. For heaven's sake, stop putting on and tell me some things, will you?

TOM. What things do you want me to tell you?

AMANDA. *Naturally* I would like to know when he's *coming!*

TOM. He's coming tomorrow.

AMANDA. *Tomorrow?*

TOM. Yep. Tomorrow.

AMANDA. But, Tom!

TOM. Yes, Mother?

AMANDA. Tomorrow gives me no time!

TOM. Time for what?

AMANDA. Preparations! Why didn't you phone me at once, as

soon as you asked him, the minute that he accepted? Then, don't you see, I could have been getting ready!

TOM. You don't have to make any fuss.

AMANDA. Oh, Tom, Tom, Tom, of course I have to make a fuss! I want things nice, not sloppy! Not thrown together. I'll certainly have to do some fast thinking, won't I?

TOM. I don't see why you have to think at all.

AMANDA. You just don't know. We can't have a gentleman caller in a pigsty! All my wedding silver has to be polished, the monogrammed table linen ought to be laundered! The windows have to be washed and fresh curtains put up. And how about clothes? We have to *wear* something, don't we?

TOM. Mother, this boy is no one to make a fuss over!

AMANDA. Do you realize he's the first young man we've introduced to your sister? It's terrible, dreadful, disgraceful that poor little sister has never received a single gentleman caller! Tom, come inside! [*She opens the screen door.*]

TOM. What for?

AMANDA. I want to ask you some things.

TOM. If you're going to make such a fuss, I'll call it off, I'll tell him not to come!

AMANDA. You certainly won't do anything of the kind. Nothing offends people worse than broken engagements. It simply means I'll have to work like a Turk! We won't be brilliant, but we will pass inspection. Come on inside.

[*Tom follows her inside, groaning.*]
Sit down.

TOM. Any particular place you would like me to sit?

AMANDA. Thank heavens I've got that new sofa! I'm also making payments on a floor lamp I'll have sent out! And put the chintz covers on, they'll brighten things up! Of course I'd hoped to have these walls re-papered. . . . What is the young man's name?

TOM. His name is O'Connor.

AMANDA. That, of course, means fish—tomorrow is Friday! I'll have that salmon loaf—with Durkee's dressing! What does he do? He works at the warehouse?

TOM. Of course! How else would I—

AMANDA. Tom, he—doesn't drink?

TOM. Why do you ask me that?

AMANDA. Your father *did*!

TOM. Don't get started on that!

AMANDA. He *does* drink, then?

TOM. Not that I know of!

AMANDA. Make sure, be certain! The last thing I want for my daughter's a boy who drinks!

TOM. Aren't you being a little bit premature? Mr. O'Connor has not yet appeared on the scene!

AMANDA. But will tomorrow. To meet your sister, and what do I know about his character? Nothing! Old maids are better off than wives of drunkards!

TOM. Oh, my God!

AMANDA. Be still!

TOM. [*Leaning forward to whisper.*] Lots of fellows meet girls whom they don't marry!

AMANDA. Oh, talk sensibly, Tom—and don't be sarcastic! [*She has gotten a hairbrush.*]

TOM. What are you doing?

AMANDA. I'm brushing that cowlick down! [*She attacks his hair with the brush.*] What is this young man's position at the warehouse?

TOM. [*Submitting grimly to the brush and the interrogation.*] This young man's positon is that of a shipping clerk, Mother.

AMANDA. Sounds to me like a fairly responsible job, the sort of job *you* would be in if you had more *get-up.* What is his salary? Have you any idea?

TOM. I would judge it to be approximately eighty-five dollars a month.

AMANDA. Well—not princely, but—

TOM. Twenty more than I make.

AMANDA. Yes, how well I know! But for a family man, eighty-five dollars a month is not much more than you can just get by on. . . .

TOM. Yes, but Mr. O'Connor is not a family man.

AMANDA. He might be, mightn't he? Some time in the future?

TOM. I see. Plans and provisions.

AMANDA. You are the only young man that I know of who ignores the fact that the future becomes the present, the present the past, and the past turns into everlasting regret if you don't plan for it!

TOM. I will think that over and see what I can make of it.

AMANDA. Don't be supercilious with your mother! Tell me some more about this—what do you call him?

TOM. James D. O'Connor. The D. is for Delaney.

AMANDA. Irish on *both* sides! *Gracious!* And doesn't drink?

TOM. Shall I call him up and ask him right this minute?

AMANDA. The only way to find out about those things is to make discreet inquiries at the proper moment. When I was a girl in Blue Mountain and it was suspected that a young man drank, the girl whose attentions he had been receiving, if any girl *was*, would sometimes speak to the minister of his church, or rather her father would if her father was living, and sort of feel him out on the young man's character. That is the way such things are discreetly handled to keep a young woman from making a tragic mistake!

TOM. Then how did you happen to make a tragic mistake?

AMANDA. That innocent look of your father's had everyone fooled! He *smiled*—the world was *enchanted*! No girl can do worse than put herself at the mercy of a handsome appearance! I hope that Mr. O'Connor is not too good-looking.

TOM. No, he's not too good-looking. He's covered with freckles and hasn't too much of a nose.

AMANDA. He's not right-down homely, though?

TOM. Not right-down homely. Just medium homely, I'd say.

AMANDA. Character's what to look for in a man.

TOM. That's what I've always said, Mother.

AMANDA. You've never said anything of the kind and I suspect you would never give it a thought.

TOM. Don't be suspicious of me.

AMANDA. At least I hope he's the type that's up and coming.

TOM. I think he really goes in for self-improvement.

AMANDA. What reason have you to think so?

TOM. He goes to night school.

AMANDA. [*Beaming.*] Splendid! What does he do, I mean study?

TOM. Radio engineering and public speaking!

AMANDA. Then he has visions of being advanced in the world! Any young man who studies public speaking is aiming to have an executive job some day! And radio engineering? A thing for the future! Both of these facts are very illuminating. Those are the sort of things that a mother should know concerning any young man who comes to call on her daughter. Seriously or—not.

TOM. One little warning. He doesn't know about Laura. I didn't let on that we had dark ulterior motives. I just said, why don't you come and have dinner with us? He said okay and that was the whole conversation.

AMANDA. I bet it was! You're eloquent as an oyster. However, he'll know about Laura when he gets here. When he sees how lovely and sweet and pretty she is, he'll thank his lucky stars he was asked to dinner.

TOM. Mother, you mustn't expect too much of Laura.

AMANDA. What do you mean?

TOM. Laura seems all those things to you and me because she's ours and we love her. We don't even notice she's crippled any more.

AMANDA. Don't say crippled! You know that I never allow that word to be used!

TOM. But face facts, Mother. She is and—that's not all—

AMANDA. What do you mean "not all"?

TOM. Laura is very different from other girls.

AMANDA. I think the difference is all to her advantage.

TOM. Not quite all—in the eyes of others—strangers—she's terribly shy and lives in a world of her own and those things make her seem a little peculiar to people outside the house.

AMANDA. Don't say peculiar.

TOM. Face the facts. She is.

[*The dance hall music changes to a tango that has a minor and somewhat ominous tone.*]

AMANDA. In what way is she peculiar—may I ask?

TOM. [*Gently.*] She lives in a world of her own—a world of little glass ornaments, Mother. . . .

[*He gets up. Amanda remains holding the brush, looking at him, troubled.*]

She plays old phonograph records and—that's about all— [*He glances at himself in the mirror and crosses to the door.*]

AMANDA. [*Sharply.*] Where are you going?

TOM. I'm going to the movies. [*He goes out the screen door.*]

AMANDA. Not to the movies, every night to the movies! [*She follows quickly to the screen door.*] I don't believe you always go to the movies!

[*He is gone. Amanda looks worriedly after him for a moment. Then vitality and optimism return and she turns from the door, crossing to the portieres.*]

Laura! Laura!

[*Laura answers from the kitchenette.*]

LAURA. Yes, Mother.

AMANDA. Let those dishes go and come in front!

[*Laura appears with a dish towel. Amanda speaks to her gaily.*]

Laura, come here and make a wish on the moon!

[*Screen image: The Moon.*]

LAURA. [*Entering.*] Moon—moon?

AMANDA. A little silver slipper of a moon. Look over your left shoulder, Laura, and make a wish!

[*Laura looks faintly puzzled as if called out of sleep. Amanda seizes her shoulders and turns her at an angle by the door.*]

Now! Now, darling, *wish!*

LAURA. What shall I wish for, Mother?

AMANDA. [*Her voice trembling and her eyes suddenly filling with tears.*] Happiness! Good fortune!

[*The sound of the violin rises and the stage dims out.*]

Scene VI

The light comes up on the fire escape landing. Tom is leaning against the grill, smoking.

[*Screen image: The high school hero.*]

TOM. And so the following evening I brought Jim home to dinner. I had known Jim slightly in high school. In high school Jim was a hero. He had tremendous Irish good nature and vitality with the scrubbed and polished look of white chinaware. He seemed to move in a continual spotlight. He was a star in basketball, captain of the debating club, president of the senior class and the glee club and he sang the male lead in the annual light operas. He was always running or bounding, never just walking. He seemed always at the point of defeating the law of gravity. He was shooting with such velocity through his adolescence that you would logically expect him to arrive at nothing short of the White House by the time he was thirty. But Jim apparently ran into more interference after his graduation from Soldan. His speed had definitely slowed. Six years after he left high school he was holding a job that wasn't much better than mine.

[*Screen image*: The Clerk.]

He was the only one at the warehouse with whom I was on friendly terms. I was valuable to him as someone who could remember his former glory, who had seen him win basketball games and the silver cup in debating. He knew of my secret practice of retiring to a cabinet of the washroom to work on poems when business was slack in the warehouse. He called me Shakespeare. And while the other boys in the warehouse regarded me with suspicious hostility, Jim took a humorous attitude toward me. Gradually his attitude affected the others, their hostility wore off and they also began to smile at me as people smile at an oddly fashioned dog who trots across their path at some distance.

I knew that Jim and Laura had known each other at Soldan, and I had heard Laura speak admiringly of his voice. I didn't know if Jim remembered her or not. In high school Laura had been as unobtrusive as Jim had been astonishing. If he did remember Laura, it was not as my sister, for when I asked him to dinner, he grinned and said, "You know, Shakespeare, I never thought of you as having folks!"

He was about to discover that I did. . . .

[*Legend on screen*: "The accent of a coming foot."]

[*The light dims out on Tom and comes up in the Wingfield living room—a delicate lemony light. It is about five on a Friday evening of late spring which comes "scattering poems in the sky."*]

[*Amanda has worked like a Turk in preparation for the gentleman caller. The results are astonishing. The new floor lamp with its rose silk shade is in place, a colored paper lantern conceals the broken light fixture in the ceiling, new billowing white curtains are at the windows, chintz covers are on the chairs and*

sofa, a pair of new sofa pillows make their initial appearance. Open boxes and tissue paper are scattered on the floor.]
Laura stands in the middle of the room with lifted arms while Amanda crouches before her, adjusting the hem of a new dress, devout and ritualistic. The dress is colored and designed by memory. The arrangement of Laura's hair is changed; it is softer and more becoming. A fragile, unearthly prettiness has come out in Laura: she is like a piece of translucent glass touched by light, given a momentary radiance, not actual, not lasting.]

AMANDA. [*Impatiently.*] Why are you trembling?

LAURA. Mother, you've made me so nervous!

AMANDA. How have I made you nervous?

LAURA. By all this fuss! You make it seem so important!

AMANDA. I don't understand you, Laura. You couldn't be satisfied with just sitting home, and yet whenever I try to arrange something for you, you seem to resist it. [*She gets up.*] Now take a look at yourself. No, wait! Wait just a moment—I have an idea!

LAURA. What is it now?

[*Amanda produces two powder puffs which she wraps in handkerchiefs and stuffs in Laura's bosom.*]

LAURA. Mother, what are you doing?

AMANDA. They call them "Gay Deceivers"!

LAURA. I won't wear them!

AMANDA. You will!

LAURA. Why should I?

AMANDA. Because, to be painfully honest, your chest is flat.

LAURA. You make it seem like we were setting a trap.

AMANDA. All pretty girls are a trap, a pretty trap, and men expect them to be.

[*Legend on screen:* "A pretty trap."]

Now look at yourself, young lady. This is the prettiest you will ever be! [*She stands back to admire Laura.*] I've got to fix myself now! You're going to be surprised by your mother's appearance!

[*Amanda crosses through the portieres, humming gaily. Laura moves slowly to the long mirror and stares solemnly at herself. A wind blows the white curtains inward in a slow, graceful motion and with a faint, sorrowful sighing.*]

AMANDA. [*From somewhere behind the portieres.*] It isn't dark enough yet.

[*Laura turns slowly before the mirror with a troubled look.*]

[*Legend on screen:* "This is my sister: Celebrate her with strings!" *Music plays.*]

AMANDA. [*Laughing, still not visible.*] I'm going to show you something. I'm going to make a spectacular appearance!

LAURA. What is it, Mother?

AMANDA. Possess your soul in patience—you will see! Something I've resurrected from that old trunk! Styles haven't changed so terribly much after all. . . . [*She parts the portieres.*] Now just look at your mother! [*She wears a girlish frock of yellowed voile with a blue silk sash. She carries a bunch of jonquils—the legend of her youth is nearly revived. Now she speaks feverishly.*] This is the dress in which I led the cotillion. Won the cakewalk twice at Sunset Hill, wore one Spring to the Governor's Ball in Jackson! See how I sashayed around the ballroom, Laura? [*She raises her skirt and does a mincing step around the room.*] I wore it on Sundays for my gentlemen callers! I had it on the day I met your father. . . . I had malaria fever all that Spring. The change of climate from East Tennessee to the Delta—weakened resistance. I had a little temperature all the time—not enough to be serious— just enough to make me restless and giddy! Invitations poured in —parties all over the Delta! "Stay in bed," said Mother, "you have a fever!"—but I just wouldn't. I took quinine but kept on going, going! Evenings, dances! Afternoons, long, long rides! Picnics— lovely! So lovely, that country in May—all lacy with dogwood, lit- erally flooded with jonquils! That was the spring I had the craze for jonquils. Jonquils became an absolute obsession. Mother said, "Honey, there's no more room for jonquils." And still I kept on bringing in more jonquils. Whenever, wherever I saw them, I'd say, "Stop! Stop! I see jonquils!" I made the young men help me gather the jonquils! It was a joke, Amanda and her jonquils. Fin- ally there were no more vases to hold them, every available space was filled with jonquils. No vases to hold them? All right, I'll hold them myself! And then I—[*She stops in front of the picture. Music plays.*] met your father! Malaria fever and jonquils and then—this —boy. . . . [*She switches on the rose-colored lamp.*] I hope they get here before it starts to rain. [*She crosses the room and places the jonquils in a bowl on the table.*] I gave your brother a little extra change so he and Mr. O'Connor could take the service car home.

LAURA. [*With an altered look.*] What did you say his name was?

AMANDA. O'Connor.

LAURA. What is his first name?

AMANDA. I don't remember. Oh, yes, I do. It was—Jim!

[*Laura sways slightly and catches hold of a chair.*]

[*Legend on screen: "Not Jim!"*]

LAURA. [*Faintly.*] Not—Jim!

AMANDA. Yes, that was it, it was Jim! I've never known a Jim that wasn't nice!

[*The music becomes ominous.*]

LAURA. Are you sure his name is Jim O'Connor?

AMANDA. Yes. Why?

LAURA. Is he the one that Tom used to know in high school?

AMANDA. He didn't say so. I think he just got to know him at the warehouse.

LAURA. There was a Jim O'Connor we both knew in high school —[*Then, with effort.*] If that is the one that Tom is bringing to dinner—you'll have to excuse me, I won't come to the table.

AMANDA. What sort of nonsense is this?

LAURA. You asked me once if I ever liked a boy. Don't you remember I showed you this boy's picture?

AMANDA. You mean the boy you showed me in the yearbook?

LAURA. Yes, that boy.

AMANDA. Laura, Laura, were you in love with that boy?

LAURA. I don't know, Mother. All I know is I couldn't sit at the table if it was him!

AMANDA. It won't be him! It isn't the least bit likely. But whether it is or not, you will come to the table. You will not be excused.

LAURA. I'll have to be, Mother.

AMANDA. I don't intend to humor your silliness, Laura. I've had too much from you and your brother, both! So just sit down and compose yourself till they come. Tom has forgotten his key so you'll have to let them in, when they arrive.

LAURA. [*Panicky.*] Oh, Mother—*you* answer the door!

AMANDA. [*Lightly.*] I'll be busy in the kitchen—busy!

LAURA. Oh, Mother, please answer the door, don't make me do it!

AMANDA. [*Crossing into the kitchenette.*] I've got to fix the dressing for the salmon. Fuss, fuss—silliness!—over a gentleman caller!

[*The door swings shut. Laura is left alone.*]

[*Legend on screen:* "Terror!"]

[*She utters a low moan and turns off the lamp—sits stiffly on the edge of the sofa, knotting her fingers together.*]

[*Legend on screen:* "The Opening of a Door!"]

[*Tom and Jim appear on the fire escape steps and climb to the landing. Hearing their approach, Laura rises with a panicky gesture. She retreats to the portieres. The doorbell rings. Laura catches her breath and touches her throat. Low drums sound.*]

AMANDA. [*Calling.*] Laura, sweetheart! The door!

[*Laura stares at it without moving.*]

JIM. I think we just beat the rain.

TOM. Uh-huh. [*He rings again, nervously. Jim whistles and fishes for a cigarette.*]

AMANDA. [*Very, very gaily.*] Laura, that is your brother and Mr. O'Connor! Will you let them in, darling?

[*Laura crosses toward the kitchenette door.*]

LAURA. [*Breathlessly.*] Mother—you go to the door!

[*Amanda steps out of the kitchenette and stares furiously at Laura. She points imperiously at the door.*]

LAURA. Please, please!

AMANDA. [*In a fierce whisper.*] What is the matter with you, you silly thing?

LAURA. [*Desperately.*] Please, you answer it, *please!*

AMANDA. I told you I wasn't going to humor you, Laura. Why have you chosen this moment to lose your mind?

LAURA. Please, please, please, you go!

AMANDA. You'll have to go to the door because I can't!

LAURA. [*Despairingly.*] I can't either!

AMANDA. *Why?*

LAURA. I'm *sick!*

AMANDA. I'm sick, too—of your nonsense! Why can't you and your brother be normal people? Fantastic whims and behavior!

[*Tom gives a long ring.*]

Preposterous goings on! Can you give me one reason— [*She calls out lyrically.*] Coming! Just one second!—why you should be afraid to open a door? Now you answer it, Laura?

LAURA. Oh, oh, oh . . . [*She returns through the portieres, darts to the Victrola, winds it frantically and turns it on.*]

AMANDA. Laura Wingfield, you march right to that door!

LAURA. Yes—yes, Mother!

[*A faraway, scratchy rendition of "Dardanella" softens the air and gives her strength to move through it. She slips to the door and draws it cautiously open. Tom enters with the caller, Jim O'Connor.*]

TOM. Laura, this is Jim. Jim, this is my sister, Laura.

JIM. [*Stepping inside.*] I didn't know that Shakespeare had a sister!

LAURA. [*Retreating, stiff and trembling, from the door.*] How—how do you do?

JIM. [*Heartily, extending his hand.*] Okay!

[*Laura touches it hesitantly with hers.*]

JIM. Your hand's *cold*, Laura!

LAURA. Yes, well—I've been playing the Victrola. . . .

JIM. Must have been playing classical music on it! You ought to play a little hot swing music to warm you up!

LAURA. Excuse me—I haven't finished playing the Victrola . . . [*She turns awkwardly and hurries into the front room. She pauses a second by the Victrola. Then she catches her breath and darts through the portieres like a frightened deer.*]

JIM. [*Grinning.*] What was the matter?

TOM. Oh—with Laura? Laura is—terribly shy.

JIM. Shy, huh? It's unusual to meet a shy girl nowadays. I don't believe you ever mentioned you had a sister.

TOM. Well, now you know. I have one. Here is the *Post Dispatch*. You want a piece of it?

JIM. Uh-huh.

TOM. What piece? The comics?

JIM. Sports! [*He glances at it.*] Ole Dizzy Dean is on his bad behavior.

TOM. [*Uninterested.*] Yeah? [*He lights a cigarette and goes over to the fire-escape door.*]

JIM. Where are *you* going?

TOM. I'm going out on the terrace.

JIM. [*Going after him.*] You know, Shakespeare—I'm going to sell you a bill of goods!

TOM. What goods?

JIM. A course I'm taking.

TOM. Huh?

JIM. In public speaking! You and me, we're not the warehouse type.

TOM. Thanks—that's good news. But what has public speaking got to do with it?

JIM. It fits you for—executive positions!

TOM. Awww.

JIM. I tell you it's done a helluva lot for me.

[*Image on screen*: Executive at his desk.]

TOM. In what respect?

JIM. In every! Ask yourself what is the difference between you an' me and men in the office down front? Brains?—No!—Ability? —No! Then what? Just one little thing—

TOM. What is that one little thing?

JIM. Primarily it amounts to—social poise! Being able to square up to people and hold your own on any social level!

AMANDA. [*From the kitchenette.*] Tom?

TOM. Yes, Mother?

AMANDA. Is that you and Mr. O'Connor?

TOM. Yes, Mother.

AMANDA. Well, you just make yourselves comfortable in there.

TOM. Yes, Mother.

AMANDA. Ask Mr. O'Connor if he would like to wash his hands.

JIM. Aw, no—no—thank you—I took care of that at the warehouse. Tom—

TOM. Yes?

JIM. Mr. Mendoza was speaking to me about you.

TOM. Favorably?

JIM. What do you think?

TOM. Well—

JIM. You're going to be out of a job if you don't wake up.

TOM. I am waking up—

JIM. You show no signs.

TOM. The signs are interior.

[*Image on screen*: The sailing vessel with the Jolly Roger again.]

TOM. I'm planning to change. [*He leans over the fire-escape rail, speaking with quiet exhilaration. The incandescent marquees and signs of the first-run movie houses light his face from across the alley. He looks like a voyager.*] I'm right at the point of committing myself to a future that doesn't include the warehouse and Mr. Mendoza or even a night-school course in public speaking.

JIM. What are you gassing about?

TOM. I'm tired of the movies.

JIM. Movies!

TOM. Yes, movies! Look at them— [*A wave toward the marvels of Grand Avenue.*] All of those glamorous people—having adventures—hogging it all, gobbling the whole thing up! You know what happens? People go to the *movies* instead of *moving!* Hollywood characters are supposed to have all the adventures for everybody in America, while everybody in America sits in a dark room and watches them have them! Yes, until there's a war. That's when adventure becomes available to the masses! *Everyone's* dish, not only Gable's! Then the people in the dark room come out of the dark room to have some adventures themselves—goody, goody! It's our turn now, to go to the South Sea Island—to make a safari —to be exotic, far-off! But I'm not patient. I don't want to wait till then. I'm tired of the *movies* and I am *about* to *move!*

JIM. [*Incredulously.*] Move?

TOM. Yes.

JIM. When?

TOM. Soon!

JIM. Where? Where?

[*The music seems to answer the question, while Tom thinks it over. He searches in his pockets.*]

TOM. I'm starting to boil inside. I know I seem dreamy, but inside—well, I'm boiling! Whenever I pick up a shoe, I shudder a little thinking how short life is and what I am doing! Whatever that means, I know it doesn't mean shoes—except as something to wear on a traveler's feet! [*He finds what he has been searching for in his pockets and holds out a paper to Jim.*] Look—

JIM. What?

TOM. I'm a member.

JIM. [*Reading.*] The Union of Merchant Seamen.

TOM. I paid my dues this month, instead of the light bill.

JIM. You will regret it when they turn the lights off.

TOM. I won't be here.

JIM. How about your mother?

TOM. I'm like my father. The bastard son of a bastard! Did you notice how he's grinning in his picture in there? And he's been absent going on sixteen years!

JIM. You're just talking, you drip. How does your mother feel about it?

TOM. Shhh! Here comes Mother! Mother is not acquainted with my plans!

AMANDA. [*Coming through the portieres.*] Where are you all?

TOM. On the terrace, Mother.

[*They start inside. She advances to them. Tom is distinctly shocked at her appearance. Even Jim blinks a little. He is making his first contact with girlish Southern vivacity and in spite of the night-school course in public speaking is somewhat thrown off the beam by the unexpected outlay of social charm. Certain responses are attempted by Jim but are swept aside by Amanda's gay laughter and chatter. Tom is embarrassed but after the first shock Jim reacts very warmly. He grins and chuckles, is altogether won over.*]

[*Image on screen: Amanda as a girl.*]

AMANDA. [*Coyly smiling, shaking her girlish ringlets.*] Well, well, well, so this is Mr. O'Connor. Introductions entirely unnecessary. I've heard so much about you from my boy. I finally said to him, Tom—good gracious!—why don't you bring this paragon to supper? I'd like to meet this nice young man at the warehouse!—instead of just hearing him sing your praises so much! I don't know why my son is so stand-offish—that's not Southern behavior!

Let's sit down and—I think we could stand a little more air in here! Tom, leave the door open. I felt a nice fresh breeze a moment ago. Where has it gone to? Mmm, so warm already! And not quite summer, even. We're going to burn up when summer really gets started. However, we're having—we're having a very light supper. I think light things are better fo' this time of year. The same as light clothes are. Light clothes an' light food are what warm weather calls fo'. You know our blood gets so thick during th' winter—it takes a while fo' us to *adjust* ou'selves!—when the season changes . . . It's come so quick this year. I wasn't prepared. All of a sudden—heavens! Already summer! I ran to the trunk an' pulled out this light dress—terribly old! Historical almost! But feels so good—so good an' co-ol, y' know. . . .

TOM. Mother—

AMANDA. Yes, honey?

TOM. How about—supper?

AMANDA. Honey, you go ask Sister if supper is ready! You know Sister is in full charge of supper! Tell her you hungry boys are waiting for it. [*To Jim.*] Have you met Laura?

JIM. She—

AMANDA. Let you in? Oh, good, you've met already! It's rare for a girl as sweet an' pretty as Laura to be domestic! But Laura is, thank heavens, not only pretty but also very domestic. I'm not at all. I never was a bit. I never could make a thing but angel-food cake. Well, in the South we had so many servants. Gone, gone, gone. All vestige of gracious living! Gone completely! I wasn't prepared for what the future brought me. All of my gentlemen callers were sons of planters and so of course I assumed that I would be married to one and raise my family on a large piece of land with plenty of servants. But man proposes—and woman accepts the proposal! To vary that old, old saying a little bit—I married no planter! I married a man who worked for the telephone company! That gallantly smiling gentleman over there! [*She points to the picture.*] A telephone man who—fell in love with long-distance! Now he travels and I don't even know where! But what am I going on for about my—tribulations? Tell me yours— I hope you don't have any! Tom?

TOM. [*Returning.*] Yes, Mother?

AMANDA. Is supper nearly ready?

TOM. It looks to me like supper is on the table.

AMANDA. Let me look— [*She rises prettily and looks through the portieres.*] Oh, lovely! But where is Sister?

TOM. Laura is not feeling well and she says that she thinks she'd better not come to the table.

AMANDA. What? Nonsense! Laura? Oh, Laura!

LAURA. [*From the kitchenette, faintly.*] Yes, Mother.

AMANDA. You really must come to the table. We won't be seated until you come to the table! Come in, Mr. O'Connor. You sit over there, and I'll. . . . Laura? Laura Wingfield! You're keeping us waiting, honey! We can't say grace until you come to the table!

[*The kitchenette door is pushed weakly open and Laura comes in. She is obviously quite faint, her lips trembling, her eyes wide and staring. She moves unsteadily toward the table.*]

[*Screen legend:* "Terror!"]

[*Outside a summer storm is coming on abruptly. The white curtains billow inward at the windows and there is a sorrowful murmur from the deep blue dusk.*]

[*Laura suddenly stumbles; she catches at a chair with a faint moan.*]

TOM. Laura!

AMANDA. Laura!

[*There is a clap of thunder.*]

[*Screen legend: "Ah!"*]

[*Despairingly.*] Why, Laura, you *are* ill, darling! Tom, help your sister into the living room, dear! Sit in the living room, Laura—rest on the sofa. Well! [*To Jim as Tom helps his sister to the sofa in the living room.*] Standing over the hot stove made her ill! I told her that it was just too warm this evening, but—

[*Tom comes back to the table.*]

Is Laura all right now?

TOM. Yes.

AMANDA. What *is* that? Rain? A nice cool rain has come up! [*She gives Jim a frightened look.*] I think we may—have grace—now . . .

[*Tom looks at her stupidly.*] Tom, honey—you say grace!

TOM. Oh . . . "For these and all thy mercies—"

[*They bow their heads, Amanda stealing a nervous glance at Jim. In the living room Laura, stretched on the sofa, clenches her hand to her lips, to hold back a shuddering sob.*]

God's Holy Name be praised—

[*The scene dims out.*]

Scene VII

It is half an hour later. Dinner is just being finished in the dining room, Laura is still huddled upon the sofa, her feet drawn under her, her head resting on a pale blue pillow, her eyes wide and mysteriously watchful. The new floor lamp with its shade of rose-colored silk gives a soft, becoming light to her face, bringing out the fragile, unearthly prettiness which usually escapes attention. From outside there is a steady murmur of rain, but it is slackening and soon stops; the air outside becomes pale and luminous as the moon breaks through the clouds. A moment after the curtain rises, the lights in both rooms flicker and go out.

JIM. Hey, there, Mr. Light Bulb!

[*Amanda laughs nervously.*]

[*Legend on screen: "Suspension of a public service."*]

AMANDA. Where was Moses when the lights went out? Ha-ha. Do you know the answer to that one, Mr. O'Connor?

JIM. No, Ma'am, what's the answer?

AMANDA. In the dark!

[*Jim laughs appreciatively.*]

Everybody sit still. I'll light the candles. Isn't it lucky we have them on the table? Where's a match? Which of you gentlemen can provide a match?

JIM. Here.

AMANDA. Thank you, Sir.

JIM. Not at all, Ma'am!

AMANDA. [*As she lights the candles.*] I guess the fuse has burnt out. Mr. O'Connor, can you tell a burnt-out fuse? I know I can't and Tom is a total loss when it comes to mechanics.

[*They rise from the table and go into the kitchenette, from where their voices are heard.*]

Oh, be careful you don't bump into something. We don't want our gentleman caller to break his neck. Now wouldn't that be a fine howdy-do?

JIM. Ha-ha! Where is the fuse-box?

AMANDA. Right here next to the stove. Can you see see anything?

JIM. Just a minute.

AMANDA. Isn't electricity a mysterious thing? Wasn't it Benjamin Franklin who tied a key to a kite? We live in such a mysterious universe, don't we? Some people say that science clears up all the mysteries for us. In my opinion it only creates more! Have you found it yet?

JIM. No, Ma'am. All these fuses look okay to me.

AMANDA. Tom!

TOM. Yes, Mother?

AMANDA. That light bill I gave you several days ago. The one I told you we got the notices about?

[*Legend on screen*: "Ha!"]

TOM. Oh—yeah.

AMANDA. You didn't neglect to pay it by any chance?

TOM. Why, I—

AMANDA. Didn't! I might have known it!

JIM. Shakespeare probably wrote a poem on that light bill, Mrs. Wingfield.

AMANDA. I might have known better than to trust him with it! There's such a high price for negligence in this world!

JIM. Maybe the poem will win a ten-dollar prize.

AMANDA. We'll just have to spend the remainder of the evening in the nineteenth century, before Mr. Edison made the Mazda lamp!

JIM. Candlelight is my favorite kind of light.

AMANDA. That shows you're romantic! But that's no excuse for Tom. Well, we got through dinner. Very considerate of them to let us get through dinner before they plunged us into everlasting darkness, wasn't it, Mr. O'Connor?

JIM. Ha-ha!

AMANDA. Tom, as a penalty for your carelessness you can help me with the dishes.

JIM. Let me give you a hand.

AMANDA. Indeed you will not!

JIM. I ought to be good for something.

AMANDA. Good for something? [*Her tone is rhapsodic.*] You? Why, Mr. O'Connor, nobody, *nobody's* given me this much entertainment in years—as you have!

JIM. Aw, now, Mrs. Wingfield!

AMANDA. I'm not exaggerating, not one bit! But Sister is all by her lonesome. You go keep her company in the parlor! I'll give you this lovely old candelabrum that used to be on the altar at the Church of the Heavenly Rest. It was melted a little out of shape when the church burnt down. Lightning struck it one spring. Gypsy Jones was holding a revival at the time and he intimated that the church was destroyed because the Episcopalians gave card parties.

JIM. Ha-ha.

AMANDA. And how about you coaxing Sister to drink a little wine? I think it would be good for her! Can you carry both at once?

JIM. Sure. I'm Superman!

AMANDA. Now, Thomas, get into this apron!

[*Jim comes into the dining room, carrying the candelabrum, its candles lighted, in one hand and a glass of wine in the other. The door of the kitchenette swings closed on Amanda's gay laughter; the flickering light approaches the portieres. Laura sits up nervously as Jim enters. She can hardly speak from the almost intolerable strain of being alone with a stranger.*]

[*Screen legend:* "I don't suppose you remember me at all!"]

[*At first, before Jim's warmth overcomes her paralyzing shyness, Laura's voice is thin and breathless, as though she had just run up a steep flight of stairs. Jim's attitude is gently humorous. While the incident is apparently unimportant, it is to Laura the climax of her secret life.*]

JIM. Hello there, Laura.

LAURA. [*Faintly.*] Hello.

[*She clears her throat.*]

JIM. How are you feeling now? Better?

LAURA. Yes. Yes, thank you.

JIM. This is for you. A little dandelion wine. [*He extends the glass toward her with extravagant gallantry.*]

LAURA. Thank you.

JIM. Drink it—but don't get drunk!

[*He laughs heartily. Laura takes the glass uncertainly; she laughs shyly.*]

Where shall I set the candles?

LAURA. Oh—oh, anywhere . . .

JIM. How about here on the floor? Any objections?

LAURA. No.

JIM. I'll spread a newspaper under to catch the drippings. I like to sit on the floor. Mind if I do?

LAURA. Oh, no.

JIM. Give me a pillow?

LAURA. What?

JIM. A pillow!

LAURA. Oh . . . [*She hands him one quickly.*]

JIM. How about you? Don't you like to sit on the floor?

LAURA. Oh—yes.

JIM. Why don't you, then?

LAURA. I—will.

JIM. Take a pillow!

[*Laura does. She sits on the floor on the other side of the candelabrum. Jim crosses his legs and smiles engagingly at her.*] I can't hardly see you sitting way over there.

LAURA. I can—see you.

JIM. I know, but that's not fair, I'm in the limelight.

[*Laura moves her pillow closer.*]

Good! Now I can see you! Comfortable?

LAURA. Yes.

JIM. So am I. Comfortable as a cow! Will you have some gum?

LAURA. No, thank you.

JIM. I think that I will indulge, with your permission. [*He musingly unwraps a stick of gum and holds it up.*] Think of the fortune made by the guy that invented the first piece of chewing gum. Amazing, huh? The Wrigley Building is one of the sights of Chicago—I saw it when I went up to the Century of Progress. Did you take in the Century of Progress?

LAURA. No, I didn't.

JIM. Well, it was quite a wonderful exposition. What impressed me most was the Hall of Science. Gives you an idea of what the future will be in America, even more wonderful than the present time is! [*There is a pause. Jim smiles at her.*] Your brother tells me you're shy. Is that right, Laura?

LAURA. I—don't know.

JIM. I judge you to be an old-fashioned type of girl. Well, I think that's a pretty good type to be. Hope you don't think I'm being too personal—do you?

LAURA. [*Hastily, out of embarrassment.*] I believe I *will* take a piece of gum, if you—don't mind. [*Clearing her throat.*] Mr. O'Connor, have you—kept up with your singing?

JIM. Singing? Me?

LAURA. Yes. I remember what a beautiful voice you had.

JIM. When did you hear me sing?

[*Laura does not answer, and in the long pause which follows a man's voice is heard singing offstage.*]

VOICE:

O blow, ye winds, heigh-ho,
A-roving I will go!
I'm off to my love
With a boxing glove—
Ten thousand miles away!

JIM. You say you've heard me sing?

LAURA. Oh, yes! Yes, very often . . . I—don't suppose—you remember me—at all?

JIM. [*Smiling doubtfully.*] You know I have an idea I've seen you before. I had that idea soon as you opened the door. It seemed almost like I was about to remember your name. But the name that I started to call you—wasn't a name! And so I stopped myself before I said it.

LAURA. Wasn't it—Blue Roses?

JIM. [*Springing up, grinning.*] Blue Roses! My gosh, yes—Blue Roses! That's what I had on my tongue when you opened the door! Isn't it funny what tricks your memory plays? I didn't connect you with high school somehow or other. But that's where it was; it was high school. I didn't even know you were Shakespeare's sister! Gosh, I'm sorry.

LAURA. I didn't expect you to. You—barely knew me!

JIM. But we did have a speaking acquaintance, huh?

LAURA. Yes, we—spoke to each other.

JIM. When did you recognize me?

LAURA. Oh, right away!

JIM. Soon as I came in the door?

LAURA. When I heard your name I thought it was probably you. I knew that Tom used to know you a little in high school. So when you came in the door—well, then I was—sure.

JIM. Why didn't you *say* something, then?

LAURA. [*Breathlessly.*] I didn't know what to say, I was—too surprised!

JIM. For goodness' sakes! You know, this sure is funny!

LAURA. Yes! Yes, isn't it, though . . .

JIM. Didn't we have a class in something together?

LAURA. Yes, we did.

JIM. What class was that?

LAURA. It was—singing—chorus!

JIM. Aw!

LAURA. I sat across the aisle from you in the Aud.

JIM. Aw.

LAURA. Mondays, Wednesdays, and Fridays.

JIM. Now I remember—you always came in late.

LAURA. Yes, it was so hard for me, getting upstairs. I had that brace on my leg—it clumped so loud!

JIM. I never heard any clumping.

LAURA. [*Wincing at the recollection.*] To me it sounded like—thunder!

JIM. Well, well, well, I never even noticed.

LAURA. And everybody was seated before I came in. I had to walk in front of all those people. My seat was in the back row. I had to go clumping all the way up the aisle with everyone watching!

JIM. You shouldn't have been self-conscious.

LAURA. I know, but I was. It was always such a relief when the singing started.

JIM. Aw, yes, I've placed you now! I used to call you Blue Roses. How was it that I got started calling you that?

LAURA. I was out of school a little while with pleurosis. When I came back you asked me what was the matter. I said I had pleurosis—you thought I said *Blue Roses*. That's what you always called me after that!

JIM. I hope you didn't mind.

LAURA. Oh, no—I liked it. You see, I wasn't acquainted with many—people. . . .

JIM. As I remember you sort of stuck by yourself.

LAURA. I—I—never have had much luck at—making friends.

JIM. I don't see why you wouldn't.

LAURA. Well, I—started out badly.

JIM. You mean being—

LAURA. Yes, it sort of—stood between me—

JIM. You shouldn't have let it!

LAURA. I know, but it did, and—

JIM. You were shy with people!

LAURA. I tried not to be but never could—

JIM. Overcome it?

LAURA. No, I—I never could!

JIM. I guess being shy is something you have to work out of kind of gradually.

LAURA. [*Sorrowfully.*] Yes—I guess it—

JIM. Takes time!

LAURA. Yes—

JIM. People are not so dreadful when you know them. That's what you have to remember! And everybody has problems, not just you, but practically everybody has got some problems. You think of yourself as having the only problems, as being the only one who is disappointed. But just look around you and you will see lots of people as disappointed as you are. For instance, I hoped when I was going to high school that I would be further along at this time, six years later, than I am now. You remember that wonderful write-up I had in *The Torch?*

LAURA. Yes! [*She rises and crosses to the table.*]

JIM. It said I was bound to succeed in anything I went into!

[*Laura returns with the high school yearbook.*]

Holy Jeez! *The Torch!*

[*He accepts it reverently. They smile across the book with mutual wonder. Laura crouches beside him and they begin to turn the pages. Laura's shyness is dissolving in his warmth.*]

LAURA. Here you are in *The Pirates of Penzance!*

JIM. [*Wistfully.*] I sang the baritone lead in that operetta.

LAURA. [*Raptly.*] So—*beautifully!*

JIM. [*Protesting.*] Aw—

LAURA. Yes, yes—beautifully—beautifully!

JIM. You heard me?

LAURA. All three times!

JIM. No!

LAURA. Yes!

JIM. All three performances?

LAURA. [*Looking down.*] Yes.

JIM. Why?

LAURA. I—wanted to ask you to—autograph my program. [*She takes the program from the back of the yearbook and shows it to him.*]

JIM. Why didn't you ask me to?

LAURA. You were always surrounded by your own friends so much that I never had a chance to.

JIM. You should have just—

LAURA. Well, I—thought you might think I was—

JIM. Thought I might think you was—what?

LAURA. Oh—

JIM. [*With reflective relish.*] I was beleaguered by females in those days.

LAURA. You were terribly popular!

JIM. Yeah—

LAURA. You had such a—friendly way—

JIM. I was spoiled in high school.

LAURA. Everybody—liked you!

JIM. Including you?

LAURA. I—yes, I—did, too— [*She gently closes the book in her lap.*]

JIM. Well, well, well! Give me that program, Laura.

[*She hands it to him. He signs it with a flourish.*]
There you are—better late than never!

LAURA. Oh, I—what a—surprise!

JIM. My signature isn't worth very much right now. But some day—maybe—it will increase in value! Being disappointed is one thing and being discouraged is something else. I am disappointed but I am not discouraged. I'm twenty-three years old. How old are you?

LAURA. I'll be twenty-four in June.

JIM. That's not old age!

LAURA. No, but—

JIM. You finished high school?

LAURA. [*With difficulty.*] I didn't go back.

JIM. You mean you dropped out?

LAURA. I made bad grades in my final examinations. [*She rises and replaces the book and the program on the table. Her voice is strained.*] How is—Emily Meisenbach getting along?

JIM. Oh, that kraut-head!

LAURA. Why do you call her that?

JIM. That's what she was.

LAURA. You're not still—going with her?

JIM. I never see her.

LAURA. It said in the "Personal" section that you were—engaged!

JIM. I know, but I wasn't impressed by that—propaganda!

LAURA. It wasn't—the truth?

JIM. Only in Emily's optimistic opinion!

LAURA. Oh—

[*Legend:* "What have you done since high school?"]

[*Jim lights a cigarette and leans indolently back on his elbows smiling at Laura with a warmth and charm which lights her inwardly with altar candles. She remains by the table, picks up a piece from the glass menagerie collection, and turns it in her hands to cover her tumult.*]

JIM. [*After several reflective puffs on his cigarette.*] What have you done since high school?

[*She seems not to hear him.*]
Huh?

[*Laura looks up.*]
I said what have you done since high school, Laura?

LAURA. Nothing much.

JIM. You must have been doing something these six long years.

LAURA. Yes.

JIM. Well, then, such as what?

LAURA. I took a business course at business college—

JIM. How did that work out?

LAURA. Well, not very—well—I had to drop out, it gave me—indigestion—

[*Jim laughs gently.*]

JIM. What are you doing now?

LAURA. I don't do anything—much. Oh, please don't think I sit around doing nothing! My glass collection takes up a good deal of time. Glass is something you have to take good care of.

JIM. What did you say—about glass?

LAURA. Collection I said—I have one— [*She clears her throat and turns away again, acutely shy.*]

JIM. [*Abruptly.*] You know what I judge to be the trouble with you? Inferiority complex! Know what that is? That's what they call it when someone low-rates himself! I understand it because I had it, too. Although my case was not so aggravated as yours seems to be. I had it until I took up public speaking, developed my voice, and learned that I had an aptitude for science. Before that time I never thought of myself as being outstanding in any way whatsoever! Now I've never made a regular study of it, but I have a friend who says I can analyze people better than doctors that make a profession of it. I don't claim that to be necessarily true, but I can sure guess a person's psychology, Laura! [*He takes out his gum.*] Excuse me, Laura. I always take it out when the flavor is gone. I'll use this scrap of paper to wrap it in. I know how it is to get it stuck on a shoe. [*He wraps the gum in paper and puts it in his pocket.*] Yep—that's what I judge to be your principal trouble. A lack of confidence in yourself as a person. You don't have the proper amount of faith in yourself. I'm basing that fact on a number of your remarks and also on certain observations I've made. For instance that clumping you thought was so awful in high school. You say that you even dreaded to walk into class. You see what you did? You dropped out of school, you gave up an education because of a clump, which as far as I know was practically non-existent! A little physical defect is what you have. Hardly noticeable even! Magnified thousands of times by imagination! You know what my strong advice to you is? Think of yourself as *superior* in some way!

LAURA. In what way would I think?

JIM. Why, man alive, Laura! Just look about you a little. What do you see? A world full of common people! All of 'em born and all of 'em going to die! Which of them has one-tenth of your good points! Or mine! Or anyone else's, as far as that goes—gosh! Everybody excels in some one thing. Some in many! [*He unconsciously glances at himself in the mirror.*] All you've got to do is discover in what! Take me, for instance. [*He adjusts his tie at the mirror.*] My interest happens to lie in electro-dynamics. I'm taking a course in radio engineering at night school, Laura, on top of a fairly responsible job at the warehouse. I'm taking that course and studying public speaking.

LAURA. Ohhhh.

JIM. Because I believe in the future of television! [*Turning his back to her.*] I wish to be ready to go up right along with it. Therefore I'm planning to get in on the ground floor. In fact I've already made the right connections and all that remains is for the industry itself to get under way! Full steam— [*His eyes are starry.*] Knowledge—Zzzzzp! Money—Zzzzzzp!—Power! That's the cycle democracy is built on!

[*His attitude is convincingly dynamic. Laura stares at him, even her shyness eclipsed in her absolute wonder. He suddenly grins.*]
I guess you think I think a lot of myself!

LAURA. No—o-o-o, I—

JIM. Now how about you? Isn't there something you take more interest in than anything else?

LAURA. Well, I do—as I said—have my—glass collection—

[*A peal of girlish laughter rings from the kitchenette.*]

JIM. I'm not right sure I know what you're talking about. What kind of glass is it?

LAURA. Little articles of it, they're ornaments mostly! Most of them are little animals made out of glass, the tiniest little animals in the world. Mother calls them a glass menagerie! Here's an example of one, if you'd like to see it! This one is one of the oldest. It's nearly thirteen.

[*Music*: "The Glass Menagerie."]
[*He stretches out his hand.*]
Oh, be careful—if you breathe, it breaks!

JIM. I'd better not take it. I'm pretty clumsy with things.

LAURA. Go on, I trust you with him! [*She places the piece in his palm.*] There now—you're holding him gently! Hold him over the light, he loves the light! You see how the light shines through him?

JIM. It sure does shine!

LAURA. I shouldn't be partial, but he is my favorite one.

JIM. What kind of a thing is this one supposed to be?

LAURA. Haven't you noticed the single horn on his forehead?

JIM. A unicorn, huh?

LAURA. Mmmm-hmmm!

JIM. Unicorns—aren't they extinct in the modern world?

LAURA. I know!

JIM. Poor little fellow, he must feel sort of lonesome.

LAURA. [*Smiling.*] Well, if he does, he doesn't complain about it. He stays on a shelf with some horses that don't have horns and all of them seem to get along nicely together.

JIM. How do you know?

LAURA. [*Lightly.*] I haven't heard any arguments among them!

JIM. [*Grinning.*] No arguments, huh? Well, that's a pretty good sign! Where shall I set him?

LAURA. Put him on the table. They all like a change of scenery once in a while!

JIM. Well, well, well, well— [*He places the glass piece on the table, then raises his arms and stretches.*] Look how big my shadow is when I stretch!

LAURA. Oh, oh, yes—it stretches across the ceiling!

JIM. [*Crossing to the door.*] I think it's stopped raining. [*He opens the fire-escape door and the background music changes to a dance tune.*] Where does the music come from?

LAURA. From the Paradise Dance Hall across the alley.

JIM. How about cutting the rug a little, Miss Wingfield?

LAURA. Oh, I—

JIM. Or is your program filled up? Let me have a look at it. [*He grasps an imaginary card.*] Why, every dance is taken! I'll just have to scratch some out.

[*Waltz music*: "La Golondrina."]

Ahhh, a waltz! [*He executes some sweeping turns by himself, then holds his arms toward Laura.*]

LAURA. [*Breathlessly.*] I—can't dance!

JIM. There you go, that inferiority stuff!

LAURA. I've never danced in my life!

JIM. Come on, try!

LAURA. Oh, but I'd step on you!

JIM. I'm not made out of glass.

LAURA. How—how—how do we start?

JIM. Just leave it to me. You hold your arms out a little.

LAURA. Like this?

JIM. [*Taking her in his arms.*] A little bit higher. Right. Now don't tighten up, that's the main thing about it—relax.

LAURA. [*Laughing breathlessly.*] It's hard not to.

JIM. Okay.

LAURA. I'm afraid you can't budge me.

JIM. What do you bet I can't? [*He swings her into motion.*]

LAURA. Goodness, yes, you can!

JIM. Let yourself go, now, Laura, just let yourself go.

LAURA. I'm—

JIM. Come on!

LAURA. —trying!

JIM. Not so stiff—easy does it!

LAURA. I know but I'm—

JIM. Loosen th' backbone! There now, that's a lot better.

LAURA. Am I?

JIM. Lots, lots better! [*He moves her about the room in a clumsy waltz.*]

LAURA. Oh, my!

JIM. Ha-ha!

LAURA. Oh, my goodness!

JIM. Ha-ha-ha!

[*They suddenly bump into the table, and the glass piece on it falls to the floor. Jim stops the dance.*]

What did we hit on?

LAURA. Table.

JIM. Did something fall off it? I think—

LAURA. Yes.

JIM. I hope that it wasn't the little glass horse with the horn!

LAURA. Yes. [*She stoops to pick it up.*]

JIM. Aw, aw, aw. Is it broken?

LAURA. Now it is just like all the other horses.

JIM. It's lost its—

LAURA. Horn! It doesn't matter. Maybe it's a blessing in disguise.

JIM. You'll never forgive me. I bet that that was your favorite piece of glass.

LAURA. I don't have favorites much. It's no tragedy, Freckles. Glass breaks so easily. No matter how careful you are. The traffic jars the shelves and things fall off them.

JIM. Still I'm awfully sorry that I was the cause.

LAURA. [*Smiling.*] I'll just imagine he had an operation. The horn was removed to make him feel less—freakish!

[*They both laugh.*]

Now he will feel more at home with the other horses, the ones that don't have horns. . . .

JIM. Ha-ha, that's very funny! [*Suddenly he is serious.*] I'm glad to see that you have a sense of humor. You know—you're—well— very different! Surprisingly different from anyone else I know! [*His voice becomes soft and hesitant with a genuine feeling.*] Do you mind me telling you that?

[*Laura is abashed beyond speech.*]

I mean it in a nice way—

[*Laura nods shyly, looking away.*]

You make me feel sort of—I don't know how to put it! I'm usually pretty good at expressing things, but—this is something that I don't know how to say!

[*Laura touches her throat and clears it—turns the broken unicorn in her hands. His voice becomes softer.*]

Has anyone ever told you that you were pretty?

[*There is a pause, and the music rises slightly. Laura looks up slowly, with wonder, and shakes her head.*]

Well, you are! In a very different way from anyone else. And all the nicer because of the difference, too.

[*His voice becomes low and husky. Laura turns away, nearly faint with the novelty of her emotions.*]

I wish that you were my sister. I'd teach you to have some confidence in yourself. The different people are not like other people, but being different is nothing to be ashamed of. Because other people are not such wonderful people. They're one hundred times one thousand. You're one times one! They walk all over the earth. You just stay here. They're common as—weeds, but—you—well, you're—*Blue Roses!*

[*Image on screen*: Blue Roses.]

[*The music changes.*]

LAURA. But blue is wrong for—roses. . . .

JIM. It's right for you! You're—pretty!

LAURA. In what respect am I pretty?

JIM. In all respects—believe me! Your eyes—your hair—are pretty! Your hands are pretty! [*He catches hold of her hand.*] You think I'm making this up because I'm invited to dinner and have to be nice. Oh, I could do that! I could put on an act for you, Laura, and say lots of things without being very sincere. But this time I am. I'm talking to you sincerely. I happened to notice you had this inferiority complex that keeps you from feeling comfortable with people. Somebody needs to build your confidence up and make you proud instead of shy and turning away and—blushing. Somebody—ought to—*kiss* you, Laura!

[*His hand slips slowly up her arm to her shoulder as the music swells tumultuously. He suddenly turns her about and kisses her on the lips. When he releases her, Laura sinks on the sofa with a bright, dazed look. Jim backs away and fishes in his pocket for a cigarette.*]

[*Legend on screen*: "A souvenir."]

Stumblejohn!

[*He lights the cigarette, avoiding her look. There is a peal of girlish laughter from Amanda in the kitchenette. Laura slowly raises and opens her hand. It still contains the little broken glass animal. She looks at it with a tender, bewildered expression.*]

Stumblejohn! I shouldn't have done that—that was way off the beam. You don't smoke, do you?

[*She looks up, smiling, not hearing the question. He sits beside her rather gingerly. She looks at him speechlessly—waiting. He coughs decorously and moves a little farther aside as he considers the situation and senses her feelings, dimly, with perturbation. He speaks gently.*]

Would you—care for a—mint?

[*She doesn't seem to hear him but her look grows brighter even.*]

Peppermint? Life Saver? My pocket's a regular drugstore—wherever I go. . . . [*He pops a mint in his mouth. Then he gulps and decides to make a clean breast of it. He speaks slowly and gingerly.*] Laura, you know, if I had a sister like you, I'd do the same thing as Tom. I'd bring out fellows and—introduce her to them. The right type of boys—of a type to—appreciate her. Only —well—he made a mistake about me. Maybe I've got no call to be saying this. That may not have been the idea in having me over. But what if it was? There's nothing wrong about that. The only trouble is that in my case—I'm not in a situation to—do the right thing. I can't take down your number and say I'll phone. I can't call up next week and—ask for a date. I thought I had better explain the situation in case you—misunderstood it and—I hurt your feelings. . . .

[*There is a pause. Slowly, very slowly, Laura's look changes, her eyes returning slowly from his to the glass figure in her palm. Amanda utters another gay laugh in the kitchenette.*]

LAURA. [*Faintly.*] You—won't—call again?

JIM. No, Laura, I can't. [*He rises from the sofa.*] As I was just explaining, I've—got strings on me. Laura, I've—been going steady! I go out all the time with a girl named Betty. She's a home-girl like you, and Catholic, and Irish, and in a great many ways we— get along fine. I met her last summer on a moonlight boat trip up the river to Alton, on the *Majestic.* Well—right away from the start it was—love!

[*Legend: Love!*]

[*Laura sways slightly forward and grips the arm of the sofa. He fails to notice, now enrapt in his own comfortable being.*]

Being in love has made a new man of me!

[*Leaning stiffly forward, clutching the arm of the sofa, Laura struggles visibly with her storm. But Jim is oblivious; she is a long way off.*]

The power of love is really pretty tremendous! Love is something that—changes the whole world, Laura!

[*The storm abates a little and Laura leans back. He notices her again.*]

It happened that Betty's aunt took sick, she got a wire and had to go to Centralia. So Tom—when he asked me to dinner—I naturally just accepted the invitation, not knowing that you—that he—that I— [*He stops awkwardly.*] Huh—I'm a stumblejohn!

[*He flops back on the sofa. The holy candles on the altar of Laura's face have been snuffed out. There is a look of almost infinite desolation. Jim glances at her uneasily.*]

I wish that you would—say something.

[*She bites her lip which was trembling and then bravely smiles. She opens her hand again on the broken glass figure. Then she gently takes his hand and raises it level with her own. She carefully places the unicorn in the palm of his hand, then pushes his fingers closed upon it.*]

What are you—doing that for? You want me to have him? Laura?

[*She nods.*]

What for?

LAURA. A—souvenir. . . .

[*She rises unsteadily and crouches beside the Victrola to wind it up.*]

[*Legend on screen:* "Things have a way of turning out so badly!" *Or image:* "Gentleman caller waving goodbye—gaily."]

[*At this moment Amanda rushes brightly back into the living room. She bears a pitcher of fruit punch in an old-fashioned cut-glass pitcher, and a plate of macaroons. The plate has a gold border and poppies painted on it.*]

AMANDA. Well, well, well! Isn't the air delightful after the shower? I've made you children a little liquid refreshment.

[*She turns gaily to Jim.*] Jim, do you know that song about lemonade?

"Lemonade, lemonade
Made in the shade and stirred with a spade—
Good enough for any old maid!"

JIM. [*Uneasily.*] Ha-ha! No—I never heard it.

AMANDA. Why, Laura! You look so serious!

JIM. We were having a serious conversation.

AMANDA. Good! Now you're better acquainted!

JIM. [*Uncertainly.*] Ha-ha! Yes.

AMANDA. You modern young people are much more serious-minded than my generation. I was so gay as a girl!

JIM. You haven't changed, Mrs. Wingfield.

AMANDA. Tonight I'm rejuvenated! The gaiety of the occasion, Mr. O'Connor! [*She tosses her head with a peal of laughter, spilling some lemonade.*] Oooo! I'm baptizing myself!

JIM. Here—let me—

AMANDA. [*Setting the pitcher down.*] There now. I discovered we had some maraschino cherries. I dumped them in, juice and all!

JIM. You shouldn't have gone to that trouble, Mrs. Wingfield.

AMANDA. Trouble, trouble? Why it was loads of fun! Didn't you hear me cutting up in the kitchen? I bet your ears were burning! I told Tom how outdone with him I was for keeping you to himself so long a time! He should have brought you over much, much sooner! Well, now that you've found your way, I want you to be a very frequent caller! Not just occasional but all the time. Oh, we're going to have a lot of gay times together! I see them coming! Mmm, just breathe that air! So fresh, and the moon's so pretty! I'll skip back out—I know where my place is when young folks are having a—serious conversation!

JIM. Oh, don't go out, Mrs. Wingfield. The fact of the matter is I've got to be going.

AMANDA. Going, now? You're joking! Why, it's only the shank of the evening, Mr. O'Connor!

JIM. Well, you know how it is.

AMANDA. You mean you're a young workingman and have to keep workingmen's hours. We'll let you off early tonight. But only on the condition that next time you stay later. What's the best night for you? Isn't Saturday night the best night for you workingmen?

JIM. I have a couple of time-clocks to punch, Mrs. Wingfield. One at morning, another one at night!

AMANDA. My, but you *are* ambitious! You work at night, too?

JIM. No, Ma'am, not work but—Betty!

[*He crosses deliberately to pick up his hat. The band at the Paradise Dance Hall goes into a tender waltz.*]

AMANDA. Betty? Betty? Who's—Betty!

[*There is an ominous cracking sound in the sky.*]

JIM. Oh, just a girl. The girl I go steady with!

[*He smiles charmingly. The sky falls.*]

[*Legend:* "The Sky Falls."]

AMANDA. [*A long-drawn exhalation.*] Ohhhh . . . Is it a serious romance, Mr. O'Connor?

JIM. We're going to be married the second Sunday in June.

AMANDA. Ohhhh—how nice! Tom didn't mention that you were engaged to be married.

JIM. The cat's not out of the bag at the warehouse yet. You know how they are. They call you Romeo and stuff like that. [*He stops at the oval mirror to put on his hat. He carefully shapes the brim and the crown to give a discreetly dashing effect.*] It's been a wonderful evening, Mrs. Wingfield. I guess this is what they mean by Southern hospitality.

AMANDA. It really wasn't anything at all.

JIM. I hope it don't seem like I'm rushing off. But I promised Betty I'd pick her up at the Wabash depot, an' by the time I get my jalopy down there her train'll be in. Some women are pretty upset if you keep 'em waiting.

AMANDA. Yes, I know—the tyranny of women! [*She extends her hand.*] Goodbye, Mr. O'Connor. I wish you luck—and happiness

—and success! All three of them, and so does Laura! Don't you, Laura?

LAURA. Yes!

JIM. [*Taking Laura's hand.*] Goodbye, Laura. I'm certainly going to treasure that souvenir. And don't you forget the good advice I gave you. [*He raises his voice to a cheery shout.*] So long, Shakespeare! Thanks again, ladies. Good night!

[*He grins and ducks jauntily out. Still bravely grimacing, Amanda closes the door on the gentleman caller. Then she turns back to the room with a puzzled expression. She and Laura don't dare to face each other. Laura crouches beside the Victrola to wind it.*]

AMANDA. [*Faintly.*] Things have a way of turning out so badly. I don't believe that I would play the Victrola. Well, well—well! Our gentleman caller was engaged to be married! [*She raises her voice.*] Tom!

TOM. [*From the kitchenette.*] Yes, Mother?

AMANDA. Come in here a minute. I want to tell you something awfully funny.

TOM. [*Entering with a macaroon and a glass of the lemonade.*] Has the gentleman caller gotten away already?

AMANDA. The gentleman caller has made an early departure. What a wonderful joke you played on us!

TOM. How do you mean?

AMANDA. You didn't mention that he was engaged to be married.

TOM. Jim? Engaged?

AMANDA. That's what he just informed us.

TOM. I'll be jiggered! I didn't know about that.

AMANDA. That seems very peculiar.

TOM. What's peculiar about it?

AMANDA. Didn't you call him your best friend down at the warehouse?

TOM. He is, but how did I know?

AMANDA. It seems extremely peculiar that you wouldn't know your best friend was going to be married!

TOM. The warehouse is where I work, not where I know things about people!

AMANDA. You don't know things anywhere! You live in a dream; you manufacture illusions!

[*He crosses to the door.*]

Where are you going?

TOM. I'm going to the movies.

AMANDA. That's right, now that you've had us make such fools of ourselves. The effort, the preparations, all the expense! The new

floor lamp, the rug, the clothes for Laura! All for what? To entertain some other girl's fiancé! Go to the movies, go! Don't think
about us, a mother deserted, an unmarried sister who's crippled
and has no job! Don't let anything interfere with your selfish
pleasure! Just go, go, go—to the movies!

TOM. All right, I will! The more you shout about my selfishness
to me the quicker I'll go, and I won't go to the movies!

AMANDA. Go, then! Go to the moon—you selfish dreamer!

[*Tom smashes his glass on the floor. He plunges out on the fire
escape, slamming the door. Laura screams in fright. The dance-
hall music becomes louder. Tom stands on the fire escape, grip-
ping the rail. The moon breaks through the storm clouds,
illuminating his face.*]

[*Legend on screen: "And so goodbye . . ."*]

[*Tom's closing speech is timed with what is happening inside
the house. We see, as though through soundproof glass, that
Amanda appears to be making a comforting speech to Laura,
who is huddled upon the sofa. Now that we cannot hear the
mother's speech, her silliness is gone and she has dignity and
tragic beauty. Laura's hair hides her face until, at the end of the
speech, she lifts her head to smile at her mother. Amanda's
gestures are slow and graceful, almost dancelike, as she comforts
her daughter. At the end of her speech she glances a moment
at the father's picture—then withdraws through the portieres.
At the close of Tom's speech, Laura blows out the candles, ending the play.*]

TOM. I didn't go to the moon, I went much further—for time
is the longest distance between two places. Not long after that I
was fired for writing a poem on the lid of a shoe-box. I left Saint
Louis. I descended the steps of this fire escape for a last time and
followed, from then on, in my father's footsteps, attempting to
find in motion what was lost in space. I traveled around a great
deal. The cities swept about me like dead leaves, leaves that were
brightly colored but torn away from the branches. I would have
stopped, but I was pursued by something. It always came upon
me unawares, taking me altogether by surprise. Perhaps it was a
familiar bit of music. Perhaps it was only a piece of transparent
glass. Perhaps I am walking along a street at night, in some strange
city, before I have found companions. I pass the lighted window
of a shop where perfume is sold. The window is filled with pieces
of colored glass, tiny transparent bottles in delicate colors, like bits
of a shattered rainbow. Then all at once my sister touches my
shoulder. I turn around and look into her eyes. Oh, Laura, Laura,
I tried to leave you behind me, but I am more faithful than I intended to be! I reach for a cigarette, I cross the street, I run into

the movies or a bar, I buy a drink, I speak to the nearest stranger
—anything that can blow your candles out!

[*Laura bends over the candles.*]

For nowadays the world is lit by lightning! Blow out your
candles, Laura—and so goodbye. . . .

[*She blows the candles out.*]

1945

Poets at Mid-Century

RICHARD EBERHART

(1904–   )

Early poems by Eberhart appeared while he was a student at Cambridge University, England, in an English anthology called *New Signatures* (1932). This "represented a new concept of poetry," whose practitioners included William Empson, C. Day Lewis, W. H. Auden, and Stephen Spender. These poets held in common a determination to enrich the language and style of poetry for the expression of their age.

Eberhart makes demands upon the reader which are unusual, but consistent with a "world too much in joint," in which only a "hard intellectual light" can restore "the moral grandeur of man." Even his simpler poems depend for their effect upon some striking extension of experience or idea, accomplished by verbal or metaphoric tension. "For a Lamb," an apparently simple lyric, is intensified by sudden violence in line 4 and complicated by the concluding enigma. William Blake may be recalled by the subject and the blending of "innocence" and "experience" in "For a Lamb"; "When Doris Danced," touched

with sensuousness and primitive wonder, may suggest both Hopkins and the Pre-Raphaelites; the metaphysical infusion in language and image evident in "Rumination" is not unlike the poetry of John Donne. But these comparisons only tend to establish the direction of Eberhart's originality, for his style is independent and his individualism is a measure of his strength.

Born in Austin, Minnesota, in 1904, Eberhart completed the baccalaureate at Dartmouth in 1926, and the M.A. at Cambridge University in 1933. From 1933 to 1942 he taught English at two private preparatory schools in Massachusetts. He served in the U.S. Navy (1942–1946) retiring with the rank of commander to enter a manufacturing business, of which he became vice-president in 1952. Since 1958 he has continued his business interests as member of the board of this and another industrial corporation.

Meanwhile his poems appeared in a variety of magazines, and in numerous volumes over a period of four decades. In

1952 he returned to academic life as professor and poet in residence at the University of Washington, then successively at Connecticut, Wheaton, Massachusetts, and Princeton. Since 1956 he has been professor of English at Dartmouth, becoming professor emeritus in 1970.

Eberhart's volumes of poetry are: *A Bravery of Earth*, 1930; *Reading The Spirit*, 1936, 1937; *Song and Idea*, 1940, 1942; *Poems, New and Selected*, 1944; *Burr Oaks*, 1947; *Brotherhood of Men*, 1949; *An Herb Basket*, 1950; *Selected Poems*, 1951; *The Visionary Farms* (drama), 1952; *Undercliff: Poems, 1946–1953*, 1953; *Great Praises*, 1957; *Collected Poems: 1930–1960*, 1960; *Collected Verse Plays*, 1962; *The Quarry*, 1964; *Selected Poems: Nineteen Thirty—Nineteen Sixty-Five*, 1966; *Thirty-One Sonnets*, 1967; and *Shifts of Being*, 1968. Full-length studies are Bernard F. Engel, *Richard Eberhart*, 1971; and Joel H. Roache, *Richard Eberhart: The Progress of an American Poet*, 1971.

For a Lamb [1]

I saw on the slant hill a putrid lamb,
Propped with daisies. The sleep looked deep,
The face nudged in the green pillow
But the guts were out for crows to eat.

Where's the lamb? whose tender plaint   5
Said all for the mute breezes.
Say he's in the wind somewhere,
Say, there's a lamb in the daisies.

1936, 1951

Rumination [2]

When I can hold a stone within my hand
And feel time make it sand and soil, and see
The roots of living things grow in this land,
Pushing between my fingers flower and tree,
Then I shall be as wise as death,   5
For death has done this and he will
Do this to me, and blow his breath
To fire my clay, when I am still.

1947, 1951

"I Walked over the Grave of Henry James" [3]

I walked over the grave of Henry James
But recently, and one eye kept the dry stone.
The other leaned on boys at games away,
My soul was balanced in my body cold.

1. First collected in *Reading The Spirit* (1936); included in *Selected Poems* (1951).
2. First collected in *Burr Oaks* (1947); included in *Selected Poems* (1951).
3. First collected in *Burr Oaks* (1947); included in *Selected Poems* (1951).

I am one of those prodigals of hell   5
Whom ten years have seen cram with battle;
Returns to what he canted from, grants it good,
As asthma makes itself a new resolution.

I crushed a knob of earth between my fingers,
This is a very ordinary experience.   10
A name may be glorious but death is death,
I thought, and took a street-car back to Harvard Square.

1947, 1951

"When Doris Danced" [4]

When Doris danced under the oak tree
The sun himself might wish to see,
Might bend beneath those lovers, leaves,
While her her virgin step she weaves
And envious cast his famous hue   5
To make her daft, yet win her too.

When Doris danced under the oak tree
Slow John, so stormed in heart, at sea
Gone all his store, a wreck he lay.
But on the ground the sun-beams play.   10
They lit his face in such degree
Doris lay down, all out of pity.

1951

"Go to the Shine That's on a Tree" [5]

Go to the shine that's on a tree
When dawn has laved with liquid light
With luminous light the nighted tree
And take that glory without fright.

Go to the song that's in a bird   5
When he has seen the glistening tree,
That glorious tree the bird has heard
Give praise for its felicity.

Then go to the earth and touch it keen,
Be tree and bird, be wide aware   10
Be wild aware of light unseen,
And unheard song along the air.

1953

4. From *Selected Poems* (1951).   5. From *Undercliff* (1953).

THEODORE ROETHKE
(1908–1963)

Roethke is distinguished among his most gifted contemporaries in having defined independently his own universe and the language appropriate for his discussion of it. Since the Second World War, American literature, even poetry, has reflected rapid changes in its sense of lost values and in negative moods of defeat, from cynicism to despair. By contrast, Roethke rediscovered the roots of life imbedded eternally in Nature. Finding himself in torturing conflict with the ingrained values of an obsolete culture, he came by painful stages back to the aboriginal sources of being—in the inert rock, in the root of a dahlia, in the flesh of man. Experience of the family greenhouse does not guarantee such discoveries: there were questions to be asked, knowledge to be attained, and some mysterious trauma to be overcome. This was evident in his early poems in which the metaphysical tension expresses itself in metaphoric luxuriance and fractured syntax. His short life was devoted to the constant discipline of his powers and to the increasing clarity and success in this expression.

He was born in 1908 in Saginaw, Michigan, where his father and his uncle had a successful business as florists. He studied locally, took the A.B. (1929) and M.A. (1936) at the University of Michigan, did further work at Harvard, and taught in several colleges—Lafayette, Pennsylvania State, and Bennington—while learning his craft as writer. He was slow at first: his first volume of poems was collected in 1941, his thirty-third year, his second in 1948. In all, eight volumes appeared before his death. He received his first Guggenheim award in 1946, his second in 1950; he also won the Pulitzer Prize, Bollingen Award, and the National Book Award. From 1947 he taught at the University of Washington at Seattle.

"I believe that to go forward as a spiritual man, it is necessary to go back," he wrote to John Ciardi in the "Open Letter" of 1950. And again he said, in retrospect, "some of these pieces * * * begin in the mire, as if man is no more than a shape writhing from the old rock." Of growing up in Michigan he declared, "sometimes one gets the feeling that not even the animals have been there before, but the marsh, the mire, the Void is always there. * * * It is America." His view of existence discards paleontology; all the life on the earth is still continuously present, as Eliot, one of his mentors, discovered of "time." So, in 1951, he wrote, "Once upon a tree / I came across a time / * * * What's the time, papaseed? / Everything has been twice. / My father was a fish." Ideas such as these remind one of Whitman, as does his rhythm, and Roethke gratefully acknowledged the influence. However, his conviction of continuity was strengthened by recent science where Whitman had to depend on an intuition originating, perhaps, in childhood. But this gift Roethke also declared: "approach these poems as a child would, naïvely, with your whole being awake, your faculties loose and alert * * * " Of his rhythms he wrote, as Lowes wrote of Whitman, "Listen to them, for they are written to be heard, with the themes often coming alternately, as in music."

It was all well and good to begin with what Kenneth Burke discerned as his "vegetal radicalism," with what a boy could learn of "being" by standing in the root cellar of the greenhouse listening to the "breathing" of roots stored for the winter. Being is proved, but what is the possibility of "becoming"? Vegetal "torpidity without cognition or coition" is not human enough. "Am I but nothing leaning toward a thing?" Early in his writing Roethke's image of the father represented continuity, the hope of becoming; but then suddenly that father "was all whitey bones." A "lost son" must wonder, ask, reply: "I'm somebody else now / * * * Have I come to always? / Not yet. / * * * Maybe God has a house. / But not here." / Something of this is in "My Papa's Waltz," but the father is also the florist, coming into the hothouse early in the morning like the new light, crying "Ordnung!" ("order"); again the father is the gardener who would "stand all night watering roses, his fat blue in rubber boots."

The evidence that Roethke's death interrupted him in mid-career is to be found in the affirmative spirit, the new amplitude of thought and form, in such late poems as "The Dying Man" and "Meditations of an Old Woman." The most significant development was that these latest poems and some posthumously published have mature faith, beyond the need of proof, the least condition on which this probing poet would have been content to accept death.

The Collected Poems of Theodore Roethke was published in 1966. Individual titles are: *Open House*, 1941; *The Lost Son and Other Poems*, 1948; *Praise to the End*, 1951; *The Waking: Poems, 1933–1953*, 1953; *Words for the Wind: The Collected Verse of Theodore Roethke*, 1958, 1961; *I Am! Says the Lamb*, 1961; *Sequence, Sometimes Metaphysical, Poems*, 1963; *The Far Field*, 1964. A collection of Roethke's critical writings, *On the Poet and His Craft: Selected Prose of Theodore Roethke*, edited by Ralph J. Mills, Jr., 1965, is the source of the self-criticism quoted in the headnote above, but see also John Ciardi, *Mid-Century American Poets*, 1950, in which first appeared the poet's "Open Letter," a remarkably objective self-analysis. *Selected Letters of Theodore Roethke*, 1968, was edited by Ralph J. Mills, Jr. *Straw for the Fire: From the Notebooks of Theodore Roethke*, 1972, was edited by David Wagoner.

A biography is Allan Seager, *The Glass House: The Life of Theodore Roethke*, 1968. Critical studies include a brief survey by Ralph J. Mills, Jr., *Theodore Roethke*, 1963; and Karl Malkoff, *Theodore Roethke: An Introduction to the Poetry*, 1966. A collection of critical commentary is Arnold Stein, ed., *Theodore Roethke: Essays on the Poetry*, 1965. William J. Martz, ed., *The Achievement of Theodore Roethke*, 1966, includes an introduction and a selection of the poetry. Gary Lane edited *A Concordance to the Poems of Theodore Roethke*, 1972.

Open House

My secrets cry aloud.
I have no need for tongue.
My heart keeps open house,
My doors are widely swung.
An epic of the eyes   5
My love, with no disguise.

My truths are all foreknown,
This anguish self-revealed.
I'm naked to the bone,
With nakedness my shield.   10
Myself is what I wear:
I keep the spirit spare.

The anger will endure,
The deed will speak the truth
In language strict and pure.   15
I stop the lying mouth:
Rage warps my clearest cry
To witless agony.

                                        1941, 1958

Cuttings

later [1]

This urge, wrestle, resurrection of dry sticks,
Cut stems struggling to put down feet,
What saint strained so much,
Rose on such lopped limbs to a new life?

I can hear, underground, that sucking and sobbing,   5
In my veins, in my bones I feel it,—
The small waters seeping upward,
The tight grains parting at last.
When sprouts break out,
Slippery as fish,   10
I quail, lean to beginnings, sheath-wet.

                                        1948, 1958

My Papa's Waltz [2]

The whiskey on your breath
Could make a small boy dizzy;

1. The second of two poems entitled
"Cuttings."
2. A zestful reminiscence of youth, not
in itself symbolic, yet Roethke's search
for meaning often invokes the symbolic
father in various guises and "the lost
son" theme.

But I hung on like death:
Such waltzing was not easy.

We romped until the pans   5
Slid from the kitchen shelf;
My mother's countenance
Could not unfrown itself.

The hand that held my wrist
Was battered on one knuckle;   10
At every step you missed
My right ear scraped a buckle.

You beat time on my head
With a palm caked hard by dirt,
Then waltzed me off to bed   15
Still clinging to your shirt.

                                    1948, 1958

Night Crow

When I saw that clumsy crow
Flap from a wasted tree,
A shape in the mind rose up:
Over the gulfs of dream
Flew a tremendous bird   5
Further and further away
Into a moonless black,
Deep in the brain, far back.

                                    1948, 1958

Elegy for Jane

My Student, Thrown by a Horse

I remember the neckcurls, limp and damp as tendrils;
And her quick look, a sidelong pickerel [3] smile;
And how, once startled into talk, the light syllables leaped for her,
And she balanced in the delight of her thought,
A wren, happy, tail into the wind,   5
Her song trembling the twigs and small branches.
The shade sang with her;
The leaves, their whispers turned to kissing;
And the mold sang in the bleached valleys under the rose.

Oh, when she was sad, she cast herself down into such a pure depth,
Even a father could not find her: 11

3. Like all fish of the pike family, pickerel have exceptionally long, narrow
heads with jaws suggesting the smile described.

Scraping her cheek against straw;
Stirring the clearest water.

My sparrow, you are not here,
Waiting like a fern, making a spiny shadow.   15
The sides of wet stones cannot console me,
Nor the moss, wound with the last light.

If only I could nudge you from this sleep,
My maimed darling, my skittery pigeon.
Over this damp grave I speak the words of my love: 20
I, with no rights in this matter,
Neither father nor lover.

                                              1954, 1958

Unfold! Unfold!

1

By snails, by leaps of frog, I came here, spirit.
Tell me, body without skin, does a fish sweat?
I can't crawl back through those veins,
I ache for another choice.
The cliffs! The cliffs! They fling me back.   5
Eternity howls in the last crags,
The field is no longer simple:
It's a soul's crossing time.
The dead speak noise.

2

It's time you stood up and asked
                —Or sat down and did.   10
A tongue without song
                —Can still whistle in a jug.
You're blistered all over
                —Who cares? The old owl?
When you find the wind
                —Look for the white fire.

3

What a whelm of proverbs, Mr. Pinch! [4]
Are the entrails clear, immaculate cabbage?   15
The last time I nearly whispered myself away.
I was far back, farther than anybody else.
On the jackpine plains I hunted the bird nobody knows;
Fishing, I caught myself behind the ears.
Alone, in a sleep-daze, I stared at billboards;   20
I was privy to oily fungus and the algae of standing waters;

4. In Dickens's novel *Martin Chuzzle-wit*, Mr. Tom Pinch was employed by Mr. Pecksniff, whose hypocritical pomposity sounded proverbial and sometimes was.

Honored, on my return, by the ancient fellowship of rotten stems.
I was pure as a worm on a leaf; I cherished the mold's children.
Beetles sweetened my breath.
I slept like an insect.   25

I met a collector of string, a shepherd of slow forms.
My mission became the salvation of minnows.
I stretched like a board, almost a tree.
Even thread had a speech.

Later, I did and I danced in the simple wood.   30
A mouse taught me how, I was a happy asker.
Quite-by-chance brought me many cookies.
I jumped in butter.
Hair had kisses.

4

Easy the life of the mouth. What a lust for ripeness!   35
All openings praise us, even oily holes.
The bulb unravels. Who's floating? Not me.
The eye perishes in the small vision.
What else has the vine loosened?
I hear a dead tongue halloo.   40

5

Sing, sing, you symbols! All simple creatures,
All small shapes, willow-shy,
In the obscure haze, sing!

A light song comes from the leaves.
A slow sigh says yes. And light sighs;   45
A low voice, summer-sad.
Is it you, cold father? Father,
For whom the minnows sang?

    A house for wisdom; a field for revelation.
    Speak to the stones, and the stars answer.   50
    At first the visible obscures:
    Go where light is.

This fat can't laugh.
Only my salt has a chance.
I'll seek my own meekness.   55
What grace I have is enough.
The lost have their own pace.
The stalks ask something else.
What the grave says,
The nest denies.   60

In their harsh thickets
The dead thrash.
They help.

1951, 1958

I Knew a Woman

I knew a woman, lovely in her bones,
When small birds sighed, she would sigh back at them;
Ah, when she moved, she moved more ways than one:
The shapes a bright container can contain!
Of her choice virtues only gods should speak,   5
Or English poets who grew up on Greek
(I'd have them sing in chorus, cheek to cheek).

How well her wishes went! She stroked my chin,
She taught me Turn, and Counter-turn, and Stand;
She taught me Touch, that undulant white skin;   10
I nibbled meekly from her proffered hand;
She was the sickle; I, poor I, the rake,
Coming behind her for her pretty sake
(But what prodigious mowing we did make).

Love likes a gander, and adores a goose: 15
Her full lips pursed, the errant note to seize;
She played it quick, she played it light and loose;
My eyes, they dazzled at her flowing knees;
Her several parts could keep a pure repose,
Or one hip quiver with a mobile nose   20
(She moved in circles, and those circles moved).

Let seed be grass, and grass turn into hay:
I'm martyr to a motion not my own;
What's freedom for? To know eternity.
I swear she cast a shadow white as stone.   25
But who would count eternity in days?
These old bones live to learn her wanton ways:
(I measure time by how a body sways).

1958

The Exorcism

1

The gray sheep came. I ran,
My body half in flame.
(Father of flowers, who
Dares face the thing he is?)

As if pure being woke,   5
The dust rose and spoke;
A shape cried from a cloud,
Cried to my flesh out loud.

(And yet I was not there,
But down long corridors,   10

My own, my secret lips
Babbling in urinals.)

2

In a dark wood I saw—
I saw my several selves
Come running from the leaves,   15
Lewd, tiny, careless lives
That scuttled under stones,
Or broke, but would not go.
I turned upon my spine,
I turned and turned again,   20
A cold God-furious man
Writhing until the last
Forms of his secret life
Lay with the dross of death.

I was myself, alone.   25

I broke from that low place
Breathing a slower breath,
Cold, in my own dead salt.

1958

Meditations of an Old Woman:
Fourth Meditation [5]

1

I was always one for being alone,
Seeking in my own way, eternal purpose;
At the edge of the field waiting for the pure moment;
Standing, silent, on sandy beaches or walking along green embank-
    ments;
Knowing the sinuousness of small waters: 5
As a chip or shell, floating lazily with a slow current,
A drop of the night rain still in me,
A bit of water caught in a wrinkled crevice,
A pool riding and shining with the river,
Dipping up and down in the ripples,   10
Tilting back the sunlight.

Was it yesterday I stretched out the thin bones of my innocence?
O the songs we hide, singing only to ourselves!

5. "Meditations of an Old Woman," five poems, first appeared as a whole in *Words for the Wind*, in 1958, the last collection of the poet's lifetime. The "Meditations" took their source in Roethke's memories of his mother's aging, but his own search for meaning —for "becoming"—inevitably entered their thought; almost the last lines are, "I'm wet with another life. / Yea, I have gone and stayed." Here he was embarking on a new phase in which, as he freely said, both the ideas and the rhythms were influenced by Whitman.

Once I could touch my shadow, and be happy;
In the white kingdoms, I was light as a seed,   15
Drifting with the blossoms,
A pensive petal.

But a time comes when the vague life of the mouth
    no longer suffices;
The dead make more impossible demands from their silence;
The soul stands, lonely in its choice,   20
Waiting, itself a slow thing,
In the changing body.

> The river moves, wrinkled by midges,
> A light wind stirs in the pine needles.
> The shape of a lark rises from a stone;   25
> But there is no song.

2

What is it to be a woman?
To be contained, to be a vessel?
To prefer a window to a door?
A pool to a river?
To become lost in a love,   30
Yet remain only half aware of the intransient glory?
To be a mouth, a meal of meat?
To gaze at a face with the fixed eyes of a spaniel?

I think of the self-involved:
The ritualists of mirror, the lonely drinkers,   35
The minions of benzedrine and paraldehyde,
And those who submerge themselves deliberately in trivia,
Women who become their possessions,
Shapes stiffening into metal,
Match-makers, arrangers of picnics—   40
What do their lives mean,
And the lives of their children?—
The young, brow-beaten early into a baleful silence,
Frozen by a father's lip, a mother's failure to answer.
Have they seen, ever, the sharp bones of the poor?   45
Or known, once, the soul's authentic hunger,
Those cat-like immaculate creatures
For whom the world works?

What do they need?
O more than a roaring boy,   50
For the sleek captains of intuition cannot reach them;
They feel neither the tearing iron
Nor the sound of another footstep—
How I wish them awake!
May the high flower of the hay climb into their hearts;   55

May they lean into light and live;
May they sleep in robes of green, among the ancient ferns;
May their eyes gleam with the first dawn;
May the sun gild them a worm;
May they be taken by the true burning;   60
May they flame into being!—

I see them as figures walking in a greeny garden,
Their gait formal and elaborate, their hair a glory,
The gentle and beautiful still-to-be-born;
The descendants of the playful tree-shrew that survived the archaic
    killers,   65
The fang and the claw, the club and the knout, the irrational edict,
The fury of the hate-driven zealot, the meanness of the human
    weasel;
Who turned a corner in time, when at last he grew a thumb;
A prince of small beginnings, enduring the slow stretches of change,
Who spoke first in the coarse short-hand of the subliminal depths,
Made from his terror and dismay a grave philosophical language;
A lion of flame, pressed to the point of love,
Yet moves gently among the birds.

3

Younglings, the small fish keep heading into the current.
What's become of care? This lake breathes like a rose.   75
Beguile me, change. What have I fallen from?
I drink my tears in a place where all light comes.
I'm in love with the dead! My whole forehead's a noise!
On a dark day I walk straight toward the rain.
Who else sweats light from a stone?   80
By singing we defend;
The husk lives on, ardent as a seed;
My back creaks with the dawn.

Is my body speaking? I breathe what I am:
The first and last of all things.
Near the graves of the great dead,   85
Even the stones speak.

1958

The Dying Man [6]

(*In Memoriam: W. B. Yeats*)

1   HIS WORDS

I heard a dying man
Say to his gathered kin,

6. The "Meditations" and "The Dying Man" represented, as Roethke told a poet friend, the resolution of his long "quest for being." See especially the present poem, Sections 4 and 5. His few posthumous poems do not suggest what direction his genius would have taken.

"My soul's hung out to dry,
Like a fresh-salted skin;
I doubt I'll use it again.   5

"What's done is yet to come;
The flesh deserts the bone,
But a kiss widens the rose;
I know, as the dying know,
Eternity is Now.   10

"A man sees, as he dies,
Death's possibilities;
My heart sways with the world.
I am that final thing,
A man learning to sing."   15

2   WHAT NOW?

Caught in the dying light,
I thought myself reborn.
My hands turn into hooves.
I wear the leaden weight
Of what I did not do.   20

Places great with their dead,
The mire, the sodden wood,
Remind me to stay alive.
I am the clumsy man
The instant ages on.   25

I burned the flesh away,
In love, in lively May.
I turn my look upon
Another shape than hers
Now, as the casement blurs.   30

In the worst night of my will,
I dared to question all,
And would the same again.
What's beating at the gate?
Who's come can wait.   35

3   THE WALL

A ghost comes out of the unconscious mind
To grope my sill: It moans to be reborn!
The figure at my back is not my friend;
The hand upon my shoulder turns to horn.
I found my father when I did my work,   40
Only to lose myself in this small dark.

Though it reject dry borders of the seen,
What sensual eye can keep an image pure,

Leaning across a sill to greet the dawn?
A slow growth is a hard thing to endure.   45
When figures out of obscure shadow rave,
All sensual love's but dancing on a grave.

The wall has entered: I must love the wall,
A madman staring at perpetual night,
A spirit raging at the visible.   50
I breathe alone until my dark is bright.
Dawn's where the white is. Who would know the dawn
When there's a dazzling dark behind the sun?

4   THE EXULTING

Once I delighted in a single tree;
The loose air sent me running like a child—   55
I love the world; I want more than the world,
Or after-image of the inner eye.
Flesh cries to flesh; and bone cries out to bone;
I die into this life, alone yet not alone.

Was it a god his suffering renewed?—   60
I saw my father shrinking in his skin;
He turned his face: there was another man,
Walking the edge, loquacious, unafraid.
He quivered like a bird in birdless air,
Yet dared to fix his vision anywhere.   65

Fish feed on fish, according to their need:
My enemies renew me, and my blood
Beats slower in my careless solitude.
I bare a wound, and dare myself to bleed.
I think a bird, and it begins to fly.   70
By dying daily, I have come to be.

All exultation is a dangerous thing.
I see you, love, I see you in a dream;
I hear a noise of bees, a trellis hum,
And that slow humming rises into song.   75
A breath is but a breath: I have the earth;
I shall undo all dying by my death.

5   THEY SING, THEY SING

All women loved dance in a dying light—
The moon's my mother: how I love the moon!
Out of her place she comes, a dolphin one,   80
Then settles back to shade and the long night.
A beast cries out as if its flesh were torn,
And that cry takes me back where I was born.

Who thought love but a motion in the mind?
Am I but nothing, leaning towards a thing?   85
I'll scare myself with sighing, or I'll sing;
Descend, O gentlest light, descend, descend.
O sweet field far ahead, I hear your birds,
They sing, they sing, but still in minor thirds.

I've the lark's word for it, who sings alone: 90
What's seen recedes; Forever's what we know!—
Eternity defined, and strewn with straw,
The fury of the slug beneath the stone.
The vision moves, and yet remains the same.
In heaven's praise, I dread the thing I am.   95

The edges of the summit still appal
When we brood on the dead or the beloved;
Nor can imagination do it all
In this last place of light: he dares to live
Who stops being a bird, yet beats his wings   100
Against the immense immeasurable emptiness of things.

1958

The Pike

The river turns,
Leaving a place for the eye to rest,
A furred, a rocky pool,
A bottom of water.

The crabs tilt and eat, leisurely,   5
And the small fish lie, without shadow, motionless,
Or drift lazily in and out of the weeds.
The bottom-stones shimmer back their irregular striations,
And the half-sunken branch bends away from the gazer's eye.

A scene for the self to abjure!—   10
And I lean, almost into the water,
My eye always beyond the surface reflection;
I lean, and love these manifold shapes,
Until, out from a dark cove,
From beyond the end of a mossy log,   15
With one sinuous ripple, then a rush,
A thrashing-up of the whole pool,
The pike strikes.

1964

Wish for a Young Wife

My lizard, my lively writher,
May your limbs never wither,
May the eyes in your face
Survive the green ice
Of envy's mean gaze;   5
May you live out your life
Without hate, without grief,
And your hair ever blaze,
In the sun, in the sun,
When I am undone,   10
When I am no one.

1964

RANDALL JARRELL
(1914–1965)

Randall Jarrell was born in Nashville, Tennessee, but spent most of his early years in Long Beach and in Hollywood, California. When he was eleven his parents separated and he stayed briefly with his paternal grandparents before joining his mother in Nashville. Prepared in high school for a business career, he attended Vanderbilt University, where he came under the influence of John Crowe Ransom. At Vanderbilt, where he returned after graduation to earn an M.A., and at Kenyon, where he followed Ransom and taught in the English Department, he wrote the early poems and reviews that appeared in the *American Review, Southern Review,* and *Kenyon Review*. Among his friends and associates in these years were Robert Penn Warren, Allen Tate, Peter Taylor, and Robert Lowell. Later academic appointments took him to the University of Texas and, for most of the last eighteen years of his life, to the Women's College of the University of North Carolina, in Greensboro.

A meticulous craftsman, Jarrell worked squarely within the tradition of English metrical verse. An admirer of Robert Frost, he shared something of Frost's ability to stretch the sound of a human voice across a metrical line without doing violence to either the line or the conversational quality of the voice. Yet the speaking voice in most instances is not his own. Although he owed much of his fame in the middle of his career to such World War II flight poems as "Eighth Air Force," "The Death of the Ball Turret Gunner," and "Losses," he had washed out of flight training and spent most of the war on the ground in Illinois and Arizona. Late in life he dispensed with his habitual reserve in order to write two strikingly autobiographic poems, "The Lost World" and "Thinking of the Lost World," but generally speaking he is not a poet who makes capital out of his direct personal experiences.

Modesty was one of his virtues. "I have tried to make my poems plain," he wrote, "and most of them are plain enough; but I wish that they were more difficult because I had known more." Yet for all their plainness, his poems are often deeply resonant; the intelligence that lay behind them was one of the keenest possessed by any of the poets of his generation. Recipient of two Guggenheim Fellowships, poetry editor or critic at various times for the *Nation*, *Partisan Review*, and *Yale Review*, and Poetry Consultant at the Library of Congress, he was not only a fine poet, but an excellent critic. A career that had been marked by a continuing capacity for growth was suddenly cut short in 1965 when he was struck and killed by an automobile.

Individual volumes of poetry include *Five Young American Poets*, 1940 (with others); *Blood for a Stranger*, 1942; *Little Friend, Little Friend*, 1945; *Losses*, 1948; *The Seven-League Crutches*, 1951; *Selected Poems*, 1955; *The Woman at the Washington Zoo*, 1960; and *The Lost World*, 1965. *Selected Poems*, 1955, has been superseded by *The Complete Poems*, 1969. A comic academic novel is *Pictures from an Institution*, 1954. Criticism is collected in *Poetry and the Age*, 1953; *A Sad Heart at the Supermarket*, 1962; and *The Third Book of Criticism*, 1971. See also *Jerome: The Biography of a Poem*, 1972. Charles M. Adams compiled *Randall Jarrell: A Bibliography*, 1958. Robert Lowell, Peter Taylor, and Robert Penn Warren edited a volume of reminiscences, *Randall Jarrell: 1914–1965*, 1967. Suzanne Ferguson, *The Poetry of Randall Jarrell*, 1971, is thorough and intelligent.

The Death of the Ball Turret Gunner

From my mother's sleep I fell into the State,
And I hunched in its belly till my wet fur froze.
Six miles from earth, loosed from its dream of life,
I woke to black flak and the nightmare fighters.
When I died they washed me out of the turret with a hose.   5

1945

Losses

It was not dying: everybody died.
It was not dying: we had died before
In the routine crashes—and our fields
Called up the papers, wrote home to our folks,
And the rates rose, all because of us.   5
We died on the wrong page of the almanac,
Scattered on mountains fifty miles away;
Diving on haystacks, fighting with a friend,
We blazed up on the lines we never saw.

We died like aunts or pets or foreigners.   10
(When we left high school nothing else had died
For us to figure we had died like.)

In our new planes, with our new crews, we bombed
The ranges by the desert or the shore,
Fired at towed targets, waited for our scores—   15
And turned into replacements and woke up
One morning, over England, operational.
It wasn't different: but if we died
It was not an accident but a mistake
(But an easy one for anyone to make).   20
We read our mail and counted up our missions—
In bombers named for girls, we burned
The cities we had learned about in school—
Till our lives wore out; our bodies lay among
The people we had killed and never seen.   25
When we lasted long enough they gave us medals;
When we died they said, "Our casualties were low."
They said, "Here are the maps"; we burned the cities.

It was not dying—no, not ever dying;
But the night I died I dreamed that I was dead,   30
And the cities said to me: "Why are you dying?
We are satisfied, if you are; but why did I die?"

1945

The Woman at the Washington Zoo

The saris go by me from the embassies.

Cloth from the moon. Cloth from another planet.
They look back at the leopard like the leopard.

And I. . . .

                    this print of mine, that has kept its color   5
Alive through so many cleanings; this dull null
Navy I wear to work, and wear from work, and so
To my bed, so to my grave, with no
Complaints, no comment: neither from my chief,
The Deputy Chief Assistant, nor his chief—   10
Only I complain. . . . this serviceable
Body that no sunlight dyes, no hand suffuses
But, dome-shadowed, withering among columns,
Wavy beneath fountains—small, far-off, shining
In the eyes of animals, these beings trapped   15
As I am trapped but not, themselves, the trap,
Aging, but without knowledge of their age,

Kept safe here, knowing not of death, for death—
Oh, bars of my own body, open, open!

The world goes by my cage and never sees me.   20
And there come not to me, as come to these,
The wild beasts, sparrows pecking the llamas' grain,
Pigeons settling on the bears' bread, buzzards
Tearing the meat the flies have clouded. . . .
                       Vulture,   25
When you come for the white rat that the foxes left,
Take off the red helmet of your head, the black
Wings that have shadowed me, and step to me as man:
The wild brother at whose feet the white wolves fawn,
To whose hand of power the great lioness   30
Stalks, purring. . . .
                 You know what I was,
You see what I am: change me, change me!

                            1960

The Lost Children

Two little girls, one fair, one dark,
One alive, one dead, are running hand in hand
Through a sunny house. The two are dressed
In red and white gingham, with puffed sleeves and sashes.
They run away from me . . . But I am happy;   5
When I wake I feel no sadness, only delight.
I've seen them again, and I am comforted
That, somewhere, they still are.

It is strange
To carry inside you someone else's body;   10
To know it before it's born;
To see at last that it's a boy or girl, and perfect;
To bathe it and dress it; to watch it
Nurse at your breast, till you almost know it
Better than you know yourself—better than it knows itself.   15
You own it as you made it.
You are the authority upon it.

But as the child learns
To take care of herself, you know her less.
Her accidents, adventures are her own,   20
You lose track of them. Still, you know more
About her than anyone *except* her.

Little by little the child in her dies.
You say, "I have lost a child, but gained a friend."
You feel yourself gradually discarded.   25

She argues with you or ignores you
Or is kind to you. She who begged to follow you
Anywhere, just so long as it was you,
Finds follow the leader no more fun.
She makes few demands; you are grateful for the few.   30

The young person who writes once a week
Is the authority upon herself.
She sits in my living room and shows her husband
My albums of her as a child. He enjoys them
And makes fun of them. I look too   35
And I realize the girl in the matching blue
Mother-and-daughter dress, the fair one carrying
The tin lunch box with the half-pint thermos bottle
Or training her pet duck to go down the slide
Is lost just as the dark one, who is dead, is lost.   40
But the world in which the two wear their flared coats
And the hats that match, exists so uncannily
That, after I've seen its pictures for an hour,
I believe in it: the bandage coming loose
One has in the picture of the other's birthday,   45
The castles they are building, at the beach for asthma.
I look at them and all the old sure knowledge
Floods over me, when I put the album down
I keep saying inside: "I *did* know those children.
I braided those braids. I was driving the car   50
The day that she stepped in the can of grease
We were taking to the butcher for our ration points.
I *know* those children. I know all about them.
Where are they?"

I stare at her and try to see some sign   55
Of the child she was. I can't believe there isn't any.
I tell her foolishly, pointing at the picture,
That I keep wondering where she is.
She tells me, "Here I am."
                              Yes, and the other   60
Isn't dead, but has everlasting life . . .

The girl from next door, the borrowed child,
Said to me the other day, "You like children so much,
Don't you want to have some of your own?"
I couldn't believe that she could say it.   65
I thought: "Surely you can look at me and see them."

When I see them in my dreams I feel such joy.
If I could dream of them every night!

When I think of my dream of the little girls
It's as if we were playing hide-and-seek.   70
The dark one

Looks at me longingly, and disappears;
The fair one stays in sight, just out of reach
No matter where I reach. I am tired
As a mother who's played all day, some rainy day.   75
I don't want to play it any more, I don't want to,
But the child keeps on playing, so I play.

1965

ROBERT LOWELL

(1917–   )

Robert Lowell's poetry has won serious critical attention and has been received with enthusiasm since the appearance of his first volume in 1944. Lowell's originality and power have greatly influenced contemporary poets and have given to his own varied works the probability of enduring merit.

Born in Boston in 1917, he was given his father's name, Robert Traill Spence Lowell, representing an inheritance of family tradition distinguished and old in New England history. His mother was a Winslow. The poet transformed his youthful embarrassment at family tradition into a literary resource: he developed a psychological interest in family situations which infuses a number of his best poems, and he allowed his tragic sense and his comic spirit to rummage in his own family attics.

After nearly two years at Harvard University Lowell completed his formal education at Kenyon College (1940) where his poetry was encouraged by John Crowe Ransom, poet-teacher, and by others, especially Randall Jarrell. Having twice been refused for enlistment, he

was later drafted, declared himself a conscientious objector, and was sentenced. He published *Land of Unlikeness*, his first volume (1944), in a limited edition. Two years later *Lord Weary's Castle* won the Pulitzer Prize (1947). Lowell was awarded a Guggenheim Fellowship in 1947–1948, the Guinness Award and the National Book Award in 1959.

As an undergraduate at Kenyon, he had been converted to Catholicism, and as Allen Tate had foreseen, Lowell became "consciously a Catholic poet"; however, he retained an earlier interest in the religious philosophy and works of learned Puritans. In Lowell the two became reconciled. This religious motivation gave his style a determined boldness, supported by complexly disciplined language, symbol, and idea.

Randall Jarrell's review of *Lord Weary's Castle* in *The Nation* (1946) gains interest because Lowell approved it, in lieu of writing his own introduction, for publication with a selection of his poems in John Ciardi's *Mid-Century American Poets*. Mr. Jarrell commented that these "poems understand the world as a sort of conflict of opposites." One force is the "inertia of the complacent self, the satisfied persistence in evil that is damnation * * * turned inward, incestuous, that blinds or binds." The opposing force "is the realm of freedom, of the Grace that has replaced the Law, of the perfect Liberator." The poems "normally move into liberation"; and in some cases "even death is seen as a liberation."

Lowell shares with Pound and other more recent poets the inclination to imitate or reconstruct poems in other languages and of other times. *Imitations* (1961) collects his versions of writings by such diverse hands as Homer, Rilke, and Pasternak. In a review, Edmund Wilson reminded his readers that while this book "consists of variations on themes provided by those other poets," it "is really an original sequence by Robert Lowell of Boston." *Imitations*, which won the Bollingen translation prize in 1962, is another search into a heritage—that of a poet's classical and European fellow-explorers.

Meanwhile, in 1959, he published *Life Studies*, newer poems with a prose fragment of autobiography. These poems are in fact "life studies" of his forebears and of his family. "It is hard not to think of *Life Studies* as a series of personal confidences, rather shameful, that one is honor bound not to reveal," wrote M. L. Rosenthal, but he concluded that "it is also a beautifully articulated poetic sequence." Clearly, Lowell has been studying, throughout his poetic life, all the materials available. In *For the Union Dead*

(1964) Lowell begins to return into our world and to New England, as in "Jonathan Edwards in Western Massachusetts," where he comes to the realization that "hope lives in doubt. / Faith is trying to do without / faith."

Drama and "imitation" were first brought together in *Phaedra* (1961), his version of Racine's *Phèdre*, and in 1964 The American Place Theatre produced, to critical acclaim, three short plays under the title *The Old Glory*. The first play (not produced, but included in the published text) combines Hawthorne's "Endicott and the Red Cross" and "The Maypole of Merrymount"; the second is based upon "My Kinsman, Major Molineux"; Melville's story "Benito Cereno" inspired the last. In his preface to the published version, the critic Robert Brustein stated that "Mr. Lowell feels the past working in his very bones. And it is his subtle achievement not only to have evoked this past, but also to have superimposed the present on it."

In *Near the Ocean* (1967) five long poems, written in deceptively simple couplets, concern his present life as it is mingled in memory and the past. That life is in a house on the Maine coast willed to the poet by Harriet Winslow. The "imitations" included in this volume are taken from Horace, Juvenal, and Dante.

Lowell's recent work culminated in 1973 with the publication of three volumes of largely personal content. *History* is a gathering into their final form of the *Notebook* poems that began to appear in 1969 in *Note-*

book 1967–68. For Lizzie and Harriet contains those *Notebook* poems that focus on the poet's second marriage. *The Dolphin* celebrates a new love in the stanza of the *Notebook* poems.

Published volumes are *Land of Unlikeness*, 1944 (now unavailable); *Lord Weary's Castle*, 1946; *The Mills of the Kavenaughs*, 1951; *Poems: 1938–1949*, 1950, which includes the two volumes above, except the title poem, "The Mills of the Kavenaughs"; and *Life Studies*, 1959, which won the National Book Award. *Imitations*, 1961, is a book of "translations." Newer poems are collected in *For the Union Dead*, 1964; *Selected Poems*, 1965; *Near the Ocean*, 1967; *Voyage, and Other Versions of Poems by*

Baudelaire, 1968; *Notebook 1967–68*, 1969; *Notebooks, Revised and Expanded*, 1970; *History*, 1973; *For Lizzie and Harriet*, 1973; and *The Dolphin*, 1973. His plays are *Phaedra* (translation), 1961; *The Old Glory* (produced, 1964), 1965, revised, and a version of *Prometheus Bound*, 1969.

A critical biography is Hugh B. Stapler, *Robert Lowell: The First Twenty Years*, 1961. More recent studies include Jerome Mazzaro, *The Poetic Themes of Robert Lowell*, 1965; Thomas Parkinson, ed., *Robert Lowell: A Collection of Critical Essays*, 1968; Philip Cooper, *The Autobiographical Myth of Robert Lowell*, 1970; and Patrick Cosgrave, *The Public Poetry of Robert Lowell*, 1972. Michael London and Robert Boyers edited *Robert Lowell: A Portrait of the Artist in His Time*, 1970.

In Memory of Arthur Winslow [1]

I. *Death from Cancer*

This Easter, Arthur Winslow,[2] less than dead,
Your people set you up in Phillips' House
To settle off your wrestling with the crab [3]—
The claws drop flesh upon your yachting blouse
Until longshoreman Charon [4] come and stab   5
Through your adjusted bed
And crush the crab. On Boston Basin, shells
Hit water by the Union Boat Club wharf:
You ponder why the coxes [5] squeakings dwarf
The *resurrexit dominus* [6] of all the bells.   10

Grandfather Winslow, look, the swanboats coast
That island in the Pacific Gardens, where
The bread-stuffed ducks are brooding, where with tub
And strainer the mid-Sunday Irish scare
The sun-struck shallows for the dusky chub [7]   15
This Easter, and the ghost
Of risen Jesus walks the waves to run [8]

1. First collected in *Lord Weary's Castle* (1946) and included in the collection of 1950.
2. In an autobiographical sketch, "91 Revere Srteet" (*Life Studies*, pp. 11–46), Lowell describes with affection Grandfather Winslow, his mother's father, a financial adventurer, Boston Brahmin, and family autocrat, proud of his descent from the Stark family of Dunbarton, N. H., as well as the colonial Massachusetts Winslows (both mentioned in the following poem).
3. "Cancer" is the Latin for "crab."

4. In Greek mythology, Charon ferried the souls of the dead across the Styx, river of death.
5. "Coxes," abbreviation for "coxswains," steersmen of racing shells or ship's boats.
6. "The Lord is risen"; the liturgical message of Easter.
7. A humble variety of carp, on Easter recalling that the fish became a Christian symbol because of miracles associated with fish and fishermen.
8. See the miracle of Jesus walking on the sea, Matthew xiv: 25.

Arthur upon a trumpeting black swan
Beyond Charles River to the Acheron [9]
Where the wide waters and their voyager are one.   20

II. *Dunbarton*

The stones are yellow and the grass is gray
Past Concord by the rotten lake and hill
Where crutch and trumpet meet the limousine
And half-forgotten Starks and Winslows [1] fill
The granite plot and the dwarf pines are green   25
From watching for the day
When the great year of the little yeomen [2] come
Bringing its landed Promise [3] and the faith
That made the Pilgrim Makers take a lathe
And point their wooden steeples lest the Word [4] be dumb.   30

O fearful witnesses, your day is done:
The minister from Boston waves your shades,
Like children, out of sight and out of mind.
The first selectman of Dunbarton spreads
Wreaths of New Hampshire pine cones on the lined   35
Casket where the cold sun
Is melting. But, at last, the end is reached;
We start our cars. The preacher's mouthings still
Deafen my poor relations on the hill:
Their sunken landmarks echo what our fathers preached.[5]   40

III. *Five Years Later*

This Easter, Arthur Winslow, five years gone
I came to mourn you, not to praise the craft
That netted you a million dollars, late
Hosing out gold in Colorado's waste,[6]
Then lost it all in Boston real estate.   45
Now from the train, at dawn
Leaving Columbus in Ohio, shell
On shell of our stark culture strikes the sun
To fill my head with all our fathers won
When Cotton Mather wrestled with the fiends from hell.[7]   50

9. The Charles, a river of Boston; Acheron, according to Greek mythology, a shade-haunted river in Hades.
1. For the Starks of Dunbarton, N. H., and the Winslows of Massachusetts, see Section I, note 2.
2. British "yeomen," that is, freeholders of land and commoners of the highest level, made up the majority in colonial New England.
3. *I.e.*, the Promised Land of the redeemed on "the day" of Judgment.

4. The Bible (Acts iv: 31) or Messiah (John i: 1, 14).
5. *I.e.*, Bible texts carved on the tombstones.
6. In placer mining the gold is washed out of superficial deposits with high-pressure hoses.
7. Industrial buildings, representing material wealth, are compared with the salvation preached by Cotton Mather (1663–1728), archetype of Puritan divines.

You must have hankered for our family's craft:
The block-house Edward made, the Governor,[8]
At Marshfield, and the slight coin-silver spoons
The Sheriff beat to shame the gaunt Revere,[9]
And General Stark's [1] coarse bas-relief in bronze   55
Set on your granite shaft
In rough Dunbarton; for what else could bring
You, Arthur, to the veined and alien West
But devil's notions that your gold at least
Could give back life to men who whipped or backed the King?   60

IV. *A Prayer for My Grandfather to Our Lady* [2]

Mother, for these three hundred years or more
Neither our clippers nor our slavers reached
The haven of your peace in this Bay State:
Neither my father nor his father. Beached
On these dry flats of fishy real estate,   65
O Mother, I implore
Your scorched, blue thunderbreasts of love to pour
Buckets of blessings on my burning head
Until I rise like Lazarus from the dead: [3]
Lavabis nos et super nivem dealbabor.[4]   70

"On Copley Square,[5] I saw you hold the door
To Trinity, the costly Church, and saw
The painted Paradise of harps and lutes
Sink like Atlantis [6] in the Devil's jaw
And knock the Devil's teeth out by the roots;   75
But when I strike for shore
I find no painted idols to adore:
Hell is burned out, heaven's harp-strings are slack.
Mother, run to the chalice, and bring back
Blood on your finger-tips for Lazarus who was poor." [7]   80

1946, 1950

---

8. Edward Winslow, their ancestor, a Mayflower Pilgrim (1622) described in his journal the earliest events in Plymouth and was three times elected governor. *Cf.* "our family's craft," l. 51.
9. Paul Revere, the midnight rider of the Battle of Lexington, was a gifted silversmith and engraver.
1. General John Stark (1728–1822), another ancestor, famous New Hampshire soldier of the Revolution.
2. The poem has proceeded from Arthur Winslow's death and burial, to memories of his material life, and finally to the stage of penitence. The two stanzas of this section are differentiated by the quotation marks enclosing the second and by the two Lazaruses—*cf.* notes 3 and 7.
3. Jesus raised Lazarus from the dead (*cf.* John xi: 11–43).
4. "You shall wash us and I shall be made whiter than snow." *Dealbabor* was erroneously printed *delabor* in the 1950 collection.
5. A very old Boston square, once a center of social refinement.
6. Fabulous island civilization presumed to have sunk beneath the ocean.
7. This "Lazarus who was poor" is the beggar in Jesus' parable of the selfish rich man (*cf.* Luke xvi: 19–31). Compare with "Lazarus" in l. 69.

After the Surprising Conversions [8]

September twenty-second, Sir: [9] today
I answer. In the latter part of May,
Hard on our Lord's Ascension, it began
To be more sensible.[1] A gentleman
Of more than common understanding, strict   5
In morals, pious in behavior, kicked
Against our goad. A man of some renown,
An useful, honored person in the town,[2]
He came of melancholy parents; prone
To secret spells, for years they kept alone—   10
His uncle, I believe, was killed of it:
Good people, but of too much or little wit.
I preached one Sabbath on a text from Kings;
He showed concernment for his soul. Some things
In his experience were hopeful. He   15
Would sit and watch the wind knocking a tree
And praise this countryside our Lord has made.
Once when a poor man's heifer died, he laid
A shilling on the doorsill; though a thirst
For loving shook him like a snake, he durst   20
Not entertain much hope of his estate
In heaven. Once we saw him sitting late
Behind his attic window by a light
That guttered on his Bible; through that night
He meditated terror, and he seemed   25
Beyond advice or reason, for he dreamed
That he was called to trumpet Judgment Day
To Concord. In the latter part of May
He cut his throat.[3] And though the coroner

8. First collected in *Lord Weary's Castle* (1949) and reprinted in *Poems: 1938–1949* (1950). The following notes, perhaps unusually full, are intended to show the poet using the words and the substance of a document to create a work of art, a new thing.
9. The source of this poem is a letter written by Jonathan Edwards on May 30, 1735. ("A Narrative of Surprising Conversions," Jonathan Edwards, *Works,* 1808). Edwards' sermon in 1734 inspired the "Great Awakening," a revival in his Northampton parish, whence revivalism spread to the surrounding Massachusetts towns. This letter to Benjamin Colman, Boston clergyman, in response to his request for information, was later amplified for publication by an account of further remarkable experiences, one of which forms the inspiration for the present poem. The "Great Awakening" continued to influence the development of Protestant denominations in the colonies until about 1750.

1. "Sensible": archaic for "evident." This line in full (Edwards' supplementary letter, May, 1735) reads: "it began to be very sensible that the spirit of God was gradually withdrawing from us." The following reported misfortunes were taken for proof of this.
2. In reporting this man's suicide to Colman, Edwards calls him "My Uncle Hawley." Joseph Hawley, who married Edwards' aunt, Rebekah, was the leading merchant of pioneer days in Northampton.
3. "He cut his throat" on June 1, 1735. Edwards wrote: "My Uncle Hawley, the last Sabbath morning, laid violent hands on himself, by cutting his own throat. He had been for a considerable time greatly concerned about the condition of his soul; by the ordering of Providence he was suffered to fall into a deep melancholy, a distemper that the family are very prone to; the devil took the advantage and drove him into despairing thoughts: he was kept very much awake a nights, so that he had

Judged him delirious, soon a noisome stir 30
Palsied our village. At Jehovah's nod
Satan seemed more let loose amongst us: God
Abandoned us to Satan,[4] and he pressed
Us hard, until we thought we could not rest
Till we had done with life. Content was gone. 35
All the good work was quashed. We were undone.
The breath of God had carried out a planned
And sensible withdrawal from this land;
The multitude, once unconcerned with doubt,
Once neither callous, curious nor devout, 40
Jumped at broad noon, as though some peddler groaned
At it in its familiar twang: "My friend,
Cut your own throat. Cut your own throat. Now! Now!"
September twenty-second, Sir, the bough
Cracks with the unpicked apples, and at dawn 45
The small-mouth bass breaks water, gorged with spawn.

1946, 1950

Her Dead Brother [5]

I

The Lion of St. Mark's upon the glass
Shield in my window reddens, as the night
Enchants the swinging dories to its terrors,
And dulls your distant wind-stung eyes; alas,
Your portrait, coiled in German-silver hawsers, mirrors 5
The sunset as a dragon. Enough light
Remains to see you through your varnish. Giving
Your life has brought you closer to your friends;
Yes, it has brought you home. All's well that ends:[6]
Achilles dead is greater than the living; 10

My mind holds you as I would have you live,
A wintering dragon. Summer was too short
When we went picnicking with telescopes

---

very little sleep for two months * * *
He was in a great measure beyond receiving advice, or being reasoned with.
The Coroner's Inquest judged him
delirious."
4. The remainder of the poem reflects
this abstruse doctrine. Perry Miller, in
Jonathan Edwards, comments on this,
passim: over "three hundred people
were converted" at Northampton "during the year" (1734–35); but after
Hawley's suicide one heard voices crying, as Edwards reports, "cut your
own throat! Now! Now!" (*cf.* the
poem, l. 43); and the initial revival at
Northampton was over. Edwards expressed current doctrine in asserting,

"The devil took advantage * * * he
seems to be in a great rage at this
* * * breaking forth of the works of
God. I hope it is because he knows
that he has but a short time." Edwards knew, as Miller observes, that
"the divine spirit has a tempo, a rise
and a fall," and will rise again to
redeem, as the poem says, "the unpicked apples and at dawn / The
small-mouthed bass."
5. In *The Mills of the Kavenaughs*
(1951) but also included in the collection published earlier, *Poems: 1938–
1949* (1950).
6. *Cf.* the title *All's Well That Ends
Well,* a comedy by Shakespeare.

And crocking leather handbooks to that fort
Above the lank and heroned Sheepscot, where its slopes   15
Are clutched by hemlocks—spotting birds. I give
You back that idyll, Brother. Was it more?
Remember riding, scotching with your spur
That four-foot milk-snake in a juniper?
Father shellacked it to the ice-house door.   20

Then you were grown; I left you on your own.
We will forget that August twenty-third,
When Mother motored with the maids to Stowe,
And the pale summer shades were drawn—so low
No one could see us; no, nor catch your hissing word,   25
As false as Cressid! [7] Let our deaths atone:
The fingers on your sword-knot are alive,
And Hope, that fouls my brightness with its grace,
Will anchor in the narrows of your face.
My husband's Packard crunches up the drive.   30

II

(THREE MONTHS LATER)

The ice is out: the tidal current swims
Its blocks against the launches as they pitch
Under the cruisers of my Brother's fleet.
The gas, uncoiling from my oven burners, dims
The face above this bottled *Water Witch*,   35
The knockabout my Brother fouled and left to eat
Its heart out by the Boston light. My Brother,
I've saved you in the ice-house of my mind—
The ice is out. . . . Our fingers lock behind
The tiller. We are heeling in the smother,   40

Our sails, balloon and leg-o'mutton, tell
The colors of the rainbow; but they flap,
As the wind fails, and cannot fetch the bell. . . .
His stick is tapping on the millwheel-step,
He lights a match, another and another—   45
The Lord is dark, and holy is His name;
By my own hands, into His hands! My burners
Sing like a kettle, and its nickel mirrors
Your squadron by the Stygian Landing. Brother,
The harbor! The torpedoed cruisers flame,   50

The motor-launches with their searchlights bristle
About the targets. You are black. You shout,
And cup your broken sword-hand. Yes, your whistle
Across the crackling water: *Quick, the ice is out.* . . .

7. Cressida's desertion of her lover, the
Trojan hero Troilus, and her amours
with the victorious Greek commanders
have made her the byword for infidelity; the story has been retold since the
twelfth century by Boccaccio, Chaucer,
and Shakespeare.

The wind dies in our canvas; we were running dead   55
Before the wind, but now our sail is part
Of death. O Brother, a New England town is death
And incest—and I saw it whole. I said,
Life is a thing I own. Brother, my heart
Races for sea-room—we are out of breath.   60

1951

Skunk Hour

(For Elizabeth Bishop)

Nautilus Island's hermit
heiress still lives through winter in her Spartan cottage;
her sheep still graze above the sea.
Her son's a bishop. Her farmer
is first selectman in our village;   5
she's in her dotage.

Thirsting for
the hierarchic privacy
of Queen Victoria's century,
she buys up all   10
the eyesores facing her shore,
and lets them fall.

The season's ill—
we've lost our summer millionaire,
who seemed to leap from an L. L. Bean   15
catalogue. His nine-knot yawl
was auctioned off to lobstermen.
A red fox stain covers Blue Hill.

And now our fairy
decorator brightens his shop for fall;   20
his fishnet's filled with orange cork,
orange, his cobbler's bench and awl;
there is no money in his work,
he'd rather marry.

One dark night,   25
my Tudor Ford climbed the hill's skull;
I watched for love-cars. Lights turned down,
they lay together, hull to hull,
where the graveyard shelves on the town. . . .
My mind's not right.   30

A car radio bleats,
"Love, O careless Love. . . ." I hear
my ill-spirit sob in each blood cell,

as if my hand were at its throat. . . . .
I myself am hell;
nobody's here—   35

only skunks, that search
in the moonlight for a bite to eat.
They march on their soles up Main Street:
white stripes, moonstruck eyes' red fire   40
under the chalk-dry and spar spire
of the Trinitarian Church.

I stand on top
of our back steps and breathe the rich air—
a mother skunk with her column of kittens swills the garbage
  pail.   45
She jabs her wedge-head in a cup
of sour cream, drops her ostrich tail,
and will not scare.

1959

The Mouth of the Hudson

(*For Esther Brooks*)

A single man stands like a bird-watcher,
and scuffles the pepper and salt snow
from a discarded, gray
Westinghouse Electric cable drum.
He cannot discover America by counting   5
the chains of condemned freight-trains
from thirty states. They jolt and jar
and junk in the siding below him.
He has trouble with his balance.
His eyes drop,   10
and he drifts with the wild ice
ticking seaward down the Hudson,
like the blank sides of a jig-saw puzzle.

The ice ticks seaward like a clock.
A Negro toasts   15
Wheat-seeds over the coke-fumes
of a punctured barrel.
Chemical air
sweeps in from New Jersey,
and smells of coffee.   20

Across the river,
ledges of suburban factories tan
in the sulphur-yellow sun
of the unforgivable landscape.

1964

The Neo-Classical Urn

I rub my head and find a turtle shell
stuck on a pole,
each hair electrical
with charges, and the juice alive
with ferment. Bubbles drive   5
the motor, always purposeful . . .
Poor head!
How its skinny shell once hummed,
as I sprinted down the colonnade
of bleaching pines, cylindrical   10
clipped trunks without a twig between them. Rest!
I could not rest. At full run on the curve,
I left the caste stone statue of a nymph,
her soaring armpits and her one bare breast,
gray from the rain and graying in the shade,   15
as on, on, in sun, the pathway now a dyke,
I swerved between two water bogs,
two seins of moss, and stooped to snatch
the painted turtles on dead logs.

In that season of joy,   20
my turtle catch
was thirty-three,
dropped splashing in our garden urn,
like money in the bank,
the plop and splash   25
of turtle on turtle,
fed raw gobs of hash . . .

Oh neo-classical white urn, Oh nymph,
Oh lute! The boy was pitiless who strummed
their elegy,   30
for as the month wore on,
the turtles rose,
and popped up dead on the stale scummed
surface—limp wrinkled heads and legs withdrawn
in pain. What pain? A turtle's nothing. No   35
grace, no cerebration, less free will
than the mosquito I must kill—
nothings! Turtles! I rub my skull,
that turtle shell,
and breathe their dying smell,   40
still watch their crippled last survivors pass,
and hobble humpbacked through the grizzled grass.

1964

For the Union Dead [8]

"Relinquunt Omnia Servare Rem Publicam." [9]

The old South Boston Aquarium stands
in a Sahara of snow now. Its broken windows are boarded.
The bronze weathervane cod has lost half its scales.
The airy tanks are dry.

Once my nose crawled like a snail on the glass;   5
my hand tingled
to burst the bubbles
drifting from the noses of the cowed, compliant fish.

My hand draws back. I often sigh still
for the dark downward and vegetating kingdom   10
of the fish and reptile. One morning last March,
I pressed against the new barbed and galvanized

fence on the Boston Common. Behind their cage,
yellow dinosaur steamshovels were grunting
as they cropped up tons of mush and grass   15
to gouge their underworld garage.

Parking spaces luxuriate like civic
sandpiles in the heart of Boston.
A girdle of orange, Puritan-pumpkin colored girders
braces the tingling Statehouse,   20

shaking over the excavations, as it faces Colonel Shaw [1]
and his bell-cheeked Negro infantry
on St. Gaudens' shaking Civil War relief,
propped by a plank splint against the garage's earthquake.

Two months after marching through Boston,   25
half the regiment was dead;
at the dedication,
William James could almost hear the bronze Negroes breathe.

Their monument sticks like a fishbone
in the city's throat.   30
Its Colonel is as lean
as a compass-needle.

He has an angry wrenlike vigilance,
a greyhound's gentle tautness;

---

8. First collected in *Life Studies*, 1959, printed last in the volume and entitled, "Colonel Shaw and the Massachusetts' 54th." In reprints it continued in the last position but bore the present title. Finally it became the title poem of *For the Union Dead*, 1964. All texts are otherwise identical.
9. "They gave all to serve the State."

1. Colonel Robert Gould Shaw (1837–1863) commanded the first enlisted Negro regiment, the Massachusetts 54th; he was killed in the attack on Fort Wagner, July 18, 1863, and buried in the grave with his men. Augustus Saint-Gaudens's monument to Shaw stands opposite the State House on Boston Common.

he seems to wince at pleasure,   35
and suffocate for privacy.

He is out of bounds now. He rejoices in man's lovely,
peculiar power to choose life and die—
when he leads his black soldiers to death,
he cannot bend his back.   40

On a thousand small town New England greens,
the old white churches hold their air
of sparse, sincere rebellion; frayed flags
quilt the graveyards of the Grand Army of the Republic.

The stone statues of the abstract Union Soldier   .   45
grow slimmer and younger each year—
wasp-waisted, they doze over muskets
and muse through their sideburns . . .

Shaw's father wanted no monument
except the ditch,
where his son's body was thrown   50
and lost with his "niggers."

The ditch is nearer.
There are no statues for the last war here;
on Boylston Street, a commercial photograph   55
shows Hiroshima boiling

over a Mosler Safe,[2] the "Rock of Ages"
that survived the blast. Space is nearer.
When I crouch to my television set,
the drained faces of Negro school-children rise like balloons. 60

Colonel Shaw
is riding on his bubble,
he waits
for the blesséd break.

The Aquarium is gone. Everywhere,   65
giant finned cars nose forward like fish;
a savage servility
slides by on grease.

1959, 1964

2. A safe that escaped destruction in
the bombing of Hiroshima was photographed; the picture was used by the
company to advertise the durability of
its products.

Fiction: The Fifties

VLADIMIR NABOKOV
(1899–   )

In the late 1950's, three decades after the publication in Russian of his first novel, *Màshen'ka* (1926; translated as *Mary*, 1970), Vladimir Nabokov began to be widely recognized as the possessor of a major literary talent. *Lolita* (Paris, 1955; New York, 1958) catapulted him to fame and financial independence. At sixty he was a celebrity, by seventy acclaimed as one of the finest stylists in English, one of the greatest novelists of his time. At an age when other writers had long since ceased to write or had turned to pale imitations of their younger selves, Nabokov continued to produce works of increasing depth and complexity. At the same time he collaborated with his son and other translators in making available in English the novels that he had originally written in Russian and published in Berlin and Paris in the 1920's and 1930's.

Much of his story, up until his emigration to the United States in 1940, is told in the remarkable autobiography *Speak, Memory* (1952; revised 1966; earlier titled *Conclusive Evi-*dence, 1951). He was born in St. Petersburg, Russia, and enjoyed the privileges of a wealthy aristocrat until forced to emigrate in 1919 as a result of the revolution. After four years at Trinity College, Cambridge, he settled in Berlin, where he lived until 1937, supplementing his income from writing by giving lessons in English, French, and tennis. In 1937 he moved to Paris, in 1940 to the United States, where he supported himself by a variety of academic positions, culminating in his eleven years as Professor of Russian Literature at Cornell (1948–1959). Since 1959 he has lived in Switzerland, devoting himself full-time to his writing.

A novelist of dazzling stylistic audacity, complex plot structures, multilayered meanings, and, with it all, a puckish sense of humor, Nabokov is not a writer who can be mastered with ease, though not all his works are difficult. Among his earlier novels, *Laughter in the Dark* (1938; a revised version of *Camera Obscura*, 1933) might well serve as an introduction to the themes and techniques of the later ones. Among those written in English, *Pnin* (1957) remains the most amusing, the most accessible. Neither approaches the complexity of *Lolita, Pale Fire* (1962), or *Ada or Ardor: A Family Chronicle* (1969). A critic, poet, playwright, translator, short story writer, composer of chess problems, and student of lepidoptera, as well as a novelist, he is a man of monumental accomplishment.

Novels written originally in Russian include *Mary*, 1926, 1970; *King, Queene, Knave*, 1928, 1968; *The Defense*, 1930, 1964; *Glory*, 1932, 1971; *Camera Obscura*, 1933, 1937 (*Laughter in the Dark*, 1938); *Despair*, 1936, 1937, 1966; *Invitation to a Beheading*, 1938, 1959; and *The Gift*, 1952, 1963. Novels written in English are *The Real Life of Sebastian Knight*, 1941; *Bend Sinister*, 1947; *Lolita*, 1955; *Pnin*, 1957; *Pale Fire*, 1962; *Ada*
* * *, 1969; and *Transparent Things*, 1972. Short story collections include *Nine Stories*, 1947; *Nabokov's Dozen*, 1958; *Nabokov's Quartet*, the source of the selection below, 1966; and *A Russian Beauty and Other Stories*, 1973. A play is *The Waltz Invention*, 1966. Collections of verse are *Poems*, 1959; and *Poems and Problems*, 1971. A critical study is *Nikolai Gogol*, 1944. The most ambitious of several translations is Aleksandr Pushkin, *Eugene Onegin*, 4 vols., 1964. A memoir is *Speak, Memory: An Autobiography Revisited*, 1966 (earlier version *Conclusive Evidence*, 1951; *Speak, Memory*, 1952). *Strong Opinions*, a collection of interviews, appeared in 1973. Selections from the works include Page Stegner, ed., *Nabokov's Congeries*, 1968; and *The Portable Nabokov*, 1971. Biographical and critical studies include Page Stegner, *The Art of Vladimir Nabokov: Escape into Aesthetics*, 1966; Andrew Field, *Nabokov: His Life in Art*, 1967; L. S. Dembo, ed., *Nabokov: The Man and His Work*, 1967; Carl R. Proffer, *Keys to Lolita*, 1968; Alfred Appel, Jr., and Charles Newman edited *Nabokov: Criticism, Reminiscences, * * ***, 1970; Alfred Appel, Jr., ed., *The Annotated Lolita*, 1970; and W. Woodlin Rowe, *Nabokov's Deceptive World*, 1971.

The Vane Sisters [1]

1.

I might never have heard of Cynthia's death, had I not run, that night, into D., whom I had also lost track of for the last four years or so; and I might never have run into D., had I not got involved in a series of trivial investigations.

The day, a compunctious Sunday after a week of blizzards, had been part jewel, part mud. In the midst of my usual afternoon stroll through the small hilly town attached to the girls' college where I taught French literature, I had stopped to watch a family of brilliant icicles drip-dripping from the eaves of a frame house. So clear-cut were their pointed shadows on the white boards behind them that I was sure the shadows of the falling drops should be visible too. But they were not. The roof jutted too far out, perhaps, or the angle of vision was faulty, or, again, I did not chance to be watching the right icicle when the right drop fell. There was a rhythm, an alternation in the dropping that I found as

1. Nabokov has written that the narrator "is supposed to be unaware that his last paragraph has been used acrostically by two dead girls to assert their mysterious participation in the story. This particular trick can be tried only once in a thousand years of fiction. Whether it has come off is another question."

teasing as a coin trick. It led me to inspect the corners of several house blocks, and this brought me to Kelly Road, and right to the house where D. used to live when he was instructor here. And as I looked up at the eaves of the adjacent garage with its full display of transparent stalactites backed by their blue silhouettes, I was rewarded at last, upon choosing one, by the sight of what might be described as the dot of an exclamation mark leaving its ordinary position to glide down very fast—a jot faster than the thaw-drop it raced. This twinned twinkle was delightful but not completely satisfying; or rather it only sharpened my appetite for other tidbits of light and shade, and I walked on in a state of raw awareness that seemed to transform the whole of my being into one big eyeball rolling in the world's socket.

Through peacocked lashes I saw the dazzling diamond reflection of the low sun on the round back of a parked automobile. To all kinds of things a vivid pictorial sense had been restored by the sponge of the thaw. Water in overlapping festoons flowed down one sloping street and turned gracefully into another. With ever so slight a note of meretricious appeal, narrow passages between buildings revealed treasures of brick and purple. I remarked for the first time the humble fluting—last echoes of grooves on the shafts of columns—ornamenting a garbage can, and I also saw the rippling upon its lid—circles diverging from a fantastically ancient center. Erect, dark-headed shapes of dead snow (left by the blades of a bulldozer last Friday) were lined up like rudimentary penguins along the curbs, above the brilliant vibration of live gutters.

I walked up, and I walked down, and I walked straight into a delicately dying sky, and finally the sequence of observed and observant things brought me, at my usual eating time, to a street so distant from my usual eating place that I decided to try a restaurant which stood on the fringe of the town. Night had fallen without sound or ceremony when I came out again. The lean ghost, the elongated umbra cast by a parking meter upon some damp snow, had a strange ruddy tinge; this I made out to be due to the tawny red light of the restaurant sign above the sidewalk; and it was then—as I sauntered there, wondering rather wearily if in the course of my return tramp I might be lucky enough to find the same in neon blue it was then that a car crunched to a standstill near me and D. got out of it with an exclamation of feigned pleasure.

He was passing, on his way from Albany to Boston, through the town he had dwelt in before, and more than once in my life have I felt that stab of vicarious emotion followed by a rush of personal irritation against travelers who seem to feel nothing at all upon revisiting spots that ought to harass them at every step with wailing and writhing memories. He ushered me back into the bar that I had just left, and after the usual exchange of buoyant platitudes came the inevitable vacuum which he filled with the random words: "Say, I never thought there was anything wrong with Cynthia Vane's heart. My lawyer tells me she died last week.".

2.

He was still young, still brash, still shifty, still married to the gentle, exquisitely pretty woman who had never learned or suspected anything about his disastrous affair with Cynthia's hysterical young sister, who in her turn had known nothing of the interview I had had with Cynthia when she suddenly summoned me to Boston to make me swear I would talk to D. and get him "kicked out" if he did not stop seeing Sybil at once—or did not divorce his wife (whom incidentally she visualized through the prism of Sybil's wild talk as a termagant and a fright). I had cornered him immediately. He had said there was nothing to worry about—had made up his mind, anyway, to give up his college job and move with his wife to Albany where he would work in his father's firm; and the whole matter, which had threatened to become one of those hopelessly entangled situations that drag on for years, with peripheral sets of well-meaning friends endlessly discussing it in universal secrecy—and even founding, among themselves, new intimacies upon its alien woes—came to an abrupt end.

I remember sitting next day at my raised desk in the large classroom where a mid-year examination in French Lit. was being held on the eve of Sybil's suicide. She came in on high heels, with a suitcase, dumped it in a corner where several other bags were stacked, with a single shrug slipped her fur coat off her thin shoulders, folded it on her bag, and with two or three other girls stopped before my desk to ask when would I mail them their grades. It would take me a week, beginning from tomorrow, I said, to read the stuff. I also remember wondering whether D. had already informed her of his decision—and I felt acutely unhappy about my dutiful little student as during one hundred and fifty minutes my gaze kept reverting to her, so childishly slight in close-fitting grey, and kept observing that carefully waved dark hair, that small, small-flowered hat with a little hyaline veil as worn that season and under it her small face broken into a cubist pattern by scars due to a skin disease, pathetically masked by a sun-lamp tan that hardened her features whose charm was further impaired by her having painted everything that could be painted, so that the pale gums of her teeth between cherry-red chapped lips and the diluted blue ink of her eyes under darkened lids were the only visible openings into her beauty.

1778 · *Vladimir Nabokov*

Next day, having arranged the ugly copybooks alphabetically, I plunged into their chaos of scripts and came prematurely to Valevsky and Vane whose books I had somehow misplaced. The first was dressed up for the occasion in a semblance of legibility, but Sybil's work displayed her usual combination of several demon hands. She had begun in very pale, very hard pencil which had conspicuously embossed the blank verso, but had produced little of permanent value on the upper-side of the page. Happily the tip soon broke, and Sybil continued in another, darker lead, gradually lapsing into the blurred thickness of what looked almost like charcoal, to which, by sucking the blunt point, she had contributed some traces of lipstick. Her work, although even poorer than I had expected, bore all the signs of a kind of desperate conscientiousness, with underscores, transposes, unnecessary footnotes, as if she were intent upon rounding up things in the most respectable manner possible. Then she had borrowed Mary Valevsky's fountain pen and added: *"Cette examain est finie ainsi que ma vie. Adieu, jeunes filles!* [2] Please, *Monsieur le Professeur*, contact *ma soeur* [3] and tell her that Death was not better than D minus, but definitely better than Life minus D."

I lost no time in ringing up Cynthia who told me it was all over—had been all over since eight in the morning—and asked me to bring her the note, and when I did, beamed through her tears with proud admiration for the whimsical use ("Just like her!") Sybil had made of an examination in French literature. In no time she "fixed" two highballs, while never parting with Sybil's notebook—by now splashed with soda water and tears—and went on studying the death message, whereupon I was impelled to point out to her the grammatical mistakes in it and to explain the way "girl" is translated in American colleges lest students innocently bandy around the French equivalent of "wench," or worse. These rather tasteless trivialities pleased Cynthia hugely as she rose, with gasps, above the heaving surface of her grief. And then, holding that limp notebook as if it were a kind of passport to a casual Elysium (where pencil points do not snap and a dreamy young beauty with an impeccable complexion winds a lock of her hair on a dreamy forefinger, as she meditates over some celestial test), Cynthia led me upstairs, to a chilly little bedroom just to show me, as if I were the police or a sympathetic Irish neighbor, two empty pill bottles and the tumbled bed from which a tender, inessential body, that D. must have known down to its last velvet detail, had been already removed.

2. "This examination is finished, along with my life. Farewell, young ladies." See, below, narrator's comments on the style of the French.
3. "My sister."

3.

It was four or five months after her sister's death that I began seeing Cynthia fairly often. By the time I had come to New York for some vocational research in the Public Library she had also moved to that city where for some odd reason (in vague connection, I presume, with artistic motives) she had taken what people, immune to gooseflesh, term a "cold water" flat, down in the scale of the city's transverse streets. What attracted me were neither her ways, which I thought repulsively vivacious, nor her looks, which other men thought striking. She had wide-spaced eyes very much like her sister's, of a frank, frightened blue with dark points in a radial arrangement. The interval between her thick black eyebrows was always shiny, and shiny too were the fleshy volutes of her nostrils. The coarse texture of her epiderm looked almost masculine, and, in the stark lamplight of her studio, you could see the pores of her thirty-two-year-old face fairly gaping at you like something in an aquarium. She used cosmetics with as much zest as her little sister had, but with an additional slovenliness that would result in her big front teeth getting some of the rouge. She was handsomely dark, wore a not too tasteless mixture of fairly smart heterogeneous things, and had a so-called good figure; but all of her was curiously frowsy, after a way I obscurely associated with left-wing enthusiasms in politics and "advanced" banalities in art, although, actually, she cared for neither. Her coily hair-do, on a part-and-bun basis, might have looked feral and bizarre had it not been thoroughly domesticated by its own soft unkemptness at the vulnerable nape. Her fingernails were gaudily painted, but badly bitten and not clean. Her lovers were a silent young photographer with a sudden laugh and two older men, brothers, who owned a small printing establishment across the street. I wondered at their tastes whenever I glimpsed, with a secret shudder, the higgledy-piggledy striation of black hairs that showed all along her pale shins through the nylon of her stockings with the scientific distinctness of a preparation flattened under glass; or when I felt, at her every movement, the dullish, stalish, not particularly conspicuous but all-pervading and depressing emanation that her seldom bathed flesh spread from under weary perfumes and creams.

Her father had gambled away the greater part of a comfortable fortune, and her mother's first husband had been of Slav origin, but otherwise Cynthia Vane belonged to a good, respectable family. For aught we know, it may have gone back to kings and soothsayers in the mists of ultimate islands. Transferred to a newer world, to a landscape of doomed, splendid deciduous trees, her ancestry presented, in one of its first phases, a white churchful of farmers against a black thunderhead, and then an imposing array of townsmen engaged in mercantile pursuits, as well as a number of learned men, such as Dr. Jonathan Vane, the gaunt bore (1780–1839), who perished in the conflagration of the steamer "Lexington" to become later an habitué of Cynthia's tilting table. I have always wished to stand genealogy on its head, and here I have an opportunity to do so, for it is the last scion, Cynthia, and Cynthia alone, who will remain of any importance in the Vane dynasty. I am alluding of course to her artistic gift, to her delightful, gay, but not very popular paintings which the friends of her friends bought at long intervals—and I dearly should like to know where they went after her death, those honest and poetical pictures that illumined her living-room—the wonderfully detailed images of metallic things, and my favorite "Seen Through a Windshield"— a windshield partly covered with rime, with a brilliant trickle (from an imaginary car roof) across its transparent part and, through it all, the sapphire flame of the sky and a green and white fir tree.

4.

Cynthia had a feeling that her dead sister was not altogether pleased with her—had discovered by now that she and I had conspired to break her romance; and so, in order to disarm her shade, Cynthia reverted to a rather primitive type of sacrificial offering (tinged, however, with something of Sybil's humor), and began to send to D.'s business address, at deliberately unfixed dates, such trifles as snapshots of Sybil's tomb in a poor light; cuttings of her own hair which was indistinguishable from Sybil's; a New England sectional map with an inked-in cross, midway between two chaste towns, to mark the spot where D. and Sybil had stopped on October the twenty-third, in broad daylight, at a lenient motel, in a pink and brown forest; and, twice, a stuffed skunk.

Being as a conversationalist more voluble than explicit, she never could describe in full the theory of intervenient auras that she had somehow evolved. Fundamentally there was nothing particularly new about her private creed since it presupposed a fairly conventional hereafter, a silent solarium of immortal souls (spliced with mortal antecedents) whose main recreation consisted of periodical hoverings over the dear quick. The interesting point was a curious practical twist that Cynthia gave to her tame metaphysics. She was sure that her existence was influenced by all sorts of dead friends each of whom took turns in directing her fate much as if she were a stray kitten which a schoolgirl in passing gathers up, and presses to her cheek, and carefully puts down again, near some suburban hedge—to be stroked presently by another transient hand or carried off to a world of doors by some hospitable lady.

For a few hours, or for several days in a row, and sometimes recurrently, in an irregular series, for months or years, anything that happened to Cynthia, after a given person had died, would be, she said, in the manner and mood of that person. The event might be extraordinary, changing the course of one's life; or it might be a string of minute incidents just sufficiently clear to stand out in relief against one's usual day and then shading off into still vaguer trivia as the aura gradually faded. The influence might be good or bad; the main thing was that its source could be identified. It was like walking through a person's soul, she said. I tried to argue that she might not always be able to determine the exact source since not everybody has a recognizable soul; that there are anonymous letters and Christmas presents which anybody might send; that, in fact, what Cynthia called "a usual day" might be itself a weak solution of mixed auras or simply the routine shift of a humdrum guardian angel. And what about God? Did or did not people who would resent any omnipotent dictator on earth look forward to one in heaven? And wars? What a dreadful idea—dead soldiers still fighting with living ones, or phantom armies trying to get at each other through the lives of crippled old men.

But Cynthia was above generalities as she was beyond logic. "Ah, that's Paul," she would say when the soup spitefully boiled over, or: "I guess good Betty Brown is dead"—when she won a beautiful and very welcome vacuum cleaner in a charity lottery. And, with Jamesian meanderings that exasperated my French mind, she would go back to a time when Betty and Paul had not yet departed, and tell me of the showers of well-meant, but odd and quite unacceptable bounties—beginning with an old purse that contained a check for three dollars which she picked up in the street and, of course, returned (to the aforesaid Betty Brown— this is where she first comes in—a decrepit colored woman hardly able to walk), and ending with an insulting proposal from an old beau of hers (this is where Paul comes in) to paint "straight" pictures of his house and family for a reasonable remuneration—all of which followed upon the demise of a certain Mrs. Page, a kindly but petty old party who had pestered her with bits of matter-of-fact advice since Cynthia had been a child.

Sybil's personality, she said, had a rainbow edge as if a little out of focus. She said that had I known Sybil better I would have at once understood how Sybil-like was the aura of minor events which, in spells, had suffused her, Cynthia's, existence after Sybil's suicide. Ever since they had lost their mother they had intended to give up their Boston home and move to New York, where Cynthia's paintings, they thought, would have a chance to be more widely admired; but the old home had clung to them with all its plush tentacles. Dead Sybil, however, had proceeded to separate the house from its view—a thing that affects fatally the sense of home. Right across the narrow street a building project had come into loud, scaffolded life. A pair of familiar poplars died that spring, turning to blond skeletons. Workmen came and broke up the warm-colored lovely old sidewalk that had a special violet sheen on wet April days and had echoed so memorably to the morning footsteps of museum-bound Mr. Lever, who upon retiring from business at sixty had devoted a full quarter of a century exclusively to the study of snails.

Speaking of old men, one should add that sometimes these posthumous auspices and interventions were in the nature of parody. Cynthia had been on friendly terms with an eccentric librarian called Porlock who in the last years of his dusty life had been engaged in examining old books for miraculous misprints such as the substitution of "l" for the second "h" in the word "hither." Contrary to Cynthia, he cared nothing for the thrill of obscure predictions; all he sought was the freak itself, the chance that mimics choice, the flaw that looks like a flower; and Cynthia, a much more perverse amateur of mis-shapen or illicitly connected words, puns, logogriphs, and so on, had helped the poor crank to pursue a quest that in the light of the example she cited struck me as statistically insane. Anyway, she said, on the third day after his death she was reading a magazine and had just come across a quotation from an imperishable poem [4] (that she, with other gullible readers, believed to have been really composed in a dream) when it dawned upon her that "Alph" was a prophetic sequence of the initial letters of Anna Livia Plurabelle [5] (another sacred river running through, or rather around, yet another fake dream), while the additional "h" modestly stood, as a private signpost, for the word that had so hypnotized Mr. Porlock. And I wish I could recollect that novel or short story (by some contemporary writer, I believe) in which, unknown to its author, the first letters of the words in its last paragraph formed, as deciphered by Cynthia, a message from his dead mother.

5.

I am sorry to say that not content with these ingenious fancies Cynthia showed a ridiculous fondness for spiritualism. I refused to accompany her to sittings in which paid mediums took part: I knew too much about that from other sources. I did consent, however, to attend little farces rigged up by Cynthia and her two poker-faced gentlemen-friends of the printing shop. They were podgy, polite, and rather eerie old fellows, but I satisfied myself that they possessed considerable wit and culture. We sat down at a light little table, and crackling tremors started almost as soon as we laid our fingertips upon it. I was treated to an assortment of ghosts who rapped out their reports most readily though refusing to elucidate anything that I did not quite catch. Oscar Wilde came in and in rapid garbled French, with the usual anglicisms, obscurely accused Cynthia's dead parents of what appeared in my jottings as *"plagiatisme."* A brisk spirit contributed the unsolicited information that he, John Moore, and his brother Bill had been coal miners in Colorado and had perished in an avalanche at "Crested Beauty" in January 1883. Frederic Myers, an old hand at the game, hammered out a piece of verse (oddly resembling Cynthia's own fugitive productions) which in part reads in my notes:

> *What is this—a conjuror's rabbit,*
> *Or a flawy but genuine gleam—*
> *Which can check the perilous habit*
> *And dispel the dolorous dream?*

Finally, with a great crash and all kinds of shudderings and jig-like movements on the part of the table, Leo Tolstoy visited our little group and, when asked to identify himself by specific traits of terrene habitation, launched upon a complex description of what seemed to be some Russian type of architectural woodwork ("figures on boards—man, horse, cock, man, horse, cock"), all of which was difficult to take down, hard to understand, and impossible to verify.

I attended two or three other sittings which were even sillier but I must confess that I preferred the childish entertainment they afforded and the cider we drank (Podgy and Pudgy were teetotallers) to Cynthia's awful house parties.

She gave them at the Wheelers' nice flat next door—the sort of arrangement dear to her centrifugal nature, but then, of course, her own living-room always looked like a dirty old palette. Following a barbaric, unhygienic, and adulterous custom, the guests' coats, still warm on the inside, were carried by quiet, baldish Bob Wheeler into the sanctity of a tidy bedroom and heaped on the conjugal bed. It was also he who poured out the drinks which were passed around by the young photographer while Cynthia and Mrs. Wheeler took care of the canapés.

A late arrival had the impression of lots of loud people unnecessarily grouped within a smoke-blue space between two mirrors gorged with reflections. Because, I suppose, Cynthia wished to be the youngest in the room, the women she used to invite, married or single, were, at the best, in their precarious forties; some of them would bring from their homes, in dark taxis, intact vestiges of good looks, which, however, they lost as the party progressed. It has always amazed me—the capacity sociable week-end revellers have of finding almost at once, by a purely empiric but very precise method, a common denominator of drunkenness, to which everybody loyally sticks before descending, all together, to the next level. The rich friendliness of the matrons was marked by tomboyish overtones, while the fixed inward look of amiably tight men was like a sacrilegious parody of pregnancy. Although some of the guests were connected in one way or another with the arts, there was no inspired talk, no wreathed, elbow-propped heads, and of course no flute girls. From some vantage point where she had been sitting in a stranded mermaid pose on the pale carpet with one or two younger fellows, Cynthia, her face varnished with a film of beaming sweat, would creep up on her knees, a proffered plate of nuts in one hand, and crisply tap with the other the athletic leg of Cochran or Corcoran, an art dealer, ensconced, on a pearl-grey sofa, between two flushed, happily disintegrating ladies.

At a further stage there would come spurts of more riotous gaiety. Corcoran or Coransky would grab Cynthia or some other wandering woman by the shoulder and lead her into a corner to confront her with a grinning embroglio of private jokes and rumors, whereupon, with a laugh and a toss of her head, she would break away. And still later there would be flurries of intersexual chumminess, jocular reconciliations, a bare fleshy arm flung around another woman's husband (he standing very upright in the midst of a swaying room), or a sudden rush of flirtatious anger, of clumsy pursuit—and the quiet half smile of Bob Wheeler picking up glasses that grew like mushrooms in the shade of chairs.

After one last party of that sort, I wrote Cynthia a perfectly harmless and, on the whole, well-meant note, in which I poked a little Latin fun at some of her guests. I also apologized for not having touched her whisky, saying that as a Frenchman I preferred the grape to the grain. A few days later I met her on the steps of the Public Library, in the broken sun, under a weak cloudburst, opening her amber umbrella, struggling with a couple of armpitted books (of which I relieved her for a moment). "Footfalls on the Boundary of Another World," by Robert Dale Owen, and something on "Spiritualism and Christianity"; when, suddenly, with no provocation on my part, she blazed out at me with vulgar vehemence, using poisonous words, saying—through pear-shaped drops of sparse rain—that I was a prig and a snob; that I only saw the gestures and disguises of people; that Corcoran had rescued from drowning, in two different oceans, two men—by an irrelevant coincidence both called Corcoran; that romping and screeching Joan Winter had a little girl doomed to grow completely blind in a few months; and that the woman in green with the freckled chest whom I had snubbed in some way or other had written a national best-seller in 1932. Strange Cynthia! I had been told she could be thunderously rude to people whom she liked and respected; one had, however, to draw the line somewhere and since I had by then sufficiently studied her interesting auras and other odds and ids, I decided to stop seeing her altogether.

6.

The night D. informed me of Cynthia's death I returned after eleven to the two-storied house I shared, in horizontal section, with an emeritus professor's widow. Upon reaching the porch I looked with the apprehension of solitude at the two kinds of darkness in the two rows of windows: the darkness of absence and the darkness of sleep.

I could do something about the first but could not duplicate the second. My bed gave me no sense of safety; its springs only made my nerves bounce. I plunged into Shakespeare's sonnets—and found myself idiotically checking the first letters of the lines to see what sacramental words they might form. I got fate (LXX), ATOM (CXX) and, twice, TAFT (LXXXVIII, CXXXI). Every now and then I would glance around to see how the objects in my room were behaving. It was strange to think that if bombs began to fall I would feel little more than a gambler's excitement (and a great deal of earthy relief) whereas my heart would burst if a certain suspiciously tense-looking little bottle on yonder shelf moved a fraction of an inch to one side. The silence, too, was suspiciously compact as if deliberately forming a black back-drop for the nerve flash caused by any small sound of unknown origin. All traffic was dead. In vain did I pray for the groan of a truck up Perkins Street. The woman above who used to drive me crazy by the booming thuds occasioned by what seemed monstrous feet of stone (actually, in diurnal life, she was a small dumpy creature resembling a mummified guinea pig) would have earned my blessings had she now trudged to her bathroom. I put out my light and cleared my throat several times so as to be responsible for at least *that* sound. I thumbed a mental ride with a very remote automobile but it dropped me before I had a chance to doze off. Presently a crackle (due, I hoped, to a discarded and crushed sheet of paper opening like a mean, stubborn night flower)—started and stopped in the waste-paper basket, and my bed-table responded with a little click. It would have been just like Cynthia to put on right then a cheap poltergeist show.

I decided to fight Cynthia. I reviewed in thought the modern era of raps and apparitions, beginning with the knockings of 1848, at the hamlet of Hydesville, N.Y., and ending with grotesque phenomena at Cambridge, Mass.; I evoked the ankle-bones and other anatomical castanets of the Fox sisters (as described by the sages of the University of Buffalo); the mysteriously uniform type of delicate adolescent in bleak Epworth or Tedworth, radiating the same disturbances as in old Peru; solemn Victorian orgies with roses falling and accordions floating to the strains of sacred music; professional imposters regurgitating moist cheesecloth; Mr. Duncan, a lady medium's dignified husband, who, when asked if he would submit to a search, excused himself on the ground of soiled underwear; old Alfred Russel Wallace, the naïve naturalist, refusing to believe that the white form with bare feet and unperforated earlobes before him, at a private pandemonium in Boston, could be prim Miss Cook whom he had just seen asleep, in her curtained corner; all dressed in black, wearing laced-up boots and earrings; two other investigators, small, puny, but reasonably intelligent and active men, closely clinging with arms and legs about Eusapia, a large, plump elderly female reeking of garlic, who still managed to fool them; and the sceptical and embarrassed magician, instructed by charming young Margery's "control" not to get lost in the bathrobe's lining but to follow up the left stocking until he reached the bare thigh—upon the warm skin of which he felt a "teleplastic" mass that appeared to the touch uncommonly like cold, uncooked liver.

7.

I was appealing to flesh, and the corruption of flesh, to refute and defeat the possible persistence of discarnate life. Alas, these conjurations only enhanced my fear of Cynthia's phantom. Atavistic peace came with dawn, and when I slipped into sleep, the sun through the tawny window shades penetrated a dream that somehow was full of Cynthia.

This was disappointing. Secure in the fortress of daylight, I said to myself that I had expected more. She, a painter of glass-bright minutiæ—and now so vague! I lay in bed, thinking my dream over and listening to the sparrows outside: Who knows, if recorded and then run backward, those bird sounds might not become human speech, voiced words, just as the latter become a twitter when reversed? I set myself to re-read my dream—backward, diagonally, up, down—trying hard to unravel something Cynthia-like in it, something strange and suggestive that must be there.

I could isolate, consciously, little. Everything seemed blurred, yellow-clouded, yielding nothing tangible. Her inept acrostics, maudlin evasions, theopathies—every recollection formed ripples of mysterious meaning. Everything seemed yellowly blurred, illusive, lost.

1966

RALPH ELLISON

(1914–   )

In a poll conducted in 1965 by *Book Week* a group of critics selected Ralph Ellison's novel *Invisible Man* (1952) as the most distinguished work of fiction to appear in the post–World War II period. That poll may be taken as a tribute not only to the power of the novel but to the continuing literary reputation of a man who, past fifty, had published only one other volume, a collection of essays called *Shadow and Act* (1964). Yet, Ellison did not come late to writing. Rather, he is a slow, painstaking author, who, after some success with short stories in his twenties, directed his attention to the completion of *Invisible Man*, which was published when he was thirty-eight. Excerpts from a second novel began to appear in magazines in 1960 and continued to appear throughout the following decade as the novel slowly progressed toward completion. Meanwhile, Ellison taught and lectured and remained a formidable literary presence.

Christened Ralph Waldo Ellison, he was born in Oklahoma City, Oklahoma, and educated at Tuskegee Institute. An early interest in music, especially jazz and blues, remains as an influence in his work. After support-

ing himself by a variety of jobs, including service in the Merchant Marine, he began teaching in 1958 at Bard College and has taught since then at Rutgers and New York University. He has also served on the Editorial Board of *American Scholar* and as a Trustee of the John F. Kennedy Center for the Performing Arts and has been the recipient of numerous awards and honorary degrees.

The effect of *Invisible Man* is due in large measure to the successful amalgamation of so many diverse elements in its structure. It is a folk novel, strong in the rhythms of jazz and blues, powerful in its projection of the dual consciousness of the American black. It is also a highly literary, and literate, novel, its epigraphs taken from Melville and T. S. Eliot, its prose polished, its episodes constructed with a care reminiscent of the practice of the greatest American and English novelists. Although the accomplishment is difficult to represent by a selection, something of the flavor of the book may be seen in the first chapter, which was originally published separately as a short story.

John M. Reilly edited *Twentieth Century Interpretations of Invisible Man*, 1970. Ronald Gottesman edited *Studies in Invisible Man*, 1971. Bernard Benoit and Michel Fabre compiled "A Bibliography of Ralph Ellison's Published Writings," in *Studies in Black Literature,* Autumn, 1971.

See also Robert A. Bone, *The Negro Novel in America,* revised edition, 1958.

From Invisible Man

Chapter I [1]

It goes a long way back, some twenty years. All my life I had been looking for something, and everywhere I turned someone tried to tell me what it was. I accepted their answers too, though they were often in contradiction and even self-contradictory. I was naïve. I was looking for myself and asking everyone except myself questions which I, and only I, could answer. It took me a long time and much painful boomeranging of my expectations to achieve a realization everyone else appears to have been born with: That I am nobody but myself. But first I had to discover that I am an invisible man!

And yet I am no freak of nature, nor of history. I was in the cards, other things having been equal (or unequal) eighty-five years ago. I am not ashamed of my grandparents for having been slaves. I am only ashamed of myself for having at one time been ashamed. About eighty-five years ago they were told that they were free, united with others of our country in everything pertaining to the common good, and, in everything social, separate like the fingers of the hand. And they believed it. They exulted in it. They stayed in their place, worked hard, and brought up my father to do the same. But my grandfather is the one. He was an odd old guy, my grandfather, and I am told I take after him. It was he who caused the trouble. On his deathbed he called my father to him and said, "Son, after I'm gone I want you to keep up the good fight. I never told you, but our life is a war and I have been a traitor all my born days, a spy in the enemy's country ever since I give up my gun back in the Reconstruction. Live with your head in the lion's mouth. I want you to overcome 'em with yeses, undermine 'em with grins, agree 'em to death and destruction, let 'em swoller you till they vomit or bust wide open." They thought the old man had gone out of his mind. He had been the meekest of men. The younger children were rushed from the room, the shades drawn and the flame of the lamp turned so low that it sputtered on the wick like the old man's breathing. "Learn it to the younguns," he whispered fiercely; then he died.

But my folks were more alarmed over his last words than over his dying. It was as though he had not died at all, his words caused so much anxiety. I was warned emphatically to forget what he had

---

1. First published in *Horizon,* October, 1947, under the title "The Invisible Man."

said and, indeed, this is the first time it has been mentioned outside the family circle. It had a tremendous effect upon me, however. I could never be sure of what he meant. Grandfather had been a quiet old man who never made any trouble, yet on his deathbed he had called himself a traitor and a spy, and he had spoken of his meekness as a dangerous activity. It became a constant puzzle which lay unanswered in the back of my mind. And whenever things went well for me I remembered my grandfather and felt guilty and uncomfortable. It was as though I was carrying out his advice in spite of myself. And to make it worse, everyone loved me for it. I was praised by the most lily-white men of the town. I was considered an example of desirable conduct—just as my grandfather had been. And what puzzled me was that the old man had defined it as *treachery*. When I was praised for my conduct I felt a guilt that in some way I was doing something that was really against the wishes of the white folks, that if they had understood they would have desired me to act just the opposite, that I should have been sulky and mean, and that that really would have been what they wanted, even though they were fooled and thought they wanted me to act as I did. It made me afraid that some day they would look upon me as a traitor and I would be lost. Still I was more afraid to act any other way because they didn't like that at all. The old man's words were like a curse. On my graduation day I delivered an oration in which I showed that humility was the secret, indeed, the very essence of progress. (Not that I believed this—how could I, remembering my grandfather?—I only believed that it worked.) It was a great success. Everyone praised me and I was invited to give the speech at a gathering of the town's leading white citizens. It was a triumph for our whole community.

It was in the main ballroom of the leading hotel. When I got there I discovered that it was on the occasion of a smoker, and I was told that since I was to be there anyway I might as well take part in the battle royal to be fought by some of my schoolmates as part of the entertainment. The battle royal came first.

All of the town's big shots were there in their tuxedoes, wolfing down the buffet foods, drinking beer and whiskey and smoking black cigars. It was a large room with a high ceiling. Chairs were arranged in neat rows around three sides of a portable boxing ring. The fourth side was clear, revealing a gleaming space of polished floor. I had some misgivings over the battle royal, by the way. Not from a distaste for fighting, but because I didn't care too much for the other fellows who were to take part. They were tough guys who seemed to have no grandfather's curse worrying their minds. No one could mistake their toughness. And besides, I suspected that fighting a battle royal might detract from the dignity of my speech. In those pre-invisible days I visualized myself as a potential Booker T. Washington. But the other fellows didn't care too much for me either, and there were nine of them. I felt superior to them in my way, and I didn't like the manner in which we were all crowded together into the servants' elevator. Nor did they like my being there. In fact, as the warmly lighted floors flashed past the elevator we had words over the fact that I, by taking part in the fight, had knocked one of their friends out of a night's work.

We were led out of the elevator through a rococo hall into an anteroom and told to get into our fighting togs. Each of us was issued a pair of boxing gloves and ushered out into the big mirrored hall, which we entered looking cautiously about us and whispering, lest we might accidentally be heard above the noise of the room. It was foggy with cigar smoke. And already the whiskey was taking effect. I was shocked to see some of the most important men of the town quite tipsy. They were all there—bankers, lawyers, judges, doctors, fire chiefs, teachers, merchants. Even one of the more fashionable pastors. Something we could not see was going on up front. A clarinet was vibrating sensuously and the men were standing up and moving eagerly forward. We were a small tight group, clustered together, our bare upper bodies touching and shining with anticipatory sweat; while up front the big shots were becoming increasingly excited over something we still could not see. Suddenly I heard the school superintendent, who had told me to come, yell, "Bring up the shines, gentlemen! Bring up the little shines!"

We were rushed up to the front of the ballroom, where it smelled even more strongly of tobacco and whiskey. Then we were pushed into place. I almost wet my pants. A sea of faces, some hostile, some amused, ringed around us, and in the center, facing us, stood a magnificent blonde—stark naked. There was dead silence. I felt a blast of cold air chill me. I tried to back away, but they were behind me and around me. Some of the boys stood with lowered heads, trembling. I felt a wave of irrational guilt and fear. My teeth chattered, my skin turned to goose flesh, my knees knocked. Yet I was strongly attracted and looked in spite of myself. Had the price of looking been blindness, I would have looked. The hair was yellow like that of a circus kewpie doll, the face heavily powdered and rouged, as though to form an abstract mask, the eyes hollow and smeared a cool blue, the color of a baboon's butt. I felt a desire to spit upon her as my eyes brushed slowly over her body. Her breasts were firm and round as the domes of East Indian temples, and I stood so close as to see the fine skin texture and beads of pearly perspiration glistening like dew around the pink and erected buds of her nipples. I wanted at one and the same time to run from the room, to sink through the floor, or go to her and cover her from my eyes and the eyes of the others with my body; to feel the soft thighs, to caress her and destroy her, to love her and murder her, to hide from her, and yet to stroke where below the small American flag tattooed upon her belly her thighs formed a capital V. I had a notion that of all in the room she saw only me with her impersonal eyes.

And then she began to dance, a slow sensuous movement; the smoke of a hundred cigars clinging to her like the thinnest of veils. She seemed like a fair bird-girl girdled in veils calling to me from the angry surface of some gray and threatening sea. I was transported. Then I became aware of the clarinet playing and the big shots yelling at us. Some threatened us if we looked and others if we did not. On my right I saw one boy faint. And now a man grabbed a silver pitcher from a table and stepped close as he dashed ice water upon him and stood him up and forced two of us to support him as his head hung and moans issued from his thick bluish lips. Another boy began to plead to go home. He was the largest of the group, wearing dark red fighting trunks much too small to conceal the erection which projected from him as though in answer to the insinuating low-registered moaning of the clarinet. He tried to hide himself with his boxing gloves.

And all the while the blonde continued dancing, smiling faintly at the big shots who watched her with fascination, and faintly smiling at our fear. I noticed a certain merchant who followed her hungrily, his lips loose and drooling. He was a large man who wore diamond studs in a shirtfront which swelled with the ample paunch underneath, and each time the blonde swayed her undulating hips he ran his hand through the thin hair of his bald head and, with his arms upheld, his posture clumsy like that of an intoxicated panda, wound his belly in a slow and obscene grind. This creature was completely hypnotized. The music had quickened. As the dancer flung herself about with a detached expression on her face, the men began reaching out to touch her. I could see their beefy fingers sink into the soft flesh. Some of the others tried to stop them and she began to move around the floor in graceful circles, as they gave chase, slipping and sliding over the polished floor. It was mad. Chairs went crashing, drinks were spilt, as they ran laughing and howling after her. They caught her just as she reached a door, raised her from the floor, and tossed her as college boys are tossed at a hazing, and above her red, fixed-smiling lips I saw the terror and disgust in her eyes, almost like my own terror and that which I saw in some of the other boys. As I watched, they tossed her twice and her soft breasts seemed to flatten against the air and her legs flung wildly as she spun. Some of the more sober ones helped her to escape. And I started off the floor, heading for the anteroom with the rest of the boys.

Some were still crying and in hysteria. But as we tried to leave we were stopped and ordered to get into the ring. There was nothing to do but what we were told. All ten of us climbed under the ropes and allowed ourselves to be blindfolded with broad bands of white cloth. One of the men seemed to feel a bit sympathetic and tried to cheer us up as we stood with our backs against the ropes. Some of us tried to grin. "See that boy over there?" one of the men said. "I want you to run across at the bell and give it to him right in the belly. If you don't get him, I'm going to get you. I don't like his looks." Each of us was told the same. The blindfolds were put on. Yet even then I had been going over my speech. In my mind each word was as bright as flame. I felt the cloth pressed into place, and frowned so that it would be loosened when I relaxed.

But now I felt a sudden fit of blind terror. I was unused to darkness. It was as though I had suddenly found myself in a dark room filled with poisonous cottonmouths. I could hear the bleary voices yelling insistently for the battle royal to begin.

"Get going in there!"

"Let me at that big nigger!"

I strained to pick up the school superintendent's voice, as though to squeeze some security out of that slightly more familiar sound.

"Let me at those black sonsabitches!" someone yelled.

"No, Jackson, no!" another voice yelled. "Here, somebody, help me hold Jack."

"I want to get at that ginger-colored nigger. Tear him limb from limb," the first voice yelled.

I stood against the ropes trembling. For in those days I was what they called ginger-colored, and he sounded as though he might crunch me between his teeth like a crisp ginger cookie.

Quite a struggle was going on. Chairs were being kicked about and I could hear voices grunting as with a terrific effort. I wanted to see, to see more desperately than ever before. But the blindfold was tight as a thick skin-puckering scab and when I raised my gloved hands to push the layers of white aside a voice yelled, "Oh, no you don't, black bastard! Leave that alone!"

"Ring the bell before Jackson kills him a coon!" someone boomed in the sudden silence. And I heard the bell clang and the sound of the feet scuffling forward.

A glove smacked against my head. I pivoted, striking out stiffly as someone went past, and felt the jar ripple along the length of my arm to my shoulder. Then it seemed as though all nine of the boys had turned upon me at once. Blows pounded me from all sides while I struck out as best I could. So many blows landed upon me that I wondered if I were not the only blindfolded fighter in the ring, or if the man called Jackson hadn't succeeded in getting me after all.

Blindfolded, I could no longer control my motions. I had no dignity. I stumbled about like a baby or a drunken man. The smoke had become thicker and with each new blow it seemed to sear and further restrict my lungs. My saliva became like hot bitter glue. A glove connected with my head, filling my mouth with warm blood. It was everywhere. I could not tell if the moisture I felt upon my body was sweat or blood. A blow landed hard against the nape of my neck. I felt myself going over, my head hitting the floor. Streaks of blue light filled the black world behind the blindfold. I lay prone, pretending that I was knocked out, but felt myself seized by hands and yanked to my feet. "Get going, black boy! Mix it up!" My arms were like lead, my head smarting from blows. I managed to feel my way to the ropes and held on, trying to catch my breath. A glove landed in my mid-section and I went over again, feeling as though the smoke had become a knife jabbed into my guts. Pushed this way and that by the legs milling around me, I finally pulled erect and discovered that I could see the black, sweat-washed forms weaving in the smoky-blue atmosphere like drunken dancers weaving to the rapid drum-like thuds of blows.

Everyone fought hysterically. It was complete anarchy. Everybody fought everybody else. No group fought together for long. Two, three, four, fought one, then turned to fight each other, were themselves attacked. Blows landed below the belt and in the kidney, with the gloves open as well as closed, and with my eye partly opened now there was not so much terror. I moved carefully, avoiding blows, although not too many to attract attention, fighting from group to group. The boys groped about like blind, cautious crabs crouching to protect their mid-sections, their heads pulled in short against their shoulders, their arms stretched nervously before them, with their fists testing the smoke-filled air like the knobbed feelers of hypersensitive snails. In one corner I glimpsed a boy violently punching the air and heard him scream in pain as he smashed his hand against a ring post. For a second I saw him bent over holding his hand, then going down as a blow caught his unprotected head. I played one group against the other, slipping in and throwing a punch then stepping out of range while pushing the others into the melee to take the blows blindly aimed at me. The smoke was agonizing and there were no rounds, no bells at three minute intervals to relieve our exhaustion. The room spun round me, a swirl of lights, smoke, sweating bodies surrounded by tense white faces. I bled from both nose and mouth, the blood spattering upon my chest.

The men kept yelling, "Slug him, black boy! Knock his guts out!"

"Uppercut him! Kill him! Kill that big boy!"

Taking a fake fall, I saw a boy going down heavily beside me as though we were felled by a single blow, saw a sneaker-clad foot shoot into his groin as the two who had knocked him down stumbled upon him. I rolled out of range, feeling a twinge of nausea.

The harder we fought the more threatening the men became. And yet, I had begun to worry about my speech again. How would it go? Would they recognize my ability? What would they give me?

I was fighting automatically when suddenly I noticed that one after another of the boys was leaving the ring. I was surprised, filled with panic, as though I had been left alone with an unknown danger. Then I understood. The boys had arranged it among themselves. It was the custom for the two men left in the ring to slug it out for the winner's prize. I discovered this too late. When the bell sounded two men in tuxedoes leaped into the ring and removed the blindfold. I found myself facing Tatlock, the biggest of the gang. I felt sick at my stomach. Hardly had the bell stopped ringing in my ears than it clanged again and I saw him moving swiftly toward me. Thinking of nothing else to do I hit him smash on the nose. He kept coming, bringing the rank sharp violence of stale sweat. His face was a black blank of a face, only his eyes alive —with hate of me and aglow with a feverish terror from what had happened to us all. I became anxious. I wanted to deliver my speech and he came at me as though he meant to beat it out of me. I smashed him again and again, taking his blows as they came. Then on a sudden impulse I struck him lightly and as we clinched, I whispered, "Fake like I knocked you out, you can have the prize."

"I'll break your behind," he whispered hoarsely.

"For *them?*"

"For *me,* sonofabitch!"

They were yelling for us to break it up and Tatlock spun me half around with a blow, and as a joggled camera sweeps in a reeling scene, I saw the howling red faces crouching tense beneath the cloud of blue-gray smoke. For a moment the world wavered, unraveled, flowed, then my head cleared and Tatlock bounced before me. That fluttering shadow before my eyes was his jabbing left hand. Then falling forward, my head against his damp shoulder, I whispered,

"I'll make it five dollars more."

"Go to hell!"

But his muscles relaxed a trifle beneath my pressure and I breathed, "Seven?"

"Give it to your ma," he said, ripping me beneath the heart. And while I still held him I butted him and moved away. I felt myself bombarded with punches. I fought back with hopeless desperation. I wanted to deliver my speech more than anything else in the world, because I felt that only these men could judge truly my ability, and now this stupid clown was ruining my chances. I began fighting carefully now, moving in to punch him and out again with my greater speed. A lucky blow to his chin and I had him going too—until I heard a loud voice yell, "I got my money on the big boy."

Hearing this, I almost dropped my guard. I was confused: Should I try to win against the voice out there? Would not this go against my speech, and was not this a moment for humility, for nonresistance? A blow to my head as I danced about sent my right eye popping like a jack-in-the-box and settled my dilemma. The room went red as I fell. It was a dream fall, my body languid and fastidious as to where to land, until the floor became impatient and smashed up to meet me. A moment later I came to. An hypnotic voice said FIVE emphatically. And I lay there, hazily watching a dark red spot of my own blood shaping itself into a butterfly, glistening and soaking into the soiled gray world of the canvas.

When the voice drawled TEN I was lifted up and dragged to a chair. I sat dazed. My eye pained and swelled with each throb of my pounding heart and I wondered if now I would be allowed to speak. I was wringing wet, my mouth still bleeding. We were grouped along the wall now. The other boys ignored me as they congratulated Tatlock and speculated as to how much they would be paid. One boy whimpered over his smashed hand. Looking up front, I saw attendants in white jackets rolling the portable ring away and placing a small square rug in the vacant space surrounded by chairs. Perhaps, I thought, I will stand on the rug to deliver my speech.

Then the M.C. called to us, "Come on up here boys and get your money."

We ran forward to where the men laughed and talked in their chairs, waiting. Everyone seemed friendly now.

"There it is on the rug," the man said. I saw the rug covered with coins of all dimensions and a few crumpled bills. But what excited me, scattered here and there, were the gold pieces.

"Boys, it's all yours," the man said. "You get all your grab."

"That's right, Sambo," a blond man said, winking at me confidentially.

I trembled with excitement, forgetting my pain. I would get the gold and the bills, I thought. I would use both hands. I would throw my body against the boys nearest me to block them from the gold.

"Get down around the rug now," the man commanded, "and don't anyone touch it until I give the signal."

"This ought to be good," I heard.

As told, we got around the square rug on our knees. Slowly the man raised his freckled hand as we followed it upward with our eyes.

I heard, "These niggers look like they're about to pray!"

Then, "Ready," the man said. "Go!"

I lunged for a yellow coin lying on the blue design of the carpet, touching it and sending a surprised shriek to join those rising around me. I tried frantically to remove my hand but could not let go. A hot, violent force tore through my body, shaking me like a wet rat. The rug was electrified. The hair bristled up on my head as I shook myself free. My muscles jumped, my nerves jangled, writhed. But I saw that this was not stopping the other boys. Laughing in fear and embarrassment, some were holding back and scooping up the coins knocked off by the painful contortions of the others. The men roared above us as we struggled.

"Pick it up, goddamnit, pick it up!" someone called like a bass-voiced parrot. "Go on, get it!"

I crawled rapidly around the floor, picking up the coins, trying to avoid the coppers and to get greenbacks and the gold. Ignoring the shock by laughing, as I brushed the coins off quickly, I discovered that I could contain the electricity—a contradiction, but it works. Then the men began to push us onto the rug. Laughing embarrassedly, we struggled out of their hands and kept after the coins. We were all wet and slippery and hard to hold. Suddenly I saw a boy lifted into the air, glistening with sweat like a circus seal, and dropped, his wet back landing flush upon the charged rug, heard him yell and saw him literally dance upon his back, his elbows beating a frenzied tattoo upon the floor, his muscles twitching like the flesh of a horse stung by many flies. When he finally rolled off, his face was gray and no one stopped him when he ran from the floor amid booming laughter.

"Get the money," the M.C. called. "That's good hard American cash!"

And we snatched and grabbed, snatched and grabbed. I was careful not to come too close to the rug now, and when I felt the hot whiskey breath descend upon me like a cloud of foul air I reached out and grabbed the leg of a chair. It was occupied and I held on desperately.

"Leggo, nigger! Leggo!"

The huge face wavered down to mine as he tried to push me free. But my body was slippery and he was too drunk. It was Mr. Colcord, who owned a chain of movie houses and "entertainment palaces." Each time he grabbed me I slipped out of his hands. It became a real struggle. I feared the rug more than I did the drunk, so I held on, surprising myself for a moment by trying to topple *him* upon the rug. It was such an enormous idea that I found myself actually carrying it out. I tried not to be obvious, yet when I grabbed his leg, trying to tumble him out of the chair, he raised up roaring with laughter, and, looking at me with soberness dead in the eye, kicked me viciously in the chest. The chair leg flew out of my hand and I felt myself going and rolled. It was as though I had rolled through a bed of hot coals. It seemed a whole century would pass before I would roll free, a century in which I was seared through the deepest levels of my body to the fearful breath within me and the breath seared and heated to the point of explosion. It'll all be over in a flash, I thought as I rolled clear. It'll all be over in a flash.

But not yet, the men on the other side were waiting, red faces swollen as though from apoplexy as they bent forward in their chairs. Seeing their fingers coming toward me I rolled away as a fumbled football rolls off the receiver's fingertips, back into the coals. That time I luckily sent the rug sliding out of place and heard the coins ringing against the floor and the boys scuffling to pick them up and the M.C. calling, "All right, boys, that's all. Go get dressed and get your money."

I was limp as a dish rag. My back felt as though it had been beaten with wires.

When we had dressed the M.C. came in and gave us each five dollars, except Tatlock, who got ten for being last in the ring. Then he told us to leave. I was not to get a chance to deliver my speech, I thought. I was going out into the dim alley in despair when I was stopped and told to go back. I returned to the ballroom, where the men were pushing back their chairs and gathering in groups to talk.

The M.C. knocked on a table for quiet. "Gentlemen," he said, "we almost forgot an important part of the program. A most serious part, gentlemen. This boy was brought here to deliver a speech which he made at his graduation yesterday . . ."

"Bravo!"

"I'm told that he is the smartest boy we've got out there in Greenwood. I'm told that he knows more big words than a pocket-sized dictionary."

Much applause and laughter.

"So now, gentlemen, I want you to give him your attention."

There was still laughter as I faced them, my mouth dry, my eye throbbing. I began slowly, but evidently my throat was tense, because they began shouting, "Louder! Louder!"

"We of the younger generation extol the wisdom of that great leader and educator," I shouted, "who first spoke these flaming words of wisdom: 'A ship lost at sea for many days suddenly sighted a friendly vessel. From the mast of the unfortunate vessel was seen a signal: "Water, water; we die of thirst!" The answer from the friendly vessel came back: "Cast down your bucket where you are." The captain of the distressed vessel, at last heeding the injunction, cast down his bucket, and it came up full of fresh sparkling water from the mouth of the Amazon River.' And like him I say, and in his words, 'To those of my race who depend upon bettering their condition in a foreign land, or who underestimate the importance of cultivating friendly relations with the Southern white man, who is his next-door neighbor, I would say: "Cast down your bucket where you are"—cast it down in making friends in every manly way of the people of all races by whom we are surrounded . . .' "

I spoke automatically and with such fervor that I did not realize that the men were still talking and laughing until my dry mouth, filling up with blood from the cut, almost strangled me. I coughed, wanting to stop and go to one of the tall brass, sand-filled spittoons to relieve myself, but a few of the men, especially the superintendent, were listening and I was afraid. So I gulped it down, blood, saliva and all, and continued. (What powers of endurance I had during those days! What enthusiasm! What a belief in the rightness of things!) I spoke even louder in spite of the pain. But still they talked and still they laughed, as though deaf with cotton in dirty ears. So I spoke with greater emotional emphasis. I closed my ears and swallowed blood until I was nauseated. The speech seemed a hundred times as long as before, but I could not leave out a single word. All had to be said, each memorized nuance considered, rendered. Nor was that all. Whenever I uttered a word of three or more syllables a group of voices would yell for me to repeat it. I used the phrase "social responsibility" and they yelled:

"What's that word you say, boy?"

"Social responsibility," I said.

"What?"

"Social . . ."

"Louder."

". . . responsibility."

"More!"

"Respon—"

"Repeat!"

"—sibility."

The room filled with the uproar of laughter until, no doubt, distracted by having to gulp down my blood, I made a mistake and yelled a phrase I had often seen denounced in newspaper editorials, heard debated in private.

"Social . . ."

"What?" they yelled.

". . . equality—"

The laughter hung smokelike in the sudden stillness. I opened my eyes, puzzled. Sounds of displeasure filled the room. The M.C. rushed forward. They shouted hostile phrases at me. But I did not understand.

A small dry mustached man in the front row blared out, "Say that slowly, son!"

"What, sir?"

"What you just said!"

"Social responsibility, sir," I said.

"You weren't being smart, were you, boy?" he said, not unkindly.

"No, sir!"

"You sure that about 'equality' was a mistake?"

"Oh, yes, sir," I said. "I was swallowing blood."

"Well, you had better speak more slowly so we can understand. We mean to do right by you, but you've got to know your place at all times. All right, now, go on with your speech."

I was afraid. I wanted to leave but I wanted also to speak and I was afraid they'd snatch me down.

"Thank you, sir," I said, beginning where I had left off, and having them ignore me as before.

Yet when I finished there was a thunderous applause. I was surprised to see the superintendent come forth with a package wrapped in white tissue paper, and, gesturing for quiet, address the men.

"Gentlemen, you see that I did not overpraise this boy. He makes a good speech and some day he'll lead his people in the proper paths. And I don't have to tell you that that is important in these days and times. This is a good, smart boy, and so to encourage him in the right direction, in the name of the Board of Education I wish to present him a prize in the form of this . . ."

He paused, removing the tissue paper and revealing a gleaming calfskin brief case.

". . . in the form of this first-class article from Shad Whitmore's shop."

"Boy," he said, addressing me, "take this prize and keep it well. Consider it a badge of office. Prize it. Keep developing as you are and some day it will be filled with important papers that will help shape the destiny of your people."

I was so moved that I could hardly express my thanks. A rope of bloody saliva forming a shape like an undiscovered continent drooled upon the leather and I wiped it quickly away. I felt an importance that I had never dreamed.

"Open it and see what's inside," I was told.

My fingers a-tremble, I complied, smelling the fresh leather and finding an official-looking document inside. It was a scholarship to the state college for Negroes. My eyes filled with tears·and I ran awkwardly off the floor.

I was overjoyed; I did not even mind when I discovered that the gold pieces I had scrambled for were brass pocket tokens advertising a certain make of automobile.

When I reached home everyone was excited. Next day the neighbors came to congratulate me. I even felt safe from grandfather, whose deathbed curse usually spoiled my triumphs. I stood beneath his photograph with my brief case in hand and smiled triumphantly into his stolid black peasant's face. It was a face that fascinated me. The eyes seemed to follow everywhere I went.

That night I dreamed I was at a circus with him and that he refused to laugh at the clowns no matter what they did. Then later he told me to open my brief case and read what was inside and I did, finding an official envelope stamped with the state seal; and inside the envelope I found another and another, endlessly, and I thought I would fall of weariness. "Them's years," he said. "Now open that one." And I did and in it I found an engraved document containing a short message in letters of gold. "Read it," my grandfather said. "Out loud!"

"To Whom It May Concern," I intoned. "Keep This Nigger-Boy Running."

I awoke with the old man's laughter ringing in my ears.

(It was a dream I was to remember and dream again for many years after. But at that time I had no insight into its meaning. First I had to attend college.)

1947, 1952

BERNARD MALAMUD
(1914–   )

The recognition of the polarity of tragedy and comedy inherent in human suffering has characterized Bernard Malamud's writing from his first novel, *The Natural* (1952), to *The Tenants* (1971) and has been brilliantly displayed in his short stories. Concerned with the essential pathos in the human condition, he has found his most congenial subjects to be the bereft, bewildered, and wandering Jew. There is a universality in his work, however, that raises him above the plane of the local colorist or racial writer. If his protagonist is an insignificant, exasperating, and pathetic old Jew lost in the maelstrom of

New York, as in the story below, he is also the focal point of the spiritual force inherent in an ancient race. Malamud makes strategic use of the tensions between comedy and terror, corrosive failure and qualified success, absurdity and high courage so accentuated in the Jewish experience but shared by all men of feeling and reflection.

Born in Brooklyn in 1914, in the spring before the outbreak of the First World War, he has shared the dislocations of that generation, his adolescence affected if not afflicted by the Depression of 1929. He attended public school in New York City and received his B.A. in 1936 from the College of the City of New York. He survived and profited from the wearing experience of teaching evening high school classes in New York for nine years, from 1940 to 1949. He received his M.A. from Columbia in 1942 and since then has taught at Oregon State University and at Bennington College in Vermont, with leaves of absence to lecture at Harvard.

His second novel, *The Assistant* (1958), is an acknowledged masterpiece, and his first collection of short stories, *The Magic Barrel* (1959), from which this story is taken, won the National Book Award.

In his review of that collection, R. C. Blackman characterized Malamud's writing in terms that are equally applicable to his later fiction: "unified by a tone of resigned and humorous wisdom and unsentimental cultural compassion. * * * The responsibility of being, first of all, a man, and then a Jew, involves all these characters. * * * Depth, but not darkness; for even hopelessness, in Mr. Malamud's hands, is infused with a kind of New World vitality."

Malamud's novels are *The Natural,* 1952; *The Assistant,* 1957; *A New Life,* 1961; *The Fixer,* 1966; *Pictures of Fidelman,* 1969; and *The Tenants,* 1971. Volumes of short stories are *The Magic Barrel,* 1958; *Idiots First,* 1963; and *Rembrandt's Hat,* 1973. Philip Rahv edited *A Malamud Reader,* 1967. Critical studies are Sidney Richman, *Bernard Malamud,* 1967; and Leslie and Joyce Field, eds., *Bernard Malamud and the Critics,* 1970.

The Mourners

Kessler, formerly an egg candler, lived alone on social security. Though past sixty-five, he might have found well-paying work with more than one butter and egg wholesaler, for he sorted and graded with speed and accuracy, but he was a quarrelsome type and considered a trouble maker, so the wholesalers did without him. Therefore, after a time he retired, living with few wants on his old-age pension. Kessler inhabited a small cheap flat on the top floor of a decrepit tenement on the East Side. Perhaps because he lived above so many stairs, no one bothered to visit him. He was much alone, as he had been most of his life. At one time he'd had a family, but unable to stand his wife or children, always in his way, he had after some years walked out on them. He never saw them thereafter, because he never sought them, and they did not seek him. Thirty years had passed. He had no idea where they were, nor did he think much about it.

In the tenement, although he had lived there ten years, he was more or less unknown. The tenants on both sides of his flat on the fifth floor, an Italian family of three middle-aged sons and their wizened mother, and a sullen, childless German couple named Hoffman, never said hello to him, nor did he greet any of them on the way up or down the narrow wooden stairs. Others of the house recognized Kessler when they passed him in the street, but they thought he lived elsewhere on the block. Ignace, the small, bent-back janitor, knew him best, for they had several times played two-handed pinochle; but Ignace, usually the loser because he lacked skill at cards, had stopped going up after a time. He complained to his wife that he couldn't stand the stink there, that the filthy flat with its junky furniture made him sick. The janitor had spread the word about Kessler to the others on the floor, and they shunned him as a dirty old man. Kessler understood this but had contempt for them all.

One day Ignace and Kessler began a quarrel over the way the egg candler piled oily bags overflowing with garbage into the dumb-waiter, instead of using a pail. One word shot off another, and they were soon calling each other savage names, when Kessler slammed the door in the janitor's face. Ignace ran down five flights of stairs and loudly cursed out the old man to his impassive wife. It happened that Gruber, the landlord, a fat man with a consistently worried face, who wore yards of baggy clothes, was in the building, making a check of plumbing repairs, and to him the enraged Ignace related the trouble he was having with Kessler. He described, holding his nose, the smell in Kessler's flat, and called him the dirtiest person he had ever seen. Gruber knew his janitor was exaggerating, but he felt burdened by financial worries which shot his blood pressure up to astonishing heights, so he settled it quickly by saying, "Give him notice." None of the tenants in the house had held a written lease since the war, and Gruber felt confident, in case somebody asked questions, that he could easily justify his dismissal of Kessler as an undesirable tenant. It had occurred to him that Ignace could then slap a cheap coat of paint on the walls and the flat would be let to someone for five dollars more than the old man was paying.

That night after supper, Ignace victoriously ascended the stairs and knocked on Kessler's door. The egg candler opened it, and seeing who stood there, immediately slammed it shut. Ignace shouted through the door. "Mr. Gruber says to give notice. We don't want you around here. Your dirt stinks the whole house." There was silence, but Ignace waited, relishing what he had said. Although after five minutes he still heard no sound, the janitor stayed there, picturing the old Jew trembling behind the locked door. He spoke again. "You got two weeks' notice till the first, then you better move out or Mr. Gruber and myself will throw you out." Ignace watched as the door slowly opened. To his surprise he found himself frightened at the old man's appearance. He looked, in the act of opening the door, like a corpse adjusting his coffin lid. But if he appeared dead, his voice was alive. It rose terrifyingly harsh from his throat, and he sprayed curses over all the years of Ignace's life. His eyes were reddened, his cheeks sunken, and his wisp of beard moved agitatedly. He seemed to be losing weight as he shouted. The janitor no longer had any heart for the matter, but he could not bear so many insults all at once so he cried out, "You dirty old bum, you better get out and don't make so much trouble." To this the enraged Kessler swore they would first have to kill him and drag him out dead.

On the morning of the first of December, Ignace found in his letter box a soiled folded paper containing Kessler's twenty-five dollars. He showed it to Gruber that evening when the landlord came to collect the rent money. Gruber, after a minute of absently contemplating the money, frowned disgustedly.

"I thought I told you to give notice."

"Yes, Mr. Gruber," Ignace agreed. "I gave him."

"That's a helluva chuzpah," [1] said Gruber. "Gimme the keys."

Ignace brought the ring of pass keys, and Gruber, breathing heavily, began the lumbering climb up the long avenue of stairs. Although he rested on each landing, the fatigue of climbing, and his profuse flowing perspiration, heightened his irritation.

Arriving at the top floor he banged his fist on Kessler's door. "Gruber, the landlord. Open up here."

There was no answer, no movement within, so Gruber inserted the key into the lock and twisted. Kessler had barricaded the door with a chest and some chairs. Gruber had to put his shoulder to the door and shove before he could step into the hallway of the badly-lit two and a half room flat. The old man, his face drained of blood, was standing in the kitchen doorway.

"I warned you to scram outa here," Gruber said loudly. "Move out or I'll telephone the city marshal."

"Mr. Gruber—" began Kessler.

"Don't bother me with your lousy excuses, just beat it." He gazed around. "It looks like a junk shop and it smells like a toilet. It'll take me a month to clean up here."

"This smell is only cabbage that I am cooking for my supper. Wait, I'll open a window and it will go away."

1. Yiddish: impudence, bravado.

"When you go away, it'll go away." Gruber took out his bulky wallet, counted out twelve dollars, added fifty cents, and plunked the money on top of the chest. "You got two more weeks till the fifteenth, then you gotta be out or I will get a dispossess. Don't talk back talk. Get outa here and go somewhere that they don't know you and maybe you'll get a place."

"No, Mr. Gruber," Kessler cried passionately. "I didn't do nothing, and I will stay here."

"Don't monkey with my blood pressure," said Gruber. "If you're not out by the fifteenth, I will personally throw you on your bony ass."

Then he left and walked heavily down the stairs.

The fifteenth came and Ignace found the twelve fifty in his letter box. He telephoned Gruber and told him.

"I'll get a dispossess," Gruber shouted. He instructed the janitor to write out a note saying to Kessler that his money was refused and to stick it under his door. This Ignace did. Kessler returned the money to the letter box, but again Ignace wrote a note and slipped it, with the money, under the old man's door.

After another day Kessler received a copy of his eviction notice. It said to appear in court on Friday at 10 A.M. to show cause why he should not be evicted for continued neglect and destruction of rental property. The official notice filled Kessler with great fright because he had never in his life been to court. He did not appear on the day he had been ordered to.

That same afternoon the marshal appeared with two brawny assistants. Ignace opened Kessler's lock for them and as they pushed their way into the flat, the janitor hastily ran down the stairs to hide in the cellar. Despite Kessler's wailing and carrying on, the two assistants methodically removed his meager furniture and set it out on the sidewalk. After that they got Kessler out, though they had to break open the bathroom door because the old man had locked himself in there. He shouted, struggled, pleaded with his neighbors to help him, but they looked on in a silent group outside the door. The two assistants, holding the old man tightly by the arms and skinny legs, carried him, kicking and moaning, down the stairs. They sat him in the street on a chair amid his junk. Upstairs, the marshal bolted the door with a lock Ignace had supplied, signed a paper which he handed to the janitor's wife, and then drove off in an automobile with his assistants.

Kessler sat on a split chair on the sidewalk. It was raining and the rain soon turned to sleet, but he still sat there. People passing by skirted the pile of his belongings. They stared at Kessler and he stared at nothing. He wore no hat or coat, and the snow fell on him, making him look like a piece of his dispossessed goods. Soon the wizened Italian woman from the top floor returned to the house with two of her sons, each carrying a loaded shopping bag. When she recognized Kessler sitting amid his furniture, she began to shriek. She shrieked in Italian at Kessler although he paid no attention to her. She stood on the stoop, shrunken, gesticulating with thin arms, her loose mouth working angrily. Her sons tried to calm her, but still she shrieked. Several of the neighbors came down to see who was making the racket. Finally, the two sons, unable to think what else to do, set down their shopping bags, lifted Kessler out of the chair, and carried him up the stairs. Hoffman, Kessler's other neighbor, working with a small triangular file, cut open the padlock, and Kessler was carried into the flat from which he had been evicted. Ignace screeched at everybody, calling them filthy names, but the three men went downstairs and hauled up Kessler's chairs, his broken table, chest, and ancient metal bed. They piled all the furniture into the bedroom. Kessler sat on the edge of the bed and wept. After a while, after the old Italian woman had sent in a soup plate full of hot macaroni seasoned with tomato sauce and grated cheese, they left.

Ignace phoned Gruber. The landlord was eating and the food turned to lumps in his throat. "I'll throw them all out, the bastards," he yelled. He put on his hat, got into his car and drove through the slush to the tenement. All the time he was thinking of his worries: high repair costs; it was hard to keep the place together; maybe the building would someday collapse. He had read of such things. All of a sudden the front of the building parted from the rest and fell like a breaking wave into the street. Gruber cursed the old man for taking him from his supper. When he got to the house he snatched Ignace's keys and ascended the sagging stairs. Ignace tried to follow, but Gruber told him to stay the hell in his hole. When the landlord was not looking, Ignace crept up after him.

Gruber turned the key and let himself into Kessler's dark flat. He pulled the light chain and found the old man sitting limply on the side of the bed. On the floor at his feet lay a plate of stiffened macaroni.

"What do you think you're doing here?" Gruber thundered. The old man sat motionless.

"Don't you know it's against the law? This is trespassing and you're breaking the law. Answer me."

Kessler remained mute.

Gruber mopped his brow with a large yellowed handkerchief.

"Listen, my friend, you're gonna make lots of trouble for yourself. If they catch you in here you might go to the workhouse. I'm only trying to advise you."

To his surprise Kessler looked at him with wet, brimming eyes.
"What did I did to you?" he bitterly wept. "Who throws out of his house a man that he lived there ten years and pays every month on time his rent? What did I do, tell me? Who hurts a man without a reason? Are you a Hitler or a Jew?" He was hitting his chest with his fist.

Gruber removed his hat. He listened carefully, at first at a loss what to say, but then answered: "Listen, Kessler, it's not personal. I own this house and it's falling apart. My bills are sky high. If the tenants don't take care they have to go. You don't take care and you fight with my janitor, so you have to go. Leave in the morning, and I won't say another word. But if you don't leave the flat, you'll get the heave-ho again. I'll call the marshal."

"Mr. Gruber," said Kessler, "I won't go. Kill me if you want it, but I won't go."

Ignace hurried away from the door as Gruber left in anger. The next morning, after a restless night of worries, the landlord set out to drive to the city marshal's office. On the way he stopped at a candy store for a pack of cigarettes, and there decided once more to speak to Kessler. A thought had occurred to him: he would offer to get the old man into a public home.

He drove to the tenement and knocked on Ignace's door.

"Is the old gink still up there?"

"I don't know if so, Mr. Gruber." The janitor was ill at ease.

"What do you mean you don't know?"

"I didn't see him go out. Before, I looked in his keyhole but nothing moves."

"So why didn't you open the door with your key?"

"I was afraid," Ignace answered nervously.

"What are you afraid?"

Ignace wouldn't say.

A fright went through Gruber but he didn't show it. He grabbed the keys and walked ponderously up the stairs, hurrying every so often.

No one answered his knock. As he unlocked the door he broke into heavy sweat.

But the old man was there, alive, sitting without shoes on the bedroom floor.

"Listen, Kessler," said the landlord, relieved although his head pounded. "I got an idea that, if you do it the way I say, your troubles are over."

He explained his proposal to Kessler, but the egg candler was not listening. His eyes were downcast, and his body swayed slowly sideways. As the landlord talked on, the old man was thinking of what had whirled through his mind as he had sat out on the sidewalk in the falling snow. He had thought through his miserable life, remembering how, as a young man, he had abandoned his family, walking out on his wife and three innocent children, without even in some way attempting to provide for them; without, in all the intervening years—so God help him—once trying to discover if they were alive or dead. How, in so short a life, could a man do so much wrong? This thought smote him to the heart and he recalled the past without end and moaned and tore at his flesh with his fingernails.

Gruber was frightened at the extent of Kessler's suffering. Maybe I should let him stay, he thought. Then as he watched the old man, he realized he was bunched up there on the floor engaged in an act of mourning. There he sat, white from fasting, rocking back and forth, his beard dwindled to a shade of itself.

Something wrong here—Gruber tried to imagine what and found it all oppressive. He felt he ought to run out, get away, but then saw himself fall and go tumbling down the five flights of stairs; he groaned at the broken picture of himself lying at the bottom. Only he was still there in Kessler's bedroom, listening to the old man praying. Somebody's dead, Gruber muttered. He figured Kessler had got bad news, yet instinctively knew he hadn't. Then it struck him with a terrible force that the mourner was mourning him: it was *he* who was dead.

The landlord was agonized. Sweating brutally, he felt an enormous constricted weight in him that slowly forced itself up, until his head was at the point of bursting. For a full minute he awaited a stroke; but the feeling painfully passed, leaving him miserable.

When after a while, he gazed around the room, it was clean, drenched in daylight and fragrance. Gruber then suffered unbearable remorse for the way he had treated the old man.

At last he could stand it no longer. With a cry of shame he tore the sheet off Kessler's bed, and wrapping it around his bulk, sank heavily to the floor and became a mourner.

1958

SAUL BELLOW

(1915–   )

Saul Bellow is a product not of the compact cities of the eastern seaboard, nor yet of the open spaces of the plains and small towns of the Midwest, but rather of the urban sprawl of Chicago. He is, in his own words, "a Chicagoan, out and out." Among post–World War II American novels his are the ones that best present the problems of the modern urban man in search of his identity. His heroes are rootless, or rooted to a past that no longer seems relevant to the present. Surrounded by friends and acquaintances who adjust, who learn to conform, they seek to be individuals in a world that appears to have little room for individuality. Convinced of the need for freedom, they do not know where to seek it except on paths that lead often to loneliness and despair. Yet there is also an affirmation in their lives. Hemmed in on all sides by society, they continue to assert the worth and dignity of the individual human spirit.

The son of Russian Jews who had settled in Canada in 1913, Bellow was born in Lachine, Quebec, in 1915. As a child he was familiar with Hebrew, Yiddish, and French, as well as English. After the family moved to Chicago in 1924 he was educated "after a fashion" in the public schools and attended the University of Chicago before graduating from Northwestern in 1937. He began graduate school at the University of Wisconsin, but did not stay long, and since that time has supported himself mainly by teaching and writing.

Dangling Man (1944) and The Victim (1947) were tightly constructed, traditional novels that earned the author some critical praise, but with the appearance of the sprawling, picaresque The Adventures of Augie March (1953) it became apparent that Bellow possessed a talent of major proportions. Henderson the Rain King (1959), in some ways Bellow's most engaging fiction, seemed self-indulgently romantic to some of his critics, but both Herzog (1964) and Mr. Sammler's Planet (1970) received general acclaim. Unlike a good many of his contemporaries, Bellow has appeared to grow with each new book, while his concern for individuality in an age of conformity has remained essentially the same.

Primarily a novelist, Bellow has also had plays produced in New York, London, and Glasgow and has written a handful of memorable short stories and novellas, the best of which are collected in Seize the Day (1956) and Mosby's Memoirs and Other Stories (1968).

Bellow's major fiction is named above. A play is The Last Analysis, 1965. Biographical and critical studies include Tony Tanner, Saul Bellow, 1965; Irving Malin, ed., Saul Bellow and the Critics, 1967; Keith M. Opdahl, The Novels of Saul Bellow: An Introduction, 1967; John J. Clayton, Saul Bellow: In Defense of Man, 1968; Irving Malin, Saul Bellow's Fiction, 1969; and Brigitte Scheer-Schäzler, Saul Bellow, 1972.

A Father-to-Be [1]

The strangest notions had a way of forcing themselves into Rogin's mind. Just thirty-one and passable-looking, with short black hair, small eyes, but a high, open forehead, he was a research chemist, and his mind was generally serious and dependable. But on

1. First published in The New Yorker in 1955. Collected in Seize the Day, 1956, and in Mosby's Memoirs and Other Stories, 1968, the source of the present text.

a snowy Sunday evening while this stocky man, buttoned to the chin in a Burberry coat and walking in his preposterous gait—feet turned outward—was going toward the subway, he fell into a peculiar state.

He was on his way to have supper with his fiancée. She had phoned him a short while ago and said, "You'd better pick up a few things on the way."

"What do we need?"

"Some roast beef, for one thing. I bought a quarter of a pound coming home from my aunt's."

"Why a quarter of a pound, Joan?" said Rogin, deeply annoyed. "That's just about enough for one good sandwich."

"So you have to stop at a delicatessen. I had no more money."

He was about to ask, "What happened to the thirty dollars I gave you on Wednesday?" but he knew that would not be right.

"I had to give Phyllis money for the cleaning woman," said Joan.

Phyllis, Joan's cousin, was a young divorcee, extremely wealthy. The two women shared an apartment.

"Roast beef," he said, "and what else?"

"Some shampoo, sweetheart. We've used up all the shampoo. And hurry, darling, I've missed you all day."

"And I've missed you," said Rogin, but to tell the truth he had been worrying most of the time. He had a younger brother whom he was putting through college. And his mother, whose annuity wasn't quite enough in these days of inflation and high taxes, needed money too. Joan had debts he was helping her to pay, for she wasn't working. She was looking for something suitable to do. Beautiful, well educated, aristocratic in her attitude, she couldn't clerk in a dime store; she couldn't model clothes (Rogin thought this made girls vain and stiff, and he didn't want her to); she couldn't be a waitress or a cashier. What could she be? Well, something would turn up and meantime Rogin hesitated to complain. He paid her bills—the dentist, the department store, the osteopath, the doctor, the psychiatrist. At Christmas, Rogin almost went mad. Joan bought him a velvet smoking jacket with frog fasteners, a beautiful pipe, and a pouch. She bought Phyllis a garnet brooch, an Italian silk umbrella, and a gold cigarette holder. For other friends, she bought Dutch pewter and Swedish glassware. Before she was through, she had spent five hundred dollars of Rogin's money. He loved her too much to show his suffering. He believed she had a far better nature than his. She didn't worry about money. She had a marvelous character, always cheerful, and she really didn't need a psychiatrist at all. She went to one because Phyllis did and it made her curious. She tried too much to keep up with her cousin, whose father had made millions in the rug business.

While the woman in the drugstore was wrapping the shampoo bottle, a clear idea suddenly arose in Rogin's thoughts: Money surrounds you in life as the earth does in death. Superimposition is the universal law. Who is free? No one is free. Who has no burdens? Everyone is under pressure. The very rocks, the waters of the earth, beasts, men, children—everyone has some weight to carry. This idea was extremely clear to him at first. Soon it became rather vague, but it had a great effect nevertheless, as if someone had given him a valuable gift. (Not like the velvet smoking jacket he couldn't bring himself to wear, or the pipe it choked him to smoke.) The notion that all were under pressure and affliction, instead of saddening him, had the opposite influence. It put him in a wonderful mood. It was extraordinary how happy he became and, in addition, clear-sighted. His eyes all at once were opened to what was around him. He saw with delight how the druggist and the woman who wrapped the shampoo bottle were smiling and flirting, how the lines of worry in her face went over into lines of cheer and the druggist's receding gums did not hinder his kidding and friendliness. And in the delicatessen, also, it was amazing how much Rogin noted and what happiness it gave him simply to be there.

Delicatessens on Sunday night, when all other stores are shut, will overcharge you ferociously, and Rogin would normally have been on guard, but he was not tonight, or scarcely so. Smells of pickle, sausage, mustard, and smoked fish overjoyed him. He pitied the people who would buy the chicken salad and chopped herring; they could do it only because their sight was too dim to see what they were getting—the fat flakes of pepper on the chicken, the soppy herring, mostly vinegar-soaked stale bread. Who would buy them? Late risers, people living alone, waking up in the darkness of the afternoon, finding their refrigerators empty, or people whose gaze was turned inward. The roast beef looked not bad, and Rogin ordered a pound.

While the storekeeper was slicing the meat, he yelled at a Puerto Rican kid who was reaching for a bag of chocolate cookies, "Hey, you want to pull me down the whole display on yourself? You, *chico*, wait a half a minute." This storekeeper, though he looked like one of Pancho Villa's bandits, the kind that smeared their enemies with syrup and staked them down on anthills, a man with toadlike eyes and stout hands made to clasp pistols hung around his belly, was not so bad. He was a New York man, thought Rogin —who was from Albany himself—a New York man toughened by every abuse of the city, trained to suspect everyone. But in his own realm, on the board behind the counter, there was justice. Even clemency.

The Puerto Rican kid wore a complete cowboy outfit—a green hat with white braid, guns, chaps, spurs, boots, and gauntlets—but he couldn't speak any English. Rogin unhooked the cellophane bag of hard circular cookies and gave it to him. The boy tore the cellophane with his teeth and began to chew one of those dry chocolate disks. Rogin recognized his state—the energetic dream of childhood. Once, he, too, had found these dry biscuits delicious. It would have bored him now to eat one.

What else would Joan like? Rogin thought fondly. Some strawberries? "Give me some frozen strawberries. No, raspberries, she likes those better. And heavy cream. And some rolls, cream cheese, and some of those rubber-looking gherkins."

"What rubber?"

"Those, deep green, with eyes. Some ice cream might be in order, too."

He tried to think of a compliment, a good comparison, an endearment, for Joan when she'd open the door. What about her complexion? There was really nothing to compare her sweet, small, daring, shapely, timid, defiant, loving face to. How difficult she was, and how beautiful!

As Rogin went down into the stony, odorous, metallic, captive air of the subway, he was diverted by an unusual confession made by a man to his friend. These were two very tall men, shapeless in their winter clothes, as if their coats concealed suits of chain-mail.

"So, how long have you known me?" said one.

"Twelve years."

"Well, I have an admission to make," he said. "I've decided that I might as well. For years I've been a heavy drinker. You didn't know. Practically an alcoholic."

But his friend was not surprised, and he answered immediately, "Yes, I did know."

"You knew? Impossible! How could you?"

Why, thought Rogin, as if it could be a secret! Look at that long, austere, alcohol-washed face, that drink-ruined nose, the skin by his ears like turkey wattles, and those whisky-saddened eyes.

"Well, I did know, though."

"You couldn't have. I can't believe it." He was upset, and his friend didn't seem to want to soothe him. "But it's all right now," he said. "I've been going to a doctor and taking pills, a new revolutionary Danish discovery. It's a miracle. I'm beginning to believe they can cure you of anything and everything. You can't beat the Danes in science. They do everything. They turned a man into a woman."

"That isn't how they stop you from drinking, is it?"

"No. I hope not. This is only like aspirin. It's superaspirin. They called it the aspirin of the future. But if you use it, you have to stop drinking."

Rogin's illuminated mind asked of itself while the human tides of the subway swayed back and forth, and cars linked and transparent like fish bladders raced under the streets: How come he thought nobody would know what everybody couldn't help knowing? And, as a chemist, he asked himself what kind of compound this new Danish drug might be, and started thinking about various inventions of his own, synthetic albumen, a cigarette that lit itself, a cheaper motor fuel. Ye gods, but he needed money! As never before. What was to be done? His mother was growing more and more difficult. On Friday night, she had neglected to cut up his meat for him, and he was hurt. She had sat at the table motionless, with her long-suffering face, severe, and let him cut his own meat, a thing she almost never did. She had always spoiled him and made his brother envy him. But what she expected now! Oh, Lord, how he had to pay, and it had never even occurred to him formerly that these things might have a price.

Seated, one of the passengers, Rogin recovered his calm, happy, even clairvoyant state of mind. To think of money was to think as the world wanted you to think; then you'd never be your own master. When people said they wouldn't do something for love or money, they meant that love and money were opposite passions and one the enemy of the other. He went on to reflect how little people knew about this, how they slept through life, how small a light the light of consciousness was. Rogin's clean, snub-nosed face shone while his heart was torn with joy at these deeper thoughts of our ignorance. You might take this drunkard as an example, who for long years thought his closest friends never suspected he drank. Rogin looked up and down the aisle for this remarkable knightly symbol, but he was gone.

However, there was no lack of things to see. There was a small girl with a new white muff; into the muff a doll's head was sewn, and the child was happy and affectionately vain of it, while her old man, stout and grim, with a huge scowling nose, kept picking her up and resettling her in the seat, as if he were trying to change her into something else. Then another child, led by her mother, boarded the car, and this other child carried the very same doll-faced muff, and this greatly annoyed both parents. The woman, who looked like a difficult, contentious woman, took her daughter away. It seemed to Rogin that each child was in love with its own muff and didn't even see the other, but it was one of his foibles to think he understood the hearts of little children.

A foreign family next engaged his attention. They looked like Central Americans to him. On one side the mother, quite old, dark-faced, white-haired, and worn out; on the other a son with the whitened, porous hands of a dishwasher. But what was the dwarf who sat between them—a son or a daughter? The hair was long and wavy and the cheeks smooth, but the shirt and tie were masculine. The overcoat was feminine, but the shoes—the shoes were a puzzle. A pair of brown oxfords with an outer seam like a man's, but Baby Louis heels like a woman's—a plain toe like a man's, but a strap across the instep like a woman's. No stockings. That didn't help much. The dwarf's fingers were beringed, but without a wedding band. There were small grim dents in the cheeks. The eyes were puffy and concealed, but Rogin did not doubt that they could reveal strange things if they chose and that this was a creature of remarkable understanding. He had for many years owned de la Mare's *Memoirs of a Midget*. Now he took a resolve; he would read it. As soon as he had decided, he was free from his consuming curiosity as to the dwarf's sex and was able to look at the person who sat beside him.

Thoughts very often grow fertile in the subway, because of the motion, the great company, the subtlety of the rider's state as he rattles under streets and rivers, under the foundations of great buildings, and Rogin's mind had already been strangely stimulated. Clasping the bag of groceries from which there rose odors of bread and pickle spice, he was following a train of reflections, first about the chemistry of sex determination, the X and Y chromosomes, hereditary linkages, the uterus, afterward about his brother as a tax exemption. He recalled two dreams of the night before. In one, an undertaker had offered to cut his hair, and he had refused. In another, he had been carrying a woman on his head. Sad dreams, both! Very sad! Which was the woman—Joan or Mother? And the undertaker—his lawyer? He gave a deep sigh, and by force of habit began to put together his synthetic albumen that was to revolutionize the entire egg industry.

Meanwhile, he had not interrupted his examination of the passengers and had fallen into a study of the man next to him. This was a man whom he had never in his life seen before but with whom he now suddenly felt linked through all existence. He was middle-aged, sturdy, with clear skin and blue eyes. His hands were clean, well formed, but Rogin did not approve of them. The coat he wore was a fairly expensive blue check such as Rogin would never have chosen for himself. He would not have worn blue suède shoes, either, or such a faultless hat, a cumbersome felt animal of a hat encircled by a high, fat ribbon. There are all kinds of dandies, not all of them are of the flaunting kind; some are dandies of respectability, and Rogin's fellow passenger was one of these. His straight-nosed profile was handsome, yet he had betrayed his gift, for he was flat-looking. But in his flat way he seemed to warn people that he wanted no difficulties with them, he wanted nothing to do with them. Wearing such blue suède shoes, he could not afford to have people treading on his feet, and he seemed to draw about himself a circle of privilege, notifying all others to mind their own business and let him read his paper. He was holding a *Tribune,* and perhaps it would be overstatement to say that he was reading. He was holding it.

His clear skin and blue eyes, his straight and purely Roman nose —even the way he sat—all strongly suggested one person to Rogin: Joan. He tried to escape the comparison, but it couldn't be helped. This man not only looked like Joan's father, whom Rogin detested; he looked like Joan herself. Forty years hence, a son of hers, provided she had one, might be like this. A son of hers? Of such a son, he himself, Rogin, would be the father. Lacking in dominant traits as compared with Joan, his heritage would not appear. Probably the children would resemble her. Yes, think forty years ahead, and a man like this, who sat by him knee to knee in the hurtling car among their fellow creatures, unconscious participants in a sort of great carnival of transit—such a man would carry forward what had been Rogin.

This was why he felt bound to him through all existence. What were forty years reckoned against eternity! Forty years were gone, and he was gazing at his own son. Here he was. Rogin was frightened and moved. "My son! My son!" he said to himself, and the pity of it almost made him burst into tears. The holy and frightful work of the masters of life and death brought this about. We were their instruments. We worked towards ends we thought were our own. But no! The whole thing was so unjust. To suffer, to labor, to toil and force your way through the spikes of life, to crawl through its darkest caverns, to push through the worst, to struggle under the weight of economy, to make money—only to become the father of a fourth-rate man of the world like this, so flat-looking with his ordinary, clean, rosy, uninteresting, self-satisfied, fundamentally bourgeois face. What a curse to have a dull son! A son like this, who could never understand his father. They had absolutely nothing, but nothing, in common, he and this neat, chubby, blue-eyed man. He was so pleased, thought Rogin, with all he owned and all he did and all he was that he could hardly unfasten his lip. Look at that lip, sticking up at the tip like a little thorn or egg tooth. He wouldn't give anyone the time of day. Would this perhaps be general forty years from now? Would personalities be chillier as the world aged and grew colder? The inhumanity of the next generation incensed Rogin. Father and son had no sign to make to each other. Terrible! Inhuman! What a vision of existence it gave him. Man's personal aims were nothing, illusion. The life force occupied each of us in turn in its progress toward its own fulfillment, trampling on our individual humanity, using us for its own ends like mere dinosaurs or bees, exploiting love heartlessly, making us engage in the social process, labor, struggle for money, and submit to the law of pressure, the universal law of layers, superimposition!

What the blazes am I getting into? Rogin thought. To be the father of a throwback to *her* father. The image of this white-haired, gross, peevish, old man with his ugly selfish blue eyes revolted Rogin. This was how his grandson would look. Joan, with whom Rogin was now more and more displeased, could not help that. For her, it was inevitable. But did it have to be inevitable for him? Well, then, Rogin, you fool, don't be a damned instrument. Get out of the way!

But it was too late for this, because he had already experienced the sensation of sitting next to his own son, his son and Joan's. He kept staring at him, waiting for him to say something, but the presumptive son remained coldly silent though he must have been aware of Rogin's scrutiny. They even got out at the same stop—Sheridan Square. When they stepped to the platform, the man, without even looking at Rogin, went away in a different direction in his detestable blue-checked coat, with his rosy, nasty face.

The whole thing upset Rogin very badly. When he approached Joan's door and heard Phyllis's little dog Henri barking even before he could knock, his face was very tense. I won't be used, he declared to himself. I have my own right to exist. Joan had better watch out. She had a light way of by-passing grave questions he had given earnest thought to. She always assumed no really disturbing thing would happen. He could not afford the luxury of such a care-free, debonair attitude himself, because he had to work hard and earn money so that disturbing things would *not* happen. Well, at the moment this situation could not be helped, and he really did not mind the money if he could feel that she was not necessarily the mother of such a son as his subway son or entirely the daughter of that awful, obscene father of hers. After all, Rogin was not himself so much like either of his parents, and quite different from his brother.

Joan came to the door, wearing one of Phyllis's expensive house-coats. It suited her very well. At first sight of her happy face, Rogin was brushed by the shadow of resemblance; the touch of it was extremely light, almost figmentary, but it made his flesh tremble.

She began to kiss him, saying, "Oh, my baby. You're covered with snow. Why didn't you wear your hat? It's all over its little head"—her favorite third-person endearment.

"Well, let me put down this bag of stuff. Let me take off my coat," grumbled Rogin, and escaped from her embrace. Why couldn't she wait making up to him? "It's so hot in here. My face is burning. Why do you keep the place at this temperature? And that damned dog keeps barking. If you didn't keep it cooped up, it wouldn't be so spoiled and noisy. Why doesn't anybody ever walk him?"

"Oh, it's not really so hot here! You've just come in from the cold. Don't you think this housecoat fits me better than Phyllis? Especially across the hips. She thinks so, too. She may sell it to me."

"I hope not," Rogin almost exclaimed.

She brought a towel to dry the melting snow from his short black hair. The flurry of rubbing excited Henri intolerably, and Joan locked him up in the bedroom, where he jumped persistently against the door with a rhythmic sound of claws on the wood.

Joan said, "Did you bring the shampoo?"

"Here it is."

"Then I'll wash your hair before dinner. Come."

"I don't want it washed."

"Oh, come on," she said, laughing.

Her lack of consciousness of guilt amazed him. He did not see how it could be. And the carpeted, furnished, lamplit, curtained room seemed to stand against his vision. So that he felt accusing and angry, his spirit sore and bitter, but it did not seem fitting to say why. Indeed, he began to worry lest the reason for it all slip away from him.

They took off his coat and his shirt in the bathroom, and she filled the sink. Rogin was full of his troubled emotions; now that his chest was bare he could feel them even more and he said to himself, I'll have a thing or two to tell her pretty soon. I'm not letting them get away with it. "Do you think," he was going to tell her, "that I alone was made to carry the burden of the whole world on me? Do you think I was born to be taken advantage of and sacrificed? Do you think I'm just a natural resource, like a coal mine, or oil well, or fishery, or the like? Remember, that I'm a man is no reason why I should be loaded down. I have a soul in me no bigger or stronger than yours.

"Take away the externals, like the muscles, deeper voice, and so forth, and what remains? A pair of spirits, practically alike. So why shouldn't there also be equality? I can't always be the strong one."

"Sit here," said Joan, bringing up a kitchen stool to the sink. "Your hair's gotten all matted."

He sat with his breast against the cool enamel, his chin on the edge of the basin, the green, hot, radiant water reflecting the glass and the tile, and the sweet, cool, fragrant juice of the shampoo poured on his head. She began to wash him.

"You have the healthiest-looking scalp," she said. "It's all pink."

He answered, "Well, it should be white. There must be something wrong with me."

"But there's absolutely nothing wrong with you," she said, and pressed against him from behind, surrounding him, pouring the water gently over him until it seemed to him that the water came from within him, it was the warm fluid of his own secret loving spirit overflowing into the sink, green and foaming, and the words he had rehearsed he forgot, and his anger at his son-to-be disappeared altogether, and he sighed, and said to her from the water-filled hollow of the sink, "You always have such wonderful ideas, Joan. You know? You have a kind of instinct, a regular gift."

1955, 1968

FLANNERY O'CONNOR
(1925–1964)

Flannery O'Connor had a realistic intelligence, an ironic and unsentimental approach to literary creativity. There is a simplicity in her novels and short stories, a basic acceptance of the human situation, that illuminates and justifies her choice of subject matter. She admitted to a preference for the vulgar and the grotesque, but her sympathetic detachment presents her characters, as in the story below, in an appealing and unforgettable light.

A native Georgian, she was born in Savannah, March 25, 1925, and spent her youth in Milledgeville where she died at the age of thirty-nine. Her creative ability was in evidence dur-

ing her college years; she began to publish before she received her M.A. in 1947, and she had a number of subsequent grants for creative writing.

She was a serious craftsman who acknowledged and exploited her southern Catholic background, yet she was genuinely concerned with the enigmatic, subconscious levels of experience. She had the gift of countering the mystical with reality. As she said, "The fiction writer presents mystery through manners, grace through nature, but when he finishes, there always has to be left over that sense of Mystery which cannot be accounted for by any human formula." The story below was collected in the volume *A Good Man Is Hard To Find* (1955).

The novels are *Wise Blood*, 1952, and *The Violent Bear It Away*, 1960. Volumes of stories are *A Good Man Is Hard to Find*, 1955, and *Everything That Rises Must Converge*, 1965. The *Complete Stories* was published in 1971. *Mystery and Manners: Occasional Prose*, 1969, was edited by Sally and Robert Fitzgerald. Critical studies include Melvin J.

Friedman and Lewis A. Lawson, eds., *The Added Dimension: The Art and Mind of Flannery O'Connor*, 1966; Carter W. Martin, *The True Country: Themes in the Fiction of Flannery O'Connor*, 1969; Josephine Hendin, *The World of Flannery O'Conner*, 1970; David Eggenschwiler, *The Christian Humanism of Flannery O'Connor*, 1972; Sister Kathleen Feeley, *Flannery O'Connor: Voice of the Peacock*, 1972; Miles Orvell, *Invisible Parade: The Fiction of Flannery O'Connor*, 1972; and Dorothy Walters, *Flannery O'Connor*, 1973.

The Life You Save May Be Your Own

The old woman and her daughter were sitting on their porch when Mr. Shiftlet came up their road for the first time. The old woman slid to the edge of her chair and leaned forward, shading her eyes from the piercing sunset with her hand. The daughter could not see far in front of her and continued to play with her fingers. Although the old woman lived in this desolate spot with only her daughter and she had never seen Mr. Shiftlet before, she could tell, even from a distance, that he was a tramp and no one to be afraid of. His left coat sleeve was folded up to show there was only half an arm in it and his gaunt figure listed slightly to the side as if the breeze were pushing him. He had on a black town suit and a brown felt hat that was turned up in the front and down in the back and he carried a tin tool box by a handle. He came on, at an amble, up her road, his face turned toward the sun which appeared to be balancing itself on the peak of a small mountain.

The old woman didn't change her position until he was almost into her yard; then she rose with one hand fisted on her hip. The daughter, a large girl in a short blue organdy dress, saw him all at once and jumped up and began to stamp and point and make excited speechless sounds.

Mr. Shiftlet stopped just inside the yard and set his box on the ground and tipped his hat at her as if she were not in the least afflicted; then he turned toward the old woman and swung the hat all the way off. He had long black slick hair that hung flat from a part in the middle to beyond the tips of his ears on either side. His face descended in forehead for more than half its length and ended suddenly with his features just balanced over a jutting steel-trap jaw. He seemed to be a young man but he had a look of composed dissatisfaction as if he understood life thoroughly.

"Good evening," the old woman said. She was about the size of a cedar fence post and she had a man's gray hat pulled down low over her head.

The tramp stood looking at her and didn't answer. He turned his back and faced the sunset. He swung both his whole and his short arm up slowly so that they indicated an expanse of sky and his figure formed a crooked cross. The old woman watched him with her arms folded across her chest as if she were the owner of the sun, and the daughter watched, her head thrust forward and her fat helpless hands hanging at the wrists. She had long pink-gold hair and eyes as blue as a peacock's neck.

He held the pose for almost fifty seconds and then he picked up his box and came on to the porch and dropped down on the bottom step. "Lady," he said in a firm nasal voice, "I'd give a fortune to live where I could see me a sun do that every evening."

"Does it every evening," the old woman said and sat back down. The daughter sat down too and watched him with a cautious sly look as if he were a bird that had come up very close. He leaned to one side, rooting in his pants pocket, and in a second he brought out a package of chewing gum and offered her a piece. She took it and unpeeled it and began to chew without taking her eyes off him. He offered the old woman a piece but she only raised her upper lip to indicate she had no teeth.

Mr. Shiftlet's pale sharp glance had already passed over everything in the yard—the pump near the corner of the house and the big fig tree that three or four chickens were preparing to roost in—and had moved to a shed where he saw the square rusted back of an automobile. "You ladies drive?" he asked.

"That car ain't run in fifteen year," the old woman said. "The day my husband died, it quit running."

"Nothing is like it used to be, lady," he said. "The world is almost rotten."

"That's right," the old woman said. "You from around here?"

"Name Tom T. Shiftlet," he murmured, looking at the tires.

"I'm pleased to meet you," the old woman said. "Name Lucynell Crater and daughter Lucynell Crater. What you doing around here, Mr. Shiftlet?"

He judged the car to be about a 1928 or '29 Ford. "Lady," he said, and turned and gave her his full attention, "lemme tell you something. There's one of these doctors in Atlanta that's taken a knife and cut the human heart—the human heart," he repeated, leaning forward, "out of a man's chest and held it in his hand," and he held his hand out, palm up, as if it were slightly weighted with the human heart, "and studied it like it was a day-old chicken, and lady," he said, allowing a long significant pause in which his head slid forward and his clay-colored eyes brightened, "he don't know no more about it than you or me."

"That's right," the old woman said.

"Why, if he was to take the knife and cut into every corner of it, he still wouldn't know no more than you or me. What you want to bet?"

"Nothing," the old woman said wisely. "Where you come from, Mr. Shiftlet?"

He didn't answer. He reached into his pocket and brought out a sack of tobacco and a package of cigarette papers and rolled himself a cigarette, expertly with one hand, and attached it in a hanging position to his upper lip. Then he took a box of wooden matches from his pocket and struck one on his shoe. He held the burning match as if he were studying the mystery of flame while it traveled dangerously toward his skin. The daughter began to make loud noises and to point to his hand and shake her finger at him, but when the flame was just before touching him, he leaned down with his hand cupped over it as if he were going to set fire to his nose and lit the cigarette.

He flipped away the dead match and blew a stream of gray into the evening. A sly look came over his face. "Lady," he said, "nowadays, people'll do anything anyways. I can tell you my name is Tom T. Shiftlet and I come from Tarwater, Tennessee, but you never have seen me before: how you know I ain't lying? How you know my name ain't Aaron Sparks, lady, and I come from Singleberry, Georgia, or how you know it's not George Speeds and I come from Lucy, Alabama, or how you know I ain't Thompson Bright from Toolafalls, Mississippi?"

"I don't know nothing about you," the old woman muttered, irked.

"Lady," he said, "people don't care how they lie. Maybe the best I can tell you is, I'm a man; but listen lady," he said and paused and made his tone more ominous still, "what is a man?"

The old woman began to gum a seed. "What you carry in that tin box, Mr. Shiftlet?" she asked.

"Tools," he said, put back. "I'm a carpenter."

"Well, if you come out here to work, I'll be able to feed you and give you a place to sleep but I can't pay. I'll tell you that before you begin," she said.

There was no answer at once and no particular expression on his face. He leaned back against the two-by-four that helped support the porch roof. "Lady," he said slowly, "there's some men that some things mean more to them than money." The old woman rocked without comment and the daughter watched the trigger that moved up and down in his neck. He told the old woman then that all most people were interested in was money, but he asked what a man was made for. He asked her if a man was made for money, or what. He asked her what she thought she was made for but she didn't answer, she only sat rocking and wondered if a one-armed man could put a new roof on her garden house. He asked a lot of questions that she didn't answer. He told her that he was twenty-eight years old and had lived a varied life. He had been a gospel singer, a foreman on the railroad, an assistant in an undertaking parlor, and he come over the radio for three months with Uncle Roy and his Red Creek Wranglers. He said he had fought and bled in the Arm Service of his country and visited every foreign land and that everywhere he had seen people that didn't care if they did a thing one way or another. He said he hadn't been raised thataway.

A fat yellow moon appeared in the branches of the fig tree as if it were going to roost there with the chickens. He said that a man had to escape to the country to see the world whole and that he wished he lived in a desolate place like this where he could see the sun go down every evening like God made it to do.

"Are you married or are you single?" the old woman asked.

There was a long silence. "Lady," he asked finally, "where would you find you an innocent woman today? I wouldn't have any of this trash I could just pick up."

The daughter was leaning very far down, hanging her head almost between her knees, watching him through a triangular door she had made in her overturned hair; and she suddenly fell in a heap on the floor and began to whimper. Mr. Shiftlet straightened her out and helped her get back in the chair.

"Is she your baby girl?" he asked.

"My only," the old woman said, "and she's the sweetest girl in the world. I wouldn't give her up for nothing on earth. She's smart too. She can sweep the floor, cook, wash, feed the chickens, and hoe. I wouldn't give her up for a casket of jewels."

"No," he said kindly, "don't ever let any man take her away from you."

"Any man come after her," the old woman said, "'ll have to stay around the place."

Mr. Shiftlet's eye in the darkness was focused on a part of the automobile bumper that glittered in the distance. "Lady," he said, jerking his short arm up as if he could point with it to her house and yard and pump, "there ain't a broken thing on this plantation that I couldn't fix for you, one-arm jackleg or not. I'm a man," he said with a sullen dignity, "even if I ain't a whole one. I got," he said, tapping his knuckles on the floor to emphasize the immensity of what he was going to say, "a moral intelligence!" and his face pierced out of the darkness into a shaft of doorlight and he stared at her as if he were astonished himself at this impossible truth.

The old woman was not impressed with the phrase. "I told you you could hang around and work for food," she said, "if you don't mind sleeping in that car yonder."

"Why listen, lady," he said with a grin of delight, "the monks of old slept in their coffins!"

"They wasn't as advanced as we are," the old woman said.

The next morning he began on the roof of the garden house while Lucynell, the daughter, sat on a rock and watched him work. He had not been around a week before the change he had made in the place was apparent. He had patched the front and back steps, built a new hog pen, restored a fence, and taught Lucynell, who was completely deaf and had never said a word in her life, to say the word "bird." The big rosy-faced girl followed him everywhere, saying "Burrttddt ddbirrrttdt," and clapping her hands. The old woman watched from a distance, secretly pleased. She was ravenous for a son-in-law.

Mr. Shiftlet slept on the hard narrow back seat of the car with his feet out the side window. He had his razor and a can of water on a crate that served him as a bedside table and he put up a piece of mirror against the back glass and kept his coat neatly on a hanger that he hung over one of the windows.

In the evenings he sat on the steps and talked while the old woman and Lucynell rocked violently in their chairs on either side of him. The old woman's three mountains were black against the dark blue sky and were visited off and on by various planets and by the moon after it had left the chickens. Mr. Shiftlet pointed out that the reason he had improved this plantation was because he had taken a personal interest in it. He said he was even going to make the automobile run.

He had raised the hood and studied the mechanism and he said he could tell that the car had been built in the days when cars were really built. You take now, he said, one man puts in one bolt and another man puts in another bolt and another man puts in another bolt so that it's a man for a bolt. That's why you have to pay so much for a car: you're paying all those men. Now if you didn't have to pay but one man, you could get you a cheaper car and one that had had a personal interest taken in it, and it would be a better car. The old woman agreed with him that this was so.

Mr. Shiftlet said that the trouble with the world was that nobody cared, or stopped and took any trouble. He said he never would have been able to teach Lucynell to say a word if he hadn't cared and stopped long enough.

"Teach her to say something else," the old woman said.

"What you want her to say next?" Mr. Shiftlet asked.

The old woman's smile was broad and toothless and suggestive. "Teach her to say 'sugarpie,' " she said.

Mr. Shiftlet already knew what was on her mind.

The next day he began to tinker with the automobile and that evening he told her that if she would buy a fan belt, he would be able to make the car run.

The old woman said she would give him the money. "You see that girl yonder?" she asked, pointing to Lucynell who was sitting on the floor a foot away, watching him, her eyes blue even in the dark. "If it was ever a man wanted to take her away, I would say, 'No man on earth is going to take that sweet girl of mine away from me!' but if he was to say, 'Lady, I don't want to take her away, I want her right here,' I would say, 'Mister, I don't blame you none. I wouldn't pass up a chance to live in a permanent place and get the sweetest girl in the world myself. You ain't no fool,' I would say."

"How old is she?" Mr. Shiftlet asked casually.

"Fifteen, sixteen," the old woman said. The girl was nearly thirty but because of her innocence it was impossible to guess.

"It would be a good idea to paint it too," Mr. Shiftlet remarked. "You don't want it to rust out."

"We'll see about that later," the old woman said.

The next day he walked into town and returned with the parts he needed and a can of gasoline. Late in the afternoon, terrible noises issued from the shed and the old woman rushed out of the house, thinking Lucynell was somewhere having a fit. Lucynell was sitting on a chicken crate, stamping her feet and screaming, "Burrddttt! bddurrddttt!" but her fuss was drowned out by the car. With a volley of blasts it emerged from the shed, moving in a fierce and stately way. Mr. Shiftlet was in the driver's seat, sitting very erect. He had an expression of serious modesty on his face as if he had just raised the dead.

That night, rocking on the porch, the old woman began her business at once. "You want you an innocent woman, don't you?" she asked sympathetically. "You don't want none of this trash."

"No'm, I don't," Mr. Shiftlet said.

"One that can't talk," she continued, "can't sass you back or use foul language. That's the kind for you to have. Right there," and she pointed to Lucynell sitting cross-legged in her chair, holding both feet in her hands.

"That's right," he admitted. "She wouldn't give me any trouble."

"Saturday," the old woman said, "you and her and me can drive into town and get married."

Mr. Shiftlet eased his position on the steps.

"I can't get married right now," he said. "Everything you want to do takes money and I ain't got any."

"What you need with money?" she asked.

"It takes money," he said. "Some people'll do anything anyhow these days, but the way I think, I wouldn't marry no woman that I couldn't take on a trip like she was somebody. I mean take her to a hotel and treat her. I wouldn't marry the Duchesser Windsor," he said firmly, "unless I could take her to a hotel and giver something good to eat.

"I was raised thataway and there ain't a thing I can do about it. My old mother taught me how to do."

"Lucynell don't even know what a hotel is," the old woman muttered. "Listen here, Mr. Shiftlet," she said, sliding forward in her chair, "you'd be getting a permanent house and a deep well and the most innocent girl in the world. You don't need no money. Lemme tell you something; there ain't any place in the world for a poor disabled friendless drifting man."

The ugly words settled in Mr. Shiftlet's head like a group of buzzards in the top of a tree. He didn't answer at once. He rolled himself a cigarette and lit it and then he said in an even voice, "Lady, a man is divided into parts, body and spirit."

The old woman clamped her gums together.

"A body and a spirit," he repeated. "The body, lady, is like a house: it don't go anywhere; but the spirit, lady, is like a automobile: always on the move, always . . ."

"Listen, Mr. Shiftlet," she said, "my well never goes dry and my house is always warm in the winter and there's no mortgage on a thing about this place. You can go to the courthouse and see for yourself. And yonder under that shed is a fine automobile." She laid the bait carefully. "You can have it painted by Saturday. I'll pay for the paint."

In the darkness, Mr. Shiftlet's smile stretched like a weary snake waking up by a fire. After a second he recalled himself and said, "I'm only saying a man's spirit means more to him than anything else. I would have to take my wife off for the week end without no regard at all for cost. I got to follow where my spirit says to go."

"I'll give you fifteen dollars for a week-end trip," the old woman said in a crabbed voice. "That's the best I can do."

"That wouldn't hardly pay for more than the gas and the hotel," he said. "It wouldn't feed her."

"Seventeen-fifty," the old woman said. "That's all I got so it isn't any use you trying to milk me. You can take a lunch."

Mr. Shiftlet was deeply hurt by the word "milk." He didn't doubt that she had more money sewed up in her mattress but he had already told her he was not interested in her money. "I'll make that do," he said and rose and walked off without treating with her further.

On Saturday the three of them drove into town in the car that the paint had barely dried on and Mr. Shiftlet and Lucynell were married in the Ordinary's office while the old woman witnessed. As they came out of the courthouse, Mr. Shiftlet began twisting his neck in his collar. He looked morose and bitter as if he had been insulted while someone held him. "That didn't satisfy me none," he said. "That was just something a woman in an office did, nothing but paper work and blood tests. What do they know about my blood? If they was to take my heart and cut it out," he said, "they wouldn't know a thing about me. It didn't satisfy me at all."

"It satisfied the law," the old woman said sharply.

"The law," Mr. Shiftlet said and spit. "It's the law that don't satisfy me."

He had painted the car dark green with a yellow band around it just under the windows. The three of them climbed in the front seat and the old woman said, "Don't Lucynell look pretty? Looks like a baby doll." Lucynell was dressed up in a white dress that her mother had uprooted from a trunk and there was a Panama hat on her head with a bunch of red wooden cherries on the brim. Every now and then her placid expression was changed by a sly isolated little thought like a shoot of green in the desert. "You got a prize!" the old woman said.

Mr. Shiftlet didn't even look at her.

They drove back to the house to let the old woman off and pick up the lunch. When they were ready to leave, she stood staring in the window of the car, with her fingers clenched around the glass. Tears began to seep sideways out of her eyes and run along the dirty creases in her face. "I ain't ever been parted with her for two days before," she said.

Mr. Shiftlet started the motor.

"And I wouldn't let no man have her but you because I seen you would do right. Good-by, Sugarbaby," she said, clutching at the sleeve of the white dress. Lucynell looked straight at her and didn't seem to see her there at all. Mr. Shiftlet eased the car forward so that she had to move her hands.

The early afternoon was clear and open and surrounded by pale blue sky. Although the car would go only thirty miles an hour, Mr. Shiftlet imagined a terrific climb and dip and swerve that went entirely to his head so that he forgot his morning bitterness. He had always wanted an automobile but he had never been able to afford one before. He drove very fast because he wanted to make Mobile by nightfall.

Occasionally he stopped his thoughts long enough to look at Lucynell in the seat beside him. She had eaten the lunch as soon as they were out of the yard and now she was pulling the cherries off the hat one by one and throwing them out the window. He became depressed in spite of the car. He had driven about a hundred miles when he decided that she must be hungry again and at the next small town they came to, he stopped in front of an aluminum-painted eating place called The Hot Spot and took her in and ordered her a plate of ham and grits. The ride had made her sleepy and as soon as she got up on the stool, she rested her head on the counter and shut her eyes. There was no one in The Hot Spot but Mr. Shiftlet and the boy behind the counter, a pale youth with a greasy rag hung over his shoulder. Before he could dish up the food, she was snoring gently.

"Give it to her when she wakes up," Mr. Shiftlet said. "I'll pay for it now."

The boy bent over her and stared at the long pink-gold hair and the half-shut sleeping eyes. Then he looked up and stared at Mr. Shiftlet. "She looks like an angel of Gawd," he murmured.

"Hitch-hiker," Mr. Shiftlet explained. "I can't wait. I got to make Tuscaloosa."

The boy bent over again and very carefully touched his finger to a strand of the golden hair and Mr. Shiftlet left.

He was more depressed than ever as he drove on by himself. The late afternoon had grown hot and sultry and the country had flattened out. Deep in the sky a storm as preparing very slowly and without thunder as if meant to drain every drop of air from the earth before it broke. There were times when Mr. Shiftlet preferred not to be alone. He felt too that a man with a car had a responsibility to others and he kept his eye out for a hitchhiker. Occasionally he saw a sign that warned: "Drive carefully. The life you save may be your own."

The narrow road dropped off on either side into dry fields and here and there a shack or a filling station stood in a clearing. The sun began to set directly in front of the automobile. It was a reddening ball that through his windshield was slightly flat on the bottom and top. He saw a boy in overalls and a gray hat standing on the edge of the road and he slowed the car and stopped in front of him. The boy didn't have his hand raised to thumb the ride, he was only standing there, but he had a small cardboard suitcase and his hat was set on his head in a way to indicate that he had left somewhere for good. "Son," Mr. Shiftlet said, "I see you want a ride."

The boy didn't say he did or he didn't but he opened the door of the car and got in, and Mr. Shiftlet started driving again. The child held the suitcase on his lap and folded his arms on top of it. He turned his head and looked out the window away from Mr. Shiftlet. Mr. Shiftlet felt oppressed. "Son," he said after a minute, "I got the best old mother in the world so I reckon you only got the second best."

The boy gave him a quick dark glance and then turned his face back out the window.

"It's nothing so sweet," Mr. Shiftlet continued, "as a boy's mother. She taught him his first prayers at her knee, she give him love when no other would, she told him what was right and what wasn't, and she seen that he done the right thing. Son," he said, "I never rued a day in my life like the one I rued when I left that old mother of mine."

The boy shifted in his seat but he didn't look at Mr. Shiftlet. He unfolded his arms and put one hand on the door handle.

"My mother was a angel of Gawd," Mr. Shiftlet said in a very strained voice. "He took her from heaven and giver to me and I left her." His eyes were instantly clouded over with a mist of tears. The car was barely moving.

The boy turned angrily in the seat. "You go to the devil!" he cried. "My old woman is a flea bag and yours is a stinking pole cat!" and with that he flung the door open and jumped out with his suitcase into the ditch.

Mr. Shiftlet was so shocked that for about a hundred feet he drove along slowly with the door still open. A cloud, the exact color of the boy's hat and shaped like a turnip, had descended over the sun, and another, worse looking, crouched behind the car. Mr. Shiftlet felt that the rottenness of the world was about to engulf him. He raised his arm and let it fall again to his breast. "Oh Lord!" he prayed. "Break forth and wash the slime from this earth!"

The turnip continued slowly to descend. After a few minutes there was a guffawing peal of thunder from behind and fantastic raindrops, like tin-can tops, crashed over the rear of Mr. Shiftlet's car. Very quickly he stepped on the gas and with his stump sticking out the window he raced the galloping shower into Mobile.

1955

The Prose Writer as Subject

HENRY MILLER

(1891–   )

Few of Henry Miller's most ardent supporters would place him in the first rank as a man of letters on literary grounds alone. His style is often tedious and his subject matter uninspired. Few of his many books approach anything like total success as artistic creations. Yet there are those who have considered him a serious candidate for the Nobel Prize in Literature and even his strongest detractors cannot deny the force of his impact on the literature of his time. He has stood squarely in the vanguard of a cultural phenomenon.

Born Henry Valentine Miller on the day after Christmas in 1891, he grew up in Brooklyn, New York, attended City College of New York for about two months, and plunged into a world of odd jobs and self-education. At thirty-three he left a position with Western Union in order to become a writer, but it was another ten years

before *Tropic of Cancer* was published (1934) and he was nearly sixty before he began to gain any substantial income from writing. Because many of his books were considered too obscene for American or British publication under the laws that then prevailed, they were printed in English in Paris; none of his novels was published in New York or London until the 1960's. In the meantime he acquired a large following among those who had become acquainted with his forbidden works in copies smuggled from abroad or borrowed from the locked shelves of university collections of erotica and his growing reputation was bolstered in the two decades after 1939 by the publication of a good many of his less sensational writings in the United States and England under the imprint of highly respected publishers such as New Directions. In 1940, after ten years in France, he returned to the United States, where he has lived, since 1942, in California.

Miller has always been a radical, a revolutionary, an outsider in a culture that he sees as inimical to the very existence of an artist. An intuitional, emotional writer, he is a descendant of the nineteenth-century individualistic tradition represented by Emerson, Thoreau, and Whitman. Lawrence he admires, but not Proust or Joyce. Always the subjective "I" of his personality comes first, with the result that even when he writes ostensibly on other subjects, the chief subject of his prose is Henry Miller. "Unconsciously I think that every great artist is trying with might and main to destroy art," he wrote in *The Cosmological Eye* (1939). "By that I mean that he is desperately striving to break down this wall between himself and the rest of humanity." Contact must be made. Conventions must be broken. The pressures toward conformity must be resisted. Certainly the obsession with sexuality that appeared so astonishing in a serious creative writer in the 1930's had come to appear considerably less so by the 1960's. Nevertheless, new ground had been broken and the influence of Miller on his younger contemporaries has been considerable. In an age characterized by the mass dissemination and standardization not only of machinery but of ideas as well, his has seemed to many a liberating and even a prophetic voice.

Novels include *Tropic of Cancer,* 1934; *Black Spring,* 1936; *Tropic of Capricorn,* 1939; *The Rosy Crucifixion* (*Sexus,* 2 vols., 1949; *Plexus,* 2 vols., 1953; *Nexus,* 1960); and *Quiet Days in Clichy,* 1956. Other titles include *Max and the White Phagocytes,* 1938; *The Cosmological Eye,* 1939; *The Colossus of Maroussi * * *,* 1941; *The Angel is My Watermark,* 1944; *Sunday after the War,* 1944; *The Air-Conditioned Nightmare,* 1945; *Remember to Remember* (vol. 2 of *The Air-Conditioned Nightmare*), 1947; *The Books in My Life,* 1952; *The Time of the Assassins: A Study of Rimbaud,* 1956; *Big Sur and the Oranges of Hieronymus Bosch,* 1957; *Stand Still Like the Hummingbird,* 1962; and *Henry Miller on Writing,* 1964. Lawrence Durrell edited *A Henry Miller Reader,* 1959. A more recent selection is *Selected Prose,* 2 vols., 1965. George Wickes edited *Lawrence Durrell and Henry Miller: A Private Correspondence,* 1964. Gunther Stuhlmann edited *Henry Miller: Letters to Anaïs Nin,* 1965.

Biographical and critical studies include Annette Kar Baxter, *Henry Miller, Expatriate,* 1961; Kingsley Widner, *Henry Miller,* 1963; George Wickes, ed., *Henry Miller and the Critics,* 1964; William Gordon, *The Mind and Art of Henry Miller,* 1967; Ihab Hassan, *The Literature of Silence: Henry Miller and Samuel Beckett,* 1968; J. A. Nelson, *Form and Image in the Fiction of Henry Miller,* 1970; and Edward Mitchell, ed., *Henry Miller: Three Decades of Criticism,* 1971.

From The Time of the Assassins: A Study of Rimbaud

PART I

Analogies, Affinities, Correspondences and Repercussions

It was in 1927, in the sunken basement of a dingy house in Brooklyn, that I first heard Rimbaud's name mentioned. I was then 36 years old and in the depths of my own protracted Season in Hell.[1] An absorbing book about Rimbaud was lying about the house but I never once glanced at it. The reason was that I loathed the woman who owned it and who was then living with us. In looks, temperament and behavior she was, as I later discovered, as near to resembling Rimbaud as it is possible to imagine.

As I say, though Rimbaud was the all engrossing topic of conversation between Thelma and my wife, I made no effort to know him. In fact, I fought like the very devil to put him out of my mind; it seemed to me then that he was the evil genius who had unwittingly inspired all my trouble and misery. I saw that Thelma, whom I despised, had identified herself with him, was imitating him as best she could, not only in her behavior but in the kind of verse she wrote. Everything conspired to make me repudiate his name, his influence, his very existence. I was then at the very lowest point of my whole career, my morale was completely shattered. I remember sitting in the cold dank basement trying to write by the light of a flickering candle with a pencil. I was trying to write a play depicting my own tragedy. I never succeeded in getting beyond the first act.

In that state of despair and sterility I was naturally highly sceptical of the genius of a seventeen-year-old poet. All that I heard about him sounded like an invention of crazy Thelma's. I was then capable of believing that she could conjure up subtle torments with which to plague me, since she hated me as much as I did her. The life which the three of us were leading, and which I tell about at length in *The Rosy Crucifixion*, was like an episode in one of Dostoievsky's tales. It seems unreal and incredible to me now.

The point is, however, that Rimbaud's name stuck. Though I was not even to glance at his work until six or seven years later, at the home of Anaïs Nin [2] in Louveciennes, his presence was always with me. It was a disturbing presence, too. "Some day you will have to come to grips with me." That's what his voice kept re-

---

1. The title of Rimbaud's first book, published in 1873, when he was nineteen.

2. American writer, born in Paris in 1903.

peating in my ears. The day I read the first line of Rimbaud I suddenly remembered that it was of *Le Bateau Ivre* that Thelma had raved so much. *The Drunken Boat!* How expressive that title now seems in the light of all I subsequently experienced! Thelma meanwhile died in an insane asylum. And if I had not gone to Paris, begun to work there in earnest, I think my fate would have been the same. In that basement on Brooklyn Heights my own ship had foundered. When finally the keel burst asunder and I drifted out to the open sea, I realized that I was free, that the death I had gone through had liberated me.

If that period in Brooklyn represented my Season in Hell, then the Paris period, especially from 1932 to 1934, was the period of my Illuminations.[3]

Coming upon Rimbaud's work at this time, when I had never been so fecund, so jubilant, so exalted, I had to push him aside, my own creations were more important to me. A mere glance at his writings and I knew what lay in store for me. He was pure dynamite, but I had first to fling my own stick. At this time I did not know anything about his life, except from the snatches Thelma had let drop years ago. I had yet to read a line of biography. It was in 1943, while living at Beverly Glen with John Dudley, the painter, that I first read about Rimbaud. I read Jean-Marie Carré's *A Season in Hell* and then Enid Starkie's work.[4] I was overwhelmed, tongue-tied. It seemed to me that I had never read of a more accursed existence than Rimbaud's. I forgot completely about my own sufferings, which far outweighed his. I forgot about the frustrations and humiliations I had endured, the depths of despair and impotence to which I had sunk time and again. Like Thelma in the old days, I too could talk of nothing but Rimbaud. Everybody who came to the house had to listen to the song of Rimbaud.

It is only now, eighteen years after I first heard the name, that I am able to see him clearly, to read him like a clairvoyant. Now I *know* how great was his contribution, how terrible his tribulations. Now I understand the significance of his life and work—as much, that is, as one can say he understands the life and work of another. But what I see most clearly is how I miraculously escaped suffering the same vile fate.

Rimbaud experienced his great crisis when he was eighteen, at which moment in his life he had reached the edge of madness; from this point on his life is an unending desert. I reached mine at the age of thirty-six to thirty-seven, which is the age at which Rimbaud dies. From this point on my life begins to blossom.

3. Rimbaud's *Illuminations* was published in 1886.   4. *Arthur Rimbaud,* 1938 (revised in 1947 and 1961).

Rimbaud turned from literature to life; I did the reverse. Rimbaud fled from the chimeras he had created; I embraced them. Sobered by the folly and waste of mere experience of life, I halted and converted my energies to creation. I plunged into writing with the same fervor and zest that I had plunged into life. Instead of losing life, I gained life; miracle after miracle occurred, every misfortune being transformed to good account. Rimbaud, though plunging into a realm of incredible climates and landscapes, into a world of phantasy as strange and marvelous as his poems, became more and more bitter, taciturn, empty and sorrowful.

Rimbaud restored literature to life; I have endeavored to restore life to literature. In both of us the confessional quality is strong, the moral and spiritual preoccupation uppermost. The flair for _language_, for music rather than literature, is another trait in common. With him I have felt an underlying primitive nature which manifests itself in strange ways. Claudel [5] styled Rimbaud "a mystic in the wild state." Nothing could describe him better. He did not "belong"—not anywhere. I have always had the same feeling about myself. The parallels are endless. I shall go into them in some detail, because in reading the biographies and the letters I saw these correspondences so clearly that I could not resist making note of them. I do not think I am unique in this respect; I think there are many Rimbauds in this world and that their number will increase with time. I think the Rimbaud type will displace, in the world to come, the Hamlet type and the Faustian type. The trend is toward a deeper split. Until the old world dies out utterly, the "abnormal" individual will tend more and more to become the norm. The new man will find himself only when the warfare between the collectivity and the individual ceases. Then we shall see the _human_ type in its fullness and splendor.

To get the full import of Rimbaud's Season in Hell, which lasted eighteen years, one has to read his letters. Most of this time was spent on the Somali Coast, in Aden a number of years. Here is a description of this hell on earth, from a letter to his mother:

"You cannot imagine the place: not a tree, even a withered one, not a sod of earth. Aden is the crater of an extinct volcano filled up with the sand of the sea. You only see lava and sand everywhere which cannot produce the slightest vegetation. It is surrounded by desert sands. Here the sides of the crater of our extinct volcano prevent the air from coming in and we are roasted as if in a limekiln."

How did a man of genius, a man of great energies, great re-

5. Paul Claudel (1868–1955), French poet and dramatist.

sources, manage to coop himself up, to roast and squirm, in such a miserable hole? Here was a man for whom a thousand lives were not sufficient to explore the wonders of the earth, a man who broke with friends and relatives at an early age in order to experience life in its fullness, yet year after year we find him marooned in this hell-hole. How do you explain it? We know, of course, that he was straining at the leash all the time, that he was revolving countless schemes and projects to liberate himself, and liberate himself not only from Aden but from the whole world of sweat and struggle. Adventurer that he was, Rimbaud was nevertheless obsessed with the idea of attaining freedom, which he translated into terms of financial security. At the age of twenty-eight he writes home that the most important, the most urgent, thing for him is to become independent, no matter where. What he omitted to add was, *and no matter how.* He is a curious mixture of audacity and timidity. He has the courage to venture where no other white man has ever set foot, but he has not the courage to face life without a permanent income. He does not fear cannibals, but he fears his own white brethren. Though he is trying to amass a comfortable fortune, with which he can travel the globe leisurely and comfortably, or settle down somewhere should he find the right spot, he is still the poet and dreamer, the man who is unadapted to life, the man who believes in miracles, the man who is looking for Paradise in one form or another. At first he thinks that fifty thousand francs will be sufficient to secure him for life, but when he almost succeeds in accumulating this sum he decides that a hundred thousand would be safer. Those forty thousand francs! What a miserable, horrible time he has, carrying this nest egg about with him! It is practically his undoing. When they carry him down from Harar to the coast in a litter—a journey, incidentally, comparable to the Calvary—his thoughts are frequently on the gold in his belt. Even at the hospital in Marseilles, where his leg is amputated, he is plagued with this nest egg. If it is not the pain which keeps him awake nights it is the thought of the money which he has on him, which he has to hide so that it will not be stolen from him. He would like to put it in a bank, but how is he to get to a bank when he can't walk? He writes home begging some one to come and take care of his precious treasure. There is something so tragic and so farcical about this that one does not know what to say or think any more.

But what was at the root of this mania for security? The fear which every creative artist knows: that he is unwanted, that he is of no use in the world. How often in his letters does Rimbaud speak of being unfit to return to France and resume the life of the ordinary citizen. I have no trade, no profession, no friends there, he says. As do all poets, he sees the civilized world as the jungle; he does not know how to protect himself in it. Sometimes he adds that it is too late to think of returning—he is always speaking as though he were an old man!—he is too used to the free, wild, adventurous life to ever go back into harness again. The thing he had always loathed was honest toil, but in Africa, Cyprus, Arabia, he toils like a nigger, depriving himself of everything, even coffee and tobacco, wearing a cotton shift year in and year out, putting aside every sou he makes, in the hope of one day buying his freedom. Even had he succeeded, we know he would never have felt free, never have been happy, never have thrown off the yoke of boredom. From the recklessness of youth he swerved to the cautiousness of old age. He was so utterly the outcast, the rebel, the accursed one, that nothing could save him.

I stress this aspect of his nature because it explains many of the malodorous traits attributed to him. He was not a miser, not a peasant at heart, as some of his biographers imply. He was not hard on others, he was hard with himself. Actually he had a generous nature. "His charity was lavish, unobtrusive and discreet," says his old employer, Bardey. "It is probably one of the few things he did without disgust and without a sneer of contempt."

There was one other bogey which obsessed him all his days and nights: military service. From the time he begins his wandering up until the day of his death he is tormented by the fear that he is not *en règle* [6] with the military authorities. Just a few months before his death, while in the hospital at Marseilles, his leg amputated, his sufferings multiplying daily, the fear that the authorities will discover his whereabouts and send him to prison rest like an incubus upon him. *"La prison après ce que je viens de souffrir? Il vaudrait mieux la mort!"* [7] He begs his sister to write him only when it is absolutely necessary, to address him not as Arthur Rimbaud but simply Rimbaud, and to post the letters from some neighboring town.

The whole fabric of his character is laid bare in these letters which are practically devoid of any literary quality or charm. We see his tremendous hunger for experience, his insatiable curiosity, his illimitable desires, his courage and tenacity, his self-flagellation, his asceticism, his sobriety, his fears and obsessions, his morbidity, his loneliness, his feeling of ostracism, and his unfathomable boredom. We see above all, that like most creative individuals, he was incapable of learning from experience. There is nothing but a repetitious round of similar trials and torments. We see him victimized by the illusion that freedom can be obtained by external means. We see him remaining the adolescent all his life,

6. In order.

7. "Prison after all that I have suffered? It would be better to die!"

refusing to accept suffering or give it meaning. To estimate how great was the failure of the latter half of his life we have only to compare his journeying with that of Cabeza de Vaca.[8]

But let us leave him in the midst of that desert which he created for himself. My purpose is to indicate certain affinities, analogies, correspondences and repercussions. Let us begin with the parents. Like Madame Rimbaud, my mother was the Northern type, cold, critical, proud, unforgiving, and puritanical. My father was of the South, of Bavarian parents, while Rimbaud's father was Burgundian. There was a continual strife and clash between mother and father, with the usual repercussions upon the offspring. The rebellious nature, so difficult to overcome, here finds its matrix. Like Rimbaud, I too began at an early age to cry: "Death to God!" It was death to everything which the parents endorsed or approved of. It extended even to their friends whom I openly insulted in their presence, even as a stripling. The antagonism never ceased until my father was virtually at the point of death, when at last I began to see how much I resembled him.

Like Rimbaud, I hated the place I was born in. I will hate it till my dying day. My earliest impulse is to break loose from the home, from the city I detest, from the country and its citizens with whom I feel nothing in common. Like him too, I am precocious, reciting verses in a foreign language while still in my high-chair. I learned to walk much ahead of time and to speak ahead of time, to read the newspaper even before I went to kindergarten. I was always the youngest in the class and not only the best student but the favorite of teachers and comrades alike. But, like him again, I despised the prizes and awards which were made me, and was expelled from school several times for refractory behavior. My whole mission, while at school, seemed to be to make fun of the teachers and the curriculum. It was all too easy and too stupid for me. I felt like a trained monkey.

From earliest childhood I was a voracious reader. For Christmas I requested only books, twenty and thirty at a time. Until I was twenty-five or so, I almost never left the house without one or more books under my arm. I read standing up, while going to work, often memorizing long passages of poetry from my favorite authors. One of these was Goethe's *Faust*, I remember. The chief result of this continuous absorption in books was to inflame me to further revolt, to stimulate the latent desire for travel and adventure, to make me anti-literary. It made me contemptuous of everything that surrounded me, alienating me gradually from my friends and imposing on me that solitary, eccentric nature which causes one to be

8. "See *The Power Within Us* by Haniel Long; Duell, Sloan & Pearce, New York" [Miller's note].

styled a "bizarre" individual. From the age of eighteen (the year of Rimbaud's crisis) I became definitely unhappy, wretched, miserable, despondent. Nothing less than a complete change of environment seemed capable of dissipating this unchanging mood. At twenty-one I broke away, but not for long. Again, like Rimbaud, the opening flights were always disastrous. I was always returning home, either voluntarily or involuntarily, and always in a state of desperation. There seemed no egress, no way of achieving liberation. I undertook the most senseless labors, everything, in short, which I was unfitted for. Like Rimbaud in the quarries at Cyprus, I began with pick and shovel, a day laborer, a migratory worker, a vagabond. There was even this similarity, that when I broke from home it was with the intention of leading an outdoor life, of never again reading a book, of making a living with my two hands, of being a man of the open spaces and not a citizen of a town or city.

All the while, however, my language and my ideas betrayed me. I was completely the literary man, whether I wanted to be or not. Though I could get along with most any type of individual, especially the common man, in the end I was always suspect. It was very much like my visits to the library; always demanding the wrong book. No matter how large the library, the book I wanted was never in or else it was forbidden me. It seemed in those days that everything I wanted in life, or of life, was proscribed. Naturally, I was guilty of the most violent recriminations. My language, which had been shocking even as a child—I remember being dragged to the police station at the age of six for using foul language—my language, I say, became even more shocking and indecent.

What a jolt I got when I read that Rimbaud, as a young man, used to sign his letters—"that heartless wretch, Rimbaud." Heartless was an adjective I was fond of hearing applied to myself. I had no principles, no loyalty, no code whatsoever; when it suited me, I could be thoroughly unscrupulous, with friend and foe alike. I usually repaid kindness with insult and injury. I was insolent, arrogant, intolerant, violently prejudiced, relentlessly obstinate. In short, I had a distinctly disagreeable personality, a most difficult one to deal with. Yet I was very much liked; people seemed over-eager to forgive my bad qualities for the charm and enthusiasm I dispensed. This attitude served only to embolden me to take further liberties. Sometimes I myself wondered how on earth I could get away with it. The people I most loved to insult and injure were those who deemed themselves my superior in one way or another. Toward these I waged a relentless war. Beneath it all I was what you would call a good boy. My natural temperament was that of a kind, joyous, open-hearted individual. As a youngster I was often referred to as "an angel." But the demon of revolt had taken possession of me at a very early age. It was my mother who implanted it in me. It was against her, against all that she represented, that I directed my uncontrollable energy. Never until I was fifty did I once think of her with affection. Though she never actually balked me (only because my will was the stronger), I felt her shadow across my path constantly. It was a shadow of disapproval, silent and insidious, like a poison slowly injected into the veins.

I was amazed when I read that Rimbaud had allowed his mother to read the manuscript of *A Season in Hell*. Never did I dream of showing my parents anything I had written, or even discussing the subject of my writing with them. When I first informed them that I had decided to become a writer they were horrified; it was as though I had announced that I was going to become a criminal. Why couldn't I do something sensible, something that would enable me to gain a living? Never did they read a line of what I have written. It was a sort of standing joke when their friends inquired of me, when they asked what I was doing. "*What is he doing?* Oh, he's writing. . . ." As though to say, he's crazy, he's making mud pies all day long.

I have always pictured the boy Rimbaud as being dolled up like a sissy, and later when a young man, as a dandy. That at any rate, was my case. My father being a tailor, it was natural for my parents to concentrate on my attire. When I grew up I inherited my father's rather elegant and sumptuous wardrobe. We were exactly the same size. But, like Rimbaud again, during the period when my individuality was asserting itself strenuously, I got myself up grotesquely, matching the inner eccentricities with the outer. I too was an object of ridicule in my own neighborhood. About this time I remember feeling extremely awkward, unsure of myself, and especially timid in conversation with men of any culture. "I don't know how to talk!" exclaimed Rimbaud in Paris when surrounded by other men of letters. Yet who could talk better than he when unrestrained? Even in Africa it was remarked of him how enchantingly he spoke at times. How well I understand this dilemma! What painful memories I have of stammering and stuttering in the presence of the men with whom I longed to hold conversation! With a nobody, on the other hand, I could talk with the tongues of angels. From childhood I was in love with the sound of words, with their magic, their power of enchantment. Often I went on verbal jags, so to speak. I could invent by the hour, driving my listeners to the point of hysteria. It was this quality, incidentally, which I recognized in Rimbaud the instant I glanced at a page of his. It registered like a shot. In Beverly Glen, when I was steeped in his life, I chalked up his phrases on the wall—in the kitchen, in the living room, in the toilet, even outside the house. Those phrases will never lose their potency for me. Each time I run across them I get the same thrill, the same jubilation, the same fear of losing my mind should I dwell on them too long. How many writers are there who can do this to you? Every writer produces some haunting passages, some memorable phrases, but with Rimbaud they are countless, they are strewn all over the pages, like gems tumbled from a rifled chest. It is this endowment which makes the link with Rimbaud indissoluble. And it is only this which I envy him for. Today, after all I have written, my deepest desire is to be done with the books I have projected and give myself up to the creation of sheer nonsense, sheer fantasy. I shall never be the poet he is, but there are vast imaginative reaches still to be attained.

And now we come to "the girl with the violet eyes." We know almost nothing about her. We know only that it was his first tragic experience of love. I do not know if it was in connection with her or the manufacturer's daughter that he used the words—"as scared as 36,000,000 new-born poodle dogs." But I can well believe that such must have been his reaction to the object of his affection. In any case I know that it was mine, and that she too had violet eyes. It is probable also, that like Rimbaud, I will think of her again on my dying bed. Everything is colored by that first disastrous experience. The strangest thing about it, I must add, is that it was not she who rejected me . . . it was I that held her in such awe and reverence that I fled from her. I imagine it must have been much the same in Rimbaud's case. With him, of course, everything—up to the eighteenth year—was packed into an incredibly short space of time. Just as he ran through the whole gamut of literature in a few years, so he ran through the course of ordinary experience quickly and briefly. He had but to taste a thing to know all that it promised or contained. And so his love life, so far as woman is concerned, was of cursory duration. We hear no mention of love again until Abyssinia, when he takes a native woman as a mistress. It is hardly love, one feels. If anything, his love was directed towards his Harari boy, Djami, to whom he tried to leave a legacy. It is hardly probable, knowing the life he led, that Rimbaud could have loved again with a whole heart.

Verlaine [9] is reputed to have said of Rimbaud that he never gave himself, either to God or to man. How true this may be each one has to judge for himself. To me it seems that nobody could have desired to give himself more than Rimbaud did. As a boy

9. Paul Verlaine (1844–1896), French symbolist poet.

he gave himself to God, as a young man he gave himself to the world. In both instances he felt that he had been deceived and betrayed; he recoiled, especially after his experience of the bloody Commune, and thereafter the core of his being remains intact, unyielding, inaccessible. In this respect he reminds me much of D. H. Lawrence, who had quite a little to say about this subject, i.e., about preserving intact the core of one's being.

It was from the moment he began to earn a living that his real difficulties set in. All his talents, and he possessed many, seemed of no use. Despite all reversals, he pushes on. "Advance, advance always!" His energy is boundless, his will indomitable, his hunger insatiable. "Let the poet burst with his straining after unheard of and unnameable things!" When I think of this period, marked by an almost frantic effort to make an entry into the world, to gain a toe-hold, when I think of the repeated sallies in this direction and that, like a beleaguered army trying to burst out of the grip in which it is held like a vise, I see my youthful self all over again. Thrice in his teens he reaches Brussels and Paris; twice he reaches London. From Stuttgart, after he has mastered sufficient German, he wanders on foot across Würtemberg and Switzerland into Italy. From Milan he sets out on foot for the Cyclades, via Brindisi, only to suffer a sunstroke and be returned to Marseilles via Leghorn. He covers the Scandinavian peninsula and Denmark with a traveling carnival; he ships from Hamburg, Antwerp, Rotterdam; he gets to Java by joining the Dutch army, only to desert after a taste of it. Passing St. Helena once in an English vessel which refuses to stop there, he jumps overboard but is brought back before he can reach the island. From Vienna he is escorted to the Bavarian border by the police, as a vagabond; from there he is brought under another escort to the Lorraine border. In all these flights and sallies he is always without money, always walking, and walking usually on an empty stomach. At Civita Vecchia he is set ashore with gastric fever brought on by inflammation of the walls of the stomach caused by the friction of his ribs against his abdomen. Excessive walking. In Abyssinia it is excessive horseback riding. Everything to excess. He drives himself inhumanly. The goal is always beyond.

How well I understand his mania! Looking back upon my life in America, it seems to me that I covered thousands and thousands of miles on an empty stomach. Always looking for a few pennies, for a crust of bread, for a job, for a place to flop. Always looking for a friendly face! At times, even though I was hungry, I would take to the road, hail a passing car and let the driver deposit me where he liked, just to get a change of scene. I know thousands of restaurants in New York, not from visiting them as a patron but from standing outside and gazing wistfully at the diners seated at the tables inside. I can still recall the odor of certain stands on street corners where hot dogs were being served. I can still see the white-robed chefs in the windows flipping waffles or flapjacks into the pan. Sometimes I think I was born hungry. And with the hunger is associated the walking, the tramping, the searching, the feverish, aimless to and fro. If I succeeded in begging a little more than was necessary for a meal I went immediately to the theatre or to a movie. All I cared for, once my stomach was filled, was to find a warm, cozy place where I could relax and forget my troubles for an hour or two. I would never save enough for carfare in those circumstances; leaving the womblike warmth of the theatre, I would set out in cold or rain to walk to the remote place where I happened to live. From the heart of Brooklyn to the heart of Manhattan I have walked countless times, in all kinds of weather and in varying degrees of starvation. When utterly exhausted, when unable to move another step, I have been obliged to turn round and retrace my steps. I understand perfectly how men can be trained to make forced marches of phenomenal length on empty bellies.

But it is one thing to walk the streets of your native city amidst hostile faces and quite another to tramp the highway in neighboring states. In your home town the hostility is merely indifference; in a strange town, or in the open stretches between towns, it is a distinctly antagonistic element that greets you. There are savage dogs, shot guns, sheriffs and vigilantes of all sorts lying in wait for you. You dare not lie down on the cold earth if you are a stranger in that vicinity. You keep moving, moving, moving all the time. In your back you feel the cold muzzle of a revolver, bidding you to move faster, faster, faster. This is your own country, too, in which all this happens, not a foreign land. The Japs may be cruel, the Huns barbarous, but what devils are these who look like you and talk like you, who wear the same dress, eat the same food, and who hound you like dogs? Are these not the worst enemies a man can have? The others I can find excuses for, but for one's own kind I can find no excuse whatever. "I have no friends there," Rimbaud often wrote home. Even in June, 1891, from the hospital in Marseilles, he repeats this refrain. "*Je mourrai où me jettera le destin. J'espère pouvoir retourner là où j'étais (Abyssinie), j'y ai des amis de dix ans, qui auront pitié de moi, je trouverai chez eux du travail, je vivrai comme je pourrai. Je vivrai toujours là-bas, tandis qu'en France, hors vous, je n'ai ni amis, ni connaissances, ni personne.*" [1] Here a footnote reads: "*Cependant la gloire littéraire*

---

1. "I will die where fate casts me. I hope to be able to return where I was (Abyssinia); I have friends there I have known for ten years who will have pity on me; I will find work with them; I will live as I can. I will always live there, whereas in France, except you, I have no friends, no acquaintances, nobody."

de Rimbaud battait alors son plein à Paris. Les admirateurs, qui lui eussent été personnellement tout devoués, étaient déjà nombreux. Il l'ignorait. Quelle malédiction!" [2]

Yes, what a malediction! I think of my own return to New York, an enforced return also, after ten years abroad. I had left America with ten dollars which I borrowed at the last moment before catching the boat; I returned without a cent, borrowing the money for the cabman from the hotel clerk who, seeing my trunk and valises, assumed I would have the money to pay for my hotel bill. The first thing I have to do, on arriving "home," is to telephone some one for a little money. Unlike Rimbaud, I have no belt full of gold hidden under the bed; but I still have two good legs, and in the morning, if help does not arrive during the night, I shall begin walking uptown in search of a friendly face again. In those ten years abroad I too had worked like a demon; I had earned the right to live comfortably for a year or so. But the war intervened, smashed everything, just as the intrigues of the European powers had blighted Rimbaud's chances in Somaliland. How familiar sounds a passage from a letter dated Aden, January 1888 . . . *"Tous les gouvernements sont venus engloutir des millions (et même en somme quelques milliards) sur toutes ces côtes maudites, désolées, où les indigènes errent des mois sans vivres et sans eau, sous le climat le plus effroyable du globe; et tous ces millions qu'on a jetés dans le ventre des bédouins, n'ont rien rapporté que les guerres, les désastres de tous genres!"* [3]

What a faithful picture this is of our dear governments! Always seeking to gain a foothold in some ungodly place, always suppressing or exterminating the natives, always clinging to their ill-gotten gains, defending their possessions, their colonies, with army and navy. For the biggest ones the world is not big enough. For the little ones who need room, pious words and veiled threats. The earth belongs to the strong, to those with the biggest armies and navies, to those who wield the economic big stick. How ironical that the solitary poet who ran to the end of the world in order to eke out a miserable living should have to sit with hands folded and watch the big powers make a mess of things in his own garden.

"Yes, the end of the world . . . Advance, advance always! Now begins the great adventure . . ." But as fast as you advance, the government is there ahead of you, with restrictions, with shac-

2. "However, the literary fame of Rimbaud was then in full swing in Paris. The admirers, who would have been devoted to him personally, were already numerous. He was unaware of it. What a curse!"
3. "All the governments have come and squandered millions (and even, taken together, billions) on all these cursed and desolate shores, where the natives wander for months without provisions and without water, under the most dreadful climate on the globe; and all those millions that have been thrown into the bowels of the Arabs have brought nothing but wars and disasters of all types."

kles and manacles, with poison gases, tanks and stink bombs. Rimbaud the poet sets himself to teaching the Harari boys and girls the Koran in their own language. The governments would sell them in slavery. "There is some destruction that is necessary," he wrote once, and what a fuss has been made over that simple statement! He was speaking then of the destruction incidental to creation. But governments destroy without the slightest excuse, and certainly with never a thought of creation. What Rimbaud the poet desired was to see the old forms go, in life as well as in literature. What governments desire is to preserve the status quo, no matter how much slaughter and destruction it entails. Some of his biographers, in describing his behavior as a youth, make him out to be a very bad boy; he did such nasty things, don't you know. But when it comes to appraising the activities of their dear governments, particularly with regard to those shady intrigues which Rimbaud inveighed against, they are all honey and whitewash. When they want to castigate him as the adventurer, they speak of what a great poet he was; when they want to subjugate him as a poet they speak of his chaos and rebelliousness. They are aghast when the poet imitates their plunderers and exploiters, and they are horrified when he shows no concern for money or for the monotonous, irksome life of the ordinary citizen. As a Bohemian he is too Bohemian, as a poet too poetical, as a pioneer too pioneering, as a man of affairs too much the man of affairs, as a gunrunner too clever a gunrunner, and so on and so forth. Whatever he did, he did too well, that seems to be the complaint against him. The pity is that he didn't become a politician. He would have done the job so well that Hitler, Stalin and Mussolini, to say nothing of Churchill and Roosevelt, would seem like mountebanks today. I don't think he would have brought about quite the destruction which these estimable leaders visited upon the world. He would have kept something up his sleeve for a rainy day, so to speak. He would not have shot his bolt. He would not have lost track of the goal, as our brilliant leaders seem to have done. No matter what a fiasco he made of his own life, oddly enough I believe that if he had been given the chance he would have made the world a better place to live in. I believe that the dreamer, no matter how impractical he may appear to the man in the street, is a thousand times more capable, more efficient, than the so-called statesman. All those incredible projects which Rimbaud envisaged putting into effect, and which were frustrated for one reason or another, have since been realized in some degree. He thought of them too soon, that was all. He saw far beyond the hopes and dreams of ordinary men and statesmen alike. He lacked the support of those very people who delight in accusing him of being the dreamer, the people who dream only when they fall asleep, never with eyes wide-open. For the dreamer who stands in the very midst of reality all proceeds too slowly, too lumberingly—even destruction.

"He will never be satisfied," writes one biographer. "Under his weary glance all flowers fade, all stars pale." Yes, there is a grain of truth in this. I know because I suffer from the same disease. *But*, if one has dreamed an empire, the empire of man, and if one dares to reflect at what a snail's pace men are advancing toward the realization of this dream, it is quite possible that what are called the activities of man pale to insignificance. I don't believe for a minute that the flowers ever faded or the stars were ever dimmed in Rimbaud's eyes. I think that with these the core of his being always maintained a direct and fervid communication. It was in the world of men that his weary glance saw things pale and fade. He began by wanting to "see all, feel all, exhaust everything, explore everything, say everything." It was not long before he felt the bit in his mouth, the spurs in his flanks, the lash on his back. Let a man but dress differently from his fellow creatures and he becomes an object of scorn and ridicule. The only law which is really lived up to whole-heartedly and with a vengeance is the law of conformity. No wonder that as a mere lad he ended "by finding the disorder of his mind sacred." At this point he had really made himself a seer. He found, however, that he was regarded as a clown and a mountebank. He had the choice of fighting for the rest of his life to hold the ground he had gained or to renounce the struggle utterly. Why could he not have compromised? Because compromise was not in his vocabulary. He was a fanatic from childhood, a person who had to go the whole hog or die. In this lies his purity, his innocence.

In all this I rediscover my own plight. I have never relinquished the struggle. But what a price I have paid! I have had to wage guerilla warfare, that hopeless struggle which is born only of desperation. The work I set out to write has not yet been written, or only partially. Just to raise my voice, to speak in my own fashion, I have had to fight every inch of the way. The song has almost been forgotten for the fight. Talk of the weary glance under which flowers fade and stars pale! My glance has become positively corrosive: it is only a miracle that under my pitiless gaze they are not blasted away. So much for the core of my being. As for the superficies, well, the outward man has gradually learned to accommodate himself to the ways of the world. He can be in it without being of it. He can be kind, gentle, charitable, hospitable. Why not? "The real problem," as Rimbaud pointed out, "is to make the soul monstrous." That is to say, not hideous but prodigious! What is the meaning of monstrous? According to the dictionary, "any organized form of life greatly malformed either by the lack, excess, misplacement or distortion of parts or organs; hence, anything hideous or abnormal, or made up of inconsistent parts or characters, whether repulsive or not." The root is from the Latin verb *moneo*, to warn. In mythology we recognize the monstrous under the form of the harpy, the gorgon, the sphinx, the centaur, the dryad, the mermaid. They are all prodigies, which is the essential meaning of the word. They have upset the norm, the balance. What does this signify if not the fear of the little man. Timid souls always see monsters in their path, whether these be called hippogriffs or Hitlerians. Man's greatest dread is the expansion of consciousness. All the fearsome, gruesome part of mythology stems from this fear. "Let us live in peace and harmony!" begs the little man. But the law of the universe dictates that peace and harmony can only be won by inner struggle. The little man does not want to pay the price for that kind of peace and harmony; he wants it ready-made, like a suit of manufactured clothes.

1956

JAMES BALDWIN
(1924–   )

"I do not think, if one is a writer," James Baldwin has written, "that one escapes it by trying to become something else." From the beginning he has been painfully aware of his identity as a black man from Harlem and almost from the time that he was old enough to possess ambitions he seems to have desired to become a writer. Because he was in some ways the most spectacularly successful of the black writers of the 1950's and 1960's and because his own rise coincided with the rise of the Negro freedom movement, there has always existed some pressure to speak for black political and social goals. His civil rights activity, however, has been secondary to his work as a writer. Seldom a spokesman for a particular cause, he has nevertheless recorded, out of the stresses of his personal situation, a memorable sense of what it means to be black and American in the second half of the twentieth century. In *The Fire Next Time* (1963) and in *No Name in the Street* (1972) he has thrown out a direct challenge to Americans. His other works present the personal vision that lies behind the challenge. His subject has been himself.

Baldwin's early years formed the basis for his first novel, *Go Tell It on the Mountain* (1953). Born in Harlem in 1924, he was raised by his mother and his foster father, a minister. While he was in high school he did some preaching, but he also continued the writing that he had begun as a child and for which he was regularly praised by his teachers. When he was eighteen he left home. World

War II provided him with a job in New Jersey, where he lived and worked with friends from high school, but New Jersey provided him also with some searing racial encounters. Before long he was living in Greenwich Village, supporting himself in any way he could, determined to become a writer. In 1948 he left the United States for Paris and for the next eight years he made his home in France. In 1957 he returned to New York and in subsequent years he traveled in the South and became active in civil rights, but he continued to see his principal role as that of a writer.

All of Baldwin's novels contain powerful passages and superior writing, but none does full justice to his talent. Usually the subject is the racial situation in the United States, but in *Giovanni's Room* (1955), for which he had difficulty finding a publisher, the subject is homosexuality, the setting is France, and race is not an issue.

In *Another Country* (1962) and *Tell Me How Long the Train's Been Gone* (1968) he returned to the themes that dominate his work. His search for a satisfactory fictional mode of presentation has also led to the production of some memorable short stories and the plays *Blues for Mister Charley* (1964) and *The Amen Corner* (1965).

His own search for personal identity plays an important role in his fiction and also forms the basis for the non-fictional prose that represents in some ways his finest work. The essays collected in *Notes of a Native Son* (1955) and *Nobody Knows My Name* (1961) stand with the best that his generation has produced.

Baldwin's novels and plays are named above. A collection of short stories is *Going to Meet the Man*, 1965. Nonfiction, in addition to titles above, includes *Nothing Personal* (with Richard Avedon), 1964; and *A Rap on Race* (with Margaret Mead), 1971. A biographical study is Fern M. Eckman, *The Furious Passage of James Baldwin*, 1966.

Notes of a Native Son

On the 29th of July, in 1943, my father died. On the same day, a few hours later, his last child was born. Over a month before this, while all our energies were concentrated in waiting for these events, there had been, in Detroit, one of the bloodiest race riots of the century. A few hours after my father's funeral, while he lay in state in the undertaker's chapel, a race riot broke out in Harlem. On the morning of the 3rd of August, we drove my father to the graveyard through a wilderness of smashed plate glass.

The day of my father's funeral had also been my nineteenth birthday. As we drove him to the graveyard, the spoils of injustice, anarchy, discontent, and hatred were all around us. It seemed to me that God himself had devised, to mark my father's end, the most sustained and brutally dissonant of codas. And it seemed to me, too, that the violence which rose all about us as my father left the world had been devised as a corrective for the pride of his eldest son. I had declined to believe in that apocalypse which had been central to my father's vision; very well, life seemed to be saying, here is something that will certainly pass for an apocalypse until the real thing comes along. I had inclined to be contemptuous of my father for the conditions of his life, for the conditions of our lives. When his life had ended I began to wonder about that life and also, in a new way, to be apprehensive about my own.

I had not known my father very well. We had got on badly, partly because we shared, in our different fashions, the vice of stubborn pride. When he was dead I realized that I had hardly ever spoken to him. When he had been dead a long time I began to wish I had. It seems to be typical of life in America, where opportunities, real and fancied, are thicker than anywhere else on the globe, that the second generation has no time to talk to the first. No one, including my father, seems to have known exactly how old he was, but his mother had been born during slavery. He was of the first generation of free men. He, along with thousands of other Negroes, came North after 1919 and I was part of that generation which had never seen the landscape of what Negroes sometimes call the Old Country.

He had been born in New Orleans and had been a quite young man there during the time that Louis Armstrong, a boy, was running errands for the dives and honky-tonks of what was always presented to me as one of the most wicked of cities—to this day, whenever I think of New Orleans, I also helplessly think of Sodom and Gomorrah. My father never mentioned Louis Armstrong, except to forbid us to play his records; but there was a picture of him on our wall for a long time. One of my father's strong-willed female relatives had placed it there and forbade my father to take it down. He never did, but he eventually maneuvered her out of the house and when, some years later, she was in trouble and near death, he refused to do anything to help her.

He was, I think, very handsome. I gather this from photographs and from my own memories of him, dressed in his Sunday best and on his way to preach a sermon somewhere, when I was little. Handsome, proud, and ingrown, "like a toe-nail," somebody said. But he looked to me, as I grew older, like pictures I had seen of African tribal chieftains: he really should have been naked, with war-paint on and barbaric mementos, standing among spears. He could be chilling in the pulpit and indescribably cruel in his personal life and he was certainly the most bitter man I have ever met; yet it must be said that there was something else in him, buried in him, which lent him his tremendous power and, even, a rather crushing charm. It had something to do with his blackness, I think —he was very black—with his blackness and his beauty, and with the fact that he knew that he was black but did not know that he was beautiful. He claimed to be proud of his blackness but it had also been the cause of much humiliation and it had fixed bleak boundaries to his life. He was not a young man when we were growing up and he had already suffered many kinds of ruin; in his outrageously demanding and protective way he loved his children, who were black like him and menaced, like him; and all these things sometimes showed in his face when he tried, never to my knowledge with any success, to establish contact with any of us. When he took one of his children on his knee to play, the child always became fretful and began to cry; when he tried to help one of us with our homework the absolutely unabating tension which emanated from him caused our minds and our tongues to become paralyzed, so that he, scarcely knowing why, flew into a rage and the child, not knowing why, was punished. If it ever entered his head to bring a surprise home for his children, it was, almost unfailingly, the wrong surprise and even the big watermelons he often brought home on his back in the summertime led to the most appalling scenes. I do not remember, in all those years, that one of his children was ever glad to see him come home. From what I was able to gather of his early life, it seemed that this inability to establish contact with other people had always marked him and had been one of the things which had driven him out of New Orleans. There was something in him, therefore, groping and tentative, which was never expressed and which was buried with him. One saw it most clearly when he was facing new people and hoping to impress them. But he never did, not for long. We went from church to smaller and more improbable church, he found himself in less and less demand as a minister, and by the time he died none of his friends had come to see him for a long time. He had lived and died in an intolerable bitterness of spirit and it frightened me, as we drove him to the graveyard through those unquiet, ruined streets, to see how powerful and overflowing this bitterness could be and to realize that this bitterness now was mine.

When he died I had been away from home for a little over a year. In that year I had had time to become aware of the meaning of all my father's bitter warnings, had discovered the secret of his proudly pursed lips and rigid carriage: I had discovered the weight of white people in the world. I saw that this had been for my ancestors and now would be for me an awful thing to live with and that the bitterness which had helped to kill my father could also kill me.

He had been ill a long time—in the mind, as we now realized, reliving instances of his fantastic intransigence in the new light of his affliction and endeavoring to feel a sorrow for him which never, quite, came true. We had not known that he was being eaten up by paranoia, and the discovery that his cruelty, to our bodies and our minds, had been one of the symptoms of his illness was not, then, enough to enable us to forgive him. The younger children felt, quite simply, relief that he would not be coming home anymore. My mother's observation that it was he, after all, who had kept them alive all these years meant nothing because the problems of keeping children alive are not real for children. The older children felt, with my father gone, that they could invite their friends to the house without fear that their friends would be insulted or, as had sometimes happened with me, being told that their friends were in league with the devil and intended to rob our family of everything we owned. (I didn't fail to wonder, and it made me hate him, what on earth we owned that anybody else would want.)

His illness was beyond all hope of healing before anyone realized that he was ill. He had always been so strange and had lived, like a prophet, in such unimaginably close communion with the Lord that his long silences which were punctuated by moans and hallelujahs and snatches of old songs while he sat at the living-room window never seemed odd to us. It was not until he refused to eat because, he said, his family was trying to poison him that my mother was forced to accept as a fact what had, until then, been only an unwilling suspicion. When he was committed, it was discovered that he had tuberculosis and, as it turned out, the disease of his mind allowed the disease of his body to destroy him. For the doctors could not force him to eat, either, and, though he was fed intravenously, it was clear from the beginning that there was no hope for him.

In my mind's eye I could see him, sitting at the window, locked up in his terrors; hating and fearing every living soul including his children who had betrayed him, too, by reaching towards the world which had despised him. There were nine of us. I began to wonder what it could have felt like for such a man to have had nine children whom he could barely feed. He used to make little jokes about our poverty, which never, of course, seemed very funny to us; they could not have seemed very funny to him, either, or else our all too feeble response to them would never have caused such rages. He spent great energy and achieved, to our chagrin, no small amount of success in keeping us away from the people who surrounded us, people who had all-night rent parties to which we listened when we should have been sleeping, people who cursed and drank and flashed razor blades on Lenox Avenue. He could not understand why, if they had so much energy to spare, they could not use it to make their lives better. He treated almost everybody on our block with a most uncharitable asperity and neither they, nor, of course, their children were slow to reciprocate.

The only white people who came to our house were welfare

workers and bill collectors. It was almost always my mother who dealt with them, for my father's temper, which was at the mercy of his pride, was never to be trusted. It was clear that he felt their very presence in his home to be a violation: this was conveyed by his carriage, almost ludicrously stiff, and by his voice, harsh and vindictively polite. When I was around nine or ten I wrote a play which was directed by a young, white schoolteacher, a woman, who then took an interest in me, and gave me books to read and, in order to corroborate my theatrical bent, decided to take me to see what she somewhat tactlessly referred to as "real" plays. Theater-going was forbidden in our house, but, with the really cruel in-tuitiveness of a child, I suspected that the color of this woman's skin would carry the day for me. When, at school, she suggested taking me to the theater, I did not, as I might have done if she had been a Negro, find a way of discouraging her, but agreed that she should pick me up at my house one evening. I then, very clev-erly, left all the rest to my mother, who suggested to my father, as I knew she would, that it would not be very nice to let such a kind woman make the trip for nothing. Also, since it was a school-teacher, I imagine that my mother countered the idea of sin with the idea of "education," which word, even with my father, carried a kind of bitter weight.

Before the teacher came my father took me aside to ask *why* she was coming, what *interest* she could possibly have in our house, in a boy like me. I said I didn't know but I, too, suggested that it had something to do with education. And I understood that my father was waiting for me to say something—I didn't quite know what; perhaps that I wanted his protection against this teacher and her "education." I said none of these things and the teacher came and we went out. It was clear, during the brief interview in our living room, that my father was agreeing very much against his will and that he would have refused permission if he had dared. The fact that he did not dare caused me to despise him: I had no way of knowing that he was facing in that living room a wholly un-precedented and frightening situation.

Later, when my father had been laid off from his job, this woman became very important to us. She was really a very sweet and gen-erous woman and went to a great deal of trouble to be of help to us, particularly during one awful winter. My mother called her by the highest name she knew: she said she was a "christian." My father could scarcely disagree but during the four or five years of our relatively close association he never trusted her and was al-ways trying to surprise in her open, Midwestern face the genuine, cunningly hidden, and hideous motivation. In later years, particu-larly when it began to be clear that this "education" of mine was going to lead me to perdition, he became more explicit and warned me that my white friends in high school were not really my friends and that I would see, when I was older, how white people would do anything to keep a Negro down. Some of them could be nice, he admitted, but none of them were to be trusted and most of them were not even nice. The best thing was to have as little to do with them as possible. I did not feel this way and I was certain, in my innocence, that I never would.

But the year which preceded my father's death had made a great change in my life. I had been living in New Jersey, working in defense plants, working and living among southerners, white and black. I knew about the south, of course, and about how southerners treated Negroes and how they expected them to behave, but it had never entered my mind that anyone would look at me and expect *me* to behave that way. I learned in New Jersey that to be a Negro meant, precisely, that one was never looked at but was simply at the mercy of the reflexes the color of one's skin caused in other people. I acted in New Jersey as I had always acted, that is as though I thought a great deal of myself—I had to *act* that way— with results that were, simply, unbelievable. I had scarcely arrived before I had earned the enmity, which was extraordinarily ingenious, of all my superiors and nearly all my co-workers. In the beginning, to make matters worse, I simply did not know what was happening. I did not know what I had done, and I shortly began to wonder what *anyone* could possibly do, to bring about such unanimous, active, and unbearably vocal hostility. I knew about jim-crow but I had never experienced it. I went to the same self-service restaurant three times and stood with all the Princeton boys before the counter, waiting for a hamburger and coffee; it was always an extraordinarily long time before anything was set before me; but it was not until the fourth visit that I learned that, in fact, nothing had ever been set before me: I had simply picked something up. Negroes were not served there, I was told, and they had been waiting for me to realize that I was always the only Negro present. Once I was told this, I determined to go there all the time. But now they were ready for me and, though some dreadful scenes were subsequently enacted in that restaurant, I never ate there again.

It was the same story all over New Jersey, in bars, bowling alleys, diners, places to live. I was always being forced to leave, silently, or with mutual imprecations. I very shortly became notorious and children giggled behind me when I passed and their elders whispered or shouted—they really believed that I was mad. And it did begin to work on my mind, of course; I began to be afraid to go anywhere and to compensate for this I went places to which I really should not have gone and where, God knows, I had no desire to be. My reputation in town naturally enhanced my reputation at work and my working day become one long series of acrobatics designed to keep me out of trouble. I cannot say that these acrobatics succeeded. It began to seem that the machinery of the organization I worked for was turning over, day and night, with but one aim: to eject me. I was fired once, and contrived, with the aid of a friend from New York, to get back on the payroll; was fired again, and bounced back again. It took a while to fire me for the third time, but the third time took. There were no loopholes anywhere. There was not even any way of getting back inside the gates.

That year in New Jersey lives in my mind as though it were the year during which, having an unsuspected predilection for it, I first contracted some dread, chronic disease, the unfailing symptom of which is a kind of blind fever, a pounding in the skull and fire in the bowels. Once this disease is contracted, one can never be really carefree again, for the fever, without an instant's warning, can recur at any moment. It can wreck more important things than race relations. There is not a Negro alive who does not have this rage in his blood—one has the choice, merely, of living with it consciously or surrendering to it. As for me, this fever has recurred in me, and does, and will until the day I die.

My last night in New Jersey, a white friend from New York took me to the nearest big town, Trenton, to go to the movies and have a few drinks. As it turned out, he also saved me from, at the very least, a violent whipping. Almost every detail of that night stands out very clearly in my memory. I even remember the name of the movie we saw because its title impressed me as being so patly ironical. It was a movie about the German occupation of France, starring Maureen O'Hara and Charles Laughton and called *This Land Is Mine*. I remember the name of the diner we walked into when the movie ended: it was the "American Diner." When we walked in the counterman asked what we wanted and I remember answering with the casual sharpness which had become my habit: "We want a hamburger and a cup of coffee, what do you think we want?" I do not know why, after a year of such rebuffs, I so completely failed to anticipate his answer, which was, of course, "We don't serve Negroes here." This reply failed to discompose me, at least for the moment. I made some sardonic comment about the name of the diner and we walked out into the streets.

This was the time of what was called the "brown-out," when the lights in all American cities were very dim. When we re-entered the streets something happened to me which had the force of an optical illusion, or a nightmare. The streets were very crowded and

I was facing north. People were moving in every direction but it seemed to me, in that instant, that all of the people I could see, and many more than that, were moving toward me, against me, and that everyone was white. I remember how their faces gleamed. And I felt, like a physical sensation, a *click* at the nape of my neck as though some interior string connecting my head to my body had been cut. I began to walk. I heard my friend call after me, but I ignored him. Heaven only knows what was going on in his mind, but he had the good sense not to touch me—I don't know what would have happened if he had—and to keep me in sight. I don't know what was going on in my mind, either; I certainly had no conscious plan. I wanted to do something to crush these white faces, which were crushing me. I walked for perhaps a block or two until I came to an enormous, glittering, and fashionable restaurant in which I knew not even the intercession of the Virgin would cause me to be served. I pushed through the doors and took the first vacant seat I saw, at a table for two, and waited.

I do not know how long I waited and I rather wonder, until today, what I could possibly have looked like. Whatever I looked like, I frightened the waitress who shortly appeared, and the moment she appeared all of my fury flowed towards her. I hated her for her white face, and for her great, astounded, frightened eyes. I felt that if she found a black man so frightening I would make her fright worth-while.

She did not ask me what I wanted, but repeated, as though she had learned it somewhere, "We don't serve Negroes here." She did not say it with the blunt, derisive hostility to which I had grown so accustomed, but, rather, with a note of apology in her voice, and fear. This made me colder and more murderous than ever. I felt I had to do something with my hands. I wanted her to come close enough for me to get her neck between my hands.

So I pretended not to have understood her, hoping to draw her closer. And she did step a very short step closer, with her pencil poised incongruously over her pad, and repeated the formula: ". . . don't serve Negroes here."

Somehow, with the repetition of that phrase, which was already ringing in my head like a thousand bells of a nightmare, I realized that she would never come any closer and that I would have to strike from a distance. There was nothing on the table but an ordinary water-mug half full of water, and I picked this up and hurled it with all my strength at her. She ducked and it missed her and shattered against the mirror behind the bar. And, with that sound, my frozen blood abruptly thawed, I returned from wherever I had been, I *saw*, for the first time, the restaurant, the people with their mouths open, already, as it seemed to me, rising as one man, and I realized what I had done, and where I was, and I was frightened. I rose and began running for the door. A round, potbellied man grabbed me by the nape of the neck just as I reached the doors and began to beat me about the face. I kicked him and got loose and ran into the streets. My friend whispered, *"Run!"* and I ran.

My friend stayed outside the restaurant long enough to misdirect my pursuers and the police, who arrived, he told me, at once. I do not know what I said to him when he came to my room that night. I could not have said much. I felt, in the oddest, most awful way, that I had somehow betrayed him. I lived it over and over and over again, the way one relives an automobile accident after it has happened and one finds oneself alone and safe. I could not get over two facts, both equally difficult for the imagination to grasp, and one was that I could have been murdered. But the other was that I had been ready to commit murder. I saw nothing very clearly but I did see this: that my life, my *real* life, was in danger, and not from anything other people might do but from the hatred I carried in my own heart.

II

I had returned home around the second week in June—in great haste because it seemed that my father's death and my mother's confinement were both but a matter of hours. In the case of my mother, it soon became clear that she had simply made a miscalculation. This had always been her tendency and I don't believe that a single one of us arrived in the world, or has since arrived anywhere else, on time. But none of us dawdled so intolerably about the business of being born as did my baby sister. We sometimes amused ourselves, during those endless, stifling weeks, by picturing the baby sitting within in the safe, warm dark, bitterly regretting the necessity of becoming a part of our chaos and stubbornly putting it off as long as possible. I understood her perfectly and congratulated her on showing such good sense so soon. Death, however, sat as purposefully at my father's bedside as life stirred within my mother's womb and it was harder to understand why he so lingered in that long shadow. It seemed that he had bent, and for a long time, too, all of his energies towards dying. Now death was ready for him but my father held back.

All of Harlem, indeed, seemed to be infected by waiting. I had never before known it to be so violently still. Racial tensions throughout this country were exacerbated during the early years of the war, partly because the labor market brought together hundreds of thousands of ill-prepared people and partly because Negro soldiers, regardless of where they were born, received their military training in the south. What happened in defense plants and army camps had repercussions, naturally, in every Negro ghetto. The situation in Harlem had grown bad enough for clergymen, policemen, educators, politicians, and social workers to assert in one breath that there was no "crime wave" and to offer, in the very next breath, suggestions as to how to combat it. These suggestions always seemed to involve playgrounds, despite the fact that racial skirmishes were occurring in the playgrounds, too. Playground or not, crime wave or not, the Harlem police force had been augmented in March, and the unrest grew—perhaps, in fact, partly as a result of the ghetto's instinctive hatred of policemen. Perhaps the most revealing news item, out of the steady parade of reports of muggings, stabbings, shootings, assaults, gang wars, and accusations of police brutality, is the item concerning six Negro girls who set upon a white girl in the subway because, as they all too accurately put it, she was stepping on their toes. Indeed she was, all over the nation.

I had never before been so aware of policemen, on foot, on horseback, on corners, everywhere, always two by two. Nor had I ever been so aware of small knots of people. They were on stoops and on corners and in doorways, and what was striking about them, I think, was that they did not seem to be talking. Never, when I passed these groups, did the usual sound of a curse or a laugh ring out and neither did there seem to be any hum of gossip. There was certainly, on the other hand, occurring between them communication extraordinarily intense. Another thing that was striking was the unexpected diversity of the people who made up these groups. Usually, for example, one would see a group of sharpies standing on the street corner, jiving the passing chicks; or a group of older men, usually, for some reason, in the vicinity of a barber shop, discussing baseball scores, or the numbers, or making rather chilling observations about women they had known. Women, in a general way, tended to be seen less often together—unless they were church women, or very young girls, or prostitutes met together for an unprofessional instant. But that summer I saw the strangest combinations: large, respectable, churchly matrons standing on the stoops or the corners with their hair tied up, together with a girl in sleazy satin whose face bore the marks of gin and the razor, or heavy-set, abrupt, no-nonsense older men, in company with the most disreputable and fanatical "race" men, or these same "race" men with the sharpies, or these sharpies with the churchly women. Seventh Day Adventists and Methodists and Spiritualists seemed to be hobnobbing with Holyrollers and they were all, alike, entangled with the most flagrant disbelievers; something heavy in their stance seemed to indicate that they had all, incredibly, seen a common vision, and on each face there seemed to be the same strange, bitter shadow.

The churchly women and the matter-of-fact, no-nonsense men had children in the Army. The sleazy girls they talked to had lovers there, the sharpies and the "race" men had friends and brothers there. It would have demanded an unquestioning patriotism, happily as uncommon in this country as it is undesirable, for these people not to have been disturbed by the bitter letters they received, by the newspaper stories they read, not to have been enraged by the posters, then to be found all over New York, which described the Japanese as "yellow-bellied Japs." It was only the "race" men, to be sure, who spoke ceaselessly of being revenged— how this vengeance was to be exacted was not clear—for the indignities and dangers suffered by Negro boys in uniform; but everybody felt a directionless, hopeless bitterness, as well as that panic which can scarcely be suppressed when one knows that a human being one loves is beyond one's reach, and in danger. This helplessness and this gnawing uneasiness does something, at length, to even the toughest mind. Perhaps the best way to sum all this up is to say that the people I knew felt, mainly, a peculiar kind of relief when they knew that their boys were being shipped out of the south, to do battle overseas. It was, perhaps, like feeling that the most dangerous part of a dangerous journey had been passed and that now, even if death should come, it would come with honor and without the complicity of their countrymen. Such a death would be, in short, a fact with which one could hope to live.

It was on the 28th of July, which I believe was a Wednesday, that I visited my father for the first time during his illness and for the last time in his life. The moment I saw him I knew why I had put off this visit so long. I had told my mother that I did not want to see him because I hated him. But this was not true. It was only that I *had* hated him and I wanted to hold on to this hatred. I did not want to look on him as a ruin: it was not a ruin I had hated. I imagine that one of the reasons people cling to their hates so stubbornly is because they sense, once hate is gone, that they will be forced to deal with pain.

We traveled out to him, his older sister and myself, to what seemed to be the very end of a very Long Island. It was hot and dusty and we wrangled, my aunt and I, all the way out, over the fact that I had recently begun to smoke and, as she said, to give myself airs. But I knew that she wrangled with me because she could not bear to face the fact of her brother's dying. Neither could I endure the reality of her despair, her unstated bafflement as to what had happened to her brother's life, and her own. So we wrangled and I smoked and from time to time she fell into a heavy reverie. Covertly, I watched her face, which was the face of an old woman; it had fallen in, the eyes were sunken and lightless; soon she would be dying, too.

In my childhood—it had not been so long ago—I had thought her beautiful. She had been quick-witted and quick-moving and very generous with all the children and each of her visits had been an event. At one time one of my brothers and myself had thought of running away to live with her. Now she could no longer produce out of her handbag some unexpected and yet familiar delight. She made me feel pity and revulsion and fear. It was awful to realize that she no longer caused me to feel affection. The closer we came to the hospital the more querulous she became and at the same time, naturally, grew more dependent on me. Between pity and guilt and fear I began to feel that there was another me trapped in my skull like a jack-in-the-box who might escape my control at any moment and fill the air with screaming.

She began to cry the moment we entered the room and she saw him lying there, all shriveled and still, like a little black monkey. The great, gleaming apparatus which fed him and would have compelled him to be still even if he had been able to move brought to mind, not beneficence, but torture; the tubes entering his arm made me think of pictures I had seen when a child, of Gulliver, tied down by the pygmies on that island. My aunt wept and wept, there was a whistling sound in my father's throat; nothing was said; he could not speak. I wanted to take his hand, to say something. But I do not know what I could have said, even if he could have heard me. He was not really in that room with us, he had at last really embarked on his journey; and though my aunt told me that he said he was going to meet Jesus, I did not hear anything except that whistling in his throat. The doctor came back and we left, into that unbearable train again, and home. In the morning came the telegram saying that he was dead. Then the house was suddenly full of relatives, friends, hysteria, and confusion and I quickly left my mother and the children to the care of those impressive women, who, in Negro communities at least, automatically appear at times of bereavement armed with lotions, proverbs, and patience, and an ability to cook. I went downtown. By the time I returned, later the same day, my mother had been carried to the hospital and the baby had been born.

III

For my father's funeral I had nothing black to wear and this posed a nagging problem all day long. It was one of those problems, simple, or impossible of solution, to which the mind insanely clings in order to avoid the mind's real trouble. I spent most of that day at the downtown apartment of a girl I knew, celebrating my birthday with whiskey and wondering what to wear that night. When planning a birthday celebration one naturally does not expect that it will be up against competition from a funeral and this girl had anticipated taking me out that night, for a big dinner and a night club afterwards. Sometime during the course of that long day we decided that we would go out anyway, when my father's funeral service was over. I imagine I decided it, since, as the funeral hour approached, it became clearer and clearer to me that I would not know what to do with myself when it was over. The girl, stifling her very lively concern as to the possible effects of the whiskey on one of my father's chief mourners, concentrated on being conciliatory and practically helpful. She found a black shirt for me somewhere and ironed it and, dressed in the darkest pants and jacket I owned, and slightly drunk, I made my way to my father's funeral.

The chapel was full, but not packed, and very quiet. There were, mainly, my father's relatives, and his children, and here and there I saw faces I had not seen since childhood, the faces of my father's one-time friends. They were very dark and solemn now, seeming somehow to suggest that they had known all along that something like this would happen. Chief among the mourners was my aunt, who had quarreled with my father all his life; by which I do not mean to suggest that her mourning was insincere or that she had not loved him. I suppose that she was one of the few people in the world who had, and their incessant quarreling proved precisely the strength of the tie that bound them. The only other person in the world, as far as I knew, whose relationship to my father rivaled my aunt's in depth was my mother, who was not there.

It seemed to me, of course, that it was a very long funeral. But it was, if anything, a rather shorter funeral than most, nor, since there were no overwhelming, uncontrollable expressions of grief, could it be called—if I dare to use the word—successful. The minister who preached my father's funeral sermon was one of the few my father had still been seeing as he neared his end. He presented to us in his sermon a man whom none of us had ever seen—a man thoughtful, patient, and forbearing, a Christian inspiration to all who knew him, and a model for his children. And no doubt the children, in their disturbed and guilty state, were almost ready to believe this; he had been remote enough to be anything and, anyway, the shock of the incontrovertible, that it was really our father lying up there in that casket, prepared the mind for anything. His sister moaned and this grief-stricken moaning was taken as corroboration. The other faces held a dark, non-committal thoughtfulness. This was not the man they had known, but they had scarcely expected to be confronted with *him*; this was, in a sense deeper than questions of fact, the man they had not known, and the man they had not known may have been the real one. The real man, whoever he had been, had suffered and now he was dead: this was all that was sure and all that mattered now. Every man in the chapel hoped that when his hour came he, too, would be eulogized, which is to say forgiven, and that all of his lapses, greeds, errors, and stray-ings from the truth would be invested with coherence and looked upon with charity. This was perhaps the last thing human beings could give each other and it was what they demanded, after all, of the Lord. Only the Lord saw the midnight tears, only He was pres-ent when one of His children, moaning and wringing hands, paced up and down the room. When one slapped one's child in anger the recoil in the heart reverberated through heaven and became part of the pain of the universe. And when the children were hungry and sullen and distrustful and one watched them, daily, growing wilder, and further away, and running headlong into danger, it was the Lord who knew what the charged heart endured as the strap was laid to the backside; the Lord alone who knew what one *would* have said if one had had, like the Lord, the gift of the living word. It was the Lord who knew of the impossibility every parent in that room faced: how to prepare the child for the day when the child would be despised and how to *create* in the child—by what means? —a stronger antidote to this poison than one had found for oneself. The avenues, side streets, bars, billiard halls, hospitals, police sta-tions, and even the playgrounds of Harlem—not to mention the houses of correction, the jails, and the morgue—testified to the potency of the poison while remaining silent as to the efficacy of whatever antidote, irresistibly raising the question of whether or not such an antidote existed; raising, which was worse, the ques-tion of whether or not an antidote was desirable; perhaps poison should be fought with poison. With these several schisms in the mind and with more terrors in the heart than could be named, it was better not to judge the man who had gone down under an im-possible burden. It was better to remember: *Thou knowest this man's fall; but thou knowest not his wrassling.*

While the preacher talked and I watched the children—years of changing their diapers, scrubbing them, slapping them, taking them to school, and scolding them had had the perhaps inevitable result of making me love them, though I am not sure I knew this then—my mind was busily breaking out with a rash of discon-nected impressions. Snatches of popular songs, indecent jokes, bits of books I had read, movie sequences, faces, voices, political issues—I thought I was going mad; all these impressions suspended, as it were, in the solution of the faint nausea produced in me by the heat and liquor. For a moment I had the impression that my alcoholic breath, inefficiently disguised with chewing gum, filled the entire chapel. Then someone began singing one of my father's favorite songs and, abruptly, I was with him, sitting on his knee, in the hot, enormous, crowded church which was the first church we attended. It was the Abyssinia Baptist Church on 138th Street. We had not gone there long. With this image, a host of others came. I had forgotten, in the rage of my growing up, how proud my father had been of me when I was little. Apparently, I had had a voice and my father had liked to show me off before the members of the church. I had forgotten what he had looked like when he was pleased but now I remembered that he had always been grinning with pleasure when my solos ended. I even remembered certain expressions on his face when he teased my mother—had he loved her? I would never know. And when had it all begun to change? For now it seemed that he had not always been cruel. I remembered being taken for a haircut and scraping my knee on the footrest of the barber's chair and I remembered my father's face as he soothed my crying and applied the stinging iodine. Then I remembered our fights, fights which had been of the worst possible kind because my technique had been silence.

I remembered the one time in all our life together when we had really spoken to each other.

It was on a Sunday and it must have been shortly before I left home. We were walking, just the two of us, in our usual silence, to or from church. I was in high school and had been doing a lot of writing and I was, at about this time, the editor of the high school magazine. But I had also been a Young Minister and had been preaching from the pulpit. Lately, I had been taking fewer engagements and preached as rarely as possible. It was said in the church, quite truthfully, that I was "cooling off."

My father asked me abruptly, "You'd rather write than preach, wouldn't you?"

I was astonished at his question—because it was a real question. I answered, "Yes."

That was all we said. It was awful to remember that that was all we had *ever* said.

The casket now was opened and the mourners were being led up the aisle to look for the last time on the deceased. The assumption was that the family was too overcome with grief to be allowed to make this journey alone and I watched while my aunt was led to the casket and, muffled in black, and shaking, led back to her seat. I disapproved of forcing the children to look on their dead father, considering that the shock of his death, or, more truth-fully, the shock of death as a reality, was already a little more than a child could bear, but my judgment in this matter had been over-ruled and there they were, bewildered and frightened and very small, being led, one by one, to the casket. But there is also some-thing very gallant about children at such moments. It has some-thing to do with their silence and gravity and with the fact that one cannot help them. Their legs, somehow, seem *exposed*, so that it is at once incredible and terribly clear that their legs are all they have to hold them up.

I had not wanted to go to the casket myself and I certainly had not wished to be led there, but there was no way of avoiding either of these forms. One of the deacons led me up and I looked on my father's face. I cannot say that it looked like him at all. His black-ness had been equivocated by powder and there was no suggestion in that casket of what his power had or could have been. He was simply an old man dead, and it was hard to believe that he had ever given anyone either joy or pain. Yet, his life filled that room. Further up the avenue his wife was holding his newborn child. Life and death so close together, and love and hatred, and right and wrong, said something to me which I did not want to hear concern-ing man, concerning the life of man.

After the funeral, while I was downtown desperately celebrating my birthday, a Negro soldier, in the lobby of the Hotel Braddock, got into a fight with a white policeman over a Negro girl. Negro girls, white policemen, in or out of uniform, and Negro males—in or out of uniform—were part of the furniture of the lobby of the Hotel Braddock and this was certainly not the first time such an incident had occurred. It was destined, however, to receive an un-precedented publicity, for the fight between the policeman and the soldier ended with the shooting of the soldier. Rumor, flowing immediately to the streets outside, stated that the soldier had been shot in the back, an instantaneous and revealing invention, and that the soldier had died protecting a Negro woman. The facts were somewhat different—for example, the soldier had not been shot in the back, and was not dead, and the girl seems to have been as dubious a symbol of womanhood as her white counterpart in Geor-gia usually is, but no one was interested in the facts. They preferred the invention because this invention expressed and corrobo-rated their hates and fears so perfectly. It is just as well to remem-ber that people are always doing this. Perhaps many of those leg-ends, including Christianity, to which the world clings began their conquest of the world with just some such concerted surrender to distortion. The effect, in Harlem, of this particular legend was like the effect of a lit match in a tin of gasoline. The mob gathered before the doors of the Hotel Braddock simply began to swell and to spread in every direction, and Harlem exploded.

The mob did not cross the ghetto lines. It would have been easy, for example, to have gone over Morningside Park on the west side or to have crossed the Grand Central railroad tracks at 125th Street on the east side, to wreak havoc in white neighborhoods. The mob seems to have been mainly interested in something more potent and real than the white face, that is, in white power, and the principal damage done during the riot of the summer of 1943 was to white business establishments in Harlem. It might have been a far bloodier story, of course, if, at the hour the riot began, these establishments had still been open. From the Hotel Braddock the mob fanned out east and west along 125th Street, and for the entire length of Lenox, Seventh, and Eighth avenues. Along each of these avenues, and along each major side street—116th, 125th, 135th, and so on—bars, stores, pawnshops, restaurants, even little luncheonettes had been smashed open and entered and looted—looted, it might be added, with more haste than efficiency. The shelves really looked as though a bomb had struck them. Cans of beans and soup and dog food, along with toilet paper, corn flakes, sardines, and milk tumbled every which way, and abandoned cash registers and cases of beer leaned crazily out of the splintered windows and were strewn along the avenues. Sheets, blankets, and clothing of every description formed a kind of path, as though people had dropped them while running. I truly had not realized that Harlem *had* so many stores until I saw them all smashed open; the first time the word *wealth* ever entered my mind in relation to Harlem was when I saw it scattered in the streets. But one's first, incongruous impression of plenty was countered immediately by an impression of waste. None of this was doing anybody any good. It would have been better to have left the plate glass as it had been and the goods lying in the stores.

It would have been better, but it would also have been intolerable, for Harlem had needed something to smash. To smash something is the ghetto's chronic need. Most of the time it is the members of the ghetto who smash each other, and themselves. But as long as the ghetto walls are standing there will always come a moment when these outlets do not work. That summer, for example, it was not enough to get into a fight on Lenox Avenue, or curse out one's cronies in the barber shops. If ever, indeed, the violence which fills Harlem's churches, pool halls, and bars erupts outward in a more direct fashion, Harlem and its citizens are likely to vanish in an apocalyptic flood. That this is not likely to happen is due to a great many reasons, most hidden and powerful among them the Negro's real relation to the white American. This relation prohibits, simply, anything as uncomplicated and satisfactory as pure hatred. In order really to hate white people, one has to blot so much out of the mind—and the heart—that this hatred itself becomes an exhausting and self-destructive pose. But this does not mean, on the other hand, that love comes easily: the white world is too powerful, too complacent, too ready with gratuitous humiliation, and, above all, too ignorant and too innocent for that. One is absolutely forced to make perpetual qualifications and one's own reactions are always canceling each other out. It is this, really, which has driven so many people mad, both white and black. One is always in the position of having to decide between amputation and gangrene. Amputation is swift but time may prove that the amputation was not necessary—or one may delay the amputation too long. Gangrene is slow, but it is impossible to be sure that one is reading one's symptoms right. The idea of going through life as a cripple is more than one can bear, and equally unbearable is the risk of swelling up slowly, in agony, with poison. And the trouble, finally, is that the risks are real even if the choices do not exist.

"But as for me and my house," my father had said, "we will serve the Lord." I wondered, as we drove him to his resting place, what this line had meant for him. I had heard him preach it many times. I had preached it once myself, proudly giving it an interpretation different from my father's. Now the whole thing came back to me, as though my father and I were on our way to Sunday school and I were memorizing the golden text: *And if it seem evil unto you to serve the Lord, choose you this day whom you will serve; whether the gods which your fathers served that were on the other side of the flood, or the gods of the Amorites, in whose land ye dwell: but as for me and my house, we will serve the Lord.*[1] I suspected in these familiar lines a meaning which had never been there for me before. All of my father's texts and songs, which I had decided were meaningless, were arranged before me at his death like empty bottles, waiting to hold the meaning which life would give them for me. This was his legacy: nothing is ever escaped. That bleakly memorable morning I hated the unbelievable streets and the Negroes and whites who had, equally, made them that way. But I knew that it was folly, as my father would have said, this bitterness was folly. It was necessary to hold on to the things that mattered. The dead man mattered, the new life mattered; blackness and whiteness did not matter; to believe that they did was to acquiesce in one's own destruction. Hatred, which could destroy so much, never failed to destroy the man who hated and this was an immutable law.

1. Joshua xxiv: 15.

It began to seem that one would have to hold in the mind forever two ideas which seemed to be in opposition. The first idea was acceptance, the acceptance, totally without rancor, of life as it is, and men as they are: in the light of this idea, it goes without saying that injustice is a commonplace. But this did not mean that one could be complacent, for the second idea was of equal power: that one must never, in one's own life, accept these injustices as commonplace but must fight them with all one's strength. This fight begins, however, in the heart and it now had been laid to my charge to keep my own heart free of hatred and despair. This intimation made my heart heavy and, now that my father was irrecoverable, I wished that he had been beside me so that I could have searched his face for the answers which only the future would give me now.

1955

Poets at
Three-Quarters-Century

JOHN BERRYMAN

(1914–1972)

John Berryman is above all a poet dedicated to bringing formal order out of chaos. As such, he is quintessentially a poet of the twentieth century. His failures are the failures of his time, writ large, his successes the personal triumphs of an individual at odds with his environment, and there is always a precarious balance between the two. A scant three years after a critic had written that Berryman had "come to poetic terms with * * * the wreck of the modern world * * * and the wreck of his personal self in that world" he jumped to his death from a bridge in Minneapolis.

He was born John Smith in McAlester, Oklahoma, the son of a schoolteacher and a well-to-do banker. The family moved to Florida when he was ten, and there, after threatening to swim out to sea with his son, drowning them both, his father shot himself outside of John's window. His mother moved to New York and remarried, Berryman taking on the name of his foster father. He attended South Kent School in Connecticut and graduated from Columbia University and Clare College, Oxford. Not long after his return to the United States he began his teaching career and was published, with Randall Jarrell and others, in *Five Young American Poets* (1940). His *Poems* (1942) came two years later, but it was not until *Homage to Mistress Bradstreet* (1956) that he developed the combination of formal structure and fractured syntax that is characteristic of the style of so many of his best poems. In the meantime, he taught at Harvard, Princeton, and the University of Minnesota and developed a reputation as a poet who had never quite fulfilled his promise. Marital problems, heavy drinking, and years spent in and out of analysis formed the chief indications in his personal life of the tensions that he attempted to resolve in his poems.

In his biographical study *Stephen Crane* (1950) his sharp insights into the work of Crane were marred by his inability to organize his thoughts into a totally satisfactory whole. In *Homage to Mistress Bradstreet*, *Berryman's Sonnets* (1967), and *The Dream Songs* (1969), too, he strives for a total coherence that he seldom achieves, but the volumes include such brilliant passages of poetry that, taken together, they had the effect of thrusting Berryman late in life into the front rank of the poets of his time. As he aged he revealed more and more of the origins of his personal anguish. A love affair of twenty years earlier formed the basis for the *Sonnets*, written, apparently years before their publication. Into *The Dream Songs* he put a decade and a half of work centering on a figure, "not the poet, not me," who shares a good many of the biographical details and philosophical outlook of the writer. He ended *Love & Fame* (1970) with a section titled "Eleven Addresses to the Lord" that hearkened back to the strict Roman Catholicism of his childhood and he continued his self-examination in *Delusions, Etc.* (1972). To the end the events of the modern world and of his presence in that world appeared to him so painfully absurd that a direct confrontation could lead to insanity. Nevertheless, he found it possible to achieve some glimpse of wholeness through the fragmented obliqueness of his poetry.

In addition to the titles named above, Berryman published verse in *The Dispossessed*, 1948; *His Thoughts Made Pockets and the Plane Buckt*, 1958; *77 Dream Songs*, 1964 (included later in *The Dream Songs*); *Short Poems*, 1967; and *His Toy, His Dream, His Rest*, 1968 (included in *The Dream Songs*). A posthumous novel, published with an introduction by Saul Bellow, is *Recovery*, 1973.

The Ball Poem

What is the boy now, who has lost his ball,
What, what is he to do? I saw it go
Merrily bouncing, down the street, and then
Merrily over—there it is in the water!
No use to say 'O there are other balls':   5
An ultimate shaking grief fixes the boy
As he stands rigid, trembling, staring down
All his young days into the harbour where
His ball went. I would not intrude on him,
A dime, another ball, is worthless. Now   10
He senses first responsibility
In a world of possessions. People will take balls,
Balls will be lost always, little boy.
And no one buys a ball back. Money is external.
He is learning, well behind his desperate eyes,   15
The epistemology of loss, how to stand up

Knowing what every man must one day know
And most know many days, how to stand up
And gradually light returns to the street,
A whistle blows, the ball is out of sight,   20
Soon part of me will explore the deep and dark
Floor of the harbour . . I am everywhere,
I suffer and move, my mind and my heart move
With all that move me, under the water
Or whistling, I am not a little boy.   25

1948

The Moon and the Night and the Men

On the night of the Belgian surrender the moon rose
Late, a delayed moon, and a violent moon
For the English or the American beholder;
The French beholder. It was a cold night,
People put on their wraps, the troops were cold   5
No doubt, despite the calendar, no doubt
Numbers of refugees coughed, and the sight
Or sound of some killed others. A cold night.

On Outer Drive there was an accident:
A stupid well-intentioned man turned sharp   10
Right and abruptly he became an angel
Fingering an unfamiliar harp,
Or screamed in hell, or was nothing at all.
Do not imagine this is unimportant.
He was a part of the night, part of the land,   15
Part of the bitter and exhausted ground
Out of which memory grows.

                     Michael and I
Stared at each other over chess, and spoke
As little as possible, and drank and played.   20
The chessmen caught in the European eye,
Neither of us I think had a free look
Although the game was fair. The move one made
It was difficult at last to keep one's mind on.
'Hurt and unhappy' said the man in London.   25
We said to each other, The time is coming near
When none shall have books or music, none his dear,
And only a fool will speak aloud his mind.
History is approaching a speechless end,
As Henry Adams [1] said. Adams was right.   30

All this occurred on the night when Leopold [2]

---

1. The American historian (1838–1918). 2. Leopold III, Belgian king (1934–1951), exiled after the war, in 1945.

Fulfilled the treachery four years before
Begun—or was he well-intentioned, more
Roadmaker to hell than king? At any rate,
The moon came up late and the night was cold,   35
Many men died—although we know the fate
Of none, nor of anyone, and the war
Goes on, and the moon in the breast of man is cold.

1948

The Dream Songs

1

Huffy Henry hid   the day,
unappeasable Henry sulked.
I see his point,—a trying to put things over.
It was the thought that they thought
they could *do* it made Henry wicked & away.   5
But he should have come out and talked.

All the world like a woolen lover
once did seem on Henry's side.
Then came a departure.
Thereafter nothing fell out as it might or ought.   10
I don't see how Henry, pried
open for all the world to see, survived.

What he has now to say is a long
wonder the world can bear & be.
Once in a sycamore I was glad   15
all at the top, and I sang.
Hard on the land wears the strong sea
and empty grows every bed.

1964

14

Life, friends, is boring. We must not say so.
After all, the sky flashes, the great sea yearns,
we ourselves flash and yearn,
and moreover my mother told me as a boy
(repeatingly) 'Ever to confess you're bored   5
means you have no

Inner Resources.' I conclude now I have no
inner resources, because I am heavy bored.
Peoples bore me,
literature bores me, especially great literature,   10
Henry bores me, with his plights & gripes
as bad as achilles,[3]

3. Achilles, in Homer's *Iliad,* is often a sulky and pathetic figure when not engaged in battle.

who loves people and valiant art, which bores me.
And the tranquil hills, & gin, look like a drag
and somehow a dog   15
has taken itself & its tail considerably away
into mountains or sea or sky, leaving
behind: me, wag.

1964

29

There sat down, once, a thing on Henry's heart
só heavy, if he had a hundred years
& more, & weeping, sleepless, in all them time
Henry could not make good.
Starts again always in Henry's ears   5
the little cough somewhere, an odour, a chime.

And there is another thing he has in mind
like a grave Sienese face a thousand years
would fail to blur the still profiled reproach of. Ghastly,
with open eyes, he attends, blind.   10
All the bells say: too late. This is not for tears;
thinking.

But never did Henry, as he thought he did,
end anyone and hacks her body up
and hide the pieces, where they may be found.   15
He knows: he went over everyone, & nobody's missing.
Often he reckons, in the dawn, them up.
Nobody is ever missing.

1964

76

Henry's Confession

Nothin very bad happen to me lately.
How you explain that? —I explain that, Mr Bones,[4]
terms o' your bafflin odd sobriety.
Sober as man can get, no girls, no telephones,
what could happen bad to Mr Bones?   5
—*If* life is a handkerchief sandwich,

in a modesty of death I join my father
who dared so long agone leave me.
A bullet on a concrete stoop
close by a smothering southern sea   10
spreadeagled on an island, by my knee.
—You is from hunger, Mr Bones,

---

4. A traditional name for a minstrel show entertainer.

I offers you this handkerchief, now set
your left foot by my right foot,
shoulder to shoulder, all that jazz,   15
arm in arm, by the beautiful sea,
hum a little, Mr. Bones.
—I saw nobody coming, so I went instead.

                                                    1964

                    145
Also I love him: me he's done no wrong
for going on forty years—forgiveness time—
I touch now his despair,
he felt as bad as Whitman on his tower
but he did not swim out with me or my brother   5
as he threatened—

a powerful swimmer, to   take one of us along
as company in the defeat sublime,
freezing my helpless mother:
he only, very early in the morning,   10
rose with his gun and went outdoors by my window
and did what was needed.

I cannot read that wretched mind, so strong
& so undone. I've always tried. I—I'm
trying to forgive   15
whose frantic passage, when he could not live
an instant longer, in the summer dawn
left Henry to live on.

                                                    1968

                    153
I'm cross with god who has wrecked this generation.
First he seized Ted, then Richard, Randall, and now Delmore.[5]
In between he gorged on Sylvia Plath.
That was a first rate haul. He left alive
fools I could number like a kitchen knife   5
but Lowell he did not touch.

Somewhere the enterprise continues, not—
yellow the sun lies on the baby's blouse—
in Henry's staggered thought.
I suppose the word would be, we must submit.   10
Later.
I hang, and I will not be part of it.

A friend of Henry's contrasted God's career
with Mozart's, leaving Henry with nothing to say

5. Theodore Roethke, R. P. Blackmur, Randall Jarrell, and Delmore Schwartz, all poets and friends of Berryman who predeceased him.

but praise for a word so apt.   15
We suffer on, a day, a day, a day.
And never again can come, like a man slapped,
news like this

1968

384

The marker slants, flowerless, day's almost done,
I stand above my father's grave with rage,
often, often before
I've made this awful pilgrimage to one
who cannot visit me, who tore his page   5
out: I come back for more,

I spit upon this dreadful banker's grave
who shot his heart out in a Florida dawn
O ho alas alas
When will indifference come, I moan & rave   10
I'd like to scrabble till I got right down
away down under the grass

and ax the casket open ha to see
just how he's taking it, which he sought so hard
we'll tear apart   15
the mouldering grave clothes ha & then Henry
will heft the ax once more, his final card,
and fell it on the start.

1968

385

My daughter's heavier. Light leaves are flying.
Everywhere in enormous numbers turkeys will be dying
and other birds, all their wings.
They never greatly flew. Did they wish to?
I should know. Off away somewhere once I knew   5
such things.

Or good Ralph Hodgson [6] back then did, or does.
The man is dead whom Eliot praised. My praise
follows and flows too late.
Fall is grievy, brisk. Tears behind the eyes   10
almost fall. Fall comes to us as a prize
to rouse us toward our fate.

My house is made of wood and it's made well,
unlike us. My house is older than Henry;
that's fairly old.   15
If there were a middle   ground between things and the soul

---

6. Ralph Hodgson (1871–1962), English poet. Two of his best-known poems
are "Eve" and "Time, You Old Gipsy Man."

or if the sky resembled more the sea,
I wouldn't have to scold

my heavy daughter.

1968

WILLIAM STAFFORD
(1914–   )

William Stafford emerged late as a poet. Of the same generation as Delmore Schwartz, Karl Shapiro, Randall Jarrell, and John Berryman, all of whom established reputations in the 1940's, he did not publish his first book of poems, *West of Your City*, until 1960. Prior to that time he had acquired a small following through publication in periodicals and anthologies and he had won some minor literary prizes, but the bulk of his reputation stems from the series of slim volumes produced in the decade when he turned fifty. His voice is quiet, even in tone, modestly self-assured, the voice of a man who has thought long and carefully about what he has to say, a man who does not waste words.

His poetry, as he has said, "is much like talk, with some enhancement." Assuming that poetry is inherent in language, he believes that the poet can best discover the poetry that exists in the sounds he hears about him if he commits himself to no preconceived notions of form. Meter and rhyme are no more to be sought than they are to be avoided: "Relying on forms or rules is always possible —is always one of the possible directions to take. But it is also possible that the everlasting process which led to discovery of forms and rules in the first place will continue to be worthy."

His subject matter reflects a life spent mostly in the open spaces of Kansas, Iowa, and Oregon. Nature bulks large. Personal relationships are important, and long-remembered. Born and raised in Hutchinson, Kansas, he graduated from the University of Kansas and some years later took his M.A. there. His service as a conscientious objector in World War II was followed by his later association with the pacifist Fellowship of Reconciliation. Possessor of a Ph.D. from the University of Iowa, he has taught for many years in the English Department of Lewis and Clark College in Oregon.

Volumes of verse are *West of Your City*, 1960; *Traveling Through the Dark*, 1962; *The Rescued Year*, 1966; *Eleven Untitled Poems*, 1968; *Allegiances*, 1970; and *Someday, Maybe*, 1973. Criticism is *The Achievement of Brother Antoninus*, 1967. A prose account of his experience as a conscientious objector is *Down in My Heart*, 1947.

Before the Big Storm

You are famous in my mind.
When anyone mentions your name
all the boxes marked "1930's"
fall off the shelves;
and the orators on the Fourth of July   5
all begin shouting again.
The audience of our high school commencement
begin to look out of the windows at the big storm.

And I think of you in our play—
oh, helpless and lonely!—crying,   10
and your father is dead again.
He was drunk: he fell.

When they mention your name.
our houses out there in the wind
creak again in the storm;   15
and I lean from our play, wherever I am,
to you, quiet at the edge of that town:
"All the world is blowing away."
"It is almost daylight."
"Are you warm?"   20

1962

Judgments

I accuse—
    Ellen: you have become forty years old,
    and successful, tall, well-groomed,
    gracious, thoughtful, a secretary.
    Ellen, I accuse.   5

George—
    You know how to help others;
    you manage a school. You never
    let fear or pride or faltering plans
    break your control.   10
    George, I accuse.

I accuse—
    Tom: you have found a role;
    now you meet all kinds of people
    and let them find the truth of your   15
    eminence; you need not push.
    Oh, Tom, I do accuse.

Remember—
    The gawky, hardly to survive students

we were: not one of us going to succeed,   20
all of us abjectly aware of how cold,
unmanageable the real world was?
I remember. And that fear was true.
And is true.

Last I accuse—   25
   Myself: my terrible poise, knowing
   even this, knowing that then we
   sprawled in the world
   and were ourselves part of it; now
   we hold it firmly away with gracious   30
   gestures (like this of mine!) we've achieved.

I see it all too well—
   And I am accused, and I accuse.

                                                    1966

One Home

Mine was a Midwest home—you can keep your world.
Plain black hats rode the thoughts that made our code.
We sang hymns in the house; the roof was near God.

The light bulb that hung in the pantry made a wan light,
but we could read by it the names of preserves—   5
outside, the buffalo grass, and the wind in the night.

A wildcat sprang at Grandpa on the Fourth of July
when he was cutting plum bushes for fuel,
before Indians pulled the West over the edge of the sky.

To anyone who looked at us we said, "My friend";   10
liking the cut of a thought, we could say, "Hello."
(But plain black hats rode the thoughts that made our code.)

The sun was over our town; it was like a blade.
Kicking cottonwood leaves we ran toward storms.
Wherever we looked the land would hold us up.   15

                                                    1966

The Farm on the Great Plains

         A telephone line goes cold;
         birds tread it wherever it goes.
         A farm back of a great plain
         tugs an end of the line.

         I call that farm every year,   5
         ringing it, listening, still;

no one is home at the farm,
the line gives only a hum.

Some year I will ring the line
on a night at last the right one,   10
and with an eye tapered for braille
from the phone on the wall

I will see the tenant who waits—
the last one left at the place;
through the dark my braille eye   15
will lovingly touch his face.

"Hello, is Mother at home?"
No one is home today.
"But Father—he should be there."
No one—no one is here.   20

"But you—are you the one . . . ?"
Then the line will be gone
because both ends will be home:
no space, no birds, no farm.

My self will be the plain,   25
wise as winter is gray,
pure as cold posts go
pacing toward what I know.

1966

JAMES DICKEY
(1923–   )

Poet, critic, and novelist, James Dickey must be counted among the most impressive of the American writers who came into prominence in the decade of the 1960's. In the eleven years from 1960 to 1970 he published seven volumes of verse, three volumes of literary criticism, a book of *Self-Interviews* (1970), and a novel. Some critics found him severely limited in his essentially visceral subject matter and prosaic style, but others perceived a mythic quality in the material and a kinetic energy in the style that heralded the presence of a major talent.

Dickey dates his real interest in poetry from his Air Force service in the South Pacific in World War II. He had come to that war from a birth and childhood in Atlanta, Georgia, where his father was a lawyer. High school in Atlanta and a year at Clemson College, where he excelled in football and track, had done little to convince him that poetry could have any meaningful relation to experience, though he had become fond of the poetry of Byron and

Shelley. In the Air Force he took to reading modern poets; when he returned he graduated Phi Beta Kappa from Vanderbilt (1949), took an M.A. there (1950), and began to teach at Rice. Recalled to service in the Korean War, he returned to teaching again briefly before turning to advertising writing in New York and Atlanta. In the meantime his poems had begun to appear in the *Sewanee Review* and *Poetry*. His first book, *Into the Stone* (1960), brought him the recognition that allowed him to end his frustratingly dual existence as businessman and poet. Since that time he has been most often a teaching poet, with appointments at Reed College, San Fernando Valley State College, the University of Wisconsin, and the University of South Carolina. He received the National Book Award for *Buckdancer's Choice* (1965) and for two years was Consultant in Poetry to the Library of Congress (1967–1969).

Dickey's novel *Deliverance* (1970) is an extraordinary tour de force, marking him as one of the very few American poets who have been able to create sustained imaginative prose of a high order of distinction. The emphasis is on sheer physical sensation, as it is often in the poems as well, and although it is possible to question the clarity of the ideas, it is difficult to deny the book's sensual impact. In the stark clarity of his images, both here

and in his verse, he touches at times the roots of human experience. His criticism, too, is so clearly etched, forceful, and perceptive that since the appearance of *Babel to Byzantium* (1968) he has been compared to T. S. Eliot and Randall Jarrell among earlier poet-critics.

Behind all that he attempts there lies a strong will to succeed. "The great joy in my life," he says, "is to do something that I love but have no particular aptitude for and become at least reasonably good at it." This joy extends not only to his literary activities, but to marksmanship with a bow and arrow, to playing the guitar, and to acting in movies (he played the sheriff in the film version of *Deliverance*). Concerning his poetry, he believes much of its strength is the result of the route by which he approached it: "I've always had the feeling that nobody really understands poetry but me because I came to it of my own free will and by a very devious and sometimes painful route; I feel that it's something I've earned."

Volumes of verse are *Into the Stone and Other Poems*, 1960; *Drowning with Others*, 1962; *Helmets*, 1964; *Two Poems of the Air*, 1964; *Buckdancer's Choice*, 1965; *Poems 1957–1967*, 1967; and *The Eye-Beaters, Blood, Victory, Madness, Buckhead and Mercy*, 1970. Critical volumes are *The Suspect in Poetry*, 1964; *Babel to Byzantium*, 1968; *The Self as Agent*, 1970, and *Sorties*, 1971. Biographical details appear in *Self-Interviews*, edited by Barbara and James Reiss, 1970. Eileen Glancy edited *James Dickey: The Critic as Poet, An Annotated Bibliography with An Introductory Essay*, 1971.

The Lifeguard

In a stable of boats I lie still,
From all sleeping children hidden.
The leap of a fish from its shadow
Makes the whole lake instantly tremble.
With my foot on the water, I feel   5
The moon outside

Take on the utmost of its power.
I rise and go out through the boats.
I set my broad sole upon silver,
On the skin of the sky, on the moonlight,   10
Stepping outward from earth onto water
In quest of the miracle

This village of children believed
That I could perform as I dived
For one who had sunk from my sight.   15
I saw his cropped haircut go under.
I leapt, and my steep body flashed
Once, in the sun.

Dark drew all the light from my eyes.
Like a man who explores his death   20
By the pull of his slow-moving shoulders,
I hung head down in the cold,
Wide-eyed, contained, and alone
Among the weeds,

And my fingertips turned into stone   25
From clutching immovable blackness.
Time after time I leapt upward
Exploding in breath, and fell back
From the change in the children's faces
At my defeat.   30

Beneath them I swam to the boathouse
With only my life in my arms
To wait for the lake to shine back
At the risen moon with such power
That my steps on the light of the ripples   35
Might be sustained.

Beneath me is nothing but brightness
Like the ghost of a snowfield in summer.
As I moved toward the center of the lake,
Which is also the center of the moon,   40
I am thinking of how I may be
The savior of one

Who has already died in my care.
The dark trees fade from around me.
The moon's dust hovers together.   45
I call softly out, and the child's
Voice answers through blinding water.
Patiently, slowly,

He rises, dilating to break
The surface of stone with his forehead.   50
He is one I do not remember
Having ever seen in his life.
The ground I stand on is trembling
Upon his smile.

I wash the black mud from my hands.   55
On a light given off by the grave
I kneel in the quick of the moon
At the heart of a distant forest
And hold in my arms a child
Of water, water, water.   60

1962

The Shark's Parlor

Memory: I can take my head and strike it on a wall   on Cumberland Island
Where the night tide came crawling under the stairs   came up the first
Two or three steps   and the cottage stood on poles all night
With the sea sprawled under it   as we dreamed of the great fin circling
Under the bedroom floor. In daylight there was my first brassy taste of beer   5
And Payton Ford and I came back from the Glynn County slaughterhouse
With a bucket of entrails and blood. We tied one end of a hawser
To a spindling porch pillar and rowed straight out of the house
Three hundred yards into the vast front yard of windless blue water
The rope outslithering its coil   the two-gallon jug stoppered and sealed   10
With wax   and a ten-foot chain leader   a drop-forged shark hook nestling.
We cast our blood on the waters   the land blood easily passing
For sea blood   and we sat in it for a moment with the stain spreading
Out from the boat   sat in a new radiance   in the pond of blood in the sea

Waiting for fins   waiting to spill our guts also in the glowing
    water.   15
We dumped the bucket, and baited the hook with a run-over
    collie pup. The jug
Bobbed, trying to shake off the sun as a dog would shake off the sea.
We rowed to the house   feeling the same water lift the boat a
    new way,
All the time seeing where we lived rise and dip with the oars.
We tied up and sat down in rocking chairs, one eye or the other
    responding   20
To the blue-eye wink of the jug. Payton got us a beer and we sat

All morning sat there with blood on our minds   the red mark out
In the harbor slowly failing us   then   the house groaned   the
    rope
Sprang out of the water   splinters flew   we leapt from our chairs
And grabbed the rope   hauled   did nothing   the house coming
    subtly   25
Apart all around us   underfoot   boards beginning to sparkle
    like sand
With the glinting of the bright hidden parts of ten-year-old nails
Pulling out   the tarred poles we slept propped-up on   leaning to
    sea
As in land wind   crabs scuttling from under the floor   as we took
    turns about
Two more porch pillars   and looked out and saw   something
    a fish-flash   30
An almighty fin in trouble   a moiling of secret forces   a false start
Of water   a round wave growing: in the whole of Cumberland
    Sound the one ripple.
Payton took off without a word   I could not hold him either

But clung to the rope anyway: it was the whole house bending
Its nails that held whatever it was   coming in a little and like a
    fool   35
I took up the slack on my wrist. The rope drew gently   jerked
    I lifted
Clean off the porch and hit the water   the same water it was in
I felt in blue blazing terror at the bottom of the stairs and scram-
    bled
Back up looking desperately into the human house as deeply as I
    could
Stopping my gaze before it went out the wire screen of the back
    door   40
Stopped it on the thistled rattan   the rugs I lay on and read

On my mother's sewing basket with next winter's socks spilling
from it
The flimsy vacation furniture   a bucktoothed picture of myself.
Payton came back with three men from a filling station   and
glanced at me
Dripping water   inexplicable   then we all grabbed hold like a
tug-of-war.   45

We were gaining a little   from us a cry went up   from everywhere
People came running. Behind us the house filled with men and
boys.
On the third step from the sea I took my place   looking down the
rope
Going into the ocean, humming and shaking off drops. A house-
ful
Of people put their backs into it   going up the steps from me   50
Into the living room   through the kitchen   down the back stairs
Up and over a hill of sand   across a dust road   and onto a raised
field
Of dunes   we were gaining   the rope in my hands began to be
wet
With deeper water   all other haulers retreated through the house
But Payton and I on the stairs   drawing hand over hand on our
blood   55
Drawing into existence by the nose   a huge body   becoming
A hammerhead   rolling in beery shallows   and I began to let up
But the rope still strained behind me   the town had gone
Pulling-mad in our house: far away in a field of sand they strug-
gled
They had turned their backs on the sea   bent double   some on
their knees   60
The rope over their shoulders like a bag of gold   they strove for
the ideal
Esso station across the scorched meadow   with the distant fish
coming up
The front stairs   the sagging boards   still coming in   up   taking
Another step   toward the empty house   where the rope stood
straining
By itself through the rooms   in the middle of the air. "Pass the
word,"   65
Payton said, and I screamed it: "Let up, good God, let up!"   to
no one there.
The shark flopped on the porch, grating with salt-sand   driving
back in

The nails he had pulled out   coughing chunks of his formless
  blood.
The screen door banged and tore off   he scrambled on his tail
  slid
Curved   did a thing from another world   and was out of his
  element and in   70
Our vacation paradise   cutting all four legs from under the dinner table
With one deep-water move   he unwove the rugs in a moment
  throwing pints
Of blood over everything we owned   knocked the buck teeth out
  of my picture
His odd head full of crushed jelly-glass splinters and radio tubes
  thrashing
Among the pages of fan magazines   all the movie stars drenched
  in sea-blood   75
Each time we thought he was dead   he struggled back and
  smashed
One more thing   in all coming back to die   three or four more
  times after death.
At last we got him out   log-rolling him   greasing his sandpaper
  skin
With lard to slide him   pulling on his chained lips as the tide
  came
Tumbled him down the steps as the first night wave went under
  the floor.   80
He drifted off   head back   belly white as the moon. What could
  I do but buy
That house   for the one black mark still there   against death   a
  forehead-
toucher in the room he circles beneath   and has been invited to
  wreck?
Blood hard as iron on the wall   black with time   still bloodlike
Can be touched whenever the brow is drunk enough: all changes:
  Memory: 85
Something like three-dimensional dancing in the limbs   with age
Feeling more in two worlds than one   in all worlds the growing
  encounters.

1965

ROBERT BLY

(1926–   )

For years Robert Bly has lived and worked in Madison, Minnesota, a town of fewer than 3,000 people located near the South Dakota border almost 150 miles from Minneapolis. He was born there in 1926 and since 1958 has edited *The Seventies* (earlier *The Fifties* and *The Sixties*) magazine and managed the Seventies Press there. He came back to Madison after spending two years in the Navy in World War II and earning degrees from Harvard (A.B., 1950) and the University of Iowa (M.A. 1956). He has also spent a year in Norway on a Fulbright award.

Unlike a good many poets of his time, he has earned his living not by teaching, but through translations and poetry readings, supplemented by stipends from fellowships and writing grants. Particularly interested in such South American and European poets as Juan Ramón Jiménez, Pablo Neruda, Antonio Machado, and Georg Trakl, he has made his magazine a showcase for their talents and has been much influenced by them in his own writing. Poetry in English, he is convinced, has for the most part gone the wrong way in modern times. Blake he admires, and Whitman, but too many other poets he sees as hampered by a respect for technique that prevents them from breaking through to the "corridors to the unconscious" where the vital symbolic roots of poetry are to be found. His poems are often composed of freely associated and elemental images; starkly simple evocations of earth, air, fire, and water tumble rapidly upon one another in the "leaping about the psyche" he admires in the ancients and perceives in too few moderns. Not only a dedicated poet, but a long-time political activist, he writes poems that range from the lyrical to the apocalyptic.

Volumes of verse are *Silence in the Snowy Fields*, 1962; *The Light Around the Body*, 1967; *The Morning Glory*, 1969; *Shadow Mothers: Poetry*, 1970; *The Teeth-Mother Naked at Last*, 1971; and *Sleepers Joining Hands*, 1972. Translations include *The Story of Gosta Berling*, Selma Lagerlof, 1962; *Hunger*, Knut Hamsun, 1967; *Twenty Poems of Pablo Neruda* (with James Wright), 1968; *Late Arrival on Earth: Selected Poems of Gunnar Ekelof*, 1968; *Forty Poems of Juan Ramón Jiménez*, 1969; and *Neruda and Vallejo: Selected Poems* (with John Knoepfle and James Wright), 1971. A brief critical introduction is by David Ray in Rosalie Murphy and James Vinson, eds., *Contemporary Poets of the English Language*, 1970.

Driving Toward the Lac Qui Parle River

I

I am driving; it is dusk; Minnesota.
The stubble field catches the last growth of sun.
The soybeans are breathing on all sides.

Old men are sitting before their houses on carseats
In the small towns. I am happy,   5
The moon rising above the turkey sheds.

II

The small world of the car
Plunges through the deep fields of the night,
On the road from Willmar to Milan.
This solitude covered with iron   10
Moves through the fields of night
Penetrated by the noise of crickets.

III

Nearly to Milan, suddenly a small bridge,
And water kneeling in the moonlight.
In small towns the houses are built right on the ground;   15
The lamplight falls on all fours in the grass.
When I reach the river, the full moon covers it;
A few people are talking low in a boat.

                                                              1962

Driving to Town Late to Mail a Letter

It is a cold and snowy night. The main street is deserted.
The only things moving are swirls of snow.
As I lift the mailbox door, I feel its cold iron.
There is a privacy I love in this snowy night.
Driving around, I will waste more time.   5

                                                              1962

Watering the Horse

How strange to think of giving up all ambition!
Suddenly I see with such clear eyes
The white flake of snow
That has just fallen in the horse's mane!

                                                              1962

The Executive's Death

Merchants have multiplied more than the stars of heaven.
Half the population are like the long grasshoppers
That sleep in the bushes in the cool of the day:
The sound of their wings is heard at noon, muffled, near the
    earth.
The crane handler dies, the taxi driver dies, slumped over   5
In his taxi. Meanwhile, high in the air, executives
Walk on cool floors, and suddenly fall:
Dying, they dream they are lost in a snowstorm in mountains,

On which they crashed, carried at night by great machines.
As he lies on the wintry slope, cut off and dying,   10
A pine stump talks to him of Goethe and Jesus.
Commuters arrive in Hartford at dusk like moles
Or hares flying from a fire behind them,
And the dusk in Hartford is full of their sighs;
Their trains come through the air like a dark music,   15
Like the sound of horns, the sound of thousands of small wings.

1967

Looking at New-Fallen Snow
from a Train

Snow has covered the next line of tracks,
And filled the empty cupboards in the milkweed pods;
It has stretched out on the branches of weeds,
And softened the frost-hills, and the barbed-wire rolls
Left leaning against a fencepost—   5
It has drifted onto the window ledges high in the peaks of
        barns.

A man throws back his head, gasps
And dies. His ankles twitch, his hands open and close,
And the fragment of time that he has eaten is exhaled from
        his pale mouth to nourish the snow.   10
A salesman falls, striking his head on the edge of the
        counter.

Snow has filled out the peaks on the tops of rotted fence posts.
It has walked down to meet the slough water,
And fills all the steps of the ladder leaning against the eaves.
It rests on the doorsills of collapsing children's houses,   15
And on transformer boxes held from the ground forever in the
        center of cornfields.

A man lies down to sleep.
Hawks and crows gather around his bed.
Grass shoots up between the hawks' toes.
Each blade of grass is a voice.   20
The sword by his side breaks into flame.

1967

ALLEN GINSBERG

(1926–   )

Allen Ginsberg was born in Newark, New Jersey, in 1926. His father, Louis Ginsberg, was a poet and high school English teacher in Paterson, New Jersey. The younger Ginsberg went to high school in Paterson and graduated in 1948 from Columbia University. At Columbia he published in the *Columbia Review;* there and elsewhere in New York in the late 1940's he participated in the activities of the group that came to be known as the Beat Generation. After experiences that included dishwashing, a stint as a welder in the Brooklyn Navy Yard, hospitalization for a nervous breakdown, reviewing for *Newsweek,* and service in the Merchant Marine, he was catapulted to fame by the obscenity charges leveled against his first book, *Howl and Other Poems* (1956).

It is difficult to dissociate Ginsberg the poet from Ginsberg the public figure. Long before he had secured any widespread reputation for his poems he had already appeared as a fictional character in two Beat novels, Jack Kerouac's *The Town and the City* (1950) and John Clellon Holmes's *Go* (1952), and William Carlos Williams had printed two of his letters in 1951 in *Paterson,* Book Four (another appears in Book Five, 1958). His travels in Europe, Asia, and South America, his advocacy of Zen Buddhism, of hallucinatory drugs, and of homosexuality, and his involvement in the Civil Rights campaign, war resistance, and attacks on the C.I.A. have done as much to keep him in the public eye since the appearance of *Howl* as has his poetry. Of his later works the best known is "Kaddish," a long poem on his mother's illness and death.

Ginsberg defines his poetry as "Beat-Hip-Gnostic-Imagist." After some early experimentation with rhymed, metrical verse in the manner of Thomas Wyatt, he began under the influence of William Carlos Williams to seek a line modeled on speech and breathing patterns. Later familiarity with the incantatory verse of Indian Mantras has strengthened his sense of the importance of parallelism and repetition. Influenced also by the Bible, by William Blake, and by Walt Whitman, Ginsberg strives for a prophetic poetry that embraces the sacred and profane.

Individual titles are *Howl and Other Poems,* 1956; *Empty Mirror: Early Poems,* 1961; *Kaddish and Other Poems, 1958–1960,* 1961; *Reality Sandwiches,* 1963; *The Yage Letters* (with William S. Burroughs), 1963; *T.V. Baby Poems,* 1967; *Ankor-Wat,* 1968; *Planet News: 1961–1967,* 1968; *Indian Journals,* 1969; *Airplane Dreams,* 1969; and *The Fall of America: Poems of These States, 1965–1971,* 1973. George Dowden compiled *A Bibliography of Works by Allen Ginsberg,* 1971. Studies are Jane Kramer, *Allen Ginsberg in America,* 1969; and T. F. Merrill, *Allen Ginsberg,* 1969.

Howl

for
Carl Solomon

I

I saw the best minds of my generation destroyed by madness, starving hysterical naked,

dragging themselves through the negro streets at dawn looking for
an angry fix,

angelheaded hipsters burning for the ancient heavenly connection
to the starry dynamo in the machinery of night,

who poverty and tatters and hollow-eyed and high sat up smoking in the supernatural darkness of cold-water flats floating
across the tops of cities contemplating jazz,

who bared their brains to Heaven under the El [1] and saw Mohammedan angels staggering on tenement roofs illuminated,

who passed through universities with radiant cool eyes hallucinating
Arkansas and Blake-light tragedy among the scholars of war,

who were expelled from the academies for crazy & publishing
obscene odes on the windows of the skull,

who cowered in unshaven rooms in underwear, burning their
money in wastebaskets and listening to the Terror through
the wall,

who got busted in their pubic beards returning through Laredo
with a belt of marijuana for New York,

who ate fire in paint hotels or drank turpentine in Paradise Alley,
death, or purgatoried their torsos night after night   10

with dreams, and drugs, with waking nightmares, alcohol and cock
and endless balls,

incomparable blind streets of shuddering cloud and lightning in
the mind leaping toward poles of Canada & Paterson,
illuminating all the motionless world of Time between,

Peyote solidities of halls, backyard green tree cemetery dawns,
wine drunkenness over the rooftops, storefront boroughs of
teahead joyride neon blinking traffic light, sun and moon
and tree vibrations in the roaring winter dusks of Brooklyn,
ashcan rantings and kind king light of mind,

who chained themselves to subways for the endless ride from Battery to holy Bronx on benzedrine until the noise of wheels
and children brought them down shuddering mouth-wracked
and battered bleak of brain all drained of brilliance in the
drear light of Zoo, [2]

who sank all night in submarine light of Bickford's [3] floated out
and sat through the stale beer afternoon in desolate Fu-
gazzi's, [4] listening to the crack of doom on the hydrogen
jukebox,   15

who talked continuously seventy hours from park to pad to bar to
Bellevue [5] to museum to the Brooklyn Bridge,

a lost battalion of platonic conversationalists jumping down the

---

1. The elevated railway.
2. The Bronx Zoo.
3. A cafeteria.
4. Greenwich Village bar.
5. Manhattan hospital; often associated with care of the insane.

stoops off fire escapes off windowsills off Empire State out
    of the moon,
yacketayakking screaming vomiting whispering facts and memories
    and anecdotes and eyeball kicks and shocks of hospitals and
    jails and wars,
whole intellects disgorged in total recall for seven days and nights
    with brilliant eyes, meat for the Synagogue cast on the
    pavement,
who vanished into nowhere Zen [6] New Jersey leaving a trail of
    ambiguous picture postcards of Atlantic City Hall,   20
suffering Eastern sweats and Tangerian bone-grindings and mi-
    graines of China under junk-withdrawal in Newark's bleak
    furnished room,
who wandered around and around at midnight in the railroad yard
    wondering where to go, and went, leaving no broken
    hearts,
who lit cigarettes in boxcars boxcars boxcars racketing through
    snow toward lonesome farms in grandfather night,
who studied Plotinus Poe St. John of the Cross [7] telepathy and bop
    kaballa because the cosmos instinctively vibrated at their
    feet in Kansas,
who loned it through the streets of Idaho seeking visionary indian
    angels who were visionary indian angels,   25
who thought they were only mad when Baltimore gleamed in
    supernatural ecstasy,
who jumped in limousines with the Chinaman of Oklahoma on the
    impulse of winter midnight streetlight smalltown rain,
who lounged hungry and lonesome through Houston seeking jazz
    or sex or soup, and followed the brilliant Spaniard to con-
    verse about America and Eternity, a hopeless task, and so
    took ship to Africa,
who disappeared into the volcanoes of Mexico leaving behind
    nothing but the shadow of dungarees and the lava and ash
    of poetry scattered in fireplace Chicago,
who reappeared on the West Coast investigating the F.B.I. in
    beards and shorts with big pacifist eyes sexy in their dark
    skin passing out incomprehensible leaflets,   30
who burned cigarette holes in their arms protesting the narcotic
    tobacco haze of Capitalism,
who distributed Supercommunist pamphlets in Union Square [8]
    weeping and undressing while the sirens of Los Alamos

---

6. Zen Buddhism was especially popular in the middle 1950's with members
of the Beat Generation.
7. Plotinus, Roman philosopher (205?–

270 A.D.); Edgar Allan Poe (1809–
1849); St. John of the Cross (1542–
1591), Spanish poet.
8. In New York City.

wailed them down, and wailed down Wall, and the Staten
    Island ferry also wailed,
who broke down crying in white gymnasiums naked and trembling
    before the machinery of other skeletons,
who bit detectives in the neck and shrieked with delight in police-
    cars for committing no crime but their own wild cooking
    pederasty and intoxication,
who howled on their knees in the subway and were dragged off the
    roof waving genitals and manuscripts,   35
who let themselves be fucked in the ass by saintly motorcyclists,
    and screamed with joy,
who blew and were blown by those human seraphim, the sailors,
    caresses of Atlantic and Caribbean love,
who balled in the morning in the evenings in rosegardens and
    the grass of public parks and cemeteries scattering their
    semen freely to whomever come who may,
who hiccupped endlessly trying to giggle but wound up with a
    sob behind a partition in a Turkish Bath when the blonde
    & naked angel came to pierce them with a sword,
who lost their loveboys to the three old shrews of fate the one eyed
    shrew of the heterosexual dollar the one eyed shrew that
    winks out of the womb and the one eyed shrew that does
    nothing but sit on her ass and snip the intellectual golden
    threads of the craftsman's loom,   40
who copulated ecstatic and insatiate with a bottle of beer a
    sweetheart a package of cigarettes a candle and fell off the
    bed, and continued along the floor and down the hall and
    ended fainting on the wall with a vision of ultimate cunt
    and come eluding the last gyzym of consciousness,
who sweetened the snatches of a million girls trembling in the
    sunset, and were red eyed in the morning but prepared to
    sweeten the snatch of the sunrise, flashing buttocks under
    barns and naked in the lake,
who went out whoring through Colorado in myriad stolen night-cars,
    N.C.,[9] secret hero of these poems, cocksman and Adonis
    of Denver—joy to the memory of his innumerable lays
    of girls in empty lots & diner backyards, moviehouses' rick-
    ety rows, on mountaintops in caves or with gaunt waitresses
    in familiar roadside lonely petticoat upliftings & especially
    secret gas-station solipisisms of johns, & hometown alleys
    too,
who faded out in vast sordid movies, were shifted in dreams,

9. Neal Cassady, the inspiration for characters in a number of Beat novels, including Kerouac's *On the Road* (1957).

woke on a sudden Manhattan, and picked themselves up
out of basements hungover with heartless Tokay and horrors of Third Avenue iron dreams & stumbled to unemployment offices,

who walked all night with their shoes full of blood on the snow-
bank docks waiting for a door in the East River to open to
a room full of steamheat and opium,   45

who created great suicidal dramas on the apartment cliff-banks of
the Hudson under the wartime blue floodlight of the moon
& their heads shall be crowned with laurel in oblivion,

who ate the lamb stew of the imagination or digested the crab at
the muddy bottom of the rivers of Bowery,

who wept at the romance of the streets with their pushcarts full of
onions and bad music,

who sat in boxes breathing in the darkness under the bridge, and
rose up to build harpsichords in their lofts,

who coughed on the sixth floor of Harlem crowned with flame
under the tubercular sky surrounded by orange crates of
theology,   50

who scribbled all night rocking and rolling over lofty incantations
which in the yellow morning were stanzas of gibberish,

who cooked rotten animals lung heart feet tail borsht & tortillas
dreaming of the pure vegetable kingdom,

who plunged themselves under meat trucks looking for an egg,

who threw their watches off the roof to cast their ballot for
Eternity outside of Time, & alarm clocks fell on their heads
every day for the next decade,

who cut their wrists three times successively unsuccessfully, gave
up and were forced to open antique stores where they
thought they were growing old and cried,   55

who were burned alive in their innocent flannel suits on Madison
Avenue amid blasts of leaden verse & the tanked-up clatter
of the iron regiments of fashion & the nitroglycerine
shrieks of the fairies of advertising & the mustard gas of
sinister intelligent editors, or were run down by the
drunken taxicabs of Absolute Reality,

who jumped off the Brooklyn Bridge this actually happened and
walked away unknown and forgotten into the ghostly daze
of Chinatown soup alleyways & firetrucks, not even one
free beer,

who sang out of their windows in despair, fell out of the subway
window, jumped in the filthy Passaic, leaped on negroes,
cried all over the street, danced on broken wineglasses
barefoot smashed phonograph records of nostalgic European
1930's German jazz finished the whiskey and threw up

groaning into the bloody toilet, moans in their ears and the blast of colossal steamwhistles,

who barreled down the highways of the past journeying to each other's hotrod-Golgotha [1] jail-solitude watch or Birmingham jazz incarnation,

who drove crosscountry seventytwo hours to find out if I had a vision or you had a vision or he had a vision to find out Eternity,   60

who journeyed to Denver, who died in Denver, who came back to Denver & waited in vain, who watched over Denver & brooded & loned in Denver and finally went away to find out the Time, & now Denver is lonesome for her heroes,

who fell on their knees in hopeless cathedrals praying for each other's salvation and light and breasts, until the soul illuminated its hair for a second,

who crashed through their minds in jail waiting for impossible criminals with golden heads and the charm of reality in their hearts who sang sweet blues to Alcatraz,

who retired to Mexico to cultivate a habit, or Rocky Mount to tender Buddha or Tangiers to boys or Southern Pacific to the black locomotive or Harvard to Narcissus to Woodlawn [2] to the daisychain or grave.

who demanded sanity trials accusing the radio of hypnotism & were left with their insanity & their hands & a hung jury,   65

who threw potato salad at CCNY lecturers on Dadaism and subsequently presented themselves on the granite steps of the madhouse with shaven heads and harlequin speech of suicide, demanding instantaneous lobotomy,

and who were given instead the concrete void of insulin metrasol electricity hydrotherapy psychotherapy occupational therapy pingpong & amnesia,

who in humorless protest overturned only one symbolic pingpong table, resting briefly in catatonia,

returning years later truly bald except for a wig of blood, and tears and fingers, to the visible madman doom of the wards of the madtowns of the East,

Pilgrim State's Rockland's and Greystone's [3] foetid halls, bickering with the echoes of the soul, rocking and rolling in the midnight solitude-bench dolmen-realms of love, dream of life a nightmare, bodies turned to stone as heavy as the moon,

with mother finally ******, and the last fantastic book flung out of the tenement window, and the last door closed at 4 AM and the last telephone slammed at the wall in reply and the

1. Scene of the crucifixion of Jesus.
2. Cemetery in the Bronx.
3. Mental hospitals in New York and New Jersey.

last furnished room emptied down to the last piece of
mental furniture, a yellow paper rose twisted on a wire
hanger in the closet, and even that imaginary, nothing but
a hopeful little bit of hallucination—   71

ah, Carl, while you are not safe I am not safe, and now you're
really in the total animal soup of time—

and who therefore ran through the icy streets obsessed with a
sudden flash of the alchemy of the use of the ellipse the
catalog the meter & the vibrating plane,

who dreamt and made incarnate gaps in Time & Space through
images juxtaposed, and trapped the archangel of the soul
between 2 visual images and joined the elemental verbs
and set the noun and dash of consciousness together jumping with sensation of Pater Omnipotens Aeterna Deus [4]

to recreate the syntax and measure of poor human prose and stand
before you speechless and intelligent and shaking with
shame, rejected yet confessing out the soul to conform to
the rhythm of thought in his naked and endless head,   75

the madman bum and angel beat in Time, unknown, yet putting
down here what might be left to say in time come after
death,

and rose reincarnate in the ghostly clothes of jazz in the goldhorn
shadow of the band and blew the suffering of America's
naked mind for love into an eli eli lamma lamma sabac-
thani [5] saxophone cry that shivered the cities down to the
last radio

with the absolute heart of the poem of life butchered out of their
own bodies good to eat a thousand years.

II

What sphinx of cement and aluminum bashed open their skulls
and ate up their brains and imagination?

Moloch! [6] Solitude! Filth! Ugliness! Ashcans and unobtainable
dollars! Children screaming under the stairways! Boys
sobbing in armies! Old men weeping in the parks!   80

Moloch! Moloch! Nightmare of Moloch! Moloch the loveless!
Mental Moloch! Moloch the heavy judger of men!

Moloch the incomprehensible prison! Moloch the crossbone soul-
less jailhouse and Congress of sorrows! Moloch whose
buildings are judgement! Moloch the vast stone of war!
Moloch the stunned governments!

---

4. "Father omnipotent, eternal God."
From a letter of the French painter
Paul Cézanne (1839–1906) in which
he commented on the nature of art.
5. "My God, my God, why hast thou
forsaken me?"—Christ's words at the
ninth hour on the Cross, Matthew
xxvii:46 and Mark xv:34.
6. In the Bible and in Milton's *Paradise Lost* an ancient god worshipped
with the sacrifice of children.

Moloch whose mind is pure machinery! Moloch whose blood is
running money! Moloch whose fingers are ten armies!
Moloch whose breast is a cannibal dynamo! Moloch whose
ear is a smoking tomb!

Moloch whose eyes are a thousand blind windows! Moloch whose
skyscrapers stand in the long streets like endless Jehovahs!
Moloch whose factories dream and croak in the fog! Moloch whose smokestacks and antennae crown the cities!

Moloch whose love is endless oil and stone! Moloch whose soul is
electricity and banks! Moloch whose poverty is the specter
of genius! Moloch whose fate is a cloud of sexless hydrogen! Moloch whose name is the Mind!   85

Moloch in whom I sit lonely! Moloch in whom I dream Angels!
Crazy in Moloch! Cocksucker in Moloch! Lacklove and
manless in Moloch!

Moloch who entered my soul early! Moloch in whom I am a consciousness without a body! Moloch who frightened me out
of my natural ecstasy! Moloch whom I abandon! Wake up
in Moloch! Light streaming out of the sky!

Moloch! Moloch! Robot apartments! invisible suburbs! skeleton
treasuries! blind capitals! demonic industries! spectral nations! invincible madhouses! granite cocks! monstrous
bombs!

They broke their backs lifting Moloch to Heaven! Pavements,
trees, radios, tons! lifting the city to Heaven which exists
and is everywhere about us!

Visions! omens! hallucinations! miracles! ecstasies! gone down
the American river!   90

Dreams! adorations! illuminations! religions! the whole boatload
of sensitive bullshit!

Breakthroughs! over the river! flips and cruxifixions! gone down
the flood! High! Epiphanies! Despairs! Ten years' animal
screams and suicides! Minds! New loves! Mad generation!
down on the rocks of Time!

Real holy laughter in the river! They saw it all! the wild eyes!
the holy yells! They bade farewell! They jumped off the
roof! to solitude! waving! carrying flowers! Down to the
river! into the street!

III

Carl Solomon! I'm with you in Rockland [7]
    where you're madder than I am
I'm with you in Rockland
    where you must feel very strange   95

7. New York psychiatric hospital.

I'm with you in Rockland
>   where you imitate the shade of my mother
I'm with you in Rockland
>   where you've murdered your twelve secretaries
I'm with you in Rockland
>   where you laugh at this invisible humor
I'm with you in Rockland
>   where we are great writers on the same dreadful typewriter
I'm with you in Rockland
>   where your condition has become serious and is reported on
>   the radio   100
I'm with you in Rockland
>   where the faculties of the skull no longer admit the worms
>   of the senses
I'm with you in Rockland
>   where you drink the tea of the breasts of the spinsters of
>   Utica
I'm with you in Rockland
>   where you pun on the bodies of your nurses the harpies of
>   the Bronx
I'm with you in Rockland
>   where you scream in a straightjacket that you're losing the
>   game of the actual pingpong of the abyss
I'm with you in Rockland
>   where you bang on the catatonic piano the soul is innocent
>   and immortal it should never die ungodly in an armed
>   madhouse   105
I'm with you in Rockland
>   where fifty more shocks will never return your soul to its
>   body again from its pilgrimage to a cross in the void
I'm with you in Rockland
>   where you accuse your doctors of insanity and plot the
>   Hebrew socialist revolution against the fascist national
>   Golgotha
I'm with you in Rockland
>   where you will split the heavens of Long Island and resur-
>   rect your living human Jesus from the superhuman tomb
I'm with you in Rockland
>   where there are twentyfive-thousand mad comrades all to-
>   gether singing the final stanzas of the Internationale [8]
I'm with you in Rockland
>   where we hug and kiss the United States under our bed-
>   sheets the United States that coughs all night and won't
>   let us sleep   110

8. Communist anthem.

I'm with you in Rockland
> where we wake up electrified out of the coma by our own
> souls' airplanes roaring over the roof they've come to drop
> angelic bombs the hospital illuminates itself imaginary
> walls collapse O skinny legions run outside O starry-
> spangled shock of mercy the eternal war is here O victory
> forget your underwear we're free

I'm with you in Rockland
> in my dreams you walk dripping from a sea-journey on the
> highway across America in tears to the door of my cottage
> in the Western night

San Francisco 1955-56   1956

W. D. SNODGRASS

(1926–   )

Born in Wilkinsburg, Pennsylvania, Snodgrass studied at Geneva College, entered the Navy for three years, was graduated from the State University of Iowa (1949), and continued to the degree of M.F.A. He has taught at Cornell University, the University of Rochester, Wayne State University, and, since 1968, Syracuse University. Snodgrass won the Pulitzer Prize for Poetry in 1960 with his first volume of poems, *Heart's Needle* (1959).

Snodgrass's verse reveals a concern for totality—a need to reveal the entirety of a given subject on a level deeper than the conscious mind. Expertise with form and rhythm play an important part. Neither the style nor the subject of his poem is likely to be complex. On the contrary, the musical fluidity of his verse is pleasing, and his themes, even when lyrical, suggest an attractive undertone of matured experience.

Snodgrass's verse is collected in *Heart's Needle*, 1959; and *After Experience: Poems and Translations*, 1968.

April Inventory

The green catalpa tree has turned
All white; the cherry blooms once more.
In one whole year I haven't learned
A blessed thing they pay you for.
The blossoms snow down in my hair;   5
The trees and I will soon be bare.

The trees have more than I to spare.
The sleek, expensive girls I teach,
Younger and pinker every year,

Bloom gradually out of reach.   10
The pear tree lets its petals drop
Like dandruff on a tabletop.

The girls have grown so young by now
I have to nudge myself to stare.
This year they smile and mind me how   15
My teeth are falling with my hair.
In thirty years I may not get
Younger, shrewder, or out of debt.

The tenth time, just a year ago,
I made myself a little list   20
Of all the things I'd ought to know;
Then told my parents, analyst,
And everyone who's trusted me
I'd be substantial, presently.

I haven't read one book about   25
A book or memorized one plot.
Or found a mind I didn't doubt.
I learned one date. And then forgot.
And one by one the solid scholars
Get the degrees, the jobs, the dollars.   30

And smile above their starchy collars.
I taught my classes Whitehead's notions;
One lovely girl, a song of Mahler's.
Lacking a source-book or promotions,
I showed one child the colors of   35
A luna moth and how to love.

I taught myself to name my name,
To bark back, loosen love and crying;
To ease my woman so she came,
To ease an old man who was dying.   40
I have not learned how often I
Can win, can love, but choose to die.

I have not learned there is a lie
Love shall be blonder, slimmer, younger;
That my equivocating eye   45
Loves only by my body's hunger;
That I have poems, true to feel,
Or that the lovely world is real.

While scholars speak authority
And wear their ulcers on their sleeves,   50
My eyes in spectacles shall see
These trees procure and spend their leaves.
There is a value underneath
The gold and silver in my teeth.

Though trees turn bare and girls turn wives,   55
We shall afford our costly seasons;
There is a gentleness survives
That will outspeak and has its reasons.
There is a loveliness exists,
Preserves us. Not for specialists.   60

1959

The Examination

Under the thick beams of that swirly smoking light,
    The black robes are clustering, huddled in together.
Hunching their shoulders, they spread short, broad sleeves like night-
    Black grackles' wings; then they reach bone-yellow leather-

y fingers, each to each. And are prepared. Each turns   5
    His single eye—or since one can't discern their eyes,
That reflective, single, moon-pale disc which burns
    Over each brow—to watch this uncouth shape that lies

Strapped to their table. One probes with his ragged nails
    The slate-sharp calf, explores the thigh and the lean thews   10
Of the groin. Others raise, red as piratic sails,
    His wing, stretching, trying the pectoral sinews.

One runs his finger down the whet of that cruel
    Golden beak, lifts back the horny lids from the eyes,
Peers down in one bright eye malign as a jewel,   15
    And steps back suddenly. "He is anaesthetized?"

"He is. He is. Yes. Yes." The tallest of them, bent
    Down by the head, rises: "This drug possesses powers
Sufficient to still all gods in this firmament.
    This is Garuda who was fierce. He's yours for hours.   20

"We shall continue, please." Now, once again, he bends
    To the skull, and its clamped tissues. Into the cran-
ial cavity, he plunges both of his hands
    Like obstetric forceps and lifts out the great brain,

Holds it aloft, then gives it to the next who stands   25
    Beside him. Each, in turn, accepts it, although loath,
Turns it this way, that way, feels it between his hands
    Like a wasp's nest or some sickening outsized growth.

They must decide what thoughts each part of it must think;
    They tap at, then listen beside, each suspect lobe;   30
Next, with a crow's quill dipped into India ink,
    Mark on its surface, as if on a map or globe,

Those dangerous areas which need to be excised.
    They rinse it, then apply antiseptics to it;

Now silver saws appear which, inch by inch, slice   35
    Through its ancient folds and ridges, like thick suet.

It's rinsed, dried, and daubed with thick salves. The smoky saws
    Are scrubbed, resterilized, and polished till they gleam.
The brain is repacked in its case. Pinched in their claws,
    Glimmering needles stitch it up, that leave no seam.   40

Meantime, one of them has set blinders to the eyes,
    Inserted light packing beneath each of the ears
And calked the nostrils in. One, with thin twine, ties
    The genitals off. With long wooden-handled shears,

Another chops pinions out of the scarlet wings.   45
    It's hoped that with disuse he will forget the sky
Or, at least, in time, learn, among other things,
    To fly no higher than his superiors fly.

Well; that's a beginning. The next time, they can split
    His tongue and teach him to talk correctly, can give   50
Him opinions on fine books and choose clothing fit
    For the integrated area where he'll live.

Their candidate may live to give them thanks one day.
    He will recover and may hope for such success
He might return to join their ranks. Bowing away,   55
    They nod, whispering, "One of ours; one of ours. Yes. Yes."

1968

Monet: "Les Nymphéas"

The eyelids glowing, some chill morning.
O world half-known through opening, twilit lids
    Before the vague face clenches into light;
O universal waters like a cloud,
    Like those first clouds of half-created matter;   5
O all things rising, rising like the fumes
    From waters falling, O forever falling;
Infinite, the skeletal shells that fall, relinquished,
    The snowsoft sift of the diatoms, like selves
Downdrifting age upon age through milky oceans;   10
    O slow downdrifting of the atoms;
O island nebulae and O the nebulous islands
    Wandering these mists like falsefires, which are true,
Bobbing like milkweed, like warm lanterns bobbing
    Through the snowfilled windless air, blinking and passing   15
As we pass into the memory of women
    Who are passing. Within those depths
What ravening? What devouring rage?
    How shall our living know its ends of yielding?

These things have taken me as the mouth an orange—   20
    That acrid sweet juice entering every cell;
And I am shared out. I become these things:
    These lilies, if these things are water lilies
Which are dancers growing dim across no floor;
    These mayflies; whirled dust orbiting in the sun;   25
This blossoming diffused as rushlights; galactic vapors;
    Fluorescence into which we pass and penetrate;
O soft as the thighs of women;
    O radiance, into which I go on dying . . .

                                                    1968

ANNE SEXTON

(1928–   )

Anne Sexton was born in Newton, Massachusetts, in 1928, and grew up in Wellesley, where she attended local schools. From her youth she was determined to learn the art she has practiced, and she early gained acceptance in a wide circle of magazines. She writes as an intensely subjective woman with the searching imagination necessary to identify with the experience of others: and she can write with the utmost subjectivity without seeming in most cases to be writing of herself. Her interests are primarily in the domestic scene or crisis, in the cycle of life and human companionship, and in nature—primarily that of the Massachusetts coast and Maine. She studied poetry with Robert Lowell at Boston University and has been awarded numerous fellowships. Her first collection of poems was made in 1960.

Volumes of her poems are: *To Bedlam and Part Way Back*, 1960; *All My Pretty Ones*, 1962; *Selected Poems*, 1964; *Live or Die*, 1966; *Love Poems*, 1969; *Transformations*, 1971; and *The Book of Folly*, 1972.

The Farmer's Wife

From the hodge porridge
of their country lust,
their local life in Illinois,
where all their acres look
like a sprouting broom factory,   5
they name just ten years now
that she has been his habit;
as again tonight he'll say
honey bunch let's go
and she will not say how there   10
must be more to living

than this brief bright bridge
of the raucous bed or even
the slow braille touch of him
like a heavy god grown light,   15
that old pantomime of love
that she wants although
it leaves her still alone,
built back again at last,
mind's apart from him, living   20
her own self in her own words
and hating the sweat of the house
they keep when they finally lie
each in separate dreams
and then how she watches him,   25
still strong in the blowzy bag
of his usual sleep while
her young years bungle past
their same marriage bed
and she wishes him cripple, or poet,   30
or even lonely, or sometimes,
better, my lover, dead.

1959   1960

The Truth the Dead Know

for my mother, born March 1902, died March 1959
and my father, born February 1900, died June 1959

Gone, I say, and walk from church,
refusing the stiff procession to the grave,
letting the dead ride alone in the hearse.
It is June. I am tired of being brave.

We drive to The Cape. I cultivate   5
myself where the sun gutters from the sky,
where the sea swings in like an iron gate
and we touch. In another country people die.

My darling, the wind falls in like stones
from the whitehearted water and when we touch   10
we enter touch entirely. No one's alone.
Men kill for this, or for as much.

And what of the dead? They lie without shoes
in their stone boats. They are more like stone
than the sea would be if it stopped. They refuse   15
to be blessed, throat, eye, and knucklebone.

1962

ADRIENNE RICH

(1929–   )

Born in Baltimore in 1929, Adrienne Rich was graduated from Radcliffe College (1951). In her senior year at college she published her first volume of poetry. She is married and has three sons.

As with many American poets, her creative sensibilities have found excitement in contact with the current impulse abroad, in older civilizations. She has discovered an affinity with contemporary Dutch poets and published a number of translations of these in *Necessities of Life*. Primarily considered, however, the inspiration of her own work has been the great tradition of American poetry from Frost and Williams to Roethke, discovering, like the latter, an individual style and technique for communicating her complex inner consciousness of the "Necessities of Life." Robert Lowell, for example, sees her most recent verse as "a poised and intact completion," deeply reminiscent of "old poets, mostly American ones, and still more * * * of our old prose writers—Hawthorne above all, with his dark and musical sense, the gaiety of his almost breathless resignation."

Her books of poetry are *A Change of World*, 1951; *The Diamond Cutters*, 1955; *Snapshots of a Daughter-in-Law*, 1963; *Necessities of Life*, 1966; *Selected Poems*, 1967; *Leaflets: Poems 1965–1968*, 1969; and *Will To Change: Poems*, 1971.

The Diamond Cutters

However legendary,
The stone is still a stone,
Though it had once resisted
The weight of Africa,
The hammer-blows of time   5
That wear to bits of powder
The mountain and the pebble—
But not this coldest one.

Now, you intelligence
So late dredged up from dark   10
Upon whose smoky walls
Bison took fumbling form
Or flint was edged on flint—
Now, careful arriviste,
Delineate at will   15
Incisions in the ice.

Be serious, because
The stone may have contempt

Loses or gains by this:
Respect the adversary,   20
Meet it with tools refined,
And thereby set your price.

Be hard of heart, because
The stone must leave your hand.
Although you liberate   25
Pure and expensive fires
Fit to enamour Shebas,
And because all you do
For too-familiar hands,
Keep your desire apart.   30
Love only what you do,
And not what you have done.

Be proud, when you have set
The final spoke of flame
In that prismatic wheel,   35
And nothing's left this day
Except to see the sun
Shine on the false and the true,
And know that Africa
Will yield you more to do.   40

1955

Necessities of Life

Piece by piece I seem
to re-enter the world: I first began

a small, fixed dot, still see
that old myself, dark-blue thumbtack

pushed into the scene,   5
a hard little head protruding

from the pointillist's buzz and bloom.
After a time the dot

begins to ooze. Certain heats.
melt it.
        Now I was hurriedly   10

blurring into ranges
of burnt red, burning green,

whole biographies swam up and
swallowed me like Jonah.

Jonah! I was Wittgenstein,   15
Mary Wollstonecraft, the soul

of Louis Jouvet, dead
in a blown-up photograph.

Till, wolfed almost to shreds,
I learned to make myself   20

unappetizing. Scaly as a dry bulb
thrown into a cellar

I used myself, let nothing use me.
Like being on a private dole,

sometimes more like kneading bricks in Egypt.   25
What life was there, was mine,

now and again to lay
one hand on a warm brick

and touch the sun's ghost
with economical joy,   30

now and again to name
over the bare necessities.

So much for those days. Soon
practice may make me middling-perfect, I'll

dare inhabit the world   35
trenchant in motion as an eel, solid

as a cabbage-head. I have invitations:
a curl of mist steams upward

from a field, visible as my breath,
houses along a road stand waiting   40

like old women knitting, breathless
to tell their tales.

1962   1966

Face to Face

Never to be lonely like that—
the Early American figure on the beach
in black coat and knee-breeches
scanning the didactic storm in privacy,

never to hear the prairie wolves 5
in their lunar hilarity
circling one's little all, one's claim
to be Law and Prophets

for all that lawlessness,
never to whet the appetite 10
weeks early, for a face, a hand
longed-for and dreaded—

How people used to meet!
starved, intense, the old
Christmas gifts saved up till spring, 15
and the old plain words,

and each with his God-given secret,
spelled out through months of snow and silence,
burning under the bleached scalp; behind dry lips
a loaded gun. 20

1965   1966

GARY SNYDER
(1930–   )

Gary Sherman Snyder was born in San Francisco and "raised up on a feeble sort of farm just north of Seattle." He graduated from Reed College in 1951 with a B.A. in anthropology and studied linguistics for a term at Indiana University before enrolling at the University of California, Berkeley (1953–1956), as a student of Japanese and Chinese culture. Recipient of a Zen Institute of America Award and a Bollingen Grant for Buddhist Studies, he spent much of his time after the mid-1950's living and writing in Japan.

One of the most successful of the poets of the Pacific Northwest, Snyder was influential in the West Coast Beat movement in the 1950's. His interest in Buddhism, in Oriental poetry and the culture of the American Indians, and in the rocks, trees, and rivers of man's physical environment helped to strengthen the beatific (as opposed to beaten-down) element in the work of such East Coast Beats as Jack Kerouac and Allen Ginsberg. In his life, as in his work, there has been implied a rejection of many of the values of western civilization. Although he was briefly a Lecturer in English at Berkeley (1964–1965), he has not pursued an academic career. His poems reflect his experiences as a logger, forest ranger, merchant seaman, and student of Zen, and are influenced as much by non-western poetic traditions as they are by the verse traditions of English. An advocate of open forms, he believes that "each poem grows from an energy-mind-field-dance, and has its own inner grain. To let it grow, to let it speak for itself, is a large part of the work of the poet."

Volumes of verse include *Riprap*, 1959; *Myths & Texts*, 1960; *Riprap and Cold Mountain Poems*, 1965; *Six Sections from Mountains and Rivers Without End*, 1965; *A Range of Poems*, 1966; *The Back Country*, 1967; and *Regarding Wave*, 1970. Literary criticism is *Earth House Hold*, 1969. A brief critical introduction is by Thom Gunn in Rosalie Murphy and James Vinson, eds., *Contemporary Poets of the English Language*, 1970.

The Late Snow & Lumber Strike of the Summer of Fifty-four

Whole towns shut down
        hitching the Coast road, only gypos
Running their beat trucks, no logs on
Gave me rides. Loggers all gone fishing
Chainsaws in a pool of cold oil   5
On back porches of ten thousand
Split-shake houses, quiet in summer rain.
Hitched north all of Washington
Crossing and re-crossing the passes
Blown like dust, no place to work.   10

Climbing the steep ridge below Shuksan
        clumps of pine
        float out the fog
No place to think or work
        drifting.   15

On Mt. Baker, alone
In a gully of blazing snow:
Cities down the long valleys west
Thinking of work, but here,
Burning in sun-glare   20
Below a wet cliff, above a frozen lake,
The whole Northwest on strike
Black burners cold,
The green-chain still,
I must turn and go back: 25
        caught on a snowpeak
        between heaven and earth
And stand in lines in Seattle.
Looking for work.

1959

this poem is for bear

"As for me I am a child of the god of the mountains."

A bear down under the cliff.
She is eating huckleberries.
They are ripe now
Soon it will snow, and she
Or maybe he, will crawl into a hole   5
And sleep. You can see
Huckleberries in bearshit if you
Look, this time of year
If I sneak up on the bear
It will grunt and run   10

The others had all gone down
From the blackberry brambles, but one girl
Spilled her basket, and was picking up her
Berries in the dark.
A tall man stood in the shadow, took her arm,   15
Led her to his home. He was a bear.
In a house under the mountain
She gave birth to slick dark children
With sharp teeth, and lived in the hollow
Mountain many years.   20
       snare a bear: call him out:
honey-eater
forest apple
light-foot
Old man in the fur coat, Bear! come out!   25
Die of your own choice!
Grandfather black-food!
          this girl married a bear
Who rules in the mountains, Bear!
          you have eaten many berries   30
          you have caught many fish
          you have frightened many people

Twelve species north of Mexico
Sucking their paws in the long winter
Tearing the high-strung caches down   35
Whining, crying, jacking off
(Odysseus was a bear)

Bear-cubs gnawing the soft tits
Teeth gritted, eyes screwed tight
         but she let them.   40

Til her brothers found the place
Chased her husband up the gorge

Cornered him in the rocks.
Song of the snared bear:
      "Give me my belt.   45
      "I am near death.
      "I came from the mountain caves
      "At the headwaters,
      "The small streams there
      "Are all dried up.   50

—I think I'll go hunt bears.
           "hunt bears?
Why shit Snyder,
You couldn't hit a bear in the ass
      with a handful of rice!"   55

                    1960

Not Leaving the House

When Kai is born
I quit going out

Hang around the kitchen—make cornbread
Let nobody in.
Mail is flat.   5
      Masa lies on her side, Kai sighs,
      Non washes and sweeps
We sit and watch
      Masa nurse, and drink green tea.

Navajo turquoise beads over the bed   10
A peacock tail feather at the head
A badger pelt from Nagano-ken
For a mattress; under the sheet;
A pot of yogurt setting
Under the blankets, at his feet.   15

Masa, Kai,
And Non, our friend
In the green garden light reflected in
Not leaving the house.
From dawn til late at night   20
      making a new world of ourselves
      around this life.

                    1970

SYLVIA PLATH

(1932–1963)

Born in Boston, Sylvia Plath was the precocious child of parents who were both teachers. Her father's German birth and his death when she was ten were to become obsessive in her poetry. At Smith College she performed brilliantly, graduating *summa cum laude* in 1955. A Fulbright Fellowship took her to Newnham College, Cambridge, where she received her M.A. in 1957. In England she married the British poet Ted Hughes and had a son and daughter. They came to this country, where she taught for a year at Smith College before the family went back to England to live.

Miss Plath's books of poetry are *The Colossus* (1960) and, posthumously, *Ariel* (1966), *Crossing The Water* (1971), and *Winter Trees* (1972). She began as a poet of great stylistic skill and somberness, but in *Ariel* she reached what Robert Lowell has called "appalling and permanent fulfillment." These are poems of intensity so great as to be painful. She committed suicide in 1963.

The volumes of poetry are named above. *The Bell Jar*, 1963, is a novel. Charles Newman edited *The Art of Sylvia Plath*, 1970.

Morning Song

Love set you going like a fat gold watch.
The midwife slapped your footsoles, and your bald cry
Took its place among the elements.

Our voices echo, magnifying your arrival. New statue.
In a drafty museum, your nakedness   5
Shadows our safety. We stand round blankly as walls.

I'm no more your mother
Than the cloud that distils a mirror to reflect its own slow
Effacement at the wind's hand.

All night your moth-breath   10
Flickers among the flat pink roses. I wake to listen:
A far sea moves in my ear.

One cry, and I stumble from bed, cow-heavy and floral
In my Victorian nightgown.
Your mouth opens clean as a cat's. The window square   15

Whitens and swallows its dull stars. And now you try
Your handful of notes;
The clear vowels rise like balloons.

1966

The Rival

If the moon smiled, she would resemble you.
You leave the same impression
Of something beautiful, but annihilating.
Both of you are great light borrowers.
Her O-mouth grieves at the world; yours is unaffected,   5

And your first gift is making stone out of everything.
I wake to a mausoleum; you are here,
Ticking your fingers on the marble table, looking for cigarettes,
Spiteful as a woman, but not so nervous,
And dying to say something unanswerable.   10

The moon, too, abases her subjects,
But in the daytime she is ridiculous.
Your dissatisfactions, on the other hand,
Arrive through the mailslot with loving regularity,
White and blank, expansive as carbon monoxide.   15

No day is safe from news of you,
Walking about in Africa maybe, but thinking of me.

1966

The Applicant

First, are you our sort of a person?
Do you wear
A glass eye, false teeth or a crutch,
A brace or a hook,
Rubber breasts or a rubber crotch,   5

Stitches to show something's missing? No, no? Then
How can we give you a thing?
Stop crying.
Open your hand.
Empty? Empty. Here is a hand   10

To fill it and willing
To bring teacups and roll away headaches
And do whatever you tell it.
Will you marry it?
It is guaranteed   15

To thumb shut your eyes at the end
And dissolve of sorrow.
We make new stock from the salt.
I notice you are stark naked.
How about this suit——   20

Black and stiff, but not a bad fit.
Will you marry it?

It is waterproof, shatterproof, proof
Against fire and bombs through the roof.
Believe me, they'll bury you in it.   25

Now your head, excuse me, is empty.
I have the ticket for that.
Come here, sweetie, out of the closet.
Well, what do you think of *that*?
Naked as paper to start   30

But in twenty-five years she'll be silver,
In fifty, gold.
A living doll, everywhere you look.
It can sew, it can cook,
It can talk, talk, talk.   35

It works, there is nothing wrong with it.
You have a hole, it's a poultice.
You have an eye, it's an image.
My boy, it's your last resort.
Will you marry it, marry it, marry it.   40

                                                  1966

Death & Co.

Two, of course there are two.
It seems perfectly natural now——
The one who never looks up, whose eyes are lidded
And balled, like Blake's,
Who exhibits   5

The birthmarks that are his trademark——
The scald scar of water,
The nude
Verdigris of the condor.
I am red meat. His beak   10

Claps sidewise: I am not his yet.
He tells me how badly I photograph.
He tells me how sweet
The babies look in their hospital
Icebox, a simple   15

Frill at the neck,
Then the flutings of their Ionian
Death-gowns,
Then two little feet.
He does not smile or smoke.   20

The other does that,
His hair long and plausive.

Bastard
Masturbating a glitter,
He wants to be loved.   25

 I do not stir.
The frost makes a flower,
The dew makes a star,
The dead bell,
The dead bell.   30

Somebody's done for.

                                                   1966

Daddy

You do not do, you do not do
Any more, black shoe
In which I have lived like a foot
For thirty years, poor and white,
Barely daring to breathe or Achoo.   5

Daddy, I have had to kill you.
You died before I had time——
Marble-heavy, a bag full of God,
Ghastly statue with one grey toe
Big as a Frisco seal   10

And a head in the freakish Atlantic
Where it pours bean green over blue
In the waters off beautiful Nauset.
I used to pray to recover you.
Ach, du.   15

In the German tongue, in the Polish town
Scraped flat by the roller
Of wars, wars, wars.
But the name of the town is common.
My Polack friend   20

Says there are a dozen or two.
So I never could tell where you
Put your foot, your root,
I never could talk to you.
The tongue stuck in my jaw.   25

It stuck in a barb wire snare.
Ich, ich, ich, ich,
I could hardly speak.
I thought every German was you.
And the language obscene   30

An engine, an engine
Chuffing me off like a Jew.
A Jew to Dachau, Auschwitz, Belsen.
I began to talk like a Jew.
I think I may well be a Jew.   35

The snows of the Tyrol, the clear beer of Vienna
Are not very pure or true.
With my gypsy ancestress and my weird luck
And my Taroc pack and my Taroc pack
I may be a bit of a Jew.   40

I have always been scared of *you*,
With your Luftwaffe, your gobbledygoo.
And your neat moustache
And your Aryan eye, bright blue.
Panzer-man, panzer-man, O You——   45

Not God but a swastika
So black no sky could squeak through.
Every woman adores a Fascist,
The boot in the face, the brute
Brute heart of a brute like you.   50

You stand at the blackboard, daddy,
In the picture I have of you,
A cleft in your chin instead of your foot
But no less a devil for that, no not
Any less the black man who   55

Bit my pretty red heart in two.
I was ten when they buried you.
At twenty I tried to die
And get back, back, back to you.
I thought even the bones would do.   60

But they pulled me out of the sack,
And they stuck me together with glue.
And then I knew what to do.
I made a model of you,
A man in black with a Meinkampf look   65

And a love of the rack and the screw.
And I said I do, I do.
So daddy, I'm finally through.
The black telephone's off at the root,
The voices just can't worm through.   70

If I've killed one man, I've killed two——
The vampire who said he was you
And drank my blood for a year,

Seven years, if you want to know.
Daddy, you can lie back now.   75

There's a stake in your fat black heart
And the villagers never liked you.
They are dancing and stamping on you.
They always *knew* it was you.
Daddy, daddy, you bastard, I'm through.   80

1966

Mystic

The air is a mill of hooks—
Questions without answer,
Glittering and drunk as flies
Whose kiss stings unbearably
In the fetid wombs of black air under pines in summer.   5

I remember
The dead smell of sun on wood cabins,
The stiffness of sails, the long salt winding sheets.
Once one has seen God, what is the remedy?
Once one has been seized up   10

Without a part left over,
Not a toe, not a finger, and used,
Used utterly, in the sun's conflagrations, the stains
That lengthen from ancient cathedrals
What is the remedy?   15

The pill of the Communion tablet,
The walking beside still water? Memory?
Or picking up the bright pieces
Of Christ in the faces of rodents,
The tame flower-nibblers, the ones   20

Whose hopes are so low they are comfortable—
The humpback in her small, washed cottage
Under the spokes of the clematis.
Is there no great love, only tenderness?
Does the sea   25

Remember the walker upon it?
Meaning leaks from the molecules.
The chimneys of the city breathe, the window sweats,
The children leap in their cots.
The sun blooms, it is a geranium.   30

The heart has not stopped.

1972

IMAMU AMIRI BARAKA

(1934–   )

Imamu Amiri Baraka (LeRoi Jones) was born in Newark, New Jersey, on October 7, 1934. Jones attended Rutgers University, Howard University, Columbia University, and The New School for Social Research. He earned his M.A. in German Literature. Of his own work, Jones has said, "'HOW YOU SOUND??' is what we recent fellows are up to. * * * MY POETRY is whatever I think I am." William Carlos Williams, Ezra Pound, and poet Charles Olson (a poet-teacher of the Black Mountain College group) have all influenced him. He has an active distaste for formalism, seeing much of it as "anaemic and fraught with incompetence and unreality." After having established a poetic reputation as LeRoi Jones, he adopted the name Imamu Amiri Baraka and became more militantly race conscious, active in politics as well as in literature. *The Toilet, Dutchman,* and *The Slave* treat black-white relationships explicitly and sometimes shockingly.

Collections of his poetry are *Preface to a Twenty Volume Suicide Note,* 1960; *The Dead Lecturer,* 1964; and *Black Magic: Poetry 1961–1967,* 1967. *The System of Dante's Hell,* 1965, is a novel. Short stories are collected in *Tales,* 1967. A study is *Blues People: Negro Music in America,* 1963. Prose is collected in *Black Music,* 1967; and *Raise Race Rays Raze,* 1971. For a full-length critical estimate, see Theodore R. Hudson, *From LeRoi Jones to Amiri Baraka: The Literary Works,* 1973.

In Memory of Radio

Who has ever stopped to think of the divinity of Lamont Cranston?
(Only Jack Kerouac, that I know of; & me.
The rest of you probably had on WCBS and Kate Smith,
Or something equally unattractive.)

What can I say?   5
It is better to have loved and lost
Than to put linoleum in your living rooms?

Am I a sage or something?
Mandrake's hypnotic gesture of the week?
(Remember, I do not have the healing powers of Oral Roberts . . .
I cannot, like F. J. Sheen, tell you how to get saved & *rich!*   10
I cannot even order you to gaschamber satori like Hitler or Goody
    Knight.

& Love is an evil word.
Turn it backwards/ see, see what I mean?
An evol word. & besides   15
who understands it?
I certainly wouldn't like to go out on that kind of limb.

Saturday mornings we listened to *Red Lantern* & his undersea folk.

At 11, *Let's Pretend/* & we did/ & I, the poet, still do, Thank
  God!

What was it he used to say (after the transformation, when he
  was safe   20
& invisible, & the unbelievers couldn't throw stones?) "Heh, Heh,
  Heh,
Who knows what evil lurks in the hearts of men? The Shadow
  knows!"

O, yes he does
O, yes he does
An evil word it is,   25
This love.

                                                      1964

An Agony. As Now.

I am inside someone
who hates me. I look
out from his eyes. Smell
what fouled tunes come in
to his breath. Love his   5
wretched women.

Slits in the metal, for sun. Where
my eyes sit turning, at the cool air
the glance of light, or hard flesh
rubbed against me, a woman, a man,   10
without shadow, or voice, or meaning.

This is the enclosure (flesh,
where innocence is a weapon. An
abstraction. Touch. (Not mine.
Or yours, if you are the soul I had   15
and abandoned when I was blind and had
my enemies carry me as a dead man
(if he is beautiful, or pitied.

It can be pain. (As now, as all his
flesh hurts me.) It can be that. Or   20
pain. As when she ran from me into
that forest.
          Or pain, the mind
silver spiraled whirled against the
sun, higher than even old men thought
God would be. Or pain. And the other. The   25
yes. (Inside his books, his fingers. They
are withered yellow flowers and were never
beautiful.) The yes. You will, lost soul, say

'beauty.' Beauty, practiced, as the tree. The
slow river. A white sun in its wet sentences. 30

Or, the cold men in their gale. Ecstasy. Flesh
or soul. The yes. (Their robes blown. Their bowls
empty. They chant at my heels, not at yours.) Flesh
or soul, as corrupt. Where the answer moves too quickly.
Where the God is a self, after all.) 35

Cold air blown through narrow blind eyes. Flesh,
white hot metal. Glows as the day with its sun.
It is a human love. I live inside. A bony skeleton
you recognize as words or simple feeling.

But it has no feeling. As the metal, is hot, it is not, 40
given to love.

It burns the thing
inside it. And that thing
screams.

1964

Recent Fiction

WILLIAM H. GASS
(1924–   )

"I think of myself as a writer of prose rather than a novelist, critic, or story-teller, and I am principally interested in the problems of style," writes Gass. "My fictions are, by and large, experimental constructions." He might as well have added that his essays, too, are experimental constructions. A professional philosopher deeply concerned with the relationships between art and life, between words and things, he writes exploratory fiction that probes the uncertain boundaries between the conventional prose narration and the discursive essay. A professional novelist, literary critic, and short story writer, he writes philosophical essays that strive toward the circular, self-contained truths of fiction.

Born William Howard Gass in Fargo, North Dakota, he had begun college at Kenyon and had briefly attended Ohio Wesleyan before serving as an ensign in the Navy in World War II. Returning to graduate from Kenyon in 1947, he attended graduate school at Cornell University for three years before accepting a position as a philosophy instructor at the College of Wooster in Ohio. Completion of his Cornell Ph.D. in 1954 led to fourteen years teaching philosophy at Purdue. In 1969 he became Professor of Philosophy at Washington University in St. Louis.

Gass's conviction that the novelist has much to learn from the philosopher is based at least partially on his insistence that "novelizing is a comparatively new, unpolished thing." His widely admired but uneven first novel, *Omensetter's Luck* (1966), displays a concern for verbal texture, sometimes at the expense of the narrative, that looks forward to the almost perfectly realized achievement of the title story of *In the Heart of the Heart of the Country and Other Stories* (1968). In publishing his third work of fiction, *Willie Masters' Lonesome Wife* (1971), as an "essay-novella" he emphasized his continuing search for a satisfactory fictional form. The essays and reviews collected in *Fiction and the Figures of Life* (1971) record the intellectual developments that parallel his fictional experiments.

Gass's books to date are named above. Sections from a novel-in-prog- ress have been appearing in literary journals.

In the Heart of the Heart of the Country

A *Place*

So I have sailed the seas and come . . .

to B . . .

a small town fastened to a field in Indiana. Twice there have been twelve hundred people here to answer to the census. The town is outstandingly neat and shady, and always puts its best side to the highway. On one lawn there's even a wood or plastic iron deer.

You can reach us by crossing a creek. In the spring the lawns are green, the forsythia is singing, and even the railroad that guts the town has straight bright rails which hum when the train is coming, and the train itself has a welcome horning sound.

Down the back streets the asphalt crumbles into gravel. There's Westbrook's, with the geraniums, Horsefall's, Mott's. The side- walk shatters. Gravel dust rises like breath behind the wagons. And I am in retirement from love.

Weather

In the Midwest, around the lower Lakes, the sky in the winter is heavy and close, and it is a rare day, a day to remark on, when the sky lifts and allows the heart up. I am keeping count, and as I write this page, it is eleven days since I have seen the sun.

My House

There's a row of headless maples behind my house, cut to free the passage of electric wires. High stumps, ten feet tall, remain, and I climb these like a boy to watch the country sail away from me. They are ordinary fields, a little more uneven than they should be, since in the spring they puddle. The topsoil's thin, but only mod- erately stony. Corn is grown one year, soybeans another. At dusk starlings darken the single tree—a larch—which stands in the mid- dle. When the sky moves, fields move under it. I feel, on my perch, that I've lost my years. It's as though I were living at last in my eyes, as I have always dreamed of doing, and I think then I know why I've come here: to see, and so to go out against new things—oh god how easily—like air in a breeze. It's true there are moments—foolish moments, ecstasy on a tree stump—when I'm all but gone, scattered I like to think like seed, for I'm the sort now in the fool's position of having love left over which I'd like to lose; what good is it now to me, candy ungiven after Halloween?

A Person

There are vacant lots on either side of Billy Holsclaw's house. As the weather improves, they fill with hollyhocks. From spring through fall, Billy collects coal and wood and puts the lumps and pieces in piles near his door, for keeping warm is his one work. I see him most often on mild days sitting on his doorsill in the sun. I notice he's squinting a little, which is perhaps the reason he doesn't cackle as I pass. His house is the size of a single garage, and very old. It shed its paint with its youth, and its boards are a warped and weathered gray. So is Billy. He wears a short lumpy faded black coat when it's cold, otherwise he always goes about in the same loose, grease-spotted shirt and trousers. I suspect his galluses were yellow once, when they were new.

Wires

These wires offend me. Three trees were maimed on their account, and now these wires deface the sky. They cross like a fence in front of me, enclosing the crows with the clouds. I can't reach in, but like a stick, I throw my feelings over. What is it that offends me? I am on my stump, I've built a platform there and the wires prevent my going out. The cut trees, the black wires, all the beyond birds therefore anger me. When I've wormed through a fence to reach a meadow, do I ever feel the same about the field?

The Church

The church has a steeple like the hat of a witch, and five birds, all doves, perch in its gutters.

My House

Leaves move in the windows. I cannot tell you yet how beautiful it is, what it means. But they do move. They move in the glass.

Politics

. . for all those not in love.

I've heard Batista described as a Mason. A farmer who'd seen him in Miami made this claim. He's as nice a fellow as you'd ever want to meet. Of Castro, of course, no one speaks.

For all those not in love there's law: to rule . . . to regulate . . . to rectify. I cannot write the poetry of such proposals, the poetry of politics, though sometimes—often—always now—I am in that uneasy peace of equal powers which makes a State; then I communicate by passing papers, proclamations, orders, through my bowels. Yet I was not a State with you, nor were we both together any Indiana. A squad of Pershing Rifles at the moment, I make myself Right Face! Legislation packs the screw of my intestines. Well, king of the classroom's king of the hill. You used to waddle when you walked because my sperm between your legs was draining to a towel. Teacher, poet, folded lover—like the politician, like those drunkards, ill, or those who faucet-off while pissing heartily to preach upon the force and fullness of that stream, or pause from vomiting to praise the purity and passion of their puke—I chant, I beg, I orate, I command, I sing—

> Come back to Indiana—not too late!
> (Or will you be a ranger to the end?)
> Good-bye . . . Good-bye . . . oh, I shall always wait
> You, Larry, traveler—
> > > stranger,
> > > > son,
> > > > > —my friend—

my little girl, my poem by heart, my self, my childhood.

But I've heard Batista described as a Mason. That dries up my pity, melts my hate. Back from the garage where I have overheard it, I slap the mended fender of my car to laugh, and listen to the metal stinging tartly in my hand.

People

Their hair in curlers and their heads wrapped in loud scarves, young mothers, fattish in trousers, lounge about in the speedwash, smoking cigarettes, eating candy, drinking pop, thumbing magazines, and screaming at their children above the whir and rumble of the machines.

At the bank a young man freshly pressed is letting himself in with a key. Along the street, delicately teetering, many grandfathers move in a dream. During the murderous heat of summer, they perch on window ledges, their feet dangling just inside the narrow shelf of shade the store has made, staring steadily into the street. Where their consciousness has gone I can't say. It's not in the eyes. Perhaps it's diffuse, all temperature and skin, like an infant's, though more mild. Near the corner there are several large overalled men employed in standing. A truck turns to be weighed on the scales at the Feed and Grain. Images drift on the drugstore window. The wind has blown the smell of cattle into town. Our eyes have been driven in like the eyes of the old men. And there's no one to have mercy on us.

Vital Data

There are two restaurants here and a tearoom. two bars. one bank, three barbers, one with a green shade with which he blinds his window. two groceries. a dealer in Fords. one drug, one hardware, and one appliance store. several that sell feed, grain, and farm equipment. an antique shop. a poolroom. a laundromat. three doctors. a dentist. a plumber. a vet. a funeral home in elegant repair the color of a buttercup. numerous beauty parlors which open and shut like night-blooming plants. a tiny dime and department store of no width but several floors. a hutch, homemade, where you can order, after lying down or squirming in, furniture that's been fashioned from bent lengths of stainless tubing, glowing plastic, metallic thread, and clear shellac. an American Legion Post and a root beer stand. little agencies for this and that: cosmetics, brushes, insurance, greeting cards and garden produce—anything —sample shoes—which do their business out of hats and satchels, over coffee cups and dissolving sugar. a factory for making paper sacks and pasteboard boxes that's lodged in an old brick building bearing the legend OPERA HOUSE, still faintly golden, on its roof. a library given by Carnegie. a post office. a school. a railroad station. fire station. lumberyard. telephone company. welding shop. garage . . . . and spotted through the town from one end to the other in a line along the highway, gas stations to the number five.

Education

In 1833, Colin Goodykoontz, an itinerant preacher with a name from a fairytale, summed up the situation in one Indiana town this way:

Ignorance and her squalid brood. A universal dearth of intellect. Total abstinence from literature is very generally practiced. . . . There is not a scholar in grammar or geography, or a *teacher capable* of *instructing* in them, to my knowledge. . . . Others are supplied a few months of the year with most antiquated & unreasonable forms of teaching reading, writing & cyphering. . . . Need I stop to remind you of the host of loathsome reptiles such a stagnant pool is fitted to breed! Croaking jealousy; bloated bigotry; coiling suspicion; wormish blindness; crocodile malice!

Things have changed since then, but in none of the respects mentioned.

Business

One side section of street is blocked off with sawhorses. Hard, thin, bitter men in blue jeans, cowboy boots and hats, untruck a dinky carnival. The merchants are promoting themselves. There will be free rides, raucous music, parades and coneys, pop, popcorn, candy, cones, awards and drawings, with all you can endure of pinch, push, bawl, shove, shout, scream, shriek, and bellow. Children pedal past on decorated bicycles, their wheels a blur of color, streaming crinkled paper and excited dogs. A little later there's a pet show for a prize—dogs, cats, birds, sheep, ponies, goats—none of which wins. The whirlabouts whirl about. The Ferris wheel climbs dizzily into the sky as far as a tall man on tiptoe might be persuaded to reach, and the irritated operators measure the height and weight of every child with sour eyes to see if they are safe for the machines. An electrical megaphone repeatedly trumpets the names of the generous sponsors. The following day they do not allow the refuse to remain long in the street.

My House, This Place and Body

I have met with some mischance, wings withering, as Plato says obscurely, and across the breadth of Ohio, like heaven on a table, I've fallen as far as the poet, to the sixth sort of body, this house in B, in Indiana, with its blue and gray bewitching windows, holy magical insides. Great thick evergreens protect its entry. And I live *in*.

Lost in the corn rows, I remember feeling just another stalk, and thus this country takes me over in the way I occupy myself when I am well . . . completely—to the edge of both my house and body. No one notices, when they walk by, that I am brimming in the doorways. My house, this place and body, I've come in mourning to be born in. To anybody else it's pretty silly: love. Why should I feel a loss? How am I bereft? She was never mine; she was a fiction, always a golden tomgirl, barefoot, with an adolescent's slouch and a boy's taste for sports and fishing, a figure out of Twain, or worse, in Riley. Age cannot be kind.

There's little hand-in-hand here . . . not in B. No one touches except in rage. Occasionally girls will twine their arms about each other and lurch along, school out, toward home and play. I dreamed my lips would drift down your back like a skiff on a river. I'd follow a vein with the point of my finger, hold your bare feet in my naked hands.

The Same Person

Billy Holsclaw lives alone—how alone it is impossible to fathom. In the post office he talks greedily to me about the weather. His head bobs on a wild flood of words, and I take this violence to be a measure of his eagerness for speech. He badly needs a shave, coal dust has layered his face, he spits when he speaks, and his fingers pick at his tatters. He wobbles out in the wind when I leave him, a paper sack mashed in the fold of his arm, the leaves blowing past him, and our encounter drives me sadly home to poetry—where there's no answer. Billy closes his door and carries coal or wood to his fire and closes his eyes, and there's simply no way of knowing how lonely and empty he is or whether he's as vacant and barren and loveless as the rest of us are—here in the heart of the country.

Weather

For we're always out of luck here. That's just how it is—for instance in the winter. The sides of the buildings, the roofs, the limbs of the trees are gray. Streets, sidewalks, faces, feelings—they are gray. Speech is gray, and the grass where it shows. Every flank and front, each top is gray. Everything is gray: hair, eyes, window glass, the hawkers' bills and touters' posters, lips, teeth poles and metal signs—they're gray, quite gray. Cars are gray. Boots, shoes, suits, hats, gloves are gray. Horses, sheep, and cows, cats killed in the road, squirrels in the same way, sparrows, doves, and pigeons, all are gray, everything is gray, and everyone is out of luck who lives here.

A similar haze turns the summer sky milky, and the air muffles your head and shoulders like a sweater you've got caught in. In the summer light, too, the sky darkens a moment when you open your eyes. The heat is pure distraction. Steeped in our fluids, miserable in the folds of our bodies, we can scarcely think of anything but our sticky parts. Hot cyclonic winds and storms of dust crisscross the country. In many places, given an indifferent push, the wind will still coast for miles, gathering resource and edge as it goes, cunning and force. According to the season, paper, leaves, field litter, seeds, snow, fill up the fences. Sometimes I think the land is flat because the winds have leveled it, they blow so constantly. In any case, a gale can grow in a field of corn that's as hot as a draft from hell, and to receive it is one of the most dismaying experiences of this life, though the smart of the same wind in winter is more humiliating, and in that sense even worse. But in the spring it rains as well, and the trees fill with ice.

Place

Many small Midwestern towns are nothing more than rural slums, and this community could easily become one. Principally during the first decade of the century, though there were many earlier instances, well-to-do farmers moved to town and built fine homes to contain them in their retirement. Others desired a more social life, and so lived in, driving to their fields like storekeepers to their businesses. These houses are now dying like the bereaved who inhabit them; they are slowly losing their senses—deafness, blindness, forgetfulness, mumbling, an insecure gait, an uncontrollable trembling has overcome them. Some kind of Northern Snopes will occupy them next: large-familied, Catholic, Democratic, scrambling, vigorous, poor; and since the parents will work in larger, nearby towns, the children will be loosed upon themselves and upon the hapless neighbors much as the fabulous Khan loosed his legendary horde. These Snopes will undertake makeshift repairs with materials that other people have thrown away; paint halfway round their house, then quit; almost certainly maintain an ugly loud cantankerous dog and underfeed a pair of cats to keep the rodents down. They will collect piles of possibly useful junk in the back yard, park their cars in the front, live largely leaning over engines, give not a hoot for the land, the old community, the hallowed ways, the established clans. Weakening widow ladies have already begun to hire large rude youths from families such as these to rake and mow and tidy the grounds they will inherit.

People

In the cinders at the station boys sit smoking steadily in darkened cars, their arms bent out the windows, white shirts glowing behind the glass. Nine o'clock is the best time. They sit in a line facing the highway—two or three or four of them—idling their engines. As you walk by a machine may growl at you or a pair of headlights flare up briefly. In a moment one will pull out, spinning cinders behind it, to stalk impatiently up and down the dark streets or roar half a mile into the country before returning to its place in line and pulling up.

My House, My Cat, My Company

I must organize myself. I must, as they say, pull myself together, dump this cat from my lap, stir—yes, resolve, move, do. But do what? My will is like the rosy dustlike light in this room: soft, diffuse, and gently comforting. It lets me do . . . anything . . . nothing. My ears hear what they happen to; I eat what's put before me; my eyes see what blunders into them; my thoughts are not thoughts, they are dreams. I'm empty or I'm full . . . depending; and I cannot choose. I sink my claws in Tick's fur and scratch the bones of his back until his rear rises amorously. Mr. Tick, I murmur, I must organize myself. I must pull myself together. And Mr. Tick rolls over on his belly, all ooze.

I spill Mr. Tick when I've rubbed his stomach. Shoo. He steps away slowly, his long tail rhyming with his paws. How beautifully he moves, I think; how beautifully, like you, he commands his loving, how beautifully he accepts. So I rise and wander from room to room, up and down, gazing through most of my forty-one windows. How well this house receives its loving too. Let out like Mr. Tick, my eyes sink in the shrubbery. I am not here; I've passed the glass, passed second-story spaces, flown by branches, brilliant berries, to the ground, grass high in seed and leafage every season; and it is the same as when I passed above you in my aged, ardent body; it's, in short, a kind of love; and I am learning to restore myself, my house, my body, by paying court to gardens, cats, and running water, and with neighbors keeping company.

Mrs. Desmond is my right-hand friend; she's eighty-five. A thin white mist of hair, fine and tangled, manifests the climate of her mind. She is habitually suspicious, fretful, nervous. Burglars break in at noon. Children trespass. Even now they are shaking the pear tree, stealing rhubarb, denting lawn. Flies caught in the screens and numbed by frost awake in the heat to buzz and scrape the metal cloth and frighten her, though she is deaf to me, and consequently cannot hear them. Boards creak, the wind whistles across the chimney mouth, drafts cruise like fish through the hollow rooms. It is herself she hears, her own flesh failing, for only death will preserve her from those daily chores she climbs like stairs, and all that anxious waiting. Is it now, she wonders. No? Then: is it now?

We do not converse. She visits me to talk. My task to murmur. She talks about her grandsons, her daughter who lives in Delphi, her sister or her husband—both gone—obscure friends—dead—obscurer aunts and uncles—lost—ancient neighbors, members of her church or of her clubs—passed or passing on; and in this way she brings the ends of her life together with a terrifying rush: she is a girl, a wife, a mother, widow, all at once. All at once—appalling—but I believe it; I wince in expectation of the clap. Her talk's a fence—a shade drawn, window fastened, door that's locked—for no one dies taking tea in a kitchen; and as her years compress and begin to jumble, I really believe in the brevity of life; I sweat in my wonder; death is the dog down the street, the angry gander, bedroom spider, goblin who's come to get her; and it occurs to me that in my listening posture I'm the boy who suffered the winds of my grandfather with an exactly similar politeness, that I am, right now, all my ages, out in elbows, as angular as badly stacked cards. Thus was I, when I loved you, every man I could be, youth and child—far from enough—and you, so strangely ambiguous a being, met me, heart for spade, play after play, the whole run of our suits.

Mr. Tick, you do me honor. You not only lie in my lap, but you remain alive there, coiled like a fetus. Through your deep nap, I feel you hum. You are, and are not, a machine. You are alive, alive exactly, and it means nothing to you—much to me. You are a cat—you cannot understand—you are a cat so easily. Your nature is not something you must rise to. You, not I, live in: in house, in skin, in shrubbery. Yes. I think I shall hat my head with a steeple;

turn church; devour people. Mr. Tick, though, has a tail he can twitch, he need not fly his Fancy. Claws, not metrical schema, poetry his paws; while smoothing . . . smoothing . . . smoothing roughly, his tongue laps its neatness. O Mr. Tick, I know you; you are an electrical penis. Go on now, shoo. Mrs. Desmond doesn't like you. She thinks you will tangle yourself in her legs and she will fall. You murder her birds, she knows, and walk upon her roof with death in your jaws. I must gather myself together for a bound. What age is it I'm at right now, I wonder. The heart, don't they always say, keeps the true time. Mrs. Desmond is knocking. Faintly, you'd think, but she pounds. She's brought me a cucumber. I believe she believes I'm a woman. Come in, Mrs. Desmond, thank you, be my company, it looks lovely, and have tea. I'll slice it, crisp, with cream, for luncheon, each slice as thin as me.

Politics

O all ye isolate and separate powers, Sing! Sing, and sing in such a way that from a distance it will seem a harmony, a Strindberg play, a friendship ring . . . so happy—happy, happy, happy—as here we go hand in handling, up and down. Our union was a singing, though we were silent in the songs we sang like single notes are silent in a symphony. In no sense sober, we barbershopped together and never heard the discords in our music or saw ourselves as dirty, cheap, or silly. Yet cats have worn out better shoes than those thrown through our love songs at us. Hush. Be patient—prudent—politic. Still, Cleveland killed you, Mr. Crane. Were you not politic enough and fond of being beaten? Like a piece of sewage, the city shat you from its stern three hundred miles from history—beyond the loving reach of sailors. Well, I'm not a poet who puts Paris to his temple in his youth to blow himself from Idaho, or—fancy that—Missouri. My god, I said, this is my country, but must my country go so far as Terre Haute or Whiting, go so far as Gary?

When the Russians first announced the launching of their satellite, many people naturally refused to believe them. Later others were outraged that they had sent a dog around the earth. I wouldn't want to take that mutt from out that metal flying thing if he's still living when he lands, our own dog catcher said; anybody knows you shut a dog up by himself to toss around the first thing he'll be setting on to do you let him out is bite somebody.

This Midwest. A dissonance of parts and people, we are a consonance of Towns. Like a man grown fat in everything but heart, we overlabor; our outlook never really urban, never rural either, we enlarge and linger at the same time, as Alice both changed and remained in her story. You are blond. I put my hand upon your belly; feel it tremble from my trembling. We always drive large cars in my section of the country. How could you be a comfort to me now?

More Vital Data

The town is exactly fifty houses, trailers, stores, and miscellaneous buildings long, but in places no streets deep. It takes on width as you drive south, always adding to the east. Most of the dwellings are fairly spacious farm houses in the customary white, with wide wraparound porches and tall narrow windows, though there are many of the grander kind—fretted, scalloped, turreted, and decorated with clapboards set at angles or on end, with stained-glass windows at the stair landings and lots of wrought iron full of fancy curls—and a few of these look like castles in their rarer brick. Old stables serve as garages now, and the lots are large to contain them and the vegetable and flower gardens which, ultimately, widows plant and weed and then entirely disappear in. The shade is ample, the grass is good, the sky a glorious fall violet; the apple trees are heavy and red, the roads are calm and empty; corn has sifted from the chains of tractored wagons to speckle the streets with gold and with the russet fragments of the cob, and a man would be a fool who wanted, blessed with this, to live anywhere else in the world.

Education

Buses like great orange animals move through the early light to school. There the children will be taught to read and warned against Communism. By Miss Janet Jakes. That's not her name. Her name is Helen something—Scott or James. A teacher twenty years. She's now worn fine and smooth, and has a face, Wilfred says, like a mail-order ax. Her voice is hoarse, and she has a cough. For she screams abuse. The children stare, their faces blank. This is the thirteenth week. They are used to it. You will all, she shouts, you will all draw pictures of me. No. She is a Mrs.—someone's missus. And in silence they set to work while Miss Jakes jabs hairpins in her hair. Wilfred says an ax, but she has those rimless tinted glasses, graying hair, an almost dimpled chin. I must concentrate. I must stop making up things. I must give myself to life; let it mold me: that's what they say in *Wisdom's Monthly Digest* every day. Enough, enough—you've been at it long enough; and the children rise formally a row at a time to present their work to her desk. No, she wears rims; it's her chin that's dimpleless. Well, it will take more than a tablespoon of features to sweeten that face. So she grimly shuffles their sheets, examines her reflection crayoned on them. I would not dare . . . allow a child . . . to put a line around me. Though now and then she smiles like a nick in the blade, in the end these drawings depress her. I could not bear it—how can she ask?—that anyone . . . draw me. Her anger's lit. That's why she does it: flame. There go her eyes; the pink in her glasses brightens, dims. She is a pumpkin, and her rage is breathing like the candle in. No, she shouts, no—the cartoon trembling—no, John Mauck, John Stewart Mauck, this will not do. The picture flutters from her fingers. You've made me too muscular.

I work on my poetry. I remember my friends, associates, my students, by their names. Their names are Maypop, Dormouse, Upsydaisy. Their names are Gladiolus, Callow Bladder, Prince and Princess Oleo, Hieronymus, Cardinal Mummum, Mr. Fitchew, The Silken Howdah, Spot. Sometimes you're Tom Sawyer, Huckleberry Finn; it is perpetually summer; your buttocks are my pillow; we are adrift on a raft; your back is our river. Sometimes you are Major Barbara, sometimes a goddess who kills men in battle, sometimes you are soft like a shower of water; you are bread in my mouth.

I do not work on my poetry. I forget my friends, associates, my students, and their names: Gramophone, Blowgun, Pickle, Serenade . . . Marge the Barge, Arena, Uberhaupt . . . Doctor Dildoe, The Fog Machine. For I am now in B, in Indiana: out of job and out of patience, out of love and time and money, out of bread and out of body, in a temper, Mrs. Desmond, out of tea. So shut your fist up, bitch, you bag of death; go bang another door; go die, my dearie. Die, life-deaf old lady. Spill your breath. Fall over like a frozen board. Gray hair grows from the nose of your mind. You are a skull already—*memento mori*—the foreskin retracts from your teeth. Will your plastic gums last longer than your bones, and color their grinning? And is your twot still hazel-hairy, or are you bald as a ditch? . . . bitch . . . . . bitch . . . . bitch. I wanted to be famous, but you bring me age—my emptiness. Was it *that* which I thought would balloon me above the rest? Love? where are you? . . . love me. I want to rise so high, I said, that when I shit I won't miss anybody.

Business

For most people, business is poor. Nearby cities have siphoned off all but a neighborhood trade. Except for feed and grain and farm supplies, you stand a chance to sell only what one runs out to buy. Chevrolet has quit, and Frigidaire. A locker plant has left its after-image. The lumberyard has been, so far, six months about its going. Gas stations change hands clumsily, a restaurant becomes available, a grocery closes. One day they came and knocked the cornices from the watch repair and pasted campaign posters on the windows. Torn across, by now, by boys, they urge you still to vote for half an orange beblazoned man who as a whole one failed two years ago to win at his election. Everywhere, in this manner, the past speaks, and it mostly speaks of failure. The empty stores, the old signs and dusty fixtures, the debris in alleys, the flaking paint and rusty gutters, the heavy locks and sagging boards: they say the same disagreeable things. What do the sightless windows see, I wonder, when the sun throws a passerby against them? Here a stair unfolds toward the street—dark, rickety, and treacherous—and I always feel, as I pass it, that if I just went carefully up and turned the corner at the landing, I would find myself out of the world. But I've never had the courage.

That Same Person

The weeds catch up with Billy. In pursuit of the hollyhocks, they rise in coarse clumps all around the front of his house. Billy has to stamp down a circle by his door like a dog or cat does turning round to nest up, they're so thick. What particularly troubles me is that winter will find the weeds still standing stiff and tindery to take the sparks which Billy's little mortarless chimney spouts. It's true that fires are fun here. The town whistle, which otherwise only blows for noon (and there's no noon on Sunday), signals the direction of the fire by the length and number of its blasts, the volunteer firemen rush past in their cars and trucks, houses empty their owners along the street every time like an illustration in a children's book. There are many bikes, too, and barking dogs, and sometimes—halleluiah—the fire's right here in town—a vacant lot of weeds and stubble flaming up. But I'd rather it weren't Billy or Billy's lot or house. Quite selfishly I want him to remain the way he is—counting his sticks and logs, sitting on his sill in the soft early sun—though I'm not sure what his presence means to me . . . or to anyone. Nevertheless, I keep wondering whether, given time, I might not someday find a figure in our language which would serve him faithfully, and furnish his poverty and loneliness richly out.

Wires

Where sparrows sit like fists. Doves fly the steeple. In mist the wires change perspective, rise and twist. If they led to you, I would know what they were. Thoughts passing often, like the starlings who flock these fields at evening to sleep in the trees beyond, would form a family of paths like this; they'd foot down the natural height of air to just about a bird's perch. But they do not lead to you.

> Of whose beauty it was sung
> She shall make the old man young.

They fasten me.

If I walked straight on, in my present mood, I would reach the Wabash. It's not a mood in which I'd choose to conjure you. Similes dangle like baubles from me. This time of year the river is slow and shallow, the clay banks crack in the sun, weeds surprise the sandbars. The air is moist and I am sweating. It's impossible to rhyme in this dust. Everything—sky, the cornfield, stump, wild daisies, my old clothes and pressless feelings—seem fabricated for installment purchase. Yes. Christ. I am suffering a summer Christmas; and I cannot walk under the wires. The sparrows scatter like handfuls of gravel. Really, wires are voices in thin strips. They are words wound in cables. Bars of connection.

Weather

I would rather it were the weather that was to blame for what I am and what my friends and neighbors are—we who live here in the heart of the country. Better the weather, the wind, the pale dying snow . . . the snow—why not the snow? There's never much really, not around the lower Lakes anyway, not enough to boast about, not enough to be useful. My father tells how the snow in the Dakotas would sweep to the roofs of the barns in the old days, and he and his friends could sled on the crust that would form because the snow was so fiercely driven. In Bemidji trees have been known to explode. That would be something—if the trees in Davenport or Francisville or Carbondale or Niles were to go blam some winter—blam! blam! blam! all the way down the gray, cindery, snow-sick streets.

A cold fall rain is blackening the trees or the air is like lilac and full of parachuting seeds. Who cares to live in any season but his own? Still I suspect the secret's in this snow, the secret of our sickness, if we could only diagnose it, for we are all dying like the elms in Urbana. This snow—like our skin it covers the country. Later dust will do it. Right now—snow. Mud presently. But it is snow without any laughter in it, a pale gray pudding thinly spread on stiff toast, and if that seems a strange description, it's accurate all the same. Of course soot blackens everything, but apart from that, we are never sufficiently cold here. The flakes as they come, alive and burning, we cannot retain, for if our temperatures fall, they rise promptly again, just as, in the summer, they bob about in the same feckless way. Suppose though . . . suppose they were to rise some August, climb and rise, and then hang in the hundreds like a hawk through December, what a desert we could make of ourselves—from Chicago to Cairo, from Hammond to Columbus —what beautiful Death Valleys.

Place

I would rather it were the weather. It drives us in upon ourselves —an unlucky fate. Of course there is enough to stir our wonder anywhere; there's enough to love, anywhere, if one is strong enough, if one is diligent enough, if one is perceptive, patient, kind enough—whatever it takes; and surely it's better to live in the country, to live on a prairie by a drawing of rivers, in Iowa or Illinois or Indiana, say, than in any city, in any stinking fog of human beings, in any blooming orchard of machines. It ought to be. The cities are swollen and poisonous with people. It ought to be better. Man has never been a fit environment for man—for rats, maybe, rats do nicely, or for dogs or cats and the household beetle.

And how long the street is, nowadays. These endless walls are fallen to keep back the tides of earth. Brick could be beautiful but we have covered it gradually with gray industrial vomits. Age does not make concrete genial, and asphalt is always—like America— twenty-one, until it breaks up in crumbs like stale cake. The brick, the asphalt, the concrete, the dancing signs and garish posters, the feed and excrement of the automobile, the litter of its inhabitants: they compose, they decorate, they line our streets, and there is nowhere, nowadays, our streets can't reach.

A man in the city has no natural thing by which to measure himself. His parks are potted plants. Nothing can live and remain free where he resides but the pigeon, starling, sparrow, spider, cockroach, mouse, moth, fly and weed, and he laments the existence of even these and makes his plans to poison them. The zoo? There *is* the zoo. Through its bars the city man stares at the great cats and dully sucks his ice. Living, alas, among men and their marvels, the city man supposes that his happiness depends on establishing, somehow, a special kind of harmonious accord with others. The novelists of the city, of slums and crowds, they call it love—and break their pens.

Wordsworth feared the accumulation of men in cities. He foresaw their "degrading thirst after outrageous stimulation," and some of their hunger for love. Living in a city, among so many, dwelling in the heat and tumult of incessant movement, a man's affairs are touch and go—that's all. It's not surprising that the novelists of the slums, the cities, and the crowds, should find that sex is but a scratch to ease a tickle, that we're most human when we're sitting on the john, and that the justest image of our life is in full passage through the plumbing.

> That man, immur'd in cities, still retains
> His inborn inextinguishable thirst
> Of rural scenes, compensating his loss
> By supplemental shifts, the best he may.

Come into the country, then. The air nimbly and sweetly recommends itself unto our gentle senses. Here, growling tractors tear the earth. Dust roils up behind them. Drivers sit jouncing under bright umbrellas. They wear refrigerated hats and steer by looking at the tracks they've cut behind them, their transistors blaring. Close to the land, are they? good companions to the soil? Tell me: do they live in harmony with the alternating seasons?

It's a lie of old poetry. The modern husbandman uses chemicals from cylinders and sacks, spike-ball-and-claw machines, metal sheds, and cost accounting. Nature in the old sense does not matter. It does not exist. Our farmer's only mystical attachment is to parity. And if he does not realize that cows and corn are simply different kinds of chemical engine, he cannot expect to make a go of it.

It isn't necessary to suppose our cows have feelings; our neighbor hasn't as many as he used to have either; but think of it this way a moment, you can correct for the human imputations later: how would it feel to nurse those strange tentacled calves with their rubber, glass, and metal lips, their stainless eyes?

People

Aunt Pet's still able to drive her car—a high square Ford—even though she walks with difficulty and a stout stick. She has a watery gaze, a smooth plump face despite her age, and jet black hair in a bun. She has the slowest smile of anyone I ever saw, but she hates dogs, and not very long ago cracked the back of one she cornered in her garden. To prove her vigor she will tell you this, her smile breaking gently while she raises the knob of her stick to the level of your eyes.

House, My Breath and Window

My window is a grave, and all that lies within it's dead. No snow is falling. There's no haze. It is not still, not silent. Its images are not an animal that waits, for movement is no demonstration. I have seen the sea slack, life bubble through a body without a trace, its spheres impervious as soda's. Downwound, the whore at wagtag clicks and clacks. Leaves wiggle. Grass sways. A bird chirps, pecks the ground. An auto wheel in penning circles keeps its rigid spokes. These images are stones; they are memorials. Beneath this sea lies sea: god rest it . . . rest the world beyond my window, me in front of my reflection, above this page, my shade. Death is not so still, so silent, since silence implies a falling quiet, stillness a stopping, containing, holding in; for death is time in a clock, like Mr. Tick, electric . . . like wind through a windup poet. And my blear floats out to visible against the glass, befog its country and bespill myself. The mist lifts slowly from the fields in the morning. No one now would say: the Earth throws back its covers; it is rising from sleep. Why is the feeling foolish? The image is too Greek. I used to gaze at you so wantonly your body blushed. Imagine: wonder: that my eyes could cause such flowering. Ah, my friend, your face is pale, the weather cloudy; a street has been felled through your chin, bare trees do nothing, houses take root in their rectangles, a steeple stands up in your head. You speak of loving; then give me a kiss. The pane is cold. On icy mornings the fog rises to greet me (as you always did); the barns and other buildings, rather than ghostly, seem all the more substantial for looming, as if they grew in themselves while I watched (as you always did). Oh my approach, I suppose, was like breath in a rubber monkey. Nevertheless, on the road along the Wabash in the morning, though the trees are sometimes obscured by fog, their reflection floats serenely on the river, reasoning the banks, the sycamores in French rows. Magically, the world tips. I'm led to think that only those who grow down live (which will scarcely win me twenty-five from *Wisdom's Monthly Digest*), but I find I write that only those who live down grow; and what I write, I hold, whatever I really know. My every word's inverted, or reversed—or I am. I held you, too, that way. You were so utterly provisional, subject to my change. I could inflate your bosom with a kiss, disperse your skin with gentleness, enter your vagina from within, and make my love emerge like a fresh sex. The pane is cold. Honesty is cold, my inside lover. The sun looks, through the mist, like a plum on the tree of heaven, or a bruise on the slope of your belly. Which? The grass crawls with frost. We meet on this window, the world and I, inelegantly, swimmers of the glass; and swung wrong way round to one another, the world seems in. The world—how grand, how monumental, grave and deadly, that word is: the world, my house and poetry. All poets have their inside lovers. Wee penis does not belong to me, or any of this foggery. It is *his* property which he's thrust through what's womanly of me to set down this. These wooden houses in their squares, gray streets and fallen sidewalks, standing trees, your name I've written sentimentally across my breath into the whitening air, pale birds: they exist in me now because of him. I gazed with what intensity . . . A bush in the excitement of its roses could not have bloomed so beautifully as you did then. It was a look I'd like to give this page. For that is poetry: to bring within about, to change.

Politics

Sports, politics, and religion are the three passions of the badly educated. They are the Midwest's open sores. Ugly to see, a source of constant discontent, they sap the body's strength. Appalling quantities of money, time, and energy are wasted on them. The rural mind is narrow, passionate, and reckless on these matters. Greed, however shortsighted and direct, will not alone account for it. I have known men, for instance, who for years have voted squarely against their interests. Nor have I ever noticed that their surly Christian views prevented them from urging forward the smithereening, say, of Russia, China, Cuba, or Korea. And they tend to back their country like they back their local team: they have a fanatical desire to win; yelling is their forte; and if things go badly, they are inclined to sack the coach. All in all, then, Birch is a good name. It stands for the bigot's stick, the wild-child-tamer's cane.

Forgetfulness—is that their object?

Oh, I was new, I thought. A fresh start: new cunt, new climate, and new country—there you were, and I was pioneer, and had no history. That language hurts me, too, my dear. You'll never hear it.

Final Vital Data

The Modern Homemakers' Demonstration Club. The Prairie Home Demonstration Club. The Night-outers' Home Demonstration Club. The IOOF, FFF, VFW, WCTU, WSCS, 4-H, 40 and 8, Psi Iota Chi, and PTA. The Boy and Girl Scouts, Rainbows, Masons, Indians and Rebekah Lodge. Also the Past Noble Grand Club of the Rebekah Lodge. As well as the Moose and the Ladies of the Moose. The Elks, the Eagles, the Jaynettes and the Eastern Star. The Women's Literary Club, the Hobby Club, the Art Club, the Sunshine Society, the Dorcas Society, the Pythian Sisters, the Pilgrim Youth Fellowship, the American Legion, the American Legion Auxiliary, the American Legion Junior Auxiliary, the Garden Club, the Bridge for Fun Club, the What-can-you-do? Club, the Get Together Club, the Coterie Club, the Worthwhile Club, the Let's Help Our Town Club, the No Name Club, the Forget-me-not Club, the Merry-go-round Club . . .

Education

Has a quarter disappeared from Paula Frosty's pocket book? Imagine the landscape of that face: no crayon could engender it; soft wax is wrong; thin wire in trifling snips might do the trick. Paula Frosty and Christopher Roger accuse the pale and splotchy Cheryl Pipes. But Miss Jakes, I *saw* her. Miss Jakes is so extremely vexed she snaps her pencil. What else is missing? I appoint you a detective, John: search her desk. Gum, candy, paper, pencils, marble, round eraser—whose? A thief. I can't watch her all the time, I'm here to teach. Poor pale fossetted Cheryl, it's determined, can't return the money because she took it home and spent it. Cindy, Janice, John, and Pete—you four who sit around her—you will be detectives this whole term to watch her. A thief. In all my time. Miss Jakes turns, unfists, and turns again. I'll handle you, she cries. To think. A thief. In all my years. Then she writes on the blackboard the name of Cheryl Pipes and beneath that the figure twenty-five with a large sign for cents. Now Cheryl, she says, this won't be taken off until you bring that money out of home, out of home straight up to here, Miss Jakes says, tapping her desk.

Which is three days.

Another Person

I was raking leaves when Uncle Halley introduced himself to me. He said his name came from the comet, and that his mother had borne him prematurely in her fright of it. I thought of Hobbes, whom fear of the Spanish Armada had hurried into birth, and so I believed Uncle Halley to honor the philosopher, though Uncle Halley is a liar, and neither the one hundred twenty-nine nor the fifty-three he ought to be. That fall the leaves had burned themselves out on the trees, the leaf lobes had curled, and now they flocked noisily down the street and were broken in the wires of my rake. Uncle Halley was himself (like Mrs. Desmond and history generally) both deaf and implacable, and he shooed me down his basement stairs to a room set aside there for stacks of newspapers reaching to the ceiling, boxes of leaflets and letters and programs, racks of photo albums, scrapbooks, bundles of rolled-up posters and maps, flags and pennants and slanting piles of dusty magazines devoted mostly to motoring and the Christian ethic. I saw a bird cage, a tray of butterflies, a bugle, a stiff straw boater, and all kinds of tassles tied to a coat tree. He still possessed and had on display the steering lever from his first car, a linen duster, driving gloves and goggles, photographs along the wall of himself, his friends, and his various machines, a shell from the first war, a record of "Ramona" nailed through its hole to a post, walking sticks and fanciful umbrellas, shoes of all sorts (his baby shoes, their counters broken, were held in sorrow beneath my nose—they had not been bronzed, but he might have them done someday before he died, he said), countless boxes of medals, pins, beads, trinkets, toys, and keys (I scarcely saw—they flowed like jewels from his palms), pictures of downtown when it was only a path by the railroad station, a brightly colored globe of the world with a dent in Poland, antique guns, belt buckles, buttons, souvenir plates and cups and saucers (I can't remember all of it—I won't), but I recall how shamefully, how rudely, how abruptly, I fled, a good story in my mouth but death in my nostrils; and how afterward I busily, righteously, burned my leaves as if I were purging the world of its years. I still wonder if this town—its life, and mine now—isn't really a record like the one of "Ramona" that I used to crank around on my grandmother's mahogany Victrola through lonely rainy days as a kid.

The First Person

Billy's like the coal he's found: spilled, mislaid, discarded. The sky's no comfort. His house and his body are dying together. His windows are boarded. And now he's reduced to his hands. I suspect he has glaucoma. At any rate he can scarcely see, and weeds his yard of rubble on his hands and knees. Perhaps he's a surgeon cleansing a wound or an ardent and tactile lover. I watch, I must say, apprehensively. Like mine-war detectors, his hands graze in circles ahead of him. Your nipples were the color of your eyes. Pebble. Snarl of paper. Length of twine. He leans down closely, picks up something silvery, holds it near his nose. Foil? cap? coin? He has within him—what, I wonder? Does he know more now because he fingers everything and has to sniff to see? It would be romantic cruelty to think so. He bends the down on your arms like a breeze. You wrote me: something is strange when we don't understand. I write in return: I think when I loved you I fell to my death.

Billy, I could read to you from Beddoes; he's your man perhaps; he held with dying, freed his blood of its arteries; and he said that there were many wretched love-ill fools like me lying alongside the last bone of their former selves, as full of spirit and speech, nonetheless, as Mrs. Desmond, Uncle Halley and the Ferris wheel, Aunt Pet, Miss Jakes, Ramona or the megaphone; yet I reverse him finally, Billy, on no evidence but braggadocio, and I declare that though my inner organs were devoured long ago, the worm which swallowed down my parts still throbs and glows like a crystal palace.

Yes, you were younger. I was Uncle Halley, the museum man and infrequent meteor. Here is my first piece of ass. They weren't so flat in those days, had more round, more juice. And over here's the sperm I've spilled, nicely jarred and clearly labeled. Look at this tape like lengths of intestine where I've stored my spew, the endless worm of words I've written, a hundred million emissions or more: oh I was quite a man right from the start; even when unconscious in my cradle, from crotch to cranium, I was erectile tissue; though mostly, after the manner approved by Plato, I had intercourse by eye. Never mind, old Holsclaw, you are blind. We pull down darkness when we go to bed; put out like Oedipus the actually offending organ, and train our touch to lies. All cats are gray, says Mr. Tick; so under cover of glaucoma you are sack gray too, and cannot be distinguished from a stallion.

I must pull myself together, get a grip, just as they say, but I feel spilled, bewildered, quite mislaid. I did not restore my house to its youth, but to its age. Hunting, you hitch through the hollyhocks. I'm inclined to say you aren't half the cripple I am, for there is nothing left of me but mouth. However, I resist the impulse. It is another lie of poetry. My organs are all there, though it's there where I fail—at the roots of my experience. Poet of the spiritual, Rilke, weren't you? yet that's what you said. Poetry, like love, is —in and out—a physical caress. I can't tolerate any more of my sophistries about spirit, mind, and breath. Body equals being, and if your weight goes down, you are the less.

Household Apples

I knew nothing about apples. Why should I? My country came in my childhood, and I dreamed of sitting among the blooms like the bees. I failed to spray the pear tree too. I doubled up under them at first, admiring the sturdy low branches I should have pruned, and later I acclaimed the blossoms. Shortly after the fruit formed there were falls—not many—apples the size of goodish stones which made me wobble on my ankles when I walked about the yard. Sometimes a piece crushed by a heel would cling on the shoe to track the house. I gathered a few and heaved them over the wires. A slingshot would have been splendid. Hard, an unattractive green, the worms had them. Before long I realized the worms had them all. Even as the apples reddened, lit their tree, they were being swallowed. The birds preferred the pears, which were small— sugar pears I think they're called—with thick skins of graying green that ripen on toward violet. So the fruit fell, and once I made some applesauce by quartering and paring hundreds; but mostly I did nothing, left them, until suddenly, overnight it seemed, in that ugly late September heat we often have in Indiana, my problem was upon me.

My childhood came in the country. I remember, now, the flies on our snowy luncheon table. As we cleared away they would settle, fastidiously scrub themselves and stroll to the crumbs to feed where I would kill them in crowds with a swatter. It was quite a game to catch them taking off. I struck heavily since I didn't mind a few stains; they'd wash. The swatter was a square of screen bound down in red cloth. It drove no air ahead of it to give them warning. They might have thought they'd flown headlong into a summered window. The faint pink dot where they had died did not rub out as I'd supposed, and after years of use our luncheon linen would faintly, pinkly, speckle.

The country became my childhood. Flies braided themselves on the flypaper in my grandmother's house. I can smell the bakery and the grocery and the stables and the dairy in that small Dakota town I knew as a kid; knew as I dreamed I'd know your body, as I've known nothing, before or since; knew as the flies knew, in the honest, unchaste sense: the burned house, hose-wet, which drew a mist of insects like the blue smoke of its smolder, and gangs of boys, moist-lipped, destructive as its burning. Flies have always impressed me; they are so persistently alive. Now they were coating the ground beneath my trees. Some were ordinary flies; there were the large blue-green ones; there were swarms of fruit flies too, and the red-spotted scavenger beetle; there were a few wasps, several sorts of bees and butterflies—checkers, sulphurs, monarchs, commas, question marks—and delicate dragonflies . . . but principally houseflies and horseflies and bottleflies, flies and more flies in clusters around the rotting fruit. They loved the pears. Inside, they fed. If you picked up a pear, they flew, and the pear became skin and stem. They were everywhere the fruit was: in the tree still— apples like a hive for them—or where the fruit littered the ground, squashing itself as you stepped . . . there was no help for it. The flies droned, feasting on the sweet juice. No one could go near the trees; I could not climb; so I determined at last to labor like Hercules. There were fruit baskets in the barn. Collecting them and kneeling under the branches, I began to gather remains. Deep in the strong rich smell of the fruit, I began to hum myself. The fruit caved in at the touch. Glistening red apples, my lifting disclosed, had families of beetles, flies, and bugs, devouring their rotten undersides. There were streams of flies; there were lakes and cataracts and rivers of flies, seas and oceans. The hum was heavier, higher, than the hum of the bees when they came to the blooms in the spring, though the bees were there, among the flies, ignoring me —ignoring everyone. As my work went on and juice covered my hands and arms, they would form a sleeve, black and moving, like knotty wool. No caress could have been more indifferently complete. Still I rose fearfully, ramming my head in the branches, apples bumping against me before falling, bursting with bugs. I'd snap my hand sharply but the flies would cling to the sweet. I could toss a whole cluster into a basket from several feet. As the pear or apple lit, they would explosively rise, like monads for a moment, windowless, certainly, with respect to one another, sugar their harmony. I had to admit, though, despite my distaste, that my arm had never been more alive, oftener or more gently kissed. Those hundreds of feet were light. In washing them off, I pretended the hose was a pump. What have I missed? Childhood is a lie of poetry.

The Church

Friday night. Girls in dark skirts and white blouses sit in ranks and scream in concert. They carry funnels loosely stuffed with orange and black paper which they shake wildly, and small megaphones through which, as drilled, they direct and magnify their shouting. Their leaders, barely pubescent girls, prance and shake and whirl their skirts above their bloomers. The young men, leaping, extend their arms and race through puddles of amber light, their bodies glistening. In a lull, though it rarely occurs, you can hear the squeak of tennis shoes against the floor. Then the yelling begins again, and then continues; fathers, mothers, neighbors joining in to form a single pulsing ululation—a cry of the whole community —for in this gymnasium each body becomes the bodies beside it, pressed as they are together, thigh to thigh, and the same shudder runs through all of them, and runs toward the same release. Only the ball moves serenely through this dazzling din. Obedient to law it scarcely speaks but caroms quietly and lives at peace.

Business

It is the week of Christmas and the stores, to accommodate the rush they hope for, are remaining open in the evening. You can see snow falling in the cones of the street lamps. The roads are filling —undisturbed. Strings of red and green lights droop over the principal highway, and the water tower wears a star. The windows of the stores have been bedizened. Shamelessly they beckon. But I am alone, leaning against a pole—no . . . there is no one in sight. They're all at home, perhaps by their instruments, tuning in on their evenings, and like Ramona, tirelessly playing and replaying themselves. There's a speaker perched in the tower, and through the boughs of falling snow and over the vacant streets, it drapes the twisted and metallic strains of a tune that can barely be distinguished—yes, I believe it's one of the jolly ones, it's "Joy to the World." There's no one to hear the music but myself, and though I'm listening, I'm no longer certain. Perhaps the record's playing something else.

1968.

JOHN BARTH

(1930–)

John Simmons Barth was born in Cambridge, Maryland, attended the Juilliard School of Music in New York, and received his B.A. in 1951 and his M.A. in 1952 from Johns Hopkins University. Briefly a Junior Instructor in English at Johns Hopkins, he moved in 1953 to Pennsylvania State University and during his twelve years teaching English there published the three novels that earned him his first critical recognition. In 1965 he became Professor of English at the State University of New York at Buffalo. He has also held a visiting appointment at Boston University (1972– 1973) and has been the recipient of grants from the Rockefeller Foundation and the National Institute of Arts and Letters.

In Barth's first novel, *The Floating Opera* (1956), the narrator reviews his life while contemplating suicide. In his second novel, *The End of the Road* (1958), Barth presents the hero with the multitudinous choices resulting from his involvement in a sexual triangle. In *The Sot-Weed Factor* (1960) he parodies the form and content of an eighteenth-century novel in detailing the life in colonial Maryland of an almost unknown poet, Ebenezer Cooke. In the immensely complicated *Giles Goat-Boy* (1966) he presents the twentieth-

century university as a metaphor for a universe managed with all the irrefutable logic and unpredictability of a computer gone insane.

Enormously inventive, Barth is also continually aware as he writes of the nature of fiction as artifice; his works abound with reminders of their imagined and therefore artificial reality. *Chimera* (1972), with its focus on Scheherazade, Perseus, and Bellerophon, emphasizes his love of myth and allegory and at the same time serves as a reminder that in Barth's eyes it has now become impossible for the novelist to return to the simpler modes of presentation of an earlier age. His comic vision and verbal fecundity, which together push his works at times beyond the edges of farce and tedium, make linear plots and traditionally realistic modes of presentation increasingly irrelevant to him. "I admire writers who can make complicated things simple," he has said, "but my own talent has been to make simple things complicated."

The Floating Opera, 1956, *The End of the Road,* 1958, and *The Sot-Weed Factor,* 1960, were revised in 1967. The other novels appeared in the single editions given above. Short stories are collected in *Lost in the Funhouse: Fiction for Print, Tape, Live Voice,* 1968, from which the following selection is taken. A brief critical introduction is by Ihab Hassan in James Vinson, ed., *Contemporary Novelists,* 1972.

From Lost in the Funhouse

For whom is the funhouse fun? Perhaps for lovers. For Ambrose it is *a place of fear and confusion.* He has come to the seashore with his family for the holiday, *the occasion of their visit is Indepen-dence Day, the most important secular holiday of the United States of America.* A single straight underline is the manuscript mark for italic type, *which in turn* is the printed equivalent to oral emphasis of words and phrases as well as the customary type for titles of complete works, not to mention. Italics are also employed, in fiction stories especially, for "outside," intrusive, or artificial voices, such as radio announcements, the texts of telegrams and newspaper articles, et cetera. They should be used *sparingly.* If passages originally in roman type are italicized by someone re-peating them, it's customary to acknowledge the fact. *Italics mine.*

Ambrose was "at that awkward age." His voice came out high-pitched as a child's if he let himself get carried away; to be on the safe side, therefore, he moved and spoke with *deliberate calm* and *adult gravity.* Talking soberly of unimportant or irrelevant matters and listening consciously to the sound of your own voice are useful habits for maintaining control in this difficult interval. *En route* to Ocean City he sat in the back seat of the family car with his brother Peter, age fifteen, and Magda G——, age fourteen, a pretty girl an exquisite young lady, who lived not far from them on B—— Street in the town of D——, Maryland. Initials, blanks, or both were often substituted for proper names in nineteenth-century fic-tion to enhance the illusion of reality. It is as if the author felt it necessary to delete the names for reasons of tact or legal liability. In-terestingly, as with other aspects of realism, it is an *illusion* that is being enhanced, by purely artificial means. Is it likely, does it vio-late the principle of verisimilitude, that a thirteen-year-old boy could make such a sophisticated observation? A girl of fourteen is *the psychological coeval* of a boy of fifteen or sixteen; a thirteen-year-old boy, therefore, even one precocious in some other respects, might be three years *her emotional junior.*

Thrice a year—on Memorial, Independence, and Labor Days —the family visits Ocean City for the afternoon and evening. When Ambrose and Peter's father was their age, the excursion was made by train, as mentioned in the novel *The 42nd Parallel* by John Dos Passos. Many families from the same neighborhood used to travel together, with dependent relatives and often with Negro servants; schoolfuls of children swarmed through the railway cars; everyone shared everyone else's Maryland fried chicken, Virginia ham, deviled eggs, potato salad, beaten biscuits, iced tea. Nowa-days (that is, in 19—, the year of our story) the journey is made by automobile—more comfortably and quickly though without the extra fun though without the *camaraderie* of a general excursion. It's all part of the deterioration of American life, their father de-clares; Uncle Karl supposes that when the boys take *their* families to Ocean City for the holidays they'll fly in Autogiros. Their mother, sitting in the middle of the front seat like Magda in the second, only with her arms on the seat-back behind the men's shoulders, wouldn't want the good old days back again, the steaming trains and stuffy long dresses; on the other hand she can do without Autogiros, too, if she has to become a grandmother to fly in them.

Description of physical appearance and mannerisms is one of several standard methods of characterization used by writers of fiction. It is also important to "keep the senses operating"; when a detail from one of the five senses, say visual, is "crossed" with a detail from another, say auditory, the reader's imagination is oriented to the scene, perhaps unconsciously. This procedure may be compared to the way surveyors and navigators determine their positions by two or more compass bearings, a process known as triangulation. The brown hair on Ambrose's mother's forearms gleamed in the sun like. Though right-handed, she took her left arm from the seat-back to press the dashboard cigar lighter for Uncle Karl. When the glass bead in its handle glowed red, the lighter was ready for use. The smell of Uncle Karl's cigar smoke reminded one of. The fragrance of the ocean came strong to the picnic ground where they always stopped for lunch, two miles inland from Ocean City. Having to pause for a full hour almost within the sound of the breakers was difficult for Peter and Ambrose when they were younger; even at their present age it was not easy to keep their anticipation, *stimulated by the briny spume*, from turning into short temper. The Irish author James Joyce, in his unusual novel entitled *Ulysses*, now available in this country, uses the adjectives *snot-green* and *scrotum-tightening* to describe the sea. Visual, auditory, tactile, olfactory, gustatory. Peter and Ambrose's father, while steering their black 1936 LaSalle sedan with one hand, could with the other remove the first cigarette from a white pack of Lucky Strikes and, more remarkably, light it with a match forefingered from its book and thumbed against the flint paper without being detached. The matchbook cover merely advertised U.S. War Bonds and Stamps. A fine metaphor, simile, or other figure of speech, in addition to its obvious "first-order" relevance to the thing it describes, will be seen upon reflection to have a second order of significance: it may be drawn from the *milieu* of the action, for example, or be particularly appropriate to the sensibility of the narrator, even hinting to the reader things of which the narrator is unaware; or it may cast further and subtler lights upon the thing it describes, sometimes ironically qualifying the more evident sense of the comparison.

To say that Ambrose's and Peter's mother was *pretty* is to accomplish nothing; the reader may acknowledge the proposition, but his imagination is not engaged. Besides, Magda was also pretty, yet in an altogether different way. Although she lived on B—— Street she had very good manners and did better than average in school. Her figure was very well developed for her age. Her right hand lay casually on the plush upholstery of the seat, very near Ambrose's left leg, on which his own hand rested. The space between their legs, between her right and his left leg, was out of the line of sight of anyone sitting on the other side of Magda, was well as anyone glancing into the rearview mirror. Uncle Karl's face resembled Peter's—rather, vice versa. Both had dark hair and eyes, short husky statures, deep voices. Magda's left hand was probably in a similar position on her left side. The boy's father is difficult to describe; no particular feature of his appearance or manner stood out. He wore glasses and was principal of a T——County grade school. Uncle Karl was a masonry contractor.

Although Peter must have known as well as Ambrose that the latter, because of his position in the car, would be the first to see the electrical towers of the power plant at V——, the halfway point of their trip, he leaned forward and slightly toward the center of the car and pretended to be looking for them through the flat pinewoods and tuckahoe creeks along the highway. For as long as the boys could remember, "looking for the Towers" had been a feature of the first half of their excursions to Ocean City, "looking for the standpipe" of the second. Though the game was childish, their mother preserved the tradition of rewarding the first to see the Towers with a candybar or piece of fruit. She insisted now that Magda play the game; the prize, she said, was "something hard to get nowadays." Ambrose decided not to join in; he sat far back in his seat. Magda, like Peter, leaned forward. Two sets of straps were discernible through the shoulders of her sun dress; the inside right one, a brassiere-strap, was fastened or shortened with a small safety pin. The right armpit of her dress, presumably the left as well, was damp with perspiration. The simple strategy for being first to espy the Towers, which Ambrose had understood by the age of four, was to sit on the right-hand side of the car. Whoever sat there, however, had also to put up with the worst of the sun, and so Ambrose, without mentioning the matter, chose sometimes the one and sometimes the other. Not impossibly Peter had never caught on to the trick, or thought that his brother hadn't simply because Ambrose on occasion preferred shade to a Baby Ruth or tangerine.

The shade-sun situation didn't apply to the front seat, owing to the windshield; if anything the driver got more sun, since the person on the passenger side not only was shaded below by the door and dashboard but might swing down his sunvisor all the way too.

"Is that them?" Magda asked. Ambrose's mother teased the boys for letting Magda win, insinuating that "somebody [had] a girlfriend." Peter and Ambrose's father reached a long thin arm across their mother to butt his cigarette in the dashboard ashtray, under the lighter. The prize this time for seeing the Towers first was a banana. Their mother bestowed it after chiding their father for wasting a half-smoked cigarette when everything was so scarce. Magda, to take the prize, moved her hand from so near Ambrose's that he could have touched it as though accidentally. She offered to share the prize, things like that were so hard to find; but everyone insisted it was hers alone. Ambrose's mother sang an iambic trimeter couplet from a popular song, femininely rhymed:

> "What's good is in the Army;
> What's left will never harm me."

Uncle Karl tapped his cigar ash out the ventilator window; some particles were sucked by the slipstream back into the car through the rear window on the passenger side. Magda demonstrated her ability to hold a banana in one hand and peel it with her teeth. She still sat forward; Ambrose pushed his glasses back onto the bridge of his nose with his left hand, which he then negligently let fall to the seat cushion immediately behind her. He even permitted the single hair, gold, on the second joint of his thumb to brush the fabric of her skirt. Should she have sat back at that instant, his hand would have been caught under her.

Plush upholstery prickles uncomfortably through gabardine slacks in the July sun. The function of the *beginning* of a story is to introduce the principal characters, establish their initial relationships, set the scene for the main action, expose the background of the situation if necessary, plant motifs and foreshadowings where appropriate, and initiate the first complication or whatever of the "rising action." Actually, if one imagines a story called "The Funhouse," or "Lost in the Funhouse," the details of the drive to Ocean City don't seem especially relevant. The *beginning* should recount the events between Ambrose's first sight of the funhouse early in the afternoon and his entering it with Magda and Peter in the evening. The *middle* would narrate all relevant events from the time he goes in to the time he loses his way; middles have the double and contradictory function of delaying the climax while at the same time preparing the reader for it and fetching him to it. Then the *ending* would tell what Ambrose does while he's lost, how he finally finds his way out, and what everybody makes of the experience. So far there's been no real dialogue, very little sensory detail, and nothing in the way of a *theme*. And a long time has gone by already without anything happening; it makes a person wonder. We haven't even reached Ocean City yet: we will never get out of the funhouse.

The more closely an author identifies with the narrator, literally or metaphorically, the less advisable it is, as a rule, to use the first-person narrative viewpoint. Once three years previously the young people *aforementioned* played Niggers and Masters in the backyard; when it was Ambrose's turn to be Master and theirs to be Niggers Peter had to go serve his evening papers; Ambrose was afraid to punish Magda alone, but she led him to the whitewashed Torture Chamber between the woodshed and the privy in the Slaves Quarters; there she knelt sweating among bamboo rakes and dusty Mason jars, pleadingly embraced his knees, and while bees droned in the lattice as if on an ordinary summer afternoon, purchased clemency at a surprising price set by herself. Doubtless she remembered nothing of this event; Ambrose on the other hand seemed unable to forget the least detail of his life. He even recalled how, standing beside himself with awed impersonality in the reeky heat, he'd stared the while at an empty cigar box in which Uncle Karl kept stone-cutting chisels: beneath the words *El Producto*, a laureled, loose-toga'd lady regarded the sea from a marble bench; beside her, forgotten or not yet turned to, was a five-stringed lyre. Her chin reposed on the back of her right hand; her left depended negligently from the bench-arm. The lower half of scene and lady was peeled away; the words EXAMINED BY—— were inked there into the wood. Nowadays cigar boxes are made of pasteboard. Ambrose wondered what Magda would have done, Ambrose wondered what Magda would do when she sat back on his hand as he resolved she should. Be angry. Make a teasing joke of it. Give no sign at all. For a long time she leaned forward, playing cow-poker with Peter against Uncle Karl and Mother and watching for the first sign of Ocean City. At nearly the same instant, picnic ground and Ocean City standpipe hove into view; an Amoco filling station on their side of the road cost Mother and Uncle Karl fifty cows and the game; Magda bounced back, clapping her right hand on Mother's right arm; Ambrose moved clear "in the nick of time."

At this rate our hero, at this rate our protagonist will remain in the funhouse forever. Narrative ordinarily consists of alternating dramatization and summarization. One symptom of nervous tension, paradoxically, is repeated and violent yawning; neither Peter nor Magda nor Uncle Karl nor Mother reacted in this manner. Although they were no longer small children, Peter and Ambrose were each given a dollar to spend on boardwalk amusements in addition to what money of their own they'd brought along. Magda too, though she protested she had ample spending money. The boys' mother made a little scene out of distributing the bills; she pretended that her sons and Magda were small children and cautioned them not to spend the sum too quickly or in one place. Magda promised with a merry laugh and, having both hands free, took the bill with her left. Peter laughed also and pledged in a falsetto to be a good boy. His imitation of a child was not clever. The boys' father was tall and thin, balding, fair-complexioned. Assertions of that sort are not effective; the reader may acknowledge the proposition, but. We should be much farther along than we are; something has gone wrong; not much of this preliminary rambling seems relevant. Yet everyone begins in the same place; how is it that most go along without difficulty but a few lose their way?

"Stay out from under the boardwalk," Uncle Karl growled from the side of his mouth. The boys' mother pushed his shoulder *in mock annoyance*. They were all standing before Fat May the Laughing Lady who advertised the funhouse. Larger than life, Fat May mechanically shook, rocked on her heels, slapped her thighs while recorded laughter—uproarious, female—came amplified from a hidden loudspeaker. It chuckled, wheezed, wept; tried in vain to catch its breath; tittered, groaned, exploded raucous and anew. You couldn't hear it without laughing yourself, no matter how you felt. Father came back from talking to a Coast-Guardsman on duty and reported that the surf was spoiled with crude oil from tankers recently torpedoed offshore. Lumps of it, difficult to remove, made tarry tidelines on the beach and stuck on swimmers. Many bathed in the surf nevertheless and came out speckled; others paid to use a municipal pool and only sunbathed on the beach. We would do the latter. We would do the latter. We would do the latter.

Under the boardwalk, matchbook covers, grainy other things. What is the story's theme? Ambrose is ill. He perspires in the dark passages; candied apples-on-a-stick, delicious-looking, disappointing to eat. Funhouses need men's and ladies' room at intervals. Others perhaps have also vomited in corners and corridors; may even have had bowel movements liable to be stepped in in the dark. The word *fuck* suggests suction and/or and/or flatulence. Mother and Father; grandmothers and grandfathers on both sides; great-grandmothers and great-grandfathers on four sides, et cetera. Count a generation as thirty years: in approximately the year when Lord Baltimore was granted charter to the province of Maryland by Charles I, five hundred twelve women—English, Welsh, Bavarian, Swiss—of every class and character, received into themselves the penises the intromittent organs of five hundred twelve men, ditto, in every circumstance and posture, to conceive the five hundred twelve ancestors of the two hundred fifty-six ancestors of the et cetera et cetera et cetera et cetera et cetera et cetera et cetera et cetera of the author, of the narrator, of this story, *Lost in the Funhouse*. In alleyways, ditches, canopy beds, pinewoods, bridal suites, ship's cabins, coach-and-fours, coaches-and-four, sultry toolsheds; on the cold sand under boardwalks, littered with *El Producto* cigar butts, treasured with Lucky Strike cigarette stubs, Coca-Cola caps, gritty turds, cardboard lollipop sticks, matchbook covers warning that A Slip of the Lip Can Sink a Ship. The shluppish whisper, continuous as seawash round the globe, tidelike falls and rises with the circuit of dawn and dusk.

Magda's teeth. She *was* left-handed. Perspiration. They've gone all the way, through, Magda and Peter, they've been waiting for hours with Mother and Uncle Karl while Father searches for his lost son; they draw french-fried potatoes from a paper cup and shake their heads. They've named the children they'll one day have and bring to Ocean City on holidays. Can spermatozoa properly be thought of as male animalcules when there are no female spermatozoa? They grope through hot, dark windings, past Love's Tunnel's fearsome obstacles. Some perhaps lose their way.

Peter suggested then and there that they do the funhouse; he had been through it before, so had Magda, Ambrose hadn't and suggested, his voice cracking on account of Fat May's laughter, that they swim first. All were chuckling, couldn't help it; Ambrose's father, Ambrose's and Peter's father came up grinning like a lunatic with two boxes of syrup-coated popcorn, one for Mother, one for Magda; the men were to help themselves. Ambrose walked on Magda's right; being by nature left-handed, she carried the box in her left hand. Up front the situation was reversed.

"What are you limping for?" Magda inquired of Ambrose. He supposed in a husky tone that his foot had gone to sleep in the car. Her teeth flashed. "Pins and needles?" It was the honeysuckle on the lattice of the former privy that drew the bees. Imagine being stung there. How long is this going to take?

The adults decided to forgo the pool; but Uncle Karl insisted they change into swimsuits and do the beach. "He wants to watch the pretty girls," Peter teased, and ducked behind Magda from Uncle Karl's pretended wrath. "You've got all the pretty girls you need right here," Magda declared, and Mother said: "Now that's the gospel truth." Magda scolded Peter, who reached over her shoulder to sneak some popcorn. "Your brother and father aren't getting any." Uncle Karl wondered if they were going to have fireworks that night, what with the shortages. It wasn't the shortages, Mr. M—— replied; Ocean City had fireworks from pre-war. But it was too risky on account of the enemy submarines, some people thought.

"Don't seem like Fourth of July without fireworks," said Uncle

Karl. The inverted tag in dialogue writing is still considered permissible with proper names or epithets, but sounds old-fashioned with personal pronouns. "We'll have 'em again soon enough," predicted the boys' father. Their mother declared she could do without fireworks: they reminded her too much of the real thing. Their father said all the more reason to shoot off a few now and again. Uncle Karl asked *rhetorically* who needed reminding, just look at people's hair and skin.

"The oil, yes," said Mrs. M——.

Ambrose had a pain in his stomach and so didn't swim but enjoyed watching the others. He and his father burned red easily. Magda's figure was exceedingly well developed for her age. She too declined to swim, and got mad, and became angry when Peter attempted to drag her into the pool. She always swam, he insisted; what did she mean not swim? Why did a person come to Ocean City?

"Maybe I want to lay here with Ambrose," Magda teased.

Nobody likes a pedant.

"Aha," said Mother. Peter grabbed Magda by one ankle and ordered Ambrose to grab the other. She squealed and rolled over on the beach blanket. Ambrose pretended to help hold her back. Her tan was darker than even Mother's and Peter's. "Help out, Uncle Karl!" Peter cried. Uncle Karl went to seize the other ankle. Inside the top of her swimsuit, however, you could see the line where the sunburn ended and, when she hunched her shoulders and squealed again, one nipple's auburn edge. Mother made them behave themselves. "*You* should certainly know," she said to Uncle Karl. Archly. "That when a lady says she doesn't feel like swimming, a gentleman doesn't ask questions." Uncle Karl said excuse *him*; Mother winked at Magda; Ambrose blushed; stupid Peter kept saying "Phooey on *feel like!*" and tugging at Magda's ankle; then even he got the point, and cannonballed with a holler into the pool.

"I swear," Magda said, in mock *in feigned* exasperation.

The diving would make a suitable literary symbol. To go off the high board you had to wait in a line along the poolside and up the ladder. Fellows tickled girls and goosed one another and shouted to the ones at the top to hurry up, or razzed them for bellyfloppers. Once on the springboard some took a great while posing or clowning or deciding on a dive or getting up their nerve; others ran right off. Especially among the younger fellows the idea was to strike the funniest pose or do the craziest stunt as you fell, a thing that got harder to do as you kept on and kept on. But whether you hollered *Geronimo!* or *Sieg heil!*, held your nose or "rode a bicycle," pretended to be shot or did a perfect jackknife or changed your mind halfway down and ended up with nothing, it was over in two seconds, after all that wait. Spring, pose, splash. Spring, neat-o, splash. Spring, aw fooey, splash.

The grown-ups had gone on; Ambrose wanted to converse with Magda; she was remarkably well developed for her age; it was said that that came from rubbing with a turkish towel, and there were other theories. Ambrose could think of nothing to say except how good a diver Peter was, who was showing off for her benefit. You could pretty well tell by looking at their bathing suits and arm muscles how far along the different fellows were. Ambrose was glad he hadn't gone in swimming, the cold water shrank you up so. Magda pretended to be uninterested in the diving; she probably weighed as much as he did. If you knew your way around in the funhouse like your own bedroom, you could wait until a girl came along and then slip away without ever getting caught, even if her boyfriend was right with her. She'd think *he* did it! It would be better to be the boyfriend, and act outraged, and tear the funhouse apart.

Not act; *be*.

"He's a master diver," Ambrose said. In feigned admiration. "You really have to slave away at it to get that good." What would it matter anyhow if he asked her right out whether she remembered, even teased her with it as Peter would have?

There's no point in going farther; this isn't getting anybody anywhere; they haven't even come to the funhouse yet. Ambrose is off the track, in some new or old part of the place that's not supposed to be used; he strayed into it by some one-in-a-million chance, like the time the roller-coaster car left the tracks in the nineteen-teens against all the laws of physics and sailed over the boardwalk in the dark. And they can't locate him because they don't know where to look. Even the designer and operator have forgotten this other part, that winds around on itself like a whelk shell. That winds around the right part like the snakes on Mercury's caduceus. Some people, perhaps, don't "hit their stride" until their twenties, when the growing-up business is over and women appreciate other things besides wisecracks and teasing and strutting. Peter didn't have one-tenth the imagination *he* had, not one-tenth. Peter did this naming-their-children thing as a joke, making up names like Aloysius and Murgatroyd, but Ambrose knew *exactly* how it would feel to be married and have children of your own, and be a loving husband and father, and go comfortably to work in the mornings and to bed with your wife at night, and wake up with her there. With a breeze coming through the sash and birds and mockingbirds singing in the Chinese-cigar trees. His eyes watered, there aren't enough ways to say that. He would be quite famous in his line of work. Whether Magda was his wife or not, one evening when he was wise-lined and gray at the temples he'd smile gravely, at a fashionable dinner party, and remind her of his youthful passion. The time they went with his family to Ocean City; the *erotic fantasies* he used to have about her. How long ago it seemed, and childish! Yet tender, too, *n'est-ce pas*? Would she have imagined that the world-famous whatever remembered how many strings were on the lyre on the bench beside the girl on the label of the cigar box he'd stared at in the toolshed at age ten while she, age eleven. Even then he had felt *wise beyond his years;* he'd stroked her hair and said in his deepest voice and correctest English, as to a dear child: "I shall never forget this moment."

But though he had breathed heavily, groaned as if ecstatic, what he'd really felt throughout was an odd detachment, as though someone else were Master. Strive as he might to be transported, he heard his mind take notes upon the scene: *This is what they call* passion. *I am experiencing it.* Many of the digger machines were out of order in the penny arcades and could not be repaired or replaced for the duration. Moreover the prizes, made now in USA, were less interesting than formerly, pasteboard items for the most part, and some of the machines wouldn't work on white pennies. The gypsy fortune-teller machine might have provided a foreshadowing of the climax of this story if Ambrose had operated it. It was even dilapidateder than most: the silver coating was worn off the brown metal handles, the glass windows around the dummy were cracked and taped, her kerchiefs and silks long-faded. If a man lived by himself, he could take a department-store mannequin with flexible joints and modify her in certain ways. *However:* by the time he was that old he'd have a real woman. There was a machine that stamped your name around a white-metal coin with a star in the middle: A——. His son would be the second, and when the lad reached thirteen or so he would put a strong arm around his shoulder and tell him calmly: "It is perfectly normal. We have all been through it. It will not last forever." Nobody knew how to be what they were right. He'd smoke a pipe, teach his son how to fish and softcrab, assure him he needn't worry about himself. Magda would certainly give, Magda would certainly yield a great deal of milk, although guilty of occasional solecisms. It don't taste so bad. Suppose the lights came on now!

The day wore on. You think you're yourself, but there are other persons in you. Ambrose gets hard when Ambrose doesn't want to, *and obversely.* Ambrose watches them disagree; Ambrose watches him watch. In the funhouse mirror-room you can't see yourself go on forever, because no matter how you stand, your head gets in the way. Even if you had a glass periscope, the image of your eye would cover up the thing you really wanted to see. The police will come; there'll be a story in the papers. That must be where it happened. Unless he can find a surprise exit, an unofficial backdoor or escape hatch opening on an alley, say, and then stroll up to the family in front of the funhouse and ask where everybody's been; *he's* been out of the place for ages. That's just where it happened, in that last lighted room: Peter and Magda found the right exit; he found one that you weren't supposed to find and strayed off into the works somewhere. In a perfect funhouse you'd be able to go only one way, like the divers off the highboard; getting lost would be impossible; the doors and halls would work like minnow traps or the valves in veins.

On account of German U-boats, Ocean City was "browned out": streetlights were shaded on the seaward side; shop-windows and boardwalk amusement places were kept dim, not to silhouette tankers and Liberty-ships for torpedoing. In a short story about Ocean City, Maryland, during World War II, the author could make use of the image of sailors on leave in the penny arcades and shooting galleries, sighting through the crosshairs of toy machine guns at swastika'd subs, while out in the black Atlantic a U-boat skipper squints through his periscope at real ships outlined by the glow of penny arcades. After dinner the family strolled back to the amusement end of the boardwalk. The boys' father had burnt red as always and was masked with Noxzema, a minstrel in reverse. The grownups stood at the end of the boardwalk where the Hurricane of '33 had cut an inlet from the ocean to Assawoman Bay.

"Pronounced with a long o," Uncle Karl reminded Magda with a wink. His shirt sleeves were rolled up; Mother punched his brown biceps with the arrowed heart on it and said his mind was naughty. Fat May's laugh came suddenly from the funhouse, as if she'd just got the joke; the family laughed too at the coincidence. Ambrose went under the boardwalk to search for out-of-town matchbook covers with the aid of his pocket flashlight; he looked out from the edge of the North American continent and wondered how far their laughter carried over the water. Spies in rubber rafts; survivors in lifeboats. If the joke had been beyond his understanding, he could have said: *"The laughter was over his head."* And let the reader see the serious wordplay on second reading.

He turned the flashlight on and then off at once even before the woman whooped. He sprang away, heart athud, dropping the light. What had the man grunted? Perspiration drenched and chilled him by the time he scrambled up to the family. "See anything?" his father asked. His voice wouldn't come; he shrugged and violently brushed sand from his pants legs.

"Let's ride the old flying horses!" Magda cried. I'll never be an author. It's been forever already, everybody's gone home, Ocean City's deserted, the ghost-crabs are tickling across the beach and down the littered cold streets. And the empty halls of clapboard hotels and abandoned funhouses. A tidal wave; an enemy air raid; a monster-crab swelling like an island from the sea. *The inhabitants fled in terror.* Magda clung to his trouser leg; he alone knew the maze's secret. "He gave his life that we might live," said Uncle Karl with a scowl of pain, as he. The fellow's hands had been tattooed; the woman's legs, the woman's fat white legs had. *An astonishing coincidence.* He yearned to tell Peter. He wanted to throw up for excitement. They hadn't even chased him. He wished he were dead.

One possible ending would be to have Ambrose come across another lost person in the dark. They'd match their wits together against the funhouse, struggle like Ulysses past obstacle after obstacle, help and encourage each other. Or a girl. By the time they found the exit they'd be closest friends, sweethearts if it were a girl; they'd know each other's inmost souls, be bound together *by the cement of shared adventure*; then they'd emerge into the light and it would turn out that his friend was a Negro. A blind girl. President Roosevelt's son. Ambrose's former archenemy.

Shortly after the mirror room he'd groped along a musty corridor, his heart already misgiving him at the absence of phosphorescent arrows and other signs. He'd found a crack of light—not a door, it turned out, but a seam between the plyboard wall panels —and squinting up to it, espied a small old man, *in appearance not unlike* the photographs at home of Ambrose's late grandfather, nodding upon a stool beneath a bare, speckled bulb. A crude panel of toggle- and knife-switches hung beside the open fuse box near his head; elsewhere in the little room were wooden levers and ropes belayed to boat cleats. At the time, Ambrose wasn't lost enough to rap or call; later he couldn't find that crack. Now it seemed to him that he'd possibly dozed off for a few minutes somewhere along the way; certainly he was exhausted from the afternoon's sunshine and the evening's problems; he couldn't be sure he hadn't dreamed part or all of the sight. Had an old black wall fan droned like bees and shimmied two flypaper streamers? Had the funhouse operator—gentle, somewhat sad and tired-appearing, in expression not unlike the photographs at home of Ambrose's late Uncle Konrad—murmured in his sleep? Is there really such a person as Ambrose, or is he a figment of the author's imagination? Was it Assawoman Bay or Sinepuxent? Are there other errors of fact in this fiction? Was there another sound besides the little slap slap of thigh on ham, like water sucking at the chine-boards of a skiff?

When you're lost, the smartest thing to do is stay put till you're found, hollering if necessary. But to holler guarantees humiliation as well as rescue; keeping silent permits some saving of face—you can act surprised at the fuss when your rescuers find you and swear you weren't lost, if they do. What's more you might find your own way yet, *however belatedly*.

"Don't tell me your foot's still asleep!" Magda exclaimed as the three young people walked from the inlet to the area set aside for ferris wheels, carrousels, and other carnival rides, they having decided in favor of the vast and ancient merry-go-round instead of the funhouse. What a sentence, everything was wrong from the outset. People don't know what to make of him, he doesn't know what to make of himself, he's only thirteen, *athletically and socially inept*, not astonishingly bright, but there are antennae; he has . . . some sort of receivers in his head; things speak to him, he understands more than he should, the world winks at him through its objects, grabs grinning at his coat. Everybody else is in on some secret he doesn't know; they've forgotten to tell him. Through simple *procrastination* his mother put off his baptism until this year. Everyone else had it done as a baby; he'd assumed the same of himself, as had his mother, so she claimed, until it was time for him to join Grace Methodist-Protestant and the oversight came out. He was mortified, but pitched sleepless through his private catechizing, intimidated by the ancient mysteries, a thirteen year old would never say that, resolved to experience conversion like St. Augustine. When the water touched his brow and Adam's sin left him, he contrived by a strain like defecation to bring tears into his eyes—but felt nothing. There was some simple, radical difference about him; he hoped it was genius, feared it was madness, devoted himself to amiability and inconspicuousness. Alone on the seawall near his house he was seized by the terrifying transports he'd thought to find in toolshed, in Communion-cup. The grass was alive! The town, the river, himself, were not imaginary; time roared in his ears like wind; the world was *going on!* This part ought to be dramatized. The Irish author James Joyce once wrote. Ambrose M—— is going to scream.

There is no *texture of rendered sensory detail*, for one thing. The faded distorting mirrors beside Fat May; the impossibility of choosing a mount when one had but a single ride on the great carrousel; the *vertigo attendant on his recognition* that Ocean City was worn out, the place of fathers and grandfathers, strawboatered men and parasoled ladies survived by their amusements. Money spent, the three paused at Peter's insistence beside Fat May to watch the girls get their skirts blown up. The object was to tease Magda, who said: "I swear, Peter M——, you've got a

one-track mind! Amby and me aren't *interested* in such things."
In the tumbling-barrel, too, just inside the Devil's-mouth entrance
to the funhouse, the girls were upended and their boyfriends and
others could see up their dresses if they cared to. Which was the
whole point, Ambrose realized. Of the entire funhouse! If you
looked around, you noticed that almost all the people on the boardwalk were paired off into couples except the small children; in a
way, that was the whole point of Ocean City! If you had X-ray
eyes and could see everything going on at that instant under the
boardwalk and in all the hotel rooms and cars and alleyways, you'd
realize that all that normally *showed*, like restaurants and dance
halls and clothing and test-your-strength machines, was merely preparation and intermission. Fat May screamed.

Because he watched the goings-on from the corner of his eye, it
was Ambrose who spied the half-dollar on the boardwalk near the
tumbling-barrel. Losers weepers. The first time he'd heard some
people moving through a corridor not far away, just after he'd lost
sight of the crack of light, he'd decided not to call to them, for
fear they'd guess he was scared and poke fun; it sounded like rough-
necks; he'd hoped they'd come by and he could follow in the dark
without their knowing. Another time he'd heard just one person,
unless he imagined it, bumping along as if on the other side of
the plywood; perhaps Peter coming back for him, or Father, or
Magda lost too. Or the owner and operator of the funhouse. He'd
called out once, as though merrily: "Anybody know where the heck
we are?" But the query was too stiff, his voice cracked, when the
sounds stopped he was terrified: maybe it was a queer who waited
for fellows to get lost, or a longhaired filthy monster that lived in
some cranny of the funhouse. He stood rigid for hours it seemed
like, scarcely respiring. His future was shockingly clear, in outline.
He tried holding his breath to the point of unconsciousness. There
ought to be a button you could push to end your life absolutely
without pain; disappear in a flick, like turning out a light. He would
push it instantly! He despised Uncle Karl. But he despised his
father too, for not being what he was supposed to be. Perhaps his
father hated *his* father, and so on, and his son would hate him,
and so on. Instantly!

Naturally he didn't have nerve enough to ask Magda to go
through the funhouse with him. With incredible nerve and to everyone's surprise he invited Magda, quietly and politely, to go
through the funhouse with him. "I warn you, I've never been
through it before," he added, *laughing easily*; "but I reckon we
can manage somehow. The important thing to remember, after
all, is that it's meant to be a *fun*house; that is, a place of amusement. If people really got lost or injured or too badly frightened in

it, the owner'd go out of business. There'd even be lawsuits. No character in a work of fiction can make a speech this long without interruption or acknowledgment from the other characters."

Mother teased Uncle Karl: "Three's a crowd, I always heard." But actually Ambrose was relieved that Peter now had a quarter too. Nothing was what it looked like. Every instant, under the surface of the Atlantic Ocean, millions of living animals devoured one another. Pilots were falling in flames over Europe; women were being forcibly raped in the South Pacific. His father should have taken him aside and said: "There is a simple secret to getting through the funhouse, as simple as being first to see the Towers. Here it is. Peter does not know it; neither does your Uncle Karl. You and I are different. Not surprisingly, you've often wished you weren't. Don't think I haven't noticed how unhappy your childhood has been! But you'll understand, when I tell you, why it had to be kept secret until now. And you won't regret not being like your brother and your uncle. *On the contrary!*" If you knew all the stories behind all the people on the boardwalk, you'd see that *nothing* was what it looked like. Husbands and wives often hated each other; parents didn't necessarily love their children; et cetera. A child took things for granted because he had nothing to compare his life to and everybody acted as if things were as they should be. Therefore each saw himself as the hero of the story, when the truth might turn out to be that he's the villain, or the coward. And there wasn't one thing you could do about it!

Hunchbacks, fat ladies, fools—that no one chose what he was was unbearable. In the movies he'd meet a beautiful young girl in the funhouse; they'd have hairs-breadth escapes from real dangers; he'd do and say the right things; she also; in the end they'd be lovers; their dialogue lines would match up; he'd be perfectly at ease; she'd not only like him well enough, she'd think he was *marvelous*; she'd lie awake thinking about *him*, instead of vice versa—the way *his* face looked in different lights and how he stood and exactly what he'd said—and yet that would be only one small episode in his wonderful life, among many many others. Not a *turning point* at all. What had happened in the toolshed was nothing. He hated, he loathed his parents! One reason for not writing a lost-in-the-funhouse story is that either everybody's felt what Ambrose feels, in which case it goes without saying, or else no normal person feels such things, in which case Ambrose is a freak. "Is anything more tiresome, in fiction, than the problems of sensitive adolescents?" And it's all too long and rambling, as if the author. For all a person knows the first time through, the end could be just around any corner; perhaps, *not impossibly* it's been within reach any number of times. On the other hand he may be scarcely past the start, with everything yet to get through, an intolerable idea.

Fill in: His father's raised eyebrows when he announced his decision to do the funhouse with Magda. Ambrose understands now, but didn't then, that his father was wondering whether he knew what the funhouse was *for*—especially since he didn't object, as he should have, when Peter decided to come along too. The ticket-woman, witchlike, mortifying him when inadvertently he gave her his name-coin instead of the half-dollar, then unkindly calling Magda's attention to the birthmark on his temple: "Watch out for him, girlie, he's a marked man!" She wasn't even cruel, he understood, only vulgar and insensitive. Somewhere in the world there was a young woman with such splendid understanding that she'd see him entire, like a poem or story, and find his words so valuable after all that when he confessed his apprehensions she would explain why they were in fact the very things that made him precious to her . . . and to Western Civilization! There was no such girl, the simple truth being. Violent yawns as they approached the mouth. Whispered advice from an old-timer on a bench near the barrel: "Go crabwise and ye'll get an eyeful without upsetting!" Composure vanished at the first pitch: Peter hollered joyously, Magda tumbled, shrieked, clutched her skirt; Ambrose scrambled crabwise, tight-lipped with terror, was soon out, watched his dropped name-coin slide among the couples. Shame-faced he saw that to get through expeditiously was not the point; Peter feigned assistance in order to trip Magda up, shouted "I see Christmas!" when her legs went flying. The old man, his latest betrayer, cacked approval. A dim hall then of black-thread cobwebs and recorded gibber: he took Magda's elbow to steady her against revolving discs set in the slanted floor to throw your feet out from under, and explained to her in a calm, deep voice his theory that each phase of the funhouse was triggered either automatically, by a series of photoelectric devices, or else manually by operators stationed at peepholes. But he lost his voice thrice as the discs unbalanced him; Magda was anyhow squealing; but at one point she clutched him about the waist to keep from falling, and her right cheek pressed for a moment against his belt-buckle. Heroically he drew her up, it was his chance to clutch her close as if for support and say: "I love you." He even put an arm lightly about the small of her back before a sailor-and-girl pitched into them from behind, sorely treading his left big toe and knocking Magda asprawl with them. The sailor's girl was a string-haired hussy with a loud laugh and light blue drawers; Ambrose realized that he wouldn't have said "I love you" anyhow, and was smitten with self-contempt. How much better it would be to be that common sailor! A wiry little

Seaman 3rd, the fellow squeezed a girl to each side and stumbled hilarious into the mirror room, closer to Magda in thirty seconds than Ambrose had got in thirteen years. She giggled at something the fellow said to Peter; she drew her hair from her eyes with a movement so womanly it struck Ambrose's heart; Peter's smacking her backside then seemed particularly coarse. But Magda made a pleased indignant face and cried, "All right for *you*, mister!" and pursued Peter into the maze without a backward glance. The sailor followed after, leisurely, drawing his girl against his hip; Ambrose understood not only they they were all so relieved to be rid of his burdensome company that they didn't even notice his absence, but that he himself shared their relief. Stepping from the treacherous passage at last into the mirror-maze, he saw once again, more clearly than ever, how readily he deceived himself into supposing he was a person. He even foresaw, wincing at his dreadful self-knowledge, that he would repeat the deception, at ever-rarer intervals, all his wretched life, so fearful were the alternatives. Fame, madness, suicide; perhaps all three. It's not believable that so young a boy could articulate that reflection, and in fiction the merely true must always yield to the plausible. Moreover, the symbolism is in places heavy-footed. Yet Ambrose M—— understood, as few adults do, that the famous loneliness of the great was no popular myth but a general truth—furthermore, that it was as much cause as effect.

All the preceding except the last few sentences is exposition that should've been done earlier or interspersed with the present action instead of lumped together. No reader would put up with so much with such *prolixity*. It's interesting that Ambrose's father, though presumably an intelligent man (as indicated by his role as grade-school principal), neither encouraged nor discouraged his sons at all in any way—as if he either didn't care about them or cared all right but didn't know how to act. If this fact should contribute to one of them's becoming a celebrated but wretchedly unhappy scientist, was it a good thing or not? He too might someday face the question; it would be useful to know whether it had tortured his father for years, for example, or never once crossed his mind.

In the maze two important things happened. First, our hero found a name-coin someone else had lost or discarded: *AMBROSE*, suggestive of the famous lightship and of his late grandfather's favorite dessert, which his mother used to prepare on special occasions out of coconut, oranges, grapes, and what else. Second, as he wondered at the endless replication of his image in the mirrors, second, as he *lost himself in the reflection* that the necessity for an observer makes perfect observation impossible, better make him eighteen at least, yet that would render other things unlikely, he heard Peter and Magda chuckling somewhere together in the maze. "Here!" "No, here!" they shouted to each other; Peter said, "Where's Amby?" Magda murmured. "Amb?" Peter called. In a pleased, friendly voice. He didn't reply. The truth was, his brother was a *happy-go-lucky youngster* who'd've been better off with a regular brother of his own, but who seldom complained of his lot and was generally cordial. Ambrose's throat ached; there aren't enough different ways to say that. He stood quietly while the two young people giggled and thumped through the glittering maze, hurrah'd their discovery of its exit, cried out in joyful alarm at what next beset them. Then he set his mouth and followed after, as he supposed, took a wrong turn, strayed into the pass *wherein he lingers yet.*

The action of conventional dramatic narrative may be represented by a diagram called Freitag's Triangle:

or more accurately by a variant of that diagram:

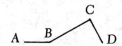

in which AB represents the exposition, B the introduction of conflict, BC the "rising action," complication, or development of the conflict, C the climax, or turn of the action, CD the dénouement, or resolution of the conflict. While there is no reason to regard this pattern as an absolute necessity, like many other conventions it became conventional because great numbers of people over many years learned by trial and error that it was effective; one ought not to forsake it, therefore, unless one wishes to forsake as well the effect of drama or has clear cause to feel that deliberate violation of the "normal" pattern can better can better effect that effect. This can't go on much longer; it can go on forever. He died telling stories to himself in the dark; years later, when that vast unsuspected area of the funhouse came to light, the first expedition found his skeleton in one of its labyrinthine corridors and mistook it for part of the entertainment. He died of starvation telling himself stories in the dark; but unbeknownst unbeknownst to him, an assistant operator of the funhouse, happening to overhear him, crouched just behind the plyboard partition and wrote down his every word. The operator's daughter, an exquisite young woman with a figure unusually well developed for her age, crouched just behind the partition and transcribed his every word. Though she had never laid eyes on him, she recognized that here was one of Western Culture's truly great imaginations, the eloquence of whose suffering would be an inspiration to unnumbered. And her heart was torn between her love for the misfortunate young man (yes, she loved him, though she had never laid though she knew him only —but how well!—through his words, and the deep, calm voice in which he spoke them) between her love et cetera and her womanly intuition that only in suffering and isolation could he give voice et cetera. Lone dark dying. Quietly she kissed the rough plyboard, and a tear fell upon the page. Where she had written in short-hand *Where she had written in shorthand* Where she had written in shorthand *Where she* et cetera. A long time ago we should have passed the apex of Freitag's Triangle and made brief work of the *dénouement*; the plot doesn't rise by meaningful steps but winds upon itself, digresses, retreats, hesitates, sighs, collapses, expires. The climax of the story must be its protagonist's discovery of a way to get through the funhouse. But he has found none, may have ceased to search.

What relevance does the war have to the story? Should there be fireworks outside or not?

Ambrose wandered, languished, dozed. Now and then he fell into his habit of rehearsing to himself the unadventurous story of his life, narrated from the third-person point of view, from his earliest memory parenthesis of maple leaves stirring in the summer breath of tidewater Maryland end of parenthesis to the present moment. Its principal events, on this telling, would appear to have been A, B, C, and D.

He imagined himself years hence, successful, married, at ease in the world, the trials of his adolescence far behind him. He has come to the seashore with his family for the holiday: how Ocean City has changed! But at one seldom at one ill-frequented end of the boardwalk a few derelict amusements survive from times gone by: the great carrousel from the turn of the century, with its monstrous griffins and mechanical concert band; the roller coaster rumored since 1916 to have been condemned; the mechanical shooting gallery in which only the image of our enemies changed. His own son laughs with Fat May and wants to know what a fun-house is; Ambrose hugs the sturdy lad close and smiles around his pipestem at his wife.

The family's going home. Mother sits between Father and Uncle Karl, who teases him good-naturedly who chuckles over the fact that the comrade with whom he'd fought his way shoulder to shoulder through the funhouse had turned out to be a blind Negro girl—to their mutual discomfort, as they'd opened their souls. But such are the walls of custom, which even. Whose arm is where? How must it feel. He dreams of a funhouse vaster by far than any yet constructed; but by then they may be out of fashion, like steamboats and excursion trains. Already quaint and seedy: the draperied ladies on the frieze of the carrousel are his father's father's mooncheeked dreams; if he thinks of it more he will vomit his apple-on-a-stick.

He wonders: will he become a regular person? Something has gone wrong; his vaccination didn't take; at the Boy-Scout initiation campfire he only pretended to be deeply moved, as he pretends to this hour that it is not so bad after all in the funhouse, and that he has a little limp. How long will it last? He envisions a truly astonishing funhouse, incredibly complex yet utterly controlled from a great central switchboard like the console of a pipe organ. Nobody had enough imagination. He could design such a place himself, wiring and all, and he's only thirteen years old. He would be its operator: panel lights would show what was up in every cranny of its cunning of its multifarious vastness; a switch-flick would ease this fellow's way, complicate that's, to balance things out; if anyone seemed lost or frightened, all the operator had to do was.

He wishes he had never entered the funhouse. But he has. Then he wishes he were dead. But he's not. Therefore he will construct funhouses for others and be their secret operator—though he would rather be among the lovers for whom funhouses are designed.

1968

JOHN UPDIKE

(1932–   )

From his first volume of poetry, *The Carpentered Hen and Other Tame Creatures* (1958), and the novel published the next year, *The Poorhouse Fair*, John Updike has been able to achieve a versatility that ranges from practiced absurdity to irony sharpened and refined by acute observation. His ear for the muted chivalry of youth brought him critical attention remarkably early in his career. A writer who has an accurate eye for the small

wonders of the commonplace, Updike can invest an international episode (as in the story below) with vivid poignancy. He has a gift for using banal phrases of domestic joy and discord to give dimension to familial situations, which he seems to absorb from the storms and brief moments of quiet in modern life.

Possessed of sharp insights and a remarkably lucid style, Updike is in some ways reminiscent of his character Henry

Bech. Highly praised in his twenties, he attained the age of forty without having satisfied his critics that the quality of his later books had fulfilled the brilliant promise of his earlier ones. The undisputed masterpiece that he seemed to many readers to be capable of producing continued to elude him, while he published book after book that all agreed were finely written but that some of his harshest critics judged to be deficient in significant content. *Rabbit, Run* (1960), his best novel, and one of the best of its decade, was published when he was twenty-eight. In *Rabbit Redux* (1971), a decade later, he advanced the central character ten years in age and, without writing a better novel than that brilliant earlier one, nevertheless reminded his readers that Harry Angstrom ("Rabbit") was one of the most interesting fictional characters of his time. "Actuality is a running impoverishment of possibility" runs a sentence from "The Bulgarian Poetess." It is Rabbit's refusal to learn, or to accept, this fact that gives him

the central place that he occupies in Updike's fiction. Time's tyranny, as theme, is the focal point for most of Updike's work.

John Updike was born in 1932 in Shillington, Pennsylvania. He attended Harvard and the Ruskin School of Design and Fine Art in England. For two years, 1955–1957, he was on the staff of *The New Yorker,* where many of his poems and short stories have appeared. In recent years he has lived and written in Ipswich, Massachusetts.

Volumes of poetry are: *The Carpentered Hen and Other Tame Creatures,* 1958; *Telephone Poles and Other Poems,* 1963; and *Midpoint and Other Poems,* 1969. Novels are: *The Poorhouse Fair,* 1959; *Rabbit, Run,* 1960; *The Centaur,* 1963; *Of the Farm,* 1966; *Couples,* 1968; and *Rabbit Redux,* 1971. Short story collections are: *The Same Door,* 1959; *Pigeon Feathers and Other Stories,* 1962; *The Music School,* 1966; *Bech: A Book,* 1970; and *Museums & Women and Other Stories,* 1972. *Assorted Prose* was published in 1965. Critical studies are Alice and Kenneth Hamilton, *The Elements of John Updike,* 1970; Rachael C. Burchard, *John Updike: Yea Sayings,* 1971; and Larry E. Taylor, *Pastoral and Anti-Pastoral Patterns in John Updike's Fiction,* 1971.

The Bulgarian Poetess

"Your poems. Are they difficult?"

She smiled and, unaccustomed to speaking English, answered carefully, drawing a line in the air with two delicately pinched fingers holding an imaginary pen. "They are difficult—to write."

He laughed, startled and charmed. "But not to read?"

She seemed puzzled by his laugh, but did not withdraw her smile, though its corners deepened in a defensive, feminine way. "I think," she said, "not so very."

"Good." Brainlessly he repeated "Good," disarmed by her unexpected quality of truth. He was, himself, a writer, this fortyish young man, Henry Bech, with his thinning curly hair and melancholy Jewish nose, the author of one good book and three others, the good one having come first. By a kind of oversight, he had never married. His reputation had grown while his powers declined. As he felt himself sink, in his fiction, deeper and deeper into eclectic sexuality and bravura narcissism, as his search for plain truth carried him further and further into treacherous realms of fantasy and, lately, of silence, he was more and more thickly hounded by homage, by flat-footed exegetes, by arrogantly worshipful undergraduates who had hitchhiked a thousand miles to touch his hand, by querulous translators, by election to honorary societies, by invitations to lecture, to "speak," to "read," to participate in symposia trumped up by ambitious girlie magazines in shameless conjunction with venerable universities. His very government, in airily unstamped envelopes from Washington, invited him to travel, as an ambassador of the arts, to the other half of the world, the hostile, mysterious half. Rather automatically, but with some faint hope of shaking himself loose from the burden of himself, he consented, and found himself floating, with a passport so stapled with visas it fluttered when pulled from his pocket, down into the dim airports of Communist cities.

He arrived in Sofia the day after a mixture of Bulgarian and African students had smashed the windows of the American legation and ignited an overturned Chevrolet. The cultural officer, pale from a sleepless night of guard duty, tamping his pipe with trembling fingers, advised Bech to stay out of crowds and escorted him to his hotel. The lobby was swarming with Negroes in black wool fezzes and pointed European shoes. Insecurely disguised, he felt, by an astrakhan hat purchased in Moscow, Bech passed through to the elevator, whose operator addressed him in German. "*Ja, vier,*" Bech answered, "*danke,*" and telephoned, in his bad French, for dinner to be brought up to his room. He remained there all night, behind a locked door, reading Hawthorne. He had lifted a paperback collection of short stories from a legation window sill littered with broken glass. A few curved bright crumbs fell from between the pages onto his blanket. The image of Roger Malvin lying alone, dying, in the forest—"Death would come like the slow approach of a corpse, stealing gradually towards him through the forest, and showing its ghastly and motionless features from behind a nearer and yet a nearer tree"—frightened him. Bech fell asleep early and suffered from swollen, homesick dreams. It had been Thanksgiving Day.

In the morning, venturing downstairs for breakfast, he was surprised to find the restaurant open, the waiters affable, the eggs actual, the coffee hot, though syrupy. Outside, Sofia was sunny and (except for a few dark glances at his big American shoes) amenable to his passage along the streets. Lozenge-patterns of pansies, looking flat and brittle as pressed flowers, had been set in the public beds. Women with a touch of Western chic walked hatless in the park behind the mausoleum of Georgi Dimitrov. There was a mosque, and an assortment of trolley cars salvaged from the remotest corner of Bech's childhood, and a tree that talked—that is, it was so full of birds that it swayed under their weight and emitted volumes of chirping sound like a great leafy loudspeaker. It was the inverse of his hotel, whose silent walls presumably contained listening microphones. Electricity was somewhat enchanted in the Socialist world. Lights flickered off untouched and radios turned themselves on. Telephones rang in the dead of the night and breathed wordlessly in his ear. Six weeks ago, flying from New York City, Bech had expected Moscow to be a blazing counterpart and instead saw, through the plane window, a skein of hoarded lights no brighter, on that vast black plain, than a girl's body in a dark room.

Past the talking tree was the American legation. The sidewalk, heaped with broken glass, was roped off, so that pedestrians had to detour into the gutter. Bech detached himself from the stream, crossed the little barren of pavement, smiled at the Bulgarian militiamen who were sullenly guarding the jewel-bright heaps of shards, and pulled open the bronze door. The cultural officer was crisper after a normal night's sleep. He clenched his pipe in his teeth and handed Bech a small list. "You're to meet with the Writers' Union at eleven. These are writers you might ask to see. As far as we can tell, they're among the more progressive."

Words like "progressive" and "liberal" had a somewhat reversed sense in this world. At times, indeed, Bech felt he had passed through a mirror, a dingy flecked mirror that reflected feebly the capitalist world; in its dim depths everything was similar but left-handed. One of the names ended in "-ova." Bech said, "A woman."

"A poetess," the cultural officer said, sucking and tamping in a fury of bogus efficiency. "Very popular, apparently. Her books are impossible to buy."

"Have you read anything by these people?"

"I'll be frank with you. I can just about make my way through a newspaper."

"But you always know what a newspaper will say anyway."

"I'm sorry, I don't get your meaning."

"There isn't any." Bech didn't quite know why the Americans he met irritated him—whether because they garishly refused to blend into this shadow-world or because they were always so solemnly sending him on ridiculous errands.

At the Writers' Union, he handed the secretary the list as it had been handed to him, on U.S. legation stationery. The secretary, a large stooped man with the hands of a stonemason, grimaced and shook his head but obligingly reached for the telephone. Bech's meeting was already waiting in another room. It was the usual one, the one that, with small differences, he had already attended in Moscow and Kiev, Yerevan and Alma-Ata, Bucharest and Prague: the polished oval table, the bowl of fruit, the morning light, the gleaming glasses of brandy and mineral water, the lurking portrait of Lenin, the six or eight patiently sitting men who would leap to their feet with quick blank smiles. These men would include a few literary officials, termed "critics," high in the Party, loquacious and witty and destined to propose a toast to international understanding; a few selected novelists and poets, mustachioed, smoking, sulking at this invasion of their time; a university professor, the head of the Anglo-American Literature department, speaking in a beautiful withered English of Mark Twain and Sinclair Lewis; a young interpreter with a moist handshake; a shaggy old journalist obsequiously scribbling notes; and, on the rim of the group, in chairs placed to suggest that they had invited themselves, one or two gentlemen of ill-defined status, fidgety and tieless, maverick translators who would turn out to be the only ones present who had ever read a word by Henry Bech.

Here this type was represented by a stout man in a tweed coat leather-patched at the elbows in the British style. The whites of his eyes were distinctly red. He shook Bech's hand eagerly, made of it almost an embrace of reunion, bending his face so close that Bech could distinguish the smells of tobacco, garlic, cheese, and alcohol. Even as they were seating themselves around the table, and the Writers' Union chairman, a man elegantly bald, with very pale eyelashes, was touching his brandy glass as if to lift it, this anxious red-eyed interloper blurted at Bech, "Your *Travel Light* was so marvellous a book. The motels, the highways, the young girls with their lovers who were motorcyclists, so marvellous, so American, the youth, the adoration for space and speed, the barbarity of the advertisements in neon lighting, the very poetry. It takes us truly into another dimension."

Travel Light was the first novel, the famous one. Bech disliked discussing it. "At home," he said, "it was criticized as despairing."

The man's hands, stained orange with tobacco, lifted in amazement and plopped noisily to his knees. "No, no a thousand times. Truth, wonder, terror even, vulgarity, yes. But despair, no, not at all, not one iota. Your critics are dead wrong."

"Thank you."

The chairman softly cleared his throat and lifted his glass an inch from the table, so that it formed with its reflection a kind of playing card.

Bech's admirer excitedly persisted. "You are not a *wet* writer, no. You are a dry writer, yes? You have the expressions, am I wrong in English, dry, hard?"

"More or less."

"I want to translate you!"

It was the agonized cry of a condemned man, for the chairman coldly lifted his glass to the height of his eyes, and like a firing squad the others followed suit. Blinking his white lashes, the chairman gazed mistily in the direction of the sudden silence, and spoke in Bulgarian.

The young interpreter murmured in Bech's ear. "I wish to propose now, ah, a very brief toast. I know it will seem doubly brief to our honored American guest, who has so recently enjoyed the, ah, hospitality of our Soviet comrades." There must have been a joke here, for the rest of the table laughed. "But in seriousness permit me to say that in our country we have seen in years past too few Americans, ah, of Mr. Bech's progressive and sympathetic stripe. We hope in the next hour to learn from him much that is interesting and, ah, socially useful about the literature of his large country, and perhaps we may in turn inform him of our own proud literature, of which perhaps he knows regrettably little. Ah, so let me finally, then, since there is a saying that too long a courtship spoils the marriage, offer to drink, in our native plum brandy *slivovica,* ah, firstly to the success of his visit and, in the second place, to the mutual increase of international understanding."

"Thank you," Bech said and, as a courtesy, drained his glass. It was wrong; the others, having merely sipped, stared. The purple burning revolved in Bech's stomach and a severe distaste for himself, for his role, for this entire artificial and futile process, focused into a small brown spot on a pear in the bowl so shiningly posed before his eyes.

The red-eyed fool smelling of cheese was ornamenting the toast. "It is a personal honor for me to meet the man who, in *Travel Light,* truly added a new dimension to American prose."

"The book was written," Bech said, "twelve years ago."

"And since?" A slumping, mustached man sat up and sprang into English. "Since, you have written what?"

Bech had been asked that question often in these weeks and his answer had grown curt. "A second novel called *Brother Pig,* which is St. Bernard's expression for the body."

"Good. Yes, and?"

"A collection of essays and sketches called *When the Saints.*"

"I like the title less well."

"It's the beginning of a famous Negro song."

"We know the song," another man said, a smaller man, with

the tense, dented mouth of a hare. He lightly sang, "Lordy, I just want to be in that number."

"And the last book," Bech said, "was a long novel called *The Chosen* that took six years to write and that nobody liked."

"I have read reviews," the red-eyed man said. "I have not read the book. Copies are difficult here."

"I'll give you one," Bech said.

The promise seemed, somehow, to make the recipient unfortunately conspicuous; wringing his stained hands, he appeared to swell in size, to intrude grotesquely upon the inner ring, so that the interpreter took it upon himself to whisper, with the haste of an apology, into Bech's ear, "This gentleman is well known as the translator into our language of *Erewhon*."

"A marvellous book," the translator said, deflating in relief, pulling at his pockets for a cigarette. "It truly takes us into another dimension. Something that must be done. We live in a new cosmos."

The chairman spoke in Bulgarian, musically, at length. There was polite laughter. Nobody translated for Bech. The professorial type, his hair like a flaxen toupee, jerked forward. "Tell me, is it true, as I have read"—his phrases whistled slightly, like rusty machinery—"that the stock of Sinclair Lewis has plummeted under the Salinger wave?"

And so it went, here as in Kiev, Prague, and Alma-Ata, the same questions, more or less predictable, and his own answers, terribly familiar to him by now, mechanical, stale, irrelevant, untrue, claustrophobic. The door opened. In came, with the rosy air of a woman fresh from a bath, a little breathless, having hurried, hatless, a woman in a blond coat, her hair also blond. The secretary, entering behind her, seemed to make a cherishing space around her with his large curved hands. He introduced her to Bech as Vera Something-ova, the poetess he had asked to meet. None of the others on the list, he explained, answered their telephones.

"Aren't you kind to come?" As Bech asked it, it was a genuine question, to which he expected some sort of an answer.

She spoke to the interpreter in Bulgarian. "She says," the interpreter told Bech, "she is sorry she is so late."

"But she was just called!" In the warmth of his confusion and pleasure Bech turned to speak directly to her, forgetting he would not be understood. "I'm terribly sorry to have interrupted your morning."

"I am pleased," she said, "to meet you. I heard of you spoken in France."

"You speak English!"

"No. Very little amount."

"But you *do*."

A chair was brought for her from a corner of the room. She yielded her coat, revealing herself in a suit also blond, as if her clothes were an aspect of a total consistency. She sat down opposite Bech, crossing her legs. Her legs were very good; her face was perceptibly broad. Lowering her lids, she tugged her skirt to the curve of her knee. It was his sense of her having hurried, hurried to him, and of being, still, graciously flustered, that most touched him.

He spoke to her very clearly, across the fruit, fearful of abusing and breaking the fragile bridge of her English. "You are a poetess. When I was young, I also wrote poems."

She was silent so long he thought she would never answer; but then she smiled and pronounced, "You are not old now."

"Your poems. Are they difficult?"

"They are difficult—to write."

"But not to read?"

"I think—not so very."

"Good. Good."

Despite the decay of his career, Bech had retained an absolute faith in his instincts; he never doubted that somewhere an ideal course was open to him and that his intuitions were pre-dealt clues to his destiny. He had loved, briefly or long, with or without consummation, perhaps a dozen women; yet all of them, he now saw, shared the trait of approximation, of narrowly missing an undisclosed prototype. The surprise he felt did not have to do with the appearance, at last, of this central woman; he had always expected her to appear. What he had not expected was her appearance here, in this remote and abused nation, in this room of morning light, where he discovered a small knife in his fingers and on the table before him, golden and moist, a precisely divided pear.

Men travelling alone develop a romantic vertigo. Bech had already fallen in love with a freckled Embassy wife in Prague, a bucktoothed chanteuse in Rumania, a stolid Mongolian sculptress in Kazakhstan. In the Tretyakov Gallery he had fallen in love with a recumbent statue, and at the Moscow Ballet School with an entire roomful of girls. Entering the room, he had been struck by the aroma, tenderly acrid, of young female sweat. Sixteen and seventeen, wearing patchy practice suits, the girls were twirling so strenuously their slippers were unravelling. Demure student faces crowned the unconscious insolence of their bodies. The room was doubled in depth by a floor-to-ceiling mirror. Bech was seated on a bench at its base. Staring above his head, each girl watched herself with frowning eyes frozen, for an instant in the turn, by the imperious delay and snap of her head. Bech tried to remember the lines of Rilke that expressed it, this snap and delay: *did not the drawing remain/that the dark stroke of your eyebrow/swiftly wrote on the wall of its own turning?* At one point the teacher, a shapeless old Ukrainian lady with gold canines, a *prima* of the thirties, had arisen and cried something translated to Bech as, "No, no, the arms free, *free!*" And in demonstration she had executed a rapid series of pirouettes with such proud effortlessness that all the girls, standing this way and that like deer along the wall, had applauded. Bech had loved them for that. In all his loves, there was an urge to rescue—to rescue the girls from the slavery of their exertions, the statue from the cold grip of its own marble, the Embassy wife from her boring and unctuous husband, the chanteuse from her nightly humiliation (she could not sing), the Mongolian from her stolid race. But the Bulgarian poetess presented herself to him as needing nothing, as being complete, poised, satisfied, achieved. He was aroused and curious and, the next day, inquired about her of the man with the vaguely contemptuous mouth of a hare—a novelist turned playwright and scenarist, who accompanied him to the Rila Monastery. "She lives to write," the playwright said. "I do not think it is healthy."

Bech said, "But she seems so healthy." They stood beside a small church with whitewashed walls. From the outside it looked like a hovel, a shelter for pigs or chickens. For five centuries the Turks had ruled Bulgaria, and the Christian churches, however richly adorned within, had humble exteriors. A peasant woman with wildly snarled hair unlocked the door for them. Though the church could hardly ever have held more than thirty worshippers, it was divided into three parts, and every inch of wall was covered with eighteenth-century frescoes. Those in the narthex depicted a Hell where the devils wielded scimitars. Passing through the tiny nave, Bech peeked through the iconostasis into the screened area that, in the symbolism of Orthodox architecture, represented the next, the hidden world—Paradise—and glimpsed a row of books, an easy chair, a pair of ancient oval spectacles. Outdoors again, he felt released from the unpleasantly tight atmosphere of a children's book. They were on the side of a hill. Above them was a stand of pines whose trunks glistened with ice. Below them sprawled the monastery, a citadel of Bulgarian national feeling during the years of the Turkish Yoke. The last monks had been moved out in 1961. An aimless soft rain was falling in these mountains, and there were not many German tourists today. Across the valley, whose little silver river still turned a water wheel, a motionless white horse stood silhouetted against a green meadow, pinned there like a brooch.

"I am an old friend of hers," the playwright said. "I worry about her."

"Are the poems good?"

"It is difficult for me to judge. They are very feminine. Perhaps shallow."

"Shallowness can be a kind of honesty."

"Yes. She is very honest in her work."

"And in her life?"

"As well."

"What does her husband do?"

The other man looked at him with parted lips and touched his arm, a strange Slavic gesture, communicating an underlying racial urgency, that Bech no longer shied from. "But she has no husband. As I say, she is too much for poetry to have married."

"But her name ends in '-ova.'"

"I see. You are mistaken. It is not a matter of marriage; I am Petrov, my unmarried sister is Petrova. All females."

"How stupid of me. But I think it's such a pity, she's so charming."

"In America, only the uncharming fail to marry?"

"Yes, you must be very uncharming not to marry."

"It is not so here. The government indeed is alarmed; our birth rate is one of the lowest in Europe. It is a problem for economists."

Bech gestured at the monastery. "Too many monks?"

"Not enough, perhaps. With too few of monks, something of the monk enters everybody."

The peasant woman, who seemed old to Bech but who was probably younger than he, saw them to the edge of her domain. She huskily chattered in what Petrov said was very amusing rural slang. Behind her, now hiding in her skirts and now darting away, was her child, a boy not more than three. He was faithfully chased, back and forth, by a small white pig, who moved, as pigs do, on tiptoe, with remarkably abrupt changes of direction. Something in the scene, in the open glee of the woman's parting smile and the unselfconscious way her hair thrust out from her head, something in the mountain mist and spongy rutted turf into which frost had begun to break at night, evoked for Bech a nameless absence to which was attached, like a horse to a meadow, the image of the poetess, with her broad face, her good legs, her Parisian clothes, and her sleekly brushed hair. Petrov, in whom he was beginning to sense, through the wraps of foreignness, a clever and kindred mind, seemed to have overheard his thoughts, for he said, "If you would like, we could have dinner. It would be easy for me to arrange."

"With her?"

"Yes, she is my friend, she would be glad."

"But I have nothing to say to her. I'm just curious about such an intense conjunction of good looks and brains. I mean, what does a soul do with it all?"

"You may ask her. Tomorrow night?"

"I'm sorry, I can't. I'm scheduled to go to the ballet, and the next night the legation is giving a cocktail party for me, and then I fly home."

"Home? So soon?"

"It does not feel soon to me. I must try to work again."

"A drink, then. Tomorrow evening before the ballet? It is possible? It is not possible."

Petrov looked puzzled, and Bech realized that it was his fault, for he was nodding to say Yes, but in Bulgaria nodding meant No, and a shake of the head meant Yes. "Yes," he said. "Gladly."

The ballet was entitled *Silver Slippers*. As Bech watched it, the word "ethnic" kept coming to his mind. He had grown accustomed, during his trip, to this sort of artistic evasion, the retreat from the difficult and disappointing present into folk dance, folk tale, folk song, with always the implication that, beneath the embroidered peasant costume, the folk was really one's heart's own darling, the proletariat.

"Do you like fairy tales?" It was the moist-palmed interpreter who accompanied him to the theatre.

"I *love* them," Bech said, with a fervor and gaiety lingering from the previous hour. The interpreter looked at him anxiously, as when Bech had swallowed the brandy in one swig, and throughout the ballet kept murmuring explanations of self-evident events on the stage. Each night, a princess would put on silver slippers and dance through her mirror to tryst with a wizard, who possessed a magic stick that she coveted, for with it the world could be ruled. The wizard, as a dancer, was inept, and once almost dropped her, so that anger flashed from her eyes. She was, the princess, a little redhead with a high round bottom and a frozen pout and beautiful free arm motions, and Bech found it oddly ecstatic when, preparatory to her leap, she would dance toward the mirror, an empty oval, and another girl, identically dressed in pink, would emerge from the wings and perform as her reflection. And when the princess, haughtily adjusting her cape of invisibility, leaped through the oval of gold wire, Bech's heart leaped backward into the enchanted hour he had spent with the poetess.

Though the appointment had been established, she came into the restaurant as if, again, she had been suddenly summoned and had hurried. She sat down between Bech and Petrov slightly breathless and fussed, but exuding, again, that impalpable warmth of intelligence and virtue.

"Vera, Vera," Petrov said.

"You hurry too much," Bech told her.

"Not so very much," she said.

Petrov ordered her a cognac and continued with Bech their discussion of the newer French novelists. "It is tricks," Petrov said. "Good tricks, but tricks. It does not have enough to do with life, it is too much verbal nervousness. Is that sense?"

"It's an epigram," Bech said.

"There are just two of their number with whom I do not feel this: Claude Simon and Samuel Beckett. You have no relation, Bech, Beckett?"

"None."

Vera said, "Nathalie Sarraute is a very modest woman. She felt motherly to me."

"You have met her?"

"In Paris I heard her speak. Afterward there was the coffee. I liked her theories, of the, oh, *what?* Of the *little* movements within the heart." She delicately measured a pinch of space and smiled, through Bech, back at herself.

"Tricks," Petrov said. "I do not feel this with Beckett; there, in a low form, believe it or not, one has human content."

Bech felt duty-bound to pursue this, to ask about the theatre of the absurd in Bulgaria, about abstract painting (these were the touchstones of "progressiveness"; Russia had none, Rumania some, Czechoslovakia plenty), to subvert Petrov. Instead, he asked the poetess, "Motherly?"

Vera explained, her hands delicately modelling the air, rounding into nuance, as it were, the square corners of her words. "After her talk, we—talked."

"In French?"

"And in Russian."

"She knows Russian?"

"She was born Russian."

"How is her Russian?"

"Very pure but—old-fashioned. Like a book. As she talked, I felt in a book, safe."

"You do not always feel safe?"

"Not always."

"Do you find it difficult to be a woman poet?"

"We have a tradition of woman poets. We have Elisaveta Bagriana, who is very great."

Petrov leaned toward Bech as if to nibble him. "Your own

works? Are they influenced by the *nouvelle vague?* Do you consider yourself to write anti-*romans?*

Bech kept himself turned toward the woman. "Do you want to hear about how I write? You don't, do you?"

"Very much yes," she said.

He told them, told them shamelessly, in a voice that surprised him with its steadiness, its limpid urgency, how once he had written, how in *Travel Light* he had sought to show people skimming the surface of things with their lives, taking tints from things the way that objects in a still life color one another, and how later he had attempted to place beneath the melody of plot a countermelody of imagery, interlocking images which had risen to the top and drowned his story, and how in *The Chosen* he had sought to make of this confusion the theme itself, an epic theme, by showing a population of characters whose actions were all determined, at the deepest level, by nostalgia, by a desire to get back, to dive, each, into the springs of their private imagery. The book probably failed; at least, it was badly received. Bech apologized for telling all this. His voice tasted flat in his mouth; he felt a secret intoxication and a secret guilt, for he had contrived to give a grand air, as of an impossibly noble and quixotically complex experiment, to his failure when at bottom, he suspected, a certain simple laziness was the cause.

Petrov said, "Fiction so formally sentimental could not be composed in Bulgaria. We do not have a happy history."

It was the first time Petrov had sounded like a Communist. If there was one thing that irked Bech about these people behind the mirror, it was their assumption that, however second-rate elsewhere, in suffering they were supreme. He said, "Believe it or not, neither do we."

Vera calmly intruded. "Your personae are not moved by love?"

"Yes, very much. But as a form of nostalgia. We fall in love, I tried to say in the book, with women who remind us of our first landscape. A silly idea. I used to be interested in love. I once wrote an essay on the orgasm—you know the word?—"

She shook her head. He remembered that it meant Yes.

"—on the orgasm as perfect memory. The one mystery is, what are we remembering?"

She shook her head again, and he noticed that her eyes were gray, and that in their depths his image (which he could not see) was searching for the thing remembered. She composed her fingertips around the brandy glass and said, "There is a French poet, a young one, who has written of this. He says that never else do we, do we so gather up, collect into ourselves, oh—" Vexed, she spoke to Petrov in rapid Bulgarian.

He shrugged and said, "Concentrate our attention."

"—concentrate our attention," she repeated to Bech, as if the words, to be believed, had to come from her. "I say it foolish— foolishly—but in French it is very well put and—*correct*."

Petrov smiled neatly and said, "This is an enjoyable subject for discussion, love."

"It remains," Bech said, picking his words as if the language were not native even to him, "one of the few things that still deserve meditation."

"I think it is good," she said.

"Love?" he asked, startled.

She shook her head and tapped the stem of her glass with a fingernail, so that Bech had an inaudible sense of ringing, and she bent as if to study the liquor, so that her entire body borrowed a rosiness from the brandy and burned itself into Bech's memory—the silver gloss of her nail, the sheen of her hair, the symmetry of her arms relaxed on the white tablecloth, everything except the expression on her face.

Petrov asked aloud Bech's opinion of Dürrenmatt.

Actuality is a running impoverishment of possibility. Though he had looked forward to seeing her again at the cocktail party and had made sure that she was invited, when it occurred, though she came, he could not get to her. He saw her enter, with Petrov, but he was fenced in by an attaché of the Yugoslav Embassy and his burnished Tunisian wife; and, later, when he was worming his way toward her diagonally, a steely hand closed on his arm and a rasping American female told him that her fifteen-year-old nephew had decided to be a writer and desperately needed advice. Not the standard crap, but real brass-knuckles advice. Bech found himself balked. He was surrounded by America: the voices, the narrow suits, the watery drinks, the clatter, the glitter. The mirror had gone opaque and gave him back only himself. He managed, in the end, as the officials were thinning out, to break through and confront her in a corner. Her coat, blond, with a rabbit collar, was already on; from its side pocket she pulled a pale volume of poems in the Cyrillic alphabet. "Please," she said. On the flyleaf she had written, "to H. Beck, sincerelly, with bad spellings but much"—the last word looked like "leave" but must have been "love."

"Wait," he begged, and went back to where his ravaged pile of presentation books had been and, unable to find the one he wanted, stole the legation library's jacketless copy of *The Chosen*. Placing it in her expectant hands, he told her, "Don't look," for inside he had written, with a drunk's stylistic confidence,

Dear Vera Glavanakova—
It is a matter of earnest regret for me that you and I must live on opposite sides of the world.

1966

JOYCE CAROL OATES
(1938–)

Joyce Carol Oates published her first collection of short stories, *By the North Gate* (1963), two years after she had received her M.A. from the University of Wisconsin and become an Instructor of English at the University of Detroit. Within ten more years she had published six novels, three more collections of short stories, three volumes of poetry, and a book of criticism. She had also had three plays produced in New York and had discarded two more novels that she decided not to publish. In the meantime, she had continued to teach, moving in 1967 from the University of Detroit to the University of Windsor, in Ontario. Reviewers admired her enormous energy, but found a productivity of such magnitude difficult to assess. Clearly her work was uneven, but clearly, also, it was distinguished by passages of brilliance.

She was born in Lockport, New York, and raised in the country nearby, "a part of the world," she has said, "and an economic background where people don't even graduate from high school." A scholarship student at Syracuse University, she wrote voluminously, graduated Phi Beta Kappa in 1960, and then spent a year on a fellowship at the University of Wisconsin.

In a decade characterized by the abandonment of so much of the realistic tradition by authors such as John Barth, Donald Barthelme, and Thomas Pynchon, Joyce Carol Oates seemed at times determinedly old-fashioned in her insistence on the essentially mimetic quality of her fiction. Hers is a world of violence, insanity, fractured love, and hopeless loneliness. Although some of it appears to come from her own direct observations, her dreams, her fears, much more is clearly from the experiences of others. Her first novel, *With Shuddering Fall* (1964), dealt with stock car racing, though she had never seen a race. In *them* (1969) she focused on Detroit from the Depression through the riots of 1967, drawing much of her material from the deep impression made on her by the problems of one of her students. Whatever the source and however shocking the events or the motivations, however, her fictive world remains strikingly akin to that real one reflected in the daily newspapers, the television news and talk shows, the popular magazines of our day. *Wonderland* (1971) opens with a family murder and suicide, from which only the main character escapes. *Do with Me What You Will* (1973), perhaps her strongest novel to date, begins with the abduction of a small girl from a school playground.

Some of her best work is in her short stories. By the time of her third collection, *The Wheel of Love* (1970), she had developed a control and an authority that placed her well ahead of most of her contemporaries. In almost all of her writing, however, she displays a healthy attitude toward the possibilities for further growth and development. In the summer of 1972, with nearly a dozen books behind her,

she was still capable of asserting that "everything I have done so far is only preliminary to my most serious work * * * ."

Novels are *With Shuddering Fall*, 1964; *A Garden of Earthly Delights*, 1967; *Expensive People*, 1968; *them*, 1969; *Wonderland*, 1971; and *Do with Me What You Will*, 1973. Collections of short stories are *By the North Gate*, 1963; *Upon the Sweeping Flood*, 1966; *The Wheel of Love*, from which the selection reprinted below is taken, 1970; and *Marriages and Infidelities*, 1972. Verse is collected in *Anonymous Sins & Other Poems*, 1969; *Love and Its Derangements*, 1970; and *Angel Fire*, 1973. Criticism is *The Edge of Impossibility*, 1972. Alfred Kazin published a perceptive critical introduction, "Oates," in *Harper's Magazine*, August, 1971, pp. 78–82.

Where Are You Going, Where Have You Been?

For Bob Dylan

Her name was Connie. She was fifteen and she had a quick, nervous giggling habit of craning her neck to glance into mirrors or checking other people's faces to make sure her own was all right. Her mother, who noticed everything and knew everything and who hadn't much reason any longer to look at her own face, always scolded Connie about it. "Stop gawking at yourself. Who are you? You think you're so pretty?" she would say. Connie would raise her eyebrows at these familiar old complaints and look right through her mother, into a shadowy vision of herself as she was right at that moment: she knew she was pretty and that was everything. Her mother had been pretty once too, if you could believe those old snapshots in the album, but now her looks were gone and that was why she was always after Connie.

"Why don't you keep your room clean like your sister? How've you got your hair fixed—what the hell stinks? Hair spray? You don't see your sister using that junk."

Her sister June was twenty-four and still lived at home. She was a secretary in the high school Connie attended, and if that wasn't bad enough—with her in the same building—she was so plain and chunky and steady that Connie had to hear her praised all the time by her mother and her mother's sisters. June did this, June did that, she saved money and helped clean the house and cooked and Connie couldn't do a thing, her mind was all filled with trashy daydreams. Their father was away at work most of the time and when he came home he wanted supper and he read the newspaper at supper and after supper he went to bed. He didn't bother talking much to them, but around his bent head Connie's mother kept picking at her until Connie wished her mother was dead and she herself was dead and it was all over. "She makes me want to throw up sometimes," she complained to her friends. She had a high, breathless, amused voice that made everything she said sound a little forced, whether it was sincere or not.

There was one good thing: June went places with girl friends of hers, girls who were just as plain and steady as she, and so when Connie wanted to do that her mother had no objections. The father of Connie's best girl friend drove the girls the three miles to town and left them at a shopping plaza so they could walk through the stores or go to a movie, and when he came to pick them up again at eleven he never bothered to ask what they had done.

They must have been familiar sights, walking around the shopping plaza in their shorts and flat ballerina slippers that always scuffed the sidewalk, with charm bracelets jingling on their thin wrists; they would lean together to whisper and laugh secretly if someone passed who amused or interested them. Connie had long dark blond hair that drew anyone's eye to it, and she wore part of it pulled up on her head and puffed out and the rest of it she let fall down her back. She wore a pull-over jersey blouse that looked one way when she was at home and another way when she was away from home. Everything about her had two sides to it, one for home and one for anywhere that was not home: her walk, which could be childlike and bobbing, or languid enough to make anyone think she was hearing music in her head; her mouth, which was pale and smirking most of the time, but bright and pink on these evenings out; her laugh, which was cynical and drawling at home—"Ha, ha, very funny,"—but high-pitched and nervous anywhere else, like the jingling of the charms on her bracelet.

Sometimes they did go shopping or to a movie, but sometimes they went across the highway, ducking fast across the busy road, to a drive-in restaurant where older kids hung out. The restaurant was shaped like a big bottle, though squatter than a real bottle, and on its cap was a revolving figure of a grinning boy holding a hamburger aloft. One night in midsummer they ran across, breathless with daring, and right away someone leaned out a car window and invited them over, but it was just a boy from high school they didn't like. It made them feel good to be able to ignore him. They went up through the maze of parked and cruising cars to the bright-lit, fly-infested restaurant, their faces pleased and expectant as if they were entering a sacred building that loomed up out of the night to give them what haven and blessing they yearned for. They sat at the counter and crossed their legs at the ankles, their thin shoulders rigid with excitement, and listened to the music that made everything so good: the music was always in the background, like music at a church service; it was something to depend upon.

A boy named Eddie came in to talk with them. He sat backwards on his stool, turning himself jerkily around in semicircles and then stopping and turning back again, and after a while he asked Connie if she would like something to eat. She said she would and so she tapped her friend's arm on her way out—her friend pulled her face up into a brave, droll look—and Connie said she would meet her at eleven, across the way. "I just hate to leave her like that," Connie said earnestly, but the boy said that she wouldn't be alone for long. So they went out to his car, and on the way Connie couldn't help but let her eyes wander over the windshields and faces all around her, her face gleaming with a joy that had nothing to do with Eddie or even this place; it might have been the music. She drew her shoulders up and sucked in her breath with the pure pleasure of being alive, and just at that moment she happened to glance at a face just a few feet from hers. It was a boy with shaggy black hair, in a convertible jalopy painted gold. He stared at her and then his lips widened into a grin. Connie slit her eyes at him and turned away, but she couldn't help glancing back and there he was, still watching her. He wagged a finger and laughed and said, "Gonna get you, baby," and Connie turned away again without Eddie noticing anything.

She spent three hours with him, at the restaurant where they ate hamburgers and drank Cokes in wax cups that were always sweating, and then down an alley a mile or so away, and when he left her off at five to eleven only the movie house was still open at the plaza. Her girl friend was there, talking with a boy. When Connie came up, the two girls smiled at each other and Connie said, "How was the movie?" and the girl said, "*You* should know." They rode off with the girl's father, sleepy and pleased, and Connie couldn't help but look back at the darkened shopping plaza with its big empty parking lot and its signs that were faded and ghostly now, and over at the drive-in restaurant where cars were still circling tirelessly. She couldn't hear the music at this distance.

Next morning June asked her how the movie was and Connie said, "So-so."

She and that girl and occasionally another girl went out several times a week, and the rest of the time Connie spent around the house—it was summer vacation—getting in her mother's way and thinking, dreaming about the boys she met. But all the boys fell back and dissolved into a single face that was not even a face but an idea, a feeling, mixed up with the urgent insistent pounding of the music and the humid night air of July. Connie's mother kept dragging her back to the daylight by finding things for her to do or saying suddenly, "What's this about the Pettinger girl?"

And Connie would say nervously, "Oh, her. That dope." She always drew thick clear lines between herself and such girls, and her mother was simple and kind enough to believe it. Her mother was so simple, Connie thought, that it was maybe cruel to fool her so much. Her mother went scuffling around the house in old bedroom slippers and complained over the telephone to one sister about the other, then the other called up and the two of them complained about the third one. If June's name was mentioned her mother's tone was approving, and if Connie's name was mentioned it was disapproving. This did not really mean she disliked Connie, and actually Connie thought that her mother preferred her to June just because she was prettier, but the two of them kept up a pretense of exasperation, a sense that they were tugging and struggling over something of little value to either of them. Sometimes, over coffee, they were almost friends, but something would come up—some vexation that was like a fly buzzing suddenly around their heads—and their faces went hard with contempt.

One Sunday Connie got up at eleven—none of them bothered with church—and washed her hair so that it could dry all day long in the sun. Her parents and sister were going to a barbecue at an aunt's house and Connie said no, she wasn't interested, rolling her eyes to let her mother know just what she thought of it. "Stay home alone then," her mother said sharply. Connie sat out back in a lawn chair and watched them drive away, her father quiet and bald, hunched around so that he could back the car out, her mother with a look that was still angry and not at all softened through the windshield, and in the back seat poor old June, all dressed up as if she didn't know what a barbecue was, with all the running yelling kids and the flies. Connie sat with her eyes closed in the sun, dreaming and dazed with the warmth about her as if this were a kind of love, the caresses of love, and her mind slipped over onto thoughts of the boy she had been with the night before and how nice he had been, how sweet it always was, not the way someone like June would suppose but sweet, gentle, the way it was in movies and promised in songs; and when she opened her eyes she hardly knew where she was, the back yard ran off into weeds and a fence-like line of trees and behind it the sky was perfectly blue and still. The asbestos "ranch house" that was now three years old startled her—it looked small. She shook her head as if to get awake.

It was too hot. She went inside the house and turned on the radio to drown out the quiet. She sat on the edge of her bed, barefoot, and listened for an hour and a half to a program called XYZ Sunday Jamboree, record after record of hard, fast, shrieking songs she sang along with, interspersed by exclamations from "Bobby King": "An' look here, you girls at Napoleon's—Son and Charley want you to pay real close attention to this song coming up!"

And Connie paid close attention herself, bathed in a glow of slow-pulsed joy that seemed to rise mysteriously out of the music itself and lay languidly about the airless little room, breathed in and breathed out with each gentle rise and fall of her chest.

After a while she heard a car coming up the drive. She sat up at once, startled, because it couldn't be her father so soon. The gravel kept crunching all the way in from the road—the driveway was long—and Connie ran to the window. It was a car she didn't know. It was an open jalopy, painted a bright gold that caught the sunlight opaquely. Her heart began to pound and her fingers snatched at her hair, checking it, and she whispered, "Christ. Christ," wondering how bad she looked. The car came to a stop at the side door and the horn sounded four short taps, as if this were a signal Connie knew.

She went into the kitchen and approached the door slowly, then hung out the screen door, her bare toes curling down off the step. There were two boys in the car and now she recognized the driver: he had shaggy, shabby black hair that looked crazy as a wig and he was grinning at her.

"I ain't late, am I?" he said.

"Who the hell do you think you are?" Connie said.

"Toldja I'd be out, didn't I?"

"I don't even know who you are."

She spoke sullenly, careful to show no interest or pleasure, and he spoke in a fast, bright monotone. Connie looked past him to the other boy, taking her time. He had fair brown hair, with a lock that fell onto his forehead. His sideburns gave him a fierce, embarrassed look, but so far he hadn't even bothered to glance at her. Both boys wore sunglasses. The driver's glasses were metallic and mirrored everything in miniature.

"You wanta come for a ride?" he said.

Connie smirked and let her hair fall loose over one shoulder.

"Don'tcha like my car? New paint job," he said. "Hey."

"What?"

"You're cute."

She pretended to fidget, chasing flies away from the door.

"Don'tcha believe me, or what?" he said.

"Look, I don't even know who you are," Connie said in disgust.

"Hey, Ellie's got a radio, see. Mine broke down." He lifted his friend's arm and showed her the little transistor radio the boy was holding, and now Connie began to hear the music. It was the same program that was playing inside the house.

"Bobby King?" she said.

"I listen to him all the time. I think he's great."

"He's kind of great," Connie said reluctantly.

"Listen, that guy's *great*. He knows where the action is."

Connie blushed a little, because the glasses made it impossible for her to see just what this boy was looking at. She couldn't decide if she liked him or if he was just a jerk, and so she dawdled in the doorway and wouldn't come down or go back inside. She said, "What's all that stuff painted on your car?"

"Can'tcha read it?" He opened the door very carefully, as if he were afraid it might fall off. He slid out just as carefully, planting his feet firmly on the ground, the tiny metallic world in his glasses slowing down like gelatine hardening, and in the midst of it Connie's bright green blouse. "This here is my name, to begin with," he said. ARNOLD FRIEND was written in tarlike black letters on the side, with a drawing of a round, grinning face that reminded Connie of a pumpkin, except it wore sunglasses. "I wanta introduce myself, I'm Arnold Friend and that's my real name and I'm gonna be your friend, honey, and inside the car's Ellie Oscar, he's kinda shy." Ellie brought his transistor radio up to his shoulder and balanced it there. "Now, these numbers are a secret code, honey," Arnold Friend explained. He read off the numbers 33, 19, 17 and raised his eyebrows at her to see what she thought of that, but she didn't think much of it. The left rear fender had been smashed and around it was written, on the gleaming gold background: DONE BY CRAZY WOMAN DRIVER. Connie had to laugh at that. Arnold Friend was pleased at her laughter and looked up at her. "Around the other side's a lot more—you wanta come and see them?"

"No."

"Why not?"

"Why should I?"

"Don'tcha wanta see what's on the car? Don'tcha wanta go for a ride?"

"I don't know."

"Why not?"

"I got things to do."

"Like what?"

"Things."

He laughed as if she had said something funny. He slapped his thighs. He was standing in a strange way, leaning back against the car as if he were balancing himself. He wasn't tall, only an inch or so taller than she would be if she came down to him. Connie liked the way he was dressed, which was the way all of them dressed: tight faded jeans stuffed into black, scuffed boots, a belt that pulled his waist in and showed how lean he was, and a white pull-over shirt that was a little soiled and showed the hard small muscles of his arms and shoulders. He looked as if he probably did hard work, lifting and carrying things. Even his neck looked muscular. And his face was a familiar face, somehow: the jaw and chin and cheeks slightly darkened because he hadn't shaved for a day or two, and the nose long and hawklike, sniffing as if she were a treat he was going to gobble up and it was all a joke.

"Connie, you ain't telling the truth. This is your day set aside for a ride with me and you know it," he said, still laughing. The way he straightened and recovered from his fit of laughing showed that it had been all fake.

"How do you know what my name is?" she said suspiciously.

"It's Connie."

"Maybe and maybe not."

"I know my Connie," he said, wagging his finger. Now she remembered him even better, back at the restaurant, and her cheeks warmed at the thought of how she had sucked in her breath just at the moment she passed him—how she must have looked to him. And he had remembered her. "Ellie and I come out here especially for you," he said. "Ellie can sit in back. How about it?"

"Where?"

"Where what?"

"Where're we going?"

He looked at her. He took off the sunglasses and she saw how pale the skin around his eyes was, like holes that were not in shadow but instead in light. His eyes were like chips of broken glass that catch the light in an amiable way. He smiled. It was as if the idea of going for a ride somewhere, to someplace, was a new idea to him.

"Just for a ride, Connie sweetheart."

"I never said my name was Connie," she said.

"But I know what it is. I know your name and all about you, lots of things," Arnold Friend said. He had not moved yet but stood still leaning back against the side of his jalopy. "I took a special interest in you, such a pretty girl, and found out all about you—like I know your parents and sister are gone somewheres and I know where and how long they're going to be gone, and I know who you were with last night, and your best girl friend's name is Betty. Right?"

He spoke in a simple lilting voice, exactly as if he were reciting the words to a song. His smile assured her that everything was fine. In the car Ellie turned up the volume on his radio and did not bother to look around at them.

"Ellie can sit in the back seat," Arnold Friend said. He indicated his friend with a casual jerk of his chin, as if Ellie did not count and she should not bother with him.

"How'd you find out all that stuff?" Connie said.

"Listen: Betty Schultz and Tony Fitch and Jimmy Pettinger and Nancy Pettinger," he said in a chant. "Raymond Stanley and Bob Hutter—"

"Do you know all those kids?"

"I know everybody."

"Look, you're kidding. You're not from around here."

"Sure."

"But—how come we never saw you before?"

"Sure you saw me before," he said. He looked down at his boots, as if he were a little offended. "You just don't remember."

"I guess I'd remember you," Connie said.

"Yeah?" He looked up at this, beaming. He was pleased. He began to mark time with the music from Ellie's radio, tapping his fists lightly together. Connie looked away from his smile to the car, which was painted so bright it almost hurt her eyes to look at it. She looked at that name, ARNOLD FRIEND. And up at the front fender was an expression that was familiar—MAN THE FLYING SAUCERS. It was an expression kids had used the year before but didn't use this year. She looked at it for a while as if the words meant something to her that she did not yet know.

"What're you thinking about? Huh?" Arnold Friend demanded. "Not worried about your hair blowing around in the car, are you?"

"No."

"Think I maybe can't drive good?"

"How do I know?"

"You're a hard girl to handle. How come?" he said. "Don't you know I'm your friend? Didn't you see me put my sign in the air when you walked by?"

"What sign?"

"My sign." And he drew an X in the air, leaning out toward her. They were maybe ten feet apart. After his hand fell back to his side the X was still in the air, almost visible. Connie let the screen door close and stood perfectly still inside it, listening to the music from her radio and the boy's blend together. She stared at Arnold Friend. He stood there so stiffly relaxed, pretending to be relaxed, with one hand idly on the door handle as if he were keeping himself up that way and had no intention of ever moving again. She recognized most things about him, the tight jeans that showed his thighs and buttocks and the greasy leather boots and the tight shirt, and even that slippery friendly smile of his, that sleepy dreamy smile that all the boys used to get across ideas they didn't want to put into words. She recognized all this and also the sing-song way he talked, slightly mocking, kidding, but serious and a little melancholy, and she recognized the way he tapped one fist against the other in homage to the perpetual music behind him. But all these things did not come together.

She said suddenly, "Hey, how old are you?"

His smile faded. She could see then that he wasn't a kid, he was much older—thirty, maybe more. At this knowledge her heart began to pound faster.

"That's a crazy thing to ask. Can'tcha see I'm your own age?"

"Like hell you are."

"Or maybe a coupla years older. I'm eighteen."

"Eighteen?" she said doubtfully.

He grinned to reassure her and lines appeared at the corners of his mouth. His teeth were big and white. He grinned so broadly his eyes became slits and she saw how thick the lashes were, thick and black as if painted with a black tarlike material. Then, abruptly, he seemed to become embarrassed and looked over his shoulder at Ellie. "*Him*, he's crazy," he said. "Ain't he a riot? He's a nut, a real character." Ellie was still listening to the music. His sunglasses told nothing about what he was thinking. He wore a bright orange shirt unbuttoned halfway to show his chest, which was a pale, bluish chest and not muscular like Arnold Friend's. His shirt collar was turned up all around and the very tips of the collar pointed out past his chin as if they were protecting him. He was pressing the transistor radio up against his ear and sat there in a kind of daze, right in the sun.

"He's kinda strange," Connie said.

"Hey, she says you're kinda strange! Kinda strange!" Arnold Friend cried. He pounded on the car to get Ellie's attention. Ellie turned for the first time and Connie saw with shock that he wasn't a kid either—he had a fair, hairless face, cheeks reddened slightly as if the veins grew too close to the surface of his skin, the face of a forty-year-old baby. Connie felt a wave of dizziness rise in her at this sight and she stared at him as if waiting for something to change the shock of the moment, make it all right again. Ellie's lips kept shaping words, mumbling along with the words blasting in his ear.

"Maybe you two better go away," Connie said faintly.

"What? How come?" Arnold Friend cried. "We come out here to take you for a ride. It's Sunday." He had the voice of the man on the radio now. It was the same voice, Connie thought.

"Don'tcha know it's Sunday all day? And honey, no matter who you were with last night, today you're with Arnold Friend and don't you forget it! Maybe you better step out here," he said, and this last was in a different voice. It was a little flatter, as if the heat was finally getting to him.

"No. I got things to do."

"Hey."

"You two better leave."

"We ain't leaving until you come with us."

"Like hell I am—"

"Connie, don't fool around with me. I mean—I mean, don't fool *around*," he said, shaking his head. He laughed incredulously. He placed his sunglasses on top of his head, carefully, as if he were indeed wearing a wig, and brought the stems down behind his ears. Connie stared at him, another wave of dizziness and fear rising in her so that for a moment he wasn't even in focus but was just a blur standing there against his gold car, and she had the idea that he had driven up the driveway all right but had come from nowhere before that and belonged nowhere and that everything about him and even about the music that was so familiar to her was only half real.

"If my father comes and sees you—"

"He ain't coming. He's at a barbecue."

"How do you know that?"

"Aunt Tillie's. Right now they're—uh—they're drinking. Sitting around," he said vaguely, squinting as if he were staring all the way to town and over to Aunt Tillie's back yard. Then the vision seemed to get clear and he nodded energetically. "Yeah. Sitting around. There's your sister in a blue dress, huh? And high heels, the poor sad bitch—nothing like you, sweetheart! And your mother's helping some fat woman with the corn, they're cleaning the corn—husking the corn—"

"What fat woman?" Connie cried.

"How do I know what fat woman, I don't know every goddamn fat woman in the world!" Arnold Friend laughed.

"Oh, that's Mrs. Hornsby. . . . Who invited her?" Connie said. She felt a little lightheaded. Her breath was coming quickly.

"She's too fat. I don't like them fat. I like them the way you are, honey," he said, smiling sleepily at her. They stared at each other for a while through the screen door. He said softly, "Now, what you're going to do is this: you're going to come out that door. You're going to sit up front with me and Ellie's going to sit in the back, the hell with Ellie, right? This isn't Ellie's date. You're my date. I'm your lover, honey."

"What? You're crazy—"

"Yes, I'm your lover. You don't know what that is but you will," he said. "I know that too. I know all about you. But look: it's real nice and you couldn't ask for nobody better than me, or more polite. I always keep my word. I'll tell you how it is, I'm always nice at first, the first time. I'll hold you so tight you won't think you have to try to get away or pretend anything ·because you'll know you can't. And I'll come inside you where it's all secret and you'll give in to me and you'll love me—"

"Shut up! You're crazy!" Connie said. She backed away from the door. She put her hands up against her ears as if she'd heard something terrible, something not meant for her. "People don't talk like that, you're crazy," she muttered. Her heart was almost too big now for her chest and its pumping made sweat break out all over her. She looked out to see Arnold Friend pause and then take a step toward the porch, lurching. He almost fell. But, like a clever drunken man, he managed to catch his balance. He wobbled in his high boots and grabbed hold of one of the porch posts.

"Honey?" he said. "You still listening?"

"Get the hell out of here!"

"Be nice, honey, Listen."

"I'm going to call the police—"

He wobbled again and out of the side of his mouth came a fast spat curse, an aside not meant for her to hear. But even this "Christ!" sounded forced. Then he began to smile again. She watched this smile come, awkward as if he were smiling from inside a mask. His whole face was a mask, she thought wildly, tanned down to his throat but then running out as if he had plastered make-up on his face but had forgotten about his throat.

"Honey—? Listen, here's how it is. I always tell the truth and I promise you this: I ain't coming in that house after you."

"You better not! I'm going to call the police if you—if you don't—"

"Honey," he said, talking right through her voice, "honey, I'm not coming in there but you are coming out here. You know why?"

She was panting. The kitchen looked like a place she had never seen before, some room she had run inside but that wasn't good enough, wasn't going to help her. The kitchen window had never had a curtain, after three years, and there were dishes in the sink for her to do—probably—and if you ran your hand across the table you'd probably feel something sticky there.

"You listening, honey? Hey?"

"—going to call the police—"

"Soon as you touch the phone I don't need to keep my promise and can come inside. You won't want that."

She rushed forward and tried to lock the door. Her fingers were shaking. "But why lock it," Arnold Friend said gently, talking right into her face. "It's just a screen door. It's just nothing." One of his boots was at a strange angle, as if his foot wasn't in it. It pointed out to the left, bent at the ankle. "I mean, anybody can break through a screen door and glass and wood and iron or anything else if he needs to, anybody at all, and specially Arnold Friend. If the place got lit up with a fire, honey, you'd come runnin' out into my arms, right into my arms an' safe at home—like you knew I was your lover and'd stopped fooling around. I don't mind a nice shy girl but I don't like no fooling around." Part of those words were spoken with a slight rhythmic lilt, and Connie somehow recognized them—the echo of a song from last year, about a girl rushing into her boy friend's arms and coming home again—

Connie stood barefoot on the linoleum floor, staring at him. "What do you want?" she whispered.

"I want you," he said.

"What?"

"Seen you that night and thought, that's the one, yes sir. I never needed to look anymore."

"But my father's coming back. He's coming to get me. I had to wash my hair first—" She spoke in a dry, rapid voice, hardly raising it for him to hear.

"No, your daddy is not coming and yes, you had to wash your hair and you washed it for me. It's nice and shining and all for me. I thank you sweetheart," he said with a mock bow, but again he almost lost his balance. He had to bend and adjust his boots. Evidently his feet did not go all the way down; the boots must have been stuffed with something so that he would seem taller. Connie stared out at him and behind him at Ellie in the car, who seemed to be looking off toward Connie's right, into nothing. This Ellie said, pulling the words out of the air one after another as if he were just discovering them, "You want me to pull out the phone?"

"Shut your mouth and keep it shut," Arnold Friend said, his face red from bending over or maybe from embarrassment because Connie had seen his boots. "This ain't none of your business."

"What—what are you doing? What do you want?" Connie said. "If I call the police they'll get you, they'll arrest you—"

"Promise was not to come in unless you touch that phone, and I'll keep that promise," he said. He resumed his erect position and tried to force his shoulders back. He sounded like a hero in a movie, declaring something important. But he spoke too loudly and it was as if he were speaking to someone behind Connie. "I ain't made plans for coming in that house where I don't belong but just for you to come out to me, the way you should. Don't you know who I am?"

"You're crazy," she whispered. She backed away from the door but did not want to go into another part of the house, as if this would give him permission to come through the door. "What do you . . . you're crazy, you. . . ."

"Huh? What're you saying, honey?"

Her eyes darted everywhere in the kitchen. She could not remember what it was, this room.

"This is how it is, honey: you come out and we'll drive away, have a nice ride. But if you don't come out we're gonna wait till your people come home and then they're all going to get it."

"You want that telephone pulled out?" Ellie said. He held the radio away from his ear and grimaced, as if without the radio the air was too much for him.

"I toldja shut up, Ellie," Arnold Friend said, "you're deaf, get a hearing aid, right? Fix yourself up. This little girl's no trouble and's gonna be nice to me, so Ellie keep to yourself, this ain't your date—right? Don't hem in on me, don't hog, don't crush, don't bird dog, don't trail me," he said in a rapid, meaningless voice, as if he were running through all the expressions he'd learned but was no longer sure which of them was in style, then rushing on to new ones, making them up with his eyes closed. "Don't crawl under my fence, don't squeeze in my chipmunk hole, don't sniff my glue, suck my popsicle, keep your own greasy fingers on yourself!" He shaded his eyes and peered in at Connie, who was backed against the kitchen table. "Don't mind him, honey, he's just a creep. He's a dope. Right? I'm the boy for you and like I said, you come out here nice like a lady and give me your hand, and nobody else gets hurt, I mean, your nice old bald-headed daddy and your mummy and your sister in her high heels. Because listen: why bring them in this?"

"Leave me alone," Connie whispered.

"Hey, you know that old woman down the road, the one with the chickens and stuff—you know her?"

"She's dead!"

"Dead? What? You know her?" Arnold Friend said.

"She's dead—"

"Don't you like her?"

"She's dead—she's—she isn't here any more—"

"But don't you like her, I mean, you got something against her? Some grudge or something?" Then his voice dipped as if he were conscious of a rudeness. He touched the sunglasses perched up on top of his head as if to make sure they were still there. "Now, you be a good girl."

"What are you going to do?"

"Just two things, or maybe three," Arnold Friend said. "But I promise it won't last long and you'll like me the way you get to

like people you're close to. You will. It's all over for you here, so
come on out. You don't want your people in any trouble, do you?"

She turned and bumped against a chair or something, hurting
her leg, but she ran into the back room and picked up the telephone. Something roared in her ear, a tiny roaring, and she was so
sick with fear that she could do nothing but listen to it—the telephone was clammy and very heavy and her fingers groped down to
the dial but were too weak to touch it. She began to scream into
the phone, into the roaring. She cried out, she cried for her mother
she felt her breath start jerking back and forth in her lungs as if it
were something Arnold Friend was stabbing her with again and
again with no tenderness. A noisy sorrowful wailing rose all about
her and she was locked inside it the way she was locked inside this
house.

After a while she could hear again. She was sitting on the floor
with her wet back against the wall.

Arnold Friend was saying from the door, "That's a good girl.
Put the phone back."

She kicked the phone away from her.

"No, honey. Pick it up. Put it back right."

She picked it up and put it back. The dial tone stopped.

"That's a good girl. Now, you come outside."

She was hollow with what had been fear but what was now just
an emptiness. All that screaming had blasted it out of her. She sat,
one leg cramped under her, and deep inside her brain was something like a pinpoint of light that kept going and would not let her
relax. She thought, I'm not going to see my mother again. She
thought, I'm not going to sleep in my bed again. Her bright green
blouse was all wet.

Arnold Friend said, in a gentle-loud voice that was like a stage
voice, "The place where you came from ain't there any more, and
where you had in mind to go is cancelled out. This place you are
now—inside your daddy's house—is nothing but a cardboard box
I can knock down any time. You know that and always did know
it. You hear me?"

She thought, I have got to think. I have got to know what to do.

"We'll go out to a nice field, out in the country here where it
smells so nice and it's sunny," Arnold Friend said. "I'll have my
arms tight around you so you won't need to try to get away and I'll
show you what love is like, what it does. The hell with this house!
It looks solid all right," he said. He ran a fingernail down the
screen and the noise did not make Connie shiver, as it would have
the day before. "Now, put your hand on your heart, honey. Feel
that? That feels solid too but we know better. Be nice to me, be
sweet like you can because what else is there for a girl like you but

to be sweet and pretty and give in?—and get away before her people come back?"

She felt her pounding heart. Her hand seemed to enclose it. She thought for the first time in her life that it was nothing that was hers, that belonged to her, but just a pounding, living thing inside this body that wasn't really hers either.

"You don't want them to get hurt," Arnold Friend went on. "Now, get up, honey. Get up all by yourself."

She stood.

"Now, turn this way. That's right. Come over here to me.— Ellie, put that away, didn't I tell you? You dope. You miserable creepy dope," Arnold Friend said. His words were not angry but only part of an incantation. The incantation was kindly. "Now, come out through the kitchen to me, honey, and let's see a smile, try it, you're a brave, sweet little girl and now they're eating corn and hot dogs cooked to bursting over an outdoor fire, and they don't know one thing about you and never did and honey, you're better than them because not a one of them would have done this for you."

Connie felt the linoleum under her feet; it was cool. She brushed her hair back out of her eyes. Arnold Friend let go of the post tentatively and opened his arms for her, his elbows pointing in toward each other and his wrists limp, to show that this was an embarrassed embrace and a little mocking, he didn't want to make her self-conscious.

She put out her hand against the screen. She watched herself push the door slowly open as if she were back safe somewhere in the other doorway, watching this body and this head of long hair moving out into the sunlight where Arnold Friend waited.

"My sweet little blue-eyed girl," he said in a half-sung sigh that had nothing to do with her brown eyes but was taken up just the same by the vast sunlit reaches of the land behind him and on all sides of him—so much land that Connie had never seen before and did not recognize except to know that she was going to it.

1970

Bibliography

The introductory essays for the authors and texts represented in this work provide fundamental bibliographies. A library collection for reference purposes should contain at least the following works: *The Literature of the American People,* edited by Arthur Hobson Quinn and others; *Literary History of the United States,* 3 vols., edited by R. E. Spiller and others; *The Oxford Companion to American Literature,* by J. D. Hart, valuable for authoritative brief references to authors and subjects; and *Harvard Guide to American History,* edited by O. Handlin and others, a comprehensive bibliography of American history, literature, and society. The bibliography which follows is a brief classified list of standard works of reference and history in the fields represented by the literature collected in the present volumes.

REFERENCE WORKS AND BIBLIOGRAPHIES

Adams, J. T., and Coleman, R. V., eds. *Dictionary of American History.* 6 vols., 1940.

American Literature, Periodical. *An Analytical Index to American Literature,* Vols. I–XXX, March, 1929–January, 1959. Thomas F. Marshall, ed. 1963.

Blanck, Jacob. *Bibliography of American Literature.* In progress. (Major writers, first editions with bibliographical descriptions.)

Carruth, Gorton, *et al. The Encyclopedia of American Facts and Dates.* 1956.

Craigie, W. A., and Hulbert, J. R., eds. *Dictionary of American English on Historical Principles.* 4 vols., 1938–1944.

Deutsch, Babette. *Poetry Handbook.* 1957. (A dictionary of terms; a comprehensive guide to the craft of poetry.)

Dictionary of American Biography. Johnson, Allen, and Malone, Dumas, eds. 20 vols. plus supplements, 1928–1958.

Gohdes, Clarence. *Bibliographical Guide to the Study of the Literature of the U.S.A.* 3rd ed., 1970.

———. *Literature and Theater of the States and Regions of the U.S.A.: An Historical Bibliography.* 1967.

Handlin, O., Schlesinger, A. M., Morrison, S. E., and others, eds. *Harvard Guide to American History.* 1954. (Includes history, fine arts, literature, philosophy, and social sciences.)

Hart, J. D. *The Oxford Companion to American Literature.* 4th ed., 1965.

International Index to Periodicals. Annual, 1907– . (Includes foreign-language periodicals and scholarly journals.)

Johnson, Merle. *Merle Johnson's American First Editions.* Revised and enlarged by Jacob Blanck, 1942.

Jones, Howard Mumford, and Ludwig, Richard M. *Guide to American Literature and Its Background Since 1890.* 1964.

Kull, Irving S., and Nell, M. *A Short Chronology of American History, 1492–1950.* 1952.

Kunitz, S. J., and Haycraft, Howard, eds. *American Authors, 1600–1900.* 1944. (A biographical dictionary.)

———. *Twentieth Century Authors.* 1942. (A biographical dictionary.) Supplement, 1955.

Leary, Lewis, ed. *Articles on American Literature, 1900–1950.* 1954. (The best guide to scholarly articles on authors and literary subjects.)

———. *Articles on American Literature, 1950–1967.* 1970.

Ludwig, Richard M., ed. *Bibliography Supplement to Literary History of the United States,* by R. E. Spiller, *et al.* 1959. *Supplement II,* 1972.

Martin, Michael, and Gelber, Leonard. *The New Dictionary of American History*. 1952.
Millet, F. B. *Contemporary American Authors: A Critical Survey and 219 Bio-bibliographies*. 1940.
Morris, R. B., ed. *Encyclopedia of American History*, 1953.
Mott, F. L. *American Journalism: A History of Newspapers in the United States through 250 Years, 1690 to 1940*. 1941. Revised, 1951.
———. *A History of American Magazines*. 4 vols., 1938–1957. (Study carried through 1905.)
Murphy, Rosalie, and Vinson, James, eds. *Contemporary Poets of the English Language*. 1970.
Nineteenth Century Readers' Guide to Periodical Literature: 1890–1899; with Supplemental Indexing 1900–1922. 1944. (For entries later than 1899 also consult the *Readers' Guide* . . .)
Poole's Index to Periodical Literature. Annual, 1802–1881. Supplements, 1882–1907. (*Cf. Readers' Guide* . . .)
Quinn, Arthur Hobson, ed. *The Literature of the American People*. 1951. (Extensive bibliographies by chapters.)
Readers' Guide to Periodical Literature. Annual, 1900–   . (Especially useful for the location of articles and literature in nonprofessional magazines.)
Report of the Committee on Trends in Research in American Literature, 1940–1950. Published by the American Literature Group of the Modern Language Association. 1951.
Sabin, Joseph, and others. *A Dictionary of Books Relating to America from Its Discovery to the Present Time*. 29 vols., 1868–1936.
Seligman, E. R. A., and Johnson, Allen, eds. *Encyclopedia of the Social Sciences*. 15 vols., 1931–1935.
Spiller, R. E., and others, eds. *Literary History of the United States*. 2 vols. in one. 3rd ed.: revised, 1963.
Stern, Madeleine B. *Imprints on History*. 1956. (American book publishers.)
Trent, W. P., Erskine, John, Sherman, S. P., and Van Doren, Carl, eds. *Cambridge History of American Literature*. 4 vols., 1917–1921. (Good bibliography to 1918.)
Vinson, James, ed. *Contemporary Novelists*. 1972.
Weimar, David R. *Bibliography of American Culture, 1493–1875*. Ann Arbor, University Microfilms, 1957.
Welsch, Erwin K. *The Negro in America: A Research Guide*. 1965.
Who's Who in America. Biennial, 1899–
Who Was Who in America. Vol. I, *1897–1942*, 1942; Vol. II, *1943–1950*, 1950; Vol. III, *1951–1960*, 1960; Vol. IV, *1961–1968*, 1968.
Woodress, James. *Dissertations in American Literature, 1891–1966*. 1968.
Wright, Lyle H. *American Fiction, 1774–1850*. 2nd ed., 1969.
———. *American Fiction, 1851–1875*. 1957.
———. *American Fiction, 1876–1900*. 1966.

LITERARY HISTORY

Aaron, Daniel. *Writers on the Left: Episodes in American Literary Communism*. 1961.
———. *American Writers on the Civil War*. 1973.
Ahnebrink, Lars. *The Beginnings of Naturalism in American Fiction*. 1950.
American Writers Series. Clark, H. H., General Editor. 1934–   . (Each volume contains representative selections of a major author, with a bibliography and critical introduction. Twenty-eight vols. have been published.)
Auchincloss, Louis. *Pioneers and Caretakers: A Study of Nine American Women Novelists*. 1965.
Baumbach, Jonathan. *Landscape of Nightmare: Studies in the Contemporary American Novel*. 1965.
Beach, Joseph Warren. *American Fiction: 1920–1940*. 1941. (Major authors only.)
Berthoff, Warner. *The Ferment of Realism: American Literature, 1884–1919*. 1965.
Blair, Walter. *Native American Humor (1800–1900)*. 1937.
Bogan, Louise. *Achievement in American Poetry, 1900–1950*. 1951.
Bone, Robert A. *The Negro Novel in America*. Rev. ed., 1965.
Brooks, Van Wyck. *The Flowering of New England, 1815–1865*. 1936.
———. *New England: Indian Summer, 1865–1915*. 1940.
Canby, H. S. *Classic Americans: A Study of Eminent American Writers from Irving to Whitman*. 1931.

Chase, Richard. *The American Novel and Its Tradition*. 1957.
Clark, H. H., ed. *Transitions in American Literary History*. 1954.
Cowie, Alexander. *The Rise of the American Novel*. 1948. (Principally eighteenth-and nineteenth-century novelists.)
Cowley, Malcolm. *After the General Tradition: American Writers, 1910–1930*. Rev. ed., 1964.
———. *A Second Flowering: Works and Days of the Lost Generation*. 1973.
Cunliffe, Marcus. *The Literature of the United States*. 1954.
Dembo, L. S. *Conceptions of Reality in Modern American Poetry*. 1966.
Edel, Leon. *The Psychological Novel, 1900–1950*. 1955.
Fiedler, Leslie. *Love and Death in the American Novel*. 1960.
French, Warren. *The Social Novel at the End of an Era*. 1966.
Frohock, W. M. *The Novel of Violence in America*. Rev. ed., 1957.
Fussell, Edwin. *Frontier: American Literature and the American West*. 1965.
Geismar, Maxwell. *American Moderns: From Rebellion to Conformity*. 1958.
———. *The Last of the Provincials*. 1947. (Modern fiction.)
———. *Rebels and Ancestors, 1890–1915*. 1953.
———. *Writers in Crisis: The American Novel Between Two Wars*. 1942. (Major novelists, 1920–1940.)
Gregory, Horace, and Zaturenska, Marya. *A History of American Poetry, 1900–1940*. 1946.
Hassan, Ihab. *Radical Innocence: The Contemporary American Novel*. 1961.
Hoffman, Frederick J. *The Art of Southern Fiction*. 1967.
———. *The Twenties: American Writing in the Postwar Decade*. 1955.
Hubbell, Jay B. *The South in American Literature, 1607–1900*. 1954.
Hughes, Glenn. *A History of the American Theatre, 1700–1950*. 1951.
Jones, Howard Mumford. *O Strange New World: American Culture, The Formative Years*. 1964.
Kazin, Alfred. *On Native Grounds: An Interpretation of Modern American Prose Literature*. 1942.
Kramer, Dale. *Chicago Renaissance: The Literary Life in the Midwest, 1900–1930*. 1966.
Krutch, J. W. *The American Drama Since 1918: An Informal History*. 1939.
Leisy, E. E. *The American Historical Novel*. 1950.
Lewis, R. W. B. *The American Adam: Innocence, Tragedy, and Tradition in the Nineteenth Century*. 1955.
Lively, Robert A. *Fiction Fights the Civil War*. 1956.
Lloyd, D. J., and Warfel, H. R. *American English in Its Cultural Setting*. 1956.
Matthiessen, F. O. *American Renaissance: Art and Expression in the Age of Emerson and Whitman*. 1941.
Margolies, Edward. *Native Sons: A Critical Study of Twentieth-Century Negro American Authors*. 1968.
Martin, Jay. *Harvests of Change: American Literature 1865–1914*. 1967.
Marx, Leo. *The Machine in the Garden: Technology and the Pastoral Ideal in America*. 1964.
Mencken, H. L. *The American Language: An Inquiry into the Development of English in the United States*. 1919. Revised to 1936. Supplement I, 1945; Supplement II, 1948.
Millgate, Michael. *American Social Fiction: James to Cozzens*. 1967.
Miller, Perry. *The New England Mind: The Seventeenth Century*. 1939.
Morgan, Edmund S. *Visible Saints: The History of a Puritan Idea*. 1963.
Murdock, K. B. *Literature and Theology in Colonial New England*. 1949.
O'Connor, W. V. *An Age of Criticism, 1900–1950*. 1952.
Parrington, V. L. *Main Currents in American Thought: An Interpretation of American Literature from the Beginnings to 1920*. 3 vols., 1927–1930.
Pattee, F. L. *A History of American Literature Since 1870*. 1915.
Pearce, Roy Harvey. *The Continuity of American Poetry*. 1961.
Pizer, Donald. *Realism and Naturalism in Nineteenth-Century American Literature*. 1966.
Poirier, Richard. *A World Elsewhere: The Place of Style in American Literature*. 1966.
Pritchard, J. P. *Criticism in America*. 1956.
Quinn, Arthur Hobson. *American Fiction: An Historical and Critical Survey*. 1936. (Comprehensive to date of publication.)
———. *A History of the American Drama: From the Beginning to the Civil War*. 1923. Rev. ed., 1943.
———. *A History of the American Drama: From the Civil War to the Present Day*. 2 vols., 1927. Reissued in 1 vol., 1936.
Quinn, Arthur Hobson, Murdock, K. B., Gohdes, Clarence, and Whicher, G. F. *The Literature of the American People*. 1951.

Rourke, Constance. *American Humor: A Study of the National Character.* 1931.
Smith, Henry Nash. *Virgin Land: The American West as Symbol and Myth.* 1950.
Spencer, B. T. *The Quest of Nationality: An American Literary Campaign.* 1957.
Spiller, R. E. *The Cycle of American Literature: An Essay in Historical Criticism.* 1956.
Spiller, R. E., Thorpe, Willard, Johnson, T. H., and Canby, H. S., eds. *Literary History of the United States.* 3 vols., 1948. 1 vol., 1953.
Stovall, Floyd, ed. *The Development of American Literary Criticism: A Symposium.* Chapel Hill, N.C., 1955.
Taubmann, Howard. *The Making of the American Theatre.* 1965.
Taylor, W. F. *The Economic Novel in America.* 1942.
Tyler, M. C. *A History of American Literature during the Colonial Period, 1607–1765.* 2 vols., 1878. Rev. ed., 1897. 1 vol., 1949.
———. *The Literary History of the American Revolution, 1763–1783.* 2 vols., 1897. Reissued in 1 vol., 1941.
Walcutt, Charles C. *American Literary Naturalism, a Divided Stream.* 1956.
Walker, Robert H. *The Poet and the Gilded Age: Social Themes in Late Nineteenth Century Verse.* 1963.
Weales, Gerald. *American Drama Since World War Two.* 1962.
Williams, Stanley T. *The Spanish Background of American Literature.* 1955.
Ziff, Larzer. *The American 1890's: Life and Times of a Lost Generation.* 1966.

POLITICAL AND SOCIAL HISTORY

Adams, J. T. *Provincial Society, 1690–1763.* 1927.
Allen, F. L. *The Big Change: America Transforms Itself, 1900–1950.* 1952.
———. *Only Yesterday.* 1931. (Social history of the 1920's.)
Beard, C. A., and Beard, M. R. *The Rise of American Civilization.* 4 vols., 1927–1942.
Billington, R. A. *Westward Expansion: A History of the American Frontier.* 1949.
Bowers, C. G. *Jefferson and Hamilton: The Struggle for Democracy in America.* 1925.
Buck, Paul H. *The Road to Reunion, 1865–1900.* 1937.
Chalmers, David M. *The Social and Political Ideas of the Muckrakers.* 1964.
Chronicles of America Series. Johnson, Allen, General Editor. 50 vols., 1918–1921. Six supplementary vols. Nevins, Allan, Editor, 1950–1951. (Brief histories of each period, authoritative in general.)
Dorfman, Joseph. *The Economic Mind in American Civilization.* 3 vols., 1946–1949. (Through World War I.)
Faulkner, H. U. *The Quest for Social Justice, 1898–1914.* 1931.
Fish, C. R. *The Rise of the Common Man, 1830–1850.* 1927.
Greene, E. B. *The Revolutionary Generation, 1763–1790.* 1943.
Hesseltine, W. B. *A History of the South.* Rev. ed., 1943.
Horton, Rod W., and Edwards, Herbert. *Background of American Literary Thought.* 1952.
Howe, Irving. *A World More Attractive: A View of Modern Literature and Politics.* 1963.
Krout, J. A., and Fox, D. R. *The Completion of Independence, 1790–1830.* 1944.
Morison, Samuel Eliot, and Commager, Henry S. *The Growth of the American Republic.* 2 vols., revised, 1950. (Excellent brief general history.)
Myrdal, Gunnar. *An American Dilemma: The Negro Problem and Modern Democracy.* 2 vols., 1944.
Nevins, Allan. *The Emergence of Modern America, 1865–1878.* 1927.
Nichols, R. F. *The Disruption of American Democracy.* 1948. (Politics and the Civil War.)
Paxson, F. L. *The History of the American Frontier, 1763–1893.* 1924.
Redding, J. Saunders. *The Lonesome Road: The Story of the Negro's Part in America.* 1957.
Schlesinger, A. M. *The Rise of the City, 1878–1898.* 1933.
———. *The Rise of Modern America, 1865–1951.* 1951.
Schlesinger, A. M., Jr. *The Age of Jackson.* 1945.
Slosson, W. P. *The Great Crusade and After, 1914–1928.* 1930.
Spielman, William C. *Introduction to Sources of American History.* 1951.
Stephenson, W. H., and Coulter, E. M., eds. *A History of the South.* 6 vols., 1948–1953. To be completed in 4 more vols.
Sullivan, Mark. *Our Times.* 6 vols., 1926–1935.
Tocqueville, Alexis de. *Democracy in America.* 2 vols., London, 1835. Bradley, Phillips, ed., 2 vols., 1942.

Van Doren, Carl. *The Great Rehearsal: The Story of the Making and Ratifying of the Constitution of the United States.* 1948.
Wecter, Dixon. *The Age of the Great Depression, 1929–1941.* 1948.
Wish, Harvey. *Society and Thought in America.* 2 vols., 1950–1952.
Wright, L. B. *The Atlantic Frontier: Colonial American Civilization, 1607–1763.* 1948.

INTELLECTUAL AND CULTURAL HISTORY

Baritz, Loren. *City on a Hill: A History of Ideas and Myths in America.* 1964.
Barker, Virgil. *American Painting, History and Interpretation.* 1950.
Cargill, Oscar. *Intellectual America: Ideas on the March.* 1941.
Cash, W. J. *The Mind of the South.* 1941.
Chase, Gilbert. *America's Music from the Pilgrims to the Present.* 1955.
Commager, Henry S. *The American Mind: An Interpretation of American Thought and Character Since the 1880's.* 1950.
Curti, Merle. *The Growth of American Thought.* 1943. (American philosophy and ideas.)
Eliot, Alexander. *Three Hundred Years of American Painting.* 1957.
Gabriel, R. H. *The Course of American Democratic Thought: An Intellectual History Since 1815.* 1940.
Guttman, Allen. *The Conservative Tradition in America.* 1967.
Hindle, Brooke. *The Pursuit of Science in Revolutionary America, 1735–1789.* 1956.
Hofstadter, Richard. *Social Darwinism in American Thought, 1860–1915.* 1944.
Howard, J. T., and Bellows, G. K. *A Short History of Music in America.* 1957.
Jackson, G. P. *White and Negro Spirituals: Their Life Span and Kinship.* 1943.
LaFollette, Suzanne. *Art in America from Colonial Times to the Present Day.* 1929.
Larkin, O. W. *Art and Life in America.* 1949.
Lasch, Christopher. *The New Radicalism in America, 1899–1963: The Intellectual as a Social Type.* 1965.
Lomax, Alan. *The Folk Songs of North America.* 1960.
Lynn, Kenneth S., ed. *The Comic Tradition in America.* 1958.
McNeill, John T. *The History and Character of Calvinism.* 1954.
Miller, Perry. *Errand into the Wilderness.* 1957.
―――. *The Life of the Mind in America: From the Revolution to the Civil War.* 1965.
Morison, S. E. *Intellectual Life in Colonial New England.* 1956.
Persons, Stow. *American Minds: A History of Ideas.* 1958.
Richardson, E. P. *Painting in America: The Story of 450 Years.* 1956.
Riley, I. W. *American Thought from Puritanism to Pragmatism and Beyond.* 2nd ed., 1923.
Rosenberg, Bernard, and White, David M. *Mass Culture: The Popular Arts in America.* 1957.
Rossiter, Clinton L. *Conservatism in America.* 2nd ed., revised, 1962.
Schneider, H. W. *History of American Philosophy.* 1946.
―――. *The Puritan Mind.* 1930.
Stewart, Randall. *American Literature and Christian Doctrine.* 1958.
Sweet, William W. *Religion in the Development of American Culture, 1765–1840.* 1952.
Warren, Austin. *The New England Conscience.* 1966.
Wood, James P. *Magazines in the United States.* 1956.

Index